The BLOOMSBURY

Guide to English Literature

The BLOOMSBURY

Guide to English Literature

Second edition

General Editor: *Marion Wynne-Davies*

BLOOMSBURY

The first edition of the *Bloomsbury Guide to English Literature* was published in 1989. The material it contained was then extensively revised and updated for use in the six companion *Bloomsbury Guides to English Literature* which were published between 1992 and 1994. The second edition of the *Bloomsbury Guide to English Literature*, published in 1995, is the result of a complete revision and expansion of both the original and subsequent guides.

This edition first published in 1995 by
Bloomsbury Publishing plc
2 Soho Square
London W1V 6HB

ISBN 0 7475 2267 7

Typeset by Hewer Text Composition Services, Edinburgh
Printed in Britain by Clays Ltd, St Ives plc

Contents

Preface

Any work which hopes to offer a stimulating and up-to-date guide to English literature cannot remain static, and the efforts involved in the production of the second edition to *The Bloomsbury Guide to English Literature* reflect the ways in which our understanding of authorship and text are developing. The canon is being expanded, both from within, through the discovery of writers and books from earlier periods, as well as from outside, as contemporary names are added to the list of established authors. For example, the works of a number of women writers from previous centuries are only just being reprinted even though the volumes were well-known during their own age; the proliferation in post-colonial studies has meant that numerous books which were written in English, but which have often been excluded from the canon, are now readily available; new poets, novelists and dramatists continually attract critical acclaim. This book sets out, therefore, to include the recent additions to English Literature, but it also covers conventional material, from well-known authors such as Shakespeare, Dickens, and Auden to popular titles like *The Canterbury Tales*, *Middlemarch*, and *Look Back in Anger*. Although the limitations of space have inevitably led to some exclusions, as a whole *The Bloomsbury Guide to English Literature* has attempted to achieve a balance between period, genre, author, text, context, tradition and innovation.

In my introduction to the first edition of *The Bloomsbury Guide to English Literature* I wrote that the guide had been 'a cumulative and democratic production' and these words are equally true of this, the second edition. Over the intervening six years the text has been gradually refined, updated and expanded by myself and, more especially, by all the contributors to this volume. In the process we have added material which represents an expansion of canonical material, for example Roger Pooley's essay on Renaissance Prose, as well as exploring fields of literature which are in the process of development today, such as Trevor Griffiths' entries on contemporary drama and Philip Shaw's essay on the relationship between critical theory and Romantic poetry. At the same time, much of the work has become collaborative, either in the sense of writing new material together, as in the case of Andrew Roberts' and my own essay on New Literatures in English, or in a process of mutual revision, as may be seen in Jane Thomas' and Linda Williams' reworking of the essay on Victorian poetry. As such, although I am writing this preface, the book as a whole must be recognised as the result of all those contributing to the essays and the alphabetical reference section, as well as to the thorough and imaginative editorial work undertaken at Bloomsbury.

The book remains divided into two parts: the first consists of a series of essays which follow a chronological order from the Middle Ages to the present day. Each period (with the exception of the first on Medieval literature) is subdivided into four parts, beginning with an overall view of the era and then moving on to a generic analysis of poetry, prose and drama. Much of this material is new, and the arrangement of the essays differs from that in the earlier edition. The second section of *The Bloomsbury Guide to English Literature* is made up of an alphabetical reference section which complements and expands upon the material found in the essays, and also incorporates several extended entries, such as English Language and Irish Literature in English. The existing entries have been updated and expanded, but, more importantly, there are over a thousand completely new topics included in this edition. Finally, the essays and A–Z entries are cross-referenced, ensuring that further areas of interest are readily accessible.

Marion Wynne-Davies

Contributors

General Editor

Marion Wynne-Davies
is a Senior Lecturer in English Literature at the University of Dundee. She is General Editor of the *Bloomsbury Guide to English Literature* and General Editor of the *Bloomsbury Guides to English Literature* series. She is the author of *The Tales of the Clerk and the Wife of Bath*, *Women and Arthurian Literature: Seizing the Sword* and has co-edited with S. Cerasano, *Gloriana's Face: Women, Public and Private, in the English Renaissance* and *Renaissance Drama by Women, Texts and Documents*. She is a regular radio broadcaster and is a popular visiting lecturer throughout Britain, in Japan, the USA and Canada.

Contributor Biographies

Janet Barron
worked with David Nokes on *Clarissa*, a three-part television adaptation for the BBC in 1991.

Clare Brant
is a Lecturer in English at King's College London.

Susan Bruce
is a Lecturer in English at Keele University. Her recent work includes an article on Rochester and *Moore's Utopia*.

Edward Burns
is Senior Lecturer in the Department of English Language and Literature at the University of Liverpool, and has edited *Reading Rochester*, 1995.

Ian Clarke
is Director of English and Drama at Loughborough University. He is the author of *Edwardian Drama: A Critical Study*.

Jonathan Culpepper
is a Lecturer in Linguistics and Modern English at Lancaster University, and is the co-author of *Drama: From Text to Context*.

Gail Cunningham
is Dean of the Faculty of Human Sciences at Kingston University. She has published *The New Woman and the Victorian Novel* (1978) and has co-edited with Sarah Sceats *Image and Power: Women in Twentieth Century Fiction*.

Professor Trevor R. Griffiths
is Director of Media and Interdisciplinary Studies at the University of North London, and was the co-editor of *British and Irish Dramatists since 1958*.

Dr Lesley Johnson
is Senior Lecturer in the School of English at the University of Leeds, and was the co-editor of *Feminist Readings in Middle English Literature*

Richard Kirkland
is a Lecturer in English at the University of Keele. He is the author of *Literature and Culture in Northern Ireland since 1965*.

Alison Milbank
is a freelance lecturer at Cambridge University. She is the author of *Daughters of the House; Modes of the Gothic in Victorian Fiction* (1992), and is the editor of *A Sicilian Romance* and *The Castles of Athlin and Dunblayne.*

David Nokes
is a Reader in the Department of English Literature at King's College, University of London, and a Fellow of the Royal Society of Literature (1994). He is the author of *Jonathan Swift; A Hypocrite Reversed* (1985), and with Janet Barron he adapted *Clarissa* for a three-part television serial in 1991.

Dr Ralph Pite
is a Lecturer in English at the University of Liverpool. He is the author of an edition of Henry Cary's translation of Dante's *Divine Comedy* (1994), and *The Circle of Our Vision: Dante's Presence in English Romantic Poetry* (1994).

Roger Pooley
is a Lecturer in English at the University of Keele, and is the author of *English Prose of the 17th Century*.

David Robb
is Senior Lecturer in English at the University of Dundee. He is the author of *George Macdonald* (1987), *God's fiction: Symbolism and allegory in the works of George Macdonald* (1989) and *Muriel Spark's 'The Prime of Miss Jean Brodie'* (1992).

Andrew Michael Roberts
is a Lecturer in English at the University of Dundee. He is the author of *Conrad and Gender* (1993), and has edited *The Bloomsbury Guide to the Novel from its Origins to the Present Day* (1993). He is also an editor of *The Conradian.*

Steven Roberts
is a Lecturer in Hispanic and Latin American Studies at the University of Nottingham. He is currently working on the articles and correspondence of Miguel del Unamuna.

Rick Rylance
is a Professor of English at Anglia Polytechnic University. He is the author of *Debating Text 1987* and *Physiological Theory in British Culture 1850-1880.*

Jonathan Sawday
is a Senior Lecturer in English at the University of Southampton. He is the author of *The Body Emblazoned* (1995), and editor of *Literature and the English Civil War.*

Philip Shaw
is a Lecturer in English at Leicester University. He is currently working on a book on Waterloo and the Romantic Imagination.

Eva Simmons
is a journalist with the BBC. She has contributed to the *Larousse Encyclopaedia – The Age of Reason.*

Jim Simpson
is a Lecturer in the German Department at Liverpool University. He has written on Matthew Arnold and Goethe, and is currently completing a work on Goethe's *Faust.*

Mercer Simpson
was formerly Senior Lecturer at the Polytechnic of Wales, and is now a freelance literary journalist. He was an editor of BWA between 1986 and 1991, and since 1993 he has been a member of the editorial board of the *New Welsh Review*. He has recently published two poetry collections, *East Anglian Wordscapes* (1993), and *Rain from a Clear Blue Sky* (1994).

Douglas Smith
is a Lecturer in French Studies at Warwick University.

Jane Thomas
is a Lecturer in English at Hull University. She is the author of *Essays in Refusal: The Plays of Caryl Churchill* and *The Death of the Playwright.*

Geoff Ward
is Professor of English at the University of Dundee. He has edited *Statutes of Liberty: The New York School of Poets* (1993), *Language, Poetry and the American Avant-garde* (1993), and the *Bloomsbury Guide to Romantic Literature* (1993).

Dr Linda Ruth Williams
is a teacher of film and modern literature at the University of Liverpool. She has written books on psychoanalytic criticism, and on D. H. Lawrence and film. She is now working on body horror cinema, and writing a book on erotic thrillers.

Acknowledgements

As the general editor to the second edition of *The Bloomsbury Guide to English Literature* first and foremost I should like to thank all those who have contributed to the book in its past and present forms. I have learned much from their erudite work and have benefited from their unfailing energies. I should like to thank Tracey Smith of Bloomsbury especially for her enthusiasm and good humour throughout this project. It has been my pleasure and privilege to work with all of them.

The publisher and editors would like to thank the following for their help in the preparation of this edition and their contribution to the project as a whole:

Jennifer Birkett; Kate Bouverie; Marilyn Butler; Katherine Cooley; Paul Crossley; John Drakakis; Richard Dutton; Alison Emmett; Tony Gibb; James Gill; Christopher Gillie; David Grant; Simon Groom; Mary Hamer; Richard Hawley; Alex Hughes; William Humphreys-Jones; Theresa Kemp; Mark Kermode; Sally Kilmister; Angela Leighton; Elizabeth Maslen; Jo Matches; Polly Napper; John O'Brien; John Osborne & Rhiannon; Jenny Parrott; Jane Parsons; Valerie Pedlar; Andrew Piasecki; Kate Quarry; Louise Robbins; Dermot Ryan; Jonathan Sawday; Neil Sinyard; Angela Smallwood; Rona Smith; Andrew Syer; John Thieme; Gareth Wakeham; Rene Weiss; Sue Wiseman; Jessica Wright.

Essay section

Medieval English literature 1

Lesley Johnson

A context for Medieval English literature

For trusteth wel, it is an impossible
That any clerk wol speke good of wyves,
But if it be of hooly seintes lyves,
Ne of noon oother womman never the mo.
Who peyntede the leon, tell me who?
By God! if wommen hadde writen stories,
As clerkes han withinne hie oratories,
They wolde han writen of men moore wikkednesse
Than al the marke of Adam may redresse.
(*The Wife of Bath's Prologue*, 688–696)

When ▷ Chaucer's Wife of Bath recounts her marital experiences with the younger clerk, Jankyn, in her *Prologue* in the ▷ *Canterbury Tales*, her story is focussed on how she confronts the intrusion of his bookish world into her private life. Jankyn, it appears, prefers the company of his book of 'wikked wyves', for him an authoritative source of reference and citation on the subject of marriage, to first-hand marital experience. In fact he substitutes one for the other and gives his wife daily readings from this book, a compilation of anti-matrimonial/anti-feminist writings from medieval and classical Latin sources. For the Wife, the stories reveal less about the experience of marriage and more about the power and prejudices of their (largely) male clerical authors, bound willingly or unwillingly to a celibate life. Her question about who wields the power of the pen is voiced through a quotation from one of ▷ Aesop's fables: 'Who peyntede the leon, tel me who?' In this fable a man tries to use a painting of a man defeating a lion to prove that men are stronger than lions. His lion companion is less impressed with the value of the picture as evidence; the painting itself is a man-made production, and if lions could paint they would offer a different view. The Wife goes on to make a similar point about wives: if they had access to the means of textual representation and production, she points out, they would produce a different image of the 'other' sex. The general point raised by the Wife here, and encapsulated in the question of 'who peyntede the leon', is an important one and applicable to any kind of representation, textual or pictorial, from any period. The answers, though, are rarely as simple and clear-cut as those found in Aesop's fable.

If we were to extend the scope of the Wife's enquiry and consider in a more general way who had access to the means of textual representation in England in the medieval period as a whole, then the Wife's conclusions about those responsible for producing Jankyn's book would still point us in the right direction. Male clerics were the literate professionals of the time. The Christian Church as an institution controlled access to literate skills, just as, of course, it exerted a pervasive influence over all areas of intellectual activity. Literacy was the privilege of the relatively small percentage of the population who formed the ranks of the clergy, and was the privilege of some members of the civil and social élite in society too. Literate women were in the minority within both these social groupings or estates.

But such generalizations about who wielded the balance of pen-power are only useful in so far as they indicate in a rough and ready way the importance of male clerics as mediators of literary culture during the four centuries or so that are traditionally held to constitute the medieval period in England (1100–1500). This clear-cut picture needs to be qualified because not all the writers in medieval England were male clerics, nor was all the literature produced in England written in English. The case of the twelfth-century writer, Marie (conventionally referred to now as ▷ Marie de France), illustrates both points. The literary signature of one 'Marie', who was probably writing in England, is incorporated into the text of a collection of *Lais*, a collection of *Fables* and a religious narrative about St Patrick, all written in French. Evidently at least one woman did leave her mark on the literary culture of her time, although very little else is known about her. But if the fact that we can identify the work of a medieval woman writer is exceptional, the fact that Marie de France was writing, perhaps in England, in French, for audiences in France and England is not. The answers to the question about who is writing and reading in England would vary to some extent according to which language and which period is under consideration.

Latin, ▷ Anglo-Norman French and English were the principal languages in use in England throughout these centuries but their respective domains of usage (as languages of public and religious ritual, law, record, of high-status culture, as vernaculars) varied considerably. Of these languages, Latin remained the language of the highest cultural authority, of the Church and Christian ritual, of academia, the preserve of the clergy. Yet as the domains of usage of the vernaculars expanded greatly in the 400-year period from 1100 to 1500, the clergy ceased to be the sole mediators of texts and textual traditions. Moreover, access to vernacular texts was not restricted to a reading public. Since textual reception was often a social, aural event rather than a private, silent experience, the question about who was reading texts needs to be reformulated as a question about who formed the audiences of literary works. Nor was access to the means of textual representation wholly restricted to the literate: a point strikingly illustrated by the *Book of* ▷ *Margery Kempe*, which is the textual record of the spiritual life of a fourteenth-century English mystic who could neither read nor write, but who dictated her story. In fact to address the question of 'who was painting the lion' during this time in a more satisfactory way would involve a consideration of who would commission artefacts, the relationship of patrons to writers, and the different kinds of relationship between writers, their texts and their audiences. This is a highly satisfactoy set of questions to which we have, at present, only a partial and fragmentary set of answers.

In the sections which follow some indication is given of the different contexts in which medieval English texts were produced and some sense too of the 'difference' of the literary culture itself. This 'difference' is part of the attraction of medieval literature for modern readers and, paradoxically, part of the modernity of medieval literary studies too. Since medieval literature resists being mapped out in terms applied to post-Renaissance literary culture, its study has received fresh impetus as those terms have been challenged over the last thirty years or so. Although the organization of this essay on medieval English literature will link up to the focus of subsequent essays in this volume (considering briefly medieval lyric, narrative and dramatic literary traditions), my emphasis throughout will be on the way in which Middle English text cannot be divided up into discrete literary categories and must be seen as part of a continuum of cultural activity that crosses apparent national, linguistic and literary divides. That spectrum of activity itself may be illustrated in the work of the more famous writers of fourteenth-century England. ⊳ John Gower's literary corpus, for example, uses the three languages of medieval England as its medium: his story collection in English, the ⊳ *Confessio Amantis*, is the final part of a literary triptych of which the first two parts are in French (*Mirour de l'Omme*) and Latin (*Vox Clamantis*). Geoffrey Chaucer's work does not literally cross linguistic divides in this way, but it does challenge any simple notions of separating out categories of literary and non-literary texts. The sheer variety of textual material included in the framework of the *Canterbury Tales* (spanning translations of classical stories, retellings of Christian legends, reworkings of Italian and Old French narratives, stories from 'olde gentil Britouns', performances of sermons and concluding with a prose treatise on penitence) illustrates the range of literary activity at this time and the diversity of the international cultural traditions from which it derives.

The purpose of this essay is not to offer a comprehensive survey, but to illustrate the range of that literary activity and to raise some questions about the term in which it is discussed. The anomalous position of this essay within the *Bloomsbury Guide* itself indicates some of the problems of fitting a discussion of medieval English literature into a wider context. The literary culture I will be considering neither began in 1100 nor ended in 1500, nor was it exclusively insular, although the emphasis, necessarily, will be texts produced during this time in England, in English.

Medieval English lyrics?

Karolles, wrastlinges, or somour games,
Who so evre haunteth any swiche shames
In cherche, other in cherche yerde,
Of sacrilege, he may be aferd;
Of entirludes, or singinge,
Or tabur bete, or other pipinge –
Alle swiche thing forboden es
Whil the preste stondeth at messe.
(Robert Mannyng, *Handlyng Synne*, 8, 991–8)

This general warning against secular diversions from religious observances prefaces a version of the story of the 'Dancers of Colbeck' in ⊳ Robert Mannyng's penitential guide *Handlyng Synne*. The story neatly illustrates the dire consequences of sacrilegious distractions, for it concerns a group of carollers who are cursed by their priest for disturbing Mass. As a result of the curse, the group find they cannot stop performing their carol in the churchyard until, having sung and danced for a whole year, they collapse at the end of their ordeal. If this story of the 'Dancers of Colbeck' allows us to glimpse the existence of a popular, secular tradition of song-making (and 'entirlude'-making too), it also illustrates the way in which we have access to that tradition only through clerical mediation of one kind or another. Snatches and fragments of English ⊳ lyrics which appear to belong to a popular tradition are preserved in sermons, chronicles and exemplary narratives, but for the most part the short poems and lyrics preserved in manuscripts are the product of learned and literary environments, and not the records of performances in churchyards. Yet that does not mean that the extant texts of poems and lyrics represent a homogeneous body of work. In fact, generalizations about their form and function are very difficult to make, such is the diversity of their range.

First, how do we recognize a medieval lyric text? Is it a literary category composed exclusively of texts designed to be sung to musical accompaniment? Or short, non-narrative texts in verse, or poems with a predominantly personal focus on a secular or religious theme? All of these kinds of texts can be found in modern editions of medieval English lyrics. The diversity of these lyric collections partly reflects the very different ways in which the term lyric can be used now. However, the very act of extracting these short poems from their manuscript text may give the impression that the literary category of 'the medieval English lyric' is more homogeneous than it really is. Some of the earliest Middle English lyrics are religious lyrics embedded as quotations in Latin sermons or are preserved in various kinds of preaching manuals, and seem to have served the ends of preaching and teaching lay audiences (the sermons themselves being preached in English). Some lyrics are collected together in manuscripts which appear to be the medieval equivalents of modern 'literary anthologies' (such as the famous manuscript, now in the British Library, known as ▷ Harley 2253). Others are squeezed as 'space-fillers' into manuscripts containing miscellaneous collections of material or preserved on scraps of parchment, and so survive for us with little indication of any contextual relations. Some musical notations are preserved, but by no means all, and it is not always clear exactly how a text is to be performed or received; in public or in private or perhaps in public and in private. This limpid twelve-line version of the Crucifixion has some of the features which would fit post-medieval definitions of lyric poetry: it is short, has an emotional focus and a first-person speaker:

Quanne hic se on rode (When I, Cross)
Jesu, mi lemman, (lover)
And besiden him stonden
Marie and Johan,
And his rig iswongen, (back scourged)
And his side istungen, (pierced)
For the luve of man,
Well ou hic to wepen, (ought)
And sinnes forleten, (abandon)
Yif hic of luve kan, (know)
Yif hic of luve kan,
Yif hic of luve kan.

But this text is not so much offering an expression of a personal experience (to adapt ▷ John Ruskin's nineteenth-century definition of a lyric), as providing a model exercise for one. The first seven lines deftly conjure up an emotive image of the Crucifixion, the last five reveal what should be the emotional response of any individual to this sight: the image is offered as a personal test of love (the logic is 'When...Then...If'). Several versions of this piece survive and one of them is preserved as a quotation in a thirteenth-century sermon text. The use of this poem in a sermon illustrates how medieval lyrics may be used to mediate between private experience and its public expression in different contexts, in different ways. In this case the poem is received, in public, for a performance in private, when the devotional exercise it sketches may be enacted. The sermon context explicitly links the poem to the clerical promotion of a devotional and empathetic kind of spirituality (and the poem itself is a translation of a Latin devotional exercise). This is a spiritual trend which is increasingly in evidence in Middle English religious literature from the twelfth century onwards, and for which the lyric form provided a particularly suitable medium of expression.

More religious lyrics survive in Middle English than secular lyrics: this is a phenomenon which, perhaps, reflects both the 'usefulness of lyrical texts as preaching and teaching devices and the predominance of Anglo-Norman as the medium for sophisticated secular culture for much of the medieval period in England. But it would be wrong to give the impression that the diverse range of Middle English lyric poems which survive can be divided into clear-cut sacred and secular categories. There is a considerable interaction between the language and the conventions of sacred and carnal love-lyrics, as even the short lyric (quoted above) suggests in its address to Jesus as a lover. Indeed, many of the Middle English poems on religious themes use a conventional language of loving drawn from a body of love poetry (a development of French literary culture of the eleventh and twelfth centuries) which celebrates the refined pleasures and pains of 'fin'amur' (▷ Courtly Love) between the sexes. The notions of using a language of carnal love as a way of expressing a spiritual relationship has a precedent in the exegetical convention of reading the Old Testament *Song of Songs* as an account of the relationship between Christ, the bridgegroom, and the Church, his bride. Using conventionalized models or refined earthly relationships to recommend (and explore) spiritual relationships is a key strategy employed in many kinds of medieval religious texts including lyrics.

What is interesting about this overlapping use of sacred and secular languages of desire is that conventionalized gender roles may be treated in rather less conventional ways in religious texts. Whereas (as might be expected) male first-person speakers predominate in the secular love lyrics, and women tend to figure more often as objects of desire rather than as desiring subjects, the gender roles in religious texts may be more fluid. Not all first-person religious love lyrics are marked as the expression of male speakers, and there are some examples of female subjects being presented as active lovers (albeit under paternal instruction). In the thirteenth-century 'Love Ron', for example, conventionally attributed to the Franciscan ▷ Thomas of Hales, a young woman is given advice in the art of spiritual loving. Couched in the form of a verse epistle from a male advisor, the twenty-seven stanzas of this text offer advice to a religious woman on how to choose the best possible lover: the candidate for that role is never explicitly named by the speaker, but is clearly identifiable from his attributes as Christ himself. The self-conscious literary quality of this religious lyric is evident in its use of the art of loving for spiritual ends, and in the way it negotiates between the private and public nature of instruction it offers. It is both a personal and a public communication, addressed to a single woman and yet sent 'open and with-ute sel' (seal), so other women may have access to it; indeed the recipient is asked to pass it on to other maidens. The last stanza acknowledges the written and performative qualities of this text, as it is a letter for singing in moments of longing:

> *Hwenne thu sittest in longynge,*
> *Drauh the forth this ilke writ;* (Draw, same writing)
> *Mid swete stephne thu hit singe,* (voice)
> *& do al so hit the bit.* (it bids you)

The 'Love Ron' provides a literary distraction for spiritual instruction and it is one of a group of early English texts, including the ▷ *Ancrene Wisse*, which are produced for, and addressed to, an audience of women who have chosen the religious life.

Our contact with medieval English literature necessarily depends on the vagaries of manuscript survival. This point is underlined by the fact that approximately half the extant texts of English secular lyrics are preserved in a single manuscript, Harley 2253, a literary anthology produced some time in the 1340s, in the Hereford area. But in this context, too, the interplay between sacred and secular literary registers is very clear; indeed some of the lyrics in the collection seem to have been physically arranged in a way which heightens the interplay between the sacred and secular poems. Thus a lyric on Christ's love for his people beginning 'Litel wot hit any man/ how love hym haveth i-bounde' is followed by one which begins in a similar way, 'Litel wot hit any man/how derne love may stǫnde': the addition of the word 'derne' (secret) signals both a change of context and referent as this lyric becomes the complaint of a disappointed male lover. But the language of sacred and carnal desire may also be played off, self-consciously, within a single text, as is the case with 'The Fair Maid of Ribblesdale'. Here, the cumulative effect of a series of religious references is to both elevate and undercut a male speaker's fantasy about a desirable woman.

A range of speaking stances is found within the love lyrics of the Harley collection: there are complaints, petitions, descriptions of reported or imagined encounters in the voice of first-person (male) speakers, but there are dialogue forms too. A wooing game is played out in one lyric (conventionally entitled '*De Clerico et Puella*' – 'About a Clerk and a Girl') between a clerical speaker who has a courtly repertoire of love-sick poses at his command and a young woman who has an equally adept command of deflationary replies. Yet the shorter poems in the collection do not merely address religious and secular emotional subjects: some encapsulate proverbial, monitory material (such as those warning of the last days); one is a poetic rendering of the parable of the vineyard while a couple address topical, contemporary issues and events (such as the corruption of the consistory courts or the death of ▷ Edward I).

The sheer variety of material and poetic forms in the Harley collection raises questions about how they can best be presented to a modern audience. Not one of the Harley lyrics is attributed to a named poet, and in this respect they are typical of much Middle English literature in general, which is working within a literary tradition that is not concerned with the promotion of literary personalities as such. So if the texts cannot be arranged as the work of particular poets or 'makers', should they then be sorted out according to their material (as love lyrics, as historical and religious poems – as has been the case in past editions), or does the very juxtaposition of diverse poems in the manuscript itself have an interest? The case of the Harley lyrics also illustrates the limitation of approaching medieval English literature solely in terms of the literature written in English, because the collection includes many short poems written in Anglo-Norman; indeed one of the religious lyrics alternates lines in English and Anglo-Norman. If these poems are the product of a bilingual literary culture of some sophistication, then should they not be presented in that context? But the Harley manuscript does not only contain shorter poems in English and Anglo-Norman, but verse narratives too, some religious narratives in Anglo-Norman and Latin prose, and even a collection of recipes in English prose, which have evidently been squeezed on to a blank leaf (including recipes on such matters as how to make iron as hard as steel).

I suggested earlier that the Harley manuscript is a medieval equivalent of a modern literary anthology, but that may be an unhelpful analogy: it is not a book written for national distribution; it is written in one of the 'Englishes' of the time (there being as yet no written standard form of the language); it reflects a regional culture of some sophistication and linguistic plurality, but it is not presented as the work of any single 'maker' or group; its composition shows that poetic form could equally provide the medium for vernacular narrative as prose (a selection of the poetry in the manuscript could include the Middle English romance ▷ *King Horn*). It is a collection which challenges some of the conventional ways in which modern texts may be organized and the terms in which they are discussed, as does that more famous book of medieval narrative poetry and prose, *The Canterbury Tales*.

Narrative poetry

III *Hwer is Paris & Heleyne*
That werenso bryht & fyre on bleo, (of face)
Amadas & Dideyne,
Tristram, Yseude and alle theo,
Ector, with his scharpe meyene, (strength)
& Cesar, riche of wordes feo?
Heo beoth i-gliden ut of the reyne
So the schef is of the cleo. (sheaf, from the cornfield)
(Thomas of Hales, 'Love Ron', 65–72)

The connections between the figures of Paris and Helen, Amadas and Idoine, Tristram and Iseult, Hector and Caesar, in the stanza of the 'Love Ron' quoted above is that these figures, drawn from different periods of the past, may illustrate the very transcience of all earthly achievements and pleasures. Presumably, though, the citation is effective because the stories of all these figures are still remembered and retold. It is useful to approach the rich narrative traditions of medieval England with some sense of the important generative story-areas, and ▷ Thomas of Hales' roll-call of names indicates some of these primary narrative subjects drawn from the stories of ▷ Troy, Rome, Gaul and Britain. The reference to Tristram and Iseult perhaps stands out here as being especially resonant of an important subject of medieval narrative (being part of the ▷ Arthurian tradition) and of an important medieval narrative form (the so-called ▷ romance) which deserve to be given special attention as an innovative part of medieval literary culture, and both subject and form will be discussed in due course. There is, however, some critical confusion over the meaning and use of the term 'romance', some of which may be avoided if the genre is aproached as part of a wider spectrum of narrative activity in which stories of Greece, Troy, Britain, and Gaul all have a place.

Translating and reworking Latin classical narratives (such as those of ▷ Thebes, Troy, ▷ Alexander the Great) in the vernacular is an important part of the literary activity of the medieval period. The same is true of English Renaissance literary culture; indeed, one important dimension of English literary cultre as a whole is its continual re-engagement with classical texts. But medieval modes of assimilating, transmitting and renewing classical culture may appear rather surprising to a modern audience whose reading habits have been shaped by the Renaissance and post-Renaissance literary ▷ humanist tradition. The medieval versions of these classical stories themselves may be unfamiliar (the medieval Troy story, for example, tends to follow a chronological design, have a strong pro-Trojan slant and focus on Hector as the greatest hero of the war), but more disorientating still for modern readers of medieval 'classics' such as ▷ Chaucer's ▷ *Knight's Tale*, the alliterative ▷ *Destruction of Troy* or *Kyng Alisaunder* is the way in which classical culture is filtered through feudal and chivalric lenses. Theseus, Hector and Alexander don the armour of the knight. In part, the assimilation of the key narratives of the classical past in the medieval period, the act of translating them into the vernacular (into French and Anglo-Norman from the twelfth century, into Middle English from the thirteenth century onwards), involved transforming some aspects of classical culture to reflect the dominant feudal/chivalric ideals of the 'present', and so to endow these ideals with the authority of the 'past'. Medieval narratives relating the Greek, Trojan and Roman past contributed substantially to the establishment of a mythology of chivalry which was developed through the medieval period and continued long after it.

The courtly patina given to medieval versions of the classics was not an unself-conscious action on the part of medieval writers. In Chaucer's *Knight's Tale*, for example, the narrator both suggests that a continuing chivalric ethos connects the world of classical Athens and that of contemporary England, but also draws attention to the potential incongruity involved in the act of representing this continuous chivalric culture. Such is the splendour of the tournament which Theseus organizes in Athens that every knight 'Were it in Engelond or elleswhere,/They wode, hir thankes, wilnen to be there' (2,113–4). But the narrator points up the anachronism of this depiction of the 'modern' chivalric world of classical Athens: when some of the knights in Athens set their sights on fashionable gear (Prussians shields!), the narrator wryly remarks on the fact that 'Ther is no newe gyse that it nas old'.

Of course not all aspects of the 'olde gyse' of classical pagan culture could be assimilated to the values and ethos of the Christian present; medieval writers were faced with great interpretative challenges when re-presenting narratives about the classical world (and material drawn from the world of classical learning). Highly elaborate strategies were evolved for reinterpreting pagan structures for contemporary audiences. The pagan framework of the *Knight's Tale* is part of the 'olde gyse' of the story, which no longer has any place in the 'newe', but it is not used as the occasion for Christian moralizing or denunciation (which is sometimes the case in other medieval versions of classical stories). Rather, the pagan gods in the *Knight's Tale* are made to function both as representatives of larger forces outside human control and government, and of those human desires and promptings which are potentially controllable by government on both a political and personal level. All the central characters of the narrative, Palamon, Arcite, Emily, Theseus, and Ageus too, have their counterparts in the pagan divinities, and these gods are interpreted as figuring abstracted human passions and powers of some kind. The gods are agents in the narrative and act on the central human figures, but they also provide a means of analysing the actions and desires of the characters themselves when faced with problems of self-government and, in the case of Theseus, the government of others.

The classical, chivalric world of the *Knight's Tale* provides an arena for exploring the interaction between the forces of individual human desire and those of the larger social, political and universal world of which they form a part. Some of the difficulties of putting into practice the conduct-book rules for knights and knight-princes are traced in this narrative, which illustrates the way in which the world of the pagan past may be used to explore, not merely to affirm and exemplify, codes of conduct.

Reworking the narratives of the past offered medieval writers considerable interpretative challenges and innovative possibilities: not only could traditional narratives be refracted through diferent kinds of generic frames in their retelling, but also new narrative subjects could be opened up within classical, historical frames. The story of ▷ Troilus and Criseyde itself is a medieval 'invention', the story of ▷ Palamon and Arcite in the *Knight's Tale* is another. In both ▷ *Troilus and Criseyde* and the *Knight's Tale*, Chaucer used narratives taken from ▷ Boccaccio to develop a new generic frame for treating classical histories, in which large-scale events were refracted through a microscosmic focus on pairs of lovers. But classical history was not the only prestigious subject for narrative development during the medieval centuries. There is, for example, a large number of Middle English narratives focussed around the activities of ▷ Charlemagne and members of his illustrious court. In these narratives, largely derived from Old French versions, chivalry serves the ends of the Christian faith, and the opposition between pagan and Christian culture (with the transforming possibility of conversion rather than extinction) provides the basic narrative and metaphysical structure of these texts. But it is, perhaps, the opening up of a new history of Britain in the twelfth century that proves to be one of the most striking and productive areas for the creation of vernacular narrative traditions, in verse and later in prose, in the medieval period.

The appearance, some time around 1138, of ▷ Geoffrey of Monmouth's ▷ *Historia Regum Britannie* (*History of the Kings of Britain*) made a significant contribution to opening up the subject of British history for narrative elaboration. This text recounts the sequence of British kings from the foundation of the kingdom of Britain by Brutus, the great-grandson of ▷ Aeneas, to the demise of British rule and the establishment of Saxon control over the island. The reign of ▷ King Arthur marks the high point of British history, for it is during this time that the island is re-established as a unified Christian nation, and becomes a great international power and chivalric centre attracting knights from all over the world. Although Geoffrey of Monmouth was not the first to suggest that British society had classical roots, he was the first to depict the illustrious history of the island in such detail and, in fact, to represent British history in a way that explores some of the political, social and cultural ideals of the twelfth century itself.

Among Geoffrey of Monmouth's academic peers and predecessors, in the early decades of the twelfth century, there was a marked interest in recovering the history of England and in bridging the gap between the narrative history provided by ▷ Bede (and the later Saxon chroniclers) and that of the twelfth-century present. Geoffrey of Monmouth's contribution to this historiographical movement was not to recover the history of Saxon and post-Conquest England but to 'recover' a marvellous pre-history. In developing his account of a relatively undocumented period of insular history, Geoffrey of Monmouth took the opportunity to comment on some aspects of the politics and values of his own, turbulent time. Establishing the political function of this act of historical fabrication (or for that matter the political function of the newly constructed histories of England) is not a simple matter, but, at the very least, a powerful argument for unified rule of the island may be drawn from Geoffrey of Monmouth's history, which is the first requirement if the English kingdom of the 'present' is to live up to the glorious achievements of its British 'past'.

Although the value of Monmouth's account (which considerably disrupted some of the established traditions of English historiography) was challenged by subsequent clerical historians, its influence was immense. Vernacular versions appeared from the mid-twelfth century onwards, and one of the earliest and most substantial verse narratives composed in Middle English, the thirteenth-century *Brut* composed by ▷ Laȝamon, is a reworking of the Monmouth tradition of British history. The way in which retelling the history of the island's past may offer a medium for investigating the cultural politics of its present may be seen in the *Brut*: this very act of retelling insular history in English, with its contrived archaic overtones, seems to be an assertion of a cultural continuity in a land which has 'i-gon from honde to honde', from Brutus' kin to 'Englisce men' and then to 'tha Frensca'.

But if Geoffrey of Monmouth gave Britain a new image and British history a new status, vernacular writers in France and England in the twelfth century opened up other areas of the British cultural heritage for formal literary treatment. The story of ▷ Tristan and Iseult has no place in the design of Monmouth's narrative, which is oriented around regnal history, but it is part of the pre-Saxon British/Celtic narrative store which French writers such as Béroul, ▷ Chrétien de Troyes and ▷ Marie de France drew on for the development of new literary subjects and from which they developed new narrative forms. It is very difficult for us, today, to recreate some sense of this ephemeral oral, Celtic tradition. However, the range of motifs, themes and subjects which Marie de France, in the late twelfth century, claims to derive from oral British traditions at least suggests that a figure like Arthur did not monopolize this tradition, and probably did not play a large part in it. Rather, vernacular writers from the mid-twelfth century onwards drew on story motifs from British/Celtic traditions to develop a corpus of narratives orientated around the chivalric ▷ Golden Age of Arthur's court, which could be given a historical location too, thanks to Geoffrey of Monmouth's historiographical efforts. Arthurian narrative, like much British historiography itself, is essentially the product of the post-Conquest period.

What seems to happen is that for writers in medieval France and England, Britain becomes a literary landscape where different narrative traditions may be located and where, for example, a historically placed Christian society may encounter otherworldly, magical forces which reflect the remnants of non-Christian cultures. The fourteenth-century verse narrative ▷ *Sir Gawain and the Green Knight* illustrates how brilliantly the narrative potential of the overlapping historical and literary landscapes of Britain may be played off against each other. The impression of Britain rising out of the ashes of Troy, which frames *Sir Gawain and the Green Knight*, offers a resonant image of the way in which new narrative areas are opened up during the period, as material from Celtic and other, hitherto, oral traditions was reworked in literary media and given formal literary status. Aeneas, Brutus, Gawain, and the Green Knight, unlikely as it may seem, form part of a narrative continuum.

I have avoided using the term 'romance' up to this point in favour of the more general term 'narrative'. Partly this is because the term 'romance', like that of 'lyric', has been used in so many different ways – both as a historically specific term and as a literary universal – that its discriminatory value is doubtful at times. The term 'romance' may still perform a useful critical function if, however, it is used of narratives *structured* in certain ways. Chivalric settings are an integral feature of medieval narratives on a wide range of subjects, with the result that the use of a chivalric/feudal setting, and the invocation of the attendant values of that milieu, are intrinsic, but not necessarily distinctive, features of 'romance'.

What is distinctive about the specific category of narratives that I would recognize as romances is that they are focussed around displaced (predominantly male) protagonists, whose social identity and status are treatened in a series of 'adventures', and who survive to reintegrate into society as members of an élite group. The structural pattern is essentially that of estrangement, risk and recovery, which is played out in a providentially ordered world in which all things shall be well, finally, for those who embody the values of the chivalric élite which are theirs by birth. The degree to which Christian providence is recognized explicitly as a controlling force in the fortunes of the protagonists is a variable factor, which is obviously related to the homiletic emphasis of the narrative as a whole.

The romances which are structured around the stories of displaced women, such as *Emaré*, and the ▷ *Man of Law's Tale* of Constance, strongly promote the notion of a providentially controlled world in which a Christian god protects those who have faith and are constant in adversity. Emaré's adventures, as the narrator points out, are firmly under providential direction: when she is put out to sea, because she resists her father's incestuous advances, 'She was dryven into a lond/Thorow the grace of Goddes sond,/That all thyng may fulfylle'. The Amazons of the classical past have few descendants in the female protagonists of medieval romance, whose virtues are predominantly those of suffering and passivity.

While this abstracted romance paradigm may provide a useful starting point for considering the 60 or so extant examples of Middle English romances (such as ⊳ *Guy of Warwick* ⊳ *Bevis of Hampton*) which make up such an important part of the vernacular narrative corpus, it is also evident from this corpus that the basic structural paradigm may be developed and refined in various ways. The episodic structure of the form, built up around sequences of adventures, gives it considerable flexibility: sequences may easily be added and interwoven to create more complex narrative structures. Indeed, what is interesting about medieval romances is the way in which variables within and beyond that basic paradigm are played out in particular narratives; the way in which generic frames may be played off against each other; the way in which the form may be used to investigate, not merely affirm, ethical codes. When Guy of Warwick, for example, has earned himself a place in the social structure, and won his wife through his chivalric prowess, the framework of values in which the narrative is working shifts to that of a transcendental Christian ethos. The narrative goes on to chart his displacement from worldly pursuits in general and his actions, thereafter, are entirely in the service of the Christian faith: the genre of romance is contiguous, here, with that of the saint's life,

The possible dimensions of the romance world in general, and the world of Arthurian romance in particular, are well exemplifed in the encyclopaedia of romance forms, in prose, which constitutes ⊳ Malory's ⊳ *Morte D'Arthur*. Here, a sequence of romance narratives is inset within a broader tragic-historic frame. The inset romances are structurally varied (some are longer and interlaced in more complex ways than others), and not all work within the same set of values. In the Quest of the Holy Grail, most notably, two different kinds of chivalric orders confront each other as a transcendent model of chivalric activity subverts the code of behaviour so carefully established through the adventures of the ⊳ Round Table knights. The series of adventures radiate out from Arthur's court and yet form part of a sequence, too, with some consequential impetus. The result is the construction of a vast narrative web, which charts the rise, consolidation and, ultimately, the fall of Arthurian society, and which defies any attempt to account for the downfall of Arthur's reign in terms of a single causal structure. In abbreviating and unlocking some of the complex strands of the larger French cycle which formed his principal source, Malory has made the relationship between actions and their consequences much more mysterious. In a world in which any individual has an imperfect knowledge of the circumstances in which she/he is operating, and lacks control over the consequences of their actions, the only measure of action becomes its adherence to a chivalric code of behaviour. But it is precisely the form and scope of that ethical code which are investigated in the epic sequence of Malory's *Morte D'Arthur* as a whole.

The spectrum of the uses (and perhaps abuses) of romance narratives and their engagement with other kinds of narrative genres (epic, saints' lives, ⊳ fabliau) is revealed in the romance collection incorporated in the *Canterbury Tales*. Alongside the epic-romance structure of the *Knight's Tale* set in classical Athens (which is set off against the fabliau imitation which follows), there is the embryonic romance-epic of the ⊳ *Squire's Tale* (situated in the marvellous east); the ⊳ Man of Law's homiletic

Tale of Constance (which moves between the world of Christian Rome and pagan societies in the east and west); Chaucer's burlesque tale of ▹ *Sir Thopas* which, though nominally set in Flanders, takes the world of romance conventions and motifs as its subject and its setting; and finally the ▹ Wife of Bath's Arthurian romance which provides a provocative analysis of sexual politics.

This Arthurian text opens with a teasing play on the idea of cultural continuity between present and past societies, which may provide both a point of return to the opening subject of this section and a point of transition to the next. The Wife begins her tale with a meditation on the relationship between the inhabitants of Britain in the 'olde dayes of King Artour' and now. The ▹ fairies and elves who once filled the land, she suggests, have been both exorcized and replaced by the wandering friars, who like the fairies can now be found 'in every bussh or under every tree'. It is to the kind of literary material produced by these wandering friars and other clerics that I shall now turn.

Pastoral literature and drama

Men yernen gestes for to here
And romaunce rede in diverse manere:
Of Alisaunder the conqueroure;
Of Julius Cesar the emperoure;
Of Grece & Troye the longe strif
There mony mon lost his lif;
Of Bruit that baroun bolde of honde
Furste conqueroure of Engelonde;
Of King Arthour that was so riche...
Mony songes of diverse ryme
As Englisshe, Frensshe, & Latyne –
To rede & here mony are prest
Of things that hem liketh best.
. . . by that thing mon draweth tille,
Men may him knowe for good or ille.

(*Cursor Mundi*, 1–46)

The opening strategy of the narrator of ▹ *Cursor Mundi*, a versified history of the world from Creation to Doomsday, is to suggest that a person's literary tastes (whether for material heard or read) are a sign of their moral and spiritual quality. Reading or hearing the stories of Alexander, Troy, Arthur, etc. is not explicitly criticized by the narrator of the *Cursor Mundi*, but the implication of the opening section is that this monumental account of Christian history offers a morally and spiritually profitable alternative to spending time on 'Stories of diverse thinges', told in 'diverse manere', in 'diverse ryme'. The alternative fare offered by this narrative, which 'courses' over the history of the world (hence its name), is an account of the ▹ Seven Ages of the World, from the first age of creation to the seventh age, which will be heralded by the coming of the 'Antichrist' and end with the Day of Judgement – the 'end' of Christian history as such. Material for this history, first compiled in English around 1300, is drawn not only from the Vulgate version of the scriptures but from supplementary material in apochryphal sources, from scriptural commentaries in Latin, biblical paraphrases, collections of saints' lives and manuals of Christian doctrine and instruction. A text such as the *Cursor Mundi* gives a literate lay audience access to a body of Christian texts and textual traditions which had been developed and consolidated within the monastic culture of the preceding centuries. It is both the product and a sign of the great pastoral movement which can be traced back to Anglo-Saxon England but which, particularly from the thirteenth century onwards, left an enormous corpus of religious instructional material in its wake.

A wide range of instructional material survives from the medieval period, addressed to different audiences and tackling different areas of Christian teaching: some texts provided the clergy with resources for lay instruction (through the medium of sermons) and guidance for pastoral care; other manuals apparently offered lay audiences direct instruction in how to cultivate their spiritual welfare by explaining the process of penitence (such as in Chaucer's ▷ *Parson's Tale*) or by providing instruction in Christian history (such as the *Cursor Mundi*).

This body of Christian literature (or 'pastoralia') did not exist in a religious vacuum but engaged with the wider spectrum of literary activity of which it formed part and which it influenced in its turn. A dramatic illustration of this engagement can be taken from the *Canterbury Tales*, where figures such as the Friar, the Nun's Priest and the Pardoner deploy the tools of their trade in the construction of tales for a story-telling competition. Though teaching was not, of course, an activity open to medieval women, the Wife of Bath borrows sermonizing techniques to organize the story of her life and lend support to her stance as a secular apologist, thus earning the title of 'noble prechour' from the Pardoner. The Pardoner himself introduces his pilgrim audience to the rhetorical art of sermonizing as he demonstrates the range of linguistic, textual and performance skills that make up his professional routine. According to the Pardoner, lay audiences 'loven tales olde/ Swiche thynges kan they wel reporte and holde' – a point borne out by his own preaching practice and affirmed by the contents of contemporary story collections compiled for preaching purposes.

Such practices of mining all kinds of literary resources for spiritual ends (favoured by the mendicant orders) was not unanimously approved by all sectors of the clergy; indeed, for Chaucer's Parson, literary fictions and 'moralitee and vertuous mateere' are incompatible. His contribution to the *Canterbury Tales* – a prose treatise on the process of penitence – both formally closes the proceedings and actually stops the story-telling game. The Parson's contribution is appropriate, perhaps, for a literary excursion that is nearing the end of the road in all senses. Yet it is clear from considering the *Parson's Tale* within the wider context of the Canterbury collection that the modes and material of spiritual guidance are not necessarily incompatible with those of secular entertainment and instruction. The Parson's rejection of the value of fables and 'switch wreccednesse' represents one position within a wider spectrum of opinion on the value of certain kinds of religious literature in particular and fictionalizing activity in general.

The alliterative poems attributed to the ▷ Gawain poet, composed some time in the late fourteenth century, offer a different view to that of Chaucer's Parson. The poems ▷ *Cleaness* and ▷ *Patience* are both structured in ways which reflect the influence of exegetical practices of reading and interpreting the Scriptures, and use those techniques to explore the interlocking nature of Christian virtues. But whereas *Patience* is focussed around the amplification and explication of a single Old Testament story (that of Jonah and the Whale), the narrative of *Cleaness* draws on more complex sermonizing techniques to investigate the lessons of Christian etiquette, through the retelling of the parable of the Wedding Feast and a further sequence of Old Testament stories. The juxtaposition of these two poems addressing the subject of Christian virtue with the brilliant reworking of Arthurian romance tradition, *Sir*

Gawain and the Green Knight, in the same manuscript, suggests that the story of Jonah and the adventures of Gawain do not necessarily belong to mutually exclusive contexts of either literary production or reception.

But it is perhaps the fourth poem in this manuscript, ▷ *Pearl*, which illustrates a merging of Christian and courtly poetics in the most spectacular way. For here the poet uses the fictional frame of a ▷ dream-vision poem as a way of approaching revelation: St John's vision of New Jerusalem in *Revelations* is incorporated into the final sections of this dream poem. The dream-vision genre traditionally offered medieval poets the licence to speculate and explore the interaction between inner and outer worlds in a fictional form. But what is remarkable about this poem is the sheer ambition of its attempt to represent the process by which an individual may come to terms with the prospect of a Christian afterlife, and literally realize and see the vision described by St John in the Bible. The occasion of the poem is one of extreme love-longing, figured in the male narrator's account of his mourning for his pearl, his most precious object, which is described in terms which suggest it represents a female form. The movement of the spiritual 'aventure' which follows is measured by the narrator's ability to see the pearl in different ways, as its possible sphere of reference expands. That expansion is figured in the form of the poem itself, in the concatenating design of every stanza and the linking pattern of the stanzas as a whole, which embodies a pearl shape. The resources of poetic and linguistic artifice, and of Christian techniques for interpreting and explicating the Scriptures, are combined in this poetic narrative, which asserts, in its very form, that fictional making and poetic artifice may serve as a wholly fitting medium for 'virtuous mateere'.

The resources and traditions of Christian teaching and preaching, described above, provide the context for some of the important vernacular dramatic traditions of late medieval England. Most of the surviving evidence for dramatic performances relates to religious drama, and this extant material is generally categorized according to whether its subject is the macrocosmic sweep of Christian history (as found in the ▷ cycle plays, sometimes referred to as 'mystery plays'), or the microcosmic history of an individual human soul (as found in the texts classed as ▷ morality plays). Texts from the first category are the remains of a widespread tradition of Christian urban drama in which select episodes from the cycle of Christian history from Creation to Doomsday were played out in the streets of towns such as York, Chester and Wakefield, which provide the settings for three of the four play cycles which survive. The textual background to this kind of dramatic tradition is provided by works such as the ▷ *Cursor Mundi*, in which a wide range of scriptural, apochryphal and instructional material is merged into a narrative of Christian history.

Considerable resources were required to make Christian history course through the streets of towns, and craft and religious guilds within the towns provided a key organizational structure for play productions. Enacting the play-cycles seems to have served both religious and civic functions: at the same time as the cycle plays celebrate the plan of Christian history, the resources and civic order of these large urban centres are evidently on display too. It is perhaps the community function of cycle drama that helps explain its survival. Performances of the cycles continued even when the religious climate became hostile to some of the doctrinal points they embodied, surviving well into the period traditionally demarcated as that of the 'Renaissance' in England: the last recorded performance of the Coventry plays were in 1579; those of Chester and York in 1569 and 1575, respectively.

If the cycle plays are an enactment of monumental Christian history, the morality plays can be seen as the dramatization of the inner history of a single soul. Whereas cycle drama sees its mundane setting as a prop in recreating a universal, cosmic playing area, the morality plays use dramatic space as an arena for mapping out the history of an inner life, or interior processes, which are less historically specific than typical and exemplary, as the names of their central characters (Everyman, Mankind, Humanum Genus) indicate. The register for morality plays such as the ▷ *Castle of Perseverance* and ▷ *Everyman* echoes that of the penitential manuals designed to provide Christians with a framework for diagnosing and correcting their inner spiritual states, and understanding the mechanics of temptation and sin. This is an analytical vocabulary built of components such as the ▷ Seven Deadly Sins and their corresponding virtues, the World, the Flesh and the Devil. It was not the only register of psychological analysis available to medieval writers: an elaborate descriptive scheme had been developed around the process of falling in love (strongly influenced by ▷ Ovid), and both of these psychological schemes (penitential and amorous) are an important element in the poetic narratives written in the dream-vision mode. But if dream-vision poetry offered a narrative space for the exploration and analysis of inner processes, the morality plays occupied this space in the dramatic tradition of late medieval England, embodying inner life and abstract modes of analysis in dramatic forms.

Although the cycle drama/morality play division offers a starting point for discussing religious drama in English, not all vernacular drama can be neatly slotted into these two categories. The focal points and interests of their cycle drama and morality plays are not mutually exclusive. The so-called ▷ 'N-Town' cycle, for example, combines the representation of Christian history with moral analysis, with the result that personified abstractions, such as 'Mors' (Death) or 'Contemplacio' (Contemplation), occupy the stage alongside figures from Christian history. Unlike the cycle drama of York, Chester and Wakefield, the N-Town sequence of plays seems not to have been designed for processional performance by guild members, and employs a much wider range of dramatic techniques for mediating the literal and symbolic narrative of Christian history.

Historical and moral perspectives could be combined in the 'Saints' Plays' of the period. Few examples of these plays survive, but the text of ▷ *Mary Magdalene* provides an example of how the historical narrative of an individual life may be turned into exemplary drama: Mary's 'fall' into 'wantoness' is represented in this play by the infiltration of the 'Bad Angel' and 'Lady Lechery' into the castle of Maudelyn. The so-called 'Creed' plays and 'Pater-Noster' plays seem to have combined dramatization of moral analysis and episodes from Christian history, too, in dramatic performances which sought to affirm and explain the power of the Lord's Prayer and the Creed. No scripts of these plays survive, but their contents can be recreated partially from records of their performance in York, Beverly and Lincoln. Clearly our picture of medieval dramatic traditions is very much dependent on the vagaries of the evidence that has survived, and much has been lost.

The spectrum of dramatic activity in medieval England is broader than that represented by plays composed in English. A tradition of Latin Church drama (that is, of acting out parts of the liturgy at key times in the Church year), continues throughout the period, and sophisticated examples of Anglo-Norman religious drama (such as the play known as ▷ *Adam*) survive from the twelfth century. Nor is the drama of medieval England wholly orientated around religious subjects, but as might be expected, far less evidence survives of secular play-making and performing than that of religious drama. Yet of the few English play texts to survive from before the fifteenth century, two of the earliest (the fragmentary account of a meeting between a clerk and a maiden and the text known as ▷ *Dame Sirith*) are humorous and concerned with love problems and tricks.

Records of accounts from noble households suggest that the playing of interludes was an important form of medieval performance art, although little evidence survives of the form and nature of these plays. We have little more idea of the nature of the interlude performed by Jakke Travail in 1427 for ▷ Henry VI than of the popular tradition of interlude-making mentioned by Robert Mannyng in his account of the 'Dancers of Colbeck'. It would be fair to say that a large part of the dramatic activity of medieval England is off the record – or only traceable indirectly through records of civic accounts, household accounts or ecclesiastical prohibitions of various kinds. But it is also fair to suggest that the boundaries between drama and other modes of literary reception were less absolute than now.

The dramatic quality of much medieval narrative, and the dramatic circumstances of its public mediation, undercut distinctions between drama and other literary media, between public and private reading experiences and performances. All kinds of vernacular narratives bear the formalized signals of performance texts ('Herkneth to me'). So the spectrum of medieval performance art is wide and may encompass sermons, readings, recitals, song-making, as well as more conventionally recognized forms of drama. When Chaucer's Pardoner describes his different voice modulations, gestures, props and text, which he deploys when preaching in parish churches, he is providing a script, and stage directions too, for one of the most common and popular forms of medieval performance art.

Chaucer, Gower and Langland

Whylome were lordes in londe that loved in thaire hertis
To here makers of myrthes, that matirs couthe fynde . . .
But now a childe appon chere, withowtten chyn-wedys, (in appearance, beard)
That never wroghte thurgh witt three wordes togedire,
Fro he can jangle as a jaye, and japes telle, (chatter like a jay)
He schall be levede an lovede...

(*Winner and Waster*, 19–26)

The narrator of the mid-fourteenth-century ▷ alliterative poem ▷ *Winner and Waster* opens with a lament for a Golden Age when literary 'makers' had status and a duly appreciative audience. Now the decline of society, in all respects, is figured by the preference for entertainment by 'boys' who 'jangle', and this decline is the focus of the rest of the text, which investigates the effects of 'winning' and 'wasting' on social structures. This complaint is a conventional preliminary to the satire which follows.

Yet looking back on the literary activity in English which followed the production of *Winner and Waster*, it may seem that a Golden Age of 'making', far from passing, was just about to begin. The fourteenth century, and the second half of the fourteenth century in particular, is hailed as the time when the English literary landscape opened up; as the time when English became recognized and proven to be a language of literature; as the time when the notion of an English literary *tradition* was born. It is certainly true that there is a massive increase in the use of English as a literary language during this time, and that the status of English – and works produced in English – is firmly established by the end of the century through the work of writers such as ▷ William Langland, ▷ John Gower and, above all, Geoffrey Chaucer. However, this does not constitute a consolidated movement, still less a simple nationalistic endeavour. The distinctive qualities of the work of Chaucer, Langland and Gower, the traditional and innovatory features of their work, derive partly from the diversity of their literary context and their mediation between different models of literary production, between classical and Christian poetics.

By way of conclusion to an essay that has emphasized the plurality of Middle English literary culture, I will discuss some features of the great encyclopaedic narratives produced by Gower, Chaucer and Langland, and briefly consider the topicality of their work. Though, as we have seen, medieval writers often used stories from the past to investigate the values of the present, these three writers also make the contemporary world a subject of their narratives.

Shared concerns, dramatic techniques, narrative strategies, can be traced between the texts of the ▷ *Confessio Amantis*, *The Canterbury Tales* and ▷ *Piers Plowman*, although these hardly fall into neat critical patterns. What is striking initially is the way in which Gower, Chaucer and Langland all use penitential occasions, motifs and processes to structure their large-scale narrative compilations. The narrative of the *Confessio Amantis* is organized around a series of confessional and instructional exchanges between a lover (Amans) and a priest (Genius), who are both servants of the Goddess of Love. These exchanges provide the medium for both an encyclopaedic collection of (largely pagan) short stories, organized to illustrate the Seven Deadly Sins, and for a narrative synthesis of other kinds of book learning and lore. Not only does the *Confessio Amantis* contain a collection of classical and Old Testament narratives, but it incorporates sections on the histories of the world, of religion, of culture and instructional material on the governance of self and society. In some respects Gower's text has the quality of a later fourteenth-century manual of culture.

In Gower's earlier works in French and Latin, the narrator assumes the stance of a social prophet and his voice is that of social, ethical and political complaint. Here in the *Confessio* the narrative voice is refracted through that of the Lover and the Priest, and the high stance of Gower's earlier work gives way to a narrative that tries a 'middel weie', between mirth and morality, addressing ethical issues through focussing on the confession and instruction of a lover, a man committed to secular values. But penitential practices are completed both in theory and in practice in this narrative as the focus shifts at the end of the collection from secular ethics to transcendental concerns. The closing stages of the *Confessio Amantis* are marked by the revelation that the Lover is too old to be a follower of Venus, and the gap between his desires and capacities is healed when Cupid's arrow is pulled from his heart. Thus the penitential process of contrition, confession and healing is completed. The state of the Lover and the maker of the *Confessio Amantis* coincide at the end of the narrative: the healing of the lover marks the end of 'love-making' for the figure of the poet, who declares his days of literary composition on the subject of love are over too.

Whereas John Gower uses a personal act of confession as the framework for his story collection, Chaucer makes a public pilgrimage the setting for his narrative drama. The pilgrimage to Canterbury becomes the arena for a tale-telling competition designed to pass the time *en route*. This was not Chaucer's first attempt at constructing a story collection. The occasion for the earlier story collection, the ▷ *Legend of Good Women*, is an act of literary penance for sins against the God of Love, which has obvious parallels with the *Confessio Amantis*. Nor was Chaucer the first writer to use the idea of story-telling as a 'pastime' as a pretext for a framed narrative collection. Before Chaucer the Italian writer ▷ Boccaccio had used a courtly retreat as the setting for a collection of 100 stories in the ▷ *Decameron*. However,

Chaucer's choice of a pilgrimage setting allows for a much greater tonal and narrative range. Unlike Boccaccio, Chaucer does not keep within the bounds of a courtly literature tradition, but incorporates a wider panorama of compositional practices and narrative genres, and trades on the social variety of the pilgrim narrators. Diversity is the governing principle of the collection.

Unlike Gower, who uses a relatively stable narrative frame for his story collection, Chaucer makes the framework of the tales a variable factor too, as narratives are generated by different kinds of interaction between the pilgrims and their games-master, the Host. The event is both organized according to certain rules and yet, at the same time, open to unexpected engagements and confrontations. The stories are refracted through a range of narrative voices which defeat any attempt to reconstitute a single, governing authorial stance from the collection. Thus the play between narrators and narrative is much greater than in Gower's *Confessio Amantis* and this ludic quality is one of the singular characteristics of Chaucer's story-collection. Whereas Gower treads a middle way between mirth and morality in the substance and organization of his story-collection, Chaucer conducts a more radical experiment into the morality of mirth at intervals in the *Canterbury Tales*. But this story competition takes place in a setting with moral and spiritual resonances too, and these are invoked at the close of the play by narratives.

The *Canterbury Tales*, though unfinished in parts, was clearly designed to end like the *Confessio Amantis*, with a radical shift of focus and a gesture that marks the end of earthly 'making' and fictionalizing. What begins as a literal and literary excursion ends, with the ▷ *Parson's Tale*, as an occasion for a spiritual journey, a 'parfit, glorious, pilgrymage' to 'Jerusalem celestial'. The time of the maker of the narrative coincides with that of the text itself: most manuscripts of the *Canterbury Tales* close with a leave-taking from the maker of the text in the form of a literary confession and retraction.

In theory and in practice, Chaucer's story-telling collection is a work in progress. Langland's ▷ *Piers Plowman* is very much a poem in progress too, built around a dynamic principle of organization and surviving in at least three different stages of revision and reformulation. If the *Confessio Amantis* and the *Canterbury Tales* bear the signs of being the last works of their respective authors, *Piers Plowman* seems to have been Langland's first and last exercise in literary making. Langland's work is much more the product of a Christian, clerical milieu than that of Gower and Chaucer: the narrative has a pervasive macaronic quality, being suffused with Latin quotations, and the conduct of Christian life in all senses is its central concern. A single penitential action does not provide the setting for the narrative of *Piers Plowman*, but penitential processes and schemes are used to organize the action within the narrative. The first major section of the poem, for example, considers how a Christian society might collectively embark on a process of contrition, confession and pilgrimage. The action of the narrative as a whole might be seen as a pilgrimage of sorts, a spiritual 'chanson d'aventure' by the narrator/dreamer Will, which encompasses a record of a macrocosmic Christian journey through history. The dream framework of the narrative means that all action in the poem is potentially translatable as inner experience, just as all inner experience in the poem may become public history. Through using the dream-vision mode, Langland is able to merge temporal and spatial perspectives, and to combine the diachronic history of an individual human 'will', that of Will, the Dreamer, in his search for Piers Plowman.

Langland's work is not a narrative collection in any obvious sense like that of the *Confessio Amantis* and the *Canterbury Tales*. Yet it has encyclopaedic qualities and synthesizes an enormous tradition of Christian literature, of *pastoralia*. If *Piers Plowman* is encyclopaedic in its scope, its mode of organizing that body of knowledge is very different from that employed by John Gower for example. Langland is concerned not only with what there is to know, but what it is to know. So at the same time as Christian history and doctrine are represented in the narrative, the process of individual assimilation and internationalization of that teaching is considered too. The dream mode allows Langland to enquire into the relationship between instruction and understanding. *Piers Plowman* is not, then, a penitential manual, or a Christian handbook, but a poetic venture, committed to the value of fictionalizing as a way of exploring spiritual issues. Yet, in its various versions, *Piers Plowmàn* exposes the problem of articulating such issues within a fallible medium, through the work of fallible human makers.

Piers Plowman, the *Confessio Amantis* and the *Canterbury Tales* all give the impression of having been produced '*in media via*', '*in medias res*', in the middle of times and traditions, under the shadow of endings which may make all literary labours irrelevant, if not damnable. All three works are given some kind of contemporary placement in late-fourteenth-century society and all three works hold a mirror up to their times, not in the sense of offering a mimesis of events, but in offering a critical assessment of their contemporary political, social and cultural context.

Although Langland opens the first dream-vision of *Piers Plowman* with a paradigmatic picture of Middle Earth, framed by the Tower of Truth and the Dungeon of Falsehood, the sense of a-temporality soon disappears as the contents of the 'fair feeld ful of folk' begin to materialize, and a complex picture emerges of contemporary social and political life. Langland cultivates a greater sense of his narrative unfolding at a particular time in the late fourteenth century than either Gower or Chaucer, and this increases the sense of the pressing urgency of the political and political-ecclesiastical issues addressed in the course of the dream-visions. Gower confronts the political and social issues of his day most directly in his earlier works in French and Latin. However, the *Confessio Amantis*, too, is framed by an extensive prologue and epilogue which places the story collection within a general framework of universal history, and with a specific historical context: the very specificity of Gower's address to his time is underlined by the changes made to parts of the opening and closing frame (notably in its address to ▷ Richard II) as that political context changed.

In comparison to Gower and Langland, Chaucer is much more guarded in his allusions to the turbulent political and social events of his time, Indeed, the topicality of his work is much more orientated towards the world of contemporary European culture. His engagement with the court culture, not only of France, but of Italy too, is unparalleled among his contemporaries. Like Langland, Chaucer open his encyclopaedic work, the *Canterbury Tales*, with a *Prologue* which gives the story-telling event some sense of historical time and place. As the pilgrims are introduced, an impression is built up of a society in which traditional social bonds are being eroded by materialistic interests. But the pilgrims do not operate within their everyday context in the *Canterbury Tales*. Rather the pilgrims are cut loose from their mundane world to become prime movers in a literary event in which contemporary social and political issues are refracted through an investigation into how literary representations are produced and received. References to such contemporary events as the ▷ Peasants' Revolt or to the deposition of Richard II are rare in Chaucer's work; a concern with the politics of representation, of 'lion painting', is much more pervasive.

When the Elizabethan critic ▷ George Puttenham came to consider the history of the *Arte of English Poesie*, he chose not to delve further back than the time of ⊳ Edward III, and mentions only a small group of writers from the fourteenth and fifteenth centuries as worthy of notice, including Chaucer, Gower, Langland, ⊳ Lydgate and ⊳ John Hardyng. For Puttenham these were not writers from a Golden Age of medieval literature, rather writers from a 'First Age' of a literary tradition which culminates, in his view, in the work of the court poets of his time. It is perhaps not surprising that Puttenham bestows the honorific title of poet on Chaucer, alone, of the writers from this first age. Some of the distinctive qualities of Chaucer's work (such as its poetic self-consciousness, its engagement with an international secular literary tradition) correspond to features of the secular, humanist, literary tradition which Puttenham promotes as *the* tradition of English poetry. But this courtly tradition of literature is part of a much broader spectrum of literary activity: it is not the *only* literary tradition of the time. Puttenham's representation of the 'First Age' of English poetry reveals how the composition of literary history itself reflects the values of its writer and its time, even as the attempt is made to engage with those of another age. Literary history was, is, and continues to be, a contingent construction. Since Puttenham wrote, John Hardyng, the fifteenth-century verse chronicler, no longer occupies a place in the high ground of medieval literary history alongside that of writers such as Chaucer and Langland. The ⊳ 'House of Fame', as Chaucer describes it, is built on a rock of partly melting ice.

In the course of the twentieth century, the study of medieval culture and the retrieval of its artefacts has expanded enormously, with the result that the medieval literary landscape has been opened up in different ways. Its features have been changed quite literally by the mapping out of wider areas of literary activity, as more medieval manuscripts have been edited and made accessible for a modern audience. But at the same time more questions have been raised about the ideological implications of these acts of retrieval, interpretation and cultural assimilation. Medieval literary studies have become the forum for debates about how texts from a half-alien literary culture may be read in a modern context. The engagement with medieval literary culture is a two-way process of critical enquiry and critical self-assessment. Reassessments are currently being made of the interplay between those texts traditionally identified as belonging to the category of 'medieval literature' and the wider spectrum of textual production of which they form a part. If medieval culture no longer speaks to modern audiences with a univocal voice, that is partly because of the greater critical sensitivity, now, to the way in which the tensions and contradictions in the dominant ideological constructions of the time are played out in the texts of the time. Although the Christian Church exerted a pervasive influence over all areas of medieval intellectual, social and political activity, that does not mean that the cultural artefacts which remain project anything like a homogeneous and unified world view. The Wife of Bath is not the only medieval figure to be interested in the politics of 'lion painting'.

My interest in this essay has not been in tracing the origin of an English tradition, so much as giving a broad impression of the range of sacred and secular literary 'making' in Middle English, and raising some questions about who was making it, and in what context. The medieval English tradition cannot be mapped out wholly in terms of individual writers, or in terms of works written just in the 'Englishes' of the time. It has a place within a literary continuum which includes works produced in Latin and French written in England, and on the continent too. This literary continuum does not end in 1500, although from this time on there is an enormous expansion in the productive and receptive contexts of English texts, as the media of page and stage are opened up.

Yet some striking lines of continuity are to be found in the relationship between the sophisticated narrative traditions of the medieval period and the dramatic traditions of the Renaissance. Not only was a great body of medieval narrative material made more readily available for private reading through printed editions, but it was also rendered more accessible through its transformation into dramatic form. Shakespeare's reworking of the medieval Troy stories is but one example of the way in which narratives formerly mediated through public and private readings become the subject of dramatic productions in the Renaissance. ⊳ *Troilus and Cressida* is a dramatic innovation which arises out of classical and medieval narrative traditions. Indeed, the homage to Chaucer at the beginning of the ⊳ *Two Noble Kinsmen*, or the appearance of Gower as a mediating figure in ⊳ *Pericles*, are only the most obvious signs of the deep-seated debt of Renaissance writers to medieval poets and 'makers' of the preceding centuries.

2 'By Any Other Name': Understanding Renaissance Literature

Marion Wynne-Davies

I

Introduction

When Juliet calls upon Romeo to reject his surname so that they will no longer owe allegiance to the warring Montague and Capulet families, she explains her argument through the metaphor of a rose:

> *What's in a name? That which we call a rose*
> *By any other word would smell as sweet.*
> (▷ *Romeo and Juliet*, II. ii. 43–4)

Juliet asserts that names are superfluities which may be discarded at will, since the substance of identity can never change – the material body of the rose will remain the same, whatever arrangement of letters or sounds we use to describe it. To a certain extent, Juliet's concerns prefigure the twentieth-century theory of semiotics, of which Ferdinand de Saussure was an important initiator. The difference between the two ideas – Juliet's simple poetic argument and de Saussure's complicated construction of a theory of language – lies in the character's insistence upon the material object and the theoretician's primary concern with the name. In other words, de Saussure pointed out that each name or 'sign' has two component parts: the sound or letters (signifier) and the concept or idea (signified). For Juliet we must take meaning a step further: to the 'referent', to the 'thing' which exists in the real world. What we are faced with as readers is the conflict between the name 'rose', which through previous cultural associations carries a romantic and beautiful signification, and the recognition of a practical argument about real objects – we must admit that if the same flower were called 'rhosyn' (Welsh for 'rose'), it would make no difference to the smell. But how do these arguments forward an understanding of what is meant by the name 'Renaissance'?

The word (and sound) 'Renaissance' is like any other signifier, a jumble of letters that may change to 'Rinascimento' in another language (Italian), or to 'renascence' when Matthew Arnold (1822–88) decided to alter the term to a more nationalistic form:

> *The great movement which goes by the name of the Renascence . . . I have ventured to give to the foreign word* Renaissance *an English form.*
> (*Culture and Anarchy*, 1869)

Indeed, the name in English does have a somewhat bastard origin in that it derives from the French verb 'renaître' (to be born again), and only began to be used commonly during the nineteenth century in scholarly tomes such as John Ruskin's *The Stones of Venice* (1851) and Walter Pater's *Studies in the History of the Renaissance* (1873). However, the name gradually developed a coherent concept (signified), which was grounded upon its original meaning of a rebirth of classical learning after the 'dark ages' of medieval scholarship. This denigration of the ▷ Middle Ages is today recognized as erroneous; in order to fashion itself, each age tends to denigrate the previous period.

Nevertheless, that there was a difference cannot be questioned. Apart from the rebirth of knowledge, the Renaissance encompasses the valorizing of the individual, the centralization of power systems and the primacy of gold, as well as discoveries in the realms of science and the New World. In this manner, we can perceive that further signifiers reverberate about the central name; ▷ humanism, neo-Platonism (▷ Platonism), alchemy, the prince and the courtier, are simply a few. Beyond this, pictorial signifiers emerge, images depicted in the most resplendent colours: the gold-clad figures of ▷ Henry VIII and ▷ Elizabeth I, the highly glazed paintings of Leonardo da Vinci, Michelangelo, Raphael and Titian, the statuesque characters from the literary works of ▷ Shakespeare and ▷ Milton, the figure of Columbus leaping ashore into a bright and vivid new world, and the rebellious ▷ Galileo confronting the Inquisition with proof that the earth moves around the sun. The complex interrelationships between these words and images – and each individual reader will be able to provide additional information – combine in various permutations to weld signifiers and signifieds into the meaning of the 'Renaissance'.

This general indeterminacy and widespread application of the term 'Renaissance' has led some critics to reject it altogether. For example, ▷ C. S. Lewis in his comprehensive *English Literature in the Sixteenth Century* (1954) complains that,

> *'The Renaissance' can hardly be defined except as 'an imaginary entity responsible for everything the speaker likes in the fifteenth and sixteenth centuries'.*

Moreover, if we take the European Renaissance as a whole into account, then we must extend the dates from the fourteenth-century Italian poet ▷ Petrarch, to mid-seventeenth-century English writers such as John Milton, ▷ Andrew Marvell and ▷ Katherine Philips. Despite Lewis' objections, however, it is both possible and necessary to draw certain margins. For example, we may accept that the Renaissance began in Italy and spread northwards and westwards, so that the English Renaissance occurred much later than the Italian. In England, we may use the commencement of the Tudor dynasty in 1495 and the end of the ▷ Interregnum in 1660 to limit the chronological extent of the Renaissance. This temporal enclosure exhibits a certain cultural and political uniformity; it begins with ▷ Henry VII's self-conscious attempts to create the court of a Renaissance prince with its panoply of entertainments and ▷ patronage, and ends with the Restoration of ▷ Charles II.

But what of Juliet's rose? For her, the names and ideas, which we so readily acknowledge, are meaningless. Instead, what is important is the material object, the referent. Juliet's understanding of the 'Renaissance' would not consist of discussing the word's etymology or of tracing the scholarly concepts which the letters imply, but would develop from discussion of the period itself, the cultural practices, the social and political events, the material circumstances of people's lives during that unique period. Although productive, we must also be aware that this approach can be unstable, since objective and timeless judgements of external reality cannot be achieved. If a text was produced in a period distant from our own, the instability is compounded. The rose is a case in point. The twentieth-century European image of a rose is most commonly the long, pointed, velvet-leafed hybrid tea, which was a development of nineteenth-century horticulture. The Renaissance rose had more in common with today's wild plants, being more globular in form and of trailing habit, with fewer petals and only two colours, red and white. The rose adopted by the Tudors as their emblem was the red version, the Rosa Gallica. Juliet's rose may be as equally romantic as those purchasable at Interflora today, but it was quite a different species. To understand the Renaissance, we too must combine historical investigation with a self-aware recognition of our own temporal distance.

Although the nineteenth century fixed the period's identity in scholarly terms, the name 'Renaissance' was probably first used by Giorgio Vasari in *The Lives of the most excellent Italian Architects, Painters and Sculptors* (1550 and 1568), where he argues that his contemporaries are not anonymous artisans like the painters of the previous period, but individualistic artists and creators. Vasari's understanding of the Renaissance subject lies at a substratum of the same seam excavated by the new historicist critic Stephen Greenblatt, with his focus upon 'self-fashioning'. Both highlight the marked increase of self-determination in Renaissance culture and society. Another twentieth-century commonplace of the Renaissance configuration, the concept of the rebirth of knowledge, was evident still earlier, when the Italian neo-Platonic philosopher Marsilio Ficino (1433–99) wrote:

> *This century, like a golden age, has restored to light the liberal arts . . . achieving what had been honoured among the ancients, but almost forgotten since.*
>
> (*Theologia Platonica*, 1482)

It seems that Renaissance men and women carried convictions about their own age which remain current, and it is these areas of convergence that we must investigate. In the remainder of this essay I shall focus upon the rebirth of knowledge; the rise of individualism; political power and patronage; and the age of gold. However, this exploration is not intended to uncover a reflection of the fifteenth to seventeenth centuries in the writing of that time. Although referents are a necessary component of meaning, literary texts are not mimetic (▷ Mimesis), reproducing exactly an external reality. Nor are we able to receive the words and images without introducing our own twentieth-century interference. Instead, we must look for ways in which literature develops a dialogue with other ▷ discourses of both periods. For example, while Ficino alerts us to the idea of the Renaissance as a golden age, he simultaneously appears to be participating in a dialogue in which that notion has been contradicted. Note: he does not write that it *is* a golden age, but *like* one. Finally, we must simultaneously be aware of our own historical and cultural positioning. As the new historicist critic Louis A. Montrose writes:

> *Integral to . . . historical criticism must be a realization and acknowledgement that our analyses and our understandings necessarily proceed from our own historically, socially and institutionally shaped vantage points; that the histories we reconstruct are the textual constructs of critics who are, ourselves, historical subjects.*
>
> ('Professing the Renaissance: The Poetics and Politics of Culture', 1987)

For example, the popularity of feminist criticism in the late twentieth century has focused readers' attention upon female authors, and several books (this guide included) have attempted to redress the gender imbalance in our canon by making contemporary readers aware of the large number of Renaissance women writers who have been neglected since the mid-seventeenth century. The recovery of authors like ▷ Lady Anne Clifford, ▷ Lady Eleanor Davies and ▷ Lady Elizabeth Cary is clearly an important historical contribution to our understanding of cultural productivity in the Renaissance. But at the same time we must not expect these women writers to have modern feminist values. ▷ Rachel Speght might well defend women against Joseph Swetnam's attack in his *Arraignment of Lewd, idle, forward, and unconstant women* (1615; ▷ *Querelle des Femmes*), but she also accepts women's inferiority to men, because they are the 'weaker vessel' (*A Mouzell for Malastomus*, 1617). Rather than condemn her out of hand, we should recognize that the increased number of women writers during the sixteenth century was partially a result of humanist edicts on education. For them, perhaps, the period was a 'naissance' and not a *re*birth of knowledge.

II

Pleasure Reconciled to Virtue

The rebirth of classical learning in the English Renaissance combined a moral and civic education of the individual together with an inspirational delight derived from the ideal beauty of words and images. Classical texts were revived not simply for their scholarly merit, but because they were in themselves pleasurable to read. Under the influence of humanism, these works were quickly absorbed by national grammar and local public schools, so that by the mid-sixteenth century writers and officials had a solid grounding in the 'classics'. One of the major influences on Renaissance poetry was ▷ Aristotle's *Poetics*, which emphasized the need for consistency; the unities of time and place may be found in Milton's ▷ *Samson Agonistes*. ▷ Homer and ▷ Virgil were seen to be the originators of the epic tradition, each celebrating his own nation and nobility for posterity; here ▷ Spenser's nationalistic epic dedicated to Elizabeth I, ▷ *The Faerie Queene*, followed their example. ▷ Seneca's drama was immensely influential upon ▷ revenge tragedy through its emphasis upon Stoical dignity and individual responsibility. Finally, the neo-Platonists replaced Aristotelian logic with ▷ Plato's rejection of the material world as transient and his belief in a higher, eternal realm in which opposites could be reconciled in an ideal and ultimate truth. This allowed writers such as ▷ Sidney to accept the poetic imagination as a powerful and mystical force for wisdom and virtue, rather than as a series of false tales or dreams (▷ *An Apologie for Poetrie*, 1595). Similarly, it facilitated the acceptance of pagan gods and goddesses into the dominant Christian ideology; ▷ Jonson relied upon classical material in much of his poetry and all of his ▷ masques, yet it is not used to contradict conventional spiritual beliefs.

Indeed, the title of this section is taken from one of Ben Jonson's masques, *Pleasure Reconciled to Virtue* (1618), which marked Prince Charles' (▷ Charles I) first court performance. In it the prince plays the classical hero, Hercules, who is faced with a choice between a life of delight, or one of toil ultimately leading to glory. The symbolic figures of Pleasure and Virtue, recalling the ▷ morality play tradition, appear on stage at the same time as Hercules, Mercury and Daedalus. A further idealized unification occurs when the two possible existences are seen to be reconcilable:

Grace, laughter and discourse may meet,
And yet the beauty not goless:
For what is noble should be sweet,

But not dissolved in wantonness.
(II. 270–3)

Political expediency made it essential that Jonson should offer the prince a delightful vista – immediately, in the courtly dances that followed the speeches, as well as a happy life in the prolonged future. However, the masque could also be used to teach both the prince and the court the value of virtue and hard work, and the last speech appears to emphasize moral endeavour:

There, there is Virtue's seat,
Strive to keep her your own;
'Tis only she can make you great,
Though place here make you known.
(II. 304–7)

Although the masque is a highly mannered court entertainment, Jonson's educative agenda and his use of the classics draw us back to the tenets of humanism mentioned briefly at the beginning of this section.

The contribution of humanism to a greater awareness of classical literature cannot be questioned, but this was not its only contribution to Renaissance culture. The central force of humanism, from the Platonist versions of the fifteenth-century Italians Ficino and Pico della Mirandola to the evangelical Christian interpretations of ▷ More and ▷ Erasmus, was the essential dignity of mankind. The key text was Pico's *Oration on the Dignity of Man* (1486), where he asserts that men are capable of self-determination, being able to choose freely between good and evil. In the *Oration*, Pico composes a speech given by God to man:

> *You shall fix the limits of your own nature according to the free choice in whose power I have placed you. We have made you neither mortal nor immortal, so that with freedom and honour you should be your own sculptor and maker, to fashion your form as you choose.*

Within Christian humanism this emphasis upon self-determination was to lead finally to Erasmus' rejection of the ▷ Lutheran theory of grace in his work *On Free Will* (1524), where he asserts that man is capable of choosing moral virtue for himself.

During the discussion of humanism I have consistently used the word 'man' or the masculine pronoun, when I could have reworked the phraseology into 'woman and man' or 'she and he'. However, while the humanists professed a belief in the importance of educating women to the same standard as men (in theory in Erasmus' *The Abbot and the Learned Woman* (1516) and in practice in the programme of studies in the More household), they were far from advocating sexual equality. Although it is essential to consider the impact of humanism upon both genders, it is at the same time important not to imbue fifteenth-century philosophers with late twentieth-century notions of political correctness. Moreover, the humanist focus upon the individual's ability to choose freely did not remain closeted within a philosophical, or even a religious, discourse. The construction of individual identity may be seen as basic to further aspects of Renaissance culture.

III

The Renaissance subject: symbolism to individualism

The relationship of the individual to his of her world underwent a radical change in the Renaissance. Seemingly, in every area of human existence there was a shift of perspective. No longer was the world linear and hierarchical, arranged neatly along the ascending rungs of a ladder, but sliced through in a horizontal cross-sectioning, allowing each component part an unprecedented degree of attention and autonomy. While the humanists focused upon the individual's spirit and intellect, parallel developments occurred in other areas: increased urbanization and freedom of the market allowed greater logistical and class mobility, and the discovery of the New World and the recognition of the earth's place in the solar system demanded that traditional religious theories about man's development be questioned. Perhaps the impact of this changing self-image may best be seen in the differences between medieval and Renaissance works of art. After all, as architecture has heralded the late twentieth-century discourse of post-modernism, so fine art appears to have encapsulated the vanguard of the Renaissance.

In medieval paintings figures are depicted in exact relation to their symbolic significance; so, in *The Wilton Diptych* (c 1400 at the National Gallery in London), for example, ▷ Richard II, as a worldly monarch, is smaller and less sumptuously arrayed than the holy figures of Saint John the Baptist, Saint Edward the Confessor and Saint Edmund who accompany him. In addition, the diptych's background makes no gesture towards naturalism; instead, its gold pattern confirms the wealth of its royal commissioner. Compare this ornate emblematic style with the meticulous secularization of ▷ Hans Holbein's pen-and-ink sketch of the More family (1527, at the Öffentliche Kunstsammlung in Basel). Here the figures are drawn in proportion to one another; their material positioning is of more importance than their relative status. Although the male heads of the household still sit centre-stage and the women stand or kneel about them, suggesting conventional gender hierarchies, these stances are simultaneously challenged by the varying gazes, foregroundings and exchanges of the family group. As Catherine Belsey writes in her article on the Holbein drawing:

> *There begins to be . . . an alternative meaning for the family in the sixteenth century . . . The home comes to be seen as a self-contained unit, a little world of retreat from the conflict of the market-place, and at the same time a seminary of good subjects, where the wife enters into partnership with her husband in the inculcation of love, courtesy and virtue in their children.*
>
> (*Disrupting Sexual Difference*, 1985)

Holbein's sketch represents the More family as a self-contained unit caught during one brief moment of activity, their books scattered upon the floor and the candle still alight upon the window-ledge. Each component of the work is given equal artistic care and imaginative value: who can judge between the delicate, inquisitive stare of Anne Cresacre and the solid triangular form of ▷ Margaret Roper?

Literary discourses echoed those of fine art. In drama the symbolic figures of the virtues and vices were replaced by the lively secularized types of the ▷ citizen comedies. Although the eponymous protagonist in Jonson's ▷ *Volpone* clearly represents the cunning fox whose greed and megalomania ultimately lead to his downfall, the audience is encouraged to admire the dexterity with which he plays upon characters who themselves can hardly be said to exemplify moral virtue. We respond automatically when Volpone begs for our approval at the end of the play:

Now, though the Fox be punished by the laws,
He yet doth hope there is no suff'ring due
For any fact which he hath done 'gainst you,
If there be, censure him; here he doubtful stands.
If not, fare jovially, and clap your hands.

(V. vii, 153–7)

The 'laws' may exact a moral and secular punishment upon Volpone, but the audience redeems him with their applause, forgiving and condoning a contravention of didactic virtue because of the pleasure awarded them. The public theatre with its fee-paying audience enabled the dramatists to evade the necessity of pleasing a single patron, whether noble or clerical. Instead, they foregrounded the concerns of other classes, challenged the validity of the law, questioned the absolutes of established religion and subverted conventional gender roles. Examples of these may be seen, firstly in *Arden of Faversham* where the central characters are the burgher Thomas Arden and his wife, Alice. Secondly, in the mode of revenge tragedy which allowed for the enactment of personal vengeance against the tenets of society and the church when both failed to see justice done. Finally, at the end of Shakespeare's comedy ▷ *As You Like It*, where the boy-actor playing Rosalind provokes homoerotic phobias when he/she offers to kiss the men in the audience:

If I were a woman I would kiss as many of you as had beards that pleas'd me, complexions that lik'd me, and breaths that I defied not; and, I am sure, as many as have good beards, or good faces, or sweet breaths, will, for my kind offer, when I make curtsy, bid me farewell.

(Epilogue)

The dynamic and vivid upsurgence of individualism, of a challenge to the dominant spiritual and secular ideologies, cannot but make the Renaissance appear like the paintings of Bruegel or Bosch, at once lively, comic, carnivalesque, grotesque and tortured.

Yet surely these elements of excess contradict the 'Renaissance' of classical rebirth discussed in Section II? A possible way of relating these opposite forces is provided by the theoretician ▷ Mikhail Bakhtin, who explained how the Renaissance both welcomed classical aesthetics and retained the bodily allegiances of the medieval period:

The new historic sense that penetrates them gives these images a new meaning but keeps intact their traditional contents: copulation, pregnancy, birth, growth, old age, disintegration, dismemberment . . . they are contrary to the classic images of the finished, completed man, cleansed, as it were, of all the scoriae of birth and development.

(*Rabelais and His World*, 1965)

It is important to recognize that beliefs as disparate as classical idealism and grotesque superfluity – Michelangelo's *David* and Bosch's demons – could, and did, coexist in a perpetual dialogue with one another. But the nature of these uneasy relationships, these disquieting dialogues, needs to be examined more closely.

IV

The prince and the courtier: power and patronage

The previous two sections have identified several interconnecting and sometimes contradictory discourses. However, in combination they open up a further line of debate, in that both humanist learning and the growth of individualism would seem to eradicate the feudal class structures of the medieval period. Yet the Renaissance was not a period of democratic liberty or of a utopian classless society. Indeed, its autocratic princes demanded absolute authority, punishing transgressions with death, rather then responding with enlightened understanding. A case in point is Sir Thomas More, the philosopher discussed earlier. More might have been one of the leading exponents of humanism, but that did not prevent Henry VIII from executing him because he would not recognize the king's divorce from his first wife, Katharine of Aragon, nor acknowledge the Act of Supremacy. Nevertheless, while the relationships between a Renaissance ruler and his noble servants could undoubtedly be fraught, their mutual dependency cannot be denied. These negotiations between governor and governed are the focus of two influential Renaissance texts, ▷ Machiavelli's *The Prince* (1513), and ▷ Castiglione's *The Courtier* (1528).

The Prince is simply one of Machiavelli's treatises on statecraft, but it best encapsulates the complex notion of an autocratic ruler who simultaneously recognizes his duty to the people. The work was not translated into English until 1640, so that it was the idea of Machiavellian power – diabolical and cunning – which carried sway in England. In ▷ Marlowe's tragedy ▷ *The Jew of Malta*, the Prologue is spoken by Machevill, who counts 'religion but a foolish toy' (l. 14) and states that,

Might first made kings, and laws were then most sure
When, like the Draco's, they were writ in blood.

(20–1)

The immense and unconditional power of the monarch is evidenced, with or without tacit criticism, throughout Renaissance literature. Examples range from Spenser's idealized vision of Elizabeth I in *The Faerie Queene*, to Shakespeare's treatment of corrupt rule and deposed monarchy in ▷ *Richard II*, with whose eponymous protagonist the queen is said to have identified:

So her Majestie fell upon the reign of King Richard II, saying, 'I am Richard II, know ye not that?'

(William Lambarde, *Memorandum*, 1601)

Of all the English Renaissance monarchs, perhaps it was Elizabeth who most appreciated the fine line of conditional autocracy along which she must practise a skilful tracery. The queen's 'Golden Speech' to Parliament in 1601, when she repealed several unpopular monopolies, is remarkable for the way in which it reminds her subjects of a prince's God-given authority, while at the same time stressing their influence over her decisions:

For myself, I was never so much enticed with the name of a King or royal authority of a Queen, as delighted that God hath made me His instrument to maintain His truth

and glory, and to defend this Kingdom (as I said) from peril, dishonour, tyranny, and oppression.

There will never Queen sit in my seat with more zeal to my country, care for my subjects, and that will sooner with willingness venture her life for your good and safety, than myself. For it is my desire to live nor reign no longer than my life and reign shall be for your good. And though you have had and may have many princes more mighty and wise sitting in this seat, yet you never had nor shall have any that will be more careful and loving.

(Elizabeth I in *Women Writers of the Renaissance and Reformation*, ed. K. M. Wilson, 1987)

Power for Elizabeth is clearly the monarch's by right, but is exercised only with the compliance of his or her populace.

The negotiation of political power was similarly recognized by the Renaissance subject. In his book of instruction on the behaviour of the ideal nobleman and -woman, Castiglione writes that,

the aim of the perfect Courtier . . . is so to win for himself, by the means of the accomplishments ascribed to him by these gentlemen, the favour and mind of the prince whom he serves that he may be able to tell him the truth about everything he needs to know, without fear or risk of displeasing him; and that when he sees the mind of his prince inclined to a wrong action, he may dare to oppose him and in a gentle manner avail himself of the favour acquired by his good accomplishments, so as to dissuade him of every evil intent and bring him to the path of virtue.

(*The Courtier*, Book Four, 5.)

Writers, like courtiers, often depended upon patronage, and they were called upon to create pleasure for their wealthy patrons, even as they attempted to inculcate certain moral lessons in them. As in Ben Jonson's masque discussed at the beginning of section II, the bitter pill of didacticism had to be sugar-coated with flattery. A mutual relationship existed, but it was hardly even-handed.

V

The age of gold

The gilded self-fashioning of the Renaissance monarch and the glorious swirl of centrifugal power in the Renaissance court cannot be better exemplified than in the meeting of Henry VIII and King Francis I of France at the ⊳ Field of Cloth of Gold in 1520. The sobriquet derived from the lavish decoration and ornamentation on the 'field' of chivalric combat, where the two kings jousted with the flower of English and French knighthood. The display was an affirmation of royal identity, a statement of personal worth, and above all, a powerful assertion of wealth. The acquisition, show and even attempted manufacture of gold provide the final glittering accoutrement of Renaissance culture. It may be seen in the neo-Platonic aspects of alchemy, in the carnivalesque power of the market-place, and in the political displays of princes and courtiers alike. Morever, it was gold that provoked the fiercest racial confrontations, from the stereotyping of Jews to the bloody massacres in the New World. Colonization was as much the product of economic enterprise as it was of the desire for discovery or of the need for glorification.

Shakespeare's play ▷ *The Merchant of Venice* is a comedy, a romantic play with marriage at its conclusion, but the idealized action takes place in the ▷ pastoral world of Belmont, while the remainder occurs in the city of Venice. The choice of setting was not random. Renaissance Venice was the market-place of the western world; its rich beauty, cosmopolitan splendour and naval superiority gave it a pre-eminence. At the hub of the mercantile republic stood the Rialto bridge; here, under the great wall map depicting Venice's major trading routes, the merchants sold goods and bought shares, Europe's busiest money market did business, and the government carefully guarded national interests. When Shylock cites Antonio's business ventures, his words evoke a goal for London's own mercantile classes:

> *he hath an argosy bound to Tripolis, another to the Indes; I understand moreover upon the Rialto, he hath a third at Mexico, a fourth for England.*
>
> (I. iii, 16–18)

England was increasingly a nation dependent upon its seaborne trade and the strength of its navy, and Elizabeth's rule encouraged an international economic expansionism similar to that of the governorship of the Doge in Venice. Investments in foreign trade to Africa, the East and the New World were central to both the Venetian and English economies, and it is especially significant that in Shylock's speech the only European country given equal weight with Venice is England. But the play also allows Antonio's diverse investments to introduce a threatening aspect to the narrative, since when his ships fail to return to port, his life becomes forfeit to Shylock, the moneylender. Indeed, although Antonio's ventures ultimately prove successful, it is through no action of his but by a 'strange accident' which he is not allowed to know about (V. i, 273–8). Thus the play interacts with the dominant social valuation of economic growth to reveal both its successes and its moral inadequacies. After all, it is Shylock's equal estimation of his ducats and his daughter that is condemned most strongly in the play. But Shakespeare also propels the audience into a confrontation with racial stereotypes – the wicked Jew – that slides in easily alongside the play's questioning of nationalist expansionism. Gold, race and colonialism reverberate through the play without any satisfying outcome, their interactions with audience expectations as mutable as the earlier dialogues between classical rebirth and individualistic regeneration, and between the creation of an independent subject and the autocratic power of a prince.

VI

Conclusion

There are several ways of re-envisaging these Renaissance power relationships. It is possible to perceive the dominant political and religious groups as exerting absolute control, with any possible challenges being seen as futile and puny in comparison with the overwhelming might of the monarchy and the Church. Here we could cite the insurmountable feudal traditions facing humanism. Alternatively, we could stress the radical changes that did occur during the Renaissance: more women were educated and more published books than in the medieval period. We could, however, follow the new historicist trend, which portrays the radical subversion of some texts as ultimately contained and suppressed by official bodies. As Jonathan Dollimore writes:

> *Subversiveness may for example be apparent only, the dominant order not only containing it but, paradoxical as it may seem, actually producing it for its own ends.*
> (*Political Shakespeare*, Jonathan Dollimore and Alan Sinfield, 1985)

What Dollimore suggests is that authority needs some form of challenge so that it may assert itself and thus retain its sense of an empowered identity. Thus the courtier's never-ending and always-failing attempts to curb the prince's power might be exactly what the monarchy requires to sustain itself. Elizabeth I's magnanimity was called into existence mainly because of her necessary response to Parliament's questioning of her absolute power. Or we could return to Bakhtin's notion of a perpetual dialogue, each discourse interacting with others, so that literature is affected by social forces as well as empowered to change that which it condemns. In *The Merchant of Venice* Shakespeare mirrors a nationalistic desire for mercantile wealth, while at the same time offering the audience an altered self-image in which gold is seen as less valuable than lead. Each interpretation may be substantiated textually and critically, leaving the reader with a sense of transience and mutability; relationships shift in perpetuity, at one minute offering harmonious homogeneity, at another radical marginality. It seems, then, that names may not be distilled to essence as easily as Juliet would wish.

This essay began with a conventional Shakespearean heroine. To conclude, I shall turn to his most unconventional female character – Katharina in ⊳ *The Taming of the Shrew*. The narrative and theme of this play turn upon the power relationship between men and women, more explicitly, between Katharina and Petruchio. During the 'taming' of his independent wife, Petruchio insists that she voluntarily accept his erroneous naming of the sun and moon. He does this to confirm overwhelmingly Katharina's total submission to his will. She responds with the tired resignation of the oppressed. Or does she?

> *Petruchio. Nay then you lie, it is the blessèd sun.*
> Katharina. *Then God be blessed, it is the blessèd sun.*
> *But sun it is not, when you say it is not,*
> *And the moon changes even as your mind.*
> *What you will have it named, even that it is,*
> *And so it shall be so for Katharine.*
> (IV. v, 18–22)

Meaning appears to be controlled by the dominant party, in this case a husband, but any of the social and religious leaders already established as conventional in this essay could easily be substituted for Petruchio. Katharina's submission to the necessity of changing meaning according to the demands of hierarchy – 'what you will have it named, even that it is' – directly refutes Juliet's innocent 'What's in a name?' Therefore, determining a meaning for the 'Renaissance' becomes a question of locating the various powerful discourses that lay claim to the definition. Classicism, humanism, autonomy, patronage, monarchy, wealth and colonization each file their petitions of ownership, engaging in an unceasing bargaining process about meaning.

But is Katharina totally submissive? When she responds to Petruchio's continual metamorphoses of meaning she appears to agree that the moon will become the sun whenever he so decides: 'And the moon changes even as your mind'. Yet she too has learnt to exploit verbal ambiguity, and with more subtlety than her husband, for this same line also suggests that Petruchio's mind is as inconstant as the moon, in other words, that he is mad – a lunatic. Katharina ceases to be an object upon whom meaning is imposed; instead she is presented as an independent subject, quite capable of making meaning for herself. So, when searching for the meaning of a 'rose', the 'Renaissance' or of any sign or text, simply recall how Katharina tamed Petruchio – remember that while meaning may appear to be already established and unchallengeable, it is in fact open to perpetual reinterpretation.

3 Reading Renaissance poetry

Jonathan Sawday

The concealed poet

Is not this excuse for mere contraries
Equally strong? Cannot both sides say so?
That thou mayest rightly obey power, her bounds know;
Those passed her nature and name is changed; to be
Then humble to her is idolatry.
As streams are, power is:

(▷ John Donne, Satire 3, 98–103)

We might begin this discussion of ▷ Renaissance poetry with an account of poetry as secrecy. In 1589, ▷ George Puttenham published *The Arte of English Poesie*, a work that was to have considerable influence on Renaissance writers. When, in Book III of this theoretical treatise, Puttenham came to consider 'Ornament' in language, the ornaments which decorate his own prose are metaphors of secrecy and duplicity. Figurative language, in this account, is inseparably caught up in a web of deceit and (to use Puttenham's word) 'doubleness'. So, the writer is:

> . . . *occupied of purpose to deceive the ear and also the mind, drawing it from plainness and simplicity to a certain doubleness, whereby our talk is the more guileful and abusing . . .*
>
> (III. ch. VII)

For Puttenham, such doubleness lay at the heart of the courtly aesthetic, and it is not difficult to understand how this awareness of poetic language as a concealing device could have a certain political efficacy. Puttenham continues:

> *And ye shall know that we dissemble, I mean speak otherwise than we think, in earnest as well as in sport, under covert and dark terms and in learned and apparent speeches, in short sentences and by long ambage and circumstance of words, and finally as well when we lie as when we tell the truth. To be short every speech wrested from his own natural signification to another not altogether so natural is a kind of dissimulation, because the words bear contrary countenance to the intent.*
>
> (III. ch. XVIII)

What Puttenham has observed here is crucial to our understanding of Renaissance writing. In trying to isolate the function of poetic language (an attempt whose result is not dissimilar to the discovery of 'defamiliarization' by the Russian ▷ formalist critics of the early twentieth century), he has focused attention not simply on the latent 'ambiguity' of all linguistic transactions but also on the struggle which takes place in all discourse. That struggle he expresses through a series of oppositions: speaking/thinking, serious/unserious, dark/apparent, lies/truths.

In reading Renaissance texts, this sense of doubleness, this possibility of concealment, and this understanding of poetic discourse as encompassing contradiction and struggle must be kept in mind. For ▷ Thomas Wyatt, courtier and diplomatic servant of ▷ Henry VIII, doubleness is itself a theme of his writing. 'What 'vaileth truth?' he asks in one of his poems, concluding:

True meaning heart is had in disdain.
Against deceit and doubleness
What 'vaileth truth?

The opposition between truth and deceit here has implications for meaning itself. Wherein can 'meaning' lie if, as Puttenham was to observe some fifty years later, we 'speak otherwise than we think'? 'Meaning', too, becomes of significance in dealing with another of Puttenham's oppositions, that between what is 'dark' or concealed, and what is 'apparent' or open to interpretation. Wyatt's poem 'My galley charged with forgetfulness', itself a version of an earlier poem by ▷ Petrarch – '*Passa la nave mia colma d'obblio*' (*Rime* CLXXXIX) – displays the problem for us:

My galley charged with forgetfulness
Thorough sharp seas in winter nights doth pass
'Tween rock and rock, and eke mine enemy alas,
That is my lord, steereth with cruelness,
And every oar a thought in readiness,
As though that death were light in such a case.
An endless wind doth tear the sail apace,
Of forced sighs and trusty fearfulness;
A rain of tears, a cloud of dark disdain
Hath done the wearied cords great hinderance,
Wreathed with error, and eke with ignorance.
The stars be hid that led me to this pain,
Drowned is reason that should me comfort,
And I remain despairing of the port.

(XXVIII)

Richard Tottel, the editor of the anthology in which this poem first appeared in published form in 1557, was in no doubt as to the meaning of the sonnet. 'The lover', he headed the poem, 'compareth his state to a shippe in perilous storme tossed on the sea' (▷ *Tottel's Miscellany*, sig. E3). Tottel is reminding the poem's sixteenth-century readers of the tradition of love poetry, stemming from Petrarch, which employs a conventional pattern of metaphors, images and formal metrical and rhythmical devices. Wyatt (together with ▷ Surrey, as has been often noted) was instrumental in importing these conventions into English verse. So, the storm-tossed lover might appear as a familiar figure to the Renaissance reader (see, for example, ▷ Edmund Spenser's ▷ *Amoretti* 63, 'After long stormes and tempests' sad assay'). We might compare Wyatt's sonnet to the 'original' (though the very question of originality is a concept to which we shall have to return):

My ship full of forgetful cargo sails
Through rough seas at the midnight of a winter
Between Charybdis and the Scylla reef,
My master, no, my foe, is at the helm;

At each oar sits a quick and insane thought
That seems to scorn the storm and what it brings . . .
(trans. Mark Musa)

Who are Petrarch's 'master' and Wyatt's 'lord'? The god of love, perhaps, and thus the enemy of reason. Yet, in Wyatt's version of the poem the character of this figure undergoes significant alterations. Where Petrarch suggests a certain unsureness as to the true nature of the helmsman ('My master, no, my foe'), Wyatt is unequivocal: at the helm is 'my enemy, alas,' who, inevitably, is also 'my lord'. And where, in Petrarch, the image was that of a blind and unreasoning steersman, rushing the ship headlong through the storm, in Wyatt he is possessed of intent – steering 'with cruelness'.

Reading Wyatt's sonnet against Petrarch's 'original' (as opposed to reading it in the way in which Richard Tottel asked his sixteenth-century contemporaries to read it) , we begin to sense that all is not quite as it appears. Once the 'code' located within conventional Petrarchan imagery has been identified, we might still feel that there is more than simply a generalized meditation on the pangs of despised love at work in the poem. At this point we might move away entirely from Petrarch and the overt conventions of sixteenth-century love poetry, to read the sonnet for what it might also be – a profoundly disturbing meditation, not on love, but on the very nature of existence within the ▷ Tudor polity. Wyatt, a diplomat, a justice of the peace, marshal of Calais, ambassador to Spain and to France, M.P. for Kent, and vice-admiral of the Fleet, would appear to represent (and to have gained) all that was most glittering in the establishment of the society in which he found himself. Yet, at the head of that society was a monarch – Henry VIII – with whom conversation, in Stephen Greenblatt's memorable phrase, 'must have been like small talk with Stalin' (*Renaissance Self-Fashioning*, 1980).

The other side of Wyatt's double existence (and the double existence of so many Renaissance writers) is what is represented in his ▷ sonnet 'My galley charged with forgetfulness'. That side – which involved, for Wyatt, imprisonment in 1534, further imprisonment and release on parole in 1536, the execution of his patron, ▷ Thomas Cromwell, in July 1540, and a final period of imprisonment in the Tower in 1541 – is one that might be drawn from any twentieth-century catalogue of existence under the conditions of absolute power. It is the realization of this existence which sends us back to the sonnet and to those key phrases – 'forgetfulness', 'mine enemy . . . my lord', 'cruelness', 'a thought in readiness', 'trusty fearfulness', 'wreathed with error', 'drowned is reason' – with a rather different sense of what this text may encode, and with an understanding, too, of the sonnet's ambiguous air of the sinister. To recall Puttenham again, we are in the presence of a text which possesses a certain 'doubleness'.

From writing to interpretation

For the poets of the ▷ Elizabethan and early ▷ Jacobean period, the contradictions involved in manoeuvring between the 'dark' and the 'apparent' produced, in turn, an awareness that the act of writing could itself be worth writing about. This self-conscious awareness of the writing process (which can be uncovered in the later parts of Petrarch's *Rime*) is the opening theme of ▷ Sir Philip Sidney's ▷ *Astrophil and Stella* (1591), and it was the status of writing, and the relationship *within* writing between meaning and truth, which was to fascinate the sonnet writers of the 1590s – ▷ Samuel Daniel, ▷ Michael Drayton, Edmund Spenser, ▷ Thomas Lodge and ▷ Shakespeare (to name but a very few). For Astrophil, in Sidney's sequence, the task is to uncover 'fit words' (I. 5) to 'entertaine' his female reader. But where are these words to be found? And once located, what process gives them utterance?

> *Thus great with child to speak, and helplesse in my throwes,*
> *Biting my trewand pen, beating my self for spite,*
> *'Foole' said my Muse to me, 'looke in thy heart and write.'*

This comic self-presentation of the poet conceals an important Renaissance theoretical problem associated with the act of writing. Sidney, here, abandons the conventional notion of male authorship 'begetting' his works upon the world (and we might recall the 'onlie begetter' of Shakespeare's sonnets here). Instead, writing is, once more, a struggle – a painful delivery rendering the author paradoxically helpless. At the same time, writing is a process by which that which was hidden within becomes manifest, and hence it entails an inward scrutiny, promoted by a voice ('my Muse') whose origin is also located within the writing self of the poet. But this inner search should not be understood as a quest for originality in the modern sense. What is at stake here is the Renaissance concept of ▷ 'imitation'. 'Imitation', as it was understood by the Renaissance writer, did not entail mere copying, but an assimilation of other voices into the unique voice of the individual poet. Writing, as ▷ Erasmus claimed in the *Ciceronianus* (1527), is therefore not an isolated utterance, but it is the product of other discourses, jostling in the mind. For the poet, working amidst these competing voices, the problem becomes one of establishing a position from which to speak, as Shakespeare's dramatic denial of other poetic voices in his sonnet 130, 'My mistress' eyes are nothing like the sun', evidences. Here, a series of Petrarchan motifs are summoned up, only to be dismissed as not answering to the reality of the woman he addresses. The paradox is, of course, that the very gesture of denial serves to evoke the competing voices of those other poetic discourses.

If writing is a proposition which involves the poet in a search for an authority with which to speak, what of reading? To the modern reader, what may be striking about Renaissance poetry is its determination both to create the reader and to control his or her response to what is read. We might understand this desire to forestall the reader's licence to interpret (for this is what it amounts to) as being a manifestation of a literary culture which is at once enclosed (in a social sense) and also profoundly anxious as to the results of unlicensed interpretive power. The freedom to interpret, as Elizabeth's ▷ Protestant divines were never tired of pointing out, could have unfortunate results. Protestant culture may, on the one hand, have championed the right to interpret scriptural texts when that interpretation seemed to support Protestant beliefs against the perceived threat of ▷ Roman Catholic ▷ Counter-Reformation, but that did not mean that the right to interpret should be invested in each and every reader. The ▷ Thirty-nine Articles, passed under Elizabeth at the Convocation of 1562, might be thought of, within this context, as an attempt at controlling the interpretation of key doctrinal issues. What the articles set out to establish was 'consent touching true religion' and the 'avoiding of diversities of opinions'. Their end, in other words, was to create a homogeneous reader.

Interpretation was understood as involving the assumption of power over the text and the experience inscribed within that text. Is this, then, the key to understanding the Renaissance poet's constant anxiety as to the way in which his secular verse is to be understood? Are the Stellas, Delias, Dianas, Licias, Zephiras, Fidessas and Chlorises (the antique names of imagined or real readers to whom sonnet collections are addressed, and whose names are inscribed in their titles) fierce interpretive presences before whom, in true Petrarchan style, the poet-writer trembled? Indeed, they are. But herein lies another paradox of Renaissance writing. In ▷ lyric poetry in particular, the relationship between the writer and the reader is above all sexual. But this sexual connection, though it involves (as we might expect) an active male author confronting a female reader (as the titles to countless sonnet sequences announce), does not position the female reader in a necessarily passive role, since she is not only a reader but an interpreter. As an interpreter she may be threatened, cajoled, persuaded, but never ignored. We can thus understand the female figure, within the dominant masculine codes of Renaissance writing, as one in whom there is invested a network of competing claims and counter-claims. She is the mainspring of the poet's invention, the object of sexual desire, the prize, the besieged fort, the source of religious or quasi-religious consolation or agony, and, most important of all, the reader and interpreter of his verses. So, Stella, in Sidney's *Astrophil and Stella*, is not only the object of Astrophil's verse (whilst his own sufferings and triumphs are the subject), she is also the final reader and interpreter of the verses laid before her. In Spenser's *Amoretti* (1595), the sequence of sonnets opens with an invocation of the reading-presence of his mistress, who is the final interpreter of what is to follow: 'Leaves, lines and rymes, seeke her to please alone, whom if ye please I care for other none' (I. 13–14).

'Politique Devotion'

It would be simple to dismiss this presence of the female reader as no more than a conventional trope of praise – a means of ensuring that the elaborate fiction of the intimacy of the lover's adoration of the beloved is sustained. Thus, the argument would continue, the true object of the sonnet-writer's fascination is himself, and the female subject is evoked only in order that she be marginalized. But to dismiss the importance attached to interpretation on the part of Renaissance poets is not only to dismiss the serious implications of interpretive power discerned by Elizabethan writers in general, but also to ignore the presence of the most important female interpreter of all – that of the queen herself.

It is almost impossible to over-estimate the awareness of late sixteenth-century poets of the abiding presence of the queen. The queen as head of state, head of the Church and ultimate source of patronage is a figure of real, not merely idealized, power. She is, moreover, a dominating presence in all forms of literary and artistic culture of the period. As such she is a protean figure, paradoxically subject herself to the transforming power of the very verses which sought to confirm her central position in the political hierarchy. But it is in the figure of the queen that the complete identification of aesthetic forms with political power is manifested. Her very name becomes an emblem of power, even whilst it is transformed, literally, through the devices of art:

E urope, the Earthes sweete Paradise:
L et all thy Kings that would be wise,
I n Politique Devotion:
S ail hither to observe her eyes,
A nd marke her heavenly motion.

B rave Princes of this civill Age,
E nter into this pilgrimage:
T his Saints tongue is an oracle,
H er eye hath made a Prince a Page,
A nd workes each day a Miracle.

R aise but your lookes to her, and see
E ven the true beames of Majestie,
G reat Princes, marke her duly;
I f all the world you do survey,
N o forehead spreades so bright a Ray,
A nd notes a Prince so truly.

These acrostic verses, written by ▷ Sir John Davies and entitled 'To all the princes of Europe', form part of a sequence entitled *Hymns of Astraea*, published in 1599. Elizabeth is addressed as the goddess Astraea, a title bestowed upon her not only by Davies, but by other poets including Spenser and ▷ George Peele. Astraea, associated with spring and with justice, is, in ▷ Ovid's *Metamorphoses* (an important source of poetic mythologizing in the period), a symbol of the former ▷ Golden Age when justice and prosperity ruled on earth, whilst in ▷ Virgil she is associated with a future Golden Age. The Golden Ages of the future and of the past thus meet in the figure of Elizabeth in the present.

To say of these verses that they are sycophantic or contrived is to miss the fundamental connection between art and political power which the poets and the queen herself sought to preserve. We might take Davies' poem as itself emblematic of the queen's presence within art. Her name and title function as the springboard for the poet – the place from which the lines themselves originate. Through her name, she is embedded within the poem – a poem which sets out to admire her, as Davies puts it, with 'Politique Devotion'. Devotional politics, indeed, are precisely what the poem produces. But the poem memorializes the queen in more than one role. Passively, she is the object of pilgrimage and devotion, moving as does the constellation Virgo (an alternative, and of course immediately appropriate name for Elizabeth/Astraea) above and beyond the earth. As an object she is, within the poem's structure of images and language, the recipient and bestower of glances and gazings. Her eyes, in a Petrarchan conceit, must be observed, her motion marked, looks raised to her. But her own glances have within them political force, and the Petrarchan conceit is itself transformed in a movement of appreciation of political reality: 'Her eye hath made a Prince a Page'.

For Sir John Davies, lawyer and aspiring politician, later (in 1603) solicitor-general to Ireland, the conjunction between the forms of art and the realities of political power meet in the multiple personae of the queen. Similarly, for the contemporaries of Davies, and as Elizabeth's reign drew to its close, the queen's continuing presence becomes itself the subject of ever-more elaborate poetic and artistic device. In ▷ Sir Walter Ralegh's poem of devotion 'The Book of the Ocean to Cynthia' (or 'The Ocean's Love to Cynthia'), a text of which only a fragment exists in manuscript form, the queen is Cynthia/Diana, goddess of the moon, hunting and chastity, whilst the poet is the ocean, subject to the moon's transforming power, a power which is absolute and, disturbingly, seemingly arbitrary:

No other power effecting wound or bliss,

She gave, she took, she wounded, she appeased.
('Ocean's Love', ll. 55–6)

What can we conclude from this assimilation within art of the realities of power? Reading the poetry of the late sixteenth century, we realize that at the very heart of the literary culture of the period lies the pervasive belief that art and the state must conspire together to affirm a vision of national identity. That it is a vision and not a reality is exemplified by the very urgency with which Renaissance writers pressed home the point that the country was a united whole. Late Elizabethan culture, rather than appearing 'monumental' (as it has been described) or as the product of a realized sense of national selfhood, begins to appear as a rather more anxious moment of history. That pressing need for unity – whether it be unity of religion, of social practices, of cultural forms, of political expression, or of interpretation (all of these being linked in any case) – like all such calls of national unity, indicates the awareness of what is potentially disuniting and positively disruptive. Within this context the 'monuments' of Renaissance culture, the poets of the late sixteenth century, begin to appear not only as poets but, at one and the same time, as ideologues of the first order. Their function was not only to adorn or beautify, but to affirm (sometimes, one feels, for the benefit of Elizabeth as well as her subjects) that the hierarchy was an established reality.

Nowhere is this awareness of the poetic text's power to sanction or authorize a sense of national selfhood more apparent than in what may appear, from the outside, to be the most monumental text of them all – Spenser's ▷ *The Faerie Queene*. Indeed, it is as a monument that the poem is approached in the first instance. On the dedicatory page of the 1596 edition of the poem appears this inscriptive address:

TO
THE MOST HIGH,
MIGHTIE
and
MAGNIFICENT
EMPRESSE, RENOW-
MED FOR PIETIE, VER-
TUE, AND ALL GRATIOUS
GOVERNMENT ELIZABETH BY
THE GRACE OF GOD QUEENE
OF ENGLAND FRAUNCE AND
IRELAND AND OF VIRGI-
NIA, DEFENDER OF THE
FAITH, &c. HER MOST
HUMBLE SERVAVNT
EDMUND SPENSER
DOTH IN ALL HU-
MILITIE DEDI
CATE, PRE-
SENT
AND CONSECRATE THESE
HIS LABOURS TO LIVE
WITH THE ETERNI-
TIE OF HER
FAME

The queen and her titles are inscribed (together with the poet's name) in the form of a memorial urn whose function is to preserve and consecrate the text which is to follow. The queen's titles, held under God (the teaching of whose works she sanctions as head of His Church in her realm), are titles of monarchy over three nations, and sovereignty over a new entity – the colony of Virginia. The poem that follows (and which will also serve to memorialize the queen and the nation, the two being, once more, inseparable) is thus approached through an elaborate token of royal power.

The Faerie Queene is, however, not only a monument to Elizabeth, but a legendary history of the nation over which she governs. It is important, here, to be fully aware of the circumstances of its composition. When Spenser embarked upon the poem (some time prior to October 1579), he was shortly to gain the position of private secretary to Lord Grey, the newly appointed lord deputy of Ireland. Ireland was to be Spenser's home throughout the period of composition and publication of *The Faerie Queene*, and it was as a diligent servant to the government in Ireland that Spenser was to fashion his own career.

The poem is, therefore, composed not close to the source of political patronage and power, but at the very margins of the Elizabethan polity. To Elizabethan authority, Ireland presented a continuing source of disruption. A Catholic and unruly nation (in the eyes of Elizabeth's government), it was not until the Battle of Kinsale (1601), where a combined Irish and Spanish force was defeated by the English under Lord Mountjoy, that the Protestant domination of the country was assured. Spenser, whose own colony of English settlers established on confiscated land was destroyed in 'Tyrone's Rebellion' (1598), was an active administrative cog in what is generally agreed to have been a brutalized (and brutalizing) regime. Indeed, Spenser was the author of two important 'policy documents' on Ireland written in the late 1590s. These works are important for what they tell us of the attitude of mind of Spenser and his contemporaries. Informing them is, above all, fear. Fear of the Irish, their alien religion, their customs, their language (which Spenser, though he lived in Ireland for nearly twenty years, never understood), and the threat which they represented to England, determines to a large extent his understanding of the country in which he found himself. They are, in short, documents of colonialism, some of the earliest we possess.

We can perceive this sense of threat, this awareness of an alien alternative to the 'civilizing' culture of the Protestant poet, at work throughout Spenser's text. In the poem we encounter an evocation of a brutal wilderness, a complex psychological state of 'otherness' which it is the task of Spenser's knights to banish from both the fantastic environment through which they move, and, more importantly, from themselves. This fear, or anxiety, which permeates the poem is, it is important to recognize, not simply a fear which can be dispelled through heroic endeavour. It is a fear, rather, of what is uncontrollable within the subject. If we need an analogy in more recent writing, then Joseph Conrad's Mr Kurtz in *Heart of Darkness* might serve. For Conrad's figure of colonial corruption, isolated from any 'civilized' values, it is the discovery that the darkness and horror lie within which is finally destructive of his own sense of integrated selfhood. So, in similar measure, with Spenser's knights. As they progress on their episodic forays into a world of alien values, their discovery of a struggle taking place within themselves is what the poem dramatizes. When, for example, at the climax of Book II (the legend of Guyon, or temperance), Guyon and his guide enter the 'Bower of Blisse' to confront a world of sensuous and artificial luxury (a world rich in images of frozen sexuality), their iconoclastic endeavour is simply to destroy the *representations* of sensuality with which they have been confronted. Yet they themselves are not untainted by what they encounter. Kurtz-like, they creep through the undergrowth to witness the strange rites from which they cannot draw their eyes. The object of their voyeuristic gaze is the enchantress Acrasia:

> *Her snowy brest was bare to readie spoyle*
> *Of hungry eies, which n'ote therewith be fild,*
> *And yet through langour of her late sweet toyle,*
> *Few drops, more clear then Nectar, forth distild,*
> *That like pure Orient perles adowne it trild,*
> *And her faire eyes sweet smyling in delight,*
> *Moystened their fierie beames, with which she thrild*
> *Fraile harts, yet quenched not; like starry light*
> *Which sparckling on the silent waues, does seeme more bright.*
> (II. xii. 78)

What, and who is Acrasia? Like the queen, she is the object of a male gaze which is fascinated by what it has alighted upon. Unlike the queen (at least overtly) a world of sensual delight is promised. Acrasia, perceived in a moment of sexual passivity, is offered as a dual object of desire. There to be consumed by 'hungry eies', thrilling 'fraile harts', she is also a place of danger and destruction. Just as Ireland, or Virginia, or America itself were represented as female figures in need of mastery, so Acrasia must be captured and her Bower destroyed by the stern masculine (and Protestant) rigour of Spenser's knights.

In externalizing this inward struggle, Spenser's poem is truly a Protestant epic. ▷ Calvinism (the official doctrine of the Church of England under the Elizabethan 'settlement') served to draw attention to the adherent's inner state of mind and promoted a seemingly obsessive curiosity as to the inner health of the individual. But even once this awareness of the poem's Protestant roots has been grasped, we also need to be aware of it as a validating text. *The Faerie Queene* glances back to other epics (to ▷ Tasso and to Virgil in particular) not out of conservatism, or a desire to emulate what previous cultures had produced, but to authorize the present. Spenser himself, in the course of a letter to Ralegh written in 1589, termed the poem a 'darke conceit' – a text which is both apparent and concealed and which might remind us, once more, of Puttenham – but he also described his own method as being that of 'a poet historical'. Within this context, Spenser's epic can be understood as part of an important Elizabethan project. That project entailed nothing less than the active creation in imaginative culture of the nation state as an understandable entity. Together with later texts such as Samuel Daniel's eight books of *The Civil Wars* (1609) and Michael Drayton's vast *Poly-Olbion* (1612–22), Spenser's epic looks back to the past (albeit in Spenser's case a legendary past) to uncover not only 'thinges forepast' but 'thinges to come'. The nation, in other words, must not only have its past created by its poets, but its future mapped out as well.

The deliberate creation of a mythopoeic past was to have enormous influence on the poets who followed Spenser. For one group in particular, the so-called 'Spenserian poets', Spenser's writing served as a model for their own attempts to creat a visionary sense of national and political identity. These writers, who include Michael Drayton, ▷ William Browne and ▷ Phineas Fletcher, discovered in Spenser's writing a readily adaptable means of expressing their own sense of both a mythical past and a wished-for future. The past which these poets created, however, was one governed by the forms and styles exploited by Spenser not only in *The Faerie Queene*, but in his autobiographical ▷ *Colin Clout's Come Home Again* (1595), and ▷ *The Shepherd's Calender* (1579). What Renaissance readers uncovered in these poems was a world determined by the conventions, inherited from ▷ classical and continental writers, of ▷ pastoral. It is important to understand that 'pastoral' poetry did not represent simply an idealized retreat into a mythic world of shepherds, shepherdesses and arcadian delight. But it did signal another form of retreat, and one that was predominantly political. The adoption of pastoral personae, the evocation of a vanished 'golden age' became, for the poets of the early seventeenth century, a means of registering their own sense of isolation under the changed conditions of the early Jacobean period. The sense of poetry occupying a central position within the political culture has begun to fragment. Instead, a new kind of poetry begins to emerge – one that we might begin to term 'oppositional'.

Pastoral has been described as an omnipresent metaphor in Renaissance writing rather than a strict genre in its own right. As such it could be endlessly adaptable, but still provide a framework which both the poet and the reader could recognize. For the poets of the seventeenth century (up to and including ▷ John Milton), pastoral forms allowed them a significant freedom. Phineas Fletcher's *The Purple Island* (written c 1614–15, but published in 1633), for example, indicates the adaptability of pastoral forms. This (to modern eyes) strangely incongruous poem – incongruous since its ostensible subject is the anatomized human body – indicates the uses to which pastoral could be put in the years after the death of Elizabeth and the accession of ▷ James I. Fletcher's twelve-canto poem is narrated by a shepherd-poet named Thirsil. Thirsil's task, to which he had been elected by his fellow-shepherds, is to become their poetic spokesman. But what is to be his subject? What role is now allotted to poetry? What kind of audience must the poet create? The answer to these questions involves Thirsil in a literary search for a subject in what he calls 'these iron daies/(Hard daies)' which 'afford nor matter nor reward' for the poet. On the surface, the theme upon which he alights is profoundly apolitical – six cantos of his poem are spent in celebrating the dissected human body. Yet we should remember Puttenham's distinction between the 'dark' and the 'apparent'. For the human body, in Fletcher's poem, is the setting for war. Just as *The Faerie Queene* had dramatized the creation of an individual identity within an alien world of uncivilized values, so *The Purple Island* represents the struggle for the human subject to define itself within a religious and political sphere. The 'Island' of the poem can be understood as the individual (and it thus offers, through allegory, an answer to Donne's famous observation that 'No man is an island', for in Fletcher's alienated world everyone is an island) and, at the same time, the potentially saved island which is Protestant England. We can call this island *potentially* saved, since the poem's function is to serve as a warning to its readers that a state of continual armed vigilance against the encroaching forces of Catholic Europe has to be maintained. Poetry, in other words, has begun to stand outside the culture of the court, serving a different function – that of warning, rather than endorsing. It is also worth remarking, in this context, that the creation of the myth with which modern British readers are familiar, of Elizabethan culture as a 'golden age' of national unity to which subsequent generations are to look for political and national definition at moments of crisis, began almost before Elizabeth herself was in her grave.

Constructing identities

If national identity is an important theme in the poetry of the late sixteenth and early seventeenth centuries, what of individual identity? Here we might remember, once more, the figure of Acrasia from *The Faerie Queene*. Acrasia represents a dual object of desire promising both sexual delight and an abyss of destruction which culminates in the loss of masculine identity. For Spenser's contemporaries – those poets of the late sixteenth century who have been celebrated for their evocation of erotic love – the figure of Acrasia seems to return, though appropriately, always in different guises. The key to these texts is not their representation of unproblematic human sexual desire, but, rather, the possibility which they uncover of confusing the boundaries of sexual identity. Shakespeare's sonnets, first published in 1609, might come to mind in this context – poems whose fascinated, and playful, confusion of the boundaries of sexual identity have presented a disturbing problem for those critics and readers who prefer a more tidy, and sanitized, national poet. But Shakespeare was not alone in preferring the confusingly playful to the depressingly ordered. Both he and ▷ Christopher Marlowe were to explore the question of sexual identity in the form of the 'brief epic', which, in the late sixteenth century, emerged as a genre in its own right. Shakespeare's ▷ *Venus and Adonis* (1593), Marlowe's ▷ *Hero and Leander* (1598), and the now largely unread *Scilla's Metamorphosis* (1589) by Thomas Lodge are usually cited as representative of this short-lived genre. Informed by the eroticism derived from the understanding of Ovidian poetry, these texts seem constantly to play with the possibility of a duality of identity. In *Hero and Leander*, the opposition between male and female – expressed in the opening opposition of the two cities which are the homes of the lovers – forms a boundary that it is not only Leander's task to cross, but the text's endeavour to confuse. Thus, Hero is at once the chaste devotee of the rites of Venus, and the tutor of the unskilled Leander. But she is also (and here we might remember Acrasia) both the voyeuristically sought-for object of sexual longing, displayed in a world of sensual (and violent) artifice, and the bestower of glances and gazes charged with erotic power. At the same moment, Leander too becomes the focus of erotic longing – an object of male sexual devotion:

> *Some swore he was a maid in man's attire,*
> *For in his looks were all that men desire . . .*
> (I. 83–4)

This sense of confusion, which Shakespeare was to take continual delight in exploiting in the playhouse, is sustained throughout that portion of the poem written by Marlowe. But was a fascination with such sexual identities the sole preserve of the male poet? What of Renaissance women themselves?

We have seen that, in the poetry of the sixteenth century, the female presence can be discerned occupying an interpretive role, and as the focus for a conflicting series of messages based on poets' experiments with language, images and forms inherited from continental models, the most important of whom was Petrarch. But this fluid female presence is largely the creation of male poets. Women as patrons are, of course, familiar figures. Not only the queen, but others such as John Donne's patron ▷ Lucy Russell, Countess of Bedford, and (most famous of them all) ▷ Mary Sidney,

Countess of Pembroke, were celebrated by writers as diverse as Sir Philip Sidney, ▷ Fulke Greville, ▷ Thomas Nashe, Edmund Spenser, ▷ Gabriel Harvey, Samuel Daniel, Michael Drayton, ▷ John Davies of Hereford and ▷ Ben Jonson. But the question of women's writing in the Renaissance period has increasingly become a subject of urgent debate. In England, the ▷ humanist endeavour of the early sixteenth century promised women a *theoretical* access to education, but whether such liberal sentiments affected any but a tiny elite is doubtful. The figure of the woman reading in the Renaissance period is one that is, as we have seen, constantly evoked. The figure of the woman writing is another matter. Elizabeth herself was, of course, a poet and scholar of some distinction. So, too, in the earlier period, was Margaret More Roper. Mary Sidney and her niece ▷ Mary Sidney Wroth (Lady Wroth) wrote not only poetry, but in the case of the latter, the first full-length work of fiction by an Englishwoman. But these were women whose access to the literary culture of the period was based on considerable fortune and political power in its own right. It is not until the turmoil of the revolutionary period of the 1640s and 1650s that a recognizably female presence begins to emerge to challenge the dominant voices of what is, by and large, an exclusively male preserve.

The question 'Did women have a Renaissance?' is an important one in this context. A powerful conclusion to this problem, on the part of contemporary feminist scholarship, is that not only was there no such thing as a 'Renaissance' for women, but that women's status and freedom actually declined in the period we are considering. Rather than looking for a female presence in the writing of the period, it is, with significant exceptions, more accurate to speak of a female absence. Absence, at a point when so much writing by men seems devoted to registering the continual presence of the female, alerts us to a further irony as we move from the period of Spenser into the very different world inhabited by the Jacobean and ▷ Stuart poets of the seventeenth century. No poet could be said to be more alive to the possible presence of the female in his writing than John Donne, but then no poet so determinedly ensures that she remains so absent when compared to the true centre of his poetry – the fascinating object of contemplation that the poet's own self presents:

Thou at this midnight seest mee, and as soone
As that Sunne rises to mee, midnight's noone,
All the world growes transparent, and I see
Through all, both Church and State, in seeing thee;
And I discerne by favour of this light,
My selfe, the hardest object of the sight.
('Obsequies to the Lord Harrington', ll. 25–30)

Thus Donne, in a meditation addressed to the soul of his dead friend (and brother of his patron, Lucy, Countess of Bedford) Thomas Harrington. These lines, though they speak in a different vein from the more familiar voices heard in the ▷ *Songs and Sonnets* or the *Holy Sonnets*, nevertheless alert us to a voice and a theme with which the reader of Donne's writing soon becomes familiar. Donne, at a moment of still quietness, contemplates the departed soul of his friend, and discovers . . . himself. The world and the poet, rendered transparent in the moment of meditation, merge together to present that 'hardest object' before the enquiring gaze of the imagination.

The urge to render things 'transparent', a desire to peer beyond surface representation, together with the triumphant discovery of the dramatic speaking voice in poetry, and the continual awareness of the poetic self as both the subject and object of his writing, combine to make Donne and Donne's poetry almost inseparable. But which Donne do we read? In an age of poetic self-creation, Donne seems to have been continuously alive to the possibility of re-creating versions of himself in his writing. Indeed, Donne's eight surviving portraits suggest an urge to record all of those different variants for the eye of posterity. Dramatically interjecting an image of himself before the reader's gaze, we must also be aware that this poetic Donne is in a state of almost continual flux and fluidity. 'Oh, to vex me, contraryes meet in one' he exclaims in his *Holy Sonnet* XIX, but the meeting of contraries was hardly a vexing possibility for the poet. In 'A valediction: of my name, in the window' Donne imagines himself to be metonymically reduced to a sign of his absence – his name, scratched in the glass of a window. But even that transparent reminder of Donne can be further reduced – the name itself is no more than a 'ruinous anatomy', waiting to be 'recompacted' at the moment of return to the mistress. In poem after poem, Donne signals his threatened absence from what is happening, imagining himself dead and waiting for dismemberment, or embarked upon a journey which leaves behind both mistress and a unified sense of selfhood, only to remind the reader that this unstable entity is, in its continuous instability, the most constant object in this poetic universe. The multiplicity of 'John Donnes' which first circulated in manuscript for the delight of his contemporaries, and which were, for the most part, first inscribed on the printed page only after his death in 1631 (itself, as ▷ Izaac Walton records, an act of controlled self-presentation) constitute perhaps the most dramatic series of poetically shifting presences of the period.

The language of God

In remarking upon this shifting poetic awareness of a created sense of selfhood, I do not wish to imply that Donne's poetry can somehow be categorized as constantly breaking across a simple binary divide – the 'religious' Donne, for example, and the 'sensual' Donne. Sensual images and language are as much to the fore in his overtly religious poetry as religious images are constantly present in his secular verses. And this was true not only of Donne, but of many of those poets of the seventeenth century who wrote on religious themes. In the writings of ▷ Richard Crashaw, for example, sensuality and eroticism combine to present a religious aesthetic which still possesses the power, within the dominant Protestant culture of Anglo-American criticism, to shock and disturb.

On the surface, Donne's contemporary ▷ George Herbert offers a rather different set of poetic values. Herbert's English poetry, all of which is devoted to religious themes, first appeared in printed form in 1633 (the same year that Donne's poetry was published) in a volume entitled *The Temple*. Reading Herbert's verses we appear to have left Puttenham's world of 'doubleness', the conjunction between the 'dark' and the 'apparent', behind. Yet has it entirely vanished to be replaced by the light of Baconian reason? Certainly, where in an earlier period the Renaissance poet delighted in uncovering a poetic language based on 'ornament', Herbert offers a manifesto for a different kind of poetry:

Who says that fictions only and false hair
Become a verse? Is there in truth no beauty?
Is all good structure in a winding stair?
May no lines pass, except they do their duty

Not to a true, but a painted chair?
('Jordan I', ll. 1–5)

Fiction, falseness, a 'winding' structure (terms in which the contemporaries of Puttenham would have delighted) are here denied. What is offered as an alternative is 'truth' – a kind of poetry which will specifically transcend the ⊳ Platonist distinction between representation and object, figured in the opposition between a 'true' and a 'painted' chair.

Yet, reading the complete collection of poems contained in Herbert's *The Temple* (a collection which was to be of profound influence on Herbert's immediate contemporaries, especially Crashaw), we encounter an elaborate structure of metaphor and formal experiment. Take, for example, the careful 'patterning' of the collection as a whole. On the title-page of the 1633 edition we read a quotation from *Psalms*: 'In his temple doth every man speak of his honour', and as we move through the collection we become aware that, in an elaborate architectural conceit, we are indeed placed within a 'temple' where speech – the words of man to God and (more problematically) God to man – is dramatized. But 'speech' is not necessarily open to all. In the opening poem of the collection we read: 'All things are big with jest: nothing thats plain,/But may be wittie, if thou hast the vein' ('Perirrhanterium', ll. 239–40), a statement which not only appears to contradict that poetic manifesto quoted above, but alerts us to a playfully ironic awareness of the resources of interpretation. In other words, beyond the seemingly artless structure of Herbert's verse lies a dense web of poetic device.

However, Herbert's dualistic conception of language – where the seemingly 'plain' may yet conceal the riddlingly 'wittie' – was to echo throughout the later part of the seventeenth century and in contexts which, to modern eyes, seem curiously inappropriate. For example, long after Herbert's collection appeared, ⊳ Thomas Hobbes was to argue for a reform of language in all areas of discourse, whilst in the 1660s ⊳ the Royal Society was to promote language reform as one of its main objectives. Underpinnning those demands was a belief that it was possible to take control of the words we use, and to uncover the very nature of external reality which (so the argument ran) had been hitherto concealed in the metaphoric (⊳ metaphor) labyrinths of poetry. The world, in other words, need no longer be understood as the product of a riddlingly (and fascinatingly) obscure God. Instead, what has been created is a God endowed not only with reason but (unlike Donne's God, and even on occasions, Milton's) reasonableness.

Retreat or engagement?

We do not, however, have to leap so far forward in time to uncover in poetry a desire to escape out of the world of brittle linguistic ornamentation. Ben Jonson, for example, in the celebration of aristocratic comfort which is depicted in his poem in praise of the Sidney family, 'To Penshurst' (published in 1616), calls for an aesthetic which is in direct contrast to that enshrined in the writings of an earlier generation. The house, Penshurst, which is the home of the family his poem celebrates, is not

. . . built to envious show
Of touch or marble, nor canst boast a row
Of polished pillars, or a roof of gold;
Thou hast no lantern whereof tales are told,

Or stair, or courts; but stand'st an ancient pile,
And these grudged at, art reverenced the while.

What is enacted here is just that revolution in taste which Herbert, in a very different context, had called for. And yet, what are the virtues of Penshurst? Essentially they are the virtues of an emergent bourgeois existence. Penshurst is a place of fruitful production, which extends outwards from its walls to embrace the surrounding countryside and its inhabitants. But Penshurst also stands in stark distinction to other houses, and other kinds of social relations, hinted at in the poem as places less benign than that which is contemplated in these verses. At the same time, as the verses quoted indicate, Penshurst represents a different set of aesthetic values. Those values might be characterized as artful without artifice, avoiding of structural complexity, at ease (as the poets of Spenser's generation plainly were not) with the history that surrounds the house and its inhabitants. 'Polished pillars', 'a roof of gold', a 'lantern whereof tales are told', the architectural equivalent, in other words, of the world of ornament and allegory which sixteenth-century poets set out to evoke, has been banished, to be replaced by a house which is 'ancient' in its own right, no longer needing the mythographic enterprises of Elizabethan culture. It is as though the frenzied *creation* of a past has finally triumphed, and Jonson's house and its inhabitants can relax in a history which has been secured.

Of course, 'To Penshurst' represents an idealized understanding of society and social relations. It is not the case that Jonson has somehow thrown off, in one swift move, the burden of creating identities and histories which Renaissance poets felt. 'To Penshurst' is, in fact, a brilliantly successful deception. It is a performance which manages to unite the present with a past discovered in Jonson's enormous reading and imitation (in the Renaissance sense) of classical literature. As such the poem manages to suggest an assimilated sense of past and present working in harmonious unity. But that Penshurst the place may be unique, and may, in fact, stand in complete isolation from the society in which it seems to rest so securely is hinted at throughout the poem.

At the same time, 'To Penshurst' signalled for the poets who came after Jonson a moment of retreat. Nestling in the idealized Kent countryside, Jonson's creation of a secure bourgeois existence was to serve as a place of pilgrimage for poets who in other respects seem very different to all that Jonson appeared to stand for in the realm of aesthetics. What these poets were retreating from was, of course, the political and ideological fragmentation of the period of the English ▷ Civil War. What they were retreating to (and whether such retreat was, in fact, possible) is open to question. On the surface, the poets of the late 1630s, 1640s and 1650s are searching for Jonson's idyll of Horatian retirement. Thus ▷ Andrew Marvell, a poet of avowedly republican sympathies (at least at certain moments), seeks a retirement from a world that appears to have fallen apart. Only behind the walls of the garden of Nun Appleton (the home of the Fairfax family, celebrated in Marvell's 'Upon Appleton House', composed c 1651) can Marvell discover 'more decent Order tame'. But is this order real, or is it an illusion? Can the world, with all its pressing engagements, in reality be fenced in behind (or outside, depending on your point of view) a garden wall? In Marvell's 'An Horatian Ode upon Cromwell's Return from Ireland' – a poem which memorializes the return of the lord protector to England in May 1650 after his bloody campaign against the Irish – the restless figure of ▷ Cromwell is imagined as being urged out of a moment of Horatian retreat into confrontation with political realities. The political reality with which it is Cromwell's task to engage is one in which the state, government, the nexus of social affiliations as a whole, would appear to have broken apart. What Marvell offers in his heroic depiction of Cromwell is an alternative and elemental figure of power – a refashioner not only of kingdoms and states, but of the very structures of thinking. It is an alternative, too (though Marvell could not have known it), to that other elemental image of power offered in the 1650s, the *Leviathan* of Thomas Hobbes. For Marvell, caught up in the turmoil of post-revolutionary thinking, any retreat into a world of disengagement is fraught with difficulties that cannot be negotiated. So, Marvell's figure of pastoral retreat – Damon the Mower – encounters in the fields not an idyll of rural innocence, but his own downfall:

While thus he threw his Elbow round,
Depopulating all the Ground,
And with his whistling Sythe, does cut
Each stroke between the Earth and Root,
The edged Stele by careless chance
Did into his own Ankle glance;
And there among the Grass fell down,
By his own sythe, the Mower mown.
('Damon the Mower', ll. 73–80)

It is not difficult to understand the self-mown mower as expressing a powerful (even if humorous) image of what seemed to many Englishmen to be the self-induced catastrophe of civil war. For Damon is a reflexive figure. He is both the victim of 'edged Stele' and the wielder of steel himself: an embodiment of death, lurking in the seemingly innocent fields, and one of death's victims.

The self-destructive double-figure of Damon can be met with again and again, in various guises, in the poetry of the Civil War period. But for other poets, other forms of retreat presented themselves. For the ▷ Cavalier poets (a misleading term since the poets who are usually denoted in the phrase were neither artistically nor politically homogeneous, though they all shared a general sense of the ultimate value of the rule of kings rather than parliaments or, worse, people), pastoralism, sensuality, drink or the mind itself offered alternatives. Thus ▷ Robert Herrick, in his volume of poetry entitled *Hesperides* (1648), evokes a world of minutely observed detail, which in its fetishistic attention to the elaborate codes of dress and food, offers a form of nostalgic sensuality to counter the breakdown in social structures. But was it possible to evade what Herrick himself in his opening poem of the collection ('The Argument of his Book') termed 'Times trans-shifting'?

For Herrick's close contemporary, ▷ Richard Lovelace, the heroic self-image of the soldier fleeing the 'nunnery' of the 'chaste breast and quiet mind' of his mistress to encounter a new 'faith' composed of 'a sword, a horse, a shield' ('To Lucasta, Going to the Wars'), breaks apart when confronted with his own form of the double-figure which Marvell's Damon seemed to represent. That figure appears most memorably in Lovelace's poem 'The Snail', a poem which, on the surface, appears to be no more than an exercise in contrived wit. Yet the poem's object of contemplation, the unlikely figure of the snail itself, is an ambiguously sinister figure – a confusion of geometric order, familial relationships, gender and questions of origin. If the snail is, as the poem claims at the opening, a 'Wise emblem of our pol'tic world', then this world is one which has become a 'deep riddle'. Fluidly mysterious, the world now conforms to no fixed model of social and political stability. By the end of the poem, the snail has dissolved into a jelly, its 'dark contemplation' of its own self no preservative against dissolution. In the directly political 'A Mock Song', Lovelace depicts the universe itself as dissolving, a response to the ultimate political cleavage of the 1640s, that which took place in Whitehall in the January of 1649:

Now the sun if unarmed,
And the moon by us charmed,
All the stars dissolved to a jelly;
Now the thighs of the crown
And the arms are lopped down,
And the body is all but a belly.
('A Mock Song', ll. 15–20)

Social dissolution, the collapse of the body politic, the transformation of an ordered world into an image of chaotic misrule – it is as if that uncivilized wilderness which Spenser and his contemporaries some fifty years earlier had struggled to keep at bay has intruded into the very heart of the culture in which Lovelace is writing.

'Recent liberty recovered'

To express the literary culture of the Civil War and post-Civil War years as a struggle against encroaching forms of social and political fragmentation is to understand the poets of the mid-seventeenth century as engaged in a desperate form of self-preservation. But to other writers (and Marvell comes to mind once more), working in an alternative political tradition – one that might be termed, broadly, republican – other problems seemed to emerge. What the short-lived experiment in a different form of government of the early 1650s represented was the possibility of engagement with a radically altered set of political co-ordinates. Within this new matrix, whose boundaries can be charted in the numberless ⊳ pamphlets and broadsheets of the period, in popular songs, ⊳ sermons, prophetic writings, political treatises and poems, and in the diaries and letters of ordinary men and women, we can locate the most dominant poetic figure of the seventeenth century – John Milton.

Milton's poetic career is one of linguistic and formal experiment. Almost no poet since Spenser had traversed with such skill such a range of possible genres – which included ⊳ masque, sonnet, ⊳ translation, ⊳ elegy, sacred drama, and, of course, ⊳ epic. But in understanding Milton's poetic achievement we also need to recognize the continual presence of Milton's political convictions – though that is not to say that those convictions, in themselves, were somehow set in rigid tablets of stone. But for Milton, read by his contemporaries as the prose defender of the great experiment in new forms of government, poetry and politics are inextricably interwoven.

At the centre of Milton's conception of political revolution stands his awareness that language is the key to ordering and understanding the world in which we live. What Milton's poetry represents, therefore, is a recognition that the language in which he is writing – indebted as it is to the language of prophecy and lyric encountered in the Old Testament, in the patristic authors, and in the classics – is one that has to be recaptured from the determining ideological structures of the moment. It is not, I think, coincidence that, at the very point when a strangely familiar (to modern ears) language of technology and utilitarian values is being demanded by the supporters of the Royal Society, ⊳ *Paradise Lost* (1667) should appear. We can glimpse the revolutionary nature of Milton's struggle on behalf of language in the 1668 preface to the poem, where Milton offers the following justification of his writing:

> *The measure is English heroic verse without rhyme, as that of Homer in Greek and Virgil in Latin, rhyme being no necessary adjunct or true ornament of poem or good verse . . . but the invention of a barbarous age . . . This neglect then of rhyme so little is to be taken for a defect, though it may seem so perhaps to vulgar readers, that it rather is to be esteemed an example set, the first in English, of recent liberty recovered to heroic poem . . .*

This, it need hardly be said, is a revolutionary poetic manifesto. And in terming it revolutionary, I have in mind the notion of a cyclical movement. Poetic form and political engagement became linked in Milton's demand for 'a recent liberty recovered'. For both poetry and political expression now seem to exist in an age which is 'barbarous' to both.

Paradise Lost is, above all, the poem of recovered poetic liberty enacted in its very language, and, just as importantly, in what the poem has to say about language. For Adam, in the poem, is the discoverer of a language which not only identifies for himself his position within the world, but initiates his own quest for self-identity. Remembering his own creation, he recalls that without language he did not know 'who I was, or where, or from what cause' (VIII. 270–1). His response is speech, and in discovering speech, he discovers not only God but an identity and a world which can be named. Against this Frankenstein-like fable is set the negative language of a 'barbarous age' – the language of Babel and of Hell, linked, in the final moments of the poem, to a 'jangling noise of words unknown', which is the language given by God 'in derision' to the followers of Nimrod: the type of human oppression. The universal history lesson with which the poem closes endeavours to demonstrate that the transgression of human and divine law involves the denial of political equality:

> *. . . man over men*
> *He made not lord; such title to himself*
> *Reserving, human left from human free.*
> (XII. 69–71)

The link between language and identity, which lies at the heart of the experience of both Adam and Eve in the poem, alerts us to Milton's other great theme of *Paradise Lost* and one with which it would be appropriate to end this account of Renaissance poetry. In terming Milton the poet of 'recovered poetic liberty', what we must also acknowledge is that Milton is, at the same time, at one with his contemporaries in seeking to establish a coherent identity for the human subject. Paradoxically, that search for a unified sense of selfhood – the discovery of an identity which has been secured – is dramatized not only in the memories of creation possessed by Adam and Eve and in gender distinction, but in the figure of Satan who claims an autonomous position in God's creation. 'Who saw/when this creation was?' Satan asks, before offering his own version of separate identity:

> *We know no time when we were not as now;*
> *Know none before us, self-begot, self-raised*
> *By our own quick'ning power . . .*
> (V. 859–61)

Milton's demonic figure of self-creation – one that entranced that other great poetic visionary and revolutionary William Blake – stands alongside Marvell's lyrical figure of self-destruction found in the fields and meadows. We do not need, therefore, to place Satan in the simple role of grand adversary, or counter-hero. For Adam, Eve and Satan are bonded to one another in a triangular design which cannot be disrupted. Satan's spiritual home, from which he cannot be excluded by God (into which, indeed, God welcomes him), is neither Heaven, nor Hell, but, disturbingly, Eden. '*Et in Arcadia ego*' – that motto of Renaissance mortality – is also Satan's motto, as the ever-perceptive Eve acknowledges in questioning what kind of freedom Eden can represent. And in ⊳ Arcadia Satan undergoes the same tormented search for identity that the human figures strive to discover rooted in one another, as, in the most famous exit in English literature, they leave Eden and the poem together, hand in hand.

This account of poetry in the Renaissance period began with Puttenham's description of a 'certain doubleness' which seemed, to the Elizabethan critic, to haunt the language of poetry. It has ended with a description of the creation of a figure of division – Milton's Satan. Doubleness, division and duplicity have become almost the themes of this essay. But I do not want to suggest, in deploying this alliterative trio, that there exists therefore a homogeneity in the writing we have been discussing. What I would argue instead is that in the enormous richness and diversity of literary forms and experience which have reached us in the twentieth century from the early modern period, we perceive a culture which is neither monumental, nor the product of a mythic golden age of national experience. The lines from Donne's satire on religion quoted at the start of this essay suggest a more complex set of possibilities. What Donne, in these lines, seems to be contemplating is the problematic status of the individual's identity within the boundaries determined by the power relationships in society. The 'nature and name' of power in fact defines, for Donne and for so many other Renaissance writers, the nature of identity itself. But Donne continues:

> *. . . those blest flowers that dwell*
> *At the rough streames calme head, thrive and do well,*
> *But having left their roots, and themselves given*
> *To the streames tyrannous rage, alas, are driven*
> *Through mills, and rockes, and woods, and at last, almost*
> *Consum'd in going, in the sea are lost:*
>
> (Satire 3, ll. 103–108)

Here is the Renaissance writer's dilemma. To obey, sometimes to celebrate, the nature and name of power is to risk that very loss of identity which so much of Renaissance poetry is designed to preserve.

Renaissance Prose 4

Roger Pooley

Much modern prose seeks anonymity, the 'prose like a window-pane' that George Orwell worked for. However, the rise of the virtuoso sentence in contemporary fiction may alert its readers to another possibility, that prose can draw on many of the resources and richness of language usually associated with poetry. Reading Renaissance prose is usually an encounter with just such a self-conscious stylishness; and this can be just as apparent in supposedly 'non-literary' modes like the sermon or the scientific report as it is in early prose fiction. Even so, there are limited pleasures in simply reading for the style, in the manner of those anthologies now out of fashion which would print short extracts from a variety of texts as if they were lyric poems. But how can one get into the really long works? This is an age of vast compendia and encyclopaedic aspirations – Burton's ⊳ *Anatomy of Melancholy* grew from three hundred and fifty thousand words in 1621 to over five hundred thousand in 1651. Most readers will have to respond to such exhaustiveness by dipping, using the index to find what Burton says about love melancholy, or lycanthropia, or stopping after the deft hundred-page introduction, where Burton establishes his satiric persona of Democritus Junior. A contemporary reader will recognise this kind of address to the reader from fiction, and the image of the theatre of the world from Shakespeare:

> *Gentle Reader, I presume thou wilt be very inquisitive to know what Anticke or Personate Actor this is, that so insolently intrudes upon this common Theatre, to the worlds view, arrogating another mans name, whence hee is, why he doth it, and what he hath to say?*

Yet there are 'poetic' effects here, too, the alliteration of 'insolently intrudes', and the neat rhetorical triplet of whence, why and what. These are prose writers who shape their sentences, who *hear* what they write.

Prose style is not just a matter of taste, though, of responding to an age where 'artifice' was not something to be ashamed of. There are times when the choice of style in this period can be an index of other kinds of loyalties. There are sharp political and doctrinal divisions between Puritans and other religious writers from the 1590s onwards, and these are sometimes echoed in arguments about the appropriate style for religious discourse. The Puritan preachers like William Perkins and Richard Sibbes, who preached in Cambridge in the late sixteenth and early seventeenth centuries, were widely published, and sought a plain discourse that would get the new Reformation doctrines over to ordinary people in an 'affectionate' (emotional) way:

> *Thus are we by nature altogether rotten and polluted; speech, fine discourse, favour, and all other outward good parts, they can put no comeliness upon us. They are but on us as flowers stuck upon a dead carcase.*
>
> (Sibbes, *The Christian Work*, 1639)

This was often contrasted to the more learned and intricate 'high Anglican' style, sometimes misleadingly labelled 'Metaphysical', whose most famous, idiosyncratic exponent is Lancelot Andrewes, eventually Bishop of Winchester. Andrewes is at his best expounding the paradoxes of the great Christian festivals, the word made flesh at

Christmas, the death and resurrection of God's son at Easter. He often took a word by word approach to the text he expounded, a text that was still quoted in Latin, even though he was one of the translators of the King James version of the Bible. Here he is on the multitude of angels praising God who appeared to the shepherds at Christmas:

> *When we heare of a multitude, we fear a confusion, But (you will observe), this multitude was* multiduo militiae; *no confused rout: No; but* acies ordinata, *a well ordered armie. There is order, in an armie: There is order, in a* Queer *[choir]: There is order among* Angells: coordinate *among themselves,* subordinate *to their head and leader. So, a* multitude without confusion.
>
> (Sermon 12 of the Nativitie, 1618)

This is intricate stuff, overlapping, step-by-step argument. The dense punctuation indicates how the words might be read out, with lots of pauses and emphases. The mixture of Latin and English makes this seem much stranger to us than it might to an educated English audience whose schooling was almost entirely Latin. It's still pretty uncompromising, though; the famous narrative bits of Andrewes, like the sentence Eliot lifts for the opening of 'The Journey of the Magi', are rare.

In view of this Puritan/Anglican contrast, it is odd that in the Restoration the positions are almost reversed. The Anglicans accused the Nonconformists (as we must call them by then) of excess, of metaphorical, passionate language which whips up the passions to rebellion; in 1669 Samuel Parker only half-jokingly proposed an Act of Parliament 'to abridge preachers the use of fulsome and luscious metaphors'. There are some specific theological and political reasons for this; Anglican theology after the Restoration stressed ethical behaviour, particularly obedience, and demoted the Reformation doctrines such as justification by faith, an inescapably metaphorical idea. The more general point is that prose style, in this period, can sometimes be regarded as the sign of allegiance to a particular political or religious point of view.

Latinity and Eloquence

For a long time, the study of Renaissance prose was influenced by a taxonomy based on Latin models of style – Cicero, Seneca and Tacitus. The distinctions were largely argued in terms of syntax, with the symmetries and lengthy subordinate clauses of the high Ciceronian style contrasted with the looser 'Senecan amble' and the more pointed, epigrammatic Tacitus. There are a number of problems with this when it comes to actual analysis; 'Senecan', particularly, is an impossibly loose description. However, two factors should stop us completely dismissing it. First is that every educated writer in the period was educated in Latin, and that Latin was the language of international scholarship. When ▷ Bacon wanted to reach a European audience with his ▷ *Advancement of Learning* (1605), he expanded it into the Latin *De Augmentis Scientiarum* (1623). Robert Burton complained that his bookseller wouldn't let him publish his *Anatomy of Melancholy* in Latin because it wouldn't sell:

> *It was not mine intent to prostitute my Muse in* English *or to divulge* secreta Minervae, *but to have exposed this more contract in* Latin, *if I could have got it*

> *printed. Any scurrile Pamphlet is welcome to our mercenary Stationers in* English, *they print all . . .*
>
> ('Democritus to the Reader')

Burton's slipping in of Latin quotations, even here, is not just revenge for this affront to his international reputation; it is the small change of intellectual discourse. The extract also points to the rising commercial and popular success of English. There is a layer of popular pamphleteering throughout the period, but its importance increases as the literate market for amusement, learning and religious devotion increases.

It may be virtually impossible for modern readers to 'hear' the Latinity beneath Renaissance prose in English. It is nonetheless there, in well-turned epigrams, in extended syntactic units, and in choices of vocabulary. It is also there in rhetoric, the art of persuasion which formed the basis of every undergraduate's early years, and which pervades almost every Renaissance text, from Hamlet's soliloquies to Boyle's scientific essays.

At the level of organisation, rhetoric is to do with the laying out of an argument. The common Renaissance figure is of logic as a closed fist, rhetoric as an open hand. The contents page of Bacon's *Advancement* is one place to look for the strengths of such an approach, the sectioning and sub-sectioning of knowledge. Bacon's work is also a reminder of the way that anti-rhetoric is still firmly in the grip of rhetoric. His well-known attack on the excesses of the Renaissance rediscovery of classical Latinity is still observably in a sentence that would have been impossible without such a rediscovery:

> *This grew speedily to an excess; for men began to hunt more after words than matter; more after the choiceness of the phrase, and the round and clean composition of the sentence, and the sweet falling of the clauses, and the varying and illustration of their works with tropes and figures, than after the weight of matter, worth of subject, soundness of invention or depth of judgement.*
>
> (*Advancement*, 1.iv.2)

The symmetry between abuses and proper uses of learning (four of each) is pointed, however. It takes longer to write 'the sweet falling of the clauses' than 'soundness of invention'; the implication is that unsound learning is wordier than the real thing.

▹ Sir Philip Sidney's *Apology for Poetry* (posthumously published in 1590) is even more obviously constructed in the manner of the Renaissance oration, with a seven-point structure (an exordium, or introduction, a narration, or statement of the facts, a proposition, division of the facts, confirmation, refutation and a peroration or summary). Rhetoric also operates at the level of local effect, of tropes. Most of the popular, English introductions to rhetoric emphasise that side of rhetoric, following the example of the most famous and influential textbook, Erasmus' *De Copia* (literally, 'of fullness').

The popular rhetorics, like Wilson, also recognise that rhetoric is a public art, an instrument of political control. One reason for writing is to display to the Renaissance ruler one's ability to persuade ambassadors or subjects of the virtues of their position. The vernacular rhetorics, paradoxically, make this instrument of power available to all who can read English; though not overtly for democratic purposes. Rhetoric as a technique was also promulgated beyond the universities by the two main professions – lawyers and preachers. By the 1650s one did not have to have a degree to be able to clinch a point in an argument in the course of a sermon, say; though the scorn of the learned might still fall.

The English Bible and its Impact

Perhaps the greatest work of English Renaissance prose is better described as a work of English Reformation prose – the ▷ Bible. Fixed for subsequent generations in 1611 as the King James version (or 'Authorised Version'), it has to be regarded as a collective effort of translation and revision over more than eighty years. However, if it were not for the courage and unusual talents of William Tyndale, whose version of the New Testament was first published, in Germany, in 1526, it would not be as distinctive as it is. Something like five-sixths of Tyndale's work survives in the King James' committees' revision.

Even at the time the Tyndale tradition of translation was regarded as 'translationese', translating word for word rather than idiom for idiom. Robert Boyle, for example, thought it underplayed the rhetoric strength of the original. The result, however, was not so much a crib as a whole series of new idioms. Tyndale himself argued that there was a good match between the biblical languages and English: 'and the properties of the Hebrew tongue agreeth a thousand times more with the English than with the Latin' – Latin being the language in which the Bible was available with the approval of the Catholic church.

The first impact the English Bible had was doctrinal rather than literary or idiomatic. The doctrines of Paul, like justification by faith and predestination, that became clear in the English translations, were of incalculable effect in shifting the focus of English politics as well as spirituality and subjectivity. If, for example, you believe that you have been predestined, either to heaven or hell, but you are not sure which, it becomes an urgent question to find out which. The key, according to Reformation practice, is self-examination. This is not entirely new in Christianity; the first autobiography in Europe is probably St Augustine's *Confessions* (397–8), in English *The Book of Margery Kempe* (d.c. 1440). However, the first explosion of prose autobiography in English dates from the mid-seventeenth century, when the Protestant emphasis on self-examination in the context of conversion (rather than the Catholic emphasis on a continuous regime of confession and penance) meets up with the need to tell one's story as a means of entrance into the separatist congregations which replaced the (temporarily) collapsed Church of England in the 1650s.

▷ John Bunyan's ▷ *Grace Abounding to the Chief of Sinners* (1666) is the most notable of these. It is a conversion story rather than a life story, although it does tell us something of his early life. The details of his marriage, and of his service in the Parliamentary army, are tantalisingly brief, and ruthlessly selected for their relevance to his unfolding spiritual awakening. It goes through a pattern characteristic of many conversion stories of the period; after a dissolute youth, some early convictions of sin lead him to church, but only in a formal way. (This distinction between outward observance and inward reality is a key factor in the construction of the early modern self, in its Christian manifestation.) Then the Word strikes again, and the central section of the book describes with great psychological intensity the interior battle between the Biblical texts that would seem to condemn Bunyan, and those that would save him. The battle is complex – there isn't a single turning point, but a gradual process of assurance with frightening relapses. Bunyan's own style isn't biblical; it doesn't have the syntactic markers, for example the binary linking of sentences like St Paul's 'For we know that the law is spiritual: but I am carnal' (Romans 7:14,

Tyndale). However, the biblical texts have a special power for him – 'that Scripture fastened on my heart', 'this Scripture would strike me down, as dead', or 'that Scripture would seize upon my Soul.'

It was much later, from the mid-eighteenth century, when the Authorised Version began to be valued for its style as well as its doctrine. In this earlier period, the echo of the English Bible is most audible in those not educated in Latin, like Bunyan, and the radicals of the 1640s and 50s, like Richard Overton the Leveller, or Gerrard Winstanley the Digger, or the female prophets like Anna Trapnel. Most extraordinary of all is the so-called Ranter Abiezer Coppe, whose *Fiery Flying Roll* (1649) combines the *persona* of the prophet Ezekiel with revolutionary zeal:

> *This saith the Lord,* I inform you, that I overturn, overturn, overturn. *And as the Bishops, Charles, and the Lords, have had their turn, overturn, so your turn shall be next (ye surviving great ones) by what Name and Title soever dignified or distinguished, who ever you are, that oppose me, the Eternall God, who am UNIVERSALL Love, and whose service is perfect freedom, and pure Libertinisme.*

With the Ranters, prophetic denunciation blends into a kind of ecstasy. Thomas Traherne, whose political instincts were quite different, achieved another impressively ecstatic, slightly heterodox devotion in his *Centuries of Thanksgiving*. Most of Traherne's work remained in manuscript until the twentieth century; and to a modern reader his recounting of childhood vision sounds more akin to Wordsworth than that of a Calvinist culture:

> *Had any man spoken of it, it had been the most easy thing in the world to have taught me, and to have made me believe, that Heaven and earth was God's house, and that He gave it me. That the sun was mine and that men were mine, and that cities and kingdoms were mine also; that earth was better than gold, and that water was, every drop of it, a precious jewel.*

It's not Wordsworth, of course; it's less moralising, less brooding. It's still recognisably within the Reformation and Counter-Reformation disciplines of meditation, defined by Bishop Joseph Hall as 'a bending of the mind upon some spiritual object, through divers forms of discourse, until our thoughts come to an issue' (*Art of Divine Meditation*, 1627). It's also a particular effect of Renaissance prose, using the arts of rhetoric sentence construction to come to a climax where the copiousness of phrase echoes the benevolent creativity of God.

Political Prose

The growth of English political debate is remarkable in the seventeenth century. The student of literature could benefit from knowing more than the arguments around ▷ Shakespeare and ▷ Marvell, although those arguments – of the limits of monarchy and the virtues or republicanism – are central. Nor is it simply a question of history of ideas, of 'background'; it is a matter of attending to considerable creativity in great prose.

Most of the arguments in the period are conducted in the language of religion; the new secular politics associated with ▷ Machiavelli make little overt impact. Machiavelli's *The Prince* was not translated into English until 1640, even if the

'Machiavell' is a bogeyman in the drama from the 1590s. Machiavelli's acuteness was sometimes recognised – Francis Bacon said that he described how men act, rather than how they ought to act – but he had to be Christianised or rejected.

The most enduring form of political writing describes the imaginary community, or Utopia. ▷ More's ▷ *Utopia* (1516), which christens the term (a pun on 'no place' and 'good place' in Greek) was written in Latin, translated into English in 1551. While it has some literary affinities with the ideal community of Plato's *Republic*, and the communitarian if not exactly communist ideals of medieval monasticism, the discovery of the New World frames its discourse. Society outside the civilised west (fictional or real) is no longer necessarily 'barbarian', primitive, there to be feared or exploited – though it is all those things in our period. It might also be admirable, a world which has escaped the Fall. So More's guide, Raphael Hythlodaeus, uses their rational society, with wealth, work and power distributed rather than concentrated, as a means of criticising the Europe of his own day. Human nature has not changed, and the Utopians are still Machiavellian in their dealings with the outside world. Inside, society is regulated, rational, cultured. Things have been arranged so that self-interest and the public interest coincide; and in doing so, as J. C. Davis points out, More lays out the problem with Utopias. If morally good decisions are always sensible decisions, doesn't this destroy the humanity, the ethical identity, of the Utopians at the same time?

Subsequent Renaissance Utopias have been less influential, and less witty; but some are still worth looking at. ▷ Francis Bacon's ▷ *New Atlantis* (1627) contains little of the circumstantial detail that makes *Utopia* such an imaginative success, but it does contain, in Salomon's House, the kind of ideal community of scientific learning that Bacon wanted to see in England. Nor is it just an annex to Bacon's scientific writing; it celebrates a society without factions, and thus forms a rebuke to the court parties in England. Sir John Harrington's *Oceana* (1656) was published while the government of England was being remade after the execution of the King. The detail in his utopia is mathematical and organisational, perhaps to emphasise the scientific validity of his schemes. Workable government depends on a well-designed framework, one that designs out the impact of human imperfection. As with More, liberty is not high on his list – a reminder that the classical republicanism of the Civil War and Commonwealth period should not be confused with modern democracy, though it opened the way for it. After the Restoration, Margaret Cavendish reinvigorated the genre with her *New World, called the Blazing World* (1666), with its imaginary fantasy of a world created by a female monarch.

The Civil War and Commonwealth period produced an explosion of debate in print at all levels, from knockabout satire to serious proposals (sometimes in the same text). This is the period of the early newsbooks, which from 1641 to 1660 gave an account of events and their meaning from various political sides in small, eight or sixteen-page pamphlets. The very first, *The Heads of Severall Proceedings in this Present Parliament*, is a summary of the proceedings in Parliament, responding to the crisis in Ireland. The various sides of the dispute had their own papers: the royalists had *Mercurius Aulicus* and *Mercurius Elencticus* amongst others, Parliament had *Mercurius Politicus*, the Levellers had *The Moderate*. Much of what we recognise as modern journalism is there – opinion pieces, astrological predictions, 'detestable outrages', strange but true stories – along with ballad poetry, even whole issues in verse, which indicates continuities with a very different culture of disseminating news and ideas.

▷ Milton's political writings begin in 1641, too, with *Of Reformation touching Church–Discipline in England, and the Causes that Hitherto have Hindered It.* (Seventeenth-century title-pages often function as brief summaries). After Charles I's execution in 1649, he becomes virtually an official apologist for Cromwell's cause: *The Tenure of Kings and Magistrates* (1649) had argued that it was lawful for a people to call a tyrant to account. The first and second 'Defences of the English People' (1651 and 1654) are written in Latin for a European readership. The word is overused about this period, but Milton is a genuinely revolutionary writer. In *The Doctrine and Discipline of Divorce* (1643) he attacks the tyrannic power of 'Custom' in domestic law; in *Areopagitica* (1644) he attacks the censorship; the attack on bishops and kings completes the republican set. Milton is not the most liberal or radical of the writers in the period, either; but the prose is certainly of more historical and artistic interest than an annex to, or diversion from, his poetry. It can be uniquely stirring:

> *He that can apprehend and consider vice with all other baits and seeming pleasures, and yet abstain, and yet distinguish, and yet prefer that which is truly better, he is the true warfaring Christian. I cannot praise a fugitive and cloister'd vertue, unexercis'd & unbreath'd, that never sallies out and sees her adversary, but slinks out of the race, where that immortal garland is to be run for, not without dust and heat. Assuredly we bring not innocence into the world, we bring impurity much rather: that which purifies us is triall, and triall is by what is contrary.*
>
> (*Areopagitica*)

Milton's prose is best seen as part of a great and various debate in the mid-seventeenth century, in a period where many assumptions were called into question. The excitement of this can still be recaptured in the writings of the Levellers, Richard Overton, John Lilburne and William Walwyn particularly, and the Digger Gerrard Winstanley. The political movements were short-lived; the ideas re-emerged. In retrospect, though, the most profound rethinking of political authority from this period is in ▷ Thomas Hobbes' ▷ *Leviathan* (1651), the first great work of political philosophy in English. Hobbes' position may at first sight seem bleak, philosophically and artistically. He reckons that human life is determined by fear on the one hand and the desire for power on the other. His intellectual drives are similarly austere; he regarded geometric as the paradigmatic procedure, and language, rhetoric and metaphor particularly, as the means to absurdity and contention:

> *The light of humane minds is perspicuous words, but by exact definitions first snuffed, and purged from ambiguity; reason is the pace; increase of science, the way; and the benefit of mankind, the end.*

Such was the rigour of Hobbes' approach that he transformed the whole level of debate. Nonetheless he was regarded as scandalously 'atheist' in his contention that civil society could hold together by contract, simply because of the fear of civil war, without any need for a theological justification like the Divine Right of Kings. Hobbes was more 'absolutist' in his analysis of the social contract than subsequent theorists, most notably Locke, whose *Two Treatises of Government* (1689) established the philosophical basis of the liberal 'Glorious Revolution'. *Leviathan* is also a more compelling read than the austere preconditions it lays down for discourse might imply ('There is nothing I distrust more than my Elocution', he wrote at the end of his masterwork). The famous Chapter 13, 'Of the Natural Condition of Mankind as concerning their Felicity and Misery' is the best example, but the whole work is based on persuasion through metaphor as much as logic. By comparison to the earlier formulations of his ideas, such as *The Elements of Law*, *Leviathan* is a blaze of rhetorical colour.

The Language of Science

Hobbes' commitment to a rigorous language purged of metaphor, even if he didn't achieve it, is often linked to the ambitions of a group he had a number of differences with, the Royal Society, founded in 1660. The Royal Society had some of the attributes of modern scientific organisation, the collective approach to knowledge according to agreed rules, a commitment to experiment rather than the authority of ancient texts, and a sense that progress could be made by accumulating facts and scientific laws. At the same time, most of their active members (Robert Boyle, John Wilkins and John Ray, for example) were at least as involved in theologico-philosophical discourse as in conducting and writing up experiments. Approaching this material simply as if it were the origins of modern science can distort its feel. It was amateur, in the best and worst sense. Nor did it supplant older ideas entirely. Boyle, Newton and Locke were exchanging alchemical secrets well into the Restoration.

The suspicion of metaphor, 'the close, naked natural way of speaking . . . bringing all things as near the mathematical plainness, as they can' (Thomas Sprat, 1667) is a key ambition of their writing. It fed the artificial language schemes of the Restoration, of which Wilkins' *Essay towards Real Character and a Philosophical Language* (1668) is the most spectacular and intricate attempt to produce a classificatory sign system which would not only describe but somehow *be* knowledge. So is the experimental narrative, the essay which describes the progress of an experiment as a story from hypothesis to conclusion. William Harvey's *De Motu Cordis* (1628, tr. 1653), on the circulation of the blood, anticipates it, but Boyle's accounts of his experiments with an air-pump, and Newton's reports on his optical experiments, define the genre.

Subsequent histories have tended to edit out the concern with the trivial and the amazing that occupied many of the early meetings. Left in, they show how Thomas Browne's *Pseudodoxia Epidemica* (1646), a fascinating compendium of popular errors, links Bacon's desire to discredit existing ignorance with the Royal Society's half-realised ambition to replace it with certain knowledge. Browne was a doctor, who had read Harvey. One might say the medical profession forms a kind of alternative source of 'modern science' in this period. Browne's *Religio Medici* (1643) is a confession of faith in a relaxed, intimate style, a reflection on God and Nature ('that universal and publike Manuscript'). Like the works of Boyle and other early scientists, it shows how scientific practice was motivated as much by a theological desire for understanding as by practical considerations. Browne may have been impatient of error, but he was tolerant and sceptical, and disarmingly aware of his own bias.

History

The chronicle histories of England and their adaptation by Shakespeare and his contemporaries show how much of an appetite for history the Elizabethans had. Not only was it a cover for debate about contemporary events, it showed how the country was still trying to define itself; and how the Tudors were establishing their version of events. Thomas More's *History of King Richard III* (1513) is an example of this, though it is also the first example of a biography in English influenced by the Humanist approach to history. The antiquarian movement was also an important methodological development. Nowadays, 'antiquarian' is a pejorative term for historians; the antiquarians of the sixteenth century, like Camden and Stowe, led the way in the critical use of sources. James I even closed down the College of Antiquaries for a while out of political suspicion.

John Foxe's *Acts and Monuments* (1570, augmented and revised until 1641) is a vast historical compilation of Protestant martyr stories; indeed it is still popularly known as 'Foxe's Book of Martyrs'. Foxe, who was a Puritan forced into exile during the reign of Mary, created an alternative hagiography to that of the Catholic saints, but more importantly created an ideal of heroic suffering that inspired Milton and Bunyan, and helped to define much of British Protestant Christianity's sense of itself as a historical and spiritual entity. Like most historians of the period, Foxe was both author and editor, reporter and polemicist. There is something of the formulaic about all those trials and burnings and last words; though the repetition has its own mesmeric effect.

▷ Sir Walter Ralegh's *History of the World* (1614) is also a sourcebook for Puritans; Cromwell and Milton admired it. Vast though it is (another individual encyclopaedia) the main text breaks off at 146 BC. Ralegh's earlier prose had addressed contemporary history in an anti-Spanish, pro-colonialist manner. Only in the Preface to the *History of the World*, with its swingeing attack on the 'merciless' Henry VIII in contrast to James I, does he hint at the dangerous practice of writing about recent events. For the most part, in the parade of English Kings in the Preface, and ancient monarchs in the body of the text, he emphasises history as a record of the judgements of God:

> *Oh by what plots, by what forswearings, betrayings, oppressions, imprisonments, tortures, poisonings, and under what reasons of State, and politic subtlety, have these forenamed Kings, both strangers and of our own Nation, pulled the vengeance of God upon themselves . . .*

In its way, Ralegh's *History* is as impressive as the historical tragedies of the period, much of whose sensibility he shares. God and great men make history; 'Eloquent, just and mighty Death', along with his historian spokesman, give the verdict.

History is what politicians write when they are out of power. Ralegh wrote his in the Tower of London. Bacon wrote his *History of Henry VI* after being dismissed from the Chancellorship. Although it is assembled from secondary sources, it is interesting as a study in power politics from an angle that owes more to Tacitus, Machiavelli and Guiccardini, not to mention his own experience, than providentialism. A similar hard-headedness, in more epigrammatic form, is available in his *Essays*, effectively the first English example of this new prose form. Closer to an eye-witness account is Clarendon's *History of the Rebellion*, not published until 1702–4, but begun in 1646 after the defeat of the Royalists. Clarendon, as Edward Hyde, had joined Charles I from a reforming, Parliamentary position, and he is able to see both sides of many questions. An old anthology of Clarendon reduced the *History* to a series of witty, judicious 'characters', which is true to one side of the text. Charles I, for example, was 'the worthiest gentleman, the best master, the best friend, the best husband and the best Christian, that the age in which he lived produced.' The beginning of the next sentence reminds us what was missing from the list: And if he were not the best king . . . 'Similarly, even as Cromwell is being consigned to hell in the final verdict, he is exonerated from being a Machiavellian and a man of blood: 'He will be looked on by posterity as a brave bad man.' Clarendon's style of history has itself had a long and continuing posterity; the judicious verdict of the participant observer can be uniquely fascinating, and the *partis pris* can be recognised and allowed for.

Prose fiction

Renaissance prose fiction has only recently emerged from a subordinate position, as a sourcebook for the drama and a preface to 'the rise of the novel' in the eighteenth century. Between five and six hundred works of prose fiction were published before 1700. Some of them are romances, heroic and/or erotic, some are allegories, some are fictional versions of non-fiction genres like the deathbed or gallows confession, the life of the rogue, or travel stories. How do you tell if they are fiction rather than fact? The title 'the true story of . . .' is usually one sign; the apparatus of fictiveness mimics that of historicity.

▷ Sir Philip Sidney's ▷ *Arcadia* (1578, first published in a revised form in 1590) is the acme of the pastoral romance, which spawned a number of imitations and continuations, most notably ▷ Mary Wroth's *Urania* (1621). The romance plot, set in ancient Greece, mixes defeated intentions and averted tragedy with disguise and doubling; the intricacies of the plot are matched by numerous opportunities for set speeches and poems. The attractions of a cultured, chivalrous aristocratic ideal – stylishness in love and in battle – are celebrated in the characteristic Elizabethan pastoral trope, where true virtue (which has to be inherited and apparent in action) is always able to shed its disguise at the final, reconciling moment.

The political and cultural complexities of *Arcadia* are never quite matched in the shorter romances of the period, of which ▷ Robert Greene's ▷ *Pandosto* (1588) and *Menaphon* (1589) and ▷ Thomas Lodge's *Rosalynde* (1590) and *A Margarite of America* (1596) are the most notable. ▷ Gascoigne's *Adventures of Master F.J.* (1573; revised and toned down 1575) uses a sophisticated battery of fictional devices, and describes a distinctively sexy and hypocritical style of 'courtly love'. In some ways it reverses romance; the virtuous sister Frances is less successful than the promiscuous tease Elinor, 'shrieking (but softly)' as she is seduced. The love debates in which F.J. takes part fail to bring him to his senses; only betrayal does that, and he takes his revenge in something close to rape.

▷ John Lyly's ▷ *Euphues: The Anatomy of Wit* (1578) began the fashion for a moralising style based on a remarkable hyper-extension of antithesis. It's not uncritical; in fact the introduction of yet another sententious pairing when the sentence ought to be over suggests a gift of self-parody:

> *This young gallant of more wit than wealth, and yet of more wealth than wisdom, seeing himself inferior to none in pleasant conceits thought himself superior to all in honest conditions, in so much as he thought himself so apt in all things that he gave himself almost to nothing but practising of those things commonly which are incident to those fine wits: fine phrases, smooth quips, merry jaunts, jesting without mean and abusing mirth without measure.*

One critical dilemma in reading Elizabethan prose is deciding what to do with its excess. Euphuism is a Humanist tale of the dangers of wit without wisdom, which values male friendship over love for a clever but deceitful woman. It is a virtuoso display of that greatest of humanist accomplishments, rhetoric, and an exposé of its limitations.

▷ Thomas Nashe, perhaps the most versatile and energetic of the Elizabethan stylists, learnt his trade as much from improvisatory satire of 'Martin Marprelate' (fl. 1588–90) that he was hired to attack as from the 'university wits' like Lyly (incidentally also an anti-Martin pamphleteer). Nashe's excess, though, mixes the verbal with the visceral. In ▷ *The Unfortunate Traveller* (1594) his picaresque hero, Jack Wilton, travels sixteenth-century Europe watching how disease, battle and torture reduce bodies to their constituent parts. Moral indignation is most often reinforced by bathos, as the proud and pretentious in love and religion are brought down.

Romance proved remarkably resilient in the seventeenth century, despite the early translation of ▷ *Don Quixote*, and its repertoire much expanded by translations from the French. The impact of this is clearest in the Restoration, where ▷ Aphra Behn's ▷ *Love Letters between a Nobelman and his Sister* (1684–7) combined contemporary allusion with a new, passionate sensationalism which her earlier translations only partially indebted to the French romances she had earlier translated.

A largely popular rather than learned tradition of religious fiction, employing allegory and dialogue, finds its most accomplished expression in Bunyan's ▷ *The Pilgrim's Progress* (1678; Part Two, 1684), ▷ *The Life and Death of Mr Badman* (1680), and ▷ *The Holy War* (1682). Arthur Dent's *The Plain Man's Pathway to Heaven* (1601) was a best seller, introducing theological and social ideas through dialogue; Richard Bernard's *Isle of Man* (1627), puts Sin on trial. Richard Overton, in *The Araignment of Mr Persecution* (1645), also uses the trial narrative, with a few hints from Foxe, to satirize the censorious Sir John Presbyter in the name of liberty of conscience. To this lively, often humorous tradition Bunyan adds his own intensity, in the first part a kind of heroic isolation, as Christian resists the blandishments of Mr Worldly Wiseman, Giant Despair, and the court of Vanity Fair, where everything exists to be sold. It's tempting to see Bunyan at a whole series of crossroads, of Puritanism and Nonconformist individualism, of popular fiction and emergent novel, of providential history and social realism. He is evidence of all these changes; but, like many of these early fiction writers, deserves to be read as more than representing a phase before the 'real' novel began.

Renaissance prose, then, often demands a disciplined attention to style, and a grasp of sometimes remote thought-forms; but it also offers tremendous examples of the beauties of sentence-form precisely attuned to logic, and some startling inventiveness that makes modern prose look po-faced and under-nourished.

5 Renaissance Drama

Susan Bruce

Introduction

Miranda: *O, wonder!*
How many goodly creatures are there here!
How beauteous mankind is! O brave new world,
That has such people in 't!
Prospero: *'Tis new to thee.*

(Shakespeare, *The Tempest*, 5.1.181–4)

If Miranda's wondrous enthusiasm at the sight of fellow Europeans points to the sense of excitement and pleasure infusing much Renaissance drama, so too her father's sardonic negation of that optimism expresses a feeling recurrent in many Renaissance plays. Indeed, it is in its conflation of these two, irreconcilable, points of view that this brief extract from ▷ William Shakespeare's ▷ *The Tempest* (c. 1611) may serve as a suitable point from which to embark on a survey of English Renaissance drama. On the one hand, the pleasure and the sense of renewal and possibility expressed by the young Miranda finds its analogue in the resolution, promise and optimism which, superficially at least, inhabits the conclusion of many Renaissance comedies. The protagonists of ▷ Ben Jonson's ▷ *Bartholomew Fair* (1614), for example, leave the play to carry on their festivities in the home of Justice Overdo, the town's magistrate, and in Shakespeare's ▷ *A Midsummer Night's Dream* (1595) the conclusion of the play points similarly to a happiness and a celebration beyond the confines of the text, as the fairy king, Oberon, speaks a blessing on the marriages of the play's protagonists. 'Now until the break of day,/ Through this house each fairy stray,' Oberon says:

To the best bride-bed will we,
Which by us shall blessed be;
And the issue there create
Ever shall be fortunate.
So shall all the couples three
Ever true in loving be;
And the blots of Nature's hand
Shall not in their issue stand.

(5.1.387–396)

For such characters, it would seem, all worlds are brave and new, peopled by many goodly creatures whose future promises more of their kind. Similarly, resolution, rebirth and the prospect of brave new worlds frequently find expression in the romances (of which *The Tempest* is one). Like *The Tempest*, for example, both ▷ *Cymbeline* (1609–10) and ▷ *The Winter's Tale* (1610–11) conclude with the reconciliation of long-divided families and the rediscovery of relations believed to be lost, or dead. A sense of miraculous rebirth underlines the ending of these plays: 'If this prove/ A vision of the island, one dear son/ Shall I lose twice,' says Alonso in *The Tempest* (5.1.175–6) as his lost son is revealed to him, and this 'most high miracle' finds its analogous moment in *The Winter's Tale* when the statue of Leontes' dead wife Hermione comes back to life, provoking from her husband the wondering expression that 'if this be magic, let it be an art/ Lawful as eating' (5.3.110–1). Similarly, in *Cymbeline*, the soothsayer's explanation of a hitherto-baffling prophecy points to rediscovery, resolution and the promise of a better future: 'The lofty cedar, royal Cymbeline,' the soothsayer explains,

Personates thee and thy lopped branches point
Thy two sons forth; who, by Belarius stolen,
For many years thought dead, are now reviv'd
To the majestic cedar join'd, whose issue
Promises Britain peace and plenty.

(5.5.454–9)

Miranda's words, then, express a structure of feeling which resonates beyond the play in which she utters them, but so too does Prospero's cynical checking of her youthful, and perhaps naive, enthusiasm. If Miranda believes like Coriolanus that 'there is a world elsewhere,' (Shakespeare, ▷ *Coriolanus* (1608?) 3.3.135) Prospero clearly does not, and his perspective, it might be argued, approximates more to the vision afforded by tragedy that it does to the (supposedly) fairy-tale perspective afforded by romance, or to the happy resolution of comedy. 'How weary, stale, flat and unprofitable/ Seem to me all the uses of this world,' 'laments Shakespeare's Hamlet (▷ *Hamlet* (c. 1601) 1.2.132–4). Not for him the pastoral conception of the world as a garden controlled and ordered by man in which, as Polixenes says in ▷ *The Winter's Tale*,

We marry
A gentler scion to the wildest stock,
And make conceive a bark of baser kind
By bud of nobler race: this is an art
Which does mend nature, change it, rather, but
The art itself is nature'

(4.4.92–97).

For Hamlet, the world appears as quite a different garden, an 'unweeded' one, which art has deserted, 'That grows to seed; things rank and gross in nature/ Possess it merely' (1.2.135–7). For him, the world is an empty place, denuded of dignity and order, as it is for Edgar, at the end of Shakespeare's ▷ *King Lear* (1605), whose world is equally hostile to the kind of transformative, youthful, perspective of a Miranda: 'The weight of this sad time we must obey;' that play concludes, 'Speak what we feel, not what we ought to say./ The oldest hath borne most: we that are young,/ Shall never see so much, nor live so long.' (5.3.322–5).

Both optimism and pessimism, then, both the sense that there is a world elsewhere and the conviction that there is not are sentiments which recur frequently in Renaissance drama. But to suggest, as I have perhaps implicitly done thus far, that such sentiments are neatly divided into two opposing genres, comedy and tragedy, is vastly to simplify the issue. To maintain, for example, that Shakespearean comedy progresses invariably to the resolution of the conflicts played out in the drama, ending in promise and the optimistic expectation of a renewed future is only one reading of that genre, and however convincing that interpretation may at first seem, what must also be accounted for are the places where such resolution is incomplete or unsatisfactory. Even in such essentially light-hearted dramas as *A Midsummer Night's*

Dream and Shakespeare's ▷ *Twelfth Night* (1599–1600) total closure remains elusive: Demetrius remains spellbound at the end of *A Midsummer Night's Dream*, for instance, whilst the 'notoriously abus'd' Malvolio exits from *Twelfth Night* expressing the desire to be 'reveng'd on the whole pack' of his fellow protagonists (5.1.376). And with the darker Shakespearean 'comedies,' such as ▷ *Measure For Measure* (1603–4) and (despite its title) ▷ *All's Well That Ends Well* (1602–3) the claim to comedic resolution is dubious indeed: those plays may deliver to their audiences the multiple marriages which are a generic convention of the endings of Shakespearean comedy, but they make it very difficult for an audience to conclude that such marriages constitute an unambiguously happy ending, that all is indeed well which ends, so superficially, well. Other comedies end with the institutionalised chastening of their protagonists: in Jonson's ▷ *Volpone*, for example, Volpone is banished to prison, to be cramped with irons until he is crippled, his accomplice Mosca is sent off to be whipped and then enslaved forever in the galleys, and the other participants in the drama similarly punished.

Renaissance comedy then, is frequently far less light-hearted and celebratory than it might at first seem. Similarly, if many tragedies seem to reflect Prospero's conviction that confidence in brave new worlds is grossly misguided, this observation must also acknowledge that many tragedies are far less essentially pessimistic, looking forward, not back, and ending with the restoration of a renewed and reempowered order. Thus Shakespeare's ▷ *Macbeth* (1605–6), for example, concludes with Duncan conferring new honours on his thanes and kinsmen, calling home his exiled friends abroad, promising to perform the tasks requisite to the re-imposition of order 'in measure, time and place', and extending thanks 'to all at once and to each one/ Whom we invite to see us crown'd at Scone' (5.7.103–4). Similarly, in ▷ Christopher Marlowe's *Edward II* (c. 1592), it is not the death of Edward with which the play concludes, but the stately, if brutal, reimposition of order on the accession of the King's son, ▷ Edward III.

History plays, of course, tend to end with the accession of a new king, even when their titles describe them as tragedies (as in ▷ *Richard III* (1593?), or when the accession of the new king is undermined by the knowledge of what is to come later, as in Shakespeare's ▷ *King Henry VI Part III* (c. 1592). In this play the celebration of the new King, Edward, is, for the audience, circumscribed by the presence on stage of the self-confessedly evil Richard, Duke of Gloucester, whose Machiavellian machinations form the subject of *Richard III*. Yet the desirability of state order is in both cases emphasised by the reconstitution of power in the single figure of the crowned head: *Richard III*, for example, ends with the accession of ▷ Henry VII, whose heirs, he promises, will 'enrich the time to come with smooth-fac'd peace' (5.5.31). The re-establishment of order, however, is not confined to the ending of the history play: in Shakespeare's ▷ *Romeo and Juliet* (1597), for example, the loss of the two protagonists becomes the occasion of the reconciliation of their respective families, as each erects a statue in memory of the other's lost child, whilst in Shakespeare's ▷ *Timon of Athens* (1607) Alcibiades promises, in the closing lines of the play, to 'use the olive with [his] sword,/ Make war breed peace, make peace stint war' (5.4.81–2).

The Tempest, then, is not alone in vacillating between a sense of infinite optimism and a sense of the ease in which such optimism might be undermined, or overlaid, by less happy perceptions. And it might be argued, as indeed I shall, broadly speaking, be suggesting here, that both of these contradictory perceptions derive from the massive and interconnected changes taking place, in all fields, during the early modern period. On the one hand, the age is one of discovery. The new world to which Miranda unconsciously refers is one of many new cultures encountered by early modern Europeans: driven by the ever-increasing exigencies of trade, profit, and eventually colonialism, they looked ever more widely for new routes and cultures to trade with and to exploit, discovering in the process new continents and new races, and extending trade and competition with those they already knew. But geographical expansion was only one of the ways in which the Renaissance was a period of discovery: in astronomy, the discoveries of Nicholaus Copernicus, Johannes Kepler, Tycho Brahe and Galileo Galilei proved that the earth is not the centre of the universe, as older theories had had it; they also showed that the universe was a much greater and emptier place than had ever been thought before. Such discoveries were driven, in part, by the compelling desire to draw conclusions about the world from empirical observation of it which also characterises ▷ Francis Bacon's inauguration, in the early seventeenth century, of a new methodology of scientific enquiry. Baconian science emphasised the centrality of experimentation and observation to our access to knowledge; it also laid out, explicitly, the claim that knowledge is power.

This scientific revolution, it may be observed, held much in common with the thinking of many of the early Protestant Reformers of the Church, as both attacked, implicitly or explicitly, older doctrines of order and hierarchy which had been central to the thinking of the old science and to established, Catholic, religion. Known as 'the Great Chain of Being,' this older doctrine is made explicit in Shakespeare's ▷ *Troilus and Cressida* (1601–2) when Ulysses argues that:

The heavens themselves, the planets, and this centre
Observe degree, priority, and place,
Institute, course, proportion, season, form,
Office, and custom, in all line of order.

(1.3.85–8)

and asks:

How could communities,
Degrees in schools, and brotherhoods in cities,
. . . The primogenity and due of birth,
Prerogative of age, crowns, sceptres, laurels,
But by degree stand in authentic place?

(1.3.103–8)

Such thinking had for centuries dominated religious, scientific and political conceptions of order, assigning a fixed and individual place in a cosmic hierarchy from God, down through the angels, man, women, and animal, to, finally, the most insignificant stone. But when Ulysses argues for its enduring truth, it is already under threat: Ulysses would not need to speak so fervently in its defence unless the view was already under attack, (as it indeed was,) from scientific, religious and, as we shall see in more depth later, political fronts.

It is no coincidence that one of the most explicit explorations of the truth or falsehood of the 'great chain of being' appears in *Troilus and Cressida*, for this play is, throughout, deeply concerned with philosophical questions about belief, and deeply sceptical of our ability to achieve secure answers to the questions that it raises. 'How do we know?' and 'on what authority can we believe?' were, as we have seen, questions raised with a compelling insistence in both religion and science; so too they inhabit the philosophical inquiry of the period, which xperienced the rise of a new kind of scepticism. The *Essaies* of Michel de Montaigne, published in 1580 and 1588, and translated into English by John Florio in 1603 brought a searching intelligence to bear on many issues which had not before even been formulated as questions, and also formulated the framework to his essays in terms of an inquiry into the nature of selfhood which was quite new: 'I desire therein,' he states in his preface to the reader,

> *to be delineated in mine owne genuine, simple and ordinarie fashion, without contention, art, or study; for it is my selfe I pourtray. . . . If my fortune had beene to have lived among those nations, which yet are said to live under the sweet liberty of Natures first and uncorrupted lawes, I assure thee, I would most willingly have pourtrayed myselfe fully and naked. Thus gentle Reader my selfe am the groundeworke of my booke: It is then not reason thou shouldest employ thy time about so frivolous and vaine a Subject.*
> (Montaigne, *Essaies.*)

And in the latter part of our period, ▷ Rene Descartes' *Meditations on First Philosophy* inaugurated an even more profound and radical scepticism, as he methodically subjected each criterion for belief in his own existence to the process of reason, holding 'back [his] assent from opinions which are not completely certain' and finding in each of them some reason for doubt, implying (although not concluding) that the answer to the question about our own existence can only be found in the interiority of the self: '*cogito ergo sum*' – 'I think, therefore I am'.

The scale and magnitude of change in the Renaissance was, then, hard to underestimate, and it is easy enough to imagine that whilst this may have initiated a sense of excitement – in the words of the narrator at the end of ▷ *Paradise Lost* 'the world was all before them; (XII, 646) – it simultaneously, may have generated a perception of profound instability: the world may lie before Adam and Eve in *Paradise Lost*, but only as they are leaving behind the security and calm which was Eden. To discover that the universe is a vast emptiness, and that man cannot pretend to the centrality in it in which he hitherto believed is a destabilising notion indeed: 'the New philosophie,' as Donne famously put it, 'calls all in doubt'.

The various developments which I have briefly detailed here could all be (and have all been) argued to play a part in the growth of the tensions which reveal themselves in Renaissance drama. The drama of the period is overdetermined, the product of a multiplicity of social and political developments which interact with each other in complex ways which we cannot easily, if at all, separate out and quantify. One way of thinking this through, perhaps, is to remember that the conclusion of the English Renaissance is conventionally marked by the outbreak of the English revolution, a social conflagration the likes of which England had never before experienced. To enter into the causes of the English revolution is way beyond the scope of this essay; what needs to be recognised, however, is that the tensions which eventually explode in so large-scale a conflict are both manifold, and in existence many years before overt conflict actually erupts. In other words, although the Renaissance is in many ways a period of extraordinary, and manifold, expansion and discovery, it also directly precedes a time of gross social upheaval, the seeds of which it must also, however unconsciously, experience and express.

In his *Modern Tragedy*, the Marxist cultural critic Raymond Williams, whose thinking underlies that of the newer cultural materialist critics of the 1980s and 90s argues that important tragedy occurs in periods 'preceding the substantial breakdown and transformation of an important culture. Its conclusion,' Williams goes on to say,

> *is the real tension between old and new: between received beliefs, embodied in institutions and responses, and newly and vividly experienced contradictions and possibilities.*
> (*Modern Tragedy*)

The English Renaissance, it is clear, constitutes such an age, poised on the verge of social disintegration, but in other senses relatively stable. And taking Williams' observation rather more liberally than he intended it, I am extending it here to encompass not just the tragedy of the Renaissance, but its drama in general, in which, I think one can see evidence both of the discoveries of the Renaissance and of its increasingly fragmentary sense of social cohesion. The remainder of this essay will attempt to touch upon some of the ways in which these various changes inhabit early modern drama: in it I shall try to raise, although not necessarily to answer, some of the many questions generated by this most fascinating period of English literature.

Trade and Expansion

'O my America, my new found land,' states ▷ Donne in 'To His Mistris Going To Bed,' 'my kingdome, safeliest when with one man man'd'. America, discovered in 1492, had by the late sixteenth century already become a figure for the possibility of expansion and colonialism, and also, in very complex ways, for the figuring of colonialism in terms of gender, and vice versa. We see this aspect of early modern Europe most clearly, perhaps, in *The Tempest* which many recent critics, especially those influenced by the New Historicism, have read as a representation of what is commonly referred to as the 'colonial encounter'. In part, *The Tempest* depicts the relation between the exiled white magician Prospero, and the 'salvage and deformed slave' Caliban, whose name is probably an anagram of the word 'cannibal'. Although Caliban's race is uncertain (as indeed is the location of the island, situated variously in the middle of the Mediterranean and adjacent to Bermuda,) he is self-evidently of non-white origin, and much of the relationship between him and Prospero is predicated on their respective, and competing, claims to the island. Caliban lays claim to the island through his mother, and through a right conferred by prior occupancy: 'this island's mine, by Sycorax my mother,' he argues (1.1.331); his claim is countered by Prospero and Miranda, who implicitly invoke their own moral superiority in their characterisations of Caliban as a lying, brutish slave 'which any print of goodness will not take' (1.2.351).

Which of the two claims is finally endorsed by the play itself is not easy to determine. Both are, in different ways, of dubious validity, and the contest between white and black in the play is complicated by the simultaneous presence in the text of other characters whose political designs align with neither. If the lower class characters of Stephano and Trinculo are as unruly and rebellious as Caliban in their plan to overthrow the aristocratic Prospero, for example, they are also quite happy to consider exploiting their 'servant monster' ally Caliban by enslaving him and displaying him for profit in the fairs and marketplaces of Europe, where 'not a holiday-fool there but would give a piece of silver' to see him (2.2.28). Indeed, *The Tempest*, it could be argued, is a kind of marketplace of discourses, a place where different races and classes meet and compete with each other, testing their respective claims to wealth and to power.

Much the same could be said of ▷ Marlowe's ▷ *The Jew of Malta* (c. 1590), which situates its action on an island which is a pivotal point of a new intercontinental trade, in which, as a consequence, colonial and conquestatory desires are played out. The opening soliloquy of the Jew, Barabas, makes it clear that it is Malta's position at the crossroads of a new, intercontinental enterprise which makes the island so important: the goods in which he trades, he tells us, come from Persia, Greece, and Spain, Egypt, Alexandria, Arabia and India. For Barabas, Malta is the place where commodities like oils, wines, spice and silks can be refined into other commodities whose value increases in inverse proportion to the commodities' volume: oils are exchanged for money, money in turn exchanged for precious stones, a gradual progressive condensation of 'infinite riches in a little room' (1.1.37) (the epitome of which, perhaps, is Malta itself). For Barabas, such exchange seems to occur almost miraculously: the Moor and the Indian (from whom the most precious of this wealth originates) can 'pick [their] riches up' (1.1.20) as they lie on the ground, the earth a cornucopia of wealth which is there for the taking. Indeed the only labour to which Barabas refers in his speech is his own, as he complains about what a 'trouble 'tis to count' the 'paltry silverings' (1.1.5) in which he has been paid, claiming that he 'all his lifetime hath been tired,/ Wearing his fingers' ends with telling it (1.1.15–6).

Barabas, then, simultaneously emphasises the centrality of trade and profit to Malta (and to the play) and mystifies the origin of that profit in labour and exploitation (miners, for instance, don't get mentioned by Barabas, only the merchants who profit from the mines). Such mystification of the shadier moral underpinnings of this new drive for profit, this new hunger for wealth, is not entirely shared by the play itself, in which, as Machevil first of all makes clear, the seemingly miraculous profusion of wealth is underpinned by the less mystical (although still mystified) designs of Machiavellian 'policy'. Trade and its consequent riches, Marlowe seems to be implying here, are inextricably linked with the systematic manipulation of power. Thus although over the course of the play wealth and Malta are removed from the Jews and the Turks respectively, to rest, finally, in the hands of the victorious Christians, the audience are not permitted the easy justification of that victory with which Ferneze, the Christian governor, concludes the play. 'Let due praise be given/ Neither to fate, not fortune, but to heaven' says Ferneze (5.5.122–3) – but this appeal to the will of God, and to right, sits uneasily with the play's exposure of the Christians' manipulation of the Machiavellian 'policy' which they have utilised, more successfully than anyone else, in the struggle for supremacy over Malta, a 'policy' in which, as Machevil points out in the prologue, 'might' (and not right) makes kings. Marlowe himself, it should be added, would certainly not have been opposed to such designs, despite his exposure of the hypocrisy with which they were frequently covered up. He was a personal player in the expansionary enterprise, with considerable vested interests in the economics of international trade; his personal involvement here may also be apparent in the impressive colonial energy with which he endows his Tamburlaine, who conquers and consumes his world in ▷ *Tamburlaine the Great 1 & 2* (published 1590).

Race

But one need not look to the Orient to see the vast impact which trade and expansion had on the Renaissance imagination: its presence is also apparent in plays whose location lies much closer to home. It is no coincidence that comedies like Jonson's ▷ *Volpone* (first acted 1605/6) and Shakespeare's ▷ *The Merchant of Venice* (1596–7) both take place in the city which was the gateway to many of the trade routes established by the Renaissance seafarer traders. Nor is it coincidental that the latter play, like *The Jew of Malta*, fuses its concern with profit with the representation of a rapacious Jew. For trade brings with it necessary contact with other races and cultures, both those which had for years existed within European societies, (such as the Jews) and those with whom the cultural encounter was relatively new, at least to England (the Moors, for example). And if in *The Jew of Malta* and *The Merchant of Venice* Jews function as the Europeans' cultural other, with whom the Europeans must compete, and whom they must contain or expel, so too, in different ways, does the eponymous hero of Shakespeare's tragedy ▷ *Othello* (1604), and his Moorish compatriots in other plays – the slave Ithamore in *The Jew of Malta*, Zanche in ▷ John Webster's ▷ *The White Devil* (1608–9), Aaron in Shakespeare's early Roman tragedy ▷ *Titus Andronicus* (1594); the Egyptian Queen Cleopatra in Shakespeare's ▷ *Antony and Cleopatra* (1606–7); and, of course, the 'salvage and deformed slave' of uncertain but undoubtedly 'Other' origins, Caliban, in *The Tempest*.

As we have seen in our discussion of *The Tempest*, however, the finer points of Renaissance attitudes to race are far from easy to determine. On the one hand, it is undoubtedly the case that on almost every occasion (with the possible exceptions of *Othello* and *Antony and Cleopatra*) where the audience is offered a representation of a character who is not white, villainy and evil are never far away. Even in plays such as *The Jew of Malta*, where all races and religions are shown to be at ease with Machiavellian policy and designs of highly dubious value, the villainy of Barabas is intrinsically associated with his race in a way that that of the Christians is not; the same could be said of the Moor Aaron in *Titus Andronicus*, whose self-confessed project of evil is expressed by him in terms of the desire to 'have his soul black like his face' (3.1.205).

But on the other hand, large-scale slavery of African races by the English only began in England in 1618, and since slavery generated, as well as stemmed from, the perception that other races were sub-human it is arguable that racist attitudes in the Renaissance were far less entrenched than they were in later years: the easy assumption of continuous political 'progress', in other words, is one which should be treated with considerable caution. We would not have to look far in our own culture, for example, to find attitudes less liberal than those expressed in the Renaissance by people such as Montaigne, who argued in his essay 'Of the Cannibales' that in condemning other cultures we simply despise what we do not understand: 'there is nothing in that [cannibal] nation,' Montaigne argues, 'that is either barbarous or savage, unless men call that barbarism which is not common to them'. The advent of large-scale slavery brought with it an ideology of the black African as a commodity, an object to be bought and sold on the international market; consequently, it might be claimed, attitudes towards black individuals became more, and not less, racist. By the end of the eighteenth century, for example, ▷ Coleridge found the thought of miscegenation in *Othello* so repellent that he denied that Shakespeare intended Othello to be black, claiming that 'it would be something monstrous to conceive this beautiful Venetian girl falling in love with a veritable negro'. And observations like this, it should be noted, continued well into the twentieth century, as Ridley's Arden edition of the play makes clear.

What of the play itself? On the one hand, attitudes similar to those of Coleridge are, undoubtedly, reflected also in the play of which he speaks. Othello himself seems progressively to internalise such attitudes in his own self-conception: at the beginning of the play he defines himself against the foreign and barbarous black Other, the

'Cannibals, that each other eat,/ The Anthropophagi, and men whose heads/ Do grow beneath their shoulders' (1.3.144–5); at the play's conclusion he seems to consider himself of a kind with those Other races to whom he had earlier opposed his own identity when he describes himself as a 'malignant and a turban'd Turk,' a 'circumcised dog' (5.2.355). And most obviously, Iago invokes a racist disgust at the thought of miscegenation very similar to that expressed by Coleridge when he rouses Brabantio with the words 'an old black ram/ Is tupping your white ewe' (1.1.88–9). But Iago's perceptions of the issue are not identical to the play's, nor, one would have thought, to its original audience's, for whom Iago is a 'hellish villain'. And whatever the answer to the old critical question of whether or not Othello and Desdemona have consummated their marriage, the play concludes with an instruction to the audience to look upon the 'tragic lodging of this bed' (5.2.364) – the marital bed, that is, one which the black and white bodies of Othello and Desdemona lie reconciled, finally, in death. Renaissance audiences, then, could at least countenance the idea that a black man might wed a white woman (and sleep with her), in a way that later audiences found very difficult to accept; the question of what vision the play itself has of the importance of race, or of what political attitudes the discourse of face in the early modern period actually denotes, remains one of great critical debate.

The City and Theatricality

The increasing interest in racial matters in the Renaissance is, then, a product at least in part of its increasing encounters with other cultures in its trade abroad. No less substantial a concern can be noted regarding trade at home. Thus comedies like Jonson's ▷ *Bartholomew Fair* and ▷ *The Alchemist* (1610) offer us, respectively, representations of an English country and an English city in which the ethos of the marketplace is both paramount and explicit (as the title of the former would lead us to expect). And the latter's setting can also point towards another development within Renaissance drama, most notable, perhaps, in Jonson, (*see also* his ▷ *The Devil is an Ass* (1616) and co-authored ▷ *Eastward Hoe* (1605) but also apparent in some of Shakespeare's plays: the Roman plays (*Coriolanus* (1608?), and ▷ *Julius Caesar* (c. 1599)) for instance; some history plays, like ▷ *Henry IV 1 & 2* (quarto editions 1598 and 1600 respectively); and in comedies like ▷ *The Merry Wives of Windsor* (1597). Like *Volpone* and *The Alchemist*, albeit in different ways, these texts are set in the new world of the city, an urban setting which is worlds apart from the pastoral locations of comedies such as Shakespeare's *A Midsummer Night's Dream*, and ▷ *As You Like It* (c. 1599); romances like his ▷ *The Winter's Tale* and (co-authored?) ▷ *Pericles* (1608–9); tragicomedies like ▷ John Fletcher's ▷ *The Faithful Shepherdess* (1610); and tragedies like Francis Beaumont's and Fletcher's ▷ *The Maid's Tragedy* (1610). Many of these, it is true, move between court and country – unlike, for example, many history plays, and many revenge and 'anti-revenge' tragedies (such as ▷ Thomas Kyd's ▷ *The Spanish Tragedy* (1587), ▷ Cyril Tourneur's ▷ *The Atheist's Tragedy* (1611) and ▷ John Marston's satirical tragicomedy of revenge ▷ *The Malcontent* (1604)), whose setting is entirely, or far more consistently, courtly. But courtly and pastoral locations differ greatly from the world of the city play, whose protagonists are often merchants, artisans, or other members of the lower classes, as in ▷ Thomas Dekker's ▷ *The Shoemaker's Holiday* (published 1600), ▷ Thomas Heywood's *The Four Prentices of London* (1600), ▷ Philip Massinger's ▷ *The City Madam* (1632), ▷ Middleton's ▷ *A Chaiste Maid in Cheapside* (1613), and Sir Francis Beaumont's parody of citizen comedy, ▷ *The Knight of the Burning Pestle* (1607). And all of these settings differ, again, from the world of the domestic tragedy, whose setting is the home, as we see for example in the anonymous ▷ *Arden of Faversham* (1592), and in ▷ Thomas Heywood's ▷ *A Woman Killed With Kindness* (1603).

City comedies are frequently characterised by an extraordinary energy and movement: characters bustle frenetically into, out of, and around the stage in a cacophonous and pleasurable medley of voices and action which reflects, perhaps, the brave new world of the urban environment. The development of that environment, indeed, is one of the most direct causatory material factors behind the hegemony of drama amongst the Renaissance literary arts, for unlike poetry and prose, (which, of course, also experienced an explosion in the Renaissance, partially as a result of the technological advance of the printing press), drama demands, and potentially gratifies, audiences of many people at once. The rise of the city guaranteed that there would be enough people in the same place to pay for the productions they consumed (the Globe theatre, for example, established in 1599, could play to audiences of almost 3,000, and was only one of several large theatres established in the period). Many plays, it is true, were still performed at Court. But the development of the city meant that the court was no longer the only, or even the dominant, form of patronage.

The exponential rise of the theatre can be read in the texts of the period in terms of the frequent, and self-conscious, theatricality with which characters and sentiments are represented, as dramatists draw similarities, or contrasts, between the world of the stage and the real world outside. Thus in one of his most famous speeches, Jacques in *As You Like It* declares that 'all the world's a stage, and all the men and women merely players' (2.7.139–40); in *The Tempest*, in a speech in which the barriers between stage-world and real world seem to dissolve and disappear, Prospero speaks of 'the great globe itself' melting into nothing, leaving 'not a rack behind' (4.1.155–6); in Kyd's *The Spanish Tragedy*, Revenge opens the play by referring self-consciously to his own role in it: 'Here we sit down to see the mystery, / And serve for Chorus in this tragedy' (Induction, 90–1); and concludes it with similarly self-referential theatricality: 'For here though death hath end their misery,/ I'll there begin their endless tragedy' (Chorus, 47–8). Plays within plays are a recurrent phenomenon in the texts: Hamlet, for example, arranges a production of a play called 'The Mousetrap' in order to 'catch the conscience of the king' (2.2.601); whilst *A Midsummer Night's Dream* concludes with the production of 'Pyramus and Thisbe' by the 'mechanicals,' (the artisanal actors who produce the play for their king), in a scene in which the comic ineptitude of the actors overlays what is in fact a profound meditation on the relation between art and reality and the phenomenon of theatrical experience. Indeed, the trope of the 'play within the play' can be extended so that, in a kind of infinite regress of theatricality, the entire play itself is embedded in another, as is for example the case with ▷ *The Taming of the Shrew* (1593–4), where the main action of the play is, explicitly, a theatrical performance, performed before the beggar Christopher Sly, who has been abducted, drunk, from a tavern, and given to believe that he is Lord of a manor.

In *The Taming of the Shrew*, as in all of the Shakespearean examples of this phenomenon I have mentioned here, Shakespeare figures theatrical performance as analogous to dreaming. Hamlet refers to acting as 'a dream of passion' (2.2.546), thus drawing further similarities between the actors and himself, 'like John-a-dreams, unpregnant of my cause' (2.2.363); Sly tries desperately (and unsuccessfully) to separate out his 'real' experience from his dreams again' (Induction 2, 122); and in *The Tempest* and *A Midsummer Night's Dream*, the distinctions between waking and dreaming, reality and theatricality, are progressively collapsed until audiences, like actors, become ethereal and unreal: 'we are such stuff / As dreams are made on,' says Prospero, 'and our little life / Is rounded with a sleep' (4.1.156–8). This kind of lyrical, philosophical meditation on the relation between the theatrical and the real world, however, is only one of many ways in which playwrights utilise self-conscious theatricality to comment on the world: in Jonson's *Bartholomew Fair*, for example, in which (like *The Taming of the Shrew*,) the main action of the play is embedded in an induction which draws explicit attention to the fact that the play is a performance, as the stage-keeper, book-holder and scrivener enter to draw up a contract between author, players, and audience. 'Not for want of a prologue, but by way of a new one, I am sent out to you here,' says the Book-holder,

> *with a scrivener, and certain articles drawn out in haste between our author, and you; which if you please to hear, and as they appear reasonable, to approve of, the play will follow presently:*
>
> (Induction, 58–62).

Jonson's satire here takes as its object not only his audience, but also other playwrights and himself. He figures himself in this introduction as being involved in an intensely competitive relation with his fellow playwrights (most notably, but not only, with Shakespeare, whose plays he represents as passé) and also as being obliged to enter into a contract with an audience whose judgement he essentially despises, but whose appreciation he is, nevertheless, obliged to gratify and solicit. In other words, he recognises the necessity of writing for this new audience of the riff-raff, instead of the crown: 'it is further agreed,' his 'contract' states,

> *that every person here have his . . . free will of censure, . . . the author having now departed with his right: it shall be lawful for any man to judge his six pen'orth, his twelve pen'orth, so to his eighteenpence, two shillings, half a crown, to the value of his place: provided always his place get not above his wit.*
>
> (Induction, 86–92)

But as he recognises that these are the new public he must please, he simultaneously chafes against having to pander to their uneducated and stupid judgement, implying that the rise of this new group of consumers of artistic production results in the prostitution of the playwright: 'if the puppets will please anybody,' he cynically promises, 'they shall be entreated to come in'.

In the Induction to *Bartholomew Fair*, then, Jonson represents the playwright as being no less immune to the temptation to prostitute his own talents in exchange for financial reward than are the many characters in his other dramas whom he satirises for the same reason. Wealth and the desire for it are frequently his targets, as for example, in *Volpone*, which opens with Volpone turning from the morning sun to apotheosize his gold, and proceeds along a plot line in which everyone is willing to sell their souls for Volpone's riches. Some are also willing to sell other people: Corvino agrees in this play to prostitute his wife for a chance of inheriting Volpone's wealth: in this new world of trade and exchange people (and perhaps especially women), become reified, turned into commodities who can be exchanged in a market of money and desires. Less easily recognisable consequences of this new economy and its contingent ideologies can also be noted in Renaissance drama. We might take, for example, the figure of the malcontent. Marston's play of that name is not quite representative of this figure, since the malcontent of *The Malcontent* is a deposed Duke, whereas the more familiar malcontent of early modern drama is generally of more uncertain social status, of a lower class than the other protagonists of the drama, like Bosola in Webster's ▷ *The Duchess of Malfi* (1613) or Thersites in Shakespeare's *Troilus and Cressida*, and very often a bastard, like Edmund in Shakespeare's *King Lear* or his predecessor, Philip, in Shakespeare's ▷ *King John* (1596–7).

Class and Gender: Bastards

It is not simply in the malcontent's dubious social status that he (for malcontents in Renaissance drama, like bastards, are almost always male) reflects a new kind of figure. Neither aristocrat nor peasant, he frequently expresses and justifies his claims and his grievances in a language that is very different from that of the aristocratic world in which he finds himself. This can best be exemplified, perhaps, in Edmund's diatribe against the injustice of the court. 'Thou, Nature, art my Goddess;' Edmund declares early on in *King Lear*,

> *to thy law*
> *My services are bound. Wherefore should I*
> *Stand in the plague of custom, and permit*
> *The curiosity of nations to deprive me,*
> *For that I am some twelve or fourteen moonshines*
> *Lag of a brother? Why bastard? wherefore base?*
> *When my dimensions are as well compact,*
> *My mind as generous, and my shape as true*
> *As honest madam's issue? Why brand they us*
> *With base? with baseness? bastardy? base, base?*
> *Who in the lusty stealth of nature take*
> *More composition and fierce quality*
> *Than doth, within a dull, stale, tired bed*
> *Go to th' creating a whole tribe of fops,*
> *Go 'tween asleep and wake? Well then,*
> *Legitimate Edgar, I must have your land:*
> . . .
> *Now Gods, stand up for bastards!*
>
> (1.2.1–22)

Edmund's words here express an ethic (or an ideology) vastly divergent from that which would underlie an aristocratic point of view. That older view of 'nature' and 'desert' (which finds its expression in the Great Chain of Being speech in *Troilus and Cressida* which I mentioned earlier in this essay) would imply that wealth, status and power are properly derived through birth, that one's intrinsic merit derives directly from one's place in society, which has been previously ordained by God. It is this view which is expressed, for example, in what is sometimes known as 'the romance convention of discovered parentage'; – the royal child, lost at birth and brought up by peasants who always know that she or he must be of higher social status because s/he is more sensitive/ courageous/ virtuous/ beautiful/ finer-limbed and so forth than the more run-of-the-mill (and lower class) specimen of a human being. A folkloric example of this convention might be 'Snow White,' a more literary one Perdita in *The Winter's Tale*. For Edmund, this view is the 'plague of custom,' to which his own ethic self-consciously opposes itself. He proposes instead a kind of meritocracy, where merit is afforded by what you make of yourself (an ideology, incidentally, far closer to our own), where status and power should derive from 'Nature,' and are not the manifestation of a divine order, and through which the baser born have as much moral legitimacy to rule as their social superiors.

It is, as I have already mentioned, no coincidence that the malcontent is so frequently a bastard. This, however, is not merely because his bastardy confers upon him an unstable social status, but also because class and gender conflicts in the plays of the period are very frequently expressed in terms of each other, as Edmund makes plain in his emphasis on the word that links both his social and sexual marginality, 'base'. The sexual product of an illicit social union, the bastard appears frequently in early modern drama, especially, but not only, in tragedy: a recent critical study has identified 71 bastards in the corpus of early modern drama. This is perhaps partially reflective of a real historical trend: the number of children born out of wedlock peaked at around 1600. But the bastard is also used to bring to the fore other social crises concerning the family and sexuality. In *King Lear*, for instance, Edmund functions to accentuate not only class, but also issues of the family. *King Lear* is organised around two incomplete families (both of which lack mothers, as do a substantial number of other families in Renaissance drama): Edmund and his brother Edgar, sons of Gloucester, whose story constitutes the subplot of the play, and King Lear and his three daughters, Cordelia, Goneril and Regan. Much of the play is thus concerned with issues of paternal authority; other forms of authority, most notably monarchical, are consistently intertwined in this play with issues of paternal power – the authority, or law, of the father. Thus in the opening scene, Lear's ill-conceived plan to divide his kingdom between his three daughters is indivisible from the love test that he sets for them, and the collapse of his regal authority set in motion by his ungovernable anger when his favourite daughter Cordelia fails this test.

Class and Gender: Fathers, daughters, sexuality and desire

It is also no coincidence that this love-test (and the division of the kingdom) occur in *King Lear* at the moment when Cordelia is about to leave the paternal home to marry and become a wife. In Lear's case, he seems unable to countenance the fact that from henceforth Cordelia's affections must be divided; she, on the other hand, insists on the necessity of this when she replies to his demands with the words,

> *You have begot me, bred me, lov'd me: I*
> *Return those duties back as are right fit,*
> *Why have my sisters husbands, if they say,*
> *They love you all? Haply when I shall wed,*
> *That lord whose hand must take my plight shall carry*
> *Half my love with him, half my care and duty:*
> *Sure I shall never marry like my sisters, to love my father all.*
>
> (1.1.95–103)

Cordelia conceives of her relation to her father in terms of a system of duties and obligations; he, though he wants her to behave like a dutiful daughter, cannot accept that on the moment when she becomes a wife those duties must be divided between her father and her spouse. The transition from paternal home to that of one's spouse, then, is one which is fraught with enormous difficulties: the conflicts consequent on this rite-of-passage underlie, for example *Othello*, Middleton's ▷ *Women Beware Women* (1614) and Middleton and Rowley's ▷ *The Changeling* (1622) as well as ▷ *Cymbeline*, and the Shakespearean comedies *The Taming of the Shrew, A Midsummer Night's Dream*, and ▷ *Much Ado About Nothing* (1598).

Not all of these plays emphasise the father-daughter relation in their treatment of this familiar moment (in *Women Beware Women*, for example, Bianca has already been 'stolen' from the paternal home when the play begins). Nevertheless, paternal authority is so important that it can go on being invoked, especially in the contexts of the daughter's marriage, even when the father is no longer there. His influence can persist long after his physical self has disappeared: as Portia sardonically laments in *The Merchant of Venice*, 'so is the will of a living daughter curb'd by the will of a dead father' (1.2.23–5). And in *The Duchess of Malfi*, the duchess' brother Ferdinand appropriates the symbol of phallic paternal authority in his attempt to control his widowed sister's sexuality and prevent her from remarrying: 'this was my father's poniard,' he tells her, 'do you see,/ I'd be loath to see't look rusty, 'cause 'twas his' (1.2.253–4).

The attempt to control female sexuality, then, and the problems and dilemmas consequent on this attempt, appear ubiquitously in Renaissance drama. Ferdinand's is only one case, useful for us here because it highlights another frequent concern of Renaissance drama: the representation of illicit sexualities, as well as their frequent juxtaposition with instances of cross-class marriages. At one extreme, the right of women to control their married lives and, if they wish, initiate divorce is supported by Elizabeth Cary in *The Tragedy of Mariam*. On the other hand, in the case of Duchess of Malfi, both her brothers contest the woman's right to marry again, but whilst her elder brother, the Cardinal, is motivated by the Machiavellian desire to control state politics and inheritances, her younger brother Ferdinand's motivation is far less easy to discern. This latter play suggests, (always implicitly) that his disgust at the thought of his sister's remarriage stems from his own incestuous desire for his sister (it is hard to understand his frenetic fantasies about his sister's intercourse with 'strong-thigh'd bargemen' (2.5.43) as anything other than a warped obsession with his sister's sexuality). Incestuous desire appears elsewhere in Renaissance drama too: it is the subject of *Women Beware Women*, it may well underlie Hamlet's vexed and probably oedipal relation to his mother Gertrude, it lurks beneath the text in Beaumont and Fletcher's ▷ *A King and No King* and is given its fullest, and arguably most sympathetic, treatment in ▷ John Ford's ▷ *'Tis Pity She's A Whore* (1632). In this play, as in *The Duchess of Malfi*, sibling incest is thematically linked with cross-class marriage, as if each if the obverse of the other, incest perhaps operating as an excessively endogamous solution to a new, and to some very threatening, exogamous social development. As has been recently suggested, this fusion of social and sexual anxieties may find expression in the plays through the metaphor of blood. Thus in *The Duchess of Malfi* Ferdinand expresses his desires in terms of their capacity to 'purge infected blood, such blood as hers,' in response to his brother's question, 'Shall our blood?/ The royal blood of Aragon and Castile,/ Be thus attained?' (2.5.21–22); in *'Tis Pity She's a Whore* Giovanni, similarly, justifies his transgressive desires by arguing that he is 'bound' to his sister 'by the links of blood' (1.1.32).

Incestuous desire is not the only form of desire which is represented in the plays of the early modern period as radically destructive. The homoerotic passion of Marlowe's *Edward II* and the self-consuming passion of *Antony and Cleopatra*, for example, are represented as equally dangerous to the state, and to stability within the family; the same is also true of desire in ▷ Mary Sidney's *The Tragedy of Antonie*. In Middleton and Rowley's *The Changeling*, the fascinatingly complicated relationship between the 'heroine' Beatrice-Johanna and her servant De Flores is used as a vehicle for an examination of the dangers of desire. Beatrice-Johanna's reaction to De Flores is characterised first by repulsion (she 'does profess herself/ The cruellest enemy to my face in town,' says De Flores, and 'at no hand can abide the sight of me' (2.1.33–5)); then by disturbance, as she can 'scarce leave trembling of an hour after' seeing him (2.1.91); and finally by compulsion: 'I'm forced to love thee now', she says to him after having slept with him (5.1.47). These mysterious, and unexplained, turns in Beatrice-Johanna's feelings for De Flores may perhaps partially be explained by De Flores' name. Beatrice-Johanna seems both to fear and desire the moment when she loses her virginity, and it is perhaps this complex of feeling which underlies the representation of De Flores (the deflowerer).

One of the reasons that desire is potentially so dangerous, and the control of female sexuality so crucial, is of course a social one: if a man does not control the sexuality of 'his' women, he can never be sure that the children he produces are his own. The production of bastards can thus threaten the very foundation of early modern property distribution, primogeniture, whereby property is passed from father to his eldest son. But however important this, it cannot explain every aspect of the representation of the relations between men and women in early modern drama, which seems frequently to pit male characters against female in a kind of battle of the sexes, as for example in Shakespeare's ▷ *Love's Labours Lost* (1594–5), and *The Merchant of Venice*, both of which end with the chastisement of the male characters by the female. In the latter play this chastisement is linked, in the plot, to the earlier trial scene, in which Portia, the heroine, sorts out the legal mess which her betrothed, Bassanio, has landed himself in, by disguising herself as a male judge. This transvesticism, or cross-dressing, in which women disguise themselves as men (for self-protection, as in *Twelfth Night* and *As You Like It*, or to effect some kind of action, as in *The Merchant of Venice*) is a recurrent trope of the plays of the period, appearing not only in the Shakespearean plays I have mentioned, but also in his ▷ *Two Gentlemen of Verona* (1593–4), in ▷ John Lyly's *Gallathea* (1585) and in Jonson's ▷ *Epicoene, or the Silent Woman* (1609) and ▷ *The New Inn* (1629), and Beaumont and Fletcher's ▷ *Philaster, or Love Lies a-Bleeding* (1611).

The complexity and depths with which cross-dressing can be used were considerable. The practice self-evidently raises issues of theatrical disguise, but it also affords the dramatist enormous possibilities for an examination of the dynamics of desire. In *Twelfth Night*, for example, the Duke Orsino experiences some anxiety when he finds himself becoming overly attached to a person whom he believes to be a young man, and similar humour surrounds Olivia's infatuation with the same person, whom the audience know to be a woman. But the issue is complicated even further in these plays by the fact that in the Renaissance, female characters were played not by women, but by boys. Thus in *The Taming of the Shrew*, Shakespeare indulges in a self-consciously theatrical joke at Sly's expense when he has a page-boy, dressed as a woman, act as though he is Sly's wife, and in *As You Like It*, he takes the dramatic and comic possibilities of cross-dressing and boy actors to an extreme when he offers us a situation in which a boy plays a girl who plays a boy who plays a girl in a (false) marriage with her unknowing beloved. And in the epilogue to the play, Rosalind steps in and out of his/her stage role to address the audience directly, commenting as s/he does so both on dramatic convention, and on the way in which the audience's own desires and identifications are complicated by the play's use of cross-dressing and boy actors. 'It is not the fashion to see the lady the epilogue,' she says,

> *but it is no more unhandsome than to see the lord the prologue. . . . I'll begin with the women. I charge you, O women, for the love you bear to men, to like as much of this play as please you. And I charge you, O men, for the love you bear to women – as I perceive by your simpering none of you hates them – that between you and the women the play may please. If I were a woman, I would kiss as many of you that had beards that pleased me, complexions that liked me, and breaths that I defied not. And I am sure, as many as have good beards, or good faces, or sweet breaths, will for my kind offer, when I make courtesy, bid me farewell.*
>
> (5.4.198–220)

Theology, Subjectivity and the Self

The cross-dressed heroine, then, can be used by the dramatist to examine profound (if generally comic) issues of social and sexual identity (one might look also, in this context, at Middleton's ▷ *The Roaring Girl* (1606). And this brings us to our final broad topic of discussion in this essay, which is the nature of identity, of the self, in Renaissance drama, its connections with what has gone before, and the ways in which its representation is revised in the face of new, and challenging, beliefs about the world.

I have, throughout most of this essay, concentrated primarily on things which are, broadly speaking, new developments in the Renaissance. But I do not want, by doing this, to imply that there is no continuity with what has gone before, for this would not be true. In the early stages of the Renaissance, especially, dramatists took their poetic models from literature of earlier ages: early tragedies, for example, such as ▷ Thomas Norton and ▷ Thomas Sackville's *Gordubuc* (1561) and Jonson's *Sejanus* (1603) experimented with Senecan tragic form, and classical models are also apparent in plays such as ▷ Nicholas Udall's ▷ *Ralph Roister Doister* (1552), ▷ Thomas Preston's *Cambyses* (1569), ▷ George Gascoigne's *Supposes* (1566), ▷ George Whetstone's *Promos and Cassandra* (1578), and Lyly's *Alexander and Campaspe* (1584), *Endymion* (1588) and *Midas* (1589). ▷ Raphael Holinshed's *Chronicles of England, Scotland and Ireland* (1578) chronicled the lives of medieval kings, which formed the subject matter of Shakespeare's history plays, as well as for tragedies like *Macbeth* and *King Lear*, and the medieval philosophy of Roger Bacon was the subject of ▷ Robert Greene's *Friar Bacon and Friar Bungay* (1589). And much Renaissance drama draws on beliefs which had a long historical precedent. The comedy of humours, for example, (whose most salient practitioner was Jonson – see his ▷ *Every Man in His Humour* (1598) and ▷ *Every Man Out of His Humour* (1599) draws upon a theory of psychology that had been current from classical times through the Middle Ages: however new the anarchic energy of Jonson's comedies are, he is working out of a theory of the self which had been around for centuries.

Do we, then, see any change in the representation of the self in the plays of the Renaissance period? Many commentators, from Jacob Burkhardt in 1860 to contemporary cultural materialist and new historicist critics (like Catherine Belsey and Stephen Greenblatt, for example), have, despite their differences with each other, argued that there is, and have claimed that the Renaissance sees the rise of a self which is recognisably modern, the precursor or origin of our own conception of human individuality. This is a view which is currently coming under attack from critics in other periods – from Medievalists, for example, who argue that many of the attributes of the self cited by Renaissance critics are recognisably present in earlier years, and conversely from Foucauldian critics, and critics of Romanticism, who variously claim that the important changes took place much later. In what follows, I'll try to elaborate some of the claims which have been made for the rise of this new subjectivity, always acknowledging, however, that the question is one which is far from decided.

Marlowe's ▷ *Doctor Faustus* (1592?) is a text which is self-evidently concerned with the obsession with new knowledge which characterises so many aspects of the Renaissance: its eponymous protagonist comes to a sticky end as a result of his pact with Lucifer's servant Mephistophilis to relinquish his soul in return for unlimited knowledge. In this play we can identify, quite clearly, two contrasting views of the world. One invokes the medieval morality play, in which vices and virtues, personified, are clearly defined, and immediately recognisable: here in *Doctor Faustus*, those vices and virtues are reflected in the Good and Bad Angels who stand on either side of Faustus, whispering their respective advice in his ears. Good and Evil here are arranged as each others' opposites, just as Heaven and Hell are clearly both inverses of each other, and situatable in a distinct and stable place in space, the one above, the other below. With the representation of Mephistophilis, it is frequently argued, we have something completely different. His account of the world refuses the literalism of the good and bad angels; for Mephistophilis Heaven and Hell, for instance, are not locateable in a specific space, but situated within the soul. Thus in the following extract, Faustus' insistent demands as to where Heaven and Hell are, in physical space, are countered by Mephistophilis' equally insistent reply that this is a misconception of the concepts implied by those terms. 'First will I question with thee about hell,' says Faustus:

> *Tell me, where is the place that men call hell?*
> Meph. *Under the heavens.*
> Faus. *Ay, so are all things else, but whereabouts?*
> Meph. *Within the bowels of these elements,*
> *Where we are tortur'd and remain for ever.*
> *Hell hath no limits, nor is circumscrib'd*
> *In one self place, but where we are is hell,*
> *And where hell is, there must we ever be;*
> *And, to be short, when all the world dissolves*
> *And every creature shall be purif'd,*
> *All places shall be hell that is not heaven.*
>
> (5.115–125)

Doctor Faustus does not resolve the questions that it raises about the 'truth' of these contradictory points of view. Dr Faustus is destroyed by devils at the end of the drama, dismembered and whisked off to a conventional Hell, full of literal fire and brimstone, existing very definitely below the earth. Yet Mephistophilis' claim that Hell is not physically locatable but carried within the soul lingers beyond the play's conclusion, undermining its adherence to the old theological order.

Mephistophilis is distanced from the Good and Bad angels with whom he appears not only by his refusal to accept their literalism about the world, but also by virtue of his interiority and depth; in *Doctor Faustus*, at least, the representation of this new way of conceiving of Heaven and Hell would appear to be linked with an emphasis on the complexity of the self. One of the dramatic devices through which this interiority is communicated to us is that of the soliloquy, which is used by Marlowe, but developed further by Shakespeare in plays such as *Macbeth, Othello, Richard III* and, most notably, *Hamlet*. Like the aside, the soliloquy can sometimes be used primarily, or ostensibly, to impart information about the plot, as it is for example at the beginning of *Richard III*, where Richard informs the audience of the depths of his Machiavellian scheming, or in Middleton's ▷ *The Revenger's Tragedy* (1607), where the revenger Vindice uses his opening soliloquy to inform us of what has gone before. But the soliloquy to inform us of what has gone before. But the soliloquy can do something much more than merely transmit to the audience necessary information about the plot, information, which, after all, might be communicated in other ways (by a chorus of a chorus figure, for example, as it is in *Romeo and Juliet* and *Pericles*). In the soliloquy, we see the construction of a new kind of relation between audience and speaker, in which the inner workings of the speaker's mind are represented to the audience in a dramatic moment of extraordinary intimacy. This intimacy can be used to establish a kind of complicity or understanding between audience and speaker, as it is, for example, in *Richard III*, and, in quite a different way, in *Twelfth Night*, where Viola occasionally, and comically, laments the complexities of her situation to the audience. The soliloquy's main generic home, however, is tragedy, in which it is frequently used to present to the audience a self at once fragmented and torn, and intensely isolated from the world that surrounds him (for again, soliloquisers are almost always male). In *Macbeth* for example, Shakespeare uses the soliloquy as one means of representing Macbeth's increasingly isolated madness, and the confusion of his conscience as he considers the imminent murder of his king. In Act 2, for example, Macbeth apostrophises a dagger:

Is this a dagger which I see before me,
The handle toward my hand? – Come let me clutch thee:
I have thee not, and yet I see thee still.
Art thou not fatal vision, sensible
To feeling as of sight? Or art thou but
A dagger of the mind, a false creation
Proceeding from the heat-oppressed brain?
I see thee yet, in form as palpable
As this which I now draw . . .

(2.1.31–40)

At this point in the play, as later in the scene when the ghost of Macbeth's murdered friend Banquo arrives to take Macbeth's place at a banquet, directors of the play on stage, as well as critics writing about it on paper, must make an interpretative choice. Do the audience, like Macbeth, see the dagger, and/or the ghost of Banquo? Or is it Macbeth alone who 'sees' them? Are they messengers from another world? Or are they manifestations of Macbeth's troubled conscience? Ghosts, for example, appear in several plays of the early modern period. But they generally speak (thus making it clear to us, since we hear them too, that they own some reality beyond the imagination of the character who sees them). Banquo's does not, which affords the director the opportunity of playing the scene entirely from a perspective which emphasises the play's interest in the main character's state of mind, a recurrent interest of *Macbeth*, which returns, for instance, in the sleepwalking scene at the end of the play, when Lady Macbeth walks in her sleep, washing her hands in the attempt to remove from them the bloodstains she imagines they carry.

The play which saw the most sustained and extensive use of the soliloquy, however, was Shakespeare's *Hamlet*. Hamlet's tortured consciousness is represented to us in this play with extraordinary complexity, as he wrestles with the opposing ethics and moralities of an age in which no course of action offers itself as clear. His problem is in one sense that he cannot tell what to believe: whether suicide is a noble or ignoble course of action, for example; whether the 'questionable shape' of the ghost in the play is 'a spirit of health or goblin damn'd' (1.4.40); whether older paradigms or revenge and honour can still hold for one who, like him, is 'pigeon-liver'd' and lacks 'gall/ To make oppression bitter' (2.2.574). Packed with questions to which they can hope to offer no answers, Hamlet's soliloquies represent him alone in his confusion and his melancholy, isolated in his profound scepticism from everyone else who surrounds him. As he himself laments,

> *The time is out of joint, Oh cursed spite*
> *That ever I was born to set it right.*
>
> (1.5.196–7)

It is Hamlet's perception of his isolation not merely from others, but from his historical moment, that has, at least in part, lent him his stature as one of literature's most paradigmatic tragic heroes. And however 'subjective' his perception of his age, it can stand, perhaps, as an epigraph at least for many current views of the Renaissance: a time out of joint with itself and its history, an age fraught with conflict and contradiction, discovery and collapse, out of which appeared some of the most compellingly fascinating drama of England's literary history.

The Augustan Age in Perspective 6

Eva Simmons

The term ▷ 'Augustan' (followed by 'England', 'age', 'era', and so on) has been applied variously, to the entire period 1660–1789 or to only parts of that time, sometimes very loosely indeed, and often without explanation. Historically, there have been repeated debates about when exactly the Augustan age occurred, what it was, or indeed whether such an age existed at all.

Lately new attention has been focused on changes in attitudes and styles of writing in the latter part of the supposed period, and on its relation to the previous and subsequent periods. Many elements more commonly associated with the Romantic (▷ Romanticism) period are already evident in numerous works from roughly the mid-18th century onwards. Some critics, such as René Wellek (*Comparative Literature*, I, 1949) and more recently Marilyn Butler (*Romantics, Rebels, and Reactionaries: English Literature and its Background 1760–1830*, 1981), have suggested that particular emphasis should be placed on these proto-romantic features, although others, such as Cleanth Brooks (*Modern Poetry and the Tradition*, 1939) and James Sambrook (*The Eighteenth Century: The Intellectual and Cultural Context of English Literature 1700–1789*, 1986), treat them simply as new directions in literature, rather than as ruptures of the past (and Sambrook dismisses the notion of 'Augustanism' entirely). One view places these works in a category of their own, labelled ▷ 'Sentiment' or ▷ 'Sensibility', while another fails to see any substantial change (see, for example, Norman Callan's 'Augustan Reflective Poetry', in Boris Ford (ed.), *The New Pelican Guide to English Literature: From Dryden to Johnson*, Vol. 4). But before these issues are discussed, it may be helpful to go back to the origins of the term 'Augustan', to understand how it came about, and what light it throws upon the times it purports to identify, as well as to consider its usefulness today.

The meaning of Augustanism

Broadly speaking, 'Augustan' has been used to signify times in which literature or, more accurately, literature in its relation to politics, supposedly resembled the literature and politics of ancient Rome under Augustan rule. Various English monarchs have been compared, in their own day and subsequently, with the Emperor ▷ Caesar Augustus, while authors of their reigns have been compared with the classical writers of Augustus' time. According to one commonly expressed formula, English monarchs from Charles II onwards have been admired as bringers of peace after periods of war, and as sponsors of the arts, just as Augustus himself was supposed to have been – encouraging the arts to flourish in a new harmonious atmosphere. But even in Augustus' own reign, this view of him, which he encouraged, was questioned, and after his death it became even more controversial. Similarly, in the 18th century, questioning and disillusionment followed the earlier idealization of Augustus, initiating a reappraisal of contemporary rulers.

Dispute arose partly due to the ambiguous character of Augustus, who became sole ruler after the defeat of Antony and Cleopatra at Actium. Even before his accession, he had shared responsibility for killing thousands of citizens thought to threaten the power of the state, under a policy known as the 'proscription'. Yet he claimed afterwards to have restored the ancient freedom of the Republic (in the name of which Julius Caesar had been murdered) and his 41-year rule was peaceful; it was a period in which Rome expanded its colonial boundaries, while the city itself was remodelled, and literature flourished. For example ▷ Virgil and ▷ Horace (▷ Latin literature), both of whom were patronized by Augustus, represented the triumphs of the age and, not surprisingly, they both praised the ruler for his bounty.

However Rome's steep decline began immediately after Augustus' death in AD 14, with a series of corrupt, cruel and incompetent rulers including Tiberius, Nero, Caligula, and Domitian. Some classical historians, especially ▷ Tacitus, presented a deeply critical vision of Augustus as a tyrant who deceived his people into thinking they were free while bringing in autocracy and paving the way for an even worse form of tyranny. Subsequent writers became fascinated with trying to interpret what had happened in this critical period of Roman history: what was the 'meaning', so to speak, of Augustus' rule, and how did his deeds compare with those of their own rulers? He could be seen either as a model for emulation, or as the embodiment of a warning; the last of the 'good' rulers, and a bulwark against chaos, or among the first of the worst: behind him the Republic, after him decay. The process of enquiry had one overriding aim, namely, to improve understanding of the writers' own times, in order to draw moral conclusions and provide moral instruction. This might make it possible to imitate Augustus' triumphs, or avoid his mistakes, depending on the outcome of the investigation.

Augustus and Augustanism in the 17th and 18th centuries

The ▷ Renaissance renewed interest in Italy and its history throughout Europe and, during the 17th and 18th centuries, concern with Augustus' era was widespread. Because European culture was seen to derive substantially from the Roman (Latin still played an important part in literature), and Augustus' reign was so pivotal in the history of Rome, and because writers of Augustus' time were so much admired, the Emperor's life and actions were carefully studied. In England his era held a special fascination, because of the country's own recent turbulent experiences, which included two major revolutions, a period of Republican rule (under ▷ Cromwell), and repeated foreign wars. English translations of ▷ Tacitus at the end of the 16th century, and again at the end of the 17th, helped to stimulate debate.

Much early writing in England, as well as in other parts of Europe, considered Augustus as a model for just and peaceful rule. At the begining of the 17th century ▷ James I encouraged comparisons of himself with the Roman, assisted by authors such as ▷ Ben Jonson, who praised him as a successor of Augustus. But at the ▷ Restoration the image of Augustus as healer and patron of the arts acquired a deeper resonance, at least in aristocratic circles. Charles II set the agenda himself, even more than his grandfather had done, in order to present himself as a symbol of Augustinian rule, almost Augustus re-incarnate. A series of triumphal arches recalling antique victories was built in what is now the City of London, and lavish entertainments were designed to celebrate his accession. Poets including ▷ Dryden rose to the occasion: his *Astraea Redux* (1660) (▷ Astraea) greeted Charles' return, 'Oh Happy Age! Oh times like those alone / By Fate reserv'd for Great *Augustus* Throne! / When the joint growth of Armes and Arts foreshew / The World a Monarch, and that Monarch *You*'. And a poem by Alexander Huish actually reworks an Horatian Ode welcoming Augustus back after long wars:

Restore thy Country her lost light, good King;
Thine own sweet face, which since like lovely Spring
W'have hop't to see, the day hath merrier gone,
The Sun hath brighter, better shone . . .

Long mayst thou live, and make long holy-day,
Good King, unto thy Country . . .

Such towering hopes were not likely to be fulfilled, on earth at any rate, and disillusion soon set in, as was expressed in such poems as ▷ *Absalom and Achitophel* (1681) and ▷ *Macflecknoe* (1682). In Dryden's own version of the story of Antony and Cleopatra, ▷ *All for Love* (1678), it has been argued, Charles is implicitly identified with Augustus' enemy Mark Antony, neglecting affairs of state in order to gratify his lusts, rather than with Augustus himself. *Macflecknoe* documents Dryden's ostensible despair at the lamentable state of letters in his time, just as ▷ Pope's ▷ *The Dunciad* (1728) was to do in the next generation. Each of these poems sets up mock monarchs of dullness to represent the supposed 'spirit of the Age', against which the poet rails, and which contrasts strongly with the heroic spirit heralded in the earlier poems. The demise of ▷ heroic drama, noted in my essay 'Restoration and 18th-century drama' (see pp. 49–50) also charts the decline from confident admiration of the monarch, and the heroic values ostensibly associated with him, to disillusionment and scepticism. At the same time, the view of Augustus deteriorated.

The critic Howard Weinbrot (*Augustus Caesar in 'Augustan' England*, 1978) suggests this process went hand in hand with the rejection of absolutism and he argues that the term 'Augustan', as a description of the period, is therefore misleading. Augustus' name, increasingly synonymous with tyranny, became a weapon in contemporary debates about artistic, social and political conditions. For example, to Whigs, ▷ James II was an Augustan tyrant, legitimately deposed by ▷ William III, while James' descendants, the ▷ Jacobite Pretenders (▷ Old Pretender, The), were seen as Augustan usurpers. But for some Tories the Augustan usurper was William himself, or else ▷ George I or George II, and the Hanoverians were represented as the destroyers of liberty (Whig and Tory). The comparison with Augustus was not confined to monarchs. In the years 1726 to 1742, the Whig Prime Minister ▷ Sir Robert Walpole was portrayed as an Augustan in the worst sense, and ▷ Chesterfield, for example, likened the imposition of the Licensing Act of 1737 (▷ theatres) to the oppressions of Augustus. But Walpole's supporters used the same epithets against their political opponents.

There is a distinction, however, between the widespread negative, Tacitean view in the 18th century of Augustus as tyrant, and the literary or cultural idea of an 'Augustan age'. For those who condemned the reign of Augustus the problem remained, how to reconcile the dark view of the ruler himself with the unquestionably sublime capabilities of the Augustan poets, who had so willingly accepted his patronage? One argument held that their artistry alleviated the pains of dictatorship, making it more bearable, as well as more palatable. ▷ Shaftesbury wrote in 1710 that although Augustus was 'a Prince naturally cruel and barbarous', his poets 'were more to him than his Arms or military Virtue; and, more than *Fortune* herself, assisted him in his Greatness, and made his usurp'd Dominions so inchanting to the World, that it cou'd see without regret its Chains of Bondage firmly riveted'. Another ingenious solution was to see the ▷ Latin poets as intellectual and moral products of the Republic, since their minds had been formed under it, even though their highest achievements took place under a later tyranny. Blackwell, in his

Memoirs of the Court of Augustus (1753 onwards) argues that 'what we loosely term the Stile of the *Augustan Age* was not *formed* under *Augustus*. It was formed under the Common-wealth, during the high struggles for Liberty'. In just such a way, he intimated, the celebrated poets ▷ Milton, ▷ Waller and ▷ Cowley, who published after the Restoration, were in fact shaped by the Commonwealth (▷ Interregnum) era in Britain. Blackwell suggested, moreover, that the Augustan poets may even have succeeded in modifying the tyrant's behaviour. Finally, even among those who abhorred the historic Augustus, there were those who, like ▷ Coleridge in the 19th century, saw the Republic itself as far from perfect, ruled by an oligarchy of senators, remote from ordinary people.

Thus the idea of Augustus and interest in his period survived despite political scepticism: somehow it was possible to hold in suspension two supposedly inimical ideas: of, on the one hand, Rome fallen under the sway of a despot and, on the other, a flowering of independent literature. In a similar vein, contrasts have been drawn between the high accomplishments of Renaissance Italy and the autocratic nature of many of her rulers; and, in modern times, between the literary achievements of Soviet Russians ('official' as well as dissident writers), and Stalinist oppression. Weinbrot gives some of Dryden's works as examples of his own anti-Augustanism, as well as generally representative of that attitude in the period. Yet the evidence regarding Dryden's and others' views, as Howard Erskine-Hill points out (*The Augustan Idea in English Literature*, 1983), is in fact very mixed. Some of the supposedly anti-Augustan writings cited by Weinbrot, such as Dryden's *Discourse Concerning the Original and Progress of Satire* (1693) and Pope's *Epistle to Augustus* (1737), display ambiguous attitudes towards Augustus which have been variously interpreted by critics, as Weinbrot himself acknowledges. Paradoxically, these works, written in classical traditions of learning and ▷ satire, with their displays of wit, elegance and erudition, are precisely those which may best be said to embody the essence of 'Augustanism' in its literary sense.

As indicated above, several other countries, notably France and Italy, whose classicism antedated that of Britain, also assigned to themselves an 'Augustan' age. Moreover, the term 'Augustan' as an expression of hope for the coming reign, was actually applied in Britain from the 16th century, and revived repeatedly thereafter. But custom has determinedly related it to a period of English literature after the Restoration. As early as 1690 the Jacobite cleric Francis Atterbury questioned, rhetorically, whether 'in Charles II's reign English did not come to its full perfection; and whether it has not had its Augustan age as well as the Latin'. ▷ Anne Finch, in *A Tale of the Miser and the Poet. Written about the Year 1709*, implied a similar view. Her poem refers nostalgically to Charles II's time, when the arts and learning were valued in their own right, and not for the money they could bring, and it ends with a plea for the revival of 'Augustean days . . . when wit shall please, and poets thrive'.

▷ Oliver Goldsmith, in *An Account of the Augustan Age in England* (1759) published in his briefly-lived periodical *The Bee*, identified a different time span for his 'Augustan Age':

> *Some have looked upon the writers in the times of Queen Elizabeth as the true standard for future imitation; others have descended to the reign of James I.; and others still lower, to that of Charles II. Were I to be permitted to offer an opinion upon this subject, I should readily give my vote for the reign of Queen Anne, or some years before that period. It was then that taste was united to genius . . . In that period of British glory, though no writer attracts our attention singly, yet, like stars lost in each other's*

[sic] *brightness, they have cast such a lustre upon the age in which they lived that their minutest transactions will be attended to by posterity with a greater eagerness than the most important occurrences of even empires which have been transacted in greater obscurity* . . .

Hopes for a new Augustan age were invoked repeatedly thereafter, notably in 1727 with the accession of George II, who conveniently carried 'Augustus' as one of his names, and again in 1760, when ▷ Hume questioned, somewhat whimsically, whether the accession of George III could also herald a new Augustan age. And Goldsmith who, writing in the third quarter of the century, as we have seen, thought the Augustan Age had coincided with the reign of Queen ▷ Anne, was himself designated an Augustan by ▷ Vicessimus Knox in 1778 and again by the Scottish essayist John Pinkerton in 1785.

However, the term 'Augustan' suggests not just a relationship between a monarch and the arts, but a standard and type of writing, or indeed a specific cultural identity. This involves ideas of ▷ taste and ▷ wit, aspired to by essayists, dramatists and poets. For example, Pope thought of himself as an Augustan, and Goldsmith sought to revive what he considered to be the flagging spirit of Augustanism. Didacticism is another recurring theme associated with the period, in secular as well as in religious writing. There is also an emphasis upon the powers of reason and scepticism, which may be seen in political and moral philosophy of the period, from ▷ Hobbes and ▷ Locke (▷ Social Contract) through to ▷ Berkeley and Hume. This was echoed by the growing involvement with science: ▷ Newton, for example, seemed to his contemporaries to represent a supreme example of what scientific reason could achieve; as Pope wrote, 'Nature and Nature's laws lay hid in night: / God said, "Let Newton be!" and all was light'.

To these qualities may be added many others widely accepted over the years, although of course not all are present in any one author, or even at any one time. They include: order, strength, dignity, propriety, symmetry, balance, erudition, classical allusion (▷ classic, classics, classical; ▷ classical education and English literature; ▷ classical mythology), refinement, harmony, grace, polite manners, and spleen. Indeed, many of the most characteristic, as well as the most famous, post-Restoration works are infused by that quintessentially Augustan quality, a compound of invective and gloom. Essays, passages in plays, and poems in the prototype Augustan form, the heroic ▷ couplet; often draw upon Horatian or Juvenalian (▷ Juvenal) satiric models, to rail against life, the universe or anything.

Gender proved one particularly fertile area for such vituperation. ▷ Rochester, for example, vilified women and marriage in heroic couplets, while women poets such as ▷ Lady Mary Chudleigh and ▷ Sarah Fyge Egerton used the form to similar purposes, but from a woman's standpoint, condemning men and marriage. Dryden and Pope also used the splenetic, satiric form to discourse on the supposedly lamentable state of literature, to condemn contemporary religion, society and the state, and for personal verbal assaults on their enemies. A bitter battle, largely conducted through verse written in classical forms, broke out between Pope and his allies on the one hand, and a group including the influential ▷ Lord John Hervey and his friend ▷ Lady Mary Wortley Montagu on the other. Pope attacked these two in a series of satiric poems, including ▷ *The Dunciad*. An anonymous author or authors, usually taken to include Lady Mary (though she herself denied responsibility), then hoisted him with his own petard. *Verses Addressed to the Imitator of the First Satire of the Second Book of Horace* (1733) retaliates against Pope in his kind of language:

> Horace *can laugh, is delicate, is clear;*
> *You, only rail, or darkly sneer:*
> *His Style is elegant, his Diction pure,*
> *Whilst none thy crabbed Numbers can endure;*
> *Hard as thy Heart, and as thy Birth obscure . . .*
>
> *If none do yet return th'intended Blow,*
> *You all your Safety to your Dullness owe;*
> *But whilst that Armour thy poor Corps defends,*
> *'Twill make thy Readers few, as are thy Friends . . .*
> (From *The Works of Lady Mary Wortley Montagu*, 5 vols., (1803))

Classical forms other than satire, such as ▷ epics, ▷ pastorals, ▷ epigrams, odes and panegyrics, were widely used throughout the period, as documented in Clare Brant's essay, 'Restoration and 18th century poetry' (see pp 13–26). Classical allusion is not, though, confined to poetry, it is also seen in drama (especially in the early part of the period) and non-dramatic prose, as well as in painting, sculpture, architecture, furniture design, landscape gardening, music and other fields of cultural endeavour.

Education, commercial writing, and the early novel

Classical practice in literature, as in the works mentioned earlier, was naturally accompanied by classical education in grammar schools (schools in England) and in universities. The knowledge of Latin, and some Greek, was considered fundamental to a good education. Writers in Augustan England looked to authors in both languages for models and inspiration. ▷ Abraham Cowley, outlining *A Proposition for the Advancement of Learning* in 1661, prescribed a curriculum dominated by Latin authors including Varro, Cato, ▷ Pliny, ▷ Seneca, ▷ Cicero, ▷ Virgil, ▷ Terence and ▷ Plautus, and supplemented by the Greeks ▷ Homer and ▷ Aristotle. He also suggested that the study of classical poetry assisted other areas of study, making the process of enquiry more palatable: 'we conceive that one book ought to be compiled of all the scattered little parcels among the ancient poets that might serve for the advancement of natural science, and which would make no small or unuseful or unpleasant volume'.

Women were usually denied a formal education in the classics, but sometimes managed to obtain it for themselves. There are various accounts of intellectual women studying Latin and Greek on their own, sometimes in secret, or perhaps aided by a sympathetic male relative or friend. Lady Mary Wortley Montagu, for example, taught herself Latin, encouraged by an uncle and by ▷ Bishop Burnet, while the Anglo-Saxon scholar ▷ Elizabeth Elstob was helped to learn her many languages by her brother. ▷ Lucy Hutchinson, who translated Virgil and ▷ Lucretius, was unusual in being highly educated at her father's expense.

But what one might call the 'high' literary tradition to which they belonged formed only one part, indeed perhaps the smaller part in numerical terms, of the writing of the Augustan age. For the 18th century was the first period in which literacy became really widespread, fuelling and feeding off the growing array of written material. In the mid-16th century only 20 per cent of men and 5 per cent of women could sign their names; these figures had increased by the mid-17th century to 30 per cent and 10 per cent respectively; by 1715 they were 45 per cent and 25 per cent; but by 1760, 60 per cent of men and 40 per cent of women were considered 'literate'. Even allowing for the possibility that some of those signing their names may have been able to do only that, for legal purposes for example, a steep rise in literacy is certainly indicated: J. A. Sharpe (*Early Modern England: A Social History*, 1987) draws on contemporary accounts to point out that reading was taught before writing, and so name-signing is probably quite a reasonable indicator of literacy.

These literacy figures point to an expansion in education for women, as well as for men. Although, as Sharpe has also noted, while the standard of education rose in general, the number in higher education and grammar schools declined. The latter, partly to combat this decrease, gradually leavened their classical diet with increasingly 'modern' and utilitarian fare. This aspect of the struggle betweeen classicism and claims for the value of contemporary learning was satirized by ▷ Swift in ▷ *The Battle of the Books* (published 1704). The growing number of charity schools, and boarding schools for girls, also emphasized the useful and moral aspects of learning (rather than the classical), as well as the study of polite manners, although a few women, including ▷ Bathsua Makin and ▷ Mary Astell, set up schools offering more serious studies to members of their sex. There were also local and informal methods that had for long existed to enable some of the poor as well as their betters to learn to read, such as teaching in village schools, or in the home. Thus while the numbers of literate people accelerated, the proportion of those with a classical education declined.

Along with the new literacy went a new demand for reading matter, both 'high' and 'low'; this included philosophical treatises and essays; ▷ periodicals and journals such as the early 18th-century ▷ *Examiner*, ▷ *Tatler*, ▷ *Spectator* and ▷ *Female Spectator*, which offered a mixed fare of gossip, news, and opinion, in the way that ▷ newspapers were increasingly to do; books; popular stories and tales; editions of popular and classic plays; and of course poetry of all kinds. The idea of the literary market-place, as product and concomitant of the century's rapid rise in trade and commercial values, is explored in 'Market, morality and sentiment; non-dramatic prose 1660–1789', by Janet Barron and David Nokes (see pp. 27–38).

Working- and middle-class authors now achieved fame writing for readers from their own classes, as well as from the traditional upper-class readership. ▷ Defoe, subsequently recognized as one of the earliest and most important contributors to what became the novel form, was from a poor tradesman's family, and changed his name to hide his humble origins. ▷ Richardson, whose ▷ *Pamela* (1740) was so successful that it went through four editions in the course of its first year, was the son of a joiner, and had received little education, certainly none of a classical kind. Even Pope, upholder of so many upper-class values, was the son of a linen-merchant, a fact which he took great pains to conceal. Insecurity about his social identity helps to explain his savage attacks on other authors forced to write for money, after he himself had risen from their ranks. Indeed, as Brean Hammond has shown (*Pope*, 1986), the continuing fight of the 'ancients' against the 'moderns', in the late 17th and early 18th centuries, was underpinned by class antagonism and class anxiety. Conservative aristocrats and their circle, many of them gentlemen-amateur authors and scholars, felt threatened by the rival new breed of professionals, whom they viewed contemptuously as low-born *arrivistes*.

Several poets of working-class origin were in fact taken up by aristocratic patrons; some examples are given by Clare Brant in her essay. On the whole, however, literary patronage declined, from the top downwards; the ▷ Stuart monarchs, notably Charles II, had encouraged the literary arts, but their Hanoverian successors, though not without aesthetic taste, had little interest in English literature. For this reason, writers had to attract a wider readership in order to get their work published, necessitating and encouraging the development of the more popular styles already discussed. The loss of patronage was deplored by Goldsmith (*The Present State of Polite Learning*, 1759), but Pope prided himself, somewhat disingenuously, on his own literary independence:

> *... Verse, alas! your Majesty disdains;*
> *And I'm not used to Panegyric strains;*
> *The Zeal of Fools offends at any time.*
> *But most of all, the Zeal of Fools in rhyme.*
> *Besides a Fate attends on all I write,*
> *That when I aim at praise, they say I bite ...*
>
> *And when I flatter, let my dirty leaves*
> *(Like Journals, Odes and such forgotten things*
> *As Eusden, Philips, Settle, writ of Kings)*
> *Clothe spice, line trunks, or fluttering in a row.*
> *Befringe the rails of Bedlam and Soho.*
> (*The First Epistle of the Second Book of Horace, to Augustus*, 1737)

This new appeal to a popular audience was noticeable in printed texts, as it was in the theatre, and gave rise to the terms ▷ 'hack' as a derogatory word for a popular writer, and ▷ 'Grub Street', as a term for the area in which such writers met, either literally or figuratively. Indeed, taste in entertainment in general, and literature in particular, appears to have been spread across a wider social spectrum at this time, than at any other time in English history.

The 18th century has been referred to as the period which saw the birth of the consumer society, in the modern sense of the term. Books and periodicals helped to create and to satisfy the urge towards consumption, as market products in themselves, and by advertising and conveying news about the latest fashions and trends. As a result, the number of books published each year quadrupled during the course of the 18th century, even though their cost was high – a novel was priced between six and ten shillings. This, for much of the period, was roughly equivalent to a day's wages for a skilled craftsman, or a week's wages for a labourer. The prohibitive pricing was, however, circumvented by both the serialization of longer works and the establishment of ▷ circulating libraries (operating in Bath from 1725, and in London from 1739). ▷ Richard Brinsley Sheridan's romantic heroine Lydia Languish, in ▷ *The Rivals* (1775), famously 'devours' books from a library in Bath (by now a fashionable city, rivalling London), with titles including *The Tears of Sensibility* (translated from the French *Les Epreuves du sentiment* in 1773), ▷ Sterne's ▷ *A Sentimental Journey* (1768), and ▷ Smollett's ▷ *Peregrine Pickle* (1751) and ▷ *Humphrey Clinker* (1771). Moreover, she is devastated to find novels including *The Reward of Constancy* (1771, author unknown), *The Fatal Connexion* (by Mrs Fogerty, 1773), *Mistakes of the Heart* (translated from French in 1769) and *The Delicate Distress* (by ▷ Elizabeth Griffith, 1769) already lent out, and therefore unavailable to her. In the same play, however, the forthright and old-fashioned Sir Anthony Absolute condemns the libraries and their effects. He declares that 'a circulating library in a town is as an evergreen tree of diabolical knowledge! It blossoms throughout the year! – and depend on it, Mrs Malaprop, that they who are so fond of handling the leaves, will long for the fruit at last!'

As this episode suggests, during the course of our period women became increasingly involved with literature as readers and as theatre-goers. But they also increased their activities as authors in their own right. It is no accident, moreover, that women pioneered or helped to inaugurate new literary forms. Most of them being deprived of classical education, apart from a handful like Hutchinson and Montagu, they had perforce to welcome innovative techniques. Nevertheless, since many kinds of experience – notably sexual and political – were denied to most of them, women usually wrote in forms acceptable to polite society, under the weight of social pressure and moral convention. Those like ▷ Aphra Behn, who wrote about sex in an almost 'masculine' (her word) voice were vilified, and eventually bowdlerized (▷ Thomas Bowdler) into oblivion. Women had therefore to find forms of expression which evaded conventional masculine ones in order to partake fully of literary life. For example, women from Behn and ▷ Delarivière Manley onwards are largely credited with the development of sentimental and romantic themes in literature (and indeed of the novel form itself) – even though men such as Defoe, ▷ Fielding and Richardson obviously made major contributions. Even in poetry, some of the characteristics we consider quintessentially romantic are already present in the poetry of ▷ Anne Finch, who died in 1720.

The growth of the novel in the period has, however, been explained in other ways. Several commentators have shown how the reading and writing of romantic literature, and associated pursuits, such as the following of fashion, and the cultivation of courtship skills, helped to occupy the leisure time now increasingly available to the middle and even lower classes. On the other hand, Janet Todd (*The Sign of Angellica*, 1989) has noted that a number of women, such as ▷ Laetitia Pilkington, wrote to support their children, or else used writing to supplement the living they earned in some other calling. This represented a considerable change, since some of the major women writers of the beginning of the period, among them ▷ Philips, Behn, and Astell, had no children, and concentrated solely upon their writing. In this sense the novel developed partly out of the relationship between social circumstance and literary impulse.

As the period developed, the novel came to perform a complex and paradoxical role in people's lives. On the one hand, romantic plot-lines and sentimental expressions of emotion afforded endless opportunities for narrative variations of suspense and intrigue; on the other, they challenged and partly ameliorated the evaluation of woman as marriage commodity and drudge, as well as offering close studies of social nuance in contemporary settings. Paradoxically, such writing may also be seen as part of the continuing effort to socialize young people of both sexes, and to overcome any resistance to marriage. For young women particularly these works served constantly to inform, or to remind them of their proper roles as maidenly objects of affection, and then as wives and mothers, and to discourage them from having ambitions outside the marital realm. The softening of parental authority, which took place during the 17th and 18th centuries, was accompanied by a new sort of propaganda campaign – to romanticize and therefore to sweeten the pill of having to assume adult responsibilities. Themes of conflict with parents, as in Richardson's ▷ *Clarissa* (1747–8), for example, map the struggles of young people to free themselves, and of their elders to retain control.

Young women also looked to novels for clues as to how to end their celibate state. Virtuous and happy heroines, as well as those seduced and abandoned, offered models of behaviour to imitate or avoid. Novels became 'how to' and/or 'how not to' guides to comportment (in affairs of the heart and other matters), which dramatized and humanized the advice offered in many ▷ conduct and ▷ advice books. Numerous plays of the period performed a similar function. In the last part of the century this advice acquired a fresh exigency, since women substantially outnumbered men; many would not marry at all, and others would marry only relatively late in life. By this time, however, a reaction against popular novels was well established; they were increasingly being attacked for their supposed impropriety or frivolity and absurdity and, in some quarters, blamed for creating dissatisfaction with life. They misled young women, it was suggested, into expecting life to be like a sentimental novel. For example, ▷ Hester Chapone said that the reading of sentimental novels 'corrupts more female hearts than any other cause whatever', and another reviewer wrote that 'the youth of both sexes . . . fondly imagine . . . that everything must yield to the irresistible influence of all-conquering love: but upon mixing with the world, . . . they find to their cost, that they have been miserably deceived . . .'. Some of the opposition was overtly class-based, part of a wider view that the education of working women would give them ideas above their station. But the social and literary historian Colin Campbell, in *The Romantic Ethic and the Spirit of Modern Consumerism* (1987), argues that the suffering and isolated heroine of so many novels in the 18th century anticipates the outcast hero of the 19th and he considers it likely that the reading of novels was a major factor in the break with traditionalism which occurred in the second half of the century.

New Directions

This brings us back to the question of how to define 'Augustan' and 'Romantic', and the shift from one to the other. This volume has followed a long-accepted practice in placing the demarcation line between the two periods, at the year of the ▷ French Revolution. Some critics have opted for an even later division, at the turn of century (see, for example, the many books with '18th-century literature' in their titles); others for an earlier one, such as 1760 (for example, Marilyn Butler, in *Romantics, Rebels and Reactionaries*), or even 1740 (Arthur O. Lovejoy, 'On the Discrimination of Romanticisms', *PMLA* XXXIX, 1924). The question of where and how to separate periods of literature has always been problematic. One convention is to separate the 'romantic' from the 'classical' in the way of H. J. C. Grierson (*Classical and Romantic*, 1923), or T. E. Hulme (*Speculations*, 1924). But one needs only to think of the many classical influences on the revolutionaries, as well as on the Romantic writers (as in ▷ Keats' *Ode on a Grecian Urn* (▷ odes, Keats'), 1819), or to look for the roots of ▷ Byron's satiric poetry in the verses of ▷ Samuel Butler, Dryden and Pope, to see the flaws in any simplistic separation. Another practice, as discussed earlier, has been to stress the continuity of ideas throughout the periods, and to argue against any sort of sharp break between one element and another.

There is a persistent view, however, shared by some of the Romantics themselves, that some kinds of change in literary taste and fashion did develop, or gathered pace, starting roughly in the middle of the 18th century, although they are not sufficient to place a clear division at that point. The mood is characterized partly by a new restlessness and searching, by a fascination with feelings, and by a sympathy with the disadvantaged in society, a general ▷ humanitarianism. The long campaign for the abolition of slavery (▷ William Wilberforce), assisted by a famous legal judgment freeing slaves in England in 1772 (▷ slavery), is an expression of the latter. These phenomena are often referred to collectively as 'sentiment' and 'sensibility'.

Other developments include a taste for the 'primitive' (▷ primitivism) including the ▷ medieval or ▷ Gothic and Celtic, and in a delight with wildness in general, from natural landscapes (▷ nature) – especially inspiring or terrifying scenes such as high mountains or deep precipices – to the idea of the 'noble savage' or 'natural' man. Images of the noble savage had existed from at least the beginning of the period well before ▷ Rousseau's famous celebration of the type. For example, Behn's ▷ *Oroonoko* describes primitive people in glowing terms, while numerous ▷ Inkle and Yarico narratives and stage plays celebrate the natural man's counterpart, the natural woman. But the idea of the natural man caught hold of the public imagination on a much larger scale in the second half of the 18th century. A succession of visitors to England from far-off countries, such as a South Sea islander called ▷ Omai, seemed to bring the symbol to life. His stay in London is described by a number of writers including ▷ Cowper, ▷ Johnson and ▷ Burney.

Finally, the transition towards Romanticism may be seen in the use of simple forms and styles, rather than the elaborate ones often admired in the earlier Augustan period; in a revival of a simpler notion of religion, including the development of Methodism from about 1739; in a love of the exotic, including the ▷ oriental, which went along with a scepticism about the superiority of one's own society in relation to the societies of others (as in Johnson's ▷ *Rasselas*, 1759, and Goldsmith's ▷ *The Citizen of the World*, 1762); in a leaning toward morbidity and pessimism, including a fascination with darkness and death; and lastly, in soaring flights of fancy. Indeed although the period saw a classical revival, as Marilyn Butler points out (*Romantics, Rebels and Reactionaries*), this time the models were primitive Greece and Rome, rather than Periclean Athens or Augustan Rome. It was at this time also that the criticism of the Roman ruler Augustus gained a new impetus, as in the eloquent castigation by ▷ Gibbon. Of course there were multiple overlaps among these categories: for example, in Omai and the characters of *Oroonoko* were represented the exotic as well as the primitive, the Gothic novel offered both primitive and gloomy elements; and Gibbon's work, while being part of the classical revival, also incorporated religious scepticism, a questioning of received ideas and a pessimistic spirit.

One of the most characteristic aspects of Romanticism was the new feeling for the wild and awesome aspects of nature. This is quite different from the cultivated and domestic kind hymned by ▷ Marvell, Dryden or Pope. It takes place in the context of a greater freedom to travel, enabling dramatic foreign scenes to become familiar to many more English people, but it also emanates from a gradual shift of the population from country-side to town. As people were driven off the land (▷ enclosures) and separated from their roots in nature and agriculture, and as agriculture itself became more mechanized, there arose a nostalgic and sentimental regard for cultivated nature, together with a new view of human existence in a natural setting. Realistic and sympathetic portraits of villagers and farm-labourers replaced the Virgilian pastoral figures that were commonplace in earlier Augustan writing. These trends are seen in the poetry of Goldsmith, ▷ Crabbe, ▷ Collins, ▷ Thomas Warton, ▷ Akenside and ▷ Gray. Mid-18th century poems, such as ▷ Young's ▷ *Night Thoughts* (1746), may be seen to have inspired Romantic writers like ▷ Wordsworth. The change is also seen in themes chosen for plays, and in stage design, as I have elaborated in 'Restoration and 18th century drama' (see pp. 42, 55–7). It is further evident in non-dramatic prose, such as in the rapturous description of the Alps written by ▷ Horace Walpole in a letter to Richard West in 1739 (▷ letter-writing), which prefigured descriptions of those mountains by ▷ Mary Shelley; just as his ▷ *The Castle of Otranto* (1764) was to form a basis for her ▷ *Frankenstein* (1817).

Walpole's phenomenally popular 'Gothic story' represents a landmark, not only in its supernaturalism, and dwelling on the elements of horror and fear (in this it is to some extent a child of ▷ Jacobean drama), but in other aspects, including its medievalism – which leads toward the Romantic and later ▷ pre-Raphaelite preoccupation with that period. Its descriptions of dark, subterranean vaults and passages are counterparts to the romantic vistas of craggy heights and vaulting skies. But its clinging atmosphere of elemental gloom and imminent disaster set a pattern for Gothic novels in general, a new form of the Augustan age which rode the transitions in political and intellectual history to survive well into the next century with its key elements intact. Compare for example this passage from *The Castle of Otranto* :

> *A clap of thunder at that instant shook the castle to its foundations; the earth rocked, and the clank of more than mortal armour was heard behind. Frederic and Jerome thought the last day was at hand ... (then) the walls of the castle behind Manfred were thrown down with a mighty force ...*

with the following from Mary Shelley's *Frankenstein* (1818):

> *As the night advanced, a fierce wind arose from the woods, and quickly dispersed the clouds that had loitered in the heavens: the blast tore along like a mighty avalanche, and produced a kind of insanity in my spirits that burst all bounds of reason and reflection ...*

There are important differences between the two, not least the shift to first-person narrative and introspection in the later piece, and the ghostly apparition, which subsequently appears heralded by nature's effects in the former. But they share a sense of nature as something wild, threatening and primitive, even as a participant in the action, influencing and commenting banefully upon it, like a Greek chorus. Once again, this is at a far remove from the early Augustan pastoral view of nature, as a carefully wrought ▷ Golden Age setting for shepherds and shepherdesses to sport and court in. Jerome at another point in Walpole's story seeks out 'the gloomiest shades, as best suited to the pleasing melancholy that reigned in his mind', anticipating the darkly mournful hero-outcasts of Byron.

In ghostly scenes such as this one, Walpole purposefully invokes ▷ Shakespeare. This is not merely a backward look, or an attempt to elevate his own material by dressing it in clothing of the Bard, but an announcement of a shift from a certain kind of ▷ neo-classic critical theory to an alternative vision of nature and of art. Since the Restoration, Shakespeare had often been condemned for mixing crude comic elements with exalted ones, as well as for failing to observe the ▷ Classical Unities; it was not until the transition from the Augustan to the Romantic periods that Shakespeare was revalued in a manner that would be familiar today. The impulse which in 1823 inspired ▷ Edmund Kean to stage ▷ *King Lear* with the tragic ending written by Shakespeare, for the first time since ▷ Nahum Tate altered it to a happy ending in 1681, was not entirely the same as that which motivated Walpole's reference to Shakespeare. Both efforts, however, were part of the same wave of so-called 'Bardolatry' which arose in the second half of the 18th century, was highlighted by a Shakespeare Jubilee in 1767, and continued into the next century. Shakespeare's works were revalued, and became appreciated, precisely because of their alleged 'wildness' and irregularity, which earlier generations had rejected. Now they seemed in keeping with, or even to embody, the newly defined spirit of nature.

Walpole, in a letter to Mme du Deffand, informed her in language extraordinarily like that of the Romantics later, that he had written *The Castle of Otranto*, to give 'reign to my imagination; visions and passions choked me. I wrote it in spite of rules, critics, and philosophers . . .'. He continued by informing her that he had composed the work 'for the future, when taste will be restored to the place now occupied by philosophy', and not for the present, 'which wants only *cold reason*'. In an epigraph attached to the second edition, he refers to the work as if to a new form. Yet the epigraph is itself a paraphrase of a passage from the Augustan 'Bible', Horace's *De Arte Poetica* ('On the Art of Poetry'), and his preface to the first edition draws attention to his use of pity and terror, those Aristotelian essentials so favoured by early Augustan dramatists, while the work itself mostly observes the rules of classical drama. A modern editor, W. S. Lewis, in his introduction to *The Castle of Otranto* (1964), describes Walpole's mission as 'to innovate', but he also adds that he wished 'to instruct, and to entertain'. These last two precepts encompass Horatian prescriptions which stand as twin Augustan ideals. Walpole himself refers to his Gothic tale as 'an attempt to blend . . . two kinds of romance, the ancient and the modern'. We might add that it links, inextricably, elements of both Augustanism and Romanticism.

Augustanism did not give way easily to the new Romantic sensibility; it survived late into the 18th century in, for example, the work of Goldsmith, who consciously and deliberately referred back to the Restoration period; in the work of Samuel Johnson, whose preoccupation with reason, 'reasonable' tone, orthodox classical standards of literature, and use of Augustan forms, allies him with writers of an earlier era (although his ▷ *The Vanity of Human Wishes* (1749), which was inspired by Juvenal's tenth satire, has a Romantic concern with futility and death); and Augustanism is even manifest, as we have seen, in some of the comic poetry of Byron – ▷ *Don Juan* (1819–24) and ▷ *The Vision of Judgment* (1821). Interestingly, the influence of the 18th century has been recognized even beyond Byron's time, for example in the poetry of ▷ Samuel Rogers, who outlived not only Byron but ▷ Wordsworth as well, and who continued to write in the Augustan style (J. R. Watson, 'Samuel Rogers: The Last Augustan', in *Augustan Worlds*, ed. Hilson, Jones, and Watson, 1978).

Conclusion

As we have seen, the idea of an Augustan age, in the sense of an era of high achievement informed by classicism and incorporating many classical models, has refused to die, and is still a convenient label for the period 1660–1789, even if incomplete as a definition and summation of all its accomplishments. Critics as careful and diverse as Pat Rogers (*The Augustan Vision*, 1974), Howard Erskine-Hill (*The Augustan Idea in English Literature*) and Margaret Doody (*The Daring Muse: Augustan Poetry Reconsidered*, 1985) insist on the continuing usefulness of the term 'Augustan'; as Doody says, it is 'the term we have . . . the one that inspires recognition'. The French Revolution, with its cataclysmic impact on English thought, marked a break with the past, inspiring fresh radicalism, and then reaction. But the intellectual seeds for those developments, as well as the development of Romanticism itself, lie further back. Thus our idea of 'Augustan' perhaps needs modifying once and for all, to allow that there is no hard line between that period and the one that follows it. We should use the term as a convenient way of marking a time-block and of implying certain ideas, but not to suggest a rigidly enclosed phenomenon.

7 Restoration and 18th-century Poetry

Clare Brant

Literary history, culture, theory

The term 'Augustan' (▷ Augustanism) properly refers to those Roman poets who celebrated, sometimes ironically, the ideals and shortcomings of civic life under the emperor ▷ Caesar Augustus. Though useful to suggest some public aspects of late ▷ 17th- and early ▷ 18th-century verse, it misrepresents the poetic diversity of the period as a whole. Nonetheless, it and other labels such as 'the Age of Reason' (▷ Rationalism) continue to be used to create an impression of poetry ruled by ideas of ▷ classical correctness. 'Reason' is often compared unfavourably with 17th-century ▷ metaphysical inventiveness or 19th-century romantic imagination: as Matthew Arnold famously remarked, 'Dryden and Pope are not classics of our poetry, they are classics of our prose'. In fact the poetry of the ▷ Enlightenment is full of ideas and experiments: from early ▷ wit to late ▷ sensibility, poets tested the limits of learning and experience with passion and humour.

Poetic variety was assisted by the expansion of print culture. New outlets for poetry, such as ▷ periodicals and ▷ magazines, appeared alongside an increased number of printed books of poetry. Though poetry still circulated in aristocratic circles in manuscript and on the street in ▷ pamphlets, ▷ ballads and songs, it was this middle ground which came to support most poetry. Its early concentration in London – represented by ▷ Grub Street, the symbolic locale of ▷ hack writers – gave way to provincial centres and networks. ▷ Thomas Gray in ▷ Cambridge, ▷ Anna Seward, 'the Swan of Lichfield', and ▷ William Cowper in rural Buckinghamshire, lived out poetry's move away from metropolitan concerns after the mid-century. It is important to remember that poetry appeared not only in books but also on buildings, tombstones and statuary, on fans and picture frames, in satirical prints and engravings. It was sung, acted and posted with presents. It was a recognized form of argument: ▷ Lady Mary Chudleigh's *The Lady's Defence* (1710) was one of many dialogues in verse. Poems turned up in novels: readers of ▷ Samuel Richardson's ▷ *Clarissa* in 1749, for instance, came across ▷ Elizabeth Carter's much-admired *Ode to Wisdom*; and ▷ Tobias Smollett included a poem by himself on Loch Lomond in ▷ *The Expedition of Humphry Clinker* (1771). ▷ Laetitia Pilkington published her poems in her memoirs in 1747. Mary Jones published her verse epistles with her prose correspondence in 1750. ▷ Joseph Addison and ▷ Sir Richard Steele used quotations from classical poets at the head of their periodical essays; and ▷ Ann Radcliffe's epigraphs used English poets to set moods to chapters in her novels. ▷ Samuel Johnson's ▷ *Dictionary* (1755) used quotations from English poets up to his own time to illustrate the meaning of words in contexts. Poetry was used in education to teach rhetoric, grammar and languages. This did not necessarily produce more talented poets, complained ▷ Charles Gildon in 1721, for though schoolboys were made familiar with the poetry of ▷ Homer, ▷ Virgil and ▷ Horace, this taught them only prosody or 'how to frame several sorts of verses in the *Greek* and *Latin* tongue, without giving them the least insight into the art of poetry it self, and therefore only qualifies them for meer versifiers'. Poetry was also connected to oratory: verse prologues and epilogues appealed to spectators to judge plays favourably. It was read aloud in small groups as well as silently by solitary readers. The look of poetry on the page, however, took on special importance in this period. It uses apostrophes to indicate precise rhythms: 'But with the odious smell and sight annoy'd / In haste she does th' offensive herd avoid' ('she' being the Muse, in ▷ Swift's *To Mr Congreve*, 1693). Poems became typographically elaborate, though always elegantly laid out, with italics, capitals and underlinings. As Swift put it,

> *To Statesmen wou'd you give a Wipe,*
> *You print it in* Italick Type.
> *When Letters are in vulgar Shapes,*
> *'Tis Ten to one the Wit escapes;*
> *But when in Capitals exprest,*
> *The dullest Reader smokes the Jest.*
> (*On Poetry: A Rhapsody*, 1734.)

The increasing presence of poetry enlarged people's ideas about the genre. In 1712, when asked to describe 'the chief Qualifications of a good Poet', Sir Richard Steele replied 'a very well-bred Man', but barriers of class and gender varied across the period. The 1730s, for instance, saw working-class poets in vogue, with the success of ▷ Stephen Duck's *The Thresher's Labour* (1735), which earned him a royal pension and a riposte from ▷ Mary Collier in *The Woman's Labour* (1739), pointing out that working-class woman's life was exhausting in specific ways to which she, as a washer-woman, could testify. Duck's exchange of agricultural work for city patronage was not, however, happy, and he committed suicide. Later working-class writers such as ▷ Ann Yearsley also struggled to survive patronage. To participate in high culture could require imitation of its forms: ▷ as Mary Leapor put it, 'You see I'm learned, and I show't the more, / That none may wonder when they find me poor' (*An Epistle to a Lady*, 1748). Though working-class writers used ▷ couplets ably enough, it was hard for them to challenge 'the Mob of Gentlemen who wrote with Ease', in ▷ Pope's phrase. A beggar's daughter in Smollett's ▷ *Peregrine Pickle* (1751) is passed off as a fine lady once she has learnt to recite 'choice sentences from Shakespeare, Otway and Pope'. Knowledge of poetry and the ability to join in games of allusion were marks of ▷ taste which self-educated poets struggled to develop.

For women, class could offset some of the disadvantages of gender. ▷ Katherine Philips and ▷ Anne Finch were recognized talents. Though John Wilmot, Second Earl of ▷ Rochester, asserted that '*Whore* is scarce a more reproachful name / Than *poetess*', women wrote continuously. Most were, however, careful to frame their productions with modest disclaimers. Anna Williams' are typical: 'Censure may be content to spare the compositions of a woman, written for amusement, and published for necessity' (*Miscellanies*, 1766). Two factors helped women. One was recognition of poetry as diverse, connected to specific, plural, various occasions: titles such as 'Miscellanies' and 'Poems on Several Occasions' were widely used by men and women, and this hint towards poetry as miscellaneous allowed for mixed abilities or mixed success. Secondly, women compensated increasingly for a lack of classical forbears as more women published. During the 18th century women cited as illustrious models first ▷ Aphra Behn and then, as a decorous private life became as much a requirement for women writers as talent, her more respectable predecessor ▷ Katherine Philips, the 'matchless Orinda'. In the later 18th century, women also increasingly looked to ▷ Shakespeare as an instance of how a poet with little Latin and less Greek could still have merit.

The dubious social status of some poetry meant that many 18th-century poems were published anonymously. But this was also a form of insurance against politically or personally motivated attack. As one anonymous writer lamented in 1779,

> *Poets and Thieves the same attention meet,*
> *Their deaths are hawk'd about from Street to Street;*
> *And the same fate attends the wretches still,*
> *Who go up Helicon or Holborn-Hill.*

Poetic stealing, or plagiarism, was one of the few forms of theft not to carry a capital charge in the 18th century, but poets policed each other vituperatively. Like Johnson's scholar, poets faced 'toil, envy, want, the patron and the jail'. John Philips' *The Splendid Shilling* (1701) was popular for its clever Miltonic ▷ burlesque, but also for its play with cliches concerning poetic penury. Poets' prospects did change: where ▷ Milton was paid £10 for ▷ *Paradise Lost*, ▷ Dryden earned a comfortable £1250 for his translation of ▷ Virgil, and Pope's translation of ▷ Homer made him financially independent. But such sums were exceptional. Swift, with his usual complicated irony, advised poets 'to hire out your Pen, to a Party, which will afford you both *Pay* and *Protection*'. Politically commissioned work mostly concealed its hired origins, but the value of public poetry was officially recognized in 1668 when John Dryden was appointed the first ▷ Poet Laureate. For all that the public bought more poetry, poets still looked to patrons for support. As the Fourth Earl of Abingdon observed about a well-placed dedication, 'it sometimes happens, that the Name of the Patron supplies the want of every other merit, and preserves the work from oblivion.' But there were a number of scandals about poets who suffered destitution or rejection; in 1782 William Hayley hoped the nation would never again see 'A future CHATTERTON by poison dead, / An OTWAY fainting for a little bread.'

Poetry was agreed to be an important proof of national greatness. Poets earned their countries peacetime laurels, and artistic alliances and rivalries evolved across Europe, though not necessarily mirroring relationships between nation-states – English and ▷ French writers, for instance, continued to read and appreciate each others' work even when their countries were at war. Writers, both English and French, attributed French regimentation to a lack of political liberty, while English social freedoms were supposed to be reflected in a less circumscribed literature. But poetic nationalism often involved informed comparisons with other countries' literature, of which travellers sought out specimens. Samples of foreign poetry were analysed both to reveal what themes if any were universal to poetry, and how particular national cultures treated them. ▷ Lady Mary Wortley Montagu, for instance, in 1717 sent Alexander Pope a specimen of Turkish poetry, first in a literal translation and then in English style. She commented on both social and linguistic determinants of poetry: 'Neither do I think our English proper to express such violence of passion, which is very seldom felt amongst us; and we want those compound words which are very frequent and strong in the Turkish Language.' Readers were particularly informed about epic poems from Spain, Portugal, France and ▷ Italy which, together with their knowledge of English ▷ epic poetry, created a European inheritance to the classics. Paradoxically, epic was prized both as the most nationalistic (▷ Nationalism) genre, promoting the poet's tribe, and also as the least nationalistic, in that epic heroes usually travelled and created new countries. So Hildebrand Jacob attempted a British epic, *Brutus*, in which the Roman founds an English colony. On a smaller scale, Pope's ▷ *Windsor Forest* (1713), a Tory celebration of the Peace of Utrecht, (▷ Spanish Succession, War of) turns local landscape into international scenery: 'The Time shall come, when free as Seas or Wind / Unbounded *Thames* shall flow for all Mankind'.

Like monarchs in this period, poets had to be secured against pretenders: versifiers, poetasters, scribblers, hacks and dunces. Correct technique was not enough in itself: Charles Gildon lamented that 'this is a Quality that gives the glorious Name of Poets to Fellows without Warmth, without Judgement, without Imagination' (1713). Literary theory used this aesthetic vocabulary consistently in the period. William Duff sums it up in a 1763 essay: 'If, on the one hand, Imagination bestows SENSIBILITY and REFINEMENT on Taste, so on the other, Taste imparts JUSTNESS and PRECISION to Imagination; while Genius is consummated by the proper union of both these faculties with that of Judgment'. Reason alone could not animate the process: 'a certain vital spirit must be infused; and in Poetry, this vital Spirit is INVENTION.' This term, from the Latin *inventio*, implies not just discovering existing forms and relations but, increasingly throughout the 18th century, thinking up new ones as well.

This distinctive combination of conservatism and passion helps to explain some parts of late 17th- and 18th-century poetic theory which are alien to a modern mind: deference to classical writers, insistence on imitating ▷ nature, and adherence to rules in doing so. In fact, not all writers were fans of the classics. Pope declared his support for the ancients: 'the highest character for sense and learning has been obtained by those who have been most indebted to *them.* For to say truth, whatever is very good sense, must have been very good sense in all times.' But Percival Stockdale, despite being in all other respects Pope's warmest admirer, took the opposite view, complaining of 'dictators [who] pay no regard to what passes in life.' ▷ Voltaire temperately suggested that 'The best modern Writers have mix'd the Taste of their Country, with that of the Ancients', but he also complicated moderate positions by upholding neo-classic systems in which French critics rather than classical poets provided guidance about rules.

Rules, according to Pope, were simply 'Nature methodiz'd'. Poetic theory constantly invoked nature, meaning not simply the visible world, but that principle which gives shape and structure to material and conceptual forms of life. Like the idea of 'human nature', it could cover a variety of behaviours, but this variety was not infinite. Nature as represented in texts was defined by the plausible. Poetry was like painting in that both arts represented something by copying it: for example, a portrait copied a person. But if the subject was an invented person, such as Hercules, then what was copied or imitated was the 'type' of a strong man. Poetry described things as they *may* be: 'whenever we speak of poetry as an imitation, we constantly call it an imitation of Nature', explained Alexander Gerard in 1780. Critics urged writers to follow nature, not to encourage slavish conformity, but to assist readers' recognition of subjects, and to make poetry as effective as other kinds of literature in offering instruction and entertainment.

Comparisons between the sister arts of 'voice and verse', as Milton called them, were common in this period. Archetypal musicians such as St Cecilia and King David interested poets from John Dryden to ▷ Christopher Smart. Besides odes and lyrics which were originally sung forms, hymns and libretti linked poetry to music. Critics used musical ideas of harmony and painterly ideas of depiction to try to represent what poetry did, though as Samuel Johnson observed, 'criticism has not yet attained the certainty, and stability of science.' It was a common jibe in the late 17th and 18th centuries that critics were failed poets, though boundaries between criticism and poetry were considered to be legitimately blurred, as when poets, usually imitating Horace's *De Arte Poetica*, wrote verse criticism of the art of poetry. Abuse of critics was colourful: James Miller, for instance, described critics as 'Those Rats, which tear Books to Pieces, only to come at the Paste they are glewed with'. But Dryden's prefaces and essays, Addison's sympathetic papers on Milton in ▷ *The Spectator* and Johnson's ▷ *Lives of the Poets* successfully developed critical theory and biography as tools for reading poetry. Various factors helped to make the critic a more prestigious figure in the second half of the 18th century: the establishment and spread of respectable magazines which had consistent policies of reviewing; London highbrow society's new interest in serious public conversation about literature, along the lines of French salons; and the necessity of agreeing critical standards as literary production expanded in the provinces.

With criticism more securely established, the formation of a native poetic canon began: Shakespeare was established as the national genius, and Milton, ▷ Spenser and Chaucer were promoted. The ▷ metaphysical poet Donne was regarded by some as uncouth, but still sufficiently interesting to be 'rectified' in Pope's re-versification. Antiquarian interests became mainstream: in 1765 ▷ Thomas Percy published his ▷ *Reliques*, a large collection of old English ballads, and ▷ Thomas Warton published his long *History of English Poetry from the Close of the Eleventh to the Commencement of the Eighteenth Century* (1779–81). Thus, throughout the 18th century, English poetry increasingly defined itself in relation to its own native history, as well as to classical inheritance.

The genres of poetry

Restoration and 18-century poetry used certain distinct genres. An ▷ epigram was a short, witty poem, often involving censure or applause. It manifested brevity, beauty or sharpness, with Martial's epigrams providing a classical model. An ▷ epitaph, a concise memorial poem, usually showed gravity, but could be jocular, like the pair of epitaphs by Pope and Lady Mary Wortley Montagu about two lovers struck by lightning. The form was challenging, since it required specific consideration of the dead person, something general on death, and all in a space short enough to be fitted onto a tombstone if need be. ▷ Elegy was a broad genre, generally about death or the coyness or cruelty of a lover. Commiseration, reproach, sympathy or tenderness predominated, but it could also show passion and restraints on passion. Pope's *An Elegy to the Memory of an Unfortunate Lady* (1717) illustrates sympathy with the griefs of people unknown to the poet, an attitude perfected in ▷ Gray's ▷ *Elegy in a Country Churchyard* (1751). Katherine Philips' *On the death of my first and dearest childe* (published 1667) is a moving example, and Elizabeth Boyd's *On the Death of an Infant of five Days old* (1733) is a powerful description of maternal grief: 'Oh! could the stern-souled sex but know the pain, / Or the soft mother's agonies sustain, / With tenderest love the obdurate heart would burn, / And the shocked father tear for tear return'. Particularly in the late 17th century, poets wrote elegies memorializing fellow poets – for example, ▷ Anne Wharton's elegy on Rochester. ▷ Pastoral, drawing on ▷ Theocritus, Virgil and sometimes Spenser, represented the doings of shepherds or rural nymphs and swains. It strained for simplicity, a contradiction which often led it into artifice. Pope's *Pastorals*, written when he was 14, were thought to be formally perfect, though by 1776 one poet, writing anonymously, complained of 'the shoals of nonsense that has been eternally written of Delias and Damons, Chloes, Strephons, &c . . . who can read such trash without disgust?' Related forms included ▷ eclogues, uninterrupted by dialogue, and ▷ georgics, poems of agricultural instruction. All these expressed interest in land which could covertly address issues of ownership and occupation through fantasy.

Poetic epistles like prose letters were able to address almost any person or subject and, again like prose letters, they were one of the most widely written forms of the late 17th and 18th centuries. Unfolding in the manner of conversation, smooth, easy and polite, they could be serious or ludicrous, satirical, heroic, descriptive, friendly or hostile. Many poets used ▷ Ovid's *Epistles* as a starting point; others, such as Pope, favoured the Horatian epistle. Descriptive poetry usually involved meditative neo-classical forms rather than the more talkative Augustan modes listed above. Following Milton's *L'Allegro* and *Il Penseroso*, poets played on tactile and aural senses as well as the visual, as in ▷ Anne Finch's study of nightfall, *A Nocturnal Reverie*. Prospect poetry organized hilltop views into narratives which used conventions comparable to those employed by landscape painters such as Claude, where the eye tracked between foreground and horizon in distinct patterns. Detail alternates with broader strokes in ▷ John Dyer's *Grongar Hill* (1726), for example: 'How close and small the hedges lie! / What streaks of meadows cross the eye!' ▷ Didactic writing made instruction palatable by concealing it in lively writing. Compendium poems, ranging over multiple aspects of a topic; were also popular, such as ▷ William Somervile's *The Chase* (1735), a poetical history of hunting. Philosophical enquiries and aesthetic analyses were often attempted: both were combined in ▷ Mark Akenside's blank-verse celebration of *The Pleasures of the Imagination* (1744). Tales and ▷ fables provided self-contained narratives, often with a disturbing twist, and allegorical discussions often involving animals or inanimates. Dryden's religious dialogue ▷ *The Hind and the Panther* (1687) and ▷ Gay's *Fables* (1727–38) brought out the form's playfulness. Extended ▷ allegories were less common: one such was ▷ James Thomson's dreamily sensual Spenserian imitation ▷ *The Castle of Indolence* (1748), in which the Knight of Arts and Industry rescues Britain from indolence with the help of a bard. But allegorical devices such as personification (▷ figures of speech) were ubiquitous.

The large category of lyric covers odes and songs. Songs were widely written in the late 17th century, since their usual subjects of love and drinking suited much Restoration self-imaging. The French critic ▷ Boileau decreed that 'Even in a Song there must be Art and Sense'; whether bawdy or sacred, songs expressed pleasure in sweetness and easy versification. Odes were ranked high in the generic hierarchy. As Boileau's *The Art of Poetry* (1683) put it, 'The Heart in Elegies forms the Discourse, / The Ode is bolder, and has greater force'. Commentators agreed that odes used disorder creatively; they were, as ▷ George Villiers, the Duke of Buckingham, put it, 'the Muse's most unruly horse'. But in odes the imagination, often depicted as Pegasus, need not be reined in. The ▷ Pindaric ode (▷ Pindar) was particularly celebrated for 'its beautiful wanderings, and its happy returns to the subject' as Charles Gildon put it. Yet the mid- to late-18th century preference for the sublime ode – bold, irregular, elevated – drew attention to its challenges. As one practitioner, Thomas Cooke, put it in 1749, 'of all Sorts of Poetry, none has been so often attempted as the *Ode*, nor with less Success'. Odes were thought to have been sung and danced in ancient times, and it was this patterning of energy which gave them appeal. The ode's importance after the mid-18th century, when many poets preferred it to couplets, is because it expressed order differently, rather than allowing a triumph of passion over reason.

▷ Epic was more discussed than practised, at least until ▷ James Macpherson's poetical prose fragments published in the 1760s, purporting to be by a third-century poet ▷ Ossian. Epic's partly real, partly fictitious stories of illustrious actions performed by heroes was turned creatively into ▷ mock heroic (Dryden's ▷ *Mac Flecknoe*, 1682) and ▷ mock epic (Pope's ▷ *The Rape of the Lock*, 1712 and ▷ *The Dunciad*, 1728). Satirical reversals of scale – in Coleridge's phrase, making the great little and the little great – pointed to communal or ideal scales of value from which the protagonists had departed. The workings of ▷ satire were much discussed in this period. The ancients provided two models, Horace and ▷ Juvenal, loosely equated with smiling and savage satire respectively. Dryden declared that 'The true end of Satyre is the amendment of Vices by Correction'. But was this end best achieved by mocking, deriding and bullying, or by teasing and humorously shaming? Poets tried out different methods of raillery and rage to discover how best for their ends 'sharpest thoughts in smoothest words' (Buckingham) might be conveyed. Not all satire was high-minded: much involved political feuding or personal abuse. Polite literature became acrimonious in satire, but the art of abuse highlighted the art of the poetry which couched it.

Poetry in context: 1660–1700

The Restoration of the monarchy in 1660 put ▷ Charles II on the throne but restored few other institutions. Besides the religious and political upheavals of the ▷ Civil War, commercial and technological innovations were changing English social life. The apparent revival of aristocratic court culture, until the ▷ 'Glorious Revolution' of 1688, distracted from the insecurities and self-inventions of poems as variously theatrical as the verse plays which many poets were also writing for the newly re-opened theatres.

Civil War poetry had been necessarily populist, taking sides, marching down the street, arguing its case, abusing its opponents. Ballads and songs continued to structure much satire, most notably in the roughly rhymed tetrameter couplets of ▷ Samuel Butler's ▷ *Hudibras*, written in four parts between 1662 and 1684. This was immensely popular: the first part ran through nine editions in its first year. Mocking everything from epic to science, it was indiscriminately caustic about faction, whether religious or political:

> *Both Parties joyn'd to do their best,*
> *To Damn the Publick Interest.*
> *And Hearded only in consults,*
> *To put by one anothers Bolts;*
> *T'outcant the Babylonian Labourers*
> *At all their Dialects of Jabberers,*
> *And tug at both ends of the Saw,*
> *To tear down Government and Law.*

As in Swift's satire later, this is not high-minded but knowing. You cannot guess where it will turn next, though many of its tropes are recognizable from earlier traditions. For example, classical satirists attacked opponents for being misers or gluttons. Culpability was illustrated by deviance from a mean: thus hospitality could degenerate into prodigality or contract into parsimony, like Butler's Puritans who 'Quarrel with *minc'd Pies* and disparage / Their best and dearest friend, *Plum-porridge*'. (Pope's miser and glutton in his *Epistle to Bathurst* continue this game.) Nor could you tell for how long such poems would go on: the ramble or survey continues until the poet has had enough. Similarly, Dryden's ▷ *Annus Mirabilis* (1666) packs into its year of wonders the naval war with Holland and the Great Fire of London, but its pace is set by the compelling nature of the various spectacles it describes rather than by strict calendar time.

This sense of 'uncovering' is common to satire, epistles, tales and fables, popular genres of this period. Dryden's ▷ *The Medall* (1682) uses the coin as an emblem of two-facedness as well as the medal struck by the Whigs to celebrate the acquittal of ▷ Shaftesbury: 'So like the Man; so golden in the Sight / So base within, so counterfeit and light'. Dryden plays with conceits established by earlier ballads about heads stamped on crowns, crowned heads and coinage as an emblem of political fortunes. In ▷ *Absalom and Achitophel* (1681–2) he goes on to use the known Biblical story of a plot against David to represent political treachery as the sinister Shaftesbury masterminds the ▷ Duke of Monmouth in a plot against Charles II. Forms of proper government are debated:

> *What shall we think! Can People give away*
> *Both for themselves and Sons, their Native sway?*
> *Then are they left Defensless, to the Sword*
> *Of each unbounded Arbitrary Lord;*

On the other hand

> *Nor is the Peoples Judgment always true:*
> *The most may err as grossly as the few,*
> *And faultless Kings run down, by Common Cry*
> *For Vice, Oppression and for Tyranny.*

This competitive play of voices carries more instability than the syntactically more complicated antitheses favoured by 18th-century couplets. Though they look smoother in Dryden's verse, both sides are open to surprise, change and disruption.

Social and political restlessness are reflected in Restoration reinvention of genres as mock genres. Parody, irony and ▷ burlesque were popular (▷ figures of speech), though recognition of the matter being reformulated also ensured that orthodoxies lingered. Burlesque distinctively dissolved grand matters into bathetic (▷ figures of speech) effects, in for instance Charles Cotton's translation of the very popular French travesty of Virgil by Paul Scarron: '*Aeneas* and his Wand'ring Mates, Were at that time, Angling for *Sprats*'. Banality was not wholly the enemy of wit, since it provided occasions for it, as in Dryden's satire of the poetic aspirations of Elkanah Settle and ▷ Thomas Shadwell in *Mac Flecknoe*. Poets who claimed merit – incessantly troped as 'laurel' or 'bays' – used surprise to guard against boredom, even in mock genres where reversals could be predicted. Rochester was particularly deft at this game, as for example in his song 'Fair Chloris in a pigsty lay', where the nymph's location burlesques pastoral. Yet the poem turns out to be an account of Chloris masturbating: a surprise not just in its frankness but in the way that its image of female self-sufficiency reverses pastoral's obsessive articulation of abandoned lovers' complaints. The incompleteness of heterosexual love is burlesqued by autoeroticism, but it ends with a further surprise by restoring Chloris to pastoral purity, though with an ironic note – ironic about both pastoral and antipastoral – 'She's innocent and pleased'.

Pastoral was especially suited to rewriting since its conventions were static. Even where lovers leave one another, order is reimposed through formulaic laments about departure. But Restoration pastoral is peculiarly dynamic, partly because women used the genre to write about desire. In the 17th century, states of semi-undress were considered more exciting than nudity; the longings and couplings of nymphs and swains thinly veil those of men and women. Love is shown as arousal, exhaustion, rearousal; where bodies mingle, moods dissolve and evolve. For example, in Aphra Behn's *On a Juniper-Tree, cut down to make Busks* (1680), after a couple make love three times,

> *. . . Chloris reassum'd her fear,*
> *And chid the Swain, for hàving prest,*
> *What she alas wou'd not resist:*
> *Whilst he in whom Loves sacred flame*
> *Before and after was the same,*
> *Fondly implor'd she wou'd forget*
> *A fault, which he wou'd yet repeat.*

The shifts between past and future, memory and desire, dizzily mimic the erotic exchange. Yet the lovers are constant: change is displaced onto the tree telling the story which (surprise) is no longer a tree but a pile of sticks for corsets and (surprise again) that transformation was anticipated at the start by the title.

Constant metamorphosis is the mark of late 17th-century poetry, as of Restoration drama, where women so often disguise themselves, as other women, even as men, usually in order to further some sexual aim. The reopening of theatres, and women's new cultural presence, created a new sense of the pleasures and threats of acting. Rochester's phrase, 'Love's theatre, the bed', points to a fascination in poetry with how sex expressed conscious performance (in every sense) rather than authenticity. This was, of course, convenient for libertines who could up and leave at any time on the grounds that no feeling was real, or if real, lasting. It is not, however, ennui which underlies Rochester's moving lyrics about transience – 'All my past life is mine noe more' – though some of his violent verse is hardly philosophical. One such poem, in which the speaker wishes to fuck out his mistress's eyes, is a mock-song, and hence could be seen to expose libertine excess by exaggerating or parodying it. But much male libertine poetry is straightforwardly anxious and violent: women are endlessly figured as towns to be attacked, besieged and conquered. In this troping of love as war, women fought back with strong mythological warriors such as Amazons or planetary deities, such as Diana, who looked down on men from a great height. Men might use the same myths as evidence of unfemininity or frigidity, but female heroism had the longer literary heritage. The popularity of poems by women about female friendship reflected not just actual supportive relations between women, but also a model of emotional constancy and trustworthiness, which misogynist poets consistently denied women showed in matters of love. Platonic love, sensual but apparently asexual, offered women an alternative to faithless heterosexual lovers, and furthermore showed women capable of reasoning philosophically. As 'Philophilippa' wrote in tribute to Katherine Philips' poems about female friendship, 'For there's requir'd (to do that Virtue right) / Courage, as much in Friendship as in Fight'.

Katherine Philips proved herself not only in contemporary, innovative, writing, but also through her display of more traditional skills. In fact she was one of many poets whose success was founded on translation – in her case, of ▷ Corneille. Translation, another form of textual metamorphosis, gave proof of skill based on intellect. Hence it was especially helpful to women, since it allowed them to show intellectual skill which was then modestly diffused through their original's pre-existing reputation. As the ▷ Earl of Roscommon put it, 'And by improving what was writ before, *Invention* labours less, but *Judgment* more'. Before Dryden translated Virgil, according to Elizabeth Thomas, translators had 'his lofty Epick Rhymes / By murd'ring Pens debas'd, to doggerel Chimes'. Rewriting Ovid, ▷ Boccaccio and Chaucer in *Fables Ancient and Modern* (1700), Dryden showed how English verse could revitalize old texts. The linguistic edge to his poetic talents was underlined by his admirers. Comparing Dryden (sprightly, energetic, various) to Pope (regular, harmonious, elevated), ▷ James Beattie in 1776 stressed how Dryden's example transformed English:

> *In Dryden's more correct pieces, we meet with no affection of words of Latin or Greek etymology, no cumbersome pomp of epithets, no drawling circumlocutions, no idle glare of images, no blunderings round about a meaning: his English is pure and simple, nervous and clear, to a degree which Pope has never exceeded and not always equalled.*

Dryden, in his use of English, showed how a poetry of restlessness could also be durable and elegant; he is said to have found it brick and left it marble.

Poetry in context: 1700–1740

Early 18th-century poetry has been most closely associated with the term 'Augustan': civilized, rational, decorous – except where wit allows it to be naughty – and with Alexander Pope as its chief exponent. There was a characteristic urbanity, not only the stability of civic architecture, but the rowdy flow of life on the streets, in for instance John Gay's *Trivia; or, the Art of Walking the Streets of London* (1716), which you might share with a Covent Garden prostitute.

> *'Tis she who nightly strolls with saunt'ring pace,*
> *No stubborn stays her yielding shape embrace;*
> *Beneath the lamp her tawdry ribbons glare,*
> *The new-scowered manteau, and the slattern air,*
> *High-draggled petticoats her travels show,*
> *And hollow cheeks with artful blushes glow;*
> *With flatt'ring sounds she sooths the cred'lous ear,*
> *'My noble captain! charmer! love! my dear!*

This interest in portraiture and types of speech was widespread in early 18th-century poetry. Material detail and social nuance created the illusion of spectatorship, in which the poet's observation appears easy. This stylistic representation of the ordinary made 18th-century poetry self-consciously literary in its appearance, even when its substance extended to low-life concerns. As Pope put it in his ▷ *Essay on Criticism* (1711), 'True Wit is Nature to advantage dressed / What oft was thought, but ne'er so well expressed'. This familiarity of poetic material and ideas also meant that poetry could become much less the prerogative of one class or gender.

Two poets from a slightly older generation showed how the commonplace could be used to reveal multiple meanings. John Philips' Georgic *Cyder* (1706) described the cultivation, manufacture and virtues of cider. It also investigated the apple's role in 'fallen states' from the theological to the drunken, as well as its political symbolism (through toasts) and association with art (through horticulture). *The Art of Cooking* (1708) by ▷ William King did for food what *Cyder* did for drink, using a Horatian ideal of temperance to investigate questions of appetite and the nationalism of gastronomy.

This conjunction of material and mythological worlds is present in Pope's *Windsor Forest*, a Tory panegyric in which the Berkshire countryside becomes the heroic birthplace of national glory, and *The Rape of the Lock*, which was ostensibly written to reconcile the families of a young woman and of a man who had cut off one of her ringlets. This sparkling mock epic has a Miltonic machinery of sylphs, but these spirits fail to protect the heroine Belinda:

Transparent forms, too fine for mortal sight,
Their fluid bodies half-dissolved in light,
Loose to the wind their airy garments flew,
Thin glittering textures of the filmy dew.

Pope's mock heroic is conventionally read as a critique of a society which confuses moral and material values, embodied in the heroine who may equally 'stain her honour or her new brocade'. Pope blames female sexuality for this confusion in his sumptuous celebration of the period's double standard over sexual behaviour. This not only excluded women from desires allowed to men, but expected them to be simultaneously innocent of sexuality, and on guard against it. Though Pope celebrates as well as condemns conspicuous consumption, he is also drawn to the shape-changing instabilities of materiality, as in the sylphs, for example. Interested in optics, Pope went to astronomy lectures: the science of seeing which exposed that what the eye could *not* see was kin to poetry, since poetry both discovered the appearances of the material world and fancifully depicted *un*real worlds. Where the metaphysical poet Donne was interested in comparative miniaturization of tears and globes, and Byron was later poignantly to compare stars and drops of ink as differently durable, Pope was fascinated by the evanescence of cultural forms in an era of innovation, corruption and change: 'And now a Bubble bursts, and now a World'. It makes his poetry surprisingly anxious and elegiac below the surface of order. For Rochester, 'a nothingness the ancients knew' was at least comforting in its continuity; for Pope, the evolution of modernity threatened irreparable rupture from the past.

The transitions between great and little in mock heroic show up physical differences of scale which raise the question of scales by which to measure moral values. Satire involved some agreement between writer and reader as to which scales were best and how to establish them. Pope conservatively evokes terms such as 'good nature', 'good humour' or 'good sense' (often rhymed with contrasting 'offence' or 'pretence'), as if they were self-evident. This approach becomes facile in his ▷ *Essay on Man* (1733–4) – 'Whatever is, is Right' – as arguments for an ordered universe and the limits of reason are sustained largely by smooth versification. Optimism drains away in his later satires: the four ▷ *Moral Essays* (1731–5) are addressed to exemplary figures whose virtues contrast with the follies and vices of contemporary individuals, historical figures and traditional types. In the ▷ *Imitations of Horace* (1733–8), Pope updates Horace but despairs of a society at best anarchic and at worst vicious. Hope is slenderly located in the community of poet and reader, provided the latter is capable of 'good taste', an alliance tested again in Pope's 1743 expanded version of *The Dunciad*, a mock epic about Grub Street's alleged threat to culture. 'Satire's my Weapon, but I'm too discreet / To run a Muck, and tilt at all I meet': Pope appears to oppose mediocrity fearlessly. However, as ▷ Colley Ciber, chief dunce in *The Dunciad*, pointed out with some dignity in his memoirs, not everyone shared Pope's definition of mediocrity. Moreover, although some writers mocked Pope for his small size, his spinal curvature and his ▷ Catholicism, in order to attack his Tory politics, not all the opposition to him was ill-founded. Pope had a talent for countering insult with feud' the effects of which made his anxieties about popular culture even harder to allay. He could be peevish and misogynist as well as an exceptionally elegant writer.

Pope's prominence tends to eclipse other poets, even Tory satirists, such as the densely topical Jonathan Swift, or Samuel Johnson, whose ▷ *London* (1738) and ▷ *The Vanity of Human Wishes* (1749) looked to Juvenal rather than Horace. Swift's *Verses on the Death of Dr Swift* (1739) were a Restoration-style joke, a mock elegy, but their mimicry of chat over cards expressed the 18th-century's interest in idiom, as well as its preoccupation with transcience. Swift's quatrains shaped irony more drily than couplets, but were used less. The couplet's compressions, comparisons and parallels suggested life as a process whose symmetries could only be provisionally stabilized. Like the ubiquitous use of irony, it suggested multiple meanings. The couplet's assurance was also useful for female and working-class poets. ▷ Mary Collier, a gardener's daughter and admirer of Pope, used it to take issue with Pope's negative views on women: 'Yet, with ten thousand follies to her charge, / Unhappy woman's but a slave at large' (*Essay on Woman*, 1746).

A number of critics pointed to the contribution of women in extending culture, but women repeatedly used tropes of ▷ slavery to describe their situation. As ▷ Sarah Egerton put it in 1703, 'Say, tyrant Custom, why we must obey / The impositions of thy haughty sway?' As Stuarts were replaced by Hanoverian dynasts, women reflected on how they were unable to change their rulers. However, many more women were writing. One particularly popular form was the epistle, where the mutual status of correspondents offered women temporary equality, with men as well as with each other. Where 17th-century epistles foregrounded friendship, 18th-century ones highlight writing as part of domestic activities. Johnson's gruff praise of Elizabeth Carter, that she could translate Epictetus and make a pudding, is acted out in women's poetry as they describe themselves 'scribbling' and running households. 'Often, from thoughts sublime as these, / I sink at once – and make a cheese', as Frances Seymour, Countess of Hertford, joked to her friend the Countess of Pomfret.

Some women achieved fame almost in spite of themselves. Lady Mary Wortley Montagu, though aristocratically reluctant to publish, was known as a wit. Her satires, some in collaboration with ▷ Lord John Hervey, prize subtlety: satire should 'like a polish'd Razor keen / Wound with a touch that's scarcely felt or seen'. Her· *Town Eclogues* (1716) are thoughtful city pastorals, one of many generic mutations which followed from a quarrel between Pope and ▷ Ambrose Philips about the proper scope of pastoral. Philips' argument that life-like rural speech or activities could modernize pastoral was playfully taken up by Gay in his Spenserian cycle *The Shepherd's Week* (1714). It also became a game in which pastoral was given oxymoronic (▷ figures of speech) locations such as the city or seaside.

High-cultural figurations of landscape were often consciously literary, but open to intellectual enquiries of all sorts. In his Miltonic ▷ *The Seasons* (1726–30), ▷ James Thomson drew together science, geography, history, philosophy and theology to celebrate and explore the natural world. Like Pope an admirer of ▷ Newton, Thomson represents both science and poetry as tracing causes, describing effects and yielding beauty. Frost illustrates the process:

The nightly Sky
And all her glowing Constellations, pour
Their rigid Influence down: It freezes on
Till Morn, late-rising, o'er the drooping World
Lifts her pale Eye, unjoyous: then appears
The various Labour of the silent Night,
The pendant Isicle, the Frost-Work fair
Where thousand Figures rise, the crusted Snow,
Tho' white, made whiter by the fining North.
(*Winter*, 1726)

For all this poem's enthusiastic natural richness, the personifications which crowd it show how early 18th-century poetry is continuously *sociable*.

Poetry in context: 1740–1790

The 1740s have been described as a decade of literary loneliness, though women writers, likely to have isolation imposed on them for writing, continued to quest for community. Poetry is still peopled, but with the deceased, including Pope, to whom many tributes were written after his death in 1744. Fashionable poems – ▷ Edward Young's ▷ *Night Thoughts* (1742–5), ▷ Robert Blair's *The Grave* (1743), Lord Lyttleton's *Monody* on the death of his wife (1747) – all involved mortality, a trend neatly parodied in William Whitehead's *New Night Thoughts on Death* (1747): 'Stop, insatiate worm! / I feel thy summons: – to my fellow-worms / Thou bidd'st me hasten! – I obey thy call, / For wherefore should I live?' Poems such as ▷ Thomas Parnell's *Night Piece on Death* (1721) had earlier considered how death levelled the already low:

Those Graves, with bending osier bound,
That nameless heave the crumbled ground,
Quick to the glancing thought disclose
Where Toil and Poverty repose.

In Thomas Gray's *Elegy Written in a Country Churchyard* thought lingered on the same nameless people's resting place:

Far from the madding crowd's ignoble strife,
Their sober wishes never learn'd to stray;
Along the cool sequester'd vale of life
They kept the noiseless tenor of their way.

Where previously poets picked out figures in crowds or sketched types, now they explored anonymity and rural community. As roads and canals improved, as travel and ▷ travel writing increased, and as publishing moved out of London, poetry became provincial, regional, exotic – almost anything but metropolitan, though town life still provided poetry with bustle.

This remoteness could be geographical or historical: for instance, in the *Persian Eclogues* (1742) and odes of ▷ William Collins, or Gray's odes *The Progress of Poesy* and ▷ *The Bard* (1757), which follow Thomson's interest in Druids, and commemorate imagination in native archetypes (▷ Welsh literature in English). The idea of the bard appealed as an image of a community poet with power: as John Brown explained in 1763, 'the Poet, though no longer a Legislator, may still occasionally exert his salutory Power, by his Influence on the Passions of the Soul'. Edward I's massacre of Welsh bards was represented almost nostalgically, since his persecution proved that poetry could have power. The bards' Celtic domains also meant a move to the margins, where Englishness was contested – literally, in the ▷ Jacobite Rebellion of 1745 and its aftermath. Northern material remained attractive in ballads, such as Jane Elliot's *The Flowers of the Forest* (1769), and Lady Anne Lindsay's *Auld Robin Gray* (1776). The distancing power of imagination itself was evoked by the controversy surrounding James MacPherson's epic fragments published under the name of ▷ Ossian, and allegedly discovered centuries after they were written. If truly discovered, the fragments would acquire historical lustre; if invented, then what they revealed would be inauthentic. This view does not express a simple suspicion of the imagination, but it supports antiquarian effort against flashy inspiration.

The commodification of poetry, partly represented by Ossian, reflected ambiguities about poetry's commercial possibilities: for instance, the footnotes which Gray strewed round his bardic poems can be seen as making his material both more and less accessible to a general readership. Controversy raged as to whether Ossian was genuine: Johnson and some others were sceptical; yet some like John Brown argued that no modern poet could come up with 'the grand Simplicity of Imagery and Diction, the strong Draughts of rude Manners and uncultivated Scenes of Nature, which abound in all these Poems'. Similar controversy surrounded the poems of ▷ Thomas Chatterton which he briefly passed off as the productions of a 15th-century monk, Thomas Rowley.

Bardic preoccupations gave way to more diverse regional interests, leading to experiments with dialect, best known in ▷ Robert Burns' poems, as in the address to a mouse whose nest had been turned up by the plough: 'Wee, sleeket, cowran, tim'rous beastie, / O, what a panic's in thy breastie!' (1785). Dialect also featured in some of the poems of Susannah Blamire, 'the Muse of Cumberland', and in the unusual poem by 'Ophelia', *Snaith Marsh. A Yorkshire Pastoral* (1754). ▷ Mary Leapor's *Crumble Hall* (1751) plays inventively with pastoral conventions; ▷ Oliver Goldsmith's ▷ *The Deserted Village* (1768) upholds them, despite addressing the effects of rural depopulation on 'Sweet Auburn! loveliest village of the plain'. Many poets attempted to reconcile pieties with social problems, but with variable success, leading ▷ George Crabbe to declare in *The Village* (1783) 'I paint the Cot, / As Truth will paint it, and as Bards will not'.

Much religious poetry of this period was not simply or sentimentally pious, but powerful, even violent. ▷ Christopher Smart's poems about the sacred bard, David, were admired for their elevated formality. His extraordinary *Jubilate Agno* (written 1759–61, but not published until 1939) brings together Biblical references and contemporary life in an idiolectic litany: 'Let Achsah rejoice with the Pigeon who is an antidote to malignity and will carry a letter. / *For I bless God for the Postmaster General and all Conveyancers of letters under his care especially Allen and Sherlock.*' More conventional liturgical pronouncements appeared in many hymns, which followed those of ▷ Isaac Watts a little earlier in the period: for instance, 'Christians, awake, salute the happy morn' ▷ (John Byrom), 'Rock of Ages, cleft for me' (Augustus Toplady), and 'God moves in a mysterious way' (William Cowper).

Where faith energized reason, reason also composed faith (visibly, in the quatrains of hymns.) Both were affected by the mid- to late- century's movement of ▷ sensibility, though since poetry had always been assumed to involve feeling, sensibility affected it less than prose. William Cowper's ▷ *The Task* (1785), written as therapy for periodic religious depression, brought the feeling mind and thinking heart together to form a poetic subjectivity which reflects on its world and narrates how that world relates to wider ones. Starting with a sofa, the poem turns expansively to books, people and the natural world, each of which contributes to poetic communication.

Fellow-feeling was promoted in a number of anti-slavery poems and in sympathy for various political struggles against tyranny. Such was *Corsica* by Anna Laetitia Aikin (later ▷ Barbauld) in 1773:

> *There yet remains a freedom, nobler far*
> *Than kings or senates can destroy or give;*
> *Beyond the proud oppressor's cruel grasp*
> *Seated secure; uninjured; undestroyed;*
> *Worthy of gods: the freedom of the mind.*

The ▷ American War of Independence attracted some interest – Anna Seward's *Monody on the Unfortunate Major André* (1781), lamenting the officer shot as a spy, was one of the poems which made its author prominent. The politics of ▷ William Blake's poems *The French Revolution* (1791) and *America* (1793) were overtly radical, despite their prophetic modes, since this was less ambiguous and dialectical than his symbolism in ▷ *Songs of Innocence and Experience* (1789; 1794).

With ideological tension increasing, moralist poets criticized mistaken sensibility: 'Tis not to mourn because a sparrow dies; To rave in artificial ecstasies', wrote ▷ Hannah More in 1782. But frivolous poetry prospered as well as the sublime: as Richard Tickell complained in 1778, 'The reigning fashion in modern poesy is *Sentimental Panegyric on Married Beauties.* This appears in a thousand various Shapes; from *Bouts Rhimées* on the *wou'd-be Sappho* of Bath, up to Doggerel Epistles to the lovely Amoret'. Provincial centres and spas, such as Bath, Tunbridge Wells, Brighthelmstone (as Brighton was then called), Cheltenham and Scarborough, provided renewable audiences. One such collection declared 'The subject of the verses written at these places of public and polite resort is generally Love and the Charms of the Fair.' There were exceptions: Christopher Anstey's constantly reprinted *New Bath Guide* (1766) mixed satire and sentiment in its epistles: thus one admirer asked, 'How came you by such an extraordinary gift / Thus to blend in one poem both YORICK and SWIFT?'

After 1740, then, some poets turned satiric and lyric energies into provincial forms. Politeness concerned cultural community rather than manners. Other poets tested the limits of nature-based genres, such as pastoral or descriptive poetry, to pursue sublime quests, escapist ideals or a more representative, gritty relation between social practices and poetry. But urbanity did not disappear: even as poets explored new areas, they continued to believe in poetry as communicative.

Modern criticism has invested heavily in the idea of ▷ Romanticism as a distinct literary era, and one whose aims and ideals are particularly associated with poetry. Late 20th-century criticism has taken a more flexible attitude perhaps to debates about dividing lines, arguing that there are multiple and sometimes competing ways of representing literary history. The map of women's poetry does not fit neatly onto that of men's. Likewise, categories of race and class, which are not necessarily the same across history, lead us to different views of literature. Historians are comfortable with the idea of a 'long 18th century', from 1660 to 1832, and the publication of

▷ Wordsworth and ▷ Coleridge's *Lyrical Ballads* in 1798 has at times been taken as the literary equivalent of the Great Reform Act in providing a convenient staging-post. But critical interest in cultural differences within periods has complicated literary history, and its relation to historical and cultural interpretation. There are many histories and many cultures involved. War, for example, was not central to the experience of all writers, but continuous conflict formed part of the public domain, and hence the public domain of poetry, from the wars against the Dutch in the 1660s and 1670s to the Napoleonic wars of the 1800s. So too imperial expeditions (▷ imperialism), colonial ventures (▷ colonialism), Grand Tours and voyages of exploration widened the horizons of some and brought oppression to others. Both war and travel stimulated literature's reflections upon national identity and modernity. Poetry's ready identification with conventions made it hospitable to conservative thought, but its association with imagination also made it the vehicle of challenging and progressive ideas.

In place of an old, reductive story of a simple opposition between reason and imagination, where Romanticism heralds the victory of the latter, recent criticism suggests that Romanticism involves responses to ideological developments precipitated particularly by the French Revolution. Similarly significant changes, particularly in the arenas of politics, religion and the economy, can be seen to be taking place from the late 17th century on. Poetry was actively engaged in these cultural transformations throughout the 18th century. In helping to engineer a dynamic cooperation between reason and passion, as well as a recognition of how they could at times contradict one another, poetry expressed one of the chief characteristics of the Enlightenment.

8 Market, Morality and Sentiment: Non-dramatic Prose 1660–1789

Janet Barron and David Nokes

No man but a blockhead ever wrote except for money
Samuel Johnson

Early prose and the origins of the novel

Secular, non-dramatic, writing in English dates back to the late 15th century and was already flourishing by the 16th. But its publication proliferated during the ▷ Civil War, when polemicists on both sides recognized the usefulness of widely distributed printed propaganda. Printing presses became cheap and relatively portable, and political ▷ pamphlets, ancestors of today's ▷ newspapers, multiplied. After the ▷ Restoration the presses continued to be used for religious and political propaganda, but also for a wide range of other secular writing, including ▷ broadsides, ▷ ballads, ▷ conduct books, books on cookery, and housewifery in general, and pamphlets on a vast range of topics, both serious and frivolous.

In addition, numerous fictional works were published, some of which look forward to the novel of the 18th century. Much ink has been spilled to determine the question of exactly where and how the novel began. As yet, no answer has emerged which seems universally acceptable. Some literary historians have looked back as far as Elizabethan writers of prose romance, such as Sidney, Nashe, Deloney, and Greene, for ancestors of the novel, or even referred to their stories as early novels. But more serious attention has been given to several post-Restoration works, including ▷ Aphra Behn's ▷ *Love Letters Between a Nobleman and his Sister* (1684–7), whose epistolary form (▷ epistolary novel) was widely taken up in the 18th century, by novelists including ▷ Richardson; and her ▷ *Oroonoko* (1688), whose first-person narrative, involving detailed accounts of the narrator-persona's own feelings in reaction to events, again anticipates many later works. Another important composition is ▷ Congreve's *Incognita*: *Or, Love and Duty Reconcil'd* (1691) which, in its playful irony, resembles the novels of ▷ Fielding. Congreve defined his own work as a novel, and in its Preface distinguished it from the earlier romance, arguing that novels, including his, 'are of a more familiar nature' than romances, and that 'Romances give more of wonder, novels more of delight'.

Most of the works described above were written for considerations other than financial gain. Some authors were inspired by passionate conviction, others by the desire to exert their influence through argument, others wrote for the sheer pleasure of the task, while others still were motivated by the simple authorial vanity of seeing the offsprings of their imagination bound up in folio or octavo volumes. A very few 17th-century writers, such as Behn, lived on the income from their writing. But it was the 18th century which really saw the emergence of the professional writer on a wide scale; the man or woman who wrote not as a genteel pastime, nor to flatter the self-esteem of a generous patron, but directly for money. For the first time, the spread of literacy, together with the emergence of commercial bookseller-publishers eager to feed the imaginations of an expanding reading public, made the trade of letters a viable, if not always lucrative, profession.

The literary market place

In the early years of the century most of the leading writers still relied more on institutional sinecures, or on a combination of public and private patronage, than on the literary market place for their support. ▷ Richard Steele was a Commissioner for stamps; William Congreve was nominally in charge of licensing hackney carriages; ▷ Daniel Defoe was a government spy; ▷ Jonathan Swift held the livings of two country parishes in Ireland; ▷ Joseph Addison was a career civil servant, finally achieving the position of Secretary of State.

Yet the qualifications required for entry to the professions excluded some authors who had to rely solely on the income from their writing. As a Catholic (▷ Catholicism), ▷ Alexander Pope was unable to hold public office, though he made a virtue of his social exclusion by celebrating his Twickenham retreat as a symbol of independence. His accomplished marketing of the subscription editions of his translations of ▷ Homer netted him an astonishing £10,000 (something in excess of £500,000 in today's terms). It was a commercial coup that other writers could only envy. By contrast, Swift was paid £200 for ▷ *Gulliver's Travels* (1726), and ▷ Oliver Goldsmith £60 for ▷ *The Vicar of Wakefield* (1761–2).

In recent years critical interpretations of 18th-century literature have increasingly questioned the traditional image of the period as an 'age of reason' (▷ rationalism), a peaceful haven of political stability and classical values. Recent studies have revealed the commercial realities that lay behind the ▷ classical façade of the 18th-century literary pantheon. By exploring the subculture of ▷ Grub Street, and by focusing attention on the many previously neglected women writers of the period, modern scholarship has provided a new perspective on this fascinating era in literary history, reminding us of the valuable contributions made by those excluded from the clubs and ▷ coffee-houses of the Augustan establishment.

Aphra Behn, debarred from the professions as a woman, attempted to attract state patronage by her political writings. The *Ode on the Coronation* would, she hoped, secure her a pension or a grace-and-favour house. But no money was forthcoming, and she turned instead to more lucrative markets for her talents in romantic fiction and theatrical comedies.

The career of ▷ Samuel Johnson demonstrates the precariousness of the literary life. Forced by poverty to abandon his studies at Oxford University, he thereby relinquished all hopes of a career in the law or the Church. After an unsuccessful attempt at school-teaching, he arrived in London, virtually penniless, and began to support himself by his writings. Regular contributions to ▷ *The Gentleman's Magazine* provided part of his income, yet his independent projects were also undertaken for commercial reasons. According to legend, ▷ *Rasselas* (1759) was written rapidly to pay the expenses of his mother's funeral; Johnson encouraged such stories as proof of his independence.

In 1755, at the culmination of his labours on the ▷ *Dictionary of the English Language*, Johnson delivered a celebrated epistolary snub to his self-styled patron, the ▷ Earl of Chesterfield: 'Is not a patron, my lord, one who looks with unconcern on a man struggling for life in the water and when he has reached ground encumbers him with help?' His letter is a declaration of literary independence that signals the end of the era of the private patron. Ironically, it was the commercial project of the *Dictionary* which brought Johnson academic recognition, as Oxford awarded him the degree he had been unable to obtain by more conventional means. In 1762, the award of a Crown pension of £300 a year relieved Johnson of some of the drudgery of

⊳ hack work, though he was careful to insist that this was not a reward for political services, but a recognition of literary achievements.

Just before the start of the century, the lapsing of the Licensing Act in 1695 provided the opportunity for a massive expansion of the printing trade. Entrepreneurial publishers ranging from society figures like Jacob Tonson to Grub Street pirates like Edmund Curll played a vital, though sometimes unrecognized, part in shaping the literary culture of the 18th century. The 'Augustan Age' (⊳ Augustanism)is often, and rightly, portrayed as a period when classical models and formal rules were of paramount literary importance; yet the commercial judgements of men like these were equally influential in promoting and developing the variety of 18th-century literature, with works ranging from translations of the classics to lurid ⊳ Newgate yarns.

It was a time when, according to Martin Scriblerus (⊳ Scriblerus Club) (alias Pope), 'paper became so cheap and printers so numerous that a deluge of authors cover'd the land'. What is remarkable about the prose writings of the 18th century, when compared with those of earlier centuries, is their sheer diversity. The rise of the novel and the development of ⊳ periodical journalism are only the two most obvious features of this expansion of the literary market. Fabulous adventures (⊳ fable), travellers' tales (⊳ travel literature), secret histories, spiritual lives, satires, ⊳ sermons, ⊳ pastorals and panegyrics and works of every conceivable style and tone, calculated to appeal to all ⊳ tastes and pockets, rolled from the presses. The pages of Pope's ⊳ *Dunciad* are filled with the names of forgotten Grub Street authors, such as Ned Ward, ⊳ Eliza Haywood and ⊳ Charles Gildon, many of whom eked out a precarious living in the kind of literary sweat-shops hilariously described by Henry Fielding in his play *The Author's Farce* (1730).

Establishment authors, like Pope and Swift, frequently deplored the promiscuous vitality of this new literary world, forseeing the death of civilized values in publishers' lists as the works of classical authors were outnumbered by the ephemeral products of those whom they dubbed the 'moderns' or 'dunces' (⊳ The Battle of the Books). The novelists themselves often appeared embarrassed at their own imaginative freedom, prefacing their works with statements which sought to legitimize the seductive appeal of fiction by appealing to some external authority. In referring to his early novels as 'comic epics in prose' Fielding endeavoured to claim a niche for them in the traditional classical pantheon. ⊳ Defoe preferred to describe his tales as 'true histories', faking his fictions to read like facts, and filling in the broad sweeps of his adventure stories with minute circumstantial details. To Samuel Richardson, the only justification for fiction was its clear commitment to moral reform, and he presented his novels as exemplary parables in which vice is routed and virtue rewarded. Yet even the sternest critics of literary self-indulgence found the lure of fictional licence irresistible. Swift's ⊳ *A Tale of a Tub* (1704) is among other things a satire on the ephemerality of modern culture. 'I have remarked,' says the *Tale*'s narrator, 'that nothing is so very tender as a modern piece of wit'. But, while affecting to deplore this cultural perishability, Swift revels in the world of literary ephemera, turning topical tit-bits into enduring metaphors (⊳ figures of speech) for human vanity.

Thus to speak of 'the rise of the novel' in the early 18th century, as if assuming that by then the novel had attained a clear, recognizable identity, is somewhat misleading. There was no single literary genre which sprang fully formed to life with the publication of ⊳ *Robinson Crusoe* in 1719. Instead, a variety of contrasting fictional forms competed for attention, ranging from the vivid Grub Street pseudo-biographies (⊳ biography) published in the down-market *Applebee's Journal* (1715–36), to witty anecdotal sketches of the ⊳ Coverley family presented in ⊳ *The Spectator* (1712);

or from salacious secret histories, such as ▷ Delarivière Manley's *The New Atalantis* (1709) to satiric fantasies, such as Swift's *Gulliver's Travels.* As late as 1711 ▷ *The Tatler* was still using the word 'novelist' to mean a newspaperman. In much the same way Johnson's *Dictionary* continued to define 'journal' as 'any paper published daily', whereas most of the periodicals so described were not in fact daily publications. In both cases it is clear that the regulatory constraints of etymology had little inhibiting influence on the dynamic growth of the genres themselves. For, despite the Augustan predilection for ▷ neo-classical rules and critical categories, the novel, like ▷ journalism, grew up happily innocent of prescriptive theories. Indeed, the emergence of the novel form in the early 18th century, which often appears an inevitable consequence of changing social conditions, can equally well be presented as the result of a series of felicitous accidents. Defoe was almost 60, and nearing the end of an indefatigably varied career during which he had tried his hand at innumerable forms of business enterprise (all failures) as well as journalism and espionage, when he published *Robinson Crusoe.* Fielding was a celebrated young playwright until ▷ Sir Robert Walpole's introduction of stage censorship with the new Licensing Act of 1737 (▷ theatres) forced him to find an alternative outlet for his literary talents. Richardson was a successful printer, whose decision to turn author was partly inspired by a prudent desire to utilize the spare capacity of his press. This process of 'serendipity', a word coined by ▷ Horace Walpole, continued throughout the century, and it was Walpole's own fortuitous success with his fantasy ▷ *The Castle of Otranto* (1764) which inspired the later vogue for ▷ Gothic fiction.

The career and reputation of Daniel Defoe offers some useful insights into one type of literary enterprise. The son of a Dissenting tallow-chandler, he was a lifelong bankrupt, a tireless entrepreneur and a prolific journalist whose collected works would fill several hundred volumes. For nine years, from 1704 to 1713 he wrote single-handedly his thrice-weekly journal ▷ *The Review*; for much of the same period he was also one of the government's leading spies, sending back secret reports from Edinburgh on the political manoeuvring surrounding the negotiations for the Act of ▷ Union between England and Scotland in 1707. Simultaneously, he was also striving to extricate himself from massive debts, and contriving to stay out of the hands of his many creditors. In both his business ventures and his journalism one finds the same spirit of brinkmanship, the same flirting with disaster. The energy and excitement of his writings co-exist with a kind of literary carelessness and an apparent impatience with more studied effects which led on occasions to disaster. His ironic pamphlet *The Shortest Way with Dissenters* (1702), which counterfeited the violent language of a High Church zealot, backfired badly when its irony was mistaken for incitement, and Defoe was sentenced to punishment at the pillory. More recently, critics have reassessed the apparent carelessness of Defoe's writing, finding in it the poker-face of a more accomplished literary gamesmanship. The 'failure' of *The Shortest Way* succeeded in exposing the covert menace of High Church policies in a way that more conventional irony (▷ figure of speech) could not have achieved. Similar subtleties may be detected in the 'mistakes' and contradictions which abound in Defoe's novels. Generations of readers have noted the glaring contradictions between what characters say in one part of a novel, and how they behave elsewhere. Well on in her narrative ▷ Moll Flanders is seized by a sudden maternal instinct and delivers a sober lecture on the depravity of mothers who neglect or abandon their offspring. Yet by this stage she herself has happily abandoned innumerable children of her own without a word or a qualm. Her flair for criminality is accompanied by a constant moral patter as she alternately presents herself as a victim of circumstances and an agent of social education. The unconvincingness of her final 'repentance', which conveniently allows her to retire in comfort on her ill-gotten gains, has often appeared to undermine the novel's moral seriousness. Contradictions like these – and there are many other celebrated examples in all the novels – have often been taken as evidence of a slap-dash journeyman approach to the business of authorship. Yet the pattern of these contradictions, in which characters preach like ▷ Puritan moralists yet act like ruthless opportunists, goes to the heart of Defoe's fiction. For all their concentration on mundane details, his novels are fantasies of survival, heroic adventures of social mobility in which individuals single-handedly confront and conquer a host of adverse circumstances. Despite the apparent crudity of their episodic narratives, Defoe's novels are animated by a quality more usually identified with a more self-consciously sophisticated form of fiction, in the characters of his unreliable narrators.

Likewise the unravelling of Jonathan Swift's ironies has been the key to the 20th-century reappraisal of his status as a writer. Earlier critics such as Thackeray viewed his writings as misanthropic and malign: 'A monster gibbering shrieks, and gnashing imprecations against mankind – tearing down all shreds of modesty, past all sense of manliness and shame; filthy in word, filthy in thought, furious, raging, obscene.'

Judgements like these derive from the tendency to identify Swift with the narrators of his satires, seeing in Gulliver's hysterical reaction to the ▷ Yahoos a representation of Swift's supposed alienation from humanity. But Swift is the master of literary disguises, and his chosen narrators are utopians or fanatics, projectors or madmen whose plausible rhetoric of half-truths lead inexorably to such savage conclusions as the eating of babies or the abandonment of human society in favour of life in a stable. As a satirist, Swift aims primarily at the irrational ▷ utopianism which founds its hopes of progress on a refusal to acknowledge the perversities and flaws of human nature itself. From ▷ *A Tale of a Tub* (1704), with its ironic epigraph 'Written for the Universal Improvement of Mankind', to the Academy of Lagado in *Gulliver's Travels*, whose scientists are engaged in projects to produce sunbeams out of cucumbers, Swift ridicules the visionary enthusiasm which finds inspiration in the belchings of a fanatical preacher, and sublime wisdom in the neighing of a horse.

Born and educated in ▷ Ireland, Swift took holy orders and became a clergyman in the Church of Ireland. Yet he spent most of Queen ▷ Anne's reign in London, pursuing an alternative career as a political journalist. His ▷ *Examiner* articles and his pamphlet *The Conduct of the Allies* (1711) provided a magisterial defence of the Tory government's policy for ending the war with France, and even today offer excellent models of the art of political journalism. Forced to return to his native land on the death of Queen Anne, Swift felt like a virtual exile, and it was several years before he could bring himself to relaunch his journalistic career with a series of powerful pamphlets deploring the miserable economic plight of Ireland. His most celebrated pamphlet, ▷ *A Modest Proposal* (1729), ironically recommends that the people of Ireland should rear their children as food for the tables of their English landlords. The scheme has a savage logic; it is methodically costed, and the arguments are financially flawless. With its plausible phrases and deadpan tone, this satire is a brilliant indictment of a society in which economic exploitation has abnegated the natural ties of humanity and love.

While it is undoubtedly true that Swift's satires dwell on the darker side of human nature, his love of jokes, riddles and *jeux d'esprit* should not be forgotten. From his *Bickerstaff Papers* (1708–9) to his *Directions to Servants* (published posthumously in 1745), a spirit of mischievous and subversive anarchy runs through all his writings. In his most famous poem *Verses on the Death of Dr Swift* (1731), he provided his own obituary, declaring, among other things, that 'fair liberty was all his cry'. The liberty that Swift cherished was less political than intellectual and his satires offer a consistent challenge to our own reasoning powers to find a way through the maze of utopian delusions and political lies.

'The female wits'

At one point in her career, Delarivière Manley worked as Swift's assistant on *The Examiner*, taking over from him as editor in 1711. Manley was already notorious for salacious society scandals: *The Secret History of Queen Zarah* (1705), using the device of a fictional history to avoid prosecution, was an instant success, with its separately published key revealing the code names. In 1709 a further *roman à clef*, *The New Atalantis*, continued this combination of transparent allegory and sexual innuendo. The Whig ministry, worried by her revelations, issued a warrant for the arrest of printer, publisher and author, and Manley was required to name her informers. Exploiting the ambiguities of fictions-as-facts, she declared her only source was divine inspiration. Her reputation as an erotic scandalmonger contributed to the stereotype of the immoral female author. Pope's image of the Grub Street hacks and booksellers as literary whores and pimps takes on further implications in the light of Manley's own life; supplementing her income by a series of affairs, she eventually became the mistress of Alderman Barber, her publisher.

Women writers anxious to avoid such notoriety often published their works anonymously, or prefaced them with humble pleas that they were written in distress. And, though scandalous works sold well, novels which conformed to social mores were more widely acceptable as serious literary efforts. The decline of the patronge system made a clear distinction between the aristocratic lady writing as a graceful accomplishment, and the woman who went against the nature of her sex and engaged in disreputable trade.

Even writers with no literary ambitions tailored their products to the changing literary tastes. Eliza Haywood's early works were titillating confections, and *Love in Excess* (1719) was, with *Robinson Crusoe* and *Gulliver's Travels*, one of the three best-selling works before Samuel Richardson's ▷ *Pamela* (1740–41). But by the 1740s and 1750s, Haywood took on a new tone of conventional conformity, and the 'women's novel' became increasingly associated with the values of hearth and home. It was a compromise which allowed the critic both to praise women for their delicate understanding, and to confine them to 'feminine' gentility which could be disparaged as frivolous.

Similar arguments were often advanced in condescending appraisal of some of the more chatty periodicals. Swift was in no doubt as to the main audience for ▷ Addison's ▷ *Spectator* when he remarked, 'let them fair-sex it to the world's end', and Eliza Haywood exploited this market with the launch of ▷ *The Female Spectator* (1744–6). If anything, Addison seems rather to have relished than repudiated his paper's reputation as providing a genteel education of ladies. When he boasted of taking philosophy out of the schools and colleges, and into 'clubs and assemblies, tea tables and coffee-houses', he made explicit the intention to mingle morality and manners, philosophy and fashion, in an urbane and witty miscellany. And despite a tinge of polite condescension in the tone of its more lightweight contributions, *The Spectator* was remarkably successful in maintaining a style of well-mannered wit. There was, however, a serious side to this endeavour to promote the refined tone and rational debate of coffee-house society to a wider reading public. In the previous century, the Puritan moralist and the fashionable ▷ Cavalier had stood on opposite sides in the ▷ Civil War. Addison and Steele endeavoured to heal this breach, by putting a smile on the face of morality, and restraining the more licentious habits of town rakes and courtly roués. In the genial atmosphere of a fictitious Spectator club, the Whig merchant Sir Andrew Freeport and the Tory squire Sir Roger de Coverley could discuss their differences over a glass of port rather than settling them on the battlefield. One form of anti-social behaviour that Addison particularly deplored was the writing of satires, which he described as 'poisoned darts' that gave 'secret stabs to a man's reputation'. In *The Spectator* he promised he would never 'draw a faulty character which does not fit at least a thousand people, or publish a single paper that is not written in the spirit of benevolence, with love to mankind'.

However, it was the growing popularity of the novel rather than Addison's benevolent pieties which gradually killed off the vogue for satire in the middle years of the century. In broad terms, one might say that satire deals essentially with types, whereas the novel presents us with individuals. 18th-century satire is concerned less with the redemption of individual sinners than with the regulation of general standards of conduct. But the novel, particularly under the influence of Richardson, was more interested in questions of moral identity and the expression of individual consciousness. The distinction between the two genres is not always as clear-cut as this might imply. When in ▷ *Joseph Andrews* (1742) Henry Fielding declares 'once for all, I describe not men but manners; not an individual, but a species', he writes as both satirist and novelist. In the preface to that book, he draws a distinction between comic fiction and satire, and like ▷ *Shamela* (1741), the first ten chapters comprise a burlesque satire on Samuel Richardson's *Pamela*. It is only after this point in the novel that Fielding attempts to transform Joseph's chastity from an absurd parody of Pamela's much vaunted virtue into a mark of fidelity for his beloved Fanny. Similarly, ▷ *Jonathan Wild* (1743), with its consistent ironic attacks on 'greatness', might be regarded more as an extended lampoon than as a novel. It is not until ▷ *Tom Jones* (1749) that Fielding finally achieved his own distinctive form of comic fiction though that novel too contains many incidental satiric and parodic moments.

In Johnson's view there was as great a difference between the literary talents of Richardson and Fielding 'as between a man who knew how a watch was made, and a man who could tell the hour by looking on the dial plate'. Although the terms of the relative judgements have sometimes altered, the temptation to draw comparisons between the literary achievements of these two men has persisted ever since. As authors, they embody two rival traditions of the English novel, appearing as contending 'fathers' of the novel, each disputing the legitimacy of the other's offspring. From Fielding we derive the tradition of comic fiction, a style of writing that revels in its own vivacity and wit, offering its readers a rich and varied diet of social comedy, urbane irony and literary sophistication. From Richardson we derive the novel of moral introspection and psychological insight; his epistolary style offers a kind of fictional confessional dramatizing the dilemmas of individual moral choice.

The morality of *Tom Jones* is based on a simple antithetical contrast: natural instinct versus social hypocrisy, goodness of heart versus cunning of head. Part of the satisfaction of the book comes from the combination of the formal symmetry of its structure (▷ Coleridge referred to it as one of the three best plots ever written) with the apparent freedom and randomness of its ▷ picaresque episodes. In the same way, Tom's artless and impulsive vitality is made acceptable by the artful manipulations of the narrator's tone.

Pamela, Richardson's inspired first-person narrative of a young servant girl's triumph over repeated attempts at seduction by her employer, was an immediate commercial success. 'If all the books in England were to be burnt, this book, next the Bible, ought to be preserved', enthused one reader. Nowadays its reputation is less secure. Modern readers are apt to side with Fielding in regarding its notorious subtitle, 'Virtue Rewarded', as evidence that Pamela is a model of policy rather than purity.

Richardson's next novel, ⊳ *Clarissa* (1747–8), is an undisputed literary masterpiece. Again using the epistolary form, Richardson interweaves four narrative voices to construct a novel of great psychological complexity. In its treatment of the contradictions between 'virtue' as reputation and virginity as an extension of moral integrity, Richardson highlights the social hypocrisies where the marriage market puts a high price on maidenhood. Anne Howe, Clarissa's friend, urges the conventional solution of marrying the seducer, but Clarissa follows the path of self-imposed martyrdom. The novel escapes any simplistic morality, reverberating beyond a reductive summary.

The distinction which Johnson drew between the novels of Fielding and those of Richardson, was reapplied by Richardson himself to the novels of ⊳ Sarah Fielding, Henry Fielding's sister. Johnson and Richardson both encouraged Sarah Fielding to publish her work. Her best-known novel, *The Adventures of David Simple* (1744), provides a notable contrast to the male novelists' treatment of female characters. Where Pamela and Clarissa struggle with threatening seducers, Sarah Fielding's heroines wryly recognize sexual harassment as a part of the social structure.

It was the development of the ⊳ circulating libraries in the later decades of the century which provided the largest market for the mass of novelistic fiction. Many critics were alarmed by the proliferation of light romantic fiction which resulted from these cheaper sources of entertainment. 'This branch of the literary trade', one reviewer remarked, 'appears, now, to be almost entirely engrossed by women.' The naive country girl who has her head turned by these frothy fantasies became a stock figure of fictional stereotypes. From ⊳ Richard Brinsley Sheridan's Lydia Languish to ⊳ Jane Austen's Catherine Morland, the harmful effects on the uneducated *ingenue* were a favourite topic for literary parody. In ⊳ Charlotte Lennox's *The Female Quixote* (1752), the heroine, Arabella, turns from the sterner labours of her father's study to while away her hours with her mother's library, a collection of lengthy French romances which she mistakes for historical accounts. By creating an ironic distance between the heroine and the narrator, Lennox uses this familiar theme to make a social comment on women's education. ⊳ Fanny Burney's major novels also focus on the entry of the *ingenue* into a potentially corrupting society. ⊳ *Evelina* (1778) uses the epistolary narrative of a woman asking her male mentor for advice. *Cecilia* (1782), her most successful novel, shows an intelligent but naive girl tricked out of her inheritance by an exploitative friend's husband. In drawing attention to the dangers faced by the good-natured but ill-advised heroine Burney contributes to the social debate on the status of women, using the novel as an entertaining medium of discussion.

Sentiment and sensation

In the second half of the century two new styles of writing became suddenly fashionable and all but dominated the fiction market. The first of these was the ⊳ sentimental novel. 'What, in your opinion, is the meaning of the word *sentimental*, so much in vogue among the polite?' Lady Bradshaigh asked Richardson. 'I am frequently astonished to hear such a one is a sentimental man; we were a sentimental party; I have been taking a sentimental walk.' Some twenty years later the Methodist ▷ John Wesley continued to protest against the word as a meaningless foreign neologism. 'Sentimental? What is that? It is not English; he might as well say Continental. It is not sense. It conveys no determinate idea.' Probably the most celebrated of sentimental novels was Henry Mackenzie's *The Man of Feeling* (1771) in which the tears of the hero, Harley, flow freely throughout the narrative. As a benevolent innocent with the most delicate ▷ sensibility, Harley is constantly cheated, deceived and hurt by the more worldly figures he encounters; yet his sufferings carry with them a *tendresse* of pleasure; his humiliations discover the exquisite sensations of injured integrity. Towards the end of the novel his apparently unrequited love for Miss Watson results in his physical decline until, on his deathbed, she reveals her love for him and he dies of sheer happiness. A similar pattern of innocent suffering can be found in Goldsmith's *The Vicar of Wakefield* (published 1766) which presents a parallel confrontation between naive benevolence and unscrupulous power. Goldsmith's vicar, Primrose, is a man who takes his 'consummate benevolence' to 'a romantic extreme'. With an authentically sentimental relish for the moral authority of suffering, Goldsmith dwells on the vicar's 'pleasing distress' at the repeated trials and tragedies heaped upon him by Thornhill, the malicious libertine squire.

Mackenzie's novel was an immediate best-seller. ▷ Burns wore out two copies of the work, calling it 'a book I prize next to the Bible'.]ohnson was less impressed, commenting scornfully on 'the fashionable whine of sensibility'. In 1773 ▷ Mrs Barbauld offered a psychological justification for this type of fiction in her *Inquiry into the kind of distress which exerts agreeable sensations*, emphasizing the evocation of a sympathetic tenderness on the part of the reader. 'Tenderness,' she wrote, 'is, much more properly than sorrow, the spring of tears.'

For modern readers the best-known fictional example of the cult of sensibility is in fact a partial parody of the genre. ▷ Laurence Sterne's ▷ *A Sentimental Journey through France and Italy* (1768) exploits many features of the sentimental style, yet does so with a tone of ironic self-consciousness that constantly trembles on the brink of satire. Like Mackenzie's Man of Feeling whose face is bathed in tears while listening to another's tale of woe, Sterne's Yorick, hearing of the death of a monk to whom he had behaved uncharitably, 'bursts into a flood of tears'. But whereas Harley's tears are the sign of his refined sensibility, Yorick's tears are produced with a sudden and comic exaggeration. Yorick is a virtuoso of the nervous system, conjuring up both tears and blushes with a facility which testifies less to his goodness of heart than to his incorrigible instinct for self-dramatization. Sterne's masterpiece, ▷ *Tristram Shandy* (1760–7), is another teasing work whose success transformed Sterne from an obscure Yorkshire clergyman into a leading literary celebrity, but whose eccentricities have divided critical opinion ever since. Johnson declared 'nothing odd will do long; *Tristram Shandy* did not last', but a formalist critic in our own century has asserted that '*Tristram Shandy* is the most typical novel of world literature'.

'In a word, my work is digressive, and it is progressive too, – and at the same time', announces Tristram in the book's first volume. It is significant that he puts the word 'digressive' first. With its black and marbled pages, its flash-backs and interpolations, its asterisks, blanks and dashes, *Tristram Shandy* is a novel which denies any conventional notions of narrative development. The first four volumes take place while Tristram, the hero/narrator, is still in the womb, and the book ends before it begins. Yet this work, which seems to break all the rules, and which consistently demonstrates the inability of rules, plans, theories and systems to cope with the accidents and vagaries of human life, is nevertheless held together by a curious pseudo-logic of its own. This is the absurd determinism of the association of ideas, as expressed in ▷ Locke's ▷ *Essay Concerning Human Understanding* (1690), which Tristram describes as 'a history-book of what passes in a man's own mind'. Each of Sterne's characters, Walter, Toby and Trim, is locked in his own private world of associations; their conversations present the collisions of words rather than the communication of thoughts; their actions are all bounded by accident.

Beside the inventiveness of Sterne, the more conventional comic skills of ▷ Tobias Smollett may seem stolid and predictable. Trained as a surgeon, Smollett published his first and some would say his best novel, ▷ *Roderick Random*, in 1748, when he was still only 26. Like all Smollett's novels, this work is a robust picaresque, episodic in form, slapstick in humour and brisk in pace. Some of its best moments are autobiographical, drawing on Smollett's own experience as a ship's surgeon. His next novel, ▷ *Peregrine Pickle* (1751), also has a nautical flavour, with its collection of old sea-dog characters such as Commodore Hawser Trunnion and the peglegged Lieutenant Hatchway. His final novel, ▷ *Humphry Clinker* (1771), is epistolary in form though the tone owes more to Fielding than to Richardson. In it a group of assorted characters including the irascible old valetudinarian Matthew Bramble and a Methodist coachman Humphry Clinker (who turns out to be Bramble's son) make a grand tour of Britain from Bristol, Bath and London, to Edinburgh and the Highlands, presenting us with a broad panorama of 18th-century society. The idiomatic clashes of the different ▷ letter-writing styles provide a constant ▷ humorous tone, and the book is rich in comic misadventures, though the plot itself is highly derivative. As one recent critic has written, 'it is as though Tom Jones has given way to Baedeker.'

The other fictional form which enjoyed considerable popularity in the later decades of the century was the Gothic novel. In terms of the market place, the date at which the Richardsonian novel of moral instruction began to give way to the Gothic novel of crepuscular phantoms can be pinpointed with some accuracy. In 1777 ▷ Clara Reeve published a novel called *The Champion of Virtue*, a title which clearly suggests a continuation of Richardsonian preoccupations. The following year, however, she reissued the same novel in a revised form and with a new title, *The Old English Baron, A Gothic Story*, evidently attempting to exploit the new trend in public tastes. However, the origins of the Gothic novel are usually traced back to Horace Walpole's *The Castle of Otranto*, a self-indulgent fantasy of fake ▷ medievalism which deliberately revels in its extravagant use of supernatural and 'marvellous' elements. One recent critic (Pat Rogers) has written: '*The Castle of Otranto* is preposterous; its setting is Hollywood-medieval, a Ruritanian version of chivalric times. Its plot is frankly incredible, jumpily constructed and flatly recounted.' Yet much of the novel's overt implausibility is a calculated device to move away from the classical symmetries and rational morality of Augustan literature. Walpole was a fashionable dilettante whose spirit of whimsicality led him to create his 'little Gothic castle' at ▷ Strawberry Hill, and also inspired this little Gothic tale. Like the young ill-fated poet ▷ Thomas Chatterton, who passed off his 'Rowley' poems as genuine medieval manuscripts, and the fraudulent ▷ James Macpherson who claimed to be 'translating' his pastiche ▷ Celtic epic ▷ *Ossian*, Walpole at first maintained a pretence that *The Castle of Otranto* was an authentic medieval story. For all of these writers, medievalism was a kind of fancy-dress, enabling them to evade the sober responsibilities of neo-classical literary forms and indulge their imaginations in a world of supernatural fantasy. For the Gothic novel entailed a reversal or rejection of many classical values. Instead of Pope's cherished landscape of 'Nature methodiz'd' with its well-proportioned country houses and Palladian villas, the Gothic landscape consists of dark forests and ruined castles, with gloomy dungeons and secret labyrinthine passageways. In place of the daylight world of rational debate and urbane ironies, Gothic fiction presents a nightmare world of torture and fantasies, irrational fears, ancient curses and nameless threats.

Gothic fiction can be divided into two broad categories, the novel of terror and the novel of horror. Practitioners of the novel of terror, from Clara Reeve to ▷ Ann Radcliffe, were interested in using the Gothic form as a means of exploring the psychology of fear. In her most famous novel, ▷ *The Mysteries of Udolpho* (1794), Radcliffe described the effect of terror on the mind: 'A terror of this nature, as it occupies and expands the mind, and elevates it to a high expectation, is purely sublime, and leads us, by a kind of fascination, to seek even the object from which we appear to shrink.' Echoing here some of the sentiments in ▷ Burke's treatise *On the Sublime and the Beautiful* (1759), Radcliffe also demonstrates an affinity with ▷ Wordsworth who, in *The Prelude* (1799–1805), describes how he 'grew up / Fostered alike by beauty and by fear'. In fact all of the apparently supernatural phenomena in Radcliffe's novels turn out to have perfectly rational, if somewhat contrived, explanations; the ghostly, diabolic presences that haunt her heroines are invariably products of illusionist trickery working on terrified imaginations. Unlike some other Gothic writers, Radcliffe has a perfect control of her plots, and part of the appeal of her novels lies in the ingenuity with which she supplies psychologically convincing explanations for the most apparently mysterious events. Nor is this merely a thriller-writer's gimmick. Radcliffe is interested in the gradations of intimidation and characteristically explores two related levels of fear. The abbeys, castles, dungeons and convents where her heroines find themselves are always reputedly cursed or haunted. Consequently when nocturnal apparitions occur, her heroines are thrown into the kind of superstitious dread satirized by Jane Austen in *Northanger Abbey* (published 1818). But typically, in the morning these imaginary terrors are replaced by a yet more insidious fear, as the heroines gradually realize that they are at the mercy not of ghosts and goblins, but of malevolent human beings. It is some indication of the popularity of Gothic fiction that Radcliffe earned £500 for *The Mysteries of Udolpho*, whereas Jane Austen was paid only £10 for her parody of the genre in *Northanger Abbey*.

A good example of the novel of horror is Matthew 'Monk' Lewis' *The Monk* (1796), which Byron described as representing 'the philtered ideas of a jaded voluptuary'. In this extravagant sadistic fantasy Lewis exploits all the charnel-house images that have since become the cliches of Hammer horror films. His heroine, Agnes, having been separated from her lover, is condemned to perpetual incarceration among rotting corpses in the vaults beneath her convent. With undisguised relish Lewis pictures bloated toads and slimy lizards crawling across her flesh and describes how, on waking, Agnes would often find 'my fingers ringed with the long worms which bred in the corrupted flesh of my infant'. The monk Ambrosio, the villain of the novel, crowns a career of vice by raping and killing Antonia, a 15-year-old girl, among these rotting bodies in the vault, having already murdered her mother Elvira. In order to escape the soldiers of the Inquisition, Ambrosio sells his soul to the Devil, who transports him to a mountain peak. There, before being hurled to his death, he is told that Elvira was in fact his mother, and Antonia his sister. Yet this conclusion is less a form of moral retribution, than a final gloating irony in this lurid sensationalist tale.

Loosely based on Arabian sources, ▷ William Beckford's *Vathek* (French edition

1782, English edition 1787) is another orgiastic tale of hedonism, sorcery and murder, that culminates in damnation. Although Beckford's work, like Lewis', is filled with a self-indulgent horror, this aspect of Gothic fiction also has its serious side. Throughout the Gothic literature of the late 18th and early 19th centuries, writers as diverse as Beckford, James Hogg (*The Private Memoirs and Confessions of a Justified Sinner*, 1824) and Mary Shelley (*Frankenstein*, 1817) explored Faustian themes and Satanic images that represented the dark side of ▷ Enlightenment thought.

Non-fictional prose

Modern critical tastes have tended to value fiction above other kinds of prose writing, but in the 18th century this was not always the case. Many of the century's most gifted prose stylists wrote not novels but ▷ histories and ▷ biographies, essays, travel books and letters. Apart from the fact that many novels were written in epistolary form and that several of Pope's satires were couched in the form of epistles, the familiar letter was itself a well-respected literary genre. Pope felt no more compunction about altering and polishing his personal correspondence for publication than he did about revising and changing his different versions of ▷ *The Rape of the Lock* or ▷ *The Dunciad*. For him, these letters were less autobiographical documents than parts of his literary *oeuvre*, to be edited and revised in the same way as any other work. Among the more notable letter-writers of the period were ▷ Lady Mary Wortley Montagu, Horace Walpole and the ▷ Earl of Chesterfield. Montagu's letters are witty, jaunty and civilized, with just an edge of malicious satire to give them bite. They reflect a life of rich variety; at the age of seven, Montagu was the infant favourite of the ▷ Kit-Cat Club; during her marriage she travelled throughout Europe and Turkey, finally retiring to live in Italy. Her letters are full of perceptive comments on the customs of the countries she visits, always animated by a tone of self-deprecating irony. Thus to one correspondent she comments, 'this letter is as long and as dull as any of Richardson's!'.

Horace Walpole was a prolific and assiduous letter writer, of whom it has been said that he organized his life to suit the needs of his correspondence. Self-consciously arranging both the occasions and the recipients of each letter, Walpole constructed a correspondence which suggests a life devoted to the delivery of *bon mots* and an experience translated into a seamless sequence of anecdotes. The Earl of Chesterfield's letters have fared least well with later readers. Their complacent tone of worldly wisdom seems designed to recommend a life of superficial elegance at the expense of more serious or humane concerns. Yet Chesterfield's notions of civilized life derive from a tradition initiated by *The Spectator* and his constant stress upon politeness and the social graces offers a useful insight into a significant strand of 18th-century thought.

Among biographers, ▷ James Boswell still holds pride of place. Although later scholars have revealed his ▷ *Life of Samuel Johnson* (1791) to be full of distortions and omissions, its quality of animation, dramatizing Johnson's oracular wit and sober sentiments in a lively series of encounters and anecdotes, captures much of his relish for conversation, for disputation and for life. Boswell's own journals, though full of the vanity of self-display, stand alongside ▷ Samuel Pepys' *Diary* and Swift's *Journal to Stella* as fascinating portraits of the day-to-day excitement of social life; all of these works weave together intimate private dramas with vivid representations of social and public issues.

Perhaps least often read now are the great works of Augustan scholarship:

▷ Edward Gibbon's ▷ *The Decline and Fall of the Roman Empire* (1776–88), the philosophical writings of Locke and ▷ Hume, Burke and ▷ Adam Smith. All of these in their different ways share certain humanist assumptions that are common to the literature of the period. Although each pursued a separate discipline of study, these authors thought of their works not as specialist treatises for students, but as philosophical essays designed for the educated general reader. While never amateurish or condescending, they are works which, in both style and tone, assume the centrality of their concerns to be human culture as a whole. As such they are expressions of that Enlightenment spirit which sought to promote the pursuit of knowledge not in the sheltered confines of universities and colleges, but in the coffee-houses, clubs and country houses of a civilized society. Johnson gave memorable expression to such sentiments. At the conclusion of the preface to his *Dictionary of the English Language* he writes: 'It may gratify curiosity to inform it that the *English Dictionary* was written with little assistance of the learned, and without any patronage of the great; not in the soft obscurities of retirement, or under the shelter of academic bowers, but amidst inconvenience and distraction, in sickness and in sorrow.' The name of Johnson has recurred several times throughout this essay, and that is hardly surprising. No one better exemplifies the achievements and anxieties, the triumphs and tribulations of the professional writer of his day. Johnson turned the life of writing into a kind of moral struggle against bigotry and ignorance, against poverty, prejudice and pretensions. Some of his more celebrated utterances may appear dogmatic or prescriptive, but this is a false impression resulting in part from Boswell's creation of him as a man of maxims. In fact, the most enduring characteristic of Johnson's writing is its tolerance in the patient exploration of the complexities and fallibilities of human nature. In his ▷ *Lives of the Poets* (1779–81) he combines balanced judgements with personal pronouncements, in assessing the writers of his own and the previous age. In *Rasselas* (1759) and in the ▷ *Vanity of Human Wishes* (1749), he explores that 'hunger of the imagination' which both fuels the creative impulse, and leads to the inevitable insufficiency of human desires. In his *Preface to Shakespeare* (1765) (▷ Shakespeare criticism) he articulates literary axioms which lie at the heart of Augustan ▷ humanism (and which, incidentally, help to explain his disparagement of *Tristram Shandy*): 'nothing can please many and please long, but just representations of general nature.'

Having begun this essay with Johnson's defence of writing for personal gain, it seems appropriate to end it with his definition of literature's public responsibilities. 'The only end of writing,' he declared, 'is to enable the readers better to enjoy life, or better to endure it.'

Restoration and 18th-century Drama 9

Eva Simmons

Introduction

The period begins with the re-opening of the theatres in 1660, after an interval of eighteen years, and in very different circumstances from before. Recent criticism has suggested that the Commonwealth Proclamation in the crisis year 1642, ordering the playhouses to be shut down, was not due merely to any ▷ Puritan objections to the theatre as such, but because numerous plays in the preceding years had been openly critical of parliamentary as well as royal policies. Thus closing them was partly what we would now call an act of political repression. The intervening period saw some productions, mostly clandestine – although from time to time the companies attempted open performances, sometimes with severe repercussions.

In the 1650s ▷ Sir William D'Avenant found a legal loophole which permitted the staging of musical performances, and he mounted, openly and successfully, four operas (▷ opera in England), including ▷ *The Siege of Rhodes* (1656) and *The Cruelty of the Spaniards in Peru* (1658). These were effectively the first entertainments of their kind in England, although they drew on earlier ▷ masques for some techniques. Despite the dearth of public performances, the taste for plays survived throughout the ▷ Interregnum, which saw the publication of large numbers of plays, including dozens of new ones. Some of the readers of these were readily assimilated into the new audiences of the 1660s, and from then on playreading as well as theatre going became an increasingly popular pastime.

The period 1660–1800 is marked by innovation from its outset. The advent of women, both as actresses and as dramatists, had a profound impact on the staging of plays and the responses to them. The shape and layout of the theatres changed, together with the style of acting, and the nature of the audiences. New themes came into prominence in the plays, partly as a reaction to new social and political conditions and partly in response to the technical changes just mentioned. Within the period also, there were discernible shifts of topic, theme and style of acting. Nevertheless, the theatres continued to operate under varying degrees of ▷ censorship. This encouraged the staging of plays expressing attitudes of loyalty to the reigning monarch and prevailing ethics, and meant that some plays considered politically or socially dangerous were suppressed. Censorship was applied most rigorously during periods of political tension, such as the Popish Plot (▷ Titus Oates) resulting in large-scale persecutions of ▷ Catholics and the ▷ Exclusion crises of the 1680s when unsuccessful attempts were made in Parliament to exclude the Duke of York (later ▷ James II) from the succession, and again in the 1730s, when satirical attacks on the Government contributed to the passing of the Licensing Act of 1737 (▷ theatres).

In the past, histories of the theatre and drama have tended to focus on so-called 'canonical' texts: those identified by generations of commentators as representing the best in their periods. In the 20th century the reinforcement of this pattern became known as the 'Leavisite' tradition, after the literary critic F. R. Leavis, who isolated certain 'great books' which he considered central to civilization. The implication has been that these and only these are worthy of serious study. But the approach has been challenged repeatedly. The Reverend Montague Summers issued new editions of plays by 'lesser' ▷ Restoration dramatists, including ▷ Aphra Behn and ▷ Thomas Shadwell, in the first decades of this century, and Leslie Hotson's *The Commonwealth and Restoration Stage* (1928) broke new ground in research on the theatre of the ▷ 17th century. More recently, writers including Robert D. Hume, Judith Milhous, Margot Heinemann, Martin Butler, Fidelis Morgan, Dale Spender and Janet Todd have contributed to a re-evaluation of many 'forgotten' dramatists and works, including many by women.

The theatres

▷ Charles II loved the theatre, and was from the beginning of his reign an enthusiastic patron of it, but when he officially re-opened the theatres, he sought to ensure political loyalty from that quarter by confirming existing monopolies to two trusted courtiers: Sir William d'Avenant and ▷ Sir Thomas Killigrew, as well as by re-establishing a system of censorship. The pattern of monopolies lasted, with interruptions, for most of the 18th century.

On confirmation of their patents, D'Avenant and Killigrew formed two companies, the ▷ Duke's and ▷ King's companies, respectively, and set about finding venues for their performances. For a brief period they used existing theatres which were re-opened for the purpose, including a few dating back to Elizabethan (▷ Elizabeth I) times. In March 1660 D'Avenant began converting Lisle's Tennis Court at ▷ Lincoln's Inn Fields. This introduced the proscenium, or framed stage, to the English theatre for the first time. But although he had extended the property, it was felt that it was still too small, and needed a substitute. D'Avenant died in 1668, and it fell to his widow, ▷ Lady Mary D'Avenant, who had inherited the patent, to carry out the work. The new theatre, designed by ▷ Christopher Wren, stood on the river front in Dorset Garden (▷ Dorset Garden Theatre), where it had access both by road and from the water by boat. The Duke's company moved here in 1671, still under Lady Mary's control, until she transferred it to her son Charles in 1673.

Killigrew meanwhile had moved his company to an old riding school in Bridges Street, Drury Lane, which he converted to a theatre – the first Theatre Royal (▷ Drury Lane Theatres). This opened in May 1663, and survived until 1672, when it was destroyed by fire. He then commissioned a new theatre, possibly also by Wren, on a site close by.

The acting area on the ▷ Restoration stage included a deep forestage or apron stage, which projected beyond the proscenium into the pit, past the side boxes. Proscenium doors admitted the actors directly onto the forestage. Here the prologue and much of the dialogue were spoken, clearly audible, and the speakers clearly visible, to the surrounding audience, some of whom might even be seated on the stage itself. The proscenium arch contained a curtain or painted cloth that could be lowered or raised to reveal the interior stage, which had receding rows of painted flats and shutters in grooves on either side. These in turn could be closed or opened, adding further depths to the set or action. Numerous Restoration plays contain 'discovery scenes', indicating that the shutters are opened to reveal behind them other settings or actors, who might then perhaps move forward to join in action nearer the audience. The result was considerable versatility, including the option to change settings in full view of the audience, and with them mood and pace during scenes. Balconies above the stage were also used for some of the action. However there was no naturalistic illusion of landscapes or interiors in the modern sense, but rather a decking of the stage with images and objects to suggest various locations.

A characteristic feature of Restoration drama was its use of elaborate effects – such as cupids or other figures floating on 'clouds' above the stage – aided by mechanical devices. Lighting, for performances were staged mainly in the afternoon, was largely daylight, admitted through the windows, as well as candelabra hung from the centre of the proscenium, and footlights or 'floats' – literally candles, or wicks threaded through corks, floating on troughs of water or oil at the front. Rows of candles and oil lamps, placed in brackets and coloured by strips of stained glass or tinted silk, as well as hand-held candles, lanterns and torches, added light to acting areas further back. Snuffers stood by because of the constant threat of fire.

In addition to the patent theatres were Court theatres, including the Cockpit at Whitehall, and the Hall Theatre, built in 1665. Two ▷ Inns of Court – the Inner Temple and the Middle Temple – put on plays, sometimes involving Duke's and King's Theatre actors, as part of their festivities. Musical performances took place in private homes and at Court. Several ▷ 'nurseries', training grounds for younger performers, also existed briefly, and mounted their own productions. Killigrew set up one of them in 1667, at Hatton Garden; another was established by Lady D'Avenant after her husband's death, in the Barbican; she was involved in the running of a third at Bun Hill in Finsbury Fields, but this lasted only nine weeks. The nurseries were the butt of opposition from several quarters, but actors sometimes succeeded in 'graduating' from them into the patent companies. Finally, strolling players performed at fairs and other venues from time to time.

Playhouses also proliferated throughout the provinces, as well as in Scotland and Ireland. Today there are only three playhouses surviving from the 18th century (the earliest still remaining): the Theatres Royal in Richmond (Yorkshire), Bristol and Margate. Another Georgian theatre, the Theatre Royal at Bury St Edmunds (opened 1819), has the distinction of preserving its original proscenium to this day.

The most important theatres in this context were the two patent houses, and these carried on a fierce rivalry. From the first the Dorset Garden specialized in staging very elaborate performances, including many operas, while the Theatre Royal concentrated on plays. In 1682 matters came to a head with the failure of the King's Company, which was effectively absorbed into the Duke's to form the ▷ United Company. The United Company continued performances of spectacles at Dorset Garden and plays at Drury Lane.

Corruption and mismanagement led three of the principal actors, headed by ▷ Thomas Betterton, to secede in 1695, returning to Lincoln's Inn Fields, which they named the 'New Theatre'. In 1705 Betterton left for Her Majesty's Theatre, also known as the Queen's Theatre, Haymarket, or simply, the ▷ Haymarket, a newly opened playhouse designed by the dramatist and architect ▷ John Vanbrugh. The company was managed in turn by Vanbrugh and ▷ William Congreve. But the theatre suffered financial problems; it proved too large for spoken drama, and in due course became the first English opera house, staging many of ▷ Handel's operas. It was burnt down in 1789, and in 1791 a new theatre was built, known first as the King's and later the Queen's.

Theatre construction and alteration continued over the next two decades. In 1714, Lincoln's Inn Fields was refurbished in grand style by the architect and designer Edward Shepherd (1670–1747), with mirrors lining the interior walls, and then run by the actor-manager ▷ John Rich – son of the late ▷ Christopher Rich whose dishonesty and incompetence had contributed to the secession of the actors mentioned above. The theatre became known by different names: sometimes the New Theatre and sometimes the Little Theatre.

In 1720 a new theatre was erected by ▷ John Potter in the Haymarket, almost opposite the Opera House. Confusingly, this was also known variously as the New Theatre, or Little Theatre in the Hay; or even as the French Theatre in the Haymarket. Scenery was still painted onto flats, and lighting was by overhead chandeliers with wax or tallow candles. As in the Restoration period, the curtain rose and fell only at the beginning and end of the play. The Licensing Act forced it to close down and it stood empty for ten years, whereupon it was taken over by the actor and dramatist ▷ Samuel Foote. In 1766 it became a 'Theatre Royal'; it stood until 1820 when the present Theatre Royal, Haymarket, was erected nearby.

In 1732 Shepherd planned the first ▷ Covent Garden Theatre, or Theatre Royal, on the site of the present Royal Opera House, to which John Rich transferred. A contemporary print shows a proscenium with two doors surmounted by balconies, and behind it an inner frame. Another device apparently surviving from the Restoration period is the 'transparent scene': a translucent surface which could be lit from behind to produce special effects. On Rich's death in 1761, the theatre was taken over by his son-in-law, John Beard (?1716–91), who passed the patent to the dramatist ▷ George Colman the Elder, and three partners, in 1767. The theatre was substantially altered in 1784 and rebuilt in 1792, mainly to allow it to hold many more spectators. It was destroyed in a great fire in 1808. A new theatre was built on the same site the following year.

The 1730s saw increasing tensions between the government and the stage. Some in high places were concerned about the rapid and apparently unchecked rise in the number of playhouses, and disputes about who should exercise control were fuelled by a number of satirical performances openly criticizing the government. Notable among these were several by ▷ Henry Fielding, who eventually sided with ▷ Sir Robert Walpole's opposition. In 1737 Walpole, precariously clinging to dwindling power, succeeded in bringing in a Licensing Act which re-established a monopoly of theatrical entertainment. This was assigned to two playhouses: Covent Garden and Drury Lane, the latter managed by ▷ David Garrick from 1747. Not surprisingly, the Act was not entirely successful in limiting theatrical activity. For example, the actor-manager James Lacy (1696–1774) defied the law at intervals after its enactment. And the ▷ Goodman's Fields Theatre in Ayliffe Street, despite being ordered like the Haymarket to close in 1737, resumed performances using subterfuges to evade the law until 1742. Here it was that Garrick made his first appearance before London audiences.

Garrick's impact on the theatre was immense not only on methods of acting, but also on the physical conditions of performance. One innovation during his tenure as manager at Drury Lane was precipitated by a number of incidents in which audience rowdiness erupted literally onto the stage, seriously interfering with the performance. In 1763 Garrick announced an increase in the capacity of the auditorium, while prohibiting seating from the area around the stage whose presence had been allowed since the Restoration. The manager of Covent Garden, John Beard, quickly followed suit.

Further, in 1765 Garrick introduced stage lighting concealed from the audience, an effect used in ▷ Richard Brinsley Sheridan's ▷ *The School for Scandal*. He also used naturalistic cut-out scenery designed by ▷ De Loutherbourg, an Alsatian who had already made his name in Paris. In the later years of the century, the ▷ Gothic revival seen in other areas of literature and culture of the period was also reflected on stage in scenes displaying dark and rugged mountains, misty and mysterious lakes, or gloomy ruined castles in the Gothic style. Some of Garrick's changes were ultimately to contribute to an effect of added unreality, as well as a loss of contact between actors and audience.

The efforts to enlarge Drury Lane continued during and after Garrick's tenure. The theatre was extensively altered and expanded by the Adam brothers (▷ Robert Adam) in 1775. In the following year, upon Garrick's retirement, it was taken over by Sheridan, who rebuilt and extended it yet again in 1794, and remained in charge until its destruction by fire in 1809. The removal of spectators from the stage effectively widened the gulf between actors and audience. The last decades of the century saw an increase in the use of the curtain to separate scenes from one another, and doors were added to the side scenes for entrances and exits, ostensibly to aid naturalism. In due course they came to replace the proscenium doors altogether, and eventually the box set, and the limiting of acting to the area behind the proscenium completed the rift between actors and audience. Plays were performed in increasingly large theatres, entirely behind the proscenium frame, and the intimacy and immediacy of drama in earlier eras was lost.

The performers, their companies and their audiences

The period is highlighted by some of the great names of theatre tradition, including some individuals of extraordinary versatility, Thomas Betterton, ▷ Charles Macklin, Samuel Foote, David Garrick and ▷ John Philip Kemble, for example, not only acted in but also wrote plays (although some were merely adaptations of older plays), as well as managing their companies. ▷ Richard Steele, in addition to contributing to and editing or co-editing at various times ▷ *The Tatler*, ▷ *The Spectator*, *The Guardian*, *The Theatre* (the first English theatrical journal) and other publications, was a theatre manager and also wrote several influential plays. ▷ Colley Cibber was a manager as well as actor and dramatist, and in his memoirs made a serious contribution to theatre history. Sir John Vanbrugh designed theatres in addition to writing successful plays. Henry Fielding managed the Haymarket during the 1730s until its closure in 1737, after which he became a celebrated novelist; another dramatist, ▷ George Colman the Elder, managed Covent Garden when the plays of ▷ Oliver Goldsmith were first produced there, and took over the Haymarket later. Sheridan, as we have seen, became a manager as well as a dramatist of lasting reputation; ▷ Susannah Centlivre started as an actress, before becoming one of the most successful dramatists of her generation. The actress ▷ Kitty Clive also wrote several plays, including some that were quite successful, and ▷ Charlotte Charke not only acted in dozens of roles, but wrote plays and managed companies as well. However, women dramatists, like other women writers, were subject to attack by men, as in the satire, *The Female Wits* (1696), and *Three Hours After Marriage* (1717) by ▷ Pope, ▷ Gay and ▷ Arbuthnot, which mocks the Countess of Winchilsea (▷ Anne Finch) through the character of Phoebe Clinket. One character says of her that 'the poor girl has a procidence [prolapse] of the pineal gland, which has occasioned a rupture in her understanding . . . instead of puddings, she makes pastorals, or when she should be raising paste [pastry], is raising some ghost in a new tragedy'.

Other important figures on the Restoration stage include ▷ Michael Mohun, ▷ Edward Kynaston and ▷ Charles Hart, all of whom had begun their careers as boy actors playing largely female roles, as well as ▷ William Smith, William Mountfort (1664–92), ▷ Elizabeth Barry, ▷ Anne Bracegirdle, for whom several of Congreve's parts were written, and of course Ellen or ▷ Nell Gwyn. She retired from the stage after she became Charles II's mistress, but remained its ardent patron and admirer. ⊳ Susanna Cibber, ⊳ Anne Oldfield, ⊳ James Quin, ⊳ Spranger Barry, ⊳ Peg Woffington and ⊳ Sarah Siddons are among major actors and actresses in the 18th century. Each era also had its noted comedians, including ⊳ James Nokes and Thomas Jevon (or Jevorn, d1688) during the early Restoration period, and ⊳ John Lacy, Thomas Doggett (1670–1721) and ⊳ William Penkethman (or Pinkethman) later on.

The most important innovation at the beginning of the period is the introduction of actresses to the stage. Before the Restoration, women had acted occasionally: the casts of court masques included some female members of royalty, and a woman had acted in D'Avenant's ⊳ *The Siege of Rhodes* in 1656. But the general rule in England had been for men and boys to act the women's parts. However, on the Continent, actresses had already become commonplace, and Charles II during his years of exile had become accustomed to seeing them. In August 1660 he ordered D'Avenant and Killigrew to place women in all female roles, and his subsequent patent suggested that it was indeed improper to do otherwise.

From a modern standpoint, the insistence on having women play women's parts may be considered as a feminist act. However, there is ample evidence that many male contemporaries saw it chiefly as adding a prurient element to their enjoyment of the theatre, Charles' ostensible views notwithstanding. The diarist ⊳ John Evelyn (1620–1706) complained bitterly that 'Foul and undecent women now (and never till now) were permitted to appear and act . . . inflaming several young noblemen and gallants . . .' More than 40 years later, ⊳ Sir Richard Steele, in quite a different frame of mind, remarked that a woman's presence was a great help to a dull production, so that 'When a poet flags in writing lusciously, a pretty girl can move lasciviously, and have the same good consequences for the author'. The dramatic motif of woman disguised as man, in order to further some – usually romantic – end, had in ⊳ Shakespeare's time relieved the burden on young actors struggling with womanish movements and vocal patterns. After the Restoration it became a means whereby actresses could put on breeches, and show off shapely ankles and calves. ⊳ Pepys commented that a woman acting in a man's role 'had the best legs that ever I saw, and I was very well pleased with it'. Many stage directions and lines in the plays, as well as the revealing dresses of the period, also contributed to an emphasis on the women's sexuality. On the other hand, wearing breeches made it possible, at least by the early 18th century, for a woman to experience briefly and without censure, freedom from cumbersome skirts in the manner of a man. Bernard de Mandeville, in *The Fable of the Bees* (1714), wrote that when a woman wore breeches 'Upon the Stage it is done without Reproach, and the most Vertuous Ladies will dispense with it in an Actress, tho' everybody has a full view of her Legs and Thighs; but if the same Woman, as soon as she has Petticoats on again, should show her Leg to a Man as high as her Knee, it would be a very immodest Action, and every Body will call her impudent for it'.

The position of the actress was ambiguous. That many actresses were kept by wealthy lovers, or performed individual sexual favours in return for gain, is undeniable. The acting profession was then, as later, a precarious one, and the temptation to reinforce their incomes in this way must have proved irresistible to many actresses. However, some dramatic historians, such as John Harold Wilson, have exaggerated the extent to which their function was synonymous with that of courtesan or even prostitute. Many actresses, including those known to be 'unchaste', also gained lasting reputations as artists; ⊳ Elizabeth Barry, for example, was said to be ruthlessly promiscuous, and was frequently condemned on this account. Yet she was much admired as both a comic and tragic actress, and as a tragedienne is reported to have performed with great dignity and pathos. It is important to note that male actors also occupied a paradoxical position during much of the period. They were considered to be relatively low down on the social scale (an Act of ▷ James I had made them technically vagabonds). Pepys, visiting the actors at one theatre backstage, remarked that 'the clothes are very poore, and the actors but common fellows'. On the other hand, actors frequently enjoyed close associations with courtiers (including several dramatists), and, in many cases, the respect of other critical theatre-goers as well. Gradually during the 18th century the status of actors and actresses rose, boosted by Garrick's success and enjoyment of public esteem, as well as the growing popularity of the theatre and interest in the performers generally. But it is clear that for a long time there were conflicts in the attitudes towards all performers, and towards actresses particularly.

The actress ▷ Katherine Corey claimed to be the first woman in her profession: she played the part of Desdemona in a production of ▷ *Othello* in December 1660. Occasionally, as with Thomas Killigrew's *The Parson's Wedding* in 1664 and again for a time during the early 18th century, plays were performed by casts made up entirely of women. Some individual women became celebrated for playing particular male roles, notably Peg Woffington as Sir Harry Wildair in ▷ Farquhar's ▷ *The Constant Couple* (1699) and, less famously, Susanna Cibber as Macheath in Gay's ▷ *The Beggar's Opera.* Colley Cibber's talented, versatile and quirky daughter Charlotte Charke, given from childhood to dressing in male attire, became as famous in her performances of men's roles as of women's. She acted the two in rapid succession, sometimes playing a man's part on one night and a woman's on the next, and occasionally, a man's and a woman's in different performances of the same play: for example she was both ▷ Macheath and Polly Peachum in *The Beggar's Opera.* During a month and half of a single season in 1734 she acted about a dozen men's roles, including Macheath in Roman dress, George Barnwell in ▷ Lillo's ▷ *The London Merchant*, Townly in Vanbrugh's and Cibber's *The Provok'd Husband*, and gay Lothario in ▷ Nicholas Rowe's *The Fair Penitent.* And once she played Sir Fopling Flutter, the part made famous by her father in ▷ Sir George Etherege's ▷ *The Man of Mode.*

Early in the 18th century the ratio of men to women in the acting profession was almost two to one. One company listed 20 men and 11 women in the first decade. At Lincoln's Inn Fields account books for the years 1724–25 bear the names 28 men and 16 women. Gradually the proportion of women rose, together with the total number of performers employed in the profession, as the number of theatres multiplied. The average for the years 1729 to 1747 was 74, and in a single season, 1729–30, over 250 named performers are listed in the bills.

As for the management structure, during the first years after the Restoration the acting profession was dominated, as already noted, by the two patent companies, which merged into the United Company in 1682. Each company had a core group of performers which shared what was left of the profits after running costs had been paid from general receipts. This group was headed by the largest shareholder, in effect the manager, and augmented by salaried 'hirelings' who might eventually become shareholders, as well as musicians, scene keepers and other non-acting personnel. In the 1690s control of the United Company passed to the unscrupulous Christopher Rich, a profiteer with little or no interest in performers or acting standards, precipitating the secession of Betterton, Barry and Bracegirdle already mentioned, to form another sharing company in 1695.

The double system of management, actor-manager on the one hand and proprietor-manager on the other, persisted into the 18th century: Rich in charge of Drury Lane, and Betterton of Lincoln's Inn Fields. After 1705 when Vanbrugh opened the Queen's Theatre in the Haymarket, companies and varieties of organization proliferated until the Licensing Act of 1737 restored the system of two patents. Meanwhile from 1705 opera, developing as an increasingly separate form of entertainment, had its own management structure.

The dominant figure on the stage during the Restoration and early 18th-century years was undoubtedly Thomas Betterton, both because of his reputation, and his ability. He was equally acclaimed in tragedies and comedies and played mostly leading roles with the Duke's Company, the United Company, and finally his own at Lincoln's Inn Fields. A contemporary portrait shows him as a stout man, quite unlike today's ideal of a romantic actor, but dignified and imposing in a silk robe wrapped and folded round his large body, a cravat loosely tied and the locks of a shiny wig flowing down his back. He excelled in Shakespearean parts, including Hamlet, Macbeth, Lear, Othello, Mercutio (*Romeo and Juliet*) and Sir Toby Belch (*Twelfth Night*), but also in contemporary ones such as Heartwell in Congreve's ▷ *The Old Bachelor*. He married Mary Sanderson (or Saunderson), one of the first English actresses and the first to play a succession of Shakespeare's great female characters, including Lady Macbeth, Ophelia and Juliet. They often appeared opposite one another on the stage, setting a precedent to be followed by other couples, from the Mountforts, Cibbers and Bullocks onwards into the 20th century. Other family members also became involved, and the 18th century saw many great acting families and dynasties, including the Bullocks, Mills, Thurmonds, Penkethmans, Kembles and Booths. Early on children also began to feature prominently in stage productions: a Miss Willis, aged five, danced at Lincoln's Inn Fields in 1704, and a ten-year-old girl played Cupid in a masque at Drury Lane later in the same year. In the third quarter of the century it became fashionable to have plays entirely acted by children. Acting became, and remained into the 20th century, a family business.

Acting styles during the Restoration era can be deduced from contemporary portraits, some written accounts, and largely from the manner of the plays themselves. For comedies it appears to have been more or less an extension of the comportment of gentlemen and women in society, that is, formal and deliberate, involving a large number of elaborate gestures and facial expressions in a curious mixture of flamboyance and decorum. The close links between the theatre and the court must have been reflected on stage, with actors and actresses modelling their performances in many plays on those of well-bred courtiers. The extremes of this style are frequently mocked, as in the characters of Monsieur de Paris, in William Wycherley's ▷ *The Gentleman Dancing Master* (1672), and Lord Foppington in Vanbrugh's ▷ *The Relapse* (1697). For tragedies the style remained solemn and declamatory, or 'theatrical . . . stiff and affected', according to a contemporary, possibly even involving chanting, until Macklin pioneered and Garrick perfected a more 'natural' approach. Betterton's method has been described as 'dignified, graceful, yet somewhat heavy and florid . . . interpreting admirably those interminable heroic generals who abound in that period of Restoration melodrama'.

Commentators on the period, such as John Harrington Smith, J. H. Wilson, Peter Holland and J. L. Styan, stress the intimate relationship between actors on stage and the audience, as shown in the many asides and direct addresses to the audience in the plays, delivered from the projecting apron. During the 18th century acting methods underwent a considerable alteration. In the first decades of the century ▷ Quin, and others in his generation, continued in the style of Betterton and his contemporaries, but Macklin and then Garrick reacted to Quin's heavy formality, introducing what seemed to theatre goers to be greater naturalism and simplicity, accompanied by a subtle expression of voice, face and gesture. Quin was eventually forced to retire from what had been an outstanding career, including the roles of Othello, Lear and Falstaff. But alongside this change came an increasing emphasis on performing skills other than acting: dancing, singing, juggling and acrobatics.

The tendency toward greater naturalism, fuelled by the rise of ▷ Romanticism, encompassed a reappraisal of some traditional roles, particularly those of Shakespeare. The part of Shylock in ▷ *The Merchant of Venice* had long been played in a low, buffoonish style. In 1741 Macklin, later to become Garrick's great rival, appeared as a tragic and dignified, though still villainous, Shylock: 'the Jew that Shakespeare drew', in ▷ Alexander Pope's words. The impact was instant; the audience applauded so much that he had to pause after each speech to allow for the interruptions, and he became famous overnight. Changes in the depiction of Hamlet happened more gradually. From Shakespeare's time he had been portrayed as an heroic 'man of action'. But in the second or third quarter of the 18th century, actors including Richard Brinsley Sheridan's father Thomas and David Ross (1728–90) are believed to have begun the trend toward playing him as the irresolute, thoughtful, melancholy personality familiar to audiences in the 20th century.

Towards the end of the 18th century came another change, moving toward the florid acting styles of the 19th century, accompanied by a tendency to rant and shout. The enlargement of the theatres and shrinking of the apron now demanded that actors and actresses raise their voices and expand their gestures if they were to be heard and seen from the top gallery. The celebrated tragic actress ▷ Sarah Siddons refused to comply, causing some criticism that she was no longer always audible. But the practice was consistent with her concept of dramatic integrity; she disdained to 'play to the gallery'. She was enormously respected as well as admired for her dignity and grace, the deep beauty of her voice, her consistent professionalism and her capacity to move audiences.

Along with changes in acting methods, came changes in the approach to dress. In 1759 ▷ John Wilkes had pleaded for a return to the Roman tradition whereby actors always dressed 'according to the fashion of the country where their scene was laid'. In 1773 Macklin dressed his ▷ *Macbeth* in tartan costumes, and played the title role with a Scottish accent. Garrick responded with a ▷ *King Lear* in old English clothing. A famous portrait shows Peg Woffington in quasi-Elizabethan costume as Mistress Ford in ▷ *The Merry Wives of Windsor*. And Siddons attempted to marry authenticity with dramatic propriety, wearing costumes not only true to their historical context but also to the genre employed: thus tragedy demanded heavy garments and simple, natural hairstyles and headgear, in contrast to some of the elaborate creations of her predecessors.

Yet at the same time as Garrick and others were attempting to instil verisimilitude into the trappings and substance of their performances of Shakespeare, they were busy rewriting many of the plays, including some scenes which had escaped onslaught from Restoration revisers. A famous example is Garrick's alteration of ▷ *Hamlet* in 1772, omitting 'scenes of low humour' (including the Grave Diggers' scene), 'improving' the character of Laertes, and altering the circumstances of the Queen's death. *King Lear*, given a happy ending by ▷ Nahum Tate in 1681, had been changed again by ▷ George Colman the Elder, although he retained much of Tate's action, including the happy ending, as did Garrick in his version. Audiences in the 18th century, like their predecessors in the 17th, could not bear to see such injustice as was done to Cordelia. ▷ Samuel Johnson wrote that Shakespeare's ending was intolerable. The philosopher ▷ David Hume said that 'An action, represented in tragedy, may be too bloody and atrocious . . . The mere suffering of plaintive virtue, under the triumphant tyranny and oppression of vice, forms a disagreeable spectacle, and is carefully avoided by all masters of the drama.' Most plays were rewritten in one form or another, and several were used as sources for short pieces focusing on just a few characters, in the manner of the time. Garrick's *Florizel and Perdita* (1756) is derived from ▷ *The Winter's Tale*, for example; his *The Fairies* (1755) from ▷ *A Midsummer Night's Dream*; and *Catherine and Petruchio* (1756) from ▷ *The Taming of the Shrew*.

Throughout the period acting was a strenuous and demanding profession, not least because of the size of a company's repertory, with programmes sometimes changing from day to day. During the season of 1721–2 John Mills (d1736) probably performed in 60 of the 70 plays put on at Drury Lane, including major roles in Marlowe, Shakespeare, Ben Jonson, Vanbrugh, Congreve and Farquhar. ▷ Robert Wilks acted at least 170 times, and Barton Booth in at least 35 roles, in addition to sharing in the company's management. Mary Porter (d1765) acted in 28 and Anne Oldfield in 26 roles in one season. Rehearsals in such circumstances were almost continuous, and inevitably scanty for any particular play. Furthermore, actors often had to double up, performing several roles in a single play and less frequently, during the 18th century, in plays in different theatres on a single night. Kitty Clive, for example, acted in Colley Cibber's *The Lady's Last Stake* at Drury Lane and ▷ Henry Fielding's *The Virgin Unmask'd* at the New Theatre on the Bowling Green on the same evening in January 1747. These factors meant that the actors had to remember huge numbers of lines, which could sometimes lead to complaints about distortions of the text and inappropriate ad-libbing. But some actors took pride in their retentive abilities: Garrick had up to 96 varied roles in his personal repertory and ▷ William Smith boasted that he could perform in any of 52 at a moment's notice.

Training facilities existed throughout the period. The Restoration nurseries have already been mentioned. In addition, senior actors and managers undertook to train the more junior recruits. In 1744 Macklin founded his own school to train actors according to his style of disciplined naturalism. Some performers in the period underwent long apprenticeships, but this did not guarantee that their careers would endure. Charlotte Charke is a prime example of an actress and dramatist who began with the best connections and hopes for her future, but ended up acting mostly in provincial theatres, or managing puppet shows, and living in terrible poverty. Income from acting was often uncertain as it depended largely on receipts. Salaried performers could not always be certain of being paid at all, and indeed payment was not made on days when there were no performances.

However, from the Restoration era onwards, leading performers could earn well: in 1694, Betterton received five pounds a week, plus a present of 50 guineas a year, and Barry received 50 shillings a week. In addition such actors, and later also some other theatre staff, were able to augment their incomes with the proceeds of 'benefits' staged on their behalf. (The profits from the third night of every production – if it survived that long – automatically belonged to the author.) The so-called 'Theatrical Fund', was established in 1765 as a form of insurance whereby a performer could claim from 30 to 65 pounds a year from retirement, or to provide a stipend for an actor's widow and surviving children on his death.

As to the audience, for many years after the Restoration it was far less heterogeneous than it had been in Shakespeare's time, containing a large number of upper-class men and women. Relatively high admission prices, ranging from one to four shillings, kept the poorest members of society away (in 1684 the average labourer's wage was only eight pence a day). But earlier views of the audience as almost exclusively aristocratic, by commentators such as Allardyce Nicoll, ▷ John Wain and A. S. Bear, have now been discounted: at present it is thought that it included a cross-section of middle- and upper-class society, including some merchants and 'citizens'. During the Restoration period, these were frequently ridiculed and actually insulted in the plays, and theories vary as to how much they joined in laughing at themselves, refused to identify with the absurd characters on stage and laughed at 'other' citizens shown as bigoted and stupid, suffered in silence, fought back or simply stayed away from plays known or presumed to be particularly offensive. A softening in dramatists' attitudes towards these classes beginning late in the 17th century, as well as the campaign to 'clean up' the stage, may represent an increasingly successful rearguard action of such individuals and/or changing social conditions. The economic strengthening and social 'legitimizing' of the bourgeois classes during the 18th century encouraged them to exercise their influence on the stage as on other cultural and social ventures. The expansion of the theatres, with the audiences gradually becoming more heterogeneous, coincided with a change in the manner of depicting the middle classes. Merchants and their families ceased to be mere objects of ridicule and were humanized into heroes and heroines, to be admired, criticized, pitied, laughed at or laughed with, according to the text.

Life in the theatre was marked by outbursts of violence during much of the period, to an extent that would seem incredible today. In 1669 Edward Kynaston was beaten up by ruffians hired by a rival, and in 1692 William Mountfort was murdered by Lord Mohun and his agents. Elizabeth Barry and ▷ Elizabeth Bowtell, required to struggle in their roles of Roxana and Statira during a revival of ▷ Nathaniel Lee's *The Rival Queens* (1677), came literally to blows, and the stabbing prescribed by the text became a real assault, with the dagger penetrating flesh. In 1735 Macklin killed a fellow-actor, Thomas Hallam, during a brawl in a green-room – the scene of frequent altercations among members of the acting profession.

Audiences were also often the source of strife. The disturbances caused by Restoration audiences are well known, but riots often took place in and outside theatres during the 18th century. These could cause substantial damage to theatres, and force closures and cancellations of runs by indigenous or visiting performers. In 1744 raised ticket prices at Drury Lane precipitated a riot there. Violent scenes occurred again in 1749, 1755, 1759, 1763, and 1789 over ticket prices and other matters. Competition to gain entry to particularly popular performances often degenerated into bloody fights, and political, religious and personal factions among the spectators also caused many outbursts, including clashes between supporters of rival performers. The riots of 1755, during performances of a ballet called *The Chinese Festival*, spread over several days. They ended with the theatre being torn apart and forced to close. The cause was 'patriotic' hostility to the French performers during a period of high tension with France, which erupted despite Garrick's efforts to pass many of the dancers off as Swiss. In the last years of the century, sentiments ran high over events associated with the ▷ French Revolution; ▷ Thomas Holcroft had to bring out some of his works anonymously, for fear of reaction because of his known links with ▷ William Blake and ▷ Tom Paine.

Apart from the complaints about violence, dramatists were frequently frustrated by their audiences' apparent indifference to their efforts. Some authors ensured applause by packing the audience with friends and even hired 'clapper-men', who would react with suitable enthusiasm to the play. But many plays and players attracted major followings, and some theatre goers were willing to pay large sums to attend particular performances of their choice. The actress ▷ George Anne Bellamy reported that several individuals, including members of the nobility, were willing to pay 100 pounds each to see her perform on a single night, whose proceeds were for her benefit.

The dramatists and the plays

The earliest plays to be performed after the Restoration were, not surprisingly, revivals of plays from earlier periods including many written shortly before the ▷ Civil War and many by Shakespeare. The latter were frequently revised to fit new notions of decorum, poetic justice, and/or French and other concepts of propriety, unity and symmetry, fostered by the ▷ neo-classical revival. For example, an early revision of ▷ *The Tempest* invents a character called Hippolytus, a man who has never seen a woman, to balance the character of Miranda, the woman who has never seen a man, other than her father. Just as, after the chaos of the preceding period, Restoration architects looked back to Greece and Rome for ideal models of order, symmetry, harmony and grace, so many Restoration dramatists looked to the ▷ classics, either directly, or via French theorists and practitioners such as ▷ Corneille and ▷ Racine, for models, precepts and subject matter, in composing their plays, rapidly expanding a process begun earlier in the century. A complex body of neo-classical dramatic theory developed, much indebted to ▷ Aristotle and ▷ Horace. This stressed the importance of preserving unities of time, place and action (▷ Classical unities). Theorists also focused on Aristotle's views that ▷ tragedy's chief task was to arouse pity (for the suffering protagonists) and fear, which the drama was to purge through a process called catharsis; and that dramatic action should imitate life, this process being defined as ▷ mimesis.

From Horace dramatists borrowed the view that drama has twin functions: to instruct, and to give pleasure (entertain). They also adopted notions of decorum, that is, a dramatic construction which is appropriate to its subject and to a genteel audience, that excludes obscenity, or anything too distasteful or revolting ('Medea must not butcher her children in front of the audience') and that avoids an awkward mixing of genres. From these theories the neo-classicists derived their own notions of poetic justice; what could be more instructive, they argued, than to reward virtue and punish vice? Shakespeare was censured for his failure to administer poetic justice, as well as his supposed rough-hewn mingling of tragic and comic elements. One of ▷ Dryden's chief criticisms of ▷ *Troilus and Cressida* was that 'Cressida is false, and is not punished'. Shakespeare was seen as a flawed genius, who could only benefit from having his works 'improved' by the present generation. Many earlier plays, by Shakespeare and others, were re-written to sanitize or even excise some of the most salacious lines, by authors conscious of post-Puritan and bourgeois criticism of the drama, and concerned in this as in other matters to observe at least some trappings of decorum (▷ Thomas Bowdler).

It is important to note, however, that theory and practice often diverged, and English drama was never as strict in preserving the 'unities', for example, as was the French. Furthermore, tragedies frequently introduced scenes of the most ghastly horror onto the stage: a famous engraving of ▷ Elkanah Settle's *The Empress of Morocco* (1673), staged at Dorset Garden, shows a backdrop with the bodies of several mutilated victims of torture, stripped and hanging on spikes and hooks upside down, while bones and dismembered bits of human remains litter the floor. ▷ Delarivière

Manley (1663–1724), in *The Royal Mischief* (1696), shows a character shot from a cannon, his lover collecting his 'smoaking Relicks' and covering them with burning kisses. ▷ Aphra Behn, one of the foremost adaptors of older comedy, repeatedly defended herself against charges of immorality in her plays. Dryden was himself accused of impropriety; in words which look forward to much of later drama, he wrote, ''Tis charg'd upon me that I make debauch'd persons . . . my Protagonists, or the chief persons of the *Drama*; and that I make them happy in the conclusion of my Play; against the Law of Comedy, which is to reward virtue and punish vice . . . But, lest any man should think that I write this to make libertinism amiable . . . I must farther declare . . . that we make not vicious persons happy, but only as heaven makes sinners so: that is by reclaiming them first.'

Other elements admitted by neo-classicists to the drama included love and the idea of 'Admiration', that is, that a character or action should be admirable. Dryden argued that love itself was admirable. A natural consequence was the writing of plays about love and honour, and about conflicts between the two, in which the period abounded. The workings of neo-classicism, though it influenced some comedy of the period, are seen most clearly in the so-called heroic plays, as well as non-dramatic poetry, exemplified in Dryden's verses. Indeed Dryden explained that he 'modelled [his] heroic plays by the rules of an heroic poem'. Plays, such as Dryden's *Tyrannic Love; or, the Royal Martyr* (1669), *The Conquest of Granada* (1670) and ▷ *Aureng-Zebe* (1675), employed the rhymed heroic ▷ couplet as their medium, with what to modern tastes often seems a ridiculous effect. D'Avenant, with *The Siege of Rhodes* and other plays, Sir Robert Howard (1626–98), ▷ John Crowne, Elkanah Settle, ▷ Thomas Otway, Nathaniel Lee and ▷ John Banks all contributed to the repertoire of heroic plays as well.

A feature of such plays was their exotic settings. Elizabethan and ▷ Jacobean tragedy was frequently set in Italy (partly because of its ▷ Italian antecedents in the theatre) and to a lesser extent in Greece. After the Restoration the growing influence of foreign novels and plays placed in distant venues, as well as the growth of trading and other links with hitherto unknown places, contributed to a taste for plays set among Christians and Moors in Spain, Morocco and several countries of the Middle East, and even among the Chinese and the Indians of North and South America. Such settings became the norm for plays of this kind: the popular understanding of the term ▷ 'oriental' (vague and undefined as that was), being almost synonymous with concepts of despotism, cruelty and luxury, made such settings ideal for plays involving spectacle, horror and scenes of high passion and intrigue, until writers such as ▷ Dr. Johnson and ▷ Goldsmith adopted more cosmopolitan attitudes to their distant fellow-beings.

The altered values and concerns of later generations have meant that today most Restoration tragedies are forgotten, and heroic dramas were mocked even in their own time, notably in Buckingham's (▷ George Villiers) ▷ *The Rehearsal* (1671), which singles out D'Avenant and Dryden for satiric attack, with devastating wit. Dryden himself recognized the potential for ridicule when he had Nell Gwyn berate an actor who would have carried her 'dead' body off the stage at the end of *Tyrannic Love*, 'hold, are you mad? you damn'd confounded Dog,/I am to rise and speak the Epilogue', thus undercutting the seriousness of his own preceding action. The modern critic Anne Righter has suggested that Restoration tragedy is 'less serious' than contemporary comedy, even 'essentially frivolous' in its penchant for easy solutions and its intellectual emptiness. A few tragedies, however, would be worthy of more attention than they have been given in recent years, especially some of the political and history plays, such as Nathaniel Lee's ▷ *Lucius Junius Brutus* (1680), and one or two tragedies of ▷ Thomas Southerne. A fine, half-forgotten, blank-verse tragedy which focuses strongly on conflicts between love and honour is Thomas Otway's ▷ *Venice Preserv'd* (1682). The play's urgent intensity, emphasis on character, chronicle of betrayals and mounting atmosphere of despair, link it with Jacobean tragedy. Tracing the failure of a rebellion against the Venetian senate, it has sometimes been viewed as predominantly Tory propaganda. But the manifest corruption of the authorities which Otway displays, and measure of (however qualified) sympathy which he allows the reluctant plotter Jaffeir, make it a more complex political statement. The play shows the moral turmoil which is produced when rulers are unjust, and that to preserve honour, let alone happiness, under them is impossible. But violent plots require violent plotters whose behaviour even toward their ostensible friends and allies is unpredictable, and whose success could presage a new era of chaos. The play may perhaps be read as ▷ Hobbesian, in that it appears ultimately to discourage rebellion, but it offers no easy solutions, and its strongest message is that the onus is on rulers to do justice by their people. Performed during a time of unrest after the so-called 'Popish Plot', the play had topical relevance.

Not only tragedies have been forgotten. Amongst the hundreds of comedies written during the period, only a handful survive today, in the sense of being widely known and regularly performed. They are the work of no more than half a dozen dramatists, including Etherege, Wycherley, Congreve, Vanbrugh, Farquhar, Dryden, and to a lesser extent Behn, although Dryden is chiefly remembered now for his poetry and non-dramatic prose. From the 18th century, the comedies of Goldsmith and ▷ Sheridan are still well known; otherwise most drama, from the Jacobeans to the late 19th century, is virtually unknown today, even though the period encompasses literally hundreds of plays of immense diversity, including many that were highly successful and acclaimed in their own time. A strange paradox has arisen: many people today have heard of Betterton, Garrick and Sarah Siddons, but few ask what – apart from the handful of Restoration comedies and plays by Shakespeare – they performed.

The reasons for this are manifold: apart from the changes in taste already mentioned, some plays fell victim to circumstances outside their authors' control: for example ▷ Thomas Shadwell, author of many fine comedies and ▷ Poet Laureate after the ▷ 'Glorious Revolution' of 1688, was pilloried by his arch-enemy Dryden who, unfortunately for Shadwell, gained the more lasting reputation. Shadwell's alleged ineptitude and dullness have been proclaimed over the years via the poem ▷ *MacFlecknoe* and kept most people from investigating his work further. Colley Cibber, a tolerable and in his way innovative, if not brilliant, dramatist, experienced the same fate at the hands of Alexander Pope and ▷ *The Dunciad*. Most so-called Restoration dramatists, and not a few that followed, suffered from the ▷ Victorian obsession with virtue and propriety. It was not deemed seemly to read, let alone perform, many of the plays from preceding generations; Restoration comedies were vilified most of all. Aphra Behn was subjected to a violently anti-feminist backlash that took hold during her lifetime, mounted in the years following her death, and eventually developed into a concerted campaign to obliterate her memory altogether. ▷ Sir Walter Scott, in a well-known anecdote, related that his grand-aunt returned some of Behn's novels which he had sent her at her own request, saying that she now felt ashamed to read a book which, 60 years before, she had heard read aloud in the best circles in London. Scott attributed the change to the gradual improvement of taste and sense of delicacy in the time leading up to his own. The publisher John Pearson was exconated when, in 1872, he published a collection of Behn's works, along with others by Restoration and early 18th-century dramatists including ▷ Susannah Centlivre.

This represented the end of a long process of decline in the attitude toward women dramatists: Behn's first play *The Forc'd Marriage*, put on at the end of 1670, has a prologue celebrating its authorship by a woman, as a sort of novelty – though Behn was not the first English woman to have a play performed (that distinction may belong to the woman better known as a poet, ▷ Katherine Philips. But opposition gathered during the 1670s, such that Behn soon felt obliged to defend herself in print, not only for the alleged bawdiness of her work, but for the mere fact that she as a woman dared to write at all. In an epilogue she asked rhetorically, 'What has poor Woman done, that she must be / Debar'd [*sic*] from Sense and sacred Poetry? . . . pray tell me then, / why Women should not write as well as Men.' She and many of her successors survived the mockery of male contemporaries, only to have their work eclipsed altogether by more narrow-minded subsequent generations. The number of women writing for the stage dwindled from about 1720, although a few prospered in each decade of the 18th century.

Behn, the first professional woman dramatist, was also among the most versatile dramatists of the era: she attempted, with varying degrees of success, virtually every genre for the stage, and portrayed almost every comic and perhaps tragic type known in her period. In many ways her plays paralleled those of the significant male dramatists of her time: she excelled at comedy, portraying the intricacies of courtship and marriage with wit and finesse. She was at her best with farcical intrigue comedy, handling multiple and complex plots without ever losing the thread of any individual one. Underlying the humour, however, was a serious vein: unlike many of her male contemporaries, she appears to have sustained a faith in the powers of true romantic love, foreshadowing many dramatists of the next century. Moreover, again unlike many male writers, she viewed the problems of love and marriage from a woman's point of view, idealizing and at the same time satirizing the typical rake character of the period, but also showing the harm which his machinations could inflict on women who took him at face value. Several plays show a sympathetic understanding of the unchaste woman, including the courtesan, or the 'wronged woman' who has rashly forfeited her chastity in the pursuit of love. Ismena in Behn's *The Amorous Prince* (1671) reproaches a suitor, 'as most gallants are, / You're but pleased with what you have not; / And love a Mistress with great Passion, 'till you find / Yourself belov'd again, and then you hate her'. In plays including this one, Behn re-examines the concept of feminine 'virtue', defining it not as virginity like most of her contemporaries, but as something we would now call integrity. Her most sustained theme is the evils of the so-called 'forced marriage': the marriage imposed on unwilling young people by greedy and ambitious relatives. Virtue consists in remaining true to one's own desires, even if that means defying the older generation and, in the case of women, giving up one's virginity to a man truly loved.

Probably the most successful and able of Behn's immediate successors was Susannah Centlivre, two of whose 19 comedies, ▷ *The Busie Bodie* (1709) and ▷ *The Wonder: A Woman Keeps a Secret* (1714), remained among the four most frequently re-printed and performed of any, except for those of Shakespeare, until late in the 19th century. Like Behn she excelled at comedy with complex intrigue plots, displaying with vitality and style young people, in pursuit of their own romantic ends, outwitting others functioning as pillars of established authority. But unlike Behn, who was a high Tory, she championed Whigs and Whig interests in several plays and, again unlike Behn, she fervently opposed Catholicism, which she referred to as 'the

Romish Yoke'. Furthermore, in keeping with her more fastidious times, the overt sexual element is omitted from her plays. Two of these, *The Gamester* (1705) and *The Basset Table* (1705), follow a contemporary convention in exposing current vice – in this case the fashionable one of gambling. She was also a fine craftswoman, creating superb acting roles, including five intended for the same actor in various disguises (▷ *A Bold Strike for a Wife*), which rendered several of her plays favourites of Garrick and Kitty Clive. Garrick chose her play *The Wonder* for the last performance of his career.

From the Restoration onwards, plays were heavily preoccupied with themes of courtship and marriage, treated in ways varying from high comedy including farce, to tragedy. Indeed the term 'Restoration Comedy' conjures up in people's minds scenes of witty courtship and flirtation, underpinned by conflict: the 'battle of the sexes' Many plays contain debates, implicit or explicit, about the value or otherwise of marriage as an institution, and discussions concerning the bases on which marriages should be contracted: whether for love or money; according to the choices of parents or lovers; between old and young ('January-May' matches); or lovers of similar age, and so forth. But these themes are not in any sense unique to the drama of the period. They permeate literature of many kinds, including a vast body of ▷ pamphlet material which was digested by increasing numbers of middle-class readers.

The genre has roots in some misogynistic writing of the ▷ Middle Ages, in which marriage was denigrated precisely because it bound men closely to women – the descendants of the flawed Eve. However it was strongly fuelled by the ▷ Reformation, with the protagonists dividing along religious lines. Increasingly, the institution of marriage was defended by Protestant Reformers, who accused Catholics of attacking marriage and sanctioning immorality ('whoring') as an alternative, so men could satisfy their sexual needs without having to resort to wedlock. A Reformist priest, Thomas Becon, in his *Boke of Matrimony* (1563), attacks 'Masse and Monckery' and its alleged opposition to matrimony, which is, he says, a state 'holy blessed . . . although counted of the Papistes neuer so Seraphicall . . .'. Catholics did not on the whole attack marriage as such, but continued to value celibacy as the highest state for those who could attain it, stimulating further attacks from Protestants for their supposed hypocrisy.

In the 17th century the debate over marriage intensified, and at the same time became secularized, erupting through the hundreds of ▷ pamphlets also written by, and largely appealing to, members of the middle-classes. Marriage was contrasted to whoring as a way of life; many pamphlets also focused on characters of courtesans or prostitutes, drawing moral conclusions from tales of their prosperity or downfall. Religious attitudes continued to inform many of the pamphlets but, increasingly, pamphlets by women responded to those by men, especially to the satiric ones attacking women. Later, women such as the polemicist poet ▷ Sarah Fyge, ▷ Mary Astell and poet and essayist ▷ Lady Mary Chudleigh attacked marriage for its patriarchal enslavement of their sex.

Images of ▷ slavery pervade both the pamphlets and the drama, with human and especially sexual relations seen in terms of the enslavement of one partner to another, or the enslavement of both to the oppressive conditions of marriage. The Civil War had heightened public concern with personal freedom, but growing censorship limited the parameters for discussion about the exercise of freedom in the political sphere. After the Restoration, the loosening of the strictures on individual sexual morality permitted a new outlet for debates about freedom, which took the form of a revived focus on the battle of the sexes. The growth of slavery in the New World also contributed to a widespread preoccupation with the metaphoric as well as literal manifestations of this institution.

Together, plays and pamphlets illustrate the debate about marriage and sexual relations in the 17th and 18th centuries. Indeed on one level, many plays may be seen as dramatized versions of a debate which constitutes a social correlative to the religio-political clash continuing in society, and exploding periodically into overt conflict. Examples are the 'Popish Plot' debacle beginning in 1678, the ▷ 'Rye House Plot' a few years later, to assassinate Charles II, and Monmouth's Rebellion (Duke of ▷ Monmouth), culminating with the so-called 'Glorious Revolution'– although the latter phenomena had distinct and various ends in view. Several late 17th-century pamphlets express concern that, because of Catholic influence on society in general and the gentry in particular, marriage as an institution was declining. But the drama shows, on the whole, no such concern. In keeping with dramatic tradition, and the reality of most people's lives, dramatists assumed that most of their characters would marry. But the plays are increasingly preoccupied with the concept of love and/or marriage as slavery, for the man or the woman, depending on the point of view. The metaphoric treatment of these themes in comedies was paralleled by more literal uses in the serious plays, of situations in which individuals are enslaved to one another via imprisonment, although they are also sometimes 'slaves of love'. So-called 'proviso scenes' in which men and women spell out the terms on which they are prepared to submit to the restrictions of marriage, and make bargains to this effect, form the climaxes to some Restoration comedies, the most famous example being the scene between Millamant and Mirabell in Act IV of Congreve's ▷ *The Way of the World* (1700). From 1670 onwards, after the first effective civil divorce, this too became a topic in some plays – seen as the only escape from an impossible union.

In the 1690s came a series of so-called 'marital discord plays', which followed more soberly in the footsteps of Behn. A major figure in this regard is the neglected dramatist, ▷ Thomas Southerne, who borrowed heavily from Behn. In several of his plays he shows the appalling situation of the wife, tied to a philandering and cruel husband, 'this hard condition of a woman's fate', in the words of one of his women characters. Vanbrugh takes up the theme in ▷ *The Relapse* (1697), written as a satiric sequel to Cibber's ▷ *Love's Last Shift* (1696), which showed the husband repenting of his unkindness to his wife, and undergoing a reform.

Today the best-known plays of the Restoration and early 18th century periods are some of the so-called wit comedies or Comedies of ▷ Manners by Etherege, Wycherley, Congreve, Vanbrugh and Farquhar. The form has an antecedent in the wooing of ▷ Beatrice and Benedick in Shakespeare's ▷ *Much Ado About Nothing*. But after the Restoration, Dryden helped develop it with what some consider the first true 'Restoration Comedy', ▷ *The Wild Gallant* (1663), in which an impoverished gallant, Loveby, is secretly supplied with money by his mistress, Constance. She articulates the plight of the woman in the period, 'tied to hard unequal laws: The passion is the same in us, and yet we are debarred the freedom to express it'.

Some plays of Etherege and Wycherley illustrate more clearly the inequalities of men and women: in Etherege's ▷ *The Man of Mode* (1676) women mistrust and betray one another. The heroine Harriet wins the appalling Dorimant away from the weak and stupid Bellinda and unscrupulous Loveit, but it is clear that her money forms a large part of her attraction in the match, making up for the ruin of his estate, and thus implicitly rescuing him from the slavery of poverty, although this is not stated in these terms. Margery Pinchwife, the title character in Wycherley's ▷ *The Country Wife* (1675), is pathetic and misguided; her denigration comes because she has not learned to guard her true interests in the harsh world of the city. The pursuit of 'interest', both financial and general, is a frequent theme in plays from a period heavily influenced not only by commercial changes in society, but also the writings of the contemporary social commentators ▷ Hobbes and François de la Rochefoucauld (1613–80), and the Greek philosopher ▷ Epicurus as adumbrated by the Roman ▷ Lucretius. Lucretius' works, translated and published during these years, contributed to a flirtation with 'atheism' by some Restoration writers and others. Denying the existence of an after-life implied, so it was thought, making the most of this one – even if that meant ignoring or downgrading the interests of others.

Many critics, such as Nicoll, J. H. Wilson, Bonamy Dobree and Clifford Leech, have attempted to organize Restoration comedies into categories, but this is a thankless task as there are so many overlaps between genres. For example, one frequently mentioned category is the Spanish Romance (▷ Spanish influence on English literature), such as Sir Samuel Tuke's *The Adventures of Five Hours*, commissioned by Charles II (1663), but in the prologue and preface to *The Wild Gallant* Dryden also acknowledges a Spanish origin. The so-called 'split-plot tragi-comedy', exemplified by Dryden's ▷ *Marriage à la Mode* and Behn's *The Widow Ranter* (1689), is another, but here the comic plots have elements from various of the supposed categories. In *Marriage à la Mode*, for example, the lovers Palamede and Doralice exchange banter normally thought of as belonging to the 'comedy of wit', as they arrange a liaison. In another scene Leonidas is identified as the son to the usurper of Sicily, Polydamas, in lines that look forward to a great deal of 'exemplary' and 'sentimental' comedy. In yet another scene illicit meetings and mistaken identities parallel those of comedy of intrigue. Congreve's ▷ *The Double Dealer* (1694), considered among the great comedies of wit because of its sparkling language, also contains many intrigue elements, as shown in its enormously complex and brilliantly managed plot. Shadwell wrote several comedies influenced by ▷ Ben Jonson's theory of 'humours' (Comedy of ▷ Humours), as suggested in the *Dramatis Personae* to *The Sullen Lovers* (1668), which lists characters including 'a morose melancholy man', 'a conceited poet' and 'a familiar loving coxcomb', and in Shadwell's own dedication to the play. But the work has 'witty' and intrigue elements as well. In fact there are often overlaps among intrigue comedy, wit comedy and farce.

Similar problems arise in discussing tragedies, which are sometimes divided into categories including heroic tragedy, horror tragedy – glorying in scenes of torture, such as *The Empress of Morocco* – and pathetic tragedies, including some of Lee and John Banks. But again, there are many overlaps between and among categories; for example, Behn's *Abdelazar* (1676) has both horror and 'heroic' elements. And there have been numerous debates about whether some of Lee's plays really were 'pathetic', and how, in any case, this term should be defined. Happier compromises than those referred to above have been achieved by such authors as Robert D. Hume in *The Development of English Drama in the late Seventeenth Century* and A. H. Scouten in *The Revels History of Drama*. Hume discusses plays according to period, although this too leaves something to be desired, because of the inevitable exceptions and overlaps. But he also discusses some individual plays according to the categories into which they supposedly fit, such as the 'French' Farce, ▷ 'Reform Comedy', 'Wit Comedy', 'Sex Comedy', 'City Intrigue Comedy', 'Augustan Intrigue Comedy' and so on. Scouten's categories are much broader ('New Drama', 'Political Plays against the Puritans', and 'Social Comedy', for example), and much of his discussion is according to author.

Behn was one of the earliest to exhibit tendencies toward what has been variously described as 'sentimental', 'exemplary', or 'reform' comedy, the 'comedy of sensibility', and more recently, 'humane comedy'. These are critics' sometimes crude attempts to define a transition between plays dominated by hard wit comic elements of the high Restoration period and the genres that followed. The terms have often been accompanied by a blanket condemnation of the new modes, as representing a loss of wit and humour without any compensatory gain. But as Shirley Strum Kenny (coiner of the term 'humane comedy') has suggested, some of the older drama had much in the way of cynicism and callousness to discredit it, and there were mitigating features of the new.

The change is attended by attacks on the stage – most famously by the Reverend ▷ Jeremy Collier in a piece entitled *A Short View of the Immorality and Profaneness of the English Stage*, written in 1698. His tirade on the alleged loose morality and profane language of the plays was the more effective, if perhaps also more puzzling, because of his evident knowledge of the texts from reading, if not seeing them performed. But the movement toward reform had been started well before: a long vituperative poem by Robert Gould, *Satyr Against the Playhouse*, written in 1685 and published four years later, is said to have heralded the controversy. Finally, the change is linked with political developments: for example, the ascendancy of the Whigs after the Revolution of 1688, bringing with them a backlash against the supposed immorality and irreligion of the Tory dramatists. Writers such as ▷ John Locke, whose works were widely distributed after the Revolution, had far more positive views of human nature than those of his predecessors Thomas Hobbes and Sir Robert Filmer (c1590–1653), whose ideas had strongly influenced many Tories. The loss of patronage by the Royal family was also an important factor: as stated above, Charles II was a keen patron of the theatre, and his cultured but wry, satiric personality had a substantial influence on its development during his reign. His brother James II, while less involved in the minutiae of play composition and performance, had also continued the tradition of patronage for the brief period of his reign.

In the 1690s and early 1700s plays began to emerge that were less overtly bawdy and had a more sympathetic and 'moral' attitude toward some of their leading characters and human nature in general. Vanbrugh and Farquhar, although often classed among, and sharing characteristics with, Restoration dramatists, also belong in many ways to this later era. For example, in Farquhar's ▷ *The Beaux' Stratagem* (1707), Aimwell, under the guise of his wealthy brother, spends most of the play courting Dorinda for the sake of her fortune. But at the crucial moment he confesses his poverty, and releases her from her vows. At this she decides to marry him anyway, moved by his 'Matchless Honesty'. This is a far cry from Etherege or Wycherley.

A feature of these plays is their softened attitude to the country, which had been seen as a wasteland of ignorance and dullness by many satiric dramatists, though not by poets, of the Restoration. Many Restoration dramatists associated the country with settled property-based marriages, contrasting them to the 'freedom' of the town. But later dramatists and audiences came increasingly to accept the conventional forms of match-making, and with them, the country seat and its environment where so many wealthy and genteel families made their home. A stock motif of Restoration comedy is young lovers refusing to accept the partners of their parents' choice, and insisting instead upon making their own choices. In the 18th century, this is replaced typically by situations in which lovers think they are choosing for themselves, but unwittingly become attracted to partners who have in fact been intended for them by their elders all along. Thus at the end conflict is avoided, and the parents are vindicated, indeed revealed as sensible and far-sighted. The effect is an affirmation of the wisdom of the older generation, and by extension, of settled social forms and values. Rebellion against such parents is unjustified, since they have the true interests of the younger generation at heart. The forced marriage motif survives, however, in some plays, including Eliza Haywood's *A Wife to be Lett* (1723), and several plays by Centlivre.

Another common feature of plays of the period is the reform of a major protagonist. This is in keeping with the more optimistic view of human nature and aspirations espoused not only by Locke, but also by ▷ Shaftesbury and later ▷ David Hume, ▷ David Hartley, Pope and others. For many decades, plays exhibited gamblers, wife-beaters and others deemed guilty of wrongdoing repenting of their ways – though usually not until the last act. Colley Cibber's *Love's Last Shift*, in which the abandoned wife succeeds in reforming her errant and impoverished husband, is generally agreed to have been a key transitional play in this regard. The husband Loveless, struck by remorse, ends by celebrating the 'chast Rapture of a Vertuous Love'. Meanwhile in a secondary plot, an older man admonishes and successfully disciplines the coquette Hillaria.

Women are also shown repenting, notably by women dramatists including Susannah Centlivre and ▷ Mary Pix. The latter, whose *The Spanish Wives* (1696) had championed women's freedom somewhat in the style of Behn, though less racily, reforms the heroine of *The Deceiver Deceived* (1697) after one bout of adultery. The genre overlaps with the so-called 'exemplary drama' or 'drama of sensibility', epitomized by Steele's ▷ *The Conscious Lovers* (1722), in which the lovers of the title agonize over the propriety of all their actions. In the second half of the century, parallel with theories about the natural 'benevolence' of human nature, the so-called 'sentimental comedy', epitomized by Hugh Kelly's (1739–77) *The False Delicacy* (1768), developed. Also ▷ Richard Cumberland's ▷ *The West Indian* (1771) contains a number of elements typical of the genre, including the reform of a rake, vice exposed and outwitted, virtue rescued from distress and honourable simplicity triumphant.

Sheridan and Goldsmith reacted against what they saw as a surfeit of pathos and morality: they consciously attempted to revive the spirit of Restoration comedy with plays such as ▷ *She Stoops to Conquer* (1773), ▷ *The Rivals* (1775) and ▷ *The School for Scandal* (1777). So successful were their efforts that many people not too well acquainted with the stage today believe them to belong to the earlier era. And yet in its more 'benign' atmosphere and softened attitude to country life, for example, as well as certain elements of the plot, *She Stoops to Conquer*, at least, belongs to a later period than true Restoration comedy, and has much more in common with Farquhar, let us say, than with dramatists like Etherege, Wycherley, Behn or Congreve.

Along with the changes in comedy came new types of serious drama, although heroic plays remained popular into the 18th century. New approaches to Shakespeare have already been referred to, providing in some cases greater authenticity and in others fresh distortions, until ▷ Edmund Kean mounted full-scale restorations of Shakespeare's own texts in the 19th century. The later 18th century may be considered as a transitional period in this regard. ▷ John Banks and others developed a variety of tragedy focusing on the sufferings of women, at a time when the numbers of women dramatists were growing, and pamphlets presenting the views and concerns of women were proliferating. Such plays of John Banks include *Vertue Betray'd: or, Anna Bullen* (1682), on Anne Boleyn; *The Island Queens* (1684), on ▷ Mary Queen of Scots; and *The Innocent Usurper* (1694), on the execution of Lady Jane Grey. Congreve experimented with the form in the ▷ *The Mourning Bride* (1697), and ▷ Nicholas Rowe took it further with *The Fair Penitent* (1703), *The Tragedy of* ▷ Jane Shore (1714) and *The Tragedy of Lady Jane Grey* (1715). There is a link between such plays and some of the comedies of Southerne, Cibber, Vanbrugh and Centlivre, which also focus on the sufferings of women, albeit in less sombre contexts.

Today Banks is usually considered a practitioner of so-called 'pathetic tragedy', encompassing elements of pathos, designed to move rather than thrill or shock the spectator, while Rowe's plays are known as ▷ 'she-tragedies'. But the two may be seen to overlap. Again negotiating with these, and developing gradually in the period, was the domestic or bourgeois tragedy, characterized by a focus on the lives of ordinary citizens, rather than the kings and queens of the heroic variety. A landmark of this genre is ▷ George Lillo's ▷ *The London Merchant: or the History of George Barnwell* (1730), which ends with Barnwell repenting of his crimes before being executed. However, as Allardyce Nicoll points out in *A History of English Drama 1660–1900*, the roots of bourgeois tragedy, like those of so many other 'new' forms, lie in the Restoration period – particularly with Otway.

▷ Burlesque plays and satires, fathered by George Villiers' *The Rehearsal*, became increasingly popular during the first decades of the 18th century. Among the most famous of these were Pope, Gay and Arbuthnot's resentful satire on contemporary women dramatists, *Three Hours After Marriage* (1717), and Fielding's ▷ *Tom Thumb* (1730), reworked as *The Tragedy of Tragedies* (1731), again mocking heroic plays. Gay's ▷ *The Beggar's Opera* (1728), technically a ballad-opera, is known to many today mainly as the source for ▷ Brecht's *The Threepenny Opera*. This comedy of low-life has antecedents in the 'rogue literature' of the 16th and 17th centuries, including some masques by Jonson. But its success was instantaneous: staged by ▷ John Rich, himself a dramatist as well as actor-manager, it is said to have made 'Gay rich and Rich gay'. This and later plays, notably by Fielding, mounted a sustained satiric attack on Sir Robert Walpole, eventually leading, as we have seen, to the Licensing Act of 1737, whereby the latter was able to subdue his critics and control the stage with a much firmer hand. It resulted in Fielding and others abandoning the stage and contributed, indirectly, to the development of the novel in the 18th century, as Fielding and others now concentrated their efforts on this less rigorously controlled, and therefore less risky, form of endeavour.

A dramatic form that developed in the 17th century, but became much more popular in the 18th is the 'after-piece', a short pantomime or farce intended to be performed after a more serious play, so the audience would be sent home laughing. Increasingly, these entertainments were considered essential to attract audiences to the theatre and, as the demand grew, many earlier plays were re-written in lighter and much abbreviated form. Just as pamphlets on marriage, written in serious or bitingly satiric vein in the 17th century were increasingly reworked into light, frivolous pieces in the 18th, so full-length, skilfully made comedies and tragi-comedies were later turned into little afterpieces. Garrick altered Wycherley's ▷ *The Country Wife* to *The Country Girl* (1766); a play by Betterton, *The Amorous Widow* (performed c1670) became a two-act farce, *Barnaby Brittle* (1782); Behn's *The Revenge* (1680), itself a sombre tragi-comic alteration of a savage satire by John Marston (?1575–1634), eventually became – via a comic and farcical adaptation by Christopher Bullock (1690–1722) called *A Woman's Revenge* (1715) – a droll, *The Stroler's Pacquet* (1742). 17th- and 18th-century dramatists were not on the whole concerned with problems of plagiarism, let alone ▷ copyright. In addition, dancing, singing, acrobatics, juggling and other forms of non-dramatic entertainment – including performances by many visiting companies from the continent – frequently functioned as entr'actes or after-pieces, as well as being staged in their own right, or integrated into plays.

Late in the century the influence of German (▷ German Influence on English

Literature) and, once again, French dramatists became important to the English stage (▷ French Literature in England), at a time when the work of German poets and philosophers, in particular, was having a growing impact on the English Romantic poets. Plays of ▷ Kotzebue and René-Charles Guilber Pixérécourt (1773–1844), for example, translated and reworked by ▷ Thomas Holcroft and ▷ Elizabeth Inchbald, became immensely popular. The translations were to include works known to us now as melodramas, at first literally containing music, from the turn of the century.

In the final years of the century, reaction against the supposed bawdiness of many plays, alluded to above, began to bite in earnest. Readers of ▷ Jane Austen may recall the horrified response of the older generation upon finding the young people in ▷ *Mansfield Park* engaged in an amateur performance of Inchbald's *Lover's Vows*. Restoration comedy, which had remained part of the repertory throughout most of the century, was attacked once again, in a period marked by the rise of the ▷ Evangelical Movement. Even ▷ Hannah Cowley's *A School for Greybeards* (1786), itself a 'refined' and 'cleaned-up' version of Behn's genuinely outspoken *The Lucky Chance* (1686), was considered shocking. The stage was set for Thomas Bowdler's edition of Shakespeare (1818), new plays in the 19th century that were even more overtly moral and religiously inspired than their predecessors of the 18th, and the disappearance of Restoration plays altogether, until the revivals of this century.

The Persistence of Romanticism 10

Geoff Ward

I

Introduction

'With what eyes these poets see nature!' ⊳ William Hazlitt's exclamatory and admiring verdict on meeting ⊳ William Wordsworth and ⊳ Samuel Taylor Coleridge, (and, as importantly, hearing them read their poetry aloud), encapsulates in precise and immediate terms the categories of pleasure and instruction through which 'these poets' entered and remain within the canon of English verse. The 'chaunt', the note of bardic exaltation which Hazlitt heard in Coleridge's voice in particular, sounded the liberation of poetry from the shackles of eighteenth-century convention. Henceforth, the tight couplets of Alexander Pope's verse, and his focus on 'What oft was thought, but ne'er so well expressed', would seem complacent and narrowly technical. The age of Pope and Samuel Johnson had been characterized by a self-doubting and frequently pessimistic retraction of artistic ambition, leaving satire as the only poetic channel for a relatively unfettered expression of energy. But now the ambition of poetry seemed limitless. The next thirty years would see the revival of ⊳ blank verse, the ⊳ epic, the ode, borrowed forms such as the Italianate ⊳ *terza rima* and ⊳ *ottava rima*, as well as more or less freshly invented forms such as Coleridge's conversation poem. Indeed, a poem such as ⊳ *Frost at Midnight*, with its blend of philosophical complexity and everyday vocabulary, is emblematic of the confidence and range of English poetry in the period from 1798 to the deaths of Shelley and Byron in the early 1820s.

In his pathbreaking poem *Lines Composed a Few Miles Above Tintern Abbey*, the closing meditation of the collection written in collaboration with Coleridge, ⊳ *Lyrical Ballads* (1798), Wordsworth wrote about landscape, and of its powers of healing and secular redemption through memory, in ways that paid more homage to both the workings of subjectivity and the features of Nature than the 'official', London-based poetry of the Augustan age would have thought either sane or desirable. Recreating a visit to the banks of the River Wye after a lapse of 'five summers', the poem's questing voice moves from description of 'mountain springs', 'lofty cliffs' and 'plots of cottage-ground' to more conceptualized sensations of being able to 'connect/ The landscape with the quiet of the sky', and hence connect it with the mind. This is done with what may strike readers of today as a perfectly musical and smooth modulation. (In a not dissimilar way, the landscape paintings of John Constable, once so radical and startling, now form a suburban cliché as mass-market prints.) But Wordsworth's poetry – at least in this early stage of his career – is above all a poetry of exploration and experiment, and even his most apparently premeditated disquisitions on the nature of identity are rarely without moments of surprised self-discovery and encounter:

These beauteous forms,
Through a long absence, have not been to me
As is a landscape to a blind man's eye:
But oft, in lonely rooms, and 'mid the din

Of towns and cities, I have owed to them,
In hours of weariness, sensations sweet,
Felt in the blood, and felt along the heart;

Gaining in both poignancy and potency from the lapse of years, the 'beauteous forms' of cliffs, woods and water become not so much ambiguous as multi-directional, existing not only in the outer world but 'in the blood', and 'along the heart', as if that organ had its own mysterious coastline. The novelty of these lines (and of many key poems by Wordsworth) lies in their proposition that the inner, personal world of bodily experience and subjective recollection matches the outer world in its complexity, beauty and depths. With this in mind, the statement by Hazlitt with which this essay begins can now be seen to be a formulation as much about 'eyes' as about 'Nature', as much about perception as landscape. This double focus animates Wordsworth's lines, and may indeed be a feature common to all Romantic poetry.

The shock of the new in Wordsworth's poetry may be hard to register in the 1990s, when nostalgia for an unspoiled rural England, and the commercialization of that sentiment by the heritage industry, have co-opted the poet, as Constable's painting has been co-opted. The nostalgic and conservative reading of a painting such as *The Haywain* (1821) views it as the faithful representation of a real and beautiful scene from England's rural past, of a kind which has had to be sacrificed to the advances of industrialization and urbanization, but which can still be visited by car at weekends, and which proposes certain values (moderation, calm, respect for continuity and ritual) which serve the interests of our political masters, particularly at a time of economic instability and underlying disquiet. This kind of interpretation of English landscape painting brings its own agenda to bear on the work, but it is not conjured out of thin air; any viewer of Constable's paintings, like all readers of Wordsworth, must respond to a rendering of Nature so vibrant as to be empathetic, deciding in consequence whether that empathy has materialist, metaphysical or social implications.

Sometimes what we see or read here are examples of what John Ruskin would term in *Modern Painters* (1834) the 'pathetic fallacy', the attribution of human feelings or aspects to non-human subjects. A painting of an English elm by Constable, done around 1821, is structured as if it were a portrait. An even more dramatic humanization of Nature can be found in the paintings of Caspar David Friedrich, or Johan Christian Claussen Dahl, about whose evocation of a birch tree in a storm the art critic Robert Rosenblum observed that 'branches almost appear to be the exposed nerves of a suffering creature'. Equally ecstatic and empathetic conjurations abound in Wordsworth's poetry, as in these famous lines from Book VI of ⊳ *The Prelude*:

The rocks that mutter'd close upon our ears,
Black drizzling crags that spake by the wayside
As if a voice were in them, the sick sight
And giddy prospect of the raving stream,
The unfettered clouds and region of the Heavens,
Tumult and peace, the darkness and the light –
Were all like workings of one mind, the features
Of the same face, blossoms upon one tree;
Characters of the great Apocalypse,
The types and symbols of Eternity,
Of first, and last, and midst, and without end.

The first wave of English Romantic poetry, and the northern European landscape painters, share a tendency to return or even relegate human figures to the sphere of Nature, whose wild storms, immeasurable vistas of sky and sea, ceaselessly changing effects of light and cloud, down to the most delicately microscopic intricacies of leaves or the colours of flowers, announce cosmic and possibly God-given mysteries beyond the constrictions – the lack of *vision* – permitted by religious orthodoxy. Yet notice how in the case of these lines from *The Prelude*, the pathetic fallacy, the attribution of human speech to the non-human 'rocks' and 'crags', undoes and reverses its own ambition of harmonization and the reintegration of humanity into Nature. It is, after all, only by the imposition of the utterly human and linguistic notion of signifying meaning through 'Characters', 'types' and 'symbols' that the wild and incoherent landscape seen by Wordsworth in the Alps can be made to cohere. The strong biblical echoes of the climactic 'first, and last, and midst, and without end' speak of what is infinitely larger than human comprehension, but do so using terms that are perfectly humanly recognizable, and so supply a satisfactory and resonant 'end' to what was alleged to be endless.

Similarly, Friedrich's Romantic evocations of the beauty or endlessness of Nature, *Monk by the Sea* (1809) for example, or *Two Men Contemplating the Moon* (1819), depict distinct consciousnesses, at least as firmly as they stage the re-entry of the human into the maternal embrace of Nature. To return John Constable's *Haywain* to this context is to divest it of late twentieth-century nostalgia, to turn it from commodified culture back into art, but then to see in it a contradiction, or at least a doubleness, that links it to both Friedrich and to Wordsworth. Constable's exploratory, conspicuous, and variously textured brushwork appeared shockingly modern – indeed, unfinished – in its time. It is precisely that quality that is most lost by mass reproduction, and that acts to separate both the painter and the viewer from any premature reinsertion of solitary human consciousness into the wider frame of Nature. Wordsworth had written in *Tintern Abbey* 'of all the mighty world/ Of eye, and ear, – both what they half create,/ and what perceive;' and Constable's brushwork reminds us likewise of the primacy of perception, and the degree to which reality is given significance by human creativity and attention, an attention that may, finally, be solitary. The larger and more idealistic projects of Romanticism co-exist with the risk that any form of search for a larger frame than the single consciousness may undo itself, unmasked as a consolatory strategy in a world that ultimately begs questions, but does not supply answers.

And so there is much in the poetry of the English Romantic movement that is new, and that has to be granted its unconventionality and even its built-in contradictions, if it is to be read with clarity after the lapse of almost two hundred years. Yet, if the poetry is shockingly new, it is important to note in passing certain ways in which Romanticism draws for its intellectual resources on a partial return to previous models and procedures. These are frequently not only non-Augustan, but anti-Augustan in spirit. For example, by combining the hypnotic and driving rhythms of the ▷ ballad with luridly colourful imagery drawn from Gothic tales and his own more feverish imaginings, Coleridge took English poetry forward by taking it back. His early poem ▷ *The Rime of the Ancient Mariner* (1798), like ▷ *Kubla Khan* and ▷ *Christabel* (both 1816), gained its novelty partly from a revivification of neglected and popular (that is, culturally low-grade) materials. Likewise, the rhetorical grandeur of Wordsworth's writing drew to some extent on the blank verse of ▷ Milton's ▷ *Paradise Lost* for its scope and intensity, leavening it with what Coleridge termed the 'divine chit-chat' of a less prophetic and more conversational poet, ▷ William Cowper.

In order to fashion itself, each age tends to denigrate the previous period; this is as true of Renaissance impatience with the benighted Middle Ages, or modernist disdain for Victorian pieties, as of the Romantic reaction against the supposed limitations of the eighteenth century. However, there has never been a major period of English literature in which the availability of literary forms drawn partly from the past coincided with the furious energies of a revolutionary present to produce a poetry so suddenly bold in scope, and wide-ranging in style. Hazlitt's reaction to the new poetry of Wordsworth and Coleridge is therefore one of the Edenic moments in English poetry and criticism. Wordsworth's lines from Book X of *The Prelude*, 'Bliss was it in that dawn to be alive,/ But to be young was very heaven', may likewise stand both for his recollection of reactions to the ▷ French Revolution in its early, inspiring phase, and as a motto for the Romantic moment.

The term 'Romanticism' has a clear etymological proximity to the word 'romance', and, although there will be much in this Introduction and in the book as a whole to complicate and darken any too simple understanding of Romanticism as the literary expression of idealism, it is worth beginning by paying heed to one of this period's dominant tones, the revolutionary hope for a better world, articulated in a visionary poetry that asks us to look at the old world through new eyes.

II

Paradises Lost and Found

All the major poems of the Romantic period, from ▷ William Blake's ▷ *The Marriage of Heaven and Hell* (c 1790–93) to ▷ Lord Byron's picaresque epic ▷ *Don Juan* (1818–24), are concerned with the accessibility or otherwise of a paradise. However, the Romantic paradise is only rarely identifiable as the Christian heaven. To Wordsworth, the paradisal perception which poetry strives to investigate and hopefully revive is closely tied to an understanding of childhood as Edenic, but blurred and progressively less available to consciousness as time and decreasing energy take their toll. His *Ode*: *Intimations of Immortality from Recollections of Early Childhood* asks 'Whither is fled the visionary gleam?/ Where is it now, the glory and the dream?' Such a privileging of the state of childhood runs quite contrary to eighteenth-century perceptions. It also diverges from, while using, Christian allegories and symbolism.

Wordsworth's relationship to Christianity appears to have been easy, in his own mind at least. Although his poetry constantly utilizes the vocabulary of redemption and the healing of the soul through submission to a higher force, it does so through a secular version of the Protestant tradition of introspection, with its plain but confessional rhetoric of self-transformation; the poet wrote cheerfully to a clergyman who had questioned his devotion to Christ that he felt no particular need for a redeemer.

It is clear that Coleridge, by contrast, strove in both his writing and his work as a lay preacher for an accommodation of his experience and his philosophical learning to orthodox Christianity, an accommodation severely undermined by the intellectual discoveries of his poetry, no less than by his opium addiction. The introduction of the deity into the phenomenology of poems such as *Frost at Midnight* (1798) and *The Eolian Harp* (1796) seems dutiful and superfluous; Coleridge's most vital perceptions are coloured by fear, guilt and nightmare. Poems such as *The Ancient Mariner* and *Kubla Khan* are so rich in symbolism as to repudiate any attempt to tie their meaning down to a single set of symbols. Coleridge's poetry is less successful when the poet is, paradoxically, most able to formulate his beliefs clearly. This was certainly noticed by ⊳ P.B. Shelley, whose poem ⊳ *Mont Blanc* is (among its other activities) a critique of the belief-system underpinning an earlier poem by Coleridge, *Hymn Before Sun-Rise, in the Vale of Chamouni.*

Both poems are set in the vicinity of Mont Blanc, and take as their subject the relationship between the awe-inspiring turbulence of the landscape, and the human mind, searching for clues to the organization and purpose of existence in a scene that seems to promise revelation while dwarfing the individual observer. In the case of Coleridge, exclamatory and strained rhetoric becomes the platform for a hierarchical and conventional, almost Sunday School, understanding of the mountainous earth reaching upward towards a deity in the sky:

Thou too again, stupendous mountain! thou
That as I raise my head, awhile bowed low
In adoration, upward from thy base
Slow travelling with dim eyes suffused with tears . . .
Great Hierarch! tell thou the silent sky,
And tell the stars, and tell yon rising sun
Earth, with her thousand voices, praises GOD.

By contrast, Shelley visits the same scene to produce, in *Mont Blanc*, a text as complex, volatile and dense with activity as the landscape itself. Shelley has none of the guilt and anxiety that pushed Coleridge into acquiescent piety. Instead, his poem is a subtle but extraordinarily self-possessed disquisition on the nature of the relationship between human perception and the 'universe of things around', which in a sense masters the landscape by using it to illustrate what are in effect a series of philosophical positions:

The everlasting universe of things
Flows through the mind, and rolls its rapid waves,
Now dark – now glittering – now reflecting gloom –
Now lending splendour, where from secret springs
The source of human thought its tribute brings
Of waters, – with a sound but half its own,
Such as a feeble brook will oft assume
In the wild woods, among the mountains lone,
Where waterfalls around it leap for ever,
Where woods and winds contend, and a vast river
Over its rocks ceaselessly bursts and raves.

Mind and landscape mirror and echo each other, bring each other significance, as in Wordsworth's phenomenology. But if Wordsworth was led to muse reflectively on what is felt in the blood and felt along the heart, Shelley presents perception as a maelstrom. The individual mind may be 'a feeble brook', but the collective unconscious, the 'One Mind' as it would be conjured in ⊳ *Prometheus Unbound*, is not only the equal of the external landscape, but what finally gives it significance. There is no God to Shelley, and the poem is atheist. (A more protracted analysis might show that even Shelley's most vehemently materialist writing is never without a mystical inflection; but it is never one that conforms to religious orthodoxy, *à la* Coleridge.)

Yet Coleridge's strongest poetry is very far from reaching definite conclusions about the nature of existence, let alone firm religious belief. Doubly sub-titled 'A Vision in a Dream' and 'A Fragment', *Kubla Khan* is best read as a collage of delightful and unfathomable mysteries, in which the reader-interpreter can wander at will without ever reaching a conclusion. As with much of the engaging literary work from this period, open-endedness or multiple, even undecideable meaning, becomes an attraction and a virtue – perhaps even a form of realism, as the world after the French Revolution seemed less stable and more malleable than before.

In Xanadu did Kubla Khan
A stately pleasure-dome decree:
Where Alph, the sacred river, ran
Through caverns measureless to man
Down to a sunless sea.
So twice five miles of fertile ground
With walls and towers were girdled round:
And here were gardens bright with sinuous rills,
Where blossomed many an incense-bearing tree;
And here were forests ancient as the hills,
Enfolding sunny spots of greenery.

The Orient in English literature (see ▷ Orientalism) tends to have been viewed ambiguously as despotic and barbarous, and therefore simpler than the West, and yet intricate, appealing to the senses, a canvas on which desires repressed by occidental culture and morals could be luridly brought to life. Do the Khan's decrees issue therefore from an absolute power, used on this occasion for benign purposes related to art and the imagination? Is it significant that X stands at the end of the alphabet, A at the beginning, and K in the middle, when the poem appears to be concerned with the origins, ending and centre of life? Does the Khan's miniature world of walls and towers and gardens symbolize the compartments of the mind? (And if so, why 'twice five miles of fertile ground'? Does 'five' have occult significance?)

Although the poem is only fifty-four lines long, what follows this – already exceedingly complex – opening takes the text in too many labyrinthine directions to be susceptible of neat analysis, in an essay of this length at least. Coleridge did nothing to solve the poem's mysteries by adding an account of its composition in an opium-reverie, in 'a lonely farmhouse between Porlock and Linton' in the West Country, after reading a seventeenth-century travel volume, *Purchas' Pilgrimage*, and in particular these phrases: 'Here the Khan Kubla commanded a palace to be built, and a stately garden thereunto. And thus ten miles of fertile ground were inclosed with a wall.' So, that might account for the twice five miles. Coleridge stated that he composed (mentally) a poem between 'two to three hundred lines' in length, of which the fragment we have is all that he could commit to paper before some nameless 'person from Porlock' distracted the poet with mundane business, driving the delicate imagining of gardens of oriental delight clean out of his head. Unfortunately for Coleridge, modern scholarship has uncovered more than one draft of the poem, and the narrative has been proved untrue in other respects.

The poem, however, is in itself concerned with the fugitive and slippery nature of truth and knowledge, the disappearance of hard fact in fiction and dream, the inability of the wandering mind to envision a paradise other than in glimpses. All that Coleridge's explanatory narrative proves, finally, is that he did not know what he had got hold of. His poem had (whether through opium or not hardly matters) written itself; and no recourse to church and scripture could possibly accommodate its sinuous, oneiric puzzles, walled gardens and blind alleys. Just as Wordsworth's project to reintegrate human life into the larger world of Nature foundered on the very agent of reintegration, perception, stressing the reality of a solitary consciousness, so in Coleridge's poem the dreams dissolve into the pathos and vulnerable isolation of the single mind, haunted by dissolving palaces. 'A damsel with a dulcimer/ In a vision once I saw': could the poet hear her song once more, he would construct the Khan's dream-dome and get back to the Garden, the oriental Eden of imagination released from moral stricture:

Could I revive within me
Her symphony and song,
To such a deep delight 'twould win me,
That with music loud and long,
I would build that dome in air,
That sunny dome! those caves of ice!
And all who heard should see them there,
And all should cry, Beware! Beware!
His flashing eyes, his floating hair!
Weave a circle round him thrice,
And close your eyes with holy dread,
For he on honey-dew hath fed,
And drunk the milk of Paradise.

The final images convey great beauty in their figure of the Poet as the incarnation of capable imagination, a construction lent considerable pathos and in a sense undone by the tenses of these magnificent final lines: ''twould', 'would', 'should'. They signify wistfulness, incapability, impotence. The vitality and effectiveness of the poem are complicated but far from diminished by the tragic shadow cast over its visions of paradise. This time it was Shelley's turn to tread the same ground, but produce a weaker poem than Coleridge. His 'West Wind' ode uses key Coleridgean terms such as 'dome', 'vaulted', 'burst' and 'towers', and seeks to elevate the prophetic figure of the Poet to an unprecedented degree, but lacks the emotional dimension which is brought to *Kubla Khan* precisely through its failure to complete the projects it initiated. It might be concluded that while the paradise motif is, in some form or other, a feature of all key Romantic poems, the shadows cast over its attainability are as much the poetry's final subject as its more positive, visionary and revolutionary elements. The explosion of creativity in English poetry at this period involves the articulation of dream, doubt and vertigo, at least as much as it does the expression of optimism and achievement.

It was Coleridge's mixed gift and curse to be able to best illuminate the workings of human psychology through the drama of his own self-estrangement and baulked creativity. If the most affecting moments in Coleridge's poetry are to do with glimpsing visionary paradises and psychological hells (see *Christabel* in particular), his experience of writing was frequently purgatorial, a career of procrastination, unworkable projects and a reliance on the verbatim incorporation of the work of others that amounts to plagiarism. (The fullest treatment of these matters is still Norman Fruman's *Coleridge: The Damaged Archangel*, 1972. For an authoritative examination of Romantic poetry in relation to religious frames of thought, see M.H. Abrams' *Natural Supernaturalism*, 1971.)

▷ Thomas De Quincey's conjurations of a visionary paradise are similarly unorthodox, and similarly conditioned by an unshakeable addiction to opium. As the author of ▷ *Confessions of an English Opium Eater* (1821; revised 1856), De Quincey has become the most celebrated drug-user in the canon of English literature. In fact he drank the drug in the form of laudanum, a solution of opium in wine or brandy. It was hard to judge the dosage; editors who complained of the illegibility or absence of certain words in De Quincey's manuscripts were not alluding to his mental state, directly; laudanum spilled from the wine glass he would have by him while writing was sufficiently acidic to burn through the ink. The author of the *Confessions* knew Coleridge well, though their relationship soured as De Quincey's fortunes declined. Discussion of their shared addiction was circumspect, and coloured by self-delusion as well as incomplete knowledge; opium was commonly available in the nineteenth century as a panacea for a wide range of conditions, but its addictive properties were not properly understood. Curiously, and again like Coleridge, De Quincey defines his sense of self through the textuality of hallucination to a degree that suggests the author would have been a hypersensitive dreamer, had he never touched drugs. Texts and the life outside them chase each other at speed in the Romantic period, and it is impossible to establish whether De Quincey wrote a drug-induced literature, now called Romantic, or whether the literary influences he followed (being a devoted and early admirer of Wordsworth and Coleridge) would have pushed his writing in certain directions with or without the drug.

Either way, his conjurations of paradisal flights of imagination in *Confessions of an English Opium Eater* are apt to turn hellish in an instant. The book is indebted to religious structures of thought, but the debt is complex and ironic. The daily ritual of opium-taking may have opened the doors to memory and imagination, but it was also a sinful and debilitating indulgence. The *Confessions*, as the title immediately suggests, both echo, parody and exceed in intellectual complexity those narratives of conversion such as those produced by sects like the Clapham Saints, of which the writer's mother was a member: 'Thou hast the keys of Paradise,' intones De Quincey, 'oh, just, subtle, and mighty opium!' Darkly witty, pedantically scholarly, suddenly acute in its proto-Freudian intuition of the importance of dreams, as labyrinthine and sonorous as a seventeenth-century sermon, revised and yet interminable, De Quincey's most important book is as orchidaceously peculiar as it is vital. In its way a spiritual autobiography, it resembles *The Prelude*, and in the mixture of drug-related orientalia, the terrors of the night and the pathos of the dreamer, it may be read as a prose sibling to Coleridge's more adventurous poems. The quotation that follows is long, of necessity:

> *Many years ago, when I was looking over Piranesi's* Antiquities of Rome, *Mr Coleridge, who was standing by, described to me a set of plates by that artist, called his* Dreams, *and which record the scenery of his own visions during the delirium of a fever. Some of them (I describe only from memory of Mr Coleridge's account) represented vast Gothic halls: on the floor of which stood all sorts of engines and machinery, wheels, cables, pulleys, levers, catapults, &c, &c, expressive of enormous power put forth and resistance overcome. Creeping along the sides of the walls, you perceived a staircase; and upon it, groping his way upwards, was Piranesi himself: follow the stairs a little further, and you perceive it come to a sudden abrupt termination, without any balustrade, and allowing no step onwards to him who had reached the extremity, except into the depths below. Whatever is to become of poor Piranesi, you*

suppose, at least, that his labours must in some way terminate here. But raise your eyes, and behold a second flight of stairs still higher: on which again Piranesi is perceived, by this time standing on the very brink of the abyss. Again elevate your eye, and a still more aerial flight of stairs is beheld: and again is poor Piranesi busy on his aspiring labours: and so on, until the unfinished stairs and Piranesi both are lost in the upper gloom of the hall – With the same power of endless growth and self-reproduction did my architecture proceed in dreams. In the early stage of my malady, the splendours of my dreams were chiefly architectural: and I beheld such pomp of cities and palaces as was never yet beheld by the waking eye, unless in the clouds.

The central allusion is to the eighteenth-century engraver, Giovanni Battista Piranesi. The plates referred to as the 'Dreams' were in truth entitled 'Imaginary Prisons', and they show classical dungeons, rather than the distinctly Gothic architecture described by De Quincey. This is in the literary sense a heavily ▷ Gothic passage, however: it resembles the currently fashionable puzzle-drawings and *trompe l'oeil* labyrinths of M.C. Escher, as the figure of poor Piranesi appears and reappears in constant aspiring labour, but it has none of the cool interest in mathematics and draughtsmanship that underpins Escher's eyecatching conundrums. The passage is full of self-directed pathos, and the figure of Piranesi is clearly intended to reflect on the figure of Coleridge, both standing finally as versions of De Quincey, trapped in his own mind between paradisal flights of aspiring imagination, and the Gothic 'malady' of his addiction to drugs and the fleeting dreams they bring. The mixture of orotundity, pathos, a sense of claustrophobic imprisonment coupled with sudden and dizzying release into the fantastic, is typical of his writing. But so is the psychological and analytical acuity: the *Confessions* is in many ways a theoretical work on the nature and importance of dreams.

De Quincey is a 'second generation' Romantic writer, who as a teenager had written an admiring letter to his hero, Wordsworth, and who in sense would always write within the parameters that the first generation had laid down. The next section will be concerned with the poets of the second generation, who variously prolonged, modified and questioned the tenets of Wordsworth and Coleridge.

III

The second generation

The importance of paradises lost and found runs through the major poetry of the three chief figures in what might be termed the second generation of Romantic poets, ▷ John Keats, Percy Bysshe Shelley, and George Gordon, Lord Byron. Racking up phenomenal scores as a fornicator with both sexes in that earthly paradise, Venice, 'mad, bad, and dangerous to know' in the words of his equally wild ex-lover Lady Caroline Lamb, and the partial source for literary vampires from Polidori's Lord Ruthven to Stoker's Count Dracula, it was Byron whose conduct most publicly and flagrantly departed from Christian norms and ideals. Yet it is Byron whose poetic questionings of the beginnings and ends of human life are most apt to leave the door open to religious answers, though not to a religious faith. The rhetorical mode of *Don Juan* is of a predominantly comic scepticism, tinged with moments of sober doubt. His paradises tend to be exotic and geographical, such as the island in the poem of that name (a reworking of the story of Fletcher Christian's mutiny on 'The Bounty') or the far-flung locations of parts of *Don Juan*. (For a rereading of Byron's poetry that lays more stress on the proto-religious nature of his thinking, see Bernard Beatty's *Don Juan*, 1984.)

Byron was made famous by ▷ *Childe Harold's Pilgrimage* (1812–18), a long and often sprawling poem in four Cantos, whose exotic locations and Hamlet-like musings on passion and mutability appealed by virtue of a turbulent self-centredness, characteristic of the time. As an image of alarm and fascination to the English imagination, the collective upheaval of the French Revolution had been replaced by the egotism and expansionist aims of ▷ Napoleon Bonaparte. Byron, the only Romantic poet to have a first-hand knowledge of armed conflict, was half-drawn to a figure he saw as fated, as tragic, yet as mastering a world of hard political actualities and the struggle for power. The more floridly rhetorical and dandyish passages in Byron have served to conceal a more sober and historically analytical intelligence with a distinctively British (and rather eighteenth-century) respect for hard fact. The ideological conflicts of his age are expressed through Byron's writing and his conduct; a libertine who had his daughter educated in a convent, a Regency fop with a liking for physically dangerous escapades, an aristocrat who backed popular uprisings. Most paradoxical of all, although the persona of the writing is the most bluff and British of the Romantic poets, it is Byron who immersed himself in European politics and culture and who has had perhaps more influence on the course of European writing than any other English poet from ▷ Shakespeare to the present day.

Byron's writing is inseparable from the figure of the man himself – or, rather, the man he invented as the Lord Byron he wished people to see. Darkly glamorous (if club-footed), exuding sexual magnetism (including an incestuous relationship with his half-sister Augusta), he was a product as well as a producer of literary genres: part Gothic, part neo-Augustan wit. Nothing in the world of *Don Juan* is safe from bathetic deflation, yet the hectic pace and love of the incongruous are tied to a sense of life's limitations and frailty:

I would to heaven that I were so much clay,
As I am blood, bone, marrow, passion, feeling –
Because at least the past were pass'd away
And for the future – (but I write this reeling,
Having got drunk exceedingly today,
So that I seem to stand upon the ceiling)
I say – the future is a serious matter –
And so – for God's sake – hock and soda-water!

Byron was the most doubtful of the Romantic poets as to the value of what the first generation had done. Canto Three of *Childe Harold* does (as Wordsworth indignantly complained) rely in part on a Wordsworthian view of Nature; but this was due to Shelley's (temporary) influence. Byron was sceptical about revolution, and about any kind of ecstasy beyond the momentary loss of self in sex. More heartfelt than *Childe Harold*'s verdict on Wordsworthian landscape are these cutting lines from *Don Juan*:

And Wordsworth, in a rather long 'Excursion'
(I think the quarto holds five hundred pages)
Has given a sample from the vasty version
Of his new system to perplex the sages;
'Tis poetry – at least by his assertion,
And may appear so when the dog-star rages –

And he who understands it would be able
To add a story to the tower of Babel.

This is wonderfully accomplished satire, however (deliberately) flip and callow; but it is also instructive, in a cautionary way. If we could go back in time, to interrogate Byron or Wordsworth, neither would understand the label 'Romantic'; the term stands for a historical-cum-critical mapping operation, that has more to do with the twentieth century than the highly individualistic standpoints from which these authors felt themselves to be writing at the time. But then individualism is the cardinal tenet of Romanticism.

Not so much famous as infamous, P.B. Shelley was Byron's friend but in many respects his antitype. Shelley prided himself on the observational accuracy of his poetry, be it in the meteorological aspect of his paean to revolution, *Ode to the West Wind* (1819), the domestic bric-à-brac of the urbane *Letter to Maria Gisborne* (1820), or the stormy landscape of *Mont Blanc* (1816). However, Shelley's preferred things are things on the move: wave-effects, clouds, dawn, things captured just as they are about to turn into something else:

Maidens and youths fling their wild arms in air
As their feet twinkle; they recede, and now
Bending within each other's atmosphere,
Kindle invisibly, and as they glow
Like moths by light attracted and repelled,
Oft to their bright destruction come and go,
Till like two clouds into one vale impelled,
That shake the mountains when their lightnings mingle
And die in rain – the fiery band which held
Their natures, snaps – while the shock still may tingle;
One falls and then another in the path
Senseless – nor is the desolation single,
Yet ere I can say where – the chariot hath
Passed over them – nor other trace I find
But as of foam after the ocean's wrath
Is spent upon the desert shore . . .
while the shock still may tingle (*The Triumph of Life*)

In one sense this is a delicate but mordant evocation of the basic human narrative of attraction, courtship, sexual union, down to the last sad stains of exchanged bodily fluids ('foam after the ocean's wrath/ Is spent') in the miniature death that follows sex . . . before the whole cycle starts up again. Shelley's is a world-weary yet compassionate summary of the most pleasant aspect of humanity's animal side; and, as always, the writing reflects on language itself and the capacities and limitations of poetry, which also allows a wild dance and copulation of verbal energies – leaving little more than spent foam behind. *The Triumph of Life* was Shelley's last, unfinished poem, and although its last line – '"Then, what is life?" I said' – would stand as a motto for all his work, the earlier work is frequently more sanguine, and convinced of the rightness of political struggle along proto-socialist lines.

The genial *Letter to Maria Gisborne* attempts, as the poetry of Wordsworth often does, to offer an Edenic perception of things seen as if for the first time. However, the brilliant quirkiness and rapidity of movement in the verse are as distant from

Wordsworth's meditative steadiness as they are from Byron's tolling rhetoric. Where Byron, typically, works from things out to a larger world-view, and Wordsworth sets self and landscape in a rolling phenomenological circularity, Shelley's world-view is more radically intellectualized and conceptual; things, in Shelley, are there to illustrate ideas. That may make him sound curiously eighteenth century, and a poem such as the *Letter* does put a quasi-Augustan urbanity and tact back into poetic circulation. In crucial respects, however, the relationship of image to idea in Shelley breaks new ground in English poetry, while utilizing in altered form the innovations of the first generation Romantics. Specifically, it is important to see that neither the 'things', the poetic images, nor the ideas they illustrate, are static. Language misses its mark, that of static representation, but in so doing generates new ideas: indeed, this is the theme of *Epipsychidion* (1821), consequently one of Shelley's most frantic yet intensely reasoned poems.

The poem is concerned with a beautiful teenage girl of the Shelleys' acquaintance, one Emilia Viviani, locked up in a convent by her parents while they sought out a suitable huband-to-be. Whatever the depths or shallows of the poet's affection for her, Emilia certainly made the ideal subject for a Shelley poem, bearing in her incarceration the related scars inflicted by church, class, gender, parents and marriage. Shelley loved to scandalize, and *Epipsychidion* contains some of his most acrid satire on the condition of wedlock. A reader might have expected it to contain a portrait of Emilia, but – and here the poem's central and more theoretical concerns come into view – the poem is partly about the failure of words to do their author's bidding. Words can describe, sketch, characterize, depict; do anything but actually *be* what they refer to. And yet the act of writing or speaking lets words develop their own life, on the page or in the mouth. Within the space of fifty lines, Emilia is called 'Seraph of Heaven', 'Sweet Benediction', a 'Moon', a 'Star', a 'Wonder', a 'Mirror', a 'Lute' and many other things, until the speaker concludes, 'I measure the world of fancies, seeking one like thee,/ And find – alas! mine own infirmity.' Emilia's humanity dissolves under the impact of 'failed' language, until she becomes a part of it, and is resurrected as achieved metaphor:

> *A Metaphor of Spring and Youth and Morning;*
> *A Vision like incarnate April, warning*
> *With smiles and tears, Frost the Anatomy*
> *Into his summer grave.*

The mutability and uncontrollable fluidity of language has become a virtue. Nothing in Shelley comes nearer the concept of paradise than this, the condition of metaphor itself.

Shelley's is a deceptive and difficult poetry. Early editions of this poem were small – 100 copies or so – and he had few admirers outside the immediate circle of Byron, ▷ Mary Shelley, and the other members of the 'Pisan Circle'. With the honourable exception of ▷ Swinburne, poets of the next generation would fail to rise to the challenge of his work. His Victorian successors disliked Shelley's morals, ignored his politics, and wilfully misread his fiery lyricism as ardent but insubstantial. To Matthew Arnold, famously, Shelley was 'a beautiful and ineffectual angel, beating in the void his luminous wings in vain'. That unfortunate and prejudiced assessment was effectively perpetuated by T.S. Eliot and F.R. Leavis in the earlier part of this century. The poet's reputation would only rise again in the 1930s, when Shelley's atheism, pacifism, call for universal suffrage and free love found sympathetic ears in the Auden generation. The proto-socialist Shelley, with whom Paul Foot's book *Red Shelley* (1984) is concerned, shows through clearly in a poem such as ▷ *The Mask of Anarchy* (1819), with its unique mixture of political allegory and the aggressive simplicity of cartoon.

A more comprehensive assessment of Shelley's achievements that takes account of his subtlety and range begins with the post-1945 generation of American critics – Earl Wasserman, M.H. Abrams – and reaches a kind of apotheosis in Shelley's adoption by the Yale Deconstructionists (▷ Jacques Derrida, ▷ Paul de Man, ▷ Harold Bloom, J. Hillis Miller and ▷ Geoffrey Hartman) who took Shelley's *The Triumph of Life*, unfinished at the time of his death, as the catalyst for a collection of essays on the (by these critical lights) interconnected topics of absence, death and writing (Harold Bloom, ed., *Deconstruction and Criticism*, 1979). This book contains a remarkable essay by the late Paul de Man, whose writings on Romanticism, collected in *Blindness and Insight* (1983) and *The Rhetoric of Romanticism* (1984), are among the most incisive pieces of criticism on the subject to have appeared in recent years.

De Man's model of Romantic literary practice is set down in a crucial essay of 1969, 'The Rhetoric of Temporality' (collected in *Blindness and Insight*). All of his subsequent writing on poetry would make a modified return to the postulates of this essay. The argument, too subtle and full to be susceptible to paraphrase on this occasion, identifies symbolism with the Romantic urge towards idealism, and towards an organicist world-view. Wordsworth's drive to reintegrate the human self into Nature, or Coleridge's divinizing of poetic utterance, would be examples of this. Allegory, the expression in rhetoric of temporality, undercuts the symbol and undoes Romantic ambition. As death, loss, change, meaninglessness – summarized by the word 'temporality' – are unavoidable forces in human existence, so even the most idealist literary text will disclose them on the page in spite of its intentions. In Wordsworth's case, for example, it is precisely a form of idealism that deconstructs his leanings towards pantheism, the attempted immersion of the self into a wider, cosmic Self. A basic contradiction runs through Wordsworth's presentation of the self, and other selves. The urge to lose discrete identity in something larger is countered by a radical prioritization of the ego, and so, to return to the admiring exclamation of Hazlitt's with which this essay began, we can see that what appeared to be a statement about Nature and then seemed to be as much a statement about perception, may finally be an egotistical statement about one man's perceptions. The lines from the *Tintern Abbey* poem quoted earlier may similarly be seen to deconstruct their own phenomenology of integrated subject – object relations by a stress on the self-centredness of experience. As de Man notes, 'Since the assertion of a radical priority of the subject over objective nature is not easily compatible with the poetic praxis of the Romantic poets, who all gave a great deal of importance to the presence of nature, a certain degree of confusion ensues.'

It will be clear that my own readings of Romantic texts are far from unfriendly to the kind of literary deconstruction that Paul de Man theorized and practised; the essay by Philip Shaw in this volume offers a more committed enquiry along de Manian lines. However, it may be worth taking issue with de Man's term 'confusion', perhaps suggesting that contradiction of meaning in Romantic texts may be a part of their conscious rather than unconscious activity. Deconstruction, like many schools of literary theory, produces its most startling results on texts which can be shown to be innocent of its approach; the nineteenth-century novel, for example. Problems arise with texts from two periods – the Romantic, and the contemporary. Contemporary literature may be written by the university-educated individual below a certain age, who may have studied literary theory, and be capable of meeting its approach forewarned and forearmed. Without suggesting that the English Romantic poets anticipated recent literary theory and braced themselves to meet it a couple of hundred years *avant le lettre*, it could still be argued that a strongly self-reflexive element in the poetry indicates that deconstruction might be viewed as a modern development of Romanticism, rather than as its anatomist.

The linguistic self-consciousness shown by ▷ Keats, for example, is hardly less than that shown by the Yale Deconstructionists (and some of his puns are as bad as Derrida's). Of all the poets from the period covered by this guide, John Keats is the writer who registers with the most lyrical poignancy the discrepancy between a paradise glimpsed, and a paradise attained. The idealistic urge to break through the confining fabric of the everyday to reach a higher or an eternal realm recurs in his poetry at all levels. It operates in miniature in Keats' use of synaesthesia – that is, the expression of experience by one of the senses in the language of one or more of the others. Examples abound, and include such lines from ▷ *Hyperion* as 'Let the rose glow intense and warm in the air', a relatively gentle conflation of the visual and the tactile. Conflation turns to deliberate confusion in these lines from *Isabella*, a poem that skirts the ludicrous in other respects: 'O turn thee to the very tale,/ And taste the music of that vision pale'; here taste, sound and sight are pushed into a weird overlap. Keats is not above a feverish and discordant levity, as in the redundant puns that are scattered throughout the *Ode on a Grecian Urn* (▷ Odes, Keats'), or the mixture of an arch tone and rabidly Gothic material that we see elsewhere. (Readers searching for a rationale behind the oddities in Keats' poetry should consult Christopher Ricks, *Keats and Embarrassment*, 1984.) But something more purposeful seems to underpin even the strangest of his synaesthetic conjunctions; for, after all, if the reader is able to stretch and bend habitual ways of seeing in order to accommodate an intensified or novel sensation at the level of metaphor, he or she may be prepared to do so in other spheres of life. Unlike Shelley or Byron, Keats had no real interest in political theory beyond the general openness to radical and libertarian thought that was current among intellectuals of his time. His idealism is centred on not the external world but the world of the senses, and the degree to which experience may or may not empathize or give itself over to what is outside itself, and with what consequences. Some theoretical reflections on this propensity for extreme and creative self-abandon that marks out the 'chameleon poet' were set down in a letter by Keats, from which the phrase 'negative capability' has come to summarize this vital aspect of his practice as a poet:

> *. . . several things dovetailed in my mind, and at once it struck me, what quality went to form a Man of Achievment especially in Literature & which Shakespeare possessed so enormously – I mean Negative Capability, that is when man is capable of being in uncertainties, Mysteries, doubts, without any irritable reaching after fact and reason . . .*

The poet should be prepared at all times to surrender to the instant of experience, without allowing the limitations of rationality or morality to get in the way of imaginative immersion in the instant. Here can be seen Keats' utter rejection of the precepts of Augustanism, and his leaning towards an art for art's sake, promoted after his death by Pre-Raphaelite and related spirits: Dante Gabriel Rossetti, or A.C. Swinburne. The association of ▷ Shakespeare with Negative Capability is very much in tune with a series of lectures on the English poets given by Hazlitt, at the Surrey Institution, at which Keats was a keen attender. He would certainly have heard Hazlitt say of Shakespeare that 'He was nothing in himself . . . He had only to think of anything in order to become that thing . . .'

Empathy is then a crucial factor in Keats' attempts to construct or find a paradise, as is clear from a brief survey of certain of the Odes. In the *Ode on a Grecian Urn*, the speaker is held by the propensity of art to keep in a frozen eternity what would otherwise die:

Fair youth beneath the trees, thou canst not leave
Thy song, nor ever can those trees be bare;
Bold lover, never, never canst thou kiss,
Though winning near the goal – yet do not grieve:
She cannot fade, though thou hast not thy bliss,
For ever wilt thou love, and she be fair!

The melancholy paradox on which the poem turns is that while positive experiences held for eternity constitute paradise, negative experience held for eternity spells death: for example, the garlanded heifer about to be slaughtered, later in the poem, may spend eternity in that odd condition, and the 'little town', emptied of its inhabitants, will be silent 'for evermore'.

The urn is not the subject so much as the catalyst of the poem; it could not be 'shifted round', turned in the hand like the marble urn of the *Ode on Indolence*. Rather it is the trigger for a flight into Negative Capability, into which (to return to Keats' original definition) an 'irritable reaching after fact and reason' necessarily intrudes, puncturing the ideal with logic. Keats, regretfully, leaves the world of the urn to its 'Cold pastoral'. A 'friend to man', it is still non-human despite being a product of human creativity in an idealist mode: in the urn's frieze, nothing can die, whereas in the larger world over which mortality holds sway, death is everywhere; and yet paradoxically it is our knowledge of death that quickens a more intense appreciation of life. The poem's closing motto 'Beauty is truth, truth beauty', has been the recipient of an untoward amount of competitive excavation by critics, but we should remember that this is the urn talking. A poem from the mid-1970s, John Ashbery's *Self-Portrait in a Convex Mirror*, exists in a Romantic tradition descending partly from Keats, and also concerns a work of art whose lessons for the living present are both profound and partial:

This is what the portrait says.
But there is in that gaze a combination
Of tenderness, amusement and regret, so powerful
In its restraint that one cannot look for long.
The secret is too plain. The pity of it smarts,
Makes hot tears spurt: that the soul is not a soul,
Has no secret, is small, and it fits
Its hollow perfectly: its room, our moment of attention.

As with Wordsworth and John Keats, the questing gaze that seeks in artwork or anything else outside the self an empathetic negation of the ego that might be the key to some larger understanding finds itself returned to itself. The Renaissance self-portrait by Parmigianino which triggers Ashbery's meditation has no reality outside 'our moment of attention', and art, it is conceded, proposes only consolatory strategies for dealing with the fight against time and mortality. Much has changed in the history of poetry between Keats' time and Ashbery's, but a certain transhistorical continuity, a persistence of Romanticism, suggests that the break between modernist and Romantic poetry is still not as great as the historical and epistemological rupture between Augustan verse and the activities of Wordsworth and Coleridge.

Where a negation of the ego in life may be fraught with problems, death may provide the ultimate abandonment of self to what is other. In Keats' *Ode to a Nightingale*, what might be termed death's analogue, death as a seductive narcotic causing loss of consciousness, is imaged in the speaker hearing the nightingale's song:

Darkling, I listen; and, for many a time
I have been half in love with easeful Death,
Called him soft names in many a mused rhyme,
To take into the air my quiet breath;
Now more than ever seems it rich to die,
To cease upon the midnight with no pain,
While thou art pouring forth thy soul abroad
In such an ecstasy.

Here the very attention to natural detail which had characterized Wordsworth's poetry or the paintings of Friedrich and Constable is wilfully abandoned in preference to a condition of not-seeing, again a Negative Capability, a resting in uncertainties. Eventually the dream is broken and the poetic voice returned to earth, as if from a drug-experience: 'Was it a vision, or a waking dream?/ Fled is that music . . . Do I wake or sleep?'

The speaker of the 'Nightingale' ode is left at last in a twilight zone, neither the realm of the everyday, nor quite the realm of the nightingale's song. Rather this is a borderline state of consciousness, arrived at by accident, but resembling what a later generation of writers, in the 1890s, would aim for on purpose; a state where, to excerpt from Arthur Symons' manifesto for a *Decadent Movement in Literature* (see ▷ Nineties Poets), 'the unseen world is no longer a dream, and the visible world no longer a reality'. Suppose however that consciousness were to be trapped in a twilight zone which was as repetitively circular as that of the urn, as close to death as the world of the 'Nightingale' ode, and yet without any of the consolations of either poem? To depict a world where the unseen is no longer a dream and the visible no longer a reality, is exactly the world of one of Keats' most important poems, *La Belle Dame sans Merci.* The speaker of most of the poem's stanzas, the knight-at-arms, may be read not as a proponent but as a victim of Negative Capability:

I

O what can ail thee, knight-at-arms,
Alone and palely loitering?
The sedge has withered from the lake,
And no birds sing.

II

O what can ail thee, knight-at-arms,
So haggard and so woe-begone?

The squirrel's granary is full,
And the harvest's done.

III

I see a lily on thy brow,
With anguish moist and fever-dew,
And on thy cheeks a fading rose
Fast withereth too.

IV

I met a lady in the meads,
Full beautiful – a faery's child,
Her hair was long, her foot was light,
And her eyes were wild.

V

I made a garland for her head,
And bracelets too, and fragrant zone;
She looked at me as she did love,
And made sweet moan.

VI

I set her on my pacing steed,
And nothing else saw all day long,
For sidelong would she bend, and sing
A faery's song.

VII

She found me roots of relish sweet,
And honey wild, and manna-dew,
And sure in language strange she said –
'I love thee true'.

VIII

She took me to her elfin grot,
And there she wept and sighed full sore,
And there I shut her wild wild eyes
With kisses four.

IX

And there she lullèd me asleep
And there I dreamed – Ah! woe betide! –

The latest dream I ever dreamt
On the cold hill side.

X

I saw pale kings and princes too,
Pale warriors, death-pale were they all;
They cried – 'La Belle Dame sans Merci
Thee hath in thrall!'

XI

I saw their starved lips in the gloam,
With horrid warning gapèd wide,
And I awoke and found me here,
On the cold hill's side.

XII

And this is why I sojourn here
Alone and palely loitering,
Though the sedge is withered from the lake,
And no birds sing.
(*La Belle Dame sans Merci. A Ballad*)

Like a number of poems of this time – Shelley's ▷ *Ozymandias* and Coleridge's *Ancient Mariner*, for example – *La Belle Dame* begins with a feint, the inclusion of a speaker who will not be the poem's real subject. The shared rationale for this might lie in stressing the depth of the gulf that can stretch between one human consciousness and another, with only language as the tightrope between; that, certainly, is the miserable lesson the knight has learned, or perhaps refuses to learn, but is still condemned to reiterate. He has been struck a devastating psychic blow, by being drawn up from the real world and, as it were, shot into paradise by an erotic obsession with a woman who may be a lamia, a vampire, a *femme fatale*, and therefore false. He is now trapped in a typically Keatsian twilight zone, alone and palely loitering, the onset of winter in the external world in effect an attribute of his wintry consciousness. Still half in love, he cannot go forward and resume his place in the real world; but he cannot go back, as paradise has turned into brutal awakening on the cold hill's side. Of all Keats' protagonists and voices, the knight in this poem is most a victim.

In a horrible and ironic sense, he is a victim of Negative Capability; he is *compelled* to rest in mysteries and uncertainties, and has no fact or reason for which to reach, irritably or otherwise. No reasons are given for La Belle Dame's conduct, and nothing we are told helps either the knight or the reader. Unlike Coleridge's Mariner, Keats' knight may leave the reader sadder, but no wiser. The view of the world implied by this text is darkly ironic, to say the least: we have freedom to act as individuals, but that may signify the chance to become ensnared. The experience of falling into the paradise of love is common – the hillside is littered with courtly predecessors to the knight – but each must travel through life alone, and none may truly help another. Peril lies in unexpected places. Perhaps the image of a knight is a fanciful externalization of exactly that state of consciousness; armed to the teeth, except against the one weapon that can penetrate armour, loss of self-possession. That abandonment of the self to empathy with the other, be it the lover or Nature, that began with Wordsworth and Coleridge, is here brought to its most vertiginous and ironic potential for danger, in the poetry of Keats.

IV

William Blake

That these matters did not entirely originate with Wordsworth and Coleridge, to be passed on to the second generation, is clear from an examination of the poems of William Blake, barely known in his own lifetime. To be sure, Blake's poetry is thoroughly perfused with Christian narrative and symbolism, but his revision of orthodox morality is as rigorously corrosive as the acid that he would apply to metal plates to fashion his engravings, while his liking for subversive epigrams and dialectical play runs as contrary to conventional reasoning as the skill in writing backward that Blake had to develop in order to incorporate his poetry onto the plates.

The early twentieth-century tendency to view Blake as an artist working in different media, literary and pictorial, undermines his intention to produce one multiform, prophetic art which would operate in the verbal and visual fields simultaneously. For example, the interplay of signification between the poems and the engravings in his ▷ *Songs of Innocence and of Experience* (1789, 1794) is often complex and ironic. The lyric beginning 'Tyger, tyger, burning bright,/ In the forests of the night' is a common anthology piece, resonating for most readers with a sense of Romantic lyricism as celebrating the more frightening and beautiful forms of life and Nature; yet the accompanying picture of the Tyger shows a sheepish and oddly diffident little beast. A similar restlessness and deployment of reversed logic inhabits all of Blake's thought, from the shocking 'Proverbs of Hell' in ▷ *The Marriage of Heaven and Hell*, such as 'Sooner murder an infant in its cradle than nurse unacted desires', to his snarling attacks on church and clergy, as in *The Garden of Love* from the *Songs of Innocence and of Experience*:

I went to the Garden of Love,
And saw what I never had seen:
A Chapel was built in the midst,
Where I used to play on the green.
And the gates of this Chapel were shut,
And 'Thou shalt not' writ over the door;
So I turn'd to the Garden of Love
That so many sweet flowers bore,
And I saw it was filled with graves,
And tomb-stones where flowers should be;
And Priests in black gowns were walking their rounds,
And binding with briars my joys & desires.

In this case, the thrust of Blake's argument is, by his standards, relatively direct. The lost paradise of *The Garden of Love* is an Edenic vision of happily promiscuous sexuality ('so many sweet flowers'), and the agents of repression are identified as the uniformed priesthood, 'walking their rounds' to police human desire. It is possible to argue not so much against this reading of the poem, as against the attitudes held by its speaker. Blake is a provocative poet, who wants the reader to argue back. It could be pointed out that no flowers last forever, and that the whole world is 'filled with graves': not even the most resolute libertarian can stave off mortality; and isn't it death that most forcefully binds our 'joys & desires', rather than the church, which does at least address itself to life-and-death matters? But in that case it might be pardonable to gather rosebuds, or 'sweet flowers', while ye may, and the case for a Romantic insurrection that pits natural desire against institutionalized repression asserts its paradisal energy once more. Such a revolving spectrum of argument is characteristic of Blake's restless engagement with ideology.

The generation of meaning in texts by Blake is generally less straightforward, however, and his investment in contrariety on principle results in lines as multidirectional as Wordsworth's, but so supercharged with possible significations as to become gnomic and opaque. The final lines of *London* are superbly resonant, but hard to pin down:

But most thro' midnight streets I hear
How the youthful Harlot's curse
Blasts the new born Infant's tear,
And blights with plagues the Marriage hearse.

Are the effects of the prostitute's curse good or bad? Perhaps infected herself with a sexually transmitted 'plague', does she 'blast' her own child's chances of a future by passing on the disease; or is the blasting away of a tear a cleansing, symbolically bracing, even a revolutionary rousing of the underclass to political action? This last reading seems to be confirmed by the attitude to the priesthood shown in *The Garden of Love*. Here can be seen a paradox central to the operations of Romantic poetry from Blake to Shelley: the greater the scope of the poetry in terms of topic, the more distant its language from customary usage. (This was something that troubled Byron: the drift of linguistic experiment into solipsism was something he debated on the page and in person with Shelley, patronized in Keats, and diagnosed in Wordsworth and Coleridge, the butts of satire in *Don Juan*.) In the twentieth century, such tendentious obscurity and a multiplication of meaning as we find in Blake has alternately been thought pleasurable and intrinsic to poetic practice, and a sign of alienation or bad writing. T.S. Eliot undervalued Romantic poetry, preferring the allegedly more unified expressiveness of the ▷ Elizabethan and ▷ Jacobean periods. F.R. Leavis followed him in undervaluing Shelley, and indicted Blake for manifesting the estrangement of an auto-didact, cut off from the nurturing influence of a literary community. This echoes Eliot's nostalgia for an age when writing counted. However, Eliot's diagnosis of a 'dissociation of sensibility', a Fall from this organic community around the time of ▷ Milton, is ironically itself a Romanticization of a historical change in the relationship between writer, audience, patronage and the means of production, which might be more accurately understood through materialist analysis of the period concerned, rather than idealized as an expression of being.

One revaluation of the Romantics begins in the 1940s, itself a period in which a form of Romanticism – dubbed the school of the 'New Apocalypse' – flourished briefly in the work of such British poets as David Gascoyne and George Barker. Critically, revaluation reached its apogee with the work of literary theorists such as Harold Bloom, Geoffrey Hartman and Paul de Man, whose writing from roughly 1960 to 1980 moves from New Criticism to deconstruction. This move, mediated by the impact of ▷ psychoanalytical, ▷ Marxist and ▷ structuralist theory on American teaching of English literature, involved a shift from viewing the generation in a poem of multiple or undecideable meaning as intentional, to seeing it as an inevitable side-effect of linguistic expression. It may be that in the Fall from various versions of paradise conjured in Romantic poetry can be seen the imagistic expression of what is at root a linguistic Fall, the slippage of expression from intention, of signifier from signified. It may be that literary criticism has now caught up with Romantic poetry, by showing how language, like all human dream-forms, is condemned to make and break itself.

V

The persistence of Romanticism

An historically limited view of Romanticism would declare it to be a bounded movement, that began (with influences as diverse as the French Revolution and the German tale of terror) with the early poetry of Wordsworth and Coleridge, and concluded with the death of ▷ Sir Walter Scott in 1832. By these lights, Victorian literature, with the burgeoning primacy of the novel, would be thought to move into a new era of ethical rather than egotistical writing, the question as to how we should live replacing the Romantic agony of who we are. The novels of ▷ Jane Austen, with which this Introduction has not dealt, might therefore be seen as important precursors of what was to come, given their emphasis on marriage and social positioning, actualities rather than dreams and desires. And yet the Victorian period, from the frequently luscious and oneiric poetry of ▷ Tennyson, Swinburne and the Pre-Raphaelites through to the Decadent poets of the 1890s, is replete with the kind of concerns that exercised Keats. The professions of artistic impersonality that accompany the seminal modernist works by T.S. Eliot, Wyndham Lewis and others by no means account for texts such as *The Waste Land* in their entirety; and the high modernist period was succeeded by literature of the 1930s, where dreams of a socialist utopia, as well as an interest in ▷ Freud, maintain a line of descent from the writing of Shelley and his generation. The bardic lyricism of the 1940s, the bulk of modern American poetry, and the 1960s cult of the self all confirm the persistence of Romanticism. The literature of Romanticism was persistent in conjuring ways through which the articulate self could empathize with something or someone outside, and was as persistently driven back into ironies and paradoxes that questioned that intention, while providing some of the most recurrently engaging and vital writings of the last two hundred years. As readers and writers of the 1990s, we are still situated in important ways within the questions that body of writing has posed.

11 Death Strolls Between Letters: Romantic Poetry and Literary Theory

Philip Shaw

I

But where has art led us? To a time before the world, before the beginning. It has cast us out of our power to begin and to end; it has turned us towards the outside where there is no intimacy, no place to rest. It has led us into the infinite migration of error. For we seek art's essence, and it lies where the nontrue admits of nothing essential . . . It ruins the origin by returning to it the errant immensity of directionless eternity.

(Maurice Blanchot, *The Space of Literature*, 1955)

What does it mean to speak 'before the beginning'; to be out of power; to be placed in exile; to have no truth beyond the sorrow of straying?

I will answer with a further question. Do we approach the 'essence' of art from the direction of literature or of philosophy? In this essay I will assume the necessity of both, not because the paths of literature and philosophy are indistinguishable – they are not, and we would be wrong to remove the distinctions that separate them – but because in the poetry of the Romantic period the two are often dangerously intertwined. The dream of Romanticism is a discourse that will encapsulate both. On the one hand, as ⊳ S.T. Coleridge puts it, we see the technical process of 'just distinction' belonging to philosophical method; on the other the 'spirit of unity' characteristic of the creative Imagination (⊳ *Biographia Literaria*, 1817). What the 'synthetic' power of Imagination effects, however, is far removed from this dream. The clash of unity with distinction, 'of sameness, with difference, of the general with the concrete, the idea with the image', is not resolved in the Romantic enterprise. And Coleridge is painfully aware of this fault. His imagination reveals itself in the flawed words and stubborn sounds of the philosophically imperfect.

To think through literature, therefore, we run the risk of repeating a great Romantic error. But that, I would argue, is our fate; for in a sense we are still Romantics, still subjects of an epoch whose 'essence lies where the nontrue admits of nothing essential'. In this sense to repeat is to err; but it is also to remind ourselves that our authenticity has its origin in what is useless, indefinite and nontrue. The Romantic epoch is 'born', to adapt ⊳ Byron, 'from the knowledge of its own desert' (⊳ *Manfred*, 1817). Here the key terms are wandering, anarchy and exile. In Romanticism, we encounter the world not as our home but as a nomadic labyrinth; a space that is truly infinite, without *arche* or *telos*, beginning or end. If truth depends on limits, on the assumption of foundations and of regulated and well-defined boundaries, then to think in this space is to commit thought to the inevitability of error. No wonder that Byron, in common with many Romantic poets, is derided for his lack of clarity, since to support this view one must cease to think in terms of the rational and the real. One must commit oneself to an event over which critical thought no longer has any control.

But from whence do we derive this rhetoric of ambiguity? In a highly influential essay, 'Literature and the Right to Death' (1949) (collected in *The Gaze of Orpheus*, 1981), Maurice Blanchot presents an analogy between literature and revolutionary action. What literature and revolution share, he argues, is a desire for the absolute: the absolute of history, the absolute of knowledge, the absolute of subjective experience – the ultimate expression of which is the absolute purity of annihilation. Literature and revolution therefore accomplish themselves in the 'freedom' of death. For Blanchot, this is the meaning of the ▷ French Revolution. The subject is liberated from external bonds (the law of tutelage); critical thought is urged on by the giddiness of the event. The modern age begins.

Two impulses are born here: on the one hand the Kantian ideals of human progress and subjective autonomy (freedom from external control through the exercise of reason); on the other hand the eruption of systematic violence allied to the bloodlust of the emergent collective (freedom from reason itself, an act of pure will). The theatre of modern consciousness begins, so to speak, with the affirmation of a convulsive duality. It stages this dualism in the tensional relation between literature and philosophy. As reason finds its justification in the progressive impulse of revolution, artistic activity is confirmed in the liberation of terror. The task in this essay, therefore, will be to unleash the latent violence of the Romantic poem so that reason may be forced to a confrontation with a range of excluded others: the random, the aberrant, the mystical and the absurd.

If philosophy attempts to explain the world in terms of unity, cohesion and universals, Romantic poetry helps us to think the unthinkable. To do so, however, requires an act as irrational as the fall of a blade; a revolt that commits thought to the infinite migration of (t)error.

II

Whence that completed form of all completeness?
Whence came that high perfection of all sweetness?
(▷ Keats, ▷ *Endymion*, I, 606–7, 1818)

Why a theory of Romanticism? On the back cover of *The Literary Absolute: The Theory of Literature in German Romanticism* (1988), the authors Philippe Lacoue-Labarthe and Jean-Luc Nancy make the following statement:

Romanticism is first of all a theory. And the invention of literature. More precisely, it constitutes the inaugural moment of literature as production of its own theory – and of theory that thinks itself as literature. With this gesture, it opens the critical age to which we still belong.

With the epoch of Romanticism we reach the stage where literature becomes the perpetual positing of its own question. Henceforth literature, ceaselessly deferred and dissembling, can never be perfected or closed in on itself: 'This is why Romanticism, which is actually a moment (the moment of its question) will always have been more than a mere "epoch", or else will never cease, right up to the present, to incomplete the epoch it inaugurated.' We are, as I have suggested, Romantics. Or rather we are not yet Romantic. For if the Romantic epoch is interminable and incomplete it can never reach the status of a 'thing'. It is more true to say that it is 'nothing'. Thus, in answer to the question what is the essence of art we might do better to reply that Romanticism, or literature, 'is that which has no essence, not even its own inessentiality'.

Because the answer to the question 'what is Romanticism' is endlessly deferred,

Romantic texts through their very dispersion demonstrate the impossibility of essence – and thus of being itself. For, as the writers of *The Literary Absolute* would claim, an epoch that begins with theory is an epoch that founds itself on the loss of being: on the supplement or the perfection of the work of art rather than with the completed work of art.

In an important sense, therefore, the question of Romanticism continues to haunt criticism. Who, for example, would deny that a correlation exists between Romanticism and ▷ deconstruction? One has only to consult the enormous variety of works on Romantic topics published in the United States in the last twenty years to find confirmation of this. A canonical book such as *Deconstruction and Criticism* (1979), with contributions by some of the most eminent theorists of deconstruction – ▷ Harold Bloom, ▷ Jacques Derrida, ▷ Geoffrey Hartman, ▷ Paul de Man and J. Hillis Miller – makes the connection between Romantic loss and postmodern absence explicit by adopting ▷ Shelley's *Triumph of Life* (1822) as a common reading text. Not the least of their concerns in treating Shelley is the problematic relation between language, literature and thought. In Derrida's essay, 'Living on: Borderlines', the problem focuses on the concept of genre. Why does the poem overflow its limits? What is it that prevents the text from maintaining the rigorous determinations of authorship, historical specificity and generic type?

The 'answer', common to Hillis Miller and de Man, is that language is a radically unstable construct. It cannot help but 'deconstruct' the imposition of borders, whether these are conceived in terms of the identity of the author, the priority of voice over writing, or the specificity of genre. If deconstruction derives this notion from the study of Romantic texts it is because Romanticism tends to demonstrate its own apparent contradictions clearly. How, for example, does one classify a 'theoretical' text such as ▷ Wordsworth's *Essay Upon Epitaphs* (1810)? As speculative meditation, prose poem, text book, autobiography or elegy? The list is potentially endless. If, on the one hand, we seek its essence in a literary genre we are led to the place where the law of genre, to recall Blanchot, 'admits of nothing essential': the text is what it is only on the condition that it excludes all of the others. Unfortunately Wordsworth's essay is incapable of such exclusion. Like all Romantic writing – here let us include the unfinished epics of Byron, Keats and Shelley; the encyclopaedic 'projects': Schlegel's *Fragments* (1798–1800), Wordsworth's *The Recluse*, Coleridge's *Biographia Literaria* (1817) – the *Essay Upon Epitaphs* struggles between comprehension and fragmentation. It wants to say everything – to reflect on the 'truth', including the truth of its own production – but it remains a fragment and 'as yet', Schlegel argues, 'no genre exists that is fragmentary both in form and in content' (*Athenaeum Fragments*).

The key phrase here is 'as yet' for the sense of the unfulfilled present strikes at the very heart of the Romantic concept of genre. Rather than to the idea of an assemblage or union the work of Romanticism points to the undefined and the illimitable: 'something evermore about to be', as Wordsworth writes in ▷ *The Prelude* (1805, 6, 542). To comprehend this fecundity, however, the energy of Romanticism must be directed toward the production of a 'literature . . . that would be a great, thoroughly connected and organized Whole, comprehending many worlds of art in its unity, and being at the same time a unitary work of art' (Schlegel, 'On the Combinatory Spirit', 1804). The Romantic work must be 'capable of containing its own reflection and of comprehending the theory of its "genre"' (*The Literary Absolute*). Literature and criticism, in other words, must become one. This prescriptiveness and conditionality, however, ultimately disfigure this aim, for if the 'essence' of Romanticism is 'that it should forever be becoming and never be perfected' (*Athenaeum Fragments*) then the process of infinite self-generation is one that is perpetually in excess of the ability of the genre to reflect and unify. The essence of the Romantic genre is therefore radically unstable. On the one hand it is fragmentary and limitless: 'No theory can exhaust it, and only a divinatory criticism would dare to characterize its ideal'; on the other encyclopaedic and holistic: 'It embraces everything' (*Athenaeum Fragments*).

But how can the essence of something not comprise a particular manifestation in space and time, with the coincidence of form and content necessary for any self-relation? Moreover, if Romantic poetry is, in some sense, the genre of genres (see again *Fragments*) what does this tell us about the relationship between literature and identity? To understand the background to this thought it is necessary to re-examine the conceptual antimonies of Enlightenment philosophy, particularly within the work of ▷ Immanuel Kant.

III

I feel I am; – I only know I am
(▷ John Clare, *I am*, c 1845)

From Descartes to Hegel philosophers have created systems of thought predicated on the autonomous existence of the thinking subject: *res cogitans*. According to this view the only thing of which we can be certain is our own capacity to doubt; *res cogitans* is that which remains when all else has been dismissed: the body, the external world and God. But the consequence of this is isolation. Like the narrator in Clare's sonnet *I am*, or the spectre of Coleridge's *This Lime-Tree Bower My Prison* (1797) the subject is deprived of its connection with 'otherness'. It has lost

Beauties and feelings, such as would have been
Most sweet to my remembrance even when age
Had dimmed mine eyes to blindness!

The Cartesian solution to this 'problem' is to insist that the subject's relationship with *res extensa* – with material space, or 'nature' – is constructed by and issues from the subject's relationship to itself. Henceforth, to quote Mark C. Taylor, 'modern philosophy becomes a philosophy of the subject. The locus of certainty and truth, subjectivity is the first principle from which everything arises and to which all must be reduced or returned' (*Deconstruction in Context*, 1986).

In the history of ideas, Descartes marks the shift from a theocentric world view to a humanist one. Humanism, however, does not imply the negation of God. For even as the conceptual significance of the divine suffers a displacement, its structural function is preserved, and possibly reinforced, by its relocation in consciousness. The subject, in other words, *is* God. And like God it possesses the ability to produce itself, to create a world and to exist alone. For Taylor, this last point is crucial. Since the subject 'relates only to what it constructs . . . What seems to be a relationship with otherness – be that other God, nature, objects, or subjects – always turns out to be an aspect of mediate self-relation that is necessary for self-consciousness'. There is, in other words, no 'other' that is not already an aspect of subjectivity. Nothing can appear to consciousness that does not confirm the subject's self-relation, constructive power and sovereign solitude.

The Cartesian subject therefore transforms the other into a mirror for itself. Like the figure of Dorothy in Wordsworth's ⊳ *Tintern Abbey* (1798), the other is present in the poem as the basis of the poet's capacity to sustain her as a mirror figure. Through catching in the sister's voice 'the language of my former heart', by reading 'my former pleasures in the shooting lights / Of thy wild eyes' (117–20), the identity of the creating subject is maintained over time. That of the sister, however, has been reduced to a creative foil; her difference has been incorporated within the circle of subjectivity's full knowledge of itself.

Discussions of Cartesian subjectivity lead, inevitably, towards a consideration of the status of knowledge. Given that in the distinguishing of the *cogito* a rift is driven between subject and object how are we to gain knowledge of anything that exists beyond the 'fact' of consciousness? If the other – which may be experienced in sensory phenomena, or felt as pleasure and pain – can never be present except as an aspect of mediated self-reflection how can we be said to have knowledge of the other? The problem is addressed by Kant in the *Critique of Pure Reason* (1781) (readers should again consult Taylor's excellent summary of the Kantian position in *Deconstruction in Context*). In brief, Kant argues that knowledge is the product of a marriage between reason and experience. The human subject makes sense of the raw data of sense experience by imposing a priori forms of intuition (*eg* the concepts of space and time) and categories of understanding (*eg* relations of cause and effect, unity and diversity and so on). In Kant's synthesizing of Cartesian and empiricist theories, to know is to exercise reason so that difference may be reduced to identity, the manifold to the one.

This still leaves unanswered the question of how the subject relates to otherness. If reason, as Kant claims, *imposes* form upon matter, does this not mean that subject and object, reason and nature, are ineluctably separate? That there was not, at some time, an original unity of theoretical and practical reason? A solution, of sorts, is offered in Kant's third *Critique*, the *Critique of Judgement* (1790). Here it is suggested that the unity of subjectivity and objectivity can be recovered in the practice and form of 'fine art'. The argument is based on the identification of two concepts of constructive activity: the work of natural organic engendering (standing for the object or other) and the work of artistic production (standing for the subject or consciousness). Kant therefore grants the art work a privileged status. If ordinary experience is random and chaotic, marked by fragmentation and loss, artistic experience is self-determining and unified, unaffected by external forces or governed by anything other than itself. Through the work of art or *poiesy* – art that is considered as 'pure' production, without use or purpose – the creating subject realizes its freedom from outside determination. Its 'finality', Kant writes, 'appears just as free from the constraint of arbitrary rules as if it were a product of mere nature'. In this way, subjectivity and objectivity – artistic activity and natural production – are related and come to completion within and through each other. Nature can only be realized through art; and art can only be realized through nature.

At this point it may be helpful to draw a further connection with Romantic verse. To take a previously cited example: in Coleridge's lime-tree bower 'the friends' who enable the poet to break out of his Cartesian isolation are both constructs of the mind and products of nature. The act of imaginative projection into the gaze of the other – 'to contemplate . . . the joys we cannot share' (67) – thus creates a reciprocal relation between subject and object, a reciprocity figured in the image of 'the solitary humble-bee' singing in the bean-flower (58–9). The solitary bee signifies the self-autonomy and constitutive labour of authentic subjectivity as well as the idealized union of natural and artistic forms of making.

This, at least, is how Coleridge (and Kant) might wish us to read the poem. And many critics have been willing to follow this tack. M.H. Abrams, for example, writes of the poetic strategy in which 'nature is made thought and thought nature both by their sustained interaction and seamless metaphorical continuity' ('Structure and Style in the Greater Romantic Lyric' in *From Sensibility to Romanticism*, 1965). Similarly, Earl Wasserman has cited Coleridge as the reconciler of 'the phenomenal world of understanding with the noumenal world of reason' ('The English Romantics, The Grounds of Knowledge' in *Studies in Romanticism*, 4). It is, however, equally arguable that in the act of synthesizing subject and object through the structures of art the poet has merely confirmed the 'natural' priority of the one over the other. As Paul de Man argues, commenting on Abrams and Wasserman in 'The Rhetoric of Temporality' (1969, collected in *Blindness and Insight*, 1983), the claim for a reconciliation of self and other in Coleridge is based on the assertion of 'affinity' or 'sympathy', terms which only make sense in the context of a relationship between subjects, not in the relationship between a subject and an object. An example of this effect occurs in the opening of ▷ *Frost at Midnight* (1798):

the thin blue flame
Lies on my low-burnt fire, and quivers not;
Only that film, which fluttered on the grate,
Still flutters there, the sole unquiet thing.
Methinks, its motion in this hush of nature
Gives it dim sympathies with me who live,
Making it a companionable form,
[With which I can hold commune.]
[With which I can hold commune.] (13–19)

To escape the solitude and silence that 'vexes meditation' the poet must find an object in nature analogous to the movements of his own mind. The fluttering film provides this function. But the assertion of unity between mind and nature is not entirely convincing, as Coleridge's manuscript revisions make abundantly clear. From a reading of these revisions it could very well be argued that the concept of organic inter-communion is meaningless without the translation of objectivity into subjectivity. Coleridge himself seems uneasily aware of the sort of paradoxes that emerge from this process:

Idle thought!
But still the living spirit in our frame,
That loves not to behold a lifeless thing,
Tranfuses into all its own delights,
Its own volition, sometimes with deep faith
And sometimes with fantastic playfullness.
(20–25; added in 1828)

Does the living spirit proceed from the self or from nature? If consciousness predominates then the relationship with otherness will turn out to be 'an intersubjective, interpersonal relationship that, in the last analysis, is a relationship of the subject toward itself'. Should, however, the subject fail to convert lifeless nature into an echo of infinity then consciousness is placed in bondage to the supremacy of the finite. The mind is a slave to external forms and thus to time. Whichever course is chosen, the supposed inter-communion of subject and object turns out to be a deceitful construct, a will-o'-the-wisp confirming consciousness in its mortal isolation.

If the link between subject and object is placed in jeopardy the fault can be traced to the dependence of speculative idealism on the structures of art. Despite Coleridge's insistence on the identity of art and nature – 'such as the life is, such the form' – the resemblance between them remains purely formal. It is possible for the work of art and the work of nature to coincide only because they have been made to partake of the same set of categories – and here the relationship is not one of subject and object, it is a relationship of signs. To put this again in Kantian terms: since, as Lacoue-Labarthe and Nancy argue, the work of auto-formation can only occur through art, the individual can only come to itself as *artifax* or, worse still, *ars*. Paradoxically then it is the very dependency on artistic form that effectuates the break between the *bildende Kraft* (creative force) of the artist and the archetype of natural organic production.

The fundamental insight of Romanticism, therefore, against Kant, is that artistic creativity predominates over the organic and the natural. Here, the subject is not transcendental, but becomes instead an effect of the art work. And in the work-of-art (to recall Blanchot) the process of auto-formation is one whereby consciousness both creates and becomes self-consciously aware of itself in creation. This, however, is a process of unfolding rather than control. Here we lose the notion of identity, of a Cartesian substratum underlying meaning. To exist in the act of writing is to commit thought to 'a non-transitive language whose task is not to speak of things . . . but to speak (itself) in letting (itself) speak, without however making itself the new object of this language without an object'. In terms, therefore, that directly anticipate the contemporary discourse of post-structuralism, the 'I' of Romanticism is one that effectively reveals and confronts its status as a linguistic 'effect'. In writing it is no longer the subject but language that speaks. The text ceaselessly unworks 'itself'.

> *Woe is me!*
> *The winged words on which my soul would pierce*
> *Into the heights of Love's rare Universe,*
> *Are chains of lead around its flight of fire –*
> *I pant, I sink, I tremble, I expire*!
> (Shelley, *Epipsychidion*, 587–91, 1821)

If the deconstruction of the subject seems alien to the official message of Romanticism – Paul de Man, for example, has been accused of the most formalistic 'misreading' of Romantic poetry – we have only to read the pronouncements of the Romantics themselves to correct this view. Schlegel, for instance, points out 'that words often understand themselves better than do those who use them' and that a certain ghost within writing will 'bring everything into confusion' ('On Incomprehensibility', 1800). Even Wordsworth, quite often miscast as the self-assured father figure of English Romanticism, seems distrustful of the claim for organicity:

> *Words are too awful an instrument for good and evil, to be trifled with; they hold above all other external powers a dominion over thoughts. If words be not . . . an incarnation of the thought, but only a clothing for it, then surely will they prove an ill gift; such a one as those possessed vestments, read of in the stories of superstitious times which had the power to consume and to alienate from his right mind the victim who put them on. Language, if it do not uphold, and feed, and leave in quiet, like the power of*

gravitation or the air we breathe, is a counter-spirit, unremittingly and noiselessly at work, to subvert, to lay waste, to vitiate, and to dissolve.

(*Essays Upon Epitaphs*. 3)

Wordsworthian ontology unfolds into an ethical imperative to maintain a rigorous defence against corruption. There is in this impassioned rhetoric a feeling that language will not incarnate thought, that the transparency of the word will turn into ghostly matter, revenging itself on the passive spirit of mind.

Romantic theory, then, in a prefiguring of modern thought, encounters language as a force from elsewhere. It becomes a 'counter-spirit' to the mastery of the self. In this connection, Wordsworth's thought is very close to that of Heidegger: 'Man acts as though he were the shaper and master of language, while in fact language remains the master of man. When this relation of dominance gets inverted, man hits upon strange manoeuvres. ('. . . Poetically Man Dwells . . .', in *Poetry, Language, Thought*, 1971). In response to this inversion, Romanticism marshals a number of strategies, the most significant of which is the valorization of symbol.

For Coleridge, the symbol 'always partakes of the Reality which it renders intelligible; and while it enunciates the whole, abides itself as a living part in that Unity, of which it is the representative' (*The Statesman's Manual*, 1830). With the emphasis on the relationship between part and whole, the structure of symbol resembles that of synecdoche. The symbol, in other words, is always 'a living part' of the totality that it stands for. The vengeful revenant is returned to the silence of the tomb. But not even the organic coherence of synecdoche can escape the effects of the inversion that Heidegger relates. As Coleridge's *The Eolian Harp* (1796) illustrates, within the alien realm of poetry, the displacement of symbolic language occurs at precisely those moments where the unity of consciousness and community, part and whole, is most needed. Throughout the poem, language draws attention to its own status as an artificial construct. In lines 3–5, for example, the symbolic significance of the 'white-flower'd Jasmin' and 'broad-leav'd Myrtle' – natural objects that would unite reason and experience – is undercut by the following parenthesis: '(Meet *emblems* they of Innocence and Love!)' (lines 4–5; my emphasis). As Tilottama Rajan suggests ('Displacing Post-Structuralism: Romantic Studies After Paul de Man', *Studies in Romanticism* 24), by bracketing the moral qualities that are meant to subsist in the landscape, reminding us that the flowers are only 'emblems', the poem discredits the claims of the symbolic style to be the 'living educt of the imagination'. It becomes, like any other trope, a supplement to the actualization of the real. By foregrounding artificiality – the synaesthesia of lines 26–7; the formal, neo-classical conceit of 32–3 – *The Eolian Harp* suggests that the work of inter-communion has more to do with aesthetic tinkering than with natural engendering.

Strangely, however, it is through the work of the aesthetic that the poem is returned to what de Man refers to as 'an authentically temporal destiny' – though time, in this case, has nothing to do with what is normally associated with authenticity, the ability to coincide, to unify and to reflect on one's self; rather, time is that which leads the subject away from itself, putting it in a relation to pure anteriority, the *outside* of selfhood. A poem such as *The Eolian Harp*, therefore, works on two levels: first to convert the violence of time into the passivity of literary or mental space; secondly, to disrupt this space through the return of time.

In the first movement the temporality of nature is reduced to metaphors of stillness and silence. These metaphors reinforce the tendency of symbol to postulate states of organic inter-fusion:

and the world so *hush'd!*
The stilly murmur of the distant Sea
Tells us of silence.

(10–12)

The suspension of movement and duration at this point dissolves the 'I' into a state of oneiric repose. Consciousness slows down. The subject is spaced out. With the return to the meditation on the subject lute, however, the flaunting of artificiality translates the poem back onto the plain of time. The temporality that the second movement of poetry restates, therefore, is the temporality of tropes, a difference signified, in this case, in the shift from a symbolic to an allegorical mode of discourse.

According to Paul de Man, language is an ⊳ allegory of its own deconstruction. He bases this claim on the structuralist distinction between the synchronic and diachronic poles of language. According to this view, formulated by ⊳ Roman Jakobson, tropes such as symbol belong to the synchronic axis. Their structure is spatial in kind. Tropes such as allegory, on the other hand, partake of the diachronic axis. Their structure is durational and thus, in a sense, 'authentically temporal'. Before going further, it is worth quoting de Man's definition of these forms:

> *Whereas the symbol postulates the possibility of an identity or identification, allegory designates primarily a distance in relation to its own origin, and, renouncing the nostalgia and the desire to coincide, it establishes its language in the void of this temporal difference.*
>
> ('The Rhetoric of Temporality')

Allegory in *The Eolian Harp*, whilst not explicitly presented as a theme of the poem, is nevertheless present in the necessarily temporal relationship that exists between signs. The symbol is no exception. Despite the appeal to organicity, the symbol, like any other sign, is able to recapture or reflect upon itself. To echo the philosophy of Merleau-Ponty, this turn of the symbol 'recuperates everything [art, nature and so on] except itself as an effort of recuperation, it clarifies everything except its own role' (from *The Visible and the Invisible*, 1968). Something, in other words, always escapes, translating the symbol back onto the plain of the diachronic, opening a gap in the text that no act of existential faith can close.

Therefore, by formulating the symbol in terms of synecdoche (part for whole), Coleridge has attempted to spatialize an essentially temporal experience. But more than this, he has attempted to exclude the time of the other. The other returns, however, in the final movement of the poem through the dialogical interference of Sara Coleridge, the wife to whom the poem has been addressed. Like Dorothy in *Tintern Abbey*, Sara can be seen as a rhetorical 'excess', an unrecuperable isotope that emerges from the failure of poetic language to realize itself. Her look of 'mild reproof' (49) subverts the poem's founding trope: the idea that the antimonies of art and nature, consciousness and the world, can be overcome through an appeal to visionary correspondence. Against the 'half-clos'd eye-lids' (36) of mental seeing, Sara's 'more serious eye' (49) is a timely reminder of corporeal limits. The darting look pierces the infinite gaze, and Coleridge is returned to the body, the mortal body in which we find our home or not at all.

Following from this, the closing address to God 'The Incomprehensible' (59) is perhaps the most moving and most pathetic statement of the entire Romantic movement. Having eschewed the symbol as a medium for self-determination, God is accepted, beyond signs, beyond temporality, as the unrepresentable horizon of a lost totality. God is what remains when all else has been closed. Faced with this knowledge, the poet's subjective freedom reverts to the pre-Enlightenment condition of tutelage, defined by Kant as 'man's inability to make use of his understanding without direction from another'.

From start to finish, therefore, the conversation poem is an allegorical disruption of the pursuit of knowledge. But Coleridge, like Kant, cannot escape his Cartesian inheritance: trapped within the *cogito*, the desired reciprocity of man and nature, self and other, turns out to be a chimera, an escape that confirms the fact of its own imprisonment. And it is one that must be repeated, like the 'rime' of the ⊳ Ancient Mariner, over and over again.

V

'violence from within'
(Wallace Stevens, 'The Noble Rider and the Sound of Words')

Within Western thought temporality is habitually excluded from the creation of systems. Time cannot be rationalized. Time is absolutely other. Given, then, that the subject through his or her relation to mortality is locked in time, how can we conceive of subjectivity as part of a system? Once again, to think the unthinkable we must look beyond philosophy toward the impure thought of poetry. Here, we may even 'see as a god sees' (Keats, *The Fall of Hyperion*, 1, 304, 1819), exchanging our mortal bodies for the immortality of mind.

But god-like vision comes at a price. To take the depth of things the self must not only pass beyond the bonds of temporality, it must also withstand the effects of human memory:

Without stay or prop
But my own weak mortality, I bore
The load of this eternal quietude
(*The Fall of Hyperion*, 1, 388–90)

In Keats' unfinished epic, the self undertakes a journey into the realm of the divine. One would therefore expect a rhetoric of self-empowerment. But Keats booby-traps the poem with pockets of irony. In the example of the lines quoted above, by juxtaposing the 'I' of 'mortality' against the 'eternal quietude' of a god, we are forced to confront what is really at stake in the dream of transcendence. Since time escapes knowledge, and since the human subject is in a perpetual process of becoming, our knowledge of the world remains partial and incomplete. This is something that the Kantian thesis, with its spatializing of human thought, cannot accept. But it is also the source of its subversive potential. For if the art work is free and indeterminate, unbounded by conceptual certainty, how can we presuppose the integrity of self-consciousness? Evermore about to be, the temporality of artistic activity denies the stability of a transcendent 'I'.

To see as a god sees, therefore, the subject must renounce its connection with process and change; it must, as Keats writes in the earlier ⊳ *Hyperion* (1819) 'Die into life' (3, 130). Only in this way can the subject attain the closure necessary for complete self-consciousness and total knowledge.

But if death closes, it does so on the condition that it closes all. For to live beyond death is a scandal that no philosophical system can bear. Philosophy, however, endeavours to preserve this fantasy by converting the absolute negativity of death into the positive reserve of a temporal dialectic. This idea is presented by Hegel in a famous passage from *The Phenomenology of Spirit* (1807). 'The life of the Spirit', he writes, 'is not the life that shrinks from death and keeps itself untouched by devastation, but rather the life that endures it and maintains itself in it. It wins its truth, only when, in utter dismemberment, it finds itself.' For Hegel, self-realization entails absolute knowledge. But this can only occur if the subject incorporates the knowledge of its own dissolution. Death, in other words, must be included as a structural element within the progressive unfolding of a temporal dialectic. To do this, however, requires an act of repression – for Hegelian thought cannot tolerate a negative that fails to preserve a kernel of positivity. Through the process of *Aufhebung* (literally a raising and suspending), therefore, death is itself negated and turned into profit. In a direct allusion to the Christian myth of death and resurrection, the subject 'dies' only to be reconstituted as historically transcendent, omnipotent and omniscient. Nothing escapes this process. The random, the senseless, the stubbornly material – in Hegel's philosophy everything is assimilated into the economics of self-realization.

This includes the Kantian concept of art. What Hegel cannot accept in the Kantian thesis is an unforeseen reliance on the irrational and the incoherent. For Hegel, art is an insufficient ground for the realization of self-consciousness. Art can never be transparent in the way that pure thought requires. What occurs in the Romantic work is a form of death that cannot be converted into profit. It retains, so to speak, the force of an absolute negativity; a pure otherness that escapes the systematic totality of dialectical reason. To maintain its integrity, therefore, Hegel's philosophy must sublimate the radical imperfection of Romantic art. It must move beyond the instability of poetic representation to the pure reflection of conceptual thought. Hegelianism must, in short, pronounce the end of Romanticism.

VI

Death Strolls Between Letters
(Jacques Derrida, 'Edmund Jabes and the Question of the Book', in *Writing and Difference*, 1978)

What happens, then, when Romantic poetry experiments with the radical negativity of death; with death considered as a literary absolute? The link between the work of the creative artist and the power of the negative may be more intimate than we might at first suppose. Take the example of *The Prelude*. For a vast majority of readers the key note of the poem is a heartfelt belief in

the life
Of all things and the mighty unity
in all which we behold, and feel, and are
(13, 253–5)

Unity, blending, interchange; the 'filial bond' between man and nature – such is the dream of Romantic perfection. But against the grain of this assumption, Romantic writing inscribes a transgressive language: a rhetoric of failure, non-sense and irreducible absence. As Geoffrey Hartman comments, within this language 'the

Imagination [which] usually . . . vitalizes and animates . . . stands closer to death than life' (*Wordsworth's Poetry*, 1965). Hence the Romantic interest in disaster; its thirst for annihilation – as in ▷ Cowper's *Castaway* (1799), Shelley's *Alastor* (1817) and Byron's ▷ *Cain* (1821), poems of despair, enervation and paradoxical pride which tease the borderline between self-affirmation and self-abnegation. The otherness of death, when it appears in these poems, is an event that cannot be accounted for, still less converted into profit. And not even Wordsworth can escape this force. When the imagination, rising 'like an unfather'd vapour' in Book 6 of *The Prelude*, releases the self from subjection to mortality, the assertion of a-temporality is made dependent on the dangerous equation of death as denial and death as possibility. At this moment, literature opens itself up 'to a time before the world, before the beginning'; to an 'outside where there is no intimacy, no place to rest' (Blanchot). This irreducible and unrepresentable 'past' opens a fissure in the text that makes presence – the assertion of the god-like, transcendent 'I' – impossible. Not even the restoration of time, through the punctual 'now' ('Halted, without a struggle to break through. "24" And now recovering', 530–1) can restore the integrity of self. 'Now' belongs to the space-time of literature, not of the world; it is an interruption that does not unify. Literary time announces the recommencement of the exodus away from self.

Perhaps this last point explains why Romantic writing continues to elicit our interest. The more philosophy struggles to attain a comprehensive view of the world, the greater the faithfulness of Romanticism to the call of the irrational and the absurd. Whether that call is heard in the cold pastoral of Keats' *Ode to a Grecian Urn* (1819), the warped lament of ▷ Thomas Hood's *Silence* (1823), or in the sorrows of ▷ Frankenstein's monster (1818), it speaks of what cannot be grasped except in fragmentary or unfinished form. But to cross the void, to forsake perfected truth for the sake of broken authenticity is a perilous, even impossible, task. In Keats, like Wordsworth, it leads to a space of pure difference; without beginning or end; without any purpose except the ceaseless affirmation of error:

No stir of life
Was in this shrouded vale, not so much air
As in the zoning of a summer's day
Robs not one light seed from the feather'd grass,
But where the dead leaf fell there did it rest:
A stream went voiceless by, still deaden'd more
By reason of the fallen divinity
Spreading more shade

(*The Fall of Hyperion*, 1, 309–16)

The difference between Keats and Wordsworth lies in their response to this void. With Keats' work, unlike *The Prelude*, the death of nature is welcomed as a source of negative inspiration. The poet draws a perverse energy from self-destroying enthralments. In the realm of Saturn, in a grotesque parody of Hegelian self-consciousness, everything comes to a productive halt. 'But where the dead leaf fell there did it rest'. A sense of immobility threatens to paralyse the poem. The subject dissolves into silence and shade. When, at last, time is restored, one would expect the syntheses of the *Aufhebung*: the subject 'dies' in order to be reborn on the altar of rational knowledge. But time in Keats' poem

> *. . . works a constant change, which happy death*
> *Can put no end to; deathwards progressing*
> *To no death*
>
> (1, 259–61)

Thus, rather than 'a-mortizing' death, Keats has made death immortal; a process to which there is no end and from which it is impossible to derive sense. Death has become useless, unworkable within any system of dialectical reason.

It is for this reason that the incompletion of the poem is so piquant and attractive. The shade of the fallen divinity is darkness *in extremis*. Thus, at the 'end', it is not the enlightenment of Apollo but the 'blank splendour' of Saturn's gaze that has most force. We are no longer faced with the desire for presence but the passivity of absence. The black hole of these eyes ('Half-closed, and visionless entire they seem'd"24" Of all external things') drains the enkindled gaze of the poet so that the dawning of the ephebe ('Knowledge enormous makes a God of me', *Hyperion*, 3, 113) is stymied, halted without a power to break through.

In the place of the dream of absolute knowledge, therefore, Keats has offered the birth of a more terrible beauty: the affirmation of death, not as mastery and endurance, but as 'Life's high meed' (*Why did I laugh to-night*, 14). In making this claim, Keats perhaps more so than any other Romantic poet points the way to a space purged of self-consciousness. As he writes in a famous letter: 'As to the poetical Character itself . . . it is not itself – it has no self – it is everything and nothing – it has no character . . . A poet is the most unpoetical of any thing in existence: because he has no Identity'. To achieve this destiny – the will to give up self – Keats utilizes the substitutions and displacements inherent in poetic language. With Keats, unlike say Wordsworth, Byron, Shelley or Coleridge, words are embraced as forces of dispersal. Here language coincides with that which does not coincide; it leads, in advance, to the *détournement* of all unity. The result is an achieved dearth of meaning; the opening of a positive void. The provocation of a time before history.

What these fragments unwittingly celebrate, therefore, is the 'power' of uselessness and failure: 'I have left "24" My strong identity, my real self' (*Hyperion*, 1, 114). And in leaving the 'real self', the poet has escaped the utilitarian world of subject-making and self-mastery. Art, to paraphrase Blanchot, has deprived the writer of the power to say 'I' – the birth of Apollo will not take place – but it has enabled him to pronounce on the nature of the other. It has allowed him to accept his death.

VII

> *Nothing, whether deed, word, thought, or text, ever happens in relation, positive or negative, to anything that precedes, follows, or exists elsewhere, but only as a random event whose power, like the power of death, is due to the randomness of its occurrence.*
> (Paul de Man, 'Shelley Disfigured', in *Deconstruction and Criticism*)

> *only nomadic affirmation remains*
> (Maurice Blanchot, *Le Pas au-delà*, 1973).

How does Romanticism manifest itself in the present age? I have argued in this essay that Romanticism continues because of the Romantic fragment's affirmation of incompletion. We must understand, however, that the fragment does not affirm its lack of perfection in relation to a lost totality. Despite the perceived official message of

Romantic poems, Romanticism is not, in essence, nostalgic. As Timothy Clark notes, whilst for Schlegel 'every part can be a whole' and conversely 'every whole can be a part', the truth of Romanticism does not reside in the recovery of an original unity or lost totality but in the moment of its interruption; the moment, that is, where the fragment 'maintains a singularity that both exceeds and resists subsumption, yet by this same token this singularity falls short of a determined identity and constitutes a lack in any putative totality.' What Romanticism affirms, therefore, is its ceaseless failure to present itself in a completed form. This is why Romanticism continues, right up to the present, to unwork the possibility that human knowledge may be articulated as a unified or total 'system'.

Where do we measure this effect in our time? One could trace it in any of the major avant-garde movements of this century: in Dada, Surrealism, Abstract Expressionism, postmodernism and so on – wherever the random or the aleatory speaks of a lack beyond the insistence of being. For the purpose of this essay I will focus on a prose fragment by the poet Paul Celan (1920–70) entitled 'Conversation in the Mountains' (1959). At the start of this text an unnamed Jew steps out of his hut to take an evening walk. The Jew, it emerges, is blind. As he shuffles along, tapping his stick on the stone, a first person stutters into life. The voice comes to us unannounced, babbling, as if from nowhere: 'Do you hear . . . here I am I, I am, I am here'. It could be the voice of the Jew, of the author, or of something entirely 'other', something at odds with the confidence and supreme virility of the eloquent 'I' – the authentic, integrated self of much Romantic literature. But whoever owns this voice and wherever it comes from, the ontological certainty of 'Here I am', the phrase with which Abraham responds to the call of God, is put into a position of extreme jeopardy. No one replies, night falls, and the voice stutters: 'I, I, I', broken and alone. Presently, another person approaches; it is the Jew's cousin, equally blind, equally uncertain. For a long time there is silence but 'it's just a pause, just a hiatus, an empty space'. At last the dialogue begins:

> *'You came from far away, came here . . .'*
> *'So I did. I came. I came like you.'*
> *'I know that.'*
> *'You do know. You know what you see: The earth has folded up here, folded over once, then twice, then three times, and split open in the middle, and in the middle there is water, the water is green, the Green is white and the White comes from still further on high, comes from the glaciers, one could say, but shouldn't, that this is a language for the here and now, the Green with the White within, a language for neither you nor me – for I ask, for whom is it meant, this earth, for I say it is not meant for you or for me – a language to be sure, without I or Thou, merely He, merely It, do you understand, merely She and nothing more'.*

In general terms, what this obscure and beautiful text acknowledges is the condition of its own belatedness. Without nostalgia and without pathos Celan draws attention to the persistence of a certain way of thinking, the presence/absence of an epistemology that might, for want of a better word, be called 'Romantic'. This is manifested in several ways. To begin with the mountainous landscape is haunted by the ghosts of Romantic agony: with Shelley's ▷ *Mont Blanc* (1816); Wordsworth's *Simplon Pass*; Büchner's *Lenz* and Byron's ▷ *Manfred*. But where, for example, in *Lenz*, the failure of the idealized unity of unity and difference, self and other, propels the 'I' into suffering and madness, here Celan manages to find a way of *affirming* that very failure in such a way that it is the voice of the overwhelming 'other' rather than of the isolated ego that has priority. By emphasizing 'babble' over eloquence, 'borrowed' language over original speech, the Green language of the 'here and now' over the White language of the timeless and transcendent, a 'Conversation in the Mountains' presents an ethical challenge to the ontological drama of Romanticism. Where Byron's ▷ *Childe Harold* expresses a hopeless desire for ownership of the 'one word' (3, 97), the unnamed Jew speaks of a language 'without I or Thou'; in so doing he enables us to welcome difference: a difference between ascent and descent, origin and anarchy, activity and passivity, mastery and subjection.

For Celan, drawing on the unacknowledged insights of Romanticism, language cannot be owned, or grasped; it comes from elsewhere, like the power of death. And like death, to adapt the words of Emmanuel Levinas, the 'He', 'She' or 'It' of language 'announces an event over which the subject is not master, an event in relation to which the subject is no longer a subject' ('Time and the Other', 1987); yet only in relation to this can the subject come into being. To signify, therefore, one must begin with annihilation, with death. I say 'a flower', and magically the concept flower appears – separated or split from the material flower. In many ways Romantic poetry 'begins' by recording this original violence – the way in which language creates meaning by negating the internal essence of things. When Celan writes, however, we are moved by silence rather than by words, by what is not there rather than by what is. The breaks and pauses in his writing gesture towards a region saturated with non-sense – a non-sense which turns out, paradoxically, to be the radical sense of poetry. Here we cannot help but supply the relations that the random event of language would deny. Death inhabits language; it is we who signify.

12 'I could a tale unfold': Women, Romanticism and the Gothic

Alison Milbank

Until recently the prose fiction of the Romantic period – least of all the ⊳ Gothic genre – would have scarcely merited a mention in a volume such as this. Poetry at the end of the eighteenth century was considered a higher form than prose, while the novel still had many years of struggle ahead before gaining equal intellectual respectability. In a letter to ⊳ Wordsworth concerning ⊳ Walter Scott's narrative poem ⊳ *Marmion*, Coleridge centres his criticism precisely in a perceived similarity to prose romances: it is a 'novel versified'. *Marmion* reminds him particularly of the Gothic, and he proceeds to classify the qualities of the latter form:

> *I amused myself a day or two ago in reading a Romance in Mrs Radcliffe's style with making out a scheme which was to serve for all Romances a priori; only varying the proportions. A baron or baroness, ignorant of their birth and in some dependent situation; castle on a Rock; a sepulchre – at some distance from the Rock – Deserted Rooms – underground passages – Pictures – a Ghost, so believed – or a written record – blood in it – a wonderful Cutthroat, etc. etc.*

Coleridge's reductive account of Gothic tropes makes them seem like a cumbersome set of stage machinery, and has the effect of distancing himself and his correspondent from the sort of literature described, even though many of the same motifs would find their way into mainstream Romantic verse, not least Coleridge's own productions. ⊳ *Christabel* (1816) is in essence a medieval romance, complete with baron, ancient castle, haunted dog, and a mysterious lady who claims to have been captured by strange warriors, and exerts seemingly magical powers, while the ⊳ *Rime of the Ancient Mariner* (1798) would itself have an influence on later Gothic writing.

However, Coleridge's scheme does fit many a Gothic tale in which the same elements are continually re-articulated, and the pleasure of repetition is itself a quality of Gothic fiction. The form was already well-established by the turn of the century, the first 'modern' Gothic fable, ⊳ *The Castle of Otranto* by ⊳ Horace Walpole, having been published thirty-six years before. For, in contrast to the ordered neo-classicism of the earlier eighteenth century ran an equally strong strain of interest in the 'Gothic' feudal past, in graveyard melancholy, and in human passions and extreme emotional states. At first, Walpole's tale was indeed presented as an authentic medieval account, so that its supernatural machinery of a giant helmet and the rapacious lusts of the tyrannical owner of the Castle were seen as of a part with a less enlightened, though fascinating, age. When its contemporary authorship was revealed, Walpole still sought to cast an aura of distance and privilege about his tale by locating its origin in a dream. (⊳ Mary Shelley was to do the same in relation to ⊳ *Frankenstein*, as Coleridge too with *Kubla Khan*, which remains unfinished because of the interruption to his opium-induced dreams by the importunate 'person from Porlock'.) Whereas Walpole – and later ⊳ William Beckford, author (in French) of the exotic *Vathek*: *An Arabian Tale* (1786) – were aristocrats with archeological interests and the money to realize their architectural and historical fantasies in Strawberry Hill's Gothic turrets and the excesses of Fonthill respectively, soon women writers began to essay 'Gothic' fables.

▷ Clara Reeve's *The Champion of Virtue* (1777), which was later revised as *The Old English Baron*, and went through many editions, was described by its author as 'the literary offspring of *The Castle of Otranto*'. However, quite deliberately, this novel eschews the spectacular supernatural effects of its fictional parent. Edmund, the true heir to the Baron Fitz-Owen's castle, does indeed evoke ghostly presences when he spends the night in a haunted room, but the visitants are his own parents, and, as in the case of Hamlet, the reader is at some liberty to interpret the haunting as an inner vision rather than an external apparition. An early specimen of the historical novel, Sophia Lee's *The Recess: A Tale of Other Times* (1783–5), charts the tragic adventures of two daughters of Mary Queen of Scots, to escape the jealous ire of Elizabeth I. The novel's historical setting and the subterranean dwelling of its sister heroines, who live immured in the underground chambers of a Tudor great house which had formerly been a convent, makes it as engendered, as it were, Gothically. As Chris Baldick's introduction to *The Oxford Book of Gothic Tales* indicates, it is the centrality of an ancient, ruinous house – imprisoning the protagonist and mediating the baleful presence of the past over all its inhabitants – which makes a novel or short story Gothic. The house in a tale like Edgar Allan Poe's 'The Fall of the House of Usher' is itself a protagonist.

So before the arrival of ▷ Ann Radcliffe's first novel *The Castles of Athlin and Dunbayne* in 1789, all the Gothic tropes that Coleridge lampooned were current and operating with different degrees of effectiveness. Radcliffe's novel already seems implicitly parodic of the genre it presents with its warring barons, plethora of captives, ambushes and secret passages, and a low-born young man who saves the life of a chief and marries the latter's sister after his nobility and heroism is finally established. Yet in the four novels which succeeded this first attempt, Radcliffe took the Gothic novel to new heights, and helped establish it as the most popular form of fiction until the 1820s.

Women writers of Gothic tended to turn away from interest in the guilty (male) tyrant and usurper towards his victims: in *The Recess* women become, as they were to remain, the central focus, so that Ellen Moers can describe the whole Gothic phenomenon as 'a device to send maidens on journeys'. At a time when the picaresque novel was becoming virtually extinct, the errant heroines of Sophia Lee – whose travels take them all over England, to the Continent and even to the Americas – seemed evidence of a new form, the episodic journey tale. The glamorous foreign locations were, however, merely changes of background to enable ever grosser treacheries and extreme dangers to assault the heroine. There is no attempt in *The Recess* to bring the settings to imaginative life as elements themselves in the story.

It was Ann Radcliffe who, in a series of novels published between 1789 (the year of the ▷ French Revolution) and 1797 (the year before Coleridge and Wordsworth's ▷ *Lyrical Ballads*), brought together these various elements of the Gothic, combining Lee's historicism and interest in enclosed spaces with Walpole's *Otranto*, with its castle and the central feud, and blending with these a strong emphasis on the natural landscape. Up to that time, in England, only the poet and novelist ▷ Charlotte Smith had employed extended natural description as a part of her fiction, though in her *Emmeline, The Orphan of the Castle* (1788) the sea-shore reveries of the eponymous heroine are but a small part of a conventional romance plot. In Radcliffe's tales, however, the landscape itself increasingly takes the part of an actor in the plot; indeed, ▷ Keats (who likened titles of two of his own poems to 'Mother Radcliffe's' style) commented on this feature in a letter recording an 1819 visit to a friend in Devon 'whence I intend to tip you the Damsel Radcliffe – I'll concern you, and grotto you, and Waterfall you, and wood you, and water you, and immense rock you, and tremendous sound you, and solitude you'. The nouns here become verbal in the same manner that the Radcliffe landscape precipitates human action. One typical example of this phenomenon occurs in *A Sicilian Romance*, when Madame de Menon, governess to the lost heroine, enjoys an evening stroll:

> *The evening was remarkably fine, and the romantic beauty of the surrounding scenery invited her to walk. She followed the windings of a stream, which was lost at some distance amongst luxuriant groves of chestnut. The rich colouring of evening glowed through the dark foliage, which spread a pensive gloom around, offered a scene congenial to the present temper of her mind, and she entered the shades. Her thoughts, affected by the surrounding objects, gradually sunk into a pleasing and complacent melancholy, and she was insensibly led on.*

Giving herself up to the rhythms and impulses of the scene, Madame de Menon seems to sleep-walk as she is 'moved' in her emotions and the windings of the stream to find a solitary figure, who proves to be her lost pupil. Others who see the girl and violate the intentions and shapes of the landscape are continually misled. They fail to notice the beauty of nature, so are unable to be helped by her benign presence or 'read' her secrets.

The locations of Radcliffe's novels are (with the exception of her first, which is set in Scotland) in continental Europe, principally France, Switzerland and Italy. It is usual to argue that the reason for the foreign nature of her locations was the more exotic terrain, the prevalence of Catholicism and the likelihood of violence and political instability. All this may be true, but it is also clear that Radcliffe had read and absorbed ▷ Rousseau's novels *Emile, ou L'Education* (1756) and *Julie, ou la nouvelle Héloise* (1760) with their depictions of the Alps and lakes, woodlands and pastoral retreats. Several of Radcliffe's novels describe the upbringing of her heroines away from the corruptions of urban upper-class life, where parents devote themselves to the education of their children in the arts and in the appreciation of nature. Rousseau's privileging of the 'natural' over the civilized, and his theories of childhood innocence were enormously influential all over Europe in the development of Romanticism. Wordsworth is often credited with bringing these ideas into the mainstream of English poetry, but Radcliffe before him, especially in *The Romance of the Forest* (1791) and *The Mysteries of Udolpho* (1794), explored the educational ideas, as well as the social vision of little quasi-familial groups in rural retreat that are found in Rousseau's two novels. *The Romance of the Forest* includes a Swiss pastor, La Luc, whose family dispense charity, nurse the sick of their village, and teach its children, taking their pleasure in rambling among the scenic wonders of their Alpine home. The landscape provides simultaneously secure protection from outside influences and imaginative and religious expansion through the aesthetic power of mountain scenery. Similarly, *Udolpho* opens with a description of Emily St Aubert's childhood home, La Vallée:

> *on the nearest banks of the Garonne, in the province of Gascony, stood, in the year 1584, the chateau of Monsieur St Aubert. From its windows were seen the pastoral landscapes of Guienne and Gascony, stretching along the river, gay with luxuriant woods and vines and plantations of olives. To the south, the view was bounded by the majestic Pyrenées, whose summits veiled in clouds, or exhibiting awful forms, seen, and lost again, as the partial vapours rolled along were sometimes barren, and gleamed through the blue tinge of air, and sometimes frowned with forests of gloomy pine, that swept*

downward to their base. These tremendous precipices were contrasted by the soft green of the pastures and woods that hung upon their skirts; among whose flocks, and herds, and simple cottages, the eye, after having scaled the cliffs above, delight to repose. To the north, and to the east, the plains of Guienne and Languedoc were lost in the midst of distance; on the west Gascony was bounded by the waters of Biscay.

This protective environment of the heroine is as safely enclosed as the Garden of Eden itself, with its 'luxuriant' vegetation 'bounded' on the south by mountains, and on the west by 'the waters of Biscay'. Conversely, 'the eye' – which is the prime mover of the scene rather than the ambulant human – has its gaze extended into a seeming infinity to the north and east, in which direction the plains are 'lost in the mist of distance'. The Edenic motif continues in the precise historical dating of the narrative in 1584, the year of the renewal of the Catholic League, which aimed to defeat French Protestants under Henry of Navarre, the next heir to the throne, and also the time when Philip of Spain's 'Catholic Enterprise' to depose Elizabeth was becoming known in Britain. Navarre is within the Pyrenees, so that all the force of Protestant religious 'purity' is enclosed in this region of natural sublimity, while the River Garonne on which the Aubert chateau is built had been the site of an earlier battle in the same Wars of Religion. Moreover, Aubert, the heroine's surname, recalls that of Navarre's mother, Jeanne d'Albret, whose lands were in Gascony. So La Vallée holds its 'repose' precariously on the Huguenot frontier, at risk from Catholic invasion, as Adam and Eve were from the serpent's grateful incursion. This admixture of the historical religio-political with the stately procession of aesthetic contrasts of an ideal landscape gives a new intensity to picturesque landscape, and energizes its portrayal. Emily St Aubert, the novel's young heroine, is soon to leave this pastoral retreat for a journey among the Pyrenees to restore the health of her bereaved father, and then for further travel, after his death among the mountains, for the gaieties of Venice, a setting which Radcliffe uses as a lovely but mystifying place of absence and false sentiment, in contrast to the stark, awful heights of the Pyrenees. Venice causes the visitor to look down, not up, as to 'the lower world', to see narcissistic reflections in the waters, rather than a presence in nature that takes one beyond the self: 'a new heaven and trembling stars below the waves, with shadowy outlines of towers and porticos'.

The Venetian scenes of *Udolpho*, with their plangent music that so moved ▷ Byron in ▷ *Childe Harold* are, in the context of the novel's aesthetic and moral scheme, ominous. Venice's physical lowness, as well as its fairy-tale illusionism, makes it a place dangerous to the imagination. For although Radcliffe anticipates the place of the mental landscape and the concept of the sublime in Romantic poetry, she is far from sharing the latter's boundless trust in the imagination. The sublime in the poetry of Wordsworth becomes a moment of direct imaginitive and moral expansion; indeed, it is the imagination itself which is sublime, as it acts to break down categories, and to unite disparate elements. But in the eighteenth-century tradition which culminates in Radcliffe and finds its most cogent expression in ▷ Edmund Burke's *Essay on the Origin of the Sublime and Beautiful* (1757), it is objects extraneous to the self that are sublime, such as great natural phenomena, mountains or cataracts, great poetry and art, architectural size and longevity, powerful heroes and, most of all, the Divine. The awful greatness of such as these overwhelms the viewer; first, the viewer is made aware of her own littleness, her subjection to forces beyond her own control, and only then, through this very negation, is a sense of imaginative access possible. So Ellena, the heroine of *The Italian*, who has been imprisoned in an Apennine convent by her aristocratic lover's powerful mother, has her prison both confirmed and yet transcended by the power of the view from her turret window:

> *Here, gazing upon the stupendous imagery around her, looking, as it were, beyond the awful veil which obscures the features of the Deity, and conceals him from the eyes of his creatures, dwelling as with a present God in the midst of his sublime works; with a mind thus elevated, how insignificant would appear to her the transactions, and the sufferings of this world.*

She concludes that her enemy was therefore 'unable to chain her soul, or compel her to fear him, while he was destitute of virtue'.

The result of this aesthetic communion is not a quietist acceptance of destiny – all Radcliffe heroines show considerable fortitude, dignity and resourcefulness under hosts of murderous attacks. But the communion is the means by which the heroine is able to maintain a sense of her value as a person by, as it were, a mental dramatization of her actual life-threatening situation, which is projected into an imaginative *agar* or conflict, where the spectator's self-hood is almost annihilated, only to be re-established on a re-ordered footing as holding its place in God's providential order. 'Thus man, the giant who now held her in captivity, would shrink to the diminutiveness of a fairy,' thinks Ellena.

This trope of the entrapped woman fleeing the sexual or murderous attentions of a male attacker is one of the most potent devices of the Gothic genre, and survives right up to literature and film of the present day. Walpole uses it in *Otranto*, but the woman writers of the 1790s and after gave it a central focus. In one sense it is a universal story, and one, in the more realist setting of contemporary seduction that formed the matter of Samuel Richardson's novels *Pamela* (1740–1) and *Clarissa* (1747–8) as well as many novels of sensibility. Despite feeding from that tradition, the Gothic novel generally gives the predatory attacks an exotic architectural setting, so that the woman is pursued through the labyrinthine passages of the tyrant's castle, monastery, or actual prison. But just as Richardson is making a mainly bourgeois critique of aristocratic ethical codes of honour and shame, Radcliffe and her host of imitators filling the lists of the ▷ Minerva Press inevitably place their villains among the relics of a decayed aristocracy. *Udolpho's* Montoni is further and further confined to his own estates and castles as his only field of force (the Byronic hero owes his pride and sense of damnation to such figures, as they owe theirs to Milton's portrayal of Satan in *Paradise Lost*). In charting the escape of women from confinement, the Gothic aligns itself to the Enlightenment project itself, though its potential political radicalism is tempered by the fact that the heroine and her associates generally go on to live a retired *Emile*-like existence in *private* life only; the public realm is eschewed for a pastoral retreat consisting of the polite arts and the social joys of the sublime.

This kind of 'female' Gothic is not necessarily to do with the gender of the author. ▷ William Godwin writes an interesting version of 'female' Gothic in *Caleb Williams, or Things as they Are* (1794), in which the hero, having found evidence of his aristocratic master's crime, is pursued by agents of that noble but flawed Falkland the length and breadth of Britain. Finally brought to account for a supposed crime against Falkland, Caleb abandons attempts to assert his innocence in favour of a version of sublime discourse dramatizing his own destitution and the impossibility of escape; the hero finally triumphs. 'Male' Gothic writers include the Marquis de Sade, M.G. Lewis (▷ 'Monk' Lewis), ▷ Charles Maturin, Francis Latham and the youthful ▷ Shelley. Their works are characterized by a doomed and guilt-ridden hero, such as Ambrosio in Lewis' *The Monk*, who breaks endless taboos by committing murder, incest and fratricide (amongst other sensational things), in a careless desire for mastery and forbidden knowledge. Ambrosio is in some ways the archetypal 'male' Gothic hero, who assaults barriers to penetrate inwards, whether into bodies, locked chambers or castles, in contrast to the female protagonists of the Radcliffean mode who seek to move beyond the 'bounds', whether of room, castle, or limited subjection as women.

In ▷ Mary Wollstonecraft's tale *Maria: or, The Wrongs of Woman* (1798) feminism and the 'female' Gothic form come together overtly in a contemporary setting, with the following opening:

> *Abodes of horror have frequently been described and castles, filled with spectres and chimeras conjured up by the magic spell of genius to harrow the soul, and absorb the wondering mind. But, formed of such stuff as dreams are made of, what are they to the mansion of despair, in one corner of which Maria sat, endeavouring to recall her scattered wits.*

The 'mansion of despair' referred to is a lunatic asylum, where Maria has been incarcerated by her husband for pecuniary gain, separating her from her young children. The story quickly develops beyond the usual confinement-escape plot: Maria falls in love with a fellow inmate, with whom she elopes, and although the loves remained unfinished at Wollstonecraft's death, her notes indicate a subsequent disillusioned parting, regret and sad decline. This is far removed from the Radcliffean 'female' Gothic, and indeed none of the three women writers most closely associated with the Romantic poets – Wollstonecraft herself, ▷ Dorothy Wordsworth and Mary Shelley – embraces the 'female' Gothic plot described above (Dorothy Wordsworth was in fact the recipient of the Coleridge letter mocking Radcliffe). Mary Shelley's powerful *Frankenstein* in particular declares its status as 'male' Gothic in its subtitle 'The Modern Prometheus', this mythological figure being the stealer of fire from the gods, and tied to a rock in eternal agonies, the archetypal damned hero of dark Romanticism. Frankenstein also transgresses the divine order in trying to create in his own image, and is explicitly associated with ▷ Milton's Satan. The story is, of course, a powerful critique of the creation of a being without mothering, without any associates, no Eve for his Garden of Eden, nor friendly angels to advise.

The prevalence of Miltonic elements in Mary Shelley's *Frankenstein* is often attributed to the influence of her husband's reading of ▷ *Paradise Lost* while she was writing her novel. There is, I believe, quite another reason why Milton's epic of the destruction of perfect human relations and the fall of nature provides a common source for Mary Shelley and for the hundreds of Gothic tales imitating Ann Radcliffe. In the late twentieth century, we may miss the radical elements in Milton's portrayal of sexual relations, being aware only of the hierarchy that makes Eve for Adam, while he is made for God – 'He for God only, she for God in him'. However, eighteenth-century feminists, reading Milton in the context of a history of extreme misogyny, latched onto the dignity and intelligence of Milton's Eve; there were even editions of *Paradise Lost* that changed the line quoted above to 'He for God only, she for God *and* him' (my emphasis). In the context of this positive reading of Milton, the 'female' Gothic plot of entrapment of the heroine by a villain whose grandeur, pride and superhuman qualities mark him as a descendant of Milton's heroic Satan takes on a new resonance. It is a re-narrating of the scene of Eve's temptation by Satan in such a way that she is freed from guilt (because it is through no fault of her own that she is in his power), and also triumphs, she escaping her persecutor's clutches and he bringing him to justice. The scene in Radcliffe's *Romance of the Forest* in which Adeline is taken by the ruffians of a Marquis to his luxurious villa, where attempts on her virtue take the form of delicious fruits and ices, sweet music, delightful smells, the arts of poetry, oratory and the vanity of mirrors, parallels the wiles of the serpent tempting Eve to eat the fruit of the tree of knowledge. Several references to the tempter of Milton's *Comus* point the moral.

The many references to the works of Milton, Shakespeare – which indeed exceed those of the later poet in frequency – and Collins, Thomson and other eighteenth-century poets suggest the literary ambitions of the Gothic novel. At a time when Romantic poetry, notably the *Lyrical Ballads*, seeks to represent the rhythms of ordinary speech and the concerns of the countryman and peasant, the Gothic novel seeks a different, and elevated, poetic expression. Novels such as Radcliffe's and Charlotte Smith's contain many verses by their authors, put into the mouths of their characters, by which their heroines reach towards literary expression of their feelings of awe and delight. Tags from the English poets furthermore seek to situate Gothic writing in a specifically native tradition, which was only beginning to enjoy the status of 'classic' awarded primarily to Greek and Latin literature. Classical learning in this sense is denied most female Gothic writers, so they reach out to an alternative genealogy. Many Gothic tales were published in *The Lady's Magazine*, and despite its subtitle – *Or, Entertaining Companion for the Fair Sex Appropriated Solely to their use and Enjoyment* – which stressed entertainment, the frontispiece engraving showed a serious intent. It shows the Goddess of Wisdom, Minerva, pointing, with a lady in a well-stocked library reading *The Lady's Magazine*, towards a Pantheon, or 'Temple of Wisdom'. The publishing house that poured out most Gothic tales was also called The Minerva Press.

The quotation in the title of this chapter is from Act I, Scene v of Shakespeare's *Hamlet*, and sounds a note of self-confidence in authorship when it heads Ann Radcliffe's *A Sicilian Romance*. Its context in the original play, however, gives it a darker meaning. The speaker is the ghost of Hamlet's father:

But that I am forbid
To tell the secrets of my prison-house
I could a tale unfold whose lightest word
Would harrow up thy soul, freeze thy young blood,
Make thy two eyes like stars start from their spheres,
Thy knotted and combined locks to part,
And each particular hair to stand on end
Like quills upon the fretful porcupine.

The most obvious effect of the Gothic novel is its ability to arouse fear and terror in its readers. Indeed, Joanna Baillie's play on the passion of fear, *Orra* (1815), concerns a girl who goes mad through giving herself up to superstitious terror, which has been fed by reading Gothic romances. In these tales, episodes of country rambling and delightful exploration of ruined abbeys which arouse elevated meditations are followed by terrifying discoveries of murdered corpses, or attacks by murderous monks. Although ghosts haunt the pages of the Gothic tale they are quite often explained away as natural phenomena. The view of critics like Coleridge (who renders the supernatural real in his own work) is that such a move to demystify shows a lack of confidence on behalf of Gothic authors, so that the whole plot collapses like a fairy palace into the air. This is, however, to miss the point of the terrific fears of the Gothic heroine, which are a form of testing. In ▷ *Northanger Abbey* (1818), ▷ Jane Austen's credulous heroine expects all the horrors of Udolpho to come true when she stays with the Tilneys in their ancient house; and she casts the General as a Montoni in wickedness, believing him to have murdered his former wife. Of course, he is nothing of the sort, and a great deal of comedy is extracted from Catherine's mistake. Yet, although her more exotic accusations are wrong, she is proved right in that Tilney is a tyrant – if a petty one – who unceremoniously throws her out of the house when he learns that she is not an heiress.

Northanger Abbey is a parody of a Gothic story, but in many ways it also possesses a true Gothic plot, in which the supernatural fear is removed only in order to reveal an actual bodily threat or deception. The castle around which ghostly sighs are expended in *A Sicilian Romance*, terrifying its inhabitants, is indeed haunted, but not by a spectre. Instead, its vaults contain the living person of the Marquis' first wife, who was immured there years before, so that he could remarry. The supernatural is demystified in order to reveal the unjust and demonic character of the Marquis, and of his order. There is an inherent feminism in the Gothic of the entrapped heroine, which is not to be found in the 'male' Gothic of Lewis and Maturin, in which the supernatural is an unquestioned reality. The heroines of 'female' Gothic learn to eschew the thrills of terror over dark passages and ghostly knocks in favour of religious awe and fear in the power of God's creation, to forego their fears of the seemingly sublime tyrant for the transposed power of the sublime. It is perhaps here that the form shows most clearly its critique of Romanticism. The heroines who become the true heirs of the tyrant's castle do not go on to inhabit their possession, but leave it to become even more ruined. There are moves today in post-structuralist literary criticism to deconstruct the claims of the Romantic poet to universality and harmony of vision and to elucidate instead an awareness of loss and the indeterminacy of meaning. This process is akin to the demystification of the sublime villain and his supernatural castle by the Gothic novel which acts to 'ruinate' his image. Perhaps we may even come to see the Gothic now not as some clumsy articulation of tropes that merely anticipates a glorious Romanticism, but rather see Romantic poetry itself, with its omnivorous claims and egotistical sublime, as merely a variation on the 'male' Gothic.

'The Babel din': Theatre and European Romanticism 13

Edward Burns

The Romantic period seems like the last place one might look for drama, at least if what one is looking for are durable dramatic texts. As far as the literary history of English drama is concerned, the period is a kind of hiatus between the comedy of manners of the ▷ Georgian stage and its revival in the ▷ Victorian period in conjunction with a new realism and the importation from France of the well-made play. At the same time, theatricality is very much a part of Romanticism, as even our cultural stereotypes of the period reveal. We imagine Romantic poets in theatrical and cinematic clichés; we *picture* them, enjoying a flamboyant self-presentation, or we cosily enshrine their quietism. Poets of no other period are dramatic characters in this sense. Behind the clichés is an intuition of the importance of theatre to the period. Yet it is a paradoxical importance, in which a distrust of and revulsion from theatre is as important as a belief in the medium, and in which the results of the writers' worrying at, subverting, deconstructing the processes of theatrical communication can be seen as fully in other forms of writing as on the stage itself.

In Britain in the late eighteenth and early nineteenth centuries, the theatre as an institution moves decisively from the position of cultural centrality it had occupied from the late Middle Ages onward. This is in sharp contrast to the role theatre played in the development of European Romanticism. The riot that took place at the first performance of Victor Hugo's *Ernani* is often seen as a pivotal moment in French culture, as a break away from classical tradition and the establishing triumph of Romantic form and feeling. The critic and philosopher Madame de Staël in *Germania* analyses the difference between northern and southern Europe in terms of opposing trends in drama, and, writing in the aftermath of the ▷ French Revolution argues that the invention of a new form of tragedy is a necessary response to the historical moment. Germany saw a revolution in standards of theatrical production and design under the patronage of the provincial courts, and the transition from classicism was again played out on the stage – in the late classical works of ▷ Goethe, in the historical plays of Schiller, and in the exploration of extremes of feeling and situation in the ironic tragedy of Kleist, and Buchner. Both in Germany and in Italy opera was the medium of politically engaged Romanticism and of the bourgeois Romanticism of private feeling – in the pathos of Donizetti's *Lucia di Lammermoor* or the popular and nationalist propaganda of Verdi's *Nabucco*, the political mythopoeia of Wagner's *Ring*, or the picturesque pathos of Weber's *Der Freischütz.* The development of theatre in Europe is very much a product of its direct engagement with political and social change. In European culture the idea of a 'theatre revolution' is by several degrees less absurd than in England.

In Britain in this period; theatre occupies a culturally marginal position, seemingly more escapist than engaged. Theatrical activity tended to the condition of pantomime, ▷ Gothic melodrama or farce. One can see this in the case of a work like the German composer Weber's opera *Oberon*, where centrally Romantic concerns – the creation of Keatsian (▷ Keats) alternative worlds of fancy from the medieval, the oriental and the faery – has to be fitted to the mixed form of an English musical entertainment, as dictated by the taste of Madame Vestris' regime at Covent Garden, and realized in a libretto of spectacular numbers sketchily linked by Planché's doggerel rhyme. It is ironic then that the major aesthetic impulse towards European Romantic form in theatre and music came from English dramatic texts, largely through the rediscovery of the plays of ▷ Shakespeare, seen as combining a powerful appeal to feeling, a broadly democratic (in the sense of non-aristocratic) representation of history, and an apparently 'natural' flexibility of form. British writers, writing for or about the theatre, are just as frustrated and exacerbated by the limits and problems of theatrical representation as they are excited by its possibilities. But the reasons for this are as much internal to the impulses and attitudes of English Romanticism as they are attributable to the contemporary state of theatrical practice. The second might as well be seen as a result of the first. To understand English Romantic theatre we should look first at the phenomenon of the anti-theatrical, not as opposition to the theatre as an institution, from a political and religious point of view (like that of the sixteenth- and seventeenth-century Puritans), but as a creative response that problematizes theatrical representation. British Romanticism turns theatre inside out, to find new theatrical forms, or to take over the formal and philosophical opportunities made visible in this process into other media.

Theatre and Anti-theatre

Charles Lamb gives the classic statement of the anti-theatrical position in his *On the Tragedies of Shakespeare, considered with reference to their Fitness for Stage Representation* (1812):

> *It may seem a paradox, but I cannot help being of opinion that the plays of Shakspeare [sic] are less calculated for performance on a stage, than those of almost any dramatist whatever. Their distinguishing excellence is a reason that they should be so. There is so much in them, which comes not under the province of acting, with which eye, and tone, and gesture, have nothing to do.*
>
> *The glory of the scenic art is to personate passion; and the more coarse and palpable the passion is, the more hold upon the eyes and ears of the spectator the performer obviously possesses . . . The sublime images, the poetry alone, is that which is present to our minds in the reading.*
>
> *So to see Lear acted, – to see an old man tottering about the stage with a walking-stick, turned out of doors by his daughters in a rainy night, has nothing in it but what is painful and disgusting. We want to take him into shelter and relieve him. That is all the feeling that the acting of Lear ever produced in me. But the Lear of Shakespeare cannot be acted.*

For Lamb the problem is the contrast between the means the stage uses to communicate a feeling or an idea, and the immensity of that idea or the intensity of that feeling. As he says later of costume and scenery:

> *I remember the last time I saw Macbeth played, the discrepancy I felt at the changes of garment which he varied . . . if things must be represented, I see not what to find fault with in this. But in reading, what robe are we conscious of? Some dim images of royalty – a crown and sceptre, may float before our eyes, but who shall describe the*

fashion of it? . . . This is the inevitable consequence of imitating everything, to make all things natural. Whereas the reading of a tragedy is a fine abstraction.

'Dim images . . . fine abstraction . . .' Lamb values reading above theatrical spectatorship for its very freedom from the specific and the material.

A split response to theatre is typical of English Romanticism, an emotionally and intellectually irreconcilable split between the limitations of theatre as a material and social phenomenon, and the transcendant possibilities, the metaphysical sublimity or psychological intensity which can be produced by certain theatrical texts or the powers of certain performers. The first is often characterized in terms of its inadequacy to the second, and that inadequacy can be presented as grotesquely comic, pitiful, sinister, or in its way rather charming. The idea that the written is of a subtlety superior to the visual seems at first almost commonsensical to us, which suggests how influential Romantic anti-theatricalism is in British culture. But to a pre-Romantic spectator, these sentiments would seem maladroit or eccentric. To make a broad contrast to eighteenth-century perceptions of theatre, one might point to the moment in Henry Fielding's *Tom Jones* (1749) when Tom and his companion Partridge go to see *Hamlet* performed by David Garrick, the great actor who above all others raised the perceived aesthetic and social status of acting, but whose revered memory is also under attack in Lamb's polemic:

. . . Partridge was all attention, nor did he break silence till the entrance of the ghost; upon which he asked Jones, 'What man that was in the strange dress; something,' said he, 'like what I have seen in a picture. Sure it is not armour, is it?' Jones answered, 'That is the ghost.' To which Partridge replied with a smile, 'Persuade me to that, sir, if you can. Though I can't say I ever actually saw a ghost in my life, yet I am certain I should know one, if I saw him, better than that comes to. No, no sir, ghosts don't appear in such dresses as that neither.' In this mistake, which caused much laughter in the neighbourhood of Partridge, he was suffered to continue, 'till the scene between the ghost and Hamlet, when Partridge gave that credit to Mr Garrick, which he had denied to Jones, and fell into so violent a trembling, that his knees knocked against each other, Jones asked him what was the matter, and whether he was afraid of the warrior upon the stage? 'O la! sir,' said he, 'I perceive it is now what you told me . . . but if that little man there upon the stage is not frightened, I never saw any man frightened in my life . . .'

The difference between Lamb and Fielding is that the joke here is on Partridge, not on the actors. Here it is the inept, not the aesthetically super-sensitive spectator who can't find the necessary mind-set, the necessary ability to be simultaneously moved by a performance and to retain a sense of its medium. A more adept pre-Romantic spectator would be able to contain his or her participation in the imaginative transaction within an acceptance of the material facts of theatrical communication. Samuel Johnson gives the most cogent expression of the pre-Romantic perception of theatre in his *Preface to The Plays of William Shakespeare* (1765):

The truth is, that the spectators are always in their senses, and know, from the first act to the last, that the stage is only a stage, and that the players are only players. They come to hear a certain number of lines recited with just gesture and elegant modulation. The lines relate to some action, and an action must be in some place.

Within these terms, the disjunction between the means of representation and the thing represented is acceptable, non-problematic, and often exploited confidently for theatrical effect.

If Romantic writers worry at the validity of theatrical representation, they never do so in quite so crude a way as to simply reject the stage altogether. Hazlitt, Keats, and ▷ De Quincey, to give just three examples, wrote powerfully of the impact on them of stage performances of Shakespeare. When Keats writes on the star Shakespearian actor ▷ Edmund Kean (in 'Mr Kean', a review in *The Champion*, 21 December 1817), he celebrates just that importation of the body into performance through the written text, which for Lamb and others is disruptive of the seriousness of theatrical texts:

> *There is an indescribable gusto in the voice, by which we feel that the utterer is thinking of the past and the future while thinking of the instant. When he says in 'Othello' 'put up your bright swords for the dew will rust them,' we feel that his throat has commanded where swords were as thick as reeds. From eternal risk, he speaks as though his body were unassailable.*

The actor's voice and presence here flesh out, literally, the written verse, in ways that parallel Keats' straining after a sense of the physical in his own writing. Hazlitt's response is not simply to an intensity of aesthetic effect and psychological insight as, when he writes of *Coriolanus*, to the immediate relevance of the politics of the plays to the public unrest of the times.

> *Shakespear [sic] has in this play shewn himself well versed in history and state-affairs. 'Coriolanus' is a store-house of political common-places. Any one who studies it may save himself the trouble of reading Burke's 'Reflections', or Paine's 'Rights of Man', or the debates in both Houses of Parliament since the French Revolution or our own. The arguments for or against aristocracy or democracy, on the privileges of the few and the claims of the many, on liberty and slavery, power and the abuse of it, peace and war, are here very ably handled . . .*

For De Quincey, in 'On the Knocking on the Gate in *Macbeth*', from the ▷ *London Magazine* of October 1823, the imaginative power of *Macbeth* allows us to share the world of the murderer, while Shakespeare's attention to the theatrical effect of the mundane ensures that the effect of the play lies in that conjunction of the imaginative and the material which, being at the heart of theatrical representation, is for Lamb the very reason for disowning the medium:

> *. . . when the deed is done, when the work of darkness is perfect, then the world of darkness passes away like a pageantry in the clouds: the knocking at the gate is heard; and it makes known audibly that the reaction has commenced; the human has made its reflux upon the fiendish; the pulses of life are beginning to beat again; and the re-establishment of the goings-on of the world in which we live, first makes us profoundly sensible of the awful parenthesis which had suspended them.*

This access to heightened experience, in a kind of retreat from, and subsequent return to the real, can be a quintessentially Romantic pursuit of intense and even forbidden feeling, but its meaning can be reversed as pure escape. Lamb himself writes engagingly of the charms of stage comedy, though in ways that neutralize it as a social event, depriving it of any critical or political force:

> *I am glad for a season to take an airing beyond the diocese of the strict consciense, – not to live always in the precincts of the law-courts, – but now and then, for a dream-while or so, to imagine a world with no meddling restrictions – to get into recessess, whither the hunter cannot follow me . . . I come back to my cage and my restraint the fresher and more healthy for it.*
>
> ('On the Artificial Comedy of the Last Century', 1822)

Theatre here has lost any power of its own, becoming instead the vehicle of a kind of pathos. Its flimsiness and evanescence are an appeal to the Romantic sensibility, through which it acquires a beauty and a meaning it does not in itself possess.

Spectacle and Meaning; Wordsworth at the Theatre

In his ▷ autobiographical poem ▷ *The Prelude* (1805), ▷ Wordsworth tracks the growth of his own poetic powers against the itinerary of his life to the date of writing. His 'Residence in London', the subject of Book Seven, takes him through a progression of 'spectacles'; life itself is a random and confusing sort of theatre. His description of the city moves from the drama of London street life –

> *. . . the quick dance*
> *Of colours, lights, and forms; the Babel din;*
> *The endless stream of men, and moving things . . .*

– through 'raree shows', 'troops of wild beasts, birds and beasts/ of every nature', panoramas in paint or modelling

> *By scale exact, in model, wood or clay,*
> *From shading colours also borrowing help,*
> *Some miniature of famous spots and things . . .*

to more established forms of theatre,

> *. . . where living men,*
> *Music, and shifting pantomimic scenes,*
> *Together joined their multifarious aid*
> *To heighten the allurement. Need I fear*
> *To mention by its name . . .*
> *Half rural Sadlers Wells?*

Wordsworth leads us through this maze with constant injunctions to 'see' – so establishing the continuity of theatrical spectatorship with our response to the wider scope of London life; so setting us up, with him, as a wondering audience. The theatre itself is an enchanting concentration of instances of human ingenuity and credulity, and the end to which it points is a loving acknowledgement of the weakness of mankind, of our need for representations of the outside world, in 'imitations, fondly made in plain/ Confession of man's weakness and his loves'. As with Lamb, the inadequacy of theatre is its charm – more than charm in this case, as it points towards a human truth.

This then is one Romantic attitude to theatre – its flimsiness is a token of our own, and recuperable by the imagination as a symbol of transience, a kind of pathos. Wordworth offers examples which identify that pathos with the feminine:

. . . I am crossed
Here by rememberance of two figures, one
A rosy babe . . . child as beautiful
As ever sate upon a mother's knee;
The other was that parent of that babe;
But on the mother's cheek the tints were false,
A painted bloom. 'Twas at a theatre
That I beheld this pair . . .

This falseness and frailty of this 'fallen woman' has been brought to his mind by his memory of a play about another, but that was

. . . too holy theme for such a place,
And doubtless treated with irreverence
Albeit with their very best of skill,
I mean, o distant friend! a story drawn
From our own ground, – the Maid of Buttermere.

The theme may be too easily profaned in its shocking transposition from private contemplation to the public stage, but its place on that stage, and the train of thought that it sets on, is typical of one Romantic association – of the fragility and falseness of theatre, and the frailty of the feminine. One might think of the centrality of the fallen woman, Verdi's eponymous *La Traviata*, for example, or its source, Dumas' *La Dame aux Camélias*, to nineteenth-century opera and to the 'well-made play' of the French and English theatre of the mid- to late century; also of the nineteenth-century cult of the ballerina, a cult that depended on the dancer's use of her own athletic ability to transcend the body in the representation of the ethereal, while at the same time inevitably offering to the spectator the spectacle of her own physical vulnerability, and/or, in certain contexts, her sexual availability. There was an appalling death rate among the star teenage ballerinas of the Paris stage caused by the vulnerability of their gauze costumes to the gas used to light the theatres, a fact that increased their star status in a morbid overlap with the roles of sylphs, butterflies and willi into which their femininity was idealized. The frailty of theatrical illusion is also the frailty – moral and physical, untrustworthy and desirable – of woman.

But this characterization of theatre can be elided with another; theatre can crystallize the troubled relation of sights to words, and thus can lead back to the problem of human knowledge. Wordsworth notes:

The champion, Jack the Giant-killer; Lo!
He dons his coat of darkness; on the stage
Walks, and achieves his wonders, from the eyes
Of living mortal safe as is the moon
'Hid in her vacant interlunar cave'.
Delusion bold! and faith must needs be coy;
How is it wrought? His garb is black, the word
'Invisible' flames forth upon his chest.

Because it relies on both spectacle and words and because, more crucially, it opens up that cultural, post-Enlightenment, shift in which the relation between the two cannot be taken for granted, theatre can make available to the Romantic writer the mystery and problems of belief inherent in our relation to other beings and to the universe.

Jack jokily anticipates a moment later in the book which Wordsworth introduces with a metaphor linking London street-life back to the theatre:

Amid the moving pageant, 'twas my chance
Abruptly to be smitten with the view
Of a blind Beggar, who, with upright face,
Stood, propped against a wall, upon his chest
Wearing a written paper, to explain
The story of the man, and who he was.
My mind did at this spectacle turn round
As with the might of waters, and it seemed
To me that in this label was a type,
Or emblem, of the utmost that we know,
Both of ourselves and of the universe;
And, on the shape of the unmoving man,
His fixed face and sightless eyes, I looked,
As if admonished from another world.

The blind man poses the problem of reading spectacle in a more serious context than does Jack. ⊳ Byron's Cain, in the play of the same name (1821), falls prey to Lucifer in his attempt to make sense of the received word in terms of his own visionary experience:

Thou speaks't to me of things which long have swum
In visions through my thought: I never could
Reconcile what I saw with what I heard.

Cain rebels against the restriction of 'the word' in that it can only tell him of a reality defined by God's law or the narrative of his father's fall. Lucifer operates in the gap between words and vision – the space of theatre, and of an ineluctable mystery. Poems in Wordsworth's ⊳ *Lyrical Ballads* (1798) turn on a similar problem of knowledge, opened up by the gap between what we see in human beings or on the landscape, and what we hear, read or say. Knowledge of the other may always be beyond our grasp. Here the sense of the failure of theatre is presented as the irreconcilable demands of word and spectacle, whose paradoxical conjunction can lead us to a more profound idea, that of the mystery that conditions our being in the world.

A third version of theatre, of spectacle given meaning in attention to its inevitable aesthetic failure, is animated at the end of the book in the description of Bartholomew Fair, the great annual summer fair that had been a London institution since the Middle Ages:

What a Hell
For eyes and ears! what anarchy and din
Barbarian and infernal, – 'tis a dream,
Monstrous in colour, motion, shape, sight, sound!

Wordsworth goes on to list:

. . . buffoons against buffoons
Grimacing, writhing, screaming, – him who grinds
The hurdy-gurdy, at the fiddle weaves,
Rattles the salt-box, thumps the kettle-drum,

And him who at the trumpet puffs his cheeks,
The silver-collared negro with his timbrel,
Equestrians, tumblers, women, girls, and boys,
Blue breeched, pink-vested, and with towering plumes.

This chaos, to be contrasted with the orderly rural celebration that starts the next book, is an image of Hell. We can find similar ideas of violent and chaotic carnival in many Romantic artists. Theatre, spectacle, masquerade, all are potentially sinister, in that nothing, or some evil violent impulse, may lurk behind masks and role play. Theatre is the domain of the monstrous, in Goya, Ensor or Poe. Perhaps there is an intuition here of the closeness of carnival and revolution. Simon Sharma in his book *Citizens* points out that many activists in the French Revolution were theatre people. Revolution is in itself a theatrical act, in that it must convince, proselytize or terrify through acts that are witnessed and have been calculated for their emblematic concision and their powerful impact. Carlyle, in *The French Revolution*, presents events visually, in a flamboyantly decorative style that suggests a kind of phantasmagoria or violent pantomime, from which the English reader is protected by the Channel, as a kind of orchestra pit. More domestically, but just as subversively, theatre in ▷ Jane Austen's ▷ *Mansfield Park* (1814) provides the outlet for anti-social energies seen, however limited their scope to work, as disruptively libidinous.

So in these three instances, reading Wordsworth for what he shares with a wider Romantic culture, we encounter a perception of theatre in which a sense of the inadequacy of dramatic representation, the uncertain relation of material means to transcendent ends, can paradoxically be recouped by the Romantic imagination as a source of pathos and charm, of epistemological mystery, or as the threat of chaos and transgressive impulse.

Poets in the Theatre

For a while Byron was a member of the sub-committee of management of the ▷ Drury Lane Theatre:

– the number of plays upon the shelves were about five hundred; . . . the Scenes I had to go through! – the authors – and the authoresses – the Milliners – the wild Irishmen – the people from Brighton – from Blackwell – from Chatham – from Cheltenham – from Dublin – from Dundee – who came in upon me! – to all of whom it was proper to give a civil answer – and a hearing – and a reading – Mrs Glover's father an Irish dancing Master of Sixty years – called upon me to request to play 'Archer' – drest in silk-stockings on a frosty morning to show his legs – (which were certainly good & Irish for his age) – & had been still better – Miss Emma Somebody with a play entitled the 'Bandit of Bohemia' – or some such title or production – Mr O'Higgins – then resident at Richmond – with an Irish tragedy in which the unities could not fail to be observed for the protagonist was chained by the leg to a pillar during the chief part of the performance . . .

The Dickensian exuberance of this description – written in Byron's self-imposed exile – has something of Wordsworth's mixture of relish and distrust for the theatrical enterprise. It must be set against Byron's panic when he heard that one of his plays, the Venetian tragedy *Marino Faliero* (1821), was to be given a London performance:

I have nothing more at heart – (that is in literature) than to prevent this drama from going upon the Stage; – in short – rather than permit it – it must be suppressed

> *altogether . . . What damned fools these speculating buffoons must be not to see that it is unfit for their Fair or their booth.*

There is an aristocratic disdain here for the compromised business of theatrical production, masking a real fear of exposure to a judging audience (a fear that motivates Faliero, a victim of slander and its obsessive avenger, within the play). The incident highlights the paradoxical conjunction of theatricality and intense privacy in Byron's own self-presentation. Like Wordsworth's worries about theatre, it raises the immediate question – then why write plays? Why do the complete works of almost any nineteenth-century poet end with a sequence of obscure, largely unread, dramas?

One answer lies in the growing reverence for Shakespeare, and the rediscovery of his contemporaries, as shown in Lamb's *Specimens of English Dramatic Poets, who lived about the time of Shakespeare* (1808). The acting of Garrick and Macklin in the mid-eighteenth century, and Garrick's interest in visually powerful stagings, aiming at a maximum of emotional impact, helped to create a cult of Shakespeare as the great dramatist of character, of individuals forced to confront metaphysical and emotional extremes. Shakespeare becomes the writer to emulate, as a genius whose imaginative powers transcend the limits of individual selfhood. As Keats puts it in a famous letter of 1817, implicitly comparing himself to Shakespeare:

> *As to the poetical character itself (I mean that sort, of which, if I am anything, I am a member; that sort distinguished from the Wordsworthian, or egotistical sublime; which is a thing per se, and stands alone), it is not itself – it has no self – it has every thing and nothing – it has no character – it enjoys light and shade – it lives in gusto, be it foul or fair, high or low, rich or poor, mean or elevated, – it has as much delight in conceiving an Iago as an Imogen; what shocks the virtuous philosopher delights the chameleon poet.*

But in emulating Shakespeare by employing dramatic form, Romantic writers tackle what they already perceive as the near-insoluble problem of imitating a supreme genius who managed to be the greatest poet *and* the greatest dramatist in one. Their aim becomes decisively unattainable – the aim of creating the art-work that combines both language and action at their highest intensity to create something which seems to transcend the material means of both. Keats achieves what he sees as the Shakespearian quality much more convincingly in his non-dramatic verse than in his plays *King Stephen* or *Otho the Great*.

It is ironic that an impetus to bardolatry that came from the theatre, particularly from Garrick, should then – as for Lamb – act towards the marginalization of theatre. But at the same time, the presence of powerful actors provided a major stimulus for writing. The Romantic theatre is a theatre of stars; Edmund Kean, William Charles Macready and ▷ Sarah Siddons all stimulated writers like Hazlitt and Keats to vivid response and reaction. Performing in large, gaslit theatres, they promoted a style of playing in which plays are conceived of as a collection of individual roles, and in which those roles are thought of as a series of moments of high-impact emotion, developed through the actors' larger-than-life presence as the unfolding of an intense, if monolithic, character. The actors were stars in that their personal charisma became part of the material through which they created characters, and through which, in a broader sense, the human and the transcendent could be linked in an event whose transience was part of its Romantic meaning. Lamb writes dismissively of 'Mrs S's . . . thrilling tones' and '. . . impressive looks'. But for Hazlitt, in 'On Mrs Siddons' and in 'Mr Kemble's Retirement' (from *A View of the London Stage*, 1818), such personal attributes point to 'something above nature':

She raised Tragedy to the skies, or brought it down from thence . . . Power was seated on her brow, passion emanated from her breast as from a shrine. She was tragedy personified. She was the stateliest ornament of the public mind. She was not only the idol of the people, she not only hushed the tumultuous shouts of the pit in breathless expectation, and quenched the blaze of surrounding beauty in silent tears, but to the retired and lonely student, through long years of solitude, her face has shone as if an eye had appeared from heaven; her name has been as if a voice had opened the chambers of the human heart, or as if a trumpet had awakened the sleeping and the dead. To have seen Mrs Siddons, was an event in every one's life.

Hazlitt's praise of Kemble points to those qualities of Romantic acting which shaped a contemporary conception of Shakespeare, and which dictated the structure and emphasis of plays inevitably conceived as star vehicles:

His person was moulded to the character. The weight of sentiment which oppressed him was never suspended . . . So in Coriolanus, he exhibited the ruling passion with the same haughty dignity of demeanour, the same energy of will, and unbending strernness of temper throughout. He was swayed by a single impulse . . . in such characters, Mr Kemble had no occasion to call to his aid either the resources of invention, or the tricks of the art: his success depended on the increasing intensity with which he dwelt on a given feeling, or enforced a passion that resisted all interference or control.

Romantic writers wanted to tap this kind of power – ▷ Shelley wrote ▷ *The Cenci* (1819) for Eliza O'Neill, ▷ Coleridge rewrote *Osorio* (1797), initially commissioned through Byron's agency as *Remorse*, after it was then rejected by ▷ Sheridan; it was performed successfully at the Drury Lane Theatre in 1813. The actors inspire the creation of an intense, internalized, often deliberately obscure vein of feeling in the central character, whose unfolding and realization in action is the dynamic of the piece. Less happily, the hierarchies of the star system ensure that other figures are more sketchily and stereotypically conceived.

Whatever level of achievement is represented by these two plays – for *The Cenci* is perhaps the most theatrically powerful of English Romantic plays, and in *Remorse* Coleridge makes intriguing use of a scenic and narrative form that is romantic in the older sense (the sense in which Shakespeare's late plays are called romances) to track his psychological and ethical interests – the most impressive body of dramatic work was produced by a writer who stayed deliberately aloof from the two overwhelming influences of the genius of Shakespeare and the charisma of the Romantic actor. Byron marks a deliberate distance not only from the English stage of his time, but from Shakespeare and his contemporaries, 'the mad old English dramatists', whom he sees as equally inimical to the creation of an aesthetically satisfying and philosophically serious theatre. Instead his models are the Italian dramatist Alfieri, and, in the case of *The Deformed Transformed* (1824), Goethe's ▷ *Faust*. But neo-classical English plays – Dryden's *All For Love* in the case of *Sardanapalus* (1821) and Otway's *Venice Preserv'd* in relation to *Marino Faliero* – allow him to place himself in an alternative tradition to the Shakespearean.

The most immediately striking feature of his dramatic *oeuvre* is the extreme energy, the voraciousness for subject matter, which shape a sequence varied in form but closely interlinked in essential concerns. Byron wrote most of the plays at Ravenna, between 1821 and 1823, in parallel to a spate of self-searching journal writing. An obsession with time, a fascination with the individual as defined against its passing, and his attempt to piece together some token against it, in fame or memory, is common to both. The protagonists of the drama are often presented as literally or figuratively 'on the brink', caught facing obliteration, but in that fact, in that moment, the more clearly defined as irreducibly individual. The two biblical plays, or 'Mysteries', show Byron at his most revolutionary in form and argument. *Cain* presents an archetypal Romantic protagonist, impelled by his dissatisfaction with the word of the father, the word of God as received by Adam; rejecting the patriarchal order that that imposes, he seeks knowledge in dialogue with Lucifer, and a flight into 'the abyss of space'. At the end, after his murder of Abel, his identity is marked ineradicably on him, 'the mark of Cain' which will protect him from human violence, but show him also as an outsider, condemned to wander the earth, exiled both by God and by the curse of his mother Eve. This individuating alienation, the expulsion not simply from society, but from 'natural' human relations, as represented here by a mother-child relationship, is repeated in other plays by Byron, and is visible too in figures like the 'Daemon' in ▷ Mary Shelley's ▷ *Frankenstein* (1817), or Coleridge's *Rime of the Ancient Mariner* (1798). In *Heaven and Earth* (1822), Byron takes up the story of Cain's descendants, as rebels against and victims of the biblical word; Anah and Aholibamah are loved by rebel angels, who rescue them from the deluge by taking them to some other planet, to form an alternative world; but the play ends with Japhet, the son of Noah who also loves Anah, contemplating the flood that has swept away all other human life except for that contained within the Ark, which, as the curtain falls, sails towards him, offering unwanted rescue.

The confident apocalyptic vision of these plays is matched by the forging of a new dramatic language, a kind of beginning-of-the-world style, transparent, flexible, and carefully freed from the conventional pseudo-Shakespearian linguistic gestures that can bring so many other Romantic plays dangerously close to pastiche. The push of the play is towards the protagonist's discovery of a language through which he can confront his universe in his own terms, and free himself from those that build oppressive imaginative structures around him. The historical plays ground a similar conflict in 'the labyrinth of statecraft'; in *The Two Foscari* (1821), a doge of Venice is forced to preside over the torture and death of his son, and in *Marino Faliero*, another elderly doge is impelled by his inability to gain legal redress for a slander on his young wife to join a rebellion against the state of which he is nominally head, and is punished not only by death, but by the official obliteration of his memory. In both plays the male characters are rendered powerless within the apparent exercise of power, by their own inability to think outside the terms that power sets for them. By contrast, the women, Marina and Angiolina, respectively, like the women in the Mysteries, stand outside these structures, are fluid and active where the men are trapped, but end unable to resist the processes they oppose. Myrrha, in *Sardanapalus*, is another of the strong, centrally placed woman characters who distinguish Byron's plays from those of most English dramatists of any period. Sardanapalus himself refuses to engage with the historical role set down for him as Assyrian emperor, preferring to exist within the unchronicled life of drink, appetite and a freely-indulged bisexuality, but in his love for Myrrha, and in his out-facing of palace revolution, he shapes a historic role for himself in the lyrical act of a flamboyant Romantic suicide.

He mounts the pile
Now, Myrrha!
Myr. Art thou ready?
Sar. As the torch in thy grasp.

MYRRHA fires the pile.
Myr. 'Tis fired! I come.
(As MYRRHA springs forward to throw herself into the flames, the Curtain falls).

The unfinished *Deformed Transformed* runs ironic, magical variations on some of those themes, in its Faustian tale of a hunchback who is granted a beautiful heroic body by a dark stranger and transported by him to fulfil an historic role in the Bourbon siege of Rome. The sardonic, puppet-like style of the play, with its casually spectacular action and arch games of historic and sexual identity, make it a kind of cartoon-strip version of Byron's most personal concerns, an improvisation for which an infinite number of endings, and therefore none at all, can be projected.

In complete contrast to Byron's practice, Shelley in *The Cenci* works consciously from within a Shakespearean and ▷ Jacobean tradition, seeking to combine this with the sacred sense of tragedy and taboo that informs his two favourite Greek plays, Sophocles' *Antigone* and *Oedipus Tyrannos*. The two lead roles, Beatrice Cenci and the Count her father – a Sadean figure whose infinite cruelty and capacity for evil is a perverse expression of his sense of himself as God's substitute within the patriarchal family – are conceived of in terms of the charisma and sustained emotionally intensity of the star Romantic actor. The subject – the Count's rape of his daughter and her parricidal revenge – again encapsulates an archetypal Romantic conflict, at the end of which Beatrice, proclaiming her innocence, becomes a radical image of idealistic revolution: 'what a world we make of it,' she says, 'the oppressor and the oppressed'. Though father-daughter incest was not representable on the London stage, the play (with *Cain*, the most frequently revived of the period) is crucially *of* the stage, in that Beatrice's appeal across time and through memory to the sympathy of an audience is close to what Shelley thinks tragedy is *for*, as he describes it in ▷ *A Defence of Poetry* (1821). Sympathy both redeems the injustices of history, and improves its audiences in an extension of their capacity for pity and love. Shelley makes sympathetic and creative use of his Jacobean precedents – particularly Webster's *The Duchess of Malfi* and Shakespeare's *Othello* and *Antony and Cleopatra* – to create a tragic heroine whose victory is her remaking of herself into a kind of icon for future generations. To that extent the sense of the past that colours the verbal style is as much a part of the effect of the play as the questioning simplicity and freshness of Byron's language in *Cain*.

There was of course a vast amount of new writing for the Romantic stage coming from outside this group of major poets; but though our interest is inevitably focused on writers we know from their work in other genres, the context of their work can be supplied from elsewhere. Questions of power are paramount in the theatre of the period. ▷ Walpole's pioneering play *The Mysterious Mother* (1768), like his Gothic novel ▷ *The Castle of Otranto*, situates power witin the family, and uses a half-serious Gothic fiction to explore the Oedipal relation of family, power, and sexuality, within a flamboyantly visual theatrical mode. Milman's *The Destruction of Jerusalem* takes on historical and biblical themes in terms of an implicitly anti-semitic Christian providentialism. Both plays are Romantic in their investment in revolutionary change, and the polarity of the two – Walpole's investment in the subversion of the family, as opposed to Milman's in the expression of an epochal moment – represents interests that Byron and Shelley were able to combine, creating dramas where familial conflict and personal crises of identity are expressions of rifts and eruptions in a social and cosmic order perceived as patriarchal; in the strict biblical sense in the case of Byron's Mysteries, in Shelley's, in the creation of a ▷ Renaissance world-view informed by his fascinated if atheistical interest in the structures of the Catholic church.

Wordsworth and Coleridge, like Shelley, create villainous protagonists who represent in some sense the opposite of their project for the play. In *The Borderers* (1797), Wordsworth centres the play on Rivers (Oswald in the 1842 revision), a character of mysterious motives, Iago-like in the terms of Coleridge's conception of Iago – a figure of 'motiveless malignancy'. Wordsworth's characters are borderers in a literal sense, living on the Anglo-Scottish borders, but they are 'borderers' in a figurative sense also. As an ex-Crusader, Oswald exists between the occidental, Christian world, and another more mysterious life. He impels the other characters towards liminal states of mind, a process that climaxes in his involving Mortimer/Marmaduke in the motiveless murder of a virtuous old man. Wordsworth denied that the play in general, and this character in particular, had anything to do with his sense of the French Revolution. It is nevertheless hard to escape a sense that new psychological and moral possibilities – particularly in relation to a perverse idealism or to an abstract villainy of self-convinced integrity – are made available to these dramatists by their own attempts to come to terms with the Revolution, the Terror, and the rise of ▷ Napoleon.

Drama by Negatives: Closet drama and the Legacy of Experiment

The Borderers is structured deictically – that is, its scenes, dialogues and narrations point to, rather than enact, an event. It is thus more like the semi-dramatic form of sections of *Lyrical Ballads* than it is like *The Cenci* or *Cain*. It points to events in the past, or to psychological events whose relation to action one has simply to take for granted. Although this builds towards a compellingly original dramatic form, it also raises the same issue as Byron's worry about performances of *Faliero*. How far are these plays *of* the stage? The term 'closet drama' seems appropriate not only to Romantic plays, but to the form Shakespeare takes in Romantic reading. Coleridge is reported to have said in a lecture that:

> *He had seen Mrs Siddons as Lady, and Kemble as Macbeth – these might be the Macbeth's of the Kembles, but they were not the Macbeth's of Shakespear; he was therefore not grieved at the enormous size and monopoly of the theatres, which naturally produced many bad and but few good actors; and which drove Shakespear from the stage, to find his proper place, in the heart and in the closet . . .*

In the 1805 version of *The Prelude* 'the imaginative power . . . slept' at the theatre despite Wordsworth's passionate response 'to the changes of the scene':

> *. . . yet all this*
> *Passed not beyond the suburbs of the mind;*
> *If aught there were of real grandeur here*
> *'Twas only then when gross realities,*
> *The incarnation of the spirits that moved*
> *Amid the Poet's beauteous world, called forth*
> *With that distinctness which a contrast gives*
> *Or opposition, made me recognize*
> *As by a glimpse, the things which I had shaped,*

And yet not shaped, had seen and scarcely seen,
Had felt, and thought of in my solitude.

In the 1850 version that last line becomes:

When, having closed the mighty Shakespeare's page,
I mused, and thought, and felt, in solitude.

This serves to clarify some very abstract reasoning, but at the same time it marks a displacement of the theatrical experience by the 'page', a decisive appropriation of Shakespeare for private 'musing'. Shakespeare's place for many of the Romantics is somewhere between stage and page, in private recitation. Wordsworth and his sister ▷ Dorothy read Shakespeare aloud in their garden at Grasmere, and readings from Shakespeare are much more acceptable at Mansfield Park than a full-scale performance of ▷ Mrs Inchbald's translation of *Lovers' Vows* (1798). The key Shakespeare texts are those that lend themselves to the solitary imagination. *A Midsummer Night's Dream*, *Romeo and Juliet* and *Hamlet* generate fantasies that colour decisively the visual arts and music of the period. All three plays are plays of fancy and introspection where the theatre, in *A Midsummer Night's Dream* and *Hamlet* especially, is as unstable an amalgam of the compelling and the inadequate as it is for the Romantics.

The term closet drama is more usefully applied to texts in dramatic form which none the less explore the unstageable, visionary imagination. In Byron's *Manfred*, the hero's solitary encounters with a spirit world, as well as the mysteries of his melancholic temperament and necromantic powers, invite us to visualize for ourselves, but baffle any attempt to fix our ideas in physical form. Byron thus exploits the half-pictorial conjuring of the imagination which Lamb found preferable to the materiality of the stage. The spirit voices are created as lyrical interventions, somehow outside the text, but not given any clear identity or placing. Shelley's *Prometheus Bound* again exploits the visionary potential of closet drama, with an aptness to an action that is essentially the action of language itself, in the shift from a tragic discourse to a language of love and liberty; the tragedy dissolves into an ideal action, as physical and mental suffering are transcended. But it would be a mistake to use this as a convenient category for plays that are simply unconventional in their theatrical demands. Even Byron's impossibly extravagant stage directions (like Wagner's) are theatrical, if in the perverse sense of the theatrically anti-theatrical, of theatre against itself. They are best seen as experimental, as attempts to remake theatre, to operate at its limits. *Cain* was admired and staged by Stanislavsky and Grotowski, *The Cenci* by Antonin Artaud; indeed these practitioners of the twentieth-century avant-garde can be seen to be the heirs of Romantic theatre. The push towards new forms in which theatre transcends itself, in which the material is somehow consumed in a spiritual or metaphysical force, is most powerfully developed in Artaud's *The Theatre and Its Double*, his manifesto for a 'theatre of cruelty':

In the anguished, catastrophic period we live in, we feel an urgent need for a theatre which events do not exceed, whose resonance is deep within us, dominating the instability of the times.

Our long habit of seeking diversion has made us forget the idea of a serious theatre, which, overturning all our preconceptions, inspires us with the fiery magnetism of its images and acts upon us like a spiritual therapeutics whose touch can never be forgotten.

Everything that acts is a cruelty. It is upon this idea of extreme action, pushed beyond all limits, that theatre must be rebuilt.

Keats, writing of Kean, and quoting Coleridge's formulation in *Christabel* (1816) of an hallucinatory exploration of sexual nightmare, celebrates the intensity of theatrical representation, its mysterious agency, its acting on its audience, in strikingly Artaudian term:

The spiritual is felt when the very letters and prints of charactered language show like the hieroglyphics of beauty; – the mysterious signs of an immortal freemasonry! 'A thing to dream of, not to tell!'

The tension between material means and transcendent ends that is at the core of Romantic theatre has a double outcome – on the one hand a struggle to achieve intensity by redefining the relation of word and image ('It is not a question of suppressing the spoken language,' Artaud writes, 'but of giving words approximately the importance they have in dreams'), and on the other an acknowledgement of the inadequacy of theatre, or rather of the gap between the semiotics it employs, in costume, set acting and so on, and the ideal – spiritual, political, sexual – to which it points. This gap can be expressed as nostalgia or charm, or it can be articulated more challengingly as camp, as a deliberate subversion of style and sexuality. In either case, the force of Romanticism is more intensely present in current theatrical experiment than the obscurity of many of the texts would suggest.

What then is the legacy of Romantic theatre? If we judge the validity of plays from the past in terms of their potential for revival on the modern stage, then a handful of these plays have proved their worth. *The Cenci* and *Cain* have each had several successful recent revivals, and a notable revival of *Marino Faliero* has confirmed the theatrical power of Byron's dramatic writing. But this is a limiting criterion. Tennyson and Browning, for example, wrote plays more professionally tailored for performance, but these scarcely work, as can even the most awkward of the earlier Romantic dramas, at the edge of Romantic aims and concerns. A work like Thomas Lovell Beddoes' *Death's Jest Book* (1825–48), a shapeless, self-generating fantasia on the themes of Jacobean drama, is much more compelling in its exploration of the twilit area between stage and page, word and vision, of the Gothic imagination in which the 'dead' text becomes 'live' fantasy. In terms of theatre, the main legacy of the Romantic period is the double-edged one of a split perception of theatre, as both transcendent and ludicrous, no longer to be taken for granted, but always an insistent question where spectacle problematizes the relation of language to perception. In terms of theatrical practice, we have the enshrinement of the actor, the star Shakespearean, whose cultural status validates the low standing of the profession as a whole. But we have also the idea, however inconsistently or implausibly realized, of a theatre that can be in some sense revolutionary. By putting the value of theatre in doubt, while simultaneously participating in a highly theatrical culture, British Romanticism forces a redefinition of the aims and means of theatre, and sows the seeds of the twentieth-century avant-garde.

14 The Construction of 'Victorianism'

Jane Thomas

Young, fair, trusted, beloved, new to business and to life, the sovereign of England commences a reign, that in the course of nature will last beyond the generations who hailed in the Reform Bill – the charter of new liberties – the transition to a new stage of British Culture.

So wrote ▷ Edward Bulwer-Lytton in the ▷ *Westminster Review* in 1840, less than three years after the eighteen-year-old Princess Alexandrina Victoria had been informed of the death of her uncle, ▷ William IV, in the early hours of 20th June, 1837. The accession of Queen ▷ Victoria was seen by many to mark a new stage in the history of the British nation, and the literature produced from the mid-1830s to the turn of the century has been indelibly stamped with her name. The term 'Victorian' functions as a convenient and historically bounded division of the cultural past, signifying the period between the decline of ▷ Romanticism and the beginnings of the cultural renaissance known as modernism. However, an examination of the literature of this period reveals the haziness of these boundaries. Lines of descent can be traced from the concerns of the major Romantics through the poetry of the ▷ 'Spasmodics', ▷ Tennyson, the ▷ Brontës, the ▷ Brownings, the ▷ Pre-Raphaelites, the ▷ sensation novels of ▷ Mary Braddon, ▷ Mrs Henry Wood and ▷ Rhoda Broughton, right up to the later novels of ▷ Thomas Hardy. Likewise, the modernist concern with narrative experiment can be detected in novels such as Emily Brontë's ▷ *Wuthering Heights* and Hardy's *The Well-Beloved* which appeared half a century later. At the same time the commonly agreed concerns of Victorianism predate Victoria and persist until World War I.

The adjective 'Victorian', denoting a variety of styles, manners and cultural forms 'typical' of a period which spans almost a century, was coined in 1875, and yet as countless critics have revealed, it is impossible to draw an objective and clear literary and cultural picture of an age that changed so rapidly that traditional certainties and ways of knowing were constantly under threat. The choice of the monarch's name as a means of labelling the period is significant. As literary historian Richard Stein has indicated it signifies an attempt to reduce a confusing and unstable world to a known and identifiable regularity (*Victoria's Year*). This essay seeks to chart that process whilst at the same time examining some of the ways in which Victorian literature of the period resists annexation.

In the early years of the 19th century, the British monarchy had seemed less than stable. By 1811, George III was acknowledged to be insane and his son became regent. For the next nine years he reigned as sovereign *de facto*, acceding to the throne on the death of his father in 1820. George IV, whose reign as king lasted less than ten years, systematically deprived the crown of any moral influence or credibility through his indolence, deviousness and profligate behaviour. He was succeeded by his brother, William IV, who died seven years later. Despite fathering ten illegitimate children by the Irish comedienne Dorothea Jordan, William was unable to produce a legitimate heir to the throne. His two daughters by Princess Adelaide of Saxe-Meningen died in infancy. His niece Princess Alexandrina Victoria, who was next in line for the throne, signified a distinct break with tradition – a new and auspicious beginning. Not only did the nation identify with her, it also elevated her into a monumental symbol of its own perceived greatness. The name Alexandrina was dropped in favour of the more anglicized and suitably exalted Victoria – instantly recognizable by her subjects as a shout of triumph. Victoria is derived from the noun 'victory', signifying supremacy or superiority.

Much was made of Victoria's youth, beauty, innocence and femininity, all of which contrasted strongly with her predecessors. England was enthralled, regarding her as a type of elder sister called upon to sacrifice her youth and desires in order to mother her recently orphaned family. Her situation began to resemble a best-selling sentimental novel of the time. On her death in 1901 ⊳ Henry James wrote, 'We all feel a bit motherless today.'

As Victoria matured, married and established her own not inconsiderable empire of nine children she became increasingly a symbol of Britain's own development. Britain's energies became focused on consolidation, expansion and economic advance. It gained in confidence, in direction, in size and in complacency. By 1851, as Victoria entered a comfortable middle age, Britain was at the height of its wealth, power and influence. T. Frederick Ball, a contemporary historian, wrote in 1886 of Victoria's ability to inspire 'a loving loyalty that seemed to thrill all classes of the community'. The politician Daniel O'Connell (known in Ireland as 'The Liberator') is quoted as having made a thunderous declaration that, if it was necessary, he could get '500,000 brave Irishmen to defend the life, the honour, and the person of the beloved young lady by whom England's throne is now filled'. On a visit to Leeds Victoria reputedly felt as though she was entering a foreign country, so limited was her knowledge of the conditions of the industrial north of England. Nevertheless a quarter of a million people came to pay their respects to her and *The Times* reported, somewhat smugly, in 1858:

> this democratic and strong-minded race, who spin and weave and forge under thick canopies of smoke – who know and care little about lords or squires or rectors, are capable, as we see, of the deepest and most heartfelt attachment to the Crown and the illustrious person who now wears it.

Not only was England consolidating its identity at home, it was also continuing to establish its presence abroad (⊳ Imperialism). Hong Kong was acquired for the nation in 1839, to be swiftly followed by New Zealand (1840), Natal and Basutoland (1843, 1868) and, most importantly Sind (1843), the Punjab (1849) and Oudh (1856). In 1877 Victoria was proclaimed Empress of India and the middle classes could congratulate themselves not so much on the extent of the British Empire, but on the philanthropy of the English who were prepared to extend their civilizing influence to the more 'backward' nations. England under Victoria gained a perception of itself as an imperial power whose successful and often violent colonization of large parts of the globe was divinely inspired. In 1883 the historian J.R. Seeley attributed the expansion of the British Empire to 'the God who is revealed in history'. In addition, Britain had become a leading industrial nation. The ⊳ Great Exhibition of 1851, initiated by Prince ⊳ Albert, was, as critic David Morse has suggested, 'the moment when England definitively proclaimed and demonstrated her superiority over the rest of the world' (*High Victorian Culture*). It was also the moment when the sovereign, and the class whose interests and achievements were celebrated in the vast glass and iron conservatory, bonded together in a new and informal way. Queen Victoria visited the Crystal Palace on over forty occasions, joining with the patriotic middle classes, who also paid repeated visits, to 'positively wallow in the image of national greatness that the exhibition represented'. By 1875 the process of identification between sovereign and subjects was so complete that they were proud to adopt the self-referential adjective 'Victorian'. The Jubilee celebrations of 1887 and 1897 were an occasion to congratulate the Queen on her extended occupation of the English throne and for the English nation to congratulate itself on its achievements, as the then Poet Laureate Alfred Tennyson proclaimed in his official tribute 'On the Jubilee of Queen Victoria':

> Fifty years of ever-broadening Commerce!
> Fifty years of ever-brightening Science!
> Fifty years of ever-widening Empire!

The term 'Victorian' became associated with confidence, direction, progress and identity, and as such functioned as a comforting amulet to ward off everything that threatened to undermine the security of the middle classes. In reality, the period of Victoria's reign was characterized by change and instability: the threat of revolution; the discrediting of old traditions; the usurpation of a God who could always be relied upon to sanction the deeds and words of the philanthropic and paternalistic, by an indifferent and mechanical natural process; the loosening of the chains of matrimony and the empowerment of women and the working classes: what ▷ Thomas Carlyle referred to as 'a boundless grinding collision of the New with the Old' (▷ 'Signs of the Times', 1829). In the very year of Victoria's accession to the throne Carlyle published his ▷ *French Revolution* (1837), with its dire warning to the upper classes that unless they provided a model of responsibility and sound leadership England would soon have a revolution of its own. In *Chartism* (1840) he drew attention to the pressures on the working classes of poverty, the ▷ Corn Laws, the ▷ Poor Law Amendment Act of 1834, *laissez-faire* economic policies and the cash nexus which, in his view, had resulted in the ▷ Chartist Movement, itself a potential catalyst for the 'English Revolution'. George Richardson Porter, a social critic of the time, warned his readers against undue complacency and optimism when surveying the nation's industrial advances:

> It must be owned that our multiple abodes of want, of wretchedness, and of crime – our town populations huddled together in ill-ventilated and undrained courts and cellars – our numerous workhouses filled to overflowing with the children of want – and our prisons (scarcely less numerous) overloaded with the votaries of crimes, do indeed but too sadly and too strongly attest that all is not as it should be with us as regards this most important branch of human progress.
>
> (J.H. Buckley, *The Victorian Temper*)

▷ Disraeli regarded England as essentially two nations, 'Rich and Poor' (▷ *Sybil*), and, like Carlyle, looked towards an enlightened aristocracy to provide the leadership and direction the nation so badly needed. ▷ Dickens lamented in the ▷ *Quarterly Review* for June 1839: 'The one half of mankind lives without knowledge of how the other half dies.' He believed that middle-class complacency and indifference to the plight of the poor was the result of ignorance, but this explanation wasn't sufficient for ▷ Mrs Gaskell's John Barton (▷ *Mary Barton*), who was to be driven to murder by bereavement and frustration at the attitudes of those in charge:

> 'Don't think to come over me with the old tale, that the rich know nothing of the trials of the poor. I say, if they don't know, they ought to know. We are their slaves

> as long as we can work; we pile up their fortunes with the sweat of our brows; and yet we are to live as separate as if we were in two worlds; ay, as separate as Dives and Lazarus.'

Despite Mrs Gaskell's best endeavours, John Barton's anarchic and revengeful voice echoes in the reader's mind long after the concilatory cooing of Jem and Mary's infant son in their Canadian haven. Tennyson's patriotic Jubilee poem seeks to dispel the nation's anxieties concerning the present time by elevating Victoria as a symbol of unity and a guiding light and, in a somewhat unsubtle play on the origins of the Queen's name, transforming her into an image of triumph over peril and lurking threat:

> Are there spectres moving in the darkness?
> Trust the Hand of Light will lead her people,
> Till the thunders pass, the spectres vanish,
> And the Light is Victor, and the darkness
> Dawns into the Jubilee of the Ages.

However, the narrator of ▷ 'Locksley Hall' exposes the schizophrenia that underlies England's bellicose nationalism. In the midst of his self-indulgent rhetoric concerning the unworthiness of women he is valedictory on the subject of the docile, democratic masses: 'Slowly comes a hungry people, as a lion creeping nigher,/Glares at one that nods and winks behind a slowly-dying fire.' The fire, whose light and heat keep the sleeper safe from the spectres of the night, is going out. The amulet is in danger of losing its charm and its owner 'nods and winks' in a gesture of concilation perhaps, or maybe as prelude to a slumber from which he may never wake. Unhappy love destroys the narrator's optimism and peace of mind but his plight is an index of a larger social malaise. For him the 'Mother-Age' is neither comforting nor secure, but wracked by an unavoidable and violent storm. Although the upheavals are incomprehensible, Tennyson's narrator confronts them with a reckless and slightly hysterical cry which registers a sense of things spiralling out of control, 'Forward, forward let us range, /Let the great world spin forever down the ringing grooves of change.' The sentiment is repeated in a more measured tone in ▷ 'The Lotos-Eaters' where the captain counsels courage to his crew helpless on a wild and stormy sea for 'This mounting wave will roll us shoreward soon'.

The foundations of society were already badly shaken before Victoria came to the throne. As early as 1831 ▷ Macaulay urged the House of Commons to 'Reform, that you may preserve, or else persist in a hopeless struggle against the spirit of the age'. In his essay of the same title, ▷ John Stuart Mill defines the 'Spirit of the Age' as one of transition 'in which worldly power must cease to be monopolized by the landed gentry'. The balance of power was shifting from the aristocracy to the middle classes and the weight of their economic prosperity fell heavily upon those whose labour helped produce it and who as yet had no parliamentary voice. Social commentators, politicians and intellectuals recognized the need for widespread changes in the status quo, a need that was emphasized by government reports of the 1830s and 1840s and by the Chartist Movement of 1837–48. Chartism, activated in the year of Victoria's accession to the throne, was largely working class in orientation and campaigned for democratic rights and improved wages and working conditions by means of mass demonstrations and, at times, mob violence. The reforms in ▷ education and the ▷ Reform Bills which enfranchised men in the industrial middle class in 1832, the urban working class in 1867 and the agricultural labourers in 1884 were designed to relieve the pressure of an increasingly militant proletariat. Much as she hated upheaval, Victoria was influenced by Carlyle's warning concerning an impending 'English Revolution' and alarmed at the sea of 'nasty faces' screaming for reform that swarmed around her carriage as she drove to open Parliament in 1867: her first state appearance since she was widowed in December 1861. In supporting the Reform Bill of 1867 Victoria sincerely believed that enfranchisement would make the nation even more favourable to a benevolent monarch. She recognized the potential of the monarchy to provide a point of stability, an icon for a society riven with tensions, carried along breathlessly in the wake of rapid industrial development and discovering the explosive potential of the unprecedented power of steam for the first time.

The situation in France was still unsettled enough for the British to take note. It seemed to dramatize in violent and shocking form the shifts in the balance of power that had been apparent in their own country for some time. Victoria and Albert were 'bourgeois' enough for the rising middle classes to claim them as their own, although, as Victoria's biographer Elizabeth Longford has shown, Albert's popularity waxed and waned throughout the period (*Victoria I*). Nevertheless Albert, the initiator of the Great Exhibition, was the driving force behind the distancing of the monarchy from the aristocracy. For Victoria, the aristocracy symbolized everything that was despicable and profligate, and she held them responsible for the wayward behaviour of Edward the Prince of Wales. Having wooed and won the middle classes she was keen to exercise her influence over the industrial working classes, or the 'lower classes' as she preferred to call them, and eclipse their differences and dissatisfactions with the regal splendour of her presence. However, there were those among Victoria's subjects who reacted strongly against the elevation of the monarchy as a panacea for all ills. In the course of her reign Victoria experienced no less than six attempts on her life. Empty and inadequate gestures though these were, they were sufficient indication that for some the monarchy was a false idol it was their duty to overthrow.

There were iconoclasts among the more moderate of her subjects also. As Richard Stein has indicated, 'Victorian society was forever subject to tensions which militated against complete spontaneity and singleness of purpose' (*Victoria's Year*), and the literature of the period, annexed by the term 'Victorian' by 1876, is riven with these tensions. Whilst Victoria's poets, novelists and social commentators are quick to defend the status quo – preferring modification to revolution – anarchy persistently haunts the margins of their texts, disrupting the stasis implied by the ubiquitous 'happy ending'. Elizabeth Gaskell's alarm at the centrality assumed by the revengeful figure of John Barton in her novel *Mary Barton* is indicated by her attempts to distract the reader with the reconciliation of Mary and Jem, and the even more unlikely understanding reached between the remorseful Barton and his victim's father. It is significant that Mary and Jem can find peace, prosperity and happiness not in England but in Canada. Charles Dickens, having raised the spectre of working class unrest and dramatized the gulf between employer and employee, undermines and demonizes supporters of the growing ▷ trade union movement: they are a 'slack bridge' between masters and men. He leaves himself with no alternative but to wallow in sentiment and homespun wisdom with his moderate, decent, working-class hero Stephen Blackpool, who gazes weakly at the stars from the bottom of his disused mineshaft, to utter with his dying breath the immortal words 'aw a muddle' (▷ *Hard Times*).

In 1830–33 ▷ Charles Lyell published his *Principles of Geology*. The disasters he catalogued, including the wholesale extermination of species, as necessary antecedents to the earth's present state of repose, had a tremendous effect on his readers. For ▷ Charles Darwin the book 'altered the whole tone of one's mind'. In ▷ *In Memoriam, A.H.H.* (1850) Tennyson's narrator is unable to sustain the heady optimism embraced by the speaker of 'Locksley Hall'. Scientific knowledge brings not wisdom but despair as the individual self is threatened with extermination in the cause of the progress of the species. The strength of much of Tennyson's poetry lies in its insistent gesture towards the dissenting individual who refuses to be blinkered by the happy lie. *In Memoriam* is one of the most powerful poems of doubt and despair to be written during the period of Victoria's reign. It acknowledges the undermining of a concept of self predicated upon the notion of a beneficent and greater 'other' whether that 'other' be God, or perhaps, by implication, Monarch. Faced with the impact of science on religious belief, Tennyson's narrator mistrusts the very ground beneath him.

> I falter where I firmly trod,
> And falling with my weight of cares
> Upon the great world's altar-stairs
> That slope thro' darkness up to God,
>
> I stretch lame hands of faith, and grope,
> And gather dust and chaff, and call
> To what I feel is Lord of all,
> And faintly trust the larger hope.

God's abdication was brought a stage nearer by the publication of Darwin's *The Origin of Species* (1859) and its vigorous defence by ▷ Thomas Henry Huxley against Bishop Wilberforce the following year. Huxley's attack was directed not only against the bishop's attempts to 'smash Darwin' but also against the innate and threatened conservatism of those members of the Church who sought 'to discredit and crush humble seekers after truth'. The post-Darwinian world was in many ways profoundly pessimistic, and the writers of the period were torn between their conviction that the purpose of art was to educate and guide the newly enfranchised and newly literate classes beneath them, and their desire to use their talents to expose what was damnably wrong with the system.

Thomas Hardy has been accused of replacing a benevolent all-seeing God with a blind, mechanical and unreasoning 'It'. It was a charge that Hardy himself resolutely denied. He regarded his novels not as manifestos of pessimism but evidence of his own practical meliorist philosophy:

> What are my books but one plea against 'man's inhumanity to man' – to woman – and to the lower animals? . . . Whatever may be the inherent good or evil of life, it is certain that men make it much worse than it need be. When we have got rid of a thousand remediable ills, it will be time enough to determine whether the ill that is irremediable outweighs the good.
>
> (▷ William Archer, *Real Conversations*)

One of the thousand 'remediable ills' that is held up for analysis in Hardy's novels is the economic, social and sexual repression of women. It isn't 'Fate' that dogs Hardy's heroines to their graves, or into the arms of unsuitable mates, it is their economic dependence on men, their lack of social and political power and their adaptation, in the interests of survival, to the forms of feminity favoured not by Nature but by society. These forms are epitomized by ▷ Coventry Patmore's ▷ 'Angel in the House' or ▷ Ruskin's 'queen' of the domestic garden: 'the centre of order, the balm of distress, and the mirror of beauty' (*Sesame and Lilies*, 1865). Once again Queen Victoria, with her selfless and very public devotion to Albert and her children, her apparent preference for the philanthropic rather than the more practical duties of state, which she preferred to leave to her husband, and her repugnance for the 'mad, wicked folly of Women's Rights', provided a model of domestic virtue which the middle-class woman was encouraged to imitate. However, by 1860 this model was already up for reconstruction. In 1866 John Stuart Mill presented an unsuccessful petition to Parliament which demanded the inclusion of women in what was to become the 1867 Reform Bill. Many women throughout the period challenged the Victorian feminine ideal and the ▷ Women's Movement of the second half of the 19th century was perhaps the most anarchic of all, for it threatened the very foundations of the domestic haven the Victorians constructed as a retreat from the vicissitudes of everyday life. Maria G. Grey writing in the ▷ *Fortnightly Review* in 1879 points to the ▷ 'Woman Question' as an issue which was to create tensions every bit as great as theories of the evolution of human beings and the democratization of the working classes:

> Among the questions agitating men's minds in this age of transition between the old world of thought and faith and custom, so rapidly disappearing, and the new world scarcely yet visible in its rudiments beneath the tide of change and destruction, there are none that go deeper to the very roots of our social life than those touching the relations between the sexes, and the position assigned to women in the family and in the State. For centuries those relations had been considered fixed as the law of nature itself and too sacred to be touched by profane hands; but, of late years, they have shared the fate of other revered institutions and have become open questions, to be tried as freely as any others in the ruthless crucible of doubt and analysis.

Thomas Hardy, for one, had no doubts about the revolutionary potential of the ▷ women's suffrage movement. In 1906, five years after Victoria's death, he wrote to Millicent Garrett Fawcett, a leading women's suffragist, outlining the reasons behind his support for the cause:

> I have long been in favour of [it] . . . because I think the tendency of the woman's vote will be to break up the present pernicious conventions in respect of manners, customs, religion, illegitimacy, the stereotyped household (that it must be the unit of society), the father of a woman's child (that it is anybody's business but the woman's own, except in cases of disease or insanity), sport (that so-called educated men should be encouraged to harass, kill for pleasure feeble creatures by mean stratagems), slaughter houses (that they should be dark dens of cruelty) & other matters which I got into hot water for touching on many years ago.

During the last two decades of the century a reaction was setting in against the cosy certainties associated with the term 'Victorian'. Faith and pride in the Machine Age in the early decades of the century had its counterpart not only in the choleric finger-wagging of Carlyle or the unctuous reasoning of Dickens, but also in the nostalgia for a bygone, simpler pre-industrial age. The ▷ medievalism of Carlyle's ▷ *Past and Present*, Tennyson's ▷ *Idylls of the King* and the work of the Pre-Raphaelite Brotherhood reached its peak in the ▷ utopianism of ▷ William Morris. For Morris art and literature had a purely ornamental and practical function. Its purpose was to improve the existing environment and to compensate for the destruction by creeping industrialization of natural beauty and to replace the ugly utility of mass-produced goods with the lasting aesthetic pleasure of the hand-made artefact. From 1883 onwards Morris was studying and then preaching revolutionary Marxism. At the same time adherents of the ▷ Aesthetic Movement sought to rise above rather than justify what they regarded as an increasingly sordid and vulgar middle-class value system. Writers like ▷ George Moore and ▷ Oscar Wilde welcomed the ridicule heaped upon them by satirists like ▷ George Du Maurier in ▷ *Punch* because it confirmed their deviation from the norm. Art was seen as an escape from rather than a means of airing intellectual conflict.

If the early years of the 19th century and the accession to the throne of England of a youthful queen encouraged a spirit of ardour and optimism, the closing decade, presided over by a fretful, dour and increasingly reclusive octagenarian, prompted a feeling of pessimism and a sense of apocalypse. Victorian England had already 'fallen prey' to the radicals, socialists and suffragettes, and conservative opinion turned its attentions to the changes threatening the British Empire. Victoria's status was elevated from Queen to Empress as she reached the height of her popularity. The façade of middle-class complacency at home gave way to jingoism: fervent support of England's imperial policy in Europe epitomized in ▷ John Davidson's 'Song for the Twenty-fourth of May':

> Sea-room, land-room, ours, my masters, ours,
> Hand in hand with destiny, and first among the Powers!
> Our boasted Ocean Empire, sirs, we boast of it again,
> Our Monarch, and our Rulers, and our Women, and our Men!

However, even the most jingoistic writers – ▷ Kipling, William Henley (1849–1903), William Watson (1858–1935) and Henry Newbolt (1862–1938) – have been reassessed by present-day critics in such a way that the tensions and schisms in their work have become apparent.

The ▷ Decadents reacted against the optimism, buoyancy and smugness of 'Victorianism' with a languid weariness and despair. Arthur Symons' 'The Pause' (1897) picks up and develops into a dirge for the dying century the bass note of regret and confusion that surfaces periodically in the more conventional literature of the period:

> Trouble has come upon us like a sudden cloud,
> A sudden summer cloud with thunder in its wings.
> There is an end for us of old familiar things
> Now that this desolating voice has spoken aloud.

The Decadents opposed 'Victorian' manliness with effeminacy, earnestness with flippancy, philanthropy with self-indulgence and moral uprightness with sexual delinquency. Anarchy no longer merely haunts the borders of their texts, it takes a central role as the marginalized working-class Chartist of the ▷ Social Problem novels gives way to the amoral aesthete, the criminally insane decadent and the 'unnatural' aristocratic foreigner epitomized by ▷ Oscar Wilde's Dorian Gray,

▷ Robert Louis Stevenson's Mr Hyde and ▷ Bram Stoker's Dracula. However, in defining themselves against 'Victorianism', the '*fin de siècle*' writers were guilty of reducing the complexities of the literature and sensibility that had preceded theirs to a simplified set of clichés. It was this 'Victorianism', floated over the cracks and fissures of Victorian society and culture like a self-levelling compound, that persisted into the 20th century as 'a shield for the conservative and a target for the modernist' (J.H. Buckley, *The Victorian Temper*).

Until relatively recently, the construction of the canon of Victorian literature has sought to determine the meaning of texts in advance by relating them to a monolithic conception of 'Victorianism' designed to resolve rather than problematize its tensions. This has resulted in the exclusion of certain groups of people from representation and the devaluing of genres perceived as aberrant or peripheral to the concerns of the age. This is clearly the case with Victorian drama, dismissed as early as 1894 by one of the period's leading dramatists, ▷ Henry Arthur Jones, as 'A Slough of Despond in the well-tilled field of English Literature'. Jones was referring specifically to ▷ melodrama, which was the dominant genre of the age, and his opinion of the form has remained largely unchallenged. However, as Ian Clarke suggests in his essay 'Drama 1837–1901' (see page 13), the rejection of a large percentage of 19th-century drama as of little worth amounts to literary critical prejudice and trivializes one of the dominant forms of popular cultural entertainment. He argues for a reglossing of the term 'melodrama' to transform it from a pejorative into a purely descriptive term. Far from functioning as mere escapist entertainment, he argues, early domestic melodrama 'offered to newly urbanized working-class audiences valid images, however indirect, of their own alienated and disempowering experience as wage slaves'. Domestic melodrama also served to highlight gender inequities by showing women, and particularly working-class women, in a hostile world 'under almost constant threat of male violence'. In this way early Victorian melodrama can be seen to dramatize for a popular audience the concerns which were to animate the middle-class novel.

The novel was indisputably the dominant literary form of the age but yet again its sheer diversity is commonly overlooked by critics in their devotion to the rise of ▷ realism. Whilst ample attention has been paid to major realists such as Dickens, ▷ Thackeray, ▷ Eliot, the Brontës, Hardy and Henry James the sensationalist writings of Mrs Braddon, Mrs Wood and Rhoda Broughton are commonly grouped together under the heading 'minor novelists'. As Gail Cunningham points out in her essay on 'The Victorian Novel' (see page 27), the single most popular novelist of the 1890s was neither Hardy nor Thackeray nor even Henry James but ▷ Marie Corelli, whose *The Sorrows of Satan* (1895) outsold any previous English novel. Throughout the Victorian period the novel was subject to a form of ▷ censorship designed to isolate the predominantly female readership from exposure to sexual corruption. Novels which failed the test risked being blacklisted by the ▷ circulating libraries, which could ruin a writer's reputation overnight. Sexuality had to be handled delicately or not at all. The ▷ sensation novels of the 1860s, with their thinly disguised eroticism and stimulating if incredible plots, were written in reaction to the morally upright and sternly prosaic atmosphere of middle-class drawing rooms. They proved so popular that their authors (who were predominantly female) were comfortably able to support themselves, their husbands and families on the proceeds. Even the ▷ historical novel and ▷ romance were regarded as subversive by Ruskin, who counselled parents to keep them from their daughters for even 'the best romance becomes dangerous, if, by its excitement, it renders the ordinary course of life uninteresting, and increases the morbid thirst for useless acquaintance with scenes in which we shall never be called upon to act' (*Sesame and Lillies*). However, as Gail Cunningham demonstrates, it was the ▷ 'New Woman' fiction of the 1890s that most effectively undermined the shrine of womanhood.

Linda Williams (see page 43) locates the strength of Victorian poetry in its acknowledgement of crisis: in particular the crisis of the relationship between the self and the material world. The poetry of the period can be seen to challenge the received wisdom of the middle classes that industrial development and technological and scientific advance served only to illustrate the supremacy of man. The myth of personal and national stability is consistently fractured by the work of Tennyson, ▷ Clough, ▷ Arnold, Anne Brontë and Hardy. At the same time women poets such as ▷ Elizabeth Barrett Browning and Emily Brontë were concerned to forge entirely new conceptions of the female self distinctly at odds with the 'Angel in the House'. As the century drew to a close the impulse toward consolidation and complacency was violently checked by the bloody and frequently blasphemous verse of ▷ Swinburne and others of the ▷ 'Fleshly School of Poetry' while the despair and bleakness of much of ▷ Hopkins and Hardy anticipates the apocalypse of World War I.

As we prepare to exit from our own calamitous century, the government and the popular media fondly invoke the 'Golden Age' of the Victorian period. However as this essay and those that follow demonstrate, we should regard the previous century not as the antithesis to our own but as its precursor. The Victorians are moderns, their conflicts are ours, and they deserve better of us than to be reduced to crass political slogans and television costume drama.

15 Victorian Poetry: 1830–1900

Linda Ruth Williams

'Dusty answers': Loss and nostalgia in Victorian poetry

Ah, what a dusty answer gets the soul
When hot for certainties in this our life!
(Modern Love; George Meredith, 1862)

The poetry of the Victorians was written largely in a state of shock. From the shock of electricity to the 'shock of the new', currents of difficulty and doubt animate poetic history, fuelled by a crisis of faith and the instability of living in a rapidly growing and urbanizing society within which values were becoming increasingly unstable. This feeling of uncertainty is indulged by the Victorians through the notion that there was once a time, well into the past, when certainty existed. In ▷ Tennyson's words, Victorian poetry is permeated with 'the quiet sense of something lost' (▷ *In Memoriam A.H.H.*).

Tennyson's long elegy, *In Memoriam A.H.H.* (1850), is perhaps the most famous poem of loss to be penned in the 19th century. Written almost as therapy over a long period, what is being mourned is not simply Arthur Hallam, the poet's greatest friend; rather his death is a pretext for an extended meditation on absence. What is lost is also a fixed personal identity, certainty of perception and judgement, and the idea of a benign or controlling divinity. ▷ Matthew Arnold's elegiac lyric ▷ *Dover Beach* (1867) sketches out this sense of loss:

The Sea of Faith
Was once, too, at the full, and round earth's shore
Lay like the folds of a bright girdle furled.
But now I only hear
Its melancholy, long, withdrawing roar . . .

Reading Tennyson's intense lament alongside the passive melancholy of Arnold gives us two perspectives on how this loss, which is of course nothing new, is characterized in a particularly Victorian way. For Tennyson, trust in God must come despite the abysmal fact that,

Nature, red in tooth and claw
With ravine, shrieked against his creed
(In Memoriam A.H.H.)

So if *Dover Beach* is an elegy, who or what has died?

In many ways the most interesting poetry of the period since 1830 can be called 'death of God' poetry, after ▷ Nietzsche's famous proclamation that 'God is dead'. In *Easter Day, Naples* 1849 ▷ Arthur Clough writes, 'Ah! "some" did well to "doubt"!', in the midst of a text which repeats an ▷ atheist incantation:

Christ is not risen, no,
He lies and moulders low;
Christ is not risen.

Ashes to ashes, dust to dust;
As of the unjust, also of the just –
Christ is not risen.

Such a strong statement runs contrary to our cherished notion that the Victorians were a nation of devout church-goers, even if read in the context of the subsequent poem by Clough, 'Easter Day II' which affirms the opposite view. Despite the explosion in church-building which took place up to the 1850s, the Religious Census of 1851 showed that a large proportion of the population did not go to church. This feeling reaches a virulent pitch later in the century with ▷ James Thomson's *The City of Dreadful Night* (1874), a poem which, in its compulsive repetition, is structured like a nightmare. *City* may be the nearest thing in English poetry to Rimbaud's *Une Saison en enfer* (1873), although its invectives against God bring it closer to Lautréamont (1846–70):

The vilest thing must be less than Thou
From whom it had its being, God and Lord!
. . . I vow
That not for all Thy power furled and unfurled, (. . .)
Would I assume the ignominious guilt
Of having made such men in such a world.
(The City of Dreadful Night)

Thomson's God is alive and actively malicious, but the God who withdraws with Arnold's Sea of Faith is conspicuous only by his absence. Tennyson wrote to fill the absences – 'if there was a blank space I would put in a poem' – and one such absence has been created by God's departure. *In Memoriam* thus confronts these absences as the grieving self confronts the Victorian 'Unreal city':

He is not here; but far away
The noise of life begins again,
And ghastly through the drizzling rain
On the bald street breaks the blank day.

As with Tennyson's ▷ *Maud* (1855), *In Memoriam* shows a self so disrupted and infiltrated that it cannot affirm ▷ Robert Browning's much quoted phrase, 'God's in his heaven – / All's right with the world' (*Pippa Passes*). This is turned inward, for if God does not exist, man cannot exist in his image, and so the self's solidity and its possibilities of self-conscious meaningful action are undermined. Two quotations, the first from *In Memoriam* (LIV), the second from the remarkable poem by John Clare (1793–1864), 'I Am' (1864), illustrate this:

. . . but what am I?
An infant crying in the night:
An infant crying for the light:
And with no language but a cry.
I am – yet what I am none cares or knows,
My friends forsake me like a memory lost;
I am the self-consumer of my woes,
They rise and vanish in oblivious host.

His 'not being here' renders the urbanized, brave new world of the mid-19th century, the world of cholera and of the Crimean war, all the more ghastly, bald and blank, a world which it seemed, for the most part, God had never visited at all.

In the wake of this appalling possibility, fragments of memory – *In Memoriam* is certainly a fragmented text – are shored up poetically against present fear and ruin,

> *. . . when the sensuous frame*
> *Is racked with pangs that conquer trust;*
> *And Time, a maniac scattering dust,*
> *And Life, a fury slinging flame.*
> (*In Memoriam A.H.H.*)

The sense that history and technology were advancing out of all rational and moral control was acutely felt by poets, characterized by feelings of alienation from home. 'A wanderer is man from his birth' writes Arnold in 'The Future' (1852), and feelings of loss serve to fill the gap between the self and its long-gone place of safety. In Clare's 'I Am' the world is a 'vast shipwreck', and the 'nothingness of scorn and noise', the 'living sea of waking dreams' renders his loved ones even 'stranger than the rest'. ▷ Anne Brontë laments to herself, 'Sad wanderer, weep those blissful times / That never may return!' ('The Bluebell'; 1840). We could turn to countless verses where this sentiment is repeated, culminating in ▷ Thomas Hardy's double vision of loss and dread right at the end of the century. An image is set up across a wide range of Victorian poems of a lost cherished past – an idyllic pre-industrial England, the innocence of childhood, a place where unproblematic faith was possible. But working in tandem with melancholic lament is the Victorian passion for more positive and elaborate retrospection.

The Victorians had a great talent for nostalgia. This means that their interpretation of the past was double-edged, countering present loss with rosily remembered bygone times. In the face of uncompromising industrial expansion and unprecedented urban squalor a sumptuous pseudo-medieval (▷ medievalism) world was erected, a counter-image of ▷ Gothic grandeur activated by the prose celebrations of ▷ John Ruskin and ▷ Thomas Carlyle. The latter looked to the Middle Ages as a point of pre-industrial authenticity where 'Antique devoutness, Antique veracity and heroism' were possible (▷ *Past and Present*, 1843); the former's celebration of the Gothic had a profound influence upon the architectural practice of the second half of the 19th century. ▷ William Morris' championing of the Arts and Crafts Movement was vehemently anti-capitalist in favouring individual production and handiwork over the mass production of advanced technology. All these were impassioned moral responses to the feeling of contemporary spiritual alienation.

For ▷ Elizabeth Barrett Browning, however, poetic nostalgia was tantamount to escapism; shirking the task of producing poetry which engaged with the moment, the nostalgic poet failed to discern 'character or glory in his times, /And trundle(d) back his soul five hundred years' (▷ *Aurora Leigh*). This poetic 'trundling-back' survives in the shadowy Arthurian world of, for example, Tennyson's ▷ *Idylls of the King* (1859–72) and the archaic images of the ▷ Pre-Raphaelite movement. Pieced into an evocative picture of traditional England, legend-spinning countered the squalid present by concentrating on a supposedly more authentic yesterday. This sentimental evocation of a mythical past acted, then, rather like what ▷ Sigmund Freud (1856–1939) calls a 'Family Romance', only on a national scale; just as an individual might pretend he or she has more glorious and romantic origins than are in fact the case, so national culture is built upon the wishful creation of images of glorious and graceful past times. By positively forging a myth of the English idyll –

Oh, to be in England
Now that April's there
('Home Thoughts From Abroad'; Robert Browning, 1845)

– or of childhood, or of God in His Heaven – personal and national stability is consolidated rather than threatened. By forging an idyllic cultural memory (a sanitized past) which acts as a kind of screen memory, blocking off far more disturbing passages of individual or national history (the dirty materiality of the real past) Victorian verse contributed to glueing together a fracturing present. In the place of what ▷ Chartist poet Gerald Massey (1828–1907) called the 'looming future', a blooming past is constructed.

One way of reading Victorian nostalgia is to assume that the strength of retrospection in a text is an index of the depth of crisis felt at the moment at which it was written. We do find frequent points where crisis is overtly acknowledged; loss in the present is as important a stated element in Victorian verse as the creation of the past. So it is wise to be as suspicious as possible when confronting these images, asking, as Anne Brontë does, why certain things have been remembered and valorized and not others:

Sweet memory, ever smile on me;
Nature's chief beauties spring from thee.

In other words, one remembers what one desires to remember:

Is childhood then so all divine?
Or, memory, is the glory thine
That haloes thus the past?
('Memory'; 1846)

What is activated in poetic remembering is, then, highly selective, evading the squalid activity of the past.

'Behind the silken-folded mask': Other voices in the 'double-breasted Age'

There cast my anchors of desire
Deep in Unknown eternity,
Nor ever let my spirit tire
With looking for What is to Be.
('Anticipation', ▷ Emily Brontë; 1845)

In her suspicious reading of the tricks of memory Anne Brontë comes close to the cynicism of Gerald Massey, whose concern is to scrutinize the 'real present' and the social contexts of idyllic images. In the ironically titled 'All's Right with the World', he shows what occurs when the 'silken-folded mask' of sweet image-making slips,

> *. . . lo, Hell welters at our very feet!*
> *The Poor are murdered body and soul, the Rich*
> *In Pleasure's chalice melt their pearl of life!*
> *Ay, all goes right, and merrily, with the world.*
> ('All's Right with the World')

Perhaps this 'silken-folded mask' is the tapestry woven by Tennyson's ▷ *The Lady of Shalott* (1832), which contains scenes of the world she cannot see first hand but only as images in her mirror. Massey's verse asks suspicious questions about who has the power to write and myth-make, and who is excluded from the process of remembering – who says what the mirror reflects? More positively, we might look for other images beneath the mask, and listen to other poetic voices.

The canon has often concealed the tears in the 'silken-folded mask' of bourgeois writing. The poetry of the 19th century is, however, extraordinarily heterogeneous. Whilst modernists were able to dismiss Victorian verse as immobile and monolithic, the terms used to discuss it could be much simpler than those which are required to do justice to its plurality and diversity. In this section I wish to point to the cracks in the idea of a Victorian poetic monolith by showing the points at which different voices call from inside the marbling.

The variety of metrical and stanzaic forms in 19th-century writing confesses both technical restlessness and openness to development – Clough's verse in parts anticipates *vers libre*, Browning and Tennyson experimented widely with metre, and as we shall see ▷ Gerard Manley Hopkins developed rhythmic forms which anticipate ▷ modernism. Voices other than that of bourgeois Victorian propriety speak in the dialect poetry of ▷ William Barnes, Thomas Hardy, and even Tennyson, in texts such as Thomas Hood's 'The Song of the Shirt' (1843) (the lament of a labouring woman – 'Would that its tone could reach the rich!'), and in the bizarre sexual delirium of ▷ Algernon Swinburne and some writers of the *fin de siècle*. The ▷ Nonsense verse of ▷ Edward Lear and ▷ Lewis Carroll plays with images from the Victorian unconscious, parodying normality to the point of absurdity, the effect of which is hilarious, provocative and disturbing. Carroll's 'The White Knight's Song' from *Through the Looking Glass* (1872), gives a world of capitalism-turned-upside-down by listing a series of utterly absurd ways of making money, a stream of words which 'trickled through my head, / Like water through a sieve'. The lament of manifest loss in Lear's 'The Dong with the Luminous Nose' (1871) parodies the grander losses of Tennyson and Arnold; 'Dong' is a melancholy pastiche, telling the story of the lost Jumbly Girl in the grandiose tones of the mock-epic:

> *But when the sun was low in the West,*
> *The Dong arose and said; –*
> *– 'What little sense I once possessed*
> *Has quite gone out of my head!' –*
> *And since that day he wanders still*
> *By lake and forest, marsh and hill,*
> *Singing – 'O somewhere, in valley or plain*
> *'Might I find my Jumbly Girl again!*
> *'For ever I'll seek by lake and shore*
> *'Till I find my Jumbly Girl once more!'*

Crucially, too, the mask slips when women take up their pens, especially when they are concerned in their writing, as was Elizabeth Barrett Browning, to inscribe literary history with visions which could not be countenanced by masculine masks. Her desire to 'catch / Upon the burning lava of a song / The full-veined, heaving, double-breasted Age' (*Aurora Leigh*) strongly contrasts with much Victorian poetry's listless return to any age but its own. Her adamant belief that poetry be relevant to its times and contemporary in its material builds up in *Aurora Leigh* into a plea for living verse, since dead images kill poems: 'death inherits death'.

The outstanding texts of this period are, not uncommonly, ways into fear, confrontations of, in Hardy's late-Victorian phrase, 'the growing gloom'. With the revolutionary year of 1848, a turbulent one for much of mainland Europe, vague uncertainties were turned into a radical sense of possibility. This was the year in which Clough published his remarkable *The Bothie of Tober-Na-Vuolich*, which interrogates class and sexual difference through the difficult problem of marriage across class barriers; in the face of a socially volatile moment, Clough asserted the necessity that poetry relate to and guide people in their urban experience. Cultural history registered the shocking dissolution of the solitary and integrated self posited by western rationality. In the British Museum Library Karl Marx was researching *Das Kapital*; 1848 had seen the publication of his and Engels' *Communist Manifesto*. It is helpful to read Victorian verse in relation to other forms of contemporary writing. Such poetry gathered itself together in the intellectual climate which also produced ▷ Charles Darwin's *On the Origin of Species* in 1859, and since the poets under discussion here never saw themselves as writing in splendid isolation from the intellectual revolutions precipitated by these texts, it would be unwise to treat poetic history as generated by a dynamic solely internal to itself.

In the ▷ 'Hungry Forties' many of the young writers which modernism cast as Victorian dinosaurs were only just beginning to reach wide audiences and capitalize most effectively on their poetic energies. The fact that the romantic paradigm was no longer applicable to an acutely altered Britain gradually became a cause for celebration rather than lament. Against a fetishized past, poets countered with a strong vision of the present, even those whose work in other places both celebrates and laments what is in truth a pastiche of medieval England. Tennyson, for instance, also makes use of images of the past to displace ▷ 'the woman question' into a space where it can be imaginatively explored. In 1847 he first published ▷ *The Princess*, that extraordinary engagement with 'the woman question' which gives us an image, albeit set up only to be undermined, of strong women of formidable intellect. The certainties of sexual difference are challenged not only by the very existence of a militantly ▷ feminist educational institution, but by the humour of the transvestite episode in which the heroes dress as women to infiltrate the enemy camp. Central to *The Princess* is the separatist University, which is both credible and credited only within a context radically different from Tennyson's own, hence his deployment of a vague medieval setting, further displaced by a variety of narrative layers. *The Princess* questions the notion that poetry springs from a singular, unified voice; it is 'A Medley', the construction of many voices, male and female, which together forge 'a sevenfold story'.

In 1855 (during the Crimean War), Tennyson published an even stranger long poem which engaged with the contemporary issues of mental aberration, sexual difference, and the war itself. This was *Maud*, subtitled 'A Monodrama', a self-undermining word since the 'one' who speaks this long complex poem is an extremely fragmented personality; he isn't 'one' – he isn't 'mono' – he speaks with many voices. The drama of the narrative is thus importantly also an effect of the dialogue between his own selves. For the speaker of *Maud* is 'Sick of a nameless fear'; disordered in his senses, he seems to speak from many positions at once. He is precipitated into paranoia, and the synaesthesia of the famous 'Come into the garden, Maud' passage, by an erotically intangible heroine who had 'fled on the roses and lain in the lilies of life'. Arnold's phrase 'the dialogue of the mind with itself' takes shape in this mad 'hero' who becomes a figure of the introspective poet, fleeing the foul fiend of horror or doubt: 'I will bury myself in myself' (*Maud*, Part II, l 75). Tennyson wrote of his character, 'I took a man constitutionally diseased and dipt him into the circumstances of the time and took him out on fire'. Along with Tennyson's more narcotic lyrics, *Maud* shows how a poetry which explored the loss of the rational self could be articulated behind the Laureate mask, even as the mask of civic poetry was held anxiously in place. But *Maud* is also in part a comment upon the circumstances of the time, of modern and mental alienation: its landscape a metaphor for psychiatric derangement, as it was to become in such later poems as Thomson's *City* and ▷ T.S. Eliot's ▷ *The Waste Land* (1922).

Aurora Leigh had a readership as enormous as *The Princess* and *Maud*, and in content deals with the questions of gender and women's power which the Tennyson texts, as well as Clough's *Bothie*, all probe from different angles. Even Queen ▷ Victoria read *Aurora Leigh*. Indeed, when the queen was faced with the task of choosing a new Poet Laureate in 1850, Elizabeth Barrett (as she then was) was a prime candidate. Stepping into ▷ Wordsworth's shoes was indeed regarded as an awesome task for any of the young poets who were penning their most interesting work at this time. Whilst no woman has ever become the Poet Laureate, in the middle of a century characterized by such acute patriarchal oppression a woman was seriously considered for the position. She was, indeed, far more popular then than her husband-to-be, Robert Browning, appropriate to an age when women wrote poetry prolifically and were highly regarded by their contemporaries, and feminist criticism recently has shown her to be a literary figure worthy of stronger recognition than she has received since her death. *Aurora Leigh* explores the boundaries between biography and fiction, identifying poetic work as a unique space for making out a woman's relationship to language and creativity. As a feminist interrogation of female friendship and sexual relations it is courageous, 'life-blood' 'wrung . . . / On every leaf . . .' (*Aurora Leigh*, Bk 5, ll. 356–7). As an exploration of how literature creates the self, it deserves its place in a tradition of poets' own critical theories. As a long narrative poem it was indeed hugely popular, fulfilling its own prescription that poetry should not flinch from history, and should partly be the space where women can begin to write their own histories, the story behind the mask. Matthew Arnold wrote that, 'Poetry is at bottom a criticism of life', and Barrett Browning's verse exemplifies this, constructively engaging with rather than retreating from her 'double-breasted Age'. As Cora Kaplan points out in her 1978 introduction to the poem, *Aurora Leigh* is a ▷ feminist bridge between two other overtly political publications, *Casa Guidi Windows* (1851) and *Poems Before Congress* (1860), forming a triptych which perhaps offers the strongest poetic analysis in English of the immediately post-1848 European situation.

As feminist criticism has shown, no mythical past could offer 19th-century women a positive image of themselves, so they set to writing it in their own way. The work of ▷ Christina Rossetti presents an intriguing exception. Her 'criticism of life' is uniquely strong in its strange combination of morbidity, painful self-denial and simplicity. Rossetti is undoubtedly ruthlessly hard on herself: much of her work is charged with absence and denial, a will to oblivion and silence, which is repeatedly invoked in a style so sparse it seems to be actively wishing to negate itself. Indeed, the word 'silence' itself is often repeated. Her 'almost Paradise' is a return to absolute equilibrium and desirelessness. In 'Rest' (1862) she calls the earth to

Lie close around her; leave no room for mirth
With its harsh laughter, nor for sound of sighs.
She hath no questions, she hath no replies,
Hushed in and curtained with a blessed dearth
Of all that irked her from the hour of birth;
With stillness that is almost Paradise.

The voice of this poem can only afford to desire the absence of pain; for Rossetti positivity isn't full energy but simply the negation of the negative. Plenitude is, perhaps, asking too much. Is this an instance of woman learning to desire her lot, internalizing the Victorian charge that she 'suffer and be still'?

But when colours and positively charged desires giddily burst into this near-silence, that which 'irked her from the hour of her birth' is quite positively broken open and challenged. Rossetti's sparse verse soars to an unnatural high when suddenly rich detail emerges, the mixture of spartan naïve form with Pre-Raphaelite decorativeness invoking a strange intoxication of deprivation and excess. The rich erotic language of ▷ *Goblin Market* (1862) pressed into a strict ▷ ballad form, or the exultation of 'A Birthday' (1862), are both good examples of this:

Raise me a dais of silk and down;
Hang it with vair and purple dyes;
Carve it in doves and pomegranates,
And peacocks with a hundred eyes;
Work it in gold and silver grapes,
In leaves and silver fleurs-de-lys;
Because the birthday of my life
Is come, my love is come to me.

In its privations Rossetti's poetry has a simple beauty, but when it brims over with rich images its singularity and strength are striking.

A more overtly positive woman's poetic voice in the earlier Victorian period is that of ▷ Emily Brontë. Hers is 'No coward soul . . ., / No trembler in the world's storm-troubled sphere' ('No Coward Soul is Mine'; 1846). The quotation which forms the epigraph to this section is typical of her immediate positivity; she would be a poet of the present moment, evoking earth-bound epiphanies which celebrate the material world rather than striving for the transcendental. Significantly, her 'anchor of desire' is cast forward into 'What is to Be' rather than nostalgically backwards. Across her corpus a theory of human freedom is constructed which needs to be read in the context of her position as a woman writer. In 'The Old Stoic' (1841) she desires only 'a chainless soul', not a heavenly transformation – 'Leave me the heart that now I bear, / And give me liberty'. Freedom is more important than heaven, a sentiment which echoes Catherine Earnshaw's dream in chapter nine of ▷ *Wuthering Heights* (1847):

Give me the hills our equal prayer,
Earth's breezy hills and heaven's blue sea;
We ask for nothing further here

But our own hearts and liberty.
('And like myself lone, wholly lone'; 1841)

Unlike the more passive mysticism of Rossetti, Brontë is anything but stoical, and her poetry's affirmation of the earth forms a strong critique of organized religion's promise of better things to come:

Let others seek its beams divine
In cell and cloister drear
But I have found a fairer shrine
A happier worship here;

By dismal rites they win their bliss,
By pennance, fasts and fear –
I have one rite – a gentle kiss;
One pennance – tender tears.

Flesh and the fin de siècle

Sexuality haunts Victorian poetry as an anxious desire, a force both attractive and repulsive, like the prostitute figure 'Jenny' (1870) in ▷ Dante Gabriel Rossetti's poem of that name. The strict a/a/b/b rhyming scheme of 'Jenny' causes her name to assonate ironically with 'guinea'; she is a fallen goddess, whose access to the 'vile text' of sexual knowledge makes her the object of simultaneous desire and denigration. Jenny's image is distorted by what men desire of her:

Yet, Jenny, looking long at you,
The woman almost fades from view,
A cipher of man's changeless sum
Of lust, past, present, and to come,
Is left. A riddle that one shrinks
To challenge from the scornful sphinx.

From ▷ Coventry Patmore's eulogies to the safe delights of married love in *The Angel in the House* (1858), to ▷ George Meredith's bitter sonnet sequence about estrangement and divorce, ▷ *Modern Love* (1862), the Victorians were covertly obsessed with the question of sex. Ahead of Nietzsche's proclamation about God, Meredith declares 'the death of love' and digs its grave with his text (*Modern Love*, (i)).

Through the Victorians' treatment of or silence regarding sexuality we can discover much about what was considered the proper subject matter for poetry. In this section I want to talk briefly about how those norms and rules of propriety gradually broke down as the century closed and as writing itself opened. Tennyson's institutionalization as Poet Laureate caused him to consolidate gradually the shifting selves and voices of his earlier verse, and by the latter decades of the 19th century he had become quite firmly the spokesman of decorum over degeneracy. By the time of 'Locksley Hall Sixty Years After' (1886), subterranean rumbles were shifting the ground beneath Tennyson's feet, causing him to castigate vehemently the author's part in inviting a new dark age in which 'Chaos, Cosmos' are interchangeable, and freedom is only 'free to slay herself':

Authors – essayist, atheist, novelist, realist, rhymster, play your part,
Paint the moral shame of nature with the living hues of Art. (. . .)
Feed the budding rose of boyhood with the drainage of your sewer;
Send the drain into the fountain lest the stream should issue pure.
Set the maiden fancies wallowing in the troughs of Zolaism, –
Forward, forward, ay and backward, downward into the abysm.
Do your best to charm the worst, to lower the rising race of men;
Have we risen from out the beast, then back into the beast again?

The force with which this sewer imagery is impressed upon us is arguably as blatant and shocking as the kind of literature it would repress; Tennyson is calling for a public health drive to counter poetic corruption as the notorious Contagious Diseases Acts of the 1860s sought to control prostitution. In its utter physical disgust this text reveals much about the bourgeois obsession with cleanliness ('next to Godliness') which ▷ psychoanalysis was beginning to encounter in its most extreme and mentally destructive forms: as Tennyson penned these words, Freud was working toward the publication, with Joseph Breuer (1842–1925), of *Studies on Hysteria* (1895), one of the founding texts of psychoanalysis. But however eloquently this poem speaks of Tennyson's own preoccupations, it is its role as a critical prescription which interests us here. For at stake in this is both the notion that 'dirty writing' messes up a literary tradition in the process of purifying itself, and also that such poetic 'foul passions' can have a profound effect on the moral welfare of the nation.

The ▷ decadent writings of the later 19th century perversely took such a stance gloriously to heart, actually affirming these powers in an indulgence of the flesh as sin. The period of the 1860s and 1870s, the High Victorian period, was a period of consolidation both politically and poetically, and writing was generally on a grander, surer scale, although this consolidation uneasily co-existed with other tendencies. In the late 1880s and early 1890s Tennyson, Browning and Arnold died, and the emphases of poetry shifted. The artists of what ▷ W.B. Yeats (1865–1939) called the 'Tragic Generation' – ▷ Oscar Wilde, ▷ Ernest Dowson, Lionel Johnson (1867–1902), ▷ Aubrey Beardsley and ▷ Arthur Symons (1865–1943) – developed an extreme form of aestheticism, strongly influenced by ▷ Walter Pater's notorious epilogue to *Studies in the History of the Renaissance* (1873). This group of bohemian poets formed ▷ The Rhymers Club in the 1890s, and published their work in a body of journals which reflected their priorities: chiefly ▷ *The Yellow Book* and *The Savoy*. As the century became more ▷ utilitarian, adamantly scientific and technologically precise, poetry turned from the prescription of social relevance and made a virtue of the notion that it was brazenly gratuitous. Perversity, superficiality and hedonism were prioritized over the socially useful, profoundly spiritual and serious. ▷ Nineties poetry in particular embraced the idea of poetry as estranged from the real world. The earlier notion of poetry as 'a weapon of strife in the social conflict', or Arnold's celebration of the moral worth of poetry, were reversed by ▷ aesthetic doctrine – as Wilde wrote, 'The man who could call a spade a spade should be compelled to use one'. Such a shift is, however, most significant in its challenging of the rules of poetic subject matter rather than in any formal innovations which decadent poets enacted. Their work is characteristically sinful rather than amoral, evil rather than atheist. Working within the structures of conventional morality *fin de siècle* writers were anti-Victorian Victorians in that they prioritized beauty over goodness, the aesthetic rather than the ethical, the body over the spirit.

This latter emphasis is what the poet, novelist and dramatist ▷ Robert Buchanan had called (in an essay on D.G. Rossetti) ▷ 'the Fleshly School of Poetry'. In the 1860s this 'school' was opened by Algernon Swinburne under the influence of the Marquis de Sade (1740–1814) and ▷ Charles Baudelaire, and bore its own bizarre progeny in the 1880s and 1890s. Certainly, the earlier obsessions of the Pre-Raphaelites had played an important role in the *fin de siècle*'s spectacular materialization of certain lurid themes, particularly in the movement's representation of *femmes fatales* like Jenny or Swinburne's Dolores. Dante Gabriel Rossetti's verse often adorns his paintings of women so that the woman becomes a fusion of verbal description and detailed visual representation on a gigantic scale.

The painting/sonnet 'Astarte Syriaca' (1877) exemplifies this, representing a woman who combines Venus and Astarte, an embodiment of an ineffable higher knowledge and thus also, an image of Victorian woman worship. Rossetti's power to frame women within a certain range of images could, perhaps, be read alongside Browning's ▷ 'My Last Duchess' (1842), the speaker of which gains power over the Duchess in the painted image of her. Together Jenny and Astarte Syriaca – woman as essentially 'Amulet, talisman, and oracle' – offer the double version of sexual fear and desire with which I began. Christina Rossetti's work supplements this masculine vision, stepping back even further than Browning from the female canvas and sharply disrupting her brother's images of essential femininity.

A more outrageous manifestation of textual fleshiness came, however, with the explosion of Algernon Swinburne on to the relatively conservative poetic scene in the mid-1860s. Swinburne is known about now more for his dissolute lifestyle and sexual excesses. His bloodstained poetry is perhaps best known for its insistence on the themes of lust and violence, not all of which even the most crusading 20th-century writers on sexuality have thought to legitimize. As *enfant terrible* to High Victorian complacency, his early Dionysian work had an intoxicating effect on his young contemporaries.

The initial impact of Swinburne's poetry stemmed in part from his technical innovation, chiefly an obsessive use of alliteration. As he became a more established literary figure his technique was conservatively consolidated. Intoxicated incantations became simply rhythmically tedious, as Swinburne's outrageous and often blasphemous themes were battered into conventional iambic shapes just as the bodies of his subjects are, 'Trodden as grapes in the wine-press of lust' ('Laus Veneris'; l 191; 1866): Thus, whilst bloodblotches are symptoms that his figures have been 'trampled' by desire, the purple effect of his writing contained in regular, conservative form signalled for later generations Swinburne's ultimate lack of poetic dynamism.

This late-Victorian prioritization of the body and the beautiful over moral and social worth may have been rebellious, challenging the moralizations of earlier politically engaged poets, but it certainly wasn't revolutionary; it may have broken the rules but it certainly didn't change the structure within which the rules worked. As well as working within a moral economy which still held matter and spirit to be diametrically opposed, the poets discussed so far were also working within a textual economy which held form and content to be separate dimensions of poetry. This, then, brings us on to another important aspect of late-Victorian writing, and in particular the poetry of those key transitional figures who were beginning to question the rules which dictated how a poem was written, just as the 'fleshly school' was questioning what a poem was written about.

The fruits of unbelief: Movements toward modernism

Much of the writing discussed so far is, in its versification and syntax at least, familiar – formally it conforms to what the reader is used to. Victorian poetry of this stylistically conventional type in part has trained our readerly sensibilities. This familiarity, however, breaks down in the more difficult verse of Robert Browning and Gerard Manley Hopkins, whose work looks forward to the formal obscurities and syntactical abnormalities of modernism.

Browning's verse is often convoluted and digressive. ▷ Ezra Pound found *Sordello* (1840) unreadable, and ▷ Jane Welsh Carlyle read the whole of it without discerning whether Sordello was a book, a man or a city. Browning is concerned to show how his verse is constructed, to leave in the traces of the psychological process he went through in writing it, to lay bare the association of ideas which lead to the final full stop. He foregrounds 'The grand Perhaps' ('Bishop Blougram's Apology', l 190 from ▷ *Men and Women*; 1855) – the doubts and equivocations of writing and modernity – to such an extent that it takes on some kind of positive identity. In the words of 'Bishop Blougram's Apology', Browning's question concerns the uses of doubt and difficulty, 'how can we guard our unbelief, Make it bear fruit to us?' Thus he overtly shows the reader the 'perhapses' of poetry writing itself, the process he goes through in trying to get from 'a' to 'b' of a narrative; the fruit that this bears is a highly unusual and difficult type of poetry. He constantly interrupts himself, leaving trails of dots for us to follow as thoughts tail off and into other thoughts. The traces of the process of a poem's construction are left on show as evidence of how it is produced, but because we are used to these traces and half thoughts being edited out, his poems are difficult reading. What aims to be a realistic representation of the flow of mental processes reads as stilted, stuttering parenthesis. In an effort to mimic the patterns of common speech Browning's verse frequently slips from self to self without formal signal:

> *Ay, because the sea's the street there; 't is arched by . . . what you call*
> *. . . Shylock's bridge with houses on it, where they keep the carnival:*
> *I was never out of England – it's as if I saw it all.*
>
> ('A Toccata of Galuppi's', *Men and Women*)

So one modernist effect of reading Browning is that he causes us to confront the process through which relevant information is usually selected or omitted, through which different textual registers are signalled. In its obscurity Browning's verse takes on the otherwise thematic problem of a dissolving subject and turns it into a question of form and syntax.

Gerard Manley Hopkins is a Victorian poet in the sense that he wrote mainly from 1875 to 1889 but his work was not published until 1918. There is a certain historical appropriateness to this delay, since his difficulty, and his interest in the ▷ Metaphysical poets, is akin to the modernists who turned to the English ▷ Renaissance as part of 'the direct current of English poetry' (T.S. Eliot). 'Difficulty' becomes the catch-word of early 20th-century writing, a strategy for marking a distinction between modern writing and the 19th-century values of the reader-friendly text. Hopkins' contorted versification, syntactic twists, and dictive and rhythmic experimentation have confounded easy readings. His 'grand Perhaps' came at the point at which he started to 'doubt Tennyson', opening up another important emphasis of poetic modernism – its concern is to move away from the preciousness of 19th-century poetic diction to something more immediate, to the rhythms of common speech. It is paradoxical, then, that readers had become used to the strict versification of the Victorians, and to a specifically poetic vocabulary and range of images, and it is this faculty which has alienated them from modernism's attempt to deploy the language and images of the everyday. Hopkins' case is highlighted by his innovative rhythmic form – ▷ sprung rhythm – which was designed to bring into his verse the energies of ordinary speech. The syllabic stresses in his lines are syncopated, as they might be in a conversation. In 1877 he wrote to ▷ Robert Bridges,

> *Why do I employ sprung rhythm at all? Because it is the nearest to the rhythm of prose, that is the native and natural rhythm of speech, the least forced, the most rhetorical and emphatic of all possible rhythms, combining, as it seems to me, opposite and one wd.* (sic) *have thought, incompatible excellences, markedness of rhythm – that is rhythm's self – and naturalness of expression ...*
>
> (21 August 1877)

His use of sprung rhythm is, however, one of the aspects of Hopkins' poetry which was considered most difficult, since difficulty is an indication of unfamiliarity.

In Hopkins' meticulous and characteristically Victorian visual powers, especially regarding the natural world, he prefigures ▷ D.H. Lawrence (1885–1930); he is not a poet of generalization, repeating tiny detail rather than broadly gesturing. But like his later imitator, ▷ Dylan Thomas (1914–53), words unroll and suggest each other uncontrollably:

> *... now, barbarous in beauty, the stooks rise*
> *Around; up above, what wind-walks! what lovely behaviour*
> *Of silk-sack clouds! has wilder, wilful-wavier*
> *Meal-drift moulded ever and melted across skies?*
>
> (*'Hurrahing in Harvest'*, 1877)

There is an (arguably unchristian) exuberance, a vision of excess, in Hopkins' verse, and in his philosophy of 'instresses' and 'inscapes' his Jesuitism becomes almost pantheistic. In touching the inscape of a thing – an image, or complex of images, a natural object or experience – poetry claims access to a vision of that thing's essential existence. This existence is communicated to the individual through an energetic pulse or channel – the 'instress' – which is opened between object and perceiver, if she or he is 'ready'. For Hopkins, poetry exceeds meaning; it is in his impulse to commune with the 'isness' of things, to allow material language to touch the thing itself through a poetic experience of epiphany, that Hopkins' modernity lies.

Hopkins' temptation to visit the dark night of the soul (particularly in the 'sonnets of desolation' of 1884–5) brings his later poems of despair close in their painful intensity to Thomas Hardy's bleakest work. Like Hopkins, Hardy is also a poet known for his use of common language and diction, and is quite literally a *fin de siècle* poet in his uniquely pessimistic and Schopenhauerian stance on passing from the old century into the new. Hardy's hopelessness looks forward and backward; a poem such as 'The Darkling Thrush' (1900) is both a poem of loss and a poem of dread, 'greeting' the 20th century from a pivotal point which also implicitly glances backwards:

> *So little cause for carolings*
> *Of such ecstatic sound*
> *Was written on terrestrial things*

Afar or high around,
That I could think there trembled through
His happy good-night air
Some blessed Hope, whereof he knew
And I was unaware.

Hardy, then, writes at the end point of a process and a century in which the self is gradually and systematically estranged from the familiar. Time is no longer simply the dimension of loss, but also that which brings the 'darkening dankness / The yawning blankness' ('The Going') of the future ever closer. His foreboding about what Yeats called (in 'Coole Park and Ballylee, 1931') the 'darkening flood' indeed prefigures much of late Yeats' feelings about the 20th century.

16 The 19th-Century Novel

Gail Cunningham

Background: Authors, Readers and Publishers

Where the ▷ Restoration and ▷ Enlightenment periods were dominated in literary terms by drama and poetry, the 19th century was indisputably the age of the novel. When ▷ Anthony Trollope noted in 1870 'that novels are in the hands of us all; from the Prime Minister down to the last appointed scullery-maid' he was drawing attention both to the pervasive cultural and social importance of fiction and, implicitly, to the immense range of novels available to what was by then a mass reading public. Not only did the novel form produce a consistent stream of major practioners (of whom an uncontroversial listing would include ▷ Jane Austen, ▷ Charles Dickens, ▷ Charlotte and ▷ Emily Brontë, ▷ George Eliot and ▷ Thomas Hardy), it also gave expression to a huge variety of discourse from writers of less established reputation. Fiction in the 19th century could address every topic, enter every dispute, reflect every ideal of an age perceived by those who lived through it to be one of unprecedented rapid change. And, significantly, an extraordinary number and variety of 19th-century novels have currency in contemporary popular, as well as scholarly, reading habits.

This enduring popularity may in part be accounted for by the novel form itself. The novel is more immediately approachable than drama or poetry, and it addresses itself directly to 'life' without the intervening artistic medium of verse or dramatic form, and in a way which other literary genres do not. It tells stories, reworks the mundane materials of everyday life into something significant, and (most 19th-century readers would add) it teaches moral lessons. More interestingly, perhaps, it could be argued that the 19th-century novel is the first art form to deal explicitly and realistically with issues which speak directly to some of the central concerns of 20th-century consciousness.

The novels of this period sprang from a society undergoing a more massive upheaval under the influence of industrialization than in any previous era (▷ Industrial Revolution). Not only was the population shifting irrevocably from an agricultural to an urban base, with all the profound changes in social, working and family patterns that this entailed, there were also the dramatic visible changes resulting from technological invention which altered people's perceptions and their world. The railway boom of the 1840s did not merely effect the landscape; its more profound repercussions lay in revolutionizing expectations of speed, mobility and permanence. When in ▷ *Dombey and Son* (1847–48) Dickens describes 'the first great shock of the earthquake' which the building of the railway brings, he is expressing a now familiar paradox inherent in such change: 'from the very core of all this dire disorder, [the railway] trailed smoothly away, upon its mighty course of civilisation and improvement'. The chaotic but human little community of Staggs's Gardens has been 'cut up root and branch' to make way for the 'crowds of people and mountains of goods' to be shifted by the railway: the individual and idiosyncratic have been sacrificed to the corporate and the homogeneous. ▷ Thomas Carlyle's famous definition of this period as 'the Mechanical Age' focused the anxieties of many of his contemporaries about the relationship of the individual to society. 'Men are grown mechanical in head and in heart, as well as in hand,' wrote Carlyle, and the development and preservation of individuality within a society dominated by various kinds of mechanistic systems (moral, social, political, economic, even historical) formed a major theme of fiction throughout the century.

However, whereas Carlyle's mechanized individual is tacitly assumed to be a man, the novel of this period belongs in certain crucial respects to women. Not only were women the major consumers of fiction, forming as they did the majority of the readership throughout the century, they were also, to a degree never seen previously, producers as well. Women novelists take at least equal status with men both as generally acknowledged 'great writers' – four of the six major practioners listed above are women – and also as part of the huge array of novel writers who produce everything from minor masterpieces to worthless pot-boilers. In the first two decades of the century Jane Austen was writing novels of sophisticated irony and realism, while ▷ Mary Shelley's ▷ *Frankenstein* (1817) represented the peak of the Gothic romance form (▷ Gothic novel). Throughout the period writers like ▷ Charlotte Yonge, ▷ Elizabeth Gaskell, ▷ Harriet Martineau, ▷ Ouida and ▷ Margaret Oliphant were producing novels ranging from serious social comment to wild sensationalism (novel of ▷ sensation). And in the 1890s the single most popular novelist (though very far from the best) was another woman, Marie Corelli, whose *The Sorrows of Satan* (1895) sold more copies than any previous English novel. The subject matter of fiction, moreover, fell characteristically into a woman's sphere: even in novels whose thematic interests lie primarily elsewhere, the standard plot and setting are almost invariably domestic and family-orientated, with courtship and marriage providing a major part of the narrative thrust. As George Eliot pointed out, the novel form, more than any other, offered opportunities to women in a society which elsewhere constrained their every activity: 'No restrictions can shut women out from the materials of fiction, and there is no species of art which is so free from rigid requirements.' The 19th-century novel was the first art form in which women could take equal status with men.

For George Eliot, though, as for many others, the unusually dominant role of women as both producers and consumers of fiction was not an unequivocally good thing. Her comments are taken from an essay entitled ▷ 'Silly Novels by Lady Novelists' in which she draws attention to the self-gratifying and unreal stereotypes which lady novelists offer to an uncritical female readership. In other respects, too, this female orientation had an unfortunate influence on the sphere of the English novel. The popular picture of the Victorian *pater familias* reading out suitable material to his devoted family was not far from the truth, and was felt by many practising novelists to be a major restriction on their art. The 'young person', made archetypal through Dickens's Miss Podsnap in ▷ *Our Mutual Friend* (1864–5), placed a crippling constraint on the material thought proper for inclusion in the novel: 'The question about everything was, would it bring a blush into the cheek of the young person? And the convenience of the young person was, that, according to Mr Podsnap, she seemed liable to burst into blushes when there was no need at all.' As ▷ Thackeray lamented in his preface to ▷ *Pendennis* (1848–50): 'Since the author of *Tom Jones* was buried, no writer of fiction among us has been permitted to depict to his utmost power a MAN'; where ▷ Henry Fielding was at liberty to portray a lovable male libertine, Thackeray and his contemporaries looked constantly over their shoulders for the blushes of the young person and the pursed lips of the symbolic guardian of morality, ▷ Mrs Grundy. This provided a focus for impassioned debate throughout the century: where Trollope recorded complacently that 'no girl has risen from the reading pages less modest than she was before', other novelists, such as the popular

▷ feminist writer of the 1890s ▷ Mona Caird, chafed furiously against such artificial restraints: 'Mrs Grundy in black silk, with a sceptre in her hand, on the throne of the Ages, surrounded by an angel-choir of Young Persons! Is this to be the end of our democracy?'

Thus, for a large part of the 19th century the English novel was significantly limited by the necessity to conform to a moral code which aimed to protect a predominantly female readership from exposure to sexual corruption. Extreme circumspection was required in the depiction of any sort of sexual contact, whether in or outside marriage, often with ludicrous results. Charlotte Brontë's unusually frank account of ▷ Jane Eyre's passionate feelings for Mr Rochester and of his sexual history brought accusations of coarseness from several critics. The scene in Hardy's ▷ *Tess of the D'Urbervilles* (1891) in which Angel Clare carries the milkmaids across a flooded lane had to be altered to expunge the image of a man lifting a personable young lady in his arms: in the serialized version, Clare had to be equipped with a wheelbarrow. And in broader terms, too, the novel upheld middle-class morality in matters of sexual conduct. Women were to be sexually pure, and morally superior to men; marriage was a sacred and indissoluble bond; women's individual emotional needs were to be subsumed in those of husband and family. Where a novel depicted deviation from these values, the appropriate moral lesson had to be firmly underlined, so that the 'fallen woman' who features in so much fiction of the period was invariably seen to be punished. ▷ Mrs Henry Wood's melodramatic and best-selling tale of adultery, ▷ *East Lynne* (1861), rammed home these lessons with almost sadistic relish, warning potential adulteresses that their fate 'will be found far worse than death' and proving the point with a story of startlingly ingenious retributive suffering. More commonly, the fallen woman was brought to a lonely death (like Lady Dedlock in ▷ *Bleak House*) or banished (like ▷ *David Copperfield's* Little Em'ly). Even in a work which pleaded for the moral rights of the fallen woman, such as Elizabeth Gaskell's ▷ *Ruth* (1853), the ultimate redemption could be attained only through death.

This circumspection had a more profound and potentially damaging effect on the portrayal of women in the 19th-century novel than it did on the representation of men. Thackeray was to some extent right to envy Fielding his Tom Jones, but he might have done better to regret his own inability to portray a ▷ Moll Flanders. Ironically, it was Thackeray himself who, in ▷ *Vanity Fair* (1847–8), encapsulated the Victorian double vision of women: the conventional ideal, destructively doting, cloyingly sentimental, passive, long-suffering and ultimately parasitical persists, as in Becky Sharp he portrays a woman of wit and initiative, who uses her sexuality and intelligence to exploit a society richly deserving her machinations, but who must finally be condemned as a neglectful mother, adulteress and, possibly, a murderer. Charlotte Brontë's ▷ *Shirley* (1849) explicitly attacks this male polarizing of supposed female attributes: 'Men are often under an illusion about women: they do not read them in a true light: they misapprehend them both for good and evil: their good woman is a queer thing, half doll, half angel; their bad woman always a fiend.' The bad woman, as we have seen, was habitually disposed of by death; but it was the good woman, half doll, half angel, who forms the common 20th-century conception of the typical Victorian heroine. Dickens' Agnes Wakefield, who in David Copperfield's image of her is 'forever pointing upward', is a typical role model for the sort of female perfection which is morally impeccable, spiritually uplifting and a well-earned reward for the world-weary hero. It was an ideal whose falsity was under constant attack throughout the period and which was largely discredited by the end of the century:

in ▷ Havelock Ellis' phrase, the stereotyped woman was 'a cross between an angel and an idiot'.

How, then, did what now appears such a patently distorted view of women retain such hold in fictional conventions? We must not dismiss out of hand the notion that Victorian portrayals of women are more reflective of their repression in reality than we would care to believe. ▷ George Gissing argued that women actually were intellectually and developmentally feebler than men, when in typically gloomy mood he stated that 'more than half the misery of life is due to the ignorance and childishness of women. The average woman pretty closely resembles ... the average male *idiot*.' In a society which, for the greater part of the century, denied women access to higher education and the professions, encased them physically in whalebone and voluminous skirts, and imbued them with the notion that their highest function was to serve and inspire men, it is little wonder that the conformist woman of the time should appear to modern eyes an unacceptably compliant creature – or, as Edward Carpenter (1844–1929) more waspishly expressed it, 'a bundle of weak and flabby sentiments, combined with a wholly undeveloped brain'. However, there is ample evidence both from the numerous examples of independent and rebellious women of 19th-century history, and from the many original and individualized heroines of fiction, that the conventional ideal was not the whole reality. More pervasively influential on characterization, as well as on the form and content of novels, were the actual conditions under which most of them were published.

At the beginning of the 19th century, the majority of novels were published in three, or sometimes four, volumes and the 'three decker' retained its popularity until almost the end of the Victorian period. The standard cost of each volume of the novel was half a guinea, a stiff enough price for most middle-class readers, and beyond the means of the working class. However, for a subscription of one guinea a year, readers could borrow a volume at a time from one of the ▷ circulating libraries, by far the most influential of which was ▷ Charles Mudie's, opened in 1842. Mudie exercised an influence over the Victorian novel which amounted to a form of censorship, for he prided himself upon selecting his stock according to its suitablility for family consumption. Just as Mudie's moral approval of an author, which could translate into mass buying of copies from the publisher and advance orders for future works, could launch a career in fiction, so his refusal to stock a novel of dubious morality might spell financial disaster. Few novelists could afford the risk of offending the circulating libraries and thus a form of guilty self-censorship constrained the creative freedom of most writers.

Alternatives to publication in three-volume form were initiated by the revival of the monthly serialization of Dickens' ▷ *Pickwick Papers* in 1836. Novels published in this manner were issued as slim volumes appearing at the beginning of each month, continuing, as a rule, for nineteen numbers. Clearly this form of publication deeply influenced the form of works in a way largely obscured by their subsequent appearance in a single volume. Writers who wished their readers to continue buying their work over a long period had to end each issue with some cliffhanging incentive to purchase the next volume, and needed also to ensure the memorability of characters whose last appearance could have occurred several months earlier. This may in part account for what is now sometimes taken to be a melodramatic form of plotting and exaggeration in characterization on the part of such habitual practioners of the monthly serial as Dickens or Thackeray. On the other hand, publication in parts did allow a writer to adjust his or her work in response to readers' preferences: a popular character could boost sales (as Sam Weller did for *Pickwick*) and a narrative red herring could be expeditiously abandoned. As single-volume serialization gradually gave way to part publication in family and literary magazines, the questions of sales and censorship moved from the author's to the editor's domain. Hardy was one of the prime sufferers from editorial restraint in the initial serial publication of his novels, and he frequently had to wait for one-volume publication before he was able to present his work in the form intended. Both Dickens and Thackeray had experience of the business from both ends, the first as editorial instigator of the family weeklies ▷ *Household Words* and ▷ All the Year Round, the second as editor of the prestigious ▷ *Cornhill*. Amongst major Victorian novelists, only the Brontës never published in any sort of serial form.

Development through the century

Given the wealth and variety of 19th-century fiction, as well as the inevitable historical shifts in critical judgements, it is hardly surprising to find widely diverging assessments of how the novel developed over the period. ▷ George Saintsbury's *A History of Nineteenth-century Literature*, first published in 1896, gives almost as much space to ▷ Maria Edgeworth as to Jane Austen and George Eliot, and treats ▷ Walter Scott more fully than Dickens: Hardy receives no mention at all. F. R. Leavis' immensely influential *The Great Tradition* (1948) opens with the characteristically combative statement: 'The great English novelists are Jane Austen, George Eliot, ▷ Henry James and ▷ Joseph Conrad'; Charlotte Brontë is noted as having 'permanent interest of a minor kind', Dickens as being a 'great entertainer' who lacks 'sustained seriousness'. Leavis' judgements, based on a vaguely defined but insistently urged criterion of 'significant creative achievement', were of course challenged almost immediately by other critics, and both he and his wife and fellow critic Q. D. Leavis later admitted Dickens and Charlotte Brontë to their higher ranks. In more recent years, the whole notion of the canon has come under attack, perhaps most notably from feminist critics. Individual writers and sub-genres of the novels which would have been relegated to areas of minor interest by many mid-20th-century critics now attract serious study, and the reputations of many well-known novelists have notably shifted. Of those most highly regarded in the 19th century itself, Scott and ▷ George Meredith have suffered the most serious depression in critical interest; neither is now much read by the general public or widely taught on literature degree courses. Dickens, on the other hand, has been reclaimed from the realm of mere entertainer and praised as an incisive social critic of profound symbolic significance. And Hardy, ignored by Saintsbury and patronizingly dismissed by Leavis, now commands as wide a critical industry on both sides of the Atlantic as any 19th-century novelist.

There is no simple way of subdividing the mass of fictional material published during the period, nor, despite Leavis' claim for a great tradition, is there any single line of development which can easily be traced. Conventionally, the pre-Victorian period, where the major figures are Scott and Jane Austen, is seen as having a separate identity, which then gives way to the explosion of talent in the first decades of Victoria's reign, with the emergence of Dickens, Thackeray and the Brontës. The mid-Victorian novel can be seen as dominated by the later Dickens and George Eliot, and the late-19th century by Hardy. These periods will be dealt with separately in conjunction with the major authors within them. However, to identify the major practitioners of the form during the period is very far from finding a consistent train of development. While there is a sense in which James' novels can be seen as a more self-consciously artistic development of Jane Austen's fictional mode, there is no obvious way in which Hardy may be said to emerge from the same tradition. Charlotte Brontë, notoriously, found little to admire in Jane Austen, and Hardy recorded that he was unable to finish reading *Wuthering Heights* (1847). Arguably, the 19th century saw the emergence in the novel of a privileging of ▷ 'realism', both in the presentation of psychological depth of characterization and in the depiction of humankind's inevitable interrelation with the newly perceived complexities of social and historical contexts. There is also a clear change, in the Victorian period at least, in the material thought permissable for inclusion in the novel. The tyranny of the circulating libraries and the family magazines was gradually eroded to allow greater frankness in the fictional portrayal of sexuality. By the 1890s outspokenness on questions of sexual behaviour – particularly in women – had become to some extent fashionable, and a host of popular novels which examined such questions in an overtly polemical manner enjoyed a brief vogue. Even so, the violently antagonistic reception of Hardy's ▷ *Jude the Obscure* (1895), which saw the novel reviled in the press and burnt by a bishop, showed how severely limited this increased tolerance could be.

More importantly, an attempt to treat 19th-century fiction as a smoothly developing series of 'great writers' severely distorts the picture of the novel as it would have been viewed by both readers and authors during the period itself. It ignores too much of what was seriously offered and received by contemporary writers and readers, and which is now the subject of increasing critical interest, both as reflections of the 19th-century consciousness and as significant and legitimate variations on the novel form. Late-20th-century taste is perhaps more open to claims of romance and fantasy, or sympathetically interested in the overt wrestling with ideas, than was the case when Leavis made high moral seriousness and mastery of form his main criteria of excellence. Minor novelists, and the sub-genres in which they frequently wrote, are an essential and illuminating part of the 19th-century fictional scene.

Sub-genres of the novel

During the early decades of the 19th century most popular fiction grew out of the traditions of ▷ romance and ▷ Romanticism. The two terms are, of course, closely linked, but should be equated. A romance, in David Masson's definition of 1859, was 'a fictitious narrative...the interest of which turns upon marvellous and uncommon incidents', and the debate between romance and realism formed a continuous part of 19th-century thinking about the theory of fiction. The influence of the Romantic movement was most apparent in the late-18th-century Gothic novel, a form not lacking in marvellous and uncommon incidents, but which also played on the Romantic interest in the supernatural and in the dark and untapped areas of the human psyche. Jane Austen, writing novels of pragmatic realism during the height of the Romantic period, mercilessly satirized the implausibility of the Gothic through the credulous Catherine of ▷ *Northanger Abbey* (1818), and neatly pinned down the possible self-indulgence of the Romantic sensibility in ▷ *Persuasion*'s Captain Brondon. ▷ Thomas Love Peacock's spoof Gothic novel ▷ *Nightmare Abbey* (1818), also lampooned the form as well as parodying the romantic excesses of some of that movement's major poets. But the Gothic was still kept vividly alive in Mary Shelley's *Frankenstein* published in the same year as Peacock's parody, and reappears, subtly transformed, in the works of Charlotte and Emily Brontë. It could also be argued that the ▷ historical novel, first popularized by Scott, and continued less successfully in the works of, for example, ▷ Harrison Ainsworth, owed much to the Romantic period and Gothic preoccupation with the past.

In many ways, though, it was romance rather than Romanticism which informed the main sub-genres of the first three decades of the 19th century. Writers of popular fiction were anxious to entertain their readers with dramatic incidents and to draw them imaginatively into worlds remote from their own. The historical novel could obviously offer limitless scope here, in terms of both high drama and (often ponderously academic) period detail. Where Ainsworth's novels catered to the contemporary taste for luridly reconstructed English history, one of the other popular practitioners of the form, ▷ Edward Bulwer, mainly remembered now for *The Last Days of Pompeii* (1834), took the wider sweep of Western historical movements as his subject. His historical romances tend to focus on the closing of eras and may thus be seen as signifying contemporary unease in the face of change and instability. But his writings are too clogged with the fruits of meticulous historical research, and too stilted in the rendering of dialogue to have lasted well. However, forms of the historical novel continued to be practised throughout the century by major as well as minor writers. George Eliot ventured into historical fiction, not wholly successfully, in ▷ *Romola*, as did Gissing in *Veranilda* (1904). And modern readers often overlook the fact that many familiar novels of the period announce themselves in their opening words as 'historical' while still being set in the 19th century: 'While the present century was in its teens...' (*Vanity Fair*); 'Thirty years ago, Marseilles lay burning in the sun...' (▷ *Little Dorrit*); 'One evening of late summer, before the nineteenth century had reached one-third of its span...' (▷ *The Mayor of Casterbridge*).

The historical novel could be both an escape from and a comment on the profound changes which were perceived to be occurring in the contemporary social order. Of less obvious relevance were the other popular sub-genres of the early 19th century, the ▷ Newgate novel and the ▷ silver-fork school. The Newgate novel played on morbid tastes for violence and death in ways which relate it to some extent to the Gothic, and in romanticizing its criminals it removed such socially disruptive elements safely into the realm of fantasy. The silver-fork school, on the other hand, displayed the sort of high society life to which increasingly prosperous members of the middle class might hope to aspire and which they could certainly be expected to envy. Novels of this class paraded details of the food, fashions and furniture of the rich and well-bred before a readership which could now begin to dream of emulating such manners. Writers of silver-fork fiction included ▷ Benjamin Disraeli in his early novel *Vivien Grey* (1826), the now largely forgotten Theodore Hook (1788–1841), and ▷ Catherine Gore. Both Dickens and Thackeray capture and to some degree satirize the mood of envious interest amongst the socially mobile on which these novels played – Thackeray in his portrayal of the *nouveau riches* Osborne and Sedly families in *Vanity Fair*, and Dickens, for example, in his parody 'The Lady Flabella' in ▷ *Nicholas Nickleby* or with the Veneerings in *Our Mutual Friend*. Interestingly, both the Newgate and silver-fork forms have counterparts in modern popular fiction in the bodice-ripping school of historical fiction (where sex replaces death as the focus) and the sex-and-shopping novel which caters for the emulative dreams of the upwardly mobile.

Of more immediate social relevance, however, as well as in general possessing more lasting literary merit, were the novels which addressed the 'condition of England' question. These works, also known as ▷ 'social problem' novels arose out of the social and political upheavals which followed the ▷ Reform Act of 1832. The 1830s and 1840s marked the beginning of a conscious effort both by Parliament and by social commentators to address the problems caused by the rapid industrialization of the preceding decades. The first Factory Act (▷ factories) and the ▷ Poor Law Amendment Act of 1834 reflected the stirrings of governmental conscience and, from the other side, the rise of ▷ Chartism marked the beginnings of concerted working-class demands for reform. The economic depression of the 1840s produced deprivation amongst the industrial workers of the north on a scale which could not be ignored, and Chartist riots and marches on Westminster made poverty and disaffection visibly threatening to the comparatively untouched middle-class southerner. It was Carlyle who first drew attention to the social effects of the Industrial Revolution in his essay ▷ 'Signs of the Times' (1829) and who, in coining the phrase 'condition of England question' in *Chartism* (1839), provided a focus for what to many novelists of the early Victorian period seemed to be the central matter for fiction. Writers like Elizabeth Gaskell, Disraeli, ▷ Charles Kingsley and the Dickens of ▷ *Hard Times* (1854), addressed themselves directly to the question and produced novels which dealt realistically and sympathetically with the new problems of the industrialized working class.

Probably the major strength of the social problem novel lay in its educational rather than its polemical function. Written by and for the middle classes, these novels laid out with passionate clarity the plight of a section of the community of which most readers, for geographical and social reasons, were simply ignorant. The new cities of the north of England, where industrial workers were herded into hastily erected housing built round smoke-belching factories, were uncharted territory for large parts of the novel-reading public, and the divisive effects of such developments were repeatedly stressed by novelists. In giving his condition of England novel ▷ *Sybil* (1845) the subtitle 'The Two Nations', Disraeli encapsulated his perception of a country tragically and dangerously split between rich and poor, and Elizabeth Gaskell's ▷ *North and South* (1854–5) explores the differences in values and living conditions between the two halves of the country. The vividly realistic descriptions of working-class life provided by many social problem novels were as educative to contemporary readers as to later social historians, and the pressing issues of Chartism, trade unions, strikes and master-worker relations receive sensitive if rarely revolutionary treatment in such novels as Gaskell's ▷ *Mary Barton* (1848), Kingsley's ▷ *Alton Locke* (1850) and Disraeli's *Sybil*. Dickens' *Hard Times*, the only one of his novels to be set exclusively in the north of England, contrasts the mechanistic, and as he sees them, inhuman principles of ▷ utilitarian philosophy with the personal and warm-hearted values of imaginative sympathy, and his handling of the question of solidarity amongst the factory hands is symptomatic of the ambivalence apparently inherent in the genre. His working-class protagonist, Stephen Blackpool, is a saintly victim, his union leader a blustering agitator and the men good-hearted innocents temporarily swayed into an unworthy form of protest against a system portrayed as patently wrong. Blackpool's repeated lament in the fact of bafflingly obvious injustice, ''Tis all a muddle', sums up the helplessness of worker and novelist alike in the face of the enormity of the problem.

Indeed, the one major criticism of the genre, levelled by contemporaries as well as by modern critics, was that it proffered inadequate and often sentimental solutions to questions of great social and political complexity. As Thackeray put it, 'At the conclusion of these tales...there somehow arrives a misty reconciliation between the poor and the rich; a prophecy is uttered of better times for the one, and better manners in the other...and the characters make their bow, grinning, in a group, as they do at the end of a drama when the curtain falls.' This is largely true of the novels mentioned: the symbolic handshake between master and man at the end of *North and South*, Mary Barton's escape to Canada with her newly-wed husband, or Stephen Blackpool's martyrdom in the cause of truth and understanding – all substitute reconciliation at a personal level for long-term political solutions. However, there is no reason to expect novelists to be in possession of answers which escaped legislators, whereas in articulating and making imaginatively immediate the social problems of the time, writers of the condition of England novels not only provided a valuable information service but also produced works of significant realism and insight.

The social condition of a newly industrialized Britain was a preoccupation of novelists during the 1840s and 1850s. During the same period the spiritual condition of the country also became of pressing concern and novels dealing with religious questions formed another recognizable sub-genre which retained its currency to the end of the century. In some sense all 19th-century novels are 'religious' in so far as they are the product of a society in which Christian observance was the norm amongst the middle classes, and thus the oral and spiritual values of Christianity are necessarily either implicit or deliberately explored by all writers of fiction. However, the crisis of faith which arose in the middle decades of the 19th century predictably gave rise to works which set out to discuss the problems explicitly, in much the same way in which the condition of England novel articulated social and political questions. The three main influences on religious thought during this time were the ▷ Oxford Movement of the 1830s and 1840s, which sought to restore High Church ideals within the Church of England, and culminated in ▷ John Newman's defection to Roman ▷ Catholicism in 1845; the new German biblical criticism, made first accessible to English readers with the publication of George Eliot's translation of Strauss's *Leben Jesu* in 1846; and, of course, the impact of ▷ Charles Darwin's *On the Origin of Species* (1859). Spiritual crises and ecclesiastical quarrellings form the subject of such novels as J. A. Froude's *The Nemesis of Faith* (1849), Disraeli's *Lothair* (1870) and ▷ Mrs Humphry Ward's *Robert Elsmere* (1883), as well as being the basis of Trollope's Barsetshire novels and Margaret Oliphant's imitations of them, 'The Chronicles of Carlingford'.

Nineteenth-century consumers of fiction were thus very much more receptive to the exposition of ideas in fiction than are most modern readers, who tend to resent being preached at under the guise of fiction. Problem novels, or 'novels with a purpose', tackled issues of all kinds throughout the period. Again, the main beneficiaries of this discursive tendency were probably women, whose problems, lumped under the catch-all phrase 'the ▷ woman question', were repeatedly examined. The fallen woman was, as mentioned above, a particularly popular subject, featuring as a dreadful warning in works such as *East Lynne* or as a repentant Magdalene figure in *Ruth*. Charlotte Yonge's *The Clever Woman of the Family* (1865) cautions young women against the temptations of the intellect as memorably as Mrs Henry Wood does against the lure of the flesh. And by the last decade of the century there had arisen a distinct class of novel, the ▷ 'New Woman fiction', which dealt with the current feminist questions of sex, marriage and work. ▷ Grant Allen's *succès de scandale*, ▷ *The Woman Who Did* (1895), marked the culmination of the genre, with its hyperbolic attack on the institution of marriage (a 'temple' where 'pitiable victims languish and die in...sickening vaults'). Nor was the problem novel exclusively the province of minor writers: almost all major novelists of the period deal with these ideas in some form or other, and in the 1890s, for example, George Gissing's ▷ *The Odd Woman* (1893), Meredith's *Lord Ormont and his Aminta* (1894) and Hardy's *Jude the Obscure* (1895) were all taken by contemporary readers to be variations of the New Woman novel.

There is, then, continuous interaction in terms of themes, issues and genres, between different writers and between recognizable sub-groups of the novel and what is now regarded as mainstream fiction. The novelists of the period should be viewed within the artistic as well as the social and political context in which they worked.

The pre-Victorian period: Jane Austen

To select Jane Austen as the single major writer of this period is at once to make a critical judgement which would not always have been accepted. For later 19th-century readers and many earlier 20th-century ones, Walter Scott would have appeared probably the more influential figure. In initiating the historical romance he popularized a form which retained its appeal throughout the century and he was read with admiration by most subsequent 19th-century novelists. Charlotte Brontë, unsurprisingly, much preferred his romantic sweep to Jane Austen's tightly controlled realism, and Henry James praised his 'responding imagination before the human scene'. Interestingly, though, it was Scott himself who was one of the first to identify and appreciate Jane Austen's particular contribution to the development of the English novel at the time. In his review of ▷ *Emma* (1816) he discusses at length the limitations and diminishing returns of the predominating romance form, praising her novels for 'presenting to the reader, instead of the striking representation of an imaginary world, a correct and striking representation of that which is daily taking place around him'.

Jane Austen was herself, as is widely known, acutely conscious of the self-imposed restrictions of her range. When she wrote of the 'little bit (two inches wide) of ivory on which I work with so fine a brush as produces little effect after much labour', she was characteristically both self-deprecating about her limitations and astute about her strengths. As a realist in an age dominated by romance, her fine brush reworked the material of fiction into tones which set standards for the investigation of the individual within a closely observed social framework for later realists to emulate if they could. For a long time her reputation was somewhat distorted by 'Janeite' critics who praised her 'gentle' irony and indulgent humour, thus creating an impression of a softly female orientation within the safe sphere of domestic concerns, untroubling to the larger issues of life. Nothing could be further from the truth. Her irony, far from being gentle, is habitually savage in its condemnation of the foolish, hypocritical and self-deceiving; her humour is razor-sharp in its exposure of human weakness in a morally flawed society. Her heroines are set painful lessons in personal knowledge and moral self-discipline which entirely deny the possibilities of sentimental or coincidental resolve to which later Victorian novelists often have recourse. If, in keeping with the comic mode, they succeed finally in securing their desirable ends, it is not through a conventional coincidence of circumstance but because moral maturity secures an appropriate partnering. Nor is Jane Austen's world as prim and restricted as is sometimes unguardedly assumed. While never condoning sexual misdemeanour, her treatment of the subject owes more to hard-headed 18th-century worldliness than to Victorian repression. Where the Victorian female innocent is habitually seduced, abandoned and condemned to a lonely fate, Lydia Bennet (▷ *Pride and Prejudice*) bounces exuberantly into Wickham's bed with no thoughts in her head beyond immediate gratification, and after her hastily patched up marriage is received, if coolly, by her family.

Jane Austen's values, then, are more 18th-century than Victorian, more ▷ classical than romantic. She portrays a society in which foolishness, hypocrisy and avarice abound, but where an agreed standard of moral principle may be assumed and where rationality may be invoked to counterbalance the disruptive lure of unbridled emotionalism. Her characters may suffer but they must also understand, and their understanding derives from a proper exercise of rational thought rather than from emotional or subconscious enlightenment. Through Marianne in ▷ *Sense and Sensibility* (1811) she attacks the idea that feeling can be a reliable guide to conduct and in ▷ *Persuasion* (1818) she satirizes, though with more sympathetic indulgence, romantic emotion. But perhaps no single factor marks Jane Austen off more distinctly from the Victorian novelists that followed her than her treatment of children. Amongst her heroines, only Fanny Price in ▷ *Mansfield Park* (1814) is portrayed in childhood, and children in general figure merely as convenient plot devices or as social distractions. By contrast, the Victorian novelist frequently makes the child, often an orphan, and the process of growth to maturity a central thematic focus. After Jane Austen, the influence of Romantic thought on ideas about childhood, innocence, imagination and feeling is everywhere apparent.

The mid-nineteenth century: Dickens, Thackeray, and the Brontës

It is notable, then, that while biographers of Jane Austen find difficulty in giving dramatic interest to a life of largely uneventful calm, those of the great mid-century novelists have a wealth of misery, neglect and misunderstanding to relate in their subjects' early years. This has the obvious effect of producing corresponding autobiographical portrayals of children in the novels, but also tends to create a sense, in marked contrast to Austen, of the fictional protagonist as alienated from or at odds with society. In the early Victorian novel the depiction of society generally expands unrecognizably from Jane Austen's little bit of ivory to a consciously panoramic perspective in which the individual is likely to be embattled and forlorn. The figure of the innocent child, often lonely and neglected, becomes a powerful symbol of society's guilt; the ▷ education and growth from childhood show the process of adjustment within a largely hostile social structure. While the Romantic movement discovered and articulated the moral potency of the child, it was the Victorian novel which produced the first sustained portrayals of children in literature.

Of the major novelists of the period, William Makepeace Thackeray is probably least directly concerned with children, though his best novel, *Vanity Fair*, does make use of significant incidents from the childhood of his protagonists in order to account for their subsequent development. Though often astute and original in his perception of his characters' psychology, his main strengths as a writer lay in his sharp eye for the particular kinds of human weakness thrown up by a newly complex society and his ability, in *Vanity Fair* as least, to bind all levels of the social structure into a comprehensive vision of moral and spiritual inadequacy. When Charlotte Brontë described him as 'the first social regenerator of the day', she was responding to qualities which were abundantly present in his early work but which faded notably in his later career. *Vanity Fair*, 'A Novel without a Hero', depicts English society in the years surrounding ▷ Waterloo as itself a battleground where money and social standing are the criteria for success and where individuals rise and fall according to their skill in playing social games as amoral and arbitrary as the Stock Exchange on which fortunes are won and lost. Though Thackeray focuses his interest on the newly emerging middle classes, his picture of society extends upwards into the metropolitan aristocracy and the landed gentry, and downwards to the working classes and ▷ Bohemia. What binds them all is the struggle for money and reputation in a cut-throat world where the clever can 'live well on nothing a year' and the weak go to the wall. It is mark of Thackeray's originality that the character who most successfully exploits the possibilities of this social struggle is a woman, the intelligent and cynical

Becky Sharp; and though he works hard to condemn her at the end of the novel, her wit and energy continue to contrast favourably with the vapid conventionality of other characters. The novel leaves a moral question mark over all its characters and in so doing forces its readers to engage actively in the process of questioning and judgement in a way calculated both to challenge and disturb.

Charles Dickens, Thackeray's more successful rival for the affections of the novel-reading public, rarely leaves such moral openness, but develops more consistantly towards a bleak view of society in which monolithic institutions (money and commerce in *Dombey and Son*, the law in *Bleak House*, the civil service in *Little Dorrit*) are potentially crushing to the strongly realized goodness of individuals. It was Dickens more than any other Victorian novelist who exploited the possibilities of the child as symbol of innocence amidst corruption, and this is one major factor which has led to accusations of sentimentality in his works. A catalogue of his maltreated but morally reformative children – ▷ Oliver Twist, David Copperfield, Paul and Florence Dombey, Jo the crossing sweeper, Little Nell, Sissy Jupe (from *Hard Times*), Little Dorrit (amongst many others) – suggests a preoccupation with the innocence of childhood which could add weight to such an accusation, and it is largely true that Dickens' children are exempt from the barbs of humorous exposure with which he mercilessly illuminates the grotesque flaws in most of his characters. But his best portrayals of childhood – those in which the child ceases to be a simple symbolic force – uniquely capture the guilts and fears as well as the pathetic helplessness of juvenile innocence.

Much modern criticism bases its praise for Dickens on a perception of the development in his later novels of a thematically coherent critique of his society which works through imagery and symbolism rather than through the creation of psychologically convincing characters. One can point, for example, to the recurrent images of imprisonment in *Little Dorrit* or to the sustained exploration of legal ramifications in *Bleak House*. Dickens' world is so richly animated, his descriptive powers so invigoratingly original as to invest the inanimate objects of his world with a vitality and significance often assumed to compensate for the lack of realism in the people which inhabit it. His women are prime targets for criticism here, since it is generally female characters who, for obvious reasons, carry the sometimes crippling weight of his moral approval. Dickens, while anatomizing the evils of his society with unique imaginative power, had a characteristically Victorian belief in the possibility of unsullied goodness and it is generally the heroines of his novels who provide examples of its morally regenerative force. Sissy Jupe in *Hard Times* works a change in the harshly utilitarian Gradgrind household 'by mere love and gratitude' and it is her 'wisdom of the Heart' which effectively counteracts the mechanistic values that the novel attacks. Her passive goodness and sweetly self-sacrificing nature exemplify the qualities often taken to be regrettably typical of Dicken's portrayal of women. However, it could also be argued that the 20th century's automatic suspicion of pure virtue blinds the modern reader to more subtle qualities in Dickens' heroines. His skill in depicting the psychological results of guilt and repression, often noted in his male characters, is present also in his portrayal of many of the women. For characters such as Florence Dombey, Esther Summerson or Little Dorrit 'becoming good' is a psychologically plausible reaction to rejection and alienation, though the modern critical eye has habitually been too prejudiced against the stereotype of the virtuous woman to note this.

Whatever may be reclaimed for Dickens' reputation in the portrayal of women, though, he can never hope to rival the Brontës in this area. ▷ Anne Brontë, less talented and original than her sisters, still writes movingly and perceptively about the loneliness of the governess in ▷ *Agnes Grey* (1847), and adds new dimensions to the depiction of marital misery in ▷ *The Tenant of Wildfell Hall* (1848). Emily Brontë's only novel, *Wuthering Heights*, is generally recognized to transcend normal moral and spiritual expectations. Though Charlotte Brontë felt it necessary in her Preface to her sister's novel to apologize for what she felt 'must appear a rude and strange production', the novel is meticulously planned and structured. Its strangeness derives partly from its unaccustomed settings, more perhaps from its extremities of violence and passion, and the central portrayal in Cathy and Heathcliff of a relationship which cannot be assimilated into any conventional framework or concept of character. That Emily Brontë was aware of the difficulties of this structure is shown by the care with which she draws her readers into the story through narrators of familiar social and psychological backgrounds; as their limitations are exposed, so their conventional judgements are progressively rejected and the reader is invited to accept an entirely unfamiliar scheme of values. At the end of the novel, Lockwood's inability to imagine 'unquiet slumbers for the sleepers in that quiet earth' seems more a reflection of his own limitations than an assurance that the grave will provide a final peace for the spirits of Cathy and Heathcliff.

However, the radical nature of Emily Brontë's vision makes her less influenced by social realities. Her main characters, being largely outside convention, make no direct comment upon it. Charlotte Brontë, on the other hand, working more within the bounds of recognizable society, produces original depictions of women which are overtly hostile to contemporary ideas. The autobiographical elements in her work create repeated images of women struggling against a world whose expectations they are unable and, indeed, unwilling to fulfil. ▷ Jane Eyre, 'poor, plain and little', and Lucy Snow (in ▷ *Villette*, 1853), wracked with the pain of unrequited love, obviously call upon Charlotte Brontë's own experiences. Her heroines all struggle in a world whose standards of female behaviour are alien to their own, and their achievements are wrenched painfully from the creation of a personal morality which is frequently at odds with the conventions of their society. Though Lucy Snow, who in *Villette*'s slightly ambiguous ending is shown as independent mistress of her own school, may seem the most obvious candidate for modern feminist approval, it is really Jane Eyre who summarizes Brontë's sustained plea for a morality in which the heroine has the right and the duty to realize her individuality independent of expectations from more moral systems. Both Charlotte and Emily Brontë participate in the Romantic's championing of the unique individual, the first within, the second largely outside contemporary social realities. The poetic intensity of their writing, together with the patent influences of the Gothic and ▷ Byronic traditions, make their works the most striking inheritors of Romanticism in the fiction of the period.

The mid-Victorian period: George Eliot

It is gratifying to reflect that the first intellectual amongst major English novelists was a woman. In an age when female education was largely limited to the acquisition of 'accomplishments', George Eliot could read French, Italian, German, Latin and Greek. Deeply involved in and influenced by the philosophical and scientific movements of the time, she lost her religious faith in early womanhood but retained a profound sense of moral imperatives in a secular context. In common with many of her counterparts, her interests focused on history and on modern attempts to arrive at systematic descriptions of social, religious and intellectual evolution. Her novels continually show her interest in the relationship between individual and historical change: as the individual is the product of social and historical forces, so society is formed and changed by the apparently inconsiderable lives of the individuals who compose it. Dorothea, who sets out at the beginning of ⊳ *Middlemarch* (1871–2) in the view of the narrator as a 'modern Saint Theresa', may be defeated in her youthful objectives of effecting visible or dramatic change in her society, but is convincingly displayed at the end as having an effect 'incalculably diffusive' on 'the growing good of the world'. The portrayal of the individual within a complex network of social and historical relationships forms a major part of George Eliot's fictional vision.

The past, and the extent to which Eliot's characters are determined by forces contained within it form a continual theme in her fiction. 'Our deeds determine us, as much as we determine our deeds,' she wrote in *Adam Bede* (1859), and her novels repeatedly display what in *Middlemarch* she described as 'the slow preparation of effects from one life on another'. Seeing her characters as largely determined by a meticulously charted individual past, and a socially and historically realized present, she nevertheless insists upon the stern exercise of personal responsibility in moral decision-making. Her characters or, more particularly, her narrators, are among the first in English fiction to be consistently portrayed in the process of rigorous *thought*, whether about personal choices or larger intellectual systems. However, George Eliot as narrator remains firmly in control of both her structures and her readers' responses. When in *Middlemarch* she comments on the unknowable significance of future developments in individual lives – 'destiny stands by sarcastic with our *dramatis personae* folded in her hand' – she could have legitimately substituted herself for destiny. George Eliot's authorial voice, omniscient, magisterial and tolerant, constantly controls our reactions and, to some extent, raises her readers to a level close to her own lofty overview. When ⊳ Virginia Woolf described *Middlemarch* as 'one of the few English novels written for grown-up people', she was deftly defining the degree to which George Eliot's fiction makes demands of serious moral response in a readership which could previously have rested happily within the safe bounds of entertaining diversion.

Hardy and the late-nineteenth century

Some contemporary reviews of Thomas Hardy's early, anonymously published work speculated that it might be by George Eliot. Presumably they were misled by the superficial similarities in the portrayal of rural communities and perhaps by Hardy's youthful pretensions to a command of contemporary intellectual issues, imperfectly assimilated. Indeed, an ability to judge his readers' tolerance of progressive moral and intellectual views was a continuing, and to modern eyes endearing, quality of Hardy's fiction, deriving as it did from his unusual combination of a countryman's pragmatism with a self-educated intellectualism. As the creator of the semi-fictional world of Wessex, Hardy became the most significant regional novelist of the age and, with his unrivalled knowledge of the local customs and accents of his native land, was in better position than any other writer to chart the changes in agricultural communities under the various dramatic shocks of 19th-century change. Hardy has, moreover, an eye for nature which is at once entirely unsentimental and supremely observant. When in ⊳ *A Pair of Blue Eyes* (1873) Henry Knight clings desperately to a cliff with a fatal drop beneath him, Hardy notes that his torments are increased by the fact that rain driven against such an obstacle moves upwards not down: and, mechanically staring death in the face, Knight's eyes actually meet the fossilized gaze of a trilobite embedded for millions of years in the rock before him. The vulnerable human in his extremity meets the indifferent but infinitely varied forces of nature, yet has contact over a gap of several million years with a fellow creature who has similarly suffered the pangs of life and death.

Such an incident is typical of the way in which Hardy's immense imaginative range and habitual preoccupation with the ironies of time are given solidity by observation of the precisely natural. It is also characteristic in that Knight's eventual rescue is effected by an incident at once stimulating and shocking to Victorian sexual tastes. The novel's heroine, Elfride, strips herself of all her undergarments in order to make a rope and, clad merely in a 'diaphanous exterior robe', hauls him to safety. Throughout his career Hardy found himself embroiled in battles against the prudish sensibilities of his readership and, as his later novels began to engage more directly with contemporary questions of sexual morality, he was drawn, apparently protestingly, into fervent debates about women, sex and marriage. His views of the human condition, though, are more comprehensively tragic than would be suggested by confining him to immediate social criticism. Frequently accused of being irredeemably pessimistic, he described himself as a meliorist who portrayed the worst in order to point towards the better. But, despite the sharpness of their social criticism, there is little in his last novels – in *Tess of the D'Urbervilles* or *Jude the Obscure* – to suggest that possible future change could effectively alleviate what a recent biographer has termed his 'obstinate intonations of doomed morality'.

Hardy was in many senses the last of the great Victorian novelists. During the final years of the century it was his reputation, together with the more warily expressed admiration for Meredith, which dominated English fiction. Amongst other novelists, though, the debate about the relationship between romance and realism continued to be waged, with Gissing and ▷ George Moore as the prime realists vying with the exotic romances of, for example, ▷ Robert Louis Stevenson and ▷ H. Rider Haggard. The vitality of the novel form was undiminished both in its challenge to social and moral convention and in its sheer inventiveness in entertainment. In literary terms, though, it was Henry James, with his infinitely sophisticated narrative and Joseph Conrad's modernism, which pointed the way forwards into 20th-century developments of the novel as a form of art.

Drama in the 19th Century: 1837–1901

17

Ian Clarke

The drama of the 19th century has often been taken to represent a fallow period in literary and theatrical history. According to this view, between the Restoration dramatists of the late 16th and early 17th centuries there is nothing much of interest (apart from slight blips in the 18th century with John Gay, Richard Sheridan and Oliver Goldsmith) until the very end of the 19th century and the arrival of ⊳ Oscar Wilde and ⊳ George Bernard Shaw. The influential *Pelican Guide to English Literature* offers a typical example of this view of 19th-century drama and theatre: 'The theatrical world was rather a shabby one, dependent largely on poor and economical translations of bad plays . . . Only with the discovery of anti-Victorian zest by Oscar Wilde and by Shaw, under the influence of Butler and a partially understood Ibsen, does the drama recover a measure of linguistic vitality and social function.' The dismissal of 19th-century drama as unworthy of consideration is compounded by the fact that its dominant genre was ⊳ melodrama and that, according to a canonical literary view, this genre itself is of little worth. Thus M. H. Abrams in *A Glossary of Literary Terms* clearly establishes a hierarchy of genres that effectively sidelines much 19th-century drama: 'The 19th century in England produced few notable tragedies but many melodramas.' Abrams, as does the essay in the *Pelican Guide*, underpins the argument by subscribing to a literary critical concept of value which cannot accommodate the structures and forms of melodrama: 'The protagonists are pure as the driven snow and antagonists luridly evil, while credibility of both character and action is sacrificed for violent effect, in a drama contrived according to an emotional opportunism.' This view is, however, a distortion and misrepresentation of the actuality of 19th-century stage melodrama; it amounts to an uninformed literary critical prejudice.

Nor is it difficult to find this sort of point of view repeated in specifically theatrical dictionaries and companions. The following examples are taken from two of the most accessible and widely available of such works:

> an extravagant drama making full use of all the possibilities inherent in music, lighting, and stage machinery for the artificial heightening of emotion) . . .
> drama of an unusually sensational type . . .
> naive popular entertainment . . .
> [a] diversion (sometimes with pretensions to social significance) . . .
> [plays] whose elements were highly coloured and larger than life – the noble outlaw, the wronged maiden, the cold-blooded villain . . .
> [melodrama indicates] everything that fed the popular appetite for horror and mystery, violence and double-dealing, but always with virtue triumphant . . .

Again the generalizations misrepresent the actuality. In effect, these reference works are not descriptive of actual cultural forms and history; rather, these theatrical dictionaries codify what is fundamentally a *literary critical* prejudice.

The consignment of 100 years of dramatic writing and theatrical history to the dustbin obscures the sheer amount of theatrical activity and writing that took place in the 19th century. Evidence of the amount and indeed the growth of theatrical activity can easily be found in the handlists of plays appended to the individual volumes of Allardyce Nicoll's *A History of English Drama 1660–1900*. The handlist for the period 1800 to 1850 runs to 395 pages, and for the period 1850 to 1900 to 617 pages.

The growth in dramatic writing was matched, particularly in the second half of the century, by the building of new theatres and the rebuilding and extensive refurbishment of existing ones in provincial towns and cities as well as in London. Technological innovation was constantly put to use in theatres often dedicated to presenting the visually spectacular. Oil lighting began to be replaced by gas soon after the start of the century, and by its end many theatres had replaced or supplemented gas with electricity. The impulses of antiquarianism and literalism resulted in sets that accurately recreated settings for which scenic artists of reputation and merit painted huge backcloths to give the effect of three-dimensionality in a two-dimensional medium. The demand for lavish and often violent spectacle grew throughout the period. Consequently, stage machinery as well as lighting effects became increasingly ingenious and technically complex. By the turn of century the stage adaptation (1899) of Lew Wallace's novel *Ben Hur* staged the chariot race with real horses, and the sporting melodrama *The Whip* (1909) represented not just the running of the Derby but also a train crash. The developing film industry capitalized on the demand for spectacle, and film's ability to present even more elaborate (and seemingly more realistic) spectacles heralded the demise of spectacular stage melodrama in the early years of the 20th century.

Throughout the whole of the 19th century the theatre represented one of the dominant forms of popular cultural entertainment. However, in the latter half of the century, actual legislation, campaigns for further legislative reform, and more general shifts in attitudes and perceptions pressured for a drama that was to have a higher cultural standing and for a mainstream theatre that was to acquire a greater social respectability. While at one level these developments represented a desire on the part of theatre managers, actors and dramatists to be taken and to take themselves more seriously, it also determined theatre-going as a class-defined social activity. From the 1860s onwards the fabric of auditoria (in the more expensive parts at least) of major provincial theatres as well as those of London's West End was designed as part of a social event, providing entertainment for a middle-class audience. The social status of the upper echelons of the acting profession rose throughout the latter half of the century to the extent that in 1895 ▷ Henry Irving was made the first actor knight for services to the theatre. This new-found conventional social respectability determined not just the tone of theatregoing but also the concept of the function of theatre and the nature of the drama it presented.

There was a similar rise in the status of the dramatist. If, in the earlier part of the century, the actor was not generally accepted into polite society, so the dramatist was often viewed as a hack churning out unfortunate adaptations of continental European dramas and farces. By the end of the century, however, a dramatist could, partly as a result of the protection provided by recent copyright legislation, view her/his profession as serious and, indeed, potentially lucrative. In the 1890s dramatists such as ▷ Henry Arthur Jones and ▷ Arthur Wing Pinero issued well-produced editions of their plays to coincide with their premieres. George Bernard Shaw, on the other hand, published his plays when there was, in some cases, little or no chance of their production on the public stage. Both enterprises indicate a reading audience for play texts. The issuing of plays by reputable publishing houses meant that the drama could stand in their lists alongside volumes of novels, poetry, and essays. A point reiterated by Jones in his collected essays, *The Renascence of the English Drama* (1895), was that if the drama were to have any intellectual respectability, dramatists had to be seen as persons of letters and that their product could bear comparison with other literary forms. The intellectual respectability of the drama was further enhanced by the seriousness with which it was taken by late-19th-century commentators and critics such as ▷ George Moore, ▷ William Archer, ▷ Henry James, A.B. Walkley, ▷ J.T. Grein, and Shaw.

According to that classist point of view that links cultural and class formations so as to validate the former by the latter, the social problem drama of the end of the century (despite its indebtedness to earlier drama) is often still viewed as a huge advance on the supposedly unfortunate popular cultural melodramatic forms of the earlier part of the century. Nevertheless, seminal works – Michael R. Booth's *English Melodrama*, and Peter Brooks' *The Melodramatic Imagination* – have done much to shift the critical ground so that the term melodrama, and more importantly its adjectival form, can be used descriptively rather than pejoratively. The re-evaluation of melodrama has also been greatly assisted by the relatively recent emergence of theatre studies and cultural studies as distinct disciplines. Melodrama and the melodramatic can now be considered as an important and, indeed, central cultural form of the 19th century.

The first play in English specifically to identify itself as a melodrama (although in the French form *mélodrame*) was Thomas Holcroft's *A Tale of Mystery* (1802), an adaptation from the French of Guilbert de Pixérécourt's *Coelina, ou l'Enfant de mystère* (1800). The ▷ Gothic elements of *A Tale of Mystery* – the creation of a sense of impending, foreboding doom; settings which included 'A Gothic Hall in the House of [the suitably foreign-sounding] Bonamo' and 'Wild mountainous country . . . with pines and massy rocks' – were to become a mainstay of early English melodrama. Such elements would become even more elaborate and spectacular to include ruined castles, dungeons, ghosts, violent storms. A feature of *A Tale of Mystery* which would remain throughout the century is its use of music – 'Violent distracted music', 'Music of Terror', 'Music to express disorder' are specifically notated, along with many other precisely discriminated types of music, in the stage directions. Music underscores the action and emotional mood, and signifies character function. The use of music in part derives from French and German dramatic antecedents, and from current English theatrical practice. Often viewed as a regrettable consequence of the monopoly of the two patent theatres (Covent Garden and Drury Lane) on the so-called legitimate drama and the legal requirement for the so-called illegitimate drama to contain a certain number of songs and pieces of musical accompaniment, the function of music in melodrama should rather be seen as central and indispensable to the creative signifying practices of the genre. A modern analogy in a popular cultural form is the use of music and song in the soundtrack of a feature film.

The exoticism of Gothic melodrama dominated in the first two decades of the 19th century, but domestic melodrama with native English settings emerged towards the end of the 1820s and became increasingly prevalent. Even in other forms of melodrama – nautical, military, temperance, criminal – domestic elements are crucial. Domestic melodrama offered a construction of domestic ideology in its ideal form so as to provide judgemental systems encoding for the spectator approbation and disapprobation of characters, incidents, and situations. Thus those characters who uphold and protect the domestic ideal are to be approved of; those who threaten it are instantly figured as villains. This places at the centre of the drama the nuclear family, and occasionally the extended family, with its attendant bonds and obligations. Within this arena the dramatic impetus derives from negotiations and intersections of class and gender, wealth and justice, and, above all, power. Far from being escapist entertainment, in the earlier part of the 19th century domestic melodrama offered to newly urbanized working-class audiences valid images, however indirect, of their own alienated and disempowered experience as wage slaves.

In this context, a key figure in the melodrama became the hard-hearted, foreclosing landlord. His activities in turning families out of their homes into the street were represented unequivocally as violating the domestic ideal. The pathos created by the presence of lachrymose children and infirm old folk confirms his behaviour as all the more heinous. The conflict between the sanctity of the family unit and the landlord's actions is brought into direct play in Douglas Jerrold's *Black-Ey'd Susan* (1829) where Doggrass, who intends to evict black-eyed Susan of the title along with the aged and dying Dame Hatley, is not only Susan's landlord but her uncle. By unwaveringly demanding his arrears of rent he jettisons his familial obligations towards, as Susan reminds him, his 'brother's orphan child'. The contradiction between the familial relationship and the relationship between landlord and tenant is made explicit in the following exchange:

> *Susan.* Uncle, the old woman is sick – I fear dangerously. Her spirit, weakened by late misfortune, flickers like a dying light – your sudden appearance might make all dark. Uncle – landlord! would you have murder on your soul?
> *Doggrass.* Murder?
> *Susan.* Yes; though such may not be the common word, hearts are daily crushed, spirits broken – whilst he who slays, destroys in safety.

Susan, whose character function of heroine earns her the support of the audience, leaves no doubt as to how the landlord's behaviour should be judged. Incidents centring on the attempted eviction form only a small part of the varied action of *Black-Ey'd Susan*; such incidents and associated issues are, however, much more dominant in the main action of Jerrold's *The Rent-Day* (1832). The problem of absentee landlords feeding their pleasures with the rents from their tenants is described thus: 'If the landlord lose at gaming, his tenants must suffer for't. The Squire plays a low card – issue a distress warrant! He throws deuce-ace – turn a family into the fields! 'Tis only awkward to lose hundreds on a card; but very rascally to be behind-hand with one's rent!' This speech is followed by advice given to the steward to pass on to the landlord:

> When you write back to the Squire, you can tell him, by way of postscript, if he must feed the gaming-table, not to let it be with money, wrung, like blood, from the wretched. Just tell him, whilst he shuffles the cards, to remember the aching hearts of his distressed tenants. And when he rattles the dice, let him stop and think of the bailiff and tax-gatherer, knocking at the cottage doors of the poor.

The ethical and emotional structuring of melodrama creates patterns of sympathy for the oppressed rather than the oppressor and might thus be described as populist. It is the disempowered – whether by wealth, class, gender, lack of access to legal redress – who form the endorsed moral and ideological centre. Yet, in the speeches above from *Black-Ey'd Susan* and *The Rent-Day*, one can hear that the populism is capable of a significant radical edge.

The radicalism potentially strikes deep. A landlord in demanding his rent and in distraining and evicting if it is not received breaks no law. Yet the ethical structures of domestic melodrama condemn him. Melodrama, therefore, sets up a system of values which come into direct conflict with the actuality of the British legal system, and offers a direct challenge to the laws relating to landlord and tenant as well as those laws which protect the ownership of property. It can be argued that the radical thrust is emolliated by narratives which suggest that it is wicked individuals administrating the system rather than the system itself that is wrong. Thus in *The Rent-Day* the problems of absentee landlords and landlord/tenant relationships are resolved when Squire Grantley reforms, makes reparation and promises to be a good landlord in the future. However, an equally valid counter-argument is that narrative closures of that order are not universal, nor do they negate the articulation of radical sentiment earlier in individual plays. The repeated endorsement in play after play of melodrama's own ethical position in relation to landlords and tenants has a cumulative effect in the ideological work the drama does, and must suggest that the expression of populist radicalism spoke powerfully to the everyday experience and imaginative needs of the audiences.

The populist class consciousness of domestic melodrama sites the central focus of the class inequity in the figure of the wealthy landowner or squire. More often than not the squire not only has unfair advantages in terms of the power that wealth and class give him, but he is repeatedly an oppressor in gender terms. In ▷ J.B. Buckstone's *Luke the Labourer* (1826), for instance, Luke may be the primary villain enacting vengeful plots against conventionally worthy Farmer Wakefield, but the Squire is a subsidiary villain who plans to abduct and take by force the virtue of Wakefield's daughter, Clara. The analogy within the nautical setting of *Black-Ey'd Susan* is the attempted rape of Susan by a naval officer. The character function of the squire figure also allows for further attacks on the administration of the legal system, for it is he who often represents justice locally. The Squire in *Luke the Labourer* is not only a potential kidnapper and rapist, he is also the local Justice of the Peace. His wrongful imprisonment of the woebegone comic man, Bobby Trott, elicits the following response from the comic woman, Jenny: 'I wish I were a queen or an emperor, for his sake: I'd see whether a Squire should not go in the cage as well as a poor man, when he deserved it'; but the Squire's escape to London where he will evade punishment offers evidence of significant corruption in the judicial system. Very different ideological work is being done here than that erroneous view of melodrama which assumes that there is 'an exact demonstration of poetic justice, in which earthly rewards and punishments are distributed in proportion to the deserts of the characters'.

Even more unrelenting in its attack on corruption in the judiciary is John Walker's industrial melodrama *The Factory Lad* (1832). Squire Westwood, the factory owner, dismisses most of his workforce after introducing steam-driven machinery, and is immediately figured in the play as the equivalent of the foreclosing landlord. It is also he who makes explicit whose interests the legal and judicial systems are designed to protect:

> I must be on the alert, and keep my doors well fastened, and have, too, an armed force to welcome these desperadoes, if they should dare to violate the laws well framed to subject them to obedience . . . What have I to fear or dread? Is England's

> proud aristocracy to tremble when brawling fools mouth and question? No; the hangman shall be their answer.

Later in the play this exchange between the aptly named Justice Bias and Rushton, the incendiarist who destroys the factory and steam machinery, articulates the populist perception of the inequity of the law:

> *Bias.* The law is open to you, is it not?
> *Rushton.* No; I am poor.
> *Bias.* And what of that? The law is made alike for rich and poor.
> *Rushton.* Is it? Why, then, does it so often lock the poor man in jail, while the rich one goes free?

The Factory Lad is remarkable for the strength of its radical sentiment and has continued to be performed seriously for its content by theatre groups and companies with left-wing political sympathies.

The construction of gender, both male and female, is enormously varied and complex in 19th-century melodrama and is beyond the scope of the present essay. However, some account of the character function of the heroine – whether as wife or daughter – in domestic melodrama is necessary. In the wake of the second women's liberation movement, the passivity of so many heroine characters is to many modern readers/spectators not only excessive but also extremely irritating. Such a reaction is understandable, but fails to do justice to the ideological work that is being done by showing women in a hostile world under almost constant threat of male violence. The violence is often specifically sexual. Already mentioned are the attempted rapes in *Black-Ey'd Susan* and *Luke the Labourer* of Susan (wife) and Clara (daughter) by upper-class characters. In *The Rent-Day* similar unwanted attentions are paid to Rachel Heywood (wife) by Silver Jack, one of the criminal characters. The most common resolution of these threats derives from the typological pattern that isolated and vulnerable women are in need of male protection. Thus Susan is saved in the nick of time by her husband, and Clara by the unintended intervention of the comic man, Bobby Trott. Rachel, on the other hand, defends herself by tricking the attacker, she then protects herself by threatening to kill her assailant with a woodcutter's bill, and eventually makes her escape. The narrative develops when she overhears a plot to rob and possibly murder the Squire, whom she goes to warn. The drama consequently utilizes the narrative expectation that squires are seducers; when she is discovered in the Squire's rooms it is immediately assumed by her husband (on the prompting of the criminals) that the assignation was a sexual one. This leads to pathos-filled scenes where she is expelled by her husband from the family home and denied access to her children. It may be unwise to extrapolate from the narrative that Rachel is being punished for an 'unfeminine' lack of passivity but the implication may remain.

Notwithstanding, the narrative developments involving Rachel indicate the centrality of the heroine character, especially in her roles of wife and mother, to the construction of domestic ideology in its ideal form; moreover, that her virtue, in conventional terms, is essential to that construction and often carries its burden. The working-class woman, further disempowered by gender and physical strength, is represented as having the consciousness of her own virtue as her only power. The articulation of this is capable, however, of development into a powerful rhetoric instrumental in the judgemental systems of the drama; thus Susan in *Black-Ey'd Susan* berates Doggrass for his suggestion that she may not be faithful to her absent husband:

> Sir, scorn has no word – contempt no voice to speak my loathing of your insinuations. Take, sir, all that is here; satisfy your avarice – but dare not indulge your malice at the cost of one, who has now nothing left her in her misery but the sweet consciousness of virtue.

Rachel's similar berating of Silver Jack can stand as axiomatic of the ethical structure of a melodramatic genre that places domestic ideology, and the heroine's vulnerability and virtue at its centre: 'He who would destroy a happy fireside, is vile and infamous; but he who insults its wretchedness, is base indeed.'

It would be wrong to assume that dramatic forms developed throughout the 19th century in clearly defined progressive movements; during the whole period aspects of the drama would appear and re-appear, would go through negotiations and re-negotiations, would re-present significant modulations of conventions and signifying practices. Nevertheless, in the 1860s a number of dramas seem to abandon the populist radicalism of the earlier domestic melodrama in favour of the endorsement of an increasingly bourgeois ideological stance. ▷ Tom Taylor's *The Ticket-of-Leave Man* (1863) is a case in point. The first act shows the heroine, May Edwards, in a hostile environment. Alone and friendless she busks with her guitar from table to table in the Bellevue Tea Gardens. Her presence causes a commotion for which she requires male assistance from the hero figure, and there are also linguistic pointers to the idea that her activity is akin to prostitution. By the second act, however, she has been able by her own efforts to set herself up in lower-middle-class domestic comfort in a rented room that is 'humbly but neatly furnished', decorated with flowers, and complete with canary. The ideological work done by the representation of isolated or independent women under threat which they are not in a position to counter has been replaced by the ideological imperative of the mid-19th-century concept of self-help. It is probably no coincidence that ▷ Samuel Smiles' *Self-Help* (1859) was published some four years before *The Ticket-of-Leave Man*. In the play the character Gibson, whose wife has employed May, makes explicit in conversation with May the ways in which approbation is apportioned: 'You've showed that you deserve her [Mrs Gibson's] kindness. For fifty people ready to help there's not one worth helping – that's my conclusion. I was telling my wife so this morning, and she insisted that I should come and satisfy myself that she had helped one person at any rate who was able and willing to help herself.' Similarly, the radical critique of the legal and penal system is now abandoned. Robert Brierly, the wrongfully imprisoned hero, is not utilized to offer such a critique; rather, his imprisonment is offered as reformative. It rescues him from bad company, cures him of his incipient dipsomania, and provides him with skills which will be useful to him in future life. The play, in its treatment of the social prejudice against ex-convicts, is often claimed to be a forerunner of the sort of social problem drama represented by John Galsworthy's *Justice* (1910). But Brierly earns his reparation not by challenging social prejudice but by thwarting the criminal plans of the villains.

The 1860s also witnessed a growth of the representation of increasingly mundane ▷ realism on stage. Thus in *The Ticket-of-Leave Man* there is a moment of playful metatheatricality; in a scene set in Gibson's bill-broking office, one of the characters looks about her at the stage set and specifically draws the audience's attention to the dressing of the stage: 'I did *so* want to see an office – a real one, you know. I've seen 'em set on the stage often but they ain't a bit like the real thing.' Plays by ▷ T.W. Robertson such as *Caste* (1867) and *Society* (1865) staged under the Bancroft management also brought into prominence domestic realism so that they were termed 'cup-and-saucer' and 'milk-and-water' comedies on account of their representation of everyday realism. Robertson's, in comparison to other drama indicates the range of visual pleasures that the 19th-century stage afforded: from large-scale antiquarian literalism; to the spectacle of the chariot race or train crash; to the interest in the everyday.

Other notable plays during this part of the 19th century were adaptations from novels by women writers, including ▷ Mary Braddon's ▷ *Lady Audley's Secret* and ▷ Ellen Wood's ▷ *East Lynne*. ▷ C.H. Hazlewood's stage adaptation (1863) of *Lady Audley's Secret* places the villainess centre stage. She is explicitly excoriated by the wronged husband. Yet the play also articulates the fact that the husband, George Talboys, was inadequate as a provider and insouciant in respect of his marital responsibilities. He leaves her in England while he goes to find his fortune in India. An unresolved point is whether he wrote to her during his period abroad. Believing herself to be abandoned, the question for Lady Audley is one of survival in a society which is represented as offering a worthwhile position for women only in relation to men. Thus Lady Audley publishes a false notice of her death in a newspaper and under an assumed name schemes to gain the affections and hand of the wealthy Sir Michael Audley. In the altercation with her erstwhile husband, Lady Audley defends herself as follows:

> I tell you, not one letter reached my hands; I thought myself deserted, and determined to make reprisals on you; I changed my name; I entered the family of a gentleman as governess to his daughters; became the patient drudge for a miserable stipend, that I might carry my point – that point was to gain Sir Michael Audley's affections; I did so, I devoted all my energies, all my cunning, to that end! and now I have gained the summit of my ambition, do you think I will be cast down by you, George Talboys? No, I will conquer you or I will die!

In conventional terms, Lady Audley, despite her justification of her behaviour and her husband's explicit admission of his failure to fulfil his marital responsibilities, is punished for her actions. Indeed, this particular stage adaptation suggests that her madness at the end of the play is a result/cause of her 'unnatural' (for a woman that is) villainy. And yet, the popularity of this narrative in its various stage adaptations suggests that, despite the overall conventional moral frame, Lady Audley's behaviour in overcoming her disadvantages possibly offered for women spectators the fantasy of a ▷ utopian resolution.

The stage adaptations of *East Lynne* were many. The one by T.A. Palmer (1874) contains the famous, but often misquoted lines: 'Oh, Willie, my child dead, dead, dead! and he never knew me, never called me mother.' Although conventionally moralistic in its treatment of the fate of the unfaithful wife, this version of *East Lynne* shows the protagonist, Lady Isabel, in a variety of roles which implicitly raise questions about the economic as well as moral position of women in society. Thus she first appears as the single woman economically dependent on her extended family; she then makes a marriage more for financial security than love, and becomes the economically dependent wife; believing her husband to be unfaithful, she leaves the family home and her children, and decamps with the villain of the piece. As a fallen woman she suffers the usual fate of the fictional kept mistress, and is discarded by her lover. Echoing interest surrounding recent divorce legislation (marriage and divorce), the play next offers Lady Isabel as divorcee. Facial disfigurement in a railway accident enables her to re-enter unrecognized the previous marital home as governess to her own children. She takes on the character function of saintly sinner/penitent; she atones and earns some reparation by maternal self-sacrifice in caring incognito for her dying child, tormented by the fact that she cannot claim the role of mother. Her ultimate expiation is through her own death brought on by her weakened state and the exertions of nursing her son.

Contemporary typological constructions of women on the stage, some of which figure in *East Lynne*, took a severe jolt with the stormy appearance of ▷ Ibsen in the English theatre, as did the range of material considered acceptable for the stage. ▷ *A Doll's House* was staged in 1889 and ▷ *Hedda Gabler* and ▷ *Ghosts* in 1891. It was the last play which particularly outraged the critics. Clement Scott in the *Daily Telegraph* was unstinting in his vituperation: it was for him 'an open drain; a loathsome sore unbandaged; a dirty act done publicly; a lazar-house with all its doors and windows open'. Now justly notorious, Scott was more vociferous than others, but his sense of outrage was shared by many. The shock waves were out of all proportion to the number of people who might have been 'contaminated' by exposure to Ibsen's play. The Royalty Theatre, where it played for one night under the auspices of the Independent Theatre Society, had a capacity of only 657. Ibsen's plays, though, with their open discussion of subjects hitherto taboo in the 19th-century English theatre and with their questioning of the traditional (and therefore supposedly natural) role of women, pricked deep-rooted late-19th-century anxieties of a general social and political disintegration.

In the 1890s Ibsen's work was presented by minority theatre ventures; it could not be accommodated to or by the commercial theatre at that time. But the commercial theatre necessarily felt the reverberations of Ibsen's intrusion on to the English stage. Shaw noted that a theatre manager 'must be very careful not to produce a play which will seem insipid and old-fashioned to playgoers who have seen *The Wild Duck*, even though they might have hissed it'. The two English commercial dramatists who seemed to take up the challenge offered to contemporary dramatic writing were Henry Arthur Jones and Arthur Wing Pinero. Jones had established his career writing strong melodramas such as *Saints and Sinners* (1884) and *The Silver King* (1882); Pinero his by writing a series of farces, including *The Magistrate* (1885) and *Dandy Dick* (1887). In 1893 Pinero produced a serious problem play, *The Second Mrs Tanqueray*. The chronology of the appearance of this play, following closely on Ibsen's turbulent entry on to the English stage, is, like Shaw's remark, misleading as well as instructive. *The Second Mrs Tanqueray*, in its examination of the double standard of morality and the unfairness with which a woman with a past like Paula Tanqueray is treated by society, superficially seems to offer a compassionate treatment of weighty moral and social issues. The debt to Ibsen is, however, more apparent than real. The play shows not a direct Ibsenite influence (both Pinero and Jones were adamant in disclaimers of such influence), but reflects an extension of tone and subject matter to which Ibsen's presence contributed. *The Second Mrs Tanqueray*, like many other dramas of the period, is a compromise between the outspokenness of Ibsen, which audiences found objectionable, and the conventional realistic play to which they were accustomed.

The Second Mrs Tanqueray examines the misalliance between Aubrey Tanqueray, upper middle class and stolidly respectable, and Paula, who has previously had several liaisons in the *demi-monde* of Europe. Tanqueray may openly articulate a condemnation of the double standard of morality, but he also articulates the idea, endorsed by what the audience actually see of Paula's behaviour, that she is somehow irrevocably damaged by her previous irregular sexual behaviour:

> There's hardly a subject you broach on which poor Paula hasn't some strange, out-of-the-way thought to give utterance to; some curious, warped notion. They are not mere worldly thoughts – unless, good God! they belong to the little hellish world which our blackguardism has created: no, her ideas have too little calculation in them to be called worldly. But it makes it the more dreadful that such thoughts should be ready, spontaneous; that expressing them has become a perfectly natural process; that her words, acts even, have almost lost their proper significance for her, and seem beyond her control. Ah, the pain of listening to it all from the woman one loves, the woman one hoped to make happy and contented, who is really and truly a good woman, as it were, maimed!

The marriage inevitably ends in disaster. Yet the inevitability arises not from the psychological mismatch of husband and wife, nor from society's hostility to the misalliance, but from a coincidence in the plot introduced by Pinero in the last act. Tanqueray's daughter returns from Paris intending to be married to a man who turns out to be a former lover of Paula. Paula's suicide ends the play and resolves the problem. Pinero's use of techniques derived in part from French models (▷ French influence) of the well-made play mediates the experience of a universe dedicated to the preservation of dominant social and moral codes and the punishment of women who have transgressed them. Similarly, in Jones' *Mrs Dane's Defence* (1900), the attempt of the eponymous woman with a past to re-enter society is foiled by an apparently chance discovery in a topographical dictionary which exposes her true identity and past indiscretion. The aesthetic of the well-made play is in essence a function of this ideological imperative. What such plays offer is a passing flirtation with the daring and the mildly risqué, but one which is safely contained by an action that provides resolutions endorsing the validity of the orthodoxies supposedly under serious discussion. Ultimately, the society drama of Jones and Pinero requires the double standard as a kingpin in its endorsement of what is a more extensive conservative ideology and sexual politics.

Other plays raise different problems to be resolved. Pinero's *The Notorious Mrs Ebbsmith* (1895) posits whether a woman of socialist and feminist beliefs can put them into practice by openly keeping house with Lucas Cleeve, a politician of some public prominence; Jones' *The Case of Rebellious Susan* (1894) asks whether a woman can openly repay her husband's infidelity in its own kind and remain in society. Mrs Ebbsmith's unconventional beliefs are rendered invalid when what is represented as her 'natural femininity' reasserts itself and she becomes a theatrically more familiar figure – the fallen woman. Her transformation in the last act to penitent fallen woman intending to retire to a life of contemplation and prayer in the north of England is not just a sign that she now recognizes the error of her ways, but allows Cleeve to return to his promising political career. In *The Case of Rebellious Susan*, Susan Harabin abandons her rebellion and returns to a patently less than perfect marriage. Jones may well have claimed that 'My comedy isn't a comedy at all. It's a tragedy dressed up as comedy', but any apparent cynicism in the idea that her rebellion can be bought off by what the Bond Street Jewellers supply and her wealthy husband can afford is subsumed by the sense of relief that not just social mores but the very fabric of society have been preserved.

The plays of Oscar Wilde, particularly ▷ *Lady Windermere's Fan* (1892), *A Woman of No Importance* (1893), and *An Ideal Husband* (1895), have, in their settings, thematic concerns and resolutions, clear affinities with the conventions of the social dramas of Jones and Pinero. Where Wilde's plays are acknowledged to differ is in the epigrammatic wit of their dialogue. The relationship between the plays' wit and their conventional theatricality creates a challenging juxtaposition. Wilde's epigrams, in their paradoxical style, logic and subject matter, undermine and subvert the assumed social hierarchies and ethical orthodoxies which are constructed in the settings and conventions of late-Victorian society drama. Similarly, his lack of concern to conceal the improbabilities and coincidences of his plotting strategies has the effect of exposing the conservative ideologies supported by the narratives of Jones and Pinero's plays: indeed, it is the very sophistication of their implementation of such strategies that tends to obscure the ideological work being done there. Wilde is often acknowledged as a satirist of social mores and a moral critic. Yet, in ▷ *The Importance of Being Earnest* (1895) the famous scene where Lady Bracknell interviews Jack Worthing to test his eligibility as a suitor is not just a display of English eccentricity or a comedic parody of theatrical convention; more importantly it also exposes the heart of the power base of the class Lady Bracknell represents. The thematic concern of contemporary society drama, the threat of misalliance, is revealed through Lady Bracknell as an issue of political as well as social and moral consequence:

> To be born, or at any rate bred, in a hand-bag, whether it has handles or not, seems to me to display a contempt for the ordinary decencies of family life that reminds one of the worst excesses of the French Revolution. And I presume you know what that unfortunate movement led to?

The political implications, which remain unstated in the work of Jones and Pinero, are here made explicit. The underlying anxiety is not of an undefined disintegration of social and moral values but is one specifically of class conflict and insurrection, of those things that, as Lady Bracknell acknowledges, might 'prove a serious danger to the upper classes . . . and lead to acts of violence in Grosvenor Square'.

The denouement of *The Importance of Being Earnest*, in keeping with the play's genre, re-establishes the previously disrupted social order: Jack really is Earnest and is of acceptable social position – his mother a Lady, his father a general. Yet the play equally suggests that this social settlement is as arbitrary and as absurd as when he was the foundling Jack Worthing and descended from hand luggage.

The society drama of the last decade of the 19th century set the stage for what would become the mainstream of English commercial theatre for at least the next 60 years. It implicitly proposed that subjects worthy or interesting enough for dramatic treatment were only to be found among members of the upper classes, and that the most appropriate way of mediating that experience would be through the conventions of realist staging. It also proposed that what would be most interesting about people from the upper classes would be their peccadilloes, most frequently their sexual peccadilloes.

The dramatist whose career begins in the 19th century but who takes English drama through to what is identifiably a 20th-century style is paradoxically Shaw. The paradox lies in the fact that, unlike progressive dramatists of the first decade of the new century such as John Galsworthy (1867–1933) and Harley Granville Barker (1877–1946) who eschewed what they considered to be outworn dramatic and theatrical conventions, Shaw was flamboyant in his declaration of indebtedness to earlier stage traditions: 'My stories are the old stories; my characters are the familiar harlequin and columbine, clown and pantaloon . . . my stage tricks and suspenses and thrills and jests are the ones in vogue when I was a boy.' Thus, despite the labelling of some of his work in his first volume of published plays as 'unpleasant'

(▷ *Plays Pleasant and Unpleasant*), *Widowers' Houses* (1892) and *Mrs Warren's Profession* (1902) owe as much to domestic melodrama and romantic comedy, and the commonplace representation of the woman with a past as they do to lbsen. Others of Shaw's plays are equally identifiable in their adaptation of the conventions of 19th-century commercial theatre: *The Devil's Disciple* (1899), melodrama as practised at the Adelphi; *Caesar and Cleopatra* (1907), large-scale historical drama; ▷ *Candida* (1900), domestic drama; ▷ *Arms and the Man* (1894), military melodrama; *Man and Superman* (1904), romantic comedy; *You Never Can Tell* (1899), farcical comedy. For traditional literary history Shaw's plays represent one of the moments where English drama once again gains recognition. The overriding irony is that Shaw's unashamed indebtedness to the vitality of 19th-century theatrical tradition represents an indication of what the canonical literary tradition has missed out on.

Notes

1 G.D. Klingopulus, 'The Literary Scene', in *The Pelican Guide to English Literature*, Volume 6, *From Dickens to Hardy*, revised edition (Harmondsworth, Middlesex: Penguin, 1969), p 116.
2 M.H. Abrams, *A Glossary of Literary Terms* (New York: Holt, Rinehart and Winston, 1957), p 98.
3 John Russell Taylor, *A Dictionary of the Theatre*, revised edition (Harmondsworth, Middlesex: Penguin, 1970), p 183; Phyllis Hartnoll (ed.), *The Concise Oxford Companion to the Theatre* (Oxford: Oxford University Press, 1972), p 347.
4 Allardyce Nicoll, *A History of English Drama 1660–1900*, 6 vols (Cambridge: Cambridge University Press, 1952–9).
5 By way of comparison the equivalent handlist in the volume covering 1750 to 1800 is only 176 pages long.
6 Dates refer to plays' first UK performances; it should be noted that in the case of Shaw's work the date of first performance often does not coincide with date of publication.
7 Michael R. Booth, *English Melodrama* (London: Herbert Jenkins, 1965); Peter Brooks, *The Melodramatic Imagination: Balzac, Henry James, Melodrama, and the Mode of Excess* (New Haven: Yale University Press, 1976).
8 Abrams, p 98; or as another dictionary has it: there is 'a happy ending in which the villain gets all he [*sic*] richly deserves', Ivor H. Evans, *Brewer's Dictionary of Phrase and Fable*, revised edition (London: Cassell, 1981), p 727.
9 At least nine different adaptations were presented on the English stage between 1866 and 1899.
10 George Bernard Shaw, *Our Theatre in the Nineties*, 3 vols (London: Constable, 1932), I, p 165.
11 George Bernard Shaw, 'Preface' to *Three Plays for Puritans*, in *The Bodley Head Bernard Shaw: Collected Plays and their Prefaces*, edited by Dan H. Laurence, 7 vols (London: Bodley Head, 1970–4), II, pp 46–7.

18 Writing from Modernism to Postmodernism

Linda Ruth Williams

> They last a second, a minute, they come and go like a moving winking light; but they have impressed their mark, deposited some kind of sensation before they vanished . . . Secret stirrings that go unnoticed in the remote parts of the mind, the incalculable chaos of impressions, the delicate life of the imagination seen under the magnifying glass; the random progress of these thoughts and feelings; untrodden, trackless journeying of brain and heart, strange workings of the nerves, the whisper of the blood, the entreaty of the bone, all the unconscious life of the mind . . .

Who speaks here, in this quotation written in 1890? Is this the statement of a peculiarly poetic psychologist, outlining the territory with which an embryonic psychoanalysis is to concern itself? Are these the ravings of an eloquent madman, the patient or subject of the analysis itself? It may seem strange to begin a book on 20th-century writing in English with a statement in translation, written by a Norwegian writer (Knut Hamsun, in 'From the Unconscious Life of the Mind') in the late 19th century. Curiouser and curiouser, it doesn't appear to be a particularly 'literary' passage at all, but rather an ephemeral account of a mind subject to (what French poet Arthur Rimbaud embraced as) 'the systematic disordering of the senses', quoted perhaps as evidence in a psychoanalytic case history written up to demonstrate the processes of derangement.

If this does not seem to be a fitting subject for literature to encounter, then the image and interpretation of 20th-century writing which this book offers should challenge that notion, along with the idea that a century's writing begins with the beginning of a century. As this book will also show, with modern writing things seldom begin when or where they're supposed to begin; moreover the very notion of beginnings and endings becomes questionable with some of the century's most radical works (as ▷ D.H. Lawrence writes, 'In the beginning – there never was any beginning'), which might loop back into themselves, Finnegan-like, beginning again in defiance of any final full stop. Indeed, ▷ James Joyce's ▷ *Finnegans Wake* actually does 'end' like this, the opening sentence being the completion of the final one, the final sentence thus turning the reader back to the start of the work again. With such challenging material in its scope, this book must offer an alternative set of boundaries and definitions which also show the origins of the century's important work in cultures and aesthetic centres quite other than that of mainland Britain, beginning, it seems, at any moment other than the turning of the year – 1900. For many, 20th-century literature begins in the mid- to late 19th century, particularly with the influence of French ▷ Symbolism; for others, like ▷ Virginia Woolf, 'in or about December 1910, human character changed', and with it forms of writing, and what is written, changed too.

This change – the 'shock of the new' – emphasized most starkly the power of *difference*, both in the sense of the mark of difference gouged into literary history by many of the writings discussed below (the difference of an innovative 'now' from a conventional 'then'), and in the sense of difference*s* within texts and subjects explored and opened up by a range of modern visions: the *self*-divisions of the painfully alienated or exuberantly 'post-impressionist' subject (like Hamsun), or the *sexual* differences of new literary voices deliberately challenging taboos concerning what can be written or who it can be written by. The former is the 'private' division within, of a self which betrays its own self-differences, which displays in language the ways in which it is divided or different from itself; using the perception of this inner division creatively, modern writers thus set about making the 'self' into the intricate object of its own scrutiny. The latter realm of difference – we might call it the 'public' differences of 20th-century writing from previous periods – made possible most strikingly by modern writing might be, respectively, transgressive writers who were keen to challenge sexual censorship laws (like D.H. Lawrence), or women writers who seized upon ▷ modernism as a formally revolutionary movement in writing. The space opened up for writers by the sense that now, artistically speaking, there is 'no map' (in the words of poet ▷ H.D., quoted in my essay on poetry below) promoted forms of women's writing which fitted closer to women's different experiences. In Virginia Woolf's phrase (writing about novelist ▷ Dorothy Richardson), what could (and should) at last be written was 'the psychological sentence of the feminine gender'. Less specifically, the writing project set out so energetically by novelists and critics such as Woolf shows modern writing to be driven by a democratic desire to listen to, use, and give voice to a variety of inner and outer selves and influences. Marking the difference between 'Modern Fiction' (the title of the essay from which this quotation comes) and older forms, she writes,

> . . . there is no limit to the horizon, and . . . nothing – no 'methods', no experiment, even of the wildest – is forbidden, but only falsity and pretense. 'The proper stuff of fiction' does not exist; everything is the proper stuff of fiction, every feeling, every thought; every quality of brain and spirit is drawn upon; no perception comes amiss. And if we could imagine the art of fiction come alive and standing in our midst, she would undoubtedly bid us break her and bully her, as well as honour and love her, for so her youth is renewed and her sovereignty assured.

This sense of use and abuse, of working with, whilst radically subverting and overthrowing, the power of traditions – the working material one has inherited – characterizes the image of 20th-century writing which this book conveys. It will be the work of this introduction to trace some of these innovative 'differences', by identifying in brief the clearest hallmarks of early and 'classic' modernism, before outlining the importance of ▷ postmodernism as the primary late 20th-century movement, in order to give readers a simple frame upon which they can map their own readings of individual writers and texts, and a way into the specific discussions of ▷ genre and theory which take place in the essays below.

Earlier in 'Modern Fiction' Woolf offers what is possibly a more familiar (because English) image of the modern obsession with the intricacies of the mind than Knut Hamsun's epigraph to this introduction. Whilst the essay is a response to James Joyce's ▷ *Ulysses*, one of the most striking things a reader of modernist work who is used to the conventions of classic realist characterizations will notice is that modern characters constantly contradict themselves; they are guided more by irrational betrayals than by rational purposefulness, through plots in which nothing very much happens. Woolf celebrates this:

> Look within and life, it seems, is very far from being 'like this'. Examine for a

> moment an ordinary mind on an ordinary day. The mind receives a myriad of impressions – trivial, fantastic, evanescent, or engraved with the sharpness of steel. From all sides they come, an incessant shower of innumerable atoms; and as they fall, as they shape themselves into the life of Monday or Tuesday, the accent falls differently from of old; the moment of importance came not here but there . . . Life is not a series of gig lamps symmetrically arranged; life is a luminous halo, a semi-transparent envelope surrounding us from the beginning of consciousness to the end.

It is this sense of the plenitude of possible images and experiences which any moment of life has the power to offer, a kaleidoscope of contradictions revealed by simply looking in a new way, which modernism most obviously explores. Woolf is careful to show that this complex, impressionistic, endlessly rewarding subject (the *human* subject) is there for everyone to explore, and find: the grand passions, cosmic paradoxes and psychological intricacies, which in previous literary eras were seen to be the preserve of the heroes of individualism, become democratized with modernism: 'the ordinary mind on an ordinary day' is precisely the proper subject of writing – and this is, indeed, exactly what *Ulysses* presents, one day in the life of Leopold Bloom, ordinary, if exemplary, Dublin citizen.

In his essay below, Andrew Roberts emphasizes the diverse roots of the modernist novel by situating 20th-century developments in the context of the influences of the mid-19th-century novel. What Woolf characterizes as the 'old' form, the 'symmetrically arranged' dictates of a ▷ realism in which 'the accent falls differently', had to be challenged, and it is this challenge which characterizes other innovative forms of modern writing (not just the novel). In prose, the realist tradition – deploying an omniscient narrator, forms of characterization which gloss over 'myriad impressions' in favour of more coherent behaviour patterns, and a sequential narrative structure which orders and forces chaotic reality into a neat chronology – was subverted by radical novelistic techniques which allowed and encouraged other forms of representation, or eschewed the notion of fiction as representation altogether. With modernism, narrators cease to be reliable, let alone all-seeing; but what they do choose to see they look at with a microscopic vision and a sense of relativity. As the essays in this book will show, the literature of this century is almost by definition recalcitrant, refusing rules of subject, coherence and accessibility in an incessant project of experimentation. Even the literature which *doesn't* do this, preferring to stick with the givens and known qualities of, say, classic realism in the novel or strict poetic versification, is paradoxically perverse in that it is forced in its conformity to older literary models to react against innovations. Rebellion is the rule, even if you want to be conventional.

Perhaps the 20th century is a century of black sheep, with the very few white ones becoming the odd ones out. Literary criticism often likes to portray the history of writing rather like a family tree, with paths of influence traced like paths of generational lineage, so that disagreements of subject matter or style, or formal rebellions against established modes of writing, are consequently read as family feuds or children's challenges to parental authority. If this is so, then in this century the family has become heterogeneous, obsessed with forging new paths in what is writable, formally (as with, say, *Finnegans Wake*) and morally (as with, say, D.H. Lawrence's sexually explicit ▷ *Lady Chatterley's Lover*), thus losing sight of literary 'normality'. In an attenuated moment which modernism traces to the mid to late 19th century, high Victorian writing (classic realism in the novel, conventionally versified or narrative poetry, both issuing a general sense that writing is and should represent a shared social, material and spiritual reality) mutated into something quite other than itself. Modernist writing – formally self-referential, difficult, often obscure, obsessed with looking at itself in the mirror of itself – is in a sense the abnormal child of a literary parentage more wholesomely concerned with accessible 'content' – conventional linear plot structures and characters who, as D.H. Lawrence puts it, behave 'according to a pattern'. For Lawrence, the 'dead' novel of the past needs to be revived with a shot of spontaneity; characters need the injection of change, and changeability, and it is this which past work was seen as unable to incorporate. Characters, then, are like lovers:

> If the one I love remains unchanged and unchanging, I shall cease to love her. It is only because she changes and startles me and defies my inertia, and is herself staggered in her inertia by my changing, that I can continue to love her. If she stayed put, I might as well love the pepper-pot.
>
> ('Why the Novel Matters')

Thus Lawrence and his diverse contemporaries set about wresting the novel from the inertia he describes, by producing characters who 'change and startle' their readers, who do not, as he famously wrote in a letter to Edward Garnett, conform to 'the old stable ego . . . of the character', thus representing a more dynamic sense of subjectivity. Literature embraced the world of relativity and defied a literary past too firmly gripped by 'absolutes':

> Once and for ever, let us have done with the ugly imperialism of any absolute. There is no absolute good, there is nothing absolutely right. All things flow and change, and even change is not absolute. The whole is a strange assembly of apparently incongruous parts, slipping past one another.
>
> ('Why the Novel Matters')

Although one strategy employed by many of the arguments and observations in this book is the setting up of modern writing against and in contrast to its past, the writers here do not presume to suggest that these images of the past – of realist fiction, or of Victorian poetry – are in fact right or accurate. It is not the aim of this present book to suggest that modernism's image of Victorianism is a true reflection of the previous century at all, but rather that many of the familiar images of Victorian writing which we might unthinkingly work with were set up for a variety of interesting reasons by modernist writers, deliberately through written polemics (such as ▷ Ezra Pound's 'A Few Don'ts by an Imagiste'; ▷ Imagism, discussed in my essay on poetry below) or used unconsciously and by implication, as necessary points of opposition. Victorian writing *needed* to be characterized as accessible, realist and psychologically coherent, so that disparate modernist writers interested in doing something quite different could have a firm point of disagreement with a past set up as a springboard into the future. I am not concerned here with challenging the early 20th-century image of the 19th century – it would be the job of one introducing readers to the complexities, the playfulness, the psychological paradoxes of Victorian writing to show how in reality it contradicts cherished modern illusions about Victorian certainty and coherence – although it is true that any discussion of modern writing may gesture toward this implied image of the previous period. However, whatever can be demonstrated as the properties of modernism's ancestry, it is nevertheless true that the avant-garde, the experimental, the transgressive have dominated this century's important works, and consequently the 'family line' has become rather twisted. To both use and subvert the traditional language of literary inheritance, it could be said that 20th-century writing is the mutant child of the 19th century. Following the path of exemplary black sheep ▷ Oscar Wilde, modernism and postmodernism have celebrated a freedom from the need to represent morally a shared image of reality:

> The final revelation is that lying, the telling of beautiful untrue things, is the proper aim of art.
>
> (*The Decay of Lying*)

The powerful perversity of this is important (and Wilde is a writer who takes perversity seriously): what is being heralded is the disruption of the realist relationship between a thing in the world and its literary representation. There need be no direct link between literature and life; indeed, the more that literature fantasizes, and cuts itself adrift from 'real events', the more 'literary' its final effect will be.

The impact of this active project to free writing from the need to represent a shared, ideal image of the world has been profound. Wilde's outrageous celebration of 'beautiful untrue things' sets the tone for a century in which what has decayed is not the art of fantasy but the more characteristically 'past' literary values which produced accessible stories, recognizable images of 'normal' reality and rational and integrated characters who move through a linear narrative with a sense of moral purpose. It's not just that there are no more happy endings, but that the endgame is often a preface, or a novel might end with a question which looks like a beginning, and so endings and beginnings cannot be found where you expect them to be, and nor can they be trusted to sit neatly in place. The reader of modern writing may often feel that she or he is being seduced into playing a game for which the rules are being written as the game proceeds. Novels can be plotless, plays can be written in which nothing happens, narrative poetry gives way to introspective or plainly nonsensical lyric poetry or 'free verse'. As Lawrence, again, has written, 'Never trust the artist, trust the tale. / As for the artist, he's usually a dribbling liar'. And since the writer here is himself an artist, this must be read as a literary version of that pop-philosophy paradox, the statement 'I am lying'. Who, in this century of perverse nonsense-speakers and rule-breakers, can we trust?

Perhaps all this at least accounts for some of the difficulty which many readers find in getting to grips with modern writing, but it also accounts for modern writing's playfulness and exuberant sense of fun. With Joyce's wordplays, ▷ Beckett's puns, Surrealism's uncanny juxtapositions of images which betray playful and sick humour by turns, ▷ Djuna Barnes' parodic, tragicomic jibes at sexual roles, the reader who braves the initial inaccessibility is offered the rewards of pleasure. It is also unfortunately true, however, that this century has seen a decline in popularity for many writing forms, and this is particularly the case with poetry, the avant-garde tendencies of modernism alienating the formerly large poetry-reading public. As John Drakakis outlines below in his essay on critical theory, dramatist ▷ Bertolt Brecht (arguably the century's dramatic mentor) celebrates the estranging powers of literature on similar lines to those marked out by the critical school of Russian ▷ Formalism, but the effect of this on readers and audiences has not been popular. 'Literariness', however, was not invented by the modernists, and modernism's consolidation or celebration of this formal self-consciousness has been famously traced back to the writings of many of this century's more eccentric, or else more untimely, literary ancestors. For instance, when Laurence Sterne draws a series of lines on the pages of *Tristram Shandy* (1760–67) as a comic visual representation of its narrative journey, one of the things that he is doing is making his readers conscious of the fact that they are reading a fiction, not a transparent or unmediated representation of a series of real events. The novel is a twisted and elaborate narrative of things which never existed, and Sterne's comic self-consciousness draws attention to the fact that the text *is a text*, a work of playful fiction which we should be prevented from 'losing ourselves' in. Amongst other things, modernism is the moment in literary history when this tendency becomes dominant. To put it crudely but clearly, form is all: as Beckett wrote about Joyce, 'His writing is not about something, it is that something itself'.

John Drakakis develops this below by showing how Brecht's *Verfremdungseffekt* (▷ alienation effect) is akin to this, in that it overtly portrays on the stage the fact that the play being performed is a work of artifice, rather than a simple representation of reality to which the audience can sacrifice its critical faculties. Brecht wanted to keep his audience sharp, self-aware and conscious of the processes through which the play is being constructed before its very eyes. This self-consciousness – also one of the hallmarks of modernist *fiction* – may have produced challenging works of invention, but it has not necessarily produced a pleasurable spectacle or read. Where the art of lying has perhaps stayed alive most obviously is in the popular forms of ▷ science fiction, fantasy and ▷ horror, in which a carnivalesque 'world turned upside down' is elaborated in a plenitude of directions. In a contemporary confirmation of Lawrence's point, horror writer ▷ Stephen King alchemically turns lying back into truth again when he argues that 'the primary duty of literature' is 'to tell us the truth about ourselves by telling us lies about people who never existed' (*Danse Macabre*).

If one thing is clear so far, it is that modern literature is knotted with paradoxes, with counter-intuitive 'truths'. This is the case even when we attempt to understand its provenance and first principles. However, this book is to some extent a work of literary history, and it is our job to trace a map of the century's literature, to give a fairly coherent range of intellectual co-ordinates as a rough guide to the literary century. The beginning of a century is not necessarily the century's *literary* beginning. It could, for instance, be argued that modernist writing actually began well into the century itself, and was engendered, was given its first breath, by war: English modernism emerged in its clearest form during the vast conflict of World War I, which gave the first kick to literary and artistic forms self-consciously characterizing themselves as 'modern' rather than 'Victorian'. It is strange that world-scale death can be understood as giving life to the creative arts. It is also strange that whilst the world was being torn in two by the divisive allegiances of the war, so modernism was becoming a cosmopolitan literary and artistic form, with its centres across Europe (and to some extent in America) staked out in defiance of enemy lines. This is not, however, to say that the arts propounded a spirit of creative harmony in a crazed world. For D.H. Lawrence, World War I intensified what Frank Kermode has called his 'apocalyptic vision'; though married to a German and physically prevented from travelling to Germany, Lawrence would at least applaud the conflict from the sidelines, not patriotically but because for him the war had the potential to sweep away the cobwebs of old worlds: 'We ought to be grateful to Germany that she still has the power to burst the bound hide of the cabbage' (*Study of Thomas Hardy*). On a different note, as philosopher and film theorist Paul Virilio has persuasively argued (in *War and Cinema*), the rise of cinema – this century's major new art form, which has had a profound and fascinating inter-relationship with literature – is intimately bound up with the development of military technology.

Another problem with definitions of this century's work in English lies in our understanding of the word 'English' itself. This book reflects the cosmopolitanism of early modernism and the multiculturalism of postmodernism in its liberal range of reference entries on writers and influences from other countries and languages. The essays also show how the century's key works were part of a wider philosophy of boundary-challenging, which has caused critics such as Marxist writer Georg Lukács to describe (particularly in *Theory of the Novel*) the modern sensibility as 'metaphysically homeless' or 'nomadic'. With the advent of modernism, literature written in English ceased to be anchored to the English landscape: Paris, Berlin, Munich, all were centres of English culture equal to London and Dublin. The battle *against* the primacy of an English literature rooted in a wholesome and parochial English landscape was *not* fought on the playing-fields of Eton, but in Berlin bars and Paris studios. This book aims to give readers a framework within which they can enjoy and understand writing this century, writing which the essays below align with the dominant but loose movements of modernism and postmodernism, and the recalcitrant writings which actively refuse to be categorized. Recent literature has had to work in a world of increased secularization and mass communications, and this too has contributed to a challenging of boundaries, both in terms of how we label (or value) works, and in terms of where those works originally situated themselves. If modernist 'wandering' promoted an inter-cultural sensibility which deployed the voices of a variety of disciplines and cultures, postmodernism radicalizes this in a rampant disregard for the integrity of the original forms it draws upon.

Late modernism and postmodernism

The initial sense of fragmentation produced by the modernistic challenge to the idea that literature written in a particular language had to be bound to a particular land or range of cultural givens was only the first step in a century-long movement. The rise of radical nationalist movements in Britain's colonial dependencies did much to change the literary map. The consequent decline of Britain's colonial hold over other parts of the world, the freer movement of people between cultures and particularly the explosion of mass communications have all made the world a smaller place. Air travel, even space travel, radio and satellite technology, computer languages – all have promoted contact between cultures and have subverted our previous sense of a specific cultural identity deriving from nationality. It is fitting that this technology should be the result of warfare; just as in military terms wars have raged in defence of national boundaries, so the two world wars have produced the means to subvert cultural boundaries.

It is the resultant sense of cultural collage which characterizes both modernism and postmodernism. If World War I prompted writers to range across the world, embracing Lukács' sense of cultural nomadism just as individual nations were closing down borders, so World War II signalled the further explosion of mass communications and the dawn of the nuclear age, and post-war literature responds to and works necessarily in the context of the resulting world-historic anxiety. What is now known as postmodernism, however, has emerged more recently for different historical and artistic reasons. The term 'postmodernism' covers a variety of disparate and often contradictory literary and cultural movements and impulses. The term itself suggests a reaction against modernism. This is only partially true, however; for many critics there are few differences between modern and postmodern writers, so much so that for some readers certain classic modernist texts exemplify, perhaps more than many postmodern ones, the postmodernist way of operating. ▷ T.S. Eliot's ▷ *The Waste Land*, for instance, deploys quotation and references from a vast collage of other texts, and one of its more unsettling qualities is the way that voices within it are at times subjectively unclear: it's hard to tell when one 'self' finishes speaking and another begins. This sense that boundaries are being constantly subverted in the poem, as subjects flow into each other or are uneasily juxtaposed, is a key postmodern motif, as well as a modern one.

However, there is a sense in which the fragmentary bits of the poem finally 'add up' to an organic conclusion, a final moment of unity and peace which causes the poem to turn back on itself, so that its early fragments are reworked and homogenized into the final whole. Postmodernism emerged at a chaotic but exhilarating time in history – the 1960s – to challenge this process of *homogenization*. By the 1960s, the radical impulses of modernism which I outlined above, which fought *against* the self-satisfaction of high Victorianism, had been appropriated by the established system, its fragmented possibilities assimilated into a great tradition of 'artistic genius' by the growing forces of Leavisite criticism (F.R. Leavis) and New Criticism. Crucially, the period from about 1930 onwards not only signalled the end of the most intensive modernist production, it was also the period in which English literature began to be studied more widely in its own right in the universities of Britain. The literature which had so excited the new young critics – who from the early 1930s onwards were establishing the terms of academic literary criticism – was to become fossilized as the final moment of cultural production worthy of study. T.S. Eliot was both one of the key poets to figure on the new syllabuses as eminently respectable, and also one of the critics who was writing the rules of the game. D.H. Lawrence had been a notorious figure for his radical and explicit descriptions of sexuality, but as a favourite of F.R. Leavis his work soon found a place as a key prop to the Leavisite canon which was to dominate the study of literature at both secondary and degree levels. In the 1960s, a new generation of writers and students reacted against the sanitization of the previously shocking forms of modernism, and sought other creative forms which were strong or bizarre enough to resist actively any re-evaluation in the wholesome, unifying terms of Leavis. *The Waste Land* may pass through an agonizing, disparate struggle, shoring fragments 'against my ruins', but it seems to conclude with all the loose ends neatly tied. Against this, in Marxist critic Fredric Jameson's terms, a composer such as John Cage offers a disharmony which cannot resolve itself into harmony. Cage's 'disconnection and fragmentation' is, for Jameson, 'related to the way we describe a text today as the production of discontinuous sentences without any larger unifying forms'. Thus *The Waste Land*, upon which critics have spent an inordinate amount of time demonstrating how its 'larger unifying forms' gather together its 'discontinuous sentences', is modernist, and that which deliberately sets out to disrupt or disavow those unities is postmodernist. Postmodernism thus takes the modernist rejection of sequential plots and develops an aesthetics of the instantaneous, of the unoriginal, of the plagiarized.

Like modernism, which had its manifesto, as I have indicated, in Pound's 'A Few Don'ts . . .', postmodernism is often defined in negative terms: as Jameson again says, 'it isn't this, it isn't that, it isn't a whole series of things that modernism was'. Reaction against the previous moment has characterized its progress, but like modernism it also has positive qualities. Critics disagree on what these are exactly, however. For instance, the postmodern technique of showing how a thing works before you show what it is – display one's formal heart on one's sleeve, as it were – is for some also evident in modernist writing. As with modernism, postmodernism is an interdisciplinary form: it is a movement in art, sculpture, music, film and architecture just as much as in writing. Indeed, in as much as postmodernism is concerned with breaking down the boundaries between disciplines, an extreme postmodernist would disregard these distinguishing generic terms. Some modernist texts play out and play with the collapse of traditional distinctions between high and low culture in a way which has been seen to be politically radical: for instance, James Joyce's novels actively incorporate speech idioms from working-class life in Dublin, or credit dream-imagery and irrational motifs with as much value as rational representation and discourse. For postmodernism, this collapse is taken to be an absolute, so that even the distinction between high and low culture becomes meaningless. As Andrew Ross, quoting Dirk Hebdige, has written:

> . . . postmodern can be used today to refer to:
> the decor of a room, the design of a building, the diegesis of a film, the construction of a record, or a 'scratch' video, a TV commercial, or an arts documentary, or the 'intertextual' relations between them, the layout of a page in a fashion magazine or a critical journal . . . the attack on the 'metaphysics of presence' . . . the collective chagrin and morbid projections of a post-War generation of Baby Boomers confronting disillusioned middle age . . . a proliferation of surfaces, a new phase in commodity fetishism, a fascination for 'images', codes and styles . . . the 'implosion of meaning', the collapse of cultural hierarchies, the dread engendered by the threat of nuclear self-destruction, the decline of the University . . .
>
> (*Universal Abandon*)

At its most extreme, postmodern writing is populated with a variety of voices, quoted or plagiarized from 'intertextual' sources to give a sense of difference and disruption, a deliberate disturbance of organic, unified representations of world or psyche, or a wider patchwork of borrowings from different genres and discourses. Postmodernism is parody and pastiche; if modernism actively makes links between disciplines, encouraging a cosmopolitanism of subject, a borrowing and connecting of ideas across an interdisciplinary network, then postmodernism transgresses this too, often flagrantly plagiarizing rather than playfully quoting and borrowing. Eliot may produce a careful collage of borrowed writings which are respectfully acknowledged, but for 1980s writer Kathy Acker past texts are there to be plundered wholesale, to the extent of copying out passages from Dickens and turning favourite authors into fictional characters to be manipulated by the whims of the plot.

However, it would be extremely misleading to offer an image of 20th-century writing as conforming to a single set of points or qualities, just as using the umbrella terms 'modernism' and 'postmodernism' to characterize all the significant works and literary movements of this century would be unhelpfully exclusive. ▷ Doris Lessing's *The Golden Notebook* is a good example of many of these techniques, although argument about where to situate it continues. It constantly draws attention to itself as a text; the heroine, Anna, is a novelist, and struggles with herself as creator in the production of five disparate notebooks which claim to 'represent' herself in various ways, but which also display themselves as material texts, and show the process of the construction of the novel as a whole. When we read each of the notebooks, which trace different aspects of Anna's past and present (such as her life in Africa or her involvement with the Commmunist Party or the 'life' of one of her characters, Ella), we are also simultaneously aware of the notebook as a material object, which has rested on a desk as the other narratives in the book have been played out. One of the notebooks disintegrates as Anna's psyche does under analysis, changing from a personal diary form to a 'diary' composed of newspaper cuttings which tell the story of national events, on a large and a trivial scale. The reader is invited to connect the historical narrative which this produces with the subjective narrative which Anna cannot speak, but the words themselves are just snippets and fragments, which display the processes through which they were edited and chosen.

The Golden Notebook does also, however, place itself within a realist tradition, because the five notebooks – black, red, yellow, blue and golden – are punctuated by sections (entitled 'Free Women') dealing much more conventionally with the events of Anna's life in the 'present' of the novel. This technique is also characteristic of the resurgence of accessible, realist post-war writing, which developed in parallel with the more popular poetry and drama of the period, discussed by myself and by Andrew Piasecki in the essays below. In fact, *The Golden Notebook* as a whole is best known as 'the Bible of the ▷ Women's Movement', a proto-feminist novel and one of the major post-war texts to represent actively its heroine's personal struggle as a political one, and vice versa, thus working through the feminist dictum coined sometime later, 'The Personal is the Political'. However, this motto in itself – which was taken up by many women in the 1960s and the 1970s as a call to consciousness-raising – is in many ways a postmodernist statement. When the boundary between 'inside' and 'outside' breaks down, or when the interconnection of subjective state and material conditions is recognized in art in a particular way, the methods of postmodernism come into play.

As is clear from this brief survey, the word 'play' used in this and in many other senses continues to be operative. Many of the texts discussed in this book are characterized more by the aesthetic *tendencies* of modernism or postmodernism than by genuine allegiance to an '-ism': they play with categories, using or ignoring them. Few could be called fully paid-up members of either 'movement'. Indeed, a polemical attempt at resisting general or totalizing categories has often been at the heart of the works and movements discussed here. It might, for instance, be helpful in one way to erect a signpost and call James Joyce's *Finnegans Wake* a modernist novel, but doing so simultaneously creates a smokescreen which might prevent us from looking creatively at the ways in which it *isn't* a 'novel' in the conventional sense, or at the ways in which *as* a novel it actively challenges and breaks open the novel form. The obvious fact that *Finnegans Wake* largely resists categories – including the category 'modernist' – is one of the things which paradoxically makes it a modernist work. The same could be said of any work we might label modernist or postmodernist: to do either is to ignore or repress the ways that literary works do as much to disrupt creatively the categories critics want to fit them into as they do to sit still in those boxes. It is one of the qualities of both modernism and postmodernism to challenge totalizing labels *per se*.

The essays: interpretation and literary movements

Literary history, like family history, is a question of how you tell it. Modern perspectives on literature counter the traditional notion that critical judgements are made through an ideal process of evaluation and emotional response, both ostensibly disregarding the processes of power; as John Drakakis writes below, 'the history of literary criticism offers many varied ways of reading: . . . how you interpret texts depends upon who is "master".' *Who* decides the patterns of literary history, and *what* has made them decide that, are questions that need to be opened up by anyone hoping to set out a fresh image of the developments of 20th-century writing.

This book offers such an image in composite through its genre essays and references, but it does not claim to escape the responsibilities which come with offering another map of modern literature. All of the essays here are more or less chronological, and all to some extent stress the violence done across this century when new writers seek to overthrow the aesthetic priorities of the old, in ways which some critics have seen as analogous to family history. My essay on the chain of poetic movements, sparked off by the initial modernist revolt against Victorianism and ▷ Georgianism, perpetuates this sense that writers often work with a strong desire to rebel against prior movements. Just as relationships between the members of families are made real by the stories that people weave around themselves and each other, so critics narrate the links and lines between writers, and turn a disparate mass of texts written across a range of historical periods into an ostensibly coherent network of relationships. Whoever tells the story is thus able to privilege certain moments, to single out 'significant' texts, to create relationships persuasively as patterns. Criticism fills in the gaps, forges the links between writers and makes connections across the writing generations, connections which look like family relationships; it traces who has influenced whom, which writings echo, repeat, or defy past works, which texts 'behave' according to the current conventions, which texts 'misbehave' and become the celebrated black sheep. Pointing out resemblances, literary criticism remembers and explains the arguments, how new generations of writing come into being, and it looks at the need for texts to argue and fall out with each other, the necessity of disagreement, refutation and contradiction between texts of different periods, differences which make new writings possible.

This position is most famously articulated by Harold Bloom in *The Anxiety of Influence*, although his is perhaps most importantly a consolidation of a multitude of positions taken across literary history. When F.R. Leavis traces a 'Great Tradition' of English novelists, he is claiming them as part of an authentic literary lineage – an elite descendancy of influence. Raymond Williams countered the Leavis lineage with his own alternative Marxist tradition, whilst feminist critics Sandra Gilbert and Susan Gubar followed both Bloom and Virginia Woolf in tracing a tradition of women writers who 'think back through their literary mothers' (after Woolf's statement 'We think back through our mothers if we are women'). Criticism has thus organized literary history metaphorically. Because Western-style family structures in a sense prototypically mark out relationships between individuals with common characteristics, or who, from shared assumptions and influences, strive to individuate themselves from their origins, these family structures have become the dominant pattern critics have imposed upon our literary heritage. It is perhaps unfortunate that even the most radical critics still represent literary movements in terms of familial metaphors. Feminists who otherwise advocate a politics which would open to question all patriarchal structures, including that of the traditional family unit, have nevertheless created an alternative literary lineage which sees patterns of influence as running between older generations of writing 'mothers' and younger women writers who become literary 'daughters'. Whilst most feminist critics seem to want to stress the non-violent continuity of this matrilineage, male critics working since Harold Bloom sometimes use a Freudian model to stress the violence of development. Distinct movements are seen as rejections of and reactions against the past, so that all innovations are deemed to be the reactions of literary adolescence, the efforts of younger writers keen to move on to something new.

All this is to say that more recent writings, as the essays below demonstrate, freely deploy techniques from a wide range of cultures and genres in their urge to inscribe differences. But marking differences has worked in tandem with the apparently contrary action of breaking down boundaries. As John Drakakis discusses in his essay on critical theory below, interpretations are powerfully determined by material factors which will prioritize different issues for different readers. Drakakis' account of the main movements of critical theory this century is included here not simply to supplement the genre-based essays, but as an account in its own right of a body of 20th-century writing which has an increasingly high profile on English syllabuses, as part of the wider discipline of English studies. Indeed, it is becoming increasingly difficult to distinguish between critically 'knowing' fictional texts and new forms of theory which are self-consciously 'literary'.

This tendency to challenge boundaries has been expressed in different forms in different genres. Andrew Roberts highlights, for instance, the importance of the ▷ stream of consciousness technique which enabled novelists to explore a more intense psychological 'realism' such as that suggested in my epigraphs by Woolf and by Hamsun. Modernism in this form disrupts the conventional discrepancy between inside and outside, in which a more or less coherent interior monologue is finally distinguishable from the 'externals' of social and material reality 'out there'. As I have begun to suggest here, and as Roberts develops below, modern writers show how in the psychological reality of character and narrator, subject and object are interrelated or, at extreme moments, indistinguishable. This sense of the interdependence of subject and object is also a primary concern for modern poets, which I discuss also in my essay on poetry. And, as Roberts argues, the rise of other powerful genres such as science fiction and fantasy writing has also problematized the notion of literature as directly representational. More recently, horror fiction, a late 20th-century version of the Gothic novel, has embraced the fantastic and the macabre possibilities of English prose, if not the linguistic pyrotechnics explored by modernists. In drama, a history of spectacular artistic and political experiment has unfolded despite the material circumstances of shameful underfunding, a factor which underpins Andrew Piasecki's history of the developments of British theatre. Experiment, and the forward-movement which embraces differences in a variety of ways, clearly drive many of the literary forms with which this book concerns itself. In a century of work which is marked by a reluctance to stay still, even nostalgia or the counter-modernism of, say, the ▷ Movement poets of the 1950s, has, ironically, been 'progressive'. Looking back in anger or in pastiche or assimilation of the past, writers have deployed nostalgia for lost forms in a way which has seldom been debilitating.

19

'Rule and Energy in View': The Poetry of Modernity

Linda Ruth Williams

'Less is more': Pound and Imagism

To mark the turn of the century as also a turning point in literature is a rather arbitrary gesture. English ⊳ modernism established itself slowly, well behind the French precedent, and the first decade of the 20th century was dominated by the popular conservatism of ⊳ Georgian poetry. People read and enjoyed the poetry of ⊳ A. E. Housman, ⊳ Rudyard Kipling and ⊳ Thomas Hardy, and eagerly bought the Georgian anthologies as they appeared from 1912 onwards. Georgianism perhaps epitomizes the popular notion of English poetry – parochial, solid and unironic, celebrating English rural life, particularly the home counties variety. Its importance lies in the way it fed into the poetry of World War I – many Georgians are better known as ⊳ War poets – which sharpened nostalgia into something that could 'draw blood', especially in the later years as the full horror became apparent.

In order to emphasize how shocking modernist poetry was after the technical familiarity of writing up to 1910, I want to focus upon the Imagist (⊳ Imagism) movement which, whilst not offering the most powerful or famous texts of the modernist period, certainly exemplifies much of what modernist verse was trying to achieve against Victorianism. '(T)he first heave' of modernism was, in poet ⊳ Ezra Pound's words, 'to break the pentameter' ('Canto 81'). Pound was a great polemicist against what he called 'the crepuscular spirit in modern poetry' ('Revolt'). Certainly, much poetry of the late Victorian period was supremely 'crepuscular', languid, pale and dreamy, and in his early so-called ⊳ 'Celtic Twilight' period ⊳ W. B. Yeats was rather prone to this. He had begun his writing career as a writer of the Victorian *fin de siècle*, and ended it as a key figure of modernist anti-decadence. His early poems are infused with an elegiac quality and peopled with mythological and heroic figures from an 'old Ireland' of ephemeral, supernatural beauty. There is a haunting sense of the inaccessible, characteristic of much ⊳ Nineties poetry, which rejected earlier Victorians' building of 'brick and mortar inside the covers of a book' (Yeats, 'The Symbolism of Poetry'; 1900). This is Yeats the 'last romantic'.

But Yeats is also arguably the first modernist of poetry, his feeling of alienation from his time strengthening his later apocalyptic poems, which 'sing amid our uncertainty' ('Per Amica Silentia Lunae'; 1917). The cultural crisis of the early 20th century turned the task of re-thinking the limits and drives of language into one of almost world-historic importance for many poets, impatient that the untenable realist notion of a shared common experience between writer and reader be exposed. If Yeats' early work is marked by a bygone aesthetic, and is metrically and syntactically conventional, his later work – particularly that written from *The Wild Swans at Coole* (1919) until his death in 1939 – would strongly assert his modernity, and was undoubtedly urged towards this point by Pound's influence.

The movement which exploded on to the poetry scene in 1912, of which Pound was initially a key member, sought to counter sloppy diction and to free verse from too much emotion. Later in the war years Imagism developed into the multi-art form movement ⊳ Vorticism, with the publication of two polemical texts edited by poet and painter ▷ Percy Wyndham Lewis, *Blast* (1914 and 1915). Vorticism was a movement which brought writing and visual art together in a futuristic celebration of energy and speed. The anti-romantic figures of the 'Great English Vortex' included Wyndham Lewis and Ezra Pound, plus artists David Bomberg (1890–1957), Henri Gaudier-Brzeska (1891–1915) and Jacob Epstein (1880–1959). Imagism in its purest form most aggressively countered Victorian versification, producing 'poetry that is hard and clear, never blurred or indefinite' (Preface to *Some Imagist Poets 1915*). Modernist poetry in this form intensifies and condenses; the poetry of modernity is written most strongly in the lyric form, rather than as narrative poems or epic novel-poems favoured by the Victorians. Imagism takes the emphasis on brevity to an extreme, its definitions being heavily reactive (just as its founders were politically reactionary), prescribing the new poetry negatively; in Pound's words modern poetry should be: 'Objective – no slither; direct – no excessive use of adjectives, no metaphors that won't permit examination . . . straight as the Greek!'

Imagism, then, rejected the use of loose simile and, like ▷ Hopkins in a different sense, strove to evoke the 'isness' of things: to present reality in a naïvely unmediated sense, avoiding flaccid re-presentation. For the Imagist, brevity is the soul of poetry: 'less is more'. Condensation counters verbiage, and so lyric poetry is put on a strict diet; in Pound's words, it is 'de-suetized'.

Whirl up, sea –
Whirl your pointed pines,
Splash your great pines
On our rocks,
Hurl your green over us,
Cover us with pools of fir.
('Oread', H. D.)

This is a poem by ▷ H. D. in its entirety; indeed, 'Oread' (1915) is often tendered as the exemplary Imagist poem, with the complex of sea, pines and nymph fusing as image. Pound had defined the image as 'that which presents an intellectual and emotional complex in an instant of time'; H. D.'s text pares down superfluity to a series of discrete, sparse phrases. What the poem 'is' is the relation between these phrases, how they build up into an image which does not come from individual key words or vague feelings but from the ways in which the component elements of the poem *relate*.

This can be clarified by looking at an even shorter Imagist poem of Pound's, 'In a Station of the Metro':

The apparition of these faces in the crowd;
Petals on a wet, black bough.

It is perhaps hard today to recapture the feelings of shock which hit the first readers of these poems. It is no wonder that at this point in literary history poetry began to become perhaps the most unpopular of art forms. The difficulty of this text lies in its requirement that we simply *accept* it on its own terms, which brings it close to the oriental form of the *haiku*, much admired by Pound.

This text is also exemplary in its peculiar atmosphere and influences. In an effort to achieve delicate clarity, Imagist poetry deployed Japanese motifs, petals, hyacinth and lotus blossoms, and clear contours, and allowed itself to become emotional only in the dexterity with which these evoke feelings. Pound's 'Fan-piece, for her Imperial Lord' (1914) is as much about loss as any Victorian elegy, but is delicately rinsed free of heavy sentiment:

O fan of white silk,
clear as frost on the grass-blade,
You also are laid aside.

Understated, it is also impersonal, a key word at this point and reinforced by ▷ T. S. Eliot's notion, in 'Tradition and the Individual Talent' (1919), that: 'Poetry is not a turning loose of emotion, but an escape from emotion; it is not the expression of personality, but an escape from personality.' Thus an Imagist poem may be poignantly posed, but it should not slide into agonized self-reflections or sentiment.

Language speaking: Eliot and the linguistic crisis

Modernist poetry not only demanded intensity, however; crucially it challenged the prevalent philosophy of language with which it was traditionally assumed 19th-century verse worked. This philosophy posited language as a transparent medium through which an unproblematic and undistorted 'reality' is represented. For the modernist poet language is emphasized and foregrounded to such an extent that it becomes the most important 'point' of the poem. Poetry scrutinizes the form, the contours, the material of the mask of language. As ▷ Samuel Beckett said of ▷ James Joyce, 'His writing is not *about* something; *it is that something itself*.'

Modernist writing is agonizingly self-conscious, probing its own limits and restrictions, foregrounding itself as text, as the interface of many texts. The process of poetry-writing becomes the object of poetry, so that the way a text is constructed, *how* it connotes many possibilities of meaning and many voices, becomes that which the poem is *about*. We can, perhaps, see why ▷ Browning was read with interest by many early 20th-century poets. Modernism foregrounds form over content, or rather, it opens up for questioning the whole economy of language through which form and content are established as distinct and separate textual dimensions. Pound's later work, especially his long sequence of ▷ the *Cantos*, continually emphasizes its own materiality betraying its own material construction. Alongside their other project of historical synthesis, the *Cantos* expose language as dirty, desirous splashes of ink; echoes of other languages intrude, typographical errors aren't edited out. Sometimes words are 'chosen' not for reasons of sense or meaning but because of the pattern they make on the page, how they sound, or how other words have suggested them. Chinese characters are included, asserting to the uncomprehending eye language's typographic existence. Pound's occasional rantings can seem more like the operation of a multi-lingual machine than a rational mind, reading rather like one enormous ▷ Freudian slip. As with many of Gertrude Stein's (1874–1946) texts and Surrealist automatic writing, words seem to suggest other words because of unconscious drives which are operating on the poem.

All of this has a profound bearing on how the role of the poet and of the reader is understood. A form of writing in which writing itself is so prioritized has also to re-write our understanding of who is 'responsible for' poetry – of who ultimately can guarantee its meaning. Despite the authoritarian postures adopted by particular modernist writers, poetry may be read as acknowledging that the position of both writer and reader is relative, non-omniscient, constructed by the forces of language. Furthermore, this sense of fragmentation has permeated the possibilities of writing to such an extent that the resultant feeling is that *all* possibilities of unity have been lost. Modernist poetry, to use the words of ▷ Lewis Carroll's *The Hunting of the Snark* (1876), spurned 'merely conventional signs', navigating itself by a map which was: 'A perfect and absolute blank!' It thus affirms – against the desires of its writers, whose quest is still towards the lost home of stable selfhood and meaning – a problematization of the individual subject somewhat analogous to that enacted by Freudian ▷ psychoanalysis and Marxist political theory.

What these breaks in poetic consciousness and linguistic coherence were signalling was the chasm in personal and national identity which World War I brought to crisis point. The War poets, particularly ▷ Siegfried Sassoon, ▷ Wilfred Owen and ▷ Isaac Rosenberg, represented this breakdown thematically, but through pre-war structures of versification and diction. Modernist poetry was more like a linguistic acting-out of the destruction of innocence which took place in the trenches.

Modernism is also identifiable as the point at which writing acknowledges that it doesn't originate purely within the soul of the author; the modernist text plagiarizes shamelessly, building itself up out of a patchwork of unacknowledged quotations from a variety of international cultural sources, fragments 'shored against my ruins' ('What the Thunder Said', from T. S. Eliot's ▷ *The Waste Land*). This is its cosmopolitanism. *The Waste Land*, to the frustration of many an undergraduate reader, straddles eastern and western cultural history in a dazzling and maddening parade of name-dropping and references, which build up into a polemical lament for fallen culture. Geographically, modernism wasn't centred on one cultural-Imperial capital, but danced from London to Paris to Vienna to Berlin to New York to Dublin and back again. It cannot be situated, and this cultural uncertainty is, in *The Waste Land* at least, a symptom of decay:

What is the city over the mountains
Cracks and reforms and bursts in the violet air
Falling towers
Jerusalem Athens Alexandria
Vienna London
Unreal

(*The Waste Land*, ll. 371–6)

Texts jump from 'home' to 'home', emphasizing how they are written 'intertextually' by a wide range of influences, and are a point at which an extraordinarily wide cultural memory is unlocked. Again, the *Cantos* are an extreme example of this in English poetry, as James Joyce's ▷ *Ulysses* is in the modern novel. The wandering poet has become poet-as-exile.

Ezra Pound was an energetic figure, tirelessly championing the modern and collaborating with T. S. Eliot in the preparation of *The Waste Land*, which is dedicated to Pound. Eliot's work is painfully aware of this crisis of the self, and its challenge to 19th-century writing is enormous. For Eliot, the lyric poem is 'the voice of the poet talking to himself, or to nobody'. But the manner of his 'talking' is quite bizarre, and shocking to our 'realist' expectations. Eliot's verse plays with and parodies traditional structures, the same poem oscillating in its versification and rhythms. Sometimes it comes near to solidity and fixity of form, only to dissolve into a much more fluid formal structure deploying, in his own words, a 'contrast between fixity and flux', and 'unperceived evasion of monotony'. *The Waste Land* exemplifies this, being an extreme example of formal eclecticism and teasing, a startling series of lyric fragments which jump schizophrenically from the sublimity of dream language to the ridiculousness of pub language and interrogate each through the other.

The problem of who writes is, then, accentuated by Pound's collaboration in the final editorial processing of *The Waste Land*, which caused Eliot to write 'I am never sure that I can call my verse my own'. So just who or what the poet's 'I' is at this stage in literary history is a painful problem, and Eliot's verse highlights this in several aspects. Thematically it often evokes disturbed mental states; in 'Rhapsody on a Windy Night' (1917), for instance, clear perception is distorted, objective reality is twisted to the point of frightening hallucination. A street-lamp tells the 'hero' about women's eyes, twisted 'like a crooked pin', and 'A crowd of twisted things' closes in. When he eventually reaches home, its safety turns out to be 'The last twist of the knife'. The figure of modernity characteristically has no home, wandering nomadically in a world stripped of values, in a shifting reality which confounds fixity in mental states. Many of Eliot's early poems seem close to the knife-edge of madness. 'Morning at the Window' (1917) consists of only two stanzas, the second an ugly, twisted re-writing of the relatively rational first, in which 'I' sits at a window looking on the street. This then becomes an experience subject to 'brown waves of fog' which toss twisted faces and tear smiles from passers-by. The 'brown fog of a winter dawn' returns as the climactic condition of *The Waste Land*'s 'Unreal City'.

For Eliot the problem of poetry feeds into the problem of culture and its role in (Christian) society. In 'The Use of Poetry' (1933) he asserts that poetry must be able to account for the sordid and the horrific, the thought that (from Pound's 'Hugh Selwyn Mauberley') 'Caliban casts out Ariel':

> *. . . the essential advantage for a poet is not to have a beautiful world with which to deal: it is to be able to see beneath both beauty and ugliness; to see the boredom, and the horror, and the glory.*

The Waste Land scrutinizes the grand dualism of beauty and ugliness and finds, in the critic and poet I. A. Richards's words, modernity's 'persistent concern with sex', which is then used as the lens through which history is seen as the history of progressive wastage. Just as 'Mauberley' reads the heroes of Victorian culture as the path to modernity's crisis, so *The Waste Land* re-reads history as a sordid parade, witnessed by the bisexual Tiresias who shuffles across its stage, and which climaxes in a series of sordid liaisons. Tiresias, an 'old man with wrinkled dugs', witnesses and foretells the sterility of a heterosexual love. The double edges of Victorian discourse on sex indelibly mark and open up modernist writing. Indeed, pleasure occupies a very warped position in Eliot's corpus, a symptom of the need for a kind of communication and communion which he perceived was no longer possible. The desperate desire for, and the impossibility of, communication, is both a 'truth' of sexual relations and of modernist writing.

However unpalatably, Eliot foregrounded a politicization of writing which aestheticism had repressed in marking out Art for Art's sake against the political engagement of High Victorian writing. His statement, 'I am sojourning amongst the termites', in a letter to ▷ Lytton Strachey, speaks eloquently of both the actual immersion of modern poetry in the most sordid aspects of social life, and the depth of his right-wing repulsion. Eliot's treatment of human beings in his poetry can be obsessively cruel and vindictive. Indeed, the extremely reactionary politics of Yeats, Pound and Eliot are problematic, and often make their work painful reading for reasons other than 'difficulty'. Yeats' advocacy of an integrated poetry as 'blood, imagination, intellect, running together' ('Discoveries'; 1906) was undoubtedly informed by the intolerant social pressures which also produced ▷ D. H. Lawrence's 'blood conscious' reactionary politics, but it is equally symptomatic of a climate which made possible the more positive politicization of writing in the 1930s. As the 1920s closed, Eliot turned to high-church Anglicanism, and the emphasis in critical theory and poetic practice became that of unity rather than disintegration. For the Eliot of 'The Metaphysical Poets', modern poetry needed to heal the 'dissociation of sensibility' which occurred at the end of the 17th century, so that it could 'devour' the plethora of modern experience. In the 1930s this was interpreted as the need for a poetry which countered obscurity and unpopularity with the addressing of relevant social issues, or what ▷ George Orwell called 'the invasion of literature by politics'.

And not before time: as the Western world spiralled towards economic breakdown, as unemployment rocketed, as Germany and Italy lurched into ▷ fascism, poets recognized that lack of commitment was tantamount to support of the right. ▷ W. H. Auden's poems of the very late 1920s are concerned with psychic landscapes, but in the 1930s his poetry became explicitly politicized and sought again to bridge the gap between theory and praxis in the pursuit of relevance, donning once more the mantle of moral guide. 'Thirties poetry' generally refers to the more politically engaged poetry of Auden, ▷ Stephen Spender, ▷ Louis MacNeice and ▷ C. Day-Lewis, the group of left-wing, psychoanalytically informed poets who met in the early 1930s at Oxford. The work of this 'school' is characterized by three collections, all edited by Michael Roberts: *New Signatures* (1932), *New Country* (1933) and the 1936 *Faber Book of Modern Verse*. Through these texts poetry can be seen to become more explicitly concerned not only with diagnosing the world historic disease, but with prescribing a cure. If modernist poetry is antihumanist, showing the human subject as already subverted by desire, the poets of the 1930s re-humanized the subject, as an effective agent of political action.

Poetry since World War II

Lay the coin on my tongue and I will sing
of what the others never set eyes on.
('Desert Flowers', Keith Douglas; 1943)

H.D. and Douglas: seer and soldier

Although H.D. had begun publishing her intense verses when she was part of the Imagist group, her most important work was written during and after World War II. She wrote *Trilogy* (1944) whilst living through the London Blitz. The war had come home; never had British people been so subjected to its extremities of violence and terror as was the urban population in the Blitz. The poets of World War I were fighters at the front; those of World War II didn't have to go to war because the war came to them, and its violence marked texts as different as ▷ Roy Fuller's *A Lost Season* (1944), T. S. Eliot's ▷ *Four Quartets (*1935–42) and ▷ Edith Sitwell's 'Still Falls the Rain' (1940). H.D.'s *Trilogy* opens with a ruined London laid out like a sacrifice, but its tone is positive. Only barriers, boundaries, proprieties are destroyed:

there, as here, ruin opens
the tomb, the temple; enter,
there as here, there are no doors . . .
ruin everywhere, yet as the fallen roof
leaves the sealed room
open to the air,
so, through our desolation,
thoughts stir, inspiration stalks us
through gloom . . .

The *Trilogy* poems, like many of H.D.'s texts, draw on a wealth of female mythological and historic/heroic figures to spin together a text of new possibilities. H.D. turns destruction into a positive value: the last section of *The Walls Do Not Fall* describes the physical effects of the bombing, but turns debilitating doubt into a clear horizon of possibilities:

we know no rule
of procedure,

we are voyagers, discoverers
of the not-known

the unrecorded;
we have no map;

possibly we will reach haven,
heaven.

Pessimistic texts have abounded since 1942 when this was written, but H.D. chooses to turn doubt into a possibility of affirmation, to stress the fact that negatives have been blasted away. Indeed, this last quotation could also be a statement about women's writing, which, in its marginalization from the canon and the difficulties of its being written at all, also knows no rule, is unrecorded, and has no map. Many post-war women poets have actively used their exclusion from the English poetic tradition as a fresh breathing space.

One of the most famous poets of World War II is undoubtedly ▷ Keith Douglas (1920–44) who was killed in Normandy, his corpus cut down but his influence disturbing writers in the post-war years. Anxious to make the right mark before it's too late, his perception is fired by the possibility of its termination, and in a clear, precise way is almost extra-sensory. On 'each side of the door of sleep' he finds a nightmare-scape in which sexual desire and unspeakable violence are inextricable. Sexuality comes into Douglas' poetry with cold images of death, corruption and violence. Rather like H.D.'s astonishment that the walls do *not* fall, Douglas finds an intensely positive desire in the midst of blasted desert and mindless military discipline. The murderer has 'a lover's face', and he is one of the

kindly visitors who meant
so well all winter but at last fell
unaccountably to killing in the spring.
('These grasses, ancient enemies'; 1941)

The poetry is in the chilling, clear, simple diction. Words themselves are militarized; poetry has always been in various guises the object of poetry, but in Douglas' case it is viewed as the soldier views his victim. In 'Words' (1943) it is scrutinized, as if (in George MacBeth's words) seen 'through the sights of a rifle':

. . . I lie in wait
for them. In what the hour or the minute invents,
in a web formally meshed or inchoate
these fritillaries are come upon, trapped . . .
The catch and the ways of catching are diverse.

Words are trapped by macabre war-scapes and dead faces:

. . . the pockmarked house . . .
whose insides war has dried out like gourds
attract words

Trap and attraction are interchangeable words for Douglas; an image has already trapped its written description and all it needs is for the poet to close in for the kill.

Dylan Thomas and the Apocalypse

Certainly World War II was a watershed in British life, and in ▷ Charles Causley's words, 'The signature of murder' (in 'I Saw a Shot Down Angel') is scrawled across the history of writing since the war. If certain experiences, cold and macabre for Douglas, actively *attract* words, we need to ask what manner of themes and experiences have words 'found desirable' in the post-war period.

Perhaps the most famous 'forties poet', Dylan Thomas, had produced much of his most interesting and characteristic work before 1940, yet his verve and style exemplify that of the so-called 'New Apocalypse', which was carried through into the dry, sardonic 1950s by Thomas' disciple, ▷ W. S. Graham. 'Apocalypse' writing was unbridled, gloriously undisciplined and heavily emotional. In consequence one can see this moment in poetic history as pitted against Eliot's impersonality, H.D.'s spartan, hard verse, or the political engagement of 1930s poetry. It is important to acknowledge the power of this poetic movement before we can really understand the significance of the philosophies of the more famous and self-conscious movements of the 1950s and the 1960s, which were very much, in turn, established in reaction to the Apocalyptics. Thomas' verse is famous for its exuberance and verbal excesses. Like the later poet ▷ Thom Gunn, Thomas often deploys syllabics to convey his sense of the natural world and himself in it rolling out of control. *Fern Hill* (1945) is perhaps typical; just as the 'I' who speaks it recalls roving and falling 'Down the rivers of the windfall light', the poem itself runs its 'heedless ways, / [Its] wishes raced through the house-high hay'; it seems to be driven, polemically and self-consciously, against the repression of formal disciplines, even though Thomas himself was in fact a meticulous and formally tight writer.

The apocalyptic poet would ostensibly free the riches, the thickness, of language from the boundaries of rationality. Thomas himself deploys bizarre juxtapositions to this end in his effort to conjure up unconscious powers; his incessant repetition connotes the power of unconscious rhythmicality when it doesn't simply irritate. In this he can perhaps be compared with Surrealist poets such as ▷ David Gascoyne or the American poet Robert Bly (b 1926), Gascoyne being a figure who continues to represent a certain disturbing undercurrent in English poetry, whose writing analyses the relationship between language and the unconscious against the empirical grain of 1930s or 1950s poetry. Indeed, it could be said that Gascoyne *is* the unconscious of the English poetic establishment, repressed and marginalized for his peculiar obsessions and failure to fit neatly into the ironic moulds of the 1950s, or the passionate egotism of the 1940s and 1960s. In asserting, in a way different from the modernists, that there is nothing commonsensical about reality, he remains resolutely anti-empirical.

In Surrealism obscurity takes on new powers. Dylan Thomas is nothing if not repetitive and obscure, but the Surrealist project is rather different in emphasis from his. Surrealism resists rational explanation; images are peculiarly juxtaposed so as to disrupt common-sense understandings and analogies. Gascoyne's 'Very Image' (1936) gathers a strange exhibition of surreal juxtapositions together:

And all these images
and many others
are arranged like waxworks
in model bird-cages
about six inches high.

Why? Empiricism can do nothing with such incongruity; reading this requires not only a suspension of disbelief but a suspension of rationality – indeed, in 1936 the Surrealist poet Hugh Sykes Davies (b 1909) supplemented the word 'surreal' with the word 'surrational'. Working through every possible permutation of a statement, rearranging its order so as to unhinge sense and cause meaning to self-deconstruct is something which we also encounter constantly in, say, Samuel Beckett's novel *Watt* (1953). This technique is frequently used to explore the outer reaches of paranoia, and the disturbing meeting of mental illness and political repression, at which point, writes Hugh Sykes Davies, 'ANYTHING YOU SEE WILL BE USED AGAINST YOU' ('Poem'; 1938).

To return to Dylan Thomas; his repetitiveness is of a different order, and his relationship with language is both more wilfully erratic than that of Surrealist poetry, and more superficial. If Douglas renders his words corpses with his rifle-pen and his sniper's eye, Thomas consciously throws himself into them as into a fierce alien element. He wants words to seduce him; he wants to be possessed. In 'Especially When the October Wind' (1934) the fact that language has already inhabited the 'I' is particularly clear: his heart sheds 'syllabic blood' on hearing the raven speak; stick-trees and 'The wordy shapes of women' have a typographical significance; the 'rows' of children are 'star-gestured'. Beeches are 'vowelled', oaks have voices, the water speaks. From this plenitude of verbal nature and life-signs – 'The signal grass', 'the meadow's signs', 'the dark-vowelled birds' – Thomas reads his poem and re-writes it. Indeed, in reading he is also trying to liberate: poetic excess and sexual freedom are inextricable. Thus the incantatory element in Thomas is linked to an attempt to allow words to bleed into a plurality of significance, meanings and connotations, spinning off of their own volition. In the 1950s this verbal free-fall was denigrated as adolescent self-indulgence, and, indeed, on its own terms, there is something inescapably restrictive about Thomas' habit of repetition.

We can, perhaps, clarify one of the positions of 1940s poetry through a statement

Thomas made about his attitude to the image, in comparison with Pound's notion that an Imagist image is 'an intellectual and emotional complex in an instant of time':

> *I let . . . an image be 'made' emotionally in me and then apply to it what intellectual and critical forces I possess – let it breed another, let that image contradict the first, make, of the third image bred out of the other two together, a fourth contradictory image, and let them all, within my imposed formal limits, conflict . . .*
> (*Fifty Modern British Poets*, Michael Schmidt)

Such an errant fecundity had to end somewhere, and one ending was a fresh return to the hardness of a confined, complex Poundian image. The re-working of modernism, especially in its American form is, then, one important strand of contemporary poetry. But immediately on Thomas' heels came the ironic self-discipline of the ▷ Movement.

'No Renaissances, please': the Movement and the 1950s

> *. . . the minipoet is basically safe.*
> *not well equipped for (but who would think of)*
> *leaving the highway, he is attuned*
> *to the temporary surface, balanced,*
> *reliable, yes, we have few regret*
> *for the archpoet, who either would not start*
> *or starting stopped; was temperamental*
> *wanted to show off, steamed up, was punctured . . .*
> ('minipoet', Miles Burrows; 1966)

The poetry of the Movement was, *par excellence*, that of post-war Anglo-Saxon rationalism. Like the famous car of the late 1950s, small but perfectly formed, the Movement poet was repulsed by grand gestures and took on the mask of a 'minipoet', 'slim, inexpensive, easy to discard/nippy rather than resonant, unpretentious' (Miles Burrows). Introducing the Movement anthology of 1956, *New Lines*, Robert Conquest (b 1917) wrote: 'It . . . like modern philosophy – is empirical in its attitude to all that comes'. Movement poetry resists 'agglomeration of unconscious commands'; banished at a stroke to the soupy ▷ Romantic past are, it seems, all poetic forms which credit unconscious selves with the power to undermine conscious, common-sense control. It has often, then, been seen as the logical reaction to 1940s excesses. Movement poetry met excess with the wisdom of tradition. But which tradition? Certainly the work of 'the Georgians cultivating their gardens' (Stephen Spender); a stable tradition of homely, pre-modernist English writers such as Thomas Hardy and Wilfred Owen, whose descendants would include ▷ John Betjeman. Conquest, again, celebrates 'rational structure and comprehensible language' in his choice of verse, as does ▷ D. J. Enright both in his own humanistic, dry, anti-Romantic verse and in the poems he collected in the equally important Movement anthology of 1955, *Poets of the 1950s*. The Bible of the Movement was ▷ Donald Davie's critical work of 1952, *Purity of Diction in English Verse*, which supported stylistic discipline and verbal austerity; words should be rationed and undue extravagance curbed. In Davie's work the obvious parallels between the 1950s and the 18th century become concrete, his role being that of the spokesperson of the anti-Bohemian poetic age when he wrote:

> *. . . there is no necessary connection between the poetic vocation on the one hand, and on the other exhibitionism, egoism, and licence.*
>
> *(Purity of Diction in English Verse)*

With the Movement English poetry again scaled itself down, and, clad in the hues of post-war Ealing movies, sardonically stated the primacy of the parochial and the provincial over the eclectic internationalism of modernism. ▷ Philip Larkin exemplifies Movement poetry, in his deflationary, perfectly formed phrases, and in his almost xenophobic stance against other cultures and cultural forms:

> *. . . to me the whole of the ancient world, the whole of biblical and classical mythology means very little, and I think that using them today not only fills poems full of dead spots but dodges the writer's duty to be original.*
>
> ('Four Conversations', *The London Magazine*)

Larkin's provincialism was adamantly rooted in his life in Hull, and his resistance to London's literary elite. The south-east's imperialization of other British cultures has since the 1960s found more energetic and positive forms in the growing importance of various regional poetic groups, from Northern Ireland, Newcastle, Scotland and Liverpool in particular. But the adamant Englishness of Larkin in the 1950s is another matter, and is itself beautifully deflated by the poet and critic ▷ Charles Tomlinson:

> *Larkin's narrowness suits the English perfectly. They recognize their own abysmal urban landscapes, skilfully caught with just a whiff of English films c. 1950. The stepped-down vision of human possibilities (no Renaissances, please), the joke that hesitates just this side of nihilism, are national vices.*

If these are vices, Larkin is an exemplary sinner, melancholically resigning himself to monochrome rather than confront the abyss. His poetic departure from the dominant romantic image of daring and heroism is beautifully epitomized by his poem 'Poetry of Departures' (1955). The 'audacious, purifying, / Elemental' movements of romantic action are parodied in implicit praise of safety, order and domestic banality which are for Larkin at least genuine:

So to hear it said
He walked out on the whole crowd
Leaves me flushed and stirred,
Like Then she undid her dress
Or Take that you bastard;
Surely I can, if he did?
And that helps me stay
Sober and industrious.
But I'd go today
Yes, swagger the nut-strewn roads,
Crouch the fo'c'sle
Stubbly with goodness, if
It weren't so artificial . . .

Larkin, then, is an ironic conformist; his poetry seems to be always already middle-aged. In 'Church Going' (1955) he responds to the divine by taking off his cycle-clips.

Even in his passion for jazz music – he was an important jazz critic as well as poet – his stance is resolutely anti-40s, preferring traditional jazz – his patience ends where the fast pyrotechnics of be-bop begin. Sexual magic is regarded dispassionately:

. . . Why be out here?
But then, why be in there? Sex, yes, but what
Is sex? Surely, to think the lion's share
Of happiness is found by couples – sheer
Inaccuracy, as far as I'm concerned.
('Reasons for Attendance'; 1955)

Other sides of nihilism: Gunn, Hughes, Plath

He tells you in the sombrest notes,
If poets want to get their oats
The first step is to slit their throats.
The way to divide
The sheep of poetry from the goats
Is suicide.
(James Fenton)

Post-Movement writers strove to break the 'minipoet' mould by formulating a poetics of irrationality and violence, reacting against genteel statements of common-sense experience. This reaction took various forms, particularly towards confessional writing, expressionism, and a further working through of the modernist techniques and internationalism which had been abandoned by the Movement. Georgian moderation was scorned, in favour of more primal passions.

Poetry has had to meet the abysmal possibilities of violence opened up after 1945 in some form or other, one way being an overt thematic acknowledgement of the exponential accumulation of military hardware and the lengthening nuclear shadow of the Cold War years. The Movement had responded by consolidating safe images of a humane England for which the violations of tradition by modernists were simply interruptions or moments of forgetting. However, writing 'death of god' poetry becomes a new and darker practice after the Holocaust, Dresden and Hiroshima, events which necessarily violated the pre-war idyll of a safe and sunny England. A. Alvarez, in his seminal introduction to the anthology of 1962, *The New Poetry*, echoes the title of Freud's pathbreaking text on the theory of the death drive (published just after World War I), *Beyond the Pleasure Principle*, when he writes that the new poetry of the early 1960s goes 'Beyond the Gentility Principle'. Alvarez collected together writing which partly reacted against the sobriety of the Movement, took more risks, was more confessional, and again explored pathological states of mind. Poet-as-man-next-door had become poet-as-victim. Alvarez's prescription was taken up particularly in the intense and grotesque work of ▷ Ted Hughes, ▷ Sylvia Plath, ▷ Peter Redgrove, and American expressionists Robert Lowell (1917–77) and John Berryman (1914–72). Both Freud and Alvarez are observing modern forces of disintegration in developing their theories of psychic and poetic development. Alvarez writes:

Theologians would call these forces evil, psychologists, perhaps, libido. Either way, they are the forces of disintegration which destroy the old standards of civilization. Their public faces are those of two world wars, of the concentration camps, of genocide, and the threat of nuclear war.

(The New Poetry)

In the 1960s British poetry begins to affirm more strongly these disturbing aspects of the human psyche and its 20th-century productions.

Given the clear rational tone of much Movement work, and the at times passionate violence of much post-Movement poetry, one is tempted to superimpose the reaction from Movement to post-Movement on to the old Enlightenment/Romantic polarity, especially since Davie's overt championing of Augustan (▷ Augustanism) values. However, the simplicity of such an opposition would be challenged by the work of someone like ▷ Thom Gunn, who uses elements from both poetic worlds. He is something of a bridging figure between the Movement poets, particularly Larkin, and the early 1960s poets, particularly Ted Hughes. On the surface, and from the point of view of his work in the 1960s, Gunn could not be further from Larkin, especially when he celebrates the heroes of rock and roll, the Hemingwayesque swaggerers, 'stubbly with goodness'. When Gunn's poetry crosses the Atlantic it goes on the road – 'On the Move' (1957), with an epigram from Marlon Brando and signed just 'California', is typical – and formally Gunn's work in the 1960s, lavish and energetic, took him towards more fluid forms and free verse. But in a couplet from his poem of 1955, 'To Yvor Winters', he anticipates this move from 'Rule' to 'Energy', and unfolds a Blakean umbrella across his corpus to cover both 1950s reason and 1960s passion – at its most effective, a 20th-century marriage of rational heaven and energetic hell:

You keep both Rule and Energy in view,
Much power in each, most in the balanced two.

What, then, of Energy? Ted Hughes is a writer known for his Romanticism, his evocations of violence and vitalistic cruelty. He is often a very disturbing writer, showing how the idyll of England reinvoked in the 1950s is already subverted or betrayed from within by the 'stirrings beyond sense' which ghost control and self-possession. 'Esther's tomcat' sleeps by day on the mat but by night 'Walks upon sleep . . . over the round world of men'; thrushes aren't safely part of an English country garden but are 'more coiled steel than living'; a skylark is 'shot through the crested head / With the command, Not die'. Hughes' verse draws strongly on mythological motifs and can seem over-written; breaking with the parochialism of the Movement, it unearths as well as savagery the sinister and harrowing visions of a volume such as *Crow* (1970).

Hughes' work serves as relief for several comparisons which could be made at this point. Conceptually it owes much to Freud and Lawrence, who meet at the point in his verse where it becomes clear that violence and human repression are inextricably part of the same mechanism, civilization engendering a more insidious violence bred of repression itself. But he is quite starkly not a liberationist writer like Dylan Thomas or Lawrence, as he bleakly emphasizes the closure or inevitability of this mechanism. Other authorial personae exist, of course, in his children's poetry, his critical essays, even in his efforts as Poet Laureate, where Hughes the painfully private poet becomes public property. As part of a new wave in poetry – confessional, naked, anguished – which looked back in anger at 1950s self-satisfaction, Hughes exemplified the savage twist which Alvarez celebrates, and in this is often compared with the work of Sylvia Plath, primarily because they were married until 1962 and worked closely together.

Hughes was also a strong champion of Keith Douglas, and marks of disintegration brought to consciousness by the war are foregrounded by their poetic relation. Finally, in his Romantic extravagance Hughes' work can be contrasted with that of those poets who picked up the loose ends of modernism.

These links coalesce at the point at which the 'I' of the poem or poet needs to be discussed. Again questions of the poet's identity and of his or her relationship to the text and its context, to writing as public or private are brought to the fore. One way into this problem is to look briefly at the work of ▷ Charles Tomlinson, whose resistance to the influences of Thomas in the late 1940s made him turn to the precision of American modernism; he wrote 'here was a clear way of going to work, so that you could cut through this Freudian swamp and say something clearly'. The image of Pound and Eliot cutting through the Georgian 'swamp' and returning to the intellectual hardness of the ▷ Metaphysical poets has an uncanny echo in Tomlinson's practice; his 'I' is a problematic entity, rather like Eliot's. It is marginalized but, since something of a process of self-conscious depersonalization is being enacted, it takes centre-stage in its impersonality. His attempt to objectify the image, resisting Thomas' emotionalism and surreal obscurity, echoes the austerity of the Imagist project: in his own words he wants to give his images 'The hardness of crystals, the facets of cut glass'. The title of his 1960 volume *Seeing is Believing* emphasizes his attempt to bring together Movement empiricism with Imagism's valuation of visual clarity.

Compare, for instance, Tomlinson's 'Fox' with Hughes' 'Thought-Fox'. Tomlinson's animal is dead in the snow, it has a sharp correctness but in the shifting romantic blizzard gives up its own existence and becomes an image of the hill itself. Tomlinson has to work hard against the drive of his poem to slide into a chaos of white and crosswinds with his mind at the confused centre:

. . . the drift still mocked
my mind as if the whole
fox-infested hill were the skull of a fox . . .

The image of hill-as-skull crystalizes from the blinding blizzard of this text. Hughes' poem begins, however, with fox-as-text; where Tomlinson's fox-skull and hill are 'out there' and the poet's job is to respect and accord them this objective autonomy, Hughes' fox finds his quickness only inside the interior of the poem, the writing of which depends upon a poetic incorporation of the natural world. For Hughes there is no critical distance which gives the image outline; the fox is already inside the self, actually entering the human skull ('the dark hole of the head'), becoming subject to the desire of writing, so that the page can be printed. Similarly, Tomlinson's hawk in 'How still the Hawk' hangs purely 'out there', innocent in its distance from human interpretation, whereas Hughes' 'Hawk Roosting' famously signifies the sinister, cold egotism of the totalitarian personality – Hughes' hawk has a subjective existence, so that it speaks the poems from the point of view of a post-war 'I'. The stillness of the hawk's image is for Tomlinson, then, a challenge to objectivism, for Hughes a point of aberrant control in the maelstrom of modern cruelty, whilst for Dylan Thomas in 'Over Sir John's Hill' it signifies an emotionally intense poise:

Over Sir John's Hill
The hawk on fire hangs still;
In a hoisted cloud, at drop of dusk, he pulls to his claws.

The dialogue between these poems, then, serves to illustrate the familiar modern dichotomy in British poetry, that of the privileging of inside or outside. Is poetic writing an attempt to clarify as succinctly as possible the autonomous and the objective, or is it an act of poetic individuation and self-definition? The Romantic question – Coleridge's notion that poet and poem are indistinguishable – often recurs at this moment in poetic history as the dilemma between confessional, violent, personal writing and a post-war form of Imagism, like Tomlinson's, or like the precise and abrupt decompositional writing of ▷ Christopher Middleton. Who, then, is the poet? Is he or she now dead, like other authors in the ▷ post-structuralist world? And how does the fresh political engagement of the 1980s affect this question? The problem of the self and its relations to writing is intensified as personal subjectivity is viewed increasingly suspiciously in recent times. The question of objectivity, of the subjectivity of the poet and the status of his or her images, which clearly Tomlinson is engaging with, became a sharper problem in the 1980s and 1990s with the increased politicization of radical poetic writing, and, in another form, with the distorted perceptions of 'Martian eye' (▷ Martian poetry) writing. I shall return to this shortly.

Sylvia Plath is, like Keith Douglas, another untimely poet, who wrote four brilliant and disturbing slim volumes of poetry in the early 1960s, three of which were published well after her suicide in 1963. It is hard to read Plath's verse outside the enormous interest in her private life which has burgeoned since her death; in modern mythology she exemplifies the self-consciously tragic poetic genius-figure. The nature of her death also evokes a more disturbing myth, that of the woman writer wracked by neurosis and too weak in body to contain her talent. Whoever Plath was, there is no doubt that her work relentlessly pursues the question of the 'I', of poetry and madness, with all Douglas' desire of words for words. The 'late mouths' of 'Poppies in October' which 'cry open / In a forest of frost' cause her to ask 'O my God, what am I?'; to whom do the poppies come, like a macabre gift, suggesting bleeding in ambulances? There is warfare in her work, a sharp killer's eye and a grotesque but erotic drive. A bleeding, fizzing cut across her thumb is the result of an Indian scalping, a sabotage, a Kamikaze act, a symptom of masochism. The image of blood as the running of 'A million soldiers . . ., / Redcoats, every one' ('Cut') is typically acute, almost humorous, but bites with paranoia as she then asks, 'Whose side are they on?' The sinister possibility that one's own flowing blood could be one's enemy speaks the psychological complexity of Plath's work, which never rests in the notion of anguish as 'authentic'. Cruel humour and ruthless self-suspicion undermine sincerity; arrogance and tragic self-glorification are deflated in 'Lady Lazarus', as suicide is paraded with the grotesque props of concentration camps:

Dying
Is an art, like everything else.
I do it exceptionally well.
I do it so it feels like hell.
I do it so it feels real.
I guess you could say I've a call.

Plath's 'reality' is not that of the every-day Movement, but that is not to say that her work can be marginalized as a depoliticized expression of private agonies; she was acutely aware of the political nature of writing for a woman, and insists on drawing parallels between her experience and disturbing political and historical reality. If she is a personal writer it is because, in the phrase coined by 1960s feminism, 'the personal is the political': 'Daddy' is as much about the powers of horror, opened up by post-war images of death camps and fascist obsession, as it is a text working through a daughter's ambivalent relationship with her father. As Plath said in an interview just before she died, poetry 'should be generally relevant, to such things as Hiroshima and Dachau'. Plath gazes straight at taboo, where a writer like ▷ Peter Porter, in 'Annotations of Auschwitz' for instance, looks satirically sideways at it. Porter's 'Your Attention Please' casts a black-comic nuclear shadow, whilst reminding us of something we meet constantly in Plath's work: 'Death is the least we have to fear'. 'Lady Lazarus' comes back,

Out of the ash
I rise with my red hair
And I eat men like air.

'A dangerous weapon': contemporary poetry

I am neither internee nor informer;
An inner émigré, grown long-haired
And thoughtful; a wood-kerne
Escaped from the massacre.
('Exposure', Seamus Heaney)

The crisis of writing and identity which is traced here as infecting British poetry has recently reached fever pitch. The problems of what constitutes a poem and of who the poet is have more recently become politicized into questions about what constitutes the *British* in 'British poetry'. Poets now, be they black, female or Irish, have felt themselves to be 'inner émigrés': as Guyanan-born poet John Agard (b 1949) writes 'I didn't graduate / I immigrate', ('Listen Mr Oxford Don', 1985). The phrase 'poetry in English' is compromised by other voices from Ireland, Scotland, regions of England, and the Commonwealth (▷ Post-colonial literature). From a traditional point of view it seems that English poetry is slowly undergoing an undignified death-process, that the incorporation of other voices into 'Eng. Lit.' constitutes the blowing into oblivion of a much-cherished friend. More energetically and optimistically we could say, rather, that what is gaining prominence is a kind of 'multiverse', a plurality of accents and experiences breaking open the poised egocentric tradition. From going 'Beyond the Gentility Principle' we reach the late 1980s with poet and critic Eric Mottram's assertion that the modern avant-garde constitutes 'A Treacherous Assault on British Poetry' (*The New British Poetry*; 1988). The critic Colin MacCabe writes, 'It is perhaps no longer appropriate to talk of English literature but of a literature in broken English':

If the members of the United Kingdom are all nominally British, it is instructive to recall that English as a language has been imposed, often by force, throughout the British Isles. And the peoples of those islands find that along with the imposed language they have acquired a literature to which their relationship is profoundly ambiguous – one need only think of Joyce or MacDiarmid to realise exactly how ambiguous.

(McCabe, 'Broken English', *Futures for English*, 1988)

This realization began to find some purchase in British poetry in the mid-1960s, although it is true that in a different way internationalist strains in modernist writing had already undermined the notion of a truly English culture. From the regional focus which constituted much poetic activity during the 1960s, to the broad cultural base of much radical poetry today, British writing now can be defined only as a space within which its vital differences are affirmed. It has many homes: Trinidad-born poet John Lyons now resides in Britain but has left a nomadic trail leading back to his 'Island Muse':

I come long years with my pen
and island hauntings
from where my navel string tree
still grows.

Thus poetry split its focus into a thriving network of regional groups, in the Mordern Tower poets of Newcastle, who found their mentor in the rediscovered ▷ Basil Bunting, and the new renaissance of poetry from Northern Ireland which has emerged as contemporaneous with the troubles, from poets such as ▷ Seamus Heaney, ▷ Paul Muldoon and ▷ Derek Mahon. The emphasis was resolutely anti-London and the cultural imperialism of the south-east. The famous 'Liverpool poets' of the early and mid-1960s – Adrian Henri (b 1932), Henry Graham (b 1930), Roger McGough (b 1937) and Brian Patten (b 1946), collected in the anthologies *The Mersey Sound* (1967) and *New Volume* (1983) – were a British version of American Beat poetry. All four had strong links with the world of pop music, and emphasized poetry as live performance, thus opening up their writing to a wide young audience. Like pop art, Mersey poetry uses the familiar images of throwaway culture in its quick-fire surreal humour, but the effect is ultimately naughty rather than revolutionary. Pop art and pop music found their way into poetry at this time as never before, and the link between rock and writing was kept bubbling underground in the late 1960s largely due to the ministrations of the poet and publisher Michael Horovitz (b 1935) – his magazine *New Departures*, founded in 1959, had long been the organ of the poetic underground, and his anthology *Children of Albion* (1969) exemplifies a late 1960s celebration of liberation politics and poetics, taking William Blake as mentor. Whilst it is true that much avant-garde writing in the 1960s and 1970s displays the preoccupations of the economically privileged young British middle classes, it also eventually encouraged a certain disrespect – against the gentility principle once more – which opened a space for the more multi-racial and working-class forms of punk, dub, reggae poetry, and New Wave performance in the late 1970s.

The regionalist movement was roughly contemporary with the establishment of a large number of small presses, through which more experimental and avant-garde work found a space outside the mainstream monolithic publishing houses, just as the high street bookshop's failure to sell marginalized writing urged poets into using local live outlets for their work. The small presses, often set up by poets themselves, have effectively countered the overwhelming influence of the major houses like Chatto & Windus and Faber & Faber – Faber in particular has long dominated poetry publication and in effect established the official canon of post-war and contemporary verse. Aesthetic valuation has seldom walked so nakedly in the profit margins. So the small presses have been vital in countering profitable orthodoxies: names such as ▷ Gael Turnbull's Migrant Press, Peterloo Poets, Stuart Montgomery's Fulcrum, Andrew Crozier's Ferry, Desmond Johnson's Akira and ▷ Ian Hamilton Finlay's Wild Hawthorn, in conjunction with small magazines like *Stand, Poetry Information* and *Agenda*, have over the years given younger and more experimental writers a space within which to work and have access to publishing facilities. In 1971 the champion of experimental and post-modernist work Eric Mottram was made editor of the Poetry Society's *Poetry Review*, an unprecedented move, as a result of which other forms of writing found a voice through the National Poetry Centre, until the scandalous dissolution of the editorial board by the ▷ Arts Council in 1977.

It must be said, however, that these energies remain fired partly by the task of countering the familiar conservatism of the poetic establishment. Two of the larger publishing houses, Anvil Press and Carcanet Press, are indeed open to more obscure and challenging types of modern writing, but Carcanet's statement of its aesthetic policy when it was established in 1969 displays a continued cherishing of bourgeois 'reasonable' traditions. Something of this survived in the compilation of the much criticized 1982 anthology, *The Penguin Book of Contemporary Poetry*, edited by ▷ Blake Morrison (b 1950) and ▷ Andrew Motion (b 1952), which collected together a chic, sophisticated body of modern verse, challenging nothing, and punctuated for bizarre effect only by sideways glances from the 'Martian eyes' of ▷ Craig Raine and Christopher Reid.

The modernist question of homelessness has recently been rearticulated by women poets as a problem of one's tradition and one's literary home; women's writing continues to disrupt the smooth contours of the traditional mask. As a woman writer, where does one come from? ▷ Denise Levertov's verse is unsettling in its sense of exile, echoing ▷ Virginia Woolf's '. . . as a woman I have no country'. ▷ Ruth Fainlight's work also knows no fixed identity; a multitude of feminine voices insinuate threats or coaxings from between its lines. Her poems are populated by female 'others' – Sibyls, forgotten sisters, 'Stone-Age' selves, Medusas, 'Sophia, Anima, Kali', 'Gloria', 'Lilith' or the faces in the mirror. They speak to free the texts 'from whomsoever's definition: / Jew, poet, woman'.

Levertov's verse protests strongly against the stench of war and her adoptive America's aggression. Like Douglas, it exults in moments lived as if at 'the last minute', intensified by the consciousness of ending. Death breathes across the still, awestruck poems, 'Living', 'Passage', '. . . That Passeth All Understanding', a finitude which concentrates; if her poetry is spiritual it is so because it exists in the shadow of oblivion:

The fire in leaf and grass
so green it seems
each summer the last summer
('Living')

a day of spring, a needle's eye
space and time are passing through like a swathe of silk
('Passage')

The intense interest in women's writing since the 1960s has, then, been important both to the ▷ women's movement and in opening up literature to a variety of other voices. Indeed, opening up the canon of contemporary poetry has occurred from inside poetry itself. Modernism's amalgamating energies, which brought many other languages and voices forth from the crevices and underbelly of the canon – its otherwise repressed voices – have been realized in a less authoritarian form since the 1960s. Almost as soon as a new contemporary canon could gather itself, it was eroded by a wave of work penned by black writers, women writers – a self-consciously politicized alternative. Canon challenging has, then, recently been more than an academic exercise, especially since poetry now is written from an acute awareness of the possibilities of academic incorporation and judgement.

MacCabe's punning phrase 'Broken English' suggests both a body terminally injured and broken open, ready for new growth – we are back, perhaps, with H.D.'s celebration of the destruction of restrictive models, which for John Agard again can be achieved armed only 'wit mih human breath / but human breath / is a dangerous weapon'. If the impetus of 1960s poetry was an urge to harmony, that of the 1980s is an affirmation of difference, as the teeming voices of other cultural forms (the language of reggae, for instance) breaks out from the broken body of 'Eng. Lit.':

I dont need no axe
to split/ up yu syntax
I dont need no hammer
to mash/ up yu grammar
('Listen Mr Oxford Don', John Agard; 1985)

'Tradition' continues to be a problem, but one which contemporary poetry encounters through a strategy of incorporation. Two recent anthologies illustrate this extremely well. Denise Riley's *Poets on Writing* (1992) places poems by new young poets alongside short prose responses and observations concerning their writing history, their influences and motivations. The collection shows the diversity of poetic 'climates' which breathe in and out of the texts included (as Riley puts it, 'what there was in the air'). The anxiety about tradition which has engendered the violent reactions of the 20th century movements I have described here has to some extent been replaced by a writing spirit which casts the net of influence culturally wider and with a greater sense of critical scepticism regarding the question of influence *per se*. Thus poet and critic Geoffrey Ward (b 1954), citing a range of elements and images (such as the Fun House at Southport, early Auden, or the whole poetic climate of his early student life) which form some of the 'troubled' origins of a poem, writes,

Writing only ever takes place at some juncture; in relation, Poetry articulates the coincidence and/or contradiction where what's heard on the radio meets what happens in the street, where what you are reading questions what you are read as doing.
('Objects That Come Alive at Night', *Poets on Writing*, ed. Denise Riley, Macmillan 1992)

Similarly, Carol Rumens' *New Women Poets* (1991) stresses the eclecticism of her writers, their variety of dialects and enthusiastic formal innovation. Citing the poetry of Briar Wood (b 1958) and Jackie Kay (b 1951), Rumens writes:

What is new is the emergence of a kind of late twentieth-century urban dialect, a montage that reverberates with the noise, colour, slanginess, jargonizing and information-glut of daily life.

In presenting this final collage, I do not wish to suggest that the project of modern poetry is a return to representation, albeit the representation of a *new* range of cultural phenomena or experiences. But perhaps modern poetry, informed by the 'climate' of popular music, films or images, and theoretical perspectives on influence, is better able to articulate its response to a wider range of materials. In this sense modern poetry comes close to ▷ postmodernism, although the term is more commonly used in relation to a range of other forms. The strategy of incorporation which I have described has, however, more clearly been deployed as a response to marginalization. Modern poetry uses its marginalization and the elements of literary crisis to form something which has not only a future but many futures, as many futures as there are cultural forms and languages to be incorporated. What is being affirmed, then, is a process of innoculation; the crisis passes as new forms of writing learn how to grow from that which formerly threatened and marginalized. The canon is being opened from within; to paraphrase Nietzsche, what doesn't kill poetry makes it stronger.

Culture and Consciousness: the 20th-century Novel in English

Andrew Michael Roberts

PART I – 1900 to 1930

Between 1900 and 1930 revolutionary developments took place in the English novel. These developments involved new subject matter, style and technique, and led ultimately to a radical rethinking of the relationship between fiction and reality. This era in the history of the novel, like the corresponding periods in the history of drama, poetry and other arts, is now widely known as ▷ modernism. The roots of modernism are exceptionally diverse, the result of cross-fertilization between cultures, between art forms and between disciplines. Like most historical generalizations, however, the concept of modernism can generate exclusions and omissions. At one time there was a tendency for critics to neglect the role of women writers in modernism (with a few exceptions such as ▷ Virginia Woolf); now, however, there is a greater (though not universal) awareness of the role played by such novelists as ▷ Katherine Mansfield, ▷ Dorothy Richardson, ▷ May Sinclair, ▷ Rebecca West and ▷ Sylvia Townsend Warner. This in turn brings a wider conception of the nature and significance of modernism as a movement in the arts. However, it is also important to recognize the considerable body of fiction from this period for which the term modernism is not appropriate. This includes fiction in the realist mode such as the novels of ▷ Arnold Bennett and ▷ John Galsworthy as well as ▷ H.G. Wells' comedies of lower-middle-class life. There was also a wide range of popular fictional genres which, without sharing the high cultural aspirations of modernist innovation, can be inventive, entertaining and revealing of early twentieth-century culture, such as the light comedies of ▷ P.G. Wodehouse, the fantasies and detective stories of ▷ G.K. Chesterton, writing for children by ▷ Kenneth Grahame and ▷ A.A. Milne, and H.G. Wells' ▷ science fiction.

Culture and reality: James, Conrad, Ford, West

▷ Joseph Conrad (1857–1924) and ▷ Henry James (1843–1916), both of whom first published in the nineteenth century, are the earliest of the great modernist novelists writing in English. One form of cross-fertilization is evident at once, in that James was born an American and Conrad a Pole. Each chose to settle in England and to become an English subject and for each the collision of different cultures was an important theme. The relation of America to Europe is a central concern of James' fiction: in major novels such as ▷ *The Portrait of a Lady* (1881) and ▷ *The Wings of the Dove* (1902), as well as ▷ novellas such as ▷ *Daisy Miller* (1879), the moral consequences of the meeting of American innocence and enthusiasm with a sophisticated but corrupt European culture are explored by means of irony, a sustained attention to the nuances of individual consciousness, and a prose style of increasing subtlety and complexity. It was not only in theme that James was cosmopolitan; influences on his work include ▷ Jane Austen ▷ George Eliot, Nathaniel Hawthorne, ▷ Balzac and Turgenev.

Conrad's life as a merchant seaman, and his upbringing in Poland and Russia, brought him into contact with a wide range of cultures. His prose style owes much to the influences of the nineteenth-century French writers Maupassant and ▷ Flaubert, and in a number of his works he explores what was to become a major concern of the twentieth-century English novel: the experience of the European in Asia, Africa or South America. In ▷ *Heart of Darkness* (1902) a supposedly enlightened colonial programme is revealed as ruthless commercial exploitation and a journey up the Congo becomes symbolic of an exploration of the darkness within man, the atrocities of history, the powerful forces of the unconscious, the mystery of evil. This work epitomizes many features of modernist fiction: the need to confront violence, nihilism and despair; the fascination with, but fear of, the unconscious; the centrality of a dramatized narrator who is not omniscient but rather himself searching for understanding; a symbolic richness which invites multiple interpretations. The last two of these features reflect the influence on modernism of the French Symbolist (▷ symbolism) movement of the nineteenth century, one of whose exponents, Rémy de Gourmont, defined the writer's purpose as being 'to unveil to others the kind of world which he beholds in his own personal mirror'. Conrad's critique of the ideology of Empire also foreshadows the many later works of fiction which use colonial or post-colonial settings to explore the European mind through its contact with what is alien and with what is shared in other cultures, while protesting against bigotry and exploitation. Examples include ▷ E. M. Forster's ▷ *A Passage to India* (1924), ▷ George Orwell's *Burmese Days* (1934), ▷ Graham Greene's *The Heart of the Matter* (1948), and, more recently, the Indian novels of ▷ Ruth Prawer Jhabvala.

But it is in their technique that James and Conrad are most revolutionary. While novelists such as Arnold Bennett (1867–1931) and John Galsworthy (1867–1933) continued to write in the accepted realist mode, using an omniscient narrator, a chronologically sequential narrative and the accumulation of details of social and public life, modernist novelists sought radical redefinitions of the real. One such redefinition is based on the view that, since the individual always perceives reality through his or her own consciousness, the contents and structure of consciousness represent the only accessible reality. A number of philosophical influences are relevant here. William James, the brother of Henry James, was an American psychologist and philosopher. In *Essays in Radical Empiricism* (1912) he elaborated the notion of a world of 'pure experience', all reality being described in terms of subjective human experience (James is also the originator of the term ▷ 'stream of consciousness'). ▷ Sigmund Freud (1856–1939), whose work began to be known in Britain around 1912, has had an enormous influence on modern literature, though less through direct application of his ideas than as a result of his contribution to the assumptions and preoccupations of modern Western society. One of his most potent ideas is also one of the simplest: that all mental phenomena have meaning. This assumption helped to validate new ways of structuring narrative based on dreams, fantasies, and chains of association. ▷ Henri Bergson (1859–1941), the French philosopher of evolution, distinguished between scientific time (a mathematical, abstract, homogeneous medium) and 'real duration' (our direct experience of time as a flowing, irreversible succession of heterogeneous and concrete states). The former, he claimed, is essentially an illusion; it is our subjective experience of time which is 'real'.

The novel was a particularly suitable form for the exploration of such perceptions, because of the possibility of manipulating the reader's experience of time by means of disruption of narrative chronology, and the possibility of representing the nature of consciousness by describing events through the awareness of one or more characters.

In the opening chapters of Conrad's ▷ *Lord Jim* (1900) a sense of foreboding is created so that the reader's expectation and interest are engaged, but at precisely the point of crisis, when an accident occurs to the ship on which Jim is first mate, the narrative jumps forward to the subsequent inquiry. Conrad thus deliberately frustrates the desire for plot satisfaction, diverting our interest from what happens, to the moral and philosophical significance of events. The narrative is structured as an investigation; an attempt, largely on the part of Marlow, who befriends Jim, to understand Jim's life. However, Marlow himself obtains much of his information at second hand, through accounts of events given to him by other characters, so that the effect is one of an enigmatic reality seen through a series of consciousnesses.

But it was Henry James above all who, in practice in his novels and in theory in his prefaces, developed the use of an observing consciousness whose viewpoint shapes the narrative. Here we need to distinguish between the narrator (the narrating 'voice' which, if it refers to itself, must do so in the first person) and the focal character or 'reflector' (the character whose point of view orients the narrative perspective). In Conrad's *Heart of Darkness* Marlow is both narrator and focal character, but the two are not identical since they represent Marlow at different points in his life. One of the subtle pleasures of the story is our sense of Marlow the narrator (middle-aged, sitting on a boat on the Thames) reflecting on and reassessing the experience of Marlow the focal character (younger, more idealistic, in the Congo). James' most favoured device is the restriction of the narrative focalization to a reflector who is not the narrator but is referred to in the third person, a prime example being Strether in ▷ *The Ambassadors* (1903). Associated Jamesian techniques include a dominance of 'scene' (the highly detailed account of particular occasions) and long accounts of the nuances of the reflector's sense of events. These reflectors become centres of interest themselves. Viewing events through their eyes, we share the limitations of their knowledge and the distortions of their viewpoint, and this is realistic in the sense that our actual experience of life is always limited in this way; we do not have all the facts, nor access to the thoughts of others. We share in the progressive illumination of Marlow and Strether. Conrad and James inaugurated a form of realism which ▷ Malcolm Bradbury (b 1932) has aptly described as 'not so much a substantiation of reality as a questing for it'.

These various manipulations of narrator and reflector are fruitful sources of irony, a primary characteristic of much modern fiction. Irony can be generated when the reader perceives more, or understands better, than the narrator and/or reflector, and can occur even when our perspective is technically limited to that of this character. James' novella *The Aspern Papers* (1888) is entirely first-person narration, but we gradually realize, through his own words and thoughts, the moral and emotional limitations of the narrator. A different form of irony is developed by Conrad in ▷ *The Secret Agent* (1907) and ▷ *Under Western Eyes* (1911): a pervasive irony of tone and event. The former is produced by a portrayal of human activity as largely futile and human nature as inherently given to self-deception and illusory beliefs. The latter occurs as characters' actions consistently go awry and produce the opposite effect to that intended. The result is a blend of black comedy with a satirical and tragic view of humanity, its pretensions, and its ideals.

A special case of the dramatized central consciousness is the unreliable narrator or reflector. One of the most fascinating examples of the unreliable narrator is Dowell in ▷ Ford Madox Ford's novel *The Good Soldier* (1915). Our initial tendency to accept a first-person narrator as an accurate source of information is exploited so that the cruelty, deception and insanity lurking beneath the genteel surface of the lives of two couples emerges with a greater sense of shock. Dowell also reflects on the nature of story-telling and its relation to truth ('I don't know how it is best to put this thing down . . .') and this novel thus anticipates two recurrent features of the twentieth-century novel. The first is the use of narrators or reflectors who are unbalanced, malevolent, of limited understanding or otherwise in an abnormal state of mind. Examples include *The Collector* (1963) by ▷ John Fowles (parts 1 and 3), and *The Spire* (1964) by ▷ William Golding. The second feature is reflexive narrative, in which the nature and purpose of writing becomes a constant secondary theme, or even the primary interest of the work. Examples include ▷ Doris Lessing's *The Golden Notebook* (1962) and William Golding's *Rites of Passage* (1980).

Rebecca West had published a study of Henry James in 1916 and her first novel *The Return of the Soldier*, which followed two years later in 1918, has marked affinities with the work of James, Conrad and Ford. Like James, she uses the device of a narrator who is a sensitive, perceptive but not impartial observer: the story of Chris, a soldier who returns from the front during the First World War having lost his memory of the last fifteen years, is told by his cousin Jenny, whose account is coloured by her own adoration for Chris. Like Conrad in *Heart of Darkness* and other of his works, West employs a narrative within a narrative, but she introduces a distinctive form of displacement between the two narrative levels: in an inset account, Jenny narrates the story of Chris' first love (which she knows only at second hand) with an instability of pronoun (shifting from 'one' to 'they') which suggests her shifting emotional identifications. Like Ford's *The Good Soldier*, West's *The Return of the Soldier* uses the play of subjectivity and projection to study loss, alienation, jealousy and the subtleties of self-deception. However, West's novel ends in partial consolation rather than the desolation evoked by Ford. In *The Return of the Soldier* modernist narrative technique contributes to the celebration of an almost mystical power of nurturing which West sees in certain women.

History, Consciousness and Gender: Lawrence, Woolf, Richardson

The relationship of history and the novel may be formulated in two ways. On the one hand, we may regard history as an objective series of public events, and the novel as an art form which may represent, ignore or fictionalize them. On the other hand, we may regard history itself as a narrative, and its relation with the novel as more reciprocal, our sense of the nature and significance of narrative influencing our sense of historical pattern and meaning and vice versa. Modernism is sometimes accused of ignoring historical and social realities. But the sense of living in a period of historical crisis is an important aspect of much modernist fiction. The apocalyptic world view which the critic Frank Kermode has identified in the work of ▷ D. H. Lawrence (1885–1930) is at once a reaction to accelerating social change and an expression of a mystical or prophetic view of the role of the artist, influenced by the Bible, and especially the Book of Revelation. ▷ *The Rainbow* (1915) describes the life of three generations of the Brangwen family in the English Midlands, and ▷ *Women in Love* (1921) (originally planned as part of the same work), continues the story of the third generation. In neither novel is there extensive reference to historical events in the conventional sense, though the effect on rural life of progressive industrialization is powerfully felt. Rather, what Lawrence writes is a history of the development of human consciousness and the unconscious life, in which the individual's relation with partner, family, work and the natural and man-made environment reflects large-scale cultural changes. The harmony achieved by Tom and Lydia, the first-generation couple living at Marsh Farm, is symbolized by the biblical image of the rainbow; by the end of *The Rainbow*, when Ursula, the modern woman, rejects marriage with Skrebensky, the representative of the mechanistic modern society, the rainbow can be only a tentative hope for a future regeneration. Just as James' novels seem to take place in a theatre of consciousness which is his unique discovery, so a considerable part of Lawrence's achievement is his development of a wholly new way of writing about human experience. The aspect of life to which he attends does not fit any of our normal categories; it cannot be summarized as the realm of the instinctual, nor of the unconscious, not of the physical, nor of the emotional, though it touches all of these. It reflects Lawrence's radically new sense of the nature of the self and his rejection of what he called 'the old stable ego of the character', and is realized by techniques of symbolism, the repetition of imagery, and the use of sustained passages of highly poetic yet often abstract language to describe the development of the individual. In *Women in Love* contemporary society is unequivocally rejected as mechanistic and destructive, and regeneration is located in personal relations of mystical intensity.

In its apocalyptic view Lawrence's work may be said to subordinate the contingency of history to a typological pattern: that is to say, a pattern of 'types' (events or persons), analogous to, and in many cases based upon, the events and persons of the Old Testament which foreshadow the dispensation of the New Testament. It is a feature of modernist narratives to order their material by symbol, pattern or metaphor rather than by the linear sequence of history. If the patterns to which history conforms are for Lawrence apocalyptic and typological, for Virginia Woolf (1882–1941) they are the patterns of art and of human sensibility. ▷ *To The Lighthouse* (1927) was described by Leonard Woolf as a 'psychological poem', and this reflects the privileging of consciousness and the work of art as a made object over the chronological sequence of conventional fiction. The novel is in three sections, of which the first and third describe the life of a family in their holiday home in Scotland on two days, one before and one after the First World War. These sections use the stream of consciousness technique developed in the English novel by Woolf, ▷ James Joyce (1882–1941) and ▷ Dorothy Richardson (1873–1957). So *To The Lighthouse* represents the thought sequences of the Ramsay family and their guests, moving freely in time and space. The middle section of the novel, entitled 'Time Passes', is concerned with the non-human, with change, with history and the ravages of time (the war takes place and several of the characters die; the house decays). An opposition is set up in the novel between, on the one hand, the destructive effect of history and of impersonal nature, and on the other the ordering power of art (represented by the painter, Lily Briscoe) and of human consciousness as a builder of social relationships (represented by Mrs Ramsay's drawing together of family and friends). The novel ends with Lily finishing her painting, completing a pattern in which the past and the dead are not lost, but reconciled in memory and in art. In so far as this painting is an analogue for the novel itself, history is mastered by art.

In Woolf's work the stream of consciousness technique moves towards a radical view of the nature of the self, which is of particular importance for ▷ feminist writing. In ▷ *The Waves* (1931) the lives of six characters are represented, and the close interaction of their consciousnesses is symbolically associated with a pattern of waves on the sea, separate yet part of a greater whole. From her first novel, *The Voyage Out* (1915), Woolf expressed a sense of the fluid nature of the self, its interdependence with the selves of others, and its relation to ▷ gender and class-based power structures. Feminists have increasingly seen the self as socially and politically constructed and have drawn inspiration from Woolf's moves towards ▷ deconstruction of the idea of immutable gender identity. Her interest in androgyny, her sense of the social protest which madness can represent and her satire on repressive psychiatric practices in ▷ *Mrs Dalloway* (1925) have also remained points of reference for feminist writers, although there is disagreement concerning her relationship to issues of class and privilege.

Woolf's ▷ *Orlando* places ideas of androgyny in a historical context through the fantasy of a single character who lives many lives, some male and some female, over four centuries. Conversely, Lawrence's wish to essentialize gender differences becomes even stronger in his later works, notably *The Plumed Serpent* (1926) and 'The Woman who Rode Away' (1928), in which his earlier vision of apocalyptic regeneration is converted into the misogynist and fascistic worship of a ritualized male sexual power. A writer who has much in common with Woolf is Dorothy Richardson, whose autobiographical novel in thirteen volumes, *Pilgrimage* (1915–67), employs a lightly-punctuated and highly poetic stream of consciousness to reveal the mind of a young woman struggling in a society where 'history, literature, the way of stating records, reports, stories, the whole method of statement of things from the beginning . . . was on a false foundation'. She herself objected to the use of the stream metaphor for consciousness, preferring the organic stability suggested by the metaphor of a tree. The life of her heroine, Miriam Henderson, is a pilgrimage in search of an indefinable fulfilment, associated with the joy of perception itself. Woolf saw Richardson's prose style as 'the psychological sentence of the feminine gender' and Richardson herself argued that men and women used language differently. Both writers, together with such contemporaries as Katherine Mansfield, have been the focus of debate concerning the existence and nature of a style and use of language specific to women's writing; an ▷ *écriture féminine*. In terms of content, much women's writing of this period emphasizes the significance to be found in the texture of experience: May Sinclair commented on the presence, in *Pilgrimage*, of a mysticism which could embrace mundane conversations and the eating of bread and butter. Sinclair's own ▷ *Bildungsroman*, *Mary Olivier: a Life* (1919) and her novel *The Life and Death of Harriet Frean* (1922) each explore, through stream-of-consciousness techniques, the development of a woman's mind and sensibility, in such a way that the details of ordinary life are informed by Sinclair's mystical, feminist and psychoanalytical interests.

Phases of modernism: Forster and Joyce

It is possible to distinguish an early phase of modernism, ending around the beginning of the First World War. In the first decade of the century James' three last great novels appeared, together with most of Conrad's major fiction and the first two novels of E. M. Forster (1879–1970), whose work is frequently regarded as containing both modernist and Victorian elements. In Forster's novel ▷ *Howards End* (1910) English society is seen as divided between the business world of action and the refined world of culture and the emotions, and a symbolic reconciliation is suggested by the marriage of the chief representatives of each group, and the inheritance of a house (the Howards End of the title), which stands for a threatened continuity in English life. The sense of threat and change is distinctively modernist, as is the location of renewal and reconciliation in the realm of the symbolic and the imagination. But Forster's social comedy, his narrative technique and his ▷ humanism associate him with more traditional strains in the English novel.

A Passage To India is at once more symbolic and less schematic than *Howards End*, and, appearing in 1924, belongs to the later post-war phase of modernism. While its satire on the arrogance and narrow-mindedness of British officials in India reflects the same belief in tolerance and liberalism as Forster's earlier work, the novel also explores at a deeper level the philosophical issues arising from the meeting of cultures. This is achieved in part through a symbolic evocation of the Indian landscape, and in particular the mysterious Marabar Caves, which call into question the identity and beliefs of several of the characters by their immitigable otherness. The novel ends with the voice of the landscape itself, on a note of ambivalent hope. While Forster made a contribution to both phases of modernism, the main figures of this post-war phase are Lawrence, Joyce and Woolf. Joyce's ▷ *Dubliners* (1914) is a seminal influence on the modern ▷ short story in English. He described his intention as that of writing 'a chapter in the moral history of my culture', using 'a style of scrupulous meanness'. Drawing on French influences, Joyce does indeed inaugurate in English the oblique, laconic short story, later developed by American writer Ernest Hemingway (1899–1961) and *The New Yorker* magazine. But the use of symbol, Joyce's mimicking of the diction and speech patterns of his Dublin characters, and his idea of the epiphany – a sudden spiritual manifestation in the ordinary – point to a more poetic and symbolic strain which culminates in the powerful yet ironic Romanticism of the last story in the collection, 'The Dead'.

▷ *A Portrait of the Artist as a Young Man* (1916) is comparable to Lawrence's ▷ *Sons and Lovers* (1913) in its semi-autobiographical nature. In each the primary interest is in the psychological and intellectual development of a young man, with great concentration on the protagonist. This is most obvious in the *Portrait*, where the other characters remain shadowy and the language and structure of the novel seeks to render the contents of Stephen's mind, but it is important that in *Sons and Lovers* much of what we learn about the other characters is essentially their roles in Paul Morel's psychological economy. The protagonists of both novels seek independence, but whereas in Lawrence's work this is primarily emotional independence, in that of Joyce it is predominantly cultural and intellectual, involving Stephen's escape from the restrictions of Irish society and the Catholic Church.

Joyce's ▷ *Ulysses* (1922) is a central text of modernism. A novel of over 600 pages concerned with one day in Dublin, it has an amazing richness of texture, combining mythical and literary allusions, parody and pastiche, punning and humour, with a powerful sense of the infinite complexity and subtlety of the individual's emotional and intellectual life. It is structured around a loose correspondence to the episodes of Homer's *Odyssey*, so that the juxtaposition of the ordinary with the heroic generates irony and wit while at the same time drawing on an archetypal level of experience comparable to that which the Swiss psychoanalyst ▷ Carl Jung located in a collective unconscious. The symbolist aspiration to imitate musical form is evident in the use of repeated words, phrases and images as forms of leitmotif. The novel encountered virulent opposition at the time of publication, being banned in England until 1936 on grounds of obscenity. Its acceptance into the canon of major works of English literature, together with the successful defence of D. H. Lawrence's ▷ *Lady Chatterley's Lover* at a 1960 obscenity trial, signalled the public endorsement of the principle that all areas of human experience could be valid subjects for the serious artist. It is in part for its combination of mundane details with a vast inclusiveness of reference that *Ulysses* is valued so highly.

The realist tradition: Bennett, Galsworthy, Wells

Despite the genuinely innovative and radical nature of modernist fiction, we should be wary of too schematic an opposition between modernists and traditionalists. We are inheritors of a distinction made by writers such as Woolf and Lawrence in order to define their artistic identity and literary programme. As Frank Kermode has pointed out, modernist programmes have the habit of claiming that they have to 'get out from under something', and Arnold Bennett, John Galsworthy and H. G. Wells were cast in the role of that 'something'. Wells himself participated in this process in his well-known comment in a letter to Henry James (8 July 1915): 'To you literature like painting is an end, to me literature is a means, it has a use . . . I had rather be called a journalist than an artist.' Nevertheless, there are some affinities between the realists and the modernists in terms of influences and subject matter: Bennett was influenced by French and Russian novelists, and Wells, in his scientific romances, shows a strong sense of the apocalyptic and of the impact of war and technology on twentieth-century society. These writers are also part of important continuities in English fiction. Wells' emphasis on ideas is continued by ▷ Aldous Huxley (1894–1963) and George Orwell (1903–50) in the 1930s and 40s, while Bennett's regional settings in the Potteries district connect him with the regional realists of the 1950s. Wells, in works such as *The War of the Worlds* (1898) and *The First Men in the Moon* (1901), was also a pioneer of science fiction, one of the most fruitful of the popular genres in the twentieth-century novel.

Bennett's best work, such as *The Old Wives' Tale* (1908) and *Riceyman Steps* (1923), contains telling studies of ordinary lives, with a strong sense of the rich detail of society, and of the passing of time. The limitations of his style include a liability to give information too directly, to 'telling' rather than 'showing'. Like Bennett, Galsworthy was extremely popular and successful during his lifetime, with works such as ▷ *The Forsyte Saga* (1906–21) which are primarily concerned with upper-class society. The most general criticism of his work is that his satire is often lacking in focus and rigour. Wells was an extremely versatile writer of fiction and journalism; his fiction included Dickensian social comedy such as *The History of Mr Polly* (1910) and studies of contemporary social issues such as *Ann Veronica* (1909), as well as his science fiction or scientific romances. George Orwell, who considered Wells' thinking to be outmoded by the 1940s, nevertheless asserted of his own generation that 'the minds of us all, and therefore the physical world, would be perceptibly different if Wells had never existed'.

1920s satire: Lewis, Huxley and Waugh

Alongside the modernist experimentation of the 1920s a vein of tragi-comic satire emerged in the English novel in the work of Aldous Huxley, ▷ Wyndham Lewis (1882–1957) and ▷ Evelyn Waugh (1903–66). These authors shared a sense of the absurdity of modern society, and one form which this takes in their novels is that of dehumanization and the dissolution of the self. Wyndham Lewis, an artist, philosopher and editor as well as a novelist, was a leading spirit of Vorticism, an anti-realist movement in art, based on jagged, rhythmical, mechanistic forms. Such principles are also reflected in the portrayal of character in Lewis' novels, such as *Tarr* (1918); he described men as comic because they were 'things, or physical bodies, behaving as persons'. Aldous Huxley's *Crome Yellow* (1921) is primarily a novel of ideas, similar in form to the novels of ▷ Thomas Love Peacock (1785–1866), in which characters carry on debates in the setting of a country house. It is based on a somewhat schematic antithesis between men of thought and men of action. The protagonist, Dennis Stone, an example of the former who wants to be the latter, is a characteristic satirical anti-hero of the period, weak and ineffectual, but both types are portrayed as inadequate. The hero of Evelyn Waugh's first novel, *Decline and Fall*

(1928), is described as a shadow; passively enduring a series of outrageous injustices and misfortunes, he ends up precisely where he started. The book describes itself as 'an account of the mysterious disappearance of Paul Pennyfeather'. Paul's adventures, however, bring him up against a large number of eccentrics, so that his shadowiness only serves to emphasize the egregious personalities which surround him.

These works contain images of the modern world as manic, mechanized and incomprehensible; they are essentially about the problem of how to live in a society which seems meaningless. The stance of the implied author (the author as manifest in the text) varies: Huxley tends to include some equivalent for himself in the novel, thereby making his own intellectual approach part of the object of his satire; Waugh is detached and invisible; Lewis is outraged, polemical and assertive. Drawing on the tradition of such European writers as Voltaire, ▷ Gogol and ▷ Swift, they represent a powerful alternative vision of the modern condition.

PART II – 1930 to 1950

In the 1930s and 40s political events were felt in English prose writing with a particular directness. The impact of the First World War and the associated social changes on the modernist novel tended to take place primarily at the level of the author's general world view, and to filter through into the content of the novel transformed by some principle of artistic shaping. From around 1930, however, there arose in many writers a sense that historical events were of such overwhelming importance in their implications for society that they demanded forms of writing which would attempt to represent, with as much immediacy as possible, the feel of contemporary experience, while also explicitly taking sides in a political or moral debate. In general terms, then, the period was one in which social or documentary realism reasserted itself; that form of realism which is concerned with an outward fidelity to the experience of the mass of individuals and an engagement with public issues. Such a generalization is, however, necessarily an oversimplification. Individual authors continued or commenced their literary careers, responding in a variety of ways to their own experiences, influences and interests as well as to the temper of the times. New works by Joyce and Woolf were still appearing during the early part of the period; Woolf's last novel was ▷ *Between The Acts* (1941) while Joyce's final work, ▷ *Finnegans Wake*, was published in 1939. ▷ Ivy Compton-Burnett (1884–1969), whose first novel had appeared as early as 1911, elaborated further her vision of power, pain and obsession in wealthy families of late Victorian and early Edwardian England, rendered almost entirely through dialogue. Evelyn Waugh's novels of the 1930s, including the hilarious *Scoop* (1938), continued and developed the satirical vein begun with *Decline and Fall.* ▷ Elizabeth Bowen (1899–1973), in novels such as *The Heat of the Day* (1949) and short stories such as 'Mysterious Kôr' (from *The Demon Lover*, 1945), combined an evocation of the atmosphere of wartime London with a Jamesian attention to the nuances of personal relations. ▷ Samuel Beckett's unique exploration of man as an isolated being confronting existential despair began with his first novel, *Murphy*, in 1938, which had been preceded by a collection of Joycean stories, *More Pricks than Kicks* (1934).

Politics, social change and war: Orwell and Gibbon

In the public sphere the 1930s were dominated by two factors. The first was the economic depression which, from the collapse of the Wall Street Stock Market in

1929, began to cause widespread unemployment and poverty. The second was the rise of ▷ fascism in Europe: Hitler seized power in Germany in 1933; in Italy Mussolini had ruled since 1922; in 1932 Sir Oswald Mosley founded the British Union of Fascists. The most coherent ideological response to both these developments came from the left wing, so that during the 1930s a considerable number of British writers and intellectuals became socialists or communists. The Left Book Club, founded in 1936, provided a focus for this tendency. It is primarily from a left-wing perspective that modernism has been rejected or criticized, both in the 1930s and since. George Orwell, a socialist, though a very independent one, described the 1920s as 'a period of irresponsibility such as the world has never before seen'. Georg Lukács, the Hungarian Marxist critic (▷ Marx, Karl), writing in 1955 from a more dogmatic perspective, attacked modernism on the grounds that it treated man as a solitary and asocial being, thus denying the reality of history.

Orwell's own writings seek to bring home to readers the human consequences of the economic and political situation: the soul-destroying nature of poverty in *Down and Out in London and Paris* (1933) and *The Road to Wigan Pier* (1937), the miseries of war and the distortions of the press in *Homage to Catalonia* (1938) and the oppressions of British imperialism in *Burmese Days* (1934). The first three of these works blend reportage and autobiography with an element of the fictional, and in each many facts are given, ranging from the minute details of daily life in the trenches of the Spanish Civil War to the income and itemized expenditure of a Yorkshire miner in 1935. This might be seen as a return to the 'materialism' which Woolf objected to in the work of Galsworthy and Bennett, but it gains new force both from Orwell's passionate indignation, and from his imaginative realization of the influence of material conditions on human consciousness and society. However, his individualism and his sometimes sentimental portrayal of the working classes have been criticized by socialist thinkers such as ▷ Raymond Williams.

Orwell's novel *Coming Up For Air* was published in 1939, on the eve of World War II, in the same year as a work by another writer of left-wing views, ▷ Christopher Isherwood's *Goodbye to Berlin*. In each there is a powerful sense of foreboding, of European civilization slipping into violence and chaos. The contrast of narrative techniques illustrates the range of 1930s realism. *Goodbye to Berlin* is a series of linked short episodes set in the decadent atmosphere of Berlin during the Nazi rise to power. The detached quality of the first-person narrator is defined on the first page: 'I am a camera with its shutter open, quite passive, recording, not thinking'; he says relatively little of his own feelings as he moves among a cast of largely manipulative, destructive or self-destructive characters. The narrator's very passivity and neutrality of stance come to epitomize the failure of the European mind to confront the rise of fascism. Orwell's narrator is George Bowling, a disillusioned insurance salesman approaching middle age who returns to the village of his childhood in an attempt to recapture something of what now seems to him to have been an idyllic Edwardian age. He is an egregiously personal dramatized narrator, who addresses the reader throughout in a conversational tone, masking a highly skilful rhetoric which persuades us to share his vision of an England of petty, narrow lives, a civilization of rubbish dumps and synthetic food, a people with fascist violence hanging over them, 'so terrified of the future that we're jumping straight into it like a rabbit diving down a boa constrictor's throat'. George's anticipation of 'the coloured shirts, the barbed wire, the rubber truncheons' looks forward to Orwell's post-war vision of totalitarianism *1984* (1949) and his political allegory *Animal Farm* (1945).

These post-war works reflect a general disillusionment with communism, resulting from the revelation of the Stalinist show trials, and the Nazi-Soviet pact of 1941. But during the 1930s many writers and intellectuals had become Marxists, and a considerable number fought for the Republicans in the Spanish Civil War. Many novels of the 1930s reflect this commitment, including ▷ Rex Warner's allegory *The Wild Goose Chase* (1937), and Edward Upward's *Journey to the Border* (1938). Both these novels have propagandist Marxist conclusions; in *Journey to the Border* the protagonist's hallucinations and fantasies are associated with a decadent society, and at the end of the novel he decides to regain reality by joining the workers' movement. Thus by the end of the 1930s 'reality' has become for many a politically defined concept, a matter of class commitment rather than of the nuances of consciousness. The experience of working-class life is perhaps most powerfully expressed in the work of writers who grew up in working-class regional communities, such as Walter Greenwood who, in *Love on the Dole* (1933), uses dialect to convey social cohesion and social deprivation in northern England.

One of the major works of Scottish fiction during this period shares a number of the features of English writing of the 30s: a left-wing political perspective, a sense of the harsh injustices and conflicts arising from the class system, and a concern with the processes of social change, in particular the fragmentation of communities in the face of modernity and war. However, ▷ Lewis Grassic Gibbon's trilogy of novels *A Scots Quair* (1932–34) is historical in setting, dealing with the period before, during and after the First World War, though it also makes an initial excursion into the early history of north-east Scotland. Written largely in Scots, a language closely related to, though distinct from, English (▷ Scottish literature in English), *A Scots Quair* combines a focus on the life of a female protagonist, Chris Guthrie, with portraits of changing rural and urban Scottish communities. The use of communal voices is a particularly original feature of the trilogy, though these are interspersed with passages focalised on Chris Guthrie which express a rich and sensitively evoked inner life. Another significant work of Scottish fiction is Neil M. Gunn's *The Silver Darlings* (1941), which looks further back in history, beginning with the Highland Clearances of the early nineteenth century and charting, in fictionalised form, the development of the communities involved in the herring industry of northern Scotland. Like Gibbon, Gunn reveals the life of a community through an individual and vice versa.

The inner and outer worlds: Greene and Lowry

The dangers of oversimplification inherent in an antithesis between a modernist concentration on the individual inner world, and a politically committed attention to social relations becomes evident when we consider the work of Graham Greene (1904–91). His early work of the 1930s, such as *It's a Battlefield* (1934) and *Brighton Rock* (1938) has a sense of the oppressive squalor of areas of modern urban life, a sense which is later translated into the more exotic settings of late colonialism; visions of seediness and corruption in such settings as Africa (*The Heart of the Matter*; 1948), Vietnam (*The Quiet American*; 1955) and South America (*The Honorary Consul*; 1973). He had a long-standing, if moderate, left-wing commitment, evident not only in his novels, with their critique of the Western role in the Third World, but also in his active friendship and support for those resisting the right-wing dictatorships of Central America, recounted in his memoir *Getting to Know the General* (1984). Yet characters such as the whisky priest of *The Power and the Glory* (1940) confront their moral choices in a condition of existential isolation and Greene himself associated his use of journeys (he was an inveterate traveller) with the methods of psychoanalysis

(▷ psychoanalytical criticism); in the introduction to *Journey Without Maps* (1936) he explains that he sought to give general significance to his travels in Liberia by using 'memories, dreams and word-associations' to suggest a parallel, inner journey. From the time of *Brighton Rock* his ▷ Catholicism became more apparent. Though he did not regard himself as a 'Catholic novelist', his work is informed by a powerful sense of good and evil, and of the sinfulness of human nature, combined with a somewhat determinist tragic irony. In these respects, as well as in his use of extreme situations which test human morality and endurance, he has links to Conrad and Dostoevsky as precursors, and to the post-war English novelist William Golding (b 1911) as a successor. Many of Greene's novels are narrated in the third person in a detached, unemotive style which serves to highlight violence, tragedy, the sordid and the grotesque. This style has affinities with American writers of the 1920s such as Ernest Hemingway and John Dos Passos.

▷ Malcolm Lowry's *Under the Volcano* (1947), like Greene's best work, endows a tragic story of human failure with metaphysical overtones. Set in Mexico, where the presence of fascist elements anticipates the approaching world war, the story of the alcoholic British Consul Geoffrey Firmin achieves a wide resonance by means of symbol, an intricate metaphorical structure and a stream of consciousness technique in which the beautiful but sinister Mexican landscape becomes an equivalent for inner turmoil. This novel belongs to the high modernist tradition in its formal experimentation and literary allusiveness, as well as in its somewhat Laurentian apocalyptic vision of political and cultural crisis. D. H. Lawrence had also previously engaged with a revolutionary Mexico in his much earlier novel *The Plumed Serpent* (1923), in his short stories, and in his travel essays, *Mornings in Mexico*. In *Under the Volcano*, however, Firmin's story is associated with that of Doctor Faustus, who sold his soul to the devil, while Mexico is presented as an archetype both of paradise and of hell. Firmin's inebriation, self-destructiveness and guilt are attributed to contemporary civilization as a whole. The novel, intended as part of a trilogy which was never completed, owes much to Joyce's *Ulysses* in its shifts of consciousness, its concentration on one day, with extended flashbacks, and its intricate, allusive structure.

The complex interplay of modernist experiment and the impulse towards social realism and political commitment was to contribute to a remarkable diversity of modes in fiction of the post-war era.

PART III – 1950 to the present

There has been a tendency among critics to see the post-war English novel as lacking in power and scope compared to the great age of modernism, and essays on the subject frequently begin by acknowledging the lack of either a great genius of the novelist's art or a single dominant movement with techniques and themes which are felt as central to contemporary culture. Gilbert Phelps, for example, in his essay 'The Post-War English Novel' (*New Pelican Guide to English Literature*, 1983), asserts that 'the trend of the English novel since the war has, on the whole, been . . . a turning aside from the mainstream of European literature and a tendency to retreat into parochialism and defeatism' and from time to time articles appear in the book pages of national newspapers, lamenting the state of the novel or predicting its demise. Several points need to be made about such views. There is the obvious but important fact that both literary achievement and cultural significance are more readily detected in retrospect. Furthermore, contemporary critical theory has made us increasingly aware that this retrospective detecting involves an element of construction. A sense of literary history, of the significance of particular works and authors, and of the existence of a canon of recognized major or serious works is necessarily a matter of a subjective, value-loaded and culturally specific process of consensus. This is not to say that such judgements are arbitrary, but only that they represent a characteristically human activity of creating patterns of meaning, of ordering and valuing cultural productions according to certain sets of values and assumptions. Post-colonial and feminist critics have questioned many of the assumptions by which the canon has been established, while theorists of post-modernism have claimed that late twentieth-century Western culture is marked by the displacement of value-laden hierarchies in favour of multiplicity, and the simultaneous availability of many forms, including imitation and pastiche of those of the past. It could therefore be argued that the diversity of contemporary fiction, by encouraging the reader to select from a huge range of available modes and styles, itself characterizes the prevailing *Zeitgeist* more effectively than could any dominant individual or group. The modernist claim to centrality depended, as we have seen, on a doctrine of experimentation and radical newness, according to which changes in novel technique accompanied changes in the nature of human experience. Works such as Joyce's *Finnegans Wake* (1939) pushed innovation along modernist lines close to the point where the coherence of the novel as a genre seemed in doubt. We have observed one form of reaction against modernism in the politically committed writings of the 1930s. Experimentation did not die out, but it increasingly came to seem one option among many, rather than an essential expression of the times. Furthermore, the shock to the idea of Western civilization administered by the Second World War, the death camps and the atomic bomb rendered the very idea of cultural centrality a dubious one. On the other hand, fictionality itself seemed an increasingly appropriate focus of attention in a culture where clear standards of truth and significance were felt to be elusive.

The awareness of fictionality

Samuel Beckett continued the Joycean line of experimentation, combining a fascination with words with an acute awareness of their limitations, and with a rich vein of parody, irony, imitation and pastiche. His vision is, however, a darker one, although humour is an essential aspect of it. In his trilogy of the 1950s, *Molloy* (1956), *Malone Dies* (1956) and *The Unnamable* (1959), isolated, aged and decrepit social outcasts of obscure identity narrate their own stories with a mixture of black humour and remorseless grimness. They are aware of themselves as story-tellers, making reference to the futility of this activity, yet continuing with the story in order to pass the time, as an act of defiance, or as an obsessive compulsion. As in Beckett's plays, there is a progressive minimalism, in which life is reduced to language, mundane and sordid physical details and the isolated human consciousness. In this respect his novels represent the ultimate breakdown of the classic realist novel, in which character is portrayed in a rich social context. In drawing attention to their own fictionality, and in playing games with language (including the game of teasing the critics by laying false clues) Beckett's narrators anticipate the contemporary fascination with the idea of fiction and of narration. This kind of metafiction is widely regarded as an aspect of ▷ post-modernism, although such concerns are not, of course, the prerogative of the twentieth century, being prominent in, for example, ▷ Laurence Sterne's ▷ *Tristram Shandy* (1759–67) and Cervantes' ▷ *Don Quixote* (1605–15). However, the current interest in this area reflects structuralist and ▷ post-structuralist scepticism about the ability of language to refer to a non-linguistic reality, and the sense that fictionality is an attribute of forms of discourse other than fiction, such as history and the social sciences. This has generated an increasing interest in narrative as a model for the structuring both of culture and of individual experience. Indeed, the philosopher of post-modernism ▷ Jean-Francois Lyotard argues for an abandonment of 'grand narratives' of history in favour of a multiplicity of small-scale narratives, while the pragmatist philosopher Richard Rorty has argued that the telling of stories is more effective than an appeal to reason as a way of overcoming prejudice and hatred.

A widespread form of self-awareness in post-modernist fiction is what the critic Linda Hutcheon terms historiographic metafiction: novels which 'are both intensely self-reflexive and yet paradoxically also lay claim to historical events and personages'. Contemporary novelists who explore this model include John Fowles (b 1926), whose book *The French Lieutenant's Woman* (1969) combines a pastiche of a Victorian novel with passages of social history and statistics about Victorian sexual habits. The author addresses the reader, discussing his own techniques and the reader's likely response, and later, appearing as a minor character, decides to abrogate his authorial power over his characters by providing two alternative endings, even going to the length of tossing a coin to decide their order. The effect is that of an intriguing, if scarcely subtle, consideration of issues of free will, determinism, power and meaning. Elements of fantasy and science-fiction are also prominent in the post-modern novel, further unsettling the boundaries of truth and fiction, text and reality. Doris Lessing's sequence of novels *Canopus in Argus: Archives* (1979–83) creates mythic narratives which are also moral allegories and which place the planet Earth and its people in a larger context of imaginary worlds. As the subtitle '*Archives*' suggests, textuality is foregrounded: for example *The Marriages of Zones Three, Four and Five* (1980) is a fable about the complimentarity of the sexes, narrated by a Chronicler who, alongside his own narration, alludes to the traditional representation of the story among his people, thus drawing attention to the shaping of the shared discourses of a culture.

Alastair Gray, perhaps the most post-modernist of contemporary Scottish novelists in terms of technique, is an artist as well as a writer, and illustrates his own books, which combine fantasy, metafiction, typographical and graphic effects with satirical, ironic and humorous treatment of contemporary Scottish society and its history. His best-known work, *Lanark*, has elements of ▷ magic realism in its combination of settings: the story of the eponymous hero (who has named himself after an area of Scotland) is partly set in Glasgow and partly in the grim and fantastical city of Unthank, a sort of Scottish urban version of hell, where the sun never shines. The novel thus combines a realist ▷ *bildungsroman* about the frustrated and embittered youth of an aspiring artist with an account of his after-death experience which is placed somewhere between science-fiction, fantasy, Swiftian political satire (▷ Jonathan Swift) and a post-modern rewriting of ▷ Dante's *Inferno*. The quirky, playful flavour of Gray's interweaving of the 'real', the textual and the imaginary is perhaps suggested by a road sign encountered by two characters crossing an 'intercalendrical zone' and which is reproduced, in a manner recalling *Tristram Shandy*, on a page of Chapter 33: it shows a left turn to New Cumbernauld (Cumbernauld is a real place near Glasgow; it is a 'new town', though not called 'New') and straight on for the imaginary cities of Imber and Unthank, via Chapter 37. The metafictional element becomes more obvious towards the end of the book, where the protagonist encounters the author, and we are provided with a hilarious 'index of plagiarisms', listing Gray's many allusions and borrowings.

Jeanette Winterson began her novel-writing career with a comparable mix of realism and fantasy, in the very popular *Oranges are Not the Only Fruit* (1985): a semi-autobiographical *bildungsroman* about a girl, brought up in a close-knit religious community in the north of England, who is rejected by that community because she is a lesbian. The story of her childhood and youth is interspersed with parodic fairy tales which parallel and comment on her experiences. These sections of the book could be naturalised as the fantasies of the protagonist, but Winterson's later work moved decisively away from realism: in novels such as *Sexing the Cherry* (1989). Here fantasy and magic dominate to the extent that we might see the novel as creating an alternative world, a view which would accord with the critic Brian McHale's conception of post-modernist fiction as 'ontological' (concerned with multiple worlds) where modernist fiction had been 'epistemological' (concerned with ways of knowing the world). There are elements of 'real' history in Winterson's novel, but with its fantastical, Gothic, carnivalesque, farcical juggling with time and place, gender and identity, it defies categorization as much as it defies summary, although showing clearly the influence of ▷ Angela Carter.

Playing games with history and fiction can of course be dangerous and controversial, since the past is so crucial to our personal and collective identities, to political and ideological programmes and to ideas of justice, justification and retribution. Within the discourses of both history and fiction it has been the Holocaust which has most acutely focused these concerns. ▷ D.M. Thomas' novels, *The White Hotel* (1981) and *Pictures at an Exhibition* (1993), both appropriate documentary records of the appalling sufferings of Jews and others under the Nazis in order to construct narratives that blend historical events, literary allusions, erotic fantasies and pseudo-Freudian theories. Many readers have found this offensive, and while theoretical expositions in terms of post-modernist and post-structuralist conceptions are readily available to support Thomas' procedures, it is not clear that these adequately deal with the ethics of voyeuristic aestheticization of violence and suffering. Another novel which has engaged with the perception of the Holocaust is *Time's Arrow* (1991) by ▷ Martin Amis. Rather than allusion, intertextuality, parody, self-interpretation and the other common devices of post-modernist fiction, this novel uses the single device of describing a world which resembles ours except that time flows backward. Inverting rather than subverting the traditional structures of cause and effect, person and responsibility which make ethical judgements possible, it presents a mirror-image of human life which has moral force as well as imaginative power.

A rather different testing of the limits and nature of fiction is apparent in ▷ B. S. Johnson's 1969 novel, *The Unfortunates*, which has twenty-seven loose-leaf sections of which twenty-five may be read in any order, the randomness of the resulting structure serving as a metaphor for the circling and shifting of the mind. Johnson saw 'truth' and 'fiction' as antithetical terms, and his last work, *See the Old Lady Decently* (1975), employs documents and photographs in an attempt to create a non-fictional novel. This aspiration is paralleled in the documentary style of Alan Burns (b 1929), some of whose novels are structured around news items or press-cuttings. A number of novelists have developed the modernist interest in multiple and unstable perspectives. These include Doris Lessing, and also ▷ Lawrence Durrell (1912–90), who, in his sequence *The Alexandria Quartet* (1957–60) portrays an intricate series of relationships in a community by means of a diversity of narratives, including third-person and first-person narratives, letters, journals and parts of an inset novel by a character. The reader's understanding of both character and event is subject to revision in the light of new information and perspectives, creating a work that has been described as 'a game of mirrors'.

In a sense, experimental novels are particularly dependent upon the traditional qualities of a good novel, such as plot interest and imaginative power in the realization of social context. In the absence of such qualities the reader is unlikely to overcome the difficulties of coming to terms with an unfamiliar form. A novelist who combines imaginative power with a wittily expressed examination of the nature of the fictional is ▷ Dan Jacobson (b 1929). *The Rape of Tamar* (1970) is set in the time of the Old Testament King David, and narrated by Yonadab, who is intensely aware of the philosophical and moral dilemmas of his role as narrator. He has knowledge of our own time as well as that of the story, and shares with us his reflections on the resulting ironies. Thus the act of narrating is a source of interest throughout, generating insights into such issues as hypocrisy, self-deception, voyeurism, the function of art, the pleasures and vicissitudes of speaking, and the culturally specific nature of modes of interpretation. But these sophisticated intellectual concerns are matched and sustained by a powerful poetic evocation of the physical and cultural context, and above all by the sheer vitality of Yonadab's personality as he addresses us with engaging frankness in what he terms 'the simulacrum of time in which you and I have managed to meet'. Self-conscious narrative, which by various means draws attention to its own fictionality, serves to question the nature of reality, and of our understanding of it, and to highlight issues of freedom and control. It has therefore held a strong appeal for writers influenced by French ▷ existentialist thought, including ▷ Christine Brooke-Rose (b 1926) and ▷ David Caute (b 1936). In the post-modernist anti-novel, practised by writers such as ▷ Gabriel Josipovici (b 1940), structures based around repeated scenes or interwoven narratives create a radical uncertainty, and the world evoked by the text disintegrates in order to fulfil the author's aim of, in his own words, 'insisting that his book is a book and not the world' (from *The World and the Book, a Study of Modern Fiction*; 1971).

Morality and art

A feature of the work of several considerable post-war novelists is a renewed attempt to present a vision of the world as a battleground of forces of good and evil. William Golding has had outstanding success in the construction of moral fables, shaped by Christian archetypes of sin, guilt, purgation and the tentative but precious hope of redemption. His novels, of which the first was ▷ *Lord of the Flies* (1954), show a powerful interest in the primitive and the physical, particularly in the examination of extreme conditions or states of consciousness in which human experience is stripped to moral and physical essentials. This description does not, however, do justice to the range of his settings and techniques. *The Inheritors* (1955) attempts to realize the mind and culture of Neanderthal man. This relatively idyllic and innocent culture is used to make us see our own nature (as represented by the arrival of *homo sapiens*) in a new and largely unflattering light. *The Spire* (1964) renders the tormented consciousness of a fanatical medieval cleric, while *Rites of Passage* (1980) uses pastiche and the ironies arising from a self-confident but mistaken narrator to portray the moral awakening of a gentleman traveller in the early nineteenth century. The limitation of Golding's work is its explicitness. The thrust of his moral vision and his mythic patterning can sometimes seem overbearing, though many readers will feel that this is a small price to pay for its power and authority.

In contrast to Golding's historical and cultural range, most of the novels of ▷ Iris Murdoch (b 1919) are set in contemporary English middle-class society, but are informed by a range of philosophical concerns centring on moral responsibility, individual freedom, the nature of love, and the possibility of actively pursuing goodness. They combine a serious, and at times tragic, exploration of these concerns with exciting plots, and elements of the comic, supernatural, and fantastic. These features have been sustained through a prolific career since the appearance of her first novel *Under the Net* in 1954. Doubts about her work focus on a sense that characters are excessively manipulated in the interest of illustrating abstract ideas, and a dissatisfaction with her use of violence and accident as a plot device. Of her early novels, *The Bell* (1958) is notable for its complex symbolic structure. The moral significance of the lives of a group of characters, brought together in a rather bizarre religious community, is examined by a pattern of interaction centred around the symbol of a convent bell, but using also animal and water symbolism. *The Sea, The Sea* (1978), a Booker Prize-winner, and one of the most acclaimed of her works, is a typically dark comedy about obsession, guilt and egotism, but is remarkable for the richness of its symbols and characters. ▷ A. S. Byatt (b 1936) shows the influence of Murdoch in her use of symbolic structures and her portrayal of the inter-relations of a large group of central characters. The latter feature is particularly evident in the opening books of a projected tetralogy: *The Virgin in the Garden* (1979) and *Still Life* (1985). Moral concerns are evident, but less explicit than in Murdoch's work, more attention being given to correspondences between experience and mythic or aesthetic patterns, and to the process of cultural change. Byatt's most popular work to date, the Booker Prize-winning *Possession*, is a cleverly interwoven pastiche of Victorian poetry, the lives of its writers, and the lives of a network of twentieth-century literary critics. The inter-relations of characters are thus wittily carried out across time, as the lives of Victorian poets intersect with those of their modern readers. The process, in *Possession*, whereby discovery of the past is crucial to the development of character and the reshaping of relationships in the present is paralleled in ▷ Alan Hollinghurst's *The Swimming Pool Library* (1988). Here a young aristocrat, part of the gay scene in London in the early 1980s, is commissioned to write a biography. In so doing he discovers the involvement of his own grandfather in the persecution of gay men, a discovery which arouses in him a new sense of defiance and political commitment in the present. As in *Possession*, literary allusions (in this instance to writers such as Oscar Wilde and E. M. Forster) and the excitement of detective work are important elements in a gripping narrative. Byatt has returned to the Victorian period in the double narrative of *Angels and Insects* (1992).

In the work of ▷ Muriel Spark (b 1918), manipulation is less a risk for the author than an explicit theme and, as in Ford Madox Ford's *The Good Soldier* (1915), the manipulative aspects of the narrating activity are exploited as a source of irony in the rendering of patterns of social and psychological control. Thus in the novella *The Driver's Seat* (1970) the use of the present tense, and an entirely external focalization on one character (the narrative recounting events from her point of view, but with almost no revelation of her feelings, thoughts or intentions) creates a grim and enigmatic vision of a woman with a psychological compulsion and a violent destiny which seem fixed and unchangeable, yet not understood either by author or reader. In *The Prime of Miss Jean Brodie* (1961) humour is more in evidence, but dark shadows of fascism and personal betrayal, evoked particularly through prolepses (jumps forward to later events), lurk around the story of a teacher's charismatic influence on a group of pupils. Spark's Catholic sensibility emerges in her portrayal of diabolic figures, such as the charming, egregiously manipulative Dougal Douglas of *The Ballad of Peckham Rye* (1960).

While Spark is a convert to Catholicism, ▷ Anthony Burgess (b 1917) has a

Catholic background, and though not a practising member of the Church, acknowledges the importance of Catholic modes of thought in his work. *A Clockwork Orange* (1962) is concerned with the relation of evil and free will. The protagonist makes a deliberate choice of a life of horrifying violence and sadistic cruelty, and attempts by a futuristic authoritarian society to reform him by brainwashing can only destroy his human identity. The novel is notable for its use of an invented teenage patois, Nadsat, reflecting Burgess's enthusiasm for Joycean linguistic multiplicity and invention. Burgess has stated that he sees the duality of good and evil as the ultimate reality, and in *Earthly Powers* (1980) the history of the twentieth century is portrayed in terms of such a moral struggle, seen through the memories of the narrator, a homosexual writer. As in Murdoch's work, a strong sense of moral patterning underlies and unifies a complexity of events. In the novels of ▷ Margaret Drabble (b 1939) moral concern is focused on social justice and the individual quest for identity, particularly on the part of women. Works such as *The Ice Age* (1977) reflect her admiration for Arnold Bennett in their realist portrayal of the state of contemporary British society.

Feminist writing

The question of what constitutes 'feminist' writing is a contentious issue, but what is certain is that novels concerned with women's experience represent a significant section of the contemporary fiction market, and make rich use of innovations in narrative technique and of a range of styles and genres. An important divide among feminist critics is between those, such as Elaine Showalter, who see the role of contemporary female writing as that of self-discovery, articulating the nature of women's personal experience within society and revealing structures of oppression, and those such as Toril Moi, who advocate rather the deconstruction of the idea of the unitary self, and the rejection of the male/female dichotomy in favour of some ideal of androgyny.

The project of articulating women's experience includes the rediscovery of the unrecorded or what has been omitted from the conventional histories and novels. Thus ▷ Eva Figes (b 1932), in *The Seven Ages* (1986), writes a fictional chronicle of the lives of seven generations of women, from pre-history up to the present, concentrating on their struggles with poverty and violence, and their experience of childbirth and child-rearing. An associative, free-floating narrative style suggests a collective female consciousness, transcending the individual self and linking women to natural forces of generation. ▷ Zoe Fairbairns' *Stand We At Last* (1983) also recounts the lives of successive generations of women, though with closer attention to the detailed historical context, while the Manawaka series of novels and stories by the Canadian writer ▷ Margaret Laurence (1926–87) are narrated by women of various ages and generations in such a way as to explore simultaneously the social history of Canada and the dilemmas and achievements of women in the context of a prairie town. ▷ Jean Rhys (1894–1979), in *Wide Sargasso Sea* (1966), writes a feminist complement to ▷ Charlotte Brontë's ▷ *Jane Eyre*, recounting the early life of the 'mad' first Mrs Rochester, from her childhood in the West Indies. Rhys gives consciousness to the character who, in the original novel, is an inarticulate symbolic location for a rejected violence of feeling. Madness is a recurrent theme of feminist writing, because, considered as a refusal to conform to an imposed social identity, it can become a potent symbol of revolt against oppression. Doris Lessing (b 1919) does not see herself as primarily a feminist writer, but her novel *The Golden Notebook* (1962) has become an important feminist text. It is built out of a skeleton narrative, entitled 'Free Women', plus four notebooks kept by Anna, one of the characters of 'Free Women'. This fragmentation reflects her fear of breakdown as she confronts political, literary and sexual problems as an independent woman, but in the fifth and final 'Golden Notebook' a new unity is achieved through a mental breakdown shared with a man, during which the collapse of divisions leads to 'formlessness with the end of fragmentation'. The Scottish novelist, Janice Galloway, uses interior monologue, dramatic dialogue and typographical effects to explore the mind of a woman suffering disturbance and alienation in *The Trick is to Keep Breathing* (1989). Her most recent novel, *Foreign Parts* (1995), explores a theme which is less dramatic than madness or breakdown but no less important to the feminist project of articulating the range of woman's experience: female friendship. This deceptively understated story about two women friends travelling together in France moves between the representation of thoughts or inner experience and more realist passages and gradually accumulates considerable power through its exploration of the subtle modulations of their relationship.

A number of writers, without adopting an overtly feminist standpoint, attend particularly to women's experience of isolation, betrayal, loss or guilt within the limitations imposed on their lives by social convention or male attitudes and behaviour. They include ▷ Edna O'Brien (b 1932), whose popular and entertaining novels are concerned particularly with the vicissitudes of sexuality and passion, and ▷ Anita Brookner (b 1928), who portrays the disillusionment of her sensitive female characters with an elegant, detached attention to the nuances of human relationships. In one sense these writers are the opposite of feminist, since their work could be held to accept as a premise the view that women seek self-fulfilment largely through relations with men. Yet in representing the tragedy or frustration which may result from such dependence, their novels raise crucial feminist issues, and are part of the context for the debate about the fictional portrayal of women.

▷ Fay Weldon (b 1931) recounts the lives of her women characters with a sort of desperate black humour. In works such as *Down Among the Women* (1971) and *Praxis* (1978), a constant shifting of relationships and roles suggests a terrifying instability of identity; both men and women move between the role of victim and victimizer, but the women are consistently the more disadvantaged, both socially and biologically. Both novels end by suggesting that a new breed of emancipated woman is emerging, but offer little convincing evidence for this hope, and Weldon's work has gradually tended towards disillusion, with an element of biological determinism. Women's sexuality, and sexual politics, have been central feminist concerns. In contrast to Weldon's cynical realism, Angela Carter (1940–92) approached these issues through fantasy, myth and symbol, reworking elements of fairytale in the stories of *The Bloody Chamber* (1979), and in her novel *Nights at the Circus* (1984) using post-modernist techniques: the disruption of narrative consistency and the blending of fiction and history. Carter's short story 'Black Venus' rewrites a piece of literary history from a feminist perspective, imaginatively exploring the life and thoughts of a Caribbean woman who became muse and mistress to the French poet Baudelaire. Through black humour and physicality the narrative resists the commodifying, voyeuristic and exoticising gaze of the male literary master. In a comparable way in ▷ Emma Tennant's *Tess*, fantasy and dream can serve as forms of experience emancipated from rational modes of thought which are seen as essentially male, and Tennant's *The Bad Sister* (1978) employs a split between realist and fantasy modes to develop this opposition, while ▷ Sara Maitland's *Three Times Table* (1990) explores the lives of three women in a mode which seems predominantly realist but which can find room for dragons in a London park. Radical perspectives on sexual relations are also a feature of the work of ▷ Maureen Duffy (b 1933), who explores particularly working-class and lesbian experience, and of novels by members of the Feminist Writers Group who share socialist as well as feminist commitment: including Sara Maitland and Michèle Roberts (both of whom are interested in the relations of religion and female sexuality) and Michelene Wandor, who co-wrote with Maitland *Arky Types* (1987), a post-modernist ▷ epistolary novel.

Realism, satire, social comedy

There is a continuing strain in the English novel which is concerned with the analysis of contemporary English culture by means of satire, humour, or irony, primarily within realistic modes. The satirical strain building on the earlier work of writers such as Waugh and Huxley, includes ▷ Angus Wilson (1913–91), whose novel, *Anglo-Saxon Attitudes* (1956), set in the late 1940s, is a portrait of academic and London life and the egotism and self-deception of a range of characters. These concerns, however, take on a broader historical and social resonance because of the novel's examination of the effect of the past on the present via the troubled personal life of an historian and the confusion arising out of an historical fraud committed in 1912. *The Old Men at the Zoo* (1961) continues the vein of satirical analysis, but moves into fantasy and allegory in its bizarre tale of the administration of the London Zoo during another war. Wilson is also a writer of short stories, which combine a sharp satirical edge with a considerable emotional charge in their exposure of cruelty, snobbishness and pretension.

During the 1950s a group of writers emerged whose work combined a realist portrayal of provincial communities with a strong sense of social injustice. Some of these writers became known by the label ▷ 'angry young men'; they include ▷ Alan Sillitoe (b 1928), ▷ Stan Barstow (b 1928), ▷ John Wain (b 1925), ▷ John Braine (b 1922) and ▷ David Storey (b 1933), and in their early novels the heroes are working-class, or in revolt against the demands of a middle-class background. Novels such as John Braine's *Room at the Top* (1957), John Wain's *Hurry on Down* (1953), Stan Barstow's *A Kind of Loving* (1960) and Alan Sillitoe's *Saturday Night and Sunday Morning* (1958) seemed to epitomize a post-war sense of futility, discontent and rebellion. Their subsequent careers have developed in various ways, as, for example, towards narrative innovation in the case of Storey, or to a reaction against radicalism in the case of Braine. They were brought up outside London, coming in most cases from working-class backgrounds, and their work continued the tradition of working-class regional writing found earlier in the novels of Walter Greenwood and Lewis Grassic Gibbon.

Of those originally seen as 'angry young men', it is perhaps ▷ Kingsley Amis (b 1922) who has most successfully sustained his popular appeal over the succeeding decades. Unlike Angus Wilson, who, influenced by Virginia Woolf, used a range of interior monologues in his sixth novel *No Laughing Matter* (1967), Amis eschews modernist experiment, though working with a number of sub-genres, such as the ghost-story (*The Green Man*; 1969) and the fantasy of an alternative world (*The Alteration*; 1976). His novels are characterised by sharp wit, inventiveness, and a considerable animus against whatever Amis sees as bogus or blameworthy. *Lucky Jim* (1954), his very entertaining first novel, inaugurated the genre of the humorous campus novel, since developed by Malcolm Bradbury (b 1932) in *Stepping Westward* (1965) and *The History Man* (1975), and ▷ David Lodge (b 1935) in *Changing*

Places (1975) and *Small World* (1984). Amis specializes in dislikeable characters, with objectionable attitudes, such as the xenophobia of the protagonists of *I Like It Here* (1958) and *One Fat Englishman* (1963), or the misogyny of Stanley in *Stanley and the Women* (1984). While these attitudes are subjected to a degree of satirical censure, they are not altogether repudiated. Amis' position is now a conservative one, marked by a distrust of the cosmopolitan and the experimental.

The influence of Jane Austen is apparent in the work of ⊳ Barbara Pym (1913–80), which enjoyed a revival in the late 1970s, and consists of subtle and ironical studies of middle-class life, combining a shrewd humour with an uncompromising sense of the commonness of frustration, isolation and ennui. The delicacy of her work might be contrasted with the satirical shock-tactics of Martin Amis (b 1949) who employs black humour to portray human fears, obsessions and desires. Surprisingly, Amis (who is Kingsley Amis' son) claims to be influenced by Jane Austen too; he shares with Pym the use of humour of some sort to reveal human weakness, but they stand at opposite ends of a spectrum stretching from gentle irony to vigorous satire.

In *London Fields* (1989) Amis draws on modernist techniques: a Joycean linguistic richness, including London slang and the ambiguous moral consequences of a narrative which is focalised on characters about whose attitudes, feelings and behaviour the reader may feel doubt or even distaste. Comparable effects are achieved by ⊳ James Kelman and ⊳ Irvine Welsh, two Scottish writers who exemplify a strong movement in contemporary Scottish fiction towards powerful, grim but often humorous portrayals of the harsh and violent conditions of working-class urban life in Glasgow and Edinburgh. Welsh's *Trainspotting* introduces a wide range of characters linked by the hard drugs culture of Edinburgh. Using various focal characters and first-person narrators it draws the reader into a lifestyle which is both repulsive and compelling: illuminated by moments of compassion and humour and above all by the energy and vitality of language, the novel nevertheless conveys powerfully a sense of destructive waste. At times Welsh seems to be setting out to subvert the tourist-board image of Scotland, as in a chapter entitled 'The First Day of the Edinburgh Festival', which culminates with a character fishing around for opium suppositaries in a blocked toilet in a Muirhouse betting shop. Another target would seem to be the myth and/or reality of the Scottish 'hard man'. This myth appears in potent form in the work of ⊳ William McIlvanney, notably in his novel *Docherty*, which portrays a Scottish mining community before and after the First World War. The central character, Tam Docherty is an heroic figure: a working class man, small in stature but of great strength, who seeks to retain his emotional and intellectual integrity and independence. He defends his family, his friends and his honourable principles with words and with force. Fistfights are a central feature of the novel and Tam's strength and skill in fighting are crucial to his character. The novel is a moving elegy for hopes and convictions largely destroyed by the war and by modern capitalism and in that sense continues elements of the work of ⊳ Grassic Gibbon. Yet McIlvanney might be accused of sentimentalising violence and the cult of the macho male. In *Trainspotting* Frank Begbie embodies all the worst features of this cult: totally selfish, randomly and wantonly brutal and an exploiter of all around him, his nickname 'Franco' hints at the fascist nature of male power; only a glimpse of his alcoholic father gives any hint of a redeeming explanation for his character. Welsh's critique of male power is developed in *Marabou Stork Nightmares* which centres on a brutal gang rape. As well as sequences of fantasy the novel uses internal monologue, and has this in common with Kelman's *How Late it was, How Late* (1994), which takes the form of an extended internal monologue by a Glasgow man who has become blind after being arrested when drunk. Kelman's rambling but gripping narrative focuses on the man's process of adjustment to his situation, on his battles with bureaucracy and officialdom and on class antagonism. The book is memorable for its rich verbal texture, with hints of black comedy and the surreal.

Multiculturalism and 'the New Internationalism'

This essay started by referring to the cross-fertilization of cultures as essential to the modernist movement at the beginning of the century. Since that time Britain's political and cultural relations with the rest of the world have changed radically. The British Empire has ended; two world wars have brought enormous social changes; technological developments have transformed the world economic system, and therefore the manner in which cultural artefacts are circulated. The diversity and plurality which have been noted as aspects of post-modern society have a particular value insofar as they promote an attention to the radical otherness of different cultures. There is thus a new, post-modern form of cross-fertilization taking place. The novel in English is now a world-wide form, with many of the finest new works of fiction emerging from post-colonial societies (▷ post-colonial writing). At the same time, the increasingly multi-cultural nature of British society as a result of immigration to Britain from former colonies since the 1950s, has prompted much fictional concern with issues of cultural identity within Britain.

Some of the contours of the theme of multicultural society and individual identity may be indicated by a comparison of three writers whose age and biography situate them differently in relation to it: ▷ Samuel Selvon, ▷ Joan Riley and ▷ Hanif Kureishi. Selvon, born and brought up in Trinidad, where he worked as a journalist, came to London in the 1950s, a period of large-scale immigration from the Caribbean to Britain. In a series of comic and satirical novels centred on a character called Moses, Selvon explored through the use of humour the personal, political and cultural development of a black community in London: these include *The Lonely Londoners* (1956), *The Housing Lark* (1965) and *Moses Ascending* (1975). In *Moses Ascending* Selvon's protagonist, long settled in London, aspires to middle-class respectability and the status of a home-owner. This brings him into conflict with his friends in the radical Black Power movement but also provides Selvon with an opportunity for a hilarious example of 'writing black': the technique of subversion through parody of the ideology encoded in literary classics, in this case *Robinson Crusoe*. Moses takes on the role of patronising Crusoe to a white Englishman called Bob, who comes from the 'black country' (an area of the West Midlands of England) and becomes Moses' domestic help and 'Man Friday'. Many racist stereotypes are invoked and inverted: for example Moses reflects on how white people are dirty, while an American character thinks that 'these English are animals'. Selvon keeps us guessing as to where he stands on the issue of 'respectable' integration versus radical action, because both sides of the debate are seen in comic terms.

In contrast, Joan Riley's *The Unbelonging* (1985) is a harrowing and tragic story of Hyacinth, a Jamaican girl sent to London to live with a father she does not know. She suffers sexual abuse, cruelty, racism and rejection and at the end of the novel tries to return to her lost childhood Eden of Jamaica, only to find that she has become a 'foreigner' there too: she has lost one identity without really gaining another, and ends in a state of 'unbelonging'. Riley, who was born in Jamaica in 1958 and attended university in Britain, belongs to a later generation than Selvon and presents with particular force the double bind of racism and gender oppression: abused by her black father, Hyacinth initially finds little help in Britain, because of perceived and actual hostility or incomprehension from teachers and social workers.

This theme has also been powerfully explored by ▷ Buchi Emecheta, who came to Britain from Nigeria to join her husband in 1962, in her novel *Gwendolen* (1989). Other writers who, like Selvon, made the journey from the Caribbean to Britain as part of the large-scale immigration of the 1950s have recorded this cultural displacement and its consequences: they include ▷ V. S. Naipaul in *The Enigma of Arrival* (1987) and ▷ George Lamming in *The Emigrants*.

Hanif Kureishi was born and brought up in Kent and *The Buddha of Suburbia* addresses multiculturalism from its first sentences: 'My name is Karim Amir, and I am an Englishman born and bred, almost. I am often considered to be a funny kind of Englishman, a new breed as it were, having emerged from two old histories'. While the novel is not post-modernist in style, since it employs a realist mode, it represents powerfully and comically post-modern ideas of hybridity and fluidity of identity. Karim's sexuality is as ambiguous as his cultural identity and, while the novel has a sharp satirical edge, it also celebrates freedoms and transformations of the self, in its portrayal of the worlds of rock music, punk, fashion, new age mysticism, political activism and fringe theatre in seventies London. Identity as role-play is prominent: Karim gets on in the theatre by acting Indian parts (despite being brought up in the London suburbs); his father, a civil servant, adopts the persona of an eastern mystic. Acting, which becomes Karim's career, is in some ways an ideal metaphor for post-modern identity, because it is anti-essentialist: life as a series of roles formed by the intersection of discourses which name or interpellate (▷ interpellation) the individual.

A thematics of identity is combined with post-modern techniques of ▷ magical realism and ▷ historiographical metafiction in Salman Rushdie's *Midnight's Children* (1981). Saleem Sinai, the protagonist and narrator of the novel, is one of 1001 children endowed with magical powers because they are born at the precise moment of India's independence in 1947. With witty and extravagant detail, the novel weaves together Saleem's life with the history of India and Pakistan as the personal and the public are subsumed in the rich instability of the narrative. Real historical events are included, but others are omitted or misplaced; Saleem admits to twisting history to suit his narrative while his listener or narratee, Padma, seeks unsuccessfully to drag him back from the digressions of oral narrative to the linear sequence of the realist novel. Rushdie is part of what Bruce King has termed 'the new internationalism' in British literature: novelists who 'write about their native lands or immigrant experience from within the mainstream of British literature' ('The New Internationalism', in *The British and Irish Novel Since 1960*, ed. James Acheson). King identifies, apart from Rushdie, ▷ Shiva Naipaul, ▷ Buchi Emecheta, ▷ Timothy Mo and ▷ Kazuo Ishiguro, representing a wide range of cultural influences: Naipaul, like his brother ▷ V. S. Naipaul, writing as an Indian brought up in Trinidad; Emecheta from Nigeria; Mo, born in Hong Kong of a Chinese father and English mother and educated in Britain and Ishiguro, born in Japan but brought to Britain when he was 6. Ishiguro's first two novels, *A Pale View of Hills* (1982) and *An Artist of the Floating World* (1986) looked back to Japan after the Second World War, exploring personal and cultural conflicts in a subtle and understated style. *The Remains of the Day* (1989) carried over some of the same concerns to an English setting. It tells the story of a butler in a great English country house before and after the Second World War, gradually revealing how his habitual restraint, propriety and rigid adherence to his duty as he sees it have starved his life of warmth and feeling, so that he lost the chance of a relationship with a woman who came to the house as housekeeper and condemned himself to emotional isolation. Simultaneously a political narrative unfolds: the pre-war master of the house was an English aristocrat who advocated appeasement of the Nazis and was disgraced when war broke out. Connections are made between the seemingly benevolent, paternalistic English aristocrat and the ruthless and supercilious Nazi leaders he entertains. The interweaving of the two stories, of the master and the butler, suggests with great subtlety how the class-based servility of the butler might have links with the passivity in the face of authority which allows fascism to develop.

Ishiguro's ability to bring a fresh perspective, informed by his interest in Japanese culture, to the study of the very English world of the country house, with its aristocracy and servants, might serve as an epitome of the way in which internationalism and multiculturalism have been rejuvenating forces, in intellectual, political and imaginative terms, within the contemporary novel in Britain. The debate which followed the publication of Salman Rushdie's novel ▷ *The Satanic Verses*, and the denunciations and death-threats which the book evoked from some elements of Muslim society, demonstrated graphically the complexity of the issues raised by multiculturalism. Yet, whatever the ideological conflicts, much contemporary fiction which grapples with the multicultural nature of contemporary Britain can be seen as striving, against powerful repressive and reactionary forces, to promote understanding, openness and tolerance.

Conclusion

The field of contemporary fiction is large and expanding. This essay attempts to provide an introduction to twentieth-century fiction by examining some perspectives on the major work of the first half of the century, and by suggesting something of the range and variety of writing since 1950, in the hope that the reader will be encouraged to explore further. Traditional features of the novel, such as satire, the pleasure of narrative, the excitement of plot and the rendering of moral distinctions still find new and original exponents. Narrative experiment and the awareness of fictionality provide powerful means for exploring the particular philosophical preoccupations of our age, while genres such as science fiction, ▷ horror and the fantasy novel offer popular alternative modes of writing. At the same time both the language and the techniques of the novel are successfully adapted to various and changing cultures. The diversity of the contemporary novel in English is a sign of the vitality of the form and of the continuing ability of fiction to engage at many levels with both intellectual issues and cultural processes.

21 Drama in the Twentieth Century

Trevor R. Griffiths

A Tale of Two Traditions

For most of the nineteenth century, theatre in Britain was neither socially respectable nor intellectually challenging – but it was immensely popular. Melodrama, music hall, farce, and spectacular Shakespeare attracted a mass audience and fulfilled some of the social functions that were later to be the preserve of cinema and television. Although increasingly mimetically realistic settings had been developed throughout the century, in both contemporary and period stagings, the vast majority of theatrical entertainment was broadly escapist in both form and content. Although the old view that nineteenth century theatre flourished while drama languished is far too sweeping, relatively little nineteenth century drama has survived the immediate occasion of its creation. By the end of the century, theatre managers were engaged in a sustained effort to bring back the middle classes to the theatre, choosing to rely on a smaller but more moneyed audience at the expense of the popular audience of the earlier period. Paradoxically, this drive towards respectability led to both a deadly theatre of social affirmation and, because there were serious minded social reformers among the middle classes, to the beginnings of a theatre of dissent. This tradition of dissent has remained a significant factor in theatre throughout the twentieth century, making a major impact in the period immediately before the First World War under the aegis of ▷ Shaw and ▷ Granville Barker and in the drama of the period since 1956.

George Bernard Shaw's championing of his somewhat idiosyncratic version of Ibsen in *The Quintessence of Ibsenism* (1891) and in his own dramatic practice, together with Granville Barker's seasons at the ▷ (Royal) Court Theatre (1904–7), were significant factors in creating an interrogative and oppositional form of theatre, associated politically and artistically with a broadly Fabian radicalism. It is precisely the drama that belongs to this tradition of intellectual and formal dissent which traditionally forms the focus of such studies as this. However, this theatre appealed only to a small class fraction who welcomed the intellectual and social challenge to prevailing norms associated with what we might now call fringe ventures. While this strand never completely died away, surfacing in many different forms over the next fifty years, it was to re-emerge most potently from the mid fifties, in a new apparently radical theatre, again centred on the Royal Court, and again associated with discontent with prevailing conditions, epitomised in the eponymous Anger of ▷ Osborne's ▷ *Look Back in Anger* (1956). This is the drama of Shaw and Granville Barker in the early years of the century, and of ▷ Arnold Wesker, ▷ Howard Brenton, ▷ Caryl Churchill, and ▷ Trevor Griffiths in the last forty years.

The drama which is valued for its 'literary' qualities is, however, largely a minority product that caters for specialised tastes in a limited number of theatres. Although the nineteenth century mass audience for melodrama, farce and the music hall has melted away, the appeal of spectacular musical comedy, farce and comedy of manners, of a theatre inherently concerned with affirmation and social consolidation has remained a major factor in the theatrical repertory throughout the century. British drama has been painfully slow to react to European developments in theatrical and dramaturgical practice such as ▷ Naturalism, ▷ Expressionism, and ▷ Epic Theatre. Mainstream theatre, the theatres in the West End of London and their counterparts throughout the country, has remained dominated by the staples of light comedy and farce, genteel melodrama in the form of the thriller, and the musical. Although the incidentals of this type of theatre may change over the years, with, for example, greater linguistic frankness about sexual matters, the use of (mainly female) nudity, and the exploitation of ever more spectacular machinery in the musicals which have dominated British theatre in the eighties, its basic strategies remain those of reinforcing its audience's self esteem by not challenging its preconceptions about the social status quo from which it benefits.

Sometimes, as in the work of ▷ Somerset Maugham, ▷ Noel Coward, ▷ Terence Rattigan, ▷ Joe Orton, and ▷ Alan Ayckbourn, popular success (at least with middle class audiences) has accompanied theatrical invention and/or social criticism. At its best, as in a work like Ayckbourn's *Woman in Mind* (1985), this type of theatre can breach the cosy circle of self congratulation by an indirect assault on the values and assumptions of its audience, administering a shock to the audience in terms which Shaw would certainly have understood. Over the century, however, the commercial imperatives of the West End have more often resulted in bland creations aimed at 'pure entertainment' or a 'good night out' in which making an audience feel good about themselves has predominated over any possibility of challenging settled assumptions.

Discussions of twentieth century drama tend to concentrate on those new plays written between the 1890s and the time of writing, and this is no exception, but it is also important to bear in mind that theatre is much more than the sum of the plays written in a certain period, since it is the most social of arts, depending on not only the writer and the printer but actors, designers, directors, theatre buildings and the whole paraphernalia of theatre. Moreover the theatre sustains itself not just on new writing, but on the selected classics of the past, so that a new play may be sharing a theatrical season with Shakespeare, Greek tragedy, musicals and Molière. Analysing only those plays written within a particular period inevitably falsifies the sense of a theatrical repertory as it appeared to the theatregoers of the period. In London in early 1995, for example, a playgoer might have attended *The Mousestrap*, a new translation of *The Women of Troy*, Stoppard's ▷ *Arcadia*, a *Macbeth* played by an all woman cast of five, *Fever Pitch*, a one man play about being a football fan, and Goldoni's *Venetian Twins*. In concentrating on new plays we must remember that this is only one aspect of the theatrical repertory.

Shaw and his Influence

By the beginning of the twentieth century, the work of a variety of small scale independent ventures had introduced London in particular to the work of such writers as Ibsen, Eugene Brieux and Gerhart Hauptmann. Serious drama was heavily influenced by the idea of the problem play, often centred on the figure of 'the woman with a past'. This reflected contemporary debates about the position of women which were to gain in strength as the campaign for women's suffrage became a major political issue in the time before the First World War period. Because of the double standard of sexual morality, it was possible to focus concern with 'the woman question' on the issue of sexual morality and the old melodramatic formula of 'the woman with a past' could be used by both conservative and radical dramatist to explore issues beyond the immediate plot line. ▷ Oscar Wilde, ▷ Henry Arthur Jones, and ▷ Arthur Wing Pinero all exploited the formula but the wages of 'sin' for the transgressive women usually remained madness, death, or social ostracism. Shaw was, then, being particularly daring in *Mrs Warren's Profession* (printed 1898, but not licensed for public performance until 1925), in allowing his (high class) brothel keeper to continue to reap the benefits of her trade, even if no-one actually says what her profession is – it is written down.

Shaw was a conscious iconoclast and his talent for publicity and his longevity meant that he dominated the British theatre for much of the first half of the century. Although his advocacy did much to establish Ibsen and Naturalistic dramaturgy in the British theatre in the face of hostile, even hysterical, reactions to such plays as *Ghosts*, his own dramatic practice was eclectic and he did not favour Naturalistic methods in his own writing. Instead, he tended to use existing forms parasitically, as Trojan horses to smuggle his controversially socialist ideas into the minds of his audience. This can be a very effective strategy, but it also has its dangers since the form has a capacity for biting back and diluting the radical message, as practitioners as diverse as T. S. Eliot, with his mid-century attempts to use drawing room drama to convey Christian messages, and ▷ Trevor Griffiths, with his 1970s attempts to use television genres to convey oppositional approaches, have found. In Shaw's case, ▷ *Arms and the Man* (1894), for example, now looks suspiciously like the Ruritarian military comedy whose form it adopts. Similarly, the success of *My Fair Lady* (1955), the musical version of ▷ *Pygmalion* (1913), is a fair indication of how readily the would-be radical can be subsumed, since it gives the play the happy ending that Shaw wriggles desperately not to give it in the final few minutes. Like the contemporary playwright ▷ David Hare, Shaw often uses female protagonists but like Hare he often has difficulty in producing them as viable motors for the dramatic action of the play. For such a prolific dramatist, Shaw was remarkably sceptical about the dramatic form and his tendency to leave the business of the play unfinished on stage, completing it in prose or in a preface, may be read either as a condemnation of contemporary theatrical practices or as a condemnation of his own dramaturgy. *Man and Superman* (1905), for example, is in some ways a fairly straightforward role reversal woman gets her man comedy, but it is blessed with a more or less self contained (and sometimes independently staged) central section 'Don Juan in Hell' which explicates the philosophy which underpins the rest of the play. Stage the play without 'Don Juan' and you miss out the philosophy; stage it with that section and the play becomes longer than many audiences will be willing to sit through. Like ▷ Howard Barker, a much later practitioner of assaults on the audience's attention span and stamina, Shaw would claim to be honouring his audience by trusting them to make the mental effort required to appreciate what he is doing.

Shaw was championed by the actor-director-dramatist-Shakespearian scholar-translator, and campaigner for a national theatre Harley Granville Barker whose decision to virtually remove himself from active theatre work after the First World War may well have changed the history of British drama for the worse. In his seasons at the Royal Court in 1904–7 Barker ran a proto-national theatre with contemporary translations of Euripides alongside work by the new dramatists: Shaw, Barker himself, ▷ Elizabeth Robins, and ▷ John Galsworthy amongst them. Barker's own plays have been overshadowed by Shaw's and by his work as a Shakespearian scholar and director, but recent productions have shown that they combine trenchant social critiques with an innovative approach to dramaturgy, operating within broadly naturalistic conventions but refusing the kinds of easy closure that can be so limiting in some versions of that form. Galsworthy, in contrast, tended to adopt a rigorous, sometimes over-schematic, naturalistic form, concentrating on a particular social issue and treating it with almost photographic realism to the extent that he contrived one of the few examples of a play that actually changed legislation, as opposed to summing up or changing a public mood: in *Justice* (1909) the presentation of a prisoner in solitary confinement apparently persuaded the then Home Secretary, Winston Churchill, to change the law. Elizabeth Robins, a powerful actress and champion of ▷ Ibsen, also wrote *Votes for Women* (1907), notable for its staging of a Trafalgar Square demonstration in favour of women's suffrage where the protagonists' personal concerns intersect with their public staging in the meeting. Although the pro-suffrage plays of such groups as the Actresses' Franchise League made little direct impact on the established theatre of the times, their work was a very effective early example of what would come to be called agitprop theatre. As well as monologues suited to political meetings and the music hall, anticipating the stand up comics of alternative comedy, the AFL often used such farce techniques as showing a world turned upside down by the application of supposedly logical (patriarchal) principles, but the AFL plays have outlived their immediate context and a play such as Inex Bensusan's *The Apple*, which is about sexual harassment in the workplace and about a father favouring his son over his daughters, remains a powerful example of its kind.

Irish, Scottish, Welsh, and Regional Theatre

The social and artistic radicalism of the period helped to plant the seeds of a national theatre in Ireland and of vigorous regional theatres in England and Scotland. In Ireland Annie Horniman's tea fortune helped to fund the creation of what became the Abbey Theatre Dublin. ▷ W. B. Yeats and Lady Gregory played a major part in establishing the theatre, but their work, like J. M. Synge's, tended to draw on the past, the mythological, and the rural. Encouraged by Yeats, Synge developed a dramatic idiom inspired by the Irish peasantry. In his master piece, ▷ *The Playboy of the Western World* (1907), he uses elements drawn from Irish, Greek, and Christian tradition to explore the difference between 'a gallous story and a dirty deed'. Christy Mahon, the playboy, wanders into a village whose inhabitants lionise him on the strength of him being a parricide but his father's arrival and apparent second death turns them against him. While the play is broadly comic with Christy emerging into a stronger new identity, the renewed isolation of Pegeen Mike, his new-found beloved, abandoned because she turned against him has a tragic penumbra which casts a shadow over the ending. While Synge's attempts to forge a new Irish English dramatic vernacular based on rural peasant speech, drew on the folk movement which was busily engaged in rediscovering (or reinventing) traditional culture across Europe, Yeats took his inspiration both from the Irish legends and from his understanding of the then fashionable Noh theatre to create chamber works of great poetic intensity aimed increasingly at an elite aristocratic audience. As a manager of the Abbey Yeats initially encouraged ▷ Sean O'Casey who found his inspiration in the urban poor and in contemporary history. Although Yeats's rejection of O'Casey's *The Silver Tassie*(1928) led him to pursue a career outside Ireland, his best known works are the three plays which form the loosely grouped Dublin Trilogy: *The Shadow of a Gunman* (1923), *Juno and the Paycock* (1924) and *The Plough and the Stars* (1926). In these evocative tragi-comedies he develops a highly flexible dramatic mode in which quasi-naturalistic narrative is heavily inflected through the ironic counterpoint of music and songs, the use of stereotypical characters, and an inventive use of stage iconography into a version of epic theatre ideally suited to explore the birth traumas of an independent Ireland. O'Casey's self-exile marks the beginnings of a divorce between British and Irish drama, although, inevitably, relations between the two islands continue to be a significant factor in Irish drama which are memorably explored in the work of such contemporary writers as Brian Friel, Tom Murphy, Christina Reid, and Ann Devlin.

A dispute about the English funding of an Irish theatre led Annie Horniman to switch her support to Manchester, where she helped to sustain a lively regional tradition drawing on the local vernacular. The so-called Manchester School included such works as Stanley Houghton's *Hindle Wakes* (1912) and Harold Brighouse's *Hobson's Choice* (1915), works which like their metropolitan counterparts show independent women choosing not to accept the constraints of traditional female roles: Houghton's young mill girl refuses to marry the mill owner's son who has 'ruined' her by taking her away for a dirty weekend, Brighouse's Maggie chooses her husband in the face of parental opposition from her drunken patriarchal father.

Theatre in Britain has largely been dominated by London, with regional theatres tending to be treated as nurseries for future metropolitan stars, but ventures likes Annie Horniman's in Manchester helped to create a strong independent regional repertory movement, which has withstood many vicissitudes and contributed significantly to the theatrical life of the whole country. ▷ Alan Ayckbourn is director of the theatre in Scarborough, ▷ John Godber operates from Hull, and ▷ Willy Russell and ▷ Alan Bleasdale are products of Liverpool. Scotland has been caught uneasily between the independent Irish model and the English regional model: for much of the century infrastructural problems limited opportunities for Scottish writers in Scotland so that, on the one hand, the talented Joe Corrie wrote mainly short plays for amateur companies and, on the other, ▷ J. M. Barrie does not have a distinctively Scottish voice. In recent years, stimulated partly by the very existence of the Edinburgh Festival, there has been a significant growth in Scottish theatre and writers such as ▷ Liz Lochhead have been able to develop a British reputation without losing their Scottish voice. Unfortunately the same has yet to be true for Welsh drama, which continues to be dominated by the working-class boy made good stereotype of Emlyn Williams and Richard Burton, and the poetic excess of ▷ Dylan Thomas' *Under Milk Wood* (radio, 1954).

After the First World War

O'Casey's dispute with Yeats owed a great deal to Yeats' unhappiness with the Expressionist-influenced second act of *The Silver Tassie* in which O'Casey resorted to stylisation and liturgical parody in order to try to convey some of the horror of the First World War. Such attempts to deal directly with the soldier's experience of war were relatively rare, and tended to appear some time after the war. R. C. Sherriff's *Journey's End*, the definitive trench warfare play, for example was staged in 1928. Conversely, the immediate post-war period saw a brief rebirth of an image-clogged verse drama from such justly forgotten writers as James Elroy Flecker and Gordon Bottomley, in which the formal qualities of verse seem to have been used as an escapist defence against the chaos of war. Similarly, J. M. Barrie's wistful whimsical tinkering with the supernatural, in *Mary Rose* (1920) may be seen as another way of coping with the aftermath of mass destruction. Towards the end of his theatrical career, Somerset Maugham, whose reputation rests largely on high comedies of manners, also applied his incisive ironic stance to the waste of human potential associated with the First World War in the bitter but much misunderstood *For Services Rendered* (1932).

Social Comedy and Farce between the Wars

Most characteristic of the period, apart from the continued attraction of musical comedy and farce, was Noel Coward's brittle social drama of hedonistic nihilism. Although Coward now tends to be remembered largely as a performer and a writer of boulevard comedies this does not do justice to his original reputation or to savage and bleak insights that characterise his early comedies. Coward secured his early reputation as what was not then called an angry young man with *The Vortex* (1924) in which family pieties are savaged in a melange of adultery, dope taking and piano playing. There is a desperate quality about the social whirl of Coward's early plays that encapsulates the post-war loss of old certainties, in contrast to ▷ Ben Travers' technically effective developments of traditional farce at the Aldwych Theatre, where the restoration of order after mistakes and misunderstanding promises a safer world than Coward's. The characters, plots, wit and construction of his comedies place Coward securely in the line of the English tradition of a comedy of manners dealing with the sexual and other morals of a leisured social elite. In *Private Lives* (1930), his protagonists are a divorced couple whose renewed attraction to one another when they meet on their second honeymoons refuels their decision to flout social convention and their new marriage partners by running away together. The action of course reflects changes in social and legal structures, but the decision to choose self gratification in the face of social strictures also reflects a pragmatic post-war hedonism. Coward was a master of subtext, of revealing the unspoken beneath a patina of almost phatic dialogue, so that a line like 'very flat, Norfolk', can reveal the underlying sexual attraction of the protagonists in *Private Lives*. Coward's homosexuality, like Wilde's and Orton's, may have been a significant factor in enabling him to produce an analysis of the mask of polite society since, as Wilde found out to his cost, society allowed homosexuals only a very limited freedom and they transgressed at their peril.

T. S. Eliot and Verse Drama

Dramatic verse in Britain had been labouring under the negative influence of Shakespeare for some 300 years, unable to break away from the powerful but imperfectly understood verse of the Renaissance dramatist, but equally unable to create an effective modern dramatic verse as the efforts of successive generations of poets, including Flecker and Bottomley, had showed. Although ▷ Naturalism had offered one way out of this dilemma by relocating the power of poetry in the theatre rather than in dramatic language, a trend which ▷ Expressionism and other post-war artistic movements furthered, experiments with dramatic verse continued to draw on both the Shakespearian and post-Romantic imitations of Shakespeare as their models. More promising initially were the experiments of T. S. Eliot. In the fragments of *Sweeney Agonistes* (1926) Eliot had found a form, inflected through Expressionism and the rhythms of Jazz, that could have constituted a decisive break with the orotund vacuousness of post-Romantic imitations of Shakespeare, and which is highly reminiscent in tone of the early ▷ Pinter. However, Eliot's growing religious convictions steered him into the religious pageant *The Rock* (1934) and then into the historical recreation of *Murder in the Cathedral* (1935) where the Canterbury cathedral setting and the medieval subject both made verse seem particularly appropriate. Eliot then tried to reach a mass audience by effecting a marriage between the conventional murder mystery of the West End and the sustaining power of Greek myth. *A Family*

Reunion (1939) contains some of his best dramatic verse but the attempt to retell the Orestes story as a drawing room drama in verse finally defeats him. Although the *Cocktail Party* (1949) has its defenders, the subsequent pattern in Eliot's plays is one of the gradual attenuation of the verse until it is scarcely possible to detect it in the late *An Elder Statesman* (1958) which looks all too anachronistic when compared to the contemporary work of ▷ Samuel Beckett, ▷ Harold Pinter, ▷ John Arden and even ▷ John Osborne. Where Eliot failed to go, ▷ W. H. Auden and ▷ Christopher Isherwood took up the cudgels with their verse plays inspired at some remove by their contacts with Expressionism and the early work of Piscator and Brecht, but their work was largely confined to what we would now call 'fringe' venues.

Dramatists of the Thirties and Forties

Neither technical innovation nor dramaturgical invention marked the majority of the mainstream output of the interwar years, though there were some relatively minor changes in subject matter in response to the First World War and there were some experiments with non-naturalistic approaches. In the thirties ▷ J. B. Priestley developed an interesting combination of socialist ideas and a dramatisation of alternative theories of time that marked a departure from some established norms. Although Priestley was to develop a convincing persona as the bluff realistic Northern conscience sent to castigate the effete south, his plays are thoughtful explorations of responsibility and causality, perhaps stretching contemporary audiences in some directions but always conscious of the probable limits of their elasticity. He used J. W. Dunne's and P. D. Ouspensky's fashionable alternative theories of time in such plays as *Time and the Conways* (1937), exploiting the gap between characters' aspirations and their outcomes to great ironic effect. Even when he did not use these theories of time overtly, he sometimes used historical settings to examine the origins of present events. In *An Inspector Calls* (1945), for example, he draws on some of the traditional apparatus of the detective thriller, a commercial staple in the hands of practitioners such as Edgar Wallace and Agatha Christie, to demand that its audience take social responsibility for each other in ways that its characters will not. Written during the Second World War, the play is set in the supposedly prelapsarian Edwardian period that is revealed both as a sham in itself and as the moment of origin of attitudes of social carelessness which have precipitated the war itself. Later generations of socialist writers would find themselves exploring precisely the period of the composition of this play in terms of their own search for the origins of their contemporary socio-political situation.

▷ Terence Rattigan, like Priestley, found some inspiration in the Edwardian period, in *The Winslow Boy* (1946), a dramatisation of a famous Edwardian court case. Whereas Priestley was an overtly didactic socialist writer, Rattigan made his initial impact with *French Without Tears* (1936), a light comedy of sexual awakening amidst funny foreigners. He was to develop into a craftsman of muted English understatement and the quiet desperations of middle class angst. Because of his concern not to offend the mythical 'Aunt Edna' whom he saw as a key element in his audience his reputation fell foul of the fifties generation, but his sympathetic treatment of a string of failed communicators and thwarted and ineffectual would be lovers (perhaps displacing his own homosexual torment onto more acceptable heterosexual targets) has led to a recent positive re-evaluation of his work.

The immediate post-war period saw little in the way of dramatic innovation: John Whiting, the most acclaimed writer of the period, never found a distinctive voice and Peter Ustinov, who was regarded at one point as a potential major dramatist, pursued other career paths. ▷ Christopher Fry's image- and colour-saturated verse offered a brief alternative to the drabness of post-war austerity but the British theatre remained dominated by attenuated society comedy of the 'anyone for tennis?' school with, as Kenneth Tynan, the key theatre critic of the period, remarked the heroic substitution of Berkshire for Loamshire in the cause of realism. Probably the most significant development was the creation of the Arts Council, a continuation of the state's wartime involvement in funding the arts, which was to change the funding base of theatre and make it possible in due course for the spread of experimental work that was unlikely to be commercially viable.

Beckett, Osborne, Brecht

In the mid fifties three decisive events helped to reinvigorate the British theatre. First, chronologically, was the 1955 British premier of ▷ Samuel Beckett's ▷ *Waiting for Godot* a play written originally in French by an expatriate Irishman that served to remind its audience of the basics of theatricality by engaging and entertaining them while, famously, nothing happened, twice. Then came the opening of ▷ John Osborne's ▷ *Look Back in Anger* in May 1956; third was the first visit to Britain of the Berliner Ensemble later in 1956, which introduced British audiences to Brecht's own company. While the excitement and controversy generated by Osborne's play may have encouraged a new generation of writers to look to the theatre, Beckett and Brecht probably had a greater long term effect on British dramaturgy. They both insisted, albeit from very different viewpoints, that the stage was a stage, opening up the possibilities of a non-naturalistic stage and effectively challenging the fourth wall conventions of ▷ Naturalism in ways which would liberate the imaginations of dramatists whether or not they shared the original authors' beliefs. In 1955 *Godot* seemed to be as minimal as theatre could be, but Beckett continued to test the frontiers of theatricality with works that pared plot, character, speech, and even the body itself to ever more attenuated depths. A typical example of this later work is *Not I* (1972) in which the protagonist is reduced to a mouth, isolated in time and space, compulsively filling a void with words designed to stave off self knowledge, while a virtually invisible 'Auditor' offers minimal gestures of help.

At the time the most controversial event was the première of Osborne's play, even if it was as Osborne himself remarked 'a rather formal old fashioned play'. Its setting, a one room flat in the Midlands with not a French window in sight, and its subject matter, a kind of sub-Strindbergian danse fatale for a male protagonist and what increasingly look like the dramatist's wish fulfilment fantasies in the guise of two unlikely women and a male friend, struck both friends and opponents as some kind of departure from accepted norms. The play, and its reception, suggested that theatre might now engage with a wider social spectrum, both in its topics and in the audiences it addressed, than it had previously. This new wave of dramatic writing was often referred to under the umbrella headings of 'kitchen sink' (in contradiction of French windows) and Angry Young Men. And at this stage they were almost exclusively young *men*.

Osborne's play was staged by the English Stage Company at the Royal Court, a theatre which resumed its earlier role as the home of new plays, a role it has continued to the present day, Osborne's energy and anger were initially mistaken for a form of socialism, but his forte turned out to be tortured heroes out of joint with their situations. His capacity for creating self-lacerating protagonists achieved its finest match between form and subject matter in *Inadmissible Evidence* (1964), where the protagonist's incipient nervous breakdown is reflected in the nightmarish population of the play where all clients merge into one and the stage picture becomes an embodiment of his hallucinatory isolation.

Brecht and Osborne each encouraged a sense of the theatre as an important public forum in ways that had not been the case since the early 1900s. It is some measure of how quickly the theatre changed that ▷ Arnold Wesker's largely autobiographical trilogy (*Chicken Soup with Barley*, 1958, *Roots*, 1959, and *I'm Talking About Jerusalem*, 1960) achieved wide critical acclaim at the turn of the decade since it is set amongst East End Jewish socialists and Suffolk labourers, living in council flats and tied cottages and using their own vernaculars. *Roots*, offers an image of a woman learning to think for herself as Beattie Bryant emancipates herself both from the deadly roots of her upbringing and from her socialist boyfriend, which many critics have found straightforwardly emancipatory, though the insights of feminism have undoubtedly complicated our understanding of the portrait.

While Osborne and Wesker began writing within broadly naturalistic boundaries, Harold Pinter's series of what became called 'comedies of menace', in which mysterious characters and unexplained events combine to unsettle the spectator with a sense of a half grasped reality which remains elusively inscrutable, were initially greeted with almost complete critical incomprehension. Pinter, like Osborne, was an actor, and where Osborne always seems to be writing leading parts for himself, Pinter seems a much more Prufrockian writer, always offering a vision of life as it might seem to an attendant lord with a minor part, always at the periphery of half understood events. His earlier writing in particular seems like the quasi-naturalism of the thriller without its characteristic closure and disclosure. Although Pinter was seen as the least political of his immediate contemporaries because he did not deal with overtly political events, his interest in the structures of power and of patriarchy was fundamentally political and it was no real surprise when he began to explore more narrowly political issues in his later writings. Perhaps the most obviously 'political' dramatist to emerge in the late fifties was John Arden, who shares both Brecht's desire for a theatre of political engagement and his non-naturalistic approach to dramaturgy. However, despite the appearance of *Serjeant Musgrave's Dance* (1959) on some school syllabuses, the British theatre has never been particularly comfortable with Arden's spare, ballad-like writing: the plays have never attracted particularly large audiences; his overtly political subject matter has sometimes led to censorship difficulties, and he has not worked in British theatre since a dispute with the ▷ Royal Shakespeare Company over their staging of *The Island of the Mighty* in 1972. He has now found himself a more secure niche writing for radio with his partner Margaretta d'Arcy.

Theatre Workshop and the Epic Theatre

▷ Joan Littlewood and Theatre Workshop played an important part in helping to demolish the old facades of British theatre by insisting on an approach to play making which, like Brecht's, was anti-naturalistic. Littlewood had been active in theatre since the 1930s with work derived from the traditions of the Workers Theatre Movement. The WTM had been far more theatrically and theoretically sophisticated than most professional theatre in Britain, gleaning an understanding of epic practices long before they reached the mainstream theatre as a result of its contacts with Workers' Theatres in other countries. Theatre Workshop was committed to ensemble production styles, to the reintegration of the writer into the theatrical process, and to the use of popular forms to engage the audience directly. In the late fifties, Littlewood developed Brendan Behan's *The Quare Fellow* (1954) and *The Hostage* (1958) and ▷ Shelagh Delaney's *A Taste of Honey* (1958) into major works, through improvisation with the company. Theatre Workshop's commitment to ensemble playing and a permanent company could not be sustained in the face of occasional commercial success which led to the siphoning off of the company into West End runs and there was always something of an element of patronage in the established critics' attitudes to their work. This is perhaps typified in the fate of the last great Theatre Workshop success, *Oh What a Lovely War* (1963). This passionate account of the horrors of war gained some of its contemporary urgency from a sense that the world was once more on the brink of extinction in the wake of the Cuban Missile Crisis. But it also located war safely in history and in using an end of the pier pierrot show format ran the risk of its songs being recycled as harmless nostalgia rather than exercises in Brechtian alienation. The Theatre Workshop style with its lack of interest in traditional forms of so-called psychologically realistic characterisation, its apparently improvisational quality, its intercutting of styles and scenes, its use of songs, and its rediscovery of the value of montage played an important part in creating a wider theatrical environment more suited to an emerging desire to break away from the narrowly deterministic qualities of Naturalism. The increasing availability of Brecht's work also played a major part in creating a new sense of dramatic and theatrical possibility.

The End of Censorship

Theatrical censorship, which had been in operation in Britain in one form or another since 1737 had long been regarded by writers and critics as a significant factor in preventing the theatre from tackling serious subjects and writers such as Shaw and Granville Barker had fallen foul of the often arbitrary proscriptions of the censor. However, despite various outbreaks of agitation against censorship, the Lord Chamberlain's powers to pre-censor plays survived until the 1960s, partly because managers felt that pre-censorship offered them some protection against the possibility of prosecution. ▷ Joe Orton, whose work fell foul of the censor in the early sixties, was another in the distinguished line of homosexual writers of comedy of manners, but he democratised the form to deal with a working class life of endemic police corruption, incest, buggery, casual promiscuity, murder, and general mayhem. The scandalised reactions which greeted his plays probably owed something to his extension of the traditional sexual and criminal pursuits of the aristocracy as represented in traditional comedies of manners and thrillers to their supposed social inferiors.

In 1968 pre-censorship was finally abolished in the wake of the Royal Court's championing of ▷ Edward Bond, a challenging radical dramatist whose play *Saved* (1965), which includes a scene where a baby is stoned to death, had become a *cause célèbre*. Bond has been much concerned with the institutional and other violence of capitalist society and the ways in which the apparatuses of power justify their own violence by defining it as 'not violence' while condemning those who commit individual acts of violence. In the case of *Saved* he compared stoning the baby to the area bombing of civilians, but since the comparison isn't enforced through the dramaturgy the linkage remains more obscure than some of his defenders would wish. In late plays Bond developed away from the residual naturalism that still characterises his earliest work in favour of a spare elliptical parable-like style reminiscent of Brecht that allows him greater freedom to stage his analysis as well as the narrative from which the analysis emerges. Like Arden, Bond has become increasingly dissatisfied with the conditions of production in mainstream theatre and his newest work is seldom to be found on national stages.

Tom Stoppard and Peter Shaffer

If many writers of the period since 1956 can be regarded as pursuing an agenda informed by a desire for some kind of social change, others have focused on less overtly political themes. Bond's fortunes contrast sharply with those of, for example, ▷ Tom Stoppard and ▷ Peter Shaffer who have proved durably successful in offering mainstream audiences theatrically inventive and intellectually challenging, but not overly political, plays over three decades.

Shaffer has used theatrical resources successfully to enrich a series of commercially successful variants on the theme of man seeking his god: in *The Royal Hunt of the Sun* (1964) the invading Spaniard Pizzaro looks to the Inca Atahualpa for a meaning that can transcend the material world; in *Equus* (1973) a psychiatrist who attempts to treat the boy who has blinded six horses in a welter of confused religious and erotic passions is only too aware that his own safe version of normality lacks the passion that has fuelled the boy's craving for transcendence; in *Amadeus* (1979) the ordinary composer Salieri looks on aghast at Mozart's scatological genius. In each case Shaffer uses variants on twinning (his twin brother Anthony is a successful thriller writer) to explore the costs of breaking away from the mundane and in each case he uses the resources of the theatre to demonstrate the attraction of the world beyond the mundane.

Born in Czechoslovakia, Tom Stoppard, unlike many of his contemporaries, initially eschewed any kind of political identification, although he did develop a strong interest in the role of dissidents in Eastern Europe in his later work. His first success, *Rosencrantz and Guildenstern are Dead* (1966), with its off-centre approach to a topic mediated through an existing dramatic work or style, set the tone of his whole career. In this case (following W. S. Gilbert) he makes two attendant lords from ▷ *Hamlet* the centre of his play, with the action of Shakespeare's play irrupting into the world of two characters who might have wandered in from *Waiting for Godot*. This method of collision between two discourses has remained central to his best work up to *Arcadia* (1993) in which he creates two sets of characters occupying the same room nearly two hundred years apart. Some of the modern characters are descendants of those who occupied the room at the beginning of the nineteenth century and Stoppard uses the contrasts between the two periods to muse on the nature of existence· using chaos theory, the randomness of sexual attraction, landscape gardening and the nature of proof.

▷ Christopher Hampton's major gift appears to be for contemporary reworking of Restoration and eighteenth century modes and topics as he showed in his brilliant reworking of Molière in *The Philanthropist* (1970) and his extraordinary adaptation of Laclos' epistolary novel *Les Liaisons Dangereuses* (1985). ▷ Michael Frayn, an accomplished translator of Chekhov, constructed a brilliant parody of the world of farce in *Noises Off* (1982), with a virtuoso dovetailing of backstage intrigues and on-stage disasters as the audience sees alternating scenes from a third rate farce and the lives of the company performing it. Frayn's technical skill in this play is close to that of Alan Ayckbourn, who stands alone as the most commercially successful dramatist of the modern theatre.

The scale of Ayckbourn's success has tended to mask the satirical bite with which he anatomises the state of modern English middle-class morals. His apparently ordinary characters soon reveal themselves to be existing in states of near mental or physical collapse as they try to tackle their problems. Ayckbourn homes in relentlessly on the quiet hysterical anomie of suburban life through a concentration on the rituals and structures that sustain the facade of respectability, from Christmas parties to the local operatic society. He tackles big themes such as the breakdown of marriages or business corruption through the meticulous observation of social detail and through the manipulation of the limits of naturalism through devices such as showing the same action in several different plays set in different locations within the same house and garden (*The Norman Conquests*, 1973), or creating a play with a fixed beginning and ending with alternative central scenes (*Sisterly Feelings*, 1979). Ayckbourn's very success has tended to obscure his trenchant social criticism and led to him being undervalued in academic circles because of his subject matter and the audiences he addresses, but it is clear that he offers just as searching an anatomy of Britain, albeit a different section of it, as many of his more apparently political colleagues.

Fringe and Alternative Theatre

Stoppard's initial success came with the staging of *Rosencrantz and Guildenstern* at the Edinburgh Festival Fringe which has played an important role in nurturing new writers and companies, to the point that 'fringe' has become a term used to describe many of the developments since the sixties. The growth in theatre writing and the creation of new theatre companies was also fuelled by the way of new theatre building in the late fifties and early sixties, partly as the result of civic redevelopment as with the Coventry Belgrade where Wesker was first staged, partly as the result of the expansion in Higher Education that involved not only the creation of new audiences for a new theatre but also the creation of new venues since most new universities created arts centres. The creation of new venues, new companies, and new audiences, together with a growth of subsidy fuelled an explosion of new writing in the late sixties and seventies which was only checked by changes in government policies after 1979. The writers who emerged towards the end of the 1960s tended to share an even greater emphasis on a politics of cultural dissent than had been the case with their immediate predecessors. This related in part to the opportunities presented for the dissemination of oppositional viewpoints through the emerging structures of alternative theatre and touring: many writers of the seventies and eighties gained significant experience with small scale touring groups such as 7:84, Joint Stock, Paines' Plough, Black Theatre Co-op, Temba, Foco Novo, Monstrous Regiment, Women's Theatre Group and Gay Sweatshop that provided high quality challenging theatrical experiences for audiences across Great Britain. ▷ Howard Barker, ▷ Howard Brenton, ▷ Caryl Churchill, and ▷ David Hare, for example, all worked with Joint Stock, although all have gone on to be staged by the ▷ National Theatre or ▷ Royal Shakespeare Company.

Hare's Joint Stock play *Fanshen* (1975), a dramatisation of William Hinton's book about the Chinese revolution, may seem to be a true heir to the epic theatre, but most of his work has been within a broadly naturalistic form and much concerned with the development of individuals within institutional frameworks. Joint Stock were one of most innovative groups of the seventies and *Fanshen* played a crucial role in their development: the play was developed through workshops which were a key element in most Joint Stock productions; each actor played many parts; and traditional naturalistic narrative and psychological realism gives way to the montage, banners, and direct address to the audience of an epic form.

In his other plays, Hare, unusually for a male dramatist, tends to concentrate on female protagonists, but they are too often sacrificial victims for him to be regarded unproblematically as a champion of the emancipation of women. Often, as in *Plenty* (1978) or *The Secret Rapture* (1988), it is a woman who carries the burden of trying to articulate a vision of the compassion that Hare is concerned with. However, this vision may be so socially deviant that she is unable to survive in the world as it is: Susan in *Plenty* retreats to a simplistic drugged recreation of the hopeful past; Isobel, the compassionate sister in *The Secret Rapture*, dies for her vision of caring.

Hare's instinctive naturalism combined with Howard Brenton's instinctive predilection for a more cartoon-like epic approach has produced two exuberant state of Britain plays: *Brassneck* (1973), about municipal corruption, and *Pravda* (1985), about the take-over of British media by an unscrupulous South African tycoon in the face of a supine Establishment, offered Jonsonian portraits of a nation's decay. Brenton has also consistently offered revisions of cultural heroes from *Wesley* (1970) and *Scott of the Antarctic* (1971) to Byron, Shelley, and Mary Shelley in *Bloody Poetry* (1984) and President Gorbachev in *Moscow Gold* (1990).

The State of the Nation

Plays anatomising the state of the nation have been a persistent strand in twentieth century British theatre from Shaw's *Heartbreak House* (1920), through Coward's less sceptical *Cavalcade* (1931) and *This Happy Breed* (1943), to Osborne's use of the music hall in *The Entertainer* (1957). In *The Entertainer* Osborne used the intercutting of scenes from a decaying music hall comedian's act to parallel his decaying offstage family life and by extention, the decay of the British empire. Alan Bennett's state of England play, *Forty Years On* (1968), was characteristic of much of his work in its mood of heavily ironic nostalgia. More recent examples include much of ▷ Peter Nichol's generally undervalued work, including the aptly titled *The National Health* (1969), which explored the discrepancy between soap opera hospital life and reality, and *Poppy* (1982) which used the traditional British genre of pantomime to investigate a little-known (to Britons) aspect of British imperial history in which Britain forced opium on the Chinese through military action.

▷ Trevor Griffiths found another apt dramatic metaphor to explore political issues through the situation of an elderly comic giving lessons to would-be stand-up comics in *Comedians* (1975): in the first act the audience are introduced to a range of conflicting views on the function of comedy, in the second, transformed into an audience watching the apprentices at a club, we experience many of the contradictions that were talked about earlier, in the third a debate about different functions of comedy widens into a debate about fundamental psychological and political issues. Griffiths, perhaps echoing Shaw in his commitment to adopting available forms to unfamiliar uses, has tended to use a developed version of Naturalism and often worked in television, in the hope of reaching a wider audience with his socialist ideas; his contemporary ▷ David Edgar has argued the contrary view that the formal structures and tight control of television make it easier to make radical points in the theatre, although the audience must inevitably be smaller. Edgar has made bold attempts to tackle issues such as the attractions of far right politics (*Destiny*, 1976) and the history of post-war dissent, juxtaposing the politics of Britain with those of the Iron Curtain in the ironically titled *Maydays* (1983), but is probably best remembered for his epic two part adaptation of *Nicholas Nickleby* (1980).

▷ Howard Barker is another dramatist of fierce political interests whose uncompromising attitudes to what can be expected of audiences have led to some of the most visceral effective, but also (and sometimes in the same play) some of the most tediously obscure scenes in contemporary drama. Perhaps the most idiosyncratic voice, however, is that of ▷ Tony Harrison, whose verse adaptations of Molière and Racine, and Greek and medieval plays combine extraordinary command of verse as a dramatic medium with a controversial socio-political outlook: in *The Trackers of Oxyrhyncus* (1988) a debate about high and low culture, the Apollonian and the Dionysiac was partly conveyed through clog dancing and an audience singalong in Ancient Greek.

Women Writers Since 1968

With the growth of a new theatre and a new politics after 1968, there also came a new and larger wave of women writers. Whereas both ▷ Shelagh Delaney and ▷ Ann Jellicoe (who utilised a far freer form in *The Knack*, 1961, than most of her male contemporaries) had been relatively isolated in the late fifties, a greater number of women succeeded in getting more than one play staged. The leader of this new wave was ▷ Pam Gems with a series of trenchant broadly feminist reappraisals of female icons, including *Queen Christina* (1977), *Piaf* (1978), and *Camille* (1984).

▷ Caryl Churchill has also established herself as one of the most effectively innovative dramatists of the period. Although her work might be seen as fitting within a socialist feminist agenda and she dealt with many of the topics that figured in much socialist and feminist drama in the seventies such as the witch crazes, seventeenth century millenarian sects, and issues of race, colonialism and gender identity, she developed new forms that appeared far more genuinely open-ended than the epic form as actually practised by Brecht. This has sometimes led to confusion about the stance of interrogative plays such as *Top Girls* (1982) in which she analysed the successful business woman who ignores her sister's (and her sisters') plight. Although much of the play is broadly naturalistic she starts with a surreal scene in which the successful career woman has invited some women from history to join her in a celebration. Perhaps most problematic was *Serious Money* (1987), a play about the London International Financial Futures Exchange: the exuberant vitality of the amoral characters and the free wheeling use of rhyming couplets tended to obscure the critiques, so much so that companies organised works outings to see the show which supposedly satirised them. Churchill has become increasing interested in working with choreographers and musicians in creating pieces that explore the boundaries of traditional theatre: *The Skriker* (1994) confused and invigorated audiences in equal measure with its extraordinarily allusive verse parable about the loss of a sense of the supernatural in modern society.

The English-domiciled Franco-American ▷ Timberlake Wertenbaker is another writer with a developing sense of the possibilities of dramatic form. Her works tend to have a particular interest in the role of art in society, the nature of myth and stereotyping. Her greatest popular success has been *Our Country's Good* (1988) in which she explores the power of art to liberate through her retelling of the story of how some of the convicts in the first white colony in Australia staged Farquhar's *The Recruiting Officer*, although the positive message about the power of art in that play is somewhat undercut in the powerful companion piece *The Love of the Nightingale* (also 1988) which retells the myth of Philomel in powerful terms. The allusive *Three Birds Alighting on a Field* (1991) is another powerful exploration of the nature of art and specifically the body as a commodity.

Marginal Voices

As well as beginning a process of empowering women, the late sixties explosion of theatrical energy encouraged other previously unheard voices including those of ethnic minorities and homosexuals, although progress has been erratic and the hostile political climate of the eighties limited some of the gains that were made in the seventies. Black writers were championed by some of the small groups such as Foco Novo which staged plays by Tunde Ikoli, Alfred Fagon, and ▷ Mustapha Matura and by companies from within the black and Asian community such as Temba, Black Theatre Co-op, Talawa, and Tara but the funding base for black theatre remains narrow and its position is unfortunately well summed up in the geographical location of Talawa's base, the Cochrane Theatre, on the physical margins of London theatreland. Although Matura and Winsome Pinnock have been staged by the National Theatre, black writers have yet to be fully accepted by white audiences as more than a minority taste.

The situation with homosexual writers is perhaps slightly better since there is a long tradition of gay writers in mainstream theatre: Wilde, Coward, Rattigan, and Orton all have secure reputations. The fringe company Gay Sweatshop has played an important role, both in staging plays on gay themes and in addressing an audience across the nation, albeit on minuscule budgets. Martin Sherman's *Bent* (1977), a play about two gay men who fall in love in a Nazi concentration camp, has been the most successful British play about male homosexuality, enjoying both a West End run and a successful revival. Even so the arrival of two gay plays in the West End in 1994 caused a press scare about 'gay domination' of the theatre.

Overtly lesbian writing has generally been confined to fringe venues, with the exception of the work of ▷ Sarah Daniels who has had some success with powerful polemic written from a radical feminist perspective. *Masterpieces* (1983) is an emotionally gripping attack on the corrosive effects of pornography and *Neaptide* (staged 1984), a modern reworking of the Demeter/Persephone, surfaced briefly at the National in its smallest auditorium.

The Thatcher Years

The 1980s saw considerable retrenchment in theatre companies committed to new writing, as funding was withdrawn from some of the more trenchantly oppositional companies under the Thatcher government. Its action in abolishing the Greater London Council, a great supporter of 'alternative' arts, left a gap which has not been filled, and the promulgation of anti-homosexual legislation (the notorious Clause 28) created an atmosphere of self censorship and fear in which some of the more innovative theatrical developments were left without funding. It was perhaps not entirely coincidental that companies with a strong commitment to new writing and to the word found themselves downgraded in favour of companies with a commitment to the classics or to the exploration of dance and physical theatre which, by virtue of their semiotic ambiguity were more difficult to criticise for their political content. Among the casualties of this period was the 7:84 company which had done invigorating populist socialist work in both England and Scotland, perhaps most notably with its founder ▷ John McGrath's sometimes sentimental but highly effective critique of successive rapes of the Scottish Highlands, *The Cheviot, the Stag, and the Black, Black Oil* (1973) in which the popular Scottish entertainment form of the ceilidh had been exploited to telling effect to comment on the state of the nation.

Epilogue

The major upsurge in the volume and quality of dramatic writing after 1956 depended on a combination of economic, social, artistic, and theatrical factors. The building of new theatres, the growth of a theatre audience interested in more challenging plays, the excitement generated by Osborne and by new approaches to staging combined with the availability of subsidy to create a vibrant exploration of theatrical possibilities. In the nineties, much of the original excitement has gone, the electronic media once more pose a powerful challenge to live performance, musicals continue to dominate the West End and the structures to sustain new writing have been battered by withdrawal of subsidy and by economic downturns. Revivals and adaptations are the order of the day and the theatre of affirmation is in the ascendant over the theatre of dissent, but the Royal Court continues to play its central role in encouraging new writers, and many other venues do continue with a commitment to staging new plays. Without such a commitment, there would be no new classics for the theatre of the future to revive.

22

The Sudden Fortuitous Discovery of the English Book: Post-colonial Writing

Andrew Michael Roberts and Marion Wynne-Davies

I

Introduction

The title of this essay is taken from an essay written by Homi Bhabha, who is one of the most perceptive and challenging critics of post-colonial literatures. In 'Signs Taken for Wonders' (*Critical Inquiry*, 1985) he calls our attention to a recurring scene in British colonial fiction where, in the middle of alien territory, the protagonist comes upon someone reading an English book:

> *It is the scenario, played out in the wild and wordless wastes of colonial India, Africa, the Caribbean, of the sudden fortuitous discovery of the English book.*

Of course, Bhabha's phrase is laced with irony and we are quickly reminded that the English book is 'an insignia of colonial authority and a signifier of colonial desire', that is, it is part of the discourse of colonialism and equipped with political as well as cultural power. In this sense, the discovery of an English book is not fortuitous (in the sense of occuring by chance), but indicative of a structure of power, and nor, for the native inhabitants who had their own well-established languages and artistic discourses, can it be regarded as fortuitous in the sense of lucky. Indeed, it is only recently that some indigenous cultures, for example Maori, have been allowed some public literary acknowledgement, while others, such as the African languages of Ewe and Zulu, still have to struggle against the overwhelming domination of English as the language of professional publication. Thus, although the term 'post-colonial' is often used to encompass the literatures written in English of, amongst others, Canada, New Zealand, Australia, Singapore, Sri Lanka, India, some African countries and the Caribbean, these nations are far from being free from the sway of European influence even though formal political control has long-since ceased to exist. Rather, as Patrick Williams and Laura Chrisman suggest, 'post' may be accurate in a chronological sense, since the British Empire has indeed been dismantled, but this does not mean to say that we have 'fully transcended the colonial . . . we are not yet post-imperialist' (*Colonial Discourse and Post-colonial Theory*, 1993). The tensions endemic to this struggle for identity did not, therefore, cease with the dissolution of the colonial empires in the years immediately following the second world war, but continue today in the theoretical and literary works of post-colonial authors. Indeed, given that the history of colonialism has been a history of exploitation and appropriation by the West, in which the suppression or marginalization of non-European cultures and languages was a major tool of oppression, the relationship between these two elements within post-colonial theory is clearly politically sensitive and of key importance if post-colonial theorising is not to repeat the colonising mentality.

A good example of how the English canon is challenged, altered and reformed in post-colonial literature may be found in the responses to ⊳ Conrad's novel *Heart of Darkness*. This work provides one of the examples given by Bhabha of the 'fortuitous discovery of the English book' when Marlow, the central protagonist, finds support and succour, while travelling through the Congo, from his reading of *Inquiry into some Points of Seamanship* which, though 'not a very enthralling book', is described as 'honest . . . humble . . . luminous . . . an old and solid friendship'. The English book for Conrad thus becomes a form of national security, which, discovered at a moment of crisis, projects an imperialist order and stability onto the dark chaos of the colonial territory. In terms of post-colonial theory such ideological contexts are a direct challenge to indigenous cultures, and *Heart of Darkness* has become something of a *cause célèbre* since 1975, when Conrad was attacked as a racist by the Nigerian writer ▷ Chinua Achebe. The ensuing debate has focused a number of the key issues of political interpretation. This is because Conrad's text uses modernist strategies of ambiguity and two-level narrative in a way that makes it difficult to identify the ideological position of the writer. Furthermore, the story combines explicit criticism of certain aspects of colonialism and racism (economic exploitation and cruelty) with the use of certain racist and colonialist clichés (Africa as a place of 'primitive' darkness, Africans as lower down the evolutionary scale). Achebe's criticism combined with his own novels, many of which study Nigerian society at various stages of its history, illustrates the fact that the double project of post-colonial criticism takes place both within the novel and through theoretical writings. Re-writing of both history and fiction plays an important role in post-colonialist literature. For example, ▷ Ama Ata Aidoo's *Our Sister Killjoy* re-writes *Heart of Darkness* in oppositional form, from the point of view of an African woman, a subject position that implies a double heritage of oppression, by colonialism and by patriarchy.

As the above example illustrates, it is difficult to identify any text as wholly within a colonial or a post-colonial discourse, for as Conrad's modernist writing simultaneously asserts and questions its own colonialist ideologies, so Achebe depends upon the imperial text to demonstrate the otherness of his own indigenous writing, and so Aidoo shifts the lines of domination to encompass both racial and gender difference. Moreover, there are huge cultural and literary variations amongst those peoples who have suffered colonisation. There is an obvious difference of historical situation between what John Theime terms the 'disrupted Third World societies' of Africa and India and the 'transplanted New World societies' of Canada, Australia and New Zealand (▷ Post-colonial Literature), although, as Theime points out, the distinction has its limitations: the Aborigine, Maori and native Canadian peoples are 'disrupted' with the 'New World' societies of the latter group, while Caribbean societies are both disrupted and transplanted. To consider the literature of both types of society under the heading 'post-colonial' is not to imagine a homogeneity but to invoke a fascinating series of similarities, contrasts and tensions, as diverse historical and geographical circumstances inflect certain broad themes, such as marginalization (both literary and political) and a divided personal and cultural identity, together with strategies such as 'writing back' and narrative of re-imagined and re-told history.

It is precisely in this multiplicity, in this flux of cultural difference, that Homi Bhabha traces the origins of the subaltern's resistance to imperial domination and the cogent articulation of indigenous culture. Bhabha points out that colonial authority sustains itself by laying claim to a universal system of values, which it imposes upon the colonised nation; in literary terms therefore, it offers them the 'English book' as a symbol of this consensual identity. However, the only way to maintain this position of power is to assert superiority over, and to discriminate against, the dominated nation, thereby stressing difference rather than similarity. This 'doublethink' of collectivity and variance produces what Bhabha terms 'hybridity' which he goes on to define as,

> *the sign of the productivity of colonial power, its shifting forces and its fixities; it is the name for the strategic reversal of the process of domination through disavowal (that is, the production of discriminatory identities that secure the 'pure' and original identity of authority).*

In other words, the imperial authority demands that the oppressed nation accepts the Western European standard as the norm, but because it can achieve this control only through asserting its superiority, the colonised subject can never perfectly replicate the 'original'. Instead, any attempt at mimesis inevitably produces a hybrid culture which is both dominant and oppressed, both archetypal and mutated. The very act of colonisation therefore encodes within it the necessity of resistance, as Bhabha writes,

> *Hybridity . . . unsettles the mimetic or narcissistic demands of colonial power but reimplicates its identifications in strategies of subversion that turn the gaze of the discriminated back upon the eye of power.*

This is perhaps the most important development in post-colonial theory, for without this recognition of the possibilities of 'writing back', of turning the gaze, and of encoding a reciprocity/confrontation within the new literatures, 'post-colonialism' becomes merely another literary term, domesticised within the imperialist culture and divorced from the effective arena of political activity.

However, before moving on to an account of the varying new literatures in English, it is important to note that not all post-colonialist critics are as Utopian about the re-emergence of the subaltern's voice as is Homi Bhabha. Another important contributor to this field of study, Gayatri Spivak, has suggested that, while worthy of praise, any attempt by Western academics to construct a voice for the repressed nations is a simplification which glosses over the problems, even the impossibility, of the creation of an independent subjectivity for the subaltern. What exists, therefore, at present is a,

> *debate between those who insist on the possibility of an effective alignment of position with the subaltern and those who insist that this, paradoxically, may serve only to construct a refinement of the system it seeks to dismantle.*
>
> Bill Ashcroft, Gareth Griffiths and Helen Tiffin,
> (*The Post-colonial Studies Reader*)

Perhaps a valid approach to the writing in English of the post-colonial nations is to aim for both an openness to the discourse of the subaltern, of the repressed peoples, and an awareness of the imperialist discourse which seeks, even now, to contain and mute those rearticulated words. In the following pages we hope to provide a brief introduction to post-colonial literature which frees these voices, albeit in a limited fashion. We have adopted divisions for the sake of clarity, but we are also aware of the dangers of totalisation inherent in such a structuring: the risk of constructing the whole around a centralising image – that of the 'English Book'. We would rather see this discussion of post-colonial literatures as an exploration which recognises both difference and connection.

II

Canada, New Zealand and Australia

The three literatures of Canada, Australia and New Zealand are often linked together as 'transplanted' forms of writing, and as countries where the English book has been readily transported with the colonisers. But in each case this is limiting classification, since Canada has its own native traditions, Australia has seen an emergence of Aborigine work and New Zealand has always had, if not always acknowledged, a very powerful Maori culture. Rather, they are a mixture of both 'transplanted' and 'disrupted'. Still, even within these broad divisions literary activity in each area has been distinctive both in the history of its development and its national characteristics.

Although the traditional songs and ritualistic drama of the native peoples, such as the Iroquois and the Inuit, can trace their roots to a much earlier period, the European (English/French) literary tradition in Canada did not begin until the early seventeenth century, although this was early in the history of North American colonisation. Robert Hayman's 'Quodlibets Lately Come Over From New Britaniola, Old Newfound-land' (1628) was probably the first book of original English verse to be written in North America and Marc Lescarbot's *Le Théâtre de Neptune en la Nouvelle-France* (1606) was the first play performed on the continent. The first English novel written in Canada, Frances Brooke's *The History of Emily Montague* (1769) came much later, but is more important in establishing national conventions, since it looks at the problems of colonisation and discusses the possibilities of cross-cultural exchange, rather than imperial domination. The establishment of a national 'voice' occurred however in poetry, where, after Canada became a nation in 1867, a group called the Confederation Poets emerged. Their primary theme was the Canadian landscape and their foremost writer was Archibald Lampman, whose Romantic sensibilities involved a powerful adherence to the specific natural environment of Canada. This reworking of European literary tradition into a form which answered the needs of the indigenous culture is exactly the kind of hybridisation Homi Bhabha writes about, and it continued to dominate Canadian literature into the twentieth century. For example, the tenets of modernism (both European and of the United States) may be traced in the poetry of E. J. Pratt, Dorothy Livesay and A. M. Klein, while the 'garrison mentality' which Northrop Frye identifies in the Canadian novel of the early twentieth century still exhibits an adherence to English cultural norms.

More potent forms of resistance have, however, emerged since the second world war. In drama the establishment of the Canadian Broadcasting Corporation (CBC) resulted in the first venue for original Canadian plays (3,500 were produced between 1939 and 1960), and playwrights have since moved from a nationalist stance (James Reaney and David French) to a more internationalist position (George Walker). The full impact of multiculturalism has been felt in Canadian poetry where the voices of the native Indians, the Anglophone/Francophone settlers and the more recent immigrants (such as those from the Caribbean and Asia) now have access to a state-funded publishing culture in which small magazines and presses abound. Finally, one of the most important sites of cultural resistance occured in the literary criticism of the novel. The best-known Canadian author is undoubtedly ▷ Margaret Atwood and it was she who widened the national identity debate to include the United States. In her seminal text *Survival: A thematic Guide to Canadian Literature* (1972) she excavates the Canadian novel in order to uncover and to challenge the 'victim' position in Canadian colonial discourses. However, her creative writing similarly foregrounds questions of national identity and links these to the dynamics of sexual politics. Symbolic and surreal elements are evident in the first-person narratives of *The Edible Woman* (1969) and *Surfacing* (1972), which centre on the internal lives of their women narrators. In *The Edible Woman* feminist issues are dominant; the metaphor of eating illuminates the narrator's reaction against both consumerism and the egotistical emotional cannibalism of men. In *Surfacing* a journey to a remote cabin in a French-speaking part of Canada is combined with the metaphor of diving into the depths of the self (with the possibilities of drowning or resurfacing). These two elements focus questions of cultural as well as personal identity. Both novels reflect the resolution stated in the last chapter of *Surfacing*: 'This above all, to refuse to be a victim.'

Canadian literature has, therefore, acquired a canon of its own, and one which follows a path from the Anglophone voices of the colonial past to the multicultural literature of today. These two elements may be combined as in the works of the novelist ▷ Margaret Laurence, who uses her fictional prairie town of Manawaka to chart Canadian social history, but who began writing in Ghana and who exemplifies a creative link between different post-colonial societies. A similar interchange may be seen in the writing of ▷ Michael Ondaatje who came to Canada from Sri Lanka; his novel *In the Skin of a Lion* (1987) blends fiction and history to focus attention on marginalised elements within Canadian life, including both the remote rural communities and the situation of an urban multicultural working class. Ondaatje, however, represents another particularly Canadian characteristic in his challenging of traditional form; innovative narrative technique is a feature of *Coming Through Slaughter* (1979) which uses transcripts of interviews, song lyrics, biographical summaries and intensely imagined subjective narration to document the life of the jazz cornet player Buddy Bolden. A comparable inventiveness is found in the less tragic but equally compelling novel by ▷ Carol Shields, *Mary Swann* (1987). This story of academics and others seeking to rediscover the life and work of an (imaginary) little-known Canadian poet contains an element of mystery, built up through four narratives: each has a different focal character, while one consists partly of letters. The novel's conclusion takes the form of a film script (including camera directions). In the present, therefore, the use of heterogeneous forms and the presence of divergent voices gives contemporary Canadian literature a feeling of uneasy multiplicity: difference is both welcomed and feared and literary forms are used to imagine unity as well as to stage conflicts.

Resistance is equally a part of New Zealand's literature, but the element of confrontation arises very much from the margins and not from the dominant cultural discourse. Indeed, until the twentieth century New Zealand had little literature of its own and instead imported traditions wholesale from Europe. The poetry of the early settlers was mediocre and often melodramatic, while theatre came under attack from the strong Puritan tradition of the colony. Prose, while commencing a little earlier than the other two genres, is initially depressing in its rehearsal of colonialist attitudes: for example, the first indigenous novel, Henry Butler Stoney's *Taranaki: A Tale of the War* (1861) justifies the oppression of the Maori as necessary and inevitable. Gradually, however, a national literature began to establish itself at the beginning of the twentieth century: a colloquial voice emerged in the poetry of R. A. K. Mason, while the concept of national identity may be seen in the writing of A. R. D. Fairburn. However, the most dominant poets of the mid-century were Allen Curnow whose technical skill and complex irony quickly established him as an authoritative voice, and James K. Baxter who linked personal experience to mythic narratives. Both writers also contributed to the growth in New Zealand of serious drama in which the Anglophone traditions were angrily overturned. Although much New Zealand fiction in the first part of the twentieth century tended towards social realism and male orientation, there was a strong if (until recently) inadequately recognised tradition of feminist fiction, of women writing from the margins. Amongst these were Edith Searle Grossman, ▷ Katherine Mansfield and Jane Mander.

However, it was not until the 1960s that a radical New Zealand literary culture emerged simultaneously in all genres. In poetry the publication of two anthologies, *Recent Poetry in New Zealand* (1965) and *The Young New Zealand Poets* (1973), introduced vibrant and diverse voices, making the work more accessible and allowing older poets, such as Curnow, to introduce fresh forms and complexities into their writing. In the field of drama, professional theatres were established and new writers challenged old conventions; these included Bruce Mason, who attacked the Puritanism of New Zealand culture, Mervyn Thompson who celebrated the working class voice, and Greg McGee, whose *Foreskin's Lament* (1981) became a byword for the country's anger at the state's conservatism. Finally, in the novel similar critical views of New Zealand society were expounded, the key text being Bill Pearson's *Coal Flat* (1963). The most exciting writer to emerge from this period was ▷ Janet Frame, whose importance to the contemporary New Zealand novel is comparable to that of Atwood in Canada. Her three-volume autobiography, *To the Is-Land* 91983), *An Angel at My Table* (1984; filmed 1990) and *The Envoy from Mirror City* (1985), is closely related to her fiction which describes, with symbolic intensity and a linguistic inventiveness, experiences – such as those of isolation, medical incarceration, and self-creation and self-healing through fiction – which are features of her own life. But Frame, like the other women writers mentioned above, still sees herself as a marginalised voice, challenging tradition and convention. Indeed, this is true for her contemporaries; ▷ Fleur Adcock's ironic poems, together with Anne French and Cilla McQueen's poetic undermining of patriarchal discourses have ensured that some of the best poetry in the 1980s has been written by women. Similar resistances are seen in Maori writing, particularly in the work of the poet and novelist ▷ Keri Hulme, whose novel *The Bone People* (1983) reacts against the consequences of colonialism, social and ecological. In her poetry Hulme adapts the strong oral tradition of Maori culture, but it is on drama that the indigenous New Zealand culture has had most impact. Despite all the oppressive forces of colonialism the ritualised performances of the Maori race could not be repressed and, with the greater recognition of their political and cultural identities, the Maoris have reintroduced their dramatic performances into everyday life. Interestingly these dramas often encode a challenge to state policies, as in the performances by 'Maranga Mai' ('Wake Up!', 1981) which were directed against South Africa's rugby tour and the works which focus upon the continuing land disputes. New Zealand is perhaps unique in being equally divided between the 'transplanted' and the 'disrupted', and in being split between a puritanical conservatism and the powerful marginal voices of the Maoris and of feminism.

Austrialia, while being closer geographically to New Zealand, has also much in common with Canada, particularly in its literary representations of the vast hinterlands, in the strength of its colonial inheritance and in its ability to produce and assimilate the voices of resistance. Because Australia simply had a larger population earlier a strong literary culture was established there before occurring in New Zealand. The eighteenth and nineteenth centuries saw the development of the bush ballad, the early melodramas, and the formative novelistic accounts of life in the penal colony, the most famous example of the latter being Henry Savery's *Quintus Servinton* (1830–1).

By the twentieth century Australian writers were confident enough to produce works which were specifically nationalistic, such as Judith Wright's poetry and Louis Esson's plays, as well as more internationalist, such as A. D. Hope's verse. After the Second World War the focus shifted more decisively to specifically Austrialian experience. Ray Lawler's play, *Summer of the Seventeenth Doll* (1957) explored the transition from the bushman myth to the urban existence of a modern society, contributing to the emergence of a new Australian character, the 'ocker' who combines the brash and crude masculinity of the bushman with the verbal dexterity and sophistication of the city business man. In poetry, Bruce Dawe's populist colloquialism, Les A. Murray's championing of the rural worker, and John Tranter's exploration of the fragmentation of city life, reflected the ironic disillusionment felt by a nation coming to terms with radical change. Evidence of this estrangement may also be found in the novel. Patrick White, who is the most widely known post-war Australian novelist, draws upon the stark polarities of his nation's identity: the polite social milieu of suburban Sydney satirised by White with a dry wit, and the starkly primitive outback, which in *Voss* (1957) becomes a spiritual testing ground. The eponymous hero of this novel is a dedicated German explorer with a compulsive though enigmatic sense of his own destiny, who leads an expedition into the Australian interior. In the early part of the novel the narrator shifts freely between realistic observation of social mores and poetic evocation of characters' inner worlds of memory, anticipation and desire. This blend is characteristic of White's idiosyncratic style, which startles by its immediacy and tonal range. Voss's journey is also an inner journey and, as in the work of Conrad, the confrontation with a harsh and alien landscape is endowed with philosophical and spiritual resonance through the questioning of personal identity; external and internal landscapes function as multiple metaphors. White was both a social satirist and a visionary, and the authority of his work was recognised by the award of the Nobel Prize for Literature in 1973.

More recently, the Australian novel has developed along more overtly post-colonial lines, as for example in the work of ▷ Janette Turner Hospital, an Australian who moved to Canada, whose novel *Borderline* (1985) explores questions of involvement, privilege and detachment with a post-modernist as well as a post-colonial self-consciousness. Similarly, Peter Carey simultaneously attacks the colonial development of Australia in *Oscar and Lucinda* (1988) as well as introducing the historical pastiche technique of post-modernist fiction. In the theatre Stephen Sewell has introduced broader issues through his Marxist perspective and in poetry non-Anglophone voices, such as those of Asian immigrants, may now be heard. Australia resembles Canada in openness to cultural multiplicity, yet, ironically, the literary reworkings in English of different cultures being welcomed by both these post-colonial states are often being repressed and silenced in the authors' countries of origin.

III

The South Pacific, Singapore, Malaysia and Hong Kong

There has not been any considerable production of literature in English in the above countries and areas but their varying responses to the post-colonial experience through poetry, drama and the novel serve to highlight the interrelated contexts in which new literatures are undertaken. For example, the authors of the South Pacific islands lay claim to a specific discourse which includes the Maori and Aboriginal writers of New Zealand and Australia, Singapore and Malaysia have a different but binding relationship, and Hong Kong negotiates an arduous and complex route between English imperialism and Chinese communism.

Although there is little written record of indigenous South Pacific literary culture, especially in prose and drama, there is a diverse and strong oral tradition in poetry which has transmuted well into the English tongue. Indeed, poems are still used at official ceremonies and, while retaining a firm base in regional culture, are open to a variety of forms and rhythms. More recently the same enthusiasm has found its way into the theatre: in Papua New Guinea after the attainment of independence in 1975 nationalistic plays were produced in the National Theatre as well as by touring companies, and in Vanuatu the Vanuatu's Wan Smolbag Theatre ('One Small Bag' theatre) stages plays which often detail the harrowing experiences of the native inhabitants under colonial rule.

Singapore parallels the South Pacific islands with its interest in poetry and relative neglect of the novel. Since the country's full independence in 1965 (national independence in 1962 and a break with Malaysia in 1965), poetry in English has established itself as an important element in Singapore's literature. The poetry ranges from the confident and ironic tone of Edwin Thumboo, through Lee Tzu Pheng's dark lyricism, to Robert Yeo's search for a national identity. Yeo is also one of Singapore's leading dramatists producing plays which have a clear political topicality and which disregard the Anglocentric tone of earlier writers. The novel has, in comparison, had a slow start, the first fictional work in English being Catherine Lim's *Little Ironies: Stories of Singapore* (1978). Increasingly, however, the English-educated readership is demanding works which are written in English but relevant to their own national experiences, and a growing number of university graduates, including Colin Cheong and Ovidia Yu, have begun writing in English in order to satisfy this desire. This last point is perhaps the key to Singapore's considerable body of imaginative literature in English: the university provides the linguistic and literary background necessary for the development of a strong literary output, while the solid English language education in Singapore's schools supplies the book-purchasing public.

The situation is very different in Malaysia, Singapore's close neighbour. Initially, Malaysian independence (1957) produced a small but interesting body of literature in English; poets such as Ee Tiang Hong and dramatic organisations such as the Malaysian Arts Theatre Group mirrored the growing nationalism of the country and attempted to find an authentic voice for the Malaysian experience. However, after the ethnic riots of 1969 English became a very subservient part of Malaysian culture and almost ceased to be taught at schools and universities. Today, there are no Malays writing novels in English, there are no interesting younger poets and there is only one significant venue for English drama, the Five Arts Centre. Perhaps this will change as English gains recognition once more, but the deep-seated political antagonisms between Britain and Malaysia make this seem a long and difficult task.

Drastic political upheaval is also at the centre of Hong Kong's cultural identity, but rather than stifling the English book the rapid approach of the Chinese take-over in 1977 has inspired many authors to examine and define Hong Kong's identity. Although there has been little poetry or drama written in Hong Kong, its novel always attained an international readership as with Han Suyin's *A Many-Splendoured Thing* (1952) and Richard Mason's *The World of Suzie Wong* (1957). More recently, the most powerful writer to emerge has been ▷ Timothy Mo, whose post-colonial novel *An Insular Possession* (1986) deals with the British annexation of Hong Kong.

The English book has had, then, a mixed reception in the South Pacific islands, Singapore, Malaysia and Hong Kong, for each nation has come to perceive, usually in conjunction with its independence or annexation, that literature cannot be divorced from political concerns and that when a post-colonial author chooses to write in English they encode an acceptance of Britain's imperial domination as well as an attempt to undermine it. Countries like Malaysia have attempted to expunge the language of colonialist control, while some writers, such as Hong Kong's Timothy Mo, make use of the size and economic strength of world publishing in English to gain an audience for work which articulates various forms of resistance or critique.

IV

Sri Lanka, India and Pakistan

Each of the countries discussed in this section has a long tradition of literature in the indigenous tongues, for example Indian poetry may be traced back over thousands of years. The relevance of the English book to their national cultures is, therefore quite limited, but at the same time authors from Sri Lanka, India and Pakistan have made a considerable impact upon the international literary scene. For example, Sri Lanka's ▷ Michael Ondaatje now lives in Canada and has won the coveted Booker Prize in Britain, India's ▷ Salman Rushdie and ▷ Rohinton Mistry emigrated to England and Canada respectively and are now highly acclaimed in their adopted countries, and Hanif Kureishi draws on a Pakistani inheritance despite being born in England. In this sense it becomes impossible to define national identity in any straightforward way, since within a post-colonial framework individuals are able to bridge difference, being simultaneously indigenous and alien, activating in themselves and in their writings a form of hybridity. Rather than only negotiating between the roles of imperial ruler and repressed subaltern as suggested by Bhabha, the concept of hybridity must be expanded to encompass the relationships between subalterns of different nations, opening out the possibility of transculturalism as well as multiculturalism.

When Sri Lanka became independent in 1948 a strong anti-English sentiment emerged resembling the experience of Malaysia, but instead of alienating contemporary authors from the English book, the policing of the language initiated a backlash and possibly the best literature to be written by native Lankans occurred in the second half of the twentieth century. One of the reasons for this seeming paradox was the influence of the department of English at the University of Ceylon, which inspired young writers and provided them with outlets for their talents through theatre groups and small literary magazines. As with Singapore, education proved a deciding factor in the continuation of English as an important cultural force, although class also plays a part in Lankan writing since the early authors were almost exclusively drawn from the upper ranks, the 'brown sahibs'. Sri Lanka's first leading novelist was probably Punyakante Wijenaike, whose ruling class origins led to a sense of alienation in her writing, as for example in *Giraya* (1971) where the central aristocratic family is shown to be corrupt and decadent. Wijenaike has now been superseded by Ediriwira Sarachchandra whose novel *With the Begging Bowl* (1986) challenges the notion of class alienation and introduces a more consensual voice into Lankan fiction. Drama in Sri Lanka is a more politicised genre than the novel with playwrights such as Nedra Vittachchi and Reggie Siriwardena favouring satire and social critiques. However, it is Lankan poetry that has excelled in its ability to relate traditional European forms and rhythms to indigenous traditions and local concerns. For example, Lakdasa Wikkramainka's poetic language draws upon an international array of voices, while Yasmine Gooneratne uses orthodox forms and Lankan content matter so as to create tension and fragmentation within her work. Gooneratne has left Sri Lanka and settled in Australia where she pursues the Lankan theme of alienation but this time from the position of the emigrant. Probably Sri Lanka's most widely known writer is ▷ Michael Ondaatje who also emigrated and has lived for many years in Canada: indeed, many Canadians would classify Ondaatje as a 'Canadian' author and not a 'Lankan' one.

India's strong and ancient traditions in poetry and drama have militated against many key developments in these genres in the English language, although writers such as Toru Dutt and Rabindranath Tagore, the latter of whom won the Nobel Prize for Literature for *Gitanjali: Song Offerings* (1912), demonstrate that Indian writers could excel in this area if they so wished. Indeed, more recently Anglo-Indian poets have revealed a multiplicity of talent; for example, P.Lal with his verbal dexterity, the contemporary Arun Kolatkar with his impressionistic political approach, and Monika Varma with her exposure of female confinement in Indian culture. Such versatility is not obvious in Anglo-Indian drama which appears to be written mainly for an elite readership rather than for public performance in the theatre.

In striking contrast the Indian novel in English has flourished alongside fiction written in Indian languages, perhaps because of a shared nineteenth-century origin, at a time when the need to explore the socio-economic conditions in India found a perfect medium in the novel genre. The early Anglo-Indian novel probably began with Bankim Chandra Chatterjee's *Rajmohan's Wife* (1864) and one of its finest exponents in this first period was Toru Dutt. The twentieth century saw the emergence of three major novelists, Mulk Raj Anand, Raja Rao and ▷ R. K. Narayan, the first two of whom focus upon political concerns. This is not true of Narayan, but on the other hand he must be acknowledged as the foremost Anglo-Indian author of his day. Writing mainly about Hindu middle-class society, Narayan takes as his main theme the transformation of the self. In an unobtrusive, lucid style Narayan's writing attends to the details of places, objects and habits, and explores subtleties of feeling and consciousness. The result is a combination of comedy and sadness as his modest, anxious, often ineffectual but highly sympathetic protagonists strive to cope with the frustrations of daily life and the elusiveness of their ambitions and desires. Broader areas of social and cultural conflict are, however, not entirely absent: *The Painter of Signs* (1976), for example, juxtaposes Western and Indian conceptions of the role of women and sexual relations in an ironic tale about a sign painter, his aunt and an emancipated woman who is seeking to promote birth control. Similarly, although Narayan's fiction can be seen within the traditions of the European novel, it can also be read in terms of plot and character elements mirroring Hindu mythological narratives: *The Man-Eater of Malgudi* (1961), for example, has a protagonist named Natara, one of the avatars of the god Shiva.

In the contemporary Anglo-Indian novel ▷ Anita Desai is pre-eminent. Desai, whose father was Bengali and mother German, was educated in India, and her work, like that of Narayan, shows the influence of both Western modernism and Indian cultural traditionalism. For example, *Clear Light of Day* (1980) has epigraphs from ▷ T. S. Eliot and ▷ Emily Dickinson and its opening scene, set in a garden, has qualities reminiscent of the novels of ▷ Virginia Woolf, while indigenous Indian literary tradition (in the form of Urdu poetry) is evident in her novel *In Custody* (1984). Desai, however, is also concerned with the plight of women in India; in *Fire on the Mountain* (1977), set in the mountains of North India, she meditates on the unfulfilled lives of a group of women characters and their quests for various forms of peace, consolation or liberation. More explicitly political themes are found in the novels written in the 1980s by ▷ Nayantara Sahgal, a member of the most prominent Indian political family. *Plans for Departure* (1986) and *Mistaken Identity* (1988) depict India in the 1910s and 1930s respectively, while *Rich Like Us* (1985) shows Sahgal's concern for human rights, using a narration from two perspectives to explore the causes and consequences of violence during the state of emergency declared by Indira Ghandi in the late 1970s. Sahgal's earlier novels, such as *Storm in Chandigarh* (1969), focused more on sexual politics, a concern which is central to the work of ▷ Shashi Despande who, in *That Long Silence* (1988), portrays the tension for a married woman between a sense of responsibility and a need for autonomy, in a story that also explores the psychic consequences of an abortion. Another radical feminist author is Bharati Mukherjee, but while she remains committed to the exposure of the patriarchal and racist repression of Indian women she left her native Calcutta, and after living for a short time in Canada now resides in New York. Similarly, Rohinton Mistry, while continuing to write about the Indian experience of post-colonialism, now lives and works in Canada. Finally, however, to compound India's immersion within this contemporary transculturalism, the legacy of the British Raj has produced two European novelists writing in India about the Anglo-Indian experience. ▷ Paul Scott's *Raj Quartet* (1966–75), a study of racial tension, corruption and violence at the time of Independence was made into a hugely popular television series, and ▷ Ruth Prawar Jhabvala's novel *Heat and Dust* (1975) juxtaposes the 1920s and the 1970s in a parallel double narrative, a technique which Jhabvala (who is a highly successful screenplay writer) describes in filmic terms as 'splicing'. Revisiting the period of ▷ E. M. Forster's *A Passage to India* and reassessing many of its political and moral concerns, this novel represents one version of the rewriting of texts of the colonial period which has been a major technique of the post-colonial novel.

In comparison with India, Pakistan's output of literature written in English is small, although it too has a fair number of highly respected expatriate authors. One of the major factors in the difference between India and Pakistan is, of course, religion, for whereas India's Hindu conventions have always encouraged theatrical performance, Pakistan's Muslim traditions have all but obliterated drama as a viable genre. Another contrast may be seen in the countries' different poetic discourses, for whereas India embraces a multitude of themes, Pakistan's poets rely heavily upon the introverted voice and nature imagery, eschewing the somewhat dangerous area of political verse. However, it is in the novel form that Pakistan attains a unique and vibrant identity; for example, in the works of Ahmed Ali who established a strong sense of nationalism after Independence in 1947, and in the writing of ▷ Zulfikar Ghose who uses landscape and location to explore the complementary and contradictory relationships between East and West. Ghose, however, now lives in the United States and writes from a position of alienation. Similarly, ▷ Hanif Kureishi's and Tariq Ali's works are based upon Pakistani experience in England, which while fascinating in their exploration of two cultures, often portrayed as equally bigoted, are far removed from an indigenous Pakistan English language novel. Perhaps, then, through the ability of individual authors to achieve success on an international scale and to bridge the differences between different cultures, the nationalist voices are becoming muted. The potency of multinational publishing houses and the development of post-colonial studies in the universities have promoted the spread of post-colonial literatures but may risk blunting conflictual edges and diluting political resistance. However, even as we acknowledge the dangers of a seemingly harmonious multiculturalism, we should also recognise its value, a value highlighted by the fact that in many countries the economic and/or political conditions that allow such multiplicity do not exist.

V

Africa and the Caribbean

Both areas considered in this final section embrace wide variations in national cultures; for example, criticism of the governments in Uganda and South Africa must be recognised as very different since the former has concerned a black dictatorship and the latter the retention of white colonialist power via apartheid. Similarly, there are diverse cultures within the Caribbean group of nations, and writing which is produced within the Caribbean islands tends to have different perspectives from that which is undertaken by the Caribbean exiles in Britain. Yet all the national cultures which come under this heading have combined their strong oral traditions with European textual conventions often producing highly political writing and creating new hybrid forms which may lay claim to being representative of post-colonial literature.

In the countries of East Africa (Kenya, Tanzania and Uganda) there was little attempt to produce national literatures in English until the period of independence in the 1960s. Even after this period in the field of poetry there have been few significant poets writing in English, with perhaps the exception of Richard Ntiru in Uganda and Jared Angira in Kenya, and it was only in the late 1980s with the publication of two impressive anthologies, *An Anthology of East African Poetry* (1988) and *Boundless Voices: Poems from Kenya* (1988) that an international readership became aware of East African poetry and its striking ability to combine the local oral tradition and immediate political concerns with British literary references. This combination also characterises the region's theatrical output, in which the playwrights attempt to promote social change through a combination of European dramatic conventions, such as Theatre of the Absurd, and native performance traditions. For example, Francis Imbuga's *Betrayal in the City* (1976) offers harsh condemnation of the post-independence Kenyan government, and John Ruganda's *The Floods* (1980) is a sharply satirical attack on the Ugandan military dictatorship. For East African drama, therefore, political content, indigenous stylistic features and international techniques of radical theatre are harnessed together to condemn the inadequacies of the present government, rather than to explore the difficulties of a colonial past. The history of the novel in East Africa is founded, unlike the poetry and drama, very much in a colonial discourse; for example, one of the early East African novels is ▷ Karen Blixen's *Out of Africa* (1964). This has led to a more complicated negotiation between the black author and the English book he or she wishes to write, since many writers in Africa, as in other parts of the post-colonial world, face a decision whether to publish in the language which is a legacy of foreign domination of their countries, or in an indigenous language, or both. For example, the Kenyan novelist ▷ Ngugi wa Thiong'o, after publishing four widely acclaimed novels in English, published a fifth in the language of his people, Gikuyu, later translating it into English himself; since 1982 he has abandoned writing in English. Still, Ngugi must be considered the most important of the post-independence East African writers in English, and his chronicling of the modern history of Kenya stands as one of the major post-colonial reviews of an oppressed past and the difficulties of creating an independent national identity in the present. His first novel *Weep Not, Child* (1964) is the story of an adolescent boy at the time of the Mau Mau rebellions, while *The River Between* (1965) goes back in time to the first nationalist rebellion of the 1920s, representing divisions in Kenyan society through the symbolic separation of two villages, on either bank of a river. *A Grain of Wheat* (1967) presents Kenyan life in the troubled period leading up to independence through the lives of four friends, and *Petals of Blood* (1977) is a powerful, realistic, but also symbolically vivid attack on the economic exploitation of the peasants in the 1970s. Ngugi's mature fiction is explicitly informed by Marxist political analysis and after writing *Petals of Blood* he was imprisoned. His work embraces both the expression of a collective social awareness and the exploration of moral uncertainty through the gradual evolution of introspective characters. Perhaps Ngugi's imprisonment goes some way towards explaining why there have been so few pathbreaking East African writers, for the political and economic conditions in the region make the publishing market a somewhat precarious arena.

Before, however, turning to the even more difficult political situation that has faced writers in South Africa, we would like to look briefly at the writing of South Central Africa (Malawi, Zambia and Zimbabwe) and West Africa (The Gambia, Ghana, Nigeria and Sierra Leone). The novel form has flourished in Zimbabwe which has used prose as the medium for its exploration of a new national consciousness both in the individual and in the state. ▷ Doris Lessing's work provided an early example of how the South Central African novel could be used to foreground racial inequality and the tensions endemic upon such imperial power structures, as for example in *The Grass is Singing* (1950). These concerns also appear in the works of Zimbabwe's two foremost black writers: Charles Mungoshi who portrays the harshness of colonial rule and who writes in both English and his native Shona, and Dambudzo Marachera who deals with his country's fragmented identity and the destabilisation of the post-modern world. If Zimbabwe is pre-eminent in the novel, then Malawi prevails in the field of poetry, with its incorporation of indigenous traditions and contemporary European and American conventions. For example, Steve Chimombo's poetry calls upon the oral tradition and Jack Mapanje's work, such as 'New Platform Dances', incorporates multiple elements of traditional Malawian culture.

West African poetry in English commenced, in common with many post-colonial cultures, with the nationalist struggles for independence after the second world war, and the most influential text of this formative period is generally accepted to be Gabriel Okara's *Black Orpheus* (1957). Okara introduced an intellectual style of poetry in which subject matter and a self-conscious stylistic approach were merged with imaginative intensity. His successors include ▷ Wole Soyinka, Christopher Okigbo and ▷ Kofi Awoonor; Soyinka's poetry, while utilising African mythology, simultaneously demonstrates an indebtedness to the European modernists, Okigbo's work encompasses the fragmentation of his own society as well as the general sense of alienation represented in international literatures, and Awoonor's verses draw directly upon Ewe songs and are perhaps some of the most authentic African poems written in English which are written and performed today. Other contemporary poets, such as Ama Ata Aidoo and ▷ Ben Okri have followed suit using experimental forms and political themes to explore the West African writer's sense of exile, alienation and dissatisfaction with the governments past and present.

Drama in English, like the poetry, developed as an important literary form after the West African countries had gained their independence from Britain, yet even now there is very little produced since English is, at best, a second language for most people, ensuring that audiences while appreciative are also quite small in number. Moreover, although in terms of content the West African plays challenged colonialist rule and highlighted the horrors of a colonial past, there remained the paradox of presenting such material, on stage, to a black audience, in the language of the oppressors. Attempts have been made to overcome this contradiction by giving the characters dialogue in a local dialect and by introducing traditional African elements such as dance and song, but the incongruity remains, permeating the plays with tensions which are not always counterproductive. Indeed, West Africa has produced some of the finest playwrights of the late twentieth century, including Ama Ata Aidoo and Wole Soyinka (both are also poets and are mentioned above). Indeed, Soyinka was the first black person to win the Nobel Prize for Literature (1986) and has an international reputation.

What Soyinka is to the West African theatre, ▷ Chinua Achebe is to the West African novel, although Soyinka and Aidoo are also important writers of prose. Along with ▷ Amos Tutuola's *The Palm-wine Drinkard* (1952), Achebe's *Things Fall Apart* (1958) initiated the rapid growth of the African novel in English. Achebe's novels articulate the impact on Nigerian culture of white colonialism and its aftermath, from the first appearance of white missionaries in *Things Fall Apart*, to Lagos in the 1960s in *A Man of the People* (1966). *Anthills of the Savannah* (1987) updates this historical chronicle, showing injustice and resistance under the rule of a 1980s African military dictator. Writing in English, Achebe incorporates African proverbs and idioms in such a way as to make the cultural context vivid and compelling for both African and English readers. Characters such as Okonkwo (the village leader who is the principle character of *Things Fall Apart*) or Christopher Oriko (the Commissioner for Information who, in *Anthills of the Savannah*, compromises with, but eventually revolts against, the one-time friend who has become a dictator) achieve psychological complexity, and a considerable tragic status.

A number of West African writers employ, however, more radical techniques than are generally used by Achebe. For example, *Our Sister Killjoy* (1970) by the Ghanaian author Aidoo uses typographical effects (such as pages with a single word on them), interposed commentaries in verse, ironic interplay between the voices of character and narrator, and a mode of address to the reader which draws on oral storytelling. The novel confronts feminist issues as well as expressing resistance to European appropriation and assimilation of African culture and African people, symbolised in the transplant of an African man's heart into a white man's body. The symbol of the heart is also structurally important to the story, in which a woman who travels to the 'heart' of Europe and is subject to its sexual and material attractions, eventually rejects it in favour of her responsibility to her African homeland. This complex inversion/subversion of the Eurocentric myth of ▷ Conrad's ▷ *Heart of Darkness* illustrates the process of 'writing back' to the centre of the Empire, a process of resistance and reappropriation which works here through intertextuality. In addition, Aidoo's criticism of aspects of the work of male African writers (in particular their use of images and ideas of motherhood) places her in a strong feminist dynamic among writers who have portrayed the 'double yoke' of black women who suffer from both racism and sexism; a concern evident in works such as Flora Nwapa's *Women are Different* (1986) and Buchi Emecheta's *Double Yoke* (1983).

Although it would be inadequate to describe the existence of contemporary authors in East, South Central and West Africa as free from the restraints of colonialism, since much of their writing in fact reacts *against* the forces of imperialism, it is South Africa that has enshrined itself in world politics as the epitome of racism and as the final bastion of the colonial way of life, although that situation has now changed radically. Unlike the other national literatures discussed in this section of the essay, South Africa's literary history begins early in the nineteenth century with the hunter-explorer poems of Thomas Pringle (the 'father' of South African poetry in English), the European touring companies with their productions of the English 'classics' and, somewhat later, the colonial adventure narratives of novelists such as ▷ H. Rider Haggard. Still, even in this formative period white writers, such as ▷ Olive Schreiner in *The Story of an African Farm* (1983) undercut the traditional colonialist view of Africa as a seductive and mysterious land by showing the 'grey pigments' of the racist and sexist realities. In the next century poets such as William Plomer and ▷ Roy Campbell used their journal *Whiplash* (founded in 1925) to attack the colonialist policies of the government, but following sharp condemnation of their attitudes both became exiles. Indeed, throughout the remainder of the twentieth century and especially after the foundation of the apartheid policy in 1948, white writers, such as Dan Jacobson and Bessie Head, challenged their government and were subsequently forced or encouraged to leave South Africa, although it is important to remember that this protest took place from a position of privilege not open to black authors. Even now, however, the two most well-known South African novelists, ▷ Nadine Gordimer and ▷ J. M. Coetzee, are non-black. The oppression of white rule in South Africa dominates the novels of Gordimer, but is addressed obliquely through its impact on private experience. Writing primarily about the white middle classes, she traces the decay resulting from their involvement in a brutal and segregated social system. Coetzee addresses similar concerns in *Age of Iron* (1990) where he combines allegory and realism in a grim picture of a violent confrontation between police and Africans and the agonised complicity of a liberal white woman.

Until the 1960s, however, black writers were not given adequate resources or recognition to access the kind of international renown built up by Gordimer and Coetzee. For example, the first novel in English to be written by a black person was Sol T. Plaatje's *Mhudi*, which although it was written in 1919 was not published until 1930. After the Sharpville massacre, the rise of the Black Consciousness Movement and the Soweto Revolt political writing by blacks in English became a powerful tool in the movement towards revolution and violent activism. At first the black authors wrote in English to shock the white reader into an appreciation of their situation, but after the mid 1970s the purpose behind the use of English had changed and was now intended to incite militancy within the disparate black South African groups and by the 1980s poetry was being used openly at political rallies to inspire those fighting for a democratic state. Drama was similarly used for political effect, combining the alienating techniques of modernist European theatre with the older African forms of song, dance and narrative recitation. The work being staged at radical venues such as the Market Theatre in Johannesburg, on university campuses and in the townships, was very different from that which was recognised by the state-controlled Performing Arts Council, and was often censored or banned. Since 1990, however, when Nelson Mandela and F. W. de Klerk began their dismantling of the apartheid system, the political situation in South Africa seems redeemable even if the economic and social legacies of imperialism still dominate. The 'English Book' of white colonial power has left a dark and indelible stain of injustice and oppression at the heart of the South African map.

The links between African and Caribbean cultures are, of course, a further testimony to the inhumanity of the colonial system, and black Caribbean writers keep returning to the traumas of transportation and slavery in their works, as for example in ▷ George Lamming's novel *Natives of My Person* (1971), in Dennis Scott's play *An Echo in the Bone* (1985) and in Grace Nichols' poetry. Yet, while the literature of South Africa remains caught within the discourse of conflict, Caribbean writing has broken free from most of its old colonialist restraints and can now lay claim to being one of the most vibrant, exciting and imaginative of the post-colonial literatures. With the Carribean canon it is, in fact, difficult to know where to begin, but surely the most dominant figure in the region's literary output is ⊳ Derek Walcott, winner of the 1992 Nobel Prize for Literature. Walcott has dominated Caribbean poetry and drama for almost half a century, reworking European forms through a multicultural articulation of local experience. His epic book-length poem *Omeros* (1990) epitomises this achievement, engaging intertextually with a founding author of the Western European literary canon, Homer (Omeros is the Greek version of the name Homer). The heroes of *The Odyssey* are transmuted into fishermen on the Caribbean island of St Lucia: like Joyce in *Ulysses*, Walcott reworks symbols and events from Homer's classical epic in a seemingly more mundane context but invests that context with heroic resonance. The poem expresses powerfully the sense of loss arising from the displacement of slavery and the poem seeks some sense of healing through a magical journey to Africa. Walcott's stance is one of tolerance and reconciliation: there is a sympathetic portrait of a retired British soldier and the poet has commented that this man's genuine love for the island gives him the right to live there. This observation might even be taken as an oblique comment on Walcott's European readership, whose genuine love for his poetry would, on this interpretation, give them the right to inhabit it. The poetic evocations of the sights and sounds of the Caribbean are one of the many pleasures of this rich and complex work. Walcott has built upon a tradition of black Caribbean writing: in poetry the early and romanticised work of Horatio Nelson Huggins and the increased access to media production as in the BBC's radio programme *Caribbean Voices* gradually formed a Caribbean voice which resounded with political urgency and verbal immediacy, while in drama, ⊳ C. L. R. James' *Toussaint L'ouverture* (1936) and the small drama groups of the 1970s promoted rebellion and the struggle for an independent identity.

The Caribbean novel also played a part in the growth of a national literature, from Tom Redcam's early attempts to found an All-Jamaica Library, through V. S. Reid's *New Day* (1949) with its use of Jamaican Creole, to the works of ⊳ George Lamming, ⊳ V. S. Naipaul, ⊳ Jean Rhys and ⊳ Wilson Harris. In this last group a more complex formulation of identity began to take place, for whereas Reid remained at home, subsequent writers left the Caribbean to settle in Britain and explored the personal and social consequences of this journey in their novels. To compound the complexity of this pattern of motion it is important to remember that the ancestors of many of these writers were brought to the West Indies from Africa as slaves, and that a return journey to the Caribbean was undertaken by several authors after experiencing deprivation and racism in Britain. It is hardly surprising therefore that the theme of journey, the sense of homelessness as a cultural condition, and a quest for a greater sense of belonging are found in much Caribbean fiction. Loss and alienation occur in ⊳ George Lamming's novel *In the Castle of my Skin* (1953) which is an autobiographical text written in the first person. It begins when the protagonist is nine with an evocation of a pre-war Barbados village dominated by the house of the white landlord and the ideology of 'little England'. A strong sense of community is implied, but also the presence of tension, violence and humiliation, and the style is poetic and symbolic; for example, a flood becomes an anticipation of chaos and disruption to come. The novel ends with the destruction of this community, with the protagonist's initiation into self-conscious black politics and his departure from the island; the concluding scene is his symbolic parting from the 'Pa' of the village – its oldest inhabitant and the emobodiment of its collective identity, who is about to be confined in an institution.

The best-known West Indian novelist is probably ▷ V. S. Naipaul, who has written about the lives of Indian people in Trinidad, but has also published novels set in other parts of the world, such as England (*The Mimic Men* 1967), Mauritius (*Guerrillas*, 1975) and Africa (*A Bend in the River*, 1979). His early novels, such as *The Mystic Masseur* (1957), evoke the life of Trinidad with an elegant clarity which emphasises both its sordid aspects and its vitality. *A House For Mr Biswas* (1961) deals with the hero's search for independence combined with the capacity to love and accept responsibility. This search is articulated by the metaphor of the building of a house, a focus of self-respect and growth in the face of the displacement which is the aftermath of colonisation. The novel is a work of considerable scope in the comic realist tradition. Naipaul's ancestors came to the West Indies from India, and in that sense he represents one of the many cultural links between different parts of what was once the British Empire.

▷ Wilson Harris stands alongside Naipaul as an internationally acclaimed novelist, but his work is very different; rather than adopting European forms and a realistic perspective as does Naipaul, Harris' novels, especially the Guyana Quartet (*Palace of the Peacock*, 1960; *The Far Journey of Oudin*, 1961; *The Whole Armour*, 1962; and *The Secret Ladder*, 1963) break down narrative progression and character consistency and search for a non-realist world in which the human psyche is the only linking force. The challenge to conventional modes is common in Caribbean fiction, for example, ▷ Jean Rhys in *Wide Sargasso Sea* (1966) employs polyphony, and ▷ Merle Collins in *Angel* (1987) writes in overtly poetic language.

Much contemporary Caribbean literature shares this thread of unconventionality which allows the author to call attention to European literary traditions while at the same time undercutting them and offering a powerful and sustained expression of indigenous culture. Ritual is important in the plays of Jamaica's Dennis Scott, especially in *An Echo in the Bone* (1985), carnival recurs in several plays, such as Sylvia Wynter's *Maskarade* (1979), while stickfighting and calypso are also used to endow West Indian drama with a unique character. However, it is Caribbean poetry that has become the most highly regarded aspect of West Indian literature. We have already commented upon Walcott's supreme achievements, but he has stiff competition from other poets such as Edward Kamu Brathwaite, Jean Binta Breeze and Linton Kwesi Johnson. Brathwaite, unlike Walcott, eschews European forms and has attempted to articulate an alternative poetic tradition founded in the African voice. Breeze and Johnson both belong to a well-known and highly acclaimed group of writers, the 'Dub' poets; like Brathwaite's poems, Dub poetry has its roots in the old oral culture of the West Indies but links these rhythms and themes with the more contemporary ones of reggae and Rastafarianism. Dub is performance-orientated poetry, although it is also available in published form in Britain. Indeed, a lot of Caribbean literature has been written away from its originating environment, in Britain, America and Canada, where there is more likelihood of economic reward and international recognition.

VI

Conclusion

In this essay we have attempted to provide an overview of some of the most exciting developments in post-colonial literature, as well as to indicate something of the colonial background and its impact in each of the nation states discussed. As we have indicated considerable tensions are invoked by those post-colonial writers who do chose to write in English, because of the involvement of the language in the colonial process. The historical role of this language, together with the history of its use and development in diverse cultures, may significantly inflect matters of genre, style, technique, form and diction, responding and contributing to the continuing evolution of the many 'Englishes' of the world. Politically and linguistically, then, 'post-colonial' designates an ambivalent, conflictual situation, in which the after effects of imperialism remain powerful and where 'post' implies a transformation rather than an absolute break; in this respect it is analagous to ▷ post-modernism. Indeed, even should the subaltern succeed in formulating strategies of resistance to the colonial discourse of the past, he or she is often ambushed by the new colonial forces of Western capitalism. The 'English book' therefore, whether used as a tool of cultural imperialism, an articulation of resistance, protest and critique or a commodity in the multinational publishing business, must remain an ambivalent institution for the post-colonial nations. While post-colonial literatures assert the right of these nations to articulate their own independent literary identities, at the same time, the glittering array of talent, the vibrant new forms, and the fascination of culturally diverse subject matter have injected a much-needed vitality into late twentieth-century English literature. If the term 'English book' is used to mean, not 'a book written by an English person', but 'a book written in English', there can be no question that the discovery of these new English books has been amazingly fortuitous for the British public and, we hope, for those reading this essay.

Reference section

Abbey Theatre, Dublin
The home of the Irish National Theatre Society from 1904 until a fire destroyed the building in 1951. The rebuilt Abbey remains a significant force in contemporary Irish theatre. The Society, usually known by the name of its theatre, grew from a fusion of the Irish National Dramatic Company, led by the actor W. G. Fay, and the Irish Literary Theatre founded by the poet ▷ W. B. Yeats, his friend ▷ Lady Gregory and others. The time was propitious: there was an intense national feeling in Ireland and an accompanying literary revival; Europe was undergoing the awakening influences of ▷ Ibsen and ▷ Strindberg; Yeats was a major poet with strong interest in the drama. Consequently the Abbey Theatre was a focus for creative energies which made it a unique institution in the history of the English-speaking theatre. However, the movement was neither the mere mouthpiece of Irish patriotism, nor just a vehicle for European fashions. Though Ibsen was a stimulus and dominated at least one of the Irish dramatists (Edward Martyn), its most outstanding contributor, ▷ J. M. Synge, was in reaction against Ibsen, as was Yeats himself. Neither of them tolerated the prejudices of the more radical nationalists. Synge's masterpiece, ▷ *The Playboy of the Western World*, caused a riot in the theatre when it was produced there in 1907. Yeats used verse of increasing vigour and austerity in a renewal of poetic drama that ranked the Abbey with the most interesting experimental theatres of the time in Europe – the Théâtre Libre in Paris and the Freie Bühne in Berlin. The heroic period of the Abbey Theatre ended with Synge's death and Yeats' retirement from its management in 1909; but under Lennox Robinson the Abbey remained a theatre of distinction. Its most notable playwright after that time was ▷ Sean O'Casey.

▷ Irish literature in English.

Bib: Mikhail, E. H. (ed.), *The Abbey Theatre: Interviews and Recollections*

Abelard, Peter (1079–1142)
Philosopher, scholar and author who taught at the University of Paris early in the 12th century. At the height of his fame he eloped with his pupil, Heloise, niece of one of the most powerful canons of Notre Dame. She bore their son Astrolabe and, to appease the anger of her uncle, Abelard proposed that they should be secretly married; open marriage was out of the question as it would obstruct Abelard's career in the Church. The marriage took place against Heloise's wishes, for she did not want her lover to risk his future prospects for her sake, and she refused to admit to it when challenged to do so. Heloise became a nun at Agenteuil and her uncle took his revenge on Abelard by causing him to be castrated. A correspondence, later famed, ensued between the separated couple. Abelard told the story of his love affair in his *Historia Calamitatum*. Abelard continued his career as a teacher but, at the instigation of Bernard of Clairvaux, he was eventually condemned for heresy (1141). Abelard died in 1141, Heloise in 1164. Their love affair became legendary and more recent literary treatments include Pope's poem *Eloisa to Abelard* (1717) and George Moore's novel *Héloise and Abelard* (1921). Helen Waddell has written a novelistic account of Abelard's life, *Peter Abelard* (1933). **Bib**: Radice, B. (ed.), *The Letters of Abelard and Eloise*.

Abergavenny, Frances Neville (?–d 1576)
Devotional writer. She wrote a collection of prayers which were originally intended for her daughter's personal use, but which were published in the first and fifth parts of Thomas Bentley's *Momument of Matrones* (1582). The prayers are written about essentially female experiences, such as childbirth. Frances Neville's writing is part of an expanding group of Renaissance women's writing which may be read both as an example of private devotion, as well as for its more general account of how women lived at that time.

Abolition literature
Literature directed towards the abolition of slavery. In Britain slave trading became a *cause célèbre* in 1788, was outlawed in 1807, and made a capital offence in 1824. While most people are aware of the anti-slavery writing in America, Harriet Beecher Stowe's *Uncle Tom's Cabin* (1852) being a prime example, similar literature in England is often neglected. The most important abolitionist in Britain during this period was ▷ William Wilberforce. Amongst other writers the most notable to write abolitionist texts are ▷ Mary Wollstonecraft, Elizabeth Benger, ▷ Hannah More, ▷ Henry Brougham, and ▷ Susannah Watts.

▷ Prince, Mary.

Abrahams, Peter (b 1919)
Novelist. Born in South Africa, which he left in 1939. After two years working as a sailor he lived in England (1941–56) and in France (1948–50) before moving to Jamaica in 1956. He has worked as an editor, journalist and broadcaster. His novels are all set in Africa (with the exception of *This Island Now*, 1966, set in Jamaica), and are concerned with social and political issues, particularly racial oppression. *Wild Conquest* (1950) deals with the historical theme of the Great Trek. *Dark Testament* (1942) is a collection of stories. His other novels are: *Song of the City* (1945); *Mine Boy* (1946); *The Path of Thunder* (1948); *A Wreath for Udomo* (1956); *A Night of Their Own* (1965); *The View from Coyaba* (1985); *Pressure Drop* (1991); *Revolution, No* 9 (1992). His non-fiction

includes: *Return to Goli* (1953); *Tell Freedom: Memories of Africa* (1954) and *Jamaica: an Island Mosaic* (1957).
Bib: Ensor, R., *The Novels of Peter Abrahams and the Rise of Nationalism in Africa*.

***Absalom and Achitophel* (1681)**
A ▷ satire in heroic couplets by ▷ John Dryden, allegorizing the political crisis of the last years of ▷ Charles II in terms of the Old Testament story of King David and his rebellious son Absalom (2 *Samuel* 13–19) (▷ Bible). Charles had no legitimate son and his heir was his brother James, Duke of York, a Catholic (▷ Catholicism), whose succession was feared by many as a menace to the ▷ Church of England and the liberty of Parliament. The Whigs, led by Anthony Ashley Cooper, the Earl of ▷ Shaftesbury, introduced a Bill excluding James from the throne and substituting Charles' illegitimate son, the ▷ Duke of Monmouth. Dryden wrote his poem at the king's suggestion, in order to influence the public against the Whigs. His handling of the biblical story glamorized the king, by paralleling his licentiousness with that of the patriarch David, and represented the Whigs as anarchic enemies of God's anointed. Monmouth becomes Absalom, Shaftesbury becomes the evil tempter Achitophel, the Duke of Buckingham appears as Zimri, and ▷ Titus Oates as Corah. Part II, which was published in 1682, is mainly by ▷ Nahum Tate, but includes a vivid passage by Dryden (ll 412–509) satirizing the poets Settle and ▷ Shadwell under the names Doeg and Og.

Abse, Dannie (b 1923)
Poet. Abse was born in Cardiff, and trained as a doctor in Cardiff and London. His volumes of verse include: *After Every Green Thing* (1949); *Tenants of the House* (1957); *A Small Desperation* (1968); *Selected Poems* (1970); *Way Out in the Centre* (1981); *Collected Poems, 1948–1976* (1977); *Ask the Bloody Horse* (1986); *White Coat, Purple Coat: Poems 1948–1988* (1989); *Remembrance of Crimes Past: Poems 1986–1989* (1990); and *On the Evening Road* (1994). He has also written novels, plays, and autobiographical material.

Absence
A term used in a variety of modern critical theories. The argument is that what is present in a text is, to a large extent, determined by features which are absent from immediate notice. For example, for ▷ psychoanalytic critics, what an author writes is determined not by what is immediately present to his or her consciousness, but by unconscious forces. However, it is in recent Marxist and ▷ deconstructionist theory that the idea has had the biggest impact. For the Marxists ▷ Louis Althusser and Pierre Macherey, a literary text is shaped by ideologies which the author often fails to understand or control. Thus, though literary texts allow us to see a pattern of ideological assumptions in reading and criticism, these often have no presence in the text itself. Althusser and Macherey note that this replicates a process experienced at a personal level where assumptions which profoundly shape a person's behaviour are often not recognised by the person who holds them. In this they were influenced by the work of the psychoanalyst ▷ Jacques Lacan (▷ interpellation).

The term absence is also used by ▷ Jacques Derrida and his fellow deconstructionists to denote what is for them the normal, fundamental condition of writing. This is the absence of ultimate truths or grounds of belief. Deconstructionists hold that all writing covers over these absences with assumptions or illusions about stable, grounding presences like, for example, God or the invincibility of human reason. But it is the ultimate absence of these things which leads language into a series of ▷ aporia and metaphorical ▷ displacements and equivocations which try to conceal this. For deconstructionists writing is always shaped by absence and plunged, therefore, into a world of ▷ difference.
Bib: Macherey, P., *A Theory of Literary Production*; Derrida, J., *Writing and Difference*.

Absurd, Theatre of the
▷ Theatre of the Absurd.

Achebe, Chinua (b 1930)
Nigerian novelist, poet and ▷ short-story writer. Born Albert Chinualumogu in Ogidi, East Central State, his mother tongue is Ibo, but he studied English from an early age and in 1953 graduated in English Literature from University College, Ibadan. He has worked in radio, publishing, journalism and as an academic, visiting universities in the U.S.A. In his five novels he has successfully incorporated African idioms and patterns of thought in a lucid English prose style. *Things Fall Apart* (1958), with its title drawn from ▷ W. B. Yeats' poem 'The Second Coming', explores a principal African dilemma: the destruction of the indigenous culture by European influence. It concerns Okonkwo, a village leader whose inflexible adherence to tradition cannot withstand the influence of white missionaries. *No Longer At Ease* (1960) continues the theme of the conflict of African and European values, but in the urban context of Lagos in the 1950s. *Arrow of God* (1964) returns to tribal society, but at an earlier stage of colonialism, in the 1920s, while *A Man of the People* (1966) is again set in Lagos, with direct reference to the turbulent political events following Nigerian independence in 1960. His most recent novel, *Anthills of the Savannah*, was published in

1987. He has published two volumes of short stories, *The Sacrificial Egg* (1962) and *Girls at War* (1972) and two volumes of poetry: *Beware Soul-Brother and Other Poems* (1971) and *Christmas in Biafra and Other Poems* (1973). He also writes children's stories.
Bib: Lindfors, B., and Innes, C. L. (ed.), *Achebe*.

Ackroyd, Peter (b 1949)
Novelist, poet and critic. Born in London and educated at Cambridge University, he has been literary editor of the ▷ *Spectator* and a reviewer of books, television and cinema for *The Times* and the *Sunday Times*. His first novel was *The Great Fire of London* (1982), followed by *The Last Testament of Oscar Wilde* (1983), which took the form of the fictional diaries of ▷ Wilde during his tragic last years in Paris, and won the Somerset Maugham award. *Hawksmoor* (1985) interweaves a police investigation in contemporary east London with a narrative set during the great plague of the 17th century, in which the architects Hawksmoor and Wren appear; the novel won both the Guardian Fiction Award and the Whitbread Prize for the best novel. *Dan Lemo and the Limehouse Golem* (1994), set in 1880s London, also involves historical characters in a mystery story and is written partly in dialogue. *Chatterton* (1987) is in part literary detective-story (in which it resembles ▷ A.S. Byatt's *Possession*) and combines historical pastiche (also a notable feature of *Hawksmoor*) with black comedy and elements of the sentimental and grotesque. *First Light* (1989) stages a confrontation between science and magic through the story of an archaeological dig in Dorset; *English Music* (1992), is a novel about Englishness and artistic traditions and *The House of Doctor Dee* (1993) a supernatural story centred on a house in London and the past. Ackroyd has published three volumes of poetry: *London Lickpenny* (1973); *Country Life* (1978) and *The Diversions of Purley* (1987). His non-fiction includes: *Notes for a New Culture: An Essay on Modernism* (1976); *Dressing Up: Transvestism and Drag: The History of an Obsession* (1979); *Ezra Pound and his World* (1980); *T.S. Eliot* (1984) (which won the Whitbread Prize for biography); *Dickens* (1990).

Acrostic
A literary game in which the initial letters of the lines of a poem spell a word when read downwards in order.

Kind sister! aye, this third name says you are;
Enchanted has it been the Lord knows where.
And may it taste to you like good old wine,
Take you to real happiness and give
Sons, daughters and a home like honied hive.

The initial letters spell 'Keats'; and it is the third verse of an acrostic poem to Georgiana Augusta Keats, by her brother-in-law ▷ John Keats. A double acrostic can also be read downwards with the last letters of each line.

Act
In drama: a division of a play; acts are sometimes subdivided into scenes. The ancient Greeks did not use divisions into acts; the practice was started by the Romans and the poet-critic ▷ Horace (1st century BC) in his *Ars Poetica* laid down the principle that the number of acts should be five. Since the renaissance of classical learning in the 16th century, most dramatists have used act divisions, and many have obeyed Horace's precepts. All ▷ Shakespeare's plays are divided into acts and scenes in modern editions, but it is certain that he did not write them in labelled scenes, and uncertain whether he thought in terms of acts; some of the first printed versions of his plays show act divisions and some do not. In the 17th century plays were divided into 5 acts as suggested by Horace, since then dramatists have used 3 acts.

Act of Settlement (1701)
An ▷ Act of Parliament excluding the heirs of the deposed Catholic monarch ▷ James II, and all other Catholics (▷ Catholicism) from the throne. The Act supplemented the ▷ Bill of Rights of 1689, which in turn confirmed in law events of the ▷ Glorious Revolution of 1688. The Act of Settlement conveyed the succession to the ▷ Protestant German House of Hanover. It was passed following the death of ▷ Queen Anne's only surviving child, the Duke of Gloucester, in 1701, and in anticipation that she would die childless, as in fact she did. In this case the throne would revert to James I's granddaughter Sophia, the Electress of Hanover and nearest Protestant relation to the ▷ Stuarts, and to her heirs, rather than to James II's Catholic son. Thus, the Act confirmed the concept of a constitutional monarchy, overriding the superior hereditary rights of James' son, who became known as the ▷ Old Pretender. In addition, the Act stipulated that the monarch must belong to the ▷ Church of England, that he or she must not leave the country without the permission of Parliament, nor involve the country in wars to defend the territories of foreign monarchs, nor appoint foreigners to Government posts. Furthermore, it provided for judges to receive fixed salaries, and prohibited their removal without the action of Parliament, except in the case of an offence proved in a court of law. These provisions assisted the separation of powers between the monarchy, Parliament and the judiciary, which ▷ Locke had thought essential to liberty.

Acting, The profession of
Acting began to achieve recognition as a

profession in the reign of Elizabeth I. The important date is the building of The Theatre – the first theatre in England – by James Burbage in 1576. It was followed by many others in London, and theatres soon became big business. Previously, actors had performed where they could, especially in inn yards and the halls of palaces, mansions, and colleges. They continued to do so, but the existence of theatres gave them a base and (though they still required an official licence) independence such as they badly needed in order to win social recognition.

Until the mid-16th century acting was practised by many kinds of people: ordinary townsmen at festivals, wandering entertainers, boys and men from the choirs of the great churches, and members of the staffs of royal or aristocratic households. It was from these last that the professional actors emerged. They still wore the liveries – uniforms and badges – of the great households, but the connection was now loose (good performers could transfer from one household to another) and was chiefly a means of procuring a licence to perform. This licence was essential because the City of London, around which dramatic activity concentrated, feared the theatre as providing centres of infection for the recurrent plague epidemics (which from time to time sent the companies away on tour) and disliked acting as a morally harmful and anomalous way of life. Moreover, the royal court, which favoured the stage, was nonetheless on guard against it as a potential source of sedition. Censorship and licensing, however, had the advantage of helping to distinguish the serious performers from the vulgar entertainers.

By the time of Elizabeth's death two great companies were dominant: the Lord Chamberlain's Men, for whom ▷ Shakespeare wrote, and the Lord Admiral's Men, headed by the leading actor of the day, Edward Alleyn. Women did not perform; their parts were taken by boys who enlisted as apprentices. Companies of boy actors from the choirs of St Paul's and the Chapels Royal also had prestige (see *Hamlet* II.2), especially in the 1570s. The establishment of the profession owed most to the dramatists, but much to the energy of actor-managers and theatre proprietors such as Philip Henslowe, Edward Alleyn, James Burbage, and his son Richard.

Actresses were allowed to perform after the Restoration of the monarchy (1660). The status of the profession continued to rise, aided by the theatre's ceasing to be the entertainment of all classes and becoming a fashionable pleasure of the London West End. In the 18th century the genius and culture of David Garrick greatly enhanced the prestige of the profession. From his time on, there is a long roll of great acting names. The first actor to be knighted was ▷ Henry Irving. Radical theatrical developments in the 20th century have challenged the traditional relationship between an actor and the audience, and the growth of improvised theatre has widened the actor's performance skills. ▷ Konstantin Stanislavsky's theories of acting, ▷ Antonin Artaud's ▷ Theatre of Cruelty and ▷ Bertolt Brecht's practice of *Verfremdungseffekt* (▷ alienation effect) have had a profound impact on the acting profession this century. More recently, actors have been seriously affected by the more material conditions of decline in public funding for theatres.
▷ Theatres; R.S.C.; Littlewood, Joan; Olivier, Laurence.

Adam Bede (1859)
A novel by ▷ George Eliot. The setting is a village in the English Midlands and the events take place at the beginning of the 19th century. Adam Bede is the village carpenter, a young man of stern morals and great strength of character; he is in love with Hetty Sorrel, the vain and frivolous niece of a farmer, Martin Poyser. She is seduced by the village squire. Another principal character is the young and beautiful Dinah Morris, a Methodist preacher whom Adam marries after Hetty has been transported for the murder of her child. The novel belongs to the early phase of George Eliot's art when her principal subject was the rural civilization which had been the background of her youth; the fine parts of the novel are those scenes, such as the Poyser household, which are directly concerned with this way of life.

Adam, Robert (1728–92)
Architect. His work is representative of the middle period of ▷ Augustan taste, as the earlier period of it is expressed in the buildings of ▷ Christopher Wren and ▷ John Vanbrugh. The earlier period was bold and dramatic in its display of shapes and ornaments; the Adam period was graceful and delicate. He was a particularly fine interior designer and is famous for the designs of his ceilings and mantelpieces. His taste was much influenced by ancient Roman architecture in Italy, for instance the ruins of the town of Pompeii and the palace of the Emperor Diocletian (AD 245–313) at Spalato (Split). The last he used as the pattern for a fine urban development (demolished in 1936) overlooking the Thames in London; he carried it out with the help of his brother James, and thus called it the Adelphi from the Greek for 'brothers'. His work in London, like most good 18th-century architecture there, has been ruined or destroyed, but Edinburgh has preserved some of his best street architecture and a number of country houses survive, either designed throughout by him or ornamented in part. These include Harewood House (Yorkshire), Mersham-le-Hatch (Kent), Syon House (near London) and Kenwood (Hampstead, London).

Adams, Sarah Flower (1805–48)
Poet, journalist and author of the hymn 'Nearer My God to Thee'. A close friend of poet Percy Bysshe Shelley (1792–1822), Adams continued to follow the ideals of ▷ Romanticism in direct contrast to the new sociological aesthetic espoused by writers such as ▷ Thomas Carlyle and ▷ Charles Dickens. She is linked with the influential but eccentric and eventually discredited school of poets satirized by ▷ William Aytoun as the ▷ 'Spasmodics'. She is chiefly remembered for *Vivia Perpetua* (1841), a dramatic poem about the life and death of an early Christian martyr. An early champion of women's rights, she insisted on a 'no housekeeping' pact with her husband and, at the age of eighteen, broke the record for the ascent of Ben Lomond by a woman.

▷ Women's Movement.

Bib: Leighton, A., *Victorian Women Poets: Writing Against the Heart*; Leighton, A. and Reynolds, M. (eds.), *An Anthology of Victorian Women Poets.*

Adcock, Fleur (b 1934)
Poet and translator. Born and educated in New Zealand, Adcock has lived in Britain since 1963. Her volumes of poetry include: *The Eye of the Hurricane* (1964); *Tigers* (1967); *High Tide in the Garden* (1971); *The Scenic Route* (1974) and *The Inner Harbour* (1970). In 1982 she edited the *Oxford Book of Contemporary New Zealand Poetry* and the *Faber Book of 20th Century Women's Poetry*, and more recent works include *The Incident Book* (1986) and *Time-Zones* (1991). A volume of her *Selected Poems* appeared in 1983. She has also translated medieval Latin poetry and Greek poetry.

Addison, Joseph (1672–1719)
Poet, politician and essayist, Addison is now best known for his contributions to two periodicals, ▷ *The Tatler* (founded by ▷ Richard Steele) and ▷ *The Spectator* (which he co-edited with Steele). *The Tatler* appeared three times a week in 1709–11, and *The Spectator* was issued daily, 1711–12 and 1714. *The Tatler* and *The Spectator* were designed as coffee-house periodicals, aiming to elevate the level of conversation by discussion of manners, morals, literature and philosophy. Addison claimed that they were enormously influential, as each printed copy could be passed around at least 20 people. The character of ▷ Sir Roger de Coverley, a country gentleman, was largely created by Addison.

Addison's first literary success was a poem, *The Campaign* (1705), celebrating the victory of ▷ Blenheim the previous year. His classical tragedy *Cato* (1713) was also a contemporary success. In his political career, Addison was a Whig Member of Parliament, and, briefly, a Secretary of State.

Bib: Samuel Johnson's life of Addison, in *Lives of the Poets*; Smithers, D., *The Life of Joseph Addison*; Otten, Robert M., *Joseph Addison.*

Addresser/addressee
Terms used in language theory to denote the sender and receiver of verbal messages. In his influential essay 'Closing Statement: Linguistics and Poetics' (1960), ▷ Roman Jakobson argues that to be effective, addresser and addressee must share a context, a code and a channel of communication.

Admiral's Men, The Lord
A company of Elizabethan actors under the protection of Lord Howard of Effingham, who became Lord Admiral in 1585. They are first heard of in 1574, and were at their height in the 1590s, when they were led by one of the two chief actors of the time, ▷ Edward Alleyn, and when their only rivals were the ▷ Lord Chamberlain's Men, who were led by the other, ▷ Richard Burbage. As Burbage was ▷ Shakespeare's leading actor, so Alleyn and the Admiral's Men were associated with ▷ Christopher Marlowe. The chief financial management of the company was under Alleyn himself and his father-in-law, ▷ Philip Henslowe, a financier. In the reign of ▷ James I (1603–25) the company came under the patronage of his eldest son, Prince Henry; and on his death under that of James' son-in-law, the Elector of the Palatinate. The company came to an end in 1628.

***Adonais* (1821)**
An elegy in ▷ Spenserian stanzas by ▷ Percy Bysshe Shelley, mourning the death of ▷ John Keats, which had been attributed to a violent attack on Keats' poem ▷ *Endymion* in the ▷ *Quarterly Review* (1818). In his preface, Shelley compares the brutal insensitivity of the reviewer to that of the wild boar which killed the mythical Adonis – hence the poem's title. Shelley was not well acquainted with Keats and the inspiration of the poem is fundamentally literary. Based in part on the *lament for Adonis* by the Sicilian-Greek poet Bion (1st century BC), the poem is elaborately rhetorical. While Keats is depicted as a symbol of creativity in a hostile world, the poem is in many important respects about Shelley himself.

***Advancement of Learning, The* (1605)**
A philosophical treatise by ▷ Francis Bacon published in 1605 in English, and expanded in a Latin version entitled *De Augmentis Scientiarium* published in 1623.

The purpose of the book is to suggest ways in which the pursuit of knowledge can be encouraged, and the methods of observation and recording of both natural and human phenomena improved. To this end, Bacon's work proposes nothing less than a taxonomy of all knowledge, a proposition strikingly familiar to that advanced by the French Encyclopaedists of the 16th century.

Perhaps the most influential aspect of *The Advancement* is the methodology that Bacon employs. In surveying all fields of knowledge Bacon offers a form of catalogue of existing fields of enquiry. This attempt at classification, whereby branches of knowledge are grouped together under common headings, relies on a system of particularization. In each subject considered, Bacon argues that the first step is the fresh observation of the detail of the phenomena. Once the detail, or particularities, had been assimilated it would become possible, through the process of induction, to assert the general propositions under which groups of phenomena could be considered. This method signalled both a break from what Bacon considered to be the traditional methods of enquiry (which involved deduction from generalized propositions) and the re-examination of observable phenomena through the process of experimentation.

As a theorist of scientific method (rather than as an experimenter in his own right) Bacon was to have considerable influence on the early founders of ▷ The Royal Society, particularly in the area of language reform. On the question of language, and the idea of an appropriate language for scientific discourse, *The Advancement of Learning* is a key text. At the same time, the importance of language to Bacon's project necessitated an exploration of poetic language which was to be influential for poets of the later 17th century, in particular ▷ Abraham Cowley.

▷ Dissociation of Sensibility.

Adventures of Captain Singleton
▷ *Captain Singleton, Adventures of.*

***Adventures of Harry Richmond, The* (1871)**
A novel by ▷ George Meredith.

***Adventures of Philip, The* (1862)**
The last completed novel of ▷ William Makepeace Thackeray, illustrated by him and published serially in ▷ *The Cornhill Magazine* during 1861 and 1862. Reiterating many of the themes of earlier novels such as ▷ *Pendennis* and ▷ *The Newcomes* it is generally regarded as evidence of its author's failing talent.

▷ Reviews and periodicals.

Adventures of Roderick Random, The
▷ *Roderick Random, The Adventures of*

Advice literature
A branch of writing related to ▷ conduct literature, but less formal, in which the author offers advice on behaviour, often to a named individual such as a son or daughter. The form developed during the late 17th century, and became increasingly popular during the 18th, when it was most often directed towards the female sex, although there are notable exceptions, such as ▷ Lord Chesterfield's *Letters* to his son and godson.

Debates about the status and nature of women altered advice literature in the 18th century. Women were still addressed as maids, wives or widows, but the debate about friendship in ▷ marriage inevitably brought up the question of the education of women (▷ education); and this fed into debates on conduct. The changes in advice on conduct are subtle, and the literature continued to advise the woman to adapt herself to circumstances, and particularly to her husband. For example, a relatively conservative advice book, *The Lady's New-Year's Gift: or, Advice to a Daughter* by George Savile, Marquis of Halifax, concentrates on the need for a woman to adapt her feelings. He recommends 'wise use of everything [one] may dislike in a husband' to transform that which might breed 'aversion' to be 'very supportable'. But he hopes that his daughter gets 'a Wise Husband, one that by knowing how to be Master . . . will not let you feel the weight of it'. In *Letters Moral and Entertaining* (1729–33), ▷ Elizabeth (Singer) Rowe has a character note the relationship between feelings and conduct when she says, 'I was sensible of the delusion and how easily vice betrays an unguarded mind.' ▷ Mary Wollstonecraft's (early) ▷ *Thoughts on the Education of Daughters* (1787) adds the perception that feelings and conduct are linked to the argument for education. She writes, 'in a comfortable situation a cultivated mind is necessary to render a woman contented; and in a miserable one it is her only consolation.'

The tradition of advice literature underlies many of the novels of the 18th and 19th centuries, among them those of ▷ Samuel Richardson and ▷ Jane Austen.

▷ Feminism; Women, status of; Women's movement, The.

Bib: Jones, Vivian, *Women in the Eighteenth Century*.

Aelfric (c 955–c 1010)
Scholar and great prose writer who was a monk of Winchester (under Bishop Aethelwold), and taught at Cerne Abbas (987–1002) before being made abbot of a new foundation at Eynsham, near Oxford. His works include two series of homilies, saints' lives, pastoral letters, translations from the Old Testament, and educational aids including a Latin grammar and a Latin textbook in dialogue form. The rhythmical prose style developed by Aelfric, above all in his *Lives of Saints*, shares some features of ▷ alliterative verse, being patterned around two-stress phrases, often linked by alliteration. The status of his work is reflected

in the number of manuscripts which survive (some from the 12th century). The scope of Aelfric's work and his pedagogical interests are a testimony of the cultural renaissance inspired by the Benedictine Reform movement of the tenth century; the status of his work is attested by the number of manuscripts which survive (some copied in the 12th century).
Bib: Godden, M. and Lapidge, M. (eds.), *The Cambridge Guide to Old English Literature*.

Aeneas
Hero of the Latin epic ▷ *Aeneid* by ▷ Virgil. Traditions about him had existed long before Virgil's poem. He was the son of Anchises and the goddess ▷ Aphrodite, and the son-in-law of Priam, king of ▷ Troy. In ▷ Homer's *Iliad* (v) he is represented as the chief of the Trojans and one of the most formidable defenders of Troy against the Greeks. Other records stated that after the fall of Troy, he set out to seek a new kingdom with some of the surviving Trojans, and eventually settled in central Italy. By Virgil's time, the Romans were already worshipping Aeneas as the father of their race.

Aeneid
An ▷ epic poem by the Roman poet ▷ Virgil (70–19BC). The poem tells the story of ▷ Aeneas, from his flight from ▷ Troy during the confusion of its destruction by the Greeks to his establishment as king of the Latins in central Italy and his death in battle with the Etruscans. The poem thus begins at a point near where ▷ Homer left off in the ▷ *Iliad*, and its description of the wanderings of Aeneas is parallel to the description of the wanderings of Odysseus in Homer's ▷ *Odyssey*. It is divided into 12 books, of which the second, fourth and sixth are the most famous: the second describes the destruction of Troy; the fourth gives the tragedy of Queen Dido of Carthage, who dies for love of Aeneas; the sixth shows his descent to the underworld and the prophetic visions of those who are to build the greatness of Rome.

Virgil wished to relate the Rome he knew, a settled and luxurious civilization which threatened to degenerate into complacent mediocrity, to her heroic past, and to inspire her with a sense of her great destiny in world history. The *Aeneid* is thus a central document for Roman culture, and inasmuch as Roman culture is the basis of the culture of Western Europe, it has remained a central document for European culture too.

The most notable English translations of the *Aeneid* are those by the Scottish poet ▷ Gavin Douglas (1553) and by ▷ John Dryden (1697). Henry Howard, ▷ Earl of Surrey translated Books II and III into the earliest example of English blank verse.

Aeolian
From Aeolus, god of the winds in ancient Greek myth (▷ Classical Mythology). An Aeolian harp is a stringed instrument, placed across a window or outside a house, so that the wind causes the strings to vibrate and make music; an example may be seen at Dove Cottage in the Lake District. The poet ▷ Samuel Taylor Coleridge possessed one; hence his poem *The Eolian Harp* (1795) and references to the instrument in *Dejection* (1802). For him, it symbolized his conception of the poet 'played upon' by Nature.

Aeolists
In ▷ Swift's satire ▷ *A Tale of a Tub* (1704), a fictional sect of believers in direct inspiration: 'The learned Aeolists maintain the original cause of all things to be wind. . .'. Swift's satire is an attack on all pretensions to truth not in accord with right reason or properly constituted authority, and the Aeolists, in Section VIII, are a kind of climax to the work. He associates them particularly with the ▷ Dissenters, who based their religious faith on belief in direct intimations from the Holy Spirit to the individual soul; Jack, who represents ▷ Presbyterianism in the *Tale*, is a leader of the sect.

Aeschylus (525–456 BC)
One of the great tragic poets of ancient Greece. Only seven of his 70 plays survive; of these the best known are *Agamemnon*, *Choephori* and *Eumenides*, making up the *Oresteia* trilogy. Aeschylus is the great starting point of all European tragedy. Shelley's masterpiece ▷ *Prometheus Unbound* (1820) was written as a kind of sequel to Aeschylus' *Prometheus Bound*.
▷ Greek Literature.

Aesop
A Greek composer of animal ▷ fables of the 6th century BC. He probably did not write them down, but fables purporting to be his were collected by later classical writers, and they and imitations of them have had a wide popularity in European literature. The most notable Aesopian fable in English literature is Chaucer's ▷ *Nun's Priest's Tale* of the Cock and the Fox in the ▷ *Canterbury Tales*.

Aestheticism
A movement of the late 19th century, influenced by the Pre-Raphaelites and John Ruskin, but its immediate inspiration was the writings of the Oxford don Walter Pater. His two most influential books were *Studies in the History of the Renaissance* (1873) and *Marius the Epicurean* (1885). These show him as a ritualistic moralist, laying emphasis on the value of ecstatic experience. Apart from Pater and his predecessors, the aesthetes owed much to the

current French doctrine of *'L'Art pour l'Art'* (Art for Art's Sake) but they retained, if sometimes not obviously, a typically English concern with moral values and issues. The outstanding aesthete was ▷ Oscar Wilde (1865–1900), and a characteristic aesthetic product was his novel *The Picture of Dorian Gray* (1891). As the movement lacked a programme, writers of very different characters were influenced by it: the naturalistic novelist ▷ George Moore; the poet Lionel Johnson who was a Catholic convert; Swinburne, a main channel for the art for art's sake doctrine; ▷ W. B. Yeats, the Celtic revivalist. A characteristic aestheticist periodical was ▷ *The Yellow Book* (1894–7), so called because French novels, conventionally considered 'daring', were printed on yellow paper. Its main illustrator was ▷ Aubrey Beardsley, whose line drawings were notorious for their sensuality. The excesses and affectations of the movement's adherents were much ridiculed in ▷ *Punch*.

Bib: Aldington, R. (ed.), *The Religion of Beauty: Selections from the Aesthetes*; Jackson, H., *The 1890s*.

Aesthetics

In general terms, the philosophical investigation of beauty, particularly artistic beauty. It is a term not often used in current critical discourse, partly because it tends to be associated with the idea of art-for-art's-sake. The word acquired this colouring through its association with the late 19th-century movement ▷ Aestheticism.

Affective fallacy, The

An influential phrase coined by the leading American New Critics W. K. Wimsatt and Monroe C. Beardsley in 1954. The affective fallacy is the belief that literature can be evaluated by assessing how it affects readers emotionally. Wimsatt and Beardsley rejected the importance of affective reactions because, they believed, these were too often contaminated by ignorance or inaccurate understanding. Instead, they believed, criticism should be based upon the analysis of so-called 'objective' features like the identification of irony and structure. Approaches to literature by way of reader-response criticism, however, are more highly regarded today.

▷ Intentional Fallacy.

Bib: Wimsatt, W., *The Verbal Icon: Studies in the Meaning of Poetry*.

Ages, Golden, Silver, etc.

The Greek poet Hesiod (8th century BC), in *Works and Days*, writes of an ideal golden age in the past, comparable to the Garden of Eden; from this period, he considered that there had been a progressive decline through the silver, bronze, and heroic ages until his own time. ▷ Virgil, in his fourth *Eclogue*, writes of a child who is to restore the golden age. This has sometimes been interpreted as a prophecy of the birth of Christ. ▷ Milton, in *On the Morning of Christ's Nativity* (1629), hopes that following Christ's birth, 'Time will run back and fetch the age of gold' (XIV. 135). The Restoration of ▷ Charles II led to suggestions that the golden age had been restored with his accession. But the image of the golden age remained a potent one, for poets, dramatists, historians, philosophers and others, among them ▷ Aphra Behn, whose ▷ pastoral poem *The Golden Age* (1684), is adapted from a translation of lines by the Italian poet Torquato Tasso (1544–95); and ▷ Pope, who laments the loss of the golden age in ▷ *Essays on Criticism* (line 478). The idea of a golden age is important in ▷ Utopian literature.

***Agnes Grey* (1847)**

A semi-autobiographical novel by ▷ Anne Brontë which first appeared under the ▷ pseudonym Acton Bell. Agnes is a rector's daughter who joins the household of the Bloomfield family to work as a ▷ governess. The vivid portrayal of the spoilt children owes much to Brontë's experience with the Ingham family, for whom she worked in 1839. Similarly, the portrait of Rosalie, the flirtatious daughter of the Murray family, draws on Brontë's experience working for the Robinsons (1841–5). The novel departs from autobiography in its later chapters, as the gentle and modest Agnes is united with the kind curate, Mr Weston, by whom she has three children.

Agnosticism

The term was invented by the biologist Thomas Huxley in 1869 to express towards religious faith the attitude which is neither of belief nor of disbelief (▷ atheism). In his own words, 'I neither affirm nor deny the immortality of man. I see no reason for believing it, but on the other hand I have no means of disproving it.' Agnosticism was widespread among writers between 1850 and 1914; it arose from the scientific thought of the time, especially that of Huxley himself, and that of another biologist, ▷ Charles Darwin.

Aguliar, Grace (1816–47)

Aguliar was born in Hackney, London, the eldest child of Spanish-Jewish parents. She is chiefly remembered today as a sentimental novelist and prose writer, although she was also a poet. She never married, and after her father's death she wrote for a profession, publishing several works on Judaism. *The Spirit of Judaism* (1842) was a controversial attack on the formalities of institutionalized religion, while *Women of Israel* (1845) and *The Jewish Faith* (1846) express a concern with the position of women within the faith. Her first novel, *Home Influence* (1847), was the only one to be published in her lifetime. Other novels include *The Mother's Recompense* (1851) and ▷ *Woman's Friendship* (1853).

Aidoo, Ama Ata (b 1942)
Ghanaian novelist, poet and playwright. Educated at the University of Ghana, she was for a time Secretary of Education for Ghana but has lived in Zimbabwe since 1983, where she has worked for the Ministry of Education and is chair of the Zimbabwe Women Writers Group. Her first novel, *Our Sister Killjoy or Reflections from a Black-Eyed Squint* (1978), uses a range of narrative techniques, including interpolated poetic commentary, the ironic use of a range of narrative voices, typographical effects and elements drawn from oral narration. The story of a Ghanaian woman who travels to Europe to encounter both racism and the appeal of affluence, it is a critique of racism and sexism, and an appeal for Africans to commit themselves to the development of their own countries. Here, as elswhere in her work, Aidoo challenges the portrayal of African women and of 'mother Africa' in the work of male African novelists such as ▷ Kofi Awoonor. *Changes: a Love Story* (1991) is similarly technically inventive. Her plays are *The Dilemma of a Ghost* (1965) and *Anowa* (1970); *No Sweetness Here* (1970) is a collection of short stories and *An Angry Letter in January* (1992) is a volume of poems. She has also written a historical study of the Asante kingdom.
Bib: James, A., *In Their Own Voices: Interviews with African Woman Writers.*

Aikin, Lucy (1781–1864)
Poet, biographer and children's author. Aikin lacked self-confidence as a creative writer, classifying herself as an editor or translator rather than as an author of original works. However, her *Epistles on Women* (1810) and *Memoirs of the Court of Queen Elizabeth* (1818) reveal that she was, respectively, a fine poet and adept political allegorist. She was acquainted with many other women authors of her age, and wrote a memoir of ▷ Joanna Baillie.
▷ Translation; Allegory.
Bib: Todd, J., *Dictionary of British Women Writers.*

Ainsworth, William Harrison (1805–82)
Novelist. His best novels are historical: *Jack Shepherd* (1839), *The Tower of London* (1840), *Guy Fawkes* (1841), *Old St Paul's* (1841), *Windsor Castle* (1843). He tended to idealize the heroic criminal, for example Dick Turpin in *Rookwood* (1834) and Jack Shepherd; this was a literary fashion in the 1830s and 1840s and censured by the ▷ Victorian novelist William Thackeray (1811–63) in his early reviews under the designation 'The Newgate School of novelists'. Ainsworth edited *Bentley's Magazine* 1840–2, *Ainsworth's Magazine* 1842–53 and *New Monthly Magazine* from 1853.
Bib: Ellis, S. M., *W. H. Ainsworth and his Friends*; Worth, G. J., *William Harrison Ainsworth.*

Akenside, Mark (1721–70)
Poet. Son of a butcher in Newcastle-upon-Tyne, and a physician by profession. He wrote the influential *The Pleasures of Imagination* (1744), a philosophical poem in Miltonic blank verse (▷ Milton, John). The assured reflective modulations of the poem influenced ▷ William Wordsworth's style in ▷ *The Prelude*, the subject matter of which – childhood impressions, the moral influence of landscape – is often the same. Akenside also wrote lyric poems and odes.
Bib: Houpt, C. H., *Mark Akenside: A Biographical and Critical Study.*

Albert of Saxe-Coburg-Gotha (1819–61)
Husband (with the title of Prince Consort) of Queen ▷ Victoria. They were cousins. The Queen was devoted to him and the marriage was of considerable political importance; Albert did much to shape the Queen's ideas of her political duties as a constitutional monarch who could not interfere directly in politics but could nonetheless exert great personal influence. ▷ The Great Exhibition of 1851 was organized on his suggestion.

Unfortunately, his foreign origin caused his influence to be regarded with considerable suspicion in Britain. His death was a cause of immense grief to the Queen; it led to her retirement from public appearances between 1861 and the Jubilee of her reign in 1887.

Albion
The most ancient name for Britain, used in Greek by Ptolemy and in Latin by Pliny. The word possibly derived from Celtic, but it was associated by the Romans with the Latin *albus* = white, referring to the white cliffs of Dover. From the ▷ Middle Ages on it has often been used poetically to stand for Britain, notably by William Blake, one of the main influences on Michael Horowitz's key poetry anthology, *Children of Albion* (1970).

***Alchemist, The* (1610)**
A comedy by ▷ Ben Jonson. The scene is a house in London during a visitation of the plague; its master, Lovewit, has taken refuge in the country, leaving his servant, Face, in charge. Face introduces two rogues: Subtle, a charlatan alchemist, and Dol Common, a whore. Together they collaborate in turning the house into a centre for the practice of alchemy in the expectation of attracting credulous clients who will believe that alchemical magic can bring them their heart's desire. Their expectations are realized, and their dupes are representative

social types. Sir Epicure Mammon dreams of limitless luxury and the satisfaction of his lust; the Puritans, Ananias and Tribulation Wholesome, hope to enrich their sect; Drugger, a tobacco merchant, wants prosperity for his business; Dapper, a lawyer's clerk, seeks a spirit to guarantee him success in gambling; Kastril, a young country squire, desires a rich husband for his sister (Dame Pliant) and knowledge of the secret of fashionable quarrelling. Only Pertinax Surly, a friend of Mammon, sees the fraudulence of the enterprise, but Face and his colleagues manage to turn the clients against him and he is routed. Each of the clients has to be deceived by a separate technique, depending on his peculiar brand of social credulity, and this requires swift changes of role by the cheats, especially Subtle. They are equal to all emergencies until Lovewit suddenly returns – a crisis which only Face survives. He expels Subtle and Common, and then wins over his master, who admires his ingenuity and is satisfied with the plunder, which includes Dame Pliant. The play is one of Jonson's best; it has energetic wit and extraordinary theatrical ingenuity. Moreover the characterization has behind it the force of Jonson's conviction that human folly is limitless and can be cured only by exposure and castigation.

Aldington, Richard (1892–1962)
Poet, critic and novelist, and key member of the early ▷ modernist ▷ Imagist group of poets. He was married to the poet ▷ Hilda Doolittle (H. D.) in 1913 (although they soon parted), and was a close friend of a number of central modernist figures, including ▷ D. H. Lawrence and, later, ▷ Lawrence Durrell (their correspondence was published in 1981 as *Literary Lifelines*). Publications include: *Images 1910–1915* (1915), *Collected Poems* (1928), *Death of a Hero* (1929) (a novel based upon his experiences of gas-attacks and shell-shock in the War), *The Colonel's Daughter* (1931) and *All Men are Enemies* (1933). Aldington was also an important biographer, author of *D. H. Lawrence: Portrait of a Genius, But...* (1950) and *Lawrence of Arabia: A Biographical Enquiry* (1955).

Aldiss, Brian (b 1925)
▷ Science Fiction.

Alexander, Mrs (Annie Hector, née French) (1825–1902)
Novelist, born in Dublin, who published over 45 novels, most of which revolve around young heroines seeking to reconcile love and financial security. They include: *Look Before You Leap* (1865), *Which Shall it Be* (1866), *The Wooing O't* (1873), *Her Dearest Foe* (1876), *The Freres* (1882), *The Admiral's Ward* (1883). *Kitty Costello* (1904) is partly autobiographical. Because of her husband's ill health and relatively early death (in 1875), she supported herself and her family by her writing.

Alexander, Sir William, Earl of Stirling (1567–1640)
Poet, dramatist, statesman, colonialist. Alexander's chief literary work was a collection of sonnets entitled *Aurora*, published in 1603. In addition to the composition of dramatic works (*The Tragedy of Darius* appeared in 1603), he accepted positions as tutor to ▷ Prince Henry, and Secretary of State for Scotland under ▷ Charles I. Alexander was also an early enthusiast for the foundation of colonies. In 1624 he published a work entitled *Encouragement to Colonies*, which was followed, in 1630, by *The Map and Description of New England*.

Alexandrine
A 12-syllable line of verse, possibly owing its name to the French medieval work, the *Roman d'Alexandre*. It is common in French poetry particularly of the classical period but unusual in English, where the commonest line length is of ten syllables. ▷ Michael Drayton used it in his long poem *Poly-Olbion* (1613–22), but its most famous use is in the last line of the Spenserian stanza, invented by ▷ Edmund Spenser for his ▷ *Faerie Queene*, and it was this form that was revived by the Romantic poets. One of the best examples is from ▷ Keats' ▷ 'The Eve of St Agnes':

Anon his heart revives: her vespers done,
Of all its wreathed pearls her hair she frees;
Unclasps her warmed jewels one by one;
Loosens her fragrant boddice; by degrees
Her rich attire creeps rustling to her knees;
Half-hidden, like a mermaid in sea-weed,
Pensive awhile she dreams awake, and sees,
In fancy, fair St Agnes in her bed,
But dares not look behind, or all the
charm is fled.

Alfred, King (848–99)
King of the West Saxons 871–99, famous for his eventually successful resistance to Viking threats to his realm and still more renowned for his institution of an educational programme to revive learning in his land and for his promotion of vernacular prose as an acceptable medium for the dissemination of Latin learning. The works credited to Alfred himself include translations of Boethius' *Consolation of Philosophy*, the *Pastoral Care* of Gregory the Great, and an important law code. His initiatives in the vernacular doubtless inspired others, but scholars no longer see any direct link between Alfred and the *Anglo-Saxon Chronicle*.
Bib: Godden, M. and Lapidge, M. (eds.), *The Cambridge Guide to Old English Literature*.

Alice's Adventures in Wonderland; Through the Looking-Glass
▷ Carroll, Lewis.

Alienation effect
Term, '*Verfremdungseffekt*', developed by the German dramatist ▷ Bertolt Brecht in his theatrical and theoretical writings. He demanded that his audiences should realize that they were not watching 'life' but a representation, and he urged that actor and audience alike should preserve a critical 'distance' from events on the stage.
▷ Defamiliarization.

***All for Love, Or the World Well Lost* (1678)**
Tragedy in blank verse by ▷ John Dryden, based on ▷ Shakespeare's *Antony and Cleopatra*, but modified in accordance with Dryden's concern for the principles of neo-classicism. Dryden concentrates on the last stage of Antony's career, after the Battle of Actium. Antony's general Ventidius, his wife Octavia, and his friend Dolabella, all plead with him to leave Cleopatra, and make peace with Caesar. Antony is on the point of complying, but then he is led to believe that Dolabella is his rival for Cleopatra's affections, and he rejects both Octavia and Cleopatra. The desertion of the Egyptian fleet, followed by a false report of Cleopatra's death, lead Antony to take his own life. He falls on his sword and dies in Cleopatra's arms, after which she kills herself with an asp. Dryden stages a meeting between Cleopatra and Octavia which does not take place in Shakespeare's version, and he softens some of Shakespeare's language. His play achieves economy, elegance, and fluency, but lacks the range of Shakespeare's. Nevertheless *All for Love* is a masterpiece of its kind, and generally considered to be Dryden's best play.

All the Year Round
A periodical published by ▷ Charles Dickens from 1859, in succession to ▷ *Household Words*, until his death in 1870. Novels which appeared in it in instalments included Dickens' own ▷ *A Tale of Two Cities* and ▷ *Great Expectations*, and *The Woman in White* and *The Moonstone* by ▷ Wilkie Collins.

Allegory
From the Greek, meaning 'speaker in other terms'. A way of representing thought and experience through images, by means of which (1) complex ideas may be simplified, or (2) abstract, spiritual, or mysterious ideas and experiences may be made immediate (but not necessarily simpler) by dramatization in fiction.

In both uses, allegory was most usual and natural as a medium of expression in the ▷ Middle Ages, ▷ Catholic doctrine prevailed as deeply as it did widely; even the physical structures of the universe and of man seemed to be living images of spiritual truth. The morality plays, notably ▷ *Everyman* (15th century), were practical applications of this doctrine to ordinary experience. But the tendency to see experience in allegorical terms extended to secular literature, for example the romances of sexual love, such as ▷ *The Romance of the Rose* (14th century) in part translated from the French by ▷ Chaucer. When Chaucer wrote a romance in which there was no overt allegory, *eg* ▷ *Troilus and Criseyde*, the allegorical spirit was still implicit within it (see C. S. Lewis, *Allegory of Love*). Such implicit allegory extended into much ▷ Renaissance drama, *eg* Shakespeare's ▷ *Henry IV, Parts I and II*.

In the Renaissance, however, explicit allegory, though still pervasive, was greatly complicated by the break-up of the dominant Catholic framework; various Christian doctrines competed with one another and with non-Christian ones such as ▷ neo-Platonism, and also with political theories. Thus in a work like Spenser's ▷ *Faerie Queene* religious, political and Platonic allegories are all employed, but intermittently and not with artistic coherence.

Since the 17th century deliberate and consistent allegory has continued to decline; yet the greatest of all English allegories, ▷ *The Pilgrim's Progress* by John Bunyan, is a 17th-century work. The paradox is explained by Bunyan's contact with the literature of the village sermon, which apparently continued to be conducted by a simple allegorical method with very little influence from the ▷ Reformation. Moreover allegory has continued into modern times, partly as an indispensable habit of explanation, partly in a suppressed form (*eg* the names of characters in Dickens' novels), and partly as a resource in the expression of mysterious psychological experience incommunicable in direct terms; here allegory merges with ▷ symbolism, from which, however, it needs to be distinguished. ▷ George Orwell's dystopian novel *Animal Farm* is an allegory of totalitarian society, and there has been a lively debate concerning the role of allegory centring on the work of ▷ Paul de Man, who wrote *Allegories of Reading* (1979) and *Blindness and Insight* (1983) in discussion of the subject.
Bib: Murrin, M., *The Veil of Allegory*.
▷ Fable.

***Allegro, L'* (c 1631)**
A poem by ▷ John Milton, published in 1645 though composed c 1631. The poem is a companion piece to ▷ *Il Penseroso*, and the title can be translated from the Italian as signifying the cheerful or happy individual. The poem's theme celebrates the active life of engagement with the world, as opposed to the reflective life depicted in *Il Penseroso*.

Allen, Charles Grant Blairfindie (1848–99)
Novelist, born in Canada, brought up there and in the USA and educated at Oxford. He is best-known for *The Woman Who Did* (1895), a ▷ New Woman novel in which the protagonist is opposed to marriage on principle, lives with the man she loves, but is left alone with a child after his death and meets a tragic end. In the 1870s he taught philosophy at the Government College in Jamaica, an experience which helped to promote his interest in questions of emancipation, a theme of many of his novels. A number of these have foreign settings, such as *In All Shades* (1886), set in Jamaica and *The Tents of Shem* (1891), an adventure story set in Algeria. He was influenced by the evolutionary theories of ▷ Herbert Spencer. His first novel was a satire, entitled *Philistia* (1884), and he wrote in a range of genres, including the detective story (*An African Millionaire*, 1897).

Alleyn, Edward (1566–1626)
Son of an innkeeper, Alleyn rose to become one of the two foremost tragic actors of the great age of English drama. In 1586 he was performing for Lord Worcester's Men; in 1592 he married the stepdaughter of the financier ▷ Philip Henslowe, and together they built up the prosperity of the ▷ Lord Admiral's Men. In this company he was celebrated for his performances of ▷ Christopher Marlowe's heroes: ▷ Tamburlaine, Faustus (▷ *Doctor Faustus*) and Barabas. He became the main owner of the ▷ Rose and the Fortune theatres, and a wealthy man by his speculation in land. He founded Dulwich College, to this day a leading public school. After the death of his first wife, he married the daughter of ▷ John Donne, the poet and Dean of St Paul's. His acting was highly praised by contemporary dramatists and other writers – ▷ Thomas Nashe, ▷ Thomas Heywood, and ▷ Ben Jonson among them – and was likened to that of the Roman actor ▷ Roscius.

▷ Acting, the profession of; Theatres.

Bib: Hosking, G. L., *Life and Times of Edward Alleyn*.

Allingham, Margery (1904–66)
Writer of ▷ detective fiction. One of the foremost women detective writers of the 20th century, Allingham's work is characteristic of the inter-war 'golden age' of detective fiction, along with the work of ▷ Agatha Christie, ▷ Ngaio Marsh and ▷ Dorothy L. Sayers. Like Christie's Poirot or Miss Marple, or Sayers' Lord Peter Wimsey, Allingham has a chief detective, Albert Campion (said to be modelled on Wimsey), who is however a rather enigmatic, mysterious character, working in a London full of atmosphere and populated by eccentrics. She began writing in the 1920s and continued until her death in 1966; her many novels include: *The Crime at Black Dudley* (1929); *Look to the Lady* (1931); *Police at the Funeral* (1931); *Sweet Danger* (1933); *Dancers in Mourning* (1937); *The Fashion in Shrouds* (1938); *The Case Book of Mr Campion* (1947); *The Tiger in the Smoke* (1952); *The Mind Readers* (1965).

Allingham, William (1824–89)
Poet, born in County Donegal, Ireland where he worked as a customs officer. He moved to Lymington in 1863 and became friends with ▷ Tennyson. Between 1874 and 1879 he edited ▷ *Fraser's Magazine*. In 1850 he published *Poems* which contains his best-known poem 'The Fairies' and the long poem 'The Music-Master', an idyll of young love set in an Irish village. Several volumes of poetry followed including *Day and Night Songs* (1854) and a verse novel of Irish life entitled *Laurence Bloomfield: or Rich and Poor* (1864), which is a plea for land reform and contains a moving account of the eviction of the population of a whole hamlet. His poetry was frequently illustrated by ▷ Dante Gabriel Rossetti, Arthur Hughes and Millais (1829–1896). His early poems are gathered together in the six-volume *Collected Poems* (1888–93) which contains some of his best work including 'The Dirty Old Man', 'George Levison, or, The School-fellows', 'The Wayside Well' and 'Wayconnell Tower'. A contemporary of George MacDonald and friends with ▷ Thomas Carlyle, Rossetti and Leigh Hunt (1784–1859), his *Diary* (1907) is an invaluable record of Victorian ▷ Aesthetic life. In 1874 he married Helen Paterson, a talented water colourist and illustrator of books such as ▷ Hardy's ▷ *Far from the Madding Crowd*.

▷ Irish Literature.

Bib: Husni, S.A, *William Allingham: An Annotated Bibliography*; Warner, A.J., *William Allingham: An Introduction*.

Alliteration

▷ Figures of Speech.

Alliterative revival
The term used to refer to a large group of poems, composed in ▷ alliterative verse between the mid-14th and mid-15TH centuries, on a wide range of subjects (histories, romances, contemporary satires, ▷ dream-visions), and employing a wide range of styles. The works of the ▷ Gawain poet and of ▷ William Langland form part of this group. Patterns of poetic and narrative techniques can be established between works using the alliterative verse mode, but it would be too simple to represent these texts as belonging to a single school or to explain the origins of the revival by a single causal model, as has been tried in the past. The production of narrative in alliterative verse seems to have been particularly concentrated in the west and

north-west regions of England, though again the 'regional' quality of alliterative poetry, and its opposition to the forms employed in the court poetry of ▷ John Gower and ▷ Chaucer, has been overstressed in the past.
Bib: Lawton, D. (ed.), *Middle English Alliterative Poetry and Its Literary Background.*

Alliterative verse
The traditional verse form of the Germanic people in which pairs of two-stress phrases are bound together by alliteration. All ▷ Old English poetry is written in this prosodic form: usually the stressed syllables of the first phrase (or half-line) and the first syllable of the second are linked by alliteration. Formalized patterns of expression are a characteristic feature of this prosodic mode. From the late Old English period onwards a wider variety of prosodic forms was in use, and the use of rhyme as a binding device for lines increases greatly in post-Conquest English poetry. Traditionally scholars have divided up the corpus of Old English poetry into that written in 'classic' alliterative form (in which a small number of variable stress patterns for phrases can be identified), and a later 'looser' alliterative verse form (in which there are more variable options in the alliterative and stress patterns of the phrases). The alliterative works of the early Middle English period are composed in this looser style which can accommodate rhyme patterns too (as illustrated in ▷ Laȝamon's *Brut*). Conventional distinctions between prose and poetry are undermined by some texts composed in rhythmical, alliterating units. The style of ▷ Aelfric's *Lives of Saints* uses some of the techniques of alliterative verse, as do a number of later prose works on religious themes (the so-called Katherine Group of saints' lives and the ▷ *Ancrene Wisse*), composed in the Worcestershire and Herefordshire areas in the late 12th and early 13th centuries. Discussions of the alliterative mode have been hampered by the desire of scholars to formulate a single model which might link classic Old English verse with the later looser traditions, and the increased use of a more disciplined verse medium in the 14th century, in the so-called ▷ Alliterative Revival. But the complex pattern of influences and associations has eluded simple explanatory models and increasingly the trend is to consider the alliterative mode as part of a continuum, as one of a number of forms available to post-Conquest writers in English, rather than as constituting a single poetic tradition.
Bib: Pearsall, D., *Old and Middle English Poetry*.

***All's Well that Ends Well* (1602–3)**
A play by ▷ Shakespeare in which the heroine, Helena de Narbon, pursues Bertram, Count of Rousillon, whom she loves but who seeks to elude her. He is misled by a dishonourable young courtier, Parolles; she eventually ensnares him by a trick. The plot is taken from Painter's ▷ *Palace of Pleasure* (1566–7) but the play is difficult to date precisely owing to its mixture of styles. Sir Edmund Chambers dates it 1602–3. This agrees with the kind of difficulty with which it faces critics: uncertainty about Shakespeare's intention; the play seems to be a romantic comedy, but the treatment of the subject is often unromantic and the comedy is often harsh. Thus *All's Well* resembles other ▷ problem plays of Shakespeare written between 1600 and 1604: ▷ *Hamlet*, ▷ *Measure for Measure*, ▷ *Troilus and Cressida*.

Althusser, Louis (b 1918)
One of the most influential French ▷ Marxist philosophers of the 1960s, whose work began to appear in English translation from 1965 onwards: *For Marx* (1965), *Reading Capital* (with Etienne Balibar; 1968), and *Lenin and Philosophy* (1971). Althusser's ideas have been influential in the area of cultural studies, where his particular brand of structural Marxism has led to a radical rethink of all social institutions, and the place of human subject within their structures. His essay 'Ideology and Ideological State Apparatuses' (*Lenin and Philosophy*) lays the foundation for a reconsideration of literature and its relationship to ▷ ideology, and has far-reaching effects also in the area of media studies.

***Alton Locke: Tailor and Poet* (1850)**
A novel by ▷ Charles Kingsley reflecting the social and political turbulence of the ▷ 'Hungry Forties' and one of the ▷ 'Social Problem' novels. Alton Locke, a shopkeeper's son, experiences the horrors of sweated labour during his apprenticeship to a tailor. Convinced of the need for social reform he joins the ▷ Chartist movement. His talent for poetry brings him into contact with Eleanor Staunton, her cousin Lillian, and Saunders Mackaye, a Scottish bookseller modelled loosely on ▷ Thomas Carlyle. At the request of Lillian and her wealthy father, Alton allows his revolutionary verse to be rendered innocuous before publication, thereby earning him the contempt of his Chartist comrades. Responding to their taunts he undertakes a mission that provokes a riot and earns him three years in prison. During that time his beloved Lillian marries someone else and it is Eleanor who nurses him back from typhus while explaining her own views on reform and the role of Christianity. Disillusioned by demagogy and violence, Alton becomes a Christian Socialist and dies on his way to the USA. Deeply flawed as a novel, *Alton Locke* did draw attention to the wretchedness of the lives of working people, suggesting Christian Socialism as a non-violent means of achieving reform. Its themes are echoed in ▷ Barratt

Browning's ▷ *Aurora Leigh*, the title of which has the same initial letters.

Amazons

A race of female warriors occuring in ancient Greek legend, and said by the 5th-century historian Herodotus to live in Scythia, north of the Black Sea. The word is often used to describe aggressive women, women who are hostile to men or women in positions of power traditionally held by men. In the late 19th century the figure of the Amazon was chosen by feminists to represent women in their struggle for the vote and as an antidote to the ▷ 'Angel in the House'. She featured in novels, poetry and ▷ utopian fiction such as Elizabeth Burgoyne Corbett's *New Amazonia: A Foretaste of the Future* (1889), which is set in the year 2472 and describes a utopian community established in Ireland, with a grant of £50 million, by 'surplus women' shipped there by the British Government. In the course of 600 years the women have grown two feet taller than the men and their waists, unrestricted by the corset, have 'thickened' to twenty-six inches. However, the success of Amazonia is predicated upon eugenics and 'compulsory self-extinction' of the old, deformed and rebellious. In 1888 ▷ Thomas Hardy used the word 'Amazon' to describe a handsome 'interesting' female smoker he met while dining at the house of ▷ Walter Pater. ▷ Arthur Wing Pinero wrote *The Amazons: A Farcical Romance in Three Acts in* 1895.

▷ Women's Movement.

***Ambassadors, The* (1903)**

A novel by ▷ Henry James. It belongs to his last period, during which he returned to his earlier theme of the interaction of the European and American character.

Lambert Strether, a conscientious, middle-aged American, is engaged to the rich American widow, Mrs Newsome. She sends him over to Paris to bring back her son Chad to run the family business. He arrives to find Chad immersed in Parisian culture, and absorbed in a love affair with the Comtesse de Vionnet, a relationship which Strether mistakenly assumes is not a sexual one. Strether, instead of persuading Chad to return, finds his sensibilities released by the freedom and richness of Parisian life, and delays his own return. Chad's sister, Mrs Pocock, and her husband, Jim, are now sent over by Mrs Newsome. Strether urges upon Chad the duty of loyalty to the Comtesse, and Mrs Newsome breaks off her engagement to Strether. After discovering the true nature of Chad's relations with the Comtesse, Strether decides to go back, abandoning his friendship with the intelligent and sympathetic Maria Gostrey, an American expatriate. Chad, however, remains.

Mrs Newsome is an authoritarian American matron, full of rectitude and prejudice. Strether has the highly developed New England conscience (it is his conscience that forces him to return) and a hitherto starved imagination. He is the ▷ focal character of the narrative throughout, so that his progressive understanding and development is a rich source of interest and irony. The Pococks stand for American philistinism, without imagination or sensibility. Together with ▷ *The Golden Bowl* (1904) and ▷ *The Wings of the Dove* (1902), the novel shows James' art at its most highly wrought and difficult stage.

***Amelia* (1751)**

A novel by ▷ Henry Fielding. Unlike ▷ *Joseph Andrews* and ▷ *Tom Jones, Amelia* deals with married love, and was Fielding's own favourite, although it was fiercely attacked by ▷ Johnson and ▷ Richardson, among others.

Set against a background of squalor and poverty, the novel opens with the imprisonment of the innocent but careless husband Captain Booth. In prison Booth meets the courtesan Miss Matthews, an old admirer who invites him to share the clean cell she has been able to afford. Booth accepts, though feeling guilty about his virtuous wife Amelia, and the two characters exchange stories about their past lives.

An old friend Colonel Bath pays Booth's bail and takes Miss Matthews as his mistress. Once out of jail, Booth turns to a life of gambling while trying to curry favour with the great. An aristocratic acquaintance assures Amelia that Booth will get his commission and invites her to accompany him to a masquerade. But 'My Lord' is a rake plotting to seduce Amelia, with the connivance of Colonel Bath and the Booths' landlady, Mrs Ellison.

Just as Amelia is about to set out to the masquerade, a fellow lodger, Mrs Bennet warns her that 'My Lord' had ruined her own life and is now threatening to destroy Amelia's 'virtue'. After several complications the plot ends happily; the Booths are rescued by their good friend Dr Harrison, and Amelia discovers that her virtue is rewarded as she will inherit her mother's fortune.

American colonies

The original thirteen colonies settled by the English which formed the first states of the United States of America (▷ American Independence, The War of), were Massachusetts, New Jersey, New York, Rhode Island, Connecticut, New Hampshire, Pennsylvania, Delaware, Virginia, Maryland, North Carolina, South Carolina, Georgia. Their population grew from 340,000 in 1700 to 1,200,000 by 1760, and to 3,000,000 by 1776.

The early colonies are now represented on the American flag by the thirteen stripes, while states established afterwards are symbolized by the stars.

American Independence, The War of (1775–83)
Also known as the American Revolution. Tensions between American settlers and their rulers in England had been building up since the 17th century: a major outbreak of hostilities, Bacon's Rebellion, had already taken place in Virginia in 1676. The intractability of George III in the later 18th century added more fuel to the fire, and conflict was precipitated by legislation favouring the London East India Company, at the expense of American shippers. Three cargoes of tea imported under the new regulations were thrown into Boston harbour by men disguised as Indians in 1773, an event described jocularly as the 'Boston Tea Party'. Fighting did not erupt until 1775, however, when the British Government attempted to arrest two American leaders at Lexington near Boston: the first shots were fired there by the British, and actual fighting broke out at Concord. On the 4th July 1776 the Congress of insurgent states issued 'The Declaration of Independence', partly inspired by the writings of ▷ Thomas Paine, and which in turn contributed to the thinking behind the ▷ French Revolution. George Washington became commander-in-chief of the insurgents. The Americans' cause was greatly helped when the French and Spanish declared war on Britain in 1777, and key defeats of the British took place along the Delaware at Trenton and Princeton (1776), Saratoga (1777) and Yorktown (1781), when the British surrendered. In 1783 peace was made in Paris and the 13 colonies (▷ American colonies) became a union of independent states, the United States of America. George Washington became the first US president, and a constitution was drawn up and ratified in 1788.

American Revolution
▷ American Independence, The War of

Amis, Sir Kingsley (b 1922)
Novelist and poet. Associated at first with the ▷ 'angry young men' of the 1950s for his novels, and with the Movement for his poetry, he has long outgrown such labelling, achieving considerable popular success with a series of sharp, ironic novels notable for entertaining incident, vivid caricatures and the comic demolition of pretension. *Lucky Jim* (1954; filmed 1957) is a hugely enjoyable novel about a young English lecturer in a provincial university and his battles against the academic establishment and a range of comically infuriating characters. It is not really a subversive work; it ends with the hero being given a good job in London by a wealthy man as well as winning the best girl. Amis' later novels tend to be less good-humoured; the protagonist of *One Fat Englishman* (1963) retains some of Jim's methods, but is fully as unpleasant as his enemies. Although Amis has remained within the format of a well-crafted plot and largely conventional modes of narration, he has employed a wide range of genres such as the detective story (*The Riverside Villas Murder*; 1973), the spy-story (*The Anti Death League*; 1966) and the ghost-story (*The Green Man*; 1969). *The Alteration* (1976), one of his most inventive works, imagines a 20th-century society dominated by the Catholic Church.

Amis' other novels are: *That Uncertain Feeling* (1955); *I Like It Here* (1958); *Take A Girl Like You* (1960); *The Egyptologists* (1965); *I Want It Now* (1968); *Colonel Sun* (as Robert Markham; 1968); *Girl, 20* (1971); *Ending Up* (1974); *The Alteration* (1976); *Jake's Thing* (1978); *Russian Hide and Seek* (1980); *Stanley and the Women* (1984); *The Old Devils* (1986); *Difficulties With Girls* (1988); *The Russian Girl* (1992); *You Can't Do Both* (1994). Story collections include: *My Enemy's Enemy* (1962); *Dear Illusion* (1972); *The Darkwater Hall Mystery* (1978); *Collected Short Stories* (1980). Poetry: *Bright November* (1947); *A Frame of Mind* (1953); *A Case of Samples* (1956); *The Evans Country* (1962); *A Look Around The Estate: Poems 1957–1967* (1967); *Collected Poems 1944–1979* (1979). Essays and criticism include: *New Maps of Hell* (on ▷ science fiction; 1960); *The James Bond Dossier* (1965); *What Became of Jane Austen?* (1975); *Rudyard Kipling and His World* (1975). He has also published his *Memoirs* (1991). Amis was knighted in 1990.
Bib: Salwak, D., *Kingsley Amis, A Reference Guide*, and *Kingsley Amis: In Life and Letters*; McDermott, S., *Kingsley Amis: An English Moralist*.

Amis, Martin (b 1949)
Novelist. Son of ▷ Kingsley Amis, he was educated at schools in Britain, Spain and the U.S.A., and at Oxford University. He has worked for the *Times Literary Supplement*, the *New Statesman* (as literary editor) and the *Observer*. His early novels are characterized by black humour, concern with the sordid, violent and absurd, and an apparent misogyny, features which he defends as satire. *The Rachel Papers* (1973) is an account of adolescence through flashbacks and memories; *Dead Babies* (1975) (paperback as *Dark Secrets*) is a tale of decadence and sadism; *Success* (1978) is closer to the hilarity of *The Rachel Papers*, while *Other People* (1981) is an experiment in ambiguity. With the linguistic wealth of *London Fields* (1989) and the experimental narrative technique of *Time's Arrow* (1991, shortlisted for the Booker Prize), Amis has emerged as a ▷ post-modernist novelist of considerable versatility. *The Information* (1995) is a black comedy of literary competitiveness. Other works: *Money* (novel; 1984); *The Moronic Inferno* (essays; 1986); *Einstein's Monsters* (stories; 1987); *Visiting Mrs Nabokov, and other excursions* (1993).

Amoretti (1595)
A sequence of 89 sonnets by ▷ Edmund Spenser, first published, together with the wedding-song ▷ *Epithalamion*, in 1595. The title of the sequence is derived from the term applied to Italian love songs which take the exploits of Cupid as their subject. *Amoretti* is unusual amongst the ▷ sonnet sequences of the period in that it moves towards an evocation of sexual love within a Christian context, which has, as its end, the sacrament of marriage. Though much of the language and many of the ideas in the sequence are derived from ▷ Petrarch, Spenser nevertheless developed the Petrarchan model in introducing a carefully organized structure to the work. Thus, the events described in *Amoretti* follow the course of the Christian year, while the work as a whole evokes the progress of the seasons. It has long been assumed that the sonnets were addressed to Spenser's second wife, Elizabeth Boyle, whom he married in 1594.

Amos Barton, The Sad Fortunes of the Rev. (1857)
The first of the three tales composing ▷ *Scenes of Clerical Life* (1858) by ▷ George Eliot.

Amphibology, Amphiboly
A sentence having two possible meanings owing to the ambiguity of its construction.

Amphibrach
In metre, a verse foot composed of a long syllable between two short ones, or an accented foot between two unaccented ones. It is rarely used in English verse.

Amphimacer
A verse foot deriving from Greek, also known as the cretic foot, it uses one short syllable between two long ones, as in the phrase 'going mad'. Rarely used in English verse, its pattern of one unstressed syllable between two stressed may be heard in ▷ Blake's poem 'Spring': 'Sound the flute!/ Now it's mute;/ Birds delight/ Day and night.' Its opposite, amphibrach (one accented foot between two unaccented ones), is even more rare.

Ana,-ana
A collection of memorable quotations from a writer, or sayings by a famous person, or anecdotes about him, *eg* Shakespeariana, Johnsoniana. Usually a suffix at the end of a name, as in these examples.

Anacoluthon
▷ Figures of Speech.

Anacreontics
Any kind of melodious verse, lyrical, and concerned with love and wine. From the Greek poet Anacreon (6th–5th centuries BC). ▷ Byron called his friend ▷ Thomas Moore 'Anacreon Moore', because he translated the Odes of Anacreon into English.

Anacrusis
The use at the beginning of a line of verse of a syllable additional to the number required by the given metrical pattern, as in the 'and' used by ▷ Thomas Campbell, in the second of these lines from 'Ye Mariners of England': 'The danger's troubled night depart/ And the star of peace return.'

Anapaest
A metrical foot having two short or unaccented syllables followed by a long or accented one. It is usually mixed with iambics. Originally a Greek marching beat, its use in English poetry frequently retains a martial resonance, as in this line from ▷ Byron's 'The Destruction of Sennacherib': 'And the sheen of their spears was like stars on the sea.'

Anatomy of Melancholy, The (1621–51)
A treatise by ▷ Robert Burton (1577–1640) on a topic which was of enduring interest, in particular to Elizabethan and Jacobean playwrights. It was first published in 1621, but by the time the sixth (posthumous) edition of 1651 appeared, Burton had expanded the original book of approximately 860 pages by about one-third. Though its ostensible theme is an enquiry into the 'symptomes, prognostickes and severall cures' of the psychological disorder of melancholy, it is also a wide-ranging exposition of the role and function of the human being in the natural order of the universe (▷ humanism). Not the least of the work's concerns is the principle of ordering and classification itself, and it thus bears comparison to ▷ Francis Bacon's ▷ *Advancement of Learning* and the work of later scientists associated with ▷ The Royal Society. But in its digressive and allusive pursuit of curious forms of knowledge, and in its stylistic delight in the piling up of quotation, modification and qualification, it stands as a work without any immediate precursors or later emulators.
▷ Humour.
Bib: Vicari, E. P., *The View from Minerva's Tower*.

Ancien Régime
A French phrase, commonly used in English, to signify the political and social order in France before the Revolution of 1789, and more loosely to indicate a former state of order.
▷ French Revolution.

Ancient Mariner, The Rime of the (1798)
A literary ▷ ballad by ▷ Samuel Taylor Coleridge first published in ▷ *Lyrical Ballads*.

The mariner kills a friendly albatross for no stated reason, and he and the crew of his ship are subjected to punishment by the Polar Spirit. The members of the crew die in agonies of thirst, while the mariner himself lives on in a state of 'life-in-death', until he 'unawares' blesses some water snakes and is absolved of his guilt. The dead albatross which the crew have hung round his neck falls into the sea, and the ship is magically driven to the mariner's home port where he is given absolution by a hermit. Thereafter he wanders the world, compulsively telling his story, and recommending a holy life in communion with all God's creatures. The story appears naively didactic: the mariner has sinned against the 'One Life' and has done penance for his sin. But the poem's moral scheme is deeply ambiguous. If the theme is one of Christian sin and redemption, it seems strange that the destinies of the mariner and the crew are determined by a game of dice played between Death and Life-in-Death. And it is unclear why the rest of the crew are punished so harshly. The mariner ends with an apparently orthodox and banal message of religious consolation: 'He prayeth best who loveth best/ All things both great and small.' But this consolation is belied by his sinister unease, as he holds the wedding guest with his 'glittering eye', preventing him from attending the marriage ceremony, and leaving him 'A sadder and a wiser man'. The poem dramatizes Coleridge's sense of irredeemable guilt, and his inability at this time to find consolation in orthodox religion or in the pantheism of his friend ▷ William Wordsworth.

Ancrene Riwle

▷ *Ancrene Wisse.*

Ancrene Wisse

Ancrene Wisse (A Guide for Anchoresses) is a devotional manual, composed in English in the West Midlands area *c* 1220, for the use (initially) of three sisters who had decided to become recluses. It seems to have been revised for a wider audience shortly afterwards and was read, recopied, readapted until the sixteenth century. Versions are extant also in French and Latin. The manual is entitled *Ancrene Wisse* in one manuscript copy: that of *Ancrene Riwle* is a modern invention. Sensitively and evocatively written, the *Ancrene Wisse* offers itself to its readers as an instructional and meditational aid. Two sections of the manual (I/VII) offer advice on how the anchoress should conduct her 'outer' life and these enclose six sections of guidance on her 'inner' spiritual conduct (II – VII). The climactic section (VII) considers how the anchoress might direct her spiritual ardour and offers a memorable portrait of Christ as a wooing-knight.

Bib: White, H. (trans.), *Ancrene Wisse*; Millett, B. and Wogan Browne, J. (eds. and trans.), *Medieval English Prose for Women*.

Andersen, Hans Christian (1805–75)

Danish author known in Britain almost entirely for ▷ fairy tales of his own composition, such as 'The Tinder Box', and 'The Princess and the Pea'. They began to appear in Denmark in 1835 and were translated into English first in 1846. Their poetic quality has been much imitated by English writers, *eg* ▷ Oscar Wilde.

▷ Children's Books.

'Andrea Del Sarto' (1855)

A dramatic monologue by ▷ Robert Browning published in ▷ *Men and Women* (1855) in which the painter admits and laments his devotion to his wife Lucrezia at the expense of his art. It was written shortly after his marriage to ▷ Elizabeth Barrett.

Andreas Capellanus (fl 1175)

Author of *De Arte Honeste Amandi (The Art of Honourable Loving)*, a manual of procedures in love. He claims to be a royal chaplain and is often said to have been attached to the court of Marie de Champagne at Troyes, but there is no evidence for this. His text is addressed to a young man called Walter and is divided into three Books which tackle (i) the nature of love and how it may be attained, (ii) how love may be retained, and finally (iii) the rejection of secular love. The debt to ▷ Ovid's work on the art of loving and the remedies for secular love is acknowledged by Andreas. The tone of the work is open to different interpretations and its divergent lines on the subject of secular love are apparent in its tripartite organization. The text seems to have been read and interpreted in very different ways by scholars and writers of subsequent centuries (as a criticism of secular love values, as a defence of ▷ courtly love); indeed, the debate about how to read Andreas' text continues among 20th-century medievalists.

Andrewes, Lancelot (1555–1626)

A bishop and leader of the ▷ Church of England during the most formative century (1550–1650) of its thought. His ▷ sermons were famous in an age when preaching was a high art; their prose was vivid and condensed, and an important contribution to the development of English prose. He took part in the translation of the King James Bible. Andrewes is compared to ▷ John Donne, poet and Dean of St Paul's, whose prose comes near his own poetry. As an intellectual defender of the Anglican religious position, Andrewes was the successor of ▷ Richard Hooker; but whereas Hooker was mainly concerned to defend Anglicanism against the ▷ Puritans, Andrewes defended

it against the Catholics. Both he and Hooker are representatives of Anglicanism as the *via media* between the two.
Bib: Eliot, T. S., 'Lancelot Andrewes' in *Selected Essays*; Higham, F., *Lancelot Andrewes*; Welsby, P. A., *Lancelot Andrewes*.

Androcentrism
Literally meaning 'male-centred', androcentrism is a term current in feminist theory to describe intellectual habits and assumptions which imply that men are the most significant agents in any process. The growth of Women's Studies can be seen as a response to androcentrism in intellectual enquiry.
▷ Phallocentrism.

Androgyny
A key term in some ▷ feminist approaches to literature, androgyny signals a balance of supposed 'male' and 'female' qualities. The word is formed from the Greek *andro* (male) and *gyn* (female). The idea has a long history, but the ideal of androgynous writing and values was particularly important to ▷ Virginia Woolf. Some recent feminist thinkers, however, criticise the idea because it does not sufficiently respect female difference.
Bib: Woolf, V., *A Room of One's Own*.

Anelida and Arcite
▷ Chaucer's poem of 354 lines, set like the ▷ *Knight's Tale* in Thebes, and drawn from material in ▷ Boccaccio's *Teseida*. The brief story of Queen Anelida's unhappy love experience with Arcite provides the preface to Anelida's epistolary complaint, addressed to her faithless lover (composed of 140 lines of varying and accomplished metrical patterns). The work is influenced by the form and format of ▷ Ovid's *Heroides* and looks forward to Chaucer's collection of stories about wronged women in his ▷ *Legend of Good Women*.

'Angel in the House, The'
A term which has come to exemplify the Victorian middle-class ideal of submissive womanhood, used originally by ▷ Coventry Patmore in his domestic epic *The Angel in the House* (1854–62). ▷ Ruskin pays homage to this stereotype of feminine behaviour in his essay 'Of Queen's Gardens', printed in *Sesame and Lillies* (1865). The Victorian feminine ideal embodied purity and selflessness, strong moral and religious principles, coupled with a willingness to submit to the will of men. Woman's realm was the home, viewed as a sanctuary from the harsh public world of capitalist competition. The 'Angel in the House' provided spiritual succour as well as domestic comforts for the middle-class male, and cherished her maternal role. In Victorian literature, characters such as ▷ Dickens' Agnes Wickfield in ▷ *David Copperfield* represent such an ideal, but as the 19th century progressed a number of writers challenged the stereotype. Well-known texts such as ▷ Charlotte Brontë's ▷ *Jane Eyre*, ▷ Elizabeth Barrett Browning's ▷ *Aurora Leigh* and George Eliot's ▷ *Middlemarch* and ▷ *The Mill on the Floss* all present anti-angelic heroines straining to be released from conventional domestic roles. The Angel in the House was nevertheless an extremely powerful idea, and the emphasis on English women's moral and spiritual superiority was crucial in the construction of national identity. In her famous work on women writers, *A Room of One's Own* (1929), Virginia Woolf (1882–1941) cites the import of the Angel in the House as a central impediment to early 20th-century women's attempts to write professionally.
▷ Feminism; 'Woman Question, The'; Imperialism; Taylor, Jane and Ann.
Bib: Poovey, M., *Uneven Developments: The Ideological Work of Gender in Mid-Victorian Britain*.

Anger, Jane (fl. 1588)
Tract-writer. Pseudonym for the author of a proto-feminist pamphlet, *Jane Anger, Her Protection for Women* (1588–9). There is no indication as to the true identity of the writer. This work is a polemical contribution to the ▷ *Querelle des Femmes* in which Anger attacks men for the way they slander women, and praises her own sex for their grace, wisdom and 'true fidelity'. It was uncommon for a woman to write for publication at this time, which perhaps explains the need to conceal her true name. However, Anger explicitly calls attention to the fact that women have been denied a public hearing and stresses that this unfair treatment has led to her own 'angry' response. Jane Anger's pamphlet is published in *Half Humankind: Contexts and Texts of the Controversy about Women in England*, 1540–1640, ed. K. U. Henderson and B. F. McManus (1985).
▷ Munda, Constantia; Sowernam, Ester; Speght, Rachel.

Angles
One of the three Germanic tribes (according to Bede) which invaded the Roman province of Britannia in the 5th century AD (the others being called the Saxons and the Jutes). English (derived from *Angle*) came to be the general term used for the Germanic language and the Germanic peoples who gained sovereignty over the central part of the island of Britain (ie England). *See* English language; Old English; Anglo-Saxon.

Anglo-Norman
The dialect of French used in the British Isles from the time of the Conquest onwards

alongside Latin and English. There were four principal domains of usage of Anglo-Norman: as a spoken vernacular; as a language of legal, administrative and business record; as a language of instruction; as a language of literary culture. It ceased to be used in these various domains at different times in the medieval period in England. From the later 12th century it was no longer a true maternal language and became increasingly a second, acquired language of the social and administrative elite, yet it continued to be learnt and used as a prestige vernacular for a further two centuries. Its function as a language of instruction, as the medium for learning Latin, seems to have been eroded by the later 14th century; its use as a language of law continued into the 15th century; its use as a language of literary culture continued through the 14th century, alongside the increasing use of English in this capacity too. Anglo-Norman literature occupies a major place in the literary culture of medieval England and a large number of English literary works translate, or rework, material from Anglo-Norman texts.
Bib: Legge, D., *Anglo-Norman Literature and its Background*; Short, I., 'On Bilingualism in Anglo-Norman England', *Romance Philology*, 33, 467–79.

Anglo-Saxon
The term which denotes the language, literature and culture of the English before the Norman Conquest of 1066 (though many scholars today use the term 'Old English' in preference). Some post-medieval writers occasionally use the term to differentiate the common people from the aristocracy of English (supposedly) Norman descent (eg. Disraeli in *Coningsby* and *Sybil*). *See* Angle; English language, Saxon.

Anglo-Saxon Chronicle
A collective term for a corpus of annals, recording events of local and national significance, organized in a more systematic way during the reign of ▷ Alfred. The annals, written in English, were kept up at a number of monastic centres and survive in seven manuscripts (which form four main versions). The subjects and length of entries in the chronicles vary considerably from version to version but collectively they provide a record of events from the beginning of the Christian era to 1154. The continuation of the chronicle for nearly 100 years after the Norman Conquest illustrates the way in which ▷ Old English literary culture did not stop abruptly in 1066, yet the changing form of the language of the later entries in the chronicle also indicates the way in which a standard written form of English could no longer be maintained in post-Conquest literary culture.
Bib: Whitelock, D. W. (ed.), with Douglas, D. C. and Tucker, S. I., *The Anglo Saxon Chronicle*; Gransden, A., *Historical Writing in England, c 550–1307*.

Anglo-Welsh Literature
▷ Welsh Literature in English.

Angria
An imaginary kingdom created by Branwell and ▷ Charlotte Brontë in 1834, matched by ▷ Emily and ▷ Anne Brontë's imaginary world, ▷ Gondal. The inspiration for Angria and Gondal came from a box of wooden soldiers given to Branwell by his father in 1826. All four children took part in the creation of a narrative that became known as the 'Glass Town Confederacy'. Charlotte and Branwell went on to develop their Angrian tales, while Emily and Anne broke away to create Gondal. Charlotte's Angrian stories of 1837–9, 'Mina Laury', 'Henry Hastings' and 'Caroline Vernon', anticipate the themes of her mature novels.
Bib: Ratchford, F., *The Brontës' Web of Childhood*.

Angry young men
A term which was loosely applied to novelists and dramatists of the 1950s who expressed a sense of dissatisfaction and revolt against established social mores. ▷ John Osborne's play *Look Back In Anger* (1956) epitomized the mood. Other authors of whom the term was used include ▷ John Braine, ▷ John Wain, ▷ Alan Sillitoe, and ▷ Kingsley Amis.
▷ Realism.
Bib: Allsop, K., *The Angry Decade*.

Anjou, House of
▷ Plantagenets.

Anne (1665–1714)
Queen of England from 1702 until her death. Anne was the younger daughter of ▷ James II by his first wife, Anne Hyde, and was educated in the ▷ Protestant faith. When in 1672 her father became a ▷ Catholic, she remained loyal to the ▷ Church of England. She joined the party of his enemy, the Protestant William of Orange (later ▷ William III) when he landed in England in 1688, although she was later drawn into some of the intrigues on her father's behalf, and toward the end of her life favoured the succession of her Catholic half-brother (the ▷ Old Pretender). In 1683 she was married to Prince George of Denmark, to whom she remained devoted. Her reign was dominated by the War of the ▷ Spanish Succession, which she inherited from William III and continued with encouragement from her confidante, the Duchess of ▷ Marlborough. She also presided over the ▷ Act of Union with Scotland in 1707. During much of her reign the Whig party was in the ascendancy, but from 1710 the Tories took over, supported by the Queen. Between 1684 and 1700 she had 17 pregnancies, but several ended with miscarriages, and none of

her children survived her. This precipitated a constitutional crisis, before the ▷ Act of Settlement was confirmed, and the monarchy reverted to the House of Hanover upon her death.

Anne of Denmark, Queen of Great Britain (1574–1619)
Patron. ▷ King James I's consort is often attacked as being light-minded and pleasure-loving. The latter is certainly true, but it is important to bear in mind that the courtly entertainments which she encouraged were not simply childlike amusements, but important pieces of political propaganda. These ▷ masques allowed Anne to participate in the public sphere, an arena that would otherwise have been denied her by the misogynous king. Numerous arguments occurred between her and James over which ambassadors should be invited to the masques, which suggests the powerful diplomatic significance of these events. Her son ▷ Henry, Prince of Wales, similarly recognized the value of court shows. Moreover, Queen Anne's commissioning of masques allowed her a certain input into the contents of the pieces and her involvement is detailed by ▷ Ben Jonson in his annotations and prefaces to various works.
Bib: Williams, E. C., *Anne of Denmark*.

***Annus Mirabilis* (1667)**
A poem by ▷ John Dryden dealing with the 'wonderful year' between the summer of 1665 and that of 1666, especially the sea battles against the Dutch, the ▷ Plague and the Great Fire of London. It is written in 'heroique stanzas', pentameter quatrains rhyming *abab*, which were felt at the time to possess an epic breadth and dignity lacking in the shorter-lined lyric metres of much 17th-century poetry. Its style is public and declamatory, the emphasis being on rapid narrative and imaginative gusto, and its epic hero is a collective one: the English people or London.

Anspach, Elizabeth, Princess of (1750–1828)
Dramatist, poet and letter-writer. Elizabeth Berkeley's first marriage was to Lord Craven, during which period she challenged convention by publishing her own poetry and allowing her play *The Miniature Picture* (1780) to be staged at ▷ Drury Lane Theatre. Although ostracized by polite society, she was accepted by other writers, and her work was admired by ▷ Horace Walpole who printed one of her early dramatic pieces, *The Sleep-Walker* (1778), and to whom she dedicated *Modern Anecdote* (1779). She was widowed in 1791 and embarked upon her second marriage, to Anspach, in the same year; after this, the remainder of her plays were acted privately. She is also known for a series of letters discussing her journeys to Russia and Constantinople (1785–6), which rival those of Lady Mary Wortley Montagu (▷ Orientalism). Her *Memoirs* offer a lively account of the age, but hardly display the proto-feminism (▷ Feminism) with which she is credited; for example, she writes that, 'whenever women are indulged with any freedom, they polish sooner than man'.
Bib: Rodgers, K. M., *Feminism in Eighteenth-century England*.

Anstey, Christopher (1724–1805)
Minor poet and author of *New Bath Guide* (1766), an extremely successful book containing letters in verse form supposedly sent by people in ▷ Bath. The letters describe in a humorous fashion the exploits of the fictitious Blunderbuss family.
Bib: Powell, W. C., *Anstey: Bath Laureate*.

Anthology
A collection of short works in verse or prose, or selected passages from longer works, by various authors. Some anthologies lay claim to authority as representing the best written in a given period, *eg* the Oxford Books (of Sixteenth Century Verse, etc.) and others are standard examples of taste at the time of compiling, *eg* Palgrave's *The Golden Treasury of the Best Songs and Lyrical Poems in the English Language* (1861). Others have had an important influence on taste, or on later literary development. Some examples of the most important poetry anthologies of the 20th century which have given shape to movements are the ▷ Georgian poetry anthologies which appeared between 1912 and 1922, A. Alvarez's *The New Poetry* (1962) and ▷ D. J. Enright's ▷ Movement collection, *Poets of the* 1950s.

Anthology, The Greek
A collection of poems begun by Meleager of Gadara (about 60 BC) and later expanded, especially by Constantius Cephalas (10th century AD), till it included selections from over 300 writers. Many of the pieces, which number over 4,500, are epigrams. The *Anthology* has been, from the 16th century onwards, an important source of information on Greek culture.

Anti-climax
▷ Figures of speech.

Anti-industrialism
A tradition of writing identified initially by the work of Raymond Williams in *Culture and Society*. 19th-century observers, the foremost of whom was Thomas Carlyle, identified a number of threats to what they saw as constructive social living brought by industrialism. The pressures of growing industrialism obliged the workforce into working in mechanical unison and consequently altered their sense

of themselves. The emphasis of industrial capitalism on material production and material acquisition changed the conditions of life and sapped the individual's powers of resistance. ▷ D. H. Lawrence was its most impassioned 20th-century opponent, and his work influenced the Romantic anti-industrialism of F. R. Leavis.

▷ Further education; Capitalism.

Anti-Jacobin, The

▷ Jacobin.

***Antiquary, The* (1816)**

A novel by ▷ Walter Scott, the third of his ▷ 'Waverley Novels', set in Scotland in the 18th century. The main story is an ordinary romance. A young officer, Major Neville, falls in love with Isabella Wardour, whose father rejects him on account of his supposed illegitimacy. Neville follows the father and daughter to Scotland, where the three have sundry adventures; Neville saves their lives and rescues Sir Arthur Wardour from impending ruin. He also turns out to be the son and heir of a Scottish nobleman. Thus the objections to the union between Neville and Isabella are removed. The distinction of the novel arises from the subsidiary characters: Jonathan Oldbuck, a learned antiquarian scholar (like Scott himself), and Edie Ochiltree, a wandering beggar who epitomizes the feelings and traditions of the Lowland Scottish peasantry. Scott states in his preface that he agrees with ▷ Wordsworth's opinion (expressed in the Preface to the ▷ *Lyrical Ballads*) that the peasantry have an eloquence in expressing the basic and most universal passions which is lost to the educated classes.

Antithesis

▷ Figures of speech.

***Antonio and Mellida* (1600)**

A play in two parts by ▷ John Marston. Part I is a transvestite, stylized and Italianate comedy about the loves of its eponymous protagonists. Part II, usually known as *Antonio's Revenge*, protrays the savage destruction of the same characters in the idiom of an Elizabethan blood tragedy.

▷ Revenge tragedy.

***Antony and Cleopatra* (1606–7)**

A tragedy by ▷ Shakespeare, probably written in 1606–7, and first printed in the First Folio edition of his collected plays in 1623. The source is ▷ Sir Thomas North's translation (1587 edition) of ▷ Plutarch's *Lives*.

Mark Antony, with Octavius Caesar and Lepidus, is one of the 'triumvirate' (43–31 BC) which rules Rome and its empire, and he is Rome's most famous living soldier. At the opening of the play, he is the lover of ▷ Cleopatra, Queen of Egypt, and, to the disgust of his officers, is neglecting Rome and his political and military duties. All the same, he cannot ignore Rome, and from time to time he reacts strongly against Cleopatra when he remembers his public position and his reputation. His strained relations with Octavius Caesar are temporarily mended when he marries Caesar's sister, Octavia, but he soon abandons her and returns to Cleopatra. Caesar is enraged, and is in any case anxious to secure sole power over the empire for himself. Open war breaks out between them, and Antony is defeated at the sea battle of Actium, largely owing to Cleopatra's attempt to participate personally in the campaign. After Antony's final defeat on land, he attempts to kill himself, and eventually dies of his wounds in the arms of Cleopatra, who has taken refuge in her 'monument'. This is a mausoleum which she had built so that she and Antony could lie together in death; it serves as a kind of miniature fortress. After Antony's death, she makes a bid for survival by pitting her wits against Caesar's. When she sees that she has failed, she takes her own life. The two death scenes, her own and Antony's, are amongst the most famous scenes in Shakespeare's work.

One of the ironies of the tragedy is that Cleopatra loves Antony just because he is a great Roman hero, and yet, in order to get full possession of him, she has to destroy this part of him. At a deeper level, Rome and Egypt are set in dramatic contrast: Rome stands for the political world, with its ruthless and calculating manoeuvring for power; Egypt stands for the heat and colour of passion, tending always to dissolution and corruption. The play belongs to Shakespeare's maturest period. As in his other 'Roman' plays, ▷ *Julius Caesar* and ▷ *Coriolanus*, Shakespeare shows an awareness of writing about the pre-Christian era, in which the hero represents the highest human type, instead of the saint.

John Dryden's (1631–1700) *All for Love* is also a tragedy about Antony and Cleopatra; a comparison of the two plays is instructive in showing the changes that came about in English verse in the intervening period.

Anxiety of influence

A term coined by the American critic ▷ Harold Bloom to describe the relationship between writers and their famous forebears. For Bloom, writers are in competition with their great precursors and their work is haunted by anxiety about over-influence. Bloom's model is explicitly ▷ Freudian, and the writer struggles against predecessors like the son struggles against the father in Freud's theory of the ▷ Oedipus Complex. A strong writer (in Bloom's parlance) absorbs the influence of his or her precursors and becomes independent. A weak writer, however, succumbs to imitation or silence.

Feminist critics have pointed out the aggressive patriarchal assumptions in the theory.
Bib: Bloom, H., *The Anxiety of Influence: A Theory of Poetry*.

Aphasia
Generally used to designate language disorder. However, in literary criticism it has been given a more specific definition by the linguistician and supporter of the ▷ Russian Formalist movement, ▷ Roman Jakobson. Jakobson begins with the observation that language functions through the *selection* and *combination* of its elements into units such as words and sentences. *Combination* is a term used to designate the process whereby a linguistic ▷ sign can generate meaning only through its relationship with other signs which provide a context for it. *Selection* permits the substitution of one element for another from the total number of elements that make up the linguistic code as a whole, and which both speaker (addresser) and listener (addressee) share. The addresser encodes a particular message, and the addressee decodes or interprets it. Any interference with either the selection or combination of linguistic units which form an utterance, such as an unusual use in a literary work, is designated as aphasia, and this disordering serves, by contrast, to reveal the ways in which language operates normally.

Aphorism, apophthegm
A terse sentence, weighted with sense; with more weight of wisdom than an ▷ epigram need have, but less elegance. For example, ▷ Wilde's comment that 'wickedness is a myth invented by good people to account for the curious attractiveness of others'.

Apocalypse
From Greek 'disclosure'. A kind of visionary literature, especially *Revelation* in the ▷ Bible. The essence of such literature, for instance, the visionary poetry of ▷ William Blake and ▷ W. B. Yeats, is that it expresses in symbolic terms truths and events which surpass the ordinary reach of the human mind. An apocalyptic mood (the expectation of the end of the world as we know it, or at least the anticipation of radical social transformation) is a feature of some ▷ modernist fiction, notably ▷ D. H. Lawrence's ▷ *The Rainbow* and ▷ *Women in Love*.

The strongest poetic movement of the 1940s was known as the 'New Apocalypse', a neo-Romantic celebration of passion and emotion, whose key figures were ▷ Dylan Thomas and ▷ W. S. Graham. Modern ▷ science-fiction writing, produced in the nuclear age, is often referred to as 'apocalyptic'.
Bib: Kermode, F., *The Sense of an Ending: Studies in the Theory of Fiction*.

Apocrypha
1 Books of the Old Testament not counted as the genuine Word of God by the Jews, nor as sacred by Protestants: *Esdras 1* and *2*; *Tobit*; *Judith*; the *Rest of Esther*; *Wisdom; Ecclesiasticus* (not to be confused with *Ecclesiastes*); *Baruch;* the *Song of the three Holy Children; Susanna; Bel and the Dragon; Manasses; Maccabees 1* and *2*.

2 Also sometimes used for works alleged on uncertain grounds to be by a given author.

'Apollodorus'
▷ Pseudonym of ▷ George Gilfillan, an ebullient Scottish reviewer and champion of the ▷ 'Spasmodic' school of poets.

Apologia, Apology
In ordinary speech, *apology* has the sense of an expression of regret for offensive conduct, but as a literary term it commonly has the older meaning still conveyed by *apologia*: defence, *eg* ▷ Sir Philip Sidney's ▷ *Apologie for Poetrie*, or explanation, vindication, *eg* Cardinal Newman's *Apologia pro Vita sua*.

***Apologia Pro Vita Sua* (1864)**
Originally entitled *Apologia Pro Vita Sua: Being a Reply to a Pamphlet Entitled: 'What Then Does Dr Newman Mean?'* this spiritual autobiography of ▷ John Henry Newman was published in seven parts with an appendix between 21 April and 2 June 1864. It began as a reply to the militantly Protestant ▷ Charles Kingsley with whom Newman had publicly quarrelled, but by the time of its publication in book form (1865) it had developed as an explanation or vindication of Newman's spiritual development, and helped to reduce anti-Catholic feeling. An example of the Victorian's enormous interest in ▷ autobiography and the confessional mode of writing it encouraged, Newman's *Apologia* is also a primary historical source for the ▷ Oxford Movement.

▷ Catholicism (Roman) in Victorian literature.

***Apologie for Poetrie, An* (1595)**
A critical essay by ▷ Sir Philip Sidney, the *Apologie* appeared in 1595, when it was also published under the alternative title *The Defence of Poesie*. Though it has long been assumed that Sidney's treatise was designed to function as a reply to a ▷ pamphlet by ▷ Stephen Gosson entitled *The Schoole of Abuse* (1579), the *Apologie* undertakes to defend imaginative writing from more general objections than those propounded by Gosson. Instead, the *Apologie* undertakes to define the role of both the artist and the literary text in respect of the society and the competing forms of alternative discourses in which they operate and are read. To this end, the *Apologie* explores the classical concept of imaginative writing, arguing that the poet

can be considered as a 'creator' or 'maker' rather than a sterile copier of forms located in the real world. The autonomy of the artist is guaranteed against the competing claims of philosophical and historical writing, and, at the same time, Sidney offers a refutation of ▷ Plato's famous condemnation of poetry in his ▷ *Republic*. The essay concludes with a survey of contemporary English writing.

The importance of Sidney's work is that it provides a clear statement of several important themes of Renaissance poetics. In particular, it deals at length with the idea of imitation and with the Platonic objection to poetry – that it is morally questionable, and that the poet is, in producing works of fiction, little better than a liar. In producing a range of arguments to deal with these two points, Sidney offers a synthesis of ▷ humanistic arguments derived from his readings in the classics and in the works of continental critics. At the same time, the *Apologie* stands as an example of the ▷ Renaissance use of the art of ▷ rhetoric, which determines the work's careful structure. For all its rootedness in late 16th-century debates on poetics, Sidney's treatise was to become, in the 17th century and later, an important statement in its own right on the nature and value of poetic discourse.

▷ *Poetics.*

Bib: Shepherd, G. (ed.), *An Apology for Poetry*.

Apophthegm

▷ Aphorism.

Aporia

In Greek *aporia* means a tangled path blocking the way, but the term has often been used in a literary context to describe a logical problem or inability to settle to a course of action as, for example, in Hamlet's 'To be or not to be' speech. More recently, the term has been used by ▷ deconstructionist critics to refer to a point of contradiction or impasse in a work when the reader is left with inconsistent or unresolvable ideas. For deconstructionist critics, the aporia is inevitable in all writing and should not be seen as a mistake or blemish in the work.

Apostrophe

▷ Figures of Speech.

Apprenticeship

A system of training undergone by youths entering on a trade or craft. The apprentice was indentured to a master in the craft, *ie* entered into a contract with him, to serve him in return for maintenance and instruction for seven years, usually between the ages of 16 and 23. The apprentice was a member of the master's household and the master was responsible for his behaviour before the law. Thus apprenticeship provided social control, as well as a form of education, and tended to maintain standards in manufacture and professional conduct. It also had the social advantage of mixing the classes and ensuring that the landed classes retained an interest in trade, for the smaller landed gentry commonly indentured their younger sons, who had no land to inherit, to master craftsmen, especially in London. Until the 18th century (when the gentry, grown richer, tended to despise trade) this mixture of classes, as well as their large numbers, made the London apprentices a formidable body of public opinion not only politically, but, for instance, in the Elizabethan theatre. Apprenticeship was systematized by law under the Statute of Artificers, 1563. It had its beginnings in the ▷ Middle Ages. Usually women were not permitted to be apprenticed; in this way they were excluded from skilled paid work, although wives, daughters and sisters often helped in the work of their male relatives. Until the 17th century, apprenticeship was the only way to enter most trades and professions.

Aquinas, St Thomas (c. 1225–74)

Dominican friar, philosopher, political theorist from Aquino (S. Italy) who produced a variety of treatises (for Christian missionaries, for the instruction of princes), commentaries on the work of Aristotle, but whose greatest (and unfinished) work, the *Summa Theologica*, attempted to harmonise the philosophy of Aristotle with Christian theology and came to be considered the most authoritative product of scholastic thinking. Aquinas was an important influence on ▷ Dante.

Bib: Knowles, D. *The Evolution of Medieval Thought.*

Arabian Nights Entertainments

Also known as *The Thousand and One Nights*, this collection of stories supposed to be told by Scheherazade was probably put together by an Egyptian story-teller around the 15th century. The stories became well-known and popular in Europe early in the 18th century. English translations have been made by Edward Lane in 1840 and, with greater literary merit, by Sir Richard Burton in 1885–88.

▷ Children's books.

Arbuthnot, Dr John (1667–1735)

Close friend of ▷ Alexander Pope, ▷ Jonathan Swift and ▷ John Gay, with whom he collaborated in the satiric sallies of the ▷ Scriblerus Club. Arbuthnot was physician in ordinary to Queen Anne and a Fellow of the ▷ Royal Society; he was widely admired for his medical science and for his genial wit. His most famous satire is 'The History of John Bull' (1712), a series of pamphlets advocating an end to the war with France which turned the arguments of Swift's *Conduct of the Allies*

into a comic allegory. He also had a hand in such collaborative Scriblerian satires as *The Memoirs of Martin Scriblerus* (1741), *The Art of Sinking in Poetry* (1727) and *Three Hours after Marriage* (1717). Among his more important scientific writings are his *Essay on the Usefulness of Mathematical Learning* (1701) and his *Essay concerning the nature of Aliments* (1731).
Bib: Aitken, G. A. (ed.), *The Life and Works of Dr John Arbuthnot*; Beattie, L. M., *John Arbuthnot, mathematician and satirist.*

***Arcades* (c 1633)**
A short ▷ masque by ▷ John Milton written c 1633. Like all masques, the title of the work indicates the occasion of its production: 'Part of an Entertainment presented to the countess dowager of Derby at Harefield by some noble persons of her family'. The work – an exercise in the ▷ pastoral – is so short that it hardly warrants the description of 'masque', being really little more than a dramatized form of brief tribute. Music for the work was composed by ▷ Henry Lawes, who was to write the music for Milton's more elaborate masque, ▷ *Comus*, when it was performed in 1634.

Arcadia
A mountainous district in Greece, with a pastoral economy, and in ancient times the centre of the worship of Pan. The country was idealized by ▷ Virgil in his *Eclogues*, and again in the Renaissance in ▷ pastoral works, notably in ▷ Sir Philip Sidney's ▷ *Arcadia*. By this time Arcadia was thought of purely as an ideal country of the imagination, uncorrupted by the sophistications of civilization.

***Arcadia, The* (1578 and 1590)**
▷ Sir Philip Sidney's ▷ pastoral romance *The Arcadia* exists in two distinct versions. The 'old' *Arcadia* was begun c 1578, and circulated widely in manuscript form before Sidney undertook to revise it in 1584 – a task interrupted by his death in 1586. This revised (though incomplete) version – the 'new' *Arcadia* – was published in 1590. In 1593 Sidney's sister, Mary Herbert, Countess of Pembroke (▷ Mary Sidney), to whom the work had been dedicated, undertook to publish a composite version of the text, which combined the two versions in existence together with her own (substantial) emendations. Thus *The Arcadia*, which enjoyed enormous popularity in the 16th and for much of the 17th century, was a curious hybrid.

In its original version the work was a mixture of love and intrigue, but in its revised form, Sidney broadened the scope of his undertaking. The episodic narrative of lovers, derived from Sidney's reading in late Greek romance, was transformed into what Sidney termed 'an absolute heroical poem', the purpose of which, in accordance with the critical precepts that had been established in ▷ *An Apologie for Poetrie*, was to instil 'delightful teaching'. From the first appearance of the work, critical opinion has been divided as to its seriousness. Some of Sidney's contemporaries understood *The Arcadia* as a profound meditation on morals and politics. For other writers, in particular ▷ John Milton, the work was no more than an exercise in escapist fantasy.
Bib: Editions include: Evans, M. (ed.), *The Countess of Pembroke's Arcadia*; Duncan Jones, K. (ed.), *The Old Arcadia*.

Archaeology of knowledge
An influential method of investigation pioneered by the French philosopher and historian ▷ Michel Foucault in which the different ▷ discourses of the leading disciplines which make up the knowledge system of a particular period are compared. The aim is to establish the common ground between them and thus establish the 'general horizon' (as Foucault terms it) of understanding. Those interested in such investigation assume that the fundamental assumptions which constitute the general horizon of knowledge change from epoch to epoch, and that knowledge in one period is organised differently from that in another. Hence it needs to be recovered as an archaeologist recovers information about 'lost' cultures. One implication of the archaeology of knowledge is that knowledge needs to be understood contextually, in a specific period, and not in the crude ▷ Positivistic sense in that it progresses over time and can therefore be judged right or wrong by the standards of the future. For Foucault, the development of knowledge is jagged and discontinuous. What is also distinctive about Foucault's conception is his emphasis on the inseparability of knowledge from social and political power. For him, knowledge develops in intimate relation to the power systems of the day which can encourage some developments, but frustrate or interdict others.
Bib: Foucault, M., *The Archaeology of Knowledge*.

Archer, William (1856–1924)
Journalist and drama critic, born in Scotland. He joined forces with ▷ George Bernard Shaw in his championship of ▷ Henrik Ibsen and helped to improve the standard of British drama at the end of the 19th century and influence its development. His translation of *Quicksands, or, The Pillars of Society*, was performed in London in 1880 and introduced Ibsen to the English audience. Later translations included *A Doll's House* (1899), *Ibsen's Prose Dramas* (1890–1), *Peer Gynt* (1892), *The Master Builder* (1893), and the *Collected Works* (1906–12).

▷ Essay.

Arden, Forest of
Formerly an extensive forest in the neighbourhood of Stratford. It gave its name to the important landed family of Arden; ▷ Shakespeare's mother, Mary Arden, may have belonged to a junior branch. The Forest of Arden in Shakespeare's ▷ *As You Like It* is the forest of the Ardennes, but Shakespeare may have had the English forest in mind as well when he used the name.

Arden, John (b 1930)
Dramatist. Barnsley born, a student of architecture and, in his own words, 'a product of English public schools and three years as a conscript in Scotland', Arden began writing plays at university. Considered one of the most influential political playwrights of his generation, Arden's output has been indelibly influenced by his meeting with Margaretta D'Arcy in 1955. Arden and D'Arcy have written many plays jointly and separately.

Most of Arden's major stage plays appeared in a ten-year period from the late 1950s to the late 1960s, ceasing abruptly after a famous if painful controversy over the RSC's handling of *The Island of the Mighty* (1972), when Arden declared he would never write again for the stage. Instead both his and to some extent D'Arcy's recent work has been more or less devoted to radio.

Although *Serjeant Musgrave's Dance* (1959) was not a popular success, it is now seen as one of the major plays of the period. Set in a bleak mining town in northern England in the 1880s, a small group of soldiers invade a village ostensibly on a recruitment drive. But the men are deserters, and their leader Serjeant Musgrave, who has become fanatically anti-war, is as terrifying in his religious zeal as the evil against which he inveighs: he demands the death of twenty-five local townspeople to match the death of a local boy who died in a colonial war and who was the trigger, in reprisal, for the death of five men. A male-oriented play, where women are seen either as whores (sexual and dangerous) or mothers (asexual and comforting), it seems hard in retrospect to see it as anything other than a passionately pacifist, anti-imperialist play.

Always a moralist, Arden's dissenting voice has increasingly swung away from the earlier anarchic detachment where there are no heroes (even the so-called pacifism of *Serjeant Musgrave's Dance* is hotly disputed by some commentators, who feel it is difficult to decide which side Arden's sympathies are on), through political activism to revolutionary socialism by the late 1970s. Others, however, argue that the seeds of Arden the revolutionary were implicit from the beginning, particularly in the fact that the plays were usually sparked off by historical and contemporary political events. *Armstrong's Last Goodnight* (1964), for example, though set in 16th-century Scotland, was inspired by the Congo War and intended as an analagous, moral parable on the subject of violence. Written in Lowland verse, it emerged as a rumbustious, sardonic study in *realpolitik*, opposing the urbane politician (Lindsay) with the highland rebel, Johnny Armstrong.

Arden, from the beginning, rejected naturalism and though his plays were *about* social, political and economic issues – small town corruption (*The Workhouse Donkey*, 1964), the welfare state (*Live Like Pigs*, 1958), violence and militarism (*Serjeant Musgrave's Dance*) – his use of bold, imagist techniques – epics, parables, sometimes grotesque comedy – and the fact that they have an obvious polemical intent, inevitably led to Arden being compared with ▷ Brecht, an influence he has always denied. Yet other observers, playing the influence game, detect a kinship with ▷ Ben Jonson and ▷ Aristophanes in such plays as *The Workhouse Donkey*. Arden / D'Arcy's work, with its increasingly anti-English, pro-Irish and community stance – *The Hero Rises Up* (1968) is an anti-heroic view of Nelson; *The Ballygombeen Bequest* (1972), an attack on absentee landlordism in Ireland; *The Non-Stop Connolly Show* (1975), a pro-Irish Republican epic which, according to Arden's biographer, Albert Hunt, should be regarded as a masterpiece – has come under increasing censorship. To the overall impoverishment of British theatre, their work remains outside the mainstream.

Arden's plays include: *Soldier Soldier* (1960); *The Happy Haven* (1960); *The Business of Good Government* (1960); *Wet Fish* (1962); *The Workhouse Donkey* (1963); *Ironhand* (1963); *Ars Longa Vita Brevis* (with Margaretta D'Arcy; 1964); *Armstrong's Last Goodnight* (1964); *Left-handed Liberty* (1965); *Friday's Hiding* (1966); *The Royal Pardon* (1966); *The Hero Rises Up* (1968); *The Ballygombeen Bequest* (1972); *The Island of the Mighty* (1972); *The Non-Stop Connolly Show* (1975); *Vandaleur's Folly* (1978); *The Little Gray Home in the West* (1978); *The Manchester Enthusiasts* (1984).

▷ Beckett, Samuel; Osborne, John; Pinter, Harold.

Bib: Hunt, A., *Arden: A Study of His Plays*; Gray, F., *John Arden*.

***Arden of Faversham, The Tragedy of* (1592)**
An anonymous Elizabethan tragedy which is sometimes attributed to ▷ Shakespeare and occupies pride of place in the 'Shakespeare Apocrypha'. The play is almost unique in the period in dealing with recent history. Its subject-matter – the murder in Faversham in 1551 of Thomas Arden by his wife Alice and her accomplices – is related in ▷ Holinshed and vividly dramatized in this early domestic tragedy about criminal passion and greed.

Bib: Belsey, C., *The Subject of Tragedy*.

Areopagitica (1644)
Title of a ▷ pamphlet, published on 28 November 1644, written by ▷ John Milton. In June 1643 Parliament had passed an ordinance which attempted to license the press – in effect it was designed as a form of covert political ▷ censorship that allowed officers of Parliament to search for, and confiscate, unlicensed books. Milton's *Areopagitica* was offered as a powerful statement on behalf of liberty of the press. In arguing for such liberty, Milton was aligning himself with radicals such as William Walwyn and Richard Overton, and entering a forceful plea for the free dissemination of information and ideas without which, in his opinion, it was impossible for individuals to make genuine political choices. In discussing this question of choice, *Areopagitica* can be thought of as being a precursor of one of the major themes of Milton's ▷ *Paradise Lost*. The title itself implicitly compares the Parliament of England, to whom Milton was addressing his comments, to the Supreme Court of ancient Athens which met on the hill Areopagos, situated to the west of the Acropolis.

▷ Levellers, The.

Aretino, Pietro (1492–1556)
Italian writer, the author of tragedies such as *Orazio* (1546) and comedies such as *La Cortigiana* (1525) – the latter containing his infamous creation, Alvigia, a bawd whose speeches are a combination of the obscene and Latin orations. He also wrote an anti-Petrarchan ▷ sonnet sequence that transmutes the conventional idealized love into eroticism and pornography. Aretino enjoyed a considerable reputation in England in the late 16th and early 17th centuries, ▷ Thomas Nashe proclaiming himself a particular admirer.

▷ Italian influence on English literature.
Bib: Lawner, L. (trans.), *Sonetti Lussuriosi*.

Ariosto, Ludovico (1474–1533)
Italian author of comedies, ▷ satires, and, most famously, the romantic ▷ epic ▷ *Orlando Furioso* (1532). Ariosto's comedies include *I suppositi* (1509), which was translated by ▷ George Gascoigne in 1572 and used by ▷ Shakespeare in the composition of ▷ *The Taming of the Shrew*. His satires owe much to ▷ Horace, but it was *Orlando* which was to have the greatest influence on English writers, in particular ▷ Edmund Spenser.
Bib: Rich, T., *Harington and Ariosto: a study in Elizabethan verse translation*.

Aristophanes (c 448–c 380 BC)
The greatest of the Attic comic poets and the most important writer of Old Comedy which is distinguished by its aggressive, bawdy satire and personalized attacks. Aristophanes' plays evolve against the background of contemporary political, philosophical and literary concerns, such as the Peloponnesian war between Athens and Sparta (*Lysistrata*), or the rivalry between the Greek tragedians (*The Frogs*). His influence on English drama is reflected in ▷ Ben Jonson's comedies, particularly in ▷ *Bartholomew Fair*, although Jonson and his contemporaries are far more dependent on the formal and thematic properties of the ▷ New Comedy idiom of ▷ Plautus and ▷ Terence.

Aristotle (384–322 BC)
A Greek philosopher, born at Stageira, and so sometimes called the Stagirite. He was first a pupil of ▷ Plato, later developing his thought on principles opposed to those of his master. He was tutor to the young ▷ Alexander (the Great). His thought covered varied fields of knowledge, in most of which he has been influential. His best known works are his *Ethics, Politics*, and ▷ *Poetics*.

The difference between Aristotle and Plato has been described as follows: Plato makes us think in the first place of an ideal and supernatural world by turning our minds to ideal forms which are the truth in terms of which imperfect earthly things can be known and judged; Aristotle turns us towards the natural world where things are what they are, perfect or imperfect, so that knowledge comes through study and classification of them in the actual world. It can thus be seen that whilst Plato leads in the direction of mysticism, Aristotle leads towards science. Until the 13th century, Christian thought tended to be dominated by Plato, but medieval Christian thought, owing to the work of ▷ Thomas Aquinas, found Aristotelianism more acceptable.

The *Poetics* is based on the study of imaginative literature in Greek from which Italian critics of the 16th century, and French dramatists and critics of the 17th century such as Corneille, ▷ Racine and ▷ Boileau constructed a system of rules. ▷ Sidney knew Aristotle chiefly through the Italians, who had derived from Aristotle some rules not to be found in him – notably the ▷ unities of time and place: ▷ Dryden and ▷ Samuel Johnson, were respectful of and deeply influenced by French neo-Aristotelianism, but they refused to be bound by it, unlike some second-rank critics such as ▷ Thomas Rymer. The 19th century reacted strongly against the attitude, but in this century the elimination of the neo-Aristotelian superimpositions of the ▷ Renaissance has revived interest in the discernment displayed in the *Poetics*.

Armada, The (Spanish), 1588
The fleet dispatched by Philip II of Spain to transport a Spanish army from Flanders to land in and conquer England. The attempt was deafeated by the English fleet under Lord

Howard of Effingham and his sea-captains, some of whom were already famous for other exploits, such as ▷ Drake, Hawkins, Frobisher. It was written up as part of the nationalist myth of both countries involved and, in consequence, contrasting accounts of it are given in Spanish and English history. For Philip II of Spain it was a holy war against the heretical English who had abandoned Rome and recently put the Catholic ▷ Mary Queen of Scots to death; under Franco the Armada was said to illustrate the Christian fortitude of Philip II and the need for stoicism in adversity. At the time the English represented it as a national triumph, a personal triumph for the queen and an inspiration for the whole people. It did have far-reaching cultural effects both for Europe and for the non-European world that Europe was about to expand into.

England was the most important country to have renounced papal authority; her defeat might have been disastrous to the Protestant side in its struggle against the Catholic powers, of which Spain was then the chief. Instead, the English victory meant a decisive check to the formidable (▷ Counter-Reformation) attempt of Catholicism to recover the northern countries of Europe. The English victory was a milestone in the shift of power from the Mediterranean region to the Atlantic powers of England, France and Holland, which henceforth increasingly led the European expansion over the globe.

Bib: Martin, C. and Parker, G., *The Spanish Armada*.

Armah, Ayi Kwei (b 1938)

Ghanaian novelist, educated at schools in Accra and Massachusetts and at Harvard and Columbia universities. He has worked as a translator, a television scriptwriter, an English teacher and an editor. His novels express nationalist feeling and a strong sense of anger, combined in *The Beautyful Ones Are Not Yet Born* (1968) and *Fragments* (1970) with elements of the comic, though the ironically-titled *Why Are We So Blest?* (1972) is a horrific and fragmented narrative of the sexual exploitation of an African man by a European woman and the violence that follows. He has drawn on Akan culture for organizing structures (generally cyclical): *Fragments* is shaped by its Akan chapter headings and *The Healers* (1978) uses the structure of Akan folk stories for an historical account of the fall of the Asante Empire; *Two Thousand Seasons* (1973) is also a historical novel.

Bib: Fraser, R., *The Novels of Ayi Kwei Armah: A Study in Polemical Fiction*; Wright, D., *Ayi Kwei Armah's Africa*.

Armstrong, John (1709–1779)

Medical doctor, friend of ▷ James Thomson, and author of didactic poems in blank verse, including the mildly erotic *Economy of Love* (1736), and *The Art of Preserving Health* (1744).

Arnold, Matthew (1822–88)

Poet, critic and educationalist, son of ▷ Thomas Arnold. Most of Arnold's verse was published by the time he was forty-five: *The Strayed Reveller* (1849); ▷ *Empedocles on Etna* (1852); *Poems* (1853); *Poems, Second Series* (1855); *Merope, a Tragedy* (1858); *New Poems* (1867). From these volumes, the best-known poems today are *The Forsaken Merman* (1849), *Sohrab and Rustum* (1853), a narrative in epic style; ▷ *The Scholar Gypsy* (1853), *Thyrsis* (1867) and the famous short lyric, ▷ 'Dover Beach' (1867 – perhaps written much earlier). His poetry is elegiac, meditative and melancholy; preoccupied with spiritual alienation and the loss of religious faith.

As Arnold began to abandon poetry writing, his essay and prose writing career took off; as a critic, he was strongly influential on early 20th-century thought, and was a crucial figure in the development of English studies as a discipline in its own right. Mediated by the works of T.S. Eliot (1888–1965), I.A. Richards (1893–1979), Lionel Trilling, F.R. Leavis (1895–1978) and the literary critical review *Scrutiny* (published between 1932 and 1953), his cultural criticism forms a lynch-pin of traditional English criticism. This influence does not come from his studies of individual writers but from his studies of contemporary culture and of the relationship, actual and potential, of literature to industrial civilization. His best known critical works are ▷ *Essays in Criticism*, First and Second Series, 1865 and 1888; *On Translating Homer*, 1861; and *Culture and Anarchy*, 1869.

Arnold's work as an inspector of schools and educationist was related to his most serious critical preoccupations, and the two worlds meet in such a work as ▷ *Culture and Anarchy*. His educational theories and absolute valuing of culture were pitted against the ▷ Utilitarianism of his historical moment. Arnold posited a system of humane education under the headship of an ideal, liberal state, as the means of ensuring the triumph of culture over social and spiritual anarchy.

▷ German influence on English literature.

Bib: Trilling, L., *Matthew Arnold*; Jump, J.D., *Matthew Arnold*; Brown, E.K., *Arnold: a Study in Conflict*; Tinker, C.B. and Lowry, H.F., *The Poetry of Arnold*; Honan, P., *Matthew Arnold: a Life*; Carroll, J., *The Cultural Theory of Matthew Arnold*; Baldick, C., *The Social Mission of English Criticism*.

Arnold, Thomas (1795–1842)

Influential Broad Church liberal Protestant, headmaster of ▷ Rugby School, and an important figure in the development of the public school system and its values. The father of ▷ Matthew Arnold, he became professor of Modern History at Oxford University in 1841. Famously characterized in Thomas Hughes' *Tom Brown's Schooldays* (1857).

Ars Poetica (Art of Poetry)
▷ Horace.

Artaud, Antonin (1896–1948)
French actor, director and poet, associated with the Surrealist theatre and founder of the Théâtre Alfred Jarry. He developed an approach to theatre which he named ▷ 'Theatre of Cruelty'. In this he downgraded the written text in favour of a theatrical language based on ritualistic gesture, movement and sound. His aim was to release in the actor and spectator the primitive human forces ordinarily suppressed by social morality and convention. His theories are explained in his collection of essays entitled *Le théâtre et son double*. He has been a strong influence on French authors, particularly Camus and Genet, and on the English director ▷ Peter Brook.
Bib: Esslin, M., *Artaud*; Hayman, R., *Artaud and After*.

Arthur, King
If there is a historical figure behind King Arthur, it may be that of a British chieftain, active some time in the 5th or 6th century, who resisted Saxon invaders after the Roman garrisons had abandoned Britain. Documentary evidence and archaeological data provide us with only a vague picture of the historical events of these centuries, and so the historical location of an Arthur figure continues to be a subject of great debate. ▷ Gildas, the 6th-century monastic chronicler, records an important British victory over the Saxons at Mount Badon, some time around 500, but there is no mention of Arthur in Gildas' narrative. However, in the 9th-century compilation, the *Historia Brittonum (History of Britain)*, attributed to ▷ Nennius, Arthur is given responsibility for leading the British side to victory at the battle of Badon, although his role here and in the 11 other battles accredited to him is that of a chieftain or general, not a British king. A 10th-century compilation, the *Annales Cambriae (Annals of Wales)*, credits Arthur with victory at the Battle of Badon in 518, and also records that in the battle of Camlan in 539, Arthur and 'Medreut' fell.

William of Malmesbury's remarks in his *Gesta Regum Anglorum (Deeds of the Kings of the English)* suggest that by 1125 much material had accreted around the figure of Arthur, some of it mere fable and lies according to William. Arthur is credited with great feats at the battle of Badon, but his family connection with Walwen (▷ Gawain) is mentioned later by William, who also comments on the legend that Arthur may yet return. Modern attempts to recreate some sense of early vernacular (Celtic) Arthurian narratives and traditions are fraught with problems. Arthur does figure in early Welsh narratives, as an important chieftain, who in one case goes on an expedition to a Celtic otherworld to obtain a magic cauldron (in the poem known as the *Spoils of Annwfn*), but although this material may be circulating from an early date, the versions that survive are in manuscripts dating from the 13th century onwards. Important Celtic Arthurian narratives, for example, are preserved in the Black Book of Camarthen, c 1200; the White Book of Rhydderch, dating from the early 14th century; the Red Book of Hengest, dating from the late 14th century.

The writer responsible for putting King Arthur firmly on the map of British history was ▷ Geoffrey of Monmouth who, in his ▷ *Historia Regum Britanniae (History of the Kings of Britain)*, c 1138, provided a continuous account of the British kings from Brutus onwards and made the reign of King Arthur the high spot of this sequence. Under Arthur's rule, Britain regains its status as a unified Christian nation, and gains international power and prestige too. This version of British history, though challenged by some late-medieval historians, appears to have been generally accepted and became a standard feature of accounts of insular history. Notable vernacular versions of Geoffrey's narrative include those by ▷ Wace (in ▷ Anglo-Norman), ▷ Laȝamon and ▷ Robert Mannyng, and material from this chronicle tradition of Arthurian narrative forms the basis for the early 15th-century English poem, the alliterative ▷ *Morte Arthure*. For the development of the tradition of Arthurian romance, we have to turn to the activities of the 12th-century French and Anglo-Norman writers who developed a body of narratives focussed on the adventures of individual members of Arthur's court. Writers such as ▷ Béroul, Thomas of Britain, ▷ Marie de France and ▷ Chrétien de Troyes, drew on Celtic story motifs to develop narratives which explored the interests and tensions of court culture and its ideals. Of these writers, Chrétien de Troyes deserves special attention: his sophisticated vernacular romances seem to have stimulated the creation of a much larger body of texts centred on the court of King Arthur, and some of his works were translated into other European vernaculars (*Yvain*, for example, is reworked in the early 14th-century Middle English verse narrative as *Yvain and Gawain*).

The 13th century sees the development of much longer, interlaced Arthurian narratives, which became organized into the so-called ▷ Vulgate and post-Vulgate cycles of Arthurian romance. A notable addition to the post-Chrétien narrative tradition of Arthurian material is the development of the quest of the Holy ▷ Grail into a narrative which celebrates transcendental Christian ideals and which provides the means for linking Arthurian history to scriptural history.

English translations and reworkings of French Arthurian romances date from the early 14th century onwards (*Sir Tristrem*, *Arthour and Merlin*, and ▷ *Morte Arthur* (stanzaic)), but the alliterative romance of ▷ *Sir Gawain and the Green Knight*, in which Arthurian chronicle and romance traditions are played off against each other, has no French precedent. ▷ Thomas Malory provided English readers with a reworking of the massive Arthurian narrative cycle in the late 15th century (drawn largely from the Vulgate cycle) and his *Works* (or rather ▷ Caxton's printed edition of Malory's text known as the ▷ *Morte D'Arthur*) provides the standard account of Arthurian narrative for later writers and reworkers of Arthurian topics and themes.

King Arthur thus became an important feature of the English literary and historical landscape, and Arthurian narrative was constantly open in the course of its development for appropriation as a means of expressing and exploring different kinds of political and cultural ideals. ▷ Spenser's epic, ▷ *The Faerie Queene*, has the figure of Prince Arthur as its central protagonist, and later writers such as ▷ Ben Jonson, ▷ Milton and ▷ Dryden all planned major works on Arthurian topics (although only Dryden actually produced an Arthurian text, his dramatic opera *King Arthur*). The history of Arthurian narrative has periods of decline and revival, though the subject of Arthur always seems to have been available as a cultural reference point. Since the 19th century, a major revival of interest in all facets of Arthurian legend, history and culture has been under way. ▷ Tennyson's composite work, ▷ *The Idylls of the King*, reaffirmed the importance of Arthurian narrative as an arena for exploring national, political and cultural values, and provided a major source of stimulation for the Pre-Raphaelite group of painters and writers. An enormous body of 20th-century Arthurian narrative is available to modern readers, including works by ▷ T.S. Eliot, ▷ John Masefield, Charles Williams, ▷ David Jones, T.H. White and Marion Zimmer Bradley (who in *The Mists of Avalon* reworks Arthurian narrative from the perspective of its central female protagonists).

Bib: Lacy, N. et al. (eds.), *The Arthurian Encyclopedia*; Loomis, R. S. (ed.), *Arthurian Literature in the Middle Ages*.

Artifice, The **(1722)**

Play by ▷ Susannah Centlivre, her last, recently revived in London. The action actually incorporates several 'artifices' spread across four linked but separate plot lines: 1 Sir John Freeman, in love with Olivia, has been disinherited in favour of his younger brother Ned, who is also courting Olivia, and has been promised her hand in marriage by her father, Sir Philip Moneylove. 2 Ned has seduced an apparently poor Dutchwoman, Louisa, who has borne him a son. She comes to England to obtain justice, and tricks Ned into marrying her. Sir John is reunited with his fortune and with Olivia, and Louisa reveals herself as an heiress. 3 Old Mr Watchit is jealous of his young wife and locks her up when he goes out. But Ned contrives to gain access to her apartments, and to court her. By another trick she humiliates her husband, and he is forced to grant her more liberty. 4 The Widow Heedless, set upon marrying a lord, is wooed by the unscrupulous gambler, Tally, and also by the Ensign Fainwell, both in disguise. Fainwell exposes Tally, wins the Widow, and reveals his true identity. The play was originally criticized as designed 'to encourage adultery, to ridicule the clergy and to set women above the arbitrary power of their husbands. . .'.

Arts and Crafts Movement, The

An English aesthetic movement, belonging to the last thirty years of the 19th century, founded to combat the effects of growing industrialization on art and culture.

The ▷ Industrial Revolution led to the mass production of decorative art leading to what many regarded as a deterioration in the standards of craftsmanship, and a vulgarization of style and public taste. In 1861 the poet and designer ▷ William Morris established a firm of manufacturers and interior decorators, which included the architect Philip Webb (1831–1915) and the painters Ford Madox Brown (1821–93), Edward Burne-Jones (1833–98) and occasionally ▷ Dante Gabriel Rossetti, who clung to the principles of medieval craftsmanship. They specialised in hand-crafted artefacts including metalwork, jewellery, wallpaper, textiles, furniture and books. The group also numbered among its members the mathematician Charles J. Faulkner and the engineer Peter Paul Marshall.

A generation of artists and designers, deeply influenced by Morris and the art critic ▷ John Ruskin, became the leading lights of the Arts and Crafts Movement: people like the architect and designer Arthur Mackmurdo (1851–1942), the painter, draughtsman, designer and author of children's books Walter Crane (1854–1915), the art critic Lewis Day (1845–1910), the designers Selwyn Image (1849–1930) and Herbert Horne (1864–1916), the architect C. F. Annesley Voysey (1857–1941), and Charles R. Ashbee (1863–1942), writer and silversmith.

The popularity of the movement was established by the 1880s and the Century Guild, an organization for craftsmen, was established by Mackmurdo in 1882. Its object was 'to render all branches of art the sphere no longer of the tradesman, but of the artist'. The Arts and Crafts Exhibition Society was founded in 1888 and actively supported by Crane and Day. The same year saw the establishment of the Guild and School of Handicraft and the National Association for the Advancement of Art and its Application to Industry.

The Arts and Crafts movement was controversial in a number of ways. In addition to reviving the art of hand printing, the movement sought to dissolve the distinction between the fine and the decorative arts. Another and perhaps deeper controversy concerned the practicality, in a mass urban and industrialized society, of the work produced by the movement. It was also viewed by many as intellectually elitist and retrogressive: looking backwards to the medieval past rather than forwards to the future.

The movement gained even wider appeal in the 1890s both in Britain and abroad, becoming more experimental and prolific. Its aims, ideals and styles found an outlet in the Art Nouveau Movement: an ornamental style of art that flourished between 1890 and 1910.

▷ Medievalism; Pre-Raphaelite Movement; Anti-Industrialism; Gothic Revival.

Bib: Madsen, S. Tschudi, *The Sources of Art Nouveau*; Pevsner, N., *High Victorian Design*.

Arts Council

This body began as the Council for the Encouragement of Music and Art in 1940, to promote theatrical and musical entertainment during World War II. It now provides funding for a great variety of arts projects, including regional and national theatres and touring companies, throughout Britain. Its purpose is 'to develop a greater knowledge, understanding, and practice of the Fine Arts, to increase their accessibility to the public, and to improve their standard of execution'. Although its distribution of funds has often been contentious, its existence helped the proliferation of theatre companies from the 1960s onwards.

As You Like It

A comedy by ▷ Shakespeare. Produced about 1599, and first printed in the folio of 1623. Its source is ▷ Thomas Lodge's romance, *Rosalynde*.

The story is romantic and ▷ pastoral. A Duke, the father of the heroine, Rosalind, has been turned off his throne by his ruthless brother, the father of Rosalind's devoted friend, Celia. He has taken refuge with a few loyal courtiers in the neighbouring ▷ Forest of Arden. An orphan son, Orlando, is tyrannized by his wicked elder brother, Oliver. Orlando and Rosalind fall in love. Rosalind is banished from court, and goes to the forest in male disguise, calling herself Ganymede; Celia goes with her as Rosalind/Ganymede's sister, Aliena, and they are also accompanied by the court jester, Touchstone. Orlando follows them. He does not discover Rosalind's disguise, however, when, as Ganymede, she makes him 'play-act' courtship with her, episodes which are used by Shakespeare as light satires on the conventions of romantic love.
Another pair of lovers in the forest are the shepherd and shepherdess Silvius and Phebe, a couple who are drawn from the most artificial pastoral mode. Phebe (true to her convention) disdains Silvius, but falls embarrassingly in love with Rosalind (in her disguise) at first sight, and in spite of Rosalind's rudeness to her. Touchstone engages the affections of an unromantic and realistic village girl, Audrey, and thus frustrates her unromantic village lover, William. There is also Jaques, a fashionable and affected young man in the Elizabethan style, attached to the court of the exiled Duke. Rosalind, who is extremely plain-spoken except when she remembers that she is in love, exposes his affectations. In the end the couples are sorted out appropriately, and Rosalind's father regains his dukedom.

Shakespeare thus plays off real life against literary convention. The play is bright, satirical and romantic, all in one. Together with ▷ *Twelfth Night* it is his best work in the style of romantic comedy.

Ascham, Roger (1515–68)

Humanist, educationalist, tutor to ▷ Elizabeth I and secretary to ▷ Mary I. In 1538 he was made Greek reader at St John's College, Cambridge, and later, in 1546, public orator of the university. His two major works are *Toxophilus* (1545) and *The Schoolmaster* (1570). The latter is an educational manual, addressed to the prospective tutors of the children of the social elite, which sets out the ▷ humanist ideal of creating the harmonious individual. His *Toxophilus* is a dialogue in praise of the sport of archery.

Bib: Ryan, L. V., *Roger Ascham*.

Ash Wednesday

1 The first day of the religious season of Lent, a day of penitence when, in the Catholic Church, the penitents had their foreheads marked with ash.

2 *Ash-Wednesday* is the title of a sequence of poems (1930) by ▷ T. S. Eliot (1888–1965), marking poetically the conversion of the poet to Christianity.

Askew, Anne (1520–46)

Protestant martyr and writer of an autobiographical account of her spiritual beliefs. She was married in her early twenties to a Catholic squire, but was expelled from his household after becoming a Protestant. She resumed her maiden name and travelled to London where she came under the protection of ▷ Queen Katherine Parr. Askew was then arrested for heresy – she believed that the Mass was a religious metaphor – and tortured. It is likely that the Lord Chancellor and his fellow nobles wished to incriminate Katherine Parr to the ageing ▷ King Henry VIII, thereby lessening her power and increasing their own. She refused to confess, however, or to incriminate any others, and was eventually burned at the stake. Her accounts were published as the *First and Lattre examinacyon of Anne Askewe, latelye martyred in Smythfelde* (1546–7). Her bravery later gained recognition in ▷ John Foxe's *Acts and Monuments* (1563) and excerpts from her work may be found in *The Paradise of Women, Writings by Englishwomen of the Renaissance*, ed. Betty Travitsky.

Aspects of the Novel (1927)
A critical work on the novel by ▷ E.M. Forster, based on his Clark Lectures delivered in the University of Cambridge. Well known for its engaging conversational style, the book anticipates aspects of ▷ narratology in its consideration of point of view and ▷ flat and round characters, but is sharply distinguished from later narratology, as well as from the more earnest and prescriptive approach of ▷ Henry James' Prefaces, by Forster's jaunty scepticism about any pretensions to abstract rigour.

Assonance
▷ Figures of Speech.

Astell, Mary (1666–1731)
Sometimes claimed as 'the first English feminist', Mary Astell was a writer and intellectual, who published influential tracts on the duties and injustices of marriage, the most famous being ▷ *A Serious Proposal to the Ladies for the Advancement of Their True and Greatest Interest* (1694), which appeared anonymously as the work of 'a Lover of Her Sex'. With the help of several patrons, most notably William Sancroft, the archbishop of Canterbury, Astell was able to live independently in London and make a career of writing. Her views on the equality of the sexes were, however, modified by her conservative politics and her religious commitment to the Anglican Church. A wife's status in relation to her husband was, she argued, in the nature of a voluntary contract, but: 'It may be any Man's Business and Duty to keep Hogs; he was not Made for this, but if he hires himself out to such an Employment, he ought conscientiously to perform it'.
Bib: Perry, Ruth, *The Celebrated Mary Astell.*

Astrophil and Stella **(1581–3)**
A sequence of 108 ▷ sonnets and 11 songs written by ▷ Sir Philip Sidney and composed c 1581–3. The collection was first published (in a pirated edition) in 1591. While early texts give the title name as 'Astrophel', the modernized 'Astrophil' is almost certainly right. The sonnets as a whole take the form of a series of poetic addresses from Astrophil (star-lover) to Stella (star), though it is not difficult to pierce this fiction and associate Astrophil with Sidney himself and Stella with Penelope Devereux, daughter of the first ▷ Earl of Essex and sister to the second. The sequence should not, however, be taken as a simple disguised autobiographical record. Instead, the sonnets are an investigation of an obsession, a complex depiction of a psychological impasse. Adopting many of the conventions of ▷ Petrarch's poetry, they catalogue not only the cumulative progress of a love affair, but raise important theoretical questions concerning the act of writing and recording a state of mind, whilst also questioning the conventions by which writer and reader are tied to one another. Though sonnet sequences were published before Sidney's collection appeared, *Astrophil and Stella* set the standard by which later sequences were to be judged.

Atalanta in Calydon **(1865)**
A verse drama by the poet ▷ Algernon Swinburne, structured like a Greek tragedy and re-telling the Greek myth of Meleager. Promised at his birth strength and good fortune by the Fates, Meleager is also warned that his life will only last as long as a stick burning in the fire. His mother Althaea removes the stick from the fire, extinguishes it and hides it. A great hunt is organized to kill a monstrous Calydonian boar sent by the goddess Artemis to punish King Oenus (Meleager's father) for his lack of reverence to her. Atalanta, the virgin huntress and one of Artemis' favourites, is one of the participants in the hunt and, when the boar is killed, the besotted Meleager grants her all the spoils. When his uncles object Meleager kills them. In revenge for the death of her brothers Althaea burns the stick that measures her son's life and kills him. In the poem Swinburne demonstrates his concern with family tensions and his impatience with orthodox religion. Several of the lyrics from the drama achieved fame outside their original context and *Atalanta in Calydon* is generally admired for its metrical versatility and emotional power.

Atheist, The: or The Second Part of the Soldier's Fortune **(1684)**
Play by ▷ Thomas Otway; his last. A comedy, with many intrigue elements. Porcia (played by ▷ Elizabeth Barry in the original version) is pursued by an unwanted suitor, her late husband's brother, who tries to force her to marry him. She approaches Beaugard (first played by ▷ Thomas Betterton) in masquerade, to take up her cause and, in effect, marry her instead, although she claims at first to hate him. Beaugard is also pursued by Lucretia, but he remains loyal to Porcia, whereupon Lucretia plots her revenge, disguising herself as

a man in the process of attempting to mismate various characters. Meanwhile Courtine and Sylvia, lovers in ▷ *The Soldier's Fortune*, have now married, but the union is unhappy, and he abandons her. Various complications are resolved after an improbable last scene, where numerous characters mistake one another's identities in the dark. It is interesting that the men in the play are largely passive, while most of the action is initiated by women.

***Atheist's Tragedy, The* (1611)**
The only extant tragedy confidently attributed to ▷ Cyril Tourneur, formerly thought to be the author also of ▷ *The Revenger's Tragedy*. The play dramatizes the evil plotting of D'Amville, the atheist, to advance his wealth through marital intrigue, and ends in a grotesque manner with the involuntary suicide of the villain and the safeguarding of true love.

Athenaeum, The
Founded in 1828, it was one of the most enlightened periodicals of the 19th century. It was honest and independent in literary criticism, and a leader of the movement to spread education among the working classes. In 1831 it reduced its price by half in order to reach this wider public, and in consequence increased its circulation six times. It was also very progressive in social reform. In 1921 it was incorporated in the *Nation and Athenaeum*, which in turn was merged in 1931 with the socialist weekly *The New Statesman*.

Atticus, T. Pomponius (109–32 BC)
Atticus was a correspondent of Cicero and learned in Greek literature. ▷ Alexander Pope refers to ▷ Joseph Addison under this name in lines which he originally sent as a reproach to the older man in a letter in about 1715. They were first published in 1722 after Addison's death, and appear in revised form in the *Epistle to Dr Arbuthnot* (1735).

Atwood, Margaret (b 1939)
Canadian novelist, poet and short-story writer. Born in Ottawa, she spent part of her early years in the wilds of northern Quebec, and her poetry makes considerable metaphorical use of the wilderness and its animals. Her first two novels are poetic accounts of the heroines' search for self-realization, and each has a dominant central metaphor: emotional cannibalism in *The Edible Woman* (1969) and drowning and surfacing in *Surfacing* (1972). *Lady Oracle* (1976) is a more comic and satirical work, portraying the limitations of middle-class Canadian life. Her poetry, which is unrhymed, shares many themes with her novels; *The Journals of Susanna Moodie: Poems* (1970) employs pioneering as a metaphor for contemporary feminist questioning of gender roles. Her more recent novels have broader social themes: *Bodily Harm* (1981) is a political satire set on a Caribbean island, while *The Handmaid's Tale* (1986) is a vision of a futuristic dystopia, influenced by ▷ George Orwell's *1984*. It focuses on the exploitation of women in a state ruled by religious fundamentalism, and the ambivalent, ironic conclusion promotes a complex sense of the novel's relevance to our own times. The novel *Cat's Eye* (1989) and the collection of short stories *Wilderness Tips* (1991) return to her Canadian background, evoking with acute irony the middle-class Canada of the 1950s, 1960s and 1970s. Atwood's interest in Canadian nationalism and in feminism have made her an important figure in contemporary Canadian culture.

Other novels include: *Life Before Man* (1979) and *The Robber Bride*. Story collections: *Dancing Girls* (1977); *Murder in the Dark* (1984); *Bluebeard's Egg* (1986). Volumes of poetry include: *Selected Poems* (1976); *Marsh, Hawk* (1977); *Two Headed Poems* (1978); *True Stories* (1981); *Notes Towards a Poem That Can Never Be Written* (1981); *Snake Poems* (1983); *Interlunar* (1984). Criticism: *Second Words: Selected Critical Prose* (1982).

▷ Post-colonial Literature.

Bib: Rigney, B. H., *Margaret Atwood*.

Aubrey, John (1626–97)
Biographer and antiquary. Aubrey was a man of endlessly fascinated speculation on every aspect of the world in which he found himself. Entirely without any form of method, he nevertheless produced (though never published) an invaluable record of people, events and happenings of the period in which he lived. Frequently the record of personalities preserved by Aubrey is highly untrustworthy in terms of its factual content, and yet his *Brief Lives* is still an important document not least because of its often penetrating assessment of his subjects' lives and works. If nothing else, Aubrey has preserved a critical running commentary on many of the figures from the 17th century whose works are read in the 20th century.

▷ Biography.

Bib: Dick, O. L. (ed.), *Aubrey's Brief Lives*.

Auchinleck Manuscript
A famous literary anthology (now kept in the National Library of Scotland, Edinburgh, Advocates' MS *19.2.1*), which was probably produced around *1330–40* in a London workshop. It contains a wide range of vernacular texts including an important collection of romances (such as ▷ *Bevis of Hampton, King Alisaunder, Richard the Lion-hear* and *Sir Tristrem).*

Auden, W. H. (Wystan Hugh) (1907–73)
Poet and dramatist. Born in York, Auden spent

much of his childhood in Birmingham, but was educated at Gresham's School, Norfolk, a public school with liberal ideas about education, and at Oxford University. The landscape of the industrial Midlands influenced his work throughout his life. Auden began writing poetry at 15, and twice edited the journal *Oxford Poetry* when he went up to Oxford in 1925. As a student he became the central figure in the 1930s group of left-wing intellectuals, which included ▷ Stephen Spender (who printed Auden's first collection of poems on a hand press), ▷ Cecil Day-Lewis, ▷ Louis MacNeice and ▷ Christopher Isherwood. His background was a middle-class intellectual one, which produced a sense of social responsibility and a strong didactic tendency in his poetry. He became a teacher and worked both in an English school and in English and American universities. He married Erika Mann, Thomas Mann's daughter and an anti-Nazi, in 1938, so that she could obtain British citizenship, although Auden was himself a homosexual. He emigrated to the U.S.A. in 1939, becoming an American citizen in 1946. In 1956 he became professor of poetry at Oxford, and died in Austria in 1973.

His first book, *Poems* (1930), was published during the great economic crisis which originated in the U.S.A. in 1929. This was followed by *The Orators* (1932), the 'charade' *The Dance of Death* (1933), *Look, Stranger!* (1936), *Letters from Iceland* (with MacNeice, 1937), *Journey to a War* (with Isherwood, 1939) and *Another Time* (1940). He also wrote plays, often with Isherwood: *The Dog Beneath the Skin* (with Isherwood; 1935); *The Ascent of F6* (with Isherwood; 1936); *On the Frontier* (with Isherwood; 1938).

His verse is full of topical reference to the social and international crises of the time; it gives direct expression to the anxieties of the contemporary intelligentsia as perhaps no other writing has done. Auden was interested in verse technique, and influenced by an extensive range of writing, extending from the alliterative styles of Old and Middle English to ▷ T. S. Eliot and the late work of ▷ W. B. Yeats. Throughout his life he was interested in ▷ Freud and psychoanalytic theory, and also absorbed Marxism, the work of Danish philosopher Søren Kierkegaard, and the 20th-century German-American theologian Niebuhr. After 1940 he became increasingly committed to Anglo-Catholic Christianity.

After his emigration to America, Auden published a wide range of poetry in different forms: *New Year Letter* (1941), *For the Time Being* (1945), *The Age of Anxiety* (1948), *Nones* (1952), *The Shield of Achilles* (1955), *Homage to Clio* (1960). He also wrote criticism (*The Enchafèd Flood* (1951), *The Dyer's Hand* (1963)), libretti for operas, and he edited a number of ▷ anthologies. Towards the end of his life he became an isolated figure, in marked contrast with the first decade of his writing when he had seemed to be the voice of a generation – although perhaps, in reality, only the generation of the younger middle class. Later works and editions include: *About the House* (1966); *City Without Walls* (1969); *Epistle to a Godson* (1972); *Thank You Fog; Last Poems* (1974); *Collected Poems* (ed. Mendelson; 1976); *The English Auden* (ed. Mendelson; 1977); *Collected Poems* (1990), *Plays and Other Dramatic Writings 1928–1938* (with Christopher Isherwood) (1989).

Bib: Hoggart, R., *Introductory Essay*; Drew, E., *Directions in Modern Poetry*; Beach, J. W., *The Making of the Auden Canon*; Spears, M. K., *The Poetry of W. H. Auden*; Everett, B., *Auden* in the Writers and Critics Series; Hynes, S., *The Auden Generation*; Mendelson, E., *Early Auden*; Smith, S., *W. H. Auden*.

Augustus
▷ Caesar, Augustus

***Aureng-Zebe* (1675)**
Heroic play by ▷ John Dryden, based on a contemporary account of the struggle between the four sons of Shah Jahan, the fifth Mogul emperor, for the succession to the throne. Dryden made several crucial changes to his source, notably to the character of Aureng-Zebe, who in Dryden's version remains loyal to his father, even though he is betrayed by him. This morality pays off in that at the end of the play he receives the crown legitimately. The character of Indamora, a captive queen whom Aureng-Zebe loves, was invented by Dryden. At the end they are united, with the blessings of the emperor who had pursued Indamora for himself.

***Aurora Leigh* (1857)**
One of ▷ Elizabeth Barrett Browning's most important works, and a key text for Victorian debates about the ▷ 'Woman Question'. Described by its author as a 'novel in verse', this 11,000-line poem is a semi-autobiographical account of the development of a female poet, exploring both the nature of sexual difference and the role of the woman writer.

Aurora is brought up in Italy until she is seventeen, then sent to England to live with an aunt. Educating herself in secret, she refuses a marriage proposal at twenty from her cousin Romney, who wishes her to abandon writing in favour of social reform. Alone and penniless on the death of her aunt, she establishes a reputation as a poet in London. Here she becomes involved with Lady Waldemar, who is in love with Romney and wishes to use Aurora to prevent him from marrying Marian Earle, a poor sempstress. Marian absconds to the continent before the marriage can take place, and Aurora finds her there with an illegitimate child, the product of a rape. The two women live happily together in Italy for some time until Aurora meets up with the now blinded and politically disillusioned Romney who acknowledges the importance of her work and whom she marries.

Although the narrative is indebted to other 19th-century texts such as ▷ Elizabeth Gaskell's ▷ *Ruth* and ▷ Charlotte Brontë's ▷ *Jane Eyre*, as well as to Madame de Staël's (1766–1817) *Corinne ou L'Italie* (1807), it is important for its discussion of art, politics, poetic tradition and women's writing. *Aurora Leigh* contains the fullest exposition of issues surrounding female creativity in Victorian literature, despite its elitist political stance and demonstrable fear of the working class. In the year of its publication it ran to three editions and remained enormously popular, achieving seventeen editions by 1882. However, some Victorian parents refused to allow their daughters to read it, fearful of the model of female independence and autonomy it presented. In its themes it echoes ▷ Kingsley's ▷ *Alton Locke*.

Aurora Leigh was republished by The Women's Press in 1978.

▷ Women's Movement.

Austen, Jane (1775–1817)
Novelist. Her novels in order of publication are as follows: *Sense and Sensibility* (1811), ▷ *Pride and Prejudice* (1813), ▷ *Mansfield Park* (1814), ▷ *Emma* (1816), ▷ *Northanger Abbey* and ▷ *Persuasion* (1818). The last two, published posthumously, are her first and last work respectively in order of composition. Fragments and early drafts include: *Lady Susan* (pub 1871), *The Watsons* (1871) and *Sanditon*, on which she was working when she died, published in 1925.

She restricted her material to a narrow range of society and events: a prosperous, middle-class circle in provincial surroundings. However, she treated this material with such subtlety of observation and depth of penetration that she is ranked among the most enduring English novelists. A French critic, Louis Cazamian, writes of her method that it is 'so classical, so delicately shaded . . . that we are strongly reminded of the great French analysts'. Her classicism arises from respect for the sane, clear-sighted judgement of the ▷ Augustan age that had preceded her, but its vitality is enhanced by the ▷ Romanticism of her own period, so that her heroines acquire wisdom by a counter-balancing of the two. She brought the English novel, as an art form, to its maturity, and the wide range which that form covered later in the 19th century owed much to the imaginative assurance which she had given it.

Her life as a clergyman's daughter was outwardly uneventful but it is probably not true that this accounts for the absence of sensationalism in her novels; her circle of relatives and friends was such as could have given her a wide experience of contemporary society. The restriction of the subject matter of her fiction seems to have been dictated by artistic considerations. D. W. Harding's essay 'Regulated Hatred: An Aspect of the Work of Jane Austen' (*Scrutiny*, 1940) credits her with being a caustic satirist and critic of society.

Bib: Austen-Leigh, J. E., *A Memoir of Jane Austen*; Butler, M., *Jane Austen and the War of Ideas*; Greg, J. D., *The Jane Austen Handbook*; Lascelles, M., *Jane Austen and her Art*; Mudrick, M., *Jane Austen: Irony as Defence and Discovery*; Southam, B. C. (ed.), *Jane Austen: The Critical Heritage*; Tanner, T., *Jane Austen*.

Austin, Sarah (1793–1867)
Translator. Primarily important for facilitating access to French and German ▷ medieval literature during a period in which the influence of ▷ Gothic literature was of primary importance. She published her translations in *Lays of the Minnesingers* (1825), with Edgar Taylor (▷ lay). She also translated: from German, Prince Puckler-Muskau's *Tour in England, Ireland and France* (1832), *Characteristics of Goethe* (1833) and *Fragments from German Prose Writers* (1841); and from French, several political and biographical works. Although committed to the education of women, she deemed it sensible to refrain from airing her feelings too strongly in her works. Nevertheless, she may have influenced J. S. Mill (1806–73) in his campaign for women's equality, as it was Austin who taught him the German language.

▷ French literature in England; German Influence on English literature.

Bib: Hamburger, L. and J., *Troubled Lives: John and Sarah Austin*.

Author
This is a very uncomplicated term when used merely to designate the person who writes the text of a work. But modern critical thought has had reservations about highlighting the author's role too prominently when analysing literary works, mainly because an over-emphasis on the author tends to block other important considerations and reduce literary commentary to biographical speculation or mindless talk about 'genius'. A number of factors have influenced this suspicion.

1 ▷ Modernist thinkers, such as ▷ T. S. Eliot, ▷ James Joyce and the Russian ▷ Formalists, emphasised the craftsmanship and impersonality of writers rather than their genius. For them, writers manipulate language, tradition and convention in a skilled way rather than by possession of special inspiration or wisdom.

2 ▷ Psychoanalytic thinkers highlight the central role of unconscious forces in human creativity rather than those of the conscious personality of the author.

3 An influential strand of critical opinion

stresses the unreliability of using the author's intentions as a benchmark for analysing literary texts for a variety of reasons (▷ Intentional Fallacy).

4 Related to this, is the view that literary texts are much too complex to be ascribed to single, personal causes: authors assume roles, for instance, they deploy ironies, set up dialogues and debates and create a plurality of voices rather than speak from a stable centre of belief or inspiration.

5 It is also argued that the emphasis on authors ignores the role of readers, and some critics stress the creativity of readers and the ways in which many literary works encourage them to use this (▷ Reader Response Criticism).

6 From a historical perspective, scholars are also unhappy that a concentration on the so-called 'timelessness' or universality of the author's genius ignores important socio-economic factors. Examples of such factors would be the role of publishers, patrons, theatre managers and the book-buying public in shaping a work for the market-place, as well as the political and ▷ ideological contexts of a period. Such scholars also point out that the ▷ Romantic idea of the genius is a 19th-century invention and, if applied to earlier periods, distorts our understanding of the social roles occupied by writers.

7 Finally, in recent times, ▷ poststructuralist thinkers like ▷ Michel Foucault and ▷ Roland Barthes have pronounced, in Barthes' famous slogan, 'the death of the author'. For Foucault, a concentration on authors as individuals neglects their social role and the way they use the ▷ discourse of their time. Foucault therefore writes about what he calls 'the author function' rather than individuals. Similarly, for Barthes, it is not authors that matter, but the ▷ text produced. However, opponents of these ideas argue that the elimination of the author disregards the fact that literature is an act of human creativity and communication, and that the isolation of free-standing, impersonal text ignores the historical and cultural circumstances of its production.

Bib: Barthes, R., *Image-Music-Text*; Foucault, M., *Language, Counter-Memory, Practice*.

Authorized Version of the Bible

▷ Bible in England.

Autobiography

The word came into English at the very end of the 18th century and by the 19th and 20th centuries the writing of the story of one's own life had become a common literary activity. However, the practice already had an ancient history, and English autobiography may be divided into three overlapping historical segments: 1 the spiritual confession; 2 the memoir; 3 the autobiographical novel.

1 The spiritual confession has as its basic type the Confessions of St Augustine of Hippo (345–430) who described his conversion to Christianity. Such records of the inner life existed in the English Middle Ages, *eg* the *Book of Margery Kempe* (15th century), but the great age for them was the 17th century, when the ▷ Puritans, depending on the Word of God in the Bible and the inner light of their own consciences, made a practice of intensive self-examination. By far the best known of these records is ▷ Bunyan's ▷ *Grace Abounding to the Chief of Sinners* (1666). However, the greater freedom accorded to women under Puritan principles allowed several women to write spiritual autobiographies, including ▷ Margaret Fell and ▷ Alice Sutcliffe. It is characteristic of such works that they contain detailed accounts of the emotional life, but little factual description of events.

2 The memoir, on the other hand, of French derivation, originates largely in the 17th century and owes much to the practice of extensive letter-writing which then developed, *eg* the letters of Madame de Sévigné (1626–96). An unusual early example of this class is the autobiography of the musician Thomas Whythorne (1528–96), published in 1964 and entitled *A Book of Songs and Sonetts*.

One of the earliest and most interesting of such secular autobiographies written by a woman was that of ▷ Lady Anne Clifford, and this was followed by ▷ Margaret Cavendish's 'A True Relation of My Birth Breeding and Life' appended to *Nature's Pictures* (1657). An example from 18th-century England is the fragmentary *Memoirs* (pub 1796) by the historian ▷ Edward Gibbon. But the objective memoir and the subjective confessions came together in the *Confessions* of the French-Swiss ▷ Jean-Jacques Rousseau, and this is the most prevalent form of the outstanding English autobiographies of the 19th century. The varieties of this form are extensive; they may be a record of emotional struggles and experiences, *eg* ▷ *The Confessions of an English Opium Eater* by ▷ Thomas de Quincey; ▷ *Sartor Resartus* by ▷ Thomas Carlyle. They may be essentially a history of the growth of ideas, convictions, and the strengthening of vocation, in the life of the writer, *eg Autobiography* (1873) by ▷ John Stuart Mill; *My Apprenticeship* (1926) by ▷ Beatrice Webb; *Apologia pro Vita Sua* (1864) by ▷ John Henry Newman. In any case, an autobiographical element becomes prominent in works which are not strictly autobiographies from the early 19th century on; *eg* ▷ Wordsworth's *Prelude, or Growth of a Poet's Mind* (first version 1805); the periodical essays of ▷ Charles Lamb in ▷ *Essays of Elia* (1820–3) and ▷ Coleridge's mixture of autobiography with philosophy and literary criticism in *Biographia Literaria* (1817). It may be said that from 1800 on it becomes the instinct of writers of many kinds to use autobiographical material, or to adopt from time to time an autobiographical standpoint. Indeed, a number of fictional works in the 18th century purport to be memoirs, or are in fact memoirs disguised as fiction, for example, ▷ Delarivière Manley's *The Adventures of Rivella* (1714).

3 Thus we come to the autobiographical novel, and while the form developed a formal identity in the 18th and 19th centuries, a prototype may be found in the mock-autobiographies of ▷ Elizabethan novels, such as ▷ Thomas Nashe's ▷ *Unfortunate Traveller* (1594). In the Victorian period we have the novels of ▷ Charlotte Brontë (▷ *Jane Eyre*, 1847, and ▷ *Villette*, 1853), and Charles Dickens' ▷ *David Copperfield* (1849–50); in addition the anti-feminist writer ▷ Eliza Lynn Linton chose to portray her life using a male protagonist in ▷ *The Autobiography of Christopher Kirkland* (1885) thereby enjoying a certain freedom to write about events which would have been denied her had she published it under her own name. ▷ Charles Darwin and ▷ Thomas Huxley both wrote autobiographies. This method of writing a novel really came into its own however, with ▷ Samuel Butler's ▷ *Way of all Flesh* (1903), which led to many successors in the 20th century, notably ▷ James Joyce's ▷ *Portrait of the Artist as a Young Man* (1916), and ▷ D. H. Lawrence's ▷ *Sons and Lovers* (1913), both autobiographical discussions of the development of the artist. More recent examples are ▷ Margaret Atwood's *Cat's Eye*, (1989), ▷ Sylvia Plath's *The Bell Jar* (1963), American writer Alice Walker's *The Colour Purple* and ▷ Jeanette Winterson's *Oranges are Not the Only Fruit*. Finally, the links between identity, culture and politics have made the autobiographical novel an important form of ▷ post-colonial and feminist fiction, *eg* ▷ George Lamming, *In the Castle of My Skin* (1953), ▷ Bessie Head, *A Question of Power* (1973).

Autobiography of Christopher Kirkland, The (1885)

The autobiography of ▷ Eliza Lynn Linton, anti-feminist journalist and author of the sensational essay ▷ 'The Girl of the Period' (1868). Although the book accurately and frankly records Linton's life, it is written from the perspective of a male. One reason for this may have been that a male persona enabled Linton to write more freely about her own close female companions without attracting speculation or scandal (especially since she had explicitly condemned ▷ lesbianism in *The Rebel of the Family*, 1880). The book was not a commercial success.

▷ Pseudonyms.

Avalon

The 'Insula Avallonis' is mentioned in ▷ Geoffrey of Monmouth's ▷ *History of the Kings of Britain* as the place where Arthur's sword was forged, and as the place to which ▷ Arthur is taken after he has been fatally wounded. More information about Avalon is given in Geoffrey's poetic account of the *Life of Merlin* (*Vita Merlini*), where it is called 'the island of apples', said to be over the Western waters and the home of Morgan la Fay. In the course of the development of Arthurian legend, Avalon has been given different geographical settings; ▷ Glastonbury, in particular, has been strongly promoted from the late 12th century onwards as being Arthur's burial place and, hence, to be identified as Avalon itself.

Avant-garde

Originally referring to the most forward part of an advanced army, this French term was used for political movements, especially revolutionary ones, from the late 19th century. It has been applied to innovative developments in the arts in all fields from the early 20th century, particularly those using experimental techniques designed to challenge their audience with their innovation or difficulty. Something of the military and political origin of avant-garde is therefore retained in the aggressive stance of much avant-garde art. The term also indicates a certain social group, largely young, urban and cosmopolitan in outlook, in which such techniques are devised and encouraged.

Avon

The river of ▷ Shakespeare's birthplace, Stratford-on-Avon, from which he is called the 'Swan of Avon' by ▷ Ben Jonson in his poem *To the Memory of Shakespeare*. The word derives from Celtic *afon* = 'river'; three other rivers with the same name exist in England.

Awkward Age, The (1899)

A novel by ▷ Henry James. Nanda Brookenham is a young girl brought up in a smart but corrupt section of London society; her mother and her mother's circle are willing to carry on immoral intrigues so long as respectable appearances are scrupulously protected. Nanda is in love with Vanderbank, who, as she learns later, is her mother's lover, and she feels some affection for Mitchett, a young man of less charm than Vanderbank, but with an attractive simplicity of heart. Unlike the other members of her mother's circle, she is free and candid in her feelings and open in her conduct; this alarms Vanderbank and inhibits him from declaring his love for her. Her elderly friend, Mr Longdon, an admirer of her dead grandmother, gives Nanda a dowry to attract Vanderbank, but this only increases the latter's fastidious reluctance to declare himself. Meanwhile, the Duchess, Mrs Brookenham's friend and rival, conspires to capture Mitchett for her own daughter, Aggie, whose appearance of immaculate innocence immediately breaks down when it has served its purpose of qualifying her for the marriage market. Vanderbank's mixture of scrupulousness and timidity remains a permanent barrier between himself and Nanda. Mr Longdon adopts her, and they remain together in their love of truthful feeling, isolated from the sophisticated but essentially trivial society which has hitherto constituted Nanda's environment.

The novel is an example of James' interest in the survival of integrity in a materialistic society blinded by its own carefully cultivated artificiality.

Awoonor, Kofi (b 1935)
Ghanaian novelist and poet, educated at University College of Ghana, University College London and the State University of New York. He has worked as a university lecturer and professor in Ghana and the U.S.A., as a film director and for the Ghana Ministry of Information. He was imprisoned in Ghana during 1975–1976 for alleged subversion; in 1983 he was appointed as Ghana's ambassador to Brazil. His first novel, *This Earth, My Brother* (1971) consists of prose chapters, interspersed with poetic fragments; a dead girl, cousin of the novel's hero, is symbolically identified with the Ghanaian nation and with the figure of 'Manny Watta', a mythical water spirit. His other works include: *Night of My Blood* (1971); *Ride Me Memory* (1973); *Guardians of the Sacred Wand* (1974); *The Breast of the Earth* (1975); *Come the Voyager at Last: A Tale of Return to Africa* (1992). Volumes of poetry: *Rediscovery and Poems* (1964); *The House by the Sea* (1978); *The Morning After: Selected Poems 1963–85* (1985).
Bib: Morell, K. (ed.), *In Person*.

Ayckbourn, Alan (b 1939)
Until recently an underestimated dramatist whose plays have often been dismissed (or presented) as light entertainment for unthinking bourgeois audiences. He often writes about the middle classes in order to explore serious issues of modern life. Ayckbourn is now one of Britain's most commercially successful playwrights, with regular West End and repertory productions, frequent televisations, and commissions both as writer and director.

After starting his theatrical career as an actor and stage-manager with Donald Wolfit's company, he moved to Stephen Joseph's Studio Theatre Company in the early 1960s, where he began directing and writing with Joseph's encouragement. Many of his most successful plays began at Scarborough where he is Artistic Director of the Library Theatre. A superb theatrical craftsman, his plays are often constructed around a tour de force of staging: *The Norman Conquests* (1973) is a trilogy of plays, each of which stands on its own, and presents the same events from the garden, sitting room and dining room; *How the Other Half Loves* (1969), *Absurd Person Singular* (1972) and *Bedroom Farce* (1975) each present more than one household on stage simultaneously; *Way Upstream* (1982) launched a riverboat onto the ▷ National Theatre stage; *Sisterly Feelings* (1979) offers alternative versions for the central section of the play. His plays have their roots in the tradition of farce rather than in experimental theatre. He has stretched the boundaries of comedy and farce as his work has developed. Increasingly, the comings and goings of married couples are injected with a note of black comedy, and social groups are fraught with the suggestions of the darker arenas of human interchange. The social niceties of the tea party in *Absent Friends* are disrupted with the inability of the participants to cope with the idea of death, and in *Just Between Ourselves* (1976) and *Woman in Mind* (1985), what begins as a familiar comic theme of a sterile marriage transforms into tragedy as the wife descends into catatonia and breakdown.

Ayckbourn's success might be accounted for in that his work is challenging, but within strict limits; his subject matter has tended to be middle-class values and lifestyle under threat (but not too much), while his dramatic form plays with theatrical convention but is always firmly rooted in the familiar structures of farce and West-End comedy. His plays include: *Relatively Speaking* (1967); *Absurd Person Singular* (1972); *The Norman Conquests* (1973); *Bedroom Farce* (1975); *Season's Greetings* (1982); *Way Upstream* (1982); *A Chorus of Disapproval* (1984); *Henceforward* (1988). In 1993, French film director Alain Resnais brought Ayckbourn's play-sequence *Intimate Exchanges* to the screen as *Smoking/No Smoking*.
Bib: Billington, M., *Alan Ayckbourn*.

Ayre
▷ Madrigal.

Aytoun, William Edmondstoune (1818–65)
Versatile Scottish satirist, poet and critic and contributor to ▷ *Blackwood's Magazine*. Provoked by the feverish ▷ Romanticism of much of the poetry of the early 1840s and by the enthusiasm of the critic ▷ George Gilfillan, he coined the term ▷ 'Spasmodic' to describe the work of ▷ Sydney Dobell, ▷ Philip James Bailey and Alexander Smith (1830–67). In May 1854, Aytoun instituted an elaborate hoax – publishing an anonymous critical review of a forthcoming production of *Firmilian, or the Student of Badajoz: A Spasmodic Tragedy by T. Percy Jones* and a preface to the work by its imaginary author in *Blackwood's Magazine*. *Firmilian* cleverly burlesqued the excesses of Dobell and Smith to such an extent that they disappeared from the literary scene. Aytoun

also wrote the *Bon Gaultier Ballads* (1855) with Theodore Martin, a series of parodies of poets such as ⊳ Tennyson and ⊳ Elizabeth Barrett Browning. His *Lays of the Scottish Cavaliers* (1849) and *The Ballads of Scotland* (1858) were very popular with their contemporary audience.

⊳ Scottish literature in English.

Bib: Martin, T., *Memoir of William Edmonstoune Aytoun*; Weinstein, M.A., *William Edmonstoune Aytoun and the Spasmodic Controversy*.

Babes in the Wood
▷ *Children in the Wood.*

Bacon, Ann (1528–1610)
Translator. Famed for her translation from Latin into English of Bishop Jewel's *Apology* (1564), and for the letters she wrote to her sons, one of whom was ▷ Francis Bacon, the Lord Chancellor. Ann Bacon was the daughter of Sir Anthony Cooke and was, with her sister Mildred (wife of William Cecil (▷ Burghley)), reputed to be amongst the most highly educated women of their age. She was a staunch Puritan and is said to have been one of ▷ Edward VI's tutors. Her relationship with her own sons was very intense and she maintained a vigorous correspondence with both. Indeed, Francis Bacon left instructions in his will that he should be buried with his mother.
Bib: Travitsky, B. (ed.), *The Paradise of Women.*

Bacon, Francis, 1st Baron Verulam and Viscount St Albans (1561–1626)
Politician, philosopher and essayist, Francis Bacon rose to the rank of lord chancellor, before being dismissed from that office in the same year in which he attained it – 1621. Bacon's offence was, technically, his conviction for accepting bribes whilst a judge in chancery suits. The cause of his conviction, however, was the ascendency of political enemies he had made in the course of his ambitious career.

It is, however, as an essayist, and, more importantly, as one of the earliest theoreticians of scientific methodology for which Bacon was to become famous. A series of works – which included ▷ *The Advancement of Learning* (1605 expanded into *De Augmentis Scientiarum* in 1623), *De sapientia veterum* (1609, translated as *The Wisdom of the Ancients* in 1619) and the incomplete ▷ *Novum Organum* (1620) – established his claims to philosophical and methodological pre-eminence amongst his contemporaries. The *De Augmentis* and the *Novum Organum* formed the first two parts of his enormous project, gathered under the title ▷ *Instauratio Magna*, which remained unfinished but which proposed nothing less than a reordering of all fields of human enquiry. In addition Bacon wrote a history of the reign of ▷ Henry VIII (published in 1622), a collection of anecdotal stories (1625) and a ▷ utopian work, based on the new scientific endeavours of the age – ▷ *The New Atlantis* (1626). His major philosophical works were written in addition to his contribution to the law and his *Essays*, which were first published in 1597 and issued in a final form (much expanded) in 1625.

Until recently, Bacon's reputation tended to rest on his *Essays*, which represent a series of terse observations in the style of Seneca rather than the more fluid meditations to be found in the writings of ▷ Montaigne, who is credited with originating the essay as a distinctly modern form. More and more attention is, however, being paid to his theoretical work in the general area of scientific methodology and taxonomy. It was Bacon who was to be celebrated in the later 17th century as the true progenitor of the ▷ 'New Science', not least because of his intense interest in the language of science, and in the forms of discourse appropriate to different rhetorical and methodological projects. As a scientist in the modern sense, his contribution to knowledge was negligible. But as the author of a series of 'manifestos' which set out to establish the basis for inductive or experimental philosophy, his influence on later generations of English philosophers was to be incalculable. The 'Baconian' method – an adherence, that is, to the importance of observation and definition of the particular, rather than a delight in deduction from the general – was to be the legacy of his work and the basis for his reputation in later periods.
▷ Bacon, Ann.
Bib: Spedding, J., Ellis, R. L., and Heath D. D. (eds.), *Works of Francis Bacon* (7 vols.); Rossi, P., *Francis Bacon: From Magic to Science* (trans.) S. Rabinovitch; Vickers, B. (ed.), *Essential Articles for the Study of Francis Bacon.*

Bacon, Roger (1210/14 –after 1291)
Franciscan scholar, student at Paris and Oxford, and author of treatises on, for example, grammar, logic, physics, mathematics and modern philosophy. He was an acute and independent thinker, and one of the leading philosophers of the ▷ Middle Ages. His originality in devoting himself to experimental methods caused him to be known in Paris as 'Doctor mirabilis' (Wonderful Doctor). He was a vociferous critic of what he saw as the inadequately based scholarship of his time and was placed in confinement at various stages in his career for his heretical propositions. In popular tradition he came to be regarded as a magician and the inventor of a brazen head that could speak. It is in such a role that he is represented in ▷ *Friar Bacon and Friar Bungay* (1594), a romantic comedy by ▷ Robert Greene.

***Badman, The Life and Death of Mr* (1680)**
A moral ▷ allegory by ▷ John Bunyan, author of ▷ *The Pilgrim's Progress*, and, apart from the more famous work, the only one of Bunyan's fictions to remain widely known. It is the biography of a wicked man told by Mr Wiseman, and contains vivid and dramatic detail. Its realism and its psychology make it one of the forerunners of the novel.

Baedeker, Karl (1801–59)
The author of famous guide-books, which were carried on by his son. Their frequent

mention in English 19th- and 20th-century fiction shows how indispensable they were to English middle- and upper-class tourists of the last 100 years, especially in visits to countries in which monuments and works of art are plentiful, such as Italy. He wrote in German but English editions were produced after his death, from 1861 onwards.
Bib: Pemble, J., *The Mediterranean Passion*.

Bagehot, Walter (1826–77)
A writer on political and economic affairs, best known for his book *The English Constitution* (1867), a classic study of the spirit of English politics and notably of the function of monarchy in providing the imaginative appeal of the state and ensuring the dignity of government without hindering desirable conflict of opinion.

Bagehot was also the author of a number of critical essays, the best known of which is *Wordsworth, Tennyson, and Browning or Pure, Ornate, and Grotesque Art in English Poetry* (1864). It is republished in *English Critical Essays* ed. by E. D. Jones (World's Classics).
Bib: Stephen, Leslie in *Studies of a Biographer*; Buchan, A., *The Spare Chancellor*; St John-Stevas, N. A. F., *Life*.

Bailey, Philip James (1816–1902)
Poet. Earliest and most significant member of a school of poets satirized by critic ▷ William Aytoun as the ▷ Spasmodics. Born in Nottingham, he was educated at Glasgow University and called to the Bar in 1840: however, he practised only as a poet. In 1839 he achieved enormous popularity with a blank verse epic drama, *Festus*, based on Goethe's (1749–1882) Faust legend. Each subsequent edition was progressively enlarged until the final *Festus* (1889) had expanded to 52 scenes and 40,000 lines. Highly emotional and religiose, *Festus* sought to portray inspiration through irregularity of form and spontaneous composition. Other, more modest, works include *The Angel World* (1850) and *The Mystic* (1855). Bailey's reputation never recovered from Aytoun's brilliant parody of his style in *Firmilian, or The Student of Badajoz: A Spasmodic Tragedy* (1854).
▷ Gilfillan, George.

Baillie, Joanna (1762–1851)
Friend of ▷ Sir Walter Scott and prolific author of plays based on the ▷ Shakespearean model (*Plays of the Passions*; 1798, 1802, 1812), five of which were acted. She also wrote poems in couplets, and lyrics on sentimental and patriotic themes (*Fugitive Verses*, 1790; *Metrical Legends*, 1821; *Poetic Miscellanies*, 1823).
▷ Aikin, Lucy
Bib: Uphaus, R.W. and Foster, G.M., *The "Other" Eighteenth Century*.

Bainbridge, Beryl (b 1933)
Novelist. Brought up near Liverpool, she worked as an actress before writing her first novel (though not the first to be published), *Harriet Said* (1972), which concerns two girls involved in a murder. Initially seen as a writer of macabre thrillers, she has gained an increasing following and has gradually attracted more serious critical attention. Her novels are characterized by black humour, economy of style and portraits of lower-middle-class manners with a strong element of the ▷ Gothic and grotesque. *The Bottle Factory Outing* (1974) centres on the relationship of two women on an increasingly sinister works outing which leads to the death of one of them. Confused and sordid lives are observed in a detached and ironic manner. *A Quiet Life* (1976) is a partly ▷ autobiographical tale of family eccentricities and the tragic precariousness of love, while *Winter Garden* (1980) draws on a visit Bainbridge made to the Soviet Union to create a chilling though comic account of confusion and intrigue on a tour of that country. Other novels are: *A Weekend with Claude* (1967); *Another Part of the Wood* (1968); *The Dressmaker* (1973); *Sweet William* (1975); *Injury Time* (1977); *Young Adolf* (1978); *Watson's Apology* (1984); *Filthy Lucre* (1986); *An Awfully Big Adventure* (1989, which was released as a film in 1995, directed by Mike Newell).

Bakhtin, Mikhail (1895–1975)
Bakhtin's first major work was *Problems in Dostoevsky's Poetics* (1929), but his most famous work, *Rabelais and His World*, did not appear until 1965. Two books, *Freudianism: a Marxist Critique* (1927), and *Marxism and the Philosophy of Language* (1930) were published under the name of V. N. Volosinov, and a third, *The Formal Method in Literary Scholarship* (1928) appeared under the name of his colleague P. N. Medvedev. Bakhtin's concern throughout is to show how ▷ ideology functions in the process of the production of the linguistic sign and to develop and identify the concept of 'dialogism' as it operates in literary texts. In Bakhtin's words 'In dialogue a person not only shows himself outwardly, but he becomes for the first time that which he is, not only for others but himself as well. To be means to communicate dialogically.' His work has in recent years enjoyed a revival, particularly among critics. Especially important is the way in which he theorizes and politicizes the concepts of festivity and ▷ carnival. Also one of his concerns is to identify the dialectal relationship between those various 'texts' of which any one literary work is comprised. This notion of ▷ 'intertextuality' is currently used within areas such as ▷ feminism and ▷ deconstruction. Much of Bakhtin's work was suppressed during his life-time and not published until after his death.

Bale, John (1495–1563)
Bishop of Ossory, dramatist and literary historian.

A staunch Protestant, Bale came under the ▷ patronage of ▷ Thomas Cromwell and wrote several anti-Catholic (▷ Catholicism) plays before the downfall of his patron. Bale himself was imprisoned for treason by ▷ Mary I and released on a fine of £300; he finally returned to Britain when ▷ Elizabeth I came to the throne. He is best known for his play *King John* (c 1540), which is acknowledged to be the first drama to bridge the gap between the ▷ morality plays of the medieval period and the history plays of the Renaissance, such as those of ▷ Shakespeare and ▷ Marlowe. The play combines moral analysis with historical representation. Bale also compiled the notes of John Leland, which led to an immensely useful index of 1,400 English writers.
Bib: Blatt, T. B. , *The Plays of John Bale*.

Balin
Balin le Savage and Balan are the two brothers who help ▷ King Arthur in his early struggles to establish power in the first book of ▷ Malory's *Morte D'Arthur*. Balin gives King Pellam the Dolorous Stroke which results in the creation of the Wasteland.

Ball, John (d 1381)
Priest and leader of the ▷ Peasants' Revolt (1381), and the subject of *A Dream of John Ball* by ▷ William Morris.

Ballad
Traditionally the ballad has been considered a folkloric verse narrative which has strong associations with communal dancing, and support for that link has been found in the derivation of the word 'ballad' itself (from the late Latin verb *ballare* – to dance). More recently scholars have viewed the association between ballads and dance forms rather more sceptically. Generally, the term is used of a narrative poem which uses an elliptical and highly stylized mode of narration, in which the technique of repetition with variation may play an important part. Often ballads contain repeated choral refrains but this is not a universal feature.

Ballad forms can be identified in early English texts: the brief narrative about *Judas* in the ▷ Harley manuscript has been hailed as the earliest English example of the form. The so-called ▷ Broadside ballads, sold in Elizabethan times, were narrative poems on a wide range of subjects printed on a single side of a broadsheet. From the 18th century onwards, collections of folk/'popular ballads' began to be made and the form was taken up by some of the most influential poets of the late 18th century as a folkloric form of expression. ▷ Wordsworth's and ▷ Coleridge's collection of poems ▷ *Lyrical Ballads* (1798) does not contain many poems in ballad form (apart from the brilliant balladic composition ▷ *The Ancient Mariner*) but the function of the title seems to be to arouse associations of oral, non-literary poetic forms. In this collection, art is used to conceal art. ▷ Walter Scott produced many adaptations and imitations of traditional Scots ballads and published a collection of ballads entitled *The Minstrelsy of the Scottish Border*. The great ballad collection of F. J. Child, *English and Scottish Popular Ballads*, was published at the end of the 19th century. Associated with oral tradition and song, ballads were a popular form for women poets in the 19th century, including Felicia Hemans (1793–1835), Letitia Landon (1802–38), ▷ Elizabeth Barrett Browning, ▷ Emily Brontë and ▷ Christina Rossetti, and they proved equally popular with readers. Victorian ballads often had a ▷ medieval setting, such as Barrett Browning's 'The Romaunt of the Page' (1839) and 'The Lay of the Brown Rosary' (1840). Twentieth-century ballads include *Miss Gee* and *Victor* by ▷ W. H. Auden, and works by ▷ Louis MacNeice and ▷ Rudyard Kipling. Arguably the clearest form in which the ballad has survived is in the work of the musicians and lyricists of the folk revival of the 1950s and 1960s; many of Bob Dylan's songs are ballads.
Bib: Bold, A., *The Ballad*.

***Ballad of Reading Gaol, The* (1898)**
A powerful poem by ▷ Oscar Wilde concerning the hanging of the murderer Charles Thomas Wooldridge during Wilde's own imprisonment in Reading Gaol for homosexual acts. In contrast to Wilde's earlier works it is less concerned with aesthetics than with the harshness of prison conditions and the Christian doctrine of forgiveness. It was his last work.
▷ Homosexuality.

Ballade
A lyrical form favoured by French court poets of the 14th century and first used in English by Chaucer (c 1340–1400). The ballade form requires three stanzas linked by a refrain and common rhymes repeated in the same order in each stanza. It was revived in the late 19th century by poets such as ▷ Swinburne and ▷ Dante Gabriel Rossetti.

Ballantyne, R.M. (1825–94)
Writer of adventure stories, aimed primarily at boys, the most famous being *The Coral Island* (1858), probably the most popular such work of the Victorian era. This story, in which a trio of boys is shipwrecked on a Pacific island, is implicitly a ▷ colonial fable, full of blood and masculine resourcefulness. Ballantyne's life was suitably adventurous: born in Edinburgh, he received little formal education but worked as a fur trader in northern Canada from the age of sixteen. This experience produced *Hudson's Bay* (1848) and *The Young Fur Traders* (1856).

After establishing himself as an author he continued to travel to research the background to his novels, which included: *Martin Rattler, Or A Boy's Adventure in the Forests of Brazil* (1858), *Pirate City* (1874), set in Algiers, and *A Tale of the London Fire Brigade* (1867).

Ballard, George (1706–55)
Writer, antiquarian, and historian, born at Campden in Gloucestershire. His mother was a midwife, and he was apprenticed to a women's clothing maker. Early in life he developed a reputation for learning, leading Lord Chedworth to provide him with a pension for life. Ballard collected books and documents, and drew up histories and genealogies of individuals, families and monuments. He was part of a circle of antiquaries, who collected and classified artifacts, books and manuscripts. He had a sister with literary interests, and this may have influenced composition of his best-known work, the *Memoirs of Several Ladies of Great Britain* (1752), which contains biographies of 64 learned and literary women from the ⊳ Middle Ages to his own day. He wrote it, as he said in the preface, in order to remove 'the vulgar prejudice of the supposed incapacity of the female sex'. His work is considered a major source of information about educated women of the past, and has been extensively used by biographers and anthologists since the 18th century.
Bib: Perry, R. (ed.), *Memoirs of Several Ladies of Great Britain.*

Ballard, J.G. (James Graham) (b 1930)
Novelist and short-story writer. Ballard is closely identified with the ⊳ science fiction genre, primarily because his more widely read novels and short stories, though essentially uncategorizable, fit most readily into the sci-fi/fantasy bracket. However, whilst his obsessions with mental decay, violence and its imagery, and the fragmentation of contemporary culture are filtered through the landscapes of more conventional fantasy writing, his allegiance with mainstream fantasy or science fiction is uneasy, and his later writing, particularly the Booker Prize shortlisted *Empire of the Sun* (1984), has moved nearer to realism, drawing upon Ballard's own childhood experiences. His works include: *The Drowned World* (1962); *The Terminal Beach* (1964); *The Drought* (1965); *The Crystal World* (1966); *The Atrocity Exhibition* (1970); *Crash* (1973); *The Unlimited Dream Company* (1979); *Myths of the Near Future* (1982); *The Day of Creation* (1987); *The Kindness of Women* (1991).

Balzac, Honoré de (1799–1850)
French novelist. His *La Comédie humaine* is a panorama of French society from the ⊳ Revolution to the July Monarchy (1830). It is bound together by the use of recurrent characters (Vautrin is one notable instance, Rastignac another) and recurrent motifs (notably the necessity of moral and social order contrasted with the pressures of the individual ego). Among the one hundred novels which Balzac completed, drafted or projected are *Eugénie Grandet* (1833), *Illusions perdues* (1837–43), *La Cousine Bette* (1846), *Le Cousin Pons* (1847), *Le Père Goriot* (1835), *Splendeurs et misères des courtisanes* (1847).

'French society was to be the historian', Balzac wrote, 'I had only to be the scribe'. His ways of depicting French society are geographical, historical, political and even geological insofar as all social strata find a place. These different representations, taken individually or in combination, bring into play a dynamic explained in *La Peau de chagrin* (1831) as the produce of desire and power, with knowledge enlisted to restrain them. But such a restraint is rare or non-existent, and society in the *Comédie humaine* is driven by a restlessness which tends to exhaustion as it competes for the fulfilment of desire. Like society, character too is open to multiple descriptions, as a machine driven by abstracts (passion, ambition, penury, for instance) or as a representative of a human or social type. In that respect, character has a potential for expansion. It is always ready to merge into symbol (more than just the performance of symbolic actions) or be exaggerated into ⊳ melodrama. Indeed, melodrama is a central Balzacian ingredient and, just as characters are actors, buildings and places too are subject to mutation into a theatre or a scene in which the novelistic events unfold. In its liking for myth and melodrama, Balzac's social realism is correspondingly more than the accumulation of surface detail, since the detail acts as an indicator of underlying causes. In turn, understanding of these causes is open only to the novelist defined by his capacity for 'second sight', the capacity to perceive pattern as well as pattern destroyed. And it is considerations of this kind which distinguish Balzac from other ⊳ *feuilleton* novelists such as Eugène Sue (1804–57) and help account for his pervasive influence on 19th century fiction, particularly in England where Balzac shaped the already strong vein of social ⊳ realism.
Bib: Prendergast, C., *Balzac: Fiction and Melodrama*; Bellos, D., *Balzac: Le Père Goriot.*

Banks, Isabella (1821–87)
Novelist, poet and journalist, born in Manchester, the daughter of a successful tradesman. She was sixteen years old when her poem 'A Dying Girl to Her Mother', was published in the *Manchester Guardian.* More of her work was published in *Bradshaw's Three* (1841–42), and her first collection of poems, *Ivy Leaves*, appeared in 1844. Banks then grew prolific, writing a series of novels set in the Manchester area, the best-known of which are *The Manchester Man*

(1876), *Caleb Booth's Clerk* (1878) and *Wooers and Winners: A Yorkshire Story* (1880). Her novels were so rooted in her native environment that she was labelled the 'Lancashire Novelist'. They are mainly of historical interest today, seeming overloaded with detailed local description and lacking narrative pace.

▷ Regional novel.

Bib: Burney, E.L., *Life*.

Banks, John (b c 1650)
Dramatist. He trained as a lawyer, but turned to the stage in 1677, when the success of Nathaniel Lee's *The Rival Queens* led him to write *The Rival Kings*. Banks specialized in writing pathetic tragedies, featuring injured heroines. He was ahead of his time as the vogue for such plays, sometimes known as ▷ She-Tragedies, did not really develop until the last decade of the century. He could not find a publisher for his *The Innocent Usurper*, or a theatre to perform it in, until 1693, ten years after it was written; it was then banned for political reasons. *The Island Queens*, concerning the execution of Mary, Queen of Scots (1684), also met with indifference until 1704, when it achieved success under the title, *Albion's Queen*. Other plays include *The Unhappy Favourite* (1681), about Elizabeth I and Essex; *Virtue Betrayed* (1682), on Anne Boleyn; and *Cyrus the Great* (1696), which had considerable success in performance at ▷ Lincoln's Inn Fields, although its run was curtailed by the death of one its leading actors.

Bankside
The south bank of the Thames in London. It was famous in ▷ Shakespeare's day for its theatres. The City of London refused to allow public theatres within its bounds; hence famous theatres such as the ▷ Globe and the ▷ Rose had to be built in Southwark on Bankside. Today, the area south of the Thames, from Southwark to Waterloo, is once more a site for the arts, including the new ▷ Globe Theatre and the ▷ National Theatre, as well as film and music complexes.

▷ Theatres; Alleyn Edward.

Bannerman, Anne (1765–1829)
Poet. She lived in penurious circumstances and poor health in Edinburgh. Her first book, *Poems* (1800) contains ▷ odes and ▷ sonnets translated from Goethe (▷ German influence on English literature), while her second, *Tales of Superstition and Chivalry* (1802) uses the ▷ ballad form to tell ▷ Gothic tales of ghosts and prophets. Other themes include nostalgic and sentimental praise for Scotland and admiration for her contemporary ▷ Joanna Baillie.

▷ Scottish Literature in English.

Bannockburn (1314)
A battle in central Scotland, in which a Scottish army under Robert the Bruce defeated a large invading English force under ▷ Edward II. The battle decided Scottish independence until the two countries became united under a Scottish king (▷ James VI and I, 1603–25). As a heroic episode, it has had a force of inspiration for the Scots similar to the victory of ▷ Agincourt for the English.

Baptists
An important sect of Nonconformist Protestants; originally one of the three principal branches of English ▷ Puritanism, the other two being the Independents (Congregationalists), and the ▷ Presbyterians (Calvinists). Their especial doctrine is to maintain that the rite of baptism must be administered to adults, and not to infants. They began as an offshoot of the Independents in the first decade of the 17th century, and made rapid progress between 1640 and 1660 – the period of the ▷ Civil War and the ▷ Interregnum, when the Puritans usurped the position of the ▷ Church of England. One of the foremost exponents of the Baptist Church in the second half of the 17th century was ▷ John Bunyan (1628–88).

▷ Protestantism; Parr, Susanna.

Barbauld, Anna Laetitia (1743–1825)
Poet, editor and writer of children's books. Her first book, *Poems* (1773), was an immediate success. It adopts an ▷ Augustan tone, imitating Samuel Johnson's (1709–84) attack on ▷ Romantic literature. She became a friend of ▷ Joanna Baillie who inspired her to turn to political writing, which resulted in the Abolitionist tract *A Poetical Epistle to Mr Wilberforce, on the Rejection of the Bill for Abolishing the Slave Trade* (1790) (▷ Abolition literature). Barbauld is rightly renowned for her fifty-volume editions of the works of English novelists (1810), for which she wrote an interesting preface on novel writing. Her *The Female Speaker* (1811), which provides selections of literature suitable as reading matter for young ladies, has generally been mocked, but she does include ▷ Coleridge's poem ▷ 'The Ancient Mariner' and refers to its 'queer, wizard-like quality'. She was also a prominent member of the ▷ Bluestocking circle and a friend of ▷ Elizabeth Montagu.

Bib: Moore, C.E., *Fetter'd or Free? British Women Novelists*. 1670–1815; Rodgers, B., *Georgian Chronicle: Mrs Barbauld and Her Family*; Schlueter, P. and J., *An Encyclopedia of British Women Writers*.

Barbour, John (c 1320–95)
Scottish poet; author of a long verse chronicle in eight-syllable couplets about the Scottish War of Indepedence – *The Bruce* (c 1375). It tells the story of the defeat of the English attempts

to conquer Scotland (1296–1328), contains a celebrated account of ▷ Bannockburn and extols the principal hero of the War – Robert the Bruce, who ended his career as king of Scotland. Other works have been attributed to Barbour, including *The Buik of Alexander*, but evidence of his authorship has been disputed.
Bib: McDiarmid, M. P. and Stevenson, J. A. (eds.), *Barbour's Bruce*, Scottish Text Society 12–13, 15.

Bard
A member of the privileged caste of poets among the ancient Celtic peoples, driven by the Romans and then the Anglo-Saxons into Wales and Ireland and, legend has it, exterminated in Wales by Edward I. The term became known to later English writers from references in Latin literature. Poets such as ▷ Shakespeare, ▷ John Milton and ▷ Alexander Pope refer to any serious poet as a 'bard'. In the 18th century, partly as a result of the growing antiquarian interest in ▷ druidism, the term came to designate a mysteriously or sacredly inspired poet, as in ▷ Thomas Gray's famous ▷ ode ▷ *The Bard* (1757).

Bard, The **(1757)**
One of ▷ Thomas Gray's two famous 'Pindaric Odes' (the other being 'The Progress of Poesy'). The last surviving Celtic ▷ bard stands on a mountain-top and calls down curses upon King Edward I and the English army, as they march below, prophesying the end of his royal house and its ultimate replacement by the (Welsh) house of Tudor. He concludes by throwing himself into the River Conway beneath. There is a stagey wildness about the work which irritated the ▷ Augustan author Samuel Johnson (1709–84), though its failure to 'promote any truth, moral or political' did not prevent it from being very popular at the time.

Barham, Richard (1788–1845)
Poet and miscellaneous prose writer. Barham is primarily known for one work: *The Ingoldsby Legends: or Mirth and Marvels* (three series collected in 1840). This collection of stories and poems was immensely successful at the time and continues to be read and valued today. The tales are often comic, but perhaps it is their ▷ Gothic quality and sexual subtext which make them enjoyable as well as intriguing.
Bib: Horne, R.H., *A New Spirit of the Age*.

Barker, Clive (b 1952)
Novelist, playwright, painter, screenwriter and director. Born, raised and educated in Liverpool, Barker wrote a number of plays (*The Magician*, *The History of the Devil*) before achieving fame as a leading light of Britain's 'new wave' of horror writers (▷ horror fiction), and in 1987, *Hellraiser* established Barker as a maverick directorial talent. He currently lives in Hollywood where he continues to write and direct. Barker's early short stories (collected in *The Books of Blood* Volumes 1 to 6, 1984–5) celebrate cultural multiplicity and sexual perversity, inverting the traditional conservatism of the horror genre. Describing himself as 'a proselytizer on behalf of horror', Barker has sought both on the page and screen to subvert concepts of 'monstrousness'. Most ambitiously, his lengthy novel *Cabal* (1988, filmed as *Nightbreed* 1990) posits a tribe of variegated shape-shifters in whose bizarre disfigurement the reader is encouraged to delight. Barker's later works (*Weaveworld* 1987, *Imajica* 1991) have eschewed the visceral revelry which characterized his short stories and explored the worlds of mythology and fantasy. Despite his huge success as a writer/film-maker, Barker maintains that painting is his first love.
Bib: Jones, S. (ed.), *Shadows in Eden*.

Barker, George Granville (1913–91)
Poet. His first collection, *Thirty Preliminary Poems*, was published in 1933, along with a novel, *Alanna Autumnal*. After that he kept up a steady output of visionary and ▷ autobiographical verse that includes *Calamiterror* (1937), *Lament and Triumph* (1940) and the two parts of *The True Confession of George Barker* (1950 and 1964). His most celebrated later volume is *Anno Domini* (1983).
Bib: Fraser, R. (ed.), *Collected Poems*.

Barker, Howard (b 1946)
One of a generation of British dramatists deeply concerned with political and social issues, Barker has never received the degree of critical acclaim given to some of his contemporaries, probably because his interest in the psychology of capitalism and patriarchy leads him to deal in much of his work with the grotesque and the distorted, often in highly scatalogical language. His plays firmly eschew naturalism in favour of an incisive and theatrically inventive cartoon-like style which juxtaposes private desires with public postures and aims for psychological and sociopolitical truth rather than the texture of everyday life. He shares with ▷ John Gay and ▷ Brecht a crucial perception of the apparent identity of interest between criminal and politician and the inherent corruptions of capitalism. The 'criminal' strand in his work is well represented by, for example, *Alpha Alpha* (1972, a study of two brothers patterned on the Kray twins), *Claw* (1975) (in which the hero acts as procurer for the Home Secretary and *Stripwell* (1975), with its judge faced both with the criminal activities of his son and a man he sentenced returning for revenge.

Barker is a history graduate and many of

his plays also pursue an interest in historical moments and their lessons for the present. *Victory* (1983), subtitled punningly 'Choices in Reaction', a fine example of this second strand, deals with the aftermath of the Restoration of Charles II, mixing historical and stereotypical characters in an extraordinary evocation of the collapse of the ideals of the Commonwealth. The play is notable for a brilliant explanation of the nature and contradictions of capitalism. *The Castle* (1985) is an extraordinary meditation on issues of gender, power, rational and emotional knowledge, war and peace, in which a returning Crusader confronts the peaceful community established by his wife in his absence. The battle lines, both medieval and contemporary, are drawn between creativity and destruction in confrontations and dialogue that are brilliantly imagined and draw to the full on Barker's ability to write with a poetic density of language, comic as well as tragic, which uses everyday idiom as much as architectural imagery to create an extraordinarily flexible language. Other plays include: *That Good Between Us* (1977); *The Hang of the Gaol* (1978); *The Love of a Good Man* (1978); *No End of Blame* (1981); *A Passion in Six Days* (1983); *Crimes in Hot Countries* (1983); *The Power of the Dog* (1984); *Scenes From an Execution* (radio, 1984; staged, 1989); *The Castle* (1985); *Downchild* (1985); *Women Beware Women* (reworking of ▷ Middleton's play; 1986); *The Possibilities* (1988); *The Last Supper* (1988); *The Bite of the Night* (1988); *Seven Lears* (1989); *The Europeans* (1993).

Barker, Jane (fl 1688–1726)
Poet and novelist. She came from a ▷ Catholic Royalist family which remained loyal to the ▷ Stuart monarchs during the ▷ Civil War and to ▷ James II after the accession of ▷ William (III) and ▷ Mary. She spent most of her life in Lincolnshire. Her poetry is both political and personal, reflecting themes such as friendship and love; it includes *Poetical Recreations* (1688), and *A Collection of Poems Referring to the Times* published in 1700. Her novels include *Love Intrigues* (1713) and *Exilius* (1715). A collection, *Entertaining Novels*, was also published in 1715. Barker remained unmarried, a fact which she discussed in *A Patchwork Screen for the Ladies* (1723). She became popular, and some of her works ran to several editions.

***Barnaby Rudge* (1841)**
A novel by ▷ Charles Dickens, published as part of ▷ *Master Humphrey's Clock*. The only other novel that he published in this proposed series was ▷ *The Old Curiosity Shop*; Dickens then abandoned it.

It is set in the 18th century and its central episodes are descriptions of the fierce anti-▷ Catholic disorders called 'the Gordon Riots', which terrorized London for several days in 1780. These vivid scenes, and the characters directly concerned in the riots (such as the half-wit Barnaby Rudge, the locksmith Gabriel Varden and his apprentice Simon Tappertit), constitute the part of the book which is most memorable and most representative of Dickens' style. The main story is a romantic one about the love affair of Emma Haredale, whose father has been mysteriously murdered, and Edward Chester, the son of Sir John Chester, a suave villain who helps to instigate the Riots. Sir John and Emma's uncle, Geoffrey Haredale, a Catholic, are enemies, but they unite in opposition to the marriage of Edward and Emma. During the riots, Geoffrey Haredale's house is burnt down but Edward saves the lives of both Emma and her uncle, and thus wins his approval of the match. The murderer of Emma's father turns out to be the father of Barnaby.

Barnaby Rudge is one of Dickens' two ▷ historical novels, the other being ▷ *A Tale of Two Cities*.

Barnard, Lady Anne (1750–1825)
Poet, artist, travel writer and prolific correspondent. Anne Lindsay, (her maiden name) was a Scottish author, descended from a ▷ Jacobite family, and acquainted with ▷ Sir Walter Scott who published several of her poems. She is known for her reworking of a Scottish ▷ ballad, 'Auld Robin Gray', and a melancholy ballad of her own composition, *Lays of the Lindsays* (▷ lay). This latter poem is reproduced in ▷ Mary Wollstonecraft's *Wrongs of Women*. In 1793 she married Andrew Barnard and in 1797 they moved to South Africa where he became the colonial secretary at the Cape of Good Hope. Her ▷ travel writings, which are accompanied by drawings, show her to have been a careful and sensitive recorder of the places she visited.

▷ Scottish Literature.

Bib: Masson, M., *Lady Anne Barnard: The Court and Colonial Service under George III and the Regency*.

Barnes, Barnabe (c 1559–1609)
Poet and dramatist. Barnes' life seems to have been as adventurous and dark as his dramatic writing; he fought alongside ▷ Essex in 1591 and was called before the Star Chamber when he tried to poison the recorder of Berwick (1598). Barnes came through both events unscathed and is known today chiefly for his lyrical ▷ sonnet sequence *Parthenophil and Parthenope* (1593). Another collection of sonnets, *A Divine Century of Spiritual Sonnets*, appeared in 1595, and a prose work, *Four Bookes of Offices*, in 1606. Barnes' only surviving drama, *The Devil's Charter* (1607), is an anti-Catholic (▷ Catholicism) account of poisoning, magic, subterfuge and evil, which is thought to have been performed before ▷ James I. His patron

was Henry Wriothesley, Earl of Southampton, and as such Barnes is one of the contenders for the role of rival poet in ▷ Shakespeare's sonnets.
Bib: Sisson, C. J., *Thomas Lodge and Other Elizabethans.*

Barnes, Djuna (1892–1982)
Novelist, poet and playwright, who was influential, but until recently little read. Barnes was born in America but lived, like many ▷ modernist artists, in the European 'cities of modernism'. Her best-known and most reprinted work *Nightwood* (1936), a poetic novel championed by ▷ T. S. Eliot (who wrote the introduction to the Faber edition), is a dark, at times surreal and deeply evocative account of decadence and transgression in Bohemian and expatriate circles in inter-war Paris and Berlin. Barnes wrote eloquently about lesbianism, both in this novel and in her other essays (particularly the Virago collection, *I could never be lonely without a husband*), and in her works of fiction. *Ladies' Almanack* celebrates lesbian sexuality in the form of a parody of a medieval calendar. Barnes also experimented in her drama, the earliest works being *Three from the Earth, An Irish Triangle* and *Kurtzy from the Sea* (1928); her last significant work was *The Antiphon* (1958), a surreal play in blank verse. Her first collection of poems was *The Book of Repulsive Women* (1915), and her first novel was *Ryder* (1929).
Bib: Hanscombe, G. and Smyers, V., *Writing for their Lives: The Modernist Women 1910–1940.*

Barnes, Julian (b 1946)
Novelist. Born in Leicester and educated in London and Oxford, Barnes has worked as a lexicographer on the O.E.D. Supplement (1969–1972), and in journalism, writing for the *New Statesman*, *The Sunday Times*, *The Observer*, and as the notorious gossip columnist 'Edward Pygge' in the journal of modern literature, the *New Review*, which ran from 1974 to 1979 under poet and critic Ian Hamilton's editorship. Barnes' work is greatly influenced by French 19th-century novelist ▷ Gustave Flaubert, the ostensible subject of the playful and very successful 1984 novel *Flaubert's Parrot*, which was shortlisted for the 1985 Booker Prize and won the Geoffrey Faber Memorial Prize. Barnes' work is typically witty and parodic: *A History of the World in* 10 Chapters (1989), an example of ▷ post-modernist historiographic metafiction, consists of a series of episodes, some comic, but with a satirical and even tragic edge. On the other hand *The Porcupine* (1992) is a realist political novel about the trial of a deposed Communist leader. Other novels: *Metroland* (1981); *Before She Met Me* (1982); *Staring at the Sun* (1986); *Talking It Over* (1991). Barnes also writes crime fiction, and under the pseudonym Dan Kavanagh published *Duffy* (1980); *Fiddle City* (1983) and *Putting the Boot In* (1985). In 1986 he won the E. M. Forster Award from the American Academy of Arts and Letters. *Letters from London 1990–1995* (1995) is a collection of journalism.

Barnes, William (1801–86)
Poet. A clergyman from the West of England (▷ Wessex), Barnes' most important work is *Poems of Rural Life, in the Dorset Dialect* (1844), but he also wrote verse in 'Standard English'. A champion of Anglo-Saxon over the Latinate element in the English language, he greatly influenced fellow Dorsetman ▷ Thomas Hardy, who wrote the poem 'The Last Signal' (1886) on his death, and prefaced and edited an edition of his poetry in 1908.
Bib: Jones, B. (ed.), *The Poems of William Barnes*; Baxter, L., *The Life of Barnes by his Daughter*.

Barnfield, Richard (1574–1627)
Poet. Barnfield wrote almost all his poetry before 1600, when he gave up writing to become a prosperous Shropshire landowner. Barnfield published three volumes of poetry, in 1594, 1595 and 1598. Of these volumes, *The Affectionate Shepherd, Containing the Love of Daphnis for the Love of Gannymede*, which appeared first, is an exercise in ▷ pastoral. The second volume, entitled *Cynthia, with Certain Sonnets and the Legend of Cassandra*, claims to imitate ▷ Edmund Spenser's ▷ *The Faerie Queene*. The third and final collection contains ▷ satire, pastoral elegy and a 'debate' entitled 'The Combat Between Conscience and Covetessnesse'. In this final collection can be found two poems by Barnfield ('If music and sweet poetrie agree' and 'As it fell upon a day') which were published in the anthology ▷ *Passionate Pilgrim* (1599) and were not recognized as being the work of Barnfield.
Bib: Klawitter, G. (ed.), *The Complete Poems of Richard Barnfield.*

Barnum, Phineas Taylor (1810–91)
A famous American showman who first made a success through the exhibition of 'George Washington's nurse', alleged to be 161 years old; he later made the American Museum, a collection of curiosities, one of the most popular shows in America. He started a circus in 1871, which, as Barnum and Bailey's in 1881, became the type and pattern of all later circuses in England and America, since he toured in both countries. The name of his famous elephant 'Jumbo' is synonymous with 'elephant' to this day.

Baroque
A term mainly applied to the visual arts, particularly architecture, and (with a somewhat

different meaning) to music, but now increasingly used in literary contexts also. It derives from the Italian word *barocco* meaning rough and unpolished, and was originally used to denote extravagance or excessiveness in the visual arts. Thence it came to designate the exuberant, florid architecture and painting characteristic of Europe during the period of absolute monarchies in the 17th and 18th centuries. The more restrained, constitutionalist climate of Britain prevented baroque architecture from taking firm hold, and the few examples (*eg* Castle Howard and Blenheim Palace, both by ▷ Sir John Vanbrugh) date from shortly after the Restoration, when French taste was in the ascendant. English ▷ neo-classicism, when it aimed at large-scale grandeur, tended to be more sober and austere, like ▷ Sir Christopher Wren's St Paul's. In domestic contexts the greater economic and political power of the lesser aristocracy, and the rising merchant class in England, meant that the modest convenience of the Palladian style (▷ Andrea Palladio) was preferred to full-blown baroque. ▷ Alexander Pope's patron Lord Burlington was the most prominent advocate of the Palladian style and Pope wrote his fourth ▷ *Moral Essay*, on the discomforts of baroque magnificence, under Burlington's influence.

In music the term denotes the new, more public, expressive and dramatic style, characterized by free recitative, and most typically seen in the new genre of opera, originating in the Italy of Monteverdi in the late 16th century. It is closely associated with the introduction of new, more expressive and louder instruments, ideal for public performance, such as the transverse flute, the violin and the harpsichord, which at this time began to supplant the softer recorder, viol and virginals, suitable to the intimate, often amateur, music-making of the ▷ Renaissance. The term is now applied to all music between this time and the onset of the classicism of Haydn and Mozart in the later 18th century. The baroque style in music came to England late, and its first great English exponent is ▷ Henry Purcell (1659–95), who wrote the first English opera, *Dido and Aeneas* (1689; libretto by ▷ Nahum Tate).

The epithet 'baroque' has recently come to be used in literary contexts by analogy with its use in the other arts. Thus the extravagant Italianate conceits of the Catholic poet Richard Crashaw who ended his life in Rome, can be called 'baroque'. The florid, public quality of ▷ John Dryden's ▷ *Annus Mirabilis*, may also be termed 'baroque', with its innocent celebration of national pride and adulation of the monarch, the literary equivalent of the mural paintings of the Italian baroque artist Verrio, who worked in England, and whose English pupil, James Thornhill, decorated the Painted Hall at Greenwich early in the 18th century. Like ▷ Classical and ▷ Romantic the word has also developed a wider application beyond its strict historical period.

Barrie, Sir J. M. (James Matthew) (1869–1937)

Scottish playwright and novelist and the ninth of ten children. He had a very close relationship with his mother, Margaret Ogilvy, who was the eponymous heroine of his novel published in 1896 and who also appears as 'the little mother' in his autobiographical novel *Sentimental Tommy* (1896). Barrie attended Edinburgh University before working for the Nottingham *Journal* for two years, and then moved to London in 1885 to become a freelance writer. In his early writing he idealized childhood and expressed disenchantment with adult life. The sketches of Scottish life he published in various papers were collected into his first successful book *Auld Licht Idylls* (1888). His novel in the same vein, *The Little Minister* (1891), was a best-seller and was adapted for the stage in 1897. From this point on Barrie devoted himself to the theatre, producing two of his best plays *Quality Street* and *The Admirable Crichton* in London in 1902. His marriage to the actress Mary Ansell in 1894 was apparently unconsummated and in 1897 he became attached to Sylvia Llewellyn Davies, telling his first Peter Pan stories to her sons and publishing some of them in *The Little White Bird* (1902). The play *Peter Pan*, about a boy who refused to grow up, followed in 1904 and the story was published in *Peter Pan and Wendy* (1911). Other plays include *What Every Woman Knows* (1908), *Dear Brutus* (1917) and *Mary Rose* (1920), and some excellent one-act pieces. He was knighted in 1913.

▷ Scottish literature in English.

Bib: Darton, F. J. Harvey, *Barrie*; Hammerton, J. A., *Barrie, the Story of a Genius*; Mackail, D., *The Story of J. M. B.*

Barry, Elizabeth (1658–1713)

The first well-known English actress, said to have been trained by the ▷ Earl of Rochester, who boasted he could make an actress of her in six months; she became his mistress and later had a daughter by him.

She began by acting at the ▷ Dorset Garden Theatre, probably in 1675, but her career blossomed in 1679–80, with a series of tragic roles which earned her 'the Name of Famous Mrs Barry, both at Court and City'.

Throughout her career she was adored for her acting talents – being admired equally in comic and tragic roles – and sharply satirized for her alleged promiscuity: a contemporary commentary describes her as 'the finest Woman in the World upon the Stage, and the Ugliest Woman off't'. She played Lady Brute in the first production of ▷ *The Provok'd Wife* (1697), Mrs Marwood in the original ▷ *The Way of the World* (1700), and dozens of important roles in plays by contemporary and earlier authors, including many of ▷ Shakespeare's. Succeeding generations of actresses viewed her as an ideal to which they aspired.

Bib: Highfill, P.H. Jr., Burnim, K.A. and Langhans, E.A. (eds.), *A Biographical Dictionary of Actors, Actresses, Musicians, Dancers, Managers, and Other Stage Personnel in London* 1660–1800; Howe, E., *The First English Actresses*.

***Barry Lyndon* (1852)**

A novel by ▷ William Thackeray serialized in ▷ *Fraser's Magazine* in 1844 under the title *The Luck of Barry Lyndon*. Written in the style of Fielding, it is set in the 18th century and concerns a boastful Irish adventurer who unwittingly reveals the extent of his own villany. Interesting as an example of rogue literature, and for its sustained use of an unreliable narrator.

▷ Historical novel; Newgate novel.

Barry, Spranger (?1717–77)

Actor, manager. He was over six feet tall and noted for his striking good looks which, added to his natural acting ability, made him one of the leading actors in his generation and a great rival of ▷ David Garrick.

Born in Dublin, he made his early reputation in the Irish theatre, acting with Garrick. Barry came to London in 1746, where he performed indifferently, first as Othello and then as Macbeth. However his next role, as Castalio in ▷ Thomas Otway's *The Orphan*, was highly acclaimed, and it became one of his most popular successes.

In 1747 ▷ Drury Lane, where he was acting, came under Garrick's management, and in the following season he and Garrick alternated as Hamlet and Macbeth, drawing large crowds. However, the growing rivalry between them caused Barry to leave for ▷ Covent Garden in 1750, after which a famous 'Romeo and Juliet War' ensued, with the two actors playing Romeo simultaneously at separate performances in the respective houses.

In 1756 Barry began ambitious plans for a theatre of his own in Crow Street, Dublin, which opened in 1758, but the theatre failed and was eventually taken over by a rival.

Barry returned to London and carried on an intermittent association with Garrick until 1774, when he left for Covent Garden, remaining there until his death.

Barsetshire

An imaginary English county invented by ▷ Anthony Trollope for a series of novels, some of which centre on an imaginary town in it, the cathedral city of Barchester. It is a characteristic southern English setting. The novels are the best known of his works.

Titles: ▷ *The Warden, Barchester Towers, Doctor Thorne, Framley Parsonage, The Small House at Allington, The Last Chronicle of Barset*.

Barstow, Stan (b 1928)

Novelist and short-story writer. His best-known work is his first novel, *A Kind of Loving* (1960), a first-person, present-tense narrative of a young man forced to marry his pregnant girlfriend. Barstow came to prominence as one of a group of novelists from northern, working-class backgrounds, including ▷ John Braine, ▷ Alan Sillitoe and Keith Waterhouse. He has retained his commitment to the realist novel (▷ realism) with a regional setting and his suspicion of metropolitan and international culture. *The Watcher on the Shore* (1966) and *The True Right End* (1976) form a trilogy with *A Kind of Loving*. Other novels are: *Ask Me Tomorrow* (1962); *Joby* (1964); *A Raging Calm* (1968); *A Brother's Tale* (1980); *Just You Wait and See* (1986); *B Movie* (1987). Story collections include: *The Desperadoes* (1961); *A Season with Eros* (1971); *A Casual Acquaintance* (1976); *The Glad Eye* (1984).

Barthes, Roland (1915–80)

Probably the best known and most influential of all the Structuralist and Post-structuralist critics. In books such as *Writing Degree Zero* (1953), *Mythologies* (1957), and *S/Z* (1970), Barthes undertook to expose how language functioned, and its relationship with ▷ ideology. Moreover, he was also concerned to uncover the distinctions between literary texts which operated on the basis of a stable relationship between signifier and signified, and those for whom the act of signification (establishing meaning) itself was of primary importance. The terms he uses to distinguish between the two types of text are 'readerly' (*lisible*) and 'writerly' (*scriptible*). In later works, such as *The Pleasure of the Text* (1975), he went on to investigate the sources of pleasure which the text affords to the reader, and distinguished between 'the text of pleasure' which does not challenge the cultural assumptions of the reader and which is therefore comforting, and 'the text of bliss' where the reader experiences a '*jouissance*' from the unsettling effect elicited from the text's representation of the crisis of language. In addition to offering penetrating analyses of literary texts, Barthes concerned himself with the structural analysis of all cultural representation, including topics such as advertising, film, photography, music and wrestling.

***Bartholomew Fair* (1614)**

A vigorous prose comedy of London life by ▷ Ben Jonson. The scene is that of a famous fair held annually in Smithfield, London, from the 12th century till 1855. The cast includes traders, showmen, dupes, criminals, a gambler and a hypocritical Puritan – the best-known character, called Zeal-of-the-land Busy. It has very lively surface entertainment, and some of Jonson's characteristic force of satire; the vicious pursue their vices with eloquence but such extravagance they they overreach themselves, and not only produce their own doom but bring ridicule on their own heads by self-caricature.

▷ Humours, Comedy of; Bakhtin, Mikhail.

Bartlett, Neil (b 1959)
Dramatist, director, actor. A determinedly anti-establishment figure, despite his first in English from Magdalen College, Oxford and a directors' traineeship at the Bristol Old Vic, much of his work has been in collaboration with friends, designer Robin Whitemore and Nicolas Bloomfield, Leah Hausman, and Simon Mellor with whom he set up his own company, Gloria, in 1988 – fulfilling a promise Bartlett had made to himself in drama school to retain autonomy over his own creativity. He has, nonetheless, also won plaudits for dazzling translations of Racine and Molière. As a director, he was responsible for the Théâtre de Complicité's *More Bigger Snacks Now*, and Annie Griffin's equally mould-breaking solo shows, *Blackbeard the Pirate* and *Almost Persuaded*. *Antibody* (1983) was one of the first plays to deal with AIDS in Britain, but *Dressing Up* (1983) began his highly flamboyant explorations into drag, followed, after *Pornography* (1985), with *A Vision of Love Revealed in Sleep* (1986) and *Sarrasine* (1990). Both spectacles featured performer Bette Bourne in ways which fused high art with low camp, and made points about the importance of the living presence of the performer, the nature of artifice and reality and the politics of gay persecution.

Bartlett's visual theatre uses text, image and music in contrapuntal abundance – satirising itself even at its most outrageous, and delighting in the contradiction. His homage to Oscar Wilde, *Who Was That Man?* and his contemporary account of gay life, *Ready to Catch Him Should He Fall*, have both been warmly received.

Base and superstructure
A key term in the cultural theory of ▷ Marx and Engels who conceptualized the function of culture in terms of this metaphor. They pictured society as being like a building in which the superstructure – culture – is dependent upon the base or foundations which support it, namely the economy. In Marxist theory, just as the economy is controlled by ruling interests, so culture – conceived in the widest terms to include, for example, art, religion, political institutions and sport – is similarly controlled. The function of culture in this theory is to ensure the co-operation of the majority and their consent to the status quo. Culture therefore is a vehicle for ideology.

There are a number of difficulties with this idea. One common objection is that it is reductionist; in other words, it reduces complex cultural activity to over-simple causes and functions. Another is that it overlooks cultural diversity, including the fact that cultural activity can often oppose the status quo. A third objection is that the model implies that cultural activity is, in a heavy sense, imposed on people rather than emerging from their genuine interests and pleasures. Nonetheless, the base/superstructure model does point to important economic and political realities in cultural activity which are sometimes forgotten.
Bib: Marx, K. and Engels, F., 'Preface' to *The Contribution to the Critique of Political Economy*; Williams, R., *Problems in Materialism and Culture*.

Basset, Mary (c 1522–72)
A translator of religious material, Basset came from the learned More family. Her mother was ▷ Margaret Roper, herself an accomplished translator, and her grandfather was ▷ Sir Thomas More, whose *History of the Passion* she translated into English (1566). She also translated the first five books of Eusebius' *Ecclesiastical History* from Greek into English and presented it to Mary Tudor (▷ Mary I), in return for which she obtained a position at court.
Bib: Hallett, P. E. (ed.), *The Works of Sir Thomas More*.

Bastard
A bastard is born out of wedlock, *ie* has no legal parents; in law, he is *filius nullius* = the son of no one. When land, and with it, status, were derived from the legal father, the bastard could inherit nothing by his own right. In early medieval times an exception was sometimes made for bastards in ruling families; thus William I of England (1266–87) took the appellation William the Bastard. But in general a bastard was by law something of a social outcast. Hence Edmund in ▷ Shakespeare's ▷ *King Lear* (1.ii) 'Why brand they us/With base? with baseness? bastardy? base, base?' However, a bastard could in exceptional circumstances acquire a position in society, acquiring land, marrying legally and bequeathing his property – all depended on his natural worth, abilities and energies. This is more apparent in the bastard Philip of Shakespeare's ▷ *King John* than in Edmund.
Bib: Findlay, A., *Illegitimate Power: Bastards in Renaissance Drama*.

Bathos
▷ Figures of speech.

Battle of Maldon
An Old English commemorative poem, written in imitation of the heroic epics of past

Germanic tradition, recounting an incident in the Scandinavian raids against England in 993 at Maldon, Essex. The late-10th-century poem recounts Ealdorman Byrhtnoth's heroic, and disastrous, attempts to oppose the Viking raiders. The text survives in an 18th-century transcript, made before the manuscript version was destroyed in a fire.

▷ Old English literature.

Bib: Scragg, D. (ed.), *The Battle of Maldon*.

Battle of the Books, The **(1697, published 1704)**
(A Full and True Account of the Battel Fought last Friday, Between the Ancient and the Modern Books in St James' Library). A prose satire by ▷ Jonathan Swift, written while he was staying with ▷ Sir William Temple. Temple's essay on 'Ancient and Modern Learning', with its praise of the Epistles of Phalaris, had been attacked by the critics Wotton and ▷ Richard Bentley, the latter proving that the Epistles were false. Swift's *Battle of the Books* satirizes the whole dispute, parodying the scholars' concern with minutiae. The ancients (*ie* the classical writers) are given the stronger claims, but overall the satire leaves the issue undecided.

Baudelaire, Charles (1821–67)
French poet. His best known work, *Les Fleurs du mal* (1857), points the way out of ▷ Romanticism towards modernism. Formally, it draws on the tradition of ▷ sonnet and song which Baudelaire inherited from the Renaissance. Conceptually, it springs from the perception of 'two simultaneous feelings: the horror of life and the ecstasy of life', periods of heightened sensitivity and sensibility alternating with the monotony of existence without meaning. Baudelaire's work is rich in suggestion, allowing sensation to transfuse the object as though the object were the source of the sensation rather than the occasion for it; and equally powerful value is bestowed upon the metaphorical expression of sense-experience. When the poet uncovers, invested with desire, an exotic and erotic universe in a woman's hair ('La Chevelure'), this moment is also an uncovering of the possible resonances which the hair triggers in the poet. The contrasting condition of 'Ennui' is a state of torpor which saps intellectual and emotional vigour and induces creative sterility. Everyday objects are here commonly used to embody feelings of failure, dejection, horror and despair. The book's five sections explore these twin conditions, in art and love (*Spleen et Idéal*), in city life (*Tableaux Parisiens*), in stimulants (*Le Vin*), in perversity (*Fleurs du mal*) and in metaphysical rebellion (*La Révolte*), ending (in the poem 'Le Voyage') with man's yearning unsatisfied but finding in death a new journey of discovery.

Baudelaire also wrote fine music and art criticism (he championed Wagner and Delacroix); his translations of Edgar Allan Poe (1809–49) helped confirm, in France, interest in tales of the fantastic; and he was the first to investigate extensively the new genre of prose poetry. In England, his influence has been constant, though at the outset it raised moral controversy. Reviewing *Les Fleurs du mal* in the ▷ *Spectator* of 1862, ▷ Swinburne responded to the sensualism of Baudelaire, and this version of Baudelaire was handed on to the late 19th-century 'decadent' poets, including ▷ Ernest Dowson and, later, ▷ Arthur Symons, who alternately regarded Baudelaire as deliciously decadent and frankly satanic. T.S. Eliot (1888–1965) 'rescued' Baudelaire and identified the French poet's sense of sin with 'Sin in the permanent Christian sense', even though Baudelaire himself in a letter to Swinburne warned against easy moral readings of his work.

▷ French influence on Victorian literature.

Bawden, Nina (b 1925)
Novelist, reviewer and writer for children. Nina Bawden is best known for her award-winning novels for children, particularly *Carrie's War* (1973) and *The Peppermint Pig* (1975). For Bawden, childhood and adolescence are times of frustration, difficulty and excitement, and her writing is both ▷ realist (*ie* not fantasy writing for children) and realistic – stories of children's perceptions of adult situations. Bawden also writes novels for adults, notably *A Woman of My Age* (1967), *Familiar Passions* (1979) and *The Ice-House* (1983).

Baxter, Richard (1615–91)
Theologian, religious writer and autobiographer. Baxter was one of the dominating figures in the period of the English ▷ Civil War. A chaplain to ▷ Oliver Cromwell's army, Baxter served after the Restoration as chaplain to ▷ Charles II, but he soon fell out with the king on religio-political grounds. Though an initial supporter of the Parliamentarian cause in the Civil War, Baxter's experiences in the New Model Army, in particular his exposure to the thinking of the ▷ Levellers, Seekers, ▷ Quakers and Behmenists, led him to adopt rather more conservative postures. In the 1650s his position changed once more and he emerged as a strong supporter of the Protectorate, dedicating his *Key for Catholics* (1659) to Richard Cromwell. Baxter's stance on religious issues has been defined as one of the earliest examples of ecumenicism or, as he put it in his *A Third Defence of the Cause of Peace* (1681): 'You could not have truelier called me than an *Episcopal – Presbyterian – Independent*.' A prolific writer, Baxter composed over 100 works on religious topics, including *The Saints Everlasting Rest* (1650) and *Call to the Unconverted* (1657). His major work, however, has come to

be recognized as his spiritual autobiography, *Reliquiae Baxterianae* (1696). This 800-page folio volume is one of the most important of 17th-century ▷ autobiographies.
Bib: Schlatter, R. B., *Richard Baxter and Puritan Politics*; Keeble, N. H. (ed.), *The Autobiography of Richard Baxter*; Webber, Joan, *The Eloquent 'I': Style and Self in Seventeenth-century Prose.*

Bayes
The name of a character in *The Rehearsal*, a play by the Duke of Buckingham (▷ Villiers, George) and others, printed in 1672. Bays, or laurels, compose the wreaths with which poets are crowned, and the character was meant as a satire on ▷ Sir William D'Avenant, and also on ▷ John Dryden, who was later created official ▷ Poet Laureate. ▷ Alexander Pope used the same name, in the form Bays, for the Poet Laureate, ▷ Colley Cibber, in *The New Dunciad* (1742), and in the 1743 version of ▷ *The Dunciad*, which has Cibber as hero.

Beaconsfield, Lord
▷ Disraeli, Benjamin.

Bear-baiting, Bull-baiting
In the ▷ Middle Ages and the 16th century a popular pastime, in which a bull or a bear was tied to a stake and then attacked by bulldogs or mastiffs. Bull-baiting continued longer and these 'sports' were only made illegal in 1835. In Elizabethan times, bear-baiting was an alternative amusement to drama; 'bear gardens' (notably the Paris Garden) were situated in the same region as the theatres – Southwark, on the south bank of the Thames. The theatres themselves were used for the purpose. It is possible that the bear which appears in ▷ Shakespeare's ▷ *The Winter's Tale* could have come from one of the Southwark bear gardens. Earlier in the century, ▷ Erasmus speaks of herds of bears being kept in the country to supply the bear gardens. The Puritans disliked the meetings as scenes likely to lead to disorder, and condemned bear-baiting alongside theatrical performances.

Beardsley, Aubrey (Vincent) (1872–98)
The leading illustrator of the 1890s and, after ▷ Oscar Wilde, the dominant figure in the ▷ Aesthetic movement of the period. He became famous for his stunning black and white illustrations to works by Wilde and ▷ Ernest Dowson (▷ Nineties' Poets). His styles were widely imitated and he was responsible for a new simplicity and directness in the art of illustrating. The flowing lines and sumptuous compositions of his drawings expressed what was considered most bold and daring in the Aesthetic movement. He was largely self-taught except for a brief spell attending evening classes at the Westminster School of Art which the artist Sir Edward Burne Jones encouraged him to attend in 1891. Two years later he was commissioned to illustrate a new edition of Sir Thomas Malory's medieval romance, ▷ *Morte D'Arthur*, (1469/70), and in 1894 he became art editor of the ▷ *Yellow Book*, designing the first four covers himself. These together with his illustrations for Wilde's ▷ *Salome* gained him widespread notoriety.

His art was influenced by the elegant, curvilinear style of the Art Nouveau movement and the bold designs of Japanese woodcuts. Added to this was the sensuality of his drawings of women coupled with an erotic morbidity which shocked his critics. His illustrations to Aristophanes' *Lysistrata* (1896) were even more graphic. Despite his distance from Wilde, Beardsley was dismissed from *The Yellow Book* when the scandal surrounding Wilde's homosexuality broke in 1895. He joined the staff of *The Savoy* magazine as its principal illustrator and during the last two years of his life he illustrated Alexander Pope's *Rape of the Lock* (1896) and Johnson's *Volpone* (1898), wrote a number of poems and part of a romantic novel, *Under the Hill*. It was privately printed in an unexpurgated version under the title *The Story of Venus and Tannhauser* in 1907. In 1896 the tuberculosis that had dogged his childhood flared up again and he became an invalid. A year later he converted to ▷ Catholicism and moved to France, where he died at the age of twenty-five.

Beatrice and Benedick
Two characters in ▷ Shakespeare's comedy ▷ *Much Ado About Nothing*. They hate each other and engage in witty exchanges of repartee. The hatred is only apparent, however, and they are brought together in love by a trick. Their witty interchanges may owe more to the convention of courtly discourse (▷ *Euphues*) than to a naturalistic portrayal of character.

Beatrice-Joanna
The deeply divided female protagonist of ▷ Middleton's and ▷ Rowley's tragedy ▷ *The Changeling*, whose refusal to marry her father's choice of a husband leads to murder and ultimately delivers her into the arms of the repellent De Flores. The combination of sexual desire and madness in Beatrice's character allows for interesting interpretations from ▷ feminist and ▷ psychoanalytical criticisms.

Beattie, James (1735–1803)
Schoolteacher and later Professor of Philosophy at Aberdeen University. His pseudo-medieval poem in Spenserian stanzas, *The Minstrel: or the Progress of Genius* (1771–4), popularized the mystique of the poet as solitary figure, growing to maturity amid sublime scenery. He also wrote a prose *Essay on Truth*, attacking the

scepticism of the philosopher ▷ David Hume from a position of orthodox piety.
▷ Bard; Romanticism.

Beau (Brummel, Nash)
'Beau' is a French word which came into use in the 18th century for an elegant young man, especially as suitor to a lady. The word also prefixed the names of certain famous men of fashion and elegance, notably Beau Nash (1674–1762), the famous Master of Ceremonies at Bath, and Beau Brummel (1778–1840), friend of George IV in his ▷ Regency days (1810–20) and leader of London fashion.

Beau Tibbs
Character in ▷ Oliver Goldsmith's ▷ *A Citizen of the World*. He boasts of familiarity with the rich and famous, but in reality is poor and obscure.

Beauclerc, Amelia (c 1810–20)
Novelist. Little is known of Amelia Beauclerc's life and her novels have occasionally been wrongly ascribed to another author. Of her eight novels, *Alinda, or The Child of Mystery* (1812) is notable for its carefully balanced scenes of transvestism and homoerotic encounters between women. Although her female characters often triumph over difficulties encountered in their dealings with men it would however be wrong to endow too radical or feminist a note to Beauclerc's writing, since much of her work is conventional and uninspired, as for example her ▷ Gothic novel, *Husband Hunters* (1816).
▷ Feminism.

Beaumont, Francis (1584–1616)
Dramatic poet and collaborator with ▷ John Fletcher. They wrote comedies (*eg The Coxcomb*); tragedies (*eg The Maid's Tragedy*); romantic dramas (*eg A King and No King* and ▷ *Philaster*). Fletcher also collaborated with other writers – ▷ Shakespeare, ▷ Massinger – and wrote plays on his own, but the general superiority of those he wrote with Beaumont has suggested to modern critics that Beaumont may have been the more talented partner. Their plays were immensely popular in the 17th century, and having undergone a decline are now being reintroduced into the theatrical canon. The tragicomedies (*Philaster* and *The Maid's Tragedy*) have been critically reassessed, revealing that the move towards self-destruction and anticlimax at the end of the plays represents a reluctance to contemplate a world in which all humanity has been lost.
Bib: Macaulay, G. G., *Beaumont: a critical study*; Appleton, W. W., *Beaumont and Fletcher: a critical study*; Finkelpearl, P. J., *Court and Country Politics in the Plays of Beaumont and Fletcher*.

Beauty and the Beast
A fairy story, best known in the French version of Madame de Villeneuve (1744). The theme is that of a young girl who learns to love a monster who holds her in his power; her freely given love transforms him into a young prince. Before she can go through this experience, however, she has to surrender her safe, tender relationship with the father who dotes on her.
▷ Fairy tales.

Beauvoir, Simone de
▷ De Beauvoir, Simone

***Beaux' Stratagem, The* (1707)**
Play by ▷ George Farquhar, one of his most successful and popular. Aimwell and Archer, two impoverished gentlemen, come to Lichfield in the guise of master and servant. They go in search of a rich wife for Aimwell, intending to split the proceeds. Aimwell courts Dorinda, daughter of Charles and Lady Bountiful. Archer carries on a flirtation with the landlord's daughter, Cherry, while at the same time, in a separate intrigue, he pursues the unhappily married Mrs Sullen. Aimwell wins Dorinda, but in a fit of honesty, admits his deception. He gives all the money he has gained from the match to Archer, who however remains single. Late in the action, Aimwell finds he has inherited a title and estate, and all ends well for him and his bride to be. The play is vigorous and at times wildly funny, with a partly unconventional ending. Its atmosphere derives largely from Restoration comedy, but several plot factors link it with the more 'moral' plays of the later 18th century. The play contains a number of incisive comments about women's position in society, particularly in the lines and character of Mrs Sullen.

Becket, St Thomas (?1118–70)
A priest who served ▷ Henry II in various offices, culminating in the highest – that of Lord Chancellor. The period was one of constant disputes between Church and Crown over spheres of power, specially in the courts of justice. When Becket reluctantly became Archbishop in 1162, he became a champion of the very rights of the Church that Henry was trying to curtail. He was exiled on the continent for seven years but, after a brief reconciliation with Henry on his return, he was killed in Canterbury Cathedral on 29 December 1170, on the orders of the King. Henry later claimed that his instructions had been misinterpreted, but he did penance for the assassination. Becket was canonized in 1173 and his shrine at Canterbury became one of the great centres of European pilgrimage, and was the destination of the pilgrims in ▷ Chaucer's ▷ *Canterbury Tales*. A large number of medieval versions of the life of St Thomas survive and his martyrdom is the subject of ▷ T. S. Eliot's play *Murder in the Cathedral* (1935).

Beckett, Samuel (1906–89)
Dramatist and novelist. Born in Dublin, he was educated at Trinity College. He became a lecturer in English at the École Normale Supérieure in Paris (1928–30) and was then a lecturer in French at Trinity College. From 1932 he lived chiefly in France, and wrote in both French and English. In Paris he became the friend and associate of the expatriate Irish novelist ⊳ James Joyce (1882–1941), whose ⊳ 'stream of consciousness' subjective method of narrative strongly influenced Beckett's own novels; another important influence upon him was the French novelist ⊳ Marcel Proust (1871–1922).

Beckett is one of the most singular and original writers to appear in English, or possibly in French, since 1945. Like Joyce an Irish expatriate, he belongs to both Ireland and to Europe; his characters are commonly Irish, and his background the desolation of European culture. In both narrative and drama (it is in the second that his achievement is perhaps the more remarkable) his method was to create art out of increasingly simplified material, reducing his images of humanity to the sparest elements. His particular view of life's absurdity is often expressed through striking theatrical images which reveal a vision of life which is both bleak and grotesquely comic. Thus, in *Happy Days* Winnie appears on stage buried up to her waist in a mound of earth; in *Not I* the audience sees only a mouth on stage struggling to deliver a monologue of reminiscences; and in *Endgame* two elderly characters, Nagg and Nell, are placed in dustbins throughout the play. In so far as he is related to an English literary tradition, it is to the generation between the wars of 1914–18 and 1939–45 when, most notably in the work of James Joyce, communication with an audience was often secondary to experiments in the medium of language. His novels have accordingly had little influence on English fiction. His plays, on the other hand, especially *Waiting for Godot* and the plays for radio, have shown new possibilities in the handling of dialogue, by which speech is used less for communication than for the expression of minds that feel themselves in isolation, or on the point of sinking into it. Such use of dialogue perhaps had its beginnings in the late 19th-century dramatists, the Russian ⊳ Chekhov and the Belgian Maeterlinck, and has superficial parallels with the work of the contemporary English dramatist, ⊳ Harold Pinter.

Poems include: *Whoroscope* (1930); *Echo's Bones* (1935).

Novels and stories include: *More Pricks than Kicks* (1934); *Murphy* (1938); *Watt* (1944); *Molloy* (1951; English, 1956); *Malone Meurt* (1952; trans. *Malone Dies*, 1956); *L'Innommable* (1953; trans. *The Unnamable*, 1960); *Comment C'est* (1961; English, 1964); *Imagination Dead Imagine* (1966, from French); *Nouvelles et textes pour rien* (1955); *Le Depeupleur* (1971; trans. *The Lost Ones*, 1972); *First Love* (1973); *Mercier et Camier* (1974).

Plays include: *En attendant Godot* (1952; trans. ⊳ Waiting for Godot, 1954); *Fin de partie (*1957; trans. *Endgame*, 1958); *Krapp's Last Tape* (1959); *Happy Days* (1961); *Play* (1963); *Eh Joe* (1966); *Breath and Other Short Plays* (1972); *Not I* (1973); *That Time* (1976); *Footfalls* (1976); *Ghost Trio* (1976); *. . . But the Clouds . . .* (1977); *Rockaby* (1980); *Ohio Impromptu* (1981); *Quad* (1982); *Catastrophe* (1982); *Nacht und Träume* (1983); *What Where* (1983). Plays for radio include: *All that Fall* (1957); *Embers* (1959); *Cascando* (1964).

⊳ Irish literature in English.

Bib: Kenner, H., *Samuel Beckett, a Critical Study*; Jacobsen, J. and Mueller, W.R., *The Testament of Beckett*; Esslin, M. in *Theatre of the Absurd*; Bair, D., *Beckett: A Biography*.

Beckford, William (1759–1844)
Novelist and travel writer, son of a Lord Mayor of London. Chiefly remembered for his ⊳ Gothic novel *Vathek*, Beckford also wrote travel books, and was an extravagant collector of Gothic curiosities. Beckford's substantial family wealth enabled him to create Fonthill Abbey, where he lived in eccentric and scandalous seclusion.

⊳ Hervey, Elizabeth.

Beddoes, Thomas Lovell (1803–49)
Poet and dramatist. Nephew of the novelist ⊳ Maria Edgeworth, and son of a physician, Thomas Beddoes. He spent most of his adult life in Germany and Switzerland, repeatedly in trouble for his revolutionary ideas. His first published work was a collection of tales in verse, *The Improvisatore* (1821). He shared the Romantic interest in the ⊳ Jacobean dramatists, and sought to revive drama in their spirit with *The Bride's Tragedy* (1822). He continued to revise his second play, *Death's Jest-Book* until his death, and it was published posthumously in 1850, as were his *Collected Poems* (1851). Despite occasional intensities his plays are unexciting dramatically, and his reputation rests chiefly on his lyric verse in the tradition of ⊳ Percy Bysshe Shelley, such as *Dream Pedlary*. Beddoes died by suicide.

Bib: Thompson, J. R., *Thomas Lovell Beddoes*.

Bede (673–735)
A native of the Angle kingdom of Northumbria and a lifelong monk in the monastery of Monkwearmouth-Jarrow, Bede was the foremost scholar of the Anglo-Saxon world. His works include scientific and grammatical tracts, a treatise on metrics, scriptural commentaries, saints' lives and a highly influential account of the *Historia Ecclesiastica Gentis Anglorum* (*History of the English Church and its People*) which was later translated into Old English.

Bib: Hunter-Blair, P., *The World of Bede*;

Sherley-Price, L. (trans.), *A History of the English Church and its People*.

Bedford, Countess of
▷ Russell, Lucy.

Bedivere
In ▷ Geoffrey of Monmouth's version of Arthurian history, he is one of ▷ Arthur's principal knights, his cupbearer and governor of Normandy. He has a less prominent role in later French and English Arthurian texts but often he is portrayed as the last knight to remain with the wounded Arthur and who has the task of returning ▷ Excalibur to the Lake (as in ▷ Malory's *Works*).

Bedlam
A famous lunatic asylum. Originally it was a priory, founded in 1247, for members of the religious order of the Star of Bethlehem. Lunatics were admitted to it in the 14th century, and in 1547, after the dissolution of the monasteries, it was handed over to the City of London as a hospital for lunatics. The name became shortened to Bedlam, and a Bedlamite, Tom o'Bedlam, Bess o'Bedlam, became synonyms for lunatics; Bedlam itself, a synonym for lunatic asylum. In modern English, 'bedlam' is a scene of uproar and confusion.
Bib: Showalter, E., *The Female Malady*.

Beer, Patricia (b 1924)
Poet. Beer was educated at Exeter and Oxford universities, has been a university teacher, and now writes full-time – she is also a novelist and critic. She grew up in Devon and her work draws strongly on West Country images. Her volumes of poetry include: *The Loss of Magyar* (1959); *The Survivors* (1963); *The Estuary* (1971); *Driving West* (1975); *Selected Poems* (1979); *The Lie of the Land* (1983).

Beerbohm, Max (1872–1956)
Essayist, cartoonist, writer of fiction. When he began his career Beerbohm belonged to the so-called 'decadent' generation of the aesthetic school in the 1890s (▷ Nineties' Poets); this included, W.B. Yeats (1865–1939) in his Celtic Twilight phase, ▷ Oscar Wilde, ▷ Aubrey Beardsley, and the poets Lionel Johnson (1867–1902) and ▷ Ernest Dowson. He showed his affiliation to this school by the playful fastidiousness of his wit, especially in his cartoons and parodies. *A Christmas Garland* (1912) contains parodies of contemporary writers including ▷ H.G. Wells, Arnold Bennett (1867–1931), and Joseph Conrad (1857–1924). But it is in his cartoons that his satirical wit is displayed with most pungency and originality, eg *Caricature of Twenty-five Gentlemen* (1896), *The Poet's Corner* (1904), *Rossetti and his Circle* (1922). As a writer he was above all an essayist; he entitled his first slim volume with humorous impertinence *The Works of Max Beerhohm* (1896), to which he added *More* (1899), *Yet Again* (1909), *And Even Now* (1920). He also wrote stories (*Seven Men*; 1919), and he is probably now most read for his burlesque romance *Zuleika Dobson* (1911), about the visit of a dazzling beauty to the University of Oxford where she is responsible for a mass suicide among the students.

Beerbohm was educated at Charterhouse and Merton College, Oxford. He contributed to the ▷ *Yellow Book*, and in 1898 succeeded ▷ George Bernard Shaw as dramatic critic on the ▷ *Saturday Review*. From 1910 he lived in Italy, except during the two world wars. He was knighted in 1939. His personal and literary fastidiousness caused him to be known as 'the Incomparable Max', and as such poet Ezra Pound (1885–1972) commemorates him as 'Brennbaum the Impeccable' in section 8 of *Hugh Selwyn Mauberley* (1920).
▷ Aestheticism.

Beeton, Mrs (1836–65)
The author of a book on cooking and household management, published serially in *The Englishwoman's Domestic Magazine* (1859–61). The book met the needs of the rapidly broadening Victorian middle class, which was strongly attached to the domestic virtues and satisfactions. It was soon regarded as an indispensable handbook.

***Beggar's Opera, The* (1728)**
By the poet ▷ John Gay, a play with numerous songs to the music of folk tunes. It is the earliest and by far the most famous of the 'ballad operas', which were light entertainments as opposed to the serious Italian operas fashionable in England, and which dealt with life in low society. In part it was a political attack on the Prime Minister, Robert Walpole. The daughter of a receiver of stolen goods falls in love with Macheath, a highwayman who is imprisoned in Newgate, where the warder's daughter also falls for him and procures his escape. As a class of literature, *The Beggar's Opera* belongs to the mock heroic; another example from the time is ▷ Fielding's novel ▷ *Jonathan Wild the Great* (1743), which is about a master criminal. The effect of such works was to make their appeal through the lawless zest for life of the characters, coupled with an ironic exposure of their baseness. *The Beggar's Opera* is a classic of the English stage, and its music has been reset by later composers such as Arthur Bliss and Benjamin Britten. It was adapted by the German dramatist Bertolt Brecht in *Die Dreigroschenoper* (*The Threepenny Opera*). *The Beggar's Opera* had an overture by the German musician Pepusch, also arranged from folk tunes.
▷ Opera in England.

Beggars, Sturdy
An expression used in the 16th century for the able-bodied poor who were unemployed and lived by begging. Unemployment was a serious social problem throughout the 16th century for a succession of causes. ▷ Henry VII (1485–1509) disbanded the private armies of the nobles; ▷ Henry VIII (1509–47) dissolved the monasteries, and threw into unemployment the numerous servants and craftsmen who had served them; the nobles enclosed extensive tracts of arable land for sheep-farming, which required less labour, or simply to surround their great houses with ornamental parks; prices rose, and periods of inflation sometimes made it impossible for poor men to support themselves without begging. The beggars were regarded as a serious social threat, since they often moved about in bands and took to robbery with violence. In the reign of ▷ Elizabeth I (1558–1603), the government made serious and fairly successful attempts to deal with the problem: they instituted a succession of ▷ Poor Laws, culminating in the Great Poor Law of 1601, in accordance with which the aged, sick and crippled were given financial relief by the parishes, but the 'sturdy beggars' were forcibly set to work. Not all the 'sturdy beggars' were from the poorer classes; in an age of enthusiastic financial speculation, richer men were sometimes suddenly ruined, and forced to take to the roads. Indeed, ▷ Orlando and Adam in ▷ Shakespeare's ▷ *As You Like It* distinctly display the plight of the sturdy beggars.
Bib: Beier, A. L., *Masterless Men: The Vagrancy Problem in England* 1560–1640.

Behan, Brendan (1923–64)
Irish dramatist. His first play, *The Quare Fellow*, was staged in Dublin in 1954, but made its impact after it was adapted by ▷ Joan Littlewood's company, Theatre Workshop, in 1956. Behan spent time in borstal, and in prison as a political prisoner, and this influenced his play about a British soldier captured by the I.R.A., *The Hostage* (1958). His last play, *Richard's Cork Leg*, was unfinished. Many of his dramatic techniques drawing on popular traditions of entertainment, such as the use of song and dance and direct addresses to the audience, are typical of the style developed by Joan Littlewood's Theatre Workshop company.
Bib: O'Connor, U., *Behan*.

Behn, Aphra (1640–1689)
English poet, dramatist and writer of fiction, also known as 'Astrea'. Little is known of her early life; the earliest record we have is the anonymous 'The Life and Memoirs of Mrs Behn Written by One of the Fair Sex' which prefaced the first collection of her writings. She may have lived in Surinam, as she presented a feather costume for the play ▷ *The Indian Queen*. She also worked as a royal spy in Holland (at the instigation of ▷ Sir Thomas Killigrew), but was not paid, despite repeated pleas for money on her return in 1667. She may have been imprisoned for debt. She began to write for money, and has been singled out by critics since Virginia Woolf (see *A Room of One's Own*) as the first Englishwoman to earn her living by writing, though the precise meaning of this description is open to dispute. She wrote eighteen plays, of which *The Forc'd Marriage* was the first, produced at the Duke's Theatre in 1670. In the preface to *The Dutch Lover* (1673), she complains that 'the day 'twas acted first, there comes to me in the pit a long, lithe, phlegmatic, white, ill-favored, wretched fop . . . this thing, I tell you, opening that which serves it for a mouth, out issued such a noise as this to those that sat about it, that they were to expect a woeful play, God damn him, for it was a woman's.' Her best-known plays are currently ▷ *The Lucky Chance* (1686) and ▷ *The Rover* (1679). *The Lucky Chance* details the plight of young women married to rich, foolish old city men. In *The Widow Ranter* she dramatizes colonial America. In prose fiction she wrote ▷ *Love Letters Between a Nobleman and His Sister* (1684–7) and ▷ *Oroonoko, or the Royal Slave* (c 1688), set in colonial Surinam. Her poems (famously) include 'The Disappointment', and she also wrote about desire in 'To the Fair Clarinda, Who Made Love to Me, imagin'd more than Woman': 'Fair lovely Maid, or if that Title be/Too weak, too Feminine for Nobler thee,/Permit a Name that more Approaches Truth: And let me call thee, Lovely Charming Youth./This last will justify my soft complaint;/ . . . And without Blushes I the Youth persue,/When so much beauteous Woman is in view.'

As a woman writer Behn was attacked for her lewd language and daring themes, and her own unconventional lifestyle has tended to obscure criticism of her work by moral condemnation.

Her works are collected in: *The Histories and Novels of the Late Ingenious Mrs Behn* (1696).
Bib: Spender, D., *Women of Ideas*; Spender, D., *Mothers of the Novel*; Spencer, J., *The Rise of the Woman Novelist*; Duffy, M., *The Passionate Shepherdess: Aphra Behn, 1640–89*; Goreau, A., *Reconstructing Aphra*.

Bell, Currer, Ellis, Acton
▷ Brontë, Charlotte, Emily, Anne.

Bellamy, George Anne (?1731–88)
Born at Fingal in Ireland on St George's Day, hence her Christian name, to the actress Mrs Bellamy and her lover, James O'Hara, second Baron of Tyrawley. She made her stage debut at Covent Garden, where her mother was engaged,

in 1741, and in 1743 she played for the first time with ▷ David Garrick. In 1745 Bellamy and her mother performed at ▷ Smock Alley in Dublin, alongside Garrick and ▷ Spranger Barry. She soon quarrelled with Garrick, and in 1748 was hired at ▷ Covent Garden, where she became one of the leading actresses. In 1749 she eloped with George Montgomery Metham to Yorkshire, giving birth to a son, George, later that year. Metham, however, reneged on a promise of marriage, and she returned to Covent Garden in 1750. Garrick determined to patch up his dispute with her and, in a famous episode, persuaded her to appear again at ▷ Drury Lane, playing Juliet to his Romeo, in competition with the *Romeo and Juliet* of Barry and ▷ Susanna Cibber. The rival performances lasted 12 nights, until Covent Garden ended its run and Drury Lane triumphed with a 13th. In 1767, now in failing health, Bellamy left the stage and moved in with the actor Henry Woodward. He died in 1777, and she afterwards lived largely off loans and gifts, pursued by creditors. During her years on the stage she played some 96 roles, excelling in those demanding pathos and grief, including Cordelia, Juliet, Calista in *The Fair Penitent*, Imoinda in *Oroonoko*, and Indiana in ▷ *The Conscious Lovers*. Her autobiography, *An Apology for the Life of George Anne Bellamy* was published in 1785.
Bib: Hartmann, C., *Enchanting Bellamy*.

Belles-lettres
A term used in the late 19th and early 20th centuries for 'fine writing', *belles-lettres*, or *belletrist* (the author of *belles-lettres*), or *belletristic* (the adjective), are all now used negatively or at best descriptively. The terms imply a privileged dilettantism and lack of intellectual rigour or seriousness of an old-fashioned kind.

Belloc, Hilaire (1870–1953)
A versatile writer (novelist, poet, essayist, biographer, historian) now especially remembered for his association with G.K. Chesterton (1874–1936) in Roman ▷ Catholic propaganda. The most important phase of his career was before 1914, when he was one of a generation of popular, vivid, witty propagandists; ▷ George Bernard Shaw, ▷ H.G. Wells, and Chesterton were his equals, and the first two (as ▷ agnostic socialists) his opponents. With Chesterton, he maintained the doctrine of Distributism – an alternative scheme to socialism for equalizing property ownership. Among his best works is his earliest: *The Path to Rome* (1902), a discursive account of a journey through France, Switzerland and Northern Italy. He is now chiefly read for his light verse, eg *Cautionary Tales* (1907), *A Bad Child's Book of Beasts* (1896).
▷ Children's literature.
Bib: Hamilton, R., *Belloc: An Introduction to his Spirit and Work*; Speaight, R., *The Life of Hilaire Belloc*.

Belphoebe
A character in Edmund Spenser's ▷ *The Faerie Queene* (1596). Belphoebe, described at some length (Book II, canto iii, stanzas 21–4), is one of the symbolic representations of ▷ Elizabeth I in the poem. Etymologically, her name signifies both beauty and, through the association with Phoebe, the moon, chastity and hunting.

Belshazzar (6th century BC)
In the ▷ Bible (*Daniel* V) the son of Nebuchadnezzar and King of Babylon. He gave a great feast where he and his nobles 'praised the gods of gold, and of silver . . .', when mysterious words suddenly appeared on the wall. Only the Hebrew prophet-in-exile Daniel could interpret that they foretold Belshazzar's overthrow, at the hands of Cyrus, King of Persia. The feast has been the subject of poems and dramas in English, including a poem by ▷ Byron.

Benedick
▷ Beatrice and Benedick.

Benedictines
▷ Monasteries.

Bennett, Alan (b 1934)
Dramatist and actor. Bennett first attracted attention as a writer and performer in revue on the ▷ Edinburgh Festival Fringe, especially with *On the Fringe* with Jonathan Miller, Dudley Moore and Peter Cook which had its long runs in London and New York. *Forty Years On* (1968) seemed to please everyone, a 'good night out' and a clever satire with songs which analyses Britain in the twentieth century via a revue put on by a boarding school (much of it began life as pastiches of literary and other styles). *The Old Country* (1977), a cerebral discussion of national identity through the image of a British defector living in the USSR, made more demands on audiences.

Enjoy (1980) manages to be illuminating about class values, town planners, the generation gap, sexual politics, and fashionable sociology in a play that continually surprises. *Kafka's Dick* (1986) in which Kafka, his parents and his publisher materialise in the suburban home of a would-be biographer, found appreciative audiences among ▷ Royal Court literati but failed to transfer to the West End. *The Madness of George III* (1991) was successfully filmed in 1994.

Bennett is a very funny writer, adept at using the techniques of farce and music hall, especially in *Habeas Corpus* (1973), but, while he will find humour in the predicament of cancer patients, geriatrics, Jewish mothers, social workers' cases or homosexual spies, his characters are not butts for laughter. He has an uncannily accurate ear for the richness of real speech. His screenplays include the ▷ Orton biography *Prick Up Your Ears* (1986).

Bennett, Anna Maria (c.1750–1808)
Novelist. Anna Bennett (she is sometimes mistakenly known as Agnes Bennett) was a Welsh writer about whose early life little is certain – mainly because she herself offered so many variations. However, in 1785 two verifiable events occurred: first the death of her lover and father to two of her children, Admiral Sir Thomas Pye, and secondly the publication of her first novel, *Anna, or memoirs of a Welch Heiress*, whose success made her economically independent. The novel's bawdy satire set the tone for her other five works, making her a ▷ Minerva best-selling author. Her most interesting work is *The Beggar Girl and Her Benefactors* (1797), which ▷ S.T. Coleridge described a 'the best novel since Fielding'. She was influenced more by the ▷ Augustan writers Samuel Richardson (1689–1761) and Henry Fielding (1707–54) than by her contemporary ▷ Romantic authors whose ▷ Gothic writings she often mocked. As a result of these allegiances her popularity, not surprisingly, waned quite quickly, although she was much admired by ▷ Scott as well as Coleridge.

▷ Welsh Literature in English.

Bib: Blakey, D., *The Minerva Press 1790–1820*; Rodgers, K. M., *Feminism in Eighteenth-century England*; Todd, J., *Dictionary of British Women Writers.*

Bennett, Arnold (1867–1931)
Novelist. His principal novels are: *The Old Wives' Tale* (1908); the Clayhanger trilogy – *Clayhanger* (1910), *Hilda Lessways* (1911), and *These Twain* (1916) – all three reprinted as *The Clayhanger Family* (1925); *Riceyman Steps* (1923); *The Grand Babylon Hotel* (1902). His distinctive characteristics as a novelist are his regionalism and his ▷ naturalism. His books mainly concern life in the industrial Five Towns of the north-west Midlands (the Potteries), the particular characteristics of which differentiate his fiction considered as an image of English society. Secondly, he was strongly influenced by the naturalism of French fiction-writers such as ▷ Zola and Maupassant. This led him to emphasize the influence of environment on character, and to build his artistic wholes by means of a pattern of mundane details. This importance that he attached to environment caused a reaction against his artistic methods on the part of novelists like ▷ Virginia Woolf (see her essay 'Modern Fiction' in *The Common Reader, First Series*; 1925) and ▷ D.H. Lawrence, who found Bennett too rigid in his notions of form and too passive in the face of environmental influence. Nonetheless, Bennett lacked the ruthlessness of the French naturalists, and softened his determination with a sentimentality that recalls ▷ Dickens.

Bib: Drabble, M., *Arnold Bennett, a Biography*; Hepburn, J., *The Art of Arnold Bennett*; Lucas, J., *Arnold Bennett: A Study of His Fiction.*

Benoît de Sainte-Maure
A 12th-century French writer, patronized by ▷ Henry II, who produced a highly influential version of the story of the destruction of Troy (*Le Roman de Troie*) and a verse history of the Dukes of Normandy down to 1135. Benoît's Troy story, amplified from the pseudo-eyewitness accounts of the Trojan war attributed to ▷ Dares and ▷ Dictys, is a rationalized, chronologically ordered history. It presents an account of the first destruction of Troy as a preface to the story of the great Greek siege of Troy, triggered by the abduction of ▷ Helen. Benoît's version was itself translated into Latin in the 13th century by ▷ Guido de Columnis, and this Latin translation superseded Benoît's text as the most popular authoritative medieval version of the Troy story. The story of ▷ Troilus and Criseyde (or Briseida in Benoît's version) appears in Benoît's narrative in an embryonic form and seems largely to have been his invention, based on a few disconnected passages in Dares' text. ▷ Chaucer used Benoît's narrative, as well as ▷ Boccaccio's version of the love story in ▷ *Il Filostrato*, in composing ▷ *Troilus and Criseyde.*

▷ Ovid; Troy.

Bentham, Jeremy (1748–1832)
An extremely influential thinker, founder of the school of thought called ▷ Utilitarianism. The basis of his thought was: **1** that human motives are governed by the pursuit of pleasure and avoidance of pain; **2** that the guiding rule for society should be the greatest happiness of the greatest number; **3** that the test of value for human laws and institutions should be no other than that of usefulness. These views he expounded in *Fragment on Government* (1776) and *Introduction to Principles of Morals and Legislation* (1780). His principal associates were James Mill (1773–1836) and John Stuart Mill (1806–73); collectively they were known as the Philosophical Radicals, and together they established a practical philosophy of reform of great consequence in 19th-century Britain. But their excessive rationalism frustrated sympathy and imagination in education and the relief of poverty. Bentham's thought derived from the sceptical 18th-century French 'philosophes' such as Helvetius and 18th-century English rationalists such as David Hartley (1705–57) and Joseph Priestley (1733–1804). It was, in fact, the outstanding line of continuity between 18th-century and 19th-century thinking.

Bentham's physical remains continue to enjoy

a high profile, preserved and displayed in the foyer of University Collegel, London.
Bib: Stephen, L., *The English Utilitarians*; Pringle-Patterson, A. S., *The Philosophical Radicals and other essays*; Atkinson, C. M., *Life*.

Bentley, E. C. (Edmund Clerihew) (1875–1956)
Journalist and writer of detective fiction and light verse. E. C. Bentley's famous detective novel *Trent's Last Case* (1903), dedicated to his friend ▷ G. K. Chesterton, was originally written as an 'exposure of detective stories', but it was soon received as a classic of the genre (▷ detective fiction). In the same spirit, he published a brilliant parody of Dorothy L. Sayers, 'Greedy Night', in 1939. Bentley is also known as the originator of the humorous, aphoristic verse form 'clerihew' (from his middle name), which aims to capture the subject of the poem in two rhyming couplets, a well-known example being,

The art of Biography
Is different from Geography
Geography is about maps,
But Biography is about chaps.

Bentley worked as a journalist for *The Daily News* and *The Daily Telegraph*, and his other books include *Trent's Own Case* (1936), *Trent Intervenes* (1938) and *Elephant's Work: An Enigma* (1950).

Bentley, Richard (1662–1742)
Distinguished as a classical scholar and noted for his despotic personality as Master of Trinity College, Cambridge. He is satirized by ▷ Jonathan Swift in *The Battle of the Books* and by ▷ Alexander Pope in ▷ *The Dunciad* (Bk. IV, 201–75).

Beowulf
The single extant text of this important ▷ Old English heroic narrative was copied about the year 1000 but there are linguistic traces of an earlier written version dating from the 8th century in the text, and the story material may derive from earlier narratives still. It deals with key events in the life of a 6th-century warrior, Beowulf, from Geatland in south Sweden, who first kills the monster Grendel, which had been ravaging the great hall of Heorot, built by Hrothgar, king of the Danes. Beowulf, nephew of the king of the Geats, slays the monster by wrestling with it and wrenching out its arm. Grendel's mother then seeks vengeance by carrying off one of the Danish nobles, but Beowulf enters the mere beneath which she lives and skills her too. Beowulf returns home and in due course becomes king of the Geats. When he has reigned 50 years, his kingdom is invaded by a fiery dragon which he manages to kill with the aid of a young nobleman, Wiglaf, when all the rest of his followers have fled. However, he receives his own death wound in the fight and as he dies, he pronounces Wiglaf his successor. His body is burnt on a great funeral pyre and the dragon's treasure is buried with his ashes; 12 of his followers ride round the funeral mound celebrating his greatness. This narrative is interlaced with digressions on historical analogues to the action, and asides concerning retrospective and prospective events, which give the poem a dense and complex narrative texture.
Bib: Swanton, M. (ed.), *Beowulf*.

***Beppo: A Venetian Story* (1818)**
A poem in ▷ *ottava rima* by ▷ Lord Byron. During the Venetian carnival Laura and her *cavaliere servente* (lover) are confronted by her long-absent husband, Beppo, who has turned Turk after being shipwrecked. The three of them discuss matters amicably over coffee, and the men remain friends thereafter. The poem reflects Byron's own position at the time as *cavaliere servente* to Teresa Guiccioli. More importantly, both its form and ambiance make it an important precursor to ▷ *Don Juan*.

Berger, John (b 1926)
Novelist, painter and art critic. His novels reflect both his Marxism (Marx, Karl), in their attention to the oppressive structures of society, and his interest in painting, in their vivid realization of sensual detail. *A Painter of Our Time* (1958), explores through the story of an émigré Hungarian painter, the role of the artist in a consumer society and the relationship of art to experience. His best-known fiction work is *G* (1972), in which authorial self-consciousness, open-ended, fragmentary narrative and documentary elements serve to resist the imposition of order on political events.

He has collaborated with the photographer Jean Mohr on a number of works which address political and social issues by combining various media and genres, including photographs, political and social analysis, poems and fictionalized case studies; these are *Ways of Seeing* (1972; which accompanied an important BBC Television series fronted by Berger); *A Fortunate Man* (1967); *A Seventh Man* (1981); *Another Way of Telling* (1982). Berger has also published two volumes of a trilogy entitled *Into Their Labours*; these are *Pig Earth* (1979), which comprises short stories and poems, and *Once in Europa* (1987). Other novels include: *The Foot of Clive* (1962); *Corker's Freedom* (1964). Drama: *A Question of Geography* (1987; with Nella Bielski); and *To the Wedding* (1995). Volumes of essays include: *Permanent Red* (1960); *The White Bird* (1985). Art criticism includes: *The Success and Failure of Picasso* (1965).

Bergson, Henri (1859–1941)
French philosopher. Bergson's work on time and consciousness had a great influence on 20th-century novelists, particularly modernist writers engaged in so-called ▷ 'stream of consciousness' work such as ▷ James Joyce, ▷ Dorothy Richardson and ▷ Virginia Woolf. His text of 1889, which was published in English in 1910 as *Time and Free Will: An Essay on the Immediate Data of Consciousness*, was particularly important. Bergson is also known as one of the key theorists of vitalism, the belief that the material progress of the world is not underpinned by determining biological or physical mechanisms but by the movements of living energy; his theory of an essential *élan vital* or *life force*, which animates material progress through its constant process of change and becoming, was taken up by ▷ George Bernard Shaw in his plays. Bergson was awarded the Nobel Prize for literature in 1928, and was married to a cousin of French novelist ▷ Marcel Proust, whose work he also greatly influenced.
Bib: Humphrey, R., *Stream of Consciousness in the Modern Novel*; Sokel, W. H., *The Writer in Extremis*; Hanna, T. (ed.), *The Bergson Heritage*.

Berkeley, George (1685–1753)
Irish churchman and a philosopher in the tradition of ▷ Descartes and ▷ John Locke but the opponent of the latter. Locke had affirmed the independence of matter and mind; Berkeley held that the reality of anything depended on its being perceived by a conscious mind; thus mind (and spirit) had primacy over matter. Nature is the experience of consciousness, and the evidence of Universal Mind, or God. He considered that Locke's insistence on external matter and physical causes led to ▷ atheism; but his own lucid and precise prose is as much the vehicle of reason as Locke's. While Locke led towards scientific scepticism, Berkeley's faith, combined with reason, maintained the religious vision in an essentially rational century. His philosophy is expressed in *A New Theory of Vision* (1709), and in *Principles of Human Knowledge* (1710). His *Dialogues of Alciphron* (1732) are distinguished for their grace of style.
Bib: Wild, J., *Berkeley: a study of his life and philosophy*; Luce, A. A., *The Life of Berkeley*; Warnock, G. J., *Berkeley*.

Berkoff, Steven (b 1937)
Dramatist and actor. Berkoff is as widely known as a performer as he is a writer. He studied mime in Paris with the École Jacques Le Coq, an emphasis very evident in his performances and plays, which rely as much for their impact on movement as on language. After working in repertory theatre Berkoff went on to found the London Theatre Group, where he began to direct and develop adaptations from literature into theatre. Kafka and Edgar Allan Poe were favoured authors for this treatment, which often involved Expressionistic sets and acting style. *Metamorphosis* (1969) was the most successful of these productions. The London Theatre Group also developed a version of ▷ Aeschylus' *Agamemnon*, and Greek tragedy became an informing principle of Berkoff's own writing. His first original play was *East* (1975), which used a juxtaposition of street language with high tragedy and blank verse to produce a vitriolic and abrasive account of East End life. *Greek* (1979) employed the Oedipus myth to polemicise about mothers, marriage and women. *West* (1983) rewrote the Beowolf legend into a scabrous attack on the British upper classes and was (ironically) a great success in the West End.

Béroul (fl 1190)
Composer of a version of the ▷ Tristan story (in ▷ Anglo-Norman), of which 4,485 lines survive. The fragment begins with the scene in which King Mark spies on the lovers from the tree and breaks off before Tristan moves away to Britanny. Little is known about the author.

Berry, James (b 1924)
Poet. Berry comes from the West Indies, but has lived in Britain since 1948, a prolific writer and great promoter of multi-cultural education. Like that of younger poets ▷ Linton Kwesi Johnson, Edward Kaman Brathwaite and Benjamin Zephaniah, his work draws strongly on West Indian vernacular and reggae rhythms, and his volumes of verse include *Chain of Days* and *Lucy's Letters and Loving* (1982). He has also edited the poetry volumes: *Bluefoot Traveller: An Anthology of West Indian Poets of Britain* (1976); *News From Babylon* (1984); and a collection from the 1983 Brixton festival, *Dance to a Different Drum*. Berry also writes widely for radio and television, short stories and children's books – his children's book, *A Thief in the Village*, won the Grand Prix Prize in 1987. In 1981 he was awarded the National Poetry Prize.

Berry, Mary (1763–1852)
Dramatist and philosophical prose writer. Mary Berry and her sister Agnes (1764–1852) were brought up by their grandmother and allowed to educate themselves. They were much admired by ▷ Horace Walpole who dedicated books to them and allowed Mary Berry to edit several of his manuscripts, although she published these editions under her father's name, rather than her own. Mary was also friendly with several contemporary female authors, including ▷ Harriet Martineau and ▷ Joanna Baillie; indeed, the latter wrote the epilogue and prologue for Berry's play, *Fashionable Friends* (1801). The sexual freedom condoned by this play, together with Mary's own rejection of

marriage, suggests that in terms of gender politics she was somewhat radical (▷ Feminism). However, her history *A Comparative View of the Social Life of England and France from the Restoration of Charles II* (1828–31) reveals a more conservative attitude.

Bib: Moers, E., *Literary Women*.

Besant, Walter (1836–1901)
Novelist, philanthropist and journalist, born in Portsea and educated at King's College, London and Christ's College, Cambridge. Many of his novels were set in east London; for example *All Sorts and Conditions of Men* (1882) is an idealistic story about an heiress and a cabinet maker who combined to bring about the dream of 'People's Palace of Delight' in the East End (a project which Besant contributed to in real life). His novel *The Revolt of Man* (1882) is an anti-feminist dystopia, part of the debate over the ▷ New Woman.

▷ Utopian Literature.

Bestiaries
Compilations of descriptions of creatures (natural and fantastic), especially popular in the medieval period, in which a brief account of the habits and appearance of the creature is usually followed by allegorical interpretations of its significance, and the moral lessons it may provide. The most accessible example of a medieval bestiary is the 12th-century Latin bestiary, translated by T.H. White, *A Book of Beasts* (1954).

Best-sellers
A transformation of the means of production in the early years of the 19th century made it possible for a single text to be printed, advertised, distributed and sold in numbers hitherto inconceivable. Charles Dickens' *Pickwick Papers* was the first work of fiction to exploit these new conditions. The financial return on this new mode of production was highly profitable, and a wide market for the commodity was opened up. In our own day the best-seller is associated not only with high sales, however, but also with quick ones. Though there is no agreement on the sales figures which define a text as a best-seller, national newspapers carry weekly charts, showing the titles which are selling most strongly in fiction and non-fiction. This may be seen as a form of advertisement, encouraging further sales of what has been guaranteed as an acceptable product by market success. Writing a best-seller may make a large sum of money for the author and some make it clear (Jeffrey Archer or Shirley Conran for instance) that they gear their fiction to the market with that intention. Recent moves, by publishers as well as authors, to aim writing and publication towards the best-seller lists inevitably threaten to narrow the range of what is published and to discourage publishers from taking chances with new authors and new kinds of writing.

▷ Detective Fiction; Horror Fiction; Science Fiction.

Betham, Mary Matilda (1776–1852)
Poet, diarist and artist. Mary Betham's family attempted to make her relinquish literary activity for the more socially acceptable activity of sewing, but she persevered, and in 1797 published her first book of poems, *Elegies*. This is hardly a sophisticated work, but marks her out as writing within a feminine tradition through, for example, her poetic indebtedness to ▷ Ann Radcliffe and the ▷ Ladies of Llangollen. Her attempt to lay claim to a genealogy of women writers continued in her finest work, the *Lay* of Marie de France (▷ lay), in which she takes on the voice of the ▷ medieval writer who, it is supposed, tells her life-story through her poetry. The poem reveals the contemporary fashion for ▷ Gothic narratives and descriptions, but is well-researched and finely done, avoiding some of the excesses of the Gothic novel. Betham was still having to fight against her family's prejudice, however, and in the 1820s they placed her in an institution for the mentally ill from which she wrote accusatory letters, as well as continuing her poetic output. Despite her family's censorious attitude, during her lifetime Betham was recognised as a fine poet, by ▷ Coleridge for example, and continued to write until her death in 1852.

Betham-Edwards, Matilda (1836–1919)
Novelist, essayist and ▷ travel writer, born on a farm in Suffolk. Her mother died when she was twelve, after which Betham-Edwards educated herself, developing early an interest in France and the French. She began her first novel, *The White House by the Sea*, while still a teenager. Eventually published in 1857, it became an immediate success, reprinting continuously for the next forty years. The author went on to write more than thirty novels, of which *Forestalled* (1880) and *Love and Marriage* (1884) were her favourites. Her travel writing includes *A Winter with the Swallows* (1866) and *Through Spain to the Sahara* (1867), which record her trips with the ▷ feminist ▷ Barbara Bodichon. Betham-Edwards was a believer in women's equality and signed the 1866 petition for female suffrage. Her sympathy to socialist perspectives is evident in *The Sylvesters* (1871). In 1884, she published *Six Life Studies of Famous Women*, which included a biographical sketch of her aunt and godmother, Matilda Betham, who wrote poetry and diaries.

▷ Travel writing; Women's suffrage.

Betjeman, Sir John (1906–84)
Poet and critic of architecture. His poetry is highly nostalgic and written in a style which

has given it wide popularity: the 1958 *Collected Poems* was a best-seller. It is largely pastiche and parody, witty and anti-modernist in its form. His works include: *Mount Zion* (1931); *Continual Dew* (1937); *Old Lights in New Chancels* (1940); *New Bats in Old Belfries* (1945); *A Few Late Chrysanthemums* (1954); *Summoned by Bells* (autobiography in verse; 1960); *The Best of Betjeman* (ed. Guest; 1978); *Uncollected Poems* (1982). Betjeman was ▷ Poet Laureate from 1972–84. He was a forceful champion of ▷ Victorian architecture, and editor of the *Shell Guides*. He published some 20 books on architectural subjects.
Bib: Brook, J., *John Betjeman, Writers and their Work*, British Council Pamphlet, *153*.

Betterton, Mary (1637–1712)
Actress, one of those competing for the title of the first professional actress. She joined ▷ Sir William D'Avenant's company, probably in 1660 and her first known appearance was as Ianthe in D'Avenant's revision of ▷ *The Siege of Rhodes* in 1661. In the same year she played Ophelia to ▷ Thomas Betterton's Hamlet, and in 1662 the two were married.

Her talents were varied: she played innocent young girls, coquettes, and forceful characters such as Lady Macbeth and the Duchess of Malfi, apparently with equal skill. In the late 1660s, she and her husband took the young actress ▷ Anne Bracegirdle into their home, virtually adopting her as a daughter. Throughout her career she maintained a reputation for 'virtuous' living: ▷ Cibber described her as leading 'an unblemish'd and sober life'. After her husband's death in 1710, she appears to have suffered some sort of mental breakdown, probably exacerbated by the poverty in which he left her. She was buried in Westminster Abbey, next to her husband.
Bib: Howe, E., *The First English Actresses*.

Betterton, Thomas (1635–1710)
The greatest English actor of his generation, he probably began acting in the late 1650s. By 1661 he had joined the ▷ Duke's Company, in which he purchased a share and so was involved in theatrical finances as well as acting for most of his career.

As an actor, he succeeded from the beginning, making a particular impression as Hamlet, coached by ▷ Sir William D'Avenant, who had seen it performed earlier by an actor under ▷ Shakespeare's tutelage, and who had himself been taught by a pupil of Shakespeare's.

In 1662 Betterton was sent by ▷ Charles II to France, on the first of several missions to research the latest developments in French drama and opera, so as to bring new ideas to the English stage. Returning to England, he proceeded to build on his reputation with a succession of great roles, especially in Shakespeare. Betterton continued acting almost to his death, dying in great poverty. He is buried in Westminster Abbey.
Bib: Milhous, J., *Thomas Betterton and the Management of Lincoln's Inn Fields* 1695–1708; Highfill, P. H. Jr., Burnim, K. A. and Langhans, E. A. (eds.), *A Biographical Dictionary of Actors, Actresses, Musicians, Dancers, Managers, and Other Stage Personnel in London* 1660–1800; Lowe, R., *Thomas Betterton*.

Between the Acts **(1941)**
▷ Virginia Woolf's last novel, published posthumously. The story concerns the staging of a pageant of English history in the grounds of a country house on the eve of World War Two. Miss La Trobe, who creates and organizes the performances, is, like Lily Briscoe in ▷ *To The Lighthouse*, a representative of the woman artist. Her pageant serves to explore issues of truth and illusion, art and reality, community and isolation, self-knowledge and deception; it briefly unites the lives of a disparate group of characters.

Bevis of Hampton
A popular metrical romance translated into English sometime in the late 13th/early 14th century. Earlier versions exist in French and ▷ Anglo-Norman. The story-type is one that is found in versions across Europe. Bevis' father has been murdered by his mother's lover, Sir Murdour. Bevis is sold as a slave and has many adventures – with his horse Arundel and his sword Morglay – before the happy ending with Bevis married to Josaine. The story was circulated in the ▷ chapbooks of the 16th century and is retold in ▷ Michael Drayton's *Poly-Olbion*.

Bible in England
The Bible falls into two parts.
1 Old Testament
The first and larger part of the Bible, consisting of the sacred writings of the Jews. It concerns the peculiar, divinely ordained destiny of the Jewish race from earliest times, and it is considered by Christians to expound the divine promise which the New Testament fulfils not merely for the Jews but for the whole of mankind. The Old Testament is divided into books which are grouped by Jews into three main sections, as follows:

1 The Torah ('Law', otherwise called the Pentateuch), consisting of five books as follows: *Genesis, Exodus, Leviticus, Numbers, Deuteronomy*. They are called 'the five books of Moses'. The first two are narrative and descriptive, and move from the creation of the world to the escape of the Jews from slavery in Egypt. The remainder contain laws and discourses.

2 The Prophets. This section is divided into two in the Hebrew Bible: the 'Former

Prophets', consisting of *Joshua*, *Judges*, the two books of *Samuel* and the two books of *Kings*; and the 'Latter Prophets', consisting of *Isaiah*, *Jeremiah*, *Ezekiel*, and the Minor Prophets. The books of the Former Prophets tell the story of the establishment of the Jews in the kingdom of Israel, and their subsequent history. The Latter Prophets contain history together with prophetic discourses.

3 The Sacred Writings, or Hagiographa, which are divided into three sections: (i) the Poetical books, consisting of *Psalms*, *Proverbs*, *Job*; (ii) the five 'Rolls', which are read at special seasons in the Jewish year: *Song of Songs*, *Ruth*, *Lamentations*, *Ecclesiastes*, *Esther* – of these *Esther* and *Ruth* are narratives; the other three are poetic meditations; (iii) *Daniel*, *Ezra*, *Nehemiah*, and *Chronicles*, all consisting mainly of historical narrative.

2 New Testament

The second and shorter part of the Bible, containing the sacred books of the Christians. It is divided into books, on the pattern of the Old Testament, and dates as a whole collection from the end of the 2nd century AD. It is customary to divide the books into four groups.

1 The three Synoptic (*ie* 'summary narrative') Gospels of Saints Matthew, Mark and Luke, and the *Acts of the Apostles*. The Gospels are narratives about Jesus Christ, and *Acts* is the narrative of the missionary careers of the apostles (including St Paul) after Christ's death.

2 The Epistles (letters) of St Paul. The four shortest of these are addressed to individuals: two to Timothy, and one each to Titus and to Philemon. The remainder are addressed to various early Christian communities. These are the Epistles to the Romans, Galations, Ephesians, Philippians, Colossians, two to the Corinthians, and two to the Thessalonians. The Epistle to the Hebrews has been ascribed to Paul, but is nowadays considered to be by a disciple of his.

3 The Catholic Epistles, so called because they were directed to Christians generally. Two of these are ascribed to St Peter, and one each to James and Jude.

4 The Johannine writings, ascribed to the Apostle John. These are the Gospel of St John, distinguished from the Synoptic Gospels as probably not intended as a historical narrative, the Epistles of John, and the poetic, visionary narrative called the *Apocalypse*, or *Revelation*.

In the Middle Ages the only version of the Bible authorized by the Church was the ▷ Vulgate, *ie* the translation into Latin by St Jerome, completed in 405. Partial translations were made into Old English before the 11th century. From the 14th century translations were made by reformers, who believed that men without Latin should have the means of seeking guidance from divine scripture without dependence on Church authority. The main translators were these: ▷ Wycliffe (14th century); ▷ Tyndale, and Coverdale (16th century). The last-named was the producer of the *Great Bible* (also called ▷ Cranmer's Bible after the Archbishop of the time), but ▷ Henry VIII, concerned for his intermediate position between Catholics and Protestants, ended by restricting its use. Under the Catholic ▷ Mary I (1553–8) English reformers produced the *Geneva Bible* abroad, with annotations suited to ▷ Puritan ▷ Calvinist opinion; and in 1568 the so-called *Bishops' Bible* was issued by the restored Anglicans to counteract Puritan influence. Finally, in 1611 the Authorized Version was produced with the approval of ▷ James I (1603–25). For three centuries it was to be the only one in general use, and it is still the prevailing version. In the 19th century it was revised (Revised Version) and recently a new translation has been authorized and produced (New Testament 1961; Old Testament 1961; Old Testament Apocrypha 1970). A Catholic translation (the Douai Bible) was issued at about the same time as the Authorized Version.

In spite of various other translations. Catholic and Protestant, in the 19th and 20th centuries the Authorized Version is by far the most important for its literary and social influence. It was based on previous translations, especially that of Tyndale, so that the cast of its prose is characteristically more 16th than early 17th century in style. Nonetheless much of it is of supreme eloquence, *eg* the Book of *Job*, and the last 15 chapters of *Isaiah*. It was for many people in the 17th and 18th centuries the only book that was constantly read, and it was familiar to all from its use in church and education. The musical cadence of Authorized Version prose can be often heard in the prose of English writers, whether or not professing Christians. It is conspicuous in John Bunyan's ▷ *Pilgrim's Progress* but it can also be heard in the prose of 20th century novelists ▷ T. F. Powys, *eg Mr Weston's Good Wine* (1927).

▷ Apocrypha

Bib: Daiches, D., *The King James Version of the Bible*.

Bidgood, Ruth (b 1922)

Poet. Born at Seven Sisters, near Neath, Glamorgan, Ruth Bidgood attended school at Port Talbot where her father was vicar, afterwards reading English at Oxford before serving as a coder with the war-time W.R.N.S. at Alexandria. After the war she worked for *Chamber's Encyclopedia* in London before returning to Wales to settle in the remote village of Abergwesyn near Llanwrtyd Wells, Breconshire, where she started to write poetry and historical articles on the history of Breconshire and Radnorshire. Her poetry is concerned with the people, the landscape and seasons of mid-Wales, the forces of nature being powerfully evoked, together with stories from local folk-lore. Her poetry collections are *The Green Time* (1972), *Not Without Homage* (1975), *The Point of Miracle* (1978) and *Kindred*

(1992), this last volume combining a selection from her previous collections with one-third new poems.
Bib: Stephens, M. (Ed.), *The Oxford Companion to the Literature of Wales.*

Bildungsroman
A novel which describes the youthful development of the central character. Prominent examples in English include ▷ James Joyce's ▷ *A Portrait of the Artist as a Young Man* (1916), ▷ Samuel Butler's ▷ *The Way of All Flesh* (1902) and ▷ D. H. Lawrence's ▷ *Sons and Lovers* (1913). In the contemporary novel, the *bildungsroman* form has often been adopted by feminist writers, as a narrative of emancipation or growing consciousness. An example is ▷ Jeanette Winterson's *Oranges are not the Only Fruit* (1985).

Bill of Rights (1689)
1 An Act passed by Parliament, according to which the powers of the king were restricted. In particular, he could no longer suspend laws without the consent of Parliament; nor could he dispense with laws in individual cases. The importance of the Act was less the specific ways in which royal power was limited than Parliament's implicit decision to take over the sovereignty of the government from the Crown. This Bill and the events that led up to it, the flight of ▷ James II (1685–8) and his replacement by ▷ William III and Mary II (the ▷ Glorious Revolution), were the real starting-points of 'constitutional monarchy' in England, *ie* a monarchy under which it is accepted by both Crown and people that the representatives of the people are the real sovereigns of the country. Because Britain does not have a written constitution, such historical traces as the Bill of Rights are the major signs of how power has been transferred and located.
2 The first ten Amendments to the Constitution of the United States, all adopted in 1791. Their guarantee of individual rights was an answer ro criticism of the Constitution, which had hindered its ratification.

Biographia Literaria (1817)
A miscellaneous work of ▷ autobiography, philosophy, and literary criticism, by ▷ Samuel Taylor Coleridge. Its psychological approach to creativity, influenced by the German philosophers Schlegel and ▷ Kant, foreshadows the ▷ Freudian concept of the unconscious, and its theory of imagination is central to the development of literary critical theory. The famous distinction between primary imagination, secondary imagination and fancy occurs in Chapter XIII. Primary imagination is seen as 'the living power and prime agent of all human perception'. Secondary imagination is the creative power to synthesize and re-express experience in new forms: 'It dissolves, diffuses, dissipates, in order to recreate; or where this process is rendered impossible, yet still, at all events, it struggles to idealize and to unify.' Fancy, on the other hand, simply juxtaposes memories and impressions and 'has no other counters to play with but fixities and definites'. Primary perception is thus not the mere passive holding of a mirror up to nature of classical literary theory, but involves an interaction between subjectivity and objective reality.

Much of the literary criticism in the book is devoted to detailed analysis and appreciation of ▷ William Wordsworth's artifice, and to pointing out that his language is not simply, as he asserted in the Preface to the *Lyrical Ballads*, 'the real language of men', but a highly individual artistic construct of his own. The 'critical analysis' of poems by ▷ Shakespeare and Wordsworth which occupies much of the second volume, displays a very modern sophistication in its treatment of metre and diction.

Biography
The chief source of inspiration for English biographers was the Greek, ▷ Plutarch (1st century AD), whose *Parallel Lives* of Greek and Roman great men was translated into English by ▷ Sir Thomas North in 1579 and was widely read. Biography had been practised before in England; there had been the lives of the saints in the Middle Ages, and in the 16th century Cavendish's life of the statesman ▷ Cardinal Wolsey had appeared. The regular practice of biography, however, starts with the 17th century, not merely owing to the influence of North's translation of Plutarch, but as part of the outward-turning, increasingly scientific interest in many kinds of people (not merely saints and rulers) which in the 18th century was to give rise to the novel. Biography is a branch of history, and the art of historical writing advanced with biography: Edward Hyde, ▷ Earl of Clarendon, included fine biographical portraits in his history of the Great Rebellion, written between 1646 and 1670. Women writers of the period also excelled at biography: the royalist ▷ Margaret Cavendish wrote a biography of her husband William Cavendish, Duke of Newcastle; ▷ Lady Ann Fanshawe wrote an account of the life she and her husband led during the ▷ Interregnum as exiles; and ▷ Lucy Hutchinson wrote a poignant record of the life and death of her Parliamentarian husband, Colonel John Hutchinson. ▷ Izaak Walton's lives of ▷ John Donne (1640), Sir Henry Wotton (1651), ▷ Richard Hooker (1665), ▷ George Herbert (1670) and Bishop Sanderson (1678) are closer to our modern idea of biography, and they are landmarks, if not originals, in the form inasmuch as the subjects, though eminent men, were humble enough to lead ordinary lives in touch with usual experience.

In the 18th century the writing of biographies became habitual; and also biography, or autobiography, became a way of disguising pure fiction, *eg* in the novels of ▷ Defoe. ▷ Samuel Johnson was a master of biography in his ▷ *Lives of the Poets* (1779–81), most notably among which is his *Life of Mr Richard Savage*, previously published in 1744. The outstanding biography of the century, however, is the life of Johnson himself by ▷ James Boswell, 1791, as an intimate and vivid account of a great man. ▷ William Godwin wrote a biography of his wife ▷ Mary Wollstonecraft, entitled *Memoirs of the author of a Vindication of the Rights of Women* (1798), which contributed to her notoriety.

In the Victorian period, the historian and social critic ▷ Thomas Carlyle regarded biography as a means of recounting 'the earthly pilgrimage of a man' (*Critical and Miscellaneous Essays*, 1838). He also regarded the history of the world as 'but the Biography of great men' (▷ *On Heroes, Hero-Worship and the Heroic in History*): His edition of *Oliver Cromwell's Letters and Speeches, with Elucidations* (1845) is an attempt to portray history through the life of one of the men who helped to make it. Carlyle's sympathetic biography helped to establish Cromwell's stature. In 1851 Carlyle wrote a *Life of John Sterling* as a tribute to his 'brilliant, beautiful and cheerful friend' and followed it with a six-volumed *History of Frederick the Great* (1858–65) which took him twelve years to complete. Both of these books are good examples of Carlyle's tendency to 'whitewash' his subjects in the service of didacticism, in that they were designed to support his claim that Britain was in need of 'strong men' with heroic leadership qualities. Carlyle's own biography was written by his great friend the historian J. A. Froude who also edited Carlyle's *Reminiscences* (1881): a series of biographical sketches of famous contemporaries (such as the poets Wordsworth and Southey), and members of his own immediate family including his father, James Carlyle, and his wife, ▷ Jane Welsh Carlyle. Other biographies of the Victorian period in which the author claims a vital relationship between him/herself and his/her subject include Thomas Moore's *Letters and Journals of Lord Byron* (1830), John Gibson Lockhart's *Memoirs* (1837–38), a biography of his father-in-law Sir Walter Scott, and ▷ Elizabeth Gaskell's study *The Life of Charlotte Brontë* (1857). In each of these cases the author had access to personal papers and information about the subject and frequently seasons the narrative with personal reminiscences.

Mrs Gaskell's life of ▷ Charlotte Brontë is characteristic of a trend among Victorian female novelists to write sympathetic and admiring lives of other women writers. A favourite subject was the French novelist ▷ George Sand. Jane Williams (1806–85), Julia Kavanagh (1824–77) and Gertrude Mayer (1839–1932) compiled surveys of women of letters, such as Williams' *Literary Women of England* (1861), or collections of articles on their lives. Anna Stoddart (1840–1911) wrote biographies of such varied individuals as the traveller Isabella Bird and *Francis of Assisi* (1903).

In contrast to the personal biography is the informative biography. This is less subjective and may be composed of a selection of events involving the subject, reported with as little interpretive comment as possible. David Masson's *Life of Milton: Narrated in Connection with the Political, Ecclesiastical and Literary History of his Time* (seven vols, 1859–94), or John G. Nicolay and John Hay's *Abraham Lincoln: A History* (ten vols, 1890) are good examples.

The 20th-century biographer Lytton Strachey regarded most biographies of the 19th century as dull monuments to the subject, whereas he considered biography to be an art form – presenting the subject as a human being and showing him or her from unexpected angles. His best-known works include *Eminent Victorians* (1918) – short biographical studies of Cardinal Manning, Florence Nightingale and General Gordon – and *Queen Victoria* (1912). ▷ Edmund Gosse wrote *The Life of Algernon Charles Swinburne* (1917) but his most famous work is the autobiographical *Father and Son* published anonymously in 1907 which sheds a personal and revealing light on the Victorian period. As such it is a classic example of the largely new form of autobiography for which the period is more outstanding.

The psychological approach and the revolutionary tone of biography had made it one of the fastest growth areas in publishing. Michael Holroyd, Victoria Glendinning and Richard Ellman are among the important biographers of the late 20th century. Biographies of women writers have played a major role in ▷ feminist analyses of the conditions and achievements of women's writing.

Bib: Gittings, R., *The Nature of Biography*.

Bishop, Isabella Bird (1831–1904)

▷ Travel writer. She was born in Boroughbridge, one of two daughters of Edward Bird, curate, and Dora Lawson, Sunday-school teacher. She began travelling abroad in 1854 with a visit to the United States. *The Englishwoman in America* (1856) was an immediate success, launching her career as a writer. *Aspects of Religion in America* (1859) was written during her second trip to North America; this was followed by *The Hawaiian Archipelago: Six Months Among the Palm Groves, Coral Reefs and Volcanoes of the Sandwich Islands* (1874). In 1878 she left for Japan, returning in 1879 after travelling through Hong Kong, Saigon,

Singapore and Malaysia. *Unbeaten Tracks in Japan* (1880) and *The Golden Cheronese* (1883) record these journeys. In 1889 she set out for the Middle East, continuing through India, Tibet, Central Asia and Persia. During this trip she organized the building of two hospitals in India, in memory of her father and sister. *Journeys in Persia and Kurdistan* was published in 1894, the year in which Bishop left Britain on a missionary trip to China. She sailed up the Yangtze River, rode 300 miles alone on a mule, and built three hospitals and an orphanage. Returning to London in 1897, she prepared *Korea and Her Neighbours* (1898), *The Yangtze Valley and Beyond* (1899) and *Chinese Pictures* (1900). Her final missionary trip was to Morocco in 1900–01. She was now severely weakened by the ill-health that had plagued her for many years, and she died of a tumour in 1904. She appears as a character in Caryl Churchill's (b 1938) play, *Top Girls* (1982).
Bib: Stoddart, A., *The Life of Isabella Bird (Mrs Bishop)*

Black Death
An epidemic which struck England in 1348–9 and reduced the population by between one-third and one-half. The economic consequences were far-reaching, especially the shortage of labour. Landowners tended to change from arable to sheep-farming, which required less labour; peasants had better bargaining power and were in a position to commute their serfdom into paid labour; the social unrest which resulted from attempts by the landed classes to keep down wages, culminated in the ▷ Peasants' Revolt of 1381. ▷ Boccaccio provides a vivid picture of the ravages of the ▷ Black Death in Florence in the introductory sequence of his ▷ *Decameron*.

Black Douglas
▷ Douglas, Black.

Black Friars (Blackfriars)
Dominican friars, called 'Black' in England owing to the colour of their robes. Their convent in London was dissolved by ▷ Henry VIII (1509–47), but the district has continued to bear their name. Part of the old convent was adapted into two distinct theatres, although they were in the same building. The first Blackfriars theatre was in the hands of boy actors – the Children of the Chapel – during the 1570s and 1580s. The second Blackfriars theatre was built by ▷ James Burbage in 1596 and initially used by the Children of the Chapel, then by the King's Men, which the Lord ▷ Chamberlain's Company had become. It was a 'private' theatre with a more affluent and probably more educated kind of audience than frequented the public theatres such as the ▷ Globe. The change of audience encouraged a change in the mode of drama. Never again would the theatre serve the whole society: its present status in this country as an entertainment for the relatively privileged is derived from the move from 'public' to 'private' theatres.
▷ Theatres.

Black Prince, The (1330–76)
Edward, Prince of Wales, eldest son of ▷ Edward III. He was famous for his military exploits, especially his defeat of a French army at Poitiers, 1356; in consequence he became a national hero comparable to ▷ Henry V. His designation 'Black' seems to originate with 16th-century chroniclers; it probably refers to his reputation as a warrior. His son was ▷ Richard II.

Blackmore, R.D. (Richard Dodderidge) (1825–1900)
Novelist and poet. Born in Berkshire, the son of a clergyman, Blackmore was educated at school in Tiverton, where he was head boy, and at Exeter College, Oxford. His mother had died when he was a baby and he spent much of his youth with an uncle in Glamorgan. A career as a barrister was cut short by epileptic fits and after an unsuccessful period as a schoolteacher, Blackmore built a house in Teddington where he lived a retired life, dividing his time between writing, and growing and selling fruit and flowers. He married Lucy Maguire in 1852; there were no children and after her death in 1888 he continued to mourn her and keep the house unchanged. He was a shy man, kind but self-centred and determined. He was fond of animals, especially dogs, and deeply absorbed in his gardening enterprise.

He published volumes of poetry, including translations of the 3rd-century Greek poet Theocritus and the Roman poet Virgil (70–19 BC). His fourteen novels include *Lorna Doone* (1869), which was rejected by eighteen publishers and is now his most famous novel, *Cradock Nowell* (1866), *The Maid of Sker* (1872), his first attempt at fiction only later finished, *Alice Lorraine* (1875) and *Springhaven* (1887). *Lorna Doone* is said to have done for Devonshire what Sir Walter Scott (1771–1832) did for the Highlands and in general Blackmore's novels abound with carefully observed and detailed descriptions of locations, wildlife and the weather along with exciting incidents, all somewhat loosely structured.
▷ Regional novel.
Bib: Burris, Q.G., *R.D. Blackmore: His Life and Novels*; Dunn, W.H., *R.D. Blackmore, The Author of Lorna Doone: A Biography*; Budd, K.G., *The Last Victorian: R.D. Blackmore and his Novels.*

Blackmore, Sir Richard (c 1655–1729)
Poet and physician to ▷ Queen Anne. The dullness of his lengthy epic, *Prince Arthur*

(1695) and *The Creation: a philosophical poem demonstrating the existence and providence of God* (1712) earned the ridicule of ▷ Alexander Pope in ▷ *The Dunciad* (Bk. II, 370ff). He also wrote a *Satyre against Wit* (1700).

Blackwell, Elizabeth (?1700–58)
Naturalist, born in Aberdeen. She eloped to London with the Scottish physician and adventurer Alexander Blackwell, who was imprisoned for debt. In order to raise money, she published *A Curious Herbal Containing Five Hundred Cuts of the Most Useful Plants Which are Now Used in the Practice of Physick* in two volumes, in 1737 and 1739. The books consisted of pictures of plants, drawn, engraved and coloured by herself, with descriptions added in Latin by her husband. The herbal was approved by leading members of the College of Physicians, became immensely popular, and was later expanded into five volumes. Alexander Blackwell was executed in Sweden in 1747, allegedly for plotting against the government.

Blackwood's Magazine
Founded in 1817 by the publisher William Blackwood as the *Edinburgh Monthly Magazine*, it was particularly influential in the first 15 years of its existence. Like the ▷ *Quarterly* it was intended as a Tory rival to the liberal ▷ *Edinburgh Review*, but called itself a 'magazine' to indicate a lighter tone than that of the 'Reviews'. It attacked ▷ Lord Byron, and ▷ Percy Bysshe Shelley on political grounds, and was, like the *Quarterly*, particularly hostile to ▷ John Keats, because of his association with the radical journalist ▷ Leigh Hunt. Hunt, Keats, ▷ Charles Lamb and ▷ William Hazlitt were stigmatized as the 'Cockney School' of literature. *Blackwood's Magazine* began with a brilliant group of contributors, especially ▷ Sir Walter Scott, John G. Lockhart (known because of his fierce criticism as 'the Scorpion'), ▷ James Hogg, and John Wilson, who wrote under the pen-name of Christopher North. Between 1822 and 1835 the magazine ran a series of brilliant dialogues, *Noctes Ambrosianae*, 'Nights at Ambrose's' (a well-known inn). In 1857 it published ▷ George Eliot's *Scenes from Clerical Life*.

Blair, Robert (1699–1746)
Scottish clergyman and author of *The Grave* (1743), a ▷ blank-verse genre piece blending ▷ Gothic sinisterness, banal piety and a pseudo-Shakespearean sublimity, imitated from *Hamlet*. Its enjoyable imaginative gusto ensured that it retained its popularity throughout the century, and beyond.

Blake, William (1757–1827)
Poet and artist. The self-educated son of a London hosier, Blake earned his living by engraving illustrations for books. His own poems are engraved rather than printed, and he wove into his text pictures which elaborated the poetic theme. His earliest poems, *Poetical Sketches* show the influence of earlier lyric writers and ▷ Macpherson's ▷ Ossianic writings. His next works, the ▷ *Songs of Innocence* (1789), and ▷ *Songs of Experience* (1794) are startlingly original. Intended, on one level, for children, they are simple but symbolically resonant lyrics 'Shewing the Two contrary States of the Human Soul'. In *Innocence* the world is unthreatening and without morality, and God is trusted implicitly. The *Experience* poems, which often parallel those of the earlier volume in setting or title, depict with fierce moral indignation, a fallen world of repression and religious hypocrisy. There is no simple relation of progression or superiority between the 'contrary states', and Blake makes no attempt to reconcile their contradictions. They remain in unresolved dialectical opposition to each other.

In later works Blake elaborates his revolutionary interpretation of Christian theology using invented characters representing psychological or spiritual forces. In *Thel* (etched c 1789), in rhythmical, unrhymed lines, usually of seven stresses, the protagonist, confronted with the interdependence of life and death, creation and destruction, flees back to the shadowy world of the unborn. *Tiriel* was written at about the same time. *The French Revolution* (1791), *America* (1793) and *Visions of the Daughters of Albion* (1793) show Blake's reaction to the American and French revolutions, which he saw as releasing the energies of humanity, so long repressed by the forces of absolutism, institutionalized religion and sexual inhibition. In ▷ *The Marriage of Heaven and Hell* (etched c 1793) Blake expressed in a series of prophetic statements and 'Memorable Fancies', mainly in prose, his contempt for 18th-century rationalism and institutionalized religion.

Because his works remained virtually unknown and he developed no lasting relationship with an audience, his later prophecies became increasingly formless and obscure. He was also unwilling to be too explicit in case he should invite trouble from the authorities. *The Book of Urizen* (1794) focuses on the tyrannical figure of Urizen, ('your reason' or 'horizon'?) who symbolizes the inhibiting powers of control and restriction. Urizen is in constant war with Orc, a Satanic force of revolutionary energy. *The Book of Ahania*, *The Book of Los* (1795) and *Vala* (1797), subsequently rewritten as *The Four Zoas* (1804) develop similar themes with increasing intricacy and elusiveness. His last two prophetic books *Milton* (1804) and *Jerusalem* (1804) are often impenetrable, but include some striking passages. They show a new emphasis on Christian humility and self-sacrifice. In *Milton* he elaborates on his famous observation that ▷ Milton was 'of the Devil's party without knowing it'. Milton is shown returning to earth in the form of Blake himself, in order to correct his earlier mistake. Blake is one of the most intellectually challenging of English poets, with a unique insight into the pieties and ideological deceptions of his time.

Bib: Ault, D., *Narrative Unbound*; Davis, M., *William Blake: A New Kind of Man*; Bronowski, J., *William Blake and the Age of Revolution*; Glen, H., *Vision and Disenchantment: Blake's Songs and Wordsworth's Lyrical Ballads*; Bottrall, M. (ed.), *William Blake: Songs of Innocence and Experience* (Macmillan Casebook); Paley, M. D., *William Blake*; Erdman, D. V., *Blake: Prophet Against Empire*; Bloom, H., *Blake's Apocalypse*.

Blank verse

Verse which is unrhymed, and composed of lines which normally contain ten syllables and have the stress on every second syllable, as in the classical ▷ iambic pentameter.

The first user of the iambic pentameter in English was ▷ Chaucer and he used it in rhyming couplets, *eg The Prologue* to ▷ *The Canterbury Tales*. The first user of blank verse was Henry Howard, ▷ Earl of Surrey (1517–47), who adopted it for a translation of the second and third books of ▷ Virgil's *Aeneid* in order to get closer to the effect of the metrically regular but unrhymed Latin ▷ hexameters. The effect in Surrey is that Chaucer's measure is being used but without rhyme:

They whisted all, with fixed face attent,
When prince Aeneas from the royal seat
Thus gan to speak.

The dramatist ▷ Christopher Marlowe (1564–93) first gave blank verse its distinctive quality. In his plays, he combined the rhythm of the verse with the normal rhythm and syntax of the sentence, so that the effect begins to be like natural speech expressed with unusual music:

Hell hath no limits, nor is circumscrib'd
In one self place: for where we are is hell,
And where hell is, there must we ever be...
(*Dr Faustus*)

Blank verse as used by Marlowe was carried on by ▷ Shakespeare, who employed it with steadily increasing flexibility and power. His contemporaries did the same, but in his immediate successors' work great freedoms are taken with the ▷ metre, and the rhythm of the sentence begins to dominate over that of the line, so that the effect is of rhythmic paragraphs of speech.

The next phase is the epic use of blank verse by ▷ Milton in ▷ *Paradise Lost* (1667), who gave the weight of Latin syntax to the long sentences and accordingly moved away from speech rhythms. ▷ Wordsworth and ▷ Coleridge at the beginning of the 19th century lightened the Miltonic effect back towards colloquialism while retaining a quasi-Miltonic gravity in order to convey the pulse of sustained meditation. Examples include Wordsworth's *Lines Composed a Few Miles Above Tintern Abbey...* (1798) and his epic of introspection ▷ *The Prelude* (1805; 1850). Twentieth-century poets such as ▷ Eliot and ▷ Pound derived from the ▷ Jacobean dramatists new free measures which cannot strictly be described as blank verse at all.

▷ Free verse; Metre.

Bleak House **(1852–3)**

A novel by ▷ Charles Dickens, published, like most of his novels, in monthly parts. It opens with an attack on the part of the legal system called the High Court of Chancery. The rest of the novel expands this opening into a dramatization, through a wide range of characters, of the various forms of parasitism that society lends itself to, and of the ways in which institutions (especially legal ones) falsify relationships and degrade human beings. Most of the story takes place in London. The telling of the story is shared by two contrasted narrators: the savagely sardonic but impersonal author who uses the present tense and the ingenuous, saccharine, unresentful girl, Esther Summerson, who is ignorant of her parentage, though she knows that she is illegitimate. She is adopted by a philanthropist, John Jarndyce, who also adopts two young orphan relatives, Richard Carstone and Ada Clare, who are 'wards in Chancery' (ie legally under the care of the Lord Chancellor) while the distribution of an estate to which they have claims is endlessly disputed in the Court of Chancery (the case of 'Jarndyce and Jarndyce'). Through Richard, Ada and Mrs Jarndyce, Esther becomes acquainted with a large number of characters, some of whom are also despairing participants in Chancery Suits, and others (such as Skimpole, the parasitic man of letters, Mrs Jellyby, a well-meaning but incompetent philanthropist, and Turveydrop, the self-styled model of fashionable deportment) who live off society without giving anything substantial in return. Another focus in the novel is Sir Leicester Dedlock, a simple-minded but self-important land-owner, whose one redeeming feature is his devotion to his wife, the beautiful and silent Lady Dedlock. Lady Dedlock is in fact the mother of Esther Summerson, a fact known to the family lawyer, Tulkinghorn, who blackmails her. Her former lover, Captain Hawdon, is still alive, but lives in destitution and misery. His only friend is the crossing-sweeper, Jo, who resembles Sir Leicester in that they are equally simple-minded and equally capable of one great love for another person. In social respects they are

so differentiated, by the lack of any advantages in the one case and by excess of privilege in the other, that it is hard to think of them as belonging to the same species. A large number of other characters contribute to Dickens' panorama of society as mainly constituted by parasites and the victims of parasites. The theme is conveyed partly through the atmosphere of contrasted houses: Bleak House, which is in fact the cordial and life-giving home of Mr Jarndyce; Chesney Wold, the vast but empty mansion of Sir Leicester; Tom-all-alone's, the slum dwelling where Jo finds his sole refuge; the clean and orderly household of the retired soldier, Bagnet; the squalid one of the money-lender, Smallweed, and so forth. For the main characters, the story ends with the corruption of Richard Carstone, the death in despair of Lady Dedlock, the murder of Tulkinghorn and Esther's marriage to the young doctor, Woodcourt. The case of 'Jarndyce and Jarndyce' was based on an actual case centring on a Birmingham millionaire, William Jennings. The character of Skimpole is partly based on journalist and poet, Leigh Hunt, (1784–1859) and another character, Boythorn, on ▷ Walter Landor.
Bib: Hawthorne, J. (ed.), *An Introduction to the Varieties of Criticism: Bleak House*.

Bleasdale, Alan (b 1946)
Dramatist. A Merseyside writer who developed a strong reputation outside the West End, Alan Bleasdale is a gritty comic satirist who has reached his widest theatre audience with what is, paradoxically, his most earnest work: *Are You Lonesome Tonight?*, an overtly hagiographic musical about Elvis Presley that aims to set the record straight about a musical legend Bleasdale thinks has been vilified. Set on the last day of the King's life, the musical is an unabashedly sentimental picture of a bloated talent looking back sardonically on his younger self, before he allowed himself to be mercilessly corrupted by managers, promoters and the press. Earlier stage plays of note include *It's a Madhouse* (1976), set in a psychiatric hospital in the northwest of England, and *Having a Ball* (1981), about four men awaiting surgery in a vasectomy clinic. *On the Ledge* (1993) is, literally, set on a window ledge. In addition, Bleasdale has written memorably for other media: Peter Smith's 1985 film *No Surrender* has a strong Bleasdale script about rival factions in a Liverpool nightclub where the tensions mirror those in Northern Ireland. His TV writing has also tapped the psychic pulse of Britain in *Boys From the Blackstuff* (a 1983 howl of rage against unemployment, set in Liverpool, that nonetheless caught a national feeling), *The Monocled Mutineer* (a 1986 parable of powerlessness in Thatcher's Britain) and *GBH* (1991) which wickedly satirised the battle for ascendency in Liverpool between the Labour Party and the Trotskyist Militant Tendency.

Blenheim (1704)
An important battle in the War of the ▷ Spanish Succession in which the forces of ▷ John Churchill, Duke of Marlborough, and Prince Eugene of Savoy defeated the French forces of Louis XIV under Marshal Tallard, near the village of Blindheim (anglicized, Blenheim) in Bavaria.

Blessington, Marguerite, Countess of (1789–1849)
Journalist and novelist. Marguerite Blessington's life was characterized by brutality and hardship, and yet she was one of the most renowned literary hostesses of the day. She received no formal education and was sold by her father as a wife to Captain Maurice Farmer when she was fifteen, but ran away after only three months. She eventually found shelter with Charles, Earl of Blessington and, when her husband died in 1817, they married. This was the happiest period of Blessington's life and she travelled on the continent, becoming acquainted with some of the most renowned literary figures of her day. It is from this period that her witty and fast-moving work *Conversations of Lord Byron* (▷ Byron) comes, of whom she wrote just before she met him: 'Am I indeed in the same town with Byron? . . . I hope he may not be fat . . . for a fat poet is an anomaly in my opinion'. It was also at this time that she made an enduring friendship with ▷ Count Alfred d'Orsay, for whom she acted as patron. She had no children by Blessington and this resulted in her rejection by his family when he died in 1829, after which she had to work hard in order to support herself, often undertaking hack journalism, although she also wrote several novels. In 1849 she was declared bankrupt and died penniless in Paris a month later.
▷ Silver-fork novels.
Bib: Marshall, W.K., *Byron, Shelley, Hunt and the Liberal*; Todd, J., *Dictionary of British Women Writers*.

Blind, Mathilde (1841–96)
Poet, biographer, translator and editor, who also wrote under the ▷ pseudonym Claude Lake. Born in Mannheim, Germany, she adopted the name of her stepfather, Karl Blind (a revolutionary who led the Baden revolt 1848–9). Educated by her mother and at schools in Belgium and England, she was politically committed from an early age. Her writings are eclectic: her first volume of *Poems* appeared in 1867, followed by *Shelley: A Lecture* in 1870. She edited a well-respected *Selection from the Poems of P.B. Shelley* (1872), translated Strauss's *The Old Faith and the New* (1873) and wrote

a long poem based on a Scottish legend, *The Prophecy of St Oran* (1881). A biography of ▷ George Eliot followed in 1883, then came a ▷ romance, *Tarantella* (1884). *Heather on Fire* (1886) was a political protest against the clearances of the Scottish Highlands. Other works include the epic poem *The Ascent of Man* (1889), a translation of the *Journal* (1890) of Russian *emigré* Marie Bashkirtseff (1858–84) and four further volumes of poetry. Always committed to raising the status of women and improving their educational opportunities, Blind left her estate to Newnham, the Cambridge women's college.

▷ Women's Movement; Scottish literature in English.

Bib: Robertson, E.S., *English Poetesses*; Symons, A. (ed.), *The Poetical Works of Mathilde Blind*; Leighton, A., and Reynolds, M. (eds.), *An Anthology of Victorian Women Poets.*

Blixen, Karen Christentze (née Dinesen) (1885–1962)

Danish novelist and short-story writer, who wrote mainly in English, using the pen-names Isak Dinesen and Pierre Andrezel. Born in Rungsted, Denmark, she studied art in Copenhagen, Paris and Rome before marrying her cousin, Baron Bror Blixen-Finecke, in 1914, and settling in Kenya where they ran a coffee-plantation (work which Blixen continued after their divorce until 1931). Her novel *Out of Africa* (1937) is based on her experiences in Africa. A number of her short stories use elements of the fantastic, the symbolic, and the ▷ Gothic: the volumes include: *Seven Gothic Tales* (1934); *Winter's Tales* (1942); *Angelic Avengers* (1944); *Last Tales* (1957); *Anecdotes of Destiny* (1958); *Shadows on the Grass* (1960); *Carnival: Entertainments and Posthumous Tales* (1979). She also published essays, some of which are collected in *Daguerreotypes and Other Essays* (1984) and *On Modern Marriage and Other Observations* (1987).

Bib: Thurman, Judith, *Isak Dinesen: The Life of a Storyteller.*

Blood, Tragedy of

▷ Revenge tragedy.

Bloody Assizes

Judicial trials of unusual ferocity held after the failure of ▷ Monmouth's Rebellion against James II. Judge Jeffreys condemned large numbers of the small rebel army to death and sentenced many more to transportation to penal colonies (▷ Botany Bay).

Bloom, Harold (b 1930)

One of the leading members of the so-called Yale school of literary criticism, along with the late ▷ Paul De Man, ▷ Geoffrey Hartman and J. Hillis Miller. In books such as *The Anxiety of Influence* (1973), *A Map of Misreading* (1975), and *Poetry and Repression* (1976) Bloom seeks to offer a revisionary account of poetry, based especially on a ▷ Freudian model of the relationship between the aspiring poet and his literary predecessors. In this way Bloom moves away from the tenets of American new criticism in his suggestion that all poetry seeks, but fails, to exclude 'precursor' texts, with which it enters into a struggle, both destructive and creative, in order to achieve its particular identity. Other books by Bloom relevant to a study of the Romantic period include: *Shelley's My Mythmaking* (1959), *The Visionary Company* (1961), *Blake's Apocalypse* (1963), *The Ringers in the Tower* (1971), *Poetry and Repression* (1976) and *The Breaking of The Vessels* (1982).

Bloomfield, Robert (1766–1823)

Poet. Bloomfield was a working-class writer who persevered in the face of great hardship, writing and publishing his poetry. His most famous work is *The Farmer's Boy* (1800), which traced the life of an orphan rustic through the natural cycle of the seasons (▷ nature). Although this book sold around 26,000 copies, the income was insufficient to live on and Bloomfield died in poverty.

Bloomsbury Group, The

An exclusive intellectual circle that centred on the house of the publisher, Leonard Woolf, and his wife, the novelist, ▷ Virginia Woolf, in the district of London round the British Museum, known as Bloomsbury. It flourished notably in the 1920s, and included, besides the Woolfs, the economist John Maynard Keynes, the biographer ▷ Lytton Strachey, the art critics Roger Fry and Clive Bell, and the painters Vanessa Bell and Duncan Grant, as well as others. The group owed much to the Cambridge philosopher ▷ G. E. Moore and the importance he attached to the value of friendship and aesthetic appreciation. The close relationships which resulted from this, in addition to the fastidiousness which arose from their critical attitude to the prevailing culture of English society, gave them an apparent exclusiveness which made them many enemies (▷ Catherine Carswell). Moore's influence also contributed to their scepticism about religious tradition and social and political conventions; they tended to be moderately left-wing and agnostic. They were innovators in art and represented an important section of the English avant-garde. Their more constructive opponents attacked them for excessive self-centredness and an aestheticism which was too individualistic and self-regarding to be really creative in social terms.

Blower, Elizabeth (b 1763)

Novelist, born in Worcester. She took to writing to help support her family. She wrote four

novels, *The Parsonage House* (1780), *Features from Life: or A Summer Visit* (1780), *George Bateman* (1782) and *Maria* (1785). They display humour and satire, as well as vivid characterization. Blower has been described as a direct predecessor of ▷ Jane Austen.
Bib: Todd, J (ed.), *A Dictionary of British and American Writers 1660–1800*.

Bluestocking
The 'Blue Stocking Ladies' were a group of intelligent, literary women in the mid 18th century who held evening receptions for serious conversation. As a setting for discussions in which both sexes were included, the evenings were a deliberate attempt to challenge the social stereotypes which confined intellectual debate to male gatherings and relegated the female sex to trivial topics. By bringing men and women together in this atmosphere, it was hoped that the 'polite' codes of gallantry could be disposed of. The chief hostesses included ▷ Elizabeth Montagu, Elizabeth Carter, ▷ Mary Delany and later, ▷ Hannah More.

The name 'bluestocking' is thought to derive from the stockings of Benjamin Stillingfleet, who, too poor to buy evening dress, attended in his daytime blue worsteds. ▷ Hannah More's poem *Bas Bleu* (1786) helped to establish the use of the term as referring to the society women, although Admiral Boscawen is traditionally credited with coining the collective noun.

Blunden, Edmund (1896–1974)
Poet and critic, and author of one of the most famous books about World War I, *Undertones of War* (1928). His lyrical poetry produced during and just after that war is drawn especially from the English countryside, and its sincerity redeemed for many readers what was becoming a hackneyed convention of 'nature poetry'. His poetry was first published in the 1914 ▷ *Georgian Poetry* anthology. His literary studies have been important especially for the 'Romantic' period, *eg Life of Shelley*, *Charles Lamb and his Contemporaries*; and he played a great part in editing and raising the reputation of the nineteenth-century poet John Clare. His best-remembered book now is probably *Cricket Country* (1944).
Bib: Hart-Davies, R., *Edmund Blunden*.

Blyton, Enid (1897–1968)
Writer for children. Blyton is one of the most famous and maligned children's novelists of the 20th century. She was phenomenally prolific, beginning with *The Enid Blyton Book of Fairies* (1924), writing school stories and the Famous Five sequence in the 1940s and 1950s, the Noddy stories in the 1950s and 1960s, as well as adaptations of classical and Uncle Remus stories, and non-fiction for children. Blyton's works are severely chastised by contemporary critics both on educational grounds (her works do not tax their young readers, their vocabulary is limited, their characters thin, and their plots simple-minded) and on political grounds (her writing is sexist, racist and nostalgic for a pre-war middle-class idyll). Despite this her novels continue to sell and most are still in print. Other works include: *Naughty Amelia Jane* (1939); *The Naughtiest Girl in the School* (1940); *Five on a Treasure Island* (1942); *First Term at Malory Towers* (1946); *Noddy and His Car* (1951) and *Noddy in Toyland* (1955).
Bib: Ray, S. G., *The Blyton Phenomenon*; Stoney, B., *Enid Blyton: A Biography*.

Boccaccio, Giovanni (?1313–75)
Italian humanist scholar and writer, born near Florence. His literary studies began in Naples, where he wrote his first works, but he later returned to Florence and was employed on diplomatic missions for the Florentine state. He publicly lectured on ▷ Dante's ▷ *Divine Comedy*, was a friend of ▷ Petrarch and the centre of a circle of humanist learning and literary activity. His works included a wide range of courtly narratives, a vernacular imitation of classical ▷ epic and a number of important encyclopaedic works in Latin which occupied the last years of his life.

Boccaccio's collection of brief tragic-narratives in Latin (*De Casibus Virorum Illustrium*) was reworked in English by ▷ Lydgate in the 15th century and provided much material for the Elizabethan compilation of short tragic-narratives, the ▷ *Mirror for Magistrates*. Tales from the *Decameron* were included in William Painter's anthology ▷ *The Palace of Pleasure*, and many Elizabethan dramatists, including ▷ Shakespeare, quarried plots from either Painter's collection or from the *Decameron* itself.
Bib: Chubb, T. C., *The Life of Giovanni Boccaccio*; Wright, H. G., *Boccaccio in England from Chaucer to Tennyson*.

Bodichon, Barbara Leigh Smith (1827–1891)
▷ Feminist and polemicist, born in London, the illegitimate daughter of a ▷ Unitarian minister and a milliner's apprentice. She enrolled in the Ladies' College in Bedford Square in 1849 and chose to study art. Later in life her drawings and paintings were widely exhibited and sold for substantial amounts. Bodichon is best-known today as an active campaigner in the fight for ▷ women's suffrage and legal reform. *A Brief Summary in Plain Language of the Most Important Laws Concerning Women* (1854) was a highly influential pamphlet that brought attention to women's powerlessness and lack of legal rights. In *Women and Work* (1857), she argued that all professions should be available to women, and in her two pamphlets on suffrage, *Reasons for the Enfranchisement of Women* (1866) and *Objections to the Enfranchisement of Women*

Considered (1866), she argued lucidly for female voting rights, substantiating her points with empirical evidence she had collected. Bodichon was also concerned with ▷ education, setting up a radical school and assisting Emily Davies in establishing Girton College, Cambridge. She left £10,000 to Girton at her death. She was involved in the editing and production of *The Englishwoman's Journal* and published her *American Diary* in 1872. In this work she protested against the injustice she had seen in the American South during a trip there in 1857–8, and drew parallels between the position of slaves and the position of women.

▷ Travel writing; Marriage.

Bib: Herstein, S.R., *A Mid-Victorian Feminist: Barbara Leigh Smith Bodichon*; Burton, H., *Life*.

Boethius, Ancius Manlius Torquatus Severinus (475–524)

Philosopher, scholar and statesman, born in Rome and educated at Athens and Alexandria. He wrote textbooks on logic and music, and was made consul in 510. His illustrious political career, as advisor to the Ostrogothic Emperor Theodoric, ended when he was accused of treason, imprisoned and executed in 524. While imprisoned, Boethius composed his most famous and influential work, *De Consolatione Philosophiae* (*The Consolation of Philosophy*). In this work, a first-person narrator who is also imprisoned recounts how he is tutored by Lady Philosophy to review his predicament and to understand the events and values of his life within a universal scheme. The text, composed in alternating verse and prose sections, deals with complex issues such as the relationship between divine foreknowledge and individual free will and was one of the most influential philosophical works of the medieval period, being translated into ▷ Old English by ▷ Alfred and later by ▷ Chaucer. The influence of Boethius pervades Chaucer's narratives. Another English translation from the Elizabethan period has been attributed to ▷ Elizabeth I.

Bib: Watts, V. (trans.), *The Consolation of Philosophy*.

Bohemian

Applied to artists and those who live a life supposedly dedicated to the spirit of the imaginative arts, it means living freely, refusing to observe social conventions, especially when they depend on mere habit, snobbery or fear of 'seeming different'. It often carries a slightly mocking tone and is rarely used now without irony. Literally, Bohemian means native to Bohemia, now the western part of Czechoslovakia. In the 15th century gipsies were supposed to have come from there; in the 19th century, French students were supposed to live like the gipsies and hence to be 'Bohemian'. The word was then introduced into English with this meaning by the novelist ▷ William Makepeace Thackeray. His novel *The Newcomers* is one of the first studies in English of Bohemianism.

Twentieth-century avant-garde movements have often been regarded as loosely 'bohemian' (*eg* ▷ the Bloomsbury Group), and the term is still in currency, used to describe a range of counter-cultural attributes and aspirations.

Boiardo, Matteomaria (?1441–94)

Italian poet who reworked the legends of ▷ King Arthur and ▷ Charlemagne. His principal work was the unfinished *Orlando Innamorato*. ▷ Ludivico Ariosto produced a sequel ▷ *Orlando Furioso*.

Boileau, Nicolas (1636–1711)

French critic and poet. The ▷ Earl of Rochester's *Satyre Against Reason and Mankind* broadly follows his Eighth Satire. Through his *Art Poetique* (*The Poetic Art*) (1674), based on ▷ Horace's *Ars Poetica*, and his translation of the Greek treatise *On the Sublime*, attributed to ▷ Longinus, he fostered in French literature the ideals of classical urbanity and regularity of form. He influenced ▷ John Dryden, who revised a translation of his *Art Poetique*, and ▷ Alexander Pope, whose ▷ *Essay on Criticism* was partly based on it, and whose ▷ *The Rape of the Lock* owes something to the French poet's mock-epic, *Le Lutrin*. In the Romantic and Victorian periods Boileau's name became synonymous with stifling (and foreign) neo-classical decadence.

***Bold Stroke for a Wife, A* (1718)**

Play by ▷ Susannah Centlivre, the only one for which she claims to have used no sources but her own invention. Anne Lovely has four guardians, all of whom must give their consent before she can marry: Sir Philip Modelove, an 'old Beau', who cares only for French fashions, and loves operas, balls and masques; Periwinkle, a 'silly half-witted Fellow . . . fond of everything antique and foreign', who dresses in the fashions of the previous century; Tradelove, a broker and cheat; and Obadiah Prim, a 'very rigid Quaker'. Colonel Fainwell is in love with Lovely, and sets out to win her by approaching each of the guardians in various disguises, and with various feigned schemes. One of his characters, Simon Pure, has given the phrase 'the real simon pure' to the English language. The means by which Fainwell succeeds in his plan forms the chief interest of the action. The play provides a wonderful vehicle for a versatile actor: three members of the Bullock family were in the original production, and many other renowned actors, including ▷ John Philip Kemble and Charles Kemble (1775–1854), have played the part of Fainwell. *A Bold Stroke for a Wife* achieved great popularity and became a stock item in the English repertory, surviving until the last quarter of the 19th century. It was acted in command performances before George II and George III.

Bolingbroke, Henry (1367–1413)
Duke of Hereford, son of John of Gaunt, who deposed his cousin, ▷ Richard II, to become King ▷ Henry IV.

Bolingbroke, Henry St John (1678–1751)
Tory politician, and writer chiefly on political matters. He favoured the ▷ Stuart (Jacobite) succession on the death of ▷ Queen Anne in 1714, and when the Whigs took power and the Hanoverian George I was declared king, he was impeached. He fled to the court of the Pretender in France, but in 1723 was pardoned and returned to England. He became a friend of ▷ Alexander Pope and his rationalist, Deist views strongly influenced the ▷ *Essay on Man* which is addressed to him. In 1749 he published *The Idea of a Patriot King*, which argued that the king's role should be as a national leader, above the corruption of politics.
▷ Deism.

Bolt, Robert (b 1924–1994)
British dramatist and screenwriter whose first major success was with the ▷ Chekhovian *Flowering Cherry* (1957). This was followed by *A Man for All Seasons* (1960), a play about the life of Sir Thomas More, which has some superficial resemblances to the style of ▷ Brecht, such as the use of a common man figure who plays a variety of roles in the play. However, the audience is not encouraged to maintain a critical distance from the action in the manner of Brecht nor are the particular historical circumstances of More's life explored in any detail. Bolt is primarily concerned with More's conflict between his commitment to himself, to his own sense of integrity, and his commitment to society, a theme which is common in his work. Other plays include: *The Tiger and the Horse* (1960); *Gentle Jack* (1963); *Vivat! Vivat Regina!* (1970); *State of Revolution* (1977). Film scripts: *Lawrence of Arabia* (1962); *Dr Zhivago* (1965); *A Man for All Seasons* (1967); *Ryan's Daughter* (1970); *Lady Caroline Lamb* (1972); *The Bounty* (1984); *The Mission* (1986).
Bib: Hayman, R., *Robert Bolt*.

Bond, Edward (b 1934)
Dramatist. Notorious for a scene in *Saved* (1965) in which a baby is stoned to death. Bond has consistently written from a Marxist perspective, and argues that the shock of such violent images is necessary to represent the violence that is done to people by capitalism.

Born in London, Bond left school at fourteen, worked in factories and offices, writing plays in his spare time, and sending them to the Royal Court. *Saved*, developed with the Writer's group at the Court, was instrumental in ridding British theatre of the censorship of the Lord Chamberlain. The theatre's attempt to stage the play under club conditions led to a prosecution which showed that such conditions did not offer any protection from censorship. In 1968, The Theatres Act abolished the powers of the Lord Chamberlain, and *Saved* and *Narrow Road to the Deep North* (1968) were toured throughout Europe under the auspices of the British Council.

Saved is a difficult play to watch; dealing with a community of young people in South London it charts their desperate and violent lives. Its first performance at the Royal Court provoked extreme, and extremely polarised, reactions. The *Daily Telegraph* critic reported 'cold disgust' and horror at the scene in which a group of men stone a baby to death (and was not alone in his reaction), while other critics and writers greeted the power of Bond's writing and imagery with acclaim. It is not only that scene which makes the play so harrowing; in one section, the baby wails unrelentingly while no one on stage responds to its cries, and the audience has to physically experience the frustration and apathy of the play's characters.

Many of Bond's plays offer radical rereadings of historical events, texts and figures that are commonly held as a source of national pride: *Bingo* (1973) confronts the dying and unheroic ▷ Shakespeare and ▷ Ben Jonson. *The Fool* (1975) is about the 'peasant poet' ▷ John Clare. Bond has described his reworking of ▷ Shakespeare's *King Lear* in *Lear* (1972) as 'an attack on Stalinism, as seen as a danger to Western revolution, and on bourgeois culture as expressed in Shakespeare's *Lear*'. He has consistently spoken out for political causes; *Black Mass* (1970) was written for the Anti-Apartheid movement; *Stone* (1976) for Gay Sweatshop; *Passion* (1971) was commissioned by the Campaign for Nuclear Disarmament.

In recent years he has insisted on directing his own new work, with the perhaps predictable result that his uniquely trenchant voice has been less widely heard. His works include: *The Pope's Wedding* (1962); *Narrow Road to the Deep North* (1968); *Lear* (1971); *The Sea* (1973); *Bingo* (1974); *The Fool* (1976); *The Bundle* and *The Woman* (both 1978); *Restoration* (1981); *The War Plays* (1985).
Bib: Hirst, D. L., *Bond*; Spencer, J. S., *Dramatic Strategies in the Plays of Edward Bond*

Bonhote, Elizabeth (1744–1818)
Novelist and poet. Bonhote was an unadventurous novelist and it was perhaps the very conservative nature of her narratives and themes which made her one of ▷ Minerva's

best-selling authors. The settings are often rural and, in *Bungay Castle* (1796), historicized; in addition, there is always a strong ▷ didactic moral at the end of the tale. Her unquestioning acceptance of traditional and conventional values is emphasized in her collection of essays, *The Parental Monitor* (1788), which contains advice for her children. Interestingly, however, while she advocates that women should stay at home and look after their families, she encourages them to write and not to be diverted from literary pursuits.
Bib: Todd, J., *Dictionary of British Women Writers*.

Book of the Duchess
▷ Chaucer's dream poem, written in octosyllabic couplets, which commemorates Blanche of Lancaster, the first wife of ▷ John of Gaunt. The date of the poem is uncertain but it is one of Chaucer's early works and seems likely to have been composed some time between 1368 (the date of Blanche's dealt) and 1372. Chaucer drew on the work of contemporary French poets, especially ▷ Jean Froissart and Guillaume de Machaut, for its material and form. The lovelorn narrator/dreamer relates how he falls asleep, having read the story of Ceyx and Alcyone as bedtime reading. He follows a hunting party in his dream-scape and, in the heart of a wood, meets a lovelorn knight, dressed in black, whom he finds lamenting the loss of his lady. In response to questions from the dreamer, the Black knight recounts the history of his courtship of his lady White, and is finally prompted to reveal, in plain terms, that she has died. At this point, the dreamer and the knight begin to move out of the wood towards the knight's castle; a bell strikes 12; the dreamer awakes, book in hand, vowing to preserve his dream experience in a literary form.

The name of the lady celebrated in the poem, 'White', obviously recalls that of Blanche of Lancaster, and various punning references are made in the text to John of Gaunt's position as Earl of Richmond and Duke of Lancaster. In the Prologue to Chaucer's ▷ *Legend of Good Women*, this ▷ dream-vision poem is listed among Chaucer's works as 'the Deeth of Blaunche the Duchesse'.

▷ John of Gaunt; Lancaster, House of. **Bib**: Phillips, H. (ed.), *Chaucer: The Book of the Duchess*; Spearing, A. C., *Medieval Dream Poetry*.

Booth, Barton (?1679–1733)
Actor, manager, poet: the leading tragic actor of his generation. Booth became interested in the theatre while performing in a play at Westminster School, and afterwards joined the profession. In 1709 he became the leading tragic actor at ▷ Drury Lane, but in the following year, after a quarrel about the distribution of management duties in the company, he helped lead a break-in to the premises which turned into a violent affray. The dispute was revived in a different form in 1713, with Booth insisting on sharing in the company's management, a position he won only after action in court. In his new position of power he was able to take on major new roles including King Lear, Jaffeir in ▷ Thomas Otway's ▷ *Venice Preserv'd* and Timon of Athens.

An admirer of ▷ Thomas Betterton, Booth is said to have imitated him – lapsing, at worst, into a monotonous intoning style of delivery; he is reported to have lacked the capacity for humour in his performances. At his best he acted with great dignity and grace, while also possessing fiery qualities enabling him to perform such roles as Othello and Hotspur with passion.

Bib: Highfill, P. H. Jr., Burnim, K. A. and Langhans, E. A. (eds.), *A Biographical Dictionary of Actors, Actresses, Musicians, Dancers, Managers, and Other Stage Personnel in London 1660–1800*.

Booth, Hester (?1690–1773)
Actress and dancer. Hester Booth (née Santlow) began her career as a dancer at ▷ Drury Lane in 1706, moving to the ▷ Queen's Theatre, Haymarket, in 1708. She began acting in the following year, with the role of Prue in ▷ Congreve's ▷ *Love for Love*. Thereafter she played a variety of comic and serious roles, major and lesser. She married ▷ Barton Booth in 1719 and left the stage around 1733, the year of her husband's death. Theatre-goers admired her more for her dancing than for her acting, commenting on its smoothness, and her interpretative abilities as a dancer.

Boothby, Frances (fl 1669)
English Restoration dramatist, whose tragicomedy *Marcelia: or the Treacherous Friend* (1670) was performed before ▷ Alpha Behn's plays – at the Theatre Royal, in 1669. It is her only known work. The plot concerns misapprehensions and deceits in love, initiated by the king's desire for a new lover, Opening, 'I'm hither come, but what d'ye think to say? / A Womans Pen presents you with a Play,' it goes on to make great play of leaving the stage, returning only to express great surprise that the audience is still there despite female authorship. The tragicomic denouement restores stability to the original relationships.

▷ Polwhele, Elizabeth.

Borges, Jorge Luis (1899–1986)
Argentinian short-story writer, poet and essayist, born in Buenos Aires and educated in Geneva. His paradoxical, metaphysical stories, which employ elements of the ▷ detective story, of ▷ science fiction, of fantasy and of philosphical speculation, helped to define the genre of

▷ magic realism, although this was not a term he himself favoured. Notable collections are: *A Universal History of Infamy* (1935), *Fictions* (1945), *Labyrinths* (1953) and *Doctor Brodie's Report* (1971). Such stories as 'The Library of Babel' (in *Fictions*), which imagines the universe as a vast library, amount to existential fables, while others, such as 'The Golden of Forking Paths' (in the same collection) are more like puzzles.

Borough
One of the synonyms of 'town', used specifically for a town which has been incorporated and given privileges of limited self-government; also used until the 20th century for a town with the right to elect a Member of Parliament.

Most constituencies had remained unchanged since the ▷ Middle Ages; in consequence, some towns had grown to great size with inadequate representation in Parliament, or none at all, while others were represented by more than one Member although they had sunk into insignificance or even, in a few cases, had ceased to exist. This meant great power for the landed aristocracy, and great deprivation of power for the large and growing middle class. Some boroughs ('towns' – but often mere villages) were called 'pocket boroughs' because they were virtually owned by one landlord, who had them 'in his pocket', *ie* caused them to elect the Members of his choice; others were called 'rotten boroughs' because few inhabitants possessed the right to vote, and they were easily and habitually bribed. The law of 1832 redistributed Members of Parliament so as to correspond to the great centres of population, but limited the franchise (right to vote) to those who possessed a level of income such as ensured that electors belonged at least to the middle class.

Borrow, George Henry (1803–81)
Born in Norfolk, Borrow was educated in Edinburgh and Norwich as his father, a recruiting officer in the militia, moved around. Borrow was articled to solicitors in Norfolk 1818–23, then when his father died he moved to London and worked for a publisher. He travelled in France, Germany, Russia, the East and Spain 1833–9, sending letters to the *Morning Herald* 1837–9, blazing a trail as effectively the first newspaper correspondent. In 1835 he published in St Petersburg *Targum*, translations from 30 different languages and dialects. In Russia and Spain he was an agent for the British and Foreign Bible Society. In 1840 he married Mary Clarke, the widow of a naval officer he met in Spain, and bought an estate on Oulton Broad in Norfolk, in which he had already inherited a share. There he allowed gipsies to pitch tents and live, and became friends with them. His books are in part based on his life. *The Bible in Spain* (1834) and *The Zincali or an account of the Gypsies in Spain* (1841) owed as much of their success to public interest in Borrow the man as Borrow the writer. *Lavengro* followed in 1851, losing Borrow much of his popularity due to its strong 'anti-gentility' tone. *The Romany Rye* (1857) and *Wild Wales* (1862) continued the mixture of fact with fiction, vivid portraits and revelations of the personality of the writer. He died largely unknown and little read.

▷ Travel writing; Anglo-Welsh literature.

Bib: Knapp, W.I., *Life, Writings, and Correspondence of George Borrow*; Collie, M., *George Borrow, Eccentric*; Williams, D., *A World of His Own: The Double Life of George Borrow*.

Bosola
A hired assassin in ▷ John Webster's play ▷ *The Duchess of Malfi* who belatedly discovers the stirrings of conscience in himself and assumes the role of revenger.

***Bostonians, The* (1886)**
A novel by Henry James serialized in *The Century Magazine* from 1885–6. It is a satirical study of the movement for female emancipation in New England. Basil Ransom, a young lawyer from the South up on business in Boston makes the acquaintance of his two cousins, Olive Chancellor, an ardent feminist, and her widowed sister, Mrs Lune, who is attracted to him. Olive introduces Basil to Miss Birdseye, an altruistic philanthopist, at a suffragette meeting where a beautiful young woman, Verena Tarrant, gives an inspired and arresting speech. Both Basil and Olive are immediately drawn to Verena. She is persuaded to share Olive's luxurious home and is groomed by Olive to become a leader of the ▷ feminist cause and to give up all marital aspirations. However, Basil falls in love with Verena and attempts to remove her from Olive's influence, thereby causing a split between himself and his cousin. The death of Miss Birdseye robs Verena of confidence in her purpose and Basil's appearance at the first of her series of lectures causes her to lose her nerve. Forced to choose she rejects the bitterly disappointed Olive and accepts Basil's proposal of marriage. A brilliantly sustained and complex novel, many critics place it second only to ▷ *The Portrait of a Lady* in James *oeuvre*.

▷ Women's movement; Lesbianism; Women's suffrage.

Boswell, James (1740–95)
Best known for his biography of ▷ Samuel Johnson whom he met in 1763, Boswell was also a copious diarist. Eldest son of Alexander Boswell, Lord Auchinleck, Boswell studied law at Edinburgh, Glasgow and Utrecht, and reluctantly entered the legal profession.

From 1760 onwards, Boswell published many pamphlets, often anonymously. After meeting

Johnson, he travelled in Europe, where he met ▷ Rousseau and ▷ Voltaire. Rousseau fired him with enthusiasm for the cause of Corsican liberty, and he cultivated a lifelong friendship with General Paoli; in 1768 he published an *Account of Corsica*, which attracted considerable international recognition.

In 1769 Boswell, by now a Scottish advocate, married his cousin Margaret Montgomerie. But Boswell longed to be part of London literary culture, and made journeys to the capital as frequently as he could. Here he was elected a member of ▷ The Club, though his habit of 'scribbling' memoranda of conversations, with the aim of writing Johnson's *Life*, irritated some of its members.

In 1773, Boswell and Johnson made their tour of the Hebrides (see ▷ *The Journal of a Tour to the Hebrides*). From 1777 to 1783 Boswell wrote a series of articles for the *London Magazine* under the pen-name of 'The Hypochondriack'. In 1782 he inherited the Scottish estate on his father's death, and his last meeting with Johnson was in 1784.

Boswell attempted, unsuccessfully, to make a career in politics, while working on the *Life of Samuel Johnson*, which appeared in 1791.

Bib: Pottle, F. A. (ed.), *Boswell's London Journal, 1762–63*; Hill, G. B. (ed.), revised Powell, L. F., *Life of Johnson and Journal of a Tour to the Hebrides*.

Bottom, Nick

A comic character in ▷ Shakespeare's ▷ *A Midsummer Night's Dream*. He is a weaver, and the most prominent of the 'Athenian artisans'.

Boucicault, Dion[ysus] (1820–96)

Dramatist and actor. Greatly admired as an actor in Britain and the U.S.A., Boucicault was a wide-ranging and prolific dramatist who wrote nearly 150 original plays and adaptations, operettas, pantomimes and melodramas (including sixteen plays in one year). The flood was aided by reworking to suit new audiences: *The Streets of London* and *The Streets of Liverpool* are almost identical to *The Poor of New York* (1857). Many of his plays offer opportunities for spectacle: the burning of a Mississippi steamer in *The Octorron* (1859) or, in *Arrah-na-Pogue* (1864), the whole scene sinking slowly as the hero climbs an ivy-clad turret to seize the villain and hurl him to his death. Though melodramas like *The Vampire* (1852) follow the pattern for the genre, his work shows careful construction and keen observation. *The Octoroon* was one of the first plays in which an American black slave was treated seriously and the social themes which often attracted him prefigured later dramas about the common people. His Irish plays, such as *The Shaughraun* (1874), provided fine vehicles for himself but, though he fought to establish copyright for dramatists in the U.S.A. and was the first to receive a royalty instead of a flat fee, he died an impoverished teacher of acting in New York. His plays are revived regularly in Ireland and a 1975 ▷ RSC production of *London Assurance*, his 1841 society comedy, restored it to the modern repertory.

Bow Street

In London; Covent Garden Opera House is in Bow Street. The chief Magistrates' Court in London has been situated there since 1735, when it opened in the house of the first Bow Street Magistrate. His successor, the novelist ▷ Henry Fielding, was given a house in Bow Street separate from the court-house. Fielding was exceptionally successful as a Magistrate in ridding London of its crime. He and his brother established the Bow Street Runners, the predecessors of the Metropolitan Police.

Bowdler, Henrietta Maria (1753–1830)

Religious writer and editor. Henrietta, or Harriet as she is better known, came from a literary family and was encouraged to write from an early age. Although her *Sermons on the Doctrines and Duties of Christianity* (1801, ▷ Sermons) were published anonymously they ran to almost fifty editions and so impressed the Bishop of London that he attempted to find out the identity of the author so as to offer 'him' a parish. Although Harriet can hardly be commended for her editorial activity, she has the singular honour of expurgating ▷ Shakespeare's plays *before* her more famous brother, ▷ Thomas Bowdler. Her most interesting fictional work is the novel, *Pen Tamar, or The History of an Old Maid* (1831) which is a curious combination of praise and harsh ridicule of women who have chosen not to marry. She may be linked with the ▷ Bluestockings and attacked Hester Piozzi (▷ Mrs Thrale) for marrying.

Bowdler, Thomas (1754–1825)

Famous for *The Family Shakespeare*, 1818; an edition in which 'those words and expressions are omitted which cannot with propriety be read aloud in a family'. He later published an edition of ▷ Gibbon's ▷ *Decline and Fall of the Roman Empire* similarly expurgated. From these we get the word 'bowdlerize' = to expurgate.

▷ Bowdler, Henrietta Maria; Shakespeare.

Bowen, Elizabeth (1899–1973)

Novelist and short-story writer. Born in Dublin and educated in England, she worked in a Dublin hospital during World War I, and for the Ministry of Information in London during World War II. Her novels are concerned with themes of innocence and sophistication, the effect of guilt and of the past on present relationships, and the damaging consequences

of coldness and deceit. Her portrayal of the inner life of female characters and her symbolic use of atmosphere and environment show the influence of ▷ Virginia Woolf, as does the structure of her first novel, *The House in Paris* (1935). Her treatment of childhood and youthful innocence owes something to the work of ▷ Henry James, especially in *The Death of the Heart* (1938), where Bowen narrates the story partly through the consciousness of a young girl. Bowen powerfully conveyed the atmosphere of World War II London during the Blitz, and the emotional dislocation resulting from the war, both in *The Heat of the Day* (1949) and in short stories such as 'In The Square' and 'Mysterious Kôr' (in *The Demon Lover*, 1945). Her other novels are: *The Hotel* (1927); *The Last September* (1929); *A World of Love* (1955); *Eva Trout* (1969). Other story collections include: *The Cat Jumps* (1934); *Look at all those Roses* (1941); *A Day in the Dark* (1965).
Bib: Glendinning, V., *Elizabeth Bowen: Portrait of a Writer*; Craig, P., *Elizabeth Bowen.*

Bowles, Caroline (1787–1854)
Poet and prose writer. Bowles was fortunate enough to have sufficient private income to enable her to devote her life to literature, and she initially consolidated this freedom by refusing to marry. Her poetry was published anonymously for over twenty years, sometimes in ▷ *Blackwood's Magazine*, where she was commonly known only as 'C'. Her poetic works consist of *Ellen FitzArthur: a metrical tale* (1820), *The Widow's Tale* (1820), *Tales of the Factories* (1833) and *The Birthday* (1836), and she is also well-known for her prose tales, *Chapters on Churchyards* (1829). The titles of these works reflect their sentimental nature, which gained her a reputation as a 'pathetic' writer. Her literary output ceased, however, in 1839 when she married ▷ Robert Southey and simultaneously lost her annuity, which had been dependent upon her remaining single. Bowles and Southey had, however, built a strong friendship based on a twenty-year correspondence, and when he became seriously ill in 1839 she married him and acted as his nurse until he died in 1843.

Bowles, William Lisle (1762–1850)
Poet and clergyman; ultimately chaplain to the Prince Regent. His *Sonnets* (1789), sentimental effusions delivered in the person of 'the wanderer', were extremely popular, and revived interest in the sonnet form. ▷ Samuel Taylor Coleridge and ▷ Robert Southey were impressed by them. The preface to his edition of ▷ Alexander Pope (1806) took its critical stance from his former teacher at Winchester, ▷ Joseph Warton, and prompted Lord Byron's 'Letter on W. L. Bowles' Strictures on Pope' (1821).

Bowtell (Boutell, Bootell), Elizabeth (c 1650–97)
Actress. Born Elizabeth Ridley she joined the ▷ King's Company at ▷ Bridges Street Theatre about 1670, afterwards specializing in the playing of 'breeches' parts, although her most famous role was as Queen Statira in ▷ Nathaniel Lee's *The Rival Queens* (1677). During one performance a quarrel between her and ▷ Elizabeth Barry, who was appearing in the play as Roxana, degenerated into genuine violence on stage. The dispute arose over the possession of a prized prop (a veil). Required to stab Statira on stage, Barry as Roxana lunged at her with such force that she pierced her flesh 'about a Quarter of an Inch', according to a near contemporary. Bowtell retired in 1696.

Boys' Own Paper
A weekly magazine for boys, founded in 1879 and published by the Religious Tract Society. It ran until 1967, reached a circulation around 250,000 and published adventure stories, often with imperialist themes, as well as essays, letters, puzzles, and competitions.
Bib: Bristow, J., *Empire Boys: Adventures in a Man's World.*

Bracegirdle, Anne (1663–1748)
Actress, singer. She came into the Bettertons' (▷ Betterton, Thomas; ▷ Betterton, Mary) household as a sort of surrogate daughter in about 1688 and in that year she became a member of the ▷ United Company, playing a succession of roles in contemporary plays, as well as speaking prologues and epilogues for many of them. In 1693 Bracegirdle acted in ▷ William Congreve's first play, ▷ *The Old Bachelor*. By the following year she had become a leading member of the United Company, but in 1695 she joined Betterton and Elizabeth Barry in seceding from the company to form a separate troupe at ▷ Lincoln's Inn Fields. There she played the first Angelica in Congreve's ▷ *Love for Love*, and in 1700 Millamant – a part written for her by Congreve – in ▷ *The Way of the World*. Congreve was among a number of prominent men who courted or admired her from a distance.

Throughout her life Bracegirdle was celebrated for her supposed virtue, some of the comments being possibly ironic. She was lauded for her abilities in both comic and tragic acting modes, her style in the latter tending towards pathos, as well as for her beauty, charm, and generosity toward fellow-performers and those in need. She was buried at Westminster Abbey.
Bib: Highfill, P. H. Jr., Burnim, K. A. and Langhans, E. A. (eds.), *A Biographical Dictionary of Actors, Actresses, Musicians, Dancers, Managers, and Other Stage Personnel in London* 1660–1800; Howe, E., *The First English Actresses.*

Bradbury, Malcolm (b 1932)
Novelist and critic. His novels include: *Eating People is Wrong* (1959); *Stepping Westward* (1965); *The History Man* (1975); *Rates of Exchange* (1983); and *Cuts* (1987). These are witty, satirical portraits of the four decades since 1950; the first three use university settings to epitomize the changing moral and political situation of western liberalism. He is often compared to ▷ Kingsley Amis for his hilarious send-ups of academic habits and pretensions, but Bradbury also has a fascination with the idea of fictionality, which he sees as central to the contemporary understanding of reality. His works are therefore informed by current critical theory (a feature which they share with the novels of ▷ David Lodge). *Rates of Exchange* draws on ▷ structuralist theories, has an eastern European setting, and a somewhat harsher tone than Bradbury's earlier work, in an attempt to register the atmosphere of the 1980s. The title of *Cuts* refers to both cuts in funding and film cutting, and the novel portrays Tory Britain in the mid 1980s through the story of a collision between an academic and a woman television executive. Bradbury has taught on the successful creative writing postgraduate course at the University of East Anglia, which has included among its graduates ▷ Ian McEwan and ▷ Kazuo Ishiguro.

Braddon, Mary Elizabeth (1835–1915)
The daughter of a solicitor and privately educated, Braddon was the author of over 80 novels, twenty of which were written between 1861 and 1871, and was dubbed by her publisher the 'Queen of the Circulating Libraries'. She was born in London and brought up by her mother, who left her husband when Mary was three. In 1856 Braddon began writing in order to support the family, the impulse also behind her taking to the stage under the name Mary Seyton. She met the publisher John Maxwell, whose wife was in a asylum, in 1860 and lived with him until they were able to marry in 1874. Her writing helped to support the five children of Maxwell's first marriage and the six from their own liaison (one of whom died in infancy). Her fourth novel, ▷ *Lady Audley's Secret* (1862), was first serialized in *Robin Goodfellow* and *The Sixpenny Magazine*, and was a sensational best-seller: a melodramatic, lurid tale of criminality and sexual passion which shocked readers by representing its deviant heroine as an angelic-looking blonde. ▷ Margaret Oliphant described Braddon as 'the inventor of the fair-haired demon of modern fiction'. Other novels include *Aurora Floyd* (1863), *The Doctor's Wife* (1864), *Henry Dunbar* (1864), *Ishmael* (1884) and *The Infidel* (1900). In addition to prolific novel writing, Braddon also wrote nine plays and edited several London magazines including *Belgravia* (1866) and *The Mistletoe Bough* (1878–92).
▷ Sensation, Novel of.
Bib: Wolff, R.L., *The Sensational Victorian: the Life and Fiction of Braddon*; Hughes, W., *The Maniac in the Cellar: Sensation Novels of the 1860s*; Pykett, L., *The Improper Feminine*.

Bradley, A. C. (Andrew Cecil) (1851–1935)
Professor of Poetry at Oxford whose books on ▷ Shakespeare, *Shakespearean Tragedy* (1904) and *Oxford Lectures on Poetry* (1909), were inspired by 19th-century idealism and had a considerable influence on the study of character in Shakespeare.

Bradley, F.H. (Francis Herbert) (1846–1924)
Brother of A.C. Bradley (1851–1935), the literary critic. He was himself an eminent philisopher, author of *Ethical Studies* (1876); *Principles of Logic* (1883); *Appearances and Reality* (1893), and *Essay on Truth and Reality* (1914). His position philosophically was an idealist one, and in this he has been opposed by most British philosophers ever since, beginning with G.E. Moore (1873–1958). Bradley, however, had a strong influence on T.S. Eliot (1888–1965), the poet and former philosophy student, whose early thesis on him was published in 1963.
▷ Realism.

Bradley, Katherine (1846–1914)
Poet and dramatist who published separately, and collaboratively with ▷ Edith Cooper under the ▷ pseudonym ▷ Michael Field.

Bradstreet, Anne (1612–72)
Poet. Bradstreet's poetic writings are noteworthy not only because she was a woman writing at a time when female authorship was actively discouraged, but also because she was one of the first poets, of either sex, to write in America. Hence, her work is included in collections of 17th-century women poets (*Kissing the Rod*, ed. G. Greer (1988)), as well as amongst 'The Poets of America' (*The World Split Open*, ed. L. Bernikow (1984)). She was born into the strongly Puritan Dudley family and for the first 18 years of her life lived in England. She received a thorough education, reading the works of ▷ Edmund Spenser and ▷ Sir Philip Sidney, and at 16 married Simon Bradstreet. The persecution of radical Puritanism determined Bradstreet's father, Thomas Dudley, to emigrate to the New World, where he, with many others of his sect, hoped to practise their religion freely. In March 1630 the family set sail on the *Arbella* and in June landed in Massachusetts. Like many of the settlers, the Dudleys and Bradstreets were dogged with ill health and economic hardship, and Anne herself probably suffered from tuberculosis. Yet in spite of bouts of sickness, having eight children, and several moves to increasingly remote settlements, she

constantly wrote poetry. At first her work was ▷ epic in nature, focusing upon political events such as the ▷ Civil War, or on spiritual concerns such as the Second Coming of Christ. The latter theme occurs in *The Four Monarchies*, which is loosely based upon ▷ Sir Walter Ralegh's *The History of the World*. *The Four Ages of Man* is another 'quaternion' and follows Joshua Sylvester's translations of ▷ Du Bartas. Both are included in *The Tenth Muse Lately Sprung up in America* (1650), which was published in London, without Bradstreet's knowledge, by her brother-in-law, John Woodbridge. After the death of her father and the birth of her last child (c 1652) Bradstreet's poems take on a more personal and contemplative tone, and these are the poems by which she is best known today. They are beautiful ▷ lyrics which address the problems of piety, marital love and parental duty; they also include accounts of actual events in her life. These later poems were published posthumously, together with a second edition of *The Tenth Muse*, as *Several Poems* (1678).

Braine, John (b 1922–1986)
Novelist. His most famous novels are *Room at the Top* (1957; filmed 1958) and *Life at the Top* (1962; filmed 1965). Both of these deal with the new kinds of social mobility and anxiety, characteristic of Britain since World War II, and led to him being thought of as one of the ▷ 'angry young men' of the 1950s. Like the heroes of his novels, however, he has become progressively more conservative in his attitudes. Other novels are: *The Vodi* (1959); *The Jealous God* (1964); *The Crying Game* (1968); *Stay with me till Morning* (1970); *The Queen of a Distant Country* (1972); *The Pious Agent* (1975); *Waiting For Sheila* (1976); *The Only Game in Town* (1976); *Finger of Fire* (1977); *One and Last Love* (1981); *The Two of Us* (1984); *These Golden Days* (1985).
▷ Realism.
Bib: Salwak, D., *John Braine and John Wain: A Reference Guide*.

Brandon, Katherine (1520–80)
Letter-writer. Katherine Brandon, Duchess of Suffolk is notable both for her own letters (which may be seen in the Public Record Office, London) and for her role as a patron. The letters are personal and colloquial, covering concerns of faith as well as the duties of parents to their children; she believed, for example, that young people should be allowed to marry for love. As part of ▷ Katherine Parr's Puritan circle she came under threat during the trial of ▷ Anne Askew, and she lived on the continent during Queen Mary's reign.
Bib: Prior, M. (ed.), *Women in English Society, 1500–1800*.

Brathwaite, E. R. (b 1912)
Novelist and autobiographer. Born in Guyana, most of Brathwaite's writing is concerned with his working life in Britain in the 1950s and 1960s. His most successful work (which was turned into a popular film), *To Sir, With Love* (1959), is concerned with his experiences as a black teacher in London, and other semi-autobiographical novels have discussed his social work and time in the RAF. He is the author of: *Paid Servant* (1962); *Reluctant Neighbours* (1972); *A Kind of Homecoming* (1962) and *A Choice of Straws* (1967).

Brathwaite, Edward Kamau (b 1930)
▷ Post-colonial literatures

Bray, Anna Eliza (1790–1883)
Novelist. Born in Newington, Surrey, she married the artist Charles Alfred Stothard in 1818. Her first published work, *Letters Written During a Tour Through Normandy, Brittany and Other Parts of France* appeared in 1820. This volume recorded travels with her husband, who died in an accident in 1821. Anna married the Rev. Edward Bray in 1822, and from 1826 to 1874 published fourteen novels, as well as historical biographies and descriptive sketches. In fiction, she favoured historical ▷ romances set in the English countryside. These were extremely popular in their day, though some literary critics considered them out of date. She is best-known for her series of letters to Robert Southey, *A Description of that Part of Devonshire Bordering on the Tamar and the Tary* (1836). Subjects of her biographies include Handel (1857) and Joan of Arc (1874). She also wrote a non-fictional work for children, *A Peep at the Pixies, or, Legends of the West* (1854).
▷ Children's literature; Travel writing.

Brecht, Bertolt (1898–1956)
One of the most significant theatre practitioners and theorists of the 20th century. His work has had a major influence on British drama since the late 1950s. Brecht's early plays were written shortly after World War I and were influenced by the Expressionist movement. From the mid-1920s he became interested in applying Marxist (Marx, Karl) ideas to plays and performance and developed his concept of ▷ 'epic theatre'. The essential characteristic of 'epic', as Brecht used the term, was the creation of a critical distance (*Verfremdungseffekt*) between the audience and the performance on stage (and a similar critical distance between the actor/actress and the role he or she performed). The purpose of this was to prevent empathy and encourage audiences instead to reflect on the relationship between social conditions and human action, in such a way that they would recognize their power and agency in the process of history. Brecht was forced to leave his native Germany during the Nazi era and continued writing in exile in Europe and later

America. After World War II he returned to Germany and formed the Berliner Ensemble company in East Berlin, where he directed a number of his plays written in exile. The Berliner Ensemble first visited London in 1956 and performed three of Brecht's plays: *Mother Courage and her Children, Drums and Trumpets* and *The Caucasian Chalk Circle*. Other plays include: *Baal* (1918); *Man is Man* (1926); *The Threepenny Opera* (1928; with music by Kurt Weill); *The Measures Taken* (1930); *St Joan of the Stockyards* (1932); *The Seven Deadly Sins* (1933; with Kurt Weill); *The Resistible Rise of Arturo Ui* (1941); *The Life of Galileo* (1943); *The Good Person of Szechwan* (1943).
Bib: Needle, J. and Thomson, P., *Brecht*; Willett, J., *Brecht in Context*.

Breeze, Jean Binta (b 1957)
Poet. Born in Jamaica, Jean Binta Breeze now lives and works in London, writing and performing live her vibrant form of dub poetry. Her works are collected in *Riddym Ravings and Other Poems* (1988), and in the collection of *the new british poetry* (ed. G. Allnutt et al.). See also Breeze's essay 'Can a Dub Poet be a Woman?' in *Women: A Cultural Review* (April 1990).

Brenton, Howard (b 1942)
British left-wing dramatist, strongly influenced by ▷ Brecht, who has worked with both ▷ fringe and mainstream theatre companies since the late 1960s. His iconoclastic plays have frequently caused controversy, particularly when they have been staged at major theatres. He began writing for the Combination, at Brighton, and The Portable Theatre, a touring company.

Recently he has worked at the ▷ National Theatre despite his having expressed doubts in the past about the value of such 'establishment' institutions. Major plays are: *Magnificence*, a ▷ Royal Court success in 1973; *Brassneck* (1973), a collaboration with ▷ David Hare; *The Churchill Play* (1974); *Weapons of Happiness* (1974); *Epsom Downs* (1977); *Romans in Britain* (1978); *The Genius* (1983); *Bloody Poetry* (1984); *Pravda* (1985), also a collaboration with David Hare; *Greenland* (1988).
Bib: Bull, J., *New British Political Dramatists*; Chambers, C. and Prior, M., *Playwright's Progress*.

Breton, André (1896–1966)
French poet, founder of Surrealism, which he launched in 1924 with the first *Surrealist Manifesto*. Prior to this, Breton had met both the poet Guillaume Apollinaire (during 1917–18) and ▷ Sigmund Freud (in 1921), both of whom provided inspiration for the movement. In 1919, he published his first collection of poems, *Mont de piété*, and in the same year he collaborated with Philippe Soupault on his first properly Surrealist text, *Les Champs magnétiques*, which preceded the official launch of Surrealism. Between 1919 and 1921, he participated in the ▷ Dadaist movement, although it was his initiative to hold in Paris the international congress which led to the break-up of Dada. Believing firmly in the radicalism of Surrealism, Breton resisted any attempt to make the movement subservient to an established political creed. In *Légitime Défense* (1926), he rejected any form of control, even Marxist control, of the psychic life and, by contrast with other members of the movement, this was to lead to his break with communism in 1935. After the war, Breton continued to campaign vigorously on behalf of Surrealist radicalism. He opposed Albert Camus' (1913–60) thesis, as expounded in *L'Homme révolté* (1952) that revolt has its limitations, and a year before his death organized a final Surrealist exhibition, *L'Ecart absolu*, which aimed to challenge the consumer society. Breton contributed to Surrealist writing not only by the three manifestoes (1924, 1930, 1934) and other polemical writing, but also by numerous collections of poetry and prose, the original editions of which were usually illustrated by leading artists connected with Surrealism.
Bib: Bozo, D., *André Breton: La·beauté convulsive*; Polizzotti, M., *Revolution of the Mind: The Life of André Breton*.

Breton Lays
A rather misleading term used by critics to refer to a group of Old French and Middle English verse narratives which claim to derive their story-material from a pre-Saxon, British literary tradition. It would be more accurate to call these texts British lays, rather than Breton lays, for the narratives claim descent from British, not specifically Breton, origins. ▷ Marie de France, writing in the late 12th century for audiences, it seems, in England and France, claims to be the first writer to produce a collection of these verse narratives, and the first vernacular writer to mediate between the old, oral-poetic traditions of the Britons (which Marie suggests had musical accompaniments) and contemporary literary traditions. Some shared themes, settings and protagonists can be traced in her story-collection. Her lays characteristically focus around emotional crises of some kind; the events are often located in Britain or Brittany; and the action tends to involve some interplay between human and otherworldly forces and places. Yet the structural patterns of the narratives vary (and may coincide with those of ▷ romances), so it is the claim to British origins which gives this group of narratives their identity, not their narrative structure. ▷ Chaucer's ▷ Franklin claims to present a British lay as his contribution to the ▷ *Canterbury Tales*.
Bib: Rumble, T. C., *The Breton Lays in Middle English*.

Breton, Nicholas (?1545–?1626)
Poet, miscellanist, pamphleteer. Little is known of the life of Nicholas Breton – a curious irony in that he was one of the most prolific writers of the ▷ Renaissance period. Still, we do know that he was the son of a wealthy London merchant, but that on his father's death his mother married ▷ George Gascoigne, who quickly spent Breton's inheritance. Between 1575 and his death he published over 30 individual collections of verse, three prose fictions and at least 25 ▷ pamphlets and miscellaneous works. From the evidence of the number of times certain of his works were reprinted (in particular his *A Post with a Mad Packet of Letters*, first published in 1602) there is the suggestion that, on occasions, he was able to secure an audience. Indeed, although he never received the court preferment he desired, he did obtain patronage from ▷ Mary Sidney.
Bib: Robertson, J., *Poems by Breton*.

Bridges, Robert Seymour (1844–1930)
Poet and dramatist. He was Poet Laureate from 1913–30. After medical training and work as a consultant at Great Ormond Street Children's Hospital, Bridges turned his energies fully to poetry in 1882. His first volume of verse was published in 1873, after which he wrote prolifically: his collected *Poetical Works* (1936), excluding eight dramas, are in six volumes. He was a fine ▷ classical scholar and in his experiments with classical rhythms, was something of an innovator. His most ambitious work was the long, philosophical *The Testament of Beauty*, which appeared in five parts from 1927 to 1929. Other works include: *Shorter Poems* (1890); *The Spirit of Man* (1916) and *New Verse* (1925). He was the chief correspondent and literary executor of the poet ▷ Gerard Manley Hopkins; the latter developed his poetic theories through their letters. A selection of Bridge's work, *Poetry and Prose*, has been edited by John Sparrow.
Bib: Smith, N.C., *Notes on The Testament of Beauty*; Guerard, A.J., *Bridges: A Study of Traditionalism*; Thompson, E., *Robert Bridges*.

Bridges Street Theatre
▷ Drury Lane Theatres.

Bridges-Adams, William (1889–1965)
Director of the Shakespeare Memorial Theatre in Stratford-on-Avon from 1919 to 1934, during which time he directed 29 of ▷ Shakespeare's plays. His productions were influenced by the work of ▷ Harley Granville Barker. Unlike his predecessor, Frank Benson, he did not act in his own productions and aimed for: 'The virtues of the Elizabethan theatre without its vices, and its freedom without its fetters: scenic splendour where helpful, but...the play to be given as written: the text unmutilated whether in the interests of the stage carpenter or the leading man.'

Bridie, James (1888–1951)
Pseudonym of Dr Osborne Henry Mavor. He was a successful playwright during the 1930s and 1940s and part-founder of the Citizen's Theatre in Glasgow. He wrote 42 plays, many of which were performed on the London stage. He was sometimes compared to ▷ George Bernard Shaw for his prolific output and range of subject matter. His best-known plays today are *The Anatomist* and *Tobias and the Angel* (both 1930), *Jonah and the Whale* (1932), *A Sleeping Clergyman* (1933), *Colonel Wotherspoon* (1934), *The Black Eye* (1935), *Storm in a Teacup* (1936), *Mr Bolfry* (1943), *Dr. Angelus* (1947) and *Daphne Laureola* (1949).
Bib: Luybem, H., *Bridie: Clown and Philosopher*.

***Brighton Rock* (1938)**
One of the best-known novels by ▷ Graham Greene. Set in Brighton, it combines elements of the thriller with the moral and religious themes prominent in Greene's later work. The story of murder, innocence and corruption set in the criminal underworld is centred on Pinkie, a 17-year-old Catholic gangster obsessed with evil, whose murder of a journalist sets him on a path to damnation. He marries Rose a 16-year-old girl, in order to protect himself from the law but Ida, an acquaintance of the murdered man, pursues Pinkie, leading eventually to his death.
Bib: Daiches, D., *The King James' Version of the Bible*.

Brink, André (b 1935)
South African novelist, playwright and critic, educated at Potchefstroom and Rhodes universities in South Africa and at the Sorbonne in Paris. He teaches Afrikaans and Dutch literature and is now professor at Rhodes University. His novels are concerned with the history, sources and consequences of racism and apartheid in South Africa. *Looking on Darkness* (1974) and *An Instant in the Wind* (1976) are both stories about sexual relationships between people of different races, though the former is set in the 20th century and the latter in the 18th. *A Chain of Voices* (1982) uses multiple narrators to recount the story of a slave revolt in Cape Colony in the early 19th century and *Rumours of Rain* (1978) is about the Soweto riots of 1976. *The Wall of the Plague* (1984), set in France, establishes parallels between apartheid and the Great Plague of the 14th century in Europe. His other novels are: *File on a Diplomat* (1965); *A Portrait of Woman as a Young Girl* (1973); *A Dry White Season* (1979); *An Act of Terror: A Novel* (1991). Brink's novels have been published in both Afrikaans and English; he moves back and forth between the two

languages in the process of writing. Several of his novels were intially banned in South Africa. He has three times won the CNA award (a South African literary prize). *Mapmakers: Writing in a State of Siege* (1983) is a collection of essays on politics and literature, and he has edited, with ▷ J.M. Coetzee, *A Land Apart: A South African Reader* (1986).

British Academy
Founded in 1901 it was intended to complement the function of the Royal Society by representing 'literary science', which was defined as 'the sciences of language, history, philosophy and antiquities, and other subjects the study of which is based on scientific principles but which are not included under the term "natural sciences"' It derived its authority from the backing of the Royal Society, the grant of a Royal Charter (1902) and the addition of bye-laws by Order in Council (1903). The British Academy elects its own Fellows, up to a total of 200: candidates have to be nominated by not fewer than three and not more than six existing Fellows. The British Academy publishes its *Proceedings* and certain lectures; research awards are annually made available for competition.

British Council
Established in 1934, it receives three-quarters of its funds, amounting to £260 million pounds in 1987–8, from the Foreign and Commonwealth Office. Its brief is to promote an enduring understanding and appreciation of Britain overseas through cultural, technical and educational exchange. The Council has staff in over 80 countries and is responsible for the implementation of more than 30 cultural agreements with other countries. It has 116 libraries world-wide and its activities include the recruitment of teachers for posts overseas, fostering personal contacts between British and overseas academics, and the placing and welfare of overseas students in Britain. It is exceptionally powerful in determining how Britain represents itself abroad in that the Council decides what is to be presented overseas as 'the best of British arts and culture'. ▷ Graham Greene, ▷ Lawrence Durrell and ▷ Olivia Manning in various novels offer a view of the early years of the Council's work.

Brittain, Vera (1893–1970)
Autobiographer, poet, novelist and journalist. Vera Brittain is best known for her autobiographical books, *Testament of Youth* (1933) and *Testament of Experience* (1957), the first detailing with great feeling her life as a nurse in France during World War I, and particularly the loss of her fiancé to the war itself, whilst the second recounts the period from 1925–1950, including an account of the therapeutic experience of writing the first book. She is also something of a war poet, offering a perspective on the conflict not represented by those usually characterized as ▷ War poets, in *Poems of the War and After* (1934). Her other novels and non-fiction writing include: *The Dark Tide* (1923); *Account Rendered* (1945); *Born 1925* (1948); *Lady into Woman: A History of Women from Victoria to Elizabeth II* (1953); *The Women at Oxford:. A Fragment of History* (1960).

Her friendship with fellow-novelist ▷ Winifred Holtby, whom she had met at Oxford after the war when the two were students, and with whom she set up house after the two graduated, was an important factor in her early life, and their friendship is represented in *Selected Letters of Winifred Holtby and Vera Brittain* (1960), and in Brittain's *Testament of Friendship* (1940), a memorial to Holtby written on her death. Brittain was also deeply committed to Labour Party politics (one of her children, Shirley Williams, became a prominent Labour, and then SDP, politician), and she was an important founder-member of CND, writing in support of the peace movement (see particularly *The Rebel Passion: A Short History of Some Pioneer Peace-Makers* (1964)).
Bib: Bailey, H., *Vera Brittain*.

Broadside Ballads
Popular ▷ ballads, printed on folio sheets. They formed a cheap method of publishing songs on topical subjects. The term 'broadside' meant that only one side of the paper was printed. They were a means of issuing news items, political propaganda, religious controversy, travellers' tales, attacks on (or defences of) women, the last words of condemned criminals, and so on. Often decorated with wood-cut prints, they were a major source of information in the 16th and 17th centuries. The British Library possesses a unique collection of broadsides amongst the 'Thomason Tracts'.
Bib: Reay, B., *Popular Culture in Seventeenth-Century England;* Shepard, L., *The History of Street Literature*.

Brome, Richard (1590–1653)
The author of two popular ▷ Caroline comedies, ▷ *The City Wit* (1629) and *The Jovial Crew* (1640). His work reflects the influence of ▷ John Fletcher, but is indebted particularly to ▷ Ben Jonson in whose service Brome spent some time, perhaps as Jonson's secretary.
Bib: Kaufman, R. J., *Richard Brome, Caroline Playwright*.

Bromley, Eliza (d 1807)
Novelist. Interesting as an early colonialist writer whose childhood in the West Indies provided her with a genuine love for the climate and mysteries of the place, but at the same time she often presents a stereotypical and patronizing view of the indigenous Indians and negro slaves.

Her most noted work in this respect was *Louisa and Augustus, An Authentic Story in a Series of Letters* (1784), which was mocked by ▷ Jane Austen in *Love and Friendship*.

Brontë, Anne (1820–49)
Novelist and poet, sister of ▷ Charlotte, ▷ Emily and Branwell Brontë. The youngest of the family, Anne was educated largely at home, though she briefly attended school at Roe Head in 1836–7. Very close to Emily as a child, together they invented the imaginary world of ▷ Gondal, the setting for several poems and a prominent feature in their lives. Anne had more experience as a ▷ governess than either Charlotte or Emily, working for the Ingham family at Blake Hall in 1839 and 1841–5 for the Robinsons of Thorpe Green Hall. Branwell followed her there but was dismissed as a result of his obsession with Mrs Robinson, and Anne followed him home. ▷ *Agnes Grey* (1847) is a semi-autobiographical novel based on her experiences as a governess. It was published under the ▷ pseudonym Acton Bell, as were her poems in the 1846 collection, ▷ *Poems by Currer, Ellis and Acton Bell*. Her second novel, ▷ *The Tenant of Wildfell Hall*, was published in 1848. Her work is considered inferior to that of Emily and Charlotte, yet it often contains vivid and powerful descriptions. She died on a visit to Scarborough in May 1849 and was buried there.
Bib: Gerin, W., *Anne Brontë: A Biography*; Langland, E., *Anne Brontë: The Other One*; Knapp, B.L., *The Brontës: Branwell, Anne, Emily, Charlotte*.

Brontë, Charlotte (1816–55)
Novelist and poet; the third of five daughters of Patrick Brontë, a Yorkshire clergyman of Irish origin, and sister to ▷ Anne and ▷ Emily Brontë. After the death of their mother in 1821, the children (including Branwell, the only son) were looked after by Elizabeth Branwell, their aunt. Charlotte attended school at Cowan Bridge, where her elder sisters Maria and Elizabeth contracted the tuberculosis from which they died in 1825, and later at Roe Head (1831–2), returning to the latter as a teacher (1835–8). She was ▷ governess to the Sidgwick family in 1839 and to the White family in 1841.
In 1842 she went with Emily to Brussels to study languages, but had to return at the end of the year due to the death of her aunt. Charlotte returned to Brussels alone in 1843 and remained there a year, forming a deep attachment to her tutor M. Heger, who was fictionalized in both *The Professor* (1857) and ▷ *Villette* (1853). She wrote a great deal as a child, inventing with Branwell the imaginary world of ▷ Angria. In 1845, according to her own account, she 'discovered' Emily's poetry and included it in ▷ *Poems by Currer, Ellis and Acton Bell* (▷ pseudonyms of Charlotte, Emily and Anne Brontë), published in 1846. The book sold only two copies but Charlotte was undeterred. She wrote her first novel, ▷ *The Professor*, in the same year (it was published posthumously in 1857), and her second novel, ▷ *Jane Eyre* (1847), was an immediate success. In 1848 both Branwell and Emily died from tuberculosis, followed by Anne in 1849. Charlotte continued to write during this traumatic period, ▷ *Shirley* appearing in 1849, followed by *Villette*, regarded by many as her most mature and accomplished novel. In 1850 she met ▷ Elizabeth Gaskell who became a great friend and who wrote her biography (1857). She married A.B. Nicholls, her father's curate, in 1854 but died from tuberculosis a few months later, in the early stages of pregnancy. She was recognized as an extraordinarily powerful and talented writer in her day, though some critics accused her of being a 'strong-minded' woman and of writing 'coarse' novels. Brontë's bold depiction of the social and psychological situation of 19th-century women has generated much late-20th-century feminist commentary which focuses on the struggle of her heroines to preserve their independence of spirit in the face of overwhelmingly adverse circumstances. In addition the confined and restless imagery of her novels is often seen as representative of the anger of suppressed and misrepresented women.
Bib: Gaskell, E., *Life*; Fraser, R., *Charlotte Brontë*; Gerin, W., *Charlotte Brontë: The Evolution of Genius*; Ratchford, F., *The Brontës' Web of Childhood*; Gilbert, S., and Gubar, S., *The Madwoman in the Attic*; Boumelha, P., *Charlotte Brontë*.

Brontë, Emily (1818–48)
Novelist and poet, sister of ▷ Charlotte, ▷ Anne and Branwell Brontë, Emily lived most of her life in Haworth, Yorkshire. She briefly attended Cowan Bridge school (1824–5) and went to Roe Head in 1835, returning after a few months suffering from homesickness. A short period spent working as a ▷ governess at Law Hill and a brief excursion to Brussels with Charlotte in 1842 were the only other occasions on which she left home. With Anne, Emily created the imaginary world of ▷ Gondal, and in many of her poems she adopts the personae of Gondal characters. Charlotte 'discovered' Emily's poetry in 1845, and ▷ *Poems by Currer, Ellis and Acton Bell* appeared in 1846. Her poetry has been overshadowed by her only novel ▷ *Wuthering Heights* (1847), but she wrote many complex and interesting lyrics exploring personal identity and the poet's relationship to language and to the natural landscape. 'Loud without the wind was roaring', 'Ah! why, because the dazzling sun' and 'I am the only being whose doom' are some of her finest poetic achievements. Other lyrics such as 'O Thy Bright Eyes Must Answer

Now' and 'I'll come when thou art saddest' represent a masculine muse figure with whom the poet establishes a dynamic relation.

Emily Brontë's originality and power were recognized when *Wuthering Heights* appeared, and she has been extensively discussed ever since. The novel is so devised that the story is told by several independent and varyingly unreliable narrators. It sets human passions (through the characters Heathcliff and Catherine Earnshaw) against society (represented by the households of Wuthering Heights and Thrushcross Grange) with extraordinary violence, while at the same time retaining a cool artistic control. This enables the reader to experience a highly intelligent criticism of society's implicit claim to absorb all the energies of the individual, who potentially is larger in spirit than society ever can be. Initially received as morbid and too violent, it has grown in critical stature, particularly with regard to its structure.

Bib: Sanger, C.P., *The Structure of Wuthering Heights*; Gerin, W., *Emily Brontë: A Bibliography*; Davies, S., *Emily Brontë: The Artist as Free Woman*; Pykett, L., *Emily Brontë*; Stoneman, P., *A New Casebook on Wuthering Heights*.

Brook, Peter (b 1925)

Director. Peter Brook is probably the most influential theatre director Britian has ever produced, though there was never a more international one, and much of his work has appeared outside his own country. Many of his productions have become legendary and his book *The Empty Space* (1968) rapidly became a set text for many theatre workers, with its crucial distinctions between 'rough' and 'holy' theatre. He has often been regarded as a theatrical guru, and by any standards he has been a key figure in exploring and developing the possibilities of drama in a career which spanned forty years of productions of theatre and opera, from the West End to Brooklyn to Persepolis to disused quarries in Australia to African villages that had never before seen a theatre company.

In 1946 he directed *Love's Labour's Lost* at Stratford, thus beginning a connection that lasted for more than twenty years. He also directed plays and operas in London and Paris. In 1962 he was appointed co-director (with ▷ Peter Hall and Michel Saint-Denis) of the newly named ▷ Royal Shakespeare Company, and there throughout the sixties he developed a range of experimental and innovative work, including the setting-up with Charles Marowitz of a group to work on ▷ Artaud's ideas. This culminated in the 'Theatre of Cruelty' season at LAMDA in 1964, which prepared the way for the exciting production of Peter Weiss's *Marat/Sade* (1966). In 1966 Brook devised with the RSC the controversial *US*, a bitter attack on American involvement in Vietnam and British government support for it, and his only overtly 'political' work. Kenneth Tyman was probably right to say that Brook's political sense was naïve. However, his 1970 production of *A Midsummer Night's Dream* is still among the most celebrated and discussed of Shakespearean productions. Staged on a bare white box set, it used acrobatics, juggling and magic tricks in a joyous response to the play's challenges.

In 1970 he left the British theatre and established an International Centre of Theatre Research in Paris to work out his ideas of a theatre laboratory along ▷ Grotowski's lines. He gathered an international company of actors dedicated to his way of working, and proceeded to experiment with Kathakali dance techniques, circus skills, masks, and a general exploration of dramatic forms, in an attempt to work out an 'international theatre language' that would transcend Western theatrical conventions.

The culmination of his work at the Centre so far has been the dramatisation, with Jean-Claude Carrière, of the Hindu epic *Mahabharata* (1985) in a cycle of three plays lasting nearly ten hours, using a multi-racial cast, many of them old Brook hands. It was played originally in a quarry near Avignon, the main features of which have now been reproduced (at considerable expense) from Australia to Glasgow. His version of Oliver Sach's *The Man Who...* has toured widely since 1994).

Bib: Brook, P., *The Empty Space, The Shifting Point*; Williams, D., *Peter Brook: A Theatrical Casebook*.

Brooke, Charlotte (d 1793)

Irish translator and poet. She nursed her father, a dramatist, until he died in 1783. She contributed an anonymous ▷ translation to *Historical Memoirs of Irish Bards* (1786), and published *Reliques of Irish Poetry* (1788) by subscription. She also wrote a tragedy, *Belisorius*, which is lost. In her translation she is concerned with the difficulty of translating not only words and genre but cultural contexts. Introducing her translation of elegies she notes, 'in the original, they are simple and unlearned, but pathetic to a great degree, and this is a species of beauty in composition, extremely difficult to transcribe into any other language'.

Bib: Gantz, K. F., *Studies in English*.

Brooke, Frances (1724–1789)

Important as the author of the first Canadian novel, she was born Francis Moore in Claypole, England, grew up in Lincolnshire and Peterborough, and was educated at home. By 1748, she had moved to London and established herself as a woman of no small literary importance, with friends like ▷ Samuel Johnson, ▷ Anna Seward and ▷ Fanny Burney. She married the Reverend John Brooke in 1755, but enjoyed a measure of freedom to pursue her literary interests. Under the name

'Mary Singleton, Spinster,' she edited *The Old Maid*, a weekly periodical (1775–6). She tried to persuade actor/manager ▷ David Garrick to produce her blank verse tragedy *Virginia*, but he was unwilling to do so, and it was finally published in 1756, with other poems and translations. She also translated, from the French, Marie-Jeanne Riccoboni's *Letters from Juliet, Lady Catesby, to her Friend, Lady Henrietta Campley* in 1760. Meanwhile, her husband had left for Canada. After the appearance of her ▷ epistolary novel, *The History of Lady Julia Mandeville* (1763), she went to join her husband, who was stationed in Quebec as military chaplain. This work, suitably concluding with the deaths of both central characters, enjoyed popular success. Frances Brooke's stay in Quebec (until 1768) informed *The History of Emily Montague*, which is popularly considered the first Canadian novel (1769). The book's major characters and correspondents, Edward Rivers and Arabella Fermor, describe in considerable detail political and social aspects of 18th-century Canada, with notable emphasis on the landscape, and on the relations between the English and the French.

After Frances Brooke's return to England, she translated Framéry's *Memoirs of the Marquis de St Forlaix* (published in 1770), and Millot's *Elements of the History of England, from the Invasion of the Romans to the Reign of George the Second* (published in 1771). There is critical debate about whether Frances Brooke is the author of the anonymous novel *All's Right at Last; or, The History of Miss West* (1774), although Lorraine McMullen's 1983 biography of Brooke supports the attribution. Brooke's next novel, *The Excursion* (1777), is about a heroine in London seeking success as a writer; David Garrick comes under direct attack for not supporting new work. From 1773 to 1778, Frances Brooke was involved, with actress Mary Ann Yates, in managing the Haymarket opera house. Three of her dramatic works were staged: *The Siege of Sinope: A Tragedy*, in 1781; *Rosina* and *Marion*, both comic operas, in 1783 and 1788. Her last novel, *The History of Charles Mandeville* (1790), was not published until after her death. She is buried in Sleaford, Lincolnshire, England.

Bib: McMullen, L., *An Odd Attempt in a Woman: The Literary Life of Frances Brooke.*

Brooke, Henry (1703–83)
Novelist, poet and playwright. Brooke's novels *The Fool of Quality* (1765–70) and *Juliet Grenville* (1774) contributed to the late 18th-century fashion for ▷ sensibility. He also published a poem, *Universal Beauty* (1735), and a ▷ tragedy, *Gustavus Vasa* (1739).

Brooke, Rupert (1887–1915)
A young poet of exceptional promise, who contributed to the ▷ *Georgian Poetry* volumes, and who died of septicaemia in the Dardanelles during World War I without having taken part in the campaign. His almost legendary physical beauty and the idealistic quality of his work caused him to be represented as the hero of the first phase of the war. 'The Soldier' (1915) and 'The Old Vicarage, Granchester' (1912) are much-anthologized poems. Just as it had been patriotically revered, Brooke's work dramatically declined in public opinion as the horror of war was fully understood, although after World War II his slim and unfinished corpus gained more critical respect.

Bib: Keynes, G. (ed.), *Poems.*

Brooke-Rose, Christine (b 1926)
Novelist and critic. Born in Geneva, of an English father and a Swiss/American mother, she is bilingual, and her best-known works are influenced by the French ▷ *nouveau roman* of Alain Robbe-Grillet and Nathalie Sarraute. *Out* (1964) uses Robbe-Grillet's technique of exhaustive description of inanimate objects. In *Such* (1966) a scientist recalls his past during the three minutes taken to bring him back to consciousness after heart failure, while *Thru* (1975) is a multilingual, playful, Joycean novel, employing typographical patterns and self-referential discussion of its own narrative technique. More recently, *Xorander* (1986) is a work of ▷ science fiction, exploring the possibilities of a computer-dominated society. Brooke-Rose lives in France, where until recently she was a professor at the University of Paris, and her resolute commitment to modernist (▷ Modernism) experimental techniques has led to her relative neglect by English-speaking readers.

Brookner, Anita (b 1928)
Novelist. Since her first novel, *A Start In Life*, was published in 1981 she has rapidly achieved popular success, confirmed by the award of the Booker Prize to her fourth novel, *Hôtel Du Lac* (1984). Her novels have an autobiographical element and somewhat similar heroines; sensitive, intelligent, but not glamorous, their search for love and fulfilment leads to disillusionment and betrayal by attractive but selfish men. Brookner's prose style is careful, elegant, lucid and mannered in a way somewhat reminiscent of ▷ Henry James. She lectures and writes on the subject of art history.

Her other novels are: *Providence* (1982), *Look At Me* (1983); *Family And Friends* (1985); *A Misalliance* (1986); *A Friend From England* (1987); *Latecomers* (1988); *Brief Lives* (1990); *A Closed Eye* (1991); *Fraud* (1992); *A Family Romance* (1993); *A Private View* (1994); and *Incidents in the Rue Langier* (1995).

Brophy, Brigid (b 1929–95)
Novelist and critic. The daughter of the novelist

John Brophy, she won immediate acclaim with her first novel, *Hackenfeller's Ape* (1953), a fable about imprisonment, rationality and the instinctive life. During the 1960s she acquired a reputation as a polemical and aggressive writer, with controversial libertarian views on sex and ▷ marriage. She campaigned for animal rights, defended ▷ pornography, and, with ▷ Maureen Duffy, set up a writers' action group in the 1970s to campaign for Public Lending Right (the Public Lending Right Bill, which provides payments to authors out of a central fund on the basis of library lending, was passed in 1979). Her novels reflect her adherence to ▷ Freudian ideas, and to the evolutionism of ▷ George Bernard Shaw. *Flesh* (1962) is a detached yet poetic study of sexual awakening; *The Finishing Touch* (1963), described as 'a lesbian fantasy', is stylistically inspired by the work of ▷ Ronald Firbank; *The Snow Ball* (1964) is an artificial, baroque black comedy of seduction; *In Transit* (1969) uses a bizarre combination of styles and characters and is set in an airport. Her works of criticism include psychological studies of creative artists: *Mozart the Dramatist* (1964); *In Black and White: A Portrait of Aubrey Beardsley* (1968); *Prancing Novelist* (on Ronald Firbank; 1973); *Beardsley and his World* (1976). Her other works of non-fiction include: *Black Ship to Hell* (1962), a Freudian account of the nature of hate; *Don't Never Forget* (1966) and *Baroque and Roll* (1987), collections of her journalism on a wide range of subjects. Other novels include: *The King of a Rainy Country* (1956); *Pussy Owl: Super Beast* (1976); *Palace Without Chairs* (1978). *The Adventures of God in His Search for the Black Girl* (1973) is a series of fables. *The Burglar* (1968) is a play.

Brossard, Nicole (b 1943)
Poet and novelist. Brossard is one of the most important writers to emerge in late-twentieth-century Canadian writing, combining, as she does, a sharp political agenda (feminism and lesbianism), an ability to shift between her native French and English which challenges preconceived ideas about Canadian linguistic divisions, and a radical approach to poetic structure and vocabulary. Her early writing was influenced by Modernism, but by the early 1980s she had combined the personal and political, the erotic and the poetic, in a manner similar to that of the French feminists, especially Hélène Cixous. Her works include: *Amantes* (1980), *Sous la Langue/Under Tongue* (1987), and the fiction/theory novel *Le Desert Mauve* (1987).

Brougham, Henry Peter, Lord (1778–1868)
Lawyer, journalist, and slave-trade ▷ abolitionist. He defended Queen Caroline brilliantly in the divorce proceedings brought against her by George IV in 1820, and later became Lord Chancellor. He was one of the founders (1802) of the ▷ *Edinburgh Review* and may have been the author of the satirical essay on ▷ Lord Byron's *Hours of Idleness* which appeared in the *Review* in January 1808 and provoked Byron to write *English Bards and Scotch Reviewers* (1809).

Broughton, Rhoda (1840–1920)
Novelist, the daughter of Jane Bennet and clergyman Delves Broughton, Rhoda Broughton grew up in Staffordshire where she set many of her ▷ best-sellers. She began to write at the age of twenty-two, inspired by her admiration for ▷ Anne Thackeray Ritchie, and was prolific and financially successful, producing novels of sexual intrigue and pathos, such as her first work *Not Wisely But Too Well* (1867), which was published serially with the help of her uncle ▷ Sheridan Le Fanu, and *Goodbye Sweetheart* (1872). After moving to Headington, Oxford in 1892, she became well-known in literary and academic circles. Altogether she wrote twenty-four novels, mostly sensational ▷ romances centring on 'strong-minded women', unhappy marriages and scandalous affairs, but featuring a new kind of tomboyish, plain-spoken heroine which helped to make her one of the best selling novelists of the Victorian period in spite of ▷ Margaret Oliphant's indignant derision. Many of her novels are witty and malicious chronicles of 'county' life, and speak out against ▷ marriage and women's economic oppression. She was paid large amounts for copyright by her publisher, Bentley. Her works include ▷ *Cometh Up as a Flower* (1867), *Alas* (1890) and *Scylla or Charybdis?: A Novel* (1895). Her last novel was *A Fool in Her Folly* (1920).
▷ Sensation, Novels of.

Brown, George Douglas (1896–1902)
Novelist, sometimes known by the pen-name of George Douglas. Born in Ayrshire in Scotland and educated at Glasgow University and Balliol College, Oxford he is known for *The House with the Green Shutters* (1901), a harshly realist story of the rise and fall of a tyrannical small-town businessman. It was acclaimed by ▷ J. B. Priestley, who described it as an 'East Wind' let into the 'cosy chamber' of ▷ Kailyard fiction; Douglas himself argued that it was 'a greater compliment to Scotland, I think, than the sentimental slop of Barrie, and Crockett, and Maclaren'. Douglas also wrote short stories and children's fiction, and left various works unfinished at his early death.

Browne, Sir Thomas (1605-82)
Physician and author. Sir Thomas Browne studied medicine at Montpellier, Padua and Leiden, and began practising medicine in 1633, before moving in 1637 to Norwich, where he

was to spend the rest of his life. Browne's most influential work was ▷ *Religio Medici* (1642, reissued in an authorized edition in 1643), a title which can be translated as *The Religion of a Physician*. The conjunction between religious meditation and an enduring fascination with the observation of the most minute details of the physical world informs the *Religio*, which stands as both a determined act of creation of an authorial persona, and as a disquisition which attempts to reconcile scepticism and belief.

In some ways, Browne can be thought of as a Baconian in his adherence to the principles of observation, and his determination to refute ideas commonly entertained by the credulous. But his Baconianism is tempered by a vein of mysticism. The two tendencies in his thought are displayed in his later works – *Pseudodoxica Epidemica*, or *Vulgar Errors* (1646); *Hydriotaphia*, or ▷ *Urn Burial* (1658); and ▷ *The Garden of Cyrus* (1658).

Bib: Keynes, Sir G. (ed.), *Works*, 4 vols.; Bennett, J., *Sir Thomas Browne*; Post, J., *Sir Thomas Browne*.

Browne, William (1591–1643)

One of the 'Spenserian' poets, Browne wrote mainly ▷ pastoral verse, and was tutor to the family of ▷ William Herbert. He contributed seven eclogues to *The Shepherd's Pipe* (1614), a work written in collaboration with ▷ George Wither. Browne also composed a ▷ masque, produced in 1614, entitled *The Inner Temple Masque* – a title which was changed to *Ulysses and Circe* when the work was staged again in 1615. In 1613 appeared the first part of Browne's *Britannia's Pastorals*, poetic accounts of familiar pastoral stories derived from Browne's reading in ▷ Edmund Spenser, ▷ Torquato Tasso and ▷ John Fletcher, and placed within an English landscape, itself a reworking of Spenser's descriptions. Subsequent parts of the work were published in 1616 and (as a Percy Society edition) in 1852. In 1613, in collaboration with ▷ Fulke Greville, Browne published *Two Elegies*, works commemorating the death of ▷ Henry, Prince of Wales.

Bib: Grundy, J., *The Spenserian Poets*.

Browning, Elizabeth Barrett (1806–61)

Poet, the eldest child of Edward and Mary Moulton Barrett, her reputation as a major Victorian poet was established long before she met ▷ Robert Browning whom she married in 1846. An experimental writer, she wrote ▷ ballads, political odes, allegories, ▷ sonnets, poetic dramas and an epic, as well as publishing essays in literary criticism and translations of Greek poetry. She spent her childhood at Hope End in Herefordshire, reading widely and schooling herself in the ▷ classics. Her juvenilia includes *The Battle of Marathon* (published anonymously when she was only fourteen), *An Essay on Mind: With Other Poems* (1826) and *Prometheus Bound: and Miscellaneous Poems* (1833) containing her translation of Aeschylus' (525–456 BC) tragedy. Her reputation was made with her first mature collection, 'The Cry of the Children', a famous plea to the social consciences of the Victorian middle classes. For six years, between 1838 and 1844, Barrett was confined as an invalid, though during this period she wrote extensively, culminating in ▷ *Poems* (1844). In 1845 Robert Browning began a correspondence with her, and a year later she ran away from her tyrannical father in order to marry Browning in secret. The couple left immediately for Italy and based themselves in Florence for the rest of Barrett's life. *Poems* (1850) incorporates the celebrated sequence of love-lyrics ▷ *Sonnets from the Portuguese* written during her courtship, including the famous and much-anthologized 'How do I love thee? Let me count the ways', and 'The Runaway Slave at Pilgrim's Point'. Elizabeth gave birth to a son, known as Pen, at the age of forty-three. In 1850 ▷ *The Athenaeum*, to which Barrett Browning was a regular contributor, recommended her for the Poet Laureateship on the death of Wordsworth (1770–1850). Although the title went to ▷ Tennyson, the fact that a woman was considered at that time is indicative of Barrett Browning's reputation.

▷ *Aurora Leigh* (1857), an epic poem concerned with the making of a woman poet, is now considered one of Barrett Browning's major achievements. Other works include *Casa Guidi Windows* (1851) and *Poems Before Congress* (1860), which testify to her passionate championship of Italian independence, and a posthumously published collection, *Last Poems* (1862). The best edition of her work is *The Complete Works of Elizabeth Barrett Browning* (eds. C. Porter and H. Clarke).

▷ Ballad; Medievalism.

Bib: Taplin, G., *The Life of Elizabeth Barrett Browning*; Hayter, A., *Mrs Browning: A Poet's Work and its Setting*; Leighton, A., *Elizabeth Barrett Browning: Woman and Artist*; Mermin, D., *Elizabeth Barrett Browning*; Stone, M., *Elizabeth Barrett Browning*.

Browning, Robert (1812–89)

Poet. The son of a clerk in the Bank of England, he married the poet Elizabeth Barrett in 1846 under dramatic circumstances, and lived with her until her death in 1861 in Italy. He spent the rest of his life in London.

From the first his poetry was exuberant, and he began as an ardent follower of Shelley (1792–1822); *Pauline* (1833); *Paracelsus* (1835); *Strafford* (a verse tragedy, 1837); *Sordello* (1840). Between 1841 and 1846 he published seven more plays, the dramatic poem *Pippa Passes*, the collection *Dramatic Lyrics* (including ▷ 'The Pied Piper'), and *Dramatic Romances* – all published together under the title *Bells and Pomegranates*. During his married life he produced *Christmas-Eve and Easter-Day* (1850) and, his best-known work, ⊳ *Men and Women* (1855).

Nonetheless, public recognition only came with ⊳ *Dramatis Personae* (1864) and *The Ring and the Book* (1868–9). The latter was his most ambitious work and consists of 10 verse narratives, all dealing with the same crime, each from a distinct viewpoint. It was based on an actual trial, the record of which he discovered in Florence. The period 1850–70 was his best; the later work has endured less well: *Prince Hohenstiel-Schwangau* (1871); *Fifine at the Fair* (1872); *The Inn Album* (1875); *Pacchiarotto* (1876); *La Saisia* (1878); *Dramatic Idylls* (1879–80); *Ferishtah's Fancies* (1884); *Asolando* (1889).

Browning was keenly aware that he was writing poetry in an age of science, of technology and of prose, particularly of prose fiction. He made poetry compete with prose in these conditions, and the curiosity and delight in detail that were part of his temperament fitted him to do so. Where other poets, notably ⊳ Tennyson, wrote in a style that moved away from and above the preoccupations of daily living, Browning delighted in the idiom of ordinary speech and in the peculiarities of minds and objects. He was not the only practitioner of the ⊳ dramatic monologue, but he is especially associated with it; he chose characters out of history or invented them in special predicaments, and made them think aloud so as to display their distinctive mentalities. He was not afraid of obscurity, and both his earlier and his later poems suffer from it (*Sordello* and *Fifine*), although *Sordello* is now increasingly recognized as one of his most extraordinary and important works, influencing, for example, Ezra Pound (1885–1972) in his conception of the *Cantos*. The influence of his monologues on Pound's and T.S. Eliot's (1888–1965) early poetry should also be noted.

⊳ Medievalism.

Bib: Griffin, H.W. and Minchin, H.C., *Life*; Miller, B., *Life*; Cohen, J.M., *Robert Browning*; Devane, W.C., *A Browning Handbook*; Duckworth, F.G.R., *Browning: Background and Conflict*; Duffin, H.C., *Amphibian: a Reconsideration of Browning*; Herford, C.H., *Robert Browning*; James, H., in *Notes on Novelists*; Johnson, E.D.H., *The Alien Vision in Victorian Poetry*; Raymond, W.O., *The Infinite Moment*; Litzinger, B. and Smalley, D., (eds.), *Browning: the Critical Heritage*; Langbaum, R., *The Poetry of Experience*; Pathak, P., *The Infinite Passion of Finite Hearts: Robert Browning and Failure in Love*.

Brownists

A ⊳ Puritan religious sect founded by Robert Browne (1550?–1633?); from about 1640 they were known as Independents, and since the 18th century they have been Congregationalists. Their best-known doctrine is that on the evidence of the New Testament each religious congregation should be self-governing, so that there should be no over-riding Church, *eg* no government through bishops under a central figure such as the Pope or, in the Anglican system, the Crown.

Bruce, Robert the

King of the Scots (1306–29) and hero of the Scottish War of Independence (1296–1328), during which he successfully resisted the efforts of ⊳ Edward I and ⊳ Edward II to conquer the country. Bruce's decisive victory was the ⊳ Battle of Bannockburn (1314).

In about 1375 a Scottish poet ⊳ John Barbour wrote an epic poem describing the war, called *The Bruce*.

⊳ Scottish literature in English.

Brunton, Mary (1778–1818)

Novelist. She married Revd Alexander Brunton in 1798 and, although she had only a meagre education, they set about studying history and philosophy together. In 1811 she published anonymously her first novel *Self-Control* with a dedication to ⊳ Joanna Baillie. Brunton was particularly keen to show how ⊳ Romantic stereotypes often acted to the detriment of women; for example, at the beginning of *Self-Control* she states that her purpose is: 'to shew the power of the religious principle in bestowing self-command: and to bear testimony against a maxim as immoral as indelicate, that a reformed rake makes the best husband'. She only completed one more work, *Discipline* (1814), before dying in childbirth, although she did leave an unfinished text, *Emmeline*. The novels focus upon the psychological development of central female characters, who are in some way made to rethink their presuppositions because of outside forces. The quality of her long-neglected novels has only recently been acknowledged, and it is now accepted that *Self-Control* influenced the work of ⊳ Jane Austen.

Bib: Moers, E., *Literary Women*; Springer, M., *What Manner of Woman?*

Bryan, Sir Francis (d 1550)

Poet and diplomat. Bryan was one of the few courtiers to maintain close and cordial relationships with ⊳ Henry VIII and was chief mourner at the king's funeral. Perhaps this unusual fact may be accounted for by his readiness to acquiesce to any of his monarch's desires, however pernicious. For example, even though he was related to the Boleyn family, Bryan faked a quarrel with George Boleyn and aided the king to condemn Queen Anne Boleyn to death. For his services Bryan accepted a pension from Henry that had belonged to one of the men he had helped execute. These actions, together with his scarred appearance (he had lost one eye while jousting) led to his being called 'the vicar of hell', a name ▷ John Milton refers to in ▷ *Areopagitica*. Bryan was also the Master of Entertainments at court, a friend of ▷ Sir Thomas Wyatt and a poet; his work was included in ▷ *Tottel's Miscellany*.

Bryden, Bill (b 1942)
Dramatist, director, film maker. Since the mid-sixties Bill Bryden has been assiduously involved in the making of drama either for stage or the screen, in Scotland and abroad. His reputation, now international, was secured when he started working away from his native land with such celebrated National productions as his promenade *Mysteries*.

Willie Rough (1972), deriving from his grandfather's experience, looked at issues of working-class life against the backdrop of shipyard politics between the wars. *Benny Lynch* (1974) was again about the aspirations and daily drudge-and-grudge of the working classes, represented by this 'bonniest o' fechters' who rose to fêted world status only to end, exploited and discarded, in the gutter.

These productions represented a conscious drive on Bryden's part to stamp the Lyceum company with a 'national' identity and to encourage new Scots writers to create for *their* nation's stage. Unfortunately, it was not the right moment for his vision. In 1981, he wrote and directed *Civilians*, a fond, anecdotal glimpse of 1940s Greenock life, for the (short-lived) Scottish Theatre Company and in 1985 he took up the post of Head of Drama Television with BBC Scotland since when works by Peter MacDougall, Ian Heggie, John Byrne and others have seen the far-reaching light of transmission.

Perhaps the work that epitomises Bryden's entrepreneurial strengths and oft-criticised weaknesses as a dramatist is *The Ship* (1990), a spectacularly staged celebration of Clyde shipbuilding in its last years of greatness. This venture turned a disused riverside engine shed into an ad hoc theatre. Thanks to designer William Dudley, the performing space was encompassed by the inner decks and shell of a liner-in-progress. The sheer persuasive showmanship of all this did much to offset the saccharine banalities of the script which reduced the hard men and hard times of post-war Clydeside to a series of ciphers and clichés.

Bryher (1894–1983)
Novelist. Bryher's historical novels, always published under the single name she legally took on (after one of the Scilly Isles) so as not to be identified with her influential industrialist father, are serious and meticulously researched works on the Greek and Roman Empires (particularly *Roman Wall*, 1954, *Gate to the Sea*, 1958, and *The Coin of Carthage*, 1963) and on the connections between early British history and contemporary life (*The Fourteenth of October*, 1951, *The January Tale*, 1966, and *Beowulf*, 1956). Bryher lived with the poet ▷ H. D. (Hilda Doolittle) for much of her life, and wrote two autobiographies, *The Heart of Artemis* (1962) and *The Days of Mars* (1972). She also wrote literary criticism (a book, in 1918, on the poet Amy Lowell), and on film, setting up the film journal *Close-Up*.
Bib: Hanscombe, G. and Smyers, V. L., *Writing For Their Lives*.

Buc, Sir George (d 1623)
▷ Master of the Revels, 1608–22. Educated at the Inns of Court, Buc pursued a political career under the auspices of ▷ Sir Francis Walsingham and Sir Robert Cecil. He was at the Cadiz expedition and later served as a Member of Parliament and an envoy. He is best remembered for his post as deputy master, and later Master of the Revels. Buc's influence on ▷ Jacobean drama was cut short, however, when he became mentally unstable. Although most of his papers were destroyed in a fire, several works survive: a history of ▷ Richard III, an ▷ eclogue (*Daphnis Polystephanos*, 1604), and a treatise arguing that London should have a university in addition to those at Oxford and Cambridge (*The Third Universitie of England*, 1615).

Buchan, John, 1st Baron Tweedsmuir (1875–1940)
Novelist. Buchan was born in Scotland and educated at Glasgow and Oxford; he contributed to the ▷ *Yellow Book* while still a student. He is best known for his adventure stories involving the character of Richard Hannay, notably *The Thirty-nine Steps* (1915), filmed by Hitchcock in 1935. Other novels include: *Scholar Gypsies* (1896); *A Lost Lady* (1899); *The Half-Hearted* (1900); *Greenmantle* (1916); *Mr Steadfast* (1918); *Sick Heart River* (1941). He had a distinguished political career and was Governor-General of Canada 1935–1940.

Buchanan, George (1506–82)
Scottish poet, classicist, educationalist. George Buchanan's life was a curious mixture of high scholarly endeavour and political intrigue. In this, he can be thought of as representing that ability, described by ▷ Thomas Browne, to live in 'divided and distinguished worlds'. As an educationalist and a classicist he was tutor to ▷ Mary Queen of Scots and James VI (later ▷ James I of England). His most illustrious pupil, however, was the French essayist ▷ Montaigne, whom Buchanan taught after fleeing to Bordeaux to escape punishment for writing ▷ satires against the Franciscans. On returning to Scotland he helped prosecute his former pupil Mary Queen of Scots for high

treason, and later, under James VI, he held high office in the Scottish government. The great majority of his works were written in Latin, and included love poems, ▷ tragedies, legal works and a history of Scotland.
Bib: Ford, P. J., *George Buchanan: Prince of Poets.*

Buchanan, Robert (Williams) (1841–1901)
Poet, novelist and playwright. Buchanan was born in Staffordshire and educated at Edinburgh University. He moved to London and published his first volume of poems *Undertones* in 1863, following it with *Idylls and Legends of Inverburn* (1865), *London Poems* (1866), *Ballad Stories of the Affections* (1866) and *North Coast and Other Poems* (1867). His work is centred on the Scottish peasantry, the rigours of northern life and, in *London Poems*, the mean and squalid nature of city life which is portrayed with some sympathy. In *The Book of Orm* (1870), *Balder the Beautiful* (1877) and *The City of Dreams* (1888) Buchanan displays his interest in the mystical and his affinity with the epic style favoured by the ▷ Spasmodic school. *Saint Abe and His Seven Wives* (1872) and *White Rose and the Red* describe life in the New World. In 1872 he published pseudonymously a pamphlet stigmatizing ▷ Swinburne and ▷ Dante Gabriel Rossetti as members of 'The Fleshly School of Poetry' because of their sensualism and lack of ethical awareness. Buchanan's plays were moderately successful and include *Lady Clare* (1883), *Sophia* (1886) an adaptation of Henry Fielding's (1707–54) *Tom Jones*, and *The Charlatan* (1894). Among his novels *The Martyrdom of Madeleine* is an attack on the French aestheticism of Théophile Gautier who had inspired the English Aesthetes.
▷ Scottish literature in English; Aestheticism.

Buckingham, Duke of
▷ Villiers, George, Duke of.

Buckingham, George Villiers, first Duke of (1592–1628)
Courtier and favourite of ▷ James I. After the death of his astute principal minister, Robert Cecil, Earl of Salisbury, in 1612, the king turned for affection and advice to handsome young courtiers, the most prominent of whom was George Villiers. James' ▷ homosexual fascination with Buckingham allowed the younger man considerable political influence, while the king lavished wealth upon his 'sweet Steenie'. As the king's power faded, however, Buckingham transferred his affections to ▷ Prince Charles, the heir to the throne. When he acceded to the throne, Charles allowed Buckingham to lead him into a series of dangerous quarrels with Parliament and to almost complete dependence upon the Duke after the king's alienation from his wife, ▷ Henrietta Maria, in 1626. Buckingham's powerful influence over the British crown was brought to an abrupt end in 1628 when he was assassinated.
Bib: Lockyer, R., *Buckingham.*

Buckstone, J.B. (John Baldwin) (1802–79)
Actor, dramatist and theatre manager, he was born in London's East End and made his debut at the Surrey Theatre in 1823–4, establishing himself as a 'low comedian'. Between 1825 and 1850 he wrote over 100 dramatic pieces including farces, operettas and domestic melodrama – his first, *Luke the Labourer* (1826), helped to establish the genre. Comedies such as *The Wreck Ashore* (1830), *The Irish Lion* (1838), *Single Life* (1839) and the sentimental *The Green Bushes* (1845) are enlivened by low-life comic characters and champion the virtues of manly fortitude and decency. Under his management the Haymarket Theatre became the home of comedy (1853–76), and played host to dramatists such as ▷ Tom Taylor, Westland Marston and ▷ W.S. Gilbert.

Bulstrode, Cecily (1584–1609)
A writer of light prose ▷ satires, which categorized women as good or bad solely in accordance with their ability to please men, often in a sexual manner. However, she was part of the small group of women who congregated about ▷ Queen Anne, many of whom were more supportive of their own sex, such as ▷ Lady Anne Clifford and ▷ Lady Frances Southwell. Bulstrode is named as the author of 'Newes of my Morning worke', which was published with other Theophrastian character sketches in the second edition of ▷ Sir Thomas Overbury's *The Wife* (1614 and 1622). ▷ Ben Jonson wrote a scathing attack of her literary ability and sexual morality in 'An Epigram on the Court Pucell', but he, ▷ Donne and ▷ Edward Herbert all wrote commendatory elegies for Bulstrode at her death.
Bib: Savage, J. E. (ed.), *Overbury's Characters.*

Bulwer-Lytton, Edward George Earle Lytton (1st Baron Lytton) (1803–73)
Novelist. He was the son of General Bulwer and added his mother's surname of Lytton on inheriting her estate in 1843. He was educated at Trinity and Trinity Hall, Cambridge, and was made a Baron in 1866. His novels were very famous in his lifetime, and their range is an indication of literary variety and changes in the Victorian period. His political outlook was radical when he was young; he was then a friend of the philosopher William Godwin (1756–1836), whose influence is evident in his early novels, *Paul Clifford* (1830) and *Eugene Aram* (1832). On the other hand, he was a member of fashionable society and his first success (*Pelham*, 1828) is closer to ▷ Benjamin

Disraeli's political novels of high society, for example ▷ *Coningsby*. Then in mid-career, under the influence of the strict Victorian moral code, he wrote domestic novels such as *The Caxtons – A Family Picture* (1848). He showed the influence of novelist Sir Walter Scott (1771–1832) on the Victorians in his ▷ historical novels such as *The Last Days of Pompeii* (1834), *Rienzi* (1835) and *The Last of the Barons* (1843), and the current ▷ German influence in the didacticism of his early novels and in fantasies such as *The Pilgrims of the Rhine* (1834). Bulwer-Lytton was a friend of ▷ Charles Dickens (see the biography of Dickens by Jack Lindsay) and satirized ▷ Lord Tennyson in his poem *The New Timon* (1846). He wrote some successful plays – *The Lady of Lyons* (1838), *Richelieu* (1838) and *Money* (1840). Like Disraeli, he combined his literary with a political career, for which he was rewarded with a peerage as Baron Knebworth (his mother's estate) but in his case literature had priority. His work is now little respected (he is considered as neither sincere nor original) but he is interestingly representative of his period.
Bib: Sadleir, M., *Bulwer: A Panorama*; Christensen, A.C., *Edward Bulwer-Lytton: The Fiction of New Regions.*

Bunting, Basil (1900–85)
Poet. Bunting's association with the poetry world began in the 1920s, but he did not achieve real recognition until the 1960s – the story of his rediscovery after years of obscurity is one of the legends of contemporary poetry. Bunting had been associated with ▷ Ezra Pound and other ▷ modernists in the 1930s, even to the extent that ▷ W. B. Yeats called him one of Pound's 'savage disciples'. *Redimiculum Matellarum* was published in Milan in 1930, followed by *Attis* (1931), *The Well of Lycopolis* (1935), and, later, *Poems* in 1950, but the text which gave Bunting enormous recognition after many years of neglect in Britain was *Briggflatts* (1966). Undoubtedly Bunting's most important and challenging work, *Briggflats* is a long, intense, mystical synthesis of Northumbrian legend, ▷ autobiography and mythology. Other works include: *Collected Poems* (1968).
Bib: Davie, D., *Under Briggflatts.*

Bunyan, John (1628–88)
Born at Elstow, near Bedford, Bunyan was the son of a tinsmith, educated at the village school. Of Baptist sympathies, he fought in the Civil War, although little is known of his military activities. With the persecution of the Puritans which followed the Restoration of Charles II, Bunyan's non-conformist beliefs came under severe censure, and in 1660 he was arrested for preaching without a licence.

For most of the next twelve years Bunyan was imprisoned in Bedford jail, where he began to write. His spiritual autobiography, ▷ *Grace Abounding to the Chief of Sinners*, appeared in 1666, and the first part of his major work, ▷ *The Pilgrim's Progress* was largely written during this period of imprisonment, though it is probable that Bunyan completed Part I during a second spell in jail in 1676; the full text, with the addition of Part II, was published in 1684. A spiritual allegory strongly in the Puritan tradition, it tells of the pilgrimage of Christian to reach the state of grace. Bunyan's other major works, ▷ *The Life and Death of Mr Badman* (1680) and ▷ *The Holy War* (1682) are also spiritual allegories.
Bib: Sharrock R., *John Bunyan.*

Burbage, James (d 1597)
Actor and theatre manager. Originally a carpenter, in 1576 he built the first English ▷ theatre, called simply The Theatre, in London's Shoreditch. In 1596 he opened the ▷ Blackfriars Theatre, where the Children of the Chapel performed.
Bib: Levi, P., *The Life and Times of William Shakespeare.*

Burbage, Richard (?1567–1619)
Son of ▷ James Burbage. On his father's death, he dismantled The Theatre and rebuilt it as the ▷ Globe on the south bank of the Thames. As a shareholder in the ▷ Lord Chamberlain's Men he took the leading part in plays by ▷ Shakespeare, ▷ Jonson, ▷ Fletcher and others, using the Globe and (after 1608) the ▷ Blackfriars Theatre. He and ▷ Edward Alleyn were the most well-known actors of the time.
Bib: Levi, P., *The Life and Times of William Shakespeare.*

Burgess, Anthony (b 1917–93)
Novelist and critic. Born John Anthony Burgess Wilson of a Roman Catholic Lancashire family, he was educated at Manchester University. After military service during World War II he worked as a schoolmaster in Oxfordshire, Malaya and Borneo. His experiences in Malaya inspired his *Malayan Trilogy* (1956–9), a rich portrait of the Malayan culture and people, employing words and expressions from Malay, Urdu, Arabic, Tamil and Chinese. A fascination with the textures of language and a ▷ Joycean inventiveness and multilingual playfulness have characterized much of Burgess's work. In 1959 Burgess returned to England with a brain tumour, expecting to survive only a year, yet in that year wrote five novels: *The Doctor is Sick* (1960), *One Hand Clapping* (1961), *The Worm and the Ring* (1961), *The Wanting Seed* (1962) and *Inside Mr Enderby* (1963). During the 1960s he worked as a music and drama critic, and produced plays, T.V. scripts, short stories and numerous book reviews. He also did

a considerable amount of university teaching, and lived in Malta, Rome and Monaco. *A Clockwork Orange* (1962), filmed in 1971 by Stanley Kubrick, is an anti-utopian novel which quickly gained cult status, centring on a viciously disaffected protagonist who deliberately chooses evil, and who is brainwashed by penal techniques based on behaviourist psychology. Its most striking feature is the use of Nadsat, an invented teenage underworld slang largely based on Russian words and English colloquialisms. *Nothing Like the Sun* (1964) is a fictional account of ▷ Shakespeare's love life, told as the parting lecture of a schoolmaster in the Far East, who progressively identifies himself with his subject. An impression of Elizabethan life is conveyed through descriptive detail and imitation of contemporary idiom. *Earthly Powers* (1980) is a large-scale consideration of the nature of evil, with extensive reference to 20th-century literary and political history. Other novels include *1985* (1978), *The Piano Players* (1986), *Any Old Iron* (1989), *The Devil's Mode* (1989) and *Mozart and the Wolf Gang* (1991). Non-fiction includes: *The Novel Today* (1963); *Language Made Plain* (1964); *Ernest Hemingway and his World* (1978); *Flame into Being: the Life and Work of D. H. Lawrence* (1985).
Bib: Aggeler, G., *Anthony Burgess, the Artist as Novelist*.

Burghley, William Cecil, Lord (1520–98)
Lord treasurer. Cecil had a successful and prolonged political career; he was secretary of state (1550–3), was employed by ▷ Mary I, and became ▷ Elizabeth I's lord treasurer and her chief minister and adviser.
Bib: Read, C., *Lord Burghley and Queen Elizabeth*.

Burgundy, Duchy of
A province in the south-east of France, with which it was united in 1477. In the phase of the Hundred Years' War associated with ▷ Henry V of England (1413–22) Burgundy was for the time an important ally of England against France.

The early ▷ Renaissance Burgundian court had a considerable artistic and cultural influence upon portraiture and court entertainments in England during the reign of ▷ Henry VII.

▷ Masque.
Bib: Kipling, G., *The Triumph of Honour*.

Burke, Edmund (1729–97)
Statesman and political philosopher; described by the ▷ Victorian writer, Matthew Arnold (1822–88) as 'our greatest English prose-writer'. Born in Dublin, he pursued his political career in England, and was a Member of Parliament for much of his life. Although never attaining high office, his political status was considerable, due mainly to his formidable powers of oratory and polemical argument. His early work *A Philosophical Inquiry into the Origin of our Ideas of the Sublime and the Beautiful* (1756) marks a transition in aesthetic theory from the neo-classicism of the Restoration and ▷ Augustan writers John Dryden (1631–1700) and Alexander Pope (1688–1744). Influenced by Milton, it emphasizes the sense of awe inspired by both art and nature. His most celebrated work, ▷ *Reflections on the Revolution in France* (1790), argues for the organic, evolutionary development of society, as opposed to the brutal surgery and doctrinaire theories of the French revolutionaries.

Burke's character reveals a number of paradoxes. His writings combine the cautious, pragmatic instincts of a conservative politician with a passionate rhetorical style. He regarded all forms of political innovation with suspicion, yet defended the cause of the American rebels in *On Conciliation with the Colonies* (1775). He attacked the corrupt practice of court patronage and the exploitative activities of the East India Company, yet retained for himself many benefits of the systems he deplored.
Bib: S. Ayling, *Edmund Burke: His Life and Opinions*; Cone, C, B., *Burke and the Nature of Politics* (2 vols); Stanlis, P. J. (ed.), *Edmund Burke: The Enlightenment and the Modern World*; Wilkins, B. T., *The Problem of Burke's Political Philosophy*.

Burlesque
A form of satirical comedy (not necessarily dramatic) which arouses laughter through mockery of a form usually dedicated to high seriousness. The word is from the Italian *burla* = 'ridicule'. One of the most well-known examples of burlesque is ▷ Pope's ▷ *The Rape of the Lock* where an elevated style is used to describe a trivial incident. Burlesque is similar to ▷ parody, but parody depends on subtler and closer imitation of a particular work.

▷ Satire.

Burnet, Gilbert, Bishop (1643–1715)
Whig cleric, who played an important part in the build-up to the ▷ Glorious Revolution of 1688 and the accession of ▷ William III and Mary II. Born at Edinburgh, Burnet entered Marischal College, Aberdeen at the age of 10, studying first law and then divinity. In 1669 he became professor of divinity at Glasgow, but resigned in 1674 because of a dispute with his former patron, the Earl of Lauderdale. He settled in London, where he was made chaplain of the Rolls Chapel and later lecturer at St Clements. Burnet incurred the hostility of ▷ Charles II, who took away his lectureship, and on the accession of ▷ James II he left for the Continent. There he allied himself with William of Orange, whom he accompanied back to England as royal chaplain. He became

Bishop of Salisbury in 1689. His *History of the Reformation* was published 1679–81 and 1714; his *History of My Own Time* (1724–34) remains a primary source of information about the period.
Bib: Clarke and Foxcroft, *Life of Bishop Burnet*; Jones, J. R., *The Revolution of 1688 in England.*

Burnet, Thomas (1635–1715)
English cleric, born at Croft in Yorkshire, became a pupil of Tillotson and Clerk of the Closet to ▷ William III, but had to resign in 1692 because of opposition incurred by his unorthodox *Archaeologica Philosophica*, which treats the Fall of Adam and Eve as an allegory. He influenced ▷ Addison, ▷ Young and ▷ Burke, and his *Telluris Theoria Sacra* (1680–89, translated into English 1684–9), was also an important source for ▷ Thomson's *The Four Seasons.*

Burnett, Frances Eliza (née Hodgson) (1849–1924)
Novelist. Burnett is known for her best-selling children's stories: *Little Lord Fauntleroy* (1886) about a boy living in New York who turns out to be the heir of an English aristocratic family, and *The Secret Garden* (1911). Burnett also wrote accomplished novels for adults: some, like *Haworth's* (1879), are set in an industrial environment in the north of England while others, like *Through One Administration* (1883), deal with American society.
Bib: Burnett, F.E., *The One I Knew Best of All*; Burnett, V., *The Romantick Lady*; Thwaite, A., *The Life of Frances Hodgson Burnett.*
▷ Children's literature.

Burney, Dr Charles (1726–1814)
Father of novelist ▷ Fanny Burney, Charles Burney was the friend of ▷ Samuel Johnson, the actor David Garrick and the painter Sir Joshua Reynolds. An organist and musical historian, he also wrote travelogues of France, Italy, Germany and the Low Countries – journeys he made to collect material for his *History of Music* (published 1776–89).

Burney, Fanny (Frances, Madame D'Arblay) (1752–1840)
Daughter of the musical historian Dr Charles Burney (1726–1814), Fanny grew up in the distinguished company of Dr Johnson (1709–84), ▷ Sir Joshua Reynolds, Garrick and the ▷ Bluestockings. In 1786 she was appointed as an attendant upon Queen Charlotte, wife of George III, and in 1793 she married a French exile, General D'Arblay. From 1802–12, interned by Napoleon, she and her husband lived in France.

Burney's major novels are ▷ *Evelina* (1778), *Cecilia* (1782) and *Camilla* (1796). Their common theme is the entry into society of a young girl, beautiful and intelligent but lacking experience of the world; during subsequent adventures the girl's character is moulded. Burney was a great admirer of Samuel Richardson (1689–1761), and his influence is apparent in her use, in her first novel, of the epistolary form. Burney was well aware, however, of the difficulties facing a woman novelist; for example, in her diary entry for 18 June 1778 she comments on the reception of her novel *Evelina*:

> *In a private confabulation which I had with my Aunt Anne, she told me a thousand things that had been said in its praise, and assured me they had not for a moment doubted that the work was a* man's. *I must own I suffered great difficulty in refraining from laughing . . .*

Burney was also well known for her diaries and letters. Her *Early Diary* (1889) covers the years 1768–78, and contains many sketches of Johnson and Garrick; her *Diary and Letters . . . 1778–1840* (published 1842–6) is a lively account of life at court. Amongst her admirers, ▷ Jane Austen shows Burney's influence.
Bib: Henlow, J., *The History of Fanny Burney*; Kirkpatrick, S., *Fanny Burney*; Simons, J., *Fanny Burney*; Todd, J., *The Sign of Angelica.*

Burney, Sarah (1772–1844)
Novelist. Overshadowed by her half-sister ▷ Fanny Burney, Sarah was a successful novelist in her own right, earning her living mainly from her writing. Her life seems to have been conventional (for example she accepted jobs as a governess and paid companion), with the exception of a five year interlude as a young adult, during which she and her half-brother left their respective homes (he was married) to live together. Sarah Burney's first novel *Clarentine* (1796), although published anonymously, received great acclaim, and a number of others followed, the most noteworthy being: *Geraldine Fauconberg* (1808), *The Shipwreck* and *Country Neighbours* (1816–20), and *The Renunciation* (1839). The novels focus upon the psychological reactions of their young heroines when confronted by some calamitous occurrence or mysterious revelation.
Bib: Hemlow, J., *The History of Fanny Burney*; Kirkpatrick, S., *Fanny Burney.*

Burns, Robert (1759–96)
Scottish poet. He was born in poverty, the son of a peasant or 'cottar', but nevertheless became well-read in the Bible, ▷ Shakespeare, 18th-century English poetry, and also learnt some French. His best work, in the Lowland Scots dialect, was precipitated by his reading of the poet Robert Fergusson (1750–74), and was written between 1785 and 1790, during most of which time he was working as a farmer, an occupation

which undermined his health. He intended to emigrate to Jamaica with Mary Campbell, but she died in childbirth in 1787. In the same year his *Poems Chiefly in the Scots Dialect* were published in Kilmarnock, and made him famous. He moved to Edinburgh where a new edition of the volume appeared in the following year, and where he was lionized as a 'natural' genius. He was a hard drinker and womanizer, and two years after Mary Campbell's death he took as his wife Jean Armour, who had already borne children by him. He leased a farm and secured preferment in the excise service in Dumfries, despite his earlier sympathies for the French and American Revolutions. He devoted himself to reworking Scottish songs, which appeared in James Johnson's *The Scots Musical Museum* (1793–1803) and George Thomson's *Select Scottish Airs with Poetry*, but he became further impoverished, and succumbed to persistent ill health.

Perhaps Burns' best-known poems are sentimental lyrics, such as *Auld Lang Syne* or love songs like *Ae fond Kiss, Highland Mary*, and 'O my love's like a red, red rose'. His *Cotter's Saturday Night* celebrates Scottish peasant life in Spenserian stanzas, and other poems express a keen sympathy with the downtrodden and oppressed. But it is his comic satires which are now considered his best work: *To a Mouse*; *The Twa Dogs*; *Tam O'Shanter*; *The Jolly Beggars*. It is significant that those poems which attack Calvinism and the hypocrisy of kirk elders, such as *The Twa Herds* and *Holy Willie's Prayer*, were omitted from the Kilmarnock *Poems* of 1786. Even during his lifetime Burns was beginning to be viewed as a kind of Scottish ▷ Poet Laureate, with all the distortions which this inevitably involved. Over the past two centuries, this status, together with the patriotism of Burns Night, have served to promote a glamorized myth, at the expense of a true appreciation of Burns' poetry.

▷ Scottish literature in English.

Bib: Daiches, D., *Robert Burns*; Jack, R. D. S., and Noble, A. (eds.), *The Art of Robert Burns*; Spiers, J., *The Scots Literary Tradition*.

Burton, Sir Richard Francis (1821–90)
Explorer and ▷ travel writer. *Scinde, or the Unhappy Valley* (1851); *First Footsteps in East Africa* (1856); *The Lake Region of Central Africa* (1860); *The Pilgrimage to Al-Medinah and Meccah* (1855). He also translated the ▷ *Arabian Nights* (*The Thousand Nights and a Night* – 1885–8) and *The Lusiads of Camoens* (1880). For the last fourteen years of his life he worked on a translation of *The Perfumed Garden*, which his widow burned after his death.

Bib: Lady Burton, *Life*; Schonfield, A.L., *Richard Burton Explorer*; Wilson, A.T., *Richard Burton*.

Burton, Robert (1577–1640)
Oxford scholar and author. Burton was born in Leicestershire, and in 1593 entered Brasenose College, Oxford, where he was to remain. Besides the anti-Catholic Latin comedy *Philosophaster* (acted in 1618), Burton's one major project was the publication of his ▷ *Anatomy of Melancholy*, a project which occupied him for the majority of his life. He wrote under the pseudonym of 'Democritus Junior', thus emulating the Greek philosopher of the 5th century BC, Democritus.

Bib: Babb, L., *Sanity in Bedlam*; Keissling, N. K., *The Library of Robert Burton*.

Bury, Charlotte (1775–1861)
Poet, novelist and diarist. Charlotte Bury was a glittering success as a literary hostess in Edinburgh, but this masked her actual poverty and she wrote because she needed to, rather than for pleasure or through dedication. Her circle included ▷ Sir Walter Scott, ▷ Susan Ferrier and Matthew Lewis; indeed, she was said to be the model for the heroine in Lewis' novel *The Monk* (▷ 'Monk' Lewis). Her own writings include *Poems on Several Occasions* (1797), seventeen unremarkable novels, and the sensational *Diary Illustrative of the Times of George IV* (1838). It was this last work, based upon her experiences as lady-in-waiting to the Princess of Wales (1810–15), that made her name, combining as it did astute political observation with salacious scandal.

▷ Diaries; Silver-fork novels.

Bib: Rosa, M. W., *The Silver-fork School*.

***Busie Body, The* (1709)**
Play by ▷ Susannah Centlivre. Sir George Airy, a wealthy young man, is in love with Miranda, but her old guardian, Sir Francis Gripe, intends her for himself. Sir Francis' son, also George's friend, Charles, is in love with Isabinda, whose father Sir Jealous Traffick wants her to marry a Spaniard. Charles' suit is additionally hindered by his impoverishment: his father has tricked him out of his inheritance, while Miranda is being denied her inheritance by Gripe. Another of Gripe's wards, Marplot, does his best to help the lovers, but invariably adds complications because of his bungling naïveté. The action proceeds by means of a series of scenes of deception and intrigue, often frustrated by Marplot. Eventually, Charles disguises himself as the Spanish suitor and marries Isabinda under her father's nose; his fortune is restored by means of writings stolen from Sir Francis by Miranda, while Miranda herself is also united with her lover. The appeal of the well-meaning but witless Marplot helped to make the play so popular that in 1710 it was played simultaneously at both ▷ Covent Garden and ▷ Drury Lane, and it survived well into the 19th century. A sequel, *Marplot in Lisbon, or, The Second Part of the Busie Body* (1710), achieved less success.

Bussy d'Ambois, The Tragedy of (1604)
The best-known tragedy by ▷ George Chapman, which dramatizes the rise and fall of Bussy d'Ambois at the court of Henri III of France. The play's complex rhetoric reflects the philosophic, particularly neo-Platonic (▷ Platonism) bent of the author's mind and sometimes inhibits its imaginative flow.

Butler, Charlotte (fl 1673–95)
Popular Restoration actress and singer, from a well-to-do family that had fallen on hard times. She specialized in playing young girls, as well as acting in breeches parts (women disguised as men and wearing men's clothes). She was alleged to be highly promiscuous, and was as famous for her supposed list of lovers as for her comic talent and beautiful voice. Between 1675 and 1692 she played at least 19 roles.
Bib: Howe, E., *The First English Actresses: Women and Drama 1660–1700.*

Butler, Samuel (1612–80)
Poet. The son of a Worcestershire farmer, he became the friend of ▷ Thomas Hobbes and ▷ Sir William D'Avenant. His mock-heroic (▷ Heroic, mock) satire on ▷ Puritanism, ▷ *Hudibras*, employs deliberately rough-and-ready tetrameter couplets, which were frequently imitated by later poets and became known as 'hudibrasticks'. Butler's other works were neglected and most of them, including the Theophrastian *Characters* and the satire on ▷ The Royal Society, *The Elephant in the Moon* (it is actually a mouse trapped in the telescope), were not published until 1759, when his *Genuine Remains* appeared.
Bib: Johnson, S., in *Lives of the Poets*; Jack, I., *Augustan Satire.*

Butler, Samuel (1835–1902)
Satirist, scientific writer, author of an autobiographical novel, ▷ *The Way of All Flesh* (1903) in a form which became a model for a number of 20th-century writers. His satires ▷ *Erewhon* (an anagram of *Nowhere*) and *Erewhon Revisited* (1872 and 1901) are anti-utopias, ie instead of exhibiting an imaginary country with ideal customs and institutions in the manner of Sir Thomas More's ▷ *Utopia* (1516), Butler describes a country where the faults of his own country are caricatured, in the tradition of Jonathan Swift's Lilliput (*Gulliver's Travels*, 1726). He attacks ecclesiastical and family institutions; in Erewhon, machines have to be abolished because their evolution threatens the human race – a blow at Darwinism.

His scientific work concerned ▷ Charles Darwin's theory of evolution, to which he was opposed because he considered that it left no room for mind in the universe; he favoured the theory of ▷ Lamarck (1744–1829) with its doctrine of the inheritability of acquired characteristics. His disagreements and his own theories are expounded in *Life and Habit* (1877), *Evolution Old and New* (1879), *Unconscious Memory* (1880) and *Luck or Cunning?* (1886).

The Way of All Flesh attacks the parental tyranny which Butler saw as the constant feature of Victorian family life (despite much evidence to the contrary); so close did he keep to his own experience that he could not bring himself to publish his book in his own lifetime.

▷ George Bernard Shaw admitted a great debt to Butler's evolutionary theories and to Butler's stand against mental muddle, self-deception and false compromise in society. Writers as different from Butler and from each other as D.H. Lawrence (1885–1930) and James Joyce (1882–1941) wrote autobiographical novels after him in which the facts were often as close to their own experience.

▷ Utopian literature.
Bib: Cole, G.D.H., *Butler and The Way of All Flesh*; Henderson, P., *The Incarnate Bachelor*; Furbank, P.N., *Samuel Butler*; Jeffers, T.L., *Samuel Butler Revalued*; Joad, C.E.M., *Samuel Butler*; Muggeridge, M., *Earnest Atheist*; Pritchett, V.S., 'A Victorian Son' in *The Living Novel.*

Butts, Mary (1890–1937)
Novelist. Mary Butts' novels, such as *Armed With Madness* (1928) and *Death of Felicity Taverner* (1932), combine stylistic innovation and an interest in myth and magic characteristic of the period of High Modernism. Indeed, Marianne Moore, HD, and ▷ Ford Madox Ford championed her writing, and at one time her reputation rivalled that of ▷ Katherine Mansfield or ▷ Virginia Woolf. The great-granddaughter of a patron of ▷ William Blake, Mary Butts grew up in Dorset, this period of her life being recorded in a vivid and poetic autobiography, *The Crystal Cabinet* (1937). Mary Butts spent the 1920s in the literary Bohemia of Paris, but returned in her last years to the south west of England.

Byatt, A. S. (Antonia Susan) (b 1936)
Novelist, critic and reviewer. Born in Sheffield and educated at the universities of Cambridge and Oxford, she has worked as a teacher and lecturer in English. The novelist ▷ Margaret Drabble is her sister. Her novels are influenced by the work of ▷ Proust and of ▷ Iris Murdoch (Byatt has published two books on Murdoch), and combine a realistic portrayal of English manners with symbolic structures and a wide range of reference to history, myth and art. *The Shadow of a Sun* (1964) is a feminist ▷ *Bildungsroman* about a girl seeking to escape from a dominating novelist father, while *The Game* (1967), a story of the tragic rivalry between two sisters, has overtones of the Fall of Man. *The Virgin in the Garden*

(1979) and *Still Life* (1985) are the first two volumes of a projected tetralogy, intended to trace the lives of a group of characters from the accession of Queen Elizabeth II in 1952 up to the 1980 Post-Impressionist Exhibition in London. Byatt's later style includes quotation, allusion, narrative prolepses (anticipations of later events) and metafictional reflections on novel writing. Story collection: *Sugar* (1987). Her 1990 novel *Possession* is an academic ⊳ detective story which splices the tale of two young scholars' researches into the love between a male and female poet in the 19th century with the story of the romance itself. It became a ⊳ best-seller and won the Booker Prize in 1990. *Angels and Insects* (1992), which consists of two ⊳ novellas, also combines 19th-century settings with literary concerns. *Passions of the Mind* (1991) is a volume of essays and *Unruly Times* a study of Wordsworth and Coleridge. Other Fiction: *The Matisse Stories* (1993); *The Djinn in the Nightingale's Eye: Five Fairy Stories* (1994).

Byrd, William (1540–1623)
Composer. Most well-known of all Elizabethan composers, Byrd is chiefly remembered for two innovative collections, *Psalmes, Sonets and Songs* (1588) and *Psalmes, Songs and Sonnets* (1611). Although these are often considered to be ⊳ madrigals, they are not influenced to any great extent by these Italian imports, and Byrd was more indebted to the writing and composition of his youth. He wrote a vast amount of music, including both sacred pieces and vocal parts for secular performance. He was a pupil of Thomas Tallis, with whom he held a monopoly on music publishing from 1575, and he also held the post of Organist of the Chapel Royal. However, although Byrd conformed to the Protestant state religion, he was a recusant and was excommunicated in 1598 for his Catholic practices. He chose, therefore, to live outside London so as not to attract attention, and this must certainly have hindered his efforts to attain valuable political patronage.

Byrom, John (1692–1763)
Poet. Inventor of a system of shorthand, Fellow of the Royal Society and student of religious mysticism. His posthumous *Miscellaneous Poems* (1773) are notable for their colloquial ease and moderate eloquence of tone.

Byron, George Gordon, Lord (1788–1824)
Poet. His childhood was dominated by a sternly ⊳ Calvinist mother, a nurse who sexually abused and beat him, and painful medical treatment for his club foot. His incestuous relationship with his half-sister, Augusta Leigh, developed into a close friendship. In compensation for his deformity he prided himself on his physical prowess, particularly in swimming. While at Harrow and Cambridge he gained a reputation for atheism, radicalism and loose-living, keeping a bear as a pet for a time. At the age of 19 he published a collection of unremarkable lyrics, *Hours of Idleness* (1807). *English Bards and Scotch Reviewers*, a vigorous but immature heroic couplet poem in imitation of Pope, followed in 1809.

He travelled across Europe to Greece in 1810, involving himself in self-consciously romantic adventures. He swam across the Hellespont like Leander in the Greek legend, and dressed in Albanian costume. He wrote in a letter, 'I smoke, and stare at mountains, and twirl my mustachios very independently.' After his return in 1811 he published Cantos I and II of ⊳ *Childe Harold's Pilgrimage* (1812), a moody, self-dramatizing poem in ⊳ Spenserian stanzas. It was an immediate success and he followed it with several hastily-written verse tales: *The Bride of Abydos* (1813) and *The Giaour* (1813), mainly in tetrameter couplets, *The Corsair* (1814) and *Lara* (1814), in loose heroic couplets. Each focuses on the characteristic Byronic hero: glamorous, haunted by the guilt of mysterious crimes, which he seeks to forget in violent and dangerous adventure. Lionized in society and pursued by various women, Byron ended by marrying the naive and inexperienced Anne Isabella (Annabella) Milbanke. Her intention to reform him failed, and the marriage broke up shortly after she had given birth to a daughter.

Byron left England for the last time in 1816, and met up with ⊳ Percy Bysshe Shelley and ⊳ Mary Wollstonecraft Godwin in Switzerland. Claire Clairmont, Mary's half-sister, gave birth to a daughter by Byron, but she died in infancy. About this time he wrote *Childe Harold* Canto III (1816) which he called 'a fine indistinct piece of poetical desolation', also ⊳ *The Prisoner of Chillon* (1816), and the gloom-laden drama, ⊳ *Manfred* (1817). He travelled to Italy where, after a period of sexual promiscuity with all kinds of women, he eventually fell in love with Teresa Guiccioli, the 19-year-old wife of an elderly Italian nobleman. His uncomfortable role of *cavaliere servente* or tolerated lover, is indirectly reflected in ⊳ *Beppo* (1818), his first poem in *ottava rima*, a form which he made peculiarly his own, employing its rattling rhymes and concluding couplet to superb effect. It is also used in ⊳ *Don Juan* (1819–24) and *The Vision of Judgement* (1822). He became restless, and after Shelley had drowned in 1822, he decided to throw himself into the cause of Greek independence.
As he had remarked in a letter of 1820:

When a man hath no freedom to fight for at home,
Let him combat for that of his neighbours;
Let him think of the glories of Greece and of Rome,
And get knock'ed on the head for his labours.

In Greece he suffered further frustrations, including a disappointed passion for a Greek youth, Loukas. He began to feel his age, and expressed this poignantly in the lyric 'On this Day I Complete my Thirty-Sixth Year'. He contracted malaria, was bled several times by his doctors, and died at Missolonghi in 1824.

Byron's popular romantic reputation, based on the first cantos of *Childe Harold, Manfred* and the verse tales, is important in literary historical terms. On the Continent Byron has been regarded as a significant philosopher of ⊳ Romanticism. However, Byron himself was dismissive of his 'Byronic' exercises in 'poetical desolation'. He preferred the brilliant wit of Pope to what he called the 'wrong poetical system' of his Romantic contemporaries. The real value of his poetry lies in his evocation of past civilizations in the fourth canto of *Childe Harold*, and in his brilliantly casual poems in *ottava rima*. Byron's letters are often more vivid than his verse. His ⊳ autobiographical journal was destroyed after his death, and many of his letters were expurgated before being published by his friend ⊳ Thomas Moore in 1830. However the correspondence with his publisher ⊳ John Murray has survived intact, and shows the same vitality as the later poetry, but expressed in less inhibited language.

Bib: Marchand, L. A., *Byron: A Portrait*; Quennell, P., *Byron*; Leavis, F. R., 'Byron's Satire' in *Revaluation*; Knight, G. W., *Poets of Action*; Read, H., *Byron*; Rutherford, A., *Byron: A Critical Study*; Rutherford, A. (ed.), *Byron*: The Critical Heritage; Calder, A., *Byron*; Kelsall, M., *Byron's Politics*; Beatty. B. and Newey, V., *Byron and the Limits of Fiction*; Beatty, B., *Don Juan*.

Cade, Jack (d 1450)
A leader of a popular rebellion in the counties immediately south of London in 1450, during the reign of ▷ Henry VI (1422–61). The rebellion had temporary success, but later grew disorganized, and Cade was killed.

Caedmon (fl 650–70)
The first English poet to be known by name. According to ▷ Bede, who provides an account of Caedmon's life in his *Historia Ecclesiastica Gentis Anglorum (History of the English Church and its People)*, Caedmon was a Yorkshire cowherd who had a mystical experience late in life and became an inspired vernacular poet. He joined the monastic community at Whitby, during the incumbency of Abbess Hild (657–80), and produced many English versifications of scriptural works. Various ▷ Old English religious poems have been linked spuriously with Caedmon's name but the only extant text which can be attributed to Caedmon is the 'Hymn of Creation', quoted by Bede, and found in English versions in two manuscripts of Bede's text.

Caesar, Augustus (Gaius Julius Caesar Octavianus) (63 BC–AD 14)
Great-nephew of Julius Caesar, and his adopted son. He adopted the surname Caesar and was awarded the title of Augustus by the Roman Senate. He overcame the political enemies and assassins of his uncle, Julius, and after defeating his other rivals (notably Mark Antony), he achieved complete power and became first Emperor of Rome. ▷ Horace, ▷ Virgil, ▷ Ovid, Propertius, Tibullus and ▷ Livy were his contemporaries; in consequence, 'an ▷ Augustan age' has become a term to describe a high peak of literary achievement in any culture, whenever such achievement shows similar qualities of elegance, restraint and eloquence. In these qualities, France in the 17th century and England in the 18th century consciously emulated the Augustan age of Rome.

Octavius Caesar, in ▷ Shakespeare's ▷ *Antony and Cleopatra*, is a portrait (based on ▷ Plutarch) of Augustus during his struggle with Antony.

▷ French literature in England.

Caesar, Gaius Julius (? 102–44 BC)
Roman general, statesman and writer. He conquered Gaul (*ie* modern France) and in 55 and 54 BC undertook two expeditions to Britain. He described these wars in *De Bello Gallico*, a work long and widely used in English education for instruction in Latin. His victories led to civil war against his chief political rival, Gneius Pompeius, generally known in English as Pompey, whom he defeated. He then became dictator in Rome, but he was assassinated by other patricians, led by Marcus Brutus, for overthrowing Roman republican institutions.

For the Middle Ages, Julius Caesar represented all that was great in Rome. His life was described by the Greek biographer ▷ Plutarch and this with Plutarch's other biographies was translated into English by ▷ Sir Thomas North. ▷ Shakespeare used it as the basis for his play ▷ *Julius Caesar*.

Caird, Mona (1858–1932)
Novelist, born on the Isle of Wight. She married J.A. Henryson in 1877 and lived in Hampstead from then until the end of her life. From 1883 to 1915 she wrote seven novels, as well as a non-fictional work, *The Morality of Marriage and Other Essays* (1897). She argued, both in this work and in her fiction, for marriage reform. Her novels focus on the oppression that women can suffer, yet Caird also creates bold heroines who defy society's expectations. Much of the fiction is polemical in tone, with long speeches calling for changes in attitude. Caird herself saw ▷ marriage as a patriarchal system of exchange, and advocated equal rights to child custody, divorce, and proper ▷ education for women. Her novels include *The Wings of Azreal* (1889), *A Romance of the Moors* (1891) and *The Daughters of Danaus* (1894). Her last work was *Stones of Sacrifice* (1915). In the 1890s, her work was considered ▷ 'New Woman' fiction.

▷ Feminism; Women's movement.

Bib: Cunningham, G., *The 'New Woman' and the Fiction of the 1890s*; Stetz, M.D., 'Turning Points: Mona Caird', *Turn of the Century Women* 2, Winter 1985.

Calvin, John (1509–1604)
French religious reformer and author of the *Institutes of the Christian Religion* (1535). He settled in Geneva, which was to become, under his influence, an important centre of one of the most disciplined and militant branches of ▷ Protestantism.

Calvin's teachings were widely influential in England, Scotland, France and Switzerland in the 17th century and later. Out of the *Institutes* and his book on predestination (published in 1552) emerged the five chief points of Calvinism, namely, its belief in: (1) 'predestination', which holds that God has determined in advance who shall be 'elected' to 'eternal life' and who shall be condemned to everlasting damnation; (2) 'particular redemption', or the choosing of a certain predetermined number of souls redeemed by Christ's death; (3) 'original sin', which holds that the infant enters the world in a state of sinfulness, carrying with it the burden of Adam's fall; (4) 'irresistible grace', which argues that those chosen to be of the 'elect' have no means of resisting that choice; and (5) the final perseverance or triumph of the 'elect'.

Taken with Calvin's views on church government and the relation between state

and ecclesiastical power, Calvinism was to be of enormous influence on the ▷ Church of England in the 16th and 17th centuries. From the early 17th century onwards his doctrines became those of the established church. Calvin's *Institutes* became a recognized textbook in the universities, and it was not until the rise of Arminianism under ▷ Archbishop William Laud in the pre-Civil War (▷ Civil Wars) years that an effective opposition to Calvin's influence was mounted.
Bib: Knappen, M. M., *Tudor Puritanism*; Dickens, A. G., *The English Reformation*.

Cambridge Platonists
▷ Platonists, The Cambridge.

Cambridge School, The
An avant-garde grouping of poets that began in the mid 1960s around J. H. Prynne, and which has continued to the present day with John Wilkinson and others. The Cambridge School has often and incorrectly been taken as a satellite of Prynne's lexical versatility and difficulty. It might more accurately be read as an English reaction first to such American writers as Charles Olson, Edward Dorn and Robert Creeley (the Black Mountain School) and latterly as a development, part welcoming and part critical, in relation to the Language group of American poets. Its chief participants include John James, Andrew Crozier, Peter Riley, and in recent years Rod Mengham, Denise Riley and Geoff Ward.

Camden, William (1551–1623)
Historian and antiquary. Camden was educated at Oxford and was appointed headmaster of Westminster School in 1593, where ▷ Ben Jonson was one of his pupils. His main works are *Britannia* (1586; an enlarged sixth edition appeared in 1607) and *Annales* (1615 and 1625), both of which were translated from the original Latin into English between 1610 and 1635 (*Britannia* was translated by Philemon Holland in 1610). All were scrupulously researched – for example, he made a tour of Britain while writing *Britannia* – and he is recognized as one of the first modern historians who demanded authenticity in his sources, rather than relying upon mythology (▷ Tudor myth). He founded a chair of history at Oxford in 1621 and was buried in Westminster Abbey.
Bib: Trevor-Roper, H. R., *Queen Elizabeth's First Historian: William Camden and the Beginnings of English Civil History*.

Campbell, Ramsey (b 1946)
Novelist and journalist. Born and raised in Liverpool, Campbell is a leading light of Britain's 'new wave' of horror writers, described by Robert Hadji as 'the finest living exponent of the British weird fiction tradition'. Has published pseudonymously under the names Carl Dreadstone and Jay Ramsay. Campbell was a young devotee of H. P. Lovecraft whose style he mimicked in his early short stories, collected in *The Inhabitant of the Lake and Less Welcome Tenants* (1964). Although his first novel *The Doll Who Ate His Mother* (1976) was a minor success, Campbell came of age with *The Face That Must Die* (1979, revised 1983) which presents a coherently grim portrait of the world through the eyes of a psychotic. His subsequent novels successfully transpose the terrors of writers such as Lovecraft, M. R. James, Robert Aickmen and Arthur Machen into starkly realistic situations of modern urban collapse. A fierce defender of the honourable tradition of horror fiction, Campbell describes himself as 'working against the innate prejudices and conservatisms of the field', using visceral horror to make people look again at things they may have taken for granted. Campbell has also edited a number of horror anthologies and critical works. Works include *Demons by Daylight* (1973); *The Parasite* aka *To Wake The Dead* (1980); *Incarnate* (1983); *Obsession* (1985); *Scared Stiff* (1987); *Ancient Images* (1989); *The Count of Eleven* (1991); and *Waking Nightmares* (1992).

Campbell, Roy (1902–57)
A South African poet, mainly resident in England, and well known in the 1930s for his opposition to the dominant left-wing school of poets led by ▷ Auden, ▷ Spender and ▷ Day Lewis whom he satirized under the composite name of Macspaunday. Much of his best verse was satirical in heroic ▷ couplets, a form otherwise very rare in 20th-century English verse. He also wrote eloquent, clear-cut lyrics. He was vigorous in all he wrote, but not distinctively original. Among his best-known works are: *The Flaming Terrapin* (1924), exalting the instinctive, vital impulses in man; *The Waygoose* (1928), a satire on South African writers; *Adamastor* and *Georgiad*. Amongst his finest works is his translation of the poems of San Juan de la Cruz, *St John of the Cross* (1951). *Collected Poems* in 3 volumes, 1960.

Campbell, The Clan
A Scottish clan, headed by the Duke of Argyll, which in the 17th and 18th centuries was one of the most powerful clans in the Highlands. The heads of the clan became dukes in the 18th century; their ancient Gaelic title is Macallum Mhor – the 'Great Campbell'. It was steadfast under its chiefs in its support of the ▷ Presbyterian Church and the ▷ Protestant succession, and in this it was opposed to other leading Highland clans who tended to support the ▷ Catholic House of ▷ Stuart.

Campbell, Thomas (1777–1844)
Author of the reflective poem *The Pleasures of Hope* (1799), which includes the well-known couplet: ''Tis distance lends enchantment to the view,/And robes the mountain in its azure hue' (II 7–8). He also wrote narrative poems such as *Gertrude of Wyoming* (1809) in ▷ Spenserian stanzas, and *Theodoric* (1824) in couplets.

Campion, Edmund (1540–81)
English Catholic. After becoming a fellow of St John's College, Oxford in 1557, Campion enjoyed the patronage of the Earl of Leicester before fleeing to Rome in 1572 as a suspected Catholic. In Rome he joined the ▷ Jesuit order in 1573, before being ordained a priest in 1578 and being chosen to return to England as a priest in 1580. In England he distributed anti-Protestant material (specifically the *Decem Rationes* in 1581) and was arrested, sent to the Tower, tortured and finally executed in 1581. His death was said to have been the cause of many former Protestants in England returning to Catholicism. He was the subject of a hagiographic biography, Evelyn Waugh's *Edmund Campion*.
Bib: Kavanagh, J., *Edmund Campion and the Elizabethan Government.*

Campion, Thomas (1567–1620)
English lyric poet and musician. He wrote and composed when the art of English song was at its height; the words do not exist merely as a pretext for the music, but are so composed that the music brings out their expressiveness. This led naturally to metrical experiment, and the resulting increase of rhythmic flexibility no doubt influenced the playwrights in the great range of expression which they achieved in ▷ blank verse. Campion wrote ayres, ▷ madrigals and ▷ masques. Despite his fine command of the rhymed ▷ lyric, he wrote an essay against the use of rhyme, *Observations in the Art of English Poetry* (1602). This provoked a reply in one of the more important Elizabethan critical essays, ▷ Samuel Daniel's *Defence of Ryme*.

Campion's reputation suffered in the early part of this century due to the championing of ▷ Donne and 'metaphysical' poetry (▷ Metaphysical poets) by critics such as T. S. Eliot (1888–1965). But his reputation has always fluctuated considerably – his contemporaries ▷ Ben Jonson and Daniel both attacked him in print. The chief difference between a poet such as Campion and the styles developed by Donne is that Campion is concerned with the auditory effects of poetry rather than concentrating on the striking effects of images. However, recent materialist criticism has highlighted Campion's awareness of the changing political situation and has suggested that his poetry and masques are more critical of the court than the previous emphasis on oral play would suggest.
Bib: Colles, H. C., *Voice and Verse*; Kastendieck, M. M., *Thomas Campion, England's Musical Poet*; Lindley, D., *Thomas Campion*; Mellers, W., *Music and Poetry*; Pattison, B., *Music and Poetry of the English Renaissance*; Warlock, P., *The English Ayre*; Smith, H., *Elizabethan Poetry*; Fellows, E. H., *English School of Lutenist Song Writers.*

***Candida* (1898)**
One of the ▷ *Plays Pleasant and Unpleasant* by ▷ George Bernard Shaw. Its theme is the conflict between two views of life: the lofty, vague one of the poet Marchbanks, and the narrow but practical one of the Christian Socialist clergyman Morell. Both men are rivals for the love of Morell's wife, Candida.

Canning, George (1770–1827)
Politician and poet. Although Canning is chiefly known for his roles as foreign secretary (1822) and prime minister (1827), he was also a fine writer of speeches and a minor poet. He was the founder of and contributor to the short-lived anti-liberal paper *The Anti-Jacobin* (1797).
▷ Jacobin
Bib: Rolo, P.J.V., *Canning: three biographical studies.*

Canon
This introduces one of the most contentious areas of contemporary critical debate. In general terms, the canon refers to a body of writing sanctioned by authority and its origins are in church law. In literary studies the term is used in two senses. In the first sense it refers to works recognized to be authentically by a particular writer when there is doubt about authorship. However the term is now more commonly used to refer to a body of work by various writers which is declared to be of the highest or most significant quality. Often this is related to a particular national literature (as in the canon of English Literature) or a trans-national group such as 'The Western Canon'. The canon is contentious today for a number of reasons. First, what is often a conservative emphasis on national identity or traditional thought is seen to exclude certain minority groups (for example, black, women or gay writers) from the canon which is therefore said to fail to reflect the full diversity of the community. But more generally, the idea of the canon has also fallen into disfavour because recent criticism is unable to agree on reliable criteria – moral, political or aesthetic – for its selection. This makes any attempt to draw up a canon appear arbitrary and/or unjust. The dispute about the canon therefore touches some central problems in modern cultural debate, including the question of whether there can be purely aesthetic criteria of judgement about art works. A third and very substantial objection to the canon simply questions any need for it in a world which is

increasingly relativistic in its ideas. This is the object of much ▷ postmodern theory.

Canon's Yeoman's Prologue and Tale, The
One of ▷ Chaucer's ▷ *Canterbury Tales*. Its authenticity as a 'Chaucerian' work has been questioned because it is not included in the early Hengwrt manuscript of the *Tales*. The Prologue to the Tale recounts how the Canon's Yeoman meets up with the pilgrims *en route* for Canterbury and decides to leave his master, the Canon, and join the company. Although the Canon's Yeoman begins by praising his master, he decides to expose the fraudulence of his alchemical practices in particular and those of alchemy in general in his Tale. His description of the alchemical art of the Canon is followed by a story (not about his master, he insists) in which a canon tricks a priest out of £40 by pretending to teach him the secret of making precious metals by alchemical means.

Canterbury Tales, The
A famed story-collection by ▷ Geoffrey Chaucer, begun sometime in the later 1380s. The General Prologue gives details of the occasion for the story-telling, relating how a group of pilgrims, bound for the shrine of ▷ St Thomas Becket at Canterbury, meet up at the ▷ Tabard Inn in Southwark. The pilgrims are introduced in a sequence of portraits which focus on the professional activities of the company (who number 31 in all). The material for these portraits derives partly from a long-standing literary tradition of social analysis and satire, but Chaucer enlarges the scope of the cross-section of society on the pilgrimage by including a broader range of bourgeois professionals in the group. The varied format and style of the descriptive cameos (in which details of dress, character or professional habits are mentioned seemingly at random) enhances the impression of the individuality of the pilgrims, who are introduced by a pilgrim-narrator whose stance is that of a reporter of events.

The list of portraits begins with that of the Knight, a representative of the higher levels of the social élite, who is travelling with his son, the Squire, and their Yeoman. The focus then shifts to the description of members of the clerical elite on the trip, including a Prioress, a Monk and a Friar. There is no clear-cut ordering principle in the sequence of portraits which follows (other than perhaps a broad downward movement through the social scale), describing a Merchant, a Clerk of Oxford, a Lawyer, a Franklin, a group of five Guild members, their wives and their Cook, a Shipman, a Physician, a Wife of Bath, a Parson and his brother, a Ploughman, a Miller, a Manciple, a Reeve and, finally, a Summoner and a Pardoner who pair up as travelling companions. The pilgrim-narrator himself is described in more detail at a later point on the journey. The General Prologue concludes with an account of how the Host of the Tabard Inn, Harry Bailey, devises a story-telling competition to take place on the round trip to Canterbury. The pilgrims agree to tell two stories each on the forward and return journeys; Harry Bailey plans to accompany the pilgrims, act as games-master and reward the pilgrim providing the best story with a meal on return to Southwark.

Diversity seems to be the organizing principle of the collection. The *Canterbury Tales* includes an extraordinarily wide range of material in verse (in rhymed decasyllabic couplets, ▷ rhyme royal verse) and prose, covering a wide range of literary genres and forms: ▷ romances, ▷ fabliaux, an animal fable, saints' lives, exemplary narratives, a moral treatise, a prose treatise on the process of penitence (which concludes the game). The relationship between 'earnest' and 'game', between serious and playful literary material, is one of the running topics of debate within and between the tales.

Judging from the condition of the extant manuscript copies of the *Canterbury Tales*, the project outlined by Harry Bailey in the General Prologue was never completed by Chaucer. The *Canterbury Tales* has the status of a 'work in progress', comprising a series of fragmentary tale-telling sequences, some of which are linked by dramatic interactions between the pilgrims and Harry Bailey, some of which begin and end without any contextual framing, and some of which show signs of being linked to other tellers at an earlier stage in the process of compilation. However, the opening and closing sequences of the *Tales* are provided and from these it seems that the literary plan was designed to change *en route* from a round journey to a one-way trip. The last tale of the sequence, the Parson's prose treatise on penitence, signals not only the end of the journey to Canterbury, but also the end of story-telling altogether, and is followed in most manuscripts by Chaucer's literary Retraction.

None of the 82 manuscripts of the *Tales* was copied during Chaucer's lifetime, and variations in form, style and tale-teller linkage are apparent. Some of the variations seem to reflect the attempts of later scribes and editors to tidy up some of the loose ends of the story-collection and provide more cohesive links for the series of fragmentary sequences left by Chaucer. Modern editions of the *Canterbury Tales* are based on two important early-15th-century manuscripts: the Ellesmere manuscript (E) and the Hengwrt manuscript (H). The form and arrangement of the text in E have provided the basis for the most accessible editions of the *Tales* (by F. N. Robinson, revised and updated by Larry Benson et al.). In E, 22 of the pilgrims mentioned in the Prologue produce a tale, beginning with the ▷ Knight, followed by the ▷ Miller, the ▷ Reeve, the ▷ Cook, the ▷ Man of Law, the ▷ Wife of Bath, the ▷ Friar, the ▷ Summoner, the ▷ Clerk, the ▷ Merchant, the ▷ Squire, the ▷ Franklin, the ▷ Physician, the ▷ Pardoner, the ▷ Shipman, the ▷ Prioress, the pilgrim / narrator (who tells two tales), ▷ *Sir Thopas*, which is rejected by the host, and ▷ *Melibeus*, the ▷ Monk, the ▷ Nun's Priest, the ▷ Second Nun, the ▷ Canon's Yeoman (who joins the pilgrimage *en route*), the ▷ Manciple and finally the ▷ Parson. It is now generally accepted that the E text has been quite extensively edited by Chaucer's literary executors and represents a later, tidied-up version of the text represented in H, and more recently, the Hengwrt manuscript has been used as the basis for new editions of the *Canterbury Tales* (by N. Blake, by Paul Ruggiers and David Baker). The differences between the two versions are mainly in the ordering and linking of the tales: the E text has more connected sequences of stories and contains the ▷ *Canon's Yeoman's Prologue and Tale*, which is not in H.

Since its publication by Chaucer's literary executors, the *Canterbury Tales* has had an active 'afterlife'. Some new tales were added to the collection by 15th-century editors (notably ▷ Gamelyn), an attempt was made to continue the narrative after the arrival at Canterbury (in the *Tale of Beryn*) and ▷ John Lydgate, the prolific court writer of the 15th century, wrote himself into the literary event of the *Tales* in his work *The Siege of Thebes*, which opens with a description of Lydgate himself joining the pilgrimage and then contributing his Theban story to the competition. Translations of selected tales were made by ▷ Dryden and ▷ Pope. The attention given to the *Canterbury Tales*, in relation to the rest of the Chaucerian canon, has varied according to the critical temper and tastes of the time, but the enormous attention given by modern scholars and critics to the phenomenon of the *Tales* is only the most recent stage in the long history of their critical reception. The *Canterbury Tales* continues to be a work in progress.

Bib: Benson, L., et al. (eds.), *The Riverside Chaucer*; Boitani, P., and Mann, J. (eds.), *The Cambridge Chaucer Companion*; Cooper, H., *The Structure of the Canterbury Tales*; Howard, D. D. R., *The Idea of the Canterbury Tales*; Pearsall, D., *The Canterbury Tales*.

Canto

Used in Italian literature as a division of a long poem, such as might be sung or chanted at one time (canto = song). The term has been borrowed for some long poems in English

▷ Pound, Ezra.

***Cantos*, The**

Long poem by ▷ Ezra Pound, unfinished at his death. The English collected edition runs to 119 ▷ cantos, and began publication with the first three cantos (later revised) in 1917. Loosely based on the 100 cantos of Dante's *Divine Comedy*, it attempts a panoramic, encyclopaedic survey of both western and oriental history, dwelling in particular on those rulers and thinkers who had exemplary significance for Pound: Confucius, Sigismondo Malatesta, Duke of Rimini, the early American presidents and Mussolini. Its main targets are usurious international finance and armament manufacturers. However, with the collapse of ▷ fascism the later stages of the poem became successively more mystical and self-consciously exploratory, and it meditates on Pound's vision of the ideal rather than on the possibilities of its earthly realization.

Bib: Bush, R., *The Genesis of Ezra Pound's 'Cantos'*; Terrell, C. F., *A Companion to the 'Cantos' of Ezra Pound.*

Canute (Cnut) (c 994–1035)

A Danish king of England with a well-documented historical reign, although he has assumed a sort of mythical status in English history. He is especially remembered for the story recorded by the 16th century chronicler ▷ Holinshed about his rebuke to his flatterers. When they declared him all-powerful, he sat down by the seashore and forbade the incoming tide to wet his royal feet. When nonetheless the waves came on, he demonstrated to his courtiers that a king had no more power over nature than an ordinary man.

***Captain Singleton, Adventures of* (1720)**

A novel by ▷ Daniel Defoe. Like the heroes and heroines of Defoe's other novels, Singleton has at first no morality and takes to a life of wandering adventure; some of this takes place in Africa (which Defoe knew only from reading and hearsay). Later he becomes a pirate in the Indian Ocean and further east; finally he settles down in England, a respectable married man, converted to a religious life. The story is told in the first person.

Carew, Jan (b 1925)

Guyanese novelist, poet and playwright. He has worked as a writer, actor, lecturer (University of London extra-mural department), radio editor (BBC Overseas Service) and broadcaster. He is now a professor of English in the USA. His novels include: *Black Midas* (1958); *The Wild Coast* (1958); *The Last Barbarian* (1961); *Moscow is Not My Mecca* (1964). His plays include *University of Hunger* (1966) and *Black Horse, Pale Rider* (1970). *Streets of Eternity* (1952) and *Sea Drums in My Blood* (1981) are volumes of poetry, and he has also published books for children, television and radio plays and historical works.

Carew, Thomas (1594–1640)

Poet. In the 1630s Carew was a member of

the court of ▷ Charles I, and his association with the court and the group of poets moving either within or on the fringe of court circles in the pre-Civil War years, has led him to be grouped as one of the ▷ 'Cavalier' poets. His first important work was his elegy on the death of ▷ John Donne, which appeared in the first edition of Donne's poems in 1633. In 1634 his ▷ masque *Coelum Britannicum* was performed by the king and his gentlemen. His *Poems* were published in 1640 with further editions in 1642 and 1651.

Carew's poetry is remarkable for its combination of eroticism, wit and logical demonstration. His elegy on Donne, as well as representing a tribute to the dead poet, also offers itself as a critical statement in its own right, and is an important commentary on the type of verse which came to be known as ▷ 'metaphysical'.

Bib: Miner, E., *The Cavalier Mode from Jonson to Cotton.*

Carey, Mary (c 1610–80)
Poet and devotional writer. Carey began her spiritual life at the age of 18 when she recovered from a serious illness, and began collecting together her meditations in verse and prose c 1653. Although these may be found in manuscript form at the Bodleian Library, Oxford, selections are published in *Kissing the Rod*, ed. G. Greer (1988). She was married twice, the second time to George Payler, a Parliamentarian paymaster whose occupation ensured that Carey was continually moving about the country from garrison to garrison. Her poems are dedicated to Payler and a number of her works, which are usually in the form of a dialogue, appear as conversations with him. She also includes exchanges with God and Satan, as well as the conventional dialogue poem between body and soul (▷ Andrew Marvell). Her tone is always modest and pious, although she often questions God as to why her babies were allowed to die.

Bib: Blain, V. et al (eds.), *The Feminist Companion to Literature in English.*

Carey, Peter (b 1943)
Australian novelist and short-story writer. He has published two volumes of short stories: *The Fat Man in History* (1974) (in the U.K. as *Exotic Pleasures*, 1981) and *War Crimes* (1979). His first two novels were: *Bliss* (1981), a bleak black comedy of the Australian suburbs about a man who believes himself to be dead and in Hell; and *Illywhacker* (1985), which combines realist elements with an outrageously ▷ unreliable narrator, who announces on the first page that he is a 'terrible liar'. These were followed by: *Oscar and Lucinda* (1988), which won the Booker Prize, and *The Tax Inspector* (1991), a sinister and violent story about abuse within a family over several generations in a suburb of Sydney. Carey is often described as a fabulist, and has acknowledged the influence on his work of the magic realism of Gabriel García Márquez.

Carey, Rosa Nouchette (1840–1909)
English novelist. The eighth child of a ship-owner, she was born in Stratford-le-Bow, London, and educated at home and at the Ladies' Institute, St John's Wood. Her first published novel was *Nellie's Memories* (1868), a story she had originally told to her sister before transcribing it several years later. Carey was deeply religious and conservative, believing strongly that woman's role was domestic and maternal. This attitude is reflected in the numerous short stories she wrote for the *Girls' Own Paper* and in the thirty-nine novels she published between 1868 and 1909. Her works include *Wee Wifie* (1869); *Not Like Other Girls* (1884); *The Sunny Side of the Hill* (1908) and *Barbara Heathcote's Trial* (1909). She also produced a volume of ▷ biographies: *Twelve Notable Good Women of the 19th Century* (1899).

Carker, James
A character in Dickens' novel ▷ *Dombey and Son*. He is a vicious character and one of Dickens' most successful depictions of villainy, and beautifully tied in with the development of the railways.

Carleton, Mary (?1633–1673)
English writer, born in Canterbury. She adapted the codes and conventions of scandalous chronicle to her own history. She was already married when she moved to London, claiming to be a German lady or princess. She soon married John Carleton, but when each discovered the other did not have the estate they pretended, he accused her of bigamy. A corpus of writings grew up, including *The Case of Madam Mary Carleton* and *A True Account* (both 1663), and *An Historical Narrative of the German Princess.*

Mary Carleton acted in a satire about her own story, called *The German Princess.* She was later convicted of theft and transported to Jamaica. She escaped, but was eventually caught and hanged.

Bib: Bernbaum, E., *The Mary Carleton Narratives.*

Carlyle, Jane Welsh (1801–66)
Woman of letters and literary personality. Jane Baillie Welsh was born in Haddington, East Lothian, the daughter of a doctor who gave her a rigorous classical education from the age of five. At school she impressed her tutor Edward Irving with her character and intelligence, and he introduced her to the historian and critic ▷ Thomas Carlyle in 1821. They married in 1826, and became the centre of an intellectual

and literary circle. Her greatest friend was ▷ Geraldine Jewsbury, and she knew such figures as ▷ John Stuart Mill and ▷ Harriet Taylor, ▷ Charles Dickens and ▷ Tennyson. She is celebrated as one of the greatest letter-writers in the English language, observant and caustic but generous and kind and a witty observer of social behaviour. Her subjects include travel, books, personalities and servants and her correspondence has been published in editions by J.A. Froude (1883); L. Huxley (1924) and T. Scudder (1931). Between 1834 and 1866, the Carlyles lived at Cheyne Row, Chelsea, though they were often apart. Their relationship was fraught and difficult; some biographers have suggested that sexual impotence contributed to the marital stress. Nevertheless she was her husband's chief protector and critic. In the early 1860s Jane's health collapsed and she lived in fear of a mental breakdown, dying suddenly in 1866.

▷ Lesbianism.

Bib: Surtees, V., *Jane Welsh Carlyle*; Hanson, J. and E., *The Carlyles*; Clarke, N., Ambitious Heights: writing, friendship, love.

Carlyle, Thomas (1795–1881)

Scottish essayist, historian, philosopher. The term 'philosopher' is inapppropriate to him if it implies the use of the reason for the logical investigation of truth; his friend ▷ John Stuart Mill, who was a philosopher in this sense, called Carlyle a poet, meaning that he reached his conclusions by imaginative intuition. In his old age he became known as 'the sage of Chelsea'; this is the kind of admiration that he received in England between 1840 and his death. He hated spiritual mediocrity, mere contentment with material prosperity, moral lassitude and the surrender to scientific scepticism and analytic reasoning. All these he regarded as characteristic of British civilization in the mid-19th century. Part of their cause was the overwhelming technical advances resulting from the ▷ Industrial Revolution; he also considered the immense popularity of the poet Byron (1788–1824) had helped to disintegrate spiritual wholeness because of the cynicism and pessimism of his poetry, and he distrusted equally the influence on the English mind of the coldly logical French philosophers. To counter Byron, he pointed to the spiritual health which he found in Goethe (1749–1832), and to counter the French he advocated the more emotional and intuitive 18th- and 19th-century German thinkers like Richter and Goethe.

Carlyle's influence derives even more, however, from his own character and the environment from which he sprang. His father had been a Scottish stonemason, with the moral energy and intellectual interests which comes partly from the influence of Scottish Calvinism (▷ Presbyterianism). This religious tradition in Scotland had much in common with 17th-century Puritanism which had left such a strong mark on the English character; the resemblance between the two traditions helps to account for the hold which Carlyle established on the English imagination. His own personality was strong and individualistic; this, combined with his intention of counteracting the abstract intellectual thought of writers like ▷ Bentham, caused him to write in an eccentric prose style, distorting natural word order and using archaic language. His ▷ *Sartor Resartus* ('Tailor Repatched', 1833–4) is a disguised spiritual ▷ autobiography in which he faces the tendencies to intellectual scepticism and spiritual denial in himself, and dedicates himself to a life of spiritual affirmation. He is unable to base this affirmative spirit on the traditional religious beliefs that had supported his father, so that he has to base it on his own will, his imaginative response to nature and the inspiration provided by the lives of great men.

History was for Carlyle the storehouse of example of these great men, his 'Heroes' – and it is in this spirit that we have to approach his historical works: ▷ *French Revolution* (1837), ▷ *On Heroes, Hero-Worship and the Heroic in History* (1841), *Oliver Cromwell's Letters and Speeches* (1845) and *Frederick II of Prussia* (1858–65). In ▷ 'Signs of the Times' (1829), *Chartism* (1839) and ▷ *Past and Present* (1843) he criticized the mechanistic philosophy which he saw underlying contemporary industrial society, and in *Latter-Day Pamphlets* (1850) he attacked the quasi-scientific treatment of social questions by the rationalist political economists. *Shooting Niagara – and After?*, written at the time of the Second Parliamentary Reform Bill in 1867, reflects his total disbelief in the efficacy of mere political reform.

As a historian, Carlyle wanted history to be related to the life of the ordinary human being; as a social thinker, his advocacy of the imaginative approach to man in society relates him to the thought of Coleridge, whom he knew through his friend John Sterling (*Life of John Sterling*, 1851), and also to his own disciple, ▷ John Ruskin.

▷ Utilitarianism; Scottish literature in English.

Bib: Seigel, J., P., *Thomas Carlyle: The Critical Heritage*; Kaplan, F., *Thomas Carlyle: a Biography*; Tennyson, G.B., *Sartor called Resartus*; Hardman, M., *Six Victorian Thinkers*; Trevelyan, G.M., *Carlyle Anthology*; Froude, J.A., *Life*; Neff, E., *Carlyle and Mill*; Harold, C.F., *Carlyle and German Thought, 1819–34*; Symons, J., *Carlyle: the Life and Idea of a Prophet*; Sanders, C.R. and Fielding, K.J. (eds.), *The Collected Letters of Thomas and Jane Carlyle*.

Carnival

The literal meaning of this term is the 'saying good-bye' to meat at the start of Lent. Traditionally it was a period of feasting during the Christian calendar which reached its climax on Shrove Tuesday, and included many forms of festive inversion of normal behaviour, often comic and mocking of authority. To this extent it signifies a spontaneous eruption of those social forces shortly to be restrained by Lent. This sense of disruption of the norm has brought the term 'carnival' into the language of contemporary critical theory. ▷ Mikhail Bakhtin first used the term to describe a form of festive language which threatens disruption and challenges the social order. The association of carnival with popular energies highlights the political tension between official ▷ ideology and potentially subversive energies. In contemporary critical theory, the carnivalesque points to the polyphonic nature of literary texts, identifying in them a series of different and frequently opposing 'voices'.

▷ Deconstruction: Discourse.

Bib: Bakhtin, M., *Rabelais and His World*.

Carpenter, Edward (1844–1929)
Late-19th-century writer and socialist reformer associated with the ▷ Arts and Crafts Movement and other forms of ▷ anti-industrialism. An undergraduate at Cambridge University from 1864 he was ordained in 1869 but from 1874 onwards he reacted against the social and religious conventions of his time, abandoning the church to follow his idiosyncratic form of primitive Communism. He became a travelling lecturer and part of the newly founded university extension movement which was designed to serve those unable to attend universities. He was greatly influenced by the sensual and passionately democratic writings of US poet Walt Whitman (1819–92) and by the essayist Henry David Thoreau, an advocate of civil disobedience in the face of unjust laws. Whitman, in particular, changed the course of Carpenter's life and his long unrhymed poem *Towards Democracy* (1883; expanded 1905) owes much to Whitman's verse forms. The two met in 1877 during Carpenter's visit to the United States.

Carpenter's form of Communism was based more on social reform and a return to rural crafts than on political revolution, and he shared many of the concerns and enthusiasms of ▷ John Ruskin and ▷ William Morris. He expounded his ideas in a number of prose works including *England's Ideal* (1887), and *Civilisation: its Cause and Cure* (1889; expanded 1912). He supported a number of other causes, many of them controversial, including: women's rights, sexual reform and vegetarianism. His unconventional ideas on sexuality – in particular ▷ homosexuality, which he openly advocated – brought him a number of admirers including the novelists E.M. Forster (1879–1970) and D.H. Lawrence (1885–1930). The psychologist and essayist ▷ Havelock Ellis was deeply impressed with Carpenter's writings on relationships between the sexes – in particular *Love's Coming of Age* (1896) – and homosexuality – *The Intermediate Sex* (1908). These and his other writings on the relationship between art and life, such as *Angel's Wings* (1898) and *The Art of Creation* (1904), were widely read and translated bringing him many visitors to his small farm at Millthorpe, near Chesterfield, where he settled in 1883. He lived there with a succession of working-class acquaintances until 1922. His autobiography, *My Days and Dreams*, was published in 1916.

Bib: Hartley, E., *Edward Carpenter 1844–1924*; Chushichi, T., *Edward Carpenter*, 1844-1929.

Carr, J.L. (1912–95)
Novelist. Carr ran his own publishing company from his home in Kettering, Northamptonshire, England, producing also children's writing, reference works and anthologies of poetry. His novel *A Month in the Country* (1980) won the *Guardian* fiction prize and was adapted for television; its several strands of plot revolve around the uncovering of mysteries from the past, and it makes characteristic use of a first-person narrative by an observing character. *The Harpole Report* (1972) is a satirical comedy about a modern primary school, which makes use of letters and journals as part of the narrative. His other novels are: *A Day in Summer* (1964); *A Season in Sinji* (1967); *How Steeple Sinderby won the F.A. Cup* (1975); *The Battle of Pollock's Crossing* (1985); *What Hetty Did* (1988); *Harpole and Foxberrow, General Publishers* (1992); *The First Saturday in May* (1993).

Carrington (1893–1932)
Carrington (who did not use her first name) was a central figure in the ▷ Bloomsbury Group, and the live-in companion of ▷ Lytton Strachey (whose homosexuality prevented her passion for him from being expressed in marriage or any sexual connection). She is best known for her letters and diaries (published as *Carrington: Letters and Extracts from her Diaries*, edited by David Garnett (1970)). Carrington studied art at the Slade School with many of the more well-known artists of the day, and was herself a gifted painter.

Bib: Carrington, N., *Carrington: Paintings, Drawings and Decorations*.

Carroll, Lewis (Charles Lutwidge Dodgson) (1832–98)
Writer for children; author of *Alice's Adventures in Wonderland* (1865) and *Through the Looking-Glass* (1872). By profession, a mathematics lecturer at Oxford University. The 'Alice' books describe the adventures of a child in dreams, and owe their distinctiveness to the combination of childlike naivety and an authentic dream atmosphere, so that events succeed and language is used with dream logic instead of daylight logic. Thus these two books mark an epoch

in the history of dream literature; the dream state is not merely a pretext for fantasy, but is shown to follow its own laws. Consequently Carroll's two masterpieces have had as much appeal for adults as for children. Dodgson was also a master of ▷ 'nonsense' verse which shows the same characteristics; his most famous poem is *The Hunting of the Snark* (1876). His other book for children, *Sylvie and Bruno* (1889), is less memorable.

▷ Children's books.

Bib: Gardner, M., *The Annotated Alice*; Collingwood, S. D., *The Life and Letters of Lewis Carroll*; Empson, W., 'Alice in Wonderland' in his *Some Versions of Pastoral*; Green, R. L., *The Story of Lewis Carroll*; Sewell, E., in *The Field of Nonsense*; Hudson, D., *Lewis Carroll*.

Carswell, Catherine (1879–1946)
Novelist and critic. Catherine Carswell was a member of the 'Other Bloomsbury' – the circle centred on ▷ D. H. Lawrence which strove to distinguish itself from ▷ Virginia Woolf's more cerebral and self-consciously bohemian group (▷ Bloomsbury). One of the first favourable critics of Lawrence's ▷ *The Rainbow* (her review of the book lost her her job at the *Glasgow Herald* in 1915), Carswell's famous *The Savage Pilgrimage* (1932) is a vindication of Lawrence against ▷ John Middleton Murry's pseudo-Freudian attack on his former friend, *Son of Woman* (1931). Lawrence encouraged Carswell in her novelistic endeavours, including *Open the Door* (1920), *The Camomile* (1922). Her autobiography appeared posthumously in 1952 as *Lying Awake*.
Bib: Delaney, P., *D. H. Lawrence's Nightmare: The Writer and His Circle in the Years of the Great War*.

Carter, Angela (1940–92)
Novelist and short-story writer. From her first novel, *Shadow Dance* (1966), her work was notable for a strain of surrealist ▷ Gothic fantasy, a fascination with the erotic and the violent, and a blending of comedy and horror. *The Magic Toyshop* (1967) is a ▷ Freudian fairy-tale seen through the eyes of an orphaned 15-year-old girl, sent, with her brother and baby sister, to live in the claustrophobic and sinister home of her uncle, a sadistic toymaker. Her new family are examples of Carter's ability to create vivid Dickensian caricatures. After *Several Perceptions* (1968) her work became unequivocally Gothic and anti-realist, centring on the reworking of myth and fairy-tale, and the exploration of aggressive and sexual fantasies. *Heroes and Villains* (1969), *The Infernal Desire Machines of Doctor Hoffman* (1972) and *The Passion of New Eve* (1977) are bizarre and fantastic visions of imaginary worlds, projections of the 'subterranean areas behind everyday experience', with picaresque and pastiche elements. One of her collections of short stories, *The Bloody Chamber* (1979), is a feminist re-working of traditional European fairy-tales; one of these stories, 'The Company of Wolves', was filmed by Neil Jordan in 1984, with screenplay by Angela Carter. Her interest in the politics of sexuality is reflected in her non-fiction work *The Sadeian Woman* (1979), an analysis of the codes of ▷ pornography. Her other novels are: *Love* (1971); *Nights at the Circus* (1984). Story collections are: *Fireworks* (1974); *Black Venus* (1985); *Come Unto These Yellow Sands* (1985) (radio plays). Her last novel was *Wise Children* (1991), a pastiche of family life in theatrical and vaudeville circles, and is perhaps Carter's most comic and accessible text, although overall her powerful work has been categorized as fantasy, ▷ science fiction and anti-realist. Two posthumous colllections have appeared: *Expletives Deleted: Selected Writings* (1992), and *American Ghosts and Old World Wonders* (1993).
Bib: *Flesh and the Mirror: Essays on the Art of Angela Carter*, ed. Lorna Sage.

Carter, Elizabeth (1717–1806)
English correspondent, poet, linguist and ▷ Bluestocking. She lived with her father (who was a preacher at Canterbury cathedral) in Deal, Kent. He taught her Latin, Greek and Hebrew, and she also learned French, Italian, Spanish, German and some Arabic. Skilled also in music, mathematics and geography, she spent her life studying. She translated Epictetus, published a volume of poetry, made ▷ translations from French and Italian, wrote for ▷ Samuel Johnson's ▷ *The Rambler* (March 1750–March 1752) and ▷ *The Gentleman's Magazine* (to which Johnson also contributed). Her correspondence with ▷ Catherine Talbot and ▷ Elizabeth Montagu display a sharp critical intellect. She regarded ▷ Katherine Philips' poetry about friendship between women as 'very moral and sentimental'.

Publications: *Poems on Particular Occassions* (1738); *Poems* (1762); *Letters from Mrs Elizabeth Carter, to Mrs Montagu, between the Years 1755 and 1800* (3 vols) (1817); *Memoirs of the Life of Mrs Elizabeth Carter,* edited by Montagu Pennington (1807); *A Series of Letters between Mrs Elizabeth Carter and Miss Catherine Talbot from the year 1741 to 1770, to which are added, letters from Mrs Elizabeth Carter to Mrs Vessey, between the years 1763 and 1787* (4 vols) (1809).

▷ Fielding, Sarah.

Cartesianism
The philosophy of ▷ Descartes.

Cartland, Barbara (b 1901)
Romantic novelist. According to the *Guinness Book of Records*, Barbara Cartland holds the record as the most prolific living author. She

has written over 300 books, including 27 in 1977 alone, and she has a deeply loyal, overwhelmingly female, readership. Her novels are remarkable for their sheer numbers and similarity of plot and theme: although she has written drama, biography and other non-fiction, she is known to many as the ▷ best-selling author of a conservative brand of romantic fiction which champions the escapist delights of marriage, monogamy and absolute sexual difference. Her heroines are nothing if not feminine, and Cartland's preference for pink is legendary. Whilst she could in no sense be deemed a feminist writer, she has been writing constantly since the 1920s (her first novel was published in 1925), and is something of a figurehead for older women in her fierce commitment to her writing career (despite her obvious wealth and connections to the British aristocracy, and despite the doctrine of her own books which suggests that a woman's identity should be found in her husband rather than in her own work), and in her active attitude to health and fitness (she has recently set up a successful health-food business, and in 1971 published her *Health Food Cookery Book*). Her books include: *Jig-Saw* (1925); *Touch the Stars* (1935); *Love is an Eagle* (1951); *Love Under Fire* (1960); *Men Are Wonderful* (1973); *A Shaft of Sunlight* (1982); *Tempted to Love* (1983); and *A Runaway Star* (1987).

Bib: Cloud, H., *Barbara Cartland: Crusader in Pink*; Radford, J., *The Progress of Romance: The Politics of Popular Fiction*; Anderson, R., *The Purple Heart Throbs*.

Cary, Anne (1615–1671)

Biographer. Anne Cary was one of the younger daughters of the prophetess ▷ Elizabeth Cary, whose ▷ biography she wrote. Anne and her three sisters escaped their father's Protestant household to live with their Catholic mother, and in time they too converted and became nuns. They also helped their two younger brothers to escape. It is most likely that Anne, later Dame Clementia, wrote the biography, although there is a slight possibility that it was another daughter, Mary, since both joined the Benedictine convent at Cambrai where the work was composed. The manuscript work remains with the nuns, but was published in 1861 as *The Lady Falkland, her Life from a ms in the Imperial Archives at Lisle*, ed. Richard Simpson.

▷ Catholicism.

Cary, Arthur Joyce Lunel (1888–1957)

Novelist. He was born in Northern Ireland, where there is a strong tradition of ▷ Protestantism; he was brought up against a background of devout Anglicanism, lost his faith, and later constructed an unorthodox but strongly ethical faith of his own along Protestant lines. He came late to the writing of novels. He studied as an art student in Edinburgh and Paris before going to Oxford University. In 1912–13 he fought, and served in the Red Cross, in the Balkan War. In 1913 he joined the Nigerian political service, fought against the Germans in West Africa in World War I, and returned to the political service after it. His first novel, *Aissa Saved*, appeared in 1932. His subsequent works were: *An American Visitor* (1933); *The African Witch* (1936); *Castle Corner* (1938); *Mister Johnson* (1939); *Charley is my Darling* (1940); *A House of Children* (1941); the trilogy *Herself Surprised* (1941), *To Be a Pilgrim* (1942) and *The Horse's Mouth* (1944); *The Moonlight* (1946); *A Fearful Joy* (1949); another trilogy, *Prisoner of Grace* (1952), *Except the Lord* (1953), and *Not Honour More* (1955); *The Captive and the Free* (1959). *Spring Song* (1960) is a collection of stories. He also produced three volumes of verse, *Verse* (1908), *Marching Soldier* (1945) and *The Drunken Sailor* (1947), and a number of political tracts – *Power in Men* (1939), *The Case for African Freedom* (1941; revised 1944), *Process of Real Freedom* (1943), and *Britain and West Africa* (1946).

In the first 30 years of the 20th century novelists tended to be open to foreign influences and experimental in expression; Cary was among the first distinguished novelists to return to English traditions and direct narrative, although he here and there uses the ▷ stream of consciousness technique of narration evolved by novelists of the 1920s, notably ▷ James Joyce. He is one of the most eclectic of modern novelists, both in method and in subject. In his comedy and his loose, vigorous narrative he has been compared to the 18th-century novelists ▷ Smollett and ▷ Defoe; in his characterization, to ▷ Dickens; in his attitude to human nature, to ▷ D. H. Lawrence; in his concern with heroic morality, to ▷ Joseph Conrad; in his endeavour to present experience with immediacy, to ▷ Virginia Woolf and Joyce; in his interlocking of human destiny and social patterns he might be compared with ▷ George Eliot. His first three novels and *Mister Johnson* are products of his African experience; *Charley is my Darling* and *A House of Children* are novels of childhood, and his two trilogies – thought by some to be his major work – are attempts, in his words, to see 'English history, through English eyes, for the last 60 years'.

Bib: Wright, A., *Joyce Cary: a Preface to his Novels*; Mahood, M. M., *Joyce Cary's Africa*: Fisher, B., *Joyce Cary, the Writer and his Theme*.

Cary, Lady Elizabeth (1585–1639)

Dramatist and translator. At 15 she was married to Henry Cary, Lord Falkland and until 1626 she tried to please her husband in all things, presenting herself as the ideal Renaissance woman – 'chaste, silent and obedient'. During this period she wrote her most well-known work,

The Tragedie of Mariam (pub. 1613), which is the first original drama in English written by an Englishwoman. Written in the ▷ Senecan mode, it recounts the story of King Herod's wife, Mariam, who is eventually executed on his orders, and the plot closely follows Cary's source text, Josephus' *Antiquities*. However, the female characters are subtly changed so that the central issue of the play becomes how an independent woman is caught between the public and political demands of queenship and her personal emotions. In the play it becomes impossible to balance these differing demands and tragedy inevitably ensues. Cary also wrote an unfinished play, *The History of King Edward II* (1627), which shows a major development in her skill at handling lengthy plot sequences and many diverse characters. This latter play was erroneously published under her husband's name in 1680. The crisis in Elizabeth Cary's own attempts to reconcile her public duty to her husband and her private religious convictions occurred in 1626 when she converted to ▷ Catholicism. She became estranged from her husband, who removed their children from her care and reduced her to poverty, but she continued to write. Cary's major scholarly achievement at this time was the translation of the complete works of Jacques Davy, Cardinal Du Perron, which remained unpublished with the exception of Du Perron's reply to James I's attack on his works. This was issued in 1630 with a dedication to Henrietta Maria, in which she clearly takes pride in her female authorship. Few copies survive, as it was ordered to be burned. Later she became reconciled to her husband and was with him at his death in 1633. One of her daughters, probably ▷ Anne Cary, wrote her biography.

▷ Lumley, Lady Joanna; Sidney, Mary.

Bib: Beilin, E.V., *Redeeming Eve*; Travitsky, B. (ed.), *The Paradise of Women*; Cerasano, S. P. and Wynne Davies, M., *Renaissance Drama by Women*.

Cary, Henry (1772–1844)
Translator. Cary's ▷ translation of ▷ Dante's ▷ *Divina Commedia* (1805–14) was immensely influential on the ▷ Romantic poets, in particular ▷ Coleridge.

Bib: King, R.W., *The Translator of Dante: the life, work and friendships of Cary*.

Casanova De Seingalt, Giacomo (1725–98)
An Italian adventurer, author of scandalous Memoirs. His name has become synonymous in English with a 'man who prides himself on his sexual attractiveness'.

'Cassandra' (1859)
A bitter and impassioned discourse on the role and position of women which concludes the second volume (entitled *Practical Deducations*) of Florence Nightingale's (▷ Crimean War) unpublished book *Suggestions for Thought to Searchers after Religious Truth*. The book was originally written in 1852, when Florence Nightingale was thirty-two years old and revised in 1859 after her visit to the Crimea. It was privately printed that year but, on the advice of ▷ John Stuart Mill, it was not published. In the 1840s, before Nightingale became engaged in hospital work, she had rejected marriage and domesticity as incompatible with her own life plan, and 'Cassandra' is a sustained critique of the domestic life of the genteel woman, in particular its 'vacuity', its 'boredom' and its 'false sentiment'. It is reprinted in full in Ray Strachey, *The Cause: a Short History of the Woman's Movement in Great Britain*.

Bib: Woodham-Smith, C., *Florence Nightingale*.

'Castaway, A' (1870)
A 600-line prose poem by ▷ Augusta Webster. The poem is concerned with the issue of prostitution and the ▷ 'fallen woman', and ranges widely in its exploration of the sexual ideology of 19th-century Britain. Unlike ▷ D.G. Rossetti's 'Jenny', published in the same year, Webster's poem speaks from the perspective of the fallen woman rather than that of the voyeuristic observer. '[T]he silly rules this silly world/makes about women' are decried by a speaker who is branded by society as a 'thing of shame and rottenness, the animal/that feeds men's lusts'.

Castiglione, Baldassare (1478–1529)
Italian humanist and author of *Il Cortegiano* (1528), translated as *The Courtier* by ▷ Sir Thomas Hoby in 1561. *Il Cortegiano* is based on Castiglione's years spent as a courtier at Urbino under Guidobaldo da Montefeltro, and takes the form of a debate on what features should be possessed by the perfect courtier. Those qualifications include: swordsmanship, nobility, military understanding, skill in virile sports (hunting, swimming, running and riding), dancing, grace, skill at repartee and telling of stories and anecdotes; the possession of the virtues of prudence, justice, temperance, and fortitude; adaptability, literary knowledge, the ability to write prose and verse, musical proficiency, and the gift of charm.

The two important features of Castiglione's book, and the ones that were to become most influential in England in the ▷ Renaissance period, were his description of *sprezzatura* and his ▷ neo-Platonic conception of love and harmony. *Sprezzatura* implies an ease of manner, a suggestion that what has been done has been achieved effortlessly and without art. Qualities such as these were to play an important role in the definition of courtly behaviour in the late 16th century in England. The neo-Platonic elements (to be found in Book IV of the work) elevate beauty, together with human and divine love, into an ideal of harmony.

Castiglione was to be of enormous importance to contemporary readers of his work in introducing the idea that individuals can create an identity and a personality for themselves. It is this idea which lies, for example, at the heart of ▷ Edmund Spenser's *The Faerie Queene*, and in the poetry, in the earlier period, of ▷ Sir Thomas Wyatt.

Bib: Greenblatt, S., *Renaisssance Self-Fashioning*.

Castle of Indolence, The **(1748)**

A poem in ▷ Spenserian stanzas by ▷ James Thomson. Its first canto deals with the 'pleasing land of drowsyhed' governed by the wizard Indolence. The poet himself ('a bard . . . more fat than bard beseems'), his friends ▷ James Quin the actor, ▷ Lord Lyttelton, and others live a life of sensuous ease in Indolence's castle, until they become bloated and are thrown into a foul dungeon. The second canto depicts the progress of the Knight of Industry from the ancient world to Britain, where he creates the new order of 'social commerce' and imperial expansion, and ends by conquering Indolence and freeing his victims. The poem presents a fascinating mixture of whimsical irony and serious ▷ 'Augustan' didacticism. Lord Lyttelton wrote the stanza describing Thomson himself (I, stanza 68) and the last four stanzas of Canto I were written by Thomson's friend ▷ John Armstrong.

▷ Bard.

Castle of Otranto, The **(1764)**

One of the first so-called ▷ Gothic novels, by ▷ Horace Walpole. The fantastic events are set in the Middle Ages, and the story is full of supernatural sensationalism. The story concerns an evil usurper, a fateful prophecy about his downfall, a mysterious prince disguised as a peasant, and his eventual marriage to the beautiful heroine whom the usurper had intended as his own bride.

Castle of Perseverance

A ▷ morality play, dating from the first quarter of the 15th century which is both the longest example of this dramatic genre (3,649 lines) and the earliest to survive in a near-complete form. The play, which is written in an East Midlands dialect, is designed for a large-scale production, with 35 speaking parts. The single extant play text is unusual in that it contains a staging plan that suggests it should be played in the round, with the Castle of Perseverance at the centre and five scaffolds arranged around the perimeter of the circle. The action depicts the life of Humanum Genus (a figure who represents humankind in general), from birth to death, as he resists and succumbs to the forces of temptation to sin. The action continues after his death and a debate follows in Heaven about whether or not Humanum Genus should be admitted. The play concludes with the acceptance of Humananum Genus into Heaven

Bib: Happé, P. (ed.), *Four Morality Plays*.

Castlereagh, Robert Stewart, Viscount (1769–1822)

Statesman, and Secretary of State for Foreign Affairs during and after the downfall of Napoleon, from 1812 to 1822. This period coincided with a phase of political reaction in Britain, and to the radicals of the time he represented the oppressiveness of the government. Hence the attack on him by ▷ Shelley in the ▷ *Mask of Anarchy*.

Catholic Emancipation, The Act of (1829)

A law by which Roman Catholics in England were awarded full political rights, *eg* to be elected as Members of Parliament. They had been deprived of these rights by legislation of various kinds since the time of the ▷ Reformation. Of particular importance for the rights of Irish Roman Catholics, who, after they lost the Irish Parliament in 1800, bitterly resented their exclusion from Westminster.

▷ Catholicism (Roman) in English literature.

Catholicism (Roman) in English literature

Until the ▷ Act of Supremacy (1534) by which ▷ King Henry VIII separated the English Church from Roman authority, and the more violent revolution in Scotland a little later, both countries had belonged to the European community of Catholic Christendom. This community was a genuine culture, allowing great unity of belief and feeling together with great variety of attitude. In the 16th century this community of cultures broke up, owing not only to the Protestant rebellions but also to the increase of national self-consciousness, the influence of non-Christian currents (especially ▷ Platonism), and the gradual release of various fields of activity – political, commercial, philosophical – from religious doctrine. ▷ The Counter-Reformation after the Catholic Council of Trent (1545–63), even more than the ▷ Reformation, tended to define Roman Catholicism in contrast to Protestantism. Thus, although the dramatists and lyric poets in England from 1560 to 1640 show a plentiful survival of medieval assumptions about the nature of man and his place in the universe, in conflict with newer tendencies of thought and feeling, the Roman Catholic writer in the same period begins to show himself as something distinct from his non-Catholic colleagues. Two clear examples in the 17th century are the poet ▷ Richard Crashaw and the dramatist ▷ Elizabeth Cary. ▷ Milton's epic of the creation of the world, ▷ *Paradise*

Lost, is in many ways highly traditional, but the feeling that inspires it is entirely post-Reformation. By the 18th century, however, religion of all kinds was becoming a mere department of life, no longer dictating ideas and emotions in all fields, even when sincerely believed; it is thus seldom easy to remember that the poet ▷ Alexander Pope was a Roman Catholic. By the 19th century, writers of strong religious conviction were increasingly feeling themselves in a minority in an indifferent and even sceptical world. They therefore tended to impress their work once more with their faith, and this was especially true of the few Catholic writers, since Catholic faith was dogmatically so strongly defined, *eg* the poet ▷ Gerard Manley Hopkins. The century also saw a revival of Anglo-Catholicism. From the time of the Reformation there had been a school of opinion which sought to remain as close to Roman Catholicism as Anglican independence allowed. This wing of the Church was important under ▷ Charles I, but lost prestige until it was revived by the ▷ Oxford Movement. Since then it has remained important in the strength of its imprint on literature. Thus in the 20th century the Anglo-Catholicism of the poet ▷ T. S. Eliot is as conspicuous as and more profound than the Roman Catholicism of the novelists ▷ Evelyn Waugh and ▷ Graham Greene. Amongst writers later in the 20th century, Catholicism is noticeable in the work of ▷ Anthony Burgess and ▷ David Lodge.

Catiline (1611)

A tragedy by ▷ Ben Jonson, about the attempt by Lucius Sergius Catilana to overthrow the government of the Republic of Rome in the 1st century BC. It is an example of Jonson's finest classical scholarship, and was, perhaps, one of the most admired plays in the scholarly and critical circles of the 17th century. Subsequently, *Catiline* has had a more chequered career: early 20th-century criticism suggested that Jonson's overt scholarship impeded the dramatic impact of the tragedy instead of enhancing it, as in the case of his other Roman tragedy, ▷ *Sejanus*. However, late 20th-century rereadings of the play have perceived more value in the political material and in Jonson's ability to present subtle challenges to dominant authority.

Cato the Censor (239–149 BC)

Marcus Porcius Cato, an austere statesman of ancient Rome, famous for his hostility to unnecessary luxury imported from Greece and for his endeavours to maintain traditional Roman simplicity. He was the first important Latin prose writer and the first of the Roman historians. His most important work was *Origines* ('Origins') in which he described the history of Rome and the rise of other Italian states. Later in the Roman Empire, Cato's emphasis on discipline and austerity in private and public life was admired as an ideal from which the sophisticated Romans of the Empire had fallen away.

▷ Latin literature.

Catullus, Gaius Valerius (?84–54 BC)

A Roman lyrical poet, famous especially for his Lesbia cycle of love poems. He was one of the Latin poets who had an extensive influence over English ▷ lyric poets in the 16th and 17th centuries. For instance, ▷ John Skelton's *Book of Philip Sparrow* (1503–7) echoes Catullus on Lesbia and the sparrow; ▷ Ben Jonson's *Song to Celia* is modelled on Catullus, and so is ▷ Andrew Marvell's *To his Coy Mistress*. Jonson, with his sensitive and profound Latin scholarship, was the most important English follower of Catullus and he transmitted the strength and delicacy of the Latin poet to the ▷ 'Cavalier' lyricists and to Marvell. The most important period for Catullus' influence on English poetry was therefore 1600–50.

Causley, Charles (b 1917)

Poet. Causley is Cornish by birth, and his writing has been compared to his contemporary ▷ John Betjeman in its usage of traditional forms, and to the Spanish poet he admires, Federico Garcia Lorca (Spanish literature), in its usage of the ballad form. He draws his influences from pre-modernist poets, particularly ▷ Victorian, ▷ Georgian and World War I poets (Causley himself fought in World War II in the Royal Navy). His first publication was *Hands to Dance* (1951); this was followed by *Union Street* (1957); *Underneath the Water* (1967); *Figure of Eight* (1969); *Figgie Hobbin* (1970); *Collected Poems* (1975).

Caute, David (b 1936)

Novelist and dramatist. Caute is one of a group of English writers, including ▷ Andrew Sinclair and Julian Mitchell, interested in formal experiment, self-referential narrative strategies and the blending of ▷ realism with elements of fantasy. He admires the work of ▷ Christine Brooke-Rose, and is strongly influenced by ▷ Jean-Paul Sartre. *The Confrontation* is a trilogy consisting of a play, *The Demonstration* (produced 1969), a critical essay supposedly by one of the characters in the play, *The Illusion* (1970) and a novel, *The Occupation* (1971). The questioning of the borders of fiction with other discourses is sustained by the competing narrators and narrative strategies within *The Occupation*. *Dr Orwell and Mr Blair* (1994) is a fictional account of the writing of ▷ George Orwell's *Animal Farm*. Caute's works reflect his commitment to Marxism in their analysis of society and history, and his novel *The Decline of the West* (1966) has been criticized as being over-didactic. He has worked as a lecturer, and as literary and arts editor of the ▷ *New Statesman*. Later novels include *News from Nowhere* (1986) and *The Women's Hour* (1991).

Cavalier

A word, meaning 'horseman', which was used for the supporters of ▷ Charles I in the ▷ Civil War. It was first used as a term of reproach against them by their opponents, the supporters of Parliament (▷ Roundheads); in this sense it meant an arrogant and frivolous man of the court. Soon, however, it was accepted with pride by the Royalists themselves. It is a mistake, however, to think of the Cavaliers merely as members of the court and of the aristocracy; many of the aristocracy supported Parliament and many of the Cavaliers were fairly modest country gentlemen who never came near the court. The Cavalier Parliament sat from 1661 to 1678 after the Restoration of ▷ Charles II and was so called because the king's supporters won most of the seats.

▷ Cavalier Poets.

Cavalier Poets

An unhelpful critical term used to encompass the group of poets associated with the court of ▷ Charles I (in particular ▷ Thomas Carew, ▷ Sir John Suckling and ▷ Richard Lovelace), often known as the ▷ Caroline poets. The term is suggestive of a homogeneity amongst this group of poets, and also contains a romanticized implication of their soldierly and martial prowess.

Cave, Jane (1757–1813)

Poet. A devout Anglican with Methodist inclinations, Cave constantly battled against the sense of duty which called her away from her poetry. She published her witty and fast-moving collection, *Poems on Various Subjects* (including an ▷ elegy on her maiden name) in 1783 and revised it in 1786 when she married Thomas Winscom, in an attempt to expunge any material in danger of being considered impious. While the 1786 version contains interesting material in relation to gender, as she focuses on the importance of marriage and motherhood, its tone is heavier and less spirited than the 1783 edition. In later editions she added some ▷ abolitionist writing.

Cavendish, Lady Jane (1621–69) and Lady Elizabeth (1626–63)

Poets and dramatists, devotional and autobiographical writers. The two sisters were the daughters of William Cavendish, Duke of Newcastle, and their stepmother was ▷ Margaret Cavendish, herself an acclaimed author. Although the writings of both women never attain scholarly heights or reveal any individualistic imagination, their work is bold, lively, sometimes satirical and often intimate. The first body of work was composed in unison during their occupation of Welbeck Castle in the ▷ Civil War period; their father was absent, mother dead, and the house passed back and forth between Royalists and Parliamentarians. To occupy their time, and possibly as a future present for their father, they wrote *Poems, Songs and a Pastoral* (1643–5) – to which they added 'a Play' – now in manuscript at the Bodleian Library, Oxford. Their linguistic and grammatical capabilities are virtually nonexistent, but the political ▷ allegory (including an unflattering portrait of their father's new wife, Margaret), the colloquial language and the proto-feminist theme (the two heroines train their suitors to desire equality with, and not domination over, their future wives) make this an important document. Excerpts are available in *Kissing the Rod*, ed. G. Greer (1988), and the play, *The Concealed Fansyes*, was published in 1931, ed. N. C. Starr. Both sisters married, Jane to Charles Cheyne in 1654, and Elizabeth to John Egerton, Earl of Bridgewater. Both continued to write. What we know of Jane's work amounts to several letters and poems, but a large canon did exist and may still be traceable. Elizabeth's devotional writings and her ▷ autobiography were collected by her husband after her death as 'True Coppies of Certaine Loose Papers Left by the Right Honorable ELIZABETH Countesse of BRIDGEWATER' (1663), which is deposited at the British Library. These writings are more sober than those written before their marriages, but still reveal an emotional and intellectual closeness between the women despite the changes in their lives.

Bib: Travitsky, B. (ed.), *The Renaissance Englishwoman in Print*; Cerasano, S. P. and Wynne-Davies, M., *Renaissance Drama by Women*.

Cavendish, Margaret Duchess of Newcastle (1623–73)

Prolific author. Margaret Cavendish wrote poetry, drama, natural philosophy, ▷ biography, orations, letters, science fiction and ▷ autobiography. She was both admired and ridiculed in her lifetime, but seems not to have cared much for either opinion. While appearing modest in her writings, she simultaneously reveals an overwhelming desire for earthly fame. A woman of contradictions and controversy, Cavendish began her life as a tongue-tied lady-in-waiting to ▷ Henrietta Maria, and she followed the queen to exile in France. There she met her husband, William Cavendish (the father of ▷ Jane and Elizabeth Cavendish by his first marriage), whose biography she was later to write. During the ▷ Interregnum, Newcastle's estates were sequestered by Parliament and Margaret was forced to visit Britain in an attempt to raise finances. It was during this stay that she wrote her first book, *Poems and Fancies* (1653), which already showed signs of her later scientific interests; for example, there is a poem on the theory of atoms. After their return to Britain during the Restoration, Margaret continued to write in several genres, covering issues such as women's oppression. Though she was lavishly entertained by the ▷ Royal Society in 1667, it was never suggested that she be elected to a Fellowship. She also wrote an autobiography, *A True Relation of My Birth Breeding and Life*, which was published with *Natures Pictures* (1656). Despite the fact that she was considered eccentric her tombstone at Westminster Abbey provides a fitting epitaph; 'wise, witty and learned lady'.

Bib: Graham, E. et al. (eds.), *Her Own Life*; Hobby, E., *Virtue of Necessity*; Greer, G. (ed.), *Kissing the Rod*; Jones, K., *A Glorious Fame*; Meyer, G. D., *The Scientific Lady in England 1650–1760*.

Caxton, William (?1422–91)
The first English printer. Caxton established his press in Westminster in 1477 (its first product was the *Dictes and Sayings of the Philosophers*) and during the years 1477–91 printed more than 100 texts, including many of his own translations of French works. Of the works he printed, some of the most important include Chaucer's *Canterbury Tales*, ▷ *House of Fame*, ▷ *Troilus and Criseyde* and Thomas ▷ Malory's ▷ *Morte D'Arthur* (the latter appearing in an edited form when printed). Caxton's extensive translation work has earned him a place in the history of the development of English prose.

Before opening his press in Westminster, Caxton worked in the Low Countries for 30 years as an agent for the cloth trade (having been apprenticed in London) and became governor of the English merchant community in Bruges from 1465–9. It was in the Low Countries that he began his other career as a translator and printer (beginning with the *Recuyell of the Historyes of Troyes*, printed in Bruges in 1475) after Caxton had spent two years in Cologne learning the art of printing. ▷ Wynkyn de Worde took over the press after Caxton's death.

Bib: Blake, N. F. *Caxton and his World*.

Celestial City
The name by which Heaven is denoted in ▷ John Bunyan's ▷ *Pilgrim's Progress*. It is contrasted with the ▷ City of Destruction.

Celtic Twilight, The
Originally *The Celtic Twilight* was a book of short stories by the poet ▷ W. B. Yeats, published in 1893. The book dealt with the widespread beliefs in magic and the supernatural which were current among Irish peasants. Since then, the term Celtic Twilight has been widely used to describe the idea that the Celts, especially in Ireland, preserve a mystical, imaginative, poetic vision which the practical and materialistic Anglo-Saxons (both in England and in southern Scotland) have lost. At the end of the 19th century and beginning of the 20th century Yeats and other Irish poets used this conception of the Celtic character as a weapon in the cause of Irish nationalism, and they cultivated ancient Irish legends about heroes such as ▷ Cuchulain and heroines such as Queen Deirdre so as to build up a distinctively Irish literary consciousness to replace the dominant English culture.

Irish literature in English.

C. E. M. A.
The Council for the Encouragement of Music and the Arts was founded in 1939, and financed by the Pilgrim Trust and the Board of Education, to provide entertainments on the home front and provide employment for artists during wartime. Its success strengthened the case for public subsidy for the theatre, and after World War II it became the ▷ Arts Council of Great Britain.

***Cenci, The* (1819)**
A tragedy by ▷ Percy Bysshe Shelley which symbolically depicts the political oppression of his own day in terms of historical events which took place in 1599. Count Francesco Cenci, a Roman nobleman, conceives an incestuous passion for his daughter, Beatrice, and in desperation Beatrice, her brother Bernard, and her stepmother Lucretia conspire to kill the Count. They are discovered, tortured, condemned to death, and executed on the orders of the Pope. Like all the dramas of the ▷ Romantic poets, Shelley's play is an artificial, literary composition. Its ▷ blank verse is highly derivative of that of the ▷ Jacobean playwrights, particularly John Webster (1578–1632).

Censorship and English literature
Systematic censorship has never been an important restriction on English writing except in times of war, but English writers have certainly not always been entirely free.

Until 1640 the monarch exercised undefined powers by the Royal Prerogative. Early in her reign, ▷ Elizabeth I ordered dramatists not to meddle with politics, though this did not prevent Norton and ▷ Sackville's ▷ *Gorboduc*, with its warnings on national disorder. However, Ben Jonson, ▷ Chapman and ▷ Marston found themselves in prison for *Eastward Hoe* (1605) because it offended the Scots friends of ▷ James I. In the reign of ▷ Charles I the term Crop-ears was used for opponents of the king who lost their ears as a penalty for criticizing the political or religious authorities. Moreover, printing was monopolized by the ▷ Stationers' Company, whose charter might be withdrawn by the Crown, so that the monopoly would cease.

In the ▷ Civil War, Parliament was in control of London, and issued an edict that the publication of any book had to be licensed, and it was during the ▷ Interregnum that censorship became most important. The edict provoked ▷ John Milton's ▷ *Areopagitica*, an appeal for freedom of expression. Its influence was not immediate; after the Restoration of the monarchy, Parliament issued a similar edict in the Licensing Act of 1663. The Act was only for a period, however, and in 1696 it was not renewed. The lapsing of the Licensing Act was the starting-point of British freedom of the press, except for emergency edicts in times of war in the 20th century, although in the early 19th century the government attempted a form of indirect censorship by imposing a tax on periodicals which restricted their sale amongst the poor. Nonetheless there are still laws extant which restrict freedom of political expression beyond certain limits.

Also serious are the English laws of libel and of obscene libel. The first exists to punish attacks on private reputation, and the second concerns the defence of sexual morals. The restrictions are serious restraints on opinion because they are vaguely defined, so that it is difficult for a publisher or writer to know when they are being infringed. Moreover, prohibition under obscenity law is frequently reversed, *eg* ▷ D. H. Lawrence's ▷ *The Rainbow* was suppressed for obscenity, but by 1965 it was a prescribed text for study in schools. One of the most celebrated challenges to public morality was the test which Penguin Books' publication of D. H. Lawrence's ▷ *Lady Chatterley's Lover* gave to the 1959 Obscene Publications Act; the 1960 'Trial of Lady Chatterley' altered the way in which the Act could be interpreted, and after it the censorship of writing on sexual grounds became much more difficult. Organizations such as Mary Whitehouse's National Viewers and Listeners Association have thus channelled their pro-censorship energies into images of violence and sexual explicitness on television and in films. The 1984 Video Recordings Act in effect raised the British Board of Film Classification 'from an industrial advisory body to legally empowered censors' (Mandy Merck).

Censorship in the theatre has been a special case since the 18th century. Henry Fielding's comedies attacking the Prime Minister, Robert Walpole, led in 1737 to the restriction of London theatres to two 'patented' ones – Covent Garden and Drury Lane – and the Court official, the Lord Chamberlain, had to license plays. In 1843 the Theatres Act removed the restriction on the theatres and defined the Lord Chamberlain's powers to the restraint of indecency. The Lord Chamberlain's censorship came to an end in 1968.

Since 1979 there has been a gradual return to the censorship of literature and this has been extended to cover the media. The Official Secrets Act is in the process of being rewritten so as to prevent both former Crown servants from revealing information – especially in autobiographies – as well as the media from printing or broadcasting, sometimes in dramatic form, any of this material. A directive was issued in November 1988 to prevent the broadcasting of statements from people of named organizations; again this may have an effect on drama. Also in 1988, the government amended the 1986 Local Government Act to forbid any Local Authority promoting homosexuality through educational means, printed material or support of gay writers. The Broadcasting Standards Council was established in 1988 in order to monitor taste and decency in the media. Finally, a non-governmental form of censorship may be found in the effects of the concentration of ownership in publishing houses and the press, which severely limit the range of writing that is commercially encouraged.

Two organizations attempt to alert people to the extent and dangers of these new censorship laws: the Campaign for Press and Broadcasting Freedom and the Writers' Guild of Great Britain.

Bib: Clare, J., *'Art Made Tongue-tied by Authority': Elizabethan and Jacobean Dramatic Censorship*; Potter, L., *Secret Rites and Secret Writing*; Patterson, A., *Censorship and Interpretation: The Conditions of Reading and Writing in Early Modern England*; Dutton, R., *Mastering the Revels: The Regulation and Censorship of English Renaissance Drama*; Findlater, R., *Banned: A Review of Theatrical Censorship in Britain*; Barker, M., *The Video Nasties: Freedom and Censorship in the Media*; Chester and Dickey (eds.), *Feminism and Censorship*.

Centlivre, Susannah (d 1723)

Actress, dramatist, essayist and poet, known in her time as 'the celebrated Mrs Centlivre'. She survived anti-feminist criticism to become the most prolific dramatist, and one of the most successful authors of either sex, of her day. Two of her comedies, ▷ *The Busie Body* (1709), and ▷ *The Wonder: A Woman Keeps a Secret* (1714), were among the four most frequently performed, apart from those of Shakespeare, in the late 19th century, and her ▷ *A Bold Stroke for a Wife* was popular for most of the 18th century. She excelled in writing intrigue comedy, somewhat in the style of ▷ Aphra Behn, but less sexually explicit, and in a softened tone.

Centlivre's origins are obscure, and her birth date has been placed variously between 1667 and 1680. Her plays suggest a knowledge of French acquired, according to contemporaries, from a tutor. One account has her masquerading as a youth and studying at Cambridge University, before coming to London as a strolling actress.

Still in her teens, Susannah married an army officer, Mr Carroll, who died soon afterwards, apparently in a duel. She began publishing poetry, as well as copies of her letters, genuine

or otherwise, to ▷ George Farquhar and others. Her first play, a cross between a tragedy and a tragi-comedy, called *The Perjur'd Husband*, appeared at ▷ Drury Lane in 1700. In 1707 she married Joseph Centlivre, the 'yeoman of the mouth' to Queen Anne, *ie* the Queen's master cook, but continued to write for most of her remaining life; her total output was 19 plays. The farcical *The Busie Body* immediately became part of the stock repertory, succeeding largely because of the engaging nature of the well-meaning but foolish character, Marplot. A sequel, *Marplot in Lisbon* (1710), was less well received. In other plays, such as *The Gamester* (1705) and *The Basset Table* (1705), Centlivre attacked the fashionable vices of gambling and card-playing. She was closely associated with many of the literary figures of the period, in addition to Farquhar, including ▷ Richard Steele, William Burnaby, ▷ Eliza Haywood, ▷ Delarivière Manley, Catherine Trotter, ▷ Nicholas Rowe ▷ Mary Pix, ▷ Colley Cibber, and the actress ▷ Anne Oldfield, who played leading roles in several of her plays. Her death came after a prolonged period of ill-health, and she was buried at St Paul's church, in Covent Garden.
Bib: Bowyer, J., *The Celebrated Mrs Centlivre*; Morgan, F. (ed.), *The Female Wits*.

Cervantes Saavedra, Miguel de (1547–1616)
Spanish novelist and dramatist, author of ▷ *Don Quixote* (1605, 1616), a satirical romance which is widely regarded as one of the first European novels and which has had a great influence on European literature. Cervantes was born at Alcalà in Spain, was injured at the battle of Lepanto (1571), and spent five years as a prisoner in Algiers after being captured by pirates. Apart from his most famous book, he wrote a pastoral novel, *La Galatea* (1585), a collection of short stories, an adventure tale, *Persiles and Sigismunda* and a number of plays.

Chamberlain's Men, The Lord
The more important of the two leading companies of actors in the reigns of ▷ Elizabeth I and ▷ James I, and the one to which ▷ Shakespeare belonged as both actor and playwright. All companies of actors had to have licences in order to perform, and this meant they had to have the patronage of some leading nobleman, or be attached to the royal household. The Lord Chamberlain's Men seems to have been formed in 1594 by a regrouping of various companies depleted by a plague epidemic. Its patron was Lord Hunsdon who held the office of Lord Chamberlain at the royal court. After the accession of James I, the king himself became its patron, and the company was known as 'the King's Men'. It played at court, and at a number of theatres in London, but its most lasting homes were at the ▷ Globe on the south bank of the Thames, and at the ▷ Blackfriars on the north bank. No doubt it was the popularity of Shakespeare's plays, both at court and among the general public, which gave the company its commanding position, though the quality of ▷ Richard Burbage's acting must also have counted. Its rival was ▷ Edward Alleyn's ▷ Lord Admiral's Men. The King's Men retained its supremacy among the acting companies until the closing of the theatres by Parliament in 1642.
▷ Acting, the Profession of.

Chambers, Sir Edmund (1866–1954)
Scholar. The exceptional breadth and exactness of his work on English literature make his books indispensable reference works for students of English literature in the medieval and Elizabethan periods. His best-known works are: *The Medieval Stage* (1903); *The Elizabethan Stage* (1923), *William Shakespeare* (1930).

Chancellor, The Lord
The office of Lord Chancellor existed before the Norman Conquest (1066) and has always been one of the most important in the state, although its outstanding political importance diminished after the resignation of ▷ Sir Thomas More in 1532, owing to his disagreement with ▷ Henry VIII's religious policy. In the ▷ Middle Ages the Chancellor was the king's secretary and keeper of the seal which authorized public enactments. This closeness to the centre of power often meant that he was second only to the king himself. In the 14th century he took upon himself the task of hearing appeals from subjects who were unable to get justice through the Common Law Courts. He thus became the head of a new Court of Law, the ▷ Court of Chancery, operating a new department of law, called the Law of Equity. The Lord Chancellor also presided over meetings of the Great Council of the Barons in medieval times, and he still presides over its historical descendant, the House of Lords, *ie* the Upper House of Parliament. As the House of Lords contains judges who meet as the highest court of judicial appeal in the country, the Lord Chancellor presides over this too, and in this capacity he is the head of the English judicial system. Finally, the Lord Chancellor is *ex officio* a member of every Cabinet and the nearest equivalent in England to a Minister of Justice.

***Changeling, The* (1622)**
A poetic tragedy by ▷ Thomas Middleton and ▷ William Rowley. Rowley seems in fact to have been responsible for the comic subplot, the value of which is contested; the play is sometimes produced without it, since the connection between the two plots has in the past been considered loose. The main plot, by Middleton, concerns the murder by ▷ Beatrice-

Joanna of her prospective husband, Alonso de Piracquo, so that she can marry another man. To execute the murder she employs one of her admirers, the servant ▷ De Flores, a man who physically revolts her, as if by employing such a man she could herself remain free of the guilt and horror of the crime. Instead, De Flores insists that they are now partners and equals in the sin of bloodshed, and blackmails her into becoming his mistress. The play is one of the most imaginative and individualistic in English after ▷ Shakespeare; it is written in sober, forceful ▷ blank verse that is one of the finest late ▷ Jacobean examples of this medium. The main plot is taken from *God's Revenge against Murther* by John Reynolds. The combination of death, sexual desire and madness makes *The Changeling* an important text for ▷ psychoanalytical criticism.

Chapbooks
The name for a kind of cheap literature which flourished from the 16th to the 18th centuries, after which they were replaced by other forms. They were so called because they were sold by 'chapmen' or travelling dealers. Their contents consisted commonly of traditional romances retold, often from the French, in crude form: ▷ *Bevis of Hampton, Guy of Warwick, Till Eulenspiegel*, ▷ *Doctor Faustus* are examples. Some of them, such as *Dick Whittington*, about the poor boy who ends up as Lord Mayor of London, have survived as children's stories to the present day, and are often the theme of Christmas pantomimes.

Chapman, George (?1559–?1634)
Poet and dramatist. As a poet he is particularly famous for one of the best-known translations of Homer's *Odyssey* and *Iliad*. It is, however, a very free translation, expressing more of Chapman himself, as an Elizabethan intellectual with strong philosophical interests characteristic of his time, than of the spirit of the ancient Greek poet. He saw the epics as heroic exemplifications of moral greatness, in accordance with Stoic ethical categories much later than Homer. In his conception, the great man had strong passions but also strong pride which raised him above the corrupting influences of society; on the other hand, this passion and pride had to be tempered by philosophical fortitude and discipline if they were not to be self-destructive. The dramatic conflicts implied in this view of Homer dominate Chapman's tragedies (1603–31): *The Tragedy of Bussy d'Ambois*; *The Conspiracy and Tragedy of Charles Duke of Byron*; *The Revenge of Bussy d'Ambois*; and *Caesar and Pompey*. Of these the first is acknowledged to be the finest. All of them contain fine passages, and none is without fairly serious imperfections. Bussy is a magnificent portrayal of the heroic man who dominates his morally mean environment but cannot control his passions; in *The Revenge*, Clermont, his brother, is a less successful example of the man of tempered passion and stoical calm. Chapman also wrote eight comedies, including ▷ *May Day*, and he completed the narrative poem ▷ *Hero and Leander*, left unfinished by ▷ Christopher Marlowe.

Bib: Bradbrook, M. C., *George Chapman*; Ide, R. S., *Possessed with Greatness*; Braunmuller, A. R., *National Fictions: George Chapman's Major Tragedies*.

Chapone, Hester (Mulso) (1727–1801)
English poet, letter-writer and ▷ Bluestocking. She learned languages, music and later, French and Latin. In 1745 she published the poem 'To Peace. Written during the late Rebellion, 1745'. For ▷ Samuel Johnson's periodical ▷ *The Rambler* (March 1750–March 1752) she wrote fictional epistles, and she also contributed to *The Adventurer* (1753). She had influence on and opinions about her contemporaries, among them ▷ Samuel Richardson – whom she admired – and Samuel Johnson, as well as ▷ Elizabeth Carter, ▷ Mary Wollstonecraft and ▷ Elizabeth Montagu. She married John Chapone in 1760 but he died within a year. She continued to write, producing *Letters on the Improvement of the Mind* (1773) dedicated to Montagu, *Miscellanies in Verse and Prose* (1775) and *A Letter to a New-Married Lady* (1777). Her works were published in six volumes in 1807.

Characters, Theophrastian
In the early 17th century a form of ▷ essay devoted to the description of human and social types grew up, and collections of such essays were known as 'Characters'. The origin of the fashion is in the brief sketches by one character of another in the comedies of the time and in the verse satires. The tone was always light and often satirical, the basic pattern deriving from the *Characters* of the ancient Greek writer ▷ Theophrastus (3rd century BC); hence the designation 'Theophrastian'.

The fashion continued, though it became less popular, throughout the 17th century and into the 18th. It was eventually superseded by the more elaborate and individualized studies and by the growth of the 18th-century novel.

'Charge of the Light Brigade, The'
A famous poem by Alfred, ▷ Lord Tennyson about the episode in the battle of Balaclava (1854) in the Crimean War, between the British and the French on one side and the Russians on the other. The charge was of great heroism, but was an act of folly based on a misunderstood order. Tennyson celebrates the heroism in vivid terms. Curiously enough his poem 'The Charge of the Heavy Brigade', about an incident in the same battle that was successful, is much less well known, although it has equal merit.

Charke, Charlotte (1713–60)
Actress, manager, puppeteer, dramatist, novelist. Youngest child of the actor, manager, and dramatist ▷ Colley Cibber and his wife, the former actress Katherine Shore (▷ Katherine Cibber). By the time she was four, Charlotte was expressing a preference for masculine clothing, which continued intermittently throughout her later career. In 1730 she married Richard Charke, a musician and actor employed at ▷ Drury Lane. She worked as an actress and dancer at Drury Lane and joined her brother ▷ Theophilus Cibber and other performers in deserting to the ▷ Haymarket Theatre in 1733. There she added more than a dozen male roles to her repertory of female ones, including ▷ Macheath in ▷ *The Beggar's Opera*, George Barnwell in ▷ *The London Merchant*, and Lothario in *The Fair Penitent*. Later she acted Polly in *The Beggar's Opera*, and Millwood in *The London Merchant*. In 1736 Charke joined ▷ Henry Giffard's company at ▷ Lincoln's Inn Fields. From 1737 she managed a succession of businesses, including a puppet theatre. In 1745 she was married again, clandestinely, to John Sacheverell. He died soon afterwards, leaving her penniless, and her subsequent series of odd jobs in London and the provinces did nothing to alleviate her distresses. Estranged from her father for many years, she attempted unsuccessfully to heal the rift in 1755. Her memoirs, *A Narrative of the Life of Mrs Charlotte Charke*, were published in eight instalments, in 1755, and again posthumously, in 1775. Her published works also include a play, *The Art of Management* (1735), the novel *The History of Henry Dumont, Esq., and Miss Charlotte Evelyn* (1756), and two short novels, *The Mercer; Or Fatal Extravagance* (1755) and *The Lover's Treat; Or Unnatural Hatred* (1758).
Bib: Highfill, P. H. Jr., Burnim, K. A. and Langhans, E. A., (eds.) *A Biographical Dictionary of Actors, Actresses, Musicians, Dancers, Managers, and Other Stage Personnel in London 1660–1800*; Todd, J. (ed.), *A Dictionary of British and American Women Writers.*

Charles, Duc d'Orléans (1394–1465)
Poet, and nephew of Charles VI of France, who was captured at the battle of ▷ Agincourt (1415) and spent 25 years as a prisoner in England. During this time he composed the ▷ ballades which form the collection known as the *Livre de Prison*. He is credited with large numbers of English translations of his French poems. On returning to France, he established his court at Blois, which became famous as a literary centre.
▷ Agincourt.
Bib: Steele, R. and Day, M. (eds.), *The English Poems of Charles of Orleans.*

Charles I
King of Great Britain and Ireland (1625–49). He had limited intellectual abilities, and the causes of religious and economic conflict were so strong during his reign that it ended in civil war, his defeat and his execution. Together with his wife, Henrietta Maria, he created around him a court of taste, refinement and distinction. His connoisseurship led to a fine collection of pictures, later dispersed by ▷ Oliver Cromwell, who sold them to obtain international currency. His patronage of the Flemish artist Van Dyck resulted in some highly flattering portraits that have done the king much good with posterity. His personal qualities, his tragic end and his nobility in its endurance were the basis of a strong sentimental, sometimes even a religious, devotion to his memory. For example, there are churches dedicated to Charles the Martyr in a few places (*eg* Tunbridge Wells) in Britain.
▷ Civil Wars.
Bib: Carlton, C., *Charles I.*

Charles II
King of Great Britain and Ireland (1660–85). The Restoration of the monarchy brought him back from exile after the ▷ Interregnum following the execution of his father, ▷ Charles I, in 1649. Politically unscrupulous, he was nonetheless one of the most intelligent kings in English history. His court was a centre of culture and wit as well as of moral licentiousness. His lack of scruple enabled him to raise the monarchy to a new pitch of popularity, in spite of the growing strength of Parliament and its increasing independence of royal authority. His was the last royal court in England to be a centre of cultural vitality.
▷ Cavalier Poets.
Bib: Fraser, A., *King Charles II.*

Chartist movement
A working-class political movement which flourished between 1837 and 1848. It arose because the Reform Bill of 1832 had reformed Parliament in favour of middle-class political rights but had left the working-class without them. The Chartists wanted Parliament to be closely responsible to the nation as a whole and to reform an electoral system according to which the poor were excluded from membership of Parliament and denied the right to vote others into membership by their lack of the necessary property qualification. Some regions were more heavily represented in Parliament than others and all voting was subject to bribery or intimidation because votes had to be declared publicly. Consequently they put forward their Charter containing Six Points: 1 votes for all males; 2 annually elected Parliaments (instead of general elections every seven years); 3 payment of Members of Parliament (so that poor men could have political careers); 4 secret voting (voting 'by ballot'); 5 abolition of the property qualification for candidates seeking election;

6 electoral districts equal in population. The movement seemed to be a complete failure, but all these points became law between 1860 and 1914 except the demand for annually elected parliaments. The Chartists attracted an ardent following but they were badly led. Allusions are made to them in those novels between 1840 and 1860 which were concerned with 'the Condition-of-the-People Question', *eg* ▷ *Sybil* by ▷ Benjamin Disraeli. This serious discussion of the social crisis of the second quarter of the 19th century was greatly stimulated by ▷ Thomas Carlyle's essay *Chartism* (1839), one of his fiercest and most influential writings.

Chaste Maid in Cheapside, A (1613)
A comedy by ▷ Thomas Middleton. It is one of the ▷ 'citizen comedies' of the ▷ Jacobean period, with a characteristic theme of a merchant (Yellowhammer) scheming against Sir Walter Whorehound, a dissolute landed gentleman, so as to secure marriage with his daughter and entry into the landowning class, while Whorehound in turn tries to marry off his mistress to Yellowhammer's son and thereby gain Yellowhammer's money. These intrigues of the gentry and the citizenry against each other were a common theme of the comedies of the time. The play makes mock of both classes, and has a characteristic robustness in the way in which it uses the social ▷ satire at a deeper level than the merely topical relationships, so as to bring out basic types of human greed, vanity and lust, in the tradition of ▷ Ben Jonson's 'comedy of humours'.

▷ Humours, Comedy of.

Chatterton, Thomas (1752–70)
Poet. Chatterton's father, a schoolmaster in Bristol, died before he was born, and he was educated at a charity school, then apprenticed to an attorney. He wrote precociously in all the genres of the day: mock-heroic couplets, ▷ Hudibrastics, political satire imitative of Charles Churchill (1731–64) oriental eclogues in the manner of ▷ William Collins (1721–59) and elegiac poetry in the manner of ▷ Thomas Gray. But his most original compositions were pseudo-medieval (▷ medieval literature) concoctions concerned with 15th-century Bristol. Influenced by the fashionable medievalism of ▷ James Macpherson, ▷ Thomas Percy, and ▷ Horace Walpole, Chatterton claimed to have discovered lyric poems and a 'tragycal enterlude' by a 15th-century monk, Thomas Rowley, among the documents of the church of St Mary Redcliffe, where his uncle was sexton. The publisher Dodsley rejected the pieces, but they deceived Walpole for a time, and the poet was encouraged to move from Bristol to London. He published some non-medieval poems in journals under his own name, and a burletta (comic opera) by him was accepted for performance at Drury Lane. Then, at the age of 17, in a fit of despondency, he poisoned himself with arsenic.

It was not until seven years later that the Rowley poems were definitively unmasked by the Chaucerian scholar, Thomas Tyrrwhitt. Their language is an artificial amalgam of medieval, Elizabethan and contemporary elements, typical of the omnivorous eclecticism of the period. But occasionally, as in 'An Excelente Balade of Charitie', Chatterton succeeds in evoking a unique exotic world of his own. During the Romantic period Chatterton's reputation lost all associations with hackwork and only the 'medieval' lyrics were remembered. His early death took on a mythical quality, making him a symbol, even a stereotype, of youthful poetic genius neglected by a prosaic world. ▷ William Wordsworth referred to Chatterton as a 'marvellous Boy' in *Resolution and Independence*. ▷ Samuel Taylor Coleridge wrote *A Monody on the Death of Chatterton*. ▷ John Keats dedicated his ▷ *Endymion* to his memory, and ▷ Percy Bysshe Shelley compared him with Keats in ▷ *Adonais*.
Bib: Kelly, L., *The Marvellous Boy: The Life and Myth of Thomas Chatterton*.

Chatwin, Bruce (1940–1989)
Novelist and travel writer. Chatwin was born in Sheffield and worked as an art consultant and journalist. His first publication, *In Patagonia* (1977), was a travel book and won the Hawthornden Prize; it was followed by *The Songlines* (1981). His novel *On the Black Hill* (1982) is about a rural community on the Welsh borders and the story is centred on two farmers who are identical twins. His other novels are *The Viceroy and Ouidah* (1980), *Utz* (1988), *What Am I Doing Here* (1990). Also: *Nowhere is a Place: Travels in Patagonia* (with Paul Theroux, 1992). A collection of his photographs and notebooks, edited by Francis Wyndham, was published in 1993.

Chaucer, Geoffrey (c 1340–1400)
Influential poet of the 14th century who occupies a privileged place in the history of English literary traditions because his work has been continuously transcribed, published, read and commented upon since his death.

He was the son of a London vintner, John Chaucer (1312–68), and served in the court of ▷ Edward III's son Lionel (later Duke of Clarence). In 1359 he was taken prisoner while fighting in France with Edward III, and ransomed. His wife, Phillipa de Roet, whom he married perhaps in 1366, was the sister of ▷ John of Gaunt's third wife, Katherine Swynford. Substantial records exist of Chaucer's career in royal service, as a member of the court and diplomat. He is first recorded as a member of the royal household in 1367 and he made several diplomatic journeys in France and Italy, which perhaps gave him the opportunity to gain access to the work of important 14th-century Italian writers (▷ Dante, ▷ Petrarch, ▷ Boccaccio). He was appointed controller of customs in the Port of London in 1374, was 'knight of the shire' of Kent in 1386 (*ie*, represented Kent in the House of Commons), and was appointed clerk of the king's works in 1389 and then deputy forester of the king's forest at Petherton in Somerset in 1391. He returned to London for the last years of his life and was buried in Westminster Abbey. His tomb, erected some time later (1555?) gives the date of his death as 25 October 1400.

The upward mobility of Chaucer's family is clear not only from the professional life of Chaucer himself but also from that of his son Thomas, who married into the nobility and became one of the richest men in England at the time. Thomas' daughter, Alice, married William de la Pole, Duke of Suffolk, and their grandson, John, Earl of Lincoln, was heir designate to the throne of ▷ Richard III. We may only speculate about the part Chaucer's literary activities played in advancing his social status and that of his family. Although more records survive of Chaucer's professional life than any other English writer of the time, the records do not contain any references to his literary labours. Thus dating Chaucer's literary works is an exercise in hypothesis and depends largely on information provided in Chaucer's own list of works, notably in the prologue to the ▷ *Legend of Good Women*, and in the prologue to the ▷ *Man of Law's Tale*.

Chaucer's literary work is notable for its range and diversity. It explores the possibilities of a number of different literary genres, and includes ▷ dream-vision poems (the ▷ *Book of the Duchess*, the ▷ *House of Fame*, the ▷ *Parliament of Foulys*, the ▷ *Legend of Good Women*), a classical love-tragedy (▷ *Troilus and Criseyde*), story-collections (the *Legend of Good Women*, and the ▷ *Canterbury Tales*, which itself encompasses a great range and variety of genres), as well as shorter lyrical texts, translations (of ▷ Boethius' *Consolation of Philosophy* and probably the first part of the English translation of the ▷ *Roman de la Rose*) and scientific treatises (on the Astrolabe, and the *Equatorie of the Planets*, which is now generally accepted as Chaucer's work).

A distinctive feature of Chaucer's literary work is that it engages not only with French and Latin literary traditions but also with the work of earlier and contemporary Italian writers (notably ▷ Boccaccio). His work became a reference point for later poets in English, and is frequently discussed in terms which suggest it played a founding role in the establishment of an English literary tradition – a point neatly underlined by the subsequent establishment of Poet's Corner in Westminster Abbey, around Chaucer's tomb.

▷ Edward III; John of Gaunt.

Bib: Benson, L., et al. (eds.), *The Riverside Chaucer*; Boitani, P. and Mann, J. (eds.), *The Cambridge Chaucer Companion*; Crow, M. C. and Olsen, C. C. (eds.), *Chaucer Life Records*.

Chekhov, Anton Pavlovich (1860–1904)

Russian dramatist and short-story writer. In his last four plays (*The Seagull, Uncle Vanya, Three Sisters, The Cherry Orchard*) he evolved a dramatic form and idiom of dialogue which were highly original and had a great influence on 20th-century drama. His originality lay in his combination of faithfulness to the surface of life with poetic evocation of underlying experience. This he achieved partly by exploiting the character of human conversation when it seems to be engaged in communication, but is actually concerned with the incommunicable. This leads on to the non-communicating dialogue in the work of playwrights such as Beckett and Pinter, when the characters on the stage alternately baffle and enlighten the audience by the undercurrents implicit in their words. The realism of Chekhov's stories is similarly subtle and original; they have similar faithfulness to surface combined with delicate artistic pattern, giving significance to seeming irrelevance and slightness of incident. An outstanding exponent of the method in English is the New Zealand writer ▷ Katherine Mansfield.

Bib: Magarshack, D., *The Plays of Anton Chekhov*; Styan, J. L., *Chekhov in Performance*.

Cheshire Cheese, The

A tavern off Fleet Street in London, and a favourite resort of ▷ Ben Jonson, and, after it was rebuilt, of ▷ Samuel Johnson and of ▷ Yeats, who liked to claim it as a haunt. It still exists.

Chester Cycle

A ▷ cycle of plays, covering episodes from Christian history from the Creation to the Last Judgement, performed at Chester in Whitsun week during the 15th and 16th centuries (over Monday, Tuesday, Wednesday), the last recorded performance being in 1575. The style and themes of its 25 pageants are more homogeneous than those found in the other major play cycles of ▷ York, ▷ Wakefield and ▷ N-Town. **Bib**: Lumiansky, R. M. and Mills, D. (eds.), *The Chester Mystery Cycle*.

Chesterfield, Philip Dormer Stanhope, 4th Earl of (1694–1773)

Statesman, diplomat and man of letters. In his youth he made 'a grand tour' of Europe, and on his return was made a gentleman of the bedchamber to the Prince of Wales, later George II. He became a Whig member of parliament for St Germains in Cornwall in

1715, and for Lostwithiel in 1722. But in 1726 his father's death brought him his title, and he moved to the House of Lords. He also served as ambassador to The Hague, 1728–32, and as Lord Lieutenant of Ireland, 1745–6. He became an opponent of ▷ Sir Robert Walpole, and changed from a Whig to a Tory in consequence. Chesterfield moved in literary circles, as a friend of ▷ Addison, ▷ Pope, ▷ Swift, ▷ Gay, ▷ Voltaire, ▷ Montesquieu and others. But he antagonized ▷ Samuel Johnson, who had vainly appealed to him for help in publishing his ▷ *Dictionary*. When Chesterfield later praised the work, Johnson revenged himself with a disdainful letter, saying Chesterfield's support had been delayed so long, 'till I am indifferent, and cannot enjoy it . . . till I am known, and do not want it'. But Chesterfield is known chiefly through his copious correspondence, and particularly the letters which he wrote to his son and his godson, both named after him. In them he offered advice (▷ advice literature) based on his own worldly experience: how to dress, how to behave, and how to succeed in society. The emphasis was on acquiring a wide range of accomplishments without becoming too learned in any particular thing and, above all, to demonstrate good breeding. His son was also advised to make good connections in order to prosper. Chesterfield's letters have been criticized for passages which appeared to defend superficiality, or even to display a less than perfect concern with morality. But he was also considered a man of great wit, who wrote with agreeable style.
Bib: Dobree, B. (ed.), *Letters of Chesterfield*, 6 vols.

Chesterton, G. K. (Gilbert Keith) (1874–1936)
An extremely versatile writer of essays, stories, novels, poems; Chesterton is best described as a polemicist, since polemics entered into everything he wrote, whether it was detective stories (the Father Brown series; 1911, 1914, 1926, 1927), fantasy (*The Man who was Thursday*, 1908), comic verse, or religious studies such as *St Francis of Assisi* (1923) or *St Thomas Aquinas* (1933). He wrote against life-denial, whether manifested in the denial of humanity in the Victorian political economy, or the sceptical withdrawal into ▷ aestheticism of the 1890s. His basis of attack was a conviction that life is to be enjoyed with all the faculties; he also had the belief that such fullness of life required a religion large enough to comprehend all the spiritual and moral potentialities in man, and he found this religion in Roman Catholicism. He was not received into the Catholic Church until 1922, but from *The Napoleon of Notting Hill* (1904) – a fantasy about a war between London boroughs – he shows the romantic medievalism which for him was a large part of the appeal of Catholicism. The period of his greatest influence was probably between 1900 and 1914, when he belonged to a group of vigorous witty polemicists, including ▷ George Bernard Shaw, ▷ H. G. Wells, ▷ Hilaire Belloc. He was from the first an ally of the Catholic Belloc against the agnostic socialists, Wells and Shaw. He had in common with both his antagonists a genius for vivid particularity strongly reminiscent of the Victorian novelist Charles Dickens; with Shaw he shared a delight in witty and disturbing paradox, which he used as Shaw did, to startle his readers out of the acceptance of platitudes into genuine thinking. In spite of his homely, zestful humanity, one notices nowadays a journalistic superficiality about Chesterton's work, as though he felt that his audience demanded entertainment as the indispensable reward for receiving enlightenment, and this may account for the neglect of his work since his death.

Politically, with Belloc, he preached an alternative to socialism in Distributism, a vision of a society of small proprietors. His critical work perhaps survives better than his other work; it included studies of Browning (1903), Dickens (1906), Thackeray (1909), ▷ Chaucer (1932), and *The Victorian Age in Literature* (1913). He is otherwise perhaps best read in selection, for instance in *Selected Stories* (ed. K. Amis) and *G. K. Chesterton: A Selection from his Non-fictional Prose* (selected by W. H. Auden).

▷ Catholicism in English literature; Detective fiction.
Bib: Belloc, H., *The Place of Chesterton in English Letters*; Canovan, H., *Chesterton, Radical Populist*; Hollis, C., *The Mind of Chesterton*.

Chettle, Henry (1560–1607)
An Elizabethan playwright and printer who collaborated with a number of his contemporaries such as ▷ Drayton, and is the sole author of a ▷ revenge drama, *Hoffman* (1602). He is best remembered for printing ▷ Robert Greene's famous attack of ▷ Shakespeare and ▷ Marlowe, *A Groatsworth of Wit* (1595). He subsequently apologized to Shakespeare in his *Kind-Heart's Dream*, praising Shakespeare's 'uprightness of dealing' and his 'honesty'.
Bib: Jenkins, H., *The Life and Works of Henry Chettle*.

Chevalier of St George
'Chevalier' is French for 'horseman' and in medieval France was equivalent to knight. After the ▷ Glorious Revolution of 1688 and the ▷ Act of Settlement of 1701 excluding the ▷ Catholic members of the House of ▷ Stuart from the English throne, James Stuart, the son of ▷ James II, was known as the Chevalier of St George as a courtesy title; he was otherwise known as the ▷ Old Pretender (*ie* claimant to the throne) in distinction from his son, Charles Stuart, known both as the 'Young Pretender' and the 'Young Chevalier'.

Chevy Chase, The Ballad of
A famous English ▷ ballad, probably dating from the 15th century. It issues from the border wars which were intermittent between England and Scotland from the 14th to 16th centuries. Lord Douglas, head of the principal Scottish border family, attacks Percy, Earl of Northumberland, who has defied him by coming for a three days' hunt on the Scottish side of the border. Both Percy and Douglas are killed in the ensuing battle. The ballad has been well known since Bishop ▷ Percy published it in his *Reliques* in 1765, but, earlier, ▷ Joseph Addison had praised the poem in the ▷ *Spectator* as had ▷ Sir Philip Sidney in his *Apologie*.

Child labour
The use of children in agricultural labour was widespread, and not necessarily pernicious, up till the 19th century, but their use in factories and mines after 1800 and during the Industrial Revolution aroused widespread indignation and led to reform. The Factory Act of 1833 limited their working hours in ▷ factories and in 1847 their hours were restricted to ten. In 1842 the Mines Act forbade the employment of women and of children under ten underground; this evil was very old, but had become much severer with the expansion of the coal industry in the 18th century after the invention of steam-powered machinery. An old abuse, too, was the employment of little boys to clean chimneys; the boys were made to climb inside the chimneys. Public indignation against the practice was aroused by ▷ Charles Kingsley's ▷ *Water Babies* (1863), but it was only effectively prohibited in 1875. The Victorian age saw the abolition of the worst abuses of children, as well as the establishment of the first universal system of ▷ education in England. Since 1939 it has been illegal to employ children under fifteen years old.

***Childe Harold's Pilgrimage* (1812–18)**
A semi-autobiographical poem in ▷ Spenserian stanzas by ▷ Lord Byron, describing the wanderings of a young man seeking escape from the *ennui* caused by over-indulgence at home. Cantos I and II (1812) describe his wanderings around the Mediterranean, ending with a lament for Greece enslaved by the Turks. The writing is sometimes very slapdash. Cantos III (1816) and IV (1818) are poetically superior, being less concerned with an affectation of solitude and mystery, and focusing on what really interested the poet: social activity and the stir of great events. In the third canto occurs the famous description of the interrupted ball in Brussels on the eve of the battle of Waterloo (stanzas xxi–xxv). In the fourth canto Byron abandons the fictional protagonist and writes in the first person, evoking the large reversals of history, as he contemplates the great Italian cities of Venice, Rome and Florence. The long meditation in the Coliseum at night, with its evocation of the dying gladiator, is very moving in a broad, rhetorical way. The poem was very popular at the time, not least for its 'Byronic' protagonist – self-regarding, proud and mysterious. Today, perhaps unfairly, it is less highly regarded than Byron's comic works in ▷ *ottava rima*.

'Childe Roland to the Dark Tower Came'
One of the most famous poems by ▷ Robert Browning. He called it a 'Dramatic Romance' and it was published in ▷ *Men and Women*, 1855. It describes a journey or 'quest' (in the tradition of medieval knightly romances) which has lasted so long that Roland is almost in despair. In the poem, he reaches his destination, the tower, which stands in the middle of a great wasteland full of the signs of death. The poem ends with his sounding his horn to signal his arrival. In spite of its sombreness, the poem has a vigour of style, characteristic of Browning, which communicates itself as the most important part of its otherwise cloudy meaning. Browning, too often associated with facile optimism, is the poet here of courage and energy in the face of desperate circumstances.

The title is a quotation from Shakespeare's *King Lear* (1605), where it may be an echo of a still older ballad.

▷ Medievalism.

Children in the Wood (Babes in the Wood)
A ballad (1593) well-known for its story, which is often retold in books of children's fairy tales (▷ Children's books). It concerns the plot of a wicked uncle to murder his little nephew and niece, whose property he means to seize. The hired murderers abandon the children in the forest, where they perish and the birds cover them over with leaves. The wicked uncle is then punished by God, with the loss of his son, his wealth and eventually his life.

Children of St Paul's
▷ Paul's, Children of St.

Children's books
Until the 19th century, children were not regarded as beings with their own kind of experience and values, and therefore did not have books written specifically for their entertainment. The literature available to them included popular versions of old romances, such as ▷ *Bevis of Hampton*, and magical folk-tales, such as ▷ *Jack the Giant-Killer*, which appeared in ▷ chapbooks. Children also read such works as ▷ John Bunyan's ▷ *Pilgrim's Progress*, ▷ Daniel Defoe's ▷ *Robinson Crusoe* (1719), and Jonathan Swift's ▷ *Gulliver's*

Travels (1726); ▷ Perrault's collection of French ▷ fairy-tales appeared in English as *Mother Goose's Fairy Tales* in 1729.

During the Romantic period it was recognized that childhood experience was a world of its own and, influenced, in many cases, by Rousseau's ideas on education, books began to be written especially to appeal to children. Such works as Thomas Day's *Merton and Sandford* (1783–9), Maria Edgeworth's *Moral Tales* (1801) and Mrs Sherwood's *The Fairchild Family* (1818) usually had a serious moral tone, but showed an understanding of a child's mind that was lacking from Anne and Jane Taylor's cautionary tales in verse (later to be parodied by ▷ Hilaire Belloc in *The Bad Child's Book of Beasts* etc.).

It was not until the Victorian period that writers began extensively to try to please children, without attempting to improve them at the same time. ▷ Edward Lear's *Book of Nonsense* (1846) and ▷ Lewis Carroll's *Alice* books combine fantasy with humour. Romance and magic had a strong appeal to the Victorians, and fairy stories from all over the world were presented in versions for children. The collection of the brothers ▷ Grimm had appeared in 1824 as *German Popular Stories* and ▷ Hans Christian Andersen's original compositions were translated into English in 1846. Andrew Lang's *Fairy Books* were published later in the century. Adventure stories for boys, such as ▷ Captain Frederick Marryat's *Masterman Ready* (1841) and ▷ Robert Louis Stevenson's ▷ *Treasure Island* (1883) became a flourishing genre, but the tradition of moral improvement persisted in such books as ▷ Charles Kingsley's ▷ *Water Babies* (1863). Children's literature is a field to which women writers have made a notable contribution; in the latter half of the 19th century enduring classics were written by Mrs Molesworth (*The Tapestry Room*, 1879), Louisa May Alcott (*Little Women*, 1868), Anna Sewell (*Black Beauty*, 1877) and E. Nesbitt (*The Story of the Treasure-Seekers*, 1899, etc.).

Animals have loomed large in children's books. Beatrix Potter's *Peter Rabbit* appeared in 1902 (doing much to establish the book where text and illustrations were of equal importance), Kenneth Grahame's *The Wind in the Willows* in 1908, the first of Hugh Lofting's *Dr Dolittle* books in 1920, ▷ A. A. Milne's *Winnie the Pooh* in 1926 and the first of Alison Uttley's *Little Grey Rabbit* books in 1929. Charges of anthropomorphism seem to have had little effect on the popularity of these books, and another writer whose lack of critical acclaim has hardly diminished her sales is Enid Blyton. Recently, allegations of racism and sexism have been laid against old favourites, and there have been efforts to bring children's literature into touch with 20th-century problems, such as single-parent families and racial prejudice. As well as writers (*eg* Noel Streatfield and Nina Bawden) who have concerned themselves with stories about everyday life, there have been others who have continued the tradition of magical fantasy. ▷ Tolkien's *The Hobbit*, Philippa Pierce's *Tom's Midnight Garden*, ▷ C. S. Lewis' *Tales of Narnia*, Ursula Le Guin's stories about *Earthsea* and the work of Alan Garner all fall into this category. In a rather different field, Rosemary Sutcliff has won recognition for the careful research underlying her historical novels. Mention should also be made of Ladybird books, which, in addition to their fiction publications, have done much to introduce children to a wide variety of topics, from music to magnetism. Following Robert Louis Stevenson's *A Child's Garden of Verses* (1885), children's verse has been written by ▷ Belloc, ▷ De La Mare, ▷ A. A. Milne, ▷ Ted Hughes and Charles Causley.

Chippendale, Thomas (1718–79)
A famous furniture designer, noted for the combination of elegance and solidity in his designs. His work was very much imitated so that 'Chippendale style' is the most familiar pattern of 18th-century furniture in England.

Cholmondeley, Mary (1859–1925)
English novelist, born in Hodnet, Shropshire, the daughter of Emily Beaumont and the Rev. Hugh Cholmondeley. She never married and lived all her life with her family. Her first novel *The Danvers Jewels* was published in 1887. *Charles Danvers* (1889); *Diana Tempest* (1893) and *The Devotee* (1897) followed. These were popular, but it was ▷ *Red Pottage* (1899) that brought Cholmondeley public recognition. Its satirical treatment of the clergy caused a minor scandal, with churchmen denouncing the book, while critics and journalists defended its humour and accuracy. None of Cholmondeley's six later novels was as successful. She faded from view, and published her last book, *The Romance of His Life* in 1921.
Bib: Lubbock, P., *Mary Cholmondeley: A Sketch from Memory*.

Chrétien de Troyes (fl 1170–90)
French writer of sophisticated and influential courtly narratives. Nothing certain is known of his life but he seems to have had the patronage of Marie, Countess of Champagne (1160–80), and then Phillip of Flanders (c 1180–90). Five of his Arthurian romances survive: *Erec et Enide, Cligés, Yvain* (later translated into Middle English and other European vernaculars), *Le Chevalier de la Charrette* (which centres on the experiences of ▷ Lancelot and which seems to have been left unfinished by Chrétien), *Perceval* (Chrétien's Grail story which was left unfinished but was continued by later writers). In the prologue to *Cligés*, he claims to have written a number of other poems on Ovidian subjects, including an art of love, and a version of the ▷ Tristan story. ▷ Arthur, King.

Bib: Owen, D. D. R. (trans.), *Chrétien de Troyes: Arthurian Romances*.

***Christabel* (1816)**
An unfinished narrative poem by ▷ Samuel Taylor Coleridge, the first part written in 1797 and the second in 1800. The story derives from the popular folk-ballad tradition. Christabel, daughter of Sir Leoline, finds a distressed lady, Geraldine, in the woods and takes her back to the castle, unaware that she is really an enchantress. Though she discovers Geraldine's nature, Christabel is forced by a spell to keep silent before her father. There is a strange confusion of sympathies in the author's treatment of the relationship between the two women, and between them and Sir Leoline. The poem is in a metrically experimental form reminiscent of Anglo-Saxon alliterative metre, each line having four stresses but a varying number of syllables. Even in its fragmentary state it achieves a compulsively anxious, but at the same time exhilarating, effect.

Christie, Agatha (1890–1976)
▷ Detective fiction writer (who also wrote romantic novels as Mary Westmacott), Agatha Christie is one of the most well known, and certainly the most widely translated, of British writers this century. Her large range of intricate but formulaic novels gained her a vast readership, and they have been widely filmed, televised and staged (*The Mousetrap*, 1952, is the longest-running stage play, still showing in London's West End). Even though she continued to write from the 1920s until her death, most of her work evidences a nostalgia for the pre-war England of the prosperous classes with which she is aptly identified, the setting for novels populated by abnormal, criminal psyches (crime is never, for Christie, socially justifiable) and brilliant, sexless sleuths (Hercule Poirot and Miss Marple being the most famous). Her books include: *The Mysterious Affair at Styles: A Detective Story* (1920); *The Murder of Roger Ackroyd* (1926); *Murder on the Orient Express* (1934); *Death on the Nile* (1937); *Ten Little Niggers* (1939), later published as *Ten Little Indians*; *Sparkling Cyanide* (1945); *Ordeal by Innocence* (1958) and *Endless Night* (1967).
Bib: Keating, H. (ed.), *Christie: The First Lady of Crime*; Sanders, D. and Lovallo, L. (eds.), *The Agatha Christie Companion*; Shaw, M. and Vanacker, S., *Reflecting on Miss Marple*.

***Christmas Carol, A* (1843)**
A story by ▷ Charles Dickens, about a miser, Scrooge, who is converted by a series of visions from a condition of mercantile avarice and misanthropy into an embodiment of the Christmas spirit, with its generosity and goodwill to humankind in general. It presents entertainingly Dickens' celebration of the virtues associated with Christmas (especially characteristic of his early work). He represented these virtues as the cure for the puritan narrowness of feeling and inhumanity of outlook which were the dark side of Victorian commerce. Compare the Christmas scenes in his ▷ *Pickwick Papers* (1837) and the comments of Sleary in ▷ *Hard Times*.

Chronicle Plays
▷ History Plays.

Chronicles of Carlingford, The
The collective title of a group of novels by ▷ Margaret Oliphant, including *Salem Chapel* (1863); *The Rector and the Doctor's Family* (1863); *The Perpetual Curate* (1864); *Miss Marjoribanks* (1866) and *Phoebe Junior* (1876). *The Chronicles* were Oliphant's most popular works, focusing mainly on religious life in a country town. They show the influence of Walter Scott (1771–1832), ▷ Anthony Trollope and ▷ George Eliot, although like much of Oliphant's work, they appear somewhat hurriedly written.

Chudleigh, Lady Mary (1656–1710)
English poet and polemicist. She replied to John Sprint's misogynist sermon *The Bride-Woman's Counsellor*. Although some modern critics think such extreme cases as Sprint's of the insistence on male superiority were read as a joke, Chudleigh replied seriously with *The Ladies Defence*, a verse defence of women, published in the second edition of her *Poems on Several Occassions* (1703). She also published a collection of *Essays Upon Several Occassions* (1710). She wrote *The Ladies Defence* for women, she says, 'out of the tender Regard I have for your Honour, joyn'd with a just Indignation to see you so unworthily us'd'. The poem borrows the character of Sir John Brute from ▷ Vanbrugh's ▷ *The Provok'd Wife*, a play dealing in the misfortunes of mismarriage. Sir John is suitably brutal, but the Parson more legalistically insidious, asserting that for women, 'Love and Respect, are, I must own, your due; / But not 'till there's Obedience paid by you.'
Bib: Ferguson, Moira, (ed.), *First Feminists*; Browne, Alice, *The Eighteenth Century Feminist Mind*.

Churchill, Caryl (b 1938)
Dramatist. After writing extensively for radio, which is traditionally more accommodating to female writers, and juggling the demands of her husband's career and childcare, Churchill moved into theatre in the early 1970s, writing intially as an individual but eventually learning different ways of working collectively as a result of her ventures with Monstrous Regiment and Joint Stock.

Churchill had tackled many of the fashionable

themes of British political and feminist theatre in the 1970s, including witches (*Vinegar Tom*, 1976), terrorism (*Objections to Sex and Violence*), and seventeenth-century revolutionary sects (*Light Shining in Buckinghamshire*, 1976), as well as more unusual topics such as the nature of ideology and repression in the all male *Softcops* (1984), inspired by a reading of the French theorist ▷ Michel Foucault. Her work has been particularly associated with treatments of sexual politics, especially in *Cloud Nine* (1978, in which the links between patriarchy and colonialisation are mercilessly and wittily exposed) and *Top Girls* (1982), a study of a 'successful' career woman. She has always been keenly aware of the socio-political dimension of oppression, which affects men as well as women, as in *Fen*, her study of the quiet horrors of rural life. Churchill uses time shifts, uneven ageing (the characters in *Cloud Nine* are twenty-five years older in part two than they were in part one, but one hundred years has passed), cross race and cross gender casting, doubling, pastiche Victorian light verse and also rhyming couplets, as part of a strategy of upsetting and destabilising conventional assumptions about both drama and life itself.

Top Girls begins with a gathering of women from different periods and cultures to celebrate the promotion of Marlene, the central character, within the Top Girls employment agency. In the first scene Marlene is apparently emancipated from the traps and entanglements of family and children that have constrained the others but much of the rest of the play is concerned with destabilising this privileged position by trapping audiences into semi-agreement with her and then encouraging them to see her putative success in a far wider context in which she is just as much a victim of the system. The play is both enormously funny and chilling in its brilliantly observed presentations of the everyday contradictions of life. Churchill, like ▷ Brecht, suggests that what we need is a new way of seeing if we are to understand and confront the pressures the characters in *Top Girls* fail to grasp. Some people interpreted *Top Girls* as a hymn in praise of its central character and the runaway success in Britain of her exposé of the financial markets, *Serious Money* (1987), owed much to its popularity with the very people it satirised, who flocked to see it both at the Royal Court and in the West End. *Mad Forest* (1990) is a fine treatment of Romania after the overthrow of the Ceausescu government.

Churchill has developed a strong interest in creating theatre with dancers and musicians. *The Skriker* (1994) is an extraordinary example of virtuoso dramatic writing coupled with music and dance in an exploration of the irrational and the need for something beyond the material world.

Bib: Cowin, G., *Churchill the Playwright*

Churchill, Charles (1731–64)
Poet and political writer. A secret marriage, contracted at the age of 17, brought an end to his academic career at Cambridge. He entered the ministry, but after several years as a curate he separated from his wife and embarked on a literary and political career, associating himself with the political aspirations of ▷ John Wilkes. In 1763 he eloped with the 15-year-old daughter of a Westminster tradesman, but died suddenly in the following year at the age of 33.

There is a distinctive vigour to Churchill's use of the ▷ heroic couplet, though he lacks refinement or nuance. His subject matter in such poems as *The Rosciad* (1761) (by which he made his reputation), *The Prophecy of Famine* (1763), *An Epistle to William Hogarth* (1763) and *The Author* (1763) remains consistently public and ▷ Augustan, at a time when other writers were turning to more intimate themes. He lacks the restraint and poise of ▷ Dryden and ▷ Pope, however, and his spontaneity anticipates in tone the couplet satires of Byron. *The Rosciad* parades the theatrical figures of the day before a judgement panel consisting of ▷ Shakespeare and ▷ Ben Jonson, and they award the laurel, predictably, to ▷ David Garrick. In other poems Churchill discusses contemporary politics and the nature of satire. He also wrote less successful works in hudibrastic tetrameters (▷ metre; ▷ *Hudibras*), such as *The Ghost* (1762–63), in which he attacked ▷ Samuel Johnson.

Bib: Smith, R. J., *Charles Churchill.*

Churchyard, Thomas (c 1520–1604)
Poet. Churchyard's career combined a marginal position at court with a near-successful attempt at professional authorship, and although his work is not well known at the present time, he was acknowledged as important by the younger ▷ Elizabethan poets such as ▷ Spenser and ▷ Ralegh. Indeed, Spenser makes Churchyard 'Palemon' in his *Colin Clout*, characterized by his long career as a poet. Churchyard began his court associations as ▷ Surrey's page and then served in several battles on the continent; these exploits were later to form the basis of his *Generall Rehearsall of Warres* (1579). He wrote a considerable amount of panegyric poetry, probably in pursuit of a perpetually elusive preferment; for example, *The Worthiness of Wales* (1587) celebrates the mythic genealogy of the Tudor dynasty (▷ Tudor Myth). His poetry is included in ▷ *Tottel's Miscellany* (1557), while his most well received work, 'The Legend of Shore's Wife', appears in ▷ *A Mirror For Magistrates* (1563 edition).

Bib: Chalmers, G., *Churchyard's Chips.*

Cibber, Colley (1671–1757)
Actor, manager, dramatist. His first known role was as a servant in *Sir Anthony Love* in 1690,

while his first opportunity at a substantial role came in 1694 in ▷ William Congreve's ▷ *The Double Dealer*. In 1696 he wrote his first play, ▷ *Love's Last Shift*, often seen as a landmark in the transition from 'hard wit' Restoration comedy to the 'comedy of ▷ sensibility'. He himself played the first of many fop parts, Sir Novelty Fashion, which he had created for himself; he later played Lord Foppington in ▷ Sir John Vanbrugh's satiric sequel to the play, ▷ *The Relapse* (1696).

In 1730 Cibber was chosen, amid great controversy, as ▷ Poet Laureate. He retired from ▷ Drury Lane in 1733, afterwards writing an opera libretto, poems, essays, more plays, and his ▷ autobiography, *An Apology for the Life of Colley Cibber* (1740), still considered a primary source of information about the theatre in his time.

Throughout his life, Cibber excited controversy, involving himself in quarrels with several prominent men, notably the authors ▷ John Dennis and ▷ Henry Fielding and, most damagingly, ▷ Alexander Pope, with whom he kept up a running battle of insults for many years. His ironic misfortune was that Pope, as the better writer, gained a more lasting reputation, so that many students today know of Cibber only through Pope's harsh satires, and his real merit is forgotten.

On the other hand, he made many loyal friends, who praised his wit and good company, and remained loyal to him in extremity. His acting was celebrated and vilified by turns; he was said to be a marvellous comic, but often execrable in tragedy, which he refused to abandon.

Bib: Hayley, R. (ed.), *The Plays of Colley Cibber*; Koon, H., *Colley Cibber: A Biography*.

Cibber, Katherine (1669–1734)

Singer, actress. Born Katherine Shore into a musical family, she studied voice and harpsichord with ▷ Henry Purcell. She married the actor ▷ Colley Cibber in 1693, much against her father's wishes, and with him had seven children, including the actress ▷ Charlotte Charke and actor-manager, ▷ Theophilus.

Katherine Cibber began acting at the ▷ Dorset Garden Theatre in the season of 1693–4, and appeared with the same company (the ▷ United Company) at ▷ Drury Lane in the following year. She specialized in romantic roles, often involving singing.

Cibber, Susanna Maria (1714–66)

Actress, singer, dramatist. Susanna Cibber was the daughter of Thomas Arne, an upholsterer. In 1732 she sang the title role in Carey and Lampe's *Amelia* at the ▷ Haymarket Theatre, and two months later, she performed Galatea in ▷ George Handel's *Acis and Galatea*. In 1734 she married the recently widowed ▷ Theophilus Cibber, with whom she had two children, although both of these died in infancy.

The marriage was a bitter failure: her husband's taste for frequenting brothels, and his general profligacy, meant that he was perpetually in debt, and he soon began to seize his wife's assets, including portions of her salary, as well as her wardrobe and personal effects, in order to satisfy his creditors.

In 1737 she began an affair with a family friend, William Sloper, egged on by her husband, who eventually forced her at gunpoint to spend the night with Sloper. This was part of Cibber's scheme to extract money from the wealthy Sloper, and in 1738 Cibber sued Sloper, but succeeded in winning only ten pounds in damages that year, and only five hundred of the ten thousand he was claiming at the end of another lawsuit in the following year.

In 1741, after a discreet absence, and the birth of her first child by Sloper, Susanna Cibber returned to the stage, both acting and singing with great success. She sang in Handel's *Messiah*, first in Dublin, and then at its London debut in ▷ Covent Garden.

Susanna Cibber seems to have been supremely gifted both as a singer and as an actress: she is said to have been Handel's favourite, and he wrote some of his best music expressly for her to perform; as an actress she played mostly in tragedy, eliciting conflicting reports as to the variety of her gestures and tones, but the general agreement was that she could wring tears out of the most hard-hearted audience. Her Juliet and Ophelia were particularly celebrated for their pathos. At her death ▷ Drury Lane stayed closed in honour of its greatest actress. She is also known to have co-authored at least one play, *The Oracle* (1752). She was buried in Westminster Abbey.

Bib: Mann, D. (ed.), *The Plays of Theophilus and Susannah Cibber*; Highfill, P. H. Jr., Burnim, K. A. and Langhans, E. A. (eds.), *A Biographical Dictionary of Actors, Actresses, Musicians, Dancers, Managers, and Other Stage Personnel in London 1660–1800*.

Cibber, Theophilus (1703–58)

Actor, dancer, dramatist, manager, the fourth child of the actor-manager ▷ Colley Cibber, and the singer and dancer ▷ Katherine Cibber. Cibber was educated at Winchester College, but left at the age of 16 to join the ▷ Drury Lane Theatre, where his father was co-manager. Still in his teens, in addition to acting in a range of established plays, he was already writing or adapting other plays and appearing in them, including *Henry VI* (1723) and *Apollo and Daphne* (1723).

Despite his unscrupulousness as an individual (▷ Susanna Cibber), Cibber maintained his reputation as an actor during most of his life: he excelled as a comedian, specializing in the playing

of fops, but was also compelling in broader roles, including that of Pistol, whose name he acquired as a nickname. Less successfully, he played some serious parts, largely ▷ Shakespeare, including Iago, Othello, Hamlet, and even (at the embarrassingly advanced age of 40) Romeo. As a manager he at times showed considerable common sense and expertise, but his career was blighted by his truculence which involved him in personal conflicts throughout his life. As an author he was undistinguished, his works showing that tendency, exhibited in other areas of his life, to prey upon the efforts of others.
Bib: Mann, D. (ed.), *The Plays of Theophilus and Susannah Cibber*.

Cicero, Marcus Tullius (106–43 BC)
Roman statesman, and writer on rhetoric, politics and philosophy. Politically he is famous for his vigorous resistance to the conspiracy of Catiline against the government of the Republic. This is the theme of ▷ Ben Jonson's tragedy ▷ *Catiline*, of which Cicero is the hero. Cicero's mastery of eloquence in his various writings, and his prestige in ancient Rome, caused him to be much admired in the ▷ Middle Ages and afterwards. Cicero's *Somnium Scipionis* (*Dream of Scipio*) influenced ▷ Chaucer's ▷ *Parliament of Foulys*, and in the 16th century the growing body of English prose writers, such as ▷ Roger Ascham, tended to take as a model either the rolling, musical sentences of Cicero or, by contrast, the terse pointed sentences of ▷ Seneca.

In the 18th century Cicero, whose murder was condoned by ▷ Augustus, came to be seen as a martyr in the cause of liberty and the Roman Republic. A *Life of Cicero* by Conyers Middleton (1741) assisted this interpretation. ▷ Bolingbroke and ▷ Thomson praised Cicero, and ▷ Cumberland wrote a play about him in 1761.

Circulating libraries
Libraries in Britain from which books were borrowed by the (mostly female) reading public. The first circulating library started in 1740 and, as the institution spread, it helped to foster the growth of literacy by bringing expensive books within the reach of ordinary people. The most famous circulating libraries in 19th-century Britain were Mudie's (▷ Charles Mudie), W.H. Smith's and Boots. The three-volume or ▷ 'triple-decker' novel of the 19th century was largely supported by these libraries, although rigorous ▷ censorship was enforced.

▷ Jewsbury, Geraldine.

Bib: Leavis, Q.D., *Fiction and the Reading Public*.

Citizen comedies
Comedies, especially between 1600 and 1640, using contemporary London and its middle class as their setting, *eg* ▷ Ben Jonson's ▷ *Bartholomew Fair* (1614), ▷ Thomas Middleton's ▷ *A Chaste Maid in Cheapside* (1611), and ▷ Philip Massinger's ▷ *The City Madam* (1632). The energy and anarchic activity of these plays seem to align with ▷ Mikhail Bakhtin's later evocation of the carnivalesque.
Bib: Gibbons, B., *Jacobean City Comedy*; Leggatt, A., *Citizen Comedy in the Age of Shakespeare*.

Citizen of the World, A **(1760–62)**
A collection of letters about life in London by ▷ Oliver Goldsmith, ostensibly the correspondence of a Chinese man living in the city, Lien Chi Altangi. It first appeared as *Chinese Letters* in John Newbery's *The Public Ledger* (1760–61). It features ▷ The Man in Black and ▷ Beau Tibbs, and was published under its present title in 1762. The letters comment on English customs and practices, the moral and ethical characteristics of English people, and on literature. Their fresh and naïve view of commonplace matters provides rich satire. The work's ironic view of the author's own culture links it with other sceptical works of the period, such as ▷ Voltaire's *Candide* and ▷ Johnson's ▷ *Rasselas*. It also displays the late 18th-century fascination with matters oriental (▷ Orientalism).

City Heiress, The; Or, Sir Timothy Treatall **(1682)**
Play by ▷ Aphra Behn. Tom Wilding, a charming Tory rake, is pursuing the rich and beautiful widow, Lady Galliard. She is attracted to him but does not trust him. He is also conducting an intrigue with the young heiress, Charlot Get-all, as well as keeping a mistress, Diana. Wilding's friend, Sir Charles Merriwill, is also interested in Lady Galliard, and becomes Wilding's rival for her affections. Meanwhile Wilding has been disinherited by his uncle, the 'old seditious Knight' Sir Timothy Treatall. Wilding schemes with Diana to pass her off to his uncle as Charlot, and Sir Timothy marries the mistress, mistaking her for the heiress. In a tempestuous scene Lady Galliard agrees to sleep with Wilding, but regrets it immediately afterwards and rejects him, opting instead for Sir Charles. Wilding turns to the faithful Charlot for solace. Writings stolen from Sir Timothy by Wilding and friends prove the old man to have been involved in treasonable activities, and he is forced to desist from them, and even to make peace with his nephew. The play is one of several with a political bent by Behn, a lifelong staunch Tory herself. A large part of its interest derives from the psychological interplay between Wilding and Lady Galliard, but it contains some hugely farcical scenes, and keeps up an entertainingly rapid pace.

City Madam, The **(1632)**
A comedy by ▷ Philip Massinger. It is about

a London merchant whose wife and daughters grow outrageously extravagant in their tastes. To teach them a lesson, the father, Sir John Frugal, temporarily retires from the world and leaves his affairs in the hands of his hypocritically humble brother, Luke. Once he has power in his hands, Luke throws off his pretence, becomes arrogant and harsh, and humiliates his nieces and sister-in-law. Like so many comedies of the age *The City Madam* ridicules the extravagance and pretentiousness of the new urban bourgeoisie.

City of Destruction, The
In ▷ Bunyan's ▷ *Pilgrim's Progress* the town from which the pilgrim, Christian, flees to the ▷ Celestial City, *ie* Heaven. The City of Destruction stands for the world divorced from spiritual values, doomed to the destruction that is to overcome all merely material creation.

City of Dreaming Spires
Oxford, from a description in ▷ Matthew Arnold's poem, *Thyrsis* (1867), an elegy for ▷ Arthur Hugh Clough.

City Wit, The **(1629)**
A fast-moving, intensely theatrical ▷ citizen comedy of manners by ▷ Richard Brome, in which the cash-nexus provides the driving force behind the plot. The play dramatizes the recovery of the fortunes and family ties of a resourceful young London prodigal, Crasy, assisted by his wily servant Jeremy.

Civil Wars, English and American
England has had two recognized periods of Civil War:

1 The more important, in the 17th century, is also called the Great Rebellion. It was fought between the king (Charles I) and Parliament, and divided into the First Civil War (1642–6) ending with the parliamentary victory at Naseby (1645) and the capitulation of Oxford (1646), the royalist capital. The Second Civil War (1648–51) also ended with parliamentary victory, this time over the Scots, who had been the allies of Parliament in the First Civil War, but took the king's side in the Second. The issues were complicated; simplified, the economic interests of the urban middle classes coincided with their religious (▷ Puritan) ideology and conflicted with the traditional economic interests of the Crown, correspondingly allied with Anglican religious belief.

2 The other occurred in the 15th century and is usually known as the ▷ Wars of the Roses.

From outside England, it appears as if the fighting in Northern Ireland, becoming overt in 1968 and still continuing in 1989, constitutes a state of civil war.

The American Civil War, or War of Secession (1861–5), was fought on the issue of whether the southern states of the United states had the right to secede from the Union and establish their independence. Their wish to do so arose from the northern opposition to the slave holding on which the southern landed economy was based.

Cixous, Hélène (b 1937)
French writer. Hélène Cixous' work has been most influential when it has actively attempted to challenge the categories of writing, and her work encompasses poetry and poetic prose, ▷ feminist theory, philosophy and ▷ psychoanalysis. She is a key player in the French feminist ▷ *écriture féminine* movement, and has written some 40 influential texts (only a few of which have been translated into English), beginning with her PhD thesis on ▷ James Joyce (published in English as *The Exile of James Joyce or the Art of Replacement* in 1972), and including *The Newly Born Woman* (with Catherine Clément), the seminal essay on women and writing 'The Laugh of the Medusa' ('*Le Rire de la Meduse*') (published in English in 1976), dramas and fiction (including ▷ *Portrait de Dora*, Cixous' vindication of ▷ Freud's famous patient, the central figure in one of his most important case histories and latter-day feminist heroine), and literary-critical works (*To Live the Orange* is a celebration of the work of Brazilian writer Clarice Lispector). Cixous is Professor of Literature at the experimental University of Paris – VIII which she co-founded in 1968, and director of the *Centre d'Études Féminine*.
Bib: Marks, E. and de Coutivron, I. (eds.), *New French Feminisms*; Conley, V. A., *Hélène Cixous: Writing the Feminine*; Sellers, S. (ed.), *Writing Differences: Readings from the Seminar of Hélène Cixous*; Wilcox, H. et al, *The Body and the Text*; Moi, T., *Sexual/Textual Politics*.

Clandestine Marriage, The **(1766)**
Comedy by ▷ George Colman the Elder, and ▷ David Garrick, inspired by the first plate in ▷ Hogarth's ▷ *Marriage à la Mode* series. The play concerns the secret marriage of Fanny Sterling to her father's clerk, Lovewell. Sir John Melvil, who had proposed to marry Fanny's affected older sister, instead falls in love with her, as does his uncle, the foppish Lord Ogleby. Eventually the complications are resolved, with the help of Lord Ogleby, who becomes an ally to the couple, and Fanny and Lovewell are able to disclose their marriage and find happiness. The play was a great success and it was revived frequently throughout the 19th century, and into the 20th.

Clanvowe, John (1341–91)
Diplomat, writer, member of the king's household, who fought in the French wars and died on a pilgrimage, near Constantinople.

He was associated with the so called 'Lollard Knights' (a group of intellectual knights with ▷ Lollard sympathies, apparently known to Chaucer), and was the author of a moralizing treatise, *The Two Ways*, and a ▷ dream-vision debate poem *The Cuckoo and the Nightingale* (which borrows lines from ▷ Chaucer's ▷ *Knight's Tale*).
Bib: Scattergood, V. J. (ed.), *The Works of John Clanvowe*.

Clare, John (1793–1864)
Poet. The son of a farm labourer in the Midlands, he was self-educated, early influences being the ▷ Bible and James Thomson's (1700–48) *Seasons*. He was unable to settle down or marry because of his poverty, and hoped that his verse might bring him security. His *Poems, Descriptive of Rural Life and Scenery*, described as being by 'a Northamptonshire Peasant' appeared in 1820, and were a great success. In that year he married, and began work on *The Village Minstrel, and Other Poems*, which appeared in 1821. This volume disappointed his hopes, despite his attempts to adjust his fresh, spontaneous style to the vagaries of literary taste. He visited London several times and made the acquaintance of ▷ Samuel Taylor Coleridge, ▷ William Hazlitt and Charles Lamb. *The Shepherd's Calendar* was published in 1827, in a version much edited by his publisher, John Taylor. (The original version of the poem, as Clare submitted it to Taylor, was published in 1964.) Under the pressure of apparent literary failure, the demands of his growing family and grinding poverty, Clare became insane in 1837. He spent the remainder of his life in lunatic asylums, periodically imagining that he was Napoleon or ▷ Lord Byron. The works which he wrote during the period of his madness were not published until the 20th century.

Clare is remarkable for his interest in nature for its own sake, rather than, as is the case with most poets, as a key to some philosophical or aesthetic illumination. During his lifetime, and since, this quality has led to the criticism that his work is merely descriptive. In his best poems however, such description conveys, in itself, a celebration of the joy of the natural scene and the changing seasons. Moreover Clare, being a farm labourer, lacks the literary idealization of nature common in other poets. In his anguished poem 'I Am' he abandons description, laments the desertion of his friends, and longs for death.
Bib: Martin, F., *The Life of John Clare*; Storey, M. (ed.), *Clare: The Critical Heritage*; Storey, M., *The Poetry of John Clare*; Howard, W., *John Clare*.

Clarendon, Edward Hyde, Earl of (1609–74)
Statesman and historian; author of *The True Historical Narrative of the Rebellion and Civil Wars in England* about the ▷ Civil War, during which he had supported ▷ King Charles I. The published history combines two separate manuscripts: a history written 1646–8 while the events were fresh in the author's mind, and an ▷ autobiography written between 1668 and 1670, in exile and without the aid of documents. In consequence, Books I–VII are superior in accuracy to Books VIII–XV, with the exception of Book IX, which contains material written in 1646. Clarendon's history is a literary classic because of its series of portraits of the participants in the war. His book is a notable contribution to the rise of the arts of biography and autobiography in England in the 17th century and contributed to the development which in the 18th century produced the first English novels.

As a statesman, Hyde was at first a leading opponent of Charles I, but his strongly Anglican (▷ Church of England) faith led him to take the Royalist side shortly before the war. He became one of the king's chief advisers. He followed the royal court into exile, and was Lord Chancellor and ▷ Charles II's chief minister at the Restoration (1660). The king's brother, the future ▷ James II, married his daughter, so that he became grandfather of Queen ▷ Mary II and Queen ▷ Anne. He was made the scapegoat for the unpopularity of Charles II's government in its early years, however, and was driven into exile in 1667. He lived the remainder of his life in France.

▷ Histories and Chronicles.
Bib: Huehns, G., *Selections from the History of the Rebellion and the Life*; Wormald, B. H. G., *Clarendon, Politics, History and Rebellion*; Firth, C., *Essays, Historical and Literary*.

***Clarissa* (1747–8)**
An epistolary novel by ▷ Samuel Richardson. The central characters are Clarissa Harlowe, Anna Howe, Lovelace and John Belford. Clarissa's family wish her to marry the odious suitor, Solmes, a wealthy man whom she abhors. The marriage is proposed to elevate the Harlowes socially, yet in the motives of Clarissa's brother and sister there is also a disturbing undertone of sadistic sexuality. As she refuses to accept Solmes the family ostracize her within their home.

Lovelace, a handsome rake, is initially the suitor of the elder sister Arabella, but his real interest is in Clarissa. When the family ill treat her he poses as her deliverer and persuades her to escape with him to London, promising that he will restore her in the esteem of her relatives. But the apparently respectable house where they stay is in reality a brothel.

Lovelace's attempts at seducing Clarissa are unsuccessful, and he eventually resorts to drugging her and then rapes her. Through this theme Richardson explores the hypocrisy of a society which equates 'honour' with virginity.

Clarissa dies after the rape, not from shame but from a spiritual integrity which cannot be corrupted. In the self-martyrdom of the heroine, Richardson achieves a psychological complexity which transcends the limitations of the purported morality.
Bib: Flynn, C., *Samuel Richardson: A Man of Letters*. Eagleton, T., *The Rape of Clarissa*; Keymer, T., *Richardson's 'Clarissa' and the Eighteenth-Century Reader*.

Clarke, Arthur C. (b 1917)
Science-fiction writer, educated at King's College, University of London. He worked as an auditor, served in the RAF 1941–46 and since then has been a scientific editor, underwater explorer and photographer, company director and television and radio presenter, as well as writing numerous novels, short stories, books for children and works of popular science. He is a Fellow of the Royal Astronomical Society and has won many prizes for his work. His science fiction draws on his wide scientific knowledge, combining exciting narrative and philosophical concerns with detailed explanations of the imagined technology of the future. Many of his fictions involve narratives of exploration and discovery, carried out by romantic individualists. His best-known work remains *2001: A Space Odyssey* (1968), the script of a hugely popular film which he subsequently turned into a novel. His other novels include: *Prelude to Space* (1951); *The Sands of Mars* (1951); *Against the Fall of Night* (1953); *Earthlight* (1955); *A Fall of Moondust* (1961); *Rendezvous with Rama* (1973); *The Fountains of Paradise* (1979); *The Songs of Distant Earth* (1986); *The Ghost from the Grand Banks* (1990). Among his many volumes of short stories are: *The Nine Billion Names of God: The Best Short Stories of Arthur C. Clarke* (1967) and *Tales from Planet Earth* (1989).

Clarke, Gillian (b 1937)
Poet. Born in Cardiff, Gillian Clarke read English at University College, Cardiff, and then worked with the BBC in London before returning to Cardiff in 1960. Many of her poems are concerned with the rhythms of the seasons, rural life and landscape. A smaller number, more prominent in her earlier work, are set in suburbia or reflect on her experiences as a mother, her poetic move towards nature being linked to her physical move to a Welsh long-house in the Dyfed countryside. Gillian Clarke was assistant editor of the *Anglo-Welsh Review* from 1971 to 1976 when she succeeded Roland Mathias as editor, an influential position which she held until 1984. Encouraged by Meic Stephens as editor of *Poetry Wales*, she began her published poetry collections with the *Triskel* pamphlet *Snow on the Mountains* (1971), this being followed by *The Sundial* (1978) and *Letter from a Far Country* (1982), and then, more recently, after her *Selected Poems* in 1985, *Letting in the Rumour* (1989) and *The King of Britain's Daughter* (1993).

Clarke, Marcus (1846–81)
Novelist. The son of a wealthy lawyer, Clarke emigrated to Australia in 1863, where he worked on a sheep station and then as a journalist. His first novel, *Long Odds* (1869), is an unremarkable ▷ sensation novel, but this was followed by *His Natural Life* (serialized 1870–2; published in a three-volume abridged form 1875), which, despite a convoluted plot concerning inheritances and impersonation, contains powerful accounts of convict life in 1840s Australia, and has become the most famous 19th-century Australian novel.
Bib: Wilding, M., *Marcus Clarke*.

Clarke, Mary Cowden (1809–98)
Critic, novelist and poet, born in London. She was the daughter of composer Vincent Novello and Mary Sabilla Hehl, and was educated at home and in France. Her father's literary acquaintances included ▷ Keats (1795–1821), Leigh Hunt (1784–1859), and Charles Cowden Clarke, whom she married in 1828. In 1829 she began a project that was to occupy her for sixteen years. *The Complete Concordance to Shakespeare* was eventually published in 1845, and remained the standard concordance until the end of the 19th century. Other work on Shakespeare includes *Shakespeare Proverbs* (1848) and a collection of stories based on *The Girlhood of Shakespeare's Heroines* (1852). She also wrote several volumes of verse biographies of her father and her husband; an autobiography, *My Long Life* (1896); a series of novels and a collection of *Short Stories in Metrical Prose* (1873). She was the editor of the *Musical Times* from 1853–6.
Bib: Altick, R.D., *The Cowden Clarkes*.

Classic, Classics, Classical
These words are apt to cause confusion. The term 'classic' has been used to denote a work about whose value it is assumed there can be no argument, *eg*, *Portrait of a Lady* is a classic. The word particularly implies a changeless and immutable quality; it has sometimes been used to deny the need for reassessment, reinterpretation and change. Because only a few works can be classics, it may be argued that the term is synonymous with the best. This is not necessarily the case, especially with regard to changes in literary taste and a constantly moving canon of texts.

'Classics' is the study of ancient Greek and Latin literature. 'Classic' is used as an adjective as well as a noun, *eg* ▷ Henry James wrote many classic novels. 'Classical' is mainly used as the adjective for 'classics', *eg* classical scholarship.

Classical education and English literature
Classical education is based on the study of the

'classics', *ie* the literature of ancient Greece and Rome, principally from ▷ Homer to the great Latin poets and prose writers (*eg* ▷ Virgil, ▷ Ovid, ▷ Cicero) of the 1st century BC – 1st century AD. Latin is more closely bound up with western history and culture, and is the easier language for English speakers to study; consequently it has been more widely used in schools than Greek, and it has been studied at earlier stages of education. Roman literary culture was, however, based on that of the Greeks.

Medieval Europe (Christendom) grew out of the ruins of the western Roman Empire; the Church, like the Empire, was still ruled from Rome; its philosophy was deeply influenced by the Greek philosophers and its language continued to be Latin. The Church controlled the universities and the classics were the basis of medieval university education, especially that part of it known as the 'Trivium' – grammar, rhetoric and logic. Nonetheless, many of the Greek and Roman writers were known principally through inferior versions of their texts and they were valued chiefly in so far as the Church could use them for its own purposes.

The movement known as the ▷ Renaissance started in Italy in the 14th century; it was, first of all, the enthusiastic rediscovery and collection by scholars of ancient classical texts, and the development of new and more accurate methods of studying them. It did not long remain merely a scholarly movement; the scholars influenced the writers and artists, and these in turn, in the 15th and 16th centuries, aroused enthusiasm in the upper classes of all western Europe. The Renaissance practice of studying the classics for their own sake and not under the direction of the Church, brought the discovery of a new principle of growth in literature and the other arts. Knowledge of the classics became a principle of discrimination: those who did not have it were by implication more primitive in their development and often from a lower social class.

The Renaissance first seriously affected England early in the 16th century. The pattern for classical education in the national public schools and the more local grammar schools was formed by such men as John Colet (?1467–1519), High Master of St Paul's School. ▷ Sir Thomas More, author of *Utopia* and Chancellor to ▷ Henry VIII, gave prestige to ▷ humanist values in the royal court. ▷ Erasmus visited England from Holland and made friends among these and other English humanists.

But ancient Greece, and Rome in its greatest days, were pagan; their values were social rather than religious. Thus there was the possibility of divided loyalty between the Rome that was the starting-point of so much European art, thought and politics, and the latter Rome that was the centre of the originally Hebrew and very unclassical religion of Christianity. The Roman Catholic Church in the 15th and early 16th centuries at first responded to the humanists favourably, even when they were critical of its traditions and practices. The thought and outlook of pagan Greece and Rome nevertheless did not agree well with the ancient Hebrew roots of Christianity as shown in the Old and New Testaments of the Bible. The 16th-century Protestant ▷ Reformation was partly the outcome of humanist criticism of the Church, but it was also a return to the Word of God as the Bible displayed it. Thus, from 1560 to 1660, much English imaginative writing has two aspects: the poets ▷ Edmund Spenser and ▷ John Milton, for example, have a Protestant aspect, which is biblical and Hebraic; and a classical aspect, strongly inspired by the classical Renaissance. The poet ▷ Ben Jonson is much more classical than Protestant, while ▷ George Herbert is strongly religious in the moderately Protestant, Anglican tradition, and despises the kind of subject matter (*eg* 'classical pastoral') which Ben Jonson accepted. Both, however, had an equally classical education.

Another division arose from the difference between native literary traditions, which continued in their non-classical character, and the classical qualities and standards which many writers felt should permeate and regulate the native tradition. This division did not correspond to religious differences: the most Latin of all English poets is the ▷ Puritan, John Milton. ▷ Shakespeare is well-known for his indifference to the classical 'rules' which critics like ▷ Sir Philip Sidney thought necessary to good drama, while his contemporary, Ben Jonson, favoured them, though not slavishly.

Classical and native traditions of literature rivalled and nourished each other until the middle of the 17th century, and so did Protestant biblical and secular classical philosophies of life. But after the Restoration in 1660, religious passions declined and sceptical rationalism began to take their place. Thus began the most classical period of English art and literature, the so-called Augustan age of the 18th century. Yet within their neo-classical horizon, the best English writers even of this period retained strong elements of native idiom; this is true of the poets, ▷ John Dryden and ▷ Alexander Pope, and of the prose writers ▷ Jonathan Swift and ▷ Samuel Johnson.

The ▷ French Revolution of 1789 was, at one level, the outcome of 18th century reason, criticism and scepticism, but it challenged the 18th-century classical qualities of order, intellectual proportion and balance, and the view of man as fulfilled only in a civilized structure of society. The English Romantic movement was partly an outcome of the French Revolution; it challenged many of the classical values, attaching more importance to the cultivation of the feelings of the individual than to the cultivation of the reason of man in society; it rediscovered the Middle Ages, which for three centuries has been despised as ▷ 'gothic', *ie* barbarous. At the same time, that part of English society which had always been more biblical than classical in its culture – the commercial middle classes – was now stronger (thanks to the ▷ Industrial Revolution) than it had ever been before. So we find the critic ▷ Matthew Arnold, in his *Culture and Anarchy* (1869), distinguishing between two categories of mind in contemporary society: the majority were the 'Hebraizers', who devoted themselves to the virtues of private conduct and practical achievement; the 'Hellenizers', like himself, valued contemplation, reason and critical discrimination. England, he considered, was becoming barbarous owing to the preponderance of the former over the latter.

Since Arnold, classical education has lost its long-held place in the centre of education. It has retained its privileged status but as education has become available to all, different skills, such as the study of English literature, have been developed as other disciplines.

Classical mythology
Ancient Greek mythology can be divided between the 'Divine Myths' and the 'Heroic Myths'.

The divine myths are known in differing versions from the works of various Greek poets, of whom the most notable are ▷ Homer and Hesiod. Hesiod explained the origin of the world in terms of a marriage between Earth (Ge or Gaea) and Sky (Uranus). Their children were the 12 Titans: Oceanus, Crius, Iapetus, Theia, Rhea, Mnemosyne, Phoebe, Tethys, Themis, Cocus, Hyperion, and Cronos. Cronos overthrew his father, and he and Rhea (or Cybele) became the parents of the 'Olympian gods', so called from their association with the sacred Olympus. The Olympians, in their turn, overthrew Cronos and the other Titans.

The chief Olympians were Zeus and his queen Hera. The other gods and goddesses were the offspring of either, but as Zeus was usually at war with Hera, they were not the joint parents. They seem to have been seen as male and female aspects of the sky; their quarrels were the causes of bad weather and cosmic disturbances. The principal offspring of Zeus were Apollo, Artemis, Athene, Aphrodite (sometimes represented as a daughter of Uranus out of the sea), Dionysus, Hermes, and Ares. Zeus had three sisters, Hestia, Demeter (the corn goddess) and Hera (also his wife), and two brothers, Poseidon who ruled the sea, and Hades who ruled the underworld. In the 3rd century BC the Olympian gods were adopted by the Romans, who used the Latin names more commonly known to later European writers. Uranus, Apollo, and some others remained the same. Gaea became Tellus; Cronos = Saturn; Zeus = Jupiter (or Jove); Hera = Juno; Athene = Minerva; Artemis = Diana; Hermes = Mercury; Ares = Mars; Hephaestus = Vulcan; Aphrodite = Venus (and her son Eros = Cupid); Demeter = Ceres; Poseidon = Neptune. There were numerous minor deities such as nymphs and satyrs in both Greek and Roman pantheons.

The Olympian deities mingled with men, and rivalled one another in deciding human destinies. They concerned themselves particularly with the destinies of the heroes, *ie* those men, sometimes partly divine by parentage, who were remarkable for the kinds of excellence which are especially valued in early societies, such as strength (Heracles), or cunning (Odysseus). Each region of Greece had its native heroes, though the greatest heroes were famous in legend all over Greece. The most famous of all was Heracles (in Latin, Hercules) who originated in Thebes. Other leading examples of the hero are: Theseus (Athens); Sisyphus and Bellerophon (Corinth); Perseus (Argolis); the Dioscuri, *ie* Castor and Pollux (Lanconia); Oedipus (Thebes); Achilles (Thessaly); Jason (Thessaly); Orpheus (Thrace). Like the Greek gods and goddesses, the Greek heroes were adopted by Roman legend, sometimes with a change of name. The minor hero of Greek legend, Aeneas, was raised to be the great ancestral hero of the Romans, and they had other heroes of their own, such as Romulus, the founder of Rome, and his brother Remus.

After the downfall of the Roman Empire of the West, classical deities and heroes achieved a kind of popular reality through the planets and zodiacal signs which are named after them, and which, according to astrologers, influence human fates. Thus in ▷ Chaucer's ▷ *The Knight's Tale*, Mars, Venus, Diana and Saturn occur, and owe their force in the poem as much to medieval astrology as to classical legend. Otherwise their survival has depended chiefly on their importance in the works of the classical poets, such as ▷ Homer, Hesiod, ▷ Virgil and ▷ Ovid, who have meant so much to European culture. In Britain, important poets translated and thus helped to 'naturalize' the Greek and Latin poems; *eg* ▷ Gavin Douglas in the 16th century and ▷ Dryden in the 17th century translated Virgil's ▷ *Aeneid*; ▷ Chapman in the 16th century and ▷ Pope in the 18th century translated Homer's epics. In the 16th and 17th centuries, poets used major and minor classical deities to adorn and elevate poems intended chiefly as gracious entertainment, and occasionally they added deities of their own invention.

While European culture was understood as a more or less distinct system of values, the poets used classical deities and heroes deliberately and objectively. In the 19th century, however, the deep disturbance of European beliefs and values caused European writers to use classical myth more subjectively, as symbols through which

they tried to express their personal doubts, struggles, and beliefs. Thus John Keats in his unfinished epic ▷ *Hyperion* tried to emulate Milton's great Christian epic, ▷ *Paradise Lost*, but instead of Christian myth he used the war of the Olympian gods and the titans to embody his sense of the tragedy of human experience. ▷ Tennyson wrote dramatic monologues in which personifications of Greek heroes (*eg* Ulysses, Tithonus, Tiresias in eponymous poems) recounted the experiences associated with them in classical (or, in the case of Ulysses, medieval) legend, in such a way as to express the emotional conflicts of a man from the Victorian age like Tennyson himself. In the 20th century, writers have used figures from the classical myths differently again; they are introduced to establish the continuity of the emotions and attitudes characteristic of modern men and women with emotions and attitudes of those from the past. It is thus that ▷ T. S. Eliot uses Tiresias in his poem ▷ *The Waste Land*, and James Joyce uses the Odysseus myth in his novel ▷ *Ulysses*. In a comparable way, modern psychologists have used the Greek myths as symbolic expressions of basic psychological conflicts in human beings in all periods. ▷ Freud's theory of the Oedipus complex is the most famous of these reinterpretations.
▷ *Odyssey; Iliad.*

Classical unities
Criteria for drama based on those of ▷ Aristotle in his *Poetics*. He argued that dramatic action should be plausible, and therefore should take place in a single location, or locations close to one another, in the space of 24 hours, and should focus on a single storyline, rather than leaping from plot to plot. Many classical Greek tragedies observe these rules, known as the 'Three Unities' – of time, of place, and of action. They were popular in the early ▷ Renaissance, especially in ▷ French literature. However, under the influence of ▷ Shakespeare the unities have been mainly disregarded, except in the 17th century when they were revived by ▷ neo-classicists, and French dramatists such as ▷ Corneille and ▷ Racine were much affected by them. In England, ▷ Thomas Rymer and ▷ John Dennis articulated neo-classical theories of tragedy which included homage to the classical unities. But most practising dramatists in England barely observed these rules. ▷ Dryden's views on the subject were complex. In his congratulatory poem, *To My Friend, the Author*, addressed to the English dramatist Peter Motteux, he praised Motteux's tragi-comedy *Beauty in Distress* (1698) for its model adherence to the unities. However, in his *Essay of Dramatic Poesy* (1668) and *Heads of an Answer to Rymer* (1677), he defended contemporary departures from neo-classical theory, including his own, on the grounds that the later plays had greater variety and interest than those of ancient times. He argued that 'although the Plays of the Ancients are more correctly Plotted, ours are more beautifully written'.
▷ Classic, classics, classical; Classical education and English literature; Nicolas Boileau.

Cleanness
One of the four ▷ alliterative poems dating from the second half of the 14th century, attributed to the ▷ Gawain poet, and preserved along with ▷ *Pearl*, ▷ *Patience* and ▷ *Gawain and the Green Knight* in a single manuscript, British Library Cotton Nero A. x. The poem's structure is influenced by contemporary sermonizing practices, in which a systematic exploration of a given theme would be made using a series of biblical narratives. In this case the narrator investigates the diverse meanings and spiritual resonances of 'cleanness' through a series of New Testament and Old Testament stories (the parable of the Wedding Feast, the story of the Flood, the destruction of Sodom and Gomorrah, Belshazzar's Feast). The poem, which has no title in the manuscript, is sometimes referred to as *Purity*.
▷ Bible, The.
Bib: Anderson, J. J. (ed.), *Cleanness*; Davenport, W. A., *The Art of the Gawain Poet*.

Cleland, John (1709–89)
Novelist and journalist, most famous for his novel *Fanny Hill: Memoirs of a Woman of Pleasure*, published in two volumes in 1748 and 1749 and immediately suppressed as pornography. An unexpurgated edition of the book published in England in 1963 was seized by police and became the subject of a trial. Cleland also wrote *Memoirs of a Coxcomb* (1751) and several other novels and dramatic pieces.

Clerihew
A lightweight epigram, usually in four lines of varying length, so called after its inventor E. Clerihew Bentley. For example:

Alfred de Musset
Called his cat 'pusset'
His accent was affected –
That was to be expected.

Clerk's Tale, The
One of ▷ Chaucer's *Canterbury Tales*. The Clerk begins his tale with a tribute to the Italian poet ▷ Petrarch who has provided him with his story of patient Griselda, who survives the trials and tortures imposed on her by her husband, the higher-born Walter, in his attempt to test the limits of her patience. The story seems to have had considerable appeal for medieval writers, and a number of other versions and analogues survive (including that of Petrarch's

source, the hundredth tale of ▷ Boccaccio's ▷ *Decameron*). In producing his version of the story in the *Clerk's Tale*, Chaucer seems to play off the possibilities of interpreting this story as a spiritual allegory and as a literal history, and the resulting narrative has a disquieting effect. Through retelling the story of Griselda, the Clerk takes up and disproves the assertion made by the ▷ Wife of Bath in her *Prologue* (that clerics cannot speak well of wives), and the tale concludes with an 'envoy' considering the lessons of Griselda's story for the Wife of Bath and all her 'sect'.

Cliché
A word borrowed from the French, used to denote a phrase or idiom employed by habit instead of meaningfully, *eg* 'her skin was *as white as snow*'. It is a stock phrase, employed without thought and heard (or read) without visualization.

Clifford, Lady Anne (1590–1676)
One of the most accomplished and fascinating diarists of her age. Lady Anne Clifford was the only child of George Clifford, third Earl of Cumberland and Margaret Russell. However, on his death in 1605 it was discovered that her father had left the family estates to his nearest surviving male relative. Much of Lady Anne's life was devoted to regaining what she considered to be her rightful inheritance, even though both her husband and ▷ King James I opposed her demands. This marriage, to Richard Sackville, Earl of Dorset, was unhappy, but she fared little better in her second attempt at wedlock, to Philip Herbert, Earl of Pembroke and Montgomery; she was widowed for a second time in 1649. At last, in 1643, she gained possession of her lands and began systematically rebuilding and refurbishing each of her six castles. During the ▷ Civil War she was a staunch supporter of the Royalist cause and continued to prove her strength of character by resisting a three-year siege by the Parliamentary forces. After 1653 she settled down to write her own and her family's history, and this work, *Great Books*, together with her diaries and letters, provides us with one of the most lively and dramatic ▷ autobiographies by a Renaissance woman. Lady Anne was a learned woman who had been tutored by ▷ Samuel Daniel and whose personal chaplain at Wilton had been ▷ George Herbert. She was celebrated in verse by ▷ Aemilia Lanyer. When she died at the age of 86 Lady Anne was a wealthy matriarch, for not only had she inherited her own estate, but she had also benefited from the rich jointures acquired at the deaths of her two detested husbands.
Bib: Sackville-West, V. (ed.), *The Diary of Lady Anne Clifford*; Graham, E. et al. (eds.), *Her Own Life: Autobiographical Writings by Seventeenth-century Englishwomen*; Fraser, A., *The Weaker Vessel*.

Climax
▷ Figures of Speech.

Clinton, Lady Elizabeth, Countess of Lincoln (c 1574–1630)
Writer on motherhood. One of the earliest female exponents of breast-feeding. Lady Elizabeth had not fed any of her own 18 children herself, but regretted this later and wrote *The Countess of Lincoln's Nursery* (1622) confessing her mistake. The treatise advises all women, but especially the Countess's daughter-in-law, to breast-feed so that they might follow the 'Ordinance of God' and strengthen the mother-baby bond. This attitude should be seen not simply as an impassioned plea by a mother denied her 'natural' rights, but as part of a theoretical debate in which humanists and reformers advocated the necessity of breast-feeding (for example, ▷ Erasmus in 'The New Mother' [1523]). Moreover, ▷ Thomas Lodge's dedicatory poem reinforces the theoretical nature of the work.
▷ Grymeston, Elizabeth; Leigh, Dorothy.
Bib: Travitsky, B. (ed.), *A Paradise of Women*.

Clive, Caroline (1801–73)
Novelist and poet. Born Caroline Meysey-Wigley, her father was an MP. She published her poems in 1840 (as 'V'), though more interest was aroused by her first (and anonymous) novel, *Paul Ferroll* (1855), whose hero murders his first wife and is able to keep his secret for eighteen years through a happy and prosperous second marriage. The novel entered into the wider debate about divorce (leading up to the 1857 Divorce Act), while the moral ambiguities arising from the author's apparent unwillingness to condemn her hero, combined with the novel's interest in secrecy, make *Paul Ferroll* an important forerunner of the ▷ sensation novel of the 1860s. In the sequel, *Why Paul Ferroll Killed His Wife* (1860), Clive adopts a more conventionally moralistic tone.
▷ Marriage.
Bib: Leighton, A., and Reynolds, M. (eds.), *An Anthology of Victorian Women Poets*.

Clive, Catherine (Kitty) (1711–85)
Actress, singer, dramatist, and pamphlet-writer. Kitty Clive (née Raftor) joined the ▷ Drury Lane Theatre in 1728 where she spent most of her career, and quickly became one of its leading comic actresses, as well as singing in operas, entr'actes, and afterpieces. Her first major success was as Polly in ▷ *The Beggar's Opera* (1728), followed by roles in *The Old Debauchees* (1732) and *The Covent Carden Tragedy* (1732), written specially for her by ▷ Henry Fielding.

She herself wrote afterpieces, farces and a pamphlet, *The Case of Mrs Clive* (1743), which attacked the managements of Drury Lane and

⊳ Covent Garden theatres. She was for many years a close friend of ⊳ Horace Walpole. In 1769, she retired, and died 16 years later, after frequent bouts of illness. Her admirers praised her for her wit, intelligence, expressive features, and comic sense of timing. She was buried in Twickenham churchyard.
Bib: Highfill, P. H. Jr., Burnim, K. A. and Langhans, E. A. (eds.), *A Biographical Dictionary of Actors, Actresses, Musicians, Dancers, Managers, and Other Stage Personnel in London 1660–1800*.

Closure
A term used to refer to the way literary works or argument are concluded. In recent critical discussion a high value is placed on works which 'resist closure', that is works which leave the events described or issues raised open at the end of the work. This preference for open-endedness is often seen as a legacy of the ⊳ Modernist movement. Though the term closure is usually used of whole narratives, it can also be used of any episode or part of a work. It is also used more abstractly to refer to the resolution by a critic of the treatment of the issues raised in a text. This is often referred to as 'interpretative closure', and again carries negative connotations at present because it implies closed or dogmatic attitudes.

Cloud of Unknowing, The
One of the most admired texts of the medieval English mystical tradition. This spiritual treatise was produced some time in the second half of the 14th century in the north-east Midlands area. The text, which explores the active and contemplative ways of living, is addressed to a young contemplative and is partly presented in dialogue form. The tutor counsels that it is only by experiencing the cloud of unknowing that God will be felt and seen. Several other spiritual treatises have been attributed to the author of *The Cloud of Unknowing* (who is otherwise unknown).
Bib: Hodgson, P. (ed.), *The Cloud of Unknowing and the Book of Privy Counselling*; Wolters, C. (trans.), *The Cloud of Unknowing*.

Clough, Arthur Hugh (1819–61)
Poet. He was the son of a Liverpool cotton merchant, and was educated at ⊳ Rugby School under ⊳ Thomas Arnold, and at Balliol College, Oxford. At Oxford he came for a time under the influence of ⊳ Newman, afterwards a Roman ⊳ Catholic but at the time one or the leaders of the Anglican religious revival known as the ⊳ Oxford Movement; later, when Clough was a senior member (Fellow) of Oriel College, he became a sceptic in religious belief. It was necessary (until 1871) to accept the doctrines of the Church of England in order to be a senior member of an Oxford College; thus Clough's religious doubts caused him to resign. He travelled in Europe, was for a short time principal of a students' hostel in London University (where no religious restrictions operated) and lectured in the USA. Finally (1853) he accepted a post under the government in the Education Office. He was the close friend and correspondent of the poet and critic ⊳ Matthew Arnold, who commemorated his death with the elegy *Thyrsis* (pub. 1867). Almost all of Clough's letters to Arnold have disappeared, but Arnold's letters to him (see *Letters to Clough*, ed. H.F. Lowry) are interesting for what they reveal of the minds of the two men. Both were religious doubters, and both were dismayed by the course of 19th-century civilization. Arnold was desolated by the loss of his friend, and attributes his death to premature despair ('Too quick despairer, wherefore wilt thou go?').

Clough's long poems have a light, though scarcely serene, spirit. The best-known ones are the two verse novels, *The Bothie of Tober-na-Vuolich* (1848) and *Amours de Voyage* (1849; pub. 1858), and the uncompleted dramatic dialogue *Dipsychus* (1850; pub. 1869). The first two are written in a metre unusual in English, the Latin hexameter. *Dipsychus* employs a wide variety of metres. The subject of the first poem is a young man of advanced intellectual opinions but emotional immaturity, and his love affair with a Scottish Highland peasant girl who has the emotional maturity that he lacks; published in the revolutionary year of 1848, it also explored ⊳ Chartism and class differences. *Amours* is about a self-doubting man who loses the girl he loves through his inability to arrive at conclusions as to the truth of his own feelings. *Dipsychus*, 'the man in two minds', is a colloquy between a self-doubter and the spirit who haunts him, who admits to the name 'Mephistophilis' and yet is not certainly evil. The other poets of the age were as much afflicted by the torments of doubt as Clough was, but Clough differed from them in relating doubt to the conduct of ordinary daily life, and in his use of a kind of irony which is much more characteristic of 20th-century poets than it is of 19th-century ones. He has consequently attracted much more critical interest in the 20th century than he received in the past; see for example the claims made on his behalf in the Introduction to Tom Paulin's *Faber Book of Political Verse* (1986).
Bib: Chorley, K., *Clough: The Uncommitted Mind*; Houghton, W.E., *The Poetry of Clough*; Goode, J., Hardy, B., essays in *The Major Victorian Poets* (ed. Isobel Armstrong).

Clout, Colin
⊳ Colin Clout.

Club, The
Later known as the 'Literary Club', an informal group founded in the winter of 1763–4 and meeting at this time in the Turk's Head, Soho.

Original members included ▷ Samuel Johnson, ▷ Sir Joshua Reynolds, ▷ Oliver Goldsmith and ▷ Edmund Burke; later, ▷ Thomas Percy, ▷ David Garrick and ▷ James Boswell were amongst those elected.

Cobbe, Frances Power (1822–1904)
Essayist and ▷ travel writer. Born in Newbridge, Dublin, she was educated by ▷ governesses until 1836 when she went to school in Brighton. Her first published work, *Essays on the Theory of Intuitive Morals*, appeared anonymously in 1855. One reviewer described it as 'the work of a lofty and masculine mind'. Cobbé wrote prolifically on religious and moral issues and was deeply involved in social reform, advocating ▷ women's suffrage and arguing that women were not contributing all that they might to society. Her works include *Essays on the Pursuits of Women* (1863); *The Cities of the Past* (1864); *Italics* (1864); *Darwinism in Morals and Other Essays* (1872); *The Moral Aspects of Vivisection* (1875); *The Duties of Women* (1881); *The Scientific Spirit of the Age* (1888) and an autobiography, *Life of Frances Power Cobbe* (1904).
▷ Women's Movement.

Cobbett, William (1762–1835)
Journalist and political leader of the working class, especially of the rural labourer. The son of a small farmer and self-educated, he remained identified with country pursuits and interests. The work by which he is especially known is ▷ *Rural Rides*, an account of tours through England on horseback, written for the enlightenment of a working-class public, and published between 1820 and 1830 in his periodical ▷ *Political Register*, which he edited from 1802 until his death. The *Rides* are famous for their racy, vigorous description of the countryside. His language is always clear, plain and lively; in an autobiographical fragment he declares that his first inspiration in the writing of prose was the work of Jonathan Swift (1667–1745), though he is completely without Swift's ironical suavity. His next most famous work is his *Advice to Young Men* (1829); his *Grammar of the English Language* (1818) is an outstanding guide to the writing of vigorous English.

Apart from the still appreciated vividness of his writings, Cobbett has remained a hero of forthright, independent political journalism. When he was in America (1792–1800) his *Porcupine's Gazette* and various pamphlets were in defence of Britain against the prejudices of the newly independent Americans; once back in England, he refused offers of government patronage, and though he started his *Political Register* in support of the Tories, then in power, in a few years he moved over to radical opposition, and spent two years in prison. In 1832 he was elected Member of Parliament in spite of his refusal to use the corrupt methods for influencing electors common at the time; in Parliament he went into opposition to the Whig government as an extreme left radical. He was excessively quarrelsome and prejudiced, but also exceedingly brave and eloquent in support of the cause of justice as, at any given time, he saw it.
▷ Paine, Thomas

Bib: Cole, G. D. H., *Life; Opinions of William Cobbett*; Lobban, J. H. (ed.), *Rural Rides*, Hughes, A. M. D., *Selections*; Hazlitt, W., in *Spirit of the Age*; Carlyle, E. I., *Cobbett*; Wilson, D. A., *Paine and Cobbett: The Transatlantic Connection*.

Cobbold, Elizabeth (c 1764–1824)
Cobbold was a northern poet, spending most of her life in Liverpool and Manchester. She began publishing when she was 19 with *Poems on Various Subjects* (1783), and followed this with *Six Narrative Poems* (1787). The poetry is bold and energetic, but the subject matter simply repeats the conventional interest in the mysterious and exotic. Her fascination with the sensational continued in her novel *The Sword, or Father Bertrand's History of His Own Times* (1791), a medieval romance which was published under her married name, Clarke. This first marriage lasted only six months, but she soon met John Cobbold, a wealthy Liverpool brewer, and married him in 1792. Her writing continued and she published several pieces of poetry including an ode on the Battle of Waterloo. Perhaps her most interesting work is *The Mince Pye* (1800), a satire of contemporary nationalistic feeling (▷ nationalism). In this later work the energies of her youthful poetry remain, but are directed with a sharp and intelligent wit.
▷ Gothic novels.

Coetzee, John Michael (b 1940)
South African novelist, translator and critic. Educated at the University of Cape Town, where he has taught literature and linguistics since 1972, having previously worked in computing in England and held an academic job at the State University of New York. Since 1984 he has been Professor of General Literature at Cape Town, and has held visiting professorships at various universities in the USA. His fiction includes *Dusklands* (two novellas, 1974); *In the Heart of the Country* (1977; published in the USA as *From the Heart of the Country*); *Waiting for the Barbarians* (1980); *Life and Times of Michael K* (1983); *Foe* (1986); *Age of Iron* (1990). Together with the novelist ▷ André Brink, he edited *A Land Apart: A South African Reader* (1986). His translations include: *A Posthumous Confession*, by Marcellus Emants (1976); *The Expedition to the Baobab Tree*, by Wilma Stockenstrom (1983). Critical writing: *White Writing: On*

the Culture of Letters in South Africa (1988). His fiction frequently works through the self-conscious transformation of established genres, such as the 18th-century novel of travel and exploration (in *Foe*, which takes as its point of departure Daniel Defoe's *Robinson Crusoe*). Coetzee's most persistent concern has been the impact on the self of colonial power-structures; many of his protagonists are compromised by their privileged position within such structures.
Bib: Dovey, T., *The Novels of J. M. Coetzee: Lacanian Allegories*; Penner, A. R., *Countries of the Mind: The Fiction of J. M. Coetzee*; Atwell, D. (ed.), *Doubling the Point: Essays and Interviews*. Attwell, D., *J. M. Coetzee: South Africa and the Politics of Writing.*

Coffee and coffee-houses
Coffee was introduced into England from the east in the mid-17th century, and from the Restoration until the mid-18th century coffee-houses were fashionable public resorts in London. Certain coffee-houses became meeting places for supporters of particular political parties, or for the members of particular professions. Will's Coffee-house became the centre for men of letters; the Cocoa Tree Chocolate-house became the home of Tory politicians, while the Whigs went to St James' Coffee-house; ▷ Lloyd's became popular with merchants; and so forth. In the later 18th century more tea was imported, and as such luxuries were now distributed more widely, ordinary people took to drinking it in their homes. So the century of the flourishing coffee-house was succeeded by that of the domestic tea-party as the typically English social occasion. Some of the coffee-houses survived in other forms; thus Lloyd's became the central office in London for marine insurance, and White's became one of London's most fashionable ▷ clubs.

Coleridge, Hartley (1796–1849)
Poet and miscellaneous author. Hartley was the disreputable son of ▷ Samuel Taylor Coleridge and is generally considered to have squandered his talents and artistic inheritance. His father wrote two poems about him: ▷ *Frost at Midnight* and *The Nightingale*. Hartley's own *Songs and Sonnets* (▷ sonnet) were published in 1833 to some acclaim, and his editions of the plays of Ford and Massinger, and Ascham's *The Scholemaster* (▷ Renaissance) are well thought-out. He spent the last part of his life in the Lake District and several of his personal effects may still be seen at Dove Cottage.
Bib: Hartman, H., *Hartley Coleridge: poet's son and poet*.

Coleridge, Mary (1861–1907)
Poet, novelist and great-great niece of poet and critic Samuel Taylor Coleridge (1772–1834). Born in London, she lived with her parents who played host to a number of distinguished literary figures including ▷ Tennyson, ▷ Browning, ▷ Ruskin and ▷ Fanny Kemble. In 1895 she taught at the Working Women's College. She wrote a number of novels including *The Seven Sleepers of Ephesus* (1893) and a historical ▷ romance *The King with Two Faces* (1897). Her poetry, which she wrote continuously throughout her life, was admired by ▷ Robert Bridges but Coleridge herself was reluctant to publish it. She produced two volumes, *Fancy's Following* (1896) and *Fancy's Guerdon* (1897), both of which appeared under her ▷ pseudonym 'Anodos'. After her death from appendicitis a collection of 200 poems was gleaned from her letters and notebooks by fellow poet Henry Newbolt (1862–1938) and published in 1907 (expanded 1954). Her themes are those of female friendship and spinsterly solidarity, love's elusiveness and the fragility of identity. Others briefly record psychic and dream states. Her most famous poem is 'The Other Side of the Mirror' which 20th-century feminist critics Sandra Gilbert and Susan Gubar regard as an examination of the monstrous alter-ego of the female (▷ *Jane Eyre*). Her other works include: a collection of short prose sketches, *Non Sequiter* (1900); three novels, *The Fiery Dream* (1901), *The Shadow on the Wall* (1904), *The Lady on the Drawing Room Floor* (1906), and a ▷ biography of Holman Hunt (1908). *Gathered Leaves* (1910) contains extracts from her letters and diaries.
Bib: Gilbert, S. and Gubar, S., *The Madwoman in the Attic*; Leighton, A., and Reynolds, M. (eds.), *An Anthology of Victorian Women Poets*, Bernikow, L. (ed), *The World Split Open*.

Coleridge, Samuel Taylor (1772–1834)
Poet and critic. Son of a Devon clergyman, he was educated in London and at Jesus College Cambridge. He left Cambridge to enlist in the Dragoons under the pseudonym Silas Tomkyn Comberbache, and although he returned after a matter of months he never completed his degree. His early religious leanings were towards Unitarianism. In 1794 he made the acquaintance of ▷ Robert Southey, with whom, under the influence of the ▷ French Revolution, he evolved a communistic scheme which they called ▷ 'Pantisocracy', and together they wrote the tragedy, *The Fall of Robespierre*. In 1795 he married Sara Fricker, Southey marrying her sister. His *Poems on Various Subjects* were published in 1796, at about the time he met ▷ Wordsworth. The two poets became friends, and lived close to each other for a time in Somerset. ▷ *Kubla Khan* and the first part of ▷ *Christabel* were written in this period, though they were not published until later. The joint publication, ▷ *Lyrical Ballads*, which included Coleridge's ▷ *The Rime of the Ancient Mariner*, appeared in 1798. Coleridge expressed his loss of faith in the French Revolution in *France, An Ode* (1798).

In 1798–9 he travelled in Germany and came under the influence of the transcendental philosophy of Schlegel and ▷ Kant, which dominates his later theoretical writing. During 1800–4 he moved near to Wordsworth in Keswick, and fell unhappily in love with his sister-in-law, Sarah Hutchinson, a relationship referred to in ▷ *Dejection: An Ode* (1802). Early in his life he had become reliant on opium and never succeeded in fully controlling the addiction. He began to give public lectures and became famous for his table talk. In 1809 he founded a periodical, *The Friend*, which was later published as a book (1818). In 1817 appeared ▷ *Biographia Literaria*, his autobiographical apologia and a landmark in literary theory and criticism. He quarrelled with Wordsworth in 1810, and in later life he lived in the homes of various benefactors, including the surgeon, James Gillman, who helped him to cope with his addiction. He became increasingly Tory in politics and Anglican in religion, developing an emotionalist conservatism in the tradition of Burke.

Coleridge's poetic output is small, diverse, but of great importance. His ▷ 'conversation poems', such as *Frost at Midnight* (1798), *This Lime-Tree Bower, My Prison* (1800), continue and deepen the reflective tradition of Gray and Cowper, culminating in the poignant *Dejection: An Ode* (1802). On the other hand his major symbolic works, such as *The Rime of the Ancient Mariner* (1798), *Kubla Khan* (1816) and *Christabel* (1816), plumb new psychological and emotional depths, and can be seen to develop along similar lines as his famous theoretical definition of imagination in *Biographia Literaria*, Chapter XIII. His perspectives are consistently more intellectually alert than those of his friend Wordsworth, though the expression of his philosophical ideas is sometimes confused. His sympathetic but discriminating analysis of Wordsworth's work in *Biographia Literaria* is a model of unfussy analytical method. As both practitioner and theorist, Coleridge is central to ▷ Romanticism.

▷ Coleridge, Hartley

Bib: House, H., *Coleridge*; Lowes, J. L., *The Road to Xanadu*; Coburn, K., *In Pursuit of Coleridge*; Holmes, R., *Coleridge*; Jackson, J. R. de J. (ed.), *Coleridge: The Critical Heritage*; Jones, A. R., and Tydeman, W., *Coleridge: The Ancient Mariner and Other Poems* (Macmillan Casebook); Fruman, N., *Coleridge: The Damaged Archangel*; Cooke, K., *Coleridge*; Hamilton, P., *Coleridge's Poetics*; Wheeler, K. M., *The Creative Mind in Coleridge's Poetry*; Sultana, D. (ed.), *New Approaches to Coleridge*; Magnuson, P., *Coleridge's Nightmare Poetry*; Holmes, R., *Coleridge: Early Visions.*

Coleridge, Sara (1802–52)
Writer, the daughter of poet and critic Samuel Taylor Coleridge (1772–1834). She educated herself, with the help of poet Robert Southey (1774–1843), acquiring six languages and a good knowledge of Classics and philosophy. Wordsworth described her as 'remarkably clever'. In 1822 she translated Dobrizhoffer's Latin *Account of the Abipones* and in 1825 the *Memoirs* of the Chevalier Bayard. She married her cousin, Henry Coleridge, in 1829, and lived in Hampstead, London, where she wrote *Pretty Lessons in Verse for Good Children* (1834) and the fantastical poem *Phantasmion* (1837). In 1843 Henry died, after which Coleridge devoted herself to organizing, editing and annotating her father's works, a task which she performed with great skill. She was greatly admired in London literary society, and her *Memoir and Letters* was published in 1873.

Bib: Wilson, M., *These Were Muses*; Woolf, V., 'Sara Coleridge' in *Death of the Moth and Other Essays*; Leighton, A., and Reynolds, M. (eds.), *An Anthology of Victorian Women Poets.*

Colin Clout
The name adopted by ▷ Edmund Spenser in his ▷ pastoral sequence ▷ *The Shepherd's Calendar* and his allegorical work *Colin Clout's Come Home Again* (1594), written to describe his visit to London and the court in 1589–91. The name became something of a code-word amongst the Spenserian poets, who, in emulation of Spenser, would refer to 'Colin' and adopt their own pastoral personae.

Collier, Jane (1710–1754/5)
English writer and social critic. She knew Latin and Greek, and numbered ▷ Sarah Fielding among her friends, as well as ▷ Samuel Richardson, whose ▷ *Clarissa* she criticized. Anonymously, she published *Essay on the Art of Ingeniously Tormenting* (1753) – 'general instructions for plaguing all your acquaintence'. This demonstrates the power of satire and burlesque in pointing to the need for social change. For instance, she advises the tormenting of female servants; 'Always scold her, if she is the least undressed or dirty; and say you cannot bear such beasts about you. If she is clean and welldressed, tell her that you suppose she dresses out for the fellows.' In the next chapter she advises on the patroness's treatment of her humble female companion, noting, 'there is some difficulty in giving rules for tormenting a dependant, that shall differ from those laid down for plaging and teazing your servants, as the two stations differ so little in themselves.' With Sarah Fielding she wrote *The Cry: a New Dramatic Fable* (1754).

Collier, Jeremy (1650–1726)
Cleric and writer. Born at Stow-cum-Quy in Cambridgeshire, Collier was educated at Ipswich and Cambridge, and became rector of Ampton near Bury St Edmunds, and a lecturer

at Gray's Inn. His life subsequently involved repeated conflicts with the authorities because of his unorthodox religious and political views and behaviour: he was imprisoned for his reply to ▷ Bishop Burnet's *Inquiry into the State of Affairs* (1688), arrested on suspicion of Jacobitism (▷ Jacobite) 1692, and outlawed for giving absolution to two condemned political criminals in 1696. However, it was his *A Short View of the Immorality and Profaneness of the English Stage* (1698) which caused the most lasting furore, this time among dramatists against whom the attack was directed. A war of words ensued, with ▷ Congreve, ▷ Dryden and ▷ Vanbrugh among those responding to Collier, and he replying in turn. Although his stance was by no means unique in its day, he is credited with influencing the development of ▷ sentimental drama. His onslaught was the more effective for the knowledge he displayed of dramatic texts, if not performances. He became a bishop in 1713. His works also include the *Great Historical, Geographical, Genealogical, and Poetical Dictionary* (1701–1721) and *An Ecclesiastical History of Great Britain* from (1708–1714).

Collier, Mary (1679-after 1762)
English poet who worked as a rural labourer, washerwoman, brewer and later, housekeeper. She paid for the publication of *The Woman's Labour* (1739), and in the reprinted version of 1762 argued that she wrote it in reply to the labourer-poet ▷ Stephen Duck's *The Thresher's Labour*. Her poem testifies to the drudgery of women's field labour: 'When night comes on, unto our home we go, / Our Corn we carry, and our Infant too; / Weary indeed! but 'tis not worth our while / Once to complain, or rest at every Stile; / We must make haste, for when we home are come, / We find again our Work but just begun.' Her poetry is a determined self-conscious articulation of the particular interlocking circumstances of gender and status. She later published, by subscription, *Poems on Several Occasions* (1762).

▷ Leapor, Mary; Little, Janet; Yearsley, Ann.
Bib: Landry, Donna, *The Muses of Resistance*; Lonsdale (ed.), *Eighteenth Century Women's Poetry*.

Collins, An
Devotional poet. Little is known about her life except that which is revealed in her one extant work, the ▷ autobiographical *Divine Songs and Meditations* (1653). It can therefore be assumed that she belonged to a reasonably well-off family, that she had suffered serious ill health since childhood and had, consequently, not been engaged in the usual female occupations or been able to have children. She was certainly antagonistic to the more radical forms of ▷ Puritanism, but it is disputed as to whether she was pro- or anti-Calvinist (see G. Greer (ed.), *Kissing the Rod* (1988) and E. Graham et al. (eds.), *Her Own Life* (1989)). Her poems are spiritual in nature, drawing upon biblical imagery and focusing upon the torments and respites of the Christian soul on earth.

▷ Calvin, John.
Bib: Hobby, E., *Virtue of Necessity*.

Collins, Merle
Caribbean poet and novelist. Collins was born and educated in Grenada, where she worked as a teacher until the US invasion in 1983. She is now a lecturer at the University of North London. Her first novel was *Angel* (1987) and was followed by *Rotten Pomerack* (1992). *Rain Darling* (1990) is a collection of stories and she edited, with Rhonda Cobham, *Watchers and Seekers: Creative Writing by Black Women in Britain* (1987). As well as poems in anthologies, she has published a collection, *Because the Dawn Breaks, Poems Dedicated to the Grenadian People* (1985).

Collins, Wilkie (1824–89)
Novelist; one of the first ▷ detective novelists in English. His two famous novels are *The Woman in White* (1860), first published in ▷ *Household Words*, a magazine edited by ▷ Charles Dickens, and ▷ *The Moonstone* (1868). These novels of ▷ sensation established a pattern for English detective fiction. His mastery was especially over plot-construction in which he influenced Dickens. His characterization is less distinguished but in *The Woman in White* he excels in this, too, and in the creation of disturbing atmosphere. He collaborated with Dickens in a few stories in *Household Words* and in ▷ *All the Year Round*: *The Wreck of the Golden Mary*, *A Message from the Sea*, *No Thoroughfare*. Collins' other novels include *No Name* (1862) and *Armadale* (1866), which has been praised for its ▷ melodrama.
Bib: Robinson, K., *Life*; Phillips, W.C., *Dickens, Reade and Collins: Sensation Novelists*; Ashley, R., *Wilkie Collins*; Eliot, T. S., Preface to *The Moonstone*, World's Classics edition; Lonoff, S., *Wilkie Collins and His Victorian Readers*; Peters, C., *The King of Inventors: A Life of Wilkie Collins*; Rance, N., *Wilkie Collins and Other Sensation Novelists*; Hetler, T., *Dead Secrets: Wilkie Collins and the Female Gothic*.

Collins, William (1721–59)
Poet. The son of a hatter in Chichester, he published his *Persian Eclogues* in 1742 while he was still an undergraduate at Oxford. Their elegant exoticism and musical use of the pentameter couplet (▷ metre) made them popular, and they were reissued in 1757 as *Oriental Eclogues*. However his *Odes on Several Descriptive and Allegorical Subjects* (1746), which includes much of his best work, achieved

little success at the time. The romantic *Ode on the Popular Superstitions of the Highlands of Scotland Considered as a Subject of Poetry* was written about 1749 but not published until 1788. In 1750 he suffered a mental breakdown and wrote no more verse before his death nine years later in Chichester. Collins' small output shows a fragile combination of exquisite classical control and intense lyricism. In such poems as *Ode* ('How sleep the Brave'), *To Evening* and *The Passions* he develops his own distinctive rococo idiom, involving the constant use of pretty personifications and classical abstraction, reminiscent of the friezes on Wedgewood pottery. His rhythms and tone are peculiarly original, and often quite haunting, though the influence of ▷ Thomas Gray, James Thomson and ▷ John Milton is often evident.
Bib: Johnson, S., *Lives of the Poets*; Garrod, H. W., *Collins*; Carver, P. L., *The Life of a Poet: A Biographical Sketch of William Collins.*

Colman, George, the Elder (1732–94)
Dramatist, essayist, theatre manager. He controlled first Covent Garden, and then the Haymarket Theatre and was responsible for staging the earliest productions of Oliver Goldsmith's (1730–74) plays, as well as writing dozens of plays, masques, and operas himself. He began writing poetry while still a pupil at Westminster School, and after receiving a degree at Oxford University and being called to the bar, he still retained his literary interests. Through his friendship with the actor David Garrick (1717–79), he became involved in the theatre, and eventually abandoned law as a career. In 1760 his first play, the farcical *Polly Honeycombe*, billed as 'a dramatic novel', was produced at ▷ Drury Lane. Six years later he collaborated with Garrick on ▷ *The Clandestine Marriage*, his most successful work.

After inheriting a fortune from his mother, Colman purchased a major interest in the Covent Garden Theatre which came under his joint management in 1767. Among his ventures there were productions of Goldsmith's *The Good-Natur'd Man*, and *She Stoops to Conquer*. In 1776 Colman acquired the Little Theatre in the Haymarket, where in 1781 he successfully staged John Gay's (1685–1732) *The Beggar's Opera* (1728), with women cast as the men and vice versa.

▷ Colman, George, the Younger.
Bib: Burnim, K. A., *The Plays of George Colman the Elder*; Wood, E. R. (ed.), *The Plays of David Garrick and George Colman the Elder.*

Colman, George, the Younger (1762–1836)
Dramatist, miscellany writer, and theatre manager. Son of ▷ George Colman, the elder. He was educated at Westminster School, and at Oxford, like his father. Again like his father, he was intended for the law, but preferred the stage, and had a musical farce, *The Female Dramatist*, produced at the Haymarket Theatre in 1782. In 1784 he underwent a clandestine marriage to the actress Clara Morris, of whom his father disapproved, and re-married her in open ceremony in 1788. In 1789, his father having been stricken with paralysis, and suffering from mental deterioration, he took over management of the Little Theatre in the Haymarket. He proved an effective manager, despite a penchant for personal extravagance which, among other factors, involved him in a series of quarrels and lawsuits. As a dramatist he was prolific, contributing more than 20 plays and musical entertainments, including several which became firm favourites, such as the comic opera, *Inkle and Yarico* (1787). In 1824 he was appointed Examiner of Plays, a title he retained to his death. He proved a fastidious censor, excising all supposedly blasphemous and indecent references, even though some of his own productions skirted close to the margins of propriety.
Bib: Tasch, P. A. (ed.), *The Plays of George Colman the Younger*; Sutcliffe, B. (ed.), *Plays by George Colman the Younger and Thomas Morton.*

***Colonel Jack* (1722)**
The History and Remarkable Life of Colonel Jacque, a novel by ▷ Daniel Defoe. Jack is abandoned by his parents, becomes a thief, a soldier, a slave on an American plantation, a planter, and eventually a rich and repentant man back in England. The sequence through crime, suffering and repentance, and from poverty to prosperity, is typical of Defoe's novels.

Colonialism
'Colonization' is normally understood to mean the process of annexation of a country or countries by an imperial power and the establishment of colonies or settlements fully or partly subject to that power. 'Colonialism' can therefore be glossed as the process by which those settlements are maintained in a subordinate relationship to that imperial power. The most aggressively colonial European countries were France, Portugal, Spain and Britain, and the areas most subject to colonization included the Indian sub-continent, Africa, Australasia, the Americas and the Caribbean.

Colonialism does not have to imply formal annexation, however. Colonial status involves the imposition of decisions by one people upon another, where the economy or political structure has been brought under the overwhelming influence of another country. Western colonialism was most active from 1450 to 1900. It began in the Renaissance with the voyages of discovery; the new territories were annexed for their material resources and for the scope they offered to missionary efforts to extend the power of the Church. By the 18th century, Britain had acquired control of India, Canada and other territories, and ranked as the greatest European colonial power. The loss of the colonies of North America in the ▷ American War of Independence was a blow, but not a devastating one. Concern about the conditions of slaves in some of the colonies fuelled the anti-slavery movement (▷ William Wilberforce). One consequence of this movement was the renewed popularity of ▷ Thomas Southerne's play ▷ *Oroonoko* (1696), based on ▷ Aphra Behn's novel of the same name, which featured a black slave as its hero. The last independent non-Western territories were parcelled out in 1900.

There was a strong tradition, founded on the imperialism myth of the Victorian era, of which ▷ Thomas Carlyle, ▷ Rudyard Kipling and ▷ Rider Haggard were the most famous exponents, that white intervention was made in the interests of the native inhabitants. Carlyle's essay 'An Occasional Discourse on the Nigger Question' (1849) claimed that the abolition of slavery in the British Empire in 1833 had led to the negroes becoming 'sluggards' and 'scoundrels'. In reality, freed slaves were refusing to work the plantations unless they were paid a decent wage. For Carlyle however, the negro was 'an idle Black gentleman, with his rum-bottle in his hand... breeches on his body, pumpkin at discretion, and the fruitfulest region of the earth going back to jungle around him'. His answer was to advocate the use of the whip to compel them back to work.

Carlyle's views alienated those more liberal Victorians such as ▷ John Stuart Mill, and his isolation was made even more acute when he demonstrated his support for the controversial British colonial officer Governor John Edward Eyre (1815–1901). Eyre emigrated to Australia for reasons of health, where he became a sheep farmer and explored much of the continent. He served as a magistrate and protector of the Australian Aborigines and was later appointed Governor of New Zealand (1846–53). In 1853 he became Acting Governor of various of the Caribbean islands (1853–64) and permanent governor of Jamaica. Shortly after his appointment to Jamaica there was a black rebellion at Morant Bay (October 11, 1865). Eyre used extreme measures to crush the rebellion and also took excessive reprisals. In all there were over 400 executions. In the end Jamaica became a crown colony and Eyre was recalled by the British government in 1866. Although he was commended for overcoming the revolt his methods were censured. Prominent British intellectuals of the time such as Mill, ▷ Herbert Spencer and ▷ Thomas Henry Huxley called for trial for murder. In addition to Carlyle, Eyre's supporters also included ▷ John Ruskin and ▷ Alfred, Lord Tennyson. Eyre was not indicted for murder and was also found innocent in a civil case brought against him by a Jamaican (▷ *Jane Eyre*).

Carlyle's friend and future biographer the novelist James Anthony Froude (1818–94) visited the Caribbean in 1886 and subsequently wrote *The English in the West Indies, or, The Bow of Ulysses* (1888) which strongly advocates government intervention to protect white settlers from being 'crowded out by the blacks'. Froude also supported Eyre, claiming he had been 'unworthily sacrificed to public clamour'. Another visitor to the West Indies was the novelist ▷ Charles Kingsley and his *At Last: A Christmas in the West Indies* (1871) is an enthusiastic account of the natural history of the West Indian colonies.

The colonization of Africa began in earnest in response to the demand for raw materials and markets caused by the ▷ Industrial Revolution. The 'scramble for Africa' between the various European powers in 1884 led to the Berlin West Africa Conference (1884–5) which agreed on an orderly partitioning of the continent and in particular the territory of the Congo. Despite this, tensions were rife between the British, Dutch and French and, towards the end of the 19th century, the Germans. The British colonial effort was aided by the explorations of David Livingstone (1813–73) from 1841 until his death, and the Welsh explorer Henry Morton Stanley in the late 1870s. The British financier and empire builder Cecil Rhodes helped to maintain a colonial presence for Britain in Africa in the mid 1880s. Kingsley's niece, ▷ Mary Kingsley, travelled extensively in West Africa between 1893 and 1895 recording her experiences in a number of books on the subject.

By 1818, after the successful resolution of the Napoleonic wars had removed the French threat, Britain was the dominant European power in India. Under the Governor Generalship of the ▷ Utilitarian Lord William Bentinck, who was instrumental in the suppression of *sati* (the sacrifice of Hindu widows on their husband's funeral pyres) and *thagi* (ritual murder and robbery by gangs), India was encouraged to absorb and adopt Western learning and culture through the medium of English and by 1857 Britain had established complete political control of the Indian sub-continent. However, in 1857 the Bengal army mutinied and what began as a military incident soon escalated into a full-scale popular revolt. Britain did not regain supremacy until 1859, threatening the fragile peace with vicious and often indiscriminate reprisals. The 60 years between the suppression of the mutiny and the end of the First World War saw both the rise of British imperial power in India, and nationalist agitation against it. It was characterized by British racial arrogance and often violent abuse of 'native' Indians. ▷ Rudyard Kipling coined the phrase 'the white man's burden' to describe the duties incumbent upon British officials sent to serve in India. The British government of India became 'the world's largest imperial bureaucracy' (Encyclopaedia Britannica) and transfer of power was effected only after partition in 1947.

British colonization of Australia began in earnest in 1788 with the landing of 730 convicts and 250 free persons at Botany Bay in January of that year. By 1830 the number of convict settlers in the country had reached 58,000, a third of which were Irish rebelling against British colonial policy in Ireland. The Australian Marcus Clarke's novel *For the Term of His Natural Life* (1874) remains a vivid description of convict experience. Between 1829 and 1859 four of Australia's six states were established: Western Australia, South Australia, and the Northern and Southern portions of New South Wales. However, led by New South Wales all the colonies achieved self-government by 1856.

▷ Karl Marx wrote articles specifically about the colonization of Ireland by England and about the British Empire in India, stressing the link between capitalism and colonialism. This was followed in the early 20th century by the link of capital to imperialism and, in the 1950s to the present day on the unequal relations between countries and the emergence of multi-national capitalism.

The recognition of difference and the awareness of inequalities in economic terms mirrored the dissolution of empires, which began in 1947 as colonial countries gained independence. This sometimes occurred through warfare, as in Kenya and Algeria in the 1950s. While there are no formal 'empires' today, the relinquishing of control has been slow and Western influence on the third world in economic and political terms is still very strong.

▷ Orientalism; Post-colonialism.

Bib: Johnston, H.H., *History of the Colonization of Africa by Alien Races*; Gopal, S., *British Policy in India*, 1858–1903; Shaw, A.G.L., *Convicts and the Colonized* (1830–60); Memmi, A., *The Colonizer and the Colonized*; Said, E., *Orientalism*; Spivak, G.C., *In Other Worlds*; Bolt, C., *Victorian Attitudes to Race*; Fieldhouse, D.K., *The Colonial Empire*; Parry, J.H., *Trade and Dominion*; Williams, P. and Chrisman, L. (eds.), *Colonial Discourse and Post-Colonial Theory*; Brewer, A., *Marxist Theories of Imperialism: A Critical Survey*.

Columba, St (c AD 521–97)
Son of an Irish chieftain, he became a Christian evangelist to Scotland, where he founded the monastery of Hy on the Island of Iona. The book of his miracles was written by Adomnan of Iona.

Combe, William (1741–1823)
Humorist, prose writer and poet. Combe is associated with the cult of the ▷ Picturesque through his most well-known works. In 1790 he published *The Devil Upon Two Sticks*, a continuation of the French comic author Alain-René Lesage's *Le Diable Boiteaux* (1707). This is a witty picturesque narrative which predates the more sentimental ▷ Romantic versions. Some time later, in 1809, he provided the poetry to accompany the comic illustrations of Thomas Rowlandson in the first of the 'Dr Syntax' series, which were crude parodies of the picturesque travel books of the day. They continued this collaboration through three works, finally collected as *The Three Tours of Dr Syntax* (1826). Syntax is a clergyman and a school teacher who is confronted with a series of strange and grotesque events which leave him open to ridicule. The character of Syntax was based on the author ▷ William Gilpin.

▷ French literature in England.

Bib: Hamilton, H.W., *Doctor Syntax: a silhouette of Combe*.

Comedy
▷ Humours, Comedy of; Manners, Comedy of.

***Comedy of Errors, The* (1592)**
An early comedy and ▷ Shakespeare's shortest play, based on Plautus' *Menaechmi*. The elements of ▷ farce and confusion in the original are enhanced in Shakespeare's taut play – it observes the neo-classical unities of time, place and action – by the addition of a second pair of twins, the Dromios, servants to the lost and separated Ephesian and Syracusan Antipholi. Shakespeare further departs from his source by foregrounding the marriage of Adriana and the Ephesian Antipholus with reference, imaginatively, to St Paul's view on marriage and sexual identity. The play is full of vitality and supersedes the reductive and mercenary view of society propounded in its classical source.

Comedy of Humour, The
▷ *Humour, Comedy of*

***Cometh Up as a Flower* (1867)**
A novel of ▷ sensation by ▷ Rhoda Broughton. The heroine, Nell le Strange, is left as the head of a motherless household and delights in her father's affection. She is later attracted to a handsome guardsman, but he is already married and Nell has to accept a marriage of convenience to a rich old man, Sir Hugh. The novel is noteworthy for its description of Nell's revulsion, both at her aged husband and her situation as a 'bought' woman. She decides not to leave Sir Hugh after reading ▷ Mrs Henry Wood's ▷ *East Lynne*, and eventually dies of consumption.

Comic verse
In direct contrast to the tendency towards

earnestness and social responsibility championed by ▷ Thomas Carlyle, the Victorians also produced a large body of light literature including excellent comic verse, parodies and ▷ nonsense. The Victorian's love of humour is perhaps best exemplified in ▷ *Punch* magazine, founded in 1841, which claimed, despite its Radical politics, to be primarily a 'Guffawgraph'.

One of the most successful and gifted parodists was ▷ William Aytoun whose *The Book of Ballads: Edited by Bon Gaultier* (1845), published jointly with Theodore Martin (1816–1909), satirizes the inflated sentiment of ▷ Tennyson among others. However, Aytoun's most influential parody was his *Firmilian, or the Student of Badajoz: A Spasmodic Tragedy by T. Percy Jones* (1854) which helped to destroy the reputation of the ▷ Spasmodic school of poets. The novelist ▷ Thackeray parodied the weaknesses of ▷ Disraeli, ▷ Bulwer-Lytton, ▷ Mrs Gore and many others in his *Mr Punch's Prize Novelists* (1847). Other parodies include C.S. Calverley's *Verses and Translations* (1862), W.S. Gilbert's *Bab Ballads* (1869), which contains a skit on Coleridge's *The Ancient Mariner*, and Lewis Carroll's *Alice in Wonderland* (1865) and *Through the Looking Glass* (1872) which contain imitations of Tennyson and ▷ Southey. W.S. Gilbert's collaboration with Arthur Sullivan, which began in 1871, resulted in the Savoy Operas which raised farce to a totally new level.

Nonsense verse was pioneered by ▷ Edward Lear, who borrowed the limerick form from an anonymous collection entitled *Anecdotes of Fifteen Gentlemen* (c 1821), and went on to popularize it. The tradition was continued by Carroll in such poems as 'The Hunting of the Snark' (1876) and *Dreamland* (1882). The Victorian age's talent for self-ridicule can be summed up in ▷ Swinburne's own *Seven Against Sense* (1880).

Bib: Henkle, R.B., *Comedy and Culture; England 1820–1900*; Huggett, E. (ed), *Victorian England as Seen by 'Punch'*; Sewell, E., *The Field of Nonsense*.

Comical Revenge, The: or, Love in a Tub (1664)

Play by ▷ Sir George Etherege, his first, with a complex and partly tedious series of plots in four different modes: 1 heroic, or mock-heroic, concerning love and honour, and including a duel, in rhymed couplets; 2 witty sparring courtship between Sir Frederick Frollick and the Widow; 3 gulling or trickery, of Sir Nicholas Cully, who is deceived into marrying a whore; 4 farce involving outright clowning, mainly by the absurd Dufoy and his associates. The title derives from the predicament of Dufoy, who has contracted venereal disease, and must sweat in a tub as part of the 'cure'.

Commedia dell'Arte

A kind of Italian comedy, developed in the 16th century, in which the plot was written but the dialogue was improvised by the actors. Certain characters regularly recurred in these plays, and by the 18th century they were adopted in England (by the way of France) and became a part of the English puppet shows (*eg* Punch and Judy) and of the pantomime tradition. Such characters, anglicized, include Harlequin, his mistress Columbine, Pantaloon, Punch.

Common metre

A four-line stanza with alternating four and three stresses and alternating rhymes. It is especially common in ▷ hymns, ▷ carols and ▷ ballads.

Common Prayer, The Book of

The first *Book of Common Prayer* was prepared under the supervision of ▷ Archbishop Cranmer and issued in 1549 to meet the needs of the ▷ Church of England for services and prayers in the vernacular. It is of great importance as a work of literature, for Cranmer succeeded in combining the plainness and directness of English with the dignity and sonority of Latin. Prayer Book language became a familiar and formative influence in speech and writing second only in importance to the Bible itself. There were revisions in 1552 and 1559. The Prayer Book authorized in 1662 was substantially the 1559 revision. A fairly extensive revision was blocked by Parliament in 1928. There are now alternative forms of the various services in use.

Companies, joint-stock

Companies whose profits are distributed among the shareholders. They began in the 16th century and largely superseded the older 'regulated company' whose members traded each on his own account and combined only for common protection. The greatest of the regulated companies was the Merchant Adventurers, founded in the 15th century; the greatest of the joint-stock companies was the ▷ East India Company founded in 1600: in the latter half of the 18th century the status of this changed from being a purely commercial concern to being an organ of imperial power, the effective sovereign power in Bengal.

▷ Colonialism.

Competence and performance

These terms, first proposed by the American linguist Noam Chomsky, are used in the study of language to refer to a speaker's overall competence to speak a language as distinct from his or her actual performance in it. The distinction is important to linguists because it allows them to analytically separate the way the system of a language operates from any individual usage. In this way it is similar to Ferdinand de Saussure's differentiation between ▷ *langue* and *parole*. For the individual language user, the competence/performance distinction is important because it helps explain how we can learn new pieces of language. Our competence in a language includes, often unconsciously, a knowledge of basic structural features which enable us to assimilate new material.

The competence/performance distinction has also been used by structuralist literary critics like Jonathan Culler with reference to our ability to interpret literary texts. Experienced readers of literature internalise the rules by which such texts operate (this is a reader's literary competence). They are therefore able to apply these when new work is presented to them (this is performance). Literary competence consists of a number of things, from a sophisticated capacity to read the language in which the texts are written, and a familiarity with the structures and conventions of literary works, to an array of more specialized cultural and literary knowledge which permits understanding and interpretation.

Bib: Culler, J., *Structuralist Poetics*.

Complaint

A term used to refer to poems (in a variety of forms), usually in the voice of a first-person speaker, which lament the vicissitudes of life, especially the pangs of disappointed or unrequited love. Used by medieval French poets, it appears to have been employed first by ▷ Chaucer, who intercalated complaints within larger narrative contexts (*eg* in Dorigen's complaint in the ▷ *Franklin's Tale*) but who also produced a number of individual complaint poems. In Renaissance literature, ▷ Spenser's ▷ *The Shepherd's Calendar* provides a good example of the complaint, but afterwards the terms elegy or lament are more frequently used to signal complaint-type poetry.

Compleat Angler, The **(1653)**

A discourse on the sport of fishing (in full, *The Compleat Angler, or the Contemplative Man's Recreation*) by ▷ Izaak Walton, first published in 1653; its 5th edition has a continuation by Charles Cotton (1630–87) and came out in 1676. The book has been described as perhaps the only handbook of art and craft to rank as literature. This is because Walton combines his practical instruction with digressions about his personal tastes and opinions, and sets it in a direct, fresh description of the English countryside which may be contrasted with the artificial pastoralism that had hitherto been characteristic of natural description. The book has the form of a dialogue mainly between Piscator (Fisherman) and Venator (Hunter), which takes place on the banks of the River Lea near London. Cotton's continuation is transferred to the banks of the River Dove between Derbyshire and Staffordshire. Throughout the text, Walton also relates moral issues to the political events of his day and, while not strictly allegorical *The Compleat Angler* does include numerous social references.

Bib: Bevan, J., *Izaak Walton's The Compleat Angler*.

Compton-Burnett, Ivy (1884–1969)

Novelist. Her first novel, *Dolores* (1911) is distinguished from all her others by an approach to the method of novel-writing similar to that of the 19th century, in particular that of George Eliot, and a disposition to accept usual conceptions of moral retribution. From *Pastors and Masters* (1925) both the method and the moral vision change radically. The novels are narrated almost wholly through dialogue; the manner derives from Jane Austen, but with even less attempt to present visualized environments. In treating occurrences such as matricide, bigamy, betrayal and incest they show affinities with Greek tragic drama, while the novels of ▷ Samuel Butler are another important influence. The period is always 1890–1914; the setting, a prosperous household of the period; the characters include some who are arrogant to the point of evil, and are able, without retribution, to dominate those who are selfless or weak; the plots are melodramatic but never break up the surface of respectability. The dialogue is epigrammatic and pungent, with the consequence that the novels are all exceptionally concentrated structures. The effect is commonly of sardonic comedy with tragic conclusion, although the comic side tends to dominate.

After 1925 the novels are as follows: *Brothers and Sisters* (1929); *Men and Wives* (1931); *More Women than Men* (1933); *A House and its Head* (1935); *Daughters and Sons* (1937); *A Family and a Fortune* (1939); *Parents and Children* (1941); *Elders and Betters* (1944); *Manservant and Maidservant* (1947); *Two Worlds and Their Ways* (1949); *Darkness and Day* (1951); *The Present and the Past* (1953); *Mother and Son* (1955); *A Father and his Fate* (1957); *A Heritage and its History* (1959); *The Mighty and their Fall* (1961); *A God and His Gifts* (1963); *The Last and the First* (1971). Few distinguished novelists have shown such uniformity of treatment and lack of development throughout their career. Probably *A House and its Head* and *A Family and a Fortune* are her two outstanding achievements.

Bib: Hansford Johnson, P., *Ivy Compton-Burnett*; Liddell, R., *The Novels of Ivy Compton-Burnett*; Spurling, H., *Ivy When Young* and *Secrets of a Woman's Heart*.

Comte, Auguste (1798–1857)

French philosopher. He sought to expound a scientifically based philosophy for human progress called Positivism, which deduced laws of development from the facts of history and excluded metaphysics and religion. His chief works were translated into English. In them he sought to establish a system that would be the scientific equivalent of the Catholic system of philosophy. In this he failed, but his work led to the modern science of sociology. In England, his chief disciple was Frederick Harrison (1831–1923). The character of his beliefs suited radically reformist and religiously sceptical English intellectuals; on the other hand, his systematization of ideas was alien to English habits of mind. His emphasis on the science of social phenomena, sociology, was intended to lay the foundations of a social and political system geared to the new age of industry. This, combined with his vision of an educational role for the priesthood, marks him as an antagonist to the dominant strains of thought in the Romantic period.

Comus (1634)

The name now given to the ▷ masque written by ▷ John Milton and performed at Ludlow Castle in 1634. The work's original title was simply *A Maske, presented at Ludlow Castle, 1634, before the Earl of Bridgewater, Lord President of Wales.* This title stresses the important features of any masque – its occasional quality, and the names of those who either witnessed or took part in the masque. Music for the masque was composed by ▷ Henry Lawes and principal parts were taken by the children of the Earl of Bridgewater. The masque endeavours to demonstrate the triumph of virtue and chastity over luxury and sensual excess, although generations of readers and critics have found it easier to identify with the anti-hero Comus, rather than with the 'Lady' who opposes his arguments.
Bib: Editions include: Diekhoff, J. S. (ed.), *A Maske at Ludlow.*

Conceit

A conceit is a ▷ metaphor or simile that initially appears improbable, but which forces the reader to acknowledge the comparison even though it is exceedingly far-fetched. The classic example comes from ▷ John Donne's poem 'A Valediction: forbidding Mourning' where he compares himself and his mistress to 'stiff twin compasses'. Comparing two lovers to a mathematical instrument at first seems strange, but the aptness is derived from the fact that even when one partner (foot of the compasses/lover) moves away from the other, they are always joined together (at the hinge of the compasses/in their hearts). This intellectual delight in complicated parallels originates in the ▷ Petrarchan influence upon ▷ Elizabethan poetry and it became an important aspect of sonnets and of ▷ metaphysical verse.

Condell, Henry (d 1627)

▷ Heming, John.

Condensation

This term is used by ▷ Freud in *The Interpretation of Dreams* (1900) to describe the compression and selection that takes place during the process of dreaming. When subjected to analysis the details of the dream can be shown to relate to a series of deeper, more extensive psychic connections. Freud distinguishes between the 'manifest content' of the dream, which is what is remembered, and the 'latent content' which can only be arrived at retrospectively through the analytical business of interpretation. Interpretation seeks to reverse the process of condensation and to investigate 'the relation between the manifest content of dreams and the latent dream-thoughts' and to trace out 'the processes by which the latter have been changed into the former' (*The Interpretation of Dreams*). The term has also become part of the language of critical theory. Applied to a literary text it was first used to afford a partial explanation of the energies which bring the text into existence, or to give an account of the unconscious motivations of represented 'characters'. More recently, the analogy between the interpretation of dreams and of texts has been used to suggest the impossibility of arriving at an original 'core' of meaning, prior to ▷ displacement or condensation. Freud speaks of the dream's 'navel' – that knotted point of enigma which indicated that there is always something unresolved, unanalysed.

▷ Displacement; Psychoanalytical criticism.

Conduct literature

During the 16th and 17th centuries there was a proliferation of books on conduct for women, such as William Gouge's of *Domesticall Duties.* These prescribed the way in which a woman should behave in all circumstances and often gave very detailed guides to personal conduct, from sexual behaviour to appropriate reading.

▷ Advice literature; Epistolary novel

Confessio Amantis

A story-collection about love and related subjects, in octosyllabic couplets, written by ▷ John Gower in the later 1380s. A confession of a lover (Amans) to Venus' priest (Genius) provides the occasion for the collection; the priest tells exemplary stories to help the lover analyse his own behaviour. Seven of the eight books of the *Confessio Amantis* are organized as illustrations of one of the ▷ Seven Deadly Sins: Book VII is devoted to advice about the government of self and society. The framework and contents of Gower's work draw together traditions of courtly love literature and of religious treatises on the processes of penitence. The collection concludes with the healing of the lover as the penitential process is completed.

The stories themselves are drawn largely from ▷ Ovid, from medieval versions of the ▷ Troy story and from the Old Testament, but large amounts of bookish lore (such as the history of religion, the history of culture) are encompassed in the confessional frame, thus giving the work an encyclopaedic quality. There is some overlap between the stories in the *Confessio Amantis* and those retold in various contexts in ▷ Chaucer's work (notably the stories of Florent, Ceyx and Alcione, Constance, Phoebus and the Crow, Pyramus and Thisbe), and the early version of the text contains complimentary references to Chaucer's work. Undoubtedly each writer knew and read the work of the other.

The Prologue and Epilogue of the *Confessio Amantis* place it in the context of universal and contemporary history. The narrator begins by suggesting that the work was commissioned by ▷ Richard II and concludes with remarks about its value for the English king and the English realm. Although the first version dates from the later 1380s, the opening and closing sections were revised to accommodate the changing political scene in England and the work was re-dedicated to Henry of Lancaster (later ▷ Henry IV). The *Confessio Amantis* was translated into Portuguese, probably in the late 14th century.

▷ Henry IV; Richard III.

Bib: Macaulay, G. C. (ed.), *The English Works of John Gower*; Minnis, A. J. (ed.), *Gower's Confessio Amantis: Responses and Reassessments.*

Confessions of an English Opium-Eater **(1822: enlarged ed. 1856)**

An ▷ autobiography, and the most famous work of ▷ Thomas De Quincey. Like ▷ Coleridge, De Quincey began taking opium to ease physical suffering, and eventually increased the dose until he became an addict. The book contains eloquent, prose-poetic accounts of his opium dreams and also graphic descriptions of his life of poverty in London. In the former aspect the prose evokes the high musical rhetoric of the 17th-century masters, such as ▷ John Milton; in the latter, it is typical of the 19th-century mode of transmitting intimate, minute personal experience, resembling the increasingly close-textured psychology of the novel. In his tenderness for and understanding of childhood suffering, De Quincey represents a development that was new in the history of literature, and which came to fruition in the ▷ Victorian novelists.

Congreve, William (1670–1729)

Dramatist and poet, born at Bardsey near Leeds, into a military family. He was educated at Kilkenny, and at Trinity College in Dublin, where he was a fellow-student of ▷ Jonathan Swift. In 1690 he entered the Middle Temple, but did not practise as a lawyer. Instead he began writing: his first published work was a novel, *Incognita* (1692), followed by three stage comedies: ▷ *The Old Bachelor* (1693), ▷ *The Double Dealer* (1694), ▷ *Love for Love* (1695). Congreve's one tragedy, ▷ *The Mourning Bride*, was written in 1697. Congreve was a particular target of the ▷ Rev. Jeremy Collier's attack on the theatre, *A Short View of the Immorality and Profaneness of the English Stage*, in 1698, and he responded vehemently in his *Amendments of Mr Collier's False and Imperfect Citations* (1698). But the assault may have helped to discourage him from writing: his interest in the stage declined after the performance of his comedy, ▷ *The Way of the World*, in 1700. This, despite its subsequent fame and lasting popularity, into our own time, was not at first a success. Congreve did not depend on the stage for his livelihood, although he retained his involvement in the management of ▷ Lincoln's Inn Fields Theatre until 1705, and managed the new Queen's Theatre in the ▷ Haymarket together with ▷ Vanbrugh after that date. He accepted some government posts, and continued to write intermittently, composing a masque, *The Judgment of Paris* (1701); an operatic piece, *Semele* (1710), which provided part of the libretto for an oratorio by ▷ Handel; a prose narrative, *An Impossible Thing* (1720); and several poems. He brought out an edition of Dryden's works in 1717. Congreve was an admirer of the actress ▷ Anne Bracegirdle, for whom he wrote several of his best roles. His friends included ▷ Steele, ▷ Pope and ▷ Swift. He went almost blind in his last years, and died following a coach accident at Bath. He is buried in Westminster Abbey. Congreve's comedies are distinguished by their verbal play and wit, in the Restoration ▷ comedy of manners mode. His art is satiric, and he created a number of memorable characters.

Bib: Johnson, S., *Lives of the Poets*; Love, H., *Congreve*; Morris, B. (ed.), *William Congreve.*

***Coningsby*, or *The New Generation* (1844)**

A political novel by ▷ Benjamin Disraeli. By means of it, the rising politician, Disraeli, expresses his contempt for the lack of principle behind the contemporary Tory (right-wing) party, whose side he nonetheless took against the expediency and materialism of the Whigs and ▷ Utilitarians. Against them he advocates a revived, platonically idealized aristocracy with the interests of the people at heart and respected by them as their natural leaders. Such a new aristocrat is the hero of the novel, Coningsby, and he and his friends form a group comparable to the Young England group which Disraeli himself led in Parliament. Coningsby is the grandson of Lord Monmouth, type of the old, unprincipled, predatory aristocracy, whose inveterate enemy is the industrialist Millbank, representing the new and vital middle class. Coningsby falls in love with Millbank's daughter, is disinherited by his grandfather and eventually is elected to Parliament with

Millbank's support. The novel is essentially one of propaganda of ideas, but written with great feeling, liveliness and intelligence. Lord Monmouth was based on the actual Lord Hertford, also used as the basis of Lord Steyne in ▷ Thackeray's ▷ *Vanity Fair*. Another excellently drawn character is the detestable Rigby, based on John Wilson Croker, politician and journalist, and author of the notoriously abusive review of Keats' *Endymion*.

Connotation and Denotation
The denotation of a word or phrase is its primary meaning, whereas the connotation is the range of associations it carries. The distinction is useful in analysing literary language because literature relies to heavily upon suggestion in, for instance, the use of imagery. Certain ▷ Figures of Speech, such as metaphor and simile, also exploit connotation to the full. 'My love is like a red, red rose' relies upon the pleasant connotations of roses to create the compliment.

Conquest, The (Norman)
The conquest of England following the defeat of Harold by the ▷ Norman invading force led by ▷ William I at the Battle of Hastings in 1066.

Conrad, Joseph (1857–1924)
Novelist. His name in full was Józef Teodor Konrad Korzeniowski. He knew hardly any English when he was 20; yet before he was 40 he had completed his first English novel, *Almayer's Folly* (1895), and ten years later he had published one of the masterpieces of the novel in English: ▷ *Nostromo* (1904). The background to Conrad as a novelist is complicated and important for understanding the richness of his art. 1 Early life. His father was a Polish patriot and man of letters, exiled from the Polish Ukraine by the Russian government, which then ruled it, for his political activity. His mother died when he was seven, and his father when he was 11, and his uncle subsequently became the main family influence in his life. 2 Life at sea. From the tales of sea life (in translation) by the English writer ▷ Captain Marryat, the American Fenimore Cooper, and the Frenchman Victor Hugo, he became fascinated by the sea and joined the crew of a French ship in 1874, and of an English one in 1878. By 1884 he was a British subject and had qualified as a master (ship's captain). In his voyages Conrad had visited the Mediterranean, South American, the Far East, and Central Africa. 3 Writing life. He began writing in about 1886 with at least as good an acquaintance with French language and literature as English. He brought to the English novel an admiration for the French ▷ realists, ▷ Flaubert and Maupassant. He also had a knowledge of many peoples, and a profound feeling of the contrast between the tightly enclosed communities of ships' crews and the loose egocentric individualism characterizing land societies. In addition, he knew, from his childhood experience in Russian Poland and Russia itself, the tragic impingement of political pressures on personal life, in a way that was unusual in the West until after the outbreak of World War I in 1914. In his preoccupation with the exploration of moral issues he was in the English tradition.

His major work is represented by the novels ▷ *Lord Jim* (1900), *Nostromo*, ▷ *The Secret Agent* (1907) and *Under Western Eyes* (1911) and the novellas *The Nigger of the Narcissus* (1898); *Youth* (1902); ▷ *Heart of Darkness* (1902); *Typhoon* (1903); and *The Shadow Line* (1917). *Lord Jim* and *The Nigger of the Narcissus* are concerned with honour, courage and solidarity, ideals for which the merchant service provided a framework. *The Secret Agent* and *Under Western Eyes* deal with political extremism, the contrast between eastern and western Europe, and human folly, cruelty, fear and betrayal. *Nostromo*, set in an imaginary South American state, shares some of the themes of the other work, but is notable for its sense of history and the power of economic forces. *Heart of Darkness* is famous for its ambiguous and resonant portrayal of evil. Conrad's earlier novels, *Almayer's Folly* and *An Outcast of the Islands* (1896) have Far Eastern settings, and a less developed prose style. His later work includes *Chance* (1914), the first to bring him a big public; *Victory* (1915); *The Arrow of Gold* (1919); *The Rescue* (1920); *The Rover* (1923); and *Suspense*, which he was working on when he died. Conrad is one of the most important modern. English novelists, both for his concerns and for his techniques. He addressed issues which have come to seem central to the 20th-century mind: the problem of identity; the terror of the unknown within and without; the difficulty of finding a secure moral base; political violence and economic oppression; isolation and existential dread. His technical innovations were particularly in the use of narrators, the disruption of narrative chronology and the employment of a powerful irony of tone.

His other works are: a number of volumes of short stories and essays, including *Tales of Unrest* (1898) and *Notes on Life and Letters* (1921). *The Mirror of the Sea* (1906) and *A Personal Record* (1912) are autobiographical. Conrad co-operated with ▷ Ford Madox Ford in the writing of two novels: *The Inheritors* (1901) and *Romance* (1903). The first three volumes of his *Collected Letters* were published in 1983, 1986 and 1988.

Bib: Baines, J., *Joseph Conrad: A Critical Biography*; Berthoud, J., *Joseph Conrad: the Major Phase*; Guerard, A. J., *Conrad the Novelist*; Najder, Z., *Joseph Conrad: A Chronicle*; Watt, I., *Conrad in the Nineteenth Century*; Hewitt, D., *Conrad: A Reassessment*; Erdinast-Vulcan, D.,

Joseph Conrad and the Modern Temper; Hawthorn, J., *Joseph Conrad: Narrative Technique and Ideological Commitment*; Hampson, R., *Joseph Conrad: Betrayal and Identity*; Roberts, A. M. (ed.), *Conrad and Gender*.

Conran, Anthony (b 1931)
Poet, translator and critic. Tony Conran was born in India where his father was a railway engineer. Because of family connections with North Wales, he was educated at Colwyn Bay and at the University College of North Wales, Bangor, returning there in 1957 to become a research fellow and tutor in the English Department until retiring from this post in 1982. The discovery of Welsh literature was a crucial event in his literary career, since he learned the rules of *cynghanedd* and wrote poems which, though they were written in the English language, were nevertheless based on Welsh metres and also celebrated births, marriages and deaths, thus undertaking the function of the Welsh *bardd gwlad*. His first collection of poetry to be published was *Formal Poems* (1960) and, omitting numerous pamphlets, his most substantial later collections are *Spirit Level* (1974), *Life Fund* (1979) and *Castles: Variations on an Original Theme* (1993). His collected poems appeared in four volumes between 1965 and 1967 and subsequently as one volume entitled *Poems 1951–67* in 1974. As a translator Tony Conran is best known for his *Penguin Book of Welsh Verse* (1967), an anthology that includes an important introduction in which he expounds his view of the poet's role in Welsh society. His volume of critical essays on Anglo-Welsh poetry, *The Cost of Strangeness* (1982) is one of the most perceptive and stimulating critical studies in this field.
Bib: Stephens, M. (Ed.), *The Oxford Companion to the Literature of Wales*; Jones, G. and Rowlands, J., *Profiles*.

Conscious Lovers, The **(1722)**
Play by ▷ Sir Richard Steele, his last, adapted from ▷ Terence's *Andria*, and sometimes considered as an archetype of ▷ Augustan 'exemplary comedy', in contrast to Restoration 'wit comedy', and a landmark in the development of the later ▷ 'sentimental comedy'. It is also seen as a vehicle for the expression of Whig attitudes and values, again in contrast to the Tory values espoused in much of Restoration comedy. Young Bevil thinks of himself as consistently virtuous, but this conflicts with his desires. He secretly supports the beautiful but impoverished Indiana, whom he also loves. However, in accordance with his father's wishes, he proposes marriage to Lucinda, while concealing the fact from Indiana. Lucinda is in turn loved by Bevil's friend Myrtle. On the wedding day Bevil regrets his commitment to Lucinda, and offers to help Myrtle to a match with her, describing it as an humanitarian act. In Act V Indiana is revealed as Lucinda's elder half-sister, and therefore heiress to half their father's fortune. She is united with Young Bevil, and Lucinda with Myrtle. The play's title derives from the thought and attention that Bevil Junior and Indiana give to their own emotions. Steele intended them to be admired, and the play as a whole to give moral guidance. But it generated a great controversy, with critics variously pointing to its supposed hypocrisy, its didacticism, and the seriousness of its tone.

Consciousness
In its most general sense consciousness is synonymous with 'awareness'. In a more specifically ▷ Freudian context it is associated with the individual's perception of reality. For Freud, of course, the impression which an individual has of his or her experience is partial, since awareness is controlled by the processes of the unconscious, which are never recognized in their true form. More recently 'consciousness' has been associated with the ▷ Enlightenment view of individualism, in which the individual is conceived of as being distinct from society, and is also held to be the centre and origin of meaning. Following from this, what distinguishes humanity is its alleged capacity for autonomy, and hence freedom of action. The ▷ Romantic equivalent of this philosophical position is that literature is the expression of the pre-existent 'self' of the writer, and that the greatest literature is that which manifests the writer's consciousness most fully. These views of consciousness should further be distinguished from the ▷ Marxist version, in which the self is 'produced' through 'material practices', by means of which social relations are generated. Theories of consciousness affect notions of the relationship between writer and reader, and it is in working out such relationships that the concept of 'consciousness' is important in current literary critical debate.

Constable, Henry (1562–1613)
Poet. Constable's early career appeared to promise him the fruits of preferment at ▷ Elizabeth I's court; he received the ▷ patronage of ▷ Walsingham and ▷ the Earl of Essex, and was the friend of ▷ Sir Philip Sidney and Sir John Harington, as well as acquainted with two court ladies, ▷ Mary Sidney and Penelope Rich (to both of whom he dedicated sonnets). However, in the late 1580s he converted to ▷ Catholicism and left the English court for France, where he was to reside until the accession of ▷ James I in 1603. At first he was well received by the king, but on the discovery of incriminating letters he was imprisoned in the Tower in 1604. Constable was released the same year, but in 1610 he

returned to the continent and died in Liège. He is mainly remembered for his sonnet sequence *Diana* (1592), which is spiritual in tone and stylistically influenced by ▷ Ronsard.
Bib: Grundy, J., *The Poems of Henry Constable*.

***Constant Couple, The: Or, A Trip to the Jubilee* (1699)**
Comedy by ▷ George Farquhar. Angelica is in love with the rake, Sir Harry Wildair, who takes her for a whore. He finds himself in a position where he must marry her or fight; he decides matrimony is the bolder course, and marries her. In the secondary plot, Lurewell has become a coquette after being apparently abandoned by Colonel Standard. The situation is found to have been based on a misunderstanding, and the couple are reunited. The play was so well received that Farquhar followed it up with a sequel, *Sir Harry Wildair* (1701), which proved far less successful.

Contagious Diseases Acts
▷ Women's Movement, The.

Contemporary Review, The
Journal, founded in 1866. Sir Percy Bunting was its most famous editor. It covered a variety of subjects and in 1955 incorporated ▷ *The Fortnightly Review*.

Contradiction
Used in literary criticism to identify the incoherences in a literary text. Derived from Hegel, Engels and ▷ Marx, contradiction, as applied to literature, implies that artistic representation is not the product of a unifying aesthetic impulse. Contradiction describes patterns of dominance and subordination and thus, in literary terms, points towards divisions within the work which challenge notions of aesthetic coherence.

Convention
Literary conventions are in many ways the building blocks of literary works. They are central to the organisation of literary form and establish the basis for communication between text and reader, performance and audience. They are usually traditional, and often highly stylised and 'unnatural' in so far as they do not correspond to forms of writing or behaviour outside literary texts. However, they are often so familiar that readers and audiences simply take them for granted. Examples include the fact that characters in Shakespeare talk in poetry and are not overheard during soliloquies, that pastoral writing is decorated with rural and classical motifs, that love is expressed in certain devotional and not sexual ways in medieval courtly literature, that villains twirl their moustaches in melodramas and that the telephone never rings unless it brings essential information to a modern plot. Conventions can either be matters of form (14 lines in a conventional sonnet, five acts in an Elizabethan play, 30 minutes in an episode of a soap opera) or matters of content, as in the ways in which certain things or people are habitually represented. In this case conventions can give home to prejudice and stereotyping. Literature, however, also makes use of the ▷ defamiliarization of conventions. Defamiliarization occurs when conventions are defied or overturned and the reader or audience is made to think again.

Conversation poem
A reflective poem, usually in ▷ blank verse, in which the poet meditates aloud, ostensibly talking to a friend. It adopts a more intimate, introspective tone than its predecessor, the 18th-century verse epistle. The term is especially associated with ▷ Samuel Taylor Coleridge, who first used it. His *Eolian Harp* (1795), *This Lime-Tree Bower* (1800), *The Nightingale* (1798) and ▷ *Frost at Midnight* (1798) are often termed 'conversation poems'.

Cook, Eliza (1818–89)
Poet, essayist and ▷ feminist. The youngest of eleven children, she was born in London and grew up in Horsham, Sussex. She educated herself and published her first verses, *Lays of a Wild Harp*, in 1835. The collection was well-received, and encouraged her to contribute poems to the *Metropolitan Magazine*, the *New Monthly Magazine* and the *Weekly Dispatch*, the last of which printed her most famous poem, 'The Old Arm Chair', in 1837. Her work varies between sentimental, domestic verse, fiery political ▷ ballads and satirical poetry. Her second collection, *Melaia and Other Poems* (1838), sold well both in Britain and North America, and three further volumes followed: *Poems: Second Series* (1845); *I'm Afloat: Songs* (1850) and *New Echoes, and Other Poems* (1864). From 1849–54 she wrote and edited ▷ *Eliza Cook's Journal*, a feminist miscellany addressing topics such as work, marriage and the law. The 1860 publication *Jottings From My Journal* includes much of this material. Cook also wrote a collection of aphorisms, *Diamond Dust* (1865). She never married, but was passionately attracted to Charlotte Cushman, an actress.
▷ Women's movement; Lesbianism.
Bib: Hickok, K., *Representations of Women: 19th Century British Women's Poetry*; Leighton, A., and Reynolds, M. (eds.), *An Anthology of Victorian Women Poets*.

Cook's Tale, The
One of ▷ Chaucer's ▷ *Canterbury Tales*. The *Cook's Tale*, set in low-life London, begins a story about 'Perkyn Revelour' before breaking off after only 58 lines. The nature of the Cook's

contribution to the story-telling competition seems rather uncertain. Later in the journey, the Host calls upon the Cook to contribute a story, but the Manciple pre-empts any response from the drunken Cook (in the Prologue to the ▷ *Manciple's Tale*). In some manuscripts of the *Canterbury Tales*, the romance of ▷ *Gamelyn* is inserted and attributed to the Cook.

Cookson, Catherine (b 1906)
Romantic novelist. Cookson is one of the ▷ best-selling writers currently working in Britain, whose stories have much in common with classic Mills and Boon plots but which also deploy historical motifs and display richer characterization. Her native Northumberland, in which most of her novels are set, has become immortalized as 'Cookson Country' by the local tourist board, which at least is testament to the rich evocations of landscape and regional feeling which her primarily romantic fiction offers.

Her wide range of novels, all written since she was in her early forties, include: *Fanny McBride* (1977); *Pure as the Lily* (1978); *The Mallen Novels* (1979); *Tilly Trotter* (1980); *Marriage and Mary Ann* (1984); *The Wingless Bird* (1990); and *A Ruthless Need* (1995).
Bib: Radford, J. (ed.), *The Progress of Romance: The Politics of Popular Fiction*; Radway, J., *Reading the Romance*.

Cooper, Edith (1862–1913)
Poet and dramatist who published separately, and collaborately with ▷ Katherine Bradley under the ▷ pseudonym ▷ Michael Field.

Cooper, William (b 1910)
Pen name of H. S. Hoff, novelist. Having already published four novels under his real name, Cooper came to prominence in 1950 with *Scenes from Provincial Life*, the story of an unconventional and sceptical schoolteacher living in a Midlands town around the outbreak of World War II. In reacting against the experimental tradition of the ▷ Bloomsbury Group and of ▷ modernism, Cooper's novel initiated the 1950s school of dissentient ▷ realism, which included such writers as ▷ John Braine, ▷ David Storey, ▷ Stan Barstow and ▷ John Wain. *Scenes from Metropolitan Life* (written in the 1950s but not published for legal reasons until 1982) and *Scenes from Married Life* (1961) complete a trilogy. Other novels include: *You Want the Right Frame of Reference* (1971), *Love on the Coast* (1973) and *Scenes from Later Life* (1983).

***Cooper's Hill* (1642)**
▷ Denham, Sir John.

Copernicus (1473–1543)
This was the Latinized form of surname of Nicolas Koppernik, a Polish astronomer. In *De Revolutionibus orbium coelestium* (*Concerning the Revolutions of the Heavenly Spheres*) (1543) he expounded for the first time since classical times the belief that the earth and other planets move around the sun. This was contrary to the hitherto accepted theory of the Egyptian astronomer ▷ Ptolemy, according to which the earth was the centre of the solar system. The Ptolemaic system suited the traditional Christian conception of the universe and the place of man within it – it is still assumed, for instance, in ▷ Milton's epic of the Creation, ▷ *Paradise Lost* – but the Copernican theory caused little scandal since at the time it was regarded merely as an ingenious hypothesis. Only when ▷ Galileo claimed its validity on demonstrable grounds after the invention of his new telescope, did the Church condemn the theory outright in 1616 and require Galileo to repudiate his findings.

Coppard, A. E. (1878–1957)
Writer of short stories. He was largely self-educated, and began serving in a shop at the age of nine. Later he began writing while working as an accountant, and his literary interests were nourished when he obtained a post at Oxford where he met and made friends with the intelligentsia. The best of his stories are chiefly in the earlier volumes: *Adam and Eve and Pinch Me* (1921); *Clorinda Walks in Heaven* (1922); *Fishmonger's Fiddle* (1925); and *The Field of Mustard* (1926). Later volumes include: *Pink Furniture* (1930); *Tapster's Tapestry* (1938); *You Never Know Do You?* (1939); and *The Dark-Eyed Lady* (1947). He also wrote poems: *Collected Poems* (1928); *Easter Day* (1931); and *Cherry Ripe* (1935), and an autobiography, *It's Me, O Lord* (1957).

Coppard had a remarkably acute ear for the spoken word, and his best tales have the freshness and simplicity of oral folk-tales. Although his subject matter was often more sophisticated than this suggests, many of his finest stories are about the life of the countryside. He was influenced by ▷ Thomas Hardy's short stories, and he often shows a stoically resigned attitude to human destiny which is similar to Hardy's outlook, but he combined this with a remarkable talent for sharp comedy, again reminiscent of peasant folk-tales.

Coppe, Abiezer (1619–72)
Religious prose writer. Coppe was born in Warwick and educated at Oxford; he became a baptist minister in the 1640s, but broke with formal religion in 1649 and was imprisoned for blasphemy in 1650 on the basis of his prophetic text *Fiery Flying Rolle* (1650). It is probable that the work was considered dangerous because of its overt Leveller ideals and its suggestion of male and female equality. A later work, *Copp's*

Return (1651) is a quasi-recantation.
Bib: Pooley, R., *English Prose of the Seventeenth Century, 1590 1700*

Copyright, The law of
The right of writers, artists and musicians to refuse reproduction of their works. The right is now established law in every civilized country. The first copyright law in England was passed under Queen Anne in 1709. Before this, it was possible for publishers to publish books without the author's permission, and without allowing him or her any profits from sale, a practice very common during the lifetime of ▷ Shakespeare. Until 1909, the laws of the United States did not adequately safeguard British authors against having their works 'pirated' there, *ie* published without their permission and without giving them suitable financial return. ▷ Dickens was a main sufferer from this state of affairs, and it greatly angered him.
▷ Shakespeare's plays; Stationers' Register.

Corelli, Marie (1855–1924)
▷ Pseudonym of novelist Mary Mackay, born in London the illegitimate daughter (though she claimed to be adopted and born in 1864) of Scottish songwriter Charles Mackay. Educated by ▷ governesses and for a while at a convent, she was a gifted pianist and had intended to take up a musical career, for which she adopted the name Corelli. In 1885 a psychic experience led her to start writing and her novels are sensational, full of trances, swoons, religious conversions and visions. Her first novel, *A Romance of Two Worlds* (1886), was so successful that she abandoned music to become a professional writer. Her great popularity occured with *Barabbas: A Dream of The World's Tragedy* (1886), despite unfavourable reviews, and of her twenty-eight best-selling novels, *The Sorrows of Satan* (1895) had a greater initial sale than any previous English novel. After 1901 she lived with her friend, Bertha Vyver, in Stratford-upon-Avon, and never married. Her popularity declined into ridicule before her death. Other novels include *The Mighty Atom* (1896) and *Boy* (1900)
▷ Sensation, Novel of.
Bib: Coates, E.G., *Life*; Bigland, E., *Marie Corelli: The Woman and the Legend*; Masters, B., *Now Barabbas Was a Rotter: The Extraordinary Life of Marie Corelli*.

Corey, Katherine (?1635–?)
Actress, Katherine Corey (née Mitchell) claimed to be the first professional English actress; she may have played Dol Common in a production of ▷ Ben Jonson's ▷ *The Alchemist* in December 1660, and certainly played the part in 1664.

***Coriolanus* (?1608)**
A ▷ tragedy by ▷ Shakespeare about a legendary Roman hero (5th century BC). Shakespeare took the story from the *Lives* by ▷ Plutarch translated into English by ▷ Sir Thomas North. A war is being waged between Rome and the neighbouring city of Corioli, capital city of the Volscians. The hero of the play, Caius Marcius, wins the title Coriolanus for his heroism against the enemy. But Rome is morally at war within herself: the arrogant patricians (aristocrats) despise the plebs, or common people, who in turn are factious and disorderly. Coriolanus differs from his fellow patricians only in being still prouder than they are, in that he cannot stoop to flatter the plebs for their votes. They succeed in expelling him from the city, whereupon he allies himself with the Volscians and returns to destroy it. His mother, Volumnia, who embodies the qualities of the arrogant patricians and has herself bred her son to value his pride above all, succeeds in deterring him; he is then assassinated by the Volscians as a traitor. The tragedy has peculiar interest for its study of social influence on the individual, and it is difficult to determine whether society, as embodied by the mob/group, is unthinking or reasonable. It is less popular than some other tragedies by Shakespeare, but it is certainly among the finest of his plays.

Corn Laws, Repeal of the, 1846
The Corn Laws existed to protect English home-grown corn from competition from imported foreign corn. Their existence made for higher food prices and assumed the superior importance of agricultural interest over urban industrial interests. In the first half of the 19th century the Tory party derived its main support from landowners, whereas the Whigs owed much of their support to the new industrialists of the rapidly growing industrial towns. The Whig Anti-Corn Law League consequently represented not merely opposition to a particular measure but rivalry between main segments of society; moreover, the workers, anxious above all for cheap food, supported the urban middle class and the Whigs. It was nonetheless a Tory Prime Minister, ▷ Robert Peel, who repealed the Corn Laws under pressure of a severe famine in Ireland. The abolition of the Corn Laws was of historic importance in several ways: 1 it divided the Tory party, sending its younger leader, ▷ Benjamin Disraeli, into opposition, with his supporters, against Peel; 2 it began the era of ▷ free trade (ie trade unrestricted by import or export taxes); 3 it acknowledged implicitly that industrial interests were henceforth to be regarded as more important than agricultural interests; 4 it relieved the almost revolutionary restlessness of the working class, so that England was one of the few countries in Europe not to undergo upheaval or serious threat of upheaval in the Year of Revolutions, 1848.
▷ Hungry Forties, The.

Corneille, Pierre (1606–84)
One of the great French classical dramatists

whose work exiled English writers encountered during the ▷ Interregnum. His dramas, *Le Cid* (1636–7), *Horace*, *Polyeucte* and *Cinna* (between 1640 and 1643), debate the conflict between duty and love, passion and honour, and highlight the difficulties posed by the heroic ethos. They show the influence also of the neo-classical conception of the unities (▷ classical unities) Corneille's critical essays (the *Examens* and the *Discours*) were pioneers in serious drama criticism. ▷ Dryden was an admirer, but his heroic dramas did not match Corneille's attainments.

Cornford, Frances (1886–1960)
Poet. Although Frances Cornford's poetic career spans the period of high ▷ modernism, she was essentially a ▷ Georgian poet, producing accessible, pastoral lyrics which often celebrate the life of and landscape around Cambridge, where she lived. She was a friend of many of the Georgians, especially ▷ Rupert Brooke, as well as being the mother of 1930s poet John Cornford and the grand-daughter of Charles Darwin. Her works include: *Poems* (1910); *Autumn Midnight* (1923); *Travelling Home* (1948); *Collected Poems* (1954); *On a Calm Shore* (1960).
Bib: Anderson, A., *A Bibliography of the Writings of Frances Cornford*; Delaney, P., *The Neo-Pagans*.

Cornhill Magazine, The
A monthly periodical, at the height of its fame soon after its foundation by ▷ William Thackeray, the novelist, in 1860. Contributors included ▷ John Ruskin, ▷ Matthew Arnold, ▷ Mrs Gaskell, ▷ Anthony Trollope and ▷ Leslie Stephen, besides Thackeray himself. It continued this century to publish the work of many writers.

Cornwall, Barry
▷ Proctor, Bryan Waller.

Corombona, Vittoria
The tragic female protagonist of ▷ *The White Devil* by ▷ John Webster. Her resilience in the face of adversity combined with her lack of sexual and moral integrity render her a fascinating and emancipated character. This is evident particularly in the famous trial scene when she emerges as morally no more guilty than her accusers, who use the full panoply of the law to pursue their spurious ends against her.

Corpus Christi, The Feast of
A festival of the Roman Catholic Church in honour of the Holy Sacrament. It was ordained in 1264 by Pope Urban IV. By the 15th century it was the principal Church feast in the year, and was associated with the performance of ▷ mystery plays.

Corpus Christi Plays
▷ Cycle plays.

***Corsair, The* (1814)**
A narrative poem in heroic ▷ couplets by ▷ Lord Byron. Conrad, who has become a pirate for some mysterious reason, disguises himself as a dervish in order to gain entry to the palace of the pasha, Seyd. In the fight which ensues he insists that his men must not invade Seyd's harem ('wrong not on your lives/ One female form'), and Seyd's wife Gulnare, described decorously as 'the trembling fair', consequently falls in love with him. All his men are killed and Conrad is thrown into a dungeon to await a slow death next day. Gulnare sets him free, but when he realizes that she has murdered her own husband, Conrad is filled with revulsion. He returns to his island to find that his faithful consort Medora has died in his absence, upon which he himself mysteriously disappears. The poem's self-indulgent blend of escapist adventure, condescending sexism and glamorous exoticism, made it one of the most popular of Byron's poems.

Cortegiano, Il (The Courtier)
▷ Castiglione, Baldassare.

Cotton, Priscilla (d 1664)
Pamphleteer. Cotton was a Quaker, who was imprisoned in Exeter gaol for preaching with her compatriot, Mary Cole. She is noteworthy as the first woman to write in defence of women preaching in *To the Priests and the People of England* (1655). This represented a general trend amongst Puritan women to speak openly of their faith, since the authority to preach (God's) was higher than that which forbade them to do so (man's). Cotton's other works provide similar forthright defences of women and Quakers (*As I was in the Prison House* (1656), *A Briefe Description* (1659) and *A Visitation of Love* (1661)).
Bib: H. Hinds in Cerasano, S. P. and Wynne-Davies, M. (eds.), *Gloriana's Face*.

Counter-Reformation
A movement in the Catholic Church to counter the Protestant ▷ Reformation. It arose from the Council of Trent (1545–63) composed of the ecclesiastical leaders of the Catholic Church. The only important English writer to be influenced by the Counter-Reformation was the poet ▷ Richard Crashaw.

***Countess Kathleen, The* (1892)**
A verse play by ▷ W. B. Yeats. Its theme is a woman who sells her soul to the devil in order to save the poor from starvation. It marks the beginning of Yeats' career as a poetic dramatist, and was one of the plays used by the Irish Literary Theatre as a starting-point.
▷ Abbey Theatre.

Country Wife, The **(1675)**
Comedy by ▷ William Wycherley. The irrational jealousy of Pinchwife, instead of keeping his naïve country wife faithful to him, puts ideas into her head which are encouraged by the libertine Horner. Horner has convinced the men of the town that he is impotent, but secretly seduces several of their wives. Most treat him merely as a means for their sexual satisfaction, and in one of the play's most famous scenes (IV, 3) Horner, pretending as a cover for his activities that he is offering china for sale, tells the women that he has sold out of china, a code meaning that he has exhausted his energy for sexual congress. Margery, the country wife of the title, cares for him more than the others, and is hurt when he rejects her and forces her to return to her husband. Meanwhile Pinchwife's sister, Alithea, is to be married to Sparkish. The latter pretends to affection but is interested only in the money which Alithea will bring as dowry, and takes her for granted. She is attracted to Harcourt, who really loves her, but resists his attentions out of duty to Sparkish. Eventually Sparkish is revealed in his true colours, and she marries Harcourt. The play's chief assets are the comedy of its scenes, heavy with dramatic irony, and the author's caustic wit. Its free treatment of sexuality drew condemnation even in its own time, and there has been critical debate about whether Horner was intended as a hero, to be admired for his cleverness, or a vicious object of Wycherley's satire. It was adapted by ▷ Garrick as *The Country Girl* (1766).

Couplet
A pair of rhymed lines of verse of equal length. The commonest form is the so-called ▷ heroic couplet of 10 syllables and five stresses in each line. It was first used in ▷ Chaucer's ▷ *Legend of Good Women*.

> *A thousand times have I herd men telle*
> *That ther is joye in heven, and peyne in helle...*

The heroic couplet had its most prolific period between 1660 and 1790 when many poets from ▷ Dryden to ▷ Crabbe used it; its master was ▷ Pope:

> *Most souls, 'tis true, but peep out once an age,*
> *Dull sullen pris'ners in the body's cage*
> *(Elegy to an Unfortunate Lady)*

▷ Leigh Hunt's 'Abou Ber Adhem' also provides a good example of the couplet:

> *Abou Ben Adhem (may his tribe increase!)*
> *Awoke one night from a deep dream of peace.*

▷ Blank verse was a derivative of the couplet. The 8-syllable (octosyllabic) couplet gives a lighter, less dignified rhythm. It was also used by Chaucer (*The Romaunt of the Rose*, ▷ *The Book of the Duchess*, ▷ *The House of Fame*) in his earlier work. It is less common after 1600 than before, but a notable later user of it is ▷ Jonathan Swift (*eg On the Death of Dr Swift*). ▷ Keats used it for *The Eve of St Mark* (1819):

> *All was silent, all was gloom,*
> *Abroad and in the homely room;*
> *Down she sat, poor cheated soul!*
> *And struck a lamp from the dismal coal.*

In the 20th century it was used by ▷ W. H. Auden for his *New Year Letter* (1941).

Courtly Love
Since the 1950s there has been considerable debate over the historical authenticity of 'courtly love', the term being coined in the late 19th century to refer to a codified, stylized expression of the experience of love, found in medieval European texts. Many of the problems have arisen from the over-rigid use of this term by literary critics. What is clear from considering the literary culture of the 12th century onwards is that the stylized expression of the lover's experience in texts cannot be assimilated and organized into a single code of behaviour or set of procedural 'rules': courtly love is a disparate phenomenon, arising out of the confluence of various literary and philosophical traditions and its definition would vary, to some extent, depending on the provenance of the medieval texts under discussion.

The notion of a refined and ennobling love experience is not a medieval invention; scholars have traced Arabic influences in the modes of expression employed by the ▷ troubadour poets of 12th-century France, whose work is often taken as the earliest expression of courtly love sentiments in medieval Europe. Classical Latin texts, especially the treatises on the arts and remedies of loving produced by ▷ Ovid, exert a great influence on medieval attempts to formalize and codify the lover's experience. What is distinctive about medieval expressions of courtly love is the development of a range of terms and conventions which portray the love experience in terms of feudal models and ethics: the male lover serves his lady as a member of a court might do his lord; the relationship is one of love service, in which the lady has the power to bestow gifts and rewards to her faithful love-servant. This love service is frequently represented as a refining, disciplined experience which has its own protocol, and there may be a sense of contiguity between the quality of the love experience for the female object of desire and the love of a trascendental, divine subject (indeed the first may lead to the second, as it does in ▷ Dante's ▷ *Divina Commedia* and in ▷ Petrarch's *Rime Sparse*).

'Fin'amor' is an important term within the more general conceptual framework signalled by 'courtly love': it derives from a tradition of moral philosophy and denotes a quality of loving which is not self-seeking, self-gratifying or possessive.

The relationship between the theory and practice of this feudalized love ethic is the subject of literary discussion and debate throughout the medieval period in a wide range of texts. The different versions of the stories of lovers such as ▷ Tristram and Isolde, ▷ Lancelot and Guinevere, illustrate how the issue of the rights and wrongs of loving is a matter for discussion and debate, and not a clear-cut or rigidly codified matter. Even those texts which may appear to offer a more theoretical guide to the rules of courtly love illustrate the way in which love remains a subject of discussion and debate, despite attempts to codify it. One of the texts frequently cited as offering an authoritative guide to courtly love, *De Arte Honeste Amandi* (*The Art of Honourable Loving*), written some time in the later 12th century by ▷ Andreas Capellanus, was itself interpreted in very different ways in subsequent centuries, as it is by more recent scholars who hope to find an interpretative key in this work. Debates about the protocol of a lover's behaviour constitute a medieval literary genre in their own right and are often set in the context of a 'Court of Love' of some kind. But considering the relationship between the theory and practice of heterosexual loving can lead to discussions of varying dimensions and import. The influential 13th-century dream-vision poem ▷ *Le Roman de la Rose* shows how the relationship between the theory and practice of refined loving can become the focal point for an exploration of all the resources of human culture itself. If courtly love is not seen by modern readers as a monolithic concept, but rather as an area of discussion and debate, a nexus point for a wide range of issues from court etiquette to the principles of universal ordering, issues trivial and profound, then the tonal range employed in such texts as ▷ Chaucer's ▷ *Parliament of Foulys* may be easier to appreciate.

How far the conventionalized modes of representing love experience and ideals in medieval texts influenced and reflected courtly practice at the time is a controversial and complex area, and generalizations are of little profit here. However, the influence of economic and political factors in determining marital arrangements should not be underestimated and, in practice, there seems little room for the exercise of female choice in the arrangements for choosing a legally recognized partner. The conceptual framework offered by the phenomenon of courtly love perhaps served a powerful compensatory function. If this feudalized love ethic arose out of the social circumstances of a specific historic moment, its power to transcend those circumstances and be used as a register for expressing and shaping ideals about loving is demonstrated by its survival through the Renaissance period and beyond.

▷ Ovid.

Bib: Boase, R., *The Origin and Meaning of Courtly Love*.

Couzyn, Jeni (b 1942)
Poet. Couzyn was born and educated in South Africa, which she left in 1965, and has since become a Canadian citizen, although she lives in Britain. Her volumes of verse include: *Flying* (1970); *Christmas in Africa* (1975); *Life By Drowning: Selected Poems* (1985). Couzyn edited the important 1985 ▷ anthology, *The Bloodaxe Book of Contemporary Women Poets*, and she also writes for children.

Covent Garden Theatres
In 1732 Edward Shepherd (1670–1747) planned the first Covent Garden Theatre, or Theatre Royal, on the site of the present Royal Opera House, to which the actor-manager ▷ John Rich transferred from Lincoln's Inn Fields. The name derives from a convent which had stood on the site previously. Following the Licensing Act of 1737 (▷ Theatres) the Covent Garden Theatre was one of only three theatres in London to be granted a licence. In 1773 Oliver Goldsmith's ▷ *She Stoops to Conquer* was staged here for the first time, and ▷ Charles Macklin mounted his innovative production of *Macbeth*, dressed for the first time in 'Scottish' costume. The present theatre opened in 1858.

Coventry Plays
▷ Cycle plays; N-Town Cycle.

Coverdale, Miles (1488–1568)
▷ Bible in England

Coverley, Sir Roger de
A fictional character invented by the essayist ▷ Sir Richard Steele for the pages of ▷ *The Spectator*, and developed by his colleague ▷ Joseph Addison. The name was taken from a north country dance, Roger of Coverley. Sir Roger was at first a member of an imaginary club, the Spectator Club, where Steele in his journalist guise of the 'Spectator' purported to be studying human nature. In the hands of Addison, Sir Roger came to take up much more space than the other members; the papers devoted to describing his life (20 by Addison, eight by Steele, and two by Budgell) are much the best known parts of *The Spectator*. In his conservatism, his devotion to the Church of England, and his kindly but despotic control of his tenants, he is a typical squire of the time, but in his civilized manners he is deliberately made

superior to the general run of country squires (compare Squire Western in ▷ Fielding's ▷ *Tom Jones*). In his simplicity and idiosyncrasies he was individual, with a literary relationship to Don Quixote. Though the 'Coverley Papers' are not a novel, the envisioning of the character is distinctly novelistic, so that they rank among the precursors of the English novel. Addison's especial aim, beyond entertainment, was to civilize the country squire; a secondary aim was the political one of making fun of the Tory English gentry.

Coward, Sir Noël (1899–1973)
British stage and film actor, dramatist and director. He began his theatrical career at the age of 12 acting in a fantasy play called *The Goldfish*. As a dramatist he gained some notoriety with his early works, *The Young Idea* (1923), *The Vortex* (1924), *Fallen Angels* (1925) and *Sirocco* (1927), which was greeted with a riot. However his partnership with the promoter and theatre manager C. B. Cochran proved his ability to work creatively and successfully within the commercial theatre. His reputation rests mainly on the six astringent comedies he wrote between 1923 and 1942: *Fallen Angels* (1925); *Hay Fever* (1925); *Bitter Sweet* (1929); *Private Lives* (1930); *Design for Living* (1932) and *Present Laughter* (1942).
Bib: Gray, F., *Noël Coward*; Kiernan, R. F., *Noël Coward*; Lahr, J., *Coward the Playwright*.

Cowley, Abraham (1618–67)
Poet and essayist. Ever since Samuel Johnson's disparaging comments on Cowley in his *Lives of the Poets* (1779–81), Cowley's reputation has suffered, and yet Cowley is one of the most important and influential of the mid-17th-century poets. A Royalist in politics, he accompanied Queen Henrietta Maria into exile in Paris in 1644–6, returned to England in 1654, was imprisoned in 1655 and later released.

His chief works include: *Poeticall Blossoms* (written 1633), a collection of poetry published in 1656 which contained Pindaric ▷ odes and ▷ elegies on William Harvey among others, and an essay on the advancement of science: *A Proposition for the Advancement of Experimental Philosophy* (1661). Cowley's attachment, after the ▷ Civil War, to the figures associated with the early ▷ Royal Society is evidenced both in his important ode celebrating the Royal Society (first published in Thomas Sprat's *History of the Royal Society*) and in his celebration of scientific figures and their works in his poetry.

As well as celebrating the advance of science, Cowley also composed an unfinished ▷ epic, *A Poem on the Late Civil War* (1679), which he abandoned at the point when the war began to turn against the Royalist forces. He also anticipated ▷ John Milton's ▷ *Paradise Lost* in attempting a biblical epic, *Davideis* ('A sacred poem of the Troubles of David', published in the *Poems* of 1656). In the 19th century and through much of the 20th, Cowley was read as a species of inferior ▷ John Donne or ▷ Thomas Carew, yet the range of his writing (which embraced science, ▷ translation and experiments in form and metre as well as critical statements on the nature of poetic discourse) make him an important figure in his own right.
Bib: Hinman, R., *Abraham Cowley's World of Order*; Trotter, D., *The Poetry of Abraham Cowley*.

Cowley, Hannah (1743–1809)
Poet, novelist and dramatist. The story goes that Cowley began writing plays after being mocked by her husband, who accused her of never actually undertaking any of the projects she planned. The result was thirteen published plays, although since she was very careless of her own writing there may well have been more. Cowley's skill was in comedy and she was adept at turning themes which had centred upon men into plots about women; examples of this gender inversion are *The Belle's Stratagem* (1780) and *A Bold Stroke For a Husband* (1783). Her awareness of the precarious role of the female dramatist is made clear in the ironic prologue to *The Belle's Stratagem*, where a male character complains about the lines she has given him:

. . . on affairs of state
I might hold faith – yet in her cursed play,
The deuce a word am I allow'd to say;
Or rather coop'd, like other folks we know,
Between two barren adverbs – Ay and no.
Tis thus we're served, when saucy women write –

Cowley also wrote a ▷ Gothic novel, *The Italian Marauders* (1810), and several long poems. In all Cowley's works the heroines are intelligent and independent women, perfectly able to control the situations in which they find themselves.
Bib: Uphaus, R.W. and Foster, G.M., *The 'Other' Eighteenth Century*.

Cowper, William (1731–1800)
Poet and letter-writer. Son of the rector of Great Berkhampstead in Hertfordshire, he was called to the bar in 1754, and through family connections was offered the post of Clerk of the Journals in the House of Lords. However, the early death of his mother, his experiences of bullying at public school and a thwarted love affair, had caused severe neurosis which led him to contemplate suicide at the prospect of the clerkship examination. He spent a year in an asylum and thereafter led a retired life on his own private income, first in the home of Morley and Mary Unwin in Huntingdonshire

and then after Morley's death with Mary Unwin in Olney. They planned to marry in 1773, but Cowper's conviction of his own personal damnation prevented this.

In Olney he came under the influence of the evangelical Rev. John Newton with whom he published *Olney Hymns* (1779), including 'Hark my soul! it is the Lord', and 'God moves in a mysterious way'. In 1780 Newton left Olney for London and Cowper's life became less spiritually strenuous. Mary Unwin encouraged him to write, in order to counteract his religious melancholia. His *Poems* (1782) contain *Table Talk*, and eight moral satires in heroic ▷ couplets which, though uneven in quality, display a distinctive unforced sententiousness which is one of his most attractive poetic characteristics. The volume also includes *Boadicea: an Ode* and *Verses supposed to be written by Alexander Selkirk* ('I am monarch of all I survey'). In the same year Cowper published his famous comic ballad *John Gilpin*. He made the acquaintance of Lady Austen, who suggested the scheme of the ▷ mock-heroic, discursive poem ▷ *The Task: A Poem in Six Books*, which appeared in 1785, and is in the more 'natural' medium of ▷ blank verse, rather than couplets. He followed this with an undistinguished translation of ▷ Homer (1791). In 1794 Mary Unwin died, and Cowper's only subsequent work is the introspective and despairing *Castaway*, published after his death, as were his *Letters* (1803), which are among the most famous in the language.

Cowper's work illustrates the movement away from the public themes of Augustanism towards a more domestic and personal poetry of sensibility. His work eschews brilliance or technical virtuosity, and can be banal. But at their best his ▷ lyrics are delicately moving, and his couplet and blank verse writing achieves an unassuming lucidity of tone, which evokes profound resonances.

▷ Romanticism.

Bib: Cecil, D., *The Stricken Deer*; King, J., *William Cowper: A Biography*; Hutchins, B., *The Poetry of William Cowper*; Priestman, M., *Cowper's Task: Structure and Influence*; Newey, V., *Cowper's Poetry: A Critical Study and Reassessment*.

Crabbe, George (1754–1832)

Poet. Crabbe was born at Aldeburgh in Suffolk and his work is intimately associated with the region. He practised medicine before taking orders in 1781. Crabbe's earliest works, *The Library* (1781) and the anti-pastoral *The Village* (1783) have an heroic ▷ couplet metre and public, discursive tone already distinctly old-fashioned at the time.

Samuel Johnson (1709–84) gave advice on the composition of the second poem, and in his grimly stoical vision of life and his distrust of pretension and excess, Crabbe resembles Johnson in temperament. *The Village* is relentless in its rejection of the conventions of literary pastoralism, showing nature with bitter realism as it was known to the poor. In his later works – *The Parish Register (*1807), *The Borough* (1810), *Tales in Verse* (1812), *Tales of the Hall* (1819) – he depicts the diverse lives of his parishioners in a series of highly original short stories in couplets, a form which he made peculiarly his own. His best work treats social outcasts and extreme psychological states, as do a number of poems by ▷ William Wordsworth. But where Wordsworth's approach is transcendental and contemplative, Crabbe's involvement with his characters is compassionate in a more down-to-earth and intimate way. In *Peter Grimes* (Letter XXII of *The Borough*) the landscape of coastal East Anglia becomes an evocative symbol for the protagonist's breakdown and despair. Crabbe's narrative artistry and uncompromising realism were admired by ▷ Jane Austen, who remarked half-seriously that he was the only man she could ever think of marrying.

Bib: Crabbe, G. (junior), *Life*; Pollard, A. (ed.), *Crabbe: The Critical Heritage*; Bareham, T., *George Crabbe*; New, P., *George Crabbe's Poetry*.

Craft Guilds

Medieval societies for the protection and regulation of trade. They grew up in the 13th century out of the already existing merchant guilds, the difference being that the merchant guilds were associations of all the traders in a town, whereas the craft guilds were each limited to a particular craft or line of business. By degrees the craft guilds eliminated the merchant guilds by making them redundant. Each town had its own guilds and part of their function was to protect the trade of that town against competition from 'foreigners'. They gave much-needed security to the exercise of trade in disorderly times, provided some social security to their members in times of need, and settled standards of work and conditions of sale. The members were ▷ master craftsmen. Guilds declined fairly rapidly in the 16th century as the capitalist, free-enterprise employers became more numerous; the guild system was too restrictive of trade to be compatible with ▷ capitalism. For the study of literature, one of the main interests of the craft guilds was their performance of ▷ cycle plays at festivals, especially ▷ Corpus Christi.

Craig, Edward Gordon (1872–1966)

Son of actress Ellen Terry and designer E. W. Godwin, and one of the most influential of early 20th-century stage designers. He began his theatrical career working with Henry Irving at the Lyceum, though disillusionment with English theatre led him to spend much of his time on the continent. Most of his highly

innovative designs were never actually put into practice, but of those that were his most famous were for a production of *Hamlet* at the Moscow Art Theatre, in 1912, and ▷ Ibsen's *The Pretenders* at the Royal Danish Theatre, Copenhagen, in 1926. His influential theories on the crucial role of the theatre designer and the importance of expressive, poetic movement are explored in his books, *The Art of the Theatre* (1905); *On the Art of the Theatre* (1911); *Towards a New Theatre* (1907); *The Marionette* (1918); *The Theatre Advancing* (1921); *Books and Theatres* (1925).
Bib: Craig, E., *Gordon Craig*; Innes, C., *Edward Gordon Craig*.

Craik, Dinah Mulock (1826–87)
Novelist and essayist, who also wrote poetry and short stories. She was born in Stoke-on-Trent, the daughter of a nonconformist clergyman who was feckless and eccentric and was committed as a pauper lunatic in the 1830s. She wrote prolifically – novels, plays, poetry, biography, ▷ travel books, didactic essays and children's stories – to help support her family. After an unsettled childhood she lived with her brother in London, becoming well-known in literary society and marrying George Craik, a partner in Macmillan's publishing house, in 1865. Her first novel was *The Ogilvies* (1849), and her most famous ▷ *John Halifax, Gentleman* (1856). Craik's fiction is predominantly sentimental and romantic, but it also questions traditional sex roles and often depicts female characters attempting to discover autonomous identities. Her novels include *The Head of the Family* (1852), *Agatha's Husband* (1853), *Christian's Mistake* (1865) and *The Woman's Kingdom* (1869). Her non-fiction includes *A Woman's Thoughts About Women* (1858), *Plain Speaking* (1882), and *Concerning Men and Other Papers* (1888). These essays address the need for female self-reliance, offering advice to women on ways to gain independence. She was not a radical writer, but nevertheless contributed to the exploration of woman's role in the Victorian period. She was also a shrewd negotiator and businesswomen, but a generous one, using a pension granted to her in 1864 to help needy authors.
▷ Women's Movement; Children's literature.
Bib: Foster, S., *Victorian Women's Fiction: Marriage, Freedom and the Individual*.

Craik, Helen (c 1750–1825)
Poet and novelist. A ▷ Scottish writer who was encouraged by ▷ Robert Burns, Craik's poetry is now hardly read and recent criticism has focused upon her ▷ Minerva novels. Her prose writing tends towards the gloomy and fantastic, but her characters are well-drawn and introduce a realistic element into the otherwise far-fetched nature of the narrative. Among her novels are: *Julia de Saint Pierre* (1796), *Henry of Northumberland, or The Hermit's cell* (1800) and *The Nun and Her Daughter* (1805).
▷ Scottish literature in English.

Cramond, Elizabeth (d 1651)
Devotional writer. Cramond was the author of *A Ladies Legacie to her Daughters* (1645) which consists of three separate sets of prayers drawn from her own personal experiences. The first consoles her daughters for their lack of monetary inheritance, the second is a series of devotions written upon the death of her second husband, and the third was meant to bring private solace during a protracted illness.

***Cranford* (1853)**
A novel by ▷ Elizabeth Gaskell (1810–65), first published in ▷ *Household Words* (ed. ▷ Charles Dickens) 1851–3. It is the best known of her novels. The town of Cranford is actually based on Knutsford, some 17 miles from Manchester. The book describes the life of the predominantly feminine genteel society of the place. Though apparently very slight, it contains graphic description, and subtle, ironic humour resembling ▷ Jane Austen's. Gaskell's moral judgments, like those of Austen, are implicated with class discriminations: the novel attempts to distinguish between the vulgar arrogance of the merely rich and the sensitive, humane pride of the gentility. Its most famous characters are the blatant and ostentatious Honourable Mrs Jamieson and, in contrast, the timid, retiring, yet distinguished Miss Matty.

Cranmer, Thomas (1489–1556)
Archbishop of Canterbury, and responsible for the *Book of Common Prayer* (1549 and 1552) containing the liturgy of the ▷ Church of England. He was made Archbishop of Canterbury by ▷ Henry VIII during the king's conflict with the Papacy, and supported his rejection of the Pope's authority (▷ Act of Supremacy, 1534), the starting-point of the Church of England. Under Henry's Roman Catholic daughter, ▷ Queen Mary I, Cranmer renounced his opinions, but repudiated his renunciation when he was burnt at the stake in 1556. He is especially important for the literary value of his Prayer Book.
▷ *Common Prayer, Book of.*
Bib: Ridley, J., *Thomas Cranmer*.

Crashaw, Richard (?1612–49)
Poet. He belongs to the ▷ Metaphysical school of English poets, but in a special sense. In 1645 he became a Roman ▷ Catholic, despairing of the survival of the Church of England at that stage of the ▷ Civil War. He earlier came under the influence of the work of the

Italian baroque poet Giovanni Battista Marino (1569–1625), whose extravagance of imagery to some extent resembled the drawing together of unlike ideas into a single image that typified the English metaphysicals. Although Crashaw was perhaps the most sensuous of the English poets of this tendency, his Catholicism and the influence of Marino give to Crashaw's ecstasy an impersonal quality quite different from the direct, very personal devotional poetry of ▷ Donne and ▷ George Herbert – the latter of whom had been Crashaw's first master. Crashaw's masterpiece is his *Hymn to Saint Theresa*; the one that shows his extravagances most obtrusively is *The Weeper*. His poems were published in 1646 in one volume under the titles *Steps to the Temple* and *The Delights of the Muses*.
Bib: Roberts, J. R. (ed.), *New Perspectives on the Life and Art of Richard Crashaw*; Warren, A., *Richard Crashaw*; White, H. C., *The Metaphysical Poets*; Williamson, G., *The Donne Tradition*.

Crécy, Battle of (1346)
The first major victory of the English in the ▷ Hundred Years' War which was brought about by the English ▷ yeomen as archers, using the longbow. For military history, this meant the beginning of the end of the domination of war by the mounted knight in armour, and the beginning of the importance of infantry. The English forces were commanded by ▷ Edward III and the French by King Philip VI.
▷ Archery.

Cresseid, The Testament of
▷ Testament of Cresseid.

Cressida
The lover of the Trojan prince Troilus in medieval and post-medieval versions of the Troy story who is involuntarily separated from Troilus when forced to join her father Calchas in the Greek camp (Calchas, a priest, has previously deserted the Trojan side). In the Greek camp she becomes the lover of Diomedes. She first appears in this role in the 12th-century text, the *Roman de Troie*, composed by Benoît de Sainte-Maure (in which she is called 'Briseida') and it is possible that the figure of Briseis, a lover of Achilles, whose story features in one of ▷ Ovid's *Heroides*, provides a precedent for the development of the Briseida character. The form of her name changes as the story of her love affair with Troilus is amplified and reworked by a series of writers from Benoît onwards, notably ▷ Boccaccio (Criseida), ▷ Chaucer (Criseyde), ▷ Robert Henryson (Cresseid), and ▷ Shakespeare (Cressida).
▷ Troy.

***Cricket on the Hearth, The* (1846)**
A Christmas book by ▷ Charles Dickens, one of a series started by ▷ *A Christmas Carol*, 1843. It is a tale in which the evil schemes of old Tackleton to injure the married love of Peerybingle and his young wife, Dot, and to marry May Fielding are frustrated by the magic of the Cricket and by a mysterious stranger.

Crimean War
A war between the Russians and the British, French and Ottoman Turkish which took place between October 1853 and February 1856, and was fought mainly on the Crimean Peninsular. It was caused primarily by an act of aggression by Russia against the Ottoman sultan and by a dispute between Russia and France concerning the holy lands in Palestine. Britain fought in defence of the Turks and major engagements took place at the Alma River on September 20, at Balaklava on October 25, and at Inkerman on November 5, 1854. In addition to high war casualties, disease accounted for the deaths of over a quarter of a million of the men lost on both sides. The British conscience was stirred by reports of the appalling conditions endured by sick and wounded servicemen, and women were urged to join the troops as nurses.

Among those who volunteered was the pioneer of the nursing profession Florence Nightingale (1820–1910). She arrived at the barrack hospital at Scutari, Turkey on November 5, 1854 where she was put in charge of nursing. Due to the initial hostility of doctors to female presence on the wards, Nightingale and her nurses were forced to stand by and watch as casualties died in overcrowded and insanitary conditions plagued by fleas and rats. When finally allowed to help she began by scrubbing down the wards and washing the patients' clothes. Her individual care of the wounded soldiers earned her the soubriquet 'The Lady with the Lamp'. Nightingale became a national hero and her efforts helped establish the Royal Commission on the Health of the Army in May 1857. This in turn led to the founding of the Army Medical School in the same year. Using her considerable private funds, and money raised by public subscription to commemorate her work in the Crimea, she set up the Nightingale School for Nurses at St Thomas' Hospital in 1860, which was the first nursing school of its kind.

The Crimean War stirred a certain amount of jingoism in England. ▷ Gladstone, then Chancellor of the Exchequer, defended it as necessary to the maintenance of public law in Europe and doubled income tax in 1854 in order to pay for Britain's involvement. Just prior to the outbreak of hostilities in the Crimea, Tennyson wrote of 'the blood-red blossom of war' in his long poem *Maud* but added six lines in 1856 to suggest that the speaker of these lines was deranged. *Maud* nevertheless retains its bellicosity and is suffused with references to the Crimean War. Tennyson also marked the disastrous events at Balaklava in his patriotic poem ▷ 'The Charge of the Light Brigade' (1854). An opposing point of view is expressed by ▷ Sydney Dobell, a member of the so-called ▷ Spasmodic school of poetry. In his *England in Time of War* (1856), jingoism gives way to compassion for the tragic personal consequences of war. In similar vein ▷ Newman, moved and enraged by reports concerning the state of the British army in the Crimea, wrote a series of letters to the *Catholic Herald* in 1855 entitled 'Who's to Blame?'. Minor novelist Thomas William Robertson (1829–71) wrote *Ours* (1866) which deals with the private lives of British officers serving in the Crimea. It also exploits the pathos and ironies of war in general, and the Crimean War in particular. The Crimean War features in the play *Birth* (1870) by Thomas William Robertson, ▷ Thackeray's *The Rose and the Ring* (1855) and ▷ Charles Kingsley's *The Heroes* (1856).

***Critic, The: Or, a Tragedy Rehearsed* (1779)**
Satiric comedy by ▷ Richard Brinsley Sheridan, using the 'play within a play' technique employed in ▷ *The Rehearsal* in order to mock contemporary dramatic technique. In the first act Dangle discusses with his wife, a fellow theatregoer called Sneer, and the author, Sir Fretful Plagiary, the fact that a new tragedy, *The Spanish Armada*, is being prepared at ▷ Drury Lane. In the second and third acts, Puff invites the three men to observe a rehearsal of his play, which concerns the approach of the Armada. Tilburnia, daughter of the governor of Tilbury Fort, expresses her love for one of the Spanish prisoners, Don Ferolo Whiskerandos. As in *The Rehearsal*, the acting of the absurd play is accompanied by the fatuous explanations and instructions of the author, and scathing comments of his guests. The play ends with the destruction of the Spanish fleet, and strains of 'Rule Britannia', ▷ Handel's 'Water Music', and the march from *Judas Maccabaeus*. The tragedy was intended to satirize the works of dramatists such as ▷ Colman and ▷ Cumberland, of whom Sir Fretful Plagiary is a caricature. The play was acted 131 times before 1800.

Critique
A term used in critical theory. Traditional conceptions of 'criticism' have privileged the acts of judgement and comparison but have often anchored them in the unspecified sensitivity of the reader. Criticism pre-supposes a direct relationship between reader and literary text; the reader responds to the stimulus of particular verbal forms which are evaluated according to their appeal to a universal human condition. The practice of 'critique', in a literary context, however, concerns itself not just with producing readings of primary texts and accounting for those social, cultural, or psychological motivations which are responsible for its appearance in a particular form, but also with appraising critical readings of those texts. Critique addresses itself to questions of why individual texts should be accorded importance at particular historical moments, and implicates 'criticism' in its more traditional guise as a process whereby meanings are constructed, as opposed to being passively discovered.

Cromwell, Oliver (1599–1658)
Chief commander of the Parliamentarian forces in the ▷ Civil War against ▷ Charles I and Lord Protector of the Realm (1653–8) in place of a king. He belonged to the landowning class in the east of England and supported the Independents among the Puritans. It was his generalship that defeated the forces of Charles I and the Scottish supporters of ▷ Charles II after the execution of Charles I. After his death, his son, Richard Cromwell, succeeded as Lord Protector for some months, after which Charles II was restored by the action of one of Oliver's generals, General Monk, in 1660. After 1660 he suffered the censure of his political opponents and it was not until Thomas Carlyle published *Oliver Cromwell's Letters and Speeches* (1845) that his stature was generally appreciated.
Bib: Fraser, A., *Cromwell Our Chief of Men*.

Cromwell, Thomas (1485–1540)
Chief minister of ▷ Henry VIII; organized the dissolution of the English monasteries in 1536 and 1539. His sister married Morgan Williams; their son adopted the name of Cromwell and was the direct ancestor of ▷ Oliver Cromwell.
Bib: Elton, G. R., *Thomas Cromwell*.

***Crotchet Castle* (1831)**
A novel by ▷ Thomas Love Peacock. The plot is unimportant, and the novel consists mainly of witty talk, burlesquing and satirizing contemporary attitudes and ideas. A crotchet is an eccentric and frivolous notion or prejudice. Some of the characters are representatives of intellectual tendencies, *eg* MacQuedy, a Scots economist whose name suggests 'Q.E.D.' (*quod erat demonstrandum*), stands for the excessive rationalism of the political economists and utilitarians of the age. On the other hand, Mr Skionar stands for the poet, critic and philosopher, ▷ S. T. Coleridge, and burlesques his transcendental mysticism. Mr Chainmail stands for the sentimental cult of the 'Gothic', *ie* the romance and sensationalism of the cult of the Middle Ages, familiar from the historical novels of ▷ Walter Scott and from the ▷ Gothic novels of the previous generation. Sanity is represented by Dr. Folliott, a clergyman, a character of robust and cheerful common sense.

Crowe, Catherine (?1800–72)
Novelist and short story writer, born in Kent. She married Lt Col John Crowe in 1822 and moved to Edinburgh until the death of her husband in 1860, after which she went to live in Folkestone. A prolific writer, she is best-known for her collection of supernatural stories, *Night Side of Nature or Ghosts and Ghost Stories* (1848), which ran to several editions. She also wrote plays, her first work being the tragedy *Aristomedus*, published anonymously in 1838. Her novel *Susan Hopley* (1841) was successfully adapted for the stage, and *The Cruel Kindness* (1853), a drama, was performed at the Haymarket Theatre. Other novels include *Manorial Rights* (1839), *Linny Dawson* (1847) and, for children, *Adventures of a Monkey* (1861).
Bib: Sergeant, A., *Women Novelists of Queen Victoria's Reign*.

Crowley, Aleister (1875–1947)
Magician, novelist and poet. Aleister Crowley, once dubbed by the *Daily Mail*, 'the Wickedest Man in the World', has become the lurid paradigm of post-Symbolist diabolism. His hedonistic sexual and pharmacological activities (leading to his famous motto, 'Do What Thou Wilt Shall Be The Whole Of The Law') have led to his celebration and denigration as a precursor to 1960s permissiveness. It is hard to separate prolificity and charlatanry in Crowley's work. However, the novels *The Diary of a Drug Fiend* (1922) and *Moonchild* (1929) have retained their power to provoke. Crowley's attempts to found an influential cult collapsed, and he died, addicted to heroin, in a Hastings boarding house.

Crowne, John (?1640–?1703)
Dramatist. Crowne published a ⊳ romance in 1665, and his first play, *Juliana, or the Princess of Poland*, a tragi-comedy, in 1671. Thereafter, he experimented with various genres: a court ⊳ masque, *Calisto*; a tragedy, *Andromache*; and a comedy based on a play by ⊳ Molière (*Le Sicilien ou L'amour peintre*), *The Country Wit*, all appeared in 1675. The heroic verse tragedy, *The Destruction of Jerusalem*, was performed in two parts in 1677. Several political plays followed. Crowne became a favourite of ⊳ Charles II, and later Queen Mary (⊳ Mary II). His greatest success, *Sir Courtly Nice; Or, It Cannot Be* (1685), modelled on a Spanish play (⊳ Spanish influence on English literature), remained popular for over a century.
Bib: McMullin, B. J., *The Comedies of John Crowne: A Critical Edition*.

Cruelty, Theatre of
⊳ Theatre of Cruelty.

Cruikshank, George (1792–1878)
Illustrator, with a strong satirical and moralistic bent: famous especially for his illustrations to ⊳ Charles Dickens' novel ⊳ *Oliver Twist*. He also illustrated works by ⊳ Burns, ⊳ Scott and ⊳ Thackeray and produced many political caricatures.

Crusades, The
Military expeditions from Western Christendom which were represented as spiritual in motivation to recover the Holy Land, and in particular the Holy City of Jerusalem, from the Muslims (though in practice, these expeditions might have a variety of political and economic motivations also). Nine crusades have attracted the attention of modern historians as the most important, from the first proclaimed by Pope Urban II in 1095, which made Godfrey of Bouillon King of Jerusalem in 1099, to that on which St Louis died (King Louis IX of France) in 1270. In the thirteenth century, the term crusade (which derives from the sign of the cross which distinguished its participants) was also used to refer to military expeditions against heretics (such as the Albigensians) and expeditions against the political enemies of the pope.

Crystal Palace
⊳ Exhibition, The Great.

Cuchulain
In Irish myth the hero of a cycle of prose legends called the Cuchulain or Ulster cycle (9th–13th centuries AD). In English, he is chiefly known by the poems and plays about him by ⊳ W. B. Yeats. Yeats' work issued from his support of Irish nationalism, which revived interest in the Irish myths, and led to the publication of English versions of them.
⊳ Irish literature in English.
Bib: Hull, E., *The Cuchulain Saga*.

Culler, Jonathan (b 1944)
Academic and critic whose works have done much to introduce English-speaking audiences to the works of ⊳ structuralist and ⊳ post-structuralist critics. His major studies include *Structuralist Poetics* (1975), *The Pursuit of Signs* (1981) and *On Deconstruction* (1983). He is Professor of English and Comparative Literature at Cornell University.

Culloden, Battle of (1746)
A battle in the north of Scotland in the 1745 ⊳ Jacobite Rebellion on behalf of the House of ⊳ Stuart in the attempt to recover the British throne from the House of Hanover, which had been installed by Parliament in 1714. The Jacobites, consisting mainly of Scottish Highland clans commanded by Prince Charles Edward Stuart ('Bonnie Prince Charlie'), were decisively defeated by the Duke of Cumberland – Butcher Cumberland to his enemies. Not only did Culloden end the rebellion but it

practically put an end to the Highland clan system, which remains chiefly in name by force of romantic nostalgia.

▷ Old Pretender, The; Scotland; Scottish literature in English.

Cultural Materialism
The most important book in the formation of cultural materialism is Jonathan Dollimore and Alan Sinfield's collection of essays *Political Shakespeare* (1985), whose foreword acts as a manifesto for this radical Marxist criticism. The authors themselves trace the origins of the theory to général dissatisfaction in the British academic world with the traditional essentialism humanism of existing criticism and the rise of numerous alternative approaches (▷ feminism, structuralism, ▷ psychoanalytic criticism). Apart from a debt to the political commitment to change, derived from Marxism, cultural materialism also draws upon Raymond Williams' cultural analysis which 'seeks to describe the whole system of significations by which a society or a section of it understands itself and its relations with the world' (*Political Shakespeare*). Thus, cultural materialism rejects any notion of 'high culture', and sets material values in the place of the idealism of conventional criticism, looking instead at texts in history. Cultural materialism also has links with new historicism (particularly the work of Stephen Greenblatt) in its emphasis upon the nature of subjectivity and the decentring of man, and with feminism, where the exploration of the gendered human subject is an overlapping interest. Antagonistic to the (allegedly) ahistorical and dangerously apolitical conclusions of ▷ deconstruction, a sceptical and combative tone, together with an interest in decentring, is nevertheless common to both, suggesting an increased disillusion with traditional, this is to say, humanist, literary criticism.

▷ Post-structuralism.

Culture
Despite its widespread use, culture remains one of the most difficult of words in the modern critical vocabulary. It is used in two, broad senses. First, it indicates a group of products (*eg* art objects or books) or personal acquisitions (*eg* 'refined tastes' or the appreciation of art) or activities (*eg* visiting the theatre or classical music concerts) which are deemed to be of considerable value or status in a society. The other sense carries different evaluative connotations and refers to the activities of a particular way of life. Thus we might speak, for example, of French culture or working-class culture. Here is indicated, therefore, a whole spread of activities which define the distinctive 'Frenchness' or 'working-classness' of a way of life and these might well include some or all of the activities mentioned above. But this second usage would tend to avoid connotations of superior, learned or elite tastes or habits.

Five different usages of the word are detectable in literary studies.

1 In the first place, culture is distinguished from ignorance or crudeness when a person becomes 'cultivated'.

2 Culture is opposed to the worlds of work and money, and is therefore associated with recreation, fine living or higher values. (The connection with aristocratic values and lifestyles in this association is obvious.)

3 Culture is opposed to popular or 'mass' forms of activity. Here, culture is often associated with the 'high-brow', the privileged or elite.

4 Culture refers to the special province of human creativity and therefore to possibilities for improvement, either personal or general

5 Finally, one tradition of radical, Marxist-influenced theory pictures culture negatively. In this line of thinking, it is associated with ▷ ideology, and its function is to shackle human thought and imagination in the interests of the status quo (▷ Myth).

It is clear, therefore, that the idea of culture is enmeshed with strong value judgements and, typically, in much literary commentary of the late 19th and early 20th centuries (for example, that of ▷ Matthew Arnold, ▷ T. S. Eliot and F. R. Leavis), the world of high, or minority, culture was opposed to the assumed degradation of moral or spiritual standards brought on by industrialization, modern commercialism and mass culture. Though lip-service was paid to the idea of culture as a 'whole way of life', in practice it was somewhat exclusively identified with traditional institutions like the Church and with the literary canon. More recent commentary, however, has taken different directions. The term 'popular culture' has flourished, and attention is given to forms of writing and cultural production which had been previously despised (film and television for example). The idea of cultural identity has also become a key term, often in relation to writing produced in societies composed of social groups with divergent traditions and interests, for example post-colonial societies (▷ Colonialism).

In contemporary literary studies several trends are therefore apparent. There is still an interest in what has been called the 'culture and society' tradition of thought based around writers of the late 19th and early 20th centuries from Arnold to ▷ George Orwell. But, more widely, a tradition of cultural studies has been established in which literary works are studied as part of the analysis of the general cultural environment of a period alongside non-literary, non-canonical or popular material. This often includes visual as well as written products. In some quarters, this has become known as ▷ 'cultural materialism' and signals an approach to cultural artefacts which stresses their social, political, intellectual and economic origins and functions rather than their aesthetic, moral or spiritual qualities.

Bib: Ross, A., *No Respect: Intellectuals and Popular Culture*; Williams, R., *Culture and Society 1780–1950*; *Culture*.

Culture and Anarchy (1869)

A volume of essays by ▷ Matthew Arnold, originally published as articles in ▷ *The Cornhill Magazine*. It is subtitled *An Essay in Political and Social Criticism* and was designed to demonstrate that culture was the best remedy for the political, social and religious unrest that, in his view, characterized England at that time. Arnold defined the main purpose of culture as the stimulation of intelligence and reason. Its advance was blocked by certain inequalities, confusions and imbalances within English life which, unchecked by an adequate centre of authority, threatened to slide towards anarchy. Arnold distinguishes between two categories of mind in contemporary society: the Hebraic, with its emphasis on the virtues of private conduct and practical achievement; and the Hellenic, which valued contemplation, reason and critical discrimination. England, he considered, was becoming barbarous owing to the preponderance of the former over the latter, with which he identified. The answer to the conflict lay in culture with its emphasis on the development of the individual within the broader framework of society, its commitment to the growth of the moral life and its aspirations towards perfection.

Cumberland, Richard (1732–1811)

Dramatist, poet, novelist, translator, essayist, associated with the rise of sentimental domestic comedy on the English stage. He began writing poetry while still a pupil at school in Bury St Edmunds. After further education at Westminster School and Cambridge University he published his first play, *The Banishment of Cicero* in 1761. Disappointed in his career aspirations in government, he turned to writing for the stage in earnest. He continued this activity even after his political fortunes improved, eventually completing over 50 plays, operas, and adaptations of plays. His first success of any consequence was with the comedy, *The Brothers*, in 1769. In 1770 he wrote his most famous play, generally considered his best, *The West Indian*, which the actor David Garrick (1717–79) staged in the following year. Even so his work was often under attack for its supposed sentimentality, and Sheridan satirized him as the vain and defensive Sir Fretful Plagiary in *The Critic* (1779). However, Cumberland was sympathetic to the causes of others, especially outcast and vilified groups. He defended the Jews in *The Jew* (1794), which was translated into several languages, including Yiddish and Hebrew, and remained popular well into the 19th century. *The Jew of Mogadore* (1808) again portrays a Jew in a kindly light, and Cumberland also defended Jews in articles in *The Observer*, written under a Jewish pseudonym. His efforts did much to rescue Jews from the villainous anti-Semitic image hitherto afforded them on the stage. In addition to plays, he wrote two novels, translations of Greek plays, ▷ epic poetry, and pamphlets expressing his views on controversial topics of the day.

Bib: Borkat, R. F. S. (ed.), *The Plays of Richard Cumberland*.

Cunningham, Lady Margaret (?–c 1622)

Scottish author of letters and an ▷ autobiography, her work is not well known, but her life story provides dramatic and romantic reading. Cunningham was married to Sir James Hamilton of Crawfordjohn in 1598, but her strong Protestant faith and moral values soon clashed with his Catholic convictions and boorish behaviour. When reconciled she wrote him passionate letters and verses in which she attempted to reform him, but after their final separation in 1608 she wrote of how he had denied her food and shut her out of their home. Cunningham had 11 children, five by Crawfordjohn and six by her second, happier marriage to Sir James Maxwell of Calderwood. Her autobiography was published in 1827 and is available at the National Library of Scotland.

Cursor Mundi

An encyclopaedic verse narrative in English, dating from around 1300, originating in the north of England, which recounts Christian history from Creation to Doomsday with a particular emphasis on the mediating role of the Virgin Mary. The *Cursor Mundi* literally 'courses over' Christian history but it also travels as a text through England; a southern version is extant. Eight manuscript copies of *Cursor Mundi* survive of varying length (the longest running to 30,000 lines of octosyllabic verse).

Curtis, Tony (b 1946)

Poet, short story writer, editor and critic. Tony Curtis was born in Carmarthen and educated at University College, Swansea, and at Goddard College, Vermont, USA. His teaching career took him to schools in Cheshire and Yorkshire before he secured a lecturer's post at Glamorgan College of Education in Barry. This institution's merger with the Polytechnic of Wales at Treforest, Pontypridd, ultimately led to his becoming the first Professor of Poetry to be appointed in Wales when the Polytechnic was elevated to the status of University of Glamorgan. Tony Curtis has been a lively crusader for the cause of poetry not only in Wales but also in Europe and North America, this contributing to a breadth of vision in his work in a historical overview that places Welshness in an international context and looks beyond the narrower and more parochial concerns that sometimes influence Anglo-Welsh poetry. This is most evident in the new poems placed first in his *Selected* volume. His poetry charts the nuances of living in the modern world, illuminating situations concerned with family or place in a compassionate and perceptive manner. His earliest poems appeared in *Walk Down A Welsh Wind* (1972) and in *Three Young Anglo-Welsh Poets* (1974) which also included poems by Nigel Jenkins and Duncan Bush. Since then, Tony Curtis' poetry collections have been *Album* (1974), *Preparations* (1980), *Letting Go* (1983), *Selected Poems* (1986), *The Last Candles* (1989), *Taken for Pearls* (1993) and *War Voices* (1995). He has also published a collection of short stories and prose poems *Out of the Dark Wood* (1977), a monograph on *Dannie Abse* in the *Writers of Wales* series (1985), and as well as editing *Madog*, an arts magazine, in his early years at the Polytechnic of Wales, he has also edited two volumes of critical essays, *The Art of Seamus Heaney* (1982) and *Wales: The Imagined Nation* (1993), and finally, with Sian James, an anthology of poetry and prose, *Love from Wales*, in 1991.

Bib: Stephens, M. (Ed.), *The Oxford Companion to the Literature of Wales.*

Curzon, Sarah Anne (1833–98)

Born Sarah Vincent in Birmingham, England, she married Robert Curzon, and emigrated with him to Canada in 1862. She was a strong advocate of suffrage and education, contributed to many journals, and wrote a column on women's issues. *Laura Secord, the Heroine of 1812: A Drama, And Other Poems* (1887) and *The Story of Laura Secord, 1813* (1891) are both historical representations of Laura Secord's heroic actions in crossing enemy lines to warn the British of impending American attack in the war of 1812. The earlier volume includes *The Sweet Girl Graduate*, a comic play about a woman who disguises herself as a man in order to graduate from the University of Toronto.

▷ Women's Movement.

Cycle plays

A type of vernacular drama, performed in England from the later 14th century until the latter half of the 16th century, composed of a sequence of episodes, or pageants, dramatizing Christian history. The scope of the sequences characteristically extends from the beginning of Christian history (the fall of the Angels, and the Creation) to the Last Judgement. These plays have been referred to by modern critics variously as 'miracle plays', 'mystery plays', 'Corpus Christi plays': each of these terms has some justification but each may lead to misconceptions of one kind or another. The term 'miracle play' has the advantage of employing a medieval dramatic term but the word 'miracle' was used during the medieval period as a very general term, applicable to any kind of religious drama, not just cycle plays. 'Mystery play' is a term (first used according to the O.E.D. in 1744) deriving from the French word for a trade or craft ('*mystère*') and is applied to the cycle plays because they were very frequently performed by the craft guild of a town, in association with the religious guilds and ecclesiastical authorities. However, not all the extant play cycles appear to be designed for performance by guild members (the so-called ▷ 'N-Town' cycle seems scripted for performance by semi-professionals) and the term 'mystery' may conjure up quite misleading, modern associations. The plays have been called 'Corpus Christi plays' with some justice, for the performance of the plays is associated with the celebration of the feast day of ▷ Corpus Christi. This feast day, which is 11 days after Whitsunday, was instituted to celebrate the Eucharist, and was marked by a procession. Precisely if, and how, this feast day stimulated the performance of cycle plays is not clear but there is evidence that by the end of the 14th century at least one major town in England (York) marked the feast day by the performance of a sequence of pageants taken from Christian history. But not all the play cycles were performed on this day: the plays at Chester, for example, were performed over three days in Whitsun week. 'Cycle play' seems the most appropriate term, therefore, for this medieval dramatic phenomenon.

There are four major play cycles extant (the ▷ York, ▷ Chester, ▷ Wakefield, and ▷ N-Town cycles), and fragments survive from play cycles associated with Coventry, Newcastle and Norwich (in addition to three cycle plays in Cornish). The central focus of the cycles is on the events leading up to the Crucifixion and Resurrection, prefaced by selected episodes from O.T. history and followed by the Day of Judgement (the source material being drawn from the Bible, supplemented by legendary and apocryphal narratives). There is some variation in the choice of episodes, as there is in the mode of production of the pageants: those at York and Chester (and probably Wakefield too) were staged on waggons and enacted at fixed points in the streets of the town; the text of the N-Town cycle seems scripted for performance on a fixed set. Necessarily, drama on this scale requires considerable resources, so it is not surprising that the cycles are associated with prosperous provincial towns. Although the efforts of the reformed English Church succeeded in suppressing performances of play cycles in the later 16th century (because they were regarded as idolatrous), the survival of the drama until this time suggests that cycle plays continued to perform a useful municipal function, displaying civic order and wealth, even if their religious function was now outmoded.

Cycle drama is drama in process: the cycles were not static events, their composition continued to change; pageants were written and rewritten, inserted and omitted. This process of composition, and indeed the context of cycle production, can only be partially recreated, since most of the play cycles (apart from Chester) exist in single manuscript copies with few indications of production details or even stage directions. However, the intense scholarly interest in the cycle plays, particularly over the last 20 years, has helped to recreate their forms and contexts, resulting in radical reassessments of this major dramatic genre of medieval Europe.

▷ Craft Guilds

Bib: Cawley, A. C., et al., *The Revels History of Drama in English: Vol I Medieval Drama*; Happé, P. (ed.), *English Mystery Plays*.

Cymbeline (1609–10)

A late tragicomedy by Shakespeare; sometimes called a romance because of its avoidance of realism. Much of the play is set in the court of the ancient British king Cymbeline (1st century AD) and the climax is the defeat of a Roman invasion; on the other hand the love triangle of Posthumus, the British princess Imogen, and the Italian Iachimo is thoroughly ▷ Renaissance; Shakespeare has in fact combined a story of ancient British history from the chronicler ▷ Raphael Holinshed with a love-story from ▷ Boccaccio's ▷ *Decameron*. Thus a victory of British patriotism over Roman imperialism is fused with a more up-to-date victory of English single-minded devotion over Italian duplicity. *Cymbeline* has also been called a reconciliation play, because, like ▷ *Pericles* before it and ▷ *The Winter's Tale* and ▷ *The Tempest* after it, it steadily darkens with murderous conspiracy from the outset to the middle, and then lightens towards a general clarification in candour and love at the end. Also like the other three plays, *Cymbeline* has as a central theme the loss to the world and, except in *The Tempest*, to the father of a young girl whose recovery expresses the recovery of the qualities of youth, purity, beauty, trust and potentiality.

▷ Romances of Shakespeare.

Cynewulf (fl 800)

Old English poet, probably working in the late 8th or early 9th century, who signed his name in runes in four poems, *Christ II, Elene, Juliana* and *The Fates of the Apostles*. The poems suggest that Cynewulf was a learned writer, familiar with Latin and thus probably a cleric, although nothing more is known about him as a historical personage.

▷ Old English literature.

Cynics, The

A school of ancient Greek philosophers founded by Antisthenes in the 4th century BC. Their belief, that the only realizable aim in life was the fulfilment of the individual by the strict application of reason to practical issues, led them to an extreme individualism, according to which social considerations were irrelevant, ambition was a distraction, pleasure a corruption, and poverty and disrepute were of active assistance in promoting self-reliance. The word 'cynic' seems to derive from the Greek word for 'dog', and they agreed in taking this animal as their emblem. The word has degenerated to imply an attitude of disbelief in the goodness of human motives and in the reality of human values.

D

Dabydeen, David (b 1955)
Guyanese novelist and poet. Dabydeen came to Britain in 1969 and studied at the universities of Cambridge, London and Oxford. During the 1980s he worked as a community education officer and as a lecturer in Caribbean Studies at the University of Warwick. His first novel was *The Intended* (1991), followed by *Disappearance* (1993), and his collection of poems, *Slave Song* (1984) won the Commonwealth Poetry Prize. He has also published critical works on the 18th-century painter Hogarth and on black writing in Britain.

Dacre, Charlotte (c 1782–?)
Novelist and poet. Dacre and her sister, the writer ⊳ Sophia King, dedicated their first work *Trifles From Helicon* (1798) to their notorious father, John King, who had just been arrested for bankruptcy. She adopted the name 'Rosa Matilda' when visiting ⊳ Rachel Despenser and in publishing her first book *The Confessions of the Nun of St Omer* (1805), which she dedicated to Matthew ⊳ 'Monk' Lewis; it was also under this name that ⊳ Byron chose to ridicule her. Her most famous work is *Zofloya, or the Moor* (1806), a ⊳ Gothic novel indebted to *The Monk*, which supposedly warns against the dangers of lust and passion, though Dacre's obvious fascination in depicting these sentiments belies the stated ⊳ didactic purpose. The final scene is a *tour de force* in which the heroine is thrown to her death from a cliff by the devil. *Zofloya* influenced ⊳ Shelley's *Zastrozzi* and was published in ⊳ chapbook format as *The Daemon of Venice* (1810). Dacre wrote several other novels, poetry, and the lyrics for popular stage songs. No evidence remains as to how she spent her later life.

Dactyl
A verse foot consisting of an accented syllable followed by two unaccented ones. It thus gives a light falling rhythm, and is commonly used with ⊳ trochees in lines which end in an accented syllable or an iambus.
⊳ Metre.

Dada
Artistic and literary movement. It arose in two distinct places at about the same time. One group was formed in Zurich in 1916 by three refugees, Tristan Tzara (1887–1968), Hans Arp (1887–1966) and Hugo Ball (1886–1927); another group was formed in New York in the years 1916–19 by Marcel Duchamp (1887–1968), Man Ray (1890–1976) and Francis Picabia (1879–1953). By 1920, both groups had united and made their headquarters in Paris where their journal was *Littérature* (1919–21). The Dada emphasis was on instinctual expression free from constraints and the consequent cultivation of destructiveness, randomness and incoherence; indeed, the very name 'Dada' (= hobby horse) was a random selection from the dictionary. The movement lasted until the early 1920s. A number of its adherents joined the ⊳ Surrealists, a movement which in part evolved out of Dada.

Daedalus
In Greek myth, an artist of wonderful powers. He made wings for himself and his son Icarus, and flew from Crete to Sicily to escape the wrath of King Minos, for whom he had built the labyrinth. The fact that he was an artist explains the use of a form of the name by James Joyce – Dedalus – in ⊳ *Portrait of the Artist as a Young Man*.

***Daisy Miller* (1879)**
A story by ⊳ Henry James. It concerns the visit of an American girl to Europe, and is one of the stories in which James contrasts American freshness of impulse, moral integrity, and naivety with the complexity and deviousness of the European mentality. The girl's innocence and candour is misinterpreted as moral turpitude by the Americans who are long settled in Europe, including the young man who acts as focal character for the narrative.

Dame schools
Schools for poor children in the 18th and 19th centuries, especially in country towns and villages. Unlike the charity schools, they were run by private initiative, especially by single women supplementing their income by teaching reading and writing.
⊳ Education.

Dame Sirith
A Middle English verse ⊳ fabliau of some 450 lines, dating from the 13th century, which survives in a single manuscript. The narrative, set in dialogue form, relates how a cleric seduces a woman with the help of the tricks of Dame Sirith.

Dance of Death
A theme of artistic and literary representation from the later medieval period, in which representative figures from different social estates were taken away to their graves by skeletal, cadaverous corpses. The earliest known representation of the Dance of Death (or *danse macabre*) was made in 1424, in the cemetery of the Innocents in Paris, and was copied in a cloister of Old St Paul's (for which ⊳ John Lydgate translated the verse inscriptions).

Dane, Clemence (1887–1965)
Playwright and novelist. Clemence Dane is the pseudonym of Winifred Ashton, a highly

prolific playwright and novelist whose work was extremely successful in her lifetime, but who has to some extent been neglected by critical history. Her career was a long one – Dane published her first novel (which deals with power and lesbianism in a girls' public school), *Regiment of Women*, in 1917, and continued writing until her death – some of her later works were dramas for BBC television. She also wrote essays, and was awarded the CBE in 1953. Her plays include: *A Bill of Divorcement* (1921); *Naboth's Vineyard* (1925); *Manners* (1927); *The Saviours* (1942); and *Call Home the Heart* (1947). Her novels include *Enter Sir John* (1930); *The Moon is Feminine* (1938); and *He Brings Great News* (1939).

Danegeld
A tax raised by Anglo-Saxon kings as tribute to the Danes to prevent their invasions of southern England.

Dangaremba, Tsitsi (b 1958)
Novelist and playwright, born and brought up in Rhodesia (now Zimbabwe). She was educated in Harare (at that time called Salisbury) before going on to study medicine and psychology at the University of Oxford and film at the Berlin film school. Her novel *Dangerous Conditions* (1988) won the Commonwealth Prize and reveals some of the psychological effects of colonialism through the lives of two young girls in pre-independence Rhodesia.

***Daniel Deronda* (1876)**
A novel by ▷ George Eliot (Mary Ann Evans). It contains a double story: that of the hero, Daniel Deronda, and that of the heroine Gwendolen Harleth. Daniel is the adopted son of an aristocratic Englishman, and a young man of gracious personality and positive values; he discovers that he is of Jewish parentage, and ends by marrying a Jewish girl, Mirah and devoting himself to the cause of establishing a Jewish homeland. Gwendolen belongs to an impoverished upper-class family and marries (under pressure from her clergyman uncle) a rich and entirely self-centred aristocrat, Henleigh Grandcourt, to redeem their fortunes. Her story is the discovery of the truth of her own nature, just as Deronda's story is the discovery of his origin and vocation. Their stories are linked by the almost casual but entirely beneficent influence of Deronda over Gwendolen, whom he saves from despair after the death of her husband in circumstances that compromise her conscience. (The theme of artistic dedication is central.) Critics have observed that the story of Gwendolen is one of the masterpieces of English fiction, but that that of Daniel is comparatively flat and unconvincing.

Daniel, Samuel (1562–1619)
Poet and dramatist. After returning from extensive travel in France and Italy (c 1586), he was employed as a tutor to the son of ▷ William Herbert, Earl of Pembroke (patron of ▷ Shakespeare) and to ▷ Mary Sidney's family, as well as to ▷ Lady Anne Clifford. His first publication was 28 sonnets included in the unauthorized edition of ▷ Sir Philip Sidney's ▷ *Astrophil and Stella* (1591). In 1592 he published his own collection of sonnets under the title of *Delia*. His dramatic work includes *The Tragedy of Cleopatra* (1594), and *Philotas* (1605), which deals with a trial, on a charge of treason, of an ambitious favourite of ▷ Alexander the Great – a theme which the authorities thought uncomfortably close to the events of the ▷ Essex rebellion of 1601 and which led to Daniel being summoned before the Privy Council to explain the play's intentions. His publications also included several ▷ masques, and a philosophical dialogue in verse form, entitled *Musophilus* (1599), which discusses the conflict between humanist theory and the value of practical arts. Daniel's masques are considered some of the most beautiful and, perhaps, challenging of the ▷ Jacobean court entertainments. Although never as scholarly as those of ▷ Ben Jonson, Daniel's shows, under the ▷ patronage of ▷ Queen Anne, presented gender roles in a disturbing light.

Daniel's major project, however, was his huge unfinished work *The Civil Wars*. This historical ▷ epic dealing with the Wars of the Roses first appeared in four books in 1592, and by 1609 eight books in all had been published, which brought his account to the marriage of ▷ Edward IV. After the project had been abandoned, Daniel turned to writing a prose history of England, which appeared in two parts between 1612 and 1617. In addition to his historical enterprises, Daniel published, in 1603, his answer to ▷ Thomas Campion's *Observations in the Art of English Poesy*.

Though Daniel's sonnets represent the major portion of his writings read in the 20th century, his attempt at creating a historical epic forms an important part of the late Elizabethan project (shared in by ▷ Edmund Spenser and ▷ Michael Drayton) to create a firmly realized sense of national identity.

▷ Histories and Chronicles.

Bib: Michel, L. (ed.), *The Civil Wars*; Rees, J., *Daniel: A Critical and Biographical Study*.

Daniels, Sarah (b 1957)
Dramatist. Daniels is one of the most controversial British playwrights, and the only radical lesbian feminist to have made it into the mainstream. She first came to prominence with *Ripen Our Darkness* (1981) which premiered, like *Byrthrite* (1987), at the Royal Court Upstairs (which also presented *Masterpieces* after its Royal Manchester Exchange opening). Her attacks on patriarchy involve the rebellion of mothers (*Ripen Our Darkness* and *The Devil's*

Gateway, 1983) and the discussion of lesbian custody of children in *Neaptide* (1984). *Byrthrite* is a warning for women about the possible consequences of modern genetic engineering and reproductive techniques and is linked to a familiar theme of the persecution of the old 'wise women' of the 17th century. *The Gut Girls* (1988) continues the historical theme with its celebration of Victorian working-class women, and *Beside Herself* (1990) tackles childhood abuse in a mythological frame.

Needless to say, Daniels' plays and her expression of unpalatable truths (especially if you are a man) have invoked, in their turn, vitriolically hostile reviews from critics (mostly but not exclusively male), particularly over *Masterpieces* (1983) and *Byrthrite*. But Daniels' early protagonists are recognisable suburban wives and mothers rebelling – wittily – against their roles as general moppers-up after men and the male value system that has put them there. In Daniels' world, the personal becomes graphically political.

Masterpieces, Daniels' best known work, is an uncompromisingly didactic play that makes a direct link between the seemingly innocuous dinner table misogynist joke and male violence against women. It is a tale of growing awareness, focused on a social worker who gradually moves from naivety to anger, from passivity to action and wholesale rejection of the man-made world in which she lives and to which she has, in the past, given tacit acceptance. The play has an irrefutable emotional force about it and has deservedly come to be regarded as a feminist classic, even if some find its philosophical links questionable. Other plays include: *Head Rot Holiday* (1992) and *The Madness of Esme and Shaz* (1994).

Dante Alighieri (1265–1321)

Poet and philosopher. Very little is known about the early life of Dante. He was born in Florence, a member of the Guelf family, and married Gemma Donati in 1285. His involvement in Florentine politics from 1295 led in 1300 to his exile from Florence, to which he never returned. He died at Ravenna in 1321. According to his own report, he was inspired throughout his life by his love for Beatrice, a woman who has been identified as Bice Portinari (d 1290).

It is difficult to date Dante's work with any degree of precision. The *Vita Nuova* (1290–4) is a lyric sequence celebrating his inspirational love for Beatrice, linked by prose narrative and commentary sections. His Latin treatise *De Vulgari Eloquentia*, perhaps begun in 1303–4 but left unfinished, is a pioneering work of literacy and linguistic commentary. Here Dante considers the state and status of Italian as a literary language, and assesses the achievements of earlier French and Provençal poets in elevating the status of their vernacular media. The *Convivio* (1304–7) is an unfinished philosophical work, a 'banquet of knowledge', composed of prose commentaries on allegorical poetic sequences. Dante's political ideas, specifically the relationship between the Pope, Emperor, and the universal Empire, are explored in *De Monarchia* (c 1310). Dante may not have begun his principal work, the ▷ *Divina Commedia*, until as late as 1314. This supremely encyclopaedic work, which encompasses a discussion of every aspect of human experience, knowledge and belief, recounts the poet's journey, with ▷ Virgil as his guide, through Hell (*Inferno*) and Purgatory (▷ *Purgatorio*) and finally, through the agency of Betarice herself, to Paradise (▷ *Paradiso*).

▷ Boccaccio (1315-75) composed an account of Dante's life and was the first to deliver a series of public lectures on the text of the *Divina Commedia* (1313-14), thus confirming the literary authority, prestige and influence of the work and its author. ▷ Chaucer, the first English poet to name Dante in his work, undoubtedly knew the *Divina Commedia*; quotations from it are scattered through his later work. Dante was read and admired by English poets in the 16th and 17th centuries (including ▷ Milton), and one of the earliest translations (of part of the *Inferno*) appeared in 1719. 19th-century poets, especially ▷ Byron, ▷ Shelley, and ▷ Thomas Carlyle much admired Dante's work and thus revived interest in the medieval poet. Of 20th century writers, ▷ T. S. Eliot in particular was profoundly influenced by Dante's work. According to Eliot, Dante has the power to make the 'spiritual visible'.

Bib: Holmes, G., *Dante*.

D'Arblay, Madame

▷ Burney, Fanny.

Dares Phrygius

A Trojan priest, mentioned in ▷ Homer's ▷ *Iliad*, who is reputedly the author of an eyewitness acount of the Trojan war, *De Excidio Troiae Historia* (*The Fall of Troy, A History*), which presents a rationalized, chronologically ordered account of events that ultimately relies on material from Homer. It is likely that Dares' account was originally composed in Greek during the 1st century but it only survives in a Latin version from the 6th century. Together with the other eyewitness account of the war, attributed to ▷ Dictys, Dares' narrative forms the basis for the most influential medieval versions of the Troy story, being used by Benoît de Sainte-Maure for his 12th-century vernacular narrative of the destruction of Troy. It was not until the beginning of the 18th century that the accounts of Dares and Dictys were conclusively exposed as forgeries.

▷ Troy.

Bib: Frazer, R. M. (ed. and trans.), *The Trojan*

War: the Chronicles of Dictys of Crete and Dares the Phrygian.

Darley, George (1795–1846)
Poet, dramatic critic and art historian. Darley was a reclusive Irish author whose sharp dramatic criticism often angered the authors of the plays he reviewed for ▷ *The London Magazine.* As a creative writer, he wrote several volumes of poetry including *Sylvia* (1827), as well as plays. His most famous work is *Nepenthe* (1835) which undertakes an allegorical description of the imagination and which is indebted to ▷ Keats and ▷ Shelley.

▷ Irish literature in English.

Bib: Heath-Stubbs, J., *In His Darkling Plain: a study of the later fortunes of romanticism in English poetry from Darley to W.B. Yeats*; Ridler, A. (ed), *Selected Poems of George Darley.*

Darwin, Charles Robert (1809–82)
Biologist. His book *On the Origin of Species by means of Natural Selection* (1859) not only expounded the theory of the evolution of natural organisms (which in itself was not new, for it had been held by, among others, Darwin's grandfather, the poet Erasmus Darwin) but presented persuasive evidence for the theory. In brief, this was that species naturally tend to produce variations and that some of these variations have better capacity for survival than others, which in consequence tend to become extinct. Darwin's conviction partly began with his study of ▷ Malthus on population, and it thus belongs to the rationalistic tradition which the 19th century inherited from the 18th. The book greatly disturbed many religious people, since it apparently contradicted the account of the creation of the world of *Genesis* in the Bible; it also raised serious doubts about the existence of the soul and its survival after the death of the body. However, it is possible to exaggerate the importance of the Darwinian theory as a cause of religious disbelief: on the one hand, ▷ Charles Lyell's *Principles of Geology* (1830–3) had already done much to upset traditional beliefs (those, for instance, of the poet ▷ Tennyson) and so had scientific scholarship on biblical texts by men like Charles Hennell (as in the case of the novelist ▷ George Eliot); on the other hand, intelligent believers such as the poet Samuel Taylor Coleridge (1772–1834) had long ceased to accept the Bible as a sacred record of fact in all its books. The effect of Darwin's ideas was probably rather to extend religious doubt from the intelligentsia (who were already deeply permeated by it) to wider circles. Another kind of effect was to produce in the popular mind a naive optimism that man was subject to a general law of progress; it thus encouraged an uncritical view of history and society.

Darwin wrote a number of other scientific works, including *The Descent of Man* (1871). His *Journal of Researches into the Geology and Natural History of the various countries visited by H.M.S. 'Beagle'*, a report of his first important scientific expedition (1831–6), is a fascinating travel book. He also wrote a brief but interesting *Autobiography* (edited with additions by Nora Barlow, 1958).

▷ Agnosticism.

Bib: Huxley, L., *Charles Darwin*; Stevenson, L., *Darwin among the Poets*; West, G., *Darwin: the Fragmentary Man*; Darwin, F., *Life and Letters*; Beer, G., *Darwin's Plots.*

Darwin, Erasmus (1731–1802)
Poet and physician; grandfather of the zoologist Charles Darwin. He wrote a lengthy poem, *The Botanic Garden* in grotesquely elaborate ▷ couplets, on the subject of the scientific classification of plants (Part II: *The Loves of the Plants*, 1789; Part I: *The Economy of Vegetation*, 1791).

Daryush, Elizabeth (1887–1977)
Poet. Daryush was the daughter of poet ▷ Robert Seymour Bridges, and her writing is a continuation and expansion of his experiments in syllabic metre. She lived for some time in Persia, and syllabically translated some Persian poetry. Publications include: Daryush's own selection of her work, *Selected Poems, Verses I–VI* (1972) and the more recent *Collected Poems* (1976).

Dathorne, O.R. (b 1934)
Novelist, poet and critic. Dathorne was born in Guyana and educated at the universities of Sheffield, London and Miami. He has taught at universities in Zaire, Nigeria, Sierra Leone and the USA, where he is now professor at the University of Kentucky. His novels are: *Dumplings in the Soup* (1963), set in London, *The Scholar-Man* (1964), set in Africa and *Dele's Child* (1986). *Kelly's Poems* (1977) and *Songs for a New World* (1988) are collections of poems. He has published a number of short stories and several critical works on African and Caribbean literature as well as editing collections of poetry, stories and essays. His novels present cultural displacement and the search for a sense of identity and history.

D'Avenant, Lady Henrietta Maria (d 1691)
Theatre proprietress, wife of ▷ Sir William D'Avenant: she took over management of the ▷ Duke's Company after his death in 1668, and saw his plans for a new theatre at Dorset Garden to completion. Lady D'Avenant was born in France, and met William during his stay there, probably in 1646. He returned about ten years later and brought her back to England as his wife in 1655. She had at least nine children by him, and also cared for

some of his children by his earlier marriages. As theatre manager she operated effectively, delegating many artistic and technical problems, ensuring the publication of her husband's works, founding Nurseries for the training of young actors and actresses, and defending the interests of the actor-manager George Jolly after a campaign by ▷ Thomas Killigrew and Lady D'Avenant's late husband to cheat him and squeeze him out of the profession. In 1673 she ceded control of the company to her son Charles, but held on to her shares in the company and various rights, including income from a fruit concession at the playhouse.
Bib: Hotson, L., *The Commonwealth and Restoration Stage.*

D'Avenant (Davenant), Sir William (1606–68)
Theatrical innovator, impresario, dramatist and poet, D'Avenant's career spanned the reign of ▷ Charles I, the ▷ Interregnum and the Restoration. A pivotal figure in the history of the English theatre, he was involved in most of the developments of this transitional period, including the dissemination of theatrical techniques associated with the aristocratic cultural form of the ▷ masque to the public stage, the creation of new genres (he is credited with the first English ▷ opera), and the introduction of actresses to the professional English stage. He adapted some of ▷ Shakespeare's plays to the new theatrical conditions, including ▷ *The Tempest* with Dryden (1667) in a version that was the basis of English productions until 1838. During the 1650s, as official Interregnum disapproval of stage plays waned, he openly mounted several musical performances, including ▷ *The Siege of Rhodes* (1656), which is often considered to be the first English opera. When the theatres reopened in 1660 D'Avenant and ▷ Killigrew obtained the only two patents granted by ▷ Charles II allowing them to stage theatrical performances in London. D'Avenant formed the ▷ Duke's Company and began converting Lisle's Tennis Court at Lincoln's Inn Fields into a theatre. After his death D'Avenant's widow, ▷ Lady Mary D'Avenant, inherited his patent.
Bib: Blaydes, S. B. and Bordinat, P., *Sir William Davenant: An Annotated Bibliography, 1629–1985.*

***David Copperfield* (1849–50)**
A novel in ▷ autobiographical form by ▷ Charles Dickens. 'Of all my books I like this the best; like many fond parents I have a favourite child and his name is David Copperfield.' Some commentators have thought that the hero is representative of Dickens himself, and point to the resemblance of initials: C.D. and D.C. It is true that in outline Copperfield's experiences – his sense of early rejection, ▷ child labour in a warehouse, experience as a journalist and final success as a novelist – are similar to Dickens' own. But Dickens' purpose was to present an imaginative picture of growth from childhood to manhood in his own period of history, using his own experience as some of its material but without intending a biographical record. The social landscape of this novel is broader than an autobiography would be likely to achieve. It includes the moralistic and sadistic oppressiveness of Copperfield's mercantile stepfather, Murdstone, and the intimate study of selfish hedonism in Copperfield's aristocratic friend, Steerforth; the spontaneous cordiality of the humble Yarmouth boatman, Peggotty, and his sister, and the cunning deviousness of Uriah Heep, whose servile humility is disguise for his total ruthlessness in making his way from bleak beginnings to a position of power. The novel is strong in dramatic contrast, and particularly interesting in the counterbalancing of the women characters in a series of feminine archetypes. Copperfield is fatherless, and his gentle, guileless mother (who becomes victim in matrimony to Murdstone) is like an elder sister to the child; both are children to the motherly, protective servant, Clara Peggotty. She is replaced by the harsh and loveless Miss Murdstone who plays the role of cruel stepmother. Copperfield runs away and takes refuge with his idiosyncratic aunt, Betsey Trotwood, who has shaped for herself an eccentric independence of men, retaining for a harmless lunatic (Mr Dick) a compassionate tenderness which she now extends to her nephew, in spite of having rejected him at birth because he was a boy. Copperfield's first wife, Dora Spenlow, is a simulacrum of his mother – a child wife, on whom ▷ Ibsen seems to have based Nora in *A Doll's House*. Two other representatives of Victorian womanhood are Agnes Wickfield (whom he eventually marries), the stereotype of defenceless womanly sanctity and nearly a victim of Heep's rapacity, and Little Em'ly who is first under the protection of Peggotty and then becomes 'the ▷ fallen woman' when she is seduced by Steerforth. Another very striking portrait is Rosa Dartle, companion to Steerforth's mother and poisoned by vindictive hatred of him because of his cool assumption of social and masculine privilege. Though not the richest and deepest of Dickens' novels, it is perhaps psychologically the most revealing, both of Dickens himself and of the society of his time.
Bib: Storey, G., *David Copperfield: Interweaving Text and Fiction.*

Davidson, John (1857–1909)
Poet. Best remembered for his ▷ ballads and songs, in particular *Thirty Bob a Week*, he also wrote plays, novels and philosophical works. A friend of poet W.B. Yeats (1865–1939) and

fellow member of the ▷ Rhymer's Club, a group of ▷ Nineties poets which met to read their poetry from 1890–94 at the Cheshire Cheese, a pub in Fleet Street. Davidson was also influenced by ▷ Nietzsche in his passionate ▷ atheism, exemplified by *God and Mammon* (1907), a trilogy of which only two parts were complete when Davidson committed suicide. He contributed to the ▷ *Yellow Book*, and was an important figure in the development of the 20th-century Scottish Renaissance (▷ Scottish literature in English).
Bib: Turnbull, A. (ed.), *Poems*; Lindsay, M. (ed.), *John Davidson: A Selection of his Poems* (Preface by T.S. Eliot).

Davie, Donald (b 1922)
Poet and literary critic. Donald Davie's rational, cool and technically pure poetry perhaps epitomizes the verse of the ▷ Movement; his critical work of 1952, *Purity of Diction in English Verse* was the Movement's bible. Davie was born in Barnsley, a place which recurs gloomily throughout his work, and has taught at universities in Britain and the U.S.A. His many publications include: *Brides of Reason* (1955); *The Forests of Lithuania* (1959); *Events and Wisdoms 1957–1963*; *Collected Poems 1950–70* (1972); *In the Stopping Train* (1977); *Under Briggflatts* (1989).

Davies, Lady Eleanor (1590–1652)
Author of prophecies and spiritual revelations. Lady Eleanor's maiden name was Audeley, but she is more commonly known by Davies, the surname of her first husband, ▷ Sir John Davies, whom she married in 1609. Although always learned, it was not until 1625 that she received her first revelation and published *A Warning to the Dragon and All His Angels*, a work replete with the contemporary fashion for anagrams (for example, she reworks her own names as 'A Snare O Devil' (Davies) and 'Reveale O Daniele' (Audeley)). She prophesied her own husband's death when he threw *A Warning* onto the fire, and immediately commenced wearing mourning clothes; he died the following year. Her second marriage, to Sir Archibald Douglas, followed the same pattern, he burning her books and she predicting his spiritual downfall. Strangely, Lady Eleanor's prophecies often came true. She predicted the death of ▷ Buckingham in 1628, the outcome of Henrietta Maria's pregnancies and, more dangerously, the downfall of ▷ Charles I and the Archbishop of Canterbury ▷ William Laud. This last work, which she published in Amsterdam, resulted in her being summoned before the Court of High Commission in 1633 and accused of writing scandalous and fanatical pamphlets. It was suggested that she be committed to Bedlam, but in the event she was fined £3,000, imprisoned for two years, her books were burned, and she was humiliated by a mocking anagram of her name, 'Never So Mad A Ladie' (Dame Eleanor Davies). Undeterred, she continued to prophesy and was incarcerated in both Bedlam and the Tower of London before the ▷ Civil War heralded a more permissive age for women writers, preachers as well as prophetesses. In 1648 she presented her 1633 prophecies, newly entitled *The Armies Commission*, to ▷ Oliver Cromwell, and finally received benign recognition from the state. She also had the sweetness of revenge, since Laud had been executed in 1645, and she was able to write to Charles I before he was beheaded, reminding him of the accuracy of her predictions. Lady Eleanor's prophecies were finally published in an uncensored form as *The Restitution of Prophecy* (1651) and she was honoured at her death, perhaps somewhat ironically, with the epitaph: 'In a woman's body, a man's spirit'.
Bib: Frazer, A., *The Weaker Vessel*.

Davies, Hugh Sykes (1909–84)
Novelist, poet and critic. Hugh Sykes Davies was an eccentric and mercurial figure, combining at various times the identities of Cambridge don and surrealist poet. He wrote the existentialist novels *No Man Pursues* (1950) and *Full Fathom Five* (1956), alongside scholarly works on ▷ Browning, ▷ Wordsworth and English grammar. His most considerable achievements are, however, the Surrealist poem-novel *Petron* (1935) and the anti-nuclear prophetic novel *The Papers of Andrew Melmoth* (1960) in which a scientist working on rats 'goes over' to join the subjects of his research. His ability to link humour, Surrealism and apocalyptic warning link his work to that of ▷ David Gascoyne.

Davies, Sir John (1569–1626)
Poet, lawyer and attorney-general for Ireland (1606–19). Sir John Davies wrote virtually all his poetry in the years 1593–9. After 1603 Davies devoted his career to advancement within the Jacobean administration of Ireland, being one of the architects of the policy of 'plantation' in Ulster which brought Scots and English to the northern parts of Ireland, a source of friction ever since. In 1609 he married ▷ Lady Eleanor Davies, the author of prophecies and spiritual revelations. In 1612 Davies published an account of Ireland, entitled *A Discoverie of the True Causes why Ireland was never entirely Subdued nor brought under Obedience of the Crown of England Untill his Majesties Happie Raigne* – a work which can be compared in its delineation of English misunderstanding of Irish culture to ▷ Edmund Spenser's accounts of Ireland at the end of the previous century. Davies died in 1626 having had his death prophesied by his wife the previous year.

Davies' chief poetic works are the two long

poems *Orchestra* (1596) and *Nosce Teipsum* (1599), a series of epigrams and the 26 acrostic poems on the name of ▷ Elizabeth I, *Hymns of Astrea* (1599). Both *Orchestra* and *Nosce Teipsum* are, in their own ways, remarkable works. *Orchestra*, composed c 1594, announces itself as 'A Poem of Dauncing', and that, in essence, is what it is: a philosophical account of the physical world in terms of a universal dance. *Nosce Teipsum*, on the other hand, develops no over-all ▷ conceit, but is instead a philosophical poem on human knowledge derived from Davies' reading in the works of ▷ Cicero, ▷ Montaigne and the two French philosophers Philippe de Mornay and Pierre de la Primaudaye. The end of the poem is to promote self-knowledge, as the title, which translates as 'Know Yourself', indicates.
Bib: Editions include: Kreuger, R. (ed.), *Poems*.

Davies, John, of Hereford (?1565–1618)
Very little is known of this prolific writer, often confused with his better-known namesake, ▷ Sir John Davies. Davies was a writing master and the author of numerous ▷ epigrams on his poetic contemporaries. He also taught ▷ Prince Henry and became part of the young prince's court. Perhaps his most ambitious project, however, was a group of three long poems, which undertook to survey existing areas of human knowledge, and which cover a vast number of disparate topics, including English history, psychology, religion and human anatomy. These poems are: *Mirum in Modum* (1602), *Microcosmos* (1603), and *Summa Totalis* (1607).
Bib: Rope, H. E. G., 'John Davies of Hereford: Catholic and Rhymer,' *Anglo-Welsh Review* II (1961), pp. 20–36.

Davies, W(illiam) H(enry) (1871–1940)
Poet. Born in Newport, Monmouthshire, adopted by his father's parents after his mother's second marriage and brought up in a dockland public house to which his sea-captain grandfather had retired, W.H. Davies not unexpectedly became a wanderer by nature. A period in the North American continent resulted in an accident that caused the amputation of his right leg but helped to inspire his first major success, *The Autobiography of a Super-Tramp* (1908) and its less well known sequel, *Beggars* (1909); and further reminiscences followed in *Later Days* (1925). Both his novels *A Weak Woman* (1911) and *Dancing Mad* (1927) were unsuccessful, but his poetry which focussed on the commonplace and deliberately eschewed complexity, expressing a delight in nature and in human companionship, gradually gained in popularity. In this he was encouraged by George Bernard Shaw and Edward Thomas. His poetry collections are *The Soul's Destroyer and Other Poems* (1905), *New Poems* (1906), *Nature Poems and Others* (1908), *Farewell to Poetry* (1910), *Songs of Joy* (1911), *Foliage: Various Poems* (1913); and all these, with the addition of many later poems previously unpublished, making up a total of 636 in number, were collected in *The Poems of W. H. Davies*, published shortly before his death. His marriage to Helen Payne in 1923 brought contentment to his later years, so that the theme of married love makes its presence felt in his later work.
Bib: Stephens, M. (Ed.), *The Oxford Companion to the Literature of Wales*; Jones, G. and Rowlands, J., *Profiles*.

Davies, (William) Robertson (b 1913)
Canadian novelist, playwright and critic. Born in Thamesville, Ontario, and educated at the universities of Queen's (Kingston) and Oxford, Davies has worked as an actor, journalist, and newspaper editor. From 1963 to 1981 he was Professor of English at the University of Toronto. His plays include: *Fortune, My Foe* (1948); *A Masque of Aesop* (1952); *A Masque of Mr Punch* (1963); *Question Time* (1975). Davies is primarily known as a novelist, however, particularly for his three trilogies: the 'Salterton' – *Tempest-Tost* (1951); *Leaven of Malice* (1954); *A Mixture of Frailties* (1958) – the 'Deptford' – *Fifth Business* (1970); *The Manticore* (1972); *World of Wonders* (1975) – and the 'Cornish' – *The Rebel Angels* (1981); *What's Bred in the Bone* (1985); *The Lyre of Orpheus*. These novels are essentially satirical comedies of manners, characterized by an often recondite allusiveness (for example, to the arcane lores of alchemy, saints, vaudeville, and fortune-telling). Despite this ▷ post-modern playfulness, Davies writes in the 19th-century moralist tradition, employing tightly constructed and interweaving plots. His most recent novels are *Murther and Walking Spirits* (1991), in which the ghost of a murdered man watches films of his ancestors, which together constitute a personalized history of Canada, and *The Cunning Man* (1994). Other books include a collection of ghost stories, *High Spirits* (1982), and *The Papers of Samuel Marchbanks* (1985), a collection of newspaper pieces.
▷ Post-colonial fiction.
Bib: Lawrence, R. G. and Macey, S. L., *Studies in Robertson Davies' Deptford Trilogy*.

Davis, Jack (b 1917)
▷ Post-colonial literature.

Davys, Mary (1674–1732)
Dramatist and novelist, originally from Dublin. Her husband was the Reverend Peter Davys, and through him she knew the satirist ▷ Jonathan Swift. Her husband died in 1698, and she came to England, where she lived by writing. Her first fiction was *Amours of Alcippus and Lucippe* (1704, republished 1725), and she wrote about Ireland in *The Fugitive* (1705, rewritten 1725).

Life in York, in the north of England, is worked into her comedy *The Northern Heiress, or the Humours of York*, which was staged in 1716. She set up a coffee-house in Cambridge, and published later works by subscription, *The Reform'd Coquet, or Memoirs of Amoranda* (1724) and *Works* (1725), which includes revisions of earlier writings. She also wrote the poem 'The Modern Poet' and other fictions and comedies, including *The Accomplish'd Rake, or Modern Fine Gentleman* (1727).
Bib: Lonsdale, Roger (ed.), *Eighteenth-Century Women Poets*.

Day, John (1574–1640)
English dramatist contemporary with ▷ Shakespeare and ▷ Ben Jonson. In his plays he collaborated with a number of other dramatists such as ▷ Henry Chettle and ▷ Thomas Dekker. His *Isle of Gulls* (1606), played by the Children of the Queen's Revels, lost them royal favour at Court because of the play's satire on the impact in the country of the ▷ Jacobean accession. Day's most acclaimed work is his ▷ masque *The Parliament of Bees* (1609).
Bib: Oastler, C. L., *John Day, the Elizabethan Printer*.

Day-Lewis, Cecil (1904–72)
Poet and critic. Day-Lewis was one of the small group of poets (with ▷ W. H. Auden and ▷ Stephen Spender) which made a considerable impact in the 1930s under the encouragement of ▷ T. S. Eliot and the political influence of Marx. His early poetry was often propagandistic, and, like many of his contemporaries, he wrote in support of the Republican cause in the Spanish Civil War (Spanish influence on English literature), using with effect the ▷ sprung rhythm and alliteration of ▷ Gerard Manley Hopkins. World War II broke up the group and tempered Day-Lewis' political aims. His later work shows the versatility which caused him to be chosen as ▷ Poet Laureate in 1968. Works include *Collected Poems* (1954; reprinted 1970) and *Poems 1925–72* (ed. Parsons). Critical essays include *A Hope for Poetry* (1934), *The Poetic Image* (1946), *The Lyric Impulse* (1965). He also translated the poetry of Virgil and wrote ▷ detective fiction under the pen-name Nicholas Blake.

De Beauvoir, Simone (1908–86)
French novelist and one of the founding 'mothers' of 20th-century ▷ feminism, long associated with ▷ Sartre and the ▷ existentialist movement, whose views she promoted in a series of novels: *L'Invitée* (1943); *Le Sang des autres* (1944); *Les Mandarins* (1954). Her uncensored *Letters to Sartre* (1991) reveal the intensity and passion of their relationship. A play, *Les Bouches inutiles* was performed in 1945. She contributed greatly to the genre of autobiography: (*Mémoires d'une jeune fille rangée* (1958); *La Force de l'âge* (1960); *La Force des choses* (1965); *Tout compte fait* (1974) (all translated). Her two-volume study of femininity and the condition of women, *The Second Sex (Le Deuxième sexe* 1949) is one of the most important feminist texts of this century, and her influence on subsequent thinkers is now eclipsing Sartre's. Contemporary feminist writers who have taken up her ideas in particular include Kate Millett (in *Sexual Politics*, 1970), ▷ Germaine Greer, Mary Ellman (in *Thinking About Women*, 1968) and Betty Friedman (*The Feminine Mystique*, 1963).
Bib: Moi, T., *Sexual/Textual Politics*; Moi, T., *French Feminist Thought: A Reader*.

De la Mare, Walter (1873–1956)
Poet, novelist, writer of short stories. He was born in Kent, and educated at St Paul's Cathedral Choir School. From 1890 to 1908 he was a clerk in the offices of the Anglo-American Oil Company; he was then given a government ('Civil List') pension to enable him to devote himself to writing. Many of his poems and his stories were addressed to children. Books of verse of this sort were: *Songs of Childhood* (1902); *A Child's Day* (1912); *Peacock Pie* (1913). ▷ Children's stories: *The Three Mulla-mulgars* (1910); *The Riddle* (1923); *The Magic Jacket* (1943); *The Dutch Cheese* (1946). He had conspicuous talent for retelling traditional ▷ fairy-tales: *Told Again* (1927); and compiled two unusual anthologies: *Come Hither* (for children, 1923) and *Love* (for adults, 1943). His most remarkable prose fiction for adults is probably *On the Edge* (stories, 1926) and *Memoirs of a Midget* (novel, 1921). His books of verse for adults include: *The Listeners* (1912); *The Veil* (1921); *Memory and other poems* (1938); *The Burning-glass and other poems* (1945); *The Traveller* (1946); *Inward Companion* (1950); *Winged Chariot* (1951); *O Lovely England and other poems* (1953); *Collected Poems* (1979). See also ▷ W. H. Auden's collection, *A Choice of De la Mare's Verse* (1963).

His poems are conservative in technique, with the melody and delicacy of diction characteristic of the poetry of the late 19th and early 20th century, but are unusual in the quiet intensity with which they express evanescent, elusive and mysterious experience. His stories have a singular quietness of tone and are written in an unassuming style, conveying material which is on the borderline of conscious experience. De la Mare's unusual combination of intensity and innocence makes the borderline between his work for children and for adults an almost imperceptible one.
Bib: Mégroz, R. L., *De la Mare: A Biographical and Critical Study*; Reid, Forrest, *De la Mare: A Critical Study*.

De Loutherbourg, Philip James (Philippe Jacques) (1740–1812)
Painter, set designer, of noble Polish descent.

In 1771 after a successful exhibition in Paris De Loutherbourg moved to London, where he met ▷ David Garrick, and presented him with proposals for co-ordinated improvements to the lighting, scenes, costumes and mechanical effects at ▷ Drury Lane.

Engaged at the theatre, De Loutherbourg 'astonished the audience', according to one observer, by his skilful and innovative use of various translucent coloured silks, lit from behind and mobile, to give changing effects of richness, subtlety, and depth to the sets. His detailed and naturalistic cut-out scenery was likened to fine paintings of contemporary and fantastic views. In 1781 he became a member of the ▷ Royal Academy.

Admired in his day by ▷ Thomas Gainsborough, De Loutherbourg is now considered one of the most influential designers for the English stage, bringing both imagination and technical abilities to bear, so as to create scenes and spectacles of unprecedented realism and magnificence. Much of his work can be seen as an important early contribution to the ▷ Romantic movement in literature and art.

De Man, Paul (1919–83)
Arguably the most rigorous of the so-called Yale School of criticism, and by the time of his death the foremost exponent in the USA of ▷ deconstruction as applied to Romantic, and other, poetry. His crucial essay of 1969, 'The Rhetoric of Temporality' (collected in *Blindness and Insight*, 1983) used texts by ▷ Wordsworth, ▷ Coleridge, ▷ Rousseau and others, in order to establish the undoing of Romantic ambition, expressed in ▷ rhetorical terms such as the 'symbol', by what de Man calls 'allegory'. His approach was extended in books such as *Allegories of Reading* (1980) and *The Rhetoric of Romanticism* (1984). De Man reflected on the whole of this process, and upon the resistance to certain sorts of theoretical enquiry, in a collection of essays, *The Resistance to Theory* published posthumously in 1986.

Paul de Man remains a controversial figure, not only because of the nihilistic conclusions of his mature work, but by the rediscovery after his death of certain pieces of 1940s journalism that express hospitality towards the intellectual consequences of Nazi occupation.

***De Profundis* (1905;1949)**
A prose piece by ▷ Oscar Wilde written during the author's imprisonment in Reading Gaol (1895–97) for ▷ homosexual practices. It takes the form of an extended letter written to Wilde's erstwhile companion Lord Alfred Douglas ('Bosie'), whose father, the Marqess of Queensberry, was instrumental in securing Wilde's incarceration. In it, Wilde upbraids Douglas for distracting him from his work and encouraging him in dissipation. He also criticizes Douglas for his shallowness and neglect and accuses him of being a petty parasite, greedy, extravagant and over-indulged. At the same time the letter praises the devotion of Robert Ross, who finally became Wilde's executor. It was sent to Douglas, who destroyed it after reading the opening pages. Afterwards he denied having received it. A drastically edited version of the letter was published by Ross in 1905 under the title *De Profundis* (taken from the opening line of Psalm 130). It was revised and reprinted in a more complete form in 1949.

De Quincey, Thomas (1785–1859)
Essayist and critic. Most famous for his autobiography ▷ *Confessions of an English Opium-Eater*. His work was mostly for periodicals and is voluminous, but only a few pieces are now much read. His strong points as a writer were his exceptionally sensitive, inward-turning imagination and his breadth of understanding. The first produced not only his autobiography but a fragment of exceptional literary criticism, 'Knocking at the Gate in Macbeth'. The English Mail Coach (1849) and 'Murder Considered as One of the Fine Arts' (1827) show the quality of an exceptional psychological novelist. His second gift produced studies of German philosophy (▷ Kant, Lessing, Richter) and able translations of German tales, besides some original historical criticism. He was very much a representative of the second generation of English ▷ Romanticism and as the poets of the first generation found new ranges of expression for their medium, so De Quincey expanded the poetic range of prose, partly by recapturing some of the quality of the early 17th-century prose writers.
Bib: Abrams, M. H., *The Milk of Paradise*; Barrell, J., *The Infection of Thomas De Quincey: the Psychopathology of Imperialism*; Clapton, G. T., *Baudelaire et De Quincey*; Eaton, H. A., *Life*; Jordan, J. E., *Thomas De Quincey, Literary Critic*; Saintsbury, G., in *Essays in English Literature*; Sackville-West, E., *A Flame in Sunlight*; Lindop, G., *The Opium Eater*.

Death and Life
An alliterative narrative, dating from the 15th century, in which a dream frame is used as a vehicle for a dramatic debate between Life and Death, over their respective powers. In the course of the debate, the notion of Life is enlarged to encompass that of Eternal Life, and Life herself evokes scriptural authorities to prove she can, therefore, circumvent the power of Death. This technique of analysing abstract concepts through a personified debate can be paralleled in other alliterative poems (including ▷ *Piers Plowman* and ▷ *Winner and Waster*). But whereas ▷ Langland's poem combines a focus on contemporary social

satire with an investigation into transhistorical Christian truths, *Death and Life* concentrates on communicating a spiritual truth.
Bib: Gollancz, I., and Day, M. (eds.), *Select Early English Poems 3.*

Decadents
A term attributed to the French poet Paul Verlaine in 1885, who contributed to a review, *Le Decadent*, founded by Anatole Baju, from 1886–9. The French Decadents were inspired by ▷ Charles Baudelaire and counted Arthur Rimbaud (1854–91), Stephane Mallarmé (1842–98) and Tristran Corbière among their number. J.K. Huysmans' novel *A rebours (Against the Grain*, 1894) was called 'the breviary of the Decadence' by poet Arthur Symons (1865–1945). In England the term 'Decadents' was applied to a group of poets at the end of the 19th century, which included ▷ Arthur Symons, ▷ Oscar Wilde, ▷ Ernest Dowson and Lionel Johnson (1867–1902), who constituted the later generation of the ▷ Aesthetic Movement and included the English followers of the French ▷ Symbolist poets. Their aim was to set art free from the claims of life and their art is characterized by a 'world weariness' brought on by the death of the century, a sense of social decline and spiritual dispossession. G.L. van Roosebroeck gives an account of the term in *The Legend of the Decadents.*

▷ Rhymer's Club; *Yellow Book*; French influence on Victorian literature.

Decameron, The
A collection of 100 stories in prose, compiled by ▷ Boccaccio in the years 1349–51. The fictional framework of the collection describes how the stories were told by a company of ten gentle-ladies and gentlemen who decide to retreat from plague-ridden Florence and spend two weeks in the country. They spend their weekdays telling short stories to pass the time, and the proceedings are organized by one member of the company who is elected anew every day. Many of the stories concern heterosexual relations of some kind, usually set in the contemporary world, and treated in a variety of serious and comic ways. Many of the short stories have ▷ fabliau-type plots. It seems likely that ▷ Chaucer knew and used the *Decameron* as a resource for the ▷ *Canterbury Tales* (though the connection has not been definitely proved and remains a controversial issue). Boccaccio's work undoubtedly provided many later writers and dramatists (including ▷ Shakespeare) with an important source of narratives. Many of Boccaccio's stories were incorporated into William Painter's ▷ *Palace of Pleasure*, and the first English translation of the *Decameron* itself appeared in 1621.
Bib: McWilliam, G. H. (trans.), *The Decameron.*

Decentring
The idea of decentring is common in much ▷ poststructuralist theory and is used in connection with either individual subjectivity or bodies of written ideas and beliefs. An individual is said to be decentred in the sense that, though most people act as though they have a consistently unified sense of identity, this is illusory and a person's self is in reality more fragmentary and unstable. It lacks, that is, a centre. This view depends heavily on the psychoanalytic theory of ▷ Jacques Lacan. In the realm of ideas, related arguments are put by ▷ Jacques Derrida who argues that even apparently stable bodies of written ideas are always internally contradictory and divided against themselves, not least by the language in which they are expressed and despite their logocentric hopes. As such they need to be ▷ deconstructed to reveal their decentred state. ▷ Postmodern theory, meanwhile, argues that contemporary culture generally is decentred in the sense that it is international rather than national, and pluralist rather than canonical.

Declaration of Independence (1776)
The assertion of independence by the American colonists, starting-point of the United States. It was signed by 13 states. Although the Committee that ordered the drafting of the Declaration included such hard-headed, 18th-century rationalists as Benjamin Franklin, their document (and the Constitution of 1787) may be seen as essentially Romantic in its idealization of freedom for the individual. The new nation demanded a new literature, and the emergence in the mid-19th-century of a truly American philosophy (promulgated by Emerson) and its corollary in poetry (supplied by Walt Whitman) may be seen as a perpetuation of Romanticism in its hospitality to experience and its emphasis on freedom of conscience, and consciousness.

***Decline and Fall of the Roman Empire, The* (1776–88)**
By ▷ Edward Gibbon; the most eloquent and imposing historical work in the English language. It begins at the height of the Roman Empire in the 1st and 2nd centuries AD – an age with which Gibbon's own era, so deeply imbued with Latin scholarship, felt strong kinship. It then proceeds to record the successive stages of Roman decline, the rise of Christianity, the struggle with the Eastern Roman Empire (the Byzantine) centred on Constantinople (Byzantium), and that empire's eventual extinction by the capture of Constantinople in 1453. As an account, it has of course become somewhat outdated, but as an imaginative epic (still regarded as substantially true) and an expression of the background to modern Europe as understood in the 18th century, it remains a much-read and very important work. Its structure is as

spacious as the subject, and is sustained by the energy of Gibbon's style. The attitude is one of 18th-century truth-seeking, and of urbane irony towards the Christian religion, whose growth Gibbon sees as one of the agents of destruction of classical civilization. Gibbon's sceptical mind is at the same time constantly critical of human pretensions to self-sufficiency, the attainment of wisdom, and integrity of motive; in such respects he is in the tradition of the great satirists of his century, ▷ Alexander Pope and ▷ Jonathan Swift.

Deconstruction
A concept used in critical theory. It has a long philosophical pedigree, but is usually associated with the work of the French philosopher ▷ Jacques Derrida. It is a strategy applied to writing generally, and to literature in particular, whereby systems of thought and concepts are dismantled in such a way as to expose the divisions which lie at the heart of meaning itself. If interpretation is a process designed to reduce a text to some sort of 'order', deconstruction seeks to undermine the basis upon which that order rests. Deconstruction challenges the notion that all forms of mental and linguistic activity are generated from within an autonomous 'centre', advancing the more disturbing proposition that such centres are themselves to be grasped textually only as rhetorical constructions.
Bib: Derrida, J., *Speech and Phenomena*; *Writing and Difference; Of Grammatology; Positions*; Norris, C., *Deconstruction: Theory and Practice*.

Dedalus, Stephen
Principal character in ▷ James Joyce's novel ▷ *Portrait of the Artist as a Young Man*; he is also a main character in Joyce's ▷ *Ulysses*. The surname derives from the mythical artist of ancient Greece, ▷ Daedalus.

Deerbrook **(1839)**
The only novel by journalist and feminist ▷ Harriet Martineau, *Deerbrook* is set in a tranquil English village in the early 19th century. Two orphaned sisters, Hester and Margaret Ibbotson, come to stay with their cousins, the Grey family. The personal lives of the sisters become entwined with the life of the village – portrayed as a hotbed of personal rivalries, gossip and intrigue. The sisters are contrasted in personality: Hester is beautiful but prone to jealousy, Margaret less physically attractive but more intelligent. Romances develop between the sisters and the two most eligible men in the village. The novel also contains ▷ feminist sentiments, expressed mainly by Maria, the crippled ▷ governess, who protests against the restricted opportunities available to middle-class women. *Deerbrook* was well-received, being favourably compared to Jane Austen's (1775–1817) novels. ▷ Charlotte Brontë later claimed that Martineau's honest portrayal of passion had influenced her own writing.

Defamiliarization
In the context of critical theory this term has its origins in Russian ▷ Formalism and in the desire to distinguish between the ▷ Aristotelian view of writing as an image of reality (▷ mimesis) and imaginative literature as a form of writing which deploys images rhetorically. The Russian term 'ostranenie' means literally, 'making strange', rendering unfamiliar that which has hitherto been regarded as familiar. It draws attention to the fact that 'reality' is never depicted in literature in an unprocessed, or unmediated way. Indeed, what literature exposes is the formal means whereby what is commonly taken to be reality itself is, in fact, a construction. In many ways, 'defamiliarization' is a form of ▷ deconstruction, although its objective is to replace one set of epistemological principles (those upon which capitalism as a particular kind of social formation rests), with other ways of organizing reality. By contrast, deconstruction has the effect of undermining all assumptions and certainties about what we know.
▷ Alienation effect.

Defence of Poesie, The
▷ *Apologie for Poetrie, An.*

Defence of Poetry, A **(1840)**
A prose essay by ▷ Percy Bysshe Shelley written as an 'antidote' to *The Four Ages of Poetry* by ▷ Thomas Love Peacock, which appeared in 1821. Shelley sent his *Defence* to Peacock in the same year, but it was not published until 1840. Peacock had argued that with the growth of scientific knowledge, the primitive metaphorical 'visions' of the poet were out of date: 'A poet in our times is a semi-barbarian in a civilized community'. Poetry only wasted time that would be better spent on 'some branch of useful study'. Shelley answered that poetry is not only useful, but essential, in enlarging 'the social sympathies' of humankind. The 'vitally metaphorical' language of the poet is the key to all morality: 'A man, to be greatly good, must imagine intensely and comprehensively; he must put himself in the place of another and of many others; the pains and pleasures of his species must become his own.' In the aftermath of the failure of the ideals of the ▷ French Revolution, Shelley is eager to envisage a political role for the poet, though inevitably this is expressed in rhetoric of an abstract and ideal kind: 'Poets are the unacknowledged legislators of the world'; 'Poetry is a sword of lightning, ever unsheathed'. However, Shelley's analysis of the totalitarian tendency of Peacock's ▷ utilitarianism anticipates Marx and post-Marxist thinking. Only 'anarchy and despotism'

he asserts, can be expected from 'an unmitigated exercise of the calculating faculty'.

Defoe, Daniel (1660–1731)
Son of a London tallow-chandler, James Foe, Defoe changed his name in about 1695 to suggest a higher social status. His writings reflect his ▷ Puritan background: Defoe was educated at Morton's academy for ▷ Dissenters at Newington Green, and his pamphlet of 1702, *The Shortest Way with Dissenters*, landed him in the pillory when its ironic attack on Dissenters was taken seriously.

Defoe's attempts to make a living form a colourful picture. Various business enterprises failed dramatically, including the scheme of marine insurance, unfortunately timed during a war, and a disastrous project to breed civet cats. Between 1703 and 1714 he worked as a secret agent for the Tory government of Robert Harley, writing many political (and anti- ▷ Jacobite) pamphlets.

Defoe produced some 560 journals, tracts and books, many of them published anonymously or pseudonymously. His reputation today rests on his novels, a genre to which he turned with great success late in his life.

The Life and strange surprising Adventures of Robinson Crusoe (▷ *Robinson Crusoe*) appeared in 1719 and its sequel, *The Farther Adventures of Robinson Crusoe*, was published some months later. 1720 saw the publication of the *Life and Adventures of Mr Duncan Campbell*, and ▷ *Captain Singleton*; 1722, ▷ *Moll Flanders*, ▷ *A Journal of the Plague Year, The History of Peter the Great*, and *Colonel Jack*; 1724, ▷ *Roxana*, the *Memoirs of a Cavalier*, and *A New Voyage round the World*; and 1726, *The Four Voyages of Capt. George Roberts*. His guide-book, *A Tour through the Whole Island of Great Britain*, appeared in three volumes, 1724–6.

Among Defoe's later works are *The Complete English Tradesman* (1726), *A Plan of the English Commerce* and *Augusta Triumphans* (1728), and *The Complete English Gentleman*, not published until 1890. Defoe died in Moorfields, and was buried in the area now called Bunhill Fields.
Bib: Moore, J. R., *Daniel Defoe: Citizen of the Modern World*; Richetti, J., *Defoe's Narratives: Situations and Structures*; Bell, Ian A., *Defoe's Fiction*.

Deism
A form of religious belief which developed in the 17th century as an outcome of the ▷ Reformation. ▷ Edward Herbert evolved the idea that, while the religion revealed in the Gospels was true, it was preceded by 'natural' religion, according to which by his own inner light a man could perceive all the essentials of religious truth. Herbert's deism was further expounded in the 18th century by others (often in such a way as to suggest that the Christian revelation as presented in the Gospels was redundant), and it suited the 18th-century cool and rational habit of mind which tended to see God as abstract and remote. Bishop Butler among the theologians and ▷ Hume and ▷ Kant among the philosophers, exposed the unsoundness of deistic arguments in the 18th century, and in the 19th century the growth of the genetic sciences demolished the basic assumptions of deism, *ie*, that human nature and human reason have always been constant, in a constant environment.

***Dejection: An Ode* (1802)**
A poem by ▷ Samuel Taylor Coleridge. The earliest version was addressed to Sara Hutchinson ('O Sara'), with whom the unhappily married Coleridge was in love. In a subsequent version this becomes 'O Wordsworth', and in the published text Sara is reinstated, but anonymously ('O Lady'). As these changes suggest, the poem reflects a complex personal unhappiness, but it was also influenced by ▷ William Wordsworth's expression of flagging inspiration in the first part of the *Immortality Ode*, written at this time. Coleridge watches a beautiful sunset, but finds that in his 'wan and heartless mood' the objective beauty of the clouds, stars and moon, inspire no response in him: 'I see them all so excellently fair,/ I see, not feel, how beautiful they are!' He reflects on the subjectivity of experience, concluding that 'we receive but what we give/ And in our life alone does Nature live'. He thus rejects the idea of the ministering benevolence of nature which was so important to Wordsworth. It is subjective imagination not objective nature which is the 'shaping spirit'. He is ambiguously cheered by reminiscences from other poets, conjured up by the wind blowing through an ▷ Aeolian harp, and the work ends, as midnight approaches, with a poignantly selfless prayer that his beloved be sleeping, safe from the storm. His love for her restores the meaning which nature had lost, but on a strictly metaphorical level: 'May all the stars hang bright above her dwelling,/ Silent *as though* they watched the sleeping Earth!'

Dekker, Thomas (?1570–1632)
Dramatist and pamphleteer. His best-known play is ▷ *The Shoemaker's Holiday*, based on ▷ Thomas Deloney's *The Gentle Craft* – a narrative about the London crafts. The play celebrates the proud traditions of the citizens, and the romantic zest of its plot and dialogue has kept it alive. His next best known play is *The Honest Whore*, Pt. I (1604). He was essentially a dramatist of middle life. He collaborated with ▷ Rowley in *The Witch of Edmonton* (1623); with ▷ Middleton in *The Roaring Girl* (1611); and with ▷ Massinger in *Virgin Martyr* (1622).

His pamphlets are as notable as his plays, especially *The Wonderful Year* (1603), a vivid account of an epidemic of plague in London, and *The Gull's Hornbook*, a satire on the manners of a fashionable young man. He was a master of the racy, vigorous, colloquial prose of his time. Dekker was immensely popular in his own time and, despite a falling off in esteem, has been critically reappraised, and it is now possible to perceive him as a politically aware and strongly Protestant dramatist.
Bib: Bowers, Fredson, *The Dramatic Works of Thomas Dekker* (4 vols.); Bose, T., *The Gentle Craft of Revision in Thomas Dekker's Last Plays*; Gasper, J., *The Dragon and the Dove*.

Delaney, Shelagh (b 1939)
One of few female dramatists to make an impact during the 1950s. Her best-known play, *A Taste of Honey* (first performed in 1958), was written when she was only 17 and is about a young woman's relationship with her mother, her black lover and a gay art student. It was performed by ▷ Joan Littlewood's Theatre Workshop company, transferred to the West End, and was later filmed. Other plays include: *The Lion in Love* (1960); *The House That Jack Built* (1978); and for radio: *So Does the Nightingale* (1980); *Don't Worry About Matilda* (1983). Her films include: *Charley Bubbles* (1968) and *Dance with a Stranger* (1985).

Delany, Mrs Mary (1700–88)
One of the famous letter writers of the 18th century. She had a wide circle of friends among the famous people of her day, and her letters give a vivid picture of contemporary life.

Deloney, Thomas (?1543–?1600)
Pamphleteer and balladeer. Little of Deloney's verse can be securely attributed to him, although in the 1590s he was the most popular ▷ ballad writer in England. It is, however, Deloney's prose narratives – *The Gentle Craft* (complete version ?1635), *Thomas of Reading* (1612, 12th edition) and *Jack of Newbery* (1619, 8th edition) – that have secured for him a reputation. These works anticipate the kind of novel which Daniel Defoe (1660–1731) was later to write. They mark the end of the tradition of producing courtly romance such as ▷ Sir Philip Sidney's ▷ *Arcadia*, and share, with the writings of ▷ Thomas Nashe, an interest in depicting the life led by those outside the elevated circles of the court.

As well as his fictional works, Deloney produced ▷ translations and ▷ anthologies, which include his *Strange Histories of Kings* (1600). Despite the diversity of his output, it is for the creation of a 'middle-class' fiction that Deloney is of importance.
Bib: Lawless, M. E., *Apology for the Middle Class: The Dramatic Novels of Thomas Deloney*.
▷ Elizabethan Novels; Pamphlet.

***Demos: A Story of English Socialism* (1886)**
A novel by ▷ George Gissing in which he questions the validity of socialism and the qualities of its leaders. The story centres on the founding of an Owenite ironworks in an unspoilt valley.
▷ Owen, Robert.

Demosthenes (4th century BC)
In ancient Greece, a great Athenian orator; he is often referred to in English literature as the pattern and ideal of all orators. He is especially famous for his speeches warning the Athenians of the danger from the growing empire of Philip of Macedon, father of Alexander the Great. Hence the word 'philippic' for an aggressive political speech.

Denham, Sir John (1615–69)
Poet and playwright. He took the Royalist side in the ▷ Civil War, translated Book II of the ▷ *Aeneid* into pentameter couplets (*The Destruction of Troy*, 1656) and published a play in ▷ blank verse, *The Sophy* (1642). His *Cooper's Hill* (1642; enlarged version, 1655), a topographical poem describing the scenery around Windsor, was much admired and imitated. In it he abandons the *enjambements* of his Virgil translation, preferring a balanced, end-stopped couplet. The passage on the Thames was cited and imitated by poets from John Dryden (1631–1700) onwards as the perfection of heroic couplet writing:

O could I flow like thee, and make thy stream
My great example, as it is my theme!
Though deep, yet clear, though gentle, yet not dull,
Strong without rage, without o'er-flowing full.

The lines are comically parodied in Alexander Pope's (1688–1744) *Dunciad* (Bk. III, ii. 163–6). Samuel Johnson (1709–84), in his *Lives of the Poets* (1781), called Denham 'one of the fathers of English poetry'.
Bib: O'Hehir, B., *Harmony from Discords: a Life of Sir John Denham*.

Dennis, John (1657–1734)
Although Dennis' efforts as a poet and playwright are undistinguished, he was one of the foremost literary critics of the ▷ Augustan era. His feud with ▷ Pope for which he is best remembered, was angry and ill-tempered on both sides, but Dennis' critical views, favouring ▷ blank-verse ▷ epics on Christian themes, are worthy of more serious attention. Among his most notable works are *The Advancement of Reformation of Modern Poetry* (1701), *The Grounds of Criticism in Poetry* (1704) and *An Essay on the Genius and Writings of Shakespeare* (1712).

Bib: Paul, H. G., *John Dennis, his Life and Criticism*; Hooker, E. N. (ed.), *The Critical Works of John Dennis*.

Dennis, Nigel (b 1912)
Novelist. He is best known for *Cards of Identity* (1955), a satirical fantasy about the nature of individual and cultural identity, influenced by the ▷ existentialism of ▷ Jean-Paul Sartre. It reflects the atmosphere of British life in the early 1950s, but combines this with a self-referential concern with the nature of fiction. His other novels are: *Boys and Girls Come Out to Play* (1949); *A House in Order* (1966).

Denotation
▷ connotation and denotation

Depression, The
A 'depression' signifies the slowing of economic activity for a considerable period of time. High unemployment and poverty usually accompany economic depression. The most significant such period in Britain was the 1930s, which is currently called 'The Depression'. It gave rise to several novels documenting the plight of the working classes, the best known being Walter Greenwood's *Love on the Dole* (1933).

Derrida, Jacques (b 1930)
Although he is primarily a philosopher, the influence of Derrida's work on the study of literature has been immense. He is the originator of a mode of reading known as ▷ 'deconstruction', the major strand in what is now regarded as the general area of post-structuralism. His main works are *Speech and Phenomena* (trans. 1973), *Of Grammatology* (trans. 1974), and *Writing and Difference* (trans. 1978). For Derrida, as for ▷ Saussure, language is composed of differences, that is, a series of non-identical elements which combine with each other to produce linguistic signs which are accorded meaning. Traditionally, this process is anchored to an organising principle, a centre, but Derrida questions this concept and rejects the idea of a 'presence' in which authority resides, thereby lifting all restrictions upon the 'play' of differences. But, in addition to the idea that language is composed of 'differences', Derrida also deploys the term '*differance*' to indicate the continual postponement of 'presence' which is located in all signifiers. Thus, signs are produced through a relatively free play of linguistic elements (difference), but what they signify can never be fully present since meaning is constantly 'deferred' (*differance*). Derrida's influence has been greatest in the U.S.A. where after his visit to Johns Hopkins and his teaching at Yale, deconstruction has become the successor to American new criticism. The thrust of literary theory in Derrida's writing bears on the question of literature itself, and opposes a traditional scholarly attachment to, and privileging of, poetry. Commissioned as an essay on Shelley, his piece 'Living On' (in Bloom (ed.) *Deconstruction and Criticism*, 1979) rapidly becomes a freewheeling meditation on death, absence and writing. *Acts of Literature* (1992) does however collect a number of essays explicitly concerned with the literary.
▷ Grammatology; De Man, Paul.

Desai, Anita (b 1937)
Indian novelist and short-story writer. Her novels offer a satirical view of social change in India since Independence, with a powerful sense of waste, limitation, self-deception and failure. *Where Shall We Go This Summer* (1975) and *Clear Light of Day* (1980) are particularly concerned with the problems of Indian women to whom westernization offers an apparent freedom. She uses visual detail and an impressionistic style in an attempt to convey a sense of the meaning underlying everyday behaviour and objects. Her other novels include: *Cry the Peacock* (1963); *Voices in the City* (1965); *Bye-Bye Blackbird* (1971); *Fire on the Mountain* (1977); and *In Custody* (1984). Story collection: *Games at Twilight* (1978). She has also written works for children, including *The Village by the Sea* (1982).

Descartes, René (1596–1650)
French philosopher, mathematician. In ethics and religious doctrine he was traditional, but in method of thought he was the starting point of the total reliance on reason – ▷ rationalism – that was pre-eminent in the later 17th and 18th centuries. In his *Discours de la Méthode* (1637) he reduced knowledge to the basic principle of *Cogito, ergo sum* (I think, therefore I am), from which intuition he deduced the existence of God and thence the reality of the external world. He also distinguished mind and matter, finding their source of combination again in God. It was the influence of Descartes' writings that drew the English philosopher ▷ John Locke, the dominant figure in English rationalism, to the study of philosophy.

Deschamps, Eustache (c 1346–1406)
French poet who, like ▷ Guillaume de Machaut his mentor, was interested in developing the technical art of vernacular lyric poetry, and was the author of one of the first treatises on the subject. ▷ Chaucer read and was influenced by his work (including his narrative poetry) but Deschamps seems to have been very aware of Chaucer's literary skills too: his ▷ ballade addressed to the English poet describes Chaucer as a writer whose learning has illuminated Britain.

***Deserted Village, The* (1770)**
A poem in heroic ▷ couplets by ▷ Oliver

Goldsmith, written in protest against the enclosure of common land by powerful landowners. The poet recalls his youth in Auburn in the traditional terms of idyllic ▷ pastoral, and laments the present desolation and depopulation. Goldsmith's conventional literary opposition between rural innocence and commercial corruption, prompted ▷ George Crabbe's realistic portrayal of the grimness of peasant life in *The Village* (1783).

Deshpande, Shashi (b 1938)
Novelist and short-story writer. Deshpande was born in Dharwad, south India and educated at the universities of Bombay and Bangalore (where she took degrees in economics and law) and the University of Mysore. Much of her fiction deals with feminist issues: the struggle of a daughter to be allowed to study medicine in *The Dark Holds No Terrors* (1983); questions of autonomy, responsibility and power within marriage in *That Long Silence* (1988). Her feminism is informed by Hindu thought and myth and by her knowledge of Sanskrit texts, as well as showing some influence of Buddhist ideas. Her other novels are: *Roots and Shadows* (1983); *Come up and be Dead* (1983); *It was the Nightingale* (1986); *The Binding Vine* (1993). Volumes of short stories: *The Legacy* (1971), *The Miracle* (1986), *It was Dark* (1986).

Despenser, Rachel Fanny Antonina (1773–1829)
Political writer and autobiographer. Despenser was an illegitimate child who, on her father's death, was sent away to a French convent where she received a ▷ classical education. She returned to Britain when the ▷ French Revolution began. Despenser's education had encouraged her democratic beliefs and she became one of the more radical writers of her day. ▷ De Quincey compared her to ▷ Shelley, and ▷ Wordsworth admired her *Essay on Government* (1808), which asserted the rights of women and the lower classes. Her personal life was, however, more complicated: she had eloped in 1794 with Matthew Lee, but left him the following year to pursue her political endeavours uninterrupted. In 1804 she either eloped with or was abducted by two brothers from the Gordon family; the stories vary, and although a case was brought against them for abduction they were cleared of the accusation. Despenser subsequently retired to the country to escape public hostility resulting from the trial. She retaliated by publishing her own version of events, *Vindication* in 1807. Her *Memoirs* (c 1812) reveal an increasingly unstable mentality and her developing paranoia led her to accuse her family of attempted murder.

***Desperate Remedies* (1871)**
▷ Thomas Hardy's first published novel in which he adopted the formulae of the popular ▷ sensation novel of the time.

Destruction of Troy, The
A Middle English translation, in ▷ alliterative verse, of ▷ Guido de Columnis' account of the first and second falls of Troy. The 14th-century English text was apparently commissioned (though the narrator does not give any precise information about the identity of the patron), and reflects considerable linguistic and metrical skill, sustained for some 14,000 lines.
Bib: Panton, G., and Donaldson, D. (eds.), *The 'Gest Historiale' of the Destruction of Troy.*

Detective fiction
This branch of literature is usually easy to distinguish from the much wider literature of crime and retribution in drama and in the novel. Unlike the latter, detective fiction seldom relies on the presentation of deep emotions or on subtle and profound character creation. Character, emotion, psychological analysis of states of mind, social reflections, will all be present as flavouring, and may even be conspicuous, but the indispensable elements are always a mysterious – but not necessarily horrible – crime, and a detective, who is commonly not a professional policeman, but who has highly developed powers of scientific deduction. It is essential that the surface details should be convincing, and that the author should keep no clues from the reader, who may thus have the satisfaction of competing with the detective at his game. In the detective story proper, as opposed to the crime novel, the criminal's identity is not revealed until the end, and provides the focus of attention. Precursors of the form are ▷ Wilkie Collins' novel ▷ *The Moonstone* (1868) and the stories of the American writer Edgar Allan Poe (1809–49), featuring the French detective Dupin. But the widespread popularity of detective fiction began with ▷ Arthur Conan Doyle's Sherlock Holmes stories, of which the first was *A Study in Scarlet* (1887). The staggering perspicuity of the amateur detective from Baker Street, and his superiority to the police and to his companion and foil, Dr Watson, won him a world-wide audience. Another early exponent of the detective short story was ▷ G. K. Chesterton, whose detective, Father Brown, is a modest and intuitive Roman Catholic priest who first appeared in *The Innocence of Father Brown* (1911).

The first women detectives in fiction appeared in the 1860s; the stereotype of women's 'nosiness' and obsessive interest in gossip and trivia was often used to explain the female detective's skill in ferreting out crimes and criminals. By the end of the 19th century a number of women writers were producing detective and mystery fiction for an increasingly profitable

market. This trend was to continue into the 20th century when some of the foremost writers of the genre were women. From the time of E. C. Bentley's classic work *Trent's Last Case* (1912) the full-length novel became the most popular form. After Conan Doyle, the dominant figure of detective fiction is Dorothy L. Sayers, whose aristocratic amateur detective, Lord Peter Wimsey, appears in works such as *Murder Must Advertise* (1933) and *The Nine Tailors* (1934); she also published a history of crime fiction in 1928 and wrote critical essays on the genre. Other prominent authors of detective fiction include Agatha Christie (the creator of Hercule Poirot and Miss Marple), Michael Innes (pseudonym of the novelist and critic J. I. M. Stewart), H. C. Bailey, P. D. James and H. R. F. Keating. The American school of tough detective fiction is exemplified by Raymond Chandler (1888–1959) and Dashiell Hammett (1894–1961).
Bib: Sleung, M., *Crime on her Mind*; Craig, P., *The Lady Investigates*; Wing, G., Ed. 'Edwin Drood and Desperate Remedies: prototypes of Detective Fiction in 1870', *Studies in English Literature* 13 677–87 Autumn 1973.

Determination
A Marxist term used in critical theory, it is often confused with 'determinism' whereby a particular action or event is wholly caused by some external agency, and must therefore be assumed to be inevitable. In 'determination', the traditional fatalistic implications of the term 'determinism' are softened considerably, to draw attention to those constraints and pressures which mould human action. Thus a distinction is to be made between a tendency which attributes all movement in the social formation to economic factors, and one which seeks to account structurally for the patterns of dominance and subordination (▷ contradictions) operating at any one moment in history. The concept of determination can also be used to ask questions about particular literary ▷ genres and their historical significance, as well as helping to account for particular elements of the rhetorical structures of text. Determination helps in seeing texts as part of a larger social context rather than as isolated verbal constructs, and it helps also to raise a number of questions concerning the inter-relationship between literature and the ways in which it represents 'reality'.

Device
▷ Formalism.

***Devil is an Ass, The* (1616)**
A satirical comedy by ▷ Ben Jonson, attacking the speculators, financial tricksters, and their dupes, in contemporary London. The young dupe, Fitzdottrel, is cheated out of his land by the 'projector' Meercraft with elaborate projects of land reclamation; Pug, an inferior devil trying his hand at deceiving and betraying humanity, finds that he is not the equal in this to human beings themselves.

Dhondy, Farouk (b 1944)
Novelist and playwright. Dhondy was born in Poona, Bombay, India and educated at Cambridge University, Bombay Engineering College and Leicester University. He has taught English in schools in London. His work includes the novel *Vigilantes* (1988) and the plays, *Mama Dragon* (1980), *Trojans* (an adaptation of the plays of Euripides) and *Kipling Sahib* (1982). He has also written television plays and fiction for children.

Diachronic
▷ Synchronic.

Dialectic
Originally used to refer to the nature of logical argument, but in the 19th century this term underwent something of a revaluation, and came to be associated with the work of the German philosophers Kant and Hegel. 'Dialectic' referred to the process whereby the 'idea' (*thesis*) was self-divided, and its internal oppositions (*antithesis*) were resolved in a *synthesis* which opened the way to a higher truth. In Marxist thinking 'dialectic' refers to the ▷ contradictions present in any one phenomenon, and to their resolution through conflict. It is the nature of the opposition and that conflict which determines movement and change.
▷ Marx, Karl.

Dialogic
▷ Bakhtin, Mikhail.

Dialogism
A term introduced by the Russian theorist and critic ▷ Mikhail Bakhtin who originally applied it to the novel, although it is now used in relation to other genres as well. A dialogical novel is one composed in multiple, interactive voices without giving particular priority to any one of them and the term originates in the idea of dialogue, as opposed to monologue. But the significance of dialogical writing for Bakhtin extends far beyond this. For him, dialogical writing is an un-hierarchical form in which the various voices are in energetic interplay in a way that is subversive of ideological structures. A monological composition, by contrast, tends in Bakhtin's view, to be hierarchical, and therefore authoritarian.
▷ Carnival; ▷ Heteroglossia; ▷ Polyphony; ▷ Univocal.
Bib: Bakhtin, M., *The Dialogical Imagination*; Dentith, S., *Bakhtinian Thought*.

***Diana of the Crossways* (1885)**
A novel by ▷ George Meredith in which the central character Diana Warwick is accused of adultery by her husband. His action for divorce fails but the couple agree to separate. Diana forms a relationship with Percy Dacier, a rising young politician, but their affair ends after Diana's betrayal of a political secret to the press. Diana eventually marries an old admirer after the death of her husband. The character of Diana Warwick has much in common with ▷ Hardy's Sue Bridehead, the heroine of ▷ *Jude the Obscure*, and is an example of the ▷ 'New Woman' fiction of the period.

Diaries
As a form of literature diaries began to be significant in the 17th century. The spirit of criticism from the ▷ Renaissance and the stress on the individual conscience from the ▷ Reformation combined with the political and social turbulence of the 17th century to awaken people to a new awareness of personal experience and its possible interest for general readers. The private nature of the diary form also led to many women taking up this form of writing. Thus the art of the diary arose with the art of ▷ biography and ▷ autobiography.

Diaries may first be divided into two classes: those clearly meant to be strictly private and those written more or less with an eye to eventual publication – although ▷ Oscar Wilde was quick to see the disingenuousness of such a division. In his play *The Importance of Being Earnest* (1895) Cecily Cardew hides her diary from Algernon claiming that it is 'simply a young girl's record of her own thoughts and impressions, and consequently meant for publication'. A further division may be made between those diaries which are interesting chiefly as a record of the time in which the writer lived and those which are mainly a record of the writer's personality.

In the ▷ Renaissance the diary became a popular form of expressing personal concerns such as ▷ Anne Clifford's diary. However, the best known of the English diaries is that of ▷ Samuel Pepys (1633–1703), which was both purely private (written in code) and entirely unself-conscious, as well as an excellent record of the time. His contemporary, ▷ John Evelyn (1620–1706), is less famous partly because his diary is a more studied, self-conscious work. ▷ Jonathan Swift's *Journal to Stella* (covering the years 1710–13) is a personal revelation but unusual in that it was addressed to the woman Swift loved. The diary of the ▷ Quaker, ▷ George Fox (1624–91), is a record of his spiritual experience for the education of his followers. In the 18th and early 19th century the most famous is that of the novelist ▷ Fanny Burney (Madame D'Arblay, 1752–1840), considered as a record of the time ingenuously imbued with her own personality. The diary of the great religious reformer, ▷ John Wesley (1703–91), is comparable to that of Fox as a spiritual record, with a wider outlook on his time. In the 19th century the diaries of Thomas Creevey (1768–1838) and Charles Greville (1794–1865) are famous as records of public affairs, and that of ▷ Henry Crabb Robinson (1775–1867) for impressions of the leading writers who were his friends. Hannah Culwick, a Victorian maidservant, wrote seventeen diaries running from 1854–74, providing a fascinating account of a life in service in the Victorian period. The socialist and reformer Beatrice Webb wrote diaries which are a major source of English social and political history and a record of the difficulties encountered by women wishing to work on an equal level with men. ▷ George and Weedon Grossmith's *Diary of a Nobody* (1892) is a comic novel of late Victorian manners which parodies the form, claiming to be the diary of city clerk Charles Pooter. In the 20th century the *Journal* of ▷ Katherine Mansfield is an intimate and vivid record of personal experience, and that of ▷ Virginia Woolf is an extremely interesting record of a writer's experience of artistic creation.

Dibdin, Charles (1745–1814)
Song-writer, dramatist and actor. Dibdin the elder is best known for his popular songs about the sea and his ▷ dramatic monologues. He also wrote an ▷ autobiography, *The Professional Life of Mr Dibdin* (1803), which contains interesting details about life in the theatre at the time and which includes transcriptions of 600 fashionable songs. One of his sons followed him into the world of entertainment, Charles Dibdin (1768–1833), who became a dramatist. His nephew ▷ Thomas Dibdin was the renowned bibliographer.

Dibdin, Thomas Frognall (1776–1847)
Bibliographer. The nephew of the actor and song-writer ▷ Charles Dibdin, Thomas had a very different career. He was the librarian to Lord Spencer of Althorp, the first secretary of the ▷ Roxburghe Club, and an erudite bibliographer. His most important works include *Bibliomania* (1809), *Bibliophobia* and *Reminiscences of a Literary Life* (1836). As the secretary of the Roxburghe Club he also supervised the editing and reissue of a number of important literary works, mainly from the ▷ Renaissance period.

Dickens, Charles (1812–70)
The most popular and internationally known of English novelists. His father was a government clerk who liked to live prosperously, and his sudden impoverishment and imprisonment for debt in the ▷ Marshalsea was a drastic shock to the boy Dickens; prisons recur literally and symbolically in many of his novels, which

are also filled with attacks on the injustice of social institutions and the inequalities between the rich and the poor. He began his writing career as a journalist, and all his novels were published serially in periodicals, especially in two edited by himself – ▷ *Household Words* started in 1850, and ▷ *All the Year Round*, started in 1859, both of them weeklies.

His first book, ▷ *Sketches by Boz* (1836), was a collection of stories and descriptive pieces written for various papers in the tradition of the essayists – Charles Lamb (1775–1834), William Hazlitt (1778–1830), Leigh Hunt (1784–1859) – of the previous generation, with the especial difference that Dickens wrote about the hitherto neglected lower middle class. ▷ *The Pickwick Papers* (1836–7), at first loosely connected but gathering unity as it proceeded, was immensely successful. There followed: ▷ *Oliver Twist* (1837–8), ▷ *Nicholas Nickleby* (1838–9), ▷ *The Old Curiosity Shop* and ▷ *Barnaby Rudge* (1840–1). This concludes the first, comparatively light-hearted phase of Dickens' writing, in which he developed his characteristic comedy and melodrama. ▷ *Martin Chuzzlewit* (1843–4) begins a more impressive style of writing in which the comedy and melodrama deepen into new intensity, though critics observe that the beginning of the novel is still in the earlier manner. In 1843 begins his series of Christmas Books, including ▷ *A Christmas Carol* and ▷ *The Cricket on the Hearth*. Thereafter come his mature masterpieces: ▷ *Dombey and Son* (1846–8); ▷ *David Copperfield* (1849–50); ▷ *Bleak House* (1852–3); ▷ *Hard Times* (1854); ▷ *Little Dorrit* (1855–7); ▷ *A Tale of Two Cities* (1859); ▷ *Great Expectations* (1860–1); ▷ *Our Mutual Friend* (1864–5). Dickens was writing ▷ *Edwin Drood* when he died.

Bib: Forster, J., *Life*; Johnson, E., *Life*; Wilson, E., in *The Wound and the Bow*; Chesterton, G.K., *Charles Dickens*; Gissing, G., *Charles Dickens: A Crucial Study*; House, H., *The Dickens World*; Leavis, F.R., in *The Great Tradition*; Collins, P., *Dickens and Crime*; *Dickens and Education*; Gross J., *Dickens and the Twentieth Century*; Leavis, F.R. and Q.D., *Dickens the Novelist*; Wilson A., *The World of Charles Dickens*; Carey, J., *The Violent Effigy: A Study of Dickens' Imagination*; Kaplan, F., *Dickens: a Biography*; Jaffe, A., *Vanishing Points: Dickens, Narrative and the Subject of Omniscience*.

Dickens, Monica (b 1915)

Novelist, children's writer and journalist. Monica Dickens is best known as the author of the popular *Follyfoot* series of books written in the 1970s (and subsequently televised), but she only began writing for children in 1970, by which time she had already published a range of (often semi-autobiographical) novels, beginning with *One Pair of Hands* in 1939. The inspiration for Dickens' writing has often come from her working life, as a nurse (*One Pair of Feet*; 1942), as a journalist (*My Turn to Make the Tea*; 1951), with the Samaritans (*The Listeners*; 1970) and more generally in her life in the countryside (*The House at World's End*; 1970, and the *Follyfoot* books). Dickens was a columnist for the *Woman's Own* magazine from 1946 to 1965, and is the great-granddaughter of the Victorian novelist ▷ Charles Dickens. Other works include: *Mariana* (1940); *The Fancy* (1943); *Flowers on the Grass* (1949); *The Winds of Heaven* (1955); *The Room Upstairs* (1966); *Follyfoot* (1971); *World's End in Winter* (1972); *Follyfoot Farm* (1973); *Stranger at Follyfoot* (1976); *The Ballad of Favour* (1985); *One of the Family* (1993).

Diction

The choice of words a writer uses in a work such as, for example, archaic, ornate or colloquial. ▷ lexis.

***Dictionary of the English Language* (1755)**

Usually known as 'Johnson's Dictionary', it was compiled by ▷ Samuel Johnson and published in 1755. It was accepted as authoritative for about a hundred years. The excellence of the work is not so much its scholarship as its literary intelligence. It is weak in etymology, as this was still an undeveloped science, but it is strong in understanding of language, and in particular the English language. In the Preface, Johnson writes a short grammar, but he points out that English simplicity of forms and freedom from inflexions make an elaborate one (as grammar was then understood) unnecessary. He makes clear that the spirit of the English language had been unduly influenced by the spirit of French, and he rejects the idea that correctness should be fixed by the authority of an Academy, since the inherent mutability of language will always cause it to follow its own laws. Johnson thus began the English habit of relying upon current English dictionaries and manuals of usage to discover the best existent expression: Fowler's *Modern English Usage* and the Oxford *New English Dictionary* are 20th-century descendants of 'Johnson's Dictionary'.

Dictys Cretensis

A supposed eyewitness of the Trojan war who kept a diary of events, *Ephemeris Belli Troiani (A Journal of the Trojan War)*, which, along with the work of the Trojan ▷ Dares, formed the basis for the most influential medieval versions of the Troy story. Dictys, as a warrior on the Greek side, provides a pro-Greek view of events and also includes an account of the homecoming of the Greeks. A small portion of a Greek version of Dictys' work has survived from the early 3rd century but all the rest of the manuscript versions are of Latin reworkings which date from the 4th century. Although the account claims to be that of an eyewitness, the material is basically a rationalized version of events drawn from ▷ Homer's ▷ *Iliad*, organized chronologically. The narratives of Dictys and Dares were shown to be forgeries in the early 18th century.

▷ Benoît de Sainte-Maure; Troy.

Didactic literature

Literature designed to teach, or to propound in direct terms a doctrine or system of ideas. In practice, it is not always easy to identify; so much literature is didactic in intention but not in form; sometimes writers renounce didactic intentions but in practice use didactic forms. Thus ▷ Spenser declared that ▷ *The Faerie Queene* was meant to 'fashion a gentleman . . . in vertuous and gentle discipline', but the poem may be enjoyed for its imaginative vision without much regard to its didacticism, and the same is true of ▷ Bunyan's ▷ *Pilgrim's Progress.* In the 18th century much poetry had at least didactic leanings, such as ▷ Pope's ▷ *Essay on Criticism* and his ▷ *Essay on Man*; minor work by other poets is much more unmistakably didactic. The prevalence of didactic poetry in the 18th century arose from the especially high regard this century had for ancient Greek and Latin literature: Hesiod's *Works and Days* (Greek, 8th century BC) and ▷ Lucretius' *De Rerum Natura* (Latin, 1st century BC) being the major examples of didactic verse. The Romantic poets of the early 19th century (▷ Wordsworth, ▷ Coleridge, ▷ Shelley, ▷ Keats) reacted against the 18th-century Augustans, and since then there has been a persistent prejudice against explicit didacticism. In fact much of Wordsworth (*eg*▷ *The Excursion*, 1814) and of Shelley (*eg* ▷ *Queen Mab*, 1813) was highly didactic, though the undisguised passion to some extent conceals the fact. The 19th-century novelists, especially ▷ Dickens and ▷ George Eliot, used didactic digressions, but in the former such passages are especially of passionate social invective, and in the latter they are usually more integrated into the imaginative art than is apparent. In the 1930s there was a revival of verse didacticism, especially in the work of ▷ W. H. Auden, *eg New Year Letter* (1941). In general, the view now is that poets and even novelists may be didactic if they choose. True didacticism, however, requires a body of assumptions commonly held by author and reader, as was true of the age of Pope, but is not so today.

Diderot, Denis (1713–84)

French philosopher, novelist, dramatist and critic, and major figure of the French ▷ Enlightenment; born at Langres in Champagne. He was educated by Jesuits and was employed as a tutor, and by a bookseller. Diderot became an ▷ atheist, and his arguments for the equality of all mankind anticipate those of the ▷ French Revolution. His was a period of ferocious censorship in France, and Diderot was persecuted by the authorities, and was for a time imprisoned because of his *Lettre sur les aveugles* ('Letter on the blind' 1749), which set out his materialistic and anti-clerical views. He was known in England particularly for his work on ▷ *L'Encyclopédie*, translated and expanded from Ephraim Chambers' *Cyclopaedia* (1728). At first, Diderot worked together with the mathematician D'Alembert, later he headed it alone. The work was published in 17 volumes between 1751 and 1765, with a further 11 volumes of plates completed in 1772. It was an anthology of 'enlightened' views on politics, philosophy and religion, and included contributions by ▷ Voltaire, ▷ Montesquieu, and ▷ Rousseau. It sought to harness all available knowledge, and to show the order and interdependence of its various branches, in a manner embodying the humanistic and rational ideals of the *philosophes*, including Diderot's own iconoclasm. The *Encyclopédie* was repeatedly banned because of its perceived challenge to the established order. Later Diderot became a favourite of Catherine II of Russia, whom he visited in 1773, and who gave him financial support. His fiction includes *La Religieuse*, a study of convent life, and *Jacques le fataliste et son maitre* (c 1774). His *Supplement aux voyages de Bougainville* (published posthumously, 1796) contrasts morals and customs of the natural inhabitants of Tahiti with those of civilized Europeans, to the detriment of the latter. *Le Neveu de Rameau* (date uncertain, probably between 1761 and 1774, published posthumously) is a satiric study of society, in the form of a dialogue between the author, in the role of a philosoper idealist, and a disillusioned beggar. The work was translated by ▷ Goethe and it influenced the philosopher Hegel, who saw in it a portrait of the 'alienated man'. Diderot's views about literature and life were also expressed in his vast correspondence with society figures and other writers. He admired ▷ Samuel Richardson, whom he described him as a 'painter of nature', to the point of adulation, and greatly helped to popularize his books on the Continent. Much in Diderot's work anticipates views of some later ▷ Romanticists: he has been described as a ▷ pantheist, as well as an atheist. His plays were mostly short melodramas.

Bib: Crocker, L. G., *Diderot, the Embattled Philosopher*.

Différance

▷ Jacques Derrida

Difference

A term introduced by ▷ Ferdinand de Saussure in his study of linguistics and used in literary theory. It is the means whereby value is established in any system of linguistic signs whether it be spoken or written. Saussure's *Course in General Linguistics* (1915) argues that in speech it is 'the phonetic contrasts' which permit us to distinguish between one word and another that constitute meaning. In writing the letters used to form words are arbitrary signs, and their values are therefore 'purely negative and differential' (Saussure). The result is that the written sign becomes important only insofar as it is different from other signs within the overall system of language. The notion of difference as a principle of opposition has been extended beyond the limits of Structuralist thinking laid down by Saussure. For example, the ▷ Marxist philosopher ▷ Mikhail Bakhtin in a critique of Saussurean Structuralism argued that 'the forms of signs are conditioned above all by the social organization of the participants involved and also by the immediate conditions of their interaction' (*Marxism and The Philosophy of Language*; 1930). Thus the clash of opposites through which meaning and value emerge is determined by the social positions of those who use the language. This means that secreted at the very heart of the form of the linguistic sign is a series of dialectical opposites whose interaction refracts the struggle taking place within the larger framework of society itself. For Bakhtin these oppositions can be defined in terms of the struggle between social classes, but the dialectical structure of these conflicts makes the notion of difference suitable for any situation which can be analysed in terms of binary opposites. For example, for ▷ feminism this would be an opposition between 'masculine' and 'feminine' as the basis upon which sexual identity is constructed. ▷ Jacques Derrida has adapted the term to form the neologism '*différance*', which denotes the deferral of meaning whereby no sign can ever be brought into direct alignment with the object that it purports to recall. This means that meaning is always *deferred*, and can never be final.

Digby Plays
A collection of three medieval plays dating from the 16th century, from the East Anglian region and found with non-literary material in a single manuscript, now kept in Oxford, MS Bodley Digby 133. Two of the plays, *Mary Magdalene* and *The Conversion of St Paul*, are rare survivals of the popular medieval genre of saints' plays. The third play, *The Killing of the Children*, is a self-contained biblical piece written, it seems, for performance on a feast day.
Bib: Baker, Donald et al (eds.), *The Late Medieval Religious Plays of Bodleian MSS Digby 133 and E. Muse 160.*

Dillon, Wentworth
▷ Roscommon, Fourth Earl of.

Dinesen, Isak
▷ Blixen, Karen.

Discourse
A term used in critical theory. Especially in the writings of ▷ Michel Foucault, 'discourse' is the name given to the systems of linguistic representations through which power sustains itself. For Foucault discourse manifests itself only through concrete examples operating within specific areas of social and institutional practice. He argues that within individual discourses a series of mechanisms are used as means of controlling desire and power, which facilitate 'classification . . . ordering [and] distribution' (Foucault). In this way a mastery is exerted over what appears to be the randomness of everyday reality. It is thus possible to investigate those discourses which have been used to master reality in the past *eg* discourses concerned with questions of 'sexuality', criminality and judicial systems of punishment, or madness, as Foucault's own work demonstrates.
Bib: Foucault, M., *The Order of Things*; *Power/Knowledge: Selected Interviews and Other Writings* (ed. C. Gordon).

Dismal science, The
Political economy; so called by ▷ Thomas Carlyle because the social thought of such writers as Adam Smith (1723–90) ▷ Jeremy Bentham, ▷ Thomas Malthus and David Ricardo tended to be pessimistic about the alleviation of poverty and inhumanly indifferent to the consequences of economic laws as they saw them.

Displacement
For ▷ psychoanalytical usage 'displacement' is associated by ▷ Freud (along with ▷ 'condensation') with the mechanisms whereby the conscious mind processes the unconscious in dreams. 'Displacement' is a form of censorship which effectively distorts the ideas which act as the controlling forces of the dream (what Freud calls 'the latent dream-thoughts'), and attaches them to other, more acceptable thoughts or ideas. This complex process is one which involves the omission or re-arrangement of detail, and modification of the dream thoughts. In order to reach the unconscious the 'manifest dream' must be interpreted as a symbolic expression of another text which lies beneath its surface and which is not readily accessible to the conscious mind. This whole mechanism rests on the assumption that psychic energy can attach itself to particular ideas, or objects (cathexis); those ideas or objects are related to the 'latent dream-thoughts', but derive their new-found significance by a process of association. Literature habitually invests objects and ideas with value, and psychic intensity, and the manner in which it does so can be

read ▷ psychoanalytically as a manifestation of deeper, more disturbing activities going on in the mind of the writer, or by analogy in the 'unconscious' of the society of which the writer is a part.

Disraeli, Benjamin (Lord Beaconsfield) (1804–81)
Statesman and novelist. He was of Spanish-Jewish descent; his grandfather settled in England in 1748. His political career was brilliant; he entered Parliament in 1837; in the 1840s he was the leader in the House of Commons of a small number of Tory politicians who, as the 'Young England' group, wanted a revival of the party and of the national spirit in an alliance between a spiritually reborn aristocracy and the common people; by 1848 he was leading the Conservatives in the House of Commons; in 1868 and in 1874–80 he had his two periods as one of the most brilliant of English Prime Ministers. Both politically (he secured the vote for the urban working class) and socially (eg his trade union legislation) he at least partly succeeded in securing support for his party from the working class. He was made Earl of Beaconsfield in 1876.

The novels which now chiefly hold attention are his 'Young England Trilogy': ▷ *Coningsby* (1844); ▷ *Sybil* (1845) and *Tancred* (1847). All were written to promulgate his doctrine of Tory Democracy and they all have imperfections, partly because for Disraeli literature was second to politics. On the other hand they have great liveliness of characterization and show keen insight into the structure of society with its cleavage between rich and poor, which Disraeli called 'the two nations'. His other novels are: *Vivian Grey* (1826); *The Young Duke* (1831); *Alroy* and *Ixion in Heaven* (1833); *The Infernal Marriage* and *The Rise of Iskander* (1834); *Henrietta Temple* and *Venetia* (1837); *Lothair* (1870) and *Endymion* (1880).

▷ Social problem novel.

Bib: Blake, R., *Life*; Moneypenny, W.F. and Buckle, G.E., *Life*; Jerman, B.R., *The Young Disraeli*; Holloway, J., in *Victorian Sage*; Dahl, C., in *Victorian Fiction* (ed. L. Stevenson); Pritchett, V.S., in *The Living Novel*; Schwartz, D.R., *Disraeli's Fiction*; Brava, T., *Disraeli the Novelist*; Harvie, C., *The Centre of Things: Political Fiction in Britain from Disraeli to the Present*.

Dissenters
A term used for those ▷ Puritans who, owing to their 'dissent' from the established ▷ Church of England, were refused certain political, educational, and (at first) religious rights from the second half of the 17th century. That is to say, they could not enter Parliament, they could not enter a university, and, until 1688, they could not join together in worship. Puritans were not thus formally restricted before 1660. They were released from their political restraints in 1828. In the 19th century it became more usual to call them Nonconformists or Free Churchmen. The term does not apply to Scotland, where the established Church is ▷ Presbyterian, not the episcopalian Church of England.

Dissenters' Schools and Academies
In the 18th century, Protestants who did not belong to the Church of England (ie Dissenters or Nonconformists) were not allowed to attend its schools. They could enter Scottish but not English universities. They therefore set up their own educational institutions which provided efficient education, often more up-to-date than that in the schools attended by Anglicans. Dissenting schools and academies became steadily less important in the 19th century, especially after London University was opened in 1828. The last restrictions on non-Anglicans at Oxford and Cambridge were removed in 1871.

Dissociation of Sensibility
A critical expression made famous by ▷ T. S. Eliot, and used in his essay *The Metaphysical Poets* (1921, included in his *Selected Essays*). He states: 'In the seventeenth century a dissociation of sensibility set in, from which we have never recovered; and this dissociation . . . was aggravated by the influence of the two most powerful poets of the century, ▷ Milton and ▷ Dryden.' Eliot's argument is that before 1660 poets, in particular the ▷ Metaphysical poets, were 'engaged in the task of trying to find the verbal equivalent for states of mind and feeling', and that after that date 'while the language became more refined, the feeling became more crude'. Poetry, henceforward, is put to more specialized purposes: ▷ 'Tennyson and ▷ Browning are poets, and they think; but they do not feel their thought as immediately as the odour of a rose. A thought to ▷ Donne was an experience; it modified his sensibility.' The implication behind the argument is that poets (with exceptions) ceased to bring all their faculties to bear upon their art: ▷ 'Racine or Donne looked into a good deal more than the heart. One must look into the cerebral cortex, the nervous system, and the digestive tracts.'

The theory has had great influence. Those who uphold it support it with the evidence provided by the rise of modern prose after 1660, and the gradual displacement of poetry from its centrality in literature thereafter; poetry either subjected itself to the rational discipline of prose (*eg* ▷ Pope), or, in the 19th century, it tended to cultivate areas of feeling to which this rational discipline was not relevant (*eg* ▷ Swinburne). However, the theory has been attacked for various reasons.

Eliot himself felt that he had used the expression in too simplified a way (*Milton*, 1974, in *Poets and Poetry*), and that the causes of the process were more complicated than his earlier essay had implied. Other writers have suggested that such a dissociation did not happen; or that it happened in different ways at different periods; or that, if it did happen, no deterioration in imaginative writing can be attributed to it. See Frank Kermode, *Romantic Image* and F. W. Bateson in *Essays in Criticism*, vol. 1.

Dithyramb
A Greek choric ▷ lyric or ▷ hymn in honour of the god Dionysus (Bacchus), and irregular and vehement in rhythm. 'Dithyrambic' is used to describe verse with similar rhythm. Not commonly used in English poetry; the best-known imitation is ▷ Dryden's *Alexander's Feast*.

***Divina Commedia* (Divine Comedy)**
The principal work of the Italian poet ▷ Dante (1265–1321). For an account of its contents, see the entries under its major sections: ▷ *Inferno*, ▷ *Purgatorio*, ▷ *Paradiso*.
Bib: Cunningham, G. F., *The Divine Comedy in English, 1090–1966*; Sinclair, J. N. (trans.), *The Divine Comedy*.

Dixon, Ella Hepworth (1855–1932)
Journalist, short-story writer and feminist. Dixon's one novel, *The Story of a Modern Woman* (1894), is an autobiographical account of the loneliness suffered by a woman who leads an independent life as a journalist. It is one of the most moving of the ▷ New Woman novels.

Dobell, Sydney (Thompson) (1824–74)
Poet, born in Kent, the son of a wine merchant. Precocious as a child, he never attended school or university but was privately educated in Cheltenham. He married at the age of twenty after a five-year engagement and was said to have never been separated from his wife for more than thirty hours during their thirty years of marriage. His dramatic poem *The Roman* (1850) supported the cause of Italian nationalism but the publication of the first part of *Balder* (1854) qualified him for inclusion in the ▷ Spasmodic school of poetry identified and ridiculed by ▷ William Aytoun, who parodied the ludicrous plot in his *Firmilian* (1854). Dobell never completed his epic poem. Other, less sensationalist, works include *England in Time of War* (1856), notable for its compassionate and non-jingoistic treatment of the ▷ Crimean War, and a collection of essays, *Thoughts on Art, Philosophy, and Religion*, which appeared posthumously in 1876.
▷ Gilfillan, George.

Doctor Faustus, The Tragical History of
A tragedy in ▷ blank verse, with comic episodes in prose, by ▷ Christopher Marlowe. The play resembles a medieval ▷ morality play in that its theme is Faustus' sacrifice of his soul to the devil (represented by Mephistophilis) for the sake of unlimited power, glory and enjoyment in this world. On the other hand, it is also thoroughly ▷ Renaissance in its treatment: the conflict of choice is made convincing as it would not have been in a medieval play, and the psychology, not only of Faustus but of Mephistophilis, is presented with moving insight. The medieval and the Renaissance outlooks fuse in *Doctor Faustus*, showing the very important continuity, as well as the contrast, between the two outlooks.

There are two uncertainties about the play. One is about its date. Marlowe uses the material of the German *Faustbuch* (*Faustbook*), which is about an early 16th-century scholar who had claimed powers of black magic, and fuses this historical figure with medieval legends about a man selling his soul to the devil. The earliest surviving English version is dated 1592, and the maturity of the poetry also suggests a date for the play late in Marlowe's live. On the other hand, some critics have found good reason to date *Faustus* at least as early as 1588. The other uncertainty concerns the extent of Marlowe's authorship. Did he have a collaborator for the comic parts? And were some of these added after his death? The edition of 1616 has considerably extended comedy, as compared with the first edition of 1604. The main reason for suspecting a collaborator is that much of the comedy is superfluous as well as trivial. It is, however, a mistake to suppose that the mere presence of comedy is injurious to the highest tragedy; the combination is frequent in Elizabethan serious drama – tragedies and history plays – including ▷ Shakespeare's; and it is one of the inheritances from medieval mystery and morality plays, with which English Renaissance drama kept a close relationship. Some of the comedy in *Faustus* enriches the tragedy by extending its relevance to common life, *eg* in the parody in which Faustus' servant, Wagner, also tries his hand at summoning the devil.
▷ Faust; Mephistopheles.

***Doctor Thorne* (1858)**
The third novel in ▷ Anthony Trollope's ▷ Barsetshire sequence. It was his most popular novel during his lifetime and extends the sequence to take account of county society.

Docwra, Anne (1624–1710)
Quaker author of numerous pamphlets in which she argued for the supremacy of God's word over human laws, and the importance of the 'inner light' as a revelation of God's love. She supported women's active involvement in the Church, and also pleaded for religious tolerance, although she was forceful in attacking those whom she felt were enemies of the Quaker cause. Among these was an apostate Quaker,

Francis Brigg, with whom she engaged in a vigorous and colourful ▷ pamphlet war. Docwra defended ▷ George Fox against accusations of indulgence.

Doggerel
Any carelessly made, irregular verse, often of a frivolous nature. The term is used by the host in ▷ Chaucer's ▷ *Canterbury Tales* in regard to the tale of ▷ *Sir Thopas*, told by Chaucer himself as one of the pilgrims: '"This may wel be rym doggerel", quod he'.

***Doll's House, A* (1879)**
A bold and controversial play by Norwegian dramatist ▷ Henrik Ibsen written in 1879 and first performed in London in 1889. In it Ibsen describes the financial and intellectual enslavement of Nora by her husband and the play discusses notions of individual freedom and social conformity, and in particular the relationship of this debate to the position of women. The play provoked a storm of controversy. It was criticized for its 'immorality' – a point of view satirized by ▷ George Bernard Shaw as 'Ibsenism' – and praised by supporters of the ▷ Women's Movement for its daring and emancipated conclusion.

***Dombey and Son* (1847–8)**
One of the earliest of the mature novels by ▷ Charles Dickens. Dombey is a proud and heartless London merchant whose sole interest in life is the perpetuation of his name in connection with his firm. For this reason he neglects his deeply affectionate daughter Florence for the sake of his little son, Paul, whom, however, he values not for himself but as the future embodiment of his firm. The boy is motherless, deprived of affection and physically delicate – he dies in childhood. To prevent Florence from marrying a mere clerk in his firm, Dombey sends her lover – Walter Gay – on business to an unhealthy colony in the West Indies. Dombey's pride makes him susceptible to flattery; he is preyed upon by Carker, his manager, one of Dickens' most notable villains, and by Major Joe Bagstock. He is led into marriage with a cold, disillusioned girl, Edith Granger, who runs away from him with Carker. Both his pride and his wealth are eventually taken from him and he finds himself in the end dependent on the forgiving Florence and Walter Gay. A particular interest of the book is that railways play an important part in it just at the time when they were transforming English life. The sombreness of Dombey's mansion is opposed to the warm-hearted if unbusinesslike environment of the shop of Solomon Gills, Gay's uncle.

Domesday Book
(Dome = doom, *ie* judgement, implying a complete and final record as on the Day of Judgement at the end of the world.) The record of a survey carried out by the order of ▷ William I and completed in 1086. It contains a description of the greater part of the landed property of England and was compiled to assist taxation and other government purposes.

Dominicans
▷ Friars.

Don Juan
The hero of legends from various European countries. His exploits were the subject of the Spanish play *El Burlador de Sevilla* by Tirso de Molina (1571–1641), who gave him his distinctive character of sensual adventurer. Plays and stories were woven round him in French and Italian, and he is the protagonist of an opera by Mozart (*Don Giovanni*). In English literature by far the most important work about him is the satirical epic ▷ *Don Juan* (1819–24) by ▷ Lord Byron.

***Don Juan* (1819–24)**
▷ Lord Byron's unfinished satirical epic in ▷ *ottava rima*, based very freely on the legendary figure of ▷ Don Juan. After a love affair in Spain (Canto I), Juan is sent abroad by his mother, but is shipwrecked and washed ashore on a Greek island where he is cared for by a Greek maiden, Haidee. Cantos III and IV describe their love and the destruction of their relationship by Haidee's pirate father, Lambro. In Canto V Juan has been sold as a slave to a Turkish princess who loves him; and in Cantos VI, VII and VIII he escapes and serves the Russian army against the Turks in the siege of Ismail. In Canto IX he attracts the attention of the Russian Empress, Catherine the Great, who in Canto X sends him on a mission to England, the setting for Cantos XI–XIII. Juan's affair with a duchess, and his deeper emotion for an English Catholic girl, are used as foci for a free-ranging satire on contemporary society. Juan has fewer mistresses in Byron's poem than in earlier versions of the legend, and is portrayed essentially as an *ingénu*, more often seduced by women than the seducer. The story-line is however subordinated to the philosophizing commentary of the poet himself, which ranges from flippant witticism ('What men call gallantry, and gods adultery,/ Is much more common where the climate's sultry'), through the moving rhetoric of the inserted lyric 'The isles of Greece', to harsh satire on 'the best of cutthroats', the Duke of Wellington ('And I shall be delighted to learn who,/ Save you and yours, have gain'd by Waterloo?'). The greatness of the poem derives from its flexible and informal metrical form which, unlike the ▷ Spenserian stanzas of ▷ *Childe Harold's Pilgrimage* and the couplets

of his verse tales, allows Byron to give full expression to his complex and contradictory personality.

Don Quixote de la Mancha (1605–15)
A satirical romance by the Spanish writer Miguel de Cervantes (1547–1616). It begins as a satire on the medieval and ⊳ Renaissance style of romance about wandering knights and their adventures in the pursuit of the rectification of injustices. It deepens into an image of idealism perpetually at odds with the pettinesss, vulgarity and meanness of the real world. Don Quixote is an impecunious gentleman whose mind has been turned by reading too many romances. He sets out on his wanderings accompanied by his servant, Sancho Panza, the embodiment of commonplace credulity and a shrewd sense of personal advantage. He takes as his patroness a peasant girl, Dulcinea del Toboso, whom he transfigures in his imagination and who is quite unaware of his devotion. The book was translated into English in 1612–20, and again a hundred years later in a more famous version by Peter Motteux. Its influence on our literature has been extensive. In the 17th century the burlesque element is emulated by Francis Beaumont in his play ⊳ *The Knight of the Burning Pestle* and by ⊳ Samuel Butler in his mock epic ⊳ *Hudibras*.

Donne, John (1572–1631)
Poet, Dean of St Paul's and prose writer. John Donne is (and was) regarded as one of the most important writers of the ⊳ Renaissance period. The early part of his life was spent at the margins of the Elizabethan court. He took part in the expeditions of the ⊳ Earl of Essex to Cadiz in 1596 and the Azores in 1597, and became private secretary to the Lord Keeper, Sir Thomas Egerton, in 1598. He travelled on the continent in 1605–6 and 1611–12. Originally a Roman Catholic, he was ordained into the Anglican Church in 1615, becoming Reader in Divinity at Lincoln's Inn in 1616, and Chaplain to Viscount Doncaster's embassy into Germany in 1619. In 1621 he was made Dean of St Paul's, and in the following year an Honorary Member of the Council of the Virginia Company.

Donne's works cover an enormous variety of genres and subjects. They include religious works such as the *Devotions on Emergent Occasions* published in 1624 and the *Essays in Divinity* (1651); anti-Catholic works such as *Pseudo-Martyr* (1610) and *Ignatius his Conclave* (1611); a considerable number of sermons (collections appearing in 1625, 1626, 1634 and 1640); a treatise on suicide entitled *Biathanatos* (1646); a collection of paradoxes (1633); and, in poetry, ⊳ satires, ⊳ lyrics, ⊳ elegies, ⊳ epigrams, verse letters and divine ⊳ sonnets.

As a preacher, Donne was justly famous in an age of famous preachers, as ⊳ Izaak Walton, his first biographer, recalled. His poetry, however, with the important exception of the two anniversary poems of 1611 and 1612, did not, for the most part, appear until after his death, when a collection was published in 1633. His poetry was, however, well known among his contemporaries, numerous manuscript versions of both his secular and his religious verse being in circulation. Donne's privileged status in the canon of English literature only came about in the first part of the 20th century (1920–50), when the highly-wrought and intellectual witticism of his verse fitted the critical tenor of the day, that is ⊳ new criticism. Recent attempts have been made to see Donne as more anxious (J. Carey), but the pre-World War II image remains entrenched. The recent discovery of the *Dalhousie Manuscripts*, which provide us with contemporary transcriptions, implies that editions of Donne's work will change over the next decade.
Bib: Grierson, H. J. C. (ed.), *Poems* (2 vols.); Smith, A. J. (ed.), *John Donne: The Complete English Poems*; Patrides, C. A. (ed.), *The Complete English Poems of John Donne*; Bald, R. C., *Donne: A Life*; Carey, J., *John Donne: Life Mind Art*; Parfitt, G., *John Donne: A Literary Life*.
⊳ *Songs and Sonnets*.

Doolittle, Hilda
⊳ H. D.

D'Orsay, Alfred Guillaume Gabriel, Count (1801–52)
Artist and dandy. A Frenchman who came under the patronage of ⊳ Marguerite, Countess of Blessington, with whose entourage he travelled on the continent, meeting ⊳ Byron, of whom he made a now famous pencil sketch.

Dorset Garden Theatre
The Dorset Garden Theatre, also known as the Duke's Theatre because of its patronage by the Duke of York, later ⊳ James II, was designed by ⊳ Sir Christopher Wren for ⊳ Sir William D'Avenant, and was considered the most magnificent public theatre when it opened in 1671.

The stage had four doors, two on each side, admitting the performers to a deep forestage or apron stage which projected into the pit, past the side-boxes. On this the prologue was spoken, and much of the acting took place, allowing great intimacy between actors and audience. Scene changes were carried out in full view of the audience, the curtain or front 'scene' being moved only at the beginnings and ends of performances; actors could step forward or backward into different, perhaps newly revealed, 'sets' as they were speaking. This made possible fast-paced, fluid action, particularly in comedy. From the first the

Dorset Garden specialized in staging the very elaborate performances, including many operas, as distinct from the Theatre Royal Drury Lane (▷ Drury Lane Theatres), which concentrated on plays. After the ▷ King's Company and ▷ Duke's Company were merged in 1682, Dorset Garden continued for a time to be the main venue for spectacles. In 1689 it was renamed the Queen's Theatre, in deference to Queen ▷ Mary II. It gradually fell out of use, and was demolished in 1709.

▷ Theatres.

Dorset, Lord

▷ Sackville, Thomas.

Dorset, Sixth Earl of (1638–1706)

Poet and patron. Charles Sackville, Lord Buckhurst, and later Earl of Dorset, was a Restoration courtier and author of ▷ satires and ▷ lyric poems (*Works*, 1714). ▷ John Dryden's *Discourse concerning the Original and Progress of Satire* is addressed to him, and contains high praise for his poetry.

Dostoevsky, Fyodor Mikhailovich (1821–81).

Russian novelist. Born in Moscow and educated at the St Petersburg Engineering Academy, he was arrested in 1849 for his socialist activities and spent eight years in a penal colony and in the army, during which period he experienced a religious conversion (to the Russian Orthodox Church), an experience which informs his major works. These include *Notes from the House of the Dead* (1869–61), *The Insulted and the Injured* (1861), *Notes from the Underground* (1864), *Crime and Punishment* (1866), *The Idiot* (1868), *The Devils* (1872) and *The Brothers Karamazov* (1880). Dostoevsky's moral and religious intensity, the compelling momentum of his narrative and his insight into extreme and disturbed states of mind have made his work highly influential in England, especially during the 20th century (much of his work was translated into English during the 1880s).

***Double-Dealer, The* (1694)**

Busy and rather bitter play by ▷ William Congreve. At its heart is the Machiavellian character of Maskwell, an arch dissembler and schemer. Setting himself up as everyone's friend and ally, he contrives to deceive and entrap each character in his single-minded plot to indulge his own lust and greed. His aim is to displace his supposed friend Mellefont, both in the fortune Mellefont is due to inherit from his uncle and aunt, Lord and Lady Touchwood, and in the hand of Cynthia as his wife. The means by which he almost succeeds are shown with infinite skill, as he manipulates other gullible and fallible characters, and situations, with breathtaking credibility. He seduces and then uses Lady Touchwood, and exploits the unhappiness of two other couples. A recurring feature is the ease with which the wives manage to allay their husbands' suspicions of their cuckoldry. Only two characters emerge from this comparatively unstained: Cynthia, and Mellefont – but even he is tainted (as Congreve points out in the preface) by his blind and stubborn adherence to Maskwell. The play's seamy and unpleasant atmosphere is mitigated by scenes of high comedy. It recalls, to some extent, ▷ William Wycherley's ▷ *The Plain Dealer*, and looks forward to ▷ Oliver Goldsmith's *The Good-Natur'd Man*.

Doubting Castle

In Part I of ▷ John Bunyan's ▷ *Pilgrim's Progress*, the castle belonging to the Giant Despair, where Christian and Hopeful lie prisoners. In Part II the Castle is destroyed by the champion Greatheart.

Douglas, Black

The Douglases were a family of the Scottish medieval border nobility, constantly at war with the English ▷ Percy family on the south side of the border. Two famous Douglases bore the epithet 'Black': James Douglas (?1286–1330), supporter of Robert the Bruce in the Scottish War of Independence, and eventually killed fighting the Moors in Spain; Archibald Douglas (also called 'the Grim'), another famous warrior, who lived later in the 14th century.

▷ *Chevy Chase, The Ballad of; Otterbourne, The Battle of.*

Douglas, Gavin (?1475–1522)

Scottish poet and Bishop of Dunkeld. Unlike many of his contemporaries, he wrote only in the vernacular, and is most famous for his translation of ▷ Virgil's ▷ *Aeneid, Aeneados*, printed in 1533, which seems to have been used by the ▷ Earl of Surrey. His allegorical poem, the *Palice of Honor* (1501), was influenced by ▷ Chaucer's *House of Fame*. Douglas, who was heavily involved in ecclesiastical and secular politics, died in exile in England.

Bib: Small, J. (ed.), *Works*; Bawcutt, P., *Gavin Douglas: A Critical Study*.

Douglas, Keith (1920–44)

Poet. Keith Douglas was born in Kent, and educated at Oxford University under the tutorship of poet ▷ Edward Blunden, before enlisting with the British Army when World War II broke out. He is the most famous English poet of that war, although he began publishing his work at the age of 16. His verse is precise, unsentimental and at times chilling, in its treatment of desire and sexuality as well as in its pervasive obsession with death and the relation of death to writing. Douglas was killed in Normandy, having also written about his involvement in the war in North Africa, his slim but intensely powerful corpus concluded at an early age. His work began to receive the acclaim it deserves only when ▷ Ted Hughes, a great admirer, edited and introduced a collection in 1964 (*Selected Poems*). See also the more recent *Complete Poems* (ed. Desmond Graham; 1978).

'Dover Beach'
A poem of religious doubt and despair by ▷ Matthew Arnold, published in *New Poems* (1867), and probably the best known of all his works. It contains the line 'Ah, love, let us be true to one another', and is a classic statement of the transitory nature of religious faith to which the speaker opposes love and faithfulness.

Dowden, Edward (1894–1913)
Critic and scholar born in Cork and educated at Queen's College and Trinity College, Dublin where he was appointed Professor of English Studies in 1867. He is distinguished for his work on Shakespeare, editing twelve plays for the original Arden edition and writing *Shakspeare: A Critical Study of His Mind and Art* (1875), which was the first book in English to attempt a study of Shakespeare's development as a dramatist, although he sentimentalized his poetry. He also wrote *A Shakspeare Primer* (1877), a study of the poet Southey (1879) and biographies of Shelley (1886) and ▷ Browning (1905). He was also one of the earliest admirers of Walt Whitman, and his own *Poems* appeared in 1876.
▷ Irish Literature in English.

Dowland, John (1563–1626)
Composer and lutenist. Refused the post of court lutenist by ▷ Elizabeth I, Dowland travelled on the continent from 1594 to 1606, becoming famous throughout Europe as a composer for the lute. He was finally given the post of court lutenist by ▷ James I, but does not appear to have composed any work of note after this overdue royal recognition. He wrote three books of *Songs or Ayres* (1597, 1600 and 1603) while abroad, from which several songs are still known today.
Bib: Poulton, D., *John Dowland*.

Dowriche, Anne
Poet. Anne Edgecombe was married to Hugh Dowriche, the rector of Honiton, and in 1589 published her major work, *The French Historie, A Lamentable Discourse of Three of the Chiefe and Most Famous Bloodie Broiles That Have Happened in France for the Gospell Of Jesus Christ*, which recounts the suffering of the Protestant martyrs in France in a manner similar to that of ▷ John Foxe's *Acts and Monuments* (1563). The poem is written in ▷ alexandrines and includes many long heroic speeches by the major characters.
▷ Protestantism.

Dowson, Ernest (Christopher) (1867–1900)
Poet, born in Kent and one of the most talented of the circle of late 1890's English poets known as the ▷ Decadents. He was an active member of the ▷ Rhymers' Club (1891–4), which included W.B. Yeats (1865–1939), ▷ Arthur Symons (1865–1943), Richard Le Gallienne (1866–1947), Lionel Johnson (1867–1902), ▷ Aubrey Beardsley and occasionally ▷ Oscar Wilde. He contributed poems to the ▷ *Yellow Book* and the *Savoy*. He left Queen's College, Cambridge without a degree, due to a decline in his family's fortunes and worked at his father's dock. His literary idols were Edgar Allan Poe, ▷ Baudelaire, Verlaine (1844–96) and ▷ Swinburne and in 1891 he met the twelve-year-old Adelaide Foltinowicz, who became the inspiration for much of his poetry and a symbol of love and innocence which counteracted his world-weariness, despite her refusal of his offer of marriage. In the same year he converted to Roman ▷ Catholicism and published his best-known poem 'Non Sum Qualis Eram Bonae sub Regno Cynarae', remembered for its refrain 'I have been true to you Cynara, in my fashion'. After the deaths of his parents in 1894 he discovered symptoms of his own tuberculosis. Adelaide married a waiter in her father's restaurant and Dowson moved to France where he was discovered wretched, penniless and addicted to absinthe by his friend R.H. Sherard, in whose house he died. The poet of ennui and idealized love, his verse first achieved attention in *Poems* (1896). *Decorations*, which included experimental prose poems, followed in 1899. Dowson's output, as were his themes, was limited, but his poems are remarkable for their lyricism and cadence and he had a significant influence on Yeats and Rupert Brooke (1887–1915). Dowson also published two novels in collaboration with Arthur Moore – *A Comedy of Masks* (1893) and *Adrian Rome* (1899) – and a one-act verse play, *The Pierrot of the Minute* (1897). His *Letters* were published in 1967.
Bib: Davidson, D., *British Poetry of the 1890s*.

Doyle, Sir Arthur Conan (1859–1930)
Novelist; chiefly noted for his series of stories and novels about the amateur detective, Sherlock Holmes, a genius in minute deduction and acute observations. His friend, Dr Watson, is represented as the ordinary, ingenuous man, who needs to have everything pointed out to him and explained; and this offsets the ingenuity of the detective. The combination of acute detective and obtuse colleague has been imitated in many detective stories ever since.

The stories include: *A Study in Scarlet* (1887); *The Adventures of Sherlock Holmes* (1891); *The Memoirs of Sherlock Holmes* (1893); *The Hound of the Baskervilles* (1902); *The Return of Sherlock Holmes* (1905). Conan Doyle also wrote historical novels of merit; eg *Micah Clarke* (1888), *The White Company* (1891), and *Rodney Stone* (1896).

▷ Detective fiction; Historical novel.

Bib: Lamond, J., *Conan Doyle: a Memoir*; Conan Doyle, A., *The True Conan Doyle*; Carr, J.D., *The Life of Conan Doyle*; Roberts, S.C., *Holmes and Watson*; Pearsall, R; *Conan Doyle: A Biographical Solution*.

Doyle, Roddy (b 1958)

Irish novelist and dramatist, who teaches English and Geography in a North Dublin school. He is best known for his *Barrytown Trilogy*, affectionate and comic portraits of the struggles, joys and frustrations of working-class Dublin life, focusing on the Rabitte family: *The Commitments* (1987), about the formation of a Dublin soul band, was filmed by Alan Parker; *The Snapper* (1990), about an initially unwanted but eventually welcomed baby, was filmed by Stephen Frears; *The Van* (1991) is the story of two friends who run a fish-and-chip van after they are made redundant. Doyle makes rich use of the nuances of the local idiom and writes extensive dialogue. *Paddy Clarke Ha Ha Ha* (1993) won the Booker Prize. Plays: *Brownbread* (1987); *War* (1989).

Drabble, Margaret (b 1939)

Novelist and short-story writer. Born in Sheffield and educated at Cambridge University. The novelist ▷ A.S. Byatt is her sister. She achieved considerable popular success with her novels of the 1960s, which dealt with the personal dilemmas of intelligent and educated heroines. In *The Millstone* (1965) Rosamund struggles for independence, and achieves relative stability and a sense of moral responsibility through her love for her baby daughter, the result of a casual liaison. Drabble's later novels broaden their scope, subsuming feminist issues in a general concern for equality and justice, and addressing wider national and international issues. *The Needle's Eye* (1972) established her as a major writer by the moral intensity of its concern with social justice. *The Ice Age* (1977) is a sombre picture of the corrupt and sterile condition of Britain in the mid-1970s. Drabble sees herself as a social historian, and admires the novelist ▷ Arnold Bennett, a biography of whom she published in 1974. The literary allusion which has been a feature of all her work becomes more marked in the 1970s, and her narrative techniques become more adventurous, as in the three points of view, alterations of style and self-conscious authorial voice of *The Realms of Gold* (1975). Her other novels are: *A Summer Bird-Cage* (1962); *The Garrick Year* (1964); *Jerusalem the Golden* (1967); *The Waterfall* (1969); *The Middle Ground* (1980); *The Radiant Way* (1987); *A Natural Curiosity* and *Gates of Ivory* (1991). Story collections: *Penguin Modern Stories 3* (with others) (1969); *Hassam's Tower* (1980). She also edited *The Oxford Companion to English Literature* (1985).

Bib: Creighton, J. V., *Margaret Drabble*.

***Dracula* (1897)**

A novel by ▷ Bram Stoker which has become, like Mary Shelley's *Frankenstein* (1818), a modern myth. The story opens with the diary of Jonathon Harker, who falls victim to Count Dracula whilst acting as his solicitor. Dracula then travels to Whitby where the story is resumed in letter form by Harker's fiancée, Mina Murray, who witnesses her friend Lucy Westenra fall under Dracula's spell. A stake through the heart restores Lucy to peace and Dracula is thwarted in his pursuit of Mina and finally destroyed. Elaine Showalter reads the novel as a 'decadent fantasy of reproduction through transfusion', with strong hints of homoeroticism, and as an attack on the sexual daring of the ▷ 'New Woman'.

▷ Horror fiction.

Bib: Showalter, E., *Sexual Anarchy: Gender and Culture at the Fin de Siècle*.

Drake, Sir Francis (?1549–96)

Built up at the end of the 19th and early 20th century as a national hero for his seafaring exploits. He engaged in numerous voyages in which he successfully raided Spain and her American colonies, and circumnavigated the world in his ship the *Golden Hind*, 1577–81. He was one of the commanders of the English fleet against the ▷ Armada during the attempted Spanish invasion of 1588.

Bib: Williams, N., *Francis Drake*.

Dramatic Irony

Dramatic irony occurs when a character in a play makes a statement in innocent assurance of its truth, while the audience is well aware that he or she is deceived.

Dramatic monologue

A poetic form in which the poet invents a character, or, more commonly, uses one from history or legend, and reflects on life from the character's standpoint. The dramatic monologue is a development from the ▷ conversation poem of ▷ Coleridge and ▷ Wordsworth, in which the poet reflects on life in his own person.

▷ Tennyson was the first to use the form, *eg* ▷ *The Lotos-Eaters* (1833), *Ulysses* (1842) and *Tithonus* (pub. 1860). In these poems, he takes the standpoint of characters in Greek myth and causes them to express emotions relevant to their predicaments. The emotions, however, are really more relevant to those of Tennyson's own age, but the disguise enables him to express himself without inhibition, and particularly without involving himself in the responsibility of having to defend the attitudes that he is expressing. His most ambitious poem in this form is the monodrama ▷ *Maud* (1855).

However it was ▷ Robert Browning who used the form most profusely, and with whom it is most associated, *eg My Last Duchess* (1845); *Fra Lippo Lippi, Andrea del Sarto, The Bishop Orders His Tomb, Bishop Blougram's Apology*, all in ▷ *Men and Women* (1855); *Mr Sludge the Medium* in ▷ *Dramatis Personae* (1864); and *The Ring and the Book* (1869). Browning used it differently from Tennyson: his characters are more detached from his own personality; the poems are attempts to explore a wide variety of attitudes to art and life. His monologues have little to do with drama, though superficially they resemble soliloquies in plays of the age of Shakespeare. They have an even closer resemblance, though still a rather superficial one, to the medieval convention of public confession by characters such as the Wife of Bath and the Pardoner in ▷ Chaucer's ▷ *Canterbury Tales*. Most of all, however, they emulate the exploration of character and society in the novel of Browning's own day, and his *The Ring and the Book* is really an experiment in the novel; the tale unfolds through monologues by the various participators in and spectators of the events. Still another use for the dramatic monologue is that to which ▷ Arthur Clough puts it in his poem *Dipsychus* (*Divided Mind*, 1850). This poem is in the form of a dialogue, but it is a dialogue between the two parts of a man's mind: that which tries to sustain moral principle, and that which is sceptical of principle, seeking only pleasure and material well-being.

A more searching irony was brought to the dramatic monologue by ▷ T. S. Eliot in *The Love Song of J. Alfred Prufrock* (1915) and *Gerontion* (1920). Since the 1930s a range of different developments have tended to make the dramatic monologue seem either false or outdated. The emphasis on authenticity of voice in poetry of the 1950s and 1960s, and the current tendency to foreground the author's ethnic origins in the language used (as in 'dub' poetry), have little use for a form to which indirectness is so intrinsic. However, the dramatic monologue has certain affinities with first-person ▷ narration and ▷ stream of consciousness in the novel.

***Dramatic Studies* (1866)**

The first collection of poetry by ▷ Augusta Webster, including the much-admired poem 'Snow-waste'. The ▷ dramatic monologues of the collection show the influence of ▷ Robert Browning, but Webster's subjects tend to be related specifically to women's experience, as in 'By The Looking Glass', a poem about spinsterhood. The ▷ realism and directness of the verse disturbed some Victorian critics.

***Dramatis Personae* (1864)**

A collection of poems by ▷ Robert Browning, including a number of his more famous ones: 'Abt Vogler', 'Rabbi Ben Ezra', 'A Death in the Desert', 'Caliban upon Setebos', 'Mr Sludge the Medium'.

***Drapier's Letters* (1724)**

A series of pamphlets by ▷ Jonathan Swift against a monopoly to issue copper coins in Ireland, granted by the English Government to the Duchess of Kendal (▷ George I's mistress) and sold by her to William Wood ('Wood's halfpence'). The Irish considered that the monopoly would be economically harmful to them. Swift wrote in their support in the semblance of a Dublin 'drapier' (= draper), *ie* an ordinary shopman. The pamphlets are an example of his apparently moderate, plain style carrying an immense force of irony; they were so effective that the Government had to withdraw the monopoly.

Drayton, Michael (1563–1631)

Poet. Little is known of the life of this prolific writer, whose works encompassed a wide range of ▷ genres and subject matter. His collection of ▷ sonnets, gathered under the title *Idea's Mirror*, first appeared in 1594, and consists of 51 sonnets, mainly in the ▷ Petrarchan mode. The sequence was continuously revised, with additions appearing in the editions of 1602, 1605 and the final version of 1619.

Apart from sonnets, however, Drayton wrote ▷ eclogues indebted to ▷ Edmund Spenser, ▷ Ovidian verses and historical poetry. Of his historical poetry, *Piers Gaveston* (1593, revised in 1596) is remarkable for its combination of the Ovidian and the homoerotic. In 1596, Drayton published the first version of a historical narrative – *Mortimeriados* – an ambitious account, in verse, of the events which ▷ Christopher Marlowe was to dramatize in his play *Edward II*.

In common with Spenser and ▷ Samuel Daniel, Drayton was alert to the importance of celebrating the idea of the nation-state. Drayton's contribution to this late Elizabethan project was the topographical verse description of England, *Poly-Olbion* (Part I, 1612; Part II, 1622). *Poly-Olbion* sets out to celebrate, in ▷ alexandrine verse, not only the geographical features of England, but the customs and histories of all the counties of the kingdom. It was an ambitious project which was never to reach completion. But *Poly-Olbion* was only one part of Drayton's desire to celebrate English history. Another aspect of his historiographical enterprise is revealed in the publication, in 1606, of his *Poems*

Lyric and Pastoral. The collection contains two verse accounts on themes of considerable national importance – a version of ▷ Richard Hakluyt's 'First Voyage to Virginia', and an account of the battle of Agincourt based mainly on ▷ Raphael Holinshed's *Chronicles*. The creation of a national past and the formation of a national identity can thus be seen as merging in the work of this writer.

▷ Histories and Chronicles.

Bib: Hebel, J. W., Tillotson, K. and Newdigate, B. H. (eds.), *Complete Works* (4 vols.); Brink, J. R., *Michael Drayton Revisited*; Hardin, R. F., *Drayton and the Passing of Elizabethan England*.

Dream of John Ball, A (1888)

A story by ▷ William Morris serialized in *The Commonweal*, 1886–7, in which the protagonist describes a dream in which he is transported back to Kent during the peasant's revolt of 1381. John Ball, a dissenting priest, inspires the peasants to victory and later discusses their hopes and plans for change with Morris. Morris describes the 19th century and the Industrial Revolution, whereupon John Ball realizes he is, in fact, dreaming of the future. *A Dream of John Ball* anticipates Morris' *News From Nowhere* (1890) in its use of the dream motif to link past, present and future.

Dream of the Rood

A highly sophisticated ▷ Old English ▷ dream-vision poem which relates the dreamer's encounter with a speaking Cross. The Cross recounts its experience of the Crucifixion, its subsequent burial and its resurrection as a Christian symbol. The poem is preserved only in an 11th-century copy but the material seems to have originated much earlier. The 8th-century preaching cross, the Ruthwell Cross preserved in Dumfriesshire has an inscription which closely resembles parts of the Cross's speech in the *Dream of the Rood*.

▷ Old English literature.

Bib: Swanton, M. (ed.), *The Dream of the Rood*.

Dream-vision poetry

An important medieval narrative form. What is distinctive about the category of medieval dream-vision poetry is not that a dream sequence is included in the narrative but that a dream sequence offers the framework for a narrative which is presented as the reported experience of the narrator/dreamer. The traditions behind medieval dream-vision poetry are as diverse as the literary dream-experiences themselves: dream-vision poetry is a distinctive, but not homogeneous, literary category. There are numerous classical and biblical precedents for the use of dreams and visions as the mediums for philosophical and/or spiritual truths, but as developed by medieval vernacular poets from the 13th century onwards, the dream-vision form appears to have offered the opportunity for self-conscious literary creation in the guise of unconscious experience. The Old French poem, the ▷ *Roman de la Rose*, provided an especially influential paradigm for later vernacular writers.

The speculative licence of dream-vision poetry is used by medieval writers in many different ways. The frequent appearance of personifications within dream-vision poetry indicates the analytical interest of many of the texts in otherwise hidden processes. Sometimes dream-vision poems investigate the workings of the individual psyche, especially the inner experience of sacred and profane kinds of love (such as in ▷ Chaucer's ▷ *Book of the Duchess*, or the ▷ Gawain poet's ▷ *Pearl*); sometimes the form is used to examine the veiled workings of contemporary society itself and the dream experience becomes the occasion for social satire. In ▷ William Langland's complex visionary narrative, ▷ *Piers Plowman*, the sequence of dream visions (including the experience of dreams within dreams) is the occasion for a highly challenging enquiry into the interaction of inner and outer worlds, personal and public history, in Christian society. A number of Middle English ▷ alliterative narratives, dating from the 14th century, use the dream-vision form for literary debates about issues of personal/public ethics (such as ▷ *Winner and Waster, Death and Life*, the ▷ *Parlement of the Three Ages*). Chaucer's dream-vision poems are especially bookish in their orientation: in the *Book of the Duchess*, the ▷ *House of Fame* and the ▷ *Parliament of Foulys*, the activity of reading a book prompts the narrators' dreams. Vernacular writers from the 15th and early 16th centuries (such as ▷ Robert Henryson, ▷ William Dunbar, ▷ John Skelton) continue to employ the dream-vision mode in their works, but the dream-vision form is less frequently used as the frame for a large-scale narrative thereafter, perhaps because fictional activity no longer required a framing justification.

Bib: Spearing, A. C., *Medieval Dream Poetry*.

Druids

The wise and holy men of the ancient Celts in Gaul, ancient Britain, and Ireland. We know about them from Roman writers (*eg* Julius Caesar in *De Bello Gallico*) and from Welsh and Irish myth. They held the oak and the mistletoe as sacred, worshipped in oak groves, and believed in the survival of the soul and its transmigration after death into other bodies. There seems to be some doubt as to whether they ever flourished in southern Britain, where in any case they were eliminated by the Roman conquest in the 1st century AD, but they were important in Ireland and in ▷ Scotland, and the early Welsh ▷ bards, or sacred poets, called themselves druids. Caesar does not mention bards but ascribes to the druids a bardic, or sacred, poetic function. In the 18th and 19th centuries a cult of the druids grew up in England, attributing to them mysterious knowledge and wisdom.

Drummond, William, of Hawthornden (1585–1649)
Scottish poet. Drummond's first publication was a eulogy on the death of Prince Henry, the eldest son of ▷ James I of England, published in 1613. A volume of poems was published in 1614, and then withdrawn, revised, and republished as *Poems: Amorous, Funeral, Divine, Pastoral, in Sonnets, Songs, Sextains, Madrigals*, whose title indicates the range of Drummond's interests. A large proportion of the verses contained in the 1616 collection are paraphrases and translations of continental writers. Other volumes of verse followed, including a celebration of the visit of James I to Edinburgh in 1618. Perhaps Drummond's most famous work is not poetic, however, but is instead his record of a series of remarkable conversations with Ben Jonson, who visited Drummond in 1618. Drummond was careful to keep a record of Jonson's conversation, though much of what was said is the product (one supposes) of a good deal of drink rather than critical insight. Nevertheless, *Conversations with Drummond of Hawthornden*, first published in 1711, does suggest something of Jonson's wit.
Bib: MacDonald, R. H. (ed.), *Poems and Prose of William Drummond of Hawthornden*.

Drury Lane Theatres
The first was an old riding school in Bridges Street, converted by ▷ Thomas Killigrew to form the original Theatre Royal, Drury Lane, also known as the King's Theatre.

In 1682 the ▷ King's Company was absorbed by the ▷ Duke's, and the resulting ▷ United Company continued to stage plays at Drury Lane, and the larger spectacles and operas at ▷ Dorset Garden. After a difficult period under ▷ Christopher Rich, the theatre prospered with ▷ Colley Cibber, ▷ Robert Wilks, Thomas Doggett (c1670–1721), and various other managers jointly in charge, and then again under ▷ David Garrick, who took over in 1747.

In 1776 upon Garrick's retirement, Drury Lane was taken over by ▷ Richard Brinsley Sheridan, who continued to run it until its destruction by fire in 1809. The present theatre opened in 1812.

▷ Theatres.

Dryden, John (1631–1700)
Poet, critic, dramatist. By family background and personal sympathies he was on the ▷ Puritan, anti-monarchical side during the Protectorate, and in an early poem, *Heroique Stanzas* (1659) he eulogized ▷ Oliver Cromwell, who had died in 1658. However, like many others, he welcomed the Restoration, composing *Astræa Redux* (1660) and *Panegyric* (1661) to welcome the king's return. With the ▷ Earl of Rochester he dominated English letters in the reign of ▷ Charles II, being appointed ▷ Poet Laureate in 1668 and Historiographer Royal in 1670. On the accession of ▷ James II in 1685 Dryden became a ▷ Catholic, and refusing to abandon his new faith after 1688, he was stripped of the Laureateship and other royal appointments.

It was in the theatre that Dryden enjoyed the greatest financial success, and between 1663 and 1681 he wrote almost a play a year. His best dramatic work, ▷ *All for Love* (1677), is an entirely new version of ▷ Shakespeare's *Antony and Cleopatra*. *The Indian Empress* (1667), *The Conquest of Granada* (1669–70), and ▷ *Aureng-Zebe* (1675) are heroic dramas on the grand model of the French dramatist ▷ Corneille. He also wrote comedies such as ▷ *Marriage à la Mode* (1673).

Dryden's first poetic works, such as his brilliant *Upon the death of the Lord Hastings* (1649), belong to the overblown decadence of 'metaphysical' wit. ▷ *Annus Mirabilis* (1667) looks at the events of 1666, including sea engagements with the Dutch and the ▷ Great Fire. It maintains a ▷ baroque elaboration of imagery, but presented in a new public, ▷ Augustan manner. His greatest works are political ▷ satires in ▷ heroic ▷ couplets, a form which his example secured in pre-eminence for several decades after his death. ▷ *Absalom and Achitophel* (1681–2) shows an ironic assurance of tone, a novelist's eye for telling characterization, a complex layering of imagery, and a virtuoso flair for fast-running narrative. Occasionally his satire is biting and cruel, as in the passage on ▷ Shaftesbury (Achitophel). Elsewhere there is good-humoured 'raillery' in the portrait of the ▷ Duke of Buckingham (Zimri) ('A man so various, that he seem'd to be / Not one, but all Mankind's Epitome'), and broad farce in the passage on Settle and ▷ Thomas Shadwell in Part II.

▷ *The Medall* (1682) continued the attack on the first Earl of Shaftesbury, while ▷ *MacFlecknoe* (1682) shows Dryden in a more relaxed, uninhibited mood, again attacking Shadwell (the man who was to succeed him as laureate) in a burlesque lampoon which is purely, even at times surrealistically, comic. The two long didactic poems ▷ *Religio Laici* (1682) and ▷ *The Hind and the Panther* (1687), on the religious question which at the time divided his sympathy, contain fine passages, but their didactic mode makes them difficult to admire today. Similarly the rhetoric of his Pindaric odes (*eg Alexander's Feast*, 1697) tends to be regarded now as artificial. Despite its public and impersonal cast, Dryden's poetry can on occasion be deeply moving, as in the elegy on his friend ▷ John Oldham. His last poetic work, *Fables Ancient and Modern* (1699), is a series of translations from ▷ Homer, ▷ Ovid, ▷ Boccaccio and Chaucer.

Dryden has been called 'the Father of English prose'. He set his own stamp on the new informal, persuasive style, which under the new constitutional system, replaced the ornamental court prose of the absolutist ▷ Tudors and early ▷ Stuarts. He also produced the first extended works of literary theory in the language. *A Discourse concerning the Original and Progress of Satire* relates the different classical styles of satire found in ▷ Juvenal and ▷ Horace to modern English writing, including his own. His celebrated essay *Of Dramatic Poesy* discusses the principles of drama and judiciously compares the qualities of ▷ Ben Jonson and ▷ Shakespeare. The *Preface to the Fables* (1700) brings a very modern sense of historical perspective to the question of the development and enrichment of literary language.

Bib: Johnson, S., *Lives of the Poets*; Ward, C. E., *Life*; Eliot, T. S., *Selected Essays*; Leavis, F. R., *Revaluation*; van Doren, M., *The Poetry of Dryden*; Bredvold, L. I., *John Dryden's Intellectual Milieu*; Nichol Smith, D., *John Dryden*; Kinsley, J. and H., *Dryden: the Critical Heritage*; Wykes, D., *A Preface to Dryden*; Rogers, P., *The Augustan Vision*; Roper, A., and Swedenborg, H.T. Jr. (eds.), *Works*.

Du Bartas, Guillaume de Saluste, Sieurdu Bartas (1544–90)

Protestant poet and soldier. The major work for which Du Bartas became famous in England in the 17th century was his ▷ epic on the story of the creation entitled *La Semaine* (1578), which was followed by a continuation, *La Seconde Semaine* (1584). This enormous poem, which celebrates the first two weeks of the biblical creation of the world, was to have a considerable influence on English writers in the period, though it is now hardly read. The ▷ translation of Du Bartas' work into English became the major undertaking of Joshua Sylvester (1562/3–1618), though he was not the only English writer to attempt translations of the work. ▷ Philip Sidney is said to have produced a translation (now lost), and ▷ James I and ▷ Thomas Lodge both translated small parts of the text. In the 17th century Du Bartas' original and Sylvester's translation became inseparably associated with one another, and a considerable number of poets were to praise the work or write under its influence. 'Divine Bartas', as he became known, was praised by ▷ Edmund Spenser, ▷ Samuel Daniel, ▷ Michael Drayton and ▷ Edmund Campion. Perhaps the high point of the reputation of the work was in the influence that it had on ▷ John Milton's *Paradise Lost*. In the 18th century, however, Du Bartas' reputation underwent a decline from which it has never properly recovered.

Bib: Sylvester, J.(trans.), Snyder, S. (ed.), *The Divine Weeks and Works of Guillaume de Saluste, Sieur du Bartas* (2 vols.).

Du Bellay, Joachim (1522–60)

Together with ▷ Ronsard, one of the most prominent of the French Renaissance group known as the ▷ Pléiade. His *Deffence & Illustration de la langue francoyse* (1549) is often regarded as their manifesto. He was the nephew of Cardinal Jean du Bellay, the protector of ▷ Rabelais, and spent the years 1553–7 in Rome in the service of his uncle. It was here that he composed the sonnet collection *Les Regrets* (based on ▷ Ovid's *Tristia*) as well as *Les Antiquitez de Rome* and the *Songe* of which ▷ Spenser's versions, *Ruines of Rome* and *The Visions of Bellay*, appeared in the 1591 *Complaints*.

Bib: Keating, L. C., *Joachim du Bellay*.

Du Maurier, Daphne (1907–89)

Novelist and short-story writer. Daphne Du Maurier began publishing in 1928, and her long career spanned and mastered a wide range of ▷ genres. She was a skilled writer of psychological suspense and supernatural tales, as well as the author of the classic romantic thriller, *Rebecca* (1938), which was filmed by Alfred Hitchcock in 1940, and has run to many editions in many different languages. Hitchcock also filmed Du Maurier's famous short story 'The Birds' in 1963, and the Hitchcock connection underlines what is perhaps most remarkable about Du Maurier's work: its concern with neo-Gothic motifs and the thin line which divides psychological obsession from supernatural possibilities. Du Maurier is also interested in exploring concepts of time in her fiction, both in the sense of how history is lived in the present (one of the concerns of her Cornish historical romances) and in concepts of non-linear time, and parallel time-scales, as the framework for her psychological thrillers. This last interest is best illustrated by the 1971 story *Don't Look Now*, which, again, was filmed, this time by Nicholas Roeg in 1973. Du Maurier's success as the originator of a number of classic modern horror films is important. She is also one of Cornwall's most famous inhabitants, and four famous Cornish historical romances, *Jamaica Inn* (1936), *Frenchman's Creek* (1941); *My Cousin Rachel* (1951) and *Rebecca* itself have become key props for the Cornish tourist industry. Du Maurier's passion for her county is also evident in her non-fictional writing, particularly *Vanishing Cornwall*.

Other works include: *The Loving Spirit* (1931); *The Apple Tree* (1952); *The Breaking Point* (1959); *The Birds and Other Stories* (1963); *The House on the Strand* (1969); *Echoes from the Macabre: Selected Stories* (1976); *The Blue Lenses and Other Stories* (1970). Autobiographical

works include: *Growing Pains: The Shaping of a Writer* (1977) and *The Rebecca Notebook and Other Memories* (1980).
Bib: Light, A., 'Rebecca' in *Feminist Review*, 1984; Radcliffe, E. J., *Gothic Novels of the 20th Century: An Annotated Bibliography*.
▷ Horror fiction; Detective fiction.

Du Maurier, George (1834–96)
Graphic artist and novelist; born in Paris. His grandparents had been refugees in England from the ▷ French Revolution; his father was a naturalized British subject; his mother was English. In 1865 he joined the staff of ▷ *Punch* and became one of the best known British humorous artists, satirizing the upper classes rather in the style of ▷ William Thackeray. He wrote three novels: *Peter Ibbetson* (1891), ▷ *Trilby* (1894) and *The Martian* (posthumous, 1896). The first two were extremely popular, but their sentimentality has put them out of fashion.
Bib: Ormond, L., *George du Maurier*.

***Dubliners* (1914)**
A volume of short stories by ▷ James Joyce. Joyce later wrote: 'My intention was to write a chapter of the moral history of my country and I chose Dublin for the scene because that city seemed to me the centre of paralysis. I have tried to present it . . . under four of its aspects: childhood, adolescence, maturity and public life. The stories are arranged in this order.' He adds that he has used in them 'a style of scrupulous meanness', but, in fact, the apparent bare realism of the stories conceals subtle mimetic and symbolic effects which render the spiritual poverty and domestic tragedy of Dublin life through its characteristic colloquial idioms. The stories are based on Joyce's theory of the 'epiphanies', by which he meant that deep insights might be gained through incidents and circumstances which seem outwardly insignificant. Their effect is thus often through delicate implication, like the stories of ▷ Chekhov. However, some of them contain sharp humour, notably 'Grace', and more have very sensitive poignancy, especially the last and longest, 'The Dead'. This story, which moves from ironical satire to a highly poetic conclusion, is often regarded as a masterpiece; it was filmed in 1987 by John Huston.

***Duchess of Malfi, The* (1613)**
With ▷ *The White Devil*, one of the two famous verse tragedies by ▷ John Webster. The plot is taken from a tale by the Italian writer Matteo Bandello in an English version included in William Painter's ▷ *Palace of Pleasure*. Set in Italy, the drama concerns the vengeance taken upon the young Duchess for marrying her steward, Antonio, against the commands of her brothers, the Cardinal, and Ferdinand Duke of Calabria, who is her twin. Ferdinand employs an impoverished malcontent soldier, ▷ Bosola, as his instrument for the mental torturing of the Duchess, but Bosola has a character of his own, and is filled with remorse. The Duchess is finally strangled, but Ferdinand goes mad with horror at his own deed, and ends by killing Bosola, who had already killed the Cardinal.

Two main problems arise in assessing the drama. The first is whether the Duchess is purely a guiltless victim. She is a young widow who marries a man of lower status for love: commentators argue that contemporary opinion was against the remarrying of widows, that the Duchess offends against the principle of degree by marrying beneath her, and that her deception of her brothers offends against the principle that a just life must be led in openness. None of these arguments is likely to have force with modern audiences, and those contemporary with the play must have been chiefly impressed by the proud dignity with which the Duchess sustains her cumulative afflictions. The more important problem is that of the brothers' motives. That of the Cardinal is intelligible: he is a cold ▷ Machiavellian who resents his sister's humiliation of the family, and no doubt the fact that by her second marriage she now has heirs to her estate. But Ferdinand's prolonged sadism, and his madness after her death, seem in excess of their ostensible causes. The natural explanation is that he is incestuously in love with his sister, and insanely jealous at her marriage; this is doubted by some critics who point out that incestuous passion is nowhere explicit in the play, which was written at a time when such motives were rarely left to the audience's inference. Webster may have preferred to leave the question open, since the bond between a twin sister and brother might itself sufficiently explain Ferdinand's extravagance. Another explanation, since the play is remarkable for its strikingly effective individual scenes, might be that Webster was more interested in opportunities for dramatizing situations than in the exposition of a dominant theme. Even this reductive judgement cannot obscure the grandeur with which Webster dramatizes extreme passion and the horror of its degradation, and, in contrast, the dignity with which an individual can outface suffering.

Duck, Stephen (1705–56)
Known as the 'Thresher Poet', and often described as 'the first proletarian author'. He was discovered working as a thresher and writing in the Wiltshire countryside, brought to London, and given a salary and accommodation near Richmond by Queen Caroline; he was also assisted by ▷ Pope. He subsequently studied and became a clergyman. His *The Thresher's Labour* is one of the early poems showing the hardships of country life and labour, in contrast to the idealized pictures painted by ▷ pastoral

tradition. It was included in *Poems on Several Occasions* (1738). Later, in poems such as *On Richmond Park, and Royal Gardens*, Duck succumbed to the same idealizing tendencies as his forbears. He ended by drowning himself.

***Duenna, The* (1775)**
Comic opera by ▷ Richard Brinsley Sheridan. Don Jerome is attempting to force his daughter Louisa to marry the rich but unpleasant converted Jew, Isaac, and locks her up to await the marriage. However, she loves Don Antonio, and uses her duenna as a go-between, to carry messages. Jerome discovers the duenna's role in their affair, and dismisses her, but Louisa escapes disguised as the duenna, while the latter impersonates her mistress and receives Isaac. Meanwhile, Louisa's brother and Antonio's friend, Don Ferdinand, has fallen in love with Donna Clara, who is to be forced into a convent. She too escapes from her father, and the two young women join forces. The duenna tricks Isaac into marrying her, and into helping Louisa and Antonio to marry. Ferdinand and Clara are also united, and Jerome is reconciled to both situations. The play was successfully performed at ▷ Covent Garden.

Duessa
Character in ▷ Edmund Spenser's ▷ *The Faerie Queen*. She is described as 'clad in scarlot red' (Book I. ii. 13), which associates her with the Catholic Church, Antichrist and the Whore of Babylon, as Protestant commentaries on *Revelation* XVII. 4 make clear. She may also be identified in the poem's contemporary political ▷ allegory as ▷ Mary Queen of Scots, and was so identified by her son ▷ James VI and I.
▷ Catholicism (Roman) in English literature.

Duffy, Maureen (b 1933)
Novelist, poet and dramatist. Her autobiographical first novel, *That's How it Was* (1962) is the account of a childhood of material insecurity and social isolation illuminated by a living relationship between mother and daughter. The themes of her fiction have been the outsider, the oppressions of poverty and class, the varieties of sexual experience and the power of love to transform and redeem. Her work reflects her socialism, lesbianism and commitment to animal rights. *The Microcosm* (1966) is a study of lesbian society using various modes of narration, including pastiche and ▷ stream of consciousness; it shows the distance between sexual creativity and ordinary life imposed by society. Duffy has lived in London for most of her adult life, and celebrated that city in *Capital* (1975). She employs colloquial language, and a laconic but vivid style. Her play *Rites*, a black farce set in a ladies' public lavatory, was produced at the ▷ National Theatre in 1969. *Rites, Solo* (1970) and *Old Tyme* (1970) rework the Greek myths of the Bacchae, Narcissus and Uranus respectively in terms of modern sexual and public life. Her other plays are: *The Lay Off* (1962); *The Silk Room* (1966) and *A Nightingale in Bloomsbury Square* (1973). Other novels are: *The Single Eye* (1964); *The Paradox Players* (1967); *Wounds* (1969); *Love Child* (1971); *I Want to Go to Moscow* (1973); *Housespy* (1978); *Gor Saga* (1981); *Scarborough Fear* (as D. M. Layer, 1982); *Londoners: An Elegy* (1983); and *Change* (1987). Poetry: *Collected Poems* (1985).

***Duke of Milan, The* (1621)**
A ▷ tragedy of court intrigue, possessive jealousy and murder by ▷ Philip Massinger.

Duke's Company, The
Acting company formed by ▷ Sir William D'Avenant after the Restoration of ▷ Charles II. It performed from June 1661 at the former Lisle's Tennis Court in ▷ Lincoln's Inn Fields, which had been converted to a theatre. In November 1671 the company moved to a new playhouse at ▷ Dorset Garden, also known as the Duke's Theatre, where it remained until its union with the ▷ King's Company to form the ▷ United Company in 1682.

Duke's Theatre, The
▷ Dorset Garden Theatre.

Dunbar, William (?1460–?1520)
Scottish poet and priest. Little is known about his life. He was employed at the Scottish court, was involved in a shipwreck off Zeeland while engaged on a diplomatic mission, and was given a pension by James IV in 1500. A relatively large corpus of his poetry survives, which is notable for its wide range of subjects and tone. The 'Thrissil and the Rose', a political allegory about the marriage of James IV to Margaret Tudor, was written in 1503. 'The Dance of the Sevin Deidly Synnis', in which the narrator sees a devil call a dance of unshriven outcasts, dates from 1507. Also dating from around this time are Dunbar's more famous pieces: 'The Golden Targe' (a dream-vision love adventure); 'The Lament for Makaris' (an elegy on life's transience and the passing of great English and Scottish poets such as ▷ Chaucer, ▷ John Gower, and ▷ Robert Henryson); and 'The Tretis of the Twa Mariit Wemen and the Wedo' (a midsummer dream experience in which a male narrator overhears three spirited women revealing their histories and their desires). Dunbar's 'Flyting of Dunbar and Kennedie' is a consummate exercise in poetic abuse.
Bib: Kinsley, J. (ed.), *Poems*; Harvey Wood, H., *Two Scots Chaucerians, Robert Henryson and William Dunbar*.

***Dunciad, The* (1728–43)**
A ▷ mock-heroic ▷ satire in pentameter ▷ couplets by ▷ Alexander Pope, satirizing his

literary enemies. In the earlier three-book version, published anonymously in 1728, the hero is the scholar Lewis Theobald (spelled 'Tibbald' in the poem), whose *Shakespeare Restored* (1726) had offended Pope by pointing out mistakes and oversights in his edition of Shakespeare's works (1725). In a brilliantly appropriate stroke, which two centuries later would have been considered daringly modernist, *The Dunciad* itself is presented in a scholarly edition, complete with learned footnotes, as though it were a classic. In the notes Pope and his friends (under the pseudonym ▷ Scriblerus) discuss the knotty textual cruxes of the work, draw attention to its various poetic excellences, and heap straight-faced praise upon the solecisms of other critics and poets. In 1742 Pope issued a fourth book under the title *The New Dunciad*, and in 1743 the whole four-book version reappeared with a new hero, the popular playwright, ▷ Colley Cibber, who to much derision had been made ▷ Poet Laureate in 1730, and thus appears as ▷ Bayes.

In Book I Cibber is snatched from his benighted labours by the goddess Dulness and is crowned Laureate in succession to Laurence Eusden, who now 'sleeps among the dull of ancient days'. In Book II the new King of the Dunces presides over a modern ▷ Grub Street version of the ancient classical games, including a pissing match (to determine 'Who best can send on high/ The salient spout, far-streaming to the sky'), a patron-tickling contest, and a competition to see who can dive deepest into the open sewer of Fleet-ditch. The book ends with the company being read to sleep by the works of John Henley and ▷ Sir Richard Blackmore: 'Soft creeping words on words, the sense compose,/ At ev'ry line they stretch, they yawn, they doze.' In Book III Cibber sleeps in the lap of Dulness and has visions, in true classical style, of the future triumph of the goddess and the destruction of civilization. Book IV traces the pantomimic progress of Dulness through the realms of science and letters ('*Art* after *art* goes out, and all is Night'), and ends in biblical solemnity with a description of the restoration of the ancient Empire of Chaos. Despite its sometimes irritating plethora of topical references, the poem is a unique masterpiece. Its nervous, ironic tone merges raucous vulgarity, exquisite sensuousness, surreal fantasy, euphoric farce and sombre despair in strange and original evocative effects.

Dunn, Douglas (b 1942)
Poet. Dunn was born in Renfrewshire, Scotland, and educated in Scotland and Hull. His first volume, *Terry Street* (1969) showed him much under the influence of ▷ Philip Larkin in its documentation of everyday provincial life; his later volumes *St Kilda's Parliament* (1981) and *Elegies* (1985) show more varied subject matter, meditating on Celtic history and on his own Scottish ancestry and on the loss of loved ones. He has trained and worked as a librarian. His other poetry includes: *Backwaters* (1971); *Love or Nothing* (1974); *Barbarians* (1979); and *Selected Poems* (1986).

▷ Scottish literature in English.

Dunn, Nell (b 1936)
Playwright and novelist. Dunn started work in the early 1960s as a key player in the British 'docudrama' movement (along with other writers and directors such as Ken Loach, ▷ David Mercer and Jeremy Sandford), which was a literary marriage of investigative journalism and naturalistic fiction. Dunn's first work, a series of short stories which observe ordinary working-class life in South London, *Up the Junction* (1963), brought her great fame in Britain, as did her early 1980s feminist play, *Steaming* (1981), about a group of women who try to keep open a public baths threatened with closure, was extremely successful. Her other works include: *Poor Cow* (1967); *Talking to Women* (1965); *I Want* (with Adrian Henri); *The Only Child* (1978); and *The Little Heroine* (1988).

Duns Scotus, John (?1265–?1308)
One of the most influential medieval philosophers. He was born at the village of Duns in Scotland, studied at Oxford, and taught at Paris and Cologne. He was the chief opponent of ▷ Thomas Aquinas in the late medieval Church. He opposed Aquinas' belief in the harmony of reason and religious faith by declaring that some doctrines were incapable of proof (*eg* the immortality of the soul); he declared, in opposition to Aquinas, that the will was not necessarily subordinate to the reason; he insisted that individual objects contain a principle of reality distinct from that of the class to which each belongs. The last doctrine was of importance to the Catholic poet ▷ G.M. Hopkins in his formation of the terms 'inscape' and 'instress'. Duns Scotus' philosophy underwent much criticism in the 16th century by both the ▷ humanist scholars influenced by Plato, and the Protestant reformers. His followers, the Scotists, were regarded as the enemies of the ▷ New Learning, and in consequence a 'Dunsman' or 'Dunce' became eventually, in common speech, synonymous with a stupid person, impervious to education.

Duration
One of the five categories in which ▷ Genette analyses narrative discourse, duration is concerned with the relationship between how long a fictional event would notionally last and how much of the text is devoted to telling of it (*eg* in Virginia Woolf's ▷ *To the Lighthouse*, the long first section of the novel tells the events of one day; the shorter second section tells the events of ten years). Duration, ▷ order

and ▷ frequency are matters of temporal arrangement or 'tense'; the other two categories are ▷ mood and ▷ voice.

D'Urfey (Durfey), Thomas (1653–1723)
Dramatist and song-writer, born in Devon, he probably trained originally for the law. He became a close friend of ▷ Charles II, who liked to hum his songs. He often stayed with the Earl of Dorset at Knowle, where there is a portrait of him painted in his sleep, according to one anecdote, for he hated the idea of being portrayed. He wrote 33 plays, including tragedies, comedies and opera, but is best remembered for his comedies, including *Madam Fickle* (1676), and *A Fond Husband* (1677), both comedies of intrigue, and political satires such as *The Royalist* (1682), and *Sir Barnaby Whigg* (1682). *Love for Money* (1691), and *The Richmond Heiress* (1693) both show tendencies toward ▷ Reform comedy. He also adapted a number of earlier works, including ▷ Shakespeare's *Cymbeline*, renamed *The Island Princess* (1682). Some of his plays' perceived bawdiness made him a target for attack by ▷ Jeremy Collier. His own and other ballads were published together in six volumes, under the title of *Wit and Mirth, or Pills to Purge Melancholy* (1720–21).

Durrell, Lawrence (1912–90)
Novelist and poet. He began writing before the war, and published an experimental novel, *The Black Book* (1938) in France which was partly the result of his fruitful and life-long friendship with American novelist Henry Miller. His present high international reputation is based in particular on the sequence *The Alexandria Quartet* comprising *Justine* (1957); *Balthazar* (1958); *Mountolive* (1958) and *Clea* (1960). *The Alexandria Quartet* has achieved fame partly through its lavishly exotic appeal, and partly through Durrell's experimental technique: a wide range of narrative forms are employed, and the same events are seen, and interpreted quite differently, by the different characters participating in them. *Tunc* (1968) and *Nunquam* (1970) together form *The Revolt of Aphrodite*, which explores the destruction of love and creativity by social pressures, embodied in the 'Firm', a vast and dehumanizing multinational enterprise. Durrell followed up the success of *The Alexandria Quartet* with a five-volume novel, *The Avignon Quincunx*, which also used exotic settings and multiple narratives, and, combining elements of myth with philosophical speculation, satirized the values of western society. It is made up of the following volumes: *Monsieur; or, The Prince of Darkness* (1974); *Livia; or, Buried Alive* (1978); *Constance; or Solitary Practices* (1982); *Sebastian; or, Ruling Passions* (1983); *Quinx; or, The Ripper's Tale* (1985).

As the titles of his two major sequences suggest, the spirit of particular places was always of importance to Durrell; he said that in *The Alexandria Quartet* he 'tried to see people as a function of place'. He published many volumes of travel writing, particularly about the islands of the Mediterranean, including: *Prospero's Cell* (about Corcyra; 1945); *Reflections on a Marine Venus* (about Rhodes; 1953); *Bitter Lemons* (about Cyprus; 1957); *The Greek Islands* (1978). Durrell also published collections of short stories, including: *Sauve Qui Peut* (1966); *The Best of Antrobus* (1974); *Antrobus Complete* (1985); a number of plays, including: *Sappho* (1959); *Acto* (1961); *An Irish Faustus* (1963) and many volumes of poetry: *Collected Poems* (1960; revised 1968) and *Collected Poems 1931–74* (1980). But his greatest achievement was to express the indeterminate and multi-faceted nature of experience through the techniques of experimental fiction.
Bib: Fraser, G. S., *Lawrence Durrell: A Critical Study*; Friedman, A. W., *Lawrence Durrell and The Alexandria Quartet.*

***Dutch Courtesan, The* (1605)**
A punitive satirical comedy by ▷ John Marston about deceit and youthful recklessness, in which the central character, Malheureux, has his values tested when he falls in love with a prostitute. Like ▷ Shakespeare's Angelo in ▷ *Measure for Measure* he is saved only at the gallows, but Marston's tone is more comic than Shakespeare's.

Dyer, John (?1700–58)
Poet and painter. Born in Carmarthenshire, Dyer studied painting under Jonathan Richardson and visited Italy in 1724–5. In 1741 he entered the Church. His most important work, *Grongar Hill* (1727), is a topographical landscape poem in the tradition of ▷ Sir John Denham's *Cooper's Hill* and ▷ Alexander Pope's ▷ *Windsor-Forest*, but its fluent use of tetrameter rather than pentameter (▷ metre) ▷ couplets gives it a lyrical *élan* all of its own. Moreover, Dyer's painterly eye leads him to focus, in a most original way, on the transient visual effects which succeed each other as he climbs up from the valley of the Towy. Dyer's feeling for the ▷ picturesque, rooted in his study of the paintings of Claude and Poussin, was influential on later poetry until well into the Romantic (▷ Romanticism) period. In 1740 appeared *The Ruins of Rome*, and in 1757, *The Fleece*, long discursive and didactic (▷ Didactic literature) poems in Miltonic (▷ Milton) ▷ blank verse. The second emulates the example of ▷ John Philips' *Cyder*, in its celebration of British scenery and British industry. It attempts to encompass all aspects of the wool trade, from the techniques of sheep-farming, modern and ancient, to the growing prosperity of Leeds and Sheffield and the growth of trade which promises to distribute British

woollen manufactures 'over the whole globe'.
Bib: Humphrey, B., *John Dyer*.

Dystopia
▷ Utopian fiction.

E

Eagleton, Terry (b. 1943)
The foremost ▷ Marxist critic writing in Britain today. Until recently Eagleton was a Fellow at Wadham College, Oxford, and he has for some time been a leading force in Marxism's encounter with a range of intellectual movements from Structuralism onwards. His book *Criticism and Ideology* (1976) laid the foundation for the introduction into British literary criticism of the work of the French critic Pierre Macherey, and is a clear development of ▷ Louis Althusser's understanding of culture. In later works, such as *Walter Benjamin or Towards a Revolutionary Criticism* (1981), *The Rape of Clarissa* (1982), *The Function of Criticism* (1984), and *William Shakespeare* (1986), he has sought to develop a sophisticated ▷ materialist criticism which is prepared to engage with, but which refuses to be overawed by, Post-structuralism.

Earle, John
▷ Characters, Theophrastian.

***Earthly Paradise, The* (1868–70)**
A poem by ▷ William Morris published in three volumes, consisting of twenty-four tales written in verse with a prologue and a linking narrative, and describing a medieval ▷ Utopia which offers an alternative to the industrial society of the mid-19th century. One of the verse tales, *Atalanta's Race*, tells the story of the legendary Atalanta, a beautiful girl famed for her speed. To win her, suitors had to beat her in a race or else be killed by her dart. She was eventually beaten by Milanion, who distracted her by throwing down three golden apples. Atalanta is also celebrated by ▷ Swinburne in ▷ *Atalanta in Calydon*. The poem proved popular with the Victorian public and helped establish Morris as one of the leading poets of the day.
▷ Pre-Raphaelite Brotherhood; medievalism.

East India Company
The best known of the Charter Companies, given a monopoly of eastern trade by Queen ▷ Elizabeth in 1600. Competition with the Dutch in the East Indian islands turned its attention to the Indian mainland, where in the 18th century its extensive commercial influence developed into political power. To protect its Chinese trade, it gained control of the Burmese and Malayan coasts down to Singapore, which it founded in 1819. After the Indian Mutiny of 1857 it was taken over by the British government, which had shared its rule in India since ▷ Pitt (the Younger)'s Indian Act of 1784. It was familiarly known as John Company and its ships as East Indiamen.
▷ Companies, joint-stock.

***East Lynne* (1861)**
A novel of ▷ sensation by ▷ Mrs Henry Wood. Lady Isabel Vane mistakenly believes her husband to be having an affair, and runs away with rakish Frank Levison. Her fate as a ▷ 'fallen woman' is one of the most appalling in Victorian literature. She has a child, is deserted, crippled in a train crash and reported dead, then returns home in disguise to become ▷ governess to her own children. In the meantime, her husband has married the woman Isabel believed he was involved with. Her final punishment is having to watch her son die without revealing her identity to him. The book was favourably reviewed in *The Times*, sold over 2.5 million copies by 1900, was translated into several languages and adapted into a stage melodrama. Conventional Victorian values towards ▷ marriage and the family are forcibly driven home, and Wood displays an almost sadistic relish in her punitive treatment of Isabel.
▷ *Cometh Up as a Flower*.

***Eastward Hoe* (1605)**
A ▷ citizen comedy about London apprentices and craftsmen written collaboratively by ▷ George Chapman, ▷ Ben Jonson and ▷ John Marston. Modern interest in this play stems not primarily from its undeniable imaginative vitality so much as from its foolhardy satire of the Scots in Act III, which led to the imprisoning and facial disfigurement (ears and noses cut) of Jonson and Chapman – Marston had decamped. The play is one of several works of the period such as ▷ Thomas Middleton's ▷ *A Game At Chess* and ▷ John Day's *Isle of Gulls* to challenge or parody the volatile contemporary political order through the theatre.

Eclecticism
In ancient Greece, a term for the kind of philosophy that did not follow any one school of thought (*eg* Platonism) but selected its doctrines from a number of schools. The term is now applied to thinkers, artists and writers who follow this principle in the formation of their thought or artistic methods.

Eclogue
A short pastoral dialogue, usually in verse. The most famous example is the *Bucolics* of the Latin poet ▷ Virgil. The word is often used as an equivalent for ▷ idyll, or a ▷ pastoral poem without dialogue. One of the most famous examples of a Renaissance poem written in the tradition of Virgilian eclogues is ▷ Spenser's ▷ *The Shepherd's Calendar*.

Ecriture
Literally the French for 'writing', but in ▷ poststructuralist theory écriture has a supercharged sense and is used instead of its English equivalent to indicate a particular attitude

to written text. Poststructuralists argue that literary writing revels in the indeterminancy of meaning. So, in écriture, meaning accumulates and disperses, but is never stable, and readers should attend to this process and not to any finished meaning or interpretation (▷ closure). ▷ Jacques Derrida and ▷ Roland Barthes are notable theorists in this area, and their work has influenced a considerable body of critical opinion (▷ Readerly and Writerly Texts). Both Derrida and Barthes were connected with the French ▷ avant-garde literary and political journal *Tel Quel* in the late 1960s and the idea of écriture is associated with a particular style of innovative, experimental writing promoted by the journal.

Ecriture féminine
A term usually reserved for a particular kind of critical writing by women, emanating from the radical ▷ feminism of contemporary French critics such as Luce Irigaray, Hélène Cixous and Julia Kristeva. What unites this form of feminist criticism is the belief that there is an area of textual production that can be called 'feminine', that it exists beneath the surface of masculine discourse, and only occasionally comes to the fore in the form of disruptions of 'masculine' language. A further assumption is that woman is given a specific identity within the masculine structures of language and power, and that she must strive to challenge it. This particular brand of radical feminism takes the view that there is an 'essential' femininity that can be recovered, and that it is also possible to distinguish between a genuine feminine 'writing' and other forms of language.
Bib: Kristeva,, J., *Desire in Language*; Moi, T. (ed.), *The Kristeva Reader*; Moi, T., *Sexual/Textual Politics*; Marks, E. and De Courtivon, I., *New French Feminisms*; Newton, J. and Rosenfelt, D., *Feminist Criticism and Social Change*; Greene, G. and Kahn, C., *Making the Difference: Feminist Literary Criticism.*

Eden, Emily (1797–1869)
The daughter of William Eden, the first Baron Auckland, Emily Eden was born in Westminster. She was a close friend of Prime Minister Melbourne, who appointed her brother George governor general of India in 1835. She went with him and her sister Frances, and acted as his hostess until their return in 1842, and in London till 1849. She was a member of the highest social circles and many celebrities visited her house where she held morning gatherings due to ill health. In 1844 she published *Portraits of the People and Princes of India*, and then in 1866 and 1872, *Up the Country: Letters Written from the Upper Provinces of India*. In 1919 her great-niece edited a further selection of her letters. Her novels, *The Semi-detached House* (1859), published anonymously, and *The Semi-attached Couple* (1860), by 'E. E.', were written some 30 years previously. They portray fashionable society with good-humoured wit and owe something to ▷ Jane Austen whom Eden much admired.

Edgar, David (b 1948)
One of Britain's major dramatists, Edgar has written for both radical touring companies and the ▷ National Theatre and the ▷ RSC. He is also active in socialist debates on theatre and culture.

Edgar was born in Birmingham, of a theatrical family, and much of his early work was written for political theatre groups (*Wreckers*, 1977, was written for 7:84, *Teendreams*, co-written with Susan Todd, 1979 for Monstrous Regiment) or in response to political events (*A Fart for Europe*, co-written with ▷ Howard Brenton, 1973, was written as an anti-EEC polemic at the time of Britain's entry into the EEC).

As a socialist dramatist Edgar has chosen to base his intervention in the theatre, believing that television is an isolating experience, while theatre has to be experienced in a collective audience. *Maydays* (1983), an epic account of dissent in Britain and Russia was produced by the ▷ RSC as one of the first new plays to be produced on the main stage at the Barbican.

Edgar's greatest success, *The Life and Adventures of Nicholas Nickleby* (1980) was developed over a long period with the cast, who thoroughly researched and devised the play with Edgar. The result was a collaborative project and a conviction in the performances and production that is rarely seen in mainstream theatre. Edgar was later invited by ▷ Ann Jellicoe to collaborate in a theatre community project in Dorset: *Entertaining Strangers* (1985) was based on research into the history of Dorchester, and devised by and for the local community. It was then given a production in revised form at the ▷ National Theatre with professional actors (1987). *That Summer* (1987), *The Shape of the Table* (1990), and *Pentecost* (1994) have continued his readiness to engage with recent political events. *That Summer*, an unusually small-scale work for Edgar, written in the form of a domestic comedy, examines culture clashes and left-wing reactions to the miners' strike of 1984. *The Shape of the Table* by contrast, although considered a static, talking-head piece by some is still a fascinating attempt to analyse the *realpolitik* behind momentous changes in Eastern Europe at the end of 1989, in an imagined capital not a million miles away from Prague.
Bib: Bull, J., *New British Political Dramatists*; Chambers, C. and Prior, M., *Playwrights' Progress*

Edgeworth, Maria (1767–1849)
Novelist. Her tales are commonly set in Ireland.

Her work is minor but still read for its vivacity, good sense and realism. *Castle Rackrent* (1800) and *The Absentee* (1812) are two of her works still in print. She was also an excellent writer for children (see *Tales* ed. by Austin Dobson). She collaborated with her father, a noted educationist, in *Practical Education* (1798), influenced by the French-Swiss thinker ▷ Rousseau. She was admired by ▷ Jane Austen, William Thackeray (1811–63) and ▷ Walter Scott, whom she influenced. She has recently been re-evaluated by ▷ feminist critics as a liberal contributor to women's social history. In her satirical *Letters for Literary Ladies* (1795) she parodies those men who opposed the education of women (▷ Women, education of), and in 'Letter from a Gentleman to his friend upon the birth of a daughter' she writes:

> *Literary ladies will, I am afraid, be losers in love as well as in friendship, by their superiority – . . . gentlemen are not apt to admire a prodigious quantity of learning and masculine acquirements in the fair sex.*

Bib: Clarke, I. C., *Life*; Newby, P. H., *Maria Edgeworth*; Butler, M. S., *Maria Edgeworth*.

Edinburgh Festival
The Edinburgh Festival, now the biggest arts festival in Britain, is actually two festivals, the official 'International Festival of Music and Drama', instituted in 1947, and the Fringe, which began in 1949. Held annually during the three weeks from mid-August to September, it is now almost a trade fair for the theatre profession. Britain's literary managers, agents, and artistic directors scour the Festival each year for new talent; and many productions offered in winter seasons at theatres all over the country will have originated at the Edinburgh Festival.

The Official Festival was initiated by the opera impresario, Rudolph Bing, then general manager of Glyndebourne, and has since imported international theatre, opera, dance companies and orchestras, and new work from British companies. ▷ T. S. Eliot, ▷ Sean O'Casey and Ionesco are among the playwrights to have had premieres of new plays at the Festival. The Official Festival now provides one of the best opportunities to see world theatre.

The Fringe Festival grew up spontaneously in response to the Official Festival, and now outnumbers it in the range of productions it offers. There is no qualification for entry in the Fringe Festival, and amateur, student and professional companies battle it out for their share of the audience.

In recent years the Fringe has become increasingly professionalised, often rivalling the Official Festival in quality and innovation of its productions. Fringe Festival awards, which are offered weekly and help to attract audiences to the otherwise hidden away and unnoticed, are now also matched by the very up-market Perrier awards given at the end of the Festival and specifically aimed at cabaret performers.

Edinburgh Review
A quarterly periodical founded by ▷ Francis Jeffrey, Sydney Smith and ▷ Henry Brougham in 1802. It introduced a new seriousness into literary criticism and generally took a moderate Whig position in politics. Jeffrey's literary taste was rigidly classicist and he had little sympathy with the 'Lake Poets', ▷ William Wordsworth, ▷ Samuel Taylor Coleridge and ▷ Robert Southey. The term originates in the *Edinburgh Review*, Oct. 1807. ▷ *Blackwood's Magazine*.

Edward I (1272–1307)
King of England. He is known for the importance of his laws, the conquest of ▷ Wales and the attempted conquest of ▷ Scotland.

Edward II (1307–27)
King of England. His reign is chiefly noted for his decisive defeat by the Scots in the Scottish War of Independence (battle of ▷ Bannockburn, 1314) and for his conflicts with the barons over his excessive indulgence of favourites, especially Piers Gaveston.

▷ Christopher Marlowe's play *Edward II* presents him as a decadent sensual prince in ▷ Renaissance style, but pitiable in his horrible death by assassination.

▷ Scotland.

***Edward III* (1596)**
An historical drama about the perverted courtship of the Countess of Salisbury by the king, and set during the French wars. It is one of the anonymous plays that, it has been argued (by Kenneth Muir, *Shakespeare as Collaborator*, and G. R. Proudfoot, *British Academy Shakespeare Lecture 1985*), on internal evidence should be attributed to ▷ Shakespeare.

Edward III (1327–77)
The king of England under whom the ▷ Hundred Years' War with France began. Up to 1360 he was notably successful, and the English armies won the battles of ▷ Crécy (1346) and Poitiers (1356). He was succeeded on the throne by his grandson, ▷ Richard II, his eldest son, the ▷ Black Prince, having died in 1376.

The play ▷ *Edward III* (1596) has sometimes been ascribed to ▷ Shakespeare, at least in part.

Edward IV (1461–83)
First of the kings of England belonging to the House of York; he was victorious in the

▷ Wars of the Roses over the last king of the House of Lancaster, ▷ Henry VI.

Edward IV plays a prominent part in ▷ Shakespeare's ▷ *Henry VI, Part III*, where he first appears as the Earl of March, and in ▷ *Richard III*, in which he dies and his throne is seized from the rightful heir, his son, by Edward IV's brother, Richard, Duke of Gloucester.

Edward V (1483)
The boy-king, son of Edward IV. He was deposed in the year of his accession to the throne by his uncle, Richard, Duke of Gloucester, who became ▷ Richard III. Edward and his younger brother were imprisoned by their uncle in the Tower of London and were never heard of again. Legend (and the 16th century chroniclers) always insisted that he had them murdered there.

Edward VI (1547–53)
The boy-king who succeeded ▷ Henry VIII. Under the regency of the Protectors (the Duke of Somerset and, later, the Duke of Northumberland) Henry's essentially political ▷ Reformation became more Protestant in doctrine, though the new ▷ *Book of Common Prayer* was a wise compromise. Persecution of Roman Catholics in Edward's reign led to a reaction against Protestantism when his sister ▷ Mary succeeded him.

Edward the Confessor (reigned 1042–66)
Edward was famed for his piety more than his political achievements and was canonized in 1161. He founded Westminster Abbey (where he was buried), but no dynasty. Edward was succeeded by Harold, Earl of Wessex, though the legitimacy of this succession was challenged by William, Duke of Normandy, who successfully prosecuted his claim to the throne of England in his military campaign of 1066.

Edwardian
A term descriptive of the political, social and cultural characteristics of the early years of the 20th century , roughly corresponding to the reign of King Edward VII (1901–1910). The period is often remembered nostalgically for its luxury and brilliance, soon to be darkened by the horror of World War I (1914–18) and obliterated by the relative austerity of the post-war years. This life of luxury, easy foreign travel, low taxation, etc. is also thought of as being relatively free from the close moral restraint commonly associated with the preceding Victorian period. It is sometimes remembered, however, that such brilliance was restricted to the upper class and the wealthier members of the middle class, and that life for four-fifths of the population was at best dull and at worst squalid and impoverished. This darker aspect of the time was responsible for the rise of the socialist Labour Party and the prominence of polemical writers, like ▷ George Bernard Shaw and ▷ H. G. Wells. Such writers attacked the social injustice and selfishness of the upper classes in an idiom designed to reach wide audiences. Another critic of the dominant materialism was the novelist ▷ E. M. Forster. ▷ Arnold Bennett was a more representative novelist: his novels were not polemical and convey a materialistic vigour and excitement which were important elements in the harsh but inspiring environments of the more prosperous provincial towns. Thus some aspect of materialism is generally associated with Edwardianism, whether it is being enjoyed, suffered or criticized. Politically, the period was one of disturbance and rapid development: trade unionism was militant, women fought for political rights (▷ Suffragette Movement), and the social conscience inspired legislation which was later to mature into the Welfare State of the 1940s.

Edwards, Amelia (1831–92)
Novelist, short story and ▷ travel writer. She was born in Weston-super-Mare and educated at home by her mother. After working as a journalist, she published her first novel, *My Brother's Wife*, in 1855. She subsequently wrote several more romantic novels and two historical works, *The History of France* (1856) and *A Summary of English History* (1858), before editing a collection of poetry, *Home Thoughts and Home Themes* (1865). She contributed a number of notable ghost stories to leading periodicals of the day before turning her attention to travel writing in the 1870s. *A Thousand Miles up the Nile* (1877) was a highly successful account of her journey through Egypt to the Nubian desert. Edwards then became an enthusiastic and learned Egyptologist, publishing a further work, *Pharaohs, Fellahs and Explorers* (1892), as well as translating a manual on Egyptian archaeology and lecturing on the subject in Britain and North America, earning herself an honorary doctorate from Columbia University.

Edwards, Richard (1523–66)
Master of the children of the Chapel Royal and author of the popular courtly drama about ideal friendship, ▷ *Damon and Pithias* (1561), as well as of an influential, posthumously published collection of poets of the early Elizabethan period, *The Paradyse of Dainty Devises* (1576).

***Edwin Drood, The Mystery of* (1870)**
A novel by ▷ Charles Dickens, unfinished at his death. The novel begins in a cathedral town (based on Rochester); the plot turns on the engagement of Edwin and Rosa Bud, who do not really love each other, and the rivalry

for Rosa's love of Edwin's sinister uncle, John Jasper, and an exotic newcomer to the town, Neville Landless. Edwin disappears and Neville is arrested for his murder; Rosa flees to London to escape Jasper; on her behalf the forces for good are rallying in the shape of Rosa's guardian, Mr Grewgious, a clergyman called Crisparkle and a mysterious stranger, Mr Datchery, when the story breaks off. The fragment is quite sufficient to show that Dickens was not losing his powers. The sombreness and the grotesque comedy are equal to the best in his previous works. There have been numerous attempts to end the novel but none of any particular note.

EFL

Teaching English as a Foreign Language: a specialist skill and a profitable enterprise. It covers both the instruction of schoolchildren and their parents whose mother-tongue is not English but who live in Britain, which is a social necessity and prime task in a multi-racial society, as well as the work done in private language schools with older people not permanently resident in Britain. This is where the money lies. The number of these schools continues to increase: overseas the ▷ British Council has also expanded its teaching of English. Material relating to EFL teaching now takes up considerable space in many publishers' lists and is a major export.

Egdon Heath

A gloomy tract of country which is the Dorsetshire setting for ▷ Thomas Hardy's novel ▷ *The Return of the Native*. As often in Hardy's novels, the place is not merely a background to the events but exercises an active influence upon them.

Egerton, George (1859–1945)

The ▷ pseudonym of novelist and short story writer Mary Chavelita Dunne. She was born in Melbourne, Australia, and travelled widely as a young woman. In 1887 she eloped with Henry Higginson to Norway. She later married George Egerton Clairmonte and moved to Ireland where she began to write seriously. Her most successful works were two volumes of short stories, ▷ *Keynotes* (1893) and *Discords* (1894). The stories challenged patriarchal attitudes, and Egerton became associated with the ▷ 'New Woman' movement. Her later writing did not live up to her early potential and she faded from view. Later works include *Fantasias* (1898); *Rosa Amorosa* (1901) and *Flies in Amber* (1905).
Bib: Cunningham, G., *The New Woman and the Fictions of the 1890s*.

Egerton, Sarah Fyge

▷ Sarah Fyge.

***Egoist, The* (1879)**

One of the most admired novels by ▷ George Meredith. The 'egoist' is the rich and fashionable Sir Willoughby Patterne, who is intolerably self-centred and conceited. The story concerns his courting of Clara Middleton and her fight for independence from his assertiveness. Willoughby is opposed by Vernon Whitford, who is austere, honest and discerning, the tutor of Willoughby's poor relation, Crossjay, a boy whose vigorous animal spirits are accompanied by deep and spontaneous feeling. Partly owing to Crossjay, Clara is eventually enabled to evade Willoughby's advances, which have been backed by her father whose luxurious tastes Willoughby has indulged. She marries Whitford, a conclusion which is a victory for integrity over deceitful subtlety. The story is told with the brilliance of Meredith's rather mannered wit and is interspersed with exuberant passages of natural description symbolically related to the theme. Though Meredith's mannerism has lost the book some of its former prestige, his analysis of self-deceit and his understanding of the physical components of strong feeling make *The Egoist* an anticipation of kinds of fiction more characteristic of the 20th century.

▷ Gentleman.

Eisteddfod

Any festival in Wales held to encourage literature in the Welsh language, music, and other aspects of Welsh national culture. Its origins are possibly 12th-century; the word is Welsh and means 'a session'. The National Eisteddfod is held annually, alternately in North and South Wales.

Ekwensi, Cyprian (b 1921)

Nigerian, novelist and short-story writer. Ekwensi's fiction, widely read in Nigeria, depicts in many cases the experience of modern urban life in Lagos. For example, *Jagua Nana* (1961) is about the life of a prostitute (its title refers to the famous novel by ▷ Zola, *Nana*) and *People of the City* (1954) is a story of journalists and jazz musicians. Ekwensi's work stresses storytelling and uses a rich variety of language and styles. His other novels include: *When Love Whispers* (1947); *Burning Grass* (1962); *Beautiful Feathers* (1963); *Iska* (1966); *Survive the Peace* (1976); *For a Roll of Parchment* (1987); *Divided We Stand* (1980); *Jagua Nana's Daughter* (1986). Volumes of short stories: *Locotown* (1966); *Restless City* (1975). He has also written fiction for children and edited an anthology of Nigerian writing.
Bib: Emenyonu, E.N. (ed.), *The Essential Ekwensi: A Literary Celebration of Cyprian Ekwensi's Sixty-Fifth Birthday*.

Elegy

An elegy is usually taken to be a poetic lament for one who has died, or at least a grave and reflective poem. In ancient Greek and Latin literature, however, an elegy was a poem written in a particular ▷ metre (line of six dactylic feet alternating with lines of five feet) and it had no necessary connection with death or gravity; the Latin poet ▷ Ovid used it for love poetry. Following his example, the English poet ▷ John Donne wrote a series of elegies with amorous or satirical themes. Most of the famous elegies in English, however, follow the narrower and more widely accepted definition: ▷ Milton's ▷ *Lycidas* is inspired by the death of his friend Edward King; ▷ Shelley's ▷ *Adonais* laments that of the poet ▷ Keats; ▷ Gray's ▷ *Elegy Written in a Country Churchyard* is a meditation on life and death; ▷ Arnold's *Thyrsis*, that of his friend ▷ Clough. All four of these are in the ▷ pastoral convention, in imitation of a 3rd-century BC Greek elegy called the *Lament of Moschus for Bion*. ▷ W. H. Auden's *In Memory of W. B. Yeats* is a famous 20th-century response to the death of Yeats. Contemporary poetry's interest in absence and bereavement has led to a renewed interest in elegy, *eg* ▷ Douglas Dunn, *Elegies*. In 1992, Nigerian writer Ben Okri's volume of verse *An African Elegy* was published to considerable critical acclaim.

Elegy Written in a Country Churchyard (1751)
A poem by ▷ Thomas Gray, in iambic pentameter quatrains, rhyming *abab* (▷ metre). Its quiet subtlety of tone raises the platitudes of conventional graveyard musing to a unique intensity, and several of its eloquent generalizations and phrases have become proverbial: 'Some mute inglorious Milton', 'the madding crowd's ignoble strife', 'Melancholy mark'd him for her own', 'Full many a flower is born to blush unseen, And waste its sweetness on the desert air.'

▷ Samuel Johnson, though contemptuous of Gray's more inspirational experiments such as the Pindaric odes, had high praise for this poem: 'The *Churchyard* abounds with images which find a mirror in every mind and with sentiments to which every bosom returns an echo.'

▷ Elegy; Sensibility.

Elements, The (Four)
The 'four elements' are the ancient Greek and medieval conception of the basic components of matter; they are air, fire, earth and water. It was a division made by ▷ Empedocles of Sicily and adopted by ▷ Aristotle. Aristotle was writing before the beginnings of chemical analysis and considered matter in regard to the 'properties' or qualities that he believed all things to possess; these he found to be 'hotness', 'coldness', 'wetness' and 'dryness'. His four elements contained these properties in different combinations: air = hot and wet; fire = hot and dry; earth = cold and dry, water = cold and wet. These, therefore, were the basic constituents of nature. Aristotle's great prestige in the Middle Ages caused his theory to dominate the thought of the time. The medieval alchemists, forbears of the modern analytical chemist, noticed that the properties of various kinds of matter change, *eg* iron becomes rust, and they deduced from Aristotle's theory that materials could be changed, provided that they retained the same basic properties, *eg* lead could be changed into gold. The theory dominated European thought until the 17th century, when the English 'natural philosopher' and chemist, Robert Boyle (1627–91) taught that an element is to be regarded as a substance in itself and not as a substance with certain basic properties. Since Boyle, chemists have discovered that elements are very much more numerous that the original four, and that air, fire, earth and water are not in fact elements at all. Nonetheless, the pervasiveness of these so-called 'four elements' in our environment has caused them to keep their hold on the modern imagination, when it is not engaged in scientific thinking, so that they are still employed as symbols for the basic constituents of our experience of the world in some imaginative literature.

The theory of the 'four elements' was connected in classical and medieval times with the medical and psychological theory of the 'humours', or four basic liquid constituents of the body. The blood humour ('hot and wet') is linked to air; choler ('hot and dry') is associated with fire; phlegm ('cold and wet') corresponds to water and melancholy ('cold and dry') to earth. The preponderance of one or other of these humours in the make-up of a person's character was supposed to determine the temperament.

▷ Humour.

Elia
▷ *Essays of Elia*.

Eliot, George (1819–80)
Pen-name of the novelist Mary Ann Evans (at different times of her life she also spelt the name Mary Anne, Marian and Marianne). She was the daughter of a land-agent in the rural midlands (Warwickshire); her father's work (the management of estates) gave her wide experience of country society and this was greatly to enrich her insight and the scope of her novels. Brought up in a narrow religious tradition, in her early twenties she adopted ▷ agnostic opinions about Christian doctrine but she remained steadfast in the ethical teachings associated with it. She began her literary career with translations from the German of two works of religious speculation (▷ German influence on Victorian literature); in 1851 she became assistant editor of the ▷ *Westminster Review*, a journal of great intellectual prestige in London. Her friendship with ▷ George Lewes led to a

union between them which they both regarded as amounting to ▷ marriage; this was a bold decision in view of the rigid opposition in the English society of the time to open unions not legalized by the marriage ceremony.

Her first fiction consisted of tales later collected together as ▷ *Scenes of Clerical Life*. Then came her series of full-length novels: ▷ *Adam Bede* (1859), ▷ *The Mill on the Floss* (1860), ▷ *Silas Marner* (1861), ▷ *Romola* (1862–3), ▷ *Felix Holt* (1866), ▷ *Middlemarch* (1871–2) and ▷ *Daniel Deronda* (1876). Up till *Romola* the novels and tales deal with life in the countryside in which she was brought up; the society is depicted as a strong and stable one, and the novelist combines in an unusual degree sharp, humorous observation and intelligent imaginative sympathy. *Romola* marks a dividing point; it is a ▷ historical novel about the society of the Italian city of Florence in the 15th century. As a work of imaginative literature it is usually regarded as scholarly but dead; however, it seems to have opened the way to the more comprehensive treatment of English society in her last three novels, in which the relationship of the individual to society is interpreted with an intelligence outstanding in the history of the English novel and often compared with the genius of the Russian novelist, ▷ Leo Tolstoy (1828–1910). Her critical reputation has varied; it declined somewhat after her death, her powerful intellect being considered to damage her creativity. She was defended by ▷ Virginia Woolf (1882–1941) in an essay in 1919, but was really re-established by inclusion in F.R. Leavis' *The Great Tradition* (1948). With the rapid strides in feminist criticism in the 1980s, however, Eliot has been reclaimed as a major influence on women's writing and her works have been the focus of numerous feminist critiques, eg S. Gilbert and S. Gubar, *The Madwoman in the Attic* (1979).

George Eliot's poetry (*The Spanish Gipsy*, 1868, and *The Legend of Jubal*, 1870) is now little regarded but her essays for the *Westminster Review* include work of distinction and she published a collection, *The Impressions of Theophrastus Such*, in 1879.

In 1880, George Lewes having died, she married John Walter Cross, but she died in the same year.

Bib: Haight, G.S., *Life*; Leavis, F.R., in *The Great Tradition*; Bennett, J., *George Eliot: Her Mind and her Art*; Harvey, W.J., *The Art of George Eliot*; Pond, E.J., *Les Idées Morales et Réligieuses de George Eliot*; Hardy, B., *The Art of George Eliot*; Roberts, N., *George Eliot: Her Beliefs and Her Art*; Newton, K.M., *George Eliot*; Norbelie, B.A., *Oppressive Narrowness: A Study of the Female Community in George Eliot's Early Writings*.

Eliot, T. S. (Thomas Stearns) (1888–1965)
Poet, critic, and dramatist. Born in St Louis, Missouri, he later settled in England, where his first important long poem – *The Love Song of J. Alfred Prufrock* – appeared in the magazine *Poetry* in 1915; his first book, *Prufrock and Other Observations* appeared in 1917. From 1917 to 1919 he was Assistant Editor of the magazine *The Egoist* (with ▷ H. D.). His most famous poem, ▷ *The Waste Land*, came out in 1922, in which year he established *The Criterion*, one of the most influential literary reviews of this century. In 1927 he became a naturalized British subject, and in the same year he demonstrated his conversion to Christianity by becoming a member of the Church of England. His remaining important volumes of poetry were *Ash Wednesday* (1930) and ▷ *Four Quartets* (1935–42). The total body of his verse is not large, but it is one of the most important collections of the century. His poetic influences were preponderantly the French 19th-century ▷ Symbolists (▷ Baudelaire, Mallarmé, Laforgue), and the early 17th-century dramatists (▷ Middleton, ▷ Webster, ▷ Tourneur, the later ▷ Shakespeare) and their contemporaries the Metaphysical poets. The great sermon writers of the same period – ▷ John Donne, Jeremy Taylor, Bishop Andrewes – exercised a double influence on his style and his thought, and so did the great Italian medieval poet ▷ Dante. The contemporary who influenced him most and, in particular, greatly contributed to his early poetic development, was his fellow American ▷ Ezra Pound. Finally, the idealist philosophy of ▷ F. H. Bradley, whom Eliot studied as a student at Harvard and Oxford, was an important formative influence on Eliot's mind; his early academic thesis on Bradley was published in 1963.

Eliot's importance as a critic is linked with his importance as a poet, inasmuch as his really influential criticism was concerned with a reassessment of the past in such a way as to lead up to his own poetic production. Thus *The Sacred Wood* (1920) came between his first two volumes of verse. The most important of these early essays were republished in *Selected Essays* (1932). His work as a critic of society and civilization, *After Strange Gods* (1933) and *Notes Towards a Definition of Culture* (1948), has been such as to produce less fruitful, more sectarian discussion than his best literary criticism.

Eliot also experimented with verse drama, *Murder in the Cathedral* (1935), *The Family Reunion* (1939) and *The Cocktail Party* (1950) being the most commercially and artistically successful. In 1981 his 1939 collection for children, *Old Possum's Book of Practical Cats*, was turned into Andrew Lloyd Webber's hit musical *Cats*, thus reaching an enormous audience.

Eliot's non-dramatic poetry and his early criticism have had the effect in this century of reordering and renewing literary taste both in this country and in America. He was not alone, but he was outstanding, in reviving admiration for the ▷ Metaphysical poets, and reducing the relative status of the ▷ Spenserian and ▷ Miltonic strains in the English tradition. His poetry enlarged the range and form of poetic expression as a medium of the modern consciousness.

Bib: Hayward, J., *Selected Prose*; Kenner, H., *Invisible Poet*; Williamson, G., *A Reader's Guide*; Smith, G., *Eliot's Poetry and Plays*; Drew, E., *T. S. Eliot: The Design of his Poetry*; Gardner, H. L., *The Art of T. S. Eliot*; Moody, A. D., *Thomas Stearns Eliot, Poet*; Smith, C. H., *Eliot's Dramatic Theory and Practice*; Çalder, A., *T. S. Eliot*.

Elision

The suppression of sounds in words with the effect of drawing words together.

***Eliza Cook's Journal* (1849–54)**

A journal written and edited (almost single-handedly), by ▷ Eliza Cook, English poet and essayist. It was aimed at middle-class women and attempted to inform and entertain as well as intervene in debates around the ▷ 'Woman Question'. It included reviews, essays, poetry and sketches, and treated such subjects as the position of working women, the need for legal reform, the social construction of the 'old maid' and the inadequacy of girls' ▷ education. It ceased publishing after five years due to Cook's ill-health, but much material was later included in *Jottings from My Journal* (1860).

Elizabeth I (1558–1603)

Queen of England. Her reign was an extremely critical one, in which the personal fate of the queen was unusually bound up with that of the nation and the national Church. As a Protestant, she broke ▷ Mary's ties with Rome and restored her father's independent Church of England, but tolerance and compromise won her the loyalty of Catholics and Puritans alike. For 30 years she successfully played off against each other the two great Catholic powers, France and Spain. While she remained single, there was always a chance that her Catholic cousin ▷ Mary, Queen of Scots and widow of a French king, might succeed her. Even when Mary, deposed by the Scots, took refuge in England and connived at plots to murder her, Elizabeth avoided reprisals for nearly 20 years. Mary's eventual execution was followed in 1588 by Philip of Spain's attempted invasion of England, which resulted in the defeat of his powerful fleet, the great ▷ Armada. This was represented as a great triumph for Elizabeth personally, and in her person the English nation saw its own triumph.

The reign saw an efflorescence of national spirit in other ways. It was the period of the first great achievements in English seamanship. Elizabeth's court was the focus of the real flowering of the English ▷ Renaissance, expressing itself through music and literature; especially, the age of English poetic drama began. Commerce expanded through the joint stock merchant companies and with it a wealthy upper class, partly landed and partly mercantile, who left their mark in the immense country mansions they built all over the land. It was also the period of nationalistic expansion and the founding of many colonies (▷ Colonialism) in the New World. The queen herself, though cautious in statesmanship, was spirited and highly cultivated. She is now recognized as an author of considerable skill and learning; her speeches and poetry are available in contemporary editions.

▷ Companies, Joint Stock; Drake, Sir Francis; Elizabethan period of English literature; Ralegh, Sir Walter; Sidney, Sir Philip; Sixteenth-century literature.

Bib: Salter, R., *Elizabeth I and Her Reign*; Travitsky, B., *The Paradise of Women*.

Elizabeth, Queen of Bohemia (1595–1660)

Poet and patron. The daughter of ▷ James I, Princess Elizabeth was more influenced by her brother ▷ Henry than by her father. Her marriage to the Elector Palatine in 1613 and their acceptance of the crown of Bohemia in 1619 confirmed her early Protestant leanings. On the loss of Bohemia in 1620 and throughout the ensuing negotiations with Spain, Elizabeth crossed the continent in search of funds and support for the Protestant cause. In Britain she was seen as a tragic heroine in exile and called 'the winter queen', while her Protestantism identified her with the old queen, ▷ Elizabeth I, and there were angry requests for James to send aid to his daughter. She also wrote some poetry.

Bib: Greer, G. (ed.), *Kissing the Rod*.

Elizabethan novels

The events in a novel or novella are not drawn directly from traditional or legendary sources but are invented by the writer, so that they are new (or 'novel') to the reader. The 'novels' of the Elizabethan period are distinguishable from the long prose romances, such as Sir Philip Sidney's ▷ *Arcadia*, by their comparative brevity, but *Arcadia* is sometimes included among them.

The Italian novella began its history in the 13th century, and one of its best practitioners, ▷ Giovanni Boccaccio, was already well known in England, especially from ▷ Chaucer's adaptation of his work. In the first 20 years of ▷ Elizabeth I's reign, various Italian 'novelle', especially those of Bandello (?1480–1562), were ▷ translated into English, notably by William Painter in his collection ▷ *The Palace of Pleasure* (1566–7). These translations created a taste for the form, and led to the production of native English 'novels'. ▷ John Lyly's ▷ *Euphues (*1578) was the first of these. Best known among those that followed are: Lyly's *Euphues and his England* (1580), Barnabe Rich's (1542–1617) collection *Farewell to the Military Profession (*1581), ▷ Robert Greene's ▷ *Pandosto* (1588) and *Menaphon* (1589), ▷ Thomas Lodge's *Rosalynde* (1590), ▷ Thomas Nashe's ▷ *Unfortunate Traveller* (1594), and ▷ Thomas Deloney's *Thomas of Reading, Jack of Newbury* and *The Gentle Craft* (all between 1596 and 1600). The style of these works varies greatly. Rich, Greene and Lodge wrote mannered and courtly tales in imitation of Lyly; Nashe's rambling narrative is sometimes strongly realistic, and his style parodies a wide range of contemporary prose styles; Deloney addressed a middle-class public and at his best (in *Thomas of Reading*) anticipates the sober vividness of Daniel Defoe (1660–1731). The taste for the form lapsed in the early 17th century. There is no continuous development between the Elizabethan novel and the novel form as we know it today: the latter has its beginnings in the work of Defoe in the early 18th century, though it had late 17th-century forerunners.

Both the Italian and the English novels were used as sources for plots by contemporary English dramatists. Shakespeare's ▷ *Twelfth Night* is drawn from *Apolonius and Silla* in Rich's collection, adapted from an Italian original; his ▷ *As You Like It* is based on Lodge's *Rosalynde*; his ▷ *Winter's Tale* draws on Greene's *Pandosto*.

Bib: Margolies, D., *Novel and Society in Elizabethan England*; Pooley, R., *English Prose of the Seventeenth Century 1590–1700*.

Elliott, Ebenezer (1781–1849)

Poet. Often called the 'Corn Law Rhymer', Elliott is best known for his political poetry, especially his attack upon unpopular Corn Laws in *Corn Law Rhymes* (1830). *The Village Patriarch* (1829) was another work which attempted to raise social consciousness with its description of a poverty-stricken old man. He was admired by Thomas Carlyle (1795–1881).

Bib: Briggs, A., *Ebenezer Elliott, the Corn Law Rhymer*.

Ellis, Alice Thomas (b before 1939)

Novelist. Alice Thomas Ellis' work has much in common with that of ▷ Beryl Bainbridge, Patrice Chaplin and Caroline Blackwood (with whom Ellis wrote *Darling, You Shouldn't Have Gone to So Much Trouble* in 1980), who have all been collectively termed 'the Duckworth gang' for the similarity of their concerns and plot: most of their novels deal (with varying degrees of irony and biting wit) with modern women negotiating their own obsessions and a bizarre range of domestic situations, often stemming from sexual and romantic traumas. Thomas Ellis' works are psychologically astute black comedies of contemporary moral dilemmas, which map the terrain between modern sexual codes and (Ellis' strongly Catholic) religious background. She is married to the director of Duckworth publishers (hence 'the Duckworth gang'), and her works include: *The Sin Eater* (1977); *The 27th Kingdom* (1982, nominated for the Booker Prize); *Unexplained Laughter* (1985); *Home Life* (1986); *Secrets of Strangers* (1986 with Tom Pitt-Atkins); *The Skeleton in the Cupboard* (1988); and *Pillars of Gold* (1992).

Ellis, Henry Havelock (1859–1939)

Psychologist and essayist. Part of his work was scientific: *Man and Woman* (1894); *Studies in the Psychology of Sex* (1897–1910). Part of it was literary and expressed in reflective essays: *Little Essays in Love and Virtue* (1922); *Impressions and Comments* (1914–23); *The Dance of Life* (1923). In the latter work he exemplified the revival of the essay as a reflective form early in this century. He was a friend of the novelist ▷ Olive Schreiner.

Bib: Calder Marshall, A., *Life*; Collis, J.S., *An Artist of Life*.

Ellmann, Lucy (b 1956)

Novelist. Daughter of the American writers Richard and Mary Ellmann, she was educated at Essex University and the Courtauld Institute and lives in Britain. *Sweet Desserts* (1988), which won the *Guardian* fiction prize, concerns the destructiveness of consumerism and the life of a young woman overshadowed by a successful academic father. Her second novel is *Varying Degrees of Hopelessness* (1991).

***Eloisa to Abelard* (1717)**

An Ovidian (▷ Ovid) monologue in heroic couplets by ▷ Alexander Pope, based on the tragic love affair between the medieval philosopher ▷ Abelard (1079–1142) and Heloise (Eloisa) the daughter of a canon at Notre Dame Cathedral. Eloisa's family, disapproving of the affair, had Abelard castrated, and she became a nun. Their later correspondence on theological and philosophical issues is famous. In Pope's poem Eloisa writes from her convent, expressing her unabated longing, with a mixture of 'romantick' melancholy and theatrical rhetoric. The poem's combination of spirituality and eroticism illustrates the emotional, ▷ Catholic side of Pope's temperament.

Elstob, Elizabeth (1683–1756)

Anglo-Saxon scholar and translator, Elstob was born in Newcastle-upon-Tyne, and by 1691 both her parents were dead. Although her guardian opposed women's education, Elstob published *An English Anglo-Saxon Homily, on*

the birth-day of St Gregory (1709), having gone to Oxford with her brother. She may have established a day school. She regarded herself as the first woman to study Anglo-Saxon, and in the preface to the *Homily* she justified women's learning: 'it will be said, What has a Woman to do with Learning? This I have known urged by some Men, with an Envy unbecoming that greatness of Soul, which is said to dignify their Sex. For if Women may be said to have Souls, and their Souls are their better part and that what is best deserves our greatest Care for its Improvement. We must retort the Question. Where is the fault in Womens seeking after Learning?' She also published *The Rudiments of Grammar for the Anglo-Saxon Tongue, first given in English with an apology for the study of northern antiquities* (1715).
Bib: Ferguson, M., *First Feminists.*

Elyot, Sir Thomas (?1499–1546)
Diplomat and scholar. A member of ▷ Sir Thomas More's circle, he was friendly with ▷ humanists such as ▷ Erasmus, Thomas Linacre and John Colet (1467–1519). His major publication was *A Book Named the Governor* (1531), dedicated to ▷ Henry VIII. The work is similar to educational and political conduct books such as ▷ Baldassare Castiglione's *Il Cortegiano* and ▷ Machiavelli's *Il Principe*, in that it sets out the humanist ideal of the educated and powerful monarch. Elyot also wrote two other works of political philosophy – *The Image of Governance* (1541) and *The Doctrinal of Princes* (composed c 1534).
Bib: Warren, L. C., *Humanistic Doctrines of the Prince from Petrarch to Sir Thomas Elyot.*

Emblem-books
Books, very popular in England in the 16th century, containing pictures of ordinary objects (compasses, bottles, flowers, etc.) together with short poems showing how the object could be used to teach a truth applicable to life or conduct. Probably the first English emblem-book was Thomas Palmer's *Two Hundred Poosees* (c 1565), created for the ▷ Earl of Leicester. The fashion influenced the imagery of the 17th-century ▷ Metaphysical poets who commonly used simple objects as more or less complex illustrations of human experience, as when the poet ▷ John Donne in 'Valediction Forbidding Mourning' compares the relationship of himself and his wife when he goes on a journey to a pair of geometrical compasses whose points can divide but which yet remain united. Poets such as ▷ Francis Quarles and ▷ George Wither wrote verses sometimes shaped like such objects – a bottle, wings, etc. George Wither's *A Collection of Emblems, Ancient and Modern* appeared in four volumes in 1635, Frances Quarles' *Emblems* also in 1635, and the slightly earlier collection by ▷ Henry Peachman entitled *Minerva Britannia* in 1612. Peacham's collection set out to proclaim not so much philosophical truths, but to celebrate English 'worthies' such as ▷ Francis Bacon. It has been argued that poets such as ▷ Richard Crashaw, ▷ George Herbert and ▷ Henry Vaughan were influenced by emblem-books. Such an influence might possibly be discerned not just in the imagery of individual poems, but in the titles and organization of their collections of poetry.
Bib: *Emblematica: An Interdisciplinary Journal for Emblem Studies.*

Emecheta, Florence Onye Buchi (b 1944)
Novelist, short-story writer, radio and television playwright. Born near Lagos, Nigeria of Ibuza parents, she moved to England in 1962 and took a sociology degree at London University. She has worked in the Library Office at the British Museum and as a youth and community worker, and, since 1972, as a writer and lecturer. She has also served on the Advisory Council to the British Home Secretary on race and equality, and on the Arts Council of Great Britain. In 1980–81 she was Senior Research Fellow in the Department of English and Literary Studies at the University of Calabar, Nigeria and she has held various visiting professorships in the United States. Her novels are: *In the Ditch* (1972); *Second Class Citizen* (1974); *The Bride Price* (1976); *The Slave Girl* (1977); *The Joys of Motherhood* (1979); *Destination Biafra* (1982); *Naira Power* (1982); *Double Yoke* (1982); *The Rape of Shari* (1983); *Adah's Story: A Novel* (1983); *A Kind of Marriage* (a novella, 1986; also as a teleplay, 1987); *Gwendolen* (1989); *The Family* (1990). She has written several teleplays, including *Tanya: A Black Woman* and *The Juju Landlord* and four works for children: *Titch the Cat* (1979); *Nowhere To Play* (1980); *The Wrestling Match* (1980); *The Moonlight Bride* (1981). *Head Above Water* (1988) is an autobiography. Much of her work contains a strong autobiographical element and deals with the situation of women confronting oppression in both African and Western value-systems and social practices, while a number of her novels are historical, set in Nigeria before and after independence.

***Emma* (1816)**
A novel by ▷ Jane Austen. The heroine, Emma Woodhouse, has wealth, social prestige, good looks and intelligence. But her good fortune and the admiration she elicits are in reality her greatest disadvantage: they blind her to the need for self-knowledge and self-criticism. In what she imagines to be pure generosity of heart, she sets about trying to control the fate of her orphan friend of illegitimate birth and insignificant character, Harriet Smith, imagining her to be the daughter of an aristocrat and

deserving a marriage socially worthy of her paternity. Later she also becomes involved with a young man, Frank Churchill, who unknown to her is secretly engaged to a girl, Jane Fairfax, who is superior to Emma in talent but much inferior in worldly fortune. Jane Austen is in fact expanding the theme of the way in which romantic fantasy can blind a character to the realities of experience, more overtly used in earlier novels, ▷ *Northanger Abbey* and *Sense and Sensibility*. Emma, who has imagination and ability but nothing on which to employ them, is first trying to make a real-life novel with Harriet Smith as heroine and then participating in a mysterious drama, which she misconceives as her own fantasy wants it to be, with Jane Fairfax as main protagonist. But Harriet decides that she is to marry the man, George Knightley, with whom Emma herself has long been unconsciously in love; Emma also discovers that Churchill, with whom she has been conducting a flirtation, has merely been using her as a tool to mask his secret engagement. She realizes, in fact, that she has caused herself to be a victim of the first of her romances and has been made to play an ignominious and unworthy role in the second. Duly repentant, Emma is ultimately rewarded by Mr Knightley's proposal of marriage. The novel is perhaps Jane Austen's finest, displaying her irony at its most subtle.

Empedocles (5th century BC)
A philosopher and statesman of the Greek colony of Agrigentum in Sicily. He is said to have led the people against the tyrannous government of a powerful class and then to have refused to become their king. According to a legend he met his death in the volcano of Etna, though in reality he seems to have died in Greece. There are various allusions to his legendary end in English literature and it is usually ascribed to dangerous curiosity. The most famous account of it is the poem *Empedocles on Etna* (1852) by ▷ Matthew Arnold; in this his death is represented as deliberate suicide by a disillusioned and banished political leader. Arnold uses the poem to express his own scepticism.

'Empedocles on Etna' (1852)
A poem by Matthew Arnold, and the most famous account of the legendary death of Empedocles, philosopher and statesman of the Greek colony of Agrigentum in Sicily, who is said to have led the people against the tyrannical government of a powerful class and then to have refused to become their king. According to legend he met his death in the volcano of Etna, though in reality he seems to have died in Greece. In the poem the philosopher is counselled by a physician, Pausanias, and a poet, Callicles, but neither is able to dispel his despair and he throws himself into the crater of Mount Etna – a disillusioned and banished political leader. Arnold's own scepticism is expressed within the poem.

Empiricism
A philosophical theory, according to which ideas are derived from experience, and the verification of knowledge must depend upon experience.

Empson, William (1906–84)
Critic and poet. Empson was born in Yorkshire and worked under I. A. Richards at Cambridge. His main critical works are: *Seven Types of Ambiguity* (1930), *Some Versions of Pastoral* (1935), *The Structure of Complex Words* (1951), and *Milton's God* (1961). Volumes of his verse include: *Poems* (1940) and *Collected Poems* (1955).

As a critic, he was very influential, especially through his analysis of the nature of language when it is used in imaginative writing, particularly poetry. His approach was influenced by the attitude to language of 20-th century linguistic philosophers, especially ▷ Bertrand Russell and Wittgenstein, who concentrated on the tendency of language, by the ambiguities inherent in it, to confuse clear thought. Empson's teacher, Richards, in his *Principles of Literary Criticism* (1924), discussed the kinds of truth that are to be found in poetic statements, and how these truths differ from, without being less valuable than, the truths of philosophical and scientific statement. Empson's first book (*Seven Types*) discusses the way in which various kinds of semantic ambiguity can be used by poets, and shows the relevance of this study to the assessment of poems. It has become a major text in what came to be known as New Criticism. His later books develop the psychological (particularly ▷ Freudian) and philosophical aspects of this approach. More recently post-structuralist and ▷ psychoanalytic critics have become interested in *Seven Types of Ambiguity*. Empson's poetry is difficult, academic – heavily annotated by him – and itself highly ambiguous. Although difficult and obscure, his poetry was greatly influential on the work of the ▷ Movement.

Enclosures, Enclosure Acts
The term 'enclosure' describes the partitioning and appropriation by individuals of land that was previously either open (▷ open field system) and farmed by communities, or uncultivated and available to anyone for gathering wood or fruit, or grazing animals. Enclosure entailed erecting physical barriers – hedges or fences – to separate land from its surroundings and transferring the responsibility for drainage and other matters onto individual caretakers. It could be done by mutual 'agreement' among owners of private land – 'sensibly dividing

the country among opulent men,' as ▷ Adam Smith wrote – or by ▷ Act of Parliament, the latter especially when large tracts of land were involved. However, sometimes wealthy people simply enclosed or sold off common land, without any negotiation or legislation at all. The process resulted in a concentration of ownership in far fewer hands than before. It led to increased crop yields, healthier and fatter livestock, and greater wealth for large-scale owners. But it also increased poverty among the dispossessed who were unable to afford the new arrangements, such as the smaller landowners, tenant farmers and agricultural labourers. They had always led a precarious existence, exercising their ancient cultivation, grazing and gathering rights on what had been common land. Many were deprived of their rights and all their property, often being driven off the land altogether. Their plight contributed to rural poverty (▷ Poor Laws), and also to the rapid growth of towns, especially London, as people flocked to them in search of work. Although enclosure is usually associated with the middle and late 18th century, it began as early as the 15th, though not on the same scale. The first part of ▷ Thomas More's ▷ *Utopia* (1516) is a stinging attack on enclosures, and their effects on poorer farmers and farmworkers. Some of his descriptions of people unable to find employment, falling into crime and ending up in prison or even hanged for theft, could as well apply to the 17th and 18th centuries.

After the ▷ Civil War, and especially after the ▷ Glorious Revolution of 1688, estates began to grow larger, aided by careful purchases of land and strategic marriages. The practice of marrying oneself or one's children for money, or to add a title and perhaps an estate to a fortune, forms the stuff of much Restoration and 18th-century comic drama and novel writing. ▷ Wycherley's ▷ *The Country Wife* (1675), ▷ Etherege's ▷ *The Man of Mode* (1676), ▷ Behn's ▷ *The City Heiress* (1682) and ▷ *The Lucky Chance* (1687), and ▷ Richardson's ▷ *Clarissa* are just some of the numerous works that deal with these subjects, with variations and sometimes ambiguities as to the precise social classes and backgrounds of the protagonists. Some families acquired enormous wealth and huge estates: a new class of ultra-rich landowners emerged whose main concern was to increase their farm yields and profits even further. Enclosures offered a way. By 1700 about half the cultivatable land had been enclosed, but there still remained a broad stretch of unenclosed land, including parts of East Anglia and much of the Midlands. A series of Acts was passed, accelerating the process of enclosure especially in the second half of the 18th century. From 1760 to 1799 enclosures brought between two and three million acres of land into cultivation.

The resulting increase in surplus wealth created a leisure class and the development of aesthetic ▷ taste, as a stimulus to consumption. But escalating rural poverty encouraged a new kind of poetry, such as ▷ Goldsmith's ▷ *The Deserted Village* and ▷ Crabbe's *The Village*, protesting against the sufferings of the rural poor and recalling happier times. This social change was a factor in the growth of ▷ Radicalism and the ▷ Romantic movement.

Bib: Plumb, J. H., *England in the Eighteenth Century*; Williams, R., *The Country and the City*; Porter, R., *English Society in the Eighteenth Century*; Sharpe, J. A., *Early Modern England 1550–1760*.

Encounter

Political and literary magazine, founded in 1953 and initially edited by the poet Stephen Spender and Irving Kirstol. During the 1950s and early 1960s it provided a prominent forum for the discussion of cultural issues, especially the condition and future of British society. Politically it was anti-communist and claimed to advocate reform on the basis of a post-ideological consensus in the West.

Encyclopaedists

The collaborators in the production of the great French encyclopaedia (▷ *L'Encyclopédia)* of the 18th century. The enterprise began with a translation of the English *Cyclopaedia* by Ephraim Chambers but the French version was intellectually altogether more impressive. Its editors were two leaders of the 'philosophers' – D'Alembert and Diderot – and its contributors were the leading male minds of France, such men as ▷ Voltaire and ▷ Rousseau. The inspiration was faith in reason and the desire to destroy superstition and beliefs thought to arise from it. The movement contributed to the influences which later led to the ▷ French Revolution, and it reinforced ▷ rationalism throughout Europe. In England the movement influenced ▷ Jeremy Bentham and through him the ▷ Utilitarians of the 19th century.

▷ French literature in England.

Encyclopédie, L'

An encyclopaedia published in 28 volumes between 1751 and 1772, under the editorship of ▷ Diderot (1713–84) and (until 1758) the mathematician D'Alembert (1717–83). Its contributors included ▷ Voltaire, ▷ Rousseau, ▷ Montesquieu, Buffon (1707–88) and Turgot (1727–81). The work originated in a translation of the English *Cyclopaedia, or the Universal Dictionary of Arts and Sciences* (1728) of Ephraim Chambers (d 1740), but the French version was intellectually more ambitious and more impressive. It was guided by a trust in reason and ▷ rationalistic explanation, and the desire to destroy superstition and the beliefs thought to arise from it. The work's fierce attacks on

Church and State proved potent criticism of the ▷ Ancien Régime (it was suppressed at various stages of its composition) and heralded the overthrow of the monarchy in the ▷ French Revolution. It reinforced European rationalism and in England influenced ▷ Jeremy Bentham and through him the 19th-century Utilitarians (▷ Utilitarianism).

End-rhyme
Rhyme occurring in the usual position, *ie* at the end of a line; internal rhymes occur in the middle of a line, and head-rhymes are the correspondence of the beginnings of words, *ie* alliteration.

End-stopped lines
Lines of verse, especially ▷ blank verse, which end at the end of a sentence or at strongly marked pauses within the sentence. The opposite effect is produced by run-on lines, when the syntax makes the voice go on to the next line without pause.

▷ Enjambment.

***Endymion* (1818)**
Poem by ▷ John Keats. It is based on an ancient Greek myth about a shepherd with whom the moon goddess fell in love. The poem has passages of great freshness and beauty, but, as Keats soon came to realize, it is immature. Its classicism is a resource for the free embroidering of fanciful stories; and the theme, the indulgence of the senses, is one that Keats quickly outgrew.

▷ Classical mythology; Greek literature.

England's Helicon
An Elizabethan verse ▷ anthology, published in 1600 and possibly edited by one Nicholas Ling. The collection mainly comprises ▷ pastoral verse, and contains poems by ▷ Sir Philip Sidney, ▷ Edmund Spenser, ▷ Michael Drayton, ▷ Thomas Lodge and others, as well as 'The Passionate Sheepheards Song' by ▷ Shakespeare. This last was taken from Act IV of ▷ *Love's Labour's Lost*, first published in quarto in 1598. The poem was republished in ▷ *The Passionate Pilgrim* of 1599. In 1614 a second edition of *England's Helicon* appeared, which included additional verses by Sidney and a poem by ▷ William Browne.
Bib: Macdonald, H. (ed.), *England's Helicon*.

English Language
English does not originate in England. English has its roots in the Germanic dialects of the peoples of north-western Europe who invaded Britain in the 5th century, after the Romans had withdrawn. According to the Venerable Bede, the bulk of the Angle, Saxon, and Jutish settlers arrived in 449, pushing back the native Celtic tribes into Cornwall, Wales and Scotland. This and subsequent invasions account for much of the current diversity in the languages of Britain. The development of the Celtic languages, notably, Cornish, Welsh and Scottish Gaelic, proceeded relatively independently of English. Each established its own literary tradition, and, excepting Cornish which died out in the 18th century, are living languages today.

The Angles settled in (and gave name to) what is now East Anglia, and also spread to Mercia (the Midlands) and further North to Northumbria (north of the Humber and south-east Scotland). The Saxons remained in the south, a fact evidenced by the area names Sussex ('south saxons'), Essex ('east saxons'), and the old name for the south-west Wessex ('west saxons'). The Jutes seem to have remained largely in Kent. Some of the dialectal differences in today's English originate in the Germanic dialects spoken by these tribes, though there is some debate about whether these differences were present before the tribes came to Britain or whether the dialectal divisions developed in England itself as a result of political, social and economic factors. Whatever the case, the differences were originally slight, and from the very beginning writers of these tribes referred to their language as 'Englisc' (derived from the name of the Angles), regardless of their own particular dialect. The most common vocabulary items in usage today come from these Germanic dialects.

In the 9th century Britain saw the beginning of a second wave of invaders – the Scandinavian Vikings. Arriving from Denmark, Norway, and Sweden, they soon took over the East of England and were only halted when King Alfred (the king of Wessex) won a decisive victory over the Danish King Guthrum in 878. The following year a treaty was drawn up whereby the Danes retreated to the east of a line running roughly from Chester to London, an area which became known as Danelaw. The significance of this boundary is that it had the effect of increasing dialectal differences between the north and the south. For example, the fact that today the words *farm* and *sir* are more likely to be pronounced as *varm* and *zir* in the south-west is partly a result of this settlement. However, the Scandinavian dialects were not greatly different from the Germanic dialects that constituted English, and in fact were readily assimilated into the core of English. For example, the word 'are' (part of the most common verb in today's English) is Scandinavian in origin.

The third wave of invaders were the Norman French who arrived in 1066. This date is an important point in the development of English. Scholars usually refer to English before 1100 as Old English; that of 1100–1500 as Middle English; and that of 1500 today as Modern English. Most surviving records of Old English are written in West Saxon, which became the principal written variety from the 9th century, largely as a result of the increasing political supremacy of Wessex. The longest work of Old English literature, and probably the best known, is the poem *Beowulf*. The arrival of French, however, diminished the cultural status of West Saxon. In the Middle English period Latin was used for highly formal texts (e.g. laws, religious texts, scholarly works), Norman French became a prestige language spoken by the upper classes and used for administration, and English was a set of largely spoken dialects. Middle English is characterised by great regional variety. In the absence of any type of standard, writers who wrote in English wrote in their own dialects. As a result, all dialects are well represented in the literature of the period. For instance, the York 'mystery plays' are good examples of the Northern dialect, the poems *Sir Gawain and the Green Knight Pearl*, *Patience* and *Purity* are written in the dialect of the north-west Midlands, and William Langland's *Piers Plowman* represents the south-west Midlands dialect. Chaucer wrote in the east Midlands dialect, and John of Trevisa wrote scholarly works in a south-western dialect.

By the end of the Middle English period, French had been displaced by English as the language of the aristocracy. Until about 1430, almost all official documentation was written in French or Latin. With an expanding population a more efficient medium for communication was needed, not a language that was understood by a very small elite. The particular variety of English that was adopted by the bureaucracy was a mixture of elements from the Midlands dialects. This development was one factor that played a role in the formation of a national standard of written English. The involvement of the Midlands dialects seems logical because of their geographical centrality: people to the north and south could understand the dialect in the middle, but not so easily each other. Moreover, the variety of English spoken in London was basically the dialect of the east Midlands. It is not surprising that London English was a key factor in the rise of this standard, given that it was the language of the capital (the centre of commerce and administration) and, importantly, that Caxton established his printing press there in the 15th century. In the 16th century we begin to see the production of English dictionaries, grammar books, and spelling books. These were adopted in schools, and became arbiters of the language. They had the effect of fixing the standard and thus stabilising the variation in written English. The development of a written standard explains why English in texts of the 18th century looks relatively familiar to us and does not vary too much from one writer to the next, whereas that of 15th-century texts and before looks alien and varies drastically.

The development of a kind of spoken 'standard' follows a very different path from that of the written standard. In Old and Middle English, writing more or less reflected speech. With the standardisation of writing, a rift opened up: writing was retarded in its natural changes, whereas speech continued to change unabated. Thus, although spelling became fixed when a written standard developed, pronunciation continued to change. In fact, from approximately 1400–1600, English saw dramatic changes in the pronunciation of long vowels; a process that is traditionally labelled 'The Great Vowel Shift'. A consequence of this is that today's spelling seems so ill matched with pronunciation. Scholars of the past, particularly in the 18th century, expressed their concern for this rift and also the apparently chaotic variability of pronunciation. Although no 'standard' (in the sense of a variety used by a majority) developed, from the 16th century onwards one variety of speech acquired particular social prestige, namely, the pronunciation of the court, based on that of the London area. Pronunciation was a marker of position in society. Just as technology (printing presses) had played a role in establishing a written standard, so technology was to play a role in promoting one variety of spoken English. In the 20th century the BBC chose 'Received Pronunciation' as the variety of spoken English they would broadcast. This was the variety spoken by the upper classes and, in particular, spoken in public schools. Today, we might well refer to it as 'BBC English', 'The Queen's English' or simple 'talking posh'. Received Pronunciation, however, has less authority now than it used to have in the first half of 20th century. It has always been spoken by a small minority, today around 3% of the population.

Successive waves of invaders brought English into contact with other languages. One important consequence of this has been the steady expansion of English vocabulary. About 1,800 words of Scandinavian origin have survived into present day English. The number of French borrowings is far greater, largely because of the great prestige enjoyed by the French language. Even after English displaced French as the language of the ruling classes, French culture exerted a powerful influence, and continues to do so today. Some 10,000 words were adopted into English in the Middle English period. In particular, French borrowings can be seen in the language of the legal system (*eg judge*, *jury*, *prison*), administration (*eg parliament*, *government*), fashion (*eg dress*, *jewel*, *cloak*), cuisine (*eg beef*, *lettuce*, *mutton*, *pork*, *sausage*, *venison*), and art (*eg art*, *beauty*, *romance*). In many cases Anglo-Saxon words were replaced by French ones (*eg stow* by *place*, *wyrd* by *fortune*). Where both survived meanings tended to drift apart (*eg house* and *mansion*, *blood* and *sanguine*).

An enormous number of the French

borrowings had originally come from Latin. There were also several thousand direct Latin borrowings, particularly towards the end of the Middle English period. Most of these were from areas such as religion, science, law and literature (*eg scripture*, *client*, *conviction*, *library*, *scribe*, *dissolve*, *quadrant*, *medicine*, *ulcer*). The main influx of Latin, and also Greek vocabulary, commenced in the 16th century. The Renaissance saw the development of new concepts and techniques, the flowering of the arts and sciences, as well as further exploration of the world. Much of this took place on the continent of Europe, and English writers often borrowed the European terms for these developments. At this time, learning was given a boost by printing: books became widely available. However, many literary, scientific and religious texts were in Latin. Latin was the language of scholarship and scholarly literature. To make these texts more widely available, people began to translate them into English, often using a Latin word in the translation when no good English equivalent could be found. The upshot of these developments was that words from many languages were adopted into English, but especially words from Latin, Greek and the Romance languages French, Italian, and Spanish. One estimate is that as many as 20,000 Latin words entered English in the 16th century alone. Examples of Latin borrowings include *absurdity*, *benefit*, *exist*, *exaggerate*, *external*, *jocular*, *obstruction*, *relaxation*, *relevant*, *vacuum*, *virus*, *excursion*, *fact*, *impersonal*, and *eradicate*.

The fact that English has a multi-sourced vocabulary has important implications for the language today. An obvious one is that English has an incredibly large vocabulary. Furthermore, words of Germanic and Latinate origin have acquired distinctive flavours of their own, and are used in different contexts and for different purposes. The basic core of everyday spoken English is Germanic, and more abstract, formal, written English tends to be Latinate. English also has many groups of near synonyms. Triple synonyms such as *fire* (Germanic), *flame* (French) and *conflagration* (Latinate) clearly vary on scale from informal to formal. Moreover, although these words might have the same basic meaning, they have developed different connotations. The word *inexpensive* (Latinate), for example, is relatively neutral when compared with the negative connotations of *cheap* (Germanic).

Authors have been able to capitalise on the resources of English vocabulary. Shakespeare made full use of both Germanic and Latinate vocabulary for purposes such as creating a particular tone, developing a character or achieving a dramatic contast. Some writers have expressed a preference for either Latinate or Germanic vocabulary. Dryden saw latin as a necessary means of giving 'ornament' to our 'old Teutonic syllables'. Milton favoured Latinate vocabulary, as did many writers of the 18th century. Others hotly debated this preference, viewing it as the abandonment of 'natural, common speech' in favour of words coming from books or the inkhorn (hence this debate which began in the Renaissance was termed the 'Inkhorn Controversy'). Recent exponents of this view have included the Dorset poet William Barnes and George Orwell.

The English language has also expanded in other respects. The uses to which English is put have multiplied over the years. By the end of the 17th century, Latin had been replaced by English as the language of scholarly works. Schools began to switch from Latin to English. Literacy improved, and in the 19th century there was a boom in publishing. Today, English dominates the world stage in a number of language uses: it is the main language of publishing, science, technology, commerce, diplomacy, air-traffic control, and popular culture. The reasons for this are to do with the political and economic power of Britain in the 19th century and America in the 20th century. These same reasons also account for a dramatic increase in the number of users of English. In the 16th century there were around three million speakers of English. today, there are over 300 million native speakers of English. To this one could add a further 300 million who regularly speak English as a second language (*ie* in addition to their native language). In fact, it has been estimated that in total around a billion people use English in varying degrees. English is the most widely used language in the world.

With the international spread of English it is perhaps more appropriate now to speak of 'World Englishes'. American and British English are the two most important national varieties, both in terms of numbers of speakers and world-wide impact. Other important varieties of English include those of Australia, Canada, Ireland, New Zealand and South Africa, where English is principally a native language, and also various countries in Africa, the subcontinent of India, the Caribbean, and south-east Asia, where English is principally a second language. In each of these countries English has acquired its own distinctive characteristics and developed its own literature. Perhaps an indication that these literatures have come of age is the fact that the 1992 Nobel Prize for Literature was awarded to Caribbean poet Derek Walcott.

Bib: Burchfield, R., *The English Language*; Baugh, A. C. and Cable, T., *A History of the English Language*; Crystal, D., *The English Language*.

Enjambment

A term describing the continuing of the sense from line to line in a poem, to the extent that it is unnatural in speaking the verse to make a pause at the line ending. The effect is that of 'run-on' lines.

▷ End-stopped lines

Enlightenment

The term was originally borrowed into English in the 1860s from German (*Aufklärung*), to designate the spirit and aims of the French philosophers of the 18th century, such as ▷ Diderot and ▷ Voltaire. But as historical perspectives have changed the word has come to be used in a much wider sense, to denote the whole period following the ▷ Renaissance, during which scepticism and scientific ▷ rationalism came to dominate European thinking. Enlightenment grew out of Renaissance at different times in different countries. In Britain, the empiricism of ▷ Francis Bacon (1561–1626) and the secular pragmatism of ▷ Thomas Hobbes (1588–1679) mark its early stages. Its golden age began however with ▷ John Locke (1632–1704) in philosophy, and ▷ Sir Isaac Newton (1642–1727) in science, and it reached its height in the first half of the 18th century. Locke argued that 'Reason must be our last judge and guide in everything', and rejected medieval philosophy as superstition. Newton's theory of gravitation seemed to explain the mysteries of the solar system. The fact that Newton had also worked on optics was ingeniously alluded to in ▷ Alexander Pope's couplet: 'Nature, and Nature's Laws lay hid in Night. God said, *Let Newton be*! and All was *Light*'.

The onset of Enlightenment in Britain coincided with the bourgeois revolution and many of its values reflect the optimistic temper of the newly dominant class, as much as any abstract philosophical system. In contrast to the previous ideology of static hierarchy, appropriate to a landowning aristocracy and its peasant underclass, the new ideology of merchants and professional men placed its emphasis on understanding and dominating the environment. God lost his numinousness, becoming a kind of divine mathematician, and the ▷ Deist thinkers of the time rejected the dogmas of the scriptures in favour of 'natural religion' based on an understanding of God's laws through science. Pope expresses this idea in classic form in his ▷ *Essay on Man* (1733–4), cleverly blending it with the older hierarchical idea of the Great Chain of Being. Pope's *Essay* stands as a compendium of popular Enlightenment ideas, expressing the expansive confidence of the middle class that 'Whatever *is*, is *right*.' It was easy for the middle-class reader of the day to feel that British philosophy, science, trade and imperialism were all working together to advance civilization throughout the world. It is a myth projected in many of the works of Pope, ▷ James Thomson and other writers of the time.

As the 18th century developed, the bourgeoisie's confidence in its progressive destiny faltered, reaching a crisis after the ▷ French Revolution in what we now call the ▷ Romantic movement. ▷ William Blake attempted to restore the pre-Enlightenment numinousness of God and nature, rejecting Newton's 'particles of light', and the idea of inert matter or empty space. Imagination, not science, was for him the key to nature: 'Every thing possible to be believ'd is an image of truth.' ▷ Percy Bysshe Shelley, using politically resonant imagery, asserted that 'man, having enslaved the elements, remains himself a slave' and warned of the dangers of 'an unmitigated exercise of the calculating faculty' (one of the characteristic institutions of the Enlightenment period was, of course, the slave trade). Even the fundamentally materialist ▷ John Keats complained about the prosaic nature of Enlightenment philosophy:

There was an awful rainbow once in heaven:
We know her woof, her texture; she is given
In the dull catalogue of common things.
Philosophy will clip an Angel's wings.
(*Lamia*; 231–4)

More recently 'Enlightenment' has been given a yet wider historical application by the German philosophers Theodor Adorno and Max Horkheimer, whose book, *Dialectic of Enlightenment* (1944) sees the manipulative, calculating spirit of Enlightenment as the identifying characteristic of western civilization. They trace its manifestations from ▷ Odysseus' tricking of the primitive bumpkin Polyphemus, to the treatment of people as means rather than ends which characterizes both modern totalitarian politics and consumer ▷ capitalism. Recent ecological movements, which advocate a respect for nature, rather than an exploitation of it, continue the same dialectic.

Bib: Willey, B., *The Eighteenth-Century Background*; Redwood, J., *Reason, Ridicule and Religion: The Age of Enlightement in England.*

'Enoch Arden'

A poem by ▷ Tennyson written in 1861 and 1862 and published in *Enoch Arden and Other Poems* in 1864, which brought its author £6000 in one year. It was one of the most popular of Tennyson's poems in its day. Based on a story furnished by his sculptor friend, Thomas Woolner, it tells of a man who returns from a voyage of many years, having undertaken to save his wife and children from penury, to find her happily remarried. Rather than destroy her happiness he conceals the fact of his return and lives alone for the rest of his life. His literal and symbolic isolation is powerfully realized in the description of his shipwreck on a lonely island, and in the moment when he renounces his wife and children after seeing the new family through the window. Enoch Arden is associated with Christ, and with Ulysses, who figures again in Tennyson's powerful lyric 'Crossing the Bar'. The theme is common to ▷ Elizabeth Gaskell's *Sylvia's Lovers* and ▷ Adelaide Anne Procter's poem 'Homeward Bound'.

Enright, D. J. (b 1920)
Poet, novelist and literary critic. Enright was an important figure in the ▷ Movement in the 1950s, and his poetry remains strongly humanistic and anti-romantic. His volumes of verse include: *The Laughing Hyena* (1953); *Bread Rather Than Blossoms* (1956); *Some Men Are Brothers* (1960); *Selected Poems* (1968); *Sad Ires* (1975); and *A Faust Book* (1979).

Ephelia
The name used by a late 17th-century poet writing in English, whose identification is made all the more difficult by the fact that it is a name frequently used by other writers, or as the name of the recipient of a poem. How much weight we give to the internal evidence of poems – such as the poems to 'Strephon' – depends on how literally we imagine these poems can be related to a 'life'. The guesses at the identity of this author have included ▷ Katherine Philips' daughter, Elizabeth Mordaunt.

Publications attributed to this name include: *Panegyric to the King* (1678); *Female Poems on Several Occassions (*1679), and *Advice to His Grace* (1681/2).
Bib: Greer, G. *et al.*, *Kissing the Rod.*

Epic
1 A narrative of heroic actions, often with a principal hero, usually mythical in its content, offering inspiration and ennoblement within a particular cultural or national tradition.

2 The word denotes qualities of heroism and grandeur, appropriate to epic but present in other literary or even non-literary forms.

Epics occur in almost all national cultures, and commonly give an account of national origins, or enshrine ancient, heroic myths central to the culture. For European culture at large, much the most influential epics are the ▷ *Iliad* and the ▷ *Odyssey* of ▷ Homer and the ▷ *Aeneid* by ▷ Virgil. ▷ C. S. Lewis in *Preface to Paradise Lost* makes a helpful distinction between primary and secondary epics: primary ones, such as Homer's, are composed for a society which is still fairly close to the conditions of society described in the narrative; secondary epics are based on the pattern of primary epics but written for a materially developed society more or less remote from the conditions described, *eg* Virgil's *Aeneid*. In English literature the ▷ Old English ▷ *Beowulf* may be counted as a primary epic. A number of attempts at secondary epic have been made since the 16th century, but ▷ John Milton's ▷ *Paradise Lost* is unique in its acknowledged greatness and its closeness to the Virgilian structure. ▷ Spenser's ▷ *The Faerie Queene* has many epic characteristics, but, in spite of the important classical influences upon it, the poem's structure is derived from the 'romantic epic' of the 16th-century Italian poets, ▷ Ariosto and Tasso; moreover, though allegory often plays a part in epics, the allegorical elements in *The Faerie Queene* are so pervasive as to present a different kind of imaginative vision from that normally found in them.

Many other works in English literature have epic qualities without being definable as epics. For example, ▷ Fielding described ▷ *Tom Jones* as a comic epic, and it is this as much as it is a novel: a series of adventures of which Tom is the hero, but of which the consequences are loss of dignity rather than enhancement of dignity. Melville's prose romance *Moby Dick* (1851) has true epic scale, seriousness of treatment and relevance to the human condition. ▷ James Joyce's ▷ *Ulysses* uses the *Odyssey* as the ground plan for a narrative about a day in the life of a Dublin citizen, and though the intention of this and of Joyce's succeeding work ▷ *Finnegans Wake* is in part comic, there is also in both books deep seriousness, such as derives from the authentic epic tradition. In fact, this tradition, in the last three hundred years, has mingled with other literary forms, such as the romance, the comic romance (*eg* ▷ *Don Quixote*), and the novel, and it is in this mixed rather than in its original pure form that it has proved most productive.

Epic, Mock
▷ Mock epic

Epic simile
Prolonged similes, commonly used in ▷ epic or heroic poetry, giving the subject described a spaciousness suited to its grandeur. Thus in *Paradise Lost* Bk. I, ▷ Milton wants to say that the fallen Satan is as big as a whale; this would be to use an ordinary simile. He expands it to an epic simile thus:

As huge as . . .
. . . that Sea-beast
Leviathan, which God of all his works
Created hugest that swim th'Ocean stream:
Him haply slumbring on the Norway foam
The Pilot of some small night-founder'd Skiff,
Deeming some Island, oft, as Sea-men tell,
With fixéd Anchor in his skaly rind
Moors by his side under the Lee, while Night
Invests the Sea, and wishéd Morn delayes:
So stretcht out huge in length the Arch-fiend lay . . .

Epic Theatre
A term used to describe dramatic and ▷ theatrical practices originally associated with Bertolt Brecht and Erwin Piscator that

attempt to combat audiences' tendencies to empathic reactions, particularly those associated with Naturalism. Brecht developed a range of strategies to achieve an Alienation effect, whereby the audience remained aware of the processes of the theatrical event and able to reflect on it rather than be consumed by it. Very little contemporary dramaturgy and staging is unaffected in some way by Epic Theatre.
Bib: Styan, J. L., *Modern Drama in Theory and Practice 3: Expressionism and Epic Theatre*; Willett, J. ed, *Brecht on Theatre*.

Epicoene, or The Silent Woman (1609)
A comedy by ▷ Ben Jonson. Epicoene means having the characteristics of either sex. The main character, Morose, who has an extreme hatred of noise, wants to disinherit his nephew and marry a silent woman if she can be found. A completely silent one is found, but after marriage she finds the use of her tongue and is anything but silent. Morose promises to reinstate his nephew as his heir, with an additional reward, if he can free his uncle of the wife who is now the opposite of what he hoped. The nephew then discloses that the wife is a boy disguised. Though not one of the greatest of Jonson's comedies, it has always been one of his most popular, owing to a large cast of lively comic characters. The play is given a close analysis in Dryden's (1631–1700) *Essay on Dramatic Poesy*.

▷ *Querelle des Femmes*.

Epigram
For the ancient Greeks the word meant 'inscription'. From this, the meaning extended to include very short poems notable for the terseness and elegance of their expression and the weight and wit of their meaning. The richest of the ancient Greek collections is the Greek ▷ *Anthology*; the greatest Latin masters were ▷ Catullus and Martial. ▷ Ben Jonson's epigrams are in their tradition; for example, *To the Reader, Pray thee, take care, that tak'st my book in hand, To read it well: that is, to understand*. After him, epigrams became shorter and most commonly had satirical content; ▷ Pope was the greatest master of this style, and his poems include many epigrams.

▷ Aphorism.

Epiphany
A Church festival celebrating the showing ('epiphany' means manifestation) of the Christ child to the Magi, otherwise known as the three Wise Men or the Three Kings (*Matthew* II). The festival is 12 days after Christmas Day, so it is also called Twelfth Night. It concludes the season of Christmas festivities.

The novelist ▷ James Joyce began his career by writing what he called 'epiphanies', *ie* sketches in which the incident, though often in itself slight, manifests or reveals the inner truth of a character. This is the method he pursues in ▷ *Dubliners*. Other 'epiphanal' experiences might be ▷ Virginia Woolf's 'moments of being' or Wordsworth's ▷ 'Spots of Time'.

Epipsychidion (1821)
▷ Shelley's turbulent poem concerning the relationship between the intellectual flights of metaphor and the felt reality of love, composed in Pisa and triggered by the incarceration of 'the noble and unfortunate lady', Emilia Viviani, in a convent. The degree to which the poet's relationship with Emilia was flirtatious or ▷ platonic is not clear to us now, and may not have been so then. What is more clear is that the imprisonment of a beautiful girl (by parents in search of a suitable husband) was a gift to Shelley as a poet, enabling him to attack favourite targets such as marriage and the church with passionate and trenchant oratory. Indeed, ▷ Romantic ▷ rhetoric in this poem begins to become its own subject, and the unfortunate Emilia becomes less a woman than a fecund figure of speech, 'A Metaphor of Spring and Youth and Morning; A Vision like Incarnate April, warning/ With smiles and tears, Frost the Anatomy/ Into his summer grave'. At once fiery and self-questioning, *Epipsychidion* not only bears on those themes that ▷ Deconstructionist critics such as ▷ Paul de Man have detected in Romantic poetry, but appears through the complexities of its language to deconstruct itself.

Episteme
The traditional meaning of the term 'epistemology' is 'the theory of science of the method or grounds of knowledge' (Oxford English Dictionary). In the work of the French philosopher ▷ Michel Foucault, 'episteme' has come to mean something more specific. He uses the term to describe 'the total set of relations that unite, at a given period, the discursive practices that give rise to epistemological figures, sciences, and possibly formalized systems,' (*The Archaeology of Knowledge*; 1972). In short the episteme is historicized as the basic unit used to describe the manner in which a society represents knowledge to itself. Foucault conceives of the episteme in dynamic rather than static terms, since knowledge is always a matter of the ways in which 'desire' and 'power' negotiate their way through the complex ▷ discourses of society. Foucault is at pains to point out, however, that the episteme does not establish a transcendental authority which guarantees the existence of scientific knowledge, but rather points towards the fact that different kinds of knowledge are inscribed in 'the process of a historical practice'.

Epistolary novel
A novel which takes the form of letters written

by one or more of the characters. One of the best-known examples in English is ▷ Samuel Richardson's ▷ *Pamela* (1740–1).

Epitaph

An inscription on a tomb, or a short verse or prose inscription that might serve such a purpose. As literary compositions, epitaphs became popular in the ▷ Renaissance, and the requirement of brevity gives epitaphs a resemblance to ▷ epigrams. The 18th century, the great age of the epigram, was also that in which the epitaph was most cultivated.

***Epithalamion* (1594)**

▷ Edmund Spenser's ode written in 1594, and published at the end of the ▷ sonnet sequence ▷ *Amoretti* (1595). The poem celebrates the marriage of Spenser to Elizabeth Boyle at Cork on 11 July 1594. ▷ *Prothalamion*.

Epyllion

A term, now largely unused, to describe the short-lived but popular Elizabethan genre of the minor or brief ▷ epic. It often, though not exclusively, denoted narrative verse which took as its model not the epics of ▷ Homer or ▷ Virgil, but the writings of ▷ Ovid. The genre flourished in England in the late 16th century, and includes works such as ▷ Thomas Lodge's *Scilla's Metamorphosis* (1589), *Ovid's Banquet of Sence* (1595) by ▷ George Chapman (?1559–1634) and ▷ Francis Beaumont's *Salmacis and Hermaphroditus* (1602). The most famous examples of the genre are undoubtedly ▷ Christopher Marlowe's ▷ *Hero and Leander* of 1598, to which Chapman and Henry Petowe (fl 1598–1612) appended 'continuations', and ▷ Shakespeare's ▷ *Venus and Adonis* (1593). Invariably, the epyllion's subject matter was erotic myth, but unlike earlier translations of Ovid, there was no attempt at placing the erotic within ▷ allegorical or moral context.
Bib: Alexander, N. (ed.), *Elizabethan Narrative Verse*.

Erasmus, Desiderius (?1466–1536)

Dutch-born Augustinian monk, translator, humanist, educationalist, biblical scholar and linguist. Erasmus was one of the most important northern European scholars of the ▷ Renaissance period. The diversity of his interests, the range of his accomplishments, and the weight of his influence on European thought in the 16th century and later are almost impossible to quantify.

Erasmus' chief works are: the *Adages* (first published in 1500), the *Enchiridion* (1503), the *Praise of Folly* (1509) and the *Colloquies* (first published in 1516). But to these popular successes can be added his editions of the Church Fathers, paraphrases, commentaries on the scripture, editions of the classics and a huge correspondence with other European scholars and thinkers, the most important of whom, in England, was his close friend ▷ Sir Thomas More. The *Praise of Folly*, a satirical work which ranges widely over all aspects of public life in the period, was conceived while Erasmus was travelling to England to see More – a circumstance preserved in the work's punning Latin title: *Encomium Moriae*.

The *Enchiridion*, on the other hand, is a manual of the Christian life which encourages knowledge of pagan (that is ▷ classical) literature as a preparative towards attaining Christian scriptural understanding. The *Adages* – a work which grew from some 800 'adages' or classical sayings into over 4,000 short essays by the time Erasmus died – provided an entry into classical literature, and into humanistic thought generally, for the public at large. Similarly, the *Colloquies* expanded as Erasmus worked at the project until they eventually formed a wide-ranging series of dialogues on a huge variety of topics, which were to include education, games, travel, parenthood, punishment and social and religious questions.
Bib: *The Collected Works of Erasmus*; Huizinga, J., *Erasmus of Rotterdam*.

***Erewhon* (1872) and *Erewhon Revisited* (1901)**

Satirical anti-utopias by ▷ Samuel Butler. ▷ Sir Thomas More's ▷ *Utopia* is a description of an ideal country as different as possible from England. Erewhon (an anagram of 'Nowhere') represents a country many of whose characteristics are analogous to English ones, caricatured and satirized. Thus Butler satirizes ecclesiastical institutions through the Musical Banks and parental tyranny through the Birth Formulae; machinery has to be abolished before it takes over from human beings. In *Erewhom Revisited*, Higgs, the English discoverer of Erewhon, finds that his previous departure by balloon has been used by Professors Hanky and Panky ('hanky-panky' is deceitful practice) to impose a new religion, according to which Higgs is worshipped as a child of the sun. Butler's method in these satires resembles ▷ Jonathan Swift's satirical technique in the Lilliput of ▷ *Gulliver's Travels*.

***Esmond, The History of* (1852)**

A historical novel by ▷ William Makepeace Thackeray. It is a very careful reconstruction of early-18th-century English aristocratic and literary society. The hero's father has been killed fighting for James II, *ie* he was a ▷ Jacobite. The politics of the book are involved with Jacobite plotting by the Roman ▷ Catholic branch of the House of ▷ Stuart to recover the throne of Britain from the Protestant branch. There are portraits of some of the distinguished personalities of the time – the Duke and

Duchess of ▷ Marlborough, and the writers ▷ Sir Richard Steele, ▷ Joseph Addison and ▷ Jonathan Swift. The style emulates that of Addison himself. The theme is the devotion of the young Henry Esmond to his relatives, Lady Castlewood, eight years older than himself, and her proud and ambitious daughter, Beatrix. These relationships are complicated by political intrigues and by family mysteries – Esmond is in reality himself the heir to the title and properties inherited by Lady Castlewood's husband. In the end, Esmond marries the widowed Lady Castlewood and emigrates to Virginia; his story continues in *The Virginians* (1857–9).

Essay concerning Human Understanding **(1690)**
A philosophical treatise by ▷ John Locke. Locke emphasizes reason as the dominant faculty of man. All knowledge is acquired through experience based on sense impressions; there are no 'innate ideas', *ie* no knowledge arises in the mind independently of impressions received from the outside world. These impressions divide into primary qualities, *ie* the measurable ones such as size, number, form, etc., and secondary ones, such as colour, sound and scent, which are not demonstrably part of the object, but dependent on the observer. Knowledge begins with perception of agreement or disagreement in the qualities observed in the objects or, as Locke calls them, 'ideas'. He distinguishes between rational judgement, which identifies and analyses ideas, and 'wit', which relates them by their resemblances; the distinction is practically one between reason and imagination and gives advantage to reason. Faith, *eg* in religious doctrine, is not distinct from reason, but the assent of the mind to a belief that accords with reason. Thus Locke appeals to clear definition in language and expression; he depreciates the intuitive and imaginative faculties of the mind and elevates the rational ones. His thesis accords with the reaction at the end of the 17th century against the intolerance and fanaticism of the religious conflicts which had prevailed during the first half of it. The influence of his philosophy is impressed on the imaginative prose literature of the first thirty years of the 18th century, for instance in the realism of ▷ Daniel Defoe. Later in the century, the novelist ▷ Laurence Sterne makes ingenious use of Locke's theory of the association of ideas in ▷ *Tristram Shandy*.

Essay on Criticism **(1711)**
Written when he was only 21 and published when he was 23, ▷ Alexander Pope's compendium of neo-classical poetic theory in ▷ heroic couplets was highly praised by ▷ Joseph Addison, and helped to make his reputation. Pope defends the poetic art by arguing, in the tradition of ▷ Aristotle, ▷ Horace, and more recently ▷ Boileau, that 'true wit' is merely an 'imitation' of nature, and is not startling and original like the 'false wit' of the discredited 17th-century ▷ 'metaphysical' poets. '*True wit* is *Nature* to Advantage drest,/ What oft was *Thought*, but ne'er so well *Exprest*'.
Moreover Nature has already been perfectly understood by the revered ancient Greek and Latin poets, and the modern poet need not go to the trouble of copying direct from it since: 'To copy '*Nature* is to copy *Them*'. Exception is however made for those of great genius who '*rise* to *Faults* true Criticks *dare not mend*; . . . And *snatch* a *Grace* beyond the Reach of Art'.

The aphoristic quality of some lines in the poem seems to bear out Pope's ideas on true wit: 'To Err is *Human*; to Forgive, *Divine*'; 'For *Fools* rush in where *Angels* fear to tread'. However the best poetry in the *Essay* is as idiosyncratic and figuratively adventurous as anything in the 'metaphysical' poets of the previous century, as for example the description of the blockheads, too dull to perceive that they are being satirized: 'Still humming on, their drowzy Course they keep,/And *lash'd* so long, like *Tops*, are lash'd *asleep*' (600–1), or the deliberately bad lines, imitating various vices of versification: 'And ten low Words oft creep in one dull Line' (347). Despite its parade of sober respectability Pope's *Essay* is best seen as the protective camouflage of a brilliant poet adapting to the prosaic temper of the times, rather than a seriously pondered theoretical system. It is however important as a summary of neo-classical and 'Augustan' maxims.

Essay on Man **(1733–4)**
After the scurrilities of ▷ *The Dunciad* (1728) ▷ Alexander Pope turned to the philosophical poem which he hoped would crown his poetic career. The *Essay* was published anonymously so as to wrong-foot his enemies, who were not sure whether to damn it as Pope's, or to praise it as superior to anything Pope could have achieved. In four heroic-couplet epistles, addressed to the Tory politician ▷ Lord Bolingbroke, the poet attempts with cheerful optimism to 'vindicate the ways of God to Man', arguing that 'Whatever *is*, is *right*'. Pope expounds the medieval and ▷ Renaissance concept of a 'chain of being', with its primitive blend of theology and natural philosophy, and reconciles it uneasily with the modern empirical science of ▷ Sir Isaac Newton. The work became a kind of handbook of popular ▷ Enlightenment notions throughout Europe and was extensively translated.

It expresses the ▷ Deist view that God can be apprehended through nature, and not only through 'revealed' scriptures. 'Lo! the poor Indian, whose untutor'd mind/Sees God in clouds, or hears him in the wind'. The 'natural religion' of the poem, influenced by Bolingbroke, and by the Whig philosopher, the third ▷ Earl of Shaftesbury, incurred a

magisterial rebuke from the Swiss professor of divinity Jean Paul de Crousaz, and Pope, a ▷ Catholic, was embarrassed to discover that his work was potentially heretical. Today Pope's facile blend of science and religion appears spiritually trivial in comparison with both the consistent 'atheist' Deism of ▷ Rochester, and the sense of original sin of an orthodox Christian such as ▷ Jonathan Swift. The poem does however give brilliant poetic expression to a mood of enlightened confidence and *élan* which characterizes the period, even when what is being said is quite unremarkable: 'Know then thyself, presume not God to scan;/ The proper study of Mankind is Man.' And it contains some fine passages and isolated ▷ couplets: 'The spider's touch, how exquisitely fine!/ Feels at each thread, and lives along the line.'
▷ Enlightenment.

Essay, The
'Essay' derives from the French *essai* meaning 'experiment', 'attempt'. As a literary term it is used to cover an enormous range of composition, from schoolboy exercises to thorough scientific and philosophical works, the only quality in common being the implied desire of the writer to reserve to himself some freedom of treatment. But the essay is also a recognized literary form in a more defined sense: it is understood to be a fairly short prose composition, in style often familiarly conversational and in subject either self-revelatory or illustrative (more or less humorously) of social manners and types. The originator of the form was the great French writer ▷ Montaigne.

Montaigne's essays were published in completed form in 1595, and translated by ▷ John Florio into English (1603). His starting-point is 'Que sais-je?' ('What do I know?') and it leads him into a serious inquiry into his own nature as he feels it, and into investigations of facts, ideas, and experiences as he responds to them. In 1597 the first great English essayist, ▷ Francis Bacon, published his first collection of essays, of a very different kind: they are impersonal and aphoristic, weightily sententious. The character writers, ▷ Sir Thomas Overbury and John Earle (?1601–65) use the classical model of the Greek writer ▷ Theophrastus, reminding one that with so indefinite a form it is impossible to be too precise about the dating of starting-points. ▷ Abraham Cowley published the first essays in English closely corresponding to what is now understood by the form, and perhaps shows the first sign of its degeneracy: easiness of tone, which in Montaigne is a graciousness of manner introducing a serious and interesting personality, but which in less interesting writers may be an agreeable cover for saying nothing in particular.

In the early years of the 18th century ▷ Addison and ▷ Steele firmly established what is now known as the 'periodical essay' – a kind of higher journalism, intended often to please rather than instruct, but in their case to instruct through pleasure. In creations such as ▷ Sir Roger de Coverley, they developed the Theophrastian character into a personal, idiosyncratic portrait anticipating the characterization of the novelists a little later in the century. Their graciousness and lightness of tone take points and interest from their serious and conscious social purpose. ▷ Dr Johnson in *The Rambler* and in his essays as ▷ 'The Idler' used the weighty, impressive style soon to be regarded as unsuitable for the medium. ▷ Oliver Goldsmith in *The Citizen of the World* (1762) perfected the graceful, witty manner which came to be considered ideal for it.

If the 18th century was what may be called the golden age of the English essay, the early 19th, in the work of ▷ Charles Lamb, ▷ William Hazlitt, ▷ Leigh Hunt and ▷ De Quincey, was perhaps its silver age. In these writers, social comment combines with a confessional, autobiographical element which had never been so prominent in the English essay before. This was true to the autobiographical spirit of so much 19th-century literature. These essayists were links between the early Romantic poets – especially ▷ Wordsworth – and the mid-Victorian novelists; they shared the close interest in material surroundings characteristic of these poets, and their essays often contained character delineations related to such environmental settings. The earliest work of ▷ Charles Dickens, ▷ *Sketches by Boz*, is in the essayists' tradition.

After 1830, the periodical essay in the tradition of Addison, Goldsmith, Hazlitt and Lamb dissolved into the morass of constantly increasing journalism; though they had emulators in the 20th century, the form was increasingly despised by serious writers, and the famous essayists of the later 19th century were the more specialized sort, such as ▷ Matthew Arnold and ▷ John Stuart Mill. Yet is is not true to say that the informal essay of serious literary interest has disappeared. In the later 19th and 20th century, essays of natural description of remarkable intensity were produced by ▷ Richard Jefferies and ▷ Edward Thomas. More important still is the use of the essay for unspecialized but serious social and cultural comment by – to take leading examples – D. H. Lawrence, ▷ George Orwell, and ▷ Aldous Huxley. With the growth in popularity of serious ▷ magazines and the extended articles in the Sunday newspapers, the essay is today having a considerable revival. These informal arguments and 'personality pieces', such as those by Bernard Levin in *The Times*, are very far, however, from the formal essay genre.
▷ Characters, Theophrastian.

***Essay to Revive the Ancient Education of Gentlewomen, An* (1673)**
A prospectus for a school at Tottenham, just

north of London, by ▷ Bathsua Pell Makin. This prospectus is also an argument for women's education, and is an early part of the debate about the education of women in literacy, numeracy and languages (see also ▷ Catharine Macaulay, ▷ Mary Wollstonecraft, ▷ Sarah Fielding). The tract confines itself to the education of gentlewomen, never suggesting that education should spread throughout society, but it does make a significant argument for broadening the accepted curriculum for girls to place more emphasis on languages and literacy. Makin also situates her argument historically (note the word 'revive' in the title) and this serves to remind readers of a tradition of women's education before the English Civil War.

▷ Women, Education of.

Essays, Bacon's

▷ Bacon, Francis.

Essays in Criticism (1865, 1888)

The two volumes (First Series 1865; Second Series 1888) that contain much of the most important of ▷ Matthew Arnold's literary critical work. The first volume opens with 'The Function of Criticism at the Present Time', a discussion of the relevance of criticism both to creative literature and to society and civilization; it is an example of what the poet T. Eliot (1888–1965) was later to call Arnold's 'propaganda for criticism', and it has been influential among 20th-century critics. The second essay, 'The Literary Influence of Academies', makes a case for authoritative standards in culture, and constitutes an implicit criticism of the habits of English culture, again in a way that is still relevant. The remainder of the first volume comprises essays on foreign writers and literature. The Second Series opens with a striking essay on 'The Study of Poetry', in which Arnold puts his view that poetry will supply to the modern world the kind of inspiration that was afforded by great religions in the past – a view which has also been put forward in the 20th century, notably by I.A. Richards in *The Principles of Literary Criticism* (1924), though he expresses the view in other terms. The remainder of the Second Series consists principally of studies of English poets of the 18th and 19th centuries. On the whole, Arnold's fame rests more on the broad themes of the relationships of literature and society than on his particular studies, though some of these, eg on the German poet Heinrich Heine in the First Series, are of great interest.

Essays of Elia (1823; 1833)

A series of essays by ▷ Charles Lamb, published in ▷ *The London Magazine* and then in a collected edition. They emulate the essays of Joseph Addison (1672–1719) and Sir Richard Steele (1672–1729) in the *Spectator* and *Tatler* of a century before, but depend less on their content than on Lamb's attempt to win the affection and interest of the reader for himself as a person. The style is whimsical and self-conscious, owing something to the musical and humorously eccentric appeal of Robert Burton's (1577–1640) *Anatomy of Melancholy* which to some extent it emulates. However, there are passages of witty observation and acute character sketches.

▷ Essay.

Essentialism

Philosophically, the notion of 'essence' refers to the proposition that the physical world embodies in it a range of fixed and timeless essences which precede existence. In Christianity this is exemplified in the division between the soul and the body, where the latter is relegated to the realm of temporal existence. In ▷ materialist accounts essentialism has come to be associated with attempts to deny the primacy of history as a formative influence on human affairs and human personality. It also challenges the emphasis upon the autonomy of the individual as a theoretically 'free' agent who is the centre of meaning. Any questioning of the notion that essence precedes existence deeply affects the issue of what is assumed to be the coherent nature of human identity. It also resists the attempt to reduce material reality to a set of mental images. To remove the human subject from the centre and to re-inscribe him or her in a series of complex historical relations is to challenge, at a theoretical level, human autonomy. It also suggests that those philosophical arguments which place the individual at the centre of meaning and authority are restrictive in that they propose a view of the world which masks the connection between knowledge and particular human interests.

Essex, Robert Devereux, Earl of (1566–1601)

Patron, poet and favourite of ▷ Queen Elizabeth I. Robert Devereux, second Earl of Essex was the stepson of the ▷ Earl of Leicester and followed him into the intimate circle of the queen's favourites. He pursued a political and martial career which won him glory throughout the 1590s; however in 1599 he was sent to Ireland to suppress Tyrone's rebellion and returned unexpectedly without Elizabeth's permission having failed in his mission. He remained under house arrest until in 1601 he attempted to seize power from the queen in an ill-fated rebellion. He was executed on 25 February of the same year. Although Elizabeth had ordered his death, even in the face of final pleas for mercy, she never recovered her old vigour and the last 18 months of her reign seem to have been shrouded in a recognition of her own mortality. Some of Essex's fellow conspirators

arranged for a special performance of what we believe to be ▷ Shakespeare's ▷ *Richard II* around the city of London on the day before the revolt. The play shows the abdication of an unpopular monarch and its enactment was supposedly to rouse the crowds into calling for a similar relinquishing of power on the part of Elizabeth. Shakespeare also refers to Essex in ▷ *Henry V*, where a successful return from the Irish campaign is hoped for.
Bib: Lacey, R., *An Elizabethan Icarus*.

***Esther Waters* (1894)**
A novel by ▷ George Moore, this sympathetic treatment of a servant girl seduced brought him instant success. Esther is a member of the Plymouth Brethren who goes into service at Woodview for the Barfield family to escape her drunken father. Aged only seventeen, she is seduced and deserted by the footman William Latch. Dismissed from her position, Esther endures a bitter and humiliating struggle to rear her son. She rejects an offer of marriage from a respectable Salvationist and marries William Latch for the sake of their son. In addition to being a good husband and father Latch is also a publican and bookmaker and is ruined both physically and financially by his involvement in horse racing. He dies leaving the family destitute, but Esther's son soon becomes independent. Esther returns to Woodview at the close of the novel and to the widowed and impoverished Mrs Barfield who was previously kind to her. Here she finds peace and fulfilment. *Esther Waters* shares many similarities with ▷ Hardy's ▷ *Tess of the d'Urbervilles* (1891) but the former is less naturalistic and its heroine is resourceful and enduring rather than tragic.
▷ 'Fallen Woman, The'.

Etherege, Sir George (?1634–92)
Dramatist, one of those who set the style of Restoration comedy after the return to the throne of ▷ Charles II. Etherege may have studied at Cambridge University, and is believed to have spent some of his early adulthood in France. He read law at the Inns of Court. His first play, *Love in a Tub; Or,* ▷ *The Comical Revenge* (1664), composed partly in rhymed ▷ couplets, established him in court circles, but his next play, ▷ *She Wou'd if She Cou'd* (1668) was a relative failure. Both these plays show the influence of ▷ Molière. In 1668 Etherege was appointed secretary to the English ambassador to Constantinople. Returning to England in 1671, Etherege continued to write and his last, most famous play, ▷ *The Man of Mode* came in 1676. Some time after 1677 Etherege married a widow, Mary Arnold, it is said for her fortune. In 1685 he was appointed Ambassador at Ratisbon (Regensburg), and abandoned his wife. He had an affair with the actress ▷ Elizabeth Barry, among his many intrigues with women; Barry bore him a daughter. In 1689 he joined the deposed King ▷ James II in Paris, where he died. Known as 'Gentleman George', Etherege epitomized to many of his contemporaries the sort of hell-raising rake depicted in his plays. The part of Bellair in *The Man of Mode* is thought to be a self-portrait, while the flamboyant Dorimant is said to have been modelled on his friend, the ▷ Earl of Rochester. His comedy depends primarily on his witty and often cynical dialogue among characters in fashionable society. Several of his comic types were used by later dramatists, such as ▷ Wycherley, ▷ Behn, and ▷ Congreve, and his fluent, easy style set a precedent for many of their plays.
Bib: Rosenfeld, S., *The Letterbook of Sir George Etherege*; Underwood, D., *Etherege and the Seventeenth Century Comedy of Manners*.

Ettrick Shepherd, The
▷ Hogg, James.

Eugenia
Name used by a writer who attacked John Sprints *The Bride-Woman's Counsellor* (1699) in *The Female Advocate* (1700), arguing that, although the woman is bound to passive obedience, yet 'I defy the meekest woman in the world, if she meets with an unreasonable, domineering, insolent creature . . . to forbear wishing it otherwise.'
▷ Chudleigh, Lady Mary
Bid: Browne, A. *The Eighteenth Century Feminist Mind*.

Euphemism
▷ Figures of speech.

***Euphues* (1578–80)**
A prose romance by ▷ John Lyly, in two parts; the first, *Euphues, or the Anatomy of Wit* was published in 1578; the second, *Euphues and his England*, in 1580. The tales have very little story; they have been described as 'pattern books' for courtly behaviour, especially in love. Their most striking quality is their elaborate style: long sentences balance clause against clause and image against image, so as to produce an effect of ornament taking priority a long way over sense. ▷ Falstaff in ▷ *Henry IV Part I* (II.iv) parodies Euphues when he is burlesquing the king, *eg* 'for though the camomile, the more it is trodden on, the faster it grows, yet youth, the more it is wasted, the sooner it wears'. Though often parodied as the language of fops, the style was much imitated, especially by Elizabethan romance writers such as ▷ Robert Greene in *Menaphon* (1589) and ▷ Thomas Lodge in *Rosalynde* (1590). Even ▷ Beatrice and Benedick in ▷ Shakespeare's ▷ *Much Ado*

About Nothing indulge in the courtly verbal play characterized by Lyly. The name 'Euphues' is from Greek, and means generally, 'well endowed by nature'. ▷ Roger Ascham in *The Schoolmaster* had already used it to designate a man well endowed for learning and able to put it to good use. Ascham was an admirer of ▷ Castiglione's *The Courtier*, and Lyly's cult of the courtly virtues is in the same tradition. Basic to it is the conception that nature is not to be imitated but to be improved upon.

Euphuism
▷ Figures of Speech.

Euripedes (480–406 BC)
The last of the three great Athenian writers of tragedy, the other two being ▷ Aeschylus and ▷ Sophocles. Like them, he had no direct influence upon the Elizabethan period of English drama, though ▷ Gascoigne's *Jocasta* (1575) is a translation of an Italian adaptation of Euripedes' *Phoenissae*. Like Aeschylus and Sophocles, however, Euripedes was admired by ▷ Milton, who emulated the Greeks in ▷ *Samson Agonistes*. Among Euripedes' surviving plays are *Alcestis, Medea, Hippolytus, Andromache, Hecuba, Bacchae, Electra, The Trojan Women, Orestes, Heracles, Iphigenia at Aulis, Iphigenia among the Tauri, Ion*.

***Europeans, The* (1878)**
A novel by ▷ Henry James, first published serially in *The Atlantic Monthly* from July to October 1878. Alongside ▷ *Daisy Miller*, which appeared in same year, it opened up the international theme in James' writing, using the ▷ 'novel of manners' style to contrast two cultures – Europe and the USA.

***Eustace Diamonds, The* (1873)**
A novel by ▷ Anthony Trollope initially serialized in ▷ *The Fortnightly Review* from 1871–73, and forming the third in the ▷ Palliser sequence. The novel shares many of the concerns of ▷ Wilkie Collins' *The Moonstone* (1868).

Evangelical Movement
A movement for Protestant revival in the Church of England in the late 18th and early 19th century. It is stimulated partly by ▷ John Wesley's Methodist revival and the activities of other sects (especially among the lower classes) outside the Church of England; it was also a reaction against the ▷ rationalism and scepticism of the 18th-century aristocracy, and against the ▷ atheism of the ▷ French Revolution. Politically, the movement tended to be conservative and was therefore strong among the Tories, whereas the Whigs (especially their aristocratic leaders such as ▷ Charles James Fox) retained more of the 18th-century worldliness and scepticism. In doctrine the Evangelicals were inclined to be austere, to attach importance to strength of faith and biblical guidance, and to oppose ceremony and ritual. Socially they developed a strong sense of responsibility to their fellow human beings, so that one of their leaders, ▷ William Wilberforce, devoted his life to the cause of abolishing slavery and the slave trade in British dominions, and later Lord Shaftesbury (1801–85) made it his life-work to alleviate the social and working conditions of the working classes. The leaders of the movement were laymen rather than clergy, and upper class rather than lower class, amongst whom the ▷ Nonconformist sects were more actively influential. As the Nonconformists were to contribute to English socialism later in the century a religious rather than a Marxist inspiration, so the Evangelicals later led to generations of highly responsible, independent-minded intellectuals such as the historians Thomas Babington Macaulay and Trevelyan, and the novelist ▷ Virginia Woolf.

Evans, Caradoc (1878–1945)
Short story writer, novelist and playwright. Born in Carmarthenshire, moving to Cardiganshire in early childhood, Caradoc Evans worked as a draper and shop assistant in Carmarthen, Barry, Cardiff and London where, after attending evening classes in English composition, he found employment as a journalist in 1906, later editing various magazines between 1915 and 1929. According to Professor Gywn Jones, the 'first distinctive ancestral voice' of Anglo-Welsh writing, Caradoc Evans gave lasting offence to the Welsh-speaking literary establishment through his presentation of Cardi peasantry with grotesqueries of character and speech, and lust, greed and hypocrisy that established a false Welsh stereotype in his short stories that amused Londoners and created both his literary reputation and his unpopularity in his native land. His short story collections were: *My People* (1915); *Capel Sion* (1916); *My Neighbours* (1919); *Pilgrims in a Foreign Land* (1942); and the posthumously published *The Earth Gives All and Takes All* (1946). His novels were: *Nothing to Pay* (1930); *Wasps* (1933); *This Way to Heaven* (1934); *Morgan Bible* (1943); and *Mother's Marvel* (posthumously, in 1949). His one play, *Taffy* (1923) attacked Welsh village life. A recently published miscellany of his writings entitled *Fury Never Leaves Us*, ed. John Harris, appeared in 1985.
Bib: Stephens, M. (Ed.), *The Oxford Companion to the Literature of Wales*); Jones, G., *The Dragon Has Two Tongues*; Jones, G. and Rowlands, J., *Profiles*.

***Eve of St Agnes* (1820)**
The 18th-century fashion for pseudo-medieval poetry in ▷ Spenserian stanzas culminated

in ▷ John Keats' masterpiece of sensuous aestheticism. Madeline retires to bed on St Agnes' Eve hoping to be granted a vision of her lover by the saint. Meanwhile her lover Porphyro, an enemy to her family, steals into her chamber, aided by an aged servant woman, and watches his beloved undress from a closet. When the girl wakes she finds that Porphyro has prepared a sumptuous banquet of 'cakes and dainties'. They make love before fleeing into the storm. The poet employs every extreme of verbal artifice to transform this flimsy escapist fantasy into a pattern of archetypal contrasts: youth and age, fire and ice, security and danger. The interwoven rhyme scheme and the final ▷ alexandrine of each stanza are each made to yield the maximum ornamental and musical effect. Dense, tactile imagery abounds ('the tiger-moth's deep-damask'd wings'). There are crowded alliterations ('the silver, snarling trumpets 'gan to chide'); inventive archaisms ('carven imag'ries', 'blue affrayed eyes'); neologisms ('jellies soother than the creamy curd'); transferred epithets ('azure-lidded sleep', 'silken Samarkand'); exotic compounds ('flaw-blown sleet', 'palsy-twitch'd'); and synaesthetic constructions ('warm gules', 'perfume light'), all designed to overwhelm and delight the reader's senses.

Evelina **(1778)**
A novel in letters by ▷ Fanny Burney. Evelina has been abandoned by her aristocratic father, and her socially much humbler mother is dead. She has been brought up by her guardian, a solitary clergyman. As a beautiful, well-bred, and intelligent young girl, she pays a visit to a friend in London, where she falls in love with a handsome aristocrat, Lord Orville, is pursued by an unscrupulous rake, Sir Clement Willoughby, and is much embarrassed by vulgar relatives, especially her grandmother, Madame Duval. The convincing and delightful part of the novel consists in its acute and lively social observation, in many ways superior to anything of the sort yet accomplished in the 18th-century novel, and anticipating the maturer art of ▷ Jane Austen in the early 19th century.
▷ Epistolary novel.

Evelyn, John (1620–1706)
Chiefly remembered as a diarist. His diary, published in 1818, covers the years 1641–97, and includes impressions of distinguished contemporaries, customs and manners, and accounts of his travels. He published ▷ translations from Greek, Latin and French, as well as essays on the practical arts (gardening, the cultivation of trees, engraving, architecture). He also wrote an interesting ▷ biography of a court lady (*The Life of Mrs Godolphin*, unpublished until 1847).
▷ Diaries.

Bib: *Diary*, ed. E. S. de Beer; Ponsonby, A., *Life*; Hiscock, W. G., *John Evelyn and his Family Circle*; Marburg, C., *Mr Pepys and Mr Evelyn*.

Every Man in his Humour **(1598)**
The first important play by ▷ Ben Jonson. By ▷ 'humour' is to be understood as a passion generated by irrational egotism and amounting sometimes to a mania. The play – which is better known in its revised form with English characters than in the first version of 1598 with Italian characters – is a comedy of misunderstandings bred largely through the deceitfulness of Brainworm, a mischievous servant, acting on the absurd humours of the other characters: the jealousy of the merchant Kitely, the credulity of his young wife, the susceptibility of her sister, the bullying boastfulness of the cowardly soldier Bobadill, etc.
▷ Humours, Comedy of.

Every Man out of his Humour **(1599)**
The second of ▷ Ben Jonson's comedies of ▷ humours, with a range of satirical portraits: Fastidious Brisk, the foppish courtier with the sharp tongue; Sordido, the landowner who delights in shortages because they increase the price of his grain; Deliro, the infatuated husband; Puntarvolo, the knight who takes out an insurance on his pets; Fungoso, the would-be courtier who is always behind the fashion, etc. The method of satire is partly through character sketches in the tradition of Theophrastus and partly through the method that Jonson developed from ▷ Marlowe (in ▷ *The Jew of Malta*) of making a character carry his extravagance to the point of self-caricature. This play is, however, too narrow in the range and depth of its satire to rank among Jonson's great ones. The opening scene includes a speech (by Asper, lines 93–120) which contains an explicit account of what Jonson meant by a ▷ 'Humour'.
▷ Characters, Theophrastian.

Everyman
A ▷ morality play dating from the end of the 15th century, which in its extant form is based on a Dutch play *Elckerlijc*. It dramatizes the final acts of Everyman's life, when he is unexpectedly summoned by Death for a journey beyond this world. Everyman looks for companions for his journey, but as Goods, Kindred et al. vanish away, he discovers that Good Deeds alone will support him. The play rehearses Church teaching on the doctine of penance and provides a vehicle for a reaffirmation of the importance of the clergy as mediators between God and the laity.
Bib: Cawley, A. C. (ed.), *Everyman*.

Ewing, Juliana Horatia (1841–85) Writer of ▷ children's literature. Born in Ecclesfield,

Yorkshire, the daughter of ▷ Margaret Gatty. Her first published story was in ▷ Charlotte Yonge's *Monthly Packet* in 1861. She also contributed to her mother's periodical for children, *Aunt Judy's Magazine*, taking over its editorship in 1873. She was an extremely prolific writer and very popular in her time, though her sentimental and moralizing tone makes her less liked by children today. Her stories include: *Mrs Overtheway's Remembrances* (1866–8); *The Brownies* (1865); *Jan of the Windmill* (1872) and *Jackanapes* (1879).
Bib: Eden, Mrs H.F.K., *Juliana Horatia Ewing and her Books.*

Examiner, The

1 A right-wing (Tory) journal, started by Lord Bolingbroke and continued by ▷ Jonathan Swift. Engaged in controversy with the left-wing writers, Joseph Addison and ▷ Sir Richard Steele.

2 A weekly periodical founded by John and Leigh Hunt in 1808, famous for its radical politics. It had no political allegiance, but criticized public affairs, in the words of Leigh Hunt's friend John Keats, 'from a principle of taste'. In 1813 the Hunts were sent to prison for two years for exposing the gross flattery of the Prince Regent (later George IV) in another paper.

Excalibur

A modification of 'Caliburnus', the name of ▷ King Arthur's sword, forged in ▷ Avalon, in ▷ Geoffrey of Monmouth's *Historia Regum Britanniae*. In later versions of Arthurian narrative, the name Excalibur is applied to the sword which Arthur receives, mysteriously, from the hand of the ▷ Lady of the Lake (as a replacement for his first sword, drawn from the stone). When Arthur is mortally wounded, he arranges for Excalibur to be returned to the lake. One of his knights (most commonly Bedevere but sometimes Girflet) is finally persuaded to throw the sword into the lake, where it is caught and brandished by a hand, before disappearing below. Both ▷ Malory and ▷ Tennyson relate this episode in their respective Arthurian narratives.

Exclusion Bills

Statutory attempts by ▷ Lord Shaftesbury and his followers to exclude the Duke of York, ▷ Charles II's brother, from succession to the throne, on grounds of his ▷ Catholic faith. Exclusion Bills were brought in each of the years 1679–81. All were unsuccessful, and the Duke duly acceded to become ▷ James II in 1685. The underlying religious and political tensions continued to simmer, however, eventually boiling up into a head-on clash, resolved with the so-called ▷ Glorious Revolution of 1688 which overthrew James. The period of strain and uncertainty surrounding the introduction of the Bills is also known as the Exclusion Crisis.

Excursion, The **(1814)**

A long ▷ didactic poem in ▷ blank verse by ▷ William Wordsworth. It was intended to be the middle part of a three-part philosophical poem, to be called *The Recluse*, but the other two parts were never written. ▷ *The Prelude*, intended as an introduction to *The Recluse*, was completed in 1805, but was not published until after Wordsworth's death in 1850. Book I of *The Excursion*, which contains the most enduring poetry in the work, comprises a piece written some years before: *Margaret or the* ▷ *Ruined Cottage.* Books II–IV contain discussion between the poem's protagonist, the Wanderer, and his friend, the Solitary, who lacks faith in man and God. In Books V–VII a new character, the Pastor, relates the histories of some of his former parishioners buried in the churchyard. The last two books are concerned with the degradation of the poor by industrial expansion, and proposes educational reforms.
▷ Education.

Exhibition, The Great

Held in 1851, in Hyde Park in London, it was the first international exhibition of the products of industry and celebrated the peak of the British ▷ industrial revolution. It was regarded as a triumph for British prosperity and enlightenment, though by some critics, *eg* the philanthropist ▷ Lord Shaftesbury, as concealing the scandal of immense urban slums. Its principal building, the Crystal Palace, was a pioneer construction in the materials of glass and cast-iron. The architect was Joseph Paxton.

Existentialism

A modern school of philosophy which has had great influence on European literature since World War II. The doctrines to which the term has been applied are in fact very various, but a number of common themes may be identified. The first is the primacy of the individual, and of individual choice, over systems and concepts which attempt to explain him or her. For instance, the ▷ essentialist notion that the human self is built on a pre-social 'essence' or core of selfhood. Existentialism argues, in ▷ Jean-Paul Sartre's words, that 'existence precedes essence': that is, that one's freely chosen individual path constitutes one's existential reality and self – the self, for the existentialist, is not *essentially* pre-ordained or God-given, but comes into being in the material world through social interactions. Sartre explores this in *Being and Nothingness.* The second is the absurdity of the universe; reality, it is claimed, always evades adequate explanation, and remains radically contingent and disordered. This absurdity causes anxiety, but also makes freedom possible, since our actions also cannot be causally explained or predicted. Neither the behaviour nor the nature of others can be understood by observation. Existentialism sees freedom of choice as the most important fact of human existence. According to Sartre, consciousness of our own freedom is the sign of 'authentic experience', as opposed to the 'bad faith' of believing oneself bound. Investigation of this freedom involves investigation of the nature of being, and this has caused existentialism to form two main streams, the first atheistic, which interprets individual existence as dependent on transcendent Being. The best-known leaders of existentialism have been the philosophers Martin Heidegger (1889–1976) and Karl Jaspers (1883–1969) in Germany, and Sartre (1905–80) and the philosopher and dramatist Gabriel Marcel (1889–1973) in France. Marcel represents the religious stream whose progenitor was the 19th-century Danish thinker Sören Kierkegaard (1813–55).

Existentialism has had relatively little influence on British philosophy, because of the strong empirical tradition in Britain, although the novelist and philosopher ▷ Iris Murdoch has termed modern British empiricists existentialist in her essay *The Sovereignty of Good*. Correspondingly, existentialism has had a less powerful influence on literature than in France, where authors like Sartre, ▷ Simone de Beauvoir, and Albert Camus have expounded its doctrines in, for example, such works as Sartre's trilogy of novels, *Roads to Freedom* (1947–9) and his play *No Exit* (1944), or Camus' novel *The Outsider* (1942), or in de Beauvoir's series of autobiographies. Nevertheless, these doctrines have been important in two ways. First, they have directly influenced a number of experimental novelists with continental affinities, such as ▷ David Caute, ▷ Nigel Dennis, ▷ Andrew Sinclair, ▷ Colin Wilson and ▷ Christine Brooke-Rose. The most important writer in this category is ▷ Samuel Beckett in whose plays and novels the isolation and anxiety of the characters combine with an awareness of the issues of manipulation and choice implicit in the narrative and dramatic modes, to present existential dilemmas with unrivalled power. Second, existentialist doctrines have contributed much to the general ethos of ▷ postmodernism, and affected a number of major writers, prompting either admiration or resistance. Thus the postmodern concern with the nature of fictionality arises in part from the sense that neither individuals nor reality as a whole can be adequately conceptualized. The author's manipulation of his or her characters has provided a fruitful metaphor for the exploration of issues of freedom, as for example in the work of ▷ John Fowles, Iris Murdoch and ▷ Muriel Spark. Existentialism speaks powerfully to the sense of the 20th century as a chaotic and even catastrophic era, in which certainties have been lost and man is faced with the abyss of nothingness, or of his own capability for evil. It lays stress on extreme situations, which produce dread, arising from awareness of freedom of choice (according to Sartre) or awareness of original sin (according to Kierkegaard). Extremity and existential dread are important in the work of ▷ William Golding and ▷ Patrick White, and, earlier in the century, ▷ Joseph Conrad, who in this respect as in others anticipates the 20th-century *Zeitgeist*.

Expedition of Humphry Clinker, The **(1771)**
▷ *Humphry Clinker, The Expedition of.*

Experience, Songs of
▷ *Songs of Innocence and of Experience.*

Expressionism
Expressionism was originally intended to define an artistic movement which flourished at the beginning of the 20th century in Europe, especially in Germany. The expressionist painters, such as Edvard Munch and Vasili Kandinsky, built upon the departure from realism of Vincent van Gogh and Henri Matisse, and developed towards the expression of feeling through colour and form. This often led to exaggeration and distortion, which induced unease in the viewing public. Similar haunting and irrational imagery were used in German expressionist cinema, such as Robert Wiene's *The Cabinet of Dr Caligari* (1919) and F. W. Murnau's *Nosferatu* (1922).

The origins of expressionism as a theatrical movement are to be found in the work of a number of German dramatists who wrote between 1907 and the early 1920s. These include Ernst Barlach, Reinhard Goering, Walter Hasenclever, Carl Hauptmann, Franz Kafka, Georg Kaiser, Oscar Kokoschka, Carl Sternheim and Ernst Toller. Even ▷ Brecht was influenced by the movement in his early days. Although their individual styles differ greatly the expressionist playwrights rejected the 'objective' approach of naturalism and developed a highly emotional and subjective form of dramatic expression which aimed to explore the 'essence' of human experience. In their view this could be revealed only by getting beyond the surface appearances of ordinary life and exploring man's subconscious desires and visions. The impulse for this was revolutionary, if politically unclear. ▷ Strindberg, Wedekind, ▷ Freud and ▷ Nietzsche were the idols of the movement. Bourgeois ideology was the enemy and the uniting vision ubiquitously advocated was the rebirth of man (with the emphasis very much on the male) in touch with his spirit and free from petty social restraints. The use of exaggerated gesture, disturbing sound, colour and movement was a vital part of the dramatists' technique of shocking the audience and conveying ecstatic or *Angst*-ridden states of being. Short disconnected scenes replaced carefully constructed plots and scenery was distorted and hallucinatory rather than realistic. Later dramatists, such as Eugene O'Neill, Elmer Rice and ▷ Sean O'Casey, have tended to borrow from the dramatic language of expressionism without necessarily sharing the fervour of their German predecessors.

Extravaganza
Any composition which relies on its fantastic content for its effect. It is usually comic and irregular in its construction although commonly used today to describe any lavish show. Unlike ▷ farce, however, it is not a defined literary mode; consequently it more often describes a critical reaction to a work than the author's intention in the work.

F

Fabian Society
A large society of socialistic intellectuals, closely bound up with the British Labour Party. It was founded in 1884 and named after the Roman general Fabius Cunctator – 'Fabius the Delayer' – who in the 3rd century BC saved Rome from the Carthaginian army under Hannibal, by using a policy of attrition instead of open battle, *ie* he destroyed the army by small attacks on isolated sections of it, instead of risking total defeat by confronting Hannibal with the entire Roman army. The Fabian Society similarly advocated socialism by piecemeal action through parliamentary reform instead of risking disaster by total revolution; this policy has been summarized in the phrase 'the inevitability of gradualness'. The Fabians were among the principal influences leading to the foundation of the Labour Party in 1900. The years between 1884 and 1900 were those of its greatest distinction; they were led by ▷ George Bernard Shaw and Sidney and ▷ Beatrice Webb, and made their impact through the Fabian Essays on social and economic problems. They always advocated substantial thinking on solid evidence, in contrast to the more idealistic and 'utopian' socialism of such Victorian writers as William Morris. The diversification of socialist thought under the combined impact of theory emanating from France and political upheavals in Eastern Europe has perhaps made the Fabian framework anachronistic.

Fabliau
Derived from 'fable', the term is applied to a medieval genre of short, humorous narratives, particularly popular in Old French poetry of the 13th century, which are usually structured around a battle of wits of some kind. Wit and ingenuity are celebrated in these stories;, their outcomes may not conform to the dictates of a Christian morality. Characteristically, fabliaux are located in contemporary settings and many, though not all, have plots centred an adulterous situations. Explicitly sexual, scatological and bawdy terms are frequently employed in these narratives, as befits the kind of action they depict. ▷ Chaucer is one of the first English writers to work in this genre (in the ▷ *Miller's Tale*, the ▷ *Reeve's Tale*, the ▷ *Shipman's Tale*, for example), but from the evidence of the Anglo-Norman fabliaux in ▷ Harley 2253, it is clear that fabliaux were circulating in England before the composition of the ▷ *Canterbury Tales*. Many of the narratives in ▷ Boccaccio's ▷ *Decameron* are reworkings of fabliaux plots.

Fabula, Sjuzet/Syuzhet
The Russian Formalist critics made a distinction between the *fabula* (the chronological series of events that are represented or implied in a fiction) and the *sjuzet* or *syuzhet* (the order, manner and techniques of their presentation in the narrative). The distinction closely resembles that made in more recent ▷ narratology between ▷ story and ▷ narrative or text; but a third category, that of the act of ▷ narrating has now been added.

Fabulation
A form of writing which playfully flaunts its own fictionality and narrative artifice. The term has been applied in particular to American novelists such as John Barth and South American writers such as ▷ Jorge Luis Borges.

Faction
A form of writing in which real persons and events are portrayed, but the detail and presentation are fictional. The form has similarities to the dramatized television documentary. The term was coined by the American novelist Truman Capote, for his book *In Cold Blood*. An example is *Coming through Slaughter* by ▷ Michael Ondaatje, which is about the life of the jazz cornet player Buddy Bolden.

***Faerie Queene, The* (1590–6)**
▷ Edmund Spenser's unfinished ▷ allegorical romance. *The Faerie Queene* was first mentioned in correspondence by Spenser in 1580, and was probably circulating in manuscript form by 1588. Books I–III were published in 1590, and a second edition which contained Books IV–VI appeared in 1596. In 1609 a folio edition of the poem appeared, which contained the first six books of the poem, together with the 'Mutabilitie Cantos'. This is all of the work which has survived, though whether any more was written is doubtful.

The design of the poem, and Spenser's general conception of what the poem should set out to achieve, is recorded in a letter from Spenser to ▷ Sir Walter Ralegh that was published in the first edition of 1590. Here Spenser explains that his intention was to 'fashion a gentleman or noble person', and we can thus understand the poem as forming part of that ▷ Renaissance desire to create and sustain a personal identity. But the work is also a legendary history and celebration of the emergent British state and its monarch, ▷ Elizabeth I. The urgency of this project is understandable given Spenser's own residence in the unstable environment of Ireland for much of the period of the poem's composition.

In structure the poem follows the adventures of six knights, representing (Spenser claimed in his letter to Ralegh) the ▷ Aristotelian virtues. But the poem is episodic rather than possessed of a cumulative narrative structure. At the same time, to mention Aristotle is to mention only one of the poem's many progenitors, which include Plato, ▷ Ludovico Ariosto's *Orlando Furioso*, ▷ Torquato Tasso, ▷ Virgil and Arthurian romance.

The Faerie Queene is perhaps best thought of as a rich synthesis of Protestant and humanist ideals, and, at the same time, an anxious declaration of faith in the vision of national identity which it is the poem's task to display. Its influence on later writers, especially ▷ John Milton, was enormous.

▷ Arthur, King; Belphoebe; Duessa; Fidessa; Florimell; Gloriana; Orgoglio; Red Cross Knight.

Bib: Hamilton, A. C. (ed.), *The Faerie Queene*; Heale, E., *The Faerie Queene: A Reader's Guide*; Miller, D. L., *The Poem's Two Bodies*.

Fainlight, Ruth (b 1931)

Poet and translator. Born in New York, Fainlight lives in Britain, although she is an American citizen. Her work is marked for its exploration of different poetic identities, and different possibilities for selfhood as a woman poet. Her volumes of poetry include: *Cages* (1966); *The Region's Violence* (1973); *Twenty One Poems* (1975); *Another Full Moon* (1976); *Sibyls and Others* (1980); *Climates* (1983); and *This Time of Year* (1993). She has also translated the Portuguese poet Sophia de Mello Breyner.

***Fair Maid of the West, The* (1600/1630)**

A romantic and ▷ picaresque comedy in two parts (1600 and 1630) by ▷ Thomas Heywood. It is set during ▷ Essex's expedition to the Azores in 1597 and dramatizes the adventures of the chivalrous Master Spencer and the beautiful Bess Bridges, whom he champions and who rescues him in turn after his capture by the Spaniards.

Fairbairns, Zoe (b 1948)

Novelist. Her novels are: *Live as Family* (1968); *Down: An Exploration* (1969); *Benefits* (1982); *Stand We At Last* (1983); *Here Today* (1984); *Closing* (1987). She uses a range of genres, such as ▷ science fiction (*Benefits*) or the crime thriller (*Here Today*; ▷ detective fiction) to explore the development of ▷ feminist consciousness. *Stand We At Last* recounts the lives of a succession of women from the middle of the 19th century up to the 1970s, and may be compared with *The Seven Ages* by ▷ Eva Figes in its project of rediscovering the unwritten history of women's experience.

Fairy-Tales

Fairy-tales have often been seen as simple narratives to amuse children, but their more pervasive significance was noted as early as the 17th century when writers used the stories for a didactic purpose. In the 19th century there was an emphasis on the moral role and related psychological impact of the tales. The major development in the theoretic treatment of fairy-tales occurred, however, with ▷ Freud and Jung: the former saw the narratives as a way in which the subjects could work out their psychic problems, while the latter looked for universal and archetypal patterns. More recently the stories have been linked to a process of socialization as well as the imposition on girls of patriarchal value judgements. ▷ Angela Carter's feminist reworking of traditional fairy-tales attempted to counter this.

Bib: Zipes, J., *Don't Bet on the Prince*.

***Faithful Shepherdess, The* (1610)**

A ▷ pastoral romance by ▷ John Fletcher which, in a short but influential preface about tragicomedy, acknowledges its indebtedness to the pastoral idiom of G. B. Guarini, the author of the seminal and famous pastoral play, *Il Pastor Fido* (1598); it thereby contributed to the vogue of English tragicomedies in the 1610s. But, whereas Fletcher's definition of tragicomedy specifically precluded death from its imaginative idiom, the English uses of the genre have tended to weld together the tragic and comic modes in a harsher manner and allowed death its full place in Arcadia.

Falconer, William (1732–69)

Author of a popular poem, *The Shipwreck* (1762; revised 1769), describing the sinking of a ship off the coast of Greece. Falconer himself drowned at sea.

'Fallen Woman, The'

A number of British women writers addressed the subject of the 'fallen woman' in the latter half of the 19th century. Sympathetic representations include ▷ Elizabeth Gaskell's ▷ *Ruth*, and Marion Erle in ▷ Elizabeth Barrett Browning's ▷ *Aurora Leigh*. Both these works brought attention to the sexual double standard, and both figure maternal love as the path of redemption for the woman. In other novels such as ▷ Mrs Henry Wood's ▷ *East Lynne* the errant woman was cruelly punished in the course of the narrative, serving as a warning to women readers.

▷ 'Castaway, A'; Orphans; Webster, Augusta; *Tess of the d'Urbervilles; Adam Bede; Esther Waters*.

Falstaff, Sir John

A character in ▷ Shakespeare's history plays, ▷ *Henry IV, Parts I and II*, and in the comedy ▷ *The Merry Wives of Windsor*. His death is described in ▷ *Henry V* (II. ii). In the history plays he is a very active comic character, embodying fleshly indulgence, and considered to be the chief injurious influence on Prince Hal (Henry), the heir to the throne. Though a fully realized character in his own right, he clearly carries also some force from medieval ▷ allegory, representing the temptations of physical indulgence or 'riot'. Accordingly Hal, once anointed as King Henry V, casts him off at the end of *Henry IV, Part II*. In *The Merry Wives* he is much less substantial, and plays the role of a comparatively commonplace buffoon.

▷ Oldcastle, Sir John.

Fanshawe, Lady Ann (1625–80)

Biographer. Although her *Memoirs* (completed 1676) ostensibly tell the life of her beloved husband for the benefit of his son, in fact they are a vivid and lively account of her own experiences, as well as those of Sir Richard Fanshawe. Lady Ann's life after she married Sir Richard in 1644 was full of the poverty-stricken turmoils and disappointments that characterized the Royalist party during the ▷ Interregnum. She was almost shipwrecked, almost abducted by pirates (she saved herself by adopting the disguise of a cabin boy), trapped in Galway during an outbreak of the plague, and bore 14 live children. Although the Fanshawes shared in the triumphal return of the monarchy, at her husband's death in 1666 Lady Ann was again left without financial support and she remained poor until her death. *Memoirs* is a dramatic account of the life of the Fanshawe family, but it is also a deeply moving account of marital love, which despite numerous trials endured undiminished.

▷ Biography; Autobiography.

Bib: Fraser, A., *The Weaker Vessel*; Wilcox, H., in Cerasano, S. P. and Wynne-Davies, M. (eds.), *Gloriana's Face*.

Fanshawe, Catherine (1765–1834)

Poet and letter-writer. Fanshawe came from a genteel background, which encouraged the education and cultural activity of women. In some ways perceptions of Fanshawe resemble those of ▷ Jane Austen, for during the 19th century she was considered a feminine, refined and respectable author, whose poetry was suitable for young women. However, on reading her work now it seems impossible that anyone could miss the sharp and incisive irony. Fanshawe parodies different ▷ discourses, satirizes political conventions and displays a worldly and somewhat cynical view about women's position in polite society. She and her sisters are also accredited with editing the memoirs of Lady Ann Fanshawe, who was an important ▷ Renaissance woman.

Fantastic

As used by the critics Tzvetan Todorov and ▷ Christine Brooke-Rose, the term fantastic denotes a situation in which the reader of a fiction cannot be sure whether an event (or a set of events) has a natural or a supernatural explanation. The classic example is ▷ Henry James' ▷ novella ▷ *The Turn of the Screw*, where the reader may remain uncertain, even after reaching the end, as to whether the ghosts were 'real' or a figment of the governess's imagination. If a natural explanation is forthcoming, the fantastic gives way to the uncanny; if supernatural explanations are explicitly required, then we are in the realm of the marvellous.

***Far from the Madding Crowd* (1874)**

A novel by ▷ Thomas Hardy. The title is a quotation from *Elegy Written in a Country Churchyard* (1751) by Thomas Gray (1716–71). It is one of Hardy's ▷ Wessex novels, and the first of real substance, following the comparatively slight ▷ *Under the Greenwood Tree*. The central character is Bathsheba Everdene, who is loved by three men: Farmer Boldwood, a solid but passionate squire; Gabriel Oak, a shepherd, who loves her with quiet constancy and wins her in the end, and the glamorous soldier, Sergeant Troy, whom she marries first. Troy combines fascinating gallantry with ruthless egoism; he allows his wife-to-be, Fanny Robin, to die in a workhouse, and is capricious and cruel to Bathsheba; he is eventually murdered by Boldwood. A crude outline such as this brings out the ballad-like quality of the story, characteristic of all Hardy's novels but more subtly rendered in later ones. Its distinction of substance is in Hardy's intimate understanding and presentation of the rural surroundings of the characters, and in the contrast between the urbane attractions of Troy and the rough but environmentally vigorous qualities of Boldwood and Oak. Bathsheba herself is a capricious and colourful heroine, not presented with psychological depth but with confident assertiveness which makes her convincing.

Farah, Nuruddin (b 1945)

Novelist and playwright. Farah was born in Somalia and educated in Ogaden (which is now in Ethiopia), at Panjab University in India and at the universities of London and Essex. The main theme of his work has been social and political change in East Africa but he chose to write in English, partly to circumvent censorship in Somalia and partly to gain an international readership. He was obliged to flee from Somalia in 1973 and subsequently lived in many parts of the world, including Nigeria, Gambia, Sudan, France, Germany, Italy and the United States. Since 1990 he has been Professor at Makere University, Kampala, Uganda. His novels have satirized the rule of dictators and the regime in Somalia as well as exploring the dilemmas of independent women living in a society where traditional gender roles are dominant. Stylistically, his fiction draws on the complex and elegant traditions of Somali poetry as well as alluding to a range of modern European writers. His novels are: *From a Crooked Rib* (1970); *A Naked Needle* (1976); *Sweet and Sour Milk* (1979); *Sardines* (1981); *Close Sesame* (1983); *Maps* (1986); and

Gifts (1993), a novel set in Mogadishu before the civil war, which deals with the political and moral issues surrounding foreign aid through the story of a nurse who wishes to resist dehumanizing dependence. Plays include *The Offering* (1975) and *Yussuf and his Brothers* (1982). He has also written for radio.

Farce
A comic dramatic genre, characteristically presenting an anarchic world in which authority, order and morality are under threat, and in which ordinary people are caught up in extraordinary goings on or extraordinary people are caught up in ordinary goings on. At its best it gives subversive expression to our wilder imaginings and rebellious instincts. Although comedy may incorporate the farcical, farce on the whole devotes less attention to character, and has more manic physical activity and accelerating momentum in its plots. In farce at its best, the successive discoveries, reversals, coincidences and repetitions are worked into an intricate and completely satisfying pattern, which persuades an audience of the logic of each successive step along the way, even if the final result seems supremely illogical. Disguising, role-playing, improvisation are forced upon the characters to keep them one step ahead of disaster, or enable them to keep up appearances as events spiral out of control. A degree of manic activity results, drawing extensively on the physical skills of the actor.

Farces often rely heavily on stereotypes – comic cleaning woman, bossy mother-in-law, apoplectic military man, etc. Inventively handled, these can be very funny and an essential part of the farcical mechanism. Uninventively handled, they can reinforce prejudice and create easy laughs.

Many of the plays of ▷ Aristophanes and ▷ Plautus offer fine examples of farcical techniques and structure, and it was also a characteristic feature of much medieval secular and religious drama. Since the ▷ Renaissance, three periods of particular creative activity in farce may be distinguished. The first is Commedia dell'arte in 16th- and 17th-century Italy, with its stock characters, situations, improvisations and comic routines. The second is France between the mid-1800s and the 1920s, where such prolific writers as Labiche and Feydeau satirized bourgeois life and the institution of marriage. Recently farce techniques and episodes have been extensively used for their subversive potential in 'serious' plays, which seek to challenge conventional sexual, political or social responses, for example, ▷ Caryl Churchill's *Cloud Nine* (1979) and ▷ Edward Bond's *Early Morning* (1968).
Bib: Davis, J., *Farce*; Smith, L., *Modern British Farce* .

Farquhar, George (1678–1707)
Dramatist, whose topics and style straddle those of the Restoration period and of the 18th century, showing some elements of ▷ Reform comedy. The son of a Church of England clergyman, Farquhar was born in Londonderry, and entered Trinity College, Dublin. Lacking funds, and the ambition to study, however, he left and turned to acting, at the ▷ Smock Alley Theatre in Dublin. There he met ▷ Robert Wilks, who became his friend and acted in several of his subsequent plays. The accidental wounding of another actor during a performance of ▷ Dryden's *The Indian Emperor* shocked him profoundly, and he left the stage and turned to writing for the theatre instead. In 1697 Farquhar went to London, where his first play, *Love and a Bottle*, was performed successfully at the Theatre Royal (▷ Drury Lane Theatres) in 1698. With ▷ *The Constant Couple; Or, A Trip to the Jubilee* (1699) he became fully established as a popular dramatist, Wilks acting the role of Sir Harry Wildair, and ▷ Susanna Verbruggen the part of Lady Lurewell. Sir Harry later became a favourite breeches part for actresses, including ▷ Peg Woffington. The play's sequel, *Sir Harry Wildair* (1701) was less successful. Farquhar obtained a commission in the army, but failed to obtain advancement. He did however travel through various parts of England, recruiting for the military, and used his experiences of army life to satiric effect in ▷ *The Recruiting Officer* (1706). The influence of changing theories about drama which took hold toward the turn of the century is evident in several of Farquhar's plays, especially *The Twin Rivals* (1702) and his last play, ▷ *The Beaux' Stratagem* (1707), which show a more humane and spontaneous attitude to life than the works of some authors of the high Restoration period. The contemporary dramatist ▷ Susannah Centlivre praised him for avoiding the risqué elements which so offended the ▷ Rev. Jeremy Collier, prompting him to write his *A Short View of the Immorality and Profaneness of the English Stage*. Centlivre's fulsome appreciation of Farquhar led to a correspondence between them, later published. In 1703 Farquhar married a woman who is said to have deceived him into believing her an heiress. He died in poverty after a lengthy illness.
Bib: Farmer, A. J., *Farquhar*.

Farrell, J. G. (James Gordon) (1935–79)
Novelist. His best work consisted of carefully researched, and powerfully imagined historical novels. *The Siege of Krishnapur* (1973), a fictitious account of the Indian mutiny, won the Booker Prize; *The Singapore Grip* (1978) recounts the collapse of British power in Malaya, culminating in the Japanese capture of Singapore in 1942; *Troubles* (1970) is set in Ireland in 1919. These three novels, which form a kind of trilogy concerned with the long demise of the British Empire, represent an ambitious attempt at historical novel-writing.

His career was ended by his early death on a fishing expedition in Ireland. Other novels are: *A Man From Elsewhere* (1963); *The Lung* (1965); *A Girl in the Head* (1967); *The Hill Station* (unfinished, 1981).

Fathers of the Church
Early Christian writers, important in the formation of Christian doctrine. They included Cyprian (3rd century), Athanasius (4th century), Gregory of Nazianzus (4th century), Augustine of Hippo (4th–5th century), Pope Gregory I, the Great (end of the 6th century). Those Fathers who were nearly contemporary with the original Apostles of Christ are often called the Apostolic Fathers; they include Clement of Rome, Polycarp of Smyrna, Ignatius of Antioch – all of the 1st century or the 1st and early 2nd centuries.

Faustus
▷ *Doctor Faustus, The Tragical History of.*

Feinstein, Elaine (b 1930)
Poet, novelist and translator. Born in Lancashire and educated at Cambridge, Feinstein has taught literature at Essex University as well as working in publishing. Her poetry is written closely from personal situations, and is deeply experiential. Her volumes of verse include: *In a Green Eye* (1966) (her first collection); *The Magic Apple Tree* (1971); *The Celebrants* (1973); *Some Unease and Angels: Selected Poems* (1977); *The Feast of Eurydice* (1980); and *Selected Poems* (1994). She has also edited an edition of Marina Tsvetayeva's poetry, and her novels include *Children of the Rose* (1975) and *The Border* (1984).

***Felix Holt the Radical* (1866)**
A novel by ▷ George Eliot. The hero is a talented young working man who makes it his vocation to educate the political intelligence of his fellow-workers. His rival for the love of Esther Lyon, the daughter of a Nonconformist minister, is the local landowner, Harold Transome, also a radical politician, though pursuing a more conventional career. George Eliot makes Holt utter high-minded speeches which weaken the reality he is supposed to possess. On the other hand, a subsidiary theme which concerns Harold Transome's mother, the secret of Harold's illegitimacy, and his hostility to the lawyer, Jermyn, who is really his father, is treated so well that it is among the best examples of George Eliot's art.

Fell, Alison (b 1944)
Poet, journalist and fiction writer. Born in Dumfries, Fell has worked as a sculptor, with women's theatre and for the feminist journal *Spare Rib*, for whom she edited the fiction ▷ anthology, *Hard Feelings*. As well as her volume of poetry, *Kisses for Mayakovsy*, in 1981 she published a children's novel, and two novels.

Fell, Margaret (1614–1702)
Pamphleteer and autobiographer. Until her 38th year Margaret Fell led an unremarkable and conventional life, having married Thomas Fell, a judge, in 1632. But in 1652 she heard the ▷ Quaker ▷ George Fox preach and instantly converted. Most of her household converted and although her husband did not he remained tolerant of her faith, allowing her to use their house, Swarthmore Hall, as a centre for Quakerism. She was never an itinerant preacher like ▷ Priscilla Cotton, but formed the pivot of a strong Quaker community and wrote numerous pamphlets and letters, some to noted personages such as Henrietta Maria and ▷ Oliver Cromwell. When she refused to abstain from Quaker practices and meetings during her trial in 1664, Margaret was imprisoned, but she used the opportunity to write and produced an important text in women's history, *Women's Speaking Justified* (1666). She married George Fox in 1669 and died within the warmth and admiration of her own family at the age of 88. Her writings were published posthumously as *A Brief Collection* (1710).
▷ Autobiography.
Bib: Fraser, A., *The Weaker Vessel.*

***Female Spectator, The* (1744–46)**
A monthly ▷ essay paper, launched by ▷ Eliza Haywood, and loosely modelled on ▷ *The Spectator*. Haywood's periodical, under the guise of a crusade against the sins of society, carried salacious gossip and scandalous accounts of individuals' indiscretions. More seriously, the editor attacked profligacy and gambling, and warned against reckless romance, while at the same time opposing arranged marriages, and arguing in favour of divorce. The paper developed a correspondence column, in which topical concerns were raised by readers, with replies by Haywood herself. After its demise, Haywood briefly ran a weekly paper with a similar format called *The Parrot*.
Bib: Adburgham, A., *Women in Print.*

Female Tatler, The
Title given to two separate journals whose names were intended to invoke ▷ *The Tatler*:
1 Publication launched in 1709 by ▷ Delarivière Manley, under the pseudonym of 'Mrs Crackenthorpe, a Lady that knows Everything'. The journal was a vehicle for her Tory views, but also contained anecdotes of contemporary life, as well as gossipy and sometimes scandalous accounts of the activities of real people, whose names were often thinly disguised. After threats of legal proceedings from some of them, Manley

resigned her editorship in November 1709, and *The Female Tatler* passed into more discreet hands. It then devoted itself to accounts of women noted for their achievements, stories, and some ▷ sentimental verses, and survived to March 1710.
2 A rival paper, also started in 1709, by the dramatist Thomas Baker, who is also thought to have produced a spurious number of Steele's ▷ *The Tatler* in 1711. His *The Female Tatler* resembled Manley's creation, and the two hurled abuse at one another for a time, before Baker's publication closed down.
Bib: Adburgham, Al., *Women in Print*.

Feminism
In literary criticism this term is used to describe a range of critical positions which argue that the distinction between 'masculine' and 'feminine' (▷ gender) is formative in the generation of all discursive practices. In its concern to bring to the fore the particular situation of women in society 'feminism' as a focus for the raising of consciousness has a long history, and can be taken to embrace an interest in all forms of women's writing throughout history. In its essentialist (▷ Essentialism) guise, feminism proposes a range of experiences peculiar to women, which are, by definition, denied to men, and which it seeks to emphasize in order to compensate for the oppressive nature of a society rooted in what it takes to be patriarchal authority. A more materialist (▷ Materialism) account would emphasize the extent to which gender difference is a cultural construction, and therefore amenable to change by concerted political action. Traditional materialist accounts, especially those of ▷ Marx, have placed the issue of 'class' above that of 'gender', but contemporary feminism regards the issue of 'gender' as frequently cutting across 'class' divisions and raising fundamental questions about the social role of women in relations of production and exchange. In so far as all literature is 'gendered', then feminine literary criticism is concerned with the analysis of the social construction of 'femininity' and 'masculinity' in particular texts. One of its major objectives is to expose how hitherto 'masculine' criticism has sought to represent itself as a universal experience. Similarly, the focus is adjusted in order to enable literary works themselves to disclose the ways in which the experiences they communicate are determined by wider social assumptions about gender difference, which move beyond the formal boundaries of the text. To this extent feminism is necessarily the focus of an interdisciplinary approach to literature, psychology, sociology and philosophy.

Psychoanalytic feminism, for example, often overlaps with socialist feminism. It approaches the concept of gender as a problem rather than a given, and draws on ▷ Freud's emphasis on the instability of sexual identities. The fact that femininity – and masculinity – are never fully acquired, once and for all, suggests a relative openness allowing for changes in the ways they are distributed. Literature's disturbance and exploration of ways of thinking about sexual difference have proved a rich source for feminist critics. In the 1990s the multiplicity of feminist criticisms has led some women to welcome this as a ▷ utopian pluralism, while others fear that this pluralism is simply a reassertion of liberal values to the detriment of political activism.

▷ Women's movement.
Bib: de Beauvoir, S., *The Second Sex*; Greene, G. and Kahn, C. (eds.), *Making a Difference: Feminist Literary Criticism*; Millett, K., *Sexual Politics*; Spender, D., *Feminist Theorists*; Wollstonecraft, M., *Vindication of the Rights of Women*.

Feminist critique
A phrase coined by Elaine Showalter in her influential essay 'Towards a Feminist Poetics' (1979) to describe an early form of modern feminist criticism. Feminist critique involves the identification and criticism of prejudiced male images or views of women in works of literature or criticism. Feminist critique aims at the identification of female stereotypes – either idealised or denigratory – and the projection of male needs and ideas onto female characters. Showalter argues, however, that though the feminist critique is a necessary beginning for feminist criticism, it is limited by its emphasis on negativity and victimization, and by the fact that, though it aims to criticise male ideas, it paradoxically remains centred on them.
▷ gynocriticism.
Bib: Showalter, E., (ed.), *The New Feminist Criticism: Essays on Women, Literature and Theory*.

Fenton, James (b 1949)
Poet. Educated at Oxford, Fenton has worked as a journalist in Britain (as theatre critic for the *Sunday Times*) and abroad, including in Vietnam. His publications include: *Terminal Moraine* (1972); *A Vacant Possession* (1978); *A German Requiem* (1980); *The Memory of War* (1982).

Fenwick, Eliza (c 1760–c1840)
Novelist and children's author. Fenwick may be associated with the development of radical women's writing at the end of the 18th century. She was friendly with ▷ Mary Wollstonecraft and ▷ Mary Lamb, and she left her alcoholic husband in 1800, supporting herself, without regrets, for the remaining 40 years of her life. Fenwick's most important and, indeed, compelling piece of work is her novel, *Secresy, or The Ruin on the Rock* (1795). It focuses on the lives of two women, Sibella and Caroline, who grow in self-awareness and recognize the

ills of their society. The ending is tragic, with both women losing what they love, but the sexual openness of the work, together with its praise of female friendship, ensure that the overall tone of the book remains challenging rather than depressing (▷ Feminism). Fenwick believed that education was the answer to social problems, a theme which she takes up in her didactic children's book, *Visits to the Juvenile Library* (1805). Her last years were spent running ▷ Godwin's library and travelling the world as a governess.
Bib: Wedd, A.F., *The Fate of the Fenwicks.*

Ferguson, Adam (1723–1816)
Scottish philosopher and historian, often thought of as the founder of modern sociology. Born at Logierait in Perthshire, Ferguson became chaplain to the Black Watch regiment, and later succeeded his friend ▷ David Hume as keeper of the Advocates' Library in Edinburgh. He was made a professor at Edinburgh University, first of Natural Philosophy, then of Moral Philosophy and finally of Mathematics. His *Essay on the History of Civil Society* (1767) analyses human existence in terms of man's social nature and tendency to form groups; it represents a landmark in the development of sociology as an academic discipline. In it he also argued that the growing division of labour encouraged individualistic pursuit of gain, and worked against the interests of the social group. Other writings include *Institutes of Moral Philosophy* (1769) and *The History of the Progress and Termination of the Roman Republic* (1782) which became a standard work.
Bib: Kettler, D., *The Social and Political Thought of Adam Ferguson.*

Fergusson, Robert (1750–74)
Poet. A clerk in the Commissary Office in Edinburgh, he died in the local ▷ Bedlam after falling ill and becoming prey to religious melancholy. He wrote extensively in English in the usual genres of the day: ▷ lyrics imitative of ▷ William Shenstone, tetrameter (▷ metre) fables and Miltonic ▷ blank verse. But his most important poetry is in the Scots vernacular and builds on the tradition begun by Allan Ramsay, often employing Ramsay's distinctive stanza forms. His *Auld Reekie* and *Hallow-Fair* depict the urban scene with pungent particularity. He intended to translate ▷ Virgil's ▷ *Georgics* and ▷ *Aeneid* into Scots, but the project was never realized because of his early death. The 1782 edition of Fergusson's works helped inspire some of ▷ Robert Burns' best poetry.

Ferrar, Nicholas
▷ *Little Gidding.*

Ferrers, George (c 1500–1579)
Poet. Ferrers was Master of the King's Pastimes at the court of ▷ Henry VIII and in this post was responsible for writing and producing several ▷ masques. He was still in the royal service during the reign of ▷ Elizabeth I and composed several verses to be recited during her visit to Kenilworth (▷ George Gascoigne). Ferrers is best known, however, for his part in the planning, with William Baldwin, of ▷ *A Mirror for Magistrates* (1559, 1563 and 1578), a work which recorded in verse the political successes and failures of historical persons.

Ferrier, Susan Edmonstone (1782–1854)
Novelist. The youngest of ten children, Susan Ferrier was born in Edinburgh. Her father was a lawyer, a principal clerk of session along with ▷ Sir Walter Scott, so Ferrier was early introduced to literary society. Through visits to Inverary Castle she also became acquainted with the fashionable world. After her mother died in 1797 her three sisters married and she kept house for her father who died in 1829. She later insisted on the destruction of correspondence with a sister, thus destroying much biographical material. Her novels of Scottish life included portraits of known people. *Marriage* (1818) was written in 1810 with a minimal contribution from her friend Miss Clavering, *The Inheritance* in 1824 and *Destiny, or the chief's daughter* in 1831. Her aim was didactic and her method keen observation, comedy and clear writing.
▷ Silver-fork novels.
Bib: Grant, A., *Susan Ferrier of Edinburgh: a Biography.*

Feuilleton
In French, a leaflet. Also used in French for that part of a newspaper devoted to literature, non-political news and gossip. In English the term was once used for the instalment of a serial story: it was the French newspaper *Le Siècle* which was the first to commission a serial novel specifically for part publication, in 1836. They were called *romans feuilletons.*

Fidessa
A character in ▷ Edmund Spenser's ▷ *The Faerie Queene* (Book I). Though the name Fidessa implies fidelity, she is, in reality, the false ▷ Duessa, and her intention is to lead the ▷ Red Cross Knight, standing for the faith of Protestant Church of England, into captivity.

Field, Michael (Katherine Bradley, 1846–1914 and Edith Cooper, 1862–1913)
Collaborative poets and dramatists. Katherine Bradley moved to the home of her niece, Edith Cooper, in 1865, and thereafter the two women were devoted and constant companions, viewing themselves as a spiritual partnership – 'closer married' than their friends the Brownings – until Edith's death in 1913. Although they

sometimes published separately under the ▷ pseudonyms Arran (Katherine) and Isla (Edith) Leigh, they first collaborated, using these pseudonyms, in a volume of poems, *Bellerophon*, and in the first 'Michael Field' play, *Callirrhoe* (1884), which was widely acclaimed. Enjoying a private income they produced twenty-seven tragic dramas and eight volumes of verse, all written in partnership and often published in limited editions. Centring mostly on classical and historical subjects, only one of their plays was ever performed, but their poetry is notable for its sensuousness, passion and mysticism, and includes love poems to each other. Their verse collections include *Long Ago* (1889) based on poems by Sappho the Greek poet; (7th–6th century BC) *Underneath the Bough* (1893); *Wild Honey from Various Thyme* (1908); *Poems of Adoration* (1912) written by Edith, and *Mystic Trees* (1913), written mainly by Katherine. The two women also co-wrote a journal, *Works and Day*, extracts from which were published in 1933 (ed. T. and D.C. Moore). In 1907 they converted to Catholicism. They lived together almost all their lives, dying of cancer within months of each other.

▷ Lesbianism

Bib: Sturgeon, M., *Michael Field*; Hickok, K., *Representations of Women: 19th Century British Women's Poetry*; Faderman, L., *Surpassing the Love of Men*; Leighton, A., *Victorian Women Poets: Writing Against the Heart*; Leighton, A., and Reynolds, M. (eds.), *An Anthology of Victorian Women Poets.*

Field, Nathaniel (1587–1633)
Actor; he was one of the most famous in the lifetime of ▷ Shakespeare. He is mentioned in the First Folio edition of Shakespeare's works as having played parts in them, and he also took leading roles in plays by ▷ Ben Jonson and the chief one in ▷ George Chapman's most famous play, ▷ *Bussy d' Ambois*. He wrote two ▷ 'citizen comedies' in the style of Jonson: *A Woman is a Weathercock* and *Amends for Ladies.*
Bib: Perry, W. (ed.), *The Plays of Nathan Field.*

Field of Cloth of Gold
The name given to the meeting-place of the English ▷ Henry VIII and the French Francis I, in France. The object of the meeting near Guisnes in 1520 was to arrange an alliance, but the encounter is less memorable politically than it is for its characteristically ▷ Renaissance splendour.

Fielding, Henry (1707–54)
Born at Sharpham Park in Somerset, the son of a lieutenant. After the death of his mother when he was II, Fielding was sent to Eton. At the age of 19, after an unsuccessful attempt to elope with an heiress, Fielding tried to make a living in London as a dramatist.

In 1728 his play *Love in Several Masques* was successfully performed at ▷ Drury Lane, and Fielding departed for university at Leyden, where he studied classical literature for about 18 months. On his return to London he continued his career as a dramatist, writing some 25 plays in the period 1729–37. His dramatic works are largely satirical, the most successful being ▷ *Tom Thumb* (performed in 1730). Fielding also edited four periodicals, *The Champion* (1739–41), *The Covent Garden Journal* (under the pseudonym Sir Alexander Drawcansir, 1752), *The True Patriot* (1745–6) and *Jacobite's Journal* (1747–8), but his major achievement is as a novelist.

▷ *Shamela*, a parody of ▷ Richardson's ▷ *Pamela*, published in 1741, was developed into the theme of ▷ *Joseph Andrews* (1742), an original and comic creation. In 1743 Fielding published ▷ *The Life of Jonathan Wild the Great*, a satire on the criminal class comparable in its inversion of values to ▷ John Gay's ▷ *Beggar's Opera*. In the same year his lesser-known satire, *A Journey From This World to the Next*, also appeared. ▷ *Tom Jones*, his greatest work, was published in 1749, and ▷ *Amelia* in 1751.

In 1748 Fielding was made Justice of the Peace for Westminster, and pursued a successful career of social reform. In 1754, his health failing, he embarked on a journey to Lisbon in search of a better climate, but died on the way. *A Journal of a Voyage to Lisbon*, his final achievement, was published posthumously the following year.

▷ Fielding, Sarah.

Bib: Alter, R., *Fielding and the Nature of the Novel*; Rogers, P., *Henry Fielding*; Rawson, C. J. *Henry Fielding and the Augustan Ideal under Stress.*

Fielding, Sarah (1710–68)
Sarah Fielding, sister of the novelist ▷ Henry Fielding, was highly praised by ▷ Samuel Richardson, who rated her achievements more highly than her brother's: 'his was but a knowledge of the outside of a clockwork machine, while yours was that of the finer springs and movements of the inside'. Her first appearance in print consisted of contributions to her brother's works.

Sarah Fielding's first novel, *The Adventures of David Simple*, began to appear in 1744, and proved a great success. In its interpretation of social conventions from a female point of view, it provides a revealing contrast with the attitudes expressed by male writers; the heroine, Cynthia, is subjected to constant sexual harassment condoned as socially acceptable behaviour. The second volume of *David Simple* appeared in 1747, and the final volume in 1753.

Sarah Fielding's concern for female ▷ education is evident in *The Governess or The Little Female Academy* (1749). Its success as a (somewhat pious) moral novel for young people ensured that it stayed in print for over 150 years.

In 1754, Sarah Fielding published *The Cry*, a dramatic fable co-written with her friend ▷ Jane Collier. In this allegorical framework the heroine tells her story to representatives of truth and justice, malice and exploitation.

Samuel Richardson was the publisher of Sarah Fielding's next work, *The Lives of Cleopatra and Octavia*, in which the two characters give different versions of their lives. In 1759 Richardson again helped with the printing of *The History of The Countess of Dellwyn*, a further critique of male-dominated society. Her later works include *The History of Ophelia* (1760) and a translation of Xenophon's *Memoirs of Socrates* (1762).

Bib: Grey, J., 'Introduction' to *The Governess*.

Fiennes, Celia (1662–1741)
English Protestant travel writer, and daughter of a regicide. She travelled around the English counties alone and accompanied, riding and using a coach. Her 'Book' was first published in part in 1888. Its descriptions combine the interests of a traveller with details which make the familiar social territory strange – for example, her vivid story of the recovery of a human relic in the abandoned monastery at York.

Fifth Monarchists
A sect of Puritans who believed, on the basis of a prophecy in the Bible (*Daniel* 2), that ▷ Oliver Cromwell's rise to power was a preparation for the Second Coming of Christ and the establishment of the great fifth and last monarchy, the previous four having been the Assyrian, the Persian, the Greek and the Roman. In disillusionment, they began to turn against Cromwell and after the Restoration of the monarchy in 1660 they tried to raise a rebellion in London. It was easily suppressed and the leaders were executed.

Fifth Monarchy Men
A sect of ▷ Puritans who believed, on the basis of a prophecy in the Bible (*Daniel 2*), that ▷ Oliver Cromwell's rise to power was a preparation for the Second Coming of Christ, and the establishment of the great fifth and last monarchy; the previous four had been the Assyrian, the Persian, the Greek and the Roman. In disillusionment, they began to turn against Cromwell and after the Restoration of the monarchy in 1660 they tried to raise a rebellion in London. It was easily suppressed and the leaders were executed.

Figes, Eva (b 1932)
Novelist and ▷ feminist writer. Born Eva Unger to a German Jewish family who escaped to England in 1939 after the imprisonment of her father by the Nazis. Educated at London University, she worked in publishing before writing her first novel, *Equinox* (1966), a partly autobiographical and largely pessimistic account of a woman's search for meaning and human relationships. The influence of ▷ Virginia Woolf is apparent in her exploration of the inner world of the self and her lyrical sense of the flux of experience and the continuity of memories. *Days* (1974) and *The Seven Ages* (1986) seek to establish an unrecorded female history, linking many generations of women, while *Waking* (1981) is structured around seven waking moments of a woman or women. These ▷ modernist techniques combine with the influence of ▷ Samuel Beckett in *Winter Journey* (1967), which represents the inner world of an old man dying alone. Figes has a sense of herself as a European, and an awareness of the Holocaust which is a part of her family history, and draws on the work of one of the great European modernists, Franz Kafka. *Konek Landing* (1969) is a Kafkaesque story of victims and executioners in a nameless country. Figes' work rejects the English realist tradition in favour of a ▷ post-modernist commitment to experiment, apparent especially in *B* (1972), a self-reflexive novel about the nature of creativity, and the problematic relations of reality and fiction. She has written short stories, radio plays, children's fiction, criticism, and a classic text of the feminist movement, *Patriarchal Attitudes: Women in Society* (1970) as well as editing a volume of *Women's Letters in Wartime 1450–1945* (1993). *Little Eden: A Child at War* (1978) is autobiography. Her other novels are: *Nelly's Version* (1977); *Light* (1983); *Ghosts* (1988); *The Tenancy* (1993).

Figures of Speech

Alliteration The beginning of accented syllables near to each other with the same consonantal sound, as in many idiomatic phrases: 'safe and sound'; 'thick and thin'; 'right as rain'. Alliteration is thus the opposite of ▷ rhyme, by which the similar sounds occur at the ends of the syllables: 'near and dear'; 'health and wealth'. Alliteration dominated the pattern of Old English poetry; after the Conquest, French influence caused rhyme to predominate. However, in the 14th century there seems to have been an 'alliterative revival', producing such important poems as ▷ *Piers Plowman* and ▷ *Sir Gawain and the Green Knight*.

An example from the latter text reveals the power of Middle English alliteration:

...the scharp of the schalk schyndered the bones,
And schrank thurgh the schyire grece, and scade
hit in twynne.
[the sharp blade shattered the man's bones and sank into the fair flesh, cutting it in two.]

Alliterative verse was accentual, *ie* did not depend

on the regular distribution of accented syllables in a line, but on the number of accented syllables in the lines.

After the 14th century, rhyme and the regular count of syllables became the normal pattern for English verse. Alliteration, however, continued to be used unsystematically by every poet. For example, ⊳ Burns used it to comic effect in 'The Twa Dogs':

His locked, letter'd, brawbrass collar
Shew'd him the gentleman and scholar.

Anacoluthon From the Greek: 'not following on'. Strictly speaking, this is not a figure of speech, but a grammatical term for a sentence which does not continue the syntactical pattern with which it starts. It may be used deliberately with the virtue of intensifying the force of a sentence *eg* by the sudden change from indirect to direct speech. Its capacity for dramatic fragmentation is used repeatedly for comic effect by ⊳ Byron in ⊳ *Don Juan*, *eg*:

Sooner shall heaven kiss earth – (here he fell sicker)
Oh, Julia! What is every other woe?
(Canto I)

Anti-climax
⊳ *Bathos* (below).

Antithesis A method of emphasis by the placing of opposed ideas or characteristics in direct contrast with each other.

Apostrophe A form of direct address often used by a narrator in the middle of his narrative as a means of emphasizing a moral lesson. Apostrophe frequently addresses a real person, living or dead, as in the opening of ⊳ Wordsworth's sonnet on Milton: 'Milton! Thou shouldst be living at this hour!'

Assonance The rhyming of vowel sounds without the rhyming of consonants.

Bathos From the Greek: 'death'. The descent from the sublime to the ridiculous. This may be the result of incompetence in the writer, but ⊳ Alexander Pope used it skilfully as a method of ridicule:

Here thou, great ANNA! whom three realms obey
Dost sometimes counsel take – and sometimes tea.
(The Rape of the Lock)

Pope wrote an essay *Bathos, the Art of Sinking in Poetry*, as a travesty of the essay by ⊳ Longinus, *On the Sublime* (1st century AD). Longinus had great prestige as a critic in Pope's time. Among the canonical Romantic poets, ⊳ Byron is the absolute master of bathos, as in the lines written on the back of his manuscript of ⊳ *Don Juan*, Canto I:

I say – the future is a serious matter –
And so – for God's sake – hock and soda-water!

Climax From the Greek: 'a ladder'. The climb from lower matters to higher, with the consequent satisfying of raised expectations.

Euphemism A mild or vague expression used to conceal a painful or disagreeable truth, *eg* 'he passed on' for 'he died'. It is sometimes used ironically.

Euphuism A highly artificial quality of style resembling that of ⊳ John Lyly's ⊳ *Euphues*, as may be seen from the following quotation:

How frantic are those lovers which are carried away with the gay glistering of the fine face, the beauty whereof is parched with the summer's blaze and chipped with the winter's blast; which is of so short continuance that it fadeth before one perceive it flourish; of so small profit that it poisoneth those that possess it; of so little value with the wise that they accompt it a delicate bait with a deadly hook, a sweet panther with a devouring paunch, a sour poison in a silver pot.

Hyperbole Expression in extreme language so as to achieve intensity, *eg* ⊳ Shelley's exclamation at the apparent failure of his own poem to achieve its target, towards the end of ⊳ *Epipsychidion*: 'I pant, I sink, I tremble, I expire!'

Innuendo A way of expressing dislike or criticism indirectly, or by a hint; an insinuation.

Irony From the Greek: 'dissimulation'. A form of expression by which the writer intends his meaning to be understood differently and less favourably, in contrast to his overt statement:

It is a truth universally acknowledged, that a single man in possession of a good fortune must be in want of a wife.

This opening sentence of ⊳ Jane Austen's *Pride and Prejudice* is to be understood as meaning that the appearance of such a young man in a neighbourhood inspires very strong wishes in the hearts of mothers of unmarried daughters, and that these wishes cause the mothers to behave as though the statement were indeed a fact.

Dramatic irony occurs when a character in a play makes a statement in innocent assurance of its truth, while the audience is well aware that he or she is deceived. Tragedies by ⊳ Byron, or ⊳ Shelley's *The Cenci*, are indebted to Elizabethan and Jacobean drama in this area.

Litotes Emphatic expression through an ironical negative, *eg* 'She's no beauty', meaning that the woman is ugly.

Malapropism A comic misuse of language,

usually by a person who is both pretentious and ignorant. The term derives from the character Mrs Malaprop in Sheridan's play *The Rivals* (1775). For example, Mrs Malaprop cries 'O mercy! – I'm quite analyzed, for my part!' when she really intends to say that she is 'amazed'. This comic device had in fact been used by earlier writers, such as ▷ Shakespeare in the portrayal of Dogberry in *Much Ado About Nothing*.

Meiosis Understatement, used as a deliberate method of emphasis by irony, *eg* 'Would you like to be rich?' – 'I should rather think so!'

Metaphor A figure of speech by which unlike objects are identified with each other for the purpose of emphasizing one or more aspects of resemblance between them. A simple example: 'the camel is the ship of the desert'. Romantic poetry abounds in more complex examples, as in the opening of ▷ Keats' 'Ode on a Grecian Urn', which employs humanized metaphor to treat an inanimate object:

Thou still unravish's bride of quietness,
Thou foster-child of silence and slow time.

The opposite approach to metaphor is adopted by ▷ Shelley in ▷ *Epipsychidion*, when the human addressee of a poem, Emilia, is called:

A metaphor of Spring and Youth and Morning;
A Vision like Incarnate April, warming,
With smiles and tears, Frost and Anatomy
Into his summer grave.

('Anatomy' here means 'skeleton'.)

Mixed metaphor is a confused image in which the successive parts are inconsistent, so that (usually) absurdity results: 'I smell a rat, I see it floating in the air, but I will nip it in the bud', *ie* 'I suspect an evil, and I can already see the beginnings of it, but I will take action to suppress it.' However, mixed metaphor is sometimes used deliberately to express a state of confusion.

Dead metaphor is one in which the image has become so familiar that it is no longer thought of as figurative, *eg* the phrase 'to take steps', meaning 'to take action'.

Metaphysical conceit
▷ Metaphysical Poets.

Metonymy The naming of a person, institution or human characteristic by some object or attribute with which it is clearly associated, as when a king or queen may be referred to as 'the Crown':

Sceptre and Crown
Must tumble down,
And in the dust be equal made
With the poor crooked scythe and spade.
('The Levelling Dust', James Shirley)

Here 'Sceptre and Crown' refer to kings, and perhaps more broadly to the classes which control government, while 'scythe and spade' stand for the humble peasantry. Metonymy has taken on additional meanings since the advent of Structuralism. One of the originators of Russian Formalism, ▷ Roman Jakobson, draws a distinction between 'metaphor' – the linguistic relationship between two different objects on the grounds of their similarity – and 'metonymy' as a means of establishing a relationship between two objects in terms of their contiguity. Where metaphor is regarded as a major rhetorical device in *poetry*, metonymy is more usually associated with *prose*. The critic and novelist ▷ David Lodge takes up this distinction in his book *The Modes of Modern Writing* (1977), and suggests that 'metaphor' and 'metonymy' constitute a structurally significant binary opposition that enables the distinction to be made between poetry and drama on the one hand, and prose on the other. Lodge emphasizes, however, that these terms are not mutually exclusive, but rather contribute to 'a theory of dominance of one quality over another'. Hence it is possible for a novel to contain 'poetic' effects and vice versa.

Oxymoron A figure of speech formed by the conjunction of two contrasting terms in a compressed paradox, such as ▷ Coleridge's 'Life-in-Death' from ▷ *The Rime of the Ancient Mariner*.

Palindrome A word or sentence that reads the same backwards or forwards, *eg*

Lewd did I live; evil I
did dwel
(Phillips, 1706)

Paradox A statement that challenges the mind by appearing to be self-contradictory.

Pathetic fallacy A term invented by the critic ▷ John Ruskin (*Modern Painters*, Vol. III, Pt. iv, Ch. 12) to denote the tendency common especially among poets to ascribe human emotions or qualities to inanimate objects, *eg* ▷ Coleridge's line 'As if this earth in fast thick pants were breathing' from ▷ *Kubla Khan*. Ruskin describes it by dividing writers into four classes: those who do not use it merely because they are insensitive; superior writers in whom it is a mark of sensitivity; writers who are better still and do not need it because they 'feel strongly, think strongly, and see truly'; and writers of the best sort who use it because in some instances they 'see in a sort untruly, because what they see is inconceivably above them'. In general, he considers that the pathetic fallacy is justified when the feeling it expresses is a true one.

Personification A kind of metaphor, by which an abstraction or inanimate object is endowed with personality. As for example in ▷ Keats' 'To Autumn', where Autumn is described as a human being:

Who hath not seen thee oft amid thy store?
Sometimes whoever seeks abroad may find
Thee sitting careless on a granary floor,
Thy hair soft-lifted by the winnowing wind;

Play on words A use of a word with more than one meaning or of two words which sound the same in such a way that both meanings are called to mind. In its simplest form, as the modern pun, this is merely a joke. In the 16th and 17th centuries poets frequently played upon words seriously; this is especially true of ▷ Shakespeare and dramatists contemporary with him, and of the ▷ Metaphysical poets, such as ▷ John Donne and ▷ George Herbert.

This very serious use of puns or plays upon words decreased in the 18th century, when ▷ Samuel Johnson censured Shakespeare's fondness for puns (or, as Johnson called them, 'quibbles'). The reason for this disappearance of the serious 'play upon words' was the admiration of educated men for what Bishop Sprat in his *History of the Royal Society* (1667) called 'mathematical plainness of meaning', a criterion emulated by poets as well as by prose writers. Poetry of the Romantic period is however characterized by daring or subtle play on words, as in Keats' reckless punning in his 'Ode on a Grecian Urn':

O Attic shape! Fair altitude! with brede
Of marble men and maidens overwrought

'Brede' and 'overwrought' are here puns, and 'Attic' calls up the word 'altitude'. ▷ Byron and ▷ Shelley play continuously on words for comic and philosophical effect respectively, and ▷ Blake's play on words in even such brief lyrics as 'The Sick Rose' and 'London' becomes so intense as to make it impossible for a reader to find less than a multitude of interpretations for them. In the 19th century, the play on words was revived by humorous writers and writers for children, such as Thomas Hood, ▷ Edward Lear and ▷ Lewis Carroll (▷ Children's books). Although their use of the pun was ostensibly comic, its effect in their writings is often unexpectedly poignant or even profound, especially in Carroll's 'Alice' books. Puns continued to be despised by the adult world of reason, but they could freely and revealingly be used in what was regarded as the childish world of nonsense and fantasy.

Modern poets and critics have recovered the older, serious use of the play on words. Ambiguity of meaning which in the 18th century was considered a vice of expression, is now seen as a quality of rich texture of expression, though of course 'good' and 'bad' types of ambiguity have to be distinguished. ▷ James Joyce used the technique with unprecedented elaboration in ▷ *Finnegans Wake*; ▷ William Empson revived the serious punning of Donne and ▷ Marvell in his poems, and investigated the whole problem in *Seven Types of Ambiguity* (1930). Just as admiration for mathematics and the physical sciences caused the decline of the play on words, so the revival of it has been partly due to the rise of another science, that of psychoanalysis, especially the school of ▷ Freud, with its emphasis on the interplay of conscious and unconscious meanings in the use of language.

Pun
▷ *Play on words* (above).

Rhyme A verbal music made through identity of sound in the final syllables of words. Several varieties of rhyme exist:

End-rhyme When the final syllables of lines of verse are rhymed.

Internal rhyme When one at least of the rhyming words is in mid-line; as in 'fair' and 'air' in the following couplet by ▷ Swinburne:

We have seen thee, O Love, thou art
fair; thou art goodly, O Love;
Thy wings make light in the air as wings
of a dove.

Masculine rhymes are single stressed syllables as in the following example from ▷ Anna Barbauld's 'Life':

Life! I know not what thou art,
But know that thou and I must part.

Feminist rhymes are on two syllables, the second of which is unaccented. As in the following from ▷ Coleridge's ▷ *Dejection: an Ode*:

Mad lutenist! who in this month of showers,
Of dark brown gardens, and of peeping flowers.

and in ▷ Marlowe's *Passionate Shepherd*:

And I will make thee beds of roses
And a thousand fragrant posies;
A cap of flowers, and a kirtle
Embroider'd all with leaves of myrtle

Half-rhymes (pararhymes) are the rhyming of consonants but not of vowels (contrast ▷ *Assonance*). They are sometimes used as an equivalent for full rhymes, since consonants are more noticeable in rhyme music than vowels. Change in pronunciation sometimes has the effect of changing what was intended as full rhyme into half-rhyme, as in the following example from Pope:

Tis not enough, taste, judgement, learning, join;
In all you speak, let truth and candour shine:

In the 18th century, 'join' was pronounced as 'jine'.

Simile Similar to metaphor, but in similes the comparison is made explicit by the use of a word such as 'like' or 'as'.

Syllepsis A figure of speech by which a word is used in a literal and a metaphorical sense at the same time, *eg* 'You have broken my heart and my best china vase'.

Synecdoche A figure of speech by which a part is used to express a whole, or a whole is used to express a part, *eg* 'fifty sail' is used for fifty ships, or the 'smiling year' is used for the spring. In practice, synecdoche is indistinguishable from ▷ metonymy. Like metonymy this figure depends upon a relationship of contiguity, and is regarded as one side of the opposition between 'poetry' and 'non-poetry'. Both metonymy and synecdoche operate by combining attributes of particular objects, therefore they are crucial rhetorical devices for the representation of reality, and are closely related to ▷ realism as a literary style insofar as they function referentially.

Transferred epithet The transference of an adjective from the noun to which it applies grammatically to some other word in the sentence, usually in such a way as to express the quality of an action or of behaviour, *eg* 'My host handed me a hospitable glass of wine', instead of 'My hospitable host handed me...'

Zeugma A figure similar to ▷ syllepsis; one word used with two others, to only one of which it is grammatically or logically applicable.

Filmer, Robert (1588–1653)
Political prose writer. Born in Kent and educated at Cambridge and Lincoln's Inn, he supported the king during the civil war and began publishing his political views in the late 1640s. However, his most influential book, *Patriarcha* (1680) was not published until after his death, although it circulated in manuscript and is known to have been influential, especially on the work of ▷ John Locke. Filmer's argument is that the origin of regal power is patriarchal, as in the father figures of the Old Testament.
Bib: Pooley, R., *English Prose of the Seventeenth Century, 1590–1700.*

Filostrato, Il
▷ Boccaccio's version of the love affair between the Trojan prince Troilo and Criseida, written in *ottava rima* in 1335, and used by Chaucer as the principal source for ▷ *Troilus and Criseyde.*
Bib: Havely, N. R. (trans.), *Chaucer's Boccaccio.*

Finch, Anne, Countess of Winchilsea (1660–1720)
English poet, at present best known for her 'A Nocturnall Reeverie', esteemed by ▷ William Wordsworth. With ▷ Anne Killigrew she was a Maid of Honour to Mary of Modena and married Heneage Finch. After ▷ James II fled, they moved to Kent and she wrote poetry. A few poems were printed, but she published *Miscellany Poems on Several Occassions* (1713). Finch uses the natural world in a distinctive and subtle way in her poetry, linking landscape and state of mind in a way that blends the features of the inner and outer worlds, politics and place. She also had a vein of sharp satire – in 'Unequal Fetters' she wrote: 'Marriage does but slightly tye men / Whil'st close Pris'ners we remain / They the larger slaves of Hymen / Still are begging Love again / At the full length of all their chain.'

Finlay, Ian Hamilton (b 1925)
Scottish poet and sculptor. Finlay works simultaneously in both words and the sculpture of physical objects, exploring the possibility of poetry as a form of visual art. His work is in certain ways representative of Concrete Poetry, the experimental movement which, since the 1960s, has sought to emphasize poetry's physical, typographical existence. Finlay has created a famous garden at Stonypath, Lanarkshire, which functions as a gallery for his work. His publications include: *The Dancers Inherit the Party* (1961); *Tea Leaves and Fishes* (1966); *Poems to Hear and See* (1971); *Heroic Emblems* (1978).

***Finnegans Wake* (1939)**
A novel by ▷ James Joyce. It is one of the most original experiments ever undertaken in the novel form, and the most difficult of his works to read. It purports to be one night in the life of a Dublin public-house keeper, H. C. Earwicker, and as he is asleep from the beginning to the end of the book, his experiences are all those of dream. The advantage of dream experience is that it is unrestricted by self-conscious logic, and operates by free association unrestrained by inhibitions. The basis of the 'story' is his relationships with his wife, Anna Livia Plurabelle, his daughter, Isobel, and his twin sons Shem and Shaun; it reaches out, however, into Irish and European myths as these are suggested to his sleeping consciousness by objects in his house and neighbourhood. Joyce intends in fact to make Earwicker a type of 'Everyman'. The language is made by fusing together words so as to cause them – as in dreams – to suggest several levels of significance simultaneously; this is a device which had already been used playfully by ▷ Lewis Carroll in his poem 'Jabberwocky' in the dream story for children *Through the Looking-Glass* (1872). Joyce, however, in his desire to universalize Earwicker, freely combines words from foreign languages with English ones, so that Earwicker's

mind becomes representatively European while remaining his own. The movement of the narrative is based on the ideas of the 18th-century Italian philosopher Vico, who believed that ages succeed each other – gods, heroes, men – and then recommence; this is followed out in Earwicker's successive identifications (as Adam, Humpty Dumpty, Christ, Cromwell, Noah, The Duke of Wellington etc.), until at the end of the book the final sentence is completed by the first sentence at its beginning. The Christian pattern of fall and resurrection also contributes to the structure of the work. Another important influence on Joyce was the psychological ideas of ▷ Sigmund Freud on the mechanism of repression and the characteristics of dream association. Study necessitates the assistance of such a work as *A Reader's Guide to Finnegans Wake* by W. Y. Tindall.

Firbank, Ronald (1886–1926)
Writer of witty fantasies whose extravagant humour derives from the subtly calculated and highly-wrought style. His best-known tales are probably *Vainglory* (1915); *Valmouth* (1919); *The Flower Beneath the Foot* (1923); *The Artificial Princess* (1934). His stylistic innovations, including his highly condensed imagery, are regarded by some critics as a major contribution to ▷ modernism.
Bib: Fletcher, I. K., *Memoir*; Forster, F. M., in *Abinger Harvest*; Brooke, J., *Firbank*.

Fisher King
The title of the Grail Keeper in Arthurian legendary narrative. The name first appears in ▷ Chrétien de Troyes' romance *Perceval* (where it is not explained), and is given a Christian interpretation in ▷ Robert de Boron's late 12th/early 13th-century version of the ▷ Grail story. In versions of the 'Quest of the Holy Grail' narrative, the Fisher King is not always the same figure as the Grail King.

Fisher, Roy (b 1930)
Poet. Born in Birmingham, Fisher's work is realist in its evocation of the Midlands industrial landscape – this is especially true of his early work, which was generally unknown until the Oxford edition *Poems 1955–1980* (1981) appeared (most of his previous work had been published by the small presses, especially by Fulcrum). Fisher is a prolific poet, and his works include: *City* (1961); *The Memorial Fountain* (1966); *Collected Poems* (1969); *Matrix* (1971); *The Thing About Joe Sullivan* (1978); *A Furnace* (1986); and *Birmingham River* (1994).

Fitz-Boodle, George Savage
The pen-name assumed by the novelist ▷ William Makepeace Thackeray for the 'Fitz-Boodle Papers' contributed to ▷ *Fraser's Magazine*, 1842–3.

FitzGerald, Edward (1809–93)
Translator and poet; chiefly known for his extremely popular translation of the Persian poem ▷ *The Rubaiyat of Omar Khayyam* (1859). He also published *Euphranor* (1851), a ▷ Platonic dialogue; translations of *Six Dramas of Calderon* (1853), and in 1865, a translation of ▷ Aeschylus' *Agamemnon*. His delicate praise of a life of pleasure and his enjoyment of beauty, evident in his *Rubaiyat*, countered the moral earnestness of the age and influenced the 'anti-Victorian' ▷ Pre-Raphaelite and ▷ Aesthetic movements later in the century.
Bib: Benson, A. C., *FitzGerald*; Terhune, A. M., *Life*; Campbell, A. Y., in *Great Victorians*, eds. Massingham, A. J. and H.

Flamineo
Brother, and ultimately pimp, of ▷ Vittoria Corombona in ▷ *The White Devil* by ▷ John Webster. Flamineo is presented as an embittered and cynical villain who spurns all the dictates of conscience and duty for self-advancement.

Flat and Round Characters
A categorization of characters, proposed by ▷ E.M. Forster in his influential study, ▷ *Aspects of the Novel*. Flat characters are 'constructed round a single idea or quality'; they are types or caricatures (such as Mrs Micawber in ▷ Dickens' ▷ *David Copperfield*). Round characters (such as ▷ Defoe's ▷ Moll Flanders) are 'capable of surprising [the reader] in a convincing way'. The idea of the flat character has passed into general use in the derogatory form of the 'two-dimensional character', but Forster himself recognized the virtues as well as the limitations of the flat character.

Flaubert, Gustave (1821–80)
French novelist. His first novel, *Madame Bovary*, involved him in a court action for immorality on its publication in 1857. The story of the adultery of a doctor's wife in Normandy, it ironizes not only the Romanticism of the principal character, but also the unappealing bourgeois values of the characters around her and the parochial milieu from which she attempts to escape. The book is equally notable for its contribution to psychological realism in the form of *style indirect libre* (▷ free indirect discourse). Flaubert's 1869 novel, *L'Education sentimentale*, intended as the moral history of his generation, portrays the fruitless love of Frédéric Moreau for Mme Arnoux, against the background of 1840s Paris and the 1848 Revolution; love and politics prove comparable in misdirected and misrecognized opportunities, which defuse both the dynamism of character and the fulfilment of plot. History, together with religion, comes under renewed investigation in *Salammbô* (1862), *La Tentation de Saint Antoine* (1874) and *Trois Contes* (1877). These end in further equivocation, with the

reader left uncertain about what values are to be derived from works so pervaded by irony and authorial impersonality. In the unfinished *Bouvard et Pécuchet* (1881), the work's eponymous protagonists are composed of the novels, guide books and folk-lore they avidly read, and conversely they take for reality what are only representations of it. In addition to foregrounding fictive processes, this novel also dwells on the stupidity of bourgeois society and the received ideas on which this society feeds, a Flaubertian theme since *Madame Bovary*.

In the 19th century, Flaubert was prized for his ▷ realism (he was also claimed by ▷ naturalism and rejected both labels), understood as psychological representation or the accumulation of circumstantial detail (called the 'reality effect' by ▷ Roland Barthes). Yet such detail in Flaubert tends to overwhelm rather than sharply define the character. Accordingly, the 20th century has valued him for his challenges to ▷ mimesis, including the traditional privileged ties between author and reader, writer and character, individual and society.

Flecknoe, Richard (17th century)
A poet who was the victim of a satire by ▷ Andrew Marvell, *Fleckno, an English Priest at Rome* (1645). Dryden chose the title ▷ *Mac Flecknoe* (son of Flecknoe) for his satire against ▷ Thomas Shadwell.

'Fleshly School of Poetry, The'
A term taken from an article by ▷ Robert Buchanan (who signed himself 'Thomas Maitland'), published in ▷ *The Contemporary Review* in October 1871. In it Buchanan links ▷ Dante Gabriel Rossetti, ▷ Algernon Swinburne and ▷ William Morris together as poets perversely loyal to each other and united against the common decencies. His main criticism was that their work was too obsessed with the body and with aesthetics in general. Buchanan also claimed that their work was morally irresponsible. Rossetti, against whom the main thrust of Buchanan's criticism was directed, replied in a dignified article entitled 'The Stealthy School of Criticism' published in ▷ *The Athenaeum* in December of the same year. However, he was deeply affected by the 'fleshly school' controversy. For Swinburne it provided yet more ammunition in his private war with Buchanan, who finally defeated Swinburne's publisher in a libel suit. However, Buchanan's literary career was irreparably damaged by the controversy. In their comic opera *Patience*, ▷ Gilbert and Sullivan based the character of Bunthorne, a 'fleshly poet', partly on ▷ Oscar Wilde, who was delighted by the association.
Bib: Buckley, J.H., *The Victorian Temper*; Doughty, O., 'The Fleshly School of Poetry: 1871–72' in *Dante Gabriel Rossetti*.

Fletcher, Giles (the elder) (?1549–1611)
Author of a book on Russia (1591), suppressed by the government at the request of the English joint stock Russia Company (▷ Companies, Joint Stock) as likely to offend the Russian government and hinder trade. He also wrote a sonnet sequence, *Licia, or Poems of Love* (1593) in emulation of ▷ Sir Philip Sidney's ▷ *Astrophil and Stella*.
Bib: Barry, L. E., (ed.), *English Works*.

Fletcher, Giles (the younger) (1585–1623)
Poet; author of ▷ allegorical religious poems, especially his ▷ epic in ▷ Spenserian stanzas, *Christ's Victorie and Triumph* (1610). He was the younger son of ▷ Giles, Fletcher the elder.
Bib: Hunter, W. B. (ed.), *The English Spenserians*.

Fletcher, John (1579–1625)
Dramatist; nephew of ▷ Giles Fletcher the elder. The 1679 edition of his work contains 57 plays – the largest of all the Elizabethan collections – but most of them were collaborations.

Among the works probably by himself alone are: *The Faithful Shepherdess* (1608), a ▷ pastoral; the tragedies *Bonduca* (▷ Boadicea) and *Valentinian* (1614); the tragicomedies, *The Loyal Subject* (1618) and *The Humorous Lieutenant* (1619); the comedies, *The Wild Goose Chase, Monsieur Thomas* and *The Pilgrim* (1621).

It was in collaboration with Beaumont that Fletcher produced his most famous work; their best plays are commonly held to be the tragicomedy ▷ *Philaster* and the tragedy *The Maid's Tragedy*. Another tragedy, *A King and No King* (1611), was greatly admired by John Dryden (1631–1700); the domestic comedy *The Scornful Lady* (1610) has also been highly praised.

Fletcher seems to have ceased collaborating with Beaumont in 1613, and to have joined briefly with ▷ Shakespeare. ▷ *Henry VIII*, formerly attributed to Shakespeare entirely, is now thought to be partly Fletcher's work, and Shakespeare is also thought to have written part of ▷ *The Two Noble Kinsmen*.

Fletcher's name has also been linked with several other dramatists, including ▷ Ben Jonson, but especially with ▷ Massinger between 1619 and 1622. Among these Massinger collaborations are *Thierry and Theodoret* and *The False One*.

Fletcher's reputation stood highest at the Restoration, when he was ranked with Shakespeare and Jonson. The opinion of most 20th-century criticism is that he was an extremely skilful theatrical craftsman, a master of striking but superficial dramatic effects; his verse, similarly, is admitted to be fluent and musical, but is felt to lack authentic depth and strength of feeling.
Bib: Waith, E. M., *The Pattern of Tragicomedy in Beaumont and Fletcher*; Bradbrook, M. C.,

Elizabethan Tragedy; Danby, J., *Poets on Fortune's Hill*; Finkelpearl, P. J., *Court and Country Politics in the Plays of Beaumont and Fletcher*; Maxwell, B., *Studies in Beaumont, Fletcher and Massinger*; Leech, C., *The John Fletcher Plays*.

Fletcher, Phineas (1582–1650)
Elder son of ▷ Giles Fletcher the elder; ▷ allegorical poet in the tradition of ▷ Edmund Spenser. Principal work: *The Purple Island, or the Isle of Man* (1633), an allegorical representation of the human mind and body.
Bib: Hunter, W. B. (ed.), *The English Spenserians*; Longdale, A. B., *Phineas Fletcher: Man of Letters, Science and Divinity*.

Flodden, Battle of (1513)
The invading Scottish forces under King James IV, fighting in alliance with France which had been invaded by Henry VIII of England, were heavily defeated by the English general, the Earl of Surrey. James himself was killed, as well as large numbers of his nobility. The battle was commemorated by a famous dirge, *The Flowers of the Forest*, the best-known version of which is by Jean Elliott (1727–1805).

Florio, John (?1553–1625)
Translator, Florio published, in 1578 and 1591, two Italian phrase books, as well as an Italian–English dictionary, *A World of Words* (1598). His best-known work, however, was his ▷ translation of the *Essays* of ▷ Montaigne, which was published in 1603.
Bib: Yates, F. A., *John Florio*.

Flowerdew, Alice (1759–1830)
Poet. After the death of her husband, Flowerdew published her spiritual and ▷ didactic work, including some interesting ▷ hymns, in *Poems on Moral and Religious Subjects* (1803), probably from financial need. The third edition (1811) of this collection carries a new preface in which the education of women (▷ Women, education of) is discussed. By this time Flowerdew was teaching in a London school and the practical nature of her argument clearly stems from personal experience. She forthrightly asserts that men and women have equal intellectual potential, but that women have been repressed by the lack of a proper education.
▷ Feminism.

Flyting
A verbal combat, in which the combatants compete against each other in satirical abuse. The device was particularly common in medieval literature, *eg* ▷ Dunbar's *The Flyting of Dunbar and Kennedy*, and Chaucer's ▷ *The Parliament of Foulys*.

Focal character
The character within a narrative 'whose point of view orients the narrative perspective' (▷ Genette). Where there is a focal character, his or her sense impressions and/or perceptions are what the narrative presents to the reader. The focal character is distinguished from the ▷ narrator, since the latter may be a different person. For example, there may be an impersonal, extradiegetic narrator, focalizing through a character in the third person, as in ▷ Henry James' ▷ *The Ambassadors*, or the narrator and focal character may be the same person, but at different points in time, as in ▷ Margaret Atwood's *Cat's Eye*.
▷ Narratology; Focalization.

Focalization
In ▷ narratology, focalization is an aspect of ▷ mood, and is adopted by ▷ Genette as a more precise term than 'point of view' to indicate the focus of a narrative. Internal focalization views events through the mind of a particular ▷ focal character, external focalization follows the experiences of a character without revealing his or her thoughts, while non-focalized narration is told by an impersonal narrator without restriction.

Folio
As applied to books, a folio is one for which the paper has been folded once, and therefore of the largest size. The expression 'the first folio' commonly refers to the first collected edition of ▷ Shakespeare's plays (1623); there were three other folio editions of Shakespeare's plays in the 17th century.

The 1623 volume is edited by two fellow actors of the King's Men – Heming and Condell – and contains a preface by them and prefatory poems, notably one by ▷ Ben Jonson. Following the poems there is a list of the 'principal actors in all these plays'; the list includes Shakespeare himself, ▷ Richard Burbage, ▷ Nathaniel Field, and of course the editors. The edition opens with the print of a rather inferior engraved portrait of the poet by Martin Droeshout. Thirty-six plays are included; ▷ *Pericles*, included by modern editors, is omitted. Eighteen of the plays had already been published in small ▷ quarto editions (some of them close to the folio version and some differing substantially), and the remainder were being published for the first time. The plays are undated, and grouped into Comedies, Histories and Tragedies; some have divisions into ▷ acts and scenes, and some are without them.

Fontenelle, Bernard le Bovyer (Bouvier) de (1657–1757)
French author, born at Rouen, a nephew of ▷ Corneille. Educated as a lawyer he followed in his uncle's footsteps by abandoning this profession in favour of literature, at first writing

for the theatre. Failing at this, despite the help of his uncle, he turned to other forms of authorship including a history of the French theatre, satires, criticism, and scientific and moral treatises. His *Dialogue des morts* (1683), in imitation of the classical Greek writer ▷ Lucian, established his reputation. He became a member of the French Academy in 1691, and of the Academy of Sciences in 1697. He was praised for his clarity and wit, as well as his ability to render complex scientific theories in simple language that could be easily understood even by non-scientists. He was admired by a number of English authors including ▷ Aphra Behn, who in 1688 translated his *Entretiens sur la pluralité des mondes* (*A Discovery of New Worlds*), and *Histoire des oracles* (*The History of Oracles and the Cheats of the Pagan Priests*).

▷ French literature in England.

Foote, Samuel (1720–77)
Actor, manager and dramatist, born at Truro to a landowning family. He trained for the law, but moved instead, like many of his contemporaries, to the stage. He studied with ▷ Macklin and played the title role in ▷ *Othello* to Macklin's Iago in 1744. He also acted at the ▷ Smock Alley Theatre in Dublin. In 1747 he leased the 'Little Theatre in the Hay' (▷ Haymarket Theatres), opening with a piece of his own called *The Diversions of the Morning*, which proved a great success, and which he followed with more of his own productions. In 1766 a riding accident caused him to lose a leg, but he was acting again only five months later. Out of sympathy, he was given a patent for life at the Haymarket. His plays, mainly social and political satires, include *Taste* (1752) and *The Minor* (1760). He was an excellent mimic, and became the subject of legal action by a number of people whom he had imitated on stage. He also wrote two pamphlets on acting and dramatic theory. ▷ Samuel Johnson praised his broad humour and wit, and he was sometimes nicknamed the 'English Aristophanes'.

Ford, Ford Madox (Ford Hermann Hueffer) (1873–1939)
Novelist, critic, poet. His father was of German origin, and became music critic for *The Times*; his mother was daughter of the ▷ Pre-Raphaelite painter, Ford Madox Brown. Ford was first known as an aesthetic writer of fairy stories, but he became deeply interested in contemporary French writing and culture, and became a propagandist for the rigorous discipline of French art, exercising a strong personal influence on ▷ Joseph Conrad and ▷ Ezra Pound. He co-operated with Conrad on two novels, *The Inheritors* (1901) and *Romance* (1903). He was a prolific writer, but is now chiefly remembered for *The Good Soldier* (1915) and for the four novels known in Britain as *The Tietjens Tetralogy* (after the name of its hero), and in America as *Parade's End*: *Some Do Not* (1924), *No More Parades* (1925), *A Man Could Stand Up* (1926), and *Last Post* (1928). The tetralogy is regarded by some critics as the most memorable fiction about the war of 1914–18 (in which Ford served, although he was 40 on enlistment), and as the most remarkable account of the upheaval in English social values in the decade 1910–20. *The Good Soldier* is a subtle and ambiguous study of the cruelty, infidelity and madness below the respectable surface of the lives of two couples, and is notable for its use of an ▷ unreliable narrator.

Ford has an undoubted importance in literary history because of his personal influence. As a poet, he played a significant part in the founding of ▷ Imagism. In 1908–9 he was editor of the brilliant but short-lived *English Review*, to which ▷ Thomas Hardy, ▷ Henry James, ▷ H. G. Wells, Joseph Conrad and the Russian novelist Leo Tolstoy all contributed. He was also an early champion of ▷ D. H. Lawrence. Brought up in the relatively narrow Pre-Raphaelite and ▷ aesthetic movements, in the 1900s he was a central figure among the writers who were thinking radically about problems of artistic form, especially in novel-writing. He regarded the 19th-century English novel as too much a product of the accident of genius, and, aligning himself with James and Conrad, was in opposition to H. G. Wells who preferred the title of journalist to that of artist. After World War I he moved to Paris and became part of a circle of expatriate writers, including ▷ James Joyce, Ernest Hemingway and Gertrude Stein. He also founded the *Transatlantic Review*.

After 1930 his imaginative writing was somewhat neglected but he is now recognized as an important figure of the ▷ modernist movement. Of present-day novelists, he has perhaps had most effect on ▷ Graham Greene. Apart from *The Tietjens Tetralogy* and *The Good Soldier*, novels selected for praise include the historical trilogy about Tudor England (*The Fifth Queen*, 1906; *Privy Seal*, 1907; *The Fifth Queen Crowned*, 1908). His *Collected Poems* were published in 1936.

Bib: Cassell, R. A. (ed.), *Ford Madox Ford: Modern Judgements*; Green, R., *Ford Madox Ford, Prose and Politics*; Meixner, J. A., *Ford Madox Ford's Novels: A Critical Study*; Mizener, A., *The Saddest Story* (biography); Ohmann, C., *Ford Madox Ford: From Apprentice to Craftsman*.

Ford, John (1586–?1640)
The best of the ▷ Caroline dramatists. He is best known for two tragedies, ▷ *'Tis Pity She's a Whore* and *The Broken Heart* (1633), and a tragic history play, *Perkin Warbeck* (1634). Less well known are *Lover's Melancholy* (1629) and *Love's Sacrifice* (1633). He collaborated with

other dramatists, notably with ▷ Dekker and ▷ Rowley in *The Witch of Edmonton* (1623). In spite of sensational themes and incidents (*eg 'Tis Pity* is about incestuous love), Ford's characteristic tone is the melancholy of private, frustrated passion; pathos rather than tragedy. Indeed, late 20th-century criticism has suggested that there are reasoned and serious themes in the plays and that far from being precious, Ford focuses on the moral judgements of his age.
Bib: Anderson, Donald K., *John Ford*; Neill, M. (ed.), *John Ford: Critical Re-Visions.*

Foregrounding
An idea originating in Russian ▷ Formalism, foregrounding refers to the way literature, despite containing multiple elements, stresses some of them while allowing others to fade into the background. As their name suggests, the Formalists were particularly interested in the formal construction of literature, and the way literature calls attention to its own language use. So for them it is certain features of literary language that are foregrounded and the term therefore has quite a technical sense. But foregrounding is now used more generally, sometimes as a mere jargon word for emphasizing.

Forest of Arden
▷ Arden, Forest of.

Form
In a simple sense, form is opposed to content, but this analytical separation has to be used with caution because, especially in literary works, the way something is said is inseparable from what is said, and the form of a work profoundly influences a reader's response to the content. In discussing form abstractly, however, it is useful to distinguish between forms which are established quite strictly and those with a more flexible organisation. An example of the former kind would be the traditional ▷ sonnet which has very exacting formal requirements. An example of the latter would be a larger ▷ genre such as ▷ tragedy whose ▷ conventions are much more malleable within certain limits. The ▷ Romantic poet ▷ Coleridge, in the early 19th century, proposed a distinction which has been influential. He distinguished between *organic* and *mechanical* form. Organic form is when a work's shape and organization evolve in relation to its content (▷ organicism). Mechanical form, by contrast, is a form determined in advance. The distinction is a useful one, but not absolute, since in practice it is often difficult to label a particular work entirely one or the other. Coleridge himself, for example, wrote a number of free-flowing odes which have an 'organic' feel. But the ode itself is of course an established form with certain expectations. One thing, however, is certain: issues of content in literature can never be separated from a consideration of the formal means by which they are communicated.

Formalism
A general name for a kind of artistic practice or criticism which emphasises form or artistic technique rather than the content of art works. As such, formalism is for many a negative description. There are, however, different varieties of formalist criticism of literature. Two schools have been especially influential in the 20th century. The first of these is the Russian ▷ Formalist school whose work has had a significant impact on recent critical thought. The second is the American movement known as New Criticism which flourished from around 1940 to around 1970. However, probably the most interesting recent work in this area relates the study of literary form to issues of historical content and development. The interest in the work of ▷ Mikhail Bakhtin, who was himself a contemporary of the Russian Formalists and much influenced by them, is one example. Another is to be found in the work of Raymond Williams and the ▷ 'cultural materialist' and 'new historicist' critics. In Williams' work on drama, for example, he traces the development of modern dramatic forms in their historical evolution and social context showing how form enables and limits the expression of a certain ▷ structure of feeling.
Bib: Thompson, E. M., *Russian Formalism and Anglo-American New Criticism*; Williams, R., *Drama From Ibsen to Brecht.*

Forman, Simon (1552–1611)
Astrologer, physician and diarist. This unusual figure is of importance to us because of his casebook or diary and his *Book of Plaies*, where he recorded personal information about prominent ▷ Elizabethan figures, as well as recounted details from the performances of several plays. For example, he has provided us with material about ▷ Aemilia Lanyer's life, as well as comments about ▷ Shakespeare's ▷ *Macbeth*, ▷ *Cymbeline* and ▷ *The Winter's Tale*. It was Forman's casebook which first gave A. L. Rowse the idea that Lanyer was the dark lady of Shakespeare's sonnets. While this hypothesis has little or no verification, Forman's personal revelations and his wide acquaintance with contemporary gossip make his work an important source of ▷ Renaissance social history and biographical detail.
Bib: Rowse, A. L., *Simon Forman: Sex and Society in Shakespeare's Age.*

Forster, E. M. (Edward Morgan) (1879–1970)
Novelist. His work is primarily in a realistic mode, and his ideas in the liberal tradition; indeed, much of his work is concerned with the legacy of Victorian middle-class liberalism. He

was educated at Tonbridge School (a public school whose ethos is characterized by Sawston in the first two novels) and then at King's College, Cambridge, of which he was later made an honorary fellow. Through contacts made at Cambridge he came to be associated with the ▷ Bloomsbury Group. He travelled in Europe, lived in Italy and Egypt, and spent some years in India, where he was for a time secretary to a rajah after World War I.

Forster's novels are: *Where Angels Fear to Tread* (1905); *The Longest Journey* (1907); *A Room with a View* (1908); ▷ *Howards End* (1910); ▷ *A Passage to India* (1924); and *Maurice* (1971). The last of these, which has a homosexual theme, was published posthumously, as was *The Life to Come* (1972), a collection of stories, many of which treat the same theme. His other two collections of short stories are: *The Celestial Omnibus* (1914) and *The Eternal Moment* (1928). These are mainly early work; they were published in a collected edition in 1947. His high reputation rests mainly on his fiction, but he has also written biographies and essays which are important for understanding his outlook as an imaginative writer. The biography of his friend Goldsworthy Lowes Dickinson (1934) is about a Cambridge scholar who was an important leader of liberal political opinion; that of his great-aunt. Marianne Thornton (1956), is enlightening about Forster's background. *The Hill of Devi* (1953) is an account of his experiences in India. The essays in *Abinger Harvest* (1936) and *Two Cheers for Democracy* (1951) include expressions of his opinions about politics, literature and society. *Aspects of the Novel* (1927) is one of the best-known critical works on the novel form. He co-operated with Eric Crozier on the libretto for Benjamin Britten's opera *Billy Budd* (1951).

Forster's dominant theme is the habitual conformity of people to unexamined social standards and conventions, and the ways in which this conformity blinds individuals to recognition of what is true in what is unexpected, to the proper uses of the intelligence, and to their own resources of spontaneous life. Spontaneous life and free intelligence also draw on traditions, and Forster shows how English traditions have on the one hand nourished complacency, hypocrisy, and insular philistinism, and on the other hand, humility, honesty, and sceptical curiosity. In several of the novels, and especially in *A Passage to India*, British culture is contrasted with a foreign tradition which has virtues that the British way of life is without. His style is consistently light and witty, with a use of irony which recalls ▷ Jane Austen and a use of comedy of situation which recalls ▷ George Meredith. *A Passage to India* stands out from his work for the subtlety and resonance of its symbolism.

Bib: Trilling, L., *E. M. Forster*; McConkey, J., *The Novels of Forster*; Bradbury, M. (ed.), *E. M. Forster: A Collection of Critical Essays*; Stone, W., *The Cave and the Mountain*; Furbank, P.N., *E. M. Forster: A Life* (2 vols).

Forster, Margaret (b 1938)

Novelist. Forster has produced a steady stream of writings since the early 1960s, as well as the screenplay (from her own novel) for one of the classic films of 'Swinging Sixties' London, *Georgy Girl* (1966, directed by Silvio Narizzano). Her works are broadly feminist, and often centre on a female protagonist or on relationships between women. Her other works include: *Dames' Delight* (1964); *The Bogeyman* (1966); *The Seduction of Mrs Pendlebury* (1974); *Mother Can You Hear Me?* (1979) and *Marital Rites* (1982). She has also written biographies of Victorian poet Elizabeth Barrett Browning and of Daphne Du Maurier, and published *Significant Sisters: The Grassroots of Active Feminism 1839–1939*.

Forsyte Saga, The

A sequence of novels constituting a study of Victorian and Edwardian society by John Galsworthy (1867–1933). They comprise: *The Man of Property* (1906): *The Indian Summer of a Forsyte* (1918); *In Chancery* (1920); *Awakening* (1920); *To Let* (1921). A television serialization of the work in 1967 was extremely popular.

Forties, The Hungry

The decade 1840–50, so called because bad harvests caused serious food shortages, leading to mass agitation for abolition of the tax on imported corn (Anti-Corn Law League) and for a more democratic political system (the ▷ Chartist Movement). It was in the years 1845–51 that the Irish Famine took place: about 10 per cent of the population died from hunger and disease, and mass emigration ensued from those remaining.

▷ Corn Laws; Free Trade.

Fortnightly Review, The

The Fortnightly Review was founded in 1865 by, among others, the novelist ▷ Anthony Trollope. It was a vehicle of advanced liberal opinion, and included amongst its contributors the scientist ▷ T.H. Huxley, the political scientist ▷ Walter Bagehot, the positivist philosopher Frederick Harrison, the critics ▷ Matthew Arnold and ▷ Leslie Stephen, the novelists ▷ George Eliot and ▷ George Meredith, the poets ▷ D.G. Rossetti and ▷ Algernon Swinburne, and ▷ Walter Pater and ▷ William Morris, the last two both leaders of social and critical thought.

Forty Shilling Freeholders

The class, outside the towns, who from the 13th century until the ▷ Reform Bill of 1832

possessed the minimum property qualification to vote for a representative in Parliament, or to be elected as one. 'Freeholder' implies owning land, not renting it from another landowner; 'forty shillings' is the annual value of the land.
 ▷ Franchise.

Forty-five, The
The rebellion or rising of 1745, *ie* the second of the two main ▷ Jacobite attempts in the 18th century to regain the throne of Great Britain for the ▷ Catholic branch of the House of ▷ Stuart. It was led by Charles Stuart ('Bonnie Prince Charlie' to his Scottish supporters, the 'Young Pretender' to his enemies), elder son of the claimant James Stuart (the ▷ 'Old Pretender'). Charles succeeded in rousing the Highlands and occupying Edinburgh. He then advanced into England and reached Derby. He had by then attracted very few English supporters, and retreated to Scotland. He was defeated by the Duke of Cumberland in 1746 at the Battle of ▷ Culloden in northern Scotland, but escaped abroad.

Fothergill, Jessie (1851–91)
Novelist, born in Chetham Hill, Manchester. She was sent to boarding school in Harrogate after her father's death, and began her literary career with *Healey* (1975). Eleven novels followed, including *The First Violin* (1877), *The Lasses of Leverhouses* (1888) and her last work, *Oriole's Daughter* (1893). Much of her fiction concerns romantic involvements between people of different social classes.
 ▷ Novel of Manners.

Foucault, Michel (1926–84)
Along with ▷ Louis Althusser and ▷ Jacques Derrida, Foucault is one of the most influential of French philosophers whose work has been taken up by the practitioners of other disciplines. Foucault rejects the totalizing explanations of human development in favour of a more detailed analysis of how power functions within particular ▷ discourses. In *Madness and Civilization* (1965) he explored the historical opposition between 'madness' and 'civilization', applying ▷ Saussure's notion of differentials (▷ Difference) to the various ways in which society excludes the behaviour which threatens it. He later took this issue up in *Discipline and Punish* (1977), and *I Pierre Riviere* (1978). In *The Order of Things* (1971) and *The Archaeology of Knowledge* (1972) he investigated the ways in which human knowledge is organized, and the transition from discourses which rely upon a notion of 'self-presence', to those which operate differentially to produce the kind of linguistic self-consciousness characteristic of ▷ post-modernism. In essays such as those translated in *Language, Counter-memory, Practice* (1977), he sought to clarify specific areas of opposition through which discourse is constructed. At the time of his death he had embarked on an investigation of the discourses of sexuality through the ages, and the three volumes of *The History of Sexuality* (1978–87) have now been published.

***Four P's, The* (1568)**
One of the amusing ▷ interludes written by ▷ John Heywood. It begins with a competition between a palmer, a pardoner and an apothecary, judged by a pedlar, to find the best liar.

***Four Quartets* (1935–42)**
Four poems written between 1935 and 1942 by ▷ T. S. Eliot, eventually published as a single work. They are contemplative, religious poems, each concerned with a distinct aspect of spiritual experience. Each has as its symbolic centre a place; each uses symbolically one of the four 'elements' of medieval physics; each has a structure analogous to the movements and the instruments of a musical quartet; the theme that unites the four is that of the human consciousness in relation to time and the concept of eternity. *Burnt Norton* (the element of air) centres on the rose garden of a ruined country house (Burnt Norton) in Gloucestershire and plays on the differences and relationships between the actual present, the past in memory, and speculation on what might have been. *East Coker* (earth) is based on a village in Somerset, whence the poet's ancestors derived, and it includes quotations from *The Governor* (1531) by ▷ Sir Thomas Elyot; the poem is concerned with man as part of the process of nature. *Dry Salvages* (water) is named after rocks off the coast of Massachusetts; the poem is concerned with racial time and memory, larger than the time of history and of the seasons, and embracing the more unconscious regions of the mind. ▷ *Little Gidding* (fire) derives its title from the religious community in the reign of Charles I, who is supposed to have visited it when broken by defeat at the battle of Naseby. Fire in this poem is used as destruction (with reference to the raids on London during World War II), purification, illumination, and as an emblem of Divine Love.

Four Quartets was Eliot's last major work in non-dramatic poetry; the remainder of his career was devoted to poetic drama.
 ▷ Gardner, Helen.

Bib: Drew, E., *T. S. Eliot: The Design of his Poetry*.

Fourteenth of July
The French annual national festival, dating from the storming of the Bastille, a state prison in Paris, on 14 July 1789. This was the first triumph of the ▷ French Revolution, and marked the end of the ▷ Ancien Régime.

Fourth Estate, The
Traditionally, and for political purposes, English society was thought until the 20th century to have three estates: the lords spiritual, the lords temporal, the commons. ▷ Carlyle alludes to a Fourth Estate, *ie* the press, implying that the newspapers have an essential role in the political functions of society. He attributed the phrase to the 18th-century statesman ▷ Edmund Burke.

Fowles, John (b 1926)
Novelist. Born in Essex and educated at Oxford University. His novels are: *The Collector* (1963); *The Magus* (1965; revised edition 1977); *The French Lieutenant's Woman* (1969); *Daniel Martin* (1977); *Mantissa* (1982); *A Maggot* (1985). He is an experimental writer, interested in the nature of fiction and its interaction with history and reality, but he combines this with a skill in story-telling and an ability to create compelling characters and a vivid sense of social context. Several of his novels have been best-sellers, and three: *The Collector, The Magus* and *The French Lieutenant's Woman* have been filmed. His reception by the critics had tended to be more enthusiastic in the U.S.A. than in Britain. The recurrent concerns of his novels are the power of repressive convention and social conformity, the enigmatic nature of sexual relations, the desire to manipulate and control and the problem of individual freedom. The last of these concerns reflects the influence of ▷ existentialism.

The Collector, the story of the kidnapping of an attractive and wealthy girl by an introverted clerk, is in part a study of a pathological desire for possession, and in part a fable about social deprivation. It is in three parts, the first and last narrated by the man, and the second by the girl. Fowles' novels are highly allusive: *The Magus*, like *The Collector*, employs parallels with Shakespeare's *The Tempest*. It also draws on the literary archetype of the quest in its story of a young man who travels to a Greek island where he is lured by a series of magical illusions into a confrontation with existential uncertainty and freedom of choice. *The French Lieutenant's Woman* employs parody of 19th-century novelistic style, quotations from sociological reports, from ▷ Darwin, Marx, ▷ Arnold and Tennyson, and authorial interruptions. Fowles' belief in the fundamental uncertainty of existence is reflected in his use of open endings; in *The Magus* the future of the main characters is 'another mystery' and *The French Lieutenant's Woman* has a choice of endings. *Daniel Martin* is more realist than his earlier work, exploiting his descriptive skill in a range of settings: it has less of the element of mystery and a more clearly affirmative ending. He has also written a volume of short stories, *The Ebony Tower* (1974) and works of non-fiction, including: *Islands* (1978); *The Tree* (1979); *The Enigma of Stonehenge* (1980) and *Land* (1985).
Bib: Conradi, P., *John Fowles*; Loveday, S., *The Romances of John Fowles*; Woodcock, B., *Male Mythologies: John Fowles and Masculinity*.

Fox, Charles James (1749–1806)
Principal leader of the Whig party from 1775 (the beginning of the ▷ American War of Independence) until his death. The crown was not then above politics and the Tories, almost continuously in power during the same period, had the support of George III. Fox's fearless opposition in the House of Commons to the policies of the government in America, in ▷ Ireland and in regard to the ▷ French Revolution caused the king to refuse his offer of participation in the government in 1804, when he became convinced of the rightness of the war against France. Fox was dissolute in private life but set a high standard of political independence of mind. His principal political opponents were the Prime Ministers Lord North during the American war and ▷ William Pitt the Younger during the French one. Though powerful in opposition, he was less effective in office; but his service as Foreign Secretary in the Whig governments of 1782 and 1806 was too brief to show results.

Fox, George (1624–91)
Religious leader. He founded the Society of Friends (▷ Quakers), and left a journal of his spiritual experience, published in 1694. Apart from its religious importance, Fox's journal is one of the classics amongst the English diaries. In 1669 he married ▷ Margaret Fell, a Quaker pamphleteer.
Bib: Foulds, E. V., *George Fox and the Valiant Sixty*.

Foxe, John (1516–87)
Author of the *Book of Martyrs*; this was the title under which it was popularly known; the correct title of the 1st edition (1563) was *Acts and Monuments of these latter and perilous days*. Foxe was a Puritan who first set out to write a history of Christian martyrdom in Latin. The first outline dealt chiefly with the 14th-century reformers, the English John Wycliffe (?1320–84) and the Bohemian John Huss. In 1554 he went abroad to escape persecution under the Catholic ▷ Mary, and completed his book there. The English version is fierce and eloquent, and had immense sales; for generations it inspired hatred for ▷ Catholicism in Britain, and was read alongside the Bible by simple folk who read little else. It is a classic of popular prose in the Elizabethan period.

▷ Reformation.
Bib: Olsen, V. N., *John Foxe and the Elizabethan Church*.

Frame, Janet (b 1942)
New Zealand novelist and short-story writer.

Her collection of stories, *The Lagoon* (1951), and her trilogy of novels *Owls Do Cry* (1957), *Faces in the Water* (1961) and *The Edge of the Alphabet* (1962) are about childhood innocence and the imagination, both threatened by bereavement and a repressive society. *Scented Gardens for the Blind* (1963) and *The Adaptable Man* (1965) explore the limitations and potentialities of language. Of her later work, *Intensive Care* (1970), written while Frame was in the U.S.A., draws on the horrors of the Vietnam War for a visionary satire on the place of war in the New Zealand consciousness. Her other novels are: *Living in the Maniototo* (1979); *A State of Siege* (1982); and *The Carpathians* (1988). Other story collections: *You Are Now Entering the Human Heart* (1983). She has also written three volumes of autobiography, and the 1991 film, *An Angel at my Table* (dir. Jane Campion), was based on her life and books.

Frame narrative, first-order narrative, extradiegetic narrative
Terms used for the outside or first narrative in a fiction, where this encloses a second-order narrative. For example, ▷ Conrad's ▷ *Heart of Darkness* has a frame narrative of a group of men sitting on a boat on the Thames; one of them, Marlow, narrates a second-order narrative about his experiences in Africa.
▷ narratology

Francis, Anne (1738–1800)
Poet and translator. Anne Francis was a distinguished scholar; she had a ▷ classical education, learning Latin, Greek and Hebrew. After her marriage to Revd Robert Francis, she published a translation of the *Song of Solomon* (1781) which she also edited, and in 1785 she brought out *The Obsequies of Demetrius Poliorcetes*, which reworked some of Plutarch's writing. Francis was also an admirer of ▷ Goethe and wrote *Charlotte to Werther: A Poetical Epistle* (1787) as a vehicle for defending him against what she felt were unjust accusations. Several more personal works remain, for example the elegies and odes to her family published in *Miscellaneous Poems* (1790). In light of this detailed and scholarly activity, it is surprising that Francis should think that such work was 'an *improper* undertaking for a *woman*' (Preface to the *Song of Solomon*).

***Frankenstein, or the Modern Prometheus* (1817)**
A philosophical romance which is also a tale of terror, by ▷ Mary Shelley. It belongs in part to the 'Gothic' tradition popular at the time and partly to a philosophical tradition going back to ▷ Rousseau, concerned with themes of isolation, suffering and social injustice. Mary Shelley originally wrote it to compete with the tales of terror being composed for their own amusement by her lover and later husband, ▷ P. B. Shelley and their friend, the poet ▷ Lord Byron. Frankenstein is a Swiss student of natural philosophy who constructs a monster and endows it with life. Its impulses are benevolent, but it is everywhere regarded with loathing and fear; its benevolence turns to hatred, and it destroys its creator and his bride. Versions of and sequels to the story have been a regular feature in the cinema from the days of silent film to Kenneth Branagh's *Frankenstein* (1994). Indeed, the English actor Boris Karloff (1887–1969) was able to found a career in the movies on his memorable performance as the Creature, for Universal Studios in the 1930s. Alongside the plethora of adaptations (and travesties) of Bram Stoker's novel ▷ *Dracula*, *Frankenstein* offers the most popular example of what might be termed the persistence of the Gothic.
▷ Gothic novels.
Bib: Hammond, R., *The Modern Frankenstein: Fiction Becomes Fact*; Baldick, C., *In Frankenstein's Shadow: Myth, Monstrosity and Nineteenth-century Writing*.

Franklin's Tale, The
One of ▷ Chaucer's ▷ *Canterbury Tales*. The Franklin suggests that his tale derives from old, insular narrative sources and introduces it as a lay which formerly circulated amongst 'olde, gentil, Britons'. In fact the tale seems to be drawn from Italian sources (from a narrative recounted by ▷ Boccaccio), which have been given a British gloss by Chaucer.

The narrative focusses on the strains placed on the marital vows of Dorigen and Arveragus, when Dorigen, unwittingly, pledges herself to her unwelcome suitor, Aurelius. Aurelius is able to fulfil Dorigen's 'impossible' condition for accepting him as a lover with the help of a clerk-magician, who appears to make the black rocks off Brittany's coast disappear. The chain of interlocking vows is broken when Arveragus and Aurelius cede their claim to exclusive rights over Dorigen's body. The clerk-magician also cedes his claim for payment for his services. The narrator concludes with a question to the audience about who was the most 'free' in the tale.
▷ Breton Lays.

Fraser, Antonia (b 1932)
Novelist and historian. Antonia Fraser is a popular writer of historical ▷ biographies, who has done much to make the lives of famous figures in British history accessible to a wide audience. Her works are meticulously researched but have been criticized for lacking historical context and finally offering a selective reading of British history. She is now married to the dramatist ▷ Harold Pinter, with whom she continues to campaign vigorously for the arts in Great Britain. She has been a member of

the ▷ Arts Council, and is a Fellow of the Royal Society of Literature. Her works include: *Mary Queen of Scots* (1969); *A History of Toys* (1966); *Cromwell, Our Chief of Men* (1973); *King Charles II* (1979); and *The Weaker Vessel: Woman's Lot in the 17th Century* (1984). Her fiction includes *Quiet as a Nun* (1977) and *The Wild Island: A Mystery* (1978).

Fraser's Magazine

It started in 1830 as an imitator of *Blackwood's*, but after the mid-19th century it became Liberal. It published ▷ Thomas Carlyle's ▷ *Sartor Resartus* in 1833–4; at this time it was under the influence of S.T. Coleridge's (1772–1834) Conservative philosophy. In 1848 it published ▷ Charles Kingsley's novel of idealistic reform, *Yeast*. The historian J.A. Froude was its editor 1861–74, and tried to publish ▷ Ruskin's radical treatise on the nature of wealth, *Munera Pulveris* (1862–3), but this proved unpopular with the public, and the treatise was left unfinished. ▷ William Allingham was its editor between 1874 and 1879. The magazine folded in 1882.

Frayn, Michael (b 1933)

British dramatist and novelist. His first plays, *Jamie* (1968) and *Birthdays* (1969) were written for television. Since then he has acquired a reputation both as a leading comic writer for the stage, particularly with his production of *Noises Off* (1982), and an important translator of ▷ Chekhov's plays. Other plays include: *The Two of Us* (1970); *The Sandboy* (1971); *Alphabetical Order* (1975); *Donkeys' Years* (1976); *Clouds* (1976); *Liberty Hall* (1980); *Make and Break* (1980); *Benefactors* (1984). Translations: *The Cherry Orchard* (1978); *The Fruits of Enlightenment* (1979); *Three Sisters* (1983); *Number One* (1984); *Wild Honey* (1984); *The Seagull* (1986); *Uncle Vanya* (1988); *Look Look* (1990); and *Here* (1993). Novels include: *The Tin Men* (1965); *The Russian Interpreter* (1966); *Towards the End of the Morning* (1967); *A Very Private Life* (1968); *Sweet Dreams* (1973).

Frazer, Sir James G. (1854–1915)

Anthropologist. His *Golden Bough* (1890–1915; abridged edition 1922) is a vast study of ancient mythology; it influenced 20th-century poetry such as T.S. Eliot's *The Waste Land* (1922). Other publications include: *Totemism (*1887); *Adonis, Attis, Osiris, Studies in the History of Oriental Religion* (1906); *Totemism and Exogamy (*1910); *Folklore in the Old Testament* (1918). Frazer was a major influence on the development of 20th-century anthropology and psychology, and in addition edited works by William Cowper (1731–1800) and Joseph Addison (1672–1719).

Free indirect discourse

A technique whereby a narrative reports the speech or thoughts of a character, referring to that character in the third person but adopting the character's own idiom. Free indirect discourse thus falls between direct speech (or thought), which quotes a character's words verbatim, and reported speech (or thought), which paraphrases the speech or thoughts of the character in the idiom of the ▷ narrator. When free indirect discourse is used there is often a productive ambiguity as to which judgements are attributable to the character and which to the narrator and/or ▷ implied author. Also known as free indirect speech and (using the French term) as *style indirect libre*.

Free verse

A way of writing poetry without use of ▷ rhyme, ▷ stanza pattern, or ▷ metre. Free verse perhaps had French origins; at all events it is often referred to as *vers libre*. It was practised, especially in the first 30 years of this century, in an attempt to escape from the rather mechanical uses of rhyme and metre by the late romantics. ▷ T. S. Eliot attacked the whole concept of free verse, declaring that it could only be defined by negatives (*no* rhyme, etc.) and that a genuine form would have a positive definition (*Reflections on Vers Libre*; 1917); 'But the most interesting verse which has yet been written in our language has been done either by taking a very simple form, like the iambic pentameter, and constantly withdrawing from it, or taking no form at all, and constantly approximating to a very simple one.' Eliot himself was as bold as any of his contemporaries in rhythmic experimentation, but his methods are clearly one or other of the two which he here describes.

Bib: Hartman, C., *Free Verse*.

French literature in England

The history of relations between English and French literature is long and complex, dating from the times before the Norman ▷ Conquest, when Latin was the *lingua franca*.

Later, in the 12th century Chrétien de Troyes' romances, as well as Marie de France's *Lais*, jointly suppose a sophisticated readership acquainted with Arthurian (▷ Arthur, King) background and named settings, usually in southern England and Wales. This period was one of intense literary activity which benefited England through the marriage of ▷ Henry II with Eleanor of Aquitaine. The civilization of the southern French courts became available throughout England and elsewhere in Europe fuelled the revolution in courtly attitudes which was to affect the Italian poets ▷ Dante and ▷ Petrarch. The English vernacular itself resorted recognition as a means of securing its own achievements. Such imitative activity reaches an apogee with ▷ Chaucer. If his prioress spoke her French 'after the scole of

Stratford atte Bowe', Chaucer himself was more fully conversant, as is attested by *The Book of the Duchess*, ▷ *The House of Fame* and ▷ *The Merchant's Tale*, the last itself stimulated by the popularity of the *lai* (▷ Lay). Similar observations could be made about ▷ Sir Thomas Malory's contacts with France. At the same time, Chaucer translated Guillaume de Lorris' ▷ *Le Roman de la Rose* and in the later ▷ Middle Ages there are also adaptations and translations of earlier epic and romance works. Thus the history of the cross-Channel literary flow from France to England is to no small degree the history of the translations and adaptations undergone by French literature.

The influence of Petrarch, felt early on both sides of the Channel, was prolonged by the Italian vogue prevalent in France in the 1550s–70s and compounded by the English admiration for Pierre de Ronsard. Ronsard's love poetry found favour with the ▷ Renaissance sonneteers, Henry Constable (1562–1613), ▷ Samuel Daniel and ▷ Thomas Lodge among them. ▷ Spenser's cultivation of the 16th-century French poet ▷ Joachim Du Bellay is untypical of his age. However, it is noticeable that poetry is the favoured genre for imitation, possibly because in France itself it is at once the most deeply exploited and the most cohesively organized. Of French drama there is no trace in England; and the fortunes of prose are the fortunes of translation, as represented most momentously in ▷ Shakespeare's recourse to ▷ John Florio for ▷ Montaigne's essay *Des Cannibales* for ▷ *The Tempest*. Yet while Montaigne can unquestionably be said to have had a hand in shaping the English essay form, ▷ Rabelais leaves more elusive traces and to discern his equivalent in English literature, one has to look as close to the Renaissance as Sir John Harington (?1560–1612), ▷ Thomas Nashe and ▷ Samuel Butler, and as far forward as ▷ Laurence Sterne and ▷ James Joyce.

Florio and Sir Thomas Urquhart (1611–60) – Rabelais' 17th-century translator – are authors in their own right. At the same period, Joshua Sylvester's (c 1563–1618) translation of Guillaume de Salluste Du Bartas was no less influential. In the later 17th and early 18th centuries, translations were supplemented by (undistinguished) adaptations, notably those which represent the barest throes of imitation of French classical drama. One such adaptation was ▷ Ambrose Philip's *The Distrest Mother* (1712), behind which stands ▷ Racine's *Andromaque* (1667). Its success is recounted in ▷ Samuel Johnson's *Life* of Philips, a success greater than the original would have had in England at that time. This exemplifies a measure of the degree to which the Restoration was culturally as well as politically out of sympathy with French classical idiom. It was left to ▷ Dryden to put ▷ Corneille back on the literary agenda, while English ▷ comedy of manners was indebted to ▷ Molière. ▷ Alexander Pope and Johnson, in the following century, attended to the criteria of taste laid down by ▷ Nicholas Boileau and René Rapin (1621–87).

If the ▷ Augustans turned to French precedents in their search for prescriptive aesthetics and decorum, the rise of the novel in England provided models for French writers – both ▷ Jean Jacques Rousseau (*La Nouvelle Héloïse*, 1765) and Pierre Laclos (*Les Liaisons Dangereuses* 1782) explored the epistolary form developed by ▷ Samuel Richardson, while ▷ Laurence Stern's ▷ *Tristram Shandy* (1759–67) established the ludic and parodic mode (itself derived in part from Rabelais) which Denis Diderot (1713–84) adopted in *Jacques le Fataliste* (1773).

Diderot was also one of the prime movers behind the collective project of the ▷ *Encyclopédie*, a platform for rationalist ideas which provided some of the intellectual foundations for the ▷ American War of Independence of 1776, the ▷ French Revolution of 1789, and contemporary political dissidence in England and Ireland. Rousseau also contributed articles to the *Encyclopédie*, but it was his autobiographical writings which were to exert an abiding influence on the first- and second-generation ▷ Romantics – William Wordsworth's ▷ *The Prelude* explores at greater length the themes of time and subjectivity broached in the *Rêveries d'un Promeneur Solitaire* (1778), devoting more space to both the role of the imagination and the interaction between self and social environment, while ▷ Lord Byron's *Childe Harold's Pilgrimage* (1812–18) and ▷ Percy Bysshe Shelley's *The Triumph of Life* (1822) both interrogate the legacy of their Swiss precursor.

Byron's portrayal of *mal du siècle* restlessness and tortured sexuality through a combination of the exotic travel narrative and Gothic locations also recalls Vicomte François René de Chateaubriand's *René* (1802), with its sibling incest plot and New World frame. Chateaubriand (1768–1848) was one of the first 19th-century French historians of English literature (*Essai sur la Littérature Anglaise*, 1836), and much of French Romanticism developed under the shadow of the second-generation English Romantics, particularly Byron, whose combination of melancholic self-dramatization and emancipatory politics appealed to Victor Hugo and Alphonse Marie Louis de Lamartime (1790–1869).

The ▷ Gothic mode was also to play a considerable role in 19th-century France. While the dissident rationalism of ▷ William Godwin (*Caleb Williams*, 1794) and ▷ Mary Wollstonecraft (*Mary*, 1788) attacked the monstrosity of the old regime and the disillusioned radical Romanticism of ▷ Mary Shelley (▷ *Frankenstein*, 1818) suggested the monstrous potential of failed revolution, Gothic fiction in France was to receive a psychological inflection in the *conte fantastique*. In the mid-19th century Gothic was re-imported into France through the work of the American ▷ Edgar Allan Poe, translated by both ▷ Charles Pierre Baudelaire and Stephane Mallarmé, who tended to stress the macabre and formalistic aspects of his work respectively.

The main mode of prose fiction in 19th-century France was of course the realist novel. Although given a kind of programme by the critic Champfleury in 1857, ▷ realism never designated a school proper and the French novel of the period retains traces of Romanticism in its delineation of society and history, largely through its reliance on young male protagonists driven by ambition for social success. In ▷ Stendhal, heroes of energy and imagination who incarnate a kind of principle of unpredictability are crushed by a conformist society which perceives them as a threat (*Le Rouge et le Noir*, 1831). Since, for Stendhal, realism as a mode is implicated in the reproduction of conformist modes of behaviour, the novel form is subject to self-conscious parody and irony.

Such irony is absent from Honoré de Balzac, whose aspiration to be History's secretary led to the conception and execution of the vast social panorama of *La Comédie Humaine* (1829–55). The cycle of novels attempts to provide a taxonomy of existing social types as well as a study of social mobility during the Restoration and the July Monarchy. As a whole, the cycle is characterized by a kind of tension between an interpretative and classificatory project premised upon the immediate legibility of signs of social class and character on the one hand and the demands of melodramatic plot requiring the mystery and suspense of deferred legibility on the other. The mixture of documentary and melodrama, together with the use of names to reveal and conceal essences, forms an obvious parallel with the work of ▷ Dickens, in spite of the gulf between Balzac's conservative cynicism and the English novelist's reformist pathos.

If Stendhal and Balzac retain certain Romantic traits, ▷ Gustave Flaubert's work, in contrast, represents a devastating critique of Romanticism – its valorization of the self and affect are debunked as a symptom of the stupidity of received opinion (*bêtise*). Thus Emma Bovary in *Madame Bovary* (1856) is a victim of having read too much ▷ Walter Scott, whose work engenders in her an insatiable desire to imitate impossible models, leading to serial affairs, compulsive consumption, mounting debts and then suicide as her creditors begin to close in. Although Flaubert's early work seems to attempt to escape the logic of *bêtise*, his later work implies that no such escape is possible. This ultimately leads to his collation of a dictionary of received opinions, quoted deadpan without quotation marks (*Dictionnaire des Idées Reçues*, 1880). His last novel *L'Education Sentimentale* (1869), set during the revolutions of 1848, tells the (non-) story of a failed generation, where no-one learns anything from the past and any notion of the genuine or the original is expunged, to the extent that the very possibility of the new is denied through 'revolutions' which are no more than cycles of repetition and devaluation. But Flaubert's technical approach allows the possibility that even this end-of-politics/end-of-history thesis may itself be nothing more than another example of received opinion. Such ambiguity is fostered through the systematic use of devices such as point of view and free indirect style, which disoriginate the voice of the narrative and question the authority of its statements. So although Flaubert was received by English contemporaries as a realist dealing with subjects such as provincial adultery, his rejection of the convention of discreet third-person omniscient narration actually served to undermine the technical basis of realism and it is this technical legacy to later writers such as ▷ Henry James and ▷ Virginia Woolf which has since identified him as a proto-modernist.

The realist tradition was extended instead by the ▷ Naturalist movement and in particular by the work of Emile Zola. The *Rougon-Macquart* cycle (1871–93) in a sense repeats the Balzacian project of a total description of society, but in terms of a different politics and a different science. Zola's liberal socialist politics were accompanied by a belief in environmental and biological determinism, hence his adoption of a family tree as a compositional schema. The picture of Second Empire France which emerges through this exercise in genealogy is not one of Balzacian energy but one of a society in entropic decay, degenerating inexorably into chaos. Hence the closing image of *La Bête Humaine* (1890) – a driverless train full of drunken soldiers hurtling towards inevitable destruction, just as the imperial regime plunges into defeat in the Franco-Prussian War. Arguably, though, Zola's influence on subsequent writers lies elsewhere. His interest in socialization and heredity, particularly with regard to working-class communities, was not only documentary and political but also sensationalist. Technically conventional, his first major novel *Thérèse Raquin* (1867) tells a story of triangular adultery and murder motivated by sex and money, thereby establishing the paradigm for much 20th-century popular narrative in book and film. In terms of immediate impact, Zola's concern with contemporary social problems was taken up by writers such as ▷ George Gissing and Arthur Morrison (1836–1945) in England Theodore Dreiser (1871–1945) and Frank Norris (1870–1902) in America.

Compared with English literature, there is a relative dearth of canonical woman novelists in 19th-century France. Revisions of the canon are in the process of redressing this, notably in the case of ▷ George Sand (1804–76), whose early novels centre on a critique of the oppressive nature of bourgeois marriage. *Indiana* (1832), the story of a West Indian woman married to an older European man explores the overlapping injustices of colonialism and patriarchy which later formed the backdrop to ▷ Charlotte Brontë's *Jane Eyre* (1847) and the subject of ▷ Jean Rhys' prequel to Brontë, *Wide Sargasso Sea* (1966).

Realism in its ▷ Naturalist guise was followed and eroded by the Symbolist novel, whose best-known exponent is Joris-Karl Huysmans (1848–1907). The episodic structure of *A Rebours* (1884), the story of a hypochondriac recluse amassing an eclectic collection of rare artefacts, reduces plot to a pretext for a catalogue of precious objects and rarefied experience. The novel was to become a cult text among ▷ Decadents on both sides of the Channel, and is cited by ▷ Oscar Wilde in *The Picture of Dorian Gray* (1890).

For the English Decadents, the most important French poet of the 19th century was ▷ Charles Baudelaire, and his reputation has survived even if the reasons for it have changed. Together with Théophile Gautier (1811–1872), he helped develop the aesthetic of art-for-art's-sake, translating his anti-Romantic allergy to nature into a cult of the artificial and the unnatural in his major collection *Les Fleurs du Mal* (1857). The emphasis on the 'unnatural' determined the lesbian and sado-masochistic content which appealed to the Decadents (▷ Algernon Swinburne, Arthur Symons), while the concern with the artificial led to an exploration of the fragmentary character of modern urban life, which was to influence the modernist project of ▷ T. S. Eliot.

Baudelaire's poetry was relatively conventional in form, and innovation in this area began modestly with Paul Verlaine's insistence on the musicality of verse ('Art Poétique', 1874), a paradigmatic emphasis echoed by Walter Pater ('School of Giorgione', 1873) and later transformed into the basis of formalist aesthetics (Roger Fry, Clive Ball). More radical change came with the experimental and iconoclastic work of Arthur Rimbaud (*Illuminations*, published 1886) whose prose poetry and fragmentary imagery prefigures the modernism of Eliot and ▷ Ezra Pound.

Equally but more quietly radical was the work of Stéphane Mallarmé (1842–1898), whose dense hermetic sonnets enact the poet's effort to control meaning, to close the gap between signifier and signified, sound and sense, through rigorous overdetermination of structure and syntax. Mallarmé was eventually to acknowledge the futility of his attempt to eliminate the arbitrary from language in his last great work, *Un Coup de Dés Jamais N'Abolira le Hasard* (published 1914). In 1890s England, Mallarmé was assimilated to art-for-art's-sake, providing a model for some of ▷ William Butler Yeats' early work. But his recognition of the paradoxical necessity of chance was to provide the starting point for the Surrealist celebration of the arbitrary in *écriture automatique*.

The Surrealist emphasis on the random encounter and chance juxtaposition as a privileged means of access to the unconscious proposed a perceptual revolution derived in part from Rimbaud. This appealed both to artists in other European countries (including in England Hugh Sykes Davis, Ronald Penrose and ▷ David Gascoyne) and to non-metropolitan francophone writers such as the Martinican poet Aimé Césaire, who saw in Surrealism a means of articulating the divided identity and experience of colonized cultures.

A further source of Surrealism was ▷ Andre Gide's notion of the *acte gratuit*, the kind of unmotivated acts which punctuate many of his narratives. In a sense, the prime *acte gratuit* for Gide was writing itself, since many of his texts revolve around the problem of motivating their own narration, hence his early use of first-person forms and his later turn to multiple-perspectives self-reflexivity (*Les Faux-Monnayeurs*, 1924). Similar techniques can be found in ▷ Marcel Proust's *A la Recherche du Temps Perdu* (1913–27), where minute attention to the detail of subjective consciousness ultimately leads to the fragmentation of the unitary identity of character and event. Of the ▷ Bloomsbury group, ▷ E. M. Forster shared Gide's criticism of the oppressiveness of convention and his interest in contingency, while Woolf, like Proust, sought to develop a style adequate to the modern experience of time and consciousness. All four writers explored the volatility of sexual identity in different ways.

Surrealism emerged from World War II largely discredited through the American exile of its major exponents and ▷ Existentialism quickly became the hegemonic movement of the 1950s. ▷ Jean-Paul Sartre's belief in the possibility and ethical necessity of self-definition through action proved a liberating notion for a generation, in France and elsewhere. Its anti-essentialism proved a useful resource both for the ground-breaking theoretical feminism of ▷ Simone De Beauvoir (*Le Deuxième Sexe*, 1949) and for Frantz Fanon's critique of colonialism (*Peau Noire, Masques Blancs*, 1962). It also provided an initial context for the writing of Jean Genet, whose analysis of the interdependent relations between identity, power and desire were to anticipate the theoretical work of ▷ Michel Foucault at the same time as his characteristic combination of polished style and tabooed content (*Journal d'un Voleur*, 1949) was to influence much later gay writing within and outside France.

The post-war ▷ Theatre of the Absurd stressed among other themes the reversibility of power relations (Genêt's *Le Balcon*, 1956), the arbitrariness and unreliability of language (Eugene Ionesco's *La Leçon*, 1951), and the theme of survival/living on through repetition with minimal variation (▷ Beckett's *Fin de Partie*, 1953). The drama of Nathalie Sarraute (b 1902) and Marguerite Duras (b 1914) dwells on pregnant silence in ways which echo ▷ Harold Pinter's work.

In a sense, the ▷ *nouveau roman* marks the culmination of a movement towards self-reflexibility which began with Gide and Proust, foregrounding the medium to the exclusion of most other content, hence Alain Robbe-Grillet's circular detective story which is also a story of writing and erasure, remembering and forgetting (*Les Gommes*, 1953). The *nouveau roman* is often closely identified with the development of structuralism in the human sciences. Fundamental to structuralism is the idea that identity has no substantive content, since it is constituted by differential relations within a systematic structure (that of kinship for human identity, that of language for the identity of meaning). Towards the end of the 1960s, structuralism developed into ▷ post-structuralism when it was pointed out that a structure of differential relations extends infinitely and is thus a structure without structure (a structure which is not a finite bounded whole). The major figures associated with structuralism included Claude Lévi-Strauss (b 1908) and ▷ Roman Jakobson (1896–1982), while post-structuralism encompassed a younger generation of thinkers including ▷ Jacques Derrida (b 1930) and Gilles Deleuze (b 1930). The careers of figures such as ▷ Jacques Lacan (1901–81), Michel Foucault (1926–84) and the single most influential French literary critic of the period in the Anglo-Saxon world ▷ Roland Barthes (1915–80) demonstrate their involvement in both projects. Broadly, in literary criticism, structuralism advanced a critique of the 'referential illusion', of realism, stressing the arbitrary relationship between a sign and what it refers to. This resulted in an attention to the autonomy and self-reflexivity of the text: Post-structuralism insists instead upon the arbitrary relationship, within the sign, between signifier and signified, word and meaning. This has resulted in some cases in the generation of an endless free play of self-cancelling meanings from a given text. Important precursors of post-structuralism include Georges Bataille (1897–1962) with his emphasis on the necessary self-immolation of identity and meaning and Maurice Blanchot (b 1907) with his stress on the impersonal and silent unworking of the work of art.

Perhaps the most important application of the critique of structuralism has been within the theory and practice of *écriture féminine*, the experimental development of kinds of writing which refuse to signify within a closed patriarchal system of meaning and seek instead to subvert language and the gender-identities constructed through it. Important figures here include ▷ Hélène Cixous (b 1937) and Monique Wittig (b 1935), whose experimentalism has clearly influenced both the theoretical agenda of British feminism, and the work of writers such as ▷ Angela Carter (1940–92) and ▷ Jeanette Winterson (b 1959). The contemporary French woman writer best-known in England is probably Marguerite Duras, whose explorations of cultural difference and apocalytic history (*Hiroshima mon Amour*, 1959) focus on traumatized subjectivity condemned to compulsive repetition (*Le Ravissement de Lol V. Stein*, 1964).

Other contemporary work which share concerns with recent French theory include ▷ John Fowles' self-reflexive and unresolved novels (*The Magus*, 1966/77, *The French Lieutenant's Woman*, 1969), Graham Swift's meditation on revolution and the end of history (*Waterland*, 1983) and ▷ Peter Ackroyd's commitment to pastiche and quotation (*The Last Testament of Oscar Wilde*, 1984). More self-conscious engagements with the French tradition include ▷ Julian Barnes' *Flaubert's Parrot* (1984), an account of a doctor's obsession with the author, and Angela Carter's *Black Venus* (1985), a re-telling of the story of Baudelaire's Creole mistress Jeanne Duval.

Like England, France is, in spite of its official reluctance to recognize itself as such, a post-colonial and multi-cultural nation, so the growth in recent British Asian writing (▷ Salman Rushdie *Midnight Children*, 1981, Hanif Kureishi's *The Buddha of Suburbia*, 1990) is echoed by the development of fiction written by French-resident or French-born (*beur*) Maghrebian Arabs (Tahar Ben Jellour's *La Nuit Sacrée*, 1987). Metropolitan connections with former or current overseas territories also form the context for the work of francophone Maghrebian and Caribbean writers such as Abdelkebir Khatibi and Edouard Glissant (b 1928), whose emphasis on cultural hybridity finds a parallel in the work of non-metropolitan anglophone writers such as ▷ Derek Walcott (b 1930).

Bib: Denis Hollier (Ed.), *A New History of French Literature* (1989).

French Revolution (1789–94)
The immediate effect of the French Revolution was to abolish the French monarchy, to reduce forever the rigid class divisions of French society, and to begin wars (lasting till 1815) which for the time being extensively altered the map of Europe. Its lasting effect was to inspire the European mind with the belief that change is historically inevitable and static order unnatural, and to imbue it with modern ideas of democracy, nationalism and equality at least of opportunity.

The immediate effect on England was confusing, for many of the changes being brought about in France had already occurred here in the 17th century, especially the establishment of the sovereignty of the elected representatives of the people in ▷ Parliament in 1688. Such changes had occurred here, however, without the same upheavals, partly because English society and politics had always been more fluid

French Revolution (1789–94)
The immediate effect of the French Revolution was to abolish the French monarchy, to reduce forever the rigid class division of French society, and to begin wars (lasting till 1815) which for the time being extensively altered the map of Europe. Its lasting effect was to inspire the European mind with the belief that change is historically inevitable and static order unnatural, and to imbue it with modern ideas of democracy, nationalism and equality, at least of opportunity.

The immediate effect on England was confusing, for many of the changes being brought about in France had already occurred here in the 17th century, especially the establishment of the sovereignty of the elected representatives of the people in Parliament in 1688. Such changes had occurred here, however, without the same upheavals, partly because English society and politics had always been more fluid than in the other larger states of Europe, and though unjustified privileges and inequalities existed, there were few definable between the Whigs on the left who were neutral or sympathetic to the revolution, and the Tories on the right who feared it from the start. Only when General Bonaparte took increasing charge of France and became Emperor Napoleon I in 1804 did Britain become united in fear of French aggression. However, ▷ Edmund Burke published in 1790 his ▷ *Reflections on the Revolution in France*, one of the most eloquent documents of English political thinking, foretelling the disasters which the Revolution was to bring, and condemning it as ruthless surgery on the living organism of society. His opponent ▷ Tom Paine answered him with *The Rights of Man* (1791), and the younger intellectuals agreed with Paine. ▷ Wordsworth wrote later in *The Prelude* 'Bliss was it in that dawn to be alive', and William Blake wore a revolutionary cockade in the streets; Robert Southey and ▷ Coleridge planned the ideal communist society, Pantisocracy; the philosophic novelist ▷ William Godwin published *Political Justice* and *Caleb Williams* to prove that reason was the only guide to conduct and society needed by man. Later Wordsworth and Coleridge came round to a view closer to Burke's, and the younger generation, ▷ Byron and ▷ Shelley, saw them as traitors; the more so because the defeat of Napoleon at Waterloo introduced a phase of political and social repression everywhere. But the older generation (except perhaps Southey) did not so much go back on their earlier enthusiasms as think them out more deeply; the philosophical conservatism of the older Coleridge was as radical in its thinking as the ▷ Utilitarianism of the philosophical radicals, ▷ Bentham and James and ▷ John Stuart Mill. Fear of revolution, prompted by the French model, is evident in ▷ Dickens' novel ▷ *A Tale of Two Cities*.

Frequency
One of the five categories in which ▷ Genette analyses narrative discourse, frequency is concerned with the relationship between how many times a fictional event took place, and how many times it is narrated. Frequency, ▷ duration and ▷ order are matters of temporal arrangement or 'tense'; the other two categories are ▷ mood ▷ voice.

Frere, John Hookham (1769–1846)
Friend of the statesman ▷ George Canning and British envoy in Lisbon and later Madrid in the first decade of the 19th century. He collaborated with ▷ Robert Southey on his translation of *The Chronicles of the Cid* (1808) contributed extensively to *The Anti-Jacobin* (▷ Jacobin) and was one of the founders of ▷ *The Quarterly Review*. His mock-romantic Arthurian poem, *The Monks and the Giants* (1817–18), written under the pseudonym 'Whistlecraft' introduced ▷ Lord Byron to the ▷ *ottava rima* style in which he wrote ▷ *Beppo* and ▷ *Don Juan*. In the 1830s and 40s Frere produced lively verse translations of four plays by the Greek dramatist Aristophanes (▷ Greek literature).

Freud, Sigmund (1856–1939)
The founder of psychoanalysis, and one of the seminal figures of 20th-century thought. Born in Moravia, then part of the Austro-Hungarian Empire, he settled in Vienna. He began his career as a doctor specializing in the physiology of the nervous system and after experimenting briefly with hypnosis, developed the technique of free association for the treatment of hysteria and neurosis. His work is based on a number of principles. The first is psychic determinism, the principle that all mental events, including dreams, fantasies, errors and neurotic symptoms, have meaning. The second is the primacy of the unconscious mind in mental life, the unconscious being regarded as a dynamic force drawing on the energy of instinctual drives, and as the location of desires which are repressed because they are socially unacceptable or a threat to the ego. The third is a developmental view of human life, which stresses the importance of infantile experience and accounts for personality in terms of the progressive channeling of an initially undifferentiated energy or libido. Important aspects of ▷ psychoanalytical theory and practice arising from these principles include the theory of infantile sexuality and its development, centred

on the ▷ Oedipus Complex, the techniques of free association and dream interpretation as means of analyzing repressed material, and the beliefs that much behaviour is unconsciously motivated, that sexuality plays a major role in the personality, and that civilization has been created by the direction of libidinous impulses to symbolic ends (including the creation of art). Freud regarded neurotic and normal behaviour as differing in degree rather than kind.

Despite his scientific orientation, Freud's thought had affinities with that of the Romantic poets (▷ Romanticism), and several features of modern literature which show his influence also have Romantic antecedents. These include a particular interest in the quality and significance of childhood experience, a fascination with memory and with what is buried in the adult personality, and a concern with disturbed states of consciousness. Such features are found in the work of ▷ James Joyce and ▷ Virginia Woolf, as well as many later writers. The ▷ stream of consciousness technique and other experimental narrative techniques which abandon external realism in favour of the rendering of consciousness, of dreams or of fantasies, owe much to Freud's belief in the significance of these areas of experience, which had been relatively neglected by scientific thought. Furthermore, the technique of free association revealed a tendency of the mind, when rational constraints were lessened, to move towards points of psychic conflict, and this discovery helped to validate new means of structuring literary works, through association, symbol, and other forms of non-rationalistic patterning (for example in the work of ▷ T. S. Eliot). The view that the individual's unconscious life is as important as his or her public and social self is crucial to much 20-th century literature, a notable example being the work of ▷ D. H. Lawrence, which rests on the assumptions that human beings live through their unconscious, and that sexuality is central to the personality. The Freudian unconscious is in particular the realm of fantasy, and Freudian thought has encouraged the belief that fantasy is of profound significance in our lives, with considerable consequences for literary forms and modes.

Psychoanalysis has developed very considerably since Freud, and continues to interact with literary practice and theory. In the field of theory, those who have studied but radically revised Freud's ideas, such as ▷ Jacques Lacan and ▷ feminist theorists, have been especially important.

Bib: Brown, J. A. C., *Freud and the Post-Freudians*; Freud, S., *Introductory Lectures on Psychoanalysis*.

Friar Bacon and Friar Bungay

A romantic comedy by ▷ Robert Greene, first acted in 1592. The title characters are based on historical figures – Franciscan ▷ friars of the 13th century whom popular tradition had made into magicians – and the play is based on a pamphlet of anecdotes about them. It has a double plot: one action concerns Bacon's manufacture of a brass head endowed (with the help of the devil) with power of speech, and the other is a ▷ pastoral love-story about the rival loves of Prince Edward and Lord Lacy for Margaret, a village maiden. The play is Greene's best; his use of the double plot to present two aspects of a theme, and his treatment of romantic love, have relevance to the later development of ▷ Elizabethan drama, including ▷ Shakespeare's.

Friar's Tale, The

One of ▷ Chaucer's ▷ *Canterbury Tales.* It is an amplified *exemplum* (or moral story) which recounts how a summoner is damned as a result of his corrupt practices, specicifically his attempt to extort money from a poor widow. It concludes with the summoner being carried off to hell by a 'summoning' colleague, a devil. This tale, which makes the pilgrim Summoner its butt, provokes the ▷ *Summoner's Tale*, a barbed narrative satire on the corrupt practices of friars.

Friel, Brian (b 1929)

Dramatist. Friel, born in Derry, is probably both the best-known and the best contemporary Irish dramatist. His work is naturally much preoccupied with the political situation in Ireland in the broadest terms, particularly with the pressures that contribute to the intractability of that situation, the difficulty of rational responses to the legacy of hundreds of years of hostility and mistrust, communities divided by religion and language and the search for a way out of the impasse. There is a strong emphasis on the theme of exile which reflects one traditional escape route from the economic and political ills of Ireland; in *Philadelphia, Here I Come!* (1965) the escape is to America, in *The Gentle Island* (1971) it is to Glasgow. The renewed violence and gradual breakdown of the political situation after 1968 is reflected in such plays as *The Freedom of the City* (1973) and *The Volunteers* (1975) which deal directly with aspects of 'the Troubles', but Friel is also concerned with the wider problems of communication and identity. He may not be a particularly daring dramatist in terms of formal experimentation but he makes effective use of splitting a character into public and private selves in *Philadelphia* and of the contrast between the judicial inquiry which 'establishes' that the civil rights marchers were terrorists in *The Freedom of the City* and their innocent behaviour in the flashbacks that show what led up to their deaths. In *The Faith Healer* (1979) three characters speak four forty-minute monologues in a hauntingly written multi-viewpoint drama which again draws on the themes of exile and return and the pains of both.

Translations (1981), the first play staged by Field Day, the company Friel co-founded with the actor Stephen Rea, is a very fine parable of the current situation in Northern Ireland which also teases out some of its cultural roots. The play is set in 1830s Donegal, in a world where tramps can read Homer in the original but not ▷ Shakespeare, a world doomed to vanish under the assault of state education (in English) and the Royal Engineers' Survey of Ireland. Although the issues are serious and the allegorical applications clear, Friel handles events with a light touch and there is much gentle comedy at the expense of two lovers failing to communicate – they both actually speak English in the play but neither understands the other – and at the expense of linguistic failures in general.

Friel's other plays include: *Making History* (1988) and *Dancing at Lughnasa* (1990)

Fringe theatre
A name which originates from unofficial theatre shows performed on the periphery of the Edinburgh Festival. The term is now used more generally and often refers to an alternative kind of theatre which provides a consciously oppositional entertainment to that on offer at mainstream establishment theatres. One of the typical fringe companies is ▷ John McGrath's 7:84 group which has always pursued a policy of touring plays and performing for working-class audiences away from conventional theatres (a policy which has been more successful in Scotland than in England). The term is useful in as much as it describes a general movement to a politically more radical kind of theatre since the late 1960s (which produced a number of dramatists, such as Howard Brenton, ▷ Caryl Churchill, ▷ David Hare and ▷ David Edgar, who now tend to work within the theatre establishment). However, 'fringe' is now used to describe such a variety of theatrical activity that it no longer has a precise meaning. Other notable groups belonging, or who have belonged, to the political fringe are: Foco Novo (1972); Belt and Braces (founded in 1974); The Women's Theatre Group (1975); Gay Sweatshop (1975); Joint Stock Theatre Group (1974); Monstrous Regiment (1976).

Froissart, Jean (c 1337–c 1410)
A French chronicler and poet, who visited England on several occasions, and recorded events at the courts of France and England, from 1325–1400, in the form of a chronicle narrative, translated into English prose by Lord Berners in 1523–5. Froissart's lyric and ▷ dream-vision poetry influenced ▷ Chaucer's work.

***Frost at Midnight* (1798)**
▷ Samuel Taylor Coleridge's ▷ conversation poem issues from the first phase of English ▷ Romantic poetry, characterized by its emphasis on spiritual ▷ autobiography, memory and the workings of the intellect and imagination, and the idealistic projection of a life of freedom for the poet's child, ▷ Hartley, under the benign tutelage of ▷ Nature. The idealism of the poem is shadowed not only by the dissipation of energies shown by the real Hartley Coleridge in later life, but by a discrepancy between what the poet desires or imagines, and what he can occupy with certainty. If this melancholy divergence reflects aspects of Coleridge's personality, as a dreamer and an opium addict, it may also express a more general truth about the fall from linguistic illusionism to a darker existential reality. ▷ Deconstructionist critics such as ▷ Paul de Man have been particularly alert to this kind of doubleness in Romantic texts.

Fry, Christopher (b 1907)
British dramatist whose first stage success was with *A Phoenix Too Frequent* (1946). *The Lady's Not For Burning*, first staged in 1948, starred ▷ John Gielgud and seemed to herald a return of verse drama to the stage. Other notable actors who played major roles in his plays include: ▷ Laurence Olivier in *Venus Observed* (1950), Paul Scofield in an adaptation of Anouilh's *Ring Round the Moon* (1950) and Edith Evans in *The Dark is Light Enough* (1954). His popularity on the commercial stage was short-lived and by the mid-1950s he was already out of favour. *Curtmantle* (1961) was performed by the ▷ Royal Shakespeare Company but was only a moderate success. His own particular brand of religious verse drama was, however, one of the few notable dramatic developments in the immediate post-war years. Film scripts include: *Barabbas* (1952); *Ben Hur* (1959); *La Bibbia* (1966).
Bib: Stanford, D., *Fry*.

Fuller, Roy (1912–91)
Poet and novelist. Fuller was born in Lancashire, and trained and worked as a solicitor. He began writing in the 1930, and published two volumes of poetry whilst he was in the Royal Navy during World War II: *The Middle of a War* (1942) and *A Lost Season* (1944) (his first volume appeared in 1939). His later publications include: *Counterparts* (1954); *Collected Poems* (1962), *From the Joke Shop* (1975) and *Last Poems* (1993). His novels are restrained in tone and style but frequently express an underlying psychological tension as well as a sharp, though understated, critique of social practices. They include: *With My Little Eye* (1948); *The Second Curtain* (1953), *Fantasy and Fugue* (1954); *Image of a Society* (1956); *The Ruined Boys* (1959); *The Father's Comedy* (1961); *The Perfect Fool* (1963); *My Child, My Sister* (1965); *The Carnal Island* (1970); *Stares* (1990).

Funds, The; The Funded Debt; Fund-holders
From the reign of ▷ William III the government sought to finance its wars by borrowing from private investors, issuing 'bonds' ('debentures') in acknowledgement of the loan and paying regular interest. This is the ▷ National Debt. It became the commonest investment for small investors and was the source of many 'private incomes' in the 19th century.

Fyge, Sarah (1669/72–1722/3)
English author of the verse *The Female Advocate, or an Answere to a late Satyr against the Pride, Lust and Inconstancy etc., of Women* (1686), which she claimed to have written when she was fourteen. This was a reply to an attack on women by Robert Gould (1683), 'written by a lady in vindication of her sex'. The defence begins with a reworking of the much-disputed question of the nature of Eve – 'The Devil's strength weak Woman might deceive, / But Adam only tempted was by Eve, / She had the strongest Tempter, and least Charge; / Man's knowing most, doth make his sin more large.' Fyge claimed in a poem (published in *Poems on Several Occassions, together with a Pastoral,* 1703) that in the 1680s her father banished her to a village far from the comfort of friends. She wrote one of the elegies in *The Nine Muses* (1700) and had two husbands, first Field, and then the Reverend Thomas Egerton, to whom she was unhappily married. In *The Liberty* she wrote 'My daring Pen, will bolder Sallies make, / and like myself, an uncheck'd freedom take.'

▷ Manley, Delarivière

Bib: Medoff, Jeslyn, 'New Light on Sarah Fyge (Field, Egerton)', *Tulsa Studies in Women's Literature*, 1, 2 (1982), pp. 155–75.

G

Gael, Gaelic
The Scottish highland branch of the Celtic race and its language. The words are sometimes used for the Scottish and Irish Celts together.

Gainsborough, Thomas (1727–88)
English painter, born at Sudbury in Suffolk, he became one of the 36 founders of the English Academy. He lacked formal training as an artist, and taught himself to paint by copying trees, rocks and other objects that he saw in the countryside around him, his style being influenced by Dutch painting. He developed into a successful landscape artist and portrait painter, whose clients included some of England's wealthiest nobility, including members of the royal family. His contemporary ▷ Sir Joshua Reynolds described him as a genius and suggested he had founded an English school of art.

Galahad
Galahad is the son of ▷ Lancelot and Elaine of Corbenic, conceived as a result of a magical trick played on Lancelot by Elaine's father, the Grail Keeper ▷ Pelles. When Galahad comes to ▷ Arthur's court he is marked out as the knight who will achieve the Quest of the Grail by marvellous signs: he alone can sit in the Perilous seat at the ▷ Round Table and draw the sword from the stone, where it has been fixed by ▷ Merlin. His role is effectively that of a knight-contemplative, whose values and actions are directed entirely towards spiritual ends. In early versions of the Grail narrative, the role of Grail seeker is played by ▷ Perceval who becomes a companion of ▷ Galahad's in later reworkings of the Grail narrative, including ▷ Malory's *Morte D'Arthur*.
▷ Arthur, King; Grail.

Galileo Galilei (1564–1642)
Italian astronomer; he was able, by improving the newly invented telescope, to confirm the theory of ▷ Copernicus that the earth revolves round the sun, contrary to the theory of Ptolemy that the earth is the centre of the solar system. The observation was made in 1610; in 1611 the English poet ▷ John Donne wrote the *Anatomy of the World*:

And new Philosophy calls all in doubt.
The Element of fire is quite put out;
The Sun is lost, and th'earth, and no man's wit
Can well direct him where to look for it.

In fact the Church was disturbed at the implications of Galileo's discovery in regard to acceptance of the Holy Scriptures, and declared it a heresy. Nonetheless Galileo's view slowly became accepted. ▷ Milton, in his epic of the Creation of the World, ▷ *Paradise Lost*, uses the Ptolemaic theory, though he had met Galileo and alludes to him in the poem ('the Tuscan Artist' of Bk. 1, lines 288–91).

Bib: Drake, S., *Galileo*.

Gallant Mavis (b 1922)
Novelist and short story writer. Gallant is one of the foremost writers of short stories in Canada, indeed, in the whole of North America, and her work is consistently published in the *New Yorker* magazine. She is fluent in English and French and began her career in the 1940s writing pieces for Canadian journals and for the Canadian Broadcasting Corporation. However by 1960 she had settled in Paris, allowing her observations upon Canadian life a certain ironic detachment. Among her most well-known collections are, *The Other Paris: Stories* (1956), *The End of the World and Other Stories* (1974) and *Home Truths: Selected Canadian Stories* (1981). Gallant continues to be immensely popular on both sides of the Atlantic, as well as influential upon younger Canadian short-story writers.

***Gallathea* (1585)**
A lyrical and courtly transvestite comedy by ▷ John Lyly about a virgin-sacrifice to Neptune and the ensuing unwitting love-affair of two disguised girls, one of whom Venus promises to transform into a boy. The play's heroine provides an early model for ▷ Shakespeare's Viola in ▷ *Twelfth Night*, and through its jewelled elegance and mythopoeia Lyly's play took English comedy to new heights in the crucial decade preceding the 1590s.

Galloway, Janice (b 1956)
Novelist. Born in Ayrshire, Galloway is one of a group of Glasgow writers that has emerged since the 1980s (▷ Gray, Alasdair; ▷ Kelman, James). She has also worked as a teacher. *The Trick Is To Keep Breathing* (1989) uses a range of discourses – first-person narrative, stream of consciousness, dialogue and typographical effects – to represent a disturbed mind. *Blood* (1991) is a collection of stories which explore feminist issues of identity and autonomy through a mixture of realism and fantasy and an inventive use of language, while *Foreign Parts* (1995) is an understated but powerful study of female friendship.

Galsworthy, John (1867–1933)
Novelist and dramatist. As a novelist, his reputation was high in the first quarter of this century for his surveys of upper-class English life, especially the ▷ *Forsyte Saga* sequence (1906–21) and *A Modern Comedy (The White Monkey*, 1924; *The Silver Spoon*, 1926; *Swan Song*, 1928). After World War I, Galsworthy underwent severe criticism by novelists of the new generation as different as ▷ Virginia Woolf ('Modern Fiction' in *The Common Reader*; 1925) and ▷ D. H. Lawrence ('John Galsworthy',

in *Phoenix*; 1927). These novelist-critics were writing in a period of rich experiment in rendering the inwardness of human experience and in testing and renewing humane values in the social context; to them, Galsworthy was artistically an obstructive conservative, severely limited to a vision of the outside of social phenomena and to a merely social definition of human beings. From such attacks, Galsworthy's reputation has never recovered among the intelligentsia; however, the popularity of a televised serial version of the *Forsyte Saga* in 1967 suggests that he may still be favoured by at least the older generation of the general public. His other novels are: *Jocelyn* (1898); *The Country House* (1907); *Fraternity* (1909); *The Patrician* (1911); *The Freelands* (1915); *Maid in Waiting* (1931); *Flowering Wilderness* (1932).

As a dramatist, Galsworthy was one of those in the first decade of the century who restored to the English theatre a substantiality of subject matter which had long been missing from it. His plays dramatized ethical problems arising from social issues. These too, however, have lost prestige, partly because of weaknesses similar to those that his novels are supposed to suffer from. Another criticism of the plays is that he brought to the theatre a novelist's vision rather than a dramatist's: during the last 50 years, British dramatists have believed that the drama requires an approach to the depiction of character and to the use of dialogue which is different to the vision of the novelist. Plays: *The Silver Box* (1906); *Joy* (1907); *Strife* (1909); *Justice* (1910); *The Pigeon* (1912); *The Eldest Son* (1912); *The Fugitive* (1913); *The Skin Game* (1920); *Loyalties* (1922); *The Forest* (1924).

▷ Realism.

Bib: Barker, D., *A Man of Principle*; Marrot, H. V., *The Life and Letters of John Galsworthy*; Fréchet, A., *John Galsworthy, A Reassessment*.

Galt, John (1779–1839)

Scottish writer of poems, travels, dramas and novels. He is chiefly remembered for his novels, especially *The Ayrshire Legatees* (1821), *Annals of the Parish* (1821), *The Provost* (1822) and *The Entail* (1823). These are vivid, realistic, humorous accounts of Scottish provincial society.

▷ Scottish literature in English.

Bib: Gordon, R. K., *John Galt*; Aberdein, J. W., *John Galt*; Parker, W. M., *Susan Ferrier and John Galt* (British Council).

***Game at Chess, A* (1624)**

A bold political ▷ allegory by ▷ Thomas Middleton. It enjoyed a short but highly successful run in London, because of its imaginative use of the pieces of chess and its appeal to popular sentiment hostile to the proposed Spanish marriage. In the play England is represented by white and Spain by black.

Gamelyn

An anonymous Middle English verse romance, dating from the mid-14th century. Gamelyn is the youngest of three brothers who is deprived of his heritage and ill-treated by his eldest brother. He takes to the forest and leads the life of an outlaw with a band of merry men. Eventually he succeeds in overthrowing the forces of the law which side with his unjust brother, retrieves his heritage and is appointed Chief Justice. The romance appears in some manuscripts of the ▷ *Canterbury Tales* as the tale told by the pilgrim Cook (which is evidently an attempt by a 15th-century editor to fill out the unfinished state of ▷ Chaucer's text). *Gamelyn* was used by ▷ Thomas Lodge for his prose romance *Rosalynde* (1590), which ▷ Shakespeare used as a source for his comedy ▷ *As You Like It*.

Bib: Sands, D. (ed.), *Middle English Verse Romances*.

Gammer Gurton's Needle

A slight but very lively verse comedy of uncertain authorship, first acted in 1566, and printed in 1575. Gammer = old woman. She loses her needle, which she had been using to mend her man's breeches. The whole village is upset, until the needle is found in the seat of the breeches.

***Garden of Cyrus, The* (1658)**

A treatise on the quincunx (a shape or pattern composed of five parts) by ▷ Sir Thomas Browne. It was published together with ▷ *Urn Burial*, or *Hydriotaphia*, and is characteristic of Browne's delight in intellectual curiosity and his interest in the relationship between science and faith.

Gardner, Helen (1908–86)

Critic. Helen Gardner was perhaps one of the most formidable literary critics of the century, publishing a number of well-respected works which did much to promote the careful reading of many poets now firmly established in the literary canon. Gardner's position, in keeping with her generation, was in line with many of the ideas of 'new criticism', in believing that the written text is the sovereign expression of its author, whose meaning must be uncovered by close readings of the text. She was later to denigrate the proliferation of modern forms of critical theory (in her last work, *In Defence of the Imagination*, 1982), but she was one of the most influential critics of her generation. Her work on the ▷ Metaphysical poets and ▷ T. S. Eliot is particularly significant. Her texts include: *The Art of T. S. Eliot* (1949); *The Metaphysical Poets* (1957); *The Elegies and the Songs and Sonnets of John Donne* (1965); *Literary Studies* (1967); *Religion and Literature* (1971).

Gareth

Gareth is the youngest son of King Lot of

Orkney and Morgause. The fourth book of ▷ Malory's *Morte D'Arthur* recounts how Gareth (nicknamed Beaumains) becomes established as a knight of the ▷ Round Table (he is a protégé of ▷ Lancelot), and how he finally wins the hand of the lady Lyones. Lancelot accidentally kills Gareth as he rescues ▷ Guinevere from the stake. ▷ Gawain, in response, vows to revenge his brother's death. Thus Gareth's death provokes the hostilities between Gawain and Lancelot which form one of the factors contributing to the break-up of the Round Table and the end of ▷ King Arthur's reign.

Gargantua
A giant, chiefly known as the hero of ▷ François Rabelais' romances *Gargantua* and *Pantagruel*, though he had a previous existence in French folklore connected with the Arthurian (▷ Arthur, King) legends. He is mentioned in ▷ Shakespeare's ▷ *As You Like It* II.2 before Rabelais had been translated into English (1653), though Shakespeare may have read Rabelais in French.

Garlick, Raymond (b 1926)
Poet, editor and critic. Raymond Garlick was born in London but as a schoolboy often visited his grandparents who had settled in Llandudno. Initially at the University of Leeds, he was later to return to Wales to read English at the University College of North Wales, Bangor, where he began to acquire a knowledge of Welsh, became aware of Anglo-Welsh literature and, above all, started to write poetry. In 1949, while teaching at Pembroke Dock Grammar School, he founded, jointly with the headmaster Roland Mathias, the literary magazine *Dock Leaves*, becoming its first editor from 1949 to 1961, and pursuing the creditable aim of building bridges between Welsh language and English language writers in Wales. He relinquished his editorship on joining the staff of an international school in Holland though he returned to Wales again in 1967, this time as a senior lecturer at Trinity College, Carmarthen. Raymond Garlick has made a major contribution to Anglo-Welsh literature which he sees (unlike Gwyn Jones) as originating from late 15th-century Welshmen writing poetry in the English language, a view developed in his seminal critical study, *An Introduction to Anglo-Welsh Literature* (1970) and supported in the chronological span of the anthology *Anglo-Welsh Poetry 1480–1980*) (1984) which he edited with Roland Mathias. In his own poetry, Raymond Garlick's verse forms are often intricately structured and his themes include a nationalist view of Wales in the wider context of European civilization, a celebration of people in the praise-tradition of Welsh poetry, a passionate concern for justice and a hatred of violence, and a preoccupation with language, in which he envisages English as one of the languages of a fully bilingual Wales. His earlier poetry collections were *Poems from the Mountain-House* (1950), *The Welsh-Speaking Sea* (1954), and a long radio poem, *Blaenau Observed* (1957) whereas his middle period produced a trilogy of poetry collections, *A Sense of Europe* (1968), *A Sense of Time* (1972), and *Incense* (1976). Recently he made a welcome return to poetry with *Travel Notes* (1992), inspired by a Mediterranean cruise which rekindled his enthusiasm for the classical world, especially that of ancient.Greece.
Bib: Stephens, M. (Ed.), *The Oxford Companion to the Literature of Wales*; Jones, G. and Rowlands, J., *Profiles*.

Garner, Alan (b 1934)
Novelist and writer for children. Many of Garner's works are set in his home territory of Cheshire, and the south Manchester landmark Alderley Edge figures particularly prominently as the setting for a series of fantasy plots which mingle contemporary reality with an uncanny sense of the mythic past, which cause alternative values and belief systems to erupt into the present. Garner draws particularly on Celtic mythology and the beliefs of pre-Christian religions (especially in his first novels, *The Weirdstone of Brisingamen*, 1960, *Elidor*, 1965, and *The Owl Service*, 1967), and is also interested in the fictional possibilities of parallel time scales and relativity, which he explores in the more adult novel, *Red Shift* (1973). More recent works include *The Stone Book Quartet* (1976–8).

▷ Children's books.

Garrick, David (1717–79)
Actor, theatre manager, dramatist, whose genius as an actor greatly enhanced the theatrical profession in social prestige, and who was also responsible for far-reaching innovations in the theatre.

In 1737 he came to London with ▷ Samuel Johnson who had been his tutor at Lichfield, and entered Lincoln's Inn, but his career there did not last. He had shown a taste for theatricals early in his youth, and in 1740 he put together a burlesque play based on characters of ▷ Henry Fielding, *Lethe*: or *Aesop in the Shades*, which was performed at a benefit night for ▷ Henry Giffard.

In 1741 Giffard took a small company including Garrick to Ipswich, and here the actor performed regularly for the first time, making his debut as Aboan in ▷ Thomas Southerne's *Oroonoko*, before returning to Giffard's Theatre at ▷ Goodman's Fields. Garrick, still unknown, played Richard III, to a rapturous reception. In 1742 Garrick travelled to Dublin with ▷ Peg Woffington, who became his mistress, and together they joined the ▷ Smock Alley Theatre. They returned to London and in 1742 Garrick opened his first season at ▷ Drury Lane. Denied their salaries by the irresponsible manager Charles Fleetwood, Garrick, ▷ Charles Macklin, and several other actors rebelled in 1743. Eventually, after a series of further disruptions, including several riots at the theatre, and a season at ▷ Covent Garden (1746–47), Garrick became a joint manager at Drury Lane in 1747. Two years later he married the actress Eva Maria Veigel.

Garrick proved a vigorous and creative manager, reviving the fortunes of Drury Lane, and adding to his own status as the leading actor of his generation. His sensitive and naturalistic acting style, inspired by that of Macklin but perfected by Garrick himself, set a standard for the period, making the previous formal and 'stagey' methods of acting seem outmoded. In 1763, after further rioting at the theatre, Garrick abolished the long practice of allowing spectators on the stage. He introduced lighting concealed from the audience which he had observed during a professional visit to Paris, and engaged the brilliant scene designer ▷ De Loutherberg, who created a series of sets in naturalistic, romantic (▷ Romanticism) style that complemented Garrick's own style of acting. He also wrote a number of plays, and rewrote others to conform with the tastes of his time, including *The Lying Valet* (1741), ▷ *Miss in Her Teens* (1747), in which he himself played the part of the fop, Fribble, ▷ *The Clandestine Marriage* (1766) (in collaboration with ▷ George Colman the Elder), *The Country Girl* (1766) (a revision of ▷ William Wycherley's ▷ *The Country Wife*), *The Irish Widow* (1772), *Bon Ton; Or High Life Above Stairs* (1775), and reworkings of several plays of ▷ Shakespeare.

Garrick retired in 1776 and died at his home in London after a long and painful illness. He was buried at Westminster Abbey, near the monument to Shakespeare who had provided him with many of his finest tragic roles, including Richard III, Hamlet (his most popular part), Macbeth, and Lear. Garrick also excelled in comedy, his best parts including Abel Drugger in ▷ Ben Jonson's ▷ *The Alchemist*, Benedick in ▷ *Much Ado About Nothing*, and ▷ Bayes in the Duke of Buckingham's ▷ *The Rehearsal* (▷ George Villiers) in which he triumphed when he imitated several well-known contemporary actors.

Bib: Murphy, A., *The Life of Garrick*; Oman, G., *David Garrick*; Kahrl, G. M. and Stone, G. W., *David Garrick, A Critical Biography*; Kendall, A., *David Garrick: A Biography*; Wood, E. R (ed.) *Plays by David Garrick and George Colman the Elder.*

Garter, The Order of the

An order of knighthood instituted by ▷ Edward III about 1344. The order was an imitation of the legendary one established by ▷ King Arthur, and Edward III built the great round tower of Windsor Castle as its meeting-place. In keeping with the ▷ Tudor myth, several panegyric poems link ▷ Elizabeth's courtiers to the chivalric idealism of Edward's and Arthur's reigns. More significantly, ▷ Spenser weaves the garter motif into his praise of Elizabethan knighthood in ▷ *The Faerie Queene*. ▷ Shakespeare alludes heavily to the garter and its ceremonies in ▷ *The Merry Wives of Windsor.*

Garth, Sir Samuel (1661–1719)

Doctor and member of the Whig clique known as the ▷ Kit-Cat Club. His ▷ heroic couplet poem *The Dispensary (*1699) is a burlesque attack on the claim of apothecaries to exclusive control over the dispensing of medicines.

Gascoigne, George (1539–77)

Poet and playwright. His chief works include the unauthorized *A Hundreth Sundrie Flowers*, published in 1573; a collection of poems republished in 1575 as *The Posies*; some of the earliest ▷ satires, including including *Glasse of Government* (1575), *The Steel Glass* (1576); and a number of plays which include *Supposes* (1566), one of the earliest comedies in English and *Jocasta* (1573) the second English ▷ tragedy. Gascoigne's talents also encompassed fiction, a treatise on prosody and a ▷ masque held at Kenilworth for ▷ Elizabeth I. Gascoigne's verse grew increasingly out of favour as he could, or would, not imitate the court wits such as ▷ Lyly, and continued with the more old-fashioned ▷ lyrical style.

▷ Ferrers, George; Breton, Nicholas.

Bib: Johnson, R. C., *Gascoigne.*

Gascoyne, David (b 1916)

Poet and translator. Gascoyne was born in Salisbury, and published his first volume of verse when he was only 16 (*Roman Balcony*; 1932). His poetry is fairly unusual in being strongly influenced by that of French Surrealists, whom he has translated; at the age of 19 Gascoyne wrote *A Short Survey of Surrealism* (1935). His publications include: *Man's Life is this Meat* (1936); *Poems 1937–1942* (1943); *Collected Poems* (1965 and 1988); *The Sun at Midnight* (1970); and *Collected Verse Translations* (1970).

▷ French literature in England.

Gaskell, Elizabeth Cleghorn (1810–65)

Novelist, short story writer and biographer. Elizabeth Cleghorn Stevenson was the daughter of a ▷ Unitarian minister and spent her childhood with her aunt in Knutsford, Cheshire after her mother's death in 1811. In 1832 she married William Gaskell, also a Unitarian minister, based in Manchester, with whom she had four daughters, and a son who died in infancy. She and her husband first intended to write the annals of the Manchester poor in the manner of George Crabbe (1754–1832, who wrote about rural life in Suffolk with uncompromising realism); and her first novel, ▷ *Mary Barton* (1848), presented the outlook of the industrial workers with justice and sympathy sufficient to anger some of the employers. It won the attention of ▷ Charles Dickens and most of her later work was published in his periodical magazines ▷ *Household Words* and ▷ *All the Year Round*. ▷ *Cranford* began to appear in 1851, and ▷ *Ruth* in 1853, the latter novel causing a scandal because of its sympathetic treatment of a ▷ 'fallen woman'. *Cranford*, a study of a small circle in a small town based on Knutsford, has been compared with the work of Jane Austen in its ability to endow smallness of circumstance with large implications. Social issues are also at the heart of ▷ *North and South* (1854–5) and many of Gaskell's short stories. In 1863 the ▷ historical novel ▷ *Sylvia's Lovers* appeared and *A Dark Night's Work: Cousin Phyllis and Other Tales*. Her masterpiece ▷ *Wives and Daughters*, though unfinished, was published posthumously between 1864 and 1866. Other works include the celebrated biography of her friend ▷ Charlotte Brontë (1857), and ghost stories, a selection of which has recently been reprinted as *Lois the Witch and Other Stories* (1989).

Mrs Gaskell's work reveals a commitment to humanitarian principles and to Unitarianism. The ▷ 'social problem' novels call for reconciliation between employers and workers, for Gaskell was always reforming rather than radical. She advocated motherhood as woman's mission in life, but her fiction often exposes the contradictions in Victorian attitudes and calls for more 'nurturing' men. Recent feminist critics have re-assessed Gaskell's portrayal of 'marginalized women' – the spinsters, widows, ▷ orphan girls and madwomen who figure largely within her work. Her novels are an interesting connecting link between those of ▷ Jane Austen and ▷ George Eliot.

Bib: Hopkins, A.B., *Life*; Cecil, D., *Early Victorian Novelists*; Haldane, E., *Mrs Gaskell and her Friends*; Tillotson, K. (on Mary Barton) in *Novels of the Eighteen-Forties*; Gerin, W., *Elizabeth Gaskell: A Biography*; Easson, A., *Elizabeth Gaskell*; Stoneman, P., *Elizabeth Gaskell*.

Gatty, Margaret (1809–73)

Writer of ▷ children's literature and a keen botanist. She was born Margaret Scott in Burnham vicarage, Essex, and moved to Yorkshire after marrying the Rev. Alfred Gatty in 1839. Of her ten children, ▷ Juliana Horatia Ewing worked most closely with her on *Aunt Judy's Magazine*, a periodical for children. Gatty's works include *The Fairy Godmothers* (1851); *Parables from Nature* (a series of five books published between 1855 and 1871); *Aunt Judy's Tales* (1859); *Christmas Crackers* (1870), and a two-volume *History of British Seaweeds* (1863), which became the standard source of information about seaweeds for the next 80 years. Gatty's writing for children reveals a good sense of humour, but contains too much moralizing to appeal to 20th-century readers. She was, however, highly popular in her day.

Gawain

One of ▷ King Arthur's principal knights, the eldest son of King Lot of Orkney and Arthur's half-sister Morgause (called Anna in ▷ Geoffrey of Monmouth's version of Arthurian history). Gawain is an established member of Arthur's entourage in early accounts of Arthur's reign, and his role as an embodiment of the chivalric ethos is developed in the romances of ▷ Chrétien de Troyes. His reputation seems to have declined in later French Arthurian narratives, especially in the ▷ Grail stories, in which he is portrayed as a knight committed to vain worldly pursuits and ends. He is, however, the central hero of the Middle English romance ▷ *Gawain and the Green Knight*, in which the question of how to judge his performance becomes one of the main issues of the narrative. The variable representation of Gawain in Arthurian narrative is illustrated by his different roles in ▷ Malory's compilation of Arthurian history. In Malory's *Morte D'Arthur* Gawain is an exemplary chivalric figure, a failed knight of the grail quest, a loyal defender of the integrity of the ▷ Round Table who resists attempts by his half-brother Mordred and brother Aggravain to break up Arthur's court, and in the later stages of the narrative, an implacable enemy of ▷ Lancelot who, after the death of ▷ Gareth, promotes Arthur's war against Lancelot and thus plays a major part in the dissolution of Arthur's court. The mysterious link between Gawain's strength and the movement of the Sun, alluded to in Malory, is perhaps a remnant of a distant connection between Gawain and a Sun-god figure of Celtic mythology. According to Malory, Gawain's skull can still be seen at Dover castle.

Gawain and the Green Knight

One of the four later 14th-century ▷ alliterative narratives attributed to the ▷ Gawain poet, which survives, along with ▷ *Patience*, ▷ *Cleanness* and ▷ *Pearl*, in a single manuscript. While the other poems address explicitly Christian topics and material, *Gawain and the Green Knight* tackles the traditions and conventions of Arthurian romance in a brilliant and complex narrative, structured around a series of interlocking games which have potentially very serious outcomes.

The story tells how a mysterious Green Knight visits ▷ King Arthur's court on New Year's Eve, offering a game. He offers any knight the opportunity to strike his head with an enormous axe if, in return, the knight agrees to submit to a return blow the following year. Gawain accepts the challenge on behalf of the court, and beheads the Green Knight, who proceeds to pick up his head and leave Arthur's court, reminding Gawain of his promise to come to his Green Chapel in a year for a return blow. The following year Gawain embarks on his quest for the Green Chapel, and takes refuge over the Christmas period in the castle of one Sir Bertilak. There Gawain gets involved in another game: for three days Bertilak is to go hunting and present Gawain with his winnings every evening. In return Gawain is to give Bertilak whatever he has won during the day at the castle. Over the next three days Gawain is subject to the attentions of Bertilak's beautiful wife as he rests in bed. His chastity, loyalty to his host, and courtesy are tested, for in defending himself against the lady's advances, Gawain has to avoid any offence to her. At the end of every one of the three days Gawain has kisses to exchange for the spoils of Bertilak's hunting expeditions. However, on the final day Gawain does not hand over the green girdle he has accepted from the wife (she has claimed it has magic qualities and will protect Gawain's life against any threat). Gawain, wearing the green girdle, leaves Bertilak's court, and eventually finds the Green Chapel and the Green Knight. There Gawain is made to submit to three feints from the axe of the Green Knight, the last just cutting the flesh of his neck. Although Gawain is overjoyed at having survived his ordeal, his mood changes as the Green Knight reveals his identity and the mechanics of the games which Gawain has played. The Green Knight and Sir Bertilak are the same figure: the outcome of Gawain's experience at the Green Chapel has depended on how honestly he has played the exchange of winnings game at the castle. Gawain's slight wound repays his retention of the girdle, which the Green Knight now excuses. Gawain is mortified, and vows to wear the girdle as a sign of his shame and failure, but is fêted as a great hero on his return to Arthur's court. Henceforth all the members of Arthur's court decide to wear a green girdle.

There are analogues in earlier French romances and Welsh narrative for the beheading game and the exchange of winnings game, but not for their combination. The power and skill of the narrative technique of *Gawain* is reflected in the enormous amount of modern critical interest in the poem, but there is hardly any evidence at all which illuminates its contemporary reception.
Bib: Burrow, J. A., *A Reading of Gawain and the Green Knight*; Tolkien, J. R. R., Gordon, E. V. and Davis, N. (eds.), *Gawain and the Green Knight*.

Gawain Poet (or Pearl Poet)
The name given to the hypothetical author of the four Middle English ⊳ alliterative poems (⊳ *Patience*, ⊳ *Pearl*, ⊳ *Cleanness*, ⊳ *Gawain and the Green Knight*), composed in the second half of the 14th century, in the north-west Midlands area. The poems are all found in a single manuscript, British Library, Nero A. x. There is no external evidence to suggest the poems are the work of a single writer: the theory of single authorship depends largely on the evidence of shared thematic interests, narrative techniques and sheer poetic skill which can be traced in all four poems.
Bib: Andrew, M. and Waldron, R. A. (eds.), *The Poems of the Pearl Manuscript*.

Gay, John (1685–1732)
Dramatist and poet, born at Barnstaple in Devon, the youngest son of William Gay. In 1708 he published 'Wine', a poem to celebrate the Act of Union between England and Scotland (⊳ Union, Act of) and in 1711 a pamphlet *The Present State of Wit*. The following year he became a 'domestic steward' to the Duchess of Monmouth, and in 1714 secretary to Lord Clarendon, Tory envoy to Hanover. However, the accession to power of the Whigs threw him again upon his own resources. His farce, *The What D'Ye Call It*, a burlesque on what he deemed to be the moral and emotional falsity of heroic tragedy, as well as the growing taste for ⊳ sentiment in comedy, followed in 1715. The play, which also satirized the idealization of country life, became a target for attack by the enemies of ⊳ Pope, whom he had befriended. Gay's *Trivia, or the Art of Walking the Streets of London* (1716), on the conditions of life in the capital, is now considered a minor classic. In 1717 he collaborated with Pope and ⊳ Arbuthnot on the satirical ⊳ *Three Hours After Marriage* caricaturing a number of contemporary literary figures. This was an initial success, but then lapsed from favour. Gay's *Poems on Several Occasions* (1720) made him some money, which he invested in the South Sea Company. When this failed, he was temporarily ruined (⊳ South Sea Bubble).

Gay is best known for his ballad opera, ⊳ *The Beggar's Opera* (1728). An instant success, the piece was said to have made 'Gay rich and Rich (the theatre manager) gay'. The so-called Newgate pastoral', with music by the German composer Pepusch, satirized the London underworld, and corruption in general. It was also read as an attack on the ruling party of ⊳ Sir Robert Walpole, who retaliated with Licensing Act of 1737, restricting the activities of the theatre (⊳ theatres). The sequel, *Polly* (1729), was banned by the Lord Chamberlain, although published by subscription. In his last years Gay lived mainly with two of his patrons, the Duke and Duchess of Queensberry in Wiltshire. He wrote the libretto for ⊳ Handel's *Acis and Galatea* in 1731. Gay returned to London in 1732, and there died suddenly. He was buried in ⊳ Westminster Abbey, where

his epitaph, written by himself, is 'Life is a jest, and all things show it; I thought so once, and now I know it'.
Bib: Johnson, S., *Lives of the Poets*; Melville L., *The Life and Letters of John Gay*; Irving, W. H., *Gay, Favourite of the Wits; Sutherland, J., Pope and his Contemporaries.*

Gems, Pam (b 1925)
British playwright, she established her reputation relatively late in life, only becoming actively involved in the theatre when she was in her 40s. Although her plays deal specifically with female issues she distances herself from direct ▷ feminist polemic. A recurrent theme in her work is the need for women to discover their own identity in a world dominated and defined by men. Major works include: *Dead Fish* (later *Dusa, Fish, Stas and Vi*; 1976); *Queen Christina* (1977); *Piaf* (1978); *Loving Women* (1984); *Camille* (1985); *The Blue Angel* (1992).
Bib: Keyssar, H., *Feminist Theatre*; Wandor, M., *Understudies*.

Gender
Originally used to distinguish between the categories of 'masculine' and 'feminine'. In modern ▷ feminist criticism it denotes something more than the different physical characteristics of both sexes. Feminist criticism regards 'masculinity' and 'femininity' as primary social constructions, supported by a range of cultural phenomena. The relationship between men and women is seen in material terms as a process of domination and subordination which functions objectively in material relations, but also subjectively in the ways in which men and women think of themselves. The concept of gender draws attention to the objective and subjective constructions of sexual difference, making possible an understanding of the mechanisms by which they operate, and offering the possibility of change.

There is a difference between the more sociological accounts and those – sometimes psychoanalytically based – which suggest there is something irreducible and specific in the nature of sexual difference. Here 'gender' is not one cultural label among others, but a firmly established basis for identity, as masculine or feminine (and not necessarily according to biological sex).

▷ *Ecriture féminine*; Feminism.

Genette, Gérard (b 1930)
French critic. His book *Narrative Discourse* (1980, translated by Jane E. Lewin) provides one of the most systematic and thorough categorizations of forms and modes of narrative.

▷ Narratology; Structuralism.

Genre
In its use in the language of literary criticism the concept of 'genre' proposes that particular groups of texts can be seen as parts of a system of representations agreed between writer and reader. For example, a work such as ▷ Aristotle's *Poetics* isolates those characteristics which are to be found in a group of dramatic texts which are given the generic label ▷ 'tragedy'. The pleasure which an audience derives from watching a particular tragedy emanates in part from its fulfilling certain requirements stimulated by expectations arising from within the form itself. But each particular tragedy cannot be reduced simply to the sum of its generic parts. It is possible to distinguish between a tragedy by ▷ Sophocles, another by ▷ Shakespeare, or another by ▷ Edward Bond, yet at the same time acknowledge that they all conform in certain respects to the narrative and dramatic rules laid down by the category 'tragedy'. Each example, therefore, repeats certain characteristics which have come to be recognized as indispensable features of the genre, but each one also exists in a relationship of difference from the general rule. The same kind of argument may be advanced in relation to particular sorts of poetry, or novel. The concept of genre helps to account for the particular pleasures which readers/spectators experience when confronted with a specific text. It also offers an insight into one of the many determining factors which contribute to the formation of the structure and coherence of any individual text.

***Gentleman Dancing Master, The* (1672)**
Play by ▷ William Wycherley, inspired partly by Calderón de la Barca's *El Maestro de Danzar* (▷ Spanish influence on English literature). 14-year-old Hyppolyta is forcibly betrothed to the stupid fop, Monsieur de Paris, but schemes to evade the watch kept on her and her woman Prue, to keep them in the house and away from men. She is attracted to Gerrard, and tricks her suitor into bringing Gerrard to her window. The pair meet secretly, but are interrupted by her father, Don Diego, alias Mr Formal. Hyppolyta passes Gerrard off as her dancing master, employed to teach her the fashionable dance the Corant, and gains permission for him to visit her again. Gerrard is confused but drawn to her beauty, and her fortune. He plans their elopement. After many more farcical episodes, the two are married. Mr Formal reveals that far from being 'of an honourable house', as he has claimed, he is descended from a long line of merchants. He accepts the marriage, while Monsieur de Paris is obliged to return to Mrs Flirt, a 'common woman of the town', with whom he has had an affair. This is one of Wycherley's least appealing plays, and was not successful.

Gentleman's Magazine, The
Founded in 1731, it was the first to call itself

a 'magazine'. It included, as later magazines were to do, a wider variety of material than the ▷ Reviews, including political reports which, in 1739–44, were contributed by ▷ Samuel Johnson.

Geoffrey of Monmouth (d 1155)
Author of the highly influential account of British history, in Latin prose, the ▷ *Historia Regum Britanniae* (*History of the Kings of Britain*), completed c 1138, which opened up a new vision of insular history, revealing Britain to be a formerly great European power. Little is known for certain about Geoffrey of Monmouth himself. He was probably born in Monmouth, of Welsh or Breton extraction, and seems to have been a resident of Oxford, probably a canon of the college of St George's, for many years of his life (?1129–51). In 1151 he became Bishop Elect of St Asaph. Before finishing his history of Britain, he produced a version of ▷ Merlin's prophecies, which were then incorporated into the history itself. At a later stage he returned to the subject of Merlin and around 1150 produced a Latin poem, the *Vita Merlini* (*The Life of Merlin*).

His history of Britain is an accomplished and complex exercise in history writing. He claims to have access to a source of British history, 'an ancient book in the British language', which has not been used by his contemporary historiographers, nor their predecessors. His narrative seems less likely to be the product of a single unidentified source, and much more the result of a careful act of compilation (using the work of contemporaries such as William of Malmesbury and earlier authorities on the history of the island, notably ▷ Gildas, ▷ Bede, and ▷ Nennius), and fabrication. In Geoffrey's narrative, a shadowy period of the island's past, covering the period before and after the Roman conquest, up to the beginnings of Saxon control in the 6th century, was given relatively detailed documentation, and a rather startling revision of Roman/British and British/Saxon power relations was advanced which disrupted some of the accepted facts of insular history. Geoffrey not only suggested that at certain stages of British history the power of Britain was a major threat to that of Rome, but that Britain was a unified realm well into the 6th century. His history also presented a picture of Britain as a world famous chivalric centre during the reign of ▷ King Arthur. A powerful argument for unified rule emerges from the history, which is a point of some relevance to the turbulent political context in which Geoffrey was writing.

The historical value of the *History of the Kings of Britain* was a controversial issue, debated and disputed by some historians of the 12th and later centuries. But Geoffrey's formulation of British history was widely used in chronicle histories of the island up to the 16th century and provided a historic foundation for the development of Arthurian narrative during the medieval period. Approximately 200 manuscripts survive of the history, and in addition there are numerous vernacular translations and adaptations extant. Poetic and dramatic versions of early British history, such as ▷ *Gorboduc* (1565), ▷ Spenser's ▷ *Faerie Queene*, ▷ Shakespeare's ▷ *King Lear* and ▷ *Cymbeline*, all use material which derives ultimately from Geoffrey of Monmouth's *History of Britain*.

▷ Laȝamon.

Bib: Thorpe, L. (trans.), *Geoffrey of Monmouth: The History of the Kings of Britain*.

George Barnwell, The History of
▷ *London Merchant, The*.

Georgian
A term for the architectural style of the period 1714–1810, under George I, II and III. Georgian architecture was severe but balanced in its proportions. It was influenced partly by the Palladian style of Inigo Jones (1573–1651) and partly by the direct experience of English travellers who made the Grand Tour of Italy and admired its classical buildings. The term is not usually applied to 18th-century literature; in other arts its suggestion of elegance and proportion is often modified by a taste for satire and caricature, as in Hogarth's paintings. It was followed by the ▷ Regency style.

Georgian Poetry
A series of verse ▷ anthologies of which five volumes appeared between 1912 and 1922. It was called 'Georgian' owing to the accession of George V (1910) and to imply a new start for English poetry, involving a degree of experiment and freshness of approach to the art. The poets represented in it included ▷ Rupert Brooke, W. H. Davies, ▷ Walter de la Mare, ▷ D. H. Lawrence, ▷ John Masefield and ▷ Robert Graves. However, the contemporary work of ▷ W. B. Yeats, ▷ Ezra Pound and ▷ T. S. Eliot, more original and more substantial than the work of the Georgian poets, quickly made their movement seem relatively unexciting. Since 1950 there has been some revival of interest in it. It was lyrical, colloquial, emancipated from some of the dead poetic convention left over from the decadent ▷ Romanticism of the previous century, but it lacked the strength and boldness of thought which marked the work of Yeats, Eliot and Pound.

Bib: Vines, S., *Movements in Modern English Poetry and Prose*; Stead, C. K., *The New Poetic*; Ross, R. M., *The Georgian Revolt: The Rise and Fall of a Poetic Ideal 1910–1922*; Rogers, T. (ed.), *Georgian Poetry, 1911–1922: The Critical Heritage*; Reeves, J. (ed.), *Georgian Poetry*.

Georgic
Virgil's *Georgics* (from the Greek word for a

farmer) comprise four poems, addressed to the Emperor Augustus (▷ Caesar, Augustus), describing the techniques of agriculture. During the 17th and 18th centuries they were extensively imitated in English, in ▷ blank verse or pentameter couplets (▷ metre), examples being ▷ John Philips' *Cyder*, ▷ John Dyer's *The Fleece*, and, in a more general way, ▷ Alexander Pope's ▷ *Windsor Forest* and much of ▷ William Cowper's *The Task*. ▷ John Gay's *Trivia*, set in London, is a humorous 'urban Georgic'.

Georgics
A poem on agricultural life by the Latin poet ▷ Virgil; it describes the peasant's year and contrasts the virtues of life in natural surroundings with the burdensomeness of urban luxury. The poem was of great influence on the tradition of ▷ pastoral poetry from the 16th to 18th centuries.

Germ, The (1850)
The literary magazine of the ▷ Pre-Raphaelite Brotherhood lasting for only four issues from January to April 1850. ▷ Dante Gabriel Rossetti, ▷ Christina Rossetti, ▷ Coventry Patmore and Thomas Woolner (▷ 'Enoch Arden') published poetry in it. Dante Gabriel Rossetti's short story *Hand and Soul* was also printed in it. It was edited by the Rossettis' brother, William Michael Rossetti.

German Princess, The
▷ Carleton, Mary

German influence on English literature
Unlike other European literatures, such as French or Italian, the literature of the German-speaking world did not begin to make itself felt in Britain to any great extent until relatively recent times. There are two reasons for this. The first is that the great flowering of a literature written in the *modern* form of the German language did not take place until the second half of the 18th century; the second is that German did not begin to assume the status of a major foreign language for the English until the second decade of the following century and even then it remained far behind French importance. However, there are isolated examples of such influence before the late 18th century, two of which are particularly interesting because they show clearly that the structural model of influencing and influenced literature falsifies what is a far more complex pattern of reciprocal interchange between two literary cultures. For many years it was a matter of debate whether the anonymous work *Der bestrafte Brudermord* was derived from one of the sources of ▷ Shakespeare's ▷ *Hamlet* or was merely a botched version of the play. It is now thought that the German play can teach us nothing about Shakespeare's sources, but another classic of the Elizabethan stage, ▷ Christopher Marlowe's ▷ *Doctor Faustus* does draw upon a German source, a legend which did not give rise to a classic in its own language until the appearance of Johann Wolfgang von Goethe's ▷ *Faust* over two centuries later.

In the cultural interchange between the two literatures Britain has on balance been the dominant partner. German men and women of letters during the 18th century were far more likely to have a lively awareness of current developments in English literature than were their English counterparts of developments in Germany. For example, the status of ▷ *Paradise Lost* as an epic poem was debated, ▷ Alexander Pope's ▷ *Rape of the Lock* was read and discussed, ▷ Oliver Goldsmith, ▷ Edward Young, ▷ Laurence Sterne and ▷ James Thomson were all known and admired. In this way English literature was able to play a crucial role in the process by which German writers of the late 18th century succeeded in exerting their independence from the prevailing standards of neo-classical decorum which French models seemed to dictate. The writers of the *Sturm und Drang* ('Storm and Stress'), as later the German romantics, looked to Britain rather than France for support and justification of their revolutionary project. Shakespeare's status as a German classic dates from this time, and the early attempts of Gotthold Ephraim Lessing (1729–81), Goethe (1749–1832) and Friedrich Schiller (1759–1805), who also translated ▷ *Macbeth*, to provide a repertoire for a German national theatre owed a great deal to the English dramatist. So when German theatre first made an impression in Britain, the new stimulus contained many, though unrecognized, indigenous elements. Interest in German theatre seems to have been kindled by the Scot ▷ Henry Mackenzie who gave an address on the subject to the Royal Society of Edinburgh in 1788. During the 1790s the English stage experienced a vogue for German plays, but the public's taste was essentially for the ▷ Gothic, and the most performed writer was the justly forgotten August von Kotzebue (1761–1819). It was not in drama, however, that the first impact of the new German literature was felt but in the novel. Goethe's epistolary novel *Die Leiden des jungen Werthers* (The Sorrows of Young Werther, 1774) was a landmark, for it was the first work of German literature to achieve European recognition. It was translated into most European languages and reached Britain in 1779, significantly via a French version. The novel's apparent defence of suicide caused a storm of righteous indignation, but the huge popularity of the novel, here as elsewhere, had much to do with the fact that it appealed to a taste for 'sentimental' literature which had already been established in Germany and Britain by, among others, ▷ Samuel Richardson. Other currents also made themselves felt. Bishop Percy's *Reliques of Ancient English Poetry* (1765) had stimulated Johann Herder and, through him, Goethe to explore their own native oral tradition of 'natural' *Volkspoesie*. This interest is reflected in the novel in Werther's admiration of ▷ *Ossian* (Oisin), ▷ James Macpherson's collection of supposed fragments of lost Celtic epics, which had appeared in 1765. The frustrations of the novel's middle-class hero were also felt to carry a political meaning, and in the early 1790s the young poet Robert Southey, still the unreconstructed democrat, always had the novel about him.

This discovery of German literature by an English audience unfortunately soon met an insurmountable obstacle in the form of war. In the wake of the ▷ French Revolution a climate of opinion was created which was deeply and indiscriminately suspicious of all mainland European influence as Jacobin, subversive and unpatriotic. The fashion of German plays was snuffed out almost instantly, and it was not until the ending of the Napoleonic wars, with England and Prussia as victorious allies, that a new climate favourable to the reception of German writers could be created. The publication of Madame de Staël's *De l'Allemagne* (1813) is rightly regarded as a crucial event in this process. When English interest was reawakened, it was once again Goethe who was at the centre of controversy. It is easy to smile now at the response to the first part of *Faust* (1808), but the work was then felt to be deeply shocking. Quite apart from a degree of frankness in sexual matters unthinkable in an English work, there were features which were regarded as highly offensive to orthodox Christian sentiment. Goethe's reputation as an immoral author was revived, and it seems likely that fear for his own reputation played some part in ▷ Samuel Coleridge not undertaking a commissioned translation of the work. It is one of the imbalances in the relations between English and German literature that while English classics found immensely talented translators in Germany – the Tieck-Schlegel version of Shakespeare, for example – many great German works have been either completely overlooked or ill-served by their English translators.

Of the first generation of English romantic poets only Coleridge, if we discount ▷ William Blake's idiosyncratic relationship to ▷ Emanuel Swedenborg and the visionary mystic Jakob Böhme (1575–1624), was deeply influenced by German culture. A cautious admirer of Goethe, translator of Schiller's *Wallensteins Tod* (Wallenstein's Death), Coleridge visited Göttingen in 1798. His thought was deeply indebted to ▷ Immanuel Kant (1724–1804), Johann Gottfried von Herder (1744–1803) and the *Naturphilosophie* of Friedrich Schelling (1775–1854). ▷ William Wordsworth, who in his view of nature was far closer to Goethe than he realized, shared the opinion of many in dismissing him as an immoral and irreligious writer, but ▷ Lord Byron and ▷ Percy Bysshe Shelley had no sympathy with such small-mindedness. Shelley valued *Faust* highly, and it is a loss to English culture that his efforts at translation never extended beyond a few small fragments of the work. As for Byron, his admiration was genuine, if not matched by any great depth of response. His esteem, however, was reciprocated. Byron, whose works, ▷ *Childe Harold's Pilgrimage* and ▷ *Don Juan* especially, were widely read and admired in Germany as in the rest of Europe, sadly did not live to see the tribute Goethe paid him in the second part of *Faust* (1832), where the English poet is represented as the child of Faust and Helen. For ▷ Thomas Carlyle, Goethe and Byron signified opposite moral and artistic poles, and it was Carlyle who was the single most important conduit of German literature and thought in the 19th century. He had already published his translation of Goethe's *Wilhelm Meister* when, in 1839, his *Critical and Miscellaneous Essays* appeared, containing the many articles on German literature which he had written for the journals of the day. The work was seminal and inaugurated what was the great age of German influence in Britain. Probably inspired by Carlyle, ▷ Matthew Arnold immersed himself in the works of Goethe and was deeply influenced by him. His discovery and admiration of Heinrich Heine (1797–1856) on the other hand was quite independent, and an appreciative essay on the later poet is included in ▷ *Essays in Criticism* (1865). For Arnold, Goethe and Heine were great modern spirits in comparison with whom the English romantics were insular and intellectually deficient. Arnold's German culture extends far beyond these two authors however, and, in scope at least, he is like ▷ George Eliot in this regard. It is now appreciated that the profound influence of the so-called 'Higher Criticism' in Britain did not commence with the publication in 1846 of Eliot's translation of David Straub's *Das Leben Jesu* (1835) but has roots which reach back into the last quarter of the 18th century, and that Coleridge was ahead of his time in his appreciation of the significance to religion and philosophy of the German school of Biblical criticism. George Eliot is less a beginning than a culmination. Arnold had recognized in Goethe a figure who was working to 'dissolve' the dogmatic Christianity which had once been the bedrock of European civilization. It is now clear, however, that it was the Higher Criticism which, by mythologizing Christianity, undermined its claims more surely even than ▷ Charles Darwin, the geologists and positivist science. From this it is clear that when considering the massive response of English writers to German literature at this time, no sharp line can be drawn between works of imagination on the one hand and works of historical scholarship, cultural history and philosophy on the other. If a novel of ideas such as ▷ *Daniel Deronda* could hardly have been written without Straub (1808–74) and Ludwig Feuerbach (1804–72), then Goethe's *Wilhelm meister* is scarcely less crucial. The relevance here of ▷ G. H. Lewes, whose *Life of Goethe* appeared in 1855, is obvious. In the last decade of the century another admirer of Goethe, Oscar Wilde, with inspired flippancy, could show in *The Importance of Being Ernest* young Cecily earnestly studying her German grammar under the eyes of Miss Prism and the Reverend Chasuble, but for many the loss of religious faith which followed the encounter with German thought gave rise to great anguish before it brought serenity.

It is one of the paradoxes of the Victorian era that, while a series such as Bohn's Standard Library made available to a reading public a large number of German classic texts in translation, there were still many gaps and absences. The imaginative literature of the middle and second half of the century, represented by writers such as the Austrian Franz Grillparzer (1791–1872), E. Mörike (1804–75), A. Stifter (1805–68), Friedrich Hebbel (1813–63), T. Storm (1817–88), Theodor Fontane (1819–98), and the Swiss writers G. Keller (1819–90) and C. F. Meyer (1825–98) did not reach the wider audience it deserved. Because some of this literature is in a sense provincial, its failure to make much impression in Britain is less surprising than the British blindness to the considerable achievements of important earlier figures such as Heinrich von Kleist (1777–1881) or E. T. A. Hoffmann (1776–1822), though the latter was not unknown and certainly influenced Edgar Allan Poe. Of this generation it was perhaps the figure of Richard Wagner (1813–83), more associated with music than literature, whose work has had most influence on English literature. In some ways he was an important precursor of the Celtic revival, and his aesthetic theories as much as his use of the *leitmotif* influenced subsequent writers throughout Europe. ▷ James Joyce associated the technique with Wagner and, of course, ▷ T. S. Eliot famously quotes *Tristan und Isolde* in ▷ *The Waste Land*.

In the 20th century, however, the European character of ▷ modernism in literature, as of romanticism before it, is impossible to mistake, and the German presence is particularly marked even if the complex and contradictory nature of modernism makes generalization hazardous. To study the poetry of Rainer Maria Rilke (1875–1926) and ▷ W. B. Yeats, however, is to be conscious of a broadly similar response to a common cultural situation rather than of indebtedness or influence. Deprived of belief in orthodox religion, both poets satisfied their need for a spiritual sense of existence by creating personal mythologies which display many striking parallels with each other. Rilke is unusual in being, after Heine, who influenced ▷ A. E. Housman, perhaps the only German writer to achieve recognition in England solely as a poet. This was certainly made possible by the Leishman, and Leishman-Spender translations, but ▷ Stephen Spender was not alone in his generation in being able to read German literature without the need for translations. ▷ Louis MacNeice himself was a co-translator of *Faust*, both ▷ W. H. Auden and ▷ Christopher Isherwood knew German, Auden translating Goethe's *Italienische Reise* and some works of ▷ Bertolt Brecht. During the 1930s the rise of ▷ fascism in Germany brought about the exile of nearly every significant writer, and resistance to this evil united many writers of both countries in a sense of common purpose. In the theatre the leading German ▷ naturalist playwright ▷ Gerhart Hauptmann (1862–1946) may not have had the impact of the Scandinavian dramatists ▷ Henrik Ibsen and ▷ August Strindberg but, in intellectual left-wing circles at least, he was read and admired. The presentation of industrial class conflict in *Die Weber* (The Weavers; 1892), where Hauptmann succeeds in creating a 'social' drama without individualized heroes, renewed interest in German theatre and in some ways foreshadowed the political commitment associated with the name of Brecht. Hauptmann is rarely performed in Britain now, but this is true of most German dramatists. German expressionist theatre swiftly found interest in Britain during the 1920s because of its radically experimental approach but only one work, G. Kaiser's (1878–1945) *Von morgens bis mitternachts* (From Morning to Midnight, 1916), achieved any success. The number of German plays one is likely to find regularly performed on the English stage now is relatively small in comparison to the presence of English works in German theatres.

Goethe's *Faust* or Schiller's *Maria Stuart* are occasionally done, but one is far more likely to see the plays *Woyzek* and *Dantons Tod* by Georg Buchner (1813–37). As in Germany, Buchner came to be valued only long after his premature death, but the vitality and continuing relevance of his plays and his justified reputation as an early forerunner of modern sensibility ensure continued interest in him. Frank Wedekind (1864–1918) has provided in his *Fruhlings Erwachen* (Spring's Awakening, 1891) a masterpiece which has triumphantly survived translation, but it was one of Wedekind's admirers, Brecht, who has had the most extensive and long-lasting influence on the theatre of the English-speaking world. His opposition to Hitler and the commitment to peace which informs all his mature work have made him more acceptable in Britain than in America where his undisguised communist sympathies have told against him. The style of his so-called Epic theatre, particularly in its rejection of naturalism and its use of music, songs and verse, has been widely imitated even where – perhaps especially where – it has been detached from its original political thrust. As clearly as any other writer Brecht shows the reciprocal forces at work in matters of cultural influence, for his Epic style received important impulses from Elizabethan theatre, especially Shakespeare. Whether his influence and reputation as a modern classic survive the collapse of communism in Eastern Europe remains to be seen.

As might be expected, it is the modern novelists who have reached the widest audiences. During the 19th century the figures of ▷ Walter Scott, ▷ William Thackeray and ▷ Charles Dickens exercised a considerable influence on the development of realist fiction in Germany, most notably on the work of Theodor Fontane. Thomas Mann (1875–1955) was closest to this tradition in his novel of the decline of a bourgeois family, *Buddenbrooks* (1901), and for many years was held in high esteem, but, perhaps because his later fiction took a rather different and more philosophical direction, his reputation has waned somewhat in recent years. Hermann Hesse (1877–1962), after a period of considerably popularity, has suffered a similar fate, but the fascination of the Czech Franz Kafka (1883–1924) is undiminished. All his writings are fables of alienation, and his name has become a byword for the bizarre and nightmarish. His unique vision is too personal for imitation, but it is hard to imagine how Joseph Heller's *Catch 22* (1961) and *Something Happened* (1974) could have been written without Kafka. A very different kind of fantastic realism characterizes the work of Gunter Grass (b 1927), and, together with Henrich Böll (1917–1985), Grass stands out among the writers of the post-war generation as one whose work has spoken most immediately to his English-speaking contemporaries. An influence on the writing of ▷ Salman Rushdie is a plausible surmise: their artistic kinship is certain.

There can be little doubt that the profoundest influence on English literature and the literatures of many other countries in the 20th century stems not from the imaginative literature of Germany but from the philosophical. Probably this should not surprise us, since a philosophical tradition which goes back to ▷ Gottfried Leibniz (1646–1716) and Kant and from which emerged the towering figures of Georg Hegel, Arthur Schopenhauer and ▷ Friedrich Nietzsche had already left its mark. In Karl Marx (1818–83) and ▷ Sigmund Freud (1856–1939), however, the German-speaking world produced two thinkers who, in contrast to Ludwig Wittgenstein (1889–1951) whose profound influence has largely been confined to specialist philosophy, have as decisively and permanently transformed the whole framework of terms within which we conceive society and the human mind, as Darwin and Einstein have transformed our understanding of the physical world. This is no less true for a writer like Vladimir Nabokov (1899–1977), who dismisses Freud as the Viennese witch-doctor, than for ▷ D. M. Thomas. For the British there is, of course, a special poignancy in this since both these radical thinkers were driven by political circumstances from their native countries and found refuge in Britain.

Goethe foresaw a time when, with the help of translation, national literatures would give way to a *Weltliteratur*. In the bookshops of Germany, where translations from English abound, one is inclined to feel that the day has arrived, but a visitor to a British bookshop in search of translations from the German is likely to reflect that here at least this consummation has still to come.

Ghose, Zulfikar (b 1935)
Novelist and poet. Ghose was born in Pakistan and educated at the University of Keele. During the 1960s he worked as cricket correspondent for the *Observer* before becoming a teacher in London and then Professor of English at the University of Texas. His trilogy, entitled *The Incredible Brazilian* and comprising *The Native* (1972), *A Beautiful Empire* (1975) and *A Different World* (1985), uses elements of ▷ magic realism to portray the cultural history of Brazil through the reincarnations of a single character named Gregório. His other novels are: *The Contradictions* (1966); *The Murder of Aziz Khan* (1967); *Crump's Terms* (1975); *The Texas Inheritance* (1980, published under the name William Strang); *Hulme's Investigations into the Bogart Script* (1981); *A New History of Torments* (1982); *Don Bueno* (1983); *Figures of Enchantment* (1986); *The Triple Mirror of the Self* (1991). Short stories: (with ▷ B.S. Johnson) *Statement Against Corpses* (1964). Poetry: *The Loss of India* (1964); *Jets from Orange* (1967); *The Violet West* (1972); *A Memory of Asia* (1984); *Selected Poems* (1991). He has also published critical works, and an autobiographical piece, *Confessions of a Native-Alien* (1965).

***Ghosts* (1890)**
A play by ▷ Henrik Ibsen originally produced in Norwegian as *Gengangere* in 1881. One of the major plays of his ▷ realist period its early performances in London caused outrage and controversy. Its main character, the widowed Mrs Alving, has vigorously suppressed the truth concerning her profligate husband. However the truth comes back to haunt her in the form of her son Oswald who returns from Paris suffering from hereditary syphilis. The play tackles such taboo subjects as incest and euthanasia, and examines the dead conventions that smother the living society.

Giaour, The (1813)
A verse tale by ▷ Lord Byron in tetrameter couplets (▷ metre) interspersed with quatrains. The word was used by the Turks as a general term for non-Muslims, especially Christians. The poem is about the love of a Turkish slave Leila for a giaour; her master causes her to be thrown into the sea, and her lover avenges her death.
▷ Orientalism.

Gibbon, Edward (1737–94)
One of the greatest English historians, author of ▷ *The Decline and Fall of the Roman Empire* (1776–88). His reputation rests almost entirely on this work, but his *Memoirs* (1796), put together from fragments after his death, are one of the most interesting biographies of the 18th century. In 1761 he published in French his *Essai sur l'Etude de la Littérature*, translated into English in 1764; it was more successful abroad than at home. He was also a Member of Parliament, 1774–81.
Bib: Low, D. M., *Edward Gibbon*; Young, G. M., *Gibbon*; Sainte-Beuve, C. A., in *Causeries dy Lundi* vol viii.

Gibbon, Lewis Grassic (1901–35)
Novelist. Lewis Grassic Gibbon is the pen-name of James Leslie Mitchell, a Scots writer whose most famous work, the trilogy of novels, *A Scots Quair (Sunset Song*, 1932, *Cloud Howe*, 1933, and *Grey Granite*, 1934) dramatizes working life in the early part of the 20th century in rural Scotland. Gibbon's work is characterized by his formally innovative combination of north-eastern Scottish dialogue and speech-rhythms, mixed with a burning belief in a rural form of socialism and feminism. Gibbon also wrote seven other novels under his own name, collaborated with poet ▷ Hugh MacDiarmid on *Scottish Scene, or, The Intelligent Man's Guide to Albyn* (1934), and, again under his own name, wrote three anthropological/archaeological texts. He died young, having produced a large body of wide-ranging work.
▷ Scottish literature in English.

Gibbons, Stella (1902–89)
Novelist. Gibbons' most famous work (perhaps more famous than its author), the novel *Cold Comfort Farm* (1932), was the first in a long series of astute, witty comedies of manners, a ▷ parody of both Lawrentian primitivism (▷ D. H. Lawrence) and rural fiction (popularized by writers such as Mary Webb, 1881–1927). It became a best-seller and has since been serialized for radio, and filmed for television. Gibbons also wrote short stories, poetry and many other novels; her works include *The Mountain Beast and Other Poems* (1930); *The Untidy Gnome* (1935); *Roaring Tower and Other Short Stories* (1937); *Nightingalewood* (1938); *Christmas at Cold Comfort Farm and Other Stories* (1940); *Westwood* (1946); *Conference at Cold Comfort Farm* (1949); *Collected Poems* (1951); *The Shadow of a Sorcerer* (1955); *The Pink Front Door* (1959); *The Charmers* (1965); *The Woods in Winter* (1970).

Gide, André (1869–1951)
French novelist. He developed an early preference for the *sotie* or *récit* (short prose piece) and in this form produced *L'Immoraliste* (1902), *La Porte étroite* (1909) and *La Symphonie pastorale* (1919). These are short, tightly-organized stories which exploit the characteristic weakness of first-person narration, in that their narrator-protagonists are without exception blind to the consequences of their words and actions (▷ narrator, unreliable). In all cases, this narrator is sharply distinguished from the author, who distances himself from his characters through irony (the title *sotie* denotes strong mockery). *Les Caves du Vatican* (1914) is a longer *récit* which develops the notion of the 'gratuitous act', an unmotivated and unpremediated act which would constitute an effect without a cause and novelistically represent an unpredictable element altering the course of the narration. The work also portrays the stifling, hidebound world of marriage, the family and religion, all objects of Gidean criticism. These concerns surface again in the only work which Gide called a novel, *Les Faux-Monnayeurs*, published in 1925. Its theme is moral and literary counterfeiting and the contrasting search for authenticity and openness (*disponibilité*) to experience. The experimental aspect of the novel is striking. Narrative orderliness and momentum are broken up by the plurality of angles of vision and the constant switching from one sub-plot to the next. Moreover, the author himself intervenes in the narrative to rupture any suspension of disbelief by declaring his own lack of control over characters and events. Above all, Gide makes crucial use of what he named the ▷ *mise en abyme* technique, a procedure by which the novel debates its own problems. In Gide's novel, this technique is exemplified in the character Edouard. Edouard is a novelist whose diary, 'quoted' by Gide, records his difficulties in writing his own novel, itself called *Les Faux-Monnayeurs*. This self-consciousness, highlighting the literariness of literature, has proved influential in the subsequent development of the novel in France.

Gide also helped found the literary magazine *La Nouvelle Revue française* and certain of his own works first appeared in its pages (*La Porte étroite*, *Les Caves du Vatican*, *Les Faux-Monnayeurs*).
▷ French influence on English fiction.

Gielgud, Sir John (b 1904)
English actor and director who first appeared

on stage in 1921 at the Old Vic. He is most famous for his performances of leading roles in ▷ Shakespeare's plays, particularly during the 1930s and 40s. He began directing in 1932 with a production of *Romeo and Juliet* for the Oxford University Dramatic Society. His production of *Hamlet* at the New Theatre in 1934 ran for 155 performances and was a landmark in West End productions of Shakespeare. He has continued a distinguished acting career up to the present day. In 1991 he fulfilled his long-held ambition to put his performance of Prospero on film, in an innovative and experimental version of *The Tempest* by British director Peter Greenaway, *Prospero's Books*.

▷ Olivier, Laurence; Littlewood, Joan.
Bib: Gielgud, J., *Early Stages*; Gielgud, J., *Stage Directions*; Hayman, R., *John Gielgud*.

Giffard, Anna Marcella
▷ Giffard, Henry.

Giffard, Henry (1694–1772)
Actor, manager. The date and place of his first stage performance are uncertain, but by 1720 at the latest he was acting at the ▷ Smock Alley Theatre in Dublin, where he remained for at least seven years, acting in a variety of young romantic lead roles. He married his second wife, Anna Marcella Lyddall (1707–77), the actress and singer, *c* 1729.

By 1731 Giffard and his wife had appeared at the ▷ Haymarket Theatre, but later that year he took over running ▷ Goodman's Fields Theatre, refurbishing it and engaging a number of new actors. He opened a new theatre, also known as Goodman's Fields, in 1733. In 1737 he took the script of a satiric play to ▷ Sir Robert Walpole, and this was used, in part, by the Government as a pretext for passing the Licensing Act (▷ Theatres). Lacking a patent, Giffard was forced out of business, although he subsequently staged some performances at the fringes of the law, including the first performance of ▷ *The Winter's Tale* for over a hundred years.

By 1740 Giffard had successfully petitioned for permission to re-open Goodman's Fields, both managing and acting at the theatre. His reputation later rested not so much on his acting talents, which were not always wholeheartedly received, as on his abilities as a manager. He was also remembered for his encouragement of other actors, not least ▷ David Garrick, to whom he gave his first acting opportunity, in 1741.

Giffard, William (1756–1826)
Journalist. He began as a shoemaker's apprentice, and rose to be an influential writer and editor of the right-wing press. He edited *The Anti-Jacobin* (1797–8) to counteract opinion sympathetic to the ▷ French Revolution, and became editor of the famous Conservative ▷ *Quarterly Review* in 1809.

Gilbert, Ann (1782–1866)
Poet, reviewer, children's author, diarist and autobiographer. Gilbert's writing equalled that of her more famous sister, ▷ Jane Taylor, and both were precocious children and prolific authors. Her first book of poems, *Original Poems* (1804–5), was immediately successful and led to her undertaking the editorship of *The Eclectic Review*. In this capacity she reviewed contemporary novels. After her marriage to Revd Joseph Gilbert in 1813, she moved to Sheffield and Nottingham and turned her literary skills to more political matters, writing against slavery (▷ Abolition literature), in favour of temperance, and offering general advice on government legislation. Gilbert had kept a diary from an early age and at 66 she began to transform some of the material into an ▷ autobiography; it was never finished, but the extant material was published posthumously in 1874.

Gilbert, Sir William Schwenck (1836–1911)
English dramatist most famous for his partnership with Sir Arthur Sullivan. Together they produced the famous Savoy operas, so called because they were produced at the Savoy Theatre; Gilbert wrote the libretti and Sullivan composed the music. The partnership began with *Thespis*; or, *The God Grown Old* in 1871 and concluded with *The Grand Duke* (1896). The best known of these light operas are *HMS Pinafore* (1878), *The Pirates of Penzance* (1880), *Iolanthe* (1882), *The Mikado* (1885) and *The Gondoliers* (1889). Gilbert's plays are rarely performed now, although *Engaged* (1887) has received attention for its influence on ▷ Oscar Wilde's ▷ *The Importance of Being Earnest*.
Bib: Cox-Ife, W., *Gilbert: Stage Director*; Sutton, M., *Gilbert*.

Gildas (d 570)
A British monk, living in the west of England, whose work, *De Excidio Britanniae* (*About the Fall of Britain*), written about 547, provides the only contemporary account of 6th-century Britain. It was written as a polemical piece, aimed at provoking the reform of British ecclesiastics and leaders. Gildas provides a preface to his complaint in which he sketches the course of British history after the Roman withdrawal. No mention is made of ▷ Arthur in his narrative, but the British triumph against Saxon aggressors at Badon (a victory later attributed to Arthur) is noted. Gildas' narrative was later used by ▷ Bede and thus indirectly helped to shape the representation of the British past in all the major insular histories of the medieval period. ▷ Geoffrey of Monmouth reworked parts of Gildas' text in his ▷ *Historia Regum Britanniae*.

Gildon, Charles (1665–1724)
English author and editor, he was an early

epitome of a ▷ hack, turning his hand to any literary endeavour that might earn him some money. His productions included ▷ pamphlets, a collection of poems, dialogues, and other items entitled *Miscellany* (1692), a *Life* of the actor ▷ Thomas Betterton (1710), and a revision of Langbaine's *An Account of the Dramatic Poets* (1696), as well as editions of works by ▷ Shakespeare and by ▷ Aphra Behn (1696). Numerous plays are attributed to Gildon himself, including *The Roman Bride's Revenge* (1696), *Phaeton* (1698), *Love's Victim* (1701), and *The Patriot* (1703); several of these involve revisions of earlier plays. He also on occasion acted as stage producer.
Bib: Backscheider, P. (ed.), *The Plays of Charles Gildon.*

Gilfillan, George (1813–1878)
An enthusiastic and exuberant reviewer and critic who frequently wrote under the name 'Apollodorus'. He championed the work of ▷ Philip James Bailey, Alexander Smith and ▷ Sydney Dobell, later satirized by ▷ William Aytoun as the ▷ 'Spasmodic' school of poetry. A Scots burgher minister in Dundee, he shared ▷ Carlyle's dogmatism and tendency to pontificate and his influence on early Victorian poetic taste was as powerful as Carlyle's, although their views on art differed significantly. He rapidly established a wide reputation with his *Galleries of Literary Portraits* (1845–54) and his articles in the *Quarterly*, the *Eclectic, Tait's Magazine* and *Hogg's Instructor.* His reputation waned, however, as a result of Aytoun's satiric portrait of him in *Firmilian, a Spasmodic Tragedy.* His *Letters and Journals* were published in 1892.
Bib: Nicoll, W. Robertson, *Gilfillan's Literary Portraits*; Buckley, J.H., *The Victorian Temper.*

Gilfil's Love-Story, Mr
One of ▷ George Eliot's ▷ *Scenes of Clerical Life.*

Gilpin, William (1724–1804)
Theorist. Gilpin's work was very important in establishing the cult of the ▷ Picturesque, as well as in heralding certain themes valued by the ▷ Romantic poets. He based his ideas upon journeys he undertook to the most 'picturesque' parts of Britain, including the Lake District and the Scottish Highlands, and published his theories in *Three Essays: On Picturesque Beauty; On Picturesque Travel; and On Sketching Landscapes* (1792). His efforts were not universally praised, and he was satirized in the figure of Dr Syntax by ▷ Combe.

Gilroy, Beryl (b 1924)
Novelist. Born and brought up in Guyana, Gilroy trained as a teacher and worked for UNICEF. In 1951 she moved to Britain where she studied at the universities of London and Sussex. She has worked as a journalist, teacher and head-teacher in London. Her novels are *Frangipani House* (1986), about the indignities suffered by an old and infirm woman in Guyana, *Boy-Sandwich* (1989) and *Sunlight on Sweet Water* (1994). She has also published fiction for children and *Black Teacher* (1970), which is autobiographical.

'Girl of the Period, The' (1868)
An essay by ▷ Eliza Lynn Linton, published in *The Saturday Review.* It caused much controversy, was sold worldwide and was described as 'an epoch-making essay'. The 'Girl of the Period' is depicted as a frivolous, extravagant creature 'who dyes her hair and paints her face . . . whose sole idea of life is fun' and who shows no respect for men, ▷ marriage or motherhood. Linton laments this 'pitiable mistake and . . . grand national disaster' and calls for a return to a past ideal of womanhood. The essay does not touch upon issues central to women's lives in the 1860s such as higher ▷ education, work, or ▷ women's suffrage, but it caused a furore and sparked numerous imitations.

▷ 'Woman Question, The'.

Gissing, George Robert (1857–1903)
Novelist; author of: *Workers in the Dawn* (1880); *The Unclassed* (1884); ▷ *Demos* (1886); *A Life's Morning* (1888); *The Nether World* (1889); *The Emancipated* (1890); ▷ *New Grub Street* (1891); *Born in Exile* (1892); ▷ *The Odd Women* (1893); *The Town Traveller* (1898); *The Crown of Life* (1899); *Our Friend the Charlatan* (1901); *By the Ionian Sea* (1901); *The Private Papers of Henry Ryecfroft* (1903). Posthumous: the historical novel *Veranilda* (1904) and *Will Warburton* (1905). Of these, much the best known is *New Grub Street*, a study of literary life in late 19th-century London. Gissing saw with deep foreboding the spread of a commercialized culture which would so oppress the disinterested artist and so encourage the charlatan that, in his view, national culture was bound to deteriorate, with concomitant effects on the quality of civilization as a whole. The partial fulfilment of his predictions has given this novel in particular a greatly revived prestige. His vision was serious and sombre, and he depicted the enclosed, deprived world of the poor of his time in *Demos* and *The Nether World. Thyrza* and *Henry Ryecroft* are other novels which are singled out from his work. He was deeply interested in ▷ Charles Dickens and his study of that novelist (1898) is among the best on the subject; but he had also been affected by the austere, scrupulous artistry of the French 19th-century novelists ▷ Flaubert and ▷ Zola. His best work often has a strong

autobiographical content, characteristic of some of his contemporaries, such as ▷ William Hale White and ▷ Samuel Butler

▷ Newspapers and periodicals.

Bib: Donnelly, M., *Gissing, Grave Comedian*; Org, J., *Gissing*; Roberts, M., *The Private Life of Henry Maitland* (novel based on Gissing's life); Poole, A., *Gissing in Context*; Pollie, M., *The Alien Art: A Critical Study George Gissing's Novels*.

Gladstone, William Ewart (1809–98)

One of the principal British statesmen of the 19th century and a leader, first of the Tories (Conservatives) and later, Prime Minister four times, of the Liberals. His strength lay in finance – he was an advocate of ▷ free trade – and domestic reform; late in life he advocated and came near to bringing about self-government for Ireland (Irish Home Rule). His personality was impressive and his ardour and energy very great, but he lacked the intimate charm and subtle wit of his opponent ▷ Benjamin Disraeli, whom he fought with almost religious dedication. Their rivalry is often recalled as a golden age of English parliamentarianism by those who see public competition and conflict between individuals as the most productive form of political activity.

Gladstone was a man of deep culture, a classical scholar who published studies of ancient Greek literature. His reforms were important in removing abuses and improving justice and equality in the universities, the army, the ▷ franchise, the right to form and maintain ▷ trade unions, and recruitment to the military and civil services.

Glasse, Hannah (1708–70)

Writer, especially on housekeeping, she was at one time 'Habit Maker' to the Princess of Wales. Glasse prided herself on the plainness and simplicity of her writing style, so that the most ignorant servant would be able to understand it. Her works include *The Compleat Confectioner* (1742), *The Art of Cookery Made Plain and Easy* (1747), and *The Servant's Directory, or House-keeper's Companion* (1760). All of these were hugely popular. Four children's books are also attributed to her.

Glastonbury

A town in Somerset where there are the ruins of a great Benedictine abbey. In prehistoric times it was almost a lake island, being set in a group of hills surrounded by low-lying country; the highest of the hills, Glastonbury Tor, appears to have figured in early myths as a point of contact with, and entry to, the Otherworld. Thus the notion of Glastonbury as a spiritual centre seems to be of great antiquity.

Many myths and legends have been generated about Glastonbury Abbey. It was the site of an early Celtic Christian community from the 6th century, but it was reputed to be the site of the first Christian church in Britain, founded by Joseph of Arimathea, the rich man described in the Gospels who buried Christ in his own sepulchre. Joseph was reputed to have planted his staff at Glastonbury, and this miraculously became the Glastonbury thorn, a tree which flowers at Christmas. The discovery and excavation of the graves of ▷ King Arthur and ▷ Guinevere at Glastonbury in 1191 encouraged the identification of Glastonbury with the island of ▷ Avalon, and the connection between Arthurian history and Glastonbury was further developed in the Arthurian narratives much recount the history and quest of the Holy ▷ Grail, which was reputed to have been brought to Britain by Joseph of Arimathea. At the end of ▷ Malory's ▷ *Morte D'Arthur*, ▷ Lancelot retires from the world to live as a hermit in the Glastonbury area.

Bib: Treharne, R. F., *The Glastonbury Legends*.

Globe Theatre

The theatre used by the Lord ▷ Chamberlain's Men; ▷ Shakespeare's plays were performed there, he acted in it, and was one of the shareholders. It was built by ▷ Richard Burbage in 1599 out of the materials of 'The Theatre' erected in 1576; the new site was at ▷ Bankside on the south bank of the Thames in Southwark. It was built of wood, open in the centre, and the surrounding galleries ('this wooden O' – Prologue, ▷ *Henry V*) were roofed with thatch. It is thought to have held about 3,000 spectators. From the roof flew a flag depicting Atlas carrying a globe with a Latin inscription equivalent to 'All the world's a stage' (▷ *As You Like It* II. vii. 138). The theatre was burnt down in 1613 during a performance of ▷ *Henry VIII*, rebuilt, and finally pulled down in 1644. Much of the information about the Globe comes from the contract for the Fortune Theatre (built in 1599), the structure of which is specified as resembling the Globe, except that the Fortune was square. A panoramic view of London dated 1616 gives a view of the Globe among other theatres. In the main, the structure of the Globe, like that of its contemporaries, derived from that of the typical inn-yard where plays were commonly performed when theatres were not available.

Under the inspired leadership of Sam Wannemaker and the auspices of the International Shakespeare Globe Centre, the Globe has risen again in Southwark, according to its original specifications and near to its old site. The original Globe's foundations have been discovered, but in the 1990s have been reconcealed within the foundations of a highrise office block. Wannemaker's Globe will be the first all-timber building licensed in London in the 20th century and will cater for international performances of Shakespeare, lectures and exhibitions.

▷ Theatres.
Bib: Orrell, J., *The Quest for Shakespeare's Globe.*

Gloriana
The ▷ Faerie Queene of ▷ Edmund Spenser's poem; she represents ▷ Elizabeth I.

Glorious Revolution
A name given to the removal by Parliament of ▷ King James II (1685–88) and the substitution of his daughter ▷ Mary II and her husband ▷ William III in 1688. The reason for the quarrel between James and Parliament was not so much that James was a ▷ Catholic as that he was using every means in his power to assert the superiority of royal power (in the name of his religion) over the power of Parliament. His policy united the whole nation against him, except for a very small minority of Catholics, and the success of Parliament finally settled the question of whether sovereign power lay with the king or with Parliament; this problem had been left unsolved when the period of republican rule (1649–60) had been succeeded by the Restoration of the monarchy. In 1688 the Revolution was a bloodless one, though there was subsequently some fighting in ▷ Ireland and Scotland. The consequences of the event were that the passionate religious and political disagreements which had so divided the nation since the beginning of the 17th century were greatly lessened, and a new temper of reasonable debate took their place; the change is typified by the *Letters concerning Toleration* (begun 1689) by the philosopher ▷ John Locke.
▷ Exclusion Bills.

Glover, Richard (1712–85)
Member of ▷ Parliament for Weymouth (1761–8), and author of epics and plays. His ▷ ballad 'Hosier's Ghost', which attacked the naval policy of the ▷ Walpole government, was printed in ▷ Thomas Percy's *Reliques.*

Glyndŵr, Owain (? 1354–? 1416)
A Welsh chieftain who rebelled against ▷ Henry IV of England, and for a time ruled most of ▷ Wales. He was eventually defeated by Henry's son, the future ▷ Henry V. Glyndŵr is a character in Shakespeare's play ▷ *Henry IV, Part I* as an ally of the English rebel Hotspur. He is there presented as a boastful poet and mystic, such being reputed qualities of the Welsh.

***Goblin Market and Other Poems* (1862)**
The first published collection of poems by ▷ Christina Rossetti. The title poem is a narrative concerning two sisters; Laura, who succumbs to the temptation to eat the luscious fruit of the rapacious goblin men which she pays for with a lock of her hair, and Lizzie, who saves her from the physical and psychological decline of unassuaged addiction by seeking out the goblins' fruit but refusing to consume it herself. Enraged by her resistance, the goblins press the fruit on to her body. When Laura eats and drinks the fruit from Lizzie it acts as an antidote, the goblins' power is defeated and she is cured. The poem is a rich blend of fantasy, allegory, fairytale and Victorian Christian morality, erotically suggestive and linguistically complex. It has generated much psychoanalytic and feminist criticism, being interpreted as a ▷ lesbian fantasy, a female myth and a poem concerned with women's relationship to language. It is Rossetti's most famous work and a strong and sinister Victorian evocation of desire, fear and compulsion.

Other notable poems in the collection include the enigmatic and elusive 'Echo', 'Winter: My Secret', and 'A Triad', in which Rossetti criticizes the amatory possibilities available to women. The collection established Rossetti as a significant voice in Victorian poetry.
Bib: Moers, E., *Literary Women*; Mermin, D., 'Heroic Sisterhood in *Goblin Market*', *Victorian Poetry*, 21 (1983), 107–18; Galligani Casey, J., 'The Potential of Sisterhood: Christina Rossetti's *Goblin Market*', *Victorian Poetry*, 29 (1991), 63–78; Leighton, A., *Victorian Women Poets: Writing Against the Heart.*

Godber, John (b 1956)
Dramatist and director. The son of a miner, Godber began writing short stories for Radio Sheffield at the age of sixteen, trained as a teacher and taught for five years, while doing postgraduate work in drama at the University of Leeds. He is most closely associated with the Hull Truck Theatre Co, of which he has been artistic director since 1984. His involvement with Hull Truck is an expression of his commitment to a 'genuinely serious popular theatre' and also to a theatre outside London.

Most of his plays are social comedies which take place in public arenas and are generally concerned with what Godber has called 'working class leisure activities'; *Up 'N' Under* (1984) and *Cramp* (1986) both take a sport as their central device. Intensely physical pieces of theatre, they draw heavily on caricature for effect as do *Bouncers* (1985) and *Putting on the Ritz* (1987), both of which are set in discos. *Up 'N' Under* uses rugby league as a means of exploring the contradictions of machismo and the energy and resources devoted to the game. It also becomes a powerful image of resources that have gone to waste in contemporary Britain (body building is used similarly in *Cramp*). *Bouncers*, similarly, adopts a fairly ambivalent stance towards its macho, working class characters. It has been produced on both the east and west coasts of the U.S.A., as well as in Australia, Germany, Belgium and Israel. Other plays include: *On the Piste* (1993) and *April in Paris* (1994)

Godwin, William (1756–1836)
Philosopher and novelist. His central belief was that reason was sufficient to guide the conduct, not merely of individuals but also of all society. His principal work was *The Inquiry concerning Political Justice* (1793). Man he believed to be innately good and, under guidance of reason, capable of living without laws or control. Punishments he declared (at a time when the English penal system was one of the severest in Europe) to be unjust; as were the accumulation of property and the institution of marriage. The Prime Minister, ▷ William Pitt (the Younger), decided that the book was too expensive to be dangerous. Godwin's best-known novel came out in 1794: *Caleb Williams* was written to demonstrate the power for injustice accessible to the privileged classes. Godwin was a brave man, not merely with the pen; but his naivety as a thinker would have left him without influence if his opinions had not agreed so well with the more extreme currents of feeling provoked by the contemporary ▷ French Revolution. As it was, he influenced a number of better minds, including, for a very short time, the poet ▷ Coleridge and, for a much longer period, ▷ Shelley, who became his son-in-law. Godwin's wife was ▷ Mary Wollstonecraft, an early propagandist for the rights of women and authoress of *A Vindication of the Rights of Woman* (1792).

Goethe, Johann Wolfgang von (1749–1832)
German poet; the greatest European man of letters of his time. His fame was due not only to the wide scope of his imaginative creation, but to the many-sidedness and massive independence of his personality. From 1770 to 1788 he was an inaugurator and leader of the passionate outbreak known in German as the *Sturm und Drang* – 'storm and stress'– movement, but from 1788 (after his visit to Italy) he represented to the world a balanced harmony inspired by the classicism he had found there. But he did not lose his sense that the spirit is free to find its own fulfilment according to its own principle of growth. At the same time, from 1775 he was prominent in the affairs of the German principality of Weimar (whose prince was his friend), concerning himself with practical sciences useful to the state, and thence with a serious study of botany and other natural and physical sciences to the point of making significant contributions to scientific thought. His commanding mind was admired in France, England, and Italy, with whose literatures Goethe was in touch; he corresponded with ▷ Byron, and ▷ Walter Scott translated his *Goetz von Berlichingen*, which dated from the romantic phase of Goethe's career.

Goethe is most famous for his double drama of ▷ *Faust*, but other works that became famous in England include the romantic drama already mentioned; the epic *Hermann and Dorothea*; a study in Romantic sensibility *The Sorrows of Young Werther*; the novel *Wilhelm Meister*, and a large body of ▷ lyrical verse.

▷ German influence on English literature.

Gogol, Nikolai Vasilyevich (1809–52)
Playwright, novelist and short story writer, Gogol was born in the Ukraine. He worked as a civil service clerk in St Petersburg, which he hated, but made notes for future use in the portrayal of characters. He was a brilliant but unbalanced man, suffering hallucinations and prone to religious extremism. At one stage he walked everywhere sideways, keeping his back to the wall for fear of being stabbed, and he had a pathological fear of eternal damnation. He admired Shakespeare, ▷ Henry Fielding and ▷ Laurence Sterne among others, and is thought to have greatly influenced Dostoevsky. His first collection of stories was *Evenings at a Farmhouse Near Dikana* (1831–2) which describe Ukranian country life. *Taras Bulba* (1834) has a Cossack tale as its title story, and *Mirgorod* and *Arabeski* followed in 1835. The play, *The Government Inspector* (1836) is a savage satire of civil servants and bureaucracy. His St Petersburg stories, including 'Nevsky Prospekt', 'Notes of a Madman' and 'The Portrait' (1835), 'The Nose' (1836) and 'The Greatcoat' (1842), have a surreal quality. The farce *Marriage* (1842) was successful. *Dead Souls* (1842), begun in Italy, combines satire, humour and brilliant characterization, but during increasing bouts of religious fervour, Gogol burnt the manuscript of the second part, along with further manuscripts. *Selected Passages from Correspondance with Friends* (1847), for which he was rebuked, was an attempt to convey his moral scruples. His work is remarkable for the power of his language and imagination.

Golden Age
▷ Ages, Golden, Silver, etc.

***Golden Bowl, The* (1904)**
A novel by ▷ Henry James. The theme is the relationship of four people: the American millionaire collector, Adam Verver; his daughter, Maggie; the Italian prince, Amerigo, whom Verver acquires as a husband for his daughter; and Charlotte Stant, whom Maggie acquires as a wife for her widowed father. To the grief of the father and the daughter Charlotte seduces the prince into becoming her lover; the story is about the defeat of Charlotte, and Maggie's recovery of the prince's affections.

The novel belongs to James' last phase, which some critics consider to be his best, and other consider to show an excessive obliquity of style. The language of the characters is charged with feeling and yet disciplined by their civilized restraint and their fear of degrading themselves and one another by damaging explicitness. It is a measure of their indirectness that the affair between the prince and Charlotte is never actually mentioned between the father and the daughter. Behind the conflict of personalities there is the theme of the clash between European and American kinds of values and consciousness; this theme is conspicuous in James' early novels, and he returned to it in his last period after a middle phase in which he was chiefly concerned with the European, and particularly the English, scene.

Golden Legend, The
A medieval collection of lives of the saints, sermons, religious commentaries, etc., begun in the 13th century. It was printed by the first English printer, ▷ William Caxton.

***Golden Notebook, The* (1962)**
Novel by ▷ Doris Lessing, an important ▷ feminist text despite its author's reservations about such a categorization. The novel is a relatively early example of the multiple narratives, indeterminacy and paradox which characterize ▷ post-modernist fiction. A series of realist episodes (entitled 'free women') from the lives of two women friends, Anna and Molly, are interspersed with excerpts from the four notebooks – red, yellow, blue and black – in which Anna records different aspects of her life and thought, including a novel that she is writing. The book culminates in a transformation of the self through traumatic mental breakdown, recorded in the final golden notebook: an important example of the feminist theme of mental disturbance as a reaction against social constraint or the oppression of a given feminine role. The conclusion of *The Golden Notebook* involves a ▷ *mise en abyme*, as different narrative levels seem to contradict each other.

Golding, Arthur (?1536–1605)
Translator. Golding's chief work was an important translation of ▷ Ovid's *Metamorphoses* (1565–67) that was instrumental in promoting knowledge of Ovidian subjects and forms in England.

Golding, Sir William (1911–93)
Novelist. His novels are: *Lord of the Flies* (1954; filmed 1963); *The Inheritors* (1955); *Pincher Martin* (1956); *The Spire* (1964); *The Pyramid* (1967); *Darkness Visible* (1979); *Rites of Passage* (1980); *The Paper Men* (1984); *Close Quarters* (1987); *Fire Down Below* (1989). *Sometime, Never* (1956) and *The Scorpion God* (1971) are collections of novellas. He has also written a play, *The Brass Butterfly* (1958), and published two collections of essays, *The Hot Gates* (1965) and *A Moving Target* (1982).

No novelist who started his career since 1945 has achieved more prestige, and this was acquired very quickly on the publication of his first book, *Lord of the Flies*. Its fame has no doubt been in part due to its pessimistic vision of human nature as inherently violent, reflecting the mood of the post-war and post-Hitler years; it also epitomizes mid-20th-century disillusionment with 19th-century optimism about human nature. Golding's father (see 'The Ladder and the Tree' in *The Hot Gates*) was a schoolmaster with radical convictions in politics, a belief that religion is outmoded superstition, and a strong faith in science. Golding's own work is strongly, but not explicitly, religious, in the Puritan tradition which emphasizes Original Sin. In 'Fable' (*The Hot Gates*) he explains how his first novel arose from his insights in the last war: 'Anyone who moved through those years without understanding that man produces evil as a bee produces honey, must have been blind or wrong in the head.' The book is also meant to counteract what may be called 'the desert island myth' in English literature, deriving from ▷ Daniel Defoe's ▷ *Robinson Crusoe*, and particularly evident in a famous book for boys, *The Coral Island* (1857) by R. M. Ballantyne. This myth nourished the belief that human beings in isolation from civilized restraints will sustain their humanity by innate virtues. Most of the boys in *Lord of the Flies* quickly degenerate into savages, and the process is made more horrifying by the convincing delineation of the characters: Golding, like his father, has been a schoolmaster. His later novels have shown variety of theme and treatment, but similar preoccupation with fundamental corruption and contradiction in human nature. They show, likewise, Golding's most conspicuous literary qualities: great inventiveness in realistic fantasy, and a disposition to use the novel form as fable. For instance, *The Inheritors* is ▷ science fiction about the remote human past: the elimination of innocent Neanderthal Man by the arrival of rapacious Homo Sapiens – a new version of the myth of the Fall. *Pincher Martin* is a dramatization of this rapacity in an individual, and a spectacular example of fantasy presented within the conventions of realism. *The Spire* shows comparable ingenuity used quite differently: it describes the building of the spire of Salisbury Cathedral and dramatizes the conflict between faith and reason. *Rites of Passage* (which won the Booker Prize) employs a characteristic shift of perspective: the narrow viewpoint of the narrator, a snobbish young aristocrat on a voyage to Australia in the early 19th century, is undermined by his gradual understanding of the devastating experiences of an awkward but sincere clergyman. The story of the voyage is continued in *Close Quarters* and *Fire Down Below* and the trilogy was collected, with revisions, as *To The Ends of the Earth* (1991). Golding received the Nobel Prize for literature in 1983 and was knighted in 1988.

Bib: Gregor, I., and Kinkead-Weekes, M., *William Golding: a Critical Study*; Johnston, A., *Of Earth and Darkness*; Medcalf, S., *William Golding*.

Goldoni, Carlo (1707–93)
Italian dramatist, much influenced by ▷ Molière and the ▷ *commedia dell'arte*, who in turn influenced the English stage. He wrote some 250 comedies, tragedies, tragi-comedies and opera librètti in French, Italian and his native Venetian dialect. He reformed the Italian theatre, modernizing both the language and the action of the drama, and increasingly reflecting middle and even lower-class values and taste, so as to bring the stage closer to its audience. He adapted the *commedia dell'arte* to make it more socially relevant, and contributed to the emerging *opera buffa*, a form of comic opera without spoken dialogue. Among Goldoni's most famous pieces are *La Locandiera* (*The Mistress of the Inn*), *and* I Due Gemelli Veneziani (*The Venetian Twins*), written between 1748–52, and *Arlecchino. Servitore di Due Patroni* (*Harlequin, the Servant of Two Masters*) (1753). In 1761 he became attached to the French court, where he stayed until the Revolution (▷ French Revolution).
▷ Italian influence on English literature.

Goldsmith, Oliver (1730–74)
Dramatist, novelist, essayist, and poet. Born in Ireland, he studied at Trinity College, Dublin, but ran away to Cork after being disciplined by his tutor. He returned, however, and graduated in 1749. He applied for ordination, but was rejected, then was given 50 pounds to study for the law, but gambled it away. After this, he studied medicine at Edinburgh and at Leyden but it is unclear whether he obtained the medical degree to which he later laid claim. In 1756 he came to London, penniless, and supported himself with a variety of occupations, including messenger, teacher, apothecary's assistant, usher, and ▷ hack writer for a periodical.

In 1758 he translated Marteilhe's *Memoirs of a Protestant, Condemned to the Galleys of France for His Religion* and in 1759 his *Enquiry into the Present State of Polite Learning in Europe*. His 'Chinese Letters', written for John Newbery's *The Public Ledger* (1760–1) were reissued in 1762 as ▷ *The Citizen of the World*, a satiric view of England written from the supposed viewpoint of a Chinaman. His first real success as a writer was with the poem 'The Traveller', published in 1764. A number of his works are now highly valued, including *A Citizen of the World*; his life of ▷ Beau Nash (1762); his novel, ▷ *The Vicar of Wakefield*; a poem, ▷ *The Deserted Village*; and the plays ▷ *The Good Natur'd Man* (1768), and ▷ *She Stoops to Conquer* (1773) written, like the plays of ▷ Richard Brinsley Sheridan, in reaction to the sentiment of many plays of the period, and with the intention to revive the spirit of Restoration comedy. He wrote much else, including histories of England, Greece and Rome, and biographies of Voltaire, ▷ Bolingbroke and ▷ Parnell.

Goldsmith was a friend of ▷ David Garrick and ▷ Samuel Johnson, and figures largely in ▷ James Boswell's *Life of Johnson* (1791). Johnson praised his writing for its 'clarity and elegance', and later generations have repeatedly praised his literary 'charm', a quality made up of humour, modesty, vitality, and graceful lucidity. These he combined with the ▷ Augustan properties of balance and proportion. He died of a fever, deeply in debt, and the Literary Club (▷ Club, The) which he had helped to found in 1764 erected a monument to him in Westminster Abbey. Garrick wrote an ▷ epitaph to comment on his greatness as an author and reputed failings in other areas: 'Here lies Nolly Goldsmith, for shortness called Noll, Who wrote like an angel, but talked like poor Poll'.

Bib: Forster, J., and Wardle, R. M. *Lives*; Balderston, K. B. (ed.), *Letters*; Ginger, J., *The Notable Man*; Danziger, M. K., *Oliver Goldsmith and Richard Brinsley Sheridan*; Swarbrick, A. (ed.), *The Art of Oliver Goldsmith*.

Goliardic
A descriptive term applied to a satirical and profane kind of Latin poetry, allegedly produced in the 12th and 13th centuries by a class of clerical writers known as goliards, named after a certain 'Golias' (whose own name derives perhaps from the Latin word for glutton '*gula*'). The notion of such a company of poets seems to be a literary myth.

Goncourt, Edmond Louis Antonine Huot de (1822–96) and Jules Alfred Huot de (1830–70)
The brothers, novelists, historians and art critics, of an old Lorraine family, collected books, pictures, manuscripts and furnishings, collaborating on several books of history and art criticism. They wrote novels which are now not much read but helped make literary history, originating the '*roman documentaire*' with its painstaking naturalistic detail, believing novelists should write 'history which might have happened'. After Jules' death, Edmond wrote some further novels and the famous *Journal des Goncourt* which portrayed literary life in Paris 1851–96. The Académie Goncourt was founded under the terms of Edmond's will; it awards the annual Prix Goncourt for imaginative prose. *Germinie Lacerteux* (1864) details the history of their maid, faithfully serving while living a life of vice and debauchery. Other novels include *Soeur Philomène* (1861) and *Madam Gervaisais* (1869). Non-fiction includes *L'Art du dix-huitième siècle* (1859–75) and *Portraits intimes du dix-huitième siècle* (1857). Novels written by Edmond alone include *Les Frères Zemganno* (1879), *La Faustin* (1882) and *Chérie* (1884).

Gondal
An imaginary world created by ▷ Emily and ▷ Anne Brontë around 1834 when they broke away from ▷ Charlotte and Branwell, who were engaged in the creation of ▷ Angria. None of the prose writings of Gondal survive, although many of Emily's poems take on the persona of a Gondal character such as Augusta Geraldine Almeda or Julius Brenzaida. Gondal continued to be a source of imaginative engagement for Emily and Anne as late as 1845, when Emily was twenty-seven and Anne twenty-five.
Bib: Ratchord, F., *Gondal's Queen*.

Gooch, Elizabeth Sarah (b 1756)
Novelist, poet and autobiographer. Elizabeth Gooch's most fascinating work is her ▷ autobiography, *Life* (1792), partly because of the difficulties she encountered and the sordid world she was forced to live in, but mainly because of the rapid-paced narrative and her penchant for vivid sensationalism. She was the daughter of a Portuguese Jewish father who died when she was three, and her stepfather never fully accepted her into his family. She was sent to school at Fountains Abbey where she entered into a romance, which was thwarted. Following this she was 'married off' to William Gooch who was more interested in her dowry than in showing her any real affection. It was not long before Gooch accused her of adultery and sent her to France, where she became a prostitute. The subsequent years saw a series of escapades in which she acted on stage, fled from debtors, disguised herself as a man so as to follow her lover into battle, and persistently tried to wring money out of her embarrassed family. By 1788 she was in prison, from where she wrote *Appeal to the Public*. Gooch's later life is obscure, but several novels and a biography of Thomas Bellamy, all written between 1795 and 1800, remain.

***Good* (1981)**
D. C. P. Taylor's last play was notable for its willingness to confront the banality of evil in its study of its protagonist's gradual drift into Nazism through all the daily minor compromises, adjustments and accommodations which take him from being an emotional advocate of euthanasia in his fiction to advising on giving the Final Solution a caring façade. We can see the terrible seductive power of Nazism as something which offers the protagonist (given a fine performance by Alan Howard in the original RSC production) the possibility of a fixed position in a sea of moral uncertainties and doubts. The idea that public postures have the configuration of private derangements achieves a memorable form: throughout the play he is haunted by snatches of music, so that the discovery that the prisoners' band which greets him at Auschwitz is real represents his complete surrender to the inverted logic of the Third Reich.

Goodman's Fields Theatres
The first Goodman's Fields Theatre of which any details survive was opened by theatre manager and dramatist Thomas Odell (1691–1749) in Whitechapel in 1729, and lasted intermittently until 1751; another theatre by the same name was opened by ▷ Henry Giffard in Ayliff Street in 1733. Like several other theatres this was ordered to close in 1737 under the terms of the Licensing Act (▷ theatres), but continued performances at the fringe of the law until 1741, the year of ▷ David Garrick's professional debut at this venue as ▷ Richard III. The theatre became a warehouse, and burned down in 1802. The present building dates from 1812.

***Good-Natur'd man, The* (1768)**
▷ Oliver Goldsmith's first play, a ▷ satire on genteel or sentimental commedy (▷ sentiment) and contemporary theories of benevolence. Young Mr Honeywood, the eponymous good-natured man, is so afraid of hurting or offending others that he entirely neglects his own interest. He runs himself into debt in order to treat his supposed friends, and even woos Miss Richland, whom he himself loves, on behalf of the vain and scoundrelly Jack Lofty, falsely believing him to be a man of honour. Honeywood's uncle, Sir William Honeywood, whose own good nature is far more discerning, vows to teach him a lesson, and arranges for bailiffs to arrest him. Miss Richland secretly pays his debts, and he is finally shamed into admitting the folly of his behaviour, while his uncle admonishes him to respect himself, for 'He who seeks only for applause from without, has all his happiness in another's keeping'.

In a related plot Miss Richland's guardian, Nicholas Croaker, wishes to force her and his son Leontine to marry. They are equally reluctant: Miss Richland loves Honeywood, while Leontine loves Olivia, whom he has brought to England masquerading as his long-departed sister as she in turn evades another odious guardian. They attempt to elope, but are discovered. Eventually all turns out well, and the various pairs of lovers are united.

The play was originally produced at ▷ Covent Garden, with the part of Sir William being played by ▷ Garrick. But at its first performance the bailiffs' scene was hissed by the audience as too 'low'. The scene was cut for a time, and the play became a success.

Gorboduc, or Ferrex and Porrex
A tragic drama by ▷ Thomas Norton (1552–84) and ▷ Thomas Sackville. The story is taken from British legendary history; the immediate source is Grafton's *Chronicle* (1556) but this in turn derives from the 12th-century ▷ *Historia*

Regum Britanniae (*History of the Kings of Britain*) by ▷ Geoffrey of Monmouth. It is the first play to be written in ▷ blank verse, and is modelled on the tragedies of ▷ Seneca.

Gorboduc is a king of Britain. His reign has been a prosperous one, when he decides to retire from government and divide his kingdom between his two sons, Ferrex and Porrex. He carries out the division against the advice of his wisest councillor. Jealousy and distrust between the two brothers break into civil war, which ends in the death of both and a rising of the whole people, who slay Gorboduc and his queen. The country is saved from final ruin only by Fergus, Duke of Albany, who, with the aid of other nobles, succeeds in restoring order under single sovereignty.

The drama has slight literary value of its own, but it has considerable historical significance. Sackville and Norton were eminent politicians who foresaw great dangers to the kingdom if ▷ Queen Elizabeth I should die without heirs. The play was first acted before the queen in 1562 and is plainly designed as a warning to her against leaving her kingdom exposed to disunity. The authors are thus using history (or legend, which was not clearly distinguished from history) as later and greater dramatists were to use it, notably ▷ Shakespeare: that is to say, as a storehouse of political lessons that could be applied to the politics of their own time. The theme of the divided kingdom resembles one of the greatest of Shakespeare's tragedies, ▷ *King Lear*, which deals with the situation in far profounder terms. The Senecan model also anticipates later Elizabethan taste, and the use of blank verse was the starting-point for the rich development of the medium by ▷ Marlowe and Shakespeare. Apart from Seneca, a literary influence upon the writers is the collection of tragic tales ▷ *A Mirror for Magistrates* (1559), to which Sackville made the most memorable contribution. This also used legend and history, recounted in a solemn style, to warn and edify contemporary courtiers and public men. The Senecan solemnity and formality of *Gorboduc* gave it peculiar dignity for the contemporary public, raising it above the (often much more lively) style of the familiar ▷ interludes and comedies of the day, and giving it the requisite impressiveness to influence the queen. It is not known what she thought of it, but ▷ Sir Philip Sidney excepted it from his general condemnation of the English drama of his day, and wrote in his *Apologie for Poetrie*: 'it is full of stately speeches, and well sounding phrases, climbing to the height of Seneca's style, and as full of notable morality . . . ' However, he goes on to complain of its failure to observe the so-called ▷ Aristotelian unities of space and time.

Gordimer, Nadine (b 1923)
South African novelist and short-story writer. She has won an international reputation and numerous prizes, including the Booker Prize for *The Conservationist* (1974). Much of her work is concerned with the situation of white middle-class liberals in South Africa, privileged by a system to which they are opposed, the relations of the private self to the political, and the failure of liberal compromise. Her work has become progressively bleaker and more disillusioned. In *A World of Strangers* (1958) she uses the perspective of an outsider coming to South Africa, while *The Conservationist* is written from the viewpoint of a rich and conservative capitalist, and employs symbolic elements in its treatment of the struggle for the control of the land. In 1991 she won the Nobel Prize for literature. Her other novels are: *The Lying Days* (1953); *Occasion for Loving* (1963); *The Late Bourgeois World* (1966); *A Guest of Honour* (1970); *Burger's Daughter* (1979); *July's People* (1981); *A Sport of Nature* (1987); *My Son's Story* (1990); and *None to Accompany Me* (1994). Story collections include: *Selected Stories* (1975); *Some Monday For Sure* (1976); *A Soldier's Embrace* (1980); *Town and Country Lovers* (1980); *Something Out There* (1984); *Jump* (1991).
Bib: Heywood, C., *Nadine Gordimer*; Clingman, S., *The Novels of Nadine Gordimer: History from the Inside*.

Gordon riots
Riots in London in 1780, led by Lord George Gordon against a law passed in 1778 to relieve the condition of Roman ▷ Catholics. The riots form the climax of ▷ Charles Dickens' novel ▷ *Barnaby Rudge*.

Gore, Catherine Grace Frances (1799–1861)
Born Moody, the daughter of a wine merchant in East Retford, Nottinghamshire, Catherine Gore showed literary ability at an early age and was nicknamed 'the Poetess' by her peers. She wrote some 70 novels between 1824 and 1862, of the 'silver-fork school'; novels of fashionable and wealthy life. They include *Theresa Marchmont or the Maid of Honour* (1824), *Manners of the Day, or Woman as the game* (1830), which was praised by George IV, *Mothers and Daughters* (1830), *Mrs Armytage: or Female Domination* (1836), possibly her best, *Cecil, or the Adventures of a Coxcomb* (1841) and *The Banker's Wife, or Court and City* (1843), which was dedicated to Sir John Dean Paul, portrayed as a swindler, as he in fact turned out to be in 1855 when Gore lost £20,000. She also wrote poems, plays – *The School for Coquettes* (1831), *Quid pro Quo or the Day of Dupes* (1844) – and short stories, and composed music. Her writing is characterized by shrewd observation and perceptive insight, together with satire and invention, and gives an interesting portrait of life in a certain class and time.

Gosse, Sir Edmund (William) (1849–1928)
Critic, biographer and poet. He is especially known for his ▷ autobiography *Father and Son* (1907), one of the classic works for interpreting the Victorian age. He was born in London, the son of Philip H. Gosse, a distinguished zoologist and devout member of the Plymouth Brethren. Privately educated, he worked as a librarian, at the British Museum and later at the House of Lords, a translator and a lecturer at Cambridge University. A central figure in London literary life, he was friends with ▷ Swinburne, ▷ Robert Louis Stevenson, ▷ Thomas Hardy and ▷ Henry James. As a critic he was one of the first to introduce ▷ Ibsen to the English stage and translated two of his plays, *Hedda Gabler* (1891) and *The Master Builder* (with ▷ William Archer, 1893). He wrote a number of critical studies of 17th-century literature, a biography of Swinburne and a study of Ibsen.

Gosson, Stephen (1554–1624)
Preacher and pamphleteer. Stephen Gosson's chief claim to a measure of literary fame is due to his being the author of *The Schoole of Abuse* (1579), a ▷ pamphlet attacking poetry and drama which is said to have occasioned ▷ Philip Sidney's ▷ *An Apologie for Poetrie*. Ironically, Gosson's career had begun as a dramatist, but he underwent a religious conversion and became a fierce Puritan critic of the drama. *The Schoole of Abuse*, if it has a somewhat nebulous relationship to the development of Sidney's critical text, nevertheless did call forth a response from ▷ Thomas Lodge, who replied to Gosson with his *A Reply to Stephen Gosson Touching Plays* (1579). Gosson, in turn, replied to Lodge with his *Plays Confuted in Five Actions* (1582). This interchange, though it added little of substance to dramatic criticism, is itself part of the continuing English debate in the 16th and 17th centuries concerning the corrupting or otherwise influence of drama.
Bib: Ringer, W. A., *Stephen Gosson: A Biographical and Critical Study*.

Gothic
A term for the style of architecture which dominated western Europe in the Middle Ages. Its main features were the pointed arch and the ribbed vault. In England, this period is divided into three: Early English (13th century), Decorated (14th) and Perpendicular (15th-16th). A fine example of the last is King's College Chapel, Cambridge.
▷ Gothic revival.

Gothic novels
A genre of novels dealing with tales of the macabre and supernatural, which reached a height of popularity in the 1790s. The term 'Gothic' originally implied 'medieval', or rather a fantasized version of what was seen to be medieval. Later, 'Gothic' came to cover all areas of the fantastic and supernatural, and the characteristics of the genre are graveyards and ghosts.

▷ Walpole's ▷ *The Castle of Otranto* is generally seen as the earliest Gothic novel. ▷ 'Monk' Lewis, ▷ William Beckford and ▷ Mrs Radcliffe are notable exploiters of the genre. The vogue for Gothic novels soon produced parodies; Thomas Love Peacock's ▷ *Nightmare Abbey* and ▷ Jane Austen's ▷ *Northanger Abbey* are among the best examples.

In the 19th century, ▷ Mary Shelley and the ▷ Brontës show the influence of the tradition. Today, the hugely successful horror novels of Stephen King (and many others) may be said to represent an affectionate modification of the Gothic novel tradition.
Bib: Baldick, C., *In Frankenstein's Shadow*; Ellis, K.F., *The Contested Castle: Gothic Novels and the Subversion of Domestic Ideology*; Meade, T., *The English Gothic Novel*; Milbank, A., *Daughters of the House*.

Gothic revival
An architectural style now chiefly associated with the reign of Queen Victoria (1837–1901). However, a taste for Gothic had in fact started in the 18th century with ▷ Horace Walpole's design of his home, Strawberry Hill (1747). The taste for Gothic spread between 1750 and 1830; it grew with the popularity of the sensationalism of the ▷ Gothic novel. In the 18th century, the taste for Gothic tended to be fanciful and sensational rather than deeply serious, although it gained seriousness from such a publication as ▷ Thomas Percy's *Reliques*; the 19th-century ▷ Romantic revival, especially the novels of ▷ Walter Scott, produced a deeper and much more genuine feeling for the ▷ Middle Ages. In poetry and fiction, ▷ Tennyson's revival of Arthurian legend in ▷ *Idylls of the King*, can be ascribed to a prevailing neo-Gothic appeal to the imagination. But in the 1870s, a reaction set in: neo-Gothic architectural styles were succeeded by a return to classicism, generally known as the new 'Queen Anne' style, though it was often much more eclectic and exuberant.
▷ Medieval literature.

Governesses
The governess was a familiar figure to Victorians, as she is to readers of ▷ *Jane Eyre* and *Agnes Grey* today. Governesses were drawn from the ranks of the middle classes; from families whose economic circumstances demanded that their daughters seek employment, yet remain respectable. The range of professions deemed suitable for middle-class women narrowed during the early 19th century so that by the Victorian period governessing was virtually the only path

open to them. Pay and conditions, however, were often poor, as the ▷ Brontë novels testify. In 1841 a Governesses' Benevolent Institution was founded to assist the unemployed and needy. It was increasingly recognized that the 'plight' of the governess was a social problem, and many periodical essayists addressed the issue during the 1840s. It was the governess's status as a middle-class woman that fired such concern; no similar attention was directed to working-class women's conditions of employment. The preoccupation with the figure of the governess was crucially linked to the ideal of womanhood that she was supposed to embody and reproduce in her charges. The anomaly of her position was that at the same time as she ideally conformed to all the standards of middle-class femininity, she was competing for jobs in the marketplace and therefore threatened to undermine the ethos of separate spheres of activity for women and men upon which Victorian society depended. Practically as well as ideologically she was often in a difficult position – barely educated herself yet required to teach others. The need for governesses to be better informed led to a series of evening lectures held at King's College, London, in 1847. These fed directly into the campaign for higher education for women, and in 1848 Queen's College for women was founded in London.

▷ Hall, Anna Maria; Jameson, Anna; Education of Women; *Deerbrook*; *Lady Audley's Secret*; *Shirley*; *Villette*; *Ruth*.

Gower, John (?1330–1408)
Poet. Only a tentative outline can be established of Gower's life. His family had Yorkshire origins and Kent connections (Gower's language bears traces of Kentish influence and he bought lands there in 1378). A reference in one of his works suggests he had a training in law, a point confirmed by other documentary evidence. Gower seems to have been based in London for most of his life. By 1398, and perhaps for some time earlier, he was living in the priory of St Mary Overy (now Southwark Cathedral), where he was buried.

He wrote extensively in three languages, French, Latin and English. Before 1374 he composed his *Cinkante Balades* and some time between 1376 and 1378 he produced the *Mirour de l'Omme*, another French work, written in octosyllabic 12-line stanzas, tackling the subject of fallen man, his vices and virtues. His Latin poem, *Vox Clamantis* (*The Voice of One Crying*), composed c 1379–81, addresses the subject of political governance and, more specifically, the disturbances of the reign of Richard II (notably the ▷ Peasant's Revolt). In his major English poem, the ▷ *Confessio Amantis*, Gower turned from overtly political and satirical subjects to take a middle way, 'somwhat of lust, somwhat of lore', recounting the experiences of a lover's confession and instruction. But here too Gower's concern with the ethics of government of self and society is very evident. His anti-war sentiments are clearly expressed in his later English poem, addressed to ▷ Henry IV, *In Praise of Peace*.

In the colophon added to the *Confessio Amantis*, Gower suggests that his major works should be seen as a triptych, as 'three books of instructive material'. His evident ambition to figure as a moral commentator and watchman of his times, and to be remembered as such, was fulfilled. His literary reputaton in the century following his death was high, and his name frequently coupled with that of ▷ Chaucer as a founding figure of the English poetic tradition. He is represented as a figure of old poetic authority in ▷ Shakespeare's play ▷ *Pericles* (which reworks the story of Apollonius of Tyre, drawn from Gower's *Confessio Amantis*). However, from the 18th century onwards, there seems to have been a decline in interest in his work and his literary reputation has only revived in recent years.

▷ Henry IV

Bib: Fisher, J. H., *John Gower: moral philosopher and friend of Chaucer*; Macaulay, G. C. (ed.), *The Works of John Gower, The English Works of John Gower*.

***Grace Abounding to the Chief of Sinners* (1666)**
The spiritual ▷ autobiography of ▷ John Bunyan, author of ▷ *The Pilgrim's Progress*. The torments undergone by Christian in the latter book are substantially those of Bunyan in the earlier one. Bunyan had a similar spiritual awakening to Christian's, being aroused by a book; he suffers the terrible conviction of sin, like Christian; he believes himself to commit the sin of blasphemy as Christian thinks he does in the Valley of the shadow of Death; at last he achieves confidence in God's mercy. Much of the narrative is an account of painful mental conflict; but Bunyan never lost the sanity of perception into the fanaticism and mental morbidity of others, such as the old man who told him that he had certainly committed the sin against the Holy Ghost (for which there is no forgiveness). The book records how he developed that compassionate understanding of other men's spiritual conflicts which makes *The Pilgrim's Progress* the antecedent of the great English novels.

Graham, W. S. (William Sidney) (1918–86)
Poet. Graham was born in Scotland (▷ Scottish literature) into a working-class family and grew up on Clydeside where he trained and worked as an engineer. His early poetry was immediately associated with ▷ Dylan Thomas and the 'apocalyptic' poetry of the 1940s – Graham's first collection was characteristically energetic and vibrant. Much of his later life was spent around St Ives, in Cornwall, a situation that

put him in contact with many of the important post-war British painters. Just as Cornwall's seascapes provided a rich source of metaphor and imagery for Graham's struggles with the opacity of language, so its equally craggy inhabitants fed his essentially Scottish wit, and later his talent for elegy. Along with ▷ David Gascoyne and ▷ George Barker, Graham wrote in a powerfully neo-Romantic style about problems of personal identity. Temporarily obscured from view by the achievements and tastes of the ▷ Movement, their poetry is among the strongest in English this century. Graham's most celebrated volume is *The Nightfishing* (1955); other works include *Malcolm Mooney's Land* (1970), *Collected Poems 1942–1977* (1979) and *Implements in their Places* (1977).
Bib: Lopez, T., *W. S. Graham.*

Grahame, Kenneth (1859–1932)
Children's writer and essayist. Grahame is remembered for his animal fable *The Wind in the Willows* (1908), which was based on stories made up for his son and which, after receiving little attention when first published, subsequently became a classic of ▷ children's fiction. Previously Grahame had contributed to ▷ *The Yellow Book* and had published several works primarily concerned with childhood experience: *Pagan Papers* (1893), *The Golden Age* (1895) and *Dream Days* (1898). He was born in Edinburgh, went to school in Oxford and worked in the Bank of England until 1908 when he retired because of ill-health.

Grail
A mysterious, sacred object of quest in Arthurian narratives which is represented and interpreted in different ways, but always linked to a conception of completion and wholeness of some kind. The Old French word 'graal' means a serving dish or platter, and in ▷ Chrétien de Troyes' romance of *Perceval*, the word is used of a richly bejewelled dish, carried by a maiden in the mysterious procession seen by ▷ Perceval in the castle of the wounded ▷ Fisher King. It transpires that this dish has life-giving and healing qualities, and the power to heal the wounded King and his Wasteland. Perceval, however, fails to release the healing power of the dish, because he fails to ask about the Grail. This dish seems to be related to the mysterious cauldrons which appear in Celtic legend and myth, which have the power to provide never-ending sources of nourishment.

▷ Robert de Boron's reworking of the Grail story (in the late 12th or early 13th century) gives an explicitly Christian interpretation to the key symbolic artefacts of the story, and provides the means of linking Arthurian history and Christian history. Here the Grail becomes the Holy Grail, and is identified with the chalice used by Christ at the Last Supper and later used by Joseph of Arimathea as the vessel to collect the blood from Christ's body at the Crucifixion. It is literally part of, and symbolically representative of, the Eucharist, a source of physical and spiritual food, and this material sign of transcendental life is kept by a series of Grail keepers, beginning with Joseph of Arimathea. In later developments of the Grail narrative, the Quest of the Holy Grail is the last and most marvellous adventure of ▷ Arthur's court, to be achieved by the Christ-knight ▷ Galahad, and the narrative becomes the vehicle for a rigorous criticism of the material values of earthly ▷ knighthood, and a celebration of a spiritual order of chivalry. Once the Grail quest has been achieved, neither the Grail knights nor the Grail itself return to Britain, and the future for Arthur's court and realm is only one of decline. The quest of the Holy Grail forms part of ▷ Malory's *Morte D'Arthur*, though in his version the criticism of the ethics and values of secular knighthood is somewhat modified. The Quest is treated rather less sympathetically by ▷ Tennyson in his ▷ *Idylls of the King*. ▷ T. S. Eliot draws on the multifaceted qualities of the Grail and its different modes of representation in Arthurian narrative, in his poetic exploration of the state of human culture ▷ *The Waste Land*.
Bib: Lacey, Norris J. et al. (eds.), *The Arthurian Encyclopaedia*.

Grammatology
This term is used by the French philosopher ▷ Jacques Derrida to denote 'a general science of writing'. As a scientific practice, its objective is to disturb the traditional hierarchical relationship between 'speech' and 'writing' where the latter is regarded as an instrument of the former. Derrida's 'science of writing' is an attempt to deconstruct (▷ Deconstruction) the metaphysical assumptions upon which the hierarchical relationship between speech and writing is based. He takes to the limit the Saussurean notion of the arbitrariness of the linguistic sign, arguing against a natural relationship between the spoken word and what it signifies.

Grand guignol
A term denoting an entertainment relying merely on sensational horror for its effect; after an old French puppet show.

Grand, Sarah (1854–1943)
▷ Pseudonym of novelist Frances McFall, née Clark. She was born in Donaghadee, County Down, and moved to Yorkshire after her father's death in 1861. At sixteen she married Major David McFall, a surgeon. She later left her husband and moved to London where she became involved in ▷ feminist activity. Her first novel was *Ideala* (1888), her second

▷ *The Heavenly Twins* (1893), which was a sensational success. It attacked the sexual double standard in marriage, called for emancipation and protested against the immorality of the Contagious Diseases Act. She is said to have coined the term ▷ 'New Woman' in 1894. In 1897 her semi-autobiographical novel *The Beth Book* appeared. In 1898 she became President of the Tunbridge Wells branch of the National Union of ▷ Women's Suffrage Societies, and between 1922 and 1929 was mayoress of Bath. She died in Bath at the age of 88.

▷ Women's Movement.

Bib: Kersley, G., *Darling Madame: a Portrait of Sarah Grand*; Cunningham, G., *The 'New Woman' and the Fiction of the 1890s*; Showalter, E., *A Literature of Their Own*.

Grant, Anne (1755–1838)
Poet, historian and letter-writer. Anne Grant (née Macvicar) was born in Glasgow, spent her childhood and teenage years in America, and returned to Britain in 1768 when she married Revd James Grant and retired with him to the Scottish Highlands. Most of Grant's work contains ▷ autobiographical elements, her *Memoirs of an American Lady* (1808) being the most clearly indebted to her own experiences of colonial life. Her *Poems* appeared in 1803 and focus on her observations of the Highland countryside and its society. Similar material emerged regularly in later works, such as *The Highlanders* (1808). There has been an attempt to reclaim Grant as an early feminist, though she herself attacked ▷ Mary Wollstonecraft in 1794 for claiming that women had equal intellectual powers, asserting vehemently the conventional view that women were clearly inferior to men.

▷ Scottish literature in English.

Granville-Barker, Harley (1877–1946)
Actor, producer, director, dramatist, dramatic critic. He began as an actor in 1891, but he achieved fame as a director (1904–21). He favoured the modern drama of ▷ Ibsen, ▷ Shaw and ▷ Galsworthy and did much to educate the public into accepting its often scandalizing themes drawn from contemporary social issues; in this he was much influenced by his close friendship with Shaw. However, his chief fame as a director was in his productions of ▷ Shakespeare. The previous generation of Shakespeare production, dominated by ▷ Henry Irving, had relied on the personalities of star actors, and Irving was continuing a tradition which went back to the 18th century. Granville-Barker concentrated on the production of the whole work, transferring the emphasis from the leading roles on to the speech and action of the entire cast. His own plays were in the Ibsen–Shaw tradition; the best known are *The Voysey Inheritance* (1905), *Waste* (which was forbidden by the censor) (1907), and *The Madras House* (1910).

In 1923 he became editor of *The Players' Shakespeare* for which he wrote prefaces to individual plays. The series was discontinued, but the prefaces were published, and because they have Granville-Barker's unique stage experience as a basis, they now constitute the crown of his reputation. However he was also a lifelong publicist for the idea of a ▷ National Theatre, which was not to be established until 1976.

Bib: Purdom, C. B., *Harley Granville-Barker, Man of the Theatre, Dramatist and Scholar*; Salmon, E., *Granville-Barker: A Secret Life*; Kennedy, D., *Granville-Barker and the Dream of Theatre*.

Graves, Richard (1715–1804)
Novelist. Graves was the rector of Claverton and a well-known figure in Bath society. He is best remembered for his novel *The Spiritual Quixote, or the Summer Rambles of Mr Geoffrey Wildgoose* (1773), which recounts the comic journeys of a Methodist preacher. The figure of Wildgoose satirizes the Methodist George Whitefield (1717–70) whom Graves had met during their student days at Oxford.

Bib: Hill, C. J., *The Literary Career of Graves*.

Graves, Robert (1895–1985)
Poet, critic, novelist. His poetry belongs to a distinctively English strain of lyrical verse which has been overshadowed by the more ambitious and more massive work of the Anglo-Irish ▷ W. B. Yeats and the American-born ▷ T. S. Eliot. Earlier representatives of this kind of verse were ▷ Thomas Hardy, Edward Thomas and the War poets such as ▷ Wilfred Owen, ▷ Siegfried Sassoon and ▷ Isaac Rosenberg. The development of Graves' work was decisively affected by his experiences as an officer in World War I, and understanding of it is helped by a reading of Owen and Sassoon. Such poetry was partly a means of preserving sanity in the face of extreme horror, partly a desire to awaken in the reader a distrust of attitudes imposed on him by convention, or adopted by himself to help him preserve his own illusions. Graves published his first poems during World War I, but he is not primarily one of the War poets; he extended the vision aroused by the war into the post-war world of human relations, especially those between the sexes, and into the impulses to self-deceive and to escape the realities of inner experience, especially by choosing to dull its image. He always wrote ▷ lyrics with skilful and precise rhythm and often poignant or pungent rhymes, and an austere yet lively, colloquial diction. A collected edition of his work was published in 1975.

As a critic he was at first a self-conscious

⊳ modernist; *A Survey of Modernist Poetry* (1927), written with the poet Laura Riding, educated the public in new kinds of poetic expression by a pioneering critical interest in subtleties and ambiguities of language. His later criticism has been less influential; it includes *The Common Asphodel* (1949), *The Crowning Privilege* (1955).

Graves engaged extensively in historical and anthropological enquiry; this resulted in work on poetry and primitive religion, *eg The White Goddess* (1948), which aroused controversy but was taken up by some ⊳ feminists in the 1960s and 70s, and in historical fiction of great popularity, *eg I, Claudius* and *Claudius the God* (1934). By far the most important of his prose works, however, is his ⊳ autobiography recounting his experiences in World War I – *Good-bye to All That* (1929).

Bib: Seymour Smith, M., *Robert Graves: His Life and Work*; Graves, R. P., *Robert Graves.*

Gray, Alasdair (b 1934)

Scottish novelist and short-story writer. Gray was educated at Glasgow Art School and works as an art teacher, painter and writer. His fiction is exuberant in style although often bleak in content, employing fantasy, myth, parable, allusion (certain of his texts include an index of plagiarisms), typographical effects, illustrations (by the author), arcane vocabulary, pseudo-historical texts and many other post-modernist devices. His work also has considerable political impact; for example *Something Leather* (1990), an erotic fantasy, also contains a biting satire on Glasgow's role as 1990 'European City of Culture'. He has been seen as a major figure of 'the new Glasgow writing', a movement involving such fiction writers as ⊳ James Kelman and ⊳ Janice Galloway, as well as poets such as Tom Leonard. His first novel, *Lanark*: *A Life in Four Books* (1981), takes its narrator from a bleak contemporary urban landscape (Glasgow is suggested but not identified) to an imaginary realm named 'unthank', while his most recent, *Poor Things* (1992), evokes late-Victorian Glasgow as a setting for the Frankenstein-like story of a doctor who tries to create his 'ideal woman' by a brain transplant. His other novels are: *1982, Janine* (1984); *The Fall of Kelvin Walker: A Fable of the Sixties* (1985, adapted from a 1968 television play); *McGrotty and Ludmilla: or, The Harbinger Report* (1990); *A History Maker* (1994). Volumes of stories: *The Comedy of the White Dog* (1979); *Unlikely Stories, Mostly* (1983); *Lean Tales* (1985), with James Kelman and Agnes Owens; *Ten Tales Tall and True* (1993). Poetry: *Old Negatives: Four Verse Sequences* (1989). Autobiography: *Self-Portrait* (1988). He has also written plays and documentaries for radio and television and a work entitled *Independence: Why Scots Should Rule Scotland* (1992).

Gray, Thomas (1716–71)

Poet and prose-writer. The sole survivor of 12 children, Gray was born in Cornhill, London. His father, a scrivener, was mentally unbalanced and Gray was brought up by his mother, who sent him to Eton where he made friends with ⊳ Horace Walpole. He went on to Peterhouse, ⊳ Cambridge, and gained a high reputation for his ⊳ Latin poetry, though he failed to take a degree. In 1739 he embarked on a tour of the continent with Walpole, but in 1741 they quarrelled and Gray returned alone. He turned to the study of law, and began a tragedy *Agrippina*, which remained unfinished. The death of Richard West, a close friend from his Eton days, in 1742, precipitated a period of poetic activity, in which he produced his *Ode on a Distant Prospect of Eton College* (published 1747), *Sonnet on the Death of Richard West* and *Ode to Adversity* (published in Dodsley's *Collections*, 1748). Also in 1742 he began ⊳ *Elegy written in a Country Churchyard*, while staying with his mother and aunt at their retirement home in Stoke Poges. The poem was carefully revised over a long period and eventually appeared in 1751, achieving instant recognition as a masterpiece.

From 1742 Gray lived in Peterhouse and later Pembroke College, Cambridge, except for a period (1759–61) in London where he pursued his studies in the British Museum. Relations with Walpole were soon restored and it was the death of Walpole's cat which inspired Gray's delightful mock-heroic *Ode on the Death of a Favourite Cat* (1748). The *Odes by Mr Gray* (1757), comprising his two Pindaric Odes, *The Progress of Poesy* and ⊳ *The Bard*, was the first book published by Walpole's Strawberry Hill press. In the same year he was offered the laureateship, but refused. In 1761 he wrote a number of poems reflecting a mixture of bookish scholarship and romantic primitivism, very characteristic of the period: *The Fatal Sisters. An Ode*, *The Descent of Odin. An Ode* (*From the Norse-Tongue*), *The Triumphs of Owen. A Fragment* (from the Welsh). They were published in 1768 in Dodsley's collected edition of his works, *Poems by Mr Gray*. In the same year Gray was appointed Professor of Modern History at Cambridge, though he never delivered a lecture. In 1769 he travelled in the Lake District and his *Journal* (1775), relates his reactions to its sublime scenery. His letters reveal a profoundly learned, but witty and entertaining personality.

Gray's reflective works, in particular the *Elegy*, are masterpieces of the hesitant, personal poetry of ⊳ sensibility. His odes, although not so successful, reflect the restless experimentalism of his period. It has been too easy to cast Gray either as a half-hearted ⊳ Augustan or a timid pre-romantic, both tendencies being encouraged by ⊳ William Wordsworth's dogmatic strictures on the language of his *Sonnet on the Death of*

Mr West, and ▷ Samuel Taylor Coleridge's corrective follow-up in ▷ *Biographia Literaria*, Chapter XVIII. It is better to see him in his own right. His particular poetic strengths are an ease of personification and abstraction (shared by his contemporary Samuel Johnson (1709–84) and emulated by ▷ John Keats in his ▷ Odes), and a restrained but eloquent felicity of phrasing, which places some of his lines among the best-remembered in the language: 'where ignorance is bliss/ 'Tis folly to be wise'; 'And Melancholy mark'd him for her own.'

▷ Bard; Romanticism.

Bib: Johnson, S., in *Lives of the Poets*; Arnold M., in *Essays in Criticism* (2nd series); Ketton-Cremer, R. W., *Thomas Gray: A Biography*; Leavis, F. R., in *Revaluation*; Tillotson, G., in *Augustan Studies*; Powell Jones, W., *Thomas Gray, Scholar*; Starr, H. W. (ed.), *Twentieth-Century Interpretations of Gray's Elegy*.

Great Exhibition, The

Held in 1851, in Hyde Park in London, it was the first international exhibition of the products of industry and celebrated the peak of the British Industrial Revolution. It was regarded as a triumph for British prosperity and enlightenment, though by some critics, eg the philanthropist ▷ Lord Shaftesbury, as concealing the scandal of immense urban slums. Its principal building, the Crystal Palace, was a pioneer construction in the materials of glass and cast-iron. The architect was Joseph Paxton.

▷ Albert of Saxe-Coburg-Gotha.

***Great Expectations* (1860–1)**

A novel ▷ Charles Dickens. Its title refers to expectations resulting from wealth anonymously donated to Philip Pirrip (shortened to Pip) who has been brought up in humble obscurity by his half-sister and her husband, the village blacksmith, Joe Gargery. His 'expectations' are to be made a ▷ 'gentleman' – understood in social terms as holding privilege without responsibility. He supposes his money to be the gift of the rich and lonely Miss Havisham, who has in fact merely used him as an experimental victim on whom her ward, Estella, is to exert her charm with the aim of breaking his heart. Pip's great crisis comes when he discovers his real benefactor to be the convict Magwitch, whom he had helped in an attempted escape when he was a child. Magwitch, who had been made into a criminal by the callousness of society in his own childhood, has built up a fortune in Australia (to which he was deported) and has tried the experiment of 'making a gentleman' out of another child. His assumption is essentially that of society as a whole – that appearances, and the money that makes them, are what matters. Magwitch returns to England illegally to see the fruit of his ambition, and Pip has to decide whether he will be responsible for his unwanted benefactor or escape from him. His decision to protect Magwitch and help him to escape again produces a revolution in Pip's nature: instead of assuming privilege without responsibility he now undertakes responsibility without reward, since he will also divest himself of his money. 'Expectations' are important in other senses for other characters: Estella expects to become a rich lady dominating humiliated admirers, but she becomes enslaved to a brutal husband; Pip's friend, Herbert Pocket, dreams of becoming a powerful industrialist, but he has no capital until Pip (anonymously) provides it; Wopsle, the parish clerk in Pip's village, imagines himself a great actor and becomes a stage hack; Miss Havisham is surrounded by relatives whom she depises and who nonetheless live in expectation of legacies after her death; Miss Havisham herself, and Magwitch also, live for expectations (in Estella and Pip) which are frustrated – in these instances fortunately. In its largest implications, *Great Expectations* is concerned with the futility of a society in which individuals live by desires powered by illusion. This view of the novel gives emphasis to those characters who are free of illusion: the lawyer Jaggers who exerts power by his cynical expectation of human folly; his clerk, Wemmick, who divides his life sharply between the harshness demanded by his profession and the tenderness of his domestic affections; Joe Gargery and his second wife Biddy, survivors from an older social tradition, who remain content with their own naive wisdom of the heart. Dickens was persuaded by his friend ▷ Bulwer-Lytton to change the end of the novel: in the first version Pip and Estella, older and wiser, meet again only to separate permanently; in the revised one, Dickens leaves it open to the reader to believe whether they will be permanently united, or not.

Greek literature

Until Greece was conquered by the Romans in 146BC, it was a country of small states, mixed racial stock and cultural origins from all round the eastern Mediterranean. These states attained a high level of self-conscious political and artistic culture, which later enriched the Roman Empire and was thence transmitted to medieval and modern Europe.

The beginnings of Greek literature cannot be dated but its first period ended about 500BC. The period contains ▷ Homer's epics, the ▷ *Iliad* and the ▷ *Odyssey*, and the poems of Hesiod. Homer's epics are the real starting-point of European imaginative literature; Hesiod's *Theogony* is one of the principal sources of our knowledge of the Greek religious system. In English literature since the 18th century, the term ▷ elegy has implied narrower limits of subject and treatment than it had for the Greeks and the Romans, but the Greek evolution of the elegy and the ▷ lyric in this period has shaped our ideas of the character and resources of the short poem. An important variety of the lyric (whose principal characteristic was originally that it was intended to have musical accompaniment) was the 'Pindaric ode', so called after its most famous practitioner, ▷ Pindar; this was much imitated by English poets from the 17th to 19th centuries.

The second period (500–300 BC) is called the 'Attic Period' because it centred on the greatest of the Greek cities, Athens, capital of the state of Attica. The outstanding imaginative achievement of the Athenians was the creation of dramatic literature. The 'choral lyric', sung by choirs on religious occasions and especially on the festival of the wine-god Dionysus, was developed into a dialogue by Thespis in the 6th century. In the 5th century this was further developed into dramatic tragedy by three writers whose works have a fundamental influence on all our ideas of the theatre: ▷ Aeschylus, ▷ Sophocles and ▷ Euripides. The primitive religion of the Greeks, based on the worship of the gods as the all-powerful forces of nature, was the origin of Greek ▷ tragedy; it was also the origin of comedy, of which the greatest Greek writer was ▷ Aristophanes. Athens, in this period, also developed Greek prose literature, in the works of the first of the historians, ▷ Herodotus, in the immensely influential philosophies of ▷ Plato and ▷ Aristotle, and in political oratory, especially that of ▷ Demosthenes.

Demosthenes achieved fame by his efforts to sustain the Greeks in their wars (357–338 BC) against Philip of Macedon, a state to the north of Greece. The war ended with the Macedonians making themselves the dominant power in Greece. They did not actually destroy the independence of the states, but the intensity and many-sidedness of Greek city life diminished. However, Philip's son ▷ Alexander the Great (ruled 336–323 BC) took Greece culture with him in his rapid conquests round the eastern Mediterranean and as far east as north-west India. The result was the 'Hellenistic Period' lasting until the Roman conquest, after which it did not cease but went into a new phase. The culture of Greece now became a climate of civilization shared by many lands; it was no longer even centred in Greece but in the university city of Alexandria in Egypt. The price paid for this expansion was that without the sustenance of the vigorous Greek city life, the literature lost its force, depth and originality, though it retained its secondary qualities such as grace and sophistication. The best known imaginative works of this period are the ▷ 'pastoral' poems by ▷ Theocritus and others; they influenced the Roman poet ▷ Virgil, and were extensively used as models by ▷ Renaissance poets in the 16th and 17th centuries.

In the Graeco-Roman period (146 BC– AD 500), the Greeks were the teachers and cultural allies of their conquerors, the Romans. ▷ Latin literature written under Greek influence now excelled what continued to be written in Greek. Yet Renaissance Europe felt so much closer to the Romans than to the Greeks that it was the Greek writers of this period who influenced it more deeply than the earlier Greeks did. The historian and biographer ▷ Plutarch, for instance, was widely read in England in the age of ▷ Shakespeare, who used him as a sourcebook for his plays. The Greek romances, the best known of which is *Daphnis and Chloe* by Longus (2nd century AD), were imitated by 16th-century writers such as ▷ Sir Philip Sidney in his ▷ *Arcadia*. To this period also belongs one of the most influential pieces of Greek literary criticism, the treatise *On the Sublime* by ▷ Longinus.

In considering the influence of Greek literature on European, and in particular on English, literature, we have to distinguish between the influence of Greek philosophy and that of Greek imaginative writing. Plato and Aristotle had profound effects on Christian thought. Plato was made dominant by St Augustine of Hippo (4th–5th century), until ▷ St Thomas Aquinas replaced his influence by that of Aristotle. In the 16th century, Plato again became most important, but now as a source of ▷ humanist as well as of religious ideas. Aristotle remained dominant as the first philosopher of literature for three centuries, and together they are still regarded as the important starting-points of European philosophy. Greek imaginative writing, on the other hand, made its impression on European, and especially English, imaginative writing chiefly through its assimilation by Roman writers. It was not, for example, the unexcelled Greek dramatists who impressed themselves on the equally unexcelled English dramatists of the age of Shakespeare, but the comparatively inferior Roman ones, ▷ Plautus in ▷ comedy and ▷ Seneca in tragedy. Only in the 30 years of the ▷ Romantic Revival that followed the ▷ French Revolution did English writers (partly under ▷ German influence) really discriminate between Greek and Roman literature, and value the Greeks more highly. Even then, such a poet as ▷ Shelley valued Greek culture as sentiment rather than as a deep influence. For such as him, the Greeks stood for freedom of spirit and of intellect, whereas Latin culture was associated with the pre-revolutionary authoritarian 'old regime' to which he and others of his generation were so much opposed. It must not be forgotten that Greek culture was based on maintaining slaves and that their women were excluded from public life and restricted to the household. Neither class was considered as capable of full humanity as free Greek males. The extraordinary privilege accorded to Greek culture in western thought has often obscured these details.

▷ Classical education; Classical mythology; Latin literature; Pastoral, Classical; Platonism and Neo-Platonism.

Green, Henry (1905–73)
Pen-name of the novelist H. V. Yorke. His novels are: *Blindness* (1926); *Living* (1929); *Party-Going* (1939); *Pack My Bag* (1940); *Caught* (1943); *Loving* (1945); *Back* (1946); *Concluding* (1948); *Nothing* (1950); *Doting* (1952). Of these, possibly the most distinguished are: *Living*, with an industrial working-class setting; *Loving*, about servants in an anachronistic great house in Ireland during World War II; *Concluding*, set in the future, about an institution for educating women civil servants, and *Party-Going*, a novel in which the events have only a few hours' duration and take place in a fog-bound London railway station. His style is condensed and poetically expressive; events are caught in movement, with a cinematic use of flash-backs to bring the past into relationship with the present. In the autobiographical *Pack my Bag* he wrote: 'Prose should be a long intimacy between strangers with no direct appeal to what both may have known. It should slowly appeal to feelings unexpressed, it should in the end draw tears out of the stone.' Green is set aside from the ▷ modernist interest in the rendering of consciousness by a belief that the novelist should not attempt to portray the inner depths of characters, but should use their spoken words to capture the opaque and shifting surface of social relations. The later novels show increasing reliance on dialogue, following the example of the novels of ▷ Ivy Compton-Burnett. Green also professed admiration for the work of the French writer, Céline. He wrote no novels in the last 20 years of his life.
Bib: Stokes, E., *The Novels of Henry Green*; Russell, J., *Henry Green*; Bassoff, B., *Towards Loving*; Sarraute, N., in *The Age of Suspicion*.

Green, Matthew (1696–1737)
Author of *The Spleen* (1737), a tetrameter (▷ metre) couplet poem advocating the simple life as a cure for boredom and 'splenetic' irritableness.

Green, Sarah (c 1790–1825)
Novelist and prose writer. Little is known about Sarah Green's personal life, but it is possible to trace through her novels a development from quiet docility to sharp feminist ▷ satire (▷ Feminism). Her *Mental Improvement for a Young Lady* (1793) is a ▷ didactic text aimed at teaching her niece correct feminine behaviour which, unsurprisingly, amounts to being chaste and obedient. Interestingly, novels are forbidden reading for the well brought-up young lady. After this incursion into print, *The Private History of the Court of England* (1808) comes as somewhat of a shock, since it describes the scandals of contemporary court life, especially the notorious affairs of the Prince of Wales, under the meagre ▷ allegorical veil of a historical setting. The actress and novelist, ▷ Mary Robinson, who was one of the Prince's many mistresses, is depicted in the novel as an intelligent woman oppressed by a misogynistic husband. Green took up this last theme again in her novel *Gretna Green Weddings, or The Nieces* (1823) which attempts to show that the abuse of women is true villainy, rather than an acceptable, although repugnant, social trait. The other butt of her satiric wit was the romance, which she attacked ruthlessly in her criticism *Romance Readers and Romance Writers* (1810–11), and which she fictionalized in the hilarious *Scotch Novel Reading, or Modern Quackery* (1824). In this latter book a father tries to save his two daughters from mental instability which has been brought on by reading ▷ Byron and ▷ Sir Walter Scott. Their madness takes the form of attempting to live out fiction in their lives; the younger daughter who is obsessed with Scott is saved, but the Byronic daughter dies tragically.

Greenaway, Kate (1846–1901)
Born in Hoxton, the daughter of a wood-engraver, Greenaway began nature drawing as a child. She went to the Royal College and the Slade, and became a writer and illustrator of children's picture books in which she portrays an idealized world of sweetly pretty children in floral surroundings. She was encouraged by ▷ John Ruskin, whom she met in 1882 and who lectured on her art at Oxford in 1883, praising its innocent view of childhood and in effect its lack of ▷ realism. ▷ George Eliot also admired her art. Greenaway liked the ▷ Pre-Raphaelites and disliked contemporaries such as James Whistler. A strong, though unorthodox, religious instinct is evident in her search for beauty and goodness. She rejected the ▷ woman's movement, and enjoyed considerable commercial success, influencing design and children's dress. Her first success was *Under the Window* (1878), a collection of rhymes she wrote and illustrated. Her later work includes *Marigold Garden* (1885) and an illustrated edition of ▷ Robert Browning's ▷ 'The Pied Piper of Hamelin'. She also wrote poetry, much of it still unpublished.
Bib: Engen, R.K., *Kate Greenaway*; Holme, B., *The Kate Greenaway Book*.

Greene, Henry Graham (1904–91)
Novelist. The son of a schoolmaster. He went to Balliol College, Oxford, and then became a journalist (1926–30) on *The Times*. He was converted to Catholicism in 1926. His first novel, *The Man Within*, appeared in 1929. It

was followed by a steady succession of novels, of which the fourth, *Stamboul Train* (1932) made him well known. It was nonetheless one of the books he called 'entertainments', meaning that they were among his less serious works; this group also includes *A Gun for Sale* (1936), *The Confidential Agent* (1939), *The Ministry of Fear* (1943), and *Our Man in Havana* (1958). In 1934 he published *It's a Battlefield*, and in 1935 a volume of stories the title story of which, *The Basement Room*, was later adapted into the film, *The Fallen Idol* (1950). In 1935 came *England Made Me*. In the same year he travelled in Liberia, on which he based his travel book *Journey Without Maps* (1936). He then became film critic for the weekly journal ▷ *The Spectator* (of which he was made literary editor in 1940). His next novel, *Brighton Rock* (1938) was the first in which there was clear evidence of Catholicism. In the same year he was commissioned to visit Mexico and report on the religious persecution there; the result was another travel book, *The Lawless Roads* (1939) and one of his most famous novels, *The Power and the Glory* (1940). During World War II he worked for the Foreign Office, and again visited West Africa. After the war he became a publisher. Later fiction: *Nineteen Stories* (1947; including eight in *The Basement Room* volume); *The Heart of the Matter* (1948); *The Third Man* (1950; also made into a film); *The End of the Affair* (1951); *The Quiet American* (1955); *A Burnt-Out Case* (1961); *A Sense of Reality* (four stories, 1963); *The Comedians* (1966); *Travels with My Aunt* (1969); *A Sort of Life* (1971); *The Honorary Consul* (1973); *Lord Rochester's Monkey* (1974); *The Human Factor* (1978); *Dr Fischer of Geneva, or the Bomb Party* (1980); *Monsignior Quixote* (1982); *The Tenth Man* (1985); *The Captain and the Enemy* (1988).

He has also written plays: *The Living Room* (1953); *The Potting Shed* (1957); *The Complaisant Lover* (1959); *The Return of A. J. Raffles* (1975), and books of critical essays, *The Lost Childhood* (1951) and *The Pleasure Dome* (film criticism, 1972). His *Collected Essays* were published in 1969 and his *Collected Plays* in 1985. His autobiographical works include *A Sort of Life* (1971), *Ways of Escape* (1981) and *Getting to Know the General* (1984).

Graham Greene's high reputation is partly due to his exploration of emotions that were particularly strong from the middle of the 20th century: the sense of guilt and frustration, impulses to violence and fear of it, pity, including self-pity. He had strong gifts for narrative and for the evocation of atmosphere, especially the atmosphere of squalid surroundings which convey deprivation and despair. His Catholicism counteracts the misery in his books by its implications of spiritual dignity remaining intact even amid degradation and abject suffering.

Bib: Allott, K., and Farris, M., *The Art of Graham Greene*; Lodge, D., *Graham Greene*; Pryce-Jones, D., *Graham Greene*; Sharrock, R., *Saints, Sinners and Comedians: the Novels of Graham Greene*; Smith, G., *The Achievement of Graham Greene*; Sherry, N., *The Life of Graham Greene*.

Greene, Robert (1558–92)

Dramatist and pamphleteer. He was one of the ▷ University Wits, having himself been at Cambridge. Four plays by Greene, apart from collaborations, have survived: *Alphonsus, King of Aragon* (?1587); ▷ *Friar Bacon and Friar Bungay* (1589); *History of Orlando Furioso* (acted 1592), *The Scottish History of James IV* (acted 1594). Of these the best known are the second and the fourth, and in them the melodious and fluent handling of the ▷ blank verse and the appealing portrayal of the heroines anticipate ▷ Shakespeare's romantic comedies of the 1590s.

Greene is more notable for his prose. This includes romances written in emulation of ▷ Lyly's ▷ *Euphues* and ▷ Sidney's ▷ *Arcadia*, including *Pandosto, The Triumph of Time*, from which Shakespeare derived ▷ *The Winter's Tale* (1610). More distinctive and very lively reading are his 'cony-catching pamphlets' (*ie* booklets about criminal practices in the London underworld), *A Notable Discovery of Cosenage* (*ie* 'cozenage' or criminal fraud, 1591) and *The Blacke Booke's Messenger* (1591) – both excellent examples of Elizabethan popular prose. A semi-fictional ▷ autobiography, *Greene's Groatsworth of Wit bought with a Million of Repentance* (1592) is notorious for containing the earliest reference to Shakespeare as a dramatist and actor, though it is an oblique one. The object of the pamphlet is ostensibly a warning to three others of the University Wits – probably ▷ Peele, ▷ Marlowe and ▷ Nashe – to amend their lives. The allusion to Shakespeare – 'an upstart crow beautified with our feathers . . . in his owne conceyt the onely shake-scene in a countrey' – comes by way of a charge of plagiarism. Thirty-five prose works, most of them short, and many containing lyrics of great charm, are ascribed to Greene.

▷ Elizabethan novels.

Bib: Provost, R., *Robert Greene et ses romans*; Crupi, C. W., *Robert Greene*.

Greenwood, Walter (1903–74)

Novelist. Born in Salford, Greenwood worked as an office boy, cab driver and salesman (among other things) before the success of his first novel *Love on the Dole* (1933). Describing the misery, poverty and squalor of life in a northern town during the Depression, the book became a *cause célèbre*, even discussed in Parliament; it was dramatized in 1934 and made into a film in 1941. His other novels include: *His Worship the Mayor* (1934); *Standing Room Only* (1936);

The Secret Kingdom (1938); *Down by the Sea* (1951); and the autobiography *There was a Time* (1967).

Greer, Germaine (b 1939)
Feminist theorist and critic. Germaine Greer is one of the most influential writers of her generation. Her groundbreaking feminist work of 1971, *The Female Eunuch*, was a brilliantly timed and characteristically outrageous critique of traditional images of femininity and women's role in Western society, as well as being a celebration of more radical female powers and talents hitherto suppressed and repressed. Greer is an incisive writer and considerable scholar, who nevertheless always exudes an intoxicating energy in her writing. She has had an enormously varied career, and is one of the foremost spokeswomen of British ▷ feminism (although she was born in Australia and continues to explore this identity in her more autobiographical writings). Greer has held university lecturing posts (at Warwick University in the early 1970s, and more recently in Cambridge and the U.S.A.), has written for the underground press (the cult journal *Oz* in the late 1960s), has edited a collection of 17th-century women's poetry (*Kissing the Rod*, 1988), has written on women's role in art history (*The Obstacle Race*, 1979), on fertility and maternity (*Sex and Destiny*, 1984), on Shakespeare (1986), and on the menopause (*The Change*, 1991).
Bib: Plante, D., *Three Difficult Women*.

Gregory, Lady (Augusta) (1852–1932)
Promoter of Irish drama, she founded the Irish Literary Theatre, with ▷ W. B. Yeats and Edward Martyn in 1898. This became the Irish National Theatre Society in 1902 and led to the establishment of the ▷ Abbey Theatre in Dublin. She wrote several plays for it and collaborated with Yeats in *The Pot of Broth* and *Cathleen ni Houlihan* (both 1902). Of her own plays the best known are *Spreading the News* (1904), *The Gaol Gate* (1906), *Hyacinth Halvey* (1906), *The Rising of the Moon* (1907) and *The Workhouse Ward* (1908). She also translated Molière into Irish idiom in *The Kiltartan Molière*.

▷ Irish literature in English.
Bib: Kohfeldt, M., *Lady Gregory: The Woman behind the Irish Renaissance*.

Grein, Jack Thomas (1862–1935)
Playwright, critic and manager who helped introduce the work of European playwrights to English audiences at the end of the 19th century. He founded the Independent Theatre Club in 1891, 'to give special performances of plays which have a literary and artistic rather than a commercial value'. The first production was ▷ Ibsen's ▷ *Ghosts* which met with a storm of abuse, and thereafter little of Ibsen's work was shown, although ▷ George Bernard Shaw's contribution to the controversy, *Widowers' Houses*, his first London production, was put on in 1892. Grein's dramatic criticism has been published in five volumes.
Bib: Orme, M., *J. T. Grein: the Story of a Pioneer*.

Greville, Sir Fulke, 1st Baron Brooke (1554–1628)
Poet, courtier, dramatist, ▷ biographer. Almost all of Fulke Greville's poetic works were published after his death. They include a collection of ▷ sonnets, religious and philosophical poems, and songs gathered under the title *Caelicia*, which appeared in the collection of his works published in 1633 as *Certaine Learned and Elegant Works*. A life-long friend of ▷ Philip Sidney, Greville wrote a life of Sidney which was published in 1652 as 'A Dedication to Sir Philip Sidney' in Greville's history of the Elizabethan era. A further volume of his work was published much later in the 17th century when *The Remains: Poems of Monarchy and Religion* was issued in 1670. His two plays – *Alaham* (written c 1600) and *Mustapha* (produced 1603–8) – though set in an exotic and remote world, are valuable attempts at dealing with the important contemporary issues of power and authority in the state. However, he also wrote a play now destroyed, *Antony and Cleopatra* (▷ Cleopatra). Greville was a member of the brilliant intellectual circle surrounding Sidney at court, and enjoyed considerable favour from both ▷ Elizabeth I and ▷ James I of England before his death in 1628 when he was murdered by an offended servant.
Bib: Rees, J. (ed.), *Selected Writings*; Rees, J., *Fulke Greville, First Lord Brooke, 1554–1628: A Critical Biography*; Gouws, J. (ed.), *The Prose Works of Fulke Greville*.

Grey, Lady Jane (1537–54)
Letter and prayer-writer as well as poet, the 'nine days' queen' of romantic legend and misty representation on canvas and celluloid is not often remembered for her small but impressive literary output. In life she became a pawn in the game of ▷ Tudor monarchy, manipulated by both her father, the Duke of Suffolk, and her father-in-law, the powerful Duke of Northumberland. Lady Jane was proclaimed queen on 10 June 1553, but when ▷ Mary Tudor entered London on 19 July, she and her husband were imprisoned in the Tower and beheaded six months later. Lady Jane was well educated and a staunch Protestant and her written work was, not surprisingly, preserved in ▷ John Foxe's *Acts and Monuments* (1563). The impassioned spiritual conviction and the acute political awareness of Lady Jane's writing suggests that conventional portrayals of her as quiet and submissive may have more to do

with feminine stereotypes than with her actual character.
Bib: Travitsky, B. (ed.), *The Paradise of Women.*

Griffith, Elizabeth (1727–93)
Dramatist, novelist, editor, and friend of the actresses ▷ Kitty Clive and ▷ Peg Woffington. Griffith was the daughter of the comedian and actor–manager Thomas Griffith, and probably born in Dublin. From 1749 to 1753 she worked as an actress at ▷ Smock Alley in Dublin, and then at ▷ Covent Garden until 1755. In 1757 she published, together with her husband Richard Griffith, *A Series of Genuine Letters Between Henry and Frances* purporting to tell the story of their own courtship. In 1764 the couple effectively separated when she moved to London, having earlier returned to Ireland. However, their correspondence continued and was published in four more volumes between 1767 and 1770. Griffith wrote three ▷ epistolary novels, *The Delicate Distress* (1769), *The History of Lady Barton* (1771) and *The Story of Lady Juliana Harley* (1776), as well as a *Collection of Novels* (1777) and *Novellettes* (1780), originally serialized in the *Westminster Magazine*. Her plays included *The Double Mistake* (1766), *The School for Rakes* (1769), *A Wife in the Right* (1772), and she translated numerous works from the French, notably some volumes of ▷ Voltaire. Many of her works were noted for their politeness and decorum, overlaid with moral comment, but she also attacked women's unequal position in marriage and society.

Griffiths, Isabella (?1713–64)
Editor and probable reviewer for the *Monthly Review*, founded by her husband in 1749. She was a target for attacks by ▷ Goldsmith and ▷ Smollett for presuming to alter their work, when she edited it for the review. Her husband denied that she had written for his journal, but his testimony is thought unreliable.
Bib: Todd, J. (ed.), *A Dictionary of British and American Women Writers 1660–1800.*

Griffiths, Trevor (b 1935)
British socialist playwright who began writing during the late 1960s. He has since written plays for television as well as the stage and collaborated with Warren Beatty on the script for the film *Reds*. His plays often dramatize a political debate between reformist and revolutionary standpoints. This is most obviously the case in *Occupations* (1970) and *The Party* (1973); it is also true of his comic work about club entertainers, *Comedians* (1975). He has expressed a preference for writing for television because of the wider audiences that can be reached than in the theatre.
Bib: Poole, M. and Wyver, J., *Powerplays: Trevor Griffiths in Television.*

Grimm's Fairy Tales
German folk-tales collected by the brothers Jacob (1785–1863) and Wilhelm (1786–1859) Grimm, and published 1812–15. They first appeared in English in a volume illustrated by ▷ George Cruickshank and containing such stories as 'Snow White', 'Hansel and Gretel' and 'Rumpelstiltskin'. They were the first collectors to write down the stories just as they heard them, without attempting to improve them.
▷ Children's literature.

Grindal, Edmund (?1519–83)
Archbishop of Canterbury. Grindal was educated at Cambridge and, as a staunch Protestant and Calvinist, received the patronage of ▷ Nicholas Ridley, but had to leave England during the ▷ Catholic reign of ▷ Mary I. At the accession of ▷ Elizabeth I he returned and became Bishop of London in 1559 and, with Cecil's support (▷ Burghley), Archbishop of Canterbury in 1575. As such Grindal should have been one of the shaping forces of Elizabethan Protestantism, but he failed to live up to his early promise. There are several reasons for this: firstly, he had little firm purpose, which he mitigated with bouts of severity, as, for example, when he denounced John Stow as a Papist; and secondly, he could not accept Elizabeth's political alliances with Catholic nations, nor curb his own zeal for prophesying and for the open discussing of scriptures, practices of which the queen disapproved. He is, however, celebrated in the 'May' and 'July' ▷ eclogues of ▷ Spenser's ▷ *The Shepherd's Calendar* (1579).
Bib: Collinson, P., *Archbishop Grindal, 1519–1583: the Struggle for a Reformed Church.*

Grocyn, William (?1446–1519)
English ▷ humanist, and one of the earliest propagators of the study of ancient Greek in England; taught at Oxford.

Grossmith, George (1847–1912) and Weedon (1853–1919)
The brothers were both involved with the theatre, coming from a theatrical family, friends of the Terrys and ▷ Henry Irving. They are remembered, however, for *The Diary of a Nobody* (1852), initially serialized in ▷ *Punch*, written by both brothers and illustrated by Weedon. The nobody in question, Mr Pooter, sensitive to the slightest humiliation, conveys the events and contemporary background detail in a life striving for gentility. The book was immediately successful, with a wide readership, and has remained popular.
▷ Diaries.

Grotowski, Jerzy (b 1933)
Polish director who established the Laboratory Theatre in Wroclaw in the early 1960s, where he developed a training process for actors which emphasized the importance of physical as well as mental skills. His rejection of the expensive

paraphernalia of traditional theatre in favour of what he called 'poor theatre' which relies more exclusively on the actor, has been a great inspiration for the British ▷ fringe theatre. He has also been an important influence on the work of the British director ▷ Peter Brook.
Bib: Grotowski, J., *Towards a Poor Theatre*.

***Group of Noble Dames, A* (1891)**
A collection of ten short stories by ▷ Thomas Hardy, published initially in various periodicals from 1889–90 and collected together in 1891. A series of historical narratives set in mansions and castles in ▷ Wessex, many of the stories were inspired by John Huchins' *History and Antiquities of the County of Dorset* (1861–73) which Hardy read. The dominant themes are taken from Hardy's earlier work, especially love between a poor man and a lady, and sexual temptation. The stories were rewritten and bowdlerized in order to make them acceptable for volume publication.
▷ Historical novels.

Group Theatre
A private play society founded in 1933 and famous for its productions of the experimental poetic plays of ▷ Auden and ▷ Isherwood: *The Dog Beneath the Skin* (1936), *The Ascent of F6* (1937) and *On the Frontier* (1939). Other notable productions include ▷ T. S. Eliot's *Sweeney Agonistes* (1935) and ▷ Stephen Spender's *Trial of a Judge* (1938). Most of its productions were directed by Rupert Doone. Group Theatre was active, apart from an interim during the war years, until 1953.
Bib: Medley, R., *Drawn from Life: a Memoir of the 1930s Group Theatre*; Sidnell, M. J., *Dances of Death: the Group Theatre of London in the Thirties*.

Grub Street
A street in London frequented in the 18th century by ▷ hack writers. Hence 'Grub-street' (adjective or noun) indicates literature or journalism of a low order. In the 19th century it was renamed Milton Street.

***Grub Street Opera, The* (1731)**
Satiric entertainment by ▷ Henry Fielding, set in Wales and featuring songs using new words to popular melodies by ▷ Purcell and ▷ Handel, among others. In it the King and Prime Minister, ▷ Robert Walpole, are mocked in the characters of Sir Owen Apshinken (Welsh *Ap* = 'son of'; German *Schinken* = 'ham'), and the butler Robin ('robbing'). At the end the butler and staff all confess to having robbed the master's household over a long period. The play, following hard on the heels of the controversial *Ballad Opera*, was banned and never performed, but has recently been staged by a touring company for the first time. It is an attack on the aristocracy in general as well as the government, and is interesting in that it reverses earlier conventions whereby servants assist (or confuse) their masters' intrigues: here the rakish and foppish young squire Owen Apshinken conspires to frustrate his servants' amours, in hopes of seducing one of them, and the servants' affairs have an importance equalling or greater than those of their masters.
▷ Grub Street.

Grundy, Mrs
A symbol of narrow-minded, intolerant, out-of-date moral censoriousness. The symbol derives from a character in an otherwise forgotten play, *Speed the Plough* (1798) by Thomas Morton. Mrs Grundy herself never appears, but her neighbour, Mrs Ashfield, is constantly worried about what Mrs Grundy's opinion will be about this or that incident or piece of behaviour.

Grymeston, Elizabeth (1563–c 1602)
Essayist. A Catholic, Grymeston had a difficult life with family feuds, ill health and the death of eight of her nine children. She found time and energy, however, to write and her work was published posthumously as *Miscelanea, Meditations and Memoratives* (1604). On the basis of this work Grymeston has become known as the first woman essayist writing in English. Her work is somewhat learned, including numerous classical references and intricate metaphors.
Bib: Beilin, E. V., *Redeeming Eve*.

Guardian, The
It was started in 1821 as a weekly paper, then called *The Manchester Guardian*, becoming daily in 1855. As the leading Liberal publication outside London, it was edited from 1872 to 1929 by C. P. Scott. Its title was changed to *The Guardian* in 1959, and since 1961 it has been published from London. It is considered to be one of the more liberal papers of the 1980s and 1990s.

Guido de Columnis (or de Columpnis, or della Colonne)
A Sicilian writer, and a judge at Messina from 1257–80, whose translation of Benoît de Sainte-Maure's verse narrative of the Troy story into Latin prose (completed around 1287) became the most popular and authoritative version of Trojan history available in the medieval period. ▷ John Lydgate's *Troy Book* is one of the many vernacular translations of Guido's *Historia Destructionis Troiae*, as is the Middle English ▷ alliterative poem, ▷ *The Destruction of Troy*.
▷ Troy.

Guild
▷ Craft Guilds.

Guinevere
The wife of ▷ King Arthur in Arthurian narratives. In ▷ Geoffrey of Monmouth's *Historia Regum Britanniae* she is from a Roman family. Mordred takes her for his lover when he usurps Arthur's throne, but the level of Guinevere's complicity in the betrayal is not made clear. In later versions of Arthurian narrative, Guinevere's relationship with ▷ Lancelot becomes the most developed aspect of her story. In ▷ Chrétien de Troyes' romance, the *Chevalier de la Charrette*, Guinevere is abducted by King Meleagant and rescued by Lancelot, her lover. Her love affair with Lancelot is later linked into the cycles of Arthurian narrative, and represented as one of the factors contributing to the break-up of Arthur's court and reign (ironically the ▷ Round Table is part of her dowry). In ▷ Malory's *Morte D'Arthur*, the quality of the love shared by Lancelot and Guinevere is celebrated, at the same time as its destructive consequences are recounted: Guinevere, in the *Morte D'Arthur* 'is a true lover, and therefore she had a good end'. She dies in the convent at Amesbury.

Gulliver's Travels **(1726)**
A satirical fable by ▷ Jonathan Swift. It exploits the contemporary interest in accounts of voyages, *eg* William Dampier's *New Voyage* (1697). ▷ Daniel Defoe's fictional account of Robinson Crusoe's voyages had been published in 1719, and had achieved great popularity; this was partly due to Defoe's strictly factual presentation, such that his book could quite well pass for a true account. Swift has his hero, Lemuel Gulliver, recount his adventures with the same sober precision for the effect of accuracy, following, as does Defoe's Crusoe, the philosopher ▷ John Locke in describing only the primary – *ie* objective, measurable – qualities of his strange environments, and ignoring the secondary qualities of colour, beauty, etc., which are more subjective, less verifiable, and so more likely to arouse a reader's disbelief. Swift's intention in doing this was of course not to deceive his readers into supposing that Gulliver's fantastic adventures were true, but to make them realize the absurdity, and worse, of accepted human characteristics when they are looked at from an unfamiliar point of view. Thus in Part I, ▷ *Lilliput*, Gulliver is wrecked on an island where human beings are little bigger than insects, and their self-importance is clearly laughable, but in Part II, ▷ *Brobdingnag*, he is himself an insect in a land of giants, and made to feel his own pettiness. In Part III, contemporary scientists of the ▷ Royal Society are held up for ridicule: science is shown to be futile unless it is applicable to human betterment – the science of Swift's day had not yet reached the stage of technology. Part IV is about the land of the ▷ Houyhnhnms, where horses are endowed with reason but human beings are not; the point here is that the horses recognize that Gulliver has reason, unlike the ▷ Yahoos of the island which he so much resembles, but they succeed in demonstrating to him that human reason is woefully inadequate for the conduct of life because of the mischievousness of the human mind. Swift was, after all, a Christian, and believed that Man would destroy himself without divine aid.

Swift was such a good story-teller that his fable became popular for the sake of the narrative, and though it was in no ordinary sense a novel, his close attention to factual detail (the way in which, especially in Parts I and II, Gulliver is continuously under the pressure of his environment) takes a long stride in the advance of novelistic art.
▷ Lagado, Luggnagg.

Gunn, Neil M. (1891–1973)
Novelist, short-story writer, playwright and journalist. Born in Dunbeath, Caithness in the north of Scotland. After a brief period in his teens when he worked as a clerk in London, Gunn was for many years a Customs and Excise Officer in Scotland until becoming a full-time writer in 1937. He was involved in politics as a Scottish Nationalist. *The Silver Darlings* (1941) depicts the development of the herring industry in the early nineteenth century, following the Highland Clearances. It centres on the story of a young mother, Catrine, whose husband disappears at sea, and her son, Finn, who, despite his mother's fears, himself turns to the sea as a living and a way of life. Other novels include: *The Grey Coast* (1926); *Morning Tide* (1930); *Butcher's Broom* (1934); *Highland River* (1937); *Young Art and Old Hector* (1942); *The Green Isle of the Great Deep* (1944). *The Atom of Delight* (1956) is autobiographical.
Bib: Hart, F. R. and Pick, J. B., *Neil M. Gunn: A Highland Life*; Gifford, D., *Neil M. Gunn and Lewis Grassic Gibbon*; McCulloch, M., *The Novels of Neil M. Gunn: A Critical Study* (1987).

Gunn, Thom (b 1929)
Poet. Educated at Cambridge and Stanford University in California, Gunn now lives in San Francisco, although he is of British origin. His work was first associated with the ▷ Movement, but gradually it drew away from comparison with ▷ Philip Larkin or ▷ Kingsley Amis through its growing violent energy in the 1960s, although formally his precise, clear style is still akin to 1950s poetry. Gunn's work in the U.S.A. has drawn him close to American beat poets in rhythm and subject matter, motorbikes

and rock music, and images of nihilism. He has experimented with syllabic, ▷ iambic and with ▷ free verse forms. His publications include: *Fighting Terms* (1954); *Poems* (1954); *The Sense of Movement* (1957) (which won the Somerset Maugham award); *Moly* (1971); *Jack Straw's Castle* (1976); *Selected Poems, 1950–1975* (1979); *The Passages of Joy* (1982); *The Man with Night Sweats* (1992); and *Collected Poems* (1993).

Gunning, Elizabeth (1769–1823)
Novelist and translator. Daughter of the ▷ Augustan novelist Susannah Gunning and the cousin of ▷ Charlotte Bury, the sensational nature of Elizabeth's family life led ▷ Walpole to entitle them the 'Gunningiad'.
Elizabeth herself rejected the husband her father chose for her to pursue a relationship with a somewhat reluctant suitor. However, it was when she was accused of forging letters that her father disowned her and she was left dependent upon the bounty of her mother, which she also came close to losing. Her novels are reminiscent of her mother's writing, both following the traditions of sentiment and ▷ melodrama, and concerning mainly aristocratic families who encounter strange and sensational events; examples of these include *The Orphans of Snowdon* (1797) and *The Gipsy Countess* (1799). Her most interesting work is *Family Stories* (1802), which purports to be a collection of magic tales for children, but which retells the traditional material from a darker and more adult perspective.

Gunpowder Plot (1605)
A conspiracy by a section of English Roman Catholics to destroy the Protestant government of ▷ James I by blowing up the Houses of Parliament at a time when the king and the members of the Houses of Lords and Commons were all in the building. The plot was inspired by the ▷ Jesuits and led by Robert Catesby, but undertaken by Guy Fawkes. The date was fixed for 5 November and the explosives were all laid, but the plot was betrayed and Fawkes was arrested on the threshold of the cellar on 4 November. This 'discovery' was somewhat stage-managed by the government, which was possibly deeply implicated in the gestation of the plot through the use of double-agents. ▷ *Macbeth* and ▷ *Catiline* both seem to allude to the incident. 5 November has since been celebrated annually with fireworks and bonfires on which Guy Fawkes is burnt in effigy.
Bib: Dehuna, B., *Jonson's Romish Plot*.

***Guy Mannering* (1815)**
A novel by ▷ Sir Walter Scott. It is set in the south of Scotland near the English border during the 18th century. The plot concerns the attempt of a criminal lawyer, Glossin, to deprive Harry Bertram, the heir to the Scottish estate of Ellangowan, of his property. Bertram is kidnapped as a child by smugglers in Glossin's pay, and carried abroad. He returns to Scotland as a young man and recovers his estate with the help of a gipsy who lives on it, Meg Merrilies. Mannering is an English officer under whom Bertram has served in the army, and with whose daughter Julia he is in love. The novel is notable partly for its romantic scene-painting, and partly for the characterization which is markedly more vivid in the lower social orders – the ▷ gipsies, the farmer Dandy Dinmont, the tutor Dominie Sampson – than in its ladies and gentlemen. There are also very good descriptions of Edinburgh.

Guy of Warwick
A very popular early 14th-century English romance, based on a 13th-century ▷ Anglo-Norman text. It recounts the story of Guy's ultimately successful attempts to prove himself as a knight and win the hand of Fenice, daughter of the Earl of Warwick. He leaves his wife to go on a pilgrimage to the Holy Land, and the narrative tells of his subsequent experiences in the guise of a pilgrim and his efforts, on his return to England, to help King Athelstan resist the Danish invaders (notably by fighting the giant Colbrand). It is only on his deathbed, having been nursed by Fenice, that the hermit, Guy, reveals his identity to his wife. There is a continuation which recounts the history of Guy's son Reinbrun. The combination of romance and saint's life story motifs in a semi-historical setting proved a popular and successful narrative formula. Many versions of the story survive, including one by ▷ John Lydgate, and the story of Guy's fight with Colbrand is retold in ▷ Michael Drayton's *Poly-Olbion*. Guy's story is the subject of several 16th-century ballads and one 17th-century play.
Bib: Barron, W. R. J., *English Medieval Romance*.

Gwynn (Gwyn, Guinn, Guin), Nell (Eleanor) (Ellen) (?1642–87)
Actress, dancer. One account of Gwynn's early years has her hawking herring in the streets of London, before she became an orange seller at the ▷ Bridges Street Theatre, under 'Orange Moll', in about 1663. By 1665 she had graduated to the stage, aided by the actor ▷ Charles Hart, who became the leading actor in the ▷ King's Company and reputedly Gwynn's lover.

Gwynn quickly gained a reputation as a brilliant comic actress and dancer, 'pretty witty Nell'. By 1667 she had become the mistress of Charles Sackville, Lord Buckhurst, and two years after that, one of the mistresses of King ▷ Charles II. She gave birth to a son, later the Duke of St Albans, in 1670. She resumed acting soon afterwards, but left the stage permanently in 1671, living in a house in Pall Mall provided for her by the king. She continued as an avid patron of the stage, bringing large parties to performances. She also gave away substantial sums to the poor, and used her influence to free some prisoners from gaol. Gwynn remained a favourite of the court circle, and of the people, despite many satiric or even venomous attacks on her.

Bib. Howe, E., *The First English Actresses*; Wilson, J. H., *All the King's Ladies: Actresses of the Restoration*; Wilson, J. H., *Nell Gwynn*; Chesterton, C., *Nell Gwynn*; Bevan, B., *Nell Gwynn.*

Gynocriticism

A concept introduced by Elaine Showalter in her influential essay 'Towards a Feminist Poetic (1979). Gynocriticism focuses on 'the newly visible world of female culture'. Instead of concentrating on restrictive male images of women as in ▷ feminist critique, gynocriticism concentrates on what is distinctive and creative about women's literary production. This might include the literary-historical relationships between women writers (a particular interest of Showalter's), the development of female sub-cultures and the dynamics of specifically female forms of creativity and ways of writing (▷ écriture féminine).

Bib: Showalter, E. (ed.), *The New Feminist Criticism: Essays on Women, Literature and Theory.*

H

Hack
Abbreviated from 'hackney', as in hackney-carriage. Since about 1700 it has been a derogatory term for an author, implying that the author can be hired for little money, to go wherever the hirer pleases; hence, a bad writer, one without originality, later often used of a journalist. The term was also a slang word for a prostitute, meaning one who could be 'ridden' for a small sum.

Haggard, Sir H. (Henry) Rider (1856–1925)
Son of a Norfolk squire, he spent several years in South Africa as a young man, writing books on its history and farming, but he is famous for his numerous adventure novels set in such exotic locations as Iceland, Mexico and ancient Egypt. They are characterized by gripping narrative and strange events, as well as evocative descriptions of landscape, wildlife and tribal society, particularly in Africa. He has had a world-wide readership and some of his stories have been filmed. *King Solomon's Mines* (1886) and *She* (1887) are the most famous novels. *The Days of My Life: an Autobiography* appeared in 1926.
Bib: Haggard, L. R., *The Cloak that I Left*; Ellis, P. B., *H. Rider Haggard: A voice from the Infinite*; Higgins, D. S., *Rider Haggard: The Great Storyteller*.

Hakluyt, Richard (?1553–1616)
Geographer. In 1589 and 1598 he published his *Principal Navigations, Voyages and Discoveries of the English Nation*, being a record of English explorations, which had lagged behind those of the French, Spanish, Portuguese and Dutch until the middle of the century, and then made prodigious progress with the nationalistic energy characteristic of England in the reign of ▷ Elizabeth I.
Bib: Parks, G. B., *Richard Hakluyt and the English Voyages*.

Halifax, George Savile, Marquess of (1633–95)
Political prose writer. Savile received his peerage in 1668, but went over to the opposition in the 1670s. Nevertheless he remained loyal to ▷ Charles II during the exclusion crisis and became Lord Privy Seal in 1682. He wrote a number of political pamphlets as well as some unpublished characters and maxims. Halifax's most well-known work is the pamphlet, *The Character of a Trimmer* (1685).

Halkett, Lady Anne (1623–99)
Devotional writer and autobiographer. Lady Anne had two unsuccessful romances before marrying Sir James Halkett in 1656, but this marriage was to last for only 14 years and, as a widow, she earned her own living by teaching and writing. Her religious meditations and ▷ autobiography ran to 50 volumes of manuscript material, but it is her life-story (edited in 1979 by J. Loftis as *The Memoirs of Anne, Lady Halkett and Ann, Lady Fanshawe* (▷ Ann Fanshawe)) that remains her most interesting work. Halkett's memoirs are practical, but carry an undercurrent of humour that allows for particularly feminine observations, as, for example, when she dresses the future James II in women's clothes to facilitate his escape in 1648.
▷ Scottish literature.
Bib: H. Wilcox in Cerasano, S. P. and Wynne-Davies, M. (eds.), *Gloriana's Face*.

Hall, Anna Maria (1800–81)
Irish novelist and journalist. Born Anna Maria Fielding in Dublin she moved to England in 1815 and married Samuel Carter Hall in 1824, who managed her literary salon from their home. She befriended many young writers including ▷ Dinah Craik and ▷ Margaret Oliphant whilst publishing her own stories of Irish character and society, such as *Sketches of Irish Character* (1829) and *Lights and Shadows of Irish Life* (1838). She also produced three dramas, some children's stories, and fiction which dealt sympathetically with the peculiar problems of women's lives. These include *Tales of Women's Trials* (1835) and *The Old Governess* (1858), which describes the miseries of the ▷ governess profession. She helped to found the Governesses' Institute and the Home for Decayed Gentlewomen, which she supported with much of the profit from her writings, although she was unsympathetic to women's rights. She was awarded a Queen's Pension in 1868.
▷ Irish literature in English; Women's Movement.

Hall, Edward (?1498–1547)
Chronicler; author of *The Union of the Noble and Illustrious Families of Lancaster and York* (1542; enlarged 1548, 1550). This tells of the bitter rivalries of the two branches of the House of Anjou (Plantagenets) from the death of the childless ▷ Richard II in 1400, and the accession of ▷ Henry IV, first of the House of Lancaster, to the death of the last of the House of York, ▷ Richard III, in 1485, and the accession of Henry Tudor as ▷ Henry VII. He idealizes Henry VII and ▷ Henry VIII, partly because they re-established dynastic harmony, and partly because, as a ▷ Protestant, Hall was strongly sympathetic to Henry VIII's reform of the Church. The Chronicle was one of ▷ Shakespeare's two main source-books for his English history plays, the other being ▷ Holinshed.
▷ Histories and Chronicles.

Bib: Kingsford, C. L., *English Historical Literature in the Fifteenth Century*.

Hall, Joseph (1574–1656)
▷ Satirist; 'character' (▷ Characters, Theophrastian) writer, religious controversialist; bishop, 1627–47. He published his *Virgidemiae* (or *Harvest of Rods*, *ie* for chastisement) in 1597–8; he claimed to be the first English satirist, but ▷ John Donne and ▷ John Marston were writing at the same time, not to mention ▷ Edmund Spenser's *Mother Hubberd's Tale*. He may have considered himself more truly a satirist than his rivals inasmuch as he was stricter in following classical Latin models, notably Juvenal. Like Juvenal, he attacked what he saw as contemporary vices. His *Characters of Virtues and Vices* (1608) was likewise in classical tradition, this time modelled on the Greek Theophrastus, and was also intended for the moral improvement of the age.
Bib: Davenport, A., *The Poems of Joseph Hall*; Huntley, F. L., *Bishop Joseph Hall*.

Hall, Marguerite Radclyffe (1883–1943)
Novelist, poet and short-story writer. Her novel *The Well of Loneliness* (1928) is perhaps the most famous lesbian novel ever published; it concerns the lesbian relationship of a writer, who eventually loses her partner to a male rival, but, having acknowledged her own sexuality, is enabled to write a successful novel. The book was banned on first appearance, despite the support of writers such as ▷ Virginia Woolf and ▷ E. M. Forster; it was republished in 1949. Born in Hampshire, England, Hall wrote poetry from an early age, and began to publish with *Twixt Earth and Stars* (1906), followed by *A Sheaf of Verses* (1908), in which she started to represent and explore her lesbianism in the poems 'The Scar' and 'Ode to Sappho'. She won the Prix Femina and the James Tait Black Memorial Prize for the novel *Adam's Breed* (1926), before the notoriety caused by *The Well of Loneliness*. Her other novels are: *The Unlit Lamp* (1924), about a destructive mother–daughter relationship; *The Forge* (1924); *A Saturday Life* (1925); *The Master of the House* (1932); *The Sixth Beatitude* (1936). *Miss Ogilvy Finds Herself* (1934) is a collection of stories.
▷ Feminism; Lesbian and Gay Writing.
Bib: Dickson, L., *Radclyffe Hall and the Well of Loneliness*; Franks, C.S., *Beyond the Well of Loneliness: The Fiction of Radclyffe Hall*; Baker, M., *Our Three Selves: A Life of Radcyffe Hall*; Troutbridge, U.B., *The Life and Death of Radclyffe Hall*.

Hall, Sir Peter (b 1930)
British director whose first major production was ▷ Samuel Beckett's ▷ *Waiting for Godot* at the Arts Theatre in 1955. From 1956 he directed at Stratford-on-Avon and became director of the theatre from 1960, when it became the Royal Shakespeare Theatre (▷ Royal Shakespeare Company). In 1972 he replaced ▷ Laurence Olivier as director of the ▷ National Theatre, from which he retired in 1988 to establish his own company.
Bib: Hall, P., *Peter Hall's Diaries: the Stories of a Dramatic Battle*.

Hallam, Arthur Henry (1811–1833)
Poet and miscellaneous writer. The son of ▷ Henry Hallam, but better known as the friend of ▷ Tennyson and famously commemorated in that poet's ▷ *In Memoriam* (1833–50). Hallam showed great promise as a scholar and was primarily influenced by the ▷ Romantic poets. His works were edited posthumously by his father as *Remains in Verse and Prose of A. H. Hallam* (1834).

Hallam, Henry (1777–1859)
Historian. Henry Hallam was the father of ▷ Arthur Henry Hallam, whom ▷ Tennyson commemorated in ▷ *In Memoriam* (1833–50). He is well known for his thorough and influential *Constitutional History of England* (1827) and his comprehensive *An Introduction to the Literature of Europe during the Fifteenth, Sixteenth and Seventeenth Centuries* (1837–9), and he edited his son's works in *Memoir of A. H. Hallam* (1834).

Hamilton, Elizabeth (1758–1816)
Essayist and satirist. Elizabeth Hamilton is known to have predicted her fate as 'one cheerful, pleased, old maid', and although she became ill during the last years of her life, this proved to be a very apt prophecy. Her many publications include *Translation of the Letters of a Hindoo Rajah* (1796), which is not a translation but a satire of contemporary British society through the eyes of the fictional character of the titular Indian Rajah, and *Memoirs of Modern Philosophers* (1800), which attacks contemporary society for its treatment of women, but simultaneously exposes the ludicrousness of women who believe they can alter anything, and in which she attacked contemporary philosophers as 'men who, without much knowledge, either moral or natural, entertain a high idea of their own superiority from having the temerity to reject whatever has the sanction of experience and common sense'. She also wrote on education and undertook historical character sketches.
Bib: Butler, M., *Jane Austen and the War of Ideas*.

Hamilton, Lady Mary (1739–1816)
Novelist, born in Edinburgh to Alexander Leslie, the fifth Earl of Leven and his wife Elizabeth. She was married twice: to Dr James Walker and, after his death, to Robert Hamilton. She spent most of her life in France, but wrote in

English, although one of her works was translated into French. Her five novels are mostly in the ▷ epistolary mode, and have ▷ romantic plots but an earnest moral tone, including appeals for women's right to ▷ education. They display considerable erudition, with a number of characters discussing the classics, science, and other serious topics, including architecture and contemporary literature.

Hamilton, Patrick (1904–1962)
Novelist and playwright. His trilogy *Twenty Thousand Streets Under the Sky* (1935), comprising *The Midnight Bell* (1929), *The Siege of Pleasure* (1932) and *The Plains of Cement* (1934), revolves around the lives of a prostitute, a barmaid and a waiter in London, and portrays a characteristically seedy world of streets and bars. He also wrote thrillers, both in the form of novels, such as *Hangover Square* (1941), and in the form of plays, most notably *Rope* (1929) (filmed by Hitchcock in 1948), and *Gaslight* (1939). His other novels include *Craven House* (1926) and *The Slaves of Solitude* (1947), both of which are set in London boarding-houses.

***Hamlet* (c 1601)**
A ▷ tragedy by ▷ Shakespeare, written in about 1601. Three early versions of it exist: the imperfect ▷ quarto of 1603, the superior quarto of 1604, and the version in the First Folio of 1623, which omits some of the material in the 1604 quarto, but also contains authentic passages not in that text. The story was a widespread legend in northern Europe. Shakespeare's immediate source is likely to have been Belleforest's *Histoires Tragiques* (1559), and Belleforest's own version came from a 13th-century Danish chronicler, Saxo Grammaticus. But Shakespeare also had another source: a play of the same name already existed and is thought to have been a lost play by ▷ Thomas Kyd. It is referred to without mention of the author by ▷ Nashe in a letter accompanying ▷ Greene's *Menaphon* (1589), by ▷ Henslowe in his Diary (1594) and by ▷ Lodge in *Wit's Misery* (1596). There are also parallels between Shakespeare's play and Kyd's ▷ *Spanish Tragedy*: both have ghosts and a play within the play; Kyd's tragedy is about a father seeking vengeance for his son, and Shakespeare's is about a son avenging his father. In both plays there are obstacles to the vengeance: in Kyd's play, the obstacle is a straightforward one, of how to bring retribution upon an offender who is so powerful as to be beyond the law; in Shakespeare it is so subtle that Hamlet's hesitations have been among the most discussed subjects in criticism.

Certain features of Shakespeare's play require special attention in assessing the play.

1 The basic situation is that Hamlet's uncle Claudius, has married Hamlet's mother, Gertrude, only a month after the death of her husband, old Hamlet. Claudius has, moreover, ascended the throne ignoring the claim of his nephew and with the consent of the court. This thoroughly distasteful situation reflects badly not only on Claudius and Gertrude, but on the court as well, and it has already plunged Hamlet into disgust at the opening of the play. We need also to remember that marriage to a sister-in-law was of at least doubtful validity: it constituted ▷ Henry VIII's legal ground for divorçe from Katharine of Aragon.

2 It is only later that Hamlet learns from his father's ghost that old Hamlet was murdered by Claudius. The revelation does not lead directly to action, but to Hamlet feigning madness, and to the 'play within the play', before which Claudius, in the audience, betrays his guilt.

3 Claudius' self-betrayal, however, is incriminating only to Hamlet and his friend Horatio, who have already learned the facts. Either Hamlet mistrusts the Ghost, who may not have been truly the spirit of his father, or it is part of his vengeance to inform Claudius that his guilt is known. One of the beliefs about ghosts current in Shakespeare's time was that they were sometimes evil spirits assuming the disguise of dead men.

4 Hamlet's hostility extends not merely to Claudius, but to the whole court, in so far as they are or may be subservient to Claudius. Thus Hamlet behaves brutally to Ophelia (the girl he loves) because he suspects (although she is entirely innocent) that she is being used as a kind of decoy by Claudius and by her father, Polonius.

5 Laertes, Ophelia's brother, is a contrast to Hamlet in being a straightforward revenger: he immediately seeks the death of Hamlet for causing the deaths of his father and sister. But his impetuosity puts him on the side of evil, for it causes him to connive with Claudius.

6 Claudius is an unusual villain for the drama of the time, for he is not *seen* to be evil on the stage; we know of his guilt indirectly. Even his conspiracy against Hamlet's life can be excused as action in self-defence.

These features of the play suggest that Shakespeare was exposing traditional beliefs about revenge as over-simplified. Revenge is difficult if we do not feel the guilty man to be guilty: 'One may smile, and smile and be a villain' (I. v. 108). Further, revenge does not solve evil, if evil lies in a complex situation: 'The time is out of joint; O cursed spite/That ever I was born to set it right' (V. i. 189–90). Finally, revenge itself may be morally wrong: what *was* the Ghost?

Hammett, Dashiell (1894–1961)
▷ Detective fiction.

Hampton, Christopher (b 1946)
British dramatist, a product of the ▷ Royal Court theatre where he was the first resident

dramatist (1968–70), while also working there as literary manager. His much acclaimed adaptation, *Les Liaisons Dangereuses* (1985), performed by the ▷ Royal Shakespeare Company, is a dramatization of a novel by Choderlos de Laclos about sexual combat and power in France just prior to the revolution of 1789. This was rewritten by Hampton for the screenplay of Stephen Frears' very successful 1988 film, *Dangerous Liaisons*. Typically of Hampton, the play does not deal explicitly with politics, though it provides a witty and vivid insight into a world of decadence and ruthlessness on the brink of collapse. Other works include: *Total Eclipse* (1968); *The Philanthropist* (1970); *Savages* (1973); *Treats* (1976); *Tales from the Vienna Woods* (1977); *Don Juan Comes Back From the War* (1978); *Tales from Hollywood* (1983); and *White Chameleon* (1993). Hampton has been described as a modern classicist, not least for his translations of plays by ▷ Chekhov, ▷ Ibsen and ▷ Molière: *Uncle Vanya* (1971); *Hedda Gabler* (1971); *A Doll's House* (1971); *The Wild Duck* (1980); *Ghosts* (1983); *Don Juan* (1972); *Tartuffe* (1984).

Handel, George Frederick (1685–1759)
Composer. Born in Germany, he was appointed chief musician to George, Elector of Hanover, who became George I of Britain (1714–27). Handel visited England in 1710 and settled there in 1712; he became a naturalized British citizen in 1726. He had studied in Italy and was deeply experienced in French music, but in many respects he was in harmony with the English tradition, whose last great master, ▷ Henry Purcell, had died in 1695. Nonetheless, Handel at first had an uneven career in England. He first attempted to establish ▷ opera in the Italian style; his opera *Rinaldo* was a success in 1711. Yet opera in the end reduced him to bankruptcy and he became the exponent of the art of oratorio, which he transformed from its original religious feeling and setting into a much more theatrical form. His first oratorio, *Esther* (1720), resembled the ▷ masques that had been popular in fashionable circles since early in the previous century. *Semele, Susanna* and *Judas Maccabus*, to mention a few of the 16 oratorios that followed, are choral dramas. His masterpiece was *Messiah*, first performed in Dublin in 1741. Handel established the oratorio as the most popular English musical form for the next two centuries. Others of his choral works included his choral settings for ▷ John Dryden's poems, *Ode on St Cecilia's Day* and *Alexander's Feast*.
Bib: Deutsch, O. E., *Handel: A Documentary Biography*.

Handlyng Synne
▷ Mannyng, Robert.

Hands, Elizabeth (fl 1785)
Poet. A neglected writer of great skill and variety, Hands had to contend with contemporary prejudice against her class (she was a servant) as well as her sex. She was sharply aware of both social barriers, writing the ▷ satirical 'Ode on a Dishclout', and inverting conventional gender roles in her pastorals, where she makes the female nymphs sing in competition describing the beauty of their lovers, the male shepherds. Her most ambitious work, *The Death of Amnon* was published in 1789 and focuses upon incest and rape.
Bib: Landry, D., *The Muses of Resistance*.

Hanway, Mary Ann (c 1775–1815)
Novelist. Little is known about Hanway's life, and she is memorable mainly for her ▷ Minerva novels. The plots of her works are predictable – beautiful, orphaned heroines discover their long-lost parents and marry happily – and the ▷ didacticism advocating unadulterated moral virtue is cloying and repetitive. But Hanway's figurative language, although unsophisticated, is passionate and ornate, and some of the passages describing physical details appear darkly obsessive. These preoccupations are coupled with an odd, but clearly stated, intention of writing so that her female readers could expunge their own emotional and bodily disorders through the process of reading. Apart from seeing novels as a form of therapy, Hanway had other ideas in advance of her time, attacking contemporary society for the way in which it treated black people, and perceiving that the education system was biased towards men.
▷ Psychoanalytical criticism.
Bib: Schlueter, P. and J., *An Encyclopedia of British Women Writers*.

Harcourt, Mary (c 1750–1833)
Diarist. Mary Harcourt married a commander in the British army, William Harcourt, in 1778, and travelled with him when he was on active duty. Her accounts of what she saw during these periods reflect the horrors of war, and show the small, and often neglected, acts of pity and heroism, as well as uncovering the political motivations behind the objectives. Her work was published by the *Harcourt Papers* in 1792–5.
▷ Diaries; Nationalism.

***Hard Times* (1854)**
A novel by ▷ Charles Dickens. It is the only one by him not at least partly set in London. The scene is an imaginary industrial town called Coketown. One of the main characters, Thomas Gradgrind, is based on the ▷ Utilitarian leader James Mill (1773–1836); as such he is an educationist who believes that education should be merely practical and hence factual, allowing no place for imagination or emotion. He marries his daughter Louisa to a ruthless manufacturer, Josiah Bounderby, who puts Gradgrind's philosophy into practice in that

he has no place for humane feeling in the conduct of his business. Louisa accepts him in order to be in a position to help her brother Tom who becomes, under the influence of his upbringing, callous, unscrupulous and meanly calculating. Louisa is nearly seduced by a visiting politician, James Harthouse, who is cynically concerned only to find amusement in a place with no other charms. The opposition to this world of calculating selfishness is a travelling circus called 'the horse-riding' owned by Sleary. Sissy Jupe, a product of the circus and the human fellowship that it engenders, is found ineducable by Gradgrind, whose dependant she becomes, but she has the inner assurance required to face Harthouse and compel him to leave the town. Gradgrind's world falls apart when he discovers that he has ruined his daughter's happiness and turned his son into a criminal. A subplot concerns a working-man, Stephen Blackpool, a victim of the Gradgrind-Bounderby system, and of young Gradgrind's heartless criminality.

▷ Social Problem novel; Anti industrialism.
Bib: Samuels, *A., An Introduction to the Varieties of Criticism: Hard Times.*

Hardwicke's Marriage Act (1753)
An Act of Parliament intended to regulate and clarify the forms of marriage. It arose because of a growing number of clandestine marriages, elopements and abductions of heiresses, as well as the ambiguities in what actually constituted a marriage owing to differences between the common law and ecclesiastical law, and contradictions within the laws themselves. The Act made it illegal to marry without a church service, required parental consent for the marriage of anyone under 21, defined times and places in which a marriage could take place in order to be legal, required all marriages to be entered into a church register, and transferred the control of marriage from the ecclesiastical to the secular courts. The Act was criticized by some for inhibiting the free expression of love among the young, and subjecting them to the tyranny of their elders. In fact parental attempts to control their children's choices in marriage were nothing new, and form the basis of the plots of many stage comedies of the Restoration and 18th century.
Bib: Stone, L., *The Family, Sex and Marriage in England 1500–1800*; Alleman, G. S., *Matrimonial Law and the Materials of Restoration Comedy.*

Hardy, Thomas (1840–1928)
Novelist and poet. Hardy was born in Higher Bockhampton, the son of a master mason and builder, Thomas Hardy senior, and his wife Jemima, who encouraged his early interest in literature. As a child he was immersed in country life, legend and folklore and became acquainted with the harshness of rural living, which contributed to his sympathy for country workers and animals. From 1856–62 he was apprenticed to a local architect and met the Dorsetshire dialect poet ▷ William Barnes, and the intellectual Horace Moule, who encouraged his intellectual aspirations and later introduced him to the theories of ▷ Charles Darwin: Hardy claimed that after reading Darwin he gave up his plan to become a country parson and he spent the rest of his life trying to reconcile the orthodox notion of a benevolent God with Darwin's theory of evolution through natural selection. At the same time he witnessed the growing, impoverishment of the south-west of England, an area which was to feature so strongly in his novels as ▷ Wessex. From 1862–7 he joined the architectural offices of Arthur Blomfield in London and published his first article 'How I built myself a House'. He also made an unsuccesful foray into poetry.

His first novel, *The Poor Man and the Lady* (1867), was rejected by ▷ George Meredith, a reader for Chapman and Hall, on the grounds that it was too socialistic. His first published novel was *Desperate Remedies* (1871), a ▷ sensation novel in the style of ▷ Wilkie Collins, and while writing it he met Emma Lavinia Gifford in St Juliot, Cornwall, where he had been sent by his employer to survey the mouldering parish church of which her father was the rector. They married in 1874 and though their relationship was extremely troubled Hardy wrote a flood of poems 'in expiation' on her death in 1912. These are collected in *Satires of Circumstance, Lyrics and Reveries* (1914), and remain amongst Hardy's finest literary works.

Between 1871 and 1898 Hardy wrote fourteen novels; three volumes of short stories: *Wessex Tales* (1888), *A Group of Noble Dames* (1891), and *Life's Little Ironies* (1894); and a volume of poetry, *Wessex Poems* (1898). His best known novels are the group he named his 'Novels of Character and Environment'. They include ▷ *Under the Greenwood Tree* (1872); ▷ *Far from the Madding Crowd* (1874); ▷ *The Return of the Native* (1878); ▷ *The Mayor of Casterbridge* (1886); ▷ *The Woodlanders* (1887); ▷ *Tess of the d'Urbervilles* (1891); ▷ *Jude the Obscure* (1895). The remaining seven he classed as 'Romances and Fantasies' (▷ *A Pair of Blue Eyes*, 1873; *The Trumpet Major*, 1880; *Two on a Tower*, 1882; *The Well-Beloved*, 1897), and 'Novels of Ingenuity' (▷ *Desperate Remedies*, 1871; *The Hand of Ethelberta*, 1876; *A Laodicean* 1881). Many of these are the subject of serious critical re-evaluation, in particular the much underrated *A Pair of Blue Eyes*. His remaining works include: *Poems of the Past and Present* (1902); *Time's Laughingstocks and Other Verses* (1909); *Late Lyrics and Earlier* (1922); *Human Shows, Far Phantasies, Songs and Trifles* (1925) and the posthumous *Winter Words in Various Moods and Metres* (1928).

Hardy's poetry is as distinguished as his novels; indeed he regarded himself primarily as a poet. His diction is distinctive and he experimented constantly with form and stresses, and the singing rhythms subtly respond to the movement of his intense feelings; the consequent poignance and sincerity has brought him the admiration of poets ever since. His lyrics nearly always centre on incident, in a way that gives them dramatic sharpness. Hardy also wrote a three-part epic verse drama, *The Dynasts* (1903–8), and a verse drama about Tristram and Iseult, *The Famous Tragedy of the Queen of Cornwall* (1923). His work is continually under scrutiny by feminist scholars, some of the more discerning of whom have interrogated the crude simplification of his works as fatalist or pessimistic and exposed the criticism of social institutions that underpins his remarkable portrayals of women.
Bib: Gittings, R., *Young Thomas Hardy*, *The Older Hardy*; Millgate, M., *Thomas Hardy: A Biography*, *Thomas Hardy: His Career as a Novelist*; Seymour-Smith, M., *Hardy*; Morgan, R., *Women and Sexuality in the Novels of Thomas Hardy*; Boumelha, P., *Thomas Hardy and Women*; Widdowson, P., *Hardy and History*; Johnson, T., *A Critical Introduction to the Poems of Thomas Hardy*.

Hardyng, John (1378–c1465)
Compiler of the verse chronicle, covering the period from the foundation of Britain by Brutus to the year 1437, referred to as *The Chronicle of John Hardyng*. The early sections of the *Chronicle* draw material from the framework of British history established by ⊳ Geoffrey of Monmouth, but in Hardyng's version ⊳ King Arthur is actually crowned Emperor of Rome. The *Chronicle* seems to have been used by ⊳ Malory for a few details of Arthurian history in his *Morte D'Arthur*. The interest in validating the claims of the kings of England to overlordship of Scotland, which is evident in the *Chronicle*, perhaps reflects one of the political motivations for its compilation.
Bib: Gransden, A., *Historical Writing in England, Vol. II*.

Hare, David (b 1947)
Dramatist and screenwriter. Hare came to prominence in the 1970s as one of a breed of committed socialist writers who included ⊳ Howard Barker, Howard Brenton, ⊳ David Edgar, Snoo Wilson and ⊳ Trevor Griffiths. He founded Portable Theatre with the dramatist Tony Bicât in 1968 and Joint Stock with William Gaskill and Max Stafford-Clark in 1974. He has also been literary manager and resident dramatist at the Royal Court Theatre and one of the companies at the ⊳ National Theatre. Hare has also carved out a singular niche in television with *Licking Hitler* (1978), *Dreams of Leaving* (1980) and *Saigon – Year of the Cat* (1983), which subtly modified traditional television techniques.

Hare has described himself in recent years as a 'commentator' on the ills of contemporary capitalism. *Fanshen* (1976), a documentary play about the Chinese Revolution, was a seminal play of the 1970s, popularising the Joint Stock rehearsal method. Unusually for Hare, the play concentrates on the processes of revolution rather than individual characters. His plays still reflect a highly charged political consciousness but recent work marks a return to a predominant interest in the topography of personal relationships. *The Secret Rapture* concentrates on the contrasting attitudes of two sisters to questions of morality and caring (it was filmed successfully in 1994); *Racing Demon* pursues similar spiritual themes in the context of modern attitudes to religious faith.

He has also written two other plays which link with *Racing Demon* to form a trilogy on religion, law (*Murmuring Judges*, 1991) and politics (*The Absence of War*), 1993). His films include: *Wetherby*, *Paris by Night*, *Strapless*, and *The Secret Rapture*.
Bib: Bull, J., *New British Political Dramatists*; Chambers, C. and Prior, M., *Playwrights' Progress*.

Harington, Sir John (1561–1612)
Poet, translator, courtier and brother to the well-respected literary patron, ⊳ Lucy Russell, Countess of Bedford. Harington's ⊳ translation of ⊳ Ludovico Ariosto's ⊳ *Orlando Furioso* (published in 1591) was undertaken, so it is said, as a punishment exacted by ⊳ Elizabeth I for his having translated part of the bawdy sections of that poem. Whatever the circumstances of its production, Harington's work established itself as one of the most important of Elizabethan translations. In addition to his work on Ariosto, Harington also wrote a humorous piece entitled *A New Discourse of a Stale Subject, called the Metamorphosis of Ajax* (1596). This work, with its punning title (Ajax = A 'Jakes' = a water closet) contains diagrams and instructions on the installation of a plumbing system. The queen suspected that the work contained a subtle allusion to the ⊳ Earl of Leicester and banished Harington from court. During this banishment he put his hydraulic theories into practice, installing the first water closet in England at Richmond Palace. A tendency to overdo a joke is suggested by the publication, again in 1596, of *An Anatomy of the Metamorphosed Ajax*.
Bib: Haughey, R., *Harington of Stepney, Tudor Gentleman: His Life and Works*.

Harley Manuscript
A rich anthology, principally of Middle English and Anglo-Norman poetry and prose (with some ecclesiastical texts in Latin), compiled

probably near Ludlow, Shropshire, c 1340; now in the British Library (Harley 2253). The pieces are of considerable literary sophistication, and include a wide variety of genres and literary forms: ▷ lyrics, a ▷ romance, ▷ fabliaux, historical poems, interludes, saints' lives, satires, biblical narratives and a guide to Holy Land pilgrimages. The texts seem to be consciously arranged to produce striking sacred/secular juxtapositions. The manuscript contains an outstanding collection of Middle English lyrics (generally referred to as 'The Harley Lyrics'), and half the extant corpus of Middle English secular lyrics (up to the end of the 14th century) are preserved in unique copies in it.

Bib: Ker, N. R., *Facsimile of BM. MS. Harley 2253*; Brook, G. L. (ed.), *The Harley Lyrics*.

Harley, Robert, 1st Earl of Oxford (1661–1724)

Statesman and Parliamentarian, originally a Whig, who changed sides to favour the Tory cause. He became Chancellor of the Exchequer in 1710, and supervised the passage of the Treaty of Utrecht (▷ Spanish Succession, War of the). In 1714 he was dismissed from office and spent a period in the Tower of London. Forced into premature retirement, he spent the rest of his life befriending literary figures and collecting literary works. His collection was added to by his son Edward, 2nd Earl of Oxford (1689–1741), and was eventually sold to become part of the library of the British Museum, now the British Library, where it is still known as the Harleian Collection, or the Harleian Manuscripts. It contains a wide variety of items from the ▷ Middle Ages onwards, including many that are rare or unique. Some tracts were edited by ▷ Samuel Johnson and William Oldys (1696–1761), and published 1744–46 as the *Harleian Miscellany*.

Harrington, James (1611–77)

Political prose writer. Born in Upton to a declining noble family and educated at Oxford, Harrington became friendly with influential figures at court such as the Elector Palatine, and with Charles I himself. However, he was a supporter of the parliamentarian cause during the ▷ Civil War and was briefly imprisoned in the tower on the restoration of the monarchy. His political writings include *The Commonwealth of Oceana* (1656) and *The Art of Lawgiving* (1659).

Harris, Wilson (b 1921)

Guyanese novelist and short-story writer. The landscape and history of Guyana play an important part in his work, which is concerned with such issues as the legacy of the colonial past and the destruction and recreation of individual and collective identity. His novels are visionary, experimental, anti-realist explorations of consciousness, employing multiple and fragmentary narrative structures, and symbolic correspondences between inner and outer landscapes. The later novels use a wider range of geographical settings, including England, Mexico and South America. His volumes of short stories, *The Sleepers of Roraima* (1970) and *The Age of the Rainmakers* (1971) locate a redemptive power in Amerindian myth. His novels are: *The Guyana Quartet: Palace of the Peacock* (1960); *The Far Journey of Oudu* (1961); *The Whole Armour* (1962) and *The Secret Ladder* (1963); *Heartland* (1964); *The Eye of the Scarecrow* (1965); *The Waiting Room* (1967); *Tutamari* (1968); *Ascent to Omai* (1970); *Black Marsden* (1972); *Companions of the Day and Night* (1975); *Da Silva da Silva's Cultivated Wilderness, and the Genesis of the Clowns* (1977); *The Tree of the Sun* (1978); *The Angel at the Gate* (1982); a trilogy consisting of: *Carnival* (1985), *The Infinite Rehearsal* (1987) and *The Far Banks of the River of Space* (1990); *Resurrection at Sorrow Hill* (1993).

▷ Post-colonial fiction.

Bib: Gilkes, M., *Wilson Harris and the Caribbean Novel*.

Harrison, Tony (b 1937)

Poet. His early volumes, *The Loiners* (1970) and *The School of Eloquence* (1978), established his recurrent subject matter – becoming distanced through education from his working-class, northern upbringing. This intensely felt sense of loss and belonging was still being explored in *V* (1985). Other volumes of poetry include: *Newcastle is Peru* (1974); *Bow Down* (1974); *Continuous* (1982); and *The Common Chorus* (1992). He has also translated Aeschylus' *Oresteia* and French drama for the theatre; see *Dramatic Verse 1973–1985* (1985). He has also begun to establish himself as a writer for the theatre with his brilliant *Trackers of Oxyrhyneus* (1988).

Harsnett, Samuel (1561–1631)

Bishop of York and religious writer. Harsnett's church career was somewhat varied in that he wrote ▷ satires against the Puritans and the Catholics (the latter, *A Declaration of Egregious Popish Inpostures* (1603), being the source for Edgar's spirit names in ▷ *King Lear*), yet was himself charged with favouring Popery, which led to his resignation from the post of master at Pembroke Hall, Cambridge. In practice he was a somewhat domineering churchman, too concerned with ceremonies to be popular. Strangely, he is best known today as the censor who failed to read ▷ Sir John Hayward's *The First Part of the Life and Raigne of King Henrie the IIII* (1599) with its eulogistic dedication to ▷ Essex. Hayward was imprisoned for the offence this gave to ▷ Elizabeth I, but Harsnett managed to convince the Attorney-General of his innocence.

Hart, Charles (?1630–83)
Actor, manager. He began his career as a boy actor, playing women's parts, at the ▷ Blackfriars Theatre. After the theatres were closed in 1642, he fought in the service of the king, and is said to have acted clandestinely in the late 1640s. Hart resumed acting openly, at the Red Bull Theatre, about the time of the Restoration, and in late 1660 he joined the ▷ King's Company under ▷ Thomas Killigrew, now performing primarily or wholly in men's roles. He is reputed to have been, during the 1660s, a lover of ▷ Nell Gwynn.

During his lifetime his reputation rested particularly on his abilities in tragic roles: he is said to have acted with great precision and concentration such that nothing could distract him from his performance; and to have been able to draw full houses. He was for a time the main rival of ▷ Thomas Betterton, who imitated his style on at least one occasion.

Hartley, David (1705–57)
A philosopher best known for his theory of association of ideas, based on the thought of ▷ Sir Isaac Newton and of ▷ John Locke in the 17th century. In his *Observations on Man* (1749) Hartley denied that moral ideas were inborn in man, holding that they derived from associations of pleasure and pain with certain behaviour. The higher pleasures derive from the lower, and culminate in the love of God. This philosophy of mechanistic psychology was very influential in the first half of the 19th century, especially on the ▷ Utilitarian school of thinkers. ▷ Coleridge was at first strongly under Hartley's influence, but later rejected it, asserting that the human personality was active in its growth, not passive as Hartley's theory implied. ▷ Wordsworth, however, based much of his feeling for ▷ nature's creative influence on human personality on Hartley.

Hartley, L. P. (Leslie Poles) (1895–1972)
Novelist. His novels and stories are: *Night Fears* (1924); *Simonetta Perkins* (1925); *The Killing Bottle* (1932); a trilogy – *The Shrimp and the Anemone* (1944), *The Sixth Heaven* (1946) and *Eustace and Hilda* (1947); *The Travelling Grave* (1948); *The Boat* (1949); *My Fellow Devils* (1951); *The Go-Between* (1953); *The White Wand* (1954) *A Perfect Woman* (1955); *The Hireling* (1957); *Facial Justice* (1960); *Two for the River* (1961); *The Brickfield* (1964); *The Betrayal* (1966); *Poor Clare* (1968); *The Love Adept* (1968); *My Sister's Keeper* (1970); *The Harness Room* (1971); *The Collections* (1972); *The Will and the Way* (1973). His reputation rests chiefly on the trilogy (especially *The Shrimp and the Anemone*) and *The Go-Between*. These both contain very sensitive child studies, and relate the influence of childhood experiences on the development of the adult. Hartley wrote in the tradition of ▷ Henry James, whom he resembles in his presentation of delicate but crucial personal inter-relationships; the influence of ▷ Sigmund Freud intervened to give Hartley a different kind of psychological depth, more concerned with the recovery of the self buried in the forgotten experiences of the past than with the self buried under the false assumptions of society.
Bib: Bien, P., *Hartley*; Mulkeen, A., *Wild Thyme, Winter Lightning*.

Hartman, Geoffrey (b 1929)
American critic. Following early essays on ▷ Wordsworth, Hopkins, Rilke, Valéry and André Malraux, Hartman produced one of the most cogent and incisive critical books on Wordsworth to date, *Wordsworth's Poetry,* (1787–1814) (1964). His writing at this stage was essentially located in new criticism, with an admixture of phenomenology.
Hartman's openness to continental European influences in the areas of philosophy and literary theory, combined with his continued engagement with English Romantic poetry, led him into a key role in the establishment of the 'Yale School' of ▷ deconstruction. His books include *Beyond Formalism: Literary Essays, 1958–70* (1970). *The Fate of Reading and other Essays (*1975), *Criticism in the Wilderness (*1980), *Saving the Text; Literature, Derrida, Philosophy* (1981) and Easy Pieces (1985).

Harvey, Gabriel (?1545–1630)
Man of letters and scholar; friend of ▷ Edmund Spenser, who presents Harvey as Hobbinol in ▷ *The Shepherd's Calendar*. Harvey argued vigorously for substituting Latin quantitative metres (based on length of syllables) for the English accentual rhythms which rely on accent. Otherwise he is chiefly known for his violent quarrels (especially with ▷ Thomas Nashe and ▷ Robert Greene), which caused his name to figure prominently in the ▷ pamphlets of the time.
Bib: Stern, V. F., *Gabriel Harvey: His Life, Marginalia and Library*.

Harvey, Jane (1776–c 1841)
Poet and novelist. A northern writer, Harvey was born in Newcastle-upon-Tyne and often included sentimental descriptions of her home town and its impoverished inhabitants in her works, as for example in *Poems on Various Subjects* (1797), written in ▷ Spenserian stanzas, and in the late *Fugitive Pieces* (1841). Otherwise, Harvey is mainly known as a ▷ Minerva novelist, whose skill lies in ingenious plots and amusing characterizations.

Harvey, William (1578–1657)
Physician and medical writer. Born in Folkestone and educated at Cambridge and Padua, he

was admitted into the College of Physicians in 1604 and began practising at St Bartholomew's Hospital in 1609. He was Charles I's physician. His most famous work is *De Mortu Cordis* (1628) and presents an original treatise on the circulation of the blood.

Hastings, Michael (b 1938)
Dramatist. Hastings began his theatrical career as a trainee actor and writer at the ▷ Royal Court. Born in London, his first play, *Don't Destroy Me* (1956), an exploration of a Jewish household in Brixton, was produced when he was only eighteen and working as a tailor's apprentice. *Lee Harvey Oswald* (1966), produced at the Hampstead Theatre Club, is an example of what was known at the time as 'Theatre of Fact', a sort of documentary account of Oswald's life up to the point of Kennedy's assasination. *Gloo Joo*, a study of a West Indian's experience of London, was produced at the Hampstead Theatre Club and then went on to transfer to the West End.

Probably Hastings' most successful play, *Tom and Viv* (1984) pursues his concern with the theatrical possibilities of biography in a study of the fraught marriage between ▷ T. S. Eliot and his first wife, Vivienne Haigh-Wood. Vivienne ended her life in a mental hospital, and the play explores her mental fragility, her tortuous relationship with Eliot, and the contemporary British upper-class culture which produced Vivienne. The play is ultimately quite unsympathetic to Eliot and his role in their relationship. *Tom and Viv* was produced in America after a successful Royal Court run under the auspices of Joe Papp, and has been successfully filmed.

Hatton, Ann (1764–1838)
Novelist. Ann Hatton (née Kemble) was the sister of the acclaimed actress ▷ Sarah Siddons, but lacking her sister's looks and build – Ann had a squint and a limp – she was apprenticed to a mantua maker by her family. Bad luck or ill-judgement seemed to dog Ann: her first husband proved to be a bigamist, she was accidentally shot in the face while in a bath house (probably one of ill-repute), and she chose to stage a suicide attempt in Westminster Abbey. However, in 1792 she married William Hatton and they began a new, and more successful, life in America, where she wrote several popular librettos. By 1806 she was once more in Britain and, having been widowed, began to write ▷ Minerva novels to make a living. Hatton took every ingredient of the ▷ Gothic novel and reproduced it in faithful stereotype; she was, as a result, one of the most popular novelists on the Minerva lists. An early work, *Poems on Miscellaneous Subjects* (1783), shows that her style was both sentimental and Gothic, but also reveal a youthful promise that was never to be fulfilled.

Hatton, Sir Christopher (1540–91)
Courtier. One of the many apocryphal stories about ▷ Elizabeth I concerns Sir Christopher Hatton; who, it is said, attained the queen's favour because she thought him an accomplished dancer. Certainly he promoted himself as ▷ Leicester's rival for the queen's affections and was to remain an ever-hopeful bachelor until his death. This role ensured him political preferment and several public posts: he was made a Gentleman Pensioner in 1564, became Lord Chancellor in 1587, and accepted the post of Chancellor of Oxford University in 1588. He was also given Ely Place in London, now the site of Hatton Garden. Like most of Elizabeth's favourites, Hatton was also interested in the arts; he was the patron of ▷ Spenser and ▷ Churchyard, and wrote Act IV of *Trancred and Gismund* (c 1567), a tragic play based on a story by ▷ Boccaccio.
Bib: Williams, N., *All the Queen's Men*.

Hauptmann, Gerhart (1862–1946)
German dramatist and exponent of a 'naturalistic' style of writing in early plays like *The Weavers* (1892), a play based on factual events relating to social struggle and revolt in the Silesian weaving industry. Much of the play is written in the Silesian dialect. *The Thieves' Comedy* (1904) was shown by ▷ Harley Granville Barker as part of his Court Theatre repertory.
Bib: Sinden, M., *Gerhart Hauptmann: The Prose Plays*.

Havelok
A Middle English verse romance, composed towards the end of the 13th century. Two 12th century ▷ Anglo-Norman versions are extant: one in Geoffrei Gaimar's *Estoire des Engleis*; the other, the *Lai d'Havelok*, claims descent from a tale told by the Britons (▷ Breton Lays). The romance tells the story of Havelok, the dispossessed heir to the Danish throne, and of Goldborough, the dispossessed heir to her father's kingdom of England. Both suffer as children from the oppression of their respective guardians who have ambitions to establish their own royal dynasties. Havelok manages to escape from the murderous designs of his guardian, Goddard, through the help of Grim the fisherman. Havelok flees Denmark with Grim and his family, and lives with them in England at the place known as Grimsby. Havelok's marriage to Goldborough is arranged by her guardian, Godrich, as a social slight to the heir to the English throne. However, through the agency of a miraculous light which shines from Havelok's mouth, and the intervention of a divine voice, Goldborough learns that her husband is not a mere kitchen boy, but of

royal descent. The narrative goes on to relate how Havelok recovers his heritage and that of Goldborough too.
Bib: Barron, W. R. J., *English Medieval Romance*.

Hawkins, Laetitia-Matilda (1759–1835)
Novelist, autobiographer and travel writer. Hawkins' early years shadowed her creative output for most of her life. Her father was the ▷ Augustan scholar John Hawkins, who produced one of the first histories of music as well as a life of Dr Johnson (1709–84). Johnson, who appointed Hawkins as his executor, found him difficult, and this is certainly the experience of his daughter who felt that her spirit had been broken by his incessant condemnation and criticism. Her first works were published anonymously, but she used her own name for *The Countess and Gertrude, or Modes of Discipline* (1811) which was dedicated to ▷ Harriet Bowdler. The narratives of her fictions often depict a repressed and self-deprecating heroine, who battles to assert herself over her male relatives. She produced a somewhat amorphous ▷ autobiography with general comments, *Anecdotes, Biographical Sketches and memoirs* (1823), which was mocked by ▷ De Quincey. Her novels, however, were admired by ▷ Jane Austen. Her ▷ travel writings remain in manuscript form.
Bib: Todd, J., *Dictionary of British Women Writers*.

Hayley, William (1745–1820)
Poet and biographer. Hayley was a popular poet, but was generally dismissed by other writers of the period, including ▷ Byron and ▷ Southey. He was befriended by ▷ Blake, however, who illustrated two of his works, *Little Tom the Sailor* (1800) and *Ballads Founded on Anecdotes Relating to Animals* (1805). Hayley also published the lives of several literary figures including ▷ Cowper and ▷ Milton.
▷ Ballad.

Haymarket Theatres
The first major theatre in the Haymarket was built in 1705 according to a design by the dramatist and architect ▷ John Vanbrugh and immediately occupied by ▷ Thomas Betterton and his company. Until Queen ▷ Anne's death in 1714 it was known as Her Majesty's Theatre or the Queen's Theatre, and then the King's Theatre, or simply the Haymarket. However, the theatre suffered financial problems since it proved too large for spoken drama, and in due course became the first English ▷ opera house, staging many of ▷ Handel's operas. After three theatres were destroyed on that site the present theatre, known as Her Majesty's, was built by Beerbohm Tree (1853–1917) in 1897.
In 1720 another theatre was erected in the Haymarket, which was known variously as the New Theatre, Little Theatre, Little Haymarket, Little Theatre in the Hay or alternatively, the French Theatre in the Haymarket, because of its frequent use by French as well as Italian performers. Eventually, confusingly, it too became known just as the Haymarket. It stood until 1820 when the present Theatre Royal, Haymarket, was erected nearby.
A third theatre in the area was in a converted tennis court built in nearby James Street in 1634.
The name Haymarket derives from an actual hay market which existed from 1664 to 1830.

Hays, Mary (1760–1843)
Radical writer. Hays was born into a family of Rational Dissenters and her early writings are concerned with religious matters; for example, in *Cursory Remarks* (1791) she attacks the prejudices of the established church. Then, in 1792 she met ▷ Mary Wollstonecraft and the main thrust of her writing became feminist (▷ Feminism). For example, in *Appeal to the Men of Great Britain in Behalf of Women* (1798; published anonymously), she wrote:

> *But for a woman to be obliged to humour the follies, the caprice, the vices of men of a very different stamp, and to be obliged to consider this as their duty; is perhaps as unfortunate a system of politics in morals, as ever was introduced for degrading the human species.*

Hays also wrote advocating vocational training for women and demanding the right to independent economic means, and she attempted to redress the pro-male balance of historical evidence by writing *Female Biography* (1803) and *Memoirs of Queens* (1821). While respected in this capacity, Hays' fictional work was ridiculed by her contemporaries, for example by ▷ Coleridge and ▷ Elizabeth Hamilton, mainly because her novels are unrepentantly ▷ autobiographical. *Memoirs of Emma Courtney* (1796) is a particularly honest and sometimes disconcertingly personal account of a woman who fails to win the love of the man she desires (in real life, William Frend).
▷ Histories and Chronicles.
Bib: Moers, E., *Literary Women*; Todd, J., *The Sign of Angelica*.

Hayward, Sir John (?1564–1627)
Historian. Hayward was the author of several learned histories: *Lives of the III Normans, Kings of England* (1613), *Life and Raigne of Edward the Sixt* (1630), *The Beginning of the Reign of Elizabeth* (1636), and *The First Part of the Life and Raigne of King Henrie IIII* (1599), and it is for this last work that he is best known today. The history of Henry III contained a eulogistic dedication in Latin to the ▷ Earl of Essex, which severely angered ▷ Elizabeth I

as it appeared to criticize her own rule, and Hayward was subsequently imprisoned.

▷ Harsnett, Samuel.

Haywood, Eliza (?1693–1756)

Haywood's literary career spanned some 30 years, from the publication of *Love in Excess or The Fatal Enquiry (1719)* to *Jemmy and Jenny Jessamy* (1753). Haywood was a prolific and highly successful writer: works known to be by her amount to almost 100 and she may also have published anonymously.

▷ Delarivière Manley and ▷ Aphra Behn, Haywood's literary reputation has been obscured by the notoriety of her personal life. ▷ Alexander Pope satirized her in ▷ *The Dunciad*, as a 'Juno of majestic size. With cow-like udders, and with ox-like eyes', her sexual favours offered as the prize in a urinating contest. Yet Pope's vituperative attack, which has been regarded as evidence of misogyny, should be read in the context of the satire on literary ▷ hacks; the rival contestants Curll and Chetwood are no less damningly portrayed.

Haywood's novels were widely acclaimed, bringing her something of the status of a 'bestseller'. Their great diversity in tone and scope reflects a period of considerable change in novelistic fashions; the earliest works use ▷ romantic names, while the later employ 'character' types such as Trueworth, Saving and Gaylord, and there is an increasing emphasis on the female experience and the heroine as central character.

Haywood was also a prolific journalist, founding, amongst other periodicals, ▷ *The Female Spectator*, a women's equivalent to the periodicals of ▷ Addison and ▷ Steele. The articles generally deal with issues of social conduct and moral behaviour, and show an advanced attitude to sexual politics. Haywood also had a brief theatrical career in both writing and acting; her play, *A Wife to Be Let* (1724), was staged at ▷ Drury Lane with the author herself as a leading actress, and in the 1730s her frequent stage appearances included roles in ▷ *Arden of Faversham* and *The Opera of Operas* (1733), her own operatic version of ▷ *Tom Thumb*.

Hazlewood, Colin Henry (1823–75)

A comedian on the Lincoln, York and western circuits, Hazlewood began his career as a dramatist in 1850 with a successful farce. He is chiefly remembered for his successful dramatization of ▷ M.E. Braddon's ▷ sensation novel ▷ *Lady Audley's Secret* in 1863.

Bib: Wolff, R.L., *Sensational Victorian: The Life and Fiction of M.E. Braddon.*

Hazlitt, William (1778–1830)

Essayist and critic. He was the son of a ▷ Unitarian minister with strong radical views, and himself took the liberal side in politics throughout his life; though he wrote for many papers and periodicals, he is most associated with John and ▷ Leigh Hunt's radical weekly, ▷ *The Examiner*. He was the early admirer and friend of ▷ Coleridge and ▷ Wordsworth (see one of his best essays, *My First Acquaintance with Poets*; 1823), and though he later resented what he considered their betrayal of the liberal cause, he continued to admire especially Wordsworth's early poetry for its integrity and disinterestedness, qualities which he exemplified in his own life. However, he did not share the simplifying, materialistic outlook of many of the radicals *eg* the ▷ Utilitarians; his best work, *The Spirit of the Age* (1825) – studies of the leading minds of the time, including ▷ Bentham and Wordsworth – shows his feeling that rational theorists like the former were really remoter from reality, though they claimed to base all their thought on experience, than were the poets who gave form to their experience directly. This regard for whole truth shows in his most perceptive criticism, especially of ▷ Shakespeare (*Characters of Shakespeare's Plays*, 1817–18). Other critical works: *Lectures on the English Poets* (1818–19); *English Comic Writers* (1819); *Dramatic Literature of the Age of Elizabeth* (1820); *Table Talk, or Original Essays on Men and Manners* (1821–2).

Though nowadays best known for his criticism, Hazlitt has always had a larger public for his miscellaneous essays, such as *On Going a Journey*, *Going to a Fight*, etc. His graphic, terse, energetic style often gives this part of his work strong character.

▷ Essay.

Bib: Howe, P. P., *Life*; Baker, H., *Life*; Schneider, E., *The Aesthetics of Hazlitt*; Brinton, C., *The Political Ideas of the English Romantics*; Stephen, L., in *Hours in a Library*; Saintsbury, G., in *Essays in English Literature*.

H. D. (Hilda Doolittle) (1886–1961)

Poet. H. D. was born in Bethlehem, Pennsylvania, educated at Bryn Mawr, where she was a contemporary of American poet Marianne Moore, and moved to Britain in 1911. She was an important figure in the ▷ Imagist group, signing her first poems, published in Harriet Monroe's *Poetry* in 1913, 'H. D. Imagiste'. She was a close associate of ▷ Ezra Pound, to whom she was briefly engaged in 1907. The 'Hellenic hardness' of her work epitomized Imagism. She married fellow writer Richard Aldington in 1913, becoming part of the network sometimes known as the 'Other ▷ Bloomsbury' which was dominated by ▷ D. H. Lawrence, who is characterized in H. D.'s novel *Bid Me To Live* (published 1960). From 1916 she co-edited, with ▷ T. S. Eliot, *The Egoist*, Dora Marsden's originally ▷ feminist journal which had published amongst other texts ▷ James Joyce's ▷ *Portrait of the Artist as a Young*

Man in serial form in 1914–15. In 1917 H. D. separated from Aldington, gave birth to her daughter Perdita, and began to travel with her friend ▷ Bryher, with whom she spent much of the rest of her life. Her first collection, *Sea Garden*, was published in 1916, followed by *Hymen* (1921), *Heliodora and Other Poems* (1924), and *Red Roses for Bronze* (1929). The trilogy, *The Walls Do Not Fall* (1944–6) and *Helen in Egypt* (1961), perhaps H. D.'s most important works, have only recently received the critical attention they deserve. Her poetry is intense, difficult, and infused with her passion for classical Greek culture. Although primarily known as a poet, H. D. wrote novels, and having undergone psychoanalysis with ▷ Freud in Vienna 1933–4, published an account of the process. *Tribute to Freud* is important both as a poetic and visionary text and as a key text in debates about psychoanalysis and feminism.
Bib: Duplessis, R. B., *H. D. The Career of That Struggle*; Buck, C., *H. D. and Freud: Bisexuality and a Feminine Discourse*.

Head, Bessie Emery (1937–86)
African novelist and short-story writer. Born in South Africa in a mental hospital, where her Scottish mother had been confined as a result of her relationship with her Zulu father, she was brought up by a foster family until the age of thirteen, then attended a mission school in Durban and trained as a teacher. She taught in South Africa, worked as a journalist for *Drum* magazine and became involved in African nationalist circles, but in 1963 went into exile in Botswana, where she worked, with other political refugees, in a village garden co-operative at Serowe, commemorated in her book *Serowe: Village of the Rain Wind* (1981), which is built around interviews. She took Botswanan citizenship in 1979. Her first three novels contain a considerable element of autobiography, most notably *A Question of Power* (1974), which is based directly on her own experience of mental breakdown, but also *When Rain Clouds Gather* (1969), about a Botswana agrarian community, and *Maru* (1971), which deals with racial prejudice through the story of an orphaned Masarwa woman, teaching in a Botswanan village where her people are regarded as outcasts. *The Collector of Treasures and Other Botswana Village Tales* (1977) is a volume of short stories, while *A Bewitched Crossroad: An African Saga* (1984) is a history of the Bamangwato tribe. *Tales of Tenderness and Power*, published posthumously in 1989, is a collection of stories, personal observations and legends, while *A Woman Alone*, published posthumously in 1990, consists of autobiographical fragments.
Bib: Vigne, R., (ed.), *A Gesture of Belonging: Letters from Bessie Head 1965–1979*; MacKenzie, C., *Bessie Head: An Introduction*; MacKenzie, C., and Clayton, C., *Between the Lines: Interviews with Bessie Head*; Abrahams, C., *Bessie Head and Literature in South Africa*.

***Headlong Hall* (1816)**
A novel by ▷ Thomas Love Peacock. It is his first and shows the main characteristics of his maturer work: witty, burlesque conversations and, innovatively, very little plot. The narrative is interspersed with attractive lyrics and songs. As in his other novels, the characters are caricatures of contemporary types.

Heaney, Seamus Justin (b 1939)
Poet. His early nature poetry, drawing on his upbringing as a farmer's son, is found in *Death of a Naturalist* (1966) and *Door into the Dark* (1969), and shows the influence of ▷ Ted Hughes. The political situation in Northern Ireland begins to be explored in *North* (1975) and *Field Work* (1979), from the standpoint of Heaney's ▷ Catholic background. The strongly individualistic, meditative and solitary vein that marks the distance between his own outlook and that of sectarianism continues to be apparent in subsequent collections: *Station Island* (1984), *The Haw Lantern* (1987), and *Seeing Things* (1991). Other recent publications include: *New Selected Poems 1966–87* (1990); *The Cure at Troy* (1990); and *Seeing Things* (1991).
▷ Irish literature in English.
Bib: Morrison, B., *Seamus Heaney*; Curtis, T. (ed.), *The Art of Seamus Heaney*; Corcoran, N., *Seamus Heaney*.

***Heart of Darkness* (1902)**
A ▷ novella by ▷ Joseph Conrad. It is narrated by Marlow, an officer in the Merchant Navy who also appears in Conrad's other works ▷ *Lord Jim, Youth* and *Chance*. Sitting on board a ship anchored in the lower reaches of the River Thames, he tells a group of friends the story of his journey up the Congo River in Africa, in the employment of a Belgian trading company. This supposedly benevolent organization is in fact ruthlessly enslaving the Africans and stripping the area of ivory, and what Marlow sees on his arrival in Africa disgusts him. At the company's Central Station he hears much about Kurtz, their most successful agent, who is apparently lying ill at the Inner Station upriver. Marlow's attempts to set out to reach him are delayed by the machinations of the manager and other agents, who are jealous of Kurtz's success. When the steamer which Marlow is to captain is finally repaired, and the party sets off, Marlow experiences a powerful sense of dread as the boat carries them deeper into the jungle, but this is combined with a strong desire to meet Kurtz. After being attacked by natives from the bank, they reach the Inner Station, where an eccentric young Russian adventurer who idolizes Kurtz tells Marlow of his power over the local inhabitants, and

the fluency and fascination of his ideas. But Kurtz's hut is surrounded by heads on poles, and it becomes apparent that, in addition to writing a report on the 'Suppression of Savage Customs', ending with the words 'exterminate all the brutes!', he has become compulsively addicted to unspecified barbaric practices, presumably involving human sacrifice. He has also acquired an African mistress. Marlow tries to get Kurtz away down river, but he dies, his last words being 'The horror! The horror!'. Back in Europe, Marlow tells Kurtz's fiancée that he died with her name on his lips.

The story has come to be regarded as a classic of 20th-century literature, and its ambiguity has made it the subject of numerous interpretations. It has also been critized by some, notably by the Nigerian novelist ▷ Chinua Achebe, for containing racist assumptions.

***Heart of Midlothian, The* (1818)**
A novel by ▷ Sir Walter Scott. Midlothian is a county in Scotland in which Edinburgh, the Scottish capital, is situated. The title refers to the old Tolbooth prison in Edinburgh, so nicknamed. The central part of the story is Jeanie Deans' journey on foot to London in order to appeal to the Duke of Argyle – a Scottish nobleman high in royal favour – on behalf of her sister Effie who has been wrongfully charged with child murder. Argyle was a historical character, and the events are linked up with the attack on the Tolbooth – known as the Porteous Riot – which actually took place in 1736. As in other novels by Scott about 18th-century Scotland, the characterization is vigorous, *eg* of Madge Wildfire who has abducted the child whom Effie is supposed to have murdered, and Dumbiedikes, the silent suitor of Jeanie. It is often regarded as the best of Scott's novels.

Heath, Roy (b 1926)
Novelist. Heath was born in Guyana, and educated at the University of London. He worked as a clerk and then as a primary school teacher in London before being called to the Bar at Lincoln's Inn in 1964; since 1968 he has taught French and German in London. His novels combine realism and mythic patterns to portray Guyanese life in the 20th century, focusing in particular on stories of personal struggle and tragic family relations among the poor and lower middle class of Georgtown. For example his *Georgetown Trilogy*, comprising *From the Heat of the Day* (1979), *One Generation* (1981) and *Genetha* (1981), chronicles the life of a single family. His other novels are: *A Man Came Home* (1974); *The Murderer* (1978); *Kwaku: or the Man Who Could Not Keep His Mouth Shut* (1982); *Orealla* (1984); *The Shadow Bride* (1988). He has also published short stories, a play and an autobiographical work, *Shadow Round the Moon: Caribbean Memoirs* (1990).

***Heavenly Twins, The* (1893)**
A novel by ▷ Sarah Grand. The first half of this immensely successful book describes the lives of two twins, Angelica and Diavolo. As children they are both irrepressible, energetic and daring, but as they grow older they are forced to take different paths. Diavolo is given a good ▷ education and finally leaves home for an army career, while Angelica follows a conventionally female path and becomes trapped in domestic routine. The second half of the book concentrates on two women, Edith and Evadne. Religious and naive, Edith unknowingly marries a syphilitic naval officer, and both she and her child contract the disease. After a period of mental degeneration, Edith dies. Evadne, who has studied anatomy, physiology and pathology, refuses to consummate her marriage after discovering that her husband has had a previous affair, and lives a sexless life. She is frustrated as a result and has a mental breakdown, but she recovers from this after the death of her husband and marries again. Like Grand's *The Beth Book*, the novel explicitly addresses sexual/political issues. The lives of the twins reflect the inequality of educational opportunity, while Edith and Evadne represent the 'old' and ▷ 'New Woman' respectively. Despite Evadne's learning, however, she becomes trapped in a life of repression after promising her husband that she will not become active in the ▷ women's movement.

Heber, Reginald (1783–1826)
Poet and religious writer. Heber's most famous works are probably the hymns 'Hark the Herald Angels Sing' and 'Holy, Holy, Holy' (*Hymns, Written and Adapted to the Weekly Church Service*, 1827), although he published several more extensive works including, *Poems and Translations* (1812) and *The Lay of the Purple Falcon: a metrical romance* (1847). In 1822 he was appointed Bishop of Calcutta, a role which inspired him to write *Narrative of a Journey through India* (1828).

▷ Hymns; Lay.

Bib: Smith, G., *Bishop Heber: Poet and Missionary*.

***Hedda Gabler* (1890)**
A play by Norwegian dramatist ▷ Henrik Ibsen which marks his development away from an expressly social and moralist mode of drama and towards a more psychological and symbolic style. The play questions the conventional ideology of womanhood through the portrayal of its central character – Hedda – who finds her potential for effective activity limited and instead is forced to exercise

an emotional power over those who enter her orbit.

Hegemony
Originally used to denote political domination. In its more modern meaning and its use in literary criticism it has come to refer to that process of political control whereby the interests of a dominant class in society are shared by those subordinated to it. Hegemony depends upon the consent of subordinate classes to their social positions, but the constraints within which that consent operates, and the ways in which it is experienced, are determined by the dominant class. This concept also offers ways of understanding the different kinds of social and personal relationships represented in literary texts. Along with a number of other concepts, it opens the way for an analysis of the different forms of negotiation that take place within texts, and between text and reader, and serves to emphasize the social context of experience, ▷ consciousness and human interaction.

***Heir of Redclyffe, The* (1853)**
A novel by ▷ Charlotte Yonge, informed by the religious principles of the ▷ Oxford Movement and much admired by prominent literary figures of the day such as ▷ Tennyson, ▷ D. G. Rossetti and ▷ William Morris. The novel contrasts genuine and superficial goodness of character through the story of two cousins, Guy and Philip Morville. Guy appears brash, but is deeply generous and ultimately self-sacrificing, whereas Philip is greatly admired but undeserving of accolades. Philip's machinations almost succeed in thwarting Guy's marriage. Guy later nurses Philip through a fever, catches it himself and dies. Philip repents of his sins and inherits the ancient house of Redclyffe.

Hemans, Felicia Dorothea (née Browne) (1793–1835)
Poet. After being deserted by her army captain husband in 1818, Felicia Hemans turned to writing to support her family, living first in Wales and then in Dublin. She published many volumes of verse, including *Translations from Camoens and other Poems* (1818), *Welsh Melodies* (1822), *Records of Women* (1828) and *Hymns on the Works of Nature* (1833). Her combination of liberalism and piety made her very popular. Her best remembered poems today are *Casabianca* ('The boy stood on the burning deck') and *The Homes of England* ('The stately Homes of England,/ How beautiful they stand!').
Bib: Hicock, K., *Representations of Women: Nineteenth-century British Women's Poetry*; Trinder, P. W., *Mrs Hemans*.

Heming, John (d 1630) and Condell, Henry (d 1627)
Acting colleagues of ▷ Shakespeare and editors of the first edition of his collected plays, known as the First Folio, 1623.

Hendecasyllabic
A metrical term meaning a line of verse having 11 syllables; decasyllabic = 10 syllables.

Henrietta Maria, Queen (1609–99)
Patron and dramatist. ▷ Charles I's queen had a significant impact upon the culture of the ▷ Stuart court. As a French princess she had had the benefit of experiencing the greater freedom allowed women in France. For example, they were able to write private plays and ▷ masques, as well as to perform in them. As a British queen she encouraged the arts and was an ardent supporter of drama, but created a scandal when she attempted to compose her own plays and act on stage, albeit only within the confines of the court. It was probably the performances of the queen and her ladies-in-waiting in Walter Montague's *The Shepherd's Paradise* that caused William Prynne's attack against actresses in *Histrio-mastix* (1632). Henrietta Maria's Catholic upbringing also brought about censure from the increasingly Puritan country, and her influence on the court was seen to create a divide between the world of London nobility and the rest of the nation. Still, the religious air that invades the ▷ Platonic masques of the ▷ Caroline court imbue them with an ethereal and delicate quality lacking in the showy entertainments of ▷ James I's reign.
Bib: Veevers, E., *Images of Love and Religion*.

Henry I (1100–35)
The third ▷ Norman king of England, fourth son of ▷ William I.

Henry II (1154–89)
King of England. Son of Geoffrey Plantagenet, Count of Anjou, and Matilda, daughter of Henry I. Henry II was thus the first king of the House of Anjou or ▷ Plantagenet. By inheritance and marriage with Eleanor of Aquitaine he acquired all western France from Normandy to the Spanish border. In England, he was an extremely efficient ruler, especially in organization of the law courts, but this brought him into his famous conflict with ▷ Thomas Becket, Archbishop of Canterbury. His relationship with his wife was largely hostile and later romancers made much of his love affair with ▷ Fair Rosamund – Rosamund Clifford – *eg* ▷ Samuel Daniel in his *Complaint of Rosamond*. During his reign the native rulers of Ireland began to be displaced by Anglo-Norman noble families, authorized by the fact that the Pope, Adrian IV, who was English, had granted Henry power over the whole of Ireland.

Henry III (1216–72)
King of England, fourth of the ▷ Plantagenet line. His reign was much disturbed by internal conflict, especially the rebellion led by Simon de

Montfort, who first secured the representation of the towns and the smaller landowners in the Great Council of the kingdom, from which ⊳ Parliament has developed.

Henry IV (1399–1413)
King of England. He was called ⊳ Bolingbroke from the name of his birthplace. His father, ⊳ John of Gaunt, Duke of Lancaster, was a younger son of ⊳ Edward III; his cousin ⊳ Richard II exiled Henry and confiscated his estates, in retaliation for which Henry succeeded in raising a rebellion and seizing the throne. Richard died mysteriously in prison. Henry thus became first of the three kings of the House of ⊳ Lancaster, really a junior branch of the ⊳ Plantagenet line. His reign was the subject of two plays by ⊳ Shakespeare, ⊳ *Henry IV, Parts I and II.*

Henry IV, Part I
A ⊳ history play by ⊳ Shakespeare, performed about 1597 and printed in a ⊳ quarto edition, 1598. The central character is Prince Hal, the king's son and later ⊳ Henry V. The king is grieved first by the opposition of some of his nobels led by the Percy family, notably Henry (Harry) Hotspur, son of the Earl of Northumberland, and secondly by the dissolute conduct of his own son, who wastes his life in taverns instead of emulating Hotspur in a career of military honour. Hal's tavern companion is ⊳ Sir John Falstaff, one of the greatest of Shakespeare's comic characters. The contrast between Hotspur and Falstaff is the prominent feature of the play: Hotspur lives only for honour, without relating it to social responsibility; Falstaff, only for pleasure, in equal indifference to social consequences. Hotspur is thus passionate but inhuman, and Falstaff all too human in his passions. At the end of the play, Hal kills Hotspur at the battle of Shrewsbury, but Falstaff manages to steal the credit for Hotspur's death. The play is close to the morality tradition in its feeling and structure, Hotspur and Falstaff standing for 'honour' and 'riot' respectively; both in their different ways are rebels, the first in political terms against the state, and the second in spiritual terms against reason. Shakespeare's main sources were the chronicles of ⊳ Hall and ⊳ Holinshed.
⊳ *Henry IV, Part II.*

Henry IV, Part II
⊳ Quarto edition 1600. A continuation of ⊳ Shakespeare's *Henry IV, Part I*, though independent in mood and dramatic structure. The Percy rebellion continues, though Hotspur is dead. A sick weariness is over the country, and the king is dying. Hal is still the central character, and again flanked by contrasting types: on the one side Falstaff, pleasure-loving still but now ageing and grasping for the power he expects when Hal becomes King Henry V; on the other side, the scrupulous and fearless Lord Chief Justice, who has faced his responsibilities so far as to send the Prince himself to prison for riot. However, when Hal becomes king at the end of the play, he unexpectedly upholds the Lord Chief Justice and dismisses Falstaff from favour. Again, the morality drama tradition is a strong influence: the just king upholds the principle of justice, and sets his face against riot and self-indulgence. Some of the best scenes are still comedy, though the mood of *Part II* is grimmer than that of *Part I*; the comedy is chiefly in Mistress Quickly's Boar's Head Tavern in London, and on the country estate of Justice Shallow. Shakespeare's sources were again the 16th-century chronicles of ⊳ Hall and ⊳ Holinshed.
⊳ History plays; ⊳ *Henry IV, Part I.*

Henry V
A ⊳ history play by ⊳ Shakespeare performed in 1599; an imperfect version printed in 1600. It records the battle of Agincourt, Henry's great victory in France; this is the triumphal conclusion to the series that had so far dramatized national disaster: ⊳ *Richard II*, ⊳ *Henry IV, Parts I and II.* This play has been censured as too much a patriotic pageant with too little genuine dramatic interest. However, there is drama in the spectacle of a small national army, united in moral purpose under a Christian king, confronting a rich and massive array of selfishly disunited nobility. The disintegrative elements on the English side are still present in the traitors Scroop and Grey, and in ⊳ Falstaff's former cronies, Pistol, Bardolph and Nym. The union of the British Isles is forecast by the presence not only of the prominent Welsh officer, ⊳ Fluellen, but of Irish and Scottish officers as well, though Scotland was in fact an ally of France at the time. The play is indeed primarily a patriotic drama, but it is by no means an uncritical one. There is, for instance, the obvious element of conflict in Henry between his dual aspects as king and man, evident especially in his dialogue with Williams and his soliloquy in IV.i; modern critics (*eg* Traversi, *Approach to Shakespeare*) find many examples of irony at the expense of Henry in the play. It is interesting to note that *Henry V* has been filmed twice, each time with the director taking the eponymous lead: by Laurence Olivier (1907–89) in 1944, and by Kenneth Branagh in 1989.

Henry V (1413–22)
King of England, and second of the House of ⊳ Lancaster. His brief reign is memorable for his brilliant victory over the French at ⊳ Agincourt. By the Treaty of Troyes (1420) he was recognized as heir to the throne of

France, his claim to which had been the cause of the war. His dissolute youth (▷ Shakespeare's ▷ *Henry IV*) was a popular legend but is probably unfounded, though he was on bad terms with his father. He modelled himself on ▷ King Arthur, the heroes of the ▷ Crusades and the ideal of the Christian monarchy (the French war, in English eyes, was a just one) and in English tradition he became a national hero.

▷ Hundred Years' War.

Henry VI (1422–61)
King of England, and last of the House of ▷ Lancaster. He was strongly religious but no man of action, and his reign was darkened by the ▷ Wars of the Roses and by the final defeat of England in the ▷ Hundred Years' War.

Henry VI, Parts I, II* and *III
Three very early ▷ history plays by ▷ Shakespeare, perhaps written between 1590 and 1592. *Parts II* and *III* were published in 1594–5 under different titles, but *Part I* not until 1623; it was possibly written, or revised, after the other two. Together they make the first three parts of a tetralogy, ending with ▷ *Richard III*, in which the spreading feuds, hatreds, crimes and vengeances finally concentrate all their force in the wickedness of one man. *Part I*: the defeat of the English in the Hundred Years' War, and the beginning of aristocratic feuds; *Part II*: the marriage of Henry to the vigorous Margaret of Anjou, Jack Cade's popular rebellion, and the opening of the civil Wars of the Roses; *Part III*: Henry's final defeat and murder at the hands of the York branch of the Plantagenets, Edward Early of March (Edward IV, 1461–83) and his brother Richard of Gloucester (Richard III, 1483–5). The Henry VI plays have vivid and poignant episodes but are inferior to the masterly *Richard III*. The 16th-century chroniclers ▷ Hall and ▷ Holinshed are the sources of the plays.

Henry VII (1485–1509)
King of England. He was the first of the House of ▷ Tudor, of Welsh origin and related to the House of Lancaster; he defeated ▷ Richard III, last of the House of York, at the battle of Bosworth (1485), with a mainly Welsh army. Henry connected his Welsh background with ▷ King Arthur, and gave this name to his eldest son (d 1502). He was a notably able ruler, and was later paralleled with ▷ Henry V as a restorer of national unity and order after civil war. At the end of ▷ Shakespeare's ▷ *Richard III* he makes an appearance as a national redeemer. ▷ Francis Bacon wrote a life of him (1622).
Bib: Chrimes, S. B., *Henry VII*.

Henry VIII
A ▷ history play written (probably) by ▷ John Fletcher and ▷ Shakespeare in 1612–13. Its main episodes concern the divorce of Katharine of Aragon, the downfall of ▷ Cardinal Wolsey, and the triumph of ▷ Thomas Cranmer. The play ends with the triumphal christening of Henry's daughter, ▷ Princess Elizabeth, the future queen. In 1613 a performance of the play at the ▷ Globe Theatre caused the destruction of the building by fire.

Henry VIII (1509–47)
King of England. He was a powerful and talented man, entitled Defender of the Faith by the Pope for his ▷ pamphlet against ▷ Martin Luther, but he replaced Papal authority with his own by the Act of Supremacy, 1534, an act important for the subsequent development of national identity and sovereign independence. He is notorious for having had six wives, two of whom he executed and two divorced. His personal power was great but he generally exerted it through Parliament.

▷ Tudor, House of; Parr, Katherine.
Bib: Smith, H. M., *Henry VIII and the Reformation*.

Henry, Prince of Wales (1594–1612)
Patron. The brief, but enormously influential, period in which Henry governed his own household and cultivated his own cultural and political circles was seen by the ▷ Jacobean court as a rebirth of the ▷ Elizabethan golden age. The disillusionment that developed after the immediate glow of ▷ James I's coronation had faded, began to focus upon his son as a possible source of integrity, honour, cultural development and staunch ▷ Protestantism. Although the burden of expectation must have been great, Henry appeared to answer these demands. His early death (probably the earliest recorded case of typhoid) make it impossible to say how far he would have continued to extend his popularity, for it is easier to maintain an idealized value system from the margins of power than from the centralized role that kingship would have necessitated. Nevertheless, Henry cultivated those courtiers and writers who had been popular in Elizabeth's day, such as the ▷ Earl of Southampton and ▷ Michael Drayton. He is also known for his participation in two of ▷ Jonson's ▷ masques, *Prince Henry's Barriers* (1610) and *Prince Oberon* (1611).
Bib: Strong, R., *Henry, Prince of Wales, and England's Lost Renaissance*.

Henryson, Robert (c 1425–? 1500)
Scottish poet. Little is known about Henryson's life: it appears that he was a master at the Benedictine abbey grammar school in Dunfermline and was evidently a well-educated man with a university training. He composed a number of short poems, mostly on devotional themes, but is best known for his short narrative poetry including a collection of 13 animal

fables (the *Morall Fabillis of Esope*), and his continuation of the story of Criseyde (⊳ *The Testament of Cresseid*). His characteristic style favours abbreviation rather than amplification and he specializes in saying much in a brief space. His collection of animal fables, drawn from the tradition of ⊳ Aesop's fables and from the corpus of stories about Reynard the Fox, explores the variety of ways in which animals can be read and interpreted according to human schemes of knowledge. Henryson's interest in problems of interpretation and understanding is evident too in the sophisticated rereadings he offers of ⊳ Chaucer's ⊳ *Nun's Priest's Tale* (in his version of the fable of the Cock and the Fox and its sequel), and ⊳ *Troilus and Criseyde* (in his *Testament*).

⊳ *Reynard the Fox*.

Bib: Fox, D. (ed.), *The Poems of Robert Henryson*; Gray, D., *Robert Henryson*.

Henslowe, Phillip (d 1616)

Theatre owner and builder. The ⊳ Rose, the Hope, and the Fortune Theatres were all at least partly owned by him, and although an efficient businessman, he was also compassionate. His son-in-law was the famous actor ⊳ Edward Alleyn of the ⊳ Admiral's Men, whose finances he looked after. His Diary, 1592–1609, is a main source for the theatrical history of the age, but is not in itself very informative.

⊳ Theatres.

Bib: Carson, N., *A Companion to Henslowe's Diary*.

Her Majesty's Theatre

⊳ Haymarket Theatres.

Heraclitus (6th century BC)

Greek philosopher. He taught that the primary element is fire and that all being is, despite appearances, the process of 'becoming', by the harmonious interaction of opposites (hot, cold; dark, light; good, evil; etc.) 'The law of things is a law of Reason universal; but most men behave as though they had a wisdom of their own.' His mysticism and his sombre view of human nature caused him to be designated 'the dark philosopher'. ⊳ Gerard Manley Hopkins' poem 'That Nature is a Heraclitean fire . . . ' is an interesting example of the 19th-century's attempt to found its beliefs in classical antecedents.

⊳ Elements, The Four.

Herbert, Edward, 1st Baron Herbert of Cherbury (1583–1648)

Poet, philosopher and diplomat. Edward Herbert (Lord Herbert of Cherbury) was elder brother of ⊳ George Herbert. A friend of ⊳ John Donne, ⊳ Ben Jonson and ⊳ Thomas Carew, and an ardent Royalist before the ⊳ Civil War, Herbert's major works were his ⊳ autobiographical *The Life of Lord Herbert Written by Himself* (published by Horace Walpole in 1765); his philosophical *De Veritate* (1624) and his volume of poems *Occasional Verses* (1665).

The *Life*, written when Herbert was in his 60s, recalls his earlier adventures as a younger man, prior to his return from Paris in 1624, where he had been ambassador. The *De Veritate*, which was of considerable influence in the 17th century, attempts to explore rationalist positions in the general field of religious experience. Herbert's own religious position was that of an orthodox Anglican, of a strongly anti-Calvinist persuasion. He is seen to be the father of Deism and a forerunner of the Enlightenment.

Although his poetry was not published until 1665, the major portion of his verses was written before 1631. His poetic contemporaries thus included both his brother and Donne, of whose verses Herbert's poetry is strongly reminiscent.

⊳ Calvin, John.

Bib: Herbert, C. A., 'The Platonic Love Poetry of Lord Herbert of Cherbury', *Ball State University Forum* II; Hill, E. D., *Edward, Lord Herbert of Cherbury*.

Herbert, George (1593–1633)

Poet. Herbert shares, with ⊳ John Donne, the distinction of being one of the most widely read of the 17th-century poets in modern times. Though he was not ordained as a priest until 1630, and though court connections ensured that the earlier part of his life was spent in cosmopolitan circles, all the extant poems are devotional in nature.

His poetry was first published posthumously, in 1633, when *The Temple: Sacred Poems and Private Ejaculations* appeared under the auspices of his friend Nicholas Ferrar shortly after Herbert's death. The collection met with enormous approval, and was a considerable influence on ⊳ Richard Crashaw, amongst others. The poems in *The Temple* are deceptively simple at first glance. Yet in his exploitation of the speaking voice, and in the complexity of the complete structure of the volume of poems, Herbert rivals Donne for a fierce logical presence in his verse. Of considerable importance to Herbert's poetic undertaking is his espousal of a direct form of poetic discourse – one that, in many respects, looks forward to the reformist projects of later 17th-century theoreticians of language.

Herbert's other major work was the prose manual *A Priest to the Temple* (1652), which is a form of conduct-guide for the ideal Anglican priest. ⊳ Izaac Walton published a *Life* of Herbert in 1651.

Bib: Hutchinson, F. E. (ed.), *The Works of George Herbert*; Vendler, H., *The Poetry of Herbert*; Summers, J. H., *George Herbert: His Religion and Art*; Strier, R., *Love*

Known: Theology and Experience in George Herbert's Poetry.

Herbert, Sir Henry (1595–1673)
▷ Master of the Revels, 1623–42. He belonged to the literary Herbert family, which included his brothers ▷ Edward Herbert, ▷ George Herbert and Thomas Herbert, as well ▷ William Herbert in whose house, Wilton, Sir Henry met ▷ King James I and was awarded the post of Master of the Revels. Initially he seems to have been the deputy of Sir John Astley (who had succeeded ▷ Sir George Buc in 1622), but by 1623 Herbert was in full control. His influence was considerable as he was a conscientious reader of all plays and made careful excisions, for example, of all blasphemous language. He resumed his post on the Restoration of the monarchy in 1660, but had lost much of his fortune during the ▷ Interregnum and never fully recovered either his wealth or his position.
Bib: Adams, J. Q., *The Dramatic Records of Sir Henry Herbert.*

Herbert, James (b 1943)
Britain's best-selling ▷ horror novelist, Herbert rose to notoriety in the 1970s as a purveyor of unabashed visceral gore set in grimy, modern urban surroundings. His first novel *The Rats* (1974) was a huge paperback hit, earning Herbert the title 'King of the Nasties'; described by the author as a metaphor for urban collapse in which 'the rats are the establishment', the novel set new standards of gruesome violence for popular horror fiction. Although subsequent works such as *The Fog*, *Lair* and *Domain* have continued this penchant for dismemberment, Herbert has also explored more subtle territory; *Fluke* (1977) is a satirical reincarnation fantasy notable for its restrained tone, while *Shrine* (1983) takes a bold swipe at organized religion and fraudulent 'miracles'. Having worked as an advertising art director before turning to writing, Herbert is unique in retaining total control of his book covers, which he designs himself. Works include: *The Survivor* (1976); *The Spear* (1978); *The Dark* (1980); *The Jonah* (1981); *Domain* (1984); *Moon* (1985); *The Magic Cottage* (1987).

Herbert, Mary
▷ Sidney, Mary

Herbert, William (1580–1630)
Poet, dramatist and courtier, William Herbert, third Earl of Pembroke is one of the candidates for 'W.H.', the young man to whom ▷ Shakespeare's ▷ sonnets are dedicated. The grounds for this identification, apart from the initials, are Herbert's noble rank, his status as a well-known patron and the fact that the First Folio is partly dedicated to him. If Herbert is identified as the young man, then Mary Fitton his mistress could be linked to the dark lady of Shakespeare's work. When Herbert came to the court of ▷ Elizabeth I, he first attempted to join her coterie of favourites, but was too melancholy and scholarly for this somewhat chivalric group. He then fell out of favour completely when he got Fitton, a lady-in-waiting pregnant and refused to marry her; he was later to have two illegitimate children by ▷ Lady Mary Wroth. Herbert was imprisoned in the Fleet and never really gained acceptance at court until the accession of ▷ James I. A supporter of ▷ Ralegh, he had interests in colonial investments. Herbert also wrote ▷ masques and poetry, which were published in 1660. He was one of the wealthiest men in England and became an increasingly significant political figure, helping to overthrow the Earl of Somerset (whom he replaced as Lord Chamberlain) and to promote another royal favourite, ▷ Buckingham. Later, however, he was central to the resistance to Buckingham's influence over James and their pro-Spanish policies. He was a major patron of the arts and literature, and was praised particularly for this by ▷ Ben Jonson.

***Hereward the Wake* (1865)**
A ▷ historical novel by ▷ Charles Kingsley written after he became Regius Professor of History at Cambridge and based on the story of a half-legendary Anglo-Saxon hero who held out against William the Conqueror until 1070 in the town of Ely. The fame of Hereward depends a good deal on Kingsley's novel which is a colourful but inadequate story of battle, disguise and witchcraft.

Hermeneutics
Used in literary criticism to denote the science of interpretation as opposed to commentary. Hermeneutics is concerned primarily with the question of determining meaning, and is based upon the presupposition of a transcendental notion of understanding, and a conception of truth as being in some sense beyond language. Hermeneutics also postulates that there is one truth, and is therefore opposed on principle to the notion of 'pluralism' that is associated with ▷ deconstruction and materialist readings.

Hero and Leander
A poem left unfinished by ▷ Christopher Marlowe and completed by ▷ George Chapman (1598). Hero was a priestess of Aphrodite, and lived at Sestos on the European shore of the Hellespont. A youth called Leander, who loved her and lived at Abydos on the opposite shore, used to swim across to her at night, until he was drowned in a storm. Marlowe's poem is one of the finest narrative poems of this period.

Herod the Great
King of Judaea under the Romans in the time of Christ. According to the ▷ Bible (*Matthew*

2), in order to eliminate the infant Christ, he ordered the slaughter of all the young children in the village of Bethlehem. This made him the villain of the medieval ▷ Mystery plays dealing with the subject. In these, he is always shown as an arrogant, boisterous, bullying character. Hence Hamlet's phrase 'it out-herods Herod' (▷ *Hamlet* III.ii), referring to acting in a violent and exaggerated manner.

Herodotus (5th century BC)
Greek historian. His main theme is the wars of the Persians against the Greeks and other nations.

Heroic drama
Type of play popular during the period after the Restoration in Britain, with central characters of exalted stature, such as kings, queens and military generals, and a florid style of verse, usually rhymed ▷ couplets. The plays were modelled on French ▷ classical tragedies, especially those of ▷ Corneille and ▷ Racine, and often featured themes of conflict between the forces of love and honour. However, they were less careful of the ▷ classical unities than their French models. ▷ D'Avenant's ▷ *The Siege of Rhodes* was one of the earliest plays to display features of heroic drama, and his dedication to an edition of 1663 discusses 'héroique Plays'. Robert Howard's ▷ *The Indian Queen* (1664) helped to establish the type in Britain, and ▷ Dryden became one of its chief exponents, with plays including *The Indian Emperor* (1665), *The Conquest of Granada* (1665) and ▷ *Aureng-Zebe* (1675). ▷ Buckingham's satire of heroic plays, ▷ *The Rehearsal*, played a large part in bringing the form into disrepute, although ▷ Congreve's ▷ *The Mourning Bride* still displays some heroic features.

Heroic, Mock
A literary mode in which large and important events are juxtaposed with small and insignificant ones for a variety of comic, satirical or more profoundly ironic effects. In its narrow sense mock heroic is the product of the Augustan, neo-classical age. As the bourgeoisie wrested cultural hegemony from the aristocracy in the late 17th century, a new, more complex attitude to the ancient aristocratic ideals of honour and nobility developed. A new irony infused their literary expression in the ▷ classical forms of ▷ epic and ▷ tragedy. Epic retained the respect of the reading public, but it was too archaic and primitive to satisfy the modern imagination in its traditional form. ▷ John Milton's ▷ *Paradise Lost*, the only significant literary epic in English (▷ *Beowulf* being an oral poem), has about it much of the complexity of the novel, and its more atavistic heroic elements (the war in heaven, the vision of future history) seem mechanical. In the generations following Milton, the major poets, ▷ John Dryden and ▷ Alexander Pope translated the ancient epics, but their own original work took the more complex form of mock epic.

Augustan mock heroic is a development from the conceit of the Tudor and ▷ 'metaphysical' poets, and its imaginative appeal derives similarly from far-fetched and unexpected comparisons and parallels. At its most basic it can be simply ▷ satirical. The poet contrasts a contemptible modern person or event with a respected heroic version. ▷ Samuel Butler's ▷ *Hudibras* works largely on this level, and there is a strong element of this kind of satire in John Dryden's ▷ *Mac Flecknoe*. The respected touchstone need not be the classical epic, but can be any admired model from the past, or even the present. In ▷ *Absalom and Achitophel* it is the Old Testament. In parts of the ▷ *Dunciad* it is Milton and other 'classic' English poets such as ▷ Edmund Waller and ▷ Sir John Denham. In parts of the ▷ *Rape of the Lock* it is the pomp of religious ritual.

Nor need the contrast imply a moral satire on the modern world, or indeed any satire at all. At the beginning of *Absalom and Achitophel* the comparison of Charles II with King David in the Book of Kings, achieves the difficult task of aggrandizing the 'merry monarch' while at the same time slyly acknowledging his libertinism. The comparison between Belinda's petticoat-hoops and Achilles' shield in *The Rape of the Lock* mocks the heroic model rather than the modern equivalent, emphasizing the delightful domestic security of Belinda's world, as against the primitive *machismo* of the ancient heroes. Often the comparison between familiar and modern on the one hand, and exotic and ancient on the other, arises from pure imaginative playfulness, as when Pope, through implied puns, compares the ceremony of preparing coffee in an English drawing-room (on 'japanned' tables), with an awesome religious ceremony in distant Japan: 'On shining Altars of *Japan* they raise/The silver Lamp; the fiery Spirits blaze' (*Rape of the Lock* III, ii.107–8).

Although mock heroic is most closely associated with the age of Dryden, ▷ Jonathan Swift and Pope, it is found in all periods. An early example is ▷ Chaucer's ▷ *Nun's Priest's Tale* in which the cock behaves like a prince, although he is merely the property of a poor widow. The 'most Lamentable Comedy' of Pyramus and Thisby, performed by Bottom and the 'mechanicals' in ▷ *A Midsummer Night's Dream*, is a particularly complex example. The low social status and eager enthusiasm of the actors contrasts not only with the stilted nobility of the characters they impersonate, but also with the unimaginative condescension of the 'audience' within the play. In the Victorian period, mock heroic can be seen in simple form in the endearing pomposity of ▷ Charles

Dickens' Pickwick, and also in the more earnest social satire of such characters as Pecksniff and Dombey. In the 20th century the full complexity of 18th-century mock heroic is again achieved in ▷ James Joyce's ▷ *Ulysses*, whose carefully worked-out parallels with ▷ Homer's ▷ *Odyssey* are designed to demonstrate the comic irrelevance to human existence of any pretension to order, hierarchy, or even meaning.

Herrick, Robert (1591–1674)
Poet. Robert Herrick's poetry was published in a collection entitled *Hesperides* (1648), which appeared together with a companion volume, *His Noble Numbers*. Numerous manuscript versions of his poetry circulated in the 17th century, but the vast majority of his verse is represented in the 1648 publication. As one of the few ▷ Renaissance poets to gather his work into a single volume, it is important to look at Herrick's poetry as a self-consciously coherent pattern.

He has long been associated with the ▷ Cavalier poets, although his writing is of a quite different kind. Indeed, Herrick's gently mocking tone shows up the ▷ Stuart utopianism as hollow dreams. Herrick's chief stylistic models were the epigrammatic Latin poetic styles to be discovered in the works of ▷ Catullus and ▷ Horace. His delight in the epigrammatic style contrasts with his other memorable poetic achievement – the creation of fantasies which combine ▷ pastoral motifs with minutely observed details of nature. The poem that opens the 1648 collection ('The Argument of His Book') sets out his poetic manifesto, which is revealed to be one of nostalgic longing for a rural ideal, probably unobtainable.
Bib: Martin, L. C. (ed.), *Robert Herrick's Poetical Works*; Rollin, R. B. & Patrick, J. M. (eds.), *Trust to Good Verses: Herrick Tercentenary Essays*.

Hervey, Elizabeth (c 1748–c1820)
Novelist. Hervey was the half-sister of ▷ William Beckford, who is thought to have had her in mind when he attacked ▷ sentimental novels in *Modern Novel Writing*, although his attack could equally well be directed at ▷ Hannah More or ▷ Mary Robinson. Whatever the intention, Hervey appears to have been genuinely upset, partly because the accusation was not particularly just. Her works exhibit some of the plot characteristics of sentimental novels, for example in *Louisa* (1789), where the heroine is selflessly devoted to the illegitimate child of her betrothed, but her character sketches and descriptive passages are sharper and more self-consciously witty than Beckford's summation suggests.

Hervey, John, Baron of Ickworth (1696–1743)
Writer and politician. Son of the Earl of Bristol, whose title he inherited in 1723. In 1720 he married the maid of honour to the Princess of Wales, Molly Lepell, who was often mentioned in the letters and verses of ▷ Pope. He became MP for Bury, and supported ▷ Sir Robert Walpole. In 1730 he became Vice Chamberlain to George II. Later he was made Lord Privy Seal, and became a confidant of Queen Caroline. His *Memoirs of the Reign of George the Second*, not published until 1848, describes the events of the period with keen satire. Pope developed a fierce animosity toward Hervey, whom he made a target for his own satire. He resented Hervey's friendship with ▷ Lady Mary Wortley Montagu, whom he himself admired, and despised Hervey's supposed 'feminine' behaviour, including taking extreme care with his diet because of ill-health, and using rouge to disguise his pallor. Pope lampooned him savagely him in the character of Sporus, in the *Epistle to Dr Arbuthnot*, and in ▷ *The Dunciad*. As with Pope's other target, ▷ Colley Cibber, the attacks were sufficient to damn him in the eyes of posterity, and even in his own time Hervey was ridiculed with another nickname used by Pope, 'Lord Fanny'.

Heteroglossia
A term introduced by the Russian theorist and critic ▷ Mikhail Bakhtin to describe the plurality of social voices in a novel (though the term is now used of other genres). For Bakhtin, one of the great virtues of a novel is that it offers a destabilising multiplicity of voices and styles which are in ▷ dialogical relationship with each other, and especially with the formal narrative voice. Heteroglossia, therefore, represents for Bakhtin a desirable and energetic plurality.
▷ Carnival; ▷ Polyphony.
Bib: Bakhtin, M., *The Dialogical Imagination*; Dentith, S., *Bakhtinian Thought*.

Hexameter
A line of verse having six metrical feet.
▷ Metre.

Heyer, Georgette (1902–74)
Novelist. Georgette Heyer was a phenomenally prolific and popular writer of detective stories and historical romances, the latter populated with a mixture of fictional characters and real historical figures, and often set in the Regency period. Whilst her writing has traditionally been criticized for its predictably escapist plots, recent feminist work on romantic fiction has emphasized its interest as fantasy and the important role that her books play in many women's lives. Her works include: *The Black Moth* (1921); *Simon the Coldheart* (1925); *The Barren Court* (1930); *The Convenient Marriage* (1934); *Regency Buck* (1935); *Royal Escape* (1937); *Beau Wyndham* (1941); *Arabella* (1949);

Bath Tangle (1955); *April Lady* (1957); *Freedom* (1965); *Lady of Quality* (1972).
Bib: Radway, J., *Reading the Romance*.
⊳ Detective fiction; romantic fiction.

Heywood, John (?1497–?1580)
Dramatist. He wrote highly entertaining short plays of the kind known as ⊳ interludes, *eg Play of the Weather* (1533), *A Play of Love* (1534), and ⊳ *The Four P's* (1568).
Bib: Johnson R. C., *John Heywood*.

Heywood, Thomas (?1574–1641)
Dramatist, actor, poet, pamphleteer; Heywood was, by his own claims, immensely prolific. His field was especially the drama of sentiment with middle-class characters, and to this belong his best-known plays, ⊳ *A Woman Killed with Kindness* and *The English Traveller*. His ⊳ blank verse, though not great poetry, benefits by the influences of a great age, and though plain, sometimes achieves poignancy. His first play may have been *The Four Prentices of London*, obviously appealing to a citizen (as distinct from a court) audience by its combination of romance and idealization of the middle class. This was perhaps acted as early as 1592. His many plays include ⊳ *The Fair Maid of the West; Edward II*; *The Wise Woman of Hogsdon*. However, Heywood had a more pervasive role in the theatre of the day, which he believed should be for public enjoyment and not as an attempt at 'literature'. He wrote several civic ⊳ pageants, was a shareholder in Queen Anne's Men, and, most importantly, wrote a sharp defence of the theatre against Puritan condemnation, *An Apology for Actors* (pub. 1612).
Bib: Boas, F. S., *Thomas Heywood*.

Hill, Geoffrey (b 1932)
Poet. His first two volumes, *For the Unfallen* (1959) and *King Log* (1968), established the characteristics of his poetry: intense moral seriousness, intellectual complexity and a concern with mythical and historical subjects, most notably with the victims of war or persecution. *Mercian Hymns* (1971), a remarkable sequence of prose poems, added elements of humour and ⊳ autobiography; *Tenebrae* (1978) is dominated by the relation of divine and human love, while *The Mystery of the Charity of Charles Peguy* (1978) is a single extended meditation on the life of the French poet. Hill's work shows many continuities with the ⊳ Modernists, especially ⊳ T. S. Eliot, and testifies to the influence of a wide range of European and American thinkers and poets. His recent work includes: *The Lords of Limit* (1984); and *Collected Poems* (1985).
Bib: Robinson, P. (ed.), *Geoffrey Hill: Essays on his Work*; Sherry, V., *The Uncommon Tongue*.

Hill, Susan (b 1942)
Novelist, short-story writer and radio dramatist. Since graduating from London University, she has worked as a literary journalist and broadcaster. Her novels are sensitive, formal and conventionally structured, and tend to explore loss, isolation and grief. *In The Springtime of the Year* (1974) recounts the gradual adjustment to bereavement of a young widow. She has written effectively of the experience of children (*I'm The King of The Castle*; 1970) and the elderly (*Gentlemen and Ladies*; 1968). Two of her novels deal with intense male friendships; these are *The Bird of Night* (1972) and, probably her best-known work, *Strange Meeting* (1971). The latter takes its title from a poem by ⊳ Wilfred Owen, and is set in the trenches of Flanders during World War I. Other novels: *The Enclosure* (1961); *Do Me A Favour* (1963); *A Change for the Better* (1969); *The Woman in Black: A Ghost Story* (1983); *Air and Angels* (1991); *The Mist in the Mirror* (1992); and *Mrs de Winter* (1993), a sequel to Daphne du Maurier's *Rebecca*. Story collections are: *The Albatross* (1971); *The Custodian* (1972); *A Bit of Singing and Dancing* (1973).

Hilliard, Nicholas (c 1547–1619)
Miniaturist. One of the most well-known artists of the Elizabethan court, Hilliard somehow managed to capture the self-fashioning golden age of this world with his sumptuous detail, delicate brush strokes and abundant use of ⊳ allegory and mythology. Even the size of the works contributes to the sense of the intimate and precocious coteries surrounding ⊳ Elizabeth I. He was praised in verse by ⊳ Donne and ⊳ Constable, and he wrote his own work, the *Art of Limning* (1603), where he argues that painting is a suitable practice for a gentleman.
Bib: Murdoch, J. (ed.), *The English Miniature;* Strong, R., *Nicholas Hilliard* and *The English Renaissance Miniature*.

Hilton, Walter (d 1396)
Mystical writer. Hilton was an Augustine canon of Thurgarton, near Southwell, Nottinghamshire, and the author of *The Scale of Perfection*, an English prose work of spiritual instruction, addressed to a single anchoress, which bears some traces of the influence of the work of ⊳ Richard Rolle and ⊳ *The Cloud of Unknowing*. It is clear from the numbers of extant manuscripts of *The Scale of Perfection* that it was a relatively popular work, and it was printed by ⊳ Wynkyn de Worde in 1494.
Bib: Sitwell, G. (trans.) *The Scale of Perfection*.

***Hind and the Panther, The* (1687)**
A didactic poem in heroic ⊳ couplets by ⊳ John Dryden, written after his conversion to ⊳ Catholicism in 1685, and counterbalancing his earlier defence of the Church of England, ⊳ *Religio Laici* (1682). It takes the form of a perfunctory ⊳ allegory, in which the Hind

(the Church of Rome) and the Panther (the Church of England) debate at length the merits of their different beliefs.

▷ Prior, Matthew.

Hippocrates (5th–4th centuries BC)
Greek physician – known as 'the father of medicine'. Reputed author of writings called the Hippocratic Collection, including the Hippocratic Oath whereby confidential information given to doctors is not to be disclosed. The theory of ▷ humours is attributed to him.

Historia Regum Britanniae (History of the Kings of Britain)
Major work of ▷ Geoffrey of Monmouth, completed around 1138, recounting the history of the kings of the island from its foundation by Brutus to the loss of British sovereignty in the reign of Cadwallader.

▷ Arthur, King.

Historical novel
A novel set in a well-defined historical context, generally before the author's own life (and therefore, in that sense at least, not based on the author's own experience, but on other sources, whether literary or historical). Historical novels often include versions of real events and persons and descriptions of social customs, clothing, buildings etc. to give an effect of verisimilitude. However, there are also more fantastical versions of the form, such as the ▷ Gothic novel (often though not always historical). Contemporary best-selling historical romances, such as those of ▷ Georgette Heyer, have a certain limited verisimilitude of detail, but a strong fantasy element as regards plot. An early example of the European historical novel is *The Princess of Clèves* by ▷ Madame de La Fayette, while later distinguished practitioners of the form include ▷ Balzac, ▷ Tolstoy, ▷ Stendhal and the German novelist Thomas Mann. In Britain it was ▷ Sir Walter Scott who established the popularity of the form, but there are examples by such novelists as ▷ Charles Dickens, ▷ George Eliot and ▷ Thomas Hardy and, more recently, ▷ William Golding and ▷ J.G. Farrell. There are also many historical novels by post-colonial writers about the colonial period, such as ▷ Patrick White's *Voss* and ▷ Chinua Achebe's *Arrow of God*. ▷ Historiographic metafiction represents a distinctively ▷ post-modernist version of the historical novel.
Bib: Lukács, Georg, *The Historical Novel*.

Historicism
A general term used in a range of disciplines and frequently found in discussions of literary theory. The meaning of historicism is complicated by three distinct usages:

1 A method of interpretation which claims that literary texts can only be properly understood in their historical context. This is the neutral, even positive usage, and is widely found in literary studies.

2 The word is also used negatively to indicate what critics take to be the fallacy of this view. Opponents argue that, in reality, we can never understand the past accurately enough to sustain this ambition, and that historicists merely project their own wishes and interests onto the past.

3 An even more negative colouring is given in the third usage. This derives from the philosopher and political theorist Karl Popper who criticised political theories based upon supposed laws of history which imply the inevitability of certain forms of development. Examples of historicist theories in this sense are those of Marx and ▷ Comte. Historicism has recently had a revival in the movement known as New Historicism.
Bib: Hamilton, P., *Historicism*.

Histories and Chronicles
Histories and chronicles are important in the study of literature in two ways: as sources for imaginative material and as literature in their own right. However, with the exception of the ▷ Venerable Bede, it was not until the 17th century that English historians began to achieve the status of major writers.

▷ Geoffrey of Monmouth (d 1154) is the most important amongst a number of medieval historians for originating two national myths in his ▷ *Historia Regum Britanniae*; the myth that Brutus, (▷ Brut), great-grandson of Aeneas, was the founder of the British race, and the myth of ▷ King Arthur as the great defender of British Christianity. Both had importance in nourishing nascent English patriotism. When England became a centralized state under the ▷ Tudor monarchs, ▷ Henry VII chose the name Arthur for his eldest son. It was the main task of Tudor chroniclers both to heighten patriotism and to identify it with loyalty to the ruling family. This was the purpose of the Latin history of England by the Italian Polydore Vergil, in the service of Henry VII and ▷ Henry VIII. More important was ▷ Edward Hall's *The Union of the two Noble and Illustrious Families of Lancaster and York* (1548), which showed the House of Tudor to be the saviour of the nation after the civil ▷ Wars of the Roses in the 15th century. ▷ Raphael Holinshed's *Chronicles of England, Scotland and Ireland* (1578) was a compilation from various sources, including Geoffrey of Monmouth, and begins in ancient biblical times. The belief of the time was that history was useful as the means by which the present could learn from the past as a source of warnings, precepts and examples. The imaginative writers used the material of the chronicles in this spirit. Geoffrey of Monmouth, Hall and Holinshed were sources for many of the historical dramas of the reign of ▷ Elizabeth including those of ▷ Shakespeare, and also for narrative poets such as those who contributed to *A Mirror for Magistrates* (1559), ▷ Samuel Daniel (*Civil Wars*, 1595–1609) and ▷ Michael Drayton (*The Barons' Wars*, 1603). Much of this new interest in history arose from the ▷ Renaissance transference of attention from heavenly destinies to earthly ones; thus the period 1500–1650 also produced the first eminent antiquarians, notably William Camden (1551–1623), and the first historical ▷ biographies: ▷ Thomas More's *Richard III* (written 1513), George Cavendish's life of ▷ Cardinal Wolsey (written shortly after the Cardinal's death but not published in full until 1667), ▷ Francis Bacon's life of Henry VII (1622) and ▷ Lord Herbert's life of Henry VIII (1648).

The True Historical Narrative of the Rebellion and Civil Wars in England by ▷ Edward Hyde, Earl of Clarendon, is the first major historical work to rank as distinguished literature in English. Clarendon began it in 1646 but it was not published until 1702–4. It is told from the point of view of an important participator in the events and is notable especially for its portraits of other participators. Clarendon was a royalist; his younger contemporary, Gilbert Burnet (1643–1715), told the story of the second half of the century from the opposing political viewpoint in his most important work, *The History of My Own Time*. Burnet was more of a professional historian than Clarendon (who was primarily a statesman who took to history partly in self-justification) and he initiated historical writing as a major branch of literary activity and scholarship. The distinguished historical writing of William Robertson (*History of Scotland during the Reigns of Queen Mary and James VI*, 1759, and *Charles V*, 1769), of ▷ David Hume the philosopher (*History of Great Britain*, pub. 1754–61) and the lighter histories of England by the novelist ▷ Tobias Smollett (1756) and by ▷ Oliver Goldsmith (1764) have been superseded by later work, but ▷ Edward Gibbon's ▷ *Decline and Fall of the Roman Empire* (1776–88) is a work not only of history but of English literature and, in the quality of its outlook on civilization, an 18th-century monument.

The 18th century was the one in which antiquarian scholarship became thoroughly established; the antiquarians were interested by the nature of their studies in the detailed life of the past. ▷ Walter Scott was one of them and his historical novels, though very uneven in quality, are important as a new kind of history as well as a new kind of imaginative literature. It was his re-creation of the daily life of the past that was one of the influences upon ▷ Thomas Carlyle, whose historical works (the most notable of which is his *French Revolution*, 1837) are more imaginative than factual. ▷ T.B. Macaulay was a better historian and not inferior as an imaginative writer; ▷ *Macaulay's History of England* is the only historical work which comes near Gibbon's *Decline and Fall* in reputation, and Macaulay was responsible for the so-called 'Whig view of history' as steady progress in material welfare and political advance. Other eminent 19th-century English historians were J.A. Froude, who is, however, notorious for his prejudices in *A History of England from the Fall of Wolsey to the Spanish Armada* (1856–70), and J.R. Green whose *Short History of the English People* (1874) was for some time a popular classic owing to the breadth of Green's social sympathies. It was, however, in the 19th century that the controversy about history as an art or as a science developed, and other distinguished historians of the period tended to become comparatively specialized scholars without the breadth of appeal of such men as Gibbon and Macaulay. The latter's great-nephew, G.M. Trevelyan (1876–1962), continued the broader humane tradition of historical writing, as did Arnold Toynbee's *A Study of History* (1934–61). Recent theoretical developments have led to renewed questioning of the terms of historical knowledge: see for example the work of Hayden White.

▷ Tudor myth; Heritage culture.

Historiographic metafiction
Term coined by the critic Linda Hutcheon to refer to 'novels which are both intensely self-reflexive (that is, they allude to their own fictional status) and yet paradoxically also lay claim to historical events and personages' (*A Poetics of Postmodernism: History, Theory, Fiction*). Examples are *The French Lieutenant's Woman* by ▷ John Fowles, and *Midnight's Children* by ▷ Salman Rushdie.

History of England from the Accession of James II
The history by ▷ Thomas Macaulay (Vols. 1 & 2, 1848; 3 & 4, 1855; 5, 1861) is a thorough, detailed account of two reigns: ▷ James II and ▷ William III. It is unfinished and was originally intended to extend to the time of George I (1714–27) and further. The period covered is perhaps the most crucial for English political development. ▷ James II, a ▷ Catholic, tried to enforce his will in the Catholic interest against Parliament, which frustrated him and expelled him from the throne in the ▷ Glorious Revolution of 1688. Parliament then summoned William from Holland to reign jointly with his wife, who was also James' daughter ▷ Mary II (1689–94). William was the champion of the ▷ Protestant cause in Europe, and Mary was also Protestant.

Macaulay's politics were strongly in the Whig parliamentary tradition and his history is an ▷ epic of the triumph of the ideas which to him gave meaning to English history. Considered as history, the work is accordingly one-sided, much more a work of historical art than of historical science; it represents what historians have come to call 'the Whig interpretation of history'.

History of Rasselas, Prince of Abyssinia, The
▷ *Rasselas, Princes of Abyssinia, The History of.*

History of Sir Charles Grandison, The
▷ *Sir Charles Grandison, The History of.*

History plays (chronicle plays)
These are especially a phenomenon of the last two decades of the 16th century, when they may have accounted for more than one-fifth of the plays written in a very prolific period of the drama. The history play is distinct from what is ordinarily called historical drama, which is a phenomenon of the 19th and 20th centuries, and, like the historical novel of the same period, involves reconstructing another period of history in awareness of its differences in customs, habits, outlook, etc. Absence of 'scientific' history in the 16th century debarred dramatists from a 'historical' sense. On the other hand, they were familiar with the dramatization of biblical events relevant to the Fall and Redemption of Man in the religious mystery plays: in a similar way history was to them and their audiences a collection of tales about the past, many of which were relevant to contemporary national predicaments. Thus in the 16th century the English Church and state had cut loose from the Roman Catholic Church, and there was consequent interest in the reign of ▷ King John (1199–1216) when there had been a comparable quarrel between king and pope; in the reign of ▷ Elizabeth I men were alarmed at the possible consequences of the queen's dying without a direct heir, and this caused them to be interested in the reign of ▷ Richard II, and so on. The morality plays also influenced the histories: until the 16th century, moralities had concerned themselves with the spiritual destinies of men in general, but the growth of national consciousness, the splintering off of national churches in the 16th century and the increased importance of the national ruler in deciding human destinies, all caused morality dramatists to extend their interest to politics and to draw on history for their subject matter. Thus ▷ John Bale, supporter of Henry VIII in his emancipation of the English Church from Rome, wrote *King John* (?1547) to make his case for Henry's policy. The morality content of Bale's play gives it coherent structure, but the chronicles of the 1580s, *eg The Famous Victories of Henry V* (?1588), relied chiefly on the eventfulness of their episodes. It was ▷ Marlowe (*Edward II*, ?1593) and ▷ Shakespeare in his two great tetralogies (▷ *Henry VI, Parts I, II* and *III* and ▷ *Richard III;* ▷ Richard II, ▷ Henry IV, Parts I and *II* and ▷ *Henry V*) and ▷ *King John*, who gave psychological and intellectual substance to the history-play form. Marlowe did little more than bring his characters vividly to his audience, but Shakespeare brought deep insights to bear on the nature of political society and its problems. His two tetralogies have been called a great national dramatic epic covering the years 1377–1485; however, it is the second half of the period (from 1422 to 1485; the reigns of Henry VI, Edward IV and Richard III) which constitutes his earlier work (perhaps 1590–93) while the plays concerning the first half (Richard II, Henry IV, Henry V) are relatively mature work (perhaps 1596–99). *King John* (?1596) is between the tetralogies in regard to maturity of style.

It becomes difficult, in the maturer Shakespeare, to draw a clear line between history plays and tragedy. ▷ *Julius Caesar* follows the Greek historian ▷ Plutarch closely, but it is also a tragedy; and ▷ *King Lear* derives from the chronicler ▷ Holinshed as does ▷ *Henry V*, though the former is not history. The history plays and tragedies in fact merge into each other; both contain politics, and both present tragic catastrophe.

Hoban, Russell (b 1925)
American novelist who has lived in London since 1969. After serving in the US army during World War II, he worked as a magazine and advertising artist and an advertising copywriter before becoming a full-time writer in 1967. His best-known work is *Ridley Walker* (1980), set 2,000 years after a nuclear war and written in an invented argot combining elements of cockney and technical language. His other novels are: *The Lion of Boaz-Jachim and Jachim-Boaz* (1973); *Kleinzeit* (1974); *Turtle Diary* (1976); *Pilgermann* (1983); *The Medusa Frequency* (1987). He has also published much fiction and verse for children, a play and a television play. He won the Whitbread Award in 1974.

Hobbes, John Oliver (1867–1906)
▷ Pseudonym of Mrs Pearl (Mary Teresa) Craigie who was born near Boston, Massachusetts and moved with her family to London as a baby. She was educated in Berkshire and Paris, read widely, and published her first stories at the age of nine. She began writing regular drama and art columns soon after her marriage to Reginald Walpole Craigie in 1887. Her first novel *Some Emotions and A Moral* (1892) established her reputation as a clever and caustic writer, and set a pattern for her subsequent fiction in its treatment of ill-matched marriages and disillusioned idealism. Her output spans ten novels, including: *The Sinner's Comedy* (1892), *The Gods, Some Mortals and Lord Wickenham*

(1895), *The Scheme For Saints* (1897), *Robert Orange* (1899), an idealized fictional portrait of ▷ Disraeli, and *The Serious Wooing* (1901); several successful plays such as *The Ambassador* (1898); sketches and ▷ travel essays as well as essays on George Eliot (*Encyclopaedia Britannica*, 1901) and George Sand (1902). She was a figure in London's literary life and was admired by writers such as ▷ Thomas Hardy. She became President of the Society of Women Journalists in 1895 – the same year as her highly publicized divorce following the birth of her son, of whom she gained custody after a public trial. Paradoxically she was also a member of the Anti-Suffrage League (▷ Women's suffrage). She converted to ▷ Catholicism in 1892 and her last novel *The Dream and the Business* (1906) deals obliquely with the 'clever' woman's predicament.

▷ 'Woman Question, The'.

Bib: Maison, M., *Life*; Richards, J.M., *Life*.

Hobbes, Thomas (1588–1679)
Philosopher. Together with the writings of ▷ Francis Bacon and ▷ René Descartes, the political and philosophical theories of Thomas Hobbes dominated thought in late 17th-century England. Yet, unlike Bacon's boundless optimism, Hobbes' philosophy appeared to be determined by an almost cynical view of human nature and society. In his great analysis of the individual and the individual's place in society, *Leviathan* (1651), Hobbes argued that human society was governed by two overwhelming individual concerns: fear (of death, other individuals, etc.) and the desire for power. For Hobbes society is organized according to these two principles, and can be rationally analysed as a 'mechanism' (an important Hobbesian concept) governed by these two concerns.

Leviathan itself emerged out of the turmoil of revolutionary upheaval in England during the ▷ Civil War, and the figure of the 'Leviathan' – the sovereign power, though not necessarily the monarch – expresses a desire for stable government. But in addition to *Leviathan* Hobbes published in various fields of philosophical and social enquiry. His interest in language and the uses of ▷ rhetoric was to be influential amongst post-Restoration thinkers. But it was his analysis of the mechanical laws (as he saw them) of production, distribution and exchange that was to be of profound importance in British economic and philosophical thought in the 18th century and later.

Hobbes' chief works include: *The Elements of Law* (written by 1640, but published ten years later); *De Cive* (1642, translated into English in 1651); *De Corpore* (1655, translated in 1656); and *De Homine* (1658). Hobbes also undertook an analysis of the causes of the English Civil War in composing *Behemoth* (1682), as well as critical work – in particular his *Answer* to ▷ Sir William D'Avenant's *Preface to Gondibert* (1650).

Bib: Molesworth, Sir W. (ed.), *The English Works of Thomas Hobbes* (11 vols.); Mintz, S. I., *The Hunting of Leviathan*.

Hobbinol
▷ Harvey, Gabriel.

Hoby, Lady Margaret (1571–1633)
Diarist. Although Lady Margaret's diary is important in generic terms in that it is the earliest diary written by an Englishwoman to have survived, its contents are repetitive and mundane. She dutifully recounts her morning prayers and the day-to-day running of a Renaissance household. Sometimes humorous juxtapostionings occur, but it is difficult to ascertain whether the irony is intentional. She was married three times before she was 30: to Walter Devereux, the brother of the ▷ Earl of Essex; to Thomas Sidney, the brother of ▷ Mary Sidney, Countess of Pembroke; and to Thomas Hoby, son of ▷ Thomas Hoby and ▷ Elizabeth Russell. Her diary was published this century: *The Diary of Lady Hoby*, ed. Dorothy M. Meads (1930).

Hoby, Sir Thomas (1530–66)
Translator. Primarily known for his ▷ translation of ▷ Castiglione's *Il Cortegiano* as *The Courtier*, which he wrote in Paris in 1552–3, but which was not published until 1561. It was an immediate success and influenced both young noblemen and women who attempted to emulate the idealized characters in the text, as well as late Elizabethan writers who portrayed similar courtly debate in their own works (▷ Spenser, ▷ Jonson and ▷ Shakespeare). Hoby was the first husband of ▷ Lady Elizabeth Russell, who was also an accomplished translator.

▷ Hoby, Lady Margaret.

Bib: Crane, T. F., *Italian Social Customs of the Sixteenth Century*.

Hoccleve, Thomas (1368–1426)
Poet. Hoccleve worked as a clerk for the Office of the Privy Seal in Westminster from c 1387–1423. He suffered a mental breakdown in 1416. His poetry covers a range of courtly topics but has a distinctive interest in the self-presentation and literary representation of Hoccleve himself. His *Letter of Cupid* (1402) is an abridgement of a work by the French writer Christine de Pisan, in which the God of Love defends women against the slanders of men. Hoccleve's most famous work, the *Regement of Princes* (1405), is a contribution to the well-established tradition of treatises which offer guides to the right conduct of princes, through a mixture of moralizing advice and exemplary stories. In the text Hoccleve represents himself as a disciple of ▷ Chaucer, whose literary skills he praises; he not only includes a verbal

portrait of Chaucer but also a visual portrait of him: Hoccleve's interest in self-portraiture is evident in the Prologue to the *Regement*: rather than cultivating the notion of a fictional first-person narrator (in the manner of Chaucer and ▷ John Gower), he fictionalizes his own identity, and describes his life and work. This interest in self-presentation is seen again in *La Male Regle de Thomas Hoccleve* (1405), where the subject is his own bad conduct and dissolute life. In the *Complaint* (1421–2), an autobiographical frame is given to a collection of narrative and didactic material, in which he alludes to his earlier illness and describes his anxieties about composing the work which follows. **Bib**: Seymour, M. C. (ed.), *Selections from Hoccleve*.

Hofland, Barbara (1770–1844)
Poet and novelist. Hugely prolific northern writer, Hofland was widowed only two years after her marriage to Thomas Hoole and was forced to write in order to keep herself and her baby. Her first book, *Poems* (1805), was successful and, although she ran a boarding school in Harrogate, she continued publishing, moving from poetry to the more lucrative novel form. In 1808 she married the young, self-centred artist, Thomas Hofland, and was forced to provide for the family by writing at night, so as not to disturb his daytime creative activities. There is an interesting portrait of an egotistical artist in Hofland's ▷ didactic text, *Son of a Genius* (1812). On the whole her work is lively and carefully presented, with some lighter touches in the later, more psychologically involved novels such as *Katherine* (1828).

Hogan, Desmond (b 1950)
Irish novelist, short-story writer and playwright. Born in County Galway and educated at University College Dublin, Hogan has worked as an actor, writer and teacher. His fiction, set in Ireland, has primarily been concerned with the tragic stories of vulnerable, isolated individuals though his most recent novel, *A Farewell to Prague* (1995), is a semi-autobiographical, fragmentary account of the travels of an Irishman in Europe and further afield, developing his explicitly autobiographic work, *The Edge of the City: A Scrapbook 1976–91* (1993). Other novels: *The Ikon Maker* (1976); *The Leaves on Grey* (1980); *A Curious Street* (1984); *A New Shirt* (1986); *A Link with the River* (1989). Volumes of short stories: *The Diamonds at the Bottom of the Sea* (1979); *Children of Lir: Stories of Ireland* (1981); *Stories* (1982); *The Mourning Thief* (1987); *Lebanon Lodge* (1988). He has also written plays for the stage, for radio and for television.

Hogarth Press, The
Publishing house. Started by ▷ Virginia Woolf and her husband Leonard, at their home, Hogarth House, Richmond, the Hogarth Press moved to Tavistock Square in 1924 and became an allied company of Chatto and Windus in 1947. John Lehmann became a partner in 1938. In the early years of its existence the press published work by, among others, Virginia Woolf, ▷ T. S. Eliot and ▷ Katherine Mansfield, as well as translations of the work of European novelists and poets.

Hogarth, William (1697–1764)
Painter. He excelled in the depiction of social life, especially the heartlessness of the richer classes permeated by social arrogance and commercial greed, with the consequent neglect of the poor. He painted sequences that followed a theme, a technique which is a pictorial equivalent of a stage drama: 'I wished to compose pictures on canvas, similar to representations on the stage; . . . I have endeavoured to treat my subjects as a dramatic writer; my picture is my stage, and men and women are my players . . .' His art became extremely popular, because he made engravings of his oil paintings, and they were to be found on the walls of inns and cottages, not merely in great country houses. In his breadth of appeal and his ▷ realism, he is in strong contrast to the fashionable portrait painters of the 18th century, ▷ Joshua Reynolds and ▷ Gainsborough, and in the quality of his social indignation and his concern with unprivileged humanity he anticipates the poet-engraver ▷ William Blake. Some of his series of what he called 'pictur'd Morals' are: *A Harlot's Progress* (1731); *A Rake's Progress* (1735); *Marriage à la Mode* (1743–5); *The Four Stages of Cruelty, Beer Street* and *Gin Lane* (1751) (2.2.3) and *Election* (1754–66).

Hogarth's literary connections were close. ▷ Jonathan Swift invokes him as natural collaborator in his own kind of savage ▷ satire in his poem *The Legion Club* (1736), and his friendship with the novelists ▷ Samuel Richardson and ▷ Henry Fielding influenced the visual element which gives their novels an advantage over those of ▷ Daniel Defoe. The ordinary people who enjoyed owning and interpreting his engravings, with their satirical edge, were the foundation of the market for later cheap serial fiction, with its engraved illustrations. The importance of the visual element in serials from Charles Dickens' *Pickwick Papers* onwards owes a debt to Hogarth and his successors.
Bib: Moore, R. E., *Hogarth's Literary Relationships*.

Hogg, James (1770–1835)
Poet and novelist. Hogg was nicknamed 'the Ettrick Shepherd' because he had been a shepherd in Ettrick Forest in southern Scotland until his poetic talent was discovered by ▷ Sir Walter Scott. He is now best known for his

powerful work of Calvinist guilt and ▷ Gothic supernaturalism, *The Private Memoirs and Confessions of a Justified Sinner* (1824).
Bib: Groves, D., *James Hogg: the Growth of a Writer*.

Holbein, Hans, the younger (c 1487–1543)
Painter. Born in Augsburg, Germany, Holbein came to England to the household of ▷ Sir Thomas More in 1526–8 on the recommendation of ▷ Erasmus, for whom he had illustrated *Praise of Folly* (1509). Several works of the More household remain, as well as sketches or paintings of ▷ Thomas Cromwell, ▷ Sir Thomas Wyatt and Henry Howard, ▷ Earl of Surrey, as well as his most famous portrait of ▷ Henry VIII. Holbein's meticulous and naturalistic style was a dramatic innovation in England and heralded the end of medieval symbolic representations in favour of the greater individuality of ▷ Renaissance art.
Bib: Robert J., *Holbein*.

Holcroft, Thomas (1745–1809)
Dramatist, novelist, actor, translator, largely associated with the introduction of continental melodrama to the English stage. In 1770 Holcroft obtained a post as prompter in the Dublin theatre and this was followed by a period of acting with strolling companies in England, and in 1778 an engagement at the ▷ Drury Lane Theatre, where his first play was performed. In 1780 his first novel, *Alwyn or the Gentleman Comedian* was published, drawing on his experiences as a strolling actor. His first comedy, *Duplicity*, was staged at ▷ Covent Garden in 1781. In 1784, on a visit to Paris, Holcroft was impressed by a production of Beaumarchais' *Le Mariage de Figaro* and, being unable to obtain a copy, he committed the entire play to memory. On his return, his translation was mounted at Covent Garden under the title *The Follies of the Day*. In 1792 Holcroft's most successful play, *The Road to Ruin*, was produced, again at Covent Garden.

An ardent supporter of the ▷ French Revolution, Holcroft became active on its behalf in England, and was imprisoned briefly for alleged treason. In 1799 he moved to Paris, where he lived for four years. In his absence his *A Tale of Mystery*, a translation from a play by Pixérécourt, was produced in London. He also published several translations of novels and wrote operas, afterpieces, and polemical essays.
Bib: Rosenblum, J. (ed.), *The Plays of Thomas Holcroft*.

Holden, Molly (1927–81)
Poet. Born in Swindon and educated in London, Molly Holden's gentle and understated poetry is now beginning to receive greater attention, but being essentially at odds with more radical poetic trends, this rather fragile 'nature poetry' (which draws on the influences of ▷ Thomas Hardy and Edward Thomas) has hitherto brought it a limited readership. She has also written three novels for children. She was a long-term sufferer of multiple sclerosis, of which she died in 1981. Her poetic works include: *A Hill Like a Horse* (1963); *The Bright Cloud* (1964); *Make Me Grieve* (1968); *Air and Chill Earth* (1971); *The Country Over* (1975); and the posthumous *New and Selected Poems* (1986).

Holdsworth, Annie (b1857–?1910)
Novelist, feminist and editor. Born in Jamaica, Holdsworth's book *Joanna Traill, Spinster* (1894) addresses the ▷ New Woman theme of female independence. She was co-editor of *The Woman's Signal*. Her later novels include: *The Years That the Locust Hath Eaten* (1896) and *The Gods Arrive* (1897).
▷ Women's Movement.

Holford, Margaret (1761–1834) and Holford, Margaret (1778–1852)
Mother and daughter. The elder Holford was a poet, dramatist and novelist, while her daughter is known for her poetry and prose. Holford senior's novels have predictable plots which rely heavily on the contemporary vogue for sensationalism and exotic mystery. Her first novel, *Fanny* (1785), is dramatic and lively, ending with the reformation of the hero from rake into model husband. Her two plays, *Neither's The Man* (1798) and *The Way to Win Her* (1814), are more challenging; they recall Restoration comedy and advocate the superiority of female 'wit'. Holford junior turned her talents towards poetry and was heavily influenced by ▷ Sir Walter Scott. Her published work, *Wallace, or The Fight of Falkirk* (1809) and *Poems* (1811) were very popular at the time, but they are too sentimental to be popular with a 20th-century readership. She also wrote a novel *Warbeck of Wolfstein* (1820), which was influenced by ▷ Shelley.
▷ Gothic novels.

***Holiday House* (1839)**
A novel for children by Scottish writer ▷ Catherine Sinclair, which helped to develop a taste for books representing mischievous rather than moral children. Sinclair described her intentions thus: 'In these pages the author has endeavoured to paint that species of noisy, frolicsome, mischievous children, now almost extinct, wishing to preserve a sort of fabulous remembrance of days long past, when young people were like wild horses on the prairies, rather than well-broken hacks on the road.'
▷ Children's literature.

Holinshed, Raphael (d ?1580)
Chronicler: *Chronicles of England, Scotland and Ireland* (1578). The history of England

was written by Holinshed himself but a vivid *Description of England* added to the history is by William Harrison. The history of Scotland is a translation of a Scottish work written in Latin – *Scotorum historiae* (1527) by Hector Boece – and the account of Ireland is by Richard Stanyhurst, Edward Campion and others. ▷ Shakespeare and other Elizabethan dramatists used the *Chronicles* as a principal source book for history plays; Shakespeare also used them for ▷ *Macbeth*, ▷ *King Lear* and ▷ *Cymbeline*.

▷ Histories and Chronicles.

Hollinghurst, Alan (b 1954)
Novelist. Educated at Magdalen College Oxford, Hollinghurst lectured at Oxford and at London University, was assistant editor of the *Times Literary Supplement* (1982–90) and poetry editor from 1990. *The Swimming-Pool Library* (1988) depicts both contemporary gay life in London and, through the researches carried out by the protagonist, who is commissioned to write a biography, the persecution of homosexual men in 1950s Britain. *The Folding Star* (1994), narrated by an English tutor in a Flemish city, is also much concerned with the relationship of art and life. *Confidential Chats with Boys* (1982) is a volume of verse. Hollinghurst has also translated Racine's *Bajazet*.

Holmes, Sherlock
▷ Detective fiction; Doyle, Sir Arthur Conan.

Holtby, Winifred (1898–1935)
Novelist and journalist. Winifred Holtby's short career was extremely prolific. She is best known as the writer of *South Riding* (1936), a study of life and rural politics in her native Yorkshire, but Holtby's career is much more varied than this suggests. She was a farmer's daughter whose first book of poetry was published when she was only 13 (*My Garden and Other Poems*). She then went on to study at Oxford (where she met and befriended ▷ Vera Brittain), worked as a nurse in the First World War, and wrote the first full-length critical study of ▷ Virginia Woolf (1932). She also lectured, and had a distinguished journalistic career (writing for, amongst others, the *Manchester Guardian* and the *News Chronicle*). Her other works include: *Anderby Wold* (1923); *The Land of Green Ginger* (1927); *Poor Caroline* (1931); *Mandoa! Mandoa!* (1933); *Women and a Changing Civilisation* (1934); *Letters to a Friend* (1937).
Bib: Brittain, V., *Testament of Friendship*; Handley-Taylor, G., *Winifred Holtby: A Concise and Selected Bibliography with Some Letters*.

***Holy War, The* (1682)**
An ▷ allegory by ▷ John Bunyan. Its subject is the fall and redemption of man. The city of Mansoul has fallen into the hands of Diabolus (the Devil) and has to be recaptured by Emmanuel (Jesus Christ), who besieges it.

Homer
Ancient Greek epic poet, author of the ▷ *Iliad* and the ▷ *Odyssey*, basic works for ▷ Greek literature. Ancient traditions exist about Homer, for instance that latterly he was blind and that seven cities claimed to be his birthplace, but nothing is conclusively known about him. Archaeological investigation has disclosed that the destruction of ▷ Troy, following the siege described in the *Iliad*, took place in the 12th century BC; linguistic, historical and literary analysis of the poems show them to date as artistic wholes from perhaps the 8th century BC. That they are artistic wholes is in fact the only evidence for the existence of Homer; efforts to show that they are compilations by a number of poets have proved unconvincing, though it is clear that Homer himself was using the work of other poets between the Trojan war and his own time. The critic ▷ Matthew Arnold in his essay *On Translating Homer* (1861) says that Homer is rapid in movement, plain in diction, simple on ideas and noble in manner; and that the translation of three eminent English poets, ▷ George Chapman (16th century), ▷ Alexander Pope and ▷ William Cowper (18th century), all fail in one or more of these qualities, however fine their verse is in other respects.

Homosexuality
Accorded a marginal place in literary representation and, when it has been shown, usually hedged about with implications of the exotic, the abnormal or at least the exceptional. According to Ronald Pearsall (*The Worm in the Bud: The World of Victorian Sexuality*) the term 'homosexual' was first used by a Hungarian physician named Benkert in 1869, and there was enormous interest in the phenomenon in the later years of the 19th century. Between 1898 and 1908 more than 1000 works on homosexuality were published. Homosexuality as a concept began to take shape in the 1880s in the work of John Addington Symonds (1840–93) and Richard von Krafft-Ebing, and in the research of Victorian sexologists such as ▷ Havelock Ellis. Legal prohibition at the time led to almost universal repression, except in the public school system where it appears to have thrived, if undercover. The editor William Stead declared in his *Review of Reviews*: 'Should everyone found guilty of Oscar Wilde's crime be imprisoned, there would be a very surprising emigration from Eton, Harrow, Rugby and Winchester to the jails of Pentonville and Holloway.' There were several attempts to make homosexuality respectable, including a number of books written by homosexuals advocating a change of terminology. Euphemisms such

as 'homogenic love', 'contrasexuality', 'homoeroticism', 'similisexualism', 'sexual inversion', 'intersexuality' and 'the third sex' were all used as substitutes. Carl Heinrich Ulrich invented the term 'uranism' in the 1860s and exponents were known as 'urnings' and 'dionings'. The philosophical form 'uranismum' indicated the female soul in the male body and the term 'urning', used to describe homosexual activity, was noted by J.A. Symonds as appearing in a number of novels of the time. Until 1828 sodomy was punishable by death if the activity had been witnessed by another, and such was the repression and fear that blackmail, especially of public figures, and self-mutilation were common.

In the 1850s Fleet Street, Holborn and the Strand were favourite places for homosexual prostitutes, who were known in early and mid-Victorian times as 'margeries' and 'pooffs'; the act itself was referred to as 'backgammon'. Politicians suspected of homosexuality but tolerated nevertheless, as people in high office tended to be, included George Canning and ▷ Disraeli. One celebrated homosexual was the painter and poet Simeon Solomon, a friend of ▷ Algernon Swinburne. He eventually died in squalor in a workhouse in 1905. J.A. Symonds and ▷ Edmund Gosse were more discreet about their sexual preferences, and the affection of ▷ Tennyson for Arthur Hallam, celebrated in ▷ *In Memoriam* (1850) has been seen by some critics as evidence of adolescent homosexual anguish. After the 1885 Criminal Law Amendment Act the penalty for procuration was two years imprisonment with or without hard labour. It was this law that ▷ Oscar Wilde fell foul of in 1895. His is perhaps the most famous example of the persecution of homosexuals at this time. Many historians follow the pioneering work of philosopher Michel Foucault (1926–84) in claiming that male homosexuality and the role of the male homosexual were 'invented', ie named and pathologized, in the 19th century in an attempt to distinguish between acceptable and abhorrent behaviour. For an account of sexual ambiguity in the literature of the late 19th century see Elaine Showalter's *Sexual Anarchy*.

▷ Lesbianism.

Bib: Montgomery Hyde, H., *The Love That Dared Not Speak its Name: A Candid History of Homosexuality in Britain*; Weeks, J., *Coming Out: Homosexual Politics in Britain from the Nineteenth Century to the Present*; Reade, B., *Sexual Heretics: Male Homosexuality in English Literature from 1815 to 1900*; Croft-Cooke, R., *Feasting With Panthers: A New Consideration of Some Late Victorian Writers*; d'Arch Smith, T., *Love In Earnest: Some Notes on the Lives and Writings of English 'Uranian' Poets from 1889 to 1930*.

Hood, Thomas (1799–1845)

Poet. His serious poetry shows strongly the influence of ▷ John Keats, but he is known chiefly for his comic and topical verse; the latter includes grim but haunting poems about contemporary social abuses, *eg The Song of the Shirt* (1843), a kind of poetic poster art which does not bear close examination but is extremely effective on first reading. In his comic verse, he was notorious for his puns which he used obtrusively but often wittily.

Bib: Jerrold, W., *Life*; Reid, J. C., *A Critical Study*.

Hook, Theodore Edward (1788–1841)

Novelist, poet and dramatist. Hook is primarily remembered as a ▷ Silver-fork novelist; his works include *Sayings and Doings* (1824–8) and *Gilbert Gurney* (1836). He was intimately acquainted with the aristocratic world which he describes, and his books were often used as behavioural guides for those who wished to enter polite society. Their narratives and characters, however, lack distinction.

Bib: Brightfield, M.F., *Hook and His Novels*.

Hooker, Jeremy (b 1941)

Poet and critic. Born at Warsash, Hampshire, Jeremy Hooker was educated at Southampton University. He lectured in English at the University College of Wales, Aberystwyth, from 1965 to 1984, subsequently moving to Winchester, to Groningen in the Netherlands, and finally back to Frome in the West Country. His poetry explores, in a highly controlled and sometimes spare style, at once probing yet reticent, the historic and mythic associations of landscape, emphasising his attachment to place, both in his native Wessex and, in the middle period of his poetic development, in Wales, these seminal themes being elaborated upon in his collection of essays *The Poetry of Place* (1973). His other critical works are a monograph on *John Cowper Powys* in the *Writers of Wales* series (1973), *David Jones: An Exploratory Study* (1975) and *John Cowper Powys and David Jones: A Comparative Study* (1979), together with a second collection of essays, on modern British and American poets, *The Presence of the Past* (1987). He also edited, with Gweno Lewis, the selected poems of Alun Lewis in 1981. His collections of poetry are *The Elements* (1972), *Soliloquies of a Chalk Giant* (1974), *Landscape of the Daylight Moon* (1978), *Solent Shore* (1978), *Englishman's Road* (1980), *Itchen Water* (1982), *Master of the Leaping Figures* (1987) and *Their Silence a Language*, which, with Lee Grandjean, explores the connections between poetry and sculpture (1993). His selected poems appeared under the title of *A View from the Source* in 1982.

Bib: Stephens, M. (Ed.), *The Oxford Companion to the Literature of Wales*.

Hooker, Richard (?1553–1600)

Theologian. His most significant work was *Laws of Ecclesiastical Polity* (1593–7). This was the first outstanding polemic expounding the ▷ Church of England viewpoint, and its main purpose was to defend the Church against attacks by Protestant reformers. Such reformers (the Puritans) trusted only the ▷ Bible as authority on matters of religion, since only the Bible was acknowledged to be inspired by God. They criticized the Church of England for being too near the Roman Catholic Church in its organization (*eg* in its retention of the authority of bishops) and for resembling the Roman Church in its excessive reliance on other kinds of authority. Hooker considered that the Puritans were making major issues out of inessentials, and that their attacks were dangerous both socially and religiously, since the state was indissolubly bound up with the Church, and it was essential for both to adapt themselves to historical change and requirement, and to draw upon the law of nature as well as upon the Holy Scriptures for guidance. Law he regarded as inherent in created nature and as the same principle, whether seen in the aspect of natural order, social order or divine order. In this view of law, Hooker is essentially a conservative thinker, inheriting from the ▷ Middle Ages the view of the universe as a system of related degrees ranging from God down to the four ▷ elements of hot, cold, moist and dry as the basis of matter. Though conservative, the outlook was not reactionary; it was the most widely accepted assumption of the time, implicit in the imaginative literature, see *eg* the speech of Ulysses in ▷ Shakespeare's ▷ *Troilus and Cressida* (I. iii. 75).

However, for all Hooker's conservatism, in the ▷ Civil War and post-Civil War period his works were widely read by radicals as well as by the more conservative-minded. Hooker's appeal to radicals was based on the posthumous publication, in 1648, of a further three books of his *Laws of Ecclesiastical Polity* – books whose authenticity has long been debated. What recommended Hooker to radicals was the role he assigned to consent in religion, and the fact that, in the later parts of the *Laws*, he offered no defence of divine-right episcopacy.

Bib: Keble, J. (ed.), *The Laws of Ecclesiastical Polity*; Cargill-Thomson, W. D. J., *Studies in the Reformation: Luther to Hooker*.

Hope, Christopher (b 1944)
Novelist, short-story writer and poet. Born in South Africa of an Irish Catholic family and educated at the universities of Witwatersrand and Natal, he moved to Europe in 1975. He served in the South African navy in 1962 and has worked as an underwriter, in publishing, as a reviewer and as an English teacher in England. His first two novels, *A Separate Development* (1980, banned in South Africa) and *Kruger's Alp* (1984) both deal with apartheid, the second in allegorical terms. *The Love Songs of Nathan J. Swirsky* (1993) is a comic satire on small-town South African life. His fiction has a satirical edge and contains strong elements of the surreal and the bizarre as well as some sinister humour. His other novels include: *The Hottentot Room* (1986); *My Chocolate Redeemer* (1989); *Serenity House* (1992). *Private Parts* (1981) is a volume of short stories and *Black Swan* (1987) a ▷ novella. His volumes of poetry include: *Cape Drives* (1974); *In the Country of the Black Pig* (1981); *Englishmen* (1985).

Hopkins, Gerard Manley (1844–89)
Poet. He was converted to Roman ▷ Catholicism in 1866, and entered the Jesuit Order in 1868. He then gave up poetry, but resumed writing in 1875 with ▷ *The Wreck of the Deutschland*, his first important poem. So unusual were Hopkins' poems that they were not published in his own lifetime; after his death they passed to his friend, ▷ Robert Bridges, who delayed their publication until 1918, and even then Hopkins' fame did not become widespread until the second edition of 1930. The date of his publication, the interest he shared with modern poets in the relationship between poetry and experience and his technical innovation and intense style, has caused him to be thought of as belonging more to the 20th century than to the 19th. His ▷ 'sprung rhythm' is a technical term meaning the combination of the usual regularity of stress patterns with freely varying numbers of syllables in each line. This was not new, but was contrary to the practice that had predominated in English poetry since ▷ Edmund Spenser (?1552–99), which required a uniform pattern of syllabic counts, as of stresses. In Hopkins' poetry, the rhythm of the verse could more easily combine with the flow and varying emphasis of spoken language, so that the two kinds of expressiveness unite. A kindred sort of concentration is obtained by his practice – natural to the spoken language but uncommon in writing – of inventing compound words, especially adjectives, eg 'dappled-with-damson west' for a sunset, 'lovely-asunder starlight' for stars scattered over the sky.

▷ Keats (1795–1821) was a strong influence upon him (as upon so many of the later Victorians) and Hopkins shared Keats' gift for evoking in words the physical response suitable to the thing they express. This was the more conspicuous in Hopkins because of his intense interest (for which he found support in the 13th-century philosopher Duns Scotus) in the qualities which give any object its individual reality, distinguishing it from other objects of the same class. For these qualities he invented the term 'inscape'. He also invented 'instress' for the force of these qualities on the mind. This intensity of response to the reality and beauty of objects was akin to the intensity of his feeling about the relationship between God and man.

All Hopkins' poetry is religious, and in quality recalls the early 17th-century devotional poets, John Donne (1572–1631) and George Herbert (1593–1633); in his 'terrible sonnets', for instance, Hopkins engages in direct dialogue with God as does Donne in his *Holy Sonnets*, or Herbert in a lyric such as *The Collar*. Thus Hopkins unites the rhythmical freedom of the Middle Ages, the religious intensity of the early 17th century, the response to nature of the early 19th, and he anticipated the 20th century in challenging conventional encumbrances in poetic form.

Bib: Gardner, W.A., *Life*; Hartman, G.H. (ed.), *Hopkins*; Bottrall, M. (ed.), *Gerard Manley Hopkins: Poems*; Bergonzi, B., *Gerard Manley Hopkins*: Roberts, G. (ed.), *Gerard Manley Hopkins: The Critical Heritage*; Oug, W.J., *Hopkins, the Self and God*; Weyland, N. (ed.), *Immortal Diamond: Studies in Gerard Manley Hopkins*.

Horace (Quintus Horatius Flaccus) (68–5 BC)
Roman poet of the Augustan age. His work divides into three classes; his Satires, Odes and Epistles. The last includes the *Ars Poetica* or *De Arte Poetica* (Concerning the Art of Poetry) which became an important critical document for Europe – for England particularly in the 18th century. It emphasizes the importance of cultivating art in poetry; he lays down the principle that if you do not understand poetry it is better to leave it alone. Art means above all the cultivation of alert judgment: expression and form must be appropriate to theme; characterization and form must be consistent with the subject and with themselves; conciseness is a virtue in didacticism; adaptation of a writer is allowed but plagiarism is not; the poet must study to be wise as a man, and he must be his own severest critic; a just critic is a severe one. The age of ▷ Alexander Pope and ▷ Samuel Johnson took these principles to heart and they also liked Horace's cultivation of balance in prosperity between wealth and poverty: he had become the friend of the rich patron of letters, Maecenas, who had provided him with a small estate in the Sabine hills. The English Augustans' concern was to cultivate proportion and balance. Criticism and satire thus became important to them as correctives of inborn human tendencies, and they cultivated the congenial spirit of Horace as Horace himself had sought to practise the virtues of the Greeks. Thus Pope entitled one of his sequences of poems ▷ *Imitations of Horace*.

Horn Childe
▷ *King Horn*.

Horror fiction
Although horror fiction has undergone astonishing changes since the earliest ▷ 'Gothic' novels (▷ Horace Walpole's *The Castle of Oranto*, 1764, ▷ M. G. Lewis' *The Castle Spectre*, 1798, ▷ Anne Radcliffe's *The Mysteries of Adolpho*, 1794 and *The Monk*, 1796) the themes of transgression with which the genre deals have remained largely unchanged. Returning obsessively to taboo subjects (death, sex, incest, decay, bodily corruption, psychosis) horror novels have been described both by critics and champions as an 'undergrowth of literature' whose function is to speak the unspeakable. In his critical work, *Supernatural Horror in Literature*, H. P. Lovecraft declares: 'The oldest and strongest emotion of mankind is fear, and the oldest and strongest kind of fear is of the unknown. These facts few psychologists will dispute, and their admittedness must establish for all time the genuineness and dignity of the weirdly horrible tales.' Sixty years later leading contemporary horror novelist ▷ Stephen King writes: 'Horror appeals to us because it says, in a symbolic way, things we would be afraid to say . . . It offers us a chance to exercise (not exorcise) . . . emotions which society demands we keep closely in hand' (*Danse Macabre*, 1981). Similarly, British horror novelist ▷ Ramsey Campbell has described the genre as 'the branch of literature most often concerned with going too far. It is the least escapist form of fantasy. It shows us sights we would ordinarily look away from or reminds us of insights we might prefer not to admit we have.'

Whilst much early Gothic fiction is rooted in American literature (▷ Edgar Allan Poe is frequently cited as the godfather of modern Gothic), Britain has produced a number of key texts. ▷ Bram Stoker's *Dracula* (1897) set the tone for future tales of vampirism, while ▷ Mary Shelley's *Frankenstein* (1818) has become the genre's single most reworked (and indeed abused) text, both on page and later screen. Of the longevity of these horror icons David Punter writes: '*Frankenstein* and *Dracula* are still granted fresh embodiments [because of] both their own imagistic flexibility and . . . the essential continuity under capitalism of the anxieties about class and gender warfare from which they sprang.' The question of whether classic horror fiction alludes to contemporary rather than timeless fears has been of central import in recent years. Following a slump in the 1960s, horror fiction was revitalized in 1971 by the extraordinary success of William Peter Blatty's occult chiller *The Exorcist*. Described by the author as 'a 350 page thankyou note to the Jesuits' for his education, *The Exorcist* rekindled modern popular religious debate, but its success was attributed by some to a contemporary fear of adolescent rebellion which the novel appeared to reflect. In the wake of Blatty's success, American short-story writer Stephen King published his first novel *Carrie*, which also dealt with aggressive adolescence. In Britain, ▷ James Herbert rapidly became the leading light of modern pulp horror fiction, producing viscerally gory tales set against a backdrop of modern urban decay. 'The rats are the establishment,' explained Herbert of the subtexts of his first best-seller *The Rats*. Although Herbert's later work became more discreet, he opened the flood-gates for a slew of writers specializing in sensationally violent fantasy; most notable is Shaun Hutson (*Spawn, Slugs, Assassin*), a connoisseur of outlandish mutilation with a recurrent sexual bent, while Guy N. Smith (*Crabs, The Sucking Pit, Crabs on the Rampage*) deserves mention for his prolific output. In the early 1980s, ▷ Clive Barker and Ramsey Campbell rose to the forefront of the British 'new wave' of horror writers. Challenging the 'innate conservatisms and prejudices of the field'. Barker and Campbell forged a new brand of horror which sought to demystify taboo subjects rather than merely revel in them. In America, Stephen King's popularity remains unchallenged, but he is outstripped in terms of invention by Peter Straub, author of *Ghost Story* (1979), and with whom King collaborated on *The Talisman* (1984). Current upcoming authors include K. W. Jeter, Kim Newman, Thomas Ligotti, Michael Marshall Smith, Nicholas Royle, Ian R. MacLeod, D. F. Lewis and Joel Lane. Recent short-story collections are: *Best New Horror* (Steven Jones and Ramsey Campbell, eds.) and *Dark Voices* (edited by Sutton, D. and Jones, S.).

Bib: King, S., *Danse Macabre* (1981); Newman, K., and Jones, S., *Horror: 100 Best Books* (1988); Sullivan, J., (ed.), *The Penguin Encyclopaedia of Horror and the Supernatural*.

Hosain, Attia (b 1913)

Novelist and short-story writer. She was born in Lucknow to an aristocratic family and educated at schools in Lucknow and at home (where she studied Arabic, Persian and Urdu). She moved to London when India was partitioned in 1947, working as a BBC presenter, an actress and a journalist. *Phoenix Fled* (1951) is a collection of short stories and *Sunlight on a Broken Column* (1961) a novel.

Hoskyns, John (1566–1638)

Poet and rhetorician. Hoskyns was educated at Winchester and New College, Oxford, but was expelled from the latter for writing ▷ satire. He was an eloquent lawyer and, finally, MP for Hereford. His poetic writing and contribution to style was for a long time unrecognized; however, it is now apparent that ▷ Jonson used Hoskyns' *Directions for Speech and Style* (1599) in *Timber*, and that several poems written by Hoskyns have been misattributed to others, such as ▷ Donne. His poetry is often witty and down-to-earth, the shorter pieces being amongst the best.

Hospital, Janette Turner (b 1942)

Novelist and short-story writer. Born in Australia and educated at the University of Queensland and at Queens University in Canada, Hospital settled in Canada in 1971 but has also lived in India, England and the USA. She has worked as a teacher, a librarian (at Harvard University), a writer-in-residence and a lecturer. The title of one of her volumes of short stories, *Dislocations* (1986), sums up a principal theme of her fiction, whether set in India, like *The Ivory Swing* (1982), or in Canada, like *Borderline* (1985), a novel of ▷ post-modernist self-consciousness in which a couple's encounter with an illegal immigrant to Canada poses issues of commitment and responsibility. *The Tiger in the Tiger Pit* (1983) is a drama of family conflict set in the USA and Australia. Her other works are: *Isobars* (short stories, 1990); *Charades* (a novel, 1989); *The Last Magician* (1992).

Hospitallers of St John of Jerusalem (Knights of St John)

A military religious order associated with the ▷ Crusades. The Hospitallers were founded in 1099 to provide a hostel for pilgrims to Jerusalem. Driven from Jerusalem, they eventually settled in Malta in 1530. They had a branch in England which was suppressed in the 16th century. The modern British order was founded in the 19th century and exists for hospital work similar to that of the Red Cross.

Hotspur (Sir Henry Percy) (1364–1403)

Eldest son of the first Earl of Northumberland. ▷ Shakespeare represented him in ▷ *Henry IV, Part I*, where he is shown as the generous, tempestuous warrior, devoted entirely to honour, but failing to relate it to any feeling for human good. He is thus, despite these qualities, a destructive force.

Hours, Book of

Certain hours of the day, called the Canonical Hours, are set aside for prayers by the Catholic Church. A Book of Hours contained the prayers to be said at the appropriate times; medieval editions were often illustrated ('illuminated') with great art and at great expense. The evidence of their illustrations has allowed some stereotyped ideas about medieval life to be challenged; see *The Medieval Woman. An Illuminated Book of Days* (1985).

House of Fame

One of ▷ Chaucer's ▷ dream-vision poems, in octosyllabic couplets, usually dated to the years 1379–80, in which the narrator records the experience of a December dream which he deems worthy of record. The dream-vision mode is used to great effect in this text, which encompasses very different dream-scapes and explores important poetic-philosophic questions without being tied to providing explanations and answers. It is a speculative work.

Book I is taken up with a retelling of ▷ Virgil's ▷ *Aeneid*, depicted on the walls of the Dreamer's first dream-room, in the temple of Venus. ▷ Dido's unhappy experience is given particular prominence by the narrator, who seems more influenced by ▷ Ovid's sympathetic treatment of her plight (in the *Heroides*) than by Virgil's representation of the incident. In Book II the narrator is given a trip to the heavens, courtesy of a Golden Eagle flown in from ▷ Dante's ▷ *Divina Commedia*. The dreamer, who is called 'Geoffrey' by the eagle, is given a chance to experience metaphysics at first hand, though his preference is for reading about the heavens in books, rather than travelling through them. The whole trip, it transpires, is a reward for the Dreamer's assiduous and bookish service to the God of Love. Book III concerns the Dreamer's visit to the aerial House of Fame (the final destination of all sounds and reports from Earth); his description of this precarious institution, its upholders, and his eyewitness report of the vagaries of Lady Fame's dispensation of her favours. From here the Dreamer is taken to the more volatile environment of the House of Rumour, a whirling house of twigs, in which he sees the generation of the stores which provide the raw material for the House of Fame. The text breaks off as a man of some authority appears on the scene. The poem provides an extremely deft exploration of the nature and scope of Chaucer's cultural heritage and the relationship between different kinds of artistic production, between the literary texts of the past and present.

Bib: Boitani, P. and Mann, Jill (ed.), *The Cambridge Chaucer Companion*.

Household Words

A weekly periodical edited by ▷ Charles Dickens from 1850 to 1859. It emulated the magazine tradition of ▷ *Blackwood's* (started 1817) but aimed at a wider public. Among works published in it were Dickens' novel ▷ *Hard Times* and ▷ Mrs Gaskell's ▷ *North and South*. It was followed by ▷ *All the Year Round*.

▷ Reviews and periodicals.

Housman, A. E. (1859–1936)

A classical scholar who published two small volumes of ▷ lyrics of enormous popularity: *The Shropshire Lad* (1896) and *Last Poems* (1922). They are very pessimistic but have an immediate musical appeal, and several have in fact been set to music by a number of composers, *eg* Vaughan Williams. His lecture *The Name and Nature of Poetry*, in which he described poetic creation as an essentially physical experience, also achieved considerable fame in his own age.

Bib: Housman, L., *AEH: Some Poems, Some Letters and a Personal Memoir*; Richards, G., *Housman 1879–1936*; Watson, G. L., *Housman: a divided life*; Graves, R. P., *A. E. Housman: the Scholar-Poet*.

Houyhnhnms, The

The horses endowed with ▷ reason in Part IV of ▷ Swift's ▷ *Gulliver's Travels*. The word imitates the whinnying of a horse. The enlightened horses are a purely reasonable aristocracy, inhabiting an island which also contains a race called ▷ Yahoos who, not endowed with reason, typify brutish and degraded behaviour. Gulliver's Houyhnhnm host recognizes that Gulliver is unlike the Yahoos in his possession of the faculty of reason, but proves to him that owing to his other qualities, which are Yahoo-like, he can only use his reason destructively.

***Howards End* (1910)**

A novel by ▷ E. M. Forster. The theme is the relationship between the Schlegel family (Margaret, Helen, and their brother Tibby) who live on an unearned income and are liberal, enlightened, and cultivated, and the Wilcoxes, who work in the commercial world which the Schlegels are inclined to despise. The Wilcoxes are snobbish, prejudiced, insensitive, and philistine; in fact they have much in common with the middle classes as described by Matthew Arnold in his critique of English culture – *Culture and Anarchy* (1869). Mrs Wilcox, however, who has bought her husband the old house, Howards End, belongs to the older, aristocratic continuity of English culture; never understood by her husband and children, on her death she bequeaths the house unexpectedly to Margaret Schlegel. Margaret comes into the inheritance at the end of the book, but only after she has married and subdued to her values Mrs Wilcox's former husband. Meanwhile Helen, moved by sympathy and indignation, has become pregnant by Leonard Bast, a poor bank-clerk who has been the victim of both the Schlegel and the Wilcox social illusions and mishandling. Bast dies after being beaten by one of the Wilcox sons, and Helen and her child come to live at Howards End with Margaret and Mr Wilcox. The house remains a tentative symbol of hope for the future of English society. The novel as a whole explores the impact of early ▷ feminist ideas, and ▷ anti-industrialism. The Merchant Ivory film *Howards End*, with a screenplay by Ruth Prawer Jhabvala, was released to critical acclaim in 1992.

***Hudibras* (1663, 1664 and 1678)**

A mock-heroic (▷ Heroic, Mock) ▷ satire in tetrameter couplets by ▷ Samuel Butler (1612–80). The Presbyterian Sir Hudibras and his Independent Squire Ralpho undergo various adventures designed to expose the hypocrisy of the Puritans, interspersed with satire on various scientific and intellectual follies. The poem's structure parodies the 16th-century ▷ epic romances of ▷ Ariosto and ▷ Spenser, and the hero takes his name from a knight in Spenser's ▷ *Faerie Queene*. In spirit it owes much to Cervantes' anti-romance satire ▷ *Don Quixote*. The poem's politics pleased ▷ Charles II, who gave Butler £300 and a pension of £100 a year. Though the work fails to sustain narrative interest it establishes its own distinctive vein of rollicking farce and homespun philosophizing:

Honour is, like a widow, won
With brisk attempt, and putting on;
With ent'ring manfully and urging;
Not slow approaches, like a virgin.
(I. ii. 911–14)

Butler's loose tetrameters with their vigorous colloquial diction and crude rhymes became an established medium for broad satire, known as 'hudibrasticks'.

Hudibrastics
Term deriving from *Hudibras* (1663, 1664 and 1678), a mock-heroic ▷ satire in tetrameter ▷ couplets by Samuel Butler (1612–80). The Presbyterian Sir Hudibras, and his Independent Squire Ralpho, undergo various adventures designed to expose the hypocrisy of the Puritans, interspersed with satire on various scientific and intellectual follies.
▷ Heroic, mock.

Hughes, Richard (1900–76)
Novelist, dramatist and poet. He published four novels: *A High Wind in Jamaica* (1929); *In Hazard* (1938); *The Fox in the Attic* (1961) and *The Wooden Shepherdess* (1971). He was educated at Charterhouse School, and at Oxford University, where he met ▷ W. B. Yeats, ▷ A. E. Coppard, ▷ T. E. Lawrence and ▷ Robert Graves. As an undergraduate he wrote a one-act play, *The Sister's Tragedy*, which was staged in 1922 and enthusiastically received, and a volume of poems entitled *Gipsy Night* (1922). In 1924 he wrote the first original radio play, *Danger* and a stage play, *A Comedy of Good and Evil*. Born in Surrey but of Welsh descent, he adopted Wales as his home, but travelled extensively around the world. His travels are reflected in his book of short stories, *In the Lap of Atlas: Stories of Morocco* (1979), as well as in his first two novels, which are set mainly at sea and are intense studies of moral issues in the context of human crisis. *A High Wind in Jamaica*, his best-known work, is the story of a group of children captured by pirates. It deals with violence, the relation of innocence and evil, and the fallibility of human justice, and takes an unsentimental view of childhood. *In Hazard* describes in great detail the events on board a cargo ship at sea during a hurricane, and has affinities with the work of ▷ Joseph Conrad. After an administrative post in the Admiralty during World War II, Hughes worked as a book reviewer and teacher. His last two novels are part of a projected historical sequence entitled *The Human Predicament*, recounting the events leading up to World War II. Other publications include: *The Man Born to be Hanged* (1923) (stage play); *A Moment of Time* (1926) (short stories); *The Spider's Palace* (1931) and *Don't Blame Me* (1940) (short stories for children); *Confessio Juvenis* (1926) (collected poems).
Bib: Thomas, P., *Richard Hughes*.

Hughes, Ted (b 1930)
One of the liveliest poets writing in Britain since 1945. His works include: *The Hawk in the Rain* (1957); *Lupercal* (1960); two volumes of verse for children – *Meet My Folks* (1961) and *Earth Owl and Other Moon People* (1963); *Wodwo* (1967); *Crow* (1970); *Poems* (1971); *Eat Crow* (1971); *Prometheus on his Crag* (1973); *Spring Summer Autumn Winter* (1974); *Cavebirds* (1975); *Gaudete* (1977); *Remains of Elmet* (1979); *Moortown* (1979); *River* (1983); *Season Songs* (1985); *Flowers and Insects* (1986); *Shakespeare and the Goddess of Complete Being* (1992); and *Rain-charm for the Duchy and other Laureate Poems* (1992). His rather violent poetry appeared when English verse was dominated by the poets of the ▷ Movement (▷ Larkin); in contrast with these restrained, disillusioned, ironic and often urban poems, Hughes' work explored and celebrated violence and the life of the unconscious, and he was a key member of the 'new poetry' group (included in A. Alvarez's important anthology of that name published in 1962). Hughes is remarkable for his evocation of natural life, in particular of animals, presented as alien and opposed to the civilized human consciousness, and for that reason, as in the poetry and prose of ▷ D. H. Lawrence, peculiarly close to sub-rational instinct in the self. Hughes married the poet ▷ Sylvia Plath in 1956. On the death of ▷ John Betjeman in 1984 Hughes was made ▷ Poet Laureate.
Bib: Sagar, K., *The Art of Ted Hughes*; *Gifford, T. and Roberts, N., Ted Hughes: a Critical Study*.

Hughes, Thomas (1822–96)
In his time a prominent public figure as a lawyer, leading Christian Socialist and Radical MP, Hughes is now remembered for his *Tom Brown's Schooldays* (1857), which launched a whole genre of boys' school tales. The novel records how Tom Brown triumphs over various schoolboy trials (including the archetypal bully, Flashman) finally to captain the school cricket team and become a solid citizen. The emphasis on sport is indicative of Hughes' affinity with the 'muscular Christianity' of ▷ Charles Kingsley.

While condemning bullying, the novel in many ways glorifies violence and is complacently sexist and chauvinistic. The book is also interesting for its first-hand (if fictionalized) account of ▷ Thomas Arnold's reform of the ▷ public school system at ▷ Rugby. The sequel, *Tom Brown at Oxford* (1861), is of interest for its evocation of the ▷ Oxford Movement.

▷ Lawrence, G.A.

Hugo, Victor(-Marie) (1802–85)
French poet, playwright and novelist. Born in Besançon, he lived in Spain and Italy as a child, where his father, a General, followed Napoleon. Despite nostalgia for the Napoleonic age, Hugo was a confirmed democrat and was elected to the Assembly in 1848 and again in 1870. He lived in exile in the Channel Isles between 1851 and 1870 after the *coup d'état* of Louis Napoleon. As a young man he refused a military career in favour of literature; he gained favour through poetry and was made Chevalier de la Legion d'Honeur by 1825. He read and admired Chateaubriand, a proto-Romantic influence, and after the publication of his play *Cromwell* (1827) with its famous Preface, became a spearhead of the French Romantic movement. He married Adèle Foucher, and was much affected by the death of his daughter in 1845. He was made a peer and became an important figure, being buried with great ceremony in the Panthéon. His plays have lasted less well than the novels and poetry which are remarkable not for intellectual content so much as beauty, faith and feeling. Hugo's output was prolific: the plays include *Hernani* (1830) and *Ruy Blas* (1838); the novels *Notre Dame de Paris* (1831), the celebrated *Les Misérables* (1862), *Les Travailleurs de la Mer* (1866), *L'Homme qui Rit* (1869). His many collections of poems include *Les Odes* (1822), *Odes et Ballades* (1826), *Les Orientales* (1829), *Les Feuilles d'Automne* (1831), *Les Chants du Crépuscule* (1835), *Les Voix Intérieures* (1837), *Les Rayons et les Ombres* (1840), *Les Châtiments* (1853), *Les Contemplations* (1856) and *La Légende des Siècles* (1859, 1877, 1883).

▷ French influence on English fiction.

Hulme, Keri (b 1947)
Novelist and short-story writer. Hulme was born in Christchurch and educated at Canterbury University, New Zealand. She has worked as a postwoman, television director and writer, as well as engaging in fishing and various forms of seasonal work on New Zealand's South Island, where she now lives in Okarito, Westland. Her family heritage includes not only Maori (the Kai Tahu tribe) but Scots and English. Maori cultural identity, language and history have been central to her work, together with environmental and feminist concerns. Her novel *The Bone People* (1983), which won the Booker Prize, is a mythic narrative of national regeneration based on Maori religious beliefs. *Lost Possessions* (1985) is a novella, *Te Kaihu/The Windeater* (1986) a collection of short stories and *The Silences Between [Moeraki Conversations]* (1982) and *Strands* are volumes of poetry.

Hulme, Thomas Ernest (1883–1917)
Poet and essayist. His attacks on 19th-century Romanticism and the verbosity that often expressed it were an important influence on the theory and practice of ▷ Imagism as a poetry of concentration and verbal compression. His writings in support of a modern classicism that should be austere and authoritarian were also important for ▷ T. S. Eliot and ▷ Wyndham Lewis. His output as a poet was tiny: *The Complete Poetical Works* were published as an addendum to the *Ripostes* of ▷ Ezra Pound in 1912, but his essays and ▷ translations of writers like the French vitalist philosopher ▷ Henri Bergson were of immense significance in the development of ▷ modernism. See *Speculations* (ed. H. Read; 1924); *Further Speculations* (ed. S. Hynes; 1955).
Bib: Kermode, F., in *Romantic Image*; Roberts, M., *T. E. Hulme*.

Humanism
The word has two distinct uses: 1 the intellectually liberating movements in western Europe in the 15th and 16th centuries, associated with new attitudes to ancient Greek and Latin literature; 2 a modern movement for the advancement of humanity without reliance on supernatural religious beliefs.

1 Humanism in its first sense had its beginnings in Italy as early as the 14th century, when its pioneer was the poet and scholar ▷ Petrarch (1304–74), and reached its height (greatly stimulated by the recovery of lost manuscripts after the fall of Constantinople in 1453) throughout western Europe in the 16th century, when it first reached England. Its outstanding characteristic was a new kind of critical power. In the previous thousand years European civilization had above all been donated – even created – by the Church, which had put the literatures of the preceding Latin and Greek cultures to its own uses and had directed movements in thought and art through its authority over the religious orders and universities. The humanists began by criticizing and evaluating the Latin and Greek authors in the light of what they believed to be Roman and Greek standards of civilization. Some of the important consequences of humanism were these: the rediscovery of many ancient Greek and Latin works; the establishment of new standards in Greek and Latin scholarship; the assumption, which was to dominate English education until the present century, that a

thorough basis in at least Latin literature was indispensable to the civilized man; the beginnings of what we nowadays regard as 'scientific thinking'; the introduction of the term Middle Ages for the period between the fall of the Roman Empire of the West (5th century AD) and the ▷ Renaissance, meaning by it a period of partial and inferior civilization. The most prominent of the European humanists was the Dutchman ▷ Erasmus, and the most prominent of the earlier English humanists was his friend ▷ Sir Thomas More. The Church was not at first hostile to humanism; indeed such a Pope as Leo X (reigned 1513–21) was himself a humanist. When, in the second 30 years of the 16th century, the critical spirit became an increasingly aggressive weapon in the hands of the religious reformers – the Renaissance branching into the ▷ Reformation – the attitude of the Church hardened, and humanists in the later 16th century found themselves restricted by the religious quarrels of Protestants and Catholics, or obliged (like ▷ Montaigne) to adopt a retiring and circumspect policy. In the 17th and 18th centuries, humanism hardened into neo-classicism.

2 Modern humanism assumes that man's command of scientific knowledge has rendered religion largely redundant. Its central principle is that 'man is the measure of all things', and elsewhere in Europe it is sometimes called 'hominism' (Lat. *homo* = man).

'Humanism' is also used as a general expression for any philosophy that proposes the full development of human potentiality. In this sense, 'Christian humanism', since the 16th century, has stood for the marriage of the humanist value attached to a conception of humanity based on reason with the Christian value based on Divine Revelation. An example of a Christian humanist movement is that of Cambridge ▷ Platonists in the 17th century. 'Liberal humanism' values the dignity of the individual and their inalienable right to justice, liberty, freedom of thought and the pursuit of happiness; its weakness lies in its concentration on the single subject and its failure to recognize the power of institutions in determining the conditions of life.

Bib: Kinney, A. F., *Continental Humanist Poetics.*

Hume, David (1711–76)

Philosopher. His first major work, *Treatise of Human Nature* (1739–40) did not arouse much interest. His *Enquiry concerning Human Understanding* (1748) and *Enquiry concerning the Principles of Morals* (1751) are revisions and developments of the first work. His theory of knowledge was distinct from the theories of ▷ John Locke and ▷ George Berkeley. Locke had said that ideas proceeded from sensations, *ie* from experience received through the senses, implying that we know mind only through matter; Berkeley that on the contrary we know matter only through our mental conceptions of it and that this proves the primacy of mind. Hume said that we cannot know of the existence of mind, except as a collective term covering memories, perceptions and ideas. He further argued that there was no necessity in the law of cause and effect, except in mathematics; what we call that law is inferred but not observed, a customary association confirmed by experience but with no provable necessity in it. Thus if Locke had seemed to validate science at the expense of religion and Berkeley the reverse, Hume seemed to drive at the roots of both. The graceful lucidity with which he expounded this extreme scepticism caused a wit to summarize his philosophy in the epigram: 'No mind! – It doesn't matter. No matter! – Never mind.' In his ethics, Hume held that virtue is what makes for happiness, both in ourselves and others, and that the two kinds of happiness are in accord with each other.

Hume also wrote the first systematic history of England, beginning, at first, with the reign of ▷ James I, when, as he considered with reasonable justice, the political differences of his own day had their start. His historical view is, however, marked by his political prejudices and, since he was a Scotsman, by his suspicion of English motives towards Scotland. His *Essays Moral and Political* (1741), and later volumes, contain acute comments on contemporary society. He differed from ▷ Rousseau by arguing against the long-established hypothesis that society is based on a 'social contract'. His economic writings were a stimulus to ▷ Adam Smith.

Bib: Mossner, E. C., *The Life of Hume*; Willey, B., *The Eighteenth Century Background*; Smith, N. K., *The Philosophy of David Hume*; Pears, D. F. (ed.), *Hume: A Symposium.*

Humour

The original meaning was 'liquid'. Ancient Greek and Latin medicine passed on to the ▷ Middle Ages the theory of four liquids (humours) in the human body: phlegm, blood, yellow bile or choler, and black bile or melancholy. Individual temperaments derived their quality from the predominance of one or other 'humour'; thus we still speak of 'phlegmatic' or very calm temperaments, 'sanguine' or ardent temperaments, 'choleric' or easily angered ones, and 'melancholy' or depressive temperaments. In the later 16th century a man's humour was his characteristic disposition, whether or not related to the original four physical humours. It could also have other meanings: his mania or obsession; his caprice or whim; his passing mood.

All these uses can be found in ▷ Shakespeare and his contemporaries; *eg* in ▷ *Julius Caesar* II.i., Portia begs her husband Brutus not to risk his health in the 'humours' (moistures) 'of the dank morning', but in the same scene Decius has declared that he can induce Caesar to go to the Capitol by giving 'his humour the true bent', *ie* by exploiting Caesar's disposition to superstition. In ▷ *The Merchant of Venice* IV.i, Shylock suggests that if an explanation is required for his preferring a pound of Antonio's flesh to 3,000 ducats, it should be put down to his caprice – 'Say it is my humour'; in ▷ *As You Like It* IV.i, ▷ Rosalind speaks of being in a 'holiday humour', *ie* in a gay mood.

▷ Ben Jonson in ▷ *Every Man in His Humour* III.i, speaks of a humour as 'a monster bred in a man by self-love and affectation, and fed by folly', *ie* produced by egotism, encouraged by fashionable ostentation, and not restrained by good sense.

▷ Humours, Comedy of; Satire; Wit.

Humours, Comedy of

A form of drama especially associated with ▷ Ben Jonson. Starting from the traditional psychology that explained a temperament as the product of its physical constitution, Jonson treats ▷ humour as the monstrous distortion of human nature by egotism and the self-regarding appetites, notably some form of greed. Partly timeless satire on human nature, the comedy of humours is also social satire since such personal extravagances are nourished by social tendencies: new prospects of wealth let loose unbounded lusts, as with Sir Epicure Mammon (in Jonson's ▷ *The Alchemist*); the rush of speculation on often fantastic 'projects' (*ie* financial enterprises requiring investment) encourages unlimited credulity in the foolish, *eg* Fitzdottrel in ▷ *The Devil is an Ass*; the prevalence of avarice causes adventurers to overreach themselves in their contempt for their victims and in their own megalomania (Volpone and Mosca in ▷ *Volpone*). Jonson's world is a jungle of predators and victims, free from the restraint of religion, reason or respect for tradition. But the passions which Jonson exposes in their excess arise from human energies that are themselves fine and belong to that exhilaration in the scope for human fulfilment which is characteristic of the ▷ Renaissance. Jonson's more massive characters, though they condemn themselves by the exorbitance of their language, make speeches of great poetic splendour and force. The hyperbole of ▷ Christopher Marlowe in ▷ *Tamburlaine* and ▷ *The Jew of Malta* provides the tradition for Jonson's eloquence. Jonson's great comedies are *Volpone* and *The Alchemist*. *The Devil is an Ass* is nearly as fine, and ▷ *Bartholomew Fair* and ▷ *Epicoene, or The Silent Woman* are memorable. The mode was first established by ▷ *Every Man in his Humour*. ▷ *Sejanus* is a satirical tragedy, with similarities to the great comedies.

Among Jonson's followers, ▷ Massinger (▷ *A New Way to pay Old Debts*, and ▷ *The City Madam*) and ▷ Middleton (▷ *A Chaste Maid in Cheapside*) are the best.

▷ Bakhtin, Mikhail.

Humphreys, Emyr (b 1919)

Novelist. Born at Prestatyn, Flintshire, but brought up in Trelawnyd, Emyr Humphreys was educated at the University College of Wales, Aberystwyth, where he read history, learnt Welsh, became a nationalist, and subsequently declared himself a conscientious objector, working first in agriculture in Pembrokeshire, later as a war relief worker in the Middle East, and afterwards in Italy. After his marriage, a brief teaching career was followed by another in BBC Wales as a drama producer, this leading to a lectureship in Drama at the University College of North Wales, Bangor, from which post he resigned in 1972 to devote himself full-time to writing. Emyr Humphreys' novels examine conscience through moral questioning within the context of realist novels, set generally in North Wales, with his characters drawn largely from the Welsh-speaking professional class, through which he impartially presents Nonconformity and refuses to indulge popular taste in novels that show concern for the future of society, in his vision of a Wales finally emerging from its betrayals. Emyr Humphreys has published a volume of short stories, *Natives* (1968), as well as four poetry collections, *Ancestor Worship* (1970), *Landscapes* (1976), *The Kingdom of Brân* (1979) and *Pwyll a Rhiannon* (1980). His novels, in chronological order, are as follows: *The Little Kingdom* (1946); *The Voice of the Stranger* (1949); *A Change of Heart* (1951); *Hear and Forgive* (1952); *A Man's Estate* (1955); *The Italian Wife* (1957); *A Toy Epic* (1958); *The Gift* (1963); *Outside the House of Baal* (1965); *National Winner* (1971); *Flesh and Blood* (1974); *The Best of Friends* (1978); *The Anchor-Tree* (1980); *Jones* (1984); *Salt of the Earth* (1985); *An Absolute Hero* (1986); *Open Secret* (1988); and *Bonds of Attachment* (1991). Important for understanding the themes in his novels, *The Taliesin Tradition* (1983) examines the development of Wales through its cultural, social and political history, especially its struggle to achieve and assert its national identity beside that of its more demographically powerful English neighbour.

Bib: Stephens, M. (Ed.), *The Oxford Companion to the Literature of Wales*; Jones, G. and Rowlands, J., *Profiles*.

***Humphry Clinker, The Expedition of* (1771)**

A ▷ picaresque novel by ▷ Tobias Smollett, written in letters. It describes a tour of England and Scotland made by Mr Matthew Bramble and his family party – his sister Tabitha, his nephew and niece Jerry and Lydia, and the maid Winifred Jenkins. Humphry Clinker is a coachman who joins the party on the way, turns out to be Mr Bramble's illegitimate son, and marries Winifred. Characterization is strongly marked but superficial, the chief object being to characterize the society of the time realistically and with an often coarse humour. This is usually held to be the most successful of Smollett's novels, and shows something of the humane sympathies of the 16th-century Spanish novelist Cervantes, whose *Don Quixote* Smollett had himself translated in 1755.

Hundred Years' War

The name given to the succession of wars between the kings of England and France between 1338 and 1453. The causes were partly territorial and partly economic. The territorial causes were especially bound up with the possession by the English kings of the large duchy of Aquitaine, first acquired through marriage by ▷ Henry II of England; as the French kings grew stronger, they increasingly coveted this large slice out of their territory. The economic causes were connected with Flanders; the Flemish cloth manufacturing towns were the importers of English wool, but they owed political allegiance to the French king; it was largely to divert this allegiance that ▷ Edward III first laid claim to the French crown. To these causes may be added the restlessness of the English and French nobility, and the popularity of the war with them as a profitable and advantageous pursuit – it was the peasantry who were the main sufferers of the campaigns. Scotland was much of the time an ally of France, either sending troops to assist the French or fighting along her own border.

Militarily, the war was notable for the great importance of the infantry soldier, especially in the form of the English ▷ yeoman archer. Hitherto the armoured knight on horseback had dominated the battlefield; the victory of the foot-soldiers at ▷ Crécy, Poitiers (1356) and above all ▷ Agincourt not only changed methods of warfare but looked forward to important social changes. The aristocracy were in future more dependent than hitherto on the support of the common people and this in turn implied a rise of national feeling.

The outstanding phases of the struggle were three:

1 The first phase under Edward III until the Treaty of Brétigny (1360) went strongly to the English advantage, though Edward renounced his claim to the French crown.

2 Under ▷ Henry V the English had another period of brilliant success and by the Treaty of Troyes (1420) Henry was recognized as heir to the French throne; his baby son was acknowledged king of France and England in 1422. Part of the English success was due to the assistance provided to Henry by the French Duke of Burgundy.

3 In the last phase, however, the English were completely defeated and driven from France except for the port of Calais, retained until 1558. This was the phase which has become memorable for the exploits of the French peasant patriot, ▷ Joan of Arc (Jeanne d'Arc), burned for heresy and sorcery at Rouen in 1431.

Hungry Forties, The

The decade 1840–50, so called because bad harvests caused serious food shortages, leading to mass agitation for abolition of the tax on imported corn (Anti-Corn Law League) and for a more democratic political system (the ▷ Chartist movement). It was in the years 1845–51 that the Irish famine took place: about 10 per cent of the population died from hunger and disease, and mass emigration ensued from those remaining.

▷ Corn Law, Repeal of the; Free Trade; Social Problem novel.

Hunt, Leigh (1784–1859)

Journalist and poet. With his brother John, he edited the boldly radical weekly periodical ▷ *The Examiner* until he gave up his share in it in 1821. His outspoken attack on the Prince Regent in 1813 brought two years' imprisonment for the brothers, but they continued to edit the journal in prison. He was joint editor with ▷ Lord Byron of the short-lived quarterly, the *Liberal*, and he edited or had a hand in several other periodicals, doing much to publicize the work of both ▷ John Keats and ▷ Percy Bysshe Shelley. His essays, popular at the time, are mostly effusions on trivial topics, though his busy and active life makes his autobiography (1850) one of his most memorable works. Later in life he was caricatured as the genial sponger, Mr Skimpole, in Charles Dickens' *Bleak House* (1852–3).

The Hunt literary circle was nicknamed the 'Cockney School' by the critic John G. Lockhart, indicating a certain vulgarity. Hunt's own poetry does indeed display a facile cosiness of tone. However, its most prominent technical features: a cloying physicality of imagery, and double or triple rhymes with feminine endings, were enthusiastically adopted by his protégé, Keats. Keats' early poem 'I stood tiptoe upon a little hill' is dedicated to Hunt and closely imitates the manner of Hunt's best work, *The Story of Rimini* (1816), from which it borrows such vocabulary as 'blisses', 'tresses', 'bower', 'blushes'. The characteristic rhyme 'blisses'/'kisses' occurs in both poems, and other rhymes of Keats ('posy'/'rosy', 'flitting'/'quitting', 'ever wrestle'/'ever nestle') recall such rhymes as 'flushes'/'blushes', 'dissemble'/'in a tremble' in *The Story of Rimini*.

Bib: Blunden, E., *Leigh Hunt's Examiner Examined*; Blunden, E., *Life*.

Hunter, Rachel (1754–1813)

Novelist. Hunter became a novelist in her 40s, and at the time her novels appeared to be somewhat self-conscious of their narrative form, and were mocked by ▷ Jane Austen. Today, however, we might call them 'metafictional', that is, writing which deliberately questions the relationship between fiction and reality by drawing attention to its own status as a linguistic construct. For example, in Hunter's *The Unexpected Legacy* (1804) the Preface is written by an author who quotes an attack on novels by a friend; both characters are fictitious, although as they appear in the Preface the reader expects them to be real. Similarly, in *Lady Maclairn, The Victim of Villainy* (1806) the author is supposedly only the editor of the letters, and, adding to the complexity, she places herself within the novel as a character, ending up as a governess to the heroine's family. In addition to the adoption of multiple authorial voices, Hunter also layers plot and time to create a complex interweaving of stories, each creating a different relationship between 'fiction' and 'reality'. Thematically, she seems to have been fascinated by the idea of mixed racial marriages; this is the concern of *Lady Maclairn* and her first published novel, *Letitia, or The Castle without a Spectre* (1801), the latter of which may also be classed as a ▷ Gothic novel.

Hutcheson, Francis (1694–1746)
Scottish philosopher, who started his own private academy of learning in Dublin, and later became professor of moral science and natural philosophy at Glasgow University. He built on ▷ Locke's distinction between sensation and reflection, and ▷ Shaftesbury's idea of 'moral sense', to argue for an innate code of conduct and ethics that has nothing to do with reason. This, he maintained, is almost as powerful as the instict for self-preservation, and ensures that the performance of virtuous action is pleasurable. He defined the greatest virtue as that most in accord with the general good, coining the phrase 'the greatest happiness for the greatest numbers', which was taken up later by ▷ Bentham and other Utilitarians (▷ Utilitarianism). He also developed a theory of aesthetics, suggesting that the appreciation of beauty, like the moral code, proceeds from an inner sense, rather than from reason or learning. His major works include *An Inquiry into the Original of Our Ideas of Beauty and Virtue* (1725), *An Essay on the Nature and Conduct of The Passions and Affections* (1726) and, his most famous, *A System of Moral Philosophy* (published posthumously in 1755). He is considered as a pioneer of the 'Scottish School' of philosophy, influencing ▷ Hume, ▷ Adam Ferguson and, in a later generation, ▷ Adam Smith, as well as the Benthamites. His ideas contributed to the growth of ▷ sensibility.
Bib: Blackstone, W. T., *Hutcheson and Contemporary Ethical Theory*; Bryson, G., *Man and Society: The Scottish Inquiry of the Eighteenth Century*; Fox, C. (ed.), *Psychology and Literature in the Eighteenth Century*.

Hutchinson, Lucy (1620–c 1675)
Prolific writer. Lucy Hutchinson displayed her immense intelligence as a child (she could read perfectly by the time she was four) and excelled her brothers at scholarly activity. Although her family thought this would repel any future husband, it was her quiet learning that attracted John Hutchinson and their marriage, which lasted from 1638 until his death in 1664 was a deeply romantic one. As a Parliamentarian, her husband was imprisoned at the Restoration, and her ▷ biography of him (*Memoirs of the Life of Colonel Hutchinson*, pub. 1806) was partly written to ensure that their children knew about and admired his life. However, she was also aware of the similar work by the Royalist ▷ Margaret Cavendish. Lucy Hutchinson also translated ▷ Lucretius and Virgil, wrote several Christian tracts (she became a ▷ Baptist in 1646), and an ▷ autobiography.
▷ Translation.
Bib: Fraser, A., *The Weaker Vessel*.

Huxley, Aldous (1894–1963)
Novelist and essayist. His novels are 'novels of ideas', involving conversations which disclose viewpoints rather than establish characters, and having a polemical rather than an imaginative theme. An early practitioner of the form was ▷ Thomas Love Peacock, and it is his novels that Huxley's earlier ones recall: *Crome Yellow* (1921); *Antic Hay* (1923); *Those Barren Leaves* (1925). *Point Counter Point* (1928) is his best-known novel and is an attempt to convey a social image of the age with more imaginative depth and substance, but his polemical and inquisitorial mind was better suited to *Brave New World* (1932), in which a future society is presented so as to bring out the tendencies working in contemporary civilization and to show their disastrous consequences. Fastidious, abhorring what he saw to be the probable obliteration of human culture by 20th-century addiction to technology, but sceptical of religious solutions – he was the grandson of the great 19th-century agnostic biologist ▷ Thomas Huxley – he turned in the 1930s to eastern religions such as Buddhism for spiritual support. This is shown in *Eyeless in Gaza* (1936). This and his last books – *After Many a Summer* (1939), *Ape and Essence* (1948), *Brave New World Revisited* (1958) – return to the discursive form of his earlier work. His novels and his essays (Collected Edition; 1959) are all concerned with how to resist the debasement of 'mass culture' and to sustain the identity of the human spirit without the aid of faith in supernatural religion of the Christian kind.
Bib: Bowering, P., *Aldous Huxley*: Ferns, C. S.,

Aldous Huxley, Novelist; Woodcock, G., *Dawn and the Darkest Hour.*

Huxley, Thomas Henry (1825–95)
Biologist. He was a supporter of ▷ Darwin's theory of evolution and combined philosophical speculation with technical exposition. His many works, essays, lectures and articles included the influential publications: *Man's Place in Nature* (1863), *The Physical Basis of Life* (1868), *Science and Culture* (1881) and *Science and Morals* (1886). He held that scientific discoveries had neither given support to nor discredited religious faith, and he invented the term ▷ agnosticism for this attitude to religion.

Hymns
The word 'hymn' is of ancient Greek origin; it meant a song of praise to the gods. Such songs have been important in all the religions that have lain behind European culture; Latin hymns were composed and sung in the Christian churches from the earliest days of Christianity, and the Jewish hymns, or ▷ Psalms, are shared by the Jewish and the Christian religions.

The English hymn began its history in the religious ▷ Reformation under ▷ Edward VI when the abandonment of the Latin form of service produced the need for hymns in English. The Psalms were the obvious resource, but they had been translated into English prose. Accordingly, in 1549, the first or 'Old Version' of metrical Psalms was published; the authors were Sternhold and Hopkins. The most famous of this collection, and the only one now generally known, is the 'Old Hundredth' (Psalm 100): 'All people that on earth do dwell'. The Old Version of the metrical Psalms was replaced by the 'New Version' (1696) by Tate and Brady. From this book, two psalms are still familiar: 'Through all the changing scenes of life' and 'As pants the hart for cooling streams'.

The majority of hymns in English, however, were not metrical Psalms, but specially composed original poems. The great period of English hymn composition was the 17th and 18th centuries. However, it is necessary to distinguish between short religious poems which have been adopted as hymns, and poems which were composed as hymns. Some of the best religious poets of the 17th century, notably ▷ Herbert and ▷ Vaughan, produced work in the first group. But the first professional hymn writer (as distinct from the composers of the metrical Psalms) was the Anglican bishop, Thomas Ken (1637–1711). His best hymns, *eg* 'Awake my soul', and 'Glory to thee, my God, this night', are distinguished poetry.

It was however, the ▷ Dissenters – the ▷ Puritan movements excluded from the Church of England by the Act of Uniformity (1662) – and their ▷ Evangelical sympathizers within the Church of England, rather than the orthodox Anglicans, who were at first most active in hymn-writing. The Church of England had a set form of worship in the Book of Common Prayer; hymns (in addition to the prose versions of the Psalms) were allowed in this service, but no special provision was made for them. But the ▷ Dissenting sects had no set form of worship; hymns for this reason alone were important to them. They were important also for three other reasons: Dissent was strong among classes in touch with traditions of ▷ ballad and folk-song; most forms of Dissenting faith demanded strong participation by the congregation in the act of worship; in the 17th century, Dissenters underwent persecution, and communal, militant hymn-singing encouraged their spirit of endurance. ▷ John Bunyan included hymns in his ▷ *Pilgrim's Progress*, written in prison; one of these – 'Who would true valour see' – is famous. But the greatest of the dissenting hymn-writers is ▷ Isaac Watts. His language combines the homeliness of the broadside ballads of the city streets with the dignity and musical cadence of biblical English. Charles Wesley, the brother of the Methodist leader ▷ John Wesley, had greater versatility than Watts, and was very prolific; his best hymns are impressive though without the power of the best by Watts. Other notable 18th-century hymn-writers were ▷ Reginald Heber, ▷ Alice Flowerdew, John Newton (1725–1807) and ▷ William Cowper. All these had at least some of the force of common speech and spontaneous emotion in their hymns. Beside them, the hymns of the orthodox Anglican, ▷ Joseph Addison, are cold, though dignified and sincere.

In the 19th century, partly under the influence of the ▷ Oxford Movement, the Church of England reversed its policy of discouraging the use of hymns in its forms of worship. Hymn-writers became numerous; 220 Church of England hymn-books were published between 1800 and 1880, including the official compilation, *Hymns Ancient and Modern* (1861). It was an age in which strong religious feeling struggled with bitter doubt, often in the same mind; the struggle is exemplified in 'Lead kindly light' by Cardinal Newman. The 20th century has produced few hymns in comparison with the 19th, but there has been a small resurgence in the last 20 years with greater freedom of language and introduction of folk-song-like melodies.

***Hypatia, or, New Foes with an Old Face* (1853)**
An ▷ historical novel by ▷ Charles Kingsley, originally published in ▷ *Fraser's Magazine* 1852–53 and set in Alexandria in the 5th century AD.

Hyperbole
▷ Figures of Speech.

Hyperion
In Greek myth, a Titan, son of the sky god Uranus and the earth goddess Ge. He was

one of the greatest of the Titans, and often identified with the sun, of whom in the original myth he was the father; the sun-god was Helios.

▷ *Hyperion* by Keats.

***Hyperion* (1820)**
***The Fall of Hyperion* (1856)**
Two fragments of an epic poem in blank verse by ▷ John Keats, written in 1818–19, the second (*The Fall of Hyperion*) unrevised. Keats' aim was to rival ▷ John Milton's philosophical profundity by treating a theme of divine conflict. The Greek myth of the war of the Olympian Gods and the primal Titans is adapted to the aestheticist idea that 'first in beauty should be first in might'. *Hyperion* (published in 1820) opens with a magnificent scene in which Saturn, chief of the Titans, mourns his lost power, while Hyperion, the only Titan as yet unfallen, roams uneasily round his palace. Apollo, the destined Olympian successor to Hyperion is confronted by Mnemosyne who begins to initiate him into godhead. At this point the fragment breaks off, Keats' explanation being that it was too Miltonic: 'I prefer the native music . . . to Milton's cut by feet.' However it is difficult to imagine how the approaching beauty-contest between Hyperion and Apollo could have been related in terms of epic conflict without absurdity, or how the moral difficulties of the theme could have been overcome. It is indeed, the highly Miltonic passages concerning the suffering of the Titans which are the most poetically moving parts of the surviving fragment.

The Fall of Hyperion (not published until 1856) escapes from narrative problems into personal preoccupations, opening with a dream in which the poet finds himself undergoing a symbolic test of dedication in the temple of (Juno) Moneta, the Counsellor. After a powerful discussion of the nature of the poetic calling, containing some of Keats' most mature verse, the story is retold as before, in the same Miltonic manner, breaking off even earlier than the previous version, as the same narrative problems loomed ahead.

Iambic foot (Iamb, Iambus)
The classical verse foot of a short syllable followed by a long one, which in English is an unaccented syllable followed by an accented one. The ▷ Alexandrine has six such feet.

Ibsen, Henrik (1828–1906)
Norwegian dramatist; his working life (1850–1900) began in a period when the literary quality of drama had fallen low everywhere in Europe, and perhaps lowest of all in Britain. By the end of the century Ibsen's example had revived interest in the drama everywhere and had profoundly influenced a number of other important dramatists, such as ▷ Strindberg in Sweden, ▷ Chekhov in Russia, and ▷ Shaw in Britain. Ibsen began by writing romantic and historical dramas. Then, in self-imposed exile, he wrote his great poetic dramas, *Brand* (1866) and *Peer Gynt* (1867). About 10 years later he started on the prose dramas, the sequence of which continued to 1900. The first group of these treated social problems with startling boldness: *Pillars of Society* (1877); *A Doll's House* (1879); *Ghosts* (1881); *An Enemy of the People* (1882). After this, his work became increasingly psychological, anticipating the 20th century in the handling of inner conflicts, self-deceptions, and frustrations: *The Wild Duck* (1884); *Rosmersholm* (1886); *The Lady from the Sea* (1888); *Hedda Gabler* (1890). Although these plays operated within ▷ Naturalistic conventions, Ibsen developed dramatic strategies to show far more than simply surface processes, through the use of dramatic metaphors and symbolism. In the last group of plays the symbolism takes precedence over the realism: *The Master Builder* (1892); *Little Eyolf* (1894); *John Gabriel Borkman* (1896), and *When We Dead Awaken* (1900). It was the social realist phase which most influenced Shaw, and it was Shaw who was the most eloquent introducer of Ibsen's art to the British public, particularly in his book *Quintessence of Ibsenism* (1891). The English dramatic revival of 1890–1914 (as distinct from the Anglo-Irish one by ▷ Yeats and ▷ Synge happening at the same time) thus consisted predominantly of realist plays dealing with social problems, by such writers as Shaw, ▷ Galsworthy, ▷ Granville-Barker. The psychological and symbolical phases of Ibsen's work have had, together with the writing of Chekhov and Strindberg, greater influence since 1920.
Bib: Beyer, E., *Ibsen: The Man and his Work* (trans. Wells, M.); Meyer, M., *Henrik Ibsen: A Biography*, 3 vols.; Williams, R., *Drama from Ibsen to Brecht*.

Idealism
In philosophy, any form of thought which finds reality not in the mind of the perceiver (the subject), nor in the thing experienced (the object) but in the idea in which they meet. In its earliest form idealism was developed by ▷ Socrates and his disciple ▷ Plato. Their influence was important in the 16th-century Europe of the ▷ Renaissance, *eg* on ▷ Edmund Spenser. A modern idealist, ▷ F. H. Bradley, had as strong an influence on the poet ▷ T.S. Eliot.

In ordinary usage, idealism means the ability to conceive perfection as a standard by which ordinary behaviour and achievement is to be judged. This view is really an inheritance from Plato, who believed that earthly realities were imperfect derivatives of heavenly perfections. To 'idealize' a thing or person is to present the image of what ought to be, rather than what experience knows in ordinary life. In imaginative art we have come to consider this as a fault, but to a 16th-century critic such as ▷ Sir Philip Sidney poetry existed for just such a purpose. This is not, however, the kind of influence which Bradley had on Eliot; Bradley maintained that no reality existed outside the spirit, and he influenced Eliot towards interpreting the phenomena and dilemmas of his age in religious terms.

In modern critical theory idealism is associated with the anti-materialist impulse to denigrate history and social context. The meaning of this term is complicated by its history within the discipline of philosophy, and by its common usage as a description of human behaviour not susceptible to the 'realistic' impulses of self-interest. The term is sometimes used in critical theory to denote the primacy of thought, and to indicate a particular kind of relationship between writer and text where it is a sequence of ideas that act as the deep structure for events and relationships.

Ideology
This term is defined by ▷ Karl Marx and Friedrich Engels (1800–95) in *The German Ideology* as 'false consciousness'. A further meaning, which Raymond Williams traces to the usage initiated by Napoleon Bonaparte, denotes a fanatical commitment to a particular set of ideas, and this has remained a dominant meaning in the sphere of modern right-wing politics, especially in relation to the question of dogmatism. The term has come to the fore again in the ▷ post-structuralist Marxism of ▷ Louis Althusser, where it is distinguished from 'science'. Ideology here is defined as the means whereby, at the level of ideas, every social group produces and reproduces the conditions of its own existence. Althusser argues that 'Ideology is a "representation" of the imaginary relationship of individuals to their real conditions of existence' (*Lenin and Philosophy*; 1971). In order to ensure that political power remains the preserve of a dominant class, individual 'subjects' are assigned particular positions in society. A full range of social institutions, such as the Church, the family and the education

system, are the means through which a particular hierarchy of values is disseminated. The point to emphasize, however, is that ideology disguises the real material relations between the different social classes, and this knowledge can only be retrieved through a theoretically aware analysis of the interrelationships that prevail within society at any one time. A ruling class sustains itself in power, partly by coercion (repressive apparatuses), but also by negotiation with other subordinate classes (▷ hegemony; Althusser's ideological state of apparatuses).

Social change occurs when the ideology of the dominant class is no longer able to contain the contradictions existing in real social relations. The function of literary texts in this process is complex. In one sense they reproduce ideology, but also they may offer a critique of it by 'distancing' themselves from the ideology with which they are historically implicated. Since all language is by definition 'ideological', insofar as it is motivated by particular sorts of social relationship, the language of a literary text can very often be implicated in an ideology of which it is not aware. The text's implication in ideology can only be excavated through a critical process which seeks to uncover the assumption upon which it is based.

Bib: Althusser, L., *For Marx*; Thompson, J.B., *Studies in The Theory of Ideology*.

Idler, The

Essays contributed weekly by ▷ Samuel Johnson to the *Universal Chronicle* or *Weekly Gazette* from April 1758 to April 1760. As compared to his ▷ *Rambler* papers, they contain more humour, and more flexible treatment of the fictional characters such as ▷ Dick Minim, but they have the same kind of emotional force and moral gravity which distinguish Johnson as a periodical essayist.

Idylls of the King, The

A series of poems by ▷ Alfred Tennyson on episodes from the legends of King Arthur. The earliest and most famous fragment is the *Morte D'Arthur* (1842), but the series really begins in 1859 with *Enid, Vivien, Elaine, Guinevere*, followed by (1869) *The Coming of Arthur*, *The Holy Grail*, *Pelleas and Ettare*, *The Passing of Arthur*; (1871) *The Lost Tournament*; (1872) *Gareth and Lynette*; (1885) *Balin and Balan*. *Enid* was later divided into *The Marriage of Geraint* and *Geraint and Enid*. *Morte D'Arthur* was included in *The Passing of Arthur*. The whole series was intended to have a loose epic structure; single-minded virtue ideally conceived is gradually overcome by evil through the sinful passion of Lancelot and Arthur's wife, Guinevere. Extremely popular at the time, the *Idylls* have chiefly harmed Tennyson's reputation since. They were written under the influence of the ▷ Pre-Raphaelite movement with its romanticization of the Middle Ages. Later the poems struck readers as bodiless, with the life neither of the Middle Ages nor of 19th century. However, parts of the *Idylls*, notably *Vivien* with its powerful evocation of unleashed sexuality and *Morte d'Arthur* with its impotent image of kingship, have recently demanded a less complacent response.

▷ Medievalism.

Igraine (Igerne, Ygerna)

Mother of ▷ King Arthur. Igraine, the wife of Gorlois, the Duke of Cornwall, is desired by ▷ King Uther, whose pursuit of her triggers a war with Gorlois. Uther, however, gains access to ▷ Tintagel and to Igraine by means of ▷ Merlin's magical powers which allow Uther to take on the appearance of the Duke of Cornwall. Arthur is conceived as a result of this trick and Igraine becomes Uther's wife after her husband's death. In ▷ Malory's *Morte D'Arthur*, Igraine has three daughters by Gorlois, ▷ Morgause, Elaine and ▷ Morgan la Fay.

Iliad

An ▷ epic by the ancient Greek poet ▷ Homer. Its subject is the siege of ▷ Troy by an alliance of Greek states; the occasion of the war is the elopement of Helen, wife of Menelaus, king of the Greek state of Sparta, with Paris, a son of Priam, king of Troy. The poem is in 24 books; it begins with the Greeks already besieging Troy. In Book I the chief Greek hero Achilles, quarrels with the Greek commander-in-chief, Agamemnon, king of Argos and brother to Menelaus. Achilles withdraws from the fighting, and returns to it only in Book XIX after the killing of his friend Patroclus by the chief Trojan hero, Hector. Achilles kills Hector in XXII, and the poem ends with Hector's funeral in Troy. Hector is the principal hero of the epic, much of which is taken up with his exploits, as well as with those of other Greek and Trojan heroes and with the intervention of the gods on either side. There is much speculation about the date of the historical events and that of the poem respectively. Present opinion seems to be that the historical city of Troy fell early in the 12th century BC and that the poem was written about 300 years later. The surviving text dates from the 2nd century BC.

The *Iliad* has had an enormous influence on the literature of Europe. With Homer's ▷ *Odyssey*, it set the standard for epic poetry, which until the 19th century was considered the noblest poetic form. Its first successor was the ▷ *Aeneid* (1st century BC) by the Roman poet Virgil. The poem has been several times translated into English verse; the most notable versions are those by ▷ George Chapman (1611) and ▷ Alexander Pope (1720).

Imagism

A poetic movement founded by a group led

by ▷ Ezra Pound in 1912; it published four anthologies – *Des Imagistes*, 1914; *Some Imagists*, 1915–16–17. The inspiration came from the ideas of ▷ T. E. Hulme (1886–1917) who was an anti-romantic, believing that words were being used by poets to obscure emotions instead of to clarify them. The kind of poet he had in mind was the Victorian ▷ Algernon Swinburne. The Imagist credo may be summarized as:

1 Use the language of common speech, but use it exactly.
2 Create new rhythms for new moods.
3 Allow complete freedom in subject.
4 Present an image, but avoid vagueness.
5 Produce poetry that is hard and clear.
6 Concentration is the essence of poetry.

Pound was an American, though he was then living in England; Imagism was an Anglo-American movement, with an English periodical, *The Egoist* (started 1914), and an American one, *Poetry* (from 1912). Pound was himself the most distinguished of the Imagists, though he separated from the movement in 1914. Notable contributors to the anthologies included ▷ D. H. Lawrence, ▷ James Joyce and ▷ H. D. The movement was more organized and distinct in its aims than most English literary movements.

▷ Vorticism.

Bib: Jones, P. (ed.), *Imagist Poetry*.

Imitation, Renaissance Theories of

Renaissance, like medieval, theories of imitation were of considerable importance to writers and rhetoricians of the 16th and 17th centuries. However, imitation did *not* mean copying or plagiarism; nor was it suggestive of ▷ translation. Instead, imitation was the process by which Renaissance writers invested their own discourse with authority, aesthetic form and structure by assimilating texts from the ▷ classical past and incorporating them into their own work. A frequently used ▷ metaphor to describe the process is that of digestion. When ▷ Ben Jonson, for example, sets out to describe an ideal of rural life and aristocratic benevolence in his poem 'To Penshurst', he not only evokes the Kentish countryside and the family who dwell at Penshurst, he organizes his description according to models found in his reading in Virgil, ▷ Juvenal, Martial (c AD 40–104) and other classical authors. Imitation is, in this sense, much more than allusion or reference. Rather, it is the means whereby the Renaissance writer could place his/her own work within a tradition of public or private utterance.

Bib: Cave, T., *The Cornucopian Text: Problems of Writing in the French Renaissance*; Greenes, T. M., *The Light in Troy: Imitation and Discovery in Renaissance Poetry*.

Imitations of Horace **(1733–78)**

Adaptations by ▷ Alexander Pope of the ▷ satires and epistles of the Latin poet ▷ Horace, who had already served as a model for satire by ▷ John Oldham, the ▷ Earl of Rochester and ▷ Jonathan Swift. The aim of the imitation is not merely to translate, but to adapt the Roman model, elaborating the parallel between Augustan (▷ Caesar, Augustus) Rome and modern Britain. Sometimes the relation between original and imitation produces ▷ mock-heroic irony as when Pope imitates Horace's verse epistle to Caesar Augustus. He addresses the stodgy Hanoverian George II (who had been christened Augustus), as though he were the great Emperor, and praises 'Your Arms, your Actions, your Repose . . .!' More usually Pope asserts a Horatian detachment from the vices of the city, and praises the self-sufficient retirement of the country gentleman: ''Tis true, no Turbots dignify my boards,/ But gudgeons, flounders, what my Thames affords'. The Tiber becomes the Thames, Rome becomes London, and Horace's estate becomes Pope's house with its five acres at Twickenham. Despite, or perhaps because of, the Latin parallel these poems are among Pope's most intimate works.

Impersonality

A key idea in much ▷ Modernist aesthetic theory and the criticism which stemmed from it. ▷ T. S. Eliot, for example, in a famous essay 'Tradition and the Individual Talent' (1919), argued that writers need to surrender their personalities in writing significant works and that craftsmanship and tradition are more important than the individual. Much early 20th-century criticism (by for example, I. A. Richards, F. R. Leavis and the American New Critics) followed this line, often under the direct influence of Eliot and others with similar views. With various emphases, all held that critics should confine their attention to 'the words on the page' and should not consider, for example, the significance of a writer's life.

▷ Author; ▷ Intentional Fallacy.

Implied author

The notional possessor of the set of attitudes and beliefs implied by the totality of a text; distinguished from the 'real' or biographical author. The distinction is necessary because a text may imply a set of beliefs (and perhaps a personality) which the author does not, in life, possess, and because different texts by the same author often imply different values.

Implied reader

A term developed on analogy with the implied author and used especially in reader-response and reception theory. It refers to the sort of reader which a novel (or other text) seems to expect or demand; the implied reader often corresponds roughly to some actual group of readers, though it is also quite possible to have an implied reader who does not correspond

even to a single actual reader. There are a range of related terms which differ in meaning to various degrees, including the ideal reader, the intended reader, the postulated reader and the inscribed reader.
Bib: Freund, E., *The Return of the Reader: Reader-Response Criticism.*

***Importance of Being Earnest, The* (1895)**
A comedy by ▷ Oscar Wilde subtitled *A Trivial Comedy for Serious People*, and first performed in 1895. The title is a subtle play on the word 'earnest' which functions as a man's name – one which 'inspires absolute confidence' – and an indication of one of the most pervading characteristics of the era. It was ▷ Thomas Carlyle who urged the Victorians to 'earnestness' in thought and deed and Wilde satirizes the condition mercilessly. The play contains sharp social observation delivered in apparently throwaway lines and covers such topics as the morals and marriages of the upper and lower classes, lady novelists and the early ▷ feminist movement. It was Wilde's last and most enduring play.

In Memoriam A. H. H.
A sequence of poems by ▷ Alfred Tennyson inspired by the death of Arthur Henry Hallam, at twenty-two, in 1833. He was a brilliant young man of great promise and hopefulness; Tennyson a year or two older, had found in his friendship with Hallam a strong resource against his own disposition to despondency and scepticism. Hallam's death crystallized for him the difficulty of spiritual affirmation in an age of upheaval in established ideas. Science was already shaking traditional certainties and contributing to the feeling that the reality of nature itself was perpertual flux: there are echoes in *In Memoriam* of ▷ Lyell's *Principles of Geology* (1830–3).

The poem was written between 1833 and 1850 and is structurally loose or fragmented – it was to be called 'Fragments of an Elegy'. It consists of 130 sections, each section being lyric in stanzas of four eight-syllable lines rhyming *abba* – a form used by Ben Jonson (1572–1637) in his elegy 'Though Beauty be The Mark of praise'. The sequence is a single poem arranged in three sections divided by Christmas Odes, and the whole concluded by a marriage-song for the wedding of Tennyson's sister; another sister, Emily, had been engaged to Hallam. Various moods of grief are expressed, and a reaching out to restored confidence and hope; in places Tennyson engages in debate between religion and science. Despite much disagreement about the work as a whole, *In Memoriam* is usually acknowledged to be Tennyson's finest achievement.

▷ Atheism; Agnosticism; Homosexuality.

Inchbald, Mrs Elizabeth (1753–1821)
Novelist, dramatist and actress. Among other plays she translated ▷ Kotzebue's *Lovers' Vows* from the German, and this is the play rehearsed in ▷ Jane Austen's *Mansfield Park*. This, and some of the other 19 plays she wrote or adapted, were popular successes: Jane Austen assumes knowledge of it by the reader. However, her best works are her two novels: *A Simple Story* (1791) and *Nature and Art* (1796).
Bib: Littlewood, S.R., *Elizabeth Inchbald and her Circle.*

Independent, The
A daily newspaper, founded in 1985 and aimed at a serious readership. As its name suggests, it aims for a relative independence of political viewpoint, which in practice means a centre position.

***Indian Queen, The* (1664)**
Rhymed ▷ heroic drama, the first such play to be staged in London, by Sir Robert Howard (1626–98) and ▷ John Dryden. The Peruvian Montezuma, having defeated the Mexicans, is offered any object of his desire in reward by the Inca. He asks for the hand of Orazia, but is scornfully refused. In a rage, he joins the Mexicans and reverses the victory. The Mexican king's sister Zempoalla is in love with Montezuma, but when she realizes he loves Orazia, she tries to kill her rival. Traxalla, a general who loves Orazia, and who aspires to the throne of Mexico, steps in and threatens to kill Montezuma if Orazia dies. Eventually Zempoalla gives up hope of winning Montezuma's love, and orders the seizure and execution of Montezuma and Orazia, as well as the execution of the now imprisoned Inca, as blood sacrifices on the altar of the gods. Her plan fails, however, and at the end Montezuma is revealed as the son of the Mexican queen, and hence as heir to the throne. He kills Traxalla in a fight, Zempoalla stabs herself, the Inca is appeased by Montezuma's new status, and gives Orazia to him, and the play ends with a speech on the vagaries of fate. Throughout, the heroism of Montezuma is contrasted with Zempoalla's disdain for honour.

Indulgences
Medieval documents bearing the seal of the Pope or of a bishop and granting the recipient remission of punishment in the next world for sins committed in this. They were freely sold in the ▷ Middle Ages by licensed 'Pardoners', and were an easy way for the Church (and also for the pardoners) to raise money. Reformers such as the Englishman ▷ Wycliffe and the German ▷ Luther were fiercely critical of them. ▷ Chaucer made grim comedy of them (▷ *Pardoner's Tale*) and his contemporary

Langland regarded them sceptically (▷ *Piers Plowman*, Passus VII).

Industrial Revolution, The
Normally understood as the succession of changes which transformed England from a predominantly rural and agricultural country into a predominantly urban and manufacturing one in the 18th and 19th centuries, and especially between 1750 and 1850. It was the first such revolution in the modern world.

England was already a great trading nation by the beginning of the 18th century, with much private capital ready for investment. Its oceanic position, which ensured easy access to overseas markets, coupled with the fact that its irregular indented coastline meant that most places were within reach of water transport, contributed to its rapid development. In addition Britain was relatively rich in natural resources such as water, salt, iron, clay and, above all, coal.

Not only was trade free to move throughout the British Isles but there was considerable freedom of movement between the social classes. English middle-class religious belief emphasized the individual conscience as the guide to conduct as well as the moral excellence of sober, industrious employment. These values encouraged self-reliance and enterprising initiative. Although those who belonged to the Nonconformist or Dissenting sects which rejected the Church of England were barred from political rights, and Parliament (controlled by the aristocracy) was far from truly representative, the political leaders of the country were extremely interested in commerce, which they were ready to participate in and profit from. The bent of the whole nation from the early 17th century had been increasingly practical and the steadily growing population provided a market which invited exploitation by various methods of improved production. Once the process started, it gathered its own momentum, which was increased by the existence of large supplies of convenient fuel in the country's coalfields. Agriculture also contributed to industrial growth: the landowners were zealous farmers and their improved methods of cultivation not only freed much labour which then became available for employment in the town factories, but increased the food supplies available for the towns. Finally, the 18th century (in contrast to the 17th) was a time of relative peace and stability in Britain, undisturbed by the wars in which her armies and money were engaged across the sea.

In the textile industry, already established since the 15th century as the principal industry, a number of machines were invented which increased production and reduced labour but were too large for the cottages where the processes had hitherto been carried out. They therefore had to be housed in ▷ factories and mills where large numbers of employees worked together. These machines were at first operated by water power. In the iron industry, the principal fuel used had been charcoal, the supply of which was becoming exhausted. However, improved methods of smelting by coal were discovered and ironmasters set up their blast furnaces in the neighbourhood of the coalfields of the north Midlands and north of England.

Most important of all, in 1769 James Watt patented an adaptation of his steam engine to the machines used in the textile industry; this consequently ceased to depend on water power and concentrated itself in the north of England to be near the coalfields. An important result was the immense expansion in the manufacture of cotton cloth. An extensive system of canals was constructed in the 18th century for the transport of goods and fuel, and the modern methods of road and bridge building were introduced, but the decisive advance in communications was the invention of the steam rail locomotive by George Stephenson (1814); by 1850 a railway system covered the country. The Industrial Revolution was a period of epic excitement, especially in the development of rail transport. It produced inventors and engineers, such as Isambard Kingdom Brunel (1806–59), who had to force their projects against established prejudice and ignorance. The other side of the epic story was the meteoric emergence of great financial speculators such as George Hudson (1800–71), the 'Railway King', who rose from being a York draper to controller of a third of the railway system, but whose career ended in disgrace. The social changes were unprecedently dramatic, in the rapid growth of the Midland and northern industrial towns and the opening of new opportunities for wealth for ambitious men from humble backgrounds. This heroic and extraordinary aspect of industrialism was a great motivating power in Victorian culture.

By 1850, Britain was the 'workshop of the world'; no other country was ready to compete with it in industrial production. The towns were the source of the country's wealth, though the landowners retained their social prestige and often became much richer by ownership of coalfields. The north of England became the most advanced region in Britain; its towns grew rapidly, unplanned and frequently characterized by ugliness and dirt. Economic motives often outran a sense of social conscience and the new urban proletariat worked and lived in evil conditions under employers who had often risen from poverty and had the ruthlessness which was the consequence of their own struggle. England was divided as never before; the industrial north from the agricultural south, the industrial working classes from their employers, and both from the long-established gentry, particularly of the south.

Many Victorian novels are eloquent testimony to the social conditions; the title of ▷ Elizabeth Gaskell's ▷ *North and South*, and the subtitle of ▷ Benjamin Disraeli's ▷ *Sybil, or the Two Nations* are evidence in themselves. Josiah Bounderby in ▷ Charles Dickens' ▷ *Hard Times* is a portrait of the unprincipled kind of industrial employer; Sir Leicester Dedlock and Rouncewell the ironmaster in ▷ *Bleak House* exemplify the old order's failure to understand the new. ▷ Charles Kingsley's ▷ *Alton Locke: Tailor and Poet* (1850), and Mrs Gaskell's ▷ *Mary Barton* drew attention to the wretched living and working conditions of the urban poor.

▷ Anti-industrialism; Hungry Forties, The; Chartist movement; Carlyle, Thomas; Child Labour; Smiles, Samuel; Social Problem novel.

Inferno, The

The first part of ▷ Dante's great poem, the ▷ *Divina Commedia*, which describes the poet's journey through Hell, under the guidance of ▷ Virgil, where he speaks to various former friends and enemies. Hell is conceived of as a conical funnel, reaching to the centre of the earth. Various categories of sinners are assigned to the nine graduated circles, where they receive appropriate punishments. The first circle is reserved for pre-Christian pagans who have not had the chance of knowing the true faith. Virgil belongs to these, whose only punishment is the hopeless desire for God. At the very bottom is Satan (Lucifer) himself, and from him Dante and Virgil pass through the earth to its opposite surface, where they arrive at the foot of the Mount of Purgatory (▷ *Purgatorio*).

Ingelow, Jean (1820–97)

Poet, novelist and writer of ▷ children's literature. Born near Boston, Lincolnshire she was educated at home and wrote poetry from a very young age. The family moved to London where, driven by financial need, Ingelow published *A Rhyming Chronicle of Thoughts and Feelings* (1850) following it a year later with *Allerton and Dreux*, the first of her five novels. She also wrote *Off the Skelligs* (1879), *Fated to be Free* (1875) and *Sarah de Berenger* (1879).

She joined a small literary group, 'The Portfolio', whose members included ▷ Adelaide Procter and ▷ Christina Rossetti, and contributed, under the ▷ pseudonym 'Oris', to the evangelical *Youth's Magazine* which she also edited for a year. These contributions were published later in book form in *Studies For Stories* (1864), *Stories Told to a Child* (1865) and *A Sister's Bye-Hours* (1868). She achieved enormous success with her twenty-five books which included verse, children's stories and novels. Her second volume of *Poems* (1863) ran to thirty editions and included the much anthologized 'Divided', and 'The High Tide on the Coast of Lincolnshire, 1571', which established her reputation as a poet. Other popular poems include 'A Story of Doom' (1867) from the collection of the same name. Her most successful children's book was *Mopsa the Fairy* (1869).

Her literary acquaintances included ▷ Tennyson, Christina Rossetti, ▷ Jane and Ann Taylor and the poet and feminist essayist Dora Greenwell (1821–82). An edition of her poems was edited in 1908 by ▷ Alice Meynell. She has been described as 'A lost Pre-Raphaelite' unjustly excluded from literary history.

Bib: Anon., *Some Recollections of Jean Ingelow* (1901); Peters, M., *Jean Ingelow, Victorian Poetess*; Hickok, K., *Representations of Women: 19th Century British Women's Poetry*; Leighton, A., and Reynolds, M. (eds.), *An Anthology of Victorian Women Poets*.

Inkle and Yarico (Yariko)

Inkle was a young English trader of the 17th century who sailed from London to the West Indies. Landing on an island on the way, he and his companions were attacked by natives and all were massacred except Inkle himself, who was saved by the native girl Yarico. She hid him in a cave, cared for him, loved him, and became pregnant by him. When an English ship passed by, Inkle boarded it, taking Yarico with him. But later he sold her into slavery. These events were reported in England and their hold on people's imaginations was part of the growing appeal of the 'primitive' (▷ primitivism), which was linked to a more general criticism of established mores in society. Inkle's actions were seen by many as archetypal of the white man's perfidy towards other races, or even simply of man's betrayal of woman, while Yarico was portrayed variously as a type of ▷ noble savage or a suffering heroine. The earliest account of their story is told by the traveller Ligon in 1657. It is elaborated by ▷ Steele in *The Spectator* (13 March 1711). Thereafter the couple's history became the subject of literally dozens of poems, plays, novels, paintings, songs, and even ballets in England and throughout Europe.

Bib: Price, L. M., *Inkle and Yarico Album*; Hazard, P., *European Thought in the Eighteenth Century*.

Innocence, Songs of

▷ *Songs of Innocence and of Experience*.

Instauratio Magna (The Great Renewal)

The title of the great philosophical work projected by ▷ Francis Bacon and left incomplete. According to Bacon's plan of 1620 it was to have consisted of six parts: I. A review of existing sciences; *De Augmentis Scientiarum*, Latin translation of ▷ *The Advancement of Learning* (1605). II. Outline of a new inductive method; ▷ *Novum Organum* (*The New Instrument*). This exists in a compressed form, unfinished. III. A Natural History to be used as a basis for inductive conclusions. The tract *Parasceve* (*Preparative*) and the *Historia Ventorum* (*History of the Winds*); *Historia vitae et mortis* (*History of Life and Death*); *Sylva Sylvarum* (*Forest of Forests*), a collection of facts and observations. IV. Examples of investigations by the new method, of which there remains only a small fragment, *Filum Labyrinthi* (*The Thread of the Labyrinth*). V. Hypotheses of Bacon's own, to be tested by inductive experiment, of which only a preface exists, though some other writings may have been intended to belong to it. VI. A synthesis of conclusions from the inductive method, none of which remains.

Intentional fallacy

A term coined by W. K. Wimsatt and Monroe C. Beardsley, two leading American New Critics. The intentional fallacy is the view (wrong in Wimsatt and Beardsley's view) that the understanding of a work of literature can usefully be directed by the authorial intentions that it is claimed motivated a particular work. There are many practical reasons why this procedure might be misleading. Sometimes a writer's intentions are now known; sometimes writers give contradictory statements about them; sometimes they change their minds; sometimes they give only partial answers; sometimes they are unconscious of some or all of their motives. But Wimsatt and Beardsley's main argument concerns the way in which an interest in authors' intentions directs attention away from the text itself towards extra-literary considerations. For them, following New Critical theory, criticism should be primarily – perhaps exclusively – concerned with 'the words on the page'.

▷ Author.

Bib: Wimsatt, W., *The Verbal Icon: Studies in the Meaning of Poetry*.

Interlude, Interludes

Interlude is a term of disputed origin, in use from the 13th century at least, for dramatic performances in general. It became the standard term for plays performed indoors, at the feasts of rich households or in the halls of ecclesiastical or educational institutions. It acquired a more specific meaning in the Renaissance when 'interludes' were short plays of a kind popular especially in the 16th century before the great flowering of Elizabethan drama. In general they were more secular than ▷ Morality plays, still being performed, but Moralities and Interludes are not always clearly distinguishable, and indeed the term 'interlude' was applied to religious plays as early as the 14th century. Nonetheless there is no other convenient term for such slight works as ▷ John Heywood's *Play of the Weather* (1533) in which an emissary of the gods tries to find out the ideal weather for humanity, only to discover that opinions hopelessly conflict. The function of such a play seems to have been entertainment after a banquet in a nobleman's hall or in a college, or during the intervals of business of a town council, etc. That it was a performance during intervals of business or other kinds of entertainment, or perhaps of long, serious plays to provide light relief, has been assumed from the usual meaning of 'interlude' in ordinary speech; however, the word has also been surmised to mean merely 'a play between' performers taking parts. One of the best known examples is the interlude of *Pyramus and Thisbe* played before Theseus and his court in the last act of ▷ Shakespeare's ▷ *A Midsummer Night's Dream*.

Interpellation

A term used by the Marxist philosopher ▷ Louis Althusser to describe the process by which ▷ ideologies present us with a version of our own subjectivity, which we are induced to (mis)recognize as our self or innate identity. The term is borrowed from the technical vocabulary of French government procedures, and should not be confused with 'interpolation', which means insertion. The concept of interpellation has been applied to literature; for example Catherine Belsey argues that 'classic realism constitutes an ideological practice in addressing itself to readers as subjects, interpellating them in order that they freely accept their subjectivity and their subjection' (*Critical Practice*).

Interpolation

A passage inserted into a text from elsewhere, usually without the permission of the author. For instance, it is claimed that some passages in Shakespeare or Marlowe were interpolated by actors, theatre managers or other jobbing writers because they are out of character with the work as a whole. The 'Hecate' scene in *Macbeth*, and the knock-about comic parts of *Doctor Faustus* are examples.

Interpretive community

Interpretive communities are the validators of meanings in literary texts according to the American critic Stanley Fish. For Fish, literary meaning does not exist in literary texts like a treasure to be found. It is something realised by readers in the course of their reading. As such, therefore, there are no settled readings of literary works. Instead the literary community either rejects or endorses certain interpretations which then pass temporarily for the settled meaning. Interpretive communities can therefore be the sources of both change or conservation depending upon their composition. Meanwhile, it is likely that several different interpretive communities will exist at any one time each validating different forms of interpretation.

▷ Hermeneutics; Reader Response Criticism.

Bib: Fish, S., *Is There A Text In This Class?: The Authority of Interpretive Communities*.

Interregnum
The term used for the period 1649–60, between the execution of ▷ Charles I and the accession of his son Charles II – the Restoration. It is divided into the period 1649–53, when England was ruled by the House of Commons and a Council of State, and the period 1553–8 when ▷ Oliver Cromwell and for a brief time his son Richard were Protectors.

Intertexuality
A term first introduced into critical theory by the French ▷ psychoanalytical writer Julia Kristeva (b 1941), relating specifically to the use she makes of the work of ▷ Mikhail Bakhtin. The concept of intertextuality implies that literary texts are composed of dialectically opposed utterances, and that it is the function of the critic to identify these different strands and to account for their oppositions within the text itself. Kristeva notes that Bakhtin's ' "dialogism" does not strive towards transcendence . . . but rather towards harmony, all the while implying an idea of rupture (of opposition and analogy) as a modality of transformation' (*Desire and Language*; trans. 1980). Similarly, no text can be entirely free of other texts. No work is written or read in isolation, it is located, in Kristeva's words, 'within the totality of previous . . . texts'. This is a second important aspect of intertextuality.
▷ Feminism.

Intimations of Immortality from Recollections of Early Childhood, Ode: **(1807)**
An ode by ▷ William Wordsworth in stanzas of varying length. The first four stanzas were composed in 1802; the rest of the poem was completed in 1806, and the whole was published in 1807. The first part laments that nature no longer appears to the poet as it did in his youth: 'Apparelled in celestial light,/ The glory and the freshness of a dream'. Wordsworth explains this in terms of the ▷ Platonic myth that the soul pre-exists the body in a perfect world of oneness with nature. At birth we come 'trailing clouds of glory . . ./ From God, who is our home'. But soon 'Shades of the prison-house begin to close/ Upon the growing Boy'. The poem thus expresses a radical Romantic reversal of accepted values: dream is more real than waking, youth is the period of wisdom and true insight. As the poem progresses, the poet's confidence revives, and he asserts a continuing oneness with nature despite his age: 'To me the meanest flower that blows can give/ Thoughts that do often lie too deep for tears'. The upbeat rhetoric is splendid, but many readers are left with the impression that Wordsworth is unnaturally forcing up his spirits towards the end of the poem, in a way which ▷ Samuel Taylor Coleridge is unable to do in his related work, ▷ *Dejection*: *An Ode*.

Ireland
A brief sketch of the history of Ireland may be divided into phases:

1150–1600 – Period of Disorder
▷ Henry II was the first English king to be acknowledged sovereign of Ireland, but at no time before 1600 did the English succeed in establishing an efficient central government. In the 12th century Ireland consisted of warring Celtic kingdoms, with a Norse settlement along the east coast. The conquest was not undertaken by Henry but by his Anglo-Norman nobility, notably Richard Strongbow, Earl of Pembroke in alliance with the Irish king of Leinster. By 1500 Ireland was ruled by a mixed English and Irish aristocracy, the former regarded as English by the Irish and as Irish by the English. English law and speech were secure only in a narrow region known as the ▷ Pale, centred on the capital city of Dublin. The first real crisis in relations arose in the 16th century, when the Irish refused to receive the English Protestant ▷ Reformation. Fierce wars against Spanish armies which landed in Ireland with a view to invading England were followed by fierce suppression under ▷ Elizabeth I, for instance under the governorship of Lord Grey de Wilton. The poet ▷ Edmund Spenser was appointed his secretary (1580) and given a grant of land in the province of Munster as part of a plan to settle the country with Protestant overlords; his castle was burnt down in 1598, a year before his death. Spenser's singularly stern view of Justice in ▷ *The Fairie Queen* (Artegall, Bk. V) is a reflection of his Irish experiences. By 1600 Ireland was a nation of mixed English and Celtic people, with an English-speaking aristocracy, and firm identification with the Roman Catholic faith. The Ulster rebellion (1595) gathered force, with Spanish aid, until in 1599 a large English army under the command of ▷ Essex was sent to crush the revolt. The expedition was, however, a miserable failure and English losses were only recouped in 1602 under the command of Mountjoy. The problem as England saw it in the next two centuries was how to subdue the country to effective Protestant rule.

1600–1800 – Irish Protestant Ascendancy
The policy of settling Protestants in Ireland was notably successful in one of the four provinces under ▷ James I (1603-25) when Ulster became the Anglo-Scottish Protestant fortress which it has remained to this day. ▷ Oliver Cromwell was savage in subjection of Catholic Ireland to his authority, and by extensive confiscations increased the class of Protestant landlords. In the 18th century, penal laws further disabled Catholic landholders, refused political rights to Catholics, and barred them from most professions and from education. The only Irish university

(founded by Elizabeth in 1591), Dublin, was a Protestant one. However, towards the end of the 18th century, partly owing to the Irish patriotism of Anglo-Irish Protestants (including the satirist ▷ Swift and the philosopher ▷ Berkeley), the penal laws were reduced in severity, and in 1782 an Irish constitution was promulgated, by which Irish Protestants were given political rights and limited powers in an Irish Parliament freed from ▷ Privy Council control. The experiment was a failure, and in 1801 Ireland was united politically and in all other respects with England and Scotland, Irish Protestants receiving for the first time representation in the English Parliament.

1801–1921 – The Union

The 19th century was the age of steady emancipation of Irish Catholics and mounting Irish patriotism. The population at the beginning of the century was four and a half million, fewer than one and a half million being of English or Scottish Protestant descent. The Anglo-Irish were the social leaders of the country; the Scots were a middle class of business men and farmers; the native Irish were largely peasants. In 1829 Catholic Emancipation removed all the important restrictions on Catholics, notably the political ones. Henceforward there was a growing party of Irish Catholics in the English House of Commons, in the last quarter of the century known as the Home Rule Party from its intention to win national independence for Ireland. In the middle of the century reform was concentrated on land matters; this was the more necessary for the misery of the Irish peasantry whose sufferings were increased by the severe famines of the 1840s, leading to deaths on a massive scale and to massive emigration to the U.S.A. In 1841 the population was over eight million, and it is now about three million; Ireland is thus one of the very few countries in the world whose population has actually diminished in the last 100 years. Attempts to obtain Home Rule through the English Parliament failed. A brief rebellion in 1916 was put down, but a severe one in 1919-21 resulted in independence within the Commonwealth. It was led by the Sinn Fein party, and the great bitterness of the fighting arose in part from their fanaticism and the brutality of the English auxiliary police (called 'Black and Tans' from their uniform) sent to suppress the rebels.

The Irish Free State

This state was formed in 1922 and included the three provinces of Munster, Leinster, Connaught, and three counties of Ulster. The remaining six counties of Ulster, being mainly Protestant and Anglo-Scottish in population, have separate status as Northern Ireland with representation in the English Parliament. The Irish Free State took the name of Eire (Ireland) in 1937, and is no longer a member of the Commonwealth. It is a republic with a president and two houses of parliament, the Dáil and the Seanad. The first official language is nominally Gaelic, but it is a minority language, since English has long been the majority language.

Ireland, Samuel William Henry (1777–1835)
Forger and poet. Ireland is infamous for having written several plays which he claimed were by ▷ Shakespeare. The deception was uncovered in 1796 when ▷ Malone published *An Enquiry into the Authenticity of Certain Papers Attributed to Shakespeare, Queen Elizabeth and Henry, Earl of Southampton*, at which Ireland confessed. However, before this revelation Ireland's play *Vortigern*, supposed by ▷ Kemble to be by Shakespeare, had been staged and generally disliked by the public. Ireland published several books of poems under his own name, including *The Fisher Boy* (1808), but his work was heavily derivative and unimaginative.
Bib: Grebanier, B., *The Great Shakespeare Forgery*.

Irish literature in English
While the concept of 'Irish literature in English' appears to be self-explanatory, its form has always adopted a fluidity relative to the strategic political pressures that have acted upon it. Moreover, the status of the category as a critical construct suggests that it is near-impossible to separate the body of texts that now constitute it as a 'tradition' from the development of an indigenous Irish literary criticism capable of challenging the appropriating strategies of British and American critics. This suggests a certain caution. While there may appear to be dominant themes running through Irish literature that foreground the importance of identity, territory and community to a sense of Irish experience, we must be aware of the extent to which these criteria have shaped the canon in the first instance according to particular perceived absences within modern Irish society itself. Indeed, it is salutary to note that, despite those who insist on the foreclosure of Irish literature as a definable entity, discordant voices and hybrid texts continually disturb such totalization and demand an audience. Ultimately then the term Irish literature has never simply been just a category that unifies a disparate range of texts (although this is part of its purpose) but rather has operated within the educational and political institution as a means of privileging certain amenable critical criteria (particularly that of a writer's political and cultural 'identity') at the expense of others. If we can construct a narrative of Irish literature – even a narrative of breakdown – it is always salutary then to keep in mind the Irish novelist ▷ Maria Edgeworth's despairing assertion that 'the truth is too strong for fiction, and on all sides pulls it asunder'.

With these preconditions we can begin such a narrative in 1171, the year of Ireland's conquest by ⊳ Henry II, and indeed until the latter years of the 19th century, the history of Irish literature in English is, largely speaking, part of the general development of English literature into a recognisable and self-validating canon. Since the Irish Literary Revival began in the 1880s, however, the existence and the memory of a literature in Ireland's original tongue, ⊳ Gaelic, has interacted with the country's adopted vernacular at every level: in the detail of syntax; in the choice – or rejection – of subject-matter; and in each writer's wrestle with a fractured and often betrayed history.

Throughout the 18th and 19th centuries – and into the 20th – writers from Anglo-Irish Ireland made a rich and vigorous contribution to English literature in its formative stages. ⊳ Jonathan Swift, ⊳ William Congreve, ⊳ Oliver Goldsmith, ⊳ Sheridan, ⊳ Oscar Wilde and ⊳ George Bernard Shaw are among the better known. Although their writings were often not primarily concerned with the matter of Ireland or their authors' own Irishness, recent Irish critics have found in their work themes that are now recognized as beholden to a typically Irish experience of cultural dislocation. Those who did write of Ireland, like Dion Boucicault (1820–90), who is held by many to be the inventor of the 'stage Irishman', and ⊳ Thomas Moore (1779–1852), the purveyor to the drawing-rooms of London of an Ireland sugared by sentiment and exile, capitalized on what looks with hindsight like caricature. All these writers of the Anglo-Irish Ascendancy, coming from their background of landed privilege, seemed to be unaware of the still surviving Gaelic tradition of native Irish literature, with its long ancestry and close connections with mainland Europe – a tradition eloquently evoked in Daniel Corkery's *Hidden Ireland* of 1924, and recently made available anew in Seán O'Tuma's and Thomas Kinsella's 1981 anthology *An Duanaire: Poems of the Dispossessed*.

Moreover, during this pre-Revival period only a handful of creative writers mirrored the growing interest that folklorists like T. Crofton Croker (1798–1849), travellers (again, many of them from Europe) and diarists were taking in Irish peasant life outside the 'Pale'. Edgeworth and William Carleton (1794–1869) stand almost alone in the seriousness with which they looked at their native land and its inhabitants. Edgeworth's *Castle Rackrent* (1800) and Carleton's *Traits and Stories of the Irish Peasantry* (1830–3) are isolated landmarks; and Carleton, an adopted member of Ascendancy culture who was born a Catholic peasant, has been read in recent years with renewed interest and recognition.

In the decades that followed the devastation of native Gaelic culture by the famine and mass emigration of the 1840s, a new sense of Ireland as an imagined nation began, paradoxically, to emerge. The poets and dramatists of the Literary Revival of the 1880s and 1890s regarded Standish O'Grady (1846–1928) as its prime mover. His two-volume history of Ireland – *The Heroic Period* (1878) and *Cuchullin and His Contemporaries* (1880) – sent them back with a new authority to the ancient matter of Ireland. And it was on this material, and on a new attention to the distinctive English actually spoken in Ireland, that the renaissance of Irish letters was founded. Its chief authors – the most notable being ⊳ W. B. Yeats (1865–1939), ⊳ J. M. Synge (1871–1909) and ⊳ Lady Gregory (1852–1932) – were still, to begin with, the sons and the daughters of the Ascendancy, but before long they were joined in this hegemonic activity by writers from the native and Catholic population. A common task was perceived.

The history of Irish literature in English is closely linked, then, to the political history of the nation that (except for the six counties in its north-east corner) won its independence from British rule in 1921, and declared its Republican status when leaving the Commonwealth in 1949. The first battle in the War of Independence had, after all, been led by a poet, Padraig Pearse (1879–1916), and inspired partially at least by his romantic ideas of blood-sacrifice:

All changed, changed utterly.
A terrible beauty is born.
(Yeats, 'Easter 1916')

Irish writers since the Revival have had to reconsider and redefine ideas of continuity and cultural identity that are quite different from those that face English writers in the post-colonial period, though there are affinities with the experience of the other Celtic nations of Britain – the Welsh and the Scots.
(⊳ Scottish Literature; Welsh Literature in English)

In the hundred-odd years since the poet and translator Douglas Hyde (1860–1949) gave a lecture to the newly formed National Literary Society in Dublin entitled 'The Necessity of De-Anglicising Ireland' (1892), Irish writers have had continually to ask themselves and each other quite how, and to what extent, de-Anglicization is to be carried out – and who they are when they have done it. Questions of national identity cross over with questions of personal identity in this distinctive version of the 20th-century artist's problematic relation to society.

Ireland's writers began by looking to their country's heroic past and its idealized idea of the west, the non-anglicized land of saints, scholars and noble peasantry; but they also looked, from the very start, to the literatures of Europe, and cast a cold and realist eye at their own urban and rural present. ⊳ James Joyce

(1882–1941) taught himself enough Norwegian as a schoolboy to write a letter to his hero, ▷ Ibsen, who was already a profound influence on the playwrights of Dublin's ▷ Abbey Theatre; George Egerton (Mary Dunne, 1859–1945) translated Knut Hamsun's *Hunger* and wrote about the 'New Woman' in her novel *Keynotes* (1893) before the old century ended. Kate O'Brien (1897–1974) and Maura Laverty (1907–66) found inspiration and objectivity by living for time in Spain, Ireland's old ally. For many Irish writers – Joyce, ▷ Samuel Beckett (b 1906) and Francis Stuart (b 1902) are early examples, followed later to Paris by the poets Denis Devlin (1908–59) and Brian Coffey (b 1905) – this looking outside Ireland necessarily became a longer physical exile: the required distance from which to practise their art – or indeed to have it published and read. For during the first half-century of independence, the Irish state's narrow, inward-looking patriotism and the tight grip of a reactionary Catholic clerisy directly impoverished cultural life within Ireland: ▷ censorship meant that most works of serious literature by Irish men and women were banned in their own country.

Those who stayed, returned, or at least kept a foothold in the place, were able to refine and multiply the means of reclaiming, repairing, or reinventing an Irish heritage. They worked from an intimate knowledge of place, like Patrick Kavanagh (1904–67), who immortalized his townland of Mucker in *The Great Hunger* (1942) and *Tarry Flynn* (1948); others, like Austin Clarke (1896–1974) and later Thomas Kinsella (b 1928), worked from a more scholarly knowledge of the Gaelic-language heritage than was available to the Revivalists. By the mid-20th century poets in particular were recognizing the impossibility of bridging the gap to the past, and were finding that the fractured state of Irish culture itself offered a fruitful area of exploration for the isolated and disillusioned artist/commentator. Flann O'Brien (Brian O'Nolan, 1911–66) created a comic and fantastic Gaelic/modernist world in his novel *At Swim-Two-Birds* (1939) as his response to this artistic dilemma.

It tended to be the novelists and short-story writers who recorded the day-to-day reality of life in the young state. ▷ Sean O'Faolain (b 1900) and ▷ Frank O'Connor (Michael O'Donovan, 1903–66) demonstrated, in their short stories of the Troubles and after, not just a consummate art, but a profound understanding of the why and the how of that wished-for 'de-Anglicization'. Written from the fringes, but courageously central in their concerns, the novels and short stories of the Aran Islander Liam O'Flaherty (1897–1984) are eloquent accounts of the dignity and constraints of life in the no-longer idealized rural west; and Patrick McGill's *Children of the Dead End* (1914) is a classic account of the reality of land-hunger and migratory labouring.

At home and abroad, then, Irish writers were grappling with the question of identity, and a body of remarkable writing was being assembled into a tradition of its own. But the achievements of three writers in particular placed a burden of success on subsequent generations. In poetry, the novel and drama, the work of Yeats, Joyce and Synge proved difficult to build on directly. Over the years a pattern can be discerned in which Ireland's vigorous – but even in the late 20th century essentially naturalistic – tradition of fiction has more in common with the elegiac and story-telling parts of Yeats' *oeuvre* than with Joyce's modernism. Conversely, poets have found in ▷ *Ulysses'* concern with the here and now of life as it is lived – and lived in the city – a more usable language than Yeats' lovely rhetoric or Synge's Gaelic-shadowed experimentalism. It is, perhaps, in drama that writers have found least constraint from the work of their predecessors. Over the years ▷ Sean O'Casey (1880–1964), Samuel Beckett (b 1906), ▷ Brendan Behan (1923–64), Brian Friel (b 1929), and Tom Murphy (b 1935) have each developed their own idiosyncratic dramatic structure and voice.

During this first century of a consciously Irish literature in English, Gaelic still often functioned as the linguistic bedrock of Irish writers. Whether through translations that are creative works in their own right, from Hyde's *Love Songs of Connacht* (1893) to Kinsella's *The Tain* (1969) and ▷ Seamus Heaney's *Sweeney Astray* (1983), or by regarding all periods of Gaelic literature as a nourishing tradition alongside other literatures, Irish poets have constantly enriched their work in English. A few have decided to write only in Gaelic – two notable poets being Sean O Riordain (1917–77) and Nuala Ni Dhomhnaill (b 1952) – but such writers are nevertheless an essential part of the English-language writing scene, both in their professional friendships and in creative translation by their peers. One excellent poet, Michael Hartnett (b 1941), publicly dedicated himself in 1975 to writing wholly in Irish; he has recently reverted to writing in both languages.

One half-century into the new state, the resurgence of violent conflict in Northern Ireland in 1968 reoriented the literary map of the island northwards often, it should be noted, to the *chagrin* of writers from the Republic. While the essentially homogeneous and quotidian nature of the Southern state following partition led to a certain complacency and narrowness of literary ambition, the challenge of writing out of a bitterly divided society has created a distinct corpus of Northern Irish literature of astonishing intensity. This is not, of course, to suggest that there is a simple correlation between literary achievement and social breakdown but rather to note that the desire to find some response to the unprecedented horror of the violence during this period led to the creation of an enduring aesthetic stance out of often meagre resources. This has been most notable in the swift rise to pre-eminence of Northern Irish poetry in both Irish and British contexts, although with this we should note the continued influence of two earlier, and neglected, Ulster poets ▷ Louis MacNeice (1907–63) and John Hewitt (1907–87). The presence of the English critic and poet Philip Hobsbaum in Belfast in the mid-1960s led directly to the precocious publication of ▷ Seamus Heaney's *Death of a Naturalist* (1966), and with this was established a poetic voice of maturity and distinction which has become perhaps the most influential of all living Irish poets as the century draws to a close. Alongside Heaney, the poetry of Michael Longley (b 1939) and Derek Mahon (b 1941) is also worthy of mention, while in the generation that followed, the work of Ciaran Carson (b 1948), Tom Paulin (b 1950), and ▷ Paul Muldoon (b 1951) now dominates the imaginative poetic terrain of Ireland as a whole.

With this activity, it is understandable that other forms of literary expression in Northern Ireland have tended to be neglected although with the recent work of two impressive young Belfast novelists, Glenn Patterson (b 1961) and Robert McLiam Wilson (b 1964), there are encouraging signs that this is being redressed. Indeed the novel form in Ireland, North and South, seems in very good health. With the emergence of the exciting ▷ Roddy Doyle (b 1958) and the continued mastery of the form displayed by John Banville (b 1945), the new social pluralism of the Republic is gaining a literary manifestation; one prefigured perhaps by the coruscating moral anger of the poet Paul Durcan (b 1944).

The North has produced one of the most exciting women poets of Ireland, Medbh McGuckian (b 1951); she, and Eavan Boland (b 1944) in the South, are the most visible of a new generation of women poets of real distinction. In the field of the novel, Irish women have managed, as women have in English generally, to make a substantial contribution; but the pressures of a conservative and patriarchal society have been less kind to women poets. As Irish women free themselves from the extremes of traditional roles, all the expected fields of women's writings are growing rapidly, and making strong connections with writing in England and the U.S.A. Particularly notable are ▷ Edna O'Brien (b 1930), Julia O'Faolain (b 1932), Jennifer Johnston (b 1930) and the promising Deidre Madden (b 1961).

Finally, as the construction of Irish literature in English as a category is driven essentially by literary criticism, it would be inappropriate to give any account of its development without acknowledging the resurgent strength of indigenous Irish itself. Central to this is the monumental three-volume *Field Day Anthology of Irish Writing* (1991), compiled under the general editorship of Seamus Deane (b 1940). Although a controversial anthology, its existence gives Irish literature a strategic location in modern Ireland that enables a much-needed revision of the Irish literary past. Deane has been joined in this desire by such diverse critics as Edna Longley (b 1940), Terence Brown (b 1944), and John Wilson Foster (b 1944), and through their lively and often passionate debates we can perceive that Irish literature is finally getting the sympathetic, thorough, and context-specific criticism it has so long deserved.

Bib: Brown, T., *Ireland's Literature*; Cairns, D. and Richards, S., *Writing Ireland: Colonialism, Nationalism and Culture*; Deane, S. (Ed.), *The Field Day Anthology of Irish Writing*; Deane, S., *A Short History of Irish Literature*; Lloyd, D., *Anomalous States: Irish Writing and the Post-Colonial Moment*; Longley, E., *The Living Stream: Literature and Revisionism in Ireland.*

Irish literature in Gaelic

Most of this is medieval (1100–1550). Two main cycles of myth are distinguished; the Ulster series, centring on Conchobar and ▷ Cuchulain; that of Leinster and Munster centring on Finn and Ossian (Oisin). *Ulster Cycle*: Cuchulain was a great warrior in the court of Conchobar king of Ulster. Other characters are Ailill and Medb (Maeve), king and queen of Connaught, against whom Cuchulain defended Ulster; Fergus, the exiled king of Ulster; Deidre, brought up to be the bride of Conchobar, who killed her lover Naoise. Such legends were versified in the Middle Ages, but are thought to have originated in pre-Christian times, *ie* before the 5th century AD. *Leinster-Munster cycle*: in their best form ▷ ballads; after 1250 these exceeded the Ulster legends in popularity. The events are supposed to take place in the 3rd–5th centuries AD. Finn was a great warrior when Cormac was king of Ireland, and commanded a band called the Fenians. He was the father of the hero Ossian, who spent many years in a kind of fairyland, and was at last baptized as a Christian by St Patrick. Such myths were used by poets and dramatists of the Irish Nationalist movement in English, *eg* especially W. B. Yeats and ▷ J. M. Synge, between 1890 and 1910.

Irony

▷ Figures of Speech.

Irving, Sir Henry (1838–1905)

Actor. His original name was Brodribb, but he adopted the name of Irving when he gave up a commercial career for acting in 1856. For ten years he performed over 500 parts in provincial companies. He made his name in London in 1871 with the part of Mathias in the melodrama

The Bells by Leopold Lewis (adapted from *Le Juif Polonais* by Erckmann-Chatrian). This was at the Lyceum Theatre, which later became famous under his management. His reputation grew by his performance in a great variety of roles (including two in plays by the poet ▷ Tennyson, *The Cup* and *Becket*), especially Shakespearean ones: his performances of Hamlet and Shylock became legendary. Irving's style was strongly romantic and powerfully eloquent; he and Ellen Terry, with whom he was associated at the Lyceum from 1878 to 1902, gave English theatre its main distinction at the time.
Bib: Bingham, M., *Henry Irving and the Victorian Theatre*.

Iseult (Isoud, Ysolde, Ysoude)
▷ Tristan and Iseult.

Isherwood, Christopher (1904–86)
Novelist and dramatist. Born in Cheshire and educated at Repton School and Cambridge and London universities. At preparatory school he met the poet W. H. Auden (1907–73), with whom he later collaborated on three plays, *The Dog Beneath The Skin* (1935), *The Ascent of F6* (1936) and *On The Frontier* (1938). These are primarily political and psychological parables. Isherwood's first two novels, *All The Conspirators* (1928) and *The Memorial* (1932), employ ▷ modernist styles and techniques. His experience of teaching English in Berlin from 1930 to 1933 is reflected in *Mr Norris Changes Trains* (1935) and *Goodbye to Berlin* (1939), which employ a more realistic mode. The latter is a series of linked tales recording the atmosphere and characters of a decadent Berlin in the last days of the Weimar Republic; the narrator is characterized by a certain passivity and detachment, summarized in his claim: 'I am a camera with its shutter open . . .' The section entitled 'Sally Bowles' was dramatized in 1951 as *I Am A Camera* and turned into a stage musical in 1968 as *Cabaret*. Isherwood visited China in 1933 with Auden, and together they wrote *Journey to a War* (1939). In 1939 they both emigrated to the USA, where Isherwood became naturalized in 1946. All his major work is written in the first person, and his American novels draw extensively on his own development as a theme. They are: *Prater Violet* (1945), *The World in the Evening* (1954), *Down There On A Visit* (1962), *A Single Man* (1964) and *A Meeting By the River* (1967). He also wrote numerous screenplays, and several autobiographical and travel pieces, including *Lions and Shadows* (1938), *Christopher and his Kind* (1976) and *The Condor and the Cows: a South American Travel Diary* (1950). He translated works relating to the mystical Hindu philosophy of Vendanta, a philosophy which is advocated in *A Meeting By the River*.
Bib: King, F., *Christopher Isherwood*; Summers, C. J., *Christopher Isherwood*; Bachards, D., and White, J.P., (eds.), *Where Joy Resides: An Isherwood Reader*.

Ishiguro, Kazuo (b 1954)
Novelist and short-story writer. Born in Nagasaki, Japan, he has lived in Britain since 1960, where he studied at the universities of Kent and East Anglia. He has worked as a grouse-beater at Balmoral Castle and as a community and social-worker in Scotland and London. He now lives in Guildford, Surrey. His work was included in *Introduction 7: Stories by New Writers, 1981*. His first two novels, *A Pale View of Hills* (1982) and *An Artist of the Floating World* (1986) explore post-war Japanese cultural displacement through the thoughts and memories of individuals: a Japanese woman living in England, stirred to retrospection by her daughter's suicide; a painter, once employed by the pre-war Imperial regime, living in a provincial Japanese town. In *The Remains of the Day* (1989), which won the Booker Prize, an English butler on a tour of Britain reassesses the lost opportunities of his life, dedicated to the service of an English aristocrat who had flirted with fascism. It was filmed by James Ivory in 1993. *The Unconsoled* (1995) picks up some of the same themes of loneliness and missed opportunity, but is more enigmatic, recounting a journey through an unidentifed country. His work has been widely praised for its delicacy of style and subtlety of psychological insight.

Isocrates (436–338 BC)
In ancient Greece, an Athenian orator who advocated a united Greece for war against the states of Asia. He advanced Greek prose style by the care he gave to his speeches.

Italian influence on English literature
Italian literature first made an important contribution to English poetry in the work of ▷ Chaucer. His ▷ *Troilus and Crisyede* is principally a translation of *Il Filostrato* and ▷ *The Canterbury Tales* may have been modelled on Boccaccio's ▷ *Decameron*. Allusions to and parodies of ▷ Dante can, similarly, be found at several points in Chaucer's work, especially in ▷ *The House of Fame*. Chaucer met ▷ Petrarch, the third great Italian poet of the medieval period, when he went as an ambassador to Italy, and he translated one of his ▷ sonnets, again for inclusion in *Troilus and Criseyde*.

In the 16th century Petrarch eclipsed Boccaccio and Dante in the minds of English writers. His sonnets were translated by ▷ Sir Thomas Wyatt and ▷ Henry Howard, Earl of Surrey in the 1520s and 1530s. In the 1580s, Petrarch's example helped create the fashion for sonnet-writing that produced ▷ Sir Philip Sidney's ▷ *Astrophil and Stella*, ▷ Edward

Spenser's ▷ *Amoretti* and ▷ Shakespeare's *Sonnets*, along with many other sonnet sequences. Petrarch's visionary poems, the *Trionfi*, were translated into English by Henry Parker, Lord Morley (*Tryumphes of Fraunces Petrarcke* (1553–6)) and into Scots by William Fowler (?1555–?) in 1587. Scottish interest in Italian literature culminated in the works of ▷ William Drummond of Hawthornden in the 17th century.

Spenser's most ambitious work, however, ▷ *The Faerie Queen*, drew much less on Petrarch than on the more recent Italian tradition of epic romance. ▷ Ariosto's ▷ *Orlando Furioso* and ▷ Tasso's *Gerusalemme liberata (*1581) suggested some of the incidents in Spenser's poem and its guileful mixture of earnestness and comedy. Similarly, Italian *novelle* (short prose fictions, often presented within a framing narrative as in Boccaccio's *Decameron*) were imitated in England in the Renaissance and provided sources for Shakespeare's ▷ *Measure for Measure* and ▷ *Othello*.

At this time, however, literary influence cannot be separated from the broader cultural importance of Italian thinking and the power of established images of Italy. ▷ Castiglione's ▷ *Il Cortegiano* (1528) became a handbook of elegant behaviour; ▷ Machiavelli's *The Prince* (1513) (designed to encourage Italian unity) offered types of deceitfulness and chicanery that were at once alluring and dreadful. Shakespeare's ▷ *Richard III* and Marlowe's ▷ *The Jew of Malta* are built around typically captivating and dastardly Machiavellian heroes. Partly because of Machiavelli and partly because of Italy's perceived cultural pre-eminence, Italian scenes and cities became glamorously corrupt. To the staunchly Protestant Elizabethan regime, moreover, Italy was the more dangerous for being the fountainhead of Roman Catholicism. In Shakespeare's ▷ *Cymbeline*, for example, when Posthumus, the downright and honest British hero, travels to Rome, he proves all too vulnerable to the artful competitiveness and deceit of the Italians. ▷ Jacobean tragedies (such as ▷ *The Malcontent* or ▷ *The Changeling*) frequently use Italian settings in a similar way.

Italian models were of less importance to 17th-century English literature; ▷ Milton is the exception to this rule. He wrote several poems in Italian and drew on Dante and Tasso for ▷ *Paradise Lost*. A widespread revival of interest in Italian literature began early in the 18th century (partly because Italian operas were so popular) and has continued until the present day. All the major medieval Italian writers were translated in the period; it became usual for educated people (particularly women) to learn Italian and read its literature; and interest gradually extended from the greats of the past to the writers of the present: in particular, the playwrights Carlo Goldoni (1707–93) and Vittorio Alfieri (1749–1803), the comic poet Casti (1724–1803) and lyric poets such as Metastasio (1698–1782).

This interest encouraged imitations and adaptations of Italian works: ▷ James Thomson's ▷ *The Castle of Indolence*, for example, is directly influenced by Tasso; ▷ Wordsworth's *Essay on Epitaphs* (1810) was inspired, he said, by his reading of epitaphs by Gabriello Chiabrera (1552–1637); ▷ Byron's ▷ *Don Juan* is modelled on the mock-heroic romances of Ariosto and Luigi Pulci (1432–84); and ▷ Sir Walter Scott's historical novels draw on the scenes and romanticism of Tasso and Matteo Boiardo (1434–94). Scott's example in turn influenced the most famous novel of the ▷ Risorgimento, *I Promessi sposi* (1827) by Alessandro Manzoni (1785–1873). Similarly, ▷ Shelley and ▷ Keats composed, in their final unfinished works, epics profoundly endebted to Dante's ▷ *Divina Commedia*.

Dante continued to grow in importance during the 19th century both as a literary influence and a cultural icon. Ugo Foscolo (1778–1827), who after 1816 became an emigré living in London, successfully promoted Italian literature; ▷ Tennyson's ▷ *In Memoriam* was, Tennyson wrote, 'a kind of Divine Comedy' and is modelled on Petrarch's *Canzoniere* as well; ▷ Dante Gabriel Rossetti translated Dante's early, autobiographical collection, *La Vita Nuova* (1292–3) plus a large number of previously obscure Italian poets in his *Early Italian Poets* (1861). Rossetti's original poetry, especially *The Blessed Damozel* (1850) and *The House of Life* (1881), is suffused with Dantean ideas and his paintings, like those by other members of the ▷ Pre-Raphaelite Brotherhood, repeatedly illustrate ecstatic moments from Dante's poetry.

Interest in Dante is an extension of interest in the medieval, pre-industrial past. Dante's poetry was attractive because it seemed not to distinguish between religious and sexual feelings. The fusion of the two was typical of a medieval world which the Pre-Raphaelites considered innocent, even pre-lapsarian. ▷ John Ruskin, similarly, read the architecture of Renaissance Venice as the embodiment of an ideal society.

For ▷ Elizabeth Barrett Browning and ▷ Robert Browning, the influence of Italy was less historical or literary than immediate and contemporary. The Risorgimento became for them, as for other English liberals, a cause and an ideal. *Casa Guidi Windows* (1851) by Elizabeth Barrett Browning is explicity concerned with events in Italy; Robert Browning's ▷ *Men and Women* and *The Ring and the Book* (1868–69) are more indirect but the poems' evocations of renaissance Italy continually suggest the mid-19th-century world. ▷ *Romola* by ▷ George Eliot recreates 15th-century Florence to similar effect. Likewise ▷ Arthur Hugh Clough's *Amours de Voyage* (1858) finds a British visitor baffled by the collision on the streets of Rome between present-day mayhem and ancient grandeur. ▷ E. M. Forster's *A Room with a View* (1908) makes Italy more pastoral but nonetheless shows the English visitors confused by the contrast of present and past. Even Colin Dexter's urbane Inspector Morse experiences the same confusion when he visits Verona and uncovers a smuggling ring and a corrupt bureaucracy right beside the Roman coliseum where Verdi is being performed.

Forster's and Clough's perspective on Italy begins in the 18th century, as soon, that is, as British travellers began to visit Italy as part of the Grand Tour. Venice and Rome were cardinal examples of greatness gone to waste and, to patriotic visitors, of the decline that England could or should avoid. ▷ Joseph Addison's *Letter from Italy* (1701), ▷ John Dyer's *The Ruins of Rome* (1740) and ▷ Tobias Smollett's *Travels through France and Italy* (1766) are all good examples of this habit of mind. It become the stock in trade of romantic period travel writers such as J. C. Eustace (?1762–1815) in his *A Classical Tour of Italy* (1813) and Lady Sydney Morgan (?1783–1859) in her *Italy* (1821), both of which proved enduringly popular. It contributed to the effect of the Italian settings of many ▷ Gothic novels. This way of thinking made Italy into a place where visitors could reflect on their cultural superiority and could observe the terrible consequences of decadence. ▷ Dickens in ▷ *Little Dorrit*, Clough and Forster all question the self-confidence that enabled visitors to use Italy in this way. ▷ Henry James' novels, especially *Roderick Hudson* (1875), ▷ *The Portrait of a Lady* and ▷ *The Wings of the Dove*, often make the clash between England and Italy symptomatic of the conflict between America and Europe.

▷ Modernism continued the Victorian revival of Dante: ▷ T. S. Eliot's ▷ *The Waste Land* is dotted with allusions to the *Commedia*, his essays on Dante (in *The Sacred Wood* (1920) and the *Selected Essays* (1928)) aim to confirm Dante's status as the key poet of the European tradition; ▷ Ezra Pound's ▷ *The Cantos* is designed as a modern version of Dante's epic as is ▷ Wyndham Lewis' less well-known trilogy of novels, *The Human Age* (1928). ▷ Samuel Beckett was deeply influenced by Dante and showed in his essay 'Dante...Bruno...Vico...Joyce' (1929) how much ▷ James Joyce drew from Dante and from the Italian philosophers, Giordano Bruno (?1548–99) and Giambattista Vico (1668–1744). Translations of Dante have multiplied and been attempted by several major poets, ▷ Seamus Heaney and Robert Lowell (1917–77) most famously. The other great medieval and Renaissance originals of Italian literature have been neglected by comparison.

Meanwhile, modern Italian poetry has become highly-respected and increasingly influential. Giacomo Leopardi (1798–1837) has gained considerable recognition only in this century. The reputation of Eugenio Montale (1896–1981) was established in the nineteen-thirties and remains very high. He and his contemporaries Umberto Sabe (1883–1957) and Giuseppe Ungaretti (1888–1970) established the European importance of Italian twentieth-century poetry. Andrea Zanzotto (b 1921) and Franco Fortini (b 1917) are among the most significant of their many successors. Italian novelists have an international readership, particularly Italo Calvino (1923–85), Primo Levi (1919–87), and Umberto Eco (b 1932). Leonardo Sciascia (1921–91) and Natalia Ginzburg (b 1916) are also the focus of intense interest and admiration. *Six Characters in Search of an Author* (1921) by Luigi Pirandello (1867–1936) and *Accidental Death of an Anarchist* (1970) by Dario Fo (b 1926) have become standards of modern theatre.

Bib: Brand, C. P., *Italy and the English Romantics*; Jack, R. D. S., *The Italian Influence on Scottish Literature*; Minta, S., *Petrarch and Petrarchism: The English and French Traditions*; Pite, R., *The Circle of Our Vision: Dante's Presence in English Romantic Poetry*; McDougal, S., *Dante Among the Moderns*.

***Ivanhoe* (1819)**

A historical novel by ▷ Sir Walter Scott. It is set in the reign of Richard I, who is one of the characters; the story concerns rivalry between the king and his wicked brother John (King, 1199–1216), and between Saxons and the ruling Norman aristocracy. Locksley (the legendary outlaw, Robin Hood) aids Richard against the rebellious Normans, and helps to bring about the union of the Saxon hero, Wilfred of Ivanhoe, and the heroine Rowena. It was the first novel by Scott to deal with an English (as distinct from a Scottish) subject, and was very popular in the 19th century. This popularity is partly due to its being one of the first attempts to write a novel about the Middle Ages with a genuine regard for history.

J

Jack and the Beanstalk
A well-known ▷ fairy tale based on a myth found all over the world. Jack exchanges his mother's cow for a hatful of beans. When thrown into the garden, the beans rapidly sprout stalks which reach above the clouds. Jack climbs one of the beanstalks and finds himself in a new land near the castle of a man-eating giant. Jack manages by cunning to steal the giant's wealth and when the giant pursues him down the stalk, he fells it so that the giant falls and breaks his neck.

Jack Wilton
▷ Nashe, Thomas.

Jacobean
Used to indicate the period of ▷ James I (1603–25) and applied especially to the literature and style of architecture of his reign. In literature, it is most commonly a way of distinguishing the style of drama under James from the style that prevailed under ▷ Elizabeth. Strictly, Elizabethan drama is experimental, expansive, sometimes ingenuous, in fairly close touch with medieval tradition but energetic with ▷ Renaissance forces. It includes the work of the ▷ University wits – ▷ Christopher Marlowe, ▷ Thomas Kyd, ▷ Robert Greene, ▷ George Peele – and also early ▷ Shakespeare. Jacobean drama is thought of as critical, sombre, disillusioned. It includes mature and late Shakespeare, ▷ Ben Jonson, ▷ Cyril Tourneur, ▷ John Webster, ▷ Thomas Middleton, ▷ Francis Beaumont and ▷ John Fletcher. The Caroline period is associated with such figures as ▷ Philip Massinger, ▷ John Ford, and ▷ James Shirley. Courts were the centre of culture, and courts depended largely on the circumstances of monarchs: while the reign of Elizabeth was prosperous at home and (mainly) triumphant overseas, that of James saw increasing disagreement at home, and experience abroad was negative or even nationally humiliating. The reign of ▷ Charles I was yet more bitter in home dissensions but his court was one of distinction and refinement. The tone of the drama varied with these differences in national fortune and court conduct. However, the labelling of literary periods is always to some extent simplifying and even falsifying.

The Jacobean period was the first that was really rich in prose, with writers like ▷ Francis Bacon, ▷ John Donne and ▷ Lancelot Andrewes. Their work contrasts especially with Restoration prose, which sacrificed the poetic qualities of the Jacobean writing for the sake of grace and lucidity. Seventeenth-century literature.

Jacobin
Originally a name given to Dominican friars in France, because their first convent was in the Rue St Jacques in Paris. The name was transferred to a political society which rented a room in the convent in the first year of the ▷ French Revolution. The society developed into a highly organized political party, led by ▷ Robespierre, who became practically dictator of France in 1793. The Jacobins were extreme in asserting the principle of equality and in their opposition to privilege. Later, when conservative reaction had set in, 'Jacobin' was used loosely for anyone with liberal political tendencies in England as well as in France. The paper *The Anti-Jacobin* was founded to combat English liberal opinion in 1797.

Jacobite
From Jacobus, the Latin form of James. ▷ James II, of the House of ▷ Stuart, was deposed in 1688 because, as a convert to ▷ Catholicism, he was considered to be conspiring against the established Protestant religion and against Parliament. His supporters were called Jacobites and this name continued for the supporters of his Catholic son and grandsons.

After the crown passed to the House of (▷ George; Windsor, House of) Hanover, a German Protestant family, in 1714, British Jacobites conspired to restore the House of Stuart. The Jacobite Rebellions of 1715 and 1745 were the two most formidable attempts; both had principally Scottish support, partly because the Stuarts had originally been a Scottish royal family. The ▷ 'Forty-five' rebellion quickly became a romantic legend chiefly because of the supposed gallantry and charm of its leader, Charles Edward Stuart, grandson of James II – 'Bonnie Prince Charlie' to his Scottish supporters and the 'Young Pretender' to his opponents. After the failure of the 'Forty-five' Jacobitism became increasingly a matter of sentiment which even persists to the present day, though the direct line of the Stuarts died out in 1807.

▷ Old Pretender, The.

Jacobson, Dan (b 1929)
Novelist, short-story writer and critic. Born in South Africa, he moved permanently to England in 1954, and is now Professor of English Literature at University College, London. His novels are: *The Trap* (1955); *A Dance in the Sun* (1956); *The Price of Diamonds* (1957); *The Evidence of Love* (1960); *The Beginners* (1966); *The Rape of Tamar* (1970); *The Wonder Worker* (1973); *The Confessions of Joseph Baiz* (1977); *Hidden in the Heart* (1991); *The God Fearer* (1992). His story collections include: *A Long Way From London* (1958); *The Zulu and the Zeide* (1959); *Beggar My Neighbour* (1964); *Through the Wilderness* (1968); *A Way of Life* (1971); *Inklings: Selected Stories* (1973). Up to and including *The Beginners*, the story of three

generations of an immigrant Jewish family, the novels are set in South Africa, and are largely naturalistic in style. *The Rape of Tamar*, which inspired the play *Yonadab* by Peter Shaffer, is a more experimental work, much concerned with the ambiguities of narration. It has an old Testament setting, and a self-conscious, and highly characterized narrator. *The Confessions of Joseph Baiz* is the fictional autobiography of a man who can love only those whom he has betrayed, and is set in an imaginary totalitarian country, somewhat resembling South Africa. Recurrent concerns of Jacobson's novels and stories include power, religion, guilt and betrayal, and his work is characterized by its inventiveness and wit. His non-fiction includes: *Time of Arrival and Other Essays* (1967); *The Story of the Stories: The Chosen People and its God* (1982); *Time and Time Again: Autobiographies* (1985); *Adult Pleasures: Essays on Writers and Readers* (1988). *The Electronic Elephant: A Southern African Journey* (1994).
Bib: Roberts, S., *Dan Jacobson*.

Jakobson, Roman (1896–1982)
Born in Moscow where he was educated. He worked in Czechoslovakia for almost 20 years, between 1920 and 1939, and after the German invasion he escaped to Scandinavia, before going to the U.S.A. where he taught in a number of universities, and became Professor of Russian Literature at the Massachusetts Institute of Technology. During his formative years he was heavily influenced by a number of avante-garde movements in the Arts, but in his own work he laid specific emphasis upon the formulation of a 'poetics' which took into account the findings of structuralism, and the work of the Russian formalists. He was an active member of the Society for the Study of Poetic Language (OPOYAZ) which was founded in St Petersburg in 1916, and in 1926 he founded the Prague Linguistic Circle. His wife Krystyna Pomorska notes, in a recent collection of his writings, that poetry and visual art became for Jakobson the fundamental spheres for observing how verbal phenomena work and for studying how to approach them (Roman Jakobson, *Language and Literature*, 1987). Jakobson's work on the relationship between metaphor and metonymy (⊳ Figures of speech) has been taken up and developed by a number of critics, with fruitful results for the understanding of Romantic poetry. The work of ⊳ Paul de Man, ⊳ Geoffrey Hartman, J. Hillis Miller and ⊳ Harold Bloom is especially noteworthy.
Bib Hawkes, T., *Structuralism and Semiotics*; Jakobson, R., *Language and Literature* and *Verbal Art, Verbal Sign, Verbal Time*; Bennett, T., *Formalism and Marxism*; Erlich, V., *Russian Formalism: History-Doctrine.*

James I, King of Scotland (1406–37)
He was not actually crowned until 1424, owing to a long period of exile in England. His literary importance is his poetry; he is generally regarded as the author of ⊳ *The Kingis Quair*, a love poem which may be autobiographical. It employs the 7-line stanza known as the ⊳ rhyme-royal perhaps because of James' use of it, though he derived it from ⊳ Chaucer.

James I of England and VI of Scotland
A member of the Scottish House of ⊳ Stuart, he ruled over Scotland alone (1566–1603) and then over England as well (1603–25). He was the first sovereign ever to reign over the whole of the British Isles. His accession to the throne of England was due to the death without children of his cousin ⊳ Elizabeth I, last of the House of ⊳ Tudor. The literature and architecture of his era is known as ⊳ Jacobean, a term transferred, especially in architecture, to the greater part of the 17th century. James was also an accomplished author in his own right. His works include *Basilikon Doron* (1599), an address to his son, ⊳ Prince Henry, on the rules of good government; *True Law of Free Monarchies* (1598), which argues that the monarch's power is absolute and God-given; and several theological treatises.
Bib: Ashton, R., *James I By His Contemporaries*.

James II of England and VII of Scotland (1685–88)
King of Great Britain and Ireland. He was deposed because, as a Catholic, he was threatening the security of the ⊳ Church of England and at the same time weakening the power of Parliament. He was succeeded by his Protestant daughter ⊳ Mary II in conjunction with her Dutch husband, ⊳ William III.
⊳ Jacobite; Glorious Revolution.

James IV (1590)
A romantic transvestite comedy by ⊳ Robert Greene which dramatizes the loves of James IV and of his English wife Dorothea against whose life he conspires. The play's main action – which is the stuff of melodrama – is framed by the choric comments of Oberon and Bohan, a misanthropic Scot. In this respect Greene's practice accords with similar dramatic strategies adopted in ⊳ Kyd's *The Spanish Tragedy*, and it also anticipates the Chinese-box structure of ⊳ *A Midsummer Night's Dream* and, to a lesser extent, ⊳ Shakespeare's use of an induction in ⊳ *The Taming of the Shrew*.

James, C.L.R. (1901–89)
Political activist, theorist, novelist, short-story writer and journalist. Born in Trinidad and educated there at Queens Royal College secondary school, Port of Spain, he began his

career in the 1920s as a professional cricket player, a school teacher and editor of the literary magazine *Trinidad*. During his long, active and eventful life he was for various periods cricket correspondent for the *Manchester Guardian*, editor of the Marxist journal *Fight* in London, a trade union organizer and Marxist activist in the USA, secretary of the West Indian Federal Labour Party in Trinidad, editor of *The Nation* (Port of Spain), a lecturer at various colleges and universities, a BBC cricket commentator and cricket columnist for *Race Today*. He was twice exiled to Britain: the first time in 1953, when the McCarthyite American government deported him because of his left-wing views, and the second time in the early 1960s when the leader of the Trinidadian Government (whose party James served as secretary and who had also once been his pupil) found his outspokeness threatening and forced him to leave. His political convictions were defined by Marxism and Pan-Africanism; in London in the 1930s he was associated with future African leaders Jomo Kenyata and Kwame Nkrumah. Pan-Africanism is explored in two of his political works: *A History of Negro Revolt* (1938), revised as *A History of Pan-African Revolt* (1969), and *Nkrumah and the Ghanaian Revolution* (1977). His response to Stalinism was to take a Trotskyist line: his book *Mariners, Renegades and Castaways: The Story of Herman Melville and the World We Live In* (1953) used a parallel with Melville's novel *Moby Dick* for a critique of Stalinism.

His own fiction writing began in the 1920s with short stories which, despite his own middle-class and British-influenced family background, were naturalistic (⊳ naturalism) studies of the life of poor Trinidadians in the Port of Spain slums. His only novel, *Minty Alley* (1936), has a similar setting, examining the lives, relationships and hopes of the inhabitants of a Port of Spain boarding house. He published a large number of political and historical works, of which the most influential is *The Black Jacobins: Toussaint L'Ouverture and the San Domingo Revolution* (1938), an account of the slave revolt, led by L'Ouverture in Haiti in the 1790s and unique in the history of slavery in that it led to independence. He also wrote a play on this subject: *Toussaint L'Ouverture*, produced in London in 1936, revised as *The Black Jacobins*, and produced in Nigeria in 1967 (published in *A Time and a Season: Eight Caribbean Plays*, ed. E. Hill, 1976). His short stories are included in *The Best Short Stories of 1928* (published by Cape) and in *Island Voices* (1970). He retained his enthusiasm for cricket and wrote several books on the game, notably *Beyond the Boundary* (1963), which examines the socio-political significance of cricket in both the West Indies and Britain. Other works include: *The Life of Captain Cipriani: An Account of British Government in the West Indies* (1932); *The Future in the Present: Selected Writings of C.L.R. James* (1977); *Spheres of Existence: Selected Writings* (1981); *At the Rendezvous of Victory: Selected Writings* (1985).

Bib: Said, E., *Culture and Imperialism*.

James, George Payne Rainsford (1799–1860)
Novelist and biographer. James was a diplomat and the historiographer of King William IV. He wrote numerous novels in the style of ⊳ Walter Scott, as well as some useful historical material such as *The Life of Edward the Black Prince* (1836). His novels are predictable and often focus upon fearless and daring horsemen, for which he was justly ridiculed.

⊳ Histories and Chronicles.

Bib: Ellis, S.M., *The Solitary Horseman: or the Life and Adventures of James*.

James, Henry (1843–1916)
Novelist. Born in New York; his father was an original writer on philosophy and theology, and his brother, William James, became one of the most distinguished philosophers and psychologists of his day. His education was divided between America and Europe. Europe drew him strongly, and he finally settled in Europe in 1875 after a series of long visits. He was naturalized British in 1915. Towards both continents, however, he had mixed emotions. As to America, he belonged to the eastern seaboard, New England, which had its own well-established traditions originating in English Puritanism, and he was out of sympathy with the American ardour for commercial enterprise and westward expansion. As to Europe, he was fascinated by the richness of its ancient societies and culture, but he brought an American, and especially a New England, eye to the corruption which such advanced development generated. The conflict was fruitful for his development as an artist, and it was not the only one; he was also aware of the contrast between the contemplativeness of his father's mind and the practical adventurousness characteristic of his brother's outlook and of Americans in general. And in his close study of the art of the novel, he felt the difference between the intense interest in form of the French tradition and the deeper moral interest to be found in the English tradition.

In the first period of his work, his theme is preponderantly the clash between the European and the American outlooks: *Roderick Hudson* (1875); *The American* (1877); *The Europeans* (1878); ⊳ *Daisy Miller* (1879); ⊳ *The Portrait of a Lady* (1881). To this period also belong two novels about American life: *Washington Square* (1881); *The Bostonians* (1886); and two restricted to English life, *The Tragic Muse* (1890); *The Princess Casamassima* (1886). His second period shows a much more concentrated and difficult style of treatment, and it concerns

English society only: *The Spoils of Poynton* and ▷ *What Maisie Knew* (1897); *The Awkward Age* (1899). Between his first and second periods (1889–95) he experimented in drama; this was his least successful episode, but the experiment helped him to develop a dramatic technique in the writing of his novels. He wrote 12 plays in all. In his last period, the most intensive and subtle in style, James returned to the theme of the contrast of American and European values: ▷ *The Wings of the Dove* (1902); ▷ *The Ambassadors* (1903); ▷ *The Golden Bowl* (1904). On his death he left unfinished *The Ivory Tower* and *The Sense of the Past*. Some of his best fiction is to be found among his short stories, and he was particularly fond of the ▷ novella form – between a story and a usual novel in length; *The Europeans* and *Washington Square* come into this class, and so does his masterpiece of ambiguity, ▷ *The Turn of the Screw* (1898).

In his criticism, James is important as the first distinguished writer in English to give the novel and its form concentrated critical attention. His essays have been collected under the title *The House of Fiction* (1957), edited by Leon Edel, who has also edited his letters (4 vols., 1974–84) and, with L.H. Powers, his notebooks (1987). James also wrote books of travel, the most notable of which is *The American Scene* (1907), and autobiographical pieces – *A Small Boy and Others* (1913); *Notes of a Son and a Brother* (1914) and *Terminations* (1917). (The last is also the title of a story published in 1895.)

Bib: Edel, L., *Henry James*; Matthiessen, F. O., *Henry James: The Major Phase*; Anderson, Q., *The American Henry James*; Leavis, F. R., in *The Great Tradition*; Dupee, F. W., *Henry James*; Bewley, M., in *The Complex Fate* and in *The Eccentric Design*; Wilson, E., in *The Triple Thinkers*; Krook, D., *The Ordeal of Consciousness in James*; Gard, R. (ed.), *James: The Critical Heritage*; Tanner, T., *Henry James*; Berland, A., *Culture and Conduct in the Novels of Henry James*; Woolf, J., *Henry James: The Major Novels*; Poole, A., *Henry James*; Horne, P., *Henry James and Revision*.

James, P. D. (b 1920)
Writer of crime stories and ▷ detective fiction. P. D. James' skilful and subtle detective novels have made her into one of Britain's most popular writers, not simply for the dexterity with which she handles her suspense plots, but for the complex characterization and social context of her writing. Like the great women crime writers of the previous generation (▷ Agatha Christie, ▷ Dorothy L. Sayers, ▷ Margery Allingham and ▷ Ngaio Marsh), James has a central sleuth who figures in many of her novels – Adam Dalgleish of Scotland Yard, who first appeared in *Cover Her Face* (1962). Her other works include: *A Mind to Murder* (1963); *Unnatural Causes* (1967); *An Unsuitable Job for a Woman* (1972); *The Black Tower* (1975); *Innocent Blood* (1980); *A Taste for Death* (1986); *Devices and Desires* (1989); and *Original Sin* (1994).

Jameson, Anna Brownell (1794–1860)
Essayist, travel writer, art historian, critic and biographer. Jameson is one of the most renowned Irish writers of her day, and she was friendly with many of her literary contemporaries, including ▷ Harriet Martineau, ▷ Mary Mitford, and Catherine Sedgwick, as well as the ▷ Victorian authors Elizabeth Barrett (1806–61) and Robert Browning (1812–89). Her work is known on two accounts: first for her book on Shakespeare's heroines, *Characteristics of Women* (1832), for which she read Samuel Johnson (1709–84), ▷ Hazlitt, ▷ Coleridge and ▷ Lamb. This book has recently been revived by ▷ feminist criticism and seen more as a vindication of the imaginative and independent women of the early 19th century than as homage to a patriarch of English literature. However, Jameson herself reported that her writing would please only those women who were 'fair, pure-hearted, delicate-minded, and unclassical'. Secondly, Jameson was praised for her travel writings which include *Winter Studies and Summer Rambles in Canada* (1838) and *Pictures of the Social Life in Germany* (1840). These are more lively and exciting than conventional ▷ travel literature and may be classified as ▷ picaresque writing.

Bib: Nestor, P., *Female Friendships and Communities*; Sherman, C., *Women as Interpreters of the Visual Arts*; Thomas, C., *Love and Work Enough: The Life of Anna Jameson*.

***Jane Eyre* (1847)**
This best-known and most popular of the novels of ▷ Charlotte Brontë is in the form of a fictionalized ▷ autobiography containing some authentic autobiographical information. The earlier and most generally admired part of the book details the experiences of the penniless and unattractive eponymous heroine, first in the household of her unfeeling aunt, Mrs Reed, and later at Lowood Asylum – a charitable school based on Cowan Bridge, which Charlotte and her sisters attended. Following this, Jane takes up the position of governess to the household of the Byronic Mr Rochester, to whom she becomes increasingly attracted, finally agreeing to marry him. Unbeknown to her, however, he has a mad wife, Bertha Mason, who is locked in the attic and who escapes the evening before the wedding and tears Jane's wedding veil before her eyes. In church the next day Rochester is exposed as a potential bigamist by his wife's brother. In the third section Jane flees, finding sanctuary with Mary, Diana and their brother St John Rivers – a cold and passionless clergyman who proposes marriage to her. Jane refuses him after a telepathic communication

from Rochester because, unlike the passionate but morally flawed Rochester, Rivers does not love her. The fortuitous bequest of a legacy by an unknown uncle in Madeira reveals the hitherto unsuspected kinship between Jane and the Rivers family and, armed with a family and independent means, she returns to Rochester to discover that his house has burned down and that he has been blinded and maimed trying to save his wife. His equal at last, she marries him.

The novel is a mixture of ▷ Romantic, ▷ Gothic and ▷ realist forms, a female *Bildungsroman* (a novel describing the youthful development of a central character, usually male) that challenged contemporary attitudes in its portrayal of a 'strong-minded' and desiring woman. *Jane Eyre* was the catalyst for feminist criticism of the 1980s, beginning with S. Gilbert and S. Gubar's *The Madwoman in the Attic* (1979), in which unstable female characters in texts written by women were seen as doubles of the sane heroine and products of the suppression of the feminine. Another re-reading occurred several years earlier in Jean Rhys' *The Wide Sargasso Sea* (1966) which tells the story sympathetically from the perspective of the first Mrs Rochester and places the novel in the context of 19th-century colonialism.

Bib: Chakravorty Spivak, G., 'Three Women's Texts and a Critique of Imperialism'; Nestor, P., *Charlotte Brontë's Jane Eyre*.

***Jane Shore, The Tragedy of* (1714)**
Play by ▷ Nicholas Rowe, based on a historic character, who was mistress of Edward IV, and afterwards of Thomas Grey, first Marquis of Dorset. Rowe stated on the title page that the play was 'Written in Imitation of Shakespeare's Style'. It traces Jane's descent, from wealth and influence as Edward's mistress, to ignominy and destitution. At her lowest ebb, she is rescued by her husband. The play is numbered among the so-called ▷ 'she-tragedies' of Rowe, which focus on the central figure of a suffering woman, and depend largely on pathos for their effect. Jane's story became symbolic of the reversal of fortune.

Janet's Repentance
One of ▷ George Eliot's ▷ *Scenes of Clerical Life*.

Jefferies, Richard (1848–87)
Essayist and novelist. He wrote about the English countryside and its life and presented it plainly, without affection but with force. This has caused his reputation to rise in the 20th century, with its intensified interest in preserving natural surroundings and in understanding their environmental influence in society. He is well known for his volumes of essays: *Gamekeeper at Home* (1878); *Wild Life in a Southern County* (1879); *Round About a Great Estate* (1880); *Wood Magic* (1881); *The Life of the Fields* (1884). His novels are *Greene Ferne Farm* (1880); *The Dewy Morn* (1884); *Amaryllis at the Fair* (1887); *After London, or Wild England* (1885). His best-known books are probably *Bevis* (1882), a children's story (▷ Children's literature), and his autobiography, *The Story of my Heart* (1883).

▷ Regional Novel.

Bib: Taylor, B., *Richard Jefferies*.

Jeffrey, Francis (1773–1850)
Critic and editor (1803–29) of the influential ▷ *Edinburgh Review* which he helped to found in 1802. His poetic taste was conservative, and he was unsympathetic to the ▷ Lake Poets, ▷ Wordsworth and ▷ Coleridge. However, in 1820 he judiciously encouraged ▷ Keats for his ▷ *Endymion*, which had been condemned by ▷ *Blackwoods* and the ▷ *Quarterly*. His weakness as a critic was not his conservatism but his susceptibility to verse of second-rate appeal such as that of Thomas Campbell and of Samuel Rogers.

As editor, Jeffrey gave the *Edinburgh* authority proportionate to its intellectual independence, and its sales reached nearly 14,000 in 1818 – a high figure at any time for a periodical of such intellectual seriousness. In politics, Jeffrey was a Whig and his journal was the mouthpiece of responsible Whig opinion.

His profession was the law, in which he excelled and was eventually made a judge.

Jeffreys, Judge
▷ Bloody Assizes; Sedgemoor, Battle of.

Jekyll and Hyde
▷ *Strange Case of Dr Jekyll and Mr Hyde, The*.

Jellicoe, Ann (b 1927)
One of few women to break into the theatre business as a writer and director during the 1950s and 60s. She was a ▷ Royal Court writer and a member of the Theatre Writers' Group organized there between 1958 and 1960, which also included ▷ John Arden, ▷ Edward Bond and ▷ Arnold Wesker. Her early plays include *The Sport of My Mad Mother* (1958), about teddy-boy violence, and *The Knack* (1961), about sexual competition. The written text of both these plays only gives a slight impression of their effect in performance since she writes in a non-literary style with clear ideas for direction in mind. Later plays such as *Shelley* (1965) and *The Giveaway* (1969) are less unconventional. More recently she has become renowned for her productions of community plays in which she has drawn on the talents of large numbers of people from single communities, bringing together professionals and amateurs, adults

and schoolchildren. An example of such work is *Entertaining Strangers* written by ▷ David Edgar and originally performed in Dorset (later re-written by him for a ▷ National Theatre production in 1987).
Bib: Jellicoe, A., *Community Plays: How to Put Them On.*

Jennings, Elizabeth (b 1926)
Poet. Published her first collection, *Poems*, in 1953, and was initially associated with the ▷ Movement, although the mystical quality of her work (Jennings is a ▷ Catholic) makes this categorization problematic. She writes prolifically, generally using traditional verse techniques, but she has also experimented with ▷ free verse. Jennings has spent much of her life living and working in Oxford. Her second book, *A Way of Looking* (1955), won her the Somerset Maugham Award, and her most important collections to date are: *A Sense of the World* (1958); *Song for Birth and Death* (1961); *Recoveries* (1964); *The Mind Has Mountains* (1966); *Growing Points* (1975); *Moments of Grace* (1979); *Celebrations and Elegies* (1982); and *Familiar Spirits* (1994). A *Collected Works* and a *Selected Works* appeared in 1967 and 1979 respectively.

Jerome, Jerome K. (1859–1927)
Novelist. Born in Walsall and brought up in the East End of London, where his father was an ironmonger, Jerome worked as an actor and journalist. His *Three Men in a Boat* (1889) is a comic ▷ picaresque tale of a rowing holiday on the Thames, and its popular success encouraged Jerome to write a sequel, *Three Men on the Bummel* (1900), in which the characters are taken to Germany. Other works include the autobiographical *Paul Kelver* (1902) and the autobiography *My Life and Times* (1926).

Jesuit
A member of the Society of Jesus, a religious order founded by Ignatius Loyola, and approved by the Pope in 1540. The Jesuits were in the forefront of combating ▷ Protestantism. In the reign of ▷ Elizabeth I they led, or were reputed to lead, the various conspiracies against her on behalf of the Catholic claimant to the English throne, ▷ Mary Queen of Scots; they were therefore regarded as national as well as religious enemies. Their advanced training made them skilled debaters and subtle negotiators. Notable English Jesuits of the English Renaissance include ▷ Edmund Campion and ▷ Robert Southwell.

Jevon (Jevorn), Thomas (1652–88)
Actor, dancer, singer, dramatist. Jevon started his career as a dancing master, and joined the ▷ Duke's Company, possibly before 1673. He had an irreverent sense of humour, and specialized in low comic parts. He was a favourite speaker of prologues and epilogues, and also wrote the highly successful *The Devil of a Wife* (1686), which was adapted several times in the 18th century.

Jew of Malta, The
A ▷ blank-verse drama by ▷ Christopher Marlowe, written and performed about 1590; published 1633. An actor impersonating the Italian political philosopher ▷ Machiavelli speaks the prologue and thereby sets the tone of the play, since to the English of Marlowe's time Machiavelli, who had sought to conduct politics amorally by scientific methods, was a godless monster. We thus expect a play dominated by evil. However, a comic tradition for the presentation of godless monsters had come down to Marlowe from the medieval mystery plays, which had presented such figures as Herod and Satan as grotesque caricatures, frightening but funny at the same time. So the Machiavellian central character, Barabas the Jew, boasting that his wealth has been acquired iniquitously, is made too impressive to be taken lightly and yet too extravagant to be taken soberly. His only philosophy is the art of gaining advantage. In the first half of the play he tries to outwit the Christians of Malta, who, scarcely less Machiavellian than himself, try to deprive him of his wealth. He eventually betrays the island to the Turks, and proceeds to try to outwit them, but he falls victim to his own plot. In a famous essay on Marlowe (*Selected Essays*), T. S. Eliot (1888–1965) described the play as an example of 'the farce of the old English humour, the terribly serious, even savage comic humour'; in his essay on ▷ Ben Jonson, Eliot points to *The Jew of Malta* as the forebear of Jonson's Comedy of ▷ Humours.

Jewsbury, Geraldine Endsor (1812–80)
Novelist, critic and journalist born in Measham, Derbyshire, the fourth of six children. Her elder sister Maria, also a writer, cared for the family until her marriage when Geraldine took over, looking after her father until his death in 1840 and her brothers until her marriage in 1853. Fêted in social and intellectual circles her friends included ▷ Charles Kingsley and his wife, the ▷ Rossettis, ▷ Ruskin and ▷ Huxley. Her first novel, *Zoë*, was published in 1845, and is one of the first Victorian novels to examine religious scepticism. It was followed by *The Half-Sisters* (1848) and *Marian Withers* (1851) both arguing strongly for changes in the upbringing of women. Jewsbsury moved to London to be close to her great friend ▷ Jane Welsh Carlyle and, despite ill-health, she contributed articles and reviews to periodicals such as ▷ *The Westminster Review* and ▷ *The Athenaeum*

and was a reader for the publisher, Bentley's, influencing the choice of books selected for Mudie's ▷ circulating library. She wrote three further novels: *Constance Herbert* (1855), *The Sorrows of Gentility* (1856) and *Right or Wrong* (1856), as well as two stories for children. She was well known for her wit and conversation, and in 1892 *A Selection from the Letters of Geraldine Jewsbury to Jane Welsh Carlyle* was published (ed. Mrs A. Ireland). Both women had wanted their letters destroyed. Virginia Woolf wrote an article, 'Geraldine and Jane', for *The Times Literary Supplement* (28 February 1929) concerning the women's friendship.

▷ Women's Movement.

Bib: Howe, S., *Geraldine Jewsbury*.

Jewsbury, Maria Jane (1800–33)

Poet. The eldest sister of the ▷ Victorian novelist Geraldine Jewsbury, Maria suffered from general ill-health, although her early death was due to an attack of cholera she suffered in India. Her first published work, *Phantasmagoria* (1825), consists of poems and some prose sketches which attack contemporary literary tastes. She dedicated the book to ▷ Wordsworth, whose daughter, Dora, was one of her friends. *Lays of Leisure Hours* (1829) was dedicated to another acquaintance, ▷ Felicia Hemans, to whom she wrote: 'the ambition of writing a book, being praised publically and associating with authors, siezed me'.

▷ Lay.

Bib: Howe, S., *Geraldine Jewsbury, Her Life and Errors*.

Jhabvala, Ruth Prawar (b 1927)

Novelist, short-story writer, and writer of screenplays. She was born in Germany of Polish parents who came to England as refugees in the year of her birth. She studied at London University and in 1951 married the Indian architect C. S. H. Jhabvala. From 1951 to 1975 she lived in India, and since then has lived in New York. Many of her novels are based on her own ambiguous position in India as a European with an Indian family. They explore the tensions of contemporary Indian society, such as the conflict of ancient and modern ideas and the interaction of Westernized and non-Westernized Indians. They are based on witty but sympathetic observation of social manners, largely in domestic settings. Some of the sharpest satire is reserved for the naive and superficial enthusiasm of certain visiting Europeans, who are frequently exploited by a manipulative swami. *Heat and Dust* (1975) employs a double narrative consisting of the experiences of a contemporary English girl in India, and the love affair of her grandfather's first wife with an Indian prince in 1923. *In Search of Love and Beauty* (1983) reflects Jhabvala's change of home; it is a story of German Jewish emigrés in 1930s New York while *Poet and Dancer* (1993) links the lives of German and Indian New York emigrés. Her other novels are: *To Whom She Will* (1955); *The Nature of Passion* (1956); *Esmond in India* (1958); *The Householder* (1960); *Get Ready For Battle* (1962); *A Backward Place* (1965); *A New Dominion* (1972); *In Search of Love and Beauty* (1983); *Three Continents* (1988). Story collections are: *Like Birds, Like Fishes* (1963); *A Stronger Climate* (1968); *An Experience of India* (1971); *How I Became A Holy Mother* (1976); *Out of India: Selected Stories* (1987). She has written a number of screenplays, some of which are based on her own works, as part of a highly successful film-making team with James Ivory as director and Ismail Merchant as producer: *The Householder* (1963); *Shakespeare Wallah* (with Ivory; 1965); *The Europeans* (1979) (based on the novel by ▷ Henry James); *Quartet* (1981) (based on the novel by ▷ Jean Rhys); *Heat and Dust* (1983); *The Bostonians* (1984) (based on the ▷ Henry James novel); *A Room with a View* (1986) and *Howards End* (1992) (based on the novels by ▷ E. M. Forster).

Bib: Sucher, L., *The Fiction of Ruth Prawar Jhabvala*; Long, R. E., *The Films of Merchant Ivory*.

Joan of Arc (Jeanne d'Arc) (1412–31)

A French national heroine for the leading part she played in turning the ▷ Hundred Years' War finally against the English invaders of France.

Politically the position was that ▷ Henry V of England had succeeded by the Treaty of Troyes (1420) in getting his son recognized as the next king of France in succession to Charles VI (1380–1422). His son was in fact proclaimed king of France in 1422 in Paris, but the English controlled only the north and east of France, and the French were still fighting, although Charles VI's son, Charles the Dauphin, had no appetite for war. The English, in alliance with the Burgundians, continued to win victories.

In 1429 Joan, daughter of a French farmer, came forward declaring that heavenly voices had directed her to relieve the city of Orleans, besieged by the English, and to lead the Dauphin to Rheims to be crowned King Charles VII. She carried out both promises and attempted to relieve Paris, which was in English hands. She was, however, taken prisoner by the Burgundians, who delivered her to the English. She was by this time regarded as a heaven-sent inspiration to the French, and the English were determined to discredit her; accordingly they secured that she was condemned for heresy by a Church court, and then burnt alive in Rouen. The war continued to go against them, however, and by 1453 they were driven from France. In 1456 the condemnation of Joan for heresy was annulled by the Church, and in 1920 she was declared a saint.

For some time the English continued to remember her as a witch and she is so represented in the early play by Shakespeare, ▷ *Henry VI, Part I,* where she appears under her French nickname of 'La Pucelle' – the Maid. By far the most striking representation of her career in English is the play *Saint Joan* (1924) by ▷ George Bernard Shaw.

Joceline, Elizabeth (1596–1622)
Tract-writer. Elizabeth Brooke was brought up by her maternal grandfather, Bishop Caderton, who was Master of Queens' College, Cambridge, and she was educated in religion, languages, history and art. She married Tourell Joceline in 1616, and died in childbirth six years later. While she was pregnant she wrote a book of moral and religious instruction for her unborn child, which is especially interesting in its gender-specific teachings. While being aware that a son would traditionally be the preferred sex, Joceline is careful to point out that a daughter will be equally welcome to her. Her touching account was published as *The Mothers Legacie To Her Unborn Childe*, with a preface by her husband, in 1624.
Bib: Travitsky, B. (ed.), *The Paradise of Women.*

***John Halifax, Gentleman* (1856)**
A highly successful novel by Dinah Mulloch Craik. The tale is narrated by Phineas Fletcher, a crippled man of sensitive character. He relates the story of John Halifax, who begins his working life as a tanner's apprentice, but rises in the world through his hard work, heroic deeds and good fortune. By the end of the novel he has married an heiress, bought property and a business, and is given the opportunity to run for Parliament. Phineas Fletcher, unable to pursue the material rewards of the world as a result of his physical disability, has been seen as symbolizing women's position in society. Phineas does not, however, revolt against his lot, but shows profound admiration for the achievements of Halifax.

John of Gaunt, Duke of Lancaster
Fourth son of ▷ Edward III. He derived the name 'Gaunt' from his birthplace, the town of Ghent in Flanders. By marrying the only daughter of the Duke of Lancaster he inherited the title and became the most powerful lord in England. He is chiefly remembered; 1 as the ancestor of the Lancastrian line of kings, beginning with his son ▷ Henry IV; 2 as the protector of the religious reformer ▷ John Wycliffe; 3 as a possible patron of the poet ▷ Geoffrey Chaucer, whose wife's sister he married; 4 for the representation of him by Shakespeare in ▷ *Richard II.*
▷ Lancaster, House of.

Johnson, B. S. (1933–73)
Novelist, poet and dramatist. His novels were highly experimental, taking as their main subject his own life as a novelist and the nature of the novel. He employed a whole range of ▷ postmodernist narrative devices for questioning the boundaries of fact and fiction. He claimed to write, not fiction, but 'truth in the form of a novel'. *Travelling People* (1963) uses a different viewpoint or narrative mode for each chapter, including a film scenario, letters and typographical effects. In *Alberto Angelo* (1964) the 'author' breaks into the narrative to discuss his own techniques, aims and sources. *The Unfortunates* (1969) is a loose-leaf novel of 27 sections, 25 of which can be read in any order. Johnson committed suicide at the age of 40, soon after completing *See the Old Lady Decently* (1975), which is based around the death of his mother in 1971, and incorporates family documents and photographs. His other novels are: *Trawl* (1966); *House Mother Normal* (1971); *Christie Malry's Own Double Entry* (1973). He also wrote plays, screenplays, television scripts and several collections of poems.

Johnson, Linton Kwesi (b 1952)
Poet and recording artist. Johnson was born in Jamaica and has lived in Britain since 1961; he read sociology at London University and was a Fellow at Warwick University. The most famous of the young Anglo-Jamaican poets to emerge since the mid-1970s (others include Benjamin Zephaniah and the older ▷ James Berry), influenced by reggae, dub and Rastafarian rhythms, his live performances and recordings with Virgin records have done much to open other forms of contemporary British poetry to a wide young audience. His three volumes of poetry have been extremely popular: *Voice of the Living and the Dead* (1974); *Dead Beat An' Blood* (1975); *Inglan is a Bitch* (1980).
▷ Post-colonial literature.

Johnson, Lionel (Pigot) (1867–1902)
Poet and critic. Born in Kent, the son of an Irish army officer, he grew up in Wales and was educated at Winchester and New College, Oxford where he enjoyed a distinguished academic career. After graduating he became a journalist contributing to the ▷ *Spectator, Academy,* and ▷ *Athenaeum* among others. He displayed an enthusiasm for medieval thought (▷ medievalism in Victorian literature), was a prominent member of the ▷ Rhymers' Club, and was a close associate of ▷ W.B. Yeats. Johnson's volume *Ireland and Other Poems* (1897) was deeply influenced by his interest in the Irish literary revival (▷ Irish literature in English) and his own Irish ancestry, which he began to investigate in 1893. He was received into the Roman Catholic church in 1891. Other works, such as *Poems* (1895), bear the mark of ▷ Walter Pater's ideas and Johnson's own ▷ classical learning. He also helped to edit

the *The Irish Home Reading Magazine* in 1894. His influences can be traced to Yeats' early work, in particular *The Wind Among the Reeds* (1899) and he is named in 'In Memory of Major Robert Gregory' as a learned man who 'brooded upon sanctity'. His chief critical books include *Postliminium* (1911), a posthumous collection of literary essays, and a pioneering study of ▷ Thomas Hardy (*The Art of Thomas Hardy*, 1894; 1923). He contributed to the ▷ *Yellow Book* and the *Book of the Rhymers' Club*. The characteristic *fin-de-siècle* remorse that informs his poetry was occasioned by his alcoholism and the poem 'The Dark Angel' is a philosophical account of his own ruined life. His *Complete Poems* (ed. I. Fletcher) appeared in 1853.
Bib: Stanfoed, D. (ed.), *Poets of the Nineties*.

Johnson, Pamela Hansford (1912–81)
Novelist. Perhaps her best-known work is the trilogy composed of *Too Dear for my Possessing* (1940), *An Avenue of Stone* (1947) and *A Summer to Decide* (1949). These extend from the late 1920s to the late 1940s, and combine observation of events and society with the study of intricate relationships arising from the attractions for each other of unlike characters. The formal quality reflects the influence of ▷ Marcel Proust, on whom Pamela Hansford Johnson composed a series of radio programmes, *Six Proust Reconstructions* (1958). Some of her later novels were more comic and satirical (*eg*, *Who is Here?*, 1962 *Night and Silence*, 1963; *Cork Street*, 1965 and *Next to the Hatter's*, 1965) but *An Error of Judgement* (1962) concerns the problem of apparently motiveless evil in modern society, and relates to her non-fictional investigation of the Moors Murder case, *On Iniquity* (1967). Pamela Hansford Johnson was married to the novelist ▷ C. P. Snow. Her other novels are: *The Survival of the Fittest* (1968); *The Honours Board* (1970); *The Holiday Friend* (1972); *The Good Listener* (1975); *The Good Husband* (1978); *A Bonfire* (1981).
Bib: Burgess, A., *The Novel Now*; Lindblad, I., *Pamela Hansford Johnson*.

Johnson, Samuel (1709–84)
Critic, poet, lexicographer, essayist. He was born at Lichfield to elderly parents, and his childhood was marred by ill health; a tubercular infection from his wetnurse affected both his sight and hearing, and his face was scarred by scrofula or the ▷ 'King's Evil'. He was educated at Lichfield Grammar School, and in 1728 went up to Pembroke College, Oxford; his studies at the university were, however, cut short by poverty, and in 1729 he returned to Lichfield, affected by melancholy depression.

After a brief period as a schoolmaster at Market Bosworth, Johnson moved to Birmingham, where he contributed articles (now lost) to the *Birmingham Journal*. In 1735 he married Elizabeth Porter, a widow greatly his senior, and using her money attempted to start a school at Edial, near his home town. The school quickly failed, and in 1737 Johnson set off to London accompanied by one of his pupils, the actor ▷ David Garrick. Lack of a university degree hindered him from pursuing a profession, and he determined to make a living by writing.

Edward Cave, the founder of ▷ *The Gentleman's Magazine*, allowed him to contribute articles, and for many years Johnson lived by ▷ hack writing. His *Parliamentary Debates* were published in this magazine, and were widely believed to be authentic. In 1738 the publication of his poem, *London*, revealed his literary abilities. But the project of compiling the ▷ *Dictionary of the English Language* which was to occupy the next nine years testifies to Johnson's concern to produce saleable material. Lacking a patron, he approached ▷ Lord Chesterfield with the plan; the resulting snub is a notorious episode in the decline of the patronage system. In 1749, the poem ▷ *The Vanity of Human Wishes* was published, and his play *Irene* staged by Garrick. In 1750 he began the twice-weekly periodical ▷ *The Rambler*, to add to his income but also as a relief from the *Dictionary* work.

The death of his wife in 1752 returned Johnson to the melancholy depression he had suffered after leaving Oxford. However, he continued to contribute to periodicals, and in 1755 the *Dictionary* was published, bringing him wide acclaim which also included, by the intervention of friends, an honorary degree from Oxford. From 1758–60 he wrote the ▷ *Idler* essays for the *Universal Chronicle*, and in 1759 ▷ *Rasselas* was published. In 1762 a crown pension relieved some of the financial pressure, and the following year he met ▷ James Boswell, who was to become his biographer.

In 1765 Johnson's spirits were much lifted as he made the acquaintance of the Thrales, and over the next few years he spent much time at their home in Streatham. In the same year, his edition of ▷ Shakespeare, for which he wrote a famous Preface, appeared.

Johnson's desire to travel was partly fulfilled by journeys made in his later years. In 1773 he and Boswell made their ▷ *Journey to the Western Islands of Scotland* (1775), and in 1774 Johnson went to Wales with the Thrale family. The following year he accompanied the Thrales to Paris, his only visit to the Continent.

In 1777 Johnson began work on ▷ *The Lives of the Poets* (1779–81), at the request of booksellers. In 1784, estranged from his friend Mrs Thrale by her remarriage, he died in his home in Bolt Court. He is buried in Westminster Abbey.
Bib: Boswell, J. (ed. Hill, G.B.; revised Powell, L.F.), *The Life of Samuel Johnson*; Bate, W.J., *Samuel Johnson*; Hardy, J.P., *Samuel Johnson: A Critical Study*.

Johnson, The Life of Samuel **(1791)**
▷ Boswell, James.

Johnson's Dictionary
▷ *Dictionary of the English Language, A.*

Jonathan Wild the Great, The Life of **(1743)**
A satirical romance by ▷ Henry Fielding. His purpose was to ridicule 'greatness' by telling the story of a 'great' criminal in apparently admiring terms. The subject makes clear that the admiration is ironical, but the reader is reminded that eminent statesmen and other 'respectable' men of power – all those, in fact, who are normally regarded as great – commonly pursue their aims with as little scruple. Wild was a historical character who had been executed in 1725, and made the subject of a narrative by ▷ Defoe.

In Fielding's fictional satire, Wild begins his career by being baptized by ▷ Titus Oates – also a criminal character – and takes to a career of crime in childhood. He becomes the leader of a gang of thieves, among whom he keeps discipline by threatening them with denunciation, while himself avoiding incrimination. The vilest of his crimes is the systematic ruin of his former schoolfriend, the jeweller Heartfree, whom he nearly succeeds in having executed. In the end it is Wild who is executed, but he is sent to his death with the same ▷ mock-heroic impressiveness as has characterized Fielding's treatment of him throughout.
▷ Picaresque.

Jones, David Michael (1895–1974)
Poet and artist. His paintings, engravings and woodcuts are probably now better known than his writing, with the exception of *In Parenthesis* (1937), an account of his experiences in World War I that combines verse and prose. See also *The Anathemata* (1952), Jones' most important work, and *Epoch and Artist* (selected writings, 1959).

Jones, Glyn (1905–95)
Poet, short-story writer and novelist. Born in Merthyr Tydfil into a Welsh-speaking family, his education in the medium of English during his creatively formative years at Cyfarthfa Castle Grammar School constrained him into writing only in the English language, though later in his life he returned to the study of Welsh to become fluent in it, reading widely in its poetry and translating it into English. This more than subliminal cultural and linguistic influence shaped his work in a distinctive manner. His teaching career provided insights into the imagination of the young, encouraging him in the use of boy-narrators in his novels and short stories. His early literary influences were D. H. Lawrence, Gerard Manley Hopkins and later Dylan Thomas, with whom he formed a close friendship, the Imagists and, most particularly, Welsh-language poetry. Thus Glyn Jones developed two tongues as a writer: one, rural, poetic and visionary, a timeless one describing the Welsh-speaking life of chapel and farm where his characters live close to nature; and the other, an Anglicized, more overtly comic one, involved in material problems, social status, possessions, money and education, of the twentieth-century industrialized valleys of South Wales, removed from the poetic into the satirical imagination. His short-story collections comprise: *The Blue Bed* (1937); *The Water Music* (1944); *Selected Short Stories* (1971); and *Welsh Heirs* (1977); his novels: *The Valley, the City, the Village* (1956); *The Learning Lark* (1960); and *The Island of Apples* (1965); his poetry: *Poems* (1939); *The Dream of Jake Hopkins* (1939); *Selected Poems* (1975); and *Selected Poems, Fragments and Fictions* (1988); and two seminal works of biography and literary criticism: *The Dragon Has Two Tongues* (1968); and *Profiles* (1980, with John Rowlands). A valedictory anthology of his best work, *Good-bye, What Were You?*, appeared in 1994, and at the time of writing *Collected* editions of his poetry and short stories are being edited by Meic Stephens and Tony Brown respectively, editions which, it is hoped, may help one of Wales' greatest writers of this century to the recognition he has so far failed to gain outside his native land.
Bib: Stephens, M. (Ed.), *The Oxford Companion to the Literature of Wales*; Jones, G. and Rowlands, J., *Profiles*; Jones, G., *The Dragon Has Two Tongues*; Simpson, M., 'Assimilation and Synthesis: Glyn Jones as Anglo-Welsh Poet', *Poetry Wales*,
XIX, 3, (1984), pp 72–89.

Jones, Gwyn (b 1907)
Novelist, short story writer, editor and scholar. Gwyn Jones was born in Blackwood, Monmouthshire, and was educated at Tredegar Grammar School and University College, Cardiff. He first taught in England before returning to Wales in 1935 as a lecturer in the English Department at University College, Cardiff. In 1939, conscious of the growing strength of Anglo-Welsh writing, he founded *The Welsh Review*, which nevertheless had to cease publication because of World War II, resuming in 1944 for a further four years.
In 1940, Gwyn Jones became Professor of English at the University College of Wales, Abertyswyth, a position he held until 1964 when he returned to Cardiff to occupy the Chair of English until his retirement in 1975. His short story collections comprise *The Buttercup Field* (1945), *The Still Waters* (1948), *Shepherd's Hey* (1953), followed by *Selected Short Stories* (1974) and his editing of three collections of *Welsh Short Stories* in 1941, 1956 and the last,

Twenty-Five Welsh Short Stories, co-editor Islwyn Ffowc Elis, 1971. He began his career as a novelist with the historical novel *Richard Savage* (1935), following this with *Times Like These* (1936), *The Nine Days' Wonder* (1937), *Garland of Bays* (1938), *The Green Island*, a novella (1946), *The Flowers Beneath the Scythe* (1952) and *The Walk Home* (1962), another historical novel. However, he is best known for his translation, with Thomas Jones, of *The Mabinogion* (1948–9) and for his seminal works on Viking exploration and conquest, *Kings, Beasts and Heroes* (1972) all of which made him world-famous. He also edited *The Oxford Book of Welsh Verse in English* (1977), produced a descriptive essay, *A Prospect of Wales* (1948) and collected, for children, *Welsh Legends and Folk Tales* (1955, 1979) and *Scandinavian Legends and Folk Tales* (1956). His most important lectures on Anglo-Welsh literature are *The First Forty Years (*1957) and the BBC Wales Annual Lecture, 1977, *Being and Belonging*, in which he traces the development of Welsh writing in English from Caradoc Evans as its 'first distinctive ancestral voice'.
Bib: Stephens, M. (Ed.), *The Oxford Companion to the Literature of Wales*; Jones, G. and Rowlands, J., *Profiles.*

Jones, Henry Arthur (1851–1929)
Dramatist. He wrote some 60 plays, and is notable for beginning an English dramatic revival in the later years of the 19th century along with T. W. Robertson, ▷ Arthur Pinero and ▷ Shaw. For instance *Saints and Sinners* (1884) was not only a dramatic success, but aroused controversy by discussing religious issues in a study of middle-class provincial life. Other plays of comparable note: *The Middleman* (1889) and *Judah* (1890). His lectures and essays on drama were collected in *The Renascence of the English Drama* (1895).
Bib: Jones, A. D., *Life*; Archer, W., *The Old Drama and the New*; Cordell, R. A., *Henry Arthur Jones and the Modern Drama.*

Jones, Inigo (1573–1651)
Architect and stage designer. He is sometimes called 'the English ▷ Palladio' because he was strongly influenced by the Italian architect of that name, and he was in fact the first important classical (Palladian) architect in English architecture. Jones and his assistant John Webb brought classical ideas into the material and commercial worlds of London architecture and the ▷ Renaissance theatre. Outstanding buildings of his design include the Banqueting Hall in Whitehall and St Paul's church in Covent Garden, both in London. He also designed sets for ▷ masques, to which words were contributed by ▷ Ben Jonson, ▷ Samuel Daniel and other poets among his contemporaries. Scenery and music were as important in the masque as poetry, and the fusion led to bitter rivalry between Jones and Jonson, who satirized him as In-and-In Medlay in *The Tale of a Tub.*
Bib: Orrell, J., *The Theatres of Inigo Jones and John Webb*; Simpson, P. and Bell, C. F., *Designs by Inigo Jones for Masques and Plays at Court*; Orgel, S. and Strong, R., *Inigo Jones: The Theatre of the Stuart Masque.*

Jones, Jack (1884–1970)
Novelist. Born in Merthyr Tydfil into a family of fifteen children, Jack Jones became, as his father had been, a miner. He later joined the army, fought in the Boer War and in World War I, became involved in post-war politics, shifting his allegiances from left to right, and then had a variety of jobs from navvy to cinema manager before he took up writing during a period of unemployment in 1928 when he was living in Cardiff. His novels exude narrative energy, humour, pathos, enlivened further by vivid scenes in which a host of bizarre characters appear, and show an understanding and sympathy with working-class life in Glamorgan's industrial valleys during the late nineteenth and twentieth centuries, with detailed research into the historical backgrounds of his settings. His most successful novels are his earlier ones from the 1930s. His novels are: *Black Parade* (1935); *Rhondda Roundabout* (1934); *Bidden to the Feast* (1938), *Off to Philadelphia in the Morning* (1947); *Some Trust in Chariots* (1948); *River out of Eden* (1951); *Lily of the Valley* (1952); *Lucky Lear* (1952); *Time and the Business* (1953); *Choral Symphony* (1955); and *Come, Night; End, Day!* (1956). He also produced three volumes of autobiography: *Unfinished Journey* (1937); *Me and Mine* (1946); and *Give me back my Heart* (1950). Three plays: *Land of my Fathers* (1937); *Rhondda Roundabout* (1939); and *Transatlantic Episode* (1947); and a biography of David Lloyd George, *The Man David* (1944).
Bib: Stephens, M. (Ed.), *The Oxford Companion to the Literature of Wales*; Jones, G. and Rowlands, J., *Profiles*; Jones, G., *The Dragon Has Two Tongues.*

Jones, Lewis (1897–1939)
Novelist. Born in Clydach Vale, Rhondda, Glamorgan, Lewis Jones became a miner at the age of 12, was married at 16, and later joined the Communist party to become a political activist, for which he was victimized, even being imprisoned for allegedly seditious public speeches. During his difficult and busy life he wrote two novels, *Cwmardy* (1937) and *We Live!* (1939), both authentic and powerful in their portrayal of the socio-economic and political situation in the South Wales Valleys between the Wars but also showing a sensitive insight into the stress-laden family relationships in this close-knit community.

Jones, Sally Roberts (b 1935)
Poet, short story writer and publisher. Born in London, but when she was thirteen the family moved to North Wales, where she was later educated at the University College of North Wales, Bangor. Having trained as a librarian in London, she returned in 1967 to Wales to take up a post as reference librarian at Port Talbot where she has since lived and where much of her poetry is set. Her work is informed by a steely sense of irony and by an ability to reveal the darker side of apparently mundane circumstances and events. Her collections of poetry are: *Turning Away* (1969); *Strangers and Brothers* (1977); *The Forgotten Country* (1977); and *Relative Values* (1985). She has also compiled a bibliography, *Books of Welsh Interest* (1977) and has provided a monograph on Allen Raine for the *Writers of Wales* series (1979). She has also recently produced a historical monograph, *Dic Penderyn, the Man and the Martyr* (1993) and has written extensively on local history in Essex, including a history of Romford, and on South Wales, especially Port Talbot. She founded the publishing business *Alun Books* in 1977.
Bib: Stephens, M., *The Oxford Companion to the Literature of Wales.*

Jones, Sir William (1746–94)
Translator. Jones occupied the post of high court judge at Calcutta for eleven years (1783–94) and during this period learned Sanskrit and embarked upon translating Indian literature into English. His most famous work of this period is *Sacontala, or the Fatal Ring: an Indian Drama by Calidas* (1779). Before Jones travelled to India, he had learned Arabic, translating several poems which were published as *The Moullakat* (1782). His works contributed to the fashion for oriental culture and he influenced ▷ Byron, ▷ Southey and ▷ Moore.
▷ Orientalism; Translation.
Bib: Cannon, G.H., *Oriental Jones: A Biography*; Mukherjee, S.N., *Jones: A Study In Eighteenth-century British Attitudes to India.*

Jonson, Benjamin (1572–1637)
Dramatist and poet; always known as Ben Jonson. In drama, he was ▷ Shakespeare's most distinguished rival, but they differed greatly in gifts and achievement. Sixteen of his plays, not including ▷ masques, have survived; 14 comedies and two tragedies. Their merits vary greatly: his universally acknowledged masterpieces are the comedies ▷ *Volpone* (1605 or 1606) and ▷ *The Alchemist* (1610), to which some distinguished critics add the satirical tragedy ▷ *Sejanus* (1603). In the second rank of importance, the following are usually included: ▷ *The Devil is an Ass* (1616), of great satirical power but less dramatic concentration; ▷ *Epicoene, or The Silent Woman* (1609) and ▷ *Bartholomew Fair* (1614), slighter in content but vigorous entertainments; and ▷ *Every Man in his Humour* (1598), the first of the comedies of ▷ humours with which his name is identified. Although all of Jonson's work contains passages of interest, his remaining plays have faults (such as excessive academicism, diffuseness of treatment or narrowness of satirical range) that usually restrict their interest to scholars. They are: *Every Man out of his Humour* (1599); *Cynthia's Revels* (1600); *The Poetaster* (1601); ▷ *Catiline* (a tragedy, 1611); *The Staple of News* (1625); ▷ *The New Inn* (1629); *The Magnetic Lady* (1632); *The Tale of a Tub* (1633); *The Case is Altered* (an early work, before he had discovered his characteristic comic medium; 1597). He left unfinished a ▷ pastoral drama *The Sad Shepherd.*

Jonson was very much a man of his age and his personal life as well as his writing both display a series of contradictions. Society was undergoing radical changes; the unsettlement of accustomed moral values gave scope to extravagance and folly. He himself was a man of strong appetites and vitality, but he understood and deeply cared for the restraining and directing qualities of civilization. His conception of civilization derived partly from his typically ▷ Renaissance admiration for ancient Roman culture, which he thoroughly assimilated through ▷ Latin literature, and partly from the traditional virtues of English society, which economic and religious changes were challenging. He was thus a moral satirist who delighted in animal vitality and human aspiration, but who made it his business to chasten the ▷ 'humours' (or, as we might say, 'manias') to which society was liable when it escaped the control of civilized discipline and reason. This made him a self-conscious artist in matters of literary form, and his plays, his prose miscellany (*Timber: or Discoveries made upon Men and Matter*, published 1640), and his conversations reported by the Scottish poet ▷ Drummond, contain much critical comment on the virtues of poetic and dramatic discipline – often at the expense of his contemporaries, including Shakespeare. At the same time he was a highly independent writer who showed no disposition to subject his work to the restriction of a code of rules.

In his non-dramatic poetry, Jonson produced a body of fine poetry which influenced the form of later ▷ lyric verse. His poems have neither the emotional extravagance of the idealizing love poets of the age, nor the rough texture of a realist like ▷ Donne; they combine the grace of manner of the former with the masculine strength of the latter, and fuse a vitality personal to Jonson with an intellectual control he learnt from Latin poets such as ▷ Catullus. ▷ Andrew Marvell was to learn from Jonson an incisiveness to temper the imaginative ingeniousness he learnt from Donne, and the school of ⊳ Cavalier Poets of the reign of ⊳ Charles I got from him much of their grace and poise.

Jonson had considerable importance as a personality who exercised influence by his talk. He was not born into the aristocratic circles of a poet like ⊳ Philip Sidney, but fashioned his career himself from bricklayer's son to proto-poet laureate. His proud and independent attitude to his noble patrons helped to enhance respect for the independence of the literary profession. His meetings and discussions with other poets at the Mermaid Tavern were commemorated by ⊳ Francis Beaumont in *Francis Beaumont to Ben Jonson* and much later by John Keats (1795–1821) in *Lines on the Mermaid Tavern* (1818), and in his old age he had a school of disciples who called themselves 'the sons of Ben'. They included such poets as ⊳ Thomas Carew and ⊳ Robert Herrick. The 1616 ⊳ Folio of his *Works* contained a carefully edited self-presentation of his career to date, with two highly selective poetry sequences (*Epigrams, The Forest*), all the court masques but no civic commissions, and only those plays he wished to preserve. He was mocked for treating play-books as serious literature, but this marks a watershed in the reception of dramatic texts in English, and set the precedent for the ⊳ Shakespeare First Folio.

Bib: Knights, L. C., *Drama and Society in the Age of Jonson*; Eliot, T. S., in *Selected Essays*; Barish, J. A., on Jonson's dramatic prose and (ed.) critical essays; Partridge, E. B., *The Broken Compass: A Study of the Major Comedies*; Barton, A., *Ben Jonson, Dramatist*; Duncan, D., *Ben Jonson and the Lucianic Tradition*; Leggatt, A., *Ben Jonson: His Vision and His Art*; Miles, R., *Ben Jonson: His Life and Work*; Riggs, D., *Ben Jonson: A Life*; Evans, R., *Ben Jonson and the Poetics of Patronage*; Dutton, R., *Ben Jonson: Authority and Criticism*, Orgel, S., *The Jonsonian Masque*.

***Joseph Andrews* (1742)**

A novel by ⊳ Henry Fielding. It was begun as a parody of ⊳ Samuel Richardson's novel ⊳ *Pamela*. In Richardson's novel the heroine, Pamela Andrews, is a chaste servant girl who resists seduction by her master, Mr B, and eventually forces him to accept her in marriage. Fielding ridicules Richardson by opening his novel with an account of the resistance by Pamela's brother Joseph to seduction by his employer, the aunt of Mr B, whose name Fielding maliciously extends to Booby ("4" clumsy fool). Joseph is dismissed for his obstinate virtue, and sets out in search of his own sweetheart. On the journey he is befriended by his old acquaintance, a clergyman, Parson Adams. At this point Fielding seems to have changed the plan of his novel; Adams, instead of Joseph, becomes the central character on whom all the interest centres. With the change, the novel becomes something like an English ⊳ *Don Quixote*, since Adams is a learned but simple-hearted, single-minded Christian whose trust in the goodness of human nature leads him into constant embarrassments.

Joseph, Jenny (b 1932)

Poet and prose writer. Joseph has been writing since 1961 (her first publication was *The Unlooked-for Season*, a volume of poetry). In 1974 she won the Cholmondely award for *Rose in the Afternoon*. Other volumes include: *The Thinking Heart* (1978) and *Beyond Descartes* (1983). She also writes for children.

Josipovici, Gabriel (b 1940)

Novelist, short-story writer and critic. Born in France, educated in Cairo, Cheltenham and at Oxford University, Josipovici is a lecturer and (since 1984) Professor of English at the University of Sussex. His novels are ambiguous and experimental works of ⊳ post-modernist fiction, conveying a sense of fragmentation and uncertainty. *The Inventory* (1968), *Words* (1971) and *The Echo Chamber* (1980) are almost entirely in dialogue; *The Present* (1975) uses a present-tense narration and interweaves a number of stories; *Migrations* (1977) and *The Air We Breathe* (1981) are structured by the repetition of scenes and images. His other novels are: *Conversations in Another Room* (1984); *Contre-Jour* (1986); *In the Fertile Land* (1987); *The Big Glass* (1991); *In a Hotel Garden* (1993). Story collections are: *Mobius the Stripper: Stories and Short Plays* (1974); *Four Stories* (1977). Plays include: *Evidence of Intimacy* (1972); *Echo* (1975); *Marathon* (1977); *A Moment* (1979); *Vergil Dying* (broadcast 1979). Criticism includes: *The World and the Book: A Study of Modern Fiction* (1971); *The Lessons of Modernism and Other Essays* (1977); *Writing and the Body* (1982); *The Book of God: A Response to the Bible* (1988); *Text and Voice: Essays 1981–1991* (1992). In 1990 he published *Steps: Selected Fiction and Drama*.

***Journal of a Tour to the Hebrides, The* (1785)**

⊳ James Boswell's account of the tour to the Hebrides which he made with ⊳ Samuel Johnson in 1773 (cf. ⊳ *A Journey to the Western Islands of Scotland*). The tour gave Boswell the opportunity to encourage Johnson's consideration of many topics, and the narrative, which he showed to Johnson, records Johnson's opinions and perorations on many matters. Boswell was partly motivated in undertaking the tour by the desire to show Johnson his homeland, but he also saw it as a good occasion to collect material for his *Life of Samuel Johnson*.

***Journal of the Plague Year, A* (1722)**

Written by ⊳ Daniel Defoe, the *Journal* purports

to be the record of 'H. F.', a survivor of the ▷ plague in London of 1664–5. The initials have suggested to critics that Defoe's uncle, Henry Foe, may have provided some of the first-hand information.

The narrative tells of the spread of the plague, the suffering of the Londoners, and the attempts by the authorities to control the disease. Defoe incorporates statistical data, some of which is taken from official sources, to demonstrate the extent of the plague and its effects on the life of the capital. The 'factual' nature of the statistics stands in grim juxtaposition to the vivid recreation of death and disease, the inhabitants imprisoned in their own homes by danger and terror, and the mass burial sites and death-carts which became a familiar part of everyday existence.

Journalism
The distinction between journalism and literature is not always clear, and before the rise of the modern newspaper with its mass circulation in the second half of the 19th century, the two forms of writing were even more difficult to distinguish than they are today. The most superficial but also the most observable difference has always been that journalism puts immediacy of interest before permanency of interest, and easy readability before considered qualities of style. But of course what is written for the attention of the hour may prove to be of permanent value; a good example is ▷ William Cobbett's ▷ *Rural Rides* in his weekly *Political Register* in the early 19th century.

The ▷ 'pamphlets' of writers such as ▷ Thomas Nashe and Thomas Dekker in the 1590s, and those on the controversial religious matters of the day such as the Marprelate pamphlets, are no doubt the earliest work with the stamp of journalism in English. However, the profession began to take shape with the wider reading public and the regular periodicals of the early 18th century. In that period we can see that it was the attitude to writing that made the difference – at least on the surface – between the journalist and the serious man of letters. Joseph Addison (1672–1719) considered himself a serious man of letters, whereas ▷ Defoe, writing incessantly on matters of practical interest without concerning himself with subtleties and elegance of style, is more our idea of a journalist. The 18th century was inclined to disparage such writing as ▷ Grub Street, though this term included all kinds of inferior, merely imitative 'literature', that we would not accept as journalism. The trade of journalism taught Defoe the realism that went into his fiction. A good example of the combination of facts and fiction is his ▷ *Journal of the Plague Year* (1722) which is both a fine example of journalistic reporting (from other people's accounts) and a fine achievement in imaginative realism. (Such a combination has a post-modernist equivalent in the form of ▷ faction, together with film and television dramatized documentaries.)

Defoe in the 18th century and Cobbett in the 19th century both assumed that the main function of their writing was to *enlighten* their readers. In the 1890s, however, the 'popular press' arose in which the desire to entertain was as strong as the desire to inform, and profitability was a major concern. The distinction between the serious and popular press is still current in the division between newspapers such as *The Times* and *The Guardian* and the tabloid press papers such as *The Sun* and *The Mirror*.

▷ Newspapers; Reviews and Periodicals.

***Journey to the Western Islands of Scotland, A* (1775)**
▷ Samuel Johnson's account of the tour which he and ▷ James Boswell made in 1773 (cf. ▷ *Journal of a Tour to the Hebrides*). The tour gave rise to Johnson's meditations on the life, culture and history of the Scottish people, as well as on the Scottish landscape. Its publication aroused the wrath of ▷ Macpherson, whose work ▷ *Ossian* Johnson rightly regarded as inauthentic.

Joyce, James (1882–1941)
Novelist. He was Irish, and born at a time when Irish ▷ nationalism was moving into its most intensive phase. Joyce was born into a ▷ Catholic family, was educated by the Jesuits, and seemed destined for the Catholic priesthood, yet he turned away from the priesthood, renounced Catholicism, and in 1904 left ▷ Ireland to live and work abroad for the rest of his life. But although he took no part in the movement for Irish liberation, he did not renounce Ireland; the setting for all his fiction is the capital city (and his home town) of Dublin. This and his own family relationships were always his centres, and from them he drew increasingly ambitious imaginative conceptions which eventually extended to the whole history of European culture.

His first important work was a volume of stories, ▷ *Dubliners*, published after long delay in 1914. The collection has artistic unity given to it by Joyce's intention 'to write a chapter of the moral history of my country . . . under four of its aspects: childhood, adolescence, maturity and public life'. The method combines an apparent objective realism with a subtle use of the symbolic and the mimesis of Dublin speech idiom and is based on Joyce's idea of ▷ 'epiphanies' – experiences, often apparently trivial, presenting to the observer deep and true insights. His first novel, ▷ *A Portrait of the Artist as a Young Man* (1916), is largely autobiographical and describes how, abandoning his religion and leaving his country, he discovered his artistic vocation. Its original method of narration causes the reader to share the hero's experience by having it presented to him with a verbal equipment which grows with the hero's development, from infancy to young manhood.

The next novel, ▷ *Ulysses* (1922), is still more original in the use of language. Its subject is apparently small – a single day in the life of three Dubliners – but Joyce's treatment of it makes it vast. The characters are made to correspond to the three main characters of Homer's *Odyssey*, and the 18 episodes are parallels to the episodes in that epic. The past is thus made to reflect forward on to the present, and the present back on to the past, revealing both with comic irony and endowing the apparently trivial present with tragic depth. In this book, modern man in the modern city is presented with unprecedented thoroughness and candour.

In his last book, ▷ *Finnegans Wake* (1939), Joyce attempts an image of modern 'Everyman' with all the forces of his experiences released – in other words it concerns one night of a character who, because he never fully wakes up, is not restricted by the inhibitions of normal daylight consciousness. To express this night consciousness Joyce uses a special dream language by which words are fused together to give instantaneous multiple allusiveness; the same technique had been used by the mid-19th-century children's writer Lewis Carroll in the poem called 'Jabberwocky' (*Through the Looking-Glass*; 1872). However, because Joyce wished to use the public-house keeper who is his hero as the representative of modern European man, he often fuses English words with those of other European languages, thus increasing the difficulty for the reader.

He published three volumes of poetry, which show his sense of poignant verbal beauty: *Chamber Music* (1907); *Gas from a Burner* (1912); *Pomes Penyeach* (1927). His *Collected Poems* appeared in 1936. His single play, *Exiles* (1918), is interesting chiefly for showing his admiration for the Norwegian dramatist ▷ Ibsen. An early version of his *Portrait of the Artist* was published in 1944 (enlarged 1955) as *Stephen Hero*.

▷ Catholicism in English literature; Irish literature in English; Dedalus, Stephen.

Bib: Ellmann, R., *James Joyce* (biography); *Ulysses on the Liffey* and *The Consciousness of Joyce*; Burgess, A., *Joysprick*; Peake, C. H., *James Joyce: the Citizen and the Artist*; Kenner, H., *Joyce's Voices* and *Ulysses*; Tindall, W. Y., *A Reader's Guide to Finnegans Wake*; Joyce, S., *My Brother's Keeper*; Levin, H., *Joyce: a Critical Introduction*; Budgen, F., *James Joyce and the Making of Ulysses*; Gilbert, S., *James Joyce's Ulysses: a Study*; Denning, R. H. (ed.), *Joyce: The Critical Heritage*; Connor, S., *James Joyce*.

Jude the Obscure (1895)

The last novel by ▷ Thomas Hardy. In Hardy's words the theme is the 'deadly war . . . between flesh and spirit' and 'the contrast between the ideal life a man wished to lead and the squalid real life he was fated to lead'. Jude Fawley is a village mason (like Hardy's father) who has intellectual aspirations. He is seduced into marriage by Arabella Donn; when she abandons him, he turns back to learning, but falls in love with Sue Bridehead, whose contradictory nature seeks freedom and yet frustrates her own desire. She runs away from her schoolmaster husband, Phillotson, who disgusts her, and joins with Jude in an illicit union. Their children die at the hands of Jude's only child by Arabella, who takes his own and their lives because he believes that he and they had no right to be born. Sue returns in remorse to Phillotson, while Jude is beguiled back by Arabella, who deserts him on his deathbed.

The setting and the four main characters are so representative that the novel is almost an allegory. Jude's native place is Marygreen, a run-down village which is a kind of emblem of decayed rural England. His ambition is to enter the University of Christminster, which is Oxford, but so named as a reminder by Hardy that the way of learning had once also been a goal of the spirit. Jude uproots himself from Marygreen but is unable to enter the university because of his social origins, though he lives in the town (where he meets Sue) and works there as a mason. Hardy's point is not so much the social one that the old universities of Oxford and Cambridge were all but closed to working men; he is more concerned to show that the decay of spiritual goals in the England of his day matches the decay of the countryside. Jude himself is a complete man – physically virile as well as spiritually aspiring; it is his very completeness which the modern world, both Marygreen and Christchurch, is unable to accept. Sue Bridehead represents the ▷ 'New Woman' of the day, emancipated in her own theory but not in body. Sue is all mind; Arabella all body, and Phillotson a kind of walking death – a man of the best intentions who is nonetheless helplessly destructive in consequence of his lack of both physical and spiritual vitality. The novel epitomizes Hardy's longing for spiritual values and his despair of them; its pessimism has a strong poetic quality, and after completing it he gave himself entirely to poetry. Like many of Hardy's novels, *Jude the Obscure* is set in the recent past – about twenty years before the time of writing. Publication of the book caused an uproar; after its hostile reception Hardy wrote no further novels.

▷ Censorship.

Julian and Maddalo (1818)

▷ Shelley's troubled and oblique narrative poem, set in Venice, concerning his relationship with ⊳ Lord Byron. The poem analyses their differences of approach to religion, politics and ethics, through the characters of Julian (Shelley) described self-mockingly in the Preface as 'rather serious', and Count Maddalo (Byron) a more worldly and sceptical figure. A long portion of the poem is taken up with their meeting, or rather overhearing the tortured outpourings of, an unnamed 'Maniac', whose tale of losing his reason through a broken love relationship may be read as a standing rebuke to both Shelley's lofty ⊳ idealism, and Byron's cynical wit. Neither can offer a remedy for the intractable recurrence of human pain, though both, as poets, must articulate it; as Maddalo is made to remark, 'Most wretched men/ Are cradled into poetry by wrong,/ They learn in suffering what they teach in song'. Although Shelley was to be misrepresented by the ⊳ Victorians and critics early this century as the purely lyrical voice of Romantic ardour, both *Julian and Maddalo* and ⊳ *Epipsychidion* (1821) are Romantic poems about the limits of Romanticism, filled with complex misgivings and self-interrogation.

Julian of Norwich (c 1343–after 1416)
English mystic and recluse whose name derives from the church of St Julian of Norwich, to which her cell was attached. Her work, the *Revelations of Divine Love*, describing her 16 visionary experiences, is extant in two versions. The short version was written first, perhaps not long after her visionary experience; the longer text was composed after some 20 years of meditation and reflection on her visions. Little is known about her life apart from the few details which appear in the *Revelations*. Her visions came, in answer to her prayer, not long after she was 30. By the time ⊳ Margery Kempe visited her (around 1413–15), Julian was established as a spiritual authority, and although she refers to herself as an unlearned woman (perhaps a reference to a lack of skills in Latin, rather than a lack of literate skills), Julian's work reveals a detailed knowledge of a wide range of scriptural and mystical texts and traditions. Her exploration of the notion of Jesus as Mother has attracted much interest, and her formulation of God's assurance to her that 'all shall be well . . . all manner of things shall be well' is one of the more famous passages of her work.
Bib: Petroff, E. A. (ed.), *Medieval Women's Visionary Literature*; Wolters, C. (trans.), *Revelations of Divine Love*.

***Julius Caesar* (c 1599)**
A historical tragedy by ⊳ Shakespeare based on the events of 44 BC, when Caesar was assassinated on suspicion of seeking to overthrow the Roman republic and make himself king. The conspiracy against him is led by Brutus, descendant of the Brutus who, according to legend, had first established the republic by throwing out the Tarquin line of kings in the 6th century. Brutus is a friend of Caesar, and his motive in organizing Caesar's assassination is his disinterested love of Rome; his chief associate, Cassius, on the other hand, is motivated by personal envy and resentment. The third outstanding character in the drama is Caesar's friend Mark Antony, who, after the assassination, treacherously but most successfully turns the Roman mob against Brutus and Cassius and drives them out of Rome. Acts IV and V show the defeat of Brutus and Cassius at the battle of Philippi (42 BC). Caesar himself plays a comparatively small part, although he is, alive and dead, the centre of the drama. The dramatic interest arises from the interplay between the characters of Brutus, Cassius and Antony, and from the conflicts in the mind of Brutus, who, as a good man, finds himself in the tragic dilemma of having to commit a horrible crime against a man he loves for the sake of the nation. Shakespeare based the events, with some interesting alterations, on ⊳ Plutarch, whose *Lives* has been translated into English by ⊳ Thomas North (1579). The play dates from about 1599.
⊳ Caesar, Gaius Julius.

Jung, Carl (1875–1961)
Swiss psychiatrist. He was part of the group surrounding ⊳ Sigmund Freud between 1907 and 1913, but because of disagreements with Freud, he left to form his own school of 'Analytical Psychology'. Jung attributed less importance to the sexual, and saw the unconscious as containing, not only repressed material, but also undeveloped aspects of the personality, which he divided into thinking, feeling, sensuous and intuitive aspects. The personal unconscious he held to be the reverse of the persona, or outer self, and to perform a compensatory function. Futhermore, beneath the personal unconscious lay the racial and collective unconscious, the repository of the beliefs and myths of civilizations, which at the deepest level were all united. Jung termed the themes and symbols which emerged from this collective unconscious, archetypes, and Jungian therapy uses dream interpretation to connect the patient with the healing power of those archetypes. Jung saw the libido as a non-sexual life force, and neuroses as imbalances in the personality. He made a comparative study of the myths, religions and philosophies of many cultures, and his thought has a religious and mystical tenor. He is also the originator of the terms 'introvert', 'extrovert' and 'complex'. Many of his ideas and experiences are referred to in the autobiographical *Memories, Dreams, Reflections* (ed. Amelia Jaffé, translated 1963).

His influence on 20th-century literature results particularly from the importance he gave to myths and symbols as universal and creative modes of understanding. The creation or reworking, of myths is a feature of the work of writers such as ▷ James Joyce (▷ *Ulysses*, about which Jung wrote an essay, 'Ulysses: A Monologue', 1923), T. S. Eliot and ▷ David Jones.

▷ Psychoanalytical criticism.

Bib: Jacobi, J., *The Psychology of C.J. Jung.*

***Jungle Book, The* (1894) and *Second Jungle Book, The* (1895)**

Two sequences of ▷ short stories and poems by ▷ Rudyard Kipling concerning the boy Mowgli, who grows up in the jungle separated from the human community. He grows from dependency into dominance over the animals and eventually returns to his kind as a forest ranger. Humanity is portrayed as crude and unrestrained in comparison with the animals who exhibit a strong sense of social responsibility in accordance with the jungle law.

Junius

The pen-name of a political polemicist who published celebrated letters attacking the government of the day in the London newspaper *Public Advertiser*, (1769–72). The letters were fiercely satirical against the ministers of George III, and were notable for their unusual eloquence. The name 'Junius' was chosen from Lucius Junius Brutus, who, in legend, overthrew the Tarquin kings of Rome in the 6th century BC. Their style shows the influence of ▷ Swift and of the Latin historian ▷ Tacitus. The real author has long been a mystery, but is now generally considered to have been Sir Philip Francis (1740–1818), a politician of the Whig party who supported the rights and privileges of Parliament against what they considered to be dangerous encroachments by the king and his supporters.

Juvenal (Decimus Junius Juvenalis) (AD ? 60–?130)

Roman satirical poet. His sixteen satires describe the society of his time and denounce its vices. ▷ Satire, as a literary form, is usually regarded as being a Roman invention, but Juvenal was the first of the Romans to associate it altogether with denunciation; his predecessor, ▷ Horace, had used it for ironic comment and discussion but was only intermittently denunciatory with the moral conviction associated with Juvenal. Like Horace, Juvenal had a strong influence on English poetry from 1590 until 1800; during these two centuries satire was increasingly practised, and Horace, Juvenal, or Horace's disciple Perseus were taken as models. Both ▷ Thomas Nashe and John Oldham (1653–83) have been described as 'the English Juvenal', but the most distinguished of his conscious followers is probably ▷ Samuel Johnson in his two poems ▷ *London* and *The Vanity of Human Wishes*, imitations of Juvenal's third and tenth satires respectively. It is interesting to compare these with Pope's ▷ *Imitations of Horace*, which Johnson was emulating. The spirit of Juvenal is also strongly present in the satirical comedies of ▷ Ben Jonson who used Juvenal in his satirical tragedy ▷ *Sejanus*. ▷ John Dryden translated Juvenal (1692).

Kailyard
A type of Scottish fiction which flourished in the last two decades of the nineteenth-century and presented a sentimental and idealized vision of small-town life: the term kailyard means a cabbage patch. ⊳ J. M. Barrie was a leading exponent in novels such as *A Window in Thrums* (1889); others were 'Ian Maclaren' (John Watson, 1850–1907) and S. R. Crockett (1860–1914). The reaction against Kailyard was inaugurated by the writer J. H. Miller, who first used the term in 1895. The main anti-kailyard novelists were George Douglas Brown, who described Kailyard fiction as 'sentimental slop' and is best known for *The House with the Green Shutters* (1901) and John MacDougall Hay, author of *Gillespie* (1914).

Kant, Immanuel (1724–1804)
German philosopher of Scottish descent. His most important works include: *Critique of Pure Reason* (1781 and 1787); *Prolegomena to every future Metaphysic* (1783); *Foundation for the Metaphysic of Ethic* (1785); *Critique of Practical Reason* (1788); *Critique of Judgement* (1790). He counteracted Leibnitzian rationalism and the scepticism of ⊳ David Hume by asserting the 'transcendence' of the human mind over time and space (hence 'transcendental philosophy'). Time and space are forms of our consciousness: we can know by appearances but we cannot know 'things in themselves'. On the other hand, it is in the nature of our consciousness to have inherent in it an awareness of design in nature, and of moral and aesthetic value under a Divine moral law. His philosophy, continued and modified by other German philosophers (Fichte, Schelling, Hegel), profoundly influenced the poet and philosopher ⊳ Coleridge; through Coleridge, it provided a line of thought which, in 19th-century England, rivalled the sceptical materialistically inclined tradition stemming from ⊳ Locke, Hume and ⊳ Bentham.
⊳ German influence on English fiction.

Katherine Group
A term used by modern critics to refer to a group of early English religious works dating from the late 12th/early 13th century, which have affinities of language and style. The group of five religious texts is found in the Bodleian Library Oxford M S Bodley 34 and includes the lives of three heroic female saints (*Seinte Katerine*, after whom the group is named; *Seinte Iuliene*; *Seinte Margerete*), a vivid treatise recommending the benefits of living a chaste, religious life and pointing out the drawbacks of living the life of a married woman and mother (*Hali Meidenhad*), and an allegorical narrative on the 'safeguarding' of the soul (*Sawles Warde*). These five texts are all written in a rhythmical ⊳ alliterative style and are highly accomplished prose works. They have linguistic, stylistic and thematic affinities with the manual for anchoresses, the ⊳ *Ancrene Wisse*, and seem particularly, though not exclusively, to cater for a specialized audience of religious women.
Bib: Ker, N. R., *Facsimile of MS Bodley* 34; Millett, B. and Nogan-Brown J. (eds.), *Medieval English Prose for Women*.

Kauffman, Angelica (1741–1807)
Swiss artist, one of the most successful women in the history of art. Recognized as a prodigy in her childhood, she was also an accomplished musician, and was for a time uncertain whether to pursue a profession in music or art. Her dilemma is reflected in an allegorical self-portrait, painted in 1791. She came to England in 1766 and grew rich and famous during 15 years in this country. Kauffman was highly versatile, working in a range of media, including oils, mezzotint, etching, engraving, and designing for decorative paintings. She used a variety of subjects and styles although ⊳ neo-classicism is a recurring theme. She received commissions for many portraits, and her work gave rise to numerous imitations. Kauffman was married briefly in 1767 to a man who claimed to be a count, but turned out to be a bigamous impostor, marrying her only in order to remain in England, and then deserting her immediately. Thereafter, she lived a single life until 1781 when she married another artist. Together they left for the Continent, where she remained until her death.
Bib: Roworth, W. W., *Angelica Kauffman, A Continental Artist in Georgian England.*

Kavan, Anna (1901–68)
Novelist. Anna Kavan's writing belongs to the subjective tradition of feminism that would include the work of ⊳ Virginia Woolf, ⊳ Djuna Barnes and Anaïs Nin. Kavan's style is both drastically experimental and yet rooted in her personal experience. She was a heoin addict for most of her life and the frozen dystopia of her novel *Ice* (1967) offers a dual symbol of her psyche and her fears of social disintegration. Other important works include the poetic prose text *Sleep Has His House* (1948). Anna Kavan was found dead, holding a syringe, in London in 1968.

Kavanagh, Julia (1824–77)
Novelist. Born in Thurles and educated at home, Julia Kavanagh was the daughter of a writer who later claimed to have written her novels and that his own worst work (a novel called *The Hobbies*) was by her. She lived with her parents in France, until they separated in 1844, when she returned to England with her mother, whom she then supported by her writing. French character and way of life are reflected in her novels, and on the death of her mother she returned to France and lived in Nice until

her death. Her first novel, *The Montyon Prizes* (1846) was very popular. The best known are perhaps *Madeleine* (1848), *Nathalie* (1850) and *Adèle* (1858). Her biographical sketches, *French Women of Letters* (1862) and *English Women of Letters* (1863), have been much praised. Her other publications include a volume of short stories, *Forget-me-nots* (1878).

Kay
Kay (Cai/Kei) is one of ▷ King Arthur's principal followers, along with ▷ Bedivere, in Welsh Arthurian narratives. In ▷ Geoffrey of Monmouth's treatment of Arthurian history he has the role of chief steward of King Arthur's household, and is killed while fighting against the Romans. In later French and English Arthurian narratives, Kay becomes a more degenerate figure, assuming the role of a knight who is a slanderer and vain boaster. In ▷ Malory's *Morte D'Arthur*, Kay is the son of Sir Ector and thus Arthur's foster-brother.

Kay, Jackie (b 1961)
Poet and dramatist. Kay was brought up in Scotland and is a graduate of Stirling University. *Chiaroscuro* (1986), commissioned by Theatre of Black Women, is a delicate but powerful piece written in a mixture of forms (dreams, songs, poetry, naturalism) in which cultural histories, friendship, 'coming out' as a lesbian and the difficulties of communication in a largely white-dominated and heterosexual world are confronted and overcome. *Chiaroscuro* as the word itself implies, is about light and shade, variation and change.

Twice Over (1988) confirmed Kay's promise as a developing playwright whose black and lesbian perspective is only a starting point to further explorations.

Kean, Edmund (?1787–1833)
One of the greatest actors of the early 19th century. He was the illegitimate son of a hawker and itinerant actress, Anne Carey. He began acting as an infant, and trained at ▷ Drury Lane so vigorously, it is said, that he had to wear irons to prevent deformity. This disadvantage was aggravated by a later fall during a circus performance in which he broke both his legs. He remained small in stature, and the actress ▷ Sarah Siddons once referred to him as 'a horrid little man'. He received some education through charity, at a school in Leicester Square, and again at a school in Soho, paid for by an aunt. Despite some early recognition as an actor, Kean long led a precarious existence, as strolling actor, singer, and tumbler, during which period he married Mary Chambers, an actress.

In 1814 Kean made his famous debut as Shylock (▷ Shakespeare's *The Merchant of Venice*), discarding the traditional red wig and playing him as a violent and tragic figure, after which his career blossomed, bringing him fame and financial reward. He followed his first success with other triumphs as Macbeth, Othello, Iago, Richard III, Lear, Barabas in Christopher Marlowe's *The Jew of Malta* (c 1590) Jaffeir in Thomas Otway's *Venice Preserv'd* (1682) and Sir Giles Overreach in Philip Massinger's *A New Way to Pay Old Debts* (1625). He toured America and Canada, receiving tumultuous acclaim. Much of his personal behaviour attracted gossip and censure; he had numerous love affairs, and drank excessively. At one time he appears to have been locked up as a lunatic. In 1829 he broke down during a performance of *Henry V*, and apologized to the audience for losing his memory. His last performance was as Othello, with his son Charles as Iago, at Covent Garden and he died a few weeks later. The most famous judgment of Kean is ▷ Coleridge's: 'To see him act, is like reading Shakespeare by flashes of lightning'.
Bib: Cornwall, B., *Life of Edmund Kean* (2 vols); Hawkins, F. W., *Life of Edmund Kean* (2 vols); Hillebrand, H. N., *Edmund Kean*; Fitzsimmons, R., *Edmund Kean: Fire from Heaven*.

Keane, Molly (b 1904)
Novelist and playwright. Born into an upper-middle-class world of country life, Keane's witty novels are concerned with the narrow interests of the privileged and leisured Anglo-Irish community. Her career has had two phases: up to her mid-30s and then from the early 1980s onwards, punctuated by 20 years of non-production. Her works include: *Taking Chances* (1929); *Conversation Piece* (1932); *Devoted Ladies* (1934); *The Rising Tide* (1937); *Spring Meeting: A Comedy in Three Acts* (1938); *Loving Without Tears* (1951); *Good Behaviour* (1981) (which was shortlisted for the Booker Prize); and *Time After Time* (1983).

Keats, John (1795–1821)
Poet. The son of a livery-stable keeper in London, he was apprenticed to an apothecary, and for a time intended to be a surgeon, but abandoned this career in his determination to be a poet. He became the protégé of ▷ Leigh Hunt, and adopted many of the older man's attitudes and literary mannerisms, though he was never, like Hunt, politically active. Through Hunt he met ▷ Percy Bysshe Shelley who helped him with the publication of *Poems by John Keats* (1817), which includes his exhilarating if callow statement of poetic ambition, *Sleep and Poetry*. The volume was not a success and Keats set himself to improve his art by writing a long poem in couplets – almost as a kind of technical exercise. *Endymion* appeared in 1818, and though its rambling allegory fails to sustain narrative interest and its poetry is of uneven

quality, it performed its function in developing Keats' style and ideas. It was severely criticized in the ▷ *Quarterly Review* and ▷ *Blackwood's Magazine*, partly with justification and partly because of their opposition to Hunt's radicalism. Its first lines show in an early immature form the aesthetic creed which preoccupied Keats throughout his short career: 'A thing of beauty is a joy forever:/ Its loveliness increases'.

Early in 1818 Keats composed *Isabella*, a macabre Italian romance in ▷ *ottava rima*, superficially similar to Hunt's work but with a sensuous complexity of Keat's own. In the same year he began work on ▷ *Hyperion*, a 'philosophical' poem in Miltonic ▷ blank verse, which remained unfinished at his death. During much of 1818 Keats was nursing his brother Tom as he died of consumption, an experience which complicated his later expressions of faith in the permanence of beauty. Towards the end of 1818 he fell in love with Fanny Brawne, and from this point on his work shows a leap in emotional depth and maturity. ▷ *The Eve of St Agnes* (1820), is a 'medieval' romance fragment in ▷ Spenserian stanzas. In 1819 Keats wrote his ▷ Odes, *To Psyche, To a Nightingale, On a Grecian Urn, On Melancholy, On Indolence, To Autumn*, and ▷ *Lamia*, a narrative romance in pentameter couplets (▷ metre). On 3 February 1820 Keats began coughing blood, and at once realized its meaning: 'That drop of blood is my death warrant. I must die.' He had consumption and knew that he would soon follow his brother. It seems that he wrote nothing from this point onwards. He travelled to Italy in September 1820 with his friend Joseph Severn and died in Rome in February 1821, directing that the epitaph on his grave should read 'Here lies one whose name was writ in water.'

Keats felt that the deepest meaning of life lay in the apprehension of material beauty, and his works are the most important embodiment in poetry of the philosophy of Aestheticism. His mature poems confront the implications of this belief in a world of disease and decay, and their most characteristic effect is the evocation of poignant transience. He is remarkable also for his intelligent awareness of his own poetic development, which enabled him to reach maturity so early in his short career. His letters are among the finest in English, not only for their discussion of his aesthetic ideas ('negative capability', 'the chameleon poet') but also simply for their humanity, spontaneity and humour.

Bib: Gittings, R., *John Keats*; Leavis, F. R., in *Revaluation*; Ridley, M. R., *Keats' Craftmanship*; Hill, J. S. (ed.), *Keats: Narrative Poems. A Selection of Critical Essays*; Fraser, G. S., *Keats: Odes. A Selection of Critical Essays*; Jones, J., *John Keats' Dream of Truth*; Ricks, C., *Keats and Embarassment*; Van Ghent, D., *Keats: The Myth of the Hero*; Hirst, W. S., *John Keats*; Allott, M., *John Keats*; Levinson, M., *Keat's Life of Allegory: The Origins of a Style*.

Kelly, Isabella (c1758–1857)
Poet and novelist. Scottish author, whose first published work was a series of confessional poems and short satirical pieces, *Collection of Poems and Fables* (c 1794). However, she soon began writing ▷ Gothic novels for ▷ Minerva Press and these followed the conventional, but highly popular, pattern, containing ruined abbeys, ghosts, ancient manuscripts and illegitimate children. *The Abbey of St Asaph* (1795) is the most accessible to 20th-century readers.

▷ Autobiography; Scottish literature in English.

Bib: Summers, M., *A Gothic Bibliography*; Tompkins, J.M.S., *The Popular Novel in England 1770–1800*.

Kelman, James (b 1946)
Novelist, short-story writer and playwright. Kelman was born and educated in Glasgow, where he attended the University of Strathclyde. He has worked in various labouring and semi-skilled jobs. He has been seen, along with ▷ Alasdair Gray, ▷ Janice Galloway and Tom Leonard, as contributing to 'the new Glasgow writing'. His fiction, like that of Gray, has its roots firmly in the urban landscape of Glasgow and combines a bleak view of contemporary culture and of human experience with linguistic exuberance and technical inventiveness, including the use of variable ▷ focalization: his novels *The Busconductor Hines* (1984) and *A Disaffection* (1989) gain some of their ironic effects from the way in which they shift between internal focalization on the narrator (using a form of stream of consciousness) and a relatively detached reporting of events, whereas the latter technique is used throughout in *A Chancer* (1985). Volumes of short stories: *An Old Pub Near the Angel* (1973); *Three Glasgow Writers* (with Tom Leonard and Alex Hamilton, 1976); *Short Tales from the Nightshift*; *Not Not While the Giro* (1983); *Lean Tales* (with Alasdair Gray and Agnes Owens, 1985); *Greyhound for Breakfast* (1987); *The Burn* (1991). Plays: *The Busker* (1985); *Le Rodeur* (adapted from a play by Enzo Corman, 1988); *In the Night* (1988). Radio play: *Hadie and Baird: The Lost Days* (1978). He has won the Cheltenham Prize (1987) and the James Tait Black Memorial Prize (1990); *How late it was, how late* (1994), the interior monologue of a man who wakes up blind in a police cell, won the 1994 Booker Prize. Other works: *Some Recent Attacks: Essays Cultural and Political* (1992).

Kemble, Frances (Fanny) (1809–93)
Actress, poet and ▷ autobiographer, born in London. She was the niece of actress Sarah Siddons and the daughter of actor-manager

Charles Kemble. In 1832 she left Britain to tour North America with her father, recording her experience in her *Journal* (1835). She married Pierce Mease Butler in 1834, but the relationship became problematic when Fanny realized that her husband was a slave-owner. She was horrified by a visit she made to his Georgia plantation in 1838, and became increasingly estranged from him. Eventually they separated in 1845 and were divorced in 1849. In 1863 she published *Journal of a Residence on a Georgia Plantation*, in which she attacks slavery, describes the living and working conditions of the people and decries her own unwitting involvement in the system. For the rest of her life she travelled between Europe and North America, writing and giving public readings. Her works include *Poems* (1844); *Records of a Girlhood* (1878); *Records of Later Life* (1882), and *The Adventures of Mr John Timothy Homespun in Switzerland* (1889).

▷ Colonialism.

Bib: Driver, L.S., *Life*, Marshall, D., *Life*; Leighton, A., and Reynolds, M. (eds.), *An Anthology of Victorian Women Poets.*

Kemble, John Philip (1757–1823)
Actor, singer, manager, dramatist. Kemble was the son of the theatrical manager Roger Kemble and actress Sarah (née Ward). His sister became known as the actress ▷ Sarah Siddons, and six other siblings also went onto the stage.

In 1777 he began acting at Liverpool, and the following year his first play, *Belisarius; or Injured Innocence* was staged there. He began the first of many seasons at ▷ Drury Lane in 1783, where his roles included ▷ Hamlet, ▷ Richard III, Shylock, (▷ *The Merchant of Venice*) and ▷ King John. Three of his sisters acted there during this time, and he played ▷ Othello to Sarah Siddons' Desdemona in 1785. In 1788 he took over management of Drury Lane, whose patent was held by ▷ Richard Brinsley Sheridan, and soon introduced elements of 'theatrical ▷ realism' into his productions, such as providing what he considered authentic Roman costumes for some of ▷ Shakespeare's Roman plays.

After 1791 when Drury Lane was declared unsafe, Kemble moved his company to the King's Theatre in the ▷ Haymarket, ▷ Covent Garden and several provincial theatres. In 1816 the advent of ▷ Edmund Kean to the stage drew from Kemble much of the public respect and admiration he had enjoyed throughout his career and he retired the following year.

Throughout his life, Kemble was admired for his good looks, elegance, and charm, and respected for his forceful professional abilities as an actor and as a manager. He had a rigorous, classical approach to acting, excelling in parts, especially those of Shakespeare, to which a grand manner and style were suited. Like many of his period he had a prodigious memory enabling him to retain many long roles in his repertoire. He lacked the emotional range of ▷ David Garrick, and later Edmund Kean, and suffered from a tendency to drink to excess, which occasionally interfered with his ability to perform. Some 58 plays, most of them alterations, are attributed to his authorship.

Bib: Baker, H., *John Philip Kemble*; Child, H., *The Shakespearean Productions of John Philip Kemble*; Donohue, J., *Dramatic Character in the English Romantic Age*; Joseph, B., *The Tragic Actor*; Kelly, L., *The Kemble Era: John Philip, Sarah Siddons and the London Stage*.

Kemp, William (fl.1593–1602)
A famous comic actor; contemporary with ▷ Shakespeare. He acted parts such as Peter, the comic servant of the Nurse in Shakespeare's ▷ *Romeo and Juliet*, and the muddle-headed constable Dogberry in ▷ *Much Ado About Nothing*, and excelled at jigs. His most famous exploit was dancing from London to Norwich (more than a hundred miles) for a bet. He and ▷ Richard Tarlton established a national reputation for themselves as comic actors, as ▷ Richard Burbage and ▷ Edward Alleyn did as tragic ones.

Bib: Wiles, D., *Shakespeare's Clown.*

Kempe, Margery (c. 1373–after 1438)
A mystic, who lived in Norwich, and whose spiritual biography is the subject of the *Book of Margery Kempe*, which Margery claims to have dictated to an amanuensis. Unlike ▷ Julian of Norwich, whom she consulted for spiritual advice at one stage, Margery was not a recluse but a married woman with 14 children who attempted to live a life devoted to Christ, and sought official Church recognition for her status as a spiritual woman, while continuing to live in the secular world. She experienced intense emotional visionary encounters with Christ, which have at times a strikingly homely quality, and the *Book* not only records these visions but also her travels in Europe and pilgrimage to Jerusalem. Her special spiritual trial, according to her book, is to be misrepresented and rejected by many of her clerical and lay peers. The recording of her spiritual life, despite severe difficulties and her own illiteracy, becomes a symbolic act in itself, representing both her claim to spiritual status and evidence of her special relationship with God.

Bib: Petroff, E. (ed.), *Medieval Women's Visionary Literature*; Windeatt, B. (trans.), *The Book of Margery Kempe.*

Keneally, Thomas (b 1935)
Novelist and playwright. Keneally was born in Sydney and educated at St Patrick's College, Strathfield, New South Wales. He studied law, trained for the Catholic priesthood, served in

the Australian armed forces, and has worked as a school teacher and university lecturer in drama. His novels employ a wide range of genres and settings: his first novel, *The Place at Whitton* (1964) is a horror story; *Blood Red, Sister Rose* (1974) is a historical novel about Joan of Arc; *Confederates* (1979) is set during the American Civil War and *Schindler's Ark* (1982) during the Second World War. However, a number of his novels have specifically Australian themes, exploring relations between Europe and Australia and between whites and aborigines in Australia: *The Chant of Jimmie Blacksmith* (1972) concerns a half-aborigine who, after experiencing racial hostility, turns to ritual killing, while *Bring Larks and Heroes* (1967) and *The Playmaker* (1987) are both set in the penal colony period in Australia. The second of these, about a group of convicts staging George Farquhar's Restoration satire of army life, *The Recruiting Officer*, has recently been adapted for the stage by Timberlake Wertenbaker as *Our Country's Good*. Keneally's other novels are: *The Fear* (1965, revised as *By the Line*); *Three Cheers for the Paraclete* (1968); *The Survivor* (1969); *A Dutiful Daughter* (1971): *Gossip from the Forest* (1975); *Moses the Lawgiver* (1975); *Season in Purgatory* (1976); *Passenger* (1979); *The Cut-Rate Kingdom* (1980); *A Family Madness* (1985); *Towards Asmara* (1989); *Flying Hero Class* (1991). His plays include: *Halloran's Little Boat* (1966); *Childermass* (1968); *An Awful Rose* (1972); *Victim of the Aurora* (1977); *Bullie's House* (1980); *Woman of the Inner Sea* (1992); *Memoirs From a Young Republic* (1993); *Jacko* (1994). He has also written plays and documentaries for television, film screenplays, books for children and non-fiction writing on Australia. He has acted in films, including the film of his own novel *The Chant of Jimmie Blacksmith*.
Bib: Quartermaine, P., *Thomas Keneally*.

Ketch, Jack (John) (d 1686)
A public executioner who made a name for himself in popular folklore, so that later executioners bore his name as a nickname. He was notorious for the clumsy brutality of his executions, which took place in public.

***Keynotes* and *Discords* (1893 and 1894)**
Two volumes of ▷ short stories by ▷ George Egerton which explore female oppression as well as celebrating women's potential. Notable stories in *Keynotes* include 'Now Spring Has Come', which deals with the transitory nature of romance, 'The Spell of the White Elf' and 'A Cross Line'. The *Discords* collection is graver and darker, focusing on women's anger and describing the effects of women's emotional and economic dependence on men. In 'Gone Under' a woman's lover arranges to have their illegitimate child murdered by the midwife, in 'Wedlock' a women murders her three stepchildren because her husband has separated her from her own child. 'Virgin Soil' describes the lasting damage caused to a young girl by her lack of sex education. Egerton's writing is characterized by a use of symbolism influenced by dramatists ▷ Ibsen and August Strindberg (1849–1912).

▷ 'New Woman, The'; Irish literature in English.

Killigrew, Anne (c1660–1685)
English poet and painter. She was praised for her piety, and was greatly admired by her circle of aristocratic contemporaries. She was Maid of Honour to the Duchess of York. *Poems by Mrs Anne Killigrew* were published the year after her death.
▷ Finch, Anne, Countess of Winchilsea

Killigrew, Thomas (1612–83)
Dramatist, actor, manager. Born in London to Sir Robert Killigrew, he became a page of honour to ▷ Charles I, possibly from 1625. Killigrew wrote his first play, *The Prisoners*, in 1635 and in the following year he married Cecilia Crofts, a maid of honour to Queen Henrietta Maria, by whom he had at least one son, before she died in 1638. Killigrew remained loyal to the king after the outbreak of the ▷ Civil War, and was imprisoned for a time. He afterwards travelled as an exile on the Continent during the 1640s, serving first the Duke of York, later ▷ James II, and then Prince Charles, later ▷ Charles II. His exploits during that period are romanticized in his play *Thomaso; Or, The Wanderer* (published 1664).

After the Restoration he was granted one of the two royal patents to form a theatre company which became known as the ▷ King's Company. In 1667 Killigrew set up a ▷ nursery to train young actors in Hatton Garden, and in 1673 he became Master of the ▷ Revels, after the death of Sir Henry Herbert (1596–1673). This made him responsible for supervising theatrical entertainment and licensing theatres and he held the post for four years before resigning in favour of his son Charles. In 1682 the King's Company, having foundered for several seasons, was effectively absorbed by the ▷ Duke's Company, but by then Killigrew had little to do with it. He was buried at ▷ Westminster Abbey, near his first wife and a sister.

Kilvert, Robert Francis (1840–79)
Diarist. He was curate in the village of Clyro, Radnorshire. His candour and responsiveness to people and environment make his ▷ diaries valuable records of rural environment in the mid-Victorian era. Selections were published in 1938–40, edited by William Plomer.

***Kim* (1901)**
A novel by ▷ Rudyard Kipling. Kim, whose

real name is Kimball O'Hara, is the orphan son of an Irish soldier in India, and he spends his childhood as a waif in the city of Lahore. He meets a Tibetan holy man in search of a mystical river, and accompanies him on his journey. Kim falls in with his father's old regiment, and is adopted by them, eventually becoming an agent of the British secret service under the guidance of an Indian, Hurree Babu. In spite of the ingenuousness of Kipling's British chauvinism, conspicuous in the later part of the book, the earlier part is an intimate and graphic picture of the humbler reaches of Indian life.

***King and No King, A* (1611)**
A tense and melodramatic tragicomedy by ▷ Beaumont and ▷ Fletcher which explores and tests the limits of courtly and romantic psychology. In the play, the king, Arbuces, falls in love with his sister, but incest is averted since at the end of the play it is revealed that Arbuces is not the king and may love his supposed sister freely.

King, Henry (1592–1669)
Poet and Bishop of Chichester. King, himself the son of a bishop, was prebend of St Paul's until his appointment as Bishop of Chichester in 1642. A year later he was expelled from his bishopric by the ▷ Puritans, but was reinstated after the Restoration. The major poetic influences on King were ▷ John Donne (with whom he was friendly) and ▷ Ben Jonson. The majority of his poetry was published in 1657, when his *Poems, Elegies, Paradoxes and Sonnets* appeared. A large proportion of King's poetic output consisted of responses to public occasions, obituaries and ▷ elegies: these included two separately published elegies on ▷ Charles I (1648 and 1649).
Bib: Berman, R., *Henry King and the Seventeenth Century*.

King Horn
One of the earliest extant English verse romances, dating from the first half of the 13th century, which has an earlier ▷ Anglo-Norman analogue. The narrative recounts the story of Horn, dispossessed from his heritage, the kingdom of Sudene, by Saracen invaders; his experiences in Westernesse and Ireland which allow him to establish his identity as a knight of skill and valour; his eventual triumph over the wicked designs of his evil companion Fikenhild, who attempts to sabotage Horn's relationship with Rymenhild, daughter of the king of Westernesse; his recovery of the kingdom of Sudene and his eventual return there as king with Rymenhild as his queen. The principle of repetition with variation provides the key to the narrative structure of *Horn*, and Horn's voyages themselves, narrated in a formulaic way, function as section-markers for the narrative. The story of Horn's loss and recovery of identity is told in a highly stylized, paratactic mode which enhances the memorability of the narrative. *Horn Childe* is a later Middle English version of the Horn story (dating from the early 14th century and written in ▷ tail-rhyme verse), which has the same plot structure as *King Horn* but differs in many points of detail. The story of Horn evidently had a wide currency during and after the medieval period. There are many balladic versions of the story, and versions of the narrative are extant in other European vernaculars too.
Bib: Barron, W. R. J., *English Medieval Romance*.

King John
A ▷ history play (*The Life and Death of King John*) by ▷ Shakespeare, perhaps derived from the anonymous *Troublesome Reign of King John*, and written before the great history plays ▷ *Henry IV, Parts I* and *II*, which first exhibit his genius in maturity. Anticipations of this maturity show themselves in the central character, Philip Faulconbridge, illegitimate son of the previous king, Richard I. The reign of the historical ▷ King John (1199–1216) was very unsettled: in the play, the disturbance arises from John's having usurped the throne from his nephew Arthur, whose cause is taken up by the king of France, the Church, and his nobles. Philip, 'the bastard', is excluded by his illegitimacy from the privileges and status of the class into which he is born, and he at first enters the king's service in a spirit of cynicism, like that of Shakespeare's other ▷ bastard, Edmund in ▷ *King Lear*. By degrees he takes to heart the dangers to the nation of the disorderly passions among the great men, and he acquires a political conscience. He is presented substantially, and stands out from the relatively flat background of the rest of the characters. However the theme that has given the play most of such popularity as it possesses centres not on the Bastard but on the child Arthur, whose pathos persuades his gaoler Hubert to spare his life. Arthur later dies from a fall in an attempt to escape.

Historically, the best-known fact about the reign of John is Magna Carta, the Great Charter which the nobles and Stephen Langton, Archbishop of Canterbury, forced the king to accept as a guarantee against tyrannical interference with the rights of the subject. Shakespeare does not mention this; it came into prominence for the national imagination only in the next reign, during the quarrels between ▷ King James I and his Parliaments.

***King Lear* (1605)**
A tragedy by ▷ Shakespeare. The play survives in two substantially different source texts: the 'Pied Bull' ▷ quarto of 1608 and the folio

edition (1623). The quarto edition contains some 300 lines which are missing from the folio, and the folio has 100 lines not in the earlier text. Most modern editions of the play conflate the two sources to make them yield a composite text which contains all the missing lines. This accommodating editorial policy has been challenged persuasively by one of the most exciting Shakespearean ventures of the second half of the 20th century, the publication of a radical edition of the complete works by Oxford University Press under the general editors Gary Taylor and Stanley Wells. Their conclusion, that Shakespeare revised and shortened *King Lear* for the folio edition, can no longer be ignored in critical discussions of the play.

The main plot of *King Lear* proceeds from the division of the kingdom of England and Lear's ill-judged rejection of his daughter Cordelia, who refuses to conform to her father's demand for a public expression of her love for him. The subplot traces the rise and fall of Edmund, the bastard and ruthless son of the Earl of Gloucester who, at Edmund's instigation, wrongfully persecutes his loyal and legitimate heir, Edgar. The double plot of the play widens its imaginative treatment of parents and alienated children and portrays a society fallen from the bias of nature, in which the old, though guilty, are more sinned against than sinning. The play offers an almost unmitigated, dark and apocalyptic vision of a universe in which good characters, particularly Cordelia, perish as well as bad ones like Goneril, Regan and Edmund. For this reason, and because Shakespeare's play contravenes poetic justice, Samuel Johnson (1709–84) preferred it in its mutilated, rewritten version by Nahum Tate (1681), which ended happily as a tragicomedy with the marriage of Edgar and Cordelia. Modern audiences have responded with empathy to the play's bleak vision.

Bib: Elton, W. R., *King Lear and the Gods*; Taylor, G. and Warren, M. (eds.), *The Division of the Kingdoms: Shakespeare's Two Versions of King Lear*.

King, Sophia (c 1782–?)

Novelist and poet. Sister to ▷ Charlotte Dacre and, like her, overawed by their powerful and infamous father, John King. Her ▷ melodramatic novels centre upon repressed heroines and dark destructive fathers and lovers. *Cordelia, or The Romance of Real Life* (1799), published by ▷ Minerva, has a daughter who devotes her life to her wicked father; *The Fatal Spectre, or Unknown Warrior* (1801) has a male protagonist who ruins his mistress and is discovered to be the devil; and *The Adventures of Victor Allen* (1805) has a hero who displays biting cruelty towards women, even though the psychological reasons for this are later uncovered. This latter work is seen to anticipate ▷ *Frankenstein*. King described her writing as a place where, 'the fantastic imagination roves unshackled'.

Bib: Tompkins, J.M.S., *The Popular Novel in England 1770–1800*.

King, Stephen (b 1947)

American novelist. The biggest-selling horror novelist of all time, King began writing short stories for American magazines in 1966; his early work is collected in the anthology *Nightshift* (1978). His first novel *Carrie* (1975) tapped into the potent vein of paedophobia uncovered by William Peter Blatty's *The Exorcist* and was marketed as an '*Exorcist*-style' work. Unlike the many contemporary plagiarists of Blatty's best-seller, however, King flourished and developed a uniquely popular personal style, using corrupted symbols of cosy suburban Americana to explore the taboos of modern life, blending elements of archaic Gothic with a new style of horrific realism. In *Salem's Lot* (1975), King transposed the traditional vampire tale to a modern setting, creating a blackly satirical modern nightmare reminiscent of *Rosemary's Baby*. Similarly, *The Shining* (1977) updated the theme of the haunted house, drawing heavily upon Shirley Jackson's *The Haunting of Hill House*. King's 1981 critical work *Danse Macabre* has become the textbook of modern popular horror fiction and films. In 1977, he adopted the pseudonym Richard Bachman to escape the demands of his growing reputation, under which he wrote a number of novels including *The Running Man* (1982) and *Thinner* (1984). Although the popularity of King's prolific output has continued to increase (he has sold over 80 million books) the quality of his writing has been inconsistent. In the early 1980s, King's creative juices dried, and his output (which he describes as 'the literary equivalent of a Big Mac') became tedious and formulaic. Ironically, this bout of artistic sterility gave birth to *Misery* (1987), perhaps King's finest novel, wherein a writer of pulp romances attempts to escape his money-making legacy and find creative fulfilment, only to be imprisoned (literally) by the stifling demands of his Number One Fan.

A few of King's novels and short stories have been successfully adapted for the screen by renowned directors: Brian de Palma (*Carrie*), Stanley Kubrick (*The Shining*), David Cronenberg (*The Dead Zone*) and Rob Reiner (*Stand by Me*, *Misery*); many more have been destroyed in translation (*Children of the Corn*, *Firestarter*, *Graveyard Shift*, *Cujo*, *Christine*). King currently lives in Maine. Works include: *The Stand* (1978); *The Dead Zone* (1979); *Firestarter* (1980); *Cujo* (1981); *Different Seasons* (1982); *The Dark Tower* (1982); *Christine* (1983); *Cycle of the Werewolf* (1983); *Pet Sematary* (1983); *The Talisman* (1984, with Peter Straub); *The Eyes of the Dragon* (1984); *Skeleton Crew* (1985); *It* (1986); *The Dark Half* (1989); *Four Past Midnight* (1990); *Needful Things* (1991). As

Richard Bachman: *Rage* (1977); *The Long Walk* (1979); *The Running Man* (1982); *Thinner* (1984).

King, William (1663–1712)
Author of satirical and burlesque works in both prose and verse, including (with Charles Boyle) *Dialogues of the Dead* (1699) and *The Art of Cookery* (1708), imitating Horace's *Art of Poetry*.

Kingis Quair
A narrative in ▷ rhyme royal, written c 1422, and attributed to ▷ James I of Scotland. The *Kingis Quair* (*King's Book*) is greatly indebted to the work of ▷ Chaucer, especially to the ▷ *Knight's Tale*. The narrative (some 1,379 lines long) recounts the experiences of a knight-prisoner who falls in love with a lady walking in the garden below his cell and in a dream-vision visits the realm of Venus, the palace of Minerva, and encounters Fortuna, and finally is assured that his suit for the lady will be successful.
▷ James I, King of Scotland. **Bib**: Norton-Smith, J. (ed.), *The Kingis Quair*.

King-maker, The
The nickname of Richard Neville, Earl of Warwick (1428–71). He was one of the most powerful English nobles during the civil wars known as the ▷ Wars of the Roses. In the early 1460s he was from time to time in a position to control the destinies of the rival claimants to the throne – ▷ Henry VI (of the ▷ House of Lancaster) and ▷ Edward IV (of York).

King's Company, The
Acting company formed by ▷ Sir Thomas Killigrew after the Restoration of ▷ Charles II. It performed from November 1660 at the former Gibbons' Tennis Court in ▷ Vere Street, near ▷ Lincoln's Inn Fields, which had been converted to a theatre. In May 1663 it moved to a purpose-built theatre at Bridges Street, ▷ Drury Lane, also known as the Theatre Royal. In January 1672 that theatre was destroyed by fire and in March 1674, after a temporary sojourn at Lincoln's Inn Fields, the company moved to a new King's Theatre, or Theatre Royal, designed at Drury Lane by ▷ Sir Christopher Wren. Here it remained until its union with the ▷ Duke's Company to form the ▷ United Company in 1682.
▷ Theatres.

King's Friends
George III tried to revive the power of monarchical government in England against the Whig aristocracy which, since the accession to the throne of the ▷ House of Hanover in 1714, had controlled the country through Parliament. Since the institution of Parliament was too strong for the king to ignore it, he tried to carry out his purpose by securing (largely through various forms of bribery) a party to support his policies and ministers from within Parliament. These became known as the King's Friends or the New Tories.

King's Men, The
▷ Chamberlain's Men, The Lord.

King's Theatre
▷ Drury Lane Theatres; Haymarket Theatres.

Kingsley, Charles (1819–75)
Novelist, clergyman, reformer. He belonged to a movement known as Christian Socialism, led by F.D. Maurice. He is now remembered chiefly for his children's book, ▷ *The Water Babies* (1863). His novels *Yeast* (1848) and ▷ *Alton Locke* (1850) are concerned with the theme of social injustice. ▷ *Hypatia* (1853), *Westward Ho!* (1855) and *Hereward the Wake* (1865) are ▷ historical novels. His retelling for the young of Greek myths, *The Heroes* (1856) is still well known.
▷ Social problem novel, Children's literature; Lawrence, G.A.
Bib: Pope-Hennessy, U., *Canon Charles Kingsley*; Martin, R.B., *The Dust of Combat*: *A Life of Kingsley*; Thorp, M.F., *Life*; Barry, J.D., in *Victorian Fiction* (ed. L. Stevenson); Chitty, S., *The Beast and the Monk: A Life of Charles Kingsley*; Collom, S.B., *Charles Kingsley: The Lion of Eversley*.

Kingsley, Mary (1852–1931)
▷ Malet, Lucas.

Kingsley, Mary (1862–1900)
▷ Travel writer and ▷ ethnologist. She was born in Islington, London, the daughter of Mary Bailey and George Henry Kingsley, and niece of the novelist ▷ Charles Kingsley. She is remembered today as an explorer of West Africa, having travelled widely in that area between 1893 and 1895. She recorded her experiences in *Travels in West Africa, Congo Francaise, Corisco, and Cameroon* (1897), in which she writes of the customs and traditions of peoples such as the Ajumba, Adooma and Fan, as well as describing natural environments in great detail. Two further works, *The Story of West Africa* (1899) and *West African Studies* (1899), are respectively historical and anthropological in focus. Kingsley died of enteric fever in Cape Town in 1900, during her third trip to Africa. She was celebrated as a great ethnologist; a society was founded in her name to promote the study of African peoples and culture.
▷ Colonialism.
Bib: Campbell, O., *Mary Kingsley: A Victorian in the Jungle*; Clair, C., 'Female Anger and African Politics: The Case of Two Victorian

"Lady Travellers"', *Turn-of-the-Century Women* 2, 1, Summer 1985.

Kipling, Rudyard (1865–1936)
Poet, short-story writer, novelist. He was born in India, educated in England, and returned to India at seventeen as a journalist. In 1889 he came to England to live.

Kipling's poetry is striking for his success in using, vividly and musically, popular forms of speech, sometimes in the ▷ Browning tradition of the ▷ dramatic monologue, eg *McAndrew's Hymn*, or in the ▷ ballad tradition, eg *Barrack-Room Ballads* (1892). He was also able to write poetry appropriate to public occasions and capable of stirring the feelings of a large public, eg his famous *Recessional* (1897). His poetry is generally simple in its components but, when it rises above the level of doggerel, strong in its impact. It needs to be read in selection: *A Choice of Kipling's Verse* (ed. T.S. Eliot) has a very good introductory essay.

Kipling's stories brought him fame, and, partly under French influence, he gave close attention to perfecting the art of the ▷ short story. The volumes include: *Plain Tales from the Hills* (1887); *Life's Handicap* (1891); *Many Inventions* (1893); *The Day's Work* (1898); *Traffics and Discoveries* (1904); *Actions and Reactions* (1909); *A Diversity of Creatures* (1917); *Debits and Credits* (1926) and *Limits and Renewals* (1932). The early stories in particular show Kipling's capacity to feel with the humble (common soldiers, Indian peasants) and the suffering. But he admired action, power, and efficiency; this side of his character brought out much of the best and the worst in his writing. Some of his best stories show his enthusiasm for the triumphs of technology, and are about machines rather than people, eg in *The Day's Work*. On the other hand he was inclined to be crudely chauvinistic, and to show unpleasant arrogance towards peoples ruled by or hostile to Britain, though he also emphasized British responsibility for the welfare of the governed peoples. Yet again, he sometimes engaged in delicate if sentimental fantasy, as in *They* and *The Brushwood Boy* (1925); some of his later stories show a sensitive and sometimes morbid insight into abnormal states of mind, eg *Mary Postgate* (1917). The stories, like the poems, are best read in selection: *A Choice of Kipling's Prose* (ed. Somerset Maugham).

Kipling is not outstanding as a full-length novelist. His best novel is ▷ *Kim* (1901), based on his childhood in India; *Stalky and Co* (1899) is well known as a tale about an English public school, and is based on Kipling's own schooldays at the United Services College. *The Light that Failed* (1890) shows his more sensitive and sombre aspect. An autobiographical fragment, *Something of Myself*, was published in 1937.

Kipling's children's stories are minor classics of their kind: ▷ *The Jungle Books* (1894–5); *Just So Stories* (1902); *Puck of Pook's Hill* (1906). *Rewards and Fairies* (1910) is less celebrated.

▷ Children's literature; Imperialism.

Bib: Birkenhead, Lord, *Rudyard Kipling* (biography); Page, N., *A Kipling Companion*; Carrington, C.E., *Life*; Dobree, B., *Kipling*; Orwell, G., in *Critical Essays*; Wilson, E., in *The Wound and the Bow*; Green, R.L. (ed.), *Kipling: The Critical Heritage*.

***Kipps* (1905)**
A novel by ▷ H. G. Wells. It describes the social rise of a shop-assistant through an unexpected legacy, his engagement to a vulgarly snobbish young lady who has hitherto been out of his reach, and his painful acquisition of the false standards and cares which are forced upon him. He escapes the marriage by marrying suddenly a girl of his own former class, but he only escapes his worries when he loses his money. The book contains acute social observation and comedy in the Dickens tradition, though Wells' style is quite his own.

Kit-Cat Club
Founded early in the 18th century by leading Whig men of letters and politicians (Whig and Tory); its members included ▷ Marlborough, ▷ Walpole, ▷ Steele, ▷ Addison, ▷ Congreve and ▷ Vanbrugh. It met at the house of a pastry-cook called Christopher Cat. Their portraits by ▷ Sir Godfrey Kneller hang in the National Portrait Gallery.

▷ Clubs.

Kneller, Sir Godfrey (1646–1723)
Painter, born at Lübeck, who trained at Amsterdam under a pupil of Rembrandt, and came to England in 1675. He was made court painter in 1680, serving under successive monarchs including ▷ Charles II, ▷ James II, ▷ William III, ▷ Anne and George I. He painted hundreds of works, including portraits of nine sovereigns and many other members of the nobility, as well as leading writers, actors, actresses and politicians. His paintings are marked by a distinctive formality and grace, in a style that is easily recognizable. His best-known works are 42 portraits of members of the ▷ Whig ▷ Kit-Cat Club, known as the Kit-Cat series (1702–17). Knighted in 1692, Kneller was the first painter in England to be made a baronet, in 1715. In 1711 he founded Kneller's Academy, the first of its kind in England.

Knevet, Ralph (1600–71)
Poet. Knevet was attached in a clerical capacity to the Paston family in Norfolk from 1628 until 1637, and wrote numerous religious poems, heavily indebted to ▷ George Herbert. Similarly, his attempt at political ▷ allegory

is confined to a 'continuation' of ▷ Spenser's ▷ *The Faerie Queene*, entitled *A Supplement of the Faery Queene* (1635). He also wrote a parodic ▷ masque, *Rhodon and Iris* (1631), for the florists' guild at Norwich. Other extant works are: *Stratiotikon, or a Discourse of Militarie Discipline* (1628) and *Funerall Elegies* (1637).
Bib: Charles, A. M. (ed.), *The Shorter Poems of Ralph Knevett*.

Knight, Frances Maria (fl1682–1724)
Actress whose career survived transitions of taste and her own aging, to remain on the stage for 35 years. She began as a child actress, playing the roles of young girls in plays of ▷ D'Urfey, ▷ Shadwell and ▷ Southerne, moving on to wives and mistresses in the 1690s and 1700s, and eventually to widows and at least one mother. She played heroines, coquettes and villainesses, and is said to have continued acting to the end of her life.
Bib: Howe, E., *The First English Actresses*.

***Knight of the Burning Pestle, The* (1607)**
A comedy by ▷ Francis Beaumont. It mocks the London middle-class taste for extravagant romances in the Spanish tradition about the adventures of wandering knights ('knight-errantry'). It also parodies a contemporary play, *The Four Prentices of London* by ▷ Thomas Heywood, who flattered this taste. It seems to owe something to Cervantes' ▷ *Don Quixote* (Pt I, 1605), itself a parody of the Spanish romances; this, however, was not translated until 1612 (▷ Spanish influence on English literature).

The play at first purports to be called *The London Merchant* but a grocer and his wife, sitting in the audience, become worried that this may turn out to be a ▷ satire on London citizens. They are determined to have something to flatter their vanity, and force their apprentice, Ralph, up on to the stage to perform the role of a 'grocer errant'; he wears on his shield the sign of a burning pestle, *ie* an implement used by shopkeepers. The play of *The London Merchant* proceeds together with Ralph's Quixote-like adventures, and the grocer and his wife, still in the audience, interpose appreciative comments.

The comedy shows the great theatrical dexterity achieved by English dramatists at the height of the Shakespearean period. A main part of this dramatic skill is the intermingling of styles – song, comic rhyme, serious ▷ blank verse, and colloquial prose.

Knighthood
A term which covers a complex historical and cultural phenomenon, referring both to members of a social estate whose role and status evolved in different ways in medieval Europe, and to a more abstract ethos, a framework of values and a code for behaviour, which is promoted in various kinds of medieval and post-medieval artistic representations and social rituals (in manuals of chivalric activity, in rituals of state and Church, in visual media, etc.), but which is perhaps more honoured in the breach than in the observance by those who claim the title of 'Sir'.

Knighthood (or chivalry – the term more favoured by modern historians of culture) cannot be summed up in a few words because it is not a homogeneous phenomenon. It seems that the role of the knight, which was defined as a military function in the early medieval period (as an armed, mounted warrior who rendered military service in return for a fief), came by the 13th century to be a socially prestigious role to which members of the nobility aspired (the military function being rendered, it seems, by financial payment). Tracing the history of that evolution requires attention to the specific power structures in operation in different countries, in different regions, during this time: the role of the knight-figure in post-Conquest England (in which Anglo-Norman and Saxon institutions were intermeshed) is not the same as that of the knight in the regions of France. However, tracing the history of the institution of knighthood also requires attention to how the cultural concept of knighthood evolved, and how a body of material on knighthood, in theory and in practice, came about. The Church had an important part to play in this: necessarily, if knights are given a role to play as defenders of the faith (and the faithful), some examination of the codes and limits of justifiable martial action is required. But all kinds of secular literature too, from romances to classical histories and conduct books, played a part in cultivating the mythology of knighthood and developing the notion of chivalry as a transhistorical phenomenon which may encode the values of the social elite of different historical times.

Attempts to generalize about medieval chivalric literature may be as misleading as attempts to generalize about knighthood. Some of the chivalric narratives most familiar to modern English audiences, such as ▷ *Gawain and the Green Knight* or ▷ Chaucer's ▷ *Knight's Tale*, are far from simple manifestos promoting the interests of chivalric culture: these texts are as much concerned with exploring the tensions in the chivalric ethos as celebrating the panopoly of knightly adventure and its civilizing effects. The trio of Knight, Squire, Yeoman, as presented in the *General Prologue* of the ▷ *Canterbury Tales*, provides both an image of the idealized structure of a feudal/chivalric hierarchy bound by notions of service, and embodies a recognition of the different models of chivalry, embodied in the single term. The Knight and the Squire represent different 'ages of Man' *and* different kinds of chivalric models: the crusading defender of the faith provides a contrast to the figure of the Squire, immersed in a world of courtly and amorous accomplishments and values. Chaucer's single foray into the world of Arthurian romance, ▷ *The Wife of Bath's Tale*, clearly shows how definitions of the knighthood might be opposed: in this tale the definition of 'courtoisie' as a moral virtue, not a 'natural' attribute of class origin, voiced by the Old Woman in the narrative, is potentially at odds with the notion of knighthood as a quality of class, voiced by the central knightly protagonist who finds it difficult to accommodate marriage to a social inferior. Many of the anonymous Middle English romances are concerned with negotiating between these two different approaches to defining knighthood. Many of their central chivalric heroes serve an 'apprenticeship' in disguise, or are dispossessed in some way from their heritage, and thus demonstrate, finally, that their membership of a social elite is justified by birth and by the moral quality of their performance as in ▷ *King Horn* or ▷ *Havelok*.

Unravelling the interrelation between the literary theory and the social practice of chivalry is no simple matter. There is no doubt, for example, that Edward III's institution of the Order of the ▷ Garter in 1348 was influenced by a model of chivalric life developed in Arthurian narratives, among others. But it is also the case that this tradition of Arthurian literature itself developed as a literary arena in which examinations of the theory and practice of the values of a social elite could take place. The chivalric world offered, and continues to offer, writers and artists an arena for the exploration of codes of behaviour and modes of social organization, even when the social and historical context of the artist's culture is far removed from the world of knights and ladies.

▷ Crusades, The.

Bib: Coss, P., *The Knight in Medieval England*.

Knights of the Shire

A term used in the 14th and 15th centuries for small landowners who elected representatives to Parliament. They were not necessarily knights in the usual sense of having had ▷ knighthood conferred on them.

▷ Forty shilling freeholders.

Knight's Tale, The

One of ▷ Chaucer's ▷ *Canterbury Tales*, which is a reworking of the *Teseida* by ▷ Boccaccio, and recounts the story of ▷ Palamon and Arcite's love for Emily, sister of Hippolyta (wife of Theseus, Duke of Athens). The two Theban knights fall in love with Emily while held as Theseus' prisoners and eventually compete for Emily in a public tournament in Athens. Although Arcite wins the tournament, he is subsequently thrown from his horse and dies. After an interval of many years, Theseus arranges the marriage of Palamon and Emily, prompted by the desire for a political alliance with Athens. The gods play an active part in the narrative, reflecting the powers and desires of the earthly characters, and partly shaping the lives of the earthly protagonists too. In Chaucer's version of the narrative, questions about how order can be achieved on a personal and political level are very much to the fore. A Chaucerian version of the story of Palamon and Arcite appears to pre-date the composition of the *Canterbury Tales*: in the prologue to the ▷ *Legend of Good Women*, composed around 1386–7, the story is mentioned as one of Chaucer's 'makyngs'. Chaucer also tackled the story of Arcite from a rather different angle in his unfinished work ▷ *Anelida and Arcite*.

▷ Theseus.

Knox, John (1505–72)

Scottish religious reformer. More than anyone else, he was responsible for the conversion of Scotland from Catholic to Calvinist Christianity, and the eventual establishment of the national Presbyterian Church there. This brought him into conflict with ▷ Mary Queen of Scots, but he was out of the country when rebellion forced her to abdicate in 1567 and seek the protection of ▷ Elizabeth I. His *History of the Reformation of Religion within the realme of Scotland* includes an account of his celebrated controversy with the queen. Knox's vehement antagonism towards the concept, as well as the actuality, of female sovereign power has recently been highlighted by ▷ feminist critics.

Bib: Ridley, J., *John Knox*.

Knox, Vicessimus (1752–1821)

English cleric and author, who became master of Tunbridge School in Kent. He wrote several volumes of sermons and theological and literary treatises, in a style noted for its elegance and correctness. Among them are *Moral and Literary Essays* (1777); *Liberal Education; or a Practical Treatise on the Methods of Acquiring Useful and Polite Learning* (1781); and *Elegant Extracts in Prose and Verse* (1789).

Koestler, Arthur (1905–83)

Novelist and philosopher. He was born in Hungary and educated at the University of Vienna. From 1932 to 1938 he was a member of the Communist Party (▷ Communism). He went to Spain as a correspondent during the Spanish Civil War, and was imprisoned by the Nationalists. Subsequently imprisoned in France during 1939–40, he joined the Foreign Legion before escaping to Britain in 1941. After World War II he became a British subject. From the 1930s to the 1950s his work was primarily concerned with political issues; his novel *Darkness At Noon* (1940) exposed Stalinist methods through the story of the imprisonment and execution of a former Bolshevik leader.

From the 1950s onwards his writings were more concerned with the philosophical implications of scientific discoveries. His non-fiction trilogy, *The Sleepwalkers* (1959), *The Act of Creation* (1964) and *The Ghost in the Machine* (1967) considered the effect of science on man's idea of himself, and defended the concept of mind. A persistent feature of his work was a sense of horror at the barbarities of 20th-century Europe. Koestler, who had advocated the right to euthanasia, and who was suffering from leukaemia and Parkinson's disease, committed suicide together with his third wife, Cynthia Jefferies, in 1983. His other novels are: *The Gladiators* (1939); *Arrival and Departure* (1943); *Thieves in the Night* (1946); *The Age of Longing* (1951); *The Call Girls* (1972). Autobiographical writings include: *Arrow in the Blue* (1952); *The Invisible Writing* (1954). Other prose writings include: *The Yogi and the Commissar* (1945); *The Roots of Coincidence* (1972).
Bib: Hamilton, I., *Koestler: A Biography*; Pearson, S. A., *Arthur Koestler*.

Kogawa, Joy (b 1935)
Poet and novelist. During the second world war, Kogawa and her family were interned in a camp for Canadians of Japanese extraction and her work circles about the uneasy sense of identity such transculturalism produces. Indeed, her most well-known work, the novel *Obasan* (1981) discusses the internment of Japanese families in Canada and combines history, autobiography, fiction and political comment in a postmodern assessment of racial difference in Canada today.

Kotzebue, August Friedrich Ferdinand von (1761–1819)
German dramatist, who directed the theatre of Vienna, and wrote some 200 plays. Several of these were translated into English, including *The Stranger*, *The Indians in England*, *Pizarro*, and *Benyowski*. One of them, adapted by ▷ Elizabeth Inchbald as *Lovers' Vows*, features in ▷ Jane Austen's ▷ *Mansfield Park*. His work greatly influenced the development of ▷ melodrama on the Continent and in England.

Kristeva, Julia (b **1941**)
French psychoanalyst, philosopher and linguistic theorist. Julia Kristeva was born and grew up in Bulgaria, and moved to Paris to study in 1966. She writes in French, and is now a naturalized French citizen, but she has often drawn on the language and psychology of exile in her work – in 1970 ▷ Roland Barthes was one of the first theorists to respond enthusiastically to her work, calling her 'L'étrangère'. Kristeva's earlier work is more strongly concerned with semiotics and linguistic theory (*Séméiotiké*, 1969, outlines Kristeva's own brand of 'semanalysis'; see also *Desire in Language: A Semiotic Approach to Literature and Art*, 1980), and as her interest in psychoanalysis has burgeoned she has undertaken a series of studies of literature, poetics and abnormal psychology, and the relationship between language and the body (particularly *Powers of Horror*, 1982 *Tales of Love*, 1983, and *Black Sun*, 1980). Her long-term interest in symbolist and ▷ modernist writers continued to animate her work (Mallarmé and ▷ Lautréamont are the subject of *Revolution in Poetic Language*, 1974, and Céline figures centrally in *Powers of Horror*), and she has also had a profound impact on the development of the so-called 'New French Feminist' movement (see essays and interviews with her in *New French Feminisms*, ed. E. Marks and I. de Courtivron, as well as *Desire in Language About Chinese Women*, trans. 1977). Kristeva is a long-term member of the editorial board of the radical journal ▷ *Tel Quel* and is a practising psychoanalyst.
Bib: Moi, T. (ed.), *The Kristeva Reader*, Lechte, J., *Julia Kristeva*; Moi, T., *Sexual/ Textual Politics*.
▷ Feminism; post-structuralism; psychoanalytic criticism; *écriture féminine*.

Kubla Khan: or, A Vision in a Dream: A Fragment **(1816)**
An ode by ▷ Samuel Taylor Coleridge, written in 1797, when he was living in Somerset. Coleridge recorded that he fell asleep after reading a description in *Purchas his Pilgrimage* (1613) of the pleasure gardens constructed in Xanadu by the 13th-century Mongol king of China, Khan (king) Kublai. While he was asleep 'from two to three hundred lines' came to him, which upon waking he hastened to write down. However he was interrupted by 'a person on business from Porlock', and afterwards could recall nothing of the remainder, 'with the exception of some eight or ten scattered lines and images'. It is difficult to know how much of this account to believe. One element Coleridge suppresses is his addiction to opium, which is certainly relevant to the hallucinatory clarity of the poem's exotic images. Because of the oddness of Coleridge's account 'a visitor from Porlock' has become a byword for any kind of intriguing, possibly evasive, excuse.

Despite its designation 'A Fragment' the work is artistically complete. The first three sections rework phrases from the ▷ Jacobean travel book, to describe a strangely primal landscape. An awesome 'mighty fountain' forms the source of the 'sacred river' Alph, on the banks of which Kubla has built a 'stately pleasure-dome' surrounded by orchards and gardens. After watering the garden the river continues its course, entering 'caverns measureless to man' and sinking 'in tumult to a lifeless ocean'. The clarity and primitiveness of these images gives the poem an archetypal resonance. The river can be seen as the river of life or creativity; the fountain symbolizes birth (of an individual, civilization, poetic inspiration), and the 'lifeless ocean' death or sterility. The dome stands for the precarious creative balance between. It is possible that the final fourth section of the poem, which seems to be a commentary upon the preceding lines, were 'the eight or ten lines or images' written after the departure of Coleridge's visitor, if he or she ever existed. The poem ends by imputing magical qualities to the poem itself and its bardic author: 'Weave a circle round him thrice,/ And close your eyes with holy dread,/ For he on honey-dew hath fed,/ And drunk the milk of Paradise.'

▷ Bard; Romanticism.

Kureishi, Hanif (b 1954)
Novelist, playwright and screenplay writer. Born in Kent and educated at King's College London, he was appointed Writer in Residence at the Royal Court Theatre in 1982 after winning the George Devine Award for his play *Outskirts* (1981). He has written two screenplays: *My Beautiful Laundrette* (filmed 1985) and *Sammy and Rosie Get Laid* (filmed 1987). He also wrote the screenplay for (and directed) the film *London Kills Me* (1991). His first novel, *The Buddha of Suburbia* (1989), is a comic, satirical story about growing up in south-east London, and was followed in 1995 by *The Black Album*.

Kyd, Thomas (1558–94)
Dramatist. He is associated with the group known as the ▷ University Wits. His only known and important contribution to the output of the group is ▷ *The Spanish Tragedy* (1587), extremely popular in its own time and the first important ▷ revenge tragedy. He was probably also the author of a lost play on ▷ Hamlet, used by ▷ Shakespeare as the basis of his own; even without this, it is clear that Shakespeare developed the revenge theme from Kyd's first handling of it. Kyd's own starting-point was the tragedies of the Roman dramatist ▷ Seneca, whose *Ten Tragedies* had been published in translation (1559–81). He was not interested in Senecan form, but in Seneca's mingling of dramatic horror and the stern restraints of ▷ Stoic philosophy, both of which were congenial to the Elizabethan age. Kyd's other surviving tragedies are only attributed to him and are much less important: *Soliman and Perseda* (?1588) and *Cornelia* (?1593), an adaptation of a Senecan tragedy by the French dramatist Robert Garnier.

Kyd was arrested in 1593 on suspicion of being involved in anti-immigrant incitement; the Socinian treatise on atheism was raised as an issue later and he implicated ▷ Christopher Marlowe by saying that the treatise really belonged to him. He was released after Marlowe's mysterious death in the same year, and seems to have died soon afterwards in poverty.

Bib: Murray, P. B., *Thomas Kyd*.

Kynaston, Edward (1643–1712)
Actor. Kynaston began his theatrical career in 1660 as a boy actor in women's roles when he was considered 'a Compleat Female Stage Beauty', by the prompter, John Downes.

Kynaston soon transferred to ▷ Killigrew's ▷ King's Company, acting first at the Red Bull Playhouse, and then at the ▷ Vere Street Theatre. He began playing men's parts in addition to women's, but with the full advent of women to the stage, and his own growing maturity, he took on men's roles exclusively.

Kynaston, Sir Francis (1587–1642)
Poet and translator. While at Lincoln's Inn, Kynaston wrote several ▷ masques, and his verse romance, *Leoline and Sydanis* (1642), displays evidence of this early theatrical involvement. The poem follows the structure of a five-act play, similar to ▷ Shakespeare's early comedies, and includes a complicated Renaissance masque set in an ancient Irish court. The language and style are reminiscent of ▷ Spenser, showing quasi-medieval influences, and indeed, Kynaston translated ▷ Chaucer's ▷ *Troilus and Criseyde* into Latin. He also opened an academy for the sons of the nobility called Museum Minervae, where he hoped to teach them a combination of languages, courtly skills and the sciences.

L

La Fayette, Marie-Madeleine Pioche de la Vergue, Comtesse de (1634–93)
French novelist, whose (anonymously published) third work, *The Princess of Clèves* (1678), represents an important early stage in the development of the European novel. As a prototype of the ▷ *Bildungsroman* and of the psychological novel, this story of an unhappy but faithful wife at the 16th-century court of Henri II of France marks the point at which the novel as such emerges in France as a form distinct from the romance. La Fayette was a member of a literary circle in Paris which included La Rochefoucauld, famous for his aphorisms.

La Guma, Alex (1925–85)
South African writer and political activist. He worked as a clerk, bookkeeper and factory hand and was a committee member of the Cape Town Communist Party until its banning in 1950. In 1956 he helped to organize the Freedom Charter and as a result was one of the 156 people accused in the Treason Trial. He began writing for *New Age* in 1960, was placed under house arrest in 1962 and, after the passing of the No Trial Act, was put in solitary confinement. He fled from South Africa in 1967, initially to Britain and then to Cuba, where he was African National Congress representative and where he died in 1985. His novels, set in the black townships and prisons of South Africa under the apartheid regime in the 1960s, are powerful works of protest, showing police violence on the streets and torture in prison, and emphasizing the development of political consciousness as necessary to any better future. The novels include: *A Walk in the Night* (1962); *And A Threefold Cord* (1964); *The Stone Country* (1967); *In The Fog of the Season's End* (1972); *Time of the Butcherbird* (1979).

Lacan, Jacques (1901–81)
French psychoanalyst whose re-readings of ▷ Freud have become influential within the area of literary criticism. Lacan's *The Four Fundamental Concepts of Psychoanalysis* (trans. 1977), and his *Ecrits: A Selection* (trans. 1977), outline the nature of his revision of Freudian psychoanalytic method. A further selection of papers has appeared under the title of *Feminine Sexuality* (trans. 1982). It is to Lacan that we owe the critical terms 'imaginary' and 'symbolic order'. Similarly, it is to his investigation of the operations of the unconscious according to the model of language – 'the unconscious is structured like a language' – that we owe the notion of a 'split' human subject. For Lacan the 'imaginary' is associated with the pre-Oedipal and pre-linguistic relationship between mother and child (the 'mirror' stage) where there appears to be no discrepancy between identity and its outward reflection. This is succeeded by the entry of the infant into the 'symbolic order', with its rules and prohibitions centred around the figure of the father (the phallus). The 'desire of the mother' is then repressed by the child's entry into language and the 'symbolic order'. The desire for 'imaginary' unity is also repressed to form the unconscious, which the interaction between analyst and patient aims to unlock. Some of the fundamental divisions that Lacan has located in the 'subject' have proved highly adaptable for a range of ▷ materialist literary criticisms, including (more controversially) ▷ feminism. As a young man, Lacan was a member of the Surrealist group in Paris, whose activities restated in modern terms a number of key Romantic interests, for example in dreams, madness and the hidden workings of the mind, all topics that his theoretical works deal with in a style frequently as opaque and challenging as poetry.

Lacy, John (?1615–81)
Actor, dancer, choreographer, manager, dramatist, Lacy came to London in 1631, probably to join the Cockpit Theatre, and became a dancer, before his career was interrupted by the ▷ Interregnum. In 1660 he joined ▷ Killigrew's ▷ King's Company, acting first at ▷ Vere Street Theatre, and soon acquired shares in the company's new building at ▷ Bridges Street, becoming a co-manager in 1663.

His first play, *Sauny the Scot* (1667), was a free adaptation of ▷ *The Taming of the Shrew*, written largely to provide a comic vehicle for himself in the part of Sauny, which became one of his major triumphs on stage. He wrote at least three other plays, all adaptations of earlier works.

His reputation was based primarily on his abilities as comedian, with a special talent for mimicry. He was the first to play ▷ Bayes in ▷ George Villiers' ▷ *The Rehearsal*, and became a favourite of ▷ Charles II.

***Lady Audley's Secret* (1862)**
A novel of ▷ sensation by ▷ Mary Braddon. Abandoned by her husband, the heroine deserts her child, leaving it to the care of her father. She adopts a new identity and gains work as a ▷ governess, later accepting an offer of marriage from Sir Michael Audley and thereby becoming a bigamist. When her first husband returns, she attempts to murder him by pushing him down a well, but he survives and Lady Audley is discovered. She is sent to a lunatic asylum, having pleaded hereditary insanity.

The novel was a huge success and has been dramatized, filmed and adapted for television. Feminist critics have read the work as a subversive attack on domestic ideals and feminine stereotypes, and commented on Braddon's use of an angelic-looking blonde as a deviant woman.

▷ Hazlewood, Colin Henry.

Bib: Showalter, E., *A Literature of Their Own*.

Lady Bountiful

A character in ▷ Farquhar's play ▷ *The Beaux' Stratagem*. She is a rich country lady who devotes her time to helping her less fortunate neighbours. She has become a proverbial figure. Farquhar portrays her satirically.

***Lady Chatterley's Lover* (1928)**

▷ D. H. Lawrence's last novel. Constance Reid ('Connie') is the daughter of late-Victorian, highly cultured parents with advanced views. She marries Sir Clifford Chatterley in 1917, when he is on leave from the army; soon afterwards he is wounded, and permanently crippled from the waist down. Connie finds herself half alive, as though she has not been fully awakened; her dissatisfaction, however, does not proceed merely from her husband's disability and sexual impotence, but from the impotence of civilization which the disability symbolizes. She turns to her husband's gamekeeper, Mellors, who fulfils her sexually and emotionally. For Lawrence, the sexual relationship was potentially the profoundest human relationship: to treat it lightly was to trivialize the whole human being, and to regard it with shame was to repress essential human energies. He saw that 'advanced' young people took the former attitude, and that the older generation took the latter; he regarded both attitudes as leading symptoms of decadence in our civilization. He did not suppose that the sexual relationship could in itself constitute a renewal of civilization, but he considered that such a renewal depended on the revitalization of relationships, and that this revitalization could never take place without the recovery of a true and healthy sexual morality. 'I want men and women to be able to think sex, fully, completely, honestly and cleanly.' (*Apropos of Lady Chatterley's Lover*, 1930).

This aim led Lawrence to use unprecedentedly explicit language in conveying the love affair between Connie and Mellors, and the novel thus acquired notoriety. In Britain, the full version was suppressed for immorality, but an expurgated version was published in 1928. An unabridged edition came out in Paris in 1929; the first British unabridged edition was published by Penguin Books in 1959. This led to an obscenity trial, the first test of the 1959 Obscene Publications Act, at which many distinguished authors and critics (including ▷ E. M. Forster) testified in defence of the novel. The acquittal of Penguin had important consequences for subsequent publishing. Lawrence's defence of the novel, *Apropos of Lady Chatterley's Lover*, is one of his most important essays.

▷ Censorship and English literature.

Lady Day

In the Church calendar, the feast of the Annunciation to the Virgin Mary, celebrating the prediction of the Birth of Christ by the Angel Gabriel (*Luke* 1). It is observed on 25 March, which is also a Quarter Day, *ie* it marks the end of the first quarter of the year on which bills, etc. have to be paid. In the ▷ Middle Ages there were other Lady Days commemorating other events in the life of the Virgin Mary.

'Lady of Shalott, The' (1832)

One of the best-known poems by ▷ Alfred Tennyson. The story is an episode from the Arthurian legend of Sir Lancelot, and is to be found in Malory's *Morte d'Arthur* (1469/70) and in the 13th-century French romance *Lancelot*. Tennyson's poem is popular as an example of his extremely musical verse; it is also an example of his recurrent theme of withdrawal from deathly reality into a world of reverie. He expanded the story in his *Lancelot and Elaine* (1859), one of the ▷ *Idylls of the King*.

Lady of the Lake

The name refers to an important role in Arthurian narratives, in origins perhaps that of an otherworldly enchantress, which may be filled by different women (including ▷ Morgan la Fay, Nimue/ Viviane). In ▷ Malory's ▷ *Morte D'Arthur* the Lady of the Lake provides Arthur with ▷ Excalibur. The Lady seems to preside over a group of 'damsels of the Lake' who may take over the central role when necessary, as does the 'damsel' Nimue (or Viviane), the woman who entraps ▷ Merlin, and becomes Lady of the Lake after Balin has beheaded the previous Lady. She is one of the company of women who appear, mysteriously, in a boat to take Arthur to ▷ Avalon. In the ▷ Vulgate version of the story of ▷ Lancelot, the 'Dame du Lac' steals Lancelot away as a child and rears him until he is ready to be knighted at Arthur's court.

***Lady of the Lake, The* (1810)**

A narrative poem by ▷ Sir Walter Scott set in the Scotland of James V (1513–42).

***Lady Windermere's Fan* (1892)**

A play by ▷ Oscar Wilde which brought him his first success in the theatre. Set in the aristocratic or upper-middle-class sections of society, it introduces many of the themes that were to characterize Wilde's later comedies: the struggle of the insiders to maintain their position and of the outsiders to break in. It also deals with the pressure placed on the individual to conform. The play centres around a fan belonging to Lady Windermere, who is revealed to be the daughter of the 'infamous' Mrs Erlynne: a woman who left her husband for a lover who subsequently abandoned her. Mrs Erlynne's attempt to break into the circle is doomed to failure. However, when Lady Windermere's fan is found in the house of the dandy Lord Darlington, Mrs Erlynne is able to save her daughter from social disgrace. The play was a huge success and was published in 1893.

Lagado
In ▷ Swift's ▷ *Gulliver's Travels* (Part III) capital of the island of Balnibarbi and its neighbouring flying island ▷ Laputa.

Lake Poets
A term coined by ▷ Francis Jeffrey in the ▷ *Edinburgh Review* (October 1807) to describe ▷ Samuel Taylor Coleridge, ▷ Robert Southey and ▷ William Wordsworth, who for a time lived in close association in the Lake District. The community of literary and social outlook in their earlier work made it natural to speak of them as a group, but in fact only Wordsworth was profoundly identified with the locality.

Lamarck, Jean-Baptiste (1744–1829)
French pioneer biologist who formulated an explanation of evolutionary change based on the supposition that physical and mental characteristics developed by an individual in response to changes in its environment were physically inherited by its offspring. His theory of evolution through the inheritance of acquired characteristics was highly influential throughout most of the 19th century, despite being usurped by ▷ Darwin's theory of evolution through natural selection. It formed the basis of much of ▷ Herbert Spencer's early thought.

Lamb, Lady Caroline (1785–1828)
Novelist and poet. The only daughter of the 3rd Earl of Bessborough, she was taken to Italy at the age of three and brought up mostly in the care of a servant. Educated at Devonshire House School, she was then looked after by her maternal grandmother, Lady Spencer, who worried about her instability and 'eccentricities'. She married the statesman William Lamb (later the 2nd Viscount Melbourne), but in 1812, just after her marriage, became desperately infatuated with ▷ Byron, of whom she wrote in her diary that he was 'mad, bad and dangerous to know'. After he broke with her, she became increasingly unstable and violent-tempered, and her husband sued for separation becoming temporarily reconciled, however, on the day fixed for the execution of the deed. Meeting Byron's funeral cortège seems to have hastened her disintegration and she ended up living with her father-in-law and only surviving son, an invalid. Her first novel, *Glenarvon* (1816), had a significant, though brief success, due no doubt to its portrayal of Byron and herself in a wild and romantic story. It was published anonymously, though she courted notoriety, being impulsive, vain and excitable to the point of insanity, as well as highly original. She wrote two further novels, *Graham Hamilton* (1822) and *Ada Reis* (1823), and poetry, some of which has been set to music.
Bib: Jenkins, E., *Lady Caroline Lamb.*

Lamb, Charles (1775–1834)
Essayist and critic. His best-known work is his two volumes of the ▷ *Essays of Elia* (1823 and 1833), in which he discourses about his life and times. His *Specimens of English Dramatic Poets who lived about the Time of Shakespeare* directed interest towards ▷ Shakespeare's contemporaries, who had been somewhat neglected in the 18th century, although perhaps not so much ignored as Lamb thought. His friends included many writers of his time, and this fact gives a special interest to his letters. He collaborated with his sister ▷ Mary in adapting Shakespeare's plays into stories for children – *Tales from Shakespeare* (1807). His poems are unimportant but one or two, *eg The Old Familiar Faces* (1798) and the prose-poem, *Dream Children*, recur in anthologies. Lamb seems to have been a man of unusual charm and of gifts which he never allowed himself to display fully and energetically, perhaps because he was haunted by the fear of insanity, to which both he and his sister were subject.
Bib: Lucas, E. V., *Life*; Tillyard, E. M. W. (ed.), *Lamb's Criticism;* Blunden, E., *Charles Lamb and his Contemporaries*; Cecil, D., *A Portrait of Charles Lamb.*

Lamb, Mary Ann (1764–1847)
Sister to ▷ Charles Lamb and daughter of a lawyer, she was brought up in poor circumstances, helping her mother, who worked as a needlewoman. In 1796, overworked and stressed, she pursued her mother's apprentice round the room with a knife in a fit of irritation, and when her mother interposed she killed her. The verdict was one of insanity and she was given into the custody of her brother Charles who took charge of her, finding suitable accommodation for her during her periodic bouts of illness and maintaining a close and affectionate relationship. With Charles, she wrote *Tales from Shakespeare* (1807), designed to make ▷ Shakespeare's stories accessible to the young; *The Adventures of Ulysses* (1808), which was an attempt to do the same for ▷ Homer; and *Mrs Leicester's School* (1809), a collection of short stories.

***Lamia* (1820)**
A poem in pentameter ▷ couplets (▷ metre) by ▷ John Keats, based on a story in Robert

Burton's *Anatomy of Melancholy* (1621–51). In ancient myth a lamia was a female demon, one of whose practices was to entice young men in order to devour them. In Keats' poem a serpent is transformed into a beautiful girl who fascinates a young Corinthian, Lycius. He takes her into his home and makes a bridal feast which is attended by the philosopher Apollonius. Apollonius recognizes the lamia and calls her by her true name, whereupon she vanishes and Lycius dies. The poem, with its rich, fluently enjambed couplets, is an ambiguous plea in favour of aestheticism and sensual escapism. Lamia should be the villain of the poem, but in fact it is Apollonius. The world to which she introduces the young Greek is one of ravishing beauty and magic, and the final triumph of philosophical truth is accompanied by the death of the imagination: 'Do not all charms fly/ At the mere touch of cold philosophy?'

Lammas
In Old English, 'loaf mass'; used formerly in the Church as a thanksgiving for harvest, or harvest festival, celebrated on 1 August. It was also (and in Scotland still is) a Quarter Day for the payment of bills, etc.

Lamming, George (b 1927)
Barbadian novelist. After teaching in Trinidad he moved to Britain in 1950. His novels are concerned with the West Indian identity, both individual and collective, and the aftermath of colonialism and slavery. *The Emigrants* (1954) is a bleak portrayal of identity sought and lost among black emigrants to England in the 1950s; *Season of Adventure* (1960) represents the awakening to a new and more liberal consciousness of the daughter of a West Indian police officer; *Water with Berries* (1971) uses parallels with the colonial symbolism of ▷ Shakespeare's *The Tempest* to represent the historical consequences of colonialism through the personal crises of three West Indian artists living in London. His other novels are: *In the Castle of my Skin* (1953); *Of Age and Innocence* (1958); *Natives of my Person* (1972); *The Pleasures of Exile* (1984).
Bib: Paquet, S. P., *The Novels of George Lamming*.

Lampoon
A personal attack in the form of a verse ▷ satire, usually motivated by mere malevolence. It was common in the later 17th and 18th centuries. A well-known example is ▷ Dryden's attack on ▷ George Villiers, 2nd Duke of Buckingham, as Zimri in ▷ *Absalom and Achitophel*. Libel laws prevented the development of the genre.

Lancelot
One of the most famous of the knights of the ▷ Round Table and lover of Queen ▷ Guinevere. Although Lancelot has no place in ▷ Geoffrey of Monmouth's version of Arthurian history (1138), by the end of the 12th century he was established as an important figure in vernacular Arthurian narratives. It is possible that an ▷ Anglo-Norman narrative about his life and adventures once existed (for it is used as the source of the late-12th century German narrative *Lanzelet*). But the earliest extant romance about Lancelot is ▷ Chrétien de Troyes' *Chévalier de la Charrete* (c 1175), which recounts how Lancelot rescues Guinevere after her abduction by King Meleagant, as well as other episodes in Lancelot's chivalric career in her service. Chrétien does not provide many details of Lancelot's background but his profile is developed considerably in the 13th-century prose *Lancelot* and in other sections of the ▷ Vulgate cycle of romances (from which ▷ Malory draws much of his material for his ▷ *Morte D'Arthur*).

Lancelot is the son of King Ban of Benoic (in western France), who is carried away as a baby and brought up by the ▷ Lady of the Lake (hence his full name Lancelot du Lac), who eventually presents him to ▷ Arthur's court. There he establishes himself, through many adventures, as a knight of superlative status. Though he is a faithful lover of Guinevere, he is induced by a trick to spend the night with Elaine, daughter of King ▷ Pelles, and ▷ Galahad is conceived from their union. He fails to achieve the Quest of the Holy Grail because of his adulterous sin, though he pledges reform. His continuing affair with Guinevere is exploited by Mordred and his company to stir up the trouble in Arthur's court which leads, in part, to the downfall of the kingdom and the court. Lancelot's accidental killing of ▷ Gareth provides a further catalyst. He spends the last years of his life as a hermit (after he has taken his leave of the penitent Queen).

Lancelot is the emotional centre of Malory's reworking of Arthurian narrative, which substantially moderates the criticism he attracts in the ▷ Grail Quest. Indeed, the whole structure of Malory's narrative affirms Lancelot's superlative status: after he has returned from the Grail Quest and resumed his affair, he nevertheless achieves the miraculous healing of Sir Urry, a feat which can only be performed by 'the beste knyghte of the worlde'. Ector's lament for Lancelot is structured around a litany of the superlative qualities of this 'hede of al Crysten knyghtes'.

Landon, Letitia Elizabeth
▷ L.E.L.

Landor, Walter Savage (1775–1864)
Poet. Of upper-class background he was expelled from Oxford University for his intemperate radicalism, and lived for many years in Florence.

He wrote the ▷ blank verse epic, *Gebir* (1798), the tragedy *Count Julian* (1812), and collections of verse: *Hellenics* (1847), *Italics* (1848), *Heroic Idylls* (1863). He was a fine classical scholar, producing a ▷ Latin version of *Gebir*, and his imagination was essentially literary in its inspiration. He is now chiefly remembered for his prose *Imaginary Conversations* (1824, 1828, 1829) between such figures of the past as Dante and Beatrice, and Elizabeth and Mary Tudor. His quarrelsome but generous personality was caricatured by Charles Dickens as Boythorn in *Bleak House* (1852–3).
Bib: Pinsky, R., *Landor's Poetry*.

Lanfranc (d 1089)
Archbishop of Canterbury, 1070–89, under ▷ William I, first of the Norman kings. Lanfranc, an Italian by origin, corrected and reformed the English church, and yet helped the king to resist papal interference.

Langham Place Group, The
▷ Women's Movement.

Langhorne, John (1735–79)
Poet, private tutor, clergyman and Justice of the Peace. He wrote sermons, translated ▷ Plutarch and edited the poems of ▷ William Collins (1765). His own poems include exercises in the numerous genres current in the 18th century: topographical verse, animal fables, ▷ pastorals, ▷ elegies and didactic epistles. His most important work, *The Country Justice* (1774–7), in pentameter couplets (▷ metre), mixes didacticism and sentimental anecdote. Its satire on the Poor Laws imitates ▷ Oliver Goldsmith's ▷ *The Deserted Village* (1770).

Langland, William (?1330–?81)
Little is known for certain about the life of William Langland, author of ▷ *Piers Plowman*, other than what can be gleaned from his literary portrait, refracted through the fictional persona of the dreamer/narrator Will. From this, especially from a passage inserted into the C text of *Piers Plowman* (Passus 6), Langland seems to have been a cleric in minor orders, originally from the West Midlands area, who made a living by saying prayers for the dead. In one manuscript of the C text there is a biographical note which identifies him as the son of Stacy de Rokayle of Shipton-under-Wychwood, in Oxfordshire. Although some other alliterative poems have been attributed to him in the past, there is no evidence for his composition of any other poems than *Piers Plowman*, which seems to have been the work of a lifetime in its own right.

Langue
This term appears throughout ▷ Ferdinand de Saussure's *Course in General Linguistics* (1915) to denote the system of signs which makes up any language structure. According to Saussure, individual utterances (parole) are constructed out of elements which have no existence 'prior to the linguistic system, but only conceptual and phonetic differences arising out of that system'. This observation is fundamental to ▷ Structuralism, which is concerned with the positioning of particular elements within a nonvariable structure. 'Langue' is the term used to denote the linguistic structure itself, that is the rules which lie behind particular linguistic events.

Lanyer, Aemilia (1569–1645)
Poet. Aemilia was the daughter of one musician, Baptista Bassani, and wife to another, Alfonso Lanyer, yet she seemed to have provided for herself through the system of ▷ patronage, being mistress to Lord Hunsdon, ▷ Shakespeare's patron, and later employed by Margaret Clifford, Countess of Cumberland, the mother of ▷ Lady Anne Clifford. Many of the details of her life come to us through the entries in ▷ Simon Forman's casebook or diary, as Lanyer consulted – and probably slept with – this well-known Renaissance astrologer. In 1611 she published *Salve Deus Rex Judaeorum* (*Hail God, King of the Jews*) in an attempt to gain economic preferment. While the poem is introduced with the usual variety of panegyric verses (including one to the Countess of Cumberland), it also contains a proto-feminist prose address to women readers, a defence of Eve and other female characters in the biblical narrative, and the earliest known English country-house poem, about Cookham, the Cumberland residence. As such, Lanyer may be read as innovative both in form and content, and as participating in the current debate about the vices and virtues of women (▷ *Querelle des Femmes*). It is also worth noting that, despite A. L. Rowse's protestations, there is no evidence to support the hypothesis that Lanyer was the dark lady of Shakespeare's sonnets (▷ Shakespeare – sonnets).
Bib: Travitsky, B. (ed.), *The Paradise of Women*; Beilin, E. V., *Redeeming Eve*; Hannay, M. P., *Silent But For The Word*.

Laputa
In ▷ Jonathan Swift's ▷ *Gulliver's Travels*, the flying island in the ▷ satire against the ▷ natural philosophers of Part III.

Larkin, Philip (1922–85)
Poet. He was the most eminent of the group known as the 'New Lines' poets (from an anthology of that name, 1956 ed. by Robert Conquest) otherwise called the ▷ Movement. Many of them held posts in universities, and their work is characterized by thoughtfulness, irony, self-doubt and humility. These qualities are in accord with the imaginative temper of ▷ Thomas Hardy's poetry; Larkin, who greatly admired Hardy, has also been compared to ▷ W. H.

Auden, though his political conservatism and concern to proclaim the pathos and humour of everyday experience rather than address the 'academic' reader represent a turning away from the technical radicalism of writers like Auden and ▷ T. S. Eliot. Publications: *The North Ship* (1945); *The Less Deceived* (1955); *The Whitsun Weddings* (1964); *High Windows* (1974); Editor *Oxford Book of Twentieth Century English Verse* (1973). Larkin also wrote two novels, *Jill* (1946) and *A Girl in Winter* (1947); see also his book of essays *Required Writing* (1983). Larkin was also known for his passion for jazz music; see *All What Jazz?: A Record Diary 1961–1968* (1970).
Bib: Thwaite, A. (ed.), *Larkin at Sixty*; Motion, A., *Philip Larkin*; Booth, J., *Philip Larkin*.

***Last Chronicle of Barset, The* (1867)**
The last of the ▷ Barsetshire novels, about the politics of the imaginary cathedral town of Barchester, by ▷ Anthony Trollope. It centres on one of Trollope's best characters – the Reverend Josiah Crawley, the curate of Hogglestock. A poor, proud, isolated man with rigorous standards, he is accused of theft and persecuted by the arrogant Mrs Proudie, wife of the bishop. A minor theme is the engagement of Major Grantly to Mr Crawley's daughter, Grace, in defiance of the wishes of his father the Archdeacon. It is often considered to be the best of Trollope's novels.

Latimer, Hugh (?1490–1555)
One of the chief English Protestant reformers. He was favoured by ▷ Henry VIII and supported the king's separation of the ▷ Church of England from papal authority. However, he went further than Henry in his independence of thought, and in 1539 he resigned the bishopric of Worcester because he could not accept Henry's conservative statement of doctrine, the Act of Six Articles. Under the more Protestant regime of ▷ Edward VI he became a very popular preacher, but in 1555 he was burnt alive as a heretic under the Catholic ▷ Mary I. Among his memorable works is his letter to Henry VIII (1530) urging the free circulation of the ▷ Bible in translation.
▷ Reformation.

Latin literature
Rome began as a small Italian city state, and grew to an empire that surrounded the Mediterranean and extended as far north as the borderland between England and Scotland. Politically, it established the framework out of which modern Europe grew. Culturally, in part by native force and in part by its assimilation and transmission of the older and richer culture of Greece, its literature became the basis of European values, and especially those values that arise from the individual's relationship to his society.

Between 300 and 100 BC, Rome began to produce literature, and at the same time, after its conquest of the rich Greek colonies in southern Italy, to expand its imaginative and intellectual vision and to increase and refine the expressiveness of the Latin language through the study of ▷ Greek literature. Primitive Roman literature had been of two kinds: that of the recording and examination of public life and conduct in annals of eminent men and in oratory, and that of the distinctively Roman art of ▷ satirical comedy. These centuries saw the production of the comic dramas of ▷ Plautus and of ▷ Terence. The orator and historian ▷ Cato the Censor upheld the virtues of Roman severity against Greek sophistication and luxury; the dominant figure, however, was the poet Ennius (239–169) who preserved a balance between Greek and Latin values by emulating ▷ Homer in a patriotic epic in Latin idiom and Greek metre, the *Annales*.

The first half of the first century BC was the last great period of the Roman Republic. Active participation in politics was still one of the principal concerns of Roman aristocrats, and by this time Romans had studied and profited from lessons in depth and force of thinking from Greece. ▷ Cicero was the great persuasive orator of public debate; such was the power of his eloquence that the period is often known as the Ciceronian age. ▷ Julius Caesar's terse, practical account of his wars in Gaul and invasion of Britain shows a different kind of prose excellence, and the vividness of Sallust's histories of episodes in recent Roman history is different again. It was thus an age of prose, but it included one of the finest of all philosophical poems, the *De Rerum Natura* ('Concerning the Nature of Things') of ▷ Lucretius, who expounded the thought of the Greek philosopher ▷ Epicurus. It included also the passionate love poems of ▷ Catullus, who gave new vitality to Greek mythology.

Julius Caesar's great-nephew, ▷ Augustus Caesar, became the first Emperor in 27 BC, and he ruled till his death in AD 14. The Republic ended, and with it the kind of moral thought and eloquence which had made Cicero so famous. Roman literature, however, entered upon its most famous period – the Augustan Age. If the Empire had not quite reached its greatest extent, its power was nonetheless at its peak; the old traditions of austerity and energy were not yet extinct; civilization, wealth and sophistication had not yet overbalanced into decadence resulting from excessive luxury. Augustus himself was a patron of letters. In prose, the outstanding writer was the historian ▷ Livy, but it was above all an age of poetry. The most famous of Roman poets, ▷ Virgil, celebrated great traditions, looked back to by a stable society, in which active political participation had become difficult or unimportant. His contemporary, ▷ Horace, celebrated the values of civilized private life. Tibullus, Propertius, and above all ▷ Ovid were poets of pleasure appealing to the refined taste of an elegant society.

The last period of Roman literature lasted approximately a hundred years from the death of Augustus. The Emperors were bad, the idea of Rome was losing much of its force, society was showing symptoms of decadence. The best writers became more detached from and more critical of Roman society. In the philosophy and drama of ▷ Seneca, the heroic poetry of ▷ Lucan, the satire of Persius (34–62), the Greek philosophy of ▷ Stoicism seemed the strongest defence of human dignity against social oppression and distress. The most powerful work, however, was the savage satire of ▷ Juvenal and the sombre history of his time by ▷ Tacitus.

Literature in Latin did not of course end here, nor did it end with the Roman Empire in the 5th century AD. Latin became the language of the Roman Catholic Church, and therefore of the early medieval educated classes. It remained a living, growing language till its style was fixed by ▷ Renaissance scholars in the 16th century. Even in the 17th century, ▷ Francis Bacon wrote much of his philosophy in Latin, and ▷ Milton wrote Latin poetry. Classical Latin was read and admired in medieval England, but knowledge of it was incomplete and inaccurate; much of this knowledge was obtained (for instance, by ▷ Chaucer) from contemporary French and Italian writers whose traditions were closer to classical Latin. Virgil retained great prestige, and Terence was studied in the monasteries for the purity of his style. After 1500, the Renaissance caused English writers to study and emulate the classical writers. Writers modelled themselves on styles of classical prose; the terse manner of Seneca and Tacitus was imitated by Bacon, whereas the eloquent flow of Cicero was emulated by ▷ Edmund Burke. More important than the study of styles was the way in which English writers again and again measured themselves against their own society by placing themselves in the position of Roman writers, and then assessed their society from a Roman standpoint. So, in the late 16th century ▷ Donne modelled his elegies on those of Ovid, and a little later ▷ Ben Jonson rewrote the lyrics of Catullus; in the 17th century Milton emulated Virgil as Virgil had once emulated Homer; in the 18th century ▷ Pope took the standpoint of Horace, and ▷ Samuel Johnson adopted that of Juvenal.

▷ Classical education.

Laud, William (1573–1645)
Archbishop of Canterbury under ▷ Charles I. He firmly resisted the desire for further reform among the religious extremists, and even tried to impose religious uniformity upon Scotland. His rigour was partly responsible for the discontent that led to the outbreak of the ▷ Civil War in 1642. Parliament, which had already secured his imprisonment in 1641, ordered his execution in 1645.
Bib: Carlton, C., *Archbishop William Laud*.

Laurence, Margaret (1926–87)
Canadian novelist and short-story writer. She wrote a series of novels and short stories centred on Manawaka, Manitoba, a fictional small town on the Canadian prairies: *The Stone Angel* (1964); *A Jest of God* (1966); *The Fire Dwellers* (1969); *A Bird in the House* (stories; 1970); *The Diviners* (1974). These works explore the social history of Canada, through the lives of several generations of women, dealing with themes such as the claustrophobia of small town life, the force of social inhibitions, the quest for identity and the importance of a sense of the past. Laurence's earlier work reflects the seven years which she spent in Somalia and Ghana between 1950 and 1957. *A Tree For Poverty* (1954) is a translation of Somali oral poetry and prose; *This Side Jordan* (1960) is a novel about racial tension in the Gold Coast (now Ghana); *The Tomorrow Tamer* (1963) is a collection of stories; *The Prophet's Camel Bell* (1963) is a travel narrative; *Long Drums and Cannons; Nigerian Dramatists and Novelists 1952–66* (1968) is literary criticism.

▷ Post-colonial literature.
Bib: Thomas, C., *Laurence*.

Lautréamont, Comte de (pseudonym of Isidore-Lucien Ducasse) (1846–70)
French writer of lyrical prose pieces which appeared under the title *Les Chants de Maldoror* in 1868, with a slightly expanded posthumous version in 1890. The hero, Maldoror, is a demonic figure and his world is one of delirium and nightmare interspersed with blasphemy and eroticism. The hallucinatory quality of this work attracted the interest of the Surrealists, who claimed Lautréamont as one of their own and promoted his work. Their interest has been carried forward into contemporary French criticism.

▷ French literature in England.

Lawes, Henry (1596–1662)
Composer. One of the most well-known English Renaissance composers after ▷ Dowland, Lawes is primarily of concern to literature students because of his close collaboration with several distinguished poets of his time. After being made a court musician to ▷ Charles I in 1631, he collaborated with ▷ Carew, ▷ Herrick, ▷ Lovelace, ▷ Suckling and ▷ Waller. But Lawes' most famous work was with ▷ Milton, for whom he composed musical accompaniments to ▷ *Arcades* and *Comus*, and he produced and acted in the latter performance. The success of Lawes' collaboration with the poets of his day resided partly in his belief that there was

an indissoluble link between musical rhythms and the metrical patterns of spoken language.
Bib: Evans, W. M., *Henry Lawes: Musician and Friend of Poets.*

Lawrence, D. H. (David Herbert) (1885–1930) Novelist, poet, critic. The son of a coal-miner, he passed through University College, Nottingham, and for a time worked as a teacher. He eloped to Italy with Frieda Weekley, the German wife of a Nottingham professor, in 1912, and married her in 1914. His hatred of World War I, together with the German origins of his wife, caused them difficulties in 1914–18; after the war they travelled about the world, visiting especially Australia, Mexico and the U.S.A. Lawrence died of tuberculosis at Vence in France in 1930. His reputation has grown gradually, and he is likely always to remain a controversial figure.

Lawrence's life, art, criticism, poetry, and teaching were all so closely related that it is unusually difficult to distinguish one aspect of his achievement from all the others. Misunderstandings about his supposed obsession with sexuality and the needless legal action for obscenity in connection with two of his novels (▷ *The Rainbow* and ▷ *Lady Chatterley's Lover*) initially distorted judgement of his work, but he is now firmly established as a major ▷ modernist novelist. On the other hand, he has been the subject of irrelevant hero-worship which is equally distorting, and which he would have repudiated. He was a deeply religious – though not a Christian – writer who believed that modern man is perverting his nature by the wilful divorce of his consciousness from his spontaneous feelings. He has been accused of social prejudice. It is true that he was keenly critical of society; but he was the first major English novelist to have truly working-class origins, and this, together with his wide range of friendships with men and women of all classes, gave him unusual perceptiveness into the contradictions of English society. His attitude to women has been severely criticized (see K. Millett, *Sexual Politics*; 1970), as have the general political implications of his ideas (see J. Carey 'D. H. Lawrence's Doctrine' in S. Spender (ed.), *D. H. Lawrence: Novelist, Poet, Prophet*; 1973).

Novels: *The White Peacock* (1911); *The Trespasser* (1912); ▷ *Sons and Lovers* (1913), an autobiographical novel, was his first distinguished work, and it was followed by what are generally regarded as his two masterpieces, ▷ *The Rainbow* (1915) and ▷ *Women in Love* (1921); *The Lost Girl* (1920); *Aaron's Rod* (1922); *Kangaroo* (1923) about Australia; *The Plumed Serpent* (1926) about Mexico; *Lady Chatterley's Lover* (1928), banned except for an expurgated edition until 1959. The unfinished *Mr Noon* was published in 1984. He also wrote several volumes of short stories and novellas which include much of his best fiction. Among the best known of these are *St Mawr, The Daughters of the Vicar, The Horse Dealer's Daughter, The Captain's Doll, The Prussian Officer, The Virgin and the Gipsy.*

One of Lawrence's most distinguishing features as an artist in fiction is his use of natural surroundings and animals realistically and yet symbolically, to express states of experience which elude direct description. This 'poetic' element in his fiction is reflected in much of his verse; some of this is in rhymed, metrical stanzas, but a great deal of it is free of verse conventions and close to the more condensed passages of his prose. Lawrence began writing poetry at the time when ▷ Imagism was seeking more concrete expression, and he contributed to Imagist anthologies. Some critics (*eg* A. Alvarez, *The Shaping Spirit*) are inclined to see his poetry as among the most important produced in the century, deserving to be set alongside the work of ▷ T. S. Eliot and ▷ W. B. Yeats.

Lawrence's descriptive, didactic, and critical prose is also important. His psychological essays, *Psychoanalysis and the Unconscious* (1921) and *Fantasia of the Unconscious* (1922) are imaginative, not scientific works, and contribute to the understanding of his creative mind. His descriptive volumes, *Sea and Sardinia* (1921), *Morning in Mexico* (1927), show his outstanding powers of presenting scenes with sensuous immediacy, and his characteristic concentration of all his interest – moral and social, as well as aesthetic – on to natural environment. The same concentration is to be seen in his critical and didactic writing; he brought moral, aesthetic, and social judgements into play together. Much of his best critical writing is contained in the posthumous volumes *Phoenix* I and II; the *Study of Thomas Hardy* is of particular importance for the understanding of Lawrence's own work. His letters are being published in seven volumes (vols 1–3, 1979–84).

Lawrence wrote eight plays including: *The Widowing of Mrs Holroyd* (1920); *Touch and Go* (1920); *David* (1927); *A Collier's Friday Night* (1965); *The Daughter in Law* (1967); *The Fight for Barbara* (1967). These have never received the attention accorded the rest of his work.
Bib: Leavis, F. R., *D. H. Lawrence, Novelist*; Lawrence, F., *Not I, but the Wind*; Hough, G. G., *The Dark Sun*; Kermode, F., *Lawrence*; Sagar, K., *The Life of D. H. Lawrence*; Macleod, S., *Lawrence's Men and Women*; Smith, A. (ed.), *D. H. Lawrence and Women*; Pinkney, T., *D. H. Lawrence*; Williams, Linda Ruth, *Sex in the Head*; Widdowson, Peter (ed.), *D. H. Lawrence.*

Lawrence, G.A. (George Alfred) (1827–76) Novelist. Lawrence's first novel was the enormously successful *Guy Livingstone* (1857), whose fighting, hunting, womanizing hero was the most extreme example of the glorification of masculinity common to a group of writers in the 1840s and 1850s sometimes known as the 'muscular' school (other novelists included ▷ Charles Kingsley and ▷ Thomas Hughes). Lawrence had attended ▷ Thomas Arnold's ▷ Rugby, and his portrayal of the school in *Guy Livingstone* is even more violent than that in Hughes' *Tom Brown's Schooldays*, published the same year. His subsequent novels were largely written in a similar vein, and include *Maurice Derring* (1864) and the nationalistic *Brakespeare* (1868), set in the Hundred Years' War.

▷ Historical novel.

Lawrence T. E. (Thomas Edward) (1888–1935)
Soldier and author, T. E. Lawrence is more popularly known as 'Lawrence of Arabia'. This title was inspired by his guerilla leadership activities in Arabia during World War I, of which he subsequently gave an epic and heroic account in the classic *Seven Pillars of Wisdom* (1926) – a shortened version of this book was later published as *Revolt in the Desert* (1927).

In many ways Lawrence epitomizes the image of the 'boy's own hero'; organizing in 1916 the Arab revolt against the Turks and developing imaginative and risky guerilla tactics, he was offered, but refused, both the Victoria Cross and a knighthood. After the war he went on to enlist in the ranks of the R.A.F. under two pseudonyms. His diaries for this period were published in 1955 as *The Mint*.

Lawrence was also something of an archaeologist and translator; in 1932 he published a translation of ▷ Homer's ▷ *Odyssey*. In 1962 the film director David Lean turned Lawrence's life and work with the Arab freedom movement into the cinema classic *Lawrence of Arabia*.

Lay
A term in use from the medieval period for a lyrical or narrative composition, especially one recited or sung to music. The 19th-century revival of interest in the Middle Ages stimulated a revival of the lay form, which may be exemplified in poems such as ▷ Walter Scott's *Lay of the Last Minstrel*.

Laȝamon
Composer of the *Brut*, a history of Britain from its foundation by Brutus to the establishment of Saxon control over the island in Middle English ▷ alliterative verse, based on ▷ Wace's *Roman de Brut* (completed 1155). Laȝamon's text is difficult to date precisely: it was composed some time between 1189 and 1275 (the date of the two extant manuscripts). Most of what is known about Laȝamon himself derives from the highly stylized prologue to the *Brut*, which introduces the writer as a priest, who lives at Arley Kings (in Worcestershire) and as which describes his process of composition (his search for books and his act of compilation from at least three sources).

The *Brut* is of great interest, not only because it contains the earliest account of Arthurian history in English (and its depiction of ▷ Arthur's reign is considerably amplified from the *Roman de Brut*), but because of its approach to the act of commemorating the past as a whole. It is composed in a style which echoes that of earlier English poetry and seems to have self-consciously archaic touches built into the text. Laȝamon's work goes against the grain of most vernacular historical narrative, in so far as it appears to cultivate a sense of the 'pastness' of the history being related, through its use of a deliberately archaic style which enhances the memorability of the history itself. Some of the archaisms of vocabulary and the stylization of descriptive passages in the British Library Cotton Caligula A ix manuscript have been revised in the text contained in the Cotton Otho C xiii manuscript the difference between the two versions is not one of date but of literary style. The *Brut*'s regional point of origin helps provide some context for this interesting literary experiment. Worcester is the centre of an area where the greatest continuity can be traced between pre- and post-Conquest literary traditions: the copying and studying of ▷ Old English works seems to have been actively fostered there for some time after the Conquest. There are echoes of phrases and expressions drawn from Old English homilies (notably by ▷ Aelfric), written in rhythmical ▷ alliterative prose, and these seem to have provided Laȝamon with some of the resources for his creation of an archaistic literary medium.

▷ Round table.

Bib: Brook, G. L., and Leslie, R. F., (eds.), *Laȝamon's Brut*; Brook, G. L. (ed.), *Selections from Laȝamon's Brut*.

Le Carré, John (David John Moore Cornwell) (b 1931)
Le Carré is one of the most intriguing of Cold War novelists, managing to write challenging and sophisticated work for a popular audience. Le Carré's work is grim, bitter and unromantic, and his characters are brilliantly bleak psychological cases of individuals (often secret service workers) in morally compromised situations. His reputation was established with his third novel, *The Spy Who Came In From The Cold* in 1963, in which Le Carré's most famous character, George Smiley, appears. Although most of his works – including *Call for the Dead* (1961); *The Looking-Glass War* (1965); *A Small Town in Germany* (1968); *Tinker, Tailor, Soldier, Spy* (1974); *The Honorable Schoolboy* (1977); *Smiley's People* (1980), *The Perfect Spy* (1986) and *Our Game* (1995) – are concerned with espionage, in *The Naive and Sentimental Lover* (1971) and *The Little Drummer Girl* (1983), he turned to the Middle East and

explored the Palestinian situation. Le Carré's work is eminently filmable, and many of his works have been translated into feature films or television dramas. In 1990 a film was made of Le Carré's 'glasnost' novel *The Russia House* (1988); scripted by Tom Stoppard, it was the first Hollywood film to be made on location in the (former) Soviet Union.
Bib: Barley, Tony: *Taking Sides: The Fiction of John Le Carré.*

Le Fanu, J. (Joseph) S. (Sheridan) (1814–73)
Novelist and journalist. Born in Dublin of an old Huguenot family related by marriage to the family of the dramatist ⊳ Sheridan, he wrote poetry as a child, including a long Irish poem at the age of 14. After education by his father and tutors, he went to Trinity in 1833, writing for the *Dublin University Magazine* and in 1837 joining the staff. He later became editor and proprietor. In 1837 he published some Irish ⊳ ballads and in 1839 was called to the bar, although he did not practise, soon turning to journalism. He bought *The Warden*, *Evening Packet* and part of the *Dublin Evening Mail*, later amalgamating the three into the *Evening Mail*. In 1844 he married Susan Bennett and withdrew from society after her death in 1858, when he wrote most of his novels, many in bed, on scraps of paper. His writing is ingeniously plotted, shows an attraction to the supernatural and has been increasingly well received this century. The novels include *The House by the Churchyard* (1863), *Wylder's Hand* (1864), *Uncle Silas* (1864), *Guy Deverell* (1865), *The Tenants of Malory* (1867), *A Lost Name* (1868), *The Wyvern Mystery* (1869), *Checkmate* (1871), *The Rose and the Key* (1871) and *Willing to Die* (1873), which was finished a few days before his death. The short stories, *In a Glass Darkly*, appeared in 1872 and a collection of neglected stories, *Madam Crowl's Ghost and Other Tales of Mystery*, in 1923.

Leadbetter, Mary (1758–1826)
Poet and story-writer. Leadbetter was an Irish Quaker who wrote poetry and short prose pieces which pictured the country life she saw about her. Her writing is often ⊳ didactic, for example, she wrote against slavery (⊳ Abolition Literature) and class prejudice. ⊳ Maria Edgeworth wrote the notes for her *Cottage Dialogues Among the Irish Peasantry* (1811).
⊳ Irish literature in English.

Leapor, Mary (1722–1746)
English poet. She was from the labouring classes, and worked as a kitchen maid. She was able to write poetry with the support of a patron, Bridget Fremantle, and *Poems upon Several Occassionns* (1748, 1751) was first published after Leapor died of measles. It included the ironical 'Essay on Woman', commenting '*Hymen* lifts his sceptered Rod, / and strikes her glories with a fatal nod.' Her verse often uses a figure called 'Mira' to explore the familial and sexual problems of women, and she strongly associates poetry with sleep and dream. In 'The Cruel Parent: a Dream' ⊳ Gothic elements interwine with labouring-class problems, including starvation. In 'a Verse Epistle to a Lady' she describes the working woman poet who 'rolls in treasures till the breaking day: . . . till the shrill clock impertinently rings,/ and the soft visions move their shining Wings'. She also wrote a blank-verse tragedy, but died while its staging was being discussed. She left a library of only sixteen or seventeen volumes, including some ⊳ Pope and ⊳ Dryden.
⊳ Collier, Mary; Little, Janet; Yearsley, Ann.
Bib: Landry, D., *The Muses of Resistance.*

Lear, Edward (1812–88)
Comic poet. He wrote *The Book of Nonsense* (1846) and *Nonsense Songs, Stories, and Botany* (1870) for the grandchildren of the Earl of Derby. Like ⊳ Lewis Carroll, who wrote the *Alice* books for children, Lear's poems for children show remarkable freedom of fantasy; in consequence, the 20th century, with its new science of psychoanalysis, has seen in them unsuspected depths of interest. The poems combine grotesque comedy with haunting melancholy. He did much to popularize the limerick. He illustrated the poems himself with extremely witty line drawings. Lear was by profession a landscape painter, but his elaborate landscape paintings have much less distinction and interest than his drawings and sketches.
⊳ Nonsense literature; Children's literature.
Bib: Davidson, A., *Life*; Noakes, V., *Life*; Sewell, E., *The Field of Nonsense.*

Leavis, Frank Raymond (1895–1978)
Critic. From 1932 till 1953 he edited ⊳ *Scrutiny*, a literary review with high critical standards, and pervaded by his personality. It maintained that the values of a society in all its activities derive from its culture, and that central to British culture is English literature; that a literature can be sustained only by discriminating readers, and therefore by a body of highly trained critics working together especially in the collaborative circumstances of a university (*Education and the University*; 1943). The need for the testing of judgements by collaborative discussion is important in Leavis' view of criticism. Unfortunately, collaboration may become uncritical discipleship, and this was one of the two unfortunate consequences of the exceptional force of Leavis' personality. The other unfortunate consequence was the hostility which this force of personality aroused in many critics who were not among his collaborators and followers. He maintained that true critical discernment can be achieved only by a total

response of mind – intellectual, imaginative and moral; thus a critical judgement reflects not only the work of literature being judged, but the worth of the personality that makes the judgement, so that Leavis' censure of critics with whom he strongly disagreed was sometimes extraordinarily vehement, as in his *Two Cultures?: The Significance of C. P. Snow* (1962). However this vehemence was a price he paid for his determination to sustain a living tradition of literature not only by assessing contemporary writers with the utmost rigour, but also by reassessing the writers of the past, distinguishing those he thought had a vital relevance for the modern sensibility from those that stand as mere monuments in academic museums. Such evaluative treatments caused him to be widely regarded as a destructive critic; his attack on the three-centuries-long prestige of ▷ Milton (*Revaluation* 1936 and *The Common Pursuit* 1952) gave particular offence.

Leavis' intense concern with the relationship between the kind of sensibility nourished by a literary culture and the quality of a society as a whole has a historical background that extends to the beginning of the 19th century. It first appears in ▷ Wordsworth's *Preface to the Lyrical Ballads* (1800), is to be felt in the writings of the 19th-century philosopher ▷ John Stuart Mill (see *Mill on Bentham and Coleridge*, ed. by Leavis, 1950), and is explicit in ▷ Matthew Arnold's writings, especially *Culture and Anarchy* (1869). Later the theme is taken up by the novelists, *eg* in ▷ Gissing's ▷ *New Grub Street* and, both in his novels and in his criticism, by ▷ D. H. Lawrence. The outstanding importance of novels in connection with the theme has caused Leavis to be foremost a critic of the novel; perhaps his most important single book is *The Great Tradition: George Eliot, Henry James, Jospeh Conrad* (1948), but this should be read in conjunction with his books on Lawrence and (with Q. D. Leavis) on *Dickens the Novelist* (1971). Although still influential, Leavis must now be considered together with more contemporary literary theory, such as ▷ post-structuralism which has tended to challenge radically and contradict vehemently his criticism.

Leavis, Q.D. (1906–81)
Literary critic, Q.D. Leavis was educated at Cambridge in the 1920s (she was a student of I.A. Richards), and became a central figure in what came to be known as 'Cambridge criticism', the 'traditional' form of moral criticism (as distinct from Richards' New criticism), which is more readily associated with her husband, ▷ F.R. Leavis. As one of the founders of the journal ▷ *Scrutiny* and writer of the influential *Fiction and the Reading Public* (1932), Q.D. Leavis helped to establish English literature as a discipline in its own right and in the form it took from the 1930s onwards, *Fiction and the Reading Public* is primarily a sociological and psychological account of popular reading patterns, which consolidates her more fundamental celebration of great literary classics as the primary source of our culture's essential humane values. Leavis' work is thus often read as the direct descendant of the cultural criticism of Victorian critic ▷ Matthew Arnold, but it is also important for a psychological dimension, and, in her essays, for a serious interest in the work of women writers, which is not generally seen as characteristic of her *Scrutiny* contemporaries. In tandem with bringing up a family, she also wrote *Dickens the Novelist* (1971) with her husband, and a wide range of essays, which are collected in three volumes as *Collected Essays* (1983).

Lee, Harriet (1757–1851)
Novelist and playwright. The sister of ▷ Sophia Lee, with whom she wrote *Canterbury Tales* (twelve tales, two by Sophia, published 1797–1805). The tales cover conventional material: for example, one is a ▷ Gothic romance and another offers a sensational account of the ▷ French Revolution. One story, however, *Kruitzer, The German's Tale* (1801), depicts the suffering of a woman unable either to escape her weak husband, or to reform her evil, but Romantic son, and was acknowledged by Byron as the source of his *Werner* (1821). Lee's dramatic output achieved much less recognition. *The New Peerage, or Our Eyes may Deceive Us* (1787) and *The Mysterious Marriage, or the Heirship of Roselva* (1795–8) are unremarkable in their plots, and the characters are somewhat ▷ flat and stereotyped. She was proposed to by ▷ Godwin, but turned him down.
Bib: Punter, D., *The Literature of Terror: A History of Gothic Fictions from 1765 to the Present Day*; Rodgers, K., *Feminism in Eighteenth-century England*.

Lee, Nathaniel (?1653–92)
Dramatist. After an unsuccessful acting career Lee turned to writing plays. He became popular for his extravagant tragedies which included *Nero* (1674), *Sophonisba* (1675) and *Gloriana* (1676), and his *The Rival Queens* (1677) heralded a return to the use of blank verse for tragedy. His most serious play, ▷ *Lucius Funius Brutus*, was considered too politically dangerous and was banned after only a few performances. Towards the end of his life Lee spent five years in ▷ Bedlam and died after a drinking bout.

Lee, Sophia (1750–1824)
English novelist and dramatist, elder sister of ▷ Harriet Lee, and friend of ▷ Ann Radcliffe. Her historical fiction included *The Recess, or a Tale of Other Times* (1783–5), and she co-wrote *Canterbury Tales for the Year 1797* with her sister.

Lee, Vernon (1856–1935)
▷ Pseudonym of essayist, novelist and short story writer Violet Paget. She was born near

Boulogne, France, and travelled around Europe as a young girl, receiving her education from various ▷ governesses. Lee's literary career was full of eccentric oscillations between fame and infamy. Her first major work was *Studies of the 18th Century in Italy* (1880), which was a great success, but her first novel (*Miss Brown*, 1884) damaged her reputation, as did the short story 'Lady Tal' (*Vanitas*, 1892), which contained an ill-considered and barely disguised portrait of novelist ▷ Henry James. Thereafter she turned her attention to essays, and *Genius Loci: Notes on Places* (1899) was a success. During the First World War she wrote a pacifist trilogy, *Satan the Waster* (1920), which was generally condemned, although it was better received when re-issued in 1930. Lee left England to avoid the disapproval of her family and friends of her ▷ lesbianism. In Paris she was a frequent visitor at Natalie Barney's (1876–1972) famous Rue Jacob salon. Other works by the prolific Lee include *Gospels of Anarchy* (1980), *The Tower of Mirrors* (1914), and two volumes of *Supernatural Tales*, published posthumously in 1955 and 1956.

Leech-Gatherer, The
Sometimes used as an alternative title for ▷ William Wordsworth's poem ▷ *Resolution and Independence*.

Legend of Good Women, The
A story-collection composed by ▷ Chaucer, probably not long after ▷ *Troilus and Criseyde*, but revised some time later (the Prologue exists in two versions known as 'F' and 'G'). Dating the poem is difficult, but it seems to be Chaucer's earliest work using the decasyllabic couplet form, the staple of the ▷ *Canterbury Tales*. The story-collection is framed by a ▷ dream-vision narrative in which Chaucer, as writer, is tried in a ▷ pastoral court of love as a sinner against the God of Love. The intervention of a legendary good woman, Alceste, helps the poet/narrator, who promises to do penance for his literary misdeeds (one of which is having written about the infidelity of Criseyde) by writing a work composed of exemplary stories of good women who are true lovers. The work is to be a secular legend, in effect, not containing stories of the lives of those who have suffered for the Faith, but of those who have suffered for their love.

Although the Prologue suggests that the *Legend* is to be a large narrative project, only nine stories are extant (including those of Cleopatra, Thisbe, Dido, Hypsipyle and Medea, Lucrece, Ariadne, Philomela, Phyllis, Hypermestra). Narrating the stories themselves is an exercise in the art of abbreviation, for only cameo narratives are provided of their lives. But the art of abbreviation has a greater thematic point in some of the stories: it is only by abbreviating half of the story of Medea, for example, that she can be given a place in the company of good women. The construction of the dream-frame is influenced by the work of French love vision poets (especially ▷ Guillaume de Machaut) and the form of the stories themselves owes much to ▷ Ovid's *Heroides*. Although the collection has not always been very sympathetically received by modern readers, it seems to have been much read and admired in the 15th century.
Bib: Frank, R. W., *Chaucer and the Legend of Good Women*.

Lehmann, Rosamond (1901–90)
Novelist and short-story writer. The poet and critic John Lehmann was her brother. Her novels depict the experience of educated and sensitive women, focusing in particular on infatuation, betrayal and the contrast between the relative safety of childhood and the disillusionment of adolescence and adulthood. They make considerable use of memories and impressions, rendered in a lyrical prose style. She was initially associated with ▷ Virginia Woolf and ▷ Elizabeth Bowen for her rendering of the consciousness of women, but her work is generally regarded as narrower in scope. Her novels are: *Dusty Answer* (1927); *A Note in Music* (1930); *Invitation to the Waltz* (1932); *The Weather in the Streets* (1936); *The Ballad and the Source* (1944); *The Echoing Grove* (1953); *A Sea-Grape Tree* (1976). Story collection: *The Gipsy's Baby* (1946). She also published an autobiography, *The Swan in the Evening* (1967).

Leibniz, Gottfried Wilhelm (1646–1716)
German philosopher and mathematician, born in Leipzig, who became one of the leading representatives of the German ▷ Enlightenment. His invention of the calculus about the same time as ▷ Newton led to a dispute as to who can be called its originator. In 1676 Leibniz met ▷ Spinoza, whose work had a considerable influence on him, along with that of ▷ Descartes and ▷ Hobbes. He persuaded Frederick I to found an Academy of Sciences in Berlin in 1700, of which he himself became the first president. Leibniz developed a theory of matter, outlined in his *Theodicee* (1710) and *Monadologie* (1714), as a finite series of indivisible particles which he called 'monads', each a concentration of energy, and each representing a microcosm of the universe. They belong to a hierarchy whose highest manifestation is God, and they move according to God's laws. Leibniz argued that God, being omnipotent and perfect, could only have created the best world possible, a view propounded by ▷ Pope in his ▷ *Essay on Man* as 'One truth is clear, Whatever IS, is Right', and satirized by ▷ Voltaire in *Candide* as 'all is for the best in this best of all possible worlds'.

Bib: Hazard, P., *European Thought in the Eighteenth Century*; Sambrook, J., *The Eighteenth Century: The Intellectual and Cultural Context of English Literature 1700–1789*.

Leicester, Robert Dudley, Earl of (?1531–88)
One of the principal favourites of ▷ Elizabeth I and for some time expected to become her husband. The *Kenilworth Festivities* were organized by Leicester in an attempt to woo the queen. This is also one example of his role as a major patron of the arts and literature in the Elizabethan period. He was also the uncle of ▷ Sir Philip Sidney, killed at Zutphen during Leicester's campaign to assist the Netherlands in their resistance to Spain. Like his nephew Essex, he showed staunch Protestant leanings through his support of the Puritans in the Privy Council during the 1570s. Leicester had the brilliance which Elizabeth liked in her personal favourites, although for her statesmen she preferred more sober types such as Cecil (▷ Burghley) and ▷ Walsingham. Scandalous stories were rumoured about his relationships with women, and in particular about his early marriage with Amy Robsart.

▷ Essex, Robert Devereux, Earl of; Gascoigne, George.

Bib: Rosenberg, E., *Leicester, Patron of Letters*.

Leigh, Dorothy (c 1616)
Writer on motherhood. Leigh was a widow who chose to write a book of instruction for her three young sons and their future wives that was published as *The Mother's Blessing* (1616). The book consists of four parts: a dedication to ▷ Elizabeth of Bohemia asking, from the precarious position of a woman writer, for the queen's protection; a letter to her sons explaining her intentions; an allegorical poem about bees; and the main body of the advice, which covers personal behaviour and spiritual practice.

▷ Elizabeth Grymeston, Lady Elizabeth Clinton.

Bib: Travitsky, B. (ed.), *A Paradise of Women*.

Leitmotif
▷ Motif

L.E.L., Letitia Elizabeth Landon (1802–38)
Poet and novelist. One of the most popular and prolific authors of her day, Landon published under the initials 'L.E.L.'. Her poetry was influenced by ▷ French literature, rather than English, although she is clearly regarded as a ▷ Romantic poet; collections include, *The Fate of Adelaide* (1821), *The Improvisatrice* (1824), *The Troubadour* (1825), and *The Golden Violet* (1827). Landon wrote of her own tendency towards sentiment:

Aware that to elevate I must first soften, and that if I wish to purify I must first touch, I have ever endeavoured to bring forward grief, disappointment, the fallen leaf, the faded flower, the broken heart, and the early grave.

Her first novel, *Romance and Reality*, appeared in 1831; it is a personalized view of London society and includes thinly disguised portraits of the ▷ Victorian novelist, Edward Bulwar-Lytton and his wife. This provided salacious information for contemporary readers, since Landon's name was linked romantically with Lytton's, as well as to the journalist William Maginn's, and when rumours of an abortion followed, her engagement with John Forster was broken off. Landon wrote of her own misfortunes:

Alas! that ever
Praise should have been what praise has
been to me –
The opiate of the mind.

Landon eventually married George Maclean, the governor of Cape Coast Castle on the Gold Coast in 1838, but died four months after reaching Africa supposedly from an overdose of prussic acid.

Bib: Aston, H., *Letty Landon*; Showalter, E., *A Literature of Their Own*.

Lely, Sir Peter (1618–80)
Painter, born in Germany to Dutch parents; his name was originally Pieter van der Faes. He studied in Haarlem, and came to England in 1641. Here he began by painting landscapes and historical and religious subjects, but then turned to portrait work, painting prolifically. He was employed first by ▷ Charles I, then by ▷ Cromwell, and then as a court painter by ▷ Charles II, who knighted him in 1679. Among his best-known works are portraits of the monarchs and their families, including a double portrait of Charles I and his brother the Duke of York, which inspired ▷ Lovelace's 'See what a clouded Majesty . . .', as well as a series of *Beauties* of the court of Charles II, including one of ▷ Nell Gwynn (now kept at Hampton Court). The 13 so-called 'Greenwich Portraits', of English admirals who fought in the second Dutch war, are also highly regarded today.

Lennox, Charlotte (?1727–1804)
Charlotte Lennox was probably born in America, and grew up in New York. From an early age she is known to have been in London trying, unsuccessfully, to make a career on the stage. In 1747 she published *Poems on Several Occasions*, and in 1750, the year in which her appearance on the stage is last reported, she brought out her first novel, *The Life of Harriot Stuart*.

Lennox's literary talent was enthusiastically supported by ▷ Samuel Johnson and ▷ Henry

Fielding. In 1752 *The Female Quixote* established her name as a writer. The novel tells of a naïve heroine, Arabella, whose view of the world is foolishly filtered through the romances she reads. Lennox uses this framework to satirize sexual stereotypes and the social conventions of courtship.

Johnson's help in finding publishers for Lennox was probably partly motivated by his knowledge of her circumstances as well as her literary achievements. Her husband, Alexander, was a constant drain on the family's finances, and Lennox's writing provided their only support. She worked on translations and adaptations to supplement their income, and produced three volumes of ▷ Shakespeare's sources, with Johnson's encouragement. Her final novel *Euphemia* (1790) explores the position of women in marriage, reflecting her own experience with the spendthrift husband she eventually left.

Lesage, Alain-René (1668–1747)
French novelist and playwright. He wrote two important ▷ picaresque narratives, both set in Spain and offering a cynical but humorous view of human desires and motives: *Gil Blas* (1715–35), which influenced such novelists as ▷ Fielding and ▷ Smollett, and *The Devil Upon Two Sticks* (1707), in which the devil removes the roofs from the houses of Madrid to reveal the greed of the inhabitants. Lesage was a professional writer who produced a large number of comic plays.

Lesbian and Gay Writing
Many major literary figures throughout history have depicted same-sex relations and/or expressed sexual desire for members of the same sex: for example, ▷ Plato, ▷ Shakespeare, Thomas Mann, ▷ Marcel Proust, ▷ Oscar Wilde, ▷ E. M. Forster, ▷ Virginia Woolf, ▷ Patrick White (to name only a few). The definitions accorded to such practices and feelings, and the extent to which they have been subject to oppression, have varied. In Ancient Greece male homosexuality was accepted within a particular framework: the teaching relationship between experienced men and boys is often depicted in the literature of the period in this way. However, criticism which has, until recently, ignored the homoerotic elements in ▷ Renaissance literature, began to acknowledge the possibility of homosexual ▷ discourses within hitherto heterosexual romanticized texts. The practice of cross-dressing in ▷ Shakespeare's ▷ comedies and the universal use of boy-actors to play female roles have been recognized as ways in which sexuality and gender-roles were questioned and challenged. For example, ▷ Rosalind's final speech in ▷ *As You Like It*, where the boy-actor acknowledges his sex while still disguised as the heroine, opens out a whole range of sexual interpretations. In poetry, ▷ Marlowe's ▷ *Hero and Leander* focuses on the male protagonist as the centre of male erotic attention, while ▷ Katherine Philips' stated love for her female friends has led to her inclusion in the lesbian canon. There are also references to homosexuality in some Restoration poetry. For example, ▷ Rochester, in a 'Song' (1672–3), refers to 'a sweet, soft page [who] does the trick [sexual intercourse] worth forty wenches'. Some lines by ▷ Aphra Behn have been interpreted as having a homosexual content, notably her 'To the Fair Clarinda, Who Made Love to Me, imagin'd more than Woman' (1688).

It was not until the 19th century, however, that the term 'homosexual' emerged and the term 'heterosexual' followed it; the tragic case of Oscar Wilde focused a great deal of public attention (and prejudice) on male homosexuality. During most of the period during which the novel has flourished there has been widespread persecution and oppression of homosexual people and homophobia in many of the discourses of culture. Hence homosexuality has tended to be accorded a marginal place in literary representation, and when it has been shown, has usually been hedged about with implications of the exotic, the abnormal or at least the exceptional. When ▷ Radclyffe Hall published her plea for the recognition and acceptance of lesbianism, *The Well of Loneliness*, (1928) – even though it had a sympathetic preface from the sexologist ▷ Havelock Ellis, testifying to its scientific accuracy – the book was condemned as obscene and banned. This is in line with official attempts to promote heterosexual activity within marriage as the healthy norm. In the 1950s and 1960s aversion therapy was used in an effort to impose or restore this norm in homosexuals – The Kinsey Reports on *Sexual Behaviour in the Human Male* (1948) and *Female* (1953), however, showed that what had been defined as deviant behaviour was far more widespread than had been believed, thus challenging the 'naturalness' of heterosexuality. Homosexual behaviour in certain circumstances defined as private was decriminalized, but not until ten years after the Wolfenden report recommended it. E.M. Forster's *Maurice*, which ends with the protagonist choosing a life of freedom rather than repression, was not published until 1971, after Forster's death. However, novelistic discussions of homosexuality tended to promote toleration. There have been important fictional presentations from outside England, for example by Jean Genet (*Our Lady of the Flowers*), William Burroughs (*The Naked Lunch*) and James Baldwin (*Giovanni's Room*). Recent scholarship has identified gay and lesbian communities as important centres of innovation; see Shari Benstock, *Women of the Left Bank*, an account of women writers in Paris in the early years of this century, which identifies a close connection between the writers' political experience as lesbians and their readiness to experiment with representation. Since the 1960s the active assertion of gay and lesbian rights and identifies in Europe and the USA have contributed to a rich and diverse field of fiction, including the work of such contemporary novelists as ▷ Sara Maitland, Michelene Wandor, ▷ Alan Hollinghurst, ▷ Maureen Duffy and ▷ Jeanette Winterson.

Bib: Dollimore, J., *Sexual Dissidence: Augustine to Wilde, Freud to Foucault*; Bristow, J., *Sexual Sameness: Textual Differences in Lesbian and Gay Writing*; Sedgwick, E., *Epistemology of the Closet*; Fuss, D., *Inside/Out: Lesbian Theories, Gay Theories*; Meyers, J., *Homosexuality and Literature 1890–1930*; Jay, K. and Glasgow, J. (eds.), *Lesbian Texts and Contexts: Radical Revisions*.

Lesbianism

The Criminal Law Amendment Act of 1885, amended to outlaw homosexual acts in private, referred only to men. Lesbianism has never been a crime in Britain. This was not due to a permissive or enlightened attitude on the part of the state, but because legislators were apparently at a loss to explain to Queen Victoria what homosexual acts existed between women, who were conventionally credited with little sexual awareness in middle-class circles. Male ▷ homosexuality came to prominence through newspaper reports of court cases but, as Ronald Pearsall (see bibliography) has suggested, if male homosexuality was 'the love that dared not speak its name', female homosexuality could not speak its name because it was undefined. There was a conspiracy of silence or professed and outraged ignorance, concerning possible sexual activity between women. ▷ Swinburn's *Poems and Ballads* (1866) violently condemned by John Morley in the ▷ *Saturday Review* because it contained poems such as 'Anactoria', in which Sappho reproaches a fickle female lover. Morley expressed relief that such poems 'will be unintelligible to a great many people, and so will the fevered folly of "Hermaphroditus", as well as much else that is nameless and abominable'. His greatest wish was that young women should remain in ignorance of the existence of such matters lest they became corrupted. Lesbianism was identified as a medical problem in Germany, but even there authors were unperceptive and inaccurate about the reality and potential of sexual love between women. Towards the end of the century passionate attachments between women were championed by the more radical New Women, a fact noted by Edward Carpenter in *Love's-Coming-of-Age* (1896). Carpenter discusses the use of the term 'urnings' (coined by the Austrian writer K.H. Ulrichs) to describe people born 'on the dividing line between the sexes... while belonging distinctly to one sex as far as their bodies were concerned they may be said to belong *mentally* and *emotionally* to the other'. Carpenter himself preferred the use of the term 'The Intermediate Sex'.

Close emotional and even physical friendships between women were sentimentalized, yet at the same time many women sought the emotional and spiritual closeness, and often the sexual satisfaction they missed in their marriages, in their friendships with other women. Novelists like ▷ George Meredith were charmed and completely unthreatened by powerful emotional relationships between women. In his ▷ *Diana of the Crossways* (1885) the passionate but possibly asexual friendship between Antonia and Lady Emma Dunstane offers sustenance and a refuge from the dismal failure of Antonia's marriage. In ▷ Charlotte Brontë's ▷ *Villette* Lucy Snowe cures herself of her passion for Dr John by 'redirecting' it to Ginevra Fanshawe under the temporary licence offered by the part she is coerced into performing in the school play.

The writer and reformer Edith Simcox was passionately involved with a largely unresponsive ▷ George Eliot who was the unwitting inspiration for much of Simcox's reforming zeal. Other such relationships that went beyond simple friendship include the attachment between ▷ Jane Welsh Carlyle and ▷ Geraldine Jewsbury, and Lillian Faderman (see bibliography) believes their love was reinforced by a 'mutual struggle to transcend the role allotted to Victorian women'. The heroines of ▷ Christina Rossetti's poem ▷ 'Goblin Market' enjoy a close and sensuous relationship which went unremarked by the censors. The same is true of Cytherea Aldclyffe's passionate response to Cytherea Graye in ▷ Thomas Hardy's novel *Desperate Remedies* (1871). The term 'Boston Marriage' was commonly used in late 19th-century New England to describe a long-term monogamous relationship between two unmarried women. ▷ Henry James' novel ▷ *The Bostonians* (1885) is a largely unsympathetic study of such a relationship between Olive Chancellor and Verena Tarrant, although James himself had no prejudice against lesbianism, having viewed it at close range in the relationship between his sister Alice and Katharine Loring in Boston. Other women who formed close, passionate and supportive relationships with each other include the sensation novelist ▷ Marie Corelli and Bertha Vyver and the poet ▷ Eliza Cook and Charlotte Cushman. Lesbianism is explicitly condemned in ▷ Eliza Lynn Linton's *The Rebel of the Family* (1880).

▷ Field, Michael; Somerville and Ross.

Bib: Pearsall, R., *The Worm in the Bud: The World of Victorian Sexuality*; Faderman, L., *Surpassing the Love of Men*;

Cox, D.R. (ed.), *Sexuality and Victorian Literature*.

Lessing, Doris (b 1919)
Novelist and short-story writer. Born in Persia (now Iran) and brought up in Southern Rhodesia (now Zimbabwe), she settled in London in 1949. Her writing spans an exceptionally wide range of genres, settings and narrative techniques, but is unified by certain persistent concerns: the analysis of contemporary culture and of social process; a sense of 20th-century history as catastrophic and an attempt to link this to personal unhappiness; a mystical and sometimes utopian emphasis on higher states of consciousness; an intense anger at social injustice; an interest in radical revisions of the self and of personal and sexual relations.

Her first novel, *The Grass is Singing* (1950) is the story of a relationship between a white woman and a black man in Rhodesia, and was followed by the *Children of Violence* series, a *Bildungsroman* about a young Rhodesian girl in revolt against the establishment, ending in England with a vision of future chaos and a tentative hope for a utopian future. The series consists of: *Martha Quest* (1952); *A Proper Marriage* (1954); *A Ripple from the Storm* (1958); *Landlocked* (1965); *The Four Gated City* (1969). ▷ *The Golden Notebook* (1962) exemplifies the element of ▷ post-modernist experiment in Lessing's work, in its use of multiple narratives and its concern with fiction and the reconstruction of the self, but it also addresses social issues of the 1960s: the crisis in radical politics, women's liberation, the value of psychoanalysis. During the 1970s Lessing started to write ▷ science fiction, and has remained a fierce exponent of its value as a literary form. Her series *Canopus in Argus: Archives* comprises: *Shikasta* (1979); *The Marriages Between Zones Three, Four and Five* (1980); *The Sirian Experiments* (1981) *The Making of the Representative for Planet 8* (1982); *Sentimental Agents* (1983). These novels attempt to set human history and human relationships in the context of a battle between good and evil in the universe and an evolutionary quest for a higher state of being. Lessing has continued to show her inventiveness and flexibility with *The Diary of Jane Somers* (1984), a critique of society's treatment of the old, *The Good Terrorist* (1985), a study of the making of a terrorist, and *The Fifth Child* (1988), which uses elements of the horror story genre to explore problems in liberal ideals. Her other novels are: *Briefing for a Descent into Hell* (1971); *The Summer Before Dark* (1972); *Memoirs of a Survivor* (1974). Story collections include: *This Was the Old Chief's Country* (1951); *Five: Short Novels* (1953); *The Habit of Loving* (1957); *A Man and Two Women* (1963); *African Stories* (1964); *Winter in July* (1966); *The Black Madonna* (1966); *The Story of a non-Marrying Man* (1972).

Her other works include: *Going Home* (1957), a study of Southern Rhodesia; *In Pursuit of the English* (1960), a study of England in (1960), *A Small Personal Voice: Essays, Reviews, Interviews* (1974); *African Laughter: Four Visits to Zimbabwe* (1992); *London Observed: Stories and Sketches* (1992); *Under My Skin* (1994) is the first volume of an autobiography. *The Making of the Representative for Planet 8* has been turned into an opera, with music by Philip Glass (1988).
Bib: Sage, L., *Doris Lessing*; Sprague, C., and Tiger, V. (eds.), *Critical Essays on Doris Lessing*; King, J., *Doris Lessing*; Sprague, C., *Rereading Doris Lessing*; Taylor, J. (ed.), *Notebooks, Memoirs, Archives*; Maslen, E., *Doris Lessing*.

***Lesson of the Master, The* (1892)**
A story by ▷ Henry James. Its theme is the barrier set up against the true artist by supposedly cultivated society, which can understand nothing about the artist's dedication and can therefore only hinder him by its unintelligent praise based on false standards.
▷ Short story.

Letter-writing
This is clearly an important branch of literature even when the interests of the letter is essentially historical (*eg* the ▷ Paston Letters) or ▷ biographical. Letters may also be, by intention or by consequence of genius, works of intrinsic literary value. For example, because of the restrictions imposed upon Renaissance women writers, their canon often exists in the form of letters rather than published works. See, for example, ▷ Ann Bacon's letters to her son ▷ Francis Bacon, Lady Margaret Cunningham, ▷ Lady Jane Grey and the correspondence between ▷ Joan and Maria Thynne.

The 18th century (the age of the epistolary novel) was more than any other period when letter-writing was cultivated as an art: see, above all, the letters of ▷ Horace Walpole and those to his son by ▷ Lord Chesterfield – the former a record of events and the latter consisting of moral reflections. Earlier than the 18th century, postal services were not sufficiently organized to encourage regular letter-writing, and the art of familiar prose was inadequately cultivated; by the mid-19th century, communications had improved enough to make frequent and full letter-writing redundant. By then letters had intrinsic, literary interest chiefly by virtue of the writers' talent for literary expression in other modes of writing, added to the accident that they found letters a congenial means of communication.

In the first 30 years of the 19th century the Romantic habit of introspection resulted in a quantity of extremely interesting letters: those of ▷ Keats, ▷ Byron, ▷ Coleridge and ▷ Lamb are outstanding. Many 20th-century writers have had large collections of

their letters published; ▷ Virginia Woolf and ▷ D. H. Lawrence wrote copious amounts, and ▷ Sylvia Plath's *Letters Home* (written to her mother) is a famous later anthology.
▷ Biography.

Levellers
An important political party during the period of the ▷ Civil War and the Commonwealth. It first became prominent in 1647; the term was first found in a letter of November of that year, describing them as people who wanted to 'rayse a parity and community in the kingdom'. Mainly found among the soldiers and opposed to kingship, the Levellers feared the Parliamentary leaders were insufficiently firm. Two documents were composed by them, *The Case of the Army Truly Stated* and *The Agreement of the People*, asking for a dissolution of ▷ Parliament and change in its future constitution. They were at odds with ▷ Oliver Cromwell, who suppressed the mutinies they engineered; Parliament declared other Leveller writings by John Liburne treasonable and in March 1649 their leaders were arrested. A public meeting in London in their support, and risings at Burford and Banbury were suppressed. Associated with them were the 'True Levellers' or 'Diggers' of April 1649, who took possession of some unoccupied ground at Oatlands in Surrey and began to cultivate it. The leaders, arrested and brought before Fairfax, denounced landowners.
▷ Civil wars; Cromwell, Oliver; Utopianism.

Lever, Charles James (1806–72)
Irish novelist. Famous in the 19th century for his vigorous comic novels about Irish country life and life in the army, eg *Harry Lorrequer* (1837), *Charles O'Malley* (1841), *Tom Burke of Ours* (1843). He was criticized for perpetuating the Englishman's comic notion of the Irish character – the 'stage Irishman' caricature – but ▷ William Makepeace Thackeray, who was a friend of Lever and parodied him in *Novels by Eminent Hands*, declared (in *A Box of Novels*) that Lever was true to Irish nature in being superficially humorous but sad at heart.
▷ Irish literature in English.
Bib: Stevenson, L., *Dr Quicksilver: The Life of Charles Lever*.

Levertov, Denise (b 1923)
Poet and prose writer. Levertov was born and grew up in Britain but has lived in the U.S.A. since 1948. Her first publication was *The Double Image* (1946), and her work was also included in Kenneth Rexroth's *The New British Poets* (1948). Her most recent work is published in Britain by Bloodaxe, and she also features in the important *Bloodaxe Book of Contemporary Women Poets* (1985). Her volumes of verse include: *Collected Earlier Poems 1940–1960*; *Poems 1960–1967*; *To Stay Alive* (1971); *Life in the Forest* (1978); *Candles in Babylon* (1982); *Selected Poems* (1985); *Oblique Prayers* (1985). Her volumes of prose essays include: *The Poet in the World* (1973) and *Light up the Cave* (1982).

***Leviathan* (1651)**
▷ Hobbes, Thomas.

Levy, Amy (1861–89)
Jewish novelist and poet, the daughter of Lewis Levy and Isabelle Levin, she was born in Clapham, London, and was the first Jewish woman to attend Newnham College, Cambridge. While still a student, she published her first volume of poetry, *Xantippe and Other Verse* (1881). *A Minor Poet and Other Verse* appeared in 1884, and in 1888 *The Romance of a Ship* and *Rueben Sachs*, a novel describing the London Jewish community in which she grew up. *Miss Meredith* and *A London Plane Tree and Other Verse*, both published in 1889, mark the end of Levy's literary career. She killed herself in the same year. She was actively involved in ▷ feminist and radical debates as well as deeply concerned about the position of Jewish people in Europe.
▷ Women's Movement
Bib: Leighton, A., and Reynolds, M, (eds.), *An Anthology of Victorian Women Poets*.

Lewes, George Henry (1817–78)
Philosopher and critic. He wrote on a wide variety of subjects but his most remembered work is his *Life of Goethe* (1855), researched with George Eliot's (1819–80) help. Other works include *The Biographical History of Philosophy* (1845–6), studies in biology such as *Studies in Animal Life* (1862), two novels, *Ranthrope* (1847) and *Rose, Blanche and Violet* (1848), critical essays on the novel and the theatre, and, his most important philosophical book, *Problems of Life and Mind* (1873–8), the last volume of which was completed by George Eliot after his death. He collaborated with ▷ Thornton Leigh Hunt in founding the *Leader* and was first editor of the *Fortnightly Review* 1865–6. In 1854 he left his wife, who had had three sons by Hunt, and lived with Mary Ann Evans (George Eliot) until his death.
Bib: Ashton, R., *G.H. Lewes*; Kitchell, A. T., *George Lewes and George Eliot*.

Lewis, Alethea (1750–1827)
Novelist. A ▷ didactic writer whose works are thoughtful but often heavily moralistic and naive in style. Her novels include *Plain Sense* (1795) for ▷ Minerva, and the ▷ Gothic *The Nuns of the Desert, or The Woodland Witches* (1805). She also wrote a philosophical treatise under the pen-name

'Eugenia De Acton', *Essays on the Art of Being Happy* (1803).

Lewis, Alun (1915–44)
Poet and short story writer. Born at Cwmaman, near Aberdare, Glamorgan, educated at Cowbridge Grammar School, University College of Wales, Aberystwyth, where he read history, and subsequently at Manchester University, Alun Lewis taught at Lewis School, Pengam, Monmouthshire, from 1938 until 1940 when he enlisted in the Royal Engineers. In his only four years of public recognition as a writer during his entire war service, Alun Lewis published four books containing 95 poems and 25 stories. His short life was fraught with intellectual and emotional tensions through his being forced into early maturity through his involvement in the war. His poetry collections were *Raiders' Dawn* (1942) and the posthumously published *Ha! Ha! Among the Trumpets* (1945); his short stories, *The Last Inspection* (1942), with the remainder collected after his death in *The Green Tree* (1948) as well as an autobiographical volume entitled *Letters from India* (1946). A recent resurgence of interest in his work some forty years after his untimely death encouraged the publication of *Letters to My Wife*, ed. Gweno Lewis (1989), a *Collected Stories*, ed. Cary Archard (1991), and a *Collected Poems*, also *ed.* Cary Archard (1994). The enigmatic circumstances of his death in Burma, at first attributed to an accidental shooting, not it appears may have been suicide through an unhappy love affair despite his deep devotion to his wife Gweno. His premature death in these circumstances was a tragedy of largely unfulfilled promise.
Bib: Pikoulis, J., *Alun Lewis – A Life*; Stephens, M. (Ed.), *The Oxford Companion to the Literature of Wales*; Jones, G. and Rowlands, J., *Profiles*.

Lewis, C. S. (Clive Staples) (1898–1963)
Novelist, critic, poet and writer on religion. Born in Belfast, Lewis served in France during World War I. From 1925 until 1954 he was a Fellow of Magdalen College, Oxford and tutor in English, and from 1954 was Professor of Medieval and Renaissance Literature at Cambridge. His fiction reflects an interest in fantasy, myth and fairytale with an underlying Christian message. He wrote a ▷ science-fiction trilogy: *Out of the Silent Planet* (1938); *Perelandra* (1943) (as *Voyage to Venus*, 1953); *That Hideous Strength* (1945). *The Lion, The Witch, and The Wardrobe* (1950) was the first of seven fantasy stories for children. His popular theological works include: *The Problem of Pain* (1940); *Miracles* (1947) and *The Screwtape Letters* (1942), which takes the form of letters from an experienced devil to a novice devil. *A Grief Observed* (1961) is a powerful autobiographical work, an account of his grief at the death of his wife. He also wrote such classics of literary history as *The Allegory of Love* (1936) and *A Preface to Paradise Lost* (1942).
▷ Children's books.

Lewis, Matthew Gregory ('Monk') (1775–1818)
Writer whose sensational novel *The Monk* (1796) had such success in its day that he was nicknamed after it.
▷ Gothic novels.

Lewis, Percy Wyndham (1882–1957)
Painter, novelist, critic and polemical journalist. Born in the USA, he came to England as a child and studied art at the Slade School in London and then in Paris. Before 1914 he was leader of the Vorticist movement in painting, which, drawing on the French Cubist movement and the Italian Futurist movement, advocated dynamic, semi-abstract representation of angular, precise and rhythmical forms. Lewis carried over this predilection for vigour and energy into literature, taking a boldly independent attitude to modern culture, rather like that of the poet Ezra Pound with whom he edited the review *Blast* (1914–15), and asserted the right and the power of the intellect to take command in the cultural crisis. He was opposed to domination by political ideology (though he wrote favourably of Hitler in 1931), by psychological cults and by the bureaucratic and welfare state; he made it his principal aim to expose the confusion of mind which he considered to be overwhelming 20th-century man, and the hollowness of humanity which he believed to be the consequence of encroaching mechanization. He had something in common with his friend T. S. Eliot (see *The Waste Land*, for example) but never became a Christian; with ▷ D. H. Lawrence whose mysticism he nevertheless despised; with ▷ James Joyce, though he was strongly opposed to his subjective ▷ stream of consciousness technique; with ▷ F. R. Leavis and the other ▷ *Scrutiny* critics, who, however, rejected him as brutally negative. He prided himself on his very distinctive style of expression, which is energetic and concentrates on presenting the externals of human nature with icy clarity.

His outstanding writings are probably his novels and stories: *Tarr* (1918); *The Wild Body* (stories; 1927); *The Apes of God* (1930 – a satire); *Snooty Baronet* (1932); *The Revenge for Love* (1937 – considered by some critics to be his best novel); *The Vulgar Streak* (1941); *Rotting Hill* (stories; 1951); *Self Condemned* (1954); and the four-part fable *The Human Age – The Childermass* (1928), *Monstre Gai* (1955), *Malign Fiesta* (1955) to have been completed by *The Trial of Man* which he did not live to finish.

His ideas are expounded in his philosophical work *Time and Western Man* (1927) and his autobiographies *Blasting and Bombardiering*

(1937) and *Rude Assignment* (1950). He wrote notable literary criticism in *The Lion and the Fox: the Role of Hero in the Plays of Shakespeare* (1927), *Men Without Art* (1934) and *The Writer and the Absolute* (1952).
Bib: Grigson, G., *A Master of Our Time*; Kenner, H., *Wyndham Lewis*; Meyers, J., *The Enemy*; Materer, T., *Wyndham Lewis: the Novelist*; Meyers, J. (ed.), *Wyndham Lewis: a Revaluation*; Jameson, F., *Fables of Aggression: Wyndham Lewis, the Modernist as Fascist*; Symons, J. (ed.), *The Essential Wyndham Lewis: An Introduction to His Work.*

Lexis
A term in linguistics denoting the total vocabulary in a language. In literary studies, however, it refers to the language used in a writer's works or in a single individual work. In practice, the word tends to be used interchangeably with ▷ diction.

***Liberty, On* (1859)**
A political essay by ▷ John Stuart Mill, in which he discusses how far and in what ways the state is entitled to interfere with the liberty of individuals. He concludes that in general this interference should be restricted to the protection of other individuals, and of individuals collectively considered as society. Mill was mainly alarmed lest a new tyranny should arise from democratic majorities who might be indifferent to minority rights.

Licensing Act
▷ Theatres.

***Life and Death of Mr Badman, The* (1680)**
▷ *Badman, The Life and Death of Mr.*

***Life of Jonathan Wild the Great, The* (1743)**
▷ *Jonathan Wild the Great, The Life of.*

***Life of Samuel Johnson, The* (1791)**
▷ Boswell, James.

Lilliput
The island in Part I of ▷ Swift's ▷ *Gulliver's Travels*; the Lilliputians are diminutive in body, and their corresponding pettiness of mind is intended as satirical comment on the pettiness of contemporary English politics and society.

Lillo, George (1693–1739)
Dramatist. Lillo owned a jewellery shop in Moorgate Street, writing plays after hours, and contemporary descriptions of his character talk of him as a modest and moral man. His first piece, *Silvia, or the Country Burial*, a ballad-opera in the style of ▷ *The Beggar's Opera*, was staged at ▷ Drury Lane in 1730, and in 1731 Lillo produced *The Merchant*, afterwards renamed ▷ *The London Merchant, or the History of George Barnwell*, based on an old ▷ ballad. *The Merchant*, with its focus on a middle-class character led astray by temptation, and the depiction of his suffering, distress, and eventual penitence and execution, helped to establish the so-called domestic or bourgeois tragedy on the English stage, and was also influential in Germany and France via ▷ Lessing and ▷ Diderot. Lillo's other plays include *The Christian Hero* (1734), *Fatal Curiosity* (1736), again based on an old ballad about a murder, and *Arden of Feversham* (1736), drawing, like its ▷ Elizabethan predecessor, on an account by ▷ Holinshed.

Lily, William (?1468–1522)
Scholar; a pioneer of Greek studies, and part-author with Colet of a famous textbook on Latin that was still in use in the 19th century.

Limerick
A kind of comic verse ▷ epigram which hardly ever varies from the following form:

There was a faith-healer of Deal
who said, 'Although pain isn't real,
If I sit on a pin
And it punctures my skin
I dislike what I fancy I feel!'

The form was popularized by the comic poet ▷ Edward Lear, though he was not its inventor. Whatever the derivation of its name, it seems to have no traceable connection with the town and county of Limerick in Ireland.

Linacre, Thomas (?1460–1524)
Physician, and a pioneer in Greek and Latin scholarship. He was chiefly responsible for founding the College of Physicians in 1518, and translated into excellent Latin some of the works of the Greek physician Galen. He is, however, less famous for his literary work than for the nobility of his character and for his zeal in promoting the study of medicine at Oxford and Cambridge.

Lincoln's Inn Fields Theatre
In March 1660 ▷ Sir William D'Avenant began conversion of Lisle's Tennis Court, built between 1656 and 1657 at Lincoln's Inn Fields, in order to house the ▷ Duke's Company under his newly confirmed patent from the king. The resulting theatre introduced the proscenium, or framed stage, to the English theatre for the first time. But increasingly the building was felt to be too small, and in 1671 the company moved to ▷ Dorset Garden. It was occupied by various companies until, in 1714, it was refurbished in grand style by Edward

Shepherd, with mirrors lining the interior walls, and reopened under the auspices of the actor-manager ▷ John Rich.

Lindsay (Lyndsay), Sir David (c 1490–1555)
Scottish poet, courtier to James IV and 'Usher' of the infant James V. He was entrusted with various overseas diplomatic missions and knighted in 1542. He is most famous for his satirical work, especially his verse ▷ morality play, *Ane Satyre of the Thrie Estaitis* (1540), which analyses the corruption of Church and State. His other works include 'The Dream' (1528), an allegorical lament on the mismanagement of the realm; *The Complaynt and Testament of the Papyngo* (Parrot) (1530), in which a parrot is used as the mouthpiece for advice to the king and warnings to courtiers; and his two-part narrative about a Scottish laird, the *Historie of ane Nobil and Vailzeand Squyer, William Meldrum* (1550).
Bib: Hamer, D. (ed.), *Poetical Works*; Kinsley, J. (ed.), *A Satire of the Three Estates*.

Linton, Eliza Lynn (1822–98)
Novelist, journalist and poet, born in Keswick, the sixth daughter and twelfth child of her mother, who died when Eliza was five months old. Self-taught, she rebelled against her conservative family background and moved at the age of twenty-three to a boarding house in London where she began a career as a journalist contributing to newspapers and periodicals such as ▷ Dickens' ▷ *Household Words*. She published two ▷ historical novels, *Azeth the Egyptian* (1846) and *Anymone* (1848), a radical attack on double sexual standards, *Realities* (1850), and wrote for the ▷ *Morning Chronicle* (1848–51) before moving to Paris where she lived until 1854. In 1858 she married William Linton in order to look after his seven children. They separated in 1867. Her later fiction, in particular *Sowing the Wind* (1867) and *The One Too Many* (1894), displays an increasingly reactionary attitude towards the early feminist movement and this tendency is even more pronounced in her journalistic writings for the ▷ *Saturday Review*. Her articles from 1866 to 1868 form a series of sensationalist attacks on the ▷ 'New Woman', and those who campaigned for women's rights, which were reprinted in 1883 under the title of her most notorious essay ▷ 'The Girl of the Period'.

Her other works include *Ourselves: Essays on Women* (1869), *Rebel of the Family* (1880), and *The True History of Joshua Davidson, Christian and Communist* (1872) which, alongside *Under Which Lord* (1879), attacks the hypocrisy of the church. Despite her intense attachments to other women she explicitly condemned ▷ lesbianism in *The Rebel of the Family*. Her ▷ *Autobiography of Christopher Kirkland* (1885) records her own life through a masculine persona. She was close friends with ▷ Walter Savage Landor, ▷ Thomas Hardy, ▷ George and Agnes Lewes, ▷ George Eliot, the novelist and suffragist Beatrice Harraden (1864–1936) and Annie Hector, and she sold the house she inherited at Gad's Hill to Charles Dickens. She was made a member of the Society of Women Authors two years before her death and became the first woman to serve on its committee. Her own memoir *My Literary Life* appeared posthumously in 1899 and contains an acid attack on George Eliot.

▷ Women's Movement.
Bib: Anderson, N.F., *Women Against Women in Victorian England: A Life of Eliza Linton*; Layard, G.S. (ed), *Mrs Eliza Lynn Linton. Her Life, Letters and Opinions*.

Literariness
The special quality of language use which differentiates from other kinds of writing according to the ▷ Russian Formalists. For them, it is not the content which distinguishes literary works, but the way they foreground their distinctive use of language. In particular, they deploy techniques of ▷ defamiliarization to mark themselves off from ordinary usage, a process ▷ Roman Jakobson famously described as 'organized violence committed on ordinary speech'.

Litotes
▷ Figures of Speech.

***Little Dorrit* (1855–7)**
A novel by ▷ Charles Dickens. It centres on the theme of imprisonment, both literal and symbolic. William Dorrit (with his children and his brother Frederick) has been so long in the ▷ Marshalsea Prison for debtors that he is known as 'the Father of the Marshalsea' – a title that gives him a spurious social prestige. Arthur Clennam, who befriends him in the belief that the Dorrit family has been victimized by the commercial interests of his own family, is eventually confined in the same prison. But outside, the characters inhabit prisons without visible walls: William Dorrit inherits a fortune, and he and his family are constricted by social ambition under the gaolership of Mrs General who instructs them in fashionable ways; Mrs Clennam, Arthur's supposed mother, inhabits a gloomy house, confined to her chair and her bad conscience, under the gaolership of her servant Flintwinch who knows her guilty secrets; Merdle, the financier of reputedly enormous wealth, is the prisoner of his false position, and his gaolers are his fashionable wife and his arrogant butler; the servant girl, Tattycoram, is at first the prisoner of the well-intentioned but misguided Mr and Mrs Meagles, and then escapes to the worse prison of Miss Wade, herself a prisoner

of her self-inflicted loneliness. The nation is under the imprisoning control of a government department, the Circumlocution Office, which exists to gratify the interests of the enormous Barnacle family. Three characters stand out in independence of this conspiracy to confine and frustrate: Frederick Dorrit, who lives out an existence of passive misery by refusing to share (in or out of the Marshalsea) the self-deceptions of his brother William; Amy ('Little Dorrit') who consistently follows the compassion of her affections and the duties this imposes on her; and Daniel Doyce, the engineer whose enterprise is baffled by the Circumlocution Office but who perseveres in his vocation with humble and disinterested reverence for the demands that it makes on him. The self-interested Circumlocution Office at the top of society is balanced by the inhabitants of Bleeding Heart Yard, people who are themselves prisoners of the exorbitant property owner, Casby, but who live in the freedom of their own equal and open-hearted society. The blackmailer Rigaud is a figure of menacing evil and a dramatic counterpart to Mrs Clennam's hypocrisy and pretence, which is at the heart of the imaginative scheme of the novel. *Little Dorrit* is often regarded as Dickens' finest work, both in dramatic impressiveness and in richness of psychological insight.

Little Gidding
A small religious community founded by the Anglican theologian Nicholas Ferrar (1592–1637) at a manor house in Huntingdonshire in 1625. It was dispersed, and the buildings destroyed, by Parliamentary soldiers at the end of the ▷ Civil War (1646). ▷ Charles I visited the community in 1633 and according to tradition he came again after his final defeat at the battle of Naseby (1645).

Little Theatre
▷ Lincoln's Inn Fields Theatre.

Little Theatre in the Hay
▷ Haymarket Theatres.

Little, Janet (1759–1813)
Scottish labouring-class poet who wrote in Gaelic and English. She did not have more than a 'common education' before becoming a domestic servant to Frances Wallace Dunlop of Dunlop, the patron of Scottish poet ▷ Robert Burns (1759–1796). She later married John Richmond. She went to work in the dairy at Loudoun Castle, and her employer showed some of her poetry to Burns. In 1792 *The Poetical Works of Janet Little* was issued. Incisively aware of her own 'impudent' status as a poet, she refused to accept received pronunciation, and threaded her writing with changes in linguistic mode. She wrote, 'But what is more surprising still, / A milkmaid must tak' up her quill; / An' she will write, shame fa' the rabble / That thinks to please with ilka bawble.' She continued to write after the publication of the book.
▷ Collier, Mary; Leapor, Mary; Yearsley, Ann.
Bib: Landry, D. *The Muses of Resistance*.

Littlewood, Joan (b 1914)
British director and founder of the Theatre Union in the 1930s with her husband Ewan MacColl. The company reformed after the war as Theatre Workshop, based firstly in Manchester and, from 1953, in East London at the Theatre Royal, Stratford East. Littlewood developed a method of working with actors which encouraged collaboration and improvisation. Her two most famous productions were ▷ Brendan Behan's *The Hostage* and *Oh, What a Lovely War*, the latter accredited to Theatre Workshop, Charles Chilton and the members of the original cast. Her aim was to provide a 'fun palace' for working-class audiences, though commercial pressures meant that the company had to rely heavily on West End transfers for survival, which destroyed her attempts to create a genuine ensemble.
Bib: Goorney, H., *The Theatre Workshop Story*.

Lively, Penelope (b 1933)
Novelist and short-story writer. Born in Egypt, Lively was sent to boarding school in England in 1945 and was educated at St Anne's College Oxford. She has worked as a reviewer and BBC radio presenter. She writes elegant and perceptive novels about the moral dilemmas and intellectual development of middle-class characters, with a particular focus on the importance of the past and its reassessment for the understanding of the present. This concern is often presented through characters professionally preoccupied with the past, such as archaeologists, biographers and historians. Her novels are: *The Road to Lichfield* (1977); *Treasures of Time* (1979); *Judgement Day* (1980); *Next to Nature, Art* (1982); *Perfect Happiness* (1983); *According to Mark* (1984); *Moon Tiger* (1987); *Passing On* (1989); *City of the Mind* (1991); *Cleopatra's Sister* (1993). Volumes of short stories: *Nothing Missing But the Samovar* (1978); *Corruption* (1984); *Pack of Cards: Stories 1978–1986* (1989). She has also written television plays, books for children and *The Presence of the Past: An Introduction to Landscape History* (1976). *Oleander, Jacaranda: A Childhood Perceived* (1994) is a memoir of her early years.

***Lives of the Poets, The* (1779–81)**
By ▷ Samuel Johnson; originally entitled *Prefaces biographical and critical to the Works of the English Poets*. Johnson began work on the

project at the request of a number of booksellers, who required essays on the poets which could be prefaced to editions of their works. The essays developed so successfully that it was decided to issue them in their own right. The essays are interesting both for their critical insight and because they embody the literary tastes of the time. They are idiosyncratic and prejudiced, but always lively; Johnson's bias against the ▷ metaphysical poets in particular has been challenged by changing literary tastes.

Livy (Titus Livius) (59 BC – AD 17)
Roman historian. He wrote the history of Rome in 142 books, 35 of which have survived, with summaries of most of the rest. His aims were partly to ensure that the achievements of 'the chiefest people of the world' should be remembered and partly to provide material for future political guidance.

▷ Latin literature.

Llangollen, The Ladies of
The 'Ladies of Llangollen' were Lady Eleanor Butler (1739–1829) and Sarah Ponsonby (1755–1831); they were close friends for ten years before pressure from their families – Butler was encouraged to become a nun and Ponsonby to accept the attentions of a male suitor – drove them to elope, and they set up house together at Plas Newydd in Llangollen. Their writings were published in *The Hamwood Papers of the Ladies of Llangollen and Caroline Hamilton* (1930), edited by G.H. Bell. It is clear from Butler's diary that they saw their retreat as a rural idyll which gave them the opportunity to study and appreciate ▷ nature. As such, they belong to the ▷ Romantic tradition. ▷ Wordsworth and ▷ Anna Seward came to visit them at Plas Newydd, the former writing them a sonnet and the latter a poem called 'Llangollen Vale' (1795). Their house, an interesting example of the ▷ Gothic Revival in architecture, may still be visited.

Lloyd's
An association of shipowners and other business men concerned with shipping. Its activities are primarily the insurance of ships and cargoes, and the dissemination of shipping information. It arose from a ▷ coffee-house kept by an Edward Lloyd in London early in the 18th century; this was frequented by merchants and insurers of ships who eventually formed their own association.

Lochhead, Liz (b 1947)
Scottish poet, dramatist, and performer. Her early poetry, with its wry observations on awry love affairs, street life and everyday folk, was full of playful, exact phrases. She has a painter's eye for local colour and situation, a wordsmith's ability to shape that perception into vital language, and underpinning all this a strong sense of how female sexuality influences actions and reactions within past history and modern society. *Blood and Ice* (1982), Lochhead's first serious attempt at playwriting, has undergone several changes since its first production but the main thrust of the piece is unchanged: the nature of female creativity. The plot concerns the hectic, febrile relationship between Byron and the Shelleys and the circumstances which led to ▷ Mary Shelley penning *Frankenstein*.

Jock Tamson's Bairns (1990), a performance piece Lochhead created with the Communicado company (it involved music, dance and mime as well as spoken text) revealed just how closely she scans the Scottish psyche as well as her fellow man and woman. Subtitled 'The Last Burnt Supper', the project took the patriotic and macho myths surrounding Scotland's national hero-bard, Robert Burns, and used them to point up the underlying sadness and inadequacy of a race that celebrates the poet's drunkenness and womanising as much, if not more than, his poems and his politics. Other plays include: *Dracula* (1985) and *Mary Queen of Scots Got Her Head Chopped Off* (1987).

Locke, John (1632–1704)
Philosopher. He follows ▷ Thomas Hobbes in his sceptical ▷ rationalism, but he is the direct opposite of Hobbes in his optimistic view of human nature and in the moderation and flexibility of his social and political ideas. Hobbes was born in the year of the attempted invasion by the ▷ Armada and was painfully aware of the human propensity to violence from the decade of civil wars (1642–52); Locke's sympathies were identified with the moderation of the bloodless revolution of 1688 (▷ Glorious Revolution) and the climate of reasonableness which followed it.

In his two *Treatises of Government* (1690), Locke, like Hobbes, presupposes a state of nature preceding a social contract which was the basis of political society. But whereas Hobbes saw the state of nature as a state of war, Locke saw it as a peaceful condition in which the Law of Nature and of Reason was spontaneously observed; his idea of the social contract was not, as for Hobbes, that human existence was intolerable without it, but that it merely provided additional assurance that life and property would be respected. For Hobbes sovereignty had to be single and absolute, but for Locke it was merely a public service always responsible to society, which may at any time remove it. Similarly, in his *Letters concerning Toleration* (1689, 1690, 1692 and a fourth published posthumously) Locke, unlike Hobbes, held that the state has no right to interfere in religious matters and that oppression of religion by governments caused religion to spark civil violence.

Locke's advocacy of religious toleration was consistent with his sceptical attitude to faith and knowledge. Man must first discover what he can know before he persecutes others for publishing false beliefs, and this inquiry he conducts in his ▷ *Essay concerning Human Understanding* (1690). This shows man's capacity for knowledge to be distinctly limited, but the existence of God turns out to be a necessary hypothesis discoverable by reason. Christianity therefore is inherently reasonable (*Reasonableness of Christianity*, 1695) and faith by revelation is indispensable only because the use of reason is unavailable to the majority of mankind; 'nothing that is contrary to . . . reason has a right to be urged or assented to as a matter of faith' (*Human Understanding*, Bk. IV).

In his *Thoughts on Education* Locke extols reason at the expense of imagination and therefore (by implication) of the imaginative arts. When he applies his philosophy to politics or education, Locke is always guided by standards of practical utility, and in his abstract speculation he refrains from carrying his reasoning so far (as ▷ David Hume seemed to do) that the logical basis for the conduct of practical life by the light of reason was undermined. His philosophy dominated the 18th century and is at the back of such 19th-century rationalist movements as ▷ Utilitarianism.

Bib: Cranston, M., *Life*; MacLean, K., *John Locke and English Literature in the Eighteenth Century*; Willey, B., *The Seventeenth Century Background*; *English Moralists*; James, D. G., *The Life of Reason: Hobbes, Locke, Bolingbroke*.

'Locksley Hall'

A poem by ▷ Alfred Tennyson, first published in *Poems* (1848). It contains the famous line 'Let the great world spin forever down the ringing grooves of change' which epitomizes the Victorian equation of change with progress. It was begun after an unhappy love affair between Tennyson and Rosa Baring and bears traces of misogyny. The poem is a ▷ dramatic monologue and its structure is unusual in that it is composed of trochaic couplets with eight stresses.

Lodge, David (b 1935)

Novelist and critic, born in London and educated at London University. Since 1976 he has been Professor of Modern English Literature at the University of Birmingham. His novels are: *The Picturegoers* (1960); *Ginger, You're Barmy* (1962); *The British Museum is Falling Down* (1965); *Out of the Shelter* (1970); *Changing Places* (1975); *How Far Can You Go?* (1980); *Small World* (1984); *Nice Work* (1988); *Paradise News* (1991); *Therapy* (1995). His earlier novels are views of English society in a light, realistic mode, but *The British Museum is Falling Down* introduces extensive use of parody and a farcical element. He is best known for *Changing Places* and *Small World*, inventive, humorous tales of academic life, full of jokes, puns, allusions, parodies and reflexive comments on the nature of narrative which reflect his interest in critical theory. They have affinities with the campus novels of ▷ Malcolm Bradbury. *Out of the Shelter* is a ▷ *Bildungsroman*, and *How Far Can You Go?* explores the personal struggles of a group of Catholics from the 1950s to the 1970s, concentrating in particular on the issue of contraception. Criticism includes: *Language of Fiction* (1966); *The Novelist at the Crossroads* (1971); *The Modes of Modern Writing* (1977); *Working With Structuralism* (1981).

Bib: Morace, R. A., *The Dialogic Novels of Malcolm Bradbury and David Lodge*.

Lodge, Thomas (1558–1625)

Poet and man of letters. He was one of the group now known as the ▷ University Wits – university scholars who used their learning to make a career as professional writers for the expanding reading public of the late 16th century. In many ways his career is representative of this new kind of Elizabethan professional writer.

He was the son of Sir Thomas Lodge, a Lord Mayor of London, and was educated at Merchant Taylors School and Trinity College, Oxford. He then became a student of law at Lincoln's Inn, London, in 1578. The law students of the Inns of Court in the reign of Elizabeth were a leading element of the literary public, and others besides Lodge found these law colleges a nursery for literary rather than legal talent. During the next 20 years he practised all the kinds of writing popular at the time. His first work (1580) was a ▷ pamphlet entitled *A Defence of Plays*, written in answer to ▷ Stephen Gosson's attack on theatrical literature, *Schoole of Abuse* (1580). Besides other pamphlets, he wrote prose romances interspersed with lyrics (*eg Rosalynde, Euphues Golden Legacy*, 1590, and *A Marguerite of America*, 1596), verse romances (*eg Scilla's Metamorphosis*, 1589, reissued as *Glaucus and Scilla*, 1610), a ▷ sonnet sequence (*Phillis*, 1593), and a collection of epistles and ▷ satires in imitation of the Roman poet ▷ Horace, *A Fig for Momus* (1595). He also wrote plays, or at least collaborated with playwrights, *eg* a chronicle play *The Wounds of Civil War* (printed 1594), and, probably with ▷ Robert Greene, *A Looking Glass for London and England* (1594). Besides this writing activity, he joined two piratical expeditions against Spain, the first to the Canary Isles in 1588, and the second to Brazil in 1591. It was on the first that he wrote his most famous work, the romance *Rosalynde*, later used by Shakespeare as the story for ▷ *As You Like It*, and on the second that he wrote *A Marguerite of America*. After 1596, when he published the penitential and satirical pamphlets (*Wit's Misery* and *World's Madness*),

he became converted to Roman Catholicism and took to the study of medicine, receiving the degree of M. D. from Oxford University in 1603. His literary works during the remainder of his life were serious and chiefly translations (*eg* of Josephus (1602) and ▷ Seneca (1614)), and religious and medical treatises.
Bib: Sisson, C. J., *Lodge and Other Elizabethans*.

Logocentrism
The Greek *logos* means word, but in philosophy it is also widely used to denote an ultimate truth, as in 'the Word of God'. Logocentrism is a key term in the thinking of ▷ Jacques Derrida and ▷ deconstruction theory. It is used to designate the way thought systems are organized around fundamental assumptions about truth. These assumptions hold the meaning of the discourse together by claiming some essential ground whose validity and truth is incontestable. The most substantial example is, of course, belief in God, but another example might be a faith in the power of reason or science. In Derrida's view, Western philosophy has taken such central, usually ▷ metaphysical presences for granted thus allowing what are merely conventional procedures for the expression of human reason and argument to appear natural and inevitable. One consequence of this has been that a certain kind of world view and mode of expression is stabilized by repressing alternative possibilities, including the possibility that we, and our habitual thought patterns, are in fact radically ▷ decentred. A particular concern of Derrida's is the Western privileging of speech over writing in which speech is held to be somehow more genuine or truthful, or to possess greater integrity, because it issues from a person's presence. However, for Derrida and other poststructural theorists, the authenticity of speech is illusory, not least because we always speak from the illusion that we possess a centred self. Meanwhile the advantage of writing is that, in the end, it suffers from no such delusion. Instead, read with due deconstructive attention, it can always be made to reveal the ▷ differences (and différances), ▷ aporia and structuring ▷ absences in which deconstruction specialises.

Lollardism
Lollard was the name (of disputed origin) given to the English followers of ▷ John Wycliffe. Their movement was widespread by the end of the 14th and beginning of the 15th century, continuing down to the ▷ Reformation. The wealth of the Church and its readiness to take money from starving peasants was what Lollardism attacked, though nobles and country gentlemen were among its supporters. Their literature was widely circulated in spite of proscription. Lollards opposed the doctrine of transubstantiation and the use of art and artifice: religious rituals and devotional practices. There were some Lollard martyrs at the beginning of the 15th century. In 1408 Convocation issued various decrees designed to control Lollard activities: a bishop's licence to preach would henceforth be necessary; preachers addressing the laity were not to rebuke the sins of the clergy; Lollard books and bibles were to be destroyed. Under ▷ Henry V they endured further persecution and in 1418 preaching in the open air was banned. In 1428, however, they were said to be as numerous as ever. Lollardism did much to shape the English Reformation: subordination of clerical to lay jurisdiction, the reduction of Church possessions and making the ▷ Bible available to ordinary people in their own language were all Lollard goals.
▷ Utopianism.

Lollards
A term (originally abusive, deriving from the Dutch word '*lollaerd*' or mumbler) used of the followers of the Wycliffite reform movement of the later 14th century onwards. The programme of the movement was aimed at reforming the materialistic corruption of the clergy, creating a ministry closer to the Gospel ideal and promoting greater access to vernacular versions of scriptural texts. The Lollards seem to have enjoyed the patronage of certain knights who appear to have sponsored a scriptorium where Lollard texts could be copied and corrected.
▷ Wycliffe, John.
Bib: Coleman, J., *1350–1400. Medieval Writers and Readers*.

London **(1738)**
A poem by ▷ Samuel Johnson in heroic ▷ couplets, written in imitation of the *Third Satire* by ▷ Juvenal. In the spirit of Juvenal, Johnson satirizes (through the character of Thales) the degenerate sophistication, the social injustice, and the crime and licence of the so-called civilization of London. The style has Johnson's typical compression and force, and the ▷ satire is more impersonal than that of his chief predecessors, ▷ Dryden and ▷ Pope who followed the more relaxed and personal style of ▷ Horace. Juvenal is not imitated slavishly but interpreted with discernment and used as a criterion for emulation.

London Cuckolds, The **(1681)**
Comedy by ▷ Ravenscroft. Three old citizens, Doodle, Dashwell and Wiseacre, are married to three young women: Arabella, Eugenia, and Peggy. Each of the men believes he has made the best choice, but the play shows how the women conspire to outwit their husbands, in order to carry on liaisons with their lovers. The atmosphere is one of farcical intrigue, with scenes of concealment, duplicity, and mistaken identity. Despite contemporary attacks on its

supposed indecency, the play was staged each year on the Lord Mayor's Day until 1751. It was revived in 1979 at the Royal Court Theatre, and more recently, at the Lyric Theatre, Hammersmith.

London Magazine, The

Three periodicals of this name have existed: the first ran 1732–85; the second, 1820–29; and the third, founded in 1954, still exists. The second is the most famous. It was founded as the political opponent of the right-wing ▷ *Blackwood's Magazine*, and its first editor, John Scott, was killed in a duel in consequence of the rivalry.

***London Merchant, The, or The History of George Barnwell* (1731)**

Play by ▷ George Lillo, thought to be the first tragedy to centre on a low-born hero and the affairs of ordinary people, and to be written predominantly in prose. In the Dedication Lillo announced a specific moral purpose, 'the exciting of the passions in order to the correcting of such of them as are criminal, either in their nature, or through their excess'. The action takes place in the reign of ▷ Elizabeth I. The virtuous and inexperienced young apprentice George Barnwell is seduced and corrupted by the predatory, man-hating courtesan Millwood. She inveigles him into stealing money from his employer, Thorowgood, and then into murdering his kindly but wealthy uncle. His resulting despair causes her to fear for her own safety, so she casts him off and betrays him to the authorities. But her servants, revolted by the depths to which she has sunk, and repenting their own part in the process, in turn betray her. Millwood is condemned to death, along with her victim. In his last moments Barnwell is visited by his master's daughter, Maria, and discovers she has loved him all along.

Barnwell's descent into crime, torn by guilt and bouts of remorse, is treated with considerable sympathy and Lillo shows how hard it is for him, once he has become an outcast, to contemplate any alternative. Even Millwood is allowed some pointed comments about men's hypocrisy, the cruelty wrought by religious bigotry, and the injustices of society. But the final scenes in the prison cell of the now repentant Barnwell are laden with ▷ sentiment.

The play, with its emphasis on Barnwell's suffering and distress, helped to establish the so-called domestic or bourgeois tragedy on the English stage. *The London Merchant* is dedicated to a wealthy merchant, Sir John Eyles, and comments on the usefulness of merchants to the nation.

The original production was a family affair, with the characters of Barnwell and Maria taken by ▷ Theophilus Cibber and his wife, and the servant Lucy by Cibber's sister, ▷ Charlotte Charke. ▷ Colley Cibber later supplied a silly, comic epilogue. The villainous Millwood was played by ▷ Charlotte Butler. The play was an enormous success, and remained popular for over a century. It also influenced ▷ Diderot and ▷ Lessing, and through them, via ▷ Kotzebue, the English stage once again.

Long Parliament, The

A parliament which was summoned by ▷ Charles I in 1640 and which continued until 1653, when it was dissolved by ▷ Oliver Cromwell. It was this parliament that broke with the king and started the ▷ Civil War in 1642. In 1648 those of its members who were disposed to come to terms with the king were expelled by Colonel Pride ('Pride's Purge') and the remainder continued to sit under the nickname of 'the Rump'. After dissolving it, Cromwell called parliaments of his own but after his death in 1658 it reassembled and in 1660, the year of the Restoration of the monarchy, it dissolved itself to make way for a new parliament under the restored king, ▷ Charles II. His government did not recognize the legality of Cromwell's parliaments, so that in law the Long Parliament was considered to have sat continuously from 1640 to 1660.

Longinus, Dionysius Cassius (1st century AD)

Greek critic. Most of his works have perished but he is the reputed author of the extremely influential treatise *On the Sublime*. This is about literary style, 'the Sublime', though the traditional rendering of the Greek title, is usually regarded as misleading. The author is concerned with the qualities of expression that make for true impressiveness, relates them to distinction of mind in the writer and discusses faults that arise from fallacious ideas of eloquence. The French critic, ▷ Boileau, made a famous translation of the treatise in 1674, and through him it influenced 18th-century English ideas on style.

***Look Back in Anger* (1956)**

A play by ▷ John Osborne, first performed at the ▷ Royal Court theatre where it immediately made a major impact. The plot and dramatic structure are fairly conventional: Jimmy Porter, from a working-class background, lives in cramped conditions with his upper-middle-class wife Alison. Alison's friend persuades her to leave Jimmy only to fall for him herself. When Alison has a miscarriage her friend obligingly makes way for her to return to her former husband. The story and subsidiary characters are really a vehicle for Jimmy's tirades against the class-ridden nature of British society in the post-war period. For many amongst the original audiences Jimmy was a kind of modern Hamlet figure, even though a modern audience would be more likely to focus on the sexist manner in which he hectors and bullies his wife. Nonetheless, the fact is that the play captured a particular mood of disillusionment in the period and established the Royal Court as a venue for drama of social protest.

▷ Angry young men.

Lord Chamberlain's Men, The

▷ Chamberlain's Men, The Lord.

***Lord Jim* (1900)**

A novel by ▷ Joseph Conrad. It is narrated by Marlow, an officer in the Merchant Navy who also appears in Conrad's other works, ▷ *Heart of Darkness*, *Chance* and *Youth*. The first 35 chapters we are to suppose recounted to companions after dinner; the rest is in the form of a letter and written narrative subsequently posted to one of these friends. Jim is a young sailor, the son of an English country parson, who dreams of being a hero. He becomes chief mate of the *Patna*, a decrepit ship with second rate officers, carrying pilgrims from Singapore to Jeddah. When the ship seems about to sink he loses his nerve and, at the last moment, jumps into a small boat with the other officers. When they reach land they discover that the *Patna* has stayed afloat and been towed to safety. The other officers disappear, but Jim stays to face disgrace at the official inquiry. He meets Marlow, to whom he tells his story and subsequently, persecuted by his sense of lost honour, Jim takes up humble employment as a water clerk in various Eastern ports (it is thus that Marlow introduces him to us at the start of the novel). Through the intervention of Marlow, Jim is sent by Stein, a benevolent trader, to a remote trading post in the jungle called Patusan. There, in alliance with a local chief called Doramin, who is Stein's friend, Jim defeats in battle the forces of Sherif Ali, a half-caste Arab bandit leader, and becomes a venerated figure. However, when a party of European adventurers led by the scoundrelly Gentlemen Brown appears in Patusan, the memory of his past dishonour fatally weakens Jim's resolve. He asks Doramin to let them go free, pledging his own life for their good behaviour. They massacre a party of the villagers, including Doramin's son, and Jim allows himself to be shot by Doramin, leaving behind Jewel, the local woman with whom he has been living, as a sad and lonely figure.

Lotos-Eaters, The

A poem by ▷ Alfred Tennyson, first published in the 1833 volume, which contains much of his most distinguished work. Its subject is the ancient Greek myth of the *lotophagi* ('lotus-eaters' – Tennyson used the Greek spelling, 'lotos') who occur in ▷ Homer's *Odyssey*. Those who visit the land where the lotus fruit grows and eat some of it lose all desire to return home. The theme of Tennyson's poem is the temptation to reject the world of activity, change and stress, in favour of a trancelike existence measured only by the more languorous rhythms of nature. It is in the tradition of Edmund Spenser (1552–99) and the more luxuriant ▷ Keats: the rhythms have hypnotic music, and the imagery is strongly and unsettlingly sensuous. Tennyson's pre-Victorian poems may be viewed as an important part of the Romantic bequest to the later 19th century.

***Love for Love* (1695)**

A comedy by ▷ William Congreve. The plot centres on an intrigue to frustrate an uncharitable father, Sir Sampson, who wishes to disinherit his extravagant elder son, Valentine, in favour of the younger brother, Ben, a hearty but ludicrous sailor. The intrigue is managed by Angelica, a rich and spirited girl in love with Valentine. A minor plot concerns Sir Sampson's attempt to marry Ben off to an equally awkward country girl, Miss Prue, the daughter of a superstitious astrologer, Foresight. The rustic embarrassment of Ben and Prue, neither of whom wants to marry the other, nicely contrasts with the wit and grace of Valentine and Angelica. The play succeeds particularly because of its skilful and witty prose dialogue.

***Love Letters Between a Nobleman and His Sister* (1684–87)**

▷ Epistolary fiction by ▷ Aphra Behn, based on the story of the adulterous and quasi-incestuous elopement and affair of Lady Henrietta Berkeley and her brother-in-law, Forde, Lord Grey of Werke, but transposing the scene to France. The novel was originally published in three volumes from 1684 to 1687. Part one concentrates on the story of Sylvia and Philander, the second part follows Philander to Cologne, and the third part ends with the execution of the ▷ Duke of Monmouth after his attempt to depose ▷ James II.

Lovelace, Richard (1618–58)

Poet. One of the so-called 'Cavalier poets', Lovelace fought on behalf of the king during the ▷ Civil War. The majority of his poetry was written before 1649, when his collection of poems entitled *Lucasta* appeared. *Lucasta* is prefaced with a commendatory poem by ▷ Andrew Marvell, and his work might be thought of as anticipating themes expressed in Marvell's poetry – in particular the search for a form of disengagement from the world. It is not, however, with the more republican Marvell that Lovelace is associated, but with aristocratic codes of love and honour embraced by the literary and military circles in which Lovelace moved. Of special note are the series of 'bestiary poems' (*eg* 'The Snail' or 'The Grasshopper') which seem often to offer

themselves as a form of disguised or encoded commentary on the political crisis of the period before the Civil War.
Bib: Wilkinson, C. H. (ed.), *The Poems of Richard Lovelace*; Weidhorn, M., *Richard Lovelace*.

Lovers' Vows **(1798)**
Play by ▷ Elizabeth Inchbald, adapted from *Das Kind der Liebe* by ▷ August von Kotzebue. Agatha has been seduced and abandoned by Baron Wildenhaim, who has married another woman. Agatha has given birth to a son, Frederic, but become separated from him. He finds her sunk in deep poverty, and learns about his birth for the first time. Eventually he persuades his father, now widowed and elderly, to marry his mother, and to allow his daughter Amelia to marry the man of her choice, instead of the wealthy man her father had chosen for her. The play is featured in ▷ Austen's ▷ *Mansfield Park* (1814).

Love's Labour's Lost **(1594–5)**
A comedy by ▷ Shakespeare, published in a ▷ quarto edition in 1598. It is a play for court taste, recalling the comedies of ▷ John Lyly; the plot is light and fantastic, and a pretext for dextrously witty dialogue and poetic flights of fancy. But the graceful artificiality is enriched by a freshness that arises from elements of rural life, both in imagery employed by the courtiers and in some of the characters. As in later comedies written by Shakespeare in the decade 1590–1600 (▷ *A Midsummer Night's Dream*, ▷ *As You Like It*, ▷ *Twelfth Night*), the witty courtiers end by making fools of themselves in their own way, much as the clowns and simple-minded pedants do – predictably – in theirs.

The King of Navarre and three of his lords vow to shut themselves away from pleasure and ladies in order to devote themselves to study. They quickly find excuses to break the vow when the king is visited by the Princess of France and three of her ladies on an embassy. A subplot concerns a group of ludicrous characters – the proud but seedy Spaniard, Don Armado; the pedantic schoolmaster Holofernes; Sir Nathaniel, the country clergyman, and Costard the rustic – who attempts to entertain the lords and ladies with a performance of the ▷ interlude of the ▷ 'Nine Worthies'. The courting of the princess and her ladies by the king and his lords is abruptly ended by the announcement of the death of the princess's father. The play ends with the ladies imposing a year's ordeal on their suitors.

Some scholars have seen in the play a light satire on the ▷ School of Night. Some of the characters are identified with living contemporaries, for instance Armado with ▷ Sir Walter Ralegh, who is said to have been one of the key members of the School.

Love's Last Shift **(1696)**
Comedy by ▷ Colley Cibber, often said to have set the stage for 18th-century ▷ Reform Comedy. Loveless, having abandoned his wife Amanda and gone abroad, returns to England deeply in debt. She has inherited a fortune, and remained loyal to him. Amanda seduces him in disguise, then reveals her true identity. Shaken by remorse, Loveless embraces the 'chast Rapture of a Vertuous Love', and the two are reunited as a couple. The ending is said to have reduced the audience to tears, and the play was a great success. Sub-plots concern the courtships of Young Worthy and Narcissa, and of the Elder Worthy, a reformed rake and the teasing woman, Hillaria. ▷ Sir John Vanbrugh's ▷ *The Relapse* (1696) was written as a sequel and sardonic 'comment' on Cibber's play, showing that Loveless' reformation is only temporary. Cibber himself performed in both plays, as Sir Novelty Fashion, who later assumes the title of Lord Foppington.

Lowry, Malcolm (1909–57)
Novelist. He was educated in England, but spent most of his later life in Mexico, the United States, and British Columbia. His first novel, *Ultramarine*, was published in 1933. His reputation chiefly rests on his second and only other completed novel, *Under the Volcano* (1947). The central character, Geoffrey Firmin, is British Consul in a Mexican city situated under two volcanoes, just as in ancient times the Underworld, Tartarus, was supposed to be situated beneath the Sicilian volcano, Etna. Firmin is an alcoholic who has rejected the love of his wife and his friends and taken to drink as escape from the inhumanity of the modern world (the events take place in 1938) and his own sense of guilt and failure. The novel is highly allusive and symbolic, with metaphysical and mythical overtones, and the narrative is partly ▷ stream of consciousness. It shows the influence of ▷ Joseph Conrad and ▷ James Joyce and it has been described as the most distinguished work of fiction produced by an English novelist since 1945. A number of works were published posthumously, including: two novels entitled *Dark as the Grave Wherein My Friend is Laid* (1968) and *October Ferry to Gabriola* (1970), which were put together from Lowry's drafts by his widow; *Selected Poems* (1962) and a volume of short stories, *Hear Us, O Lord, from Heaven Thy Dwelling Place* (1961). This *Selected Letters* have been edited by Harvey Breit and Margerie Bonner Lowry (1965).
Bib: Woodcock, G., *Lowry: the Man and His Work*; Day, D., *Lowry, a Biography*; Cross, R.

K., *Malcolm Lowry: a Preface to His Fiction*; Binns, R., *Malcolm Lowry*.

Lucan (Marcus Annaeus Lucanus) (AD 39–65)
A Roman poet; author of the poem *Pharsalia* about the struggle for power between ▷ Julius Caesar and ▷ Pompey. ▷ Christopher Marlow translated the first book (1600). The translation by Rowe (1718) was greatly praised by ▷ Samuel Johnson. In ancient times Lucan was noted for his florid style, and for his gift for ▷ epigram.

Lucian (2nd century AD)
Greek satirist. He is especially known for his satirical dialogues and for his *True History*, an account of imaginary voyages which ▷ Jonathan Swift may have used as a model for his ▷ *Gulliver's Travels*.

***Lucius Junius Brutus* (1680)**
Tragedy by ▷ Nathaniel Lee, based on the historic overthrow of Tarquin and establishment of a republic in Rome, using ▷ Livy as a major source. It contains strong libertarian and egalitarian speeches, as when Brutus accuses Tarquin of arbitrary rule (Act II) and looks forward to a time when 'no man shall offend because he's great' (Act V). Staged at a time of high political tension in England, with the Whigs pressing the ▷ Exclusion Bill, the play was considered too dangerous and was suppressed.

***Lucky Chance, The* (1686)**
Comedy by ▷ Aphra Behn. The title plot concerns the fortunes of Julia, Lady Fulbank, married to an old man, Sir Cautious Fulbank, but in love with the poverty-stricken Gayman. She secretly conveys money to Gayman, and then visits him disguised as an old crone. Later Sir Cautious gambles with Gayman, and stakes a night with his wife as the prize. Gayman wins, and is brought to Julia's chamber, where he makes love to her in the guise of her husband. In the secondary plot, Bellmour, having killed a man in a duel, flees to Brussels, leaving behind his fiancée Leticia. In his absence Sir Feeble Fainwou'd, an old alderman whose name describes his condition, convinces Leticia that her lover is dead, and she agrees to marry Sir Feeble, but the wedding is forestalled when Bellmour returns, and manages to thwart his rival's plans. The play ends with Lady Fulbank announcing that she is leaving her husband, and both women being united with the men of their choice. In an extended and vivid speech, Lady Fulbank defends the right of women to love where they please, even if it means cuckolding their husbands. The play was successfully staged at ▷ Drury Lane, and formed the source of ▷ Hannah Cowley's *School for Greybeards* (1786). It was revived at the Royal Court Theatre in 1984.

Lucrece (Lucretia)
A Roman lady of outstanding virtue and beauty. She was the wife of Tarquinius Collatinus but Sextus, the son of Tarquin, king of Rome, tried to seduce her and, when she resisted, raped her. She told her father and her husband of the outrage and exacted an oath of vengeance from them, after which she killed herself. In consequence, a relative of her husband, Lucius Junius Brutus, led a rebellion against the ▷ Tarquin monarchy and expelled them from the city. Lucrece was thus traditionally the occasion for the foundation of the ancient Roman Republic. The tale has been reworked many times, notably in a poem by ▷ Shakespeare, and in the play ▷ *Lucius Junius Brutus*, by ▷ Nathaniel Lee, because it poses questions about guilt and innocence that are of enduring concern.
Bib: Donaldson, I., *The Rapes of Lucrece*.

Lucretius (Titus Lucretius Carus) (1st century BC)
Roman poet; author of the great didactic poem *De Rerum Natura* ('Concerning the Nature of Things'). It outlines the philosophy of the Greek thinker ▷ Epicurus, which is based in the atomic theory of Democritus. The poet seeks to expound that all reality is material. The gods exist but they also are material, though immortal, and they are not concerned with the affairs of men; the soul exists but it, too, is material and mortal like the body, dissolving into its original atoms after death. Lucretius is not, however, a cynical poet; he testifies to the beauty of the natural world and the poem opens with an eloquent invocation to Venus, the conception of whom is followed by ▷ Edmund Spenser in ▷ *Faerie Queene* Bk. IV, x, stanza 44 onwards. Lucretius' love of the natural world and his reverence for reason caused him to be greatly admired during the ▷ Renaissance and the succeeding two centuries; parts of the poem were finely translated by ▷ Dryden and by Thomas Creech (1659–1700).

Lucretius is a late ▷ dramatic monologue by ▷ Tennyson, in which the poet philosopher expounds his dying vision of the world.

Lucy Poems
A group of five ▷ lyrics by ▷ William Wordsworth, composed between 1799 and 1801. There is no clear evidence that the figure of Lucy represents any actual person, though her ambiguity may be an expression of the poet's intense relationship with his sister ▷ Dorothy. In 'Strange fits of passion I have known' the lover approaches Lucy's cottage as the moon sinks behind it, and suddenly imagines, for no apparent reason, that she might

be dead. In 'Three years she grew' Lucy is a child who has died young, and in 'A slumber did my spirit seal' the poet consoles himself with the idea that the dead Lucy is now part of inanimate nature, 'Rolled round in earth's diurnal course,/ With rocks, and stones, and trees'. The sublime, almost mystical, simplicity of style of these poems has incurred parody. The poem which begins 'She dwelt among the untrodden ways/ Beside the springs of Dove,/ A Maid whom there were none to praise/ And very few to love', was delightfully rewritten by ⊳ Samuel Taylor Coleridge's son, ⊳ Hartley, to apply to the poet himself: 'He lived amidst th'untrodden ways/ To Rydal Lake that lead;/ A bard whom there were none to praise,/ And very few to read'.

Luggnagg
A country in Part III of ⊳ Swift's ⊳ *Gulliver's Travels*. It is inhabited by the Struldbrugs who have immortality, and find it a curse.

Lumley, Lady Joanna (1537–76)
Translator and dramatist. Lumley is interesting in that she is one of only three Renaissance Englishwomen to translate or compose complete dramas, the other two being ⊳ Elizabeth Cary and ⊳ Mary Sidney. Like her cousin ⊳ Lady Jane Grey she was well educated, and had access to one of the finest libraries in England, owned by her father, Henry Fitzalan, Earl of Arundel. Her prose ⊳ translation of ⊳ Euripides' tragedy *Iphigenia at Aulis* was transcribed into a notebook, together with several Latin pieces (a modern edition was published in 1909, ed. Harold H. Child). The work is notable in several ways: it is the first known attempt to translate a Greek drama into English; it adopts a strongly pro-women stance and reveals the possible abuses of women within a patriarchal society; and, finally, it is all the more remarkable an achievement since she could only have been 15 or 16 when she undertook the translation.
Bib: Travitsky, B. (ed.), *The Paradise of Women*.

Luther, Martin (1483–1546)
German religious reformer, and the chief figure in the European movement known as the ⊳ Reformation. The beginning of this is often dated from 1517, when Luther fixed on the church door at Wittenberg his 95 'Theses' against the sale of 'indulgences'; a consequence of this was his condemnation by the Pope at the Diet of Worms (1521).

Luther's influence on the English Reformation is a matter of dispute. Before he separated the English church from the authority of the Pope, ⊳ Henry VIII wrote a treatise against Luther, for which the Pope awarded him the title Defender of the Faith (*Fidei Defensor*), still used by English monarchs. Lutheran influences were felt by humanists such as John Colet and ⊳ Sir Thomas More, and inspired ⊳ William Tyndale's translation of the ⊳ Bible, the first of several in the 16th century. They certainly operated on the doctrines represented by the second Prayer Book, introduced by ⊳ Archbishop Cranmer under ⊳ Edward VI. However, reformist influences had been current in England since ⊳ John Wycliffe in the 14th century.
Bib: Brecht, M., *Martin Luther*.

Lyall, Edna (1857–1903)
⊳ Pseudonym of novelist Ada Allen Bayly. She was born in Brighton, Sussex, and after the deaths of both her parents moved to her uncle's home in Caterham. Lyall supported women's suffrage, was a committed Liberal and involved herself in charitable and social work. Her novels reflect her Christian religious views, but are more than simple moral tracts. With her second work, *Donavan* (1882), she became an extremely popular writer and her subsequent works ran to numerous editions. *We Two* (1884) and *Hope the Hermit* (1898) were especially successful. Other works include *Doreen* (1894), in which she supported the movement for Irish Home Rule, and her last novel *The Hinderers* (1902), which protested against the Boer War.
Bib: Escreet, J.M., *Life;* Payne, G.A., *Life*.

***Lycidas* (1637)**
A ⊳ pastoral ⊳ elegy by ⊳ John Milton, written in 1637. It is in the form of a monody, *ie* modelled on the ⊳ odes sung by a single actor in ancient Greek ⊳ tragedy. Line lengths vary between three and five feet, and the rhymes follow no regular pattern, but the mournful, majestic sonority is consistently sustained. Milton is lamenting the death of his college friend Edward King, a gifted young man who was drowned at sea, but it is not a poem of personal loss. The theme is the tragic loss of promise: King is seen as a young man of talent and serious endeavour in an age whose spiritual laxity requires the reforming zeal of such a spirit. Greek pastoral imagery is used – gods, muses, nymphs, including Camus, invented for the occasion as the god of the river that flows through Cambridge where Milton and King had studied. More important, however, is the pastoralism of the ⊳ Bible: King was a good shepherd; the clergy are spiritual shepherds by their function, but mostly bad ones.

Lydgate, John (c 1370–1449/50)
A prolific 15th-century writer who seems to have enjoyed a higher contemporary literary reputation than he does now. He was born in Lydgate, Suffolk, and entered the famous and well-endowed monastery of Bury St Edmunds c 1385. He successfully aspired to noble and

royal patronage, and his vast literary output provides a cultural 'barometer' of his time. He translated a number of key texts on classical, historical and moralizing subjects, including his monumental *Troy Book* (composed over 8 years, 1412–20), which is a translation of ▷ Guido de Columnis' Troy story; the *Siege of Thebes* (1420–2), which he presents as a contribution to the ▷ *Canterbury Tales*; the *Pilgrimage of the Life of Man* (1426–30); and the *Fall of Princes* (1431–8), which is a translation of a French version of ▷ Boccaccio's compilation of tragedies (*De Casibus Virorum Illustrium*). He also composed ▷ dream-vision poems (including the *Temple of Glass*, modelled on ▷ Chaucer's ▷ *House of Fame*), large numbers of lyric poems and a selection of dramatic pieces (including Mummings), designed for performance on various ceremonial occasions or to mark court festivities. His development of a Latinate, aureate poetic register influenced the style of court poetry in the 15th century.

Lydgate styled himself as a follower of Chaucer, and his reputation as a leading man of letters was evidently established during and after his lifetime: from the later 15th century onwards, his name is coupled with that of Chaucer's as a founding figure of the English literary tradition. Although his enormous output finds less favour with modern readers, he is undoubtedly a writer of monumental dimensions, who assimilated some of the important, authoritative narratives of medieval European court culture and made them available to a prestigious English audience. The scale of his work is daunting, but that is also his strength.

Bib: Norton-Smith, J. (ed.), *Poems*; Pearsall, D., *John Lydgate*.

Lyell, Sir Charles (1797–1875)

Geologist. His principal work, *The Principles of Geology* (1830–33) revolutionized ideas about the age of the earth, and was a challenge to current theological thinking as ▷ Darwin's *Origin of Species* (1859) was to be. He also contributed the idea of change as continuous and ceaseless instead of sudden, intermittent and catastrophic, which had been the prevailing view. This added to the sense of flux and instability which haunted such contemporary imaginative writers as ▷ Matthew Arnold and Tennyson, whose *In Memoriam* (1850) shows traces of Lyell's influence.

Lyly, John (1554–1606)

Poet, writer of romances, dramatist. He was a popular writer for the cultivated society of court and university circles.

His prose romances, ▷ *Euphues, or the Anatomy of Wit* (1578) and *Euphues and his England* (1580), contain little story and are mainly pretexts for sophisticated discussion of contemporary manners and modes in a style whose graceful ornateness is really an end in itself. Its artificiality, now regarded as its fault, was at the time regarded as a virtue of high cultivation. It was much imitated in the last 20 years of the 16th century, and it was also parodied, *eg* by ▷ Shakespeare in his early comedies and, through ▷ Falstaff, here and there in ▷ *Henry IV, Part I*.

Lyly's comedies are in the same elaborately sophisticated style, and are in fact the first *socially* sophisticated comedies in English. The plays were performed by boy-actors in private theatres; they were not intended for the socially mixed audiences of public theatres such as the ▷ Globe. *The Woman in the Moon* (before 1584) was the only one of these in verse. He followed it with prose plays interspersed with graceful lyrics: *Sapho and Phao* (1584); *Alexander and Campaspe* (1584); ▷ *Gallathea* (1585); *Endimion* (1588); *Midas* (1589); *Mother Bombie* (1594); and *Love's Metamorphosis* (published 1601). The best known of these are *Alexander and Campaspe, Endimion* and *Mother Bombie*. They have grace and wit, and were closer to popular taste than was Restoration comedy a century later. Lyly's writing was an adjunct to his search for preferment from his early patron, the Earl of Oxford, and from the queen; he was given hope of becoming Master of the ▷ Revels, but died a disappointed man.

▷ Theatres.

Bib: Hunter, G. K., *John Lyly*.

Lyonesse

A legendary country in Arthurian narratives which came to be identified with a tract of land extending westwards and southwards from Cornwall, now submerged under the sea, according to the legends. ▷ Tristan is the son of the king of Lyonesse.

Lyric

In Ancient Greece the name given to verse sung to a lyre (from the Greek *'lurikos'* – 'for the lyre'), whether as a solo performance or by a choir. In English usage, the term has had different associations in different historical literary periods. Elizabethan critics first used the term in England: ▷ George Puttenham, for example, describes a lyric poet as someone who composes 'songs or ballads of pleasure to be sung with the voice, and to the harpe'. From the illustrative quotations in the O.E.D. (sv. lyric), it is clear that in later usage musical accompaniment was no longer considered essential to the definition of the form. In the 17th century lyric forms were widely used in poetry. Among the chief exponents were ▷ Shakespeare, Jonson, ▷ Herrick ▷ Lovelace, ▷ Marvell, ▷ Herbert, ▷ Milton and ▷ Behn. Lyric poetry was less popular in the 18th century, but is found, for example, among the works of ▷ William Collins, and ▷ Thomas Gray.

▷ Blake contributed greatly to a revival of lyric poetry, which gathered pace in the 19th century.

It was in the 19th century that Ruskin offered a different definition of lyric poetry as 'the expression by the poet of his own feelings'; a definition which has the virtue of drawing attention to the personal and emotional focus of many lyric poems, but rather obscures any recognition of the highly stylized modes of mediating between personal experience and its public expression employed in lyric texts, which, like all literary conventions, may change over time. This definition owes a great deal to the personalization of the lyric in the Romantic period, *eg* ▷ Keats' 'When I have fears that I may cease to be', and ▷ Shelley's 'To a Skylark'.

In modern English, the term lyric has a very general range of reference: it may be used to cover most forms of short poetry, especially that which has a personal focus of some kind, or is non-narrative. But the very generality of its reference undermines its value as a critical term since it may refer to many different kinds of poetic genres and sub-genres (as modern collections of lyric poetry reveal). The term 'lyrics' now describes verbal arrangements for musical accompaniment.

Bib: Lindley, D., *Lyric*.

***Lyrical Ballads, with a Few other Poems* (1798)**
A collection of poems by ▷ William Wordsworth and ▷ Samuel Taylor Coleridge, often seen as the starting point of the Romantic movement, the term 'lyrical ballad' indicating the combination of primitive simplicity (▷ ballad) and literary elevation (▷ lyric) at which Wordsworth in particular aimed. The volume first appeared anonymously in 1798. Most of the poems were by Wordsworth, Coleridge's contributions being *The Rime of the* ▷ *Ancient Mariner*, *The Foster Mother's Tale*, *To the Nightingale*, and *The Dungeon*. The second edition (1800) appeared under Wordsworth's name only, and included the famous *Preface* and his poem ▷ *Michael*. Coleridge's poem *Love* was added in place of Wordsworth's *The Convict*. In the third edition of 1802 the *Preface* was enlarged. The fourth and final edition appeared in 1805.

In Chapter XIV of his ▷ *Biographia Literaria*, Coleridge describes how the collaboration came about. He and Wordsworth had been discussing 'two cardinal points of poetry, the power of exciting the sympathy of the reader by a faithful adherence to the truth of nature, and the power of giving the interest of novelty by the modifying colours of the imagination'. They projected a volume in which Coleridge should direct himself to characters 'supernatural' or at least romantic; yet so as to transfer from our inward nature a human interest . . . sufficient to procure . . . that willing suspension of disbelief for the moment, which constitutes poetic faith'. Wordsworth's object would be to 'excite a feeling analogous to the supernatural' for everyday things the beauty of which was normally concealed by the 'film of familiarity'.

Wordsworth's *Preface* (1800) is a poetic manifesto attacking the 'gaudiness and inane phraseology' of poets such as ▷ Thomas Gray, who attempt to separate the language of poetry as far as possible from that of real life. Wordsworth proposes instead to fit 'to metrical arrangement a selection of the real language of men in a state of vivid sensation'. 'Humble and rustic life' is the chosen subject 'because in that condition, the essential passions of the heart find a better soil in which they can attain their maturity, are less under restraint, and speak a plainer and more emphatic language'. It is important not to oversimplify Wordsworth's aims or practice here. His language in the volume does sometimes affect the flat plainness of prose (in *The Thorn* for example), and at other times he employs the sing-song metre and artless repetitions of the primitive ballad ('Her eyes were fair, and very fair,/ – Her beauty made me glad'). Sometimes however, as in the non-ballad ▷ blank verse poem *Lines Composed a Few Miles Above Tintern Abbey*, the philosophical, literary vocabulary of earlier reflective verse is in evidence ('tranquil restoration', 'somewhat of a sad perplexity'). At first Coleridge felt entirely at one with Wordsworth's *Preface*, but later, in *Biographia Literaria*, Chapters XVII–XX, he subjected Wordsworth's theories of poetic language to incisive analysis.

Lyttelton, George, Lord (1709–73)
Politician and poet. Opponent of ▷ Sir Robert Walpole and for a time in 1756 Chancellor of the Exchequer. ▷ James Thomson apostrophizes him in ▷ *The Seasons* and he was a friend of ▷ Alexander Pope, ▷ Henry Fielding and ▷ William Shenstone. His own poems include *The Progress of Love* (1732), *Monody to the Memory of a Lady* (1747), and *Dialogues of The Dead* (1760–5). He also published a *History of Henry II* (1767).

Lytton, Edward George Earle Lytton Bulwer- (1st Baron Lytton) (1803-73)
▷ Bulwer-Lytton, Edward.

M

Mabinogion
A collection of medieval Welsh tales, some from the 14th-century *Red Book of Hergest*. A *mabinog* was a bard's apprentice. 11 tales were translated by Lady Charlotte Guest (1838); four of these are versions of still older Celtic myths and are called the 'Four Branches of the Mabinogi'. These are the true *Mabinogion*. The others are old British tales of Roman times, British tales of ▷ King Arthur, and later tales of medieval romance.

▷ Wales.

***Mac Flecknoe, or a Satyr upon the True-Blew-Protestant Poet, T. S.* (1682)**
A ▷ mock-heroic satire by ▷ John Dryden in ▷ pentameter ▷ couplets, written about 1678 and published in 1682. The poem attacks ▷ Thomas Shadwell, who is designated as the successor, or 'son' of Flecknoe, a Catholic poet previously the butt of a satire by ▷ Andrew Marvell. Shadwell had replied to Dryden's attack on ▷ Lord Shaftesbury in ▷ *The Medal*, with *The Medall of John Bayes*, accusing the Laureate (hence ▷ Bayes) of atheism. Dryden countered by attacking Shadwell in ▷ *Absalom and Achitophel*, Part II, and in this poem. It is a masterpiece of high-spirited lampoon, in which Dryden mocks Shadwell by making Flecknoe eulogize his 'son's' literary ineptitude and corpulence: 'The rest to some faint meaning make pretence,/ But Shadwell never deviates into sense . . . Besides his goodly Fabrick fills the eye,/ And seems design'd for thoughtless Majesty.' Its conclusion, in which two specialists in the new theatrical gimmicks of pantomime send 'the yet declaiming Bard' through a trapdoor, is purely farcical, and helps to make this one of the best comic poems in the language.

Macaulay, Catharine (1731–1791)
English historian and Whig (▷ Whig and Tory) radical. In 1760 she married the physician George Macaulay, and in 1763 began to publish her long 'anti-Royalist' *History of England from the Accession of James I to that of the Brunswick Line* (1763–1783) (compare, for example, ▷ Mary Astell's Tory history). Her husband died in 1766, and she became ill, but went to France in 1777 and visited the US in 1784, staying with President ▷ George Washington (1732–1799). She was abused for her second marriage to the younger William Graham. She responded to philosopher ▷ Thomas Hobbes and ▷ Edmund Burke, and again took issue with Burke's ▷ *Reflections on the Revolution in France* (1790). Her *Letters on Education* (1790) influenced ▷ Mary Wollstonecraft's ▷ *Vindication of the Rights of Woman*. In the *Letters* (addressing 'Hortensia') she wrote, 'The situation and education of women . . . is precisely that which must necessarily tend to corrupt and debilitate both the powers of mind and body.'

▷ *Essay to Revive the Antient Education of Gentlewomen, An*.

Bib: Ferguson, M. (ed.), *First Feminists*.

Macaulay, Thomas Babington (1800–59)
Historian, essayist, politician and poet. He was actively on the Whig side politically; that is to say, without being a radical reformer, he had strong faith in the virtue of British parliamentary institutions. He was, from the publication of his essay on the poet John Milton (1608–74) in 1825, a constant contributor to the main Whig periodical, the ▷ *Edinburgh Review*, and his *History of England* (1848 and 1855) is strongly marked by his political convictions. He was trained as a lawyer and became an eloquent orator; his writing has corresponding qualities of persuasiveness and vividness. As a historian he was best at impressionistic reconstruction of the past, and the same gift served him in his biographical essays on writers John Bunyan (1628–88), Oliver Goldsmith (1730–74), Samuel Johnson (1709–84), Fanny Burney (1752–1840) and the younger William Pitt. He represented the most optimistic strain of feeling in mid-19th-century England – its faith in the march of progress.

Macaulay's *Lays of Ancient Rome* (1842) were an attempt to reconstruct legendary Roman history in a way that might resemble the lost ▷ ballad poetry of ancient Rome. Though not major poetry, they are very vigorous verse with the kind of appeal that is to be found in effective ballad poetry.

Macaulay was raised to the peerage in 1857.

▷ *Macaulay's History of England*.

Bib: Trevelyan, G.M., *Life and Letters*; Bryant, A., *Macaulay*; Firth, C., *A Commentary on Macaulay's History of England*; Trevelyan, G.M. in *Clio: a Muse*; Stephen, L., in *Hours in a Library*; Clive, J., *Thomas Babington Macaulay: The Shaping of the Historian*.

Macaulay's History of England from the Accession of James II
The history (Vols. 1 & 2, 1848; 3 & 4, 1855; 5, 1861) is a thorough, detailed account of two reigns: James II (1685–8) and William III (1689–1702). It is unfinished and was originally intended to extend to the time of George I (1714–27) and further. The period covered is perhaps the most crucial for English political development. James II, a ▷ Catholic, tried to enforce his will in the Catholic interest against Parliament, which frustrated him and expelled him from the throne in the Revolution of 1688. Parliament then summoned William from Holland to reign jointly with his wife, who was also James' daughter, Mary II (1689–94). William was the champion of the Protestant cause in Europe, and Mary was also Protestant.

Macaulay's politics were strongly in the Whig parliamentary tradition and his history is an epic of the triumph of the ideas which to him gave meaning to English history. Considered as history, the work is accordingly one-sided, much more a work of historical art than of historical science; it represents what historians have come to call 'the Whig interpretation of history'.

▷ Histories and Chronicles.

Macauley, Dame Rose (1881–1958)
Novelist, poet, travel writer and critic. Born in England, she spent part of her childhood in Italy, but returned to England for her education at Oxford High School and Somerville College Oxford. She had early experience of loss: her brother was murdered and the poet Rupert Brooke, who was her friend, died in 1915 on his way to the front in the Dardanelles. During World War I she worked as a civil servant and began a long-term relationship with a married man (until his death in 1942), which caused her exile from the Anglican Church. In London from 1916 she attended a literary salon where she met such writers as W.B. Yeats, ▷ Arnold Bennett, ▷ Aldous Huxley and ▷ Walter de la Mare. In the 1930s she became a close friend of ▷ Virginia Woolf. She wrote war fiction, including the autobiographical *Non-Combatants and Others* (1916) and *Told By an Idiot* (1923) and, later, *And No Man's Wit* (1940), set in civil war Spain; a historical novel, *They Were Defeated* (1932); satire, in *Potterism* (1920). During the 1940s she published no fiction, but returned to the novel with *The World My Witness* (1950) and *The Towers of Trebizond* (1956), the first about the after-effects of World War II, as seen in the mind of a young woman living in London, and the second a more humorous work about Islam and Anglicanism.
Bib: Babington Smith, C. (ed.), *Letters to a Friend* (1961–62); *Rose Macauley* (1972); Kime Scott, B. (ed.), *The Gender of Modernism.*

***Macbeth* (1605–6)**
A ▷ tragedy by ▷ Shakespeare; it probably dates from 1605–6, and was first printed in the First Folio edition of Shakespeare's collected works, 1623.

The material for the tragedy comes from ▷ Raphael Holinshed's *Chronicle of Scottish History* (1578). Macbeth was an historical king of Scotland who reigned approximately 1040–58. He seems to have been a capable and beneficent sovereign in spite of his usurpation of the throne and sundry acts of cruelty, and Holinshed so records him. Shakespeare blackens his character, elevates his predecessor Duncan into a kind of saint, and makes a virtuous figure out of Macbeth's associate Banquo. Banquo was the legendary ancestor of James VI of Scotland, who ascended the English throne as ▷ James I in 1603. The relative idealization of Banquo, the prominence of witchcraft – a subject that was one of King James' hobbies – and other indications show that the play was written to appeal to the king's interest. They are all put to artistic purpose by Shakespeare, however, and enhance rather than deflect from his imaginative intention.

The tragedy is the conversion of a good man into a wholly evil one. Macbeth begins as the heroic warrior who defends Scotland against a triple enemy: the king of Norway has invaded Scotland in alliance with the open rebel Macdonwald and the secret rebel Cawdor. After his victory, Macbeth is confronted by a triple enemy assailing his own soul: the witches; his own evil desires; and his wife, who reinforces these desires. He first encounters the witches, who predict that he is to be king of Scotland, after being made Thane (Lord) of Cawdor. As Macbeth knows nothing of Cawdor's part in the rebellion and invasion, both prophecies are to him equally incredible. The second is, however, immediately confirmed by emissaries from Duncan, king of Scotland. Macbeth is now lord of Cawdor and finds himself haunted by thoughts of bloodthirsty ambition: he becomes his soul's own secret enemy. The witches and his own desire would not in the end have been sufficient to cause him to murder the king, but Lady Macbeth dedicates herself to reinforcing his ambition. Macbeth is thus brought to murder Duncan, though in a state of horror at the deed, and becomes king on the flight of Duncan's son Malcolm. After the murder, however, he becomes a hardened man, though a restless and desperate one; he proceeds to the murder of Banquo, whose children the witches have predicted will succeed him on the throne, and then degenerates into massacre and tyranny. The play exemplifies one of the beliefs of Shakespeare's time, that the soul of man is the pattern of the state, and that where evil breaks into the soul of a king it will extend over the state he rules.

Macbeth was written in Shakespeare's maturest period; together with *Othello*, ▷ *King Lear*, and ▷ *Antony and Cleopatra*, it is accounted one of his finest tragedies.

MacCaig, Norman (b 1910)
Poet. A Scottish writer, educated at Edinburgh University, and often compared to fellow Scot ▷ Hugh MacDiarmid, MacCaig uses mainly traditional poetic forms for his witty verse, although he has also been drawn towards ▷ free verse. His publications include: *Far Cry* (1943); *Riding Lights* (1955); *A Common Gate* (1960); *Surroundings* (1967); *Selected Poems* (1971); *Tree of Strings* (1977); *The Equal Skies* (1980); *A World of Difference* (1983); *Voice-Over* (1988).

▷ Scottish literature in English.

MacDiarmid, Hugh (Christopher Murray Grieve) (1892–1978)
Poet and critic. A Marxist, and a leading Scottish nationalist. His outstanding contribution has been the revival of the Lowland Scottish branch of English (once called Inglis, now for literary purposes, Lallans, and still the medium of speech) as a poetic medium. The language had a distinguished literary phase about 1500, and reached another peak in the work of Robert Burns in the 18th century, but thereafter was overwhelmed by southern English. In the earlier and greater period, Scots poetry was part of the wide European tradition; Burns' excellence drew from the surviving vigour of Lowland Scots culture. MacDiarmid's success arose from his ability to follow the example of Burns in far less promising conditions, and to resist southern English modes by his awareness of the wider context of Europe. His best-known poem in Lallans is *A Drunk Man Looks at the Thistle*. He also wrote in southern English. *Complete Poems 1920–1976*, ed. M. Grieve and W. R. Aitken.

▷ Scottish literature in English.

Bib: Glen, D., *Hugh MacDiarmid and the Scottish Renaissance*.

MacDonald, George (1824–1905)
Novelist and children's author (▷ children's literature), his father was a weaver in rural Aberdeenshire. Educated at Aberdeen University, MacDonald worked as a tutor in London and later trained as a Congregational minister. He served the community at Arundel from 1850 to 1853, but was dismissed from his job for heresy, whereupon he turned to journalism and lecturing for a living. MacDonald also began to produce fairy stories which were deeply influenced by his theological training in their blending of elements of Christian ▷ symbolism and mysticism. He eventually settled in London in 1859 as Professor of English Literature at Bedford College. His first three novels, *David Elginbrod* (1863), *Alec Forbes* (1865) abd *Robert Falconer* (1868), were set in his native Aberdeenshire and are remarkable for their attack on Calvinsim. (▷ John Calvin). He is chiefly remembered for ▷ allegorical fantasies such as *Phantasies, A Faerie Romance for Men and Women* (1858) and *Lilith* (1895) and, more so, for his children's books: *At the Back of the North Wind* (1871), and *The Princess and the Goblin* (1872) and *The Princess and Curdie*, which are allegories of good (personified by the miner's son Curdie) and evil (goblins and other misshapen figures). These have since become children's classics. He wrote over twenty novels, many of which merge theological argument with Scottish rural manners, and he is often regarded as a precursor of the 1890s 'Kailyard' school of novelists (▷ Scottish Literature in English). He also produced several volumes of verse. MacDonald was a close friend of ▷ Lewis Carroll, and his children were the first to hear the story of ▷ *Alice in Wonderland*. His influence can be traced in the work of ▷ G.K. Chesterton, ▷ C.S. Lewis and ▷ J.R.R. Tolkein.

Bib: Wolff, R.L., *The Golden Key, A Study of the Fiction of George MacDonald*; Collins, R.A. and Pearce, H.D. (eds.), *The Scope of the Fantastic – Culture, Biography, Themes.*

McEwan, Ian (b 1948)
Novelist and short-story writer. His first collection of stories, *First Love, Last Rites* (1975) gained immediate notoriety for its erotic, perverse and macabre concerns, which also figure in *In Between the Sheets* (1978). His first novel, *The Cement Garden* (1978) is a story of adolescent guilt, while *The Comfort of Strangers* (1981) is a dream-like narrative set in Venice and ending in violence. His recent work includes *The Child in Time* (1987); *The Innocent* (1990); and *Black Dogs* (1992). He has also written a television play, *The Imitation Game* (1981) and a screenplay, *The Ploughman's Lunch* (1983).

McGahern, John (b 1934)
Irish novelist and short-story writer. Educated at University College Dublin. After his second novel, *The Dark* (1965) was banned, he lost his job as a schoolteacher in Ireland and was obliged to move to London. He has been a Research Fellow at the University of Reading, a visiting professor in the USA and Northern Arts Fellow at Newcastle University. He now lives in Ireland and teaches at University College Galway. In one of his short stories a character makes television documentaries about 'the darker aspects of Irish life' and this might serve as a description of McGahern's own fiction, which explores family tensions, and minor, mundane tragedies of loss, alienation and unfulfilment in domestic Irish settings, using a language which is generally sparse and understated, but is illuminated by colloquial vividness and humour and sometimes modulates into lyricism. His other novels are: *The Barracks* (1963); *The Leavetaking* (1974); *The Pornographer* (1979); *Amongst Women* (1990). Volumes of short stories: *Nightlines* (1970); *Getting Through* (1978); *High Ground* (1985); *The Collected Short Stories* (1992).

McGrath, John (b 1935)
One of the foremost writers of the political fringe during the 1970s and 80s. In 1971 he founded the 7:84 company (the name is based on a statistic which revealed that 7 per cent of the population owned 84 per cent of the country's wealth). The company was divided into two, between Scotland and England, in 1973. One of McGrath's most successful works was the popular entertainment *The Cheviot, the Stag and the Black, Black Oil* (1973), written for 7:84 Scotland. In this he compared the plundering of

Scottish oil assets with the Highland Clearances. He has consistently insisted on disassociating himself from the theatre establishment and once said he would 'rather have a bad night in Bootle' than write a play for the ▷ National Theatre. His radical ideas about the politics of entertainment are recorded in his book, *A Good Night Out* (1981). Other plays are: *The Game's a Bogey* (1974); *Fish in the Sea* (1977); *Little Red Hen* (1977); *Yobbo Nowt* (1978); *Joe's Drum* (1979); *Blood Red Roses* (1981); *Swings and Roundabouts* (1981).

Machaut, Guillaume de (c 1330–77)
French poet and musician. Machaut was a prolific and influential composer of lyric poems and songs, using and developing a number of poetic forms (eg ▷ ballade, ▷ rondeau). His narrative poetry includes several ▷ dream-vision poems, exploring problems of love and its literary representation, which influenced the form and structure of ▷ Chaucer's dream-vision poetry, especially the ▷ *Book of the Duchess*.
Bib: Wimsatt, J., *Chaucer and the French Love Poets: the Literary background of the 'Book of the Duchess'*; Windeatt, B. (trans.), *Chaucer's Dream Poetry: Sources and Analogues*.

Macheath
Central character in ▷ Gay's ▷ *The Beggar's Opera*. Macheath is a highwayman and sexual adventurer, who bigamously marries ▷ Polly Peachum and Lucy Lockit, at the same time conducting a series of other amours. Betrayed by one of his other women, he is sentenced to be hanged. He is reprieved at the last minute, when one of the players in the comedy demands a happy ending, and throws in his lot with Polly. The resolution is a ▷ satiric reversal of the contemporary dramatic vogue for administering poetic justice.

Machen, Arthur (1863–1947)
Novelist and short story writer. Born in Caerleon, Monmouthshire, Arthur Machen migrated to London to become a journalist. He is best known for his tales of the occult, influenced by his interest in Arthurian legend and Celtic and pre-Christian religions. This permeates much of his work, a section of his output appearing first in the *London Evening News* between 1910 and 1914. His short story collections comprise: *The House of Souls* (1906); *The Shining Pyramid* (1925); *The Green Round* (1933); *The Cosy Room* (1936); and *The Children of the Pool* (1936); a novella, *The Great Return* (1915); and his novels: *The Hill of Dreams* (1907); *The Terror* (1917); and *The Secret Glory* (1922). His autobiography appeared in two volumes, *Far Off Things* (1922) and *Near and Far* (1923).
Bib: Stephens, M. (Ed.), *The Oxford Companion to the Literature of Wales*; Jones, G. and Rowlands, J., *Profiles*.

Machiavelli, Nicolo di Bernardo dei (1469–1527)
Italian political theorist and historian. Machiavelli can be thought of as having two discrete existences. One is that of the Florentine diplomat, author of the comedy *La Mandragola* (1518) and of a series of important treatises on politics and statecraft: *The Prince* (1513), *Art of War* (1520) and *The Discourses* (1531). The other existence, however, is that which haunted the imagination of English writers in the 16th century and later, when Machiavelli's reputation as a cynical, cunning and diabolic figure emerges. In fact, Machiavelli's own works were very little known in England (other than by unreliable report) until a translation of *The Prince* appeared in 1640, though translations of his *Art of War* and portions of his historical works had been translated and published in 1560 and 1593 respectively. Nevertheless, it is this image of Machiavelli which became influential in England, as is evidenced by ▷ Christopher Marlowe's creation of the stage-figure Machevill in his play ▷ *The Jew of Malta*. We can perhaps best understand this image of the Italian thinker in England as the embodiment, or focus, of a network of anxieties experienced within the emergent Protestant state, and directed outwards on the threatening presence of continental (and Catholic) Europe.
Bib: Gilmore, M. P. (ed.), *Studies on Machiavelli*.

McIlvanney, William (b 1936)
Novelist. Born in Kilmarnock in Scotland he attended Glasgow University and after teacher training college worked as a school teacher from 1959 until 1977, when he turned to writing full time. *Docherty* (1975) is the story of Tam Docherty, a miner of great strength, courage, integrity and political conviction. Within a close-knit working-class community he struggles against poverty, war and a harsh economic system in support of his family and friends and is worn down but never wholly defeated. Other novels: *Remedy is None* (1966); *A Gift from Nessus* (1968); *Laidlaw* (1977); *The Papers of Tony Veitch* (1983). *The Longships in Harbour* (1970) is a volume of poems and 'Growing up in the West' (in *Memoirs of a Modern Scotland*, 1970, ed. K. Miller) is an autobiographical essay.
Bib: Murray, I. and Tait, B. (eds), *Ten Modern Scottish Novels*.

Mackenzie, Compton (1883–1972)
Novelist. Son of a British actor-manager and an American actress. A very prolific writer of great popularity; his best-known novels are probably *Sinister Street* (1913–14) and *The Four Winds of Love* – a sequence composed of *The*

East Wind (1937), *The South Wind* (1937), *The West Wind* (1940), *West to North* (1940), *The North Wind* (1944–5). When he began writing, ▷ Henry James regarded him as one of the most promising of younger novelists, and ▷ Ford Madox Ford thought *Sinister Street* perhaps a work of genius. However, other critics have rarely given him extensive attention.
Bib: Dooley, D. T., *Compton Mackenzie*; Linklater, A., *Compton Mackenzie: A Life*.

Mackenzie, Henry (1745–1831)
Scottish novelist and magazine editor. His novel *The Man of Feeling* (1771) epitomized the 18th-century cult of ▷ sensibility. His second novel, *The Man of the World* (1773), has a villainous hero in contrast to the sensitive, benevolent and unworldly hero of his first book. He also published *Julia de Roubigné* (1777), which shows the influence of ▷ Richardson, and a play, *The Prince of Tunis* (1773).

McKerrow, R. B. (Ronald Brownlees) (1872–1940)
Editor and bibliographer who was co-founder of the Malone Society (1906), dedicated to the study and editing of early and often neglected English drama. He wrote the seminal *An Introduction to Bibliography for Literary Students* (1927). He was one of the driving forces behind the 'New Bibliography' and is the author of the important *Prolegomena* (1939) for an Oxford edition of ▷ Shakespeare's works. This latter, which aimed at discovering an editorial methodology from ten selected texts, has proved an important milestone on the road to the new and revisionary Oxford University Press Shakespeare edited by Gary Taylor and Stanley Wells.

Macklin, Charles (1699–1797)
Actor, manager, singer, dancer, dramatist. Macklin began employment as a scout at Trinity College Dublin, and came to London as a waiter before 1720. Some of his early stage performances were at ▷ Lincoln's Inn Fields, and in the next few years, he acted at ▷ Goodman's Fields Theatre, the ▷ Haymarket Theatre and ▷ Drury Lane.

In 1741 he astonished audiences with a radical new interpretation of the role of Shylock in ▷ *The Merchant of Venice*, hitherto played for many years in low buffoonish style. Macklin presented him as a harsh, stern character, dressed 'authentically' with a red Venetian-style hat and red beard, and a long black gown. The response was repeated thunderous applause, such that he had to stop at the ends of several speeches to allow it to die away. His performance was recalled in detail by some spectators for decades afterwards. Its naturalism helped to render ▷ James Quin's elaborate and stylized methods obsolete, and set a precedent for the ultimately more successful actor, ▷ David Garrick, whom Macklin then began to sponsor and coach.

Subsequent years of Macklin's career were mainly divided between Dublin and London, but in 1773 he caused another sensation by creating a ▷ Macbeth in 'the old Caledonian habit', instead of the scarlet coat and wig worn, for example, by Garrick in the role. By the 1780s, Macklin's advanced age and failing health began to interfere seriously with his performances and he was finally forced to retire in 1789, after a career lasting nearly 70 years.

Macklin's achievements, and his reputation, have been somewhat obscured by those of his younger, more personable and physically more attractive contemporary, David Garrick, who perfected the acting style which Macklin initiated. Macklin trained a generation of actors and actresses in his methods, and he is credited with turning acting into a 'science', a tribute to the seriousness with which he took his profession, and to his imaginative abilities. His career was constantly interrupted by squabbles with other actors and managers, fuelled by his notorious temper.
Bib: Appleton, W., *Charles Macklin an Actor's Life*; Kirkman, J. T., *Memoirs of the Life of Charles Macklin*; Congreve, F., *Authentic Memoirs of the Late Charles Macklin*.

Macmillan's Magazine
It was founded in 1859 and published a variety of material, including pieces by ▷ Tennyson, ▷ Matthew Arnold, ▷ Henry James and ▷ Thomas Hardy. It folded in 1907.

MacNeice, Louis (1907–63)
Poet. He was born in Northern Ireland, the son of an Anglican clergyman who became a bishop. During the 1930s he was associated by the reading public with a group of left-wing poets led by ▷ W. H. Auden. They were certainly his friends, but, although he had socialist sympathies, he never committed himself politically; in politics, as in religion, he was ▷ agnostic. He excelled in witty, sensuous verse of rhythmical versatility and with a strong element of caustic pessimism. He also wrote criticism, notably *The Poetry of W. B. Yeats* (1941), numerous plays for radio, and translated the *Agamemnon* of Aeschylus (1936) and Goethe's *Faust* (1951). He collaborated with Auden in *Letters from Iceland* (1937). *Collected Poems*, ed. E. R. Dodds (1979).
Bib: Fraser, G. S., in *Vision and Rhetoric*; Thwaite, A., *Essays on Contemporary English Poetry*.

Macpherson, James (1736–96)
The son of a farmer, educated in Aberdeen and at Edinburgh University. In 1760 he published 16 prose poems under the title *Fragments of*

Ancient Poetry, Collected in the Highlands of Scotland, and translated from the Gaelic or Erse Language. He attributed them to the 3rd-century poet ▷ Ossian, an attribution which was accepted by most readers at the time, though some scholars were sceptical. After travelling in the Western Isles in 1760–61 at the expense of his supporters in Edinburgh, he published 'translations' of two complete epics by Ossian: *Fingal* (1762) and *Temora* (1763), which he claimed to have similarly 'collected'. The cloudy rhetoric and dramatic character simplification of Macpherson's prose-poetry caught the mood of the moment. ▷ Thomas Gray was enraptured by 'the infinite beauty' of the *Fragments*, ▷ William Blake was adulatory about them, and Macpherson's *Ossian* retained its popularity throughout the ▷ Romantic period, particularly on the continent. ▷ Goethe admired it; ▷ Napoleon carried a copy of Macpherson on his campaigns and took it into exile with him to St Helena. ▷ Samuel Johnson was amongst those who attacked the authenticity of Macpherson's sources, replying when asked if he believed that any modern man could have written such works: 'Yes Sir, many men, many women, and many children.' The indignant poet threatened him with physical violence. In later years Macpherson became a political ▷ journalist, wrote history with a ▷ Jacobite bias, and was elected MP for Camelford. After his death the Highland Society of Scotland undertook an inquiry into his work and in 1805 declared it to be an amalgam of freely adapted Irish ballads and original compositions by Macpherson himself.

▷ Percy, Thomas.

Madrigal

A poem composed to be sung, with or without instrumental accompaniment. It derived from the Italian '*canzone*', and flourished in England especially between 1580 and 1630; one of its main practitioners is said to be ▷ William Byrd, although he himself did not consider his songs to be madrigals. It was sung chorally, and had three forms:

1 The Ayre. This had a melody composed for the top voice, which was accompanied by the other voices to the same melody.

2 The Ballet. This resembled the ayre, but was distinguished by its dance-like melody and refrain.

3 The Madrigal proper. This had different 'parts', *ie* melodies, for the individual voices, and was so composed that the melodies interwove. The parts were sometimes composed with the effect of dramatic contrast, *eg* by Thomas Weelkes (?1575–1623). Great attention was paid by composers to bringing out the meaning of the words, so that poets and musicians worked in close collaboration. Only ▷ Thomas Campion is known to have composed music for his own words, but others are believed to have done so. Ayres and madrigals are common in the plays of the period, and most of the poets wrote them.

Maeterlinck, Maurice (1862–1949)

Belgian ▷ symbolist dramatist, influential in the development of 'serious' drama at the end of the 19th century. His most famous work is *Pelleas et Melisande*, produced in London in 1898, and again in 1904 with Sarah Bernhardt as Pelleas and Mrs Patrick Campbell as Melisande. His plays were admired by the poet W.B. Yeats (1865–1939) and actor and dramatist Harvey Granville Barker (1877–1946); *Aglavaine and Selysette* was given six performances at the Court Theatre in 1904.

Bib: Knapp, B., *Maurice Maeterlinck*.

Magazine

Originally meaning 'storehouse', the word has also denoted, since the 18th century, a periodical containing miscellaneous material, *eg* the *Gentleman's Magazine* (founded 1731): 'a Monthly Collection to store up, as in a Magazine, the most remarkable pieces on the subjects above-mentioned' (from the introduction to the first number). In the 18th and early 19th century magazines only differed from other serious periodicals (*eg* the ▷ *Edinburgh Review* and the ▷ *Quarterly*) in having greater variety of content and being open to imaginative writing. Distinguished magazines of this kind include ▷ *Blackwood's* and the second ▷ *London Magazine* (1820–29). Later in the 19th century, magazines became predominantly popular periodicals devoted principally to fiction. However, serious magazines still exist, *eg* the current *London Magazine*, the third to bear the name. Since World War II magazines have often been seen as synonymous with reading matter specifically directed at women; examples are *Vogue, Cosmopolitan*, and the feminist magazines *Spare Rib* and *Everywoman*. Whilst literary magazines have declined in popularity, one of the current best-selling magazines in Britain is the TV listings publication, *Radio Times*. See *Wellesley Index to Periodicals*.

Magic realism

A term applied in literature primarily to Latin American novelists such as ▷ Jorge Luis Borges (1899–1987), Gabriel García Márquez (b 1928) and Alejo Carpentier (b 1904), whose work combines a realistic manner with strong elements of the bizarre, supernatural and fantastic. This technique has influenced novelists such as ▷ John Fowles, ▷ Angela Carter and ▷ Salman Rushdie.

▷ Spanish influence on English fiction.

Magna Carta

The Great Charter which ▷ King John was

forced by his barons to accept in 1215. It has long been popularly regarded as the foundation of English liberties, guaranteeing such rights as freedom from arbitrary imprisonment. However, 16th-century plays on King John, *eg* ▷ Shakespeare's, omit mention of the Charter, which came to have its modern symbolic importance only in consequence of the conflicts between kings and parliaments in the 17th century.

Mahon, Derek (b 1941)
Poet. Mahon was born in Belfast and educated at Dublin, and has lectured at the universities of Sussex and Ulster. Along with fellow poets James Simmons, ▷ Paul Muldoon, ▷ Seamus Heaney and Michael Longley, he is an important figure in the Northern Irish renaissance in contemporary poetry. See *Night Crossing* (1968); *Beyond Howth* (1970); *Lives* (1972); *The Snow Party* (1975); *Light Music* (1977); *Poems 1962–1978* (1979); and *Selected Poems* (1991).

▷ Irish literature in English.

Maid Marian **(1822)**
▷ Thomas Love Peacock's parody of ▷ medieval romances (such as ▷ Scott's ▷ *Ivanhoe*, 1819) fashionable in the early 19th century. It contains very good songs in comic opera style.

Maids Tragedy, The **(1610)**
A play by ▷ Francis Beaumont and ▷ John Fletcher. It takes place in the town of Rhodes, and the story concerns the attempt of the king to conceal his relationship with his mistress, Evadne, by forcing one of his most loyal courtiers, Amintor, to marry her. Aspasia, the 'maid' of the tragedy, is the girl whom Amintor has to give up. Evadne's brother, Melantius, discovers the unhappy secret and compels his sister to murder the king; she then commits suicide on finding that Amintor will not forgive her.

The tragedy is generally considered to be Beaumont and Fletcher's masterpiece. It is typical of later ▷ Jacobean tragedy in relying for its effectiveness on individual scenes rather than on its totality, which is unconvincing. It is typical of Beaumont and Fletcher in the accomplished melody of its ▷ blank verse and the skill of its theatrical craftmanship.

Maitland, Sara (b 1950)
Novelist, short-story writer. She was educated at St Anne's College Oxford, and is a member of the Feminist Writers Group, a group of women writers who share socialist and feminist convictions. Another member is ▷ Michèle Roberts, who shares with Maitland an interest in the relations of Christianity with feminism and women's sexuality, an interest reflected in Maitland's novel *Virgin Territory* (1984), about tension between lesbian love and Christianity. The group also includes Michelene Wandor (with whom Maitland co-wrote a post-modernist epistolary novel, *Arky Types*, 1987), ▷ Zoë Fairbairns and Valerie Miner. They collectively produced a volume of short stories, interspersed with direct political statements and entitled *Tales I Tell My Mother* (1978); the stories were written individually but discussed and revised collectively. The blending of realism and fantasy which has emerged as an important feminist strategy (for example in the work of ▷ Angela Carter) is apparent in Maitland's novel *Three Times Table* (1990), which explores the lives of three women in London but includes dragons as well as dialogue. *Home Truths* (1993) is a novel about family conflicts and memory lost and regained. Maitland's other works include her novel *Daughter of Jerusalem* (1978), *Very Heaven: Looking Back at the Sixties* (1988) and *The Rushdie File* (1989), edited with Lisa Appignanesi. Maitland joined the Roman Catholic Church in 1993.

Makin, Bathsua (1612–c 1680)
Educationalist and poet. Her poetry, *Musa Virginea* (1616), is a multilingual collection dedicated to various members of the royal family, but it is for her role as a teacher of women that Makin is best known. In the early 1640s she was appointed tutor to Princess Elizabeth, the sister of ▷ Charles II, and following the Restoration of the monarchy she opened a school at Tottenham High Cross and advertised it with the publication of *An Essay to Revive the Antient Education of Gentlewomen* (1673). Dedicated to the princesses Anne and Mary (somewhat inappropriately, since their father opposed the education of women), this treatise sets out the benefits of a scholarly education for women and cites numerous examples, including ▷ Elizabeth I, ▷ Ann Bradstreet and ▷ Katherine Philips, to prove her argument. Oddly, Makin takes on a male persona in the book and is very careful to assert that schooling for girls will not make them equal with boys, but better wives. Rather than dismiss Makin as simply accepting the renewed repression of women in Restoration monarchist circles, it is important to realize that she was attempting to win custom for her school and was, within certain confines, offering women the education necessary for independent and fulfilled lives.
Bib: Hobby, E., *Virtue of Necessity*; Fraser, A., *The Weaker Vessel.*

Malaprop, Mrs
A character in ▷ Richard Brinsley Sheridan's comedy ▷ *The Rivals*. She is the aunt and guardian of the heroine, Lydia Languish. Her principal comic effect is her habit of

misusing words; this has given rise to the term 'malapropism'.

***Malcontent, The* (1604)**
A ▷ tragicomedy by ▷ John Marston, with additions by ▷ John Webster. An intrigue engineered by the villainous Lord Mendoza has caused the deposition of Giovanni Altofronto, the noble Duke of Genoa, and substituted the weak Pietro Jacomo, who is married to Aurelia, daughter of the Duke of Florence. Altofronto, however, has returned to his own court in disguise as Malevole (the 'malcontent'). He is tolerated as a witty though sour court jester and commentator on the times and its corrupt manners. Meanwhile he awaits his chance for revenge and the recovery of his dukedom. Mendoza continues to conspire against the new duke, whose wife is Mendoza's mistress, and Malevole in turn conspires against Mendoza. In the end, Mendoza is exposed, and Pietro and Aurelia penitently resign the duchy back to the rightful duke.

The play is part ▷ satire and part ▷ revenge play, midway between ▷ Ben Jonson's comedies of ▷ humours (*eg* ▷ *Volpone*) and ▷ Tourneur's ▷ *Revenger's Tragedy*. The malcontent role of bitter commentator on society is a common onc in ▷ Jacobean drama; ▷ Bosola in ▷ Webster's ▷ *Duchess of Malfi* is a well-known example, but ▷ Hamlet, Iago (in ▷ *Othello*) and Thersites in ▷ *Troilus and Cressida* all have some aspects of the malcontent in their parts. The essence of the role is that the malcontent is somehow frustrated from satisfying his ambitions or being accepted by the rest of society; such exclusion gives him the motives (morally acceptable or otherwise) and the detachment for his satire.

Malet, Lucas (1852–1931)
▷ Pseudonym of novelist Mary Kingsley, the daughter of novelist ▷ Charles Kingsley. The pseudonym was adopted to avoid capitalizing on the family's literary fame. *Mrs Lorimer: A Sketch in Black and White* (1882) was Malet's first novel, and she continued to write until her death, producing more than twenty works, including *Colonel Enderby's Wife* (1885); *The Wages of Sin* (1891); *The Gateless Barrier* (1900); *The Far Horizon* (1906); *Deadhum Hard* (1919); *The Survivors* (1923) and *The Dogs of Want* (1924). Her style is prolix and often sentimental, her characterization and detail typically 19th- rather than 20th-century, yet her contribution to literature was recognized when she was awarded a civic pension in 1930.

Malgonkar, Manohar (b 1913)
Indian novelist and short-story writer. Educated at Bombay University, he has been an officer in the Maratha Light Infantry, a big game hunter, a civil servant, a mine owner and a farmer, as well as standing for parliament. He is primarily a novelist of action and adventure, with a Conradian (▷ Joseph Conrad) stress on the stuggles of the individual; he uses Indian historical settings such as the Indian Munity, the last years of the Raj and the aftermath of Independence and Partition in 1947. His novels are: *Distant Drum* (1960); *Combat of Shadows* (1962); *The Princes* (1963); *A Bend in the Ganges* (1964); *The Devil's Wind: Nana Saheb's Story* (1972); *Shalimar* (1978); *The Garland Keepers* (1980); *Bandicoot Run* (1982). Volumes of short stories: *A Toast in Warm Wine* (1974); *In Uniform* (1975); *Bombay Beware* (1975); *Rumble-Tumble* (1972). He has also written biography, popular history and a screenplay.
Bib: Naipaul, V.S., *An Area of Darkness*; Dayananda, J.Y., *Manohar Malgonkar*.

Mallarmé Stéphane
▷ Symbolism.

Mallet (Malloch), David (?1705–65)
Poet. On moving from ▷ Edinburgh to London he expunged the Scotticisms from his speech and changed his name from the Scottish Malloch to the English Mallet. He is remembered for his collaboration with ▷ James Thomson on the ▷ masque *Alfred* (1740), and also for his ▷ ballad *William and Margaret* (1724), which anticipates the ▷ Gothic fashion in popular taste, and was reprinted in ▷ Thomas Percy's *Reliques* under the title *Margaret's Ghost*.

Mallock, W. H. (William Hurrell) (1849–1923)
A ▷ Catholic controversialist now best known for his satirical novel *The New Republic* (1877), portraying leading members of the Victorian intelligentsia, including John Ruskin, Matthew Arnold, Walter Pater and Thomas Huxley. He wrote a number of books on social questions against socialism. His *Memoirs of Life and Literature* was published in 1920.
Bib: Adams, A. B., *The Novels of W. H. Mallock*; Wolf, R. L., *Gains and Losses: Novels of Faith and Doubt in Victorian England*.

Malone, Edmund (1741–1812)
The greatest early editor of ▷ Shakespeare's works, many of whose textual emendations and editorial principles are still widely used. His greatest work remains his posthumously published edition of the complete Shakespeare (1821) and his research on the order in which Shakespeare's plays were written. He was also the first to denounce the Shakespearean forgeries of William Henry Ireland (1775–1835), one of whose fake plays, *Vortigern and Rowena*, was performed as Shakespeare's at ▷ Drury Lane.
▷ Shakespeare editions.

Malory, Thomas
Identifying which Thomas Malory produced the work known as the ▷ *Morte D'Arthur* in

around 1469/70 remains a controversial issue. Sir Thomas Malory of Newbold Revel (c 1446–71) is the most generally accepted candidate for the role. He was in the service of the Earl of Warwick in the French wars (c 1414), and by 1440 was established as a country gentleman, being knighted in 1442. After 1450 his public standing seems to have radically declined. His extensive spells in prison (on a range of charges including rape) after 1450 may have provided the opportunity for his literary labour. Although it is possible to recreate the public life of this Sir Thomas Malory, there is no documentation which sheds any light on his literary career.
Bib: Lacy, N. et al. (ed.), *The Arthurian Encyclopaedia*; Riddy, F., *Sir Thomas Malory*.

Malthus, Thomas Robert (1766–1834)
Economist; particularly famous for his *Essay on Population* (1798), which he reissued in an expanded and altered form in 1803. Its original title was: *An Essay on the Principle of Population as it affects the Future Improvement of Society, with Remarks on the Speculations of Mr Godwin, M. Condorcet, and other Writers.*

The essence of his view was that social progress tends to be limited by the fact that population increases more rapidly than the means of subsistence, and always reaches the limits of subsistence, so that a substantial part of society is doomed to live beyond the margin of poverty. The 'natural checks' which prevent population increase from exceeding the means of subsistence are war, famine, and pestilence, to which he added human misery and vice. In the second edition he added a further possible check by 'moral restraint', ie late marriages and sexual continence. These arguments made a strong impression on public opinion; an important practical consequence of them was the replacement of the existing haphazard methods of poor relief by the harsh but reasoned and systematic ▷ Poor Law system of 1834.

Malthus' relentless and pitiless reasoning led to political economy becoming known as the ▷ 'dismal science'. His conclusions were contested by humanitarians, and later seemed belied by factors he did not foresee, such as cheap imports of food from newly exploited colonies like Canada. Since 1918 'Malthusian' theories of the dangers of over-population have revived.

▷ Darwin, Charles Robert.

Man in Black, The
A character in the collection of essays by ▷ Oliver Goldsmith entitled *The Citizen of the World* (1762). He is prodigiously generous, but his sensibility causes him to conceal this virtue by pretending to be mean.

Man of Law's Tale, The
One of ▷ Chaucer's *Canterbury Tales*, written in ▷ rhyme royal, recounting the story of Constance, daughter of a Christian emperor, whose adventures are triggered by her marriage to the Sultan of Syria (who agrees to convert to the religion of his wife). Constance becomes the victim of a plot organized by the Sultan's mother, a confirmed pagan, and is cast adrift on the sea. She is providentially protected on her journey but becomes a victim of yet another plot by a pagan mother-in-law, after her conversion of, and marriage to, the King of Northumberland. After further ordeals she is eventually reunited with all members of her family in Rome. The basic narrative paradigm has analogues in other examples of pious romances which have a constant woman at their centre (notably the Middle English romance *Emaré*), and ▷ John Gower tells a version of the story of Constance in Book II of the ▷ *Confessio Amantis*. The tale is prefaced by a wry complaint from the Man of Law, who claims to have difficulty in finding a story to tell because Chaucer has told them all before.

***Man of Mode, The: Or Sir Fopling Flutter* (1676)**
Third and last play by the Restoration dramatist, ▷ Sir George Etherege, written in the ▷ Comedy of Manners' style, and generally held to be his best. It concerns the amours of Dorimant, a rake whose character is probably based on that of the ▷ Earl of Rochester. He pursues, and then rejects, first the infatuated Mrs Loveit and then her supposed friend, the weak and stupid Bellinda, who intrigues with him in secret. He ends up with the wealthy and beautiful Harriet, who has held out against his wiles until he has promised to marry her. A subplot concerns the wooing of Young Bellair and Emilia. The title derives from the foolish Sir Fopling Flutter, a minor figure who personifies slavery to fashion. Dorimant's chief charm is his acerbic wit; otherwise he is a portrait of a misogynist, who takes as much delight in hurting women as in seducing them. The play's tone is cynical rather than satirical, and the overall effect one of brilliance, but with a deeply disturbing note.

Manchester Guardian, The
It was started in 1821 as a weekly paper, becoming daily in 1855. As the leading Liberal publication outside London, it was edited from 1872 to 1929 by C. P. Scott. Its title was changed to *The Guardian* in 1959, and since 1961 it has been published from London. It is considered to be one of the more liberal or left-wing papers.

Manciple's Tale, The
One of ▷ Chaucer's ▷ *Canterbury Tales*, an animal fable which tells the story of the metamorphosis of a tell-tale crow (based

primarily on ▷ Ovid's *Metamorphoses* ii, though ▷ John Gower also tells the story in the ▷ *Confessio Amantis*). The Manciple recounts how Phoebus fosters a white crow whom he teaches to speak and through whom he learns of his wife's adultery. In his rage, Phoebus kills his wife, and then blames the crow for his action. He plucks out all its feathers, deprives it of the faculty of speech and throws the bird to the Devil: from that time onwards, the narrator explains, all crows are black. The *Tale* concludes with a moralizing rant about the need to keep 'mum' and never to pass on stories.

Mandeville, Bernard de (1670?–1733)
Of Dutch birth, Mandeville made his career in London as a doctor. His satire in Hudibrastic (▷ *Hudibras*) ▷ couplets *The Grumbling Hive, or Knaves turn'd Honest* (1705) was reissued with accompanying prose essays in 1714 as *The Fable of the Bees; or Private Vices, Public Benefits.* Mandeville followed through the economic implications of the new bourgeois individualistic ethic with enthusiastic gusto, arguing that the greatest social good was generated by allowing the individual the maximum freedom to pursue private self-interest. The hive thrives so long as this principle is respected: 'Thus every Part was full of Vice,/Yet the whole Mass a paradise'. But once the ▷ Puritan moralist camp among the bees takes control, demand for luxuries and corrupt pleasures disappears, enterprise declines and the hive is ruined. The prose ▷ essays defend public brothels, argue that without the wasteful luxury of the rich the poor would starve, and doubt the utility of Christian morality in the conduct of war. Mandeville delighted in driving uncomfortable wedges between the economic and religious components of the new bourgeois consensus, and, like a kind of conservative George Bernard Shaw he expounded unpalatable truths with unabashed vigour. His pungent intellectual honesty offended optimistic ▷ Deists and pious Puritans alike, and it proved easier for writers such as the cleric William Law (1686–1761) to attack him as a scoffing blasphemer, than to answer his impressive logic.

***Manfred* (1817)**
A dramatic poem in ▷ blank verse by ▷ Lord Byron, set in the Alps. It focuses on the typical Byronic hero, outcast from society and haunted by the guilt of unnamed crimes. Manfred conjures up the Spirits of earth and air, the Witch of the Alps, the Destinies and Nemesis, and beseeches them in vain for oblivion. He eventually dies absolved, however, saved from the clutches of the evil spirits who claim his soul by the intervention of Astarte, the spirit of the woman whom he had loved. The poem, reminiscent of ▷ Goethe's *Faust*, was very popular throughout the 19th century, Schumann and Tchaikovsky basing major musical compositions upon it. Byron himself referred to it in a letter as 'a sort of mad drama'.

Mankind
A ▷ morality play, dating from c 1465–70, seemingly designed for performance by a small professional or semi-professional group (the collection of money for performance is built into the play text). The plot recounts an exemplary incident in the life of its central character, Mankind, who allows himself to be distracted almost to damnation by a rowdy, bawdy trio (New-Guise, Now-a-Days, Nought) directed by the devil Titivellus (a demonic figure traditionally associated with loose speech). Mankind's repentance brings the aid of Mercy. The play draws attention to the pleasures and dangers of the dramatic medium itself, and toys with its own audience's commitment to dramatic distraction.
Bib: Eccles, M. (ed.), *Macro Plays.*

Manley, Delarivière (?1663–1724)
Playwright and novelist. Manley's unconventional lifestyle led to many scandalous strictures. She married her cousin John Manley at an early age, only to find he was already married, and on making this discovery left him, although she was pregnant and had no means of support. For some months she lived in the household of the Duchess of Cleveland, acting as secretary and companion, but left her patronage after rumours of an affair with the Duchess's son.

For some time she seems to have lived in the country, returning to London in 1696, when two of her plays were performed: *The Lost Lover or the Jealous Husband* and *The Royal Mischief.* At this time she became the mistress of John Tilly, the Warden of Fleet Prison.

In 1705 Manley's novel *The Secret History of Queen Zarah* appeared, and proved an enormous success. In its use of a mythical society to satirize contemporary English life, it set the pattern for her later *roman à clef*, *The New Atalantis* (1709). In 1711 Manley succeeded ▷ Jonathan Swift as editor of ▷ *The Examiner*, and in the course of her writing career produced many political pamphlets. In 1714 *The Adventures of Rivella*, apparently a fictionalized autobiography, appeared. Her final achievement was a series of novels, *The Power of Love*, published in 1720.

Manners, Comedy of
A form in which laughter is provoked by exaggerations of fashionable behaviour, absurdities in fashion itself, or departures from what is considered to be civilized normality of behaviour. Thus a comedy of manners can only arise in a highly developed society, in which there is a leisured class which not only has standards of politeness and good sense in human

relationships but tends to give such standards first importance in social life. The ▷ Comedy of Humours of ▷ Ben Jonson and his younger contemporaries dealt with fundamental human appetites, and was therefore concerned with much more than what was regarded as civilized behaviour by fashionable society, though that was often included in their purview. In the court of the French king Louis XIV in the second half of the 17th century, a highly civilized society held to a code of behaviour which was also a code of morals; the comedies of ▷ Molière were the first true examples of the Comedy of Manners, and had profundity as well as surface brilliance. His comedy influenced dramatists in England. The Comedy of Manners in England is not so much a pure variety of drama, as a framework for plays with a witty, ▷ satiric atmosphere, and social comment, which may also contain other elements, such as ▷ Spanish Intrigue, Humours, ▷ Reform, etc. The bestknown comedies of this type were written after the Restoration of ▷ Charles II in 1660. Many involve a critique of marriage, and re-assessment of relations between the sexes, and of women's role in society. The plays are often sexually explicit, contributing to a growing reaction against them in the 18th and 19th centuries when, as standards of polite and rational behaviour extended through society, and audiences became more heterogeneous, drama tended to become more middle class, and to show more propriety. ▷ Goldsmith and ▷ Richard Brinsley Sheridan reacted to what they considered excessive sentimentalism in the works of some of their contemporaries, and consciously revived the spirit of Comedy of Manners in their plays, though these were never as bawdy as those of any of their predecessors.

Manning, Olivia (1915–80)
Novelist and short-story writer. Her major work is *The Balkan Trilogy* set in Romania, Greece and Egypt during the early stages of World War II, and which consists of: *The Great Fortune* (1960); *The Spoilt City* (1962) and *Friends and Heroes* (1965). It is told primarily through the consciousness of a newly married Englishwoman, and builds up a strong sense of place and of history through the portrayal of a wide range of characters and the accumulation of details of daily experience. The story is continued in *The Levant Trilogy*: *The Danger Tree* (1977); *The Battle Lost and Won* (1978); *The Sum of Things* (1980). Other novels: *The Wind Changes* (1937); *Artist Among the Missing* (1949); *School for Love* (1951); *A Different Face* (1953); *The Doves of Venus* (1955); *The Rain Forest* (1974). Story collections: *Growing Up* (1948); *My Husband Cartwright* (1956); *A Romantic Hero* (1967).

Mannyng, Robert (fl 1288–1338)
Writer and chronicler. Robert Mannyng is one of the few Middle English writers to offer autobiographical details in their work. From the information he provides in the prologues of his two works, it seems Mannyng (a native of Bourne in Lincolnshire) entered the Gilbertine order at an early age, was sent to Cambridge and then began his translation (*Handlyng Synne*) of the ▷ Anglo-Norman *Manuel de Pechiez* in 1303. Some time later, at the Gilbertine house of Sixhills, he produced a chronicle history of England, which he finished in 1338. *Handlyng Synne* is a book of doctrinal instruction, describing and illustrating the Ten Commandments/ Seven Deadly Sins/ Sacrilege/ Seven Sacraments/ Shrift; it follows the model of its Anglo-Norman source but Mannyng adds new exemplary narratives which liven the text considerably. His expanded story of the 'Dancers of Colbeck' appears in the Sacrilege section.

Mannyng's *Chronicle* covers the foundation and history of Britain (following ▷ Wace's *Roman de Brut* with additions from ▷ Geoffrey of Monmouth and ▷ Bede) and the history of England up to 1307 (following the Anglo-Norman *Chronicle* of Pierre de Langtoft). In both works he comments on the sources he uses, acknowledges his additions and remarks on the function of his translations into English. In the *Chronicle* he adds some interesting comments on the paucity of Arthurian material available in English and defends the historicity of ▷ King Arthur.
Bib: Sullens, Idelle (ed.), *Handlyng Synne*; Furnivall, F. J. (ed.), *The Story of England by Robert Mannyng of Brunne*.

Mansfield, Katherine (1888–1923)
Short-story writer. Born (Kathleen Mansfield Beauchamp) in Wellington, New Zealand; married the critic ▷ John Middleton Murry in 1913. Her story collections (several of which were published posthumously) are: *In a German Pension* (1911); *Je Ne Parle Pas Français* (1918); *Bliss* (1920); *The Garden Party* (1922); *The Dove's Nest* (1923); *Something Childish* (1924); *The Aloe* (1930); *Collected Stories* (1945). Her *Journal* (1927, enlarged edition 1934) and *Letters* (1928) were edited by Murry. The stories resemble in their form those of the Russian writer ▷ Chekhov, and ▷ James Joyce's ▷ *Dubliners*; they do not have a distinct plot with a definite beginning and ending and a self-sufficient action, conveying instead an impression of continuity with ordinary life, and depending for their unity on delicate balance of detail and feeling. She contributed to the development of the ▷ stream of consciousness technique, and to the ▷ modernist use of multiple viewpoints.
Bib: Alpers, A., *The Life of Katherine Mansfield*; Hanson, C., and Gurr, A., *Katherine Mansfield*.

***Mansfield Park* (1814)**
A novel by ▷ Jane Austen. The theme is the

conflict between three different styles of moral feeling. The first is that of Sir Thomas Bertram, owner of Mansfield Park; it stands for a system of conservative, orderly principle, a tradition inherited from the 18th century, emphasizing stability and discounting the feelings. The second style of moral feeling is embodied in Fanny Price, Sir Thomas' niece whom he takes into his household because her parents are poor and their family too large; although she is timid, withdrawn and overawed by her new surroundings, she possesses a highly developed sensibility and capacity for affection both of which are foreign to the Bertrams, except to the younger son, Edmund, who to some degree appreciates her. The third style is represented by Henry and Mary Crawford, half-brother and half-sister to the wife of the village parson. They are rich, independent, attractive; they do not share Sir Thomas' cold theories, and they do possess Fanny's capacity for ardent feeling; on the other hand, they are without Sir Thomas' dedication to conscience and without Fanny's reverence for consistency of moral with affectionate and aesthetic sensibilities. The difference between the three styles of life becomes overt while Sir Thomas is absent in the West Indies; the Crawfords virtually take over Mansfield Park in order to rehearse, with the Bertram children and two guests, a performance of Kotzebue's *Lovers' Vows*. Henry Crawford is by this time conducting a flirtation with Maria Bertram, who is engaged to one of the guests, Mr Rushworth, and Mary Crawford is in love with Edmund; these relationships are in effect parodied in the play (popular in Jane Austen's time) so that the characters can perform on the stage what they desire to enact in real life. Fanny, knowing that Sir Thomas would disapprove of amateur acting, refuses to take part, but the situation is painful to her because she is secretly in love with Edmund herself. The rehearsals are stopped by Sir Thomas' sudden return, but a new crisis occurs in Fanny's life when Henry, awakened to the reality of her diffident charms, proposes marriage to her. She refuses him, much to Sir Thomas' uncomprehending disapproval, and is not in a position to explain to him the grounds of her refusal: that she disapproves of Henry morally and is in love with his son. She is exiled to her own family at Portsmouth, where disorder and strong emotion, often reduced to callous bad temper by poverty and overcrowding, are the rule. Henry is for a time constant, but he disgraces himself, the Bertrams and his sister by eloping with Maria after she has married. By degrees, both Sir Thomas and Edmund came to appreciate Fanny at her true value, and at the end of the novel she is to become Edmund's wife.

Of Jane Austen's completed works *Mansfield Park* is the most direct criticism of the ▷ Regency style of sensibility (represented by the Crawfords), with its tendency to reject continuity with the best elements of the past; at the same time the criticism is balanced by a recognition of the importance of the sensibility if morality is to receive true life from the feelings. It is also a bold challenge to the romantic style of fiction: Mary Crawford, antagonist to the heroine Fanny, is not only shown as friendly to her and in all but the deepest sense appreciative of her; she is also the possessor of genuine social attractions which Fanny lacks. The reader is made to like both her and her brother, and at the same time obliged to acknowledge Fanny's ultimate human superiority.

Margaret of Anjou (1430–82)
The queen of ▷ King Henry VI. Owing to the weakness of her husband, it was she who was the effective leader of the Lancastrian party in the ▷ Wars of the Roses. As a woman with exceptional power and responsibilities, she became famous for her determined leadership, the ferocity with which she defended the rights of her husband and son, and her pitiless vengefulness. She is a prominent character in the three ▷ *Henry VI* plays by Shakespeare, and reappears in his ▷ *Richard III,* IV, iv, where she joins with the Yorkist ladies in a common lament for the dead of both families, since Richard has now laid waste his own, as well as contributing to the destruction of the Lancastrians.

Marginality
A widely-used metaphor to describe social groups or cultural practices which are on the edges of the mainstream. In much modern thinking, marginality carries two implications, one negative, the other neutral or even positive. Negatively, to be marginalized means to be excluded or ignored as, for example, work by women or black writers has been in literary studies. But in the other sense – widely used in ▷ postmodern theory – it is argued that contemporary societies and contemporary cultures are in fact largely cultures of the margins in which there is no settled sense of the centre. Thus, for example, 'English Literature' can no longer be used as a collective term in a world in which English is a global language used by very diverse cultural groups, and in which we are powerfully conscious of diversities of region, ethnicity, class and gender. As a result, there can be no accepted canon of great works, only works which speak to diverse ▷ interpretive communities. In 'the postmodern condition', inevitable marginality is a cause for some celebration because it guarantees diversity and plurality. Opponents of this idea, however, insist that this benign view underestimates the realities of power and disadvantage, while conservative critics deplore

the relativism of this idea and the loss of settled, central values.
▷ Decentred.

Marian Withers (1851)
A novel by ▷ Geraldine Jewsbury. Considered to be her best work of fiction, it is concerned with issues such as female ▷ education and societal expectations of women. Set in Manchester, the narrative focuses on the life of Marian Withers, detailing her social background and describing her passage to maturity.

Mariana
A character in ▷ Shakespeare's ▷ *Measure for Measure*; she was betrothed to Angelo, the deputy of the Duke of Vienna, and after being cast off by him she lives forsaken in 'the moated grange' until the Duke compels Angelo to marry her. She is the subject of one of the most famous poems by Alfred Tennyson (1809–92) – *Mariana*.

Marie de France (fl. c 1180)
One of the earliest known women writers of vernacular poetry, working in French, some time during the years 1160–1215, for, it seems, audiences in France and England (judging by the provenance of the extant manuscripts of her work). Little is known about her life; indeed the principal record of her existence derives from the signatures built into her work: her collection of *Lais*, her collection of *Fables*, and her version of *Espurgatoire S. Patrice (St Patrick's Purgatory)* all contain references to their composition by one 'Marie' who is, according to the epilogue of the *Fables*, from France. She was clearly an educated woman, acquainted with Latin and likely, therefore, to have had an ecclesiastical training of some kind. The image she develops in her work is of something of a cultural polymath, mediating between British/English/Latin culture of the past in the production of her poetry: she claims to have taken material for her *Lais* from British sources; claims to be translating her collection of *Fables* from an Old English work of ▷ King Alfred; and translates her account of St Patrick's Purgatory from Latin. She remains something of a literary enigma, despite scholarly hypotheses about her life and her possible connection with the court of Henry II.
Bib: Burgess, G. and Busby, K. (trans.), *The Lais of Marie de France*; Wilson, K. (ed.), *Medieval Women Writers*.

Marina
A character in ▷ *Pericles, Prince of Tyre*, a play written wholly or in part by ▷ Shakespeare. She is the daughter of King Pericles, who loses her at sea and later recovers her (V. i) in a scene described by T. S. Eliot (1888–1965) as one of the most beautiful by Shakespeare. She is the subject of one of Eliot's Ariel Poems, *Marina*.

Marius the Epicurean (1885)
A philosophical novel by ▷ Walter Pater tracing the spiritual journey of a young Roman of the second century AD who moves from Epicureanism (the doctrine of the philosopher Epicurus, 342–270 BC, who is best known for his principle that pleasure is the beginning and end of life – although for him pleasure meant the acquisition of a mind at peace), through Stoicism (a philosophy founded in 4th-century-BC Greece which underlined the significance of the soul and advocated indifference to bodily suffering) and finally to the aesthetic pleasure of Christianity. However Marius remains faithful to his Epicurean philosophy to the end. The novel was enormously influential on Pater's contemporaries, as well as on later writers such as W.B. Yeats (1865–1939) as an analysis of aesthetic religiosity.

Markandaya, Kamala (b 1924)
Pen name of Kamala Durnauja, Indian novelist. Educated at Madras University, she has worked as a journalist, but is now a full-time writer and lives in London. Her novels are set in contemporary India; they deal with a range of subjects and settings, but tend to emphasize relationships and personal dilemmas, including the tension between Indian and European cultural influences. Her novels are: *Nectar in a Sieve* (1954); *Some Inner Fury* (1955); *A Silence of Desire* (1960); *Possession* (1963); *A Handful of Rice* (1966); *The Coffer Dams* (1969); *The Nowhere Man* (1973); *Two Virgins: A Novel* (1974); *The Golden Honeycomb* (1977); *Pleasure City* (1982).
Bib: Banerji, N., *Kamala Markandaya: A Critical Study*.

Marlatt, Daphne (b 1942)
Poet, critic and editor. Marlatt's hugely prolific output and her ability to span a range of Canadian literary interests makes her one of the most important women writers in Canada today. She is truly 'post-colonial' having been born in Australia and then lived in Malaysia and England before finally emigrating to Canada in 1951. Her early poetry, such as *Rings* (1971) and *Steveston* (1974), already reveals her commitment to innovative form with the fluency of the long line and her merging of prose and poetry, as well as her interest in the interconnected texture of place and language. In the 1980s she increasingly used her own experiences to combine a personal eroticism with a sharp political sentiment, as for example in *Double Negative* (1988; written with Betsy Warland) and *Touch to My Tongue* (1984).

Marlatt's ability to work across generic frontiers has led her to experiment with poetic prose, such as in *Ana Historic* (1988), and to evolve an editorial role in the influential and radical feminist journal *Tessera*.

Marlborough, John Churchill, Duke of (1650–1722)
Son of Winston Churchill, a minor country gentleman. At fifteen he became a page of honour to James, Duke of York, and in 1667 he received an officer's commission in the Guards. In 1672 he showed distinction in various sieges in the Netherlands, in a campaign in which the English were allied with the French against the Dutch, and in 1685 he was made a Baron and promoted to the rank of Major General. It was largely due to his efficiency that the Monmouth rebellion, against ▷ James II (formerly the Duke of York) was defeated at the ▷ Battle of Sedgemoor. When William of Orange landed in England in 1688, however, Marlborough deserted James, and thus facilitated the bloodless Revolution by which William became ▷ King William III (▷ Glorious Revolution). Churchill was made Duke of Marlborough on the accession of Queen ▷ Anne in 1702, and his wife, Sarah, was the Queen's chief favourite. On the outbreak of the War of the ▷ Spanish Succession in the same year, Marlborough commanded the armies of the allied states against France, and won victories at ▷ Blenheim (1704), Ramillies (1706), Oudenarde (1708) and Malplaquet (1709). The country was tiring of the war, however, and the Queen was tiring of the Duchess. Marlborough was relieved of his command in 1711. In the meantime the great mansion of Blenheim Palace had been built for him in honour of his first and most remarkable victory in the war. The architect was ▷ Sir John Vanbrugh.

Marlborough, Sarah Churchill, Duchess of (1660–1744)
Essayist, letter writer and Whig politician. She married John Churchill, son of Winston Churchill, in 1678. They had eight children, five of whom survived infancy. Sarah was a confidante of Princess Anne, later the queen (▷ Anne), and was able in 1702 to persuade her, despite strong opposition from the Tories, to continue the War of ▷ Spanish Succession, being conducted by Sarah's husband the Duke. Toward the end of Anne's reign, the Duke and Duchess fell out of favour, and lived abroad until they were able to regain positions with ▷ George I. The Duchess survived her husband by 22 years, during which she wrote *An Account of the Conduct of the Dowager Duchess of Marlborough* (1742), a volume of her *Opinions* (published posthumously in 1788), and a substantial correspondence. She variously befriended and antagonized many contemporary writers, including ▷ Samuel Johnson, who attacked her, and ▷ Fielding, who defended her.

Marlowe, Christopher (1564–93)
Dramatist and poet. Son of a Canterbury shoemaker; educated at King's School, Canterbury, and Corpus Christi College, Cambridge. He most likely began writing plays on leaving Cambridge. Most of them eventually entered the repertoire of the Lord ▷ Admiral's Men, with ▷ Edward Alleyn taking leading roles such as Tamburlaine and Faustus. Marlowe probably became a government agent, and his mysterious death in a fight in a tavern at Deptford – nominally about who should pay the bill – may have had a political cause. When he died, he was under shadow of charges of atheism on the evidence of his fellow dramatist, ▷ Thomas Kyd.

His four major plays were written between 1585 and 1593; ▷ *Tamburlaine the Great, Parts I and II*; ▷ *The Jew of Malta*; *The Tragical History of* ▷ Doctor Faustus; *Edward II. Dido, Queen of Carthage* (with ▷ Nashe 1594) and *The Massacre at Paris* (1593) are attributed to him. His non-dramatic poetry is famous for the narrative ▷ *Hero and Leander*, based on the Greek of Musaeus (5th century AD) and completed by ▷ Chapman, and the lyric *The Passionate Shepherd*. Little else has survived, apart from his translation of ▷ Ovid's *Amores* (printed 1596) and of *The First Book of Lucan* (printed 1600). It has been suggested, without evidence, that he had a share in the writing of a number of other plays, including ▷ Shakespeare's ▷ *Henry VI*, ▷ *Titus Andronicus*, and ▷ *Richard III*.

Marlowe was much the most innovative dramatic writer in the 16th century after Shakespeare, and much the most important influence upon Shakespeare. His importance is due to the energy with which he endowed the ▷ blank-verse line, which in his hands developed an unprecedented suppleness and power. His plays have great intensity, but they show a genius that is ▷ epic rather than dramatic – at least in *Tamburlaine* and *Doctor Faustus*, his acknowledged masterpieces; his best-constructed piece of theatre, *Edward II*, is also the least typical of his poetic genius. On the other hand the final scene of *Doctor Faustus* is one of the most intensely dramatic in English literature. In the musical handling and control of the ten-syllable line, he learned from ▷ Spenser and contributed to ▷ Milton as well as to Shakespeare.

▷ Faust.

Bib: Boas, F. S., *Christopher Marlowe*; Levin, H., *The Overreacher*; Steane, J. B., *Marlowe: a critical study*; Leech, C. (ed.), *Essays on Marlowe*; Eliot, T. S., in *Selected Essays*; Kelsall, M., *Christopher Marlowe*; Masington C. G., *Christopher Marlowe's Tragic Vision*; Robinson, J. H., *Marlowe, Tamburlaine and*

Magic; Shepherd, S., *Marlowe and the Politics of Elizabethan Theatre*.

Marmion, A Tale of Flodden Field **(1808)**
An historical romance in tetrameter ▷ couplets (▷ metre) by ▷ Sir Walter Scott, set in 1513, the year of the catastrophic defeat of James IV of Scotland by the English. The story concerns the attempts of Lord Marmion to marry the rich Lady Clare, and to dispose of her lover by making false allegations of treason against him. Marmion is eventually killed in the battle and the lovers are reunited. The poem contains the famous lyrics 'Where shall the lover rest', and 'O, young Lochinvar is come out of the west'.

Marprelate, Martin
The pen-name for an anonymous author or authors of a series of ▷ pamphlets that appeared 1588–90. They were written from a Presbyterian standpoint denying the validity of bishops, and they attacked the religious establishment, by which the Church was governed by crown-appointed bishops. The bishops were satirized so vigorously in such expressive, popular prose that the authorities were alarmed into commissioning such gifted writers as ▷ Thomas Nashe, ▷ John Lyly and ▷ Robert Greene to reply to them. The leaders of the movement were arrested in 1593, and the government of ▷ Elizabeth I imposed severe restrictions on sermons and on the press. (Marprelate: mar = damage, ruin; prelate = bishop.)

Marriage
According to Laurence Stone, in England marriage only gradually acquired its function of regulating sexual chastity in wedlock: up to the 11th century polygamy and concubinage were widespread and divorce was casual. Even after that time divorce by natural consent followed by remarriage was still widely practised. In the 13th century, however, the Church developed its control, asserting the principles of monogamy, defining and outlawing incest, punishing fornication and adultery and ensuring the exclusion of ▷ bastards from property inheritance. In 1439 weddings in church were declared a sacrament and after 1563 in the Roman Catholic Church the presence of a priest was required to make the contract valid. In this way, what had been a private contract between two families concerning property exchange – Claude Levi-Strauss was the first to point out in 1948 women's universal role in such transactions between men – became regulated. Ecclesiastical law always recognized the formal exchange of oral promises (spousals) between the parties as a legally binding contract; as the Church got more powerful it exerted greater control over the circumstances in which those promises were made. In 1604 the hours, place and conditions of church weddings were defined and restricted; notice and publicity (the calling of the banns) were required, as a guard against bigamy and other abuses. One effect of this was to create a demand for clergymen willing to perform weddings outside the specified conditions. In 1753 Lord Hardwicke's Marriage Act was designed to close these loopholes: weddings had to be in church, duly registered and signed, verbal spousals would not be legally binding and marriages already contracted in breach of the 1604 conditions were declared invalid. No-one under 21 could marry without parental consent and there were heavy penalties for clergymen who defied these injunctions. The first significant Marriage Act of the Victorian period was the Marriage Act of 1836 which permitted legal wedding ceremonies to be held in ▷ Catholic or Protestant Dissenting churches, provided that the registrar was notified. Prior to this only a Church of England parson had the legal right to marry people. No one under the age of twenty-one could marry without parental consent and there were heavy penalties for clergymen who defied these injunctions. Divorce with the option of remarriage was not available except by private Act of Parliament, which only the rich could afford. For the poor the only substitutes for divorce were ritualized wife-sales (as in ▷ Thomas Hardy's ▷ *The Mayor of Casterbridge*: the last recorded example was in 1887) or desertion. In 1857 the Matrimonial Causes Act introduced civil divorce for adultery: again only the rich could afford it and only men could petition for divorce. Wives were not permitted to divorce their husbands for adultery until 1923.

Before the Married Women's Property Acts of the late Victorian period a woman's property became her husband's on marriage, despite the wedding vow, in which the man promised to endow his wife with all his worldly goods. The review of the English marriage laws, which stated that a wife, her property, earnings and children were all in the power of her husband, was initiated in 1836 by ▷ Caroline Norton, who separated from her husband after his unsuccessful petition for divorce on the grounds of her adultery with Lord Melbourne. Prevented from having access to her children she published a number of pamphlets condemning the marriage laws and in particular the obliteration of a woman's legal personality on becoming a wife. These coupled with the publicity surrounding her trial gave impetus to the first organized ▷ feminist effort to challenge the marriage laws and became one of the great women's rights campaigns of the Victorian period. Norton induced Thomas Talford to introduce the Infant Custody Act allowing women to sue for custody of children under seven and access to those under sixteen. It became law in 1839. The Infant Custody Act of 1886 made separated or divorced parents jointly responsible for their children; however, the children of parents living together were still under the control of the father.

In 1854 Barbara Leigh Smith, inspired by Norton's case and that of Anna Murphy Jameson, wrote *A Brief Summary in Plain English of the Most Important Laws of England Concerning Women*, which was a plea for married women's rights. She formed a small committee to draw up and circulate a petition to Parliament asking for the amendment of the laws of property affecting wives. This group was the core of the Langham Place Group (▷ Women's Movement). From the spring of 1856–7 the issues of married women's property and divorce law reform were inextricably linked, although proposals for divorce reform were issued quite independently of women's rights activists. Women had to wait until the 1870 Married Women's Property Act before their right to earn money and keep it for their own use was recognized by the law. However, in 1870 most middle-class women were unable to obtain remunerative occupations. After 1870 improvement in the status of married women was closely allied with the ▷ women's suffrage campaign, each hampering the progress of the other. A full Married Women's Property Law was not passed until 1882. This was the single most important change in the legal status of women in the Victorian period and allowed women to act as independent legal personages. It was fought for by women's rights campaigners such as ▷ Elizabeth Wolstenholme-Elmy and Ursula Bright.

Although men could divorce women from 1857, it was not until the 20th century, in 1923, that wives were permitted to divorce their husbands for adultery. In 1937 three additional grounds for divorce were introduced, cruelty, desertion and insanity. Further liberalization of the divorce laws took place in the 1960s: recognition of the concept of marital breakdown has allowed a less punitive and accusatory procedure.

▷ 'Woman Question, The'.

Bib: Shanley, M.L., *Feminism, Marriage and the Law in Victorian England: 1850–1895*; Holcombe, L., *Wives and Property: Reform of the Married Women's Property Law in 19th Century England*; Stone, L., *Family, Sex and Marriage in England, 1500–1800*.

***Marriage à la Mode* (?1671)**

Play by ▷ John Dryden, sometimes described as a 'split-plot tragi-comedy', setting a serious unrhymed 'heroic' plot against a witty love plot. In the serious plot, Polydamas has usurped the throne of Sicily from the rightful prince, Leonidas, who is unaware of his rights. Leonidas is in love with Palmyra. She is courted by Argaleon, while he is loved by Argaleon's sister, Amalthea. The comic plot concerns the adulterous love between Rhodophil, a captain of the guards, and Melantha, 'an affected lady', and Rhodophil's wife Doralice and Palamede. Palamede is also a suitor to Melantha. The play's action essentially revolves round the complications arising from these situations, and has scenes of mistaken identities, including women disguised as men. A factor unifying the two plots is the theme of longing for the apparently unattainable. The play represents an attempt by Dryden to resist what he saw as the coarsening and cheapening of contemporary comedy. In his dedication he claimed to have preserved the 'Decencies of Behaviour', but this did not prevent him from inserting a number of very bawdy songs between some serious scenes.

***Marriage of Heaven and Hell, The* (c 1793)**

A composition mainly in poetic prose by ▷ William Blake. It was engraved, with designs woven into the text in the early 1790s, at the time he was working on ▷ *The Songs of Experience*. The text consists of a series of symbolic, caustically humorous anecdotes, and terse aphorisms. Blake's thesis, influenced by the thought of the mystic ▷ Emanuel Swedenborg, is that the rationality of John Locke (1632–1704) and ▷ Sir Isaac Newton, and the piety of established hierarchical religion, are repressive and sterile. He thus presents Hell as a region of dangerous but vital energies, and Heaven, without them, as a lifeless, ▷ Deistic abstraction. The most famous section of the work is the 'Proverbs of Hell', 70 aphorisms asserting flux and creativity against the stasis and hierarchy of Heaven: 'The road of excess leads to the palace of wisdom', 'The tygers of wrath are wiser than the horses of instruction', 'Sooner murder an infant in its cradle than nurse unacted desires.'

▷ *Songs of Innocence and Experience*.

Marryat, Florence (1838–99)

Novelist, the daughter of ▷ Captain Frederick Marryat, author of *Children of the New Forest* (1847). Florence was educated by ▷ governesses and at sixteen married T. Ross Church, with whom she had eight children. A prolific writer of ▷ sensation novels, her first work, *Love's Conflict*, was published in 1865. Between 1865 and 1899 she wrote over forty volumes, including works on spiritualism, such as *There Is No Death* (1891) and *The Spirit World* (1894). Marryat's novels are mostly melodramatic ▷ romances with stereotypical characters who become involved in crimes of passion. They include *Woman Against Woman* (1865); *Her Lord and Master* (1871); *A Crown of Shame* (1888) and *How Like a Woman* (1892).

Marryat, Captain Frederick (1792–1848)

Novelist. He was a Captain in the Royal Navy and his novels are chiefly about the sea. The best known of them are: *Frank Mildmay*

(1829); *Peter Simple* (1834); *Jacob Faithful* (1834); *Mr Midshipman Easy* (1836). *Japhet in Search of a Father* (1836) is the story of a child of unknown parents who eventually achieves prosperity. Others of his books were intended for boys; the best known of these is *Masterman Ready* (1841). Marryat continued the 18th-century realistic tradition of narrative, the most famous examples of which are the novels of Tobias Smollett (1721–71). Marryat's other well-known novel, *Children of the New Forest* (1847), was one of the first ▷ historical novels to be written for children.

▷ Realism; Children's literature.

Bib: Marryat, F., *Life and Letters of Captain Marryat*; Conrad, J., 'Tales of the Sea' in *Notes on Life and Letters*; Warner, O., *Captain Marryat: a Rediscovery*.

Marsh, Ngaio (1899–1982)
Detective novelist. Her works include: *A Man Lay Dead* (1934); *Enter a Murderer* (1935); *Death in Ecstasy* (1936); *Death at the Bar* (1940); *Died in the Wool* (1945); *Opening Night* (1951); *Singing in the Shrouds* (1958); *Hand in Glove* (1962); *Black Beech and Honeydew* (1965); *A Clutch of Constables* (1968); *Tied up in Tinsel* (1972); *Last Ditch* (1977); *Photo Finish* (1980). Ngaio Marsh is frequently bracketed with her three female detective-writing contemporaries (▷ Margery Allingham, ▷ Agatha Christie, Dorothy L. Sayers) who together comprise the formidable bed-rock of classic inter-war crime writing. Although she was born, educated and lived in New Zealand (her name is Maori), Marsh's novels are nevertheless often set in the English country house, or in the theatre, which she loved and dedicated much of her working life to: she was a successful director, and the action of her last novel (*Light Thickens*, 1982) takes place in the middle of a production of *Macbeth*. Marsh's 'serial detective' is Roderick Alleyn, a character of some complexity whose role is nevertheless always set out as a function of plot and narrative mystery, for Marsh the primary factors in detective writing.

Marshalsea
A prison in Southwark, London. It was opened in the 13th century as a prison for the Marshalsea Court, which dealt with cases involving a member of the royal household. After the Restoration it was kept for petty debtors. ▷ Dickens' father was imprisoned there for debt, and it is described in ▷ *Little Dorrit* (1858). The prison was abolished in 1849.

Marston, John (?1575–1634)
Satirist and dramatist. His father was a lawyer. John Marston was educated at Brasenose College, Oxford; lectured in the Middle Temple (one of the Inns of Court); entered the Church in 1609. His writing life runs from 1598 to 1607. During this period he engaged in literary warfare with ▷ Ben Jonson ('the war of the theatres') who satirized Marston and ▷ Dekker in *The Poetaster* (1601) and elsewhere. The two men were, however, intermittently friends, and collaborated (with Chapman) in writing ▷ *Eastward Hoe* (1605), for which they were imprisoned for offending the king's Scottish friends.

In 1598 Marston published *The Metamorphosis of Pygmalion's Image* and, under the pen-name of W. Kinsayder, a collection of ▷ satires entitled *Scourge of Villainie*. The satires are modelled on those of the Roman poet Persius. Their language is coarse and vigorous, and the violence and disgust they exhibit become a feature of Marston's dramatic writing. His plays are his most successful work, but they are very uneven. ▷ *Antonio and Mellida* and *Antonio's Revenge* (1599 – *Antonio*) are ▷ revenge plays in the tradition of Kyd's ▷ *The Spanish Tragedy*, and exhibit a mixture of ▷ Stoic idealism and melodramatic sensationalism, with passages of intense poetry. ▷ *The Malcontent* is a tragicomedy and usually considered to be Marston's most effective work; its satirical qualities and the role of the central character suggest comparisons with ▷ Shakespeare's ▷ *Measure for Measure* and ▷ *Hamlet*. ▷ *The Dutch Courtesan* (1605), *The Parasitaster, or the Fawne* (1606) and *What You Will* (1607) are comedies; *Sophonisba, Wonder of Women* (1605) and *The Insatiate Countess* (?1606) are tragedies.

It was Marston's lack of critical control and the bad taste of his extravagance which caused the satirical attacks on him by Jonson. His violent revulsion from sensuality and worldly vice inspired some of his best passages as well as his worst ones.

Bib: Ellis-Fermor, U. M., *The Jacobean Drama*; Caputi, A., *John Marston, Satirist*; Finkelpearl, P., *John Marston of the Middle Temple*.

Martian poetry
The name of the so-called 'Martian' school of poetry derives from the second collection of ▷ Craig Raine, *A Martian Sends a Postcard Home* (1979). Everyday objects are described in an unusual, often highly striking manner, as if being seen for the first time by an alien visiting earth. The poet attempts to write from a position of innocence, radically outside of the society he or she observes, reading things from a position of exile, or as an anthropologist. The ordinary or commonsense world is twisted, often by an outrageous use of simile (▷ Figures of speech):

Rain is when the earth is television.
It has the property of making colours darker.
(Raine, 'A Martian Sends a Postcard Home')

Much contemporary poetry makes use of

'Martian eye' techniques, but the chief poets of the school are Raine and Christopher Reid (b 1949).

Martin Chuzzlewit, The Life and Adventures of *(1843–4)*

A novel by ▷ Charles Dickens. The Chuzzlewit family includes old Martin, a rich man grown misanthropic owing to the selfishness and greed of the rest of his family; young Martin, his grandson, who begins with the family selfishness but is eventually purified by hardship and the good influence of his servant, Mark Tapley; Anthony, old Martin's avaricious brother, and Jonas, Anthony's son, who, by the end of the book, has become a figure of the blackest evil; Pecksniff, at first a trusted friend of old Martin, is one of Dickens' most effective hypocrites; Mrs Gamp, the disreputable nurse, is one of his most famous comic creations. The novel is divided rather sharply by the episode in which young Martin temporarily emigrates to America. This episode is a self-sufficient satire on American life; moreover, not only is young Martin's character radically changed by it but the story thereafter takes on a denser substance. Pecksniff, Jonas and the fraudulent financier Tigg Montague cease to be merely comic and become substantially evil. These changes mark the transition from the earlier Dickens, the comic entertainer, into the later Dickens, of sombre power. The novel is thus a transitional work but it is also, as his comic masterpiece, the climax of Dickens' first phase.

Martineau, Harriet (1802–76)

Critic, novelist, journalist, essayist and biographer. Born in Norwich, the sixth of eight children, her youth was marked by illness, poverty and morbidity and increasing deafness; her Huguenot parents insisted on educating the children to earn their own living, which became essential after their father went bankrupt in 1826. She supported herself initially by writing reviews for the *Monthly Repository* and by needlework. A devout ▷ Unitarian, she published *Devotional Exercises for the Use of Young Persons* in 1823, followed by *Addresses with Prayers* (1826). In 1830 she won all three prizes in a competition set by the Central Unitarian Association to write essays aimed at converting the Roman Catholics, Jews and Mahommedans. Between 1832 and 1834 she published a series of social reformist tales, *Illustrations of Political Economy*, influenced by the ideas of ▷ J.S. Mill, ▷ Jeremy Bentham, and David Ricardo (1772–1823). The tales were highly successful, as were her stories for 'Brougham's Society for the Diffusion of Useful Knowledge', which sold some 10,000 copies. She became a literary celebrity, turning increasingly away from religion, and was consulted on social and economic matters by her friends including ▷ Malthus and Sydney Smith; she suggested and managed ▷ Thomas Carlyle's first course of lectures in 1837.

She travelled to North America in 1834, supporting the Abolitionists despite threats to herself, and published *Society in America* (1837) and *A Retrospect of Western Travel* (1838). A trip to Venice in 1839 was cut short by illness and from 1839–44 she was an invalid, but produced her first and best novel, *Deerbrook*, in 1839, an historical work which celebrates women's intellectual aspirations and bonds. *The Hour and the Man* (1840), on Toussaint l'Ouverture, and children's stories collected in *The Playfellow* (1841) followed. *Life in the Sickroom* appeared in 1843, followed by *Letters on Mesmerism*, an account of the treatment she claimed had cured her illness, in 1845. She settled in the Lake District in a house she designed and built herself, where she received William Wordsworth (1770–1850), ▷ Matthew Arnold, ▷ Charlotte Brontë, and ▷ George Eliot. She visited Palestine in 1845.

Other publications include numerous articles for the *London Daily News* and the ▷ *Edinburgh Review*, supporting divorce reform and attacking the Contagious Diseases Act (▷ Women's Movement); a radical *History of the Thirty Years' Peace* (1849–50), and the anti-theoretical *Laws of Man's Social Nature and Development* (1851). She was influenced by ▷ Comte, and her free translation, *The Positivist Philosophy of Comte*, appeared in 1853. Her *Autobiography*, begun in 1855, was eventually published in 1877. A staunch advocate of ▷ education for women, she also supported ▷ women's suffrage movements in England and the US.

▷ Children's literature; Travel writing; Feminism.

Bib: Miller, F., *Life*; Pichanick, V.K., *Harriet Martineau: The Woman and Her Work*; Webb, R.K., *Harriet Martineau: A Radical Victorian.*

Marvell, Andrew (1621–78)

Poet. He was educated at Hull Grammar School (where his father was master) and Trinity College, Cambridge. He travelled in Europe, and in 1650 became tutor to the daughter of Lord Fairfax, the ▷ Civil War Parliamentary general. In 1653 he became tutor to ▷ Cromwell's ward, and in 1657 ▷ John Milton's assistant in the foreign secretaryship. In 1659 he became Member of Parliament for Hull, which he continued to represent after the Restoration of the monarchy in 1660, apart from a period in which he was secretary to Lord Carlisle.

The main body of Marvell's ▷ lyric poetry is to be found in *Miscellaneous Poems* of 1681, which contains his best-known verse. He published, in addition to the lyric poetry for which he is famous, a number of satirical works and, in 1672–3, the curious amalgam of theological controversy and prose satire which is *The Rehearsal Transprosed* – the work for which he was most famous in the 17th century. But it is the lyric poetry that has attracted most modern critical attention. Of enduring fascination to modern criticism has been the question of the relation of Marvell's poems of the 1650s to the poet's own political sympathies. Is, for example, his celebration of the return of Cromwell from Ireland ('An Horatian Ode upon Cromwell's Return from Ireland') enlisting sympathy for Cromwell, or ▷ Charles I? Or is it, as some modern critics have argued, simply disinterested? Similarly, to what extent does his poetry represent a struggle to escape out of the turmoil of civil war? More radically, does the poetry dramatize the impossibility of any such retreat?

Together with the poetry of ▷ John Donne and ▷ George Herbert, Marvell's poetry has come to be appreciated as some of the most important to have been written in the 17th century. But modern criticism has, itself, not been disinterested in championing Marvell's work. For ▷ F. R. Leavis, Marvell became an ideological touchstone, while for Marxist literary historians Marvell's work represents a continually fascinating test-case of the relationship between literature and history.
Bib: Legouis, P. (ed.), *The Poems and Letters of Andrew Marvell*; Patterson, A., *Marvell and the Civic Crown*; Chernaik, W., *The Poet's Time*; Stocker, M., *Apocalyptic Marvell*.

Marx, Karl (1818–83)
Born in Trier of German-Jewish parentage, and attended university in Berlin and Bonn where he first encountered Hegelian dialectic. He met Friedrich Engels (1820–95) in Paris in 1844, and in 1848, the Year of Revolutions, they published *The Communist Manifesto* together. In that year Marx returned to Germany and took part in the unsuccessful revolution there before fleeing to Britain where he was to remain until his death in 1883. In 1867 he published *Capital*, the voluminous work for which he is best known. Marx is justly renowned for his adaptation of the Hegelian dialectic for a materialist account of social formations, which is based upon an analysis of the opposition between different social classes. He is, arguably, the most prolific thinker and social commentator of the 19th century whose work has had far-reaching effects on subsequent generations of scholars, philosophers, politicians and analysts of human culture. In the political ferment of the 1960s, and especially in France, his work has been subject to a series of extraordinarily productive re-readings, especially by philosophers such as ▷ Louis Althusser which continue to affect the understanding of all aspects of cultural life. In Britain Marx's work is what lies behind a very powerful literary and historical tradition of commentary and analysis, and has informed much work in the areas of sociology, and the study of the mass media. *Capital* and a range of earlier texts, have come to form the basis of the materialist analysis of culture.

Marxism
Founded on the school of thought espoused by Karl Marx (1818–83).

Mary I (1553–58)
Queen of England. She was the eldest child of ▷ Henry VIII, who had used his divorce from her mother, Katharine of Aragon, as a pretext for taking the control of the English Church out of the hands of the Pope and into his own. Under her brother ▷ Edward VI England had swung further into ▷ Protestantism but Mary restored the Roman Catholic religion of her mother. In 1554 she married the most fanatically Catholic sovereign in Europe, Philip II of Spain; this involved her in wars with France and the loss of the last English possession there – the town of Calais. Her reign, not bloodthirsty by comparison with that of Philip in his own dominions, was nonetheless severely repressive of Protestantism, and some 300 English Protestants were burnt alive, including ▷ Cranmer and the eloquent Bishop Latimer. ▷ John Foxe's *Book of Martyrs* (1563) consigned her memory to national hatred, and she has come down in school books as 'Bloody Mary'. Her sister and successor ▷ Elizabeth I restored a moderate form of Protestantism.

▷ Tudor, House of.
Bib: Loades D., *Mary Tudor: A Life*.

Mary II (1662–94)
Queen of Great Britain from 1689 to her death. She was the daughter of ▷ James II by his first wife, and was educated in Protestant doctrine, which she retained when her father became converted to ▷ Catholicism. She married William of Orange, ruler of the Netherlands, in 1677. When James was removed from the throne in the ▷ Glorious Revolution of 1688 Mary was summoned to rule the nation jointly with her husband, who assumed the throne as ▷ William III.

▷ Stuart, House of.

***Mary Barton* (1848)**
The first novel by ▷ Elizabeth Gaskell, subtitled *A Tale of Manchester Life*, and written to counteract her deep distress at the death of her infant son. The background to the story is Manchester during the ▷ 'Hungry Forties', a decade during which working-class protest came to the attention of the middle classes. Mary Barton is the daughter of John Barton, a man employed by the Carson family as a mill hand and driven by desperation to join a militant ▷ Chartist group which requires him to assassinate Harry Carson, one of the most

unpopular employers. However, Jem Wilson becomes the principal suspect. Mary has been involved with Carson, lured by the appeal of his wealth, but is in danger of following her beloved Aunt Esther's inevitable descent into prostitution. Ultimately she saves working-class Jem from the death penalty and recognizes her real love for him. The novel provoked much hostility from Manchester mill owners and the Tory press, yet it has also been criticized by Marxist commentators for its naive treatment of class struggle and its sentimental ending. Recent feminist readings have emphasized the novel's critique of masculinist politics of confrontation, its exploration of the process of socialization and its call for an ethic of caring and nurturing in the community, which is seen to bind women and the working class. It was admired by ▷ Charles Dickens and ▷ Thomas Carlyle.

▷ Social Problem novel

Bib: Tillotson, K., *Novels of the Eighteen-Forties*; Williams, R., *Culture and Society 1780–1950*, Spencer, J., *Elizabeth Gaskell*; Stoneman, P., *Elizabeth Gaskell*; Homans, M., *Bearing the Word*; Nestor, P., *Female Friendships and Community*; Stoneman, P., *Elizabeth Gaskell*.

Mary Queen of Scots (1542–67)

Queen of Scotland. She was born a few days before the death of her father, James V. In 1548, when she was five years old, she was betrothed to Francis, heir to the French throne, and was sent to France. She returned to Scotland only after the death of her husband in 1560; she was Catholic, but in the meantime the Scottish Protestants had with English help overthrown the Catholic establishment in their country. Mary in consequence found herself opposed to her people, led by the reformer ▷ John Knox. She was dangerously involved in English politics not only because she would be heir to the English throne should ▷ Elizabeth of England die childless, but because in the eyes of Catholics she was already legitimate Queen of England, since the Catholic Church did not recognize the legality of the marriage between Elizabeth's father, ▷ Henry VIII, and her mother. For diplomatic reasons, Mary married her cousin, Lord Darnley, a worthless young man who treated her abominably. In 1567 Darnley was murdered. The evidence for Mary's complicity in the murder is in the so-called 'casket letters', but their authenticity is uncertain. However, three months later she married his murderer, Lord Bothwell. Her subjects rebelled, and Mary was imprisoned but escaped and fled to England. Elizabeth gave her shelter, but the succession of plots against her on Mary's behalf eventually drove the English queen to authorize the Scottish queen's execution. Her son, already recognized as James VI in Scotland, became in 1603, on the death of Elizabeth, ▷ James I of England as well.

Owing to her charm, beauty, intelligence and misfortune, Mary became a legend in Europe. The greatest imaginative work about her is the tragedy *Maria Stuart* by the German poet Schiller; in English literature she is the subject of a dramatic trilogy by ▷ Algernon Swinburne (1837–1909) and of ▷ Walter Scott's (1771–1832) novel, *The Abbot* (1820).

Bib: Fraser, A., *Mary Queen of Scots*.

Masefield, John (1878–1967)

Poet and novelist. He went to sea in 1893, and published his first volume of poems, *Salt-Water Ballads* in 1902. He was a prolific poet; the first edition of his *Collected Poems* came out in 1923, and the collection increased steadily until 1964. His work has immediate appeal, and is strongest in narrative verse: *The Everlasting Mercy* (1911); *The Widow in the Bye Street* (1912); *Dauber* (1913); *The Daffodil Fields* (1913); *Reynard the Fox* (1919). He was chosen as Poet Laureate in 1930. His novels have romantic charm, *eg Sard Harker* (1924); *Odtaa* (1926). *The Midnight Folk* (1927) is a classic of children's literature.

▷ Children's books.

Bib: Babington Smith, C., *John Masefield, a Life*; Spark, M., *John Masefield*.

Masham, Damaris, Lady (1658–1708)

▷ Rationalist theological writer, born in Cambridge where her father, the well-known philosopher Ralph Cudworth, taught. She herself studied philosophy and divinity with ▷ John Locke, who described her as having one of the most learned and original minds of his day, and who moved in with her family when he became ill in 1691. She became involved in a theological discussion between Locke and the philosopher and theologian John Norris, and in 1696 published *A Discourse Concerning the Love of God*, where she argues that the development of the mind is an essential part of Christianity, rather than adjunct or even antithetical to it. She was also, along with ▷ Mary Astell, an early defender of women's education. In *Occasional Thoughts in Reference to a Vertuous or Christian Life* (1700) she urges women to learn, in spite of resistance from relatives fearful that this would alienate potential husbands. Although the path of knowledge is hard, she says, only an educated woman could teach true Christianity to her children.

Bib: Reynolds, M., *The Learned Lady in England 1650–1760*; Todd, J., (ed.), *A Dictionary of British and American Writers 1660–1800*.

***Mask of Anarchy, The* (1832)**

A poem by ▷ Percy Bysshe Shelley, written in 1819, after he had heard news of the ▷ 'Peterloo Massacre' in Manchester, when soldiers fired on a peaceful demonstration in favour of parliamentary reform. He sent the poem to ▷ Leigh Hunt for publication in his radical periodical ▷ *The Examiner*, but Hunt dared not print it at the time, and withheld publication until 1832. The poem was intended for popular reading, and Shelley used quatrains and five-line stanzas, similar to those of the popular ▷ ballad. He identifies Anarchy with the lawless tyranny of the British government, and exhibits its leaders in a garish pageant of Anarchy's minions: 'I met Murder on the way – / He had a mask like Castlereagh – / Very smooth he looked, yet grim; / Seven blood-hounds followed him.' Shelley ends with a magnificent address to the 'Men of England, heirs of Glory', exhorting them to throw off their chains: 'Ye are many – they are few.' Its rough, angry style and passionate rhetoric give the poem a prophetic resonance which anticipates the *Communist Manifesto* of Karl Marx and Friedrich Engels (1848).

Mason, William (1725–97)
Poet and biographer. A minor poet, Mason was heavily influenced by his friend ▷ Gray, whose poems he edited with an appended ▷ biography, *The Poems of Gray with Memoirs* (1775). Mason's own works, *Elfrida* (1751) and *Caractacus* (1759) use ▷ Pindaric odes. He was also interested in the ▷ Picturesque, publishing a three volume poem on gardening called *The English Garden* (1771–81), which despite its uninspired poetry reveals an understanding of design and form. He had numerous friends in the literary world, including ▷ Walpole.

Masque
A form of dramatic entertainment which combined verse, music, dancing and scenic effect in about equal proportions. In England it flourished between 1580 and 1630, and was essentially an aristocratic style of entertainment, especially popular at the royal court. The performers were commonly professional actors, while the masquers themselves, who remained silent, were played by ladies and gentlemen of the court. The subject was often symbolic – a conflict between virtue and vice (as in ▷ John Milton's *Comus*) – or ceremonial, celebrating a great personage, *eg* Milton's ▷ *Arcades* in honour of the Countess of Derby. The masque was often preceded by an anti-masque, the content of which was comic and often satirical; the anti-masque was always performed by professionals.

Masques were sophisticated entertainments for carefully selected audiences. They were in keeping with many forms of imaginative expression of the age, and may be regarded as a synthesis of them. First of all, the visual sense had been highly developed by the great ▷ Renaissance schools of painting and architecture in Italy and France, and a favourite activity of artists was to translate into visual terms the allegorical vision that the Renaissance had inherited from the ▷ Middle Ages. This visual ▷ allegory influenced the poets; much of the best of ▷ Edmund Spenser's ▷ *The Faerie Queene* consists of brilliantly visualized allegorical scenes such as the House of Busirane (Book III, canto 12). Secondly, the age attached great importance to spectacles such as ▷ pageants (*ie* ceremonial processions), which often contained symbolic, masque-like features; a famous example (which still survives) was the annual Lord Mayor's Pageant in the City of London, for which the dramatist ▷ George Peele was more than once employed as designer. Thirdly, masques appealed to the contemporary taste for imaginative extravagance, delighting in the fairy tales of English folklore and in classical mythology as well as in grand pageantry. Fourthly, the fantastical styles of many Elizabethan plays – attributable partly to popular taste and partly to the explorations of humanist scholars – made them either akin to masques (*eg* ▷ Robert Greene's *James IV*, Peele's *The Old Wives' Tale*, ▷ John Lyly's *Mother Bombie*), or capable of including masques as part of the dramatic ingredient, *eg* ▷ Shakespeare's ▷ *Love's Labour's Lost* and ▷ *The Tempest*. Finally, it was an age of close musical and literary collaboration, and masques provided opportunities for musicians and poets to collaborate on a large scale, just as they already did on a small scale in the ▷ madrigal.

Dramatists who were eminent for their composition of masques included ▷ George Chapman, ▷ John Fletcher and ▷ James Shirley, but the greatest of them – in his own estimation and probably that of others – was ▷ Ben Jonson. He collaborated with the composer Alfonso Ferrabosco the younger, and the great architect ▷ Inigo Jones; with the latter he had bitter quarrels as to which of them had artistic control of the production. Amongst Jonson's most celebrated masques are those performed under the authority of ▷ Queen Anne: *Masque of Blackness* (1606), *Masque of Beauty* (1608) and *Masque of Queens* (1609). The most famous of all masques, however, is Milton's *Comus*, composed for the Earl of Bridgewater, whose children acted the main parts, when he was installed as Lord President of Wales. Part of the fame of *Comus* is due to its untypical quality of containing much larger speaking parts than most masques did; thus Milton allowed himself more poetic scope than was usual. For this reason, some critics prefer to call *Comus* a ▷ pastoral drama, like Jonson's *The Sad Shepherd* (1637) and Fletcher's *The Faithful Shepherdess* (1610). However, pastoral dramas and masques had much in common; both were spectacular and symbolic rather than dramatic.

Though designed as a form of lavish court entertainment, it is true that, in the 1630s

especially, the masque also played a significant political role in the culture of the court. It existed to legitimize, through spectacle and pageantry, the authority of the monarch and the central position of the court in the affairs of the nation. At the same time, however, the masque form is implicated in the cultural breakdown that preceded the ▷ Civil War. Not only were masques extravagantly expensive to produce (as critics of the court pointed out), but they may also have served to suggest to the monarch and those around him that a harmony pertained in the affairs of the nation, and in the court's relationship to the world outside, when no such harmony in fact existed.
Bib: Lindley, D. (ed.), *The Court Masque*; Orgel, S. and Strong, R., *Inigo Jones: The Theatre of the Stuart Masque*.

Massinger, Philip (1583–1640)
Dramatist. His father was in the service of the great Herbert family. He left Oxford University without a degree in 1607. He has been suspected of Catholic sympathies, largely on the strength of four plays: *The Virgin Martyr* (1620), ▷ *The Duke of Milan* (1621), *The Maid of Honour* (1621), and *The Renegado* (1624). He collaborated extensively with other dramatists, especially ▷ Fletcher, but 16 or 18 plays are attributed to him alone; of these, the two usually regarded as being of the most enduring value are the comedies, ▷ *A New Way to Pay Old Debts* (1625) and ▷ *The City Madam* (1632). He himself regarded his tragedy ▷ *The Roman Actor* (1626) as his masterpiece. The dates of these plays show them to belong to the last, or ▷ Caroline, phase of what is commonly called Elizabethan drama because it started in the reign of ▷ Elizabeth I. Two plays by Massinger are central to our understanding of the ▷ censorship of drama in the period: *Sir John Von Olden Barnavelt* (with ▷ Fletcher, 1619) and *Believe as you List*, both of which survive in manuscript. The latter was only allowed a licence after changes to disguise contemporary applications. The comedies mentioned still show a lively influence from ▷ Ben Jonson; they deal with contemporary politics and theatre and detail the latest scandals of the time. On the other hand, Massinger's tragedies have been accused of a lack of that intensity which gave grandeur to the work not only of ▷ Shakespeare but of ▷ Chapman, ▷ Tourneur and ▷ Webster. Massinger's ▷ blank verse is in the late Shakespeare tradition, but grown so flexible as almost to have lost its rhythms into prose. However, he handled his sustained periods skilfully and sometimes impressively, anticipating ▷ Milton.
Bib: Eliot, T. S., in *Selected Essays*; Knights, L. C., *Drama and Society in the Age of Jonson;* Dutton, R., *Mastering the Revels: The Regulation and Censorship of English Renaissance Drama*.

Master Craftsman
In the ▷ Middle Ages, a full member of a ▷ Craft Guild and usually an employer of ▷ apprentices and journeymen. Originally every apprentice could theoretically hope to become 'a master' after a specified period of 'apprenticeship' or training and the production of a 'masterpiece' to prove his skill in the craft. By the 14th century, however, the master craftsmen of the guilds were already becoming a comparatively rich class of employers, which the apprentices could not hope to enter unless they themselves had money, or married the master's daughter. Most apprentices could by then only hope to become trained journeymen.

Master Humphrey's Clock
The title of what ▷ Charles Dickens intended to be an inclusive serial linking distinct tales – ▷ *The Old Curiosity Shop* and ▷ *Barnaby Rudge*. Master Humphrey is the narrator of the early pages of the former, but Dickens abandoned the idea.

***Master of Ballantrae: A Winter's Tale* (1889)**
A novel by ▷ Robert Louis Stevenson set immediately after the Jacobite Rebellion of 1745, telling the story of the Marquis of Tullibardine. Stevenson intended it as 'a drama in a nutshell', a chronicle of domestic enmity.
▷ Historical novel.

Master of the Revels
▷ Revels, Master of the.

Materialism
The philosophical theory that only physical matter is real and that all phenomena and processes can be explained by reference to it. Related to this is the doctrine that political and social change is triggered by change in the material and economic basis of society.
▷ Marx, Karl.

Mathias, Roland (b 1915)
Poet, editor and critic. Roland Mathias was born at Talybont-on-Usk, Breconshire, and was educated first in military schools in Germany where his father was an army chaplain and subsequently at Caterham School and at Jesus College, Oxford, where he read Modern History. After teaching in England he returned to Wales as headmaster of Pembroke Dock Grammar School in 1948. The following year, with Raymond Garlick, he founded *Dock Leaves*, later the *Anglo-Welsh Review*, and between 1961 and 1976 he was its editor, contributing a large number of poems, reviews, articles,

and substantial editorials. In 1958 he moved on to headmasterships at Belper, Derby, and subsequently at King Edward VI School, Five Ways, Birmingham, a post from which he retired in 1969 so that he could devote all his time to writing, editing and lecturing on returning to his Welsh roots in Brecon. His poetry is highly personal, erudite in its allusiveness and notable for its vivid language, honesty and craftsmanship. His first collection was *Break in Harvest* (1946), followed by *The Roses of Tretower* (1952), *The Flooded Valley* (1960), *Absalom in the Tree* (1971) and *Snipe's Castle* (1979), his selected poems appearing in *Burning Brambles* (1983). With Raymond Garlick he was co-editor of the anthology *Anglo-Welsh Poetry 1480–1980* (1984). Further studies of poets included that of *Vernon Watkins* in the *Writers of Wales* series (1974) and another, of John Cowper Powys, *The Hollowed-Out Elder Stalk* (1979), and he also edited a collection of essays on David Jones as writer and artist in 1976. Roland Mathias' prose works include a collection of his short stories, *The Eleven Men of Eppynt* (1956), and he has also been co-editor with Sam Adams in both a selection of short stories by Anglo-Welsh writers, *The Shining Pyramid* (1970), and in the collected monograph on his co-editor, *Sam Adams*, in the *Writers of Wales* series (1995). Another monograph, but a historical one, was his *Whitsun Riot* (1963). Indeed, the historical perspectives in his writing, allied to his impeccable scholarship, have done much to promote a critical awareness of, and to stimulate the development of Welsh writing in English. His finest critical work in that field, his essays in *A Ride Through the Wood* (1985), were followed by the more popularist *Anglo-Welsh Literature: An Illustrated History* (1987).
Bib: Stephens, M. (Ed.), *The Oxford Companion to the Literature of Wales*; Jones, G. and Rowlands, J., *Profiles*.

Matura, Mustapha (b 1939)
Dramatist. Trinidad-born Matura settled in England in the 1960s, and eventually established himself as one of Britain's major (not to mention most prolific) black dramatists and co-founded the Black Theatre Cooperative with Charlie Hanson. Matura's early works were given exposure at the Royal Court and a variety of fringe venues often under the aegis of Roland Rees; his writing for television – particularly the series *No Problem* and *Black Silk* – helped widen his audience in the 1980s. His work has concentrated both on the black experience in Britain and on Trinidadian issues, with a recent development into versions of classics adapted to his own interests. The common thread that links both the Trinidadian and the British-set plays is Matura's interest in the contradictions that arise when people drawn from different social and racial groups interact.

Like many contemporary writers Matura is particularly interested in colonialism as a state of mind as well as a physical institution. Thus in *Play Mas* (1974) people of Indian and African descent work out power relations against the background of Carnival and of independence; in *Independence* (1979) different versions of independence are mobilised in contradiction; and in *Meetings* (1981) we see the tensions between old and new focused in a wealthy couple, one nostalgic for traditional cooking (and, by extension, a life rooted in the old values), the other enslaved to the values of American economic colonialism. Matura has a great gift for witty and revealing diologue which he put to particularly good use in his adaptations of the classics; *The Playboy of the West Indies* (1984) is an adaptation of ▷ J. M. Synge's *Playboy of the Western World. Trinidad Sisters* (1988) is a particularly poignant relocation of ▷ Chekhov's *Three Sisters*, as a statement of 'mother country' and its mental stranglehold.

Maturin, Charles Robert (1782–1824)
Irish novelist and dramatist. Like ▷ 'Monk' Lewis and ▷ Mrs Radcliffe he belonged to the school of writers who exploited the emotions of terror and love of mystery among readers in the late 18th and early 19th centuries. *The Fatal Revenge, or The Family of Montorso* (1807), *The Wild Irish Boy* (1808) and *The Milesian Chief* (1812) were ridiculed but admired for their power by ▷ Walter Scott. Scott and ▷ Byron secured the production of Maturin's tragedy *Bertram* in 1816, which was a great success. His other tragedies were less successful, and he returned to the novel. The best of his later novels is *Melmoth the Wanderer* (1820), to which the French novelist ▷ Balzac wrote a sequel *Melmoth réconcilé à l'église* (1835).
▷ Irish literature in English.

***Maud* (1855)**
One of the best-known poems by ▷ Alfred Tennyson. It is called 'A Monodrama', and is in fact an example of the ▷ dramatic monologue, a form particularly characteristic of Victorian poetry, especially in the work of ▷ Browning and Tennyson.

It is in three parts. Part I tells of the mysterious death of the narrator's father, who has been ruined by the contrivances of 'that old man, now lord of the broad estate and the Hall'. But the narrator gradually falls in love with the old lord's daughter, and here occurs the famous lyric 'Come into the garden, Maud'. The young lord, her brother, treats him with contempt, however, and Part II opens with their duel and the death of the brother. The narrator flies abroad, and falls into the depths of morbid despair. In Part III he recovers, and seeks salvation through the service of his country in war: the poem was written in the year in which the Crimean War broke out.

Maud exemplifies the versatility of Tennyson's craftsmanship by the variety of its metrical and stanzaic form, and the brilliant distinctness of his vision in some of the imagery. It contains bitter criticism of the temper of the age. The poem has been held to betray Tennyson's confusion about his age; criticizing it, yet swimming with its tide. *Maud* is a Gothic conflation of images of disease, mental aberration and sexual repression.

Maugham, (William) Somerset (1874–1965)
Novelist, short-story writer and dramatist. Educated at King's School, Canterbury, and Heidelberg University; he then studied medicine in London. His first novel, *Liza of Lambeth* (1897) shows the influence of Zola, an example of the growing importance of French influence on English fiction at the end of the 19th century. His semi-autobiographical novel *Of Human Bondage (*1915) made his name. Other novels include: *The Hero* (1901); *The Moon and Sixpence* (1919); *The Painted Veil* (1925); *The Casuarina Tree* (1926); *Cakes and Ale* (1930). The professional accomplishment of his novels gave him a wide foreign public, and after 1930 his reputation abroad was greater than at home, though interest in him revived towards his 80th birthday. He celebrated his 80th year by the special republication of *Cakes and Ale*, a novel which satirizes the English propensity for admiring the 'Grand Old Men' among their writers. Some of his best fiction is in his short stories, in volumes such as *The Trembling of a Leaf* (1921), *The Mixture as Before* (1940). His twenty-two plays, mainly neatly constructed comedies, are entertaining and witty. They often tend to moralise, but, though set in the fashionable middle class to whom he was seeking to appeal, he by no means toes the establishment line. Indeed *The Circle* (1921) was booed for its 'immorality' at its premiere. Although his closet homosexuality does not figure in his plays, his unsatisfactory marriage may have influenced the criticism of the divorce laws found in *Home and Beauty* (1919) and the debate on economic and social sexism in *The Constant Wife* (1926).

In *For Services Rendered* (1932) his cynical wit is put aside to show the caustic effect of war on family life and in *Sheppey* (1933) he shows hostile public reaction to a barber who, on winning a lottery, attempts to use his winnings according to Christ's teaching. *The Sacred Flame* (1928) probably the best of his serious dramas, shows his greatest depth of feeling in a study of unrequited love, part of a murder story that offers a defence of euthanasia.
Bib: Maugham, R., *Somerset and All the Maughams*; Morgan, T., *Somerset Maugham*; Brander, L., *Somerset Maugham: A Guide*.

***May Day* (1611)**
A complex, multiple-plot comedy by ▷ George Chapman which skilfully interweaves a wealth of romance and native ▷ pastoral motifs with stock characters from Plautine (▷ Plautus) and Terentian (▷ Terence) comedy. Unlike Chapman's tragedies, *May Day* is unimpeded by an overly inflated and abstract rhetoric.

Mayor, Flora M. (1872–1931)
Novelist and ▷ short story writer who also wrote under the ▷ pseudonym of Mary Stafford. The twin daughter of intellectual parents, and born into an Anglican clerical household that respected women's ▷ education, Mayor was educated at Surbiton High School and Newnham College, Cambridge. She initially pursued an acting career without parental consent. Mayor's first publication appeared during this period, a collection of short stories entitled *Mrs Hammond's Children* (1901). Mayor's career as an actress was terminated through illness, brought on by the sudden death of her fiancé in 1903. Mayor never married, and lived largely in the company of members of her family.

Mayor's writings champion the rights of middle-class unmarried women and widows at a time when the English spinster was regarded as a problem by political commentators and the ▷ women's movement alike. Her first two novels take as their central theme different facets of spinsterhood, focusing particularly on psychological issues. In *The Third Miss Symons* (1913) Mayor explores the stereotype of the 'spurned' and unlikeable spinster in relation to a sensitive apprehension of the self-destructive effects of apparent social, sexual and emotional failure. *The Rector's Daughter* (1924) redresses the stereotype, detailing the complexity of the unconsummated but reciprocated passion between Mary Jocelyn and the neighbouring clergyman. *The Squire's Daughter* (1929) formulates an analysis of the disintegration of late-Victorian class boundaries, a concern which draws attention to Mayor's own conservative political beliefs. Mayor's novels are significant in their close examination of the inner life of women, and interestingly straddle late 19th- and early 20th-century gender ideologies. Mayor's only other publication is *The Room Opposite and Other Tales of Mystery and Imagination* (1935).
Bib: Oldfield, S., *Spinsters of this Parish*; Williams, M., *Six Women Novelists*.

***Mayor of Casterbridge, The* (1886)**
A novel by ▷ Thomas Hardy. Its hero is the country labourer, Michael Henchard. At the beginning of the book, when times are hard, he gets drunk at a fair and sells his wife and child (▷ marriage) to a sailor called Newson. He bitterly repents and renounces strong drink for twenty years. His wife returns after eighteen years, supposing Newson to be drowned, and by this time Henchard has prospered so far as to have become Mayor of

Casterbridge (Dorchester). At the same time as her return Henchard takes on as his assistant in his business of corn-dealing a wandering Scotsman, Donald Farfrae. The rest of the novel is the story of the rivalry between Farfrae and Henchard. Farfrae is never deliberately his enemy, yet merely by virtue of living in the same town he deprives Henchard of everything, and the latter leaves the place at the end of the novel as poor as when he started, and far more wretched. Hardy seems to have intended a kind of ▷ Darwinian study of the survival of the fittest among human beings. Henchard is a monolithic character, who puts all his energy and passion into every relationship and activity; Farfrae has a flexible personality and is able to devote to every predicament exactly what it demands, without excess. Henchard's crowning sadness is the loss of the girl he has supposed to be his daughter but who is in fact Newson's; he loves her nonetheless, but Newson returns and claims her.

Meaning and significance
A distinction made by the American theorist E. D. Hirsch. Hirsch argues that most literary works have a meaning which the ▷ author intended. But they also have a significance which readers experience in relation to these texts. This significance, for Hirsch, should be directly related to the meaning and not be merely idiosyncratic; that is, it represents for him the arena of legitimate interpretation in literary criticism. Some critics however object that literary works should be so tied to an ▷ author's intention (▷ Intentional Fallacy; Reader-Response Criticism; Text).
Bib: Hirsch, E. D., *Validity in Interpretation.*

***Measure for Measure* (1603–4)**
A play by ▷ Shakespeare. It was probably written in 1603–4, and was first printed in the First Folio of 1623. Its plot derives from *Promos and Cassandra* (1578), the translation by ▷ George Whetstone of a tale by the Italian Cinthio. In the Folio it is grouped with the comedies, but modern critics are inclined to call it a ▷ problem play, a modern classification that includes ▷ *Troilus and Cressida*, ▷ *All's Well that Ends Well*, and sometimes ▷ *Hamlet.*

Vincentio, Duke of Vienna, is faced with the difficulty of enforcing severe laws against unchastity after they have fallen into disuse; he finds that the claims of justice and virtue conflict with those of mercy and compassion. He makes the experiment of pretending to leave the country so as to depute the task to Angelo, a man of austere life and rigid principle. In fact, the Duke remains on the scene, disguised as a friar, to watch the experiment. Angelo condemns Claudio to death for seducing his betrothed before marriage. Claudio's sister Isabella, a novitiate nun, comes to plead for her brother's life, urged on by Lucio, a man of loose life but a friend of Claudio's. Angelo is appalled to find that his lust is aroused for Isabella. His strict principle is transformed into brutal hypocrisy when he attempts to blackmail Isabella into surrendering herself in return for her brother's life. The disguised Duke induces her to pretend to consent, while he substitutes for her ▷ Mariana, whom Angelo has cold-heartedly discarded in spite of his engagement to her. Even after Isabella's apparent consent, Angelo orders Claudio's execution in order that no witness of his brutal conspiracy shall survive. Finally the Duke reveals himself, and exposes his deputy, but spares his life on the appeals of Isabella and Mariana.

It is necessary to remember the biblical text (*Matthew* 7:1) from which the title is taken: 'Judge not that ye be not judged. For with what judgement ye judge, ye shall be judged: and with what measure ye mete, it shall be measured to you again.' The three main problems that perplex critics are:

1 The Duke is evidently intended to be a virtuous ruler, who even plays the role of God, the invisible witness of our most secret thoughts and actions. Viewed realistically, however, he escapes from his duty and then plays the role of a mean spy on Angelo's actions. The mistake here is to confuse the conventions of modern, realistic drama with the conventions of Shakespeare's drama. The latter saw character in terms of role, or social function, first, and in terms of individual psychology only second. Vincentio is a ruler as God is the Ruler; by taking on the role of the omnipresent witness who has ultimate power of judgement, he is extending his function, not escaping from it. Recently, connections between the Duke and ▷ James I, who also pursued pacifist policies, have been asserted, adding a historicist approach.

2 Isabella is presented as a virtuous woman, and yet she seems inexcusably callous in her refusal to put her brother's life before her own chastity. This is not a problem if we understand that Isabella's religious vocation is the meaning of life to her (I. iv); she has to be educated into seeing that virtue can never retain its value if it is segregated from life, just as law can never operate widely if it is isolated from knowledge of the human heart; this is Angelo's mistake.

3 Although the death penalty on Claudio is cruel, no one disputes that he has committed an offence, and yet later Angelo (by the contrivance of the Duke) is made to commit the same offence with Mariana, for which neither of them is held guilty. An answer to this is the difference between Claudio's and Angelo's actions. Claudio had offended against the law, but not against his betrothed, Juliet, whereas Angelo had previously offended against Mariana by renouncing his engagement to her, though not against the law. Morally, the play shows that Angelo's offence is the worse, and

is in fact made good by his 'sin' of the Duke's contrivance.

For an adverse view of the play, see A. P. Rossiter in *Angel with Horns*; for favourable ones, see F. R. Leavis in *The Common Pursuit* and Wilson Knight in *The Wheel of Fire*; for a historical approach, see L. Marcus, *Puzzling Shakespeare*.

Bib: Hawkins, H., *Measure for Measure*.

***Medall, The, A Satyre against Sedition* (1682)**
A ▷ satire in ▷ heroic couplets by ▷ John Dryden. The ▷ Earl of Shaftesbury, leader of the Whig party which opposed the succession of the Catholic James, Duke of York, to the throne, had been acquitted on a charge of treason. Dryden found an ideal focus for his ▷ mock-heroic ridicule in the medal struck to celebrate the Whig victory, which shows Shaftesbury's head on the obverse, and on the reverse the sun rising over the Tower of London (where Shaftesbury had been imprisoned), with the legend *Laetamur* ('Let us rejoice').

Medieval, medievalism
The later 18th century saw a revival of interest in the art and literature of the ▷ Middle Ages, as part of an incipient reaction against ▷ Renaissance and ▷ neo-classical ideals of symmetry and order. It coincided to a large degree with interest in the ▷ Gothic and the ▷ primitive, and with a growing taste for the wilder forms of ▷ nature. In politics there was a harking back to the ideas of Alfred the Great, whose balanced constitution, giving equal powers to the king, lords and commons, was seen as a model; many essays and plays refer to him. ▷ Thomson's patriotic hymn 'Rule Britannia' was sung for the first time in a masque called *Alfred* (1740). Druids were idealized as early patriots in, for example, Thomson's *Liberty*, ▷ Collins' *Ode to Liberty*, and ▷ Gray's *The Bard*. The ancient British queen Boudicca, or Boadicea, was also held up as a symbol of courage and patriotism, as in ▷ Cowper's *Boadicea*. Admiration for ancient ▷ Welsh, ▷ Irish and ▷ Scottish literature is also part of the medieval revival, as is revealed in the ▷ Ossian or Oisin saga. The quest for old English as well as Celtic literature resulted in such works as ▷ Thomas Percy's *Reliques of English Poetry* (1765), which was much admired by the ▷ Romantic poets later on, and ▷ Thomas Warton's *History of English Poetry* (1774–89), which involved exploring hundreds of examples of medieval verse. The development of the ▷. Gothic novel, with its medieval associations and a renewed interest in Spenser, ▷ Shakespeare and ▷ Milton, who were thought to have drawn their inspiration from medieval romance, formed a part of the movement. Shakespeare became admired precisely for the 'crude' elements of speech and plot structure which had alienated earlier generations, particularly immediately after the Restoration, and elements of his plays which had been excised for a hundred years or more were gradually restored to the texts performed on stage. In the 19th century the ideas sown in the 18th developed into a full-blown extended movement.

The nostalgia for an idealized medieval period that animated several writers of the Victorian period had its roots in a profound dissatisfaction with and rejection of aspects of the society and culture of the time. Enthusiasm for things medieval was stimulated by the ▷ Oxford Movement's interest in the medieval background of the Church. For ▷ Thomas Carlyle the 12th century was epitomized by everything he found missing in his own society: universal religious belief, a society based on community feeling rather than cash, electoral systems which resulted in the appointment of the best candidate, and a benevolent and uncorrupted dictatorship free from what he saw as the inefficiency of parliamentary democracy. His essay ▷ *Past and Present* (1843) contains a finely realized study of the 12th-century Abbot Samson of Bury St Edmunds.

The poet ▷ Elizabeth Barrett Browning disguises her analysis of contemporary sexual politics by placing the action of her ▷ ballad 'The Romaunt of the Page' (1839) in a picturesque medieval setting. 'The Lay of the Brown Rosary' (1840) is also set in the medieval period as are many of ▷ Robert Browning's poems, such as 'The Statue and the Bust', which deals obliquely with the possessiveness, both in material and sexual terms, which he saw as characteristic of his age. ▷ Tennyson was likewise possessed by 'the Passion of the past' and reacted to the problem of producing 'contemporary poetry' by adapting ancient genres to the treatment of modern subjects. His poem 'Morte d'Arthur', based on Sir Thomas Malory's long prose romance of the same name written around 1469/70, uses a medieval form to examine contemporary issues such as the collapse of political, intellectual, and religious orthodoxy. Tennyson developed this project in his ambitious Arthurian epic ▷ *The Idylls of the King*. Malory's original text was reprinted at the end of the 19th century with illustrations by ▷ Aubrey Beardsley.

However, it was the ▷ Pre-Raphaelites – ▷ William Morris, ▷ Dante Gabriel Rossetti and ▷ John Ruskin – who raised nostalgia for the Middle Ages to a creed. They upheld the strong moral tone of Victorian art and believed in a medieval world (largely of their own invention) in which culture was serious, satisfying, and integrated into the fabric of society. 'Apart from the desire to produce beautiful things,' wrote Morris in 1894, 'the leading passion of my life has been and is hatred of modern civilization.' Much of Morris' early verse such as 'The Defence of Guinevere' has a medieval setting. At the same time he was dedicated to the revival of domestic crafts, in reaction to an increasingly mechanized age. The Pre-Raphaelites were also attracted to the ideals of courtly love (passionate yet unconsummated love which could take on a sacramental quality as the sublime experience) embodied in the Medieval period. The Aesthetes, influenced by ▷ Pater, supplanted an idealized Middle Ages as a source of inspiration with an equally idealized Renaissance. Since the 19th century, however, Medievalism has dropped out of fashion.

Bib: Morris, K. L., *The Image of the Middle Ages in Romantic and Victorian Literature*; Cheney, L.D.G. (ed.), *Pre-Raphaelitism and Medievalism in the Arts.*

Meiosis

▷ Figures of Speech.

Melibee, The Tale of

The second of ▷ Chaucer's own contributions to the ▷ *Canterbury Tales*, which follows the narrative of ▷ *Sir Thopas* rejected by the Host. This allegorical prose narrative concerns the counselling of the impetuous Melibeus, by his wise wife Dame Prudence. The treatise derives from a French source, itself a translation of an earlier 14th century Latin composition.

***Melincourt, or Sir Oran Haut-ton* (1817)**

A novel by ▷ Thomas Love Peacock. Sir Oran Haut-ton is an orang-outang of delightful manners and a good flute-player for whom the young philosopher, Mr Sylvan Forester, has bought the title of baronet and a seat in Parliament. 'Haut ton' is a French phrase then used in English for 'high tone', *ie* fashionable, refined, and aristocratic. Peacock is developing the idea of Lord Monboddo (1714–90), an early anthropologist, who describes such a creature in his books, as an example of 'the infantine state of our species'; Peacock's ape, however, compares favourably with the aristocracy. The book is a satire on the right-wing (Tory) establishment, and especially those writers who had once been Radicals but now favoured it: ▷ Southey (Mr Feathernest); ▷ Wordsworth (Mr Paperstamp); ▷ Coleridge (Mr Mystic). Mr Vamp and Mr Killthedead are Tory reviewers, and Mr Fax may represent ▷ Malthus. Sylvan Forester may be the poet ▷ Shelley; and Simon Sarcastic, Peacock himself.

Melodrama

The prefix 'melo-' derives from the Greek 'melos', music. Originally, melodrama was a play in which there was no singing but the dialogue had a musical accompaniment; the first example is said to be ▷ Rousseau's *Pygmalion* (1775). The musical accompaniment gradually ceased; the word came to denote romantic plays of extravagantly violent action, and it is now applied to sensational action without adequate motivation, in any work of fiction.

The word has also been used to denote popular ballad operas in which spoken dialogue is used extensively. This use, however, is much less common.

Melville, Lady Elizabeth Culross (c 1603)

Poet. Her poem, *Ane Godly Dreame* (1603), is a Calvinist account of the horrors of hell in store for all those except God's anointed. It is a first-person dream vision of a pilgrimage through smoking pits and damned souls, which combines strong imagery with graceful eight-line stanzas. It belongs to the Scottish tradition of ▷ Presbyterian texts in which individual prophesying and personal interpretations of the ▷ Bible were increasingly encouraged.

▷ Calvin, John; Scottish literature in English.

Bib: Greer, G. (ed.), *Kissing the Rod.*

Memoir novel

A novel which is presented as an autobiographical account but is in fact partly or wholly fictitious, such as ▷ Defoe's ▷ *Moll Flanders* (1722) or ▷ Charlotte Brontë's ▷ *Jane Eyre* (1847).

***Memoirs of a Cavalier* (1724)**

A work of fiction by ▷ Daniel Defoe, but it was thought that the memoirs were possibly genuine. They describe the career of a professional soldier, Colonel Andrew Newport, born in 1608. He sees military service in Europe during the ▷ Thirty Years War, and then joins the English Royalist army in the ▷ Civil War.

***Men and Women* (1855)**

A volume of poems by ▷ Robert Browning. It contained fifty pieces, nearly all ▷ dramatic monologues, a form in which a character soliloquizes about himself, his predicament or his relationship with another. The book contains much of Browning's best-known work, such as 'Any Wife to Any Husband', 'Andrea del Sarto', 'Fra Lippo Lippi'. In the *Collected Works* of 1868, the poems were dispersed, and only thirteen remained under the title *Men and Women.*

Menander (342–293 BC)

An Athenian comic poet whose plays were popular in the classical world and provided the characteristic matrix of ▷ New Comedy, which became the model for both ▷ Plautus and ▷ Terence. Menander is widely acknowledged by the Roman dramatists as their mentor, but it was not until the 20th century (1905) that substantial parts of manuscripts of his plays and one complete work (*Dyskolos*, 1955) were discovered. These confirmed the high regard in which Menander was held by his contemporaries.

Mephistopheles
An evil spirit whose name first occurs in the German *Faustbuch* (1587), a collection of tales about the necromancer ▷ Johann Faust. He is one of the seven great princes of hell. As Mephostophilis he is best known in English through Marlowe's ▷ *Doctor Faustus* (1592).

Mercantile system
A term used by the economist ▷ Adam Smith (*Wealth of Nations*, 1776) and later writers to denote the assumptions behind the practice of commerce from the later ▷ Middle Ages until the 18th century. In its extreme form, it identified wealth with money so that the main object of governments was to accumulate large stocks of precious metals. Smith advocated a contrary theory of ▷ free trade, which became the dominant policy by the middle of the 19th century.
Bib: Foucault, M., *The Order of Things*.

Mercer, David (1928–80)
British dramatist renowned for his television work as much as his stage plays, some of which have been performed by the ▷ Royal Shakespeare Company. He was one of the first to write serious plays for television dealing with the working class. Mercer's treatment of this subject has been accused of being excessively nostalgic and only his middle-class, not his working-class, characters are generally given any intellectual depth. Social alienation and madness are commonly the fate of those who move away from their class origins. Although he wrote from a Marxist perspective, there is little optimism about the modern world in his plays. Television plays include: *The Generations* (1961–3); *Morgan, A Suitable Case for Treatment* (1962); *For Tea on Sunday* (1963); *In Two Minds* (1967); *On the Eve of Publication* (1968); *The Cellar and the Almond Tree* (1970); *Emma's Time* (1970). Stage plays include: *Ride a Cock Horse* (1965); *Belcher's Luck* (1966); *After Haggarty* (1970); *Duck Song* (1974); *Cousin Vladimir* (1978); *The Monster of Karlovy Vary* (1979); *Then and Now* (1979).
Bib: Trussler, S. (ed.), *New Theatre Voices of the Seventies*.

Merchant of Venice, The **(1596–7)**
A comedy by ▷ Shakespeare. It is dated by external evidence 1596–7. Its two outstanding incidents – the winning of a bride by undergoing a test, and the demanding of a pound of human flesh by the usurer – occur in a number of earlier narratives, but Shakespeare seems to have depended principally on a collection of Italian novels called *Il Pecorone* (*The Blockhead*) and the *Gesta Romanorum* (*Tales of the Romans*). ▷ Quarto edition, 1600; included in the First Folio (1623).

The play has a double plot.

1 An impoverished young Venetian, Bassanio, seeks to marry a wealthy heiress, Portia of Belmont. For the expense of the courtship he has to borrow 3,000 ducats from his friend, the merchant Antonio. When Bassanio and Portia meet, they fall in love at first sight, but before she can surrender herself, Bassanio has to pass the test of the caskets, ordained by her dead father. The test is to choose between a gold, a silver, and a lead casket; the right casket contains her portrait. He passes the test, but their rejoicing is interrupted by the arrival of a letter from Antonio.

2 Antonio's money is all invested in mercantile expeditions, so that to help Bassanio he has had to borrow from the Jewish usurer, Shylock. Shylock has made the strange stipulation that Antonio will have to surrender a pound of flesh in default of repayment. Antonio's letter now relates that his voyaging ships have all been lost, he is penniless, and will have to pay the pound of flesh. The two plots join in the trial scene of IV. i. The issue has come before a court of law at which Portia appears disguised as a young lawyer instructed to judge the case. She appeals to Shylock to show mercy, but when he insists on the letter of the law she lets him have it: he may take his pound of flesh, but there is no mention of blood in the bond; if he sheds any, the law of Venice is clear: his lands and goods are to become the property of the state. Antonio is saved, and Shylock has to undergo certain severe penalties, including compulsory conversion to Christianity. Act V concludes the play with light comedy and the lyrical union of several pairs of lovers.

Like others of Shakespeare's earlier comedies, the play is a mixture of courtly sophistication, light fantasy, and moving realism. The plot belongs to fable and fairy story, and the love affairs to the tradition of courtly romance. On the other hand, Shylock is a very powerful, sombre figure and brings a sharp criticism to bear on the otherwise glibly accepted value judgements of the court. His bond, however, is counterbalanced by Antonio's arrogant treatment of him and the eloquent irony with which Shylock protests against it. The trial scene is one of the elements of fable in the play: in real terms, Shylock is being treated with gross unjustice, but the real theme is the contrast between Mercy and the Law. It is the function of mere Law to be merciless; he who refuses mercy and insists on law must abide by the consequences.

Bib: Danson, L., *The Harmonies of Merchant of Venice.*

Merchant's Tale, The
One of ▷ Chaucer's ▷ *Canterbury Tales.* Prompted by the *Clerk's Tale* of patient Griselda, the Merchant tells a contrasting story of married life, set in Italy, involving the tricking of an old jealous husband, January, by his young wife, May, and her lover, Damian (who is January's squire). The tale is built up from a mixture of different styles, registers, and generic conventions. It begins in a debate mode with a long discussion about the theory and practice of married life, which injects a tone of Christian idealism into the narrative; the relationship between May and Damian is described using the register of a courtly romance (although the two lovers hardly live up to romance role models); the characters' names give the narrative a semi-allegorical quality; the intervention of the classical gods in January's garden endows the action with an epic touch (since the gods function as a domestic *deus ex machina*); while the plot structure itself is basically that of a ▷ fabliau. The climax of the tale comes when the old, now blind, knight January miraculously recovers his sight, only to see his wife making love with Damian in a pear tree. This climactic scene has many European analogues but none has the elaborate build-up which distinguishes Chaucer's version.

Mercia
One of the ancient ▷ Anglo-Saxon kingdoms from the 6th to the 9th centuries. From the 10th century to the ▷ Norman Conquest (1066) it was an earldom in the kingdom of England. It roughly corresponded to the modern Midlands.

Meredith, George (1828–1909)
Novelist and poet. Born at Portsmouth, the son of a tailor and naval outfitter; his grandfather, Melchizedeck, had had the same business and is the basis of the character Old Mel in the novel *Evan Harrington* (1861). George Meredith was educated in Germany and his writings were influenced by ▷ Germans, especially the novelist Jean Paul Richter (1763–1825), who stimulated his conception of comedy. Meredith was even closer to ▷ French culture, especially the radical thinking of the 18th-century Philosophes. On his return to England he began to study law but soon took to journalism and serious literature.

He began by publishing verse: *Poems* (1851). In 1855 he published his eastern romance *Shaving of Shagpat*, and in 1857 a romance in German style, *Farina, a Legend of Cologne.* ▷ *The Ordeal of Richard Feverel* (1859) was his first real novel, followed by *Evan Harrington*, which is now regarded as one of his best. In 1862 he produced his most famous volume of poems, ▷ *Modern Love*. Other publications included: *Sandra Belloni* (1864; originally called *Emilia in England*); *Rhoda Fleming* (1865); *Vittoria* (1867 – a sequel to *Sandra*); *The Adventures of Harry Richmond* (1871); *Beauchamp's Career* (1875 – his own favourite); *The Idea of Comedy* (1877 – a critical essay, important for understanding his work); ▷ *The Egoist* (1879 – one of his best known novels); *The Tragic Comedians* (1880); *Poems and Lyrics of the Joy of Earth* (1883); ▷ *Diana of the Crossways* (1885 – the first of his novels to reach a wide public); *Ballads and Poems of Tragic Life* (1887);.*A Reading of Earth* (1888 – verse); *One of Our Conquerors* (1891); *The Empty Purse* (1892 – a poem); *Lord Ormont and his Aminta* (1894); *The Amazing Marriage* (1895). His concluding works were all poetry: *Odes in Contribution to the Song of French History* (1898); *A Reading of Life* (1901); *Last Poems* (published in 1910 after his death). His unfinished novel, *Celt and Saxon*, was also published posthumously.

Meredith's reputation at present rests chiefly on his novels but, like ▷ Thomas Hardy, he seems to have been a novelist who preferred poetry. His prose is poetic in its use of metaphor and ▷ symbolism, and both his poetry and his prose are often expressed in concentrated and difficult language which invites comparison with ▷ Robert Browning. The impulsiveness and ruggedness of his prose also recalls ▷ Thomas Carlyle, whom Meredith resembled in his hostility to the mechanistic qualities of his age. Of all the Victorian novelists who ever had a major reputation, his has perhaps sunk the lowest in this century: both his prose and his poetry tend to be regarded as intolerably mannered and he is accused of fixing his attention on style as an end, instead of using it as a medium. Nonetheless, his intense interest in psychological exploration (again recalling Browning), his use of metaphor and symbol from the natural world to express states of mind and the freshness of some of his characters (especially women) were all original in his own time and keep him from being forgotten.
Bib: Stevenson, L., *Life*; Lindsay, L., *Life*; Trevelyan, G.M., *Poetry and Philosophy of George Meredith*; Sassoon, S., *Meredith*; Sitwell. O., *Novels of Meredith*; Lees, F.N., in *Pelican Guide 6: Dickens to Hardy*; Cline, C.L., *Letters*; Woolf. V., in *Common Reader*; Williams, D., *George Meredith: His Life and Lost Love.*

Meres, Francis (1565–1647)
Author of *Pallados Tamia, Wit's Treasury* (1598), a book of moral and critical reflections. One chapter is an account of English writers, and his comments are interesting for estimating their reputations at the time.
Bib: Smith, G. G., *Elizabethan Critical Essays.*

Merlin
Prophet and enchanter who comes to play

a central role in directing the early stages of Arthurian history. Merlin first appears in the guise of prophet of British history and magic worker in ▷ Geoffrey of Monmouth's version of British history (completed c 1138). There, a whole book is devoted to his veiled predictions about the future shape of British history; he is also responsible for the removal of Stonehenge from Ireland to Britain, and he engineers ▷ King Arthur's conception by allowing ▷ Uther to take on the guise of ▷ Igraine's husband. His name, 'Merlinus', is an adaptation of 'Myrddyn', the bard who features in Welsh legendary narratives, and is credited with the prophecy of a future Celtic revival. So although Merlin first appears in Geoffrey's work, there are earlier precedents for his role. In Geoffrey of Monmouth's poetic account of the *Vita Merlini* (the *Life of Merlin*), completed c 1150, the seer is presented as a former battle leader who has gone mad after a great defeat, and lives as a man of the woods, endowed with prophetic insight.
In ▷ Robert de Boron's version of Arthurian narrative, which gives a pronounced Christian bias to the history, Merlin is conceived as part of the Devil's plot to oppose Christ; however, the goodness of his mother ensures that his magical powers are used for positive ends. He is credited with the founding of the ▷ Round Table and with the arrangements for Arthur's fostering. In ▷ Malory's *Morte D'Arthur* Merlin has a key role to play in setting up the Arthurian kingdom and mapping out the shape of later events but he is prevented from playing any further part in the history because he is entrapped in a rock by Nimue (or Viviane), after he has taught her his magical secrets.

Mermaid Tavern
A 16th-century tavern in London's Bread Street. According to legend the Bread Street, or Friday Night, Club was founded by ▷ Sir Walter Ralegh, and was one of the earliest English clubs and meeting-places of writers.

Merry Wives of Windsor, The **(1597)**
A comedy by ▷ Shakespeare, probably written 1597 in connection with the celebrations of the ▷ Garter Knights, to whose order the younger Lord Hunsdon, patron of Shakespeare's acting company, was elected that year; an imperfect edition came out in 1602 and a corrected version was published in the First Folio of 1623. The critic John Dennis (1657–1734) states that it was written at the request of ▷ Queen Elizabeth I, who wanted a play about ▷ Sir John Falstaff in love. Falstaff had been a great popular success in the two ▷ *Henry IV* plays. It has also been suggested that Shakespeare was emulating the realistic comedy of ▷ Thomas Dekker (▷ *Shoemaker's Holiday*, 1600) and ▷ Ben Jonson (▷ *Every Man in his Humour*, 1598; ▷ *Every Man out of his Humour*, 1599). *The Merry Wives* is the only play by Shakespeare to be written mainly in prose.

Falstaff makes love to two married women, the wives of Ford and Page; but the wives and their husbands finally expose him in Windsor Forest, after he has been beset by neighbours disguised as fairies. A subordinate plot concerns the wooing of Anne Page by three suitors, and how she and Fenton, the suitor she prefers, contrive their elopement.

Apart from Falstaff, other characters recur from the *Henry IV* and *V* plays: Nym, Pistol, Slender, Mistress Quickly. Falstaff in *The Merry Wives* bears little resemblance to the creation of the earlier plays.

Metafiction
This term is applied to fictional writing which questions the relationship between reality and fiction through deliberately and self-consciously drawing attention to its own status as a linguistic construct. Examples would include ▷ John Fowles' *The French Lieutenant's Woman*, ▷ Salman Rushdie's *Midnight's Children* and ▷ Dan Jacobson's *The Rape of Tamar*.
▷ Historiographic metafiction.

Metalanguage
A term coined by the linguist L. Hjelmslev to describe a language which refers to *another language* rather than to non-linguistic objects, situations or events. In the words of ▷ Roland Barthes it is 'a second language in which one speaks about the first' (*Mythologies*). In this sense, metalanguage can be used as a means of reflecting on language itself.
▷ Metafiction.

Metamorphoses
Poems in Latin by ▷ Ovid. They are a series of mythological tales whose common subject is miraculous transformation of shape, beginning with Chaos into Cosmos, ending with ▷ Julius Caesar into a star, and including such tales as Baucis and Philemon, the peasants who unawares gave hospitality to the gods, who granted them immortality as a pair of trees. They were popular in medieval Europe and afterwards, up till the 19th century, and have often been translated, in whole or in part, into English *eg* by ▷ Arthur Golding in the 16th century and by George Sandys in the 17th.

Metaphor
▷ Figures of Speech.

Metaphysical
A complex philosophical term used in some contemporary critical discourse as the opposite of materialism, usually with negative connotations. Metaphysical ideas are ideas which posit a

level of reality or causation which is beyond the physical world. A belief in God would be an example of a metaphysical belief.

Metaphysical conceit
▷ Metaphysical Poets; Conceit.

Metaphysical Poets
The accepted designation of a succession of 17th-century poets, of whom the following are the principal names: ▷ John Donne, ▷ George Herbert, ▷ Richard Crashaw, ▷ Andrew Marvell, ▷ Henry Vaughan, ▷ Abraham Cowley. The term came to be applied to them in a special sense; that is to say, they were not so described because their subject was the relationship of spirit to matter or the ultimate nature of reality; this is true of ▷ Lucretius, ▷ Milton and ▷ Dante, who have little else in common. It is true that some of them – Donne, Herbert, Vaughan and Crashaw especially – were metaphysical in this generally accepted sense, but the adjective is applied to them to indicate not merely subject matter, but qualities of expression in relation to subject matter.

Samuel Johnson (1709–84) was the first so to classify these poets: 'The metaphysical poets were men of learning, and to show their learning was their whole endeavour' (essay on Cowley in *Lives of the Poets*). The sentence shows that he is using the term disparagingly, and this disparagement had already been expressed by John Dryden (1631–1700): 'Donne affects the metaphysics not only in his satires but in his amorous verses . . . [he] perplexes the mind of the fair sex with nice speculations of philosophy' (*Discourse concerning the Original and Progress of Satire*, 1693). Dryden and Johnson were antagonistic to Donne and his followers because they valued above all the assurance, clarity, restraint and shapeliness of the major Augustan poets of ancient Rome. Critics and poets of the 20th century have on the other hand immensely admired Donne, Herbert and Marvell, but they still use 'Metaphysical' as the term under which to group them. H. J. C. Grierson (Introduction, *Metaphysical Poetry: Donne to Butler*) justifies it because it indicates 'the peculiar blend of passion and thought, feeling and ratiocination which is their greatest achievement.' However, they have also been labelled '*The Fantasticks*' (an anthology edited by W. S. Scott) and L. B. Martz has suggested *The Poetry of Meditation* (the title of his book). The first of these alternative designations suggests a resemblance between the English poets and their so-called 'baroque' contemporaries in Italy (Marino), Spain (Góngora) and France (Théophile de Viau and Saint-Amant); the second emphasizes the difference – the greater balance and control among the English poets; it may be said that Crashaw, at one extreme, belongs more to the former, and Herbert, at the other extreme, is much better described as 'meditative'.

The distinctiveness of the Metaphysicals was their use of the so-called 'metaphysical ▷ conceit' – *ie* paradoxical metaphor causing a shock to the mind by the unlikeness of the association, *eg* Donne's

her pure and eloquent blood
Spoke in her cheeks, and so distinctly wrought,
That one might almost say her body
thought.
(*Second Anniversary*)

or Herbert's

Only a sweet and virtuous soul
Like season'd timber, never gives;
But though the whole world turn to coal
Then chiefly lives.
(*Virtue*)

In most respects, therefore the term is so broad, and embraces poetic styles and forms so disparate, that its use is nearly meaningless, being little more than an anthologist's convenience.
Bib: Smith, A. J., *The Wit of Love*.

Metonymy
▷ Figures of Speech.

Metre
From the Greek word meaning 'measure'. In poetry, metre is the measure of the rhythm of a line of verse, when the line is rhythmically systematic, *ie* can be divided into units of 'metrical feet'. The names for these feet all derive from ancient Greek verse. The commonest feet in use in English are as follows:

Iambus ˘ ˊ *eg* the words
'again', 'revenge', delight'.
'Iambics march from short to long.'

Trochee ˊ ˘ *eg* the words
'never', 'happy', 'heartless'.
'Trochee trips from long to short.'

Anapest ˘ ˘ ˊ *eg* the words
'entertain', 'supersede', 'engineer'.
'With a leap and a bound the
swift anapaests throng.'

Spondee ˊ ˊ *eg* the words
'maintain', 'heartbreak', 'wineglass'
'Slow spondee stalks, strong foot. . .'

Dactyl ˊ ˘ ˘ *eg* the words
'melody', 'happiness', 'sorrowful'.
'. . . yet ill able
'Ever to come up with dactyl trisyllable.'

The illustrative lines are taken from ▷ Coleridge's mnemonic rhyme 'Metrical Feet' (the dactyl example in particular being a joke).

It is important to remember three points when analysing ('scanning') English verse:

1 Despite Coleridge's use of 'long' and 'short' for iambic and trochaic feet, these words are inappropriate to English metrical feet, which are composed of accented and unaccented syllables (two accented ones in the case of the spondee) irrespective of their length.

2 Except in the case of the iambus, it is unusual to find lines of verse composed entirely of the same foot; this is especially true of the spondee and the dactyl.

3 It is unwise to think of metre at all when reading a great deal of English verse. Old and Middle English ▷ alliterative verse was not metrical. ▷ Chaucer's is metrical, but not consistently so; his verse depends more on the natural rhythms of the English speaking voice. This is also true of ▷ Sir Thomas Wyatt in the early 16th century, of the mature dramatic verse of ▷ Shakespeare and his contemporaries, of ▷ John Donne, of ▷ Gerard Manley Hopkins in the 19th century, and of many 20th-century poets.

Verse lines have names according to the number of feet they contain; much the commonest English line is the iambic pentameter (five feet). The hexameter has six feet, and is called an ▷ Alexandrine when they are iambic. Other lengths: monometer = one foot; dimeter = two feet; trimeter = three feet; tetrameter = four feet; heptameter = seven feet; octameter = eight feet. Some minor 16th-century poets used lines of 14 syllables known as 'fourteeners'; a couplet consisting of a fourteener and an Alexandrine, first used by Wyatt, is known as the ▷ poulter's measure.

▷ Blank verse; Free verse; Ode; Sonnet.

Mew, Charlotte (1869–1928)
Poet and ▷ short story writer, born in London to a genteel but oppressive middle-class family. Mew's life was overshadowed by the mental illness of two siblings and the death of her father, which was to leave her impoverished in her late twenties. Despite limited educational advantages she published her first poems and a short story, 'Passed', in the ▷ *Yellow Book* shortly before the public scandal of ▷ Oscar Wilde's arrest in 1895 left the magazine greatly discredited. She also published in *The English Woman* and *The Egoist*. Her work was well received by ▷ Thomas Hardy, John Masefield (1878–1967), publisher Harold Monro (1879–1932) and Walter de la Mare (1873–1956), whose combined influence secured her a civil list pension in 1923. She committed suicide in 1928 by drinking Lysol after the death of her closest sister, Anne. Because of its naturalistic form, her work is frequently linked with the early 20th-century Georgian school, despite her exclusion from representative anthologies of this poetic movement. However, her immunity from the stylistic innovations of modernism, as well as from the sexual and political freedoms of the 20th century, coupled with her thematic concerns with female self-repression, lost childhood and the past has led critics to regard her as a late Victorian in spirit. She published only two volumes of poetry and her reputation rests on twenty-eight poems, most of which were written before 1916. Her work is characterized by a complex use of the ▷ dramatic monologue, in poems such as 'The Farmer's Bride', 'In Nunhead Cemetery', 'The Quiet House' and 'Madeleine in Church', to explore gender relations, frustrated and obsessive sexuality, loss and extreme psychological isolation. In the 1920s both Hardy and Virginia Woolf (1882–1941) regarded her as the greatest living woman poet.

Bib: Leighton, A., *Victorian Women Poets: Writing Against the Heart*; Fitzgerald, P., *Charlotte Mew and Her Friends*; Leighton, A., and Reynolds, M. (eds.), *An Anthology of Victorian Women Poets.*

Meynell, Alice (1847–1922)
Poet and essayist, born in Barnes, London, and educated at home by her father. She converted to ▷ Catholicism in 1868, a faith shared by her concert-pianist mother. Her first volume of verse, *Preludes*, was published in 1875, attracting praise from ▷ George Eliot and from the author and editor Wilfred Meynell, whom she married in 1877. Further volumes followed, including *Poems* (1893); *Other Poems* (1896); *Later Poems* (1902); *Poems on the War* (1916) and *Last Poems* (1923). Meynell's lyrical and mystical poetry gained her a high reputation, particularly among writers, and after ▷ Tennyson's death she was proposed as Poet Laureate. She had eight children, and supported the family by writing for periodicals and newspapers, including *The National Observer* and *The Pall Mall Gazette*. Her essays were collected under various titles, which include *The Rhythm of Life* (1893), *The Colour of Life* (1896) and *The Spirit of Place* (1899). She also wrote translations, produced editions and wrote biographies of Holman Hunt (1893) and ▷ Ruskin (1900). She was active in the ▷ women's suffrage movement in the early years of the 20th century.

Bib: Michalik, K., *Meynell: Her Life and Works*; Badeni, J., *Life*; Leighton, A., and Reynolds, P. (eds.), *An Anthology of Victorian Women Poets.*

***Michael* (1800)**
A poem in ▷ blank verse by ▷ William Wordsworth concerning the austere life of a shepherd in the Lake District, whose only son Luke goes away to work in town, meets disgrace, and then disappears. The emptiness of Michael's life without his son is symbolized,

in an image of characteristic simplicity, by the unbuilt sheepfold, whose first stone Luke had laid before his departure as a covenant between them. Michael spends the last seven years of his life brooding over it and leaves it still unfinished at his death.

▷ Lake Poets.

Microcosmographie

▷ Characters, Theophrastian.

Middlemarch, A Study of Provincial Life (1871–2)
A novel by ▷ George Eliot, considered by many to be her finest work. It is set in the years immediately preceding the 1832 ▷ Reform Bill, a time of unrest, agitation and intense political discussion, but its ideas are more relevent to the mid-Victorian period when it was written. The material was originally intended for two novels, one centred on Dorothea Brooke and the other a study of provincial life in the town of Middlemarch, based on Coventry. Unity is achieved by the fusion of the two senses of 'provincial': the geographical sense of 'situated outside the capital' and the cultural one of 'ignorant of the central current of ideas'. Dorothea, the daughter of a country gentleman, aspires to a life of high spiritual conduct; she is, however, isolated geographically, socially and intellectually, and she finds no scope for her ambitions. In consequence she is led to an infatuation with Mr Casaubon, an elderly parson-scholar whose life's work is the writing of his *Key to all Mythologies*, in which he expects to demonstrate the centrality of the Christian scriptures. Unfortunately his work is rendered futile by his ignorance of the leading (German) scholarship in his field, and his egoism and narrowness of human experience prevent him from appreciating the quality of Dorothea's ardour and potentiality. He dies having failed in his ambition.

The disillusionment and failure of their marriage runs parallel to that of Tertius Lydgate, a young doctor engaged in radical research, and the materialistic Rosamund Vincy. Unlike Casaubon, Lydgate is alert to the intellectual centre of his thought (Paris) and he has chosen to live in a provincial town only because he supposes that by so doing he can escape the social involvements and professional rivalries of the metropolis. Rosamund is the daughter of a Middlemarch manufacturer who has the typically provincial ambition to raise his family to the level of metropolitan fashion, and she is attracted to Lydgate only because he has aristocratic relations. She has no understanding of his intellectual promise and does nothing but frustrate it. Moreover, Lydgate's arrogance in viewing women as ornamental reflections of himself blinds him to Rosamund's real personality. Lydgate's career is virtually ruined when he becomes involved in a scandal concerning Bulstrode, a banker and bigoted ▷ Dissenter.

Dorothea's youthful desire is similarly thwarted, but at the end of the novel she seems to find happiness with Will Ladislaw, a young relative of her husband's who differs from the other characters by being essentially cosmopolitan in his background and outlook. Another centre of judgement is the Garth family, who acknowledge their provinciality and, by avoiding illusions, achieve balanced insights and clear directions for their energies in ways that are less provincial than those of their superiors. A minor character, but central to George Eliot's valuations, is the free-thinking parson Farebrother, condemned to a life of self-sacrifice by external causes. He is neither bitter nor unctuous, and is also capable of great sympathy for others. Through the portrayal of these characters, and others such as Cadwallader, Chettam and Brooke, Eliot analyses the social and political upheavals of the early 19th century and exposes the sexual prejudice that permeated the society of the day. The limitations imposed upon women's lives are highlighted in the case of Dorothea, while the dangers of contemporary ideologies of femininity are explored in Rosamund. The detailed and thorough analysis of gender in the novel has not prevented some critics from arguing that at the heart of Eliot's vision is a conservatism that emphasizes the need for individuals to curb their own desires in the face of social duty.

▷ Realism.

Bib: Peck, J., (ed) *Middlemarch: Casebook*; Brady, K., *George Eliot*.

Middleton, Christopher (b 1926)
Poet, literary critic and translator. Middleton was born in Cornwall, educated at Cambridge and became a university lecturer in Germany, England and then America. He teaches German studies, and his work is influenced by German and French literature, although it is notoriously eclectic, drawing also on English ▷ Victorian poets, ▷ Dada and ▷ Spanish poetry. Middleton's work is both technically precise and extremely difficult – it employs highly disruptive techniques, disturbing conventional syntax and rhythm and in this lies its obscurity. His texts include: *Torse 3: Poems 1949–1961* (1962); *Our Flowers & Nice Bones* (1970); *The Lonely Suppers of W. V. Balloon* (1975); *Pataxanadu* (1976).

Middleton, Elizabeth (c 1637)
Poet. Little is known about Elizabeth Middleton, although G. Greer in *Kissing the Rod* (1988) suggests that she might belong to the Myddleton family of Denbighshire and includes detailed genealogical material to that effect. We know

of her existence through one extant devotional poem, 'The Death and passion of Our Lord Jesus Christ' (1637). It has 173 six-line stanzas which take the form of an oratorio, the biblical narrative event being followed by a passionate statement of one speaker's emotional response. Her imagery is simple, but strong, and her language is clearly influenced by other religious writers such as ▷ Robert Southwell.

Middleton, Thomas (1580–1627)
Dramatist. Little is known about his life; he may have been a student of law in London and in the 1590s he was at Oxford University. Later he was often employed to write ▷ pageants to celebrate civic occasions, and in 1620 he was appointed city chronologer (historian).

His masterpieces were two tragedies: ▷ *Women Beware Women* (1614) and ▷ *The Changeling* (1622), with a subplot by ▷ William Rowley. The latter play is one of the finest tragedies in English since ▷ Shakespeare. In his comedies he was one of the two notable successors to ▷ Ben Jonson, the other being ▷ Philip Massinger. His best are probably: *A Trick to Catch the Old-one* (1604), ▷ *The Roaring Girl* (with ▷ Dekker, 1606), and above all ▷ *A Chaste Maid in Cheapside* (1611). These, like others of his comedies, are ▷ citizen comedies, *ie* about London middle-class life, like the comedies of Dekker, but presented with more substantial realism. ▷ *A Game at Chess* (1624) was a political satire provoked by the king's failure to marry his son to a Spanish princess; its performance was stopped by the protest of the Spanish ambassador. *The Witch*, a ▷ revenge play of uncertain date, may have influenced Shakespeare's ▷ *Macbeth* but was more probably influenced by it, and Middleton has been thought by some to have contributed Act III, Sc. v in *Macbeth*.

With Rowley, Middleton also wrote *A Fair Quarrel* (1614); *The World Tost at Tennis* (1620); *The Spanish Gipsy* (1623). Plays ascribed to Middleton alone: *The Old Law* (1599); *Blurt, Master-Constable* (1601–2); *The Family of Love* (1602); *Michaelmas Term* (1605); *The Phoenix* (1607); *A Mad World, my Masters* (1606); *Your Five Gallants* (?1607); ▷ *No Wit, No Help like a Woman's* (?1613); *Anything for a Quiet Life* (?1617); *More Dissemblers besides Women* (before 1622); *The Widow* (uncertain date). Eleven of his ▷ masques have survived. He also wrote some minor poetry and prose ▷ pamphlets.
Bib: Bradbrook, M. C., *Elizabethan Tragedy*; Knights, L. C., *Drama and Society in the Age of Jonson*; Barker, R. H., *Thomas Middleton*; Heinemann, M., *Puritanism and Theatre*; Mulryne, J. R., *Thomas Middleton*.

***Midsummer Night's Dream, A* (1595)**
A comedy by Shakespeare. From internal evidence it has been dated about 1595; it was printed in 1600. The title refers to the fantastic quality of events, resembling a dream on Midsummer night, when fantastic dreams were supposed to be commonly experienced.

The characters are in four distinct groups. The background is the court of a character from Greek mythology, King Theseus of Athens, on the eve of his marriage to Hippolyta, queen of the Amazons. The four lovers whose confusions form the bulk of the action, Helena and Demetrius, Hermia and Lysander (as they are eventually paired), have classical names, but their story is a typical comedy of ▷ Renaissance romantic love, in which they are all victims of blind passion. The third group is made from the Athenian artisans whose names – ▷ Bottom, Quince, Snout, Flute and Starveling – show them to be English types of Shakespeare's own day. They celebrate Theseus' wedding night (and that of the other lovers) by performing the interlude ▷ 'Pyramus and Thisbe' – intended to be tragic but, as they carry it out, decidedly comic. The fourth group is the ▷ fairies. In general (especially ▷ Puck, or Robin Goodfellow) these are drawn from English folklore, but their king, ▷ Oberon, comes from *Huon de Bordeaux* (a medieval French romance) and Titania from ▷ Ovid's ▷ *Metamorphoses*. Oberon, through Puck, confuses the lovers as they wander through the wood near Athens, and causes Titania to fall in love with Bottom, who, for the night, is given an ass's head. The fantasy is deftly contrived.

Mildmay, Grace (1552–1620)
Autobiographer. Despite an extremely strict upbringing, during which she was regularly beaten, Mildmay gained confidence in her writing and educational capabilities through her tutoring by a poor relation. At 15 she married Anthony Mildmay and later in life ran the large estates at Apethorpe. It was not until she became a grandmother that she attempted to record her life for the benefit of her daughter, Mary Fane, so that the younger woman could learn from the example of her mother. The ▷ autobiographical diary focuses mainly upon the bringing up of children and how to educate the young, its ultimate end being a preparation for the eternal life in heaven. The work exists in manuscript at Northants public library, but extracts are published in 'An Elizabethan Gentlewoman', ed. R. Wiegall, in *Quarterly Review* (1911).
Bib: Travitsky, B. (ed.), *The Paradise of Women*.

Mill, John Stuart (1806–73)
Writer on economics, politics, psychology, logic and ethics. He did not invent the word ▷ Utilitarian, but was the first to apply it to the reform movement started by his father's friend ▷ Jeremy Bentham and of which his father James Mill was one of the leaders.

The movement derived from 18th-century ▷ rationalism, and the group was known as 'the philosophical radicals' because of the intellectual thoroughness with which they reasoned out their political and social standpoints. James Mill educated his son strenuously from a very early age but the education, wide as it was, ignored his son's imaginative and emotional needs. J.S. Mill describes in his *Autobiography* (1873) how this neglect produced in him a spiritual crisis when he was twenty-one, after he had already made a brilliant start to his career. He discovered that he was emotionally indifferent to the ends for which he was working. He recovered partly through his discovery of the poetry of ▷ William Wordsworth and the crisis enabled him to develop a far more sympathetic and balanced outlook on human needs than had been possessed by his father or Bentham. Mill's personal development reflects the change from ▷ Enlightenment rationalism to a renewed interest in feeling and emotion characteristic of the ▷ Romantics. His essays on Bentham and ▷ Samuel Taylor Coleridge published in the ▷ *Westminster Review* in 1838 and 1840 respectively neatly epitomize this conflict.

After the passing of the 1832 ▷ Reform Bill, Mill worked to establish a radical party and harnessed the *London and Westminster Review* (which he owned from 1836–40) to this end.

Mill's literary and philosophical output was very large, and his essays and books were extremely influential. These included *System of Logic, Ratiocinative and Inductive* (1843; 1930) and *Essays on Some Unsettled Questions of Political Economy* (1844; 1949). This was followed in 1849 by his influential *Principles of Political Economy*; in which he discusses the growth and importance of the working class. Mill's life and career were deeply affected by his marriage in 1851 to Harriet Taylor, with whom he had enjoyed an intimate frienship during her first husband's lifetime. Together they produced one of Mill's most important works, *The Subjection of Women* (1859) which argued, amongst other things, for the extension of the franchise to women. Other works include *On Liberty* (1859) a liberal manifesto on the rights of the individual; *Considerations on Representative Government* (1860) and *Utilitarianism* (1863). In 1865 he was elected to Parliament for Westminster but was defeated in 1868. He died in Avignon.

Bib: Moller-Okin, S., *Women in Western Political Thought*; Packe, M. St J., *Life*; Hayek, F.A., *J.S. Mill and Harriet Taylor: Their Correspondence and Subsequent Marriage*; Hamburger, J., *Intellectuals in Politics: J.S. Mill and the Philosophic Radicals*.

Mill on the Floss, The (1860)

A novel by ▷ George Eliot, set in the Midlands. Its central characters are Maggie Tulliver and her brother Tom – children of the miller of Dorlcote Mill on the River Floss. She is headstrong, intelligent and richly imaginative beyond the understanding of her family – particularly that of Tom, a boy of limited intelligence and sympathies to whom she is devoted. The novel is divided into seven parts; the first three lead up to Mr Tulliver's bankruptcy and form a rich and comic study of English country life in the mid-19th century with deep insights into the psychology of the rural middle-class. The last three deal with the tragic love of Maggie for Philip Wakeham, the disabled son of the lawyer through whom Mr Tulliver has been ruined, the compromising of her reputation by the educated and agreeable Stephen Guest and her rejection by and alienation from her brother. In a ▷ melodramatic denouement Maggie rescues Tom from the flooded mill and they are reconciled before they drown. Although much is left unresolved, it is a powerful novel, particularly in terms of Eliot's representation of Maggie's psychological turmoil. In the provincial environment in which she grows up Maggie is prevented from following her desires and is forced to internalize all her intellectual and spiritual energies. Many women, including ▷ Simone de Beauvoir (1908–86), have identified with Eliot's semi-autobiographical portrayal of Maggie.

Miller, Anne (1741–1781)

English poet, patron and travel writer. She held poetry evenings in her excessively expensive villa at Bath, during which poems would be thrown into an antique vase and then each taken out and read aloud. Some were published in *Poetical Amusements at a Villa near Bath* (1775–1781), and the preface emphasizes 'the Vase, and Sprigs of Bay and Myrtle alluded to in these poems are not emblematical, but real'. When ▷ Fanny Burney visited her, she called her 'a round plump coarse-looking dame'. Miller also wrote *Letters From Italy* (1776–7).

▷ Seward, Anna

Miller, Jonathan (b 1934)

Director, performer, doctor. Jonathan Miller qualified as a doctor at Cambridge where he co-wrote and performed in a legendary Footlights revue *Beyond the Fringe* (1960) with ▷ Alan Bennett, Peter Cook, and Dudley Moore. He has directed contemporary plays, many works from classical repertory, contemporary work, and opera. He was Artistic Director of the Old Vic in 1988–90. His book *Subsequent Performances* (1986) is a brilliantly sustained meditation on the theatrical production of the classics.

Bib: Romain, M., *A Profile of Jonathan Miller*

Miller's Tale, The

One of ▷ Chaucer's ▷ *Canterbury Tales*. Following the ▷ Knight's story about competing lovers, set in classical Athens, the Miller insists on 'quiting' this story with a tale of love rivalry set in Oxford. Double trickery is at the heart of this ▷ fabliau. An old jealous husband, John, a carpenter, is deceived as a result of believing his lodger's prediction about the coming of a second flood, and gullibly accepting the chance offered to play the role of Noah. His lodger, the clerk Nicholas, thus plots a means of spending the night with the young Alison, John's wife. In the course of the evening, Alison spontaneously plays a trick on another of her admirers, Absolon, and gets him to kiss her 'nether.eye'. Nicholas is branded with a ploughshare as a result of attempting to repeat the trick.

Milne, A. A. (Alan Alexander) (1882–1956)
Novelist, dramatist, children's writer. He was for many years assistant editor of *Punch*, and he became widely popular as the author of light comedies and novels. His earliest play is *Wurzel-Flummery* (1917) and his best known *Mr Pim Passes By* (1919). However he achieved fame by four ▷ children's books, centring on his son, Christopher Robin. Two of these are verse: *When We Were Very Young* (1924) and *Now We Are Six* (1927). The other two are prose stories, with Christopher Robin's teddy bear Winnie the Pooh as hero: *Winnie the Pooh* (1926); *The House at Pooh Corner* (1928). They have been translated into many languages; *Winnie the Pooh*, rather to its advantage, into Latin.

Milton, John (1608–74)
Poet and prose polemicist. Milton was born in London, the son of a scrivener and musician, and educated at St Paul's School and Christ's College, Cambridge. After leaving Cambridge in 1632, Milton lived for the next five years at his father's house in Horton. During this, his early poetic career, he wrote the companion pieces *L'Allegro* and *Il Penseroso*, two ▷ masques, ▷ *Arcades* and *Comus*, and the ▷ elegy ▷ *Lycidas*. From 1638 to 1639 Milton travelled abroad, chiefly in Italy. His Italian journey was to have a lasting influence on his later development, not least in the contact he established among Florentine intellectuals. But more than that, it reaffirmed his distaste – loathing even – for Roman ▷ Catholicism, and focused his intense opposition to the Laudian (▷ Laud, William) regime in England.

Milton's continental journey was interrupted early in 1639 at Naples, where he claims to have first heard news of the political crisis in England. He was later to claim that he thought it 'base that I should travel abroad at my ease for the cultivation of my mind while my fellow citizens at home were fighting for liberty' (*Defensio secunda*). Returning to England, Milton embarked upon what has now come to be seen as the second phase of his career – that of a political prose writer and propagandist for the anti-Royalist cause in the English ▷ Civil War. Between 1640 and 1655, Milton was to write little poetry. His energies and his sympathies were now to be engaged fully on the side of the republican forces in England – though he was not an uncritical supporter of the new experiment in government. From this period can be dated the series of great prose declarations dealing with political and religious questions – *Of Reformation* (1641), his attack on episcopacy in the *Apology for Smectymnuus* (1642), his statement on personal liberty contained in *The Doctrine and Discipline of Divorce* (1643). These works were followed by ▷ *Areopagitica* (1644), *Tenure of Kings and Magistrates* (1649), *Eikonoklastes* (1649), the two 'defences' of the English people (1651 and 1654), *A Treatise of Civil Power* (1659) and, almost at the moment when ▷ Charles II returned to England to re-establish the claims of monarchy, *A Readie and Easie Way to Establish a Free Commonwealth* (1660). The list of topics upon which Milton wrote in this period is bewildering, but running through all his prose writings is a stable belief that the English people have been chosen, by God, to perform a necessary political act – the establishment of a state based on principles of choice and, within certain bounds, freedom.

▷ *Paradise Lost*, Milton's great religious and political poem, was begun at some point in the mid-1650s – perhaps in the growing awareness that although there had been political choices in England, the wrong choice had been made. The poem was not published, however, until 1667, with a second (revised) edition appearing in 1674, shortly before Milton's death in November of that year. But the period after 1660 is usually recognized as the third and final phase of Milton's career. It is the period of the publication of ▷ *Paradise Regained* and ▷ *Samson Agonistes*. Though it has long been claimed that Milton's absorption in the task of writing these works marked an end to his career of political engagement, it is probably truer to say that these works signal a renewed, and possibly deeper, investigation of the themes which had occupied him for most of his life – the questions of political and religious liberty, the problems associated with choice and rule, and the problematic nature of government and obedience.
Bib: Carey, J. and Fowler, A. (eds.), *The Complete Poems of John Milton*; Wolfe, D. M. (ed.), *Complete Prose Works of John Milton*; Parker, W. R., *Milton: A Biography*; Hill, C., *Milton and the English Revolution*; Nyquist, M. and Ferguson, M. (eds.), *Re-membering Milton*.

Mimesis
In ▷ Plato's *Republic* 'mimesis' is used to designate 'imitation', but in a derogatory way. The term is given a rigorous, positive meaning

in ▷ Aristotle's *Poetics* where it is used to describe a process of selection and representation appropriate to tragedy: 'the imitation of an action'. Literary criticism from ▷ Sir Philip Sidney onwards has wrestled with the problem of the imitative function of literary texts, but after structuralism with its questioning of the referential function of all language, the term has taken on a new and problematic dimension. Mimesis has frequently been associated with the term ▷ 'Realism', and with the capacity of language to reflect reality. At particular historical moments, *eg* the Renaissance, or the present time, when reality itself appears to be in question, then the capacity of language to represent reality is brought to the fore. The issue becomes even more complex when we realize that 'reality' may be something other than our experience of it. The debate has been carried on most vigorously at a theoretical level in the exchanges earlier this century between the Hungarian critic Georg Lukács, and the dramatist Bertolt Brecht. The nub of the debate between these two Marxist thinkers (▷ Marx, Karl) was how best to represent 'the deeper causal complexes of society' (Brecht). Brecht rejected the view propounded by Lukács that the novel was the literary form which pre-eminently represented social process, arguing that realism was a major political, philosophical and practical issue and should not be dealt with by literature alone. Such a view rejected the metaphysical implications which lay behind the Aristotelian notion of mimesis, in favour of a more historical analysis which saw literature as part of the process of social change.

In ▷ narratology, the distinction between mimesis (showing) and diegesis (telling) is considered under the heading of ▷ mood. For example, if the speech of a fictional character is given in full, in quotation marks, this is considered mimetic, whereas a summary of what was said would be relatively diegetic.
Bib: Auerbach, E., *Mimesis*; Genette, G., *Narrative Discourse*.

Minerva Press
Established in London in 1790 by William Lane, it combined a press with a ▷ circulating library, and published mainly women authors for a primarily female readership. It is often identified with ▷ Gothic and sentimental excess, and probably equates most closely to the Mills and Boon pulp novels published in the late 20th century. Yet the authors did produce some interesting work, and Minerva certainly provided the means for women to earn their living as authors.
Bib: Blakey, D., *The Minerva Press 1790–1820*.

Minim, Dick
A character in ▷ Samuel Johnson's ▷ *Idler* essays for the *Weekly Gazette*. Dick Minim is a ▷ satirical representation of the kind of person who seeks a reputation for critical acumen by praising what is in fashion and sneering at what is unfamiliar.

Miracle plays
▷ Cycle plays.

***Mirror for Magistrates, A* (1559)**
A collection of verse monologues spoken by characters in English history and legend. The collection was inspired by ▷ John Lydgate's *The Fall of Princes* (1494), and written by William Baldwin, ▷ George Ferrers and others. Nineteen verse monologues are spoken by historical figures from the reigns of ▷ Richard II to ▷ Edward IV, and in the main the intention of these verse accounts is to warn rulers and subjects against (respectively) tyranny and rebellion. After the first edition of 1559, numerous editions appeared throughout the 16th century and well into the 17th. With each edition, the work expanded, though the edition of 1563 (with contributions by ▷ Thomas Sackville) is claimed to be, artistically, the most satisfactory. The edition of 1610 (the last, though there were reissues of 1619, 1620 and 1621) is the largest of what had become a series rather than a sequence of editions.

Though the *Mirror* was perhaps not an artistically distinguished enterprise, it nevertheless exerted a considerable thematic influence on the writing of history plays in the period, and on the conception of ▷ tragedy pursued by ▷ Elizabethan and ▷ Jacobean writers. It partakes, too, in that Elizabethan attempt at creating a sustained account of national history of which the work of ▷ Samuel Daniel, ▷ Michael Drayton and ▷ Edmund Spenser is also, in part, representative.

▷ Histories and Chronicles.
Bib: Campbell, L. B. (ed.), *A Mirror for Magistrates*.

Mise en abyme
The *mise en abyme* is a feature specially characteristic of the French ▷ *nouveau roman* and of metafiction. It means a throwing into the abyss, and occurs when some element within the text mirrors the structure of the text as a whole, creating an interpretative 'abyss' as the part seems to contain the whole. A visual analogy would be a painting of a room, in which a copy of the same painting hangs on the wall. The device and the term were developed by the French novelist ▷ André Gide, whose novel *The Counterfeiters* (1949) contains a clear example: a character who is writing a novel resembling *The Counterfeiters*.

Misrule, Lord of
Title given to the master of revels for the 12

days of the Christmas festivities, which mark a licensed period of disorder and which may be celebrated in medieval noble and royal households.

▷ New Historicism.

***Miss in Her Teens* (1747)**
A shortened (two-act) comedy by ▷ David Garrick, one of the first of its type (also known as 'petite pièce' or 'petite comédie'), adapted from D'Ancourt's *La Parisienne*, and staged as an 'afterpiece' at ▷ Covent Garden. The main plot concerns Captain Loveit's competition with his miserly father, Sir Simon Loveit, for the hand of the 16-year-old country girl and heiress, Biddy Bellair. She is also courted by two other suitors: a braggart and a fop. The Captain is assisted in his plans by the girl's own cunning and determination, and by two clever servants. A sub-plot concerns the rivalry between two of the servants for the attentions of a third. The Captain chases away the absurd rivals and confronts his father, who gives up his claim to Biddy voluntarily. The play has various patriotic elements referring to the contemporary War of the Austrian Succession: its last line, spoken by Biddy, is, 'Who fails in honour, will be false in love'. Garrick himself played the effeminate suitor, Fribble, who has some of the wittiest lines in the play; it was one of his most popular roles. The rest of the dialogue and the action are simple but very funny, and the piece was staged repeatedly.

Mistry, Rohinton (b 1952)
Indian novelist. Mistry was brought up in Bombay, and moved to Canada in 1975, where he studied at the University of Toronto and has since worked in a bank. His first work was *Tales from Firozsha Baag* (1987), a collection of short stories set in the middle-class Parsi suburbs of Bombay. His first novel, *Such a Long Journey* (1991), is the story of a Bombay family; it has an extravagant plot, vivid, often humorous characters and elements of ▷ magic realism.

Mitford, Mary Russell (1786–1855)
Poet, dramatist, letter-writer, autobiographer and sketch-writer. Mary Mitford remained living with her parents in the country, supporting her family, especially her father who was laden with gambling debts, by her prolific writing. Her first publication, *Miscellaneous Poems* (1810), was well received and she was encouraged by ▷ Coleridge to continue writing. She produced several acclaimed and lucrative dramas, *Julian* (1823), *Foscari* (1826) and *Rienzi* (1828). Even more successful were her prose sketches of country life, in particular *Our Village* (1824–32). Her style was lucid and direct, and Mitford herself stated that she 'always wrote on the spot and at the moment and in nearly every instance with the closest and most resolute fidelity to the place and the people'. While rightly lauded for her work, Mitford felt isolated with her family in the country and entered into correspondence with some of the other well-known authors of her day; these included Elizabeth Barrett Browning (1806–61), ▷ Felicia Hemans, ▷ Charles Lamb, ▷ Harriet Martineau, and ▷ Amelia Opie. Today it is these letters which provide the most valuable insight into Mitford's own life and work, as well as presenting us with a picture of the literary world at the beginning of the 19th century. More formal ▷ autobiographical material may be found in her *Recollections of a Literary Life*, (1857).
Bib: Astin, M., *Mary Russell Mitford*; Edwards, P.D., *Idyllic Realism from Mary Russell Mitford to Hardy*.

Mo, Timothy (b 1953)
Novelist. Born in Hong Kong of an English mother and a Cantonese father and educated at St John's College, Oxford. He has worked as a journalist. His first novel was *The Monkey King* (1978), a lively story of family and business intrigue, set in Hong Kong and New Territories on the Chinese Mainland. *Sour Sweet* (1982) is the touching story of a Chinese family, first-generation immigrants in London, whose initial isolation is mitigated when they open a take-away, leading to comic cross-cultural confusions, until the father accidentally becomes involved in the world of the Triad gangs in Soho (the subject of a parallel narrative in the novel). *An Insular Possession* (1986) blends history and fiction in its account of conflicts between Britain and China over the opium trade in the 1830s and 1840s, as does *The Redundancy of Courage* (1991), which concerns an initially uncommitted Chinese hotel-proprietor who becomes involved in the resistance movement, after the American-backed Indonesian invasion of East Timor in 1975. In 1995, Mo took the unusual step of publishing his latest novel, *Brownout on Breadfruit Street*, himself rather than putting it through a conventional publishing house.

▷ Post-colonial literature.

Mock epic
A form of ▷ satire practised with most success in English by ▷ Alexander Pope. The method is to employ the dignified expression associated with epic about subjects in themselves either trivial or base. Thus ▷ *The Rape of the Lock* describes a family quarrel provoked by a young man robbing a girl of a lock of her hair; it uses a dignity of style appropriate to the Rape of Helen which gave rise to Homer's ▷ *Iliad*, and applies it to the minute detail and obviously trivial scale of emotion appropriate to the slightness of the episode. In Pope's ▷ *Dunciad*

the method is rather different, because here Pope is describing what is base rather than what is petty; the contrast is not, as with *The Rape*, an ironic one between grandeur of treatment and pettiness of subject, but between the nobility of the style and the depth of meanness in the subject.

Another form of mock epic is the ▷ mock heroic poem, in which a bad man committing base deeds is described in epic style, without disguising the badness.

The mock epic is especially the product of the century 1660–1760, when admiration for Greek and Latin satire and epic was particularly high.

▷ Epic.

Mock heroic

A literary mode in which large and important events are juxtaposed with small and insignificant ones for a variety of comic, ▷ satirical or more profoundly ironic effects. In its narrow sense mock heroic is the product of the ▷ Augustan, ▷ neo-classical age. As the bourgeoisie wrested cultural hegemony from the aristocracy in the late 17th century, a new, more complex attitude to the ancient aristocratic ideals of honour and nobility developed. A new irony (▷ figures of speech) infused their literary expression in the classical forms of ▷ epic and ▷ tragedy. Epic retained the respect of the reading public, but it was too archaic and primitive to satisfy the modern imagination in its traditional form. ▷ John Milton's ▷ *Paradise Lost*, the only significant literary epic in English (▷ *Beowulf* being an oral poem), has about it much of the complexity of the novel, and its more atavistic heroic elements (the war in heaven, the vision of future history) seem mechanical. In the generations following Milton the major poets, ▷ John Dryden and ▷ Alexander Pope, translated the ancient epics, but their own original work took the more complex form of mock epic.

Augustan mock heroic is a development from the conceit of the ▷ Tudor and ▷ 'metaphysical' poets, and its imaginative appeal derives similarly from far-fetched and unexpected comparisons and parallels. At its most basic it can be simply satirical. The poet contrasts a contemptible modern person or event with a respected heroic version. ▷ Samuel Butler's ▷ *Hudibras* works largely on this level, and there is a strong element of this kind of satire in Dryden's ▷ *Mac Flecknoe*. The respected touchstone need not be the classical epic, but can be any admired model from the past, or even the present. In ▷ *Absalom and Achitophel* it is the Old Testament (▷ Bible). In parts of the ▷ *Dunciad* it is Milton and other 'classic' English poets such as ▷ Edmund Waller and ▷ Sir John Denham. In parts of the ▷ *Rape of the Lock* it is the pomp of religious ritual.

Nor need the contrast imply a moral satire on the modern world, or indeed any satire at all. At the beginning of *Absalom and Achitophel* the comparison of ▷ Charles II with ▷ King David in the Book of Kings achieves the difficult task of aggrandizing the 'merry monarch' while at the same time slyly acknowledging his libertinism. The comparison between Belinda's petticoat-hoops and Achilles' shield in *The Rape of the Lock* mocks the heroic model rather than the modern equivalent, emphasizing the delightful domestic security of Belinda's world, as against the primitive *machismo* of the ancient heroes. Often the comparison between familiar and modern on the one hand, and exotic and ancient on the other, arises from pure imaginative playfulness, as when Pope, through implied puns, compares the ceremony of preparing ▷ coffee in an English drawing-room (on 'japanned' tables), with an awesome religious ceremony in distant Japan: 'On shining Altars of *Japan* they raise/ The silver Lamp; the fiery Spirits blaze' (*Rape of the Lock*, III, II. 107–8).

Although mock heroic is most closely associated with the age of Dryden, ▷ Swift and Pope, it is found in all periods.

Mode of literary production

A term used to indicate the material circumstances in which literature is produced. For example, work written for the modern commodity market is produced under very different conditions, and with different results, from that produced for a wealthy patron in the seventeenth century or for a small, local community. However, the use of the term is sometimes extended beyond the economic level. For instance, in discussions of why authorship has been so difficult for women in earlier periods, feminist critics highlight not just the problems women experience in gaining access to publication but a range of other factors inhibiting to writing such as child-bearing and other family pressures, lack of education and cultural prejudice.

Bib: Eagleton, T., *Criticism and Ideology*; Woolf, V., *A Room of One's Own*.

***Modern Love* (1862)**

A series of sixteen-line poems resembling sonnets, by ▷ George Meredith. The poems tell the story of the breakdown of a marriage ending in the suicide of the wife. The tone is strongly emotional and the attitude to the emotions is self-scrutinizing; in these ways Meredith's *Modern Love* suggests comparison with the ▷ dramatic monologues of ▷ Robert Browning and ▷ Alfred Tennyson, for example Browning's *Any Wife to Any Husband* and Tennyson's ▷ *Maud*.

Modernism

Twentieth-century English literature may be divided into two phases: modernism and ▷ postmodernism. In both phases, changes in literary technique and subject matter are closely linked with comparable transformations in music, art and architecture. Modernism and postmodernism were also inspired by, and contributed to, social changes, and developments in philosophy, psychology, anthropology and science. Since the term 'modernism' was first used earlier in the 20th century, its meaning has developed and been revised. It is now agreed to mean the influential international movement in literature, drama, art, music and architecture which began in the latter years of the 19th century and flourished until at least the 1920s. Modernism was felt to be a reaction to ▷ realism and ▷ naturalism, undermining the representationalism (▷ mimesis) associated with those movements.In fiction the ▷ stream of consciousness novel was a prime example of modernism. In critical terms, modernist writing challenged the approaches of students and critics alike and so contributed to the development later in the century of new approaches to literature and reading. Literary modernism in England started during the first decade of the century, but World War I played a major part in its development, contributing especially to the sense of radical newness, of the apocalyptic and of destruction and desolation. The prolonged and massive slaughter of the war put paid to the Victorian sense of progress. In poetry, it was ▷ T. S. Eliot and ▷ Ezra Pound who were the leading spirits of modernism, Eliot through his poetry and his criticism; Pound to some extent in his poetry, but even more through his role as man of letters, theorist, starter of movements and champion of artists and writers. Reacting against the ▷ Romantics, and against the conventions of Edwardian poetry, these writers introduced ▷ free verse, fragmentary and innovative structures and allusive and eclectic modes of thought. The best-known example of these developments is Eliot's ▷ *The Waste Land* (1922). Powerful accounts of the experience of war are found in the work of the ▷ War poets, in particular ▷ Isaac Rosenberg, ▷ Wilfred Owen, ▷ Siegfried Sassoon, ▷ Edmund Blunden, Ivor Gurney and Charles Sorley, and later in ▷ David Jones' *In Parenthesis* (1937). Some of the War poets had also been associated with the ▷ Georgian Poets, whose work appeared in Edward Marsh's five anthologies of 1912–22 and who, in technical terms, represented a relatively traditional strain in poetry. Three poets are best considered independently of movements (which are anyway somewhat arbitrary and temporary phenomena): ▷ W. B. Yeats, ▷ Thomas Hardy and ▷ Gerard Manley Hopkins. Yeats, the greatest of modern Irish poets, followed a unique line of development, from the aestheticism of his early work to the eloquent symbolic power of his major poetry of the 1920s and 30s. Hardy, though born in 1840, did not publish his poetry until 1898 (it appeared in eight volumes between 1898 and 1928). His idiosyncratic diction and metrical experiment were to influence, among others, ▷ Philip Larkin. Hopkins had died in 1889, but his lyrical and visionary work had appeared only in anthologies prior to 1918. Other poets who published major work before 1930 included ▷ D. H. Lawrence, ▷ Robert Graves and the Scottish poets ▷ Hugh MacDiarmid and ▷ Edwin Muir.

In the novel the modernist period is dominated by six major figures: ▷ Henry James, ▷ Joseph Conrad, ▷ James Joyce, ▷ Virginia Woolf, ▷ D. H. Lawrence and ▷ E. M. Forster. Each made a distinctive contribution to the modernist transformation of fiction. James' work is notable for a fine moral sense, a complex style, and subtle studies of human consciousness (▷ *The Ambassadors*; 1903); Conrad's for narrative experiment, irony, sense of history and tragic moral vision (▷ *Nostromo*; 1904); Joyce's for linguistic exuberance, broad humanity and structural richness (▷ *Ulysses*; 1922); Woolf's for the representation of the texture of consciousness and for symbolic and poetic qualities (▷ *To The Lighthouse*; 1927); Lawrence's for the exploration of the unconscious and a unique and unrelenting vision of human nature and history (▷ *The Rainbow*; 1915); Forster's for a blend of liberalism with human insight and symbolic power (▷ *A Passage to India*; 1924). Other writers who made significant contributions to modernism include ▷ Ford Madox Ford and ▷ Dorothy Richardson. Alternative modes of fiction were the popular, realistic, relatively conventional works of ▷ Arnold Bennett and ▷ John Galsworthy, the ▷ science fiction and social realism of ▷ H. G. Wells, and the tragicomic satire of ▷ Evelyn Waugh, ▷ Wyndham Lewis and ▷ Aldous Huxley.

In the theatre the early decades of the century were dominated by ▷ George Bernard Shaw, who created a drama of ideas which questioned prevailing assumptions and expounded his socialist views. The concern with contemporary social and moral problems in Shaw's work reflected the influence of the Norwegian dramatist ▷ Henrik Ibsen. In Ireland the ▷ Abbey Theatre, Dublin, became the centre of an Irish dramatic revival. In the first decade of the century the theatre staged ▷ J. M. Synge's poetic dramas of Irish peasant life, and in the 1920s the more naturalistic and overtly political tragicomedies of ▷ Sean O'Casey. In the 1930s, and again in the 1950s, ▷ T. S. Eliot attempted to revive verse drama in English, while ▷ W. H. Auden and ▷ Christopher Isherwood co-operated on plays which, while mixing verse and prose, owed something to the early expressionist work of the German dramatist ▷ Bertolt Brecht.

In the 1930s political concerns predominated in both fiction and poetry. A group of poets led by W. H. Auden employed the ideas of Marx and

▷ Freud and dealt directly with contemporary social issues such as unemployment, class conflict and the approach of war, as well as exploring psychological states. The main members of this group were ▷ Stephen Spender, ▷ Cecil Day-Lewis and ▷ Louis MacNeice. In the 1940s the Welsh poet ▷ Dylan Thomas achieved considerable popularity with his lyrical and rhetorical style of poetry. Novelists of importance who emerged during the 1930s and 40s included ▷ Graham Greene, ▷ George Orwell, Christopher Isherwood, ▷ Elizabeth Bowen, ▷ Joyce Cary and ▷ C. P. Snow.

Since 1945 two tendencies have been evident in English literature. One of these is identifiable with postmodernism considered as a phase of western culture, and is characterized by a continuing interest in experimental techniques, the influence of philosophy and literary theory (in particular ▷ existentialism, ▷ structuralism and ▷ post-structuralism) and a creative interchange with continental, American, Latin American and other literatures. The second tendency is a reaction against aesthetic and philosophical radicalism in favour of the reassertion of more traditional modes: this tendency has an English and anti-cosmopolitan streak. This division does not necessarily entail a polarization into opposed camps; both tendencies are sometimes found in the work of the same writer.

The reassertion of traditional modes was especially evident in the 1950s. The group of poets who became known as the ▷ Movement favoured clarity, irony, scepticism and a no-nonsense tone: these included ▷ Philip Larkin, ▷ Donald Davie and ▷ John Wain. Just as the Movement was a reaction against the influence of Symbolism, of Ezra Pound and of Yeats, so the modernist novel provoked a comparable reaction. The value of the realistic and satirical novel was reasserted by the work of the so-called ▷ 'angry young men', (such as ▷ John Osborne, ▷ John Braine, ▷ Alan Sillitoe and ▷ Kingsley Amis) who expressed a mood of alienation and revolt. Both these movements are, however, partly journalistic inventions, and of less importance than the individual bodies of work which emerged from them: Philip Larkin's sceptical, poignant and witty poetry; Kingsley Amis' entertaining and often acrimonious tales of English life. In the satirical and realistic vein, ▷ Angus Wilson is one of the most considerable post-war novelists, while ▷ Iris Murdoch, another writer who emerged in the 1950s, combines intricate tragicomic plots with philosophical and artistic concerns. Murdoch's sense of life as a battle of good and evil is shared by ▷ William Golding, ▷ Muriel Spark and ▷ Anthony Burgess; these writers blend elements of realistic narrative with post-modernist techniques such as intertextuality (sustained allusion to another literary work) and devices which draw attention to the contingency of narrative and its interpretation. In the novel, postmodernism has taken the form of a foregrounding of fictionality which undermines the mimetic illusion, or a multiplication of perspectives which emphasizes uncertainty and subjectivity. Such features are found particularly in the work of ▷ John Fowles, ▷ Lawrence Durrell, ▷ Bryan S. Johnson and ▷ Salman Rushdie. Rushdie also employs the mode of ▷ magic realism, developed primarily by Latin American novelists like Gabriel García Márquez (b 1928). The prose writings of ▷ Samuel Beckett have a Joycean linguistic playfulness, but their experimentalism is dominated by a relentless and progressive minimalism. Other notable areas of development in the post-war novel have been the feminist novel, ▷ science fiction, the fantasy novel, and ▷ horror fiction.

During the 1960s a number of major poetic talents emerged: ▷ Ted Hughes, ▷ Sylvia Plath, ▷ Charles Tomlinson, ▷ Geoffrey Hill and ▷ Seamus Heaney. All of these poets except Heaney were included in the anthology *The New Poetry* (1962). In the polemical introduction, Al Alvarez championed the cause of poetry which, absorbing the implications of psychoanalysis and World War II, abandoned the gentility of the Movement. Hughes' poetry of extremity, physicality, anthropomorphism and the creation of myth rapidly gained him popularity and a place on the school syllabus. Plath, like Eliot and Pound, came to England from the U.S.A.; she is best known for her powerfully sensuous and symbolic explorations of disturbed states of mind, which associate her with fellow Americans such as Robert Lowell and John Berryman. Charles Tomlinson and Geoffrey Hill are poets with smaller, but devoted followings. Tomlinson is very much a cosmopolitan poet, influenced by American and continental models, and by the painting of Cézanne; his poems render the process and significance of visual perception with an unerring subtlety. Hill's work combines religious and historical subject matter and an almost overpowering sense of tradition with an intensely physical imagination and a postmodernist scepticism about the ability of language to engage with reality. Heaney's work, with its sensuous precision, its involvement with Irish political issues and its deeply personal yet highly accessible concerns, has made him one of the most popular and admired of contemporary poets, pre-eminent among a flourishing group of Ulster poets, including ▷ Paul Muldoon, John Montague, ▷ Derek Mahon and Michael Longley.

The power of English drama to confront contemporary experience was revived in the 1950s by a new generation of dramatists who employed colloquial speech with an expressive and symbolic power which showed the influence of the leaders of modern European drama: ▷ Ibsen, ▷ Strindberg, ▷ Chekhov and Brecht. Foremost among them was Samuel Beckett, whose play *Waiting for Godot* (first published in Britain in 1955) initiated a new era with its existentialist preoccupations and anti-realist techniques. The ▷ Theatre of the Absurd of Beckett and Eugene Ionesco influenced the work of another of this generation, ▷ Harold Pinter, whose plays explore the ambiguities and failures of everyday communication through terse, minimalist dialogue and significant silences. Blending realism and sinister fantasy, they suggest the fear and violence underlying mundane experience. The dramatists of the 1950s reacted against the upper-middle-class milieu of the work of ▷ Noël Coward and ▷ Terence Rattigan. In the work of ▷ John Osborne and ▷ Arnold Wesker this took the form of so-called 'kitchen-sink drama', which deals with working-class life and social conflict. Since 1950 it has been the drama, more than any other form of English literature, which has directly addressed public issues and exhibited political commitment, frequently of a radical nature. These features were evident in the 1950s and 60s in the work of Wesker, ▷ John Arden and ▷ Edward Bond, and more recently in that of ▷ Howard Brenton, ▷ Howard Barker, ▷ Trevor Griffiths and ▷ David Edgar. Many of the dramatists mentioned here have been brought to public notice by the productions of the English Stage Company, whose home at the ▷ Royal Court Theatre in London has been a centre for innovatory drama since 1956. Another important development has been the success of fringe theatre in exploiting the dramatic potential of small, open performing spaces. Feminist drama has flourished, prominent exponents being ▷ Ann Jellicoe, ▷ Nell Dunn, ▷ Shelagh Delaney and ▷ Caryl Churchill. Three of the most popular of contemporary dramatists are ▷ Peter Shaffer, ▷ Alan Ayckbourn and ▷ Tom Stoppard. Shaffer's work has a wide range, embracing comedy, studies of obsession and creativity, and historical epic. Ayckbourn and Stoppard both make use of humour; Ayckbourn in farces of middle-class life, pervaded by a lurking desperation; Stoppard in witty, playful, parodic and allusive dramas which explore political and metaphysical issues.

Across the range of literary forms an increasing contribution is being made by writers from India, Africa, Australia, New Zealand, Canada, and the West Indies (▷ Post-colonial literature). A primary characteristic of postmodernism as an era is the diversity and rapid circulation of culture, evident not only in the multi-cultural nature of contemporary literature in English, but also in the success of fringe theatre and small poetry presses and in the sheer range of styles and modes of literature currently available to a large public. But theories of postmodernism also suggest that cultural artefacts function increasingly as commodities, and this emphasizes the extent to which such diversity is dependent upon economic forces and political decision-making, and in these respects the future of literature is highly unpredictable.

▷ Postmodernism; Deconstruction; Symbolism; Aestheticism.

Modernity
▷ Modernism

***Modest Proposal, A* (1729)**
A ▷ satirical ▷ pamphlet by ▷ Jonathan Swift, written when he was Dean of St Patrick's Cathedral, Dublin. The full title is *A Modest Proposal for Preventing Children of Poor People from being a Burden to their Parents or the Country*. Indignant at the extreme misery of the Irish poor under English government, Swift, in the guise of an economic 'projector', calmly recommends that it would be more humane to breed up their children as food for the rich. The pamphlet is an example of the controlled but extreme savagery of Swift's irony, and the fierceness of his humanitarianism.

Mohun, Michael (?1616–84)
Actor-manager. Mohun trained as a boy actor under Christopher Beeston (?1570–1638) at the Cockpit Theatre, in Drury Lane, and graduated to adult roles before the theatres closed in 1642. He joined the army on the royalist side during the ▷ Civil War, reaching the rank of major. Shortly after the theatres reopened, he became the leading actor of the newly formed ▷ King's Company under ▷ Killigrew. He created several roles in tragedy and comedy, and his Iago in ▷ *Othello* was especially admired.

Molesworth, Mary Louisa (1839–1921)
Children's writer and novelist. Born Stewart, in Rotterdam where her father was a merchant, she was educated at home by her mother in Manchester where they moved in 1841. In 1861 she married Major Richard Molesworth, and first told stories to her own seven children, writing stories for and about them from a child's viewpoint, in which she portrayed a disciplined but loving world. In 1878 she separated from her husband, whose personality had been changed by a head wound sustained in the Crimean War, and from then on wrote to support her family. Using the pseudonym Ennis Graham, she wrote a large number of novels and stories. Her own childhood is described in *The Carved Lions* (1895) but perhaps the most famous and popular children's book is *The Cuckoo Clock* (1877). Others include *The Tapestry Room* (1879), *Tell Me a Story* (1875), *Carrots* (1876) and *Two Little Waifs* (1883).

▷ Children's books.

Bib: Avery, G., *Nineteenth-Century Children*; Lancelyn Green, R., *Tellers of Tales*.

Molière (pseudonym of Jean Baptiste Poquelin) (1622–73)
French dramatist. Born in the middle class,

the son of an upholsterer, he became one of the most favoured playwrights at the court of Louis XIV. With one exception his plays are comedies, and a basic influence behind English comedy from 1660 to 1800. His *Les Précieuses ridicules* (1659), a satire upon an extremely fashionable, excessively sophisticated circle in contemporary Paris, marks the beginning of the ▷ comedy of manners tradition in which the English dramatists ▷ Etherege, ▷ Wycherley, ▷ Vanbrugh, ▷ Congreve and ▷ Sheridan all worked. He wrote over 30 plays, of which the best known are: *Sganarelle* (1660); *l'Ecole des maris* (The School for Husbands, 1661); *L'Ecole des femmes* (The School for Wives, 1662); *Tartuffe* (1664); *Le Festin de Pierre* (Don Juan, 1665); *Le Misanthrope* (The Misanthropist, 1666); *Le Médecin malgré lui* (The Reluctant Physician, 1666); *L'Avare* (The Miser, 1668); *Le Bourgeois Gentilhomme* (The Middle-Class Nobleman, 1670); *Les Femmes savantes* (The Learned Women, 1672); *Le Malade imaginaire* (The Hypochondriac, 1673). His nearest equivalent on the English stage is William Congreve, but the only achievement in English literature comparable with Molière's kind of excellence is in the Augustan ▷ satire of ▷ Dryden (▷ *Absalom and Achitophel*) and ▷ Pope, and the novels of ▷ Jane Austen.

Moll Flanders **(1722)**
A novel by ▷ Daniel Defoe, and his most famous, after ▷ *Robinson Crusoe* (1719). Its full title was *The Fortunes and Misfortunes of the Famous Moll Flanders*, and its substance is the adventures of an orphan girl from her early seduction through her various love affairs and her career of crime, to her transportation to Virginia and her final prosperity there. It is a realistic, episodic narrative with keen social and psychological perception in certain incidents. The book has no unifying structure, however, and none of the characters is fully established imaginatively. The conclusion is an example of Defoe's crude and superficial morality, ▷ Puritan in its tradition, but much less profound and subtle than that of his predecessor ▷ John Bunyan. The Puritanism has become simplified to commercialism, especially evident in Moll's final 'repentance'.
▷ Picaresque.

Monasteries and Monasticism
The practice of monasticism arose in the lands about the eastern Mediterranean in the early centuries of Christianity, and was inspired by the belief that the holy life could be lived only in isolation from the practical interests of worldly society. This early monasticism consisted of hermits each living in his own cell, and Irish monasticism of the 6th-8th centuries had similar characteristics. However, in the 6th century St Benedict founded in Italy the ▷ Benedictine order which, during the ▷ Middle Ages, dominated western Europe including the British Isles, and had immense consequences for Western civilization; the monks lived in community, and followed a regular rule of life which included a great deal of practical activity. They were artists, architects, scholars and writers – especially historians, such as the Venerable ▷ Bede, William of Malmesbury, and Matthew Paris (13th century); monasteries such as the Cathedral Priory at Canterbury were seats of learning which rivalled universities such as Paris and Oxford. Corporately, the monasteries were great landowners, and some of the abbots managed these estates with great constructive efficiency; an example is the 12th-century Abbot Samson of Bury St Edmund, – see ▷ Carlyle's fine study of him in *Past and Present* Bk II (1843). The Cistercian Order, a reformed version of the Benedictine, established their monasteries in the wilder places of England, and set up sheep farms. In medieval England the monasteries were the only source of poor relief, and they provided the only hospitals until the 14th century. Politically, the great abbots ranked with the Bishops in the Great Council of the realm; in the 12th and 13th centuries monks were the intelligentsia, owners of at least 10 percent of the national income, and the largest employers.
monks were often us. When ▷ Henry VIII dissolved the monasteries (1536–9) the measure met with little resistance in the south-east, but it provoked the rebellion known as the ▷ Pilgrimage of Grace in the north.

There were no monasteries in Britain after the middle of the 16th century, but since the second half of the 19th century some have been re-established.

'Monk' Lewis (1775–1818)
Matthew Gregory Lewis, whose sensational novel *The Monk* (1796) had such success in its day that he was nicknamed after it.
▷ Gothic novels.

Monk's Tale, The
One of ▷ Chaucer's ▷ *Canterbury Tales*. The Monk produces a collection of short verse narratives recounting the fall of individuals from high estates, spanning subjects as diverse as Adam and Ugolina of Pisa. The shape of the narratives corresponds to that of the *'de casibus'* model of tragedies in which the falls of individuals are attributed either to moral weakness or to fortune, or to both, and is modelled on ▷ Boccaccio's collection of tragic exemplum in his *De Casibus Virorum Illustrium (Concerning the Falls of Famous Men)*. The Monk does include a few examples of the fall of famous women too. His sequence is halted by the intervention of the Knight, who

objects to the tone and subject of the Monk's contribution.

Monmouth, James Scott, Duke of (1649–85)
An illegitimate son of ▷ Charles II. Charles had no legitimate son, and the heir to the throne was consequently James, Duke of York, his brother. James, however, was an open Catholic, and fear of Catholicism in England and Scotland was still very strong. Thus a movement arose in both countries to persuade Charles to exclude James from the succession, and to recognize Monmouth, who had been educated a Protestant. Exclusion Bills to secure this change were introduced into Parliament, where the Exclusionists were led by ▷ Lord Shaftesbury. Charles, however, resisted the movement, and in 1681 a reaction of opinion in the country came to the support of the King and his brother. In 1685, Charles died, and James succeeded him as ▷ James II. Some of his more fanatical Protestant opponents, such as the Scottish Duke of Argyll, persuaded Monmouth to attempt rebellion. The Monmouth Rebellion was defeated at the single ▷ Battle of Sedgemoor (1685) and Monmouth himself was executed.
▷ *Absalom and Achitophel*; Bloody Assizes.

Monologic
▷ Bakhtin, Mikhail.

***Mont Blanc* (1816)**
Poem by ▷ Shelley, inspired by the view from the Bridge of Arve in the valley at Chamouni, Switzerland. It was first printed at the end of his *History of a Six Week's Tour* (1817), in which the poet describes this work as 'composed under the immediate impression of the deep and powerful feelings excited by the objects it attempts to describe; and, as an undisciplined overflowing of the soul'. This emphasis on a subjective and emotional reaction to a turbulent landscape scene recalls the work of the first-generation ▷ Romantic poets ▷ Wordsworth and ▷ Coleridge, vividly present in the poem's evocation of the human mind, which 'renders and receives fast influencings,/ Holding an unremitting interchange/ With the clear universe of things around'. Equally important however is *Mont Blanc*'s revisionary and antagonistic relationship to Coleridge's *Hymn Before Sunrise in the Vale of Chamouni* (1802), which describes the same landscape. Where Coleridge attributes the splendours of the scene to the workings of divinity, the atheist Shelley views the significance of landscape as produced by the human mind alone.

Montagu, Elizabeth (1720–1800)
An eminent ▷ Bluestocking and famous ▷ epistolarist, Montagu's early intellectual abilities were widely remarked upon, and ▷ Samuel Johnson hailed her as 'Queen of the Blues'.

Montagu began to hold her formal receptions in the early 1750s, and she boasted to ▷ David Garrick that, whatever the social status of the guests, 'I never invite idiots'. Her patronage of young authors aided ▷ James Beattie and Richard Price.

In 1769 her *Essay on the Writings and Genius of Shakespeare*, challenging ▷ Voltaire's theories, was widely admired, though Johnson perceived its critical failings.

Montagu, Lady Mary Wortley (1689–1762)
Poet and letter-writer. In 1716–18 her husband was Ambassador to Constantinople, where she came across the practice of inoculation against smallpox, which she popularized in England. In 1716 the publisher Edmund Curll produced an unauthorized edition of her poems, from a manuscript which she had dropped in the street, under the title *Court Poems by a Lady of Quality* (the authorized edition of 1747 was entitled *Town Eclogues*). ▷ Alexander Pope took her side against Curll but they later quarrelled for some reason, and she appears in *Moral Essay II* as Sappho in her 'dirty smock'. She lived in Italy during her later years and her lively and informative *Letters* were published in 1763–7.
Bib: Halsband, R., *The Life of Lady Mary Wortley Montagu*.

Montaigne, Michel de (1533–92)
French essayist, and inventor of the ▷ essay form. His life was lived partly at court, or performing the office of magistrate in the city of Bordeaux, and partly in retirement. During retirement, he wrote his *Essais* ('experiments'), the first two volumes of which were published in 1580, and the third in 1588. He was a scholar, well-read in ▷ humanist literature and in the works of the ancient Greeks and Romans. His favourite author was Plutarch.

The Essays seem to have been begun as commentaries on his reading, perhaps to assist his exceptionally bad memory. From this grew a desire to arrive at a complete image of man; as a means to this, he tried to develop a portrait of himself, since 'each man bears the complete stamp of the human condition'. The sentence shows the still-prevailing view of his time, that human beings followed general principles in the structure of their personalities – a view quite unlike the view that grew up in the 18th century and came to predominate in the 19th, that each individual is unique (see ▷ Rousseau). He recognized, however, the difficulties in arriving at conclusive ideas about human nature, and the essays are characterized by the scepticism with which he weighs contradictions and opposing views.

Montaigne was translated into English by John Florio in 1603. The essays had an extensive influence upon English literature and the Montaigne tradition of essay writing was taken up by Abraham Cowley (*Essays in Verse and Prose*, 1668), ▷ Sir William Temple (*Miscellanea*, 1680, 1692, 1701) and, after the more formal period of the 18th century, ▷ Charles Lamb's *Essays of Elia* (1823).

Montesquieu, Charles de Secondat de, Baron de la Brède et de (1689 –1755)
French philosopher and historian. He came to England in 1729, and studied English institutions and the ideas of English philosophers, including ▷ John Locke. He argued that human history reflects a process, influenced by many factors including geography and climate, which in turn affect such factors as religion, culture and society. He identified and discussed three sorts of government, the republican, the monarchical and the despotic, and held up the English constitution as a model of freedom. These ideas, expounded in *Considérations sur les causes de la grandeur et de la décadence des Romains* (1734) and *De l'esprit des lois* (1748), had a considerable influence on English, Scottish and Continental thinkers.
French literature in England.

Montgomerie, Alexander (c 1545–98)
Poet. Montgomerie was a ▷ Scottish court official, man of action and writer; he was admired by ▷ James II (James VI of Scotland) and was granted a pension in 1583. After having been suspected of involvement in a Catholic plot, he left Scotland in 1586 to travel in Europe. His most well-known work is *The Cherrie and the Slae* (1597), an ▷ allegorical work contrasting the cherry's elevated and valued position with the sloe's lowly and despised growth. It is meant to be sung aloud. He also wrote ▷ sonnets in which a ▷ Petrarchan influence is clear, *Flyting of Montgomery and Polwart* (published posthumously in 1621), and a general output of ▷ lyrics and songs.
Bib: Jack, R. D. S., *Alexander Montgomerie*.

Montrose, James Graham, Marquess of (1612–50)
Scottish patriot, general and statesman. He was one of the most gifted of Charles I's supporters in and after the Civil War. After spasmodic but brilliant successes, he was caught by Parliament forces and executed. ▷ Walter Scott's novel *A Legend of Montrose* (1819) concerns his career. John Buchan wrote a biography of him.

Mood
One of the five categories in which ▷ Genette analyses narrative discourse, mood is described by him as 'the regulation of narrative information' through the control of 'distance' and 'perspective'. The analysis of mood in a novel therefore includes the question of ▷ focalization.
▷ Narratology.

Moodie, Susanna (1803–85)
The youngest of the literary Strickland sisters, born in Suffolk, England, Susanna Moodie lived near Southwold until her emigration to Canada in 1832. Her sisters, Agnes and Elizabeth, wrote *Lives of the Queens of England* and other biographies; her other sister, Catherine Parr Traill (1802–1899), wrote many natural history books. Moodie published early, contributing her stories, poems and sketches to various annuals. Susanna and Agnes collaborated on a poetry volume called *Patriotic Songs* (1830), and Susanna published her own *Enthusiasm; and Other Poems* in 1831, the same year she married John Wedderburn Dunbar Moodie. A year later the couple emigrated to Upper Canada (Ontario). In *Flora Lyndsay; or, Passages in an Eventful Life* (1854) Moodie offers a fictionalized version of the arduous journey, concluding with the trip up the St Lawrence River. Her best known works are *Roughing it in the Bush; or, Life in Canada* (1852) and *Life in the Clearings Versus the Bush* (1853), considered autobiographical but written using strong elements of fiction. Susanna Moodie as writer is effectively able to distance herself from Susanna Moodie as narrator. Both books detail the harshness of trying to wrest a living out of the uncleared wilderness. In essence, the Moodies were ill-equipped to deal with the demands of pioneer life, failed at farming, and moved to the town of Belleville in 1840, where Dunbar Moodie was appointed sheriff.

Despite her isolation, Susanna Moodie did not curtail her literary aspirations. She wrote serialized fiction for *The Literary Garland*, which was published in Montreal. In 1847 to 1848, the Moodies together edited *The Victoria Magazine* in Belleville. Susanna also wrote a number of sentimental novels, much less interesting than her Canadian material: *Mark Hurdlestone; or, the Gold Worshipper* (1853), *Matrimonial Speculations* (1854), *Geoffrey Moncton; or, the Faithless Guardian* (1855) and *The World Before Them* (1868). Although Moodie has been the recipient of much critical vitriol for her desire to warn potential settlers of what awaited them in Canada, her story is remarkable for its courageous endurance in the face of hardship. After her husband's death in 1869 she lived mostly with her family in Toronto.
Bib: Dahl, E.H., *'Mid Forests Wild': A Study of the Concept of Wilderness in the Writings of Susanna Moodie, J.W.D. Moodie, Catherine Parr Traill and Samuel Strickland*; Fowler, M., *The Embroidered Tent: Five Gentlewomen in early Canada*; Morris, A., *The Gentle Pioneers: Five Nineteenth-Century Canadians*; Murray, H., in

A Mazing Space; Shields, C., *Voice and Vision*; Thomas, Clara, in *The Clear Spirit*.

Moonstone, The **(1868)**
A novel by ⊳ Wilkie Collins. It is one of the earliest stories of detection and concerns the mysterious disappearance of a valuable diamond, formerly sacred to the Moon-god in one of the Indian temples. The novel is told in the first person by various participants in the events; it is plotted with skill, psychological ingenuity and a typically Victorian delight in characterization. Sergeant Cuff, the first detective in English fiction, appears in it.
⊳ Detective fiction.

Moore, Brian (b 1921)
Novelist. Born in Belfast, Moore emigrated to Canada in 1948 and now lives in California. His Northern Irish Catholic upbringing provides the background for much of his work, which deals with themes of Irish migration, failure, guilt, isolation and loss of faith. His novels are characterized by narrative clarity and a sensitivity to the female point of view (notably his first and perhaps most famous novel, *The Lonely Passion of Judith Hearne*, 1955). *Black Robe* (1985) reflects contemporary Ulster by describing the confrontation between the settlers and native Indians in 17th-century Canada. Other novels include: *I Am Mary Dunne* (1968); *The Revolution Script* (1971); *Catholics* (1972); *The Great Victorian Collection* (1975); *The Doctor's Wife* (1976); *The Colour of Blood* (a political and theological thriller, 1987); *Lies of Silence* (1990); *No Other Life* (1993); and *The Statement* (1995). Moore also writes detective fiction as Michael Bryan and Bernard Marrow.
Bib: Dahlie, H., *Brian Moore*; Flood, J., *Brian Moore*.

Moore, G. E. (George Edward) (1873–1958)
Philosopher. He lectured on philosophy at Cambridge from 1911 to 1925, when he became Professor. His principal book is *Principia Ethica* (1903); he also wrote *Ethics* (1912) and *Philosophical Studies* (1922). His philosophy was that of the 'New Realism', in opposition to the ⊳ idealism of ⊳ F. H. Bradley whose work was in the tradition of Hegel. Where the Idealists tended to a poetic conception of truth and ethics, rhetorically expressed and appealing to the emotions as much as to the reason, Moore appealed to the reason only, basing his arguments on common sense, and holding it to be the function of philosophy to clarify statements and arrive at fully intelligible definitions. At the same time, he argued that all experience is to be enjoyed, and that the richest possessions are aesthetic experience and personal friendship. He consequently had two kinds of influence, philosophical and literary. Philosophically, he was one of the starting points for ⊳ Bertrand Russell and the Logical Positivists such as A. J. Ayer, but in literary circles he had considerable personal influence on the ⊳ Bloomsbury Group, centred on the novelist ⊳ Virginia Woolf and her husband Leonard. The Bloomsbury Group owed its cohesiveness to a cult of personal relations such as Moore advocated, and some of its members regarded the state of mind of perfect aesthetic appreciation as one of the aims of life.
Bib: Schilpp, P. A., *The Philosophy of Moore*; Johnstone, J. K. *The Bloomsbury Group*.

Moore, George (1852–1933)
Irish novelist. He combined an ⊳ aestheticism in tune with the aesthetic movement at the end of the 19th century, and the Celtic revivalism that went with a part of it, with a ⊳ naturalism which showed the influence of late 19th-century French literature, especially from the novelist Zola. His most famous novels are: *A Mummer's Wife* (1885); *Esther Waters* (1894); *Evelyn Innes* (1898); *Sister Theresa* (1901); *The Brook Kerith* (1916); *Héloise and Abélard* (1921). He was equally well known for his autobiographical studies: *Confessions of a Young Man* (1888); *Avowals* (1919, 1926); *Hail and Farewell* (1911–14) and *Conversations in Ebury Street* (1924). His carefully worked style was more admired in his own day than it is now.
⊳ *Celtic Twilight*.
Bib: Korg, J., in *Victorian Fiction* (ed. L. Stevenson); Brown, M. J., *Moore: a Reconsideration*; Sechler, R. P., *George Moore: 'a Disciple of Walter Pater'*; Yeats, W. B., in *Dramatis Personae*; Hough, G., in *Image and Experience*.

Moore, Thomas (1779–1852)
Born in Dublin, Moore studied law at the Middle Temple and became a popular drawing-room singer. Later he was for a time Admiralty Registrar in Bermuda. His early pseudonymous volume, *The Poetical Works of the late Thomas Little Esq.* (1801) was referred to by Lord Byron in *English Bards and Scotch Reviewers* (1809), and the two poets became close friends. Moore received many letters from Byron, though he shamefully expurgated them after Byron's death, and agreed to destroy the *Memoirs* which Byron had left to him. Moore's own writings range from lyric to satire, from prose romance to history and biography. The extremely popular *Irish Melodies*, which contain his most enduring work, appeared in ten parts between 1807 and 1835, and in 1813 he published a group of satires aimed at the Prince Regent, *The Twopenny Post Bag*. His long narrative peom in the Byronic mode, *Lalla Rookh: An Oriental Romance* (1817), achieved an international reputation, but in his next work *The Fudge Family in Paris* (1818) he returned to satire, aiming his shafts against the Englishman abroad. His *Loves of*

the Angels (1823) became notorious for its eroticism. He also wrote a prose romance set in 3rd-century Egypt, *The Epicurean* (1827), a *History of Ireland* (1835–46), and biographies of Thomas Sheridan (1825), and (ironically in view of his destruction of his friend's own autobiographical work) of Byron (1830).
Bib: White, T. de V., *Tom Moore: The Irish Poet*.

Moral Essays **(1731–5)**
Four epistles in heroic ▷ couplets by ▷ Alexander Pope, concerned with large ethical and philosophical issues. Epistle I elaborates a simplistic philosophy of 'the ruling passion' as an explanation of human psychology, and its poetic value lies in the occasional witty vignette of human folly, rather than in any profundity of thought. Epistle II, *To a Lady*, concerns the characters of women, and is addressed to Pope's close friend Martha Blount. Though the work has many memorable lines it is little more than a series of crudely sexist jibes at particular women, or at women in general: 'Nothing so true as what you once let fall, 'Most Women have no Characters at all'; 'ev'ry Woman is at heart a Rake'. Epistle III treats the right use of riches, and ends with an idealized portrait of John Kyrle, the 'Man of Ross', a celebrated philanthropist. Epistle IV, addressed to Lord Burlington, was the first to be published (1731) and is the most impressive. It again satirizes the wrong use of wealth, but focuses specifically on architecture, Burlington being an active promoter of the convenient decency of the Palladian style (▷ Andrea Palladio) as opposed to the large-scale exuberance of ▷ baroque, so much in vogue in absolutist France. Pope follows his patron also in advocating a 'natural' style of garden rather than the artificial geometricality of continental taste. The description of the discomfort of Timon's villa brilliantly satirizes such un-English grandiosity as Blenheim Palace or Castle Howard, both recently built by ▷ Sir John Vanbrugh.

Morality plays
A term used by modern critics to distinguish plays expounding points of moral doctrine, extant from the 15th century, from other kinds of contemporary vernacular drama which commemorate the events of Christian history (such as the ▷ cycle plays or saints' plays). The plots of morality plays are allegorical narratives of one kind or another; the human protagonists tend not to be individualized or given a historical identity. The scope of the plays may vary: whereas the ▷ *Castle of Perseverance* dramatizes the epic story of 'Humankind's' life from birth to beyond the grave, and requires great dramatic resources, ▷ *Mankind* focuses on an exemplary episode in Mankind's life, and seems designed as an itinerant production by a smaller acting group. Generally, however, the genre is associated with plays like *Mankind*, which can be performed in halls by smaller acting groups. Behind plays such as *Castle of Perseverance, Mankind* and ▷ *Everyman* is a long tradition of Christian instruction and teaching: sermons addressed to lay audiences and manuals of instruction may employ similar devices of analysis and instruction to those dramatized in these morality plays, which endow abstract notions, concepts, processes, with a tangible form.

But this kind of drama is not confined to expounding points of religious doctrine. In the morality plays dating from the late 15th century (such as Henry Medwall's *Fulgens and Lucres*), or from the 16th century (such as John Rastall's *Of Gentilness and Nobility*), issues of social order (in these cases the relationship between social rank and moral virtue) come under scrutiny. The instructional impetus of this kind of drama can be used for secular as well as religious ends. This dramatic form has had more impact on the drama of the Renaissance than the ▷ cycle plays, due to the flexibility of its form and the use of allegory for ethical and moral analysis.

Although the term 'morality' play is useful for locating a distinctive dramatic form which seems popular in the 15th and 16th centuries, it should not be regarded as a fixed and wholly distinctive dramatic genre. Allegorical personages appear in the cycle drama, and saints' plays too, and many plays confound rigid generic categories: ▷ John Bale's play, *King John* (c 1536), for example, presents a historical narrative and an allegorical commentary on the action at the same time.
Bib: Cawley, A. C. et al., *The Revels History of Drama in English: Vol. I Medieval Drama*; Davenport, W. A., *Fifteenth Century English Drama: the Early Moral plays and their Literary Relations*.

Mordred
In the 10th century *Annals of Wales* (*Annales Cambriae*), a figure called Medraut is reported as having fought and fallen in a battle against ▷ King Arthur in 539. In ▷ Geoffrey of Monmouth's version of British history, Mordred is Arthur's nephew, who usurps the throne and takes ▷ Guinevere for his lover while Arthur is fighting against the Romans. In later developments of Arthurian narrative, Mordred is Arthur's illegitimate son, conceived through a brief, incestuous relationship with ▷ Morgause. He provokes trouble over the affair between ▷ Lancelot and ▷ Guinevere.

More, Hannah (1745–1833)
An eminent ▷ Bluestocking, More settled in London in 1774, where she became the friend of ▷ Garrick, ▷ Johnson, ▷ Burke, ▷ Richardson, ▷ Reynolds, ▷ Percy and ▷ Montagu. She

was a conservative Christian feminist who opposed ▷ Mary Wollstonecraft on women's rights. Her tragedy *Percy* was produced by Garrick in 1777, and established both her literary reputation and her social status. A tragedy, *The Fatal Falsehood*, appeared in 1779.

▷ Horace Walpole became her great admirer, printing *Bishop Bonner's Ghost* at the Strawberry Hill press in 1789. In 1784 her earlier poem *Bas Bleu* was published.

More used her writing to express concern about social reform. *Village Politics* appeared in 1793, and the *Cheap Respository Tracts* of 1795–8 sold two million copies. *Thoughts on the Importance of the Manners of the Great* (1788) also ran into several editions. In 1809 More published *Coelebs in Search of a Wife*, a novel which, despite hostile reviews, proved an immense success. Her correspondence is lively and entertaining.

Bib: Jones, M. G., *Hannah More*.

More, Sir Thomas (St Thomas More) (1478–1535)

Scholar, thinker and statesman. He was the leading humanist of his day, and a friend of ▷ Erasmus. For some time he was a particular favourite of ▷ Henry VIII, who raised him to the Lord Chancellorship, the highest office in the state. However, More firmly refused to recognize the king's divorce from Queen Katharine and the ▷ Act of Supremacy (1534). For this the king executed him, and the Catholic Church canonized him exactly 400 years later.

More's *History of King Richard III* (1513) has been called the first masterpiece of ▷ history and ▷ biography in English, but his principal work, ▷ *Utopia* (1516), was in Latin, translated into English in 1551. While More's idealized characteristics have often been emphasized, recent criticism has detected a darker side to his writing, which may be seen in his intemperate tone, detailing of extreme forms of conduct, and biting irony. Famous as a ▷ patron of letters and arts, he invited the painter ▷ Holbein to England.

▷ Catholicism (Roman) in English literature; Roper, Margaret More.

Bib: Surtz, E. (ed.), *Selected Works*; Sylvester, R. S. and Harding, D. P. (eds.), *The Life of Sir Thomas More*; Hexter, J. H., *More's Utopia: The Biography of an Idea*; Greenblatt, S., *Renaissance Self-fashioning*; Martz, L. L., *Thomas More: the Search for the Inner Man*.

Morgan, Sydney (1776–1859)

Novelist. Lady Sydney Morgan (née Owenson) was a prolific Irish author, whose ▷ nationalist politics were reflected in her fictional recreations of Irish history and legend. Her novels, which include *St Clair* (1803) and the popular *Wild Irish Girl* (1806), did much to establish the idea of Ireland's past as fashionable and romantic both in her own country and in England. Moreover, she contributed to the Celtic revival of the mid-19th century. Her novel *The Missionary* (1811) influenced both ▷ Byron and ▷ Shelley.

▷ Macpherson, James; Ossian; Irish literature in English.

Bib: Spender, D and Todd, J., *Anthology of British Women Writers*; Stevenson, L., *The Wild Irish Girl: the life of Sydney Owenson, Lady Morgan*.

Morgan La Fay

In ▷ Geoffrey of Monmouth's account of the life of ▷ Merlin, Morgan is introduced as a ▷ Lady of the Lake figure, who has magic powers and is in charge of nine women who live on ▷ Avalon and who receive ▷ King Arthur after he has been wounded. She is perhaps a literary form of a much older Celtic goddess. Her role becomes much more ambiguous in later versions of Arthurian narrative (including ▷ Malory's version), in which she both assists and obstructs the foundation of Arthurian society. She becomes identified as Arthur's half-sister, wife of Lucan and daughter of ▷ Igraine, and is portrayed as a frustrated woman who uses her magical powers to ensnare men. But she continues to be one of the women who escort Arthur away to Avalon, after his last battle. In recent Arthurian fiction, Morgan has become a more complex figure; she has been used by some writers as the focus of feminine power and independence in the legends.

Morgause

Half-sister of ▷ King Arthur in Arthurian narratives (post ▷ Geoffrey of Monmouth's version of Arthurian history), who marries King Lot and is the mother of ▷ Gawain, Gaheris, Agravain and ▷ Gareth. She conceives ▷ Mordred as a result of a brief affair with Arthur (who is unaware of his familial connection with her), and she is killed by Gaheris when discovered in bed with Lamorak.

Morier, James Justin (1780–1849)

Travel writer and novelist. Morier was a diplomat stationed in Persia and his ▷ travel books, *A Journey Through Persia* (1812) and *A Second Journey Through Persia* (1818) describe his experiences while there. In 1817 he resigned his post and devoted himself to writing novels, including *The Adventures of Hajji Baba of Ispahan* (1824), a ▷ picaresque tale of an ordinary Persian artisan, which made an important contribution to the growing popularity of ▷ Orientalism.

Morning Chronicle

A London Whig ▷ newspaper founded in 1769; its contributors included Sheridan, ▷ Lamb, James Mill, ▷ John Stuart Mill,

▷ Dickens, and ▷ Thackeray. It came to an end in 1862.

Morning Herald, The
A London ▷ newspaper, 1780–1869. It had a large circulation, and published police cases, illustrated by the famous artist ▷ George Cruikshank, illustrator of Dickens' novel ▷ *Oliver Twist*.

Morning Post, The
A conservative but highly independent London newspaper, founded 1772, ceased 1936. Wordsworth, ▷ Coleridge and Southey contributed to it.

Morris, Sir Lewis (1833–1907)
The most famous ▷ Anglo-Welsh poet of his time, Sir Lewis Morris reached the height of his fame in the last twenty years of the 19th century and was second only to ▷ Tennyson in public acclaim. Indeed, Lewis was expected to succeed him as ▷ Poet Laureate.

Born in Carmarthen, South Wales, Morris' social class and education insulated him from the Welsh-speaking community of his home town. The Welsh language was, in fact, ruthlessly suppressed during his lifetime, due to Victorian government policy which ruled that the language was detrimental to the educational and moral progress of the Welsh people. However, Morris developed a keen interest in his Welsh ancestry and in Welsh traditions in his later years. He moved to Sherborne in Dorset at the age of seventeen before entering Jesus College, Oxford in 1851, where he took a double first. He went on to practise as a conveyancing counsel in London. Morris published his first three series of poems *Songs of Two Worlds* (1871, 1874, 1875) anonymously. A combination of graphic social comment and metrical virtuosity tempered with vague moralizing and naive anecdotalsim, his poetry was extremely well received. *The Epic of Hades* (1877), was enthusiastically reviewed by Oliver Wendell Holmes and *The Times*, and by 1896 the book had sold 40,000 copies. His popular ▷ dramatic monologue, *Gwen* (1879), has much in common with his great friend Tennyson's ▷ *Maud*, and his sixth volume of poems, *Songs Unsung* (1883), was highly praised by ▷ Gladstone. Other volumes include *Songs of Britain* (1887), *Songs Without Notes* (1894) and *Idylls and Lyrics* (1896).
Bib: Phillips, D., *Writers of Wales: Sir Lewis Morris.*

Morris, William (1834–96)
Poet, socialist thinker, designer and printer. He was one of the leading artists of his day, associated with, though not a member of, the ▷ Pre-Raphaelite Brotherhood, which sought to recover the cultural unity of ▷ medieval society. It is as a designer of textiles and wallpapers that he is most admired today. His aim was to counteract the industrial squalor of Victorian England, and to correct the major social injustice by which the proletariat were cut off from beauty of any sort by the nature of their environment: 'I don't want art for a few, any more than education for a few, or freedom for a few.' Paradoxically his campaign against aesthetic barbarism went with rejection of the machine and insistence on handwork, which cut him off from the economic realities of his age.

This withdrawal from social and political complexities is in keeping with his poetry, which expresses withdrawal into the romances of the Middle Ages (*Defence of Guinevere*, 1858; *Earthly Paradise*, 1868–70); into ancient Greek epic (*Life and Death of Jason*, 1867; translation of Virgil's *Aeneid*, 1875, and of Homer's *Odyssey*, 1887); and into Icelandic epic (*Sigurd the Volsung*, 1876). His verse (the majority of it translation) was voluminous, fluent, decorative and musical in the Spenserian tradition current in the Victorian period.

Nonetheless, his socialism was a reality. He was one of the founders of the Socialist League (1884) and edited its monthly periodical *Commonweal*, until in 1890 the anarchist wing of the movement drove him out. His *News from Nowhere* (1891 – previously contributed to *Commonweal*) is a prose ▷ 'utopia' describing England at a future date after the establishment of socialism. It is one of the most read of his works today. Another work of socialist inspiration, in mixed prose and verse, is *A Dream of John Ball* (1888).

Morris had some influence on the young ▷ W.B. Yeats (1865–1939), who remarked 'The dream-world of Morris was as much the antithesis of daily life as with other men of genius, but he was never conscious of the antithesis and so knew nothing of intellectual suffering' (*Autobiographies*, 1955).

▷ Arts and Crafts Movement.
Bib: Henderson, P., *Life*, Mackail, J.W., *Life*; Hough, G., *The Last Romantics*; Jackson, H., *Morris: Craftsman-Socialist*: Thompson, E.P., *Morris: Romantic to Revolutionary*; Lewis, C.S., in *Rehabilitations*. Thompson, P., *The Work of William Morris*; Kirchoff, F., *William Morris: The Construction of a Male Self: 1856–1872*; Harvey, C., *William Morris: Design and Enterprise in Victorian Culture*.

Morrison, Arthur (1863–1945)
Novelist and short-story writer. Born in Poplar, Morrison worked as a journalist, contributing tales of East End life to ▷ *Macmillan's Magazine* (published as *Tales of Mean Streets*, 1894). His subsequent novels *A Child of the Jago* (1896) and *The Hole in the Wall* (1902) are also naturalistic accounts of slum life. Morrison also wrote ▷ detective fiction (*The Dorrington Deed Box*,

1897, in the manner of ▷ Conan Doyle), and later became a distinguished Orientalist. A conservative but highly independent London newspaper, founded 1772, ceased 1936. Wordsworth, ▷ Coleridge and Southey contributed to it.

Morrison, Blake (b 1950)
Poet and critic. Morrison is a prominent figure in contemporary British poetry, perhaps more as a critic than a poet, and he has taught at London University and the Open University, as well as writing on poetry and fiction for *The Observer* and the *Times Literary Supplement*. He has published critical studies of ▷ the Movement and of ▷ Seamus Heaney, and is co-editor (with ▷ Andrew Motion) of *The Penguin Book of Contemporary British Poetry* (1982). His poetic works include *Dark Glasses* (1984) and *The Ballad of the Yorkshire Ripper* (1987).

***Morte Arthur* (stanzaic)**
Stanzaic poem, dating from the mid/late 14th century, which recounts events from the later stages of Arthurian narrative, specifically those leading up to the break-up of the ▷ Round Table. This narrative follows the framework of the 13th-century Old French Arthurian narratives in which the love affair between ▷ Lancelot and ▷ Guinevere, and the enmity between ▷ Gawain and Lancelot are important catalysts in the destruction of Arthurian society, in addition to the treachery of Mordred. It was used by ▷ Malory in the final books of his *Morte D'Arthur*.
▷ Arthur, King.
Bib: Benson, L (ed.), *King Arthur's Death*.

***Morte Arthure* (alliterative)**
▷ Alliterative poem, dating from c 1400, recounting events in the second half of ▷ King Arthur's career, from his campaign against Rome to his final battle against ▷ Mordred, concluding with his death. The narrative follows the basic frame ultimately provided by ▷ Geoffrey of Monmouth's version of Arthurian history but events are elaborated and a remarkable dream sequence is added (just before Arthur returns to fight Mordred) which features a vision of the ▷ Nine Worthies, organized around Fortune's wheel. The dream, in effect, provides a meditation on the nature of the forces which shape Arthur's history. The *Morte Arthure* was used by ▷ Malory in Book 2 of his *Morte D'Arthur*
Bib: Benson, L. (ed.), *King Arthur's Death*.

Morte D'Arthur
The *Morte D'Arthur* is the conventional title for a highly influential prose narrative, completed in 1469/70 by a Sir Thomas ▷ Malory, which recounts the foundation, history and destruction of ▷ King Arthur's court and the knights of the ▷ Round Table. Until 1934 Malory's narrative was known only through ▷ Caxton's edition (first printed in 1485) entitled the *Morte D'Arthur*, but the discovery of a manuscript version of the text in 1934, and its publication in 1947 as Malory's *Works*, revealed the extent of Caxton's editorial intervention. Whereas Caxton's text is divided into 21 books, the *Works* is composed of eight narratives (called 'Tales', or 'Books'), which are relatively self-contained, but taken together form an overall history of Arthur's reign. The first recounts the founding of Arthur's kingdom and the Round Table; the second concerns Arthur's campaign for Rome; the third is devoted to the adventures of ▷ Lancelot; the fourth is taken up with the romance of ▷ Gareth; the fifth is predominantly concerned with a version of ▷ Tristan's history; the sixth recounts the Quest of the Holy ▷ Grail; the seventh relates the events which follow Lancelot's return to court and his love affair with ▷ Guinevere; the eighth recounts events leading up to the break-up of the Round Table and the end of all Arthur's knights. This organization into eight Tales/Books helps point up Malory's narrative strategy: he has not chosen to present events in a continuous narrative sequence, organized chronologically. Rather he has cultivated a looser structure that enables his reader to follow a number of narrative lines, which make up the sequence of Arthurian history.

Malory drew material for his work principally from the massive cycles of Arthurian narrative which had been compiled in France in the 13th century and in which accounts of the adventures at Arthur's court were organized in interlaced narrative forms (▷ Vulgate Cycle). Malory has abbreviated and reorganized this material, drawing out some of the narrative threads from the interlaced sequences, and reordering some of the adventures. His narrative is structured as an investigation into the meaning of the codes and ethos of that world. The institution of the Round Table is meant to introduce a civilizing code of behaviour to Arthur's kingdom, but the stories of the knights' adventures reveal the difficulty of working out a chivalric ethos in practice. The narrative explores and celebrates chivalric values, but it does not present a narrow moralizing account of Arthurian history, nor a simple explanation of why the brave new world of Arthur's court eventually collapses in such disarray. Malory's narrative is structured in such a way that no single chain of actions 'causes' the breakdown of the Round Table: the relationships between events and actions are more mysterious than in the Old French sources.
Bib: Vinaver, E. (ed.), *Malory: Works*; Riddy, F., *Sir Thomas Malory*

***Mother Hubberd's Tale, or Prosopopeia* (c 1579)**
A verse ▷ satire by ▷ Edmund Spenser, in ten-syllable couplets, presented in the form of

a fable; 'Prosopopeia' means 'endowing things or animals with personalities'. It was published with other poems in *Complaints (*1591) but written at about the same time as ▷ *The Shepherd's Calendar* (1579). It was written at a time when ▷ Elizabeth I seemed inclined to marry the Duke of Anjou, brother of Henry III of France. He was hated by the more convinced Protestants in England (of whom Spenser was one) because he was a Catholic and a member of the family responsible for the Massacre of St Bartholomew, 1572, in which French Protestants had been slaughtered. The fable tells how the ape and the fox steal the lion's crown while he sleeps. The ape is Anjou, and the fox is William Cecil, Lord Burghley, Spenser's enemy.

***Mothers and Daughters: A Tale of the Year* 1830 (1831)**

A novel by ▷ Catherine Gore, belonging to the 'silver-fork' school of fashionable fiction, like Gore's earlier work *Women as They Are* (1830). The central characters are Lady Maria Willingham and her two daughters, Claudia and Eleanor. The action revolves around the women's schemes for attracting aristocratic or wealthy men, and goes into great detail about the fashions of the day and the social milieu of the wealthy and privileged.

Motif

Generally, a recurrent, often well-known feature or idea occurring across a work or a number of literary works, for example the symbolic representations of life as a journey. When a pattern of such symbols or images are found in a work it is called a *leitmotif.* In some narrative theory (for example, the ▷ Russian Formalist Boris Tomashevsky's essay 'Thematics'), motif has a more specialized sense pertaining to the units which make up a narrative, but this usage is not common.

Motion, Andrew (b 1952)

Poet and critic. Motion is a prolific writer, who has also worked as a lecturer in English (at the University of Hull), and has edited the *Poetry Review*. His publications include (poetry): *The Pleasure Steamers* (1978); *Independence* (1981); *Secret Narratives* (1983); *Dangerous Play* (1984) and *Natural Causes* (1987); and (criticism): *The Poetry of Edward Thomas* (1978) and *Philip Larkin* (1982). Motion has written the official biography of ▷ Larkin, who died in 1985.

***Mourning Bride, The* (1697)**

Congreve's only play with a tragic action, though a happy ending, set in Granada. Almeria, Princess of Granada, has secretly married Alphonso, Prince of Valentia, when she was a captive in the Valencian palace. In battle the King of Valentia, Anselmo, dies, and Alphonso disappears and is presumed dead. While mourning at his tomb, Almeria is interrupted by the prisoner Osmyn, who turns out to be Alphonso in disguise. Meanwhile the captive queen Zara has fallen in love with 'Osmyn' but, failing to win him, plots to have him killed. Belatedly she tries to save him, but unknown to her, he escapes, and the tyrant King of Granada, Manuel, is mistakenly murdered in his place. Zara, finding his headless body, believes it to be that of Osmyn, takes poison and dies. Almeria is about to do the same when Alphonso enters, and the couple are reunited. The play ends with the assurance that 'blessings ever wait on virtuous deeds'. *The Mourning Bride* was hugely successful, and survived well into the 18th century. It contains two quotations which remain famous: 'Music has charms to soothe a savage breast' and 'Heav'n has no rage, like love to hatred turn'd,/Nor Hell a fury, like a woman scorn'd'.

Movement, The

One of the most important 'movements' in post-war British poetry, *the* Movement was really made into a coherent poetic body with the publication of three important anthologies: ▷ D. J. Enright's *Poets of the 1950s* (1955), Robert Conquest's *New Lines* and G. S. Frazer's *Poetry Now* (both 1956). As with any poetic school all of the prominent members of the Movement can ultimately be linked only through a tenuous range of connections, and indeed by 1957 its cohering impulse was dissolving. Some of its major figures are generally understood to be ▷ Kingsley Amis, Conquest and Enright, ▷ Donald Davie, ▷ Thom Gunn, ▷ Elizabeth Jennings, ▷ Philip Larkin and ▷ John Wain. The work which is covered by this umbrella term is sardonic, lucid and self-consciously ironic. Opposed to the romantic and apocalyptic tone of much 1940s poetry, especially that of ▷ Dylan Thomas and ▷ W. S. Graham, Movement poetry is meticulously crafted and witty, controlled and commonsensical.

Bib: Morrison, B., *The Movement.*

Mphahlele, Es'kai (b 1919)

South African novelist, short-story writer and critic. He was educated at the University of South Africa in Pretoria and the University of Denver, USA. He worked as a clerk and as an English teacher in South Africa and was fiction editor of *Drum* magazine (1955–57) before leaving on an exit permit (which forbade re-entry to the country) in 1957; he was not to return for 20 years. In the 1960s he was director of African cultural programmes in Paris and in Nairobi, Kenya and then edited the journals *Black Orpheus* and *Journal of New African Literature and the Arts* in Ibadan, Nigeria. He held lecturing posts at universities in Nigeria, Kenya, Zambia and the USA before returning to South Africa in 1987, where he lectured at the University of Witwatersrand, Johannesburg and became director of a community education project in Soweto. His early short stories, collected in *Man Must Live* (1947), portrayed life in the urban black ghettos of South Africa with a degree of humour; later stories, in *The Living and Dead* (1961) and *In Corner B* (1967), have a stronger element of protest. He has written two novels, *The Wanderers* (1971), a partly autobiographical account of South African intellectuals in exile, and *Chirundu* (1979), a political novel about a post-independence African state. His critical work *The African Image* (1962) was an early and influential account of African fiction and he also edited *Modern African Stories* (1964, with E. Komey) and *African Writing Today* (1967); Mphahlele has played an important role in developing and promoting African literature. His most recent work of fiction is the volume of short stories *Renewal Time* (1988). He has published two autobiographical works: *Down Second Avenue* (1959) and *Afrika My Music: An Autobiography 1957–1983* (1984) as well as essays, books for children and works on education and creative writing; see *The Unbroken Song: Selected Writing of Es'kai Mphahlele* (1981). His letters have been published as *Bury Me at the Crossroads: Selected Letters of Es'kai Mphahlele* (1984).

Bib: Barnett, U. A., *Es'kai Mphahlele*; Manganyi, N. C., *Exiles and Homecomings: A Biography of Es'kai Mphahlele*.

***Mrs Dalloway* (1925)**

A novel by ▷ Virginia Woolf. Set in London, it is the story of one day in the life of Clarissa Dalloway, the wife of Richard Dalloway, a Member of Parliament (the Dalloways appeared in Woolf's earlier novel, *The Voyage Out*). Clarissa spends the day preparing for a party she is to give that evening, a party which provides the culmination of the novel. The ▷ stream of consciousness narrative represents the thoughts of Clarissa and a range of other characters with whom she is acquainted, or connected by chance occurrences of the day. Throughout the novel, memories of the past are blended with present sensations, and the narrative builds up a highly poetic evocation of the atmosphere of London and of the interaction of different lives. The principal characters, apart from the Dalloways, are: their daughter Elizabeth and her embittered and envious tutor, Miss Kilman; Peter Walsh, with whom Clarissa was in love during her youth; Sally Seton, Clarissa's girlhood friend, and Lady Bruton, a society hostess. In contrast to this group, whose lives are linked, are Septimus Warren Smith and his wife Rezia; Septimus is in a highly disturbed state after his experiences during World War I and the news of his suicide intrudes on Clarissa's party, brought by Sir William Bradshaw, a manipulative psychiatrist whom Septimus had consulted. The novel ends with the affirmation of life joined to an awareness of loss and death.

***Much Ado about Nothing* (1598)**

A comedy by ▷ Shakespeare. It was acted in 1598, and printed in 1600. The main plot is drawn from ▷ *Orlando Furioso* (Bk V) and from a novel by Bandello. The scene is Messina, at the court of the governor, Leonato, who receives a visit from the Prince of Aragon, his evil-minded brother, Don John, and the Prince's friend, Claudio. The main plot concerns Claudio's indirect courtship of Hero, Leonato's daughter, the frustration of their marriage plans by Don John, who plants a slander on Hero, the eventual exposure of the slander, and the reconciliation. A subplot concerns the relationship between Benedick and Beatrice, who are famous in the court for their war of wits in which they declare mutual detestation; a plot is devised which enables each to recognize that their war is really a mask disguising their real love, and they acknowledge this to each other. The subplot joins the main plot when Beatrice tests Benedick's feelings for her by demanding that he challenge Claudio (his friend) to a duel for slandering Hero. The play is more famous for its subplot (and for ▷ Dogberry and Verges, the comic constables) than for its main plot, owing to the vividness of the characters in the former and the comparative colourlessness of those in the latter. However the comedy has more unity and impressiveness once the reader sees in it a strong current of satire. The court, like other ▷ Renaissance courts, is an environment in which witticism is valued without regard to true feeling, disguise of some sort is normal, artifice has more prestige than nature, and carefully cultivated appearances take the place of reality. In such a world, it is natural that Claudio should be a superficial lover easily deceived by a stratagem and that a mere game played in mockery of Beatrice and Benedick should lead to their stumbling on the truth. Their moment of truth stands out with dramatic poignancy. Similarly, Dogberry's naïve stumbling over language is a contrast to the courtiers' artificial perversion of it.

Mudie, Charles Edward (1818–90)

Son of a bookseller, Mudie founded Mudie's Circulating Library, which loaned books to the public for a fee. Beginning in Bloomsbury, he expanded to Oxford Street, where the business ran for many years. Along with other ▷ circulating libraries, Mudie's exercised a noticeable moral ▷ censorship in the selection of books.

Muir, Edwin (1887–1959)

Autobiographer, critic, poet, and novelist. He

spent his childhood on a farm in the Orkney Islands, from which his father was compelled by economic hardship to move to Glasgow. For several years Muir struggled to earn his living in Glasgow as a clerk in various businesses; he became interested in socialism, and started writing. In 1919 he married, moved to London, and became a journalist. Thereafter, he travelled widely in Europe, and held a number of teaching posts. In 1940 he produced the first version of his autobiography, *The Story and the Fable*, expanded, revised and republished as *Autobiography* in 1954. The experiences of his own lifetime afforded him deep insight – social, cultural, spiritual. He had moved from a pre-industrial society in Orkney to 20th-century industrialism at its grimmest in Glasgow. He was deeply aware of the Scottish roots of his culture, and was liberated from their limitations partly through ▷ German literature and thought – ▷ Nietzsche, Heine, Hölderlin; in the 1930s he and his wife Willa translated Kafka. Experience of ▷ psychoanalysis liberated the deeper levels of his imagination, and led him, through illumination about the relationship of man to his natural environment, to strong and unusually lucid religious feeling. His *Autobiography* is a modern classic.

His birthplace, Orkney, has had some measure of detachment from the history of the rest of Scotland, and it is partly this that enabled him to show some of the most penetrating perceptions about modern Scottish culture in *Scottish Journey* (1935) and *Scott and Scotland* (1936). His critical works include: *Latitudes* (1924); *Transition* (1926); *The Structure of the Novel* (1928); *The Present Age* (1939); *Essays on Literature and Society* (1949).

Poetry: *First Poems* (1925); *Journeys and Places* (1925); *Chorus of the Newly Dead* (1926); *Variations on a Time Theme* (1934); *The Narrow Place* (1943); *The Voyage* (1946); *The Labyrinth* (1949); *Prometheus* (1954); *One Foot in Eden* (1956); *Collected Poems 1921–1958* (1960). He came to writing poetry late, through urgency of personal feeling rather than a professionally poetic concern with the medium. Nonetheless his later volumes embody some of his most moving insights, *eg* 'The Combat' from *The Labyrinth*.

His novels are: *The Marionette* (1927); *The Three Brothers* (1931); *Poor Tom* (1932). Biography: *John Knox* (1929).

▷ Autobiography; Scottish literature in English.

Bib: Knight, R., *Edwin Muir; an Introduction to His Work*; Butter, E., *Edwin Muir, Man and Poet*.

Mulcaster, Richard (c 1530–1611)
Educationalist. Mulcaster was the first head-master of Merchant Taylors School, London, where he taught ▷ Andrewes, ▷ Kyd, ▷ Lodge and ▷ Spenser, and in 1596 he became the high master at St Paul's School. His views on education were humanist; he believed, for example, that girls should be educated to as high a standard as boys. Mulcaster wrote two books on education, *Positions* (1581) and *The Elementarie* (1582), and he also contributed ▷ masques, entertainments and commemorative verses to state and city occasions, such as the funeral orations on ▷ Elizabeth I in 1603.

Bib: Elsky, M., *Authorizing Words*.

Muldoon, Paul (b 1951)
Poet. Born in County Armagh and educated at Queen's University, Belfast, Muldoon is one of the younger generation of poets to emerge from Northern Ireland in the last two decades (see also ▷ Seamus Heaney and ▷ Derek Mahon). His publications include: *Names and Addresses* (1978); *New Weather* (1973); *Mules* (1977) and *Why Brownlee Left* (1980).

▷ Irish literature in English.

Mummers' Plays/Mumming
Although many Mummers' plays survive from various parts of the country, all of the texts date from the 18th century or later. Characteristically they take the form of a fight between a Champion (often St George) and an Antagonist, who is killed but resurrected at the end through the agency of a Doctor. The plays often conclude with a Dance and the opportunity for a collection of money. Archetypal patterns are ritually enacted within these plays, though the texts as we have them may themselves be the product of folkloric revivals. Access to folk-drama and rituals of the past is necessarily difficult because by its very definition this kind of cultural activity does not depend on written records or texts. Information about medieval folk-drama is derived from the records of attempts by ecclesiastical authorities to ban, curb, or suppress it.

Mummings, as their name suggests, are dumb-shows, particularly masquerades and disguisings associated with the festivities of the New Year and Shrove-Tide. Again, though there are records of prohibitions on mummings from the early medieval period, the texts that survive from the 15th century are of mummings contrived as occasions of civic and aristocratic entertainment, such as those composed by ▷ John Lydgate (in which a dumb-show is accompanied by a verse commentary).

Bib: Brody, A., *The English Mummers and their Plays*.

Munda, Constantia (c 1617)
Polemical tract-writer in the debate about women. 'Constantia Munda' is a pseudonym for a female response to Joseph Swetnam's attack upon women (▷ *Querelle des Femmes*), which was published as *The Worming of a Mad Dogge* (1617). The treatise begins with a poem

thanking her mother for setting an example of virtue and piety, and continues with a prose defence of women asserting them to be valued equally with men by God. It also accuses Swetnam of praising only masculine virtues and of classifying all women as the same when there are many different levels of moral virtue to be found.

▷ Sowernam, Ester; Speght, Rachel.
Bib: Henderson, K. U. and McManus, B. F. (eds.), *Half Humankind*.

Munday, Anthony (1553–1633)
Poet, dramatist, translator and ▷ pamphlet writer. Munday's somewhat prolific career is marked by a keen interest in narrative, but little imaginative skill in his use of language. Of his life outside the theatre we know little, and can only speculate about his being a boy-actor and a double agent (moving between the Protestant state and Catholic insurgents). Of his many pamphlets, several are staunchly Protestant, and the contents of the others are general, appealing to popular rather than specific tastes. He also wrote poetry, some of which is included in ▷ *England's Helicon*, and while employed as London's official poet (1592–1623), he composed several civic entertainments. However, Munday is better known for his dramatic collaborations and his ▷ translations of prose romances. He was one of the revisers of ▷ *Sir Thomas More* (c 1596) and collaborated with ▷ Henry Chettle on two plays about Robin Hood, *The Downfall of Robert, Earle of Huntington* and *The Death of Robert, Earle of Huntington* (both 1598). Munday may now be seen as an important contributor to the ▷ Elizabethan novel through his translations of the prose romances *Palladine of England* (1588) and *Amadis of Gaule* (c 1590). He is satirized by ▷ Jonson as Antonio Balladino in *The Case is Altered*.
Bib: Hayes, G. R., *Anthony Munday's Romances of Chivalry*; Turner, C., *Anthony Munday: An Elizabethan Man of Letters*.

Murdoch, Iris (b 1919)
Novelist and philosopher. Her novels are: *Under the Net* (1954); *Flight from the Enchanter* (1955); *The Sandcastle* (1957); *The Bell* (1958); *Bruno's Dream* (1960); *A Severed Head* (1961; dramatized 1963); *An Unofficial Rose* (1962); *The Unicorn* (1963); *The Italian Girl* (1964; dramatized 1967); *The Red and the Green* (1965); *The Time of the Angels* (1966); *The Nice and the Good* (1968); *A Fairly Honourable Defeat* (1970); *An Accidental Man* (1971); *The Black Prince* (1973); *The Sacred and Profane Love Machine* (1974); *A Word Child* (1975); *Henry and Cato* (1976); *The Sea, The Sea* (1978); *Nuns and Soldiers* (1980); *The Philosopher's Pupil* (1983); *The Good Apprentice* (1985); *The Book and the Brotherhood* (1987); *A Message to the Planet* (1989); and *The Green Knight* (1993).

Iris Murdoch is one of the most prolific and the most popular of serious contemporary novelists. Born in Dublin and educated at Somerville College Oxford and Newnham College Cambridge, she has lectured in philosophy. Her husband is the critic John Bayley. Her profession as a philosopher is reflected in many aspects of her fiction. She has written a study of the work of Jean-Paul Sartre (*Sartre, Romantic Rationalist*, 1953) and her interest in, and dissent from Sartre's ▷ existentialism is evident in her first two novels, which treat existential issues of identity and freedom. These concerns have persisted in her work, but *The Bell* and *The Time of the Angels* introduce religious themes, while since *The Nice and the Good* many of her novels have directly addressed ethical questions. *The Good Apprentice*, for example, explores the idea of a character who, without explicit religious faith, sets out to be good. Although her works are novels of ideas, they combine this with exciting and sometimes macabre plots, elements of the grotesque and supernatural and touches of social comedy. They are highly structured, both by the use of symbolism, and by the patterning of shifting personal relationships.

Her plays include: *The Three Arrows* (1970); *The Servants and the Snow* (1973); *Art and Eros* (1980). Other works are: *The Sovereignty of Good* (1970); *The Fire and the Sun: Why Plato Banished the Artists* (1977); *Acastos: Two Platonic Dialogues* (1986); *Metaphysics as a Guide to Morals* (1992).
Bib: Conradi, P., *Iris Murdoch: the Saint and the Artist*; Johnson, D., *Iris Murdoch*; Todd, R., *Iris Murdoch*; Byatt, A.S., *Degrees of Freedom: The Novels of Iris Murdoch*.

Murphy, Arthur (1727–1805)
Dramatist. Murphy's prolific output includes tragedies, comedies and farces. He adapted the works of the French dramatists Molière and Voltaire (▷ French literature in England), and his own plays include the witty ▷ satire, *Three Weeks After Marriage* (1764). Murphy is also known for writing biographies of Fielding (*An Essay on the Life and Genius of Henry Fielding*, 1762), Garrick (*The Life of David Garrick*, 1801), and his friend Dr Johnson (*An Essay on the Life and Genius of Samuel Johnson*, 1792).
Bib: Dunbar, H.H., *The Dramatic Career of Murphy*.

Murray, John (1778–1843)
Publisher. He founded the ▷ *Quarterly Review* in 1809, and published works by ▷ Lord Byron, ▷ Jane Austen and ▷ George Crabbe, among others. Alone among Byron's correspondents he refused to cooperate with the conspiracy to destroy the poet's *Memoir* and expurgate his letters after his death. Byron's correspondence with Murray thus provides our best insight into

Byron's actual language in informal contexts. Murray's father (1745–93) and his son (1808–92), both named John, were also publishers of note.

Murry, John Middleton (1889–1957)
Critic. His own struggles to achieve personal integration, his close relationship with ▷ D. H. Lawrence, and his marriage to ▷ Katherine Mansfield, led him to write about a number of writers relating their personal lives to their art: *Dostoevsky* (1916), *Keats and Shakespeare* (1925), *Studies in Keats* (1930), *William Blake* (1933), *Shakespeare* (1936), *Jonathan Swift* (1954). He is perhaps best known for his controversial study of D. H. Lawrence, *Son of Woman* (1931) (▷ Catherine Carswell), and for *The Problem of Style* (1922). He was editor of the *Athenaeum* from 1919 to 1921, and published the work of a number of major writers, including ▷ T. S. Eliot and ▷ Virginia Woolf.
Bib: Lea, F. A., *The Life of John Middleton Murry*.

Musgrave, Agnes (fl 1800)
Novelist. Almost nothing is known of Musgrave's life, but she was a best-selling ▷ Minerva novelist from 1795 to 1801. Intriguingly, her first work purports to be a history of the Musgrave family through the female line from ▷ medieval times to her own age; it is supposedly discovered and recounted by the author. *Edmund of the Forest* (1797), *The Solemn Injunction* (1798) and *The Confession* (1801) followed Musgrave's first novel, but they are all rather predictably sensational and quasi ▷ Gothic.

***'Mutabilitie Cantos', The* (1609)**
When the 1609 folio edition of ▷ Edmund Spenser's ▷ *The Faerie Queene* was published, two further cantos of the poem, and two stanzas of a fragmentary third canto, were printed. These, the putative cantos vi, vii, and a fragment of viii of Book VII of the poem, were described in the 1609 edition in the following way: 'TWO CANTOS of *Mutabilitie*: Which, both for Forme and Matter, appeare to be parcell of some following Booke of the *FAERIE QUEENE* under the legend of Constancie'. The precise relationship between these cantos and the main body of the poem has been a subject of dispute ever since their first appearance. The fragmentary nature of the material, together with the theme of the verses (not simply constancy, but a dispute between mutability or 'change' and nature) might, it has often been thought, provide a key to the interpretation of Spenser's complete project, *The Faerie Queene*. Whatever the theological or artistic nature of these final cantos, in reading them after the main body of the poem many modern readers have concluded that they are evidence for the resistance of Spenser's text to any form of 'closure'.

'My Last Duchess'
A poem by ▷ Robert Browning and one of his most powerful and successful ▷ dramatic monologues. It was first published in *Dramatic Lyrics* (1842). Ostensibly the poem describes an incident in the life of Alfonso II, Duke of Ferrara during the 16th century, but its interest lies mainly in the complex psychological portrait of the Duke that unfolds during its course. In an attempt to impress the envoy of a Count whose daughter he intends to marry with his knowledge of art and love of beautiful things, Alfonso draws back the curtain on a strikingly lifelike portrait of his first wife. As he describes her it becomes clear that he was jealously obsessed with the duchess and in order to possess her exclusively he arranged for her portrait to be painted and then for her murder.

Myers, Leopold Hamilton (1881–1944)
Novelist. His father, F. W. H. Myers (1843–1901) was a characteristic product of the 19th-century ▷ agnosticism so prominent among the educated classes; his reaction against it took the form of attempts to prove the existence of the soul by scientific experiment; he was one of the founders of the Society for Psychical Research. The son's concern with the spiritual life took the form of seeking answers to the question 'Why do men choose to live?'. His chief opponents in his pursuit of the answer were not scientific rationalists in the tradition of ▷ T. H. Huxley, but aesthetes of the Bloomsbury tradition, who left moral experience to look after itself while they cultivated enjoyment of 'states of mind'. He also regarded the great influence on English writing of the French novelist, ▷ Marcel Proust (1871–1922) as pernicious, because Proust likewise esteemed experience aesthetically and not morally. Myers considered that this led to the trivializing of life, and his novels dramatize the opposition between those who interpret experience through moral discrimination and those who vulgarize it by regarding it as a means to aesthetic experience only; from the latter evil arises. He regarded civilized society as corrupted by its moral indifference.

His first novel, *The Orissers* (1922) presents the issue in bare terms, but his principal work was the sequence of novels about 16th-century India, published together as *The Near and the Far* in 1943. Myers chose the remote setting of India under the Emperor Akbar because he wanted to escape from the secondary preoccupations of daily life in modern England, and to treat moral and spiritual issues with the large scope which the India of that date, with its multiplying religions and philosophies, afforded him. Evil is represented in the novel through Akbar's son Prince Daniyal, intelligent, artistic, but morally nihilistic, and rival of his merely stupid brother Salim for succession to the throne. Good is expressed through the character of the Guru (teacher) of the last section (*The

Pool of Vishnu): 'All communion', he says, 'is through the Centre. When the relation of man and man is not through the Centre it corrupts and destroys itself.' In his later years he became a ▷ Communist. He committed suicide in 1944. Other novels include: *The Clio* (1925); *Strange Glory* (1936).

▷ Bloomsbury Group.

Bib: Bantock, G. H., *L. H. Myers: A Critical Study*.

***Mysteries of Udolpho, The* (1794)**
A novel by ▷ Mrs Ann Radcliffe. It achieved great fame in its own day, and is often cited as the typical ▷ Gothic novel. It is mainly set in a sombre castle in the Apennine mountains in Italy. The atmosphere is of secret plots, concealed passages, abductions, and the supernatural. ▷ Jane Austen satirized the taste for such sensational literature in ▷ *Northanger Abbey*.

Mystery plays
▷ Cycle plays.

Myth
Three modern uses of this term can be distinguished. The traditional meaning refers to the body of supernatural stories often either inspire works of literature or can be used as source material for them. In writing in English, those most commonly found are the Greek and Roman myths (▷ Classical mythology), though there is also a strong tradition which treats Christian stories as myths. The second, more modern usage relates to the development by the psychoanalyst Carl Jung. A third, contemporary usage follows that of the influential French critic ▷ Roland Barthes' book *Mythologies* (1957). Barthes argued that modern media systems – films, television, advertising, popular writing and journalism – create and indulge myths about our world by investing ordinary behaviour with extra significance (for example, that steak, chips and red wine represent a quintessential Frenchness). Barthes' model, which is carefully explained in a concluding theoretical essay, but which is embodied in the inventive and witty short essays originally written for magazines which make up the body of the book, is now widely accepted. For him, modern mythologies propagate ▷ ideology.

▷ Naturalization

Bib: Barthes, R., *Mythologies*.

N

Naden, Constance (1858–89)
Poet, painter and journalist. She was educated at the Birmingham Midland Institute and the Mason Science College where she studied the philosophy of ▷ Herbert Spencer. She wrote articles for the *Journal of Science* and lectured on scientific subjects. ▷ Darwinian theories of evolution also influenced her writing, which is distinctly ▷ atheist but nevertheless humorous. Her pamphlet *What is Religion? A Vindication of Freethought* anticipates a time when religious values will be superseded by scientific ones. Poems such as 'Evolutional Erotics' dispense with notions of 'romantic love' in favour of more Darwinian methods of selection and others confront the difficult choice between love and work as it affects women. Her overriding themes, however, concern the challenge to religious faith posed by Darwinian evolutionary theories as in poems such as 'The New Orthodoxy' and 'Poet and Botanist'.

In 1887 she travelled to Palestine, Egypt and India and retained an active interest in the medical needs of Indian women. In this she was encouraged by pioneer female doctor Elizabeth Garrett Anderson, and she was a loyal supporter of the new Garrett Anderson hospital for women in London. Literary acquaintances included ▷ Michael Field and ▷ Edith Cooper. She died at the age of thirty-one, after a major operation, of an infection possibly contracted in India. She was mourned by both the scientific and the literary communinity, and was highly praised as a woman poet by ▷ Gladstone in the ▷ *Spectator*.
Bib: Leighton, A. and Reynolds, M., *An Anthology of Victorian Women Poets.*

Naipaul, Shiva (1945–85)
Trinidadian novelist, travel writer and journalist. Born in Port of Spain, Trinidad, the brother of ▷ V. S. Naipaul, he was educated at Queens Royal College, Trinidad, St Mary's College, Trinidad and at University College Oxford. His first two novels are both set among the Hindu community in Trinidad: *Fireflies* (1970) and *The Chip-Chip Gatherers* (1973), which won the Whitbread Award. *A Hot Country* (1983) is a study of English expatriates in a fictional South American country. *North of South: An African Journey* (1978) presents a critical view of East African societies, showing racism, corruption and inequality. *Journey to Nowhere: a New World Tragedy*, first published as *Black and White* (1980), is about the 1978 Jonestown Massacre in Guyana, in which 900 sect members committed suicide on the orders of their leader. *Beyond the Dragon's Mouth: Stories and Pieces* (1984) includes essays, stories and autobiographical fragments.

Naipaul, V. S. (Vidiahar Surajprasad) (b 1932)
Trinidadian novelist of Indian descent. Educated at Queens Royal College, Port of Spain, Trinidad, and Oxford University, he settled in England in 1950. His brother was the novelist ▷ Shiva Naipaul. V. S. Naipaul is the most admired of contemporary Caribbean novelists writing in English and has won many literary awards, including, in 1993, the first David Cohen British Literature Prize. His work is concerned with personal and political freedom, the function of the writer and the nature of sexuality, and is characterized by fastidiousness, clarity, subtlely, and a detached irony of tone. His earlier novels, *The Mystic Masseur* (1957), *The Suffrage of Elvira* (1958) and *Miguel Street* (1959) convey both the vitality and the desolation of Trinidadian life. *The Mimic Men* (1967) is a satirical examination of the economic power structure of an imaginary West Indian island. *A House for Mr Biswas* (1961), often regarded as his masterpiece, tells the tragicomic story of the search for independence and identity of a Brahmin Indian living in Trinidad. His other novels are: *Companion* (1963); *In A Free State* (1971); *Guerillas* (1975); *A Bend in the River* (1979); *The Enigma of Arrival* (1987); *A Way in the World* (1994). Naipaul has also produced essays, criticism, journalism, autobiography and travel writing, including: *The Middle Passage* (1962); *An Area of Darkness* (1964); *A Congo Diary* (1980); *The Return of Eva Peron* (1980); *Among the Believers: An Islamic Journal* (1981); *India: A Million Mutinees Now* (1981); *Finding the Centre* (1984). He was knighted in 1990.
Bib: Hamner, R. D. (ed.), *Critical Perspectives on V. S. Naipaul*; Theroux, P., *V. S. Naipaul: An Introduction to His Work.*

Namjoshi, Suniti (b 1941)
Indian short-story writer and poet. Namjoshi was born in Bombay and educated at the University of Poona in India and at Missouri University, USA, and McGill University, Canada. Drawing on Indian legends, fables, poems and oral story-telling traditions, she has written feminist fables and versions of fairy-stories, a practice she shares with a number of English feminists such as ▷ Angela Carter. Prose works: *Feminist Fables* (1981); *The Conversations of Cow* (1985); *Aditi and the One-Eyed Monkey* (1986); *The Blue Donkey Fables* (1988); *The Mothers of Maya Diip* (1989). Her volumes of poetry include: *The Jackass and the Lady* (1980); *The Authentic Lie* (1982); *Flesh and Paper* (1986); *Because of India* (1989).

Napoleon I (Napoleon Bonaparte, originally Buonaparte, 1769–1821)
A Corsican whose unique career began in the ▷ French Revolution, when he joined the French army defending the first French Republic against European alliances. His military successes brought him to dictatorship in 1799, with the title of First Consul, and in 1804 he

became Emperor. His armies dominated the greater part of Europe until 1812, when his campaign against Russia failed. His final defeat at the hands of the British and the Prussians under ▷ Wellington and Blücher at ▷ Waterloo (1815) led to his exile on the Atlantic island of St Helena, where he died.

His unprecedented success aroused contrasted feelings amongst the British. For the great majority he was a nightmare figure; mothers used his name to frighten naughty children into discipline. To a man like ▷ Wordsworth he was the tyrant who revealed the illusoriness of the ideals of universal freedom which the Revolution had seemed to express. For ▷ Byron and ▷ Shelley he was the first man in Europe to have risen to the summit of power by intrinsic merit and not at least partly through privilege; his downfall and the restoration of the traditional kinds of government that he had overthrown was for them a defeat of the new hopes for mankind. Byron described him memorably in ▷ *Child Harold* Canto III, stanzas 36–44.

▷ French literature in England.

Napoleon III (lived 1808–73)
The nephew of ▷ Napoleon I. He became Emperor of the French in 1852, after previously being elected to the office of President of the second French Republic in 1848. His revival of the Napoleonic title caused him to take the title of Napoleon III, out of respect for his uncle's dead son who had in fact never succeeded to the title. He was without his uncle's genius in war and statecraft, but among the British the mere fact of his succession to power renewed fears of French aggression. His regime was overthrown by the Germans in the Franco-Prussian war of 1870, and he died in England.

Narayan, R. K. (Rasipuran Krishnaswami) (b 1906)
Indian novelist and short-story writer. His novels are: *Swami and Friends* (1935); *The Bachelor of Arts* (1937); *The Dark Room* (1938); *The English Teacher* (1945); *Mr Sampath* (1949); *The Financial Expert* (1952); *Waiting for the Mahatma* (1955); *The Guide* (1958); *The Man Eater of Malgudi* (1961); *The Vendor of Sweets* (1967); *The Painter of Signs* (1976); *A Tiger for Malgudi* (1983); and *Talkative Man* (1986). His novels are set in the imaginary southern Indian community of Malgudi, based on the town of Mysore, which he uses to epitomize Indian culture from the days of the Raj to the present. The early novels show the continuing influence of British culture, in particular on the education system, and contain elements of ▷ autobiography. His work attains a new seriousness with *The English Teacher*, which is based on his own marriage and the early death of his wife. His mature work deals with spirituality and with human weakness, corruption, failure and lack of fulfilment in an ironic and sceptical manner, supported by the vivid realization of the life of the town. *The Guide*, the story of a con man who becomes a saint, is one of his outstanding works, while *A Tiger for Malgudi* represents an excursion into a fantasy mode; drawing on the Hindu doctrine of reincarnation, it has a tiger as its hero and narrator. Story collections are: *Malgudi Days* (1943); *Dodu* (1943); *Cyclone* (1944); *An Astrologer's Day* (1947); *Lawley Road* (1956); *A House and Two Goats* (1970); *Old and New* (1981); *Malgudi Days* (1982) (not the same as the 1943 volume); *Under The Banyan Tree* (1985). Narayan has also written travel literature, memoirs, essays and versions of the Indian epics *The Ramayana* and *The Mahabharata*.
Bib: Walsh, W., *R. K. Narayan: a Critical Appreciation*.

Narrating or narration/*narration* (French)
Terms in ▷ narratology denoting the act of telling a story, which takes place in a ▷ narrative.

Narrative or text/*récit* (French)
Terms denoting the objects of study in ▷ narratology. The narrative informs the reader of the story and implies the existence of the act of ▷ narrating.

Narratology
The systematic study of the structures, forms and modalities of narrative, including questions of temporal arrangement or tense (▷ order, ▷ duration, ▷ frequency), ▷ mood (the manner of narration and point of view, including ▷ focalization), and ▷ voice (the identity and relationship to the action of the ▷ narrator and narratee). Early considerations of narratological questions are found in ▷ Henry James' Prefaces (1907–9) and ▷ E.M. Forster's book ▷ *Aspects of the Novel* (1927). Wayne Booth's *The Rhetoric of Fiction* (1961) inaugurated a more wide-ranging and systematic approach, while the influence of structuralism produced the rigorous analysis of categories of narrative typified by ▷ Gérard Genette's *Narrative Discourse* (1980). There is a more accessible summary of this approach in Shlomith Rimmon-Kenan's *Narrative Fiction: Contemporary Poetics* (1983).

Narrator
A fictional person or consciousness who narrates all or part of a text. A narrator may be a character within a story, who then tells a story, such as Marlow in ▷ Conrad's ▷ *Heart of Darkness*; this is known as an intradiegetic narrator. Alternatively, a narrator may be extradiegetic, that is, outside the story that he or she narrates, like the narrator of ▷ Fielding's ▷ *Tom Jones* (who has a strong personality, but does not participate in the story as such), or like the

largely impersonal and uncharacterized narrator of ⊳ Henry James' ⊳ *The Ambassadors*. Such extradiegetic narrators are different from the ⊳ implied author since they may be unreliable narrators (⊳ Narrator, unreliable).

Narrator, unreliable
A ⊳ narrator who cannot be relied upon to provide accurate information, so that the reader is obliged to try to deduce, from the possibly misleading account given by such a narrator, the true facts of the case. A narrator may be unreliable because of limited knowledge or understanding (*eg* the idiot Benjy in the first section of William Faulkner's *The Sound and the Fury*), because of being in a disturbed state of mind (*eg* the governess, in one possible reading of ⊳ *The Turn of the Screw* by ⊳ Henry James), because of personal bias or dubious moral values (*eg* Dowell in ⊳ Ford Madox Ford's *The Good Soldier*), or out of sheer wilfulness (*eg* the narrator of ⊳ Peter Carey's *Illywhacker*). Unreliable narration tends to emphasize the subjective nature of truth and the technique often tends towards the implication that there is no such thing as an objective viewpoint.

Nashe, Thomas (1567–1601)
Pamphleteer, poet and playwright. He spent six years at St John's College, Cambridge, and is numbered among the ⊳ University Wits who made the decade 1590–1600 an unusually lively period in literature. Two features of this liveliness were ⊳ satire and prose romance (sometimes misleadingly called ⊳ 'the Elizabethan novel'). Nashe contributed to both: his best-known work, ⊳ *The Unfortunate Traveller, or the Life of Jack Wilton* (1594), is one of the outstanding romances of the decade, and it includes some of his best satire, often in the form of a ⊳ parody of some of the contemporary styles of fine writing. Most of the rest of his satire was also in prose. *Pierce Penniless, His Supplication to the Devil* (1592) is a satire in the tradition of the allegorical ⊳ morality plays, an attack on the qualities that made for success in the London of his day, and a denunciation of them as new versions of the ⊳ Seven Deadly Sins; the method looks forward to ⊳ Ben Jonson's comedy of humours (⊳ Humours, Comedy of). His last work, *Lenten Stuff* (1599), is a comic extravaganza on Yarmouth, a fishing town, and the red herring. Other prose work includes his early ⊳ pamphlets attacking the Puritan side in the ⊳ Marprelate controversy amd vigorous disagreement with ⊳ Gabriel Harvey on literary and moral questions between 1593 and 1596. His *Christ's Tears over Jerusalem* (1593) records his repentance for religious doubts.

Nashe escaped being sent to prison in 1597 for an attack on abuses in his play *The Isle of Dogs*, which has been lost. His co-author Jonson and the other actors were imprisoned – Nashe fled. The only play of his sole authorship which survives is *Summer's Last Will and Testament* (1592). This defends the traditional festivities of the countryside against Puritan condemnation of them, and at the same time attacks the useless extravagance of courtiers. It includes some very fine lyrics especially *In Plague Time* and *Autumn*.

Nashe is chiefly known as a prose-writer; his prose is notable for the abundance of its energy and its carnivalesque spirit, which compensate for the confusion of its organization. His gift for parody and the rapidity and vividness of his expression show that the greater coherence and lucidity which English prose was to achieve in the 17th century was not all gain. The freedom and zest of his comic writing owe something to earlier ⊳ Renaissance writers – the Italian poet and comedian ⊳ Pietro Aretino and the great French satirist ⊳ François Rabelais. However, recent criticism has suggested that there is a clear ideological centre to Nashe's works, and this revival of interest must be set alongside the idea of his writing being incoherent and uncontrolled.
Bib: McKerrow, R. B. (rev.), *The Works of Thomas Nashe* (5 vols); Hibbard, G. R., *Nashe: A Critical Introduction*; Hutson, L., *Thomas Nashe in Context*; Nicholl, C., *A Cup of News*.

National Theatre, The
The idea of a national theatre in London had existed since the 18th century. Serious efforts to create such an institution began early this century with the publication in 1903 of *The National Theatre: A Scheme and Estimates*, by ⊳ William Archer and ⊳ Harley Granville-Barker. Enthusiastic lobbying of governments continued after World War I and by 1938 a fund of £150,000 had been raised. However, it was not until 1962 that a National Theatre Board was established. This body created a National Theatre company led by ⊳ Sir Laurence Olivier, which was based at the ⊳ Old Vic whilst a new theatre was built for it on the South Bank at Waterloo. This was finally completed in 1976; the theatre has three auditoria: the Lyttelton, Olivier and Cottesloe theatres, providing a proscenium stage, an open stage and a workshop studio. The first general director was ⊳ Sir Peter Hall, who was replaced by Richard Eyre in 1988. The company policy is to present a diverse repertoire, embracing classic, new and neglected plays from the whole of world drama and to give audiences a choice of at least six different productions at any one time.
Bib: Elsom, J. and Tomalin, N., *The History of the National Theatre*.

Natural History and Antiquities of Selborne
⊳ White, Gilbert.

Natural Law
According to theologians (*eg* ⊳ Richard Hooker), that part of the Divine Will that

manifests itself in the order of the material world: distinguishable from but a piece with human and divine law. Modern scientists define it as the principles of uniformity discernible in the behaviour of phenomena, making such behaviour predictable. For the 18th century, the existence of Natural Law was important as the basis for ▷ Natural Religion.

Natural Philosophy
In the 17th and 18th centuries, the study of physics and kindred sciences. Interest in Natural Philosophy became organized and heightened with the establishment in 1662 of the ▷ Royal Society, which took the whole of knowledge as its province. The natural philosophers included such eminent persons as ▷ Isaac Newton, the chemist Robert Boyle (1627–91), and the naturalist John Ray (1627–1705). They were religious men and made their religion accord with their science. However, in spite of the respect accorded to some of them, especially Newton, intellectuals in the period 1660–1730 tended to react against natural philosophy with angry contempt. They were provoked not so much by the fear of the injury such thought might do to religious faith – this was much more a 19th-century reaction – as by disgust at the triviality of much scientific inquiry, the technical fruits of which were slow to appear. The most notable satire was Swift's 'Laputa' in Part III of ▷ *Gulliver's Travels*. Other examples were Samuel Butler's *Elephant in the Moon*, some of the ▷ *Spectator* essays of Addison and Steele, and the *Memoirs of Martinus Scriblerus*, published with the works of ▷ Pope in 1741, though the principal author seems to have been John Arbuthnot (1667–1735).

Natural Religion
A belief first taught by ▷ Lord Herbert of Cherbury; according to him, belief in God and right conduct are planted in human instincts. This Christian doctrine was the basis for deistic thought (▷ *Deism*) in the later 17th and 18th centuries, and contributed to the growth of religious toleration, though also to passivity of religious feeling and hence to indifference. Herbert's aim was to resolve the doubts arising out of the religious conflicts of his time – see *eg* ▷ Donne's *Third Satire*. For the reaction against Deism, see ▷ William Blake's propositions *There is No Natural Religion* (1788).

Naturalism
In literature, a school of thought especially associated with the novelist ▷ Emile Zola. It was a development of ▷ Realism. The Naturalists believed that imaginative literature (especially the novel) should be based on scientific knowledge, and that imaginative writers would be scientifically objective and exploratory in their approach to their work. This means that environment should be exactly treated, and that character should be related to physiological heredity. Influential in France and Germany, the movement counts for little in Britain; the novelists ▷ George Gissing and ▷ Arnold Bennett show traces of its influence in the treatment of environment in relation to character.

Naturalization
A process, described in much structuralist and ▷ post-structuralist theory, whereby cultural sign systems come to be taken for reality. The process occurs in, for example, journalism and other news media, and in realist forms of literary writing, all of which claim to represent 'the truth' often simply by virtue of their ▷ conventionality or 'taken-for-grantedness'. As such they are vehicles for ▷ ideology. According to ▷ Roland Barthes, naturalized signs repress the fact that they are signs, and pretend to be real and true instead of artificial and constructed. It is here that they are most dangerous. Fears about the ideological contamination of 'realism' led Barthes and other post-structuralist thinkers to prefer writing in experimental or ▷ avant-garde modes which flaunts their constructedness and deliberate artificiality.
▷ Myth; ▷ Realism
Bib: Barthes, R., *Mythologies*.

Nature
The word is used throughout English literature with meanings that vary constantly according to period or to mode of expression, *eg* philosophic, religious or personal. This note is intended to guide the student by showing some of the basic approaches to the idea.

1 *Creation and the Fall*. Fundamental to all conceptions of Nature is traditional Christian doctrine. This influences English writers even when they are using a more or less agnostic or atheistic approach. The doctrine is that Nature is God's creation, but by the fall of man, symbolized by the story of ▷ Adam's disobedience in the book of *Genesis*, earthly nature is self-willed and destructive though not to the extent that the Divine Will and Order is obliterated in it.

2 *All-embracing Nature*. Nature is sometimes seen as the whole of reality so far as earthly experience goes. For instance, the opening 18 lines of ▷ Chaucer's ▷ *Prologue to the Canterbury Tales* show Nature as the great reviver of life. This use of the word has a different kind of significance in the 18th century when scientific Reason has replaced the religious imagination as the familiar vehicle for the interpretation of reality. See 4 *Nature and Truth*.

3 *Nature and God*. In line with traditional Christian doctrine, Natural Law is linked to Human Law and Divine Law as a manifestation

of the Divine Will, in such works as ▷ Hooker's Laws of Ecclesiastical Polity (1597). However, from the beginning of the 17th century, there was a new interest in the function of human reason as an instrument for the acquisition of knowledge independently of religious feeling. Men like ▷ Ralegh (*History of the World*, 1614) and ▷ Bacon (▷ *The Advancement of Learning*) began to ask what, given that God was the Primary Cause of Nature, were the Secondary, or Immediate, Causes of natural phenomena. ▷ Newton's work on gravitation (*Principia Mathematica*, 1687) and ▷ Locke's ▷ *Essay Concerning Human Understanding* seemed to solve the problem causing people to see God as the Divine Artificer whose Reason could be discerned in the government of even the smallest phenomena, as well as in the great original act of Creation.

4 *Nature and Truth*. Nature is in the 18th century Truth scientifically considered. 'To follow Nature' (*eg* in works of imaginative literature) may mean: (i) to present things and people (*eg* an imagined character) as they really are; (ii) to reveal truths that lie beneath appearances; (iii) to follow rational principles. It was the attempt to 'follow Nature' in these ways that constituted the main discipline of the novelists ▷ Defoe, ▷ Richardson, ▷ Fielding, ▷ Smollet.

5 *Nature as Moral Paradox*. The Christian conception of Nature as both God-created and spoilt by the fall of man led at various times to the problem that Nature is both good and evil. According to the medieval conception, maintained until the middle of the 17th century, human society was itself the outcome of the Divine Natural Order, so that it was by Natural Law that children should honour their parents, subjects their sovereigns, etc. On the other hand, the natural passions of men and beasts, unrestrained by reason, were the source of rapacity and ruin. Thus ▷ Shakespeare's King Lear begins by relying on the former conception of Nature, but he is exposed to the reality of the latter.

19th-century natural science revived the feeling that Nature was essentially destructive, and hostile or at best indifferent to men; this is the 'Nature red in tooth and claw' image of ▷ Tennyson's ▷ *In Memoriam*, set against the idea of the love of God. The atheistic ▷ Thomas Hardy saw men as subjected to the irony of indifferent fates, and the natural environment as governed in the same way.

6 *Nature for Man's Use*. Implicit in Christian doctrine was the belief that Nature was created *for* man; that it was his birthright to exploit and use it. This begins with the conception of Nature as the Great Mother originating in pre-Christian times but pervasive in medieval verse and later, *eg* in much Elizabethan ▷ pastoral poetry. It took a more active significance when the 17th- and 18th-century 'Natural philosophers' from ▷ Bacon onwards sought methods by which man could increase his power over Nature; 18th-century poetry commonly shows Nature as beautiful when she is productive under the ingenuity of human exploitation.

7 *Nature and Art*. 'Art' in earlier contexts often includes technology, *eg* in Polixenes' remarks on cultivation to Perdita in *The Winter's Tale* IV. iii; here art is seen as itself a product of nature. But art was often set against nature in Shakespeare's time and afterwards, *eg* in Sidney's ▷ *Apology for Poetry*; 'Her (*ie* Nature's) world is brazen; the Poets only deliver a golden'; here the function of imaginative art seems to be the opposite of the 18th-century poets' and novelists' conception of 'truth to nature', but Sidney meant that poetry should improve on Nature, not falsify it; the creation must be ideal, but consistent with Nature.

8 *Nature opposed to Court and City*. 'Art', however, was not necessarily an improvement. The city and the court, in Shakespeare's time, were the centres of new financial forces generating intrigue and 'unnatural' (*ie* inhuman) behaviour. There was also a kind of pastoral made by idealizing the life of the great country houses, *eg* ▷ Ben Jonson's ▷ *Penshurst* and ▷ Aemelia Lanier's *Salve Deus Rex Judaeorum*. In the 18th century poets like ▷ James Thomson wrote about natural surroundings for their own sake, and sometimes included wild nature as their subject, but it was ▷ Wordsworth who gave to wild nature its importance as the principal subject of what later came to be known as 'nature' poetry.

9 *Nature in Communion with the Individual*. Wordsworth was to some extent anticipated in the 18th century by such a poet as ▷ William Cowper, and his teacher was especially ▷ Jean-Jacques Rousseau. It was Wordsworth above all, however, who gave to Nature its modern most familiar sense – as the non-urban, preferably wild environment of man, to which the depths of his own nature always respond. Here he finds a communion which refreshes the loneliness of his spirit in a relationship which underlies and gives meaning to his human relationships.

▷ French literature in England.

Négritude

A literary movement begun amongst black writers from the French colonies in Paris in the 1930s, négritude was widely-influential among colonial and post-colonial writers in Africa and the Caribbean especially. Négritude emphasises the blackness of black writing and the need for such writers to return to indigenous black themes and culture. Its leading figures were the poets Aimé Césaire from Martinique (who coined the term) and Léopold Sédar Senghor from Senegal. Négritude ideas were particularly influential during the large-scale European de-colonization after World War Two and were championed in Europe by some leading dissident intellectuals like Jean-Paul Sartre. The journal *Présence Africaine*, founded in 1947, was a force in the propagation of négritude ideas, but they started to fall from favour in the 1960s when they were criticized for being too limited in political ambition and too European in intellectual and artistic orientation.

Nelson, Horatio, Viscount (1758–1805)
English admiral, and a national hero. His naval successes against ▷ Napoleon culminated in the Battle of Trafalgar (1805) at which he lost his life in gaining victory over the combined French and Spanish fleets, thus saving England from French invasion. As an officer he was strongly independent and unconventional; one of the famous anecdotes about him tells how he put his telescope to his blind eye at the battle of Copenhagen in 1801 in order not to see his superior officer's signal ordering him to withdraw. Equally famous are the signal to his ships before Trafalgar: 'England expects every man to do his duty', and his dying words: 'Now I am satisfied; thank God I have done my duty.' His love affair with the beautiful Lady Hamilton was a notorious romance. In 1813 the poet ▷ Robert Southey published his life, one of the best known of English biographies.

Nennius
Welsh monk and reputed compiler of a 9th-century *Historia Brittonum (History of the Britons)*, which provides an outline of British history, from the founding of the island by Brutus, used by ▷ Geoffrey of Monmouth as a framework for his historical narrative. ▷ Arthur is mentioned as a British battle leader (not a king), who fights 12 battles, culminating in the battle of Badon, in which he fells 960 men at one charge.

▷ Arthur, King.

Neo-classicism
This term can be understood for the purposes of English literary culture in two senses: (1) the broad sense, which refers to the ▷ Renaissance of Classical culture and its influence on English literature down to the end of the 18th century. This influence operated mainly by the cultivation of Latin culture, and was mediated first by Italy and later by France. (2) The narrow sense of neo-classicism refers to a European artistic movement which originated in Germany and lasted approximately from 1750 until 1830.

In the first sense, neo-classical culture affected English literature in two phases:

1 In the 16th century England developed a fine school of classical scholars, of whom the best known was ▷ Thomas More. Through travellers and scholars such as ▷ Sir Thomas Wyatt and Henry Howard, ▷ Earl of Surrey, poetry and prose received strong influences from Italian writers such as ▷ Petrarch and French ones such as ▷ Ronsard who already belonged to the classic revival. A critic like ▷ Sidney showed the influence of Italian critics who in turn were developing 'rules' out of classical writers for dramatic construction, etc. All these influences matured in the last decade of the 16th century but their effect was uneven; the greatest of the rising dramatists, ▷ Shakespeare, ignored the neo-classical rules for dramatic construction, whereas ▷ Ben Jonson, his chief rival in the theatre by 1600, was deeply affected by classical principles and classical culture generally. ▷ Pastoral poems, deriving from Italian influences and more directly from Virgil, were numerous from Spenser's ▷ *The Shepherd's Calendar* (1579) onwards, and in the 1590s there was a widespread production of ▷ Sonnets under the influence of Petrarch. Much of the classical influence was on the level of ornament, however, as it was in English architecture in the same period. Jonson was outstanding in his absorption of classical influence to a deep level, and it was deeper in his lyrical work than in his drama. He is, in fact, an important link with the next phase of English neo-classicism – that which began in 1660 and lasted throughout the 18th century.

2 The second phase was much influenced by contemporary French literature, which was marked by distinguished achievement. English culture was entering a relatively aristocratic period by reaction from the Republican decade of the 1650s; it was also undergoing an increasingly strong revulsion against religious and political passions such as produced the ▷ Civil War. The result was admiration for philosophy, reason, scepticism, ▷ wit and refinement – all qualities conducive to neo-classic culture. Significantly this was also the first important period of English criticism. Yet thoroughly neo-classic critics like ▷ Thomas Rymer were the exception. The restlessness of English society, the increasing importance of the middle class, the difficulty of making such a large exception to neo-classical principles as Shakespeare, and the hostility the English literary tradition has always shown to authoritative doctrines, all help to explain the refusal of the leading critics, ▷ Dryden and ▷ Samuel Johnson, to adopt neo-classic theory unquestioningly. Nonetheless, such a figure as the French neo-classicist ▷ Boileau was deeply respected, and the best poets and essayists (though hardly the novelist) – ▷ Addison, ▷ Swift, ▷ Pope, Johnson – all exhibited the neo-classic virtues of clarity, order, reason, wit and balance.

Neo-classicism in the narrow sense was the cultivation of Greek culture in opposition to Roman culture, and originated partly in the German movement to emancipate German culture from France. It can be said that whereas Renaissance classicism sought to emulate the culture of Rome, this 'New Humanism' sought inspiration in the originality of the Greeks. This difference enabled the new Neo-classicism to merge with Romanticism, whose progenitor was above all ▷ Rousseau. In England, it is thus impossible to distinguish Neo-classic from Romantic writers in the period 1790–1830. It is clear, however, that ▷ William Blake shows neo-classic inspiration in his graphic art, and that the poems by ▷ Keats on classical themes (▷ Endymion and the two ▷ Hyperions) are in a romantic-classical style, very different from Augustan classicism of the previous century. Neo-classicism is more distinguishable in the architectural style known as ▷ Regency, and in the sculpture of an artist such as Flaxman (as well as in ▷ costume), than in imaginative literature.

▷ Classic, Classics, Classical; Unities; French literature in England; Italian influence in English literature.

Bib: Honour, H., *Neo-classicism*.

Neo-Platonism

▷ Platonism.

Nesbit, Edith (1858–1924)

Nesbit was born in London and educated in France and Germany as well as England. Through her elder sister, Mary, she meet the ▷ Rossettis, ▷ Swinburne and ▷ William Morris, and published her first poem in *The Sunday Magazine* in 1876. She married the journalist Hubert Bland in 1880, and both became founder members of the ▷ Fabian Society in 1884. Hubert was a notorious womanizer, but Edith allowed his illegitimate offspring to live in the household along with her own four children (▷ H.G. Wells satirized the couple's unconventional lifestyle in his *Experiment in Autobiography*). Financial difficulties forced Nesbit to abandon poetry and write popular fiction and books for children – her first stories about the Bastable family appeared in 1898. Three 'Bastable' novels quickly followed: *The Story of the Treasure Seekers* (1899), *The Wouldbegoods* (1901) and *The New Treasure Seekers* (1904). Her blend of ▷ realism and magic proved highly popular, and her other famous children's novels include *Five Children and It* (1902); *The Phoenix and the Carpet* (1904); *The Railway Children* (1906) and *The Enchanted Castle* (1907). Her other published work includes early collections of poetry, political verse such as *Ballads and Lyrics of Socialism* (1908), a study of childhood, *Wings and the Child* (1913) and several ghost stories. Her last novel, *Lark*, appeared in 1922.

▷ Children's literature.

Bib: Moore, D.K., *Life*, Briggs, J., *A Woman of Passion*; Leighton, A., and Reynolds, M. (eds.), *An Anthology of Victorian Women Poets*.

***New Atlantis, The* (1626)**

A philosophical tale by ▷ Francis Bacon, in the tradition of ▷ Sir Thomas More's ▷ *Utopia* (1615). It was left unfinished at Bacon's death, and published in 1626. The title is an allusion to the mythical island described by ▷ Plato in his dialogue *Timaeus*. Bacon's island is called Bensalem (*ie* an analogous place to Salem or Jerusalem, the holy city) and its chief glory is its university, 'Solomon's House'. Unlike the English universities of Bacon's day, this is devoted to scientific research – 'the knowledge of causes, and secret motions of things; and the enlarging of the bounds of human empire, to the effecting of all things possible'. The boundless optimism of this Baconian ideal was to be reflected in the work of 17th-century science in general.

New Comedy

Unlike ▷ Aristophanes' Old Comedy, New Comedy as extant in the writings of ▷ Menander, ▷ Plautus and ▷ Terence does not address specific and topical issues so much as focus on general moral and imaginative motifs. Its formulae consist of stock characters such as the young rake, the wily servant (*servus dolosus*), the courtesan, the braggart soldier (*miles gloriosus*) and the irascible old man (*senex*). The plays are populated by lost children and siblings. The genre of New Comedy proved highly influential for English literature. It could more readily accommodate the ▷ neo-classical Horatian moral stance that distinguishes much Elizabethan drama, and its generalized approach proved politically safe in a theatre where every play needed a licence for performance from the Lord Chamberlain's office.

New criticism

This term is given to a movement which developed in the late 1940s in the U.S.A., and which dedicated itself to opposing the kind of criticism that is associated with ▷ Romanticism, and 19th-century realism. The 'practical criticism' of I. A. Richards was an influential stimulus to this movement in which emphasis was placed upon the self-contained nature of the literary text. In the work of 'new' critics such as Cleanth Brooks, W. K. Wimsatt, John Crowe Ransom, Allen Tate, and R. P. Blackmur, concern with the 'intention' of the writer was replaced by close reading of particular texts, and depended upon the assumption that any literary work was self-contained. New criticism placed a particular emphasis upon poetry, and asserted that the individual poem 'must not mean but be'.

Although the methods of new criticism now seem insufficiently historical, the tradition of close reading is perpetuated in ▷ Deconstruction (though hardly in a form which the 40s generation would have relished). Since its inception, English Literature as a university discipline has been marked by alternating fashions for either close reading or historicization.

New Grub Street (1891)
A novel by ▷ George Gissing. The title refers to Grub Street, which was inhabited in the 18th century by journalists of a low order, who wrote to gain a living without seriousness of intention or artistic standards. The living they earned was generally a mean one, but since 1875 the new periodicals and newspapers had found a way to achieve massive circulations by printing material which had an immediate appeal although its intrinsic quality was trivial or merely sensational. This commercialization of journalism had spread to the production of books. Gissing's novel is about the difficulties of the serious literary artist faced by successful competition from the now very well rewarded commercial writer without scruples, either moral or artistic. The serious writer in the book is Edwin Reardon (a self-portrait) and his successful competitor is Jasper Milvain. Commercial success is also illustrated by Whelpdale, editor of the magazine *Chit-Chat* (based on the actual magazine *Titbits* founded in 1881) which never publishes articles longer than two inches in length. At the other extreme is the novelist Biffen, who has the artistic fastidiousness of the French novelist ▷ Flaubert and writes the same kind of book. Biffen and Reardon both end in failure but Gissing's novel was fairly popular, which perhaps argues against the extreme pessimism of his thesis.
▷ Newspapers.

New historicism
A theoretical movement which developed in America in the 1980s, partly as a reaction against the ahistorical approaches of New Criticism and the unselfconscious historicism of earlier critics. New historicism draws upon Marxist criticism in its emphasis upon political and social context and rejection of individual aspiration and universalism, but at the same time it insists that historical context can never be recovered objectively. New historicists do not assume that literature reflects reality and that these 'reflections' enable the reader to recover without distortion the past presented in the texts. Rather, they look for an interplay between text and society, which can never be presented neutrally. Moreover, readers must be aware of their *own* historical context: we read texts from the perspective of our own age and can never perfectly re-create history.
▷ Cultural materialism; Marx, Karl; Poetics.
Bib: Greenblatt, S., *Renaissance Self-fashioning*; Howard, J. E. and O'Connor, M. F., *Shakespeare Reproduced*; Tennenhouse, L, *Power on Display*; Veeser, H. A., *The New Historicism.*

New Inn, The (1629)
A late play by ▷ Ben Jonson which attempts to work native romance motifs into the fabric of a contemporary ▷ citizen comedy. More than any Jonson play, *The New Inn* has been the particular discovery of the 1970s, when several leading Jonson scholars championed its claim to being a masterpiece of mixed genre and a Jonsonian tribute to ▷ Shakespeare.

New Learning, The
Study of the Bible and the Greek classics in the original languages instead of through Latin versions (▷ Greek literature; classical education). This study in the 15th–16th centuries was an important influence in the ▷ Renaissance and the ▷ Reformation.

New Model Army, The
Formed by Parliament in 1645 towards the end of the ▷ Civil War between itself and ▷ King Charles I. The war had so far been indecisive owing to the amateurish soldiering on both sides. Parliament now ensured that its own army should be highly professional. The result was the decisive victory of Naseby in June 1645. The commander was Sir Thomas Fairfax, but its most gifted general was ▷ Oliver Cromwell, who between 1646 and 1660 made the English army one of the most formidable in Europe. Cromwell's special contribution was his highly trained force of cavalry, the Ironsides.

New Monthly Magazine
It started in 1814 and had editors of considerable literary note such as the poets Thomas Campbell (1777–1844) and Thomas Hood (1799–1845), the novelists ▷ Harrison Ainsworth and ▷ Bulwer-Lytton, and the essayist Theodore Hook. It gave considerable space to criticism. It closed in 1884.

New Philosophers, The
▷ Nouveaux Philosophes, Les.

New Science
The term 'New Science' or 'New Philosophy' is something of a catch-all phrase, but one which usually is used to suggest the revolution in scientific understanding in Europe generally in the 16th and 17th centuries. On the continent, the work of ▷ Galileo in the field of astronomy and Andreas Vesalius (1514–64) in the area of human anatomy signalled a reassessment of the study of the natural world. In England the influence of ▷ Francis Bacon in the area of scientific methodology was to be of considerable importance. English science in the 16th century, however, lagged behind the work that was taking place on the continent. But, with the publication of William Harvey's discovery of the circulation of the blood (1628), an age of remarkable scientific innovation began in the British Isles.

The influence on literature of the 'New Science' of the age is a much-debated topic.

Certainly poets such as ▷ John Donne and ▷ Henry Vaughan were aware of the changes taking place in the ordering and understanding of the natural world – and this awareness is reflected in their writings. Others, such as ▷ Abraham Cowley, were enthusiastic in promulgating ideas and experimental attitudes associated with new scientific methodology. ▷ Thomas Traherne, on the other hand, found himself in the paradoxical situation of being fascinated with the products of scientific enquiry while being deeply suspicious of the anti-fideistic tendency of much of the work that was undertaken.

Bib: Debus, A. G., *Man and Nature in the Renaissance*.

New Statesman and Society, The

The leading left-wing weekly periodical of the intelligentsia. It was founded in 1913; its Conservative counterpart is ▷ *The Spectator*. In politics it has always followed a general line of ▷ Fabian socialism.

New Theatre, The

The present Albery Theatre in St Martin's Lane was known as the New Theatre from its opening in 1903 to 1973.

***New Way to Pay Old Debts, A* (1625)**

The best-known comedy by ▷ Philip Massinger. The main character is Sir Giles Overreach, a man of powerful energy and unlimited rapacity, who has no scruples in his schemes to increase his own wealth and social greatness. He is, however, outwitted by those very social superiors, Lord Lovell and Lady Allworth, whom he attempts to flatter and use; they take the side of the young people whom he tries to victimize, his nephew Wellborn and his daughter Margaret. Overreach thus 'overreaches' himself, in the manner of ▷ Ben Jonson's characters, and he is in fact the last vigorous representative of the comedy of ▷ humours tradition. The weakness of the play is that Overreach's opponents are colourless characters, so that the play is artistically unbalanced in Overreach's favour. Massinger's use of ▷ blank verse is extremely flexible to the point sometimes of insipidity, although in the best passages it regains much of the concentrated force of Jonson himself. Overreach is based on a contemporary profiteer, Sir Giles Mompesson.

Newcastle, Duchess of

▷ Cavendish, Margaret, Duchess of Newcastle.

***Newcomes, The* (1853–5)**

A novel by ▷ William Makepeace Thackeray; it was published in instalments. The characters are drawn from the middle and upper classes, and the book is a study of the vices and virtues of such mid-19th-century society. The vices are shown in the worldly cynicism of Lady Kew who seeks a fashionable marriage for her grand-daughter Ethel Newcome; in the mean snobbery of Ethel's brother Barnes, who frustrates her marriage with her cousin Clive Newcome; in the hypocrisy, intrigue and viciousness of Clive's eventual mother-in-law Mrs Mackenzie, and in the philistinism and arrogance of the social world as a whole. The virtues are less successfully presented. Clive Newcome's father, Colonel Newcome, is the honourable, single-minded soldier who loses his fortune and is subjected to the tyranny of Mrs Mackenzie. Thackeray was inclined to see decency as overwhelmed by materialism.

▷ Bohemian.

Bib: McMaster, R.D., *Thackeray's Cultural Frame of Reference: Allusion in The Newcomes*.

Newgate

In the Middle Ages, the principal west gate of the City of London. The gate-house was a prison from the 12th century, enlarged in the 15th century and burnt down in the ▷ Gordon Riots in 1780. Its destruction is described in ▷ Dickens' novel ▷ *Barnaby Rudge*. It was rebuilt and finally demolished in 1902, when the present Central Criminal Court (Old Bailey) was built on its site.

▷ Newgate novel.

Newgate novel

Strictly speaking, a novel in which the characters and/or elements of plot are taken from *The Newgate Calendars*, which were records of notorious crimes, named after Newgate Prison in London, and published at various dates between 1773 and 1826. Examples are *Rookwood* (1834) by ▷ William Harrison Ainsworth and *Paul Clifford* (1830) by ▷ Bulwer-Lytton. The term is applied more loosely to novels about criminals, such as ▷ *Oliver Twist* (1837) by ▷ Charles Dickens. Newgate novels provoked a furious debate in the 1830s and 40s, because they often showed some sympathy for criminals and suggested that social conditions contributed to crime. They were attacked as morally corrupting by some critics, including the novelist ▷ Thackeray, who satirized the form in his novel ▷ *Barry Lyndon* (1844).

Newman, John Henry (1801–90)

Writer on religion and education. From 1833 to 1842 he was one of the most influential and controversial leaders of the Church of England, but in 1845 he was received into the Roman ▷ Catholic Church. As a Catholic convert he was even more influential, and he was made a Cardinal in 1879.

His first period of activity (1833–42) was as leader of the Tractarian Movement – more or less identical with the ▷ Oxford Movement, whose aim was to defend the Church of England against encroachments by the state on the one hand, and against adulteration of its doctrines by the Broad Church tendencies on the other. The Church of England was founded in the 16th century on a central position between the Catholicism of Rome and the whole-hearted ▷ Protestantism of Martin Luther (1483–1546) and John Calvin (1509–1604). This had always been both its strength and its weakness; it was able to accommodate a variety of believers, but it was inclined to lose itself in vagueness and become subservient to the state. Newman's *Tracts for the Times* tried to secure a firm basis for Anglican doctrine and discipline, as against supporters of the Broad Church party (such as ▷ Thomas Arnold) who cared less for doctrine than for social ethics. Newman's tracts led him steadily towards Roman Catholicism, however, until his *Tract XC* went so far as to say that the Anglican 39 Articles – which all clergy had to accept – were not incompatible with essential Roman Catholic beliefs, but only with distortions and exaggerations of them.

As a Roman Catholic, Newman's first valuable literary work was *The Scope and Nature of University Education* (1852), a collection of lectures to the new Catholic University of Dublin, of which he became Rector in 1854. These were combined with further lectures delivered in 1859 to make *The Idea of a University Defined* (1873). His spiritual ▷ autobiography, defending the sincerity of his Catholic beliefs against the accusations by the Broad Churchman, ▷ Charles Kingsley, came out with the title ▷ *Apologia Pro Vita Sua* (*Defence of his Life*) in 1864. It was not only very persuasive in convincing the public of the genuineness of his faith; it was also an eloquent and lucid presentation of the nature of religious belief at a time when much religious thinking in English was muddled, superficial and entangled in irrelevant controversies with scientific ▷ agnostics such as ▷ T.H. Huxley. His *Grammar of Assent* (1870) was a more strictly philosophical account of religious belief.

Newman also wrote some minor poetry, including the famous hymn *Lead Kindly Light*, and the ▷ dramatic monologue *The Dream of Gerontius*, better known for the music set to it by Elgar. He also wrote two religious novels, *Loss and Gain* (1848) and *Callista* (1856).

As a writer he is famous for the lucidity and grace of his style. His wide influence, still very powerful, arose from his ability to understand the tragic extremity of the emotional and intellectual bewilderment of his contemporaries, while refusing to compromise his beliefs.

Bib: Harold, C.F., *Newman: an Expository and Critical Study of his Mind, Thought and Art*.

Newspapers

Periodicals resembling newspapers began in a small way in the reign of James I; in the decades of the Civil War and the Interregnum they increased in number owing to the need of either side to engage in propaganda. From 1695 press ▷ censorship was abandoned; newspapers and weekly periodicals began to flourish.

The first English daily, the *Daily Courant*, a mere news-sheet, began in 1702, but in the earlier part of the 18th century papers more nearly resembling what we now know as the weekly reviews were of greater importance, and leading writers conducted them, *eg* ▷ Defoe's *The Review* (thrice weekly – 1704–13); ▷ Steele's *Tatler* (thrice weekly – started 1709); Steele and Joseph Addison's ▷ *Spectator* (daily – started 1711); and the ▷ *Examiner* (started 1710), to which the chief contributor was ▷ Jonathan Swift. ▷ Samuel Johnson's ▷ *Rambler* (1750) was of the same kind. Of these men, only Defoe resembled fairly closely what we nowadays regard as a journalist as distinct from a man of letters.

The first attempt to reach a mass circulation was made through this kind of periodical by ▷ William Cobbett with his *Weekly Political Register* (started 1802), and in 1808 Leigh Hunt's weekly *Examiner*, directed to a more educated public through with less remarkable literary merit, began to rival Cobbett's paper as a medium of radical comment and criticism.

Of daily papers founded in the 18th century, the ▷ *Morning Post* (started 1772) survived until 1936, and *The Times* (started 1785) is today the daily with the greatest prestige, though it has a comparatively small circulation. Other important dailies with a shorter life were the ▷ *Morning Chronicle* (1769–1862), and the ▷ *Morning Herald* (1780–1869). Both reached peak circulations of about 6,000. To reach the very large circulations of today, newspapers had to await the abolition of the stamp duty – a tax on newspapers – in 1855. The Stamp Tax was started in 1712. It was a method of restricting circulations by raising the prices of newspapers. The government of the day resented criticism of its policies but did not dare revive the Licensing Act, the lapsing of which in 1695 was really the start of the British freedom of the press. The abolition of the tax, together with the advent of cheap paper and a nationwide potential public thanks to universal literacy, led to a new kind of newspaper at the end of the 19th century. Alfred and Harold Harmsworth, later Lord Northcliffe and Lord Rothermere, founded the *Daily Mail* in 1896; by 1901 it was selling a million copies. Other popular newspapers followed it with steadily increasing circulations.

Several unfortunate consequences have followed this development:

1 Much ▷ journalism has degenerated into mere commerce, so that news is regarded as what is most saleable, *ie* what appeals most readily to the baser and more easily roused human appetites.

2 Newspapers, in order to keep their prices

down, have come to rely on advertising revenue, which is attracted chiefly to those with very large circulations so that some with smaller circulations have been eliminated.

3 The British newspapers have divided rather sharply into the serious ones with a large influence but a small circulation, and the popular ones or tabloids, which often achieve their large circulations by irresponsible appeals to the baser public tastes. Finally, modern newspapers, as great capitalistic enterprises, tend to be right-wing politically, so that left-wing opinion is under-represented in the daily press. However, British newspapers are jealous of their independence: they are quick to resist any tendency by the government to check their freedom of expression. Since the war, the Press Council has been established for the purpose of limiting the abuse of this freedom by, for instance, the infringement of personal privacy; however, its powers are limited to public rebuke, and it has no power to penalize or censor newspapers. In 1990 the Press Complaints Commission was established.

The 20th-century weekly reviews have seldom been able to compete with the daily papers in the size of their circulations. However, the strong tradition of weekly journalism inherited from the 18th and 19th centuries ensures that the 'weeklies' have large influence among the intelligentsia. The oldest of the influential weeklies is the *Spectator* which has no connection with Addison's periodical, but was founded in 1828. It is conservative and is counter-balanced by ▷ *The New Statesman and Society* on the left. The most influential literary periodicals in Britain are *The Times Literary Supplement*, a weekly which is published by *The Times* newspaper and the *London Review of Books*, published every two weeks.

Newton, Sir Isaac (1642–1727)
Mathematician and natural philosopher. He entered Trinity College, ▷ Cambridge, in 1661, became a fellow of the college in 1667, and Professor of Mathematics in the university in 1669. He resigned the professorship in 1701; in 1703 he was made President of the ▷ Royal Society, and was re-elected annually until his death. Queen ▷ Anne knighted him in 1705.

His principal work was *Philosophiae Naturalis Principia Mathematica* (1687), written in Latin. By the application of mathematical calculation, it explained the force of gravity in its operation through the solar system. His book on *Optics* (1704) was less important, but it aroused new interest in vision and colour and influenced descriptive writing throughout the 18th century. His scientific and mathematical discoveries did not shake his religious convictions, which were very strong, and he also wrote on theology and biblical chronology. On the other hand, he did not understand and had no use for the imaginative faculty and, like ▷ Locke (whose ▷ *Essay concerning Human Understanding* was published in 1690) he dismissed poetry as an unimportant and irrelevant activity.

Despite this indifference to poetic literature, Newton's discoveries, combined as they were with his religious piety, had a great influence on 18th-century poets. He caused them to revere ▷ Reason in both Man and God, who, seen through Newton's writings, became the Divine Artist of the Universe. ▷ Pope's ▷ *Essay on Man* was a restatement of the traditional vision of the natural order newly shaped to accord with Newton's rational harmony, and it was Pope who composed for Newton the famous epitaph:

Nature and Nature's laws lay hid in night:
God said, 'Let Newton be!' *and all was Light.*

The most famous poet of the natural scene in the 18th century, ▷ James Thomson, wrote his ▷ *Seasons* in accordance with Newtonian principles. In the revised ▷ *Prelude* (1850) ▷ Wordsworth wrote of the statue in Trinity College:

Of Newton with his prism and silent face,
The marble index of a mind for ever
Voyaging through strange seas of Thought, alone.

Wordsworth thus chooses to emphasize the mysteriousness of science, whereas Pope had emphasized its power to clarify mystery.
Bib: Nicholson, M. H., *Newton Demands the Muse*.

Ngcobo, Lauretta (b 1932)
South African novelist and critic. Ngcobo now lives in Britain having escaped from South Africa during the 1960s, when she was threatened with arrest as a member of the Pan-African Congress. Her two novels are about black resistance to the apartheid regime and to white oppression in South Africa: *Cross of Gold* (1981) is about a revolutionary fighter, while *And They Didn't Die* (1990) is about a woman's struggle for life and autonomy. Ngcobo edited *Let It Be Told* (1987), a collection of essays by black women writers in Britain.

Ngugi wa Thiong'o (b 1938)
Kenyan novelist, short-story writer and playwright. Educated at the universities of Makere in Kenya and Leeds in Britain, Ngugi was a fierce critic of the Kenyan regime and campaigner for the rights of the rural poor in Kenya, and was held in solitary confinement after the performance of his play *Ngaahika Ndeenda* (written with Ngugi wa Mirii, translated as *I Will Marry When I Want*, 1982) and the publication of his novel *Petals of Blood* (1977), which attacks economic exploitation from a Marxist perspective. Ngugi has lived in exile

since 1982. He published four novels in English, a fifth in both English and Kikuyu (the language of the people of the Kenyan highlands) and since 1982 has not written in English. Some of his work was published under the name James T. Ngugi. *Weep Not, Child* (1964) and *The River Between* (1965) were both written while the author was still a student; the first is the story of a boy growing up during the period of the Mau Mau rebellions, while the second is based around the symbolic separation of two villages and set during the rebellion of the 1920s; *A Grain of Wheat* (1967) portrays the time leading up to Independence. These novels combine realism with elements of the symbolic and of parable and explore collective values through the thoughts and experiences of individuals. *Devil on the Cross* (1982) represents a shift towards a more allegorical and fantastic mode, used for a direct polemical attack on bourgeois exploitation. The novel *Matigari* (1986) was translated into English in 1987. Plays: *The Black Hermit* (1962); *This Time Tomorrow* (1966); (with Micere Githae Mugo) *The Trial of Dedan Kimathi* (1976). Short stories: *Secret Lives* (1975). Other writings include: *Homecomings: Essays on African and Caribbean Literature, Culture and Politics* (1972); *Writers in Politics: Essays* (1981); *Detained: A Writer's Prison Diary* (1981); *Barrel of a Pen: Resistance to Repression in Neo-Colonial Kenya* (1983); *Decolonising the Mind: The Politics of Language in African Literature* (1986).

Nicholas Nickleby (1838–9)
A novel by ▷ Charles Dickens; like his other novels, it was first published in serial parts. Nicholas, his sister Kate and their mother are left penniless, and struggle for a living under the oppressive guardianship of Ralph Nickleby, an avaricious financier, the dead Mr Nickleby's brother. Morally, the tale is in black and white; Nicholas stands for ardent and youthful virtue, Ralph for meanness and cruelty. Nicholas is sent to teach at Dotheboys Hall, an iniquitous school run by Wackford Squeers to whom Nicholas gives a vigourous thrashing. Kate is apprenticed to Madame Mantalini, a dressmaker, where she is exposed to the vicious advances of Ralph's associate, Sir Mulberry Hawk. Nicholas beats him too. Ralph's evil intentions are eventually exposed by his eccentric but right-minded clerk, Newman Noggs, and the Nickleby family are befriended by the Cheeryble brothers. The novel is in Dickens' early, episodic and melodramatic style but many of the episodes are presented with great vividness and comedy. It was dramatized, with huge success, by the Royal Shakespeare Company in 1980.
▷ Education.

Nichols, Grace (b 1950)
Poet and novelist. Born in Guyana where she worked as a teacher, journalist and information assistant, and educated at the University of Guyana, Nichols came to live in Britain in 1977. Her publications include a biting attack on colonialism in *i is a long memoried woman* (1983) (which won the Commonwealth Poetry Prize), and the playfully ironic *The Fat Black Woman's Poems* (1984). Her first novel was *Whole of a Morning Sky* (1986), set in Guyana in the 1960s. She also writes ▷ children's books.
▷ Post-colonial fiction.

Nichols, John (1745–1826)
Historian. Nichols' antiquarian activities provided a useful source for literary activity; for example, his *The Progresses and Public Processions of Queen Elizabeth* (1788–1821) were used by ▷ Scott in his novel *Kenilworth*. He also provided a fascinating account of the literary activity of his day in *Literary Anecdotes of the Eighteenth Century* (1812–16) and *Illustrations of the Literary History of the Eighteenth century* (1817–58; completed by his son). During his lifetime, however, Nichols was considered somewhat old-fashioned and his editorship of ▷ *The Gentleman's Magazine* (1792–1826) led to it being dismissed by younger writers such as ▷ Hazlitt.
▷ Histories and Chronicles.

Nichols, Peter (b 1927)
British dramatist whose first major success was with *A Day in the Death of Joe Egg* in 1967, a serious comedy about the struggles of a family with a spastic child. This was first seen at the Glasgow Citizen's Theatre and later transferred to London. In 1969 *The National Health* was produced at the ▷ National Theatre. Again Nichols used comedy to dramatize a serious subject, in this case terminal illness and undignified death. His more recent plays are: *Passion Play* (1980); *Poppy*, a musical, (1982); *A Piece of My Mind* (1986).

Nietzsche, Friedrich Wilhelm (1844–1900)
German philosopher. He challenged the concepts of 'the good, the true, and the beautiful' as, in their existing form of abstract values, a decadent system at the mercy of the common man's will to level distinctions of all kinds. Instead he developed a number of counter-models – the will to power, the doctrine of eternal recurrence, the importance of self-overcoming. Among his more famous works are writings on the philosopher Schopenhauer and the composer Wagner, whom he regarded as his own teachers: *Unzeitgemässe Betrachtungen* ('Thoughts out of Season'; 1876); *Die Fröhliche Wissenschaft* ('The Joyful Wisdom'; 1882); *Also sprach Zarathustra* ('Thus spake Zarathustra'; 1891).

Critic Walter Kaufmann has argued for Nietzsche's position as one of the important progenitors of ▷ existentialism, and he had a considerable influence on some of the major

English writers in the first quarter of this century. His ideas inspired ▷ George Bernard Shaw in the latter's belief in the Superman-hero as the spearhead of progress, *eg* his conception of Joan of Arc in his play *Saint Joan*, and ▷ D. H. Lawrence wrote in Nietzsche's spirit in his affirmation of spontaneous living from deep sources of energy in the individual – human 'disquality' (see ▷ *Women in Love*, ch. 8) as opposed to democratic egalitarianism, although Lawrence also criticized (his conception of) Nietzsche's notion of Will to Power. Nietzsche also had a strong influence on the development of ▷ Freudian psychoanalysis, and this is indicative of the contradictory responses he has provoked in his readers: Lawrence was a vehement critic of Freud, and Freudian psychoanalysis is incompatible with existentialism, yet Nietzsche is said to have influenced all three. The Irish poet ▷ W. B. Yeats also affirmed a natural aristocracy of the human spirit, and saw in Nietzsche a continuation of the message of the poet William Blake (1757–1827), who preached the transcendance of the human 'identity' over the 'self', which is defined and limited by the material environment. In recent criticism Nietzsche's work has been re-evaluated by ▷ post-structuralist theory, especially with regard to his discussion of metaphor and metonymy and the privileging of a rhetorical reading of philosophical texts.

Nietzsche is also an important figure in the development of ▷ deconstruction, and (although deeply critical of the whole notion of 'influence'), has strongly influenced the writing of Georges Bataille, ▷ Michel Foucault and ▷ Jacques Derrida.

▷ German Influence on English Literature.

Bib: Deleuze, G., *Nietzsche and Philosophy*; Descombes, V., *Modern French Philosophy*; Kaufmann, W., *Nietzsche: Philosopher, Psychologist, Antichrist.*

Night Thoughts on Life, Death, and Immortality

▷ Young, Edward.

Nightingale, Ode to a

▷ Odes, Keats'.

Nightmare Abbey (1818)

A novel by ▷ Thomas Love Peacock. It is a satire on the current taste for ▷ Gothic mystery and romantic despair. Mr Glowry and his son Scythrop own the Abbey; Scythrop is in love with two girls, like Peacock's friend, the poet ▷ Shelley. Mr Flosky is a satirical portrait of ▷ Coleridge in his aspect as a transcendental mystic, and Mr Cypress represents ▷ Byron's self-centredness. There are other characters of cheerful temperament to counteract the romantic sombreness of these. The plot is slight, but the comic fantasy is sustained by it and by the conversations, which are always the greater part of a Peacock novel.

Nine Worthies

The subject of literary, artistic and dramatic representation from the later medieval period onwards, the so-called 'Nine Worthies' is a group representing the best knights of all time, made up of three figures each from the periods of pagan, Old Testament and Christian history. Composition of the list, especially the Christian representatives, may vary somewhat but most of the versions found in England include Hector, ▷ Alexander, ▷ Julius Caesar, Joshua, David, Judas Maccabeus, ▷ King Arthur, ▷ Charlemagne, Godfrey of Bouillon. The 'Nine Worthies' theme promotes the notion of chivalry as a transhistorical phenomenon and is part of the developing mythology of knighthood, in evidence throughout the medieval period (and after). The list of Nine Worthies is first recorded in an Old French Alexander narrative of the early 14th century, and a dramatized pageant of the 'Nine Worthies' is included in ▷ Shakespeare's ▷ *Love's Labour's Lost.*

Nineteenth Century, The

A monthly review founded in 1877 by J.T. Knowles, its first editor. It was renamed *The Nineteenth Century and After* in 1900, and *The Twentieth Century* in 1950. It was distinguished for bringing together leading antagonists of opposing views. Contributors included ▷ Ruskin, ▷ Gladstone, ▷ T.H. Huxley, ▷ Beatrice Webb, ▷ William Morris, ▷ 'Ouida' and ▷ Oscar Wilde.

Nineties' Poets

The group of poets centred around the ▷ Rhymer's Club in the 1890s, including ▷ Lionel Johnson, ▷ Ernest Dowson and ▷ Arthur Symons. The Rhymer's Club met at the Cheshire Cheese tavern near Fleet Street, immortalized by W.B. Yeats (1865–1939) in *The Trembling of the Veil* and 'The Grey Rock,' and published two volumes of its members' verse in 1891 and 1894. Nineties poetry was part of the *fin-de-siècle* ▷ Aesthetic movement. Strongly influenced by ▷ French culture and particularly French ▷ Symbolist poetry, it was also a development of the work and ideas of ▷ Algernon Swinburne, ▷ Walter Pater and the ▷ Pre-Raphaelite Brotherhood. The confessional and ▷ decadent quality of their work, together with the incidence of untimely death in their lives, led Yeats to label them 'The Tragic Generation' in his *Autobiographies.* They were important in their influence on poets like Yeats and Ezra Pound (1885–1912). Much of their work was published in the journals ▷ *Yellow Book* and *The Savoy* (which Symons edited).

Bib: Stanford, D., *Poets of the Nineties*; Thornton, R.K.R., *Poetry of the 'Nineties.*

Nisbet, Robert (b 1941)
Short story writer. Born at Haverfordwest, Pembrokeshire, educated at University College, Swansea, and at the University of Essex, subsequently becoming a teacher of English at Milford Haven, Robert Nisbet is the author of six collections of short stories, in chronological order as follows: *Dreams and Dealings* (1973); *The Rainbow's End* (1979); *Sounds of the Town* (1982); *Stories of Sheepskin* (1983); *Downmarket* (1988); and *The Ladybird Room* (1991). He has also edited two anthologies of stories, *Dismays and Rainbows* (1979) and *Pieces of Eight* (1982) and has published a collection of poetry, *Pastoral* (1983). His short stories evoke an inner life behind their details, thus celebrating the richness of the ordinary.

***No Wit, No Help Like a Woman* (1613)**
A high-spirited comedy by ▷ Thomas Middleton which evolves on a complex double-plot level and reworks material from ▷ Ben Jonson's ▷ *Epicoene* and ▷ Shakespeare's ▷ *Twelfth Night*. The play's heroine, Kate Low-water, a disguised married woman intent on recovering her lost fortune, is one of the most charismatic female characters in the drama of the period. The extent to which the play's idiom of mercenary ▷ citizen comedy becomes submerged in Shakespearean romance depends largely on Kate's magnetic personality.

Noble Savage, The
▷ Primitivism.

Noh plays
A kind of drama practised in Japan since the 15th century. It is highly formal, austere, and ritualistic, making a great part of its effect through ▷ symbolism. Its artistic economy and symbolism have greatly interested some Western writers in the 20th century – see the book, *Noh, or Accomplishment* by Fenollosa and ▷ Pound. The poet ▷ W. B. Yeats imitated the form in some of his experiments to revive the verse drama, *eg At the Hawk's Well* (1917).

Nokes, James (d 1696)
Actor. Nokes performed briefly at the Cockpit in Drury Lane, largely in women's roles, before joining the ▷ Duke's Company under ▷ William D'Avenant in 1660 as actor and shareholder. He usually played in low and crude comic roles, specializing as foolish old husbands, nurses, and fops.

Nominalism
One of the two main schools of late medieval philosophy, the other being ▷ realism. The nominalists argued that terms naming things according to their kinds ('animal', 'vegetable', etc) and abstract terms ('beauty', 'goodness', etc) are merely names describing the qualities of things and do not refer to things that have reality in themselves. The realists argued that on the contrary such 'universals' alone have an ultimate reality and that the reality of individual objects depends upon them. The nominalist viewpoint is represented in modern philosophy by such thinkers as ▷ John Stuart Mill and other 'empiricist' philosophers who reason that reality can only be known by particular experience of it, and argue against any theory of implanted ideas such as the Deists believed in. In 20th-century political philosophy, nominalism has been opposed to essentialism (which resembles realism by believing in transcendent universals); see Karl Popper, *The Poverty of Historicism*.
Bib: Knowles, D., *The Evolution of Medieval Thought*.

Nonsense literature
This covers several kinds of literature, which have in common that they all in some way deliberately defy logic or common sense, or both. In English folk literature, many ▷ nursery rhymes come into the category. The most important kind, however, is undoubtedly in ▷ children's literature, especially the poems of Edward Lear and the *Alice* stories by Lewis Carroll, both of which are to be taken seriously as literature. Both writers are ▷ Victorian and this perhaps accounts for their imaginative depth; they wrote in a period of intense mental restlessness before the time of ▷ Freud and thus they gave themselves wholly to their fantasies, undisturbed by the idea that they might be betraying secrets of their own nature. Modern writers, *eg* ▷ James Joyce in his ▷ *Finnegans Wake*, will as fearlessly reveal their depths, but it will not be to children. Another reason why nonsense literature reached its peak in the Victorian period is perhaps that this was almost the earliest period when intelligent minds considered that children were worth writing for merely in order to amuse them, and not to elevate their minds. Twentieth-century writers in plenty have thought children worth amusing but the child-public is now a recognized one, whereas Lear and Carroll wrote for a few young friends; they were thus as much concerned with their own interest and amusement as with that of their audience.

Norman Conquest, The
▷ Conquest, The (Norman).

Norris, Leslie (b 1921)
Poet and short story writer. Leslie Norris was born on a farm near Merthyr Tydfil, Glamorgan, and was educated (as was Glyn Jones) at Cyfarthfa Castle Grammar School in Merthyr, and afterwards at Coventry College

of Education and Southampton University. His teaching career, as teacher, headmaster, college lecturer and Visiting Professor, has taken him to England and thence to the USA, though since 1974 he has earned his living as a full-time writer. The emotional base of his writing is his childhood experiences in Merthyr, then in its last phase of 'metropolitan' vitality, where in poems about boxers, horses, greyhounds, birds, and especially the colourful characters of the town, he responds to an integration of literary and physical life in that community which World War II was to terminate. Nevertheless, Leslie Norris is an exile at two removes – to England, where he lectured at Bognor Regis College of Education in West Sussex, and more recently to the University of Washington, Seattle and the Brigham Young University of Utah, though maintaining until recently a cottage in North Carmarthenshire to keep alive his Welsh roots. Thus it is not surprising that Welsh poetic influences, such as Vernon Watkins, and English ones, such as Edward Thomas and Andrew Young, the latter a close friend, merge in his poetry about natural life, birds, beasts and flowers, expressed often in formal, almost Georgian metric. A deep melancholy is more overtly discernable in his later work and adds poignancy to his reminiscences of childhood. His American experiences have made his poetry more diffuse and urbane, the emphasis being more descriptive, but his contact with Wales has not been diminished. His collections of poetry are: *The Tongue of Beauty* (1941); *Poems* (1944); *The Lord Winter* (1967); *Finding Gold* (1967); *Ransoms* (1970); *Mountains Polecats Pheasants* (1974); *Islands off Maine* (1977); *Merlin and the Snake's Egg* (1978 – poems for children); *Water Voices* (1980); and *A Sea in the Desert* (1989). His collected poems have been published in an American edition under the title of *Walking the White Fields* (1980) and his *Selected Poems*, in Britain, in 1986. A *Collected* volume is in course of preparation and includes many new poems which show exciting developments both in his poetic technique and in his thematic material. His prose works include two volumes of short stories, *Sliding* (1978) and *The Girl from Cardigan* (1988), and he also published a monograph on Glyn Jones in the *Writers of Wales* series in 1973.
Bib: Stephens, M. (Ed.), *The Oxford Companion to the Literature of Wales*; Jones, G. and Rowlands, J., *Profiles.*

***North and South* (1854–5)**
A novel by ▷ Elizabeth Gaskell, published serially in ▷ Charles Dickens' periodical ▷ *Household Words. North and South* explores the contrast between the rural south and the industrial north of England, as the heroine, Margaret Hale, moves from Hampshire to Lancashire. During a dispute between workers and employers, she encounters Mrs Thornton and her son John, an inflexible and unsympathetic manufacturer. Margaret finds Thornton's attitudes repellent at first, but gradually the couple move closer together and are finally united. Margaret comes to appreciate and respect both the mill owner and his workers, while Thornton, through Margaret's influence, adopts a more humane attitude towards his employees. Like Gaskell's ▷ *Mary Barton, North and South* was an important ▷ 'social problem' novel of the mid-Victorian period, but the work achieves an added richness through its exploration of religious doubt and its use of industrial unrest as a symbolic register of sexual awareness. Recent feminist critics have argued that it promotes the spread of maternal values outside the sphere of the home and into the commercial world.

North Briton, The
A radical political weekly, started in 1762 by ▷ John Wilkes and ▷ Charles Churchill. It opposed the government of ▷ George III and his Prime Minister, the Scotsman Lord Bute, and was aimed particularly against Bute's journal *The Briton*, edited by the Scottish novelist ▷ Tobias Smollett. After 45 issues it was suppressed.

North, Sir Thomas (?1535–?1601)
Translator. He is especially known as the translator of ▷ Plutarch's *Lives* of the ancient Greek and Roman heroes. The translation was from the French of Amyot, and was published in 1579. It was not close, but very clear and vigorous, and constituted one of the masterpieces of English prose. It was widely read in ▷ Shakespeare's day, and was used by Shakespeare himself as the basis for his plays ▷ *Julius Caesar*, ▷ *Antony and Cleopatra* and ▷ *Coriolanus*. Other translations by North were the *Dial of Princes* (from *Reloj de Principes* by Guevara) published in 1557, which set the fashion for ornate writing culminating in ▷ Lyly's ▷ *Euphues*; and *The Moral Philosophy of Doni* (1570), an Italian collection of eastern fables.
Bib: Cowley, C. H., *The First English Translators of the Classics*.

***Northanger Abbey* (1818)**
A novel by ▷ Jane Austen. It was started in 1798 and incompletely revised when it was published (in 1818 after her death) with her last completed novel ▷ *Persuasion*.

The book is in part a satire on the sensational and sentimental literature of the time, particularly of the enormously popular ▷ *Mysteries of Udolpho* by ▷ Mrs Radcliffe. The heroine is an ingenuous young girl, Catherine Morland, who visits the fashionable resort of Bath and afterwards, with some friends she has made there, the country house of Northanger Abbey. She is healthy-minded and trusting but very suggestible; on the one hand she is entirely deceived by the worldly flattery of her scheming friend, Isabella Thorpe, who tries to marry Catherine's brother under the mistaken impression that he is very rich, and on the other hand she suspects (under the influence of Mrs Radcliffe's novel) that Northanger Abbey conceals terrible secrets. Its owner, General Tilney, is the father of the man she loves and is in fact almost as cold-hearted and inhumane as she suspects him of being, but in quite a different way; he has not, as she at first suspected, murdered his wife, but he turns Catherine out of the house at very short notice from purely mercenary motives. The theme of the book is partly the danger of confusing literature and life, a theme to which Jane Austen returns in *Sense and Sensibility* and ⊳ *Emma*; it is also that life is as surprising and remorseless as the most romantic literature but in quite a different way.

⊳ Roche, Regina Maria.

Northcliffe, Alfred Harmsworth, Viscount (1865–1922)
One of the principal founders of the 'popular press' with its very large circulation, and in particular of the *Daily Mail* (1896).

⊳ Newspapers.

Norton, Caroline (1808–77)
Poet, novelist, dramatist and campaigner. She was the granddaughter of the dramatist Richard Sheridan (1751–1816), and married George Norton in 1827. The marriage was disastrous, and in 1836 her husband brought an action for adultery against Lord Melbourne, who had frequented Caroline Norton's literary salon. The divorce case collapsed for lack of evidence, but Norton's sexual reputation was severely damaged. She then began a long struggle to gain access to and custody of her children, publishing *A Plain Letter to the Lord Chancellor on the Infant Custody Bill* (1839) under the ⊳ pseudonym Pearce Stevenson. Her efforts resulted in a change in the law in 1839. She later campaigned for the property rights of divorced women in *English Laws for Women in the 19th Century* (1854). She cannot be described as a ⊳ feminist, however, since she believed in male superiority and sought legal change only on the basis that individual cases existed in which men had failed in their responsibilities. Norton's novels, which were admired in her day, include *The Wife and Woman's Reward* (1835); *Stuart of Dunleath* (1851); *Lost and Saved* (1863). Poetry includes *The Sorrows of Rosalie* (1829); *The Undying One* (1830) and *The Dream* (1840).

⊳ Marriage.

Bib: Ackland, A., *Life*: Perkins, J.G., *Life*.

Norton, Sir Thomas (1532–84)
Poet and dramatist. A staunchly ⊳ Protestant barrister, Norton participated in the questioning of Catholics during ⊳ Elizabeth I's reign, as well as translating ⊳ Calvin's *Institutes* (1561). He is best known to literature students, however, for his collaboration with ⊳ Thomas Sackville in the composition of ⊳ *Gorboduc* (1561), which is assumed to be the first 'English' ⊳ tragedy. Written in ⊳ blank verse, it was enormously influential. Norton's poetry was included in ⊳ *Tottel's Miscellany*.

***Nostromo* (1904)**
A novel by ⊳ Joseph Conrad. The setting is an imaginary South American state called Costaguana, intended to be typical of that continent; all the events occur in or near Sulaco, capital city of the Occidental Province in Costaguana. At the beginning of the novel, Costaguana is ruled by a brutal and corrupt dictator after a short period of enlightened and liberal rule. The Occidental Province, however, remains a refuge of enlightenment and comparative prosperity, thanks partly to its geographical isolation from the rest of the country, and mainly to the existence of a large silver mine, run by an Englishman, Charles Gould, who secures the financial support of an American millionaire. In outline, the story is the history of how the Occidental Republic establishes its independence of the rest of the country, but at the same time loses the ideals which inspired it in the struggle.

Each of five main characters serves as a focus for a strand of narrative:

1 Charles Gould (nicknamed 'King of Sulaco'), in his struggles to save the mine from ruin by the corrupt government, becomes the centre of the party of freedom and justice; but he becomes increasingly dehumanized by his preoccupations, and estranged from his wife, whose values of humaneness and compassion are betrayed, despite the eventual triumph of her husband's party.

2 Captain Mitchell, the Harbourmaster, is another Englishman; stupid, but honest and courageous, he is unable to see beneath the surface of events, and is used by Conrad to record these deceptive appearances.

3 Gian'Battista Fidanza, the Italian chief of the dockworkers, is universally known as 'Nostromo' ('Our Man'). He has a romantic pride in the devotion of his men, and in the knowledge that Mitchell, Gould, and their associates have complete confidence in his integrity. His spiritual downfall, unknown to any but himself, is due to his desire to preserve the appearance of integrity while yielding to secret dishonesty.

4 Martin Decoud is the journalist of the Sulacan revolution; he is totally French by education and culture, though not by descent. He is cynically entertained by the spectacle of Costaguaneran politics, but romantically attached to Antonia Avellanos, daughter of José, a Sulacan scholar and liberal politician. He

dies of the physical isolation brought upon him by circumstances, since his highly cultivated consciousness is incapable of sustaining a sense of his own reality when the spectacle of events and the woman he loves are removed from him.

5 Dr Monygham is an Irishman, embittered by his self-contempt arising from his betrayal, under torture, of his political associates. His humanity is preserved by his devotion to Mrs Gould, who is for him the uncontaminated embodiment of what is good in human nature.

These are only the chief characters, and they do not exhaust the novel's large cast. They are united by the theme of individual isolation even in co-operation with one another, and by a discrete pattern of symbols, of which the chief is the silver of the mine. This operates at first as an instrument of liberation, and later as a force of corruption; all the time it is a symbol of the illusiveness of human idealism. The novel depicts the pervasive and debasing effects of 'material interests' (primarily the economic power of US business). The narrative structure is highly complex, and uses shifts of chronology and retrospective narration to combine a detailed account of 17 days of crisis with a sense of the broad sweep of historical events.

***Nouveau roman* (new novel)**

A French literary movement originating in the late 1950s and associated principally with Nathalie Sarraute (b 1902), Claude Simon (b 1913), Michel Butor (b 1926), Robert Pinget (b 1919) and Alain Robbe-Grillet (b 1922). Their common concern was a challenge to narrative assumptions based on strictures of the orderly unfolding of plot and life-like characters moving in a recognizable universe. These assumptions, however widely held, suppose that literature is mimetic, that it imitates life. The *nouveau roman* set out to challenge the illusion of reference (that the novel 'refers' to life) insofar as reference is tied to representation. It held that the so-called naturalness of narrative was a set of artifices to which we had become accustomed and that narrative order and significance were an illusion fostered by the omniscient author. For the 'new' novelists, representation is not an a priori given; it is produced. Drawing on the work of ▷ André Gide and ▷ Marcel Proust, notably Gide's ▷ *mise en abyme* technique, the *nouveau roman* will therefore expose its own means of production and raise the problem of its own narrative existence. Correspondingly, the role of the reader is also revised. He or she is called upon to co-author the text, to act not as a passive recipient of information, but as an active producer of meanings. Indeed, given the fragmentary or elliptical nature of *nouveau roman* narrative presentation, the reader's search for meaning is often thematized as an (impossible) attempt to solve an enigma (the *nouveau roman* frequently adopts the detective story format).

The impact of the *nouveau roman* was greatly magnified by the fact that the practice of novel writing was accompanied by thorough-going critical reflection on that practice. The novelists themselves were also heavily engaged in theory and frequently worked alongside professional academic theoreticians or were allied to magazines such as *Tel Quel*. Of the original group of new novelists, Robbe-Grillet and Simon are still strong practitioners. While the mainstream of the English novel has been little affected, the techniques of the *nouveau roman* have influenced writers such as ▷ Christine Brooke-Rose and ▷ Brigid Brophy. In the 1970s there emerged the new new novel (*nouveau nouveau roman*), centring on the novelist and theorist Philippe Sollers (b 1936) and displaying many of the traits of ▷ deconstructive and ▷ post-structuralist principles.

Bib: Robbe-Grillet, A., *Pour un Nouveau Roman*.

Nouveaux Philosophes, Les

A title coined by the magazine *Les Nouvelles littéraires* in June 1976 to describe a group of writers among whom the most prominent are André Glucksmann (*Les Maîtres penseurs*, 1977; reviewed by Michel Foucault) and Bernard-Henri Lévy (*La Barbarie à visage humain*, 1977; *L'Idéologie française*, 1981). The group combined certain traits of Foucault and ▷ Jacques Lacan (often simplified and distorted) with right-wing views – hostility to Marxism, vague spiritual yearning and finding the source of all value in the individual. As a group, their influence was at its height in the late 1970s and is now played out (it was in any case media-promoted), but Glucksmann and Lévy are still well known.

Novel in verse

The novel in verse is not a recognized or clearly defined genre; most candidates for inclusion in this category belong to other, well-established genres: ▷ *The Odyssey* is an epic; ▷ *Sir Gawain and the Green Knight* (late 14th century) is an alliterative romance; Wordsworth's autobiographical *magnum opus*, *The Prelude* (1805), is a philosophical poem; Byron's ▷ *Don Juan* (1819–24) is a mock-epic satire. The category is worth proposing only because it indicates a fruitful area of overlap between the novel and other genres, including some curiosities such as *Amours de Voyage* (1858) by Arthur Hugh Clough, which is a short ▷ epistolary novel in verse. ▷ David Jones' *In Parenthesis*, a sustained narrative about the First World War, is partly in verse and partly in prose that is so poetic it might be termed a prose poem; the poet Ezra Pound described his modernist sequence of poems, *Hugh Selwyn Mauberley* (1920), as 'an attempt to condense the [Henry] James novel'. There have been some remarkable recent achievements in this area: *Omeros* (1990), by the poet Derek Walcott, is a lyrical and poetic reworking of Homeric epic in a Caribbean context, but contains some richly novelistic description, characterization and episode. *Love, Death and the Changing of the Seasons* (1987), by the American poet Marilyn Hacker, is the story of a lesbian relationship, recounted with a witty intensity that places it in the tradition of the Renaissance sonnet sequence, whereas ▷ Vikram Seth's *The Golden Gate* (1986), although written entirely in a variation of sonnet form, is essentially a novel: plot and character predominate, rather than linguistic artifice and meditation.

Novel of manners
This term is often used to designate a particular genre within 19th-century ▷ realism exemplified in the work of such authors as Jane Austen (1775–1817), ▷ Balzac, ▷ Turgenev, ▷ Trollope, ▷ Thackeray and ▷ Henry James. The novels characteristically analyse the individual and the social by bringing together representatives of two different social groups in such a way as to highlight the other's behaviour code by contrast. The plot mechanism usually hinges on love relationships between these representatives (who may stand for town and country; north and south; the *nouveau riche* and the aristocracy or, in Henry James' case, the United States and Europe) and whether the differences in their code of manners can be resolved by marriage. The mode is therefore an excellent vehicle for dissecting the marital economy, relations between the sexes and the social determination of love. It was perceived by hostile critics, including the ▷ naturalist writers of 1870 onwards, as overly genteel. The US novelist Frank Norris characterized the style as 'the tragedy of the broken teacup'. This is a misapprehension however, as, in the hands of its major exponents, larger aspects of the human condition such as love, sex, class and war are not so much avoided as refracted through social behaviour codes in a subtle, heavily nuanced and psychologically complex fashion. The genre continued in the 20th century with novels such as E.M. Forster's *A Passage to India* (1924) and is negotiated in Virginia Woolf's *To the Lighthouse* (1927) and *Mrs Dalloway* (1925).

Novella
In modern usage the novella is a long short story or short novel, such as ▷ Joseph Conrad's ▷ *Heart of Darkness* (1902), or ▷ Henry James' *The Aspern Papers* (1888). The French term '*nouvelle*' is sometimes used with the same meaning. The *novella* (Italian), or *nouvelle* (French), was also a Renaissance genre, a short prose narrative of the sort found in ▷ Boccaccio's ▷ *Decameron*, and was one of the forms out of which the novel developed.

***Novum Organum* (1620)**
A philosophical treatise by Francis Bacon, the *Novum Organum* (*New Instrument*) was written in Latin and published in the ▷ *Instauratio Magna* (1620) in an incomplete form. His aim was to describe a method of gaining power over nature through a complete and correctly founded system of knowledge. Knowledge must be acquired by experience and experiment, *ie* inductively. The obstacles to true knowledge are false assumptions, which Bacon calls 'Idols'. These are of four kinds: the Idols of the Tribe are common human weaknesses such as allowing the emotions to interfere with the reason; the Idols of the Cave are individual weaknesses arising from individual upbringing; Idols of the Market-place arise from erroneous uses of language, such as using names for non-existent things, or for concepts which have been inadequately defined; Idols of the Theatre are caused by false philosophical principles and by incorrect reasoning. The object of speculative science must be to discover the true 'forms' of things, beginning with the forms of 'simple natures', *ie* the true manifestations of the most elemental phenomena such as heat and light. By inductive experiment certain axioms will be made of increasing generality and abstractness. Thus Bacon sought a method of recognizing what he called 'an alphabet of nature' so that a reliable language could be built up from it. The method of discovery proved too slow to be scientifically useful in the coming centuries, but his approach was a development from the too exclusively deductive methods of medieval thought towards the modern scientific combination of deduction and experiment.

N-Town Cycle
A collection of plays, recounting episodes from Christian history, formerly called the *Ludus Conventriae Cycle* because it was mistakenly linked to the town of Coventry. But unlike the other examples of cycles from the late medieval period in England (such as ▷ York, ▷ Chester), this sequence of plays cannot be linked to any specific town. The Banns announce that it will be performed at 'n town'; which suggests the sequence was scripted to be performed at different towns, using a fixed stage setting, not pageant waggons. The text seems to have originated from the East Midlands area, but there are no records of its performance. The scholarly consensus currently is that this collection is a fifteenth-century compilation made up from parts of longer plays about the life of Mary and the Passion with additional pageants from an earlier sequence.
Bib: Spector, S. (ed.), *The N-Town Play.*

Nuns and Nunneries
Monastic orders in the Middle Ages had female as well as male branches; most English nuns belonged to the ▷ Benedictine Order. They lived in 'nunneries', later increasingly known as 'convents', though originally a convent might house either sex. They were ruled by elected

prioresses or abbesses. Until the 14th century nuns were usually from aristocratic families; among the lower classes it was generally possible for a woman to work; but in the upper classes, a nunnery was the only alternative to marriage. Before the ▷ Norman Conquest (1066) nunneries compared with monasteries as places of learning, but afterwards the nuns were seldom as learned, though they excelled in such accomplishments as embroidery. From the 14th century merchants' daughters as well as girls from noble families were increasingly admitted. Nunneries were sometimes used as places of confinement for girls who refused to marry the husbands of their parents' choice, etc. Manual work was neglected from the 13th century and conducted by lay servants, as in monasteries, but nunneries sometimes ran small schools for the children of well-to-do families. Nuns who wished to live a life dedicated to solitary meditation were called 'anchoresses'; such was the mystical writer ▷ Juliana of Norwich.

Nun's Priest Tale, The

One of ▷ Chaucer's ▷ *Canterbury Tales*. The Nun's Priest, who is barely mentioned in the General Prologue, contributes a brilliant animal fable to the competition which greatly amplifies the traditional story of the cock who is captured by the fox, but who manages to escape by exploiting the fox's pride in his achievement. The story has analogues in ▷ Marie de France's collection of fables, and in the 13th-century beast epic, the *Roman de Renart* (▷ Reynard the Fox), but Chaucer's version is distinguished by its enormous build-up to the fox's assault. Much of the early section of the *Tale* is taken up with an argument over the value of dreams between Chauntecleer, the cock, and his hen-consort, Pertelote, which is prompted by the cock's dream of being attacked by a large red animal. Problems about how to extract meaning from dream narratives, raised in their debate, are relevant to the *Tale* as a whole, which ends with a challenge to the reader to extract the moral 'fruit' from this brilliantly inflated, mock-heroic animal fable.

Nurseries

Training establishments for actors and actresses in the Restoration period.

Nut-Brown Maid, The

A 15th-century anonymous poem, first printed in 1502. It is in 30 12-line stanzas, spoken by a young man and woman alternately, with the respective refrains 'Alone a banished man' and 'I love but you alone', and their debate focuses on the faithfulness of women. Although the woman believes her lover to be an outlaw, she remains true.

Nwapa, Flora (b 1931)

Nigerian novelist and short-story writer. Much of Nwapa's fiction is concerned with questions of isolation, support and autonomy, as they bear on women. Her novels are: *Efuru* (1966); *Idu* (1970); *One is Enough* (1981 – the title refers to husbands); *Women Are Different* (1986). Volumes of short stories: *This Is Lagos* (1986); *Wives at War* (1980).

Bib: James, A., *In Their Own Voices: Interviews with African Women Writers*.

O

Oates, Titus (1649–1705)
An English conspirator. He was the son of a Puritan preacher, and himself professed to stand for the defence of ▷ Protestantism against supposed Catholic dangers, but he was really a disreputable adventurer who used the religious passions of the time for his personal advantage. In 1678 he fabricated the Popish Plot, by which he pretended without factual basis to expose a Catholic conspiracy against the ▷ Church of England. Popular suspicion of ▷ Charles II, and the fact that the Queen and his brother James were avowed Roman Catholics, caused a national panic, and a large number of Catholics were put to death. His evidence was eventually proved false, and he was imprisoned. He is satirized under the name of Corah in Dryden's ▷ *Absalom and Achitophel*.

Oberon
In Germanic myth, king of the elves, or fairies. A French 13th-century romance, *Huon of Bordeaux*, in which he occurs, was translated into English in 1534. From this ▷ Robert Greene introduced him into his romantic play ▷ *James IV* (1594), and ▷ Shakespeare into his comedy ▷ *A Midsummer Night's Dream*. He was used thereafter in a number of works, including a ▷ masque by ▷ Ben Jonson (in which ▷ Prince Henry is identified with Oberon) and the poem *Nymphidia* by ▷ Michael Drayton.
▷ Fairies.

Objective correlative
An expression first used by the critic and poet ▷ T. S. Eliot, in his essay on ▷ Shakespeare's play, *Hamlet* (1919). Eliot describes Shakespeare's play as an artistic failure because it 'is full of some stuff that the writer could not drag to life, contemplate, or manipulate into art'. He goes on: 'The only way of expressing emotion in the form of art is by finding an "objective correlative"; in other words, a set of objects, a situation, a chain of events which shall be the formula of that *particular* emotion; such that when the external facts . . . are given, the emotion is immediately evoked'. He then instances the sleep-walking scene in *Macbeth* as a successful 'objective correlative', and adds: 'The artistic "inevitability" lies in this complete adequacy of the external (*ie* the event on the stage is witnessed by the audience) to the emotion; and this is precisely what is deficient in *Hamlet*.'

Eliot's adverse judgement of *Hamlet* has not been widely accepted, but the term 'objective correlative' has passed into critical currency.

O'Brien, Edna (b 1932)
Novelist and short-story writer, born in County Clare, Ireland. Novels include: *The Country Girls* (1960); *The Lonely Girl* (1962) (as *Girl With Green Eyes*, 1964); *Girls in Their Married Bliss* (1964); *August is a Wicked Month* (1965); *Casualties of Peace* (1967); *A Pagan Place* (1970); *Night* (1972); *Johnny I Hardly Knew You* (1977); and *The High Road* (1988). Her novels are concerned primarily with women's experience of loss, guilt and self-division; they are characterized by a certain lyricism and nostalgia, combined with a detached humour which has become more bitter as her work has developed.

Her first three novels form a trilogy about the lives of two contrasted women, and use a realistic mode which is replaced by internal monologues in some of her later work. Her style is very effective in the short-story form: *The Love Object* (1968); *A Scandalous Woman* (1974); *Mrs Reinhardt* (1978); *Returning* (1982); *A Fanatic Heart: Selected Stories* (1984). She has also written plays, screenplays and T.V. plays.

O'Brien, Flann (1911–66)
Pseudonym of Brian Nolan, author of hilarious, learned, parodic, linguistically exuberant novels, which anticipate many features of ▷ post-modernist metafiction: *At Swim-Two-Birds* (1939), which incorporates pastiche and parody of Irish folklore; *An Béal Bocht* (1941 in Gaelic, translated 1973 as *The Poor Mouth*); *The Third Policeman* (written 1940, published 1967). O'Brian was born in County Tyrone and educated at University College Dublin; he was a civil servant and also wrote a weekly satirical column in the *Irish Times*.

Observer, The
A ▷ newspaper published only on Sundays, started in 1792. It is central in its politics, and aims to appeal to a liberal and left-wing readership. In 1993 it was bought by the daily newspaper The *Guardian*.

O'Casey, Sean (1880–1964)
Irish dramatist best known for his three plays about tenement life in Dublin around the time of Irish independence in 1921. These were first performed at the ▷ Abbey Theatre: *The Shadow of a Gunman* (1923), *Juno and the Paycock* (1924) and *The Plough and the Stars* (1926). The last of these was greeted with a riot on its opening night. His next play, *The Silver Tassie* (1928), was an anti-heroic piece which experimented with expressionistic techniques. The play was rejected for performance at the Abbey by ▷ W. B. Yeats. After this O'Casey lived in England in self-imposed exile until his death. With *The Star Turns Red* (1940), *Purple Dust* (1940), *Red Roses for Me* (1943), *Oak Leaves and Lavender* (1947), *Cock-a-Doodle Dandy* (1949) and *The Bishop's Bonfire* (1961), he continued experimenting with non-

naturalistic theatrical devices. These later plays deserve greater recognition than they have been given to date.

▷ Irish literature in English.

Bib: Kosok, H., *O'Casey the Dramatist*; Krause, D., *Sean O'Casey: The Man and His Work*.

Ockham (Occam), William of (?1300–?1349)
Philosopher and Franciscan friar. He was one of the leaders of the Nominalist school of philosophy, according to which individual things were considered to be real, but the names for kinds and classes referred to qualities of individuals only, and not to independent realities. This prepared the way for the thought of ▷ Francis Bacon which was in itself the starting point of modern scientific thinking, since Ockham's ideas implied building generalizations from the knowledge of individual objects instead of arguing from pre-established generalizations, as the more typically medieval Realists had reasoned.

The principle known as 'Ockham's Razor' lays down that 'entities' must not be unnecessarily invented, implying that abstractions must be somehow proved to have a necessary relationship with known realities. The principle makes for exact thinking, and also for scepticism. He went so far as to say that the existence of God could not be proved, though he did not mean by this that God did not exist.

▷ Nominalism; Realism.

O'Connor, Frank (pen-name of Michael O'Donovan) (1903–66)
Irish writer, especially famous for his short stories. He was born in Cork, received little education, and for some time worked as a librarian in Cork and Dublin. He was encouraged to write by the Irish poet AE (George Russell), and his publisher, Harold Macmillan (later the British Conservative Party leader) influenced him in deciding for a literary career. He participated in the Irish Rebellion after World War I. His first volume of short stories, *Guests of the Nation*, was published in 1931. Other volumes are: *Bone of Contention* (1936), *Three Tales* (1941), *Crab Apple Jelly* (1944), *The Common Chord* (1948), *Traveller's Samples* (1951), *My Oedipus Complex* (1963). His translation of poetry and legends from the Irish are also famous: *A Golden Treasury of Irish Poetry* (1967). He wrote two novels which have less repute than his short stories: *The Saint and Mary Kate* (1932) and *Dutch Interior* (1966). His critical works include one of the best studies of the art of the short story, *The Lonely Voice*, and a study of the novel, *The Mirror in the Roadway*. He also published two volumes of an uncompleted autobiography, *An Only Child* and *My Father's Son*. From 1952 he taught in an American university.

O'Connor's stories are remarkable for their insight, comedy, pathos and compassion. His field was the lower ranges of Irish society, which he understood profoundly, and which he universalized by his generous intelligence and sympathies in a way that recalls Chekhov's treatment of Russian life.

Bib: Sheehy, Maurice (ed.), *Michael/Frank*.

Octavia
Half-sister of Octavius Caesar, who became the first Roman Emperor, ▷ Caesar Augustus (ruled 27 BC–AD 14) She married her brother's rival, Mark Antony, and occurs as a character in ▷ Shakespeare's tragedy *Antony and Cleopatra* and in ▷ Dryden's tragedy ▷ *All For Love*.

***Odd Women, The* (1893)**
A novel by ▷ George Gissing which deals with many of the issues found in the ▷ 'New Woman' novels of the 1890s. Three 'odd' or 'surplus' women – spinsters – are left penniless by their improvident father, and the story concerns the limited choices each is forced to make. Monica Madden is pretty enough to marry for economic security rather than love, while her sisters Alice and Virginia become worn out and dispirited working in the only available jobs of teacher and ▷ governess, supported by the vain belief that they will start a school one day. Rhoda Nunn and Mary Barfoot are placed in direct contrast to them. Energetic, resourceful and committed to women's independence and emancipation, they run a business school to train women for work in commerce. Their plans are disrupted by a mutual affection which grows up between Rhoda and Everard Barfoot, Mary's cousin, and Rhoda has to reconcile love with her desire for independence. Gissing's Rhoda foreshadows ▷ Thomas Hardy's Sue Bridehead in ▷ *Jude the Obscure*.

▷ *The Bostonians*; Lesbianism; Women's Movement.

Ode
The Pindaric ode is modelled on the works of ▷ Pindar, a Greek poet of the 5th century BC, best known for his odes celebrating the victors at the Olympic games. These were accompanied by music and dance, and were disposed in a threefold pattern corresponding to the movements of the Greek dramatic chorus (*strophe, antistrophe, epode*). From the 17th century onwards English poets took Pindar as a model for lyric and declamatory verse expressive of high-wrought emotion. ▷ Thomas Gray's *Progress of Poesy* follows Pindar's stanza forms with scholarly exactness, but ▷ Abraham Cowley had earlier established the more usual 'irregular ode', which sanctions unpredictable variations in line-length, rhyme and ▷ metre within each stanza. Early examples of this form are ▷ John Dryden's *Alexander's Feast*

and *Ode to the Memory of Anne Killigrew*. 'Pindarics' remained popular throughout the 18th century and became a natural vehicle for the new ▷ 'romantick' sensibility. Gray's use of them in ▷ *The Bard* and *The Progress of Poesy*, for all its scholarly meticulousness, is intended to sound bold and inspirational. The form remains essentially the same in such ▷ romantic works as ▷ William Wordsworth's ▷ *Ode: Intimations of Immortality* and ▷ Samuel Taylor Coleridge's ▷ *Dejection*, though by now it has lost its classical, 'Pindaric' associations, and is fully naturalized.

The Roman poet ▷ Horace imitated Pindar, but his odes employ unvarying stanza forms. The 'regular' Horatian ode was imitated by ▷ Andrew Marvell in his *Horatian Ode upon Cromwell's Return from Ireland*, and by ▷ William Collins in *How Sleep the Brave* and *To Simplicity*. ▷ John Keats' Odes, with their long and complex, but regular stanzas, lie somewhere between the Pindaric and Horatian form.

Odes, Keats'
▷ John Keats' six Odes: *On Indolence*, *On a Grecian Urn*, *On Melancholy*, *To Psyche*, *To a Nightingale*, and *To Autumn*, were all written in 1819. They are in regular stanzaic form, but the length of stanza and complexity of rhyme-scheme recalls the freer ▷ Pindaric tradition of the ode. They constitute the most complex expression of Keats' aestheticist approach to life. In each poem a celebration of sensuous beauty of the material world is rendered the more intensely poignant by an acknowledgement of transience and decay.

On a Grecian Urn and *To a Nightingale* are companion pieces, one concerned with Art, the other with Nature. Both urn and bird persuade the poet for a while that their beauty is permanent. The urn's message to Man is 'Beauty is truth, truth beauty', and the Nightingale seems an 'immortal bird', 'not born for death'. However the urn's comfort remains on its beautiful surface. Though a 'friend to man' it is a 'Cold Pastoral'. The beautiful figures depicted upon it, preserved from time by art, can never reachieve the trembling elusive life which they possessed when really alive. Their death and distance is paradoxically only accentuated by Keats' ecstatic, even hectic, celebration of its artistic immortality. Similarly, the nightingale's song, though unchanged through history, fades as the particular bird to which he is listening flies away, and Keats is returned to his 'sole self', admitting that 'the fancy cannot cheat so well/ As she is fam'd to do, deceiving elf'.

The Ode to Autumn contains no explicit philosophizing, and seems purely descriptive. It provides, however, an emotional answer to the problems of the previous odes. The images of the poem are beautiful precisely because the scene described is a transient moment in the flux of time. The poignant pleasure they give derives from their lack of permanence or stability: 'And gathering swallows twitter in the skies'. Keats is here expressing in his own way the paradox of the great prophet of ▷ Romanticism, ▷ William Blake: 'He who binds to himself a joy/ Does the winged life destroy;/ But he who kisses the joy as it flies/ Lives in eternity's sun rise.'

Odyssey
An ▷ epic by the ancient Greek poet ▷ Homer. The hero, ▷ Odysseus King of Ithaca, is on his way home after the Trojan war, but he is blown off course and the return journey takes him ten years. The principal episodes of his voyage are as follows:

1 The land of the Lotus-Eaters. Those who eat of the lotus plant forget their homeland.

2 The land of the ▷ Cyclops. These are a race of one-eyed giants. Odysseus puts out the eye of the Cyclops Polyphemus, who is son of ▷ Poseidon, god of the sea; it is to punish him for this that Poseidon sends him wandering for ten years.

3 The Isle of Aeolus, king of the winds. Odysseus steals from him the bag in which the winds are contained, but his companions open it too soon, and the winds escape.

4 Telepylus, the city of the cannibal Laestrygonians. They destroy his fleet except one ship, in which he escapes.

5 The Isle of ▷ Circe. She transforms his men into swine, but with the aid of the god ▷ Hermes, he resists her enchantments, compels her to restore his men, and remains in the island as her lover for a year.

6 He visits the Underworld, ▷ Hades, to learn from the prophet ▷ Tiresias the way home. Tiresias warns him against harming the cattle of the sun-god, Helios.

7 He evades the enchanting songs of the ▷ Sirens, who try to lure him on to the rocks.

8 He passes through the strait of Scylla and Charybdis – a treacherous rock and a whirlpool.

9 He comes to the Island of Thrinacia (Sicily) where the cattle of Helios live, which the ghost of Tiresias has warned him not to harm, but overcome by hunger, his companions devour them.

10 In punishment, his ship is wrecked and all his men perish, but Odysseus reaches the island of the goddess ▷ Calypso, who keeps him prisoner for seven years as her lover. He eventually escapes, with the aid of the goddess ▷ Athene, and reaches the lands of the Phaeacians where Nausicaa and her father, the king of the country, befriend him. The narrative of all the above events comes to the reader through Odysseus, who tells them to the king. The king helps him back to Ithaca. There, with the help of his son Telemachus, he kills the suitors who have been pestering the chaste Penelope, his queen. The *Odyssey* has had a considerable influence

upon the novel most notably ▷ *Ulysses*, by ▷ James Joyce.

Oedipus complex
In ▷ Freudian psychoanalysis Sophocles' story of Oedipus who killed his father and married his mother, is used as a model of the way in which human desires and feelings are structured during the passage from infancy to adulthood. The triangular relationship modelled on Sophocles' text can be used to explain relationships within the family which is the model of socialization available to the child. In order for successful socialization to occur, the child must emerge from the position of desiring an incestuous relationship with individual parents – for which in the case of the male, the penalty would be castration – and to transfer the affections for the mother on to another. The difficulties which this sometimes causes are illustrated in novels such as ▷ D. H. Lawrence's ▷ *Sons and Lovers* where Paul Morel is faced with having to transfer his affections for his mother onto other women. The Oedipus complex, and the model of triangulated desire upon which it is built, must be overcome in order for individual gendered human subjects to take their place in a world of which they are not the centre. This process of 'decentring' is explained by ▷ Jacques Lacan as an acceptance of the repression of desire imposed upon the subject by the father, an acceptance of a 'symbolic castration'. This raises a number of difficulties in the case of the gendered *female* subject who can never break free of the castration complex imposed upon her by a phallocentric ▷ symbolic order. Basically the Oedipus complex is used to account for a particular hierarchy of relationships within the family unit. It is a process through which the male is expected to pass in order to reach mature adulthood, and it seeks to offer an explanation of the ways in which authority operates as a system of constraints and laws.

▷ Psychoanalytic criticism.

Bib: Laplanche, J. and Pontalis, J. P., *The Language of Psychoanalysis*.

O'Faolain, Sean (b 1900)
Irish novelist and writer of short stories. He was born in Dublin and attended the National University of Ireland and Harvard University in the U.S.A. He participated in the Irish Rebellion following World War I, and later lived in England as a teacher. His novels include *A Nest of Simple Folk* (1933) and *Bird Alone* (1936). His first volume of stories, *Midsummer Night Madness* (1932), vividly reflects the atmosphere of the Irish disturbances. A collected edition of the stories was published in 1958, and in 1966 he published a further volume, *The Heat of the Sun*. Among his other writings are two biographies which are studies of Irish leaders, one on Daniel O'Connell entitled *King of the Beggars* (1938), and *The Great O'Neill* (1942). His critical work includes *The Short Story* (1948). His autobiography *Vive Moi!* appeared in 1965. He was made Director of the Arts Council of Ireland in 1957.

O'Flaherty, Liam (1897–1984)
Irish novelist and writer of short stories. Born in the Aran Islands he was educated for the Roman Catholic priesthood, but did not enter it. He fought in World War I, and settled in England in 1922. His first volume of stories, *Spring Sowing*, was published in 1926; it contains stories of Irish peasant life and wild nature. At his best, his stories have the intensity of fine lyric poetry, and he is peculiarly gifted at representing the exhilaration and poignancy of life directly exposed to natural forces. Other volumes of stories include: *The Mountain Tavern* (1929), *The Wild Swan* (1932), *Two Lovely Beasts* (1948). His novels include *The Informer* (1925 – made into a film in 1935) and the historical *Famine* (1937). His autobiography is entitled *Shame the Devil* (1934).

Og, king of Bashan
▷ *Absalom and Achitophel*.

Oisin
Also known as Ossian. In 1760–63, James Macpherson published a series of blank verse epics which he attributed to Ossian and claimed to have translated from the Gaelic. His version had an immense success and a wide influence; however, Macpherson was later proved not to have translated the poems, but to have synthesized them from a number of genuine Celtic legends, in which the hero Oisin occurs. Dr Johnson was among the earliest sceptics; when asked whether he thought any man 'of the modern age' could have written the poems, he replied: 'Yes, Sir, many men, many women, and many children.'

▷ W. B. Yeats wrote a narrative poem *The Wanderings of Oisin* (1889), the earliest of his attempts to create a new literature out of Celtic mythology. In the ancient legends Oisin bridged the gap between the heroic pagan age and Irish Christianity; his longevity was due to a long sojourn in Fairyland.

▷ *Celtic Twilight*; Irish Literature in English.

O'Keeffe, Adelaide (1776–1865)
Novelist and children's author. Daughter and amanuensis of the Irish dramatist ▷ John O'Keeffe, Adelaide would have certainly written down his most famous play, *Wild Oats* (1791), since she began copying for him when he became blind in 1788. O'Keeffe's father was the centre of her affections, and she wrote in order to sustain her family when he had to retire,

penning a touching memoir to him after his death (published with his poems as *O'Keeffe's Legacy to his Daughter*, 1834). She is best known for her *Original Poems for Infant Minds* (1804–5), which although ▷ didactic, are also spiced with a certain sense of disrespectful fun. Her novels are far more adventurous works for an adult readership, and include *Dudley* (1819) and *The Broken Sword* (1854), which deal with the emotional problems besetting families and are both perceptive and gently humorous.

O'Keeffe, John (1747–1883)
Actor and dramatist, who wrote many popular comedies and comic operas in the late 18th century. O'Keeffe was drawn to the stage by reading the plays of George Farquhar (1678–1707) and he wrote his first play, *The Gallant*, at the age of 15, later obtaining a post as an actor. In 1773 he took up writing seriously, and his farce, *Tony Lumpkin in Town*, based on Oliver Goldsmith's (1730–74) *She Stoops to Conquer*, was staged in Dublin, and afterwards at the Haymarket Theatre in London. His *Wild Oats, or the Strolling Gentleman* (1791) was revived by the Royal Shakespeare Company in 1976, with great success, largely because of the magnificent acting vehicle provided in the character of Rover. This play would have been written down by his daughter, the novelist ▷ Adelaide O'Keeffe, since John had become blind in 1788. O'Keeffe's autobiography was published in 1826.

Okri, Ben (b 1959)
Novelist and short-story writer, educated in Nigeria and at the University of Essex. During the 1980s he was poetry editor of *West Africa* magazine and worked for the BBC World Service 1984–5. *The Famished Road* (1991), which brought him widespread recognition, is narrated by a 'spirit child' and combines social realism with elements of the supernatural and of ▷ magic realism, producing a dream-like quality also found in many of his short stories, collected in *Incidents at the Shrine* (1986) and *Stars of the New Curfew* (1989). His other novels are: *Flowers and Shadows* (1980); *The Landscape Within* (1981); *Songs of Enchantment* (1993, sequel to *The Famished Road*); *Astonishing the Gods* (1995).

***Old Bachelor, The* (1693)**
Comedy by ▷ Congreve. After being seduced and abandoned by Vainlove, Silvia sets out to marry, pretending to be sexually inexperienced. Heartwell, the aged and surly 'old bachelor' of the title, falls in love with Silvia, and marries her. He later discovers to his relief that the marriage is a sham, as the parson was only Vainlove's friend Bellmour in disguise. Afterwards Silvia traps Sir Joseph Wittol into a genuine marriage. Bellmour loves Belinda, but at first she keeps him at a distance, knowing him to be a rake: eventually they marry. In another intrigue, Bellmour is attracted to the uxorious Fondlewife's wife Laeticia, whom Vainlove has wooed, as he woos any pretty woman. In this instance Vainlove allows Bellmour to reap the fruit of his labours: Bellmour goes to Laeticia's house, disguised as a Puritan preacher, and seduces her in her husband's absence. Fondlewife returns, but the lovers convince him that she has remained chaste. Araminta, another woman whom Vainlove pursues, loves him but resists him. At last they seem near to marrying, but the ending of their plot-line remains ambiguous. The play is lively and entertaining, but cynical in tone.

Old Comedy
▷ Aristophanes.

***Old Curiosity Shop, The* (1840-1)**
A novel by ▷ Charles Dickens; it was serialized as part of ▷ *Master Humphrey's Clock* in 1840–1 (published in book form in 1841).

The Curiosity Shop (a shop which sells second-hand goods of ornamental or rarity value) is kept by the grandfather of little Nell, Trent. The old man has been impoverished by the extravagances of his son-in-law and those of Fred Trent, Nell's brother. He is forced to borrow money from Quilp, a grotesque and malevolent dwarf, who believes the old man to be a miser with a hidden store of wealth. Quilp gets possession of the shop, and Nell and her grandfather take to wandering about the countryside. Eventually Nell dies, too late to be saved by her grandfather's brother, who has returned from abroad and finds them after a long search. Quilp is drowned while attempting to escape arrest. Other characters include Sampson Brass, Quilp's unscrupulous lawyer, his sister Sally and 'the Marchioness', a child whom the Brasses keep as a servant in vile conditions.

The novel shows Dickens' extraordinary vitality of imagination and also exemplifies the vulgarity which was part of his vitality. This vulgarity tended to display itself in melodrama and in sentimentality, here exhibited in the characters of Quilp and Little Nell respectively. The death of Little Nell is often regarded as Dickens' most notorious sentimental indulgence.

Old English
The name is practically identical with Anglo-Saxon is denoting the language, literature and culture of the English before the Norman conquest of 1066, and also afterwards until it becomes fused (Middle English) in the 13th century with the insular Anglo-Norman; it was later occasionally used to differentiate

the common people from the aristocracy of (supposedly) Anglo-Norman descent.

▷ English language; Saxons.

Old English Baron, The (1778)
Historical and ▷ Gothic ▷ romance by English writer ▷ Clara Reeve, first published as *The Champion of Virtue: A Gothic Story* (1777). Sir Philip Harclay returns to England after serving ▷ Henry V, to discover that there have been strange deeds in the family of his friend, Lord Lovel, whose castle is now occupied by Lord Baron Fitz-Owen. A mystery begins to be unravelled around the well-bred but impoverished Edmund, and his banishment by an evil relative. Ultimately, the rightful claims of inheritance are asserted. In a preface, Reeve asserts that Gothic effects must 'be kept within certain limits of credibility'.

▷ *Mysteries of Udolpho, The*; Radcliffe, Ann

Old English literature
The four centuries preceding the Norman Conquest of 1066 were a period during which the Teutonic tribes who invaded Britain in the 5th century, after the fall of Roman dominion, achieved a level of organization capable first of resisting, then assimilating, the 8th-century invaders from Scandinavia. The conversion to Christianity of the Angles in the north and east of England, the Saxons in the south and the Jutes in Kent, partly by Irish, partly by Continental missionaries, led to the establishment of monasteries which became centres of learning and literate culture. Partly as a result of initiatives taken by ▷ Alfred to cultivate the use of English as a literary medium (to compensate for the decline in Latin learning during the period of the Danish invasions), partly as a result of the pastoral impetus of the ▷ Benedictine Revival, English achieved a status as a literary language surpassing that of any other European vernacular. By the 11th century a standard written form of English (West Saxon) was being cultivated as a medium for pastoral instruction, for literary culture, for the purposes of administration and record (although Latin remained the language of the highest cultural authority and scholarship). Old English literary culture may be roughly classified as follows:

1 The Latin work of monastic scholars. Monastic, Latin culture occupied a central and crucial position within Anglo-Saxon, and European, culture as a whole. From this context, the Latin work of ▷ Bede, Alcuin, and Aldhelm deserves special recognition. Bede (673–735) was the foremost scholar of Anglo-Saxon culture and the most enduringly influential of this group. Alcuin (735–804) was the most famous Saxon scholar of his time, as a result of his important position in the court of the Emperor Charlemagne (from about 781) as an educational reformer and pioneer. His works cover a range of topics (historical, grammatical, and scientific) in Latin verse and prose. Aldhelm (640–709) was Abbot of Malmesbury and later Bishop of Sherbourne. His works include florid treatises in verse and prose in praise of virginity, and a treatise on metrics. His English poetry, apparently admired by Alfred, is lost.

2 Old English poetry. The bulk of this is preserved in just four manuscripts, dating from the second half of the 10th century (the so-called Junius ms, the Vercelli Book, the Exeter book and the ▷ Beowulf ms). The prosodic form of Old English poetry is ▷ alliterative verse, and the extant poetic corpus is one of considerable formal sophistication. The blend of traditions and values from Germanic and Christian culture gives it a distinctive quality. The heroic narratives rework material from a historical-legendary Germanic past, preserved through the efforts of literate Saxon monks. Most of the material cannot be attributed to a single writer, nor dated with any degree of precision. A list of the subjects will give some idea of its range:

i Heroic narratives about the legendary-historical past (such as ▷ *Beowulf*, *Deor*, *The Battle of Finnsburh*, *Waldere*, *Widsith*).

ii Commemorative historical poems (*The Battle of Brunanburh* and the ▷ *Battle of Maldon*).

iii Poems on biblical and scriptural themes (retelling O.T. narratives such as *Genesis A*, *Genesis B*, *Judith*, *Exodus*; retelling N.T. events such as ▷ Cynewulf's *Christ II* or those contained in apocryphal gospels, such as *Andreas*; meditations on Christian iconography, such as the ▷ *Dream of the Road*, the *Phoenix*; hymns of praise, such as the famous, earliest extant example of O.E. poetry, ▷ Caedmon's 'hymn').

iv Lives of saints (such as *Guthlac A and B*, *Juliana*, *Elene*).

v Short elegies (complaints written from the stance of a first-person speaker on the hardships of separation and isolation of one kind or another, such as *The Wanderer*, *The Seafearer*, *The Wife's Lament*).

vi Riddles and gnomic verse (the riddles, such as those collected in the Exeter Book, are characteristically in the voice of objects who pun on their identity, using clever metaphorical and metonymical twists).

3 Old English prose. There was a well-developed prose tradition in Old English, stimulated by the initiatives taken by Alfred to produce translations of those books 'most necessary for men to know': translations by Alfred, or attributed to the Alfredian school, include Gregory the Great's *Pastoral Care*, ▷ Boethius' *Consolation of Philosophy*, Augustine's *Soliloquies*, ▷ Bede's *Ecclesiastical History*. Prose was used as the medium for homiletic instruction (most notably by ▷ Aelfric

and Wulfstan, and in the *Blicking Homilies*), and for translations from the Old and New Testaments. Classical narratives, such as the story of Apollonius of Tyre and parts of the ▷ Alexander legend, also survive in vernacular prose translations. The ▷ *Anglo-Saxon Chronicle* illustrates the use of Old English prose as a medium of historical record, and there are also extant examples of laws, charters, wills, scientific and medical writings in O.E. prose.

A number of factors contributed to the demise of English as a prestige vernacular in the later 11th century. With the Conquest, the English administrative, ecclesiastical and social elite was replaced by Norman personnel. The effect was to confirm Latin as the language of official administration and record, and to encourage the use of Norman-French (▷ Anglo-Norman) as a vernacular of status. There seems to have been no attempt to prevent English being used in official contexts: it simply was no longer practical to do so in many cases. But Latin culture underwent an enormous renaissance from the late 11th century onwards, as did French culture from the mid-12th century, which influenced their use across Europe as cultural and literary mediums. The tradition of O.E. learning was kept up at some monastic centres through the 12th century, particularly at Worcester, but a standard written form of the language could no longer be maintained. The early written forms of English which survive from the 12th century reflect regional variations in usage and the enormous changes in the spoken forms of the language that had not permeated the standard written forms of O.E.. Thus the so-called Middle English period begins. The study of O.E. texts never entirely died out through the medieval period in England, but it increasingly became an area of antiquarian scholarship. The revival of substantial scholarly interest in Anglo-Saxon culture in the 16th century (reflected in the work of scholars such as ▷ John Bale and ▷ Matthew Parker) was stimulated in part by religious-political issues, and the desire to find evidence of an autonomous national, ecclesiastical tradition in the pre-Norman era that could be used to refute Papal claims to ecclesiastical and spiritual authority. In the next century, Anglo-Saxon traditions and culture became a reference point for pro-Parliamentarians anxious to locate the roots of English political institutions firmly in the Saxon past. The subsequent history of Anglo-Saxon scholarship reflects a similarly complex merging of academic, political, national and racial interests.

▷ Alfred, King; Heptarchy.

Bib: Mitchell, B. and Robinson, F., *A Guide to Old English*; Shippey, T., *Old English Verse*; Swanton, M., *English Literature before Chaucer*.

Old Pretender, The

James Francis Edward Stuart (1688–1766), son of ▷ King James II who had been deposed for reasons connected with his ▷ Catholicism. He was a pretender to (*ie* he claimed) the British throne on the death of his half-sister Queen ▷ Anne in 1714, but his claim was rejected because like his father he was a Catholic. Instead, George of Hanover became king as ▷ George I. In 1715, James led a rebellion on his own behalf in ▷ Scotland, but this failed. His followers were called ▷ Jacobites from the Latin 'Jacobus' = James, and he was termed the 'Old' Pretender to distinguish him from his son, Charles Edward Stuart, the Young Pretender, who attempted a similar Scottish rebellion in 1745.

▷ Stuart, House of.

Old Vic Theatre. The

Situated in Waterloo Road, this is one of London's most famous theatres. Built in 1816–18, during the 19th century it drew on the local working-class population for its audiences, with productions of popular ▷ melodramas. In 1880 it was converted into a temperance amusement-hall. From 1881 to 1883 it was managed by the Shakespearean actor and director William Poel.

Oldcastle, Sir John (1378–1417)

Sir John Oldcastle became Lord Cobham and died a martyr for Wycliffite (▷ Wycliffe, John) heresy which rejected the doctrine of John) transubstantiation. There is cogent evidence to suggest that ▷ Falstaff in ▷ *Henry IV* was originally called Oldcastle, notwithstanding ▷ Shakespeare's explicit disclaimer of this in the 'Epilogue' to *Henry IV, Part II*. The complete works of Shakespeare edited by Gary Taylor and Stanley Wells retains (uniquely) Oldcastle for Falstaff in *Henry IV, Part I*, on the basis that the name was changed for reasons of political accommodation, not for aesthetic ones.

Oldfield, Anne (?1683–1730)

Actress. She served in a tavern where, according to tradition, her talents as an actress were recognized by the playwright ▷ George Farquhar, who heard her reciting some lines behind the bar. She was engaged at ▷ Drury Lane from 1699 where apart from a brief sojourn at the Queen's Theatre (▷ Haymarket Theatres), she remained to the end of her career. She gradually supplanted the previous leading actress, ▷ Anne Bracegirdle.

Throughout her career Oldfield preferred comic to tragic roles, excelling in the performance of coquettes and women of fashion such as Lady Betty Modish in ▷ Colley Cibber's *The Careless Husband* (1704).

Bib: Robins, E., *The Palmy Days of Nance Oldfield*; Melville, L., *Stage Favourites of the Eighteenth Century*.

Oldham, John (1653–83)

Poet. Some of his early poems were written under the influence of the ▷ Earl of Rochester, and

his *Ode, Suppos'd to be spoken by a Court-Hector at Breaking of the Dial in Privy-Garden*, also known as *A Satyr against Vertue*, concerns one of Rochester's drunken exploits. His *Satyrs upon the Jesuits*, in heroic ▷ couplets (1681), ridicule ▷ Catholic superstition. He was a pioneer of the 'imitation' form, writing versions of poems by ▷ Horace, ▷ Juvenal and ▷ Boileau in urbane couplets, adapting the original to an English contemporary context. His *Poems and Translations* appeared in 1683. He died early from smallpox, and ▷ John Dryden wrote an elegy to his memory.
Bib: Zigerell, J., *John Oldham*.

Oliphant, Margaret (1828–97)
▷ Scottish novelist, biographer and critic, born in Wallyford, Midlothian; also known as M.O.W. She married her cousin Francis Oliphant in 1852, but in 1859 he died of consumption, leaving Margaret with two children and expecting a third. She supported her family (and that of her widowed brother and his three children) by writing prolifically, becoming the author of over 100 works. She wrote fiction, biography and reviews, her best-known novels today being the ▷ *Chronicles of Carlingford* series (1863–76). Her first work, *Passages in the Life of Mrs Margaret Maitland* (1849) was well-received, and this was followed by the ▷ historical novel *Caleb Field* (1851) and *Merkland* (1851). *The Athelings* (1857) was a huge success, and is the best of Oliphant's many domestic ▷ romances. In 1862, her biography of Edward Irving appeared, and in 1863 the first of the *Chronicles, Salem Chapel.* The other four novels in the series were *The Rector and the Doctor's Family* (1863); *The Perpetual Curate* (1864); *Miss Marjoribanks* (1866) and *Phoebe Junior* (1876). Another group of books, *Stories of the Seen and Unseen*, dealt with matters of death and the soul, and include *A Beleaguered City* (1880) and *A Little Pilgrim in the Unseen* (1882). Also in 1882, her much admired *Literary History of England* appeared, and, in 1897–8, *Annals of a Publishing House*, which commemorated her long association with ▷ *Blackwood's Magazine*, to which she was a frequent contributor. Oliphant's best writing is sharply humorous and vivid in description, and she has been compared to ▷ George Eliot and ▷ Trollope, but the financial pressure to keep producing inevitably affected her work, not least since she was compelled to write scores of popular romances. Her posthumously published ▷ autobiography (1899) reveals the strain she was under, and records her struggle to meet financial obligations.
Bib: Coghill, H. (ed.), *Margaret Oliphant: the Autobiography and Letters*; Williams, M., *A Critical Biography*; Colby, V. and R., *The Equivocal Virtue: Margaret Oliphant and the Victorian Literary Market Place*; Cunningham, V., *Everywhere Spoken Against: Dissent in the Victorian Novel.*

***Oliver Twist* (1837–9)**
A novel by ▷ Charles Dickens, published in instalments in 1837–9. Oliver is a child of unknown parents, born in a workhouse where he leads a miserable existence under the tyranny of Bumble, a beadle, ie a parish council official. He runs away to London and becomes mixed up in a gang of thieves led by Fagin and including the brutal burglar, Bill Sikes, Nancy his whore and a young pickpocket called the 'Artful Dodger'. He is temporarily rescued by the benevolent Mr Brownlow but a mysterious character called Monks, who has an interest in keeping Oliver's parentage a secret, induces the gang to kidnap him. He is finally rescued through the action of Nancy, who in consequence is brutally murdered by Sikes.

The novel shows the mixture of sentimentality and ▷ melodrama characteristic of early Dickens but in Bumble especially he exhibits keen social satire, and the London underworld is presented vividly. It was written at a time when a number of novelists (eg the ▷ 'Newgate School', especially ▷ Harrison Ainsworth) had written romances about crime, but Dickens dissociated it from these in the preface to the 3rd edition, and was realistic enough to startle the educated public into a new consciousness of the unprivileged and the criminal level of society, and to show how lack of compassion in the more privileged helped to make poverty a nursery of crime.

Olivier, Laurence (1907–89)
Actor and producer, knighted in 1947, and created a life peer in 1970. He established his reputation at the ▷ Old Vic Theatre during the 1930s, especially with his performance of *Hamlet* in 1937. The range and success of his career on stage and in films mark him as the leading English actor of this century. In 1961 he was appointed director of the Chichester Festival Theatre and made the first director of the ▷ National Theatre.
Bib: Gourlay, L. (ed.), *Olivier*; Olivier, L. *Confessions of an Actor.*

***Olney Hymns* (1779)**
A collection of religious poems by the Rev. John Newton and ▷ William Cowper, so called from the village of Olney where they lived.

Omai
Tahitian, brought to England with James Cook's second voyage in 1774, and shown around as the epitome of a 'noble savage' (▷ Primitivism), one of a series of such visitors including American Indians and Eskimos. His dignified bearing and

conduct, as he moved in the highest English circles, were marvelled at and seemed to bear out theories of natural virtue, compared with the corruptions of civilization. A painting by ▷ Reynolds depicts him in a turban and flowing garment, standing erect, with his right hand outstretched, in the pose of a statesman or oriental prince. His visit is mentioned by several contemporaries, including ▷ Cowper, ▷ Johnson and ▷ Burney.

On Heroes, Hero-Worship and the Heroic in History (1841)
Frequently abridged to *On Heroes and Hero-Worship*, this book by ▷ Thomas Carlyle was cited by the liberal press of the time as evidence of his anti-democratic views. It is actually a study of the way in which the 'heroic' as a phenomenon evolves and changes throughout history. Originating as a series of lectures the book moves from the pagan god Odin through Italian poet Dante (1265–1321), religious leaders John Knox (1505–72) and Martin Luther (1483–1546), Scottish poet Robert Burns (1756–96), Critic Samuel Johnson (1709–84), thinker Jean-Jacques Rousseau (1712–78), the prophet Mahomet and others, ending with Napoleon Bonaparte (1769–1821), and discusses each man's ability to discern new truths which, for Carlyle, is characteristic of a true hero. True heroism is the ability to act on these 'truths', to modify them and to discover new ones that will supersede them. Carlyle's heroism therefore appears progressive in its capacity for perpetual renewal and in its tolerance.
Bib: Rosenberg, J.D., *Carlyle and the Burden of History*.

On Liberty (1859)
A political essay by ▷ John Stuart Mill, in which he discusses how far and in what ways the state is entitled to interfere with the liberty of individuals. He concludes that in general this interference should be restricted to the protection of other individuals, and of individuals collectively considered as society. Mill was mainly alarmed lest a new tyranny should arise from democratic majorities who might be indifferent to minority rights. The novelist ▷ Thomas Hardy numbered the essay among his 'cures for despair'.

Ondaatje, Michael (b 1943)
Novelist and poet, born in Sri Lanka (then Ceylon). At the age of eighteen he arrived in Canada, where he attended Bishop's University in Quebec, the University of Toronto and Queen's University, Kingston, Ontario. He taught at the University of Western Ontario (1967–71) and subsequently at York University in Toronto. His fiction has a strong element of technical experiment, combined with strong feeling and political concerns: *Coming Through Slaughter* (1976) uses a form of ▷ faction, portraying the life of the jazz cornet player Buddy Bolden through a combination of narrative techniques, including transcripts of interviews, song lyrics, biographical summaries and subjective narration. Ondaatje has written a stage version of this novel. *In the Skin of a Lion* (1987) explores the lives of marginalized people in Canadian society using both mythic and metafictional devices. His most recent novel is: *The English Patient* (1992), which was joint winner of 1992's Booker Prize. His volumes of poetry include: *The Dainty Monsters* (1967); *The Man With Seven Toes* (1969); *The Collected Works of Billy the Kid: Left Handed Poems* (1970); *Rat Jelly* (1973); *Elimination Dance* (1978); *Secular Love* (1984); *The Cinnamon Peeler: Selected Poems* (1989). He has also directed films and edited books of verse and stories. *Running in the Family* (1982) is autobiographical.
Bib: Solecki, S., (ed.), *Spider Blues: Essays on Michael Ondaatje*.

Onomatopoeia
The use of verbal sound to evoke the sound of what the word represents. Thus a cuckoo is a bird whose song resembles the two syllables of its name, which is therefore onomatopoeic.

Open and closed texts
▷ Closure; Readerly/Writerly

Open field system
That system of land use especially typical of medieval English agriculture. Land under cultivation was divided into strips, and distributed among the peasants of the village or manor. The strips were not surrounded by hedges or fences, so that good farmers suffered from the effects of the bad farming of their immediate neighbours. The system began to be replaced in the 16th century, when landowners preferred sheep-farming, and it was effectually abolished in the 18th century when, in the course of 'the agricultural revolution', the open fields were enclosed in larger arable units by the landlords.
▷ Enclosures.

Open University
The Open University was established in 1969, began teaching in 1971 and is now based at Milton Keynes. Its aim is to provide degree courses for those students who do not have formal qualifications, who are not of a standard, and who do not have the opportunity or the finance to enter for full-time university degrees. The courses are based at home and the teaching is done mainly through

television and radio. Its popularity continues to increase.

Opera in England

Opera, in the sense of a staged drama in which the words and music are of equal importance, began in Italy at the end of the 16th century. It was an integral part of the ▷ Renaissance, arising out of the attempt to revive what were thought to be the performance practices of Greek drama. Subjects, therefore, were tragedies drawn from classical mythology and the words were set to a declamatory style of singing known as recitative. The first English opera was *The Siege of Rhodes*, with a libretto by ▷ William D'Avenant and music (now lost) by Matthew Locke and others. It was first produced in 1642, at a time when the ▷ Puritans had closed the theatres, and seems to have been an attempt to circumvent the ban on plays. The convention of recitative, however, does not seem to have been to the English taste, so that, apart from Blow's *Venus and Adonis* and ▷ Purcell's *Dido and Aeneas*, the main contribution of composers in the 17th century was in the genre now known as dramatic or semi-opera. After the theatres reopened in 1660, many plays were given with musical interludes, ▷ Shakespeare being adapted for this purpose by ▷ D'Avenant and ▷ Dryden. Two sets of ▷ *Tempest* music exist, one by Locke, the other sometimes thought to be by ▷ Purcell. *The Fairy Queen* (1693), an adaptation of ▷ *A Midsummer Night's Dream*, is Purcell's best-known work in this field.

In the 18th century Italian opera was imported, as well as the German composer, Handel, who wrote operas in the Italian style, but the fashion for such entertainment proved to be short-lived. ▷ Addison, amongst others, ridiculed the conventions of opera in the ▷ *Spectator*. Nor, despite its popularity at the time, did ▷ Gay's ▷ *The Beggar's Opera* (1728) lead to a significant tradition of ballad opera. The romantic operas that held the stage in the first half of the 19th century are, apart from Balfe's *The Bohemian Girl*, little known nowadays. More lasting fame, however, has attached to the comic operas written by ▷ Gilbert and Sullivan between 1875 and 1896.

Until the 20th century, London had a virtual monopoly of opera performances, the only touring company that lasted for any time being the Carl Rosa Opera Company. In recent years the establishment of regional companies who tour, as well as performing at their home base, has brought opera to a much wider public, although cuts in public subsidies are now threatening this expansion. Improved standards of production and a general policy of singing in English if possible have helped to make it a more popular art form. Two English composers in particular have enriched the repertoire: Benjamin Britten and Sir Michael Tippet. Britten tended to find inspiration in classic texts, as, for instance, in ▷ *Peter Grimes* (▷ George Crabbe), *Billy Budd* (Herman Melville), ▷ *The Turn of the Screw* (▷ Henry James), *A Midsummer Night's Dream* (▷ Shakespeare), *Death in Venice* (Thomas Mann), whereas Tippett writes his own, very individual, libretti. Of the younger composers, Harrison Birtwhistle has contributed a variety of dramatic pieces (including *Punch and Judy*, *Down by the Greenwood Side*, *The Mask of Orpheus* and *Yan Tan Tethera*) which are largely concerned with re-working myth, whilst Peter Maxwell Davies has written several chamber and children's operas, as well as the large-scale *Taverner* and *Resurrection*.

Opie, Amelia (1759–1853)

Novelist and poet. Opie began to participate in London society in 1794 and she soon became acquainted with and admired by the most radical members of the literary groups, in particular, ▷ Elizabeth Inchbald, ▷ William Godwin and ▷ Mary Wollstonecraft (whom Opie depicts in her novel, *Adeline Mowbray, or The Mother and Daughter*, 1804). Her other novels include, *The Father and Daughter* (1801), *Valentine's Eve* (1816) and *Madelaine* (1822); they are all sentimental novels set in unremarkable domestic circumstances and fully corroborate her own stated purpose in writing novels: 'I like to make people cry, indeed, if I do not do it, all my readers are disappointed'. Her ceaseless literary outpouring is of questionable quality, and this led to her being ▷ satirized as Miss Poppyseed by ▷ Peacock in his novel *Headlong Hall*. She married the painter John Opie in 1798 (her maiden name was Alderson), but at his death in 1807 moved to Norwich where, in 1825, she became a Quaker, devoting herself to spiritual writing, e.g. *Lays for the Dead* (1833).

Bib: James, A. H., *Best Sellers of Jane Austen's Age*; Menzies, J., Wilson and Lloyd, H., *Amelia: The Tale of a Plain Friend*.

Orange, House of; Orange Free State; Orangemen

The town of Orange in southern France was originally an independent principality. Philibert of Orange (1502–30) was rewarded by the Emperor Charles V (who ruled the Netherlands amongst his other territories) with large estates in the Netherlands for his help in statesmanship and war. The Princes of Orange thus became Dutch nobles, and later William 'the Silent' of Orange established the Dutch (Netherlands) Republic by defeating the armies of the territory's former ruler, Philip II of Spain. William's leadership, and the importance of the Orange family in the Netherlands, gave the House of Orange special eminence in the Republic, and successive members of it held the high office of Stadtholder. They twice married into the ▷ Stuart family reigning in Britain: William II married Mary, daughter of ▷ Charles I, and in 1677 their son, ▷ William III, married Mary (▷ Mary II), daughter of ▷ James II. William and Mary became joint sovereigns of Britain in 1689 after the expulsion of James II. After William III's death in 1702, the family continued to be pre-eminent in Dutch politics, and were kings of Holland (the Netherlands) from 1814. In the same year the Dutch colony in South Africa was ceded to Britain; in 1836 some of the Dutch colonists, fleeing from British sovereignty, set up the Orange Free State Republic to the north of the colony.

Throughout the 17th century the House of Orange was a champion of ▷ Protestantism against the ▷ Catholic powers, first of Spain and then of France; the religious conflict was also a fight for Dutch national survival, and from 1690–1700 it was in addition one for the survival of the British system of politics. The issue was then felt most keenly in ▷ Ireland, where the northern province of Ulster was Protestant, and the southern three provinces were Catholic. Religious hostility between the north and the south continued throughout the 18th century, when it died down in most of Europe, and it is still a political issue at the present day. In 1795 'Orange Societies' were founded in Ulster, in memory of the great Protestant king William III, who had saved Ulster from being overrun by the Catholic south by defeating James II's army at the Battle of the Boyne (1690). Orangemen (*ie* members of these societies) are still an important political force in Northern Ireland, although the societies are nominally religious and not political.

***Ordeal of Richard Feverel, The* (1859)**
A novel by ▷ George Meredith. Sir Austin Feverel prides himself on the 'system' which he has devised for the upbringing and education of his motherless son, Richard; he is, however, a self-satisfied egotist who lacks disinterested understanding of his son's character. The 'system' breaks down in Richard's adolescence, when the boy falls in love with Lucy Desborough, a girl of lower social background than Sir Austin's ideal for his son's bride. They are secretly married but Sir Austin manages to separate them by egotistically exploiting Richard's love for him. Richard becomes involved with a beautiful woman of loose morals; he begins this new relationship with characteristically romantic and idealistic motives of redeeming her but he partly falls under her spell. Lord Mountfalcon, who is interested in permanently separating Lucy and Richard, is chiefly responsible for Richard's betrayal of her, and in remorse for his infidelity Richard fights a duel with him and is wounded. Lucy has meanwhile become reconciled with Sir Austin but the shock of the duel kills her. The novel – Meredith's first important one – exemplifies his combination of romantic intensity with psychological analysis.

Order
One of the five categories in which ▷ Genette analyses narrative discourse, order is concerned with the relationship between the chronological order of fictional events and their order in the narrative (*eg* 'flashbacks'). Order, ▷ duration and ▷ frequency are matters of temporal arrangement or 'tense'; the other two categories are ▷ mood and ▷ voice.

▷ Narratology.

Orfeo, Sir
An early Middle English narrative, dating from the 13th century, which claims to be a reworking of a lay composed by British harpers (▷ Breton Lays). In *Sir Orfeo*, the classical story of ▷ Orpheus and Euridice is translated into a feudal/chivalric Celtic world in which Orfeo is a former British king whose court is at Winchester (which, the narrator explains, was formerly called Thrace). The Underworld of the classical story becomes an Otherworld, presided over by the King of the Fairies. Heurodis is eventually rescued by Orfeo, who enters the Otherworld disguised as a minstrel, and after an absence of many years from their kingdom, the couple return and resume their positions as king and queen. **Bib**: Barron, W. R. J., *Medieval English Romance*.

Organicism
A social theory entertained by a number of writers, especially in the 19th and early 20th centuries. Organicist theories picture society as developing like a natural organism in which each part is integrated functionally with the rest to compose the whole. As such, organic theories stress the mutual dependency of the various parts of society (for example rich and poor), but they can also have a conservative colouring because they imply that whatever is is natural and right, including inequalities. As such, organicist theories are often criticized by ▷ Marxist critics (eg Terry Eagleton, *Criticism and Ideology*). Organicist theories were popular among conservatives during and after the ▷ French Revolution (▷ Edmund Burke was a key thinker) but, as the argument developed, evolutionary theory complicated and enriched the picture, as in the work of ▷ George Eliot. Radical organicists, such as ▷ D. H. Lawrence, took the argument still further. For them, the individual is natural and healthy, but society and the state are unnatural and corrupting. Such thinkers opt instead for an organic primitivism, finding positives only in pre-industrial cultures. In literature there is also the important notion of organic ▷ form developed by ▷ S. T. Coleridge. Here it is

argued that literary works are at their best when they grow like natural organisms following the flow of emotion and idea. This was a key idea of the ▷ Romantic movement.

Orgoglio
A character representing Arrogance in ▷ Edmund Spenser's ▷ *Faerie Queene*. He occurs in Book I. cantos vii and viii; he captures the ▷ Red Cross Knight and is slain by Prince Arthur (▷ Arthur, King). The name derives from the Italian for pride.

Oriana
A name sometimes used for ▷ Elizabeth I by Elizabethan poets. It comes from the 15th-century Spanish-Portuguese romance *Amadis de Gaula*, in which Oriana is a British princess beloved by the hero, Amadis.
▷ Spanish influence on English literature.

Orientalism
Narratives of the East, in verse and prose, were immensely popular in the 18th and 19th centuries, ranging in style and theme from the dry analytical wit of Samuel Johnson's *Rasselas* (1759) to the galloping romance of ▷ Byron's 'Turkish Tales', ▷ *The Giaour* (1813) or ▷ *The Corsair* (1814). With their interest in lust, slavery, abduction and the exotic, the latter had a huge popular appeal related in part to the image of Lord Byron himself, variously portrayed in oils as rapaciously and broodingly ▷ Gothic, or got up to fight in Albanian costume. That such hectic and flashy adventure-poetry says more about the ▷ Romantic libido than about any real Oriental place seems to be confirmed by Captain Benwick in ▷ Jane Austen's novel ▷ *Persuasion* (1818), whose interest in the star-crossed and storm-tossed leads Anne Elliot to remark, 'that she thought it was the misfortune of poetry, to be seldom safely enjoyed by those who enjoyed it completely'.

Less self-mythologizing than Byron, ▷ Southey in *The Curse of Kehama* (1810), and ▷ Moore in *Lalla Rookh* (1817) make forays into similar territory, while in a more complex and indirect way ▷ Coleridge's ▷ *Kubla Khan* (1797) shows that the poetic associations of Oriental imagery might be paradisal and delicate, and not wholly to do with despotism and wildness. Many of the hallucinations and dream-visions recorded in ▷ Thomas De Quincey's ▷ *Confessions of an English Opium-Eater* (1822) involve the Oriental, and the author's drug-induced conflation of different periods and cultures may typify a general British reaction to the non-occidental world as there to be pillaged for its images, whether by artists, explorers, or more obvious agents of imperialism. The drug makes De Quincey temporary victim, rather than oppressor: 'I fled from the wrath of Brama through all the forests of Asia: Vishnu hated me: Seeva laid wait for me. I came suddenly upon Isis and Osiris: I had done a deed, they said, which the ibis and the crocodile trembled at.'

Despised for its illiberal forms of government, explored and exploited, the Orient fell victim to a garish literary tradition, stretching from ▷ Beckford's *Vathek* (1786) to Sax Rohmer's devilish criminal genius, Dr Fu Manchu. Yet to Western eyes it remained the geographical and racial expression of what is Other; desirable, Edenic, malleable by the individual imagination.
Bib: Barrell, J., *The Infection of Thomas de Quincey: the Psycopathology of Imperialism*; Said, E., *Orientalism*.

Origin of Species, The
▷ Darwin, Charles.

Orinda', The 'Matchless
▷ Philips, Katherine.

***Orlando* (1928)**
A fantasy by ▷ Virginia Woolf in which the evolution of poetic genius is traced through the Sackville family and their country mansion of Knole from Thomas Sackville (1536–1608) to the poet Victoria Sackville-West (1892–1962). This is done through an immortal character Orlando, who changes sex from a man into a woman in the 17th century, after growing to male adulthood in Elizabethan times. She then discovers that life as a woman in the 18th and 19th centuries offers different and limited freedoms. The book is a parodic combination of historical novel and biographical fantasy which explores the themes of androgyny and women's creativity. It is thus perhaps the closest Woolf gets in her fiction to an exploration of the ideas she outlines in *A Room of One's Own* (1931) and *Three Guineas* (1938).

Orlando
The Italian form of the name Roland, hero of the Old French *Chanson de Roland* (*Song of Roland*). From the Italian 16th-century romantic epics by ▷ Ariosto, the name passed into English romance narratives, being used, for example, for the hero of ▷ Shakespeare's romantic drama ▷ *As You Like It*.

***Orlando Furioso* (1532)**
A romance epic by the Italian poet ▷ Ludovico Ariosto. It is in the tradition of Italian developments of the legends centring on the French hero Roland, who in the reign of ▷ Charlemagne (768–814) repelled the Muslim invasion of Europe. Ariosto invents fantastic episodes and complicated romantic intrigues

and adventures. Orlando goes mad because his lady, Angelica, marries a Moorish youth, but he is cured in time to defeat Agramante, king of Africa, who has been besieging Paris. Many linked tales and episodes accompany this central theme, as is usual in the 16th-century romantic ▷ epic, of which Ariosto is the master and ▷ Edmund Spenser (▷ *The Faerie Queene*) one of his chief emulators.

Ormond, John (1923–90)
Poet and film-maker, born at Dunvant near Swansea, Ormond, though he read English and philosophy at University College, Swansea, nevertheless retained his early interest in painting throughout his life, his painterly eye influencing both his poetry and his film-making. Friendships with Dylan Thomas and Vernon Watkins drew him into poetry, his early work *Indications* (1943) being strongly influenced by the former. He joined the London staff of *Picture Post* in 1945 before returning to Swansea and eventually becoming a director and producer of documentary films for BBC Wales in 1957. His major poetry collections appeared much later after slow gestation and careful revision. These were *Requiem and Celebration* (1969), *Definition of a Waterfall* (1973), with a further selection of his work in *Penguin Modern Poets 27* (1978) before additional new poems appeared in his *Selected Poems* (1987) which brought all his finest work together.
Bib: Stephens, M. (Ed.), *The Oxford Companion to the Literature of Wales*; Jones, G. and Rowlands, J., *Profiles*.

***Oroonoko, Or, The Royal Slave* (1688)**
Novel by ▷ Aphra Behn. Oroonoko is an African prince, sold into slavery and transported to Surinam. He is separated from his beloved wife, Imoinda, who undergoes a similar fate to his own: they are re-united in Surinam. The novel is in two parts: the first tells of their lives at the court of Coromantien (now Nigeria), where Oroonoko clashes with his lustful grandfather the king, who wants Imoinda for himself, before they are parted and each one is sold to slave-traders. The second part tells of their meeting in Surinam, where Oroonoko has been given the name Caesar, of the abortive slave uprising which he leads, and of their eventual deaths. The novel is part romance, part exotic travel tale, part polemic, with a wealth of critical commentary about the hypocrisy and treachery of the white man, and his practice of Christianity, and of the corruption of colonial government – a theme Behn returned to in her play, *The Widow Ranter, Or, Bacon's Rebellion in Virginia* (1696). Oroonoko and Imoinda are 'noble savages' (▷ primitive, primitivism), whose virtue and beauty are extolled as being far superior to the qualities of the white people around them, and their sufferings are portrayed very movingly. On the other hand, the argument is not against slavery as such, but against the presumptious and cruel treatment of the high-born by their social and moral inferiors. The novel is told by a first-person narrator, ostensibly Behn herself, who claimed to have witnessed the events in Surinam. For many years this was taken as an invention, with descriptive details about the colony being cribbed from other works. But recent scholarship accepts that Behn lived in Surinam, and based much of her narration on first-hand experience.

▷ Thomas Southerne's play *Oroonoko* (1695) is based on Behn's novel.
Bib: Duffy, M., (ed.), *Oroonoko and Other Stories*.

Orphans
In mid-Victorian fiction, orphans frequently appear as central characters. In an age when the reading public responded to sentiment, the representation of orphans was sometimes used by writers as a catalyst for pathos. This was often the case with ▷ Elizabeth Gaskell, for example, whose novel ▷ *Ruth* creates sympathy for the ▷ 'fallen woman' by stressing initially the heroine's lack of parental guidance. Alternatively the effects of disinheritance and exclusion were illustrated through an orphan, as ▷ Emily Brontë demonstrates with Heathcliff in ▷ *Wuthering Heights*. Authors seeking to challenge the conventions of society often created orphaned central characters in order to speak from a marginalized position, to view society from 'outside'. The heroine of ▷ Charlotte Brontë's ▷ *Jane Eyre* is an example, although Jane, like many other fictional orphans, eventually discovers familial connections and financial support, thereby gaining both security and power. The necessary independence of orphans could also give rise to the theme of individualism and self-help which ran through the literature of the age, registering an unacknowledged complicity with the values of the middle classes. This paradoxical position is exemplified by the heroine of ▷ Elizabeth Barrett Browning's ▷ *Aurora Leigh*, who both resists as a woman the constraints imposed upon her by society and simultaneously advocates the conservative ideology that has oppressed her.

▷ *Professor, The*.

Orton, Joe (1933–67)
British dramatist renowned for his black humour, witty and savage verbal dialogue in the tradition of ▷ Oscar Wilde, and iconoclastic attacks on social conventions. He was murdered by his homosexual partner when his career had barely begun. His first play, *Entertaining Mr Sloane* (1964), is a comedy about suburban sex. In this, as in his other plays, much of the humour is derived from the disparity between what characters say and what they actually mean or do. This was followed by two farces, *Loot*

(1966) and *What the Butler Saw* (produced in 1969); the former about money, death and police corruption and the latter about sex and institutionalized corruption. Other plays are: *The Ruffian on the Stair* (staged 1966), *The Erpingham Camp* (staged 1967) and *Funeral Games* (staged 1970). In 1987 Stephen Frears directed a film adaptation (by Alan Bennett) of Lahr's biography of Orton, *Prick Up Your Ears*.
Bib: Bigsby, C. W. W., *Joe Orton*; Lahr, J., *Prick Up Your Ears*; Shepherd, S., *Because We're Queers*.

Orwell, George (pseudonym of Eric Blair) (1903–50)
Novelist, journalist and critic. Born into a poor but proud middle-class family, he was sent to a private school, from where he won a scholarship to Eton. His snobbish upbringing, and the uneasiness he felt in living with boys richer than himself, gave him a distaste for middle-class values and, in relation to the working classes, a sense of guilt which was intensified by the large unemployment of the 1930s. He served in the Burma Police (1922–7), and then resigned from dislike of what he interpreted as ⊳ imperialist oppression – *Burmese Days* (1934). He then tried to appease his sense of social guilt by living for 18 months in the utmost destitution – *Down and Out in London and Paris* (1933). At the height of the economic ⊳ depression in the 1930s, he was commissioned by a left-wing publisher, Gollancz, to make a personal investigation of conditions in the north of England – *The Road to Wigan Pier* (1937). By the time of its publication, Orwell was fighting for the Republicans in Spain, where he was wounded in the throat – *Homage to Catalonia* (1938). He came to regard himself as an independent and democratic socialist. During World War II, he was rejected for the army on medical grounds, and worked for the Indian service of the B.B.C. In 1945 he published his masterpiece, the fable *Animal Farm* a satire on Stalinism. After the war he wrote his most famous work, *1984* (1949), a vision of a world ruled by dictatorships of the Stalinist style, taken to an extreme in which private life and private thought are all but eradicated by surveillance, propaganda, and the systematic perversion of language.

His other novels are: *A Clergyman's Daughter* (1935); *Keep the Aspidistra Flying* (1936); *Coming Up For Air* (1939). Among his best works are his social and literary critical essays: *Inside the Whale* (1940); *The Lion and the Unicorn* (1941 – subtitled *Socialism and the English Genius*); *Critical Essays* (1946); *Shooting an Elephant* (1950). Recurrent themes in his work are the effect of poverty on the spirit, the difficulty of reconciling public demands with private desires and conscience, and the danger of corrupted language. He was literary editor of *Tribune* 1943–5. His *Collected Essays, Journalism and Letters* were published in 1968 (ed. S. Orwell and I. Angus).
Bib: Woodcock, G., *The Crystal Spirit*; Williams, R., *Orwell*; Crick, B., *George Orwell, a Life*; Meyers, J., *George Orwell: The Critical Heritage*.

Osborne, Dorothy (1627–95)
Wife of ⊳ Sir William Temple, statesman, diplomatist and author. Their marriage was delayed for seven years owing to the disapproval of her family, and her letters to him during a part of this time are famous social documents.

Osborne, John (1929–94)
Dramatist. He is widely thought of as the leader of the dramatic revival which started in the 1950s, through the great popular success of ⊳ *Look Back in Anger* (1956), which found an infectious contemporary idiom for the frustration of the younger British generation since World War II, and for their rejection of the traditional values of 'the Establishment'. The play gave currency for a decade to the term ⊳ 'the angry young men'. His later plays include: *The Entertainer* (1957); *Epitaph for George Dillon* (1958); *The World of Paul Slickey* (1959); *Luther* (1961); *The Blood of the Bambergs* (1962); *Under Plain Cover* (1962); *Inadmissible Evidence* (1965); *A Patriot for Me* (1965); *A Bond Honoured* (1966); *Time Present* (1967); *West of Suez* (1972); *A Sense of Detachment* (1972); *A Place Calling Itself Detachment* (1972); *The Picture of Dorian Gray* (1973); *Watch It Come Down* (1975); *The End of Me Old Cigar* (1975); *Déjà vu*, a sequel to *Anger* (1992). For television: *A Better Class of Person* (1985); *God Rot Tunbridge Wells* (1985). Osborne published two volumes of autobiography: *A Better Class of Person* (1981) and *Almost a Gentleman* (1991).
Bib: Allsop, K., *The Angry Decade*; Banham, M. *Osborne*; Trussler, S., *The Plays of Osborne*.

Osmond, Gilbert
A principal character in ⊳ Henry James' novel, ⊳ *Portrait of a Lady*; he is a poor, expatriate American dilettante living in Italy and secures in marriage the rich young heroine, Isabel Archer, whose life he then ruins by his moral triviality and cold-heartedness.

Ossian
James Macpherson (1736–96) was the author of a series of blank verse epics which he attributed to Ossian, son of Finn, and which he claimed to have translated from the Gaelic. There was considerable interest in ⊳ primitivism in the 1760s, and works such as *Fingal, an Ancient Epic Poem in Six Books* (1762) and *Temora* (1763) caused a great sensation, particularly among patriotic Scots. Ossian's fame also spread to the European continent, where the poetry

was read with enthusiasm by ▷ Napoleon I, and quoted by ▷ Goethe in *The Sorrows of Young Werther*. ▷ Samuel Johnson was among the earliest sceptics; when asked whether he thought any man 'of the modern age' could have written the poems, he replied: 'Yes, Sir, many men, many women, and many children.' Following Macpherson's death, an investigating committee concluded that the poetry was a collage of edited and newly-written material. Despite this exposure, ▷ Matthew Arnold defended the poetry as late as 1866 for its 'vein of piercing regret and sadness'. In the ancient legends Oisin (Ossian) bridged the gap between the heroic pagan age and Irish Christianity; his longevity was due to an extended residence in Fairyland.

Othello (1604)

A ▷ tragedy by ▷ Shakespeare, first acted in 1604. It was based on an Italian tale in *Hecatommithi* by Giraldi Cinthio (1565; translated into French 1584).

The full title of the play is *Othello, the Moor of Venice*: the extended title emphasizes Othello's position as commander of Venetian forces against the Turks and his race, both clues to the understanding of his tragedy. Othello is highly valued by the Venetians for his military prowess, but he is not a member of Venetian society; he is first and last a soldier, a member of a military community, trusting and trusted by his brother officers. Consequently it is as astonishing to him when Desdemona, a conventional Venetian aristocratic girl, leaves her home to marry him, as it is outrageous to her indignant father, Brabantio. Venice urgently needs Othello to defend Cyprus against the Turks, so Brabantio is forced to accept the match; however he warns Othello that a girl who has behaved so unpredictably once may prove as unreliable a wife as she has been a daughter. Othello is in rapture; his bliss is the greater for its incredibility, so that he naïvely imagines himself transported into a heaven on earth. But his junior officer, Iago, has motives of resentment against him; the most concrete of these is that the Florentine, Cassio, has been promoted over his head. Moreover, he is himself a cynic who has a low opinion of human nature and of the scope for genuine happiness. Partly as a double revenge against Othello and Cassio, partly as a cynical game the object of which is to bring Othello down to his own level of reality, he contrives first to disgrace Cassio temporarily, and then to insinuate into Othello's mind the suspicion, mounting by degrees to certainty, that Cassio and Desdemona are conducting a secret love affair. In Othello's mind the circumstances make this affair more than plausible: he has the habit of trusting Iago as his confidential officer; Desdemona has come to him out of a foreign society; Cassio is the sort of man who would have been considered an eligible husband for her. Until their marriage, Othello had had a single-minded dedication to his military vocation. The marriage has enriched this dedication, since it was Desdemona's admiration for him as a soldier that attracted her to him, but he now finds that his jealousy has divided his single-mindedness and is destroying his integrity. Accordingly he murders her, in the belief that heavenly justice is on his side. Desdemona, however, has been presented as one of the most innocent of all Shakespeare's heroines, for whom adultery is unimaginable, and her innocent goodness has won the heart of her lady companion, Emilia, who is Iago's wife. Emilia, who has been ignorant of Iago's plot but has unintentionally assisted him in it, realizes his guilt and publicly exposes him; Othello, restored to his dignity, makes a final speech of self-assessment, and kills himself.

Othello follows ▷ *Hamlet* in the sequence of Shakespeare's tragedies and is another masterpiece in the tradition of ▷ revenge tragedy. It is psychologically much more lucid, though perhaps not a more sophisticated play, than *Hamlet*, and is one of the most eloquent of Shakespeare's dramas.

Ottava rima

An Italian stanza of 8 lines rhyming *a b a b a b c c*. It was used by ▷ Boccaccio in the 14th century. Pulci in the 15th century used it for the mock-heroic, ironic style with which the stanza is chiefly associated in English through ▷ Byron's ▷ *Don Juan* and his *Vision of Judgement*. In *Don Juan*, the form is frequently exploited for the possibilities it allows for playing off long syntactical units against the bathos (▷ Figures of speech) of the closing couplet:

What is the end of fame? 'tis but to fill
A certain portion of uncertain paper:
Some liken it to climbing up a hill,
Whose summit, like all hills, is lost in vapour;
For this men write, speak, preach, and heroes kill,
And bards burn what they call their 'midnight taper',
To have, when the original is dust,
A name, a wretched picture, and worse bust.
(Canto I, CCXVIII)

Otterbourne, The Battle of

A famous medieval ▷ ballad about a battle fought in 1388 between the English and the Scots near the English castle of that name. The English commander was ▷ Henry Hotspur, Lord Percy, and the Scottish one, James Earl of Douglas. The ▷ Percy family and the Douglases were the chief rival familes on either side of the Scottish-English border in the later Middle Ages. The battle was a Scottish victory but Douglas was killed; Hotspur was taken prisoner. Another version of the battle is the ballad ▷ *Chevy Chase*.

The Hotspur of the ballad is the same as the character in ▷ Shakespeare's ▷ *Henry IV, Part I*; the Douglas in that play is another member of that family, whom Hotspur had just taken prisoner in the battle of Homildon Hill (1402).

Otway, Thomas (1652–85)
Dramatist and poet. He made a single attempt as an actor, when ▷ Aphra Behn gave him an opportunity as the old King in her *The Forc'd Marriage* (1670). Paralysed with stage fright, he broke down, and the next night the part had to be given to another actor. Otway turned instead to writing, and had immediate success with his tragedy, *Alcibiades* (1675), in which ▷ Elizabeth Barry made her first appearance. Otway is said to have fallen in love with her at that time, though she did not reciprocate his feelings. Otway nevertheless wrote several of his finest parts for her.

Otway followed his first play with the rhymed tragedy *Don Carlos* (1676); adaptations of a comedy by ▷ Molière as *The Cheats of Scapin* (1676) and ▷ Racine's tragedy *Titus and Berenice* (1677); and another comedy, *Friendship in Fashion* (1678). In 1678 Otway went to Flanders as a soldier, and drew on his experiences for ▷ *The Soldier's Fortune* (1681) and its sequel, ▷ *The Atheist* (1684). His best-known and most admired plays are two blank-verse tragedies, *The Orphan; Or, The Unhappy Marriage* (1680), and ▷ *Venice Preserv'd; Or A Plot Discovered* (1682). Otway also wrote prologues and epilogues, and a few poems. He died in poverty.
Bib: Taylor, A. M., *Next to Shakespeare*; Ham, R. G., *Otway and Lee*; Summers, M. (ed.), *The Complete Works of Thomas Otway*; Ghosh, J. C. (ed.), *The Complete Works of Thomas Otway*.

Ouida (1839–1908)
The pseudonym of Marie Louise de la Ramée, 'Ouida' originates in a childish failure to say 'Louise'. She was born in Bury St Edmunds of an English mother and French father, was educated in local schools and then in Paris, where her father disappeared during the Paris Commune of 1871. From 1860 she lived mostly in Italy, an expensive and affected life with dogs and frequent hopeless infatuations. She had a high opinion of her own genius, writing 45 novels of an unreal fashionable world, rebelling against the moral tone of contemporary literature. Her powerful novels were very popular for a time, despite their extravagance and inaccuracies, and her ridiculous portrayals of men. However, she became less popular from 1890 and ultimately died in destitution in Viareggio. Her stories appeared in *Bentley's Miscellany* 1859–60. Her first success was *Held in Bondage* (1863) but *Strathmore* (1865) really established her reputation. Her other novels include *Under Two Flags* (1867), *Folle-Farine* (1871), *Two Little Wooden Shoes* (1874), *A Village Commune* (1881) dealing with peasant life, *In Maremma* (1882) and the animal stories, *A Dog of Flanders* (1872) and *Bimbi, Stories for Children* (1882).
Bib: Ffrench, Y., *Ouida: A Study in Ostentation*; Bigland, E., *Ouida: The Passionate Victorian*; Stirling, M., *The Fine and the Wicked: The Life and Times of Ouida*.

***Our Mutual Friend* (1864–5)**
The last complete novel by ▷ Charles Dickens, published serially 1864–5. The principal plot starts from the will of a deceased refuse-collector, Old Harmon, who bequeaths his fortune to his son, John Harmon, on condition that he marries a certain girl, Bella Wilfer. Young Harmon wishes to discover what she is like before he discloses himself. He intends to adopt a disguise but his identity is obscured beyond his intention when circumstances point to his death by murder. Since he is believed dead, the father's property goes instead to Mr Boffin, old Harmon's foreman. Boffin adopts Bella, and young Harmon, disguising himself as John Rokesmith, becomes engaged as Boffin's secretary. Bella becomes spoilt by wealth and contemptuously rejects Rokesmith-Harmon as a lover; she is, however, reformed by Boffin, who pretends himself to undergo complete debasement of character through his accession of wealth and thus gives Bella, who has been devoted to him, a violent distaste for the evils of money. Rokesmith's true identity as young Harmon is at length brought to light. With this main plot goes a minor story of Silas Wegg's attempt to blackmail Boffin. In addition there is a parallel main plot concerning the rival lovers of Lizzie Hexam, daughter of a Thames boatman; one of her lovers is the aristocratic young barrister, Eugene Wrayburn, and the other the embittered schoolmaster of low social origins, Bradley Headstone. Headstone tries to murder Wrayburn and nearly succeeds, but he is drowned in a struggle with Rogue Riderhood, another waterman who is also a blackmailer. Wrayburn, physically wrecked, marries Lizzie for whom he at last comes to have a real need. The two main plots are linked through the waterside characters who are connected with young Harmon's supposed murder at the beginning of the book. The novel extends through the Wrayburn-Lizzie story into upper-middle-class circles which include the arrogant Podsnaps, the Veneerings who attempt to climb into wealthy society and fall out of it again, the fraudulent social adventurers Mr and Mrs Lammle, the mean and ruthless financier Fledgeby. Through Fledgeby on the one side and Lizzie on the other, the lower social circles include Riah, the

benevolent Jew, and Jenny Wren, the bitter-sweet doll's dressmaker. The book is thus given an unusually wide variety of character and social environment, even for Dickens, and it is pervaded by a rich symbolism arising from the use made of the River Thames and the dust-heaps out of which the Harmon fortunes have been made. The motive of special social reform, more characteristic of early Dickens (eg ▷ *Oliver Twist*, 1838) is evident in the episode of Betty Higden, the poor woman who dies by the roadside sooner than enter a workhouse.

Overbury, Sir Thomas (1581–1613)
Essayist and poet; as a writer he is chiefly remembered as the author of one of the most widely read collections of 'Theophrastian' character sketches (▷ Characters, Theophrastian), published in 1614. ▷ John Webster, ▷ Thomas Dekker, ▷ John Donne, ▷ Cecily Bulstrode, ▷ Lady Frances Southwell and others made additions to subsequent issues of the collection between 1614 and 1622.

Overbury was also the victim of one of the most sensational murders in English history. He tried to oppose a love intrigue between ▷ James I's royal favourite, Thomas Carr, Earl of Somerset, and the young Countess of Essex. The lovers conspired to have Overbury poisoned; the crime came to light, and the prosecution was conducted by ▷ Francis Bacon. Carr and the Countess were convicted and disgraced, but their agents who actually administered the poison were hanged.

Overton, Richard (fl. 1631–64)
Religious prose writer. Little is known for certain about Overton, but it is probable that he was the son of a clergyman, joined a ▷ Baptist community in the Netherlands in 1615–6 and matriculated from Cambridge in 1631. During the early 1640s he wrote a number of tracts against ▷ Laud, ▷ Catholicism and monopolies, following these with six anti-Presbyterian (▷ Presbyterianism) tracts and works supporting the ▷ Levellers. His most well-known work is *Mans Mortalitie* (1644) which argues that the soul is not immortal between death and resurrection (▷ Hobbes and ▷ Milton also argue this). Overton's tone is a combination of satire and parody and links him closely in style to ▷ Martin Marprelate.
Bib: Pooley, R., *English Prose of the Seventeenth Century, 1590–1700*.

Ovid (Publius Ovidius Naso) (43 BC – AD 17)
Roman poet, and the last of the greatest period of Latin poetry, the Augustan Age. He wrote for the sophisticated and elegant society of the capital of the Empire, but the immorality of his *Ars Amatoria* ('Art of Love') offended the Emperor ▷ Augustus who (for this and some other more mysterious offence) exiled him to the Black Sea about AD 9. The works by which Ovid is principally known are: the *Amores*, love poems in what is called the 'elegiac' couplet; the *Ars Amatoria*; the *Remedia Amoris*, in which he tries to redeem himself for the offence he caused by the *Ars Amatoria*; the *Heroides*, in which he makes the heroines of myth give tongue to their misfortunes; the ▷ *Metamorphoses*, a collection of tales about miraculous transformation of shape; the *Fasti*, a poetic account of the Roman calendar; and the *Tristia*, verse epistles lamenting his exile.

Ovid was one of the most read and influential poets in later centuries, in England this is especially true from the 16th to 18th centuries. his most popular work was the *Metamorphoses*; these were repeatedly imitated and translated, memorably by ▷ Golding in the 16th century and by Sandys and ▷ Dryden in the 17th. ▷ Shakespeare was called in 1598 'the English Ovid' because the source of his *Venus and Adonis* was the *Metamorphoses* and that of *The Rape of Lucrece* was the *Fasti*; moreover the quality of these two poems was felt to be Ovidian. ▷ Marlowe translated Ovid's love elegies, and the freedom and vigour of his kind of love poem influenced ▷ Donne in his Elegies. As early as the 14th century ▷ Chaucer got the tales in his ▷ *Legend of Good Women* from the *Heroides*, and these poems set a tradition in 'Heroic Epistles' which began with ▷ Drayton in the early 17th century and culminated in ▷ Pope's *Eloisa to Abelard*. Ovid's influence is traceable repeatedly in the work of ▷ Spenser and touched ▷ Milton. Thus he may be said to have affected, either in subject matter or in style, almost all the major poets from Chaucer to Pope, and his influence was equally extensive among lesser figures. The influence was not always deep, however, and it can be ascribed partly to his being the liveliest and most beguiling of the Roman poets who were regarded as the basis of a cultured understanding of literature.
▷ Elegy; Latin literature.

Owen, Robert (1771–1858)
Social reformer, and a leading socialist thinker in the early 19th century. He became part-owner of the New Lanark Cotton Mills in 1800, and found that its workers were living in the degraded and nearly desperate conditions common in the earlier phase of the ▷ Industrial Revolution. He set about improving their housing and working conditions, and established infant schools. His reforms were a success, but his expenditure on them caused resentment among his partners, and in 1813 he established a new firm, with ▷ Jeremy Bentham as one of his partners. In the same year he published a volume of essays, *A New View of Society*, in which he sought to prove that the human character is entirely created by its environment. In 1817, in a report to the House of Commons, Owen pointed out that

the existing social misery was caused by men competing unsuccessfully with machines, and he recommended the establishment of socialist working communities in the country; they were to vary from 500 to 3,000 in size, and were to be partly industrial. His views were received favourably by, among other people, the Duke of Kent, the father of Queen Victoria, but Owen spoilt his case with public opinion in general by mixing his proposals with anti-religious propaganda. Nonetheless two experiments were attempted in 1825, one in England and one in America; both failed in under two years. Owen now became the leader of a socialist-secular movement, through which he sought to replace the emphasis on political reform by emphasis on economic action. His influence led to the Grand National Consolidated Trades Union in 1833, but this also failed owing to bad organization. The word 'socialism' originated through discussions centred on the Association of all Classes of all Nations, which Owen founded in 1835. The only permanent success among Owen's experiments was his establishment of the Co-operative Movement, which nowadays is affiliated to the Labour Party.

Owen, Wilfred (1893–1918)
The best known of the so-called 'War poets' of World War I: *Poems* (1920). He served as an infantry officer, was awarded a decoration for bravery, and was killed a week before the armistice. Before the war he was already writing mildly sensuous poetry influenced by John Keats; for some time during the war he continued to write in this late-Romantic tradition. But he then adapted his technique so as to express the intensity of the suffering of the Western Front, deliberately introducing elements of discordance and harshness into his style especially by the use of 'para-rhyme', *ie* the repetition of consonants but changing the vowels, as in the words 'hall'-'hell'. The best known of his poems is *Strange Meeting* – a dream about an encounter with an enemy soldier who is, humanly, a friend, in surroundings which are both those of the war and of hell. Owen's poems were used by the composer Benjamin Britten in one of his major musical compositions, *War Requiem*.

▷ War poets.

Bib: Owen, H., *Life*; critical study by D. S. R. Welland; Hibberd, D., *Owen the Poet*.

Owl and the Nightingale, The
A Middle English anonymous debate poem, dating from the early 13th century. It is a sparkling, highly sophisticated piece in which the two birds take opposing views first on their respective arts of song-making, but then on a wide range of religious and moral issues. The natural song-making ability of the birds is used to represent the clash between different kinds of lyrical literary traditions; indeed the question of whether literature should be used as a medium of entertainment or instruction becomes part of the grounds of their quarrel. The author makes full use of the range of shifting symbolic and figural associations of owls and nightingales, and plays with the possibilities of their anthropomorphic and naturalistic representation. Neither of the two birds is a wholly positive or negative figure, neither is clearly right or wrong, though generally the nightingale takes the lighter role whereas the owl espouses a more solemn stance. Their dispute is not resolved: the narrative concludes with their departure to seek judgement from one Master Nicholas of Guildford.

Bib: Stanley, E. G. (ed.), *The Owl and the Nightingale*.

Oxford Movement (Tractarian Movement)
A religious movement within the ▷ Church of England; it had its origin and main centre in Oxford and ran from 1833, when it began with a sermon by Keble until 1845 when its most eloquent leader, ▷ John Newman, entered the Roman Catholic Church. Some of the leaders of the Church of England realized (especially after the Act of Catholic Emancipation, 1829) that the Church was by its constitution largely at the mercy of the state, and was in danger of becoming in essentials a department of the state. The Oxford Movement preached that the Church had its independent, spiritual status, was in direct descent from the medieval Catholic Church, and represented a 'middle way' between post-Reformation Catholicism and ▷ Protestantism. The movement's propaganda was conducted through ▷ tracts, many of them by John Newman, and culminated in *Tract XC* which asserted that the Thirty-Nine Articles, on which Anglican doctrine is based, are compatible with Roman Catholic doctrine. The tracts divided Anglican opinion severely, and Newman's secession to the Church of Rome, followed by the secession of other High Anglican clergy, brought the movement into discredit with the majority of Anglican opinion. Edward Pusey, Professor of Hebrew at Oxford, was the leader of the Oxford Movement, which was in consequence often called Puseyite. An indirect result of the movement was to focus attention on the medieval background of the Church, and to encourage that reification of the Middle Ages which emerged in much victorian literature, in the artistic movement known as Pre-Raphaelitism and in Victorian neo-Gothic architecture.

Oxymoron

▷ Figures of Speech.

***Ozymandias* (1818)**
A witty sonnet by ▷ Percy Bysshe Shelley concerning the vanity of human ambition. An ancient statue stands broken and isolated in

the desert, its boastful inscription now carrying an ironically different meaning from that first intended: 'My name is Ozymandias, king of kings: Look on my works, ye Mighty, and despair!' The ancient Greek historian Diodorus Siculus (1st century BC) calls the tomb of the great Egyptian Pharoah Rameses II the tomb of Ozymandias.

Paean
In ancient Greece, a hymn of thanksgiving, obscurely linked with the god of health (or perhaps ▷ Apollo in one of his aspects), perhaps through the practice of chanting sacred healing spells.

Page, Louise (b 1955)
Dramatist. A graduate of Birmingham University's drama course (where she was taught by ▷ David Edgar), she has been writer-in-residence at the ▷ Royal Court, a Fellow in Drama and TV at Yorkshire Television, and associate Director at Theatre Calgary in Alberta, Canada.

Something of a minimalist and a writer of spare dialogue, her plays reflect a generation of women where feminism is assumed, if not overt. Her plays have ranged from the unpredictable and surreal time-warp of *Salonika* (1982) to the hermetic domesticity of *Real Estate*, and the large-scale and ambitious re-working of the old fairy tale *Beauty and the Beast* (1985). An early play, *Tissue* (1978), touches sensitively on the trauma of a young woman facing breast cancer whilst *Golden Girls* (1984), about women and sport, takes a leaf out of ▷ Caryl Churchill's book in tackling women and ambition. Much of her reputation rests on *Salonika* with which she won the 1982 George Divine award at the age of twenty-four. *Slaonika* is a surrealistic account of the effect of World War I on a widow returning to the Grecian beach where her husband died sixty-five years earlier (he reappears during the course of the play), and on her elderly spinster daughter. Critics hailed it as 'haunting' and a remarkably mature piece of work on the themes of futility and the frictions of mother/daughter relationships. Her plays have been produced all over the world, in New Zealand, the U.S.A., Denmark, Greece, Australia, Norway.

Pageant
The word derives from the name of a kind of stage used in medieval ▷ Mystery plays which moved in procession to prearranged positions in the town and exhibited scenes from the Bible dramatizing the fall of man and his redemption by Christ. In modern England, a pageant is a display, commonly in the form of a procession, celebrating a historical or legendary event, usually with patriotic significance. This sense of the word 'pageant' has a clear relationship with the Mystery plays, and illustrates a particular dramatic viewpoint. The Mysteries were dramatic inasmuch as they represented conflicts between good and evil, but the stories and their outcome were fully known to the audience, so that there was small place for the unexpected. The modern pageant is an undramatic spectacle, and such pageants existed in the 16th century, symbolizing non-biblical legends of patriotic significance like the story of ▷ St George and the Dragon. Thus the traditions of the pageant are twofold: in one sense it is purely spectacle, but in another it may be a spectacle combined with the narrative of a conflict, which is dramatic only because the conflict is seen as symbolic of a permanent truth of human experience. The second sense of the pageant tradition is important for understanding Elizabethan ▷ history plays, especially those of ▷ Shakespeare. Thus, in ▷ *Henry IV, Part I* the modern audience is inclined to see the drama as a conflict of the soul of Prince Hal, who on the one hand is faced with the temptations of self-indulgence through Falstaff, and on the other with the task of winning 'honour' from Hotspur. Yet the audience is misled by this approach, since in I.ii Prince Hal declares that he is in no danger of yielding to Falstaff, and his acquisition of honour is also foreknown through the historical fact of the battle of ▷ Agincourt; Hal is thus not the hero of an inner moral and an outer physical conflict, at least in the sense that there is the smallest uncertainty in the audience's mind about the outcome. On the other hand, Falstaff and Hotspur – the self-indulgent favourite and the self-centred politician – are dangers to which any nation is everlastingly exposed. Thus the dramatic interest of the play is not Hal but the nation, and the play is essentially the re-enactment of a conflict to which the nation is perpetually exposed – a dramatic pageant in the Mystery and ▷ Morality tradition. Pageants, even informal ones, continued to be important in the social life of communities: ▷ Virginia Woolf's *Between the Acts* is based on one.

***Pageant, and Other Poems, A* (1881)**
A collection of poems by ▷ Christina Rossetti, including the sonnet sequence 'Monna Innominata' and the important poems 'The Thread of Life' and 'An Old World Thicket', in which Rossetti explores her poetic and religious identity. Other noteworthy lyrics include 'An Immurata Sister', spoken from the perspective of a nun who seeks release from worldly (and gender-specific) constraints, and 'A Life's Parallels', an enigmatic poem addressing the mystery of death.

Paine, Thomas (1737–1809)
Political author. The son a small farmer, his early career in England as an official ended in failure, and he sailed for America in 1774. In 1776 he published the republican pamphlet *Common Sense*, which set the colonists openly on the road to independence. After the start of the American War of Independence, he maintained the morale of the rebels with a series of pamphlets called *The Crisis* (1776–83). The opening sentence was 'These are the times that try men's souls' – words which became a battle-cry.

In 1787 he returned to Europe to carry on his fight for republican democracy. When ▷ Burke published his ▷ *Reflections on the Revolution in France* in 1790, Paine replied with Part I of his ▷ *Rights of Man* (1791). The Government was making the preparations for his trial for treason in 1792 when the poet ▷ William Blake got him out of the country to France, where the French revolutionary government had elected him a member of the republican Convention. In France he published his *Age of Reason* (1793) which defended a rational, abstract form of ▷ deism against orthodox Christianity. This caused him to lose his popularity in England and in America. He also lost favour with the French for his injudicious criticisms, and for a time he was imprisoned, though he was later restored to his seat in the Convention. In 1802 he returned to America to find that he had lost his influence there and he died at his farm in New Rochelle in 1809. Ten years later the English radical ▷ William Cobbett returned to England with Tom Paine's bones. For some time his works remained a text-book for English radicalism.
Bib: Wilson D.A., *Paine and Cobbett: The Transatlantic Connection*; Philip, M., *Paine*.

***Pair of Blue Eyes, A* (1873)**
▷ Thomas Hardy's third and much underrated novel, often unfairly overshadowed by ▷ *Tess of the d'Urbervilles* (1891) which, in many ways, it anticipates. Echoing the circumstances of Hardy's courtship of his first wife Emma Gifford it deals with the story, and consequences, of the abortive love affair and elopement of Elfride Swancourt, an isolated rector's daughter living in Endlestowe on the North Cornish coast, and a young architect from London, Stephen Smith. Stephen's lowly class origins are the reason for the Reverend Swancourt's opposition the marriage, and the couple elope on an impulse, only for Elfride to lose heart and return home on the next train. However, she has been seen in a compromising situation by Mrs Jethway who believes that Elfride's light-hearted flirtation with her son caused his death. Stephen goes off to India to make his fortune and promises to return to claim Elfride. As a result of her father's marriage to a wealthy widow, and her attempts at novel writing, Elfride meets and falls in love with the curiously fastidious Henry Knight and breaks off her engagement with Smith. Terrified that Knight might discover her previous relationship with Smith, Elfride is haunted by Mrs Jethway, who threatens to betray her. Finally confessing to the elopement she is immediately rejected by Knight whose cruel judgement of her leaves her heartbroken. Knight meets Smith, his former friend and protégé, and both men betray their love for Elfride hurrying down to Cornwall to reclaim her, unaware that the train on which they are travelling is also carrying Elfride's copse back to Endlestow. Her marriage to the wealthy Lord Luxellian has not prevented her decline and she has died in childbirth. ▷ Tennyson, ▷ Coventry Patmore and Marcel Proust (1871–1922) were wildly enthusiastic about the novel which is now the subject of critical re-evaluation. The scene on the Cliff Without a Name is one of Hardy's most magnificent depictions of man's relationship to an indifferent Nature, and is deeply influenced by evolutionary theory.
▷ Darwin, Charles.

Pakington, Dorothy, Lady (d 1679)
Moralist, considered one of the most learned ladies of her time, she remained loyal to the ▷ Church of England, and to the ▷ Stuart cause throughout her life. A number of popular conduct books (▷ conduct literature) have sometimes been attributed to her, including *The Whole Duty of Man* (1658), *The Gentleman's Calling* (1660) and *The Lady's Calling* (1673), a textbook of virtue, modesty, and duty. But nowadays doubt has been thrown on her authorship of the first two works, which are believed to be by the cleric Richard Allestree, and he may have composed the third as well. Nevertheless, her influence was considerable in her day. Lady Pakington was part of a circle of educated and devout men and women, and before the Restoration she held in her home a sort of salon for those who shared her concerns.
Bib: Reynolds, M., *The Learned Lady in England and 1650–1760*.

'Palace of Art, The' (1832)
Poem by ▷ Alfred Tennyson published in *Poems* (1832). It is an allegory of the aesthetic soul that vainly shrinks from the encroachment of 'uncertain shapes', the lengthening shadows of a dark reality. It is evidence in Tennyson of the struggle between a personal 'art for art's sake' philosophy and art linked to the interests of 19th-century society. It is a reaction to the anti-romantic bias of the Victorian period that produced a sociological aesthetic, and considers the question of whether art should function as an escape from or a means of considering broader cultural and intellectual problems.
▷ Aestheticism.

Palace of Pleasure, The
An anthology of tales translated from the Italian and Latin, compiled by William Painter (?1540–94) and published 1566–7. Writers include Bandello, ▷ Boccaccio, Herodotus and Livy. It was used as a source book for plots by ▷ Elizabethan dramatists, including ▷ Shakespeare who drew on it, at least to some extent, for ▷ *All's Well that Ends Well*, and perhaps some other plays.

Palamon and Arcite
Rivals for the love of Emily in ▷ Chaucer's ▷ *Knight's Tale*, the first of the ▷ *Canterbury*

Tales, Shakespeare and Fletcher dramatised their story in *The Two Noble Kinsmen*. ▷ Dryden paraphrased Chaucer's tale as *Palamon and Arcite*, published in his *Fables Ancient and Modern* (1699).

Palindrome
▷ Figures of Speech.

Palinode
The withdrawal in a piece of writing of ideas or attitudes expressed in another by the same writer; or the expression in one work of ideas which are in direct opposition to those which the author has expressed in a previous one. As, for example, ▷ Geoffrey Chaucer does in the *Retraction* at the end of ▷ *The Canterbury Tales*, where he rejects his romances and love poetry:

> *my translacions and enditynges of worldly vanitees, the whiche I revoke in my retracciouns:/ as is the book of Troilus; the book also of Fame; the book of the XXV. Ladies; the book of the Duchesse; the book of Seint Valentynes day of the Parlement of Briddes; the tales of Caunterbury, thilke that sownen into synne;/ the book of the Leoun; and many another book, if they were in my remembrance, and many a song and many a leccherous lay, that Crist for his grete mercy foryeve me the synne.*

Palladio, Andrea (1508–80)
Italian architect. Palladio's villas, public buildings and churches – built between 1540 and 1580, and to be found in Venice, Vicenza and the countryside around these two important Italian ▷ Renaissance cities – were to have a lasting effect on English and American architectural styles. The first great English classical architect ▷ Inigo Jones was strongly influenced by Palladian ideals of design. These ideals – usually manifested in symmetrical fronts and applied half-columns topped by a pediment – were themselves derived from Palladio's intense study of architectural styles to be found in the surviving antiquities of ancient Rome. Indeed, Palladio was himself the author of one of the earliest guidebooks to the city's remains when he published his *Le Antichita di Roma* in 1554. This work, together with his *Quattro Libri dell' Architecttura* (1570), served to publicize the classical forms of architecture that came to dominate design in the 17th and 18th centuries.

The 'Palladian' style expresses key Renaissance aesthetic ideas. Those ideas, which encompass proportion, harmony and balance, were to become of great importance during the 18th century when Palladio's designs, and studies of his works, were much in vogue.
Bib: Wittkower, R., *Architectural Principles in the Age of Humanism*; Ackerman, J. S., *Palladio*.

Palliser Novels, The (1864–80)
A sequence of novels by ▷ Anthony Trollope which is composed of *Can You Forgive Her?* (1864–65), *Phineas Finn* (1867–9), *The Eustace Diamonds* (1871–3), *Phineas Redux* (1873–4), *The Prime Minister* (1875–6) and *The Duke's Children* (1879–80). Trollope described them as 'a series of semi-political tales'.

***Pamela* (1740–1)**
Subtitled 'Virtue Rewarded', *Pamela* is an ▷ epistolary novel by ▷ Samuel Richardson. The story of a young servant girl who evades her master's attempts at seduction, Richardson's novel was a great contemporary success, yet sophisticated readers were quick to see its ambiguous message. By her insistence on her country simplicity, Pamela persuades the squire to marry her; yet her self-conscious parade of 'artless' virtue suggests a level of sexual innuendo of which Richardson may or may not have been aware. ▷ Henry Fielding's ▷ *Shamela* and ▷ *Joseph Andrews* parody this element of *Pamela*.

Pamphlet
Any short treatise published separately, usually without hard covers. It is usually polemical, *ie* written to defend or attack some body of ideas, especially religious or political ones. In the 16th century and especially towards the end of the reign of ▷ Elizabeth I pamphleteering became a widespread literary industry, the beginning of journalism. ▷ Thomas Nashe and ▷ Thomas Dekker were amongst the most famous pamphleteers and the ▷ Marprelate controversy was the most famous of the 'pamphlet wars'. In the 17th century Milton was the most famous writer of pamphlets, and his ▷ *Areopagitica* is his masterpiece. In the 18th century some of ▷ Swift's finest prose was in pamphlet form, *eg* ▷ *A Modest Proposal* (1729), and ▷ Defoe was a prolific pamphleteer. The 18th century, however, saw the rise of the weekly periodicals, which reduced the need for the pamphlet form of literature.
▷ Journalism.

***Pandosto, The Triumph of Time* (1588)**
A prose romance by ▷ Robert Greene, used by ▷ Shakespeare as the basis for his late play, ▷ *The Winter's Tale*.

Panjandrum
The word first occurs in a sentence devised by the actor-playwright Samuel Foote (1720–77) to test the memory of another actor-playwright, Charles Macklin (d 1797): '. . . and there were present the Picninnies, and the Joblillies, and

the Garyulies, and the Grand Panjandrum himself, with the little round button on top.' The word came to be used for any pompous person, or for someone of supposed power.

Pankhurst, Sylvia (1882–1960)
Poet and political writer. Sylvia Pankhurst's extraordinary career as a political activist, first for women's suffrage and later in wider socialist causes (for women in London's East End, and for Ethiopian independence) has overshadowed her equally extraordinary writing. She produced strong biographical and historical accounts of the suffrage movement (for example, the definitive biography of her mother, the *Life of Emmeline Pankhurst*, 1935, and *The Suffrage Movement*, 1931), and published two volumes of passionate, radical poetry in her lifetime: *Writ on a Cold Slate* (1922) and a translation of the Romanian poems of M. Eminescu *Poems* (1931).
▷ Feminism.
Bib: Castle, B., *Sylvia and Christabel Pankhurst* (1987); Pankhurst, R. K. P. *Sylvia Pankhurst: Artist and Crusader* (1979); Romero, P. W. E., *Sylvia Pankhurst: Portrait of a Radical* (1987).

Pantagruel
A comic romance by ▷ François Rabelais, published in its first version in 1532. Pantagruel is the son of ▷ Gargantua.

Pantheism
A term used to cover a variety of religious and philosophical beliefs, which have in common that God is present in nature, and not separable from it in the sense in which a cause is separable from its effect, or a creator from his creation. Pantheism is implicit in doctrines derived from ▷ Plato, *eg* in some of the neo-Platonists of the 16th century, and in some poetry inspired by the natural environment. Amongst English poets, the most famous example is ▷ Wordsworth in his earlier phase (1797–1807), notably in the first two books of his 1805 version of ▷ *The Prelude*. In his revised version of this autobiographical poem, Wordsworth tried to eliminate the pantheistic tendencies, since they are not in accordance with most forms of Christian doctrine.

Pantisocracy
The name given by ▷ Samuel Taylor Coleridge and ▷ Robert Southey to the ideal anarchistic society which preoccupied them in 1794–5 during the first phase of the ▷ French Revolution (from the Greek: *pan* = 'all', *isos* = 'the same', *cratos* = 'power'). They hoped to establish a community on the banks of the River Susquehanna in the United States in which motives of gain would be replaced by brotherly love. They were unable to raise money, however, their ideas changed, and they abandoned their plan.

Pantomime
Originally, in ancient Rome, a representation by masked actors, using gestures and dance, of religious or warlike episodes. One actor played many parts, male and female, with changes of mask and costumes. It was often accompanied by music. It was used for episodes in medieval religious drama, and as the 16th-century Italian ▷ *commedia dell'arte* it became a form of popular drama that spread all over Europe together with a number of traditional characters such as Harlequin and the Clown. In the 18th century it established itself in England. Nowadays the children's pantomimes performed in Britain after Christmas are usually musical plays representing traditional folk-tales (*Puss in Boots, Dick Whittington,* etc.) in a vulgarized form, but sometimes introducing traditional characters from the *commedia dell'arte*. Certain conventions are peculiar to it: the hero of the story or 'principal boy' is always performed by an actress, and a comic character known as the 'pantomime dame' is performed by an actor, a gender-reversal which is a direct inheritance of the 'world-turned-upside down' ▷ carnivalesque mode.
Bib: Bukhtin, M., *Rabelais and his World*.

Paradigmatic
The terms paradigmatic and syntagmatic were used by the linguist Ferdinand de Saussure to indicate two axes for the understanding of language. The syntagmatic axis is controlled by the way units in any given language are combined sequentially. Specifically, this refers to the rules governing the combination of sounds (phonemes) to make meaningful sequences and therefore words, and, at higher levels, the grammatical and syntactical rules which structure the way words are put together in sentences. The paradigmatic axis, by contrast, is sometimes called the 'associative' axis. It refers (to stay at the level of words) to the network of associations connected to the actual word selected, that is, words which belong to the same class. The linguist is primarily interested in formal connections at the level of sound and structure (cat is associated with bat, fat, hat and so on), but such formal connections link with more nebulous levels of behaviour or cultural association which interest the literary critic (for example, cat is associated with mat and hence hearth and home). It is from the associative or paradigmatic axis, it is argued, that imagery and metaphor are derived and much of literature gains its energy thereby. The rules which shape syntagmatic and, especially, paradigmatic selection is of interest to structuralist literary critics.
Bib: Lodge, D., *The Modes of Modern Writing*.

***Paradise Lost* (1667)**
An ▷ epic poem by ▷ John Milton, first published in ten books in 1667, but

reorganized and published in 12 books in a second edition of 1674. The composition of *Paradise Lost* was possibly begun in the mid-1650s, but the idea for an epic based on scriptural sources had, in all probability, occurred to Milton at least as early as 1640, when the four drafts of an outline ▷ tragedy were composed. These drafts, contained in a Trinity College, Cambridge manuscript, indicate that in its original conception, *Paradise Lost* (or, to give the poem its draft title, *Adam Unparadized*) was to have been a sacred drama, rather than an epic. This hint at a dramatic origin, on the lines of classical Greek tragedy, helps to explain the undoubtedly dramatic qualities to be found in the poem – for example the soliloquizing habits of Satan, and the *perepeteias*, or discoveries, where new ▷ ironies in the narrative are allowed to unfold.

The chief source of the poem is the ▷ Bible, but the Bible as glossed and commented upon by the Patristic (early Christian) authorities, and by Protestant theologians. But also important to Milton's project were the classical writers – ▷ Homer and ▷ Virgil – from whom Milton's conception of 'epic' was principally inherited. ▷ Edmund Spenser's ▷ *The Faerie Queene* was also vital to Milton's handling of language and imagery. To these principle sources can be added the epics of ▷ Ludovico Ariosto and ▷ Torquato Tasso, ▷ Ovid's *Metamorphoses*, the *De rerum natura* of ▷ Lucretius, and the once popular, though now little read, *La Semaine* by ▷ Guillaume de Saluste Du Bartas. Once these sources have been remarked upon, however, the possible progenitors of Milton's poem still remain numberless, since *Paradise Lost* draws upon the whole field of intellectual endeavour open to a classically trained European scholar in the 17th century.

For all that it is a poem rooted in Milton's literary experience, it is also a poem of, and for, its times. The poem's chief theme is rebellion – the rebellion of Satan and his followers against God, and the rebellion of Adam and Eve against divine law. Within this sacred context, Milton sets himself the task of justifying God's creational will to his 17th-century readers. But, in confronting questions such as choice, obedience and forms of government, Milton also raises the issues of freedom, social relationships and the quality and definition of power – whether almighty, satanic or human. We can thus understand the poem as confronting political questions that, in the moment of its composition and eventual publication following the English ▷ Civil War and the Restoration of the monarchy, were of real urgency to both the republican Milton and his readers. This is not to say that, as some of Milton's commentators have claimed, the poem operates as a veiled ▷ allegory of events in mid-17th-century England. But the issues faced by the protagonists in *Paradise Lost* are also issues that were at the heart of contemporary political debate. To entwine matters of theology and political theory was by no means a strange grafting to Milton's contemporaries. Religion and politics were inseparably twinned, and *Paradise Lost* confronts that conjunction at every point.

The history of the poem's critical reception since the date of its publication is itself a commentary on the history of English literary 'taste'. For all that 18th-century writers admired Milton's grand scheme, their admiration was tinged by a certain uneasiness. Both Joseph Addison (1672–1719) and Samuel Johnson (1709–84) felt that Milton's achievement was undoubtedly immense, but that it was also an achievement which could not and should not be replicated. For the poets of the Romantic period – William Blake (1757–1827), Percy Bysshe Shelley (1792–1822), John Keats (1795–1821) and the William Wordsworth (1770–1850) of *The Prelude* – *Paradise Lost* was read as a significant text in the history of the individual's struggle to identify him or herself within the political and social sphere. But rather than understand the poem as a theological epic, they tended to read it as a text of human liberty, with Satan, rather than God, as the focus of the poem's meaning. In the 20th century, following the re-evaluation in poetic taste prompted by W. B. Yeats (1865–1939), T. S. Eliot (1888–1965) and ▷ F. R. Leavis, *Paradise Lost* was seen, once more, as a masterpiece of questionable stature. Was it, perhaps, removed from what Eliot and Leavis in particular cared to identify as the 'English tradition'? The debate initiated by Leavis and his followers was to be answered in a series of important accounts of the poem by ▷ C. S. Lewis, ▷ William Empson and Christopher Ricks. In the 1970s and 1980s attention has been refocussed, by Marxist and feminist critics especially, on what have long been unexamined aspects of the poem: its treatment of patriarchal authority and its relationship to the continuing historical debate on the intellectual culture of the revolutionary period. At the same time, Milton's themes of language and identity have rendered the poem a fruitful text for ▷ psychoanalytical criticism. We might conclude, then, that whilst perhaps the greatest achievement of the English literary ▷ Renaissance, *Paradise Lost* is also a text open to continuous re-reading and revision.

Bib: Carey, J. and Fowler, A. (eds.) *The Complete Poems of John Milton.*

Paradise Regained **(1671)**

An ▷ epic poem by ▷ John Milton in four books, it was first published (together with *Samson Agonistes*) in 1671. Begun after the publication of ▷ *Paradise Lost* in 1667, the poem can, in some sense, be thought of as a sequel to *Paradise Lost*. In particular, the poem's treatment of Christ, his resistance to temptation, and the redeeming nature of his ministry on earth, cast him in the theologically traditional role of the 'Second Adam' – a regenerative and redeeming force in the world.

Where *Paradise Lost*, however, was conceived of along lines inherited from classical epic, *Paradise Regained* is in the form of the 'brief epic' in the style of the book of *Job*. The chief subject matter of the poem is the temptation of Christ in the wilderness, described in the gospel of *St Luke*.

Paradiso
The third and final section of ▷ Dante's great poem, the ▷ *Divina Commedia*. Dante has been led through the Inferno and the Purgatorio by the spirit of the Roman poet ▷ Virgil. Now his guide is Beatrice, the woman who had inspired Dante's love. As the Inferno was divided into circles, so Paradise is divided into spheres: the sphere of the Moon, of Mercury, Venus, the Sun, Mars, Jupiter, Saturn, the Fixed Stars, and the Primum Mobile, or First Mover. Each sphere contains the kind of spirit the ancient Greek and Roman myths had caused to be associated with it: Mars, the Christian warriors and martyrs; Jupiter, the just rulers; Saturn, the holy contemplatives, etc. The spheres are in ascending order of merit, and culminate in Dante's remote, ecstatic vision of God Himself. In each, Dante has conversations on philosophical and spiritual matters with the men and women from history whom he conceives to have been assigned there.

▷ *Inferno: Purgatorio.*

Paradox
▷ Figures of Speech.

Pardoner's Prologue and Tale, The
One of ▷ Chaucer's ▷ *Canterbury Tales*. As his contribution to the storytelling competition, the Pardoner offers an exposé of his standard preaching routine in theory and in practice. His performance may be compared to that of Faus Semblant (False Seeming) in the ▷ *Roman de la Rose*. His prologue outlines the range of techniques he employs to persuade his lay audiences to buy his (self-confessedly) worthless relics, and contains verbatim extracts from his routine. The theme of his performance as a whole is '*Radix malorum est cupiditas*' ('covetousness is the root of all evil'), but the maxim is graphically illustrated in his tale of the three 'riotoures' who set out to kill Death (who has killed one of their companions). They meet a mysterious old man on their quest, who directs them to a spot where they might find Death, but when they arrive they simply find a pile of gold. As a result of their plotting to cheat each other out of their shares in the gold, all three are killed. Although the Pardoner has exposed his mercenary motives to the pilgrim audience, he ends his performance apparently with a serious attempt to sell them his relics. His invitation to the Host to have the first choice is violently and abusively rejected. The game limits have been transgressed and the Knight steps in to heal the breach so that the *Canterbury Tales* may continue.

Parker, Matthew (1504–75)
Became Archbishop of Canterbury on the accession of ▷ Elizabeth I, and was her main ally in her policy of keeping the ▷ Church of England on its unique midway course between the Roman Catholic Church and the more decidedly Protestant sects such as the Lutherans and Calvinists, represented in England by the Puritans. He was a notable scholar, and promoted the 'Bishop's Bible' (1568), which became the basis for the 'Authorized Version' of 1611.

▷ Bible in England; Reformation; Catholicism (Roman) in English literature.

Parlement of the Thre Ages, The
A 14th-century alliterative poem, recounting a ▷ dream vision experience in which the narrator witnesses a debate between Youth, Middle Age, and Old Age. These figures describe the different occupations and preoccupations of the successive stages in a man's life (the focus is on masculine pursuits); the pursuit of courtly pleasures advocated by Youth, gives way to the materialistic concerns which obsess Middle Age, and finally the *contemptus mundi* views of Old Age are ushered in. Old Age eclipses the views of Youth and Middle Age, because for him any engagement in worldly pleasures or materialistic gains is vain and futile. There is a correlation between the different attitudes and interests of the figures and different kinds of literary traditions, so the narrative offers a summary view of a range of literary themes and subjects at the same time as it epitomises the stance of Youth, Middle Age and Old Age.
Bib: Offord, M. Y. (ed.), *The Parlement of the Thre Ages*.

Parliament of Foulys, The
A ▷ dream-vision poem by ▷ Chaucer, in ▷ rhyme royal, which concludes with an account of a bird parliament, held on St Valentine's Day, when the birds meet to decide their mates for the year. The poem begins with an account of the melancholic narrator's reading matter, ▷ Cicero's *Dream of Scipio*, and then proceeds to recount a marvellous dream-experience in which the narrator is taken into a garden of love by Africanus, an important guide figure of the *Dream of Scipio*. Inside the garden, the narrator first explores Venus' temple and then moves on to witness the bird parliament, presided over by Dame Nature. Proceedings are delayed by a debate over which of three tercel eagles is the most fitting mate for a

formel eagle. Representatives from the three bird estates offer their views, but the decision is finally given to the formel eagle herself, who defers making a choice for another year. The rest of the birds are then free to choose their partners and the dream ends with a bird song (a ▷ roundel) welcoming Spring. The dreamer awakes and returns to his books, still hoping to learn something of value from them.

In just 699 lines, Chaucer explores the continuum of love and its literary expression, evoking the philosophical and ethical dimensions of love as a literary subject, yet keeping the tone of this *tour de force* light and comic, through using a slightly ineffectual narrator, and giving floor space to the down-to-earth views of geese and cuckoos on the subject. It is a poem which wittily negotiates quotations from ▷ Dante and from ducks.

▷ Courtly Love.

Bib: Brewer, D. S. (ed.), *The Parliament of Foulys.*

Parnell, Charles Stewart (1846–91)
Irish political leader. He entered Parliament in 1875, and led the Home Rule party in its fight for Irish self-government. He converted ▷ Gladstone and the Liberal Party to the support of Home Rule, but was politically ruined by becoming involved in a scandal with the wife of Captain O'Shea in 1890. His success was the more remarkable because he was a ▷ Protestant; the scandal finally turned the ▷ Catholic Church in Ireland against him. His downfall caused a deep split among the Irish nationalists.

Parnell, Thomas (1679–1718)
Member of the Tory (▷ Whig and Tory) clique associated with the ministry of Harley and ▷ Bolingbroke and participant with ▷ Jonathan Swift, ▷ Alexander Pope, ▷ John Gay and ▷ John Arbuthnot, in the shortlived ▷ Scriblerus Club. He translated a comic ▷ epic then attributed to ▷ Homer, *Battle of the Frogs and Mice*, into heroic ▷ couplets (1717). He also composed moral and allegorical ▷ fables including *The Hermit*, and the drearily sexist *Hesiod: or, The Rise of Woman*, 'A creature fond and changing, fair and vain,/ The creature woman, rises now to reign.' His versification has a facile elegance which was greatly valued at the time. In *A Night-Piece on Death*, first published in his posthumous *Poems* (1722), the characteristic tetrameter (▷ metre) couplet of 17th-century reflective poetry is smoothed out and polished, transforming religious intensity into conventional piety: 'There pass with melancholy State,/ By all the solemn Heaps of Fate,/ And think, as softly-sad thou tread/ Above the venerable Dead,/ Time was, like thee they Life possest,/ And Time shall be, that thou shalt Rest.' Later graveyard musings in the 1740s and 1750s add ▷ Gothic or ▷ sentimental elaborations to Parnell's model. Parnell's *Essay on the Different Stiles of Poetry* (1713) gives a rigid exposition of the ▷ Augustan doctrine of literary kinds.

Bib: Woodman, R., *Thomas Parnell.*

Parody
Parody consists of mocking a style of literary production through an exaggerated imitation. It is close to ▷ satire in its criticism of eccentricites, but it must always refer to literature or a way of writing, rather than satire's more open scope. For example, Cervantes' ▷ *Don Quixote* is a parody of chivalric romance and ▷ Shakespeare includes some parody of ▷ Lyly's ▷ *Euphues* in ▷ *Much Ado about Nothing.*

In the 18th century ▷ Fielding's ▷ *Joseph Andrews* is partly a parody of ▷ Richardson's ▷ *Pamela*, and ▷ Pope's ▷ *Rape of the Lock* is a parody of grand ▷ epic in the style of ▷ Homer and ▷ Virgil. In the ▷ Romantic period an example of parody is ▷ James and ▷ Horatio Smith's ▷ *Rejected Addresses* (1812) which contains witty attacks against ▷ Wordsworth, ▷ Coleridge, ▷ Southey, ▷ Byron, ▷ Crabbe and ▷ Scott. It is difficult to draw a line between parody and ▷ burlesque; the latter is more obviously comic in its style of imitation. For example, ▷ Stella Gibbons' *Cold Comfort Farm* uses parody (of the primitivism of writers such as D. H. Lawrence) as well as burlesque; less famous short examples of 20th-century parody can be found in *The Faber Book of Parodies.* Together with pastiche, parody has played a significant role in ▷ post-modernist fiction.

Parole
In the work of ▷ Ferdinand de Saussure, the founder of Structuralism, this is usually translated as 'speech' or 'speech act'. It refers to a particular instance of speech. '*Parole*' is to be distinguished from ▷ '*langue*' (language) which is the linguistic system which underpins every utterance (*parole*). Speakers of a language (*langue*) avail themselves of parts of that system and reactiviate it each time they engage in speech (*parole*).

▷ Sign.

Paronomasia
▷ Figures of Speech.

Parr, Queen Katherine (1512–48)
Devotional writer. Last of ▷ Henry VIII's six wives, Katherine was widowed twice before she married the aging king. She immediately influenced the court towards a more contemplative and Protestant character, while initiating religious debate with Henry himself. Katherine was especially concerned with education and was a known protector and patron

of the new Protestant universities; moreover, she personally directed the education of the future ▷ Edward VI and ▷ Elizabeth I. Her religious activities became somewhat radical and she was in danger of being executed over the ▷ Anne Askew affair, but being forewarned of the plot against her she skilfully manipulated the king into supporting her. Katherine Parr's two works are devotional in nature: *Prayers and Medytacions* (1545) and *Lamentacion of a Sinner* (1547).
Bib: Travitsky, B. (ed.), *The Paradise of Women*.

Parr, Susanna (c 1659)
Religious writer and autobiographer. Known for one work, *Susanna's Apologie Against the Elders* (1659), we may deduce that Susanna Parr was attacked by the elders of her Baptist church in Exeter when she left, and that they tried to have her excommunicated. She was angered by their attack and, rather than accept the more conventional female role of victim, decided to defend herself in print. Interestingly, she attributes the more radical position to the minister who opposed her, Lewis Stuckley, but even though she appears to position herself within the main body of Baptist beliefs, her views on the rights of women to speak in church are clearly not conventional. She uses biting irony to ridicule her attackers, but also includes detailed descriptions of church practices and contemporary theological arguments.
▷ Autobiography.
Bib: Graham, E. *et al.* (eds.), *Her Own Life*.

Parson's Tale, The
The last of ▷ Chaucer's ▷ *Canterbury Tales*. It is prefaced by a call from the Host for the Parson to complete the sequence with a 'fable'. Although the Parson rejects this request (indeed he rejects the value of literary fictions altogether), he offers instead a 'myrie tale in prose', which will complete the journey by showing the pilgrims the way to that 'parfit, glorious pilgrimmage that highte Jerusalem celestial'. What he presents is a treatise on the art of penance (drawn in fact from two well-known penitential handbooks of the 13th century), which includes a review of the ▷ Seven Deadly Sins and concludes with an emphatic call for repentance. Chaucer's 'Retraction' follows the Parson's treatise (in most manuscripts). In this the 'maker' takes leave of his book, and asks forgiveness for any literary sins he may have committed in his writing career. In concluding the *Canterbury Tales* in this way, Chaucer is both affirming the ultimate values propounded in *The Parson's Tale* (the Parson's call for repentance is followed by an act of repentance) and following a long tradition of literary endings in which writers distance themselves from the non-religious aspects of their work.

Pascal, Blaise (1623–62)
French religious philosopher and mathematician. In 1646 he became a devout adherent of the Jansenist movement which had its headquarters at the nunnery of Port-Royal near Paris. Jansenism (started by Cornelius Jansen, 1585–1638) maintained, like the Protestant predestinarians (▷ Predestination), that salvation through the love of God was possible only for those whom God pleased to love, *ie* an individual was predestined to salvation or to damnation; however it also emphasized the necessity of belonging to the Roman Catholic Church. The movement was strongly attacked by the ▷ Jesuit order, and when its leading exponent, Antoine Arnauld, was being threatened with dismissal from his academic post, Pascal wrote *Provincial Letters* (1656) in his defence. This was his first important work, a masterpiece of lucid, ironical controversy; in particular, Pascal advocated moral austerity and criticized Jesuit libertinism. His *Pensées* ('Thoughts' – pub. 1670) is his more famous work; it consists of notes for a book on religion intended to demonstrate the necessity of the religious life. Though fragmentary, the notes have great aphoristic power; with an intellect as powerful and a style as lucid as that of ▷ Descartes, Pascal criticizes the earlier philosopher's notion of the supreme power of human reason, and shows the limitations of reason in dealing with ultimate mysteries.

***Passage to India, A* (1924)**
A novel by ▷ E. M. Forster. It had originally been planned ten years earlier, and its picture of India belongs partly to that period. The scene is the city of Chandrapore on the banks of the Ganges, and India is under British rule. The background characters consist mainly of the British officials and their wives, and the local Indian intelligentsia. The main characters are as follows: Aziz, a Muslim Indian doctor; Godbole, a Hindu professor; Fielding, the headmaster of the Government College; Ronald Heaslop, another of the British officials; and two visitors from Britain, Mrs Moore, the mother of Heaslop by her first marriage, and Adela Quested, who is engaged to him. Both women have strong liberal principles, and make friends easily with Fielding, the only liberal in the resident British colony. Fielding is also a friend of Aziz, and a colleague of Godbole. Aziz issues an impulsive invitation to the British visitors to visit the local Marabar Caves; these have a strong significance for the Hindus, although Godbole, when he is asked about them, is unable to explain it. The climax of the book occurs when this visit takes place. Heat, discomfort, and the caves themselves

cause Mrs Moore and Adela to suffer traumatic experiences. Mrs Moore loses all her faith and idealism; Adela has an attack of hysteria which temporarily convinces her that Aziz has attempted to rape her. This supposed rape brings the already strained relations between the British and the Indians to a crisis, but the crisis is resolved (not without disgracing the more reactionary British officials) by Adela's return to sanity in the witness-box. Mrs Moore, although she is now selfish, hard and disillusioned, whereas before she had been generous, kind and idealistic, is in touch with a new kind of truthfulness which helps Adela's restoration. Only Mrs Moore and Godbole understand the true nature of Adela's experience in the caves, and they understand it from opposite, though complementary, points of view.

The novel has psychological, political, and religious dimensions. The Christianity, or the sceptical liberalism, of the more enlightened of the British is shown to be adequate for normal relationships and practical affairs, but they have become too shallow for the interpretation of deeper human experience; Aziz's Muslim faith is stronger, but it is more an aesthetic and cultural tradition than a binding spiritual faith. Godbole's Hinduism, on the other hand, is profound and intelligent, though it is no guide to the daily conduct of affairs. This religious dimension is presented by constant symbolism, ranging in character from unobtrusive (though often important) details, to the conspicuous and suggestive image of the caves themselves. *A Passage to India* is Forster's most ▷ modernist work and is usually regarded as his masterpiece.

***Passionate Pilgrim* (1599)**

An anthology of poetry containing odes by ▷ Richard Barnfield (1564–1627) formerly attributed to ▷ Shakespeare.

***Past and Present* (1843)**

An example of ▷ Thomas Carlyle's immensely influential social criticism in which the 'past' is epitomized by a medieval chronicle of the monastery of Bury St Edmunds, describing everyday life and recording the procedure for electing a new abbot. In this document Carlyle finds evidence of all that he saw as missing from Victorian society: spiritual power, organic community and personal responsibility. Carlyle used the fashion for ▷ medievalism, current at the time, in order to make a diagnosis of the contemporary world. The 'present' was typified by a sensational news item which told of the murder of three children by their parents in order to defraud a burial society of £3 8s due on the death of each child. Using classical allusions such as the myth of King Midas, and Dante's myth of Ugolino who was driven by starvation to eat his own children, Carlyle mounted an attack on industrial England, which had the power to make money but could only produce starvation. The present is also portrayed in the form of a morality play with representative characters such as Plugson of Undershot, an unscrupulous industrialist, and Pandarus Dogsdraught, a corrupt politician. ▷ Charles Dickens was to develop this technique in his own novels. ▷ Matthew Arnold was also influenced by the style of *Past and Present* which put a number of useful terms into currency such as 'mammonism', 'dilettantism', 'windbag', 'cash-nexus' and 'captains of industry'.

Paston Letters

The general name for a large collection of correspondence by, or to, members of the Paston family of Norfolk, dating from 1422–1509. The letters, written at times with great vigour, provide an interesting insight into the political and domestic life of this rising Norfolk family, during the turbulent reigns of Henry VI, Edward IV, and Richard III.

▷ *Edward IV; Henry VI; Richard III.*

Bib: Davis, N. (ed.), *The Paston Letters*.

Pastoral

A form of literature originally developed by the ancient Greeks and Romans in the ▷ idylls of the former (*eg* ▷ Theocritus') and the ▷ eclogues of the latter (*eg* ▷ Virgil's). Ancient pastoral idealized the Greek state of ▷ Arcadia which had a rustic population of shepherds and herdsmen. The ▷ Renaissance of the 16th century, deeply interested in the literature of the Greeks and Romans, revived the pastoral mode; the earliest forms of it date back in Italian literature to the 15th century, but it was the romance *Arcadia* (1504), by the Italian poet Sannazaro, which was particularly influential throughout Europe. The appeal of the pastoral kind of literature was partly to human wishfulness – the desire to conceive of circumstances in which the complexity of human problems could be reduced to its simplest elements: the shepherds and shepherdesses of pastoral are imaged as having no worries, and they live in an ideal climate with no serious physical calamities; love and death, and making songs and music about these experiences, are their only preoccupations. Another function of pastoral, however, was as a vehicle of moral and social criticism; the shepherds and shepherdesses sought the pleasures of nature and despised or were innocent of the corrupting luxury of courts and cities. Finally, pastoral presented a means of offering, allegorically, thinly disguised tributes of praise and flattery to real people whom the poet admired or wanted to please. The satirical, moral and eulogistic functions of Renaissance pastoral all tended to make it allegorical, since it was through ▷ allegory that the poet could most safely make his criticism felt, and could most eloquently convey his praise. Allegory also suited the ▷ neo-Platonic, idealizing cast of mind so characteristic of 16th-century writers. When we remember that the tradition of romantic love was one of the most ardently pursued inheritances from the Middle Ages, and that the circumstances of pastoral lent themselves to its expression, it is not surprising that the pastoral mode was so extensively cultivated in 16th-century Europe. To England it came late, by way of influences from France, Spain and Italy, but it lasted longer; it was especially pervasive in the last quarter of the 16th century, and continued till the mid-17th; there was a minor revival early in the 18th century.

The first important English pastoral poem is ▷ Edmund Spenser's ▷ *The Shepherd's Calendar* which consists of an ▷ eclogue for each month of the year; the tone is morally didactic in some, satirical in others, and eulogistic of the queen in a third group. ▷ Philip Sidney's ▷ *The Arcadia* is a pastoral romance whose purpose is entertainment, but it idealizes the courtly virtues, as does Book VI of Spenser's ▷ *The Faerie Queene*, about Sir Calidore, the Knight of Courtesy. ▷ The University Wits, ▷ Peele, ▷ Lyly, ▷ Greene and ▷ Lodge, wrote pastoral dramas in verse and romances in prose, and one of the best pastoral works of the 1590s is Shakespeare's ▷ *As You Like It*, based on Lodge's romance *Rosalynde* (1590). Shakespeare dramatized the pastoral mode, however, with a difference: the fanciful world of pastoral romance is contrasted with the world of common sense, and the fairyland pastoral country of shepherds and shepherdesses with Greek names is juxtaposed to the real English countryside and its commonplace peasants, so that his pastoral romance is also antipastoral. It was not unusual, however, to salt pastoral with elements from real country life – Spenser does it in *The Shepherd's Calendar*, and Shakespeare does it most skilfully in ▷ *The Winter's Tale* IV. iii. More conventional pastoral dramas were ▷ John Fletcher's *Faithful Shepherdess* (1610) and ▷ Ben Jonson's *The Sad Shepherd* (1635). The artificiality of pastoral lent itself to the ▷ masque form which combined music, poetry, dancing and the decor in equal proportions; Jonson, the master of masque, wrote a number of pastorals for it, but by far the most famous pastoral masque is ▷ Milton's *Comus*.

Of the various forms of pastoral, the prose romance had the shortest life, and ended with the 16th century; the last pastoral drama was Elkanah Settle's *Pastor Fido* (1677). In non-dramatic poetry, pastoral lasted much longer. ▷ Michael Drayton is the next pastoral poet of note after Spenser with *Idea: The Shepherd's Garland* (1593) and *Endimion and Phoebe* (1595); ▷ Marlowe's famous pastoral lyric *Come Live With Me* was first printed in 1599, and pastoral lyric writers in the tradition of Spenser were numerous from 1590 up to 1650; they included Nicholas Breton (?1545–?1626), ▷ George Wither (1588–1667), ▷ William Browne (1591–1643), and above all ▷ Robert Herrick. However, the most famous poems in 17th-century pastoral are Milton's: ▷ *L'Allegro* and *Il Penseroso* and his ▷ elegy ▷ *Lycidas*. In the 18th century, ▷ Pope's early *Pastorals* (1709) were a small masterpiece influenced by Virgil, but his ▷ *Windsor Forest* (1713) is a more impressive work, using pastoral to extol the Peace of Utrecht (1713) which ended the long War of the Spanish Succession, and to celebrate peace, prosperity and civilization.

Classical pastoral has not been practised notably since the first half of the 18th century. However, ▷ William Empson (*Some Versions of Pastoral*, 1935) sometimes uses the term more widely than classical pastoral denotes. Even so, pastoral – even of the non-classical kind – is not synonymous with 'nature poetry' or poetry of country life: ▷ Wordsworth, ▷ Clare, ▷ Hardy, ▷ Blunden, and ▷ Heaney are not writers of pastoral in any usually accepted sense.

Bib: Patterson, A., *Pastoral and Ideology*; Chaudhuri, S., *Renaissance Pastoral and its English Developments*.

Pater, Walter Horatio (1839–94)
Scholar, essayist and critic. He was elected to a fellowship in Brasenose College, Oxford, in 1864. He was connected with the Pre-Raphaelite group, shared their idealistic worship of beauty and became an important influence in the cult of art which led to the ▷ Aesthetic Movement at the end of the century; ▷ Oscar Wilde was among those profoundly affected by the Paterian sensibility. His most important work was *Studies in the History of the Renaissance* (1873), a collection of essays on Italian painters and writers from the 14th to 16th centuries; the Conclusion to these essays, in which he advocates a fusion of psychic, moral and sensuous ecstasy, became a kind of manifesto of the aesthetic movement. His next most famous work is the philosophic romance *Marius the Epicurean* (1885). Other works: *Imaginary Portraits* (1887); *Appreciations with an Essay on Style* (1889); *Plato and Platonism* (1893); *The Child in the House* (1894); *Greek Studies and Miscellaneous Studies* (1895); an unfinished romance, *Gaston de Latour* (1896). Pater wrote with immense care for beauty of style, which became for him and end in itself.

Bid: Levey, M., *The Case of Walter Pater*; Monsman, G., *Walter Pater*; Iser, W., *Walter Pater: The Aesthetic Moment*; Seiter, R. M. (ed.), *Walter Pater: The Critical Heritage*; Loesberg, J., *Aestheticism and Deconstruction: Pater, Derrida and De Man*; Brake, L., *Walter Pater*.

Pathetic fallacy
▷ Figures of Speech.

Patience
The conventional title given to a 14th-century ▷ alliterative poem, found in the same

manuscript as ▷ *Gawain and the Green Knight*, ▷ *Cleanness* and ▷ *Pearl*, and so attributed to the ▷ Gawain poet. This relatively short composition explores the active and passive meanings of patience, through a reworking of the story of the Old Testament prophet, ▷ Jonah.
Bib: Anderson, J. J. (ed.), *Patience*.

Patmore, Coventry Kersey Dighton (1823–96)
Poet. He contributed to the ▷ Pre-Raphaelite periodical *The Germ*; in 1864 he became a ▷ Catholic. The two books by which he is most remembered are ▷ *The Angel in the House* (comprising *The Betrothed*, 1854; *The Espousals*, 1856; *Faithful for Ever*, 1860; *The Victories of Love*, 1862) and *The Unknown Eros* (1877). The former is about his first marriage and celebrates married love; the latter, consisting of forty-two irregular odes, is on a similar theme but more mystical. Both poems are examples of the type of philosophy in verse characteristic of William Wordsworth's famous *Prelude* (1850). Patmore had independent ideas on poetic technique, and has been considered by some critics to bear resemblance to the 17th-century Metaphysical poets. As much as for his own poetry, he is known today for being the friend and correspondent of the poet ▷ Gerard Manley Hopkins, whose work, however, he seems not to have properly appreciated. Other works include: *Amelia* (1878), which was his own favourite among his poems; the critical essays *English Metrical Law* (1878); *Principle in Art* (1879); *Religio Poetae* (1893); the religious meditations *Rod, Root and Flower* (1895).
Bib: Patmore, D., *Life*; Oliver, E.J., *Life*; Page, F., *Patmore: a Study in Poetry*; Reid, J.C., *The Mind and Art of Coventry Patmore*: Hopkins, G.M., (ed. Abbott, C.C.) *Further Letters*.

Patriarchy
A key term in ▷ feminist theory, patriarchy literally means rule by the father and is hence taken as short-hand for any male-dominated society. As such, it is sometimes criticized for being too universalist a term because it neglects differences of, for example, race and social class in the experience of the oppression of women.

Patronage in literature
A system by which the king or a nobleman afforded protection and livelihood to an artist, in return for which the artist paid him special honour, or returned him service in the form of entertaining his household and his guests. The great period for this system was the 16th century, but patronage continued to be an important cultural and social institution until the end of the 18th century. In the ▷ Middle Ages the writer or scholar might work under the protection of a religious order, but already ▷ Chaucer was dependent on the patronage of ▷ John of Gaunt. After the 18th century, through ▷ circulating libraries and wide circulation of periodicals, writers could rely on support from the general public; but from the 16th to 18th centuries failure to secure a patron might mean oblivion, or at least starvation, as in the case of ▷ Chatterton. In the 16th century patronage was a commonly found institution since noblemen and women still kept large households and it was assumed that these would include entertainers (such as a band of actors) and scholars who performed educational and secretarial functions. In this century actors ('players') who were not attached to some household were regarded as vagabonds liable to punishment or shutting up in houses of correction by the public authorities; by the end of the century, however, the ▷ Lord Chamberlain's Men, the Lord Admiral's Men etc. were attached to their patrons only in name, and they performed in public theatres or at court. The Earl of Essex (patron of ▷ Ben Jonson), the Earl of Southampton (patron of ▷ Shakespeare), and ▷ Sidney's sister, ▷ Margaret Countess of Pembroke, were among the great patrons in the reign of ▷ Elizabeth I, but the most valuable patron was the sovereign. Disagreeable necessities of patronage were the flattering 'dedications' which commonly preceded works of literature, and poems written specially to honour or gratify the patron, such as ▷ Donne's *First* and *Second Anniversary* commemorating the death of Elizabeth Drury, daughter of his patron Sir Robert Drury – though Donne's poems are evidence that such work was by no means necessarily bad or insincere. The status of men and women of letters steadily gained in esteem, moreover, freeing the writer of the necessity of servility, and Ben Jonson was one of the most vigorous in upholding its dignity and independence. Nonetheless, it tended to be true under Elizabeth and her successor, ▷ James I, that writers were either 'gentlemen amateurs' like Sidney and ▷ Ralegh, able to work independently, or professional writers like Jonson and Shakespeare, for whom patronage was important, if not indispensable. By the 18th century, thanks largely to the increased reading public and the growth of periodicals like Addison's ▷ *Spectator* and Jonson's ▷ *Rambler*, patronage was obsolescent, and chiefly required when a writer of slender means, such as ▷ Samuel Johnson, attempted a major task, such as his Dictionary. Johnson's famous letter to Lord Chesterfield is a classic example of rebuke to a neglectful patron. Political parties and leaders by this time provided extensive patronage, *eg* Harley and the Tories to ▷ Defoe. Many writers gained a livelihood through the system by which the universities and landlords inherited from the monasteries (dissolved in the 1530s) the right to appoint parish priests;

one example among many is the poet ▷ Crabbe whose verse tale *The Patron* (*Tales* of 1812) illustrates the unhappy side of patronage.
Bib: Brennan, M., *Literary Patronage in the English Renaissance*; Lytle, G. F. and Orgel, S., *Patronage in the Renaissance*; Rosenberg, E., *Leicester, Patron of Letters*.

Paul's, Children of St
A company of boy-actors, chosen from the choirboys of St Paul's Cathedral, who were very popular with audiences at the end of the 16th century. Their chief rivals among boy-actors were the Children of the Chapel Royal. Both were to some extent serious rivals of the adult actors (see ▷ Shakespeare's ▷ *Hamlet* II. ii). The boy companies were used especially for ▷ pastoral plays, such as those of ▷ John Lyly and ▷ George Peele.
▷ Acting, The profession of.
Bib: Gair, R., *The Children of Paul's*.

Payn, James (1830–98)
Novelist. Educated at Eton and Cambridge, Payn launched his literary career by contributing to ▷ Dicken's ▷ *Household Words*. His highly popular novels tapped into the vogue for the ▷ sensation novel of the 1860s and 1870s, melodramatically dealing with scheming relatives, disputes over wills and strange disappearances; of these, the best known are *Lost Sir Massingberd* (1864) and *By Proxy* (1878). Between 1883 and 1896 Payn edited the ▷ *Cornhill Magazine*.

Peacham, Henry (c 1576–1643)
Author and artist. Although Peacham was interested in writing, he may be seen as an example of the ideal 'Renaissance man' whose interests and skills covered a wide range of topics and fields, for he was also proficient at music, drawing and mathematics. It is perhaps no surprise that one of his most popular works, *The Complete Gentleman* (1622), is a manual for young ▷ gentlemen on how to behave and on what scholarly accomplishments they should set out to achieve. He combined his own literary and artistic skills in *Minerva Britanna* (1612), an ▷ emblem-book, and wrote a treatise on the practical skills of artistry, *Graphice* (1606). He was well connected at the court of ▷ James I, being associated with ▷ Jonson and ▷ Byrd; however, his own aesthetic leanings brought him closer to ▷ Henry, Prince of Wales, the king's elder son. Peacham has left the only contemporary picture of a ▷ Shakespeare play in performance, a scene from ▷ *Titus Andronicus*.
Bib: Cawley, R. R., *Henry Peacham: his contribution to English poetry*.

Peacock, Thomas Love (1785–1866)
Novelist and poet. After unsuccessful attempts in poetry and the theatre, he found his special form in the 'discussion novel': *Headlong Hall* (1816); ▷ *Melincourt* (1817); ▷ *Nightmare Abbey* (1818); ▷ *Maid Marian* (1822); *The Misfortunes of Elphin* (1829); ▷ *Crotchet Castle* (1831); *Gryll Grange* (1861). These consist almost entirely of conversation and have very little plot; the characters represent outlooks, ideas, and attitudes such as arouse Peacock's derision, and the prevailing tone is comic and satirical. The conversations are interspersed with songs, often of great charm, and hilarious and extravagent episodes. His sceptical essay *The Four Ages of Poetry* (1820) provoked ▷ Shelley's famous ▷ *Defence of Poetry* (1821).
Bib: Van Doren, C., *Life*; Priestley, J. B., *Life*; Able, A. H., *Meredith and Peacock – A Study in Literary Influence*; House, H., in *All in Due Time*; Brett-Smith, H. F. B. (ed.), *Life and Works*, Vol 1; Mayoux, J. J., *Un Epicurien Anglais: Peacock*; Jack, I., Chap VII in *Oxford History of English Literature*.

Peake, Mervyn (1911–68)
Novelist, dramatist, poet and painter. Peake was born in China, but his family returned to England in 1923, where he subsequently trained as an artist. He is best known for his trilogy *Gormenghast*, a fantasy epic set in a grotesque world, consisting of *Titus Groan* (1946), *Gormenghast* (1950) and *Titus Alone* (1959). In form it is a ▷ *Bildungsroman* with multiple subplots, and it is distinguished by a rich vocabulary and by the effects of Peake's strong visual imagination. Peake's work met a mixed critical reception, but gained a considerable cult following, aided by the increasing popularity of fantasy fiction associated with the work of ▷ J. R. R. Tolkien.
Bib: Batchelor, J., *Mervyn Peake: A Biographical and Critical Exploration*.

Pearl
A 14th-century ▷ dream-vision poem attributed to the ▷ Gawain poet, preserved in the same manuscript as ▷ *Gawain and the Green Knight*, ▷ *Patience* and ▷ *Cleanness*. It draws on the diverse traditions behind this literary form (as a medium for analysing abstract concepts, secular and religious, as a medium for insight into higher truths) and literally incorporates a scriptural vision into the narrative: the vision of New Jerusalem in *Revelation* becomes part of the personal experience of the Dreamer in *Pearl*. This translation of material from the Bible to the personal experience of the Dreamer, the realization of a prospect of an afterlife, epitomizes the subject of the narrative as a whole, which explores how spiritual truths may be represented by necessarily imperfect material means.

The pearl is the central object of meditation in the poem, providing both the means and end of the dream-vision. The movement of the narrative is shaped by the process of revealing layers of meaning in the form of a pearl. It opens with the narrator lamenting the loss of his prize possession, a pearl. But as he meets his lost pearl in his dream, the relationship between the man and his pearl is reinterpreted as that between a father and a daughter who has died in infancy. Retrospectively, the garden spot where the dreamer lost his pearl, and fell asleep, takes on the aspect of a grave. But the Pearl-maiden in the dream tries to redefine their relationship again and to convince the Dreamer that she is not lost, rather she has found a much better setting in New Jerusalem. In a series of exchanges she tries to tutor the Dreamer out of his materialistic values. The Dreamer finally sees his Pearl as one of the 144,000 virgin companions of Christ in New Jerusalem, but breaks his visionary experience when he tries to get closer and join the maiden.

The poem is itself pearl-shaped: the opening line is reworked as the closing line and this overall linking structure is repeated in the organization of the stanzas into groups of five, which are linked by echoing first and last lines. Each stanza is structured by a combination of alliterative lines and an elaborate rhyme scheme. It is an exercise in formal artifice of the highest order, and suggests that poetry may serve the ends of spiritual vision, but some recognition of the limitations of art are also built into the poem's structure, for one of its 12 sections contains six not five stanzas. The poem appears to be constructed as a pearl with a flaw of the most self-conscious literary kind.
Bib: Gordon, E. V. (ed.), *Pearl.*

Peasants' Revolt
A popular uprising in 1381, which attempted to force the reform of an outmoded manorial system. The immediate stimulus of the revolt was an attempt to levy a further poll tax (on every head of the population), but it is clear from the demands finally presented to ⊳ Richard II that the grievances arose from injustices in the manorial system, and from the 1370s onwards there had been growing signs of unrest with the restrictions of villeinage (the system whereby a tenant held land in return for manorial services). ⊳ John Ball and ⊳ Wat Tyler were among the leaders of the protest movement which mobilized disaffected labourers and peasants in 1381. The protesters, gathered from the counties around London, finally entered the city (having had no answer to their demand to meet the king), and opened prisons and attacked the property of nobles and civic administrators. ⊳ John of Gaunt's palace of Savoy, in the Strand, was gutted, and the Archbishop of London and several councillors were later executed. Risings occurred outside London at the same time, notably in the eastern counties. Richard II met the protesters, discussed their grievances, and agreed to their demands to abolish villeinage, to allow labour services to be engaged on the basis of free contract, and to the right to rent land for 4d an acre. At a later meeting with the king, Wat Tyler was killed by the Lord Mayor of London. The promises made by the king were not honoured and subsequently the Chief Justice toured the disaffected areas dispensing severe punishments to those involved in the uprisings.
Bib: Hilton, R., *The English Peasantry in the Later Middle Ages*; McKisack, M., *The Fourteenth Century*.

Peel, Sir Robert (1788–1850)
British Prime Minister 1834–5 and 1841–56, responsible for repealing the ⊳ Corn Laws in 1846, thereby freeing imports. Earlier in his career he was persuaded by the rising crime statistics that legal reform should be coupled with better crime prevention. In 1829, as Home Secretary, he carried through the Metropolitan Police Act that was responsible for the first disciplined police force for the Greater London area. Blue-coated, with top hats and truncheons, Peel's police helped to protect London from the riots that occurred in Bristol and elsewhere during the ⊳ Reform Bill agitation in the early 1830s. From this point on the police force was gradually established throughout the whole country. 'Bobby', meaning policeman, derives from his name.

Peele, George (1556–96)
Poet and dramatist and one of ⊳ University Wits, Peele was educated at Christ's Hospital and Oxford University. His work comprised various forms of dramatic entertainment characteristic of the taste of the time. His best-known plays are the ⊳ pastoral play *The Arraignment of Paris* (?1584), acted by the Children of the Royal Chapel, and *The Old Wives' Tale* (1590), which is something like a dramatized folk-tale. He also wrote a biblical play, *The Love of King David and Fair Bethsabe* (1587), and patriotic ⊳ history plays, *The Famous Chronicle of King Edward I* (printed 1593) and *The Battle of Alcazar with the Death of Captain Stukeley* (?1588), and a number of other plays have been attributed to him. In 1585 and 1591 he designed ⊳ pageants for London's Lord Mayor's Show. As a precursor of ⊳ Shakespeare he has a similar importance to ⊳ Robert Greene; he helped to give greater smoothness and flexibility to the use of the ⊳ blank-verse line, and combined elements appealing to popular taste with qualities of courtly refinement. He can thus be regarded as a contributor to the rich variety of tone that is unique to the best Elizabethan drama.
Bib: Prouty, C. T., *Life and Works*; Cheffaud, P. H., *George Peele*.

Pelagian
The adjective from Pelagius, the Latin name of an early British theologian (4th–5th century

AD). He is associated with a doctrine ('the Pelagian heresy') held to be false by most branches of the Christian Church – that it is within human power to be good; this is contrary to the Christian doctrine of 'Original Sin', according to which human beings relying on their own efforts must inevitably sooner or later do wrong, since moral goodness depends on the aid of Divine Grace.

Pellam
A Grail-keeper in the Quest of the Holy ▷ Grail narratives, the father of ▷ Pelles and Pellinore, who is wounded by ▷ Balin (with the Dolorous Stroke) but healed much later by his great-grandson ▷ Galahad.

Pelleas, Sir
In ▷ Malory's version of Arthurian narrative Pelleas first appears in hopeless pursuit of Ettard. ▷ Gawain promises to assist Pelleas in his quest but becomes Ettard's lover himself. Pelleas is helped by Nimue's spell to recover from his love sickness and subsequently marries this ▷ Lady of the Lake.

Pelles, Sir
A ▷ Fisher King, Lord of Corbenic, descended from Joseph of Arimathea. Sir Pelles engineers the conception of ▷ Galahad, the knight who is to achieve the ▷ Grail Quest.

Pembroke, Countess of
▷ Sidney, Mary.

Pendennis, The History of
A novel by ▷ William Makepeace Thackeray, published serially 1848–50. It is about worldly upper-class society in London and the fortunes of a young man, Arthur Pendennis, whose 'bad angels' are his cynical, materialistic uncle, Major Pendennis, and the pretty but selfish Blanche Amory whom he nearly marries. Blanche's father, an escaped convict who is thought to be dead but is in fact – as Major Pendennis knows – still alive, haunts the book in the guise of Colonel Altamont. Arthur's 'good angels' are his widowed mother, Helen; Laura Bell, whom he eventually marries and whom his mother has adopted; and George Warrington, a friend with whom he shares rooms. The good influences are, however, less imaginatively presented than the bad ones, and the distinctiveness of the novel depends on its amusing portrayal of the vulgarity, intrigue, and materialism of London society and the journalistic and literary world of Fleet Street.

Penkethman (Pinkethman), William (?–1725)
Actor, singer, dancer, manager. Penkethman is believed to have begun acting in about 1692 with the ▷ United Company at ▷ Drury Lane where he remained for most of his career. Penkethman's forte as an actor was comedy, and he was often asked to speak prologues and epilogues. Much of his humour was conveyed through clowning and mobile facial expression, although he was accused, on numerous occasions, of over-acting, and ad-libbing to excess.

Pennington, Sarah, Lady (d1783)
Author. She married Sir Joseph Pennington, a gentleman of Yorkshire, in 1746, and separated from him in acrimonious circumstances twelve years later. Thereafter she drew on her own experiences in writing conduct-books (▷ conduct literature), letters and ▷ epistolary fiction. These include *An Unfortunate Mother's Advice to her Absent Daughters; in a Letter to Miss Pennington* (1761), her most popular and successful work, *Letters on Different Subjects* (1766), and *The Child's Conductor* (1777).
Bib: Todd, J., (ed.), *A Dictionary of British and American Women Writers 1660–1800*.

***Penseroso, Il* (c 1631)**
A poem by ▷ John Milton, published in 1645 though composed c 1631. The poem is a companion piece to ▷ *L'Allegro*. The title can be translated from the Italian as signifying the thoughtful or reflective individual. The poem celebrates the retired life of thought and contemplation.

Pentameter
In English verse, usually five iambic feet, *ie* with the stress coming on every second syllable. The line has been the commonest in use since ▷ Chaucer, *eg* the *Prologue to the Canterbury Tales*:

He knéw the távérns wéll in évery tówn.

The commonest English uses of the iambic pentameter are in ▷ blank verse and in ▷ heroic couplets (as in the *Prologue*).
▷ Metre.

Pepys, Samuel (1633–1703)
Diarist. He was an industrious and highly efficient official in the Admiralty Office, and a man who had musical culture and persistent, if amateurish, scientific and literary interests. As secretary to his cousin, Edward Montagu, Earl of Sandwich, he was aboard the fleet which brought ▷ Charles II back to England at the Restoration in 1660. His official position in the Admiralty gave him the confidence of the king's brother, James Duke of York, who was Lord High Admiral, and an opportunity for direct observation of court life. He was elected to Parliament and knew the world of politics, was a friend of a number of leading writers and musicians, and held distinguished

appointments in the ▷ City of London. He was thus centrally placed to observe his age, and with all his seriousness he was pleasure-loving and witty.

His diary (kept 1660–9) is a unique document not only because he brought to it these qualities and advantages (many of which were shared by his friend the diarist ▷ John Evelyn) but because he kept it for his eye alone, and consequently wrote with unusual candour and objectivity. To prevent his servants and family from prying into it, he used a kind of shorthand cypher, which was not interpreted until 1825, when part of the diary was first published. The first more or less complete edition was in 1896. Of all diaries in English, it has the greatest appeal to the general reader, as well as having outstanding value for the historian.

▷ Diaries.

Bib: Lives by J. R. Tanner, A. Bryant, and J. H. Wilson. Letters edited by J. R. Tanner, A. Bryant, and J. H. Wilson. Marburg, C., *Mr Pepys and Mr Evelyn*; Latham, R. and Mathews, W., (eds.), *Diary*.

Perceval

One of the members of the court of ▷ King Arthur. There is some variation in the treatment of Perceval's adventures and achievements in the Arthurian narratives of medieval Europe: Perceval is the hero of the ▷ Grail Quest before ▷ Galahad takes over his role. The earliest extant Perceval narrative is that composed by ▷ Chrétien de Troyes (left unfinished but the subject of later continuations). The basic story of Sir Perceval is that of a child of noble origin who is brought up outside a court context but becomes fascinated with chivalry (despite his mother's attempts to keep him away from the world of knights). He is gradually educated in the chivalric code through a series of blunders, caused by his literal-minded application of helpful advice about how to be a knight. One of his missed opportunities involves his failure to heal the ▷ Fisher King because he does not ask any questions about the mysterious Grail procession at the Fisher King's castle. Perceval attempts to make up for this mistake by searching for the Grail castle, and is successful in some versions of his story. In *Parzival*, composed in the 13th century by Wolfram von Eschenbach, Parzival is the knight who finally achieves the mystical Grail quest. In ▷ Malory's version, he becomes a companion of Galahad and dies as a hermit in Sarras after Galahad has achieved the Quest. The 14th-century Middle English romance *Sir Perceval* concentrates on Perceval's over-literal attempts to follow the advice of his mother and others, and exploits the comic possibilities of Perceval as a non-ideal hero.

Percy, Thomas (1729–1811)

Clergyman and antiquarian; he became Bishop of Dromore in 1782. Along with ▷ James Macpherson, ▷ Horace Walpole and ▷ Thomas Gray, Percy was a pioneer of the literary exoticism which flourished in the later 18th century. In 1761 he published *Hau Kiou Choaan*, a translation of a Portuguese version of a Chinese romance, and in 1763 *Five Pieces of Runic Poetry*, translated from Latin versions of Old Icelandic texts. His most influential work, *Reliques of Ancient English Poetry* (1765), includes poems from a 17th-century manuscript now in the British Museum and known as 'The Percy Folio'. This manuscript contains many ballads of ancient origin which Percy edited according to 18th-century taste, adding also some modern compositions in the archaic style. Although his editorial approach was not that of a modern purist, the volume marks a significant phase in the revival of interest in early poetry, and exerted a strong influence on later poets such as ▷ Thomas Chatterton, Sir Walter Scott, ▷ William Wordsworth and ▷ Samuel Taylor Coleridge.

Bib: Davis, B. H., *Thomas Percy*.

***Peregrine Pickle, The Adventures of* (1751)**

A novel by ▷ Tobias Smollett. The hero is an adventurer seeking his fortune in England and on the Continent. Its form is a succession of episodes without a uniting structure, depending for its interest on the vigour of depiction of the characters and incidents. It contains famous eccentric characters, especially the retired sailor and his associates, Commodore Trunnion, Lieutenant Hatchway, and Tom Pipes. The episodes give opportunity for much social and political satire, from English village life upwards, and show an awareness of social structure like that found in the novels of ▷ Henry Fielding. Trunnion and his circle were an inspiration to ▷ Laurence Sterne's Uncle Toby in ▷ *Tristram Shandy*.

Perfectibilism

The optimistic doctrine that individuals and society are capable of achieving perfection in living. The ▷ French Revolution, with its reliance on reason for the solution of all human problems, encouraged perfectibilism, and the philosopher ▷ William Godwin was an English example. ▷ Peacock, in ▷ *Headlong Hall* (1816), presents a humorous version of a perfectibilist in Mr Foster.

Performance

▷ Competence.

***Pericles, Prince of Tyre* (1608–9)**

A play, acts III–V of which are considered to be by ▷ Shakespeare; acts I–II are mainly or entirely by another writer. The play was published in 1609 in an untrustworthy edition, but it was not included in a collected edition of Shakespeare's works until (in the same version) the third Folio of 1664. The story is based on a well-known late classical romance, Apollonius of Tyre, used by John Gower in his 14th-century cycle of poems, ▷ *Confessio Amantis* (Book VIII). Gower appears in the play to speak the chorus, but the play does not follow his version in all respects; another source book was Lawrence Twine's *The Pattern of Painful Adventures*, first published in 1576.

In the first two acts, the play has a very rambling structure, but from Act III it follows a pattern characteristic of Shakespeare's last four plays. Although in each of these the pattern is varied, they have in common a central relationship between a prince and his daughter – in this case Pericles and ▷ Marina. Pericles is separated from her and is led to believe that both she and her mother, Thaisa, are dead. By the end of the play, however, he recovers them both, and the recovery restores him to happiness and health. The scene (V. i) in which Marina, at first unrecognizing of and unrecognized by her father, restores him from his stupor of sorrow, is of remarkable beauty, and recalls the scene in ▷ *King Lear* (IV. vii) in which Cordelia restores her father.

Periodicals
▷ Reviews and Periodicals, Newspapers.

Perrault, Charles (1628–1703)
French author, known in England chiefly for his collection of fairy tales published in 1697, *Histoires et Contes du Temps Passé* (Stories and Tales from the Past) subtitled *Contes de ma Mère l'Oie* (Tales of Mother Goose). They were translated into English by Robert Samber (1729), and have remained the best known fairy tales among English children. They were retold by Perrault from popular sources, and are as follows: *Sleeping Beauty*; *Red Riding Hood*; *Blue Beard*; *Puss in Boots*; *The Fairy*; *Cinderella; Riquet with the Tuft*; *Hop o' my Thumb*. Several of them provide the themes for modern Christmas ▷ pantomimes.

Personification
▷ Figures of Speech.

***Persuasion* (1818)**
The last completed novel by ▷ Jane Austen; it was published, incompletely revised, in 1818, the year following her death. The theme is the coming together of the heroine, Anne Elliott, and the hero, Captain Wentworth, in spite of social obstacles, the selfishness and foolishness of her father (Sir Walter) and sisters, and the rival attraction of the more obviously seductive Musgrove sisters. Anne, before the novel begins, had already refused Wentworth on the counsel of Lady Russell, who stands in place of mother to her; Lady Russell had misunderstood Wentworth's character and feared his poverty. Anne's personality is diffident and humble but at the opening of the story she has begun to realize that the refusal was a mistake, likely to ruin her happiness. The renewal of Wentworth's love and his eventual marriage to Anne is a victory: their strong and distinctive but quiet and reticent qualities overcome the cruder and shallower social characteristics of their circumstances.

***Peter Bell: A Tale* (1819)**
***Peter Bell the Third* (1939)**
The first is a 'lyrical ballad' by ▷ William Wordsworth, written in 1798 but not published until 1819. Peter, a hard-hearted hawker of earthenware, finds an ass gazing down at its drowned master in the River Swale. He seeks out the man's widow, and on his journey is reformed by the spiritual influence of nature. The poem possesses that deliberate flatness which characterizes some of Wordsworth's most original early works.
▷ Percy Bysshe Shelley, in his *Peter Bell the Third* (1819; published 1839), having read a review of the poem, used its title (somewhat inappropriately) in a ▷ satire on the older poet's descent into respectability and conservatism. As Shelley says in his Dedication: 'He was at first sublime, pathetic, impressive, profound; then dull; then prosy and dull; and now dull – oh so very dull! it is an ultra-legitimate dulness.'

Peter Grimes
A tale in heroic couplets (▷ metre) by ▷ George Crabbe, Letter XXII in the series composing *The Borough* (1810). Peter is the son of a poor fisherman who tries to bring him up kindly and religiously. However, the boy is violent and wilful, and causes the death of his father by ill-treatment. He then lives a solitary life, distrusted and feared by the neighbourhood, with only a boy from an orphanage for company. He treats the boy brutally and finally causes his death, after which he misuses two other boys in the same way. The magistrates forbid him to employ any more pauper boys as apprentices, and his life becomes increasingly solitary, until he is found drifting distractedly along the desolate coast in his boat. As he dies he tells how he has been haunted by the ghosts of his dead father and the three boys, who never leave him, and ceaselessly condemn him to an eternity of lonely drifting. The poem is remarkable for its social realism and psychological power. It was made into an opera by Benjamin Britten (1945).

***Peter Pan* (1904)**
A children's play by ▷ J. M. Barrie, originally called *Peter Pan, or the Boy who wouldn't grow up*. It became, and remains, extremely popular

for its whimsical charm and its ingenious use of some traditional features of children's romances, such as Red Indians, the pirate Captain Hook who lives in fear of a crocodile which has already consumed one of his hands, and the fairy Tinkerbell.

▷ Children's books.

Peterloo Massacre, The

At a political meeting advocating the reform of parliamentary elections at St Peter's Field, Manchester, in 1819, the magistrates took alarm and ordered soldiers to attack the crowd. A small number of people were killed, and a large number were injured. The event caused intense resentment against the government of the time, and was nicknamed 'Peterloo' in ironic reference to the Anglo-Prussian victory over Napoleon at ▷ Waterloo in 1815. It provoked ▷ Shelley's fierce poem ▷ *The Masque of Anarchy*. It was also one of the causes of the establishment of the Metropolitan Police Force by Robert Peel in 1829, so that there should be a possibility of keeping order among crowds without the use of soldiers and firearms.

▷ Reform Bills, Parliamentary.

Petition of Right

A demand leading to a law forced on ▷ King Charles I by Parliament in 1628; it ended imprisonment without trial, the raising of taxes without Parliamentary authorization, martial law (*ie* legal judgements enforced under military authority), and the billeting of troops in private houses as an indirect means of forcing political obedience. It was the first major clash between Charles and Parliament in the conflict that ended in the ▷ Civil War of 1642–6.

Petrarch (Francesco Petrarca) (1304–74)

Italian poet and scholar. Petrarch's influence on English ▷ Renaissance poetry is incalculable. Petrarch's early years were spent in the Papal court at Avignon, but his life was one of constant movement – he described himself as *peregrinus ubique*, a wanderer everywhere. He travelled throughout Provence and Italy, living for eight years in Milan (1353–61), but visited in that time centres as far afield as Prague and Paris.

Travelling was to become a central metaphor in Petrarch's writing. The idea of the journey in his own life seemed to imitate great journeys of the past – those of the Apostles, St Augustine of Hippo (345–430), and the Homeric heroes. Life itself could be represented as a journey, or pilgrimage or, on occasion, a flight. This ▷ metaphor of transience was to be one of the many 'Petrarchan' motifs that English poets were to assimilate with such delight (cf ▷ Sir Thomas Wyatt's sonnet 'My galley charged with forgetfulness')

Petrarch's chief works are his *Africa* (a Latin ▷ epic on *Scipio Africanus*), the *Secretum* (a self-analytical dialogue), and his collection of poetry, the *Canzoniere*. The *Canzoniere* (also known as the *Rime* or *Rime sparse*) contained, by the end of his life, some 366 poems in all, the majority of which deal with the poet's love for 'Laura' – the unobtainable ideal of womanhood – whom Petrarch claimed to have first seen in church on 6 April 1327. In addition to the *Canzoniere*, he composed imitations of ▷ Virgil's *Eclogues* and the six *Trionfi* (*Triumphs*) poems – the triumphs of Love, Chastity, Death, Fame, Time and Eternity.

The *Trionfi* and the *Canzoniere*, were medieval best-sellers. Both circulated widely in manuscript form before their first publication in 1470. The *Trionfi* were to have a huge influence upon all forms of Renaissance representation – poetry, painting, tapestry, medals, emblems, ▷ pageants and theatre. At the same time, the introspective self-analysis, and the depiction of a female ideal who is both mistress and saint in the *Canzoniere*, were to influence European poets of the 16th and 17th centuries. The ▷ sonnet sequences of ▷ Sir Philip Sidney, ▷ Samuel Daniel, ▷ Michael Drayton and others, as well as the poetry, in an earlier period, of Sir Thomas Wyatt and ▷ Henry Howard, Earl of Surrey, all took Petrarch as a starting-point. Similarly the anti-Petrarchism of some of ▷ Shakespeare's sonnets or ▷ Donne's poetry, is, in its vigorous denial of Petrarchan modes, a tribute to the pervasive influence on the Renaissance sensibility of the Italian poet's work.

Bib: Durling, R. M., (ed.), *Petrarch's Lyric Poems*; Minta, S., *Petrarch and Petrarchism*.

Pfeiffer, Emily (1827–90)

Welsh poet and polemical writer, born in Montgomeryshire. Pfeiffer wrote ten volumes of poetry, including *Gerard's Monument* (1873); *Poems* (1876); *Sonnets and Songs* (1880); *The Rhyme of the Lady of the Rock* (1884) and *Flowers of the Night* (1889). Her work is informed by a Victorian ▷ feminist perspective, is sympathetic to marginalized women and addresses subjects such as ▷ marriage, rape, ▷ education, sexuality and work. Pfeiffer also wrote political essays including *Flying Leaves from East and West* (1885), written after a tour of Asia and America, and *Women and Work* (1887), where she protests against the limited vocational opportunities available to women. She died in 1890, leaving £2000 for higher education for women, which was used to build accommodation for female students at University College, Cardiff.

▷ Welsh literature in English.

Bib: Hickok, K., *Representations of Women: 19th Century British Women's Poetry*; Leighton,

A., and Reynolds, M. (eds.), *An Anthology of Victorian Women Poets.*

Phallocentrism
This term is used generally to mean 'male-centred' and therefore overlaps with ▷ androcentrism, but the strict meaning is 'centred on the phallus'. In this sense it is used by feminists to indicate the way power is invested in male symbolism and activity.

***Philaster, or Love lies a-bleeding* (1611)**
A romantic play by ▷ Francis Beraumont and ▷ John Fletcher; it was produced in 1611, and is in ▷ blank verse. It is the first in a style of ▷ tragicomedy that became characteristic of the English theatre during the next 30 years. Of all Beaumont and Fletcher's collaborations, it is perhaps the most famous; it derives from the prose romances of chivalry popular in France and Spain, and to some extent (*eg* ▷ Philip Sidney's ▷ *The Arcadia*) in England. The plot is characteristic: Philaster is rightful king of Sicily, but his throne has been usurped by the king of Calabria, with whose daughter, Arethusa, he is in love. He keeps communication with her through his page, Bellario. Her father wants her to marry Pharamond of Spain, and to avoid this she reveals to him the love affair between Pharamond and Megra, a lady of her father's court. In revenge Megra makes out that Arethusa has been having an affair with Bellario, whom Philaster accordingly dismisses. It then turns out that Bellario is a girl disguised as a page for love of Philaster. This situation seems to be borrowed from ▷ Shakespeare's ▷ *Twelfth Night*, but Shakespeare combined poignant truth to natural feelings with the romantic extravagance of the plot. Beaumont and Fletcher's emotion is obviously 'poetic' but not convincing.

Philemon and Baucis
A tale by the Roman poet ▷ Ovid, from the eighth book of his ▷ *Metamorphoses.* They are an aged peasant couple and very poor, but they give hospitality to the gods Zeus and Hermes, disguised as travellers. In reward, their cottage is transformed into a temple, of which they are made priest and priestess; they are also permitted to die in the same hour, and after death they are transformed into trees with intertwining boughs. ▷ Dryden's version (1693) of Ovid's poem is one of his best ▷ translations; ▷ Swift also wrote a poem on the subject (1709).

Philips, Ambrose (1675?–1749)
Poet. Associate of ▷ Joseph Addison and ▷ Richard Steele, and member of the Whig clique which frequented ▷ Button's ▷ Coffee-house. His ▷ couplet epistle, describing a snow scene addressed from Copenhagen to the ▷ Earl of Dorset, is a brilliantly evocative work, which was admired by ▷ Alexander Pope. His *Pastorals* (1709) were published in the same year as those of Pope, and the coincidence prompted a theoretical debate, which now seems quite arid, concerning the correct understanding of the form. Philips, it was felt, preserved the authentic rusticity of the ancient genre, while Pope polished it into a modern elegance. When the Buttonian ▷ Thomas Tickell pointedly praised Philips' pastorals in *The Guardian*, Pope submitted an anonymous piece *On Pastorals* to the same journal, in which with straight-faced irony he prefers Philips' poems to his own. The irony was so fine that, as ▷ Samuel Johnson relates, 'though Addison discovered it, Steele was deceived, and was afraid of displeasing Pope by publishing his paper'. Philips also edited a periodical (▷ reviews and periodicals), *The Freethinker* (1718–21), wrote several plays, Pindaric ▷ odes, and poems addressed to children, whose archness led his contemporary Henry Carey to attack him in *Namby-Pamby* (1725), from which the epithet in current use derives.

Philips, John (1676–1709)
Poet and physician. A pioneer of poetry in Miltonic ▷ blank verse. *The Splendid Shilling* (1701), described by ▷ Joseph Addison as 'the finest burlesque poem in the British language' presents a rueful self-portrait of the down-at-heel poet, without a shilling to his name. 'But I, whom griping penury surrounds,/ And Hunger, sure Attendant upon Want,/ With scanty Offals, and small acid Tiff/ (Wretched Repast!) my meagre Corps sustain:/ Then Solitary walk, or doze at home/ In Garret vile, and with a warming puff/ Regale chill'd Fingers'. The poet hides in a cupboard from a dun, then writes moody poems about disappointed love, and the work ends with an ▷ epic simile comparing the splitting of his ageing breeches to a shipwreck in the Aegean. Philips' obvious delight in self-dramatization gives the poem permanent appeal. He also wrote a serious ▷ epic, *Blenheim* (1705), but his most influential work was *Cyder* (1708), a Georgic poem in two books blending landscape description (often focused on Hereford, where he practised medicine), historical and philosophical reflection, and detailed advice on orchard-management. Its assured handling of blank verse, and its easy discursiveness of tone, were emulated and developed further by ▷ James Thomson in his *Seasons.*

Philips, Katherine (1632–1664)
Welsh poet and dramatist working during the ▷ Interregnum (1649–1660), known as 'Orinda'. Her parents were ▷ Presbyterians, and in 1647 she married James Philips, a supporter of ▷ Oliver Cromwell (1599–1658). Katherine Philips herself was a Royalist, and her poems record the difference between her own views and those of her husband. She was fluent in several languages, and a prolific writer. Thus

far, 116 poems, five verse ▷ translations and translations of two plays comprise her canon. The performance of her translation of French dramatist ▷ Pierre Corneille's *Pompey* in 1663 make her the first woman to have a play staged professionally in London. In 1651, her poems began to circulate in manuscript, and they were first published in 1651, prefixed to the poems of ▷ Henry Vaughan and Thomas Cartwright. In 1664 an unauthorized edition of her poems was published, but an authorized edition appeared in 1667. Philips' 'Society of Friendship', a correspondence circle, seems to have begun in 1651 and lasted until 1666, and included Henry Vaughan, among others. Within the circle, each member was assigned a name from classical literature, and Philips was dubbed 'Matchless Orinda'. Her letters to Sir Charles Cotterell were published as *Letters from Orinda to Poliarchus* (1705). She also corresponded with ▷ Dorothy Osborne. When she died of smallpox, her translation of *Horace* was unfinished. Philips was praised by her contemporaries as the ideal woman poet because of her modest choice of subjects (compare, for example, ▷ Aphra Behn). The majority of her poetry is written for particular occasions or persons, and in many of them she transforms the conventional language of courtship and applies it to friendships between women: 'Our hearts are mutuall victims lay'd, / While they (such power in friendship ly's) / are Altars, Priests, and off rings made, / And each heart which thus kindly dy's / Grows deathless by the sacrifise.'

▷ Polwhele, Elizabeth

Bib: Greer, G., *et al.*, Kissing the Rod; Hobby, E., *Virtue of Necessity*.

Phillips, Caryl (b 1958)
Novelist, playwright, travel writer. Born in St Kitts, West Indies, brought up in Leeds, England, and educated at Oxford, he has been writer-in-residence at the Factory Community Centre, London, at the Literary Criterion Centre, Mysore, India and at the University of Stockholm, Sweden. Both *Cambridge* (1991) and *Crossing the River* (1993) consist of several narratives linked by the theme of slavery, and both are written in an imitation of 18th and 19th-century English. His other novels are: *The Final Passage* (1985); *A State of Independence* (1986); *Higher Ground* (1989). Plays: *Strange Fruit* (1981); *Where There is Darkness* (1982); *The Shelter* (1984); *The Wasted Years* (1985); *Playing Away* (1987). Travel writing: *The European Tribe* (1987).

Philosophes
▷ Encyclopaedists.

Phiz (Browne, Hablot Knight) (1815–82)
Illustrator. He was the principal illustrator for the novels of ▷ Charles Dickens (especially ▷ *David Copperfield*, ▷ *The Pickwick Papers*, ▷ *Dombey and Son*, ▷ *Martin Chuzzlewit*, ▷ *Bleak House*). He also illustrated the works of other Victorian novelists, notably ▷ Harrison Ainsworth and ▷ Charles Lever.

***Phoenix and the Turtle, The* (1632–64)**
A poem by ▷ Shakespeare included in an anthology *Love's Martyr* (1601) assembled by Robert Chester. The book includes other poems on the love and death of the phoenix and the turtle (turtle-dove); some of these are anonymous and others (including Shakespeare's, and verses by ▷ Ben Jonson, ▷ George Chapman and ▷ John Marston) are signed.

Shakespeare's poem consists of 13 quatrains followed by five triplets (stanzas of three lines) as a concluding 'threnos' (*ie* threnody, or song of lament). The phoenix represents Beauty, and the turtle, Truth; they are united by love; by their death, Reason (personified as the singer of the threnos) declares that the world has been deprived of real truth and real beauty:

Truth may seem, but cannot be;
Beauty brag, but 'tis not she;
Truth and beauty buried be.

Beauty and Truth, the poem says, have therefore no meaning separable from Love. The poem is idealist in the style of ▷ Renaissance ▷ Platonism, it is also metaphysical in its concepts, but not in the style of the ▷ Metaphysical Poets who owe their name to ways of thinking rather than to the concepts they invoke.

Physician's Tale, The
One of ▷ Chaucer's ▷ *Canterbury Tales*. It is an exemplary narrative, set in the Roman past, recounting the history of Virginia, a beautiful young woman who is beheaded by her father Virginius. He chooses to murder his daughter, rather than allow her to be placed in the care of a corrupt and lascivious judge, Appius. The judge is later publically executed for his corruption of the law: Virginius is publically reprieved. Several other versions of this disturbing narrative were available to Chaucer (in ▷ John Gower's ▷ *Confessio Amantis*, in the ▷ *Roman de la Rose*), but the version in the *Physician's Tale* is distinctive for its emphasis on the pathos of Virginia's murder, subversive of the apparent lesson of the narrative, which purports to show how sin has its rewards.

Picaresque
From the Spanish *picaro*, 'rogue' or 'cunning trickster'. The term is especially applied to a form of prose fiction originating in Spain in the 16th century, with such works as the anonymous *Lazarille de Tormes* (1553), and dealing with the

adventures of such characters in loose episodic form, often involving a journey.

The first distinctive example in English is ▷ Thomas Nashe's *The Unfortunate Traveller* (1594). In the 18th century, examples include ▷ Daniel Defoe's ▷ *Moll Flanders*, ▷ Henry Fielding's ▷ *Jonathan Wild* and ▷ Tobias Smollett's *The Adventures of Ferdinand Count Fathom*. Other traditions combine with the picaresque: the mock romance in the tradition of ▷ *Don Quixote*, and the tradition of religious pilgrimage (cf. ▷ *The Pilgrim's Progress*).

Bib: Sieber, H., *The Picaresque*.

Pickwick Papers, The **(1836–7)**
The first novel by ▷ Charles Dickens, published serially 1836–7. The story is the adventures of Mr Pickwick and his friends Tupman, Snodgrass and Winkle, who go on a journey of observation of men and manners on behalf of the Pickwick Club, of which Mr Pickwick is the founder and the chairman. The episodes are predominantly comic and Mr Pickwick seems at first to be intended as a mere figure of fun, destined always to be made a fool of owing to his extreme innocence of the ways of the world. Fairly early on, however, he acquires a servant, Sam Weller. Sam is the ideal servant; he is practical, good-humoured, resourceful and devoted. Pickwick now begins to be endowed with a new dignity; still very innocent, he is no longer a mere figure of fun, for he is also shown to have positive moral qualities, such as a determination to stand by the values of truth and justice. He becomes, in fact, a kind of 19th-century English middle-class Don Quixote with Sam Weller as a Sancho Panza, without any of the ridiculousness of Sancho, but with a great deal of comedy derived from his highly developed and typically Cockney sense of humour. At first there is a story but no plot; about half-way through, however, a semblance of a plot develops with Mrs Bardell's conspiracy to obtain £750 from Mr Pickwick for breach of promise of marriage. Assisted by a firm of unscrupulous lawyers, she is at first successful and Mr Pickwick goes to prison. This is the beginning of Dickens' constant preoccupation with prison and with the parasitic qualities of the legal profession. Various episodes illustrate the kinds of social viciousness which Dickens was to enjoy ridiculing or dramatizing – the cheerful roguery of Mr Jingle; the hypocrisy of the 'shepherd', Mr Stiggins; the demagogic Mr Potts in the parliamentary election at Eatanswill, etc. By contrast, Mr Wardle represents the opulent philanthropy and cordial 'religion of Christmas' which were also to figure in Dickens' novels to the end but especially in the earlier ones. In the outcome, Mr Pickwick and Sam Weller emerge as a kind of ideal alliance between the middle and working classes – complete sincerity and integrity in moral guidance on Pickwick's part, total devotion and most useful practical capacity on Weller's side.

Picture of Dorian Gray, The **(1890)**
A novel by ▷ Oscar Wilde which updates ▷ Goethe's ▷ Faust legend. Tempted by the selfish sybarite Henry Wotton, Dorian trades his soul for eternal youth and beauty while his portrait, painted by Basil Hallward, who appeals to the better side of his nature, bears the ravages of time and Dorian's decadent living. It was meant as an examination of the consequences of regarding sensual indulgence and moral indifference as aesthetic ends in themselves. Another version of the *doppelgänger*, it has much in common with ▷ Stevenson's ▷ The Strange Case of Dr Jekyll and Mr Hyde.

▷ Aestheticism.

Picturesque, The Cult of the
A term used in the late 18th and early 19th centuries to describe a certain kind of scenery, where cultivation was employed to produce artificially 'wild' nature. Landscape gardeners incorporated 'wildernesses' into their prospects, often with fake ruins suggesting the decay of classical civilization. The writer most identified with the 'picturesque' was William Gilpin (1724–1804), who wrote a series of illustrated picturesque tours. ▷ Jane Austen in ▷ *Mansfield Park* parodies the cult, and ▷ Thomas Love Peacock's *Headlong Hall* satirizes a contemporary dispute about its qualities.

'Pied Piper of Hamelin, The' (1845)
A poem by ▷ Robert Browning. It retells an ancient legend: a piper promises to rid the town of Hamelin in Germany of its plague of rats in return for a thousand guilders from the Council. The rats follow the music of his pipe as far as the river Weser, where they are drowned. The Council, however, refuse to pay the piper, whereupon he similarly plays the children out of town and into the side of a mountain which opens to receive them. The origin of the legend may be the Children's Crusade of 1212, when thousands of young people were persuaded to join an expedition to the Holy Land, and many of them perished on the journey.

Piers Plowman
Attributed to ▷ William Langland, *Piers Plowman* is a major ▷ alliterative narrative poem, composed in the later 14th century and extant in three versions, conventionally known as the A, B and C texts. It is now generally accepted that Langland is responsible for each of these versions, and it seems the composition of the poem must have occupied some 25 years of his life: the A text, consisting of a Prologue and 12 Passus (the 'steps' or divisions of the

poem), dates from c 1367–70; the B text, which reworks and develops material from A and is about three times as long, dates from c 1377–9; the C text, a partial revision of B, dates from c 1385–6.

The ▷ dream-vision mode frees medieval poets from the conventional time and space limitations of other narrative genres, and facilitates literary speculations of all kinds. Langland uses these possibilities to the full in *Piers Plowman*, which is made up of a series of dream-vision sequences (ten in all in the B and C texts, two of which occur as dreams within dreams). The dreams of Will, the narrator, provide the medium for a wide-ranging investigation into the theory and practice of Christian conduct – in Christian society as a whole, and in the life of its individual members. The current corrupt state of clerical and ecclesiastical practice is an insistent topic of the text. The dreamscapes shift from overviews of a whole society (as seen in the 'field ful of folk' with which the poem opens) to a more introspective landscape (as when Will encounters other personified faculties such as Wit and Thought in later Passus) to a visionary experience of major events in Christian history (such as Will's vision of the Crucifixion and Resurrection sequence in the B and C texts). The context of Will's dreams shifts too in the course of the poem: he begins dreaming alone in the Malvern hills but after a later dream he wakes up to call his wife and daughter to church.

Through using the dream medium Langland is able to locate the events of his poem in different times as well as places: attention is focussed on the status quo of 14th-century English society (in the Prologue), on a projected future state of its reform, on the stages in the life of an individual member of that society (in the history of Will, the Dreamer/ narrator), on the history of the Church itself and on the place of the individual and society within the overarching framework of Christian history (Will witnesses a replaying of events leading up to, and following, the Crucifixion). In fact Langland progressively complicates the temporal dimension of the action in the B and C texts, so that individual, social and Christian history intermesh. By the end of the narrative, the end of the Dreamer's life approaches, as the institution of the Christian church itself seems set to crumble as the time of Antichrist draws near.

The poem does not however end with universal collapse, but with the Dreamer renewing his quest for Piers Plowman, the linking character of the narrative, who appears in different roles (as leader of social reform, as a model for the spiritual life), and who seems able to make the connections between the divisions the Dreamer sees all around him (between Christian theory and practice, between knowledge and understanding, between the different stages of Christian life, Do-wel, Do-bet, Do-best). In *Piers Plowman* the dream medium is used not only as a means of analysis and debate (as it is in many other dream-vision poems of his time) but also as a medium for experiences of insight and integration when manifold connections can be made, although not sustained.

The language of the Church and the Bible (Latin) is woven together with the language of the laity (English): the question of how the former should be translated into the latter creates one of the crisis points in the B text (Passus 7), when Piers Plowman and a priest debate how the text of a pardon should be interpreted. Partly the issues at stake in the poem come down to questions of semantics, as the Dreamer tries to find out what words mean, and is sometimes enlightened, but is often confused. The result is a text which pays extraordinary attention to the resources of verbal expression, and in which puns, metaphors and word-play of all kinds abound, as Langland explores ways of making the spiritual visible.

Over 50 manuscripts are extant, which suggests that Langland's work enjoyed considerable popularity in the 15th century among clerics and members of the educated middle classes. An edition of the B text was printed in 1550. George Puttenham's response to Langland's work (in the *Art of English Poesy* c 1589) suggests he read it less as 'poesy', more as social satire, and that view has tended to predominate in critical studies of Langland's work until very recently.

Bib: Alford, J. (ed.), *A Companion to Piers Plowman*; Pearsall, D. (ed.), *Piers Plowman by William Langland: An Edition of the C text*; Schmidt A. V. C. (ed.), *William Langland: the Vision of Piers Plowman.*

Pilgrimage of Grace, The

A rebellion provoked by the closing of the ▷ monasteries in 1536. It arose in and was chiefly supported by the north of England, and this fact shows that it had a social and political basis as well as a religious one. The south of England was economically and socially much more advanced as well as more closely in touch with movements of religious reform on the continent of Europe; in consequence, monasteries were not only becoming redundant there in their social functions, but were to some extent actively resented. In the north of England they were more respected on religious grounds, and still served social functions of poor relief and large employment of labour. In addition to these causes directly related to monastic institutions, there were other social causes bound up with the resentment of the old landed nobility of the north for the newer nobility of the south, who were encouraged and advanced in public service by ▷ King Henry VIII. The closing of the monasteries was a pretext for rebellion such as the northern nobility had been looking for. The rebellion was formidable, and the government, through its representative the Duke of Norfolk, had to come to terms; the terms, however, were not kept, and once the rebel army had dispersed, its leaders were executed.

Pilgrim's Progress, The
A prose ▷ allegory by ▷ John Bunyan. *The Pilgrim's Progress from this World to that which is to come* is in two parts: Part I (1678) tells of the religious conversion of Christian, and of his religious life – conceived as a pilgrimage – in this world, until he comes to the River of Death, and the Heavenly City which lies beyond it; Part II (1684) describes the subsequent conversion of his wife Christiana and their children, and their similar journey with a group of friends.

Both parts contain episodes which symbolize real life experiences: thus, Christian, soon after the way has been pointed out to him, falls into the ▷ Slough of Despond – a bog which represents the depression which overcomes the new convert when he has passed the stage of first enthusiasm; later he has to pass through phases of spiritual despair and terror, symbolized by the ▷ Valleys of Humiliation and the Shadow of Death; he has to face the derision and anger of public opinion in the town of Vanity Fair, and so on. Christiana and the children have an easier time; perhaps Bunyan wished to show that God in his mercy shields the weaker pilgrims, or perhaps that public opinion is harsher to pioneers than to those that follow them.

The 'pioneer pilgrims' – Christian and his associates – belong to the Puritan sects, of one of which Bunyan was himself a member, who were undergoing persecution in the reign of Charles II, especially during the earlier years, when English society was in strong reaction against the previous Puritan regime of Oliver Cromwell. Yet *The Pilgrim's Progress* is much more than merely a dramatization of the Puritan spirit. By its allegorical content, it is related to the tradition of the allegorical sermon which, in village churches, survived the Reformation of the 16th century, and some of the adventures (Christian's fight with Apollyon, the Castle of Giant Despair, the character of Greatheart) are related in spirit to popular versions of medieval and 16th century romances, surviving in the ▷ chapbooks. These aspects give it a close relation with popular traditions of culture to an extent unequalled by any other major literary work. Another element of popular culture shows in Bunyan's assimilation of the English translation of the ▷ Bible, and this reminds us that for many households the Bible was the only book constantly read, and that during the next century Bunyan's allegory took its place beside it. Still more important than these links with the past is Bunyan's anticipation of the kind of vision of human nature which in the 18th and 19th centuries was to find its scope in the novel: his allegorized characters do not, as in past allegories, merely simplify human virtues and vices, but reveal how an individual destiny can be shaped by the predominance in a personality of an outstanding quality, good or bad; the adventures of the pilgrims are conditioned by the differences of these qualities. Thus, Christian and Faithful, fellow pilgrims, have radically different temperaments and correspondingly different experiences.

▷ Celestial City; City of Destruction; Doubting Castle; Vanity Fair.

Pilkington, Laetitia (c 1708–1750)
Irish poet and memoirist, born to parents of Dutch origin in Dublin. In 1725 she married the Reverend Matthew Pilkington and met satirist ▷ Jonathan Swift and others. Swift helped Matthew Pilkington to a chaplaincy in London and when Mrs Pilkington followed she found that her husband was involved with an actress. In 1733 she returned alone to Dublin, already regarded as a woman of dubious character. In 1738 Pilkington divorced her for adultery. Pilkington did not supply much maintenance, and she and her children moved to London, where she tried to live by her writing. She began with the subject of masculine infidelity in *The Statues*: *Or*, *the Trial of Constancy* (1739) and accompanied writing with wild living. She found it hard to survive by her pen, and was imprisoned for debt, escaping to open a bookshop in St James'. She returned to Dublin in 1747, and began to publish her *Memoirs* featuring stories of Swift and ▷ Samuel Richardson, some of which settled old scores.

Her other publications include: *An Excursory View on the Present State of Things and Memoirs* (1748–1754).

Pinckney, Eliza Lucas (c1722–1793)
North American letter-writer. Born in Antigua, West Indies, and educated in England, she was the daughter of wealthy South Carolinan plantation owners. An astute and imaginative businesswoman, she managed the family plantations in the West Indies beginning in 1740. Her experiments to improve the cultivation of indigo were major contributions to that crop's importance in the West Indian and American South's economies. The *Journal and Letters of Eliza Lucas* details her life in the West Indies, her experiments with indigo, her attitudes towards ▷ marriage and her religious beliefs. After a life in which she continued her various agricultural experimentations and raised a family in South Carolina, she died in Philadelphia.

Pindar (5th century BC)
Greek poet. He is famous for his lyrical ▷ odes, *ie* poems to be sung to the accompaniment of

musical instruments and dancing. The odes had a strong religious tone and were designed for solemn occasions, including sporting celebrations. The fact that their composition was influenced by their musical and dance accompaniment gives the odes an appearance of irregularity. This, and the loftiness of their emotion, made them tempting models, from the 17th to 19th centuries, for English poets when they were writing on themes of deep emotional power and felt the need of an ample form which would allow them considerable licence in the treatment of the subject. Pindar's odes were not really as unsystematic as they seemed, however, and many English poems in 'Pindarics' have only a superficial resemblance to the kind of ode that Pindar wrote. Notable examples are ▷ Dryden's *Alexander's Feast*, and *Ode to the Memory of Anne Killigrew*.

Pindaric Ode
▷ Ode.

Pindarics
▷ Pindar.

Pinero, Sir Arthur Wing (1855–1934)
Dramatist. His earliest plays were farces, but in 1889 *The Profligate* showed a great advance in seriousness over earlier plays in the century, when the English theatre had been practically bankrupt of contemporary drama of interest. At about this time, largely owing to the influence of ▷ Ibsen, drama was being revised radically in Europe. Pinero's *The Second Mrs Tanqueray* (1893) was at the time of its production a conspicuous contribution to the new movement; it was translated into French, German and Italian, and attracted the leading European actress of the age, Eleonora Duse. Pinero followed this success with other plays which sustained his reputation in Britain at least, such as *Trelawny of the 'Wells'* (1898) and *The Gay Lord Quex* (1899). He was, in fact, a prolific writer, publishing thirty-nine plays between 1891 and 1930. His plays are now seldom produced and little studied: in wit and dramatic ingenuity he was soon excelled by ▷ George Bernard Shaw. Like Tom Robertson (1829–71) before him, his brilliance was like that of a candle in the dark: he was conspicuous in contrast to the dullness that preceded him.
Bib: Dunkel, W.D., *Life*; Boas, F.S., *From Richardson to Pinero*; Lazenby, W., *Pinero*.

Pinter, Harold (b 1930)
British dramatist. Major works: *The Room* (1957); *The Birthday Party* (1958); *The Dumb Waiter* (1957); *A Slight Ache* (radio 1958, stage 1961); *A Night Out* (1960); *The Caretaker* (1960); *The Homecoming* (1964); *Old Times* (1971); *No Man's Land* (1975); *Betrayal* (1978); *A Kind of Alaska* (1982); *Mountain Language* (1988).

His distinctiveness among contemporary dramatists arises from his use of dialogue. Words are used less for communication than for justification by the speaker's self to himself, and as weapons against others. He has been claimed as a British exponent of the Theatre of the Absurd, although his plays often begin from an ostensibly naturalistic context, which breaks down into a threatening, and sometimes surreal world. The plays are often structured around the intrusion of a menacing stranger into an apparently safe world, who then becomes a catalyst for the return of the repressed. The theatre critic Irving Wardle has termed Pinter's work the 'Comedy of Menace'. Pinter has said that his fascination with oblique communication was something that he learned as a Jew brought up in an anti-semitic area of London, where evasion was a means of survival.

Born in the East End, the son of a Jewish tailor, Pinter worked as an actor before turning to writing and still performs occasionally as well as directing. The first London production of a Pinter play was received with critical incomprehension, and was a commercial disaster. *The Birthday Party*, in which two menacing figures threaten the banality of a seaside boarding house, was variously described in the national papers as: 'half-gibberish', 'puzzling' a 'baffling mixture'. Consequently, *The Dumb Waiter* had its first performance in Hamburg, and it was not until *The Caretaker* in 1960 that Pinter was recognised as a major writer.

All the plays sound an enigma, the threat in them is all the more frightening for never being directly explained. Pinter's work has been interpreted in a host of different ways; among other theories, Freud and the Bible have been hauled in to account for their obscurity, but Pinter resolutely insists that the plays mean no more than they say: 'I can sum up none of my plays. I can describe none of them, except to say: That is what happened. That is what they said. That is what they did.'

Pinter is also a major film writer, whose credits include *The Servant* (1963), *The Quiller Memorandum* (1966), *The Go-Between* (1971), *The French Lieutenant's Woman* (1981) and *The Handmaid's Tale* (1990).

Piozzi, Hester Thrale
▷ Thrale, Hester Lynch.

Pitt (the Elder), William, Earl of Chatham (1708–78)
English politician. He led the government during the major part of the ▷ Seven Years' War, during which the British won Canada from the French, and established themselves as the dominant political influence on the subcontinent of India. The successes of this war are usually attributed to Pitt's statesmanship.

Pitt (the Younger), William (1759–1806)
Politician. The son of ▷ William Pitt, Earl of Chatham. He led the government from 1783 to

1801, and again in the years 1804–6. He first became Prime Minister when he was only 24, at a time when ▷ George III's government had been deeply discredited by defeat in the ▷ American War of Independence, brought to an end by the Peace of Versailles, 1783. Moreover, politics were thoroughly corrupted by various systems of bribery, and Parliament represented only the interests of various sections of the privileged classes. Pitt was as prudent a statesman as his father had been a dynamic one, and he was famous for his strict integrity. His first ministry was one of cautious reconstruction such as Britain needed for the long wars with France (War of the ▷ French Revolution, 1793–1801, and the ▷ Napoleonic War, 1803–15). Politically he was conservative 'Tory', but he was the first political leader to rely on public opinion as expressed in the electoral constituencies instead of on more or less bribed backing among Members of Parliament.

Pitter, Ruth (1897–1992)
Poet. Pitter's long writing career began with the publication of *First Poems* in 1920, and developed through traditional routes: her poetry is accessible, simple and anti- ▷ modernistic. She has also written on gardening. In 1955 she became the first women to win the Queen's Gold Medal for Poetry. Her works include: *Persephone in Hades* (1931); *A Mad Lady's Garland* (1934); *The Rude Potato* (1941); *On Cats* (1947); *Still By Choice* (1966); *Poems 1926–1966* and *End of Drought* (1975).
Bib: Gilbert, R., *Four Living Poets*; Russell, A. (ed.), *Ruth Pitter: Homage to a Poet*; Watkin, E. I. *Poets and Mystics*.

Pix, Mary (1666–1709)
Dramatist and novelist, one of the so-called 'Female Wits' satirized in a play of that name in 1696. Pix's first play, a heroic tragedy called *Ibrahim, the Thirteenth Emperor of the Turks*, was produced at Drury Lane in 1696, the same year as her novel, *The Inhuman Cardinal, Or: Innocence Betrayed*, and a comedy following ▷ Aphra Behn, *The Spanish Wives*. Another comedy, *The Innocent Mistress*, was staged at Lincoln's Inn Fields in the following year. Later plays include *The Deceiver Deceived* (1697), *The False Friend* (1699), *The Beau Defeated* (1700), *The Double Distress* (1701); and *The Conquest of Spain* (1705); Pix wrote a dozen plays in all, of which the comedies are generally considered far superior to the tragedies.
Bib: Steeves, E. L. (ed.), *The Plays of Mary Pix and Catharine Trotter*; Clark, C., *Three Augustan Women Playwrights*; Morgan, F. (ed.), *The Female Wits*.

***Plain Dealer, The* (1676)**
Dark comedy by ▷ William Wycherley, based on ▷ Molière's *Le Misanthrope*. Manly, an 'honest' but dour sea captain, has put his trust in the duplicitous Vernish and brittle Olivia, to whom he has been betrothed. In his absence the two have secretly married, and she has appropriated the fortune that he had entrusted to her care. Manly returns from the Dutch Wars and, on learning of her marriage to an unknown man, determines to revenge himself on her by seducing her, with the help of his page. Also unknown to him, the page is a woman in disguise, Fidelia, who has loved him and gained employment with him in order to be near him. The 'youth' reluctantly agrees to address Olivia on Manly's behalf, but Olivia becomes attracted to Fidelia, and attempts to make love to her, in a scene recalling the one between Viola and Olivia in ▷ Shakespeare's ▷ *Twelfth Night*. Manly overhears Olivia acknowledge that she deceived him deliberately. Later Vernish witnesses an assignation between the women and on discovering Fidelia's sex, attempts to rape her, but is interrupted. In the final scene, Fidelia is wounded in a skirmish, defending Manly from Vernish, who is revealed as Olivia's husband. Fidelia's true identity, and status as an heiress, are also made known, and she and Manly are united. A subplot involves the litigations of the Widow Blackacre and her doltish son Jerry. The play was considered by ▷ Dryden to be Wycherley's best, and from it he derived the frequent appellation 'Manly Wycherley'. The play survived to the late 18th century, when it disappeared from the stage, but has been revived (several times) in the 20th century, including the 1988–9 production by the RSC.

Plantagenet (Anjou), House of
A medieval royal family which reigned over England from 1154 until 1399; ▷ Henry II 1151–89; ▷ Richard I 1189–99; ▷ John I 1199–1216; ▷ Henry III 1216–72; ▷ Edward I 1272–1307; ▷ Edward II 1307–27; ▷ Edward III 1327–77; ▷ Richard II 1377–99. The first of the line, Henry II, succeeded to the English throne through his mother, Mathilda, daughter of the last ▷ Norman king, Henry I. Henry II's father was Geoffrey, Count of Anjou, a province in France; hence the family was known either as the House of Anjou or as Plantagenet, from the plant broom (in Latin, *planta genista*) which Geoffrey used to wear in his cap. The families of Lancaster and York, which ruled England successively in the 15th century, were junior branches of the Plantagenet family.

Plath, Sylvia (1932–63)
Poet and novelist. She was brought up in the U.S.A.; her father, who died when she was nine, was of Prussian origin and her mother Austrian. Her university education was at Smith College, Massachusetts, and Newnham College, Cambridge. She married the English

poet ▷ Ted Hughes in 1956. For a time she taught at Smith College, but in 1959 she settled in England. In 1960 she published her first volume of poetry, *The Colossus*, and in 1963 her only novel, *The Bell Jar*, under the pen-name of Victoria Lucas. Her reputation was established on the posthumous publication of her book of poetry, *Ariel* (1965). This volume aroused more interest in Britain than any other since ▷ Dylan Thomas' *Deaths and Entrances* (1946). The poems combine bold imagery and original rhythms with strenuous artistic control; their themes concern states of mind in extremity. In a commentary recorded for the ▷ British Council, she declared: 'One should be able to control and manipulate experiences, even the most terrifying . . . with an informed and intelligent mind.' Plath committed suicide in 1963. Other important posthumous publications are *Crossing the Water* (1971) and *Winter Trees* (1972); Plath also wrote a radio play, *Three Women*, broadcast in 1962. *Collected Poems* (ed. Ted Hughes; 1981); *Letters Home* (1978).
Bib: Alvarez, A., in *Beyond All This Fiddle* and *The Savage God*; Uroff, M. D., *Sylvia Plath and Ted Hughes*; Rose, J., *The Haunting of Sylvia Plath*; *The Art of Sylvia Plath: A Symposium* (ed. Charles Newman) contains a bibliography.

Plato (? 428 – ? 348 BC)
Greek philosopher. He was a follower of the Athenian philosopher ▷ Socrates, and his dialogues represent conversations in which Socrates takes the lead. The most famous of these 'Socratic' dialogues are *Protagoras, Gorgias, Phaedo, Symposium*, ▷ *Republic, Phaedrus, Timaeus*. His longest work, the *Laws*, does not include Socrates as a character. His central conception is that beyond the world of transient material phenomena lies another eternal world of ideal forms which the material world represents in the form of imitations. His figure for this in the *Republic* is that men in the material world are like people watching shadows moving on the wall of a cave; they see only these shadows and not the realities which cast the shadows. Plato is one of the two most influential philosophers in European thought, the other one being ▷ Aristotle, who was at first his pupil.
▷ Platonism.

Platonic Love
A term that has come to possess three distinct, if related, senses: 1 A love between individuals which transcends sexual desire and attains spiritual heights. This is the most popularly understood sense of the term. 2 The complex doctrine of love which embraces sexuality, but which is directed towards an ideal end, to be found discussed in ▷ Plato's *Symposium*. ▷ John Donne's poem 'The Extasy' explores this form of love. 3 A reference to homosexual love (▷ Katherine Philips). This third sense is derived from the praise of homosexual love to be found in the *Symposium*.

Platonism and Neo-Platonism
The term 'Platonism' is applied to the school of thought derived immediately from the Greek philosopher ▷ Plato. 'Neo-Platonism' names schools of thought that adapted his philosophy by adding to or modifying it. Two main periods of revival of Plato's thought are described as neo-Platonism: 1 that initiated by the pagan Plotinus (3rd century AD) in Rome, and at first a revival of Christianity, into which it was to some extent carried by St Augustine of Hippo (345–430) when he was converted; 2 that which Marsilio Ficino initiated by his studies of Platonic philosophy in Florence (15th century). The 17th-century group known as the Cambridge Platonists (▷ Platonists, Cambridge) were true Platonists rather than Neo-Platonists.

1 Plato taught that beyond the world of transient phenomena surrounding us is one of permanent and imperishable ideas, but he relied on logical reason for the development of his philosophy. Neo-Platonism added a religious aspect that depended on revelation; it derived this influence from other philosophies and from eastern religions. The elements that St Augustine transferred to Christianity remained dominant until the 13th century, when Platonic influence was succeeded by that of ▷ Aristotle.
2 Sixteenth-century neo-Platonism in Italy revived the ancient neo-Platonist conception that the universe is peopled by many supernatural beings, and maintained that these existed in addition to the angels and devils allowed by Christian doctrine. It also taught that men, being essentially spirits, could, by the acquisition of wisdom and virtue, immensely increase their power and knowledge, and could control for their good and wise purposes the non-human supernatural spirits. Thus arose the idea of 'the Mage', or master of high magic: in ▷ Shakespeare's ▷ *The Tempest*, Prospero is such a neo-Platonic Mage, and Ariel is a spirit such as the neo-Platonists believed could be controlled and used. Neo-Platonism also influenced poetic conceptions, whereby the beloved lady of a sonnet sequence (*eg* ▷ Sir Philip Sidney's ▷ *Astrophil and Stella*) was a sublime image of her ideal soul, and virtues (*eg* those allegorized by ▷ Edmund Spenser in ▷ *The Faerie Queene*) could exist as ideal realities. In criticism, Sidney shows neo-Platonic influence in his conception that poetry should not merely represent but improve on nature, in accordance with the Platonic idea that the world of ordinary realities is an inferior imitation of the eternal idealities. This outlook emphasized the importance of the imagination as the faculty that could create ideal images and not merely

imitate the general qualities common to classes of actual objects, in accordance with Aristotle's critical theory.

Platonists, The Cambridge
A group of thinkers at Cambridge University in the mid-17th century. Their aim was to combine reason with revealed religion, and to counteract the religiously destructive tendencies of the thought of ▷ René Descartes and ▷ Thomas Hobbes. Their concern with true religion was combined with a care for both clarity of thought and religious tolerance. Their chief representatives were Henry More (1614–87), Ralph Cudworth (1617–88), Benjamin Whichcote (1609–83) and John Smith (1618–52).
▷ Platonism and Neo-Platonism.
Bib: Patrides, C. A. (ed.), *The Cambridge Platonists.*

Plautus, Titus Maccius (? 254–184 BC)
Roman comic dramatist. His comedies are based on situation and intrigue; they had a high reputation in his own time, but unlike the other outstanding Roman comedian, ▷ Terence, he was ignored during the Middle Ages. In the 16th century his reputation revived, and his style of comedy was emulated throughout Western Europe. The play which is often called the first English comedy, Nicholas Udall's ▷ *Ralph Roister Doister*, is based on Plautus' *Miles Gloriosus* ('The Boastful Soldier') and Shakespeare's ▷ *Comedy of Errors* on Plautus' *Menaechmi*, which, using a confusion between twins, may also have influenced Shakespeare's ▷ *Twelfth Night*. Again, Shakespeare's ▷ *Taming of the Shrew* may be partly based on Plautus' *Mostellaria*, and the last act of Jonson's ▷ *The Alchemist* is also indebted to it. Certain of Plautus' comic characters, such as that of the boastful soldier as in Udall's play, started a tradition, exemplified by Captain Bobadill in Jonson's ▷ *Every Man in his Humour* and Parolles in Shakespeare's ▷ *All's Well that Ends Well.* These are the most important examples, but traces, at least, of Plautus in the background of English plays can be found in other works of Ben Jonson, and in plays by ▷ Thomas Heywood, ▷ Dryden and ▷ Fielding.

Play on words
▷ Figures of Speech.

***Playboy of the Western World, The* (1907)**
A play by ▷ John Millington Synge. The scene is a remote part of rural Ireland. The hero, Christy Mahon, arrives at a village inn in flight from the law, since he believes himself to have killed his tyrannical father. Instead of being handed over to the police or regarded with abhorrence, he is treated with admiration, and the innkeeper's daughter, Pegeen Mike, falls in love with him. He is at first a miserable youth with no belief in himself, but the universal admiration and Pegeen's love build up his confidence, until he behaves like a true hero. This fiction is destroyed momentarily when his father, who has merely been injured, suddenly appears on the scene. The assault on the father is then suddenly removed from fiction into fact, and the village, including Pegeen, turn against Christy. However, Christy turns into yet a third type of person; he defies the village, through sheer desperation at the idea of sinking back into subservience to his father, and makes his departure in the bullying style which has always been his father's character. The play is thus a mixture of ironic comedy, poetic tragedy, and exuberant farce.

The language is that of the superstitious Irish peasantry, musical and imaginative in its idiom, and though the dialogue is prose, it reaches an intensity that is unique in drama in the English language since the days of ▷ Shakespeare. Irish nationalist opinion was deeply angered by Synge's refusal to idealize the Irish character, and its early performances at ▷ W. B. Yeats' ▷ Abbey Theatre in Dublin caused riots.
▷ Irish literature in English.

***Plays for Puritans* (1901)**
The title for a volume of three plays by ▷ George Bernard Shaw: *The Devil's Disciple*; ▷ *Caesar and Cleopatra*; *Captain Brassbound's Conversion.* Shaw was himself a declared ▷ Puritan in the sense that he shared the Puritan insistence on the importance above all of a sensitive conscience, but he was concerned that the public should be clear-thinking about it. Hence each of these plays treats the conscience and its workings from an original and ironic angle.

***Plays Pleasant and Unpleasant* (1898)**
A collection of seven plays by ▷ George Bernard Shaw. The four 'pleasant' plays are comedies with serious themes (the character of the true soldier, what constitutes moral strength, the nature of greatness, etc.) but nothing likely to dismay or shock the conventional moral sense of the audiences of the day. These are: ▷ *Arms and the Man, Candida, The Man of Destiny, You Never Can Tell.* The three 'unpleasant' plays dealt with social topics (sexual morality and the ownership of slum property) such as were generally felt to be unsuitable for presentation in the theatre. These are: *Widowers' Houses, The Philanderer, Mrs Warren's Profession.*

Pléiade
The name given to the group of 16th-century poets led by ▷ Ronsard and ▷ Du Bellay, supposedly seven in total, although early mentions of poet comrades are far in excess of this number. Du Bellay's *Deffence & Illustration de la langue francoyse* (1549) sets out a credo

common to the group as a whole: wholehearted promotion of the vernacular, imitation of the Ancients, rejection of medieval forms of ▷ lyric verse such as the *ballade* or *rondeau*, establishment of the 12-syllable ▷ alexandrine as the staple of French verse. Their cultivation of the ▷ sonnet stimulated the major English writers of the last decade of the 16th century such as ▷ Sidney, ▷ Spenser and ▷ Shakespeare.

Pleonasm
The use of unnecessary words in the expression of a meaning, *eg* in the phrase 'a deceitful fraud', 'deceitful' is pleonastic, since a fraud is by definition a kind of deceit.

Pliny
There were two Roman writers of this name. Pliny the elder (1st century AD) was the author of a famous *Natural History*, in which fantastic myths about animals are mixed up with some sound early science. His nephew, Pliny the younger, was the author of letters which are an interesting source of information on the ancient Roman world under the Emperor Trajan, especially about the treatment of Christians.

Plot (and Story)
▷ Russian Formalism.

Plotinus
▷ Platonism and Neo-Platonism.

Plumptre, Anne (1760–1818) and Annabella (1761–1838)
Translators and novelists. The two Plumptre sisters were well educated and were prolific authors, usually in tandem, for most of their lives. They probably began by sending poems to periodicals, but the first certain works by them are two ▷ Minerva novels. Anne wrote *Antoinette* (1796), the story of a beautiful and intelligent woman philosopher, while Annabella (commonly known as Bell) published *Montgomery, or Scenes in Wales* (1796). Shortly afterwards they began translating from German, Anne undertaking seven plays by Kotzebue and Bell, Iffland's play, *The Foresters* (1799) and Kotzebue's *The Guardian Angel* (1802). They then returned to novels, producing Bell's *The Western Mail* (1801) and Anne's *Something New* (1801). It was only in 1802, when Anne travelled to France to see the effects of the ▷ French Revolution with ▷ Amelia Opie that the two sisters parted ways, Anne to commence writing ▷ travel and ▷ autobiographical works (*Narrative*, 1810, and *History of Myself and My Friends*, 1813), and Bell to concentrate on children's stories and domestic material (*Stories for Children*, 1804, and *Domestic Management, or the Healthful Cookery Book*, 1804). They collaborated once again just before Anne's death in 1818 writing the strange and fascinating collection, *Tales of Wonder, of Humour, and of Sentiment*.

Pluralism
A pluralist conception of literary criticism claims that the meanings of works are not fixed but are open to revision by multiple interpretative approaches which are not themselves to be hierarchically ranked. The idea of critical pluralism also implies that critics are free to borrow from many sources and should not be fixed by the protocols of any one critical method.

Plutarch (AD 46–? 120)
Greek biographer and moralist. He is chiefly famous for his 46 *Parallel Lives* in which he matches 23 famous men from Greek history with 23 famous Romans. The *Lives* were presented in an English version by ▷ Sir Thomas North in 1579; North did not translate them from the original Greek but from the French version by Jacques Amyot. North's book was as popular and influential in England as Amyot's was in France; Plutarch's conception of the great and many sided man was in harmony with the 16th-century conception of the public virtues and personal accomplishments that should go to make the full man and the perfect courtier. The *Lives*, in North's version, were used as a source-book by dramatists - notably by Shakespeare in ▷ *Julius Caesar*, ▷ *Antony and Cleopatra* and ▷ *Coriolanus*. Plutarch also wrote a number of treatises on moral and physical subjects known as the *Moralia* – a precedent for the essays of ▷ Bacon as well as the very different ones of the great French essayist, ▷ Montaigne.
▷ Translation.

Poel, William (1852–1934)
Actor, director and Shakespeare scholar. He founded the Elizabethan Stage Society in 1894. Poel's influential productions of the plays of Shakespeare and his contemporaries rejected the traditional techniques of stage realism dominant at the end of the 19th century. Characteristic of his productions was an attempt to recreate Elizabethan stage conditions by performing on a bare apron stage. He also pursued a policy, not always successfully, of restoring full uncut texts for production. Though it is now accepted that he overstressed the notion of the 'bare' Elizabethan stage, he was, with Harley Granville Barker (1877–1946), a great influence on the development of Shakespeare productions in this century.
▷ Old Vic Theatre.
Bib: Speaight, R., *William Poel and the Elizabethan Revival*.

***Poems* (1844)**
A collection of poetry by ▷ Elizabeth Barrett Browning, published after six years of invalidism

during which Barrett (as she was then) focused her energies on poetic experiment. *Poems* (1844) is notable for its formal innovation (half-rhymes, metrical irregularity, compound words) and for the range of voices that surface in the collection. There is a mystical, opium-inspired voice in poems such as 'The House of Clouds' and 'A Vision of Poets'; a sentimental voice, found in the popular ▷ ballads and in poems such as 'To Flush, My Dog'. A concern with social class is evident in 'The Cry of the Children', a strategically sentimental protest poem about the working conditions of children. 'A Drama of Exile' reviews the Fall 'with a peculiar reference to Eve's alloted grief', while 'L.E.L.'s Last Question' and the pair of sonnets 'A Desire' and 'A Recognition' are poetic tributes to Letitia Landon (1802–38) and ▷ George Sand respectively. The collection established Barrett as a major Victorian poet.

***Poems by Currer, Ellis and Acton Bell* (1846)**
The first published work by the ▷ Brontë sisters, which included poems by Charlotte (Currer), Emily (Ellis) and Anne (Acton). Charlotte organized the publication after 'discovering' Emily's poetry, which she considered 'not at all like the poetry women generally write'. The collection sold only two copies, but received a few favourable notices.

▷ Pseudonyms.

Bib: Leighton, A., and Reynolds, M. (eds.), *An Anthology of Victorian Women Poets.*

Poet Laurate
The laurel, also known as the bay (*Laurus nobilis*), was sacred to Apollo, the god most associated with the arts. The Greeks honoured Olympic victors and triumphant generals, by crowning them with a wreath of laurel leaves. In the 15th century the universities of Oxford and Cambridge gave the title 'laureate', meaning worthy of laurels, to various poets including ▷ John Skelton, and it was later given to court poets like ▷ Ben Jonson. In 1668 the title gained its modern status when ▷ John Dryden was granted a stipend as a member of the royal household charged with writing court odes and celebrating state occasions in verse. Since the time of Dryden the laureateship has been awarded to a few poets of lasting worth and to many of mediocre talent, chosen for reasons of fashion or political acceptability. The list is as follows: ▷ Thomas Shadwell, ▷ Nahum Tate, ▷ Nicholas Rowe, Laurence Eusden, ▷ Colley Cibber, William Whitehead, ▷ Thomas Warton, Henry James Pye, ▷ Robert Southey, ▷ William Wordsworth, ▷ Alfred Tennyson, Alfred Austin, ▷ Robert Bridges, ▷ John Masefield, ▷ Cecil Day Lewis, ▷ John Betjeman and ▷ Ted Hughes. Poets who were offered the laureateship but declined it include ▷ Thomas Gray, ▷ Sir Walter Scott, ▷ Samuel Rogers, ▷ William Morris and ▷ Philip Larkin. Wordsworth was the first Poet Laureate to make his acceptance of the office conditional on his not being obliged to honour official occasions with specially composed poems, though some later laureates have continued the practice, notably Tennyson, Betjeman and Hughes.

Poetics
A treatise on poetry by the Greek philosopher ▷ Aristotle. He had already written a dialogue *On the Poets*, which has only survived in fragments, and a treatise on rhetoric; knowledge of both is to some extent assumed in the *Poetics*. The *Poetics* is considered to have been an unpublished work, resembling notes for lectures addressed to students rather than a full worked-up treatise for the general public, like the *Rhetoric*. This accounts for its fragmentary character. Thus Aristotle distinguishes Tragedy, Epic and Comedy as the chief kinds of poetry, but Comedy is practically omitted from fuller discussion. Lyric, though it is referred to, is not included among the chief kinds, either because Aristotle considered it to be part of music or because he considered it to be taken up into Tragedy. The main part of the work is therefore concerned with Tragedy and Epic – the former more extensively than the latter. Aristotle's method is essentially descriptive rather than prescriptive; that is to say, he is more concerned with what had been done by acknowledged masters such as ▷ Homer and ▷ Sophocles, than with what ought to be done according to so-called 'rules'.

Nonetheless, the *Poetics* became the most authoritatively influential of all critical works. Its dominance in European critical thought from the 16th to the 18th centuries was partly due to its influence on the most widely read of the Roman critics, ▷ Horace, and partly because it was rediscovered at the end of the 15th century when the ▷ Renaissance was at its height, and the spirit of the Greek and Latin writers was felt to be civilization itself. Critics such as the 16th-century Italian Scaliger took what are mere hints in Aristotle and erected them into important rules of art, such as the 'neo-Aristotelian' ▷ unities of time and place. In England, the important critics, such as ▷ Dryden and ▷ Johnson, regarded Aristotle and neo-Aristotelianism with strong respect rather than total reverence, but the complete submission of minor critics such as ▷ Thomas Rymer is exemplified by his obtuse treatment of Shakespeare's *Othello* in the essay *Short View of Tragedy* (1692). Neo-Aristotelianism was set aside by the Romantics, who cultivated literary virtues which are different from Aristotelian shapeliness and order, but the influence of the *Poetics* is still evident in Wordsworth's Preface to the ▷ *Lyrical Ballads*.

Today the *Poetics* remains one of the most outstanding works of European thought. Critics still use Aristotle's terminology in classifying poetic forms; his theory of art as imitation (different from ▷ Plato's) is still the starting-point of much aesthetic discussion; such terms as 'harmatia', for the element in human nature which makes it vulnerable to tragedy, 'peripeteia' for the reversal of fortunes common in tragic narrative, and 'katharsis' for the effect of tragedy on the mind of the audience, have been useful for a long time. It continues to be widely studied as one of the earliest works of critical theory.

Poetics
In Aristotle's ▷ *Poetics* the rules of 'tragedy' are abstracted from a collection of specific instances to form a theoretical model. The function of 'poetics', therefore, has always been to organize formally details of poetic structures, and to this extent it is both prescriptive and descriptive. This Aristotelian usage persists, though in considerably extended form, in the titles of works of critical theory, such as Jonathan Culler's *Structuralist Poetics* (1975). The theoretical works also address the issue of an organized system of analytical methods, as well as aesthetics of artistic construction. More recently, for example in the work of ▷ new historicist critics such as Stephen Greenblatt, the phrase 'cultural poetics' is used to designate an investigation into 'how the boundaries were marked between cultural practices understood to be art forms and other, contiguous, forms of expression' (*Shakespearean Negotiations*; 1988). Such investigations seek to explain how particular aspects of general cultural life are given artistic expression. Whereas Aristotle's *Poetics* can be said to have a ▷ formalist bent, one of the ways in which the term has come to be used today locates the formal aspects of literary texts within a social context.

Point of view
Term often used in the analysis of ▷ narrative to refer to the perspectives from which the events are seen and narrated. Since these two may be different (the ▷ focal character may differ from the ▷ narrator), the term 'point of view' has been abandoned in more recent ▷ narratology, and its elements separated out into aspects of ▷ mood and ▷ voice.

Poliakoff, Stephen (b 1952)
Dramatist. Although he began writing plays in 1969 Poliakoff first came to prominence with *Hitting Town* and *City Sugar* (both 1975) as a result of the understated precision with which he evoked the sham comforts of anonymous shopping malls, fast-food outlets and motorway service areas, while exploring readily identifiable, unlikeable and deeply alienated characters. He is particularly effective in capturing the curious absence of real passion in people smothering in webs of superficiality, and the sense of conscious distress behind even the most glibly desperate – exemplified by the radio DJ in *City Sugar*. The plays are notable for a strong sense of isolation and of communication replaced by half-hearted buzz-words and slogans. He conveys – rather surprisingly given his settings – an accurate sense of particular physical spaces, underlined by their actual emptiness: public spaces deserted at night; the enclosed but lonely world of the late-night radio phone-in; surveillance cameras and unseen observers render even his most aggressive characters exposed and vulnerable. Other plays include: *Strawberry Fields* (1977); *Stronger Than The Sun* (1977); *Shout Across The River* (1978); *American Days* (1979); *The Summer Party* (1980); *Breaking The Silence* (1984); *Coming In To Land* (1987); *Playing with Trains* (1989); and *Sienna Red* (1991).

Polidori, John (1796–1821)
Polidori emerged from a literary background in Soho's Italian community, his father Gaetano having translated the complete works of ▷ Milton and ▷ Walpole's ▷ *Castle of Otranto* into Italian. He studied medicine at the University of Edinburgh, graduating at the age of 19: his dissertation, on such topics as somnambulism and mesmerism, showed an interest in the ▷ Gothic as well as the medical, a combination that may have been peculiarly appropriate to his next spell of employment, as ▷ Lord Byron's physician. Their relationship was volatile and short-lived. Polidori was however a crucial member of the 'Pisan Circle' whose shared enthusiasm for horror and the fantastic was to produce, most famously, ▷ Mary Shelley's novel ▷ *Frankenstein* (1817). Scarcely known to modern readers, Polidori's short tale *The Vampyre* (1819) was hugely popular, and is the first text to fuse the hitherto disparate features of the vampire myth into a coherent literary whole. Bram Stoker's novel *Dracula* (1897) shows that the influence of Polidori's 'Lord Ruthven' was still powerful many decades later. Indeed, the presentation of Count Dracula in, for example, the Hammer films of the late 1950s and 1960s is closer to Polidori's version of the suavely aristocratic vampire than it is to the bewhiskered, Slavic ancient of Stoker's novel. It is possible to see the image of Lord Byron in Polidori's Lord Ruthven, and it was falsely assumed at the time of first publication that Byron was the author of *The Vampyre*. Its real author, troubled not only by debt but by brain damage sustained in a carriage accident, died (perhaps by his own hand) at the age of 25.

Political Register, The
A weekly journal started by ▷ William Cobbett in 1802, and continued until the year of his death, 1835. It was singularly bold and independent in opinion, and had a wide circulation especially

among the poor of rural England. In 1803, Cobbett was fined £500 for his criticism of the government's Irish policy, and in 1809 he was sent to prison for two years for his criticism of military punishments. He continued to edit the paper from prison. From 1821 it included serial publication of ▷ *Rural Rides*.

▷ Journalism.

Pollard, A. W. (1859–1944)
Influential bibliographer and ▷ Shakespearean scholar who is best known for his work on the *Short-Title Catalogue of Books Printed in England . . . 1475–1640* (1926), which was revised by Katharine Pantzer and others in 1927 (Vol. II) and 1985 (Vol. I).

Polo, Marco (?1254–?1324)
Italian traveller. At a time when Europe was in almost total ignorance of the majority of Asia, he travelled from Venice across central Asia as far as China where he remained for 17 years. On his return to Italy after an absence of 24 years, he wrote an account of his journeys. This became very popular, particularly in the 16th century, when contacts with eastern Asia were renewed. The book was first translated into English in 1579.

Polwhele, Elizabeth (?1651–1691)
English Restoration dramatist. Polwhele seems to have written three plays, *Elysium* (now lost), the rhymed tragedy *The Faythfull Virgins* (manuscript), and the comedy *The Frolicks*, performed at the Duke's Theatre in 1671 (▷ Dorset Garden Theatre). The play features a rake, Rightwit, who is the father of illegitimate children, and Claribell, a witty heroine. With ▷ Katherine Philips and ▷ Frances Boothby, she was one of the women writing for the stage in the early Restoration period.
Bib: Milhouse, J. and Hume R. D. (eds), *The Frolicks* (1977).

Polyphonic
▷ Bakhtin, Mikhail.

Polyphony
A term used by ▷ Mikhail Bakhtin which is broadly equivalent to ▷ dialogism. Literally, polyphony means 'many voiced' and Bakhtin regarded this as one of the most enriching features of the novel because it enables the dramatization of an open plurality of voices and perspectives.

▷ Heteroglossia; Univocal.
Bib: Bakhtin, M., *The Dialogical Imagination*; Dentith, S., *Bakhtinian Thought*.

Polysemy
Literally, polysemy means 'many meanings' and refers to the ability of texts (or words) to carry multiple meanings at the same time. For many modern commentators, polysemy is a defining characteristic of literary works as opposed to ▷ univocal works which offer only parsimonious or stereotyped meanings.

▷ Closure; Readerly and Writerly Texts.

Pomfret, John (1667–1702)
Rector of Maulden in Bedfordshire and author of *Poems on Several Occasions* (1699), a collection of ▷ Pindaric ▷ odes, narrative poems, ▷ pastorals, and epistles. His most important poem, *The Choice* (1700), treats the ▷ Horatian theme of rural retirement with a bland cosiness which exactly hit the popular taste of the time. 'Near some fair Town I'd have a private Seat,/ Built uniform, not little nor too great'. He eschews aristocratic splendour in favour of comfortable amenity: 'I'd have a Clear and Competent Estate,/ That I might live Genteelly, but not Great', and advocates benevolent charity towards 'the Sons of Poverty'. *The Choice* presents an ideal of the private life to which both the aristocrat and the successful new bourgeois could subscribe, and it was immensely popular. ▷ Samuel Johnson remarked in his ▷ *Lives of the Poets* (1781): 'Perhaps no composition in our language has been oftener perused.'

Pope, Alexander (1688–1744)
Poet. The son of a Catholic linen-draper in London, born significantly in the year of the ▷ 'Glorious Revolution' of 1688, which heralded the new era of optimism and national confidence reflected in much of his work. In childhood his father encouraged him to produce 'rhymes', insisting that they be perfect, and by his early teens he was already writing polished imitations of such diverse models as ▷ Chaucer, ▷ Edmund Spenser, ▷ Edmund Waller and ▷ Abraham Cowley. His *Pastorals* (1709) established his reputation, followed by the ▷ *Essay on Criticism* (1711), and ▷ *Windsor Forest* (1713). The last line of this poem is virtually identical with the first line of his *Pastorals*, indicating an ▷ Augustan parallel with ▷ Virgil, the last line of whose ▷ *Georgics* is the same as the first line of his *Eclogues*. The ▷ mock heroic ▷ *Rape of the Lock* appeared in 1712, and in an enlarged form in 1714. The characteristic miniaturizing effect of Pope's use of mock heroic can be related to the fact that he was only 4 ft 6 ins high, and suffered from curvature of the spine.

During the early years of his career he had associated with ▷ Joseph Addison, the magisterial arbiter of the new moderate bourgeois taste. But Pope's volatile temperament and Tory (▷ Whig and Tory) leanings drew him towards the more heady intellectual circle of ▷ Jonathan Swift, ▷ John Gay and ▷ John Arbuthnot, with whom in 1713 he formed the ▷ Scriblerus Club, whose object was to 'ridicule all false tastes in learning'. In 1717 Pope produced a collected volume of *Works*, in which appeared ▷ *Eloisa to Abelard* and *Elegy to the Memory of an Unfortunate Lady*, which shows a bold and unorthodox sympathy for a suicide.

Meanwhile he capitalized on his growing reputation by inviting subscriptions for a translation of ▷ Homer's ▷ *Iliad*, a new practice at the time. The work, published in instalments between 1715–20, served to make him financially secure. Several commentators remarked at the time on the failure of his brisk pentameter ▷ couplets to capture the rugged grandeur of Homer's unrhymed hexameters (▷ metre), but most were happy to have an 'English Homer', adapted to contemporary taste. He followed up his success by an advertisement 'undertaking' a translation of the ▷ *Odyssey*, which appeared in 1725–6. It leaked out, however, that much of the labour had been subcontracted to two minor poets, Elijah Fenton and William Broome, and for a time Pope was nicknamed 'the undertaker'. Unlike his original compositions, his Homer has not outlived its age. In 1725 he published an edition of the works of ▷ Shakespeare, based on textual comparisons between ▷ Quarto and Folio versions, and is thus one of the earliest editors to apply the scholarly techniques previously reserved for ancient ▷ classical literature to an English 'classic' (▷ Shakespeare editions.)

In ▷ *The Dunciad* (1728), itself a parody of a scholarly edition, Pope attacked his literary enemies, including the Shakespeare scholar Lewis Theobald, who had corrected errors in his edition. In 1733–4 he turned away from translation and editing and the squabbles in which these had involved him, and published his philosophical poem ▷ *An Essay on Man* and the four ▷ *Moral Essays* (1731–5). Between 1733 and 1737 he produced his ▷ *Imitations of Horace*, and in 1735 appeared the *Epistle to Dr Arbuthnot* which contains some of his most polished satire. In 1742 he produced the *New Dunciad*, a continuation of the earlier poem, and in 1743 this was added as Book Four to a new edition of *The Dunciad*, the hero being changed from Theobald to ▷ Colley Cibber, the ▷ Poet Laureate.

Pope's last years were spent in a rented riverside house at Twickenham, where he played out his own version of ▷ Horatian retirement. Imitating a landed gentleman, he indulged in a mock heroic, miniaturized version of landscape-gardening, designing a whimsically romantic 'grot' in a tunnel which linked the waterfront with his back garden. It was walled with shells and pieces of mirror, so as to reflect fragments of the river scene in the day, and after dark the light of a flickering lamp which was hung from the roof. Before his death he received the last sacrament, never having abandoned his Catholic religion, despite his ▷ Deist leanings and the double taxation which his ▷ recusancy incurred. He left his property to his lifelong friend Martha Blount.

All Pope's important poetry, with the exception of the Deist *Universal Prayer* (1738), is in heroic couplets, a form which he used with an idiosyncratic perfectionism, not attempted by any other poet of the period. He refined his own personal 'rules': on the exact positioning of the caesura, on the choice of diction and on perfection of rhymes (monosyllabic nouns or verbs containing long vowels are preferred). The reader's ear quickly adapts to this hyper-regularity and thus any variation in tone or rhythm, or any deliberate 'irregularity' has an explicit precision of effect virtually unknown in other poets. This characteristic is found cloying by some readers. But, particularly in his more flexible, later verse, it creates one of the most expressive and versatile literary media in the English language.

Bib: Johnson, S., in *Lives of the Poets*; Mack, M., *Alexander Pope: A Life*; Leavis, F. R., in *Revaluation*; Tillotson, G., *On the Poetry of Pope*; Rogers, P., *An Introduction to Pope*; Gooneratne, Y., *Alexander Pope*; Hill, H. E., and Smith, A. (eds.), *The Art of Alexander Pope*; Hammond, B., *Pope*; Bateson, F. W., and Jukovsky, N. A. (eds.), *Pope* (Penguin Critical Anthology); Hunt, J. D. (ed.), *The Rape of the Lock* (Macmillan Casebook).

Popish Plot

▷ Oates, Titus.

Pornography

This is generally understood to mean representations or literature which is intended to produce sexual excitement. There is, however, a considerable degree of dispute about pornography and it has become the subject of legal cases and public campaigns.

In the 17th and 18th centuries pornographic literature circulated widely. There is an overlap between true pornography, however, and a variety of so-called 'rogue literature', which depicted the pranks and schemes of low-life characters, such a beggars, thieves, prostitutes and pimps. The characters of the whore Lucetta and her pimp Sancho in ▷ Behn's ▷ *The Rover*, for example, are in this tradition. Some of the earliest pornography in England was imported from the Continent, and some was translated. A volume called *Ragionamenti*, by the Italian Petro Aretino (1492–1557), which included illustrations of sexual activity, circulated in England from the 16th century onwards under the title *Aretin's Postures*, or simply, *Postures*. For many years the name 'Aretin' was used as a byword for matters pornographic, both humorously and otherwise. Another Italian import was *La Puttana errante*, translated as *The Wandering Whore*. A common formula for pornographic literature is the purported account of a prostitute's life, or life in a brothel, including 'advice' given by one prostitute or bawd to another. Such a one is *La Retorica delle Puttane* ('The Whore's Rhetoric') by the dissident priest Ferrante Pallavicino, who was executed in 1644, two years after its publication. This work generated various translations and adaptations; a very good one was published in 1683.

▷ Pamphlets with titles such as *The Fifteen Plagues of a Maidenhead, The Fifteen Comforts of Whoring, The Fifteen Comforts of Matrimony*, etc., were published from the early 17th century onwards. These parody a religious original from the 15th century. Interestingly, much pornographic literature in England was associated in some way with religion, particularly the ▷ Catholic faith, and this added to its *frisson*, and also provided ammunition to anti-Catholic forces. Another popular production was *Venus dans le cloître* ('Venus in the Cloister: or the Nun in Her Smock'), (1724), which earned a prosecution for its publisher, Edmund Curll. Dialogues in Latin called *Satyra Sotadica*, by Nicolas Chorier, appeared in 1660 and were translated into several other languages including English.

▷ Pepys records in his diary for 13 January 1668 finding *L'Ecole des Filles* (published 1655) in a bookshop. On the 9th February he read it, 'in plain binding', because he was embarrassed to be seen with it. The book is mentioned again by Horner in Act I of Wycherley's ▷ *The Country Wife*, and in ▷ *The London Cuckolds* by ▷ Ravenscroft. But pornography also originated in Britain. A play, *Sodom*, often attributed to ▷ Rochester, circulated clandestinely in the 1680s. There are pornographic elements in a number of Rochester's poems, as well as in those of contemporaries including Wycherley and ▷ Behn.

In the 18th century pornography entered the novel. ▷ Cleland's *Fanny Hill* (1748 and 1749) was suppressed as pornography; this book was the subject of a trial after a revived edition was published in 1963. The works and activities of the Marquis de Sade attracted considerable attention, and scandal, in the later 18th and 19th centuries.

In the 20th century, the most notorious of the legal cases about pornography must be the trial concerning ▷ D. H. Lawrence's ▷ *Lady Chatterley's Lover* in 1960.

Generally speaking, today, on the right wing are those moralists who wish to police public standards and ban all sexual material, arguing that it depraves and corrupts. Some ▷ feminists also attack pornography at all levels, saying that it is male violence against women; they have particularly broad categories, including advertising; other feminists have sought to offer alternative erotic representations in literature, photography and art, which will be appealing to women. The liberal viewpoint, summed up by the Williams Committee of 1979, draws a distinction between public and private pornography, and if it is not hurting anyone will not interfere legally, though definitions of what is 'private' and what constitutes hurt remain contentious.

▷ Censorship.

Bib: Dworkin, A., *Pornography: Men Possessing Women*; Kappeller, S., *Pornography of Representation*; special *Screen* edition on Pornography (1982); Lawrence, D. H., 'Pornography and Obscenity' in *Phoenix*; Betterton, R. (ed.), *Looking On: Images of Feminity in the Visual Arts and Media.*

Porter, Endymion (1587–1649)

Poet and patron. No published writing survives, if it existed at all, but Endymion Porter was recognized as one of the influential figures in the cultural world of his day. He was known and respected by ▷ D'Avenant, ▷ Donne and ▷ Herrick, and would have been made a member of the proposed ▷ Royal Society. Some work has survived, a commemoration for D'Avenant, an epitaph for Donne, and several manuscript poems and letters to his wife. Although politically influential under the reign of ▷ Charles I (he was part of the ▷ Buckingham faction), during the ▷ Interregnum Porter and his Catholic wife were exiled and lived abroad in poverty.

Bib: Huxley, C., *Endymion Porter: the life of a courtier, 1587–1649.*

Porter, Peter (b 1929)

Poet. Born in Brisbane, Australia, Porter has lived in Britain since 1951. His work is most famous as an acutely satirical, witty analysis of the decadence of post-war society, and was included in A. Alvarez' 1960 ▷ anthology *The New Poetry*. His work includes: *Once Bitten, Twice Bitten* (1961); *Poems Ancient and Modern* (1964); *A Porter Folio* (1969); *The Last of England* (1970); *Living in a Calm Country* (1976) and *English Subtitles* (1981).

***Portrait of a Lady, The* (1881)**

A novel by ▷ Henry James. The heroine, Isabel Archer, is brought from the US to England by her aunt, Mrs Touchett, the wife of a retired American banker. Isabel has the candour and freedom conspicuous among American girls of the period; she also has beauty, intelligence, and a spirit of adventure and responsiveness to life. She refuses offers of marriage from both Lord Warburton, a 'prince' of the English aristocracy, and Caspar Goodwood, a 'prince' of American industry. In the meantime her cousin, Ralph Touchett, has fallen in love with her, but he is slowly dying of consumption and dare not become her suitor. Instead, he tries to play the 'fairy godmother' by persuading his father to leave her the money which would have been due to himself. His action has two unfortunate results: it awakens Isabel's New England Puritan conscience through the sense of responsibility which the possession of wealth entails, and it attracts the rapacious Madame Merle, whose guilty secret is that she is looking for a rich stepmother for her daughter by her former lover, Gilbert Osmond. Osmond (like Madame Merle herself) is an artistic but cold-blooded and totally self-centred expatriate American. Isabel in her humility is easily made to feel her own cultural inferiority to the exquisite exterior qualities of Osmond, whom she sees as the prince she has been looking for – a man deprived of noble potentialities by the unjust circumstance of his poverty. She marries him, only to discover his hollowness, and that her marriage is imprisonment in the ogre's castle.

The novel, sometimes regarded as James' masterpiece, shows his conception of the relationship of the US and European consciousnesses; the Americans have integrity, the will to live, and good will towards humanity, but they lack richness of tradition and are restricted by the limitations of the New England puritan inhibitions; the Europeans (especially some of the American expatriates) have rich cultural awareness but this commonly corrupts their integrity, and instead of good will they have immense rapacity. On the other hand the best kind of US expatriate (Ralph Touchett) combines the best of both worlds.

▷ Novel of manners.

Bib: Kirby, D. (ed.) *An Introduction to the Varieties of Criticism: The Portrait of A Lady.*

Portrait of the Artist as a Young Man, A (1916)

An autobiographical novel by ▷ James Joyce. The theme is the life of a middle-class Irish boy, ▷ Stephen Dedalus, from his infancy in the strongly Catholic, intensely nationalistic environment of Dublin in the 1880s to his departure from Ireland some 20 years later. In his boyhood he sees his elders bitterly divided in consequence of the Church's rejection of Parnell, the nationalist leader, owing to the scandal of his private life. As he grows up he is repelled by the pettiness, treacheries and vindictiveness of Irish nationalism, and for a time is drawn towards the rich spirituality of the Catholic tradition. The Irish Catholic Church, however, also suffered from provincialism and narrowness, and a moment of revelation on the seashore shows him that the largeness of an artistic vocation will alone suffice for him to harmonize the spiritual and fleshly sides of his nature, and enable him to rise above the vulgarity of his environment; but the choice brings with it the decision to leave Ireland.

The originality of the novel consists in its presentation of the hero's experience from within his own consciousness. The language gradually expands from the fragmentary diction of an infant on the first page through the connected but limited range of expression characteristic of a schoolboy to the sophistication of a fully articulate university student.

▷ Irish literature in English.

Positivism

▷ Comte, Auguste.

Postmodernism

The break away from 19th-century values is often classified as ▷ modernism and carries the connotations of transgression and rebellion. However, the last 30 years have seen a change in this attitude towards focusing upon a series of unresolvable philosophical and social debates, such as race, gender and class. Rather than challenging and destroying cultural definitions, as does modernism, postmodernism resists the very idea of boundaries. It regards distinctions as undesirable and even impossible, so that an almost ▷ Utopian world, free from all constraints, becomes possible. Postmodernism remains a controversial term, but may be linked to a transformation of European culture at the end of World War II. This war produced the death camps and the atomic bomb, and thus generated a new sense of man's propensity to evil, of the destructive potential of scientific knowledge, and of the perils of political totalitarianism. The end of Empire and the post-war changes in the world economy and power-structure involved new relationships between Britain and other cultures.

It must be realized, though, that post-modernism has many interpretations and that no single definition is adequate. Different disciplines have participated in the postmodernist movement in varying ways, for example, in architecture traditional limits have become indistinguishable, so that what is commonly on the outside of a building is placed within, and vice versa. In literature, writers adopt a self-conscious ▷ intertextuality sometimes verging on pastiche, which denies the formal propriety of authorship and genre. In commercial terms postmodernism may be seen as part of the growth of consumer capitalism into a multi-national and technological identity.

Its all-embracing nature thus makes postmodernism as relevant to street events as to the avant-garde, and as such is one of the major focal points in the emergence of interdisciplinary and cultural studies.

Bib: Jameson, F., *Post-modernism and Consumer Society*; Lyotard, J.-F., *The Post-modern Condition.*

Post-structuralism

At first glance, the term post-structuralism seems to imply that the post-structuralists came after the structuralists and that post-structuralism was the heir of structuralism. In practice, however, there is not a clear-cut division between structuralism and post-structuralism. Although the two have different focuses of interest and preoccupations, many of their concerns bind them together. Structuralism encompasses approaches to criticism which use linguistic models to enable critics to focus not on the inherent meaning of a work but on the structures which *produce* or generate meaning. Post-structuralism focuses on the ways in which the texts themselves subvert this enterprise; the structuralist emphasis on ▷ difference as constructing relatively stable systems of meaning is displaced in post-structuralism by ▷ Derrida's concept of *différance* a French term which puns on the words for 'difference' and 'deferral', thus suggesting the endless displacement of unstable meaning along a chain of signifiers. Leading post-structuralists include ▷ Derrida, ▷ Lacan, Gilles Deleuze, J. Hillis Miller and ▷ Paul de Man.

▷ Deconstruction; Feminism.

Bib: Culler, J., *On Deconstruction*; Norris, C., *Deconstruction: Theory and Practice*; Sturrock, J. (ed.), *Structuralism and Since*.

Potter, Beatrix (1866–1943)

Writer for children. One of the most famous and widely translated writers of children's stories, Potter's anthropomorphic tales of animal adventures have been famously praised by ▷ Graham Greene for their lack of sentimentality. Beginning with *The Tale of Peter Rabbit* (1901) (published and printed – as well as, of course, illustrated – by Potter herself), her simple stories have become classics of ▷ children's writing. Potter was also an accomplished naturalist, artist (illustrating all her own work), and (later) sheep farmer. Her numerous works hardly need listing; they include: *The Tale of Squirrel Nutkin* (1903); *The Tailor of Gloucester* (1903); *The Tale of Jemima Puddle-Duck* (1908); *The Tale of Mr Tod* (1912). See also *The Journals of Beatrix Potter* (1966) and *Dear Ivy, Dear June: Letters from Beatrix Potter* (1977).

Bib: Godden, R., *The Tale of the Tales*; Greene, G., 'Beatrix Potter' in *Collected Essays*; Linder. L., *The History of the Writings of Beatrix Potter*; Taylor, J., *Beatrix Potter: Artist, Storyteller, Countrywoman*.

Potter, John (?–1749)

Theatre proprietor, and craftsman. Potter entered the theatre in or after 1708, probably as a carpenter and/or scene painter. He erected a playhouse known as the French Theatre as well as the Little Theatre in the Hay, and eventually, the Haymarket Theatre (▷ Haymarket Theatres).

Poulter's Measure

A verse metre used by some 16th-century poets, it consisted of a 12-syllable line (▷ Alexandrine) alternating with a 14-syllable one. 'Poulter' = 'poulterer' – an allusion to variations in the number making up a dozen in the poultry trade. It was used by ▷ Thomas Wyatt, ▷ Henry Howard, Earl of Surrey and less distinguished poets.

When Dido feasted first the wand'ring
Trojan knight,
Whom Juno's wrath with storms did force
in Lybic sands to light,
That mighty Atlas did teach, the supper
lasted long
With crispéd locks, on golden harp, Jopas
sang in his song.
(*Wyatt, 'Jopas' Song'*)

Pound, Ezra (1885–1972)

American poet. He came to Europe in 1907, and made London his home during the period 1908–20. His influence on English poetry during this period, especially on that of his fellow American, ▷ T. S. Eliot, was very great. English poets had become insular, and they tended (with some exceptions) to occupy themselves with a marginal field of experience left over to them by the novelists, abstaining from the issues that were central to the destiny of their thoroughly industrialized society. They also restricted themselves to a limited diction, consecrated as 'poetic', with an obvious emotional appeal. The recent British poets who interested Pound were Robert Browning for his direct and 'unpoetic' address to the reader, and the Irish poet ▷ W. B. Yeats, for his austere seriousness and energy. In his campaign to reform diction he became the leader of the ▷ Imagist Movement, though he later abandoned it; this phase is illustrated by his *Ripostes* (1912) and *Lustra* (1916). It also drew him to Chinese poetry, from which he made excellent English verse, although his are not such accurate translations as those of his contemporary Arthur Waley.

In his campaign to free English poetry from insularity, Pound accepted the concept, which he shared with some other American writers (*eg* ▷ Henry James and ▷ T. S. Eliot), that European culture is a whole, not segmented into national cultures. Thus he offered fresh insights into ▷ French and ▷ Italian poetry back to the ▷ Middle Ages (see his critical essays, *Make It New*) and into the Latin classics. In his poetry he used the diction of everyday speech with a subtle ear for its rhythms. Like Eliot, he abandoned the logical continuity of prose in favour of a juxtaposition of ideas and images whose continuity appears through their psychological association. Also like Eliot, he used quotation frequently, thereby relating his treatment of his themes with the treatment accorded by past poets to similar themes, and thus illuminating the fundamental alterations in outlook and assumption brought about in the course of history. This technique of quotation is conspicuous in Eliot's poem ▷ *The Waste Land*, which Pound heavily revised. A comparable poem by Pound is *Hugh Selwyn Mauberley* (1920), which heralded his departure from Britain by offering an assessment of the state of culture there at the time. He moved to Paris, and in 1924 to Italy, where he became increasingly sympathetic to ▷ Fascism, partly in consequence of his strongly held and eccentric economic theories (see his *ABC of Economics*).

From this time onwards, his poetry output consisted almost entirely in working on his extended poem ▷ the *Cantos*, which was not finished at his death. The *Pisan Cantos* (1948) are the most famous section, recording his incarceration in Pisa by the American forces at the end of World War II, while waiting to stand trial for treason. Found unfit to plead at his trial in 1948, he was committed to St Elizabeth's Hospital, Washington D.C., from where he was released in 1958, spending the rest of his life in Italy. See also his *Literary Essays* (ed. T. S. Eliot), and *The Translations of Ezra Pound* (ed. H. Kenner).

Bib: Kenner, H., *The Poetry of Ezra Pound* and *The Pound Era*; David, D., *Ezra Pound: Poet as Sculptor*; Bush, R., *The Genesis of Ezra Pound's 'Cantos'*.

Powell, Anthony (b 1905)

Novelist. He writes sophisticated comedy of upper-class life in England since 1920; his approach may be compared with the different treatment of the same society by ▷ Aldous Huxley, ▷ Evelyn Waugh, and by ▷ D. H. Lawrence in *St Mawr*. Early novels are: *Afternoon Men* (1931); *Venusberg* (1932); *From A View to a Death* (1933); *Agents and Patients* (1936); *What's Become of Waring* (1939).

In 1948 he produced a study of John Aubrey, the 17th-century anecdotal biographer, author of *Brief Lives*. He then began his major work which, it has been suggested, owes something to Aubrey as it clearly does to the sequence *A la recherche du temps perdu* by the French novelist ▷ Marcel Proust. Powell's sequence of novels is called *A Dance to the Music of Time*. The narrator, whose personality is kept in detachment but not eliminated, is an upper-class young man with whose life various circles of friends intertwine in a kind of dance, and in a way that is only conceivable in the upper levels of any society. The characters make a pattern of contrasts, the most serious and interesting being that of the man of distinction – Stringham – who evokes the high style of an Elizabethan courtier such as Ralegh, but who is in the wordly sense a failure, and Widmerpool, the man of grotesque and crude manners and feeling, who is yet a worldly success owing to his insensibility and the force of his ambition. *A Dance to the Music of Time* consists of: *A Question of Upbringing* (1951); *A Buyer's Market* (1952); *The Acceptance World* (1955); *At Lady Molly's* (1957); *Casanova's Chinese Restaurant* (1960); *The Kindly Ones* (1962); *The Valley of Bones* (1964); *The Soldier's Art* (1966); *The Military Philosophers* (1968); *Books Do Furnish a Room* (1971); *Temporary Kings* (1973); *Hearing Secret Harmonies* (1975). The sequence begins in 1921 at the narrator's public school; it ends after the war with the death of Widmerpool in circumstances of sinister pathos. Powell has followed up his novel sequence with a sequence of memoirs entitled *To Keep the Ball Rolling: Infants of the Spring* (1978); *Messengers of Day* (1978); *Faces in My Time* (1980); *The Strangers All Are Gone* (1982). Other novels: *O, How the Wheel Becomes It!* (1983); *The Fisher King* (1986).

Bib: Bergonzi, B., *Anthony Powell*; Spurling, H., *Invitation to the Dance*; Tucker, J., *The Novels of Anthony Powell.*

Powys, John Cowper (1872–1963)

Novelist, poet and essayist. Principal novels are: *Wolf Solent* (1929); *A Glastonbury Romance* (1932); *Weymouth Sands* (1934); *Maiden Castle* (1936); *Owen Glendower* (1940); *Porius* (1951). Works of criticism and thought: *Visions and Revisions* (1915; revised 1935); *Psychoanalysis and Morality* (1923); *The Religion of a Sceptic* (1925); *The Meaning of Culture* (1929); *In Defence of Sensuality* (1930); *The Art of Happiness* (1935); *The Pleasures of Literature* (1938). One of his most famous books is his *Autobiography* (1934), developed from his contribution to the *Confessions of Two Brothers* (1916) written with Llewelyn Powys.

Like his brother, ▷ T. F. Powys, his fiction is influenced by his background in the English West Country, but his prose is contrasted with his brother's by its expansiveness and diffuseness. His writing combines a strongly physical sensationalism with a fascination for the intangible and mysterious reaches of human experience. He is concerned with the transformation of ordinary life by a contemplative intensity which generates a mythical sense of the individual's relation to his natural environment. His work shows the influence of ▷ Thomas Hardy, with whom he was acquainted, although Powys is more clearly identified with ▷ modernist forms than Hardy. Critics are divided as to whether Powys is an overrated or an underrated novelist.

Bib: Graves, R. P., *The Brothers Powys*; Cavaliero, G., *John Cowper Powys, Novelist*; Churchill, R. C., *The Powys Brothers*.

Powys, T. F. (Theodore Francis) (1875–1953)

Novelist and short-story writer; brother of ▷ John Cowper Powys. His novels and fables are set in the rural south-west of England; the characters are presented with a simplicity and poetry resembling the style of the Old Testament

of the ▷ Bible, but the individuality of the expression is too distinct for the resemblance to be obvious, and the tone is naïve on the surface but sophisticated in its pagan, often cynical implications. At its best, *eg* in *Mr Weston's Good Wine* (1927) and *Fables* (1929), Powys' art rose to exquisite tragic poetry; at its worst it descended to brutality and cruelty. His fiction is a very late and unusual example in English of a writer using purely rural traditions and environment; the tragic pessimism, less humane and more sophisticated than ▷ Thomas Hardy's, is perhaps a reflection of the disappearing vitality of that way of life. Some other works: *Mark Only* (1924); *Mr Tasker's Gods* (1925); *Kindness in a Corner* (1930). *Fables* was republished as *No Painted Plumage* in 1934.
Bib: Coombes, H., *T. F. Powys*; Hunter, W., *The Novels and Stories of T. F. Powys*.

Practical criticism
A term coined by I. A. Richards in the 1920s to describe a critical method which concentrated on the close reading of texts rather than, for example, attention to biographical, historical or other contextual modes of interpretation. Practical criticism has probably been the most influential Anglo-American critical method of the twentieth century and formed the basis for much critical practice and literary education in both Britain and the United States for half a century. The aims of practical criticism were to train students in close reading skills which fully respected nuances of meaning and avoided 'stock responses'. The methods of practical criticism and close reading were well suited to short lyric poetry, but were less successful on longer or dramatic texts. Practical criticism, however, came increasingly to be criticized for the dogmatic outlook of many of its supporters, the prescriptiveness of its methods and the narrowness of the concerns it addressed.
Bib: Richards, I. A., *Practical Criticism*.

Precious women, *Précieuses, préciosité*
Translation of the French term *Précieuses*, applied to a group of literary women in the 17th century. The *Précieuses* were closely associated with the salon movement in the decade 1650 to 1660 and placed ever greater emphasis on refinement, or *préciosité*, in matters of social etiquette, literature and language in a bid to raise the status of women. Among the most notable were ▷ Madeleine de Scudéry and the *bourgeoises* who frequented her *Samedis* or Saturday salons. The original sense of the term was positive, reaffirming that women were 'full of value', and designating such a woman as '*celle qui raffine sur le langage, qui sait quelque chose*', ('a woman who uses refined language and knows something'). The Precious Women accordingly placed great value on women's independence from men and questioned the institution of ▷ marriage. For their *romanesque*, or ▷ romantic, ideas and linguistic excesses, they were much ridiculed by the dramatist ▷ Molière and others. In his *Dictionnaire des Précieuses* ('Dictionary of the Precious Women', 1659), Somaize (b1639) distinguished three sorts of women in French society: those with 'no knowledge and no conversation' ('*aucune connaissance, aucune conversation*'); those who were just as ignorant but engaged readily in conversation ('*aussi ignorantes, mais parlent avec promptitude*'); and those who, using their exceptional beauty to distinguish themselves from the crowd, read all the novels and verse they could in a bid to learn how to speak well. In his dictionary, Antoine Furetière (1619–88) gives the following definition: 'The epithet *Précieuse* was formerly applied to exceptionally virtuous women, who were particularly knowledgeable about society and language. The word has been devalued by the excesses and affected manners of others, who have been called false *Précieuses* or ridiculous *Précieuses*, about whom a comedy has been written.' ('*Précieuses est aussi une épithète qu'on a donné ci-devant à des filles de grande vertu, qui savoient bien le monde et la langue: mais parce que d'autres ont affecté et outré leurs manières, cela a décrié le mot, et on les a appelées fausses précieuses, ou précieuses ridicules, dont on a fait une comédie.*')
Bib: Backer, D. and Liot, A., *Precious Women*.

***Prelude, or Growth of a Poet's Mind, The* (1805: 1850)**
A ▷ blank verse ▷ autobiographical poem by ▷ William Wordsworth. The first version, in 13 books, was written between 1799 and 1805, but remained unpublished. Wordsworth continued to revise the poem at intervals throughout his life, and a version in 14 books appeared in 1850, after his death. With the encouragement of ▷ Samuel Taylor Coleridge, Wordsworth originally hoped to achieve a great philosophical poem (provisionally entitled *The Recluse*) 'on man, on nature, and on human life', to which *The Prelude* was intended as an introduction. Only one further part of the project, the vastly inferior ▷ *Excursion*, was completed. In *The Prelude* Wordsworth takes stock of his experience and resources, and traces the events of his early life. Books I–II, which concern 'Childhood and School-Time' contain some of his best-known work, illustrating the interaction between his growing mind and nature, as he climbs up to a raven's nest, rows a boat out on to a lake at night, or skates under the stars. Later books concern his time at Cambridge, in London and in revolutionary France (▷ French Revolution). The heading of Book VIII sums up a constant theme: 'Love of Nature Leading to Love of Man'.

In a sense the work is a continuation of the ▷ epic tradition in a bourgeois form, the heroic adventures of the aristocratic warrior hero being replaced by the inner adventures of the individual poet. This helps to explain the epic grandeur of the poem's tone and scope, though this is not always sustained in practice. The revisions in the 1850 version, though they frequently improve the phrasing and pace of the 1805 text, impose upon it a Christian orthodoxy which muffles the immediacy of Wordsworth's original idiosyncratic ▷ pantheism.

Pre-Raphaelite Brotherhood
A movement of painters and poets which began just before 1850; it was more important in painting than in poetry, but one of its leading members, ▷ Dante Gabriel Rossetti, was equally famous in both arts. The essence of the movement was opposition to technical skill without inspiration. This made it anti-Victorian, inasmuch as industrial techniques (illustrated by the ▷ Great Exhibition of 1851) were producing vast quantities of work which were products of engineering. Technical skill without inspiration was deemed to be an aspect of the neo-classical art of the 18th century, against which the ▷ Romantics had already protested, and behind neo-classicism lay the 16th-century Renaissance of Greek and Roman art, and the paintings of the Italian artist Raphael (1483–1520), who had produced religious pictures of extraordinary perfection in technique but (in the opinion of the Pre-Raphaelites) with an almost cynical disregard of spiritual feeling. This tenderness of the spirit had existed in ▷ medieval art; hence the Brotherhood, by no means hostile to highly polished technique, cultivated the artistic spirit of the Middle Ages. The principal painters of the Brotherhood were Rossetti, John Millais and Holman Hunt; its poets were Rossetti and his sister ▷ Christina Rossetti, and, a little later, ▷ William Morris.

The movement drew for its poetical inspiration on the ardour of the Romantic poet John Keats (1795–1821), who had also cultivated the Middle Ages, and it greatly revered the contemporary poet ▷ Alfred Tennyson, whose art owed much to Keats. But Pre-Raphaelitism was not merely an aesthetic movement; a great influence upon it was the work of the art critic ▷ John Ruskin, who had a strong social conscience about the duty of art to society, and especially of the duty of redeeming the squalid life of the urban working classes. Less close to the movement, but still in harmony with it, was the poet critic ▷ Matthew Arnold, with his attack on the philistinism of the middle classes and the barbarism of the upper classes. Finally, the ground of Pre-Raphaelitism had been prepared by the ▷ Oxford Movement in the Church of England; this had rejected the interfering state, and by its cultivation of ritual in religious worship asserted that it had brought beauty back into religion.

However, Keats had not been dismayed by the world of his time so much as by the inevitability of desperate suffering as part of the human lot in every age. Arnold and Tennyson, in their poetry, were dismayed by the surface hideousness and the apparently irremediable injustices of their society. They had tended to write a 'poetry of withdrawal', creating an inner world of unassailable dreams (Tennyson) or a transcendent fortress of lofty feeling (Arnold). The Pre-Raphaelites followed this example. The poetry of D.G. Rossetti and of Morris is a 'literary' art, ie it depends on the proved poetic stimulus of a special 'poetic' language and imagery which was alien to the ordinary man of the age, and had no relationship to the economically productive genius of the age itself. (The intensely pious Christina Rossetti had a more authentic, religious inspiration, but even in her work the feeling is subjectively personal as compared to the work of a 17th-century religious poet such as George Herbert, 1593–1633, whom in some respects she resembled.) Thus, whatever the social consciences of Rossetti and Morris, they tended to take poetry to be an autonomous activity, largely independent of the political and social issues of the time. The poet ▷ Algernon Swinburne had the courage to take this autonomy seriously; with him, 'art for art's sake' was born, and the aesthetic movement (▷ Aestheticism). The only poetry which was moving strongly in another direction was that of ▷ Gerard Manley Hopkins from 1865 to 1889, and he was regarded as unpublishable. Another poet, W.B. Yeats (1865–1939), owed much to the Pre-Raphaelites and especially to Morris, but the bitter realities of Irish politics made him, in the next century, one of the leaders of the reaction against the whole direction of art as the worship of Beauty. This reaction has lasted to the present day. The Pre-Raphaelites had their own periodical ▷ *The Germ*; it first appeared in January 1850, and ran for only four numbers.

Bib: Stanford, D. (ed.), *Pre-Raphaelite Writing*; Pearce, L., *Woman, Image, Text: Readings in Pre-Raphaelite Art and Literature*.

Presbyterianism
A ▷ Protestant doctrine of church organization devised by John Calvin (1509–1604) and other Reformers during the 16th-century Protestant Reformation. The word 'Presbyter' comes from a Greek word meaning 'elder', and Presbyterianism is a system of church government by councils of elders. It became dominant in Scotland under the leadership of John Knox (1505–72) and had wide support in England between about 1570 and 1648 when Oliver Cromwell (1599–1658) alienated the Presbyterian puritans and terminated the Presbyterian establishment because of their support for King Charles I. Briefly re-established after Cromwell's death it seceded extensively to ▷ Unitarianism during the 18th century. It was revived by Scottish

settlers in England who began organizing their own congregations. In 1847 some Scottish and English Presbyterian congregations merged to form the United Presbyterian Church. The Presbyterian Church of England was formed in 1876 from a further amalgamation of the United Presbyterian Church and other such congregations. ▷ Thomas Carlyle was raised in Scotland as strict Presbyterian within the Burgher sect (which attempted to cling to a belief in an extreme Protestant theocracy throughout Cromwell's governance). His parents intended him to become a minister in the Burgher church, but he renounced his calling in 1817. By 1820 the sect had ceased to exist as an independent body.

Presence
▷ Absence.

Press Council, The
A body established by the British Government to maintain good and responsible standards of ▷ journalism. When newspapers seem to abuse their powers by interfering with private life and liberty, complaints may be made to the Council which can then, if it thinks the abuse is genuine, administer a public rebuke to the newspaper concerned. It has no powers of censorship.

Preston, Thomas (1537–98)
Author of the early Elizabethan ▷ tragicomedy *Cambyses, King of Persia* (1569). He may also have written the popular and influential romance *Sir Clyomon and Sir Clamydes.*

Pretender
▷ Old Pretender, The; Jacobite.

Pride and Prejudice **(1813)**
A novel by ▷ Jane Austen. Mr and Mrs Bennet belong to the minor gentry and live at Longbourne near London. Mr Bennet is witty and intelligent, and bored with his foolish wife. They have five daughters, whose marriage prospects are Mrs Bennet's chief interest in life, since the estate is 'entailed' – *ie* by the law of the period it will go on Mr Bennet's death to his nearest male relation, a sycophantic clergyman called Mr Collins. The main part of the story is concerned with the relationship between the witty and attractive Elizabeth Bennet and the haughty and fastidious Fitzwilliam Darcy, who at first considers her beneath his notice and later, on coming to the point of asking her to marry him, finds that she is resolutely prejudiced against him. His friend Charles Bingley is in love with the eldest daughter, Jane, but they are kept apart by the jealous snobbishness of his sisters and (at first) the fastidious disapproval of Darcy. Meanwhile, Elizabeth is subjected to an insolent offer of marriage by Mr Collins and the arrogant condescension of his patroness, Lady Catherine de Bourgh, Darcy's aunt. Those who regard the Bennet family as foolish and vulgar have their opinion justified when Lydia Bennet elopes with an irresponsible young officer, George Wickham. By this time, however, Darcy and Elizabeth have been chastened by finding in one another a fastidiousness and pride that equal their own and, despite the family scandal, they are united.

The novel has always been one of the most liked of Jane Austen's, and it contains excellent social comedy, but in some respects it stands apart. She herself said of it 'The work is rather too light, and bright, and sparkling; it wants to be stretched out here and there with a long chapter of sense.' Elizabeth Bennet was, however, her own favourite heroine.

Priestley, J. B. (John Boynton) (1894–1984)
Dramatist and novelist. Priestley wrote forty-seven plays, an opera libretto, films, television and radio plays and twenty-eight novels – quite apart from a much greater number of books of travel, political comment, literary biography, etc. Most of his plays are carefully plotted and mainly conventional in form, even allowing for the split, serial and circular theories of time which shape the three 'time plays': *Dangerous Corner* (1932), *Time and the Conways* (1937) and *I Have Been Here Before* (1937). More unconventional in breaking out of the domestic box set are: *Johnson Over Jordan* (1939), which follows its protagonist through the fourth dimension of immediate after-death; *Music at Night* (1938), which explores the thoughts and lives of the audience at a concert; *They Came to a City* (1942), which pictures a socialist utopia; and *Desert Highway* (1943), written for army actors, which shows a tank crew marooned in the desert with a flash-back to their prototypes in ancient times. Priestley was much more adventurous than most dramatists being performed on Shaftesbury Avenue at the time, but he quite consciously sought to work within the limits acceptable to contemporary society and behaviour and a presentation of ideas beyond the humour and narration of their surface. Their optimism now dates his more overtly political pieces, but *Time and the Conways*, the comedy *When We are Married* (1938) and *An Inspector Calls* (1945) are frequently revived.
Bib: Evans, G. L., *Priestley the Dramatist*; Klein, H., *J. B. Priestley's Plays.*

Priestley, Joseph (1733–1804)
A nonconformist minister, scientist and teacher. He was partly educated at a nonconformist academy at Daventry; such academies existed in the 18th century to give a university education

to non-conformists, who for their religious views were not admitted to the recognized universities of Oxford and Cambridge. They were commonly more advanced scientifically than the real universities; Priestley eventually became the first chemist to isolate oxygen. In 1768 he published his *Essay on the First Principles of Government*, advocating 'the happiness of the majority' as the criterion by which government must be judged. This line of thought was developed by ▷ Jeremy Bentham and his 19th-century followers, the ▷ Utilitarians. Priestley's house in Birmingham was destroyed by the mob in 1791 owing to his well-known sympathy with the ▷ French Revolution, and in 1794 he emigrated to the United States.

Primitive, primitivism
From a literary viewpoint, the concept of primitivism revolves around the figure of the 'noble savage'. Descended from the classical notion of a ▷ Golden Age, the concept gains most popularity and intellectual resonance in the 18th century, anticipated by the figure of Man Friday in ▷ Defoe's ▷ *Robinson Crusoe* (1719) and ▷ Aphra Behn's novel ▷ *Oroonoko, or the History of the Royal Slave* (1688), successfully adapted for the stage by ▷ Thomas Southerne in 1695. Based partly on the author's experiences of Surinam, Behn's novel is one of the earliest examples of primitivism in imaginative literature, describing primitive people in 'the first state of innocence, before men knew how to sin': the whole primitivist tradition may be read as a varied series of laments for, and objections against, the myth of *Genesis* and the Fall of mankind. Primitivism expresses an optimistic belief in the essential goodness of human beings, corrupted and deformed by so-called civilization. The chief conduit for debate in this area was the philosopher ▷ Rousseau. His writings of the 1750s contrast the harmonious existence of primitive man in a 'state of nature' with the indolence, profligacy and selfish obsession with private property experienced by Europeans. *Emile* (1762) attempted to establish the principles of a new educational system, through which a child could develop rational independence of mind, while preserving a natural innocence, while the *Social Contract* of the same year argued for equality before the law, a more fair distribution of wealth, and a democratic subscription to the common good. While the resonance of these ideas for ▷ the French Revolution is self-evident, their influence on ▷ Romantic literature runs deep, persisting well beyond a point when the Revolution itself had been compromised by slaughter.

▷ Inkle and Yarico; Omai.

Bib: Tinker, C. B., *Nature's Simple Plan*, Fairchild, H. N., *The Noble Savage*, Whitney, L., *Primitivism and the Idea of Progress*, Roszak, T., *Towards a Counter-Culture*.

Primose, Diana (c 1630)
Poet. The only reference extant to this writer is on the title-page of her book *A Chaine of Pearls* (1630), ostensibly a panegyric to ▷ Elizabeth I. The queen, however, had been dead for 27 years and the poem is more likely an attack on ▷ Charles I, whose shortcomings are shown up by contrast with Elizabeth's virtues. Her narrative source is ▷ William Camden's *Annals of Queen Elizabeth* (1615; published in English in 1625), while the list of virtues are commonplace, such as chastity, temperance, justice and fortitude.

Bib: Greet, G. (ed.), *Kissing the Rod.*

Primrose League
A Conservative political society founded in memory of ▷ Benjamin Disraeli, Lord Beaconsfield, whose favourite flower was said to be the primrose. The society was founded in 1883 and achieved large membership; it was one of the earliest successful attempts at permanent organization of public opinion in support of a political party.

Prince, Mary (c 1788–c 1833)
Autobiographer. Mary Prince was a slave who, on being abandoned in London in 1831, was befriended by Susannah Moodie (one of the first Canadian women writers) who acted as her amanuensis, and by Thomas Pringe who campaigned for her emancipation. Her story was published in that year as part of the campaign, and makes for dispiriting, although compelling, reading. Prince was born in Bermuda in the household of a kindly family, but she was sold separately from her family when she was 11 and her new owners were savagely cruel to her. Over the next 18 years Prince was flogged, put to work at salt production (particularly harsh), and probably sexually abused. But by 1826 she was in Antigua, had converted to Methodism, had learned to read and had married Daniel Jones, a free man. Her owners appeared to have attempted to break this new sense of independence by taking her to London, but when that failed they simply threw her out on to the streets. Prince's narrative is part of a tradition of slave narratives which began at the beginning of the 18th century and were an important contribution to the political movement against slavery.

▷ Abolition literature; Autobiography.

***Princess, The* (1850)**
Poem by ▷ Alfred Tennyson, originally titled *The Princess, A Medley* (1847), enlarged and revised in 1850. Despite bad reviews, *The Princess* was immensely popular and sold well

on publication. Like ▷ Elizabeth Barrett Browning's ▷ *Aurora Leigh*, it was a key text in the so-called ▷ 'woman question' debate, displaced on to a pseudo-medieval scene. The tale of Princess Ida, champion of women's rights who rejects ▷ marriage and sets up a women-only university, is collectively told by a group of friends entertaining themselves. Ida was betrothed in infancy to the Prince, who narrates the tale of how he defies 'the inscription on the gate, LET NO MAN ENTER IN ON PAIN OF DEATH'. He and two friends dress as women and infiltrate the university. The men's identities are discovered by the women, and the university is attacked by the prince's father, who demands that they be released unharmed. In the ensuing battle between Ida's father and the Prince's, the three young men fall. Ida calls for the women to nurse them, and the women's university is turned into a hospital. When the Prince recovers he proposes a progressive marriage of equality to Ida, to which she yields:

My bride
My wife, my life. O we will walk this world,
Locked in all exercise of nobel end . . .

▷ Education of women; Feminism; Medievalism.
Bib: Killham, J., *Tennyson and 'The Princess'*.

***Prince's Progress, and Other Poems, The* (1866)**
The second published collection of poetry by ▷ Christina Rossetti, including the quest narrative 'The Prince's Progress', 'The Iniquity of the Fathers Upon the Children' (a narrative poem spoken from the perspective of an illegitimate child) and 'L.E.L.', a lyric dedicated to the poet Letitita Landon (1802–38). The simple diction and controlled poetic form which characterizes the collection reflects Rossetti's developing aesthetic of personal and artistic renunciation.

Prior, Matthew (1664–1721)
Poet and diplomat. The son of a joiner, Prior was educated under the patronage of the ▷ Earl of Dorset. While an undergraduate at ▷ Cambridge he collaborated with the Earl of Halifax on a parody of ▷ John Dryden, *The Hind and the Panther transvers'd to the Story of the Country Mouse and the City Mouse* (1687), and in 1700 he celebrated the arrival of ▷ William III from Holland in *Carmen Saeculare*. After a period as secretary to the ambassador at the Hague he allied himself to the Tory camp of ▷ Harley and ▷ Bolingbroke and was involved in secret negotiations with the French government over the Treaty of Utrecht (1713) (▷ Spanish succession, War of, which was nicknamed 'Matt's Peace' after him. When ▷ Queen Anne died in 1714 and the Tories fell from power he was impeached and imprisoned for two years. His *Poems*, published by his friends in 1718, helped to restore his fortunes. His best work is marked by an easy-going humour. *Alma: or the Progress of the Mind*, (1718), a long poem in loose Hudibrastics (▷ Hudibras), mocks the systematic philosophy of ▷ Aristotle and ▷ Descartes and elaborates the proposition, borrowed from ▷ Montaigne's essay 'On Drunkenness', that the mind begins in youth in the toes, and rises by degrees until it reaches the head in old age. It is in his shorter, occasional poems that Prior achieves his most satisfying poetic effects. 'Jinny the Just' (published in 1907), an elegy for his housekeeper and mistress, employs an unheroic ▷ metre of anapaestic triplets to characterize its uneducated subject, and to create a moving personal tribute:

Tread Soft on her grave, and do right to
her honour
Lett neither rude hand nor Ill tongue light upon her
Do all the Small favours that now can be don her.

Other poems of importance are *Solomon on the Vanity of the World* (1718), in heroic ▷ couplets; *Henry and Emma* (1707), a travesty of the old ▷ ballad *The Nut-Brown Maid*; and *Down-Hall, a Ballad* (1723). Prior was a brilliant exponent of the epigram, a memorable example being 'A True Maid':

No, no; for my Virginity,
When I lose that, says Rose, *I'll dye:*
Behind the Elmes, last Night, cry'd Dick,
Rose, *were you not extreamly Sick?*

Bib: Johnson, S., *Lives of the Poets*.

Prioress's Tale, The
One of ▷ Chaucer's ▷ *Canterbury Tales*, which derives from the popular tradition of devotional narratives celebrating the miraculous interventions of the Virgin Mary. It is an anti-Semitic story, set in Asia, which recounts how a young Christian boy is murdered by Jews as he walks through their quarter singing a Christian hymn. His body is discovered because he continues to sing the hymn, miraculously, even after his death. The narrative, written in ▷ rhyme royal, is narrated in an emotive and pathetic style.

***Prisoner of Chillon, The* (1816)**
A poem by ▷ Lord Byron in tetrameter ▷ couplets (▷ metre) interspersed with quatrains. It is based on the story of François de Bonnivard (1496–1570), prior of the monastery of St Victor, near Geneva, who participated in a revolt against the Duke of Savoy and attempted to set up a republic in Geneva. He was imprisoned from 1530 to 1536 in the castle

of Chillon. Byron's work is prefaced by a facile sonnet extolling Liberty as the 'Eternal Spirit of the chainless Mind!' The poem itself, however, contradicts this optimism, describing the slow pining away of the narrator's two brothers, and the disintegration of his own mind under the strain of solitude: 'It was at length the same to me,/ Fetter'd or fetterless to be,/ I learn'd to love despair.' The historical Bonnivard was given a pension after his release, and was married four times.

Pritchard, Hannah (1709–68)
Actress, singer. She joined ▷ Theophilus Cibber and other performers who seceded from the company at ▷ Drury Lane, and opened at the ▷ Haymarket Theatre in 1733, only to return to Drury Lane in the following year. By now she was frequently cast in major roles, including Phaedra in ▷ Dryden's *Amphitryon* (1690), Isabella in ▷ Sir Richard Steele's ▷ *The Conscious Lovers*, and Dol Common in Jonson's ▷ *The Alchemist*.

In 1740 Pritchard played Desdemona to ▷ James Quin's ▷ Othello, but her performance as Rosalind in ▷ *As You Like It* from the end of that year is said finally to have established her as one of the leading actresses of her generation. She appeared as Nerissa in the production of ▷ *The Merchant of Venice* in which ▷ Charles Macklin revolutionized the portrayal of Shylock, and later acted in several plays with ▷ Garrick.

In 1749 her popularity forced a change in the ending of ▷ Samuel Johnson's *Mahomet and Irene*, to the author's chagrin: she was to have been strangled on stage, but the audience would not have it, and the action was modified so that she was 'killed' away from their view instead. She was noted for the intelligence of her interpretations, her versatility, and her dedication to her profession.
Bib: Vaughan, A., *Born to Please: Hannah Pritchard, Actress.*

Pritchett, Sir V. S. (Victor Sawdon) (b 1900)
Novelist, short-story writer, critic and travel writer. He left school at 15 to work in the leather trade, and also worked in the photographic trade in Paris before becoming a journalist. Since 1926 he has been a regular critic for the ▷ *New Statesman*, and since 1946 a director. He is best known for his short stories, which are economical and understated, employing colloquial dialogue. His work is primarily in a ▷ realist mode, and consists of ironic observation of society and human eccentricity. Story collections are: *Collected Stories* (1982); *More Collected Stories* (1983). His novels are: *Clare Drummer* (1929); *Shirley Sanz* (1932); *Nothing Like Leather* (1935); *Dead Man Leading* (1937); *Mr Beluncle* (1951). Criticism includes: *The Living Novel* (1946); *Balzac: A Biography* (1973); *The Myth Makers: Essays on European, Russian and South American Novelists* (1979).
Bib: Baldwin, D. R., *V. S. Pritchett.*

Privy Council
With a history going back to the king's council which in the 13th century gave the sovereign private ('privy') advice on the government of the country, this is now a body with largely formal work, mainly carried out by committees since the membership – now conferred as a special honour – is large. The former powers of the Privy Council are now exercised by the Cabinet.

▷ Orders in Council.

Problem plays (of Shakespeare)
A term first used in the late 19th century by critics of ▷ Shakespeare to designate a group of his plays written between 1600 and 1604. These are: ▷ *Troilus and Cressida*, ▷ *All's Well that End's Well* and ▷ *Measure for Measure*. What makes these all 'problem plays' in the view of some critics is that it is difficult to discern the individual play's overall thematic direction. *Troilus and Cressida* is regarded as a problem because, while the Trojans are shown to be intrinsically nobler than the Greeks, they are also shown to be wrong, although the Greeks are not conclusively shown to be right in their outlook. Thus no positive value is preached by the play, nor does it seem to be light-hearted enough to be simply a comedy. *All's Well*, the slightest of the three, is a problem because the noble heroine uses means that nowadays we would despise to gain her lover, who does not, in any case, seem to be worth her trouble. The play is thus a 'romantic comedy', but one in which the romance has gone sour. *Measure for Measure* is a comedy which, in the opinion of some critics, is both too serious and too cynical in some of its characteristics to be successful either as a comedy or as a serious critique of society. Not every critic agrees that all these plays, or any of them, are really 'problematic'.
Bib: Tillyard, E. M. W., *Shakespeare's Problem Plays.*

Procter, Adelaide Anne (1825–64)
Poet and ▷ feminist, also wrote under the ▷ pseudonym Mary Berwick. She was born in London, the daughter of the poet Barry Cornwall. In 1853 she began to contribute poetry to ▷ *Household Words* and found an admirer in ▷ Charles Dickens, who wrote a foreword to her *Complete Works* (1905). A collected two-volume edition, *Legends and Lyrics* (1858 and 1861) includes her most popular verse, much of which is sentimental. Procter was a dedicated feminist and helped to found the Society for Promoting the Employment of Women. The proceeds from *Chaplet of Verses* (1862) went to a homeless women's refuge. Procter also

edited an anthology of miscellaneous verse, *Victoria Regia*, which was published by Emily Faithful's Victoria Press in 1861.

▷ Women's Movement; Feminist publishing.

Bib: Leighton, A., and Reynolds, M. (eds.), *An Anthology of Victorian Women Poets*.

Proctor, Bryan Waller (1787–1874)
Poet, dramatist and biographer. Proctor, a lawyer, wrote under the pseudonym of 'Barry Cornwall'. His work, including *Dramatic Scenes* (1819) and *Marcian Collona* (1820), was very popular with the public, but generally dismissed by other poets, such as ▷ Keats and ▷ Shelley. He was, however, on friendly terms with ▷ Lamb, who had admired *Dramatic Scenes*, and Proctor undertook his biography, *Charles Lamb: A Memoir* (1866).

***Professor, The* (1857)**
A novel by ▷ Charlotte Brontë, written in 1846 but not published until after the author's death. In many ways it is an early version of ▷ *Villette*, although it is not as sophisticated. The central character, William Crimsworth, is an ▷ orphan who leaves England to seek his fortune in Brussels. He falls in love with Frances Henri, an Anglo-Swiss pupil-teacher, and eventually marries her. Their relationship is analogous to that of Lucy Snowe and Paul Emmanuel in *Villette*, although it is not drawn with as much complexity.

Prolepsis
The technique used when a narrative forecasts or anticipates its conclusion in events described at the beginning. This might be done explicitly, or implicitly by symbol or suggestion. It is the opposite of 'flashback'.

Prologue to The Canterbury Tales
▷ *Canterbury Tales, The*.

Prometheus
In Greek myth, one of the Titans. In the war between the gods and the Titans, he remained neutral, and was still on terms with Zeus when the gods were victorious. He was, however, very cunning and skilful.

According to legend Zeus was angry at a deception practised on him by Prometheus and deprived mankind of fire. Prometheus, however, stole fire from the gods, and gave it to man. Zeus then tried to punish man by sending the first woman (Pandora) with her jar of misfortunes; Hope, however, was left to man when the misfortunes were released to plague humanity. Zeus now tried to drown the human race in a great flood, but again Prometheus came to the rescue. To punish Prometheus for repeatedly outwitting him, Zeus had him bound to Mount Caucasus, and sent an eagle which gnawed incessantly at his liver. Prometheus, however, refused to ask pardon, and withheld a secret affecting Zeus' destiny. Eventually, Zeus allowed Heracles to free the Titan, who told the secret, and enabled Zeus to save himself. Prometheus was mortal, and on his death descended to the underworld. However, at the prayer of the centaur, Cheiron, he was eventually released, and permitted by Zeus to join the company of the gods. ▷ Shelley's lyrical drama ▷ *Prometheus Unbound* completes the Promethean trilogy by the Greek poet ▷ Aeschylus, and places the figure of Prometheus in a contemporary political context.

***Prometheus Unbound* (1820)**
A 'lyrical drama in four acts' by ▷ Percy Bysshe Shelley, written to correspond to the final lost play of the Promethean trilogy by the Greek poet, ▷ Aeschylus. The demigod Prometheus, having stolen the secret of fire from the gods and given it to man, is punished by being chained to a rock and subjected to everlasting torture. Nevertheless, comforted by his mother, the Earth, and consoled by thoughts of his bride, Asia, the Spirit of Nature, he remains defiant against Jupiter, king of the gods. At the appointed hour Demogorgon, the primal life-force, defeats Jupiter, frees Prometheus, and an era of love dawns, in which all cruelty and oppression are banished: 'the man remains/ Sceptreless, free, uncircumscribed, but man/ Equal, unclassed, tribeless, and nationless,/ Exempt from awe, worship, degree, the king/ Over himself'. The original Greek myth in which Zeus (Jupiter) and Prometheus are reconciled, is thus transformed into a political allegory of modern revolution. The style is elaborately abstract, and the play is to be read rather than acted. In his Preface the poet refers to his desire 'to familiarize the highly refined imagination of the more select classes of poetical readers with beautiful idealisms of moral excellence'. Despite its cloyingly consistent elevation of tone, it is a strangely powerful work.

Protestant succession
The belief that the throne should not pass to a Roman Catholic. The arguments about the royal succession became bitter when ▷ Charles II was succeeded by his brother ▷ James II. James' Catholicism was only one reason for the ▷ Glorious Revolution of 1688 but the fear of a return of James or of later succession by other Catholics caused further controversy and led to the ▷ Act of Settlement of 1701 and later ▷ Acts which made it impossible for a Catholic to succeed to the throne.

▷ Protestantism.

Protestantism
A term used for all varieties of Christian belief which broke away from Roman Catholicism

during the ▷ Reformation in the 16th century, or for religious communities not in agreement with Roman Catholicism but originating since the Reformation. It was first used in regard to those who protested against the Emperor Charles V's condemnation of the reformers in Germany at the Diet of Spires, 1529. Protestants in Britain include ▷ Anglicans, ▷ Presbyterians, ▷ Methodists and ▷ Baptists.

***Prothalamion* (1596)**
A wedding song, written by ▷ Edmund Spenser and published in 1596. *Prothalamion* is roughly half the length of Spenser's other wedding song – ▷ *Epithalamion*. The ode celebrates the double wedding of two sisters – Lady Elizabeth and Lady Katherine Somerset in August 1596.

Proust, Marcel (1871–1922)
French writer. Early in his career, he was the author of critical works, *Les Plaisirs et les jours* (1896; translations from Ruskin), *Pastiches et mélanges* (1919) and two posthumously published works *Contre Sainte-Beuve* (1981), and the incomplete novel *Jean Santeuil* (1952). Proust is nonetheless known for one book, his major work, *A la recherche du temps perdu*. It runs to 3,000 printed pages and was originally published in eight parts between 1913 and 1927. The novel was first translated by C. K. Scott-Moncrieff under the title *Remembrance of Things Past*, but a recent and much improved version has been completed by Terence Kilmartin.

A la recherche is the story of an artistic vocation, the attempt to write a novel which is similar to (though not the same as) that which the reader has before him. The novel itself is full of artist-figures, and the narrator's own endeavours to perceive pattern in disorder and fragmentation centre crucially on a discovery, a discovery about time and memory. The attempt to resurrect and recapture time past through voluntary memory cannot but fail, for voluntary memory is sifted for its relevancies. The past can consequently only be reached by involuntary memory, itself triggered by the most apparently innocuous and circumstantial of objects: a madeleine dipped in tea, a starched napkin, an uneven paving-stone. These objects are associated with forgotten events in the past, and those instants when the bond between past and present is recovered and the past reborn are 'privileged moments' (*moments privilégiés*). The novel jettisons a unilinear plot, while the central focus for narration is restricted to that of Marcel (not to be confused with Proust himself); impressions and sensations are fed through his consciousness which evolves over time and constitutes a devolved, perceptually-limited human subject. Proust's portrayal of social and above all sexual relations, moreover, intensify the sense of a self unable to know others, until the narrator realizes that only art gives access to others, since only in art is there the 'real residue' of the personality.

Proust's novel aroused two kinds of reactions. His minuteness in rendering human consciousness, for example, recalls both ▷ Henry James and ▷ James Joyce. His perception that the insignificance of an incident at the time of experiencing it contrasts with the importance it may come to have in the memory anticipates ▷ Virginia Woolf. The design by which relationships amplify through a lifetime into a pattern evocative of musical composition was emulated by ▷ Anthony Powell in *A Dance to the Music of Time*. On the other hand other 20th-century novelists, such as ▷ D. H. Lawrence and ▷ L. H. Myers, have rejected Proust on the grounds that his principles are merely aesthetic.

Proviso scene
Scene in a play showing bargaining between lovers, typically those featured in so-called ▷ Comedies of Manners, of the ▷ Restoration, wherein they set their terms before agreeing to be married. The most famous such scene is that between Millamant and Mirabell in ▷ William Congreve's ▷ *The Way of the World* (1700), in which they guarantee one another independence within marriage, before announcing their engagement (IV, 2).

***Provok'd Wife, The* (1697)**
Play by ▷ Sir John Vanbrugh. The drunken, boorish and misogynistic Sir John Brute, married but hating ▷ marriage, conducts a deliberate campaign to abuse and humiliate his wife and her niece Bellinda. In revenge, Lady Brute determines to cuckold him with the amorous Constant, who has been courting her for the past two years. In a parallel plot Heartfree, another misogynist, at first woos the affected Lady Fanciful, then falls in love, for the first time in his life, with Bellinda. A series of intrigues brings the pairs of lovers together in amorous assignations, although Lady Brute refrains from adultery with Constant. In the final scene Lady Fanciful attempts, but fails, to defame the reputations of both Bellinda and Heartfree, with whom she is now in love. Bellinda and Heartfree are united, while Sir John undergoes a supposed but unconvincing change of heart, and vows to be a better husband in future. The play's comedy barely sweetens its bitter comments on marriage, and especially the vulnerability of women in marriage. But it affirms the value of true love: Constant says, 'Though marriage be a lottery, in which there are wondrous many blanks, yet there is one inestimable lot in which the only heaven on earth is written'. Ironically however, he, the only admirer of women, apparently remains

unmarried at the end, while the misogynists are matched.

Prynne, J. H. (Jeremy Halward) (b 1936)
Poet. Prynne's poetry is densely allusive, complex, and includes terms and ideas drawn from the sciences and other discourses far removed from the conventional precincts of British poetry. He is a fellow of Gonville and Caius College, Cambridge, and lectures in the English Faculty. His teaching as well as his poetry has been an important influence upon younger writers and academics. His books include: *Brass* (1971), *The Oval Window* (1983) and *Not-You* (1993).

Psalms, The
A book of the Old Testament composed of the sacred songs of the ancient Jewish religion. In ancient Hebrew, they were called 'Praise-songs', indicating the predominant function of the collection, though other functions – lament, meditation, imprecation etc. – were included. Authorship was traditionally attributed to ▷ King David, but it is evident that the psalms either date from after the Babylonian Captivity (6th century BC) or were re-edited then; in any case they originated at different periods.

In the 16th century under the inspiration of the ▷ Protestant Reformation, the psalms were translated into English. There are two prose versions in official use in the ▷ Church of England: that of the Authorized Version of the ▷ Bible of 1611, and the older translation in the Book of ▷ Common Prayer dating from 1549. Both include some of the well-known masterpieces of English prose of the ▷ Renaissance. In addition, there are the metrical and rhymed versions especially favoured by the more extreme Protestants. The so-called 'Old Version' by Sternhold and Hopkins was published in its complete form in 1562. Another version, principally the work of Francis Rouse, came into general use in Scotland in the mid 17th century, and in 1696 Nicholas Brady and ▷ Nahum Tate produced the so-called 'New Version'. More distinguished attempts to versify the prose psalms were made in the 16th century by ▷ Sir Philip Sidney and his sister the ▷ Countess of Pembroke; in the 17th, by George Sandys, ▷ George Wither and ▷ John Milton; in the 19th, by John Keble.

▷ Bible in England.

Pseudonyms
A 'pseudonym' or false name is mostly used by writers wishing to protect their identity and enjoy the freedom to express their ideas openly. As such pseudonyms are often used by writers in marginal positions, such as women and racial minorities. While this usage has occurred through many periods, as for example with Jane Anger's attack against men, the 19th century is the key period for the emergence of the pseudonym, especially during the 1840s when female novelists were becoming a recognizable professional group. The ▷ Brontë sisters first published under the androgynous pseudonyms Currer, Ellis and Acton Bell. Charlotte Brontë later admitted that 'a vague impression that authoresses are liable to be looked on with prejudice' had influenced the decision. ▷ George Eliot pleaded with Charles Gray not to expose her identity after she published an article in the ▷ *Westminster Review* in 1855. 'The article appears to have produced a strong impression,' wrote Eliot, 'and that impression would be a little counteracted if the author were known to be a *woman*.' Other examples might include the French writer ▷ George Sand (who had an enormous influence on Eliot), ▷ John Oliver Hobbes and ▷ George Egerton: the pseudonyms of Aurora Dupin, Pearl Craigie and Mary Chavelita Dunne respectively, and ▷ Augusta Webster, whose first volumes of poetry were published under the name Cecil Home. ▷ Eliza Lynn Linton chose to write her ▷ autobiography under the name Christopher Kirkland. The collaborative poets Katherine Bradley and Edith Cooper wrote under the pseudonym ▷ Michael Field and entreated ▷ Robert Browning to guard the secret of their controversial dual authorship (which seemed to strike at the very notion of the sanctity of the writer), and most importantly their gender. 'We have many things to say that the world will not tolerate from a woman's lips,' declared Katherine Bradley. Edith Somerville and Violet Martin also wrote collaboratively, but their pseudonym, ▷ Somerville and Ross, was designed only to protect their identities as women. At the same time the market for women's literature was a lucrative one and some male authors such as ▷ William Sharp (Fiona Macleod) were not above changing sex – in name only – in order to exploit it. Women poets and novelists in the 19th century often favoured the use of enigmatic pseudonyms such as 'Speranza' (▷ Jane Wilde) and ▷ 'Ouida' (Marie Louise de la Ramée).

Many contributors to reviews and periodicals, such as the novelist ▷ Thackeray ('Charles James Yellowplush', 'Michael Angelo Titmarsh' and 'George Savage Fitz-Boodle'), disguised their names to conceal their ubiquity. At the same time the use of a *nom de plume* sometimes implied a second identity and allowed a writer to experiment with a variety of subject matter. ▷ Dickens published his first book ▷ *Sketches by Boz* using a pseudonym derived from his own infant attempts to pronounce the name 'Moses'.

In the 20th century pseudonyms have largely

dropped from use unless for idiosyncratic purposes. Perhaps the most famous post-2nd-World-War use of the pseudonym was 'Pauline Réage' the author of *The Story of O* whose real name is Dominique Aury. The reason for this use was the pornographic (⊳ pornography) nature of the text.

Psychoanalytical criticism
Psychoanalysis and literary criticism both seek to interpret their respective objects of enquiry, and both involve the analysis of language. In its early manifestations psychoanalytical criticism (*eg* Ernest Jones' *Hamlet and Oedipus*; 1949) sought to apply the methods of psychoanalysis to particular texts, in order to uncover their 'unconscious'. Jones' claim was to reveal the causes of Hamlet's behaviour beginning from the assumption that 'current response is always compounded partly of a response to the actual situation and partly of past responses to older situations that are unconsciously felt to be similar'. The French psychoanalyst ⊳ Jacques Lacan's re-reading of ⊳ Freud has sought to render problematical this relationship between patient and analyst, and, by implication, between text and reader. Lacan's description of the unconscious as being structured 'like a language' raises fundamental questions of the authoritative role usually ascribed to the literary critic. To this extent the 'unconscious' of the literary text is brought into confrontation with the unconscious of the critic.

Many of the terms taken from psychology which are associated with Lacan's reading of Freud have been incorporated into the language of literary criticism; for example, the decentred subject of psychoanalysis, ⊳ condensation, ⊳ displacement, the realm of 'imaginary', the symbolic order, all refer in some way to textual mechanisms.

Bib: Laplanche, J. and Pontalis, J-B., *The Language of Psychoanalysis;* Lacan, J., *The Four Fundamental Concepts of Psychoanalysis*; Wright, E., *Psychoanalytical Criticism.*

Ptolemy (Claudius Ptolemaeus) (2nd century AD)
Astronomer, geographer and mathematician. He was a native of the Egyptian city of Alexandria, and may have been of Greek origin. His theory of the structure of the universe, according to which the planets, sun and stars all revolved round the earth, remained the accepted opinion until replaced by the theory of ⊳ Copernicus in the 16th century and the observations of ⊳ Galileo in the 17th. This is the Ptolemaic System summarized in the *Almagest*, his treatise on astronomy.

Punch
A weekly comic periodical, founded in 1841. Thomas Hood (1799–1845) and ⊳ Thackeray were early members of its staff, and it employed a number of distinguished illustrators in the 19th century including Leech, Tenniel, Keene, and George Du Maurier (1834–96). From 1849 for a century it kept the same cover picture – of Punch of the puppet-shows. It was at first a radical paper, but as it became more and more an upper-class 'institution', so in politics, tone and taste it began to represent an influential but increasingly narrow section of the upper middle class. It has published the work of many famous cartoonists, including, in recent years, Ronald Searle, Michael Heath, Bill Tidy and Gerald Scarfe. The magazine was closed in 1993.

Purbeck, Elizabeth and Jane (c 1789–1802)
Novelists. The Purbeck sisters wrote collaborative novels which balanced romantic narratives with gentle social and political comment. *History of Sir George Warrington, or The Political Quixote* (1797) and *Neville Castle* (1802) show a certain sympathy for the ideals of equality and use characters from real life, such as ⊳ Tom Paine, and historical backdrops, like the ⊳ French Revolution, in order to test their protagonist's devotion to their political and philosophical commitments. The latter novel also provides interesting critical material on ⊳ Fanny Burney, Henry Fielding (1707–54), ⊳ Sophia Lee, and Samuel Richardson (1689–1761).

Purcell, Henry (1659–95)
Composer. His father and uncle held musical appointments at the Chapel Royal, and his father was also master of the choristers of ⊳ Westminster Abbey. He became a chorister in the Chapel Royal as a young boy, and as a young man was made 'composer in ordinary to the king' and organist at the Abbey. He composed some instrumental pieces, but is expecially famous for his choral compositions. Some of these were church music, *eg* the *Te Deum and Jubilate* (1694), which was the first English religious work to be scored for both strings and brass. His official appointments also caused him to set choral odes written for official occasions, such as the odes to St Cecilia. In addition, he collaborated with a number of Restoration dramatists in writing for the theatre, including a musical setting for a ⊳ masque in ⊳ Betterton's drama *Diocletian* and musical numbers in several dramas by ⊳ Dryden: *Tyrannic Love* (1687), *Amphitryon* (1690), *King Arthur* (1691). This work for the theatre included a musical version of ⊳ Shakespeare's ⊳ *A Midsummer Night's Dream* entitled *The Fairy Queen* (1693), and his opera *Dido and Aeneas* (1689), with a libretto by ⊳ Nahum Tate.

Purcell's career concluded the period of

English music which had begun in the mid-16th century. In his youth one of his principal teachers had been the English composer John Blow, but he was also a close student of French and Italian musical development. As a composer he had great freedom of imagination and strong gifts for dramatic writing.

▷ Opera in England.

Purgatorio

The second book of the ▷ *Divina Commedia* by ▷ Dante. Having emerged from the Inferno, the poet, still accompanied by ▷ Virgil, follows a spiral up to the Mount of Purgatory, where the souls of the dead are purged of the stains of their sins as they await release into Heaven. They encounter various groups of repentant sinners on the seven circular ledges of the mountain, who suffer punishments and pain, but do so more willingly, knowing the suffering will pass in the end. On its summit is the Earthly Paradise where the poet meets Beatrice, who is to guide him through the spheres of Heaven.

▷ *Inferno; Paradiso.*

Puritanism

The term is used in a narrow sense of religious practice and attitudes, and in a broad sense of an ethical outlook which is much less easy to define.

1 In its strict sense, 'Puritan' was applied to those Protestant reformers who rejected Queen Elizabeth's religious settlement of 1560. This settlement sought a middle way between Roman Catholicism and the extreme spirit of reform of ▷ Geneva. The Puritans, influenced by Geneva, Zurich, and other continental centres, objected to the retention of bishops and to any appearance of what they regarded as superstition in church worship – the wearing of vestments by the priests, and any kind of religious image. Apart from their united opposition to Roman Catholicism and their insistence on simplicity in religious forms, Puritans disagreed among themselves on questions of doctrine and church organization. The principal sects were: ▷ Presbyterians, Independents (at first called ▷ Brownists, and later ▷ Congregationalists), ▷ Baptists, and (later) ▷ Quakers. They were strong in the towns, especially in London, and in the University of Cambridge, and socially they were widespread, and included members of the aristocracy and of the working classes, as well as the middle, commercial classes where they had their chief strength. Puritanism was very strong in the first half of the 17th century and reached its peak of power after the ▷ Civil War of 1642–6 – a war which was ostensibly religious, although it was also political. Matters of church government were much involved with matters of state government, since Presbyterians and Independents, who believed in popular control of the church, were not likely to tolerate royal control of Parliament's political affairs. Puritanism was both religiously and politically supreme in the decade 1650–60, but on the Restoration of the monarchy Puritans were denied participation in the Church of England, and refused rights of free religious worship. The last was granted them by the Toleration Act of 1689, and during the 18th century both Puritanism and the official attitude to it were modified under the influence of Rationalism. Nonetheless, the ▷ Methodist movement of that century had many of the characteristics of the older Puritan sects. It was, moreover, only in 1829 that Nonconformists (as they were now called) were allowed to offer themselves as candidates for seats in Parliament, and only in 1871 did the Universities of Oxford and Cambridge cease to be the monopoly of the Church of England.

2 In the broader sense of a whole way of life, puritanism has always represented strict obedience to the dictates of conscience and strong emphasis on the virtue of self-denial. In this sense individuals can be described as 'puritan' whether or not they belong to one of the recognized Puritan sects, or even if they are atheists.

The word 'Puritan' is often thought to imply hostility to the arts, but this is not necessarily true. In the reign of ▷ Elizabeth I poets such as ▷ Spenser and ▷ Sidney combined a strong puritan moral tone (without any Puritan doctrine in the sectarian sense) with an intense delight in artistic form; in the 17th century ▷ John Milton was an ardent Puritan, but his poetry is one of the climaxes of English ▷ Renaissance art. However, it is true that the strict Puritans of the age of Shakespeare were commonly opponents of the art of the theatre; this was partly because the theatres were sometimes scenes of moral licentiousness and disorder, and partly because the strict puritan, in his intense love of truth, was very inclined to confuse fiction with lying. Thus in the later 17th century Bunyan was criticized by some of his Puritan comrades for writing fiction in his allegory, ▷ *Pilgrim's Progress*, and in the early 18th century ▷ Defoe had to defend his ▷ *Robinson Crusoe* against similar charges. Nonetheless, in the 18th and 19th centuries, Puritanism, or attitudes derived from it, did tend to encourage 'philistinism', or contempt for culture. This was because Puritanism had always encouraged an essentially practical attitude to worldly affairs, and when religion slackened as a driving force, the practical virtues came to be regarded as the principal, if not the only ones. Art, on the other hand, encourages the contemplative virtues, which the practical man of Puritan tradition was inclined to regard as unnecessary, therefore frivolous, and so, in a puritan sense, 'sinful'. There is continuity of development from Priestley, the 18th-century scientist and preacher, through the practical philosophy of ▷ Bentham, to James Mill, the ▷ Utilitarian leader, who was an atheist.

What is called the 'Puritan conscience', on the other hand, had an important influence on one kind of art form – the novel. Puritans believed that the good life could only be lived by 'the inner light' – the voice of God in the heart – and to discern this light it was necessary to conduct the most scrupulous self-enquiry. This produced the kind of spiritual autobiography that was common in the mid-17th century, and of which the best example is Bunyan's ▷ *Grace Abounding*. Such self-knowledge had two important consequences: it increased interest in, and understanding of, the human heart in others as well as the self, and the first results of this are apparent in Bunyan's *Pilgrim's Progress*; but it also encouraged a sense of the loneliness of the individual – a sense that was supported by the growing economic individualism of the later 17th century. These are important constituents of the novelist's vision, and when one adds to them the preoccupation with moral values with which puritanism is so bound up, and which are such a permanent feature of the English novel, it is possible to think that without Puritanism the novel form would never have developed indigenously in England.

▷ Reformation.

Purity

▷ *Cleanness.*

Puttenham, George (d 1590)

The reputed author of *The Arte of English Poesie* (1589). The book is a thorough treatise on English poetic technique at the time, on the threshold of one of the great decades of English short poems. It discusses the various forms of metrical verse, discusses – without deciding between them – the rival merits of metrical and non-metrical forms and presents an enlightened review of English verse. With ▷ Sidney's ▷ *Apologie for Poetrie*, Puttenham's book is one of the two most important critical works of the Elizabethan period. It is more scholarly, if less eloquent than Sidney's essay, but like Sidney, Puttenham is trying to establish civilized standards for the composition of poetry, and is opposed to the 'vulgar', popular traditions of a poet such as ▷ Skelton.

Bib: Willcock, G. D. and Walker, A. (eds.), *The Arte of English Poesie.*

Pym, Barbara (1913–80)

Novelist. Educated at Oxford University, she served with the W.R.N.S. during World War II, and subsequently worked at the International African Institute in London. Between 1950 and 1961 she published six novels: there then followed 16 years during which she could not find a publisher. After praise from Lord David Cecil and the poet Philip Larkin in 1977 her work received renewed attention, and she published a further three novels. Since then her work has enjoyed considerable popularity. Her novels are sensitive, shrewd, ironical portraits of English middle-class life, with a particular focus on the lives of women; the social contexts are frequently academic and clerical. She is often said to write in the tradition of ▷ Jane Austen. A further three novels were published posthumously. Her novels are: *Some Tame Gazelle* (1950); *Excellent Women* (1952); *Jane and Prudence* (1953); *Less Than Angels* (1955); *A Glass of Blessings* (1958); *No Fond Return of Love* (1961); *Quartet in Autumn* (1977); *The Sweet Dove Died* (1978); *A Few Green Leaves* (1980); *An Unsuitable Attachment* (1982); *Crampton Hodnet* (1985); *An Academic Question* (1986).

Bib: Benet, D., *The Life and Work of Barbara Pym*; Weld, A., *Barbara Pym and the Novel of Manners*; Liddell, R., *A Mind at Ease: Barbara Pym and Her Novels.*

Pyramus and Thisbe

The hero and heroine of a love story by the Roman poet ▷ Ovid (▷ *Metamorphoses* iv). The lovers are forbidden marriage by their parents, but they exchange vows through a hole in the wall that separates their respective houses. They agree to meet outside Babylon at the tomb of Ninus, but Thisbe, who arrives first, is frightened by a lion and hides in a cave, the lion meanwhile covering her dropped veil with blood. When Pyramus arrives and finds the bloody veil, he supposes Thisbe to be dead, and kills himself; Thisbe follows his example. In Shakespeare's play ▷ *A Midsummer Night's Dream* the artisans give a comically bungled performance of the tragedy before King Theseus of Athens.

Pythagoras (6th century BC)

Greek philosopher. He is important in the histories of religion, mathematics and astronomy. In religion he founded the Pythagorean brotherhood, which believed in the immortality of the soul and its migration into another body, perhaps that of an animal, after death; for this reason they practiced vegetarianism. In mathematics, he discovered the mathematical relations of musical intervals; he or his followers believed that the sun and the planets were divided by comparable intervals – hence the tradition of 'the music of the spheres' inaudible to earthly hearing. In geometry, he is credited with the theorem called after him, that the square on the hypotenuse of a right-angled triangle is equal to the sum of the squares on the other two sides. In astronomy, he discovered that day and night are caused by the revolution of the earth about its own axis.

Many legends grew up round Pythagoras, amongst others that he was of extraordinary beauty and had golden thighs. Historically, his ascetic philosophy, based on the belief that the body was the tomb of the soul and that denial of the flesh was the way to its final release, is considered to foreshadow ▷ Platonism.

Quadrille
1 A game of cards which replaced ▷ ombre in fashion about 1726, to be succeeded about 20 years later by whist.

2 A dance of French origin; it was first used in ballet, and then became popular in the ballroom. Introduced into England in the late 18th century.

Quadrivium and Trivium
In the medieval educational syllabus the 'seven liberal arts' were divided into the Trivium – grammar, rhetoric, logic – followed by the Quadrivium – arithmetic, geometry, astronomy, music.

Quakers
Originally a derisive name for the members of a religious society properly called the Society of Friends; the Friends are still known as Quakers, but the term has lost its contemptuous significance. The Society was founded by ▷ George Fox, who began his preaching career in 1647. He preached that the truth came from an inner spiritual light, and declared that no special class of men (*ie* churches) should be set apart for religious purposes. This individualism at first attracted a number of mentally disturbed followers whose ecstasies are perhaps responsible for the nickname 'Quaker', though Fox himself declared that it was first used in 1650 because he taught his followers to 'Tremble at the Word of the Lord'. They held a view, unusual among ▷ Puritans, that it was possible to gain complete victory over sin in this life. Such a doctrine, in addition to their refusal to accept those religious institutions that the other Puritans accepted, made them intensely unpopular for the first ten years of their existence. Later they became influential far beyond their numbers, which have remained comparatively few. Owing to the freedom of mind which is the essence of the movement, it is difficult to define their doctrine, which seems to vary greatly among individuals. On the other hand they are well known for a range of characteristic virtues: humanitarianism (they were amongst the first to protest against slavery – 1688); non-resistance to violence; respect for individuals regardless of race, sex, or religion; sobriety of conduct and tranquillity of mind. One of the most important of their early members was William Penn (1644–1718), the founder of the American colony of Pennsylvania. Like other Puritans, they were prominent in commerce, but took care to engage in activities that were not harmful; in consequence, Quaker names are particularly well known in connection with the manufacture of chocolate. However, in the 18th century their outstanding importance was in banking: their sober-mindedness and strictness of morality counteracted the speculative manias of the time, and did much to establish secure financial foundations for the rapid expansion of British trade.

Quarles, Francis (1592–1644)
Poet, emblematist, pamphleteer, Francis Quarles was a prolific author, producing not only a number of verse collections, but also a play, biblical paraphrases, a romance and two remarkable ▷ emblem-books: *Emblems* (1635) and *Hieroglyphics of the Life of Man* (1638). His earlier verse publications, such as *A Feast for Worms* (1620), *Hadasa: or, The History of Queen Esther* (1621) and *Sion's Elegies* (1624), were, in the main, adaptations of biblical themes. In the 1630s his attention was devoted to the production of his emblem-books and to occasional pieces. With the outbreak of the ▷ Civil War, Quarles published a series of anti-Puritan ▷ pamphlets. But it is for his emblematic work that Quarles is chiefly remembered; indeed, *Emblems* is said to have been the most popular book published in the 17th century.
Bib: Grosart, A. B. (ed.), *Complete Works in Verse and Proses* (3 vols); Hasan, M., *Quarles: A Study of His Life and Poetry*.

Quarterly Review, The
Founded by ▷ John Murray in 1809 as a moderate Tory rival to the ▷ *Edinburgh Review*. The first editor was the irascible traditionalist ▷ William Gifford, and later editors included ▷ Samuel Taylor Coleridge's nephew, Sir J. T. Coleridge, and John Lockhart. ▷ Sir Walter Scott, ▷ Robert Southey, and ▷ Samuel Rogers were early contributors. Scott's approving review of ▷ Jane Austen's ▷ *Emma* appeared in the *Quarterly* in March 1816, and a hostile article by John Wilson Croker on ▷ John Keats' ▷ *Endymion* (Sept. 1818) provoked ▷ Lord Byron's squib (written in 1821):

> *Who kill'd John Keats?*
> *'I,' says the* Quarterly,
> *So savage and Tartarly;*
> *'Twas one of my feats.'*

Quarto
A term used in publishing to designate a size of volume, made by folding the standard paper twice instead of only once (▷ folio size). The quarto editions of ▷ Shakespeare's plays are those published in his lifetime, as distinct from the folio editions published after his death. 18 of his plays appear in separate quarto editions.

Quatrain
A stanza of four lines, usually rhyming *a b a b* or *a b c b*.

Queen's Theatre
▷ Haymarket Theatres.

Querelle des Femmes
The ▷ Renaissance debate about the virtues and vices of women ('the quarrel about

women') was a continuation of a medieval argument which in literary terms may be dated from Jean de Meun's attack on women in his section of *Roman de la Rose* (c 1277) and Christine de Pisan's response, *The Book of the City of Ladies* (1405), in which she defends women. The 'woman question' became a focus of attention again in the late 16th and early 17th centuries, commencing with the publication of Joseph Swetnam's *The Arraignment of Lewd, idle, froward, and unconstant women* (1615). ▷ Rachel Speght, who was primarily a devotional writer, challenged his arguments in a serious and theoretical manner, basing her own arguments upon God's, rather than man's, law. Two other women wrote more angry ripostes to Swetnam's vituperative outpourings: ▷ Constantia Munda and ▷ Ester Sowernam, who adopted pseudonyms to protect their reputation, and, one suspects, to ensure their physical safety in a society hardly renowned for its championing of women's rights. An earlier defence of women occurs in ▷ Jane Anger's *Jane Anger, Her Protection for Women* (1588–9).
Bib: Henderson, K. U. and McManus, B. F. (eds.), *Half Humankind*.

Quid Pro Quo, or, the Day of the Dupes **(1843)**
A play by ▷ Catherine Gore, which won a £500 prize for an 'English comedy'. The plot concerns social climbing, class division,
and the political machinations of county folk. Although it was admired by the judges of the competition, it was a box-office failure, unpopular with both audiences and critics. It was Gore's last play.

Quin, James (1693–1766)
Actor, manager, singer. Born in London, Quin was the product of a bigamous union between James and Elizabeth Quin, and the grandson of a former Lord Mayor of Dublin. After 1713 he began acting at the ▷ Smock Alley Theatre in Dublin, and by early 1715 he had reached the ▷ Drury Lane Theatre in London, where he later helped to manage the company. In 1746 and 1747 Quin acted with ▷ Garrick at Covent Garden (▷ Covent Garden Theatres), and the two became friends despite their ostensible rivalry. But Garrick's light, naturalistic style made Quin's acting appear absurdly formal, pompous, and monotonous to many observers, and the older man gradually retired from the stage, to ▷ Bath.

Quin was noted for his 'strong passions', including a violent temper, but also good humour and dignity. He was a friend of ▷ Pope and ▷ Swift, and was admired by ▷ Horace Walpole and the Prince of Wales (later ▷ George III). He held his own in parts ranging from ▷ Othello, ▷ Macbeth, ▷ Richard III, ▷ Coriolanus, Comus, Bajazet in ▷ Rowe's *Tamerlane*, and Pierre in ▷ Thomas Otway's ▷ *Venice Preserv'd*, to his most celebrated role as Falstaff. Garrick's innovations hurt his reputation more substantially, perhaps, than that of any leading actor of the period, quite suddenly making him seem outmoded. But even at the end of his career, Garrick and other colleagues continued to respect him, and he was still able to draw large crowds.
Bib: Taylor, A. M., *Life of Mr James Quin, comedian*.

Rabelais, François (?1495–1553)
French comic writer. He was successively a Franciscan friar, then Benedictine monk, before abandoning the religious life and turning to the study of medicine (he became a Bachelor of Medicine at Montpellier in 1535). He was protected by the powerful Du Bellay family in his censorship disputes with the Sorbonne. His famous works are all in prose, but difficult to classify because of their kaleidoscopic forms of narrative and plot. ▷ *Pantagruel* (1533) and ▷ *Gargantua* (1535) were later reversed in sequence, Gargantua being the father of Pantagruel. Ten years and more later come *Tiers Livre* (*Third Book*, 1545) and *Quart Livre* (*Fourth Book*, first version 1548, expanded version 1552). The authenticity of the *Cinquiesme Livre* (1564) remains disputed, though the opening section, *L'Isle Sonnante* ('Ringing Island'), was published separately in Rabelais' lifetime and is accepted by some as his work.

There is in Rabelais an exuberant command of linguistic mechanisms which underpin the entire range of comedy he deploys, from simple pun to obscenity, and slapstick and absurdity to invective and satire. Among English writers consciously indebted to Rabelais, Sir John Harington's *Metamorphosis of Ajax* and *Anatomy* follow his style, using coprological humour and mock encomia; the Elizabethan journalist ▷ Thomas Nashe has much of Rabelais' vitality; Robert Burton's *Anatomy of Melancholy* has a comparable amplitude of language; and Samuel Butler's bitter attack on the Puritans (▷ Puritanism), the mock-epic *Hudibras*, is more than Rabelaisian in its bitter humour. Rabelais was notably translated by the Scotsman, Sir Thomas Urquhart (c 1611–60) (Books I–II, 1653; Book III, 1693), with continuations by Peter Motteux (1663–1718) (Books IV–V, 1693–94).
Bib: Bakhtin, M., *Rabelais and his World*.

Racine, Jean (1693–99)
French dramatist. His principal sources of inspiration were either ▷ classical (the larger group of his works, including *Andromaque* (1667), *Britannicus* (1669), *Bérénice* (1670), *Mithridate* (1673), *Iphigénie* (1674) and *Phèdre* (1677)) or biblical (*Athalie*, (1690)). Racine examines the nexus of passion and power, and the distorting effect these invariably have upon the heroic values which his characters inherit or purport to represent. He delineates the moral and political blindness which can all too easily sway human judgement and conduct and he highlights with particular force the destructiveness of passion from which ▷ tragedy will proceed. His dramas are tightly constructed according to classical criteria of the ▷ unities and display a virtuoso command of the 12-syllable Alexandrine line combined with a strong sense of rhyme and rhythm and a lucid, economical style. Racine was admired in England by ▷ John Dryden and ▷ Thomas Otway, whose ▷ 'heroic drama' is nevertheless no serious rival to its French counterpart.

Radcliffe, Ann (1764–1823)
Novelist. She was one of the most famous of the writers of ▷ Gothic novels, which sought to gain their effect through mystery and the supernatural in a setting of grand scenic description. She was immensely popular in her own day for her four novels: *The Sicilian Romance* (1790) *The Romance of the Forest* (1791) ▷ *The Mysteries of Udolpho* (1794) and *The Italian* (1797). *Udolpho* is the best remembered, owing to ▷ satirization through an account of its effect on a young girl in ▷ Jane Austen's ▷ *Northanger Abbey*.

***Rainbow, The* (1915)**
A novel by ▷ D. H. Lawrence. It is set in Lawrence's own background, the English Midlands; the subject is three generations of the Brangwen family extending from the middle of the last century to the early years of the present one.

The Brangwens are a family of farmers and have for generations lived on their own land which, as the novel begins, is near an encroaching industrial area. Tom Brangwen, the first of the main characters, is sent to a grammar school by his ambitious mother; the experience both frustrates him and arouses him. His awakened need for what is strange and mysterious attracts him to Lydia Lensky, an aristocratic but impoverished Polish exile, a widow, and the mother of a small daughter. They marry and although their marriage meets difficulties it becomes a happy one. Lydia and Tom remain ignorant of much in each other's nature, but Lydia finds confidence in Tom's established way of life, while he finds enlargement precisely in what, for him, is mysterious in his wife. Tom's stepdaughter, Anna, is attracted to his nephew, Will Brangwen, who has had an urban upbringing and has a strong artistic imagination and profound religious instincts. This marriage is more troubled but they are united in a passionate night-time sensuality. Their daughter, Ursula, belongs to the first generation of modern women: she sets out to be a teacher, and after an intense struggle in an inhuman English board school, she succeeds in affirming her independence. But her love affair with Skrebensky, a thoroughly Anglicized descendant of another Polish exile, ends in frustration. She inherits from her mother a capacity for passion which expresses her full nature, whereas his nature is divided between a dead conformity to society and a sensuality which is incapable of real passion. The relationship ends with Ursula pregnant, although in the novel's climactic scene, Ursula miscarries, but then finds reconciliation through the image of the rainbow.

The story of Ursula and her sister Gudrun is continued in ⊳ *Women in Love*, originally conceived as part of the same novel. The novel was for a time suppressed on grounds of immorality, seized and burnt in 1915 primarily for its representation of Ursula's lesbian affair with her schoolteacher. It is now regarded as one of Lawrence's greatest achievements.

Raine, Craig (b 1944)
Poet. His first two collections, *The Onion, Memory* (1978) and *A Martian Sends a Postcard Home* (1979), established a vogue for ⊳ 'Martian' poetry in this country. *Rich* (1984) shows him extending his work into areas such as prose ⊳ autobiography. He has also written an opera libretto and work for the theatre.

Raine, Kathleen (b 1908)
Poet and critic. Raine has been prolifically publishing poetry since the 1930s; in 1943 *Stone and Flower: Poems 1935–43* appeared. In 1956 *Collected Poems* appeared, followed by *The Hollow Hill* (1964). The 1981 *Collected Poems, 1935–80* gathered together much of her important work. Raine is also well known as a scholar of William Blake, and has also written on ⊳ Yeats and Coleridge. Recent collections include: *The Lost Country* (1971); *On A Deserted Shore* (1973); *The Oracle in the Heart* (1980), and *World Within a World* (1982), as well as three volumes of her ⊳ autobiography. In 1991 she gave what she announced as her last public lecture, at Liverpool University.

Ralegh (Raleigh), Sir Walter (1552–1618)
Poet, historian, courtier, explorer, colonist. The career of Sir Walter Ralegh has been taken as almost symbolic of the 'Renaissance ideal' of the complete individual – one who, with an easy grace, excels in all forms of endeavour. In addition to the pursuits listed above, for example, one might add: seaman, soldier, chemist, philosopher, theologian, even pioneer in naval medicine and dietetics, diplomat and (somewhat unsuccessful) politician. Ralegh's military experience included soldiering in France (1569) and Ireland (1580). While in Ireland Ralegh met ⊳ Spenser, who approved of his slaughter of Spanish troops at Smerwick. As an explorer and colonist (⊳ Colonialism) Ralegh was the driving force behind the project to found a colony on the eastern seaboard of the North American continent in 1585. The project was abandoned in 1586 and, after several unsuccessful expeditions, the patent for what had become the Virginia settlement lapsed to the Crown in 1603. In 1595, following a period of imprisonment in the Tower due to Elizabeth I's displeasure at his relationship with a member of her court, Ralegh led an expedition to South America – an enterprise which was to be repeated in a further unsuccessful expedition to the Orinoco in 1616. Ralegh's South American exploits were directed chiefly towards gaining treasure at the expense of the Spaniards, and it was as a member of the expeditions to Cadiz (1596) and the Azores (1597) that his military reputation in fighting the Spanish was established. With the accession of ⊳ James I in 1603, however, Ralegh's brand of vigorous expansionism became unfavourable. With the exception of the Orinoco expedition, the period between 1603 and his execution in 1618 was spent in confinement in the Tower, to which he had been committed following his being found guilty of conspiring against the king in November 1603. His execution on the charge for which he had been sentenced in 1603, was in fact due to his pursuit of an anti-Spanish policy when such attitudes were no longer favourably perceived at court.

Ralegh's life was, in some measure, his greatest achievement, for it became one of the foundation stones of the myth of Elizabethan accomplishment. The fact that almost every project in which he was involved (exceptions being the Cadiz and Azores expeditions) failed was conveniently ignored. As a myth-maker, however, Ralegh was a potent force: not only his own life, but his earlier written works served to underline the Elizabethan self-image. In particular *A Report of the Fight about the Azores* (1591) and *The Discovery of the Large, Rich, and Beautiful Empire of Guiana* (1596) can both be read as attempts at promoting an ideal of national endeavour. Ralegh's poetry also contributed to the romantic legend, tinged as it is with a melancholic awareness of the transitory nature of existence. Perhaps his most significant poetic achievement, though, is the fragmentary 'Ocean's Love to Cynthia' – a brooding, obscure and allusive text of loss and longing. A rather different proposition is his *History of the World* (1614), which, in its all-inclusiveness, might stand as an apt commentary on its author. The *History*, though it draws veiled comparisons between the present and the past, concludes at the date 130 BC. It is yet another unfinished enterprise.

⊳ School of Night.

Bib: Oldys, W. and Birch, T. (eds.), *Works* (8 vols); Greenblatt, S., *Ralegh: The Renaissance Man and His Roles*; May, S. W., *Sir Walter Ralegh*.

Ralph Roister Doister **(1552)**
A comedy by Nicholas Udall, printed in 1566, and written in about 1552. It is sometimes called 'the first English comedy', presumably because the earlier 'comic interludes' notably by ⊳ John Heywood (*eg The Play of the Weather* and *The Four P's*) were too slight to count, whereas Udall's play, which may have been written for the boys of Westminster School, is an adaptation of the *Miles Gloriosus* (*The Boastful Soldier*) by ⊳ Plautus. The

basic situation is the same in both plays: vain but foolish and boastful soldier makes love to a respectable woman (Christian Custance in Udall's play), who is betrothed to a merchant, Gawin Goodluck, and Ralph is encouraged in his misguided enterprise by a mischievous associate, Matthew Merygreek. But the play has a kind of farcical humour which has more in common with the popular ▷ interludes and even the May Games of English country life, and it reads as a thoroughly native product. The rhymed verse is rather primitive, but the dialogue has realistic freshness. The comedy is an example of humanistic learning married to popular entertainment.

Rambler, The

A twice-weekly periodical produced by ▷ Samuel Johnson from March 1750 to March 1752. All except five were written by Johnson himself. The papers were in the tradition of ▷ *The Tatler* and ▷ *The Spectator* essays by ▷ Addison and ▷ Steele 40 years before. The essays cover a wide variety of subjects, including eastern tales, criticism and ▷ allegories. Johnson's moral seriousness in the work is indicated by the prayer that he wrote on its commencement. *The Rambler* was pirated and copied, evidence of its great popularity, and in Johnson's lifetime ran to ten reprintings.

Ramsay, Allan (1686–1758)

Edinburgh wig-maker and father of the portrait painter of the same name. He was a prolific poet in both English and Scots, using a variety of ▷ metres, from intricate stanzas to pentameter and tetrameter ▷ couplets. His marriage of Scottish and English literary traditions, together with his earthy realism of language and dramatic flair, laid down the foundations on which ▷ Robert Fergusson and ▷ Robert Burns were later to build.

Randolph, Thomas (1605–35)

Poet and dramatist. Randolph revealed his literary skills early on, writing poetry at the age of ten, and then becoming renowned for his Latin and English verses while a student at Cambridge. The plays do not live up to his early promise, however, and he is most successful at short satiric pieces. For example, although *The Jealous Lovers* (1632) was performed before ▷ Charles I and ▷ Henrietta Maria, it is an uninspired and glib romance. He is more skilful with country scenes: the ▷ pastoral poems are beautifully lyrical and his pastoral play, *Amyntas* (1630), has some good rustic comedy pieces. Randolph's most interesting work, *The Muse's Looking Glass*, was written while he was still at university, although only published in 1638; it contains an actor who defeats a Puritan's anti-theatre arguments and it is gratifyingly ▷ Jonsonian in tone.

Bib: Smith, G. C. M., *Thomas Randolph*.

***Rape of the Lock, The* (1712/1714)**

A ▷ mock-heroic poem in ▷ pentameter ▷ couplets by ▷ Alexander Pope. Its immediate stimulation was a quarrel between two families with whom Pope was acquainted, caused by Lord Petre cutting off a lock of Miss Arabella Fermor's hair. Pope hoped to place this act of sexual harrassment in a trivial light by his comic and burlesque treatment, which owes something to the example of ▷ Nicolas Boileau's *Le Lutrin* (*The Lectern*, 1674), ▷ a mock epic concerning an ecclesiastical quarrel over the placing of a lectern. However Pope only succeeded in giving further offence. The first published version (1712) comprised two cantos, but Pope continued to work on it after the immediate occasion had passed, and in 1714 it was issued in a much enlarged five-canto version, incorporating the epic machinery of the sylphs.

The work has been interpreted as a severe moral ▷ satire. By describing this transient quarrel in the heroic language of ▷ Homer's ▷ *Iliad*, Pope could be said to be ▷ ironically mocking the selfish vanity of fashionable society. However, the sensuous beauty of the verse and the elaborateness of the poem's imagery suggest that the young Pope was no Puritan moralist. The most vivid passages in the poem celebrate the new ease and amenity of the English middle class in its first confident phase of capitalist ▷ imperialism. The heroine's exotic cosmetics and beauty aids, brought from the farthest corners of the earth by British ships, are described with delight. The sylphs, fanciful projections of the secular drawing room, are substituted for the awesome gods of the ancient Greeks (▷ Greek literature), and the primitive *machismo* of Hector and Achilles becomes the feminine 'armour' of stays and petticoats, or the elegant 'triumph' of a game of cards. Counterpointing this delight in social life is an elegiac lament over its transience, and the poem is at its most moving when it laments the imminent decay of Belinda's 'frail beauty', 'When those fair Suns shall sett, as sett they must,/ And all those Tresses shall be laid in Dust'.

Raphael the Painter

▷ Pre-Raphaelite.

***Rasselas, Prince of Abyssinia, The History of* (1759)**

A prose work by ▷ Samuel Johnson. Tradition has it that Johnson composed the work rapidly to pay for the cost of his mother's funeral. Its theme has often been compared by critics to that of Johnson's poem ▷ *The Vanity of Human Wishes*.

The theme of *Rasselas* is 'the choice of life', a phrase which occurs repeatedly. The prince, son of the emperor of Abyssinia, is tired of the pleasant life in the 'happy valley' and, in the company of his sister Nekayah, her attendant Pekuah, and the philosopher Imlac, escapes to Egypt.

Imlac's advice demonstrates to the youth the transient nature of human happiness, a state which is in any case unobtainable. Imlac also voices Johnson's views on 'the business of a poet', which is to 'examine not the individual, but the species'. The poet should aim to be 'the interpreter of nature, and the legislator of mankind', not to 'number the streaks of the tulip'. *Rasselas* often parallels ▷ Voltaire's *Candide*, published in the same year, and when Johnson later read this work he commented on the similarities.

▷ Orientalism.

Rationalism
1 In philosophy, the belief that reason, rather than sensation, is the only certain guide to knowledge.

2 In religion, the practice of seeking explanations which satisfy reason for what had been accepted as supernatural.

Rattigan, Sir Terence (1911–77)
British dramatist whose first stage success was with the light comedy *French Without Tears* (1936). This was followed by such plays as *Flare Path* (1942), *While the Sun Shines* (1943), and *Love in Idleness* (1944), the last of these a modern treatment of Hamlet and Claudius. *The Winslow Boy*, a play about a father's struggle to defend his son on a charge of theft, won the Ellen Terry Award for the best play of the year in 1946. *The Browning Version* (which has recently been filmed for a second time, directed by Mike Figgis [1994]) received the same award in 1948. *The Deep Blue Sea* (1952), a piece about passion and suicide, might have been more interesting had Rattigan been able to deal openly, in the play, with his own tragic homosexual love which inspired him to write it. But English repression is a subject which he knew and wrote about well. Rattigan was well aware that his commercial success depended on the appeal of his plays to 'Aunt Edna', as he called the middle-brow members of his audience. His sound judgement of the market ensured continued success with *Separate Tables* (1955), *Variations on a Theme* (1958), *Ross*, a dramatization of the life of T. E. Lawrence (1960), *A Bequest to the Nation* (1970) and *Cause Célèbre* (1977).
Bib: Darlow, M. and Hodson, G., *Rattigan: The Man and His Work*.

Ravenscroft, Edward (?1650–97)
Dramatist, popular mainly for his farces. A lawyer by training, he was a member of the Middle Temple in 1671, where he composed his first play, *Mammamouchi, or the Citizen Turn'd Gentleman*, based on ▷ Molière's play *Le Bourgeois Gentilhomme*; Ravenscroft used Molière as a source several more times. *The Careless Lovers* followed in 1673, and *The Wrangling Lovers* in 1676, again using French as well as Spanish sources. A play inspired by the ▷ Commedia dell'Arte, *Scaramouch a Philosopher, Harlequin a Schoolboy, a Bravo, Merchant and Musician*, and a play based on George Ruggle's 1615 Latin comedy, *Ignoramus, or the English Lawyer*, were produced in 1677, and *Titus Andronicus, or the Rape of Lavinia*, an alteration of the play by ▷ Shakespeare, in 1678. His most celebrated play, ▷ *The London Cuckolds*, another farce in the French manner, was staged in 1681. It became a tradition to perform this at both ▷ Drury Lane and ▷ Covent Garden on the Lord Mayor's Day (9 November) every year; the play was revived in 1782 and again by the Royal Court Theatre in 1979. Ravenscroft's great rival, Dryden, referred to his works with contempt.

Raworth, Tom (b 1934)
Poet. His first books *The Relation Ship* (1967) and *The Big Green Day* (1968), show the emerging influence of post-war avant-garde American poetry on British writing. Internationalism has remained an important part of Raworth's life and work, and he has lived in, among other places, France, America and Mexico. He currently lives and works in Cambridge. His more recent books include: *Writing* (1982) and *Eternal Sections* (1993). Raworth's poetry is characterized by microscopic verbal precision, though the breaking apart of syntax and words themselves paradoxically works to multiply meaning.

Reade, Charles (1814–84)
The seventh of eleven children, Reade was born in Oxfordshire and educated largely at home; he excelled in sports and was self-motivated in study. In 1831 he went to Oxford and in 1843 was called to the Bar, but preferred music and the theatre. In 1845 he was made Dean of Arts at Magdalen College, Oxford, where he upset some members by wearing a green coat with brass buttons. In 1846 he tried medicine in Edinburgh, and in 1847 obtained a DCL and began to deal in violins. In 1851 he was made vice-president of his college, and began a long and prolific career as writer and dramatist. He met the actress Mrs Seymour in 1854 and they lived together until her death in 1879, after which he wrote little, turning to religion. He was a philanthropic man, helping the poor, distressed gentlefolk, lunatics, and waifs and strays; both impulsive and impatient, he was generous, boisterous and kept dogs, horses and other animals. He remained a theatre manager to 1882.

His writing career began with a stage version of Tobias Smollett's *Peregrine Pickle* (1751) in 1851. He co-wrote and produced *Masks and Faces* in 1852, turning it into the novel *Peg Woffington* the following year, when the 'reforming' novel about prisons, *Christie Johnstone*, also appeared. *It is Never Too Late to Mend*, in similar vein, followed in 1856, as well as the play *Gold!*; the novel was later dramatized and the play rewritten as the novel *Foul Play* (1869). He wrote short stories, pieces of journalism and plays at the same time. In 1858 he published *The Autobiography of a Thief* and *Jack of all Trades*, and in 1859 *Love Me Little, Love Me Long*. *The Cloister and the Hearth* was published in 1861. *Hard Cash* (1863) tackled the disgrace of lunatic asylums and in 1866 *Griffith Gaunt* triggered scandal and litigation by its frank attitude to sexual problems.

From this time on, Reade was a controversial and litigious figure. *Put Yourself in His Place* (1870) attacked enforced trade union membership; *The Simpleton* (1873) gave rise to a libel action and a quarrel with ▷ Anthony Trollope. Other novels and plays include *The Wandering Heir* (1873) and *A Woman Hater* (1877). Reade was both famous and successful, being regarded as the natural successor to ▷ Charles Dickens, and by ▷ Henry James and ▷ Swinburne as superior to ▷ George Eliot. He commented on himself, 'I am a painstaking man, and I owe my success to it.' His writing is now considered overburdened with detail, ▷ melodramatic and superficial in characterization. His most successful work was *The Cloister and the Hearth*.

Bib: Elwin, M., *Charles Reade: A Biography*; Burns, W., *Charles Reade: A Study in Victorian Authorship*; Hughes, W., *The Maniac in the Cellar: Sensation Novels of the 1860s*.

Reader response criticism

This term refers to a number of different schools of criticism which stress the central role of the reader in making literary meanings. The most influential of these schools are ▷ Reception theory, which originates in Germany, and the approach associated with the American critic Stanley Fish. Fish argues that literary texts do not conceal their meanings like treasure from readers, but offer what are in effect endless interpretative possibilities which are realised in the interaction between text and reader. What validates an interpretation therefore is not its ultimate 'rightness' or 'wrongness' but the verdict of the ▷ interpretive community in which it is produced.

Bib: Tompkins, Jane P. (ed.), *Reader Response Criticism*.

Readerly and writerly texts

A distinction made by ▷ Roland Barthes to indicate the difference between forms of writing which are plural in their meanings and effects, which he calls 'writerly' texts (*scriptible* in French), and those geared towards the quick consumption of easy, narrow meanings which he calls readerly (*lisible*). Readerly writing indulges the simple, the conventional, the stereotypical and the expected and does not present a challenge. Writerly texts, on the other hand, make demands of their readers and force them to, in a sense, write their own text because this kind of writing gives little in terms of fixed or secure meaning. For this reason, Barthes considers them politically and psychologically liberating. Barthes identified this kind of writing with that of the ▷ avant-garde, and his followers have tended to reject works considered to be merely representational or ▷ realistic.

Bib: Barthes, R., *S/Z*.

Realism

A term used in various senses, both in philosophy and in literary criticism. Three principal meanings, two of them philosophical and one literary, are particularly worth distinction.

1. In medieval philosphy, the realists were opposed to the ▷ nominalists. Realism here means that classes of things ('universals') have reality whereas individuals have not, or at least have less: *eg* individual birds take their reality from the classification 'bird'. The nominalists considered that only the individual bird has reality, and that the classification 'bird' in only a formulation in the mind.

2. Since the Middle Ages, realism has become opposed to ▷ idealism. Here realism means that reality exists apart from ideas about it in the mind, and idealism represents the view that we can know nothing that is not in our minds.

3. Realism was first used as a literary term in France, where it was applied to literary and visual forms which aim for the accurate reproduction of the world as it is. Literary realism emerged in the late 18th and 19th centuries concomitantly with the rise of the novel and coterminous with industrial capitalism. In general, it means the use of the imagination to represent things as common sense supposes them to be. It does not only apply to 19th-century literature; Daniel Defoe (1660–1731) is commonly called a realist because of his factual description and narration. 19th-century realism in literature arose, however, from a reaction against 19th-century ▷ Romanticism, and is related to ▷ naturalism; for a discussion of late 20th-century critiques of realism as a vehicle of ideology, see Catherine Belsey, *Critical Practice*. ▷ George Eliot's ▷ *Middlemarch* (1871–2), with its carefully observed representation of the forces which structure society, is a notable example of English 19th-century realism. Many realist novelists chose to depict the lives and sufferings of the lower classes in texts that combine fiction with documentary. ▷ Elizabeth

Gaskell's ▷ *Mary Barton* (1848) is a good example of this. Realism was often associated with the representation of immoral or transgressive behaviour, notably in the fiction of French 19th-century realist novelists such as ▷ Balzac and ▷ Flaubert, who defended themselves from charges of immorality by claiming fidelity to realism.

19th-century novels are often described, from a 20th-century perspective, as classic realist texts, a term devised by the film critic Colin McCabe in 1974 to describe *Middlemarch*. Classic realism, according to McCabe, who reverses the terms of Lukacs' socialist realist attack on modernism, works by a sleight of hand, to hide the constructedness of the world; the world of the novel is presented to the reader as if it were a direct mirroring or reflection of the real world, rather than an ideologically saturated interpretation of the real. The term most often used to describe the strategy of the realist text is transparency. The illusion of transparency created by realism is contrasted with modernist writing which supposedly foregrounds its textuality.

Naturalism is a late 19th-century form of realism, associated with the French novelist ▷ Emile Zola. It emerged out of an attempt to marry literary and scientific discourses, and demanded a scientific and empirical objectivity from writers, whose novels were supposed to be laboratory experiments to show how character is determined by environment. In practice, naturalism remained focused on the world as external material appearance, and imposed a rigid set of normalizing causal narratives. ▷ Thomas Hardy's ▷ *Tess of the d'Urbervilles* (1891) and ▷ *Jude the Obscure* (1895), ▷ George Gissing's ▷ *New Grub Street* (1891) and ▷ George Moore's ▷ *Esther Waters* (1894) are all influenced by naturalism. It is important to distinguish between different forms of realism – for example, classic realism, naturalism, socialist realism – and to recognize that they pre-suppose different kinds of relationship between the literary text and the world.

Realism is also used in modern literature in opposition to what is regard as sentimentalism – the disposition to represent feelings (*eg* the various forms of love) as nicer than we know them to be; an illogical extension of this use of the term is sometimes to apply it to literature that represents experience as nastier than we know it to be. Finally, realism in literature is sometimes related to nominalism, *ie* the realist writer is he who represents individuals rather than types; in this sense, modern literary realism is the opposite of the realism of medieval philosophy.

Dominant 20th-century critiques of realism regard it as a naturalization of ideological positions, presenting them as if they were commonsense perceptions or views. Latterly it has been argued that the polarization of realism and modernism, and the rejection of realism, has been too absolute. More work is being done on the many varieties of realism, and work on reading and fantasy suggests that earlier views of how the classic realist text operated assumed too simplistic a model of reading practices and modes of reception.

▷ Stendhal.

Bib: Levine, G., *The Realistic Imagination*.

Reason

▷ Rationalism.

Rebellion, The Great

▷ Civil Wars.

Reception theory

This movement is associated pre-eminently with the German contemporary literary theorists Wolfgang Iser and Hans-Robert Jauss, and is often linked with reader-response criticism. Reception theory emphasizes the reader's consumption of the literary text over and above the question of the sum total of rhetorical devices which contribute to its structure as a piece of literature. The work of reception (*Rezeptionästhetik*) causes the reader constantly to rethink the canonical value of texts, since it involves noting the history of a text's reception as well as the current value which it may possess for the critic. Insofar as reception theory concerns itself with larger historical questions, it emphasizes histories of response which help to account for the reception of particular texts in the present. The approach to 'history' outlined here is pragmatic, and the emphasis is laid firmly on the matter of the interaction between text and reader and on the way cultural context is required to make sense of literature.

Recluse, The

▷ *Excursion, The*

***Recruiting Officer, The* (1706)**

Comedy by ▷ George Farquhar. Captain Plume recruits men to the army by courting the women with whom they are in love, and his sergeant, Kite, poses as an astrologer to lure men into service. Sylvia, the daughter of Justice Ballance, loves Plume but has promised not to marry him without her father's consent. She disguises herself as a man and contrives to get herself arrested for scandalous conduct. She appears before her father, who hands her over to Plume as a recruit, and eventually the two are married. In a secondary plot, Captain Brazen seeks to marry the wealthy Melinda but is deceived into almost marrying her maid, while Melinda herself marries Mr Worthy.

The play draws on Farquhar's own experiences as a recruiting officer at Lichfield and Shrewsbury in 1705–6, and there is some amusing ▷ satire on the law in the courtroom scenes. The play captures much of the spirit of the Restoration, but its ▷ realism, rural setting (unlike the urban settings of most Restoration comedies), and broader humour, give it the hallmark of its later period.

Recusancy
A term used under ▷ Elizabeth I for refusal, usually by Roman Catholics, to attend religious worship in the ▷ Church of England. The recusancy law continued to exist until the Toleration Act (1689), which permitted freedom of worship.

Red Cross Knight, The
The central figure of Book I of ▷ Edmund Spenser's ▷ *The Faerie Queene*. He represents Holiness, the ▷ Church of England and St George, whose red cross on a white ground is the national emblem of England. His adventures are connected with two women: Una, the true religion from which he is separated, and ▷ Duessa, the Roman Catholic Church which beguiles him. He is eventually united to Una with the assistance of Prince Arthur (▷ Arthur, King), who rescues him from the House of Pride.

***Red Pottage* (1899)**
A novel by ▷ Mary Cholmondeley. It centres on the lives of two women, Hester Gresley and Rachel West. Hester is a writer who lives with her bigoted clergyman brother and his narrow-minded wife. Her efforts at literary achievement are defeated when her brother burns the only copy of her novel, claiming it is immoral. The story of Hester's friend, Rachel, is a more conventional ▷ romance. The novel caused a minor sensation, being simultaneously denounced by clergymen and celebrated as a brilliant satire by journalists. Recent feminist readings have emphasized the strength of the relationship between Hester and Rachel, and praised the novel's defence of women's friendship.
Bib: Showalter, E., *A Literature of Their Own*.

Red Riding Hood, Little
A popular fairy tale, originally derived from the French version by ▷ Perrault, translated into English in 1729. The little girl is so called because of the red hood that she wears. A wolf meets her in the forest while she is on her way to her grandmother. Having discovered the purpose of her journey, he goes on ahead and eats the grandmother and takes her place in bed; when Red Riding Hood arrives he eats her as well. In modern versions, she and her grandmother are subsequently cut out of the wolf's stomach, alive and well, by her father, a woodcutter.

Redgrove, Peter (b 1932)
Poet and novelist. Redgrove is a prolific writer whose work straddles many forms – he has worked as a scientific journalist, and has written many novels, poems, plays (he won the Italia prize in 1981) and non-fiction (including *The Wise Wound* with poet Penelope Shuttle, with whom he lives in Cornwall). His poetic work was originally associated with that of the Group, the 'school' of post-Movement poets which included his contemporaries at Cambridge in the late 1950s, Ted Hughes and ▷ Sylvia Plath. Redgrove is now also a lay psychoanalyst. His poetry publications include: *The Collector* (1960); *The Force* (1966); *Sons of my Skin* (1975); *The Weddings at Nether Powers* (1979); *The Applebroadcast* (1981); *The Man Named East* (1985); *Poems 1954–1987* (1989); *Dressed As For a Tarot Pack* (1990); and *The Laborators* (1993). His fiction includes: *In the Country of the Skin* (1973); *The Beekeepers* (1980); *The Cyclopean Mistress: Selected Short Fiction* (1993); and, with Shuttle, *The Terrors of Dr Treviley* (1974). Both fiction and poetry are notable for powerful, dense images and a preoccupation with both physicality and spirituality.
Bib: Roberts, N., *The Lover, the Dreamer and the World: The Poetry of Peter Redgrove*.

Reeve, Clara (1729–1807)
Novelist, poet and critic who wrote the well-known ▷ Gothic novel ▷ *The Old English Baron* (1778). The daughter of a rector from near Ipswich, one of eight children, who started writing in the 1750s. She translated Barclay's romance, *Argenis*, as *The Phoenix* (1772), and in *The Progress of Romance* (1785) her characters comment on romance in its different historical and geographical incarnations – a process which involves a discussion of women writers, including Hortensius' opinion that the dead ▷ Aphra Behn is too risqué – 'I shall not disturb her, or her works' – but a woman speaks up for ▷ *Oroonoko*.

Other publications included *Original Poems on Several Occassions* (1769), *The Two Mentors* (1780), *The School For Widows* (1791) and *Plans of Education* (1792).

▷ Radcliffe, Ann; Haywood, Eliza.

Reeve's Tale, The
One of ▷ Chaucer's ▷ *Canterbury Tales*, it is told by the Reeve to 'quite' the Miller for the personal insult he perceives in the ▷ *Miller's Tale* about a cuckolded carpenter (the Reeve being a carpenter by trade). So the Reeve replies with a tale about a cuckolded Miller, set just outside Cambridge (whereas the *Miller's Tale* had been set in Oxford). This ▷ fabliau charts a battle of wits between

a thieving miller and two northern clerks, students at Cambridge University. Neither side displays much intellectual vigour but the clerks manage to sleep with the Miller's wife and daughter in order to avenge the theft of their corn. The Miller emerges as the loser in the contest, although the clerks only narrowly escape from a physical battle with the Miller through the chance, and mistaken, intervention of the Miller's wife. Several analogues to this tale are extant in French and Italian (one in the ▷ *Decameron*) but Chaucer's version is distinctive for its detailed development of the setting of the story and for the number of verbal puns built into the text. Chaucer is one of the earliest writers to present a conscious imitation of another English dialect: the clerks in this tale are characterized by their use of northern English forms.·

Referent
In the theory of language associated with Ferdinand de Saussure, the sign is divided into the signifier (the graphic mark or sound) and the signified (the mental concept attached to that sign or mark). The reference is the extra-linguistic reality to which the sign refers. The distinction between sign and referent is important because the sign is not created primarily by a naming process with reference to the real world, but by the internal dynamics of the structure of the language. As a result it is said to be 'arbitrary', or only attached to the referent by convention.

***Reflections on the Revolution in France* (1790)**
A political treatise by ▷ Edmund Burke. Burke attacks the principles on which the ▷ French Revolution was being conducted, denies that the English ▷ Glorious Revolution of 1688 was based on the same principles, and insists that a society is an organic growth like a tree, requiring the same kind of careful surgery in accordance with its principles of growth. The book was provoked by a ▷ sermon in praise of the French Revolution, preached by a Nonconformist minister, Dr Price; Burke is in effect not merely attacking the French revolutionaries, but the reverence for abstract, rational, scientific ▷ enlightenment which had increasingly transformed the 17th-century Puritans into the 18th-century rationalistic ▷ Dissenters or Nonconformists, and had found disciples among many others of the educated classes. The *Reflections* is a great work of conservative political philosophy, as well as a masterpiece of polemical prose. It represents the French Revolution as a turning-point in history: 'The age of chivalry is gone. That of sophisters, economists and calculators has succeeded; and the glory of Europe is extinguished for ever.'

Reform comedy
Comedy whose *dénouement* is dominated by a major character repenting some wrong-doing, and promising to reform. The type became prominent toward the end of the 17th century, especially after ▷ Colley Cibber's ▷ *Love's Last Shift* (1696), in which the central figure of Loveless repents, after leading a debauched life and abandoning his wife, leaving his debts unpaid. Attacks on the supposed immorality and profanity of the stage by ▷ Jeremy Collier and others encouraged the writing of more such plays. Other early exponents, besides Cibber, include ▷ Steele, ▷ Centlivre, Wilkinson, and ▷ Pix. ▷ Farquhar also incorporates some elements of the type in a few of his plays. Reform comedy became more prevalent during the 18th century, eventually overlapping with sentimental comedy, in which ▷ didactic considerations are paramount.
Bib: Loftis, J., *Comedy and Society from Congreve to Fielding*; Hume, R. D., *The Development of English Drama in the Seventeenth Century*.

Reformation
An important religious movement in the 16th century; its aim was to protest in a variety of ways against the conduct of the Catholic church, which had hitherto remained undivided. The outcome was division: the Roman Catholics remained dominant in the countries bordering on the western Mediterranean and in south Germany; the new ▷ Protestant churches became supreme in northern Europe. The causes of the movement were political (the rise of the new nation-state); moral (resentment at the low example set by many of the clergy); and doctrinal (disagreement, stimulated by the new critical spirit of the ▷ Renaissance, over points of doctrine hitherto imposed by the authority of the Church).

The reformation in England proceeded in three phases.

1 ▷ Henry VIII carried out the first in merely political terms. His desire to divorce Katharine of Aragon was merely a pretext; he himself sought complete control over the Church of England, and needed money; he resented the authority of the Pope in Rome and the internationalism of the monastic orders; he welcomed the opportunity to increase his wealth by confiscating their property. He declared himself Supreme Head of the Church of England by the ▷ Act of Supremacy, supported by Parliament and passed by it in 1533; he dissolved the monasteries in 1536–39. On the other hand, his ▷ Six Articles of 1539 tried to keep the Church fully Catholic on all points except that of papal sovereignty. As the support by Parliament showed, he had popular opinion behind him, at least in southern England; the English Church had long been restive against the sovereignty of the Pope, particularly when, in the 14th century, he had reigned from Avignon in France, the home of the national enemy.

2 The second phase, under his son

▷ Edward VI, went further and aroused more national disagreement. The clergy were permitted to marry, and the ▷ *Book of Common Prayer* included 42 articles of faith (later reduced to 39) which defined the doctrine of the Church of England in Protestant terms; there was extensive destruction of religious images in churches throughout the country. Henry's daughter ▷ Mary I undertook a complete reaction back to Catholicism, but her persecution of the Protestants and her subservience to her husband, Philip II of Spain, the most fanatical of the Catholic sovereigns, confirmed the country in a Protestant direction.

3 Henry's remaining daughter ▷ Elizabeth I contrived religious settlement that was a compromise between the reforms of her father and those of her brother. The intention was to be inclusive: Catholics were not to be driven out of the Church of England if she could help it, and she wanted to keep as many of her Protestant subjects within it as possible. The result, however, was disunion: Catholics could not subscribe to the Church of England after the Pope had excommunicated the Queen in 1571, and the more extreme Protestants were constantly pressing for further reforms, especially in the structure of church government (they mostly wanted the abolition of rule through bishops) and in the conduct of worship, which they wanted in full austerity. These ▷ Puritans, as they were called by their enemies, eventually established their own religious organizations, but not until after 1660. The vagueness of the Elizabethan settlement also gave rise to disagreement within the Church of England, and this has lasted until the present day: the High Church is the section which emphasizes the more Catholic interpretation of the settlement (*ie* more in keeping with Henry VIII's intentions), and the Low Church is the section which insists that the Church of England is essentially Protestant. This disagreement, however, has never disrupted the organization of the Church, which, under the headship of the sovereign, is still that of the Catholic church of medieval England.

The reformation in Scotland proceeded side by side with the Elizabethan phase in England, and helped to bring about a reconciliation of the two nations which had been hostile to each other for three centuries. The Scottish reformation, however, was extreme, under the leadership of ▷ John Knox, a disciple of the French reformer ▷ Calvin. The national Church of Scotland has remained Calvinist (▷ Presbyterian) to this day. Ireland remained Catholic, and in consequence suffered severe persecution by its English rulers in the 16th and 17th centuries. The only excuse for this tyranny was the real danger that Ireland might become a base for one of England's more powerful Catholic enemies – France or Spain.

Regency

In English history, the period 1811–20 when George, Prince of Wales, later George IV (1820–30), took the title of Prince Regent during the final illness of his father, George III (1760–1820). In British cultural history, the term is often applied to cover the first 20 years of the 19th century during which a certain style of taste in art and architecture prevailed. It was inspired by the taste of the first French Empire (▷ Napoleon I) which itself arose from French revolutionary cultivation of ancient Greece, especially the republic of Athens. Architecture was austerely classical (the 'Greek style'), and dress was similarly modelled on long, graceful lines suitable for men and women with slender figures.

In literature, the term covers the working life of the second generation of Romantic poets (▷ Byron, ▷ Shelley and ▷ Keats), the work of the essayists ▷ Lamb and ▷ Hazlitt, and that of the novelists ▷ Jane Austen and ▷ Walter Scott. The best work of the essentially Augustan poet ▷ Crabbe also comes into the Regency period. The word is applied, however, more to architecture, dress and furniture than to literature, the principal architects being John Nash (1752–1835) and John Soane (1753–1837), architect of the Bank of England.

Regional novel

A novel (often one of a series) which portrays the life of a specific region. For a novel to be termed regional, the specific characteristics of that region generally need to be a significant focus of attention in the text. Examples are the Potteries novels of ▷ Arnold Bennett (for example, *Anna of the Five Towns*, 1902) and the ▷ Wessex novels of ▷ Thomas Hardy (for example, *The Return of the Native*, 1878).

Register of language

A term used to indicate the type of language used in an utterance, for example something might be spoken or written in a formal or an informal register. Literary critics use the term when analyzing the style or tone of a piece of writing.

***Rehearsal, The* (1671)**

Burlesque play attributed to George ▷ Villiers, Duke of Buckingham, satirizing the heroic ▷ tragedies of the day. ▷ Bayes (a name implying that he is ▷ Poet Laureate) takes two friends, Johnson and Smith, to see a rehearsal of his latest play, which concerns the struggle for the Kingdom of Brentford. Most of the action consists of scenes from the absurd play within a play, punctuated by the two spectators' incredulous, sardonic or contemptuous questions and comments, and Bayes' ridiculous explanations to them and instructions to the players. Finally, the two observers, and then the actors themselves, steal off before the play is finished, and the piece ends with Bayes vowing to revenge himself on 'the Town' for its ill-use of him and his plays. ▷ D'Avenant and ▷ Dryden are thought to have been the main targets of the satire; the figure of Drawcansir has been viewed as a parody of Almanzor in ▷ Dryden's *The Conquest of Granada*. His name became symbolic of blustering, bragging characters.

***Rejected Addresses* (1812)**
When the ▷ Drury Lane theatre was rebuilt after having been destroyed by fire, the committee in charge, which included ▷ Lord Byron, advertised for an address to be recited at the reopening. None of those submitted was judged suitable, and Byron himself composed the lines which were actually delivered. *Rejected Addresses*, by ▷ James and ▷ Horace Smith, purports to include the unsuccessful submissions of all the major poets of the day. It contains often brilliant ▷ parodies of ▷ William Wordsworth, ▷ Samuel Taylor Coleridge, ▷ Robert Southey, ▷ Lord Byron, ▷ George Crabbe and ▷ Sir Walter Scott, among others.

***Relapse, The; Or, Virtue in Danger* (1696)**
Play by ▷ Sir John Vanbrugh, written as a sequel to, and gentle satire on, ▷ Colley Cibber's ▷ *Love's Last Shift* (1696), in which the central character stages a repentance which Vanbrugh found unbelievable. This did not prevent Cibber himself from acting the part of Lord Foppington in *The Relapse* with relish and to great acclaim. Loveless is now living quietly in the country with his faithful and virtuous wife Amanda, whom he had abandoned and then rejoined in *Love's Last Shift*. They return to the town for the winter season, whereupon he falls in love with Amanda's gayer cousin, Berinthia. Meanwhile, Worthy, an old flame of Amanda's, begins a new pursuit of her. Berinthia becomes an accomplice in his plan to seduce Amanda, so as to clear the path for her affair with Loveless. The affair is consummated, but Amanda summons her resources to resist Worthy's advances. A separate plot involves the impoverished Young Fashion's scheme to impersonate his older brother Lord Foppington, so as to marry the wealthy and lustful country girl, Miss Hoyden. At the end Worthy is shown unfulfilled and now in love with Amanda, while she achieves another uncertain reunion with her husband. The play's humour resides more in comic action than in witty dialogue, and there is a good deal of crude ▷ farce. Amanda's sobre virtue is somewhat at odds with the rest of the play, while the consequences of Loveless' intrigue with Berinthia are left unclear.

Relativism
A philosophical theory, according to which beliefs and truths are neither universal nor timeless, but dependent upon the assumptions and situation of the individual or group that maintains them. A moderate form of relativism holds that an objective world exists, but that it must always be seen and interpreted differently by different persons. A more extreme form, adopted by ▷ Nietzsche and sometimes termed perspectivism, holds that it is only perspectives which exist and that there is no objective reality, knowable or otherwise.

***Religio Laici* (1682)**
A poem in heroic ▷ couplets by ▷ John Dryden, defending the tenets of the ▷ Church of England against the extremes of ▷ Deism and Roman ▷ Catholicism. It is frequently compared with ▷ *The Hind and the Panther* which Dryden published five years later after becoming a Catholic.

***Religio Medici* (1635)**
(*The Religion of a Physician.*) A work of spiritual and autobiographical reflection by ▷ Sir Thomas Browne. It was written c 1635, and seems not to have been intended for publication but for circulation among the author's friends. After its publication without Browne's permission in 1642, however, an authorized text was issued in 1643 that was subsequently translated into Dutch, German, Latin and French. As a form of ▷ autobiography, the work presents the image of a relaxed, sceptical, philosophic and endlessly self-intrigued author. Informed by a desire to reconcile religious belief with the kind of scepticism associated with the ▷ 'New Science' of the mid-17th century, Browne's work became something of a best-seller. Stylistically, in its engaging enjoyment of digressive, curious and highly intellectualized speculation, the work can be compared to the poetry of ▷ John Donne or, later, ▷ Henry Vaughan. But it also forms part of the trend towards sceptical enquiry that was to be fostered by ▷ Thomas Hobbes.

Reliques
▷ Thomas Percy's *Reliques of Ancient English Poetry* (1765) contains a mixture of genuine and ancient ballads, edited to conform to the tastes of the later 18th century, and contemporary offerings in an archaic style. Although Percy's approach to editing lacked stringency, it is important to distinguish his important labour of retrieval from the element of fakery and

fantasy to be found in the ▷ Ossian poems of ▷ James Macpherson.

Renaissance in England, The
'Renaissance' (or 'Renascence') derives from Latin 'renascentia' = 'rebirth'. The word was first used by Italian scholars in the mid-16th century to express the rediscovery of ancient Roman and Greek culture, which was now studied for its own sake and not used merely to enhance the authority of the Church. Modern scholars are more inclined to use the term to express a great variety of interdependent changes which Europe underwent politically, economically and culturally between 1450 (although the starting-points were much earlier) and 1600. The religious outcome of these changes is expressed through the terms ▷ Reformation and ▷ Counter-Reformation, a sequence of events closely bound up with the Renaissance.

In England, the Renaissance is usually thought of as beginning with the accession of the House of ▷ Tudor to the throne in 1485. Politically, this marks the end of the period of civil war amongst the old feudal aristocracy (the Wars of the Roses) in the mid-15th century, and the establishment of something like a modern, efficient, centralized state; technically, the date is close to that of the introduction of printing into England – an invention without which the great cultural changes of the Renaissance could not have occurred. Culturally, the first important period in England was the reign of the second Tudor monarch, ▷ Henry VIII. This was the period of the English ▷ humanists ▷ More, ▷ Grocyn, ▷ Linacre and the poet ▷ Sir Thomas Wyatt.

Several distinctive features characterize the English Renaissance. The first is the lateness of its impact. Italian, French, German, Dutch and Spanish scholars had already worked on the ancient Greek and Latin writers, and had produced works of their own inspired by the classics; in consequence, English culture was revitalized not so much directly by the classics as by contemporary Europeans under the influence of the classics. ▷ Castiglione's *The Courtier*, ▷ Machiavelli's *The Prince*, ▷ Ariosto's *Orlando*, were as important in the English Renaissance as ▷ Virgil's ▷ *Aeneid* or the plays of ▷ Seneca, and it was characteristic that ▷ North translated ▷ Plutarch's *Lives* not from the original Greek but from a French version. Such an influx of foreign influences, both contemporary and ancient, might have overwhelmed the native English literary tradition but for two more distinctive features: England as an insular country followed a course of social and political history that was to a great extent independent of the course of history elsewhere in Europe, for example in the peculiarity of the English Reformation, and this assisted the country in preserving its cultural independence; and owing to the example of the works of the 14th-century poet ▷ Chaucer, the native literature was sufficiently vigorous and experienced in assimilating foreign influences without being subjected by them. A fourth characteristic of English Renaissance literature is that it is primarily artistic, rather than philosophical and scholarly, and a fifth is the coinciding of the Renaissance and the Reformation in England, in contrast to the rest of Europe, where the Reformation (or, in countries that remained Roman Catholic, the Counter- Reformation) succeeded the Renaissance.

The English Renaissance was largely literary, and achieved its finest expression in the so-called Elizabethan drama, which began to excel only in the last decade of the 16th century and reached its height in the first 15 years of the 17th; its finest exponents were ▷ Christopher Marlowe, ▷ Ben Jonson and ▷ William Shakespeare. Non-dramatic poetry was also extremely rich, and reached its peak in the same period in the work of ▷ Edmund Spenser, ▷ Philip Sidney, Shakespeare and ▷ John Donne, but it is typical of the lateness of the Renaissance in England that its most ambitious product, John Milton's ▷ epic ▷ *Paradise Lost*, was published as late as 1667. Native English prose shaped itself more slowly than poetry; More wrote his ▷ *Utopia* in Latin, which was the vehicle of some other writers, including ▷ Francis Bacon (in much of his work), owing to its advantages (for international circulation) over English at a time when the latter was little learned in other countries. Nonetheless English prose developed with vigour in native English writers such as ▷ Roger Ascham, Thomas North, ▷ Richard Hooker, in the English works of Francis Bacon, and in the translators of the ▷ Bible.
Bib: Braden, G. and Kerrigan, W., *The Idea of the Renaissance*.

Renault, Mary (1905–83)
Writer of popular historical novels. Renault was born and educated in England, working as a nurse during World War II, after which she emigrated with her life-long partner Julie Mullard to South Africa, where she was an active anti-apartheid campaigner until her death in Cape Town. Most of Renault's highly successful novels deal with the classical world, and, in their exploration of the transition from matriarchal social systems and religion to more modern partriarchy, they show the influence of ▷ Robert Graves' *The White Goddess*. All of Renault's novels are distinguished by the meticulous research and accuracy of historical details which underpin them. Her best-known books are the Alexander trilogy (which covers the life of Alexander the Great: *Fire from Heaven*, 1970, *The Persian Boy* 1972, and *Funeral Games* 1981), and two novels narrated by Theseus (*The King Must Die*, 1958, and *The Bull from the Sea*, 1962). Her other works include: *Purposes of Love* (1939); *The Charioteer* (1953); *The Last*

of the Wine (1956); *The Mask of Apollo* (1966); *The Praise Singer* (1978).
Bib: Dick, B. F., *The Hellenism of Mary Renault*; Wolf, P., *Mary Renault*.

Republic, Plato's
A philosophical dialogue by the Greek philosopher ▷ Plato. ▷ Socrates discusses with his friends the nature of justice, and the conversation leads to an outline of the ideal state. Public life must exhibit the highest virtues of private life, and justice is achieved if the classes work together to contribute to society the virtues in which each excels. Democracy (the rule of the people), oligarchy (the rule of a small powerful group), and timocracy (the rule of men of property) are in turn rejected, in favour of aristocracy – the rule of the best, trained by an exacting system of education. The aristocrat will seek wisdom, whereas the man of action seeks honour, and the merchant gratifies his appetites. Wisdom is a direct apprehension of the good conceived as a system of ideal forms; Book VII contains the famous parable of men sitting with their backs to these forms (the only substantial reality) watching the shadows on the wall of the cavern – *ie* phenomena apprehended by the senses – and supposing these shadows to be the only reality. Book X contains Plato's notorious rejection of poetry: poets must be expelled, though with honour, because they frustrate the pursuit of true wisdom by extolling the illusory phenomena of this world, and weaken the mind by stimulating wasteful sympathy with the misfortunes of men.

***Resolution and Independence* (1807)**
A poem by ▷ William Wordsworth, sometimes known as *The Leech-Gatherer*, composed in 1802, published in 1807, and subsequently revised. It uses a reduced version of ▷ Spenserian stanzas, rhyming *ababbcc*, the first six lines being pentameters and the last an Alexandrine (▷ metre). Travelling across the moor the poet finds that the freshness of nature fails to raise his spirits. He reflects on ▷ Thomas Chatterton and ▷ Robert Burns, and the 'despondency and madness' to which the poetic vocation seems to lead. In his reverie he encounters the portentous figure of 'a Man', 'in his extreme old age', standing 'Beside a pool bare to the eye of heaven'. At first he seems part of inanimate nature, like a 'huge stone', but when approached he explains that he earns 'an honest maintenance' by roaming from pond to pond collecting leeches (much in demand by doctors of the day for blood-letting). The man's equanimity dispels the poet's moodiness: 'I could have laughed myself to scorn to find/ In that decrepit Man so firm a mind'. Despite its elements of conventional piety, the poem is remarkable for its sense of awe and spiritual humility before a man who in social terms is of no account.

***Return of the Native, The* (1878)**
A novel by ▷ Thomas Hardy. Its setting is Egdon Heath, a wild tract of country in Dorset, in the south-west of England. The atmosphere of the Heath prevails over the whole book; as an environment, it repels some characters and absorbs others; those who are absorbed achieve a sombre integration with it but those who are repelled and rebel suffer disaster. The central character – 'the Native' – is Clym Yeobright, a Paris diamond merchant who has returned to the Heath in revulsion from the futility of his urban life and occupation. He intends to become a schoolmaster and marries the restless, self-seeking Eustacia Vye who is unfaithful to him; her affair with the unscrupulous Damon Wildeve leads to the death of both. Other charactes include Thomasin Yeobright whom Wildeve marries, to her misfortune and the grief of Diggory Venn, the travelling sheep-dyer (or 'reddleman') who represents a primitive sincerity and truthfulness, and Mrs Yeobright, Clym's mother, whom Eustacia estranges from her son. Clym becomes a furze-cutter on the Heath and eventually a travelling preacher. The novel is an example of Hardy's preoccupation with the relationship of characters with natural environment but it suffers from a weak conception of the central character, Clym.

Revels, Master of the
An official at the royal court in the 16th and 17th centuries; his function was responsibility for court entertainments, *eg* ▷ masques, cf. Philostrate in ▷ *A Midsummer Night's Dream*. This function later involved the ▷ censorship of plays and licensing of theatres in the London region.
Bib: Dutton, R., *Mastering the Revels: the Regulation and Censorship of English Renaissance Drama*.

Revenge tragedy
A kind of tragedy that was particularly popular during and just after the lifetime of ▷ Shakespeare, *ie* 1590–1620. The plot of such plays was commonly the murder by a person in power of a near relative, wife, or husband of the central character, who is then faced with the problem of how, or sometimes whether, to carry out revenge against a murderer who, because of his social importance, is out of reach of ordinary justice. The literary inspiration for this kind of play came from the plays of the Roman poet ▷ Seneca, whose *Ten Tragedies* were translated into English between 1559 and 1581. Seneca's plays would doubtless have been insufficient in themselves, however, to get going the great English series of revenge tragedies, if the theme had not been relevant

to English society. This society was in a stage midway between primitive lawlessness, in which justice is beyond the reach of the weak and unprivileged, and the modern state, in which justice is impartial and police are numerous and efficient. The tradition that revenge for an injury to a member of his or her family was a duty for the individual was still widely maintained; against it, the state maintained that revenge not carried out as due punishment through a court of law was a crime, and the Church taught that it was a sin. On the other hand, the law was unreliable, though not helpless, against the powerful and the powerfully protected, and in the face of the religious prohibition the revenger might consider himself to be the instrument of Divine Vengeance.

This state of conflict in the Elizabethan conscience made for different styles of revenge play. The first of those offering straightforward treatment of the theme was ▷ Thomas Kyd's ▷ *The Spanish Tragedy*; Shakespeare's early ▷ history plays ▷ *Henry VI, Parts I, II* and *III* and ▷ *Richard III* are revenge plays as well, and another early example by Shakespeare is his ▷ *Titus Andronicus*. Later examples: ▷ *The Revenger's Tragedy* by ▷ Cyril Tourneur (or perhaps ▷ Thomas Middleton) and Thomas Middleton's ▷ *Women Beware Women*, to mention only plays of distinction. Another style might be called the 'anti-revenge' drama, in which the hero is too enlightened to seek revenge – examples are Tourneur's ▷ *The Atheist's Tragedy* and ▷ Chapman's *Revenge of Bussy d' Ambois*, both about 1611. The finest of all tragedies of revenge, Shakespeare's ▷ *Hamlet*, is between the two styles, inasmuch as the hero both accepts the obligation to revenge and has to fight against his revulsion from it. A third style might rather be called the tragedy of retribution, inasmuch as a crime is avenged but the drama is not centred on a specific avenger; such plays include ▷ Webster's ▷ *The White Devil* and ▷ *The Duchess of Malfi* and Middleton's masterpiece ▷ *The Changeling*. Revenge and retribution are of course akin, and the importance of revenge tragedy, apart from its intrinsic interest, is that it is the starting-point for the development of some of Shakespeare's greatest tragic themes, *eg* his ▷ *Othello* and ▷ *Macbeth*, though these are not usually placed in the same category.

Bib: Mercer, P., *Hamlet and the Acting of Revenge*.

Revenger's Tragedy, The **(1607)**

A drama in ▷ blank verse attributed to ▷ Cyril Tourneur, although modern scholars incline increasingly to attribute it to ▷ Thomas Middleton. The scene is a dissolute ▷ Renaissance court in Italy. The sensual Duke has a vicious legitimate son, Lussurioso, by his first wife; the Duchess, his second wife, is in love with his illegitimate son, Spurio, who uses his bastardy as a pretext for general sensual rapacity; her own sons, Ambitioso and Supervacuo, are consumed with envy, and she herself is totally without moral restraint. This evil family is not so much a group of characters in the ordinary, realistic sense as an array of allegorical representations of the fleshly vices; their Italianate names suggest their ▷ allegories – Lussurioso = Luxury, Spurio = Falseness, etc. They are predatory on one another, and the downfall of the whole family is plotted by Vindice (= Revenger), whose betrothed has been poisoned by the Duke; he is assisted by his brother Hippolito. Disguised, Vindice enters the service of Lussorioso, and pretends to procure his own sister, Castiza (= Chastity) as mistress for his master; he finds to his horror that their own mother is prepared to sell her for the price of becoming a court lady. Vindice carries out his revenge on the Duke in a scene of great emblematic ferocity, and eventually contrives the bloodthirsty destruction of the whole family. He himself, however, is sent to his death by the Duke's virtuous successor: a Revenger, in however just a cause, is a criminal too dangerous to leave alive.

The violence of the action is redeemed from crudity by the energy, compression and conviction of the language, and by the way in which Tourneur fuses three modes of feeling into original art. One of these is the tradition of medieval allegory, which was becoming diluted and abstract in much Renaissance poetry, but which in this play keeps its old power of condensing emotion into powerful images. Tourneur uses the allegorical form to substantiate Puritan detestation of sensual vice, which was the evil extreme of the Renaissance liberation of the physical appetites. At the same time, both these vices and Vindice's vindictiveness are expressed with an energy that is itself a rich manifestation of Renaissance feeling. In uniting these disparate resources, the play is one of the masterpieces of ▷ Jacobean drama.

▷ Revenge tragedy.

Review, The

A periodical, written by ▷ Daniel Defoe and published three times weekly from 1704 to 1713. It expressed Defoe's opinion on current political events, and also on literature and manners. Defoe has been called the inventor of the leading article, a feature of modern newspapers.

Reviews and Periodicals

The English periodical press arose gradually from the controversial religious and political pamphleteering of the late 16th and 17th centuries. It became established as a recognized institution early in the 18th century, and it was also in the 18th century that the review, which expresses opinion, became distinguished from the newspaper, which gives priority to information on current events. The great age for the periodical press was, however, 1800–1914; this was the period when the quarterlies and the monthlies had their widest influence, and the weeklies their largest circulation proportionately to the size of the reading public. Since 1914, the influence of the quarterlies and monthlies has declined; the weeklies have remained important, but they have had to compete on the one side with the tendency of newspapers to include a large amount of material originally restricted to reviews, and on the other with the medium of broadcasting.

Revolution of 1688
▷ Glorious Revolution.

Reynard the Fox
The hero of a cycle of animal fables or ▷ bestiaries, begun about 1200, and very popular during the Middle Ages. The animals stand for basic characteristics of human nature, especially as it betrays itself in social relationships. Reynard is the cunning self-seeking individualist who betrays everyone and preys on society, always escaping justice. ▷ Caxton published an English translation of a Flemish version of the tales in 1481, but there is no native version of the cycle in English. The most famous work in which Reynard makes an appearance is Chaucer's ▷ *Nun's Priest's Tale*, one of the *Canterbury Tales*.

Reynolds, G. W. M. (George William MacArthur) (1814–79)
Novelist and journalist. A political radical, Chartist sympathizer and republican, Reynolds built up a substantial niche for himself in publishing and the newspaper business by writing specifically for the growing urban working-class readership: in 1846, he founded the penny weekly magazine *Reynolds' Miscellany* and in 1850 launched *Reynold's Weekly Newspaper* (which ran until 1967). One of the most successful purveyors of the so-called 'penny-dreadful' fiction (sensational stories issued in 1d serial form), he initiated the series *The Mysteries of London* (1846–50; based on Eugene Sue's *Les Mystères de Paris*, 1842–3), the Regency romance *The Mysteries of the Court of London* (1849–56), and various of the many ▷ Dickens plagiarisms and continuations that poured out in the 1840s, including *Pickwick Abroad* (1839), *Pickwick Married* (1841) and *Master Timothy's Book-Case* (1842).
Bib: James, L., *Fiction for the Working Man*; Sutherland, J., *The Longman Companion to Victorian Fiction*.

Reynolds, John Hamilton (1796–1852)
Recipient of some of ▷ John Keats' most important letters, and of the verse epistle *To J. H. Reynolds Esq.* He published several volumes of poetry, including *The Garden of Florence and Other Poems* (1821).

Reynolds, Sir Joshua (b1723–92)
One of the leading portrait painters of the 18th century, the great age of English portrait painting. He was the first President of the ▷ Royal Academy, and the author of *Discourses*, *ie* lectures, delivered to its students between 1760 and 1790, on the principles of art. The friend of ▷ Samuel Johnson, he was a founder-member of the Literary Club of which Johnson was the centre. Reynolds was strongly representative of 18th-century aristocratic ▷ taste, and in the opinion of ▷ William Blake, writing about 1808, 'This man was Hired to Depress Art'. However, his *Discourses* were admired by the greatest 19th-century English art critic, ▷ John Ruskin.

Rhetoric
Rhetoric in the medieval period was a formal skill of considerable importance. It was taken to mean the effective presentation of ideas with a set of rules or style, and was founded in the classical tradition of ▷ Aristotle and ▷ Cicero. It was taught in monastic schools as part of the *trivium*, Rhetoric, Logic and Grammar, which used as its basic text Geoffrey de Vinsauf's *Poetria Nova* (1200). Rhetoric not only formed patterns in which texts should be written, but it also governed how the works should be received and allocated them to particular categories, *eg* epic, debate or sermon. The system of rhetoric was paramount to the operation of literature in the medieval period.

Similarly, almost all of the practice or theory of writing in the ▷ Renaissance period was touched by what became known as the 'Art of Rhetoric'. Rhetorical theory formed an important part of the educational syllabus at the universities, and almost every major writer of the 16th and 17th centuries would have undergone some training in rhetoric. Rhetoric was learned first through reading the classical text-books on rhetoric, in particular the works of Quintilian (especially the *Institutio Oratore*) and Cicero. Secondly, practical rhetorical exercises were performed by the student in which a particular topic was debated. In these debates, the student was expected to be able to organize an argument according to set formulae, producing examples with which to sustain the analysis which themselves would be derived from a suitable store of words, images, fables and metaphors discovered in reading classical texts.

But the production of arguments was only one part of the rhetoricians' skills. Rhetoric also involved the classification of language – in particular the classification and analysis of ▷ figures of speech. Further, it was understood as an enabling tool by which ▷ discourse could be reproduced. In essence, therefore, it offered a system for producing both speech and writing. This system can be considered under five distinct parts: 1 'invention', which signifies the discovery of arguments applicable to a given case; 2 'arrangement' or 'disposition', which governed the ordering of the arguments to be used; 3 'style' on the actual choice of words and units of expression; 4 the important area of 'memory', which helped the rhetorician develop skills in recalling the order and substance of the argument being deployed; 5 'delivery', which was applicable mainly to spoken discourse but which governed such details as the appropriate facial expressions or gestures which might be used.

Whilst rhetoric was understood as a way of facilitating the classification of the various parts of an argument it was also a powerful tool in the analysis of discourse and it can thus be understood as a form of literary criticism. It was, however, in its abiding influence on stylistic forms that it was of most importance to the Renaissance writer. Numerous textbooks on rhetoric were published throughout the 16th century in England. Perhaps the most important were: Leonard Cox, *The Art or Craft of Rhetoric* (1624); Richard Sherry, *A Treatise of Schemes and Tropes* (1550); Thomas Wilson, *Art of Rhetoric* (1553); Henry Peacham, *The Garden of Eloquence* (1577); and Abraham Fraunce, *Arcadian Rhetoric* (1584). But many other texts were written with the art of rhetoric either governing the structure or informing the language. ▷ Sir Philip Sidney's ▷ *An Apologie for Poetrie*, for example, is structured according to rhetorical principles of organization.

Recent developments in critical theory have sought to re-emphasize rhetoric as a form of critical practice, particularly in relation to the *effects* that any verbal construction may have on those to whom it is addressed. In this respect rhetoric is closely associated with some of the larger issues which surface in relation to the theory of 'discourse'. The recent emphasis upon the *structure* of discourse draws attention away from language as a means of *classifying* to one of examining the way discourses are constructed in order to achieve certain effects. Here the emphasis would be on the different *ways* in which particular figures are presented in language, and what that presentation may involve. This form of rhetorical analysis has been undertaken by ▷ Jacques Derrida in volumes such as *Of Grammatology* (1974), by ▷ Paul De Man in his *Blindness and Insight* (1971), by ▷ Terry Eagleton in *Criticism and Ideology* (1976), and in a whole range of texts by ▷ Michel Foucault.

Rhyme

▷ Figures of speech.

Rhyme Royal

▷ Chaucer seems to have been the first English poet to use the rhyme royal form in his narrative poetry but it is conventionally named after its use in the ▷ *Kingis Quair*, attributed to ▷ James I of Scotland. In rhyme royal, seven decasyllabic lines form a stanza, rhyming ababbcc. Chaucer's use of this form suggests that it was used for narrative subjects of a sophisticated courtly or devotional kind (the ▷ *Second Nun's Tale* and ▷ *Troilus and Criseyde* are both composed in rhyme royal). It became an extremely popular form in the 15th century for courtly poetry.

The following example of rhyme royal is taken from *Troilus and Criseyde* and describes the moment Troilus first sees his lady:

Withinne the temple he wente hym forth pleyinge,
This Troilus, of every wight aboute,
On this lady, and now on that, lokynge,
Wher so she were of town or of withoute;
And upon cas bifel that thorugh a route
His eye percede, and so depe it wente,
Til on Criseyde it smot, and ther it stente.

Rhymer's Club, The

Founded in 1891 at the Cheshire Cheese tavern near Fleet Street, it consisted of a group of poets including ▷ W.B. Yeats, ▷ Ernest Dowson, ▷ Lionel Johnson, ▷ John Davidson, Ernest Rhys, Richard Le Gallienne (1866–1947), ▷ Arthur Symons, ▷ Aubrey Beardsley and occasionally ▷ Oscar Wilde. Discussions centred on their own lyrics, which they read aloud, and poetry in general. They issued two anthologies (1892, 1894) of verse which exhibited many of the characteristics of the ▷ Decadent and ▷ Aesthetic movements.

▷ Nineties' Poets.

Bib: Yeats, W.B., *Four Years: 1887–1891*; Hough, G., *The Last Romantics*.

Rhys, Jean (1894–1979)

Adopted name of novelist, born Jean Williams on the West Indian island of Dominica. Brought up speaking both English and the Dominican French dialect, she lived in Europe from the age of 16, moving between London, Vienna and Paris before finally settling in Devon. *The Left Bank* (1927), a series of sketches of Bohemian life in Paris, was followed by four novels which tell the stories of isolated, poor, victimized women, adrift in London or Paris, in a laconic, lucid style which combines the tragic and the absurd. These are: *Postures* (1928) (in the U.S.A. as *Quartet*; 1929); *After Leaving Mr Mackenzie* (1931); *Voyage in the Dark* (1934) and *Good Morning Midnight* (1939). After a considerable period of critical neglect, *Wide Sargasso Sea* (1966) reawakened widespread interest in her work, especially among ▷ feminists. It recounts the early life of the first Mrs Rochester from ▷ Charlotte Brontë's ▷ *Jane Eyre*, rendering the alienation and suffering of an isolated consciousness with

great power. Set mostly in the West Indies, it is richer in imagery and symbolism than her earlier work, combining lyricism and psychological insight with an exploration of political, racial and sexual oppression. She wrote two books of short stories: *Tigers Are Better Looking* (1968) and *Sleep It Off Lady* (1976). *Quartet* was made into a film (with a screenplay by ▷ Ruth Prawer Jhabvala) by the director James Ivory in 1981.
Bib: Stanley, T. F., *Jean Rhys: A Critical Study*; Carr, H., *Jean Rhys*; Howells, C. A., *Jean Rhys*.

Rich, Christopher (1657–1714)
Theatre manager. Rich assumed full control of the ▷ United Company in 1693, but his mismanagement contributed to the defection of the leading actors, including ▷ Thomas Betterton, ▷ Elizabeth Barry, and ▷ Anne Bracegirdle, in 1695. Even so, he succeeded in building up an able company in their place, including the young ▷ Colley Cibber, William Bullock, Joe Haines, ▷ John and ▷ Susannah Verbruggen, ▷ Anne Oldfield and ▷ William Penkethman, as well as bringing in foreign performers as attractions.

In 1701 Rich weathered an attempt to oust him from control of ▷ Drury Lane, but he continued to invite conflict with both actors and dramatists, and in 1709 he was forced to close Drury Lane on an order from the Lord Chamberlain, after his attempt to deny his actors their full profits from benefit performances. Rich was not allowed to form a new company until 1714, but he died just six weeks before the scheduled opening.
Bib: Highfill, P. H. Jr., Burnim, K. A. and Langhans, E. A. (eds.), *A Biographical Dictionary of Actors, Actresses, Musicians, Dancers, Managers, and Other Stage Personnel in London 1660–1800*.

Rich, John (1692–1761)
Actor, manager, dancer, dramatist, son of ▷ Christopher Rich. John inherited the largest share of the theatrical patent owned by his father, and took over the refurbished ▷ Lincoln's Inn Fields Theatre opened by his father before his death in 1714. He soon began acting and dancing at the theatre, and built up its repertory of dance, variety, and pantomime programmes, for whose growing popularity he was largely responsible.

During the following years he gained a mixed reputation for, on the one hand, allegedly degrading the stage, and on the other hand, providing popular entertainment by talented performers in settings of great magnificence. He was also complimented for reviving the best of the old plays, and encouraging new authors. It was under his auspices that ▷ John Gay's ▷ *The Beggar's Opera* was first staged in 1728, making (according to a well-known quotation) 'Gay rich and Rich gay'. The profits from *The Beggar's Opera* helped finance a new theatre in Covent Garden on the site of the present Royal Opera House (▷ Covent Garden Theatres), which opened in 1732 with a cast headed by ▷ James Quin. A fierce rivalry developed between Covent Garden and ▷ Drury Lane under ▷ Garrick's management, highlighted in 1750–51, when the ▷ theatres staged *Romeo and Juliet* simultaneously. For decades after his death, theatres continued to honour Rich in tributes on stage, or by borrowing devices from his shows.
Bib: Highfill, P. H. Jr., Burnim, K. A. and Langhans, E. A. (eds.), *A Biographical Dictionary of Actors, Actresses, Musicians, Dancers, Managers, and Other Stage Personnel in London 1660–1800*.

Richard I Coeur de Lion (Lionheart) (1189–99)
King of England. He spent most of his reign out of the country, engaged in various wars, especially the third ▷ Crusade. His exploits made him into a figure of romance and legend, and as such he appears in two very popular novels by ▷ Walter Scott: ▷ *Ivanhoe* and ▷ *The Talisman* (1825). He belonged to the House of ▷ Plantagenet (Anjou) and was the son of his predecessor ▷ Henry II and the brother of his successor, ▷ John.

Richard II (1377–99)
King of England, and last of the direct line in the ▷ House of Plantagenet (Anjou). He was the son of the ▷ Black Prince and the grandson of his predecessor, ▷ Edward III. His neglect of the war against France, his youthfulness (he came to the throne at the age of 11), and his capricious, inconsistent character all helped to make his reign appear to be a period of disorder; the throne was eventually usurped by his cousin, Henry Bolingbroke, who became first king of the House of Lancaster as ▷ Henry IV.

Richard II, King
An historical drama in ▷ blank verse by ▷ Shakespeare, based on the Chronicles of ▷ Holinshed. First performed in 1595, and published in a first ▷ quarto in 1597, it is the first of the second tetralogy of ▷ history plays by Shakespeare, the other three being ▷ *Henry IV, Parts I* and *II* and ▷ *Henry V*.

The theme of all four is kingship; ▷ Richard II is treated as a king whose sacred claim to the throne is beyond doubt, but is tragically unaccompanied by any capacity to rule. The leading story is about his relationship with his cousin, Henry Bolingbroke (▷ Henry IV); he drives Henry (not altogether without justification) into exile, and then quite unlawfully confiscates Henry's land. Henry returns to England to defend his right, and receives so much support that he is driven to making himself king. Usurpers, however, were considered to be opposing God, since kings held the throne by God's authority, and so Henry does his best to persuade Richard to abdicate publicly. Richard does so, but he skilfully makes it clear to all the witnesses that his abdication is involuntary (IV. i), so that the public abdication only emphasizes, instead of relieves, Henry's guilt. Concerned as it is with the ritualistic aspect of monarchy – the ceremonies that are the signs of the sacredness of the office – the whole play has been observed by critics to have a ritualistic style in the formal patterning of much of the verse and the pageant-like ceremony of a number of the important scenes. Richard is imprisoned in the Tower, and is later assassinated; thus the effect of criminality in Henry's action in seizing the throne is confirmed.

Richard III **(?1593)**
An historical drama in ▷ blank verse by ▷ Shakespeare based on ▷ Holinshed's Chronicles, and the last of Shakespeare's first historical tetralogy, the other plays being the three parts of ▷ *Henry VI*. The ▷ Henry VI plays are about the Wars of the Roses, and the accumulation of hatred, vengefulness and crime that those wars brought about. *Richard III* opens in the reign of Edward IV, Richard's brother, and shows the attempts of the king to induce his nobles to be reconciled. Fear and war-weariness make them comply, but Richard is still filled with ambition and cold-blooded cruelty. In spite of his appearance – he is a hunchback and has a withered arm – he has a magnetic personality and manages to win friends to help him in his conspiracies. By consistent treachery and ruthlessness he acquires the throne, but is shortly after defeated and killed by Henry Tudor (▷ Henry VII), who is shown in the play to have right and divine aid on his side. Though totally evil, Richard is presented as a character of energy and wit, the source of much sardonic comedy. Dramatically he is in the tradition of both ▷ Machiavelli's *The Prince* – a treatise of evil for Englishmen of Shakespeare's day – and of Herod in the medieval mystery plays. The play is the masterpiece of the earliest group of Shakespeare's plays, *ie* those probably written before 1594.
▷ History plays.

Richard III (1483–85)
Last King of England in the House of York, which seized the throne from the ▷ House of Lancaster in 1461. The first of the short line was ▷ Edward IV (1461–83), Richard's brother; he was succeeded by his son, the boy king ▷ Edward VI, whose throne Richard usurped. He was himself defeated and killed at the Battle of Bosworth (1485) by Henry Tudor, who succeeded as ▷ Henry VII the first sovereign of the ▷ Tudor line. It was very much in the Tudor interest to blacken the character of Richard III, and 16th-century historians (Polydore Vergil, ▷ Thomas More, ▷ Holinshed) depict him as satanically evil. Modern historians have found it difficult to discover whether this account is just, and there have been some attempts to rehabilitate his character. One of the chief charges against him is the murder of his two nephews Edward V and Richard of York, the 'princes in the Tower'. That they were murdered is almost certain, but there is no proof that Richard was guilty.
▷ Histories and Chronicles.

Richard Feverel
▷ *Ordeal of Richard Feverel, The.*

Richards, Alun (b 1929)
Novelist, short story writer and playwright. Alun Richards was born in Pontypridd, Glamorgan, and was educated at Pontypridd Grammar School and then at Gwent College of Education and University College, Swansea. Drawing on his experiences as a probation officer, hospital patient for two years, sailor, and teacher for ten years in Cardiff before moving to Swansea in 1967 to devote his life to full-time writing, he rejects the portrayal of a romanticized Welsh past of myth and anecdote and is concerned instead with the modern Wales of rugby, beauty queens, television, the language question and the industrial and spiritual decline in the South Wales Valleys. In an updated view of Valleys society, Alun Richards illumines social tensions, especially among the migratory professional classes, in subtle regional nuances between the Valleys and Cardiff, and also between Cardiff and London, in a delineation that is lively, sharply observed, deeply understanding and extremely funny. His novels are: *The Elephant You Gave Me* (1963); *The Home Patch* (1966); *A Woman of Experience* (1969); *Home to an Empty House* (1973); *Ennal's Point* (1977); and *Barque Whisper* (1979). His collections of short stories are: *Dai Country* (1974); and *The Former Miss Merthyr Tydfil* (1976); and he has edited *The New Penguin Book of Welsh Short Stories* (1993) as well as writing about Welsh rugby in *A Touch of Glory* (1980) and in his memoir of Carwyn James in 1984. His theatre plays, performed in England, include *The Big Breaker*, *The Victuallers' Ball* and *The Snowdropper*, and were later published in 1973 as *Plays for Players*, but he became well-known for radio and television drama, for which he has adapted work by H. G. Wells, Somerset Maugham, Georges Simenon and Alun Lewis, as well as providing many of the scripts for the popular sea story series *The Onedin Line*.
Bib: Stephens, M. (Ed.), *The Oxford Companion to the Literature of Wales*; Jones, G. and Rowlands, J., *Profiles*.

Richards, I. A. (1893–1979)
Critic. His approach to poetry was philosophic, linguistic and psychological. One of his

important insights was that we are inevitably influenced by some kind of 'poetry', even if it is only that of bad films and magazine covers, or advertisements. In *Principles of Literary Criticism* (1924) and *Science and Poetry* (1926) he discusses what kind of truth is the subject-matter of poetry, the place of poetry in the context of the rest of life, and what is the nature of critical judgements of poetry. He worked to his conclusion on Benthamite (▷ Utilitarian) lines, of asking what is 'the use' of poetry, but his conclusion was not far from that of ▷ Matthew Arnold, that poetry's function in the modern world is that formerly provided by religion – to provide a 'touchstone' of value, and hence, if only indirectly, a guide to living (see Arnold's 'Study of Poetry', in ▷ *Essays in Criticism* 2nd Series, 1888). This view resembles the judgements of other writers of the 1920s and 30s, such as ▷ Pound, ▷ Wyndham Lewis, ▷ Eliot, ▷ Leavis, though each of them arrives at his judgement by a different approach. Richards' *Practical Criticism* (1929) is a teaching manual for the study of poetry with the aim of training students to judge poems presented anonymously, without being influenced by the author's reputation; its ideas have been extensively followed in English and American schools and universities. Much of his later work has been purely linguistic, *eg Basic English and its Uses* (1943). Other works: *The Meaning of Meaning* (with Ogden, 1923); *Coleridge on Imagination* (1934); *The Philosophy of Rhetoric* (1936); *Speculative Instruments* (1955); *Goodbye Earth and other poems* (1959); *The Screens* (1961).

▷ New Criticism.

Bib: Hyman, S., *The Armed Vision*.

Richardson, Dorothy (1873–1957)
Novelist. Born in Abingdon, Berkshire, she worked as a governess from the age of 17, before moving to London where she became an intimate of ▷ H. G. Wells and part of a circle of socialists and intellectuals. She took up journalism, and for the rest of her life earned a meagre living by this means, while dedicating herself to her long novel, *Pilgrimage*, which consists of the following volumes: *Pointed Roofs* (1915); *Backwater* (1916); *Honeycomb* (1917); *The Tunnel* (1919); *Interim* (1919); *Deadlock* (1921); *Revolving Lights* (1923); *The Trap* (1925); *Oberland* (1927); *Dawn's Left Hand* (1931); *Clear Horizon* (1935); *Dimple Hill* (1938); *March Moonlight* (1967). It is a semi-autobiographical work, recounting the life of the heroine, Miriam Henderson, through concentration on her continuous subjective experience of the present moment. Richardson, together with ▷ Virginia Woolf and ▷ James Joyce, was responsible for the development of the ▷ stream of consciousness technique (though she disliked this term) which was an important aspect of the ▷ modernist revolution in narrative.

Bib: Watts, C., *Dorothy Richardson*; Radford, J., *Dorothy Richardson*.

Richardson, Henry Handel (1870–1946)
Pseudonym of Australian novelist and short-story writer Ethel Florence Lindesay Richardson Robertson. She studied music in Leipzig from 1887–90, lived in Strasbourg 1895–1903, and in England from 1903. Her trilogy *The Fortunes of Richard Mahony* uses elements of her father's life, and is the sombre tale of an emigrant doctor's rise to riches and unexpected loss of fortune. It consists of *Australia Felix* (1917); *The Way Home* (1925); *Ultima Thule* (1929). Her work shows the influence of ▷ Goethe and the German Romantic tradition. Her other novels are: *Maurice Guest* (1908); *The Getting of Wisdom* (1910); *The Young Cosima* (1939). Story collections include: *The End of Childhood and Other Stories* (1934). The autobiographical *Myself When Young* was published posthumously in 1948.

Bib: Mcleod, K., *Henry Handel Richardson: A Critical Study*.

Richardson, Samuel (1689–1761)
Novelist. Richardson was the son of a furniture-maker, born near Derby, though most of his childhood was spent in London as the family returned to live there. Little is known of his education, though by the age of 13 he is known to have written love letters on behalf of his friends, an activity relevant for his later choice of the ▷ epistolary genre.

In 1706 Richardson was apprenticed to a printer, and in 1715 became a freeman of the ▷ Stationers' Company. In 1721 he began his own business, which proved successful for the rest of his life. In the same year he married the daughter of his former master. His wife died ten years later, and in the early 1730s he suffered the deaths of all the six children born to the marriage.

In 1733 he remarried, again to the daughter of a colleague, and four of their daughters survived. In the same year he published *The Apprentice's Vade Mecum*, a conduct guide to moral behaviour. In 1739 his own, deliberately moral, version of *Aesop's Fables* appeared.

The moral intention of his early works is evident in his fiction, though the creations of his imagination frequently escape any strict schemata. ▷ *Pamela*, begun in the same year as *Aesop's Fables* appeared, started as a series of conduct guides or 'Familiar Letters', which his friends encouraged him to write. Richardson's professional life, meanwhile, was proving rewarding. In 1723 he had begun to print *The True Briton*, an influential Tory 9▷ Whig and Tory) journal, and in 1733 the House of Commons was using his presses. In 1742 he gained a lucrative contract as printer of the ▷ Parliamentary Journals.

His social life was proving equally enjoyable. He particularly relished the company of young women, whom he referred to as his 'honorary daughters', and while writing ▷ *Clarissa* (probably begun in 1744) he frequently asked them for their comments and teased them with speculations about the fate of his heroine. The first two volumes appeared in 1747 and were widely acclaimed; five more followed in 1748. The novel was praised, but readers were uneasy about its sexual elements, and its popularity proved less than that of *Pamela*.

About 1750 Richardson embarked on a new project, which was to be centred on the 'good man'. In 1752 ▷ Samuel Johnson read the draft manuscript of the work, ▷ *The History of Sir Charles Grandison*, and the novel appeared in seven volumes in 1753–4. Again, there was some doubt about the morality of the book, an ironic fate for a writer with Richardson's intentions.

In 1755 Richardson published a volume of selections from his three novels, in a form which he considered contained the essence of his writing; he was constantly concerned about the length of his fictions, and continually worked on revisions. His novels develop the ▷ epistolary style to a great degree of psychological subtlety, and he has long been regarded as one of the chief founders of the English novel.

Bib: Eaves, T. C. D. and Kimpel, B. D., *Samuel Richardson*; Kinkead-Weekes, M., *Samuel Richardson, Dramatic Novels*; Flynn, C. H., *Samuel Richardson, A Man of Letters*.

Ridley, Nicholas (?1500–55)
One of the leading religious reformers in the reign of ▷ Henry VIII and, with ▷ Cranmer and ▷ Latimer, one of the three principal martyrs in 1555 under the Roman Catholic reaction of ▷ Mary I. He helped Cranmer compile *The Book of Common Prayer* of 1549 and 1552, and thus contributed to one of the first English prose masterpieces. He became Bishop of London in 1549.

Ridolfi plot (1570)
Organized by the Italian Roberto di Ridolfi against ▷ Elizabeth I. He planned to marry the Catholic ▷ Mary Queen of Scots to the Duke of Norfolk and place her on the throne of England with Spanish help. The plot was discovered by Elizabeth's spies, but Ridolfi was himself in safety in Paris.

Ridotto
A kind of public social gathering, with dancing and music, introduced into England in 1722, and very popular in the 18th century.

***Rights of Man, The* (1791–2)**
▷ Thomas Paine's *The Rights of Man* is a political treatise in two parts, first published in 1791 and 1792 respectively. Part I is essentially a reaction to ▷ Edmund Burke's ▷ *Reflections on the Revolution in France* of 1790. Burke is attacked for indulging in dramatic writing at the expense of truth: 'Mr Burke should recollect that he is writing history, and not *plays*.' Part II makes a comparison between the new constitutions of France and America, and the hidebound British attachment to hereditary succession. Paine's progressive and egalitarian proposals were labelled seditious, and Paine, who had already escaped to France with the assistance of ▷ William Blake, was convicted of treason and sentenced to banishment.

Riley, Denise (b 1948)
Poet and theorist. Denise Riley was active in the nascent women's liberation movement of the late 1960s and early 1970s. She collaborated with the poet Wendy Mulford on the collection *No Fee* (1978): in the previous year, Mulford's avant-garde press, Street Editions, had published her collection of poetry, *Marxism for Infants*. Since that time Riley has made an important contribution to literary theory, feminism and poetry, often by allowing these categories to interfuse. For example, *War in the Nursery* (1983) was followed in 1985 by the Virago collection of poems *Dry Air*. The 1987 feminist analysis, *Am I That Name?*, was succeeded by her most wide-ranging and intense sequence of poems, *Mop Mop Georgette* (1994). A lecturer at Goldsmith's College, London, Riley is active in a variety of fields including creative and editorial writing.

Riley, Joan (b 1958)
Novelist. Born in Jamaica, and educated at the universities of Sussex and London, she teaches black history and culture and works for a drugs advisory agency. Her novels are: *The Unbelonging* (1985); *Waiting in the Twilight* (1987); *Romance* (1988). Her work is concerned with the hardships, and the search for a sense of meaning and identity, of people born in Jamaica and living in Britain.

▷ Post-colonial literature.

Rime of the Ancient Mariner, The
▷ *Ancient Mariner, The Rime of the*

Risorgimento
Italian for 'resurrection'. The name given to the movement for the unification of Italy in the mid-19th century, led by Victor Emmanuel, king of Sardinia, his Prime Minister Cavour, the agitator Mazzini, and the soldier Garibaldi. In 1847 Cavour founded a newspaper called 'Risorgimento'. The movement appealed to English sympathies, which were strongly liberal at that time; references to it are common in mid-19th-century literature.

Ritchie, Lady (Anne Thackeray) (1837–1919)
Novelist, ▷ short story writer and essayist, the daughter of ▷ William Makepeace Thackeray and aunt of Virginia Woolf (1882–1941). Almost

all the literary celebrities of the day were known to the family, including ▷ Dickens, ▷ Tennyson, ▷ Robert and ▷ Elizabeth (Barrett) Browning, ▷ Charlotte Brontë and ▷ George Eliot. Ritchie wrote five novels: *The Story of Elizabeth* (1863); *The Village on the Cliff* (1867); *Old Kensington* (1873); *Miss Angel* (1875) and *Mrs Dymond* (1885). Her non-fiction includes *Toilers and Spinsters* (1874), which called attention to the plight of single, unemployed women, and *A Book of Sibyls* (1883), a collection of essays on women writers. Other works include *Records of Tennyson, Ruskin and Browning* (1892), and *Alfred Tennyson and his Friends* (1893). The *Letters of Anne Thackeray Ritchie* was published in 1924. The character of Mrs Hilbery in Virginia Woolf's *Night and Day* is based on Ritchie, and she was well-known to the Bloomsbury Group.
Bib: Gerin, W., *Life*; Woolf, V., 'The enchanted organ: Anne Thackeray Ritchie' in *Collected Essays*, Vol. 4.

Ritson, Joseph (1752–1803)
Editor and literary scholar. Joseph Ritson was an idiosyncratic scholar who suffered from ill health and who eventually went mad. He produced, however, important editions of early English poetry, including *A Select Collection of English Songs* (1783) and *Ancient English Metrical Romances* (1802). His demanding editorial standards led him to dismiss the works of ▷ Warton and ▷ Percy, but he remained a close and admiring friend of ▷ Walter Scott.
Bib: Johnston, A., *In His Enchanted Ground*.

***Rivals, The* (1775)**
A prose comedy by ▷ Richard Brinsley Sheridan. It is set in the fashionable city of Bath, and the plot concerns parents and guardians at cross purposes with their children. The central situation is that the young and ▷ sentimental Lydia Languish, a great novel reader, prefers the idea of marrying a young, penniless officer to the possibility of a rich young heir as a husband. Captain Absolute is such an heir and genuinely in love with her, but to win her affections he disguises himself as the penniless Ensign Beverley. His father, Sir Anthony Absolute, a rich baronet, is determined to make an unromantic marriage of convenience between his son and Lydia, but the Captain dare not disclose his disguise and so seems to be disobeying his father's wishes. Mrs Malaprop, Lydia's guardian, is equally anxious for the worldly match and disapproves of Beverley, but at the same time she is making love by letter to the aggressive Irishman, Sir Lucius O'Trigger, who supposes that the letters come from Lydia, and is one of her suitors. An additional complication is that the so-called Beverley and Sir Lucius have as another rival an absurd young country squire, Bob Acres. A sub-plot is another love affair between Julia Melville and the morbidly jealous Faulkland.

Sheridan's comedies – of which *The Rivals* is the first – are, like those of ▷ Goldsmith at about the same time, above all a reaction against the sentimental tradition, and recall the wit and theatrical deftness of Restoration drama without its sexual explicitness.

***Roaring Girl, The, or Moll Cut-Purse* (1606)**
A buoyant and big-hearted comedy of gender ambiguity by ▷ Thomas Middleton, structured around the benevolent figure of Moll Cutpurse whose function in the play it is to smooth the course of true love. She is described by her detractors as a 'woman more than man, / Man more than woman,' and becomes the play's moral centre of reference. More than anything Middleton's Moll Cutpurse seems to be conceived of as a ▷ Jacobean ▷ citizen comedy version of ▷ Shakespeare's ▷ Rosalind from ▷ *As You Like It*.

***Rob Roy* (1817)**
A novel by ▷ Sir Walter Scott, giving a picture of Scotland just before the first ▷ Jacobite rebellion of 1715. The plot concerns the rivalry in love of the cousins Francis and Rashleigh Osbaldistone for Diana Vernon. Rashleigh, the villain, is involved in Jacobite intrigue. Their adventures are interwoven with the fortunes of Rob Roy, a historical character whom Scott romanticizes. He is the chief of the Macgregor Clan in the Scottish Highlands, and a convicted outlaw who lives by plunder. In the novel he acts on the side of the hero, Francis, at Diana's earnest appeal. As usual in Scott's novels, the notable parts are those which concern Scottish common life, and such characters as Bailie Nicol Jarvie and Francis' servant Andrew Fairservice.

Robert de Boron
French writer, working in the late 12th/early 13th century, who substantially developed the early history of the ▷ Grail (in his *Roman de Graal/Joseph d'Arimathie*), giving it a Christian interpretation as the vessel used by Christ at the Last Supper and by Joseph of Arimathea to collect Christ's blood at the Crucifixion. He thus provided the means whereby Arthurian history could be seen as another key chapter in Christian history. Robert seems to have taken the Grail story further in his narratives of *Merlin* (of which only a fragment survives) and *Perceval*, which is not extant. Both verse narratives stimulated further reworkings and continuation. The 13th-century continuation of *Merlin* (known as the *Suite de Merlin*) provides the basis for ▷ Malory's version of the foundation of Arthur's court. The prose reworkings of Robert's work (the prose *Joseph*, the prose *Merlin*, and the so-called *Didot*

Perceval) were used substantially in the later composition of the ▷ Vulgate Cycle.

Roberts, Emma (c 1793–1840)
Poet and travel writer. Roberts' most interesting writing focuses on India where she travelled for three years after moving there with her married sister in 1828. On her return to London, she published her first book of poems, *Oriental Scenes, Sketches and Tales* (1832) and dedicated it to ▷ L.E.L. with whom she had lived before travelling abroad. A prose work, *Scenes and Characteristics of Hindostan, with Sketches of Anglo-Indian Society* (1835), followed, and in both works Roberts shows herself to be an acute and impartial observer of injustice and cruelty. She attacked both Indian and English bigotry and intolerance, especially where women were the victims. In 1839 she returned to India and began editing *The Bombay United Service Gazette*. Two further travel books on India followed before her death in 1840.
▷ Orientalism; Travel literature.

Roberts, Michèle (b 1949)
Poet, short-story writer and novelist. Roberts is a prolific writer, has appeared widely on television, radio and in anthologies, and regularly gives readings of her work. She was very influential on the development and recognition of contemporary poetry in her capacity as poetry editor of the London listings magazine *City Limits*. Her recent publications include *The Mirror of the Mother* (1986), a volume of poetry, *The Book of Mrs Noah* (1987) and *In the Red Kitchen* (1990).

Robertson, T. W. (1820–71)
Dramatist. Plays include *Society* (1865), *Ours* (1866), *Caste* (1868). *M. P.* (1870). He is memorable chiefly for restoring to the drama some degree of relevance to contemporary social life at a time when contemporary plays had very little serious interest. His best-known play is the social comedy *Caste*.
Bib: Nicoll, A., in *A History of Late Nineteenth Century Drama* 1850–1900; Rowell. G., *The Victorian Theatre*.

Robespierre, Isidore Maximilien de (1758–94)
A leader of the extremist ▷ Jacobins during the ▷ French Revolution. He exercised virtual dictatorship from July 1793 to July 1794, during which he conducted the Reign of Terror and tried to establish the worship of the deistic Supreme Being in opposition to Catholicism on the one side and atheism on the other. His reputation for fanatical integrity caused him to be known as the Incorruptible. Represented in Anthony Trollope's *La Vendée* (1850), where considerable emphasis is placed on his integrity.
▷ Deism.

Robins, Elizabeth (1862–1952)
Actress and novelist whose play *Votes for Women* was performed at the Court Theatre in 1907. In this she introduces an innovatory crowd scene of a suffragette rally at Trafalgar Square; the rest of the play is written within the conventions of society drama. She worked mainly in London and belonged to the group of Ibsenites encouraging the development of an English drama of ideas. She performed in the first productions of several of ▷ Ibsen's plays during the 1890s, including *Pillars of Society* (1889). *A Doll's House* and *Hedda Gabler* (both 1891).
▷ Women's suffrage.
Bib: Robins, E., *Ibsen and the Actress*; Robins, E., *Both Sides of the Curtain*.

***Robinson Crusoe, The Life and Strange Surprising Adventures of* (1719)**
A novel by ▷ Daniel Defoe. The first part was based on the experiences of a sailor, ▷ Alexander Selkirk, who went ashore on the uninhabited island of Juan Fernandez in 1704, and remained there until he was rescued in 1709. Crusoe runs away to sea (as Selkirk had done) and after a number of adventures is wrecked on an uninhabited island, where he remains for 20 years. Defoe describes the industrious and methodical way in which he builds up a life for himself, how he is endangered by the periodic visits of a race of cannibals, how he tames one of them into an ideal servant, Man Friday. The island is eventually visited by a ship in the hands of mutinous sailors; he subdues the mutineers and rescues the officers, who take him back to England, leaving the repentant mutineers behind as a colony, together with some Spaniards whom he had previously rescued from the cannibals.

In *The Farther Adventures of Robinson Crusoe*, published in the same year, Crusoe revisits the colony and relates its fortunes; he also travels elsewhere, visits China, and returns to England across Siberia and Russia. The third part, *The Serious Reflections of Robinson Crusoe* (1720), consists of moral essays in which Defoe represents the book as an ▷ allegory of his own life. This was partly a defence against the disapproval of his fellow Puritans who regarded fiction as hardly distinguishable from lies; on the other hand, Defoe's tale is certainly an image of the loneliness and arduousness of the life of individual economic enterprise which was becoming increasingly typical of society; Crusoe is made to say that he has been more lonely since his return to London than he ever was on his island.

Modern critics have noticed how Crusoe sees human beings merely in terms of their economic virtues. The book has always been praised for its detailed verisimilitude, which caused it to be received at first as an authentic account; the descriptions are almost entirely in terms of what the philosopher ▷ John Locke had distinguished as the objectively discernible 'primary qualities' (▷ *Essay concerning human understanding*) as opposed to the subjectively experienced 'secondary qualities' (colour, beauty, etc.) which it is difficult to verify. The style of the writing is extremely plain, in keeping with the principles that Thomas Sprat had laid down for the ▷ Royal Society in 1667 (*History of the Royal Society*): 'the language of Artisans, Countrymen, and Merchants'. That Crusoe appears much less religious than Defoe intends is also often remarked; on the other hand, if there is a principle of unity in the long, episodic narrative, it is the function of God as the basic Providence, subjecting chaos so that man may use his constructive virtues for the building of an orderly world.

Robinson, Henry Crabb (1775–1867)
Diarist. Robinson studied at Jena University where he met ▷ Goethe and Schiller. He was one of the first foreign ▷ newspaper correspondents, becoming foreign editor of *The Times*. In later life he practised as a barrister, and helped found the Athenaeum Club and University College London. His extensive diaries and correspondence throw much light on the literary scene of his time, in particular on ▷ William Blake, ▷ William Wordsworth, ▷ Samuel Taylor Coleridge, ▷ Charles Lamb and ▷ William Hazlitt. They were partly published in 1869, and since then further selections have appeared.

Robinson, Mary (1758–1800)
Novelist, poet and actress. Although Mary Robinson is now known for her ▷ Gothic novels, during her lifetime she was infamous for her affair with the Prince of Wales. He saw her act the role of Perdita in 1779 and fell in love with her. The relationship lasted just over a year, leaving Robinson the butt of crude satire and with the lasting nickname 'Perdita'. In 1783 she became paralysed from the waist down after a miscarriage and from then on she was forced to earn her living by writing. Her poetry was never very original, picking up populist sentiment in relation to current events, such as the storming of the Bastille, and when her collection *Lyrical Tales* (1800) was published, Wordsworth considered changing the title of his own work. In comparison her novels are sharp and witty, tinged with liberal sentiment; they include *Vancenza* (1792), *Angelina* (1795) and *Hubert de Sevrac* (1796).
Bib: Bass, P., *The Green Dragon*; Rodgers, K., *Feminism in Eighteenth-century England.*

Roche, Regina Maria (1764–1845)
Novelist. Prolific Irish novelist, Roche wrote sentimental tales about the injustices done to her various protagonists and their families. The tone, however, was predictably ▷ Gothic, and she became one of the stalwarts of the ▷ Minerva Press. Her novels include *The Vicar of Lansdowne, or Country Quarters* (1789), *The Children of the Abbey* (1796) and *Clermont* (1798). This last work was satirized by ▷ Jane Austen in ▷ *Northanger Abbey*.
▷ Irish literature in English.

Rochester, John Wilmot, Second Earl of (1647–80)
Poet and libertine. His father had been ennobled by ▷ Charles II for his support during his exile and he enjoyed a privileged position at the Restoration court, being more than once banished (and later pardoned) for his unruly behaviour and verses. His reputation among his contemporaries can be gauged from the portrait of the elegant and witty Dorimant in ▷ Sir George Etherege's ▷ *The Man of Mode* (1676) which is based on the poet. He showed conspicuous courage in battle during sea-engagements with the Dutch. Later, however, he was suspected of acting less honourably in having ▷ John Dryden set upon in an alley, believing him to be the author of an anonymous ▷ satire in a poem by the Earl of Mulgrave. Rochester's motive for refusing to fight a duel with Mulgrave is unclear. It is unlikely to have been the simple lack of courage which his enemies attributed to him at the time, though he did recommend cowardice in his poetry.

Rochester's combination of aristocracy and rigorous intellectual honesty set him at odds with the emergent bourgeois ethos of the time. He followed ▷ Hobbes and the ancient philosophers ▷ Lucretius and ▷ Seneca in consistent philosophical materialism. He was a Deist who believed that God, if He existed, could take no interest in petty human affairs, that there was no life after death and that the soul was merely a function of matter. His translation of lines from ▷ Seneca's *Troades* dismisses Hell and the afterlife as 'senselesse Storyes, idle Tales/Dreames, Whimseys, and noe more.'

Also he wrote freely about sexual intimacy, both in its pleasurable and disgusting aspects, flouting bourgeois prudery and linguistic censorship. There is sometimes a trivial, unpleasant tone to his writing in this vein, for example in *Signior Dildo* and the Chloris lyrics. But his obscenity is more often psychologically profound and philosophically disturbing, as in *A Ramble in St James' Park* and *The Imperfect Enjoyment*. Moreover, as an aristocrat, he was contemptuous of the proprietorial sexism of the new bourgeoisie. His friend ▷ Gilbert Burnet, later bishop of Salisbury, showed the orthodox attitude when he argued that Rochester's libertinism amounted to 'theft' by one man from another: 'men have a property in their wives and daughters, so that to defile the one, or corrupt the other, is an unjust and injurious thing'. In contrast, though Rochester could scarcely be called ▷ feminist, his ambiguous satire on the Earl of Mulgrave, *A Very Heroical Epistle in Answer to Ephelia*, shows an insight into what we would now call male chauvinism, which is most unusual for the period.

Rochester's Puritan mother and his friend Burnet refused access to his libertine friends as he lay dying of syphilis, and apparently persuaded him to turn to orthodox religion. After the poet's death Burnet published *Some Passages of the Life and Death of the Earl of Rochester* (1680), and over the next two-and-a-half centuries Rochester's poetry (much of it suppressed) was overshadowed by the edifying legend of the atheist's death-bed repentance. The argument over whether he 'really' repented as he lay in his syphilitic delirium is, however, irrelevant to his poetry, all of which is consistently ▷ materialist and libertine. The pious poems attributed to his last days are not by him and lack the quality of his genuine work.

His poetry is diverse, reflecting the social and cultural transitions of his time. He wrote some exquisite lyrics in the 'cavalier' tradition, including the movingly philosophical *carpe diem* poem 'All my past life is mine noe more' (sometimes called *Love and Life*). Much of his best work, however, is in the new medium of heroic ▷ couplets, a form which he uses, in such poems as *A Satyr against Reason and Mankind*, *Timon*, and *Tunbridge Wells*, with a conversational ease and freedom much admired and imitated by later ▷ Augustans. His *An Allusion to Horace, the Tenth Satyr of the First Book* is the first example of the characteristically Augustan genre of the 'imitation', also adopted about this time by ▷ John Oldham.

Bib: Johnson, S., *Lives of the Poets*; Pinto, V. de S., *Enthusiast in Wit*; Adlard, J., *The Debt to Pleasure*; Treglown, J., *Spirit of Wit: Reconsiderations of Rochester*; Farley-Hills, D., *Rochester's Poetry*.

Roderick Random, The Adventures of (1748)

A novel by ▷ Tobias Smollett. It is based on Smollett's own experience as a naval doctor at the siege of Cartagena in 1741; it is episodic in form, and vivid but somewhat brutal in manner. In the Preface, the author pays tribute to the comic genius of ▷ Cervantes, author of ▷ *Don Quixote*.

Rogers, Samuel (1763–1855)

Poet. The wealthy son of a banker from Stoke Newington, he wrote an *Ode to Superstition* (1786) and the popular reflective poem, *The Pleasures of Memory (1792)*. *Columbus*, a fragment of an ▷ epic, appeared in 1810, and a narrative poem, *Jacqueline*, was published together with ▷ Lord Byron's *Lara* in 1814. He was offered the ▷ Poet Laureateship on the death of ▷ William Wordsworth in 1850, but declined. He has been referred to as 'the last ▷ Augustan'.

Roland

Hero of the Old French *chanson de geste*, the *Chanson de Roland*, dating from the first half of the 12th century, an epic account of the battle between the rearguard of ▷ Charlemagne's army, led by his nephew Roland, and the large Saracen forces who ambush the rearguard in the valley of Roncevaux. The ambush is arranged with the treacherous connivance of Roland's stepfather, Ganelon. Roland takes up the challenge to fight against the odds and refuses to summon help from Charlemagne, as his companion, Oliver, advises. When many of the French side have been slaughtered, Roland finally summons Charlemagne's aid. The French king returns to find his rearguard massacred but goes on to rout the pagan army and avenge his nephew's death. The narrative is structured around a series of binary oppositions, the most obvious being that between the forces of the west and east, between righteous Christians and sinful pagans. Yet within that clear-cut antagonism, the heroic ethos of the narrative is made more complex, not only by Ganelon's perfidy, but by the juxtaposition of Roland and Oliver's response to the prospect of fighting against the odds: the necessary rashness which constitutes heroism is contrasted with a more pragmatic response to the prospect of a hopeless, if glorious, battle. The earliest extant copy of the text was copied in England (1125–50). Roland is the hero of ▷ Boiardo's *Orlando Innamorato* and ▷ Ariosto's *Orlando Furioso*.

Bib: Sayers, D. (trans.), *The Song of Roland*; Whitehead, F. (ed.), *La Chanson de Roland*.

Rolle, Richard (1300–49)

One of the most prolific of the English mystical writers, who lived as a hermit in Yorkshire and became a spiritual advisor to a group of nuns at Hampole. He composed devotional works in Latin, and his English work includes a commentary of the Psalter, meditations on the Passion and a guide to the spiritual life, *The Form of Living*, written for a single recluse but circulated more widely. His prose style makes frequent use of alliteration. Although never canonized, he was widely regarded as a saint until the time of the Reformation.

Bib: Allen, H. E., *The English Writings of Richard Rolle*; Riehle, W., *The Middle English Mystics*.

Roman à these/Tendenzroman

A novel which is dominated by its treatment of a particular issue (French '*these*' = proposition, argument; German '*Tendenz*' = tendency, trend). Frequently this involves an attack on a particular social injustice. The ▷ social problem novels of the 1840s in England are examples of the *roman à these*.

Roman Actor, The **(1626)**
A bloody ▷ tragedy by ▷ Philip Massinger set at the time of the emperor Domitian. The play dramatizes Domitian's marriage to the resourceful Domitia, whose husband he has executed. During a play-within-the-play he kills the actor Paris with whom she has fallen in love, which leads to her conspiring against him and his assassination.

Roman de la Rose
An immensely influential French ▷ dream-vision narrative, composed during the 13th century. The first 4,058 lines of the poem were written by Guillaume de Lorris, c 1237; the remaining 17,622 lines were a later addition of Jean de Meun (le Clopinel), c 1277. The whole narrative is framed as an allegorical account of a love affair, reported as a dream-vision experience by the narrator/lover. Guillaume de Lorris' section provides an exemplary account of the protocol of loving, from the viewpoint of a male lover who courts the object of his desire, a beautiful Rosebud, in the garden of Love, presided over by Mirth. The love garden is the arena of courtly society itself; the dreamer, appropriately, is ushered in by Oiseuse (Leisure), for leisure is a necessary prerequisite for the refined courting which goes on in the garden, as is Richesse; Poverty and Old Age figure among the undesirable qualities kept out by the garden wall. The desired woman is represented as an object to be plucked, but aspects of her response to the lover's advances are represented in a series of personified figures (including Fair Welcoming, Shame and Danger) which surround the Rose, just as some aspects of the Lover, notably Reason, are figured in personified forms. Guillaume's poem ends, unfinished, with the lover in an impasse, having only kissed the Rose which now is protected in a castle by Jealousy. As it stands, the poem provides a manual of the art of ▷ courtly loving in a narrative form, and this dreamscape and mode of working out love's protocol through an allegorical narrative were imitated and reworked in many courtly love poems in French, and in English too (including ▷ Chaucer's dream-vision poems).

Jean de Meun's continuation remains set within the garden but substantially expands the subject of the narrative, and its philosophical and moral dimensions. The expansion comes in the form of a new cast of personified figures (including a Friend, an Old Woman, Nature and Genius her priest) who step in to advise, and assist, or to educate the Lover. The precious and rarified atmosphere of the garden is subverted, as the Lover's desire is subjected to a rigorous appraisal by Reason (who assumes a far larger role in the action), and made into a much more pragmatic quest for satisfaction, through the intervention of the Friend and the Old Woman (who brings a temporal perspective to the action which Guillaume de Lorris deliberately excluded). Rather than being a delicate embodiment of love theory in practice, the narrative beomes an arena for large-scale debates about social organization in theory and in practice, including what part sexual desire has to play in society and how it is being abused. In the end the Lover gets the chance to pluck his Rose and the narrative concludes with a barely disguised description of a sexual assault. Jean de Meun's section of the poem provides a different kind of cultural handbook: it subverts the 'givens' in the structure of Guillaume's love garden and embarks on a broader, more intellectual and philosophical discussion, which considers different kinds of loving (including divine love), but it does so through dramatized debates and monologues. It provides an example of how the clash of opposing ideas can be given dramatic expression but not necessarily a resolution (a point which seems to have profoundly influenced the construction of much of Chaucer's narrative poetry).

The poem as a whole was immensely influential throughout the 14th, 15th and even the 16th centuries. It provoked controversy as well as literary imitation and was the subject of a public debate in France at the end of the 14th century in which Christine de Pisan was a leading figure (who objected to its misogynistic polemic and its blatant representation of a sexual attack). Chaucer translated the poem into English but his relationship to the extant Middle English translation (▷ *The Romaunt of the Rose*) is not clear. There are three extant fragments (two translating sections from Guillaume's section, the third an excerpt from Jean de Meun's) and most critics seem to accept that fragment A (covering the first 1,700 lines of the poem) is Chaucer's work. **Bib**: Dahlberg, C. (trans.), *The Romance of the Rose*.

Roman feuilleton
A novel published in serial form in a newspaper.

Roman-à-clef
A novel which describes real people and events, but using invented names, so that it can be decoded using a key (French, '*clef*'). Examples are ▷ Peacock's *Nightmare Abbey* (1818), which contains caricatures of Shelley, Byron and Coleridge, and ▷ Aldous Huxley's *Point Counter Point*, which includes characters based on ▷ Middleton Murry and ▷ D.H. Lawrence. Since novelists very frequently base their characters to some extent on real people, the boundaries of the form are not clearly

defined, although some authors have actually published a key.

Romance

The term romance is derived from the Latin word *romanice*, meaning 'in the Romance language' and is used, somewhat confusingly, in a range of literary senses, of which at least five can usefully be distinguished, although they are historically related in various ways:

1 Medieval romances, such as ▷ *Sir Gawain and the Green Knight*, were verse narratives on courtly and chivalric subjects, in most cases based on legends and stories about the courts of King Arthur and the Emperor Charlemagne or classical tales of heroism. Many were translations or versions of French originals. Generically and historically distinct from the novel, they nevertheless, as extended fictional narratives, can be seen as one of its antecedents. Chivalric romance made a major contribution to the novel via ▷ *Don Quixote*, partly a satire on the form.

2 Prose romances became common in English from the 15th century and flourished in the Elizabethan era; for example ▷ Thomas Lodge's *Rosalynde, Euphues Golden Legacy* (1590) and ▷ Mary Wroth's *Urania*. These tend to be notable for elegance of style, elaborate description and intellectual discussions rather than plot interest, but ▷ picaresque romances, such as ▷ Thomas Nashe's ▷ *The Unfortunate Traveller* have stronger links to the novel.

3 17th-century French romances, or *romans de longue haleine* (literally, 'romances of long breath'; *ie* sustained romances), such as ▷ Madeleine de Scudéry's ten-volume *Artamène, or the Great Cyrus*, were interminable episodic narratives of love and honour; they were part of the literary context out of which the French novel emerged (▷ Marie-Madeleine de La Fayette), and a form with which English novelists of the 18th century, such as ▷ Samuel Richardson and ▷ Clara Reeve, were given to contrasting with their own works.

4 The term romance has continued to be applied, regularly though not systematically, to novels involving fantastic or supernatural events, such as the ▷ Gothic novel, and to adventure novels, such as the historical romances of ▷ Sir Walter Scott, ▷ Robert Louis Stevenson's *Kidnapped* or the novel simply entitled *Romance*, by ▷ Joseph Conrad and ▷ Ford Madox Ford. ▷ H.G. Wells called his science fiction novels 'scientific romances', and science fiction is one of the contemporary inheritors of this tradition of writing.

5 In post-war fiction, romances, more often termed romantic fiction, are novels about love, sex and adventure, written for a mass market and in many cases aimed particularly at women readers. This form of writing has traditionally been given a low valuation by literary critics, but some feminist critics have sought to revise this (see Modleski, T., *Loving with a Vengeance: Mass-Produced Fantasies for Women*; Elam, D., *Romancing the Postmodern*).

▷ Romanticism.

Romances of Shakespeare

A term often used to express the character of four of the last plays by Shakespeare: ▷ *Pericles* (1608–9); ▷ *Cymbeline* (1609–10); ▷ *The Winter's Tale* (1610–11); ▷ *The Tempest* (1611).

The following are some of the qualities that distinguish these plays:

1 Extravagance of incident. Shakespeare abandons the comparatively realistic presentation characteristic of his tragic period, 1604–8. Events are extraordinary, and in *Pericles* and *The Winter's Tale* they are widespread in place and time; in *Pericles* and *Cymbeline* they are loosely related in plot. In *Cymbeline* and *The Winter's Tale* there is no consistency of period, and classical history mingles with 16th-century social settings. In *The Tempest* Shakespeare makes a freer use of magic than in any of his other plays, but in its strict unity of time and place this play is otherwise in contrast to the other three plays of the group.

2 Although *The Tempest* is again here to some extent a contrast to the others, the group belongs to a category known as ▷ 'tragicomedy'; that is to say *Pericles, Cymbeline* and *The Winter's Tale* each deepen into tragedy, which reaches a climax midway in the story, and then lighten towards a happy conclusion. *The Tempest* is different in that the tragedy has all taken place before the play has begun; the whole play is thus devoted to restoring happiness out of tragedy already accomplished.

3 In each play the theme concerns an ordeal undergone by the main character; in this respect, however, the plays show a progression. Pericles does no wrong; he is a passive sufferer, with no power of his own to relieve his suffering. Cymbeline commits errors, and the tragedy arises from them, but he is not called on to act in order that the errors shall be redeemed. In *The Winter's Tale* Leontes' error amounts to a terrible crime, and this has to be expiated by a long period of unremitting repentance. Prospero, in *The Tempest*, has committed no error beyond severing himself from his worldly responsibilities; he is a powerful and virtuous man who could wreak vengeance on his enemies but chooses instead to reconcile himself to them by acts of godlike mercy.

4 In the first three plays, the ordeal of the hero is characterized by the loss of his family, and in each of them it is a daughter who is chiefly instrumental in bringing about the reunion which constitutes the happy ending. *The Tempest* is again somewhat different from the others. Here father and daughter remain together, but they are both cast off from the rest of the world; it is again the daughter who is instrumental in the final reunion.

In the romances the imaginative emphasis is on reconciliation. Prospero's statement in *The Tempest* that 'the rarer action is/In virtue than in vengeance' epitomizes the distance Shakespeare has travelled since ▷ *Hamlet* and the other tragedies, all of which are to some extent reworked in the late plays.

Roman-fleuve

A sequence of novels in which some of the same characters reappear, and in which the plot of each novel continues or complements that of others in the sequence. Well-known examples are ▷ Balzac's *The Human Comedy* and ▷ Galsworthy's *The Forsyte Saga* (1922); the latter, since it is about a family, could also be termed a saga novel.

Romantic Fiction

▷ Romance.

Romaunt of the Rose, The

The Middle English translation of the ▷ *Roman de la Rose*, which has been attributed, in part, to ▷ Chaucer.

Romeo and Juliet (1597)

A romantic ▷ tragedy by ▷ Shakespeare. It was published in ▷ quarto in a corrupt form in 1597, and in a better edition in 1599. The story is an old one; Shakespeare's version is based on the poem *Romeus and Juliet* (1562) by Arthur Brooke, itself based on a French version of an Italian tale by Bandello (1554). The story is of the romantic love of Romeo, belonging to the family of Montague, and Juliet, of the Capulet family, both living in the Italian city of Verona. The affair has to be kept secret owing to the bitter hostility of the two families, and only Juliet's nurse and Friar Laurence, who marries them, know of it. Even so the affair is not allowed to continue peacefully; Juliet's cousin Tybalt provokes an affray that leads not only to his own death but to that of Mercutio, friend of Romeo and relative of the Prince of Verona, with the result that Romeo is exiled from the city. Moreover, Juliet's father, in ignorance of his daughter's secret marriage, proposes to marry her off in haste to a young nobleman, Paris. To enable her to escape this, Friar Laurence gives Juliet a potion that sends her into a profound sleep and causes her family to suppose her dead; the Friar's design is that she shall be placed in the family burial vault, and that meanwhile a message is to be sent to Romeo directing him to come by night and steal her away. However, by an accident the message is not sent, and Romeo hears only of her death; he returns to Verona, but only to take poison and die by her side. A moment later, the effect of the potion wears off and Juliet recovers; she sees her lover dead beside her, and kills herself in turn.

The play is one of Shakespeare's early masterpieces, and is famous for its exquisite poetry and the dramatic excellence of some of its scenes (*eg* II. i where the lovers declare their love to each other in the 'balcony scene'), and of three of its characters, namely Juliet, her nurse, and Romeo's friend Mercutio. It is not, however, a tragedy in the sense in which we understand the term 'Shakespearian tragedy', in regard to the plays written after 1600. In these plays, tragedy is the outcome of the nature and situation of the central character (*eg* ▷ *Othello*), whereas in *Romeo and Juliet* the unhappy ending is more the result of accident – notably the failure to send the message to Romeo. On the other hand, it is possible that the usual response to the play is more sentimental than Shakespeare intended: Brooke's poem is puritanical and reproves the lovers for their passion; Shakespeare presents them sympathetically, but there are signs – *eg* the Friar's soliloquy opening II. iii – that he intended the passion to be regarded as a misfortune in itself. Whatever one's views on this, the excellence of the play arises above all from the actuality with which Shakespeare presents Juliet: the tradition of courtly romance is brought, as in ▷ Chaucer's ▷ *Troilus and Criseyde*, closely into relationship with real life.

▷ Courtly love.

Romola (1863)

A historical novel by ▷ George Eliot, serialized in ▷ *Cornhill Magazine* (1862–3). It is set in late-15th-century Florence at the time of the predominance of the reforming monk ▷ Savonarola. Romola is a high-minded girl who marries a self-indulgent and unscrupulous Greek, Tito Melma. Repelled by her husband and disillusioned by the course of Savonarola's career, she eventually finds her salvation in self-denial. In writing the novel, George Eliot was putting forward the principle that it is as important to actualize the society in which the characters move as to give reality to the characters themselves. The novel has been praised for the thoroughness of research which established the Florentine scene; on the other hand, by comparison with the later novels (▷ *Middlemarch* and ▷ *Daniel Deronda*) set in England, modern readers feel that medieval Florence did not touch the author in the sense that she participated imaginatively in its life, with the result that of all her novels, *Romola* is probably the least read.

▷ Historical novels.

Rondeau

A form of short poem originated in 16th-century France. It consisted of 13 eight- or ten-syllable lines, divided into stanzas of unequal length, with the addition of short refrains, and only two rhymes throughout. The form was little used in England until the late 19th century when a taste developed for the more artificial forms of short poem among poets like ▷ Swinburne *eg* his *Century of Roundels.*

Rondel
A form of short poem similar to the rondeau, but consisting of 14 lines instead of 13, and with a somewhat different rhyme scheme. It was not much used in English until the end of the 19th century in the work of such poets as ▷ Bridges, Dobson and Henley. It originated in France in the 14th century.

Ronsard, Pierre de (1524–1585)
French poet, leader of the ▷ Renaissance group known as the ▷ 'Pléiade'. His output was wide-ranging (▷ odes, ▷ hymns, ▷ epic, ▷ elegies), but he is particularly famous for his love ▷ sonnets, Petrarchan (▷ Petrarch) in style, and it was in this form that Ronsard was influential among English sonneteers of the Renaissance, *eg* ▷ Henry Constable (1562–1613) and ▷ Samuel Daniel.
Bib: Langer, V., *Invention, Death and Self-definitions in the Poetry of Pierre de Ronsard.*

Roper, Margaret More (1505–44)
Margaret Roper, the daughter of ▷ Thomas More, became renowned in England for her learning. As a member of More's household, her education was of great importance, indeed she was perhaps the intellectual star of what has been sometimes termed the 'School of More', which included More's children, wards, relatives and friends. In a letter written in 1521, ▷ Erasmus records that it was the education and intellectual capacities of Margaret Roper that convinced him of the value of education for women in general. Indeed, Margaret Roper may well have formed the basis for Erasmus' sympathetic portrait of the learned woman in one of his *Colloquies*. Many of Margaret Roper's works are now lost, but what is known of her is derived mainly from the letters she and her father exchanged while he was in prison prior to his execution, and from her husband's account of More's life, which is also an account of his wife. Her major surviving published work is her ▷ translation of Erasmus' commentary on The Lord's Prayer, which was published (though its translator was not acknowledged) as *A Devout Treatise Upon the 'Pater Noster'*, probably in 1524. Her daughter, ▷ Mary Basset, was also a learned translator.
Bib: McCutcheon, E., 'Margaret More Roper: The Learned Woman in Tudor England', *Women Writers of the Renaissance and Reformation* (ed.) K. M. Wilson.

Rosalind, Rosalynde
1 The central character in ▷ Shakespeare's comedy ▷ *As You Like It*. She is based on the heroine of ▷ Thomas Lodge's romance *Rosalynde, Euphues Golden Legacy* (1590)
2 A character in *January*, the first month of Spenser's ▷ *Shepherd's Calendar*; she has been thought to represent Rosa Daniel, the sister of the poet ▷ Samuel Daniel, and wife of ▷ John Florio, translator of the *Essays* of ▷ Montaigne.

Roscoe, William (1753–1831)
Poet. Famous for his children's book, *The Butterfly's Ball and the Grasshopper's Feast* (1806). He also wrote other poems, and biographies of Lorenzo de Medici (1796) and Pope Leo the Tenth (1805).

Roscommon, Wentworth Dillon, Fourth Earl of (?1633–85)
Critic and Restoration courtier. His translation of ▷ Horace's *Art of Poetry* (1680) in blank verse, and his *Essay on Translated Verse* (1684), in heroic ▷ couplets, were greatly admired at the time, and his versification was praised by ▷ Alexander Pope.

Rose Theatre
Opened by the theatre manager, ▷ Philip Henslowe, in 1587 on Bankside in Southwark. ▷ Shakespeare may have been a member of his company at the time. Henslowe managed the theatre together with his son-in-law, ▷ Edward Alleyn, until 1603. The foundations of the Rose were uncovered in 1990.
▷ Theatres.

Rosenberg, Isaac (1890–1918)
Poet. He was born in Bristol, and educated at an elementary school in London. He then became apprenticed to an engraver, and entered the Slade School of Art in 1911. He joined the army in 1915, serving as a private soldier, and was killed in action. He was the most original of all the 'War poets'. His work is full of rhythmic energy, less sombre than ▷ Wilfred Owen's, and bolder in imagery. Owen reacted with indignation and compassion against the war; in the Preface to his poems he wrote: 'Above all I am not concerned with Poetry. My subject is War, and the pity of War. The Poetry is in the pity.' Rosenberg wrote in a letter (1916): 'I will not leave a corner of my consciousness covered up but saturate myself with the strange and extraordinary new conditions of this life, and it will all refine itself into poetry later on.' Works include: *Night and Day* (1912); *Youth* (1915); *Poems* (ed. G. Bottomley, with a Memoir by L. Binyon; 1922). *Collected Poems* (ed. G. Bottomley and D. Harding, 1937). Rosenberg's definitive *Collected Works* appeared in 1979.
▷ War poets.
Bib: Cohen, J., *Journey to the Trenches: The*

Life of Isaac Rosenberg; Liddiard, J., *Isaac Rosenberg: The Half-Used Life*.

Roses, Wars of the
▷ Wars of the Roses.

Rosicrucianism
A system of philosophical and mystical beliefs professed by an organization known as the Ancient Mystic Order of Rosa Crucis (the 'red cross'). Its origins are obscure; it is first mentioned in 1614. Part of its doctrine has consisted in the belief that the universe contains a hierarchy of spirits governing the various elements. ▷ Pope, in his second version of ▷ *The Rape of the Lock*, used this system for ▷ satirical purposes; he needed for his ▷ mock epic a supernatural system comparable to the ancient Greek gods and goddesses of ▷ Homer's ▷ *Iliad*, but adapted, as they would not be, to the pettiness of his theme. He used the Rosicrucian system because it provided spirits of all degrees of importance.

Ross, Mrs (fl 1811–25)
Novelist and writer of short stories. Published by ▷ Minerva among others, Mrs Ross is one of few prose writers to balance rationalism and ▷ Romanticism, 'sense and sensibility' as it were, and combine them with relatively direct descriptions of sexuality. Her plots and characters are ingenious and she clearly expects her readers fully to appreciate her novels' tough moral conclusions. Her work includes: *The Cousins, or A Woman's Promise and A Lover's Vow* (1811), *The Balance of Comfort, or The Old Maid and Married Woman* (1817), and *The Woman of Genius* (1821).

Rossetti, Christina (1830–94)
Poet, younger sister of ▷ Dante Gabriel and William Michael Rossetti. Her father, Gabriele, was an Italian patriot who came to England in 1824, her mother Frances Polidori was half-English and a former ▷ governess. Italian influence, particularly that of Dante, is noticeable in much of Rossetti's work. She was educated largely at home, her first poetry being published privately when she was twelve. Five poems appeared under the ▷ pseudonym Ellen Alleyne in the ▷ Pre-Raphaelite Brotherhood's journal *The Germ* (1850). She broke off an engagement to the painter James Collinson when he joined the ▷ Catholic Church in 1850, for she was a devout High Anglican, much influenced by the ▷ Oxford Movement. Although she was high-spirited as a child, she became increasingly reclusive and was plagued by illness, contracting Grave's disease in 1873.

Rossetti's best-known poem today is the sensual and complex ▷ 'Goblin Market', published with other poems in 1862. ▷ *The Prince's Progress, and Other Poems* appeared in 1866; ▷ *Sing Song, A Nursery Rhyme Book* in 1872 and ▷ *A Pageant, and Other Poems* in 1881. She also wrote religious prose works such as *Seek and Find* (1879); *Called to be Saints* (1881); and *The Face of the Deep* (1892). Her poetry often dwells on loss, renunciation and death, yet she is not limited to these subjects. The work ranges from fantasy verses to lyrics, ▷ ballads, ▷ nonsense poems, devotional verse and sonnets, including the 'Monna Innominata' series (1881). The 'simple surface' of the poetry often conceals the complications beneath: Rossetti's best work engages profoundly with epistemological, spiritual and psychic concerns. Her work has suffered from reductive interpretations, but she is increasingly being reconsidered as a major Victorian poet.
Bib: Crump, R. (ed.), *The Complete Poems of Christina Rossetti* (3 vols); Kent, D.A. (ed.), *The Achievement of Christina Rossetti*; Rosenblum, D., *Christina Rossetti: The Poetry of Endurance*; Harrison, A., *Christina Rossetti in Context*; Jones, K., *Learning not to be First: The Life of Christina Rossetti*.

Rossetti, Dante Gabriel (1828–82)
Poet and painter; the son of an Italian political refugee and a half-English mother. In 1848 he started the ▷ Pre-Raphaelite Brotherhood with a number of fellow-painters, but the inspiration of his painting, as of his poetry, was essentially literary. The poetry is a continuation of the English ▷ Romantic movement, particularly the work of John Keats (1795–1821), inasmuch as its central impulse is the sensuous response to beauty. Another main inspiration for Rossetti and the Pre-Raphaelites was the direct appeal of detail in ▷ medieval painting. Rossetti also inherited, however, the feeling for the mysteriousness of the Middle Ages which both he and Keats shared with the taste for 'Gothic' which was an aspect of Romanticism at the beginning of the century. In addition, he inherited some of the feeling for ▷ aestheticism in sanctity which had been part of the ▷ Oxford Movement in the Church of England during the 1830s and 40s. The triumph of English industrialism, with its admiration for technology, tended to disregard values which were not practical ones. Thus poets like Rossetti were tempted to use their poetry as a dream world of refuge from external squalor and commercial struggle and this led to a self-regarding nostalgia. This meant that fields of inspiration such as the Middle Ages and religion are not so much expressed in their own vitality as used as a defence against other, objectionable realities; Rossetti is accused of being 'religiose' rather than 'religious', and of having falsified the past. On the other hand, Rossetti's poetry, within these limitations, is sumptuous and melodious. He was at first much better known for his paintings, but his poem 'The Blessed Damozel' was published

in the Pre-Raphaelite journal ▷ *The Germ* in 1850. Later came his translations from Dante, *The Early Italian Poets* (1861); *Poems by D.G. Rossetti* (1870); and *Ballads and Sonnets* (1881), including a sonnet sequence, *The House of Life*, which was expanded from a version in the 1870 volume, and is sometimes called his masterpiece.
Bib: Doughty, O., *A Victorian Romantic*; Winwar, F., *Poor Splendid Wings*; Holman Hunt, W., *Pre-Raphaelitism and the Pre-Raphaelite Brotherhood*; Boas, H.O.B., *Rossetti and his Poetry*; Cary, E.L., *The Rossettis*; Pater, W., in *Appreciations*; Hough, G., in *The Last Romantics*; Rees, J., *The Poetry of Dante Gabriel Rossetti*.

Round Table, The
The Round Table is first mentioned in ▷ Wace's *Roman de Brut* (1155), where it is described briefly as a construction devised by ▷ King Arthur, to pre-empt rivalry for a place at the hall table among members of his fast-expanding entourage. ▷ Laȝamon amplifies the story of how a marvellous table was introduced to Arthur's hall: after a riot breaks out at one of Arthur's feasts, a witty Cornish woodworker devises a table which can be expanded to accommodate any number of guests (it is not specifically round). In later Arthurian narrative, the Round Table frequently provides a way of demarcating the elite members of Arthur's court (as the Knights of the Round Table) but the significance and size of the table itself may vary considerably: it is not a fixed artefact by any means.

In the Christianized version of the ▷ Grail legend (first formulated by ▷ Robert de Boron), the Round Table is invested with a mystical significance, as a successor to the earlier Holy Tables of the Last Supper and the Grail Table (of Joseph of Arimathea). Its round shape is symbolic of the universe, and one place at the Table is reserved only for the knight who will achieve the Grail quest (known as the 'Perilous Seat'). ▷ Merlin constructs this Table for ▷ Uther, who passes it on to ▷ Guinevere's father; Arthur receives it as part of Guinevere's dowry.

In ▷ Malory's version of Arthurian narrative, the Table (Guinevere's dowry) can accommodate up to 150 knights, and it becomes symbolic of the chivalric ethos itself, and Arthur outlines the rules for its members in the first tale of Malory's *Morte D'Arthur*. The import of its round shape is later explained by ▷ Perceval's Aunt in the course of the Grail Quest but it is not identified as a successor to the Grail Table, which is made of silver and found in ▷ Pelles' castle.

The Round Table still preserved at Winchester, though identified by ▷ John Hardyng in his *Chronicle* as *the* Round Table, is a manufactured relic: it was built some time around the mid-13th century and repainted sometime in the mid-16th century. It is largely responsible for the popular modern notion of the Round Table as one which has a strictly fixed number of places. It is, however, just one of the many shapes which the Round Table assumes in medieval Arthurian narratives.

Roundel
▷ Chaucer seems to have been the first English poet to compose roundels in imitation of the French ▷ rondeau form. Roundels have a varying number of lines (8–14), but use only two rhymes. The opening line recurs as the refrain. The bird song at the end of the ▷ *Parliament of Foulys* is in the form of a roundel.

Roundheads
A name for Puritan supporters of the Parliamentary party in the ▷ Civil Wars of 1642–51. They were so called because they habitually cut their hair close to their heads, whereas the Royalists (▷ Cavaliers) wore their hair ornamentally long. This Cavalier habit was regarded by the Puritans as a symptom of worldliness. The word has been traced back to 1641, when a Cavalier officer was quoted as declaring that he would 'cut the throats of those round-headed dogs that bawled against bishops'. Earlier than this, a ▷ pamphlet against long hair was published under the title of 'The unloveliness of lovelocks'.

Rousseau, Jean-Jacques (1712–78)
French-Swiss thinker. His chief works were: *Discourse on the Influence of Learning and Art* (1750), in which he argues that progress in these has not improved human morals; *Discourse on Inequality* (1754), in which society is considered to have spoilt the liberty and virtue natural to primitive peoples; a novel, *The New Héloïse* (1761), in which the return to primitive nature is considered in relation to the relationships of the sexes and the family; ▷ *The Social Contract* (1761), a political treatise with the theme that the basis of society is artificial, not binding on individuals when society ceases to serve their interests; *Emile* (1762), advocating education through the evocation of the natural impulses and interests of the child, and the *Confessions*, an autobiography which was self-revealing without precedent, published after his death.

Rousseau was immensely influential, not only in France but throughout Europe. His praise of nature and protests against society were significant contributions to the creation of a revolutionary state of mind, culminating in the ▷ French Revolution of 1789. Education from nature, his conception of nature as a life-giving force, was of great importance in the background of Wordsworth, and through Wordsworth, of much of English 19th-century imaginative thinking, and linked with his devotion to nature was his equally influential reverence for childhood. As an autobiographer, Rousseau was one of the first to base the importance of individual experience on its uniqueness, not on its moral excellence or intellectual attainment. This was quite contrary to the characteristic 18th-century view, expressed in works like Samuel Johnson's ▷ *Rasselas*, in which the valuable experience was conceived to be only that which was true of and for humanity at large.

***Rover, The* (1679)**
Comedy by ▷ Aphra Behn, reworked from ▷ Thomas Killigrew's play *Thomaso* (1663–4). The play concerns four cavaliers, exiled in the cause of the future ▷ Charles II, and the women whom they meet during a sojourn in Naples. Penniless Willmore (the Rover) is accompanied by the English Colonel Belville, his friend Frederick, and an English country gentleman called Blunt. Hellena, a 'gay young woman design'd for a Nun', is determined to avoid her fate and find a husband, while her sister Florinda is equally determined to avoid marrying the man intended for her by her brother. She has fallen in love with Belville, while Hellena, attending a carnival in disguise with her sister and two other women, falls in love with Willmore. He, however, is attracted by the wealthy and beautiful courtesan Angelica Bianca, and determines to gain her services without payment. Hellena pursues him, at one time disguised as a boy, while he woos Angelica Bianca, whom he eventually manages to bed. No sooner has this happened than he loses interest in her, while she is now painfully in love with him. She plans to kill him, but at the last moment is interrupted, and then finds herself unable to pull the trigger. Willmore marries the wealthy and virtuous Hellena, while Florinda, after a series of incidents, is united with Belville. Frederick marries Florinda's and Hellena's kinswoman Valeria, and the foolish Blunt, after being deceived and robbed by the prostitute Lucetta, remains unattached. The play takes place at carnival time, and there are colourful scenes of dancing and singing, ▷ wit and clowning. But the anguished character of Angelica Bianca adds a solemn note to the action, which also contains some ugly episodes, as when the enraged Blunt attempts to revenge himself for Lucetta's perfidy by raping Florinda. The other men join him, and only the appearance of Valeria saves her. The play achieved great success, and remained popular until late in the 18th century. It generated a sequel, *The Rover, Part II*, and some imitations, including ▷ John Kemble's *Love in Many Masks* (1760).

Rowe, Elizabeth (Singer) (1674–1737)
English poet and journalist from Somerset – where her father had settled after being imprisoned for religious Nonconformity. Of ▷ Dissenting religious principles, she began to publish, and the Thynnes became her patrons (▷ Frances Seymour, Countess of Hertford). Her *Poems on Several Occasions* (1696) contains several different kinds of poetry. In her preface she writes that male writers have the traditions of writing, and try to 'Monopolize Sence too' so that not 'so much as Wit should be allowed us'. She sees such assertion as 'Violations of the liberties of Free-born English women' – language which recalls the radical political associations of Nonconformist religion with the English ▷ Civil War (1642–6) and (1648–51). She married the writer Thomas Rowe (1710), and after his death in 1715 she lived in Frome, Somerset, working as a teacher. Religion became her topic in the *Friendship in Death* (1728) – letters from the dead to the living. More letters followed, *Letters Moral and Entertaining* (1729–33) and the verse *History of Joseph* (1736).
▷ Scott, Mary (Taylor)

Rowe, Nicholas (1674–1718)
Poet and dramatist, known today chiefly for his so-called ▷ 'she-tragedies', in which the distresses of female victims are displayed, and for his edition of Shakespeare (▷ Shakespeare, editions). Rowe was initially a barrister in the Middle Temple, but gave this up for the ▷ theatre when his father died leaving him an inheritance, in 1692. He became in due course a friend to ▷ Pope and ▷ Addison. Rowe's ▷ blank-verse tragedy *The Ambitious Stepmother* was staged successfully at ▷ Lincoln's Inn Fields in 1700, with ▷ Betterton, ▷ Barry and ▷ Bracegirdle in the cast. His *Tamerlane* (1702), a tragedy whose figures of Tamerlane and Bajazet were modelled on those of ▷ William III and Louis XIV, became a stock play. *The Fair Penitent (*1703), based on Massinger's *The Fatal Dowry* followed, to great acclaim. The heroine Calista, abandoned by the 'gallant, gay Lothario', and eventually committing suicide, drew enormous sympathy from audiences; she was played first by ▷ Elizabeth Barry and later by ▷ Sarah Siddons. The characters formed part of ▷ Richardson's inspiration in his writing of ▷ Clarissa (1747–8). Rowe's edition of Shakespeare (1709; reissued in 1714) is often considered the first attempt to edit Shakespeare in the modern sense, dividing the plays into acts and scenes according to fixed principles, marking actors' entrances and exits, clarifying the texts, and supplying lists of characters. ▷ *The Tragedy of Jane Shore* (1714), was written 'in Imitation of Shakespeare's Style', although as Odell and others have pointed out, many would barely discover Shakespeare among the lines. Both this and *The Tragedy of Lady Jane Grey* (1715), continued Rowe's tradition of suffering heroines. The former, like *Tamerlane* and *The Fair Penitent*, lasted into the 19th century, and all three became well-known in translation, in France. In 1715 Rowe became ▷ Poet Laureate.

Bib: Canfield, J. D., *Nicholas Rowe and Christian Tragedy*.

Rowley, William (1585–1637)
English actor and dramatist who collaborated with ▷ Thomas Middleton on several plays, including ▷ *The Changeling* to which he almost certainly contributed the subplot. He also collaborated with ▷ Thomas Heywood and ▷ John Webster, among others, on *The Witch of Edmonton* (1608). However, Rowley's work is uneven and he is often thought to have produced the weakest portions of those plays he worked on.
Bib: Stork, C. W., *William Rowley*.

Rowson, Susanna Haswell (1762–1824)
British/North American novelist, dramatist, poet and essayist. Born in Portsmouth, England, she was brought to North America at the age of five. Although she returned to England periodically thereafter, because of political persecution or economic need, she became one of North America's earliest and most popular novelists. Extraordinarily diverse in her literary talents, she published ten novels, including ▷ *Victoria* (1786), *Charlotte, a Tale of Truth* (1791), *Mentoria* (1791), *Rebecca* (1792) and *Lucy Temple: a Sequel to Charlotte Temple*; a dozen plays, most notably *Slaves in Algiers* (1794); several collections of poetry, including *A Trip to Parnassas* (1788); and numerous other miscellanies, including textbooks and historical accounts of famous women. Her novels combined traditional ▷ didactic seduction plots with a more ▷ 'feminist' treatment of women's situation. Acknowledging the power of sexuality and the dangers of women's economic dependency (especially dependency on those who prove unreliable), Rowson's fiction shows links with the later 19th-century woman's novel formula.

She pursued various other careers during her life, including actress and songwriter; but, in addition to her literary career, her role as head of the Young Ladies' Academy was her most influential position. Intellectually demanding and yet warm and caring, she is cited in numerous private journals of the era as an excellent teacher. Although her life was one of constant financial hardship, it was also notable for her extraordinary literary productivity and attention to women's lives.

Roxana, or the Fortunate Mistress **(1724)**
A novel by ▷ Daniel Defoe presented as a fictional ▷ autobiography. 'Roxana', the daughter of French Protestant refugees, is deserted and left destitute by her first husband, and, with a taste for the finer things in life, sees prostitution as her only lucrative profession. A second marriage to a Dutch merchant leaves her widowed, but she climbs to a state of social importance by a series of increasingly grand affairs, one of which is hinted to be with the king. As in ▷ Defoe's ▷ *Moll Flanders*, the whore repents; but the penitence of Roxana is also ambiguous, and her thoughts are haunted by the illegitimate daughter whose death is on her conscience.

Roxburghe Club
Book Club. The Roxburghe was the first book club and took its name from John Ker, third Duke of Roxburghe (1740–1804), who had acquired a vast collection of antiquarian books. When his 1471 edition of ▷ Boccaccio was sold for £2,260, a phenomenal sum in those days, several book enthusiasts celebrated the event with a dinner during which the club was initiated. Its first president was Lord Spencer of Althorp and its first secretary was his librarian, ▷ Thomas Frognall Dibdin. The Roxburghe Club continues to this day, each member financing the production of an important and unjustly neglected work.

Roxburghe, John Ker, Third Duke of
▷ Roxburghe Club.

Royal Academy of Arts
Founded with the approval of King George III in 1768 'for the purpose of cultivating and improving the arts of painting, sculpture and architecture'. The first President (P.R.A.) was a portrait painter ▷ Sir Joshua Reynolds. Angelica Kaufmann was a founding member, although women were not permitted to study in the life classes. An elected council of 40 Royal Academicians are entitled to place R.A. after their names, and a further number of associates bear the letters A.R.A. The Royal Academy runs schools of art to which women have been admitted since 1867 and holds an annual exhibition of about 1,000 works submitted to it and approved by it; the opening is an important social occasion. The Academy is further the manager of financial trusts on behalf of artists, and organizes exhibitions of foreign artists. Until the mid-19th century the Academy included distinguished artists amongst its number, such as the landscape painter, Turner, but for the last 100 years its policy has been conservative to the point of mediocrity, so that the livelier movements of English art have occurred without its patronage. Nonetheless, apart from the ▷ Royal Society, it is the only official institution in the arts to have achieved national prestige. It has occupied its present site, Burlington House, Piccadilly, London, since 1869.

Royal Court Theatre
A theatre of this name has existed in Sloane Square since 1871. The first outstanding period of its history was between 1904 and 1907 when,

under the management of J. E. Vedrenne and ▷ Harley Granville Barker, the work of new writers such as ▷ Shaw and ▷ Galsworthy was presented, as well as works by Euripides, ▷ Ibsen, Hauptmann and Maeterlinck. Since 1956, when ▷ John Osborne's ▷ *Look Back In Anger* was performed by George Devine's company, the English Stage Company, the theatre has consistently supported the work of new writers, helping to establish, amongst others, the reputations of John Osborne, ▷ John Arden, ▷ Edward Bond, ▷ Christopher Hampton, ▷ Caryl Churchill, Bill Gaskill, Peter Gill and Max Stafford-Clark.
Bib: Browne, T., *Playwright's Theatre*; MacCarthy, D., *The Court Theatre*; Roberts, P., *The Royal Court Theatre 1965–1972*.

Royal Martyr, The
▷ Charles I, so called by his supporters in consequence of his trial and execution by the revolutionary Parliament of 1649. Charles was devout, and the ▷ Civil Wars broke out for reasons which were partly and ostensibly religious; the victory of Parliament was also that of the Puritans, and entailed the temporary overthrow of the ▷ Church of England. Charles was consequently not only regarded as a martyr for the Anglican Church, but even by some as a saint, and a few churches exist dedicated to King Charles the Martyr.

The Royal Martyr is also the subtitle of a play otherwise called *Tyrannic Love* (1669) by ▷ John Dryden.

Royal Shakespeare Company
The resident company at the Royal Shakespeare Theatre (formerly the Memorial Theatre) in Stratford-upon-Avon since 1960. The first general director was ▷ Peter Hall who was replaced by Trevor Nunn in 1968. Recent directors for the company include Bill Alexander, John Barton, Terry Hands, Barry Kyle and Adrian Noble now the artistic director. Although the company mainly produces ▷ Shakespeare's plays, there is a policy of showing the work of his contemporaries and encouraging new modern writers. The company now has a second theatre in Stratford, The Swan, which contains a scaled-down imitation of an Elizabethan stage; the Other Place is used for more overtly experimental work. It also has two theatres for large- and small-scale productions in the Barbican Centre in London.
Bib: Beaumann, S., *The R.S.C., A History of Ten Decades*; Chambers, C., *Other Spaces: New Theatre and the R.S.C.*

Royal Society, The
Founded with the authority of ▷ Charles II in 1662; its full name was 'The Royal Society of London for Promoting Natural Knowledge'. It grew out of a philosophical society started in 1645 and was composed of 'divers worthy persons, inquisitive into natural philosophy and other parts of human learning, and particularly of what hath been called the New Philosophy or Experimental Philosophy', in other words of men whose minds were moving in the way opened up by ▷ Francis Bacon. The Society took the whole field of knowledge for exploration; one of its aims was to encourage the virtue of intellectual lucidity in the writing of prose, and Thomas Sprat, writing the *History of the Royal Society* in 1667, defined the standards which writers were to emulate. The Royal Society was thus central in the culture of its time; it was promoted not only by scientists such as the chemist Boyle, but by writers as well.

▷ Porter, Endymion.

R. S. C.
▷ Royal Shakespeare Company

Rubaiyat of Omar Khayyam, The
Verses by Omar Khayyam, a Persian scholar and poet who died in 1123. He was an outstanding mathematician and astronomer, but is still more famous for his verse epigrams written in 'rubai', ie four lines, the first, second and fourth of which have the same rhyme while the third is usually rhymeless. The rubai had been invented for the epitomizing of subtle thoughts on Islamic belief, but Omar used them to satirize religious bigotry with a free-thinking irony. This has caused him to be referred to as 'the Voltaire of the East'.

The English poet ▷ Edward FitzGerald published a translation of the Rubaiyat in 1859 (75 verses); he enlarged this to 110 verses in a new edition in 1868, and issued other versions (101 verses) in 1872 and 1879. FitzGerald emphasizes the pleasure-loving aspect of the Persian poet, and the poem was extremely popular in Victorian England both for its musicality and for its expression of a liberated way of life which contrasted with the narrow and bigoted codes of mid-Victorian respectability. The poet Robert Graves (1895–1985) also published a translation of the Rubaiyat.

Rubens, Bernice (b 1927)
Novelist. Born in Cardiff into a talented musical family, and educated at University College, Cardiff, Bernice Rubens has lived in London for many years. A prolific novelist whose work is original and exciting, she has written 19 novels to date, in the following order: *Set on Edge* (1960); *Madame Sousatzka* (1962); *Mate in Three* (1966); *The Elected Member* (1969); *Sunday Best* (1971); *Go Tell the Lemmings* (1973); *I Sent a Letter to My Love* (1975); *The Ponsonby Post* (1977); *A Five Year Sentence* (1978); *Spring Sonata* (1979); *Birds of Passage* (1982); *Brothers* (1983); *Our Father* (1987); *Set on Edge* (1987); *Kingdom Come* (1989); *A*

Solitary Grief (1991); *Mother Russia* (1992); *Autobiopsy* (1993); and *Yesterday in the Back Lane* (1995).

Rudkin, David (1936)
British dramatist whose first major play, *Afore Night Come* (1962) explored mysterious dark forces affecting apparently ordinary life in the modern British countryside. This, and later plays, have been performed by the ▷ Royal Shakespeare Company. For some years Rudkin turned his back on the stage and worked for television, his two best-known plays during this time being *Children Playing* (1967) and *Blodwen Home from Rachel's Wedding* (1969). *Cries from Casement as His Bones Are Brought to Dublin* (1973) and *Ashes* (1975) marked his return to the stage with dramatizations of events in Northern Ireland (a subject often avoided by modern British dramatists). Rudkin is clear about the political purpose behind his work: 'I believe the dramatist's function in a society to be to transmute the idiosyncracies of personal life experience into metaphors of public, political value to mankind.' Other plays include: *The Sons of Light* (1977); *The Triumph of Death* (1981); a translation of *Peer Gynt* (1983); *The Saxon Shore* (1986).

Rugby School
One of the most famous of the English Public Schools. It was founded in 1567, but its importance begins with the headmastership of ▷ Thomas Arnold (father of the poet and critic ▷ Matthew Arnold) from 1828 to 1842. Hitherto, the ancient Public Schools had imparted education (chiefly in the Greek and Latin languages and literatures) but without any consistent moral instruction. Rugby became a pioneer of 'character-building', which came to be regarded as the most typical quality of the English 'public school tradition'. The virtues were supposed to be those of physical and moral discipline, leadership and fair-mindedness. A large number of public schools were founded in the second half of the 19th century, and they were modelled on Arnold's ideals. Since the large Empire of which Britain was the centre required an extensive class of administrators, these ideals were eminently useful in producing them. A once-popular novel, *Tom Brown's Schooldays* (1857) by Thomas Hughes, describes life at Rugby under Arnold.

***Ruined Cottage, The, or The Story of Margaret* (1814)**
A poem in ▷ blank verse by ▷ William Wordsworth, written in 1797, and included in Book I of ▷ *The Excursion* (1814). It tells the poignant story of a woman whose husband is driven by grinding poverty to join the army. He never returns, and eventually grief and poverty take Margaret's life. Contemplating her cottage, now derelict and overgrown, the narrator is overcome by 'the impotence of grief', and reflects on:

That secret spirit of humanity
Which 'mid the calm oblivious tendencies
Of nature, 'mid her plants, and weeds, and
flowers,
And silent overgrowings, still survived.

'Runaway Slave at Pilgrim's Point, The' (1850)
A poem by ▷ Elizabeth Barrett Browning. The speaker of the poem is a black woman slave who relates how she was torn from her lover and then raped by a white slave-owner. She bears a child, whom she murders and buries in a forest. The rage, grief and pain of the woman is chillingly conveyed in the first person narrative. The speaker cannot bear to see 'the *master's* look' on the child's face, yet is driven to frenzied distraction after the murder. Reconciliation is offered for the mother and child only 'In the death-dark where we may kiss and agree'. Barrett Browning's impassioned protest against slavery made a considerable impact upon her contemporaries; it is still a powerful read.

Runnymede
The place on the south bank of the Thames, where the Barons forced ▷ King John to accept ▷ Magna Carta in 1215.

Rupert, Prince (Count Palatine of the Rhine, and Duke of Bavaria) (1619–82)
Son of Frederick of the Palatinate and ▷ James I's daughter Elizabeth. Rupert was an able cavalry commander on the Royalist side in the ▷ Civil Wars, and after the Restoration, an enthusiastic supporter of the ▷ Royal Society.

***Rural Rides* (1820–30)**
Reports of rural conditions by ▷ William Cobbett. He disapproved of certain remedies proposed by an official body to the Government for agricultural distress resulting from the Napoleonic War. He decided to make a number of tours on horseback in order to find out the facts for himself, and published his impressions in his journal, the ▷ *Political Register*, between 1820 and 1830, when they were collected into book form. The essays are in vivid, direct prose, full of acute comments, lively incident, and strong if prejudiced argument. They are early examples of direct journalistic reporting and are raised to permanent value as literature by the energy of Cobbett's conviction and the simplicity and vigour of his prose, which he had modelled on the writings of Jonathan Swift (1667–1745).

Rushdie, Salman (b 1947)
Novelist. Born in Bombay and educated at Cambridge University, his second novel, *Midnight's Children* (1981) won the Booker Prize

and became a best-seller. It is a voluminous work, ranging in time from World War I to 1977, and combining a realistic portrayal of poverty and suffering with magic, fantasy, farce, symbolism and ▷ allegory in a manner which associates it with ▷ magic realism. Its many narrative strategies compete with, and undermine, each other, and serve to question the relation of history to fiction; in this respect Rushdie is a ▷ postmodernist writer. In particular, narrative multiplicity functions in his work as a form of resistance to the unitary nature of ▷ imperialist ideology and political control. He is an inventive, self-conscious and versatile writer, with a flamboyant and indulgent style. His other novels are: *Grimus* (1975); *Shame* (1983), and ▷ *The Satanic Verses* (1988) which aroused worldwide controversy and criticism from Muslims for its alleged blasphemy. Following the death sentence imposed upon Rushdie by the Ayatollah Khomeini, Rushdie went into hiding in 1989, and produced his children's book (▷ children's books), *Haroun and the Sea of Dreams* in 1990. Travel writing: *The Jaguar Smile: A Nicaraguan Journey* (1987).

Ruskin, John (1810–1900)
Writer on art and on its relationship with society. His central inspiration was that great art is moral and the corollary that the working men of industrial England were spiritually impoverished. Like the ▷ Pre-Raphaelites (he was a patron of ▷ D.G. Rossetti, their leader), he found the contrast to the England of his day in the freedom of individual response to environment among the medieval artists, and he expressed this view in the famous chapter called 'The Nature of Gothic' in *The Stones of Venice*. In the field of design, Ruskin, like ▷ William Morris, advocated a return to handicrafts and to medieval conditions of production.

The latter part of his life was much concerned with attacks on the social philosophies of political economists, such as ▷ John Stuart Mill, to whom he did less than justice, and in endeavours to awaken the working classes to the nature of their combined artistic and moral impoverishment. He wrote his artistic books in a style of elaborate but precise and delicate eloquence but his social gospel had more concentrated and direct fervour. His puritanical mother (he was an only child) had given him a concentrated education in the Bible and though his religious views as an adult were not explicit, his conception of art as fundamentally spiritual arose out of the intensity of his early religious training. Though a supporter of the Pre-Raphaelites, Ruskin did not lean like them towards 'art for art's sake' but towards 'art for the spiritual health of man'. In his campaign against the mediocre aspects of industrial culture, he was a disciple and admirer of ▷ Thomas Carlyle but he extended Carlyle's vision of greatness and has proved to be a writer of more permanent interest.

His principal works are: *Modern Painters* (1843–60) in which he champions Turner, one of the greatest of English painters and at the time one of the most controversial; *The Seven Lamps of Architecture* (1849) leading to *The Stones of Venice* (1851–3) in which he makes his discovery of 'the Nature of Gothic'; this took him towards problems about the nature of civilized society in *The Political Economy of Art* (1857), *The Two Paths* (1859) and, one of his most famous books, ▷ *Unto This Last* (1862). *Sesame and Lilies* (1865), *Ethics of the Dust* (1866), *The Crown of Wild Olive* (1866) are essays in criticism on the age, and *Fors Clavigera* (1871–84) is composed of 96 letters to an educated artisan in which he shows himself distrustful of liberal democracy. *Praeterita* (1885–9) is one of the celebrated ▷ autobiographies in English, although it is fragmentary and incomplete. Its most famous section is the first, in which Ruskin describes his unusual, in some ways unnatural, yet fertilizing childhood.

▷ Gothic architecture; Medievalism.
Bib: Selections by Quennell, P.; Clark, K.; Rosenberg, J.D.; Leon, D., *Life*; Evans, J., *Life*; Ladd, H., *The Victorian Morality of Art*; Rosenberg, J.D., *The Darkening Glass*; Wilenski, R.H., *John Ruskin*; Lippincott, B., *Victorian Critics of Democracy*.

Russell, Bertrand Arthur William, Lord (1872–1970)
Philosopher. Russell's important work on mathematical philosophy and logic is one of the foundations of 20th-century Anglo-Saxon philosophy. His most influential texts are *The Principles of Mathematics* (1903); *Principia Mathematica* (1910–13, written in collaboration with his Cambridge tutor, A. N. Whitehead); *The Problems of Philosophy* (1912); his epistemological works *Mysticism and Logic* (1918), *Analysis of Mind* (1921) and *Human Knowledge* (1948); and the accessible *History of Western Philosophy* (1945). As this indicates, Russell's working life was long and illustrious; he was a fringe member of the ▷ Bloomsbury Group (writing on aesthetics, and a famous sparring-partner for ▷ D. H. Lawrence). Later in life Russell was a founder member of CND. He was married to writer ▷ Dora Russell.

Russell, Dora (1894–1986)
Feminist writer and activist. Russell's dynamic campaigning life began during and after World War I when she became committed to pacifism and socialism, causes which continued to motivate her throughout her life. In 1921 she married philosopher ▷ Bertrand Russell, and the two worked together on socialist causes, co-wrote *The Prospects of Industrial Civilization* (1923),

and set up a progressive school at Petersfield, which Dora Russell continued to run when her husband left her in 1932. She was central in establishing a number of important issues at the heart of the British social and political agenda throughout her long career, including the Worker's Birth Control Group in the 1920s, the Women's Caravan for Peace and the Campaign for Nuclear Disarmament in the late 1950s, and the National Council for Civil Liberties. Her publications include: *Hypatia, or, Women and Knowledge* (1925), *The Right To Be Happy* (1927), and *In Defence of Children* (1932), *The Religion of the Machine Age* (1983). A good collection of her work appeared in 1984 as *The Dora Russell Reader: 57 Years of Writing and Journalism*. Her autobiography has been published in three volumes as *The Tamarisk Tree* (1977–85).

Russell, Lady Elizabeth (1528–1609)
Translator, letter-writer and poet. Lady Russell was sister to ▷ Ann Bacon and wife to ▷ Sir Thomas Hoby, themselves both learned translators. After Hoby's death, she married Lord John Russell, but continued the supervision of her Hoby children, and her ▷ translation of John Poynet's *A Way of Reconciliation of a Good and Learned Man* (1605) is dedicated to her daughter. She wrote verse epitaphs, some in Greek and Latin, for her family, and corresponded with Sir William Cecil (▷ Burghley).
Bib: Travitsky, B. (ed.), *A Paradise of Women.*

Russell, Lucy, Countess of Bedford (d 1627)
Together with ▷ Mary Sidney, Countess of Pembroke and ▷ Mary Wroth (Lady Wroth), Lucy, Countess of Bedford was one of the most important patrons of poetry in the early 17th century. However, since her husband, Edward, third Earl of Bedford, came rarely to court (he had been exiled from court for his part in the ▷ Essex rebellion and later, in 1612, suffered partial paralysis from a fall), this role was based entirely upon her own talents and upon her Harington family connections – she was the sister of ▷ Sir John Harington. Herself a poet, she was also the patron of ▷ Ben Jonson, ▷ George Chapman, ▷ Samuel Daniel and ▷ Michael Drayton. Perhaps the poet who benefited most from her interest, however, was ▷ John Donne. Donne addressed seven of his verse letters (published in 1633) to the Countess, who was godmother to Donne's second daughter, Elizabeth.
Bib: Byard, M. M., 'The Trade of Courtiership: The Countess of Bedford and the Bedford Memorials – A Family History from 1585 to 1607', *History Today* (January, 1979), pp. 20–28; Hannay, M. P., *Silent But for the Word: Tudor Women as Patrons, Translators, and Writers of Religious Works.*

Russell, Lady Rachel (1636–1723)
Letter-writer. Married at 17 to Lord Vaughan she was widowed in 1665 and left rich by the death of her father, the Earl of Southampton, in 1667. In 1669 she married William Russell, a man three years younger, in a passionate love match which became a deeply happy marriage. But Russell, a zealous Protestant (▷ Protestantism) and Whig got involved with a group of people who discussed rising up against the king, ▷ Charles II, and replacing him with his illegitimate son, the Duke of Monmouth, in a conspiracy known as the ▷ Rye House Plot. Arrested and convicted on flimsy evidence of treason, Russell was beheaded in 1683. Throughout his arraignment and trial Lady Russell supported him, collecting evidence to defend him, standing next to him in the courtroom, and appealing to the king for clemency. After her husband's death she focused her attention on restoring his reputation (a task achieved when his attainder was reversed in 1689), and seeing to her children's marriages. She remained inconsolable for her husband's death, and achieved heroic stature among her contemporaries for her fidelity and fortitude. Her letters, describing her life in detail, were published in 1773 and 1817.
Bib: Fraser, A., *The Weaker Vessel.*

Russell, Willy (b 1947)
Dramatist. One of the most often produced contemporary dramatists, Russell's work is closely linked with Liverpool (he was born in nearby Whiston) and the Everyman Theatre which mounted his first professional production and has commissioned other plays from him, including *John, Paul, George, Ringo and...Bert* (1974). This musical about the Beatles brought him national success. *Educating Rita* (1979), a two-hander about a middle-aged lecturer and a 'raw diamond' working-class woman student – especially in its film version – put Russell on the international map. Russell himself left school at fifteen, returning to college years later because he had decided to become a teacher and a playwright, although the play probably owes as much to his regional background and time spent as a ladies' hairdresser. He is totally unpatronising about the working class, and his female characters are particularly vivid. In both *Educating Rita* and *Shirley Valentine* (1986) – a Liverpudlian monologue with marvellous jokes (but little feminist consciousness) – he makes use of minimal resources, but he is equally adept at handling large groups of characters. A good example is *Stags and Hens* (1978) (filmed as *Dancing Thru' the Dark*), in which bride and groom, each with their own friends on a last, prenuptial night out both choose the same

club for their celebration. Loosely based on the old 'Corsican Brothers' story of twins brought up in different classes, *Blood Brothers* (1981; musical version 1983) is a deeply felt picture of different social backgrounds. Its middle-class characters are perhaps less convincing than the working-class, despite the parable-like nature of its overall construction. The songs are able to succeed outside the show, but they are an integral and necessary part adding to our understanding of the characters. A smash hit that offered a social document disguised as melodrama.

Russian formalism
A school of literary criticism which flourished in the period leading up to the Russian Revolution of 1917 and for a brief time thereafter. It had strong connections with Futurism in both literature and the visual arts. There were two main groups: the Moscow Linguistic Circle (founded 1915) and the St Petersburg-based OPOJAZ (Society for the Study of Poetic Language) which began a year later. During Stalin's reign the movement was forced into retreat and several of its most able thinkers moved abroad, to Czechoslovakia first, where the Prague Linguistic Circle was founded, and then, in the late thirties, to Britain and the United States as the German invasion of Czechoslovakia threatened. Among Russian Formalism's most significant thinkers were ▷ Roman Jakobson, Victor Shklovsky, Boris Eichenbaum, Boris Tomashevsky and Yury Tynyanov.

The Russian Formalists analyzed literature not in terms of its content, but in terms of the way of organized language; that is, the Formalists defined ▷ literariness as essentially a type of language use. Literary language, they believed, is used in a fundamentally different way to ordinary language. Literary language foregrounds the device, that is, language features which call attention to themselves specifically as language use rather than as mere bearers or a message. One crucial function of the device is ▷ defamiliarization, a term coined by Shklovsky to describe literature's power to make the conventional appear strange. For the Russian Formalists, literature roughens or impedes the ordinary flow of language to make the reader reconsider habitual perceptions. Russian Formalist work was therefore done on the functions of language features like rhyme and metaphor, but they also made a major original contribution to the study of narrative where the work of Tomashevsky was particularly important. His distinction between *fabula* or story (the bald events in chronological sequence) and *syuzhet* or plot (how those events are told in, for instance, a novel) has been widely adopted.

The Formalists are criticized for ignoring the significance of the content of the literature they analyzed (▷ Formalism), and of underestimating the importance of social context, but their work gave a powerful impetus to the much more socially-engaged work of ▷ Mikhail Bakhtin. It has also been very influential in the West after its rediscovery from the mid-1960s when it formed a component of the Structuralist approach to literature and influenced some recent forms of Marxist criticism.
Bib: Lemon, L. and Reis, M. (eds.), *Russian Formalist Criticism: Four Essays*.

Russian influence on English literature
The international importance of Russian literature belongs chiefly to its achievements in the 19th century. Until the middle of the 19th century, the influence was chiefly from Britain upon Russia: Laurence Sterne, Walter Scott, Lord Byron and, later, Charles Dickens all made an important impression on Russian writers. Since about 1850, however, the balance of influence has been in the opposite direction, although Russian literature has chiefly been known in translation, which has limited extensive public knowledge to prose works, especially the novels. These have been widely read, especially in the famous translations by Constance Garnett, who translated Tolstoy, Dostoevski, Turgenev, ▷ Chekhov and Gogol in the decades before and after 1900.

Tolstoy and Turgenev were the first Russian novelists to receive wide acclaim in Britain and Tolstoy is still considered by many the supreme novelist. His reputation in Britain owed much to Matthew Arnold, whose essay in praise of Tolstoy appeared in 1887, and is included in *Essays in Criticism, Second Series*, 1888. His tribute is the more noticeable because he otherwise ignored novelists in his criticism, and it made its mark because he was the most influential critic of his day. However, other critics contributed their admiration for the Russians in the last quarter of the 19th century. This interest was awakened by the feeling that the Russians, besides the French, were the only nation to produce a range of major novelists comparable to those writing in English and that, unlike the French they shared with the British and Americans a moral concern with human nature in society. There was also the feeling that the Russian novelists went beyond the British and Americans, excelling in their rendering of religious experience, though the full force of this was not felt until Constance Garnett produced her translation of Dostoevski's *Brothers Karamazov* in 1912.

In America, interest in Russian writing seems to have gone deeper, because of a feeling that these two great continental nations shared comparable experiences in the disorderly variety of their rapid growth. It was not merely this, however that made the great Anglo-American novelist ▷ Henry James a lifelong admirer of Turgenev. Turgenev was already well known in

England from the middle of the century when he became the friend of ▷ George Eliot. These two novelists were the predominant influences on James' own work. He admired both for the depth of their moral insights but he admired Turgenev for what he saw as his superior artistic strictness in handling the elusive novel form. Turgenev thus combined for James the virtues of the French novelists with those of the English novelist he most admired. Gilbert Phelps, in *The Russian Novel in English Fiction* (1956), traces Turgenev's influence in some of the detail of James' novels and suggests his further influence on George Gissing, George Moore, Arnold Bennett, ▷ John Galsworthy and ▷ Joseph Conrad. Conrad is the most doubtful instance of these writers showing the Russian influence; as a Pole, he felt antagonistic to Russia and he did not know Russian, and yet it is impossible not to think of both Turgenev and Dostoevski when reading ▷ *Under Western Eyes*.

Chekhov's influence on the short story and on drama seems evident, although it may be that the distinctive development of the ▷ short story in English (for instance in ▷ James Joyce's ▷ *Dubliners* and in ▷ Katherine Mansfield) is as much an example of parallel development in the form as owing to Chekhov's initiation. In the drama, Chekhov's original handling of human speech as a medium has been developed in the works of ▷ Samuel Beckett and ▷ Harold Pinter.

The prestige of Russian literature in the mid-20th century remains very high in Britain, especially Boris Pasternak's *Doctor Zhivago* (1957) and the works of Alexander Solzhenitsyn. What is admired is the rendering of human experience and suffering on an heroic scale, and the courage and vitality of literary productivity in the face of adverse and repressive conditions. In the 1980s, however, with the more liberal regime in Russia, more, frequently dissident, literature has become available to the west, for example the poetry of Irina Ratoslinskaya.

In late 1991 and early 1992, the Soviet Union began to break up as ▷ communism ceased to be a dominant and cohering political force in Eastern Europe. Writing in Russian will thus cease to be identified with the U.S.S.R in its old form.

Ruth (1853)
A novel by ▷ Elizabeth Gaskell. Ruth Hilton, an ▷ orphan, is seduced by wealthy and self-interested Mr Bellingham and abandoned after a brief affair. She is taken in by the Dissenting minister, Mr Benson, and his sister, and assumes the identity of Mrs Denbigh, a widow, so that she and her illegitimate son will be accepted in society. Ruth finds employment as a ▷ governess to the Bradshaw family, and later re-encounters her seducer, who is now the local MP, re-named Mr Donne. He offers to marry her, but she refuses, having determined to seek redemption for her sin. Later, her true identity is discovered, and Mr Bradshaw casts her out (Donne is not known to be the seducer). After many futile attempts to find employment she offers her services as a sick-nurse during a typhus epidemic, and through her devoted work becomes revered in the eyes of the community. Her last unselfish act is to nurse delirious Mr Donne through his fever, after which she catches typhoid and dies a martyr's death. The novel was burned by members of Gaskell's congregation and criticized both for its sympathetic treatment of the ▷ 'fallen woman' and for its unrealistically saintly portrayal of Ruth, who is throughout a picture of innocence, humility and Christian submissiveness. Flawed as it is by religiosity and narrative contrivance, *Ruth* nevertheless reveals the ideological contradictions of Christian and Victorian attitudes towards women.

Rutherford, Mark
▷ White, William Hale.

Rye House Plot (1683)
A plot led by the ▷ Ist Earl of Shaftesbury, the leader of the Whig Party, to kidnap ▷ Charles II and force him to summon a parliament. The plot was discovered, and the consequent discredit of the Whigs, together with Charles II's popularity, caused a public reaction against them, and enabled ▷ James II to succeed peacefully in 1685, in spite of his open Roman ▷ Catholicism.

Rymer, Thomas (1641–1713)
A rigidly ▷ neo-classical critic, chiefly known for his obtuse though witty and amusing *Short View of Tragedy* (1692) in which he condemned ▷ Shakespeare's tragedy ▷ *Othello* for a barbaric failure to observe the ▷ classical unities.

S

Sackville, Charles
⊳ Dorset, Sixth Earl of.

Sackville, Thomas, first Earl of Dorset (1536–1608)
Poet, statesman, diplomat; created first Earl of Dorset in 1604. He contributed the *Induction* and the *Complaint of Buckingham* in the verse compilation ⊳ *Mirror for Magistrates*; the *Induction* is the main basis for his fame as a poet. He also collaborated with Thomas Norton in writing the first ⊳ tragedy in ⊳ blank verse, ⊳ *Gorboduc*.
Bib: Berlin, N., *Thomas Sackville*.

Sackville-West, Hon. Victoria Mary ('Vita') (1892–1962)
Poet, novelist, travel writer, gardener. Born at Knole, Kent, to one of the oldest families in England, she married Harold Nicolson and travelled with him during his diplomatic career before settling at Sissinghurst Castle, Kent in 1930, where she created an important garden, which still exists. From 1918 until 1921 her relationship with Violet Keppel (later Violet Trefusis) was of great importance in her life. In 1922 she met ⊳ Virginia Woolf and began a correspondence, and a friendship that inspired Woolf's novel, ⊳ *Orlando* (1928). Her earlier novels were: *Heritage* (1919); *The Dragon in Shallow Waters* (1921); *Challenge* (1923); *Grey Wethers* (1923); *Seducers in Ecuador* (1924). Her next three novels were best-sellers: *The Edwardians* (1930); *All Passion Spent* (1931); *Family History* (1932). *Thirty Clocks Strike the Hour* (1932) was a collection of short stories, while her remaining four novels were: *The Dark Island* (1934); *Grand Canyon* (1942); *The Easter Party* (1953); *No Signposts in the Sea* (1962). Her fiction evokes a social world in realistic detail and, while largely traditional in form, explores themes such as duality within the gender identity of the individual and the assertion of women's rights. Her volumes of poetry were: *Constantinople* (1915); *Poems of West and East* (1917); *Selected Poems* (1941); *Collected Poems* (1933). *The Land* (1926), which belongs to the pastoral genre, *Solitude* (1938) and *The Garden* (1946) were all long poems. Her other works include a family history, entitled *Knole and the Sackvilles* (1922), travel books on Persia, gardening books and biography.
Bib: Watson, S. R., *V. Sackville-West*; Nicolson, N., *Portrait of a Marriage*; Nicolson, N. and Trautman, J., (eds.), *The Letters of Virginia Woolf, Vol. III 1923–1928*; De Salvo, L. and Leaska, M. A., *The Letters of Vita Sackville-West to Virginia Woolf*; MacKnight, N. (ed.), *Dearest Andrew: Letters from Vita Sackville-West to Andrew Reiber, 1951–1962*; Leaska, M. A. and Phillips, J., *The Letters of Violet Trefusis to Vita Sackville-West*; Glendinning, V., *Vita: The Life of Vita Sackville-West*; Raitt, S., *Vita and Virginia*.

Sade, Donatien Alphonse, Marquis de (1740–1814)
French novelist and poet. His belief that his destructive impulses were part of his nature, and yet uncontrollable, counterbalanced the doctrine of ⊳ Rousseau, according to whom man undistorted by social forces was naturally good. Sade's ideas profoundly influenced the dark side of ⊳ romanticism.

Saga
An old Norse word meaning 'oral story'. The sagas were a body of Norwegian and Icelandic prose epics (11th–13th centuries). However, the term has also come to refer to any large and long familial narrative such as ⊳ Galsworthy's ⊳ *Forsyte Saga*.

Sahgal, Nayantara (b 1927)
Indian novelist and journalist, born in Allahabad, Uttar Pradesh, India and educated at schools in India and at Wellesley College, Massachusetts, USA. She is a member of one of India's most powerful political families, the Nehrus, the niece of India's first prime minister, Jawaharlal Nehru, and daughter of a prominent politician and diplomat, Nehru's sister Vijaya Lakshmi Pandit. Her earliest writings were autobiographical, drawing on her experience of Indian politics before and after Independence: *Prison and Chocolate Cake* (1954); *From Fear Set Free* (1962). Most of Sahgal's earlier novels concern the lives of upper-middle-class women, with political events providing the context: *A Time to be Happy* (1958); *This Time of Morning* (1965); *Storm in Chandigarh* (1969); *The Day in Shadow* (1971); *A Voice for Freedom* (1977); *A Situation in New Delhi* (1977). Her later fiction is more explicitly focused on the political and historical: *Rich Like Us* (1985), which won the Sinclair Prize for fiction, shows concern for human rights issues in its portrayal of political violence during the state of emergency of the late 1970s. *Plans for Departure* (1985), which won the Commonwealth Prize for fiction (Eurasia category) is set in India during the period of World War I, with a Danish suffragette as protagonist, while *Mistaken Identity* (1988), about a woman who rejects a life in *purdah*, is set in the 1930s. Sahgal has also written historical and political non-fiction, including two books on Indira Ghandi and *The Freedom Movement in India* (1970).
Bib: Krishna Rao, A.V., *Nayantara Sahgal: A Study of Her Fiction and Non-Fiction*.

St Paul's Cathedral
The cathedral of the ⊳ City of London, and its principal church. The old cathedral was burnt down in the Great Fire of London (1666) and the present one was built according to the design of ⊳ Sir Christopher Wren. Until the 18th century not only the churchyard but

the building itself was a public meeting-place for much besides Christian worship; news was exchanged there, servants were hired, and business was conducted. The central aisle was called Paul's Walk, and a Paul's Man was a term for one of its frequenters.

Saintsbury, George Edward Bateman (1845–1993)
Literary historian and critic. His works include: *A Short History of French Literature* (1882); *A Short History of English Literature* (1898); *A History of Criticism* (1900–04); *A History of English Prosody* (1906–21); *The History of English Criticism* (1911); *A History of the French Novel* (1917–19). He also wrote studies of Dryden, Walter Scott, and Matthew Arnold. His treatment of literary study was historical; that is to say, principles of evaluation or critical theory were for him secondary to coherent narration.

Saladin (1138–93)
Sultan of Egypt. His conquest of the Christian Latin Kingdom of Jerusalem (1187) provoked the Third Crusade under ⊳ Richard I of England and Philip II of France, with whom he made a truce. He was famous for his fierce piety compounded with chivalrous generosity; in English history and legend these qualities are made to represent him as a suitable antagonist to Richard, himself a legend for his courage and chivalry. Their rivalry is the subject of ⊳ Scott's novel *The Talisman* (1825). Historically, Saladin is important for halting the invasion of the East by the Christian West, and starting a counter-movement against the West which lasted until the 17th century.
⊳ Crusades.

Salisbury, Sir Thomas (d 1643)
Poet. Salisbury studied at Oxford and the Inner Temple, but then left London at the death of his father to look after his family estates. He later became a Member of Parliament for his local constituency, Denbigh. A staunch Royalist, he was imprisoned for supporting ⊳ Charles I at Edge Hill. Although he was a prolific poet, all that remains is *The History of Joseph* (pub. 1636).

***Salome* (1891)**
A play by ⊳ Oscar Wilde centred on the destructive love of Salome for John the Baptist. It was written first in French and translated by Lord Alfred Douglas, whose edition appeared in 1893 illustrated by ⊳ Aubrey Beardsley. Although the play went into rehearsal in 1893 it was banned by the Lord Chamberlain for representing a biblical subject, and was not performed in Britain until 1931. It was first staged in Paris in 1896 with Sarah Bernhardt in the leading role: by that time Wilde was in prison for 'homosexual acts'. Salome has been called the 'Goddess of Decadence', the symbolic incarnation of undying lust. Wilde imagined her dressed in green 'like a curious poisonous lizard', contrasting strongly with the yellow costumes of the other characters. New Women writers such as ⊳ George Egerton appropriated the image of Salome to represent sexual desire.

***Samson Agonistes* (1671)**
A ⊳ tragedy in ⊳ blank verse by ⊳ John Milton, published (with ⊳ *Paradise Regained*) in 1671. It is an example of Milton's blended Puritan-biblical and ⊳ Renaissance-classical inspiration; the subject is drawn from the Old Testament (*Judges* 16) and the form from the ancient Greek tragedies of ⊳ Aeschylus and ⊳ Sophocles.

Samson, the Jewish hero, has been betrayed by his Philistine wife Dalila (spelt Delilah in the Authorized Version of the ⊳ Bible, where she is not his wife) to her people, who are the foes of the Jews. His hair, on which depended his exceptional God-given strength, has been cut off; he has been blinded and cast into prison in Gaza, where his hair is allowed to recover its former length and he is subjected to slavery by his enemies. The play opens while he is resting from his enormous labours and he is approached by a chorus of lamenting Jews. In his mood of extreme despair, he is visited by his father Manoa, who hopes to negotiate his release from the Philistines; Samson, however, has the moral strength to refuse Manoa's suggestions, on the grounds that his lot is a consequence of his own moral weakness in betraying the secret of his strength to his wife. His next visitor is Dalila herself, who seeks his forgiveness in return for alleviation of his sufferings; he replies, however, that if he cannot pardon himself, her crime is still more unpardonable. This double moral victory heartens him enough to enable him to frighten away his third visitor, the Philistine giant Harapha, who comes to mock at him. Next a messenger arrives with an order that he is to come before the Philistine lords in order to entertain them with feats of his strength. To the dismay of the chorus, he accepts the order, but we learn from a messenger that it is only to destroy the entire assembly (including himself) by rooting up the two pillars which support the roof of the building. The chorus is left to chant praise of the hero and of the wisdom of God, who sustains his people.

It has long been assumed that *Samson Agonistes* was written after Milton had finished ⊳ *Paradise Lost* (*ie* between 1667 and 1671). This traditional dating reinforces the connection between the blind and defeated hero of the work, and the blind and (ideologically) defeated figure of Milton after the Restoration. However, strong reasons have now been advanced for dating Milton's drama to a much earlier period of his career between 1647 and 1653. The two principle themes of modern criticism of the work have centred on the question of 'structure', and the question of whether the guiding spirit of the play is 'Hellenic', 'Hebraic' or 'Christian'. In essence, both of these questions address a problem that *Samson Agonistes* has long posed to readers – that interpretation of the work rests on locating it in relation to other texts (Greek tragedy or the Old Testament, for example) and to a specific historical moment.

Sand, George (1804–76)
French Romantic novelist and the best known French woman writer of the 19th century. Her influence on Victorian writers and the Victorian reading public was enormous and her work was a formative influence on the Victorian consciousness. Sand was born Aurore Dupin and brought up at her paternal grandmother's country property at Nohant. After a convent education in Paris she returned to Nohant where her independent spirit was encouraged. She read Jean-Jacques Rousseau (1712–78), Byron (1788–1824), Shakespeare and Vicomte de Chateaubriand (1768–1848), the greatest French writer of his generation and the father of French Romanticism. She married the baron Dudevant with whom she had two children, but in 1831 was living with a young writer Jules Sandeau whose surname she adapted as her pen-name. She subsequently enjoyed a stream of extra-marital affairs, the most famous of which were with the poet Alfred de Musset (1810–57), recorded in her novel *Elle et Lui* (1859), and with composers Franz Liszt (1811–86) and Frédéric Chopin (1810–49). She played an active role during the political upheavals of 1848, but disassociated herself from radical ▷ feminist attempts to get her elected to the National Assembly, as she was a reformist rather than a revolutionary at heart. She enjoyed a period of bourgeois respectability towards the end of her life and died peacefully at Nohant in 1876.

The ▷ *Athenaeum* mentioned her work in February 1833 with a mixture of moral outrage and admiration and from that point on she was widely read and reviewed in England, and very much a talking point in middle-class drawing rooms. Her main impact was made with works written during the first twenty years of her career when her doctrines were *avant garde* and challenging. In works such as *Indiana* (1832), *Valentine* (1833), *Léila* (1833) and *Jacques* (1834) she described ▷ marriage as 'one of the most barbaric institutions [society] has ever invented'. Her views were bold and outspoken, especially on the subject of relationships between the sexes and she was widely credited with having introduced passion as a major theme in the novel.

The 'second' phase of Sand's writing coincided with her increased enthusiasm for humanitarianism, socialism and Christianity. During this period she produced novels in which her desire to see humanity regenerate itself through a combination of social change and adherence to the teachings of Christ is very apparent. These include *Spiridion* (1838), *Les Sept Cordes de la Lyre* (1839), *Consuelo* (1842–3) and *La Comtesse de Rudolstadt* (1843–4). They were followed by a series of pastoral and/or socialist novels – *La Mare au Diable* (1846), *La Péché de M. Antoine* (1847), *La Petite Fadette* (1849), *François le Champi* (1850) and *Les Maitres Sonneurs* (1853) – for which their author is most famous, and which reveal her tendency to idealize working-class rural life. In the mid-1850s she produced her less successful novels and her twenty-volume ▷ autobiography *Histoire de ma Vie* (trans. 1855).

▷ Matthew Arnold went on a pilgrimage to the middle of France in order to meet her and ▷ Clough drew inspiration for a poem from her novel *Jeanne*. For ▷ Jane Carlyle, ▷ George Eliot, Geraldine Endsor, the ▷ Brontës, and ▷ Elizabeth Barrett Browning, George Sand was the model of a dedicated professional writer who held her own with men, asking for no allowance to be made for her sex. Elizabeth Barret found her novels intense and liberating in their testimony to the irresistible power of human passion. The Brontës valued her resistance to received doctrines which forbade women equality, frankness and the right to a similar intensity of love to that enjoyed by men. ▷ Kingsley and ▷ Samuel Smiles also admired her work and ▷ George Lewes claimed she and Jane Austen (1775–1817) were the two touchstones for feminine literary greatness. Arnold and Clough identified with her idealism, her revolt against contemporary social norms, her delight in natural scenery and her faith in humanity. ▷ Thomas Carlyle, however, coined the term 'George Sandism' to describe tolerance of immorality, romantic effusiveness, lack of common sense, high flown sentiments and an obsession with love. ▷ Thomas Hardy and ▷ Henry James were deeply impressed with her work and James was singing her praises well into the 20th century.

▷ French influence on Victorian literature.

Bib: Thomson, P., *George Sand and the Victorians*; Blount, P.G., *George Sand and the Victorian World*; Cate, C., *George Sand: A Biography*; Crecelius, K.J., *Family Romances: George Sand's Early Novels*.

Sandys, George (1578–1644)
Translator and travel writer. Son of the Archbishop of York, Sandys travelled extensively and published accounts of his journeys to Italy and the Near East in *A Relation of a Journey* (1615). He then moved to America as treasurer of the Virginia Company (1621) and began translating ▷ Ovid's ▷ *Metamorphoses*, the

work for which he is best known. This text was published in 1626, with the first book of the ▷ *Aeneid* added at its reissue in 1632. He also translated Grotius' *Christ's Passion; A Tragedy* (1640) and rendered several parts of the ▷ Bible into verse. Sandys' Ovid was immensely influential on the Augustan writers (it had reached eight editions by 1690), and it was an important factor in establishing the heroic couplet as their preferred poetic metre.

▷ Turberville, George; Translation.

Bib: Davis, R. B., *George Sandys: Poet Adventurer*.

Sanger, John (1816–89)
The founder of the most famous of the British travelling circuses. He began with a conjuring exhibition in Birmingham in 1845, and reached the height of his fame as a circus proprietor in the 1870s and 80s. In his later years he was known as Lord John Sanger, though he never received a peerage.

Sangreal
A name for the Holy ▷ Grail.

Sansculottes
The name for recruits from the poorer classes to the ▷ French Revolutionary army. The word means 'without breeches' – kneebreeches being then the wear of all but the poorest. The sansculottes wore loose trousers or 'pantalons'.

Sansom, William (1912–76)
Short-story writer, novelist and travel writer. He served in the London Fire Brigade in World War II, an experience which gave rise to *Fireman Flower* (1944), a volume of short stories, which was the form in which he was most successful. His work covers a wide range of subject matter and styles, from documentary realism to macabre fantasy. In *The Body* (1949) the mental stability of the first-person narrator gradually disintegrates as a result of obsessive jealousy.

Bib: Michel-Michot, P., *Sansom: A Critical Assessment*.

Sappho (Psappho) (7th–6th century BC)
Greek poet from Lesbos. Daughter of Scamandronymus and Cleis, and sister of three brothers. At some time she visited Sicily. The many anecdotes about Sappho's life, drawn from her works and from comic dramas written about her, make accurate biography impossible. She may have had a daughter, Cleis, although Sappho refers to her with a word that may simply be a term of affection. The stories that she committed suicide for love of Phaon probably come from 4th-century BC comic drama.

Her work is the largest corpus written by an ancient Greek woman, although very fragmentary. It shows, in a variety of metres, Sappho as leader of a band of young girls in worship of the goddess of love Aphrodite. The *Hymn to Aphrodite*, in a metre called 'sapphic', after her, is an address to the goddess to aid her seduction of a young girl whom Sappho loves. It neatly employs traditional hymnic commonplaces to describe a female object of desire. A second fragment was preserved which evocatively describes the symptoms of one in love, as she watches the woman she loves beside her bridegroom. Sappho wrote many marriage songs and was famous for them in antiquity.

Other fragments include a description of the beauty of the woman Anactoria, a poem to her 'daughter' Cleis, good wishes to her brother as he sets out on a voyage, a narrative poem on the marriage of Hector and Andromache (▷ epic characters) and a poem for a girl, Lydia, who is compared to the moon outshining the stars.

Sappho occasionally used epic metaphors and images of war to describe love, and thus played an important part in the development of the theme of 'love as war' in later Latin elegiac poetry. This literary transference of male war imagery to female love poetry is one further sign of her literary ability. Another is the variety of metres employed in her lyric poetry. Her poetry was translated into Latin and imitated by Roman poets such as ▷ Catullus and ▷ Horace in the 1st century BC. Antipater of Thescalonica (2nd century BC) includes her in his list of nine women poets, and another Greek ▷ epigram styles her 'the tenth Muse'. In the 17th and 18th centuries, a woman poet was somtimes referred to as 'Sappho'. A notable Sappho was ▷ Katherine Philips. Another was ▷ Madeleine de Scudéry.

Bid: (text & trans.) Campbell, D. A., *Greek Lyric*; de Jean, J., *Fictions of Sappho* 1546–1937.

Sargeson, Frank (b 1903)
New Zealand novelist, short-story writer and dramatist. His stories tend to deal with a small group of characters and to be narrated from within the consciousness of one of them, often a character with limited powers of self-expression, like the narrator of the ▷ novella *That Summer* (1946). His novels are more various in tone, but render the sense of a claustrophobic and somewhat Puritan New Zealand society by means of irony, comedy and a skilful rendering of idiom. His novels are: *I Saw In My Dream* (1949); *I For One . . .* (1954); *Memoirs of a Peon* (1965); *The Hangover* (1967); *Joy of the Worm* (1969); *Sunset Village* (1976). Story collection: *Collected Short Stories* (1965).

Bib: Copland, R. A., *Frank Sargeson*.

Sartor Resartus: The Life and Opinions of Herr Teufelsdröckh
A disguised spiritual ▷ autobiography by ▷ Thomas Carlyle. It was serialized (1833–4)

in *Fraser's Magazine* and published in book form in Boston, USA, in 1836 and in Britain in 1838. Carlyle was under the influence of the German ⊳ Romantics, eg Jean Paul Richter. The title is Latin for 'the tailor re-patched': Carlyle offers the fable that human beliefs and institutions are like clothes and need renewing. Against the poet Byron's (1788–1824) attitude of doubt, isolation and suffering, Carlyle calls for the affirmativeness of the German poet ⊳ Goethe; heroic qualities such as sacrifice and devotion to duty must redeem the inner man and, through men, the directionless age in which Carlyle felt himself to be living – the age of flux and the decay of unquestioning religious faith. Besides the drive of ⊳ German influence, Carlyle felt the force of the old-fashioned Scottish Calvinism such as had animated his father. The three crucial chapters are 'The Everlasting No', 'Centre of Indifference' and 'The Everlasting Yea'. Despite the difficulty he had in getting the book published in Britain, it marks the beginning of his exposition of the creed of heroism, which made Carlyle an inspiring figure in commerce-dominated mid-19th-century Britain.

Sartre, Jean-Paul (1905–80)
French writer. His areas of activity and influence covered philosophy, the novel, drama, literary criticism and political commitment. He was the major exponent of atheistic ⊳ existentialism in France and made an early impact with his novels *La Nausée* (1938) and *Les Chemins de la liberté*, a projected tetralogy of which only three volumes were published: *L'Age de raison* (1945), *Le Sursis* (1945) and *La Mort dans l'âme* (1949). In *La Nausée*, the central character, Roquentin, discovers that far from being central to the nature of things, man is metaphysically superfluous (*de trop*) in the universe. *Les Chemins de la liberté* are set at the outbreak of World War II and portray the urgent necessity of commitment, especially in the form of political action, to secure personal and collective freedom. The same themes run through Sartre's drama, which is more accessible than the fiction and has proved more enduringly popular (*Les Mouches*, 1943, a version of the Orestes story; *Huis Clos*, 1945; *Les Mains sales*, 1948). The philosophical background to existentialism was expounded in *L'Etre et le néant* (1943) and *Critique de la raison dialectique* (1960).

Satre also wrote a number of existentialist-orientated biographies, of Baudelaire, of Jean Genet (1910–86) and of ⊳ Flaubert. His volumes of *Situations* contain mainly essays on politics, literature and society and in 1945 he founded the important literary and political review, *Les Temps modernes*. In 1964 he published his autobiography, *Les Mots*, which seeks to expose the ideology of the autobiographical genre and views with irony his years of childhood under his grandfather Charles Schweitzer (Sartre was the cousin of Albert Schweitzer, (1875–1965). In the same year, Sartre was awarded and refused the Nobel Prize for Literature.

Sassoon, Siegfried (1886–1967)
Poet and autobiographer. His *Memoirs of a Foxhunting Man* (1928) and *Memoirs of an Infantry Officer* (1930) are accounts of his life as a country gentleman before World War I, and of his experiences during it. He also became famous for his savagely satirical poems written during his military service, his first and most famous volume of anti-war poems being *Counter-attack* (1918). He was a friend of Wilfred Owen, and influenced Owen's writing. The two volumes of memoirs were put together as *The Complete Memoirs of George Sherston* (1937), which includes an additional section, *Sherston's Progress*. His poems, including volumes published since World War I, are in a collected edition (1961).

***Satanic Verses, The* (1988)**
Novel by ⊳ Salman Rushdie which received mixed reviews on its publication in 1988. Controversy erupted when Muslims protested that the book was blasphemous. Copies were burned in Bradford and demonstrations took place there and elsewhere in Britain, Pakistan and the USA. In Iran mass demonstrations against the author, book and publisher caused international tension to rise. The Ayatollah Khomeini passed a death sentence on Rushdie, who went into hiding. The novel returned to the ⊳ best-seller lists in the wake of the controversy, which raised many issues of freedom of speech and expression, and the freedom to publish.

Satire
A form of attack through mockery; it may exist in any literary medium, but is often regarded as a medium in itself. The origins of the word help to explain the manifestations of satire. It derives from the Latin 'satura' = a vessel filled with the earliest agricultural produce of the year, used in seasonal festivals to celebrate harvest; a secondary meaning is 'miscellany of entertainment', implying merry-making at such festivals, probably including verbal warfare. This primitive humour gave rise to a highly cultivated form of literary attack in the poetry of ⊳ Horace, Persius (1st century AD) and ⊳ Juvenal. Thus from ancient Roman culture two ideas of satire have come down to us: the first expresses a basic instinct for comedy through mockery in human beings, and was not invented by the Romans; the second is a self-conscious medium, implying standards of civilized and moral rightness in the mind of the poet and hence a desire on his or her part to instruct readers so as to reform their moral failings and absurdities. The two kinds of satire are inter-related, so that it is not possible to

distinguish them sharply. Moreover, it is not easy to distinguish strict satire in either of its original forms from other kinds of comedy.

1 Strict satire, *ie* satire emulating the Roman poets. This was one of the outcomes of ▷ Renaissance cultivation of ancient Latin literature. Between 1590 and 1625 several poets wrote deliberate satires with Juvenal, Persius and Horace in mind; the most important of these were ▷ Donne and ▷ Ben Jonson, but ▷ Joseph Hall claimed to be the first, and another was ▷ Marston. The great age of the strict satire was the 18th century, notably in the work of ▷ Pope who emulated the relatively genial satire of Horace, and ▷ Samuel Johnson, who emulated the sombre style of Juvenal. Satire of this sort makes its object of attack the social forms and corruptions of the time, and its distinctive medium is the 10-syllable rhymed couplet, perfected by Pope and used with different force by Johnson.

2 ▷ Comedy of Humours and ▷ Comedy of Manners. These are the most easily distinguishable forms of dramatic satire. The former is associated chiefly with Ben Jonson, and has its roots in the older ▷ Morality drama, which was only intermittently satirical. The 'humours' in Jonson's conception are the obsessions and manias to which the nature of human beings invites them to abandon themselves; they have a close relation to the medieval ▷ Seven Deadly Sins, such as lust, avarice and gluttony. The Comedy of Manners belongs to the period 1660–1800, and, especially, to the first 40 years of it. Its most notable exponents are ▷ Congreve at the end of the 17th century and ▷ Sheridan at the end of the 18th. This comedy is less concerned with basic human dispositions and more with transient social ones; rational social behaviour is the standard in the mind of the dramatist. Both these forms of satire were taken over by novelists; the 18th-century novelist ▷ Fielding began as a writer of dramatic comedies of manners, but Dickens in the 19th century writes more distinctly in the tradition of the comedy of humours, with a strong addition of social stagnation. Satire in the theatre has, since the 1960s, been replaced by television satire, with radical programmes such as *Beyond the Fringe* and more recently, *Spitting Image*.

3 Satire of ▷ Parody and ▷ Irony. This includes the most skilful and powerful satire in the language; its most productive period is between 1660 and 1750. Parody at its most powerful implies the writer's complete respect for the serious form which he or she is using in a comic way; thus in this period (which included the very serious ▷ epic ▷ *Paradise Lost*) the prestige of the epic form was still high, and ▷ Dryden (▷ *Absalom and Achitophel*) and ▷ Pope (▷ *The Rape of the Lock* and ▷ *The Dunciad*) used their appreciation of epic to make ironic contrast between the grandeur of its style and pettiness, meanness and destructiveness of their chosen subject. The most notable practitioner in prose of ironic and parodic satire was ▷ Swift. Works such as ▷ *A Modest Proposal* and ▷ *Gulliver's Travels* aim to ambush the reader's expectations and to undermine complacency through shock, laughter and incongruity. Similarly ▷ Samuel Butler used the mode of romantic epic to attack the ▷ Puritans in ▷ *Hudibras*.

Irony does not necessarily use parody, but even when it does not, it operates in a similar way, by addressing the reader in terms which he has learnt to receive as acceptable at their face value, and then shocking him into recognition that something quite unacceptable is the real subject.

4 ▷ Flytings, and other traditional forms. The Middle Ages took from its popular festivals a strong tradition of verbal combat (flytings) and sardonic criticism of the established social order. One aspect of this emerges in popular ▷ ballads (especially in the printed form of broadsides which developed after the medieval period) and in the work of educated writers such as ▷ Langland and ▷ Chaucer – grimly in the former's ▷ *Piers Plowman*, and genially in the latter's ▷ *Canterbury Tales*. Dunbar was another eminent practitioner of flytings, *eg* his *Flyting of Dunbar and Kennedy*.

5 Novelistic satire. Much satire in novels from the 18th to the 20th century cannot be summed up under comedy of manners. The novels of ▷ Peacock, for example, establish a tradition of comic discussions mocking at contemporary trends of thought; Peacock's example was partly followed by ▷ Meredith and ▷ Aldous Huxley. Another variant is the 'anti-utopia', using an imaginary country to satirize actual tendencies in contemporary Britain. The most notable examples of this are ▷ *Erewhon* by ▷ Samuel Butler and *Brave New World* by ▷ Aldous Huxley. Apart from these examples, it is difficult to find a novelist who does not use satire at least intermittently, usually as social comment. Eminent examples are: Fielding, ▷ Jane Austen, ▷ Thackeray, ▷ Dickens, ▷ Wells, ▷ Foster, and more recently ▷ Angus Wilson, ▷ Evelyn Waugh, ▷ George Orwell, and the 'campus novels' of ▷ Kingsley Amis and ▷ David Lodge.

Saturday Review
It was founded in 1855 and noted for the brilliance of its contributors and the severity of its criticism. Later it took a greater interest in literature and included contributions from ▷ Thomas Hardy, Max Beerbohm, Arthur Symons and ▷ H. G. Wells. George Bernard Shaw was dramatic critic from 1895 to 1898 and Agate from 1921 to 1923.

Saussure, Ferdinand de (1857–1913)
Swiss linguist, generally regarded as the founder of Structuralism. Saussure's *Course in General*

Linguistics, was published two years after his death, in 1915, and represents a reconstruction of three series of lectures which he gave at the University of Geneva during the years 1906–7, 1908–9, and 1910–11. It was Saussure who pioneered the distinction between ▷ 'langue' and 'parole', and who sought to define the operations of language according to the principles of combination and ▷ difference. Although ▷ deconstruction has done much to undermine the Structuralist base of Saussure's thinking, the concept of 'difference' as a determining principle in establishing meaning ('signification') remains one of the key concepts in modern critical theory. Moreover, Saussure's work provided the foundation for the methodological analysis of sign systems (semiotics), and the types of linguistic investigation which he undertook have been successfully appropriated by literary critics, as well as by social anthropologists such as Claude Lévi-Strauss (b 1908).

Savage, Richard (?1697–1743)
Poet. Savage claimed to be the illegitimate son of the Countess of Macclesfield, and spent his life in petulant complaint against her, and in cultivating wealthy patrons. He was accused of being ▷ Alexander Pope's spy at the time of the composition of ▷ *The Dunciad*, and after his death was the subject of an intimate ▷ biography by ▷ Samuel Johnson. His monologue in heroic ▷ couplets, *The Bastard* (1728) dramatizes his situation following the death sentence passed on him after he had killed a man in a brawl. It contains some vigorous lines:

Blest be the Bastard's *birth!* . . .
No sickly fruit of faint compliance he;
He! stampt in nature's mint of extasy!
He lives to build, not boast, a gen'rous race:
No tenth transmitter of a foolish face.

On the intervention of his friends he was pardoned and a long poem, *The Wanderer*, appeared in 1729. Savage also wrote satirical poems in couplets, including *The Progress of a Divine* (1735).

Savonarola, Fra Girolamo (1452–98)
In Italian history a Florentine monk who led a revolt against the worldly excesses of the ▷ Renaissance. His own reforms went to excess, and he was eventually condemned and executed as a heretic.

Saxons
The name of a Germanic people which invaded southern Britain from their homeland around the mouth of the Elbe in the 5th and 6th centuries, after the departure of the Roman occupying forces. They eventually shared what came to be known as England (Angle-land) with the Angles and the Jutes. Their principal kingdom was Wessex (*ie* West Saxons) in the south-west. Other Saxon kingdoms are commemorated in the names of modern English counties: Sussex (South Saxons); Middlesex (Middle Saxons, in London and to the immediate north of it); and Essex (East Saxons). ▷ Wessex itself has disappeared as a geographical name, except in the novels of ▷ Thomas Hardy.
▷ Anglo-Saxon.

Sayers, Dorothy L. (Leigh) (1893–1957)
▷ Detective fiction.

***Scenes of Clerical Life* (1857)**
Three tales by ▷ George Eliot, and her earliest work in fiction: *The Sad Fortunes of the Rev. Amos Barton; Mr Gilfil's Love-Story*; and *Janet's Repentance*. The hero of each is a clergyman. They were published first in ▷ *Blackwood's Magazine* in 1857 and collected as *Scenes of Clerical Life* in 1858.

'Scholar Gipsy, The'
A poem by ▷ Matthew Arnold, first published in 1853. He took the subject from a legend reported by Joseph Glanvill in *The Vanity of Dogmatizing* (1661). The Scholar of the legend renounced the anxiety of seeking a career through his scholarship, and took to wandering with the gipsies, dedicating himself to learning their lore. Arnold regards him as an immortal figure, and uses him as the type of a man who has happily escaped the anguish of the 19th-century intellectual's loss of faith and controlling convictions. The poem is not always considered to be Arnold's best, but it is one of his most famous, since it expresses the distress and doubt that is widely evident in mid-Victorian writing. It is written in twenty-five ten-line stanzas resembling those of John Keats' (1795–1821) Odes. It is like the Odes too in its sensuous evocation of natural surroundings, though Arnold's tone is often nostalgic and insular. In 1867 Arnold published a companion-piece to 'The Scholar Gipsy' entitled *Thyrsis*, an elegy to his friend ▷ Clough, who died in 1861.

School for Scandal, The
A comedy by ▷ Richard Brinsley Sheridan, first produced in 1777. Two of the central characters are brothers: Charles Surface, whose character is open-hearted but reckless and extravagant, and Joseph Surface, a meanhearted hypocrite. The principal women are Lady Teazle, the young, gay wife of the elderly Sir Peter Teazle, and Maria, his ward, with whom Charles is in love and whom Joseph is trying to marry for her money, while he also makes love to Lady Teazle. Sir Oliver Surface, rich uncle to the two brothers, returns from India in disguise in order to spy on his nephews, thereby to discover their

true characters. In the background, a group of scandal-lovers (Lady Sneerwell, Mrs Candour, Sir Benjamin Backbite) do their worst to damage as many reputations as possible. Sir Oliver satisfies himself, in scenes of extremely successful theatrical comedy, about which of his nephews truly deserves his affection: Charles marries Maria, and the deceitfulness of Joseph is exposed.

The comedy is Sheridan's masterpiece, and the last notable play in the tradition of the English ▷ Comedy of Manners until ▷ Oscar Wilde at the end of the 19th century.

School of Night
A term used to designate a circle of intellectuals that centred on ▷ Sir Walter Ralegh in the early 1590s. It derives from ▷ Shakespeare's play ▷ *Love's Labour's Lost* (IV. 3. 251–2). The courtier Berowne has just been praising the lady Rosaline who has a dark complexion: 'No face is fair that is not full so black', whereupon the king breaks in:

O paradox! Black is the badge of hell,
The hue of dungeons and the School of Night.

'School of Night' has puzzled editors, who have variously amended it to 'scowl' and 'stole'. Some modern scholars, however (see especially the Cambridge Shakespeare edition and M. C. Bradbrook's *The School of Night*), consider that Shakespeare was alluding to Ralegh's dark complexion and to the reputation of himself and his circle for atheism. At about the time the play was written (1594–5), Ralegh, in disgrace at court, had retired to his country house and declared his preference for a life of study over the active and public life. The rival claims of the studious and retired and the active and public life is the theme of *Love's Labour's Lost*.

Ralegh's circle seems to have consisted of himself, the famous mathematician Thomas Harriot, the poets ▷ Christopher Marlowe and ▷ George Chapman, the Earls of Northumberland and Derby, and a few others. Marlowe and Harriot shared Ralegh's atheistic reputation, Chapman had highly developed philosophical interests, and Northumberland and Derby had esoteric interests in alchemy.
Bib: Bradbrook, M. C., *The School of Night*.

Schreiner, Olive (Emilie Albertina) (1855–1920)
Daughter of a ▷ Methodist missionary of German descent and an English mother, Olive Schreiner was born in Basutoland, in South Africa, the sixth of twelve children. Self-educated, she became governess to a Boer family at the age of fifteen and began to write. She came to England in 1881 to seek a publisher and in 1884 met ▷ Havelock Ellis with whom she developed a close friendship. Ten years later she returned to South Africa and married the politician Samuel Cronwright who became her literary assistant and later literary executor. They took trips to England and travelled around Africa together. Her first and most acclaimed work is *The Story of an African Farm* (1883), which was published under the ▷ pseudonym Ralph Iron. Its unorthodox religious views and ▷ feminist standpoint caused a considerable stir. She wrote most after her return to South Africa: *Trooper Peter Halket of Mashonaland* (1897), *From Man to Man* (1926) and *Undine* (1929), all with feminist themes, and short stories, *Dreams* (1891), *Real Life* (1893) and *Stories, Dreams and Allegories* (1920). She also wrote *Woman and Labour* (1911). See also: *Letters* (1924).
Bib: Schreiner, S. C. C., *The Life of Olive Schreiner*; First, R. and Scott, A., *Olive Schreiner: A Biography*.

Schuurman (Schurman), Anna Maria van (1607–1678)
Prose writer and poet from the northern Netherlands. The daughter of a nobleman from Antwerp who settled with his family in Utrecht in 1615, she received an excellent education. In an era when the ▷ Renaissance adoration of women came into vogue, van Schuurman, with her considerable knowledge of languages and her artistry, attracted the attention of many people, including Queen Christina of Sweden, and ▷ René Descartes. She completed her theology studies in Utrecht, attending lectures in a small room adjacent to the classroom of the male students. Her *Amica dissertatio inter Annam Mariam Schurmanniam et Andr. Rivetum de capacitate ingenii muliebris ad scientias* (1638) (A Friendly Discourse Between Anna Maria Schurmann and A. Rivetus Concerning the Capacity of Women for Scholarly Pursuits) is a learned dialogue on the question of whether women are capable of studying the sciences and the arts. *A Learned Maid*, written in 1641, was translated into English by Clement Barksdale. She devoted herself to Calvinism, and later to Labadism. On her life and theological views she composed in Latin *Eucleria* (1684, Dutch translation *Eucleria of uitkiezing van het beste deel*, 1684) (Eucleria or Selection of the Best Part). Apart from poems and letters, she wrote *Paelsteen van den tijt onzes levens* (1639) (Boundary Stone of Our Lifetime), and a festive song on the occasion of the inauguration of the University of Utrecht.

Science Fiction
The term 'science fiction' was coined in the mid 19th century, though it was 'reinvented' and given wider currency in the late 1920s by the American magazine editor Hugo Gernsback, who pioneered the stories deriving from, pre-

eminently, ▷ H. G. Wells and Jules Verne. To Gernsback a science fiction story was 'a charming romance intermingled with scientific fact and prophetic vision' (editorial, *Amazing Stories*, 1926). Wells had called what would now be dubbed his science fiction 'scientific romances', and the relation between romance, particularly Gothic romance (▷ Gothic novels), and science fiction has often been remarked on by definers of the form. ▷ Kingsley Amis in *New Maps of Hell* (1960), a work which did much to encourage serious critical attention to this branch of popular literature, allows for a broadening of the speculative base of science fiction through reference to sciences, or 'pseudo-sciences', like sociology, psychology, anthropology, theology and linguistics.

Darko Suvin (*Metamorphoses of Science Fiction*, 1979) remarks that 'cognition' would be a more appropriate word than science in defining this literary genre, and his emphasis on estrangement, or alienation, provides a useful direction for the discussion of science fiction in terms of recent critical theory, which has given new life to the Russian Formalist assertion that literature 'defamiliarizes' conventional assumptions. Science fiction, which is a product of and response to an era of rapid scientific and technological development, has often been concerned to promote new ways of seeing appropriate to, for example, the human consequences of industrialization, the implications of Darwinian (▷ Charles Darwin) evolutionary theory, Einstein's theory of relativity, and the second law of thermodynamics concerning the ultimate entropy of a closed system like the universe. Though the popularity of science fiction may result from the withdrawal of much modern mainstream fiction from traditional forms of storytelling, its concerns as speculative, defamiliarizing literature set it apart from the conventions of classic realism with its emphasis on, for example, characterization. Critics hostile to the science fiction genre have complained that its presentation of human character compared unfavourably with that of realist fiction, whereas others have argued that this represents a response to a world dehumanized by technology, or a radically different viewpoint for asking the question 'What constitutes the human?'

▷ Mary Shelley's ▷ *Frankenstein, Or The Modern Prometheus* (1817) is centrally concerned with this question of defining the human through its treatment of artificially created life and offers the polar opposites of the human as idealist romantic hero and as mere mechanism. This duality is figured in a wide range of subsequent science fiction, most obviously in the genre's obsession with robots and other forms of artificial life and intelligence. In constructing a nameless 'other', Frankenstein's creation or 'monster', *Frankenstein* deals with another obsessively pursued theme of science fiction – confrontation with the alien. Mary Shelley's text, in its repeated patterns of dualism, of attempted completion of incomplete individuals, suggests the possibility, dear to much recent science fiction, that Earth is the alien planet and 'otherness' is the repressed in the human psyche or in human society.

Frankenstein may be regarded as a significant root work of science fiction, but it is the scientific romances of ▷ H. G. Wells which established the genre in the 1890s. Many of these share with *Frankenstein* an unsettling pessimism deriving from a perception of the destructive and alienating uses to which technological development might be put, while much American science fiction, at least in the period before World War II, suggested an optimistic faith in the possibilities of scientific and technological development, springing, perhaps, from a culture defining itself through reference to an expanding frontier. Wells established an influential British tradition of bleaker Darwinism, emanating from an imperial culture already in decline.

Wells' *The Time Machine* (1895) provides a model for a range of subsequent science fiction. It introduces, in almost comic pseudo-scientific discourse, a technological means of travel through time; it facilitates sociological criticism and prediction through the use of utopian and dystopian discourses; it treats the theme of confrontation with the alien, of the last man on earth, of the entropic death of the world; it provides new contexts for old myths; and it defamiliarizes the cosy certitudes of the late Victorian male world in which it starts. *The War of the Worlds* (1898), repeatedly adapted and imitated in the 20th century, may be regarded as the genesis of the bulk of science fiction treatments of interplanetary war or invasion by the alien. *Mr Blettsworthy on Rampole Island* (1928), which employs the traditional device of the dream as a means of transport in place of a time-machine, involves an inversion of dream and reality of a kind familiar in a wide range of science fiction. *The Shape of Things to Come* (1933), widely known through the Alexander Korda film version, represents a more optimistic element in Wells' science fiction in that it suggests the possibility of redemption through an enlightened, technologically oriented élite; yet images of global disorder and collapse are, perhaps, most vividly projected in this text.

Mark Rose, in *Alien Encounters: Anatomy of Science Fiction* (1981), approaches the definition of science fiction through its phases of development. Thus the scientific romances of such as Wells transform earlier kinds of romance, like the Gothic, and fill a gap left by the predominance of realistic fiction. Later phases manifest a generic self-consciousness, in that science fiction texts come to be based on an explicit form. Rose provides the example of ▷ C. S. Lewis, whose science fiction output is in part a response to the fiction of

Wells. The settings of Lewis' space trilogy, *Out of the Silent Planet* (1943), *Perelandra* (1943) and *That Hideous Strength* (1945), are respectively Mars, Venus and Earth, but Lewis' preference for angels rather than space-ships as a means of interplanetary travel has led to some questioning of their status as science fiction. The trilogy evinces an attachment to supernatural Christianity rather than to science, in opposition to the element of pessimistic materialism in Wells; but some variant of such mysticism is not uncommon in the genre. For example, Lewis' near-contemporary, Olaf Stapledon, in works like *Last and First Men* (1930), *Last Men in London* (1932) and *Star-Maker* (1937), projected what he called 'myths' of future history on a scale that goes beyond Wells' scientific romances.

▷ Aldous Huxley acknowledged that his *Brave New World* (1932) started out as a parody of H. G. Wells' *Men Like Gods*, and it has become, in the words of Brian Aldiss (b 1925) (*Billion Year Spree*, 1973) 'arguably the Western World's most famous science fiction novel'. The status accorded this satirical dystopian text, like that enjoyed by the still controversial *Nineteen Eighty-Four* (1949) by ▷ George Orwell, may result from the fact that, in the context of the author's novel output outside the field of science fiction, it can be regarded as somehow 'mainstream' fiction. Both of these works have been regarded as more 'serious' than most science fiction, though this may be based on questionable assumptions about intrinsic literary merit.

A number of British writers were regular contributors to the pre-World War II American science fiction magazine which did much to create a persistent downmarket image for the genre in the popular imagination. The first magazine devoted entirely to science fiction was Hugo Gernsback's *Amazing Stories* (published from 1926), which made an effort to appear respectably scientific and educational in a market which often relied upon lurid presentation. It was followed by such titles as *Science Wonder Stories, Wonder Stories* and *Astounding Stories* in the late 1920s and early 1930s. Besides Wells, British contributors included John Russell Fearn, Eric Frank Russell and John Beynon Harris. Fearn, whose work appeared in *Amazing Stories* first in 1933, produced a staggering quantity of novels and short stories under no less than 25 pseudonyms as well as editing two British science fiction magazines. Russell, whose output was modest compared to Fearn's, began publishing in *Astounding Stories* in 1937 and went on to contribute to British magazines like *Tales of Wonder* and *Fantasy*. Harris is better known as John Wyndham, though he also wrote as John Beynon, J. B. Harris and Johnson Harris. He published short stories and novels from 1930 on, though his reputation rests on the novels he produced as John Wyndham from 1951, the year in which *The Day of the Triffids* was published.

'Exiles on Asperus' (in *Wonder Stories Quarterly*, 1933) by John Beynon Harris demonstrates how Wyndham was not temporarily drawn to the 'space-opera' conventions of the American magazines or to their attachment to science fiction 'gadget' stories. He was happier, and more successful, developing the Wellsian tradition of science fiction novels centring on an imagined disaster arising from the upsetting of the natural and social orders generally through the agency of technology. His catastrophe stories, including *The Day of the Triffids, The Kraken Wakes* (1953) and *The Midwich Cuckoos* (1957), belong to a class of British science fiction from Wells to the present, including New Wave science fiction which in some ways represented a reaction against Wyndham's formulae. *The Day of the Triffids* makes use of the traditional science fiction theme of the Last Man/Last Woman, a new Adam and Eve faced with the arduous complexities of an unfamiliar world. The treatment evokes a characteristically English romantic nostalgia, reminiscent of ▷ Richard Jefferies' vision of the ruined capital in *After London* (1885). The remaking of a new world out of the scraps of the old in *The Day of the Triffids* also suggests a debt to ▷ Daniel Defoe's ▷ *Robinson Crusoe* (1719), but Wyndham's novel is predominantly Wellsian, though it retains a safe, genteel quality not so typical of Wells.

Arthur C. Clarke (b 1917), one of the most celebrated science fiction writers of the 20th century, combines meticulous attention to the scientific and technological aspects of the genre, in the tradition of Jules Verne, with a lyrically didactic commitment to the benign evolutionary potential of technology that owes much to the impact of Clarke's early reading of Stapledon. Both were powerfully expressed in Stanley Kubrick's film *2001* (1968), for which Clarke wrote the screenplay. The kind of wondering transcendence conveyed at the end of that film is characteristic of Clarke's work, encountered in, for example, one of his most popular novels, *Childhood's End* (1953); while *The Deep Range* (1957) develops into a lesson in respect for the non-human creatures of the earth as the prospect of contact with beings from other worlds approaches.

The first novel of Brian Aldiss, *Non-Stop* (1958), gave an indication of the exhilarating variety which has proved a feature of his subsequent fictional output. *Hothouse* (1962) and *Greybeard* (1964) treat the well-established theme of imagined catastrophe, but combine a playful abundance of exotic science fiction invention with romantic nostalgia. A Swiftian satirical mode characterizes *The Dark Light Years* (1964), while the alienating detachment of *Report on Probability A* (1968) draws the techniques of the French ▷ *Nouveau roman* into the orbit of science fiction. *Frankenstein Unbound* (1973) and *Moreau's Other Island* (1980) reinvent seminal science fiction texts for a new context, while the abundance of Aldiss's Helliconia trilogy (1982–5) defies brief categorization. The epilogue to the third volume, *Helliconia Winter* (1985), a translated extract from ▷ Lucretius, *De Rerum Natura*, might be applied to Aldiss's *oeuvre*: 'Everything must pass through successive phases. Nothing remains forever what it was'.

Aldiss's commitment to science fiction, his urge to experiment and enjoy, and to extend the possibilities of the genre, gave him a respected place in the so-called New Wave science fiction writing associated with the magazine *New Worlds* under the editorship of Michael Moorcock (b 1939) from 1964. Until then *New Worlds* had been edited by E. J. Carnell, who was also responsible for *Science Fantasy*. Carnell's magazine published a wide range of British science fiction, including the work of such prolific authors as Kenneth Bulmer, who employed 15 pen-names in addition to his own name, and John Brunner, who began publishing science fiction at the age of 17. The scale of Brunner's output may have resulted in his work being critically underrated, though his dystopian novels *Stand on Zanzibar* (1968), *The Jagged Orbit* (1969) and *The Sheep Look Up* (1972) achieved critical acclaim. Like Brunner, Moorcock is a prolific author who started young; he was editing *Tarzan Adventures* at the age of 17. His 'sword and sorcery' fantasies embody the apocalyptic theme which runs through much of his later science fiction, in which he reconstructs the past as well as imagining the future; this kind of reconstruction may be seen as a way of deconstructing the present. Works like *War Lord of the Air* (1971) and *The Land Leviathan* (1974) present a past manufactured from a range of literary reference, to, for example, Verne, Wells and ▷ Joseph Conrad, and demonstrate Moorcock's attachment to the concept of the 'multiverse', which proposes a variety of separate realities which can sometimes interact. His fondness for series of novels and a modernist tendency to fragment his narratives are particularly evident in his Jerry Cornelius novels, including *The Final Programme* (1969), *A Cure for Cancer* (1971), *The English Assassin* (1972) and *The Condition of Muzak* (1977).

New Worlds under Moorcock represented a spirited reaction against the continuing influence of American pulp science fiction, and a number of American authors were attracted to its programme. But it was a British author, J. G. Ballard (b 1930), who was championed most consistently by the magazine. The Conradian tone of much of Ballard's science fiction contrasts with the racier products of some *New Worlds* writers, influenced by the current 'rock' culture; he has never been much interested in the traditional science fiction fare of space travel and the distant future, preferring to focus on something challengingly closer to the present, defamiliarizing the familiar earth into the alien planet, and insisting that the outward thrust of science fiction be matched by an inward journey. The estranging, detritus-strewn landscapes of much of his fiction indicate Ballard's fascination with surrealist art, though his *Empire of the Sun* (1983), a novel drawing on his boyhood experience of World War II in the Far East, reveals a source closer to home for his images of collapse and desolation. Ballard's catastrophe novels, like *The Drowned World* (1962), *The Drought* (1965) and *The Crystal World* (1966), bear some relation to the disaster stories of John Wyndham and John Christopher, though there is little in the way of romantic nostalgia in his treatment of 'biospheric' disasters. What might be seen as his post-imperial pessimism has not generally endeared Ballard to an American audience. His experimental 'condensed' novels, which first began appearing in *New Worlds*, were published together in *The Atrocity Exhibition* (1970) and, again, did not find favour in the U.S. The disturbing presentation of perverse urban nightmares in *Crash!* (1973), *Concrete Island* (1974) and *High Rise* (1975) bring the concept of the science fiction catastrophe even closer to our own time, as if the irreversible disaster had already occurred in our culture.

▷ Doris Lessing, who turned to science fiction in the early 1970s when her reputation as a mainstream novelist was already established, is also drawn towards visions of the decline and breakdown of society. The last volume of the 'Children of Violence' novels, *The Four-Gated City* (1969), ultimately projects into the future, but from the publication of *Briefing for a Descent into Hell* (1971) Lessing has shown a firm commitment to the exploratory, speculative potential of science fiction, with particular reference to questions of gender and the theme of spiritual awakening. The evocations of collapse and depletion in Lessing's science fiction, which, in the 1980s, turns to space fiction on the grand galactic scale, are set against the possibility of a utopian alternative, and its emphasis is more mystical than scientific. In *Briefing* and *Memoirs* the alternative might amount to no more than dreams; but in *Shikasta* (1979) utopian society is destroyed by a malign galactic empire, while in *The Marriages between Zones Three, Four, and Five* (1980) it is confirmed that the project of utopian evolutionary development, through, for example, the use of psychic powers, lies within the province of women.

A number of ▷ Angela Carter's novels may be classed as science fiction, though, like Lessing, she tends not to focus primarily on science. *Heroes and Villains* (1970) is set in the familiar terrain of a post-catastrophe world and, using the structure of romantic fantasy, explores a variety of dualities, including fantasy/reality, beauty/barbarism, love/hate, male/female. Carter's particular skill, evident in *The Infernal Desire Machines of Dr Hoffman* (1972), *The Passion of New Eve* (1977) and *Nights at the Circus* (1983), lies in her exuberantly self-conscious, inventive storytelling in which romance, satire, horror and comedy interact exotically.

Ian Watson is also adept in exotic narrative, for example, *Whores of Babylon* (1988), but his reputation has been for intellectual, speculative brilliance. His texts, like Lessing's, have a tendency to the mystical and transcendent, and approach the possibility of such transcendence through the discourses of science, linguistics, mysticism and myth, as is impressively demonstrated by his first four novels: *The Embedding* (1973), *The Jonah Kit* (1976), *The Martian Inca* (1977) and *Alien Embassy* (1977).

Christopher Priest also built up during the 1970s a reputation as a thoughtful and inventive science fiction author through such works as *Inverted World* (1974) and *A Dream of Wessex* (1977).

Science fiction might be said to have begun with the work of a woman and, looked at one way, Mary Shelley's *Frankenstein* is a coded analysis of female experience. The women's movement of recent years, with a strong lead from the United States, has led to a powerful reaction against science fiction's traditional marginalization of women, and Lessing is not unique in turning to science fiction from a different novel tradition. Michèle Roberts, for example, adopts the dystopian mode in *The Book of Mrs Noah* (1973), while ▷ Zoë Fairbairns uses science fiction's speculative resources to consider the issue of wages for housework in *Benefits* (1979). The Women's Press boasts a growing list of feminist science fiction, and one of the editors responsible for this, Sarah Lefanu, has written a study of feminism and science fiction, *In the Chinks of the World Machine* (1988). Commenting on the value of science fiction, Lefanu has said: 'It deals with the possibility of change, and allows the investigation of radical ideas.'

The more male-oriented, technological tradition of science fiction has been re-invigorated through the 1980s and into the 1990s by the writers of 'cyberpunk' fiction. The formative influence in establishing this sub-genre is the American William Gibson, in whose *Neuromancer* (1984) the term 'cyberspace', now routinely used in writings on contemporary information technology, was coined. Fredric Jameson has called cyberpunk 'the supreme literary expression if not of postmodernism, then of late capitalism itself'. His assertion is symptomatic of a convergence of the discourses of science fiction, of the kind of critical writing now loosely termed 'theory', and of technological discussion, particularly in fields related to the concept of virtual reality. This concept is as much the invention of the science fiction genre as of the information industry, and it is the ground on which the novels of Jeff Noon, pre-eminent among British writers of cyberpunk, are constructed. His *Vurt* (1993) and *Pollen* (1995), for all the appearance of novelty which has been claimed for cyberpunk, draw, like the work of Gibson, on long-standing traditions of science fiction and of related popular forms, like the hard-boiled detective story. *Frankenstein*'s obsession with the ambiguous distinction between human and mechanical is, in new guises, fundamental to cyberpunk; and the works of William Burroughs, Philip K. Dick and J. G. Ballard cast long shadows into the fiction of such as Noon.

In the same period that has seen the rise of cyberpunk, the tradition of space opera has been kept alive in the prolific output of Ian M. Banks, the galactic expansiveness of whose plots contracts with cyberpunk's world of 'nonspace'. In works like *The Player of Games* (1988) and *Against a Dark Background* (1993) Banks elegantly recycles a wide range of science fiction conventions, sometimes with a parodic edge which recalls the witty and popular fictions of Douglas Adams and Terry Pratchett. The popularity of this parodic strain is some indication of how deeply embedded the narratives of science fiction have become in our culture, not just through literature, but also through other popular media influenced by and, in turn, influencing literary production.

Scotland

The northern kingdom of Great Britain. Geographically, racially, linguistically and culturally, it has two parts.

The northern and north-western half, known as the Highlands and the Islands, is Celtic in race, with a Norse admixture. The native language was originally the Celtic one called ▷ Gaelic, but this is now spoken only by a small minority. Until the middle of the 18th century its social structure was of the semi-tribal clan system under hereditary chieftains. Its culture was chiefly oral and Gaelic-speaking, and much of it has been lost. The so-called Scottish national dress, of the kilt woven into chequered designs known as tartans, was peculiar to this region; it was forbidden after the second Jacobite rebellion of 1745, when the British government started its policy of colonizing the Highlands, but it was revived in the 19th century as a sentimental fashion for the upper classes and is now an extremely profitable export item. This region of Scotland, though extremely beautiful, has had a torn history; centuries of clan warfare were followed by a century and a half of economic neglect and depopulation, during which the small farms or 'crofts' were steadily replaced by 'grouse moors', preserved by rich landlords for hunting and shooting. In the 20th century the economy has to some extent revived, thanks to the tourist industry and efforts by successive governments to cultivate forests.

The southern and eastern half of the country is called the Lowlands, and contains all the important cities including the capital, Edinburgh, and the largest, Glasgow. These two cities are respectively at the east and west ends of the narrowest part of the country, and the plain between them is a rich coal-mining area. The Lowlands are geographically hilly, in spite of their name. Racially, the population is as Germanic in origin as that of most of England, and with small exceptions it has always been English-speaking. It has never been subjected to the clan system of the Highlands, although the great families along the border with England had, until the 17th century, an influence comparable to that of the clan chieftains of the Celtic north. Economically and politically, the Lowlands have always been the richer and more important part of the country. When we speak of Scottish culture, we are nearly always thinking of the literature of the Lowlands; this has had its distinctive tradition, but it has become increasingly absorbed into English culture since the 16th century.

Scott, Hugh Stowell (1862–1903)
Writer of adventure ▷ romances, which he published under the name 'Henry Seton Merriman'. Most of them have rapid, exciting plots and exotic settings, which Scott researched on his extensive travels. The son of a shipowner in Newcastle-upon-Tyne, Scott abandoned a business career early on to pursue writing and travelling; it has been suggested that he worked for the British intelligence services, and some of his work is strongly pro- ▷ imperialist. His novels include: *The Slave of the Lamp* (1892); *With Edged Tools* (1894); *The Grey Lady* (1895); *In Kedar's Tents* (1897); *The Isle of Unrest* (1900); *Barlasch of the Guard* (1902); *The Last Hope* (1904).

Scott, Mary (Taylor) (1752–1793)
English poet. She lived in the same house as ▷ Elizabeth Rowe in Somerset, and who knew ▷ Anna Seward. She wrote in favour of women's ▷ education. In *The Female Advocate* (designed as a sequel to John Duncombe's *Feminiad*) she praises past and contemporary women writers, saying of ▷ Sarah Fielding, ''Twas *Fielding's* talent, with ingenious Art, / To trace the secret mazes of the Heart', and of ▷ Anne Killigrew, 'in thee . . . we find / The Poet's and the Painter's arts combin'd'. In the same text she reserves a special place for ▷ Lady Mary Chudleigh, who had the courage to assert that women were naturally equal to men and to 'plead thy hapless injured sex's cause'. She married John Scott in 1788, when her mother died. In the same year she published *The Messiah*, and she also wrote hymns. Her son founded the Manchester *Guardian*.

▷ Astell, Mary; Williams, Helen Maria

Scott, Paul (1920–78)
Novelist. He served in India, Burma and Malaya during World War II and subsequently worked in publishing. His major achievement was *The Raj Quartet*, a tetralogy consisting of: *The Jewel in the Crown* (1966); *The Day of the Scorpion* (1968); *The Towers of Silence* (1971); *A Division of the Spoils* (1975). A portrait of Indian society at the time of Independence in 1947, it uses a range of narrative forms, including letters, journals, reports and memories. The story is built around the consequences of the rape of an English girl; consequences which serve to reveal corruption and racism in the Raj adminstration and the roots of the political unrest and intercommunal violence at the Partition of India. Scott was accorded little critical recognition until *Staying On* (1977), a gentle satire set after Independence, won the Booker Prize. His work is notable for its combination of complex narrative technique with historical accuracy. *The Raj Quartet* was televised as *The Jewel in the Crown* in 1984 and *Staying On* was adapted for television in 1981. Scott's earlier novels include *The Birds of Paradise* (1962).

Scott, Sarah (Robinson) (1732–1795)
English novelist, writer of ▷ utopias and historian. She was the sister and correspondent of ▷ Elizabeth Montagu, the ▷ Bluestocking. She wrote for money after leaving her husband (whom she had married in 1751) and moved with Barbara Montagu to launch a female community at Bath Easton, where they taught poor children. They lived here from 1754 to 1756. Scott wrote six novels, but her well-known *Description of Millenium Hall* (1762) uses this idea of a woman's community. This secular separatist community based around ▷ rational virtues provided at least one answer to the unstable social and economic place of the unmarried or – particularly – separated woman. The novel opens with a man whose coach has broken down in Cornwall impressed by the rational yet pleasurable employments of the women. He first sees them engaged in their rational pursuits: 'in the bow [window] sat two ladies reading, with pen, ink and paper on a table before them, at which was a young girl translating out of the French.'

Other publications: *The History of Cornelia* (1750); *A Journey Through Every Stage in Life* (1754); *Agreeable Ugliness, or the Triumph of the Graces* (1754); *Sir George Ellison* (1766), and *The Test of Filial Duty* (1772).

Scott, Sir Walter (1771–1832)
Scottish poet and novelist. The son of an Edinburgh lawyer, he was descended from

famous families on the Scottish side of the border with England. This ancestry early attracted him to the drama and tragedy of Anglo-Scottish border history; he became an antiquarian, and a very Romantic one. His ▷ Romanticism was stimulated further by reading the poetry of the contemporary Germans, Bürger and ▷ Goethe; he hoped to do for the Scottish border what they had done for the German Middle Ages, and make its past live again in modern romance. A widespread taste was already developed for the Middle Ages and was manifesting itself in the ▷ Gothic novel. He collaborated with the most famous of the Gothic novelists – ▷ 'Monk' Lewis – in producing *Tales of Wonder* in 1801. A little later ▷ S. T. Coleridge's poem ▷ *Christabel* inspired him to write poems in the same metre, and between 1805 and 1815 he produced the succession of narrative poems which made him famous. He began to feel himself outdone as a narrative poet by ▷ Byron, however, and from 1815 he devoted himself to the novels for which he is now better known. Publishing enterprises in which he had begun to involve himself in 1809 left him with a debt of £130,000 to pay off, when the London publisher Constable went bankrupt. Scott was immensely proud, and determined to pay off the debt by his own literary efforts. By writing very prolifically for the rest of his life, he nearly succeeded; he was by then a very sick man, and his efforts are a legend of literary heroism.

Scott's most famous poems are *The Lay of the Last Minstrel* (1805); ▷ *Marmion* (1808), and ▷ *The Lady of the Lake* (1810). The first two are from Anglo-Scottish border history and legend; the third is about the equally bitter enmity of Scottish Highlander for Scottish Lowlander. The readability of these poems makes it easy to account for their popularity, but the kind of interest they offer – the dramatization of the life of a whole society – was not such as Scott was able to work out in the verse-narrative medium.

His novels show a double interest: he was the first novelist in English to present characters as part of a society, and not merely against the background of a particular society, the nature of which is taken for granted; he was also the inventor of the true historical novel. His best work is contained in the Waverley novels and in the first three series of *Tales of My Landlord*: ▷ *Waverley* (1814), *Guy Mannering* (1815), *The Antiquary* (1816), *Old Mortality* (1816), *Rob Roy* (1817), ▷ *The Heart of Midlothian* (1818), *The Bride of Lammermoor* and *The Legend of Montrose* (1819). All these concern 17th- and 18th-century Scotland, and the religious and dynastic struggles that shaped the nation as Scott knew it. From then onwards he was writing with excessive haste in order to pay off his debts, and he commonly chose English and medieval subjects, *eg* ▷ *Ivanhoe* (1819), *Kenilworth* (about English Elizabethan times – 1821), *Quentin Durward* (1823) and some 16 others, only one of which, *St Roman's Well* (1823), was set in Scott's own time.

Not only was Scott's influence, both in Britain and Europe, very large in shaping literary taste, but he had an extensive influence in encouraging non-literary taste, such as that for wild landscape (especially of the Highlands) and more intelligent interest in the past. As a critic he was among the first to recognize the genius of ▷ Jane Austen. In politics he was a staunch Conservative, and he helped to found the great Tory review, the ▷ *Quarterly*, in 1809.

Bib: Buchan, J., *Life*; Davie, D., *The Heyday of Sir Walter Scott*; Hayden, J. O., *Scott: The Critical Heritage*; Hillhouse, J. T., *The Waverley Novels and their Critics*; Lewis, C. S., in *They Asked for a Paper*; Lockhart, J. G., *Memoirs*; Muir, E., *Scott and Scotland*; Goslee, N. M., *Scott the Rhymer*.

Scottish Chaucerians

A rather over-generalized term, applied to a diverse group of Scottish poets of the 15th and 16th centuries (including ▷ William Dunbar, ▷ Robert Henryson, ▷ Gavin Douglas, and James I of Scotland, author of the *Kingis Quair*), on the grounds that their work shows signs of Chaucerian influence.

Scottish literature in English

Despite its origins in Old English and in twelfth century Northern English, Scots (the language of lowland Scotland since the Middle Ages) can be seen as a language in its own right, rather than as simply a dialect of English, closely related as the two undoubtedly are. Both Scottish and English people generally regard the two speeches as markedly different, with the Scottish vernacular largely incomprehensible to most southerners; Scots has a range of features which is sufficiently copious to mark it out as something more than a dialect; it has been associated for most of its history with a distinctive political entity; it possesses a long and rich literary tradition of its own. Throughout its history, however, it has variously interacted with English, a language which has often exerted a powerful influence on Scottish speech and writing. These related languages, in fact, constitute two of Scotland's principal languages, Gaelic being the third.

The war of independence against England (1296–1328), prompted two early heroic poems. ▷ John Barbour's *The Bruce* (1375–8), an epic in 8-syllable couplets, was written at a time when Scottish political fortunes were low; its intention is to inspire the national spirit, less by rhetorical eloquence than by the facts of the heroic struggle. Blind Harry's *Wallace* (1476–78) was equally nationalistic. Both remained favourite reading amongst ordinary

Scots until the 18th century. Very different in method and subject is *The Kingis Quair* (*c* 1424), perhaps by James I of Scotland, some of whose reign was spent in imprisonment in England: partly an account of James' love and marriage, it is also a dream-vision in the tradition of Boethius. In Scotland, the 15th century saw the beginning of a golden age, covering the careers of Robert Henryson, William Dunbar, Gavin Douglas, and David Lindsay – the 'makars'. The climax of this period was the reign of the exceptionally able James IV (1488–1513). Henryson's versions of *The Fables* of Aesop mix comic realism, satire and moral comment; his masterpiece is *The Testament of Cresseid*, a continuation of ▷ Chaucer's ▷ *Troilus and Criseyde*, but with a tragic quality which is quite un-Chaucerian. Dunbar wrote in contrasting styles – the courtly and the colloquial; his finest work is perhaps the latter, notably, the *Tretis of the Tua Mariit Wemen and the Wedoe* (Treatise of the Two Married Women and the Widow). Douglas' finest work is his translation of Virgil's *Aeneid*, and Lindsay is best known for his *Ane Pleasant Satyre of the Thrie Estaitis* (*c* 1540), a political morality which is still regularly and successfully revived and which is perhaps even yet Scotland's greatest play.

Despite the religious Reformation and all the political troubles attendant on it from 1550 till the early 18th century, Scotland continued to produce poetry of value by such writers as Alexander Scott, Alexander Hume, Alexander Montgomerie and William Drummond of Hawthornden. The first three wrote within a tradition of 'art' poetry but continued to use vernacular Scots; Drummond is usually seen as reflecting in verse that shift towards increasing use of English by Scots (especially of the upper classes) consequent upon the move of the court to London in 1603, and also consequent upon the church use of English translations of the Bible after 1560 – no major translation of the Bible in Scots was available until that of the New Testament by W. L. Lorimer (1983). The poetic use of Scots, however, was kept alive in the 17th century by the reprinting of heroic and comic poems of the 15th and 16th centuries, and by a continuing tradition of writing new, often occasional, comic and satire verses such as the astonishingly popular and influential poem *The Life and Death of Habbie Simson, the piper of Kilbarchan* by Robert Sempill (*c* 1595–*c*1665) with its six-line stanza known to Ramsay and Burns as 'standard Habbie', and to us as 'the Burns stanza'. Equally important was the ballad and folksong tradition, strongly alive from the middle ages until the 20th century, and capable both of producing individual ballad texts of greatness and also of influencing novelists such as Scott, Hogg, Stevenson, Gibbon and Gunn.

Early in the 18th century, stimulated in part by Scotland's final loss of political independence with the Treaty of Union in 1707, there occurred a revival of antiquarian interest in Scotland's distinctive heritage. Collections of earlier poetry were compiled and published: ballads and folksongs, poems by the makars and by the 16th-century court poets, and poetry of the 17th century. Stimulated by this antiquarian activity, there was a major revival of new poetry by Scottish poets. ▷ Allan Ramsay (1684–1758) was both anthologist and original poet, using both Scots and English. His most influential work was a Scottish pastoral play, *The Gentle Shepherd*, which like the works of Barbour and of Blind Harry became a favourite with ordinary Scottish readers for generations after Ramsay's death. The best of Ramsay, however, is in his poems of Edinburgh city life. A greater poet, though with a smaller body of poems as a result of his early death, was ▷ Robert Fergusson (1750–74). He, too, is particularly the author of poems reflecting life in Edinburgh during the Scottish Enlightenment – not merely his long poem surveying the city through twenty-four hours, *Auld Reekie*, but also a series of occasional poems describing and commenting upon the scenes and issues of the day. Some of his poems describe rural life, however, including *The Farmer's Ingle*, which was a model for one of Burn's best-known poems, *The Cotter's Saturday Night*. Fergusson's greatness lies in his ability to combine an ear for spoken Scots with the formal requirements of his verse. Like Burns after him, Fergusson was a master of Scots vernacular who wrote with a confident knowledge of the poetry of the great English Augustans.

▷ Robert Burns (1759–96) is perhaps the first internationally famous Scottish poet since the 16th century. He is the culmination of the major trends in 18th century vernacular verse, and is also the fountainhead of much that occurred, for good or ill, in Scottish literature for a century after his death. It is still possible to find the view being expressed that Burns was an instinctive master when he wrote in Scots, and the creator of lifeless verse when he wrote (as he regularly did) in English. In fact, Burns could be fallible when writing Scots verse, and could write impressively in English, as in the final section of *The Cotter's Saturday Night*. The tradition, begun in his own lifetime, that his palpable greatness was a mystery in view of his presumed lack of educational opportunity – that he was a 'heaven-taught ploughman', in fact – accords neither with what we know of his substantial education and reading, nor with the evident conscious artistry of his poems. Best known now for his love-songs and for the verse narrative *Tam o' Shanter* (a late and uncharacteristic piece), Burns was also the author of poems of many types, including a number of fine satires, often deriving from ecclesiastical disputes but at their best, as in *Holy Willie's Prayer*, transcending their narrow and unappealing origins to attain to a compelling, and entertaining, universality.

18th-century Scottish verse seems so dominated by the Ramsay-Fergusson-Burns triumvirate that it is easy to lose sight of the existence of much vigorous, if secondary, writing, from other users of Scots such as Alexander Ross, and from practitioners in English such as James Beattie and James Thomson. Hugely influential, also, was ▷ James MacPherson (1736–96), whose alleged translations of ancient Gaelic material aroused controversy even when they first appeared: viewed as reflections of an 18th-century cultural moment, some of their contemporary power and appeal can still be sensed.

Burns' example was a powerful one in colouring much 19th writing in prose and verse: not only did many lesser poets adopt too easily his most popular modes, in poems of sentimental love, or comic booziness, or commonplace sententiousness, but the association of quintessential Scottishness with rural life, naturally arising in a country transformed by the industrial explosion and population shifts of the 19th century, was given an extra confirmation by the popularity of his work. Yet, the long-held view that Scottish poetry between Burns and MacDiarmid is a sorry picture of embarrassing vapidity is increasingly difficult to sustain. While the major poems of Walter Scott have yet to undergo the modern re-evaluation from which his novels have benefited, James Hogg (1770–1835) and William Tennant (1784–1848) have re-emerged as individualist minor poets, and Byron himself is regularly claimed as an essentially Scottish poet. Much work remains to be done, not only in re-evaluating such poets as ▷ James Thomson (1834–82), author of *The City of Dreadful Night*, and ▷ John Davidson (1857–1909), but also in exploring the wealth of local and working-class poetry produced by a population for whom both the reading and writing of verse seem to have been frequent and favourite activities.

Important prose works in Scots exist from the 15th and 16th centuries, but prose proved to be far more susceptible than verse to erosion from English influence. While ▷ John Knox's writing contains more Scottish features than is often assumed, it is true to say that most of the important prose works of the 17th and 18th centuries are in English. The peaks of this writing are in the works of Sir Thomas Urquhart of Cromarty (c 1611–1660), and of such Enlightenment luminaries as David Hume (1711–76) and Adam Smith (1723–90). Much vigorous writing, however, lies in works of historiography, and of memoir, and of controversial prose. ▷ Boswell's ▷ *Life of Johnson* (1791) and Lockhart's *Life of Scott* (1837–8), the two great classic biographies in English, were written by Scots. The writings of ▷ Thomas Carlyle (1795–1881) were amongst the most influential of the 19th century, and Hugh Miller (1802–56), perhaps the most gifted writer living and writing in Scotland during the 1840s and early 1850s, was a journalist, a local antiquarian, a scientist and an autobiographer.

Scotland had important novelists in the 18th century, but while Tobias Smollett (1721–71) is still read, at least to some extent, ▷ Henry Mackenzie (1771–1832), 'the Man of Feeling', is now regarded by most readers as an example of the unaccountable taste of a previous age. The Scottish novel, as a powerful and distinct fictional tradition, begins with Scott and his generation. ▷ Walter Scott (1771–1832) remains Scotland's greatest novelist, but while his achievement is widely recognised, the very individual artistries of Hogg, especially in *The Private Memoirs and Confessions of a Justified Sinner*, and of ▷ John Galt (1779–1839), especially in *Annals of the Parish, The Provost* and *The Entail*, are still insufficiently realised by English-speaking readers. All three novelists use English narrative but each succeeds in writing, where appropriate, fine Scots speech which is both true to the language yet accessible to non-Scots. The necessity of being simultaneously true to the linguistic realities of Scotland, while retaining accessibility and appeal to non-Scots, has been a condition of writing facing most major Scottish novelists from Scott's time to the present. Some have realised, with Galt, that it is possible to write prose which is clearly Scottish while using few if any uniquely Scots words or expressions: rhythm, intonation and syntax can do the work alone. 19th-century Scottish fiction is increasingly being seen, not as a desert in which only ▷ Robert Louis Stevenson (1850–94) can be discerned (as it was until recently), nor yet as the domain of a few other recently rediscovered worthy (if still secondary) authors such as ▷ Margaret Oliphant (1828–97) and ▷ George MacDonald (1824–1905), nor even as merely a one-way road to the sentimentality of the Kailyard writers ('Ian Maclaren', S. R. Crockett, J. M. Barrie). Rather, it is perceived as embodying the cross-currents, contradictions and self-examinations of a small country coming to terms (at last) with its changed economic and political circumstances, and clinging to as much of its distinctiveness as it can.

The late-Victorian sentimentality of Kailyard fiction was vigorously countered by the grim and melodramatic realism of ▷ George Douglas Brown (in *The House with the Green Shutters*, 1901) and J. MacDougall Hay (in *Gillespie*, 1914). The 20th century has seen what is often described as the Scottish Renaissance, which suggests a revival in cultural production and political identity. There have been several phases in this rejuvenation of Scottish writing. The first, in the early part of this century, was associated with a growth in nationalistic settlement. In this period the work of C. M. Grieve (▷ Hugh MacDiarmid) (1892–1978) is most seminal. MacDiarmid's first major publications were two collections of modernistic lyrics (1925, 1926) in a Scots heavily enriched by words and phrases from a wide range of Scottish dialects and from earlier phases of the language. While clearly written in artificial literary Scots (to which the ancient term 'Lallans' was reapplied), the resulting poems are of great power and beauty. From more (mainly) short poems, MacDiarmid fashioned his most famous work, a long poem dealing with modern Scotland and with the human condition in general, *A Drunk Man Looks at the Thistle* (1926). In the 1930s, MacDiarmid began to use English once more and to explore the poetic possibilities of other areas of specialised language, such as the geological terminology in his later masterpiece *On a Raised Beach* (written 1933). Varied and unequal as MacDiarmid's output was, he was successful in his aim of placing Scottish literature firmly in the European modernist movement.

Other important writers of the first phase include the poet and critic ▷ Edwin Muir (1887–1959), and the novelists James Leslie Mitchell (▷ Lewis Grassic Gibbon) (1901–35) and ▷ Neil M. Gunn (1891–1973). Writing poems mainly in English, Muir adopts a mythopoeic discourse; in his important critical work *Scott and Scotland* (1936) he dissociates himself from some of the theoretical assumptions underpinning MacDiarmid's 20th-century Renaissance enterprise. Gibbon's writing is perhaps the most deeply and intelligently political of a very politicised group of writers; nevertheless, he is remembered by many readers primarily for the powerfully elegaic treatment of Scottish rural life in *Sunset Song* (1932), the first part of his trilogy *A Scots Quair* (1932–4). Gunn writes of his native northern highlands in an impressive body of work in which the history and pain of Highland life in the 19th and 20th centuries become means for expressing his deeper insights into the psychology of human experience.

The second phase, in the 1940s and 1950s, produced poems such as Sydney Goodsir Smith (1915–75), Alexander Scott (1920–89) and Robert Garioch (1909–81), inspired by MacDiarmid's example to further establish the poetic use of Scots. Such writers saw themselves as continuing the programme of cultural nationalism which MacDiarmid had begun. In this period however poets also appeared whose poetic language is English. These include Norman MacCaig (b 1910) and George Mackay Brown (b 1921). Iain Crichton Smith (b 1928) must be grouped with these, although his writing in Gaelic (a language also enjoying a 20th-century poetic renaissance thanks to the MacDiarmid-like achievement of Sorley Maclean) is an equally important part of his life's work.

Emerging from this second phase, however, is the period which still broadly continues, a period in which nationalistic commitment is scarcely if at all stressed by many writers. The 'renaissance' has done its job. Scottish writers now, with a new self-confidence and ease, write about, and from, Scotland; 'Scotland' is no longer a quaint literary domain which must be presented to the world with awkward self-consciousness. This ease can be sensed in the work of such diverse poets as ▷ Douglas Dunn (b 1942), Don Patterson, Kathleen Jamie (b 1962) and Carol Ann Duffy (b 1955).

Important elements of MacDiarmid's programme are still visible, but the sense of the programmatic has gone. Thus the national and regional are still celebrated in novels by Robin Jenkins (b 1912) and Jessie Kesson (1915–95), while a powerful left-wing vision is still articulated by, for example, the playwright ▷ John McGrath in *The Cheviot, the Stag and the Black, Black Oil*, and by such diverse novelists as ▷ William McIlvanney (b 1936), ▷ Alasdair Gray (b 1934) and ▷ James Kelman (b 1946). These three writers, with others such as Agnes Owens (b 1926), Jeff Torrington and the poet Edwin Morgan (b 1920), form a distinctively Glasgow/West-Coast school of current Scottish writing; the best-known work emanating from this group is Gray's *Lanark* (1981). Edinburgh's answer is in the bleak but vital and comic treatments of the city's underside by Irvine Welsh, Kelman and Welsh, who along with poets such as Tom Leonard (b 1944) and W. N. Herbert (b 1961), embody a new willingness to use the Scots vernacular – not, however, the literary 'Lallans' of MacDiarmid and his disciples, but the rough, vigorous, inventive, rhythmic and often foul-mouthed language of urban working-class life.

MacDiarmid's commitment to high aesthetic ideals is echoed in the novels of ▷ Muriel Spark (b 1918), perhaps the best-known, internationally, of 20th-century Scottish novelists. Women writers are often overlooked in brief accounts of Scottish literature, but the achievements of 18th-century poets such as Lady Nairne (1766–1845), of such bearers of folk-tradition as Anna Gordon (1747–1810) and Jeannie Robertson (1908–75), of 19th-century writers like the novelists Susan Ferrier (1782–1854) and Margaret Oliphant and the autobiographer Elizabeth Grant (1797–1885), of a host of earlier 20th-century poets and novelists (Violet Jacob, Marion Angus, Helen Cruickshank, Nan Shepherd, Naomi Mitchison, Willa Muir among others) can perhaps be seen as prefiguring those of such important current writers as A. L. Kennedy (b 1965), ▷ Janice Galloway (b 1956), Dilys Rose (b 1954), etc. Several women writers are distinguished practitioners of the short story, a genre of some importance in current Scottish writing.

Bib: Craig, C. (gen. ed.), *The History of Scottish*

Literature (4 vol.); Watson, R., *The Literature of Scotland*.

Scriblerus Club
Formed in 1713 by ▷ Alexander Pope, ▷ Jonathan Swift, ▷ John Gay, ▷ Thomas Parnell, ▷ John Arbuthnot, and the Tory politician, Lord Oxford. The aim was to satirize 'false tastes' through the fictional memoirs of a conceited and arrogant 'modern' writer, Martinus Scriblerus. The club's members were scattered when the Tories fell from power after Queen ▷ Anne's death in 1714. Only the first volume of the memoirs was completed, and this was published in Pope's works in 1741. However, the ideas initiated at this time saw fruit in various later works, in particular Pope's ▷ *Dunciad*, many of the notes of which are signed 'Scriblerus', and in the ▷ satire on science and learning in the third book of Swift's ▷ *Gulliver's Travels*.

Scrutiny
A literary critical review published in Cambridge from 1932 to 1953; its principal editor was ▷ F. R. Leavis. *Scrutiny* was famous for its intellectual energy, the coherence of outlook among its contributors, and the urgency and purposefulness of its tone. This purposefulness was a response to a Leavisite analysis of the contemporary cultural scene which may be summarized as follows. The quality of Western (more particularly, British) civilization was deteriorating because of the influence upon it of commercial vulgarization. Such vulgarization could only end in the complete loss of those standards by which life in any organized society can be seen and felt to be valuable. The importance of a great literary tradition is that it constitutes a form of spiritual life that sustains high values and withstands vulgarization. However, such a tradition must itself be sustained by constant, sensitive and scrupulous critical activity carried on by alert and active intellects within the society. But the British literary tradition no longer possessed this kind of cultural leadership; the leading men of letters, on the contrary, with a few exceptions, regarded literature as an elegant pastime for a fashionable elite (such as the ▷ Bloomsbury Group) and they employed slack and inadequate standards in their judgements. *Scrutiny*, therefore, was intended to demonstrate the exacting standards which are required of criticism if a lively and effective literary tradition is to be sustained. The example to be followed was that of the recently defunct review, *The Calendar of Modern Letters* (1925–27) edited by Edgell Rickword.

The strongest part of *Scrutiny's* critical attack was directed towards literary education. It sought to counteract the kind of academic inertia which tends to the passive acceptance of some literary reputations and the equally passive neglect of other writers. This policy led to an extensive revaluation of the writers of the past. In regard to poetry, this revaluation took the direction already pursued by T. S. Eliot (*Selected Essays*, 1932); in regard to the novel, the dominant influences were those of F. R. Leavis himself, and his wife ▷ Q. D. Leavis. *Scrutiny* had a pervasive influence in Britain and the USA, especially among teachers at all levels of education.
Bib: Mulhern, F., *The Moment of Scrutiny*; Baldick, C., *The Social Mission of English Criticism*.

Scudéry, Madeleine de (1607–1701)
French writer of ▷ epic novels, *nouvelles* (short fiction), letters and occasional verse, and a notable *précieuse* (▷ Precious Women). In her youth, she frequented the *Chambre bleue*, the salon of the Marquise de Rambouillet (1588–1665), with her brother, the dramatist and Academician Georges de Scudéry (1601–67). Madeleine lived with her brother in Paris and Marseilles until his marriage to Marie-Madeleine du Moncel de Martinval in 1654, writing a series of *romans-à-clef*, set in exotic locations; the characters, though in disguise, could easily be identified from among their friends and acquaintances. Although mercilessly mocked by the writers Charles Sorel (c 1600–1674), Jacques-Bénigne Bossuet (1627–1704) and others, these novels were of great importance for raising the status of women and fiction.

Ibrahim, ou l'illustre Bassa (1641) contains one of the few theoretical prefaces to be written by a novelist in the 17th century. It seeks to give fiction ▷ classical antecedents, by aligning the novel with the epic poem and identifying history as the mainstay of *vraisemblance* (verisimilitude) in the novel. The success of this four-volume novel encouraged Madeleine de Scudéry to use wider canvases for her next two novels, *Artamène, ou le Grand Cyrus* (1649–1653, translated as *Artamenes, or The Grand Cyrus*, 1653–5), which contained a *mise en abyme* of the Hôtel de Rambouillet and her own *samedis* (Saturday *salons*) at the rue de Beauce in Paris, and *Clélie, histoire romaine* (1654–60, translated as *Clelia: An excellent new romance*, 1661). Both these novels also appeared under Georges de Scudéry's name, though there is a marked change of tone after their separation at the end of volume 2 of *Clélie*, which is the most ▷ 'feminist' of Madeleine de Scudéry's writings and includes the celebrated '*Carte de Tendre*', an allegorical map of love. Known as the 'incomparable ▷ Sappho', Madeleine de Scudéry was noted for her intellect and learning even among the most respected scholars of her day, though her lack of Latin and Greek meant that she could not consult the many classical historians on whom she loosely based her fiction in the original. Despite the innumerable anachronisms in her novels, she may be regarded as the 'mother of the historical novel in France'. She also wrote

Les Femmes illustres, ou les Harangues héroïques (The Illustrious Women, or The Heroic Speeches), *Célinte, nouvelle première* (1661), *Mathilde d'Aguilar* (1667) and *Célanire* (1669), which includes *La Promenade de Versailles*.

In 1657, Mademoiselle de Scudéry received a pension from the superintedent of finances, Nicolas Fouquet (1615–80), to whom she remained a loyal friend. Among her other benefactors were the First Minister, Mazarin (1602–61), Queen Christina of Sweden (1626–89) and Louis XIV (1638–1715), though she always had difficulty making ends meet. Madeleine de Scudéry was elected to the Academy of the Ricovrati in 1684 and is said to have been the first woman to have been considered for election to the French Academy. Her ugliness was frequently remarked upon. She admits to having received three proposals of marriage, but, in keeping with the theory of *amitié tendre* (loving friendship) developed in her novels, she refused even to marry the Academician Paul Pellisson (1624–93), who was devoted to her. A series of influential selections from the dialogues in her novels was published during the 1680s.
Bib: Tallemant des Réaux, *Historiettes*: Aronson, N., *Mademoiselle de Scudéry*.

Scudéry, Marie-Madeleine du Moncel de Martinval (1627–1711)
French correspondent and co-author of a novel. She helped her husband, the dramatic poet Georges de Scudéry (1601–67), to write the novel *Almahide, ou l'esclave reine* (Almahida, or The Slave Queen, 1661–3 and is noted for her cultivated correspondence with, among others, the exiled writer Roger de Bussy-Rabutin (1618–93). The main theme of her letters is the value of friendship. She appears in Somaize's *Dictionnaire des Précieuses* (Dictionary of the Precious Women, 1659) under the pseudonym Sarraïde, as '[*l*]' *une des plus grandes précieuses du royaume*, ('one of the greatest *précieuses* of the realm') (▷ Precious Women). The memoir-writer Tallemant des Réaux (1619–1692) portrays her as a romantic woman yearning to work on a novel, and who married late in life under the mistaken illusion that Georges de Scudéry had written the great novels published under his name. Of her relationship with her husband, Tallemant writes: 'their marriage was made in their writings rather than in the normal way, for their mutual inclination was a question of the similarities in their style of writing which came before their wedding.' It was generally felt that her prose was better than his verse, and her letters have recently been reappraised.
▷ Scudéry, Madeleine de
Bib: Tallemant des Réaux, *Historiettes*; Mesnard, J., 'Mme de Scudéry', *Actes de Caen* (1980).

Seasons, The **(1726–30)**
Four ▷ blank-verse poems by ▷ James Thomson. *Winter* was published in 1726, followed by *Summer* (1727), and *Spring* (1728). *Autumn* first appeared in the collected *Seasons* in 1730, which also contained a concluding *Hymn on the Seasons*. The work blends numerous strands: the ▷ classical spirit of ▷ Virgil's *Pastorals* and ▷ *Georgics*, a self-conscious sublimity which comes from ▷ John Milton, and the topographical genre popularized by ▷ Sir John Denham's ▷ *Cooper's Hill* (1642) and ▷ Alexander Pope's ▷ *Windsor Forest* (1713). Thomson's blank verse is an extremely flexible and capacious medium, though always affecting a somewhat mechanical Miltonic dignity. On the one hand there are charming descriptions of the natural scene (▷ nature), such as the famous snow scenes in *Winter*, the nest-building passage in *Spring*, and the *Summer* thunderstorm. There are discussions of philosophy and morality, such as the condemnation of blood-sports in *Autumn*, and the expression of ▷ 'natural religion' in the concluding hymn. There are celebrations of British history, industry and commerce in *Summer* and *Autumn*, and ▷ sentimental vignettes of rural life, such as the man dying in the snow in *Winter* and Amelia struck by lightning as she is embraced by her astonished lover in *Summer*.

An important element is Thomson's scientific and practical approach to nature. In *Summer* he describes the beginning of the Newtonian universe, as the 'unwieldy planets' are 'launched along/ The illimitable void'. In *Autumn* he speculates on the migration of birds, and throughout the poems he is concerned to use a kind of poetic version of Linnaean taxonomy, stressing the generic qualitics of animals and plants: 'plumy people' (birds) 'the finny drove' (fish) and 'woolly people' (sheep). Typically nature is seen as providing a livelihood to man. Despite their influence on later more ▷ romantic 'nature poets', such as ▷ Mark Akenside, ▷ William Collins, ▷ William Cowper, ▷ Thomas Gray and ▷ William Wordsworth, the *Seasons* in themselves are peculiarly smug and inert in their ▷ Augustan optimism. Thomson's is a world in which, without a qualm, 'Man superior walks/ Amid the glad creation', where farm labourers are picturesque adjuncts of the landscape, and where British industry and commerce subject the world. Its ideal for living smacks of bourgeois self-congratulation:

An elegant sufficency, content,
Retirement, rural quiet, friendship, books,
Ease and alternate labour, useful life,
Progressive virtue, and approving Heaven!

Second Nun's Tale, The
One of ▷ Chaucer's ▷ *Canterbury Tales*. A saint's life, written in ▷ rhyme royal, recounting the life and martyrdom of St Cecilia, a noble

Roman maiden, who publically affirms the power of the Christian faith and opposes the pagan practices of the Deputy, Almachius. Her husband and brother become martyrs for the faith but Cecilia defies Almachius' attempts to kill her by boiling her in a bath. Even when her throat is cut, Cecilia miraculously manages to continue preaching for three days before dying. Her testimony converts many to Christianity, both during her lifetime and afterwards. The story of her life follows the outline of her life in the ▷ *Golden Legend*.

Secret Agent, The (1907)

A novel by ▷ Joseph Conrad. The subject is revolution and counter-revolution in western Europe; the scene is London; the 'secret agent' is Mr Verloc, of mixed nationality. He is employed by the embassy of an unnamed foreign power (Czarist Russia) to mix with anarchist conspirators who have taken refuge on British soil, and to report their activities. Between the embassy and the conspirators are the London police, represented by Chief Inspector Heat, whose work is to watch the anarchists but not to interfere with them until they commit crimes. The embassy wishes to force the British government and its police to suppress the anarchist colony, and uses Verloc to organize a bomb outrage (against Greenwich Observatory) so as to incriminate them. Verloc's seedy shop in Soho is a meeting place for the motley group of political fanatics, including Karl Yundt, a malevolent old terrorist, Ossipan, a scientific materialist who lives off women, Michaelis, a utopian Marxist, and the Professor, the most ruthless of the anarchists, who always carries with him a bomb to prevent arrest. The Professor is disquieted by the inability of the British masses to see politics in terms of violence; if violence were used by the government, the masses would believe that counter-violence was their only hope, and a revolutionary situation would exist in Britain. In addition to this political level, the novel has a psychological one: if either revolution or counter-revolution is to be accomplished successfully, the human instruments must be disinterested, but in fact both the revolutionaries and their opponents are dominated by self-regard. The only characters capable of full disinterest are those who are so wretched as to be incapable of reflecting on their own condition. Mrs Verloc's half-witted brother Stevie rises to one idea only: 'bad life for poor people'. He thus becomes the willing tool of Mr Verloc, who charges him with the task of placing the bomb. In the event, Stevie causes no damage to the Observatory but he is himself blown up. Mrs Verloc, who has married Mr Verloc solely to provide support for Stevie, though her husband supposes her entirely devoted to himself, murders him from rage and grief. She tries to flee the country with Ossipan and, when he deserts her, she throws herself overboard from a Channel ferry. In contrast to Winnie Verloc and Stevie, characters simplified by misery and elementary development, is the Assistant Commissioner of Police, who neither acts disinterestedly nor has any belief that he can, but lives by the awareness that self-knowledge is the only antidote to the poison of self-regard. He solves the mystery of the outrage, and thus frustrates the destructive folly of Mr Vladimir, the ambassador. The novel is distinguished by the use of a pervasive irony to expose the futility of political extremism, the strength of human illusions, and the suffering and chaos prevailing in a supposedly civilized society.

Sedgemoor, Battle of (1685)

The culmination of a rising of west-of-England Puritans against ▷ Charles II's openly Catholic brother ▷ James II. It was led by Charles' illegitimate son, the Duke of Monmouth. The battle was won by the government troops, and was followed by the ferocious punishment of the rebels by Judge Jeffreys in his notorious ▷ Bloody Assizes. Sedgemoor was the last battle fought on English (as distinct from British) soil.

Sejanus (1603)

A satirical tragedy by ▷ Ben Jonson. The central character is an historical figure, a favourite of the Roman emperor Tiberius (reigned AD 14–37). The play is a study of a man driven by extreme ambition; he first eliminates all his rivals to power in the Senate, and then, exploiting the emperor's love of luxurious indolence and inclination for retirement, he conspires to murder Tiberius' heirs in order to occupy the throne himself. Tiberius, however, is too cunning for him; he employs Macro, a new favourite, to bring about the downfall of the old, and Sejanus ends up being torn to pieces by the Roman mob, leaving Macro, equally ambitious and unscrupulous, in his former seat of power. The sensuality of Tiberius and his court, and the violence of the politicians, are contrasted with a group of grim commentators led by Arruntius, remnants of the old stoical (▷ Stoics) Romans whose austere virtues had made Rome great. Ben Jonson presents through Sejanus one of the ▷ Renaissance 'men of power', glorying in the consciousness of unlimited resources, the pattern for whom is ▷ Christopher Marlowe's ▷ Tamburlaine. Sejanus is also the diabolical ▷ Machiavellian politician, without conscience and capable of any crime, such as recurs in many ▷ Elizabethan and ▷ Jacobean dramas. Yet in his unbounded appetites, he is almost a grotesque figure, like the ludicrous sensualists in Jonson's great comedies, ▷ *Volpone* and ▷ *The Alchemist*. The play may have been an attempt to rival ▷ Shakespeare's ▷ *Julius Caesar* of a few years before; it is much more learned in its use of ancient authors, and dramatically it is perhaps the more impressive work. The play was not liked at its first performance, and offended the Earl of Northampton; Jonson had to answer for it before the Privy Council.

Selborne, Natural History and Antiquities of
▷ White, Gilbert.

Selden, John (1584–1654)
Historian and antiquary. Selden was educated at Oxford and the Inns of Court and became a Member of Parliament in 1623, in which capacity he voiced sharp criticism of the crown, withdrawing, however, before the execution of ▷ Charles I. His main works include the *History of Tithes* (1618), which attacked the clergy and was suppressed, and *Table Talk*, which was gathered together by his secretary Richard Milward and published in 1689. Selden was also a friend of ▷ Ben Jonson and ▷ Michael Drayton; indeed, he provided the 'illustrations' or notes for the latter's *Poly-Olbion* (1612 and 1622). He was also admired by ▷ John Milton for his interest in historical facts and authenticity, rather than relying upon myth and popular custom.
▷ Camden, William.
Bib: Fletcher, E. G. M., Sir, *John Selden, 1584–1654*.

Selkirk, Alexander (1676–1721)
A sailor, whose experiences on the uninhabited island of Juan Fernandez, where he was landed at his own request and remained from 1704 to 1709, are the basis of the desert island part of ▷ Daniel Defoe's ▷ *Robinson Crusoe*.

Selvon, Sam (b 1923)
Novelist, playwright (radio and theatre), screenwriter and short-story writer. Born in Trinidad, he served in the Royal Naval Reserve in the Caribbean during World War II, worked as a journalist for the Trinidad *Guardian* from 1946 until 1950, and then moved to London, working for three years as a civil servant in the Indian High Commission and then as a freelance writer, particularly for B.B.C. drama. Since 1978 he has lived in Canada. His novels are: *A Brighter Sun* (1952); *An Island is a World* (1955); *The Lonely Londoners* (1956); *Turn Again Tiger* (1958); *I Hear Thunder* (1963); *Housing Lark* (1965); *The Plains of Caroni* (1969); *Those Who Eat the Cascadura* (1972); *Moses Ascending* (1975); *Moses Migrating* (1983). *Ways of Sunlight* (1958) is a collection of short stories. His work is set in Trinidad and London, and many of his novels are concerned with the experience of cultural displacement, racism and the economic hardship of those moving to Britain from the West Indies, an experience treated with wit, humour and affirmation of growing confidence and assertion, as well as with indignation. Similar themes, and some of the same characters, appear in *Eldorado, West One*, a sequence of seven one-act plays (written 1969; published 1988). He has also written many radio plays, and *Switch* (1977), a play for the theatre. He was co-author of the film *Pressure* (1978) and has published a prose collection, *Foreday Morning: Selected Prose 1946–1986* (1989).

Semiology, Semiotics
The term 'semiology' was used in ▷ Ferdinand de Saussure's *Course in General Linguistics* (published 1915) to describe 'a science of signs', whose objective is 'to investigate the nature of signs and the laws governing them'. The more current term, semiotics, was associated originally with the American philosopher C. S. Peirce. Peirce's tripartite division of signs into 'icon' (a sign possessing a similarity to its object), symbol (a sign arbitrarily linked to the object), and 'index' (a sign physically associated with its object), has more recently been revised in Umberto Eco's *A Theory of Semiotics* (1976) where the emphasis throughout is upon the complex mechanisms and conventions which govern the production of signs.

Seneca, Lucius Annaeus (? 4 BC - AD 65)
Roman philosopher and dramatist. He belonged to the ▷ Stoic school of philosophy, which taught that men should seek virtue, not happiness, and that they should be superior to the influences of pleasure and pain. As an orator, he was famous for the weight and terseness of his expression – the 'Senecan style'. He was tutor to the emperor ▷ Nero during the latter's boyhood, but later was suspected of being involved in a conspiracy against him; Nero accordingly ordered him to end his life which he did with true stoical dignity. His nine tragedies were modelled on those of ▷ Aeschylus, ▷ Sophocles and ▷ Euripides, but there is much doubt whether they were ever intended to be performed in a theatre; they seem to be designed for declamation to small circles. They contain no action, though the subjects are of blood-thirsty revenge. Their titles: *Hercules Furens; Thyestes; Phoenissae; Phaedra (Hippolytus); Oedipus; Troades (Hecuba); Medea; Agamemnon; Hercules Oetaeus* A tenth, *Octavia*, has proved to be by another author.

Neither as a philosopher nor as a dramatist was Seneca one of the most important figures of the ancient Mediterranean world, but he had great importance for the 16th-century ▷ Renaissance in Europe, and particularly for English poetic drama between 1560 and 1620. This influence was of three kinds: 1 Seneca's dramas provided inspiration for Elizabethan ▷ revenge tragedy or 'tragedy of blood'; 2 at a time of English literature when there was keen interest in modes of expression but no settled standards about them, Senecan style was one of the favourite modes, both inside and outside the drama; 3 at a time when inherited ideas about the ordering of society and the ethical systems that should control it were undergoing alarming transformations, Senecan stoicism had an appeal for thoughtful men that harmonized with ▷ Protestant strictness and individualism of conduct. The three influences were more related than might appear. The translator of Seneca's *Ten Tragedies* (1559–81) declares in his preface that their effect was 'to beat down sin', and Protestants were familiar with the vengefulness of Old Testament religion. Sensational drama could unite with serious social purpose, and thus mingle learned sober conceptions of drama (*eg* ▷ *Gorboduc*) with the demands of popular taste. Outside the drama, the terse sententiousness of Senecan style is best found in the *Essays* of ▷ Francis Bacon.

Senior, Olive (b 1943)
Jamaican short-story writer, novelist, poet and dramatist. She was born one of ten children of a poor family living in a rural part of Jamaica and brought up by a relative. She has worked as a Publications Officer at the University of West Indies Institute of Social and Economic Studies and as editor of *Jamaica Journal*. Senior has stressed her interest in orality, oral narrative and the sound of the speaking voice, and her short stories, collected in *Summer Lightning* (Commonwealth Writers Prize, 1987) and *Arrival of the Snake Woman* (1989), make rich and complex use of the variety of forms of spoken English in Jamaica to explore social and personal relations. Poetry: *Talking of Trees* (1985). Plays: *Down the Road Again* (1968). Other works: *The Message is Change: A Perspective on the 1972 General Election*; (1972); *A–Z of Jamaican Heritage* (1983); *Working Miracles: Women's Lives in the English-Speaking Caribbean* (1989).
Bib: Pollard, V., 'Mothertongue Voices in the Writing of Olive Senior and Lorna Goodison', in Nasta, S. (ed.), *Motherlands*.

Sensation, Novel of
A genre that emerged in Britain from about 1860, influenced by Gothic literature and characterized by extravagant, passionate and sometimes horrific events. It is often considered the precursor of the modern thriller. Sensation novels were extremely popular with the reading public and formed a large part of the stock of ▷ circulating libraries. Examples of the genre include ▷ Mary Braddon's ▷ *Lady Audley's Secret* (1862); ▷ Mrs Henry Wood's ▷ *East Lynne* (1861) and ▷ Rhoda Broughton's ▷ *Cometh Up as a Flower* (1867). In *A Literature of Their Own* (1977), Elaine Showalter argues that sensation novels form a significant part of the tradition of 19th-century women's writing. Novelists such as Mary Braddon subverted the stereotype of the 'blonde angel'; others brought a wide range of suppressed female emotions to the surface of their texts and constructed powerful fantasies of escape and protest.

▷ Collins, Wilkie; Corelli, Marie.
Bib: Hughes, W., *The Maniac in the Cellar: Sensation Novels of the 1860s*; Pykett, L., *The Improper Feminine*.

Sense and Sensibility **(1811)**
A novel by ▷ Jane Austen. A youthful version, *Elinor and Marianne*, has been lost. The revised novel was published in 1811.

The two heroines, Elinor and Marianne Dashwood, are fatherless sisters who live with their mother in comparative poverty, having been defrauded of more substantial income by their stepbrother, John Dashwood, and his arrogant and selfish wife. The title of the novel indicates the difference between the sisters: Elinor is practical and watches after the family affairs with sober good sense, and Marianne prides herself on the strength of her feelings and her contempt for material interests. Elinor is in love with a depressed and apparently dull young man, Edward Ferrars (brother of Mrs John Dashwood), while Marianne loves the handsome and glamorous John Willoughby. The superficial contrast between the sisters and their lovers is shown to be deceptive: Elinor's feelings are as deep as Marianne's but her sense of responsibility is greater and she keeps her sorrows to herself, whereas Marianne makes almost a virtue of the public exhibition of her grief, thus becoming a burden on her sister and her mother. In the end, the romantic-seeming Willoughby turns out to have given up Marianne from fear of losing a legacy, while the prosaic Edward gladly sacrifices the favour of a rich relative for the sake of marriage to Elinor.

Sensibility
The term 'sensibility', indicating the tendency to be easily and strongly affected by emotion, came into general use in the early 18th century. At this time writers and thinkers, such as the third ▷ Earl of Shaftesbury, in reaction against the practical, materialist philosophy of ▷ Hobbes, began to promote an idealistic, spiritual alternative, based on personal feeling. ▷ Joseph Addison in 1711 defined modesty as 'an exquisite Sensibility', 'a kind of quick and delicate Feeling in the Soul'. By the middle of the 18th century the word 'sensibility' had grown in stature, indicating the capacity for compassion or altruism, and also the possession of good ▷ taste in the arts. ▷ Joseph Warton in 1756 declines to explain a subtle point since 'any reader of sensibility' will already have taken it. ▷ Laurence Sterne in his ▷ *Sentimental Journey* (1768) eulogizes 'Dear Sensibility! source unexhausted of all that's precious in our joys or costly in our sorrows!'

The word remained fashionable in this sense in the early 19th century when ▷ Jane Austen used it in the title of her novel ▷ *Sense and Sensibility* (1811).

Recently some critics have begun to refer to the period from about the time of the death of ▷ Alexander Pope in 1744 until the publication of ▷ *Lyrical Ballads* in 1798 as the 'Age of Sensibility'. This label is preferred to 'late Augustanism' or 'pre-▷ Romanticism', since it stresses the distinctive characteristics of the period rather than relating it by negative contrast to a different one. The poets of this time, ▷ Thomas Gray, ▷ William Collins and ▷ William Cowper, share a distinctive emphasis on feeling as an end in itself, rather than as part of some larger philosophical scheme. This can be seen both in the resonant truisms of Gray's ▷ *Elegy* and *Eton College Ode*, and in the descriptive delicacy of Collins' *To Evening* or Cowper's *The Poplar-Field*. Even the conservative ▷ neo-classicist ▷ Samuel Johnson shows something of this sensibility in the emotional intensity of his Christian stoicism.

However, the cultivation of sensibility also led to experiment and restlessness in poetic form. Emotional novelty was sought in exoticism and ▷ medievalism. The oral ▷ ballad was given respectability by ▷ Thomas Percy's *Reliques*, while ▷ James Macpherson, ▷ Thomas Chatterton, and ▷ Thomas Warton all adopted various medieval, ▷ 'Gothic' tastes or literary forms. These developments in poetry were paralleled in the 'Gothic story', ▷ *The Castle of Otranto* (1765) by ▷ Horace Walpole. The new intensity of feeling took a less exotic form in the profuse sentiment of ▷ Samuel Richardson's novels, and also in the cult of sentimentalism promoted by Sterne's *A Sentimental Journey* and Henry Mackenzie's *The Man of Feeling* (1771).
Bib: Todd, J., *Sensibility*; Hilles, F. W. and Bloom, H. (eds.), *From Sensibility to Romanticism*; Frye, N., *Towards Defining an Age of Sensibility*.

Sentiment or sensibility, novel of
▷ Sensibility.

Sentiment, sentimental
False, exaggerated or superficial feeling, where the focus is on the feeling itself or on the person experiencing the feeling, rather than on any object or person supposedly stimulating the feeling. In literature this often results in formulaic expressions of grief, sympathy or remorse. Examples in the 17th and 18th centuries are in some of the poems of ▷ Cowper and ▷ Gray, the novels of ▷ Richardson, especially ▷ *Pamela*, and in the plays of ▷ Cibber, ▷ Steele, and ▷ Cumberland.
▷ Sensibility; Reform Comedy; Bathos.

***Sentimental Journey through France and Italy, A* (1768)**
A narrative, part novel and part travel book, by ▷ Laurence Sterne (under the pseudonym of 'Mr Yorick' – the same of a character in Sterne's ▷ *Tristram Shandy*), based on his stay in France, 1762–4. It was intended to be longer, but Sterne died after the publication of the first two volumes in 1768.

***Serious Proposal to the Ladies for the Advancement of Their True and Greatest Interest, A* (1694)**
Polemical essay by ▷ Mary Astell, arguing the case for women's ▷ education, in a developing tradition of serious writing by and for women. A second part of the *Serious Proposal* was published in 1697. Astell prescribes learning to raise women's understanding, develop their self-esteem and give them what we would now call confidence in their own judgement, the better to live a Christian life. 'There is a sort of bravery and greatness of soul', she says, 'which does more truly ennoble us than the highest title, and it consists in living up to the dignity of our natures, scorning to do a mean, unbecoming thing . . .'. Astell proposes to set up a seminary or retreat for women, which she calls a 'religious retirement', for contemplation and study. Thus, she says, women would be equipped to 'see through and scorn those silly artifices which are used to ensnare and deceive them . . . (then) She would know, that not what others *say*, but what she herself *does*, is the true commendation and the only thing that exalts her'. The book was criticized by some who, like ▷ Bishop Burnet, interpreted it as merely advocating a type of convent. But it encouraged and influenced numerous women contemporaries, such as ▷ Lady Mary Chudleigh, ▷ Lady Damaris Masham and ▷ Lady Mary Wortley Montagu, and contributed to a flood of treatises in women's defence.
Bib: Perry, R., *The Celebrated Mary Astell, An Early English Feminist*; Rogers, K. M., and McCarthy, W. (eds.), *Meridian Anthology of Early Women Writers: British Literary Women from Aphra Behn to Maria Edgworth 1660–1800*.

Sermons
The word 'sermon' is used in English to denote a speech from a church pulpit for the edification of the audience, always in this context called a 'congregation'. The sermon considered as a means of communication had a central importance in English life until the 19th century, when universal literacy and the rise of the mass-circulation newspaper tended to eclipse it. At a popular level, it reached a larger audience than any other form of public communication. ▷ Chaucer's Pardoner in the ▷ *Canterbury Tales* demonstrates the power that a medieval preacher felt that he had over an ignorant and superstitious audience, but ▷ *The Pardoner's Tale* is partly a satire about

how the sermon could be abused. The sermon was a means of religious and governmental (*eg* Elizabethan *Book of Homilies*) propaganda. Doctrine, speculative philosophy, social criticism, and ethical problems of daily life were all within the sphere of the sermon, and interested all ranks of society in one way or another.

The sermons of ▷ Hugh Latimer, who lived through the most dramatic phase of the English Reformation, are some of the earliest examples in English of vivid prose in the popular and spoken idiom. Three famous preachers of the golden age of Anglicanism in the first half of the 17th century have left sermons addressed to the Court or to other highly educated audiences. The best known of these is the poet ▷ John Donne, who became Dean of St Paul's in 1621. His sermons have massive learning, but his style is richly personal and persuasive, with a depth of feeling comparable to that of his great religious verse. ▷ Lancelot Andrewes was a subtle and elaborate analyst in language, and appealed more exclusively to the intellect, and ▷ Jeremy Taylor was described by ▷ Coleridge as the 'Spenser of prose' because of his command of musical cadence and linguistic flow.

The change that came over English in the middle of the century emphasized flexibility, control, and lucidity at the expense of poetic emotive power. It is heralded by John Wilkins' book on preaching, *Ecclesiastes* (1646), which teaches the virtue of strict method in organizing a sermon. The main Anglican preachers of the next hundred years, were Robert South (1634–1716), notable for his succinctness and ▷ satire, Isaac Barrow (1630–77), whom ▷ Charles II called 'the best scholar in England', John Tillotson (1630–94), famous for the elegance of his prose, and Joseph Butler (1692–1752), an acute thinker. The virtues of this kind of sermon, and the vices that it sought to combat, are tersely expressed by ▷ Swift (whose own sermons are exemplars of the ideal) in his *Letter to a Young Gentleman entered into Holy Orders* (1721). The best of the ▷ Puritan preachers followed a similar course in a more popular idiom, for instance, the Presbyterian Richard Baxter (1615–91) who declared 'The Plainest words are the profitablest oratory in the weightiest matters', and this is a criterion which ▷ Bunyan exemplifies at its noblest. The preaching by women began to be accepted in Puritan circles, and Priscilla Colton, a ▷ Quaker, wrote the first work defending women's rights to preach, *To the Priests and People of England*.

During the 18th century there was a tendency for sermons to lose touch with the common people. The sermons of William Paley (1743–1805) owed their fame to his talents as a teacher, but they show mediocrity of thought and tepidity of feeling. Those of the novelist ▷ Laurence Sterne (*Sermons of Mr Yorick*, 1760), of the poet ▷ George Crabbe and of the editor ▷ Henrietta Maria Bowdler have merit (especially Sterne's) as literary essays in ethics, but that is what they are, rather than spiritual discourses. It was left to those outside the Anglican tradition, ▷ John Wesley, the founder of Methodism, and George Whitefield (1714–70) to address themselves to the less educated.

In the 19th century there were still preachers of great influence, some on the popular level, such as the enormously popular ▷ Baptist clergyman, ▷ Charles Spurgeon. But ▷ J. H. Newman, the leader of the ▷ Oxford Movement who later became a Catholic and a cardinal, was perhaps the last preacher to be also a major literary figure. It was not merely the competition of the Press that displaced the sermon from its central influence in English life by the end of the 19th century, but the growth of agnosticism among the intelligentsia and the corresponding decline in the prestige of the pulpit.

Bib: Henson, H. (ed.), *Selected English Sermons* (World's Classics); Sampson, A. (ed.), *Famous English Sermons*.

Serres, Olivia (1772–1834)

Miscellaneous writer and artist. Olivia Serres claimed to be the daughter of the Duke of Cumberland by a secret marriage, and in 1822 published *Statement to the English Nation* setting out her evidence for this declaration. Nothing came of it, however, and she died penniless leaving a vast collection of manuscripts on numerous subjects. Her published work includes a collection of poems, *Flights of Fancy* (1805), which is ostensibly sentimental but often idiosyncratically radical. *St Julian* (1808) is also sentimental in tone, but interesting for its indebtedness to ▷ Rousseau.

Seth, Vikram (b 1952)

Poet, novelist, travel writer. Born in Calcutta, India, and educated at Corpus Christi College, Oxford, Stanford University and Nanjing University, China, he was trained as an economist. His volumes of poetry are *Mappings* (1980); *The Humble Administrator's Garden* (1985); *All You Who Sleep Tonight* (1990). *The Golden Gate* (1986) is a witty and accomplished novel, written in a form of sonnet borrowed from Pushkin's *Eugene Onegin*, and portrays the Californian life-style through the story of the relationships of a group of young professionals. His epic novel *A Suitable Boy* (1993) won much popular acclaim. Seth has also published *From Heaven Lake: Travels through Sinkiang and Tibet* (1983).

Settle, Elkanah (1648–1724)

Restoration dramatist, at one time rivalling ▷ Dryden in popularity. His wrote a number of ▷ heroic dramas noted for their blood and

bombast, of which the best known is *The Empress of Morocco* (1673). This was performed at court under the auspices of the ▷ Earl of Rochester, but earned the contempt of Dryden, ▷ Crowne, and ▷ Shadwell; Dryden ridiculed it as a 'Rapsody of none-sense'. A bitter and personal war of words ensued, with Settle attacking plays of Dryden's, Dryden satirizing Settle as Doeg, 'whom God for Mankind's mirth has made', in ▷ *Absalom and Achitophel*, and Settle replying with more counter-attacks. In 1691 Settle became official poet to the ▷ City of London. He took to writing ▷ operas, such as *The Fairy Queen* (1692), which was set to music by ▷ Purcell, *The World in the Moon*(1697), and *The Virgin Prophetess* (1701). Settle also wrote ▷ pageants, and comic scenes, known as drolls, for London's annual ▷ Bartholomew Fair. He died in poverty.
Bib: Brown, Frank C., *Elkanah Settle, His Life and Works*; Nonak, Maximilian E., *The Empress of Morocco and its Critics.*

Settlement, Act of
▷ Act of Settlement.

Seven Years' War (1756–63)
Frederick the Great of Prussia, in alliance with Great Britain and Hanover, fought an alliance of France, Austria and Russia. Frederick kept his dominions by the Treaty of Hubertusberg. The importance of the war for Britain was that it left her predominant in North America and in India (Treaty of Paris, 1763). An indirect consequence of this was that the American colonists, no longer afraid of conquest by the French, now felt free to resist the British policy of taxing them without allowing them representation in ▷ Parliament; this led to the ▷ American War of Independence (1775–83) and the establishment of the United States.

The Seven Years' War produced three war-leaders: in India, Robert Clive, victor of the battle of Plassey, 1757; in America, James Wolfe, captor of Quebec, 1759; and ▷ William Pitt the Elder, Earl of Chatham, the minister who controlled the strategy of the Franco-British struggle.

Seward, Anna (1742–1809)
English poet. Known as 'the Swan of Lichfield', she was born and brought up in the historic village of Eyam in Derbyshire, where her father was rector. In 1754 he became Canon of Lichfield, and Anna looked after him there in his old age. She began to write in her mid-thirties, attending ▷ Anne Miller's poetry evenings. Her elegies on ▷ David Garrick and Captain Cook brought her to public notice. Her novel *Louisa* was published in 1784, and she continued to publish verse, letters and poems in periodicals, including ▷ *The Gentlemans Magazine*. She was very well known in the 1780s, and a formidable (if ridiculed) figure throughout this and the next decade. Her *Poems* was published in 1810. She knew ▷ Helen Maria Williams, the Ladies of Llangollen, and ▷ Hester Lynch Thrale. ▷ Scott, Mary
Bib: Lonsdale, R., *Eighteenth Century Women Poets.*

Sewell, Anna (1820–78)
Famous for the one book she wrote, *Black Beauty* (1877), whose success was largely posthumous. Sewell was paid only £20 for the book, which was published just before her death. The story, of a black mare's unhappy adventures, ending happily, has remained a children's classic.
▷ Children's literature.
Bib: Chitty, S., *Life.*

Sewell, Elizabeth (1815–1906)
Novelist and polemical writer. She was born in Newport on the Isle of Wight and went to school in Bath until recalled home at the age of fifteen. She began to write partly to help the family finances, publishing her first work, *Amy Herbert*, in 1844. A keen supporter of the ▷ Oxford Movement, her novels are deeply religious and moral, yet their focus on women's lives has aroused recent feminist interest. Works include: *Laneton Parsonage* (1846); *Margaret Percival* (1847); *Katherine Ashton* (1854); and *Ursula* (1858). Sewell also wrote devotional works, including *Thoughts for Holy Week* (1857) and *A History of the Early Church* (1861), as well as an *Autobiography* (1907).
Bib: Foster, S., *Victorian Women's Fiction: Marriage, Freedom and the Individual*; Showalter, E., *A Literature of Their Own.*

Seymour, Frances, Countess of Hertford (1669–1754)
English poet, aristocratic patron and correspondent and editor of ▷ Elizabeth Singer Rowe. After her first marriage in 1715 to Algernon Seymour, she moved in court circles, and in 1723 became Lady of the Bedchamber to the Princess of Wales. In 1748 she became the Duchess of Somerset on her marriage to the Duke of Somerset. Her poems were published in anthologies. She was related to ▷ Ann Finch.
Bib: Hull, T. (ed.), *Selected Letters.*

Shadwell, Thomas (?1642–92)
Dramatist and poet. Born in Norfolk. Shadwell was educated at Bury St Edmunds and at Cambridge and entered the Middle Temple in 1658. However, he decided on a literary career instead of the law. He travelled on the Continent, and married Ann Gibbs, an actress in the ▷ Duke's Company. Shadwell was a disciple of ▷ Ben Jonson and admirer of ▷ Molière, on whose play *Les Facheux*

he based *The Sullen Lovers* (1668). Shadwell wrote 17 plays, of which the best known are *Epsom Wells* (1672), ▷ *The Virtuoso* (1676), an engaging satire on the Royal Society, and *The Squire of Alsatia* (1688) (the latter refers to Whitefriars, a London district where those liable to arrest took sanctuary, and the play makes free use of the cant language of thieves and their associates).

A convinced Whig, unlike most of his leading contemporaries in the theatre, Shadwell incurred the fierce enmity of the Tory ▷ John Dryden. At first the two men were on good terms, but they took opposite sides when ▷ Lord Shaftesbury clashed with ▷ Charles II on the issue of the Protestant succession to the throne. Dryden attacked Shaftesbury in ▷ *Absalom and Achitophel* and *The Medal*; Shadwell retorted with *The Medal of John Bayes*: *A Satire Against Folly and Knavery* (1682). Dryden then stigmatized Shadwell in ▷ *Mac Flecknoe, Or A Satire on the True Blue Protestant Poet, T.S.* (1682) as one who 'never deviates into sense', and as Og in the second part of *Absalom and Achitophel*. Shadwell attempted counter-attack in an adaptation of ▷ Juvenal's tenth satire, but Dryden's proved the more lasting reputation, and Shadwell has retained an unfair image as a dull author. However, he had some revenge by superseding Dryden as ▷ Poet Laureate after the Protestant triumph in the ▷ Glorious Revolution of 1688. A regular user of opium, Shadwell died suddenly, supposedly after an overdose. His daughter Anne became an actress, the celebrated ▷ Anne Oldfield, and a son, Charles, became a dramatist.

Bib: Dobree, B., *Restoration Comedy*; Summers, M. (ed.), *Works*; Borgman, A.S., *Thomas Shadwell: His Life and Comedies.*

Shaffer, Peter (b 1926)

British dramatist who has established his reputation with a number of major successes: *The Royal Hunt of the Sun* (1964); *Black Comedy* (1965); *Equus* (1973); *Amadeus* (1974) and *Lettice and Lovage* (1987). The first is a spectacular play about the Spanish conquest of Peru; the second a short farce; the third an exploration of the disturbed psyche of a violent youth who puts out the eyes of a horse; *Amadeus* looks at the court composer Antonio Salieri's jealousy (and possible murder) of Mozart; *Lettice and Lovage* is a comedy written especially for the actress Maggie Smith.

Bib: Klein, D., *Peter Shaffer.*

Shaftesbury, Lord (Anthony Ashley Cooper, 1st Earl of Shaftesbury, 1621–83)

Politician. He first took the side of the king in the ▷ Civil War of 1642–46, but changed sides because he considered that Royalist policy threatened the Protestant religion. He later became a parliamentary opponent of ▷ Cromwell, however, and after the Restoration he became one of ▷ Charles II's chief ministers. Charles II, however, was Catholic in sympathy, and Shaftesbury again went into opposition in 1673. By the Exclusion Bills, he tried to exclude Charles' openly Catholic brother, James, Duke of York, from succession to the throne, advancing the claims of Charles' illegitimate son, the ▷ Duke of Monmouth, in James' place. The alliance of Shaftesbury and Monmouth is satirized in Dryden's ▷ *Absalom and Achitophel*, one of the best-known ▷ satirical poems in the English language. Charles II's statesmanship outwitted Shaftesbury, who fled to Holland and died in exile.

Shaftesbury, Lord (Anthony Ashley Cooper, 3rd Earl of Shaftesbury, 1671–1713)

A moral philosopher, with great influence in the first half of the 18th century. His main beliefs are contained in his *Characteristics of Men, Manners, Opinions, Times* (1711; revised edition, 1713). He was a Deist (▷ Deism), a Churchman, and a ▷ Platonic idealist. His optimistic philosophy was in direct opposition to that of ▷ Thomas Hobbes, author of ▷ *Leviathan*. He believed that men have 'natural affections' which are capable of going beyond self-interest. The cultivation of disinterested affection for others will produce virtue and the true social morality. His concept of these 'natural affections' seemed to make the supernatural elements of Christian doctrine unnecessary to the acquirement of true religion. On this ground he was opposed by Bishop Butler in his *Analogy of True Religion* (1736). On a purely theoretical level, Shaftesbury anticipated the beliefs about ▷ Nature of the poet ▷ William Wordsworth, and he encouraged the growing emphasis on ▷ sentiment and ▷ sensibility in criticism and poetry in the 18th century.

Bib: Willey, B., *Eighteenth-century Background* and *The English Moralists*; Brett, R. L., *The Third Earl of Shaftesbury: a Study in Eighteenth-century Literary Theory.*

Shaftesbury, Lord (Anthony Ashley Cooper, 7th Earl of Shaftesbury, 1801–85)

Statesman and philanthropist. His politics were right wing, but he devoted his career to improving the condition of the working classes. It was largely owing to him that the Ten Hours Bill, restricting hours of work in ▷ factories, became law in 1847, and in the same decade his efforts led to improvement in the mines. After 1846, he gave his attention to the London slums; clearance of the squalid district of Seven Dials led to the building of Shaftesbury Avenue, called after him; the statue of Eros in Piccadilly Circus also commemorates him. Shaftesbury was an adherent of the religious revival known as the ▷ Evangelical Movement, working against the ▷ Utilitarian theories of the political economists (Adam Smith, ▷ Jeremy Bentham, ▷ Thomas Malthus) in the shaping of the industrial changes and urban expansion of the mid-19th century.

▷ Anti-industrialism.

Shakespeare – criticism

As with any exceptionally popular author, different ages have appreciated different aspects of Shakespeare. In his own day, popular taste, according to ▷ Ben Jonson, particularly enjoyed ▷ *Titus Andronicus*, now regarded as one of the least interesting of his plays. John Dryden (1631–1700) (*Essay on Dramatic Poesy*), picked out ▷ *Richard II*; Samuel Johnson (1709–84) (*Preface to Shakespeare*, 1765) admired the comedies. It is possible to understand these preferences: *Titus* is the most bloodthirsty of all the plays, and suited the more vulgar tastes of an age in which executions were popular spectacles. Dryden and Johnson both belonged to ▷ neo-classical periods. Johnson, like Dryden, was troubled by the differences in Shakespeare's tragedies from the formalism of ancient Greek and 17th-century tragedy that the spirit of their period encouraged them to admire, and Johnson's warm humanity caused him to respond to the plays which displayed wide human appeal while their mode permitted some licence of form. Both Johnson and Dryden rose superior to the limitations of their period in according Shakespeare such greatness. The 19th-century inheritor of Johnson's mantle as the most perceptive critic of Shakespeare is S. T. Coleridge (1772–1834), whose seminal lectures on Shakespeare were inspired by German Romanticism. In his letters John Keats (1795–1821) offers some of the most enduringly valuable comments on Shakespeare's works before A. C. Bradley published *Shakespearean Tragedy* in 1904, which was to prove the most influential text on Shakespeare for two generations.

In the 20th century Wilson Knight (*The Imperial Theme, The Crown of Life*), Harley Granville-Barker (*Preface to Shakespeare*) and others such as D. A. Traversi (*An Approach to Shakespeare*) and H. C. Goddard (*The Meaning of Shakespeare*) have all contributed to our understanding of the plays and poetry. Shakespeare's education has been closely scrutinized by T. W. Baldwin in two volumes, *Shakespeare's Smalle Latin and Lesse Greeke*, and Geoffrey Bullough's eight volumes on Shakespeare's sources, *Narrative and Dramatic Sources of Shakespeare*, are indispensable to Shakespearean critics. Increasingly the critical debate has been conducted in a number of specialized journals, particularly the long-established *Shakespeare Jahrbuch, Shakespeare Survey, Shakespeare Studies*, and *Shakespeare Quarterly*. A few books are outstanding in their focus on particular aspects of Shakespeare, such as C. L. Barber's influential essay on Shakespearean comedy and the rituals of English folklore and country customs, *Shakespeare's Festive Comedy*, and Northrop Fry's archetypal study of comedy and romance, *A Natural Perspective*. Howard Felperin's distinguished book on Shakespeare's last plays, *Shakespearean Romance*, and Janet Adelman's thought-provoking study of *Antony and Cleopatra* and its mythopoeic imagery in *The Common Liar*, both reflect the influence of Frye in their sober and formally predicated approaches.

Of a more radical bent is Jan Kott's famous essay on ▷ *King Lear* in '*King Lear*, or *Endgame*' (1964), which argued the case for Shakespeare as our contemporary, with his finger imaginatively on the pulse of a dark, modern human predicament. On the same lines Peter Brook's famous production of ▷ *A Midsummer Night's Dream* in 1970 emancipated the play from its putative operatic and conformist frame and irretrievably altered our perception of it. By thus indicating the extent to which the theatre can influence interpretation of plays, Brook materially contributed to redirecting critical attention back to the stage.

Modern social and critical movements have made their impact felt in the field of Shakespeare studies: ▷ deconstruction, in the guise of a creative disintegration of the texts' organic status, and ▷ feminism provide the impetus for some of the most controversial writing on Shakespeare at the end of the 20th century, as do ▷ 'cultural materialism', particularly ▷ 'new historicism' and ▷ psychoanalytical theory. New historicism in particular seems set to command a wide audience in the works of Stephen Greenblatt and Louis Montrose, whose work combines the scholarly scruples of the older tradition with an acute sceptical and self-critical awareness of the historical and epistemological contexts of literary criticism in society.

Bib: Bradley, A. C., *Shakespearean Tragedy*; Barber, C. L., *Shakespeare's Festive Comedy*; Coleridge, S. T., *Shakespearean Criticism*; Dollimore, J., *Radical Tragedy*; Dryden, J., *Essays*; Frye, N., *A Natural Perspective*; Greenblatt, S., *Renaissance Self-Fashioning*; Jardine, L., *Still Harping on Daughters*; Johnson, S., *On Shakespeare*; Parker, P. and Hartman, G., *Shakespeare and the Question of Theory*, Ryan, K., *Shakespeare*.

Shakespeare – history of textual study

Apart from a scene sometimes ascribed to Shakespeare in the play ▷ *Sir Thomas More* (c 1596), none of Shakespeare's work has survived in manuscript. In his own lifetime, 18 of his plays were published in separate volumes (the ▷ Quartos), but this was probably without the author's permission, and therefore without his revisions and textual corrections. His non-dramatic poems, including the ▷ sonnets, were also published during his lifetime. After his death, his fellow actors Heming and Condell published his collected plays (except ▷ *Pericles*) in the large, single volume known as the First Folio, and this was succeeded by the Second Folio (1632), and the Third (two editions) and Fourth in 1663, 1664 and 1685. The Second Folio regularized the division of the plays into Acts and Scenes, and the second issue of the Third added *Pericles*, as well as other plays certainly not by Shakespeare. In several important respects the Folio editions were unsatisfactory:

1 The texts of some (though not all) of the smaller quarto volumes of the plays published during the poet's lifetime differed materially from the text of even the First Folio, which in turn differed from the later folios.

2 The First Folio arranged the plays according to their kinds (Comedies, Histories or Tragedies) and gave no indication of the order in which the plays were written.

3 There was no evidence that even the first editors had had access to the best manuscript texts, and there were evident errors in some passages, the fault of either the editors or their printers, and editors of the later Folios made alterations of their own. Consequently, there was plenty of work during the next two centuries for scholars to re-establish, as nearly as possible, Shakespeare's original text. Work also had to be done on the chronological order of the plays, discovery of the sources of their plots, philological investigations of linguistic peculiarities, and research into the conditions in which the plays were originally acted.

Two of the most eminent 18th-century writers published editions of the plays; these were Alexander Pope (in 1725 and 1728), and Samuel Johnson (in 1765). Neither, however, was a sound scholarly edition, though Johnson's was important for its critical Preface and annotations. Lewis Theobald (1688–1744) attacked Pope's poor scholarship in his *Shakespeare Restored* (1726), and published his own edition in 1734. He was the first enlightened editor, and did permanently useful work both in removing post-Shakespearean additions and alterations and in suggesting emendations of corrupt passages. After him came Steevens and Capell, who compared the original Quarto texts with the Folio ones, and ▷ Edmond Malone (1741–1812), the most eminent of the 18th-century Shakespeare scholars. In 1778 he made the first serious attempt to establish the chronological order of the plays, and in 1790 he brought out the best edition of them yet established.

Shakespearean scholarship in the 18th century was more the work of individuals than a collaborative enterprise. They saw many of the problems involved in estimating the relative values of the early texts, the possibilities of scholarly emendation of corrupt passages, and the necessity of eliminating the errors of unscholarly 17th- and 18th-century editors. This work culminated in the publication of 'Variorum' editions of the plays, 1803–21. But the establishment of a really sound text required the study of wider subject-matter. Shakespeare's work had to be estimated as a whole so that his development could be understood; philological study of the state of the language in his time was needed; historical events had to be examined for their possible relevance; many sources for the plots remained to be discovered; theatrical conditions and the relationship of Shakespeare to dramatists contemporary with him needed exploration; even handwriting was important, for the detection of possible misprinting. All this was the work of the collaborative scholarship of the 19th century. It was carried out by German scholars, by the English Shakespeare Societies led by Halliwell and Furnivall, and by the universities.

In the later 18th century Shakespeare became an inspiration to the movement in Germany for the emancipation of German culture from its long subjection to French culture. A. W. Schlegel's remarkable translations (1797–1810) were fine enough to enable Germans to adopt Shakespeare as something like a national poet. German scholars such as Tieck, Ulrici, Gervinus and Franz adopted Shakespearean studies with thoroughness and enthusiasm. They stimulated the foundation of Shakespeare Societies in England, and in 1863–6 the Cambridge University Press was able to publish an edition of Shakespeare's works, which, in its revised form (1891–93), is substantially the text now generally in use.

There has been considerable editorial activity in the 20th century, and it was to be expected that the 'New Bibliography', spearheaded by ▷ A. W. Pollard, ▷ R. B. McKerrow and W. W. Greg would produce a major reconsideration of the Shakespearean text. In the end the fruit of their research, and particularly of McKerrow's brilliant *Prolegomena for the Oxford Shakespeare* (1939), needed to wait for nearly 40 years before they were put to use by the editors of the *Oxford Shakespeare*, Gary Taylor and Stanley Wells. In the meantime Charlton Hinman produced two seminal volumes on the collations of the extant Folios in *The Printing and Proof-Reading of the First Folio*, and incorporated his findings in *The Norton Facsimile: The First Folio of Shakespeare*, which remains a standard work of reference. All the major university and other presses turned their attention to re-editing Shakespeare in the late 1960s and early 1970s. At a time when Oxford University Press were printing two complete one-volume Shakespeares (one old spelling and another modern spelling) as well as a huge textual companion and the entire works in separate editions for the Oxford English Texts, Cambridge University Press published the first volume of Peter Blayney's exhaustive survey of the 'origins' of the First

Quarto of ▷ *King Lear: The Texts of 'King Lear' and their Origins*. Cambridge, Methuen (New Arden), Macmillan and Longman have pursued similar goals, updating and editing afresh Shakespeare's works, each bringing to the canon a different approach. Whereas most of the editions have followed basically conservative principles, most have embraced to a greater or lesser degree the Oxford view of the plays as primarily works for the theatre. Increasingly, Oxford's view of Shakespeare as a dramatist who regularly reshaped his plays in line with theatrical and aesthetic demands is gaining ground. The particular focus for this hypothesis has become the two-text (Quarto and Folio) *King Lear*, which most editors now agree reflects two different versions of the play. The same editorial principles are being applied to other texts reflecting similar source situations, such as ▷ *Richard III*, ▷ *Hamlet* and ▷ *Othello*. Among Oxford's most radical proposals are the printing of two versions of *King Lear*, the calling of ▷ Falstaff ▷ 'Oldcastle' in ▷ *Henry IV, Part I*, as well as boldly recreating the text of ▷ *Pericles*.

The history of Shakespeare editing in Britain towards the end of the 20th century is ultimately one of the creative disintegration of the shibboleths of traditional editorial policy, even if all the changes proposed by contemporary scholars do not find favour with posterity.

Bib: Bowers, F., *On Editing Shakespeare*; Greg, W. W., *The Shakespeare First Folio: Its Bibliographical and Textual History*; Honigmann, E. A. J., *The Stability of Shakespeare's Text*; McKerrow, R. B., *Prolegomena for the Oxford Shakespeare*;Wells, S., *Re-Editing Shakespeare for the Modern Reader*.

Shakespeare – Sonnets

First published in 1609, but there is no clear evidence for when they were written. They are commonly thought to date from 1595–9; ▷ Francis Meres in *Palladis Tamia* (1598) mentions that Shakespeare wrote ▷ sonnets. There are 154 sonnets; numbers 1–126 are addressed to a man (126 is in fact not a sonnet but a 12-line poem) and the remainder are addressed to a woman – the so-called 'dark lady of the sonnets', since it is made clear that she is dark in hair and complexion. There has been much speculation about the dedication: 'To the only begetter of these ensuing sonnets Mr. W. H. all happiness and that eternity promised by our everliving poet Wisheth the well-wishing adventurer in setting forth T. T.' 'T. T.' stands for Thomas Thorpe, the stationer (*ie* bookseller and publisher of the sonnets); speculation centres on what is meant by 'begetter' and who is meant by 'W. H.' W. H. may stand for the man (William Hughes?) who *procured* the manuscript of the sonnets for Thorpe, if that is what 'begetter' means. But if 'begetter' means 'inspirer', it has been conjectured that W. H. may be the inverted initials of Henry Wriothesley, ▷ third Earl of Southampton, to whom Shakespeare had dedicated his ▷ *Venus and Adonis* and *The Rape of Lucrece*, or they may stand for ▷ William Herbert, Earl of Pembroke or for someone else. Guesses have also been made as to the identity of the 'dark lady', who has been thought by some to be Mary Fitton, a maid of honour at court and mistress of William Herbert, or by A. L. Rowse to be ▷ Aemelia Lanyer. There is too little evidence for profitable conjecture on either subject.

Critics and scholars disagree about the extent to which the sonnets are autobiographical (and if so what they express), or whether they are 'literary exercises' without a personal theme. A middle view is that they are exploratory of personal relations in friendship and in love, and that some of them rehearse themes later dramatized in the plays – for instance 94 suggests the character of Angelo in ▷ *Measure for Measure*, and the recurrent concern with the destructiveness of time seems to look forward to ▷ *Troilus and Cressida* and the great tragedies. Since it is unknown whether the edition of 1609 is a reliable version, there is also some doubt whether the order of the sonnets in it is that intended by Shakespeare; most scholars see little reason to question it.

One of the most valuable recent editions of the *Sonnets* is Stephen Booth's, which uses the 1609 text, rightly accepting its ordering of the poetry as binding. Booth's edition compares the modern text with the ▷ Quarto versions at each stage. But if his extensive notes are instructive, they also tend to be too comprehensive in their suggestions of infinite and ultimately meaningless ambiguities in the text. John Kerrigan's edition of *The Sonnets and A Lover's Complaint* provides a sensitive text, informative notes and does justice to the often neglected *A Lover's Complaint*. Kerrigan authoritatively attributes the poem to Shakespeare and offers the best commentary on it to date.

Bib: Leishman, J. B., *Themes and Variations in Shakespeare's Sonnets*; Schaar, C., *Elizabethan Sonnet Themes and the Dating of Shakespeare's Sonnets*; Smith, H., *The Tension of the Lyre: Poetry in Shakespeare's Sonnets*; Fineman, J., *Shakespeare's Perjured Eye*.

Shakespeare, William (1564–1616) – biography

Dramatist and poet. He was baptized on 26 April 1564; his birth is commemorated on 23 April, which happens also to be St George's Day, the festival of the patron saint of England. His father, John Shakespeare, was a Stratford-on-Avon merchant who dealt in gloves and probably other goods; his grandfather, Richard Shakespeare, was a yeoman, *ie* small farmer, and his mother, Mary Arden, was the daughter of a local farmer who belonged to the local noble family of Arden, after whom the forest to the north of Stratford was named. John Shakespeare's affairs prospered at first, and in 1568 he was appointed to the highest office in the town – High Bailiff, equivalent to Mayor. A grammar school existed in Stratford, and since it was free to the sons of burgesses, it is generally assumed that William attended it. If he did, he probably received a good education in the Latin language; there is evidence that the sons of Stratford merchants were, or could be, well read and well educated. He married Anne Hathaway in 1582, and they had three children: Suzanna, born 1583, and the twin son and daughter, Hamnet and Judith, born in 1585.

Thereafter Shakespeare's life is a blank, until we meet a reference to him in *A Groatsworth of Wit* (1592), an autobiographical pamphlet by the London playwright ▷ Robert Greene, who accuses him of plagiarism. By 1592, therefore, Shakespeare was already successfully embarked as a dramatist in London, but there is no clear evidence of when he went there. From 1592 to 1594 the London theatres were closed owing to epidemics of plague, and Shakespeare seems to have used the opportunity to make a reputation for himself as a narrative poet: his ▷ *Venus and Adonis* was published in 1593, and *The Rape of Lucrece* a year later. Both were dedicated to Henry Wriothesley, ▷ Earl of Southampton. He continued to prosper as a dramatist, and in the winter of 1594 was a leading member of the Lord ▷ Chamberlain's Men, with whom he remained for the rest of his career. In 1596 his father acquired a coat of arms – the sign of a ▷ gentleman – and in 1597 William bought New Place, the largest house in Stratford. There he probably established his father, who had been in financial difficulties since 1577. In 1592, John Shakespeare had been registered as a recusant (▷ Recusancy); this might mean that he was a Catholic, but may equally show that he was trying to escape arrest for debt.

In 1598, ▷ Francis Meres, in his literary commentary *Palladis Tamia, Wit's Treasury*, mentions Shakespeare as one of the leading writers of the time, lists 12 of his plays, and mentions his ▷ sonnets as circulating privately; they were published in 1609. The Lord Chamberlain's Men opened the ▷ Globe Theatre in 1599, and Shakespeare became a shareholder in it. After the accession of ▷ James I the company came under royal patronage, and was called the King's Men; this gave Shakespeare a status in the royal household. He is known to have been an actor as well as a playwright, but tradition associates him with small parts: Adam in ▷ *As You Like It*, and the Ghost in ▷ *Hamlet*. He may have retired to New Place in Stratford in 1610, but he continued his connections with London, and purchased a house in ▷ Blackfriars in 1613. In the same year, the Globe theatre was burnt down during a performance of the last play with which Shakespeare's name is associated, ▷ *Henry VIII*. His will is dated less than a month before his death. The fact that he left his 'second-best bed' to his wife is no evidence that he was on bad terms with her; the best one would naturally go with his main property to his elder daughter, who had married John Hall; his younger daughter, who had married Thomas Quiney, was also provided for, but his son, Hamnet, had died in childhood. His last direct descendant, Lady Barnard, died in 1670.

Owing to the fact that the subject-matter of ▷ biography was restricted until mid-17th century to princes, statesmen and great soldiers, the documentary evidence of Shakespeare's life is, apart from the above facts, slight. His contemporaries ▷ Christopher Marlowe and ▷ Ben Jonson are in some respects better documented because they involved themselves more with political events. Many legends and traditions have grown up about Shakespeare since near his own day, but they are untrustworthy. He was certainly one of the most successful English writers of his time; his income has been estimated at about £200 a year, considerable earnings for those days. After the death of Marlowe in 1593, his greatest rival was Ben Jonson, who criticized his want of art (in *Discoveries*, 1640), admired his character, and paid a noble tribute to him in the prefatory poem to the First Folio collection of his plays (1623).

Bib: Chambers, E. K., *William Shakespeare: A Study of Facts and Problems* (2 vols); Dutton, R., *William Shakespeare: A Literary Life*; Schoenbaum, S., *Shakespeare's Lives; William Shakespeare: A Documentary Life*.

Shakespeare's plays

Earliest publications. The first collected edition was the volume known as the First Folio (1623). This included all the plays now acknowledged to be by Shakespeare with the exception of *Pericles*. It also includes *Henry VIII*. Stationers (the profession then combining bookselling and publishing) were glad to bring out individual plays in ▷ quarto editions in his lifetime, however, and since there was no law of copyright these were often 'pirated', *ie* published without the permission of the author. On the whole, Shakespeare's company (the Lord ▷ Chamberlain's Men) did not want such publication, since printed editions enabled other acting companies to perform the plays in competition. Eighteen of Shakespeare's plays were published in this way, sometimes in more than one edition, and occasionally in editions that varied considerably. Since none of the plays has survived in the original manuscript, the task of modern editors is often to reconcile different quartos (where they exist) with each other, and any quartos that exist with corresponding versions in the First Folio. The following is a list of the separate editions of the plays, published while Shakespeare was alive or soon after his death, with dates of different editions where they substantially disagree with one another:

Titus Andronicus (1594)
Henry VI, Part II (1594)
Henry VI, Part III (1595)
Richard II (1597, 1608)
Richard III (1597)
Romeo and Juliet (1597, 1599)
Love's Labour's Lost (1598)
Henry IV, Part I (1598)
Henry IV, Part II (1600)
Henry V (1600)
A Midsummer Night's Dream (1600)
The Merchant of Venice (1600)
Much Ado About Nothing (1600)
The Merry Wives of Windsor (1602)
Hamlet (1603, 1604)
King Lear (1608)
Troilus and Cressida (1609)
*Pericles (*1609)
*Othello (*1622)

Order of composition. The First Folio does not print the plays in the order in which they were written. Scholars have had to work out their chronological order on three main kinds of evidence: 1 external evidence (*eg* records of production, publication); 2 internal evidence (*eg* allusions to contemporary events); 3 stylistic evidence. The following is an approximate chronological arrangement, though in some instances there is no certainty:

1590–91	*Henry VI, Parts II and III*
1591–92	*Henry VI, Part I*
1592–93	*Richard III*
	The Comedy of Errors
1593–94	*Titus Andronicus*
	The Taming of the Shrew
	Two Gentlemen of Verona
1594–95	*Love's Labour's Lost*
	Romeo and Juliet
1595–96	*Richard II*
	A Midsummer Night's Dream
1596–97	*King John*
	The Merchant of Venice
	The Merry Wives of Windsor
1597–98	*Henry IV, Parts I and II*
1598–99	*Much Ado about Nothing*
	Henry V
1599–1600	*Julius Caesar*
	As You Like It
	Twelfth Night
1600–1	*Hamlet*
	Measure for Measure
1601–2	*Troilus and Cressida*
1602–3	*All's Well that Ends Well*
1604–5	*Othello*
	King Lear
1605–6	*Macbeth*
1606–7	*Antony and Cleopatra*
1607–8	*Coriolanus*
	Timon of Athens
1608–9	*Pericles*
1609–10	*Cymbeline*
1610–11	*The Winter's Tale*
1611–12	*The Tempest*

Shakespeare is now believed to have written all of *Henry VIII* and to have collaborated with ▷ Fletcher on *Two Noble Kinsmen.*
▷ Romances of Shakespeare; Problem plays (of Shakespeare).

Shamela (1741)
An Apology for the life of Mrs Shamela Andrews, published pseudonymously by ▷ Henry Fielding, parodies ▷ Samuel Richardson's ▷ *Pamela* of the preceding year. The plot and characters are taken from Richardson's novel, yet the tone reveals what Fielding saw as Richardson's hypocritical morality, where virtue is rewarded by worldly wealth and status.

Sharp, William (1855–1905)
Scottish novelist and poet, who published much of his better work in the 1890s under the name 'Fiona Macleod', supposedly his cousin, an alter ego whose real existence he always maintained (she appeared in *Who's Who*) and may even have believed in. The novels of Fiona Macleod are mystical, nostalgic tales of Celtic peasant life, such as *Pharais: A Romance of the Isles* (1894), *The Mountain Lover* (1895), *The Sin Eater* (1895) and *Green Fire* (1896). Sharp also wrote novels under his own name, including the epistolary novel *A Fellowe and his Wife* (1892), jointly authored with the US writer Blanche Willis Howard. After early, uncongenial work as a clerk, Sharp had begun his literary career in the 1880s as a journalist, and by writing commissioned biographies and poetry, but in the 1890s spent much of his time travelling. The dual personality provoked a nervous crisis in 1897.
▷ Scottish literature in English.

Shaw, George Bernard (1856–1950)
Dramatist, critic, social thinker. His family belonged to the Irish Protestant gentry. His father was an unsuccessful businessman; his mother was a musician of talent. Apart from the musical education he received from her, he was practically self-educated. He came to London in 1876, and set to work as a novelist. The novel proved not to be his medium, but his efforts in the form were an apprenticeship for dramatic writing in which he excelled. He wrote five novels in all: the best known are *Cashel Byron's Profession* (pub. 1885–6) and *The Admirable Bashville* (pub. 1901). In 1884 he joined the newly formed socialist ▷ Fabian Society, of which he became a leading member; he edited *Fabian Essays* (1887) which was influential in forming socialist opinion in Britain. Between

1885 and 1898 he wrote much criticism for a number of papers; he was probably the most astute music and dramatic critic of his time.

His career as a dramatist began in 1892 and lasted substantially until 1939, though he wrote his last play when he was over 90. He was profoundly impressed by the work of the Norwegian dramatist ▷ Henrik Ibsen, especially by Ibsen's plays of social criticism such as *A Doll's House*. In 1891 came his study *The Quintessence of Ibsenism*, and then he embarked on plays of social purpose on his own account. Shaw's art is, however, very different from Ibsen's; whereas for Ibsen the characters are always more important than the ideas in a play, and the characters engage in convincing talk, in Shaw's plays it is the ideas that really matter, and his characters don't talk – they make speeches. The speeches are composed in the operatic tradition of Mozart; Shaw once said that it was Mozart who taught him to write. As a dramatic critic and a student of Ibsen, he had learnt stagecraft thoroughly, and he knew how to achieve theatrical effect, to which his unique talent for wit, surprise, and paradox strongly contributed. In regard to ideas, he was concerned to shock his audiences out of their unthinking acceptance of social conventions, but he was careful (unlike Ibsen) never to scandalize them beyond their willingness to listen. Apart from socialism, his leading doctrine (derived partly from the French philosopher ▷ Bergson and partly from the German philosopher ▷ Nietzsche) was his belief in the 'Life Force' – that the progress of humanity depends in every generation on the evolution of geniuses, who constitute the spearheads of advance but inevitably arouse the hostility of their contemporaries. He was the first dramatist to realize that the reading public for plays was now larger than the theatre-going public; accordingly he published his own plays with long prefaces, which are commonly as famous as the plays themselves, and with elaborate stage directions intended not only for stage producers but for readers accustomed to the kind of detail provided by novels.

His most famous plays are probably: *Man and Superman* (1903); *Major Barbara* (1905); *Pygmalion* (1912); *Heartbreak House* (1917); *Back to Methuselah* (1921); *Saint Joan* (1924). Other plays: in *Plays Pleasant and Unpleasant* (1898) – *Widowers' Houses* (first staged 1892); *The Philanderer; Mrs Warren's Profession*; *Arms and the Man; Candida; The Man of Destiny; You Never Can Tell.* In *Plays for Puritans* (1901) – *The Devil's Disciple; Caesar and Cleopatra; Captain Brassbound's Conversion.* Other plays before 1914; *John Bull's Other Island; How He Lied to Her Husband; Press Cuttings; The Doctor's Dilemma; Getting Married; The Showing up of Blanco Posnet; Misalliance; Fanny's First Play; Androcles and the Lion; Overruled; Great Catherine.* After 1918: *The Apple Cart; In Good King Charles' Golden Days.*

Among Shaw's extensive political writings are his attack on the British government, *Common Sense about the War* (1914), and *The Intelligent Woman's Guide to Socialism and Capitalism* (1928).

Bib: Pearson, H., *Life*; Henderson, A., *Life*; Chesterton, G. K., *George Bernard Shaw*; Bentley, E., *George Bernard Shaw*; Meisel, M., *Shaw and the Nineteenth Century*; Morgan, M., *The Shavian Playground.*

She Stoops to Conquer

A comedy by ▷ Oliver Goldsmith, first acted in 1773. The basic comedy is that of a morbidly shy man misled into a situation in which he behaves in a way such as to horrify him when he awakes to the true circumstances. The young man is Marlow, sent by his father to court in marriage the daughter of his friend Hardcastle. Marlow loses his way, and is deceived into supposing the Hardcastle house to be an inn. In a gentleman's house he is horribly embarrassed, but in an inn he is at ease; he proceeds to behave off-handedly to old Hardcastle as to a landlord, and to make love to his daughter, as to a waiting maid. The arrival of his father clears up the situation, and the mistake turns out to Marlow's advantage. The play is one of Goldsmith's best works, and an example of the brief revival of the Comedy of ▷ Manners in the 1770s.

***She Wou'd If She Cou'd* (1668)**

Play by ▷ Sir George Etherege, with a cynical and bawdy atmosphere. Two gallants, Courtall and Freeman, are out to seduce and ruin women, but fall in love with Gatty and Ariana in spite of themselves, and are united with them after several scenes of bantering flirtation. The character referred to in the title is Lady Cockwood who, being badly treated by her despicable husband, longs to cuckold him. Courtall and Freeman make sport with her, openly leading her on, but privately mocking and insulting her. The play is derogatory of ▷ marriage, despite its endings in espousal, and heavy with race-course imagery, with women seen as horses for men to ride.

Shelley, Mary Wollstonecraft (1797–1851)

The only daughter of feminist ▷ Mary Wollstonecraft and radical philosopher ▷ William Godwin, her mother having died a few days after her birth. Her father remarried in 1801 but Mary found her stepmother unsympathetic and remained rather close to her father despite his cold manner. She idolized her own mother, and educated herself through contact with her father's intellectual circle and her own hard study. She met ▷ Percy Bysshe Shelley in 1812 and on return from an extended visit to friends in 1814 became very close to him. He was in the midst of separating from his wife Harriet, and within a couple of months he and Mary left England together, marrying in 1816 after Harriet's suicide. They had a devoted but difficult relationship, only one of their children surviving childhood, Godwin pressing them for loans and Shelley's father Timothy making only a small allowance for the child, Percy. After Shelley's death in 1822 Mary stayed a short while in Italy, then returned to London where she continued to write novels, produced an account of her travels with Percy in Europe and edited Shelley's poetry and prose, but proved too exhausted to write his biography, which she abandoned. ▷ *Frankenstein, or the Modern Prometheus* (1817) was her first and most famous novel, apparently inspired by a dream. *The Last Man* (1826) has characters based on Shelley and ▷ Byron, and *Lodore* (1835) contains much that is autobiographical. *Mathilda* (1819) and *Valperga* (1823) are among her other novels; *Rambles in Germany and Italy* (1844) was well received; she also published many short stories in annuals like *The Keepsake*. Her ▷ diary, recently published as *The Journals of Mary Shelley*, provides a fascinating account of her life and her attitudes to writing.

▷ Feminism.

Bib: Jones, F. L. (ed.), *Mary Shelley's Journal* and *The Letters of Mary Shelley*; Lyles, W. H., *Mary Shelley: An Annotated Biography*; Nitchie, E., *Mary Shelley*; Poovey, M., *The Proper Lady and the Woman Writer*; Gilbert, S. and Gubar, S., *The Madwoman in the Attic*; Fleenor, J., *The Female Gothic*.

Shelley, Percy Bysshe (1792–1822)

Poet. He was born into an aristocratic family in Sussex, and was educated at Eton and Oxford, from which he was expelled in 1811 for circulating a pamphlet, *The Necessity of Atheism*. He eloped with and married Harriet Westbrook, who was then only 16, and whom he left after three years. He travelled abroad in 1814 with Mary Wollstonecraft Godwin, daughter of the ▷ feminist ▷ Mary Wollstonecraft and the philosopher ▷ William Godwin, whose extreme rationalism had attracted the young poet. At one point, in accordance with his idealistic notions of free love, Shelley proposed that both Harriet and Mary should live together with him. Accompanied by Mary's step-sister, Claire Clairmont, he and Mary travelled to Switzerland where they joined ▷ Lord Byron, with whom Shelley made a close friendship. Harriet drowned herself in the Serpentine in 1816 and Shelley married Mary, though he continued to develop intense platonic relationships with other women. They moved to Lerici in Italy and in 1822 he was drowned while sailing, in circumstances which suggested that he made no attempt to save himself.

Shelley's earliest writings, produced while he was at Eton and Oxford, are ▷ Gothic romances in the style of ▷ 'Monk' Lewis. His first important poem was the atheistic *Queen Mab* (1813) in the tradition of the irregular ode. In 1816 appeared the ▷ blank verse *Alastor; or the Spirit of Solitude*, in which an exquisitely sensitive young poet is drawn by a highly erotic vision, representing 'truth and virtue . . . And lofty hopes of divine liberty', across exotic eastern landscapes, only to die, disappointed. *The Revolt of Islam* (1817) in ▷ Spenserian stanzas, preaches bloodless revolution, and has a similar beautiful youth as its protagonist. ▷ *Mont Blanc*, published in the same year, is a less self-indulgent work, in which Shelley turns his intellectual scepticism on the conventional piety of such poems as ▷ Samuel Taylor Coleridge's *Hymn Before Sun-rise in the Vale of Chamouni* (1802), which describes the same landscape. Where Coleridge attributes the sublime beauty of nature to a 'Great Hierarch', the atheist Shelley attributes it (like Coleridge himself in ▷ *Dejection: An Ode*) to 'the human mind's imaginings'. In ▷ *Julian and Maddalo* (written 1818, published 1824), he describes in irregularly rhyming ▷ couplets a visit to a madhouse in Venice in the company of Byron, who appears in the guise of an Italian nobleman.

In 1819 Shelley published *The Cenci*, a play in the Elizabethan style, and composed the 'lyrical drama', ▷ *Prometheus Unbound* (1820). He also wrote the *Ode to the West Wind* in which his abstract symbolism is, for once, brilliantly controlled, and makes the natural force of the wind into a convincing metaphor for political revolution. The news of the ▷ 'Peterloo Massacre' in Manchester on August 16, 1819, prompted ▷ *The Mask of Anarchy* (published 1832), a poem of superb rhetoric, calling upon the men of England to overthrow their oppressors. This was followed by *To a Skylark* (1820), the famous elegy on ▷ John Keats, ▷ *Adonais* (1821), *The Witch of Atlas* (published 1824), and another 'lyrical drama', *Hellas* (1822), inspired by the struggle for Greek independence from Turkey. He was working on *The Triumph of Life* when he died, a grimly garish dream-allegory in ▷ *terza rima* in which the poet contemplates the gory but awesome pageant of history, in company with the spirit of ▷ Jean-Jacques Rousseau. Shelley's prose ▷ *Defence of Poetry* (written 1821; published 1840) was written in answer to *The Four Ages of Poetry* by his friend ▷ Thomas Love Peacock, who argued that poetry was an obsolete art. Shelley retorts boldly that poets are 'the unacknowledged legislators of the world'.

Shelley can be an extremely irritating poet, particularly when congratulating himself on the exquisiteness of his own sensibility, or indulging in dreamy abstraction and elaborately theatrical symbolism. In his best work, however, he actually achieves the sublimity about which he talks so

much, and when dealing with intellectual or political issues he can be eloquently lucid and incisive.
Bib: Blunden, E., *Life*; Barcus, J. E., *Shelley: The Critical Heritage*; Rogers, N., *Shelley at Work*; Webb, T., *Shelley: A Voice Not Understood*; Leighton, A., *Shelley and the Sublime*; Foot, P., *Red Shelley*; Dawson, P. M. S., *The Unacknowledged Legislator: Shelley and Politics*; Swinden, P. (ed.), *Shelley: Shorter Poems* (Macmillan Casebook); Everest, K., *The Poems of Shelley*.

Shenstone, William (1714–63)
Poet and landscape gardening (▷ Gardens and literature) enthusiast. He wrote *The Schoolmistress* (revised version 1742), a ▷ Spenserian ▷ burlesque, celebrating Sarah Lloyd, the schoolmistress of a village near Shenstone's family estate. The condescending ▷ sentimentalism of this poem, and the facile lyricism of such works as *A Pastoral Ballad*, in anapaestic quatrains (*Poems on Various Occasions*, 1737), make Shenstone an important representative of the new post-▷ Augustan ▷ sensibility of the time. ▷ Thomas Percy consulted him in the preparation of his *Reliques*, and he wrote several ▷ essays on landscape gardening. His estate at Leasowes near Halesowen, Staffordshire, because famous for its ingenious 'natural' effects.

***Shepherd's Calendar, The* (1579)**
A pastoral poem by ▷ Edmund Spenser in 12 parts, one for each month of the year, published in 1579. The series is written in the tradition of the ▷ 'eclogues' of ▷ Virgil, *ie* verse dialogues in a rural setting, with shepherds and shepherdesses with classical, French or (more frequently) English peasant names, *eg* ▷ Colin Clout (for Spenser himself) and Hobbinol (for his friend ▷ Gabriel Harvey). The intention is not that of 19th-century nature poetry to give a description of the countryside as it actually is at any particular time of the year, but to use the simplified conditions of an ideal rural setting as a standpoint for commenting on life, often that of the court. Four of the dialogues ('January', 'June', 'November' and 'December') are ▷ complaints, *ie* laments for such things as lost love ('January') or advancing age ('December'). Three of them are cheerful: 'March' in praise of love; 'April' in praise of ▷ Elizabeth I, and 'August', a shepherds' song competition, again in praise of love. 'February', 'May', 'July', 'September' and 'October' are 'moral' eclogues on such topics as respect for age ('February') or a Protestant attack on Roman Catholicism ('May'). The three main themes are love, poetry and religion. The verse is sophisticated and varied, owing much to the examples of Virgil and ▷ Theocritus, and also to the French 16th-century pastoralist Clement Marot, but paying tribute to ▷ Chaucer as well and following the free rhythms of medieval English poetry. The poem set a fashion for pastoral in England, and inaugurated the great lyrical period of the last 20 years of the 16th century.

***Shepherd's Calender, The* (1827)**
▷ Clare, John.

Sheraton, Thomas (1751–1806)
Next to Thomas Chippendale (1718–79) the most famous English furniture designer. His reputation, which began about 1790, was built up on his severe and graceful style; later, under the influence of French Empire furniture, his designs became much more elaborate. He had many imitators, and the name 'Sheraton' is usually associated with a general style rather than with the works of the original master.

Sheridan, Frances (1724–66)
Novelist and dramatist, born in Dublin. Forbidden by her father to study, Sheridan was taught in secret by her brothers, and clandestinely went with them to the theatre. In 1746 she published a ▷ pamphlet supporting the actor-manager ▷ Thomas Sheridan, in a dispute over his Dublin Playhouse, and they married in the following year. They had four children, one of whom was the future dramatist ▷ Richard Brinsley Sheridan. They moved to London in 1754. Frances Sheridan's best-known work was the novel *The Memoirs of Miss Sidney Biddulph*, published anonymously in 1761, in three volumes. A two-volume sequel, *Conclusion of the Memoirs of Miss Sidney Biddulph*, followed in 1767. These were very well received, and were translated into French, by the Abbé de Prevost (author of *Manon Lescaut*). Incidents from the novel feature in Richard Brinsley Sheridan's ▷ *The School for Scandal*. In 1763 Garrick staged, very successfully, Mrs Sheridan's comedy *The Discovery*, with himself and Thomas Sheridan in the cast. The draft of another comedy, *A Journey to Bath*, was rejected by Garrick, but eventually published in 1902. Her last work, *The History of Nourjahad* (published posthumously in 1767), a didactic story with an ▷ oriental setting, was another success, translated into several languages, and staged as a musical play in 1813.
Bib: Hogan, R., and Beasley, J. C. (eds.), *The Plays of Frances Sheridan;* Todd, J. (ed.), *A Dictionary of British and American Women Writers 1660–1800*.

Sheridan, Richard Brinsley (1751–1816)
Dramatist and politician. Like many dramatists of note writing in English during the 18th and 19th centuries, he was of Irish (Irish literature in England) extraction, born in Dublin. His

courtship of his future wife, Elizabeth Linley, began with his carrying her off to a French nunnery to save her from the attentions of a suitor to whom she objected; he returned to fight two duels with his rival; in 1773 his secret marriage to her in France was publicly recognized. In 1776 he became principal director and, a little later, sole proprietor of the ▷ Drury Lane Theatre in London; it was twice burnt down and rebuilt during his proprietorship. He entered ▷ Parliament in 1780 and was famous for his oratory there; his opposition to the ▷ American War of Independence caused the American Congress to offer him £20,000, which he refused. His most famous oratorical exploit was his impeachment of Warren Hastings in 1787. During the ▷ French Revolution he supported the Whig leader, Fox, in opposing military intervention against France. Later he held an independent position politically, but he was influential, partly owing to his friendship with the Prince Regent (later ▷ George IV). He ended his life deeply in debt.

His memorable plays are ▷ *The Rivals* (1775), ▷ *The School for Scandal* (1777), and ▷ *The Critic* (1779); they show a reaction against the ▷ sentimental comedy which had dominated the English theatre for much of the 18th century, and the first two belong to a revival of the Comedy of ▷ Manners which had been dominant at the beginning of it. They are still appreciated for the freshness of their dialogue and the ingenuity of their comic situations. Other plays: *St Patrick's Day* (1775); *The Duenna* (a comic opera, 1775); *A Trip to Scarborough* (1777), an adaptation of ▷ Vanbrugh's ▷ *Relapse* (1696), and the tragedy *Pizarro* (1799).

Bib: Sichel, W., *Life*; Nicoll, A., *A History of Late Eighteenth-century Drama*; Sadleir, T. H., *The Political Career of Sheridan*; Danziger, M. K., *Oliver Goldsmith and Richard Brinsley Sheridan*.

Sheridan, Thomas (1719–88)
Actor-manager, teacher and author, born in Dublin. He was a godson of ▷ Swift, husband of ▷ Frances Sheridan, and father of ▷ Richard Brinsley Sheridan. His parents intended him to be a schoolmaster, but his preference for the stage was confirmed in 1743, with the success of his performance of ▷ *Richard III*. He became manager of the Theatre Royal in Dublin, to which he returned after a period acting at ▷ Covent Garden in London. By then a theatre opened in Dublin by his rival, ▷ Spranger Barry, reduced his audiences, and he moved to England with his family for good. He began a new career as a teacher and lecturer on elocution, travelling around the country to speak. His house became a gathering-point for literary figures, including ▷ Samuel Johnson. But the two men quarrelled, and Johnson later described Sheridan as 'dull, naturally dull'. Sheridan wrote extensively on grammar and language in general, as well as ▷ education and elocution. He published the *Works of Swift, with Life* in 18 volumes in 1784.

Sherman, Martin (b 1938)
Dramatist. Born in Philadelphia, and educated at Boston University, Sherman was resident playwright at Playwrights' Horizons in New York from 1976–77 before going to England where his *Passing By* was one of half a dozen plays in the 1975 lunchtime season of gay plays put on by Ed Berman at the Almost Free. Sherman is probably best known however for *Bent* (1977), a play about the Nazi persecution of homosexuals, one of the plays that arose out of Gay Sweatshop's production of *As Time Goes By* (1977) which looked at homosexual persecution in three different periods.

One of the early plays to show gays in a sympathetic and unsensationalistic light, *Bent* used two quite distinct styles: a first half of a *Boys in the Band* type bitchery and a second act set in Dachau with a Beckettian-type duologue between the central character, the tormented Max, and his lover, Horst. This may be partly due to the fact that though ostensibly set in the 1940s, the play is informed by and exudes a 1970s Gay Liberation consciousness and is therefore as much concerned with issues of changing personal politics as it is with historical perspective.

Bent subsequently turned up at the ▷ Royal Court and on Broadway with some star names – Ian McKellen and Tom Bell in Britain, Richard Gere and briefly Michael York on Broadway – and scored considerable success. It has gone on to be performed all over the world.

Sherwood, Mary Martha (1775–1851)
Novelist, diarist, autobiographer, but mainly known as a children's author. Mary Sherwood began writing at seventeen in order to help fund the school in which she was a pupil (*The Traditions* was published by ▷ Minerva in 1795), and she continued working on novels in order to support, first her parents and siblings, and later her husband and children. She married her cousin Henry Sherwood in 1805 and they went to India as missionaries. Her two most famous books are *Little Henry and His Bearer* (1815) and *The Fairchild Family* (1818; second and third parts were published in 1842 and 1847). This last book was immensely popular, partly because its overtly moralizing tone is neatly undercut with a delight in gruesome details and genuinely scary passages. In the later, ▷ Victorian, editions these parts were considered too unpleasant for the young and were expurgated. From then on, the book declined in popularity.

Bib: Cutt, M.N., *Mrs Sherwood and Her Books for Children*.

She-tragedy
Type of pathetic ▷ tragedy, related to ▷ heroic tragedy, and popular in the last decade of the 17th century and in the early 18th, focusing on the distresses of exalted women characters. Women's sufferings form an important element in plays such as ▷ Cibber's ▷ *Love's Last Shift*, Vanbrugh's ▷ *The Provok'd Wife*, and ▷ Southerne's ▷ *The Wives Excuse*. But the women in these plays are more ordinary than those in true she-tragedies. The form is exemplified in plays including ▷ Banks' *Virtue Betrayed* (1682), on Anne Boleyn, and *The Island Queens* (1684), on the execution of Mary Queen of Scots, performed under the title *Albion's Queen* in 1704, ▷ Mary Pix's *Queen Catharine: or The Ruines of Love* (1698), Motteux's *Beauty in Distress* (1698), and ▷ Nicholas Rowe's *The Fair Penitent* (1703), ▷ *The Tragedy of Jane Shore* (1714), and *The Tragedy of Lady Jane Grey* (1715).

Shields, Carol (b 1935)
Novelist and short-story writer, born in America and educated at Hanover College. In 1957 she married a Canadian and settled in Canada, where she attended the University of Ottowa and wrote an MA dissertation on the nineteenth-century Canadian writer Susanna Mudie, published as *Susanna Moodie: Voice and Vision* (1976). Many of her novels are concerned with marriage, love and the details of domestic experience, including *Small Ceremonies* (1976), *The Box Garden* (1977), *Happenstance* (1980), *A Fairly Conventional Woman* (1982) and *The Republic of Love* (1992), the last of these with a suggestion of the magical. *Mary Swann* (1987) is a literary mystery story which uses a range of narrative forms: letters, diaries, poems, a film script; generically it is comparable to ▷ A. S. Byatt's *Possession*. Shields' work shows a fondness for enigmas with hinted solutions: the sender of a bizarre wedding present in *The Republic of Love*; the identity and motives of a literary thief in *Mary Swann*; *The Stone Diaries* (1993) is the story of a woman who 'just let her life happen to her' and includes photographs of her family (she is absent). Shields has also written a novel jointly with Blanche Howard, *A Celibate Season* (1991), and drama. She has lived in Vancouver, Toronto and Ottowa, and now lives in Winnipeg, Manitoba. Volumes of short stories: *Various Miracles* (1985); *The Orange Fish* (1989). Poetry: *Others* (1972); *Intersect* (1974).

Shinebourne, Janice (b 1947)
Novelist. Shinebourne was born in Guyana of Chinese and Indian ancestry, and educated at the University of Georgetown and in Britain, where she moved in the early 1970s. She has worked as a lecturer, editor and community worker. Her first novel, *Timepiece* (1986) is about the move from rural to urban Guyana and its effect on the consciousness of the young woman protagonist. Her second novel is *The Last English Plantation* (1989). She has also written short stories.

Ship Money
An ancient tax for providing ships to defend the country in time of war. ▷ Charles I revived it in 1634 in time of peace and without the consent of Parliament. His action caused great resentment, but 12 judges gave their verdict that it was legal. Nonetheless, repeated revivals of the tax aroused positive resistance, notably from John Hampden, and it was one of the contributory causes of the ▷ Civil War that broke out in 1642. In 1641 Parliament passed a law declaring Ship Money an illegal tax.

Shipman's Tale, The
One of ▷ Chaucer's ▷ *Canterbury Tales*. This ▷ fabliau, set in Flanders, involves marital and financial trickery on the part of a wife and a monk, at the expense of the husband, a merchant. A series of bargains between different pairs of the three central protagonists makes up the plot sequence, which concludes with the wife offering sexual credit to her husband, in order to cover his lost loan to the monk. An analogue to the story is found in the ▷ *Decameron* (8.1) but Chaucer's version is distinctive for its detailed development of the mercantile backdrop to this story of a domestic economy.

***Shirley* (1849)**
A novel by ▷ Charlotte Brontë. It is set in Yorkshire at the time of the Napoleonic wars and is concerned, like several novels of the 1840s, with labour relations. Robert Gerard Moore is a half-English, half-Belgian mill owner who introduces the latest labour-saving machinery to the workplace, ignoring the protests of his employees. They turn against him and attempt to destroy the mill and to take his life. In an effort to raise funds Robert proposes to the spirited Shirley Keeldar, an heiress. She refuses him and eventually marries Robert's brother, Louis, a tutor in her family. Robert marries Caroline Helstone, his cousin. The novel protests against the limited opportunities available to women, demonstrated particularly in the life of Caroline, confined in her uncle's rectory and prohibited even from working as a ▷ governess. In the character of Shirley, Brontë claimed she was drawing a portrait of her sister ▷ Emily Brontë, 'had she been placed in health and prosperity'.

▷ Historical novel; 'Woman Question, The'; Social Problem novel.

Shirley, James (1596–1666)
Dramatist. He was one of the last dramatists of the great ▷ Elizabethan-▷ Jacobean-▷ Caroline period of English drama, a period which lasted from 1580 to 1640 and included the career of ▷ Shakespeare. Shirley wrote fluent, graceful ▷ blank verse and is at his best in social comedy; in many ways he anticipated the Restoration writers of Comedies of ▷ Manners after 1660. His audience, as in Restoration comedy, was that of the elegant, refined court; it was not drawn from all social classes like the audiences for Shakespeare and ▷ Ben Jonson, so that his plays have a comparatively narrow, though sophisticated, range of interests. He wrote over 40 plays of which the best known are the tragedies *The Traitor* (1631); and the *Cardinal* (1641); and the comedies *The Lady of Pleasure* (1631) and *Hyde Park* (1632).

Shoemaker's Holiday, The
A comedy by ▷ Thomas Dekker, published in 1600. It is a ▷ citizen comedy, *ie* designed to appeal to the taste and sentiment of the London merchant class, with a strong romantic flavour. The time of the story is mid-15th century, and the principal character is Simon Eyre, shoemaker and, at the end of the play, Lord Mayor of London. The story concerns the courtship by the young nobleman, Rowland Lacy, of Rose, the daughter of the existing Lord Mayor. The courtship is opposed both by his uncle, the Earl of Lincoln, and by Rose's father. Lacy disguises himself as a shoemaker, takes employment with Simon Eyre, and eventually, with the support of the king, they are successfully married. The play is mainly in prose, with blank verse interspersed; it has no profundity but its happy mood has kept it popular.

Short Story
This very early kind of fiction was first taken seriously in the 19th century as an independent literary form, making different demands on the writer and the reader from the demands of longer works of fiction such as the novel. Three writers originated this serious practice of the art of the short story: the American, Edgar Allan Poe (1809–49); the Frenchman, Poe's disciple, Guy de Maupassant (1850–93); and the Russian, ▷ Anton Chekhov. These writers evolved the qualities especially associated with the short story: close texture, unity of mood, suggestive idiom, economy of means. Such qualities associate the short story with the short poem, and we find that in English the verse story anticipated the prose story in works such as the tales of George Crabbe and Arthur Hugh Clough's *Mari Magno* (1862). However, no relationship can be established between the verse of such writers and the prose of ▷ Rudyard Kipling, with Maupassant behind him, or that of ▷ Katherine Mansfield, who was strongly influenced by Anton Chekhov. These two wrote little else in prose except stories (Kipling wrote two novels), but the greatest masters of the short story form – ▷ Henry James, ▷ Joseph Conrad, ▷ James Joyce, and ▷ D. H. Lawrence – were predominantly novelists. Their stories were perhaps formed less by the example of the foreign writers mentioned than by the structure of their own novels. These had a less distinctly marked plot line than those of earlier novelists, and yet a closer coherence; chapters from them can be extracted showing many of the essential qualities of short stories (*eg* 'Rabbit' in Lawrence's ▷ *Women in Love*, or the Christmas dinner in Joyce's ▷ *Portrait of the Artist*) in spite of their relationship to their respective novels as wholes. It seems therefore that the best stories of these writers were by-products of their novels, which by their structure suggested the evolution of stories as separate entities.

It is difficult to make a clear distinction between the short story and the *nouvelle* (novella or long story); it is difficult also to say at what point a *nouvelle* stops short of being a novel; on the whole the *nouvelle* or 'long short story' seems to share with the short story as generally understood a unity of mood, which is not so likely to be found in a true novel, however short. All the masters of the short story who have been mentioned were also masters of the *nouvelle*, but not necessarily (*eg* Chekhov) of the novel form.

The period 1880–1930 was the flowering time of the short story in English; besides the English writers already mentioned, it included the early and best work of ▷ A. E. Coppard, who was one of the few English fiction-writers of any note (Katherine Mansfield being another) who have restricted themselves to the short-story form. Later short-story writers have been numerous, but they have mostly practised the art as an alternative and often subsidiary form to that of the novel. In Ireland, where the art of the novel has scarcely taken root, the art of the short story has flourished more distinctively. It begins with the stories of ▷ George Moore (*The Untilled Field*, 1903), but the Irish tradition becomes really outstanding in the first books of Liam O'Flaherty (*Spring Sowing*, 1926), ▷ Sean O'Faolain (*Midsummer Night Madness*, 1932), and ▷ Frank O'Connor (*Guests of the Nation*, 1931). In his book on the art of the short story, *The Lonely Voice* (1964), O'Connor offers an explanation as to why the short story should be the more natural form of fiction for Irish literary culture.

Since O'Connor, William Trevor has continued the Irish connection with the short story. Other contemporary writers who excel

at the form include ▷ Peter Carey, whose early stories are collected in *Exotic Pleasures* (1980) and ▷ Ian McEwan, whose collections *First Love, Last Rites* (1975) and *In Between the Sheets* (1977) attracted great critical attention. ▷ Angus Wilson, ▷ Muriel Spark, ▷ Nadine Gordimer, ▷ Margaret Atwood, ▷ Desmond Hogan and Shena Mackay have also used the genre to interesting effect.
Bib: Bates, H. E., *The Modern Short Story*; O'Connor, F., *The Lonely Voice*; O'Faolain, S., *The Short Story*; Bayley, J., *The Short Story: Henry Ian to Elizabeth Bowen*; Lohafer, S. and Clarey, J. E., *Short Story Theory at a Crossroads*.

Shorthouse, Joseph Henry (1834–1903)
Novelist, whose *John Inglesant* (1880), a historical and philosophical ▷ romance set in England and Italy during the 17th century, was initially rejected by publishers but later became a ▷ best-seller and acquired something of a cult following. Shorthouse was brought up as a Quaker but converted to the Church of England, and religious loyalties and conversion play a large part in the novel. Shorthouse worked in business despite poor health; his other literary works were relatively minor historical romances, such as *The Countless Eve* (1888) and two novels set in the present: *Sir Percival* (1886) and *Blanche Lady Falaise* (1891).
▷ Historical novel.

Shuttle, Penelope (b 1947)
Poet. Shuttle's forceful, strong verse has brought her considerable critical recognition, as has her 1978 book on feminine creativity and menstruation, *The Wise Wound* (written with her husband, ▷ Peter Redgrove). Her works include: *An Excusable Vengeance* (1967); *Wailing Monkey Embracing a Tree* (1973); *Photographs of Persephone* (1974); *The Dream* (1975); *Period* (1976); *Prognostica* (1980); *The Child Stealer* (1983).

Siddons, Sarah (1755–1831)
Actress. The most celebrated woman on the stage in the 18th century. She was the eldest child of the actor-manager Roger Kemble and Sarah (née Ward), and was born into what became an important acting dynasty. Siddons began acting as a child, including the part of Ariel in a performance of the ▷ Dryden/▷ D'Avenant version of ▷ *The Tempest* (1667), in which her future husband, William Siddons (1744–1808), played Hyppolito. She fought her parents' disapproval in order to marry him in 1773, and the couple continued acting in the provinces. ▷ Garrick engaged her for a season at ▷ Drury Lane, 1775–6, but her first appearances there were poorly received. Her fortunes turned during a visit to Manchester, and her reputation as an actress was consolidated at Bristol and at Bath. In 1782 she appeared again at Drury Lane, playing Isabella in Garrick's version of ▷ Thomas Southerne's *The Fatal Marriage*. Her triumph was immediate, and she went on to play a succession of major roles with the company, including Belvidera in ▷ Otway's ▷ *Venice Preserv'd*. It is said that people breakfasted near the theatre, so as to be first in the queue for tickets to see her, some coming from as far away as Newcastle, and prices rose to as much as a hundred guineas. Contemporaries commented on her beauty, stately dignity, and expressiveness, as well as her articulacy, so that not a word was lost. Her capacity to convey passion and grief was legendary. But she was sometimes criticized for her lack of variety, was poor in comic roles, and although she had many friends in high places, she had a reputation for being difficult to work with, and mean with money.

In 1785 Siddons played her most famous part, Lady Macbeth (▷ Macbeth), for the first time, later performing it on occasion by royal command. She added to her repertoire Cordelia (▷ King Lear), Cleopatra (▷ Antony and Cleopatra), Desdemona (▷ Othello), Rosalind in ▷ *As You Like It*, other major ▷ Shakespearian roles and many other roles, some written especially for her. Her career was interrupted only for brief intervals by the births of her seven children. In 1803 she followed her brother ▷ John Philip Kemble to ▷ Covent Garden. In old age she became fat and had to be helped out of a chair, the fact disguised by other actresses being similarly treated. Widowed in 1805, Siddons retired in 1812, afterwards appearing only at special benefits.
Bib: Boaden, J., *Memoirs of Mrs Siddons* (2 vols); Campbell, T., *Life of Mrs Siddons*; Manvell, R., *Sarah Siddons*; Kelly, L., *The Kemble Era: John Philip and the London Stage*.

Sidney, Mary, Countess of Pembroke (1561–1621)
Writer, translator and literary patron. Mary was born Mary Sidney, and was a member of the remarkable family which included ▷ Sir Philip Sidney, her eldest brother. Her early years were spent at Penshurst Place, in Kent (later to be celebrated in ▷ Ben Jonson's 'To Penshurst') and at Ludlow Castle, the setting for ▷ John Milton's ▷ masque *Comus*. In 1577 she married Henry Herbert, Earl of Pembroke, and took up residence in her husband's great estate of Wilton Place. Wilton was to become, in the words of ▷ John Aubrey, '. . . like a college, there were so many learned and ingenious persons. She was the greatest patroness of wit and learning of any lady in her time.' Amongst her protégés were ▷ Edmund Spenser, ▷ Sir Fulke Greville, ▷ Thomas Nashe, ▷ Gabriel Harvey, ▷ Samuel Daniel, ▷ Michael Drayton, ▷ John Davies of Hereford, ▷ Ben Jonson and ▷ John Donne.

So great was her influence on the writers of

the late 16th century that it is easy to forget that she was an accomplished author and translator in her own right, and one, moreover, who used her own literary efforts as well as the reworkings of her brother's texts to advance her own Protestant and political causes. She revised and published an altered version of her brother's ▷ *Arcadia*, completed his translations of the ▷ Psalms and translated the French Protestant thinker Philippe de Mornay's *Discourse of Life and Death*, ▷ Petrarch's *Trionfo della Morte*, and Robert Garnier's French ▷ neo-classical tragedy *Marc Antoine*.

▷ Patronage in literature; Cary, Elizabeth; Lumley, Lady Joanna.

Bib: Hannay, M. P., *Philip's Phoenix: Mary Sidney, Countess of Pembroke;* Waller, G. F., *Mary Sidney, Countess of Pembroke: A Critical Study of Her Writings and Literary Milieu.*

Sidney, Sir Philip (1554–86)

Poet, courtier, soldier and statesman. A member of a distinguished noble family, he was a fine example of the ▷ Renaissance ideal of aristocracy in his ability to excel in all that was regarded as fitting for a nobleman. He thus became a pattern for his age, as is shown by the numerous ▷ elegies to him, including one by ▷ Edmund Spenser (*Astrophel*) and one by ▷ James I of England. He was wounded at the battle of Zutphen in Flanders in characteristic circumstances, having discarded leg armour on finding that a comrade in arms had neglected to wear any; as he lay mortally wounded in the leg, he is reputed to have passed a cup of water to a dying soldier with the words, 'Thy need is greater than mine.'

Sidney's writings date mostly from the period 1580–83, when he was temporarily out of favour with ▷ Elizabeth I for political reasons, and was living with his sister ▷ Mary Sidney, Countess of Pembroke, at Wilton House near Salisbury; they were published after his death. Indeed, his work is permeated with political material and, as such, has become a focus of interest for ▷ cultural materialist and ▷ new historicist critics. His most famous poetry, the ▷ sonnet sequence ▷ *Astrophil and Stella*, was published in 1591, and inspired the numerous other sonnet sequences of the 1590s including ▷ Shakespeare's.

Apart from his sonnets, Sidney's poetic reputation rests on the verse interludes in ▷ *The Arcadia*, his prose romance, started in 1580 and published in 1590. His prose work also includes the most famous piece of Elizabethan criticism, ▷ *An Apologie for Poetrie*, published in 1595. A collaboration with his sister, the verse paraphrase of the Psalms, was not published until 1823. He also wrote two ▷ pastoral poems published in Davison's *Poetical Rhapsody* (1602) and partly translated from the French Du Plessis Mornay's *A Work Concerning the Trueness of the Christian Religion* (1587).

Bib: McCoy, R. C., *Sir Philip Sidney: Rebellion in Arcadia*; Hamilton, A. C., *Sir Philip Sidney*; Waller, G. F. and Moore, M. D. (eds.), *Sir Philip Sidney and the Interpretation of Renaissance Culture.*

***Siege of Rhodes, The* (1656, revised in 1661)**

Opera-cum-▷ heroic drama by ▷ Sir William D'Avenant, thought to have been written originally as a play, with music added later in order to circumvent the Commonwealth (▷ Interregnum) law against purely dramatic entertainment, and gain the Government's permission to mount it at Rutland House. The performance helped pave the way for the re-opening of the theatres, and for D'Avenant's own receipt of one of the monopoly patents as theatre manager. The action concerns the siege of Rhodes by Soleyman the Magnificent, and Duke Alphonso's unreasonable jealousy of his wife, the virtuous Ianthe, who eventually saves her husband and the island. D'Avenant said he wrote it partly to illustrate 'the Characters of Vertue in the shapes of Valor and Conjugal Love'. The staging as with the earlier court ▷ masque was accompanied by lavish spectacle.

Sign

This is the term used by ▷ Ferdinand de Saussure in his *Course in General Linguistics* (1915) to refer to any linguistic unit through which meaning is produced. In Saussure's theory, the *sign* is the combination of two discrete elements, the *signifier* (form which signifies) and the *signified* (idea signified). In the phrase 'A rose by any other name would smell as sweet', the word 'rose' is the signified.

Signifier and signified are distinct aspects of the sign, but exist only within it. One important aspect of Saussure's definition of the sign is that any particular combination of signifier and signified is *arbitrary*. So a 'rose' could be called a 'chrysanthemum' or a 'telephone', but would still be as aromatic. Saussure's perceptions have been extremely influential in the development of ways of discussing the processes through which meaning is achieved.

▷ Langue; Parole; Structuralism; Post-structuralism; Discourse; Barthes, Roland; Derrida, Jacques.

'Signs of the Times' (1829)

A highly influential and analytical essay by the historian and social critic ▷ Thomas Carlyle which originated as an anoymous article in the *Edinburgh Review*. In it Carlyle claims that the mechanical age and its reverence for moribund institutions has led to a lack of spirituality among men and women. Carlyle proposed heroic individualism as the solution to the problem. It was a specific attack on ▷ Utilitarianism, which it condemned as a 'mechanical' rather than a 'dynamic' system of thought. The essay

influenced a number of Victorian writers, in particular ▷ Charles Dickens, who dedicated his novel ▷ *Hard Times* (1854) to Carlyle.
▷ Anti-industrialism.

Silas Marner (1861)
A novel by ▷ George Eliot. Silas Marner is a weaver who has been driven out of his religious community as a result of a false charge of theft. He loses his religious faith and moves to a Midland village, Raveloe, where he re-establishes his trade, but maintains a self-imposed exile from the community. He lives only for money, hoarding his gold until it is stolen from his cottage by Dunstan Cass, son of the local squire. Dunstan then disappears, leaving Silas in despair. A transformation in Silas' life occurs following the mysterious arrival of a young child who finds her way into his cottage. Silas, initially, sees the child as a substitute for his lost wealth, and adopts her. But the relationship soon draws him from his miserly ways and he and the child, whom he calls Eppie, become devoted to one another. It is later revealed that Eppie is the daughter of Dunstan's brother, Godfrey, and Molly Farran, a working-class woman whom Godfrey had married, but refused publicly to acknowledge. Molly and her child had been forced to live in squalor and wretchedness, and Molly eventually dies, abandoned, in a ditch. When Eppie is almost grown up, Godfrey finally acknowledges his paternity, but Eppie refuses to leave the man who has cared for her. She refuses, also, to be seduced by Godfrey's wealth, and remains loyal to the working-class values of her closest friends. In *Silas Marner*, Eliot is critical of the rigid system of patriarchal law and its associated ethics of individualism, and argues for an alternative morality based upon more malleable and socially responsible codes.

Sillitoe, Alan (b 1928)
Novelist and poet. The son of a labourer in a cycle factory, he left school at 14 to work in a similar factory. His birthplace was the Midlands town of Nottingham, near which ▷ D. H. Lawrence also grew up. Sillitoe, like Lawrence, writes from the standpoint of one whose origins are outside London and the middle classes, and he is the best known of a group of post-war novelists from similar backgrounds, including ▷ Stan Barstow, ▷ John Braine and ▷ David Storey. The influence of Lawrence on these writers is inevitably strong, and especially so in the case of Sillitoe, but he presents a narrow spirit of social rebellion from which Lawrence is free. At present, his fame rests chiefly on his first novel, *Saturday Night and Sunday Morning* (1958), which has been filmed. The novel's hero, Arthur Seaton, has become a type-figure of the post-1945 industrial, welfare state working man, born into an economic fabric against which his strong impulses rebel. More original and equally well known is the tale *The Loneliness of the Long-Distance Runner* (1959), a kind of fable of anarchic social rebellion. He has also written stories: *The Ragman's Daughter* (1963); *Guzman Go Home* (1968); *Men Women and Children* (1973); *Down to the Bone* (1976); *The Second Chance* (1980); and poems: *The Rats* (1960); *A Falling Out of Love* (1964); *Snow on the North Side of Lucifer* (1979); *Sun before Departure: poems 1974 to 1982* (1984); *Tides and Stone Walls* (1986); and more novels: *The General* (1960), about the war in Malaya, in which Sillitoe served; *Key to the Door* (1961); *The Death of William Posters* (1965); *A Tree on Fire* (1967); *A Start in Life* (1970); *Travels in Nihilon* (1971); *Raw Material* (1972); *The Flame of Life* (1974); *The Widower's Son* (1976); *The Storyteller* (1979); *Her Victory* (1982); *The Last Flying Boat* (1983); *Down From the Hill* (1984); *Life Goes On* (1985); *Out of the Whirlpool* (a novella; 1987); *Snowstop* (1993). In 1978 he published three plays: *This Foreign Field* (1970), *Pit Strike* (1977), *The Interview* (1978).
▷ Realism.
Bib: Atherton, S., *Alan Sillitoe: a Critical Assessment*.

'Silly Novels by Lady Novelists' (1856)
An article by ▷ George Eliot, printed in the ▷ *Westminster Review*. With scathing ridicule, Eliot attacks the unreality of many women's novels, criticizing their false portrayals of character and sexual relationships, their romantic wish-fulfilment and ludicrous representations of female learning. Eliot argues that the effect of such 'Silly Novels' is to make female aspirations appear risible and to undermine female achievement. '[R]otten and trashy books' depreciate 'the sacredness of the writer's art' and obscure a genuine women's tradition. 'For there is a distinctive women's writing,' Eliot asserts, '"a precious specialty", lying quite apart from masculine aptitude and experience.'

Silver-fork novels
A genre popular in Britain between 1825 and 1850. Typically, these novels concentrate on describing the lives of the wealthy, and feature glamorous heroines in search of love, marriage and luxury. A significant aspect of the genre is its focus on contemporary fashion; the novels often served as handbooks for the latest styles, explicitly naming particular London shops and dressmakers. Even at the time there was debate as to whether these novels unquestioningly praised the seemingly empty lives of their heroes and heroines (the term comes from 'silver-fork polisher', which means to compliment those wealthy enough to possess such cutlery), or whether they

were in fact subtle satires revealing upper-class hypocrisy. These two aspects may seen to be represented by ▷ William Hazlitt, who referred to silver-fork novelists as 'dandy writers' (*The Examiner*, 1827), and by the ▷ Victorian novelist Edward Bulwer Lytton (1803–73) himself described as such an author, who defended his work as an exposé of the fashionable classes rather than an accolade to them. Other silver-fork novelists include: ▷ Marguerite Blessington, ▷ Charlotte Bury, ▷ Susan Ferrier, ▷ Catherine Gore, ▷ Lady Caroline Lamb, ▷ Frances Trollope.
Bib: Adburgham, A., *Silver Fork Society: Fashionable Life and Literature 1814–1840*; Rosa, M.W., *The Silver-fork School*.

Simile
▷ Figures of Speech.

Simnel, Lambert (?1477–1525)
An imposter, used by Yorkist opponents of ▷ Henry VII, first king of the ▷ Tudor family; they declared Simnel to be Edward, Earl of Warwick, whose father, George, Duke of Clarence, was the younger brother of ▷ Edward IV. The true Earl of Warwick (1475–99) had been imprisoned by ▷ Henry VII. Simnel received extensive foreign support, but his army was defeated by Henry VII at Stoke-on-Trent in 1487. Henry spared Simnel's life, and made him a humble servant in the royal household.

Simon Pure
Character in ▷ *A Bold Stroke for a Wife* (1718), the comedy by ▷ Susannah Centlivre, who is described in the list of *Dramatis Personae* as 'a Quaking Preacher'. He is impersonated by Colonel Fainwell, as part of the latter's plot to impress the guardians of Mrs Lovely, and gain their permission to marry her. The scene in which this occurs is interrupted by the arrival of Simon Pure himself, giving rise to the expression, 'the real Simon Pure', meaning the real, genuine, or authentic person or thing.

Simpson, N. F. (Norman Frederick) (b 1919)
British dramatist sometimes classified as an absurdist writer, although his work is strongly influenced by a bizarre and zany humour in the English tradition of Lewis Carroll and the Goon Show. He wrote several short plays before his more famous *One Way Pendulum* in 1959, in which 500 weighing machines are taught to sing the Hallelujah Chorus. This was followed by a spy comedy, *The Cresta Run* (1965). Although he is not considered a major dramatist his work helped the development of drama away from conservative conventions during the 1950s and early 60s.
▷ Theatre of the Absurd.

Sinbad the Sailor
The hero of one of the Eastern tales called ▷ *Arabian Nights*. Also spelt Sindbad. His best-known adventure is that with the huge sea-bird called the Roc.

Sinclair, Andrew (b 1935)
Novelist. Like ▷ David Caute, Sinclair is interested in ▷ postmodernist experimental narrative. *Gog* (1967), the epic journey through England of an alienated, semi-mythical character, blends realism and fantasy, and employs a variety of narrative forms, including critical essay, comic strip and film script. Sinclair's work has affinities with that of American writers such as Kurt Vonnegut. Other novels include: *Magog* (1972); *A Patriot for Hire* (1978).

Sinclair Catherine (1800–64)
Scottish novelist and writer of ▷ children's literature. She was born in Edinburgh and lived there for most of her life, concerning herself with philanthropic work in the city. Her famous novel for children is ▷ *Holiday House* (1839), while her adult novels include *Jane Bouverie or, Prosperity and Adversity* (1846, reissued as *Jane Bouverie or, How She Became an Old Maid*, in 1855). Most of Sinclair's writings are moralistic and religious, and she published a tract in 1852, *A Letter on the Principles of the Christian Faith*.
▷ Scottish Literature in English.

Sinclair, May (1863–1946)
Novelist, poet and critic. She was brought up by her mother and educated largely at home, though she spent one year at Cheltenham Ladies College. Her novels include: *The Divine Fire* (1904); *The Judgment of Eve* (1907); *The Helpmate* (1907); *Kitty Tailleur* (1908); *The Creators: A Comedy* (1910); *The Combined Maze* (1913); *The Three Sisters* (1914); *The Tree of Heaven* (1917); *Mary Olivier: a Life* (1919); *The Romantic* (1920); *Anne Severn and the Fieldings* (1922); *The Life and Death of Harriet Frean* (1922); *The Dark Night* (1924); *The Rector of Wyck* (1925); *Far End* (1926); *The Allinghams* (1927); *The History of Anthony Waring* (1927). They reveal her interest in psychoanalysis, philosophy and feminist issues and her concern with problems of social and psychological repression faced by women; some, such as the ▷ *Bildungsroman, Mary Olivier* and *The Life and Death of Harriet Frean* use ▷ stream of consciousness narrative (a term which Sinclair herself applied to the work of ▷ Dorothy Richardson). Sinclair supported herself financially by writing reviews and translations; she published *The Three*

Brontës (1912), a biography; *Feminism* (1912); two works on idealist philosophy, *Defense of Idealism* (1917) and *The New Idealism* (1922); and articles and reviews about the work of contemporary poets such as T.S. Eliot and ▷ H.D.

Bib: Boll, T.E., *Miss May Sinclair, Novelist*; Zegger, H., *May Sinclair*; Gillespie, D.F., in Kime Scott, B. (ed.), *The Gender of Modernism*.

***Sing Song, A Nursery Rhyme Book* (1872)**

A collection of ▷ nonsense verse and nursery rhymes by ▷ Christina Rossetti. Written for children, the poems explore the imaginative possibilities of language, emphasizing sound, repetition and word play. Notable lyrics include 'Who has seen the wind?' and 'How many seconds in a minute?'. *Sing Song* has been compared to William Blake's *Songs of Innocence and Experience* (1789 and 1794)

▷ Children's literature.

***Sir Charles Grandison, The History of* (1753–4)**

The last of the three novels presented through letters by ▷ Samuel Richardson. It is an attempt to present the type of the perfect gentleman, just as its predecessor, ▷ *Clarissa* had represented the perfect woman. It prescribes the kind of behaviour which ▷ Addison had preached in his periodical ▷ *The Spectator*. However, it suffers much more than does *Clarissa* from the excessive idealization of its central character. The theme is right conduct in acute ▷ sentimental and ethical dilemma; Grandison is in love with Harriet Byron (whom he rescues from the vicious Sir Hargrave Pollexfen), but has obligations to Clementina Porretta, member of a noble Italian family. Among other lessons, Sir Charles shows how a gentleman can avoid fighting a ▷ duel without losing his honour. The book has some good minor characters, and is an interesting study in manners, though Richardson did not understand the Italian aristocracy of his period. As a psychological study, it is much inferior to *Clarissa* but it influenced the work of ▷ Jane Austen.

Sir Patrick Spens

An old Scottish ▷ ballad describing the loss at sea of a Scottish ship, its commander Sir Patrick and all the crew. It exists in several versions; in the shortest, the ship puts to sea in bad weather at the order of the king and Sir Patrick foresees the disaster – brought about, apparently, by royal vanity. In the longest version, the ship goes to Norway to bring back a princess possibly based on the Maid of Norway who died at sea in 1290, or possibly the Scandinavian queen of James VI (16th century); the Norwegian lords complain about the behaviour of the Scottish nobility, who leave suddenly, in bad weather, having taken offence. Both versions are fine examples of the art of the ballad, but the shortest exhibits that form at its most economical and dramatic.

***Sir Thomas More* (c 1596)**

Although the play has been roughly dated to 1596, there is no actual record of production and it exists in manuscript in the British Library, London. It follows the story of ▷ Sir Thomas More's life from his rise to favour in the court of ▷ Henry VIII to his friendship with ▷ Erasmus, his political downfall, and his execution. It is interesting primarily to students of English literature because ▷ Shakespeare may have been one of the contributors to the play, together with ▷ Henry Chettle, ▷ Thomas Dekker, ▷ Thomas Heywood, and ▷ Anthony Munday. The manuscript contains additions and revisions, possibly in response to heavy ▷ censorship of the original text by the Master of the Revels (▷ Revels, Master of the), and these may be as late as 1601.

Sir Thopas

▷ *Thopas, Sir*.

Sitwell, Edith (1887–1964), Sir Osbert (1892–1969), Sir Sacheverell (1897–1988)

An eminent literary family, of whom Edith is best known as a poet, and her brothers (both of whom were also poets) as an autobiographer and a writer of travel books respectively.

Edith is the most celebrated of the three. Born of repressive and disapproving aristocratic parents, Edith's eccentric beauty and unconventionality set her apart. As an adolescent she encountered the work of Rimbaud, who influenced her greatly. Her first volume of poems was *The Mother and Other Poems* (1915). Her poetry is distinctive for her interest in elaborately contrived sound effects, experiments in rhythm, and startling imagery. Her sequence *Façade* (1923) is her most popular work; it was set to music by the composer William Walton. Osbert Sitwell indicates its character in his autobiography, *Laughter in the Next Room*: 'The idea of *Façade* first entered our minds as the result of certain technical experiments at which my sister had recently been working: experiments in obtaining through the medium of words the rhythm of dance measures such as waltzes, polkas, foxtrots. These exercises were often experimental enquiries into the effect on rhythm, on speed, and on colour of the use of rhymes, assonances, dissonances, placed outwardly, at different places in the line, in most elaborate patterns'. The tone of *Façade* is light-hearted or satirical. From *The Sleeping Beauty* (1924) a more romantic tone predominated, and in 1929 *Gold Coast Customs* opened her most ambitious phase of philosophic verse with majestic themes. These include *Street Songs* (1942), *The Song of the Cold* (1945) and *The Shadow of Cain* (1947). Her prose works and

criticism include a biography of Alexander Pope (1930). From 1916 to 1921 she edited *Wheels*, a magazine which represented a resistance to the ▷ Georgian poets.
Bib: Glendinning, V., *Edith Sitwell*; Pearson, J., *Façades*.

Six Articles
A law passed through Parliament on the authority of ▷ Henry VIII in 1539. Having removed the English Church from the authority of the Pope and abolished the ▷ monasteries, Henry was concerned to prove himself a true Catholic 'without the Pope'. He therefore ordained that the traditional doctrines should be reaffirmed, especially 'the real presence' of Christ in the bread and wine taken in Holy Communion. Protestants, by then numerous in southern England, disliked the law, which they called 'the whip with six strings'.
▷ Reformation.

Skelton, John (c 1460–1529)
Poet; awarded the title of ▷ 'poet laureate' by the universities of Oxford and Cambridge; tutor to Prince Henry, later ▷ Henry VIII (1494–1502); ordained in 1498 and Rector of Diss from 1502. Skelton composed poetry in Latin but is most famous for his satirical English poetry, in which the corruption and corrupting influence of ▷ Cardinal Wolsey are frequent targets. He is a brilliant stylist, who seems to delight in the juxtaposition of learned and popular registers (often inserting Latin verses or tags into his work). He developed the 'skeltonic' verse form: lines containing 2/3 accented syllables which often alliterate, linked in couplets or sometimes longer rhyme runs of up to 14 lines. His work is highly self-conscious, playful, sometimes parodic, and reveals a wide acquaintance with the work of late 14th- and earlier 15th-century court poets. The *Bowge of Court* (1498) is a barely veiled attack on court corruption through a reworking of the 'ship of fools' convention.

His *Phyllype Sparrow* (c 1505) is in two parts: the first represents an attempt by a young convent girl to compose a fitting memorial for her dead sparrow, using the resources of classical and Christian culture, which includes a parodic bird Mass; the second is a lengthy praise poem outlining the attractions of Jane herself, and the fantasies she arouses in the speaker. The *Tunnyng of Elinour Rummyng* (c 1517) is an exercise in creating the female grotesque which describes the establishment and the female patrons of Elinour's ale house. Skelton's later satires, *Speke Parrot, Colin Clout, Why Come Ye Nat to Court*, (all written c 1521–2) attack Wolsey's abuse of power in particular, and state and ecclesiastical corruption in general. Indeed, recent criticism suggests that his early vocation as a priest constantly affects his literary work, but towards social criticism and not inward contemplation like later spiritual writers (*eg* ▷ George Herbert). The *Garlande or Chapelet of Laurell*, heavily indebted to ▷ Chaucer's *House of Fame*, is Skelton's witty projection of his place, as a poet laureate, in the Hall of Fame. He is also the author of a ▷ morality play, *Magnyfycence* (c 1515–16), which examines the dangers of materialistic corruption at court.
▷ Catullus.
Bib: Carpenter, N., *John Skelton*; Fish, S., *John Skelton's Poetry*; Kinney, A. F., *John Skelton, Priest as Poet*; Scattergood, J. (ed.), *John Skelton: The Complete Poems*.

***Sketches by Boz* (1836)**
Early journalism by ▷ Charles Dickens. The sketches, 'Illustrative of Everyday Life and Everyday People', were begun in 1833, published in various magazines, and collected into book form in 1836.
▷ Short story.

Slavery
Slavery grew during the 17th century, and people of colour entered England through the ports, especially Bristol, which was the centre of the slave trade. African slaves were taken to English colonies in the West Indies, where the slaves and the colonized native population might not share a language, so the new forms of English from these regions did not emerge as written discourses until after the 18th century. Writers from ▷ Aphra Behn to ▷ Hannah More wrote about slavery, and abolitionist activity began towards the end of the 18th century, by which time there was an active oral culture among slaves using song in African and English languages (see Sir Hans Sloane, *A Voyage to the Islands Madera, Barbados, Nieves, S. Christophers and Jamaica*, 1707). Women writers in the 17th and 18th centuries also had a keen awareness of slavery as a ▷ feminist issue. Many identified the condition of women in society, and particularly in ▷ marriage, as one of slavery; *eg* ▷ Sarah Fyge's, 'From the first dawn of life into the grave, / Poor Woman kind's in every state a slave'.
▷ Wilberforce, William; Feminism, Augustan.
Bib: Pratt, M. L., *Imperial Eyes*.

Sleath, Eleanor (c 1800)
Novelist. Sleath wrote six ▷ Gothic novels for ▷ Minerva. While mocked by ▷ Jane Austen for her unsophisticated style, Sleath's novels are packed full of all the usual Gothic ingredients (ghosts, castles, disguises and villainy), have fast-paced narratives, and are altogether enjoyable, mainly because they are so utterly unpretentious. *Orphan of the Rhine* (1798) and *The Nocturnal Minstrel, or The Spirit of the Wood* (1810) have historical settings

and beautiful heroines who although crossed by fate and deceived by scoundrels triumph in the end. *The Bristol Heiress, or The Errors of Education* begins slowly and seems to be a satire of polite society, but quickly improves when the plot transfers to a strange, haunted castle in Cumberland.

Sleeping Beauty, The
A famous fairy story in the collection made by ▷ Charles Perrault, translated into English in 1729. A baby princess is doomed by a wicked fairy to prick herself on the finger and die, but a good fairy changes death into a hundred years' sleep, from which the princess is awakened by the kiss of a prince.

Slough of Despond
A boggy place in ▷ John Bunyan's allegory ▷ *Pilgrim's Progress*. Christian sinks into it immediately after taking flight from the ▷ City of Destruction. It signifies the period of depression into which a convert is liable to fall after the first enthusiasm of his conversion.

Smart, Christopher (1722–71)
Poet. He showed early poetic gifts, and received support from the aristocratic Vane family, on whose estates his father was a steward. He made a precarious living through his early poems, which followed the fashions of the time. His *Poems on Several Occasions* (1752) include *The Hop-Garden*, a ▷ blank-verse ▷ Georgic in the manner of ▷ John Philips' *Cyder*, and a ▷ satirical poem, *The Hilliad* appeared in 1753. In the 1750s he developed a religious mania which drove him to continuous prayer, and he was for a time locked up in an asylum (▷ Bedlam) where he developed the original poetic style for which he is now best known. After his release he published *A Song to David* (1763), an ecstatic poem in praise of David as author of the ▷ *Psalms*. It is written in six-line stanzas rhyming *aabccb*, and owes something to the ▷ biblically inspired poetry and hymns of such writers as ▷ Isaac Watts and ▷ Charles Wesley. Smart's work was ignored at the time and much of it, including *Jubilate Agno*, *A Song from Bedlam*, was not published until 1939.
Bib: Ainsworth, E. G., and Noyes, C. E., *Life*.

Smart, Elizabeth (1913–1986)
Canadian novelist and poet. Smart is best known for *By Grand Central Station I Sat Down and Wept* (1945), a novel in an extravagant, highly poetic style influenced by the surrealist poetry of George Barker, with whom she had four children, though she never became one of his several wives. This relationship, begun when Smart wrote to Barker and continued over many years, is portrayed in the latter part of the novel. Smart moved to England in 1943, working as a journalist, an advertising copy-writer and literary editor of *Queen*. Her later works include two volumes of poetry, *A Bonus* (1977) and *Eleven Poems* (1982); an autobiographical prose piece, *The Assumption of the Rogues and Rascals* (1977); *In the Meantime* (1984), poems and prose pieces. Her journals have been published as *Necessary Secrets* (1991) as well as her *Early Writings* (1987)
Bib: Sullivan, R., *By Heart. Elizabeth Smart: A Life*.

Smectymnuus
A name under which five ▷ Presbyterian writers wrote against episcopacy – rule of the Church by bishops – in the 17th century. The name was suggested by the initial letters of the names of the writers: Stephen Marshall, Edward Calamy, Thomas Young, Matthew Newcomen, and William Spurstow. Their ▷ pamphlet was attacked by ▷ Bishop Joseph Hall, and was defended in two pamphlets by ▷ John Milton in 1641 and 1642. ▷ Samuel Butler, in his poetic satire *Hudibras*, written against the Puritans, calls the Presbyterians the 'Legion of Smec'.

Smiles, Samuel (1812–1904)
Journalist: philosopher of 'self-help'. Born at Haddington in Scotland, one of eleven children, his early life was a struggle, dominated by the vigour of his widowed mother. He graduated in medicine at Edinburgh University in 1832, and began practising as a doctor in his home village. Competition was severe however, and he exchanged medicine for journalism, becoming editor of the *Leeds Times*. He also became secretary to railway companies, and in this capacity he made acquaintance with George Stephenson (1781–1848), inventor of the steam railway engine. His *Life of Stephenson* was published in 1857, and was followed by the lives of other famous 19th-century engineers: *James Brindley* (1864); *Boulton and Watt* (1865); *Telford* (1867). But the book that made him famous was *Self-Help* (1859); it sold 20,000 copies in the first year and was translated into at least seventeen languages. He followed it by similar books, all demonstrating the worldly advantages of certain moral virtues: *Character* (1871); *Thrift* (1875); *Duty* (1880). The success of these books was due to their optimism, and to the simple, practical expression of his ideas. His international prestige is illustrated by his reception of the Order of St Sava from the King of Serbia in 1897. Smiles represents the vigorous and hopeful aspect of the Industrial Revolution, as it affected ordinary people, in contrast to the sceptical view of it taken by many other writers.

Smith, Adam (1723–90)
Political economist. His important work was *An Enquiry into the Nature and Causes of the*

Wealth of Nations – always referred to as *The Wealth of Nations* – published in 1776, at the outbreak of the rebellion of the colonists in America (▷ American colonies; American Independence, The War of) which he predicted, 'will be one of the foremost nations of the world'. The especial influence of this book comes from his discussion of the function of the state in the degree and kind of control it should exercise over the activities of society, and in particular, of trade. He concluded that the traditional ▷ mercantile system (nowadays called 'protection') was based on a misunderstanding of the nature of wealth, and that nations prospered to the extent that governments allowed trade to remain freely competitive, unrestrained by taxes intended to protect the economy of a nation from competition from other nations. His opinions became increasingly influential and eventually dominant in British economics during the first half of the 19th century; his opposition to *unnecessary* interference by the government in trade and society became harmful in that it was interpreted by later governments as an excuse not to remedy social abuses arising from industrialism.

▷ Free trade.

Smith, Charlotte (1749–1806)
Poet, novelist and translator, born in London. She began writing for the *Lady's Magazine* when she was only 14. Married in 1764 or 1765 she had two pregnanicies before she was 17. Her *Elegiac Sonnets* (1784) was moderately successful, her first novel, *Emmeline* (1788), much more so, and this was followed by another nine novels, including *Ethelinde* (1789), *Celestina* (1791), *The Old Manor House* and *The Wanderings of Warwick* (both 1794), *Montalbert* (1795), *Marchmont* (1796), *The Banished Man* and *The Young Philosopher* (1798). The novels contain elements of ▷ satire, ▷ sentiment and the ▷ Gothic, and were compared favourably with those of ▷ Fanny Burney, and ▷ Anne Radcliffe, whom she influenced. Smith was also sympathetic to the ▷ French Revolution and ▷ American War of Independence, and comments on these in several of her works. She wrote a number of children's books, and made translations from the French.

Smith, Horatio (1779–1849)
Poet and novelist. Horatio Smith (also known as 'Horace') collaborated with his brother ▷ James Smith on ▷ *Rejected Addresses* (1812) and *Horace in London* (1813), extremely popular imitations of ▷ Horace's odes. Horatio went on to write historical romances in the style of ▷ Scott, including *Brambletye House* (1826) and *The Tor Hill* (1846).

Smith, James (1775–1839)
Poet. James was the brother of ▷ Horatio Smith, with whom he wrote ▷ *Rejected Addresses* (1812) and *Horace in London* (1813), odes in imitation of ▷ Horace.

Smith, Stevie (Florence Margaret) (1902–71)
Poet and novelist. The 'unpoetic' life of Stevie Smith, who worked in an office and spent her life caring for her elderly aunt in a London suburb, is well known as the context for the production of her concise but anarchic poetry. Much of her work is animated by themes of sexual anxiety and an ambivalence towards Christianity which belies its popular image of comic whimsy. Of her novels, *Novel on Yellow Paper* (1936) is the most widely known. Several of her collections of witty, understated poems are accompanied by her own drawings. Works include: *Collected Poems* (1975); *Me Again: Uncollected Writings* (ed. Barbera, J. and McBrien, W.; 1983).

Smith, W. H. and Sons
A firm of newsagents, stationers, booksellers and (from 1860 until 1961) owners of a ▷ circulating library, the rival of Mudie's (▷ Mudie, Charles Edward). Founded in 1792 in a small newsvendor's shop in London, the firm flourished through its station bookstall concessions (the first at Euston in 1848) and its involvement in publishing. Like Mudie's, Smith's exercised some moral censorship over the material they sold (and still do). The two firms were rivals but combined to kill off the ▷ triple-decker novel in 1894. Unlike Mudie's, however, Smith's are still flourishing and in 1959 established the W.H. Smith Literary Award.

Smith, William (d 1696)
Actor. Smith joined the ▷ Duke's Company under ▷ Sir William D'Avenant in 1662, where he became one of its leading actors, and created many prestigious roles of the period, including Sir Fopling Flutter in ▷ Sir George Etherege's ▷ *The Man of Mode*, Pierre in ▷ Thomas Otway's ▷ *Venice Preserv'd*, a part written for him, and Willmore in ▷ Aphra Behn's ▷ *The Rover* (*Parts I and II*). Tall and handsome, Smith was viewed by his contemporaries as a gentleman, of high moral reputation. He is said to have acted in both comedy and tragedy with dignity and flair.

Smock Alley Theatre, Dublin
This was important not only in its own right, but also to the London theatre as a venue for preview performances. In addition, many of the great names in the English theatre began their careers in Dublin, including ▷ Spranger Barry, ▷ Kitty Clive, Thomas Doggett (c1670–1721), ▷ George Farquhar, ▷ Charles Macklin, ▷ James Quin, ▷ Richard Brinsley Sheridan (whose father ▷ Thomas acted at Smock Alley for many years), ▷ Robert Wilks, and ▷ Peg Woffington. Others like ▷ David Garrick and

▷ Barton Booth acted in Dublin on various occasions.

Smollett, Tobias (George) (1721–71)
Born near Dumbarton, the son of a Scots laird, Smollett studied at Glasgow University and was then apprenticed to a surgeon. In 1739 he moved to London, trying to stage his play *The Regicide*, but the attempt was unsuccessful, and he joined the navy as a surgeon's mate, sailing for the West Indies.

In 1744 Smollett returned to London and set up a medical practice in Downing Street, though he never made a living out of medicine. His first publication, a poem entitled *The Tears of Scotland*, appeared in 1746, and later that year he published a satire on London life, *Advice*. In 1747 a further satire, *Reproof*, appeared, and he wrote the novel *The Adventures of* ▷ Roderick Random, published to great acclaim in 1748. Further novels, which draw on his experiences in the navy and his continental travel, include *The Adventures of* ▷ Peregrine Pickle (1751) and *The Adventures of Ferdinand Count Fathom* (1753).

Smollett, now married and a father, struggled to support his family by editorial work, working on *The Critical Review* (1756–63) and publishing his translation of ▷ *Don Quixote* in 1755. Finally, his *Complete History of England* proved a commercial success, and was followed by *Continuation* volumes. In 1760 Smollett began *The British Magazine*, where *The Life and Adventures of Sir Lancelot Greaves* was run as a serial; in the same year he was fined and imprisoned for a libellous article in the *Critical Review*.

Smollett had been suffering from ill health for several years, and in 1753 he began to show symptoms of consumption. In 1763 his daughter died, and he abandoned literary work to travel with his wife in Italy and France. On their return in 1765 he wrote the ▷ epistolary work *Travels through France and Italy*, which drew from ▷ Sterne the nickname 'Smelfungus'. His final major work was *The Expedition of Humphry Clinker*, published shortly before his death in 1771.
Bib: Knapp, L. M., *Tobias Smollett: Doctor of Men and Manners*; Boucé, P. G., *The Novels of Tobias Smollett*.

***Snobs, The Book of* (1848)**
A collection of satirical sketches by the novelist ▷ William Makepeace Thackeray, first published in the periodical ▷ *Punch* in 1846–7 as *The Snobs of England by one of themselves*. The title is based on a Cambridge student paper, *The Snob*, to which he contributed as an undergraduate in 1829.

Snow, C. P. (Charles Percy) (1905–80)
Novelist; author of the sequence *Strangers and Brothers* (1940), *The Light and the Dark* (1947), *Time of Hope* (1949), *The Masters* (1951), *The New Men* (1954), *Homecomings* (1956); *The Conscience of the Rich* (1958); *The Affair* (1960); *Corridors of Power* (1964); *The Sleep of Reason* (1968); *Last Things* (1970).

He also played a large part in public affairs; he was created Baron (Life Peerage) in 1964, and served as a junior minister (Ministry of Technology) from 1964 till 1966. Trained as a scientist, he held strong views about the intellectual cleavage between men trained in the sciences and those trained in liberal studies in the modern world. His Rede Lecture at Cambridge, *The Two Cultures and the Scientific Revolution* (1959), became famous, partly because it provoked an exceptionally ferocious retort from the critic F. R. Leavis. Other novels include: *The Malcontents* (1972); *In Their Wisdom* (1974). He was married to the writer ▷ Pamela Hansford Johnson.
Bib: Cooper, W., *C. P. Snow*; Leavis, F. R., *Two Cultures? The Significance of C. P. Snow*.

Social Problem novel (Condition of England novel)
A type of novel which came to prominence in the 1840s (known as the ▷ 'Hungry Forties' because of starvation among the urban working classes). These novels addressed the social and economic problems arising from the Industrial Revolution, including urban poverty, unemployment and industrial conflict, and attempted to promote reform. Notable examples are ▷ *Mary Barton* (1848) and ▷ *North and South* (1854–5) by ▷ Mrs Gaskell, ▷ *Coningsby* (1844) by ▷ Disraeli and ▷ *Alton Locke* (1950) by ▷ Charles Kingsley. The phrase 'condition of England' was coined by ▷ Carlyle in his work *Chartism* (1839) (▷ Chartist movement).
Bib: Winn, S.A. and Alexander, L.M. (eds.), *The Slaughter-House of Mammon: An Anthology of Victorian Social Protest Literature*.

Socrates (? 470–399 BC)
Greek philosopher. He taught entirely by word of mouth, the so-called 'Socratic method' being the discovery of the truth by putting appropriate questions. Because he wrote nothing, all information about him depends on the writing of two contemporaries – the historian ▷ Xenophon (*Memorabilia*) and the philosopher ▷ Plato, who stands in relation to Socrates somewhat as St Paul does to Jesus Christ, except that Plato was personally taught by Socrates. Plato puts his own ideas into the mouth of Socrates in his philosophical dialogues, and it is of course difficult to know just how much and in what ways he expanded the Socratic philosophy. This philosophy declared that the true end of philosophy was not to discover the nature of the world but the nature of goodness and how to lead the good life; related to this is the doctrine of Forms, according to which

reality is seen as fundamentally spiritual, and the real in a person is their soul.

Socrates is said to have had a beautiful soul in an ugly body; he was married to a woman called Xanthippe. He fell out of favour with the ruling party of Athens, his native city, because he befriended enemies of the party; he was accordingly made to put himself to death by drinking hemlock.

Soldier's Fortune, The **(1681)**
Comedy by ▷ Thomas Otway. Beaugard and Lady Dunce have loved one another for seven years, but during his absence in France, she has been prevailed on by her family to marry Sir Davy Dunce. Aided by the unpleasant pander, Sir Jolly Jumble, the former lovers plot to cuckold Dunce, duping him into carrying their messages and even facilitating their adulterous liaison unwittingly. This intrigue is offset against the witty courtship of Sir Jolly's adopted daughter Sylvia and the impoverished Courtine. She quite literally snares him in a noose, in order to win him. In a comical ▷ proviso scene, full of *double entendre*, he undertakes to farm her lands and keep other tenants away, unless he finds the property 'too common' already. The play is fast-moving, but rather episodic in structure. It is expressly royalist, but there are elements of social comment, as in the references to the poverty of the king's loyal soldiers and servants (▷ Charles II was notoriously bad at paying his debts to those whom he employed). A sequel, ▷ *The Atheist*, appeared in 1684.

Some Reflections on Marriage **(1700)**
Polemic by ▷ Mary Astell, attacking the contemporary conditions of ▷ marriage; it was occasioned by reading about the forced marriage of the Duchess of Mazarin to a man she disliked, which led to the marriage's breakdown, and a series of extra-marital affairs, including one with ▷ Charles II. Astell analyses the causes of the many unhappy unions in her day, identifying the unequal power relations between men and women, and men's contempt of women, as the major factors. These, she says, deprive women of a proper choice before marriage, and keep them as slaves or prisoners within it. Astell argues that too often the man's motive in marrying is to gain possession of a woman's estate, rather than love, and that tyranny in marriage ought not to be tolerated any more than despotism in a state. And echoing her own arguments in ▷ *A Serious Proposal to the Ladies* Astell advocates education to strengthen women's capacity for judgment, and men's respect. She herself resolved the problem, however, by remaining single.
Bib: Perry, R., *The Celebrated Mary Astell. An Early English Feminist*; Rogers, K. M., and McCarthy, W. (eds.), *The Meridian Anthology of Early Women Writers: British Literary Women from Aphra Behn to Maria Edgworth 1660–1800.*

Somerville and Ross (Edith Anne Oenone Somerville, 1858–1949, and Violet Florence Martin, 1862–1915)
Collaborative novelists and second cousins, both of them belonging to the wealthy Anglo-Irish ascendancy. Edith Somerville grew up at the family seat in County Cork, and went on to study art in Düsseldorf, Paris and London. Violet Martin was born in West Galway. Somerville exhibited as an artist from 1920–38 but began her literary career in 1889, three years after meeting her cousin. Their first collaborative book was *An Irish Cousin* (1889), which charts the decline of the Irish land-owning classes. They were very successful and popular for their portrayal of the humour of the indigenous Irish at the expense of their landed masters. Their comic masterpiece, *Some Experiences of an Irish RM* (1908), details the experiences of a resident magistrate in Ireland in the form of a series of ▷ short stories. This was followed by more tales of Irish life in *A Patrick's Day Hunt* (1902), *All on the Irish Shore* (1903) and *Further Experiences of an Irish RM* (1908). They also published ▷ travel books including *Through Connemara in a Governess Cart* (1892) and *In the Vine Country* (1893), which described their travels in France. *Beggars on Horseback* (1895) recounts a riding tour of North Wales. Their novels include *The Real Charlotte* (1894), which overturns the stereotype of the 'good' and beautiful woman, *The Silver Fox* (1898) and *Dan Russell the Fox* (1911), which was the last collaboration before the death of Martin. Somerville continued to publish novels under their ▷ pseudonym right up until 1938, believing that she retained a spirit connection with Martin. Somerville became the first female Master of Fox Hounds in 1903 and both women worked for the ▷ women's suffrage cause in Ireland, although they distanced themselves from the militant activity and anti-Home Rule stance of the English suffragists. Towards the end of her life Somerville was awarded the Gregory Medal for her contribution to ▷ Irish literature.
▷ Lesbianism.
Bib: Cronin, J., *The Lives of 'Somerville and Ross'*; Robinson, H., *A Critical Study of Somerville and Ross*; Keane, M. (ed.), *Selected Letters of Somerville and Ross.*

Somerville, William (1675–1742)
Author of *The Chace* (1735), a poem in ▷ Miltonic ▷ blank verse celebrating the various branches of hunting. He followed this in 1740 with *Hobbinol*, a ▷ mock heroic piece set in rural Gloucestershire and a poem on hawking, *Field Sports* (1742).

Songs and Sonnets **(Donne) (c 1633–5)**
A heading given to 55 love poems by ▷ John Donne. Though the poems themselves first appeared in the 1633 edition of Donne's *Poems*

(with the exception of 'Breake of Day' and 'The Expiration', which had been published earlier), the category of 'Songs and Sonnets' did not appear until the publication of the second edition of Donne's poetry in 1635. Despite the title, very few of the poems gathered under the heading are songs, or, in the technical sense, ⊳ sonnets. Modern editors have questioned the authorship of two of the poems attributed to Donne (though not published either in 1633 or 1635), these being 'The Token' and the poem known as 'Self-Love'. Again, some modern editors have felt the need to add to the category by transferring other poems of Donne's into the group. Various attempts at arranging the poems into a sequence according to their presumed date of composition have been made, but with little real success.

***Songs and Sonnets* (Tottel)**
⊳ *Tottel's Miscellany*.

***Songs of Innocence and Experience* (1789–1794)**
Two collections of lyric poems by ⊳ William Blake, engraved and illuminated by hand. The *Songs of Innocence* were completed in 1789, and the *Songs of Experience* were added in an enlarged edition in 1794. They were intended to be read by children, and although frequently profound and complex, are perfectly lucid and easy to comprehend. They present 'the Two Contrary States of the Human Soul', and are thus complementary, since in Blake's dialectical view 'Without Contraries is no progression'. The world of Innocence is without morality, repression or fear, and in Blake's dynamic interpretation of Christian mythology, 'unfallen'. Inevitably some of the *Innocence* poems, such as 'The Lamb' and 'A Cradle Song' seem sentimental and oversweet to the adult, 'fallen' reader, while others, such as 'Holy Thursday' and 'The Chimney Sweeper' can seem highly ironic in their trusting attitude towards corrupt parental and political authority. But irony is no part of Innocence, and the Experience counterparts to these poems are in no sense a debunking of the *Innocence* versions. However it must be admitted that the bitter social criticism and moral indignation of *Experience* produce more memorable verse (though again perhaps this is more the case for the adult reader than the child). 'The Tyger', 'The Clod and the Pebbles', and 'The Sick Rose' are the most concentrated symbolic poems in the language, remarkable for their combination of emotional complexity and intellectual clarity. It is characteristic of Blake's dialectical approach that the later poem 'To Tizrah', added to *Experience* in the 1801 edition, flatly contradicts the sexual libertarianism of the other poems in the *Experience* collection, depicting the freeing of the soul from its physical bonds.

Sonnet
A short poem of 14 lines, and a rhyme scheme restricted by one or other of a variety of principles. The most famous pattern is called the 'Petrarchan sonnet', from its masterly use by the Italian poet ⊳ Petrarch. This divides naturally into an eight-line stanza (octave) rhyming *abba abba*, and a six-line stanza in which two or three rhymes may occur; the two stanzas provide also for contrast in attitude to the theme. The origin of the sonnet is unknown, but its earliest examples date from the 13th century in Europe, although it did not reach England until the 16th century. The immense popularity of the form perhaps derives from its combination of discipline, musicality and amplitude. The subject-matter is commonly love, but after the 16th century it becomes, at least in England, much more varied. The first writers of sonnets in England were ⊳ Sir Thomas Wyatt, and ⊳ Henry Howard Surrey; the popular anthology ⊳ *Tottel's Miscellany* (1559) made their experiments widely known. The first really fine sonnet sequence was ⊳ Sir Philip Sidney's ⊳ *Astrophil and Stella*. Its publication in 1591 set an eagerly followed fashion for its distinctively English form. This consisted of a single stanza of 14 lines concluding in a ⊳ couplet; it is thought that the comparative scarcity of rhyming words in the English language may be the explanation of the greater number of rhymes and freedom in the rhyming scheme in contrast to the Petrarchan form. The greatest of the succeeding sequences was undoubtedly ⊳ Shakespeare's (⊳ Sonnets, Shakespeare's), but notable ones were produced by ⊳ Samuel Daniel, ⊳ Michael Drayton, and ⊳ Edmund Spenser. The first sonnet sequence to be written in English by a woman was ⊳ Lady Mary Wroth's *Panpuilia to Amphilanthus*.

The sonnet form continued to be used after 1600, notably by ⊳ John Donne and ⊳ John Milton, but much less for amorous themes and more for religious ones (*eg* Donne's *Holy Sonnets*) or by Milton for expressions of other forms of personal experience (*eg On his Blindness*) or for political declamation (*On the Late Massacre in Piedmont*). Milton used the Petrarchan rhyme scheme, but he kept the English form of using a single stanza. From the mid-17th to mid-18th century the different style of thought and feeling suggested by the heroic couplet kept the sonnet out of use; the cult of sentiment by poets such as ⊳ Thomas Gray and ⊳ William Cowper then brought it back, but a real revival had to wait for the first 30 years of the 19th century in the work of the ⊳ 'romantics' – especially ⊳ William Wordsworth, who used it freely, ⊳ John Keats, who wrote few but some of them among his best short poems, and ⊳ Percy

Bysshe Shelley whose ▷ *Ozymandias* sonnet is one of the best of all his poems. The romantic poets tended to follow the Miltonic example both in form and subject-matter. After 1830, the form continued to be popular in the 19th century, notably in the work of ▷ Christina Rossetti, ▷ Dante Gabriel Rossetti, ▷ Elizabeth Barrett Browning *(Sonnets from the Portuguese,* 1847). ▷ G. M. Hopkins experimented very boldly in the form, and produced some of his best work in what he claimed to be sonnets, though they are often scarcely recognizable as such. Though in the earlier part of the 20th century the sonnet form appeared to have lost favour, in the later part of this century there has been a revival of interest in the form. The most notable example of this re-awakening of interest is perhaps the two 'sonnet sequences' by John Berryman (1938–68) published in 1952 and 1967. Other important 20th century sonnet writers are ▷ W. H. Auden and ▷ Tony Harrison.

***Sonnets from the Portuguese* (1850)**
A sequence of forty-four sonnets by ▷ Elizabeth Barrett Browning, written during her courtship with ▷ Robert Browning in 1845–6. In the course of the *Sonnets* Barrett Browning writes about love from a series of different perspectives, at times positioning her lover as a muse, at other times expressing her willingness to be his inspirational figure. She disrupts the conventions of amatory poetry in her treatment of the lovers' relationship, substituting a fluid and shifting relation for the gendered fixture characteristic of courtly love-poetry. The *Sonnets* were not originally intended for publication, and it was only on Robert Browning's insistence that they were included in Barrett Browning's *Poems* of 1850. Although they attracted little critical attention during the 19th century, they are now considered a major achievement.

Sonnets, Shakespeare's
▷ Shakespeare – Sonnets.

***Sons and Lovers* (1913)**
The first of ▷ D. H. Lawrence's major novels. It is based on his own early life in the Midlands coal-mining village of Eastwood (Nottinghamshire), on his relationship with his mother and father, and on those with his early women friends.

Eastwood is called Bestwood in the novel; the character who corresponds to Lawrence himself is Paul Morel. The strongest relationship is the close tie between Mrs Morel and Paul, who has two brothers and a sister. Mrs Morel comes of a proud, Dissenting middle-class family; though her family has been impoverished, she has an inherent aristocracy of temperament derived from her family tradition of high standards. The father, Walter Morel, a miner, is a contrast to his wife, both in his background (he is the grandson of a French refugee and an English barmaid) and in his easy-going, pleasure-loving, spontaneous temperament. The marriage is an unhappy one: Mrs Morel's strictness and truthfulness are outraged by her husband's slackness and deceitfulness. In the war between them, the children take the side of the mother.

The closeness between Mrs Morel and Paul develops after the death of her eldest son, William, and Paul's own serious illness. He goes to work in a Nottingham factory, but he has his mother's intellectual seriousness and artistic sensitivity, and has ambitions to become an artist. Mrs Morel invests in him all her pride of life and the hopes and passions that her marriage has disappointed. She finds a rival in Miriam Leivers, the shy and intensely serious daughter of a local farmer, and bitterly opposes her friendship with Paul. He is affected by his mother's opposition, and at the same time he resents what he considers to be Miriam's excessive spirituality and her emotional demands upon him, since he believes these to be a barrier to the sensual release for which he craves. He reacts against Miriam by engaging in a sensual love affair with Clara Dawes, a married woman who has quarrelled with her husband. This relationship is not opposed by Mrs Morel, since it is a physical one and does not compete with her own emotional possessiveness. Paul, on the other hand, finds that Clara affords him no more release than Miriam had done; he is unconsciously subjected, all the time, to his mother. The mother's protracted illness and death, and Paul's fight with Baxter Dawes, Clara's husband, are complementary climaxes of the novel. Both together constitute his release, although the death leaves him with a sense of complete dereliction: he has to face the choice of willing himself to live or surrendering to his own desire for death.

The book was early regarded as a vivid presentation of the working of the ▷ Oedipus complex. Lawrence was not acquainted with ▷ Freud's theories when he started work on the novel in 1910, but had come into contact with them before completing the final version in 1912. It is in its own right a major novel, but it certainly constitutes Lawrence's attempt to release himself from the problems of his own early development. He later declared that his study of his father had been unfair and one-sided. Jessie Chambers, the woman on whom Miriam was based, wrote a study of Lawrence as a young man as a reply to her characterization as Miriam; this was published as *D. H. Lawrence, A Personal Record* by E. T. (1935).

Sophia (fl 1739–41)
English writer. Sophia was the name attached to two out of three essays on the relative merits of the sexes. *Woman not Inferior to Man* (1739) and *Woman's Superior Excellence over Man*

(1740) are adaptations of publications by the French ex-Catholic cleric, François Poulain de la Barre, first translated into English in 1677. She wrote, 'surely the *Women* were created by Heaven for some better end than to labour in vain their whole life long.' The whole exchange took the same shape as the French when a reply to the first tract appeared, purporting to be by a man. Sophia refers to her attacker in *Man Superior to Woman* (1740) as 'one of those amphibious things between both, which I think they call a Wit'.

▷ Astell, Mary; Chudleigh, Lady Mary; Feminism; Feminism, Augustan.

Bib: Ferguson, M (ed.), *First Feminists*; Seidel, M, *Journal of the History of Ideas* 35, 3 (1974), pp. 499–508.

Sophists

In ancient Greece of the 5th century BC, professional educators, who claimed to train men for civic life, but not for any particular trade or profession. They differed from philosophers in that they professed to teach, whereas philosophers professed to know; it is the difference between victory by argument and discovery through argument. By degrees the Sophists fell into disrepute, and today the term 'sophistry' means an ingenious argument deliberately intended to mislead the audience.

Sophocles (495–406 BC)

One of the three foremost ancient Greek dramatists, the other two being ▷ Aeschylus and ▷ Euripides. He wrote about 100 dramas, of which only seven survive: *Oedipus the King; Oedipus at Colonus; Antigone; Electra; Trachiniae; Ajax; Philoctetes*. His poetic language shows more flexibility than that of Aeschylus – their relationship in this respect has been compared to that of ▷ Shakespeare and ▷ Marlowe – and he used three actors on the stage instead of only two (not counting the Chorus). In his relationship to Euripides, he is quoted by ▷ Aristotle as saying that he depicted men as they ought to be whereas Euripides depicted them as they were. The Irish poet ▷ W. B. Yeats made free English renderings of his *Oedipus the King* (1928) and *Oedipus at Colonus* (1934).

South Sea Bubble

The name given to a series of extensive speculations in 1720 involving the South Sea Company, founded in 1711. In 1720 individuals who had lent money to the government through the Bank of England were invited to exchange their claims for shares in the Company, which had a monopoly of trade with Spanish America and was very prosperous. This project led to irresponsible financial speculation in a number of dishonest companies, financial scandals in which ministers of the Crown were involved, and a major financial collapse in which thousands were ruined. The South Sea Company survived until the 19th century. Its headquarters, South Sea House, was for a time the place of employment of the essayist ▷ Charles Lamb, and is the subject of one of his essays.

Southampton, Henry Wriothesley, third Earl of (1573–1625)

Chiefly famous as a ▷ patron of letters, and particularly as a patron of ▷ Shakespeare. He was educated at St John's College, Cambridge from 1585 to 1589, where he made friends with the chief favourite of ▷ Elizabeth I, the ▷ Earl of Essex, and was shown special favour by the queen herself. Shakespeare dedicated to him his poems ▷ *Venus and Adonis* (1593) and (in terms of warm devotion) *The Rape of Lucrece* (1594). There has long been much speculation about whether the young man in the sonnets (▷ Shakespeare – Sonnets) is Southampton, and whether the initials of 'Mr W. H.' in the dedication ('To the Onlie Begetter of These Insuing Sonnets') stand for 'Henry Wriothesley' reversed. Southampton accompanied Essex on his two naval expeditions against Spain in 1596 (to Cadiz) and 1597 (to the Azores), and distinguished himself by his daring on the second of them. In 1598 he had to make a hasty marriage with Essex's cousin Elizabeth Vernon, and this angered the queen against him. He was later concerned in Essex's conspiracy against Elizabeth, and is thought to have arranged a special performance of Shakespeare's ▷ *Richard II* on the eve of the rebellion. In 1601 he was sentenced to death; however the sentence was commuted to life imprisonment and when ▷ James I acceded in 1603, Southampton returned to court. He died of a fever when serving, with his son, as a volunteer on the side of the Dutch in their war with Spain. Other writers with whom he was associated as patron included ▷ John Florio, the translator of ▷ Montaigne, and ▷ Thomas Nashe, who dedicated ▷ *The Unfortunate Traveller* to him.

Bib: Akrigg, G. P. V., *Shakespeare and the Earl of Southampton*.

Southcott, Joanna (1750–1814)

A religious fanatic who attracted a following of about 100,000 early in the 19th century. She is particularly known for her sealed box, which she declared should be opened in the presence of the assembled bishops at a time of national crisis. It was opened in 1927, in the presence of only one bishop but was found to contain unimportant objects.

Southerne, Thomas (1659–1746)

Dramatist. A Tory (Whig and Tory), Southerne wrote his first play, *The Loyal Brother; Or, the Persian Prince* (1682), to honour the

Duke of York, later ▷ James II, and satirize ▷ Shaftesbury and the Whigs. Southerne found his path to an intended military career blocked because of his political sympathies, and he turned more seriously to writing plays. He became a friend of ▷ Dryden, whose tragedy, *Cleomenes*, he was asked to complete in 1692, and of ▷ Aphra Behn, whose work he used repeatedly for source material. His *The Fatal Marriage*; Or, *the Innocent Adultery* (1694) and *Oroonoko* (1695) are based on two of her novels, with added material from one of her plays, and several other works drew on plays attributed to her, or sources used by her. Southerne is identified with a wave of so-called 'marital discord comedies' of the 1690s (other writers include ▷ Vanbrugh and ▷ Farquhar) which focused on the problems of ▷ marriage, as much as on courtship. Southerne had a capacity for seeing difficulties from a woman's point of view; for example, his ▷ *The Wives Excuse*: Or *Cuckolds Make Themselves* (1691) presents the dilemma of the woman trapped in an unhappy marriage to a shamelessly unfaithful husband, while she restrains herself from accepting the advances of another man.
Bib: Root, R. L., Jr., *Thomas Southerne*.

Southey, Robert (1774–1843)
Poet and historian. He was a friend of ▷ Samuel Taylor Coleridge (they married sisters) and also of ▷ William Wordsworth. Southey shared their revolutionary ardour in the 1790s, but his opinions, like theirs, became conservative at about the turn of the century, and when the Tory ▷ *Quarterly Review* was founded in 1809 he became one of its leading contributors. He was made ▷ Poet Laureate in 1813. In 1839 he married the poet ▷ Caroline Bowles with whom he had been friends for twenty years; she nursed him through his last years of ill-health. Southey wrote long heroic ▷ epics (*Thalaba*, 1801; *Madoc*, 1805; *Roderick*, 1814) which at the time were much admired. The best known of his shorter poems is *The Battle of Blenheim*. He wrote several historical works in prose, including *The Life of Nelson* (1813) and *A History of the Peninsular War* (1823–32). His change in political opinion, and in particular his position as Poet Laureate, drew the fire of the second generation of Romantic poets, and he lacked the poetic originality which partially redeemed Wordsworth and Coleridge in their eyes. In 1821 his poem ▷ *A Vision of Judgement*, describing the admission of George III into heaven, provoked ▷ Byron's ▷ *The Vision of Judgement*, with its brilliant caricature of Southey as servile turncoat and bumbling hack: 'He had written much blank verse, and blanker prose,/ And more of both than anybody knows.' He also features as Mr Featherнest in ▷ Thomas Love Peacock's satirical novel ▷ *Melincourt* (1817).
▷ Pantisocracy.
Bib: Curry, K., *Southey*; Madden, L. (ed.), *Robert Southey: The Critical Heritage*.

Southwell, Lady Frances (c. 1615)
Essay-writer. Lady Frances, like her friend ▷ Cecily Bulstrode, wrote Theophrastian character sketches which consisted of short satirical essays on exaggerated personality 'types'. Her 'Certain Edicts from a Parliament in Eutopia' were published with ▷ Sir Thomas Overbury's *The Wife* (1615) – Overbury was one of the foremost writers of such 'characters'. 'Certain Edicts' reveals a sharp appreciation for some of the artifices and mannerisms of the day, especially those adopted by women wishing to seem 'feminine' at the expense of their intelligence. Lady Frances was also central to the court world, being a favoured lady-in-waiting to ▷ Queen Anne and a friend of ▷ Lady Anne Clifford.

Southwell, Robert (?1561–95)
Poet and Roman Catholic priest. He worked in England as a member of the ▷ Jesuit order at a time when this was illegal; in 1592 he was arrested and tortured for evidence of other priests, which he did not disclose. He was executed after three years in prison, where he wrote some fine religious poems (*St Peter's Complaint with Other Poems* and *Maconiae*, 1595). His most famous poem is *The Burning Babe*. He also wrote a long poem, *Fourfold Meditation of the Four Last Things* (1606), and a number of religious tracts, one of which, *Mary Magdalen's Tears*, was imitated by ▷ Thomas Nashe in his *Christ's Tears over Jerusalem*.
Bib: Devlin, C., *The Life of Robert Southwell: Poet and Martyr*.

Sowernam, Ester (fl. 1617)
Tract-writer. One of the defenders of women in the ▷ *Querelle des Femmes*, who answered the attacks in Joseph Swetnam's *The Arraignment of Lewd, idle, froward, and unconstant women* (1615). 'Sowernam' is a pseudonym that plays partly upon Swet*nam*'s name, and partly upon one of his catch-phrases – 'every sweet hath his sowre' (meaning every good man has his wicked female counterpart). 'Ester' is taken from the fearless character in the ▷ Bible who, to protect the Jews, hanged Haman, the man who attacked them. Her work, *Ester Hath hanged Haman* (1617), is written in a lively style and sets out to prove the nobility of women with erudition and humour. Today it is assumed that this anonymous author was female, since we are now aware that middle-class women could have had an education that would equip them with the classical and scholarly allusions evident in the text. Sowernam's defence should be compared with that of ▷ Rachel Speght's, since she herself draws parallels between the works, saying that

Speght's work 'doth rather charge and condemn women'.

▷ Anger, Jane; Munda, Constantia.

Bib: Henderson, K. U. and McManus, B. F. (eds.), *Half Humankind*; Travitsky, B. (ed.), *The Paradise of Women*; Beilin, E. V., *Redeeming Eve*.

Soyinka, Wole (b 1934)
Nigerian playwright, novelist and poet, educated at the Government College, Ibadan and the University of Leeds. After his degree at Leeds, he worked as a reader for the Royal Court Theatre in London before returning to Nigeria in 1959, where he subsequently held various research and teaching posts in drama at the universities of Ibadan, Ife and Lagos as well as working for Nigerian radio and television. His account of this period is found in his book *Ibadan: The Penkelemes Years: A Memoir 1946–65* (1994). He was imprisoned 1967–69 for alleged pro-Biafra activities, an experience recorded in his *The Man Died: Prison Notes* (1972). In 1975 he became Professor of Comparative Literature at the University of Ife. Soyinka is primarily a dramatist, his work ranging from the early comedy of village life, *The Swamp Dwellers* (1958), to *The Road* (1965), a Beckettian drama set in a Lagos 'motor park', and *The Bacchae: A Communion Rite* (1973), based on the classical tragedy by Euripides. Much of his drama uses mime, dance, myth and supernatural elements; for example, *The Road* involves characters, masks and ceremonies from the Yoruba Festival of the Dead. Other plays include: *The Lion and the Jewel* (1959); *The Invention* (1959); *A Dance of the Forests* (1960); *The Jero Plays* (1960 and 1968); *Madmen and Specialists* (1971); *A Play of Giants* (1984). Soyinka has also published two novels: *The Interpreters* (1965), which explores hopes for the future of Africa through the activities of a group of young Nigerian artists, and *Season of Anomy* (1973), a bleak portrayal of war, tyranny and poverty in post-colonial Africa, using ▷ modernist techniques such as highly symbolic and figurative language and an open ending. Poetry: Idanre (1967); A Shuttle in the Crypt (1972); *Mandela's Earth* (1989). Soyinka has also published critical works such as *Myth, Literature, and the African World* (1976). In 1976 he became the first African to win the Nobel Prize for Literature.

Bib: Maja-Pearce, A. (ed.), *Wole Soyinka: an Appraisal* (1994).

Spanish Influence on English Literature
Spanish literature, especially that of the so-called Golden Age of the sixteenth and seventeenth centuries (which paralleled in quality, but greatly exceeded in abundance of texts, the creativity of the Elizabethan and Jacobean ages in England), has provided many writers in English with plots, characters and themes.

This can be seen first of all in drama. The most popular play of the Elizabethan age, Thomas Kyd's *The Spanish Tragedy* (*c* 1588), made full use of Spanish settings and attitudes, as did John Marston's *Antonio and Mellida* (1602) and *Antonio's Revenge* (1602). During James I's reign and for much of the seventeenth century, English playwrights such as Middleton, Beaumont, Rowley and Shirley adapted Spanish works. John Fletcher and Philip Massinger, for example, based their *The Custome of the Countrey* (*c* 1619)on Cervantes' novel *Persiles y Sigismunda* (1617) while Massinger's *The Renegado* (1624) combines material from Cervantes' *Don Quixote* (1605/15) and his play *Los baños de Argel* (1615). Some drew directly or indirectly on other Spanish plays, many of which are now lost. Visitors to Spain brought back news of the work of Lope de Vega (1562–1635), the author of '*capa y espada*' (cape and sword) plays, and of Pedro Calderón de la Barca (1600–81), who perfected the genre. Although it has proved impossible to trace the exact sources, it seems certain that Samuel Tuke's *The Adventures of Five Hours* (1663) and George Digby's *Elvira, or The Worst Not Always True* (1667) are direct adaptations of works by Calderón.

But it is probably in prose fiction that Spanish literature has had its most lasting influence. Both the picaresque tradition and ▷ Cervantes' ▷ *Don Quixote* were to play an essential role in the development of the English novel. Here the influence was mediated through early translations of key works. The seminal picaresque text, the anonymous *Lazarillo de Tormes* (1554), was translated into English by David Rowland in 1586 while Mateo Alemán's (1547–1615) *Guzmán de Alfarache* (1599/1604) was translated by James Mabbe in 1622 and published with introductory verses by Ben Jonson. Later in the seventeenth century, Captain John Stevens rendered Quevedo's *Historia de la vida del Buscón* (1626) as *Pablo de Segovia, the Spanish Sharper*. Meanwhile, in 1612, Thomas Shelton translated Part 1 of Cervantes' *Don Quixote* (1605) and followed it up with Part 2 (1615) in 1620. The hardworking Mabbe also translated Fernando de Rojas' (c. 1465–1541) early dialogue novel *La Celestina* (*c* 1499), calling it *The Spanish Bawd* (1631), and Cervantes' *Novel as ejemplares* (1613; *Exemplarie Novells*, trans. 1640).

The Spanish picaresque novels, first-person narratives which deal with the adventures of low-life characters and contain vividly realistic and satirical descriptions of contemporary life and social mores, appealed to generations of English writers. Their influence can be felt in some Restoration comedies, such as Farquhar's ▷ *The Beaux' Stratagem* (1707), and in many of the novels written in the eighteenth century: ▷ Defoe's ▷ *Moll Flanders* (1722), ▷ Smollett's *The Adventures of Roderick Random* (1748), *The Adventures of Peregrine Pickle* (1751), and Fielding's ▷ *Tom Jones* (1749), to name just a few.

But it was *Don Quixote* which, more than any other single work, influenced the development of the novel, not just in England but throughout Europe. Thanks mainly to the Romantics, the nineteenth century took the knight to be a quasi-tragic figure, an idealist lost in an increasingly materialistic world. The seventeenth and eighteenth centuries, however, saw the tale of Don Quixote and his faithful squire Sancho Panza as an adventure story and a comic masterpiece which broke new ground as far as narrative techniques, irony and satire were concerned. As well as in Samuel Butler's mock-heroic poem *Hudibras* (1663), its influence can be felt in Fielding's *Don Quixote in England* (1734) and *Joseph Andrews* (1742) which was 'Written in Imitation of the Manner of Cervantes, Author of Don Quixote'. Smollett's *The Adventures of Sir Launcelot Greaves* (1762) was a poor imitation of *Don Quixote*, while many of the situations and narrative devices in Sterne's ▷ *Tristram Shandy* (1760/67) grew out of the author's reading of Cervantes' novel. But the humour and sense of adventure continued to attract novelists well beyond the eighteenth century: echoes of *Don Quixote* can be found in Scott's *Redgauntlet* (1824), Dickens' ▷ *Pickwick Papers* (1836/37), George Eliot's ▷ *Daniel Deronda* (1876) and Stevenson's ▷ *Treasure Island* (1883). More recently, Graham Greene produced a modern reworking of the novel in *Monsignor Quixote* (1982) which, in its questioning of the nature of faith, also drew on the religious writings of Miguel de Unamuno (1864–1936).

In the nineteenth century, Spain was perceived throughout Europe as the Romantic country par excellence, a place which was exotic, picturesque and still rooted in age-old traditions. A typically Romantic interest in things Medieval led the poet Robert Southey to translate the chivalric romance *Amadís de Gaula* (1496 / 1508) in 1803 and, shortly after, to bring out his translation of three Medieval texts under the general title *Chronicles of the Cid*. His contemporary J. G. Lockhart published his carefully crafted versions of the popular *Spanish Ballads* in 1822. Two other Romantic poets showed their indebtedness to Spanish literature at this time. Just like the German Romantic theorists, Shelley 'rediscovered' the work of Calderón, learning Spanish in order to read his plays and partially translating his famous religious drama, *El mágico prodigioso* (The Wonder-Working Magician, 1634). Shelley also admired *La cisma de Inglaterra* (*The Schism of England*, perf. 1627), a play dealing with the same subject as Shakespeare's ▷ *Henry VIII*. Byron worked on his ▷ *Don Juan* between 1818 and 1824, examining the life and loves of yet another Spanish literary archetype who had first appeared in Tirso de Molina's (1583–1648) *El Burlador de Sevilla* (c 1630).

The nineteenth century also saw the increased popularity of travel writing. George Borrow's *The Bible in Spain* (1843) and Richard Ford's *Handbook for Travellers in Spain* (1845) appealed to the Victorians' love of the exotic and the picturesque. The tradition of the travelogue which sets out to shed light on the Spanish character has continued into this century with Havelock Ellis' *The Soul of Spain* (1908), V. S. Pritchett's *Marching Spain* (1928) and *The Spanish Temper* (1954), Gerald Brenan's *South from Granada* (1957) and Laurie Lee's *A Rose for Winter* (1955) and *As I Walked Out One Midsummer Morning* (1969).

But it was the Spanish Civil War of 1936–39 which focused the attention of writers on Spain. For many, such as W. H. Auden and Stephen Spender who were involved in the war, the conflict became a testing-ground for their left-wing sympathies. Most of these writers were not influenced by individual Spanish authors but rather by the country and its tragic predicament. Out of the war came Hemingway's *For Whom the Bell Tolls* (1940) and George Orwell's powerful political study *Homage to Catalonia* (1938). Orwell's sense of disillusionment with the events in Spain probably had some bearing on the writing of his two anti-totalitarian novels, *Animal Farm* (1945) and *Nineteen Eighty-Four* (1949).

Nowadays, Spanish texts in English have become more readily available. The plays of Lope de Vega and Calderón and those of Federico García Lorca (1898–1936), especially *Blood Wedding* (1933) and *The House of Bernarda Alba* (1936), enjoy regular revivals in Britain. The works of the philosopher Jose Ortega y Gasset (1883–1955), in particular *La deshumanización del arte* (The Dehumanization of Art, 1925) and *La rebelión de las masas* (The Revolt of the Masses, 1929), continue to influence both art critics and political thinkers.

In recent years, it is Latin American literature which has had the most pronounced effect on English writing and on the reading public in Britain. Charles Tomlinson collaborated with the Mexican poet Octavio Paz (b 1941) on *Renga: A Chain of Poems*; British and North American critical theorists find the philosophical and metafictional short stories of the Argentinian Jorge Luis Borges (1899–1986), especially his *Ficciones* (*Fictions*, 1935–44), to be an essential reference point; and the novels of the Peruvian Mario Vargas Llosa (b 1936), the Cuban Guillermo Cabrera Infante (b 1929) – both of whom have spent time living in England – the Mexican Carlos Fuentes (b 1928) and the Chilean Isabel Allende (b 1942) are now internationally famous in English as well as Spanish. Their work, and especially that of the Colombian Gabriel García Márquez (b 1928) whose *Cien años de soledad* (One Hundred Years of Solitude, 1967) established the vogue of what has become known as 'magic realism', has influenced a number of novelists in English, most notably ▷ Salman Rushdie.

Spanish intrigue comedy
English comedy influenced by, or using as its source, a type of Spanish play known as the 'comedia de capa y espada' (comedy of cape and sword). The originals include works by Pedro Calderón de la Barca (1600–81), Lope de Vega (1562–1635), and Tirso de Molina (1571–1648). The plays frequently turn on conflicts of love and honour and are dominated by busy intrigue plots involving problems of mistaken identity, duelling, and concealment. One of the first of this variety was Sir Samuel Tuke's *The Adventures of Five Hours* (1663), based on a play by Calderón, and commissioned by ▷ Charles II. Other elements of the type include rigid father, brothers and uncles attempting to force young relatives into unwelcome marriages, and high-spirited women active in determining their own fates. This helped to make the form popular with women dramatists, including ▷ Aphra Behn, ▷ Susannah Centlivre, and ▷ Mary Pix.
▷ Spanish influence on English literature.
Bib: Loftis, J., *The Spanish Plays of Neoclassical England.*

Spanish Succession, The War of (1702–13)
A war fought to determine the succession of the Spanish throne, and ultimately the balance of power in Europe, after the death of Charles II of Spain. The French king ▷ Louis XIV supported the candidacy of his grandson Philip of Anjou. England, whose interests had changed since the accession of the Protestant ▷ William III in 1689, and which feared the expansion of French power, supported instead the claim of the Archduke Charles, son of the Holy Roman Emperor (▷ Holy Roman Empire) Leopold I. A third claimant was the Bavarian Prince Joseph Ferdinand. England formed the Grand Alliance with the Holy Roman Empire and the Netherlands, while Bavaria joined with France, Spain, Savoy and Portugal. The last two, however, quickly changed sides. England achieved a series of successes under the ▷ Duke of Marlborough. England's involvement in the war ended with the Treaty of Utrecht in 1713–14. Philip's accession as Philip V was confirmed, but major transfers of territory in Canada, from France to Britain, were also part of the settlement.

Spanish Tragedy, The
A drama by ▷ Thomas Kyd, probably written around 1587. It is the earliest important ▷ revenge tragedy, and both by date and by influence it is one of the principal starting-points of the great age of ▷ Elizabethan drama. The plot has no known source and is presumably Kyd's invention. The scene is Spain, just after the Spanish-Portuguese war of 1580. Andrea, a Spanish nobleman, has been unchivalrously killed in a battle by Balthazar, a Portuguese prince, who in turn is captured by Lorenzo, nephew of the King of Spain, and Horatio, son of Hieronimo, Marshal of Spain. The ghost of Andrea and the spirit of Revenge sit above stage and watch the action throughout: Andrea is to witness how his death is to be avenged. This process is most intricate, and centres on Bel-imperia, Lorenzo's sister. She and Andrea have been lovers, and in consequence she detests Balthazar, who nonetheless seeks her in marriage with Lorenzo's support. She deliberately slights Balthazar by cultivating the affections of Horatio, who is in consequence murdered by Lorenzo and Balthazar. Hieronimo – hitherto a background figure – discovers the identity of his son's murderers; half crazed with grief, he seeks justice, but his pleading is brushed aside by the king. He eventually secures it by contriving a play (within the play) in which the guilty parties suffer real deaths instead of simulated ones. Hieronimo then takes his own life after biting out his tongue. Thus Andrea (after displaying some impatience) watches how his own death is avenged. The audience sees how justice is brought about when it is left to mere human motives: not as Heaven would bring it, cleanly and economically, but wastefully and brutally, hatred breeding hatred, and callous contrivance countered by contrivance still more ruthless. Only Lorenzo can be described as an evil character – a Machiavellian schemer – the other characters are driven out of their natural virtue by vindictive bitterness. Hieronimo himself is momentarily checked by biblical authority – '*Vindicta mihi*': 'Justice is mine, saith the Lord' (*Romans* 12:19) – but he is driven on by the energy of his grief.

Kyd's poetry is undistinguished, but the play is theatrically so effective that it remained popular for a generation. In 1602 the play was expanded by some more effective verse, probably by ▷ Ben Jonson, whom the theatre manager ▷ Philip Henslowe paid for additions. However, these obscure rather than enhance Kyd's essential drama.

Kyd was certainly influenced by the plays of ▷ Seneca, for instance in his use of ▷ stichomythia and in the role of the ghost. Kyd's own influence was great, and can be seen in ▷ *Hamlet*. The dilemma of revenge, in one aspect seen to be a duty and in another an acknowledged sin, deeply preoccupied the Elizabethans. At the lowest level it was a pretext for the violence that appealed to them in the theatre – the 'tragedy of blood' – at a higher level it presented the problem of how it could be executed against evil-doers who were men of power or who were protected by such men; at a higher level still it was a natural vehicle for dramatizing the theme of the corrupted conscience, which both ▷ Renaissance and ▷ Reformation ideas brought to the forefront of social attention. *The Spanish Tragedy* was effective on all these planes.

Spark, Muriel (b 1918)
Before becoming a novelist, Spark was a poet (*Collected Poems*, 1967). Her first novel was *The Comforters* (1957), which she has described as 'a novel about writing a novel', *ie* an experiment in, and exploration of what it means to write fiction. At about the same time she became a convert to Roman Catholicism, and her novels since have tended to take a parabolic form (characteristic of other contemporary novelists, *eg* ▷ Iris Murdoch, ▷ William Golding) combining overt, often wittily satirical ▷ realism with implications of an extra-realist, spiritual dimension. One of her best-known works is *The Prime of Miss Jean Brodie* (1961), the story of the influence over a group of schoolgirls of a progressive spinster schoolteacher in Edinburgh. It is characteristic of Spark's work in its combination of the comic and the sinister, and the skilful use of anticipations of later events. Her three ▷ novellas, *The Public Image* (1968); *The Driver's Seat* (1970) and *Not to Disturb* (1971) exemplify the economy, precision and hardness of her work; they invite little sympathy for their characters, but rather convey a strong sense of pattern and fate underlying an apparent contingency of events. Her other novels are: *Robinson* (1958); *Mememto Mori* (1959); *The Ballad of Peckham Rye* (1960); *The Bachelors* (1960); *The Girls of Slender Means* (1963); *The Mandelbaum Gate* (1965); *The Hothouse by the East River* (1972); *The Abbess of Crewe* (1972); *The Takeover* (1976); *Territorial Rights* (1979); *Loitering with Intent* (1981); *The Only Problem* (1984); *A Far Cry From Kensington* (1988).

Other writings include a stage play *Doctors of Philosophy* (1962), radio plays collected in *Voices at Play* (1961), a further volume of poetry, *Going Up to Sotheby's* (1982) and short stories in *Collected Stories I* (1967); and *The Stories of Muriel Spark* (1985). Her recent work includes *Symposium* (1990).

Bib: Stanford, D., *Muriel Spark: A Biographical and Critical Study*; Stubbs, P., *Muriel Spark* (Writers and their Work series); Kemp, P., *Muriel Spark*; Bold, A., *Muriel Spark*.

'Spasmodic' school of poetry
The 'Spasmodic' poets espoused a crude ▷ Romanticism which revered the poet as a divinely inspired being whose eccentricities should be humoured and encouraged, especially in the realm of accepted social conventions, and whose observations were projected through the lens of a melancholy solipsism. It was their bursts of ranting emotion, often ill-disguised as spontaneous feeling, that earned them their sobriquet. Pioneered by ▷ Philip James Bailey in his dramatic poem *Festus* (1839) and indulged by Alexander Smith (1830–67) in *A Life Drama* (1853), the style reached its height in ▷ Sydney Dobell's *Balder* (1854), the excesses of which led the literary critic and satirist ▷ William Aytoun to coin the term 'Spasmodic' in his brilliant parody *Firmilian, or The Student of Badajoz: A Spasmodic Tragedy by T. Percy Jones* (1854). *Firmilian* mimicked the extravagant imagery of Smith and Dobell and burlesqued their plots, even managing a sideswipe at their champion, the critic ▷ George Gilfillan. Others of the 'Spasmodic' school included John Stanyan Bigg (1826–65), Ebenezer Jones and Gerald Marston. It is possible to detect the influence of the 'Spasmodics' on ▷ Emily Brontë, Elizabeth Barrett Browning and ▷ Tennyson. After *Firmillian* the 'Spasmodic' tragedy disappeared from serious verse and much of its energy may have been channelled into the ▷ sensation novels of the 1860s.

Spectator, The
The name of two periodicals, the first appearing daily (1711–12 and 1714), and the second a weekly founded in 1828 and still continuing. The earlier is the more famous of the two, owing to the contributions of its famous editors, Addison and Steele; it had an important influence on the manners and culture of the time. The later *Spectator* has also had a distinguished history, however; it began as a radical journal, but is now the leading intellectual weekly periodical of the right.

▷ Reviews and periodicals.

Speght, Rachel (c 1598–1630)
Devotional and tract-writer. One of the respondents to Joseph Swetnam's attack on women (the other two being ▷ Constantia Munda and ▷ Ester Sowernam). Speght came from a learned family – her father edited ▷ Chaucer – and her ▷ pamphlet *A Mouzell for Malastomus* ('a muzzle for Black-Mouth'), published in 1617, is a serious and theoretical defence. It is divided into two sections, the first being a well-organized refutation of Swetnam's arguments, and the second a livelier and more wide-ranging disputation. To 20th-century readers Speght's hesitancy over asserting female virtues appears to defeat her own argument, and, indeed, she was accused of being irresolute by her contemporary, Sowernam. It is interesting to note, however, that Speght chose to write under her own name ('Sowernam' is a pseudonym) and that she was prepared to face any repercussions her open argument should incur. Primarily, Speght should be seen as a devotional writer and she is concerned with the plight and salvation of all humankind, rather than either sex in isolation. Her later work, the devotional poem *Mortalities Memorandum* (1621), is probably more representative of her true beliefs.

▷ *Querelle des Femmes*.

Bib: Beilin, E. V., *Redeeming Eve*; Travitsky, B. (ed.), *The Paradise of Women*; Nyquist, M. and Ferguson, M. (eds.), *Re-membering Milton*.

Spence, Elizabeth Isabella (1768–1832)
Novelist and travel writer. Spence began writing for amusement, but when she was orphaned in 1786 she gradually began to use her writing as a means of support. Her early work consists of rather banal accounts of her travels within Britain and of the people she met, including *Summer Excursions* (1809; England and Wales) and *Letters From the Highlands* (1816; Scotland). The novels which followed attempted to retain the tone of ▷ travel writing by mixing regional history and descriptions of local scenes with fictional characters and narrative, and include *A Traveller's Tale of the Last Century* (1819), *Old Stories* (1822) and *How to be Rid of a Wife* (1823).
▷ Picturesque.

Spencer, Herbert (1820–1903)
Philosopher. He was representative of an important aspect of the Victorian period in his faith in evolutionary theory and his trust in scientific progress. He is most notably associated with the phrase 'Social Darwinism', which can be roughly glossed as extreme *laissez-faire* economics endowed with a supposed biological sanction. Basing his ideas on the evolutionary theories of the French scientist ▷ Lamarck (1744–1829), a forerunner of ▷ Darwin, Spencer concluded that everything was in the process of development, interaction, change, growth and progress. In this way, the laws of science, nature and evolution could only be beneficial. Spencer regarded society as an organism which was evolving from a simple primitive state to a complex heterogeneous form according to the designs of an unknown and unknowable absolute force. The same theory was applied to the development of knowledge from an undifferentiated mass into the various separate sciences. Spencer's scientific determinism was extremely popular in the latter half of the 19th century. He formulated his ideas independently of Darwin and was responsible for coining the phrase 'survival of the fittest' which he used as early as 1852. In that year Spencer heard ▷ Thomas Huxley's paper on oceanic hydrozoa and used some facts from it in his 'Theory of Population deduced from the General Law of Animal Fertility'. He also helped to put the word 'evolution' into common parlance in the 1850s. Some of his more influential books were *Social Statics* (1850), in which he developed his idea of progress as inevitable rather than accidental, and *Education: Intellectual, Moral and Physical* (1861) in which he claimed that science (including social science, psychology, economics, sociology and political theory) was the only discipline worth studying. The best-selling *The Man Versus the State* (1884) proclaimed the popular notion that individual freedom depended on the absence of all forms of interference including government intervention. In 1857 Spencer decided on a massive system of philosophy, beginning with the humble biological origins and ending with the highest ethical principles, that was to be his life's work. The ten volumes of his *System of Synthetic Philosophy* took him nearly forty years to produce and included *First Principles* (1862), and volumes on biology, psychology, morality and sociology. It was completed in 1896. At the height of his popularity he influenced ▷ George Eliot (with whom he was romantically linked for a time) who applied his *Principles of Psychology* to the detailed creation of her characters. The character of Casaubon in ▷ *Middlemarch* is based on Spencer. Others he influenced included T.H. Huxley, ▷ John Stuart Mill, and ▷ Beatrice Webb.
Bib: Peel, J.D.Y., *Herbert Spencer: The Evolution of a Sociologist*; Low-Beer, A., (ed.) *Spencer*; Wiltshire, D., *The Social and Political Thought of Herbert Spencer*.

Spender, Sir Stephen (1909–95)
Poet and critic. Son of a distinguished journalist, J. A. Spender, who was editor of the liberal *Westminster Gazette*. Educated at University College School, London, and University College, Oxford, where he became friendly with the poets ▷ W. H. Auden, ▷ C. Day-Lewis, and ▷ Louis MacNeice. The four, together with the novelist ▷ Christopher Isherwood, formed an influential group of left-wing writers in the 1930s. Spender was a passionately political poet, working as a propagandist for the Republicans in the Spanish Civil War and, in *The Destructive Element* (1935), partly defending poetry's addressing of political subjects through a discussion of fellow poets ▷ W. B. Yeats and ▷ T. S. Eliot. As his career progressed Spender's political orientation changed; though briefly a member of the ▷ Communist Party, in 1950 he contributed to the anti-Communist collection of essays, *The God that Failed* (ed. R. H. S. Crossman). His volumes of verse include *Nine Entertainments* (1928), *Twenty Poems* (1930), *The Still Centre* (1939), *Ruins and Visions* (1942). As a critic he wrote two studies of modern literature: *The Destructive Element* (1935) and *The Creative Element* (1953). His ▷ autobiographical writings include *World within World* (1951). In 1953 he became co-editor of *Encounter*, a monthly review of culture and world affairs. In 1969 he published a study of student politics: *The Year of the Young Rebels*. In 1970 he became Professor of English Language and Literature at University College, London. Later works include *Love–Hate Relations* (1974), *The Thirties and After* (1978), a critical study of T. S. Eliot and *Collected Poems 1928–85* (1985). Spender

was also an important translator, particularly of ▷ German literature, and collaborated with painter David Hockney in the 1982 account of their trip to China, *China Diary*. In 1988 he finally published his first novel, *The Temple*, the revised version of a novel concerning homosexuality first written more than 50 years previously.

Spens, Sir Patrick
▷ *Sir Patrick Spens.*

Spenser, Edmund (?1552–99)
Poet. Spenser's poetry, and in particular ▷ *The Faerie Queene*, was possibly the single most influential body of writing to appear in the ▷ Renaissance period in England. Throughout the 17th century his influence was immense, not least on ▷ John Milton. In the 20th century, however, his reputation began to decline – readers preferring the so-called ▷ 'metaphysical' school of writing represented by ▷ John Donne. Yet, in recent years, there has been a revival of interest in Spenser, particularly among ▷ 'new historicist' and ▷ psychoanalytical critics for whom *The Faerie Queene* has become an endlessly fascinating text.

Spenser was born in London, but lived for most of his adult life in Ireland. He first visited Ireland in 1577, becoming in 1580 private secretary to Lord Grey, the newly appointed lord deputy of Ireland. From 1580 onwards Spenser's fortunes were connected with his progress through the ranks of the colonial administration of Ireland, and by 1588 Spenser had occupied the forfeited estate of the Earl of Desmond. The estate, at Kilcolman in County Cork, Spenser developed as a small 'colony' of six English householders and their families. Kilcolman was to be Spenser's home until 1598, when, in October of that year, the castle of Kilcolman was destroyed in the course of 'Tyrone's Rebellion'. Following the upheaval, Spenser returned to London for the last time, where he died, according to ▷ Ben Jonson, 'for lack of bread' in 1599.

Spenser's first published works were anonymous translations from ▷ Petrarch and the French poet ▷ du Bellay which appeared in a violently anti-Catholic collection in 1569. It was not, however, until the publication of ▷ *The Shepherd's Calendar* (1579 with five editions by 1597) that Spenser's poetic reputation became established. In 1580 he published a correspondence with ▷ Gabriel Harvey, an old friend from his Cambridge days, which set out his views on metrics and prosody. The correspondence is not, perhaps, of startling critical force. Further collections of poetry appeared in 1591, followed by his ▷ sonnet sequence ▷ *Amoretti* together with ▷ *Epithalamion* in a single volume in 1595. The ▷ autobiographical *Colin Clout's Come Home Again* (1594) (▷ Colin Clout) was followed by the ▷ Platonic *Fowre Hymnes* of 1596 and his celebration of the marriage of the daughters of the Earl of Worcester, ▷ *Prothalamion*, also in 1596. Spenser's major poetic work, *The Faerie Queene*, begun prior to 1579, appeared first in 1590 when the first three books of the poem were published. The second edition of Books I–III appeared together with Books IV–VI in 1596, and the final version (as we have it) of the poem after Spenser's death, when a folio edition including the 'Mutabilitie Cantos' was published in 1609.

In the late 16th century, Spenser was the dominating literary intellect of the period, and his reputation was sustained throughout the 18th century, reaching an apotheosis amongst the Romantic poets. To the modern reader he presents a complex set of problems and responses. As a 'source' for wide areas of Renaissance intellectual culture he has been continuously explicated and re-explicated, his texts being examined for their Platonist, numerological, Lucretian (▷ Lucretius) and Calvinist elements. But he is also a writer whose engagement with the creation of a national myth of identity was part of a vital Elizabethan project.

Bib: Greenlaw, E. et al. (eds.), *Works of Edmund Spenser* (10 vols.); Nohrnberg, J., *The Analogy of 'The Faerie Queene'*; Sale, R., *Reading Spenser*; Goldberg, J., *Endlesse Worke: Spenser and the Structures of Discourse*; Shepherd, S., *Spenser.*

Spenserian stanza
A verse form devised by ▷ Edmund Spenser for his poem ▷ *The Faerie Queene*. It consists of eight ten-syllable lines, plus a ninth line of 12 syllables (▷ alexandrine), an iambic rhythm and a rhyme scheme as follows: *a b a b b c b c c*. Example from *The Faerie Queene*:

And as she looked about, she did behold,
How over that same door was likewise writ,
'Be bold, be bold,' and everywhere 'Be bold',
That much she mused, yet could not construe it
By any riddling skill, or common wit.
At last she spied at that room's upper end,
Another iron door, on which was writ,
'Be not too bold'; whereto though she did bend
Her earnest mind, yet wist not what it might intend.

(Book III, Canto xi, 54)

The stanza was used by Spenser's poetic disciples ▷ Giles and ▷ Phineas Fletcher early in the 17th century.

Spinoza, Baruch (1632–77)
Philosopher, theologian and mathematician, born in Amsterdam of a Portuguese Jewish family. He was excommunicated from the Jewish community because of his unorthodox beliefs and became a Christian. After an attempt was made to assassinate him, he left his home and earned a living grinding lenses for microscopes

and telescopes. At the same time he became the leader of a philosophical circle. Building on the ▷ rationalism of ▷ Hobbes and ▷ Descartes, Spinoza speculated that matter is eternal, and the universe is God. His ▷ pantheistic belief that minds and bodies are both aspects of God resolves the Cartesian (▷ Descartes, René) dualism of mind and matter as inhabiting separate systems, the spiritual one ordered by God, the material one by secondary causes. Spinoza also suggested that everything happens according to a 'logical necessity' determined by God, which restricts the possibility of free will, except insofar as acting according to the will of God makes man free. Among his most famous works are the *Tractatus Theologico-Politicus* (1670) and *Tractatus Politicus* (1677).

Spleen, The

1 Title of a Pindaric poem by ▷ Anne Finch, Countess of Winchilsea, published in 1713. She uses the term variously, sometimes to mean melancholy, and sometimes anger or ill-humour. In the poem she examines its place in history, then describes her personal struggle with recurring bouts of it, and finally discusses its manifestations in marriage, and in religious practice, which can result in religious melancholia.
2 Poem by ▷ Matthew Green, which uses a ▷ pastoral framework to celebrate rustic simplicity.

Spondee

In ancient Greek and Latin poetry, a unit of verse measure composed of two long syllables; in English verse, two accented syllables.

Words like 'maíntaín'

and 'wíneglass' in English may be spondees, just as

'ăgaín' is an iambus, and 'ónlў' is a trochee. It is possible to find whole lines of verse in trochee (falling) rhythm, and usual to find lines in iambic (rising) rhythm, but whole lines in spondaic rhythm have to be artificially contrived, *eg*

Slów spón/ dée stálks; / stróng fóot.

▷ Metre.

Spoonerism

Derived from the name of the Rev. W.A. Spooner (1844–1930) of New College, Oxford, who was reputed to have made such errors when speaking. The term describes the transposition of the initial letters of two or more words as in 'You have hissed the Mystery lectures' (OED). The technical term for this is metathesis.

Sprung rhythm

A term used by the poet ▷ Gerard Manley Hopkins to denote the method by which his verse is to be scanned. In his time most English verse was written in running rhythm, *ie* ▷ metres with regular stresses in the line:

Tonight the winds begin to rise

And roar from yonder dropping day
(▷ Tennyson – ▷ *In Memoriam*)

Hopkins wished to free English verse from this rhythm, so as to bring verse into closer accord with common speech, to emancipate rhythm from the linear unit, and to achieve a freer range of emphasis. His theory of sprung rhythm (contained in the Preface to his *Poems*) is complicated, perhaps because he felt he had to justify himself to rather academic metricists like his friend ▷ Robert Bridges. In fact he was reviving the rhythm of Old English alliterative verse (he cites ▷ Langland's ▷ *Piers Plowman* as being in sprung rhythm) and in folk poetry including many ▷ ballads and ▷ nursery rhymes. In sprung rhythm the number of stresses in each line is regular, but they do not occur at regular intervals, nor do the lines have a uniform number of syllables. The rhythm also drives through the stanza, and is not basically linear. The following is an example:

Summer ends now; now, barbarous in beauty, the sticks rise
Around; up above, what wind-walks! what lovely behaviour
Of silk-sack clouds! has wilder, wilful wavier
Meal-drift moulded ever and melted across skies?
(Hopkins – *Hurrahing in Harvest*)

Spurgeon, Charles Haddon (1834–92)

An extremely popular Baptist preacher, for whom the Metropolitan Tabernacle, Newington, London, was built to hold audiences of 6,000. His sermons were in the old Puritan tradition, with strong appeals to the emotions and the conscience, but also varied by a bold and unusual kind of humour. In doctrine he was thoroughly traditional, and eventually he left the Baptists because of his distrust of the new biblical criticism.

Squire

▷ Knighthood.

Squire's Tale, The

One of ▷ Chaucer's ▷ *Canterbury Tales.* It is set in the exotic east and begins with an account of how Cambyuskan, King of Tartary, receives magic gifts on his birthday, including a magic ring for his daughter Canace. The ring allows her to understand the language of birds and through it she hears the sad lament of a female falcon who has been deserted by a faithless tercelet. The tale is unfinished but from the plot résumé given before it breaks off, it seems that the Squire was embarking on a romance of epic length, involving several major narrative lines in an interlaced structure (of the kind found later in the works of ▷ Boiardo, and ▷ Ariosto).

Both ▷ Spenser and ▷ Milton admired the tale, which is related in a highly self-conscious manner by its narrator. The Franklin follows on with praise for the Squire's contribution and there is no indication that the Franklin's response is designed to interrupt the Squire, although the *Squire's Tale* is left unfinished.

▷ *Franklin's Tale, The.*

Stanislavsky, Konstantin (1863–1938)
Russian actor and director, and founder of the Moscow Art Theatre in 1898 with Nemirovich-Danchenko. He rejected the declamatory acting style of the Imperial Theatres and developed a rigorous actors' training which explored, among other things, character psychology and motivation. These ideas about acting can be studied in his published works: *My Life in Art*; *An Actor Prepares*; *Building a Character*; *Creating a Role*. The principle was that the actor should explore all aspects of the character, often through improvisation: his or her history, attitudes and way of behaving outside the frame and events of the play should be as much a part of the actor's knowledge as the lines and responses in the play. The aim was to accquire what Stanislavsky termed 'inner realism' to 'be' rather than to 'do' a character. His sytem is based on two main parts; inner and outer work of actors on themselves and the inner and outer work of the actor on the part.

Unfortunately, only part of Stanislavsky's theories was available in translation for many years and led to an over emphasis on the 'inner' element of the method. This accounts for some of the ways in which American interpretations of the Method differed from the Russian original. Stanislavsky's was the informing principle of Lee Strasberg's enormously influential Actors' Studio, which trained such diverse performers as Marilyn Monroe, Shelley Winters and Marlon Brando. Strasberg taught a method that put more emphasis on psychology and emotions than on the body and voice. Stanislavsky's methods still form the basis of much British and American drama school training and his Moscow Arts Theatre inspired the philosophies of many of the most important twentieth-century companies.

Bib: Benedetti, J., *Stanislavsky: An Introduction*; Magarshack, D., *Stanislavsky on the Art of the Stage*.

State funding
This is an important source of income for much of the 'arts' in Britain. Theatre, as for example the ▷ R.S.C, and ▷ opera, like the Royal Opera at Covent Garden, are subsidized by the state, while on a smaller scale local authorities provide grants for writers, bookshops and courses.

▷ Arts Council of Great Britain; Censorship.

Stationers
In modern English, sellers of writing materials. In the Middle Ages and until the mid-17th century, however, they were booksellers, and were so called from their practice of taking up stalls or 'stations' at suitable places in cathedral towns (*eg* against the walls of St Paul's Cathedral in London) and universities. In the 16th and early 17th centuries they not only sold books, but printed and published them as well. The absence of a law of ▷ copyright (until 1709) made it lawful for stationers to publish author's manuscripts whenever and however they could procure them, without the authors' permission. This kind of unauthorized publishing is now called 'pirating'. 18 of Shakespeare's plays were possibly pirated before the publication of the first collected edition of his plays in the First Folio of 1623, and the fact has caused some difficulties to scholars; there is no assurance that their publication was authorized by the poet, that he had revised the plays for publication, or even that the stationer had procured a reliable version.

The Stationers' Company was formed in 1557 by royal charter; by this charter, no one not a member was entitled to publish a book except by special privilege, and all stationers had to record the titles of books they published; the Company's record of books is thus an important source of information for the literary historian, and particularly valuable evidence in dating many Elizabethan plays. The Company gradually lost its publishing monopoly in the 17th century.

The modern institution, Her Majesty's Stationery Office, publishes official government documents.

▷ Stationers' Register.

Stationers' Register
An important source of bibliographical information for the 16th and 17th centuries. In 1557 ▷ Mary I granted the Worshipful Company of ▷ Stationers and Papermakers of London the monopoly of printing. Under the charter granted to the company, all printers were enjoined to record the titles of any works intended for publication for the first time in a register. Once a title had been recorded, no other member of the company was allowed to publish the book. The Stationers' Register thus *should* include the titles of all books intended for publication between 1554 and 1709. In practice, however, the record is incomplete. First, records for the years 1571–6 have been lost. Secondly, titles were sometimes entered but the book never published. Thirdly, on

occasion a book was published without being entered. Finally though titles were usually entered shortly before the actual publication of a book, there are cases where a period of years elapsed between the entering of a title and the final publication of a work. Nevertheless, the Stationers' Register is an important record of the English book trade in the period. Not least, it provides a valuable indication of what works were being considered for publication at a particular moment.

Bib: Arber, E. (ed.), *A Transcript of the Register of the Company of Stationers of London,* 1554–1640, 5 vol.; Eyre, G. E. B. (ed.), *A Transcript of the Register of the Worshipful Company of Stationers from 1640 to 1709*, 3 vol.

Stead, Christina (1902–83)
Australian novelist. Educated at Sydney University Teachers' College, she moved to Europe in 1928, and to the U.S.A. in 1935, travelling with the American political economist William James Blake, whom she married in 1952. She worked as a Hollywood screenwriter before moving to England and, in 1968, returning to Australia. Many of her novels are concerned with the experience of women, and in particular the quest for love. They are notable for their stylistic power, richness of observation, and vivid characterization, and contain an element of the fantastic. Her first works were collections of stories: *The Salzberg Tales* and *Seven Poor Men of Sydney*, both published in 1934. Of her novels, *House of All Nations* (1938) reflects her left-wing views in its account of a glittering, amoral world of financial speculation, while *The Man Who Loved Children* (1940), a novel of American family life, shows an interest in the causes of genius. In *For Love Alone* (1944) a girl escapes to Australia in search of love and freedom.

▷ Post-colonial literature.

Steel, Mrs Flora Annie (1847–1929)
Novelist. Brought up in London and Scotland, she married at twenty and lived for some twenty-one years in the Punjab, India, where her husband was a civil servant. She worked extensively for the health and education of Indian women, founding a school for Indian girls and working as a school inspector. She started writing after returning to England in 1889, and most of her fiction is set in India: *On the Face of the Waters* (1896), about the Indian mutiny; *Wide Awake Stories* (1884), tales set in the Punjab; *Hosts of the Lord* (1900), about Indian religions; and *The Curse of Eve* (1929), which advocates birth control. She was involved with the ▷ women's suffrage movement and wrote an ▷ autobiography, *The Garden of Fidelity* (1929).

Bib: Powell, V., *Flora Annie Steel: Novelist of India*.

▷ Colonialism.

Steele, Sir Richard (1672–1729)
Essayist and journalist. He was educated (with ▷ Addison) at Charterhouse School (▷ Carthusians) and at Oxford University. On graduation he entered the army. His prose treatise *The Christian Hero* (1701) attracted the favour of the king, ▷ William III, but caused Steele the inconvenience of finding that he was expected to live up to his own precepts. This his pleasure-loving nature did not find convenient, and he redressed the balance by his comedy *The Funeral* (1701). He wrote other comedies: *The Lying Lover* (1703); *The Tender Husband* (1705), an imitation of ▷ Molière's *Sicilienne*; and ▷ *The Conscious Lovers* (1722). It is not, however, for his comedies that he is now read, but for a new kind of ▷ periodical ▷ essay of which he was practically the inventor, and which he published in ▷ *The Tatler*, started in 1709, and appearing three times weekly. Although since the lapsing of the Licensing Act (▷ theatres) in 1695 there was no active ▷ censorship of political opinion, Steele found it safer to avoid politics, at least after the Tory party came to power in 1710, since he was a consistent Whig (Whig and Tory). His essays treated daily life, manners and behaviour, in a way calculated to educate middle-class readers and win the approval of people of virtue, and yet always to entertain them. These motives, and the kind of interest that his essays inspired, anticipate the character of later 18th-century novels, especially those of ▷ Samuel Richardson. *The Tatler* was already a success when Joseph Addison started to collaborate with Steele, but they closed it down in 1711, and started the still more famous ▷ *Spectator* (1711–12). The crisis of succession to the throne grew intense in 1713–14: the Whigs favoured the Protestant House of Hanover and a powerful Tory faction was ready to support ▷ Anne's half-brother James if he would turn Protestant, though other Tories remained loyal to the Act of 1701 in favour of Hanover. Steele was consequently attacked by the Tory journalist ▷ Jonathan Swift, both for his conduct of his next paper, *The Guardian* (1713), and for his ▷ pamphlet in favour of the Protestant succession, *The Crisis* (1714). In 1714 the Whigs returned to power and Steele's political fortunes revived; he was knighted in 1715, and received various official posts. In 1714 he produced his autobiographical *Apology for Himself and his Writings*; he also edited a number of other periodicals, all of them short-lived, and none with the fame of *The Tatler* and *The Spectator*: *The Englishman*, *The Reader*, *Town Talk*, *Tea-Table*, *Chit Chat*, *Plebeian*. The last, a political paper, led to a quarrel with Addison in 1718.

▷ Coverley, Sir Roger de.

Bib: Aitken, G. A., *Life*; Hazlitt, W., *The English Comic Writers*; Dobree, B., *Variety of Ways*; Bateson, F. W., *English Comic Drama, 1700–50*.

Stendhal (pseudonym of Henri Beyle) (1788–1842)
French writer, known for his novels *Armance* (1822), *La Chartreuse de Parme* (1839), *Le Rouge et le Noir* (1830) and *Lucien Leuwen* (unfinished and published posthumously in 1894). Considered the first of the French ▷ realists, Stendhal is renowned for his exact depiction of milieu and for his close attention to psychological verisimilitude and motivation. However, his realism is neither a simple fidelity to detail nor does it underwrite the values and representations which aristocratic and bourgeois society make of themselves. Stendhal does depict the conflict of social verisimilitudes with narrative inventions which contravene such verisimilitudes; so the mainspring of *Le Rouge et le Noir* is the socially unacceptable love of the aristocratic Mathilde and the commoner Julien, while *Armance* raises the 'shocking' issue of ▷ homosexuality before its Byronic conclusion. On the author's side, irony is his means of refusing to endorse such values. Irony here is not a purely corrosive negativity. It discreetly raises the issue of the ethics of representation itself, moving outwards from the hero and society to ask whether the novel can hold together that encounter of social and individual forces it narrates.

Stendhal's interests were wide and he was the author of travel books, journalism and controversial literary pamphlets (*Racine et Shakespeare*, 1823 and 1825, in which he declared his support for the ▷ Romantics). Three volumes of autobiographical writings were published after his death: his *Journal* (1888), *La Vie de Henry Brulard* (1890) and *Souvenirs d'égotisme* (1892).

▷ French influence on English literature.

Stephen, Sir Leslie (1832–1904)
Critic and biographer. He began his career as a tutor at Trinity Hall, Cambridge, and university rules demanded that he should be in orders as an Anglican clergyman. His philosophical studies led him to the religious scepticism so frequent among intellectuals of the middle and later 19th century, and he renounced his orders in 1875. From 1866 he contributed critical essays to the ▷ *Cornhill Magazine* and political ones for the *Nation*; he also wrote for the ▷ *Saturday Review* and helped to found the *Pall Mall Gazette* (1865). In 1871 he became editor of the *Cornhill*; the eleven years of his editorship made it one of the most distinguished literary reviews of the later 19th century. His critical essays were published in book form in *Hours in a Library* (1874–9). He wrote philosophical essays, defining his agnostic position: *Essays on Free Thinking and Plain Speaking* (1873). He contributed a number of biographies to the *English Men of Letters* series: *Johnson* (1878); *Pope* (1880); *Swift* (1882); *George Eliot* (1902), and *Hobbes* (1904). His most distinguished work is firstly his editorship of the *Dictionary of National Biography*, started in 1882, to which he contributed many of the articles, and his book on *The English Utilitarians* (1900). His last book was *English Literature and Society in the Eighteenth Century* (1904).

Today, Stephen is one of the most respected among critics of the later 19th century; the rigour and sincerity of his thinking make him a link between the Victorians and 18th-century rationalist traditions of thought which continued into the 19th century in the ▷ Utilitarian school of thinkers. He has twice been used as the basis of character in the masterpieces of distinguished novelists: Vernon Whitford in ▷ *The Egoist* by ▷ Meredith, and Mr Ramsay in *To the Lighthouse* (1927) by Virginia Woolf (1882–1941), his daughter by his second wife. His first wife had been a daughter of the novelist ▷ Thackeray.

▷ Agnosticism; Reviews and periodicals.

Bib: Lives by F.W. Maitland; Noel Annan.

Stephens, Meic (b 1938)
Poet and editor. Meic Stephens was born at Treforest, near Pontypridd, and was educated at the University College of Wales, Aberystwyth, and at the University of Rennes in Brittany. Initially teaching French at Ebbw Vale, he later settled in Merthyr Tydfil where he founded the *Triskel Press* and *Poetry Wales*, editing the magazine from 1965 to 1973. In 1967, he became the Literature Director of the Welsh Arts Council, a post he held for over twenty years. His early poems were published with those of Harri Webb and Peter Gruffydd in *Triad* (1963) and he also contributed a booklet, *Exiles All* (1973), to the *Triskel Press* series. Among his other work, *Linguistic Minorities in Western Europe*.(1976) examines the interaction between culture and politics in sixteen states, whereas in a contrasting context, in *The Curate of Clyro* (1983), he made a selection from the diary of Francis Kilvert. However, the main thrust of his work has been as an editor and as an anthologist, promoting other writers' work at the expense of his own. His greatest achievement has been his editing and compiling *The Oxford Companion to the Literature of Wales* (1986), published in both Welsh and English language editions, a work of intensive but entertaining scholarship. Among his considerable list of publications are three Anglo-Welsh poetry anthologies, *The Lilting House* (co-editor John Stuart Williams, 1969), *Green House* (co-editor Peter Finch, 1978), and *The Bright Field* (1991); two anthologies of poetry and prose, based on locality, *A Cardiff Anthology* (1987) and

Rhondda Anthology (1993); *The Welsh Language Today* (1973), *A Reader's Guide to Wales* (1973), *Artists in Wales* (in three volumes, 1971, 1973, 1977), *The Arts in Wales, 1950– 1975* (1979) and the *Writers of Wales* series (co-editor, R. Brinley Jones, from 1970). More recently Meic Stephens has edited *The Oxford Literary Guide to Great Britain and Ireland* (1992) and he is at present preparing a revised and enlarged second edition of *The Oxford Companion*, as well as editing the posthumous *Collected Poems* volumes of both Glyn Jones and Harri Webb.

Sterne, Laurence (1713–68)
Sterne was born at Clonmel in Ireland, the son of an improvident army officer. After leaving Cambridge University he became an Anglican priest near York, where his great-grandfather had been Archbishop. His celebrated novel ▷ *The Life and Opinions of Tristram Shandy* appeared in successive volumes from 1760 until 1767. Opinions have always been divided about the qualities of this book, although Sterne's reputation rests principally upon it. ▷ Samuel Johnson found it eccentric and shallow, declaring, 'Nothing odd will do long. *Tristram Shandy* did not last'; but in the 20th century the critic Viktor Schlovsky has argued that '*Tristram Shandy* is the most typical novel of world literature.' ▷ *A Sentimental Journey through France and Italy*, which demonstrates many of the same stylistic idiosyncracies, appeared in 1768, the last year of Sterne's life. His *Journal to Eliza*, published posthumously, is a curious, quasi- ▷ autobiographical work that hovers uneasily between fact and fiction, ▷ tragedy and farce. The same blend of seriousness and whimsicality is evident in Sterne's ▷ sermons, he published under the name of one of the characters from *Tristram Shandy* as *The Sermons of Mr Yorick*. A contemporary review took offence at this jesting allusion. 'We have read of a Yorick likewise in an obscene romance,' it thundered. 'But are the solemn dictates of religion fit to be conveyed from the mouths of buffoons and ludicrous romancers?'

Sterne's characteristic blending of ▷ sentimentality and farce, although distinctive in style, is not without precedent. His main literary influences can be found in ▷ Rabelais, Cervantes (1547–16), and ▷ Montaigne, although there are also debts to Burton's ▷ *Anatomy of Melancholy* (1621–51), ▷ Locke's ▷ *Essay on Human Understanding*, and ▷ Swift's ▷ *Tale of a Tub*. From Rabelais Sterne derived not only his bawdy humour, but also his fascination with exuberant word-play, his love of lists and puns, his delight in the sonorous malleability of words and his absurd parodies of learned debates. From Locke he borrowed and parodied the theory of the association of ideas, a theory which allows him to present each of his characters trapped in a private world of allusions. ▷ Thackeray objected to the self-indulgence of Sterne's wit; 'He is always looking on my face, watching his effect, uncertain whether I think him an impostor or not; posture-making, coaxing and imploring me.' Yet it is precisely this fictional virtuousity that has recommended Sterne as a model to later writers keen to assert not only that all art is artifice, but that history and ▷ biography too are merely varieties of elaborate fiction.

Bib: Cash, A. H., *Laurence Sterne*; New, M., *Laurence Sterne as Satirist*.

Stevenson, Anne (b 1933)
Poet. Stevenson was born in Britain, and now lives here, but was brought up and educated in the U.S.A. She has written critical texts as well as poetry, and has worked as a teacher. Her publications include: *Living in America* (1965); *Travelling Behind Glass: Selected Poems* (1974); *Enough of Green* (1977); *Minute by Glass Minute* (1982); *The Fiction-makers* (1985); *Selected Poems* (1986). Stevenson's biography of poet ▷ Sylvia Plath, *Bitter Fame: A Life of Sylvia Plath*, was published in 1989.

Stevenson, Robert Louis Balfour (1850–94)
Novelist, essayist, poet. The son of an engineer, he intended to take up the same profession, for which he showed early talent, but bad health prevented this. Partly because of his health and partly for love of travel, he spent much of his life abroad and some of his best writing is in essays of travel, eg *An Inland Voyage* (1878) and *Travels with a Donkey in the Cevennes* (1879). His most famous works, however, are the fantasy, so often used as an emblem of divided personality, ▷ *The Strange Case of Dr Jekyll and Mr Hyde* (1886) and his adventure story ▷ *Treasure Island* (1883). Still well known are his Scottish historical romances, in the tradition of Walter Scott (1771–1832): *Kidnapped* (1886), ▷ *The Master of Ballantrae* (1889), and *Catriona* (1893); it has been said that *Weir of Hermiston*, also in this style but left unfinished, would have been his masterpiece. Other works of fiction: *New Arabian Nights* (1882); *Prime Otto* (1885); *The Black Arrow* (1888); *The Wrong Box* (1889); *The Wrecker* (1892); *Island Nights Entertainments* (1893); *The Ebb Tide* (1894); *St Ives*, also left unfinished at his death. Essays: *Virginibus Puerisque* (1881); *Familiar Studies of Men and Books* (1882); *Vailima Letters* (1895). His *A Child's Garden of Verses* (1885) was for long considered a minor children's classic (▷ Children's literature), and he published other poetry in *Underwoods* (1887). Stevenson was strongly influenced by French ideas of literary style and to a lesser extent by ▷ aestheticism. He has had a wide popular readership which has perhaps denied him critical attention: critics have detected a darker side to his writing beneath the swashbuckling, and dualism is a theme in evidence.

Bib: Balfour, G., *Life*; Daiches, D., *Robert Louis Stevenson*; Elwin, M., *The Strange Case of Stevenson*; Furnas, J.C., *Voyage to Windward* (life); Eigner, E.M., *Robert Louis Stevenson and Romantic Tradition*; Calder, J. (ed.), *Stevenson and Victorian Scotland*.

Stichomythia
A terse but artificial style of dramatic dialogue, used in disputes between two characters, each speaking in turn a single line of verse. It originated in ancient Greek tragedies; from them it passed to ▷ Seneca whose influence caused it to be used by some of the early Elizabethans.

The following example of Stichomythia is taken from ▷ Kyd's ▷ *The Spanish Tragedy* and shows a love-dialogue between two of the characters in the play:

BEL-IMPERIA
Set forth thy foot to try the push of mine.
HORATIO
But first my looks shall combat against thine.
BEL-IMPERIA
Then ward thyself: I dart this kiss at thee.
HORATIO
Thus I retort the dart thou threw'st at me.

Stoics
A school of philosophy founded by the Greek Zeno of Citium, in the 4th century AD. It later extended to Rome, where its leaders became Epictetus and ▷ Seneca (both 1st century AD) and the Roman Emperor Marcus Aurelius (2nd century AD). They reasoned that all being is material, and therefore the soul is, and so are the virtues. The soul, however, is an active principle which sustains the body, and proceeds from God; only the active principle has significance, and the wise person is therefore indifferent to material suffering and cares only for virtue governed by judgement which is in accordance with the principles of wisdom. Some of the ethical principles of Stoicism were in accordance with Christianity (which Marcus Aurelius nevertheless persecuted) and, abstracted from religious doctrine, they appealed to the ▷ Renaissance ideal of the noble soul; hence the recurrence of Stoic attitudes in the drama of ▷ Shakespeare and his contemporaries.

Stoker, Bram (1847–1912)
Irish novelist and ▷ short story writer, now remembered principally for the universally known, much parodied and frequently filmed ▷ *Dracula* (1897), which was influenced by ▷ J. S. Le Fanu's vampire novel *Carmilla* (1872). Stoker spent most of his career as secretary and business manager to the actor Henry Irving; he wrote many ▷ horror stories, other novels of the supernatural, such as *The Lady of the Shroud* (1909), and adventure novels such as *The Snake's Pass* (1890).
▷ Irish literature in English.

Stoppard, Tom (b 1937)
Czech-born British dramatist and something of an eclectic who has experimented with a variety of forms in his writing for stage and television. Characteristic of his plays is a heavy reliance on intellectual wit and allusion, which would appear to make his appeal rather esoteric, yet he is now established as a leading comic playwright. His work is always full of verbal fireworks, intellectual references and literary jokes. Most of his plays are constructed around elaborate conceits; *Jumpers* puts a philosophical discussion of logic together with a troupe of acrobats; *Every Good Boy Deserves Favour* has a full scale orchestra on stage in a play about Soviet dissidents; *Hapgood* relates the complexities of spying and double agents to nuclear physics. This method of highly improbable juxtaposition owes a lot to Surrealism, and, in *After Magritte*, Stoppard wrote a play around the elements of a Magritte painting (umbrellas, bowler hats, skies, etc) located in a suburban household. *Arcadia* juxtaposes chaos theory and literary detection in a compelling conjunction of verbal wit and intellectual games. His major works include: *Rosencrantz and Guildenstern Are Dead* (1966); *The Real Inspector Hound* (1968); *Jumpers* (1972); *Travesties* (1974); *Dirty Linen* (1976); *Every Good Boy Deserves Favour* (1977); *Night and Day* (1978); *On the Razzle* (1981); *The Real Thing* (1982); *Rough Crossing* (1985); *Hapgood* (1987); *Arcadia* (1993); *Indian Ink* (1995). Television plays include: *Professional Foul* (1977); *Squaring the Circle* (1984).
Bib: Bigsby, C. W. E., *Tom Stoppard*; Hunter, J., *Tom Stoppard's Plays*.

Storey, David (b 1933)
Novelist and dramatist. His novels include: *This Sporting Life* (1960); *Flight into Camden* (1961); *Radcliffe* (1963); *Pasmore* (1972); *A Temporary Life* (1973); *Saville* (1976); *A Prodigal Child* (1982); *Present Times* (1984).

Before he became a novelist and playwright Storey was an art student, and to pay for his studies in London he played at weekends in professional Rugby League football for a northern team. The son of a miner, Storey is one of a group of novelists who rose to prominence in the 1950s and 1960s, who have in common that their social viewpoint is outside the middle class and centred geographically outside London; they include ▷ Alan Sillitoe, ▷ John Braine and ▷ Stan Barstow. Their obvious antecedent is ▷ D. H. Lawrence. Storey is distinguished from his contemporaries with a similar background by the absence of social belligerence and an ability to reach across from a provincial–industrial world denuded of art to a world of highly cultivated sensibility without

playing false to the social experience that shaped him. His first novel, which has been filmed, is about his background world, in which sport is the principal cultural force; the next two are in different ways more ambitious and less successful, but their faults are interesting as the price paid for their serious experimental boldness. *Radcliffe* modifies 1950 ▷ realism with elements of the Gothic, allegorical and fantastic, while retaining a concern with class and social mobility; *Pasmore* continues this development by linking social instability to a personal crisis of identity. His plays often explore class antagonism and social dislocation. In his play *The Contractor* (1969) the process of manual work is presented dramatically as the action centres on the construction of a huge marquee on stage. This bold if somewhat sentimental gesture about the worth of work originally made a strong impression. Yet Storey's plays tend to avoid simplistic idealization of the working class or indeed any kind of simple obvious 'meaning'. The ▷ Chekhovian *Home* (1970) is set in a mental hospital, perhaps a metaphor for modern Britain, whose communication is painfully reserved. Much is hinted at but little is directly expressed. The later plays, *Mother's Day* (1976) and *Sisters* (1978) both have working-class settings and deal with what Storey termed the 'delusions, illusions and fantasies' of domestic life. Other plays include: *The Restoration of Arnold Middleton* (1966); *In Celebration* (1969); *The Changing Room* (1971); *The Farm* and *Cromwell* (both 1973): *Life Class* (1974); *Early Days* (1980).
Bib: Taylor, J. R., *David Storey*.

Story and plot
▷ Russian Formalism.

Story of an African Farm, The
▷ Schreiner, Olive.

Story/*histoire* (French)
Term used in ▷ narratology for the chronological series of events described in a fiction, as the reader deduces them from the ▷ narrative (which may not recount them in chronological order).
▷ Narrating.

Stow, John (1515–1605)
Historian and antiquary. Stow's first interest was in literature rather than history, and he produced an edited version of ▷ Chaucer's poetry, *The Workes of Geoffrey Chaucer* (1561). His historical texts include the detailed and authoritative *Chronicles of England* (1580; later known as *Annales*) and *A Survey of London*, which is an invaluable account of the capital city during the Elizabethan period. He was suspected of ▷ recusancy and charged with owning Popish documents (Edmund Grindal), but managed to convince the ecclesiastical commission of his innocence.

Stow, Randolph (b 1935)
Australian novelist, born in Western Australia and educated at the University of Western Australia and the University of Sydney. He has worked as a storeman in an Anglican Mission, as an anthropologist in Papua New Guinea and as a lecturer in English at the universities of Leeds and Western Australia. In 1966 he moved to Britain, living in Suffolk and later in Essex. He won the Patrick White Award in 1979, and Stow's portrayal of a spiritual journey in *To the Islands* (1958), which is about the quest of an ageing Christian missionary for the aboriginal 'island of the dead', invites comparison with ▷ Patrick White's *Voss*. His other novels are: *A Haunted Land* (1956); *The Bystander* (1957); *Tourmaline* (1963); *The Merry-Go-Round in the Sea* (1965); *Visitants* (1979); *The Girl Green as Elderflower* (1980); *The Suburbs of Hell* (1984). His volumes of poetry include: *Act One* (1957); *Outrider: Poems 1956–1962* (1962); *A Counterfeit Silence: Selected Poems* (1969). He has also written opera libretti for the composer Peter Maxwell Davies (*Eight Songs for a Mad King*, 1969, and *Miss Donnithorne's Maggot*, 1974), edited *Australian Poetry* (1964), and written for children.
Bib: Hassall, A. J. (ed.), *Visitants, Episodes from Other Novels, Poems, Stories, Interviews and Essays*; Hassall, A. J., *Strange Country: A Study of Randolph Stow*.

Strachey, (Giles) Lytton (1880–1932)
Biographer. His best-known works are *Eminent Victorians* (1918) – short biographical studies of Cardinal Manning, Florence Nightingale and General Gordon – and *Queen Victoria* (1921). He also wrote *Elizabeth and Essex* (1928), and criticism: *Landmarks in French Literature* (1912) and *Books and Characters* (1922). Strachey regarded most biographies of the 19th century as dull monuments to the subject, whereas he considered biography to be an art form, presenting the subject as a human being and showing him or her from unexpected aspects. Strachey was a prominent member of the ▷ Bloomsbury Group, living with diarist and painter ▷ Carrington.
▷ Biography.
Bib: Sanders, C. P., *Strachey: His Mind and Art*; Johnstone, J. K., *The Bloomsbury Group*; Holroyd, M., *Lytton Strachey*.

Strafford, Sir Thomas Wentworth, first Earl of (1593–1641)
Statesman, and one of ▷ Charles I's chief ministers. He began his career as an opponent of the king; as Member of Parliament for Yorkshire in 1625, he opposed the attempt of Charles' minister, The Earl of Buckingham, to

raise taxes for war against Spain, and in 1627 he was imprisoned for refusing to contribute a forced loan to the king. His opposition to Charles was different in motive from that of other members; theirs was based on the desire to assert the power of Parliament, whereas Wentworth's motive was to secure efficient government. Consequently, when in 1628 Parliament asserted itself by forcing on the king the ▷ Petition of Right, he changed sides. In 1632 Charles sent him to Ireland to reform the administration there. He was never consulted on English affairs until the major crisis brought about by the defeat of the royal troops by the Scots in 1639. Wentworth was then recalled, and made Earl of Strafford in 1640. Events, however, had gone so far that he could no longer help the king, and merely focused public hostility upon himself. Parliament condemned him to death by an Act of Attainder (*ie* a law effecting death of a subject without using the normal judicial process), and he was executed accordingly.

***Strange Case of Dr Jekyll and Mr Hyde, The* (1886)**
A novel by ▷ Robert Louis Stevenson which, along with ▷ *Treasure Island*, is probably his best known work. The story of Dr Jekyll, who discovers a drug that reduces him periodically to an embodiment of his purely evil impulses – Mr Hyde – is told to the reader through a series of disparate narratives. It has attracted much commentary in recent times, being read as a case study of male sexual hysteria, a fable of late 19th-century homosexual panic, a variant on the *doppelgänger* myth and a pre-Freudian study of ego and libido.
Bib: Showalter, E., *Sexual Anarchy*.

Strawberry Hill
▷ Walpole, Horace.

Stream of consciousness
A term which was used by William James in his *Principles of Psychology* but was first applied to literature in a 1918 review by May Sinclair of volumes of ▷ Dorothy Richardson's *Pilgrimage*. Since then it has been used for the narrative technique which attempts to render the consciousness of a character by representing as directly as possible the flow of feelings, thoughts and impressions. The term 'interior monologue' is also sometimes used. The classic exponents of the technique, apart from Richardson, are ▷ Virginia Woolf, ▷ James Joyce and the American novelist William Faulkner (1897–1962). Joyce attributed his initial discovery of the technique to his reading of the novel *Les Lauriers sont coupés* by the French novelist Edouard Dujardin.

Stretton, Hesba (Sarah) (1832–1911)
Novelist and writer of ▷ children's literature. She contributed to ▷ Dickens' periodicals, ▷ *Household Words* and ▷ *All the Year Round*, and had much work published by the Religious Tract Society. An ▷ Evangelical Christian, she wrote a large number of novels with religious messages, which were extremely popular. *Jessica's First Prayer* (1867) made her internationally famous and was translated into several languages. Her works include *Little Meg's Children* (1868), *Alone in London* (1869) and *Pilgrim Street* (1872).

Strindberg, August (1849–1912)
Swedish dramatist and novelist. His father, a shipping agent, married his servant who had been his mistress during his first marriage. The unpromising circumstances of this parentage, intensified by his bad relations with his father, were the beginnings of a psychologically tormented life for Strindberg; he was married and divorced three times, and had a mental breakdown in 1895–6, described in *Inferno*, one of several vivid autobiographical fragments. Intellectually he was immensely versatile: a student of Chinese, botany, chemistry, alchemy and painting. He had comparable literary versatility, and wrote radical journalism (1872–80), prose fiction (notably *The Red Room*, 1879), and his varied, original dramas. He is chiefly famous, at least outside Sweden, for the last. He wrote historical dramas (*Master Olof*, 1872; *Saga of the Folkungs*, *Gustavus Vasa*, *Eric XVI*, 1899) which show the influence of ▷ Shakespeare's history plays; tragedies influenced by Zola's ▷ Naturalism and the philosophy of ▷ Nietzsche; fantasies (*Easter*, 1900; *Dream Play*, 1902) under the influence of the Belgian dramatist, Maurice Maeterlinck (1862–1949); and, at the end of his career, highly symbolic dramas often called ▷ 'expressionist', of which the best known is *The Ghost Sonata* (1907). Two partly autobiographical works, *To Damascus* (1898) and *The Great Highway* (1909–12) can also be termed 'expressionist'.

Strindberg's dramatic inspiration was to epitomize human experience as the experience of conflict, and he sought to dramatize this conflict at its deepest and most intense. This shows most clearly in his naturalist phase, especially the two plays by which he is best known in Britain: *The Father* (1887) and *Miss Julie* (1888). To these may be added the double play *The Dance of Death* (1901), a Naturalist tragedy verging towards the expressionist symbolism of his later work. One of his strongest preoccupations at the time was the theme of conflict in relationships between women and men, since he considered women to be undergoing a fundamental change in their nature in their struggle for emancipation. He was aware of the possibilities of dramatic experiment on stage and enhanced the visual aspect of his plays. In dialogue he was also experimental, though not with such decisive

success as his Russian contemporary, ▷ Anton Chekhov.
Bib: Lamm, M., *August Strindberg*.

Strophe
A Greek word meaning 'turn'. It is used as a term in Greek versification, for example, the ▷ Pindaric Ode, for a passage which is sung and danced (or 'turned') by a chorus. When another passage succeeds it, to be danced and sung by another part of the chorus, this second passage is known as an 'antistrophe'. This is sometimes followed by a third part, the 'epode' when the chorus stood still, thus forming, altogether, a triadic passage. More generally, 'strophe' means a stanza or subdivision of a poem.
▷ Ode.

Structuralism
This influential school of criticism grew out of the ideas of ▷ Ferdinand de Saussure as they appeared in his *Course in General Linguistics* (1915). Saussure established the role of ▷ difference, the relationship between linguistic elements (signs), as the major determining principle in the establishment of meaning (signification). Thus structuralism encompasses approaches to criticism which use linguistic models to enable critics to focus not on the inherent meaning of a work, but on the structures which produce or generate that meaning or meanings.

As a critical method Saussure's insights were developed subsequently in a wide range of areas, from anthropology, especially by the social anthropologist Claude Levi-Strauss (b 1908), to language, in particular by the Russian ▷ Formalists such as ▷ Roman Jakobson and Tzetvan Todorov (b 1940). In addition, Saussure's insights into sign systems were applied to phenomena as varied as folk tales by the Russian critic Vladimir Propp and menus and traffic lights, in the work of the French critic ▷ Roland Barthes. ▷ Post-structuralism and ▷ deconstruction have developed from the basis of structuralism.
Bib: Culler, J., *Structuralist Poetics*.
▷ Derrida, Jacques; discourse; Foucault, Michel.

Structure of feeling
A term coined by Raymond Williams to denote the connections between various works in a given period or literary ▷ genre. The term is deliberately oxymoronic, suggesting something both structurally ▷ determined but also responsive to more nebulous feeling. In this way, though himself a socialist, Williams resisted the dogmatic emphasis on determination found in some Marxist accounts of culture. The term has the further advantage of uniting personal feeling with social structure, and Williams insisted that literature always presented human experience in a specific social context. In this way he tried to eliminate the abstraction of conventional coverage of 'background' or 'world-view'. Williams also insisted that the ▷ form of a work was as important as its content in the expression of feeling and experience, and that, in their development, literary forms both enable and limit (i.e. structure) the expression of certain kinds of historically and socially specific feeling and experience.
Bib: Williams, R., *The Country and the City; Marxism and Literature*.

Stuart (Stewart), House of
The family from which came the sovereigns of Scotland between 1371 and 1603, and the sovereigns of Scotland, England and Ireland between 1603 and 1714. The family originated in Brittany, from where they migrated to England in the 11th century and to Scotland in the 12th, where they acquired the surname 'Stuart' (variously spelt) by serving the kings of Scotland as Stewards. They came to the Scottish throne by intermarriage with the Bruce family, and the reigns until 1603 were as follows: Robert II (1371–90); Robert III (1390–1406); James I (1406–37); James II (1437–60); James III (1460–88); James IV (1488–1513); James V (1513–42); Mary (1542, deposed 1567); James VI (1567–1603). In 1603 ▷ Elizabeth I of England died childless, and James VI inherited the crown of England by virtue of his descent from Elizabeth's aunt Margaret, who had married James IV. James VI thus became also ▷ James I of England, and ruled over the two countries until 1625. The succession during the ▷ Renaissance period continued as follows: Charles I (1625–49), after whom there was an ▷ Interregnum until 1660 when the monarchy was restored in his son, Charles II (1660–85).

Stubbes, Philip (?1555–?1611)
Puritan author of *The Anatomie of Abuses* (1583) who censured stage plays and wrote a strong and colourful prose. He may have been involved in the ▷ Martin Marprelate controversy, and was attacked in pamphlets by both ▷ John Lyly and ▷ Thomas Nashe. He is most valued now for his contribution to our understanding of the popular customs and festivals of the time.

Subjectivity
In its use in the language of literary criticism this concept is not to be confused with the notion of 'individual response' with which it has customarily been associated. ▷ Louis Althusser and ▷ Jacques Lacan develop the notion of human beings as 'subjects', that is points at which all of those social, cultural and psychic forces which contribute to the construction of the individual, come together. Implicit in the concept of the 'subject' is the idea

of the grammatical positioning of the personal pronoun in a sentence: the 'I' being referred to as 'the subject of discourse'. Also, implicit in the concept of 'subjectivity' is the notion of 'subjection', which raises fundamental questions about the ways in which the behaviour of individual 'subjects' is conditioned by external forces. Within the boundaries of critical theory the 'subject' is never unified (except through the functioning of an ▷ ideology which is designed to efface contradiction), but it, in reality split, or 'decentred'. This is part of a movement away from the kind of philosophical ▷ humanism which would place the individual at the centre of attention. It would attribute to him or her an autonomy of action as well as an authority arising out of the suggestion that he or she is the origin and source of all meaning. 'Subjectivity' is an indispensable category of analysis for ▷ feminism, ▷ psychoanalytical criticism and for the various kinds of materialist analysis of texts.

Sublimation
This term is used in ▷ Freudian psychoanalysis to describe the process whereby activities which have their origins in the unconscious, and which can be traced to primal issues of sexuality, are diverted and surface in other areas of human endeavour, as something else. This concept is of particular use to literary criticism, not only because it can provide an explanation of the mechanisms of artistic creation itself, but because it assists in the analysis of literary representations of human motives and actions. Implicit in sublimation is the notion of an unconscious whose operations, distorted as desires, rise to the level of the conscious.

Subversion
This is a term usually associated with the sphere of political action, but applied to literary texts it points towards the relationship between a particular text, or even a part of a text, and what is generally regarded as the prevailing order. Individual texts are capable of challenging dominant orthodoxies (*eg* ▷ James Joyce's ▷ *Ulysses* or ▷ D. H. Lawrence's *Lady Chatterley's Lover*), either at the level of literary form, or at the level of discernible content. Thus, they may be said to subvert expectations or dominant values. A more complex kind of subversion may take place within the boundaries of a particular text which otherwise would be accepted as conforming to prevailing values and attitudes. Where this happens, negotiation takes place (which can be analysed as part of the text's structure) whereby that which is dominant in the text seeks to contain and control those forces which could subvert it. Such a process is particularly evident in relation to sexual difference, where a potentially subversive 'femininity' is often seen to threaten the dominant masculine discourses which seek to contain it. Very often potentially subversive energies are only ever permitted to enter a text in marginalized forms, *eg* female promiscuity, as various forms of 'evil' all of which are shown to be a danger to the status quo. An acceptance of the judgements implied in these moral categories is usually a precondition of a reading which is complicit with its dominant discourses and structures. A more critical reading will seek to reinstate the text's 'subversive' elements in order to show precisely how certain values, and the literary structures which sustain them, are produced.

Suckling, Sir John (1609–41)
Poet and dramatist. Suckling has been grouped with the ▷ 'Cavalier' poets associated with the Royalist cause during the ▷ Civil War. Closely associated with the court, his military career was marked by an ostentatious delight in the appearance rather than the reality of a campaign: he is said to have paid £12,000 from his own pocket to have 100 cavalrymen decked out in striking uniforms for the war against the Scots in 1639. The king's army, of which Suckling and his troops were a part, were routed. Following the abortive attempt to rescue the king's favourite, the ▷ Earl of Strafford, from the Tower, Suckling, who took part in the plot, fled abroad, where he died, possibly committing suicide and probably in the autumn of 1641.

Although the author of four plays, the most successful of which was *Aglaura* (first produced in 1637 as a ▷ tragedy, and revised and produced as a comedy in 1638), Suckling's reputation rests on his short ▷ lyric poems, written in an anti-Petrarchan style and calculated to strike the pose of a cynical rake.
Bib: Berry H. (ed.), *Sir John Suckling's Poems and Letters from Manuscript*.

Suffragette Movement
Colloquial term for the Women's Suffrage Movement which pursued violent action to secure political rights for women before and during World War I. The suffrage movement has often been seen as the origin of the modern women's movement; it developed out of the campaigns led in the 1860s and 1870s by Josephine Butler against the notorious Contagious Diseases Acts. The origin of the Women's Suffrage Movement thus lies in the late 19th century. Specifically, the suffragettes wanted equal rights with men to have the vote (suffrage) in parliamentary elections and to be candidates for election. Among the famous leaders of the movement were Mrs Pankhurst and her two daughters, ▷ Sylvia and Christabel. The movement ended in 1918 when votes were given to women at the age

of 30; in 1928 they received equal rights with men.
Bib: Tickner, L., *The Spectacle of Women.*

***Summer's Last Will and Testament* (1592)**
A lyrical ▷ allegory and ▷ pageant by ▷ Thomas Nashe, and his only surviving dramatic work.

Summoner's Tale, The
One of ▷ Chaucer's ▷ *Canterbury Tales.* It is delivered as a riposte to the ▷ *Friar's Tale*, has a strong scatalogical emphasis and contains a devastating picture of the corrupt practices of Friar John, who uses his profession and professional skills to procure material comforts for himself and his colleagues. The basic plot follows a ▷ fabliau structure, and recounts the gulling of Friar John by one of his lay clients, who appears to promise him a significant gift, but this turns out to be no more than sound and wind (and provides a fitting comment on the Friar's principal qualities). However, the Friar has promised to distribute the gift among his colleagues, and the tale closes with an investigation into how the offensive gift might be divided into 12: a squire of the local lord solves this difficult problem of 'arsmetrike' and thus completes the total humiliation of the Friar.

Supremacy, Acts of
1 The law passed through ▷ Parliament on the initiative of ▷ King Henry VIII in 1534; it established the King as Supreme Head of the Church in England, and thus displaced the sovereignty of the Pope. The Act was the immediate consequence of Henry's dispute with the Pope over his attempt to divorce his Queen, Catherine of Aragon; however, this immediate cause was insufficient by itself to bring about the break. Deeper causes include the growth of national feeling; longstanding resentment against some forms of papal taxation; distrust of Roman Catholic doctrine, first roused by ▷ Wycliffe and now reawakened by the German reformer, ▷ Luther; growing dislike of the international religious orders of monks and friars who were ultimately subject to the Pope. Nonetheless, Henry was a conservative in doctrine, and the act did not entail doctrinal reformation.

2 The similar law passed through Parliament on the initiative of ▷ Elizabeth I in 1559. Since the act of 1534, the English nation had undergone ▷ Protestant doctrinal ▷ reformation in the reign of ▷ Edward VI and had reverted to full Roman Catholicism under headship of the Pope in the reign of ▷ Mary I. In consequence Elizabeth's Act of Supremacy was deliberately vague, so as to gain the widest possible national support, from both Protestant and Roman Catholic sympathizers. Elizabeth abandoned the title 'Supreme Head' and adopted that of 'Supreme Governor'.

Surrealism
Inaugurated in Paris in 1924 by ▷ André Breton's first *Surrealist Manifesto* (two further manifestos were to follow in 1930 and 1934), its founding members included Louis Aragon (1897–1982), Robert Desnos (1900–45), Paul Eluard (1895–1952), Benjamin Péret (1899–1959) and Philippe Soupault (b 1897). The movement's ambition was a radical programme, extending beyond art and literature to embrace social and political reform. To advertise and propagate their aims, the Surrealists created a 'Bureau de recherches surréalistes' and a number of reviews: *Littérature* (1919), *La Révolution surréaliste* (1924), *Le Surréalisme au service de la Révolution* (1930) and *Minotaure* (1932). Purely with France, Surrealism's roots lay in Guillaume Apollinaire's (1880–1918) experiments with poem-objects and in the cubist poetry of Pierre Reverdy (1889–1960). More broadly, as the first *Manifesto* made clear, it was especially indebted to Freudian (▷ Freud) theories of dream and sought to overthrow rationalism in favour of unconscious mental states, so giving rise to an expanded sense of the psychic life. Such unconscious processes could best be liberated by activities such as 'automatic writing'. By this technique, a writer's faculty of conscious censorship is laid aside, allowing the chance encounter between two otherwise unrelated elements which might produce the surreal image and intimate the incursion of dream into reality.

Just as Surrealism travelled easily between forms of artistic production and ostensibly external forms such as psychology and philosophy, so its own artistic manifestations span poetry, prose and painting, though it is best known for and possibly most representatively manifested in the first and last of these. Max Ernst (1891–1976), René Magritte (1898–1967) and Joan Miró (1893–1983) helped establish the movement in art and Salvador Dali (1904–89) provided greater impetus still when he associated himself with Surealism in 1929; his dream-like work was plainly inspired by Freud, while his surreal objects such as the lobster-telephone amuse and shock our sense of the everyday propriety of such objects. Louis Aragon (1897–1982), the foremost of Surrealism's several communists (Eluard was another), made an early contribution with his *Feu de joie* (1920) and *Le Mouvement perpétuel* (1925) as well as major novels. However, Aragon's commitment to communism from 1927 onwards finally led to his break with Surrealism in 1932, even though Breton's *Second Manifesto* of 1930 had called for the harmonization of Freud and ▷ Marx. World War II caused an hiatus in Surrealism's activities and despite the success of the various Surrealist Exhibitions (*eg*

London, 1936; Paris 1938, 1947, 1959), by the 1950s the movement's force was to all intents and purposes spent.

The widespread influence of French Surrealism between the Wars gave rise to two corresponding movements, Belgian Surrealism and English Surrealism.

Surrey, Henry Howard, Earl of (?1517–47)
Poet. He was the son of the Duke of Norfolk, the senior nobleman of England. Surrey and his father were both arrested by ▷ Henry VIII on a ridiculous charge of high treason. Surrey was executed, Henry's last victim; his father, also condemned to death, survived Henry and was reprieved. In character Surrey was a man of the ▷ Renaissance, with the Renaissance conception of the courtier as the complete man in all worthy things – art, learning and action. His poetry was thus a cultivation of poetic ideals on the model of the poets of the Italian Renaissance, and he shares with his older contemporary ▷ Sir Thomas Wyatt the distinction of being the first poet to naturalize Renaissance poetic modes in English; their work was published by ▷ Tottel in his *Miscellany* of 1557. Like Wyatt, Surrey cultivated the ▷ sonnet, and he was the first poet to use ▷ blank verse, in his translation of ▷ Virgil's *Aeneid*, Books 2 and 3. However, Surrey was respected for these contributions more by modern critics who have in the past pointed out that the merit of his poetry is much slighter than Wyatt's and that the flowering of the English short poem in the 1590s owed more to the sonnets of ▷ Sir Philip Sidney (▷ *Astrophil and Stella*) and to ▷ Edmund Spenser's pastorals (▷ *The Shepherd's Calendar*) than to the work of either Wyatt or Surrey.
Bib: Jones, E. (ed.), *Poems*.

Surtees, Robert Smith (1805–64)
Novelist. In 1832 he helped to found the *New Sporting Magazine*, which he edited for five years and to which he contributed sketches collected in 1838 under the title of *Jorrocks' Jaunts and Jollities*. It was this book which suggested to the publishers, Chapman and Hall, the idea that ▷ Charles Dickens might write a similar series of sketches about a Nimrod Club of amateur sportsmen. Dickens adapted this idea to the Pickwick Club and thus started ▷ *The Pickwick Papers*, issued in twenty parts in 1836–7 and published in book form in 1837. Surtees' most famous fox-hunting novel is probably *Handley Cross* (1843), still regarded as a minor classic. He published eight novels in all.
Bib: Cooper, L., *R.S. Surtees*; Welcome, J., *The Sporting World of R.S. Surtees*.

Sutcliffe, Alice (c 1633)
Poet. Alice Sutcliffe published only one work that we know of, *Meditations of Man's Mortalitie* (1633); it includes several panegyric poems written by men praising the extraordinary skill of the author – extraordinary in that she is a woman. Two of these were written by ▷ Ben Jonson and ▷ George Wither, and these, together with her dedication to Katherine, Duchess of Buckingham, reveal Sutcliffe's court associations. Her husband, John Sutcliffe, was Groom of the royal chamber. The poems stand for themselves, however, regardless of any social connections, since they combine religious allusions with deeply passionate, grotesque and overtly physical language. Their admonition against sin and their warning of the Day of Judgement reside uneasily with a gothic sensuality.
Bib: Greer, G. (ed.), *Kissing the Rod*.

Swedenborg, Emanuel (1688–1722)
Swedish scientist, philosopher and theologian. The earlier part of his life was dedicated to the natural sciences, and his theories anticipate important discoveries in geology, cosmology, and especially in the physiology of the brain. Later he devoted himself to religion and had mystical experiences: his religious beliefs led to the founding of the New Jerusalem Church and the English Theosophical Society. According to Swedenborg's beliefs, God is Divine Man, whose essence is infinite love; there are correspondences between spiritual ▷ nature and material nature, but the former is alive and the latter is dead; both in God, and in man and nature there are three degrees, those of love, wisdom and use, or end, cause and effect; by a love of each degree man comes into relation with them, and his end is to become the image of his Creator, God. Swedenborg's *Heaven and Hell* and *True Christian Religion* were translated into English in 1778 and 1781, and amongst his followers were the father of the poet ▷ William Blake, and Blake's friend, the sculptor John Flaxman. Swedenborg's doctrines are the starting point of much of Blake's thinking. But Blake, who wrote comments on Swedenborg's doctrines, came to disagree with the philosopher in important respects.

Swift, Graham Colin (b 1949)
Novelist and short-story writer. Born in London and educated at the universities of Cambridge and York, he worked as a part-time teacher of English in London colleges from 1974 to 1983. *Waterland* (1983) reflects on the significance of historical knowledge and the influence of the environment on human identity, through the tragicomic story of several generations of a Fenland family, interspersed with material about the history and geography of the area. His other fiction is: *The Sweet-Shop Owner* (1980); *Shuttlecock* (1981); *Learning to Swim*

and Other Stories (1982); *Out of This World* (1988); *Ever After* (1992).

Swift, Jonathan (1667–1745)
▷ Satirist. He was of an old English family, but his grandfather seems to have lost his fortune on the ▷ Cavalier side in the ▷ Civil Wars of the mid-17th century. The poet ▷ Dryden was his cousin. Swift was educated in Ireland, where he had the future playwright ▷ Congreve as a schoolfellow, and took his degree at Trinity College, Dublin. He began his working life as secretary to the statesman and writer ▷ Sir William Temple in 1689, left him to take orders as a priest in the Church of England in 1694 (receiving a small ecclesiastical office in Ireland), and returned to remain in Temple's service until Temple's death in 1699. Throughout the reign of Queen ▷ Anne (1702–14) he played a large part in the literary and the political life of London, though he was dividing his time between England and Ireland. He contributed some numbers to ▷ Addison's and ▷ Steele's journals ▷ *The Tatler* and ▷ *The Spectator*, and together with ▷ Pope and ▷ Arbuthnot founded the ▷ Scriblerus Club. Politically he at first served the Whig party, but in 1710 he changed over to the Tories, led by Edward Harley, Earl of Oxford, and the brilliant but unreliable ▷ Bolingbroke (Whig and Tory). He served the Tories by his ▷ pamphlet *The Conduct of the Allies* (1711) advocating peace in the War of the ▷ Spanish Succession, and by his conduct of the journal *The Examiner* (1710–11). His assistance was invaluable to the Tory party, who held power from 1711 until the death of the Queen; in 1713 Swift was rewarded by being made Dean of St Patrick's Cathedral, Dublin, an office which he at first held as an absentee. By this time, however, the Queen was dying, and Harley and Bolingbroke, divided over the succession to the throne, were opponents: Bolingbroke offered Swift great rewards for his support, but Swift preferred to remain with Harley, who had lost power and for a time was even in danger of losing his life. In 1714 the Queen died, the Whigs returned to power, Bolingbroke fled, and ▷ George I came over from Germany as king. Swift left England for his Deanery in Ireland. At first he had few friends there, but between 1720 and 1730 he wrote a number of eloquent pamphlets in the interests of the oppressed Irish, and ended by achieving great popularity. The same decade saw the crisis of his relationships with the two women who loved him: Esther Johnson, the 'Stella' of his *Journal to Stella*, compiled 1710–13, and Esther Vanhomrigh, whom he called 'Vanessa'. The relationship with the latter was tragically concluded with her death in 1723; Stella died in 1728. Swift lived as a conscientious and efficient Dean almost to the end of his life, unselfishly disposing of most of his wealth for the poor, but he went out of his mind in 1742.

Swift wrote a great deal of prose, chiefly in the form of pamphlets, and not all of it is satire; *The Conduct of the Allies* is not, for instance, nor are his ▷ sermons. However his great reputation rests principally on his prose satire, and he is especially admired for the very subtle and powerful form of his irony (▷ Figures of speech). The surface of his prose is limpidly clear and beguilingly placid, but his use of it is to enforce by close logic an impossible and often very shocking proposition, which is driven home with distinct and startling imagery. His position was that of a sincere Christian who advocates reason; he despised alike the emptiness of the ▷ Deists and the emotionalism of Puritans. He was at the same time a strong humanitarian, revolted by injustices leading to so much suffering, but despairing of the capacity of the human race to rid itself of its tendency to bestiality and heartlessness. Though a believer in reason (▷ rationalism), he despised the pedantry of so many scholars, and the irrelevances of the 'natural philosophers' in their pursuit of science. He has been censured on two grounds: first, the minor but undoubted one that his disgust at some aspects of human existence derived from his own morbidity, and secondly, the much more controversial one that his vision is in the end negative and destructive. His most famous works are as follows: ▷ *The Battle of the Books* (written 1697, published 1704), a contribution to the dispute between the relative merits of the ancients and the moderns in literature; ▷ *A Tale of a Tub* (1704), a satire on 'corruption in religion and learning' and one of his masterpieces; *Argument against Abolishing Christianity* (1708), a satire on the irreligion of the time; ▷ *Drapier's Letters* (1724), against the monopoly granted by the English government to William Wood to provide the Irish with a copper coinage; ▷ *Gulliver's Travels* (1726); and ▷ *A Modest Proposal* (1729), a most forceful exposure of the conditions of the Irish poor. Swift's poetry has only recently received the critical attention that it deserves. His most admired poem is *Verses on the Death of Dr Swift* (1731), a partly satirical piece in which he imagines public reaction to the news of his death, and then gives his own deliberately deceptive assessment of his life and achievements. *Cadenus and Vanessa* is an equally deceptive poem which purports to give an account of his love affair with Esther Vanhomrigh. It was published, at her request, after her death in 1723. ('Cadenus' is an anagram of 'Decanus' = Dean.)
Bib: Ehrenpreis, I., *Swift, The Man, His Works and The Age*; Nokes, D., *Jonathan Swift, A Hypocrite Reversed*.

Swinburne, Algernon Charles (1837–1909)
Poet and critic. His family background was aristocratic: his father was an admiral and his grandfather a baronet. He was educated at Eton

and at Balliol College, Oxford. The style of his poetry is very distinctive, and his literary sympathies were wide. Swinburne led a dissolute, wild life (his predilection for flagellation is infamous), and produced poetry which shocked those who read it carefully, and intoxicated his youthful contemporaries, especially ▷ Thomas Hardy and the ▷ Pre-Raphaelites. He read eclectically, absorbing ▷ classical literature, the Elizabethans, the US poet Walt Whitman, William Blake (1757–1827), the Marquis de Sade (1740–1814) and ▷ Baudelaire. In his first dramas *The Queen Mother* and *Rosamond* (1860), he was, like most English 19th-century verse dramatists, in the Elizabethan tradition, but his more famous ▷ *Atalanta in Calydon* (1865) as well as his much later *Erectheus* (1876) were in the style of the ancient Greek tragedy of Sophocles. The eroticism of his lyrics in *Poems and Ballads* (1866) owed something to the Latin poet Catullus, and more to Pre-Raphaelite poetry of his own day, chiefly that of ▷ Dante Gabriel Rossetti. In this book he is rebelling against the moral repressiveness of the dominant middle-class attitude to sex; in the *Song of Italy* (1867) and *Songs before Sunrise* (1871) he is siding with Italian political revolt against oppression, in the spirit of the French 19th-century poet Victor Hugo (1802–85). *Chastelard* (1865) and *Bothwell* (1874) are the first two plays, again in Elizabethan style, on Mary Queen of Scots, and were completed by *Mary Stuart* in 1881. A second series of *Poems and Ballads* in 1878 contains tributes to the contemporary French poets, Baudelaire and Théophile Gautier and translations of the medieval French poet François Villon. *Songs of the Springtides* and *Studies in Song* (1880) show the strong inspiration he drew from the sea, and the Arthurian legend *Tristram of Lyonesse* (1881) is a romance of the Middle Ages (▷ medievalism) comparable to those of ▷ William Morris and ▷ Alfred Tennyson, amongst other mid-Victorians. In *Marino Falieri* (1887) he produced a drama on a theme drawn from medieval Venice already used by the poet Byron (*Marino Falieri*, 1821); it was published with another drama, *Locrine*. His later works are: the dramas *The Sisters* (in prose, 1892) and *Rosamund, Queen of the Lombards* (1899); poems – *Poems and Ballads*, 3rd series (1889); *Astrophel* (1894), *A Tale of Balen* (1896), *A Channel Passage* (1904), *The Duke of Gandia* (1908).

Swinburne was thus a poet who drew on a wide range of influences and interests, and was prolific in output. Against the prejudices of his time, which declared that poets should be morally serviceable, he asserted the right to pursue the poetic vocation to express beauty, but this in itself isolated him from contemporary English culture, especially the novel, which emphasized the search for deeper moral experience. Swinburne's influence was strong on his younger contemporaries of the ▷ aesthetic movement.

In his criticism, Swinburne is notable for studies of dramatists who were contemporaries of Shakespeare as well as of Shakespeare himself: *Study of Shakespeare* (1880); *The Age of Shakespeare* (1990). He also wrote a study of William Blake (1868), *A Note on Charlotte Brontë* (1877), *A Study of Victor Hugo* (1886), amongst other criticism.

Swinburne also wrote novels, which are very little known; they have been praised by the distinguished US critic Edmund Wilson in *The Bit between my Teeth*. One of them, *Love's Cross-Currents*, was published in 1905. They show the influence of the Marquis de Sade.

Bib: Gosse, E., *Life*; Lafourcade, G., *La Jeunesse de Swinburne*, literary biography (in English); Chew, S.C., *Swinburne* (critical study); Nicolson, H., *Swinburne*; Welby, T.E., *A Study of Swinburne*; Winwar, P., *The Rossettis and their Circle*; Eliot, T.S., 'Swinburne as a Poet' in *Selected Essays*; Hyder, C.K., *Critical Heritage*.

Sybil, or The Two Nations (1845)

A novel by ▷ Benjamin Disraeli. The 'two nations' are the rich and the poor. The country is shown to be governed by the rich in the interests of the rich – ie the landlords and the employers. Sybil is the daughter of Gerard, a ▷ Chartist leader; she is loved by an enlightened young aristocrat, Charles Egremont, younger brother of an oppressive landlord, Lord Marney. Disraeli gives romantic historical background to his theme by causing Sybil to belong to the same family as the last abbot of Marney, whose lands Lord Marney's ancestors had seized at the time of the dissolution of the monasteries under Henry VIII (1509–47). The poor nation is likewise identified with the Anglo-Saxons, despoiled of their land by the Norman conquerors of the 11th century. This novel, like ▷ *Coningsby* (1844), is part of Disraeli's campaign to renew the Tory party through the Young England movement by inspiring it with a true and disinterested ideology. The novel combines a rather comic element of operatic Romanticism with shrewd observation and social satire.

▷ Social Problem novels.

Syllepsis

▷ Figures of Speech.

Sylvia's Lovers (1863)

An ▷ historical novel by ▷ Elizabeth Gaskell, set in the whaling port of Monkshaven during the Napoleonic wars. The plot revolves around the activities of press-gangs who capture men and force them to work on naval warships. Daniel Robson, Sylvia's father, is hanged after leading an attack on the press-gang's headquarters. Her lover, Charley Kinraid, is seized by the gang, but he sends a note pledging his love and faithfulness via Sylvia's cousin,

Philip Hepburn. Philip conceals the message as he loves Sylvia himself, and she later agrees to marry him, believing Charley to be dead. Years later Charley returns, Philip's treachery is revealed, and Sylvia swears lifelong enmity to her husband. The novel explores gender relations through the marriage of Sylvia and Philip and analyses the interaction of public and private events in its focus on aggression, revenge and rivalry.

Symbolic order

A psychoanalytical term now frequently used in literary criticism. 'Symbolic' in this context refers initially to the notion that language itself is comprised of symbols which stand for things. But, the French psychoanalyst ▷ Jacques Lacan observes that: 'It is the world of words that creates the world of things', and in so doing introduces an 'order' into what would otherwise be disparate units. That process of ordering is motivated by a series of impulses and desires which are not usually available to the conscious mind. Thus, the symbolic order is that order of representations through whose organization the child enters into language and the social order as a gendered human 'subject'. In the case of ▷ Freudian psychoanalysis each symbol refers back to an Oedipal stage (▷ Oedipus complex) which the infant passes through on the way to maturity. In Lacan, the 'unconscious' is said to be structured like a language, already a system of representations through which the individual gendered subject realizes his or her identity. In some respect all literary texts traverse the realm of the symbolic order in that they represent and articulate those images through which reality is grasped discursively.

Symbolism

A name primarily associated with a school of French poets writing in the second half of the 19th century. The movement grew out of the work of ▷ Baudelaire (1821–67) and is above all associated with Paul Verlaine (1844–96), Arthur Rimbaud (1854–91) and ▷ Stephane Mallarmé (1842–98). In addition to Baudelaire, the American writer Edgar Allan Poe (1809–49) and the German music-dramatist Richard Wagner (1813–83) contributed to the shaping of Symbolism. It constituted a development from Romanticism inasmuch as it was poetry of the feelings as opposed to the reason, but it was a reaction against it inasmuch as it was more intellectual in its conception of the way poetry operates. This intellectualism did not imply that the content of poetry should be one of what is ordinarily called ideas: Mallarmé's affirmation was that 'Poetry is not made with ideas; it is made with words'. This looks forward to much 20th-century thought in all the arts, requiring that the artist should above all have respect for the medium in which he has chosen to work; it also anticipates ▷ T. S. Eliot's praise of the English 17th-century ▷ Metaphysical poets that 'they were, at best, engaged in the task of trying to find the verbal equivalent for states of mind and feeling'. Since 'states of mind and feeling' are ultimately mysterious and elusive, the Symbolists emphasized the suggestiveness of poetic language, but though this emphasis on suggestiveness makes much of their poetry obscure, their care for the organization and operation of language kept it from vagueness, in the sense in which the poetry of their English contemporary, the late Romantic ▷ Algernon Swinburne, is very commonly vague. Swinburne is also much concerned with the poetic medium of words, but in such a way that his verse subdues the reader into a state of passive receptivity, whereas the French Symbolists evoke active participation; Swinburne relies for his effect on stimulating emotions already latent in the reader, whereas the Symbolists incite extension of these emotions. T. S. Eliot's essay on Swinburne (in *Selected Essays*) is a help in elucidating the distinction.

The French Symbolists are particularly important in English literature for their decisive influence on the two most important poets writing in English in the first half of the 20th century: T. S. Eliot and ▷ W. B. Yeats. Eliot's understanding of them was much the more intimate and profound, but A. Symons' *The Symbolist Movement in Literature* (1899) acted on them both.

Symons, Arthur (William) (1865–1945)

Poet, critic and leading light of the ▷ Decadent movement in the 1890s. His friends included ▷ Ernest Dowson, ▷ Lionel Johnson and ▷ Oscar Wilde, with whom he socialized at the ▷ Rhymer's Club. He contributed to the ▷ *Yellow Book* and became editor of ▷ *The Savoy* in 1896. His volumes of poetry include *Days and Nights* (1889), *Silhouettes* (1892), *London Nights* (1895) and *Images of Good and Evil* (1899). He introduced ▷ French ▷ Symbolism to English readers in his influential study *The Symbolist Movement in Literature* (1899) and also translated Baudelaire's *Les Fleurs Du Mal* (originally published 1857) and Zola's *L'Assommoir* (originally published 1878). His other critical studies include *An Introduction to the Study of Robert Browning* (1886), *William Blake* (1907), *Charles Baudelaire* (1920) and *Studies in Elizabethan Drama* (1920). He particularly influenced the work of W.B. Yeats (1865–1939).

Synchronic

Adjective used by ▷ Ferdinand de Saussure to describe the analysis of the meaning of a ▷ sign in relation to the other current elements of the language system (▷ *langue*). Saussure juxtaposes the synchronic study of language with the *diachronic* study of language which looks at the historical development of language. This is one of the important polarities in Saussure's theories.

▷ Parole.

Synecdoche

▷ Figures of speech.

Synge, J. M. (John Millington) (1871–1909)
Irish dramatist. He belonged to the Protestant Anglo-Irish segment of Irish society, but at the suggestion of ▷ W. B. Yeats in 1899, he devoted his career to interpreting Irish Celtic peasant life. From this proceeded his remarkable series of dramas which were the chief glory of the drama of the Irish literary renaissance, and of the ▷ Abbey Theatre in Dublin (under the direction of Yeats) through which this movement expressed itself. Part of the Irish dramatic endeavour was to revive poetic drama; Synge wrote in prose, but he exploited with great sensitivity the poetic suggestiveness of the rhythms, diction, and imagery of Irish peasant speech. At the same time he avoided the sentimentalities of late 19th-century romanticism and the falsifications which Irish nationalistic vanity required; the result was that his masterpiece, ▷ *The Playboy of the Western World* (1907) was received with rage and uproar. His other plays are: *The Shadow of the Glen* (1903); *Riders to the Sea* (1904); *The Well of the Saints* (1905); *The Tinker's Wedding* (1907), and his last play – drawn unlike the others from Irish myth – *Deirdre of the Sorrows*, published in 1910 after his death.

Synge also wrote descriptions of Irish peasant life in *The Aran Islands* (1907), *In Wicklow*, and *In County Kerry* (both published 1910).

▷ Irish literature in English.

Bib: Greene, D. H. and Stephens, E. M., *Life*; Price, F., *Synge and Anglo-Irish Drama*; Thornton, W., *J. M. Synge and the Western Mind*.

Syntagmatic

▷ Paradigmatic.

T

Tabard Inn

An inn on the south bank of the Thames, in the borough of Southwark. It was here that ▷ Chaucer's pilgrims assembled before setting out to Canterbury in the ▷ *Canterbury Tales*. The inn was pulled down in 1875.

A tabard was a sleeveless coat worn by heralds and by knights over their armour. The coat was painted or embroidered with armorial bearings, *ie* the crest and emblems of the knight's family or the king whom the herald represented.

Tacitus, Cornelius (AD ? 55 – ? 120)

Roman historian. He was eminent in Roman political and social life, and the son-in-law of Gnaeus Julius Agricola, the governor of Britain who effectively transformed the island into an orderly Roman province. His surviving works are the *Dialogue on Orators*, consisting of conversations about the decay of Roman education; the *Life of Agricola*, including an account of Britain under the rule of his father-in-law; *Germany*, an account of the characteristics of the land and its people, contrasting their freedom and simplicity with the degeneracy of Rome; the *Histories*, a fragment of an account of the Roman Empire during the last 30 years of the 1st century; the *Annals*, a fragment of a history of the Empire in the first half of the century.

Tacitus was a contemporary of the satirical poet ▷ Juvenal; together they represent the last significant phase of classical ▷ Latin literature; both have a strong ethical concern with the condition of Roman civilization, and Tacitus reveres the austere virtues of the pre-imperial republic, though he accepts the Empire as a political necessity. His style is distinguished for its brevity, and his works were an outstanding constituent of English education from the 16th to 19th centuries.

▷ Classical education.

Tail-Rhyme

A verse form used in a number of Middle English romances, which is structured around the repetition of a 'tail' line (often shorter than the rest), after at least two rhyming lines. In ▷ Chaucer's ▷ *Sir Thopas*, for example, the stanzas are built up from a pattern of six lines rhyming aabaab:

Sire Thopas wax a doghty swayn;
Whit was his face as payndemayn,
His lippes rede as rose;
His rode is lyk scarlet in grayn,
And I yow telle in good certayn
He hadde a semely nose.

Talbot, Catherine (1721–70)

Poet, essayist and ▷ letter-writer, admired by contemporaries for her learning. Almost all her works were published posthumously, by her close friend ▷ Elizabeth Carter, including her collection of essays *Reflections on the Seven Days of the Week* (1770), and by Carter's nephew Montagu Pennington, who brought out the *Series of Letters between Mrs Elizabeth Carter and Miss Catherine Talbot* and Talbot's *Works*, both in 1809.

Tale of a Tub, A (1704)

A prose satire by ▷ Jonathan Swift. The title is the same as that of one of the last and least interesting comedies by ▷ Ben Jonson, but Swift ironically explains it in his Preface as derived from the practice of sailors of tossing a tub to a whale in order to divert it from attacking the ship. The ship, Swift explains, is an image of the state, and the whale is ▷ *Leviathan*, ▷ Hobbes' political treatise, from which the ▷ wits of the age drew their dangerous armament of scepticism and ▷ satire; he pretends that he has been employed to divert these attacks by his engaging nonsense. For the next edition (1710), Swift added *An Apology*, in which he discloses his true aim – to satirize 'the numerous and gross corruptions in Religion and Learning'. The real meaning of the title is that Swift is beguiling readers so as to expose them the more effectively to the ferocity of irony (▷ Figures of speech). The central ▷ fable of the *Tale* is the story of three brothers, Martin, Peter and Jack, who inherit three simple coats from their father, whose will enjoins that the coats must in no way be altered. Under the leadership of Peter, however, the brothers find it convenient to alter the coats beyond recognition to comply with fashion. Peter's authority eventually becomes so insanely domineering that Martin and Jack revolt against him; Martin tears off the ornaments on his coat, but stops before he altogether disfigures it; Jack, however, reduces his to a squalid rag. The fable is an ▷ allegory of the ▷ Reformation: Peter represents the Church of Rome, Martin the Church of England, in which Swift was a priest, and Jack the extremer ▷ Protestants, or ▷ Dissenters; the coat is the Word of God as expressed in the New Testament (▷ Bible). Swift's main object of attack is Jack, since he regarded the Dissenters, with their claim to receipt of divine inspiration and their resistance to authority, as the principal threat to the rule of right reason, true religion, and fine civilization in his time. The fable is interspersed with digressions, satirizing the arrogance of those who set up their private intellects or privileged inspiration as guides to their fellow-men; by Section XI the digressions come together with the fable, and Jack is declared to be the leader of the ▷ Aeolists, who expound their doctrines through 'wind', from Aeolus, Greek god of the winds. The satire is essentially an attack on the 'windiness' that Swift discerned in the more pretentious philosophical and religious teaching of his time.

Tale of Two Cities, A (1859)

A novel by ▷ Charles Dickens. The cities are London and Paris, and the tale is a ▷ romance of the French Revolution (1789–94). The hero is a young French nobleman, Charles Darnay, who has renounced his status as nephew of the Marquis de St Evrémonde from hatred of the pre-revolutionary aristocratic oppression, exemplified by his uncle. He marries the daughter of Dr Manette, who at the beginning of the novel has just been released from the Paris prison of the Bastille, where he was confined eighteen years before by the secret influence of the Marquis. Darnay, owing to his aristocratic descent, nearly falls victim to the Terror (a period in the French Revolution when many people were executed without trial), but he is saved by the dissolute Englishman, Sydney Carton, who redeems himself by sacrificing his life for Darnay; this is made possible because Carton and Darnay exactly resemble each other, so that the former is able to substitute himself for the latter. The novel is notable for its scenes of revolutionary violence, for which Dickens was indebted to ▷ Thomas Carlyle's *History of the French Revolution* (1837). The revolutionaries Monsieur and Madame Defarge, and the English body-snatcher Jerry Cruncher, who makes a living by stealing corpses and selling them for medical dissection, are memorable characters.

▷ Historical novels.

Taliesin

A Welsh poet of the 6th century AD whose Welsh name translates as 'bright brow'. Various poems are attributed to him, of which the tales of Urien and Owain (in the legends of ▷ King Arthur called Ryence and Yvain) may be genuine. Taliesin is a half-legendary figure. ▷ Thomas Love Peacock introduces him into his parody of Arthurian romance, *The Misfortunes of Elphin* (1829), and ▷ Tennyson includes him as one of the Knights of the Round Table in his ▷ *Idylls of the King* (1859–72).

Tam O'Shanter (1791)

A poem by ▷ Robert Burns in Lowland Scots dialect. Tam, a drunken farmer, riding home late at night, passes 'Aloway's old haunted Kirk' which he sees lighted up. He creeps nearer to find witches and warlocks dancing to the tune of the bagpipes played by Old Nick. He admires one of the prettiest of the witches and in his excitement cries out: 'Weel done, cutty-sark!' ('short-shirt'). The witches come rushing after him, but he is able to reach the middle of the bridge over the River Doon, beyond which they cannot follow him, though they wrench off his horse's tail. The work shows an effortless adaptation of the mock heroic (▷ heroic, mock) pentameter ▷ couplet to the vigorous and earthy Scots language.

Tamburlaine the Great, Parts I and II

Two dramas in ▷ blank verse by ▷ Christopher Marlowe, published in 1590. The subject is the life of the 14th-century central Asian Timur, who by his conquests rose from obscurity to become one of the most powerful men in Asia. A life of Timur by Pedro Mazia was translated into English and published in 1571.

Part I is a drama of conquest. Tamburlaine is an obscure shepherd chieftain who defeats Mycetes, king of Persia, and subsequently the king's brother, Cosroe, as well. He is next victorious over Bajazet, Emperor of Turkey, and finally captures Damascus from the Soldan (Sultan) of Egypt. His victories are a triumph of immense natural energy and ruthlessness over equally cruel but weak and decadent civilizations. However, Tamburlaine's barbarity is not merely brutish – he worships the potentialities of the human mind, and he falls passionately in love with his bride, Zenocrate, the daughter of the Soldan. Tamburlaine is, in fact, a product of Marlowe's characteristically ▷ Renaissance imagination, fascinated by the earthly magnificence available to men of imaginative power who have the energy of their convictions. The play is essentially non-moral; Tamburlaine is not judged, but presented as though he were a natural force.

Part II was probably written in consequence of the success of Part I, rather than foreseen as a sequel, though critics differ in their opinions about this. Tamburlaine is forced to face the truth that although he feels his energies to be inexhaustible, he cannot triumph over death – first that of Zenocrate, and then his own. This play is, therefore, a tragedy, that man feels himself to be infinite but is nonetheless mortal.

The plays are a most important advance in the use of blank verse as a medium of drama. Hitherto it had been used stiffly and unimaginatively; Marlowe, in these plays, made blank verse eloquent for the first time.

Taming of the Shrew, The

An early comedy by ▷ Shakespeare; probably written 1593–4, and first published in the First Folio of 1623. It may be partly a recasting of an anonymous play, *The Taming of a Shrew* (of uncertain date), and both are based on ▷ George Gascoigne's comedy *Supposes* (1566), itself a translation from the Italian of Ariosto's *Suppositi* (1509).

In a prologue of 'induction', a drunken tinker, Chistopher Sly, is subjected to a practical joke: a nobleman picks him up in his stupor, brings him to his mansion, and causes his servants to explain to him that he is himself a great lord who has for some time been out of his wits. The play is then performed by the nobleman's actors for Sly's benefit. The scene is Verona, and the plot concerns the successful attempts of a gentleman, Petruchio, to tame into obedience and love the wilful and ferocious Katharina, thought to be unmarriageable because of her shrewishness. A subplot concerns the courting of Katharina's sister, Bianca, by Lucentio (who is successful) and by Hortensio, who marries a widow instead. At a feast that concludes the play, Petruchio proves that he has, after all, the most affectionate and docile wife of the three. The play is essentially a comedy of situation, and may be regarded as one of several experiments in different kinds of comic form by Shakespeare in the years 1592–95. However, due to Katharina's complete submission in the closing scene, it has become problematic in 20th-century stage productions and for feminist criticism.

▷ *Querelle des Femmes.*

Tarlton, Richard (d 1588)
A famous comic actor, mentioned in 1583 as one of the Queen's Players, and a favourite clown of ▷ Elizabeth I. He dressed as a rustic ('a clown' was originally a term for a simple-witted country peasant) and was gifted at composing the rough, comic kind of verse known as 'doggerel'; he popularized on the London stage the mixture of song and dance, something like light opera, called country jigs. He wrote a comedy, *The Seven Deadly Sins*, for the Queen's Players, and after his death a number of volumes of popular humour – not necessarily his – were published under the title of *Tarlton's Jests*. He was one of the first actors to become a national figure. He was probably an innkeeper before he became an actor.

▷ Acting, The profession of; Yorick.

Bib: Levi, P., *The Life and Times of William Shakespeare.*

***Task, The* (1785)**
A long ▷ blank-verse poem by ▷ William Cowper, combining ▷ mock heroic with ▷ Georgic and ▷ sentimental elements. It begins in heavily ▷ Miltonic vein with an account of the history of Cowper's own sofa. Later passages concern the joys of rural retirement, gardening, the peculiarities of various local characters, and the moral and religious corruptions of the day, which are condemned at great length. The poem manages to achieve a distinctive and engaging tone, despite the miscellaneousness of its literary elements, and its simplicity of diction foreshadows that of ▷ William Wordsworth in ▷ *Lyrical Ballads.*

Tasso, Torquato (1544–95)
Italian poet. He continued the tradition of the romance ▷ epic, already made famous by ▷ Ludovico Ariosto's ▷ *Orlando Furioso* (1532), in his two major works, *Rinaldo* (1562) and *Jerusalem Delivered* (1581). Tasso's imagination was romantic but in his literary ideal he was ▷ classical, and the thought of the second poem is elevated by the high seriousness of the Catholic ▷ Counter-Reformation. His seriousness made his work very attractive to the English romance epic poet ▷ Edmund Spenser, whose very Protestant ▷ *The Faerie Queene* is also an attempt to rival Ariosto by a poem of similar form but imbued with strong religious feeling. Tasso's impress is strong on parts of *The Faerie Queene*, especially in its ▷ Platonism. *Jerusalem Delivered* was finely translated by Sir Edward Fairfax and published under the title of *Godfrey of Bulloigne or the Recovery of Jerusalem* in 1600.

Tasso was locked up for insanity by Alphonso II, Prince of Ferrara, between 1579–86; subsequent legend attributed his imprisonment to a love affair with the Princess Leonara d'Este.

▷ Translation; Italian influence on English literature.

Bib: Brand, C. P., *Torquato Tasso: a study of the poet and of his contribution to English literature.*

Taste
The 18th century saw the development of 'taste' as an ideal, accompanying the growth and spread of wealth among the middle and upper classes. Among the *nouveaux-riches* especially, good taste seemed to demonstrate good breeding, creating a distance between the person of good taste, and the class from which he or she might have come. Thus, by expressing taste, they could appear to overcome any deficiencies of birth.

Discussions of taste grew partly out of a philosophical concern to identify universal aesthetic criteria. Thinkers including ▷ Hutcheson and ▷ Hume believed in ideal standards of taste, although they did not agree about what these were. Addison, in ▷ *The Spectator* in 1712, likened 'mental taste' to taste of the palate. He also defined taste as 'that faculty of the soul which discerns the beauties of an author with pleasure, and the imperfections with dislike', implying that beauties and imperfections existed in and of themselves, and taste was only a matter of being able to recognize them for what they were. Later in the century, however, more subjective criteria were applied, as when a reviewer in the ▷ *Gentleman's Magazine* in 1767 commented that 'in questions of taste . . . everyone must determine for himself'.

Yardsticks of taste could be applied to almost any sphere of life that lends itself to consumption, including art and literature as well as goods. But a persistent view of 18th-century taste strongly associates it with new appetites for consumer durables, including fashionable houses, furniture, household effects, paintings, sculptures, clothes, jewellery and other possessions. A growing breed of professional

designers, such as ▷ Robert Adam, ▷ Thomas Sheraton and ▷ Josiah Wedgwood, catered to such demands. Taste is also associated with codes of behaviour, such as gentility and displays of ▷ sensibility in order to demonstrate fine feeling. Good taste was thought by many to be a guide to character, so that fine taste in fashion and moral refinement went hand in hand.
Bib: Lynes, R., *The Tastemakers*; Williams, R., *Keywords: A Vocabulary of Culture and Society*; Campbell, C., *The Romantic Ethic and the Spirit of Modern Consumerism.*

Tate Gallery, The
A public gallery for modern paintings and sculpture on the north bank of the Thames in London. It was established by a sugar-merchant, Sir Henry Tate, and opened in 1897. A 'Tate of the North' opened in Liverpool's Albert Dock in 1989; a 'Tate of the West', based on the work of the St Ives school of modern British painting, opened in Cornwall in 1993.

Tate, Nahum (1652–1715)
Educated in Dublin. He assisted ▷ John Dryden with the second part of ▷ *Absalom and Achitophel*, and wrote the libretto of ▷ Purcell's opera *Dido and Aeneas* (performed 1689). His metrical version of the psalms, written with Nicholas Brady, appeared in 1696, and his revised version of *King Lear*, with a happy ending, was that performed through most of the succeeding century. His *Panacaea – a Poem on Tea* appeared in 1700.

Tatler, The
A periodical published three times a week, between 1709 and 1711, by the ▷ Whig author and editor ▷ Richard Steele. It contained ▷ essays and ▷ reviews on topical issues, including politics, entertainment, and fashionable gossip, at first supposedly emanating from the popular chocolate and ▷ coffee-houses of the day. Most of these were written by Steele himself, others by ▷ Joseph Addison. Steele borrowed from ▷ Swift the name 'Isaac Bickerstaffe' as his editorial pseudonym, and became for a time the chronicler and even arbiter of ▷ taste. Increasingly moral issues, such as the evils of drinking and of ▷ duelling, were discussed. In 1711 the *Tatler* was succeeded by ▷ The Spectator.

Taylor, C. P. (Cecil) (1929–81)
Dramatist. Born in Glasgow, but long time resident in the Northeast, Taylor wrote some fifty plays for virtually every type of theatre – from the local village to the West End, via community theatre, television and the ▷ RSC. Much of his work, from his first play to his last, included music, and his wry imagination and capacity for what ▷ Brecht called 'complex seeing' is exemplified in *Ophelia* (1977), which is *Hamlet* from Ophelia's viewpoint, or *Withdrawal Symptoms* (1978) which parallels its heroine's drug withdrawal treatment with the pangs of withdrawal from empire. ▷ J. M. Barrie was the inspiration for *Peter Pan Man* (1979) and *Peter Pan and Emily* (1977) in which Peter Pan becomes involved with a Newcastle working-class family. It is typical of the paradoxical nature of Taylor's career, and of the split in theatre-going audiences, that the majority of those who went to see Harry Secombe in the retitled *The Plummer's Progress* (1974, an adaptation of Carl Sternheim's *Schippi*) and the majority of those who went to see *Good* (1981) would have been extremely unlikely to recognise him as the author of both plays.

Taylor, Harriet (1807–58)
Writer, philosopher and poet and leading light of the early ▷ feminist movement. Her friends included ▷ Harriet Martineau, ▷ Sarah Flower Adams and later ▷ John Stuart Mill, whom she eventually married after an extended friendship. It was Taylor who influenced Mill's views on female emancipation and the political education of the working classes; all his work from 1840 onwards including *The Principles of Political Economy* (1848) and ▷ *On Liberty* (1859) was written in collaboration with her. She is best remembered for her eloquent essay 'The Enfranchisment of Women' published in the ▷ *Westminister Review* in 1851.
Bib: Hayek, F.A., *John Stuart Mill and Harriet Taylor.*

Taylor, Jane (1783–1824) and Ann (1782–1866)
Authors of popular children's books in verse: *Original Poems for Infant Minds* (1804), *Rhymes for the Nursery* (1806), in which appears 'Twinkle twinkle, little Star' (parodied by ▷ Lewis Carroll in *Alice in Wonderland*, 1865), and *Hymns for Infant Minds* (1810).
▷ Children's literature.

Taylor, Jeremy (1613–67)
Clergyman and religious writer. He was one of the representatives of Anglicanism in its most flourishing period, and his career shows the vicissitudes of the ▷ Church of England in the 17th century. The son of a barber, he was educated at a Cambridge grammar school and in the University of Cambridge. His talent for preaching attracted the favour of ▷ Archbishop Laud, to whom (and to ▷ King Charles I) he became chaplain. In 1645 he was captured by Parliamentary troops, and until 1660, while the Church of England was in abeyance, he was private chaplain to the Earl of Carbery. It was during this period that he wrote much of his best work. Later, he was made Bishop of Dromore in Ireland, where, contrary to his inclination, he was obliged to discipline clergy

hostile to the Anglican establishment. He thus stands in contrast to his former patron, the authoritarian Archbishop Laud, and the change marks not merely a difference in personalities but the growth of the spirit of Anglican tolerance in the later 17th century. His *A Discourse of the Liberty of Prophesying* (1646) was a plea for religious toleration; his other outstanding works were his *The Rule and Exercises of Holy Living* (1650) and *The Rule and Exercises of Holy Dying* (1651).

▷ Sermons.

Bib: Stranks, C. J., *Jeremy Taylor*; Gosse, E., *Jeremy Taylor*; Smith, L. P., *The Golden Grove: Selected Passages from Jeremy Taylor*.

Taylor, John (c 1580–1653)

Poet and miscellanist. John Taylor was apprenticed, in early life, to a London waterman (ferryman). He enlisted in the Navy, making several voyages, and then returned to London to ply his trade as a waterman. Hence he became known as 'The Water Poet'. Taylor was an extraordinarily prolific writer. His large collected edition – *All the Works of John Taylor the Water Poet* (1630) – though it contains over 60 separate works, does not begin to represent his complete *oeuvre*. Almost any topic attracted his attention, and almost every topic did. He was famous for proposing preposterously difficult travel-projects, such as travelling from London to Edinburgh and back without spending any money, or rowing a paper boat. On the strength of these proposals, he would solicit subscriptions from the curious, who would then read his accounts of his difficulties and dangers. His death followed his last trip from London to Gravesend and back: a journey made all the more difficult by the fact of his being lame.

Bib: Notestein, W., *Four Worthies*.

Taylor, Tom (1817–80)

Dramatist, editor and critic, Taylor was born in Sunderland the son of a self-educated farmer turned brewer. He attended Glasgow University and was made a fellow of Trinity College, Cambridge. He became a professor of English literature at University College, London from 1845–7 and also practised briefly as a barrister before taking up a position in the Health Department where he remained for twenty years. From 1874 until his death in 1880 he was editor of ▷ *Punch* magazine. He was also an enthusiastic amateur actor. In addition he wrote 80 plays, leading articles for ▷ newspapers such as ▷ *The Morning Chronicle* and *The Daily News* and was an art critic for *The Times* and *The Graphic* as well as contributing regularly to *Punch*. He was the resident dramatist at the Olympic Theatre (1853–60) and the Haymarket (1857–70). His dramatic styles included farce, pantomine, historical verse drama and comedy, but he excelled in ▷ melodramas such as *Plot and Passion* (with John Lang, 1853) and *The Ticket-of-Leave Man* (1863). His comic plays, including *Masks and Faces* (with ▷ Charles Reade, 1852), *To Oblige Benson* (1854), *The Overland Route* (1860) and *New Men and Old Acres* (with A.W. Dubourg, 1869), also contain a degree of social perception. In addition to tempering melodrama with ▷ realism, Taylor's *The Ticket-of-Leave Man* (1863) focuses on the rehabilitation of ex-criminals and presents an accurate picture of lower middle-class culture. Others, including *Birth* (1870), rework his favourite themes of class-prejudice and the conflict between industrialists and the landed aristocracy.

Bib: Tolles, W., *Tom Taylor and the Victorian Drama*; Banham, M. (ed.), *Plays by Tom Taylor*.

Tel Quel

A magazine, for many years the leading French *avant-garde* journal. Its name was taken from a work by Paul Valéry (1871–1945) and it was edited by Philippe Sollers (b 1936), novelist, theorist and husband of the feminist writer, Julia Kristeva. In political terms, the magazine's sympathies were Marxist-Leninist-Maoist. It welcomed the student demonstrations of May 1968 with an issue entitled 'The Revolution, here and now' and its programme for a French 'Cultural Revolution' was backed by figures such as the composer Pierre Boulez (b 1925) and the novelist and theoretician Jean Ricardou (b 1932). *Tel Quel* provided a forum for left-wing intellectuals and gave rise to the *Tel Quel* group. Their joint publication, *Théorie d'ensemble* (1968), contained *inter alia* ▷ Jacques Derrida's essay 'La Différance', ▷ Michel Foucault's piece 'Distance, aspect, origine' (discussing Alain Robbe-Grillet and Sollers) and ▷ Roland Barthes' 'Drame, poème, roman' (on Sollers). Alongside its support for radical political and theoretical positions, the magazine did much to promote the cause of a literary counter-orthodoxy, represented by ▷ Sade, ▷ Lautréamont, George Bataille and Robbe-Grillet.

In the late 1970s, *Tel Quel* began to lose its radical impetus. Sollers renounced his theoretical persuasions, sympathised with the right-wing group, ▷ Les Nouveaux Philosophes, and embraced ▷ Catholicism. From 1982, the magazine changed its name to *L'Infini* and found itself a new publisher.

***Tempest, The* (1611)**

A play by ▷ Shakespeare probably written in 1611, and regarded by some as the last completely by his own hand. The plot does not derive from any known principal source. The setting of the island with its aboriginal inhabitant Caliban, and the shipwreck with which the play opens, owe details to travel books of the time, especially a ▷ pamphlet by

Sir George Somers (1609) about his voyage to and shipwreck on the Bermudas.

Prospero, Duke of Milan, with his daughter Miranda, has been expelled from his duchy, where he had avoided the task of government for the sake of devoting himself to secret learning, by his wicked brother, Antonio. At the opening of the play Prospero and Miranda have lived on a lonely island for many years, served by the brutish savage Caliban and the sprite Ariel. By his magic powers, Prospero contrives the shipwreck on the island of his enemies – his brother Antonio, Alonso, King of Naples, who had conspired with Antonio, Alonso's wicked brother Sebastian and a few courtiers. Also shipwrecked, but separated from the others, is Ferdinand, the virtuous son of Alonso; each believes the other to be drowned. The situation is such that Prospero, if he wishes, can use his supernatural powers to execute vengeance on his enemies; instead he uses it to bring about reconciliation and forgiveness. Ferdinand, after a brief trial in which he is subjected to austere labours, is united with Miranda. Alonso's company is also subjected to trials, but finally reunited with Ferdinand and reconciled to Prospero, who discloses himself. A subplot concerns the farcical attempt of Trinculo and Stephano, Alonso's servants, to rob Prospero of his instruments of magic, with the aid of Caliban.

The play is the most symbolic of Sheakespeare's plays. Prospero is in the tradition of the ▷ Platonic mage, who, according to one line of ▷ Renaissance thought, could achieve extraordinary power by uniting exceptional wisdom with exceptional virtue. Miranda unites the innocence of nature with the nobility of high breed; her union with Ferdinand and their restoration to a corrupt world symbolize the renewal of vital forces. Caliban, on the other hand, represents the unredeemably brutal side of nature, and also the inherently vicious propensities of the body: he can be forced to serve, but he cannot be elevated. The other characters represent degrees of redeemability: the 'good old lord' Gonzalo has always been virtuous though he has been made to serve evil ends; Alonso has done evil but is capable of repentance; Antonio and Sebastian do not repent and can only be intimidated; the rest are merely passive and, in Antonio's words, 'take suggestion as a cat laps milk'.

The Tempest is the last of the four plays sometimes called ▷ romances, the others being ▷ *Pericles*, ▷ *Cymbeline*, ▷ *The Winter's Tale*. An interesting feature of it is that while the other plays in the group are very loosely constructed in terms of time and place, *The Tempest* has the greatest unity in these respects of all Shakespeare's plays: the action is restricted to the island, and occupies only three hours.

▷ Colonialism.

Temple, Dorothy
▷ Osborne, Dorothy; Temple, Sir William.

Temple, Laura Sophia (1763–c 1820)
Poet. A neglected writer whose work was admired at the time (for example, by ▷ Coleridge) and whose poetry marks her out as central to the ▷ Romantic tradition. Three collections remain extant: *Poems* (1805), *Lyric and Other Poems* (1808) and *The Siege of Zaragoza and Other Poems* (1812). She and her husband became destitute towards 1820 and they appealed to the Royal Literary Fund for support, but nothing is known of them after this date. The request mentions another long poem in manuscript, but this has been lost. Temple used a wide range of forms, including ▷ ballads, ▷ sonnets, ▷ lyrics, and the ▷ dramatic monologue, and her subject matter was fittingly Romantic, in that she focused on ▷ nature, temporality, and the power of poetry, with occasional excursions into ▷ orientalism.

Temple, Sir William (1628–99)
Statesman, diplomatist, essayist. In English literature Temple is especially known as the patron of ▷ Jonathan Swift, who lived at his house (Moor Park) as his secretary from 1689 to 1694, and again from 1696 till Temple's death. Temple's most famous ▷ essay was his contribution to the controversy about the relative merits of ancient (*ie* Greek and Latin) and modern literature. Entitled *Of Ancient and Modern Learning*, it praised the *Letters of Phalaris* as a notable example of ancient work. Unfortunately the great scholar ▷ Bentley exposed the Letters as a forgery. Temple's embarrassment provoked Swift to come to his aid with his first notable essay, ▷ *The Battle of the Books*. Temple was a model of the cultivated aristocracy of his time, and his essays (chiefly on political matters) were regarded as setting standards for correctness and elegance of expression. His wife was ▷ Dorothy Osborne and her letters (▷ A letter writing) to him before their marriage (in 1655) were first published in 1888; her position resembled that of ▷ Samuel Richardson's heroine in his novel ▷ *Clarissa*, inasmuch as her parents were opposed to the marriage. Temple's memoirs were published by Swift in 1709.
Bib: Lives by C. Marburg and H. E. Woodbridge.

***Tenant of Wildfell Hall, The* (1848)**
A novel by ▷ Anne Brontë, first published under the ▷ pseudonym Acton Bell. The tenant of the title is Helen Graham, who has recently moved

into the neighbourhood with her son, Arthur. The narrator, Gilbert Markham, falls in love with her, but is puzzled by her relationship with her landlord, Lawrence. Markham ignores the village rumours until he overhears Helen and Lawrence in intimate conversation, after which he assaults Lawrence. Helen reveals the story of her past in a lengthy journal which tells of her unfortunate marriage to Arthur Huntingdon, who, after a short period of happiness with Helen, slipped back into a life of drunkenness and infidelity. It is revealed that Helen has left Arthur to seek refuge with Lawrence, who is in fact her brother. She later returns to Arthur to nurse him through a fatal illness. After his death, Markham and Helen are able to pursue their relationship, and finally agree to marry. The novel was received as a morbid story, especially since it came from a woman's pen. Anne Brontë's comment in the Preface to the 1850 edition highlights the double standards imposed on women writers: 'I am at a loss to conceive how a man should permit himself to write anything that would be *really disgraceful* to a woman, or why a woman should be censured for writing anything that would be proper and becoming for a man.'

Tennant, Emma (b 1937)
Novelist. Her work combines a ▷ feminist perspective with a ▷ postmodernist use of allusion, parody, and fantasy, and in these respects has some affinity with that of ▷ Angela Carter. *The Time of the Crack* (1973) and *The Last of the Country House Murders* (1974) are both set in the future; the former is an apocalyptic satire, while the latter is a black comedy which parodies country house detective fiction. *The Bad Sister* (1978) satirizes the divisive effect upon women of social roles and expectations: the heroine finds herself inhabited by a demented other self, and the book itself is split between a prosaic account of contemporary society and a realm of dreams and fantasy. The expression of feminist revolt through a disturbed mental state has antecedents in *The Golden Notebook* by ▷ Doris Lessing, and in the work of ▷ Virginia Woolf. Tennant's other novels are: *The Colour of Rain* (1964); *Hotel de Dream* (1976); *Wild Nights* (1979); *Alice Fell* (1980); *Queen of Stones* (1982); *Woman Beware Woman* (1983); *Black Marina* (1985); *The Adventures of Robina, by Herself* (1986); *The House of Hospitalities* (1987).

Tennyson, Alfred (1809–92)
Poet, usually known, after he was made a baron in 1884, as Alfred, Lord Tennyson. Fourth of twelve children (two others of whom, Frederick and Charles, were also poets) of a Church of England clergyman. The family was long established among Lincolnshire landowners, but the poet's father had been disinherited by his grandfather, and Alfred's childhood and youth were spent in comparative poverty; he was partly educated by his father but later he went to Trinity College, Cambridge. Tennyson's family background does not conform to the 20th-century ideal of the family in the 19th century. His father was a violent alcoholic rector, his mother was distressed and wretched, two of his brothers became insane and a third was also an alcoholic. Images of mental illness, doubt and conflict thus naturally fracture Tennyson's work, especially the most interesting and intense poems. His earliest work (*Poems by Two Brothers*, in which his brother collaborated) is unimportant, and he did not begin to win fame until the 1840s. Thereafter he achieved popularity unequalled by any other English poet in his own lifetime. In 1850 he was made Poet Laureate (in succession to William Wordsworth, 1770–1850) and in 1884 he was made a Baron – the only English poet ever to have been ennobled purely for his poetry. This popularity arose from two facts: he had, on the one hand, exquisite poetic skill; he was, on the other hand, in his mental and emotional outlook, very representative of his age. He had a characteristically Victorian insular patriotism; he was both exhilarated and disturbed, like so many of his contemporaries, by the social and industrial changes of the age, and he was distressed by the shaking of traditional religious beliefs by the scientists – in his youth, the geologist ▷ Charles Lyell (*The Principles of Geology*, 1830–33), and in his middle age, the biologist ▷ Charles Darwin (*The Origin of Species*, 1859). He countered this threat from the intellect by an emotional, sometimes sentimental, idealism which was extremely acceptable to the middle-class reading public. His idiom was that of the ▷ Romantics – Wordsworth, Shelley (1792–1822), and especially Keats (1795–1821) – but his formal technique was as meticulous as that of the 18th century poets; the combination was both beguiling and reassuring. Physically and in his dress, he was imposing and romantic, and with this appearance he typified the poet for the nation.

The first three books of his sole authorship (1830, 1832, 1842) include much of what is now considered his best, most disturbing and challenging work – eg *Mariana*, ▷ 'The Lady of Shalott', *Ulysses*, ▷ *Morte d'Arthur*, ▷ *The Lotos-Eaters*. In 1833 his great friend, Arthur Hallam, died, and the great grief of this loss produced the series of elegies which are usually considered to be his masterpiece – ▷ *In Memoriam* A.H.H., eventually published in 1850. Queen Victoria declared that she valued it next to the Bible; however, it was the mixture of picturesque Romanticism and acceptable idealism in ▷ *The Princess* (1850) which greatly extended Tennyson's popularity with the general public. In 1852 he produced the most impressive of his public poems, *Ode on the Death of the Duke of Wellington*, and in

1854, the most popular of English patriotic poems, the ▷ *Charge of the Light Brigade*. ▷ *Maud* (1854) is one of the most singular of his works, evoking mentally deranged states, and written at the time of the Crimean War.

Other works: his immensely popular cycle of tales, ▷ *Idylls of the King* (1859–72); dialect poems, eg *The Northern Farmer* (1864); narrative, in the tradition of Wordsworth, ▷ 'Enoch Arden' (1864); ▷ ballads, notably *The Revenge* (1880), and a number of verse dramas, of which the most successful is *Becket* (1884).

Taste in the early 20th century on the whole turned against his poetry; the accusation of one of his earliest critics, ▷ John Stuart Mill, (reviewing the 1832 volume) that Tennyson's poetry is deficient in power of thought anticipated modern opinion, which has been until recently, attuned to T.S. Eliot (1888–1965) and the 17th-century Metaphysical poets. It was still admitted that he had an extraordinary ear for cadence and rhythm, but it was implied that this virtue did not compensate for the mediocrity of his intelligence. However, this tribute to his 'fine ear' amounted to acknowledgement that Tennyson was a fine artist. His first three books and *In Memoriam* contain poems in which some of the deeper emotional conflicts of his time are beautifully articulated. In recent years readings of Victorian poetry have freed themselves from modernist valuations, and Tennyson's work has been re-read with interest for its strong acknowledgement and analysis of problematic areas of psychic and social existence; questions of mental health, the role of women, war and economic conditions.

Bib: Sinfield, A., *Alfred Tennyson*; Nicholson, H., *Tennyson*: *Aspects of his Life*, *Character and Poetry*; Palmer, D.J. (ed.), *Tennyson*; Killham, J., *Tennyson and The Princess*; Killham, J. (ed.), *Essays on Tennyson*; Ricks, C., *Tennyson*; Ricks, C. (ed.), *Poems*.

Terence (Publius Terentius Afer), (? 190 – ? 159 BC)

Latin dramatist. His six comedies are adaptations of older Greek comedies, especially those of Menander (342–291 BC). They have been praised for the purity of their Latin and criticized for their deficiency of comic power. They were known, read and imitated throughout the Middle Ages and afterwards, eg his *Heautontimorumenos* (163) was adapted by ▷ Chapman into *All Fools* (1605), and his *Andria* (166) was adapted by Steele into *The Conscious Lovers* (1722). Other dramatists such as ▷ Ben Jonson used some of his themes and his comic devices such as the role of the crafty slave (*eg* in ▷ *Volpone*). The time-act structure apparent in Terence's comedies eventually came to be the model for publication of plays in England, though it is debatable how much influence it ever had on their composition and production.

Terror, The (Reign of)

The period in the ▷ French Revolution from June 1793 to July 1794 under the dictatorship of Robespierre, when many people were executed without trial merely because they were suspected of opposition to the Revolution. The term has since been applied to similar regimes in other periods and countries.

Terza rima

The pattern used by the Italian poet ▷ Dante in his long poem the ▷ *Divine Comedy*. Each line is of 11 syllables, the last syllable unaccented, and the rhyme scheme follows the pattern *aba bcb cdc ded* etc. Examples in English are rare, and consist of 10-syllable lines. One reason for the scarce use of *terza rima* in English is the paucity of rhyming words in the language, by comparison with Italian. The form was first used in English by ▷ Thomas Wyatt in his *Satires* and paraphrases of the ▷ Psalms, an example from which follows:

My Poyntz, I cannot frame my tune to feign,
To cloak the truth for praise without desert
Of them that list all vice for to retain.
I cannot honour them that sets their part
With Venus and Bacchus all their life long;
Nor hold my peace of them, although I smart.

Sir Thomas Wyatt, 'Of the courtier's life, written to John Poyntz'.

In the ▷ Romantic period ▷ Shelley used the form with great success in his long poem *The Triumph of Life*, unfinished at his death in 1822.

***Tess of the D'Urbervilles, A Pure Woman* (1891)**

A novel by ▷ Thomas Hardy. The heroine is Tess Durbeyfield, daughter of a poor west-country peasant who learns that he may be a descendant of the aristocratic D'Urbervilles. The novel is about her tragic predicament between her brutal seducer, Alec Stoke D'Urberville, and her husband Angel Clare. Both Alec and Angel are intruders into Tess's environment; Alec (who has no proper title to his aristocratic surname) is the son of a north-country businessman who has bought his way into the class of gentry; Angel is the son of a conventional clergyman and has dissociated himself from his background by acquiring vague liberal ideas. When Tess confesses to him her seduction, his old-fashioned prejudices overcome him and he casts her off, repenting when it is too late. Forsaken by her husband, Tess is faced by renewed assaults from Alec, whom she eventually murders. After a period of hiding with Angel, Tess is tried, condemned and executed for murder. The finest passages of the book are the episodes set in the peaceful environment of Talbothays Dairy Farm, where

Tess meets Alec, and the grim surroundings of Flintcomb Ash, where she works when Angel has forsaken her. Tess is represented as the victim of cruel chance – an example of Hardy's belief that the world is governed by ironical fate – but as usual in his work it is the intruders who are the instruments of the destructive force.

Testament of Cresseid, The
A poem by ▷ Robert Henryson (late 15th century), which provides an ending to Criseyde's story. In ▷ Chaucer's ▷ *Troilus and Criseyde*, there is little account of Criseyde's life in the Greek camp, after her affair with Diomede has begun: the narrative focus in Book V is on ▷ Troilus' history and his end. However, the old narrator of Henryson's poem, who finds his pleasures in books, discovers another 'quair' (book) containing 'the fatall destenie/Of fair Cresseid, that endit wretchitlie' (61–2).

The contents of that 'quair' form the substance of Henryson's poem, which relates how Cresseid is abandoned by Diomede, is stricken with leprosy and has a final meeting with Troilus, in which neither wholly recognizes the other. Something about the leper's glance triggers a memory of Cresseid for Troilus (and he throws her a purse of money) but Cresseid does not discover the identity of her generous patron until he has left. She has time only to compose a testament (a will), leaving a ring to Troilus, before she dies.

The poem is a consummate exercise in the art of abbreviation: it is only 616 lines long and contains a collection of short poetic forms, being called a 'ballet' and encompassing a visionary sequence (in which the classical gods descend to judge Cresseid), two formal complaints and an epitaph. The significance of Cresseid's affliction with leprosy is open to a number of interpretations, and in the poem final endings and definitive judgements about Cresseid are juxtaposed with speculation and hearsay about her life and death. The *Testament* does not end Cresseid's life as a narrative subject. Although Henryson's poem disrupts rather than continues Chaucer's text, it was printed in the 1532 edition of Chaucer's work as if it formed the sixth book of *Troilus and Criseyde*: thus it was well known to subsequent readers of Chaucer's work, including ▷ Shakespeare.

▷ Troy.

Bib: Fox, D. (ed.), *The Poems of Robert Henryson*.

Text
The word text is employed in several specific ways alongside a general, rather modish use to refer to pieces of literary writing and some other kinds of cultural production (e.g. 'filmic text').

1 It is used to refer expressly to the words on the page as distinct from any interpretation that might be given of them in processes of 'close reading' (▷ Practical Criticism).

2 In textual editing, it indicates a particular version of the work when there are textual variants.

3 Finally, in ▷ poststructuralist theory, particularly that of ▷ Roland Barthes, text is opposed to work. Barthes' distinction here is similar to the one he made between ▷ writerly and readerly. The writerly text is adventurous, plural, open, surprising and ▷ avant-garde; it is where ▷ écriture is to be found. The work, however, is closed (▷ closure), stereotyped, un-demanding and captive to mundane representations.

Bib: Barthes, R., *Image-Music-Text*.

Thackeray, William Makepeace (1811–63)
Novelist. He had a conventional upper-class education at a public school – Charterhouse – and Cambridge University, which he left in 1830 without taking a degree. For the next sixteen years he worked as a comic illustrator and journalist, writing satirically humorous studies of London manners in *The Yellowplush Correspondence* (▷ *Fraser's Magazine* 1837–8), and *Snob Papers* (▷ *Punch* 1846–7) – later published as ▷ *The Book of Snobs*; parodies of the contemporary fashion for the criminal-hero (*Catherine*, 1839, and ▷ *Barry Lyndon*, 1844); humorous travel books (*The Paris Sketch-Book* and *The Irish Sketch-Book*, 1840 and 1843), tales of humour and pathos (*The Great Hoggarty Diamond*, 1841).

His first major novel, ▷ *Vanity Fair*, came out in the year 1848 (it was published serially, as were most of his novels, and the date given is that of completion); it was a social panorama of the English upper-middle classes, satirizing their heartlessness and pretentiousness at the height of their prosperity; it was followed by novels in a similar field: ▷ *Pendennis* (1850), and ▷ *The Newcomes* (1853–5). ▷ *Henry Esmond* (1852) is an historical novel set in the reign of Queen Anne (1702–14) and represents Thackeray's strong taste for the 18th century; *The Virginians* (1859) is its sequel in 18th-century England and North America. The same taste for 18th-century England is expressed in his historical lectures, *The Four Georges*, published in 1860. In 1855 he published his comic-romantic ▷ children's story, *The Rose and the Ring*. In 1860 he became editor of the famous ▷ *Cornhill Magazine*, and contributed to it ▷ *The Adventures of Philip* (1861–2), his essays *Roundabout Papers* and the novel, unfinished at his death, *Denis Duval*.

Thackeray was once considered the great counterpart to ▷ Charles Dickens in the mid-Victorian novel (the years 1850–70). Dickens conveyed a panorama of the lower half of society and Thackeray of the upper half; both were great humorists, with a strong bent for satire and a capacity for social indignation. Thackeray is now chiefly remembered for *Vanity Fair*. His imaginative intensity is seen to be less than that of Dickens and the sentimentality with which he counterbalanced his satire is the more conspicuous. Like Dickens, he opposed the ▷ utilitarianism of his age by an appeal to spontaneous affection and he tried to counterbalance it by an appeal to 18th-century proportion and elegance, but he also felt impulses of ▷ Romanticism, which in Dickens are far more uninhibited.

Bib: Ray, G.N., *Life*; Tillotson, G., *Thackeray the Novelist*; Stevenson, L., *The Showman of Vanity Fair*; Stevenson, L., ed. in *Great Victorians*; Studies by J. Dodd, L. Ennis, J.Y. T. Greig and G.N. Ray; Tillotson, G., and Hawes, D. (eds.), *The Critical Heritage*; Carey, J., *Thackeray: Prodigal Genius*; Shillingsburg, P.L., *Pegasus in Harness: Victorian Publishing and W.M. Thackeray*.

Theatre of Cruelty

A style of theatre developing out of the work of ▷ Antonin Artaud, introduced to English audiences in 1964 by a 'Theatre of Cruelty' season at the LAMDA Theatre arranged by ▷ Peter Brook and Charles Marowitz. These experiments were developed in Brook's productions of Peter Ulrich Weiss's *Marat/Sade* in 1964 and the improvised play *US* in 1966. Theatre of Cruelty aims to shock the audience out of its complacency and restricted conventional behaviour into an awareness of the primitive forces within human nature. To do this it requires a committedly non-rationalistic approach to acting.

Bib: Artaud, A., *The Theatre and its Double*; Styan, J. L., *The Dark Comedy*.

Theatre of the Absurd

A name given by the critic Martin Esslin to describe the work of a number of dramatists, including Ionesco, Genet, ▷ Beckett and ▷ Pinter. These and other authors do not belong to any 'school' as such but their plays often have in common the sense that human existence is without meaning. The idea is reflected in the form as well as the content of the plays, by the rejection of logical construction, and the creation of meaningless speeches and silences. Such devices helped to develop new forms of theatre during the 1950s and 60s no longer reliant on outmoded dramatic conventions.

Bib: Esslin, M., *The Theatre of the Absurd*.

Theatres

No special buildings were erected in England for dramatic performances until late in the 16th century. The earliest form of regular drama in England was the ▷ Mystery Plays, which began as interpolations in religious ritual in the churches. By the 15th century these plays were being performed at religious festivals in towns on movable stages or ▷ pageants, conveyed from point to point on wagons. In country districts at seasonal festivals such as ▷ May Day, primitive dramas of pagan origin – jigs, May games, Morris dances – were performed in the open air. The absence of theatres did not indicate scarcity of drama, but its wide pervasion of ordinary life.

Secular dramas of entertainment, such as we know today, grew up in the 16th century; they were performed in the courtyards of inns and in the great halls of country mansions, royal palaces, Oxford and Cambridge colleges, and the ▷ inns of court of London. The performers were professional actors who were usually incorporated in companies attached to noble or royal households, but by degrees this attachment became increasingly nominal, and actors required places where they could work independently and permanently. Hence the first playhouse, known as The Theatre, was erected by ▷ James Burbage in Shoreditch outside the City of London, in 1576–7. It was followed by many others, including the ▷ Globe (1598) which is the most famous owing to its association with Shakespeare. None of these theatres survived the middle of the 17th century, but a contemporary sketch of one of them (The Swan) exists, and there is a detailed description in the contract for the Fortune (1600).

The designs owe nothing to those of ancient Greece and Rome (unlike contemporary Italian theatres) but seem to be based on a mixture of the typical inn-yard and the bear-pits, *ie* the arenas for fights between animals. The structures were usually of wood, and round or hexagonal, though they might be rectangular. The centre was an arena exposed to the open air, where the poorer spectators stood; the richer ones sat in galleries surrounding the arena. The stage was probably divided into two or three parts; the main ('apron') stage projected into the arena, so that spectators surrounded it on three sides. The wall at the back of this stage was flanked by doors for exits and entries, between which there was probably a rear stage, though the sketch of the Swan does not include this. Above the rear stage there was probably an upper stage (to represent *eg* a castle wall); above this again, possibly a musicians' gallery. A canopy may have extended partly across the apron stage. The projection of the apron stage – upon which spectators sometimes actually sat – shows that the theatre of Shakespeare's day was not adapted to convey illusion like the typical modern theatre; scenery was scarcely used, though 'props' (*ie* thrones, objects representing flowery banks, etc.) were brought on and off.

Such were the 'public theatres'; there were also 'private theatres' such as the Blackfriars which came into the hands of Shakespeare's company in 1608. Pictures or accounts of these do not survive, but they were roofed, probably used some kind of artificial lighting, and may have provided more opportunity for scenery.

Scenic spectacle was certainly not unknown or despised by Shakespeare's contemporaries; in the reign of ▷ James I there was a pronounced fashion for ▷ masques, an early form of opera, in which a poet such as ▷ Ben Jonson and a designer such as ▷ Inigo Jones collaborated.

It was only after the Restoration of the Monarchy in 1660 that the theatre began to assume its modern shape, with a proscenium arch dividing the audience from the stage, thus providing greater scope for scenery and illusion. One of the earliest English theatres of this style was ▷ Drury Lane, which had already been a theatre in the reign of James I and was rebuilt in 1662. From this time the theatre became the special entertainment for the middle and upper classes, largely cut off from the mass of the people, and it has, on the whole, remained that way. It was still, however, a place of influence, and in 1737 the government found it convenient to pass a Licensing Act which had the effect of restricting the theatres in London to three – the Haymarket opera house, Drury Lane and Covent Garden – until the act was repealed in 1843, though licences were issued for a few theatres in the provinces, at Bath, Bristol and Liverpool. The law greatly hindered the development of a creative drama in 18th-century England, though it was a period of great actors and actresses.

The repeal of the Licensing Act in 1843 was followed by widespread building of theatres, but there was no live taste for intelligent new plays until ▷ George Bernard Shaw, in the last decade of the 19th century, began to create one. In the 20th century there has been a sharp division between the commercial theatres which provide intellectually commonplace entertainment, and the theatres of the intelligentsia. Two companies of the latter kind have an official national status, ▷ The Royal Shakespeare Company and the ▷ National Theatre. The Royal Shakespeare Company produces Shakespeare's and other dramatists' plays at Stratford-on-Avon and, formerly, at the Aldwych Theatre in London. Since 1982 the Royal Shakespeare Company have performed at their new base in the Barbican Centre near ▷ St Pauls, where they are spaciously accommodated in a London home of their own, similar to that of the National Theatre which, after opening at the Old Vic Theatre in 1963 transferred to a new site on the South Bank in Waterloo in 1976–77. Under the guidance of Trevor Nunn and Sir Peter Hall respectively, the two national companies have inventively produced the English repertoire from Shakespeare and his contemporary dramatists to classical and modern European and American drama. They have increasingly benefited from funding by the Arts Council whose key role in freeing the British theatre since World War II from the shackles of economic success at the expense of art cannot be underestimated. To the extent that both the great companies have enjoyed a certain artistic franchise, the gap between them and the more radical theatrical groupings has narrowed.

Of these the English Stage Company, founded in 1955 and housed for years in the Royal Court Theatre in London, is the most important. It pioneered new modes of dramatic expression and encouraged new dramatists by giving them a space for their writings. John Osborne's *Look Back in Anger* (1956) was launched at the Royal Court and went on to become a milestone in the history of modern British drama. The 1960s saw the blossoming in London and in Britain of ▷ fringe theatre which corresponded to the New York Off Broadway and Off-Off Broadway. It was associated with Americans such as Charles Marowitz and Jim Haynes, mostly working at different improvised venues in London. Their work, and that of many of the dramatists of the 1960s and 1970s, above all shows the influence of ▷ Brecht and ▷ Artaud. The theatrical scene in 1980s Britain was bleak, as resources were dwindling and funding bodies like the Arts Council were increasingly reluctant to underwrite commercially non-viable plays. The re-emergence in the metropolis of a new theatre of farce and social comedy is an indication that the age which was once hailed as that of the new radical Elizabethans is on the wane, as new norms of quietist conformism are endorsed in the theatre.

Thelwall, John (1764–1834)
Poet and essayist. Thelwall was a radical writer who published tracts and ▷ essays explaining his political views. His radicalism led to his arrest in 1794, but he was acquitted at the trial, and wrote about the experience in *Poems Written in Close Confinement in the Tower and Newgate Upon a Charge of Treason* (1795). Thelwall is also known for his acquaintance with ▷ Wordsworth and ▷ Coleridge whom he visited in the Lake District, having walked all the way from London.

Theocritus
A Greek poet of the 3rd century BC. Little is known about him, but his importance is that he originated ▷ pastoral poetry in his 'idylls' – short poems about shepherds and shepherdesses living in primitive simplicity in the rural parts of Sicily. He may have written these in the Egyptian city of Alexandria for urban readers; one of the characteristics of pastoral has been that it has expressed the town-dwellers' fantasy of the beauty of country surroundings, the simplicity of country living and the purity of country air. Theocritus was emulated by the Roman poet ▷ Virgil, and both Theocritus and Virgil were taken as models by the 16th-century ▷ Renaissance poets in Western Europe, of whom the most notable English example is

▷ Edmund Spenser, and by poets in the 17th and 18th centuries including ▷ Behn, ▷ Pope and ▷ Thomson.

Theophrastus
A Greek philosopher, follower of ▷ Aristotle, of the 4th century BC. Amongst other writings, he composed a series of descriptions of moral types called *Ethical Characters*. These were the original pattern for the minor literary form of character-writing, widely practised in England in the early 17th century. The most notable example is John Earle's *Microcosmography* (1628). Other examples: ▷ Joseph Hall's *Characters of Virtues and Vices* (1608); ▷ Thomas Overbury's *Characters* (1614).
▷ Characters, Theophrastian.

Thespis (6th century BC)
A Greek poet of the 6th century BC; he is usually regarded as the originator of tragic drama. Choric songs were already sung at festivals; Thespis is said to have introduced an actor who engaged in dialogue with the leader of the chorus.

Thiong'o, Ngugi wa
▷ Ngugi wa Thiong'o.

Thirty Years' War
A European religious war, lasting from 1618 to 1648, between nearly all the Catholic and Protestant nations of Europe. It was fought principally in Germany, to the ruin of that country, and was concluded by the Peace of Westphalia. Britain was one of the few important countries that took hardly any part in it.

Thirty-nine Articles
The code of religious doctrine which all clergy of the ▷ Church of England have to accept. In 1553, 42 articles were laid down; these were reduced to 39 in 1571.

Thomas (fl c 1170)
Composer of an influential version of the ▷ Tristan story, which only survives in fragmentary form (totalling about 3,150 lines). Little is known about the author, although modern scholars have suggested he was writing for the royal household of ▷ Henry II. The Middle English version of the Tristan story, *Sir Tristrem*, reworks material deriving from Thomas' poem.

Thomas Becket
▷ Becket, St Thomas.

Thomas, D. M. (Donald Michael) (b 1935)
Novelist and poet. His best-known work is *The White Hotel* (1981), a fictional account of the life of one of ▷ Freud's patients, making extensive use of fantasy. It also contains poetry and a pastiche of a case study by Freud. His other works include *Ararat* (1983); *Swallow* (1984); *Selected Poems* (1983); *Flying in to Love* (1992); and *Eating Pavlova* (1994).

Thomas, Dylan Marlais (1914–53)
Poet. He was born in the Welsh town of Swansea; much of his work shows the impression on his early life of grim Welsh religious puritanism contrasting with the equally Welsh characteristic of strong emotion combined with his own sensuality. His *18 Poems* (1934) and *Twenty-five Poems* (1936) bring together conflicting images in startling association, with pronounced and emotive verbal rhythms. The method has superficial resemblances to those of the 19th-century poet ▷ Gerard Manley Hopkins and the 17th-century ▷ Metaphysicals, but it presents less access than they do for the analytical intellect. Thomas' theme is characteristically the relationship between the disorderliness of sexual impulses and the forces of growth in nature. *The Map of Love* (1939) is mixed prose and poetry; it includes one of his most remarkable poems, *After the Funeral*, in which the striking rhythm and images cohere round the figure of the woman for whose death the poem is an ▷ elegy. *Deaths and Entrances* (1946) contains most of Thomas' most famous work. The poems show the impression made on him by World War II (during which he remained a civilian) in *A Refusal to Mourn*, a more overt use of religious emotion in *The Conversation of Prayer*, and delight in natural environment (*eg Poem in October*, *Fern Hill*). These poems are often less obscure than earlier ones, but the method remains a strong attack on the emotions, achieved by the shock of the imagery and the sweep of the rhythm.

Thomas also wrote prose works – notably the stories entitled *Portrait of the Artist as a Young Dog* (1940) and the play *Under Milk Wood* (1954) published after his death. The prose has no obscurity and exhibits, as the poems do not, Thomas' strong humour. The play shows a mastery of the medium of drama for sound broadcasting which remains unexcelled.

Thomas' wide fame derives especially from three qualities: his unashamed appeal to latent emotionalism in the common reader, on whom he made a direct impact perhaps greater than that of other modern poets; his remarkable talent as a public reader of verse; his personality, which became a legend during his own lifetime, especially in America. On the other hand, his exuberance ran counter, before the war, to the intellectual fastidiousness of ▷ T. S. Eliot and the emotional scepticism of ▷ W. H. Auden, the two poets with the greatest prestige amongst the intelligentsia in England during the 1930s; again, he has been regarded with suspicion since 1945 by younger poets.

▷ Welsh literature in English.

Bib: Jones, T. H., critical study in *Writers and Critics* series; Fraser, G. S., in British Council *Writers and their Work* series; Holbrook, D., *Llaregyb Revisited.*

Thomas, Gwyn (1913–81)

Novelist, short-story writer and playwright. Born at Porth in the Rhondda Valley, the youngest of the twelve children of an unemployed miner, he won a scholarship to Oxford to read Modern Languages, subsequently continuing his Spanish studies at the University of Madrid. He gave up teaching as late as 1962 to become a full-time writer. Most of his work is set in a working-class ambience in the South Wales mining valleys in the first half of the twentieth century, during the social deprivation and unemployment of the 1930s. Paradoxically, despite the grimness and poverty of this background, his novels are outpourings of comic invention with plot less important than hilarious incident, character and language. Life is only made bearable by the wit with which he invests it, together with a farcical gigantism informed by compassion, thus creating a completely original literary milieu. His eleven published novels (two posthumously), comprise: *The Dark Philosophers* (1946); *The Alone to the Alone* (1947); *All Things Betray Thee* (1949); *The World Cannot Hear You* (1951); *Now Lead Us Home* (1952); *A Frost on my Frolic* (1953); *The Stranger at my Side* (1954); *A Point of Order* (1956); *The Love Man* (1958); and the posthumously published *Sorrow For Thy Sons* (1986) and *The Thinker and the Thrush* (1988). His collections of short stories are: *Where did I put my Pity?* (1946); *Gazooka* (1957); *Ring Delirium 123* (1960); and *The Lust Lobby* (1971); a volume of *Selected Short Stories* (1984) was followed by a second posthumous collection, in the latter instance including hitherto uncollected material, in *Meadow Prospect Revisited* (1992). His six stage plays were: *The Keep* (1960); *Loud Organs* (1962); *Jackie the Jumper* (1963); *Sap* (1974); *The Breakers* (1976); and *Testimonials* (1979). He also wrote a great many talks, plays and features for radio and television, two volumes of essays, *A Welsh Eye* (1964) and *A Hatful of Humours* (1965), and an autobiography, *A Few Selected Exits* (1968). In his latter years, Gwyn Thomas, through his increasing amount of work for radio and television, became a media personality, an activity that reflected the ephemeral but provided a vehicle for his spontaneous wit though inevitably and regrettably diverted his creative energies away from the written word.

Bib: Parnell, M., *Laughter from the Dark: A Life of Gwyn Thomas* (1986); Stephens, M. (Ed.), *The Oxford Companion to the Literature of Wales*; Jones, G. and Rowlands, J., *Profiles*; Jones, G., *The Dragon Has Two Tongues*; Jones, G., *Random Entrances to Gwyn Thomas* (Annual Gwyn Thomas Lecture, 1982).

Thomas of Hales (fl 1250)

A Franciscan preacher, possibly from Hailes, Gloucestershire, who composed at least one Anglo-Norman sermon and is identified as the author of the poem known as the 'Love-Ron' (which survives in a single manuscript version, dating from the late 13th century). The 'Love-Ron' is a verse epistle, addressed ostensibly to a young religious woman who has requested spiritual advice. It offers a guide to the art of spiritual 'fin'amor' and recommends Christ as the best lover of all.

Bib: Brown, C. (ed.), *English Lyrics of the Thirteenth Century*.

Thomas, Philip Edward (1878–1917)

Poet and essayist. He was educated at St Paul's School and Lincoln College, Oxford, and was killed at the battle of Arras during World War I. He made his living by writing a long series of prose works, beginning with *The Woodland Life* (1897) and including ▷ biography, criticism and essays on natural surroundings. The last are in a tradition that extends back through ▷ Richard Jefferies, about whom Thomas wrote a critical assessment (1909), to the poetry of ▷ William Wordsworth. It was not until 1914 that Thomas began to write poetry, under the influence of the American poet Robert Frost, whom he first met the year before. His poems are continuous with his prose studies of nature, but it is by the poems rather than the prose that his reputation has grown since his death. English 'nature poetry' at its best has never been merely descriptive, but has concerned the power of the natural environment to elicit the purest human responses, not only to the environment but to elemental human relationships, including the relationship of the poet with himself. Thomas' poems show integrity of responsiveness and sensitivity to the language of his day; they are without the weakening nostalgia and sensibility which showed the decadence of the nature poetry tradition in some of his contemporaries. After his death, his poetic achievement was at first overshadowed by the reaction against the decadence of his contemporaries. ▷ Ezra Pound and ▷ T. S. Eliot led public taste away from the whole tradition, in both its good and its bad aspects, in which Thomas wrote. However, *New Bearings in English Poetry* (1932) by ▷ F. R. Leavis contains an intelligent reassessment of his work. Since 1945, Thomas' austere honesty and delicacy of perception have caused his work to appeal strongly to English poets striving for the same virtues; with ▷ Thomas Hardy, he is seen as representative of distinctly English sensibilities in contrast to the partly alien sensibilities of Pound and ▷ W. B. Yeats.

Bib: Lives by Eckert, R. P., Moore, J., and Farjeon, E.; Thomas, H., *As It Was* and *World Without End*; Coombes, H., *Edward Thomas*; 'Hardy, De la Mare and Thomas' in *The Modern Age* (Pelican Guide); Leavis, F. R., *New Bearings in English Poetry*; Day Lewis, C., in *Essays by Divers Hands* (Transactions of the Royal Society of Literature Vol. XXVIII, 1956); Motion, A., *The Poetry of Edward Thomas*; Thomas, R. G., *Edward Thomas, A Portrait*.

Thomas, R. S., (Ronald Stuart) (b 1913)
Poet. Since his first volume, *The Stones of the Field* (1946), he has maintained a regular and substantial output, including *Song at the Year's Turning* (1955), *Laboratories of the Spirit* (1975) and *Experimenting With an Amen* (1986). He is best known as a recorder of the rigorous beauty of the Welsh landscape, and of the duress of farming-community life there and the religious sensibility that evolves in such a context. In 1936 Thomas was ordained as a Church of Wales clergyman. *Selected Poems 1946–68* (1973), *Later Poems: a Selection* (1983), *Selected Prose* (revised ed. 1986).

▷ Welsh literature in English.

Bib: Dyson, A. E., *Riding the Echo: Yeats, Eliot and R. S. Thomas*; Phillips, D. Z., *R. S. Thomas*; Ward, J. P., *The Poetry of R. S. Thomas*.

Thompson, Francis (1859–1907)
Poet. He gave up the study of medicine in Manchester to seek his fortunes in London, where he nearly starved. He published his *Poems* in 1893. Thompson was a ▷ Catholic; the most famous of his poems (included in the above volume) was the intensely religious *Hound of Heaven*. Its bold, extravagant style recalls the work of the 17th-century Catholic poet ▷ Richard Crashaw (?1612–49), one of the English Metaphysicals. On the other hand, Thompson was more in the tradition of his immediate predecessors in his employment of sensuous, ornate ▷ symbolism; in this he resembles the ▷ Pre-Raphaelites of the mid-19th century, and another Catholic poet – one of the first of his admirers – ▷ Coventry Patmore. In this respect, a comparison of the *Hound of Heaven* with ▷ *The Wreck of the Deutschland* (1875) by yet another Catholic, ▷ Gerard Manley Hopkins, is instructive; Hopkins shows equal emotional intensity with much more of the intellectual rigour of the 17th-century poets. Thompson's other volumes were *Sister Songs* (1895) and *New Poems* (1897). His prose work includes his *Essays on Shelley* (1909).

Bib: Lives by Meynell, E., Meynell, V., and Thompson, P. van K.; critical study by Reid, J.C.

Thomson, James (1700–48)
Poet. Born in the Scottish border country, the son of a minister. He studied divinity at Edinburgh University, but in 1725 sought his fortune in London, where he became tutor in an aristocratic family. His poem *Winter* was published in 1726 and its success encouraged him to write poems on the other three seasons during the following years, the ▷ *Seasons* being completed in 1730. Thomson's artificially dignified ▷ Miltonic ▷ blank verse, and the miscellaneousness of his subject matter, struck the new bourgeois ▷ taste exactly, and the *Seasons* were extremely popular. He possesses a facility, almost amounting to genius, for holding together in loose, artificial suspension all the characteristic elements of the popular culture of his day: ▷ Augustan patriotism, ▷ Classicism in diction and tone, ▷ Gothic excess, ▷ sentimentalism. His most original passages elaborate ▷ Virgilian ▷ pastoral into a pleasantly self-indulgent enthusiasm for the natural scene. Rhetorical patriotism, of which he is the period's most unembarrassed exponent, features also in his next large-scale poem, *Liberty* (1735–6), and also in the ▷ masque *Alfred*, written and produced with ▷ David Mallet in 1740 , which contains the song ▷ *Rule Britannia*. Thomson also wrote ▷ tragedies, which were very successful at the time, but are now forgotten (*Sophonisba*, 1730; *Agamemnon*, 1738; *Edward and Eleanora*, 1739; *Tancred and Sigismunda*, 1745; *Corolianus*, 1749). His ▷ Spenserian imitation, ▷ The Castle of Indolence (1748) is far more successful, eclectically combining ▷ mock-heroic ▷ burlesque, sensuous description, whimsical self-mockery, patriotism and didactic moralizing.

Bib: Johnson, S., *Lives of the Poets*; Grant, D., *Thomson, Poet of the Seasons*; Cohen, R., *The Art of Discrimination*; Cohen, R., *The Unfolding of the Seasons*.

Thomson, James (1834–82)
Poet. He was the son of a sailor in the merchant navy, and of a deeply religious woman who belonged to one of the narrower ▷ Protestant sects. He was an army schoolmaster, 1850–62, during which period he had a tragic love affair, and made friends with Charles Bradlaugh, who became a well-known ▷ atheist radical. Thomson is chiefly known for a long, sombre, atheistic poem, *The City of Dreadful Night* (1880), which expressed in the most uncompromising terms the darkest aspect of the loss of religious belief common among Victorian intellectuals. He was also capable of gaiety (*Vane's Story and Other Poems*, 1881). A Voice from the Nile and other Poems was published posthumously in 1884. He commonly wrote under the initials B.V. (Bysshe, from Percy Bysshe Shelley, and Vanolis, anagram for the German poet, Novalis).

Bib: Dobell, B., *The Laureate of Pessimism*; Walker, E.B., *James Thomson*.

Thopas, Sir
One of ▷ Chaucer's ▷ *Canterbury Tales*. Chaucer's own contribution to the tale-telling

competition is a burlesque ▷ tail-rhyme romance, which the Host stops after only 200 lines or so. Although nominally set in Flanders, the narrative is placed in the world of romance conventions and motifs itself, and its orientation is signalled by the cast list of romance heroes with whom Sir Thopas is compared in the second 'fitt' (a conventional name for the sectional division of a poetic narrative). *Sir Thopas* is built up from a series of anti-climaxes, both in terms of action and style. When the Host steps in to halt proceedings, Sir Thopas has neither found a fairy lover nor fought the giant who challenges him, and though he has contemplated the possibility of doing both, has actually achieved very little in the course of his furious ride across the meadows. For the Host, this tale with its 'drasty rymyng' is 'nat worth a toord'. Chaucer's own contribution to his own tale-telling contest is thus a brilliant anti-climax: it is the only tale of the whole collection which is rejected on aesthetic grounds.

He counters with a second tale, ▷ *Melibee*, a prose moral treatise which could not be more different to *Sir Thopas*.

***Thoughts on the Education of Daughters* (1787)**
English writer ▷ Mary Wollstonecraft's earlier publication on ▷ education. She advocates the education of women both for material reasons – to enable them to obtain such work as is permitted to women, if they have need – and for spiritual and intellectual comfort.

▷ *Vindication of the Rights of Women.*

Thrale, Hester Lynch (1741–1821) (later Hester Thrale Piozzi)
Born Hester Salusbury, she married Henry Thrale in 1763. Thrale was a wealthy brewer with political ambitions, and when in the following year they made the acquaintance of Samuel Johnson (1709–84), Johnson assisted Thrale by writing election addresses. The friendship between Johnson and Hester Thrale became very close, and at various times Johnson lived with the family in their home at Streatham. When Thrale died in 1781, Hester Thrale remarried. Gabriel Piozzi, her second husband, was an Italian musician, and her friends and family vociferously disapproved. The marriage ended the friendship with Johnson, who sent her an anguished letter on the subject.

Hester Thrale's biography of Johnson, *Anecdotes of the late Samuel Johnson*, was strongly contested by James Boswell (1740–95) when it appeared in 1786; his motives in challenging her account probably stem from literary rivalry. Hester Thrale was also an energetic letter writer, and *Thraliana*, a selection of anecdotes, poems, jests and journal entries, covers the period 1776–1809.

Bib: Clifford, J. L., *Hester Lynch Piozzi.*

Thraliana
Journal of ▷ Hester Lynch Thrale, covering the years 1776–1809, and including many of her poems. They began as a set of six blank books presented to her by her husband Henry Thrale as an anniversary gift. The journal contains vivid and often humorous portraits and anecdotes concerning her many friends and acquaintances, including ▷ Samuel Johnson and her two husbands, as well as accounts of contemporary life and customs. Passages from it read like extracts from novels or plays. Johnson's other biographer ▷ Boswell admired but also disparaged her as a rival whom he feared.

***Three Hours After Marriage* (1717)**
▷ Burlesque comedy by ▷ Pope, ▷ Gay, and ▷ Arbuthnot, satirizing several contemporary literary figures, including ▷ John Dennis (Sir Tremendous), ▷ Colley Cibber (Plotwell), and the Countess of Winchilsea (▷ Anne Finch) (Phoebe Clinket). The play was at first a success, but its production occasioned a furious hostility between Gay and Cibber, and it was not revived for another 20 years.

Through the Looking-Glass and What Alice Found There
▷ Carroll, Lewis.

Thucydides (5th–4th centuries BC)
Greek historian of the ▷ Peloponnesian war. It is one of the earliest historical works in European literature in its distinct care for accuracy. Nearly a quarter of the book however, is devoted to political speeches, including the great Funeral Oration by ▷ Pericles; these give an important insight into Greek attitudes to politics. Thucydides has been a principal text for English ▷ classical education.

Thynne, Joan (1558–1612) and Maria (c 1578–1611)
Letter-writers. Joan Thynne was the first mistress of Longleat and Maria was her daughter-in-law. Unfortunately, in personal terms, the two women were never reconciled to one another, but fortunately for present-day readers, they left a collection of dramatic, complex and intimate letters written over a period of 30 years (their correspondence is available in a modern version, edited by A. D. Wall). Joan is much cooler and more reticent, both to her daughter-in-law and her husband, but Maria ranges from conventional submissiveness to angry diatribe and writes tender, sometimes erotic, letters to her spouse.

Tickell, Thomas (1686–1740)
Member of the clique which frequented ▷ Button's Coffee-house and whose leader was ▷ Joseph Addison. He contributed to *The*

Guardian and ▷ *The Spectator*. ▷ Alexander Pope suspected that Addison had attempted to spoil his success by inciting Tickell to publish his translation of the first book of ▷ *The Iliad* just before the appearance of Pope's translation of the first two books (1715). Tickell edited Addison's works after his death, his edition being prefaced by a moving ▷ elegy in heroic ▷ couplets (1721).

Tighe, Mary (1772–1810)
Poet. The life of Mary Tighe (née Blachford) accords with the archetypal biography constructed for the ▷ Romantic poet. Although she had a strict religious upbringing, she married her cousin (Henry Tighe), with whom she was passionately in love, against her mother's wishes, and they moved into the social and literary London scene. Her first book of poems, *Psyche, or the Legend of Love* (1805), was an ▷ allegory in six cantos written in ▷ Spenserian stanzas and depicting Psyche's experiences in Cupid's palace. In her preface she apologizes for her focus upon passion, but when the poem begins with its languorous exploration of space and emotion, no qualms surface to halt the steady sensuous flow of the poetry. Two other works exist, *Mary, A Series of Reflections During 20 Years* (1811) and an ▷ autobiography, *Selina*, which is in manuscript form in the National Library of Ireland. Even as *Psyche* was published, Tighe knew she was suffering from consumption, and died when she was thirty-eight.

Tilney (Tylney), Edmund (d 1610)
Master of the ▷ Revels, 1579–1608. Tilney was appointed to the post of Master of the Revels after his prose tract, *A Briefe and Pleasant Discourse of Duties in Mariage called the Flower of Friendshippe* (1568), which was dedicated to ▷ Elizabeth I, was well received. Tilney's influence on court and public drama of the Elizabethan period was immense: he chose the works to be performed before the queen, and, more importantly, read every play composed for publication or public presentation that needed a licence. Thus, he was on familiar terms with ▷ Philip Henslowe and the other theatrical managers of the day, and he would have examined critically the manuscripts of a number of ▷ Shakespeare's plays in order to license them. At the accession of ▷ James I, Tilney seems to have given over many of his duties to ▷ Sir George Buc (possibly his nephew), and he retired fully in 1608.

Timber
A collection of commentary, paraphrase and ▷ translation by ▷ Ben Jonson, *Timber* was first published in the two-volume edition of Jonson's works that appeared after his death. As a record of Jonson's reading in the classics, it is invaluable. More than this, however, is the insight it provides into questions which inform Jonson's own aesthetic theories, in particular his use of ▷ 'Imitation'.

Times, The
British newspaper. It was founded in 1785 as *The Daily Universal Register*, and took its present name in 1788. In the 19th century it took the lead in contriving new methods of collecting news (notably throught the employment of foreign correspondents), and its succession of distinguished editors and contributors gave it an outstanding status among British newspapers. Though always in private ownership, it has always claimed to be an independent newspaper rather than a party one. The literary style of one of its staff writers caused it to be nicknamed 'The Thunderer' in the 19th century; the novelist ▷ Anthony Trollope consequently refers to it as *The Jupiter* in his novels, since this king of the gods was known as the Thunderer by the ancient Romans. *The Times* publishes *The Times Literary Supplement* and *The Sunday Times* weekly. Its outlook is traditional and often conservative in political terms. In 1981 it was bought by Rupert Murdoch's News Internatinoal Group, which also publishes the tabloid newspaper *The Sun*.
▷ Newspapers.

Timon
A rich citizen of Athens of the 5th century BC; he was celebrated for his hatred of mankind. He is referred to by a number of ancient Greek writers, including ▷ Aristophanes, and notably by ▷ Plutarch in his life of Mark Antony, and ▷ Lucian in his dialogue *Misanthropos*. ▷ Shakespeare (▷ *Timon of Athens*) makes him a rich, ostentatious philanthropist who becomes a misanthropist through disillusionment at men's ingratitude.

***Timon of Athens* (1607)**
A tragedy by ▷ Shakespeare, written about 1607 and concerning ▷ Jacobean ▷ patronage and material power. The material is probably taken from ▷ Plutarch's life of Mark Antony (written 1st century AD), ▷ Lucian's dialogue *Misanthropos* (2nd century AD), and an anonymous play of Shakespeare's own day.

Timon is an Athenian nobleman who delights in the prodigal entertainment of his guests. In spite of his great wealth, he presently finds himself in debt; he is then outraged to discover that none of those to whom he has been so generous is prepared to help him. He invites his friends to one more banquet, but the steaming dishes, uncovered, contain only hot water; throwing the dishes and water at them, he drives his guests out of the house. In a frenzy of hatred, he then takes to a life of solitude in the wilderness, where he is visited by the cynical philosopher Apemantus, his devoted steward Flavius, the general Alcibiades, who is rebelling against the meanness of the Athenian government, and other characters from his past life of opulence. This part of the play consists of a series of dialogues that leave Timon resolute in his hatred of humanity, though he is obliged to make an exception of his disinterestedly loyal steward. The dialogue with Apemantus is the most striking. Apemantus has always forseen that Timon would be deceived by his friends, since he has a low opinion of human nature; Timon, however, retorts that Apemantus' cynicism is groundless except for the mean motive of jealousy, whereas he, Timon, has proved that humanity is inferior after testing it on the opposite hypothesis. Alcibiades is afflicted by the public meanness of the Athenian state, as Timon has been afflicted by private ingratitude; thus he regards Timon as an ally, though he cannot persuade him to join forces with the rebels. The rebellion of Alcibiades is successful, and when Timon dies, the Athenian rulers penitently acknowledge their ill-treatment of him.

▷ Timon.

Tintagel
In ▷ Geoffrey of Monmouth's version of British history, Tintagel features as the castle where ▷ King Arthur is conceived. In later Arthurian romances it is identified as the castle of King Mark, overlord of Cornwall and uncle to ▷ Tristan. Today there are remains of a medieval castle on the headland, but archaeological evidence suggests that there may have been a stronghold on the site in the late 5th century.

Tintern Abbey
One of the most famous remains of the medieval abbeys, dissolved by Henry VIII in 1536–39. It stands in a particularly beautiful natural setting, in the valley of the River Wye, near the border of England and Wales. The poet ▷ William Wordsworth used this setting for one of the best known of his early poems, *Lines Composed a Few Miles Above Tintern Abbey* (in ▷ *Lyrical Ballads*), in which he meditates on the influence of natural surroundings on the formation of his mind.

***Tintern Abbey, Lines Composed a Few Miles Above* (1798)**
A reflective poem in ▷ blank verse by ▷ William Wordsworth, not itself a lyrical ballad but one of the 'few other poems' included in ▷ *Lyrical Ballads* (1798). The poet returns to a spot on the river Wye visited five years earlier, and reflects upon the moral influence its beauty has exerted upon him in the meantime, inspiring 'little, nameless, unremembered, acts/ Of kindness and of love'. He goes on to describe himself as 'A worshipper of Nature', and this is his most ▷ pantheistic work.

Tiresias (Teiresias)
In Greek myth, a sage of Thebes whom the gods afflicted with blindness but then compensated with the gift of prophecy. In the most familiar form of the legend, he spent part of his life as a woman.

▷ Tennyson's poem *Tiresias* is one of those ▷ dramatic monologues which are now among the most admired of his poems; here, Tiresias speaks with the voice of the lonely, timeless sage. He also occurs in Part III of ▷ T. S. Eliot's poem ▷ *The Waste Land*; here he is more the impartial witness of the crises of the human mind, and is described in a note as 'the most important personage in the poem, uniting all the rest'.

***'Tis Pity She's a Whore* (1632)**
▷ John Ford's greatest ▷ tragedy, which treats the passionate and incestuous love-affair between the siblings Giovanni and Annabella – and their relationship's inevitable progress towards destruction – with remarkable empathy and tact. When Annabella finds she is pregnant by her brother she marries a suitor, Soranzo, who discovers the truth about the child's paternity and conspires to revenge his own humiliation. The play concludes in a mass killing after a grotesque scene during which Giovanni enters with his sister's heart on the point of his dagger.

Tithonus
In Greek myth, the son of Laomedon, king of Troy. Such was his beauty that Eos (Aurora), goddess of the dawn, fell in love with him and made him her husband. She secured for him from Zeus the gift of immortal life, but forgot to require also immortal youth. ▷ Tennyson's poem *Tithonus* is a ▷ dramatic monologue representing Tithonus in the agony of his eternal old age.

***Titus Andronicus* (1594)**
A tragedy by ▷ Shakespeare, published in 1594. The origin of the plot is not known; it may owe something to ▷ Ovid's Procne and Tereus, one of his ▷ *Metamorphoses* translated by Golding, 1565–7, and to ▷ Seneca's drama *Thyestes*, translated between 1559 and 1581. It is in any case a violent ▷ revenge tragedy of the kind that Shakespeare and his contemporaries derived from Seneca. The setting is imperial Rome; the plot concerns the revenge of Titus, a Roman general, for the atrocities committed by Tamora, the Queen of the Goths, against his family. She is aided by a villainous slave, Aaron the Moor. Much doubt has been expressed by scholars as to whether the play is entirely by

Shakespeare, by Shakespeare in collaboration, or not by Shakespeare at all; the last opinion arises partly from the low esteem in which the play is usually held, although, according to ▷ Ben Jonson, it was popular among the contemporary public. However, the play has been revived to great success in the late-20th century, and scholars now perceive the themes of gender, race and power to be key issues often dealt with by Shakespeare.

***To the Lighthouse* (1927)**
A novel by ▷ Virginia Woolf. The setting is a house used for holidays by Mr and Mrs Ramsay. The household consists of themselves, their eight children, and a number of their friends, of whom the most important is the painter Lily Briscoe. The novel dispenses with plot and is organized into three parts, dominated by two symbols – the lighthouse out at sea, and Lily's painting of the house, with Mrs Ramsay sitting in the window with her son James. The parts are entitled 'The Window', 'Time Passes', and 'The Lighthouse'. The first part is dominated by Mrs Ramsay, who is intuitive, imaginative, and possesses a reassuring and vitalizing influence upon people and their emotions. The mysterious lighthouse flashing through the darkness is associated with her. In the interval represented by the second part of the novel, corresponding to the war years 1914–18, she dies, and the third part is dominated by Mr Ramsay who is intellectual, philosophical, and lonely. The lighthouse seen as a practical instrument, close at hand and by daylight, is associated with him. The middle section concerns the empty house, subject to the flux of time and its changes. Lily Briscoe, the artist, stands aloof from Mrs Ramsay's embracing influence and seeks to fix the constantly changing relationships of people and objects in a single composition; she completes the picture in the last sentence of the book, when the Ramsay son, James, achieves reconciliation with his father and with the lighthouse seen as fact. Mrs Ramsay, in her role as wife and mother, and Lily, single and an artist, represent alternative possibilities for a woman's way of life.

The story is told through the ▷ stream of consciousness technique – in the minds of the characters, especially James, Lily, and Mrs Ramsay. The novel, one of the most original of the many fictional experiments in the 1920s, is partly autobiographical, and based on Virginia Woolf's own family. Mr and Mrs Ramsay are her father and mother, Leslie Stephen and his second wife.

Toft, Eric John (b 1933)
Novelist and short-story writer. Born and brought up in Hanley, Stoke-on-Trent, in the Potteries district of the English Midlands, he was educated at Hanley High School and Magdalen College Oxford, and taught at Brighton College of Education. In a sequence of powerful realist novels, set primarily in the Potteries, he has created a story of change and development in English working-class life from 1917 to the present: *The Bargees* (1969); *The Wedge* (1972); *The Underground Tree* (1978); *The Dew* (1981). *The House of the Arousing* (1973), a volume of short stories, draws on the author's experience of travelling in Malaysia.

Toleration, Act of (1689)
▷ Act of Parliament which granted freedom of worship to ▷ Dissenters, one of the first Acts passed by the Protestant monarchs ▷ William III and ▷ Mary II after their accession. It went some way to eliminating the discrimination against non-conformists of the years preceding, and the resentment this caused. Dissenters were still not allowed to hold official positions, but many of them succeeded in doing so without retribution. Catholics continued to be forbidden to vote or to hold office.

▷ Puritanism.

Tolkien, J. R. R. (John Ronald Reuel) (1892–1973)
Novelist, philologist and critic. From 1925 to 1945 he was Professor of Anglo-Saxon at Oxford University, and during the 1930s belonged to 'The Inklings', a literary society whose other members included ▷ C. S. Lewis. From 1945 to 1959 he was Merton Professor of English Language and Literature at Oxford. His large-scale fantasy of another world *The Lord of the Rings* (1954–6) has gained enormous popularity. His other novels are: *The Hobbit* (1937) and *The Silmarillion* (1977).

Tolpuddle Martyrs
In 1834 six farm labourers from Tolpuddle in Dorset were transported to Australia for swearing men into a trade union lodge. The men were respectable – five were Wesleyans – and were returned home after three years of the seven-year sentence. But the lack of Whig support revealed the limits of common interest between the middle and working classes. The event nourished the ▷ Chartist movement and the men were seen as martyrs to the cause of unskilled-labour trade unions.

Tolstoy, Count Leo Nikolaevitch (1828–1910)
Russian novelist, dramatist and moral philosopher. What are usually considered his two greatest novels, *War and Peace* (1865–9) and *Anna Karenina* (1875–7), have a spaciousness, profundity and balance of sanity which have caused them to be used as a standard by which the achievements of other novelists can be measured. The scale of greatness is to be accounted for not only by the depth

of Tolstoy's mind but by the breadth of his experience, which in turn owes something to Tolstoy's position in Russian society and the critical phase of history through which Russia was passing during his lifetime. He belonged to the class of Russian landed gentry and was partly educated by French tutors, a fact which, taken with the sensitivity of the Russian intelligentsia to West European culture, gave him a broader understanding of the issues of civilization in his time than was characteristic of most Western novelists. Tolstoy frequented the intellectual and fashionable classes of Russian society, travelled abroad and spent the years 1851–7 in the Russian army, seeing service in the Crimean War against Britain, France and Turkey. Two other absorbing aspects of his experience were the problems of Russia's vast peasantry, emancipated from serfdom in 1861, and the prominence of religion in Russian life.

Tolstoy was early influenced by the thought of ⊳ Jean-Jacques Rousseau and this, combined with his own direct experience of peasant life, developed in him a strong faith in spontaneous, simple living in contrast to the sophisticated, fashionable, educated society which he also knew well. From 1876, disillusioned by worldliness and inspired by the example of the peasants, he thought increasingly about the religious interpretation of experience, but his thinking turned him away from the Russian Orthodox Church to a religion of his own, based on the words of Christ (in *Matthew* 5:39) 'that ye resist not evil'. Tolstoy's religion was thus pacifistic and on the side of self-abnegation; it did not admit the existence of life after death nor a personal God, his belief being that the kingdom of God is within man. He described his religion in *What I believe in* and *A Short Exposition of the Gospels*; a complete account of his conversion is given in *A Confession* (1879–82), and he also published stories inspired by his inner life at the time, *The Memoirs of a Madman* and *The Death of Ivan Ilyich*. In *What is Art* (1896), he expounded his doctrine that good art works by re-creating in the reader the fine emotions of the writer, bad art by similarly conveying the bad ones. Tolstoy's influence may be seen in the works of G.B. Shaw, ⊳ E.M. Forster and ⊳ D.H. Lawrence.

Tom Brown's Schooldays
⊳ Hughes, Thomas; ⊳ Rugby School.

***Tom Jones, a Foundling* (1749)**
A novel by ⊳ Henry Fielding. The central character begins life as a baby of unknown parentage (*ie* 'a foundling') who is discovered in the mansion of the enlightened landowner, Squire Allworthy. Allworthy adopts him, and he grows up a handsome and generous-hearted youth, whose weakness is his excess of animal spirits and inclination to fleshly lusts. He falls in love with Sophia Western, daughter of a neighbouring landowner, Squire Western, who is as gross, ignorant and self-willed as Allworthy is refined and enlightened. Western intends Sophia for Blifil, Allworthy's nephew, a mean and treacherouly hypocitical character, who is supported against Tom by two members of Allworthy's household, the pedantic chaplain Thwackum and the pretentious philosopher, Square, who counterbalance each other. They succeed in disgracing Tom, whom Allworthy is persuaded to disown. The central part of the novel describes his travels and amorous adventures in the company of a comic follower, Partridge. Sophia also leaves home, to escape from Blifil, and nearly falls victim to a plot by Lady Bellaston, with whom Tom has become amorously entangled, to place her in the power of Lord Fellamar. Tom is eventually identified as the son of Allworthy's sister; the plots against him are brought to light; he is received again by Allworthy, and marries Sophia.

The novel, like its predecessor by Fielding, ⊳ *Joseph Andrews*, is a 'comic ⊳ epic', offering a wide range of social types of the age, all of whom are presented as permanent human types rather than as unique individuals, as 19th-century novelists would show them. Fielding's method is expository; he does not attempt to create illusions of characters with interior lives of their own, but expounds behaviour, with the aid of prefatory ⊳ essays to his chapters, always light-heartedly, but always with a view to exhibiting basic human motives as they have always existed, rather in the manner of the 17th-century Comedies of ⊳ Humours and of ⊳ Manners. He owes much to ⊳ Cervantes' comic romance ⊳ *Don Quixote* and to the studies of contemporary morals and manners by the painter ⊳ William Hogarth. To some extent the book was written in rivalry to ⊳ Samuel Richardson's ⊳ *Clarissa*, a novel written in a tragic spirit and in a strenuous and idealistic moral tone. It was Fielding's tendency to 'correct' Richardson's idealism and partly self-deceiving moral rigour by reducing events to more usual human experience and interpreting this in the light of tolerant comedy instead of grand ⊳ tragedy; for instance, Lovelace, in *Clarissa* is a human fiend (though also an interesting psychological study) where Tom is merely a healthy young man whose licentiousness is bound up with his virtue of outgoing sympathy and generosity. Thus, *Tom Jones* is both one of the first important English novels, a new kind of imaginative work, and one that embodies highly traditional values.

***Tom Thumb the Great* (1730)**
⊳ Burlesque play by ⊳ Fielding, expanded and performed as *The Tragedy of Tragedies, or, The Life and Death of Tom Thumb the Great* in 1731. The piece satirizes heroic ⊳ tragedy, somewhat in the manner of ⊳ *The Rehearsal*, but in ⊳ blank verse rather than ⊳ heroic couplets.

In addition, the ▷ satire works entirely through the absurdity of the lines, and the device of having the tiny Tom Thumb as 'hero', without the benefit of commentary from sources outside the 'tragic' action. Fielding acknowledged his debt to ▷ Pope's *The Art of Sinking in Poetry* by attributing the play to 'Scriblerus Secundus'.

Tomlinson, Charles (b 1927)
Poet and literary critic. Tomlinson has been a university lecturer since 1956, and he also paints and translates. His work is precise and aspires to technical objectivity, influenced by both ▷ Donald Davie (who taught him at Cambridge and introduced Tomlinson's 1955 volume *The Necklace*), and by ▷ Imagists and American ▷ modernists, especially William Carlos Williams and Marianne Moore. He has experimented with ▷ free verse and rhythmic irregularities, and is constantly expanding his technical range. His later volumes include: *The Way of a World* (1969); *The Shaft* (1978); *Selected Poems 1951–1974* (1978); *The Flood* (1981).

Tonks, Rosemary (b 1932)
Poet and novelist. Rosemary Tonks was a poet of considerable innovation and originality, until her conversion to fundamentalist Christianity stopped her writing career short in the early 1970s. Her work is cosmopolitan, often parodic, and European in its influences and themes, drawing particularly on the concerns of French ▷ Symbolism and Surrealism (▷ French literature in English). Her works include: *Notes on Cafés and Bedrooms* (1963); *Opium Fogs* (1963); *Illiad of Broken Sentences* (1967); *Businessmen as Lovers* (1969); her last published work was *The Halt during the Chase* (1972).

Torquemada, Tomas de (1420–98)
A Dominican friar who was appointed in 1483 as the first Inquisitor-general to investigate religious heresies in Spain. His zeal has made him a symbol of cruelty in England.

***Tottel's Miscellany* (1557)**
An influential ▷ anthology of verse published by Richard Tottel, a bookseller, and Nicholas Grimald, a translator and scholar. It was originally entitled *Songs and Sonnets*, and included the work of the ▷ Earl of Surrey and ▷ Sir Thomas Wyatt. Their poems, the first of any distinction in English to show characteristics of ▷ Renaissance style, had never before been printed, though they had circulated in manuscript, and the great popularity of the anthology helped to shape the short poem so much cultivated in the last 20 years of the century; their success led to the publication of many similar anthologies.

Tourneur, Cyril (?1575–1626)
Dramatist. Not much is known of his life, except that he was employed abroad in military and diplomatic service, and died in Ireland on the return of the unsuccessful naval expedition under ▷ Buckingham to capture Cadiz. He is well known for two plays, one of which, ▷ *The Revenger's Tragedy* (1606–7), is regarded as one of the finest achievements of the period, and is attributed by most scholars to another dramatist, ▷ Thomas Middleton. The other, ▷ *The Atheist's Tragedy* (1611), an interesting anti-revenge play, is much less esteemed. The case for Tourneur being the author of the more admired of the two plays is partly based on the resemblance to an obscure religious poem by him, *The Transformed Metamorphosis* (1600). He also wrote a number of ▷ elegies.
▷ Revenge tragedy.
Bib: Murray, P. B., *Tourneur*; Eliot, T. S., in *Selected Essays*; Bradbrook, M. C., in *Themes and Conventions of Elizabethan Tragedy*.

Towneley Plays
▷ Wakefield Cycle.

Tract
An ▷ essay or treatise, usually short but published singly and usually on a religious subject. The most famous in English are the *Tracts for the Times* (1833–41) by a group of devout Anglicans, Hurrell Froude, Pusey, Keble, and ▷ Newman. Their purpose was to increase the spiritual dignity and independence of the ▷ Church of England by the revival of doctrines stressed in the 17th century but since then largely neglected, with the consequence, as the authors believed, that the Church was losing its spiritual identity and was exposing itself more and more to secular ▷ utilitarianism and domination by the state. Newman's was the predominating spirit in the group; he started the series, and he wrote *Tract XC*, which caused scandal by emphasizing the closeness of the Anglican to the older Catholic tradition, and thus ended it.
▷ Oxford Movement.

Tractarian Movement
▷ Oxford Movement; Tract.

Tradition
In literary studies, tradition or traditional is used in a number of ways. Generally, it refers to the established rather than the innovative or experimental and, depending on viewpoint, can carry connotations of being old-fashioned or settled and reliable. In another sense, it can also refer to a body of works or conventions which share significant features of technique or outlook handed down from the past and made use of in later work – for example, work produced in the Christian tradition, or the oral tradition, or the epic tradition. But there is also a more contentious usage in which tradition refers to a restricted body of works, often

declared to be *the* tradition in the singular and then promoted exclusively as of supreme value. In this line of thought, the traditional is often identified with a small number of styles and tastes, or particular forms of writing, or works which favour particular beliefs. (An example is F. R. Leavis' book *The Great Tradition* which reduces British writers of fiction to a class of five.) Often, this usage is closely related to the idea of the canon and some objections to it are discussed in that entry.

Trafalgar, Battle of (1805)
The chief sea-battle of the war against ▷ Napoleon, in which the British fleet under ▷ Nelson defeated a joint French and Spanish fleet under Villeneuve. The victory made impossible an invasion of Britain by the French army, but Nelson was killed in the action.

Tragedy
Tragedy as it is understood in Western Europe has its origins in the Greek dramas by the Athenian dramatists ▷ Aeschylus, ▷ Sophocles and ▷ Euripides, in the 6th-5th centuries BC. Essentially the spirit of this writing was that inevitable suffering overwhelms the characters, and yet the characters maintain their dignity in the face of this suffering, and prove their greatness (and the capacity of human beings for greatness) by doing so. Greek tragedy arose out of their religious interpretation of the nature of human destiny. When Christianity prevailed over Western Europe, a much more hopeful interpretation of human destiny dominated the thoughts of writers, and tragedy, in the Greek sense, became difficult to imagine and unnatural: if good men suffer in this world, they are rewarded in Heaven, and this is not tragic; wicked men who happen to suffer in this world may be damned in the next, but this is also not tragic because they are wicked. Hence medieval tragedy was on the whole reduced to the conception of the Wheel of Fortune – that chance in this world is apt to take men from prosperity to misfortune, whatever their spiritual merits.

In the late 16th century the tragic vision of human experience was rediscovered by some English dramatists, notably by ▷ Marlowe and ▷ Shakespeare. Insofar as it had a literary ancestry, this was not the tragedy of the ancient Greeks, which was scarcely known, but the comparatively debased imitation of it by the Roman poet ▷ Seneca, which helped to give rise to Elizabethan ▷ Revenge Tragedy or 'Tragedy of Blood'. More interesting was the growth of conceptions of human destiny which did not usurp the Christian conception, but existed side by side with it, as an alternative, or perhaps rather as a complementary, vision. Although, as C. Belsey points out, 'human tragedy' more often than not means male, English, middle-class tragedy.

The first important English tragedy is Marlowe's ▷ *Doctor Faustus* in which the hero forgoes eternal happiness after death for the sake of earthly ecstasy; Marlowe sets in opposition the Christian doctrine of the soul and ▷ Renaissance delight in earthly experience. ▷ *Hamlet*, in which Shakespeare for the first time makes the task of revenge a genuine moral dilemma, is perhaps the next. The best known achievements of English tragic drama are Shakespeare's five plays: ▷ *Othello*, ▷ *Macbeth*, ▷ *King Lear*, ▷ *Anthony and Cleopatra* and ▷ *Coriolanus*. These cannot be summed up in a phrase, but they have in common that the hero's hope of some form of supreme earthly happiness collapses into terrible misery, brought about less by the hero's character than through the nature of earthly reality of which his character forms a part. Among Shakespeare's later contemporaries and his successors, several dramatists wrote distinguished plays in the tragic style *eg* ▷ Middleton's ▷ *The Changeling* and ▷ Webster's ▷ *The Duchess of Malfi* and ▷ *The White Devil* and ▷ Elizabeth Cary's *Tragedy of Marian*.

This period, from 1590 till about 1625, was the only one in English literature in which there were more than isolated examples of distinguished theatrical tragedy. The single important example of a work written in the Greek style is Milton's *Samson Agonistes*, but critics disagree as to whether it can be called truly dramatic. Numerous attempts were made to write tragedy in the Greek style, or in the neoclassical French style of ▷ Corneille and ▷ Racine, after 1660, but they lacked conviction; perhaps the best is ▷ Dryden's *All for Love*. Various attempts were made by 19th-century poets to revive the Shakespearean mode of tragedy. Of these, Shelley's *The Cenci* is the only noteworthy example, but even that was only a minor success.

Some of the plays of ▷ Synge and ▷ Yeats were genuinely remarkable and original tragedies, but their scale is unambitious. However, in the 1960s the work of such dramatists as ▷ Pinter, ▷ Osborne and ▷ Arden has revived dramatic tragedy in a more recognizable form.

Bib: Belsey, C., *The Subject of Tragedy*; Callaghan, D., *Women and Gender in Renaissance Tragedy*; Dollimore, J., *Radical Tragedy*; McAlindon, T., *English Renaissance Tragedy*.

Tragedy of Arden of Faversham, The
▷ *Arden of Faversham, The Tragedy of.*

Tragical History of Doctor Faustus, The
▷ *Doctor Faustus, The Tragical History of.*

Tragicomedy
Drama in which the elements of both ▷ tragedy and comedy are present. Examples are the ▷ romances of ▷ Shakespeare, particularly

▷ *Pericles*, ▷ *Cymbeline*, and ▷ *The Winter's Tale*, each of which reaches a tragic climax halfway through and then lightens towards a happy conclusion. A peculiarly English form of tragicomedy developed in the years 1610 to 1640, particularly in the works of ▷ Beaumont and ▷ Fletcher.

Traherne, Thomas (c 1638–74)
Poet and religious writer. In the 17th century, the only works published by Traherne were three religious pieces, all of them in prose. In 1896, however, the Victorian editor A. B. Grosart discovered a collection of manuscripts in a London bookshop which he believed to be by ▷ Henry Vaughan. The manuscripts were identified as being those of Traherne, and comprised religious poems and the remarkable mystical prose work *Centuries of Meditation*. The latter constitutes a spiritual ▷ autobiography, tracing the author's progress towards 'felicity' (a key term for Traherne). Criticism of Traherne's poetry has in the 20th century concentrated on his affinity with ▷ George Herbert, and on his visionary delineation of childlike experience. Understsood as a mystic and an intellectual conservative in comparison to the rationalism of 17th-century science, Traherne has been closely linked with the Cambridge ▷ Platonists – almost as though he were the poetic 'voice' of that group. Yet for all Traherne's concern with 'the inward eye', in fact his approach to language, his undoubted fascination with the possibilities of rational science (particularly as it had unfolded a new perspective in which to understand the human body) and his experimental verse forms make him one of the most remarkable of later 17th-century writers.
Bib: Margoliouth, H. M. (ed.), *Traherne's Centuries, Poems, and Thanksgivings*; Clements, A. L., *The Mystical Poetry of Thomas Traherne*.

Traill, Catherine Parr (1802–99)
Novelist and botanist. One of the early pioneer writers of Canadian literature, together with her sister ▷ Susannah Moodie. Traill was born in London to the Strickland family, and only moved to Canada in 1832, at the same time as Moodie, to take up a land grant. Although the life was hard, Traill made every effort to make a home in the new world and her optimistic endeavours are described in *The Backwoods of Canada* (1836) which was written to encourage others to emigrate. Her work contrasts sharply with the patronizing and discontented tone of her sister's book, *Roughing it in the Bush* (1852) which chronicles the same period and events. Indeed, Traill's resolutely bright and cheerful approach was satirized by ▷ Margaret Laurence in her novel *The Diviners*. In addition to her accounts of the early settlement of Canada, Traill is also known for her important contribution to the study of Canadian plant life.

Transference
This is the term used in ▷ Freudian psychoanalysis, along with others such as ▷ 'condensation' and ▷ 'displacement', to describe one of the mechanisms whereby unconscious desires enter into ▷ consciousness. It is given a more specific meaning in the relationship between analyst and patient (analysand) in psychoanalysis, as part of the process of removing those impediments to the recollection of repressed impulses on the part of the latter. Situations and emotions are relived during the treatment and these ultimately express the indestructibility of unconscious fantasies. In the structure of a literary work, repetitions of particular situations and events, and even the duplication of 'character', can be explained as kinds of transference of the 'unconscious fantasies' of the writer. In this way desires and feelings which in psychoanalysis occur in the life of the patient, are *transferred* onto the analyst/reader, producing a repetition or re-enactment of them. For example, in Shakespeare's ▷ *Hamlet* 'madness' is transferred from the hero onto Ophelia, and an analysis of that process situates the reader/spectator within a complex process of the construction of male/female subjectivity as a result. The issue can be complicated further if the writer 'Shakespeare' is taken to be the 'analysand' projecting unconscious desires and feelings through his 'characters' onto the 'analyst' (reader/spectator).

Transferred epithet
▷ Figures of speech.

Transgression
As a term used in contemporary literary criticism, it is generally associated with the concept of 'subversion' insofar as it denotes the act of crossing accepted boundaries. Applied to literary texts it is usually taken to refer to any form of behaviour or representation which challenges the dominant values encoded within the text. A classic example of the process might be the introduction of the act of 'cross-dressing' in a number of ▷ Renaissance drama texts, and the resultant challenge which is posed to the issue of a stable sexual identity. Here, the practical constraints of the ▷ Elizabethan or ▷ Jacobean theatre, involving the impersonation of female roles by male actors, serve to highlight what in the world outside the theatre was becoming a controversial issue as the relative positions of men and women in 17th-century society underwent re-evaluation.

Translation
The life of English literature has always issued from a combination of strong insular traditions

and participation in wider European traditions. Translation has always been the principal means of assimilating European literatures into the English idiom, and it was particularly important before the 18th century, when the main streams of European cultural life were flowing through other languages. The aim of translators was then less to make an accurate rendering than to make the substance of foreign work thoroughly intelligible to the English spirit; the character of the translation thus proceeded as much from the mind of the translator as from the mind of the original writer. If the translator had a strong personality, the translation often became a distinguished work of English literature in its own right. Translators with less individuality often produced work of historical importance because of its contemporary influence on English writing.

From the 14th to the 18th centuries, English writers were constantly absorbing the ancient and contemporary Mediterranean cultures of Europe, and worked on the literatures of France, ancient Rome, Italy, ancient Greece, and Spain. There is no distinct boundary between translation and adaptation; ▷ Chaucer brought English poetry into accord with French and Italian poetry partly by freely adapting work in those languages. His outstanding work of translation is his version of Guillaume de Lorris' *Roman de la Rose*. French ceased to be the first language of the English upper classes in Chaucer's lifetime, but the English nobility continued to have strong ties with French aristocratic culture, and thus translations from French prose were in demand in the 15th and 16th centuries. ▷ Caxton, the first English printer, published many English versions of French romances. The outstanding 15th-century work of English prose was ▷ Malory's ▷ *Morte d'Arthur*, which Caxton published, and which is partly a translation and partly an adaptation. The work of translation was an important influence on the development of a fluent English prose medium, and this is evident in the difference between Wycliff's 14th-century translation of the Latin Bible and ▷ Tyndale's version of the New Testament from the Greek (1515). Lord Berner's translation of ▷ Froissart's *Chronicles* is another distinguished example of English prose development in the 15th and early 16th centuries.

Printing, the ▷ Renaissance, and the rise of new educated classes, all helped to expand translation in the 16th century, which was the first major period for translation of classical writers. These had been of central importance in the Middle Ages too (King Alfred and later Chaucer had translated ▷ Boethius' *De Consolatione Philosophiae*) but knowledge of them had now widened and standards of scholarship had advanced. The first important rendering in English of a great classical poem is that of ▷ Virgil's ▷ *Aeneid* by the Scots poet, ▷ Gavin Douglas (1553). ▷ Chapman's *Iliad* (1611) and *Odyssey* (1615) are impressive, but have less intrinsic merit as English literature. ▷ Ovid had long been a favourite poet, and translations were made of his poems by ▷ Arthur Golding (1565–67) and ▷ Christopher Marlowe (pub 1597). But in the 17th and 18th centuries the best-known English version of Ovid was George Sandys' version of ▷ *Metamorphoses*, completed in 1626. Ovid had an extensive influence on poets, including ▷ Shakespeare; ▷ Seneca's influence on the poetic drama, both as a philosopher and as a dramatist, was equally conspicuous, and it was no doubt helped by the historically important but otherwise undistinguished *Ten Tragedies*, translated by various hands and published between 1559 and 1581. Among the most distinguished prose translators of ancient literature in this period was Philemon Holland, remembered especially for his version of ▷ Pliny's *Natural History*, which he published in 1601. The best known of all, especially for his value to Shakespeare but also for the quality of his writing, is ▷ Thomas North, whose version (1579) of ▷ Plutarch's *Lives* was made not from the original Greek but from the French of Jacques Amyot. Several women also produced excellent translations in this period, perhaps because of a reluctance to face the censure inevitable upon the production of their own writing. These female translators include ▷ Ann Bacon; ▷ Mary Basset; ▷ Lady Elizabeth Cary; ▷ Katherine Philips; and ▷ Margaret Tyler.

Translations from the contemporary European languages were also numerous in the 16th and early 17th centuries, and indicate the constant interest of English writers in foreign literatures. ▷ Sir John Harington translated ▷ Ariosto's ▷ *Orlando Furioso* in 1591: ▷ Tasso's *Jerusalem Delivered* was translated as *Godfrey of Bulloigne* or *The Recovery of Jerusalem* (1600); ▷ Castiglione's very influential ▷ *Il Cortegiano* was translated by Sir Thomas Hoby (1561). The best known of all these contemporary works is ▷ John Florio's rendering of the ▷ *Essays* of ▷ Montaigne, published in 1603. Part I of Cervantes' ▷ *Don Quixote* was translated in 1612 before Part II was written; the whole work was three times translated in the 18th century, by Motteux (1712), Jarvis (1742) and ▷ Smollett (1755). The first three books of ▷ Rabelais' *Gargantua and Pantagruel* were translated notably by Thomas Urquhart; two were published in 1653, and the third in 1694. The fourth and fifth books were added by Motteux in 1708.

Many of the translations made before 1660, especially those in prose, were marked by a superabundance of words, characteristic of much English writing in the 16th and 17th centuries; the originals tended to be amplified rather than closely rendered. After the Restoration in 1660, writers attached importance to discipline and control, and to emulating these virtues as they were exemplified in the old Latin poets and in contemporary French writers of verse and prose. In consequence, ▷ John Dryden accomplished some of his best work in translating Latin poetry, especially Ovid (*eg* ▷ *Philemon and Baucis*) and the Aeneid of Virgil, whose works he translated entire, completing them in 1697. ▷ Pope's translations of Homer's *Iliad* and *Odyssey*, which appeared in 1720 and 1726, greatly enhanced his reputation, but despite the skill of the versification, they are obviously much further from the spirit of Homer than Dryden's renderings are from the Latin poets; the British Augustans were much closer in feeling to the Roman Augustans than they were to the ancient Greeks. As the century went on, writers became restless under Augustan restraints, and became interested in literatures that had hitherto been ignored or despised; ▷ Thomas Gray imitated Icelandic and Celtic verse. Macpherson's versions of Gaelic legends, which he alleged to be by the legendary poet ▷ Ossian, were more inventions and adaptations than translations, but they probably had a wider influence in other countries than any other English work going under the name of translation, with the exception of the English Bible. Sir William Jones (1746–94), the first important British Oriental scholar (▷ Orientalism) published in 1783 a version in English of the ancient Arabic poems called *Moallakat*, as well as other work from Persian and from Sanskrit.

Some of the more distinguished translations of the first 30 years of the 19th century, such as Cary's translation in ▷ blank verse of Dante's *Divine Comedy* (1805–12), ▷ Coleridge's version of Schiller's *Wallenstein* (1800), and ▷ Shelley's fragments of ▷ Goethe and ▷ Calderón (▷ Spanish influence on English literature), show the new kinds of influence on the Romantic writers. After 1830, translation became a kind of net for hauling in exotic writings, and its field became very wide, *eg* ▷ Fitzgerald's version of the Persian poem, *The Rubaiyat of Omar Khayyam* (1859), ▷ Richard Burton's ▷ *Arabian Nights* (1885–88), ▷ William Morton's translation of the Icelandic Sagas (beginning in 1869), ▷ Swinburne's versions of Villon, as well as many new versions of the ancient Greek and Latin authors. Two vices of the period were a tendency to make a foreign work express essentially English 19th-century sentiment (*eg* Fitzgerald's *Rubaiyat*), and to use peculiarities of style under the mistaken impression that because they gave strangeness to the work, therefore they gave the translation an air of authenticity – a fault which ▷ Matthew Arnold criticizes in his fine essay *On Translating Homer* (1861). The really influential translations were more often of contemporary writers, such as those by Constance Garnett of the Russian novelists ▷ Tolstoy and ▷ Turgenev (▷ Russian influence on English literature); William Archer's translations of ▷ Ibsen; and Scott Moncrieff's fine rendering of ▷ Proust's great novel under the title of *Remembrance of Things Past*. These works bring us into the 20th century, in which translation has been cultivated with a new sense of its importance and difficulties. Among the most eminent of modern translations are ▷ Ezra Pound's *Cathay* (from the Chinese) and his version of the Old English *The Seafarer* (1912), and Willa and ▷ Edwin Muir's translations of Kafka (1930–49). In the 20th century translation has become more widespread, making texts in many languages readily available, and this has included critical as well as fictional works. However, while providing us with an international ▷ best seller list, regularly including writers such as Umberto Eco (▷ Italian influence on English literature) and Gabriel Garcia Márquez (▷ Spanish influence on English literature), there is a danger that a new saleable canon will be created and more marginal texts will remain trapped by linguistic barriers.

Bib: Cowley, C. M., *The First English Translators of the Classics*.

Trapnel, Anna (c 1622–c 1660)
Devotional and prophetic writer. Trapnel is one of the most well-known ▷ Baptist and ▷ Fifth Monarchist writers. She discovered her vocation in 1654, when she fell into an 11-day trance at the examination of Vavasor Powell, a fellow Fifth Monarchist. During this time she sang, chanted and spoke in tongues, and upon her recovery her prophecies were published in *Strange and Wonderful Newes* and *The Cry of a Stone* (both 1654). Her writings take the form of verse and prose prophecies, which also contain a fair amount of ▷ autobiographical material, such as her being accused of witchcraft. Although Trapnel asserts that she is simply the mouthpiece of God, her prophecies, given in a dramatic, trance-like state, clearly satisfied her own desire to be the centre of attention. Her other two works, also published in 1654 (*Report and Plea* and *A Legacy for Saints*), carry a similar mixture of self-dramatization and Fifth Monarchist propaganda.

Bib: Graham E. et al. (eds.), *Her Own Life*; Hobby, E., *The Virtue of Necessity*; Greer, G. (ed.), *Kissing the Rod*.

Travel literature
This large branch of English literature may be conveniently discussed under these headings: **1** fantasy purporting to be fact; **2** factual accounts; **3** travel experiences regarded as material for art.

1 *Literature of fantasy purporting to be fact*. So long as extensive travel was rarely undertaken, it was possible for writers to present accounts of fantasy journeys and to pass them off as fact without much fear of being accused to lying. Thus a 14th-century French writer wrote the *Travels of Sir John de Mandeville*, which is a work of fiction or compilation from narratives by other travellers, but purporting to be an account of genuine journeys written by Mandeville himself. The work was translated into English in 1377, became extremely popular, and was long regarded as genuine. Long after the extravagances of the story were seen to be falsehoods, Mandeville, a purely fictional English knight, was thought to be the genuine author.

2 *Literature of fact*. By the second half of the 16th century, the great Portuguese, Spanish and Italian explorers had discovered the Americas and greatly extended knowledge of eastern Asia. Liars could still find large, credulous audiences, but the facts were marvellous enough to require no distortion. Writers also began to feel strong motives for publishing truthful accounts. Thus ▷ Richard Hakluyt published his *Principal Navigations, Voyages and Discoveries of the English Nation* in 1589, partly for patriotic reasons. The English had been slow to start on exploratory enterprises, although by this time they were extremely active. Hakluyt, finding that the reputation of his nation stood low among foreigners in this field, wanted to demonstrate the reality of the English achievement, and at the same time to stimulate his fellow-countrymen to further endeavours. His book is really a compilation of accounts by English explorers; an enlarged edition came out in 1598, and a still further enlarged edition was published under the title of *Hayluytus Posthumus*, or *Purchas his Pilgrims* by Samuel Purchas in 1625. The accounts vary from those by accomplished writers like ▷ Sir Walter Raleigh to others by writers with little or no experience of writing; they constitute an anthology of early English descriptive writing in which the writers are concerned with the truthfulness of their accounts rather than with entertaining or deceiving the reader. Other examples of this new kind of honest and truthful handling of description language are Captain John Smith's history of the founding of the colony of Virginia, *General History of Virginia, New England, and the Summer Isles* (1624). The contrast between this newer, plainer style and the extravagant and whimsical style more characteristic of the ▷ pamphleteers can be seen in accounts of travels in Europe by Thomas Coryate (?1577–1617), author of *Coryate's Crudities*, and Fynes Morison (1556–1630), author of *Itinerary*: Coryate is deliberately strange and fanciful, though an acute observer, but Morison is much more straightforward.

The steady growth of English overseas trade kept alive a taste for accounts of great voyages throughout the 17th and 18th centuries. At the end of the 17th century Captain William Dampier published three books which included the imaginations of ▷ Defoe and ▷ Swift: *New Voyage Round the World* (1697), *Voyages and Descriptions* (1699), and *Voyage to New Holland* (1703). Dampier was an excellently direct and clear writer of his own books, but Lord George Anson's voyage round the world (1740–44) was written up from his journals by his chaplain, R. Waters, and depends on the singularly dramatic events for its force of interest. The last of these outstanding accounts of great voyages were the three undertaken by Captain James Cook, *A Voyage Round Cape Horn and the Cape of Good Hope* (1773), *A Voyage Towards the South Pole and Round the World* (1777), and *A Voyage to the Pacific Ocean* (1784).

3 *Travel literature as material for art*. Mungo Park's *Travels in Central Africa* preserves the plain, unaffected style of 18th-century travel literature, but with the discovery by Europeans of the coastlines of Australia and New Zealand, the main outlines of world geography became known to the West, and the interest both of explorers and their readers passed from accounts of great voyages, such as those undertaken by Captain James Cook, to the mysteries of the great undiscovered interiors of the continents. With this change in subject matter, a change also came over the style of travel literature. ▷ Sir Richard Burton's book about India, *Scinde or the Unhappy Valley* (1851), and his later books about his exploration of East and Central Africa (*First Footsteps in East Africa*, 1856; *The Lake Regions of Central Africa*, 1860) bear the stamp of the author's personal feelings and reactions. Partly, no doubt, this arose from the new importance attached to authorial personality due to ▷ Romanticism; also the contact with strange physical environments and peoples (in contrast to the emptiness and impersonality of the ocean) inevitably drew out authorial response. At all events, travel literature began to draw nearer to ▷ autobiography. Not only 'darkest Africa', but the Arabian peninsular fascinated writers. Burton was one of the first Englishmen to visit the holy city of Mecca, and wrote an account of it in *Pilgrimage to Al-Medinah and Mecca* (1855). Later Charles Doughty tried to restore the vividness of 16th-century language to 19th-century prose in his *Arabia Deserta* (1888), and T.E. Lawrence's *Seven Pillars of Wisdom* (1926) belongs to the same tradition of art made from travel in Arabia. ▷ George Borrow (1803–81) did not go so far for his material, but he went a stage further than these writers in combining travel literature and imaginative art, so that it is difficult to know whether or not to classify his books with the novel. They are full of personal encounters with individuals, chiefly among the common people; he was particularly interested in the gypsies (*The Gypsies in Spain*, 1841; *Lavengro*, 1851; *Romany Rye*, 1857) and he was talented at conveying the intimate texture of the life of a country (*The Bible in Spain*, 1843; *Wild Wales*, 1862). James Kingslake's

account of his travels in the lands of the Eastern Mediterranean, *Eothen* (1844), and Lafcadio Hearne's *Glimpses of Unfamiliar Japan* (1894) are two other examples of travel literature which owe their classic status as much to the author's art and personality as to their subject matter. Thus travel literature became a natural subsidiary form for the novelists; it is among the best writing of ▷ R.L. Stevenson.

Many 19th-century British women writers travelled abroad and recorded their experiences in published accounts. ▷ Anna Eliza Bray (1790–1883) and ▷ Frances Power Cobbe (1882–1904) were tourists primarily, and travelled mainly within Europe. Others, including ▷ Frances Trollope (1780–1863), Anna Jameson (1794–1860), ▷ Harriet Martineau (1802–76) and ▷ Barbara Bodichon (1827–91) visited North America and wrote about their experiences in the 'New World'. Bodichon also travelled to the Sahara with ▷ Matilda Betham-Edwards (1836–1919), who published a record of the trip. Another group of women, including ▷ Isabella Bird Bishop and ▷ Mary Kingsley were genuine 'explorers'. Bishop journeyed through China, Japan and India; Kingsley in West Africa.

In the 20th century modernist travel writing may be seen in the works of ▷ D.H. Lawrence and ▷ Joseph Conrad, who, as a sailor, was a professional traveller during the first part of his adult life, and may be said to have completely assimilated the literature of travel into the art of the novel.

Increasing ease of travel since World War II has greatly increased the amount of travel writing. Eric Newby's *A Short Walk in the Hindu Kush* (1959) has become a classic. Other important contemporary travel writers include Bruce Chatwin (1940–89). In critical terms travel writing has increasingly been examined in relation to gender, ▷ colonialism and Imperialism.

Bib: Foster, S., *Across New Worlds: 19th Century Women Travellers and Their Writings.*

Travers, Ben (1886–1980)

British dramatist famous for his 'Aldwych farces', performed at the Aldwych Theatre by casts which included Mary Brough, Robertson Hare, Ralph Lynn, and Tom Walls. The first of these was *A Cuckoo in the Nest* (1925), followed by several others including *Rookery Nook* (1926), *Thark* (1927) and *Plunder* (1928). At the age of 89 he wrote the 'sex comedy' *The Bed Before Yesterday*, which was first performed in 1975, by which time Travers was able to deal explicitly with matters which he had previously only written about implicitly.

Bib: Smith, L., *Modern British Farce: a Selective Study.*

***Treasure Island* (1883)**

A romance by the novelist ▷ Robert Louis Stevenson, perhaps his best known work. It is set in the 18th century and the plot concerns the search for hidden treasure buried in a desert island by an actual 18th-century pirate, Captain Kidd. The story contains the basic elements of a traditional English ▷ romance – treasure, pirates, adventure, a desert island – and belongs to a line of desert island literature descending from Defoe's *Robinson Crusoe* (1719).

Treatise of Human Nature

▷ Hume, David.

Treatises of Government

▷ Locke, John.

Tree, Sir Herbert Beerbohm (1853–1917)

English actor-manager famous for his productions at the Haymarket and Her Majesty's theatres, and for founding the Royal Academy of Dramatic Art. Productions at the Haymarket included ▷ Oscar Wilde's *A Woman of No Importance* (1893), Shakespeare's *The Merry Wives of Windsor* (1889) and *Hamlet* (1892). Most successful was an adaptation of a George Du Maurier novel, ▷ *Trilby* (1895), the proceeds from which enabled him to build Her Majesty's. The repertoire at Her Majesty's was dominated by Shakespeare and historical verse drama. His Shakespeare productions were illustrative of the fashion of the period for spectacular 'romantic realism'. Detailed ostentatious sets, busy stage action and sometimes bizarre stage additions were all characteristic of these productions, disparagingly referred to by designer Gordon Craig as 'beautiful copies of Irving' (▷ Henry Irving). Tree combined the qualities of the showman and pioneer. The Shakespeare festivals at Her Majesty's from 1905 to 1913 matched those being given by actor-manager Frank Benson at Stratford. He also championed the cause of ▷ Ibsen, by running matinée performances of *An Enemy of the People*.

Bib: Bingham, M., *The Great Lover.*

Tremain, Rose (b 1943)

Novelist, playwright and short-story writer. Educated at the Sorbonne and the University of East Anglia, she has worked as a teacher, assistant editor and researcher and since 1980 has been a full-time writer and part-time lecturer in creative writing. Her novels are in most cases unsentimental accounts of the loneliness and emotional relationships of ageing or unfulfilled characters: *Sadler's Birthday* (1976); *Letter to Sister Benedicta* (1978); *The Cupboard* (1981); *The Swimming Pool Season* (1985); *Sacred Country* (1992). *Restoration* (1989) is a historical novel, set in the Restoration period and narrated by the King's fool. Volumes of short stories: *The Colonel's Daughter* (1984); *The Garden of the Villa Mollini* (1987). Drama: *Mother's Day* (1980);

Yoga Class (1981); *Temporary Shelter* (1984); *Evangelista's Fan* (1994). She has also written books for children, a biography of Stalin and *The Fight for Freedom for Women* (1973).

Tressell, Robert (pseudonym of Robert Noonan) (? 1870–1911)
Novelist. Tressell worked as a painter and decorator, and is remembered for his posthumously published novel *The Ragged Trousered Philanthropists* (1918; first full edition 1955). A ▷ naturalistic account of a year in the life of a town's working men (in the decorating and undertaking businesses), the novel is a powerful attack on the greed of employers (the philanthropy in the title is an ironic reference to the exploited workers), and has become a classic of working-class and left-wing fiction.
Bib: Alfred, D. (ed.), *The Robert Tressell Lectures, 1981–88.*

Tricoteuses
The 'knitters', from the French *tricoter* = to knit. A name given to the women who brought their knitting to the debates in political assemblies during the ▷ French Revolution. In English fiction, Madame Defarge in Dicken's novel ▷ *A Tale of Two Cities* knits the names of those who are to meet death by the guillotine into an endless scarf. A symbolic modern incarnation of the *tricoteuses* is found in ▷ Conrad's ▷ *Heart of Darkness.*

***Trilby* (1892)**
Novel, written and illustrated by ▷ George du Maurier. It tells the story of Trilby O'Ferrall, an artists' model in Paris with whom all the art students fall in love. She comes under the mesmeric influence of Svengali, a German-Polish musician who makes her famous. His spell is so strong that when he dies she loses her voice, fails and dies herself. The novel enjoyed enormous popularity and was dramatized in 1895. Trilby's soft felt hat with an indented crown is the original 'trilby'.

Triolet
A graceful verse form of eight lines and two rhymes with a rhyme scheme *abaaabab*. It was invented in France in the 13th century, and was not used in England till the 17th century. Like other verse forms which have little merit beyond their gracefulness, it has seldom been used in English except by minor poets, and those chiefly of the late 19th and early 20th centuries.

Triple-decker/three decker
A novel published in three volumes. This was the dominant form of fiction during the period from the 1820s until 1894, and the novels were distributed primarily via the ▷ circulating libraries, such as ▷ Mudie's.

Triplet
In verse, three lines rhyming together, occasionally used among ▷ couplets to introduce variety. A good example may be found in ▷ Dryden's ▷ *MacFlecknoe*; the '}' was often used to link the 3 lines:

Where unfledg'd Actors learn to
  laugh and cry,
Where infant Punks their tender Voices try,
And little Maximins *the Gods defy.* }

Tripp, John (1927–86)
Poet. Born at Bargoed, Glamorgan, and brought up in Cardiff. After working as a journalist in London, Tripp returned to Wales in 1969, becoming the literary editor of *Planet* from 1973 to 1979. His main poetic themes are the history of Wales and the present condition of its people, its focal point his denunciation of the shoddy materialism that has severed the Welsh people's links with their past, so that his work often describes how the once great and famous have fallen on harder times. John Tripp refused to compromise his strong left-wing and pacifist convictions; often abrasive in his personal relationships through frustration with the national condition, he used a contemporary vocabulary and a vigorous style in his poetry, though he could stand back and cast a critical eye on himself as poet-observer, obliged to suffer suburban living but still capable of humour, anger and compassion. His collections of poetry are: *Diesel to Yesterday* (1966); *The Loss of Ancestry* (1969); *The Province of Belief* (1971); *Bute Park* (1971); *The Inheritance File* (1973); *For King and Country* (1980); and *Passing Through* (1984). A selection of his poetry appeared in the *Penguin Modern Poets* series (1979) and his *Collected Poems 1958–1978* was published in 1978.
Bib: Stephens, M. (Ed.), *The Oxford Companion to the Literature of Wales.*

Tristan and Iseult
There are many medieval and post-medieval versions of the tragic love affair between Tristan (Tristram/Tristrem) and Iseult (Iseut/Isolde/Isolt/Isode); however, if the lovers' tragedy is a fixed element in their history, details of why and how it happened are not. It seems likely that their love story has a source in early Celtic legendary narrative: Tristan seems to be a transfiguration of the 8th-century Pictish Prince Drust, and there are Irish analogues to the story of the erotic triangle which forms the basis of the Tristan and Iseult narrative. But there are no Celtic versions of the love story which pre-date the

French versions, composed in the later 12th century.

In the mid-12th century Tristan is mentioned as an ideal lover in the lyrics of the ▷ troubadours, which suggests some version of his story was circulating at this time. Fragments of longer vernacular narratives about Tristan and Iseult are extant by ▷ Thomas (c 1175) and ▷ Béroul (c 1190). ▷ Marie de France also included an episode from the lovers' history in her collection of *Lais*, and ▷ Chrétien de Troyes claimed to have produced a version of the story too, though no trace of the text has survived (his romance, *Cligés*, contains many references to the affair between Tristan and Iseult). From the fragments by Thomas and Béroul, and from their subsequent reworkings (especially in early medieval German versions), some idea of the overall story-line may be established.

Tristan is the son of Rivalen and Blancheflor (the sister of King Mark of Cornwall). Blancheflor dies the day her son is born, and he is brought up as an orphan until he is old enough to go to Mark's court, where he kills the Irish champion, Morholt. Later he is given the task of finding a bride for Mark. Tristan travels to Ireland, is wounded in a fight against a dragon, and is nursed by the king of Ireland's daughter, Iseult. She manages to identify Tristan as the killer of her brother Morholt; however, she saves Tristan's life on condition that he rescue her from an unwanted marriage. Tristan takes Iseult back to be Mark's wife, but on the voyage to Cornwall they accidentally drink a love potion which had been designed for Iseult and her future husband, and so they fall passionately in love. Their love affair continues after Iseult's marriage to Mark (with the help of Iseult's maid), but rumours about their adultery finally reach Mark. Later, after the affair has been exposed, Tristan goes into exile in Brittany, and marries another Iseult (of the White Hands), although the marriage is never consummated. When, at a later stage, he is wounded by a poisonous weapon, he calls for Iseult of Ireland to come to heal him: if she consents, the ship which carries her is to have white sails; if not, her message is to be carried in a ship with black sails. Although Iseult comes to Tristan's aid, Iseult of the White Hands tells Tristan that a ship with black sails is approaching. At this news Tristan dies. Iseult, realizing she has come too late, dies of grief beside Tristan.

The status of the love potion (whether it is a permanent or temporary spell, whether it is a metaphor for their love, rather than a literal love potion) is a variable element in the love story. So too is the means by which the lovers are exposed and punished by Mark: in some versions the lovers are condemned, but Tristan manages to escape and rescue Iseult from a group of lepers to whom she has been given for their pleasure; in some versions Iseult survives a truth ordeal by swearing an equivocal oath, and the lovers subsequently run away to live together for a time in a forest. The story of frustrated and passionate love arouses very different ethical responses, too, from medieval poets and prose writers: Tristan and Iseult have an equivocal status as exemplary lovers, being famous and infamous, a subject for praise and blame. Gottfried von Strassburg's *Tristan* (c 1210) provides one of the most celebratory versions of the story, which strongly affirms the metaphysical status of the bonds between these two lovers (and this, in turn, is the source for Wagner's opera of 1865, *Tristan und Isolde*).

The experience of Mark, Iseult and Tristan clearly offers a parallel to, and perhaps a prototype for, the other major erotic triangle of Arthurian romance involving ▷ King Arthur, ▷ Guinevere, and ▷ Lancelot. And in the later French prose versions of the Tristan story (dating from the 13th century), the friendship between Tristan and Lancelot is developed: in these versions, substantial accounts are added of Tristan's adventures as a Knight of the Round Table, and in these versions he is killed, finally, by King Mark himself. ▷ Malory's long 'Book of Sir Tristram' is a reworking of the French prose *Tristan* (c 1225). The 13th-century English verse romance, *Sir Tristrem* (in the ▷ Auchinleck manuscript), provides an incomplete reworking of Thomas' 12th-century *Tristran*.

▷ Tennyson, ▷ Matthew Arnold, and ▷ Swinburne are among the later poets to take Tristan and Iseult as their subjects, and of these, Tennyson presents the least sympathetic, and most critical interpretation of the lovers' experience.

Bib: Ferrante, J., *The Conflict of Love and Honour: The Medieval Tristan Legend in France, Germany, and Italy*; Lacy, N. et al (eds.), *The Arthurian Encyclopaedia*.

Tristram Shandy, The Life and Opinions of (1760–7)

A novel by ▷ Laurence Sterne, published in successive volumes, I to IX from 1760 to 1767. Any attempt to paraphrase the 'plot' of this eccentric masterpiece would be doomed, like trying to net the wind. Sterne deliberately flaunts his freedom to tease and surprise the reader with his interruptions and digressions. 'If I thought you was able to form the least judgement or probable conjecture to yourself, of what was to come in the next page,' he writes, 'I would tear it out of my book.' Tristram, the nominal hero, plays little part in the action of the book, though as the authorial voice of the narrative his random associations determine its form. As a character he is not born until volume IV, and never gets beyond infancy. The bulk of the novel is taken up with the theories and hobby-horses of Tristram's father,

Walter Shandy, and his uncle Toby; these two brothers appear like comic caricatures of ⊳ Locke's theory of the association of ideas. Each of them is trapped in his own private world of associations; for Walter these centre on his obsessions with noses and names; for Toby they are based on military science and his quest to determine the circumstances of the wound in the groin which he suffered at the seige of Namur. The other characters, Dr Slop, Corporal Trim, parson Yorick, Mrs Shandy and the Widow Wadman are swept up in the general associations – many of them sexual – of noses and wounds, breeches and ballistics.

'Shandy' is an old Yorkshire dialect word meaning crackbrained, odd or unconventional, and it suits this book perfectly. With its black and marbled pages, its flash-backs and interpolations, its asterisks, blanks and dashes, this novel defies any attempts to unscramble a straightforward narrative theme. The effect on the reader is to suggest that the conventional notion of a biographical narrative, with a distinct beginning, sequence of events and ending, is untrue to human experience which finds that beginnings do not really exist, and orderly sequences are frustrated by every kind of distraction. Tristram Shandy has been called 'the greatest shaggy-dog story in the language' and a ⊳ satiric ⊳ essay on human misunderstanding. It is a joyous, exuberant cock-and-bull story, in which the juggler Sterne shamelessly leads the reader by the nose on an endless quest for the elusive copula that links cause and effect, intention and achievement.

Trochee
⊳ Metre.

***Troilus and Cressida* (1601–2)**
A play by ⊳ Shakespeare, written 1601–2, and first printed in 1609. Its position in the first collected edition of Shakespeare's plays, the folio of 1623, is curious, inasmuch as it was placed by itself and not in one of the three groups of histories, tragedies and comedies. Shakespeare used as sources ⊳ Caxton's *Recuyell of the Histories of Troy* (1474), translated from the French of Raoul le Febvre; ⊳ Chaucer's ⊳ *Troilus and Criseyde*, especially for Pandarus and the love story; ⊳ Chapman's translation of the ⊳ *Iliad* (for Thersites); and possibly ⊳ Lydgate's *Troy-book*.

Troilus, son of King Priam of Troy, woos Cressida, with the help of her uncle, Pandarus. Meanwhile the war continues between the Trojans and the Greeks; the latter are doing badly, because their chief warrior, Achilles, is sulking in his tent. The subtle Ulysses contrives a plan to rouse Achilles by provoking his vanity; he chooses the brutishly stupid Ajax to fight the Trojan champion, Hector; the ruse is successful. A pact is made of an exchange of prisoners, and the Trojans consent to hand over Cressida, whose father has deserted to the Greeks; she and Troilus part, with many promises of fidelity, but she quickly becomes the mistress of the Greek Diomed, to the bewildered disillusionment of Troilus, who sees her in Diomed's arms during a truce. The end of the play is a chaos of fighting, in which all higher emotions are lost in a rage of murderous hatred, and Hector, the noblest character in the play, is treacherously murdered by Achilles.

What bewilders critics is the hopelessness of the play. Two of the finest episodes are debating scenes, during the first of which (I. iii) the Greeks discuss their failure in the cold light of reason; in the second (II. ii) the Trojans defy reason for the sake of emotional dedication to 'honour'. But the play shows that reason alone conduces to ignobility and treachery, while honour alone is defeated by the facts of human nature. The voice of truth seems to be the mocking one of the Greek clown Thersites, who despises everybody and respects nothing. A possible view is that the much-prized virtue of honour, so cultivated by ⊳ Renaissance courtiers, is an idealistic value, a literary growth in terms of which real life cannot be evaluated, whereas the 'reason' of politicians by itself destroys the value of living. This interpretation makes the play more an affair of light-hearted mockery than it is commonly taken to be; it is frequently interpreted as a grim and despairing ⊳ satire.

⊳ Problem plays (of Shakespeare).

Bib: Adamson, J., *Troilus and Cressida*.

Troilus and Criseyde
⊳ Chaucer composed *Troilus and Criseyde* some time in the 1380s (before 1388). His contribution to the medieval Troy story was not to produce an English version of the history of Troy, from beginning to end (in the tradition of Benoît de Sainte-Maure and ⊳ Guido de Columnis), but to refract the Troy story through that of the relationship between Troilus ('little Troy') and Criseyde, organized as an epic love-tragedy, with a five-book division and elaborate apostrophes and a palinode. The siege of Troy and past Trojan and Greek history form a significant backdrop to, and determining influence on, the conduct and outcome of their affair.

The outline of Chaucer's narrative is taken from ⊳ Boccaccio's ⊳ *Il Filostrato* but in addition to developing the background to their story, Chaucer changes some aspects of the presentation of its key characters, not least in the role of the narrator himself, who no longer presents Troilus' experience as a cipher for his own but adopts the familiar 'ineffectual' Chaucerian role. Pandaro, the go-between figure in Boccaccio's version, is a cousin of Criseida and a peer of Troilus; in Chaucer's version, Pandarus is Criseyde's uncle and, though still a lover himself, plays the role of an avuncular confessor to Troilus. His engineering power is increased on a local domestic scale and his role as stage-manager of their affair is enhanced, but his controlling powers are markedly circumscribed at the same time: he may be on hand literally to help Troilus into bed with Criseyde but his resources diminish as the larger context of the siege intervenes in the lovers' lives. Criseyde is more vulnerable, naive and sensitive to the pressures around her than her counterpart in Boccaccio; there is no precedent for her presentation as a woman under siege within a siege. Troilus is a more bookish lover in Chaucer's version, who has a lyrical tradition of love sentiments at his command, and his songs and monologues in Book III celebrate his relationship with Criseyde in metaphysical terms. However, Chaucer is not presenting a Divine Comedy in this narrative but a pagan history, and one in which human love is subject to the forces of time and change.

The organization of the poem into five books reflects the progress of the love affair: the broad opening panorama of Book I gives Troilus and Criseyde a place in the wider history of Troy; the focus narrows in Books II and III, which chart the increasing self-involvement of the lovers as they create their own private world within Troy. Book IV marks the interruption of the historical world into their affairs, with the plan to exchange Criseyde; and the final Book sketches the 'changing' of Criseyde, her transferral to the Greek camp and engagement with Diomedes, Troilus' reluctant perception of her change, and his final change, as he ascends the spheres after his death and laughs at the behaviour of mortals, their loves and longings, on little earth. The book ends with its 'maker' committing it to the care of his peers 'Moral ▷ Gower', and 'philosophical Strode'.

▷ Troy.

Bib: Windeatt, B. (ed.), *Troilus and Criseyde*; Salu, M. (ed.), *Essays on Troilus and Criseyde*.

Trollope, Anthony (1815–82)

Novelist. The unbusinesslike qualities of his father, a barrister who forsook the law and ruined himself in farming, caused his childhood to be poverty-stricken, although his mother ▷ Frances Trollope kept her family from the worst hardships by writing. Trollope himself was a prolific novelist, and though he worked seriously his *Autobiography* (1883) deeply offended the taste of the time by his frank statement that the writing of novels was a craft and a business, like making shoes, with nothing exalted or inspired about it. He was a strong admirer of the novels of ▷ Thackeray and shared Thackeray's contempt for the commercial arrogance of the British upper-middle classes. On the other hand, unlike Thackeray, Trollope had also strong faith in the traditional virtues and values of the English gentry, and several of his novels are about how the gentry class opened its ranks (through marriage, and after a struggle) to the best elements of less-privileged classes. His first novel was published in 1847, but it was in 1855 that he published the first of his most famous series, the ▷ Barsetshire novels – ▷ *The Warden*. The series continued with *Barchester Towers* (1857); ▷ *Dr Thorne* (1858); *Framley Parsonage* (1864); *The Small House at Allington* (1864); ▷ *The Last Chronicle of Barset* (1867). It is in these books that he displays his very conservative values most winningly and convincingly; they present a world of very solidly portrayed church dignitaries and landed gentry and show a loving care for fully-rounded characterization. The world he shows with such conviction was perhaps already passing, and in presenting it Trollope does not forget the weaker side of its values nor the assaults and encroachments upon it of political adventurers and the more vulgar of the middle class. His later work became more political, for instance *Phineas Finn* (1869); ▷ *The Eustace Diamonds* (1873); *Phineas Redux* (1874); *The Way We Live Now* (1875); *The Prime Minister* (1876); *The Duke's Children* (1880). Some critics consider that this group of his novels is unduly neglected; the setting is commonly London, which Trollope thought a source of evil, and the tone is more critical of society. *The Way We Live Now* reflects his disillusionments most strongly; it includes a powerful portrait of a fraudulent tycoon in Melmotte, and is not so much political as a devastating social study.

Trollope lost favour after his death, but regained strong popularity in the mid-20th century. This was because this period of insecurity and war made Trollope's world of traditional values seem very reassuring. Yet critics seldom allow him rank equal to his contemporary ▷ George Eliot; he does not even pretend to insight as deep, or tragic vision, though he is often subtle and fond of pathos.

Bib: Sadleir, M., *Life*; Bowen, E., *Trollope: a new Judgement*; Cockshut, A.O.J., *Anthony Trollope: a Critical Study*; Gerould, W.G. and J.T., *Guide to Trollope*; Smalley, D. (ed.), *The Critical Heritage*; Wall, S., *Trollope and Character*.

Trollope, Frances (1780–1863)

Born Frances Milton in Somerset, the daughter of a vicar, she married in 1809 and had six children, including the novelist ▷ Anthony Trollope. She began writing when she was over fifty to support the family in the face of her husband's financial disasters and published in all some 114 books on ▷ travel, and novels. Despite the financial success of her first book she worked extremely hard, from before dawn each day, writing and caring for her family. She visited North America for an extended period and lived in France, Austria and Italy (meeting the ▷ Brownings, ▷ Dickens and ▷ Walter

Landor) for a few years. Her writing owed its popularity perhaps to her scathing views of Americans, also to its exuberant quality and her rather coarse, humorous women. *Domestic Manners of the Americans* (1832) brought her fame and popularity; *Paris and the Parisians* (1835), *Vienna and the Austrians* (1838) and *A Visit to Italy* (1842) were also successful. Her novels include *The Vicar of Wrexhill* (1837), portraying a mixture of vice and religion, *The Widow of Barnaby* (1838) and *The Life and Adventures of a Clever Woman* (1854).
Bib: Trollope, F.E., *Frances Trollope: Her Life and Literary Work from George III to Victoria*; Johnston, J., *The Life, Manners and Travels of Fanny Trollope: A Biography*.

Trotter (Cockburn), Catherine (1679–1749)
English dramatist and, after her marriage to the Reverend Patrick Cockburn in 1708, writer of theological works. Until 1707 she was a Roman Catholic. She began publication very young with the ⊳ epistolary novel *Olinda's Adventures or, The Amours of a Young Lady* (1793), and her verse dramatization of ⊳ Aphra Behn's story *Agnes de Castro* was acted at ⊳ Drury Lane in 1695. *The Fatal Friendship* (1698) was her most admired play. She contributed to *The Nine Muses* (1700). In 'To Mrs Manley' on ⊳ Delarivière Manley's play *The Royal Mischief* (1696) she wrote 'Th' Attempt was brave, how happy your success, / The Men with Shame our Sex with Pride confess.'

Her other publications include: *The Unhappy Penitent* (1701).

⊳ Pix, Mary
Bib: Greer, G. *et al.*, *Kissing The Rod*.

Troubadour and Minstrels
Court poet-composers of southern France (*trouvères* is the term for their northern French counterparts), who produced a sophisticated poetic corpus which reflected and promoted an emerging secular court culture in early medieval France. The troubadours are renowned for their love poetry, and their highly formalized descriptions of the experience of love and desire, often expressed in terms of a relationship of feudal service between the male speaker and his desired lady (⊳ Courtly Love). But their work is far from homogeneous: it includes a wide variety of lyrical genres and sub-genres (laments, dawnsongs, ⊳ pastoral poems and debates), may be satirical (⊳ Satire) as much as celebratory, and is always highly self-conscious about the literary nature of the experience it provides.

Some of the early poet-composers (as opposed to *jongleurs* who performed the work of others) were from the ranks of the social elite: the earliest poet whose name and work has survived is that of Guilhelm IX, Duke of Acquitaine (fl 1071–1127), but although their milieu was undoubtably that of the court most troubadour poets were not aristocrats themselves but professionals who made their living from their art. Some work by women troubadours has survived too, though this has attracted less attention than that of their male counterparts.

The legendary status of some of the 12th-century poets in particular was promoted by the appearance in the 13th century of prose 'Lives' (*Vidas*), which provided idealized histories of the poets to match the substance of their poems. But the high status of these court poets also derives from their influence on later medieval writers, including ⊳ Dante and ⊳ Petrarch.
Bib: Bogin, M., *The Woman Troubadours*; Dronke, P., *The Medieval Lyric*; Press, A. (ed. and trans.), *Anthology of Troubadour Poetry*; Patterson, L., *Troubadours and Eloquence*.

Troy
Ancient capital city of the Troad, a region on the north-west coast of Asia Minor; strictly, the capital was Ilium (in Homer's ⊳ *Iliad*) and Troy and Ilium have become alternative names for the same city. Troy is the subject of legends which began in ancient Greek times and were added to by the Romans, and further expanded by medieval writers in Western Europe. Somewhere behind the legends is a background of historical fact, but this is very obscure.

1 *Historical background.* Archaeologists and historians doubted whether a real city of Troy ever existed, until the German archaeologist Heinrich Schliemann discovered its remains near the modern Hissarlik, very near the traditional site. Subsequently, excavations uncovered nine cities in successive levels; the earliest (Troy I) dates from 3000–2500 BC, and the latest (Troy I) faded away in about the 5th century AD. Opinion has been divided about whether the Trojan war was fought against Troy 6, which in fact was destroyed by earthquake and fire about 1800 BC, or the rebuilt city known as Troy 7A, destroyed by similar causes in about 1200 – nearer the traditional date of the Trojan War in which the city is supposed to have been destroyed by the alliance of Greek princes.

2 *Greek myths of the fonding of Troy.* These recount a succession of mythical princes, the earliest being of divine or semi-divine origin: Teucer, Dardanus, Ericthoneus, and Tros – from whom the name of the country and its people originated. Tros' son Ilus was the founder of the city of Ilion (Ilium) or Troy. In the reign of Laomedon, son of Ilus, the walls of Troy were built by the ocean god Poseidon, to whom Laomedon refused the agreed reward; he was in punishment killed, together with most of his family, by the hero ⊳ Heracles. One of his two surviving children was ⊳ Priam, who was king of Troy in the Trojan war and met his death after the capture of the city. Priam's children included:

▷ Hector, the Trojan hero of Homer's *Iliad*; ▷ Paris, whose elopement with ▷ Helen was the cause of the war; ▷ Cassandra, the sombre prophetess; and ▷ Troilus, around whom legends were to be constructed in medieval times. Ilus' brother Assaracus was ancestor of another line of heroes who were to become more important in Roman and medieval European myth: this line of descent went through Capys, Anchises and Aeneas, who according to the Roman poet ▷ Virgil was the ancestor of the Roman people.

3 *Troy epic*. The legendary Trojan war led to three epics: Homer's *Iliad*, about the siege; Homer's ▷ *Odyssey* about the wanderings of Odysseus after the siege; and Virgil's ▷ *Aeneid*, about the wanderings of Aeneas until he finds his destination in Italy. Homer's epics arise out of still more ancient legends, but their own date is uncertain, as, to some extent, is their authorship; scholars do not think that they can be later than the 7th century BC. Virgil's poem dates from the 1st century BC, and is a deliberate attempt to emulate Homer. The three poems are the pattern of a tradition of European ▷ epic – *eg* Milton's ▷ *Paradise Lost*.

4 *Trojan myth in western Europe to AD 1500*. The prestige of Homer and Virgil kept Trojan myth alive and growing in the Middle Ages of Europe, but these poets were not the only source of its growth. Two collections of writing, alleged to be records of the Trojan war, and to be by ▷ Dictys the Cretan and ▷ Dares the Phrygian, are the source of new legends, including indirectly that of ▷ Troilus and Cressida. Virgil's view that the Romans were descendants of the Trojan Aeneas led to legends that other European nations have similar ancestry. For instance, *The History of the Britons* by the Welsh chronicler Nennius (8th–9th centuries) declares the ancestor of the British race to have been Brutus (▷ Brut), the great-grandson of Aeneas: this is repeated by the 12th-century ▷ Geoffrey of Monmouth.

Tudor, House of
The name of a family that ruled over England and Wales from 1485 until 1603. The succession was as follows: ▷ Henry VII; his son, ▷ Henry VIII; Henry VIII's three children, ▷ Edward VI, ▷ Mary I and ▷ Elizabeth I. Elizabeth died childless, and the throne passed to the Scottish family of ▷ Stuart, one of whom (James IV) had married a daughter of Henry VII.

The Tudors were of Welsh origin; Henry VII was the grandson of Owen Tudor, who married a member of the Lancastrian branch of the royal Plantagenet family. Henry thus acquired the claim of the House of Lancaster to the English throne, which he won at the Battle of Bosworth, the concluding battle of the Wars of the Roses, where he defeated ▷ Richard III of the House of York.

The Tudor family was notable for its abilities. Henry VII was a cautious ruler, who reconstructed the government's finances. Henry VIII started the ▷ Reformation in England by founding the ▷ Church of England, and this became distinctively Protestant under the boy king Edward VI. Mary I was a Catholic, married Philip II of Spain, and re-established Catholicism in England, but she died childless, and Protestantism was restored by her sister Elizabeth, possibly the most successful sovereign ever to sit on the English throne. The last ten years of Elizabeth's reign saw the beginnings of the literary flowering known as the 'Elizabethan age'. Her reign was also remarkable for victory over Spain and the beginnings of English overseas enterprise.

Tudor myth
A term used by historians to express the 16th-century belief, encouraged by the royal House of ▷ Tudor, that the Tudors were national saviours from the horrors of the Wars of the Roses and restorers of legendary national greatness. The first Tudor, ▷ Henry VII, took the throne from ▷ Richard III in 1485 by force of conquest, and since usurpation of a kingdom from its rightful king was a deadly sin, it was important for the Tudors to prove that they had not been guilty of it. Henry maintained that his was the rightful claim, but this was too clearly open to doubt; however, if Richard III was a proved tyrant, the usurpation was justified. Sixteenth-century historians made it their business to blacken Richard's character, not only to please the Tudors, but in reflection of national relief that they had brought the civil wars to an end, with the consequence that Richard is the legendary evil man of English history. Such is the picture given by ▷ Thomas More's *Richard III* (1513), ▷ Edward Hall's *Union of the Noble and Illustrious Families of Lancaster and York* (1548), and ▷ Holinshed's *Chronicles* (1578). The Tudors also encouraged the belief that, as a Welsh line of princes, they could trace themselves back to King ▷ Arthur, the hero of the mythical British golden age. Henry VII called his eldest son Arthur, but he did not live to succeed to the throne. The impress of the Tudor myth is strong on ▷ Shakespeare's ▷ history plays.
Bib: Anglo, S., *Spectacle, Pageantry, and Early Tudor Policy*.

Turberville, George (c 1540–1610)
Poet and translator. Turberville was secretary to ▷ Thomas Randolph, and during 1568–9 went with him on a political mission to Russia, where he met Ivan the Terrible. An account of this journey was reprinted by ▷ Hakluyt. He also knew ▷ Drummond, ▷ Gascoigne and ▷ Harington. Turberville is chiefly known for his translations of ▷ Ovid, early experiments with ▷ blank verse (*Epitaphes, Epigrams, Songs*

and Sonets (1567)), and a book on hunting (*The Noble Art of Venerie or Hunting* (1575)).

▷ Sandys, George; Translation.

Bib: Hiller, G. (ed.), *Poems of the Elizabethan Age*.

Turgenev, Ivan Sergeevich (1818–83)
Novelist and dramatist. Born in Orel, central Russia, educated at Moscow and St Petersburg Universities and Berlin. After a brief spell in the civil service he devoted himself to literature. In 1852 he was imprisoned for a month for his article on the death of Ukrainian writer Gogol (1809–52), and was subsequently banished to his estate. He left Russia in 1861 and, apart from a few visits, remained in self-imposed exile, largely in Baden Baden and Paris, where he died, although he continued to write of Russia and his own class, which he perhaps sensed was doomed. The novels have something of an autumnal character. He fell in love with the singer Pauline Garcia Viardot who did not give him an easy life, and this is also reflected in the novels in the theme of a strong woman and rather weak man. He knew ▷ Flaubert, ▷ George Sand and other French writers, and from 1847 visited England. He was widely read in English, admiring ▷ Shakespeare greatly; he knew and valued ▷ Charles Dickens and ▷ George Eliot, and was acquainted with ▷ William Thackeray, ▷ Anthony Trollope, ▷ Thomas Carlyle, ▷ Robert Browning, ▷ Alfred Tennyson, the ▷ Rossettis and others. He admired, met and influenced ▷ Henry James, and influenced many writers including ▷ George Moore, Joseph Conrad (1857–1924) and Virginia Woolf. He published a little poetry in 1838 but his first published prose was *A Hunter's Notes* (1847–51). He wrote a series of novels illuminating social and political issues: *Rudin* (1856), *A Nest of Gentlefolk* (1859), *On the Eve* (1860), *Fathers and Sons* (1862), *Smoke* (1867) and *Virgin Soil* (1877). His short stories include 'Asya' (1858), 'First Love' (1860) and 'Torrents of Spring' (1870); his most famous and critically acclaimed play is *A Month in the Country* (1850).

▷ Russian influence on English literature.

***Turn of the Screw, The* (1898)**
A novella by ▷ Henry James, published in *The Two Magics*. It is a ghost story, about a governess given sole charge of two children, Miles and Flora, in a country house named Bly. She comes to believe that she has to contend with the evil, ghostly influence of two dead servants, Peter Quint and Miss Jessell, over the children, who are ostensibly angelic but invisibly corrupted. Flora is taken away to London by the housekeeper, but Miles, when confronted by the governess with her belief, dies in her arms. The possibility that the governess is an hysteric who hallucinates the ghosts and herself manipulates the children provides a second layer of meaning. This layer is, however, absent in Benjamin Britten's opera of the same title. James' story, which he described as 'a trap for the unwary', is a masterpiece of ambiguity throughout.

Bib: Kirby, D. (ed.), *An Introduction to the Varieties of Criticism: The Portrait of A Lady/ The Turn of the Screw*.

Turnbull, Gael (b 1928)
Poet. Born in Edinburgh, Turnbull has long been a passionate champion of contemporary writing, especially visible since he set up the small but influential Migrant Press in the late 1950s. He has also been important in bringing ▷ Basil Bunting's work to prominence in Britain. His works include: *A Trampoline, Poems 1952–1964* (1968); *Scantlings* (1970); *A Gathering of Poems 1950–1980* (1983); and *A Winter Journey* (1987).

Turpin, Dick (Richard) (1706–39)
A famous English highwayman and thief, hanged at York for horse-stealing. He was greatly romanticized by the novelist ▷ Harrison Ainsworth in his novel *Rookwood* (1834), in which Turpin's famous ride from London to York on his mare, Black Bess, is described. The ride, like other romantic episodes told about him, is fictional.

Tutuola, Amos (b 1920)
Nigerian novelist. Tutuola was born in Abeokuta, Western Nigeria, where he was educated at an Anglican school. He served in the RAF in Lagos (1943–46) and later worked for the Nigerian Broadcasting Corporation. His first novel, *The Palm-Wine Drinkard and His Dead Palm-Wine Tapster in the Dead's Town* (1952), was one of the first Nigerian novels in English and received praise for its vivid and playful use of language. The patronizing tone of some early critical treatments of his work provoked hostility to it in Africa, but it was defended by ▷ Chinua Achebe in *Morning Yet on Creation Day* (1975). His other novels are: *My life in the Bush of Ghosts* (1954); *Simbi and the Satyr of the Dark Jungle* (1955); *The Brave African Huntress* (1958); *The Feather Woman of the Jungle* (1962); *Abaiyi and His Inherited Poverty* (1967); *The Witch-Herbalist of the Remote Town* (1981); *Pauper, Brawler and Slanderer* (1987). Stories: *The Village Witch Doctor* (1990). Other publications: *Yoruba Folktales* (1986).

Bib: Lindfors, B., *Critical Perspectives on Amos Tutuola*.

***Twelfth Night, or What You Will* (1599–1600)**
A comedy by ▷ Shakespeare, probably written 1599–1600 or possibly a little later. Its main source is a prose tale, *Apolonius and Silla* (1581)

by Barnabe Rich, an English version of an Italian tale by Cinthio (▷ Elizabethan Novels). The comic situations arising from confusion between twins come down from *Menaechmi* by the Roman playwright ▷ Plautus; Shakespeare had already adapted this play into ▷ *The Comedy of Errors*. Two 16th-century Italian plays, *Inganni* (*Deceits*) and *Gl'Ingannati* (*The Deceived*) have also been suggested as possible sources. The setting is the court of Orsino, Duke of Illyria, and the house of the wealthy Countess Olivia, whom he is courting. He uses as a go-between his page Cesario, really a girl, Viola, disguised as a boy. The page has already fallen in love with Orsino, and expresses sentiments on love so elequently to Olivia that the Countess believes herself in love, but with the page, not with the Duke. Meanwhile, Viola's twin brother, Sebastian, turns up, wearing the same style of clothes that his sister has chosen to wear as Cesario; he has been rescued from shipwreck by a sea-captain, Antonio, who feels a deep affection for him. The possibility of confusion is clearly various and great, and every possible confusion occurs. A subplot centres on Olivia's drunken kinsman, Sir Toby Belch, and her conceited steward, Malvolio; Sir Toby takes revenge on Malvolio for an insult, and incidentally gets mixed up in the confusions occurring round Viola and Sebastian by playing a trick on his friend, Sir Andrew Aguecheek, who is also courting Olivia. Sir Toby's interference ends in a clearing-up of the confusions of identity, and a subsequent suitable pairing off of Orsino and Viola, Sebastian and Olivia.

The comedy can be regarded as being about different forms of love, or imagining oneself to have fallen in love, and though the plot is bewildering in summary, it is deftly worked out theatrically and beautifully balanced, with finely cadenced poetry and a more unifying theme than any earlier comedy by Shakespeare. The title, like ▷ *A Midsummer Night's Dream* and ▷ *The Winter's Tale*, indicates the sort of occasion for which the story is suitable: Twelfth Night was the last night of the Christmas festival and a time of licensed disorder presided over by a Lord of ▷ Misrule, such as Sir Toby Belch. Although this title has often been seen to have little to do with the thematic content of the play, recent criticism suggests that the sense of misrule may be seen in attempts to cross class barriers (Malvolio), success at so doing (Maria), and the general economic self-sufficiency of Feste (▷ New Historicism).

***Two Gentlemen of Verona, The* (1594)**
An early romantic comedy by ▷ Shakespeare, probably written about 1594.

Shakespeare's source seems to have been a Spanish tale, Montemayor's *Diana*. The plot is a double love-affair with complications: Proteus is in love with Julia, and Valentine with Silvia, but Proteus plays both Valentine and Julia false in his efforts to win Silvia. Julia follows Proteus, disguised as a page, while Valentine, by the contrivance of Proteus, has to flee and takes refuge as the captain of a band of robbers. Proteus in the end is confronted by both Valentine and Julia, and happiness is restored by his suitable repentance. In plot, poetry and characterization the play is clearly very immature, though it has a limpid charm. There is an element of low-life comedy in the role of Launce, servant to Proteus, accompanied by his dog. Julia's disguise and the sentiment of the play look forward to the much more interesting ▷ *Twelfth Night*.

Two Noble Kinsmen, The
A play of romantic love chiefly by ▷ John Fletcher, perhaps in collaboration with ▷ Shakespeare. It was probably written in 1612–13, and was printed in 1634. The plot derives from ▷ Chaucer's *Knight's Tale* (▷ *The Canterbury Tales*) about the tragic rivalry in love of Palamon and Arcite.

Tyler, Margaret (c 1578)
Translator. Little is known of Margaret Tyler's life, the only biographical information coming from the dedicatory letter to her *A Mirrour of Princely Deedes and Knighthood* (1578), where she states that she belongs to the rich, ▷ Catholic Howard household. The preface to *A Mirrour* is important for students of women's history since it forthrightly states that women may write imaginative literature as well as men: 'my perswasion hath bene thus, that it is all one for a woman to pen a story, as for a man to addresse his story to a woman'. She also deals with the importance of female ▷ patronage.
Bib: Travitsky, B. (ed.), *The Paradise of Women*.

Tyler, Wat
The leader of the ▷ Peasants' Revolt of 1381. He was killed in the street by the Lord Mayor of London in the presence of ▷ Richard II.
▷ Ball, John.

Tyndale, William (?1492–1536)
A translator of the Bible; his version was a principal basis for the Authorized Version of 1611. He was a convinced Protestant. His other works include: *Parable of the Wicked Mammon* (1528), *Obedience of a Christian Man* (1528), and *Practice of Prelates* (1530). These works influenced the forms that the extreme Protestantism of ▷ Puritanism took in England. In 1535, while on a visit to the Netherlands, he was arrested and later burned as a heretic.
▷ Bible in England; Reformation.

Bib: Daniell, D. (ed.), *The New Testament, translated by William Tyndale*.

Tyrwhit, Elizabeth (c 1530–78)
Devotional writer. Lady-in-waiting to ▷ Katherine Parr, she belonged to the queen's circle of Puritan women and only narrowly escaped being arrested for her outspoken ▷ Protestantism. Her *Morning and Evening Praiers, with divers Psalms, Himnes and Meditations* (1574) were published in Thomas Bently's collection of works by pious women, *The Monument of Matrones* (1582). The work consists of several unimaginative verses and a series of prose meditations; overall Tyrwhit's concern is more with the plain presentation and interpretation of female piety and spiritual learning than with literary skill or finesse. She was governess to ▷ Elizabeth I and the queen's own copy of *Morning and Evening Praiers* survives (in the British Library); it is bound with gold, has enamelled portraits of Solomon and Moses on the covers, and is furnished with rings to attach it to a woman's girdle.
Bib: Beilin, E. V., *Redeeming Eve*; Blain, V. et al. (eds.), *The Feminist Companion to Literature in English*.

U

Udall, Nicholas (1505–56)
Dramatist and translator. Udall began his career as a school master (most famously becoming headmaster at Eton College), but won favour at court in 1533 when he wrote ▷ masques for the coronation celebrations of Anne Boleyn. His work as a translator was encouraged by ▷ Katherine Parr for whom he translated ▷ Erasmus' version of the New Testament. Although a staunch Protestant he remained in favour at the accession of the Catholic ▷ Mary I. It was during this period that he wrote ▷ *Ralph Roister Doister*, the first English comedy.

Ulysses
A novel by ▷ James Joyce, and one of the key texts of ▷ Modernism. It was first published in Paris in 1922, but was banned in England for its alleged obscenity until 1936. In a number of ways the book is an innovation in methods of presenting human experience through the novel form, and it is also the most ambitiously comprehensive attempt to do so, except perhaps for Joyce's next book, ▷ *Finnegans Wake* (1939). It is an attempt to present a character more completely than ever before. The story shows in immense detail the life of a man during a single day of 24 hours. The man is Leopold Bloom, a Jew of Hungarian origin living in Dublin; the day is 16 June 1904. To do this requires a method of conveying the process of thinking; Joyce's method has become known as the ▷ stream of consciousness technique, suggested to him by the work of a French novelist, Dujardin, and deployed by his contemporaries ▷ Dorothy Richardson and ▷ Virginia Woolf (▷ Henri Bergson). At the same time as seeking to create imaginatively 'a whole individual', Joyce seeks to make this individual representative, by setting him against the background of the oldest extended portrait of a man in European literature. He does this by making Bloom analogous with ▷ Homer's Odysseus, and by dividing the book into episodes, each of which corresponds to one in the ▷ *Odyssey*, though not in the same order. Joyce varies the technique of written expressions so as to make his language as close an analogy as possible to the modes of modern human experience. Thus in the fierce drunken episode 15 (Circe), the method is dramatic dialogue; in the fatigued anti-climax of 17 (Ithaca), the questionnaire is used; in the final episode 18 (Penelope), the stream of consciousness is used to the full, without punctuation.

No human experience is complete without relationship; Bloom is a lonely man, with numerous casual acquaintanceships. However, two deeper relationships dominate his story: there is the physical relationship with his wife, Molly, whose fidelity he more than mistrusts, and a spiritual affinity with ▷ Stephen Dedalus, whom he does not meet till near the end, but who is a lonely young man unconsciously seeking a father, as Bloom is a lonely middle-aged man wanting a son. Molly is analogous to Penelope in the *Odyssey* and Stephen relates to Telemachus, the wife and son respectively of Odysseus.

In some respects Joyce is carrying the artistic devotion of the French novelists to an extreme: *Ulysses* is an elaborate formal construction of immense seriousness, showing a dedication to art for its own sake comparable to that of the novelist ▷ Flaubert; it is also a realistic exercise, carrying to extreme the ▷ Naturalism of ▷ Zola. It is also remarkable for its parodic comedy and ▷ carnivalesque sense of fun and its radical image of a 'world turned upside down', which is developed fully in *Finnegans Wake*. Finally, it is a vivid tribute to Joyce's Dublin, from which he had become self-exiled.

▷ Irish literature in English.

Uncommercial Traveller, The
A collection of tales, sketches and essays, descriptive of places, society and manners, by ▷ Charles Dickens. They were published in ▷ *All the Year Round* and reissued in book form in 1861 and 1868.

Under the Greenwood Tree (1872)
The first of the ▷ Wessex novels by ▷ Thomas Hardy. The story is a village love affair between a schoolmistress, Fancy Day, and Dick Dewy, son of a 'tranter' or carrier of goods. It includes the theme of the rivalry of the village orchestra, who have hitherto played the music in church services, with Fancy, who takes over from them by substituting the harmonium. The story is thus slight and idyllic compared to Hardy's later Wessex stories but it is written with delicacy and insight. The title is the first line of a song in Shakespeare's *As You Like It*.

Under the Volcano
▷ Lowry, Malcolm.

Under Western Eyes (1911)
A novel by ▷ Joseph Conrad. It is set in pre-revolutionary Russia and in Switzerland, and is told through the character of the English language teacher, who witnesses many of the events in Switzerland, and reconstructs those in Russia from the notebooks of the central character, Kyrilo Sidorovitch Razumov. Razumov is the illegitimate son of a Russian nobleman, and has been brought up in the household of a Russian priest. He is given to understand that if he behaves well, his real father will assist him in his career; accordingly he is studious at the university, and keeps himself rigorously isolated from student politics. His enigmatic silence on political subjects, however, is misinterpreted by the radical students as signifying that he is a

strongly committed supporter of revolutionary activity; thus, when one of them, Victor Haldin, commits a political assassination and takes refuge with him, Razumov tries to disembarrass himself by betraying Haldin to the police. The police, however, will not allow him to return to his solitary studies; instead they send him to Switzerland, ostensibly as a revolutionary emissary, but actually to spy on the Russian revolutionaries in exile there. He finds them to be a circle composed partly of flamboyant or brutal self-seekers, such as Peter Ivanovitch, Madame de S., and Nikitin (nicknamed Necator, the killer). But there are also idealists of complete integrity, including Victor Haldin's sister, Nathalie Haldin. Nathalie is a pupil and friend of the English language teacher, who thus becomes involved in the story. She welcomes Razumov as a revolutionary hero, and the friend of her brother, for whose death he has in fact been responsible. Razumov is tormented by his guilt, his love and admiration for Nathalie, his horror and contempt of the debased elements among the revolutionaries, and the seeming impossibility of recovering his integrity and living otherwise than by false appearance. Eventually he confesses the truth to Nathalie and to the revolutionaries, and is reduced to total deafness by two blows from Nikitin. Nathalie is appalled, but understands him. She has told her English friend: 'You belong to a people which has made a bargain with fate, and wouldn't like to be rude to it.' The Western (British and Swiss) attitude to politics and the individual is such that fateful choices such as the one forced on Razumov are not demanded. His drama 'under the Western eyes' of the English language teacher is the drama of a nation where the individual is not permitted to withdraw from political decision into private life. Razumov spends the rest of his days as a sick man in Russia, respected by the best of the revolutionary circle whom he has known in Switzerland, and cared for devotedly by one of them.

Underhill, Cave (1634–?1710)
Actor. Underhill joined John Rhodes' company before the Restoration, and afterwards became a member of the ▷ Duke's Company under ▷ Sir William D'Avenant, specializing in comic roles, including the eponymous Cutter, in ▷ Abraham Cowley's *Cutter of Coleman Street*, the first Gravedigger in ▷ *Hamlet*, and the Clown in ▷ *Twelfth Night*. Tall, with a large face, flat nose, and 'unwandering eye', coupled with an apparently stolid, stupid, or lugubrious manner, he is said to have inclined people to laugh, merely by looking at him.

***Underwoods* (1640–1)**
Title of a collection of poems by ▷ Ben Jonson, published in the second folio edition of his *Works* in 1640–1. In the first edition of his works (1616) a collection of his poems had been given the title 'The Forest'.

***Unfortunate Traveller, or the Life of Jack Wilton, The* (1594)**
A romance by ▷ Thomas Nashe, published in 1594. Wilton begins as a page in the court of ▷ Henry VIII, and then travels through Europe as adventurer, soldier of fortune, and hanger-on of the poet Henry Howard, ▷ Earl of Surrey. It is one of the first notable ▷ picaresque tales in English. Among other historical figures, apart from Surrey, Wilton meets ▷ Sir Thomas More, ▷ Erasmus and ▷ Pietro Aretino; he witnesses historical events, such as the struggle between the Anabaptists of Munster and the Emperor Charles V, and describes a plague in Rome. The book is extremely episodic, and Jack himself has no consistent character. The narrative begins as a sequence of mischievous pranks in the manner of the popular 'jest-books' of Nashe's time, and at the other extreme goes into brutally realistic descriptions of rape and of the plague in Rome. Nashe's story is remarkable for its creation of a self-conscious narrative voice, and in its awareness of its status as a text that is created by the activity of a reader. At the same time, its delight in the grotesque, and in a constantly re-iterated ▷ discourse of bodily distortion and pain, serves to make the work one of the most vivid attempts at linguistic refashioning in the 16th century.
Bib: Rhodes, N., *Elizabethan Grotesque*.

Uniformity, Acts of
Laws passed by Parliament during and after the ▷ Reformation to secure religious union in England. The first was that of 1549 (under ▷ Edward VI) and the second and more important in 1559, under ▷ Elizabeth I. Both required the common use in church worship of ▷ *The Book of Common Prayer*. In 1662, under ▷ Charles II, another Act of Uniformity insisted on its use by all clergy and schoolmasters, and marks the beginning of the dissenting sects as formally separate religious bodies, distinct from the ▷ Church of England.

Union, Act of (1707)
Government Act by which ▷ Scotland was united with England, and given representation at Westminster. The Act was imposed on Scotland as an English reaction, during a period of war with France (▷ Spanish Succession, War of), to continuing Scottish efforts to achieve greater independence from England, and to restore to the throne the deposed ▷ James II, and then his descendants. The aim was to pacify Scotland, and prevent any possibility of an alliance between that partly Catholic nation and France. Under the legislation, the Scots were

allowed to vote on all issues in both the House of Commons and the House of ▷ Lords, and in return they had to agree to the Hanoverian (▷ George; Windsor, House of) succession. Much bitterness was created by the loss of Scottish autonomy which the Act entailed.

Unionist
A name used by politicians from 1886 to express opposition to Home Rule for Ireland, ie a separate Parliament for that country. The word at first united Conservatives with a number of Liberals who resisted the Home Rule policy of their leader, ▷ Gladstone. Later 'Unionist' became synonymous with 'Conservative', and it is still used by members of that party, though it officially accepts the existence of the Irish Republic.

Unitarianism
A doctrine of religion that rejects the usual Christian doctrine of the Trinity, or three Persons in one God (the Father, the Son, and the Holy Ghost), in favour of a belief in the single person of God the Father. It originated in Britain in the 18th century and was in accord with the rationalistic approach to religion of that century. The first Unitarian church opened in London in 1774; many English ▷ Presbyterians (in the 16th and 17th centuries one of the largest sects outside the Church of England) became Unitarians.

United Company, The
Acting company formed by the union of the ▷ King's Company with the ▷ Duke's Company in 1682. In effect the stronger Duke's Company absorbed what had been its rival for 21 years, because of the latter's ailing state. The United Company lasted until 1695, when its leading players, including ▷ Thomas Betterton, ▷ Elizabeth Barry, and ▷ Anne Bracegirdle, defected, because of a dispute with the theatre management, and moved to the remodelled ▷ Lincoln's Inn Fields Theatre. Until that time the United Company occupied both the Theatre Royal at ▷ Drury Lane and the ▷ Dorset Garden Theatre, using the Theatre Royal mainly for plays and Dorset Garden for the larger spectacles and musical performances.
▷ Theatres.

Unities, Classical
▷ Classical Unities.

Unity Theatre
A left-wing amateur theatre group founded in London in 1936, with the aim of dramatizing current affairs such as the Spanish Civil War, the popular front against war and Fascism, and the problems of unemployment. The use of theatrical documentary and group composition was innovatory at the time. The company was influenced by European developments in the theatre, but more so by the Living Newspaper method developed in America, 'a method which makes a continual claim to observed truth, to verified fact, whilst at the same time ordering and shaping these facts dramatically so they are charged with emotion'. Notable productions were: Clifford Odets' *Waiting for Lefty* (1936); ▷ Brecht's *Señora Carrar's Rifles* (1938); *Busmen* (1938), a collectively written piece; and ▷ Sean O'Casey's *The Star Turns Red* (1940). A left-wing amateur company of the same name was formed in Glasgow in 1941.
Bib: Chambers, C., *The Story of Unity Theatre*.

University Wits
A group of young men in the reign of ▷ Elizabeth I who were educated at either Oxford or Cambridge Universities, and then embarked on careers as men of letters. Their names were ▷ John Lyly, dramatist and writer of the kind of romance known as the ▷ Elizabethan novel; ▷ George Peele, dramatist; ▷ Robert Greene, dramatist; ▷ Thomas Lodge, who tried most of the branches of contemporary literature; ▷ Thomas Nashe, novelist and pamphleteer; ▷ Christopher Marlowe, dramatist. To these, the name of ▷ Thomas Kyd is sometimes added, although he is not known to have attended a university. Lyly was a writer for court circles, but the others were representative of a new kind of writer (of which ▷ Shakespeare was also an example) who sought his fortune with the general public. Most of them had some kind of influence on, or relationship with, Shakespeare: Lyly used the kind of sophisticated diction which Shakespeare partly emulated and partly parodied in ▷ *Love's Labour's Lost* and elsewhere; Green wrote a mellifluous ▷ blank verse that anticipates some qualities in the earlier verse of Shakespeare, and was the author of the 'novel' *Pandosto*, source of ▷ *The Winter's Tale*; Lodge wrote *Rosalynde*, the source of ▷ *As You Like It*; Marlowe was the architect of the dramatic blank-verse medium; Kyd possibly wrote the first version of ▷ *Hamlet*.

Univocal
Having one clear meaning. A univocal text might be considered an opposite of a 'writerly' text (▷ Readerly and writerly texts). Such writing would discourage attention to ambiguity, ▷ polyphony or polysemy.

Unreliable narrator
A ▷ narrator who cannot be relied upon to provide accurate information, so that the reader is obliged to try to deduce, from the possibly misleading account given by such a narrator,

the true facts of the case. A narrator may be unreliable because of limited knowledge or understanding (*eg* the idiot Benjy in the first section of William Faulkner's *The Sound and the Fury*), because of being in a disturbed state of mind (*eg* the governess in one possible reading of ▷ *The Turn of the Screw* by ▷ Henry James), because of personal bias or dubious moral values (*eg* Dowell in ▷ Ford Madox Ford's *The Good Soldier*), or out of sheer wilfulness (*eg* the narrator of ▷ Peter Carey's *Illywhacker*). Unreliable narration tends to emphasize the subjective nature of truth and the technique often tends towards the implication that there is no such thing as an objective viewpoint.

Unsworth, Barry (b 1930)
Novelist. Unsworth was born in Durham and educated at Manchester University. He worked for several years for the British Council in Athens and Istanbul, and Greece and Turkey have often provided the settings for his fiction, which deals with the passions and moral ambiguities arising from the meetings of cultures and ideologies. His novels include: *The Partnership* (1966); *The Hide* (1970); *Mooncranker's Gift* (1974); *The Big Day* (1976); *Pascali's Island* (1980); *The Rage of the Vulture* (1982); *Stone Virgin* (1985); *Sugar and Rum* (1988). The Booker Prize winning *Sacred Hunger* (1992) is a sea-tale in the tradition of ▷ Conrad and ▷ Golding, recounting the voyage of an 18th-century slaver; its wealth of historical detail and strongly sustained narrative make for a powerful indictment of the slave trade, and, by implication, the exploitation engendered by an unfettered and amoral free market.

***Unto This Last* (1860–2)**
Four essays on political economy by ▷ John Ruskin. They were intended to be part of a larger treatise, but their publication in the ▷ *Cornhill Magazine* aroused so much hostility that the editor (▷ William Thackeray) discontinued them. The reason for the anger was that Ruskin (an art critic) was, as it seemed to the public, stepping out of his professional function in order to attack the predominant economic theory of trading relationships, which he was considered by the middle-class public unqualified to do. The middle classes were inclined to believe that the subject had been reduced to the clear elements of a science by the political economists and ▷ Utilitarian thinkers of the first half of the 19th century – men such as ▷ Jeremy Bentham, David Ricardo, (1772–1823), ▷ Malthus, James Mill (1773–1836) and ▷ John Stuart Mill. Ruskin pointed out that what was called 'political economy' was really 'commercial economy' and that it was untrue since it omitted facts of human nature, unjust since it unduly favoured the employing middle class and uncivilized since it omitted the cultural values that ought to underlie wealth. He found space to praise ▷ Charles Dickens' novel ▷ *Hard Times*, itself an attack on Utilitarianism. In spite of the hostility and scorn of Ruskin's contemporaries, much of his thinking in these essays has been accepted by later sociologists and economists. The Indian leader Mahatma Gandhi admitted a debt to *Unto This Last*, as did a number of the early leaders of the British Labour Party.

Upward, Edward (b 1903)
Novelist. He was educated at Repton School and Cambridge University with ▷ Christopher Isherwood, with whom he invented a fantasy world, Mortmere, a setting for bizarre and anarchic stories which survive only in Upward's *The Railway Accident* (1969). *Journey to the Border* (1938) reflects Upward's commitment to Marxism; it ends with the neurotic protagonist rejecting his fantasies in favour of the 'real world' of the Worker's Movement. *In the Thirties* (1962), which ▷ Stephen Spender described as 'the most truthful picture of life in that decade', is the first part of a trilogy, *The Spiral Ascent*, which examines the conflict between private fulfilment and political activism. The trilogy concludes with *The Rotten Elements* (1969) and *No Home But the Struggle* (1977). Story collection: *The Night Walk* (1987).

Urizen
▷ Blake, William.

***Urn Burial*, or *Hydriotaphia* (1658)**
A treatise by ▷ Sir Thomas Browne, published in 1658. Its starting-point is the discovery of ancient burial urns in Norfolk; this leads to an account of various ways of disposing of the dead, and meditations on death itself.

Uther Pendragon
King of Britain, father of ▷ King Arthur. In ▷ Geoffrey of Monmouth's version of British history, his title 'Pendragon' (lit. 'head of dragon') derives from his commissioning of two dragon banners, which commemorate the dragon-shaped portent which appeared to him at the moment of his father's death. ▷ Merlin is on hand to explain the significance of the dragon sign, which anticipates both Uther's and Arthur's great achievements.

Utilitarianism
A 19th-century political, economic and social doctrine which based all values on utility, ie the usefulness of anything, measured by the extent to which it promotes the material happiness of the greatest number of people. It is especially associated with ▷ Jeremy Bentham, at first a jurist concerned with legal reform and later a social philosopher. Followers of the

movement are thus often called 'Benthamites' but Bentham's disciple ▷ John Stuart Mill used the term 'Utilitarians'. Owing to their habit of criticizing social concepts and institutions on strictly rational tests, the leaders of the movement were also known as Philosophical Radicals.

Utilitarianism dominated 19th-century social thinking, but it had all its roots in various forms of 18th-century rationalism. In moral philosophy David Hume (1711–76) had a strong influence on Bentham by his assumption that the supreme human virtue is benevolence, ie the disposition to increase the happiness of others. Psychologically, Bentham's principle that humans are governed by the impulses to seek pleasure and avoid pain derives from the associationism of David Hartley (1705–57). But Bentham and his associates believed that the virtue of benevolence, and human impulses towards pleasure, operate within social and economic laws which are scientifically demonstrable. Bentham accepted Adam Smith's reasoning in *The Wealth of Nations* (1776) that material prosperity is governed by economic laws of supply and demand, the beneficial operation of which is only hindered by governmental interference. ▷ Malthus, in his *Essay on the Principle of Population* (1798), maintained that it is mathematically demonstrable that population always tends to increase beyond the means of subsistence, and David Ricardo (1772–1823), a friend of Bentham's, applied Malthus' principle to wages, arguing that as the population increases wages will necessarily get lower, since the increase is more rapid than that of the wealth available to support the workers. Smith, Malthus and Ricardo were masters of what was called the science of political economy, and the inhuman fatalism with which they endowed it caused to be known as the ▷ dismal science. However, it was not dismal for the industrial middle class of employers, whose interests it suited; they were already 'utilitarians' by self-interest and thus willing converts to the theory.

Thus the operation of Utilitarianism in the 19th century was paradoxical. It liberated society from laws which were inefficient survivals from the past (the Elizabethan Poor Laws) but it replaced them by laws that often operated with cold inhumanity (eg the ▷ Poor Law of 1834). It reduced senseless government interference with society but its concern with efficiency encouraged a bureaucratic civil service. It liberated the employers but it was often unsympathetic to the interests of the employees. Its principle was benevolence but its faith in reason often made it indifferent to individual suffering. The inhumanity of the creed, and its indifference to cultural values unless they could be shown to be materially useful, caused it to be vigorously attacked by leading writers between 1830 and 1870, including ▷ Thomas Carlyle, ▷ Charles Dickens, ▷ John Ruskin and ▷ Matthew Arnold. But perhaps its sanest and most lucid critic was John Stuart Mill; though himself a Utilitarian to the end of life, he saw the philosophical limitations of the movement and exposed them in his essays in 1838 on Bentham and on ▷ Samuel Taylor Coleridge (1772–1834) whom he admired as the father of the opposing tendency of thought. Mill's essay *Utilitarianism* (1863) emphasized that some kinds of pleasure are better than others – a distinction Bentham failed to make – and that the highest virtue in humanity is 'the desire to be in unity with our fellow creatures'. Mill was aware, as Bentham had not been, of the importance of the artistic imagination, in particular of poetry, in a civilization.

Our society is still in many ways utilitarian but as a systematic philosophy Utilitarianism did not outlast the 19th century. The last important figures connected with the movement are the philosophers ▷ Herbert Spencer and ▷ Leslie Stephen.

▷ *Unto This Last.*

Utopia (1516)
A political and philosophical treatise by ▷ Sir Thomas More, in the form of an account of an imaginary, newly discovered country. It was written in Latin, and translated into English (after More's death) in 1551; it had already been translated into French (1530), and such was the European fame of the book that Italian, Spanish and German versions also appeared.

The idea of a fictional country was no doubt stimulated by recent Italian, Portuguese, and Spanish exploration, and in particular by ▷ travel literature such as Amerigo Vespucci's account of his travels (1507). Philosophically, the book is a pure product of ▷ Renaissance ▷ humanisim, and like other products of that movement, it was inspired by the ancient Greek philosopher ▷ Plato. The land of Utopia is the Platonic ideal of a country, only to be realized on the assumption that man is basically good. Private property is replaced by communal ownership; there is complete freedom of thought; war is regarded as abominable, and to be used only in the last resort, when it should be waged as effectively as possible, even, if necessary, by unscrupulous means. Earthly happiness is glorified; the good life is the life of mental and physical fulfilment, rather than the medieval Christian life of self-denial and asceticism, but the Utopians are humane and benevolent, not self-indulgent. There is perfect mutual respect, and women receive the same education as men.

Utopian fiction
More's ▷ *Utopia* introduced into the English language the word 'utopian' = 'imaginary and ideal', and started a succession of 'utopias' in English literature. The idea of inventing an imaginary country to be used as a 'model'

by which to judge earthly societies did not, however, originate with More, but with his master the Greek philosopher ▷ Plato, who did the same in his dialogues *Timaeus* and the *Republic*. *Utopia*'s most notable successors in the 17th century were Bacon's unfinished *New Atlantis* (1626), in which science is offered as the solution for humanity, and James Harington's *Oceana* (1656), which put forward political ideas that were to have a powerful influence in America. In the 20th century, ▷ H. G. Wells was, in his earlier days, a vigorous utopian: *Anticipations* (1901), *A Modern Utopia* (1905), and *New Worlds for Old* (1908). Just before Wells, ▷ William Morris' *News from Nowhere* (1890) is a noteworthy socialistic utopia.

However, from the 18th century, much utopian literature is satirical, intended to give warning of vicious tendencies of society rather than to exemplify ideals. An example of this is Bernard de Mandeville's (1670–1733) *Fable of the Bees* (1714), about the downfall of an ideal society through the viciousness of its inhabitants; and Swift's ▷ *Gulliver's Travels* (1726) can be put in the same class. In the 19th century the best known examples are Samuel Butler's ▷ *Erewhon* (1872) and *Erewhon Revisited* (1901). In the 20th century, fears for the future of mankind have predominated over the optimism about inevitable progress which was more typical of the 19th century, and this has led to a new kind of utopian writing, portraying our own society set in the future, showing our fears realized. For this kind of work, the term 'dystopia' has been invented. The first striking example was ▷ Aldous Huxley's *Brave New World* (1932), about the deadness of a civilization which has come to be dominated by scientific technology; ▷ E. M. Forster's tale *The Machine Stops* has a similar theme, and both are written in reaction against H. G. Wells' optimism about technology. ▷ George Orwell's *1984* is a nightmare about 20th-century political totalitarianism, the grimmer, because Orwell brought the date of his anticipated society so close to the time of writing. A number of 20th-century women writers have explored utopian and dystopian worlds as a means of satirizing or criticizing sexual relations in the modern world, or as a way of exploring new possibilities for gender relations and identities. ▷ Doris Lessing's science fiction explores utopianism, while Marge Piercy's *Woman On The Edge of Time* juxtaposes an ideal future with the grim present. American feminist writer Charlotte Perkins Gilman's *Herland* (1916) is perhaps the most famous feminist utopia, whilst ▷ Margaret Atwood's *The Handmaid's Tale* is a feminist dystopia.

▷ Science Fiction.

Utrecht, Treaty of

▷ Spanish Succession, War of.

V

Vagabonds and vagrants

Generally known today as 'tramps'; men and women who have no settled residence or work, but live by begging or 'casual labour', wandering from place to place, finding shelter where they can. The 16th century was a period when vagrancy was a critical problem, for special causes: the dissolution of the ▷ monasteries (1536–9) caused unemployment among monastic servants and tradesmen, and ▷ enclosures of land for sheep-farming and parks evicted peasants from their farms. Some of the vagabonds (also called 'rogues') were wandering entertainers, including actors ('players') unattached to noble households; some were pedlars (like Autolycus in ▷ Shakespeare's ▷ *The Winter's Tale*) with goods for sale; a special class were the gipsies who appeared in England early in the 16th century. Many, more or less inevitably, became part of the underworld of crime, for which a large slang language of 'cant' grew up: Abraham men = pretended lunatics (Mad Tom, in Shakespeare's ▷ *King Lear*); 'hookers' or 'anglers' = thieves who extracted goods from houses with a hooked stick; 'rufflers' = highway robbers; 'priggers of prancers' = horse thieves. 'Prig' was at this time a common word for thief. This underworld was the subject of a class of popular literature known as 'rogue pamphlets', the most notable examples of which are ▷ Robert Greene's 'cony-catching' ▷ pamphlets, 1591–2.

The government tried to deal with the problem of vagrancy by constructive legislation (*eg* the ▷ Poor Law of 1601) and by severity – imprisonment, whipping, and, in the 17th century, branding.

Bib: Beier, A. L., *Masterless Men: The Vagrancy Problem in England 1560–1640.*

Valley of Humiliation; Valley of the Shadow of Death

Two places of trial through which pilgrims had to pass in ▷ John Bunyan's ▷ *Pilgrim's Progress*. The Valley of the Shadow of Death is a reference to Psalm 23 in the ▷ Bible (Authorized Version).

Vanbrugh, Sir John (1664–1726)

Architect and dramatist, who designed Blenheim Palace for the Duke of ▷ Marlborough, the Queen's Theatre in the ▷ Haymarket, and (with Nicholas Hawksmoor) Castle Howard in Yorkshire. He also wrote several plays of distinction. The son of a London tradesman whose father was a ▷ Protestant refugee from Ghent, Vanbrugh became a captain under Marlborough, and was imprisoned from 1690 to 1692 in the Bastille, where he wrote parts of his play, ▷ *The Provok'd Wife*, eventually staged in 1697. His first performed play was ▷ *The Relapse: Or Virtue in Danger* (1696), ▷ a satiric response to ▷ Colley Cibber's ▷ Reform comedy, ▷ *Love's Last Shift*. He wrote several other lively comedies, mostly adaptations from the French, including *The False Friend* (1701), *The Country House* (1703), *Squire Trelooby* (1704), and *The Confederacy* (1705), performed by ▷ Thomas Betterton's company at the newly opened Queen's Theatre, which Vanbrugh managed for a time with ▷ William Congreve.

Vanbrugh was one of the dramatists singled out for attack by ▷ Jeremy Collier in his *A Short View of the Immorality and Profaneness of the English Stage* (1698), to which he responded vigorously in *A Short Vindication of the 'Relapse' and 'The Provok'd Wife' from Immorality and Profaneness* in 1698. He was knighted and became Clarencieux king-of-arms in 1705, and was made comptroller of royal works in 1714. His last play, *A Journey to London*, was left unfinished at his death, and was completed by Cibber as *The Provok'd Husband* (1728). ▷ Richard Brinsley Sheridan reworked *The Relapse* as *A Trip to Scarborough* (1777). The original version was revived in 1947 and again by the ▷ Royal Shakespeare Company in 1967.

Bib: Whistler, L., *Sir John Vanbrugh, Architect and Dramatist*; Berkowitz, G. M., *Sir John Vanbrugh and the End of Restoration Comedy*; Beard, G., *The Work of John Vanburgh*; Downes, K., *Sir John Vanbrugh: A Biography.*

Vanessa

▷ Jonathan Swift's name for Esther Vanhomrigh who was in love with him between the years 1708 and 1723.

Vanity Fair (1874–8)

A satirical ▷ historical novel by ▷ William Thackeray published in monthly issues. The title, borrowed from John Bunyan's *Pilgrim's Progress* (1678 and 1684), shows that Thackeray's subject matter is the worldly, materialistic society of his time. He shows his men of religion to be either hypocrites or deluded. ▷ Dissenters, the descendants of Bunyan, include old Osborne, the arrogant, sombre and unfeeling businessman; ▷ Evangelicalism is represented by the hypocritical Bute Crawley.

The novel is subtitled 'A Novel without a Hero' and there is in fact nothing heroic about the society that Thackeray presents. However, its heartlessness and snobbery are skilfully manipulated by the central character, Becky Sharp, an ingenious and vigorous adventuress of poor parentage. She begins her socially ambitious career with a friendship with Amelia Sedley, the soft-hearted, weakly sentimental heroine of the book. Becky tries to marry Jos Sedley, Amelia's brother, a foolish but rich 'nabob'. Frustrated in this, and reduced to being a ▷ governess, she then makes love to the mean and avaricious Sir Pitt Crawley, but makes the mistake of marrying his second son,

Rawdon, a gallant but ignorant and dissolute man who, despite his incapacity, is later made Governor of the unhealthy Coventry Islands. Her marriage does not prevent her from pursuing her social ambitions still further by becoming the mistress of the aristocratic and degenerate Lord Steyne. Her ambitions are eventually defeated but she manages to end up as a respected member of society.

Amelia Sedley first marries the worthless young officer, George Osborne, who is killed at the battle of Waterloo. The only fine human values are characterized by his friend, Dobbin, an English ▷ gentleman in the moral rather than the social sense, who eventually becomes Amelia's second husband. The novel is an impressive, if negative, landscape of upper-class society in the first half of the 19th century; its best parts are those that concentrate on Becky Sharp and are written with a keen, sardonic humour. The novel is commonly regarded as Thackeray's most successful work.

***Vanity of Human Wishes, The* (1749)**
An imitation of ▷ Juvenal's Tenth Satire in heroic ▷ couplets by ▷ Samuel Johnson. Where the tone of the imitations of ▷ Horace by other poets is detached and urbane, Johnson's poem affects the moral earnestness and ruggedness of Juvenal. The poet reflects upon the vanity of ambition as illustrated by the lives of various historical figures, including ▷ Cardinal Wolsey the statesman, a number of famous scholars, and the 'warrior' Charles XII of Sweden. The poem is remarkable for its sonorous authority of tone, exemplified by the famous first lines: 'Let observation with extensive view, / Survey mankind, from China to Peru'. It is packed with memorable generalizations, expressing a kind of Christian stoicism. All human activity ends in disappointment and all life ends in death: 'From Marlb'rough's eyes the streams of dotage flow. / And Swift expires a driv'ler and a show.' The universality of the poem can descend to mere platitude, and its unremittingly emphatic gloom risks lugubriousness. It has consequently been felt to embody a decadent, mechanically inauthentic Augustanism. In fact, it shows a morally hypersensitive poet taking refuge from despair in satisfyingly rhetorical pessimism and pious abjection: hence its surprisingly moving, personal intensity. It is as much a product of the age of ▷ sensibility as a 'late Augustan' work.

Vaughan, Henry (1622–95)
Poet. Henry Vaughan, together with his brother Thomas Vaughan (1622–66) the alchemist and poet, was born at Newton-by-Usk in Wales. Vaughan's Welsh roots were to feature prominently in his writing. He termed himself 'The Silurist' after a local Welsh tribe termed the Silures by Tacitus, and his third published collection of poems was entitled *Olor Iscanus* (1651), which can be translated as 'The Swan of Usk', a reference to Vaughan's native river. In addition to *Olor Iscanus*, three collections of Vaughan's poetry appeared in his lifetime: *Poems with the Tenth Satire of Juvenal Englished* (1646), *Silex Scintillans* (1650, revised ed. 1655), and *Thalia Redivivia* (1678).

Silex Scintillans perhaps provides a clue as to Vaughan's intellectual identity. The title means 'The Flashing Flint' – an image which was given emblematic significance on the title-page of the collection where a hand, issuing from a cloud, is shown striking fire from a flintstone, fashioned in the shape of a heart. The image, which signifies a 'stony' heart surrendering flames of divine love when struck by God's spiritual force, suggests ▷ George Herbert's influence on Vaughan. But the image, with its conjunction of stone and fire suggestive of a religious awakening (a theme explored in the collection of poems as a whole), also alerts us to another side of Vaughan's writing. In 1655 Vaughan published a translation of an 'Hermetic' work entitled *Hermetical Physick* and in 1657 appeared his *The Chymists Key*. Hermeticism – the linking of alchemy, magic and science – might also be thought of as represented in the physical image of the flint flashing with fire. These two elements in Vaughan's intellectual life combine in his poetry in a way reminiscent of ▷ Thomas Traherne's concern for expressing the physical and spiritual worlds.

Bib: Martin, L. C. (ed.), *Works*; Hutchinson, F. E., *Henry Vaughan: A Life and Interpretation*; Post, J., *Henry Vaughan: The Unfolding Vision*.

***Venice Preserv'd: or, A Plot Discovered* (1682)**
▷ Tragedy by ▷ Thomas Otway, his sixth and last, set in Venice, and based on an original work by Cesar Vischard, Abbé de Saint Real. Jaffeir, married to Belvidera, pleads with her father Priuli, a wealthy Venetian senator, to make peace with him. Priuli adamantly refuses; he is outraged because Jaffeir, having been made welcome in Priuli's house after saving Belvidera's life, 'stole' her from him, and married her secretly. Jaffeir's friend Pierre enters, and privately they commiserate over the tyranny of the Senate. Pierre's beloved Aquilina has been taken from him by the rich, elderly senator Antonio, and Pierre tells Jaffeir his property is being confiscated by Priuli, leaving him and his wife destitute. The two plot rebellion and revenge, but the conspiracy fails, and Jaffeir betrays Pierre, who is taken and condemned to death. But at the end Jaffeir repents, stabs Pierre to preserve him from a shameful death, then stabs himself. Belvidera is driven mad and dies. The tragedy was topical: the character of Antonio is a ▷ satire on the ▷ Earl of Shaftesbury, and the 'plot' referred to in the sub-title was related by many to the

▷ 'Popish plot' to murder ▷ Charles II and reinstate ▷ Catholicism, in which Shaftesbury played a large part. The play has been seen as transitional in the move toward the domestic ▷ tragedy of the 18th century.

***Venus and Adonis* (1593)**
A narrative poem in six-lined stanzas by ▷ William Shakespeare. It is dedicated to Henry Wriothesley, ▷ Earl of Southampton. It is based on the Romano-Greek myth of the love of Venus, the goddess of sexual beauty, for the beautiful youth ▷ Adonis. The poem probably emulates the love poem ▷ *Hero and Leander* by ▷ Marlowe (completed by ▷ Chapman) and is Shakespeare's earliest published work. The poem reflects the extent to which Shakespeare was indebted to ▷ Ovid, particularly to the ▷ *Metamorphoses.*

Verbruggen, John (d c1707)
Actor, singer, dancer, manager, dramatist. He joined the ▷ United Company in 1688, acting at first under the name of Alexander.

A handsome man, Verbruggen was often in trouble because of his fiery temperament: on one occasion he got into a brawl with the Duke of St Albans behind the scenes at ▷ Drury Lane, and afterwards apologized publicly for hitting and insulting the Duke. He created many important roles, including Loveless in ▷ Colley Cibber's ▷ *Love's Last Shift* and ▷ Sir John Vanbrugh's ▷ *The Relapse*; Constant in Vanbrugh's ▷ *The Provok'd Wife*; the King of Granada in ▷ William Congreve's ▷ *The Mourning Bride*, and Mirabel in his ▷ *The Way of the World.*

His wife was the actress ▷ Susanna Verbruggen.

Verbruggen, Susanna (?1667–1703)
Actress. Susanna Verbruggen (née Percival) acted at the Theatre Royal, and later at ▷ Dorset Garden, with the ▷ United Company, and in 1686 married the popular actor and dramatist William Mountfort (1664–92). By 1690 she was recorded as being one of the leading actresses of the company. Two years after Mountfort's death, she married the actor ▷ John Verbruggen, and died in childbirth.

Susanna Verbruggen excelled in comedy, was a superb mimic, and according to ▷ Cibber 'gave many heightening touches to Characters but coldly written, and often made an Author vain of his Work, that in it self had little merit.' She was famous for her special talents in men's parts, playing ▷ Bayes in ▷ George Villiers' ▷ *The Rehearsal* to great acclaim, and in the roles of hoydens and female fops. Cibber described her performance as Melantha in ▷ Dryden's ▷ *Marriage à la Mode* as '(containing) the most compleat System of Female Foppery, that could possibly be crowded into the tortur'd Form of a Fine Lady'.

Vere Street Theatre
One of the first venues used for stage performances after the Restoration, before the construction of purpose-built theatres, and, like ▷ Lincoln's Inn Fields, it involved conversion of a former tennis court.

Verfremdungseffekt
▷ Alienation effect.

Vergil, Polydore
▷ Histories and Chronicles.

Verne, Jules (1828–1905)
French author of adventure stories and ▷ science fiction, notably *Voyage to the Centre of the Earth* (1864), *Twenty Thousand Leagues Under the Sea* (1869) and *Round the World in Eighty Days* (1873).

Vers de société
A kind of poetry originating in France in the 17th century, distinguished by its content, and the treatment of it: light, graceful, witty comment on current manners. In England it was particularly characteristic of the early 18th century – much of the work of ▷ Prior, ▷ Gray and ▷ Swift. An example is Swift's *A Soldier and a Scholar* (1732).

Vers Libre
▷ Free Verse.

Vicar of Bray, The
The title of an anonymous 18th-century song in which a parish priest boasts of having changed his views to fit every political and religious regime from the time of ▷ Charles I to that of ▷ George I. The figure may be based on Simon Aleyn, who actually belongs to an earlier period. He was vicar of Bray in Berkshire from about 1540 to 1588, and changed his religion several times to suit the policies of ▷ Henry VIII, ▷ Edward VI, ▷ Mary I, and ▷ Elizabeth I. 'Vicar of Bray' has become a byword for a time-server.

***Vicar of Wakefield, The* (1761–2)**
A novel by ▷ Oliver Goldsmith written 1761–2 but not published until 1766. Dr Primrose, a good-natured and innocent vicar, lives in comfortable circumstances with his wife and six children. Then their life is overturned by a series of disasters, reducing them to poverty and disgrace; the vicar endures his troubles with sweetness and stoicism. Eventually, they are restored to prosperity by the friendship of a benefactor, Mr Burchill, who turns out to be Sir William Thornhill, whose nephew had originally caused their misfortunes. The novel has conventionally been interpreted as a simplistic moral ▷ fable, the chief virtue of which is its ▷ sentimentality. Recent critics

however suggest an element of ▷ satiric irony (▷ Figures of speech), drawing parallels with Goldsmith's complex creations in other genres.

Vice, The
A 16th-century term for a type of tempter found in 16th-century ▷ interludes, used for the first time in ▷ John Heywood's *Play of the Weather* (1533), in which Merry-report is called the 'vice of the play'. The figure has precedents in the devil-tempters which appear in earlier medieval drama, and descendants in the individualized tempters in Elizabethan drama.

Victoria, Queen (1837–1901)
Born in 1819, Victoria came to the throne at the age of seventeen and was the longest reigning monarch in British history. In addition to re-establishing the prestige of the monarchy, she became a monumental symbol for the nation during the 60 years of the greatest power and influence Britain had ever known. The British Empire grew and was consolidated, with her as its figurehead. Her effectiveness as such was recognized by her Prime Minister ▷ Benjamin Disraeli when he induced her to adopt the title Empress of India in 1877. Victoria's jubilees of 1887 and 1897 were great national occasions, on which the sovereign was identified with the nation as never before since the reign of Elizabeth I (1558–1603). Victoria was also seen as an exemplary wife and mother, having nine children with her husband ▷ Prince Albert of Saxe-Coburg-Gotha, whom she married in 1840 and to whom she was devoted. When he died in 1861 she entered a period of mourning that was to end only with her death. She was responsible for setting a standard for the domestic virtues of rectitude of personal conduct and devotion to her husband and family, virtues greatly esteemed by the middle classes at a time when these classes dominated national life. Needless to say she was a life-long opponent of 'women's rights'.

Victoria was well-read; her diaries record her reading of ▷ the Brontës, ▷ Elizabeth Gaskell and ▷ George Eliot, as well as many male writers. She was especially fond of the works of ▷ Tennyson, who became her Poet Laureate in 1850. The Queen wrote scores of letters, which are published in five volumes edited by Roger Fulford, and accumulated over 100 volumes of diaries and journals. Selections from her jounals (subsequently destroyed) along with some edited correspondence, have been published in three volumes edited by A.C. Benson and Viscount Esher (1907). The only writings published during her lifetime were *Leaves from a Journal of Our Life in the Highlands (1848–61)* (1868) and *More Leaves* (1883), in which she records her travels in Scotland.
Bib: Longford, E., *Victoria R.I.*

Villanelle
Originally a rustic song; made into a regular form of courtly grace and sweet tunefulness by the French poet Passerat (d 1602). The form was not much used in England until the period 1880–1910, when a fashion developed – chiefly among minor poets – for all such graceful forms (the ballade, rondeau, triolet, etc.). It consists of five three-line stanzas and a final four-line one; the first and third lines of the first stanza recur, alternately, as refrains and make a concluding couplet to the last stanza.

***Villette* (1853)**
Novel by ▷ Charlotte Brontë. Like her earlier novel, ▷ *The Professor*, *Villette* is based on the author's experiences in Brussels, where she worked as a teacher. The narrator, Lucy Snowe, loses her family and means of financial support early in the novel, and leaves for Villette (the name Brontë chose for Brussels) to find employment with Mme Beck, initially as a nursery ▷ governess and later as a teacher in Mme Beck's school. Lucy's pupils are mostly vain, frivolous and shallow, unlike her in personality, but she succeeds in establishing authority. Much of the novel is devoted to the tempestuous relationship between Lucy and the professor M. Paul Emmanuel, Mme Beck's cousin. Ultimately M. Paul establishes Lucy in a school of her own before leaving on a business trip to the West Indies. The ending is ambiguous, for the reader is left to decide whether he returns to marry Lucy or is drowned on the way back to Belgium. The novel fuses Gothic elements with 19th-century ▷ realism, and the narrative strategy is unusual for its time. Recent feminist criticism has focused on the instability of the narrator's discourse and the gaps, ellipses and psychological projections which appear in *Villette*'s exploration of subjectivity.
Bib: Newton, J., 'Villette' in *Feminist Criticism and Social Change*, ed. Newton and Rosenfelt; Jacobus, M., 'The Buried Letter: Romanticism in *Villette*' in *Women Writing and Writing About Women*.

Villiers, George, 2nd Duke of Buckingham (1627–87)
Courtier and dramatist, son of the statesman, the 1st Duke of Buckingham, who had been a favourite of ▷ James I, and who was assassinated in 1628. Villiers, the 2nd Duke, accompanied ▷ Charles I to Scotland during the ▷ Civil War, and again into exile later. In 1657 he returned secretly to England, and married the daughter of Lord Fairfax, the parliamentary general who had charge of his confiscated estates. These were returned to him after the Restoration. He became one of ▷ Charles II's 'cabal' of intimates, and wrote a number of plays, of which the ▷ burlesque ▷ *The Rehearsal* is the best known. He was parodied by ▷ Dryden as Zimri in ▷ *Absalom and Achitophel*.

***Vindication of the Rights of Woman* (1792)**
Tract by English writer ▷ Mary Wollstonecraft. It follows her *Vindication of the Rights of Man* (1790). She returns to the question of women's ▷ education (which she had addressed in ▷ *Thoughts on the Education of Daughters*, 1787) to argue that uneducated girls are often 'cruelly left by their parents without any provision, and, of course, are dependent on not only the reason but the bounty of their brothers'. She speaks of such women as 'unable to work, and ashamed to beg'. Thus in Wollstonecraft's polemic, work and the ability to work are increasingly seen as important in terms of a woman's self-definition and survival in the world. This shifts the debate from the terrain of provision to one of rights, but it is coupled with a spiritual and psychological polemic – she wants women to 'acquire strength of mind and body' to combat their situation physically, but also to resist psychologically the categories constructed for them. She asks, 'Why are girls to be told that they resemble angels; but to sink them below women?' In the same work, Wollstonecraft expresses radical views on ▷ marriage, including the view that seduction should be regarded as marriage (she was writing after ▷ Hardwicke's 1753 Marriage Act made it harder for women to sue for breach of promise) and that 'the man should be legally obliged to maintain the woman and her children, unless adultery, a natural divorcement, abrogated the law.'

Virgil (Publius Vergilius Maro) (70–19 BC)
Roman poet. He was born on a farm not far from Mantua in northern Italy, and is often referred to as 'the Mantuan'. He greatly esteemed the farming section of society to which he belonged, and valued the farming way of life. He was not, from the place of his origin, of Roman descent, but belonged to the first generation of Italians who felt a consciousness of nationhood, with Rome as their capital. By 40 BC he was in Rome, under the patronage of the wealthy Roman patrician (nobleman), Maecenas. He wrote the first work for which he is famous, the *Eclogues* or *Bucolics* (▷ Eclogue), between 42 and 37 BC; their title merely means short, selected pieces, but his intention was to praise the Italian countryside as the Greek poet ▷ Theocritus had praised the countryside of Sicily. The ▷ *Georgics* (37–30 BC), written at the instigation of Maecenas to encourage a sense of the value of a stable and productive society, is devoted to the praise of the farming way of life. The ▷ *Aeneid* written during the remainder of his life, is an ▷ epic about the travels of Aeneas the Trojan, and emulates Homer's ▷ *Odyssey*. Its purpose is not merely this, but to relate the Romans to the great civilization of the Greeks, on which their own civilization was so much based, by making Aeneas the ancestor of the Roman nation. The *Aeneid*, with the epics of Homer, is one of the basic poems in the culture of Europe and is taken as a standard for what was, perhaps until the 19th century, regarded as the noblest form of literature.

Not even Homer exceeds Virgil in the extent of his influence and prestige in the 20 centuries of European culture. He did not, like all the Greek poets and many of the Roman ones, have to wait for the ▷ Renaissance to 'discover' him, for he was esteemed in the Middle Ages, when, indeed, he became a legend. This was partly owing to his *Fourth Eclogue* which celebrated the birth of a child who was to restore the Golden Age (▷ Ages, Golden, Silver), a poem which in the Christian centuries was supposed to be a prophetic vision of the birth of Christ. He was thus regarded as more than merely a pagan poet, and ▷ Dante chose him as his guide through Hell and Purgatory in his 13th-century Christian epic, the *Divine Comedy* (▷ Divina Commedia). In direct literary influence, he was, even more than Theocritus, the pattern for ▷ pastoral poetry, and even more than Homer, for the epic, although he was himself a student of both.

Virgin Queen
A name for ▷ Elizabeth I of England, on account of the fact that she never married. The title enabled poets and other writers to associate her with Diana, the Roman goddess of chastity. The first English colony in America was called Virginia by ▷ Sir Walter Ralegh in her honour. The iconography associated with the public persona of Elizabeth is elaborate: see Frances Yates, *Astraea: The Imperial Theme in the Sixteenth Century*, and Roy Strong, *Gloriana: the Portraits of Elizabeth I* and *The Cult of Elizabeth I*.

***Virtuoso, The* (1676)**
▷ Comedy by ▷ Shadwell, which satirizes contemporary scientific endeavour, and the efforts of the ▷ Royal Society in particular. The virtuoso of the title, Sir Nicholas Gimcrack, conducts absurd experiments on respiration, for example, which mock researches carried out by the physicists Robert Boyle, Robert Hooke and other members of the ▷ Royal Society. In the same famous scene, Gimcrack demonstrates swimming upon a table, without the use of water, which he abhors and considers unnecessary to the purpose. The episode ridicules excessive reliance on scientific theory. There is also some serious romantic action involving two pairs of lovers: Longvil and Clarinda, and Bruce and Miranda, as well as scenes which involve the aged Lady Gimcrack's attempts to flirt with the young lovers. An historically interesting element is the besieging of Sir Nicholas' house by weavers, enraged by his purported invention of a mechanical loom.

***Vision of Judgement, A* (1821)**
***Vision of Judgement, The* (1822)**
▷ Robert Southey's poem *A Vision of Judgement*,

which shows the soul of the dead king George III being received into heaven, provoked ▷ Lord Byron's comic masterpiece *The Vision of Judgement*. Byron's poem changes Southey's ponderous classical hexameters (▷ metre) into racy ▷ *ottava rima* stanzas, and reduces George's ascent into heaven to the familiar genre of a 'Saint Peter sat at the celestial gate' story. George arrives, 'an old man/ With an old soul, and both extremely blind' and has to wait at the gate while Satan and St Michael argue over his immortal destiny. Satan claims him, since despite his 'neutral virtues' he was the constant enemy of political liberty: 'The New World shook him off; the Old yet groans/ Beneath what he and his prepared, if not/ Completed'. The debate is interrupted by the arrival of the devil Asmodeus who, hovering over Skiddaw, has caught the ▷ Poet Laureate scribbling away at 'some libel' (Southey's *Vision*) and snatched him up to heaven to give an account of himself. After offering to write both Michael's and Satan's biographies for a good profit ('Mine is a pen of all work'), Southey insists on reading his 'grand heroics' to the assembled throng, and in the ensuing desperate scramble to escape, King George slips into heaven unnoticed.

In his poem Byron finally achieved his ambition to rival his literary idol Alexander Pope (1688–1744), and the imaginative *élan* and iconoclastic inventiveness of the earlier poet's *Dunciad* are brilliantly emulated. Byron's *ottava rima* form, however, generates a freer, looser tone than Pope's ▷ couplets, allowing for some touches of magnificent political rhetoric. Moreover, Byron's wittily blasphemous treatment of religion shows a characteristically ▷ Romantic insight. Theology is converted into politics: the angels 'all are Tories', Peter is jealous of Paul as a *parvenu*, and Satan is compared to an impoverished Castilian nobleman, wary of the 'mushroom rich civilian', Michael, who has supplanted him. Though Southey's gauchely painstaking poem is now quite unread, Byron's parody remains one of the most imaginative comic works in the language.

Vision of Piers Plowman, The
▷ *Piers Plowman.*

Voice
One of the five categories in which ▷ Genette analyses narrative discourse, voice is concerned with the way in which the act of narrating is 'implicated in the narrative'; the study of voice in a novel therefore attends to the identity and nature of the ▷ narrator and the real or implied audience or narratees.

Volpone
A comedy in ▷ blank verse by ▷ Ben Jonson. First acted in 1605 or 1606 and printed in 1607, it is often considered Jonson's masterpiece. The names of the principal characters signify their roles in the comedy: Volpone = fox; his servant Mosca = fly, since he is a parasite who tries to take advantage of the vicious natures of everyone; the lawyer Voltore = vulture, Corbaccio = crow, and Corvino = raven, because all three birds feed on dead bodies, and all three men hope to gain from Volpone's will when he dies. Volpone is well aware of this, and pretends to be very ill in order to extract gifts from his so-called friends; Corvino, a jealous husband, is even prepared to sacrifice his wife, the pure-hearted Celia. Mosca tries to outdo his master by blackmailing Corvino, and this leads Voltore the lawyer to bring them both to judgement. A subplot concerns an absurd Englishman and his wife, Sir Politick and Lady Would-Be, who are on a visit to Venice (the scene of the play) and are ▷ satires on the contemporary English enthusiasm for financial speculation through fantastic 'projects'. The concentrated satire in the ▷ morality tradition of the main plot rises to heights of great poetry: the play is not, as it first seems, a piece of savage cynicism, because the characters, especially Volpone, have a vivid zest for living which is morally condemned only because they carry it to the point of mania.

▷ Humours, Comedy of.

Voltaire (pseudonym of François Marie Arouet, 1694–1778)
French writer. He wrote prolifically, and in his own day was regarded as above all a poet and a philosopher, but his international fame rests more on his prose work – satirical essays and the ironical romance, *Candide* (1759). He is even better known as the pattern of humane intellectuals: he was the determined opponent of beliefs and institutions sanctified by tradition but really disguising the selfishness and inhumanity of privileged classes of society. His dictum '*Ecrasez l' Infâme*' (Crush the Evil) is not, as it has often been thought to be, a slogan against religion as such, but against intolerance, superstition and unjustified privileges supported by religious institutions. He gained immense prestige all over Europe, and corresponded with Frederick II of Prussia and Catherine II of Russia. *Candide* was published at almost the same time as ▷ *Rasselas* by ▷ Samuel Johnson, and Johnson himself remarked on the extraordinary similarity of their themes, although there was no direct exchange of ideas between the two men. In general, Voltaire had strong sympathies with English trends of thought, and his long visit to England (1726–9) was an important episode in his development. In his *Lettres sur les Anglais* he used his English experiences as a basis for his attack on the French establishment. Correspondingly, Voltaire

was admired in England and his influence is pervasive in English 18th-century writing.

▷ Encyclopédie, L'.

Vorticism

Art movement which to some extent characterizes visual ▷ modernism in Britain, as one of the few discrete and self-conscious avant-garde movements in the British art world. To some extent Vorticism resembles the more famous European movements of futurism, cubism and expressionism, both in its celebration of German aesthetics and the principles of energy, speed, visual violence and dynamism, and in its close relationship with the literary world, particularly with the primarily poetic movement ▷ Imagism. Vorticism was furiously anti-Romantic and anti-representational, with the Vorticist 'mental emotional impulse' (in ▷ Percy Wyndham Lewis' famous words) 'let loose on a lot of blocks and lines', paralleling ▷ Ezra Pound's uncompromising series of poetic rules which would 'break the pentameter' and produce a genuinely new form of writing; the artistic impulse was to unlock the dynamic energy at the heart of images and visual objects. Together, these creative ideas formed (again in Lewis' words) 'the Great English Vortex'. The Vorticists opposed the aesthetics of the ▷ Bloomsbury Group, their less dynamic contemporaries whose arts-and-crafts movement-inspired works strove for visual harmony and integrity; the Rebel Arts Centre was the Vorticists' answer to Bloomsbury's Omega Workshops. The Vorticist magazine-manifesto, *Blast*, which ran to two famous issues in 1914 and 1915, has recently been republished. Key figures in the movement also include painters and sculptors William Roberts, David Bomberg, Edward Wadsworth, Jacob Epstein, and Henri Gaudier-Brzeska.

Vulgate Cycle

The conventional modern name for a 13th-century compilation of Arthurian prose narratives which collectively provide an encyclopaedic account of Arthurian history, quests and adventures, comprising the *Lancelot en prose* (which is nearly half the length of the cycle as a whole), the *Queste del Saint Graal*, the *Morte (le roi) Artu*, and two Arthurian pre-histories which recount the early history of the ▷ Grail, going back to its place in the Last Supper, the *Estoire del Saint Graal*, and the early history of ▷ Merlin and the foundation of ▷ Arthur's kingdom, the *Estoire de Merlin*.

A matrix of cross-references and prophecies gives cohesion to this massive narrative cycle, and allows access to the comprehensive scope of the material through any one of its parts. The cycle is sometimes called the 'Lancelot-Grail' cycle, or the 'Pseudo-Map cycle' (because parts are attributed to the 12th-century writer Walter Map).

Vulgate, The

From the Latin 'vulgatus' = 'made public or common'. The name of St Jerome's Latin version of the ▷ Bible, completed in AD 405. For a long time it was the only authorized text for the Catholic Church. The ▷ Protestants in the 16th century insisted on extending Jerome's principle of making the Word of God common to all, by translating it into other languages, a principle now accepted by the Catholic Church itself.

▷ Catholicism (Roman) in English literature.

Wace (c 1100–c 75)
Composer of one of the most influential vernacular versions of the history of Britain, the *Roman de Brut* (completed 1155), which is a close reworking of ▷ Geoffrey of Monmouth's ▷ *Historia Regum Britanniae*. In Wace's version, however, the sophisticated court environment over which ▷ Arthur presides is particularly developed. The earliest record of Arthur's ▷ Round Table appears in Wace's text too. What little is known about Wace derives largely from comments included in his other major work of vernacular history, the *Roman de Rou* (an unfinished verse history of the Dukes of Normandy). It seems that he was born in Jersey, had a clerical education, and was made canon of Bayeux by ▷ Henry II. He aspired to court patronage, but he complains in the *Rou* of too little material support for his literary labours. The *Roman de Brut* was reworked in Middle English by ▷ Laȝamon.

Wain, John (1925–94)
Novelist, poet and critic. Prose fiction: *Hurry on Down* (1953); *Living in the Present* (1955); *The Contenders* (1958); *A Travelling Woman* (1959); *Nuncle and Other Stories* (1962); *The Young Visitors* (1965); *Death of the Hind Legs and Other Stories* (1966); *The Smaller Sky* (1967); *A Winter in the Hills* (1970); *The Life Guard* (1971); *The Pardoner's Tale* (1978), *Young Shoulders* (1982). Criticism: *Preliminary Essays* (1957); *Essays on Literature and Ideas* (1963); *The Living World of Shakespeare* (1964). His first novel showed him to be a leading member of the school of novelists who concern themselves with the changed surface and social texture of the post-war world. His novels are distinguished by unusual narrative force and economy, and his criticism by the clarity and forthrightness of his judgements. As a poet, Wain's work has been associated with that of the ▷ Movement and with later 'movements' of the 1960s, publishing *A Word Carved on a Sill* (1956); *Weep Before God* (1961); *Wildtrack* (1965); and *Feng* (1975).

***Waiting for Godot* (1953)**
A play by ▷ Samuel Beckett which could be categorized as a modern tragicomedy. The plot is utterly absurd, which is the point of the play, since it is implying that life itself is absurd (▷ Theatre of the Absurd). Two tramps, Estragon and Vladimir, wait for the mysterious Godot who never arrives. Their only visitors are Lucky and Pozzo, who are locked in a sadomasochistic bonding of master and servant from which there seems to be no escape. Despite its bleak view of life the play has great wit, drawing on the traditions of music hall and popular clowning. It was first performed in Britain in 1955 and is an undisputed landmark in British drama.

Wakefield Cycle
A ▷ cycle of 32 plays (commonly referred to as the *Towneley Cycle* after an 18th-century owner of the manuscript), which was performed at Wakefield, Yorkshire in the 15th and 16th centuries, and which is indebted for some of its plays to an early form of the ▷ York cycle. Parts of the cycle were rewritten and revised in a distinctive nine-line stanzaic form, and modern critics have discussed this revision as the work of a so-called 'Wakefield Master', a dramatist of considerable skill with an interest in the possibilities of black comedy. Six plays, including the 'Second Shepherd's play' are wholly in his distinctive stanzaic form, but traces of his influence can be seen in several other plays too. The cycle exists in a single manuscript copy, dating from the mid to late 15th century. Performance of the plays was prohibited in 1576.
Bib: Cawley, A. C. (ed.), *The Wakefield Plays in the Towneley Cycle*; Pollard, A. (ed.), *The Towneley Plays.*

Wales
A mountainous country to the west of England; it has been united to England politically since 1536, but it has preserved a national individuality and its native Celtic language. In 1989, 20% of Wales' population of 2.8 million spoke Welsh, but by 1995, this figure had increased to 21.5%. The geography of the country has always been a hindrance to its unity, and before the English conquest it tended to divide into separate northern and southern regions. Just before the ▷ Norman Conquest of England (1066), however, Gruffudd ap Llywelyn, a Welsh prince, succeeded in briefly uniting the country, and Wales in consequence seemed formidable enough for the first Norman king of England, ▷ William I, to establish three strong earldoms for the defence of England along the Welsh frontier. These earldoms correspond to the former English counties of Hereford, Shropshire and Cheshire, long known as the Marches.

After his conquest of Wales, ▷ Edward I in 1301 gave his eldest son the title of Prince of Wales, a custom which has been followed by many English monarchs since then. However, until the 16th century, they did very little else to govern Wales. The Welsh have twice been influential in English history: once they rebelled with considerable success under ▷ Owain Glyndŵr against ▷ Henry IV (see ▷ Shakespeare's play *Henry IV, Part I*), and it was a mainly Welsh army that won the Battle of Bosworth (1485) and thus established on the English throne a dynasty of Welsh descent – the ▷ Tudors. The second king of this dynasty,

▷ Henry VIII, passed an Act of Union in 1536 which united Wales administratively with England. Since then, the most notable differences between the two countries have been in language and religion.

The ▷ Reformation made slower headway in Wales than in England, but it was effectively established by the end of the 16th century. In the 18th and 19th centuries, Methodism became very strong in Wales, to the extent that the Church of England was disestablished (*ie* it ceased to be the state Church) by a law passed in 1914. The Welsh Nonconformist churches are thus not 'nonconforming' in the English sense; the country is divided among a number of religious denominations (of which Anglicanism is only one), none of which have any official pre-eminence over the others. The Methodist churches in particular have done much to keep the Welsh language alive and vital. Education is conducted in the Welsh language, mainly in state schools in those regions where families are predominantly Welsh-speaking: one or more subjects are taught in the medium of Welsh in 20% of primary and 16% of secondary schools, whereas Welsh is taught as a language in 80% of primary and 88% of secondary schools (these statistics relate only to the state system throughout Wales). The S4C television channel began transmitting late in 1982, its Welsh-language programmes being concentrated in peak-viewing times. The annual cultural festival of the National ▷ Eisteddfod exists to keep literature in the Welsh language alive and healthy. The chief opponent of this nationalism is not English, but industrialism; the main industrial regions are in the south-east, around the capital city of Cardiff, and in the south, around the port of Swansea. In this area, once dominated by coal mining, where steel still plays an important though reduced role, light industries, especially electronics, (sometimes through Japanese and American investment) have relieved some of the problems of unemployment created by post-war pit closures. Historically, however, where there are large towns and urban ways of life, the essential rural and working-class characteristics of Welsh life have tended to anglicization.

Whereas, since 1350, the principal output of literature in ▷ Scotland and ▷ Ireland has been in English, though with Scottish and Irish national colouring, Welsh literature has chiefly been in the native Welsh language. It is thus scarcely possible to say that English literature has been distinctively modified by the literature of Wales, as can be said of the literatures of Scotland and Ireland. Occasionally a writer of English arises with a distinctively Welsh personality, and this is true of two 20th century poets, though they are of very different character: ▷ Dylan Thomas (1914–53) and ▷ R. S. Thomas (b 1913), the former rejecting Wales' language, religion and society, the latter embracing it, learning Welsh as his second language, becoming an Anglican priest, a convinced nationalist and a powerful upholder of Welsh cultural identity. Nor is it common for an English writer to learn Welsh so as to receive influence from Welsh literature, though this is to some extent true of ▷ Gerard Manley Hopkins (1844–89). Unfortunately the strength of Welsh literature is especially its poetry, and poetry is never fully translatable. Its best period was the Middle Ages. The majority of Arthurian legend (▷ Arthur) as we know it is of French, not Welsh, creation, but the oldest parts (*eg* the figure of ▷ Gawain) have their roots in Welsh myth.

▷ Welsh literature in English.

Walford, Lucy (1845–1915)
Scottish novelist, born in Portobello, near Edinburgh. Her first work, *Mr Smith: A part of His Life*, was published in 1874, and resulted in Walford being presented to ▷ Queen Victoria, who had asked to meet the book's author. Walford went on to write more than thirty works, including *Pauline* (1877); *Troublesome Daughters* (1880); *A Pinch of Bubble* (1895); *A Dream's Fulfilment* (1902) and *The Enlightenment of Olivia* (1907). She also published two non-fictional works: *Recollections of a Scottish Novelist* (1910) and *Memoirs of Victorian London* (1912).

Wallace, Sir William (?1270–1305)
A Scottish national hero of the Scottish War of Independence (1296–1328). He cleared most of the country of the English and then gained a major victory over them at the Battle of Stirling (1297), but he was defeated by ▷ Edward I at Falkirk in 1298. Taken prisoner in 1305, he was brought to trial by the English as a traitor; he replied to this charge that he owed no allegiance to the English king and therefore could not be a traitor to him. He was executed. Wallace was one of the first patriots in a nationalistic sense in British history; he received comparatively little help from the Scottish nobility, who wanted to stand well with Edward. He is the subject of a long poem by Henry the Minstrel ('Blind Harry') written about 1461.

▷ Scotland.

Waller, Edmund (1606–87)
Poet. As with so many of his contemporaries, Waller's career reflects the vicissitudes of public life in the revolutionary period of the mid-17th century. As a member of Parliament prior to the ▷ Civil War, he opposed the bishops, but, on the outbreak of hostilities, he was on the Royalist side. In 1643 he was found guilty of plotting to surrender London to the Royalist armies, and was banished. In exile in Paris he became friendly with ▷ Thomas Hobbes, before returning to

England (having secured permission) in 1651. On his return he wrote a 'Panegyric to my Lord Protector' (1655) addressed to ▷ Oliver Cromwell, but with the Restoration in 1660 Waller was fully restored to the king's favour, and proceeded to write a second panegyric, this time to ▷ Charles II.

Waller's chief verse collections were his *Poems* of 1645 (a second part being published in 1690) and his collection of religious verse, *Divine Poems* (1685). After 1660 he produced numerous occasional verses, including *To the King, Upon His Majesty's Happy Return* (1660) and *To the Queen, Upon Her Majesty's Birthday* (1663). But it is as a transitional figure that he has attracted critical comment. Waller's poetry can be seen as marking the transition from the 'witty' ▷ conceits of poets such as ▷ John Donne to the smoother ▷ neo-classicism of 18th-century poetry. Indeed, John Dryden (1631–1700), ignoring figures such as ▷ Robert Herrick and ▷ Ben Jonson, claimed that if Waller had not written, 'none of us could write'.

Bib: Thorn-Drury, G. (ed.), *Poems*, (2 vols.); Chernaik, W. L., *The Poetry of Limitation: A Study of Waller*.

Walpole, Horace (1717–97)

Letter-writer, antiquarian, connoisseur. He was son of the powerful statesman ▷ Robert Walpole, and for a short time followed a political career, but he abandoned it, though he continued his interest in politics. His father's influence procured for him three sinecures (*ie* posts under the government which carried salaries though they required very little work) and these enabled him to pass his life as an assiduous spectactor and man of pleasure. He developed a strong taste for the ▷ Gothic style in all its forms, converting his house (Strawberry Hill, Twickenham, where he settled in 1747) into what he called 'a little Gothic castle', and writing the first of the ▷ Gothic novels, ▷ *The Castle of Otranto* (1764). He is chiefly famous for his letters, however, and is regarded as one of the best correspondents in the best period of ▷ letter-writing. Their main quality is their liveliness, humour, and vividness of observation.

Bib: Lives by Ketton-Cremer and Lewis, W. S.; Stephen, L., in *Hours in a Library*.

Walpole, Sir Robert (1676–1745)

Statesman. He is sometimes called 'the first Prime Minister', meaning that he was the first statesman to hold chief power in the state and at the same time to base this power on the House of Commons. His practice of consulting his ministers in a private office or 'cabinet' and of insisting that they should comply with his policies or resign their posts has also caused him to be credited with the invention of the cabinet system of government. In both, he is a figure of importance in the history of the development of the British constitution. He held power continuously from 1721 to 1742, and was enabled to do so partly by his financial ability (he came to office at the time of the ▷ South Sea Bubble crisis), and partly by the incapacity of the German-born kings, ▷ George I (1714–27) and George II (1727–60), to manage English politics.

▷ Parliament.

Walsh, William (1663–1708)

Minor poet, called by ▷ John Dryden the best critic in the language. The youthful ▷ Alexander Pope was encouraged by his advice that 'though we had several great poets, we never had any one great poet that was correct; and he desired me to make that my study and aim'.

Walsingham, Sir Francis (?1530–90)

Statesman. Walsingham was educated at the Inns of Court and, as a ▷ Protestant, was forced to leave the country during the Catholic reign of ▷ Mary I. He returned under ▷ Elizabeth I and acted as the queen's principal secretary, as well as being an excellent foreign diplomat. He was, however, too blunt for Elizabeth and she never treated him with the respect he deserved, although she did knight him in 1577. He was the main force behind the execution of ▷ Mary Queen of Scots for her implication in the Babington plot. His letters and papers remain extant and are an invaluable source for the history of Elizabethan politics.

Walton, Izaac (1593–1683)

Biographer. Izaac Walton's popular reputation has rested on his ▷ *The Compleat Angler* (1653, with revised editions in 1658 and 1661) – ostensibly a fishing manual. The comprehensive nature of the work is, however, hinted at in its subtitle: *The Contemplative Man's Recreation* – an evocation of an idyllic, reflective, ▷ pastoral nostalgia. As a biographer Walton was the author of a series of important 'lives' of 17th-century poets and divines. His *Life of John Donne* was published in 1658, and was followd by lives of ▷ Richard Hooker (1665), ▷ George Herbert (1670) and Robert Sanderson (1678). *The Life of Sir Henry Wotton* (▷ Henry Wotton) first appeared appended to a posthumous edition of Wotton's poetry in 1640 and was published separately in 1651. The two biographies of ▷ Donne and Herbert are the most renowned. Walton is concerned with recording his subjects' piously Anglican Christian virtue, but they are, nevertheless, important statements concerning the contemporary perception of these major writers and instances of a 17th-century art of hagiographic ▷ biography.

Bib: Keynes, G. L. (ed.), *The Compleat*

Walton; Novarr, D., *The Making of Walton's Lives.*

Walwyn, William (1600–81)
Religious prose writer. Born into the gentry, Walwyn was apprenticed to a silk merchant in 1619 and had risen to become a member of the Merchant Adventurers by 1632. At first he supported a moderate Anglican cause (as in *New Petition For Papists*, 1641), but began to write pamphlets supporting the ▷ Levellers in the late 1640s. He was arrested in 1649 when the Leveller movement was suppressed. Walwyn consistently upheld the liberty of conscience in all his works, most notably in *The Compassionate Samaritan*.
Bib: Pooley, R., *English Prose of the Seventeenth Century, 1500–1700*.

Wandor, Michelene (b 1940)
Dramatist, poet, fiction writer, critic and theoretician. Michelene Wandor's unique position is well summed up by Helene Keyssar: 'More than any single figure, Wandor is responsible for articulating and supporting the interaction of feminism, theatre, socialism and gay liberation in Britain.' Active in the reborn women's movement from its earliest days – *The Day After Yesterday* (1972) attacks the sexism of the Miss World contest, *Care and Control* (1977) is about the issue of lesbian mothers having custody of their children – Wandor has made significant contributions at both the theoretical and practical level, as one of the few theatre practitioners with a strong academic background. As editor of the first four volumes of the Methuen anthologies of *Plays by Women*, she made a significant body of women's dramatic writing available to those who were unable to see the plays in their first productions and in *Understudies, Carry on Understudies* and *Look Back in Gender*, she documented and analysed the undervalued contribution of women to the contemporary theatre, and the representation of women in the theatre.

A prolific radio dramatist, she has never achieved comparable critical success in the theatre, although *Aurora Leigh* (1979) is a fine adaptation of Elizabeth Barrett Browning's verse novel and deserves a wider audience.

War poets
A group of poets who served in the army in World War I, and made poetry out of the experience. The three who are most commonly thought of as 'war poets' are ▷ Wilfred Owen, ▷ Siegfried Sassoon and ▷ Isaac Rosenberg. ▷ Rupert Brooke, who wrote with feeling about the outbreak of war, died before he saw much action; his poetry does not in consequence reflect the shock and violence so evident in the work of the other three. ▷ Edward Thomas was killed in action, but little of his poetry is about the war. ▷ Edmund Blunden and ▷ Robert Graves both survived to write memorable prose works about the war, but their poetry was only indirectly affected by it.

The effect of the war on the verse of Owen, Sassoon and Rosenberg was to cause them to turn away from the rather tepid ▷ romanticism of much pre-war poetry, and to adapt their language to the new and terrible experiences. They thus played a significant part in the renewal of poetic language.

Warbeck, Perkin (1471–99)
The son of a poor citizen of Tournai in Flanders, he pretended to be Richard, Duke of York, one of Edward IV's two sons whom ▷ Richard III had imprisoned in the Tower of London, and whose fate was unknown. He was supported by a number of enemies of ▷ Henry VII, including Charles VIII of France and James IV of Scotland. Eventually he landed in the west of England in 1497, but was soon captured by Henry's troops and hanged. The dramatist ▷ John Ford wrote a moving play about him, *Perkin Warbeck* (1634).

Ward, Edward ('Ned') (1667–1731)
Tavern-keeper and ▷ Grub Street writer, specializing in doggerel verses and humorous sketches of London life. His prose work *The London Spy* (1698–1709) takes us on a tour of the sights of London, and is full of humorous anecdotes and eccentric characters. His *Hudibras Redivivus* was published 1705–7 (▷ *Hudibras*).

Ward, Mrs Humphrey (1851–1920)
Novelist, born Mary Augusta Arnold, the granddaughter of ▷ Thomas Arnold. She was born in Tasmania but moved with her family back to England in 1856, where she was educated in private boarding schools. In 1872 she married Thomas Humphrey Ward, an Oxford don. She contributed to the *Dictionary of Christian Biography* in 1877, and in 1881 moved to London and wrote for *The Times*, *Pall Mall Gazette* and ▷ *Macmillan's Magazine* as well as publishing a children's story, *Milly and Olly* (1881). Her first novel for adults, and her most famous, was *Robert Elsmere* (1888). It is the story of a clergyman who loses his faith through a study of the 'higher criticism' of Bible texts (the novelist ▷ George Eliot lost her faith in the same way). The purport of the book is that the revitalization of Christianity requires more attention to the social obligations of the Church and the abandonment of its supernatural – or at least its miraculous – constituents of belief. The novel was an immediate success, and she wrote twenty-four more, including: *The History of David Grieve* (1892); *Marcella* (1894); *Sir George Tressady* (1896); *Helbeck of Bannisdale* (1898); *Lady Rose's Daughter* (1903); *The Marriage of William Ashe* (1905);

Diana Mallory (1908); *Delia Blanchflower* (1915) and *Cousin Philip* (1919). Her novels deal principally with social and religious themes, often contrasting tradition with progress. She was a leading intellectual figure and an active philanthropist, yet although she campaigned for higher ▷ education for women, she strongly opposed the ▷ women's suffrage movement. She generated support for an 'Appeal Against Female Suffrage', published in 1889, and became the first President of the Anti-Suffrage League in 1908. Like many Victorians, she believed that women should set a moral example, issuing firstly from the home. Ward was also known to be a severe critic of other women writers. Her ▷ autobiography, *A Writer's Recollections*, was published in 1918.

Bib: Trevelyan, J.P., *The Life of Mrs Humphrey Ward*; Jones, E.H., *Mrs Humphrey Ward*; Huw Jones, E., *Mrs Ward*; Peterson, W.S., *Victorian Heretic: Mrs Humphrey Ward's Robert Elsmere*.

Ward, Mary (1558–1645)
Religious writer and educationalist. Mary Ward's name has become associated with the history of female education. She set up a Catholic boarding school for girls at St Omer in the Netherlands (1609) and in 1639, under the auspices of ▷ Henrietta Maria, she returned to Britain, where she hoped to promote scholarly studies for young women. During the intervening years abroad, Mary Ward had frequently visited her home country on 'recruiting drives' for pupils, and such was her skill and that of her companions at evading arrest as Catholics that they were nicknamed the 'Galloping Girls'. Born into a recusant family, Ward eventually became a nun (1606) and established several religious communities in connection with her schools. Persecuted in Britain for her faith, on the continent she was attacked and even imprisoned for her radical views on the equality of women by the Catholic Church she gave her allegiance to. Her hopes for reform in Britain were crushed by the Civil War, and she died in a safe house outside York. Throughout her trials, which were made worse by ill health, Mary Ward retained her strong religious and educational convictions together with a seemingly indomitable sense of humour. These qualities come through in her writings and in her last recorded words, 'it matters not the who, but the what'. Extracts from her work may be found in M. C. Chambers, *The Life of Mary Ward* (1882–7).

Bib: Fraser, A., *The Weaker Vessel*; Prior, M. (ed.), *Women in English Society 1500–1800*.

***Warden, The* (1855)**
A novel by ▷ Anthony Trollope, the first to be a success with the public, and the first of his ▷ Barsetshire series.

The theme of the novel is the two aspects of the problem of the reform of public abuses. It shows how an office which brings to its holder an income much in excess of his duties may nonetheless be conducted usefully and with integrity, so that to abolish the office may be an act of personal injustice although the abolition may be justifiable on public grounds.

The novel is set in the cathedral city of Barchester in Barsetshire. A clergyman, the Reverend Septimus Harding, is Warden of Hiram's Hospital, a long-established charitable institution for maintaining twelve poor old men in comfort. For this he draws an income which in the course of time has increased to £800 a year, although his actual duties are almost non-existent. However, he maintains with the old men affectionate relationships which are inestimable financially. The wardenship is attacked as a public abuse by John Bold, a Barchester surgeon, although Bold is in love with Harding's daughter Eleanor. Bold is opposed (on the wrong grounds) by the worldly churchman Archdeacon Grantly, who is Harding's son-in-law. Harding resigns his office as a matter of conscience, but the Bishop refuses to appoint a new Warden, and the old men of the Hospital lose the chief solace of their old age.

Warner, Marina (b 1946)
Novelist, critic and cultural historian, educated at Lady Margaret Hall, Oxford. Her novels are much concerned with history and its bearing on the present: *In A Dark Wood* (1977) is about a Jesuit who is writing a biography of a 17th-century missionary; in *The Lost Father* (1988) the narrator is writing a novel, set in Italy and based on her own family history. Other novels: *The Skating Party* (1982); *Indigo, or Mapping the Waters* (1992). Television play: *Tell Me More* (1991). Libretto: *The Legs of the Queen of Sheba* (1991). She has also written cultural criticism, studies of history and myth, biography and children's writing.

Warner, Rex (1905–86)
Novelist, poet and translator. He was educated at Oxford University, where he met ▷ W. H. Auden and ▷ Cecil Day-Lewis. His allegorical first novel, *The Wild Goose Chase* (1937), examines the political issues of the 1930s through a fantastic imaginary world and concludes with a ▷ communist ▷ Utopia. *The Professor* (1938) and *The Aerodrome* (1941) are similarly concerned with political power, and the conflict of love and personal integrity with totalitarianism. Warner's work is frequently compared with that of Kafka, but also shows the influence of classical literature, of which he made many translations. He also wrote several historical novels, including *The Young Caesar* (1958) and *Imperial Caesar* (1958),

which are written in the form of supposed autobiography.

Warner, Sylvia Townsend (1893–1978)
Novelist, poet, short-story writer, musicologist and biographer. Born in Harrow, Middlesex, she worked in a munitions factory during World War I and in 1922 became one of the editors of the Oxford University Press *Tudor Church Music*. She lived in Dorset with the poet Valentine Ackland from 1932 until the latter's death in 1969; together they served as Red Cross Volunteers in Spain in 1930. Her novels are: *Lolly Willowes; or, The Loving Huntsman* (1926); *Mr Fortune's Maggot* (1927); *The True Heart* (1929); *Summer Will Show* (1936); *After the Death of Don Juan* (1938); *The Corner That Held Them* (1948); *The Flint Anchor* (1954). Her work is notable for its imaginative scope, including elements of the supernatural, mystical and historical and embracing fantasy, comedy and satire; the novels' settings include a South Sea Island, a medieval nunnery, the Paris of the 1848 revolution and the Essex marshes. She also published ten volumes of short stories, books on Somerset (1949) and on Jane Austen (1951), a biography of T. H. White (1967) and volumes of poetry, including: *The Espalier* (1925); *Time Importuned* (1928); *Opus 7* (1931, a long narrative poem); *Rainbow* (1932); *Whether a Dove or a Seagull* (1933, with Valentine Ackland); *Boxwood* (1957); *Two Poems* (1945); *King Duffus* (1968); *Azrael* (1978); *Twelve Poems* (1980). Her *Collected Poems* were published in 1982, edited by Claire Harman, and her *Letters* in 1982, edited by William Maxwell.
Bib: Harman, C., *Sylvia Townsend Warner: a biography*; Mulford, C., *The Narrow Place: Sylvia Townsend Warner and Valentine Ackland: Life, Letters and Politics 1930–1951*.

Wars of the Roses, The
A name for the civil wars that were waged intermittently between the two branches of the ▷ Plantagenet family, the House of Lancaster and the House of York, between 1455 and 1485. The name derives from the emblems chosen by either side: the Lancastrians chose the red rose, and the Yorkists chose the white. The ▷ Tudor rose was a red and white emblem, to signify the reconciliation of the two sides by the marriage of Henry Tudor on the Lancastrian side (▷ Henry VII) with Elizabeth of York, daughter of ▷ Edward IV.

The immediate causes of the war were dynastic; the underlying ones were social. ▷ Richard II, the last Plantagenet king by direct succession, died without heirs, having lost his throne by usurpation to ▷ Henry IV, his cousin and the first king of the Lancastrian line, so called because Henry was the son of John Duke of Lancaster (▷ John of Gaunt). There was always some doubt whether the descendants of another of Richard's uncles, Edmund Duke of York, had not a better claim to the throne, and the disagreement broke into open war in 1455 owing to the drop in Lancastrian prestige when England was at last defeated in the ▷ Hundred Years' War against France (1453). It is here that the social causes become important. In the first place, power in England was in the hands of a number of rich, self-interested and ambitious nobles, whose energies were now no longer taken up by the wars in France. They sought new outlets for their ambition by an attempt to dominate the government at home. Secondly, the ending of the French wars let loose upon England a mass of unemployed soldiers who urgently needed occupation. The interests of the majority of the common people were not deeply engaged, though the towns were disposed to be Yorkist and the rural areas to be Lancastrian. Consequently the Wars of the Roses were felt to be a profitless evil by the majority of the nation. The reign of ▷ Elizabeth I was haunted by the fear that civil wars might recur because the queen (like Richard II) had no direct heirs.

The House of Tudor was correspondingly revered because it brought the wars to an end. An important social consequence was that the medieval nobility which was responsible for their outbreak was much weakened and discredited at the end of them. The Tudor sovereigns raised up their nobility from men of lesser family, from whom the aristocratic families of modern England, *eg* the Cecils and the Russells, commonly descended.

▷ Shakespeare used the Wars of the Roses as the material for his first tetralogy of historical dramas, the three plays on ▷ Henry VI and one on ▷ Richard III. The first three are national tragedies of mounting conflict and destructive hatred; the last shows the evil which has afflicted the country concentrated in one king of diabolic proportions, with Henry Tudor presented in religious terms as the saviour of the people at the conclusion.

Warton, Joseph (1722–1800)
Critic and poet; headmaster of Winchester School and the brother of ▷ Thomas Warton. His *Essay on the Genius and Writings of Pope* (vol. I, 1756; vol. II, 1782) distinguishes the 'true poet' from the mere 'man of wit' and is often seen as a 'pre-▷ Romantic' document, though Warton himself admired ▷ Alexander Pope and edited his works (1797).

Warton, Thomas (1728–90)
Professor of Poetry at Oxford (1757–67) and later (1785–90) ▷ Poet Laureate. His *Poems* (1777) include several ▷ sonnets, a form neglected in previous decades. His *The Suicide: An Ode* and *Verses on Sir Joshua Reynolds' Painted Window*,

toy with 'romantick' excess and ▷ Gothic medievalism, without ever having the courage of their convictions, and his comic verse is perhaps more successful. He edited the humorous miscellany, *The Oxford Sausage* (1764). It is in his criticism, with its scholarly approach to early literature that his real importance lies. His *Observations on the Fairie Queene of Spenser* (1754) shows a sensitive historical perspective, and his *History of English Poetry* (1774–81), conveys his fascination with the ▷ 'Gothic' ▷ Middle Ages more convincingly than the dilettantism of his poems. Breaking off at the death of ▷ Elizabeth I, it complemented ▷ Samuel Johnson's ▷ *Lives of the Poets*, and despite their aesthetic differences the two men were on friendly terms. In 1785 he published an edition of ▷ John Milton's early poems.
Bib: Pittock, J., *The Ascendancy of Taste: The Achievement of Joseph and Thomas Warton*; Rinacker, C., *Thomas Warton: A Biographical and Critical Study*.

Washington, George (1732–99)
Leader of the American rebel forces in the War of Independence (1775–83); president of the American convention, 1787; first President of the United States, 1789. He served in the British forces during the wars against the French and Indians in the 1750s and was a rich and efficient tobacco planter, but did not play a leading part in American politics until relationships with Britain became critical in the 1770s. He was however noted a 'a young man of an extraordinary and exalted character'. Washington's great-grandfather had emigrated from Britain in 1657.

***Waste Land, The* (1922)**
A poem by ▷ T. S. Eliot. It is 433 lines long, and is divided into five parts: I. *The Burial of the Dead*; II. *A Game of Chess*; III. *The Fire Sermon*; IV. *Death by Water*; V. *What the Thunder Said*. There is no logical continuity between the parts, or within each part except for the very short Part IV. The lines vary in length and rhythm and are usually unrhymed, but the poem is not written in ▷ 'free verse'. The author contributed his own (often cryptic) explanatory notes.

The theme is the decay and fragmentation of Western culture, conceived in terms of the loss of natural fertility. Despite the absence of logical continuity, *The Waste Land* possesses artistic coherence brought about by four closely related methods.

1 The use of symbols derived from two anthropologists: Jessie L. Weston (*From Ritual to Romance*) and ▷ James Frazer (*The Golden Bough*). These books relate to ancient myths about the alternation of fertility and barrenness. Although study of them undoubtedly helps the reader to understand the poem, it is not entirely necessary; Eliot intended the symbols to be imaginatively convincing, by their own force, to a sufficiently responsive reader.

2 The juxtaposition of passages with contrasting rhythms, diction, and imagery to accomplish 'a music of ideas . . . arranged not that they must tell us something, but that their effects in us may combine into a coherent whole of feeling and attitude'. (See ▷ I. A. Richards. Compare Eliot in *Shakespeare and the Stoicism of Seneca*: 'The poet who "thinks" is merely the poet who can express the emotional equivalent of thought.')

3 The use of past history in contrast to the present time, as a means of demonstrating the peculiarities of the present. This method is paralleled by ▷ James Joyce in ▷ *Ulysses* and ▷ Ezra Pound in his ▷ *Cantos*.

4 The use of literary quotation and parody in order to bring out the contrasts of past and present states of culture. At least 35 writers are quoted or parodied in *The Waste Land*.

The poem caused great controversy when it was published, and is often considered to mark the effective beginning of a distinctively 20th-century style of verse, although Eliot had already published verse in the new idiom with *The Love Song of J. Alfred Prufrock* (1915) and *Gerontion* (1920). *The Waste Land* is dedicated to Ezra Pound, whose extensive revisions of the poem can be seen in the facsimile of the original drafts edited by Valerie Eliot and published in 1971.
Bib: Williams, H., *T. S. Eliot: 'The Waste Land'*.

***Water Babies, The* (1863)**
A moral fantasy for children, by ▷ Charles Kingsley, subtitled *A Fairy Tale for a Landbaby*. The little boy Tom is employed as a chimney-sweep by the brutal Mr Grimes; he falls into the river, gets turned into a water baby and is carried down to the sea. He meets a number of fabulous creatures and undergoes ordeals which effect moral instruction. He emerges purified, on equal terms with Ellie, the little girl in whose house he once swept the chimneys. Grimes is sent away to a penance of sweeping out Etna. The book is partly an attack on the exploitation of child labour and on the brutalization of the poor, and partly a fable about their moral education. Some of the moralizing is offensive, socially and psychologically, to modern readers but the book remains a children's classic for the sake of the ingenuity of its fantasy.

▷ Child labour; Children's literature.

Waterloo, Battle of (1815)
An army of British, Dutch, Belgians and Germans under the ▷ Duke of Wellington and the Prussian army under Blücher finally defeated a French army under ▷ Napoleon and thus ended the Napoleonic Wars (1803–15). Waterloo is a village in Belgium to the south

of Brussels. Wellington's army took up its position in squares, which the French attacked unavailingly all day, until Blücher's army came to Wellington's assistance. Wellington's own comment on the battle was that 'it was a damn near thing', and Napoleon's defeat is partly attributable to his failing health. He surrendered to the British and was exiled for the remainder of his life to the island of St Helena. English history represents this as a victory for the English army: in Germany it is seen as an occasion retrieved by the Prussian force from defeat.

Watkins, Vernon (1906–67)
Poet. Born at Maesteg, Glamorgan, Watkins' father's occupation as bank manager necessitated several family moves before Swansea became their settled home in 1913. Vernon Watkins was sent away to an English public school education at Repton, after which he went up to Magdalene College, Cambridge, to read modern languages. Nevertheless, by that time he had already nurtured a powerful ambition to become a poet, in furtherance of which he wished to travel to Italy, abandoning his university course for what became an unfulfilled dream, parental opposition ensuring that his next move was to a Cardiff bank whose uncongenial surroundings precipitated a nervous breakdown. It was his illness that prompted a return to the St Helen's branch of the bank in Swansea where he remained for the rest of his life except for his military service in World War II. From the pagan influence of the Romantic poets he developed into a modern metaphysical whose insight-symbols from the Gower shoreline frequently surface in his work, in poetry that is always meticulously crafted, the most successful of which appeared before 1960. His considerable poetic output was initiated with *Ballad of the Mari Llwyd* (1941) and *The Lamp and the Veil* (1945), followed by an early *Selected Poems* (1948), *The Lady and the Unicorn* (1948), *The North Sea* (translations from Heine, 1951), *The Death Bell* (1954), *Cypress and Acacia* (1959) and *Affinities, Fidelities* (1968) appearing posthumously, though he himself had put this collection together just before his death. After his death, *Uncollected Poems* (1969), *Selected Verse Translations* (1977), *The Breaking of the Wave* (1979) and *The Ballad of the Outer Dark* (1979) were all assembled from a mass of unpublished material, with *I That Was Born in Wales* (1976) and *Unity of the Stream* (1978) being selections from his published works.
Bib: Stephens, M. (Ed.), *The Oxford Companion to the Literature of Wales*; Jones, G. and Rowlands, J., *Profiles*.

Watt, James (1736–1819)
Scottish engineer, inventor, and scientist. His outstanding achievement was the improvement of the steam engine, the principles of which (apart from ancient Greek experiments) had been discovered in the 17th century. Newcomen's improvements on existing models in 1705 enabled it to be put to practical use, but it was Watt in 1763 who made it commercially successful and one of the main instruments for the ▷ Industrial Revolution, the beginnings of which are sometimes dated from his time. Watt's engine made deep mining for coal possible when it was applied to pumping; it could be used for driving machines in factories, and it led in the 1820s to the invention of railway locomotives.

Watts, Isaac (1674–1748)
Poet and ▷ hymn writer. He was minister of an Independent church in London until in 1712 ill health forced him into an early retirement in the household of the Whig merchant Sir Thomas Abney in Hertfordshire. His verse appeared in *Horae Lyricae* (1706), *Hymns* (1707), *Divine Songs for Children* (1715), *Psalms of David* (1719). Later in life he turned to prose tracts on theology. Much of his work is charged with a ▷ Puritan dogmatism, but sometimes more literary instincts prevail. Watts experimented with ▷ classical ▷ metres, and wrote bold ▷ Pindaric ▷ odes and distinctive ▷ blank verse. Some of his hymns, for instance 'O God, our help in ages past' and 'When I survey the wondrous cross' are famous. His songs for children became a part of popular British culture, and form the basis of some of ▷ William Blake's ▷ *Songs of Innocence and Experience*.

Watts, Susanna (1768–1842)
Poet, prose writer and artist. ▷ Evangelical writer whose humble origins and powerful moral beliefs endowed her with an interesting character, which combined self-depreciation with the zeal of a crusader. Her poetry was generally well thought of, including *Original Poems and Translations* (1802) and the posthumous *Hymns and Poems* (1842). She settled in Leicester, and her *Walk Through Leicester* was published as a guide to the town in 1804; the City Library there still holds her original manuscript. Watts' fictional work always had a barely concealed ▷ didactic purpose, from trying to help suffering animals (*The Humming-Bird*, 1824–5) to attacking the middle classes (*The Wonderful Travels of Prince Fan-Feredin in the Country of Arcadia*, 1828).
▷ Hymns; Travel literature.

Waugh, Evelyn (1903–66)
Novelist. Born in London and educated at Hertford College Oxford, he worked for a while as an assistant schoolmaster, an experience which provided the basis for his first novel, *Decline and Fall* (1928). His satires of the late

1920s and 1930s up to and including *Put Out More Flags* (1942), present the modern world as anarchic and chaotic, and are a blend of farce and tragedy. His technique included the extensive use of dialogue, and rapid changes of scene. Many of the early novels recount the ▷ picaresque and outrageous experiences of a naive central character, such as Paul Pennyfeather in *Decline and Fall*, and William Boot in *Scoop* (1938), a hilarious story of Western journalists in Africa. Waugh became a Catholic in 1930; this was initially reflected in his work only in a sense of the transience and emptiness of worldly concerns. But World War II, during which Waugh served with the Royal Marines in Crete and Yugoslavia changed the character of his work; it became more explicitly Catholic, serious to the point of sombreness, and more three-dimensional in his portrayal of his characters. The first novel to show these qualities was *Brideshead Revisited* (1945). In 1961 he completed his most considerable work, a trilogy about the war entitled *Sword of Honour*. Among others of his novels that have achieved fame are *The Loved One* (1948), a satire on American commercialism, extending to the commercialization of death, and *The Ordeal of Gilbert Pinfold* (1957), a pseudo-autobiographical caricature of a 50-year-old Catholic novelist. His post-war work expresses a distaste for, and rejection of, modern civilization, and a pervasive sense of the vanity of human desires. All Waugh's work is marked by an exquisite sense of the ludicrous and a fine aptitude for exposing false attitudes. His comedy is closely dependent on the carefully calculated urbanity of his style. Other novels are: *Vile Bodies* (1930); *Black Mischief* (1932); *A Handful of Dust* (1934); *Scott-King's Modern Europe* (1947); *Tactical Exercise* (1954); *Basil Seal Rides Again* (1963). Story collections are: *Mr Loveday's Little Outing* (1936); *Work Suspended* (1949).

Waugh also wrote travel books, selections from which have been collected under the title *When the Going Was Good* (1946), and biographies of the 19th-century poet and painter D. G. Rossetti (1928), and of the 16th-century Catholic martyr, Edmund Campion (1935).

▷ Catholicism in English literature.

Bib: Bradbury, M., *Evelyn Waugh* (Writers and Critics Series 1964); Stannard, M., *Evelyn Waugh: the Critical Heritage*; Sykes, C., *Evelyn Waugh: a Biography*.

***Waverley* (1814)**

The first of ▷ Sir Walter Scott's novels, subtitled *'Tis Sixty Years Since*. The hero, Edward Waverley, is a young English officer who visits the Highlands of Scotland just before the ▷ Jacobite Rebellion of 1745. Here he falls in love with Flora, the Jacobite daughter of a Highland chieftain. He joins the Jacobite forces. When these are eventually defeated, Waverley is saved from execution by a senior English officer on the other side, whom he has saved in a battle. *Waverley* is the first historical novel of distinction in English literature, and Scott's vivid description of Scottish society and scenery caused it to be received with great enthusiasm.

***Waves, The* (1931)**

A novel by ▷ Virginia Woolf. It is the story of six characters, each of whom tells his or her own story in monologue, and reflects images of the others in his or her own mind. The monologues occur in groups, at different stages of their lives, and each group is preceded by a passage describing a time of day, from dawn to nightfall. It is a poetic, lyrical and highly patterned work, and presents human existence as an organic process, uniting individuals like waves in the sea. *The Waves* is the climax of Virginia Woolf's experiments in fictional form. (▷ Modernism)

***Way of All Flesh, The* (1903)**

A novel by ▷ Samuel Butler, written 1873–5 and published after his death, in 1903. It is one of the few purely satirical works of distinction of the Victorian period; the satire is directed against the Victorian cult of the family as the sacred and blessed nucleus of society, and (as so often in ▷ Charles Dickens) the refuge from the harshness of the world. The arrogant, self-righteous, intolerant and stupid kind of Victorian parent is exemplified in the clergyman Theobald Pontifex, father of Ernest Pontifex. Victorian authoritarianism and repressiveness is also attacked in Theobald, seen as a religious humbug, and in Dr Skinner, headmaster of the public school that Ernest attends. The first fifty chapters of the book are autobiographical; Butler even includes actual letters in the text. The narrative is not told through Ernest (Butler as a boy) but in the first person through his friend the middle-aged Overton, who represents a more tolerant aspect of Butler; by this means, Butler conveys criticism of his intolerant younger self, in the person of Ernest. The book was much praised, especially by ▷ G.B. Shaw.

▷ Autobiography.

Way of the World, The (1700)

A comedy by ▷ William Congreve, produced in 1700. The plot is a complicated succession of intrigues which surround the love affair between the sparkling young rake, Mirabell (a hero in the tradition of ▷ Etherege's Dorimant in ▷ *The Man of Mode*), and the urbane and witty heroine, Millamant. Mirabell's aim is to trick or persuade Millamant's aunt, Lady Wishfort, into consenting to their marriage; and his efforts include pretending to make love to Lady Wishfort herself. This intrigue is frustrated by Mrs Marwood, embittered against Mirabell because he has previously rejected her. Mirabell then attempts further intrigue, and this leads to counter-intrigues by Mrs Marwood in alliance with Mirabell's treacherous friend Fainall, who combines them with conspiracies against his wife, a former mistress of Mirabell's, and blackmail of Lady Wishfort. Mirabell finally succeeds in defeating his enemies and saving Lady Wishfort from the threats against her; in gratitude, she consents to his marriage to Millamant. The intrigues serve as a framework for theatrically very successful comic scenes and imaginatively witty dialogue. Millamant and Mirabell set out the conditions on which they agree to relinquish their freedom and submit to marriage, in a famous ▷ Proviso scene (IV, vi). Millamant's charm and independence have made her role a star part for great actresses, and supply a main reason for the play's lasting reputation.

▷ Manners, Comedy of.

Weak ending
In ▷ blank verse an unstressed syllable in the place of the normally stressed one at the end of a line; also, a word such as a conjunction or preposition which may bear metrical stress but cannot bear speech stress.

Wealth of Nations
▷ Smith, Adam.

Webb, Beatrice (1858–1943)
Sociologist. She was the daughter of Richard Potter, a railway director and friend of the philosopher ▷ Herbert Spencer, who exercised a guiding influence over her education. Her mother was a product of the 19th-century ▷ Utilitarian school of thought. She early developed a strong social conscience, which led her to choose as her career the almost unprecedented one of 'social investigator'. Victorian sensitiveness to social abuses was strong amongst the intelligentsia, but she realized that constructive action was hampered by lack of exact information: 'The primary task is to observe and dissect facts.' In order to do so, she took bold steps for a Victorian girl of the prosperous middle class, such as disguising herself as a working girl and taking employment under a tailor in the East End of London. She and her husband were among the early members of the ▷ Fabian Society, and among the founders of the Labour Party. Her autobiographies *My Apprenticeship* (1926) and *Our Partnership* (1948) are in the tradition of ▷ John Stuart Mill's *Autobiography* (1873) in being essentially histories of the growth of opinions and ideas; *My Apprenticeship*, however, is very enlightening about social backgrounds in the 1880s, and a valuable addition to the Victorian novels, which, she said, were the only documents for the study of society available in her youth. She and her husband were among the founders of the weekly journal *New Statesman*, still a leading left-wing journal.

Webb, Harri (1920–94)
Poet, journalist, television script-writer, pamphleteer and public speaker. Born in Swansea of a Gower family related to the *bardd gwlad* Cyril Gwynne who was to influence him towards simple rhyming ballads (especially in his later work), Harri Webb read Romance Languages at Oxford. He subsequently became librarian at Dowlais and later at Mountain Ash. Formerly a member of the Welsh Republican movement, he edited its newspaper *Welsh Republican* from 1950 to 1957 and afterwards Plaid Cymru's English language newspaper *The Welsh Nation* from 1961 to 1964. In 1965 he assisted Meic Stephens in the launching of *Poetry Wales*, after which his poetry collections *The Green Desert* (1969) and *A Crown for Branwen* (1974) ranged through history and mythology to satirical political poems, this powerfully nationalist motivation providing the context for his later collections *Rampage and Revel* (1977) and *Poems and Points* (1983), all to be garnered – including a large number of previously unpublished poems – by Meic Stephens who is currently editing a *Collected* volume. Because much of Harri Webb's work gained greater impact and influence from his own public performance of it, his poetry had become an effective medium for a political message, thus effectively widening the scope of Anglo-Welsh poetry.
Bib: Stephens, M. (ed.), *The Oxford Companion to the Literature of Wales*; Jones, G. and Rowlands, J., *Profiles*.

Webster, Augusta (1837–94)
Poet, dramatist and essayist, who also wrote under the ▷ pseudonym Cecil Home. After marrying Thomas Webster at the age of twenty-six, she published her first collection of verse, *Blanche Lisle and Other Poems* (1860). A committed ▷ feminist, much of her work focuses on female subjects. ▷ *Dramatic Studies* (1866) includes poems about spinsterhood, ▷ marriage and motherhood; ▷ 'A Castaway' (1870) is concerned with prostitution; 'Circe' (1870) is a psychological portrait of the mythological figure; *A Housewife's Opinions* (1878) is a collection of essays on the lives of married women. Webster was at times criticized for her forthrightness and unabashed ▷ realism, but she was also favourably compared to ▷ Elizabeth Barrett Browning, ▷ Christina Rossetti and ▷ Jean Ingelow. Her unfinished sonnet sequence, *Mother and Daughter* (1895), was published posthumously, edited by William Michael Rossetti, Christina and ▷ Dante Gabriel's brother. Dramatic works include *The Auspicious Day* (1872); *Disguises* (1879) and *In a Day* (1882).

▷ Women's Movement.

Bib: Hickok, K., *Representations of Women: 19th Century British Women's Poetry*; Leighton, A., and Reynolds, M. (eds.), *An Anthology of Victorian Women Poets.*

Webster, John (1578–1632)
English dramatist about whom little is known, although his father's life is well documented. He is the author of two of the most famous ▷ Jacobean tragedies, ▷ *The White Devil* (1612) and ▷ *The Duchess of Malfi* (1613), and collaborated with ▷ Dekker, ▷ Fletcher, ▷ Ford and others on a number of plays. Webster excels in constructing richly metaphorical passages and iconographic scenes, but he is less satisfactory on form and in overall conception. His works have been accused of lacking moral fibre in their pursuit of grotesque and titillating images of death.
Bib: Morris, B. (ed.), *John Webster.*

Wedgwood
The name of a firm of distinguished manufacturers of china. The founder of the firm, Josiah Wedgwood (1730–95), was the son of a potter of Burslem. He perfected an English style of pottery called cream ware, and later Queen's ware. He then developed a new style of ▷ classical designs, inspired by contemporary interest in ancient Greek pottery and by the discovery of the Roman city of Pompeii in southern Italy. The most famous of the Wedgwood designers in this style was the friend of the poet ▷ William Blake, John Flaxman. The Wedgwood factory near Hanley is called Etruria; the firm continues in production at the present day. Josiah's son, Thomas Wedgwood (1771–1805), was a generous patron to the poet ▷ Coleridge.

Welch, Denton (Maurice Denton Welch) (1915–48)
Novelist and painter. Denton Welch wrote three novels, around sixty short stories and an extensive journal. Perhaps his most powerful writing is to be found in the novels *Maiden Voyage* (1943) and *A Voice Through a Cloud* (1950), in which a perfumed and acutely literary style combines with unusually exacting powers of observation. Welch had trained at the Goldsmith's School of Art as a painter, a career that was cut short at the age of twenty by a cycling accident from which he never fully recovered and which drove him inwards to meet the resources and anxieties of his own imagination. A sign of the revival of interest in Welch's writing is the biography *Denton Welch: the making of a Writer* by Michael De-la-Noy.

Weldon, Fay (b 1931)
Novelist, dramatist and television screenwriter. Her novels include: *The Fat Woman's Joke* (1967); *Down Among the Women* (1971); *Female Friends* (1975); *Remember Me* (1976); *Words of Advice* (1977); *Praxis* (1978); *Little Sisters* (1978); *Puffball* (1980); *The President's Child* (1982); *The Life and Loves of a She-Devil* (1983); *The Shrapnel Academy* (1986); *The Rules of Life* (1987); *The Heart of the Country* (1987); *Leader of the Band* (1988). Story collections are: *Watching Me, Watching You* (1981); *Polaris* (1985). The ▷ feminism of her work is concentrated in the portrayal of the exploitation of women by men in domestic situations, and in relationships. Her tragicomic novels are powerful stories of pain, loss and betrayal, and their desperation is accentuated by the sense of a controlling social and biological pattern which negates the characters' attempts to make choices about their lives. The endings of her books, however, often hint at the emergence of a new and more liberated woman.

Well of Loneliness
▷ Hall, Radclyffe.

Well-Beloved, The (1897)
A novel by ▷ Thomas Hardy. It was originally published in serial form as *The Pursuit of the Well-Beloved* in the *Illustrated London News* in 1892 in place of ▷ *Tess of the d'Urbervilles*, which Hardy withdrew from periodical publication in deference to the qualms of the newspaper syndicate Tillotson and Son. The story concerns the sculptor Jocelyn Pierston, the son of a wealthy stone merchant on the ancient Isle of Slingers (Portland), who spends his life in a wasted search for a woman who embodies his ideal. His search leads him to a fruitless courtship of Avice Caro, her daughter and, subsequently, her grand-daughter (both named Avice). Eventually, age and illness leave him disillusioned with his ideal and he marries his early love Marcia Bencomb, who by this time is also old and withered. In a letter to the *Academy* in March 1987, Hardy wrote that *The Well-Beloved* was 'a phantasmal narrative of the adventures of a Visionary Artist in pursuit of the unattainable perfect in female form.' Consistently classed as a 'minor' novel, *The Well-Beloved* is slowly gaining the critical attention it deserves, not least for its contribution to the debate on art, ▷ aesthetics and the role of women that characterized the *fin-de-siècle*.

Wellington, Arthur Wellesley, 1st Duke of (1769–1852)
General and statesman. By origin, of Anglo-Irish aristocracy. He joined the army in 1787, and between 1796 and 1805 he had a distinguished military career in India, where his eldest brother was Governor-General. Arthur Wellesley then returned to Britain. Between 1808 and 1814 he gained fame for his resistance to the French armies of ▷ Napoleon I on the Spanish

Peninsula. He was created Duke in 1814. In 1815, with the Prussian general Blücher, he inflicted the final defeat on ▷ Napoleon at ▷ Waterloo.

He took part in the Congress of Vienna, which made the peace treaty with France, and his influence did much to prevent the partition of the country. Thereafter, his career was in British politics, where he was one of the principal leaders of the Tory (Whig or Tory) (Conservative) party. He gave way, however, over one issue, that of Catholic Emancipation (*ie* granting Catholics full political rights) because he understood its political inevitability; he was less clear-sighted about ▷ Parliamentary reform, and was forced to resign in 1830. He again held ministerial posts, though not that of Prime Minister, in 1834, and 1841–6, under the leadership of Robert Peel. After his death, ▷ Tennyson commemorated him with one of his best poems, his *Ode on the Death of the Duke of Wellington*. He was popularly known as 'the Iron Duke', and used proudly to call his London mansion at Hyde Park Corner, 'Number One, London'.

Wells, H. G. (Herbert George) (1866–1946)
Novelist and journalist. He was brought up in the lower middle class, the son of a professional cricketer; in 1888 he took an excellent degree in science at London University. His social origins and his education explain much of his approach to life as a writer. The great novelist of the 19th-century lower middle classes is ▷ Dickens and some of H.G. Wells' best fiction is about the same field of society; novels such as *Kipps* (1905) and *The History of Mr Polly* (1910) are of this sort, and they have the kind of vigorous humour and sharp visualization that is characteristic of early Dickens. On the other hand, rising into the educated class at a time of rapid scientific and technical progress, he ignored the values of traditional culture and art, and became fascinated with the prospects that science offered, for good as well as for ill. This side of him produced a different kind of writing: Wells was one of the inventors of ▷ science fiction. *The Time Machine* (1895), *The Invisible Man* (1897), *The War of the Worlds* (1898) and *The First Men in the Moon* (1901) are examples of his fantasies. But his social experience and his interest in technology also drew him to writing fictional-sociological studies in which he surveyed and analysed, often with the same Dickensian humour, the society of his time; *Tono-Bungay* (1908) is perhaps the best of these. Other examples are *Ann Veronica* (1909) about the problems connected with newly emancipated women, *The New Machiavelli* (1911) about socialist thinking – Wells had joined the ▷ Fabians in 1903 – and *Mr Britling Sees It Through* (1916) about World War I seen from the point of view of the 'Home Front'. But the interest in science also made him a ▷ utopian optimist, and this point of view caused him to write such didactic works as *A Modern Utopia* (1905) and *New Worlds For Old* (1908). There was always a great deal of naivety in Wells' optimism, and later in his life he paid the penalty by reacting into excessive gloom, in *Mind at the End of its Tether* (1945). He declared that *The Open Conspiracy* (1928) contained the essence of his philosophy. He was never a deep thinker, however; his work lives by the vitality of his humour and by the urgency with which he pressed his ideas. This urgency necessarily made him a popularizer, and his most notable work of popularization was *The Outline of History* (1920).

In some ways Wells resembles his contemporary, the dramatist ▷ George Bernard Shaw; both were socialists, both felt the urgency to enlighten mankind as quickly as possible, and both cared more that their works should have immediate effect than that they should be works of art – Wells told the novelist ▷ Henry James that he would rather be called a journalist than an artist. Possibly the most penetrating remark on Wells was that addressed to him by the novelist Joseph Conrad (1857–1924): 'You don't really care for people, but you think they can be improved; I do, but I know they can't.'
Bib: Mackenzie, N. and J., *The Time Traveller: Life of H.G. Wells*; Bergonzi, B., *The Early H.G. Wells* and *H.G. Wells: Twentieth-Century Views*; Parrinder, P. (ed.), *H.G. Wells; the Critical Heritage*.

Welsh, Irvine (b 1958)
Novelist and short-story writer. Born in Leith and brought up in Muirhouse, these two areas of Edinburgh feature prominently in his work. Leaving school at 16, he worked in various jobs, including training officer for Edinburgh District Council and took a degree in business administration. His first novel, *Trainspotting* (1993) attracted rapid acclaim and debate: written primarily in Scots urban working-class vernacular, it is a grim but comic narrative of the Edinburgh drugs scene, largely realist in style though interweaving various narrative voices. *Marabou Stork Nightmares* (1995) is more technically inventive, switching as it does between the memories and fantasies of a coma victim, but its core is again a macho world of football, drink, drugs and violence. *The Acid House* (1994) is a collection of short stories. Welsh now lives in Amsterdam.

Welsh literature in English
Writers' claims on Welsh ancestry vary enormously. Some even adopt Welshness as, for example, Raymond Garlick (b 1926), an Englishman who identified with Welsh political causes and became founder-editor of the literary magazine *Dock Leaves* (later *The Anglo-Welsh Review*, 1957–88) and a critic and poet firmly

within the Welsh context. Thus poet and novelist Glyn Jones' criterion of Anglo-Welshness – expressed in his critical work *The Dragon Has Two Tongues* as involvement in the Welsh situation – seems justifiable. So is ▷ George Herbert, brought up in the Marches (▷ Wales) and an influence on ▷ Henry Vaughan, acceptable? Does ▷ Gerard Manley Hopkins' three-year residence at St Beuno's seminary, during which he learnt Welsh, admit him? His assimilation of *cynghanedd* (▷ Welsh terms) into English poetry transmitted Welsh metric to ▷ Dylan Thomas who could not speak Welsh. For poet and critic Anthony Conran, W. H. Davies qualifies as Anglo-Welsh because his *New Poems* conforms to the thematic divisions of the *bardd gwlad* (▷ Welsh terms). Nevertheless, Conran concedes only two Anglo-Welsh poems to Edward Thomas, who is included on parentage, emotional attachment to Wales, and his belated influence on Anglo-Welsh poets. Richard Hughes and ▷ John Cowper Powys have received the accolade of critical studies in the *Writers of Wales* series through their eventually permanent residence in, and lifelong empathy for Wales. From Powys' Wessex came Jeremy Hooker (b 1941), whose 19 years in Wales made him a leading critic in the Anglo-Welsh field and temporarily changed his poetic direction. Thus a widely debatable area of Anglo-Welsh acceptability exists.

Historically, poetry is the dominant genre of Anglo-Welsh literature, prose a mainly 20th-century growth. The poetic origins can be traced to the 15th century, but excepting George Herbert, Henry Vaughan and John Dyer, all the major work belongs to the present century. What is significant, to cite Anthony Conran, is the 'seepage' from Welsh-language culture into English. For example, the traditional function of the Welsh-language poet was to commemorate the society he lived in whether, as earlier, in 'praise poems' for princes or, later, the local community. In the last-named instance, the *bardd gwlad*'s categories of poems included nature, love, beer, hunting songs, poems to individuals and moral poems. Some were in complex traditional metres, others in less exacting free metres, so form is an overriding concern. In serving his community, the Welsh poet is perceived as a craftsman, cultivating an objectivity that contrasts with English poetry from the ▷ Romantic revival onwards and particularly that of contemporary confessional egocentricity. The formal preoccupations of Welsh-language poetry assimilated by Anglo-Welsh practitioners over four centuries revealed affinities by the early 20th century with the English ▷ Georgians' objective descriptions of nature, in birds, flowers, landscapes, and of people and their working lives in an essentially rural setting. The legacy of this is Anglo-Welsh poetry's perseverance with tighter forms and greater objectivity than English contemporary poetry. Welsh-speaking Anglo-Welsh poets such as Glyn Jones (1905–95), Harri Webb (1920–94) and Anthony Conran (b 1931) have translated Welsh-language poems into English, often following the Welsh metric of the originals, such as *traethodl*, *cywydd*, or *englyn*, sometimes including the internal rhymes and alliterations of *cynghanedd*, and the accretion of comparisons known as *dyfalu* (▷ Welsh terms). As Welsh metric poses almost insurmountable technical problems when grafted onto the English language, any assimilation through the centuries has been gradual, and it is more the common thematic inheritance that unites Welsh and Anglo-Welsh poetry and differentiates the latter from English poetry. However, the growth of Anglo-Welsh literature is a concomitant of the historical process that weakened the influence of the Welsh language.

Anglo-Norman settlements of the Marches and South Wales were followed by Henry I's 12th-century Flemish settlement of South Pembroke, subsequently augmented by English settlements in Gower and around Laugharne. Edwardian castles protected English merchants who were granted privileges within town walls, as at Caernarfon and Conwy. Itinerant drovers and weavers soon forged linguistic links with England. The establishment of the Tudor dynasty brought Welsh influence into England, though Henry VIII's Acts of Union insisted on Welsh office-holders' proficiency in English, eventually producing an anglicized squirearchy. Three centuries later, Victorian government policy further weakened the hold of the Welsh language by encouraging 'The Welsh Not', prohibiting Welsh-language conversation in schools. A piece of wood or slate with the letters 'WN' cut into it was hung round the neck of the last pupil caught speaking Welsh in class – whoever was left wearing it at the end of the school day would be punished. From the early 19th century, the increasing influx into the South Wales valleys not only drained the rural areas of the west and north but brought in labouring or technological expertise for pit-sinking, blast furnace, canal, tramroad, railway and docks construction. The ultimate figure of English-speaking immigrants in the South Wales valleys accounted for at least 40% of the population, swamping the native Welsh speakers. The subsequent foundation of county schools from 1895 onwards provided secondary education in the medium of English. This explains why Glyn Jones, an early pupil at Merthyr's Cyfarthfa Castle Grammar School, though from a Welsh-speaking family, developed into an Anglo-Welsh writer. It was these socio-economic pressures that helped to create the 'first flowering' of Anglo-Welsh literature.

Many young provincial writers departed for London between the wars to find publishers who encouraged them to adapt their work for the metropolitan market. Caradoc Evans

(1878–1945), according to the 'first distinctive ancestral voice' of Anglo-Welsh writing, produced the first London-published best-seller. In *My People* (1915) and subsequent short-story collections, Caradoc Evans invented grotesqueries of character and speech for his Cardi peasantry whose lust, greed and hypocrisy established a false Welsh stereotype that amused Londoners but gave unmitigated and lasting offence to the Welsh-speaking literary establishment. Notwithstanding, Caradoc Evans' commercial success encouraged a vein of fantasy among the 'first flowering' of Anglo-Welsh writers, Rhys Davies, Glyn Jones and Dylan Thomas, continued in the post-war period by Gwyn Thomas. Moreover, the eccentric and grotesque provided a diversion from painfully harsh living conditions in decaying rural and unemployment-ravaged industrial communities. Beneath this surface, however, industrial realism encapsulates a political message – socialist in the 'first flowering', nationalist in the 'second flowering' in the 1960s. This idealism motivates an inevitably doomed nationalist military uprising in Glyn Jones' ▷ novella, *I Was Born in the Ystrad Valley*, as early as 1937. Communist political activism inspires Lewis Jones' *Cwmardy* (1937) and *We Live!* (1939), Jack Jones paints panoramic historical canvases behind his family epics in *Black Parade* (1935) and *Rhondda Roundabout* (1934), whereas Gwyn Jones employs a briefer time-scale in *Times Like These* (1936) where he examines the social and familial crises precipitated by the General Strike. However, it was Richard Llewellyn's *How Green Was My Valley* (1939) which became the popular stereotype of the Valleys' industrial novel despite its inaccuracies and sentimentality, a far cry from Gwyn Thomas' rejected pre-war novel *Sorrow For Thy Sons* (eventually published in 1986, five years after his death). Gwyn Thomas' post-war hyperbolic wit, farcical situations and eccentric characters create a Valleys' world where laughter is the only antidote to poverty and unemployment. Meanwhile, short stories between the wars mediate between a poetic vision of Welsh-speaking Wales, Lawrentian-influenced in Rhys Davies and Geraint Goodwin, and the realistic depiction of industrial communities, infused with wit and humour. Only one poet identifies with the industrial milieu: Idris Davies, despite a ▷ Georgian vocabulary and the formal strait-jacket of the ▷ Housman quatrain, brings his strike-bound communities to life when he uses local vernacular speech and escapes into free verse.

The two most original poets to appear in the 1930s were very different from Idris Davies in theme and technique. David Jones achieved the critical recognition due to him as a major poet only in the 1980s, shortly after his death. *In Parenthesis*, for example, encapsulated his experiences in World War I but appeared only two years before World War II. His juxtaposition of prose passages with poetry, all loaded with mythopoeic reference, represented an exciting new poetic dimension, though it received scant notice at the time. Very different was the critical reception for Dylan Thomas, who alienated himself from the Welsh concept of community-serving poet and escaped from Swansea to literary London as early as possible to promote his self-advertising poetic image. Nevertheless, his indisputable success and originality gave fresh impetus to Anglo-Welsh writing which found a mouthpiece in Keidrych Rhys' literary magazine *Wales*, published in three intermittent series between 1937 and 1960, and in Gwyn Jones' more academically respectable *Welsh Review* published first in 1939 and then between 1944 and 1948. Unlike other Anglo-Welsh poets, Dylan Thomas flowered early because his poetry was self-created. Influenced by his work, some young poets published prematurely shortly after the war, including Leslie Norris and John Ormond, who then waited for 20 years for their individual, mature and successful voices to be heard. Inevitably, the war had limited publishing so that the tragically brief war-time appearance of Alun Lewis' work was all the more remarkable.

In post-war years, attempts to revive *Wales* and the *Welsh Review* were short-lived through lack of funds, though *Dock Leaves* (founded 1949) survived in Tenby, thanks to Raymond Garlick and Roland Mathias. Despite the growing reputation of Vernon Watkins (1906–67) as a poetic visionary, Dylan Thomas' untimely self-destruction left a void that was eventually filled by ▷ R.S. Thomas (b 1913), whose major poetic status was rapidly endorsed by critics in England despite their disregard of most Anglo-Welsh literature. R.S. Thomas' concern for rural and urban poverty in Wales, reflected in his sympathy for the uncouth hill farmer, is revealed in firmly structured, emotionally restrained poems of arresting imagery. For him, nationalism would answer Wales' problems: God he listens for in answer to his own problems as priest-poet. Another major poet Emyr Humphreys (b 1919). Humphreys, of North Walian orientation, examines conscience among the Welsh-speaking professional class, and impartially presents Nonconformity, while never seeking to depart from his fictive high seriousness or to indulge popular taste.

Meic Stephens (b 1938) was the prime mover behind the 'second flowering' which gather momentum in the 1960s when nationalist ideas were superseding socialist politics. He founded *Poetry Wales* in 1965 with support from Harri Webb, thus providing a nationalist conscious poetic forum, fostering mutual interest between Wales' two languages, especially reinvigorating Anglo-Welsh poetry through John Ormond, Harri Webb, John Tripp, Raymond Garlick, Roland Mathias, Leslie Norris and Gillian Clarke.

In 1967 he became Literature Director of the newly constituted *Welsh Arts Council* whose financial support for writers and publishers gave tremendous impetus to Welsh and Anglo-Welsh writing. An unfortunate effect, however, was that London publishers and reviewers disregarded Anglo-Welsh writing when it developed independently from metropolitan influences, leading to a critical undervaluing that still persists in England. In 1968 Meic Stephens led a move to create the English section of *Yr Academi Gymreig*, originally a literary society founded for Welsh-language writers only, but from then on providing invaluable encouragement to Anglo-Welsh writers. Concluding an exciting decade, Ned Thomas launched *Planet* in 1970, a magazine whose political thrust was left-wing and nationalist, and which also published literary material.

Recently, an updated view of Valleys society has informed the short stories and novels of Alun Richards (b 1929) and Ron Berry (b 1920). Alun Richards illuminates social tensions among the migratory professional classes, nuances between the Valleys and Cardiff, and Cardiff and London. His sensitive ear for dialogue contributed to the effectiveness of his work for the theatre (published in *Plays for Players*, 1975) and television. Ron Berry has explored Valleys sexual mores with lively humour. Closely associated with the border country of his upbringing, Raymond Williams' novels present the tensions of nationalism, social mobility, working-class solidarity and conflicting loyalties, though the political and socio-economic dimensions of his critical *oeuvre* are more familiar. The novelists with Anglo-Welsh connections who have achieved the most recent critical acclaim are Bernice Rubens, Alice Thomas Ellis, Stuart Evans and Peter Thomas, a newcomer as a novelist extending Gwyn Thomas' hyperbolic vision.

Anglo-Welsh literature has produced no playwright to emulate Emlyn Williams (1905–88), though the recent emphasis has shifted from theatre via radio into television, as reflected in the careers of Gwyn Thomas, Alun Owen, Alun Richards and Elaine Morgan.

Although disappointment with the result of the referendum on devolution did not affect the republican nationalist views of some of the younger poets such as Nigel Jenkins and Mike Jenkins, a widening of poetic horizons has been taking place. Its trailblazer ▷ Dannie Abse (b 1932) has exploited a series of fruitful tensions in his work which reflect contrasting life-styles: Cardiff/London; Welsh/Jewish; poetry/medicine. His sympathy for oppressed minorities reveals a humanitarianism and compassion haunted by the horror of the Holocaust. His range of themes ensures his international, as well as Anglo-Welsh, status. Another poet who has broadened his Anglo-Welsh context through exposure to the influence of American 'confessional' poets (such as Robert Lowell, ▷ Sylvia Plath, John Berryman and Anne Sexton), thereby producing many transatlantic poems, is Tony Curtis (b 1946) whose recent work invokes historical perspectives through condemnation of war and nuclear weapons. Peter Finch (b 1947) has experimented with concrete and multilingual, occasionally almost surreal, poetry. John Davies, Steve Griffiths, Robert Minhinnick, Mike Jenkins, Nigel Jenkins, Duncan Bush, Sheenagh Pugh and Chris Meredith are all acutely conscious of their present social reality while rejecting traditional Welsh stereotyping. Moving towards English influences, Oliver Reynolds (b 1957) has embraced the ▷ Martian 'new heartlessness', his poetic incisiveness deriving also from ▷ W.H. Auden. Hilary Llewellyn-Williams' rural, mythopoeic vision owes something to Gillian Clarke and Ruth Bidgood in that it is personal, familial and rooted in the Welsh landscape, its inhabitants and their history.

With a higher concentration of writers in Wales than anywhere else in Britain, the vigorous growth of Anglo-Welsh literature is assured, particularly since, though it has retained its traditionally distinguishing characteristics, it has developed a more outward-looking stance. Happily, as this text proves, there are indications that the Anglo-Welsh literary movement may eventually receive its long overdue recognition from the English critical establishment.

Bib: Stephens, M. (ed.), *The Oxford Companion to the Literature of Wales*; Adams, S. and Hughes, G. R., *Essays in Welsh and Anglo-Welsh Literature*; Conran, A., *The Cost of Strangeness*; Garlick, R., *An Introduction to Anglo-Welsh Literature*; Hooker, J., *The Poetry of Place*; Jones, G., *The Dragon Has Two Tongues*; Jones, G. and Rowlands, R., *Profiles*; Mathias, R., *A Ride Through the Wood*; Mathias, R., *Anglo-Welsh Literature*; Curtis, T. (ed.), *Wales: the Imagined Nation*.

Welsh terms

bardd gwlad Country poet or folk poet. There were instances of their skills being practised in the English language, as, for example, in Gower, which was predominantly English-speaking.

traethodl Seven syllable lines with rhymed couplets, an accented syllable usually rhyming with an unaccented one.

cywydd traethodl With the addition of a form of *cynghanedd*.

cynghanedd Internal rhymes with alliteration in a fixed metrical pattern.

englyn The most common is a four-line stanza of ten, six, seven and seven syllables. There is a break, like a caesura, after the seventh syllable of the first line, and it is on this syllable that the rhyme usually occurs with the end syllable of the second, third and fourth lines. Thus each line rhymes with the others, though the

first-line rhyme is internal. Most commonly occurring on the seventh syllable, it may occur on the eighth or ninth.
dyfalu A series of comparisons.
▷ Welsh literature in English.

Wertenbaker, Timberlake
British resident Anglo-French-American dramatist. Although Timberlake Wertenbaker is American by birth, and French educated, her work has all been created within the British theatre. Her most successful plays, *The Love of the Nightingale* (1988) and *Our Country's Good* (1988) offer an exhilarating contrast in their treatment of theatrical techniques. Like ▷ Caryl Churchill she has shown a persistent interest in how notions of normality and self are constructed and many of her plays contain a Faustian bargain in which knowledge is purchased at the expense of innocence. *The Grace of Mary Traverse* (1985), set in a picaresque eighteenth-century, is primarily an exploration of the possibilities for women when they step outside their own environment. Wertenbaker had already engaged with this topic in *New Anatomies* (1981), a sprawling, ambitious account of two rebellious women who broke the conventions of gender by dressing in male attire: the nineteenth-century explorer Isabelle Eberhardt and the music hall performer Vesta Tilley. *Our Country's Good* owed its success at the ▷ Royal Court, in Australia and the West End, to its reaffirmation of the power of theatre to change lives and influence people for the better. The play, based on Thomas Keneally's novel *The Playmaker*, shows convicts from the First Fleet staging the first theatrical production in Australia, ▷ Farquhars' *The Recruiting Officer*. The play uses familiar backstage situations to debate the aesthetics and politics of the theatre and the philosophy of punishment, and the original production used devices such as cross-casting, multiple doubling and onstage changes of identity to further the debate about the relationship between environmental and genetic influences on character and behaviour. *The Love of the Nightingale* is a powerful and spare reworking of the myth of Philomel and Procne, which includes a staging within the play of the Phaedra story and an enactment of Bacchic rituals. Its use of the theatre within its design relates dialectically to that in *Our Country's Good*, where the theatre is regarded in terms of its power to transform the performers, rather than its audience. *Nightingale* is much more concerned with the making of myths, the power of language, gender roles, and the role of fantasy in more negative terms. Here the power of theatre is questioned alongside a powerful exploration of the construction of male and female roles. With these two plays Wertenbaker established herself as one of Britain's most challenging and intellectually stimulating dramatists. In 1991, *Three Birds Alighting in a Field* confirmed her growing reputation as a bold and original theatre practitioner.

Wesker, Arnold (b 1932)
British dramatist, born in London's East End and son of a Russian Jewish tailor. After military service, he became a professional pastry cook, and then entered the London School of Film Technique. ▷ John Osborne's ▷ *Look Back in Anger* (1956) influenced him to concentrate on the theatre. In 1961, he became Director of Centre Forty-two, intended to break down such barriers to popular appreciation of the arts as commercialism and intellectual and social snobbery, or social fragmentation due to restricted ways of life and inarticulacy in the shaping of goals. These obstacles to communication in the mass of society are the subject matter of his plays which are pervaded by a search for cordial understanding and sympathy. *The Wesker Trilogy*, firmly set in an East End world of the Jewish family, uses a form of social realism to depict working-class life. *Chicken Soup with Barley* (1958) charts the experience of the Khans, a Jewish family in the East End over twenty years, beginning in 1936 with the threat of Moseley's Blackshirts, and ending with the 1956 Soviet invasion of Hungary. These events are experienced from within a domestic world; the play traces the decline of the family, a group of people who come to stand for the disillusion of the post-war generations, as their hopes for the future turn to a loss of faith. The play was enormously influential. *Roots* (1959) focuses on the socio-political enlightenment of its heroine. In the last play of the trilogy, *I'm Talking about Jerusalem* (1960), Wesker returns to the Khan family; the Jerusalem of the title represents the hopes for the future in the face of the failure of socialist idealism (a reference to the call 'Next year in Jerusalem!' of the Passover ritual). In *Chips with Everything* (1962) Wesker began to move away from a strictly naturalist form, and employed folk and popular song, a device he was to pursue in his later plays. Wesker's more recent work has tended to move away from the broad chronology and canvases of his earlier work. In *Caritas* (1981) he explores the phenomenon of a fourteenth-century woman anchorite (a religious mystic and recluse) who literally walls herself up in a cathedral wall. *Annie Wobbler* (1983) and *Mothers* (1982) take the form of dramatic monologue. His *The Merchant* (1977) is an intelligent reworking of ▷ Shakespeare's *The Merchant of Venice* from a Jewish viewpoint.
Bib: Taylor, J. R., *Anger and After*; Ribalow, H. U., *Arnold Wesker*; Leeming, G., *Arnold Wesker*.

Wesley, Charles (1707–88)
▷ Hymn writer. Brother of the evangelist, ▷ John Wesley, he was the poet of the

▷ Methodist movement. He wrote about 6,500 hymns of unequal merit. Some of them, such as 'Hark the Herald Angels Sing', 'Jesu, lover of my soul', and 'Love divine all Loves excelling' show genuine poetic feeling, and are well known.

Wesley, John (1703–91)
Evangelist and founder of the ▷ Methodist religious movement. At Oxford, with his brother ▷ Charles, he became the centre of a society which regulated the lives of its members; this led to their being described as 'Methodists'. He was at first a strict Anglican, conforming rigidly to ▷ Church of England liturgies and doctrines, but on a voyage to America in 1735 he became deeply impressed by the purity and undogmatic spirit of fellow-passengers belonging to the German sect known as the Moravians. On his return to England, Wesley preached up and down Britain. Both the Church of England and the ▷ Dissenters who were heirs of the 17th-century Puritans had by now relatively little to offer to the minds of the simple people; reaction against the violent conflicts of the previous century had caused the clergy of all denominations to obscure the sense of religion as a power in individual lives. Wesley taught both that every man was naturally a sinner, and that the power of God was available to all for spiritual salvation. In this he followed the Arminian tradition of religious belief, instead of the belief in ▷ Predestination more prevalent among the 17th-century Puritans. Wesley's direct challenge to the hearts and the wills of his hearers caused deep psychological disturbances, and the Methodists were despised by many for the hysteria and emotionalism of their meetings. Nonetheless, the influence of Wesley was extensive and profound, and bore fruit in other religious revivals in the 19th century. He was courteous and had a pleasant wit. When confronted by an arrogant opponent in a narrow street who declared 'I never make way for fools!', Wesley stood aside politely, replying: 'I always do.'

▷ Sermons.

Wessex
The kingdom of the West Saxons from the 6th century till the reign of Alfred at the end of the 9th, after which it developed into the kingdom of England. The capital was the town of Winchester in Hampshire, and the area also included Dorset, Somerset, Wiltshire, and Berkshire. The name of Wessex was revived by the novelist and poet ▷ Thomas Hardy for his ▷ regional novels.

▷ Barnes, William.

***West Indian, The* (1771)**
Comedy by ▷ Richard Cumberland. Belcour has been brought up in the West Indies; he is honest but unsophisticated. Arriving in London, he falls in love with Louisa, the daughter of the impoverished Captain Dudley, but is deceived into thinking her the mistress of Charles, who is in fact her brother. He makes advances to her as if she were a whore and she repels him with the classic phrase, 'Unhand me, sir!' Meanwhile, Charles loves his wealthy cousin Charlotte, but will not acknowledge the fact because of his own poverty. Belcour comes to the aid of Captain Dudley. Eventually Charles and Louisa are revealed as heirs, Belcour and Louisa become reconciled and are married, and Charles marries Charlotte. The play contains references to the workings of Providence in refusing to allow 'innocence to be oppressed', or cruelty and cunning to prosper; it has often been cited as an archetypal example of ▷ sentimentality in the drama of the period.

West, Jane (1758–1852)
Poet, novelist and dramatist. A prolific author, whose restrained prose style and dry sense of humour brought admiration from ▷ Jane Austen and ▷ Mary Wollstonecraft. West's self-deprecating wit may be seen in her mocking self-description:

You said the author was a charmer,
Self-taught, and married to a farmer;
Who wrote all kinds of verse with ease,
Made pies and puddings, frocks and cheese.

Her poetry and plays were published in 1791, but thereafter she concentrated upon novels. Her work includes material that is anti-sentimental (*The Advantages of Education, or The History of Maria Williams*, 1793), anti-radical (*A Tale of the Times*, 1799) and anti-feminist (*Letters to a Young Lady*, 1806). Her historical novels, *The Loyalists* (1812) and *Alicia de Lacey* (1814), are perhaps the most readable today.
Bib: Butler, M., *Jane Austen and the War of Ideas*; Rendall, J., *The Origins of Modern Feminism 1780–1860*.

West, Dame Rebecca (1892–1983)
Novelist, journalist, feminist writer and critic. Born Cecily Isabel Fairfield, she named herself Rebecca West at the age of 19, after the strong-willed and independent protagonist of *Rosmersholm*, a play by the Norwegian dramatist Ibsen. She was educated in Edinburgh and began her writing career with work for feminist and socialist journals such as *The Freewoman* and *Clarion*. She had a long affair with the novelist ▷ H.G. Wells (after writing a highly critical review of his work) and had a son by him; in 1930 she married a banker. In 1916 she published a study of ▷ Henry James and in 1918 her first novel, *The Return of the Soldier*, appeared. This uses ▷ modernist narrative techniques to explore the psychological and

social nuances of the relationship between three women and a man who returns from World War I with memory loss. Much of her fiction is centred on the contemporary experience of women and emphasizes the special qualities of women as she sees them: *Harriet Hume* (1929); *The Harsh Voice* (1935); *The Thinking Reed* (1936); *The Fountain Overflows* (1956). She also deals with political issues, such as the suffrage movement in *The Judge* (1922) and the Russian Revolution in *The Birds Fall Down* (1966). A journey to Yugoslavia resulted in a travel diary, *Black Flag and Grey Falcon: A Journey through Yugoslavia* (1941), and she published *The New Meaning of Treason* (1949), based on her observation of the Nuremberg trials, *McLuhan and the Future of Literature* (1969) and a biography of St Augustine (1933). See also: *Rebecca West: A Celebration* (1977); *The Strange Necessity: Essays by Rebecca West* (1928); *The Young Rebecca: Writings of Rebecca West 1911–1917* (1982, ed. Jane Marcus).
Bib: Glendinning, V., *Rebecca West: A Life*; Weldon, F., *Rebecca West*; Deakin, M., *Rebecca West*; Wolfe, P., *Rebecca West: Artist and Thinker*; Orel, H., *The Literary Achievement of Rebecca West*; Ray, G.N., *H.G. Wells and Rebecca West*.

Westminster Review
It was founded in 1823 as a vehicle for the Benthamite (▷ Jeremy Bentham) otherwise known as the ▷ Utilitarian school of thought, and at first kept severely to its principles. Its politics of ruthless, scientific institutional reform made it not only a strong opponent of the Tory *Quarterly Review* but put it well to the left of the ▷ *Edinburgh Review*. It appealed to a narrower public, and tended, in the Utilitarian manner, to regard the arts with disdain. In 1836 it combined with the now livelier Utilitarian *London Review* and continued as the *London and Westminster Review*, under the editorship of the distinguished Utilitarian ▷ John Stuart Mill. Mill wanted to broaden Utilitarian thinking, and writers who were not followers of the movement were brought in, such as ▷ Carlyle and the novelist ▷ George Eliot, who was assistant editor 1851–4. Later contributors varied as greatly as ▷ Walter Pater, father of the ▷ Aesthetic movement, and the positivist Frederic Harrison. It continued to advocate scientific progress, and by the end of the century it ceased to be literary.

Wharton, Anne (1659–1685)
English dramatist and poet, niece of John Wilmot, ▷ Earl of Rochester. In 1673 she was married to Thomas Wharton, later Whig politican, who ignored her. Some of her letters to him survive. When Rochester died, she became close to ▷ Bishop Gilbert Burnet, who was critical of her poetry. Her tragedy, *Love's Martyr, or Witt Above Crowns* was not acted, but is a political allegory of the ▷ Exclusion Crisis. Her poetry circulated during her lifetime, but it only began to appear in print after her death. She paraphrased the letter from Penelope to Ulysses in Ovid's *Heroides*: 'Would Troy were glorious still, so I had you.'

Her other publications include: *Poems by Several Hands* (ed. ▷ Nahum Tate 1685); *Idea of Christian Love* (1688); *A Collection of Poems* (1693), and *Whartonia* (1727).
Bib: Greer, G. *et al.*, *Kissing the Rod*.

***What Maisie Knew* (1897)**
A novel by ▷ Henry James. Its theme is the survival of innocence in a world of adult corruption, the influence of adults on a child, and her influence on them.

Maisie Farange is a small girl whose parents have divorced each other with equal guilt on both sides. The parents are heartless and indifferent to their daughter, except as a weapon against each other and in their farcical, though not wholly vain, struggles to maintain acceptable social appearances. Maisie is passed from one to the other, and each employs a governess to take responsibility for her welfare. Both parents marry again, and eventually relinquish Maisie herself. By the end of the book Maisie finds herself torn between two prospective 'step-parents', each formerly married to her real parents, divorced from them, and about to marry each other, Maisie herself having been the occasion of their coming together. Her 'stepfather', Sir Claude, is charming and sweet-natured, but weak and self-indulgent; her 'stepmother', Mrs Beale, is genuinely fond of Maisie (as Sir Claude is) but is basically selfish and rapacious. In addition, the child has a simple-minded, plain and elderly governess, Mrs Wix, who is herself in love with Sir Claude, and devoted to Maisie. The affection of none of them, however, is single-minded, as hers is for each one of them. The pathos of the novel arises from the warm responsiveness, deep need, and pure integrity of Maisie, from whose point of view all the events are seen. Its irony arises from the way in which the child's need for and dependence on adult care and love is transformed into responsibility for the adults themselves, who become dependent on her decisions. In the end these decisions lead her to choose life alone with Mrs Wix, who naively hopes to imbue her with a 'moral sense', unaware that beside Maisie's innocence her own idea of a moral sense represents modified corruption.

The novel is written in James' late, compressed and dramatic style, and is one of his masterpieces.

Wheathill, Anne (c 1584)
Devotional writer. Little is known about Wheathill's life except that she was an unmarried gentlewoman at the time she composed her one

known work, *A Handfull of Holesome (though homelie) Hearbs Gathered Out of the Goodlie Garden of Gods Most Holie Word* (1584). This text consists of 49 prayers arranged symbolically in accordance with the title; their concerns are conventional, for example how to avoid the sin of pride, how to evade the temptations of the devil, and prayers for faith and repentance. The book itself has an attractive title-page, but the contents are not exceptional.
Bib: Travitsky, B. (ed.), *A Paradise for Women*.

Wheatley, Phillis (?1753–1784)
The first black poet in English. As a child she was sold as a slave to the Wheatley family in Boston, who treated her well and encouraged her inclination to write. Her *Poems on Various Subjects, Religious and Moral*, published in London in 1773, comprises derivative and conventional verses on ▷ didactic themes: 'Remember, *Christians*, *Negroes*, black as *Cain*,/ May be refin'd, and join the angelic train.'

Whetstone, George (1550–87)
English poet and dramatist who is mostly remembered for the comedy *Promos and Cassandra* (1578), which ▷ Shakespeare used in *Measure for Measure*.

White, Antonia (1899–1980)
Novelist and translator. She was intially named Eirene Botting, White being her mother's surname. Her parents were converts to Catholicism and she was sent to the Convent of the Sacred Heart, Roehampton; after she began writing her novel *Frost in May* (1933) at the age of 15 her father withdrew her from the school (telling her she had been expelled) and sent her to St Paul's School for Girls (where he was classics master). After doing some teaching and clerical work she attended drama school in 1919 and worked as an actress. She was married three times, two of the marriages being annulled; she experienced periods of mental disturbance (and spent nine months in an asylum) but also supported herself and her children for periods through work as a journalist and advertising copy-writer. She is best known for her four autobiographical novels: *Frost in May*; *The Lost Traveller* (1950); *The Sugar House* (1952); *Beyond the Glass* (1954). These depict her experiences at school and her subsequent mental disturbances as well as her continuing complex and ambivalent relationship with Catholicism. *The Hound and the Falcon* (1965) describes, in letter form, her reconversion to Catholicism. Her other writings include: *Strangers* (1954), a volume of short stories; *Three in a Room* (1957); *Minka and Curdy* and *Living with Minka and Curdy* (1970) about her much-loved cats. *As Once in May* (1983) includes stories, essays, poems, autobiographical fragments and parts of a sequel to her tetralogy of novels and was edited by her daughter Susan Chitty, who also published *Now to My Mother: A Very Personal Memoir of Antonia White*.
Bib: Marcus, J., in Kime Scott, B. (ed.), *The Gender of Modernism*; Showalter, E., *A Literature of their Own*.

***White Devil, The* (1608–9)**
A tragedy by ▷ John Webster, published in 1612 with the subtitle *Vittoria Corrombona*, written in 1608–9. It is based on the story of the actual murder of Vittoria Accoromboni (1585) as told in William Painter's ▷ *Palace of Pleasure*. Vittoria is the wife of Camillo. The Duke of Brachiano, husband to Isabella, the sister of the Duke of Florence and of Cardinal Montecelso, falls in love with her and is assisted in winning her by her brother, Flamineo. Flamineo causes the death of Camillo, and Brachiano poisons his own wife. In Act III, Vittoria is on trial before Cardinal Montecelso for adultery and murder; she is proudly defiant, and condemned to confinement in a convent, where Brachiano continues to visit her, and whence he eventually steals her away and marries her. In Act V, Flamineo kills his brother, Marcello, who is upbraiding him for his wickedness, and their mother sings over her dead son the lovely dirge 'Call for the robin redbreast and the wren'. The Duke of Florence's hireling, Lodovico, avenges the death of Isabella by killing Flamineo and Vittoria. 'My soul, like to a ship in a black storm, is driven, I know not whither'; the spirit of the stormy play is expressed by this line spoken by the dying Vittoria. The play contains many passages of intense poetry, no virtuous characters among the outstanding ones, and a number of fine theatrical episodes which are difficult to perform because they are long drawn out. The unifying tone is of desperation produced by destructive and self-destroying passions.

White, Gilbert (1720–93)
Writer on natural history. He was born at Selborne, a village in Hampshire. After spending some years as a Fellow of Oriel College, ▷ Oxford, he became a country curate, and spent the last nine years of his life in the village of his birth. His *Natural History of Selborne* (1789) is a record of the plant, animal and bird life there, inspired by genuine scientific curiosity and showing great delicacy and charm of expression. The book has been described as the first to raise natural history to the level of literature, and is the fruit of the development of 17th- and 18th-century natural science, partly initiated by the greatest of English naturalists, John Ray (1627–1705), author of *The Wisdom of God Manifested in the Works of his Creation* (1691), a scientist who shared ▷ Newton's intellectual curiosity and his religious awe at the spectacle of divine organization in the

universe. Another tradition leading to White was the newly awakened ▷ sensibility for natural surroundings in the poetry of ▷ William Collins, ▷ Oliver Goldsmith and ▷ William Cowper. The poetic movement culminated in the 19th century in the work of ▷ Wordsworth and ▷ Clare.

Bib: Holt-White, R., *Life and Letters.*

White, Henry Kirke (1785–1806)

Poet. White came from a poor family but won a scholarship to Cambridge after being encouraged and helped by ▷ Southey. His first book of poetry, *Clifton Grove* (1803), showed great promise, but he died while still at university and Southey published his papers together with a small biography in *The Remains of Kirke White* (1807).

White, Patrick (1912–90)

Australian novelist, dramatist and poet. Born in London, educated in Australia, and at Cheltenham College and Cambridge University. He travelled widely in Europe and the U.S.A., served in the Royal Air Force during World War II, and then returned to live in Australia. His work combines an intense spirituality with social comedy and a distaste for human pretension and egotism. His first novel, *The Happy Valley* (1939), set in remote New South Wales, shows the influence of ▷ Joyce, while *The Living and the Dead* (1941) is primarily a condemnation of English society of the 1920s and 1930s. White established his reputation with *The Tree of Man* (1955) and *Voss* (1957). Both concern man's confrontation with the inhuman forces of nature in Australia, the former through the struggles of a young farmer, the latter through the journey among the Aborigines of a mid-19th-century German explorer. White's last works of fiction were two collections, each containing three short pieces: *Memoirs of Many in One* (1986) and *Three Uneasy Pieces* (1988). His other novels are: *The Aunt's Story* (1948); *Riders in the Chariot* (1961); *The Solid Mandala* (1966); *The Vivisector* (1970); *The Eye of the Storm* (1973); *A Fringe of Leaves* (1976); *The Twyborn Affair* (1979). Drama includes: *Return to Abyssinia* (1947); *Four Plays* (1965) (*The Ham Funeral,* 1961; *The Season at Sarsaparilla,* 1962; *A Cheery Soul,* 1963; *Night on Bald Mountain,* 1964); *Big Toys* (1977); *Signal Driver* (1983). Story collections are: *The Burnt Ones* (1964); *The Cockatoos* (1974). Verse: *The Ploughman and Other Poems* (1935).

▷ Post-colonial fiction.

Bib: Walsh, W., *Patrick White's Fiction*; Marr, D., *Patrick White: A Life*; Bliss, C., *Patrick White's Fiction: The Paradox of Fortunate Failure*; Tacey, D. J., *Patrick White: Fiction and the Unconscious.*

White, William Hale (1831–1913)

Novelist who used the ▷ pseudonym Mark Rutherford. His father was a ▷ Dissenter and intended his son to be a Dissenting clergyman. However, William White could not reconcile his ideas and the religious doctrines that he was required to believe, and instead he had a civil service career in the Admiralty. His three famous novels were *The Autobiography of Mark Rutherford* (1881), *Mark Rutherford's Deliverance* (1885) and *The Revolution in Tanner's Lane* (1887). The first two are ▷ autobiographical and concerned with loss of faith. White makes Rutherford more outwardly unfortunate than he was himself, since he had a successful career both as a writer and as a civil servant; the reason seems to be that he makes his character represent not only his own loss of Christian faith but the sense of impoverishment that accompanied it. In his study of John Bunyan (1905), he makes the statement: 'Religion is dead when imagination deserts it.' White's own questioning of his belief started from reading William Wordsworth (1770–1850) in *Lyrical Ballads* (1798–1800) and the subsequent feeling that nature stirred him as 'the God of the Church' could not. As studies of spiritual loss and contention with it, the Mark Rutherford novels have wide human relevance. The third novel is concerned with radical movements in the early 19th century and shows White's political intelligence, which comes out directly in his pamphlet on the political franchise. His other novels are *Miriam's Schooling* (1890), *Catherine Furze* (1893) and *Clara Hopgood* (1896). Other works: *Pages from a Journal* and *More Pages from a Journal* (1900 and 1910); *Last Pages* (1915).

▷ Agnosticism.

Bib: Maclean, C.M., *Life*; Stone, W., *Life*; Stock, I., *William Hale White*; Lucas, J., *The Literature of Change: Studies in the Nineteenth-Century Provincial Novel* (chapter).

Whitgift, John (c 1530–1610)

Archbishop of Canterbury. Whitgift rose to prominence at Cambridge University, where he was appointed Regius Professor of Divinity in 1567, and in the same year he became chaplain to ▷ Elizabeth I. He was Bishop of Worcester (1577–83) before being made Archbishop in 1583, after the death of ▷ Edmund Grindal. Whitgift's firm Anglican policy and his belief in conformity – he reversed his predecessor's policy of conciliation with the ▷ Puritan sects – brought him into close alliance with the queen, who appointed him to her Privy Council and insisted that he attend her at her deathbed. Subsequently, Whitgift was responsible for ▷ James I's ready acceptance of the Anglican church at his accession in 1603. Whitgift's most well-known work is an attack against ▷ Presbyterianism, *An Answere to a Certen Libel Intituled, An Admonition to the Parliament* (1572).

Bib: Dawley, P. M., *John Whitgift and the Reformation*.

Whiting, John (1917–63)
British damatist and actor. Although his plays are now rarely performed, he is important as a pioneer of serious drama during the immediate post-war period. Plays include: *A Penny for a Song* (1951), *Saint's Day* (1951), *Marching Song* (1954) and *The Devils* (1961), based on ▷ Aldous Huxley's *The Devils of Loundon*. Both *A Penny for a Song* and *The Devils* were performed by the ▷ Royal Shakespeare Company.
Bib: Salmon, E., *The Dark Journey*.

Whitney, Isabella (c 1567)
Poet. The first known professional woman poet writing in English, her two extant books, *Copy of a Letter* . . . (c 1567) and *A Sweet Nosegay* (1573), both contain moralizing poetry which is primarily secular in tone. Thematically, Whitney concentrates upon the constancy of women and the fickleness of men, using classical allusion to back up her light-hearted arguments and following the tradition of ▷ Ovid's *Heroides*. In *A Sweet Nosegay* she is indebted especially to Sir Hugh Platt's *Flours of Philosophie* whose maxims she translates into verse, although she also participates in the contemporary vogue for 'flower poetry', for example ▷ George Gascoigne's *A Hundreth Sundrie Flowres*. Her work also includes interesting material that is assumed to be ▷ autobiographical and is useful as such, since little about Whitney's life is known. It is probable that she was the sister of Geoffrey Whitney, the author of *A Choice of Emblemes* (1586), and that she had several sisters in service in London to whom she dedicated poems. She clearly knew London intimately since her last poem, 'Wyll and Testament', consists of a mock bequest to all the streets and buildings of London; it is entirely secular in tone and is reminiscent of the travel pieces in ▷ Thomas Nashe's ▷ *The Unfortunate Traveller* (1594).
▷ Emblem-books.
Bib: Travitsky, B. (ed.), *The Paradise of Women*; Beilin, E. V., *Redeeming Eve*.

Whittington, Richard (d 1423)
A rich and famous Lord Mayor of London in 1397–8, 1406–7, and 1419–20. He made substantial loans of money to the kings ▷ Henry IV and ▷ Henry V, and used his wealth for public works, including a legacy for improving Newgate Prison. His almshouses for the poor are still maintained. According to popular legend, he was originally a poor orphan and became the ill-treated servant of a rich merchant. He ran away from London, with his cat, until he heard Bow bells calling him back:

Turn again, Dick Whittington,
Lord Mayor of London.

The legend is a popular subject of Christmas ▷ pantomimes, in which the cat plays a principal part.

Who's Who
An annual biographical dictionary of eminent contemporary men and women. First published in 1849.

Wickham, Anna (1884–1947)
Poet. Anna Wickham (pseudonym of Edith Harper) published her first volume of poetry in 1911 as *Songs of John Oland* (another of her pseudonyms), and whilst her writing career spanned the period of high ▷ modernism, her poetry is more characteristic of ▷ Edwardian and ▷ Georgian styles (so much so that it appeared in two important collections of the 1930s, *Edwardian Poetry* and *Neo-Georgian Poetry*, 1937). She committed suicide in 1947. Her published works include: *The Contemplative Quarry and the Man with a Hammer* (1921); *The Little Old House* (1921); *Thirty-Six New Poems* (1936), and the 1984 Virago Press publication of *The Writings of Anna Wickham: Free Woman and Poet* (ed. R. D. Smith).

Wide Sargasso Sea, The
▷ Rhys, Jean.

Wife of Bath's Prologue and Tale, The
Part of ▷ Chaucer's ▷ *Canterbury Tales*. The Wife of Bath contributes both the story of her life and an Arthurian (▷ Arthur, King) romance to the story-telling collection. Her *Prologue*, of some 856 lines, gives an account of her marital career, spanning five marriages, and borrows sermonizing techniques for its thematic organization, structure and mode of argument. The Wife's history outlines the economic laws of the marriage market: it is only after three marriages to old, but financially well-endowed men that the Wife has gained the economic independence to find more pleasing partners. She challenges some of the clerical attitudes to marriage both in theory (in her opening comments) and in practice (in her physical confrontation with her fifth husband Jankyn, the clerk, and his book, an anti-feminist compilation). The Arthurian narrative which follows is a version of the 'Loathly Lady' story (which has parallels in ▷ Gower's ▷ *Confessio Amantis*, and the *Weddynge of Sir Gawen and Dame Ragnell*), and offers an equally complex view of power relations between the sexes, but refracted through the lens of the romance genre.

Unlike the analogues, the Wife's story begins with a rape of a young woman by a knight. The female members of King Arthur's court agree to commute the knight's death sentence for the offence, if he can answer the question 'What do women most desire?'. The winning answer (sovereignty) is supplied by a mysterious old woman whom the knight meets on his quest. In return for saving the knight's life, the old woman demands that the knight should marry her. He does so, but she is transformed into a beautiful woman (after the knight has ceded sovereignty to her over the choice she offers him between a wife who is beautiful or one who is faithful), and they enjoy, according to the narrator, a happy harmonious life together. No explanation is offered for the mechanics of this transformation in the Wife's version of events (again, unlike the other analogues). The Wife's contribution provides a catalyst for further tales, a debating point for the pilgrims, and a subject of modern critical controversy. A debate between the Friar and the Summoner is provoked in the course of her tale, which continues after she has finished; she is referred to an authority on marriage in the ▷ *Merchant's Tale*; and the clerk explicitly replies to her criticism of the clerical representation of secular women in his tale.

Wilberforce, William (1759–1833)
Philanthropist and politician. He devoted much of his life to the campaign to abolish the slave trade and ▷ slavery in overseas British territories. In 1807, the slave trade was made illegal, and so was slavery itself in the year of his death. He was leader of the ▷ Evangelical Movement, particularly of a group known as the Clapham Sect because it met in his house at Clapham.

Wild Gallant, The **(1663)**
Play by ▷ John Dryden, which has been seen by some as the first Restoration Comedy of ▷ Manners. Constance, a rich heiress, is in love with the charming but penniless Loveby. She steals money from her father in order to supply her lover secretly; he, however, thinks it is a gift from the devil. He expresses his appreciation of the devil in a number of lines bordering on blasphemy. Eventually, by pretending to be pregnant Constance gains leave to wed the man of her choice, and marries Loveby. In a separate but linked plot Isabella, a witty and charming relative of Constance's, wants to marry a man with money and chooses the wealthy Timorous, to whom she is somewhat attracted, although she does not love him. She wins him by means of various intrigues and disguises, including passing herself off as Constance. The play has some farcical comic business: in one sequence Constance persuades the men in the play that they too are pregnant. There is also some ▷ feminist comment, as when Constance complains that 'Women are tied to hard unequal laws: the passion is the same in us, and yet we are barred the freedom to express it'.

Wilde, Jane Francesca (1826–96)
Irish writer, born in Wexford, the daughter of an archdeacon. In 1851, she married a surgeon, Sir William Wilde, and was widowed in 1871. She died in considerable poverty in London in the year her son, ▷ Oscar Wilde (1856–1900), was publicly tried and disgraced on grounds of ▷ homosexuality. Frequently using the ▷ pseudonym Speranza, she contributed regularly to *The Nation*, and published a collection, *Poems*, in 1864. Her writings about folklore and collections of Irish legends include: *Driftwood from Scandinavia* (1884), *Ancient Legends of Ireland* (1887) and *Ancient Cures* (1891). Her other books are *Men, Women and Books* (1891) and *Social Studies* (1893).
▷ Irish literature in English.
Bib: Leighton, A., and Reynolds, M. (eds.), *An Anthology of Victorian Women Poets.*

Wilde, Oscar Fingal O'Flahertie Wills (1856–1900)
Dramatist, poet, novelist and essayist. He was the son of an eminent Irish surgeon and ▷ Jane Francesca Wilde. At Oxford University his style of life became notorious; he was a disciple of ▷ Pater, the Oxford father of ▷ aestheticism, and he carried the doctrine as far as to conduct his life as an aesthetic disciple – a direct challenge to the prevailing outlook of the society of his time, which was inclined to regard overt aestheticism with suspicion or disdain. In 1888 Wilde produced a volume of children's fairy tales very much in the melancholy and poetic style of the Danish writer ▷ Hans Christian Andersen – *The Happy Prince*. He followed this with two other volumes of stories, and then the novel, ▷ *The Picture of Dorian Grey* (1891), whose hero is an embodiment of the aesthetic way of life. More commonly known were his comedies, ▷ *Lady Windermere's Fan* (1892), *A Woman of No Importance* (1893), *An Ideal Husband* (1895), and above all the witty ▷ *Importance of Being Earnest* (1895). The plays are apparently light-hearted, but they contain strong elements of serious feeling in their attack on a society whose code is intolerant, but whose intolerance is hypocritical. In 1895, by a libel action against the Marquis of Queensberry, he exposed himself to a countercharge of immoral ▷ homosexual conduct, and spent two years in prison. In 1898 he published his ▷ *Ballad of Reading Gaol* about his prison experience, proving that he could write in the direct language of the ▷ ballad tradition, as well as in the artificial style of his *Collected Poems* (1892). His *De Profundis* (1905) is an eloquent statement of his grief after his downfall, but modern critics are equally as impressed by the intelligence of his social essays, such as *The Critic as Artist* (1891) and *The Soul of Man under Socialism* (1891). The paradox of Wilde is that, while for his contemporaries he represented degeneracy and weakness, there is plenty of evidence that he was a brave man of remarkable strength of character who made an emphatic protest against the vulgarity of his

age and yet, artistically, was himself subject to vulgarity of an opposite kind.
Bib: Critical studies by Roditi, E., Ransome, A.; Lives by Ellman, R.; Lemmonier, L.; Ervine, St J.; Pearson, H.; Bentley, E.R., in *The Playwright as Thinker*; Beckson, K. (ed.), *The Critical Heritage*; Bird, A., *The Plays of Oscar Wilde*; Worth, K., *Oscar Wilde*.

Wilkes, John (1727–97)
Journalist and politician. He was dissolute, and notorious for his membership of the scandalous Hell-Fire Club at Medmenham Abbey, with its motto 'Fay ce que voudras' = 'Do as you will'. Politically he was radical and courageous, and a popular hero. In 1762 he attacked ⊳ George III's administration under Lord Bute in *The North Briton*, a periodical which countered *The Briton* edited by the novelist, ⊳ Tobias Smollett. As an MP, he was twice expelled from the House of Commons for libel, and in 1769 he was three times elected to ⊳ Parliament by the county of Middlesex, the election each time being annulled. He was allowed to sit in 1774, in which year he was Lord Mayor of London. His character was such as to win the respect of ⊳ Dr Johnson, a man of opposite moral and political principles: 'Jack has great variety of talk, Jack is a scholar, Jack has the manners of a gentleman.' (Quoted in ⊳ Boswell's *Life of Johnson*.)

Wilkinson, John (b 1953)
Poet. Wilkinson's poetry aims to combine analytical traditions of thought, including the psychoanalytic, with a fierce commitment to the lyric as the fundamental mode for poetic expression. His poetic career began while he was a student reading English at Jesus College, Cambridge, and his early work shows the influence of ⊳ J. H. Prynne, as for example in *Useful Reforms* (1976). More recent texts, such as the 1994 collection *Flung Clear*, are both more encyclopaedic in subject and more personal in tone.

Wilkinson, Sarah (?–c 1830)
Novelist. By Wilkinson's own account she published a novel, *The Thatched Cottage*, opened a school on the proceeds, and taught intermittently after that time. Her own novels, of which *The Spectre of Lanmere Abbey* (1820) is perhaps the best, include all the required ⊳ Gothic ingredients and she was much influenced by ⊳ Ann Radcliffe. However, Wilkinson was unable to take the ghosts, hauntings and other paraphernalia seriously and a mocking irony always undercuts, quite pleasurably, the overladen and exaggerated tone expected of the genre. Wilkinson is also known for her ⊳ chapbooks, which consist of condensed forms of popular works as well as simplified ⊳ translations of foreign literature. She scrupulously acknowledged the authors of the works she treated in this manner (Henry Fielding, ⊳ 'Monk' Lewis, Ann Radcliffe and ⊳ Sir Walter Scott), but her own irrepressible ironic tone creates a witty self-consciousness.

Wilks, Robert (?1665–1732)
Actor, manager. Wilks made his first public appearance, as ⊳ Othello, at the ⊳ Smock Alley Theatre in Dublin in 1691, and in the following year he was employed as an actor by ⊳ Christopher Rich in London. He became noted for his gentlemanly style of acting, and was the original Sir Harry Wildair, in his friend, ⊳ George Farquhar's ⊳ *The Constant Couple*.

Wilks became co-manager first of the ⊳ Haymarket, and then, from 1709, of ⊳ Drury Lane, in combination with several others including, at various times, Owen Swiney (1675–1754), ⊳ Colley Cibber, Thomas Doggett (c1670–1721), Richard Estcourt (1668–1712), ⊳ Sir Richard Steele, ⊳ Barton Booth, and ⊳ Anne Oldfield. He shared control for the rest of his career, while at the same time continuing to strengthen and build up his repertoire as a leading actor, succeeding more in comedies than in tragedies.

Throughout his life Wilks maintained a reputation for sobriety and conscientiousness. Cibber also speaks of his superb memory which, coupled with his diligence, meant that he was almost invariably word-perfect, in an age when ad-libbing on stage was common. However, he could be unduly exacting of others and at times quarrelsome. Wilks is generally credited with a large share of responsibility for Drury Lane's prosperity during the 1710s and 1720s.

William I (1066–87) the Conqueror
As Duke of Normandy he came to power in 1035, and proved himself an effective soldier and ruler. In 1051, he may have received some sort of promise from ⊳ Edward the Confessor, his relative, that the English throne should pass to him, and Harold Earl of ⊳ Wessex promised his support in 1064. When, nonetheless, Harold himself succeeded Edward, William invaded England and defeated Harold near Hastings in Sussex, 1066. By 1070 he had reduced the whole country. William's government was remarkably thorough and efficient. There was an extensive redistribution of land, with the result that the ⊳ Anglo-Saxon nobility were effectively dispossessed. At the same time, William so managed this redistribution that the royal authority could be more effectively maintained throughout the country than was usual in 11th-century western Europe.

⊳ Domesday Book; Lanfranc; French literature in England.

William II (1087–1100)
King of England. His nickname William Rufus arose from the reddish colour of his complexion

and hair. He continued the policy of his father, William I, but was much more unpopular owing to his wilful tyrannies. According to legend he was killed while hunting in the New Forest by an arrow shot by Walter Tirel.

William III (1689–1702)
King of Britain, reigning jointly with his wife ▷ Mary II until her death in 1694. As William of ▷ Orange, Stadtholder of Holland, he was leader of the European opposition to the power of Louis XIV, which also menaced Britain. His wife was the daughter of ▷ James II, deposed for his Catholicism and his threat to the liberty of Parliament. His reign was largely taken up with war against France. The political power of Parliament was further increased by his foreign preoccupations, and by the fact that, as a foreigner, he lacked experience of English political affairs.

William IV (1830–37)
He was brother of his predecessor, ▷ George IV, and uncle to his successor, ▷ Victoria. He was a well-meaning man of small ability, but the most popular member of a royal family which was otherwise very unpopular.

Williams, Helen Maria (1762–1827)
English poet, novelist and correspondent. Brought up in Berwick-on-Tweed, she first published the verse romance *Edwin and Eltruda*, and *Peru* (1784) and sonnets in 1786. Her *Poem on the Slave Trade* (1788) was commented on by ▷ Mary Scott. After she settled in France she reworked ▷ Jean Jacques Rousseau's *Julie: ou, la nouvelle Héloïse* (1761) in *Julia* (1790). Her radical letters from France describing the Revolution (▷ French Revolution) were published in 1790. In France she lived with the divorced John Hurford Stone. She translated the popular bestseller *Paul et Virginie* – the text chosen for its apolitical status in case of raids. She writes, 'no danger could be more imminent than that of living under the very tyranny which I had the perilous honour of having been one of the first to deprecate and to proclaim.' She was lucky enough to get a passport to Switzerland, which resulted in *A Tour in Switzerland* (1798).
Bib: Scheffler, J., *The Wordsworth Circle*, No. 19 (1988).

Williams, Raymond (1921–87)
The most influential of all radical thinkers in Britain in the 20th century. Williams' work spans literary criticism, cultural studies, media studies, communications and politics, and he also wrote plays and novels. In *Culture and Society 1780–1950* (1958) and *The Long Revolution* (1961) he laid the foundation for a wide-ranging analysis of modern cultural forms, and can justly be accredited with the foundation of cultural studies as an interdisciplinary field of enquiry. In books such as *Modern Tragedy* (1966) and *Drama from Ibsen to Brecht* (1968), which was a revision of his earlier *Drama from Ibsen to Eliot* (1952), he challenged accepted ways of evaluating drama and dramatic forms and in 1968 was a guiding spirit behind the New Left's *Mayday Manifesto* (1968). For Williams writing was always and primarily a social activity, deeply implicated in politics. Through books such as *The Country and The City* (1973), *Marxism and Literature* (1977), *Politics and Letters* (1979), *Problems in Materialism and Culture* (1980), *Writing in Society, Towards 2000* (1983) and his *John Clare's Selected Poetry and Prose* (1986), he pursued these themes with an intellectual rigour which refused easy formulations. His was the intellectual force behind the current movement of cultural ▷ materialism, the British equivalent of American ▷ new historicism. His novels are now belatedly receiving the critical attention they have long deserved. They begin with *Border Country* (1960), *Second Generation* (1964), and *The Fight for Manod* (1979) in a partially autobiographical trilogy mainly set in Wales, showing a growing identification with the then newly emerging Welsh consciousness of nationhood, a theme continued in *The Volunteers* (1978) and in *Loyalties* (1985). At his death Raymond Williams left an unfinished historical trilogy *People of the Black Mountains*, of which the first and second volumes *The Beginning* (1989) and *The Eggs of the Eagle* (1990) were prepared for publication by his widow Joy and his daughter Merryn.

Will's Coffee-house
Named after its owner William Unwin, it was the haunt of such authors as ▷ John Dryden, ▷ William Wycherley, ▷ Joseph Addison and ▷ Alexander Pope. It became dominated by the older, mainly Tory (▷ Whig and Tory) set in the early years of the 18th century and ▷ Button's Coffee-house was set up as a fashionable rival, with a more Whiggish clientele.

Wilmot, John
▷ Rochester, John Wilmot, Second Earl of.

Wilson, Angus (1913–91)
Novelist and short-story writer. Born in Durban, South Africa, Wilson was educated at Westminster School in London and at Merton College, Oxford. He worked for many years in the British Museum Reading Room, served in the Foreign Office during World War II, and, from 1963, taught English literature at the University of East Anglia. He was primarily a satirist (▷ satire), with a particularly sharp ear for the way in which hypocrisy, cruelty and smugness are betrayed in conversation.

His first published works were short stories, *The Wrong Set* (1949) and *Such Darling Dodos* (1950), depicting English middle-class life around the time of World War II. His early work was traditional in form, inspired by his respect for the 19th-century English novel and a reaction against the dominance of post-Jamesian (▷ Henry James) narrative techniques in the ▷ modernist novel. *Hemlock and After* (1952), *Anglo-Saxon Attitudes* (1956) and *The Middle Age of Mrs Eliot* (1958) deal with such issues as responsibility, guilt and the problem of loneliness. The surface is satirical, and at times highly comic, but, as the protagonist of *Anglo-Saxon Attitudes* comments, 'the ludicrous was too often only a thin covering for the serious and the tragic'. *The Old Men at the Zoo* (1961) represented a considerable change of mode: it is a bizarre fable concerning personal and political commitment, set in the London Zoo at a time of international crisis. From this point on Wilson's work became more experimental: *Late Call* (1964) makes use of pastiche, while *No Laughing Matter* (1967) reflects the influence of ▷ Virginia Woolf, employing multiple interior monologues, as well as parodic dramatic dialogue and stories by one of the characters. It has a broad historical and social sweep, setting the story of a family between 1912 and 1967 in the context of British society as a whole. Like *Anglo-Saxon Attitudes* and *Late Call* it traces personal and public concerns back to the period immediately before World War I. *Setting the World on Fire* (1980) was another new departure in form; it is a complex and highly patterned work in which the myth of Phaeton is re-enacted in modern London. His other novels are: *As If By Magic* (1973). Story collections: *Death Dance* (1969); *Collected Stories* (1987). Travel writing: *Reflections in a Writer's Eye* (1986). Critical works include: *Émile Zola* (1952); *The World of Charles Dickens* (1970); *The Strange Ride of Rudyard Kipling* (1977).
Bib: Cox, C. B., *The Free Spirit*; Halio, J. L. (ed.), *Critical Essays on Angus Wilson*; Gardner, A., *Angus Wilson*; Faulkner, P., *Angus Wilson, Mimic and Moralist.*

Wilson, Colin (b 1931)
Novelist and critic. He is known primarily as the author of the ▷ existentialist work *The Outsider* (1956), which was much acclaimed at the time of its publication. He is the author of 15 novels, and over 50 works of non-fiction. His novels feature violence, sexuality and the idea of the outsider in society, and seek to acknowledge fictionality by using genres such as the detective story with a deliberate incongruity.

Wilson, Harriette (1786–1845)
Autobiographer. Infamous for her racy ▷ autobiography, *Memoirs* (1825), in which she describes her life as a courtesan and her affairs with many of the leading figures of her day. She planned the book with her husband, William Henry Rochfort (whom she had married in 1823), as a form of blackmail and, indeed, when it was published it caused an immediate commotion amongst those mentioned (including Beau Brummel and the ▷ Duke of Wellington), as well as amongst the outraged upholders of morality. She followed this with two *romans-à-clef* which are immensely readable accounts of London life: *Paris Lions and London Tigers* (1825) and *Clara Gazul* (1830).

Wilson, John (1785–1854)
Scottish journalist, chiefly known under the pseudonym 'Christopher North' which he used when writing for ▷ *Blackwood's Magazine*, for which he was the principal writer from 1817. He wrote very lively, semi-dramatic discussions called *Noctes Ambrosianae* which became famous. In 1820 he was elected to the professorship of moral philosophy in Edinburgh University. He had no special qualifications for the post, but was backed by ▷ Walter Scott. Nonetheless he filled the post very effectively. He contributed much other journalism to *Blackwood's*, and was also a poet: *The Isle of Palms* (1812) and *The City of the Plague* (1816).
Bib: Swan, E., *Christopher North – John Wilson.*

Wilson, Robert (d 1600)
Dramatist and actor. We know little of Wilson's life, except that he joined the acting companies of the Earl of Leicester's Men after 1572 and of Queen Elizabeth's Men after 1583; he is also known for his brilliant extemporizing during dramatic performances. His dramatic writing includes *The Ladies of London* (c 1581), *The Three Lords and Ladies of London* (c 1589), and *The Cobbler's Prophecy* (c 1594). Wilson's dramatic output represents the bridge between writing for the medieval ▷ morality tradition and for the ▷ Renaissance public theatres.

Wilson, Thomas (c 1525–81)
Theorist and politician. Thomas Wilson had a successful public career as well as writing one of the most important ▷ Renaissance books on literary style, *Arte of Rhetorique* (1553 and 1560). An ardent supporter of ▷ Elizabeth I, he was appointed as Privy Councillor (1572) and Secretary of State (1578), and was involved in the successful prosecution of the Duke of Norfolk and ▷ Mary Queen of Scots. He was also a confirmed ▷ Protestant and spent most of ▷ Mary I's reign on the continent. His two most noted works are *Arte* and *Rule of Reason* (1551), the latter concerning itself with logic, rather than focusing on ▷ rhetoric as his later writing does. Wilson's *Arte* gives a series of epistles and orations in different styles, some are meant to be copied, others are more akin to parodies, so that the whole text conforms

to the Renaissance doctrine of both teaching and amusing – 'pleasure reconciled to virtue'.
Bib: Medine, P., *Thomas Wilson*.

Winchilsea, Countess of
▷ Finch, Anne, Countess of Winchilsea.

***Windsor Forest* (1713)**
A poem by ▷ Alexander Pope in heroic ▷ couplets describing the landscape around his home, and reflecting on its history and economic importance. It blends ▷ Georgic, ▷ pastoral and topographical elements in an engaging expression of ▷ Augustan optimism.

***Wings of the Dove, The* (1902)**
A novel by ▷ Henry James. The scene is principally London and Venice. Kate Croy and Merton Densher, a young journalist, are in love, but without the money to marry. Kate's rich aunt, Maud Lowder, takes into her circle Milly Theale, a lonely American girl of great single-mindedness, eagerness for life, and capacity for affection, and also a millionairess. Milly is travelling in Europe with Susan Stringham, an old friend of Mrs Lowder's. Mrs Stringham learns from Milly's doctor that the girl is suffering from a fatal illness, that her death cannot be long delayed, and that it can only be delayed at all if she achieves happiness. Mrs Stringham communicates this to Kate, who conceives a plot with a double purpose: Merton is to engage Milly's love, thus bringing her the happiness that she needs, and at the same time securing her money when she dies, so that Kate's own marriage to Merton can at last take place. Milly's love for Merton is very real; because of it, however, she refuses another suitor, Lord Mark, who knows Kate's plot and in revenge betrays it to Milly. She dies, broken-hearted, but she leaves Merton her money. Merton and Kate, however, find that they are for ever separated by the shadow of the dead Milly between them.

The story is an example of James' 'international theme': in this case, the openness and integrity which he saw as strengths of the American personality are opposed to the selfishness and deviousness which he saw as part of the decadent aspect of European culture. It is written in the condensed, allusive style which is characteristic also of ▷ *The Ambassadors* and ▷ *The Golden Bowl*.

Winner and Waster
An ▷ alliterative ▷ dream-vision poem, composed in the mid to later 14th century, which investigates the relationship between the earning (winning) and dispending (wasting) forces in a society, by dramatizing a confrontation between the martial forces of Winner and Waster. The narrator describes how, in his dream, he sees the two sides in full martial array, drawn up before a king (whose emblems suggest he is ▷ Edward III). The two leaders from either side embark on a war of words, attacking the principles of the other and defending their own position, and present their respective cases for the judgement of the king (and thus defer physical combat). The debate is the vehicle for a wry assessment of various kinds of materialistic corruption in contemporary society, and of the injustices which result from the misuse of money. The last lines of the poem are missing so the king's judgement, if he offered one, is not known. It may have influenced the techniques of social satire developed by ▷ Langland in ▷ *Piers Plowman*, but Langland's poem takes the debate very much further.
Bib: Gollancz, I. (ed.), *Winner and Waster*.

Winter, John Strange (1856–1911)
▷ Pseudonym of novelist Henrietta Palmer (she also wrote as Violet Whyte). She was born in York, the daughter of a rector who came from a military family. Winter's writings show the army influence, often describing the lives of wives and children of military heroes. The pseudonym was adopted on the advice of her publishers, who considered that works such as *Cavalry Life* (1881) and *Regimental Legends* (1883) would be more credible if thought to have been written by a man. Winter's most successful work was *Bootle's Baby: A Story of the Scarlet Lancers* (1885), which was serialized in the *Graphic* and adapted for the stage, playing at the Globe theatre in London in 1889. Other works include *He Went for a Soldier* (1890), *A Soldier's Children* (1892), and *A Summer Jaunt* (1889). Winter also founded the *Golden Gates* magazine in 1891, was President of the Writer's Club (1892) and President of the Society of Women Journalists (1901–3).

***Winter's Tale, The* (1610–11)**
A play by ▷ Shakespeare; one of his ▷ romances, dated 1610–11, and based on ▷ Robert Greene's *Pandosto*. Leontes, king of Sicilia, is married to Hermione, whom he deeply loves, and at the opening of the play is receiving a visit from Polixenes, king of Bohemia and the intimate friend of his childhood. Leontes becomes consumed by an insane jealousy, and is convinced that the child with which Hermione is pregnant has been fathered by Polixenes. He orders Camillo, a courtier, to poison Polixenes, but instead Camillo and Polixenes flee the country together. Leontes orders the trial of Hermione for adultery and, to appease his indignant courtiers, he sends to the oracle of Delphi in order to obtain what he believes will be confirmation of her guilt. The baby is born, but Leontes orders another courtier, Antigonus, to leave it in a desolate place to perish. At this point a succession of

catastrophes is heaped on Leontes: he learns from the oracle that his wife is innocent, from Paulina, wife of Antigonus, that Hermione has died, and that his little son has also died, of grief at the suffering of his mother. The last scene of Act III shows Antigonus depositing the baby on the coast of Bohemia and her discovery by two shepherds. Thus far the play is tragic; Acts IV and V show recovery. The baby grows up into a beautiful girl, Perdita, who believes herself to be a shepherd's daughter. Florizel, son of Polixenes, courts her at the shepherds' sheep-shearing feast, but they have to flee to Sicilia to escape the anger of his father. Polixenes follows them, and at Leontes' court once more a great reconciliation takes place. Paulina discloses that Hermione is not dead, but has been kept in hiding until the return of Perdita, in accordance with the prediction of the oracle; in the last scene she is shown to Leontes as a statue of her supposedly dead self, but at the command of Paulina the statue gradually comes to life to the sound of music.

The summary shows that the play has no pretence to external realism; it is a fable about the destructiveness of the passions and the healing power of time. The symbolism is especially of the seasons: 'a winter's tale' is about deprivation, but the play ends in autumn, the season of recovered fulfilment, while the sheep-shearing scene (IV. 3) has springlike qualities, with Perdita reminding one of Persephone in her lines about the spring flowers. The ▷ pastoral aspect of the play shows pastoralism in a new light – not as an escape from change and decay into day-dream, but as a phase of development which must be outgrown if capacity for growth is to be fulfilled. The process of growth implies desire, fear and possessiveness, which form the state of mind of the jealous Leontes at the beginning of the play when he finds that he has outgrown his pastorally innocent friendship with Polixenes. From this false development, he can recover only by repentance.

Winterson, Jeanette (b 1959)
Novelist. Winterson's works have been praised for their originality of subject matter and form. Her first novel, the autobiographical *Oranges are not the only fruit* (1985), is a witty account of her upbringing as the child of fundamentalist Christians and her development as a lesbian in a town in the north of England; it won the Whitbread Award for First Novel and was translated into an enormously popular television series. Her subsequent novels have been more experimental and formally complex; these are *Boating for Beginners* (1986); *The Passion* (which won the John Llewelyn Rhys Prize in 1987); *Sexing the Cherry* (1989); *Written on the Body* (1992); *Art and Lies* (1994) interweaves multiple voices to create an imaginary world.

▷ Lesbian and gay writing.

Wit
This word has a number of distinct, though related, meanings. 1 The oldest meaning is identical with 'mind', as in ▷ Wycliffe's 14th-century translation of the Bible: 'Who knew the wit of the Lord?' (*Romans* 11:34). This use of 'wit' rarely occurs in the literature of the last hundred years. 2 Another long-established meaning is 'a faculty of the mind'. This is still in use today, as when we speak of someone having 'lost his wits', *ie* lost the use of his mental faculties. 3 A common meaning in the 17th and 18th centuries was the capacity to relate unlike ideas, as in Locke's definition: 'Wit lying in the assemblage of ideas, and putting these together with the quickness and variety wherein can be found any resemblance or congruity, thereby to make up pleasant pictures in the fancy' (*Essay concerning Human Understanding*, 1690). ▷ Cowley, in his poem *Of Wit* (1656), wrote 'In a true piece of wit all things must be. Yet all things there agree.'

▷ Lyly, John; University Wits, The.

Witches
People supposed to be in league with the devil, who gives them supernatural powers. The name 'witch' was sometimes used for both sexes, though those accused of being witches were usually women. They commonly had 'familiars' in the form of spirits disguised as animals of bad or sinister reputation – toads or cats of certain colours. To work their magic, witches uttered 'spells' of specially devised words, or they used objects ('charms') supposed to have magical properties; witches used to gather in small communities known as 'covens', and they assembled on one day of the year (a 'witches' Sabbath') to worship the Devil.

The common explanation of witchcraft is that, in Europe at least, it represents the long survival of pre-Christian pagan religions in which the gods were the embodiments of the powers of nature, usually in the forms of animals, often a goat, but in Britain commonly the bull, the dog, or the cat. More recently witchcraft, or the accusation of witchcraft, has been regarded as a 17th-century mechanism of social control, used to discourage women from living alone outside the authority of a male-dominated household.

That witchcraft was common in the Middle Ages is not surprising; it is at first sight surprising that it was conspicuous in the later 16th and early 17th centuries, and that not merely the ignorant and uneducated but some of the learned believed in it. ▷ James VI of Scotland and I of England, who has been called 'the greatest scholar who ever sat on the English throne', was himself deeply interested in it and wrote a denunciation of it – his *Daemonologie* (1599). The pamphlet *News from Scotland* (1591) describes his conversion from scepticism to belief in it, and seems to have been used by ▷ Shakespeare in the portrayal of the witches in ▷ *Macbeth*. James later, however, moved to a more sceptical position again. The first law making witchcraft an offence punishable by death in England was passed in 1603 (though causing death by witchcraft had been so punishable since 1563) and it was not repealed until 1736. Sir Thomas Browne declares his firm belief in it in ▷ *Religio Medici* (1643); the last learned defence of the belief was *Saducismus Triumphatus* (1681) by the scholar and clergyman Joseph Glanville. The belief seems to have been particularly strong among ▷ Puritans and in Puritan countries, for instance in Scotland, 17th-century New England, and England under the ▷ Long Parliament. Rare survivals of it have been found in 20th-century England. It has been suggested that the prevalence of the belief in the 17th century and among Puritans is that their superstitious impulses were no longer satisfied by the Catholic system of mysteries (miracles, lives of the saints, etc.) which they had expelled from their faith by its 'purification'.

In the reign of James I, a number of plays besides *Macbeth* dealt with witchcraft, *eg* ▷ Dekker and ▷ Ford's *Witches of Edmonton* (1623) and ▷ Middleton's *The Witch* (1615). ▷ William Golding's *The Spire* (1964) deals with medieval pagan survival.

Bib: McFarlane, A., *Witchcraft in Tudor and Stuart England*; Thomas, K., *Religion and the Decline of Magic*.

Wither, George (1588–1667)
Poet. Between 1612, when Wither's first publication appeared, and the poet's death in 1667, there were very few years that were not marked by the publication of at least one volume of verse or prose from this prolific author. Wither was possibly the most imprisoned writer in the history of English literature. In 1613 his ▷ satiric work *Abuses Stripped and Whipped* earned him a period of imprisonment, a punishment he earned once more in 1621, when *Wither's Motto* appeared, and which was to befall him again in 1646 (on publication of his ▷ pamphlet *Justiarius Justificatus*) and in 1660 (appearance of unpublished satire: *Vox Vulgi: A Poem in Censure of Parliament*). His later works were written in the belief that he was God's prophet. Of note, however, are several volumes of earlier verse, and his collection of emblems (▷ Emblem-books), which appeared in four volumes in 1635.

Bib: Hunter, W. B., *The English Spenserians*.

***Wives and Daughters* (1864–6)**
A novel by ▷ Mrs Gaskell, published serially in the ▷ *Cornhill Magazine* and not completed at her death. It is a study of two families, the Gibsons and the Hamleys, in a small country town and the relationships of the parents and the children in each. The central character is Molly Gibson, whose liberal, frank, sincere and deeply responsible nature is painfully tested by the marriage of her widowed father (a country doctor) to a silly, vain widow. The widow brings with her, however, her own daughter, Cynthia, a girl with her mother's outward charm but without her silliness and with feelings guided more by her discerning intelligence than by spontaneous loyalties. Cynthia at sixteen has become engaged to a coarse but astute man, Mr Preston, who is a local land-agent. The two girls become involved with the two sons of Mr Hamley, the local squire. The elder boy, Osborne, is superficially brilliant and charming, and much overestimated by his father. The younger son, Roger, has much less showy qualities but a deeper nature and eventually wins the academic success expected of but not achieved by the elder, who makes an unfortunate marriage, is cast off by the father and dies young. The novel thus brings out the differences between superficial and deep natures, and the perils that result from consequent false estimates of character, made even by the intelligent.

***Wives Excuse, The: Or Cuckolds Make Themselves* (1691)**
Play by ▷ Thomas Southerne, identified with a wave of so-called 'marital discord comedies' of the 1690s by writers including ▷ Vanbrugh and ▷ Farquhar, which focused on the problems of ▷ marriage, as much as on those of courtship. Southerne concentrated on showing up the sexual double standard and its effects on women. *The Wives Excuse* bleakly presents the dilemma of the woman trapped in an unhappy marriage to a man whose shameless infidelity goes unpunished, while she stands to lose her dignity, reputation, and remaining peace of mind if she succumbs to the advances of her would-be lover. Mrs Friendall wrestles with temptation in the form of the attractive but unscrupulous Lovemore, while Mr Friendall pursues an affair with Mrs Wittwoud. At the end, the couple agree to separate. Southerne implies that Mrs Friendall will eventually give in to Lovemore, only to be abandoned when he tires of her. The play was unsuccessful, but is now considered one of the great plays of the period, its polish and sophistication serving only to point up the hypocrisy underlying the situation which it portrays.

Wodehouse, (Sir) P. G. (Pelham Grenville) (1881–1975)
Writer of humorous short stories and novels. Born in Guildford, Surrey and educated at Dulwich College, London, he was brought up

partly by aunts in England, since his father was a judge in Hong Kong. Known always as P. G. Wodehouse, his most famous creations were the good-natured but disaster-prone young man about town, Bertie Wooster, and his ever-resourceful 'gentleman's gentleman' (manservant), Jeeves, first introduced in *The Man With Two Left Feet* (1917). The Jeeves and Wooster books include: *My Man Jeeves* (1919); *The Inimitable Jeeves* (1923); *Carry On Jeeves* (1925); *Right Ho, Jeeves* (1934); *The Code of the Woosters* (1938); *Jeeves in the Offing* (1960); *Stiff Upper Lip, Jeeves* (1963). Wodehouse depicted a range of other comic characters, evoking a charming escapist myth of the upper-class England of the 1920s. He also wrote school stories such as *Mike* (1909), sentimental romances such as *Love Among the Chickens* (1906), song lyrics and works for the theatre and cinema. Despite a scandal when he broadcast from Germany during World War II, after having been captured, he remained immensely popular. He lived in Britain, France and the U.S.A., becoming an American citizen in 1945.
Bib: Donaldson, F., *P. G. Wodehouse*.

Woffington, Peg (Margaret) (?1714–60)
Actress. At the ▷ Smock Alley Theatre, Dublin, in 1740, she played the first of many performances as Sir Harry Wildair in ▷ George Farquhar's ▷ *The Constant Couple*. She repeated the role at ▷ Covent Garden and at ▷ Drury Lane, and became so celebrated in it that even ▷ Garrick could not equal her when he took on the same part.

The rest of her career from 1741 was spent largely at Drury Lane, but with further appearances at Covent Garden and in Dublin. She became the mistress of Garrick, and a theatrical rival of ▷ Kitty Clive, and ▷ George Anne Bellamy, whom she literally stabbed during a performance of Nathanial Lee's ▷ *The Rival Queens*, just as ▷ Elizabeth Barry had done to ▷ Elizabeth Bowtell more than half a century before.

Peg Woffington was described as the most beautiful woman to have appeared on the stage in her own day. She was said to be full of vitality, elegance, and ▷ wit. During a career lasting over 30 years, she took on major roles in well over a hundred plays, sometimes acting different parts in the same play, at different periods in her life. She was especially famous for her talent in men's roles.
Bib: Daly, A., *Life of Peg Woffington*; Molloy, J. F., *The Life and Adventures of Peg Woffington*.

Wolcot, John (1738–1819)
Poet. After a career as a doctor in Jamaica and Cornwall, Wolcot accompanied the painter Opie to London, intent on a career in literature. His poems, published under the pseudonym Peter Pindar are crude if vigorous ▷ satires on respectable public figures and institutions: *Lyric Odes to the Royal Academicians* (1782–5), *The Lousiad* (1785), *Instructions to a Celebrated Laureat* (1787). His *Bozzy and Piozzi* (1786) is a whimsical poem in which ▷ James Boswell and ▷ Hester Lynch Thrale are shown reminiscing about ▷ Samuel Johnson, who had died two years earlier.

Wolley (Woolley), Hannah (?1621–?1676)
English writer on household management and ▷ conduct, who wâs a servant and then married a headmaster (and others), and published a sequence of books on cooking, medicine and the household. She writes in *The Cook's Guide* (1664) that she has 'sent forth this book, to testifie to the scandalous world that I do not altogether spend my time idly'.

Her other publications include: *The Ladies Directory* (1661); *The Queen-Like Closet* (1670), and *The Ladies Delight* (1672).

Wollstonecraft, Mary (1759–97)
Pamphleteer and novelist. Wollstonecraft is notable for her outspoken views on the role of women in society, and on the part played by ▷ education in woman's oppression. After running a school in London with her sister, she set out her ideas in the early pamphlet *Thoughts on the Education of Daughters* (1787). The following year her novel *Mary* developed this theme, together with a satirical perspective on the manners of the aristocracy, possibly based on her own experiences as governess with the family of Lord Kingsborough in Ireland.

Wollstonecraft's most famous work, ▷ *A Vindication of the Rights of Woman* (1792) now stands as one of the major documents in the history of women's writing. Attacking the 'mistaken notions of female excellence' which she recognized in contemporary attitudes to 'femininity' and the cult of the ▷ sentimental, Wollstonecraft argued that women were not naturally submissive, but taught to be so, confined to 'smiling under the lash at which [they] dare not snarl'. Although widely caricatured by critics for her own 'immoral' life – an affair with Gilbert Imlay, and subsequent marriage with ▷ William Godwin – Wollstonecraft's ideas are closely related to the moralist tradition of writing addressed to young women. Arguing that the true basis of ▷ marriage must be not love but friendship, she continues the rational proposals outlined by the 17th-century pamphleteer ▷ Mary Astell in such works as ▷ *A Serious Proposal to the Ladies*. The most radical of her thoughts concern the treatment by society of unmarried mothers, whom she believed were worthy of the respect and support of their families and lovers. Her novel *Maria*: *or*, *The Wrongs of Woman* (1798) remained unfinished and was published posthumously, but develops the ideas of *A Vindication* in a more complex and experimental context. The philosophical tradition behind her writings is evident in *A Vindication of the Rights of Man* (1790), a reply to ▷ Burke, and in the dedication of *Rights of Woman* to Talleyrand.

▷ Feminism; Women, Status of.

Bib: Tomalin, C., *The Life and Death of Mary Wollstonecraft*.

Wolsey, Thomas (?1475–1530)
Statesman and churchman. He was born of comparatively humble parents in Ipswich, but with the aid of various patrons he received rapid promotion in the Church. In 1507 he became chaplain to ▷ King Henry VII, who employed him on diplomatic affairs. In the next reign he was for 20 years practically the sole ruler of the country, having the full confidence of ▷ Henry VIII. He became Bishop of Lincoln, Bishop of Tournai in France, Archbishop of York, Cardinal, within reach of becoming Pope. At home he was a firm and able administrator. His foreign policy was skilful, but his personal ambitions led to its ultimate failure. In his anxiety to become Pope, he sought the favour of Emperor Charles V and allowed him to become too powerful in Europe. Charles was nephew to Henry VIII's queen, Katharine of Aragon, whom in 1528 Henry wanted to divorce. Since Charles had Rome in his hands, the Pope could not consent, and in 1529 Wolsey lost the favour of the king; his downfall was the more complete because he had no other powerful supporters in the country. His life was written by a member of his household, George Cavendish, but it was not published until 1641. His downfall was dramatized by ▷ Fletcher and ▷ Shakespeare in ▷ *Henry VIII*.

Bib: Ridley, J., *The Statesman and the Fanatic: Thomas Wolsey and Thomas More*.

Wolstenholme-Elmy, Elizabeth (1834–1913)
Essayist and poet, who also wrote under the pseudonyms E. Ellis, Ellis Ethelmer, and 'Ignota'. ▷ Orphaned as a child and deprived of an adequate ▷ education, she became an ardent ▷ feminist and vigorous campaigner. She was Honorary Secretary to the Manchester ▷ Women's Suffrage Society (1865), Secretary to the Married Women's Property Committee (1867–82), a founding member of the Women's Franchise League (1899) and the founder of the Women's Emancipation Union (1891). She published a long feminist poem, ▷ *Woman Free* (1893); two sex education manuals (*The Human Flower*, 1894, and *Baby Buds*, 1895) and many pamphlets, including her last work, *Woman's Franchise: The Need of the Hour* (1907).

▷ Women's Movement.

Bib: Strachey, R., *The Cause*.

***Woman Free* (1893)**
A long poem by ▷ Elizabeth Wolstenholme-Elmy, concerned with women's subordination. The poem attacks the 'brainless bondage' to which women are subjected in ▷ marriage, and protests against male sexual aggression, claiming that women must be 'Free from all uninvited touch of man'. The poem also contains many notes which supplement the author's ▷ feminist perspective. The author writes: 'Anyone who has looked a little below the surface of women's lives can testify to the general unrest and nervous exhaustion or malaise among them, although each would probably refer her suffering to some cause peculiar to herself and her circumstances, never dreaming that she was the victim of an evil that gnaws at the very heart of society, making almost every woman the heroine of a silent tragedy.'

▷ Women's Movement.

***Woman Killed with Kindness, A* (1603)**
A powerful domestic ▷ tragedy by ▷ Thomas Heywood, which explores the marriage, adultery and death of Anne Frankford, the wife of a gentle and upright man, who kills her with his 'kindness' by refusing her his and her children's company. The seduction of Anne by Frankford's friend Wendoll and the husband's subsequent discovery of the lovers are presented with great sympathy and understanding. The play's subplot is informed by a similar range of domestic detail and is not without tenderness.

'Woman Question, The'
From the 1830s onwards Victorian Britain was obsessively concerned with the 'Woman Question', as they called it. The arguments in this debate were complex and multivocal; the issue of woman's role in society was discussed in newspapers, magazines, and literary, philosophical, educational and medical journals; in Parliament, in church and in the home. No single cultural myth prevailed, and the idea of 'Woman', her 'mission', her 'sphere' and her 'influence' became a site of struggle where competing ideologies strove for dominance. Some commentators challenged the constraints placed upon middle-class women's lives and argued for greater vocational and educational opportunity; others argued passionately that women and men should operate in separate spheres of existence. Recent critical examination of the 'Woman Question' has explored the interrelationships between the Victorian preoccupation with history, national identity and Empire, and the widespread concern with the status and function of women (see Christina Crosby's *The Ends of History*, 1991). Numerous extracts from contemporary writings on the 'Woman Question' can be found in Helsinger et al. (eds.), *The Woman Question: Society and Literature in Britain and America 1837–1883*.

▷ Feminism; Linton, Eliza Lynn.

Bib: Crosby, C., *The Ends of History: Victorians and 'The Woman Question'*; Rubenstein, D.,

Before the Suffragettes: Women's Emancipation in the 1890s.

***Woman Who Did, The* (1895)**
A novel by ▷ Grant Allen which openly engaged with the ▷ 'Woman Question' and the issue of 'free union'. It was attacked, along with ▷ Thomas Hardy's ▷ *Jude the Obscure*, by ▷ Margaret Oliphant for being 'anti-marriage'. The heroine of the novel, Herminia, is martyred in the cause of free union, a fact which was seen to militate against Allen's message of 'free love' and feminine emancipation. The book and its author were convincingly attacked by Millicent Garrett Fawcett in ▷ *The Contemporary Review* in 1895. Allen's novel, which was a best-seller in its time, was mercilessly parodied in *The Woman Who Didn't* by 'Victoria Crosse' and *The Woman Who Wouldn't* by 'Lucas Cleeve'.

***Woman's Friendship* (1853)**
A novel by ▷ Grace Aguilar, concerned with the importance of female bonding. The central character, Florence, becomes friendly with Lady Ida Villiers, a woman whose social status is considerably higher than her own. Florence is warned by her 'mother' (who turns out to be a foster-parent) that this friendship cannot be mutual because Lady Villier's class position prohibits it. Later, Florence's true parentage is revealed, and after a period of estrangement from one another Florence and Lady Villiers are re-united in friendship. Aguilar writes at the end of the book that although female bonding is 'in general scorned and scoffed at . . . [it] may be the invisible means of strengthening in virtue'.

***Women Beware Women* (1614)**
A baroque and vindictive ▷ tragedy of misdirected desire which ends in a bloodbath, by ▷ Thomas Middleton. Like ▷ *The Changeling* the play features a skilfully integrated subplot, which here dramatizes the incestuous love of Hippolito for his brother's daughter Isabella, whom he hopes to seduce with the help of her aunt. The most famous scene in the play concerns the seduction of Bianca by the Duke of Florence in a series of moves that parallel those of a game of chess played simultaneously between Bianca's mother-in-law and a corrupt go-between, Livia. Like ▷ Webster's ▷ *The White Devil*, *Women Beware Women* evinces a cynical and erotic awareness of the role of power and money in human relationships, and their ability to destroy even marriage.

***Women in Love* (1921)**
A novel by ▷ D. H. Lawrence. It continues the lives of the characters in ▷ *The Rainbow*. Ursula Brangwen is a schoolteacher, and her sister Gudrun is an artist. The other two main characters are Gerald Crich, a mine-owner and manager, and Rupert Birkin, a school-inspector. The main narrative is about the relationships of these four: the union of Rupert and Ursula after conflict, the union of Gerald and Gudrun ending in conflict and Gerald's death, the affinities and antagonisms between the sisters and between the men. The settings include Shortlands, the mansion of the mine-owning Crich family; Breadalby, the mansion of Lady Hermione Roddice, a meeting-place of the leading intellectuals of the day; the Café Pompadour in London, a centre for artists; and a winter resort in the Austrian Tyrol. The theme is human relationships in the modern world, where intelligence has become the prisoner of self-consciousness, and spontaneous life-forces are perverted into violence, notably in Gerald, Hermione, and the German sculptor Loerke. Symbolic episodes centred on animals and other natural imagery are used to present those forces of the consciousness that lie outside rational articulation, and personal relationships are so investigated as to illuminate crucial aspects of modern culture: the life of industry, the life of art, the use and misuse of reason, and what is intimate considered as the nucleus of what is public.

Women's movement
The women's movement – under many names – is dedicated to the campaign for political and legal rights for women. It wishes to prevent the discrimination on the grounds of gender and is, generally, a movement for social change.

There is no single source, although the history of women's quest for equality is a long one. The *Querelle des Femmes* is the medieval period, ▷ Aphra Behn and ▷ Mary Astell in the 17th century, and ▷ Mary Wollstonecraft in the Romantic Age all furthered women's rights. In the Victorian period feminism became linked with other social movements such as anti-slavery campaigners, evangelical groups and ▷ Quakers. The suffragette movement (1860–1930) united women and this solidarity was to re-emerge in the radicalization of the 1960s.
Bib: Mitchell, J. and Oakley, A. (eds.), *What is Feminism?*; Eisenstein, H., *Contemporary Feminist Thought*.

Women's suffrage
The first National Association for Women's Suffrage was formed in Manchester in 1865, and in 1866 a petition of 1500 signatures was presented to ▷ J.S. Mill, whose essay 'On the Subjection of Women' had been published that year. Signatories of the petition included ▷ Barbara Bodichon, ▷ Harriet Martineau and ▷ Matilda Betham-Edwards. Mill presented a motion to Parliament to include female suffrage in the 1867 ▷ Reform Bill, but he was defeated

by 196 votes against 73. Throughout the rest of the 19th century women continued to campaign for the vote. Societies were formed in London, Edinburgh, Birmingham and Bristol in the late 1860s, and the first Women's Suffrage Bill was presented to Parliament by Jacob Bright in 1870. The first reading was carried by 124 votes to 91, but the government then opposed the Bill, and on the second vote it was defeated by 220 to 94. Although hopes were running high when a new government (led by ⊳ Disraeli) came to power in 1874, no significant change of policy occurred. In 1880 ⊳ Gladstone succeeded as Prime Minister, and the first women-only demonstration was held in Manchester's Free Trade Hall. The next major event was the new Parliamentary Reform Bill of 1884 – a crushing defeat for the suffragists since Gladstone made it clear that he was inexorably opposed to the inclusion of women in the Bill. It was defeated by 271 to 135. Among the MPs who voted against the Bill were 104 Liberals who had pledged support.

In 1889 ⊳ Mrs Humphry Ward led an 'Appeal Against Female Suffrage', stating that 'The political ignorance of women is irreparable and is imposed by nature.' Although Ward had many notable supporters, the tide of public opinion was slowly beginning to turn. Another Women's Suffrage Bill was presented in 1892, and was only defeated by twenty-three votes. In 1897 Millicent Fawcett became President of the new National Union of Women's Suffrage, and the campaign for the vote was boosted after the Boer War, which bridged the end of the 19th and the beginning of the 20th centuries.

The first decade of the 20th century marked a shift towards violent action as a means to secure the vote. Among the leading figures of the movement was Emmeline Pankhurst (1858–1928), who campaigned with her daughters Christabel and Sylvia. The arrest of Christabel and the Irish trade unionist Annie Kenney during their protest at a Liberal Party meeting in 1905 marked the turning point in the movement's strategies and public profile. Emmeline Pankhurst was first arrested in 1908, and consistently thereafter.

The suffrage movement ended in 1918 when votes were granted to women at the age of thirty. In 1928 Parliament decreed that women should have equal voting rights with men.

⊳ Cobbe, Frances Power; Grand, Sarah; Lyall, Edna; Meynell, Alice; 'New Woman, The'; Ouida; Wolstenholme-Elmy, Elizabeth; 'Woman Question, The'; Yonge, Charlotte.

Bib: Pankhurst, S., *The Suffragette Movement*; Rubenstein, D., *Before the Suffragettes*.

***Wonder, A Woman Keeps a Secret, The* (1714)**
Comedy by ⊳ Susannah Centlivre, partly based on ⊳ Ravenscroft's *The Wrangling Lovers* (1677), and often considered her best play. It is set in Lisbon, where Don Felix, son of a Portuguese grandee, Don Lopez, wounds Antonio in a duel, after refusing to marry Antonio's sister. He goes into hiding, but secretly visits Donna Violante, a young woman intended for a nun, with whom he is in love, and who loves him. In the secondary plot, Don Lopez wants his daughter, Isabella, to marry the wealthy but foolish Don Guzman, and locks her into a room to await her suitor. She escapes into the arms of Colonel Britton, a Scotsman on his way back to England. He takes her to another house, which turns out to be Violante's, and asks for her to be cared for. Violante recognizes her and agrees to hide her and keep the secret. In fact she conceals not only Isabella, but Felix as well, and, further, hides Isabella from Felix. All the lovers are united at the end. The title is gently ironic for in the play's final triplet Felix remarks that Violante's steadfastness has shown 'That Man has no Advantage but the Name'. *The Wonder* was first produced at ⊳ Drury Lane with ⊳ Robert Wilks as Don Felix and ⊳ Anne Oldfield as Violante, to whom Centlivre paid tribute as being largely responsible for its success. But it was revived numerous times during the 18th and 19th centuries, notably with ⊳ Garrick as Felix, from 1756 onwards, and ⊳ John Philip Kemble in the part afterwards. Garrick chose the play to end his theatrical career in 1776. It survived to 1897.

Wood, Mrs Henry (Ellen) (1814–87)
Novelist, who also wrote under the ⊳ pseudonym Johnny Ludlow. She was born in Worcester, the daughter of a manufacturer. Wood's early short stories appeared in the *New Monthly Magazine* and her first novel, *Danesbury House*, was published in 1860. Her second, ⊳ *East Lynne* (1861), was hugely successful, selling over 2.5 million copies by 1900. The conservatism of this book is also apparent in the rest of Wood's *oeuvre*, with *Mrs Halliburton's Troubles* (1862) and *A Life's Secret* (1867) exhibiting extreme hostility to working-class activism. She was prolific, writing over thirty novels and 300 short stories, as well as editing a periodical, *Argosy*. Most of her works are novels of ⊳ sensation underscored by a rigid Victorian morality. They include *The Channings* (1862); *The Shadows of Ashlydyat* (1863); *Lady Adelaide's Oath* (1867) and *The Master of Greylands* (1873). Her last work was *Ashley and Other Stories* (1897). *A Life's Secret* (1867) portrayed a negative side of trade unionism and caused her publisher's office to be mobbed by a hostile crowd. The *Johnny Ludlow* series of stories (1868–9) drew on local and family history from her early life, and lacked some of the melodramatic and sensational elements of many of her other novels.

Bib: Hughes, W., *The Maniac in the Cellar: Sensation Novels of the 1860s*.

***Woodlanders, The* (1887)**
A novel by ⊳ Thomas Hardy. The setting is Dorset in the south-west of England and the

human relationships are a kind of movement upwards, downwards and upwards again from the primitive rural base. The primitive peasant girl, Marty South, is in love with the young cider-maker, Giles Winterbourne, who is as simple in his background as she is herself but has great natural delicacy of feeling. Giles is himself in love with Grace Melbury, the daughter of a local timber merchant, who has had a 'lady's' education (▷ education of women). She has not been spoiled by this but her sensibilities have spoiled her for the primitive environment to which Giles belongs. Her parents marry her to the young doctor, Edred Fitzpiers, who, however, is enticed away by the great lady of the district, Felice Charmond. Grace takes refuge in the woods with Giles, who, though a sick man, abandons his cottage to her and lives in a hut nearby, where he dies. Grace and Marty South mourn together over his grave but Grace becomes reconciled to Fitzpiers and Marty is left to mourn alone. Neither Fitzpiers nor Mrs Charmond belongs to the rural background and their intrusion into it is disruptive of its values, embodied above all in Giles Winterbourne.

Woolf, Virginia (1882–1941)
Novelist and critic. She was the daughter of Leslie Stephen, the literary critic; after his death in 1904, the house in the Bloomsbury district of London which she shared with her sister Vanessa (later Vanessa Bell) became the centre of the ▷ Bloomsbury Group of intellectuals, one of whom, the socialist thinker Leonard Woolf, she married in 1912. Together they established the ▷ Hogarth Press which published much of the most memorable imaginative writing of the 1920s. She experienced recurrent bouts of mental illness and during one of these took her own life by drowning herself in the River Ouse, near her home at Rodmell, Sussex.

Her first two novels, *The Voyage Out* (1915) and *Night and Day* (1919), are basically ▷ realist in their technique, but in the next four – *Jacob's Room* (1922), ▷ *Mrs Dalloway* (1925), ▷ *To the Lighthouse* (1927) and ▷ *The Waves* (1931) – she became increasingly experimental and innovatory. Her attitude was formed by three influences: the negative one of dissatisfaction with the methods and outlook of the three novelists who, in the first 20 years of this century, dominated the contemporary public, ▷ H.G. Wells, ▷ Arnold Bennett, and ▷ John Galsworthy (see Woolf's essay 'Mr Bennett and Mrs Brown', 1923); the outlook of the Bloomsbury circle, with their strong emphasis on the value of personal relations and the cultivation of the sensibility; the sense of tragedy in the 19th-century Russian novelists, ▷ Tolstoy and ▷ Dostoevsky, and the dramatist and short-story writer ▷ Chekhov. She sought to develop a technique of expression which would capture the essence of the sensibility – the experiencing self – and to do this, she reduced the plot-and-story element of novel-writing as far as she could and developed a ▷ stream of consciousness narrative to render inner experience. The last two of the four experimental novels mentioned are usually considered to be her most successful achievements, especially *To the Lighthouse*. In her later novels, *The Years* (1937) and *Between the Acts* (1941), she again used a more customary technique, though with stress on symbolism and bringing out the slight incident as possibly that which is most revelatory. She is now generally regarded as one of the greatest of the ▷ modernist innovators, and is also an important focus for ▷ feminist debate.

▷ *Orlando* (1928) is a composite work, ostensibly a biography of a poet (a tribute to ▷ Vita Sackville-West), but in part a brilliantly vivid historical novel (though her subject was her contemporary) and in part literary criticism. Her more formal literary criticism was published in two volumes, *The Common Reader* (1925) and *The Common Reader, 2nd Series* (1932). In these she expressed her philosophy of creative writing (for instance in the essay 'Modern Fiction', 1925) and her response to the writers and writings of the past that most interested her. She had a partly fictional way of re-creating the personalities of past writers which is sensitive and vivid. In her social and political attitude she was feminist, *ie* she was much concerned with the rights of women and especially of women writers. This is one of the basic themes of *Orlando* but it comes out most clearly in *A Room of One's Own* (1931). *Flush* (1933) is another experiment in fictional biography (of ▷ Elizabeth Barrett Browning's spaniel) and she wrote a straight biography of her friend the art critic Roger Fry (1940). Apart from *The Common Reader*, her volumes of essays and criticism include: *Three Guineas* (1938); *The Death of the Moth* (1942); *The Captain's Death Bed* (1950); *Granite and Rainbow* (1958). Her *Collected Essays* were published in 1966, her *Letters* between 1975 and 1980 and her diaries (*The Diary of Virginia Woolf*) between 1977 and 1984. *Moments of Being* (1976) is a selection of autobiographical writings. Her stories are collected in *A Haunted House* (1943).

Bib: Woolf, L., *Autobiography*; Bell, Q., *Virginia Woolf, A Biography*; Bowlby, R., *Virginia Woolf: Feminist Destinations*; Gordon, L., *Virginia Woolf: Writer's Life*; Clements, P., and Grundy, I. (eds.), *Virginia Woolf: New Critical Essays*; Marcus, J. (ed.), *New Feminist Essays on Virginia Woolf*; Naremore, J., *The World Without a Self*; Rosenthal, M., *Virginia Woolf*; Marcus, L. *Virginia Woolf*.

Wordsworth, Dorothy (1771–1855)
Diarist, letter-writer and poet. The sister of ▷ William Wordsworth and consequently one of the few women writers acknowledged by traditional criticism. Although Dorothy grew

up with distant relatives, in 1794 she rejoined her brother and lived with him, and later his wife and children, until her death. She devoted herself entirely to William's creative genius and even her own journal was written to 'give William pleasure by it'. Her descriptions of the friendship she and William shared with ▷ Coleridge, of their long discussions and observations of nature, and of the daily routine and surroundings of Dove Cottage are valuable to literary historians. But because her own writing does not fall into a conventional literary classification, it has often been neglected by critics and biographers. Recently, however, she has been reclaimed by ▷ feminist criticism which has pointed towards the parallels between her writing and her brother's, often making it impossible to tell who originated certain phrases, vocabulary and images.
Bib: Homans, M., *Women Writers and Poetic Identity*; Levin, S.M., *Dorothy Wordsworth and Romanticism*.

Wordsworth, William (1770–1850)
Poet. He was born in Cumberland, the son of a law-agent. His mother died when he was only eight, and when his father died five years later, he was sent to school at Hawkshead, where he led a life of solitary freedom among the fells. In 1787 he went to Cambridge, but more inspiring in their influence were his two visits to revolutionary France: the first in 1790, and the second, lasting a year, from November 1791. During the second visit his love affair with a surgeon's daughter, Annette Vallon, resulted in her pregnancy, and she gave birth to a daughter. Forced to leave Annette behind on his return Wordsworth underwent a period of turmoil, intensified when England went to war with France in 1793. The emotional trauma of this period in his life seems to have been displaced into the searching anxiety which underlies much of his early poetry. The love affair is not mentioned explicitly in his work but is recounted at one remove in the story of *Vaudracour and Julia* (written c 1804; published 1820).

Wordsworth's relatives intended him for the Church, but his religious views at this time tended towards an unorthodox ▷ pantheism, evolved during his strangely lonely but happy childhood. Moreover, the writings of the extreme rationalist philosopher ▷ William Godwin influenced him still further against the possibility of a career in the Church of England. Fortunately in 1795 a friend left him a legacy sufficient to keep him independent, and he settled down in Somerset with his sister ▷ Dorothy, one of the most sustaining personal influences of his life. By 1797 he had made the friendship of ▷ Samuel Taylor Coleridge, who came to live nearby, and in 1798 the two poets collaborated in producing ▷ *Lyrical Ballads.* In 1799 William and Dorothy moved to Dove Cottage, Grasmere, and in 1802 Wordsworth married Mary Hutchinson. By this time, he was disillusioned with France, now under dictatorship, had abandoned Godwinism, and was beginning to turn back to orthodox religion. He also became more conservative in politics, to the disgust of younger men such as ▷ Byron and ▷ Shelley. The great decade of his poetry ran from 1797 to 1807. Thereafter it declined in quality while his reputation slowly grew. By 1830 his achievement was generally acknowledged, and in 1843 he was made ▷ Poet Laureate.

Wordsworth's first volumes (*Descriptive Sketches*, *An Evening Walk*, 1793) show the characteristic tone and diction of 18th-century topographical and nature poetry. They were followed by a tragedy, *The Borderers* (not published until 1842). The *Lyrical Ballads* collection marks a new departure however, in the uncompromising simplicity of much of its language, its concern with the poor and outcast, and its fusion of natural description with inward states of mind. These qualities have often caused the volume to be viewed as the starting point of the ▷ Romantic Movement. The *Preface* to the 1800 edition of *Lyrical Ballads* also contained Wordsworth's attack on the 'gaudiness and inane phraseology' which he felt encumbered contemporary verse. With the encouragement of Coleridge, he planned a long philosophical poem to be called *The Recluse*, and in preparation for it, wrote ▷ *The Prelude.* This was completed by 1805, but not published until 1850, and then in a revised form. In 1807 Wordsworth published *Poems in Two Volumes*, and in 1814 ▷ *The Excursion*, the only part of *The Recluse* to be completed besides *The Prelude*. These were followed by *The White Doe of Rylstone* (1815); *Peter Bell* (1819); *The River Duddon* (1820); *Ecclesiastical Sketches* (1822); *Sonnets* (1838).

Wordsworth's greatness lies in his impressive, even stubborn authenticity of tone. Sometimes this is achieved through the use of primitive or simplistic literary form as in such lyrical ballads as *We are Seven* and *The Thorn*, and also the ▷ Lucy poems. Sometimes Wordsworth develops the discursive ▷ blank verse manner of the 18th-century ▷ Georgic into an original, profoundly introspective vehicle for what ▷ John Keats called his 'egotistical sublime', as in *The Prelude*, ▷ *The Ruined Cottage* and ▷ *Tintern Abbey*. Frequently he succeeds in convincing the reader that subject matter which in other poets would be merely banal or even comic, is in fact of mysterious portentousness. This technique is particularly impressive in poems which treat the poor, the mad, the senile, members of humanity generally disregarded in earlier poetry. In these works his diction and tone brush aside the class-based doctrine of kinds, and the related conceptions of 'high' and 'low' language which dominate much 18th-century verse. Such poems as *Simon Lee*, *The Idiot Boy*, and ▷ *Resolution and Independence* (1807) seem to challenge the reader's humanity, by their empathy with the wretched, the abject, and the poverty-stricken.

Another characteristically Romantic idea, that 'the child is father to the man', that youth is essentially richer in wisdom and insight than age, is developed into a full-scale philosophy in the early books of *The Prelude*. It is significant however that the illustrative reminiscences of the poet's own youth are far more effective as poetry than the passages of explicit theorizing. The *Ode*: ▷ *Intimations of Immortality from Recollections of Early Childhood* (1807) is often thought to show Wordsworth's uneasy recognition that his inspiration was leaving him. It is a mistake, however, to suppose that he wrote no good poetry after 1807, though his spiritual earnestness increasingly declines into orthodox piety, and his bold austerity of tone into mere banality.

Bib: Moorman, M., *Life*; Bateson, F. W., *Wordsworth, A Reinterpretation*; Knight, G. W., in *The Starlit Dome*; Sherry, C., *Wordsworth's Poetry of the Imagination*; Beer, J., *Wordsworth and the Human Heart*; Wordsworth, J., *William Wordsworth: The Borders of Vision*; Watson, J. R., *Wordsworth*; Hartman, G., *Wordsworth's Poetry 1787–1814*; Jacobus, M., *Tradition and Experiment in Wordsworth's Lyrical Ballads (1798)*; Jones, A. R., and Tydeman, W. (eds.), *Wordsworth: Lyrical Ballads* (Macmillan Casebook); Harvey, W. J., and Gravil, R., *Wordsworth: The Prelude* (Macmillan Casebook).

Wotton, Sir Henry (1566–1639)
Poet and courtier. Wotton was educated at Oxford, where he became acquainted with ▷ Donne, whose biography he wished to write (the task actually fell to ▷ Izaak Walton, who also wrote a memoir of Wotton himself). At court Walton became attached to the ▷ Essex faction and performed several intelligence-gathering tasks for the earl. He was welcomed by ▷ James I at his accession, since Wotton had carried secret messages to James when he was king of Scotland. He was given a diplomatic role by the king, and, among other duties, was ambassador to Venice. Although well known, it is worth recording Wotton's definition of an ambassador as an honest man who has to lie when abroad for the sake of his country. In 1624 he became Provost of Eton. The only work to be published during his lifetime was *The Elements of Architecture* (1624), but his many poems were gathered together after his death, together with Walton's memoir, as *Reliquiae Wottoniae* (1651). The lyrical pieces are characterized by a searching for honest, spiritual truth, and his panegyric poems – one to his patron, ▷ Elizabeth of Bohemia, is particularly fine – appear more honest than many of their kind.

'Wreck of the Deutschland, The'
A poem by ▷ Gerard Manley Hopkins, written in 1875, but not printed until the first editions of his collected poems (edited by ▷ Robert Bridges) was published in 1918, apart from a short extract in Bridges' anthology *The Spirit of Men* (1918). Hopkins had ceased writing poetry when he entered the Jesuit Order in 1868. He broke his silence in consequence of being deeply moved at the news of the loss of the ship *Deutschland* at the mouth of the Thames in the winter of 1875, and of the drowning of five German nuns, who were passengers and exiles on account of Bismarck's anti-Catholic legislation (the Falk Laws).

It is the first of Hopkins' important poems to be written in what he called ▷ sprung rhythm, which he employed for most of his subsequent poetry; the lines have a regular count of rhythmic stresses but a varying count of syllables. This rhythm enabled Hopkins to combine the emphasis and syntax of the spoken language with the musical devices of the verse, and his use of it illustrates his statement that the language of poetry is 'that of current speech heightened'. The technique was very foreign to 19th-century ideas of poetic decorum, and explains why the poem was not published until much later: Hopkins offered it to the Jesuit journal *The Month*, but the editor declared that he dared not publish it.

Wren, Sir Christopher (1632–1723)
Architect. He was also a distinguished mathematician and astronomer, a member of the circle which in 1662 became the ▷ Royal Society. He was in fact a representative of his age, which regarded the great cultural tradition of Europe as descending from ancient Rome and Greece and immensely valued the scope and power of the human reason. His masterpiece is ▷ St Paul's Cathedral in London; even before the old Cathedral was burnt down in 1666, he proposed to remodel it 'after a good Roman manner' not following 'the ▷ Gothic rudeness of the old design'. Wren's cathedral is an example of an English version of the ▷ classical style known as ▷ Baroque elsewhere in contemporary Europe. He also proposed a replanning of the City of London, in an arrangement of wide streets radiating from a central space, but difficulties in agreeing about property valuations with the existing landowners prevented this. He did, however, rebuild 52 London churches after the Great Fire of 1666, giving them towers and spires of ingeniously varied and graceful designs in white stone that stood out against the black dome of the cathedral – an effect now entirely ruined by the alteration of the skyline by commercial

buildings. Wren also contributed fine buildings to ▷ Oxford and ▷ Cambridge.

Wriothesley, Henry
▷ Southampton, Henry Wriothesley, third Earl of.

Writing
▷ Ecriture.

Wroth, Mary (Lady Wroth) (?1586–?1652)
The niece of ▷ Philip Sidney and ▷ Mary Sidney, Countess of Pembroke, Mary Wroth was a member of court, where she danced with ▷ Queen Anne in ▷ Ben Jonson's ▷ masque, *The Masque of Blackness*. Jonson was a particular admirer of her talents, dedicating his play ▷ *The Alchemist* to her and enthusiastically acclaiming her poetry. In 1614, following the death of her husband, Sir Robert Wroth, Mary Wroth was left with over £20,000 in debts, which she undertook to pay off. Financial difficulties stalked her for most of her life, a factor which may have induced her to publish the first part of her work *Urania* in 1621. The second part of this work, together with a ▷ pastoral ▷ tragicomedy entitled *Loves Victorie*, circulated in manuscript. *Urania* is the first prose romance written in English by a woman. Soon after its publication it was withdrawn, because various passages touched upon court intrigues. Like Philip Sidney's ▷ *Arcadia*, *Urania* contains poetry, including a sequence of songs and ▷ sonnets entitled *Pamphilia to Amphilanthus*, the title being derived from the names of the two protagonists of *Urania*. The sequence is important because, while participating in the ▷ Petrarchan tradition, it is also written from the perspective of a woman.
Bib: Roberts, J. A. (ed.), *The Poems of Lady Mary Wroth*; Hannay, M. P., 'Mary Sidney: Lady Wroth' in *Women Writers of the Renaissance and Reformation*, (ed.) Wilson, K. M.; Cerasano, S. P., and Wynne-Davies, M., *Renaissance Drama by Women*.

Wuthering Heights **(1847)**
A novel by ▷ Emily Brontë, first published under the ▷ pseudonym Ellis Bell. The story is narrated by two characters, Lockwood and Nelly Dean, who recount the tale of Heathcliff and his involvement with the Earnshaw and Linton families. The arrival of the foundling Heathcliff disrupts the lives of Catherine Earnshaw and her brother, Hindley. Catherine and Heathcliff develop an intense bond, but Heathcliff overhears her saying to Nelly Dean that marrying him would degrade her. He then leaves Wuthering Heights, returning three years later, by which time Catherine has married Edgar Linton. In revenge, Heathcliff marries Edgar's sister, Isabella, mistreating and brutalizing Hindley and his son, Hareton. Catherine dies shortly after giving birth to a daughter, Cathy. After Edgar's death, Cathy is lured to the Heights and subjected to Heathcliff's terrible will. At the end of the novel, Heathcliff dies and Cathy and Hareton are united. *Wuthering Heights* has generated an enormous body of criticism, and has always been recognized as a novel of great power and originality. Recent interpretations have focused on the complex narrative structure, the novel's treatment of temporarility, its transgression of conventional sexual and moral codes, and its intense examination of the nature of desire.
▷ Orphans; Gothic novel; Romanticism.

Wyatt, Sir Thomas (1503–42)
Poet, courtier, diplomat. Wyatt's life, with its changes in fortune, perfectly represents the uncertain conditions of existence in the court of ▷ Henry VIII. Imprisoned several times (once because he was suspected of being the lover of Anne Boleyn), he brought to his writing an awareness of continental European styles and manner to which his life as a diplomat exposed him. His best-known poems appeared in ▷ *Tottel's Miscellany* (1557) together with poems by Henry Howard, ▷ Earl of Surrey, though his first printed works were his translations and adaptations of the ▷ Psalms (1549). His complex, ambiguous lyrics, with their development of ▷ Petrarchan motifs and images, are not only some of the earliest attempts at writing in a recognizably 'modern' (that is, non-medieval) style, but are important statements in their own right on the uncertain quality of life in the ▷ Renaissance polity.
Bib: Daalder, J. (ed.), *Collected Poems*; Foley, S., *Sir Thomas Wyatt*; Greenblatt, S., *Renaissance Self-Fashioning*.

Wycherley, William (1640–1716)
Dramatist of the Restoration period. Born at Clive near Shrewsbury, the son of a lawyer, and educated first in France, where he became a Catholic, and then at Oxford. He studied law at the Inner Temple, but preferred to write for the stage, and to mix in courtly literary circles, associating with such individuals as the ▷ Earl of Rochester, ▷ Sir George Etherege, and Sir Charles Sedley (1639–1701). His first play, *Love in a Wood; Or St James's Park* (1671), is dedicated to one of ▷ Charles II's mistresses, the Duchess of Cleveland, who later became his mistress as well. After this he served for a time in the fleet, and was present at a sea-battle. His second play, ▷ *The Gentleman Dancing Master* (1672) is an adaptation of a play by Calderón, and written in the ▷ Spanish intrigue style.

It is for his last two plays that Wycherley is now best remembered: ▷ *The Country Wife* (1675) and ▷ *The Plain Dealer* (1676), in which his deep cynicism lends savagery to his wit. ▷ Dryden praised the 'satire, strength and wit of Manly Wycherley', punning on the name of Manly, the chief character in *The Plain Dealer*, and Wycherley was often referred to in this way thereafter. In 1676 he stopped writing for the stage, and in 1679 married the Countess of Drogheda, a wealthy widow. She died in 1681, leaving him her fortune, but the bequest involved him in litigation, and he was reduced to poverty and imprisoned for debt for four years (1682–6). During this period he wrote *Epistles to the King and Duke* (1683), expressing his need. James II secured his release from prison, paid his debts, and awarded him a pension.

Bib: Nicoll, A., *Restoration Comedy*; Dobree, B., *Restoration Comedy*; McCarthy, E. B., *William Wycherley: A Biography*; Thompson, J., *Language in Wycherley's Plays: Seventeenth Century Language Theory and Drama*.

Wycliffe (or Wyclif), John (c 1320–84)
Religious reformer and theologian who provided the academic inspiration for the church reform programme of the Lollards (sometimes called Wycliffites). Educated at Oxford, he became master of Balliol *c* 1360, but later left this academic environment to become rector at Lutterworth in 1374. Wycliffe's views were developed in a series of Latin treatises. In these he argued (amongst other things); against the doctrine of transubstantiation (in Wycliffe's view, material bread and wine remained after the consecration of the Host); that oral confession was not necessary for the truly contrite person; that the true Pope is the most righteous man on earth and not to be necessarily identified with the clerics who claim or compete for that title in Rome. Wycliffe attacked the power of the established clergy in many ways and explicitly rejected the ideals of monasticism and fraternalism. The Gospels were the most important source of Christian instruction for Wycliffe and he argued for their accessibility in the vernacular. He was responsible for inspiring the systematic vernacular translation of the ▷ Bible into English (a text banned by Bishop Arundel in 1409), though it is unlikely that he ever played any part in the translation process itself (the combined work of a number of clerics and scholars) as has been commonly supposed. Although Wycliffe's views were banned by a church council in 1382 and his followers judged to be heretics in the early fifteenth century, his beliefs continued to attract interest and support and there is undoubtedly some continuity between early sixteenth-century Lollards and those open to the reformist ideas of Luther and Tyndale.

Wynkyn de Worde (d 1534)
Jan van Wynkyn moved to England with ▷ Caxton in 1476, and in 1491 took over Caxton's press, which he ran until his death c 1534. He published the first illustrated edition of ▷ Malory's ▷ *Morte D'Arthur* in 1498.
▷ Carol.

X

Xanadu
▷ *Kubla Khan*.

Xenophon
Ancient Greek (Athenian historian and philosopher, born about 430 BC. He was a disciple of ▷ Socrates, and greatly embittered against ▷ Athens, which had put his master to death. Because of this, although he had been an Athenian general, he left the city and served the ▷ Spartans. His writings on Socrates, the *Memorabilia* and the *Symposium*, are the principal records we possess of Socrates besides those of ▷ Plato. Xenophon's *Anabasis* is an account of the war against Artaxerxes; his *Hellenica* is a continuation of the history by ▷ Thucydides down to 362 BC. He wrote other works on household management, history, the duties of a cavalry officer, and on the elder Cyrus, founder of the Persian monarchy.

Yahoos
Primitive and filthy creatures with the bodies of humans but base and simple minds, whose barbarism is contrasted, in ▷ Swift's ▷ *Gulliver's Travels*, with the civilized behaviour of the ▷ Houyhnhnms, a race of gentle and intelligent horses. The Yahoos are used by Swift to satirize the human race in general. The term became synonymous with a boor or brute.

Yates, E.H. (1831–94)
Novelist, dramatist, journalist and editor. A prolific and versatile literary figure, who was drama critic of the *Daily News*, edited various journals before founding the society magazine *World*, was gossip columnist for the *Illustrated Times*, published numerous novels and plays, gave lecture tours and worked for the General Post Office into his forties. His career was profitable but controversial; in 1858 he was expelled from the Garrick Club for insulting ▷ Thackeray in *Town Talk* and in 1885 he was imprisoned for a libellous article in *World*. He was a friend and admirer of ▷ Dickens. His novels are sensational stories of intrigue and crime, including *Running the Gauntlet* (1865), *Land at Last* (1866) and *The Black Sheep* (1876)
▷ Sensation, novel of.
Bib: Sutherland, J., *The Longman Companion to Victorian Fiction*.

Yearsley, Ann (1752–1806)
English poet, novelist and dramatist. Originally a milkwoman, she was taught to read and write by her brother. She married John Yearsley in 1774, and in 1784, when her family were living in terrible conditions, she showed her verses to ▷ Hannah More, who arranged for the publication by subscription of *Poems on Several Occasions* (1785). However, More kept control of Yearsley's access to the proceeds, and in a later edition she complains of this. More's attitude seems to have been very patronizing – *Poems on Several Occasions* carries a letter from her to Mrs Montagu, in which she discusses Yearsley's 'wild wood notes', and goes out of her way to mention that Yearsley's husband was 'honest and sober'. Eventually, Yearsley rejected More's attempts at intellectual control. She published *Poems on Various Subjects* (1787), including a poem (like More) on the ▷ slave trade. Her play *Earl Goodwin* was acted and published, she wrote a novel, *The Royal Captives* (1795), and she ran a ▷ circulating library. Her final publication was *The Rural Lyre*.
▷ Collier, Mary; Leapor, Mary; Little, Janet
Bib: Landry, D., *The Muses of Resistance*.

Yeats, W. B. (William Butler) (1865–1939)
Anglo-Irish poet. He was of a Protestant family, a fact of importance in 19th-century Ireland where nationalism was so bound up with ▷ Catholicism. His father was an eminent painter. He spent his boyhood between school in London and his mother's native county of Sligo, a wild and beautiful county in north-western Ireland which is a background to much of his poetry. His youth was passed during the upsurge of Irish political nationalism represented by the Home Rule movement led by Parnell. He shared the antagonism felt by English writers of ▷ Pre-Raphaelite background – notably William Morris – to the urban and industrial harshness and materialism of contemporary English culture. He sought a basis for resistance to it in Irish peasant folk traditions and ancient Celtic myth. His first work was on a theme from this mythology – *The Wanderings of Oisin* (▷ Oisin). Yeats was indeed fortunate in having such a cultural basis at hand for his anti-materialistic poetry, while his English contemporaries had further to look. His career divides naturally into four phases:

1 *1889–99*. During this period he was a leading member of the ▷ Aesthetic Movement in London, an outcome of Pre-Raphaelitism, but especially indebted to the Oxford scholar, Walter Pater. In its revolt against ▷ Victorian materialism, it tended to Catholicism and to mysticism. Its meeting-place was the Rhymers' Club, and its public voice the ▷ *Yellow Book*. Yeats shared its mystical sympathies, which in his case brought together Celtic and Indian mythology; these come out in his works of the period: prose – ▷ *The Celtic Twilight* (1893), *The Secret Rose*, *The Tables of the Law*, *The Adoration of the Magi* (1897); verse – *Crossways* (1889), *The Rose* (1893), *The Wind Among the Reeds* (1899); verse plays – *The Countess Cathleen* (1892) and *The Land of Heart's Desire* (1894).

2 *1899–1909*. Yeats, with the help of ▷ Lady Gregory, built up the Irish National Theatre, which found a home in the ▷ Abbey Theatre, Dublin. Until 1909, he was its manager, and he wrote plays for it, predominantly based on Irish myth. The period was disillusioning for him so far as his hopes for Irish culture went, but it was formative in his development as a major poet. He hoped to make the theatre the voice of a distinctively Irish modern culture, and at least he succeeded in creating one of the most interesting dramatic movements in contemporary Europe. In personal terms, the theatre business brought out new strength and realism in his character and in his writing; he was the first poet writing in English since the 17th century to seek intelligently and purposefully for an effective dramatic idiom and for new methods of dramatic production. His only volume of verse during these ten years was *In the Seven Woods* (1904); amongst his plays are *Cathleen ni Houlihan* (1902), *The King's Threshold* (1904), *Deirdre* (1907).

3 *1910–18 – the Period of Transition*. He had begun his career in the tradition of ▷ Spenser, ▷ Shelley and the Pre-Raphaelites, and he had always been interested in the mysticism

of ▷ Blake, but he now became one of the poets, including ▷ Ezra Pound (whom he met at this time) and ▷ T.S. Eliot, drawn to the intellectually more vigorous tradition associated with the 17th-century ▷ Metaphysicals, especially ▷ Donne. He was no longer a ▷ romantic, at least in the decadent sense of a dreamer, but though his mood was harsher and he had lost some of his faith, he searched no less assiduously for symbols which could give meaning to history and life. At first he turned away from Ireland, but the Irish Rebellion of 1916 turned him back to the country which was after all the human context of his emotions. His books *The Green Helmet* (1910) and *Responsibilities* (1914) represent the new austerity of his poetry.

4 *1919–39*. It is in this period that Yeats grows into one of the most important poets of the 20th century, with the publication of *The Wild Swans at Coole* (1919), *Michael Robartes and the Dancer* (1921), *The Tower* (1928) and *The Winding Stair* (1933). This work is marked by strong rhythms, by stanza and rhyme patterns which enforce thought, by severe diction with few adjectives, and by a range of symbols each of which is a nucleus of meanings. The symbols are part of an elaborate theory of history (explained in the prose *A Vision*, 1925) derived from the Italian philosopher Vico (1668–1744) and the neo-Platonism of Plotinus (3rd century AD). Whatever the faultiness of the system considered apart from the poetry, it constituted for Yeats a mythology which he could use poetically to embody human experience widely and deeply. It is scarcely helpful to try to 'learn' this mythology in order to understand Yeats' poetry; it is elucidated by the poetry itself, if it is read in bulk. With these symbols (the tower, the moon, etc.) Yeats had a wide mythology of persons, some drawn from his own friends, some from history and myth, and some invented, *eg* Crazy Jane in *Words for Music Perhaps*. This, like *A Woman Young and Old, A Full Moon in March* (1935) and *Last Poems* (1936–39), has more bitterness and less richness than the previous volumes of this period. Yeats continued to write plays and to improve his dramatic idiom, partly under the influence of the Japanese ▷ Noh drama; his best play is nearly his last – *Purgatory* (1939). After 1910, Yeats' prose is also distinguished, notably his *Autobiographies* (1915 and 1922), some of his critical essays, *eg Per Amica Silentia Lunae* (1918) and his essays on drama, *Plays and Controversies* (1923).

▷ Irish literature in English.

Bib: Hone, J. M., *Life*, Ellmann, R., *Yeats, the Man and the Masks*; *The Identity of Yeats*; Henn, T. R., *The Lonely Tower*; Stock, *W. B. Yeats*; Unterecker, J., *A Reader's Guide to Yeats*; Kermode, F., *Romantic Image*; Hall and Steinmann (eds.), a collection of essays; Larrissey, E., *Yeats the Poet*; Leavis, F. R., *New Bearings in English Poetry*; Ure, P., *Yeats the Playwright*; Smith, S., *W. B. Yeats*.

Yellow Book

An illustrated quarterly review, 1894–7. It was a main organ of the arts during the period, and although it was especially the voice of the ▷ Aesthetic Movement, it also published writers who did not belong to this movement, eg ▷ Henry James.

▷ Nineties' Poets.

Yeoman

Originally the word probably meant 'countryman', but by the 14th century it was used for a peasant freeholder, *ie* a man below the class of gentry, but an independent owner of land, or at least 'a tenant at will', *ie* a man who owed rent for his land but who could abandon his tenancy when he pleased. Yeomen thus formed a class between the gentry and the hired labourers or serfs (who were few after the 14th century). The younger sons of yeomen would be landless, and commonly took service with the gentry, often bearing arms for them, like the Yeoman who follows the Squire in Chaucer's ▷ *Canterbury Tales*. As a class they were substantial and independent; their skill as archers caused them to be invaluable to the 14th- and 15th-century kings (especially ▷ Edward III and ▷ Henry V) engaged in wars with the French, who relied on cavalry. The success of the yeoman archers at the battles of ▷ Crécy (1346), Poitiers (1356) and ▷ Agincourt (1415) indeed brought about a military revolution; from the 15th century the cavalryman declined in importance and the importance of the infantryman increased.

The ▷ Wars of the Roses and the policy of the ▷ Tudor sovereigns reduced the power of the old nobility and encouraged the prosperity of the yeomen, who flourished throughout the 16th and 17th centuries, and often improved their condition so as to rise into the class of the gentry. In the 18th century the tide ran the other way; the richer landowners were anxious to enclose land into large farms, and to buy out the freeholding yeomen whose small farms stood in the way. This freeholding class thus declined, or joined the ranks of the tenant farmers under the big land-owners. Often they went to work in the rapidly growing industrial towns By the mid-19th century, the term 'yeoman' practically disappeared but it is now used for a nostalgic concept of the sturdy independent Englishman, full of common sense and natural patriotism.

The Yeomen of the Guard were established in 1485, and now guard the Tower of London; they are popularly known as Beefeaters. Yeomanry Regiments were regiments of volunteers who in peacetime trained as soldiers in their spare time; after 1920 they were known as the Territorials.

Yeoman's Tale, The Canon's
▷ *Canon's Yeoman's Tale, The*

Yonge, Charlotte (1823–1901)
Editor, historian, biographer, translator and hugely successful novelist. She was born in Otterbourne, near Winchester, where she remained for the rest of her life, apart from visiting Paris briefly in 1869. In 1838 she came under the influence of John Keble and adopted the religious views associated with the ▷ Oxford Movement, which influence all her writing. Her most famous novel, ▷ *The Heir of Redclyffe*, was published in 1853. Other tales of contemporary life include *Heartsease* (1854); *The Daisy Chain* (1856); *The Clever Woman of the Family* (1865) and historical ▷ romances for children (*The Prince and the Page*, 1865, and *The Dove in the Eagle's Nest*, 1866). For forty years she edited the girls' magazine, *The Monthly Packet*.

Yonge was highly religious and conservative, opposed to ▷ women's suffrage and socialism, and a great defender of traditional Victorian standards and morals. The message of *The Clever Woman of the Family* is that women should not pursue intellectual subjects, but accept their inferiority to men.

▷ Women's Movement; Historical novels; Children's literature.
Bib: Battiscombe, G., *Charlotte Mary Yonge: An Uneventful Life*; Mare, M. and Percival, A.C., *Victorian Best-Seller: The World of Charlotte M. Yonge*.

York Cycle, The
A ▷ cycle of plays on pageant waggons, at stations in the streets of York, on Corpus Christi day from the late 14th century until performances were suppressed in the late 16th century. The earliest record of the performance of plays on Corpus Christi day comes from York (1378), and if it was one of the oldest cycles, it seems also to have been one of the longest. There are 48 plays in the single extant manuscript of the cycle, but there are signs that texts of more plays in the cycle have not survived. The cycle underwent several revisions, and the work of some distinctive revisers (the 'York metrist', the 'York realist' have been identified by critics). Bib: Beadle, R. and King, P. (eds.), *York Mystery Plays: A Selection in Modern Spelling*; Beadle, R. (ed.), *The York Plays*.

***Yorkshire Tragedy, A* (1608)**
A domestic ▷ tragedy published in 1608, and based on actual murders occurring in 1605. The play was ascribed to ▷ Shakespeare on its publication, but he is not now thought to have had any hand in it and ▷ Middleton is now the leading candidate for authorship. It is a forceful work, in a tradition of domestic tragedy that is an important subordinate line of the drama of Shakespeare's time: ▷ *Arden of Faversham*; *Warning for Fair Women* (Anon., 1599), and ▷ Thomas Heywood's ▷ *A Woman Killed with Kindness* (1603). They have in common that they deal with men and women of the middle classes (not, like the grand tragedy of the age, with the courts of princes), that they are realistic, and that they convey a strong moral warning.
Bib: Cawley, A. C. and Gaines, B. (eds.), *A Yorkshire Tragedy*.

Young, Edward (1683–1765)
Royal chaplain and later Rector of Welwyn in Hertfordshire. He wrote three tragedies which were successfully acted in ▷ Drury Lane, and a series of ▷ didactic ▷ satires: *The Force of Religion* (1714) in ▷ couplets, and *The Love of Fame* (1725/18), *The Vindication of Providence* (1728) and *Resignation* (1762), all in ▷ Miltonic ▷ blank verse. His most important work, the melancholy and reflective poem *The Complaint or* ▷ Night Thoughts on Life, Death and Immortality (1742–5), consisting of 10,000 lines of ▷ blank verse, was considered by ▷ Samuel Johnson to display 'the magnificence of vast extent and endless diversity', and became immensely popular both in Britain and on the continent. As their titles suggest, Young's poems are marked by a crushing orthodoxy of religious sentiment, and their turgid rhetorical dogmatism makes them very difficult to read today. Young's influential prose essay *Conjectures on Original Composition* (1759) focuses on the nature of artistic 'genius' and marks an important stage in the development of pre-▷ romantic literary theory.
Bib: Wicker, C. V., *Edward Young and the Fear of Death*.

Yvain
One of the Knights of the ▷ Round Table, the son of King Urien, who appears in early Welsh legendary narratives as Owein. His story is the central focus of ▷ Chrétien de Troyes' 12th-century romance *Yvain*, which charts events by which Yvain wins, loses, and regains his chivalric identity. He wins a wife and a rich court as a result of his encounter with the Knight of the Fountain; but forfeits his wife and reputation when he fails to return, as promised, from more than a year away in the company of the Round Table. A period of madness ensues, but he gradually builds up a reputation through his adventures as the Knight of the Lion (so called because his companion and aide is a Lion). The Lady of the Fountain reluctantly accepts him back finally, largely as a result of the plotting of her maid. Chrétien's narrative forms the basis for the 14th-century Middle English romance, *Yvain and Gawain*.

Z

Zany
A court fool or jester, from the Italian 'zani' for actors or clowns in the ▷ Commedia dell'Arte.

Zeal-of-the-land Busy
A hypocritical ▷ Puritan in ▷ Ben Jonson's comedy ▷ *Bartholomew Fair*. It was common for Puritans of the period to give themselves names that were phrases derived from biblical texts.

Zeugma
▷ Figures of Speech.

Zimri
▷ *Absalom and Achitophel.*

Zola, Emile Edouard Charles Antoine (1840–1902)
French novelist. He carried the ▷ realism of ▷ Flaubert a stage further into the doctrine of ▷ naturalism. He believed that the biological sciences (notably the discoveries of ▷ Darwin) had changed the conditions under which the human character should be presented and interpreted, and that in future the novelist should present his characters in relation to the influences of heredity and environment. This he carried out in the succession of novels about the Rougon and Macquart families (1871–93) including *La Fortune des Rougon* (1871), *La Curée* (1874), *Le Ventre de Paris* (1874), *La Conquête de Plassans* (1875), *La Faute de l'Abbé Mouret* (1875), *Son Excellence Eugène Rougon* (1876), *L'Assommoir* (1878), *Nana* (1880), *Germinal* (1885), *La Terre* (1888), *La Débâcle* (1892) and *Docteur Pascal* (1893). Zola's influence was healthy in England inasmuch as his doctrine counteracted an English prejudice against the ugly, the 'indecent' and the horrible in art. He had English imitators, eg ▷ George Moore, and he influenced such realists as ▷ George Gissing and ▷ H.G. Wells.